Dictionary
OF THE Old Testament
Wisdom, Poetry & Writings

Editors:

Tremper Longman III

Peter Enns

IVP Academic

An imprint of InterVarsity Press
Downers Grove, Illinois

Inter-Varsity Press
Nottingham, England

InterVarsity Press, USA
P.O. Box 1400, Downers Grove, IL 60515-1426, USA
World Wide Web: www.ivpress.com
Email: email@ivpress.com

Inter-Varsity Press, England
Norton Street, Nottingham NG7 3HR, England
Website: www.ivpbooks.com
Email: ivp@ivpbooks.com

InterVarsity Press®, USA, is the book-publishing division of InterVarsity Christian Fellowship/USA®, a student movement active on campus at hundreds of universities, colleges and schools of nursing in the United States of America, and a member movement of the International Fellowship of Evangelical Students. For information about local and regional activities, write Public Relations Dept., InterVarsity Christian Fellowship/ USA, 6400 Schroeder Rd., P.O. Box 7895, Madison, WI 53707-7895, or visit the IVCF website at <www.intervarsity.org>.

Inter-Varsity Press, England, is closely linked with the Universities and Colleges Christian Fellowship, a student movement connecting Christian Unions in universities and colleges throughout Great Britain, and a member movement of the International Fellowship of Evangelical Students. Website: <www.uccf.org.uk>.

All Scripture quotations, unless otherwise indicated, are the author's own translation.

Design: Cindy Kiple
Images: Reunion des Musees Nationaux/Art Resource, NY

USA ISBN 978-0-8308-1783-2
UK ISBN 978-1-84474-306-3

Printed in the United States of America ∞

 InterVarsity Press is committed to protecting the environment and to the responsible use of natural resources. As a member of the Green Press Initiative we use recycled paper whenever possible. To learn more about the Green Press Initiative, visit <www.greenpressinitiative.org>.

Library of Congress Cataloging-in-Publication Data

Dictionary of the Old Testament: wisdom, poetry & writings/editors,
Tremper Longman III, Peter Enns.
    p. cm.
  Includes bibliographical references and index.
  ISBN 978-0-8308-1783-2 (cloth: alk. paper)
  1. Bible O.T.—Dictionaries. I. Longman, Tremper. II. Enns, Peter,
  1961-
  BS440.D53 2008
  221.3—dc22
                       2008005967

British Library Cataloguing in Publication Data

A catalogue record for this book is available from the British Library.

P	23	22	21	20	19	18	17	16	15	14	13	12	11	10	9	8	7	6	5	4	3	2
Y	28	27	26	25	24	23	22	20	19	18	17	16	15	14	13	12	11	10	09			

InterVarsity Press

Project Staff

Reference Book Editor/Project Editor
Daniel G. Reid

Managing Editor
Allison Rieck

Copyeditor
Robert G. Maccini

Editorial Assistant
Jeff Reimer

Administrative Support
Taryn Bullis

Design
Cindy Kiple

Design Assistant
Mark Eddy Smith

Artist
Greg Deddo

Typesetters
Gail Munroe
Marj Sire
Maureen Tobey

Proofreaders
Drew Blankman
Keith Williams

InterVarsity Press

Publisher
Robert A. Fryling

Associate Publisher for Editorial
Andrew T. Le Peau

Associate Editorial Director
James Hoover

Production Manager
Anne Gerth

Print Coordinator
Jim Erhart

Contents

Preface _____ *vii*

How to Use This Dictionary _____ *ix*

Abbreviations _____ *xi*

Transliterations _____ *xx*

List of Contributors _____ *xxi*

Dictionary Articles _____ *1*

Scripture Index _____ *942*

Subject Index_____ *960*

Articles Index _____ *967*

Preface

The editors are honored to present the seventh in a series of critically acclaimed IVP Academic dictionaries on the various parts of the biblical canon. By the time we began our work some years ago, we had already benefited personally from the dictionaries that had seen publication. These dictionaries were helpful to our research because they provided a ready summary of the best thinking on the most important subjects in the areas of their coverage, and they advanced the discussion with fresh insights and ideas. We were excited at the prospect of helping to produce the same quality research tool as our predecessors on a part of the canon that has received spotty attention—the Psalms, Wisdom and Writings.

The delineation of this corpus of biblical books is difficult. The first volume in the Old Testament series presents no problem in this regard, the Pentateuch being a clearly defined unit, the Torah of the Hebrew Bible. The Historical Books are a bit more problematic to define since not all the historical books fall into a particular part of the Hebrew or Greek canon. The Former Prophets of the Hebrew canon (Joshua, Judges, Samuel, Kings) are all included, but so are Chronicles and Ezra-Nehemiah, which are found in the Writings (*Kĕtûbîm*) of the Hebrew canon. One could mount an argument for the inclusion of Ruth and Esther in the Historical Books volume. Nonetheless, they instead are included in our volume in order to treat all the Megillot (or Festal Scrolls: Ruth, Song of Songs, Ecclesiastes, Lamentations and Esther) together. The Megillot and all the other books covered in this volume are from the Writings, though not all the Writings are found here. We have already commented that Chronicles and Ezra-Nehemiah are in the Historical Books volume, and Daniel will be treated in the forthcoming volume on the Prophets.

After determining which books would be included in this volume, it was necessary to choose what topics would be given article-length treatment. As with previous volumes, each biblical book gets a long article. But a new feature of this volume is that for each book there is also an article focused on its ancient Near Eastern background and on its history of interpretation. Major characters are also the subject of longer treatment as well as the most significant theological themes. Different methods of study are described and then applied to the text. While this list does not capture all the different types of articles in this dictionary, special mention should be made of those articles that cover the literary qualities of the Psalms, Wisdom and Writings. All told, the topics were chosen to give full coverage to the important tools, concepts and content needed for the study and interpretation of these books.

The success of such a project depends mainly on the quality of the contributors, and the editors were extremely fortunate to have had the participation of the leading experts on this corpus of biblical writings. We want to thank the contributors for their hard work, careful research and stimulating writing. One of the advantages of editing a dictionary like this one is that we learned and deepened our own knowledge in the process. We trust that our readers will have the same experience.

Besides the contributors, we want to thank InterVarsity Press and especially Dan Reid, our fellow editor, for his vision for this series and his huge imprint on the final form of this particular book. Further, we thank Robert Maccini, Jeff Reimer, Taryn Bullis and the others who have attended to the production of the book.

Tremper Longman III
Peter Enns

How to Use This Dictionary

Abbreviations
Comprehensive tables of abbreviations for general matters as well as for scholarly, biblical and ancient literature may be found on pages xiii-xxii.

Authorship of Articles
The authors of articles are indicated by their first initials and last name at the end of each article. A full list of contributors may be found on pages xxiii-xxvi, in alphabetical order of their last name. The contribution of each author is listed following their identification.

Bibliographies
A bibliography will be found at the end of each article. The bibliographies include works cited in the articles and other significant related works. Bibliographical entries are listed in alphabetical order by the author's name, and where an author has more than one work cited, they are listed chronologically by date. In articles focused on the biblical books, the bibliographies are divided into the categories "Commentaries" and "Studies."

Cross-References
This *Dictionary* has been extensively cross-referenced in order to aid readers in making the most of material appearing throughout the volume. Five types of cross-referencing will be found:

1. One-line entries appearing in alphabetical order throughout the *Dictionary* direct readers to articles where a topic is discussed, often as a subdivision of an article:

ANAT. *See* CANAANITE GODS AND RELIGION.

2. An asterisk before a word in the body of an article indicates that an article by that title (or closely worded title) appears in the *Dictionary*. For example, "*David" directs the reader to an article entitled **DAVID**. Asterisks typically are found only at the first occurrence of a word in an article.

3. A cross-reference appearing within parentheses in the body of an article directs the reader to an article by that title. For example, (*see* God) directs the reader to an article by that title.

4. Cross-references have been appended to the end of articles, immediately preceding the bibliography, to direct readers to articles significantly related to the subject:

See also DESTRUCTION; HONOR AND SHAME; LAMENT, PSALMS OF; RETRIBUTION; WARFARE IMAGERY.

5. Occasionally references are made to articles in the companion volumes, primarily the *Dictionary of the Old Testament: Pentateuch (DOTP)* and *Dictionary of the Old Testament: Historical Books (DOTHB)*. Others include *Dictionary of Jesus and the Gospels (DJG)*, *Dictionary of Paul and His Letters (DPL)*, *Dictionary of the Later New Testament and Its Developments (DLNTD)* and *Dictionary of New Testament Background. (DNTB)* These references are found within the body of the text of articles. For example, a reference such as (*see DOTP*, Law) refers to the article on "Law" in the *Dictionary of the Old Testament: Pentateuch*.

Indexes
Since most of the *Dictionary* articles cover broad topics in some depth, the *Subject Index* is intended to assist readers in finding relevant information on narrower topics that might, for instance, appear in a standard Bible dictionary. For example, while there is no article entitled "Vanity," the subject index might direct the reader to pages where vanity is discussed in the article on "Ecclesiastes 1: Book of."

A *Scripture Index* is provided to assist readers in gaining quick access to the numerous Scripture texts referred to throughout the *Dictionary*.

An *Articles Index* found at the end of the *Dictionary* allows readers to review quickly the breadth of topics covered and select the ones most apt to serve their interests or needs. Those who wish to identify the articles written by specific contributors should consult the list of contributors, where the articles are listed under the name of each contributor.

Transliteration

Hebrew has been transliterated according to the system set out on page xii.

Abbreviations

General Abbreviations

/	parallel text
§ or §§	section or paragraph numbers
Akk	Akkadian
Aram	Aramaic
BCE	Before the Common Era
c.	circa
CE	Common Era
cf.	*confer*, compare
chap(s).	chapter(s)
contra	against
d.	died
DSS	Dead Sea Scrolls
e.g.,	*exempli gratia*, for example
esp.	especially
ET	English translation
fem	feminine
fl.	*floruit*, flourished
frg(s).	fragment(s)
Gk	Greek
Heb	Hebrew
i.e.	*id est*, that is
Lat	Latin
lit.	literally
masc.	masculine
mg.	margin
MS(S)	manuscript(s)
NT	New Testament
OT	Old Testament
pace	with all due respect to
par.	parallel text(s)
passim	in various places
pl.	plural
repr.	reprint
rev. ed.	revised edition
sg.	singular
Sum	Sumerian
Ugar	Ugaritic
v(v).	verse(s)

Texts and Translations of the Bible

BHK	*Biblia Hebraica Kittel*	*BHS*	*Biblia Hebraica Stuttgartensia*
BHQ	*Biblia Hebraica Quinta*	ESV	English Standard Version

GNB	Good News Bible	NET	New English Translation
HSCB	Holman Christian Standard Bible	NJB	New Jerusalem Bible
JB	Jerusalem Bible	NIV	New International Version
JPS	*The Holy Scriptures according to the Masoretic Text: A New Translation with the Aid of Previous Versions and with Consultation of Jewish Authorities*	NJPS	*Tanakh: The Holy Scriptures: The New JPS Translation according to the Traditional Hebrew Text*
KJV	King James Version	NKJV	New King James Version
LXX	Septuagint	NLT	New Living Translation
MT	Masoretic Text	NRSV	New Revised Standard Version
NAB	New American Bible	REB	Revised English Bible
NASB	New American Standard Bible	RSV	Revised Standard Version
NEB	New English Bible	TEV	Today's English Version
		TNIV	Today's New International Version

Books of the Bible

Old Testament	1-2 Kings	Is	Mic	Mk	1-2 Thess
Gen	1-2 Chron	Jer	Nahum	Lk	1-2 Tim
Ex	Ezra	Lam	Hab	Jn	Tit
Lev	Neh	Ezek	Zeph	Acts	Philem
Num	Esther	Dan	Hag	Rom	Heb
Deut	Job	Hos	Zech	1-2 Cor	Jas
Josh	Ps	Joel	Mal	Gal	1-2 Pet
Judg	Prov	Amos		Eph	1-2-3 Jn
Ruth	Eccles	Obad	*New Testament*	Phil	Jude
1-2 Sam	Song	Jon	Mt	Col	Rev

Ancient Near Eastern Literature

CH	Code of Hammurabi	MAL	Middle Assyrian Laws
CT	Cuneiform Texts from Babylonian	NBL	Neo-Babylonian Laws
Tablets		RS	Ras Shamra tablet (Field identification
	in the British Museum		of tablets excavated from Ras Shamra
HL	Hittite Laws		[Ugarit] are identified by RS followed
LE	Laws of Eshnunna		by number.)

Later Jewish Literature

ʾAbot	ʾAbot	*m.*	Mishnah
ʾAbot R. Nat.	ʾAbot de Rabbi Nathan	*Mak.*	*Makkot*
Add Esth	Additions to Esther	*Meg.*	*Megillah*
Ag. Ap.	*Josephus, Against Apion*	*Mek.*	*Mekilta*
Aḥiqar	*Ahiqar*	*Midr.*	*Midrash (+ biblical book)*
ʿArak.	ʿArakin	*Nid.*	*Niddah*
b.	Babylonian Talmud	*Pesiq. Rab.*	*Pesiqta Rabbati*
Bar	Baruch	*Pesiq. Rab Kah.*	*Pesiqta de Rab Kahana*
B. Bat.	*Baba Batra*	*Pesaḥ.*	*Pesahim*
B. Qam.	*Baba Qamma*	*Ps.-Phoc.*	*Pseudo-Phocylides*
Ber.	*Berakot*	*Pss. Sol.*	*Psalms of Solomon*
Beṣah	*Beṣah*	*Qidd.*	*Qiddušin*
1 En.	*1 Enoch (Ethiopic Apocalypse)*	*Rab.*	*Rabbah (+ biblical book)*
1-2 Esdr	1-2 Esdras	*Šabb.*	*Šabbat*
4 Ezra	*4 Ezra*	*Sanh.*	*Sanhedrin*
. ag.	*Hagigah*	*Sipre*	*Sipre*
Ḥul.	*Hullin*	*Sir*	*Sirach*
Jub.	*Jubilees*	*Sop.*	*Soperim*
J.W.	*Josephus, Jewish War*	*Soṭah*	*Soṭah*
Let. Aris.	*Letter of Aristeas*	*t.*	Tosefta

Taʿan.	*Taʿanit*	Wis	Wisdom of Solomon
Tg. Esth. I, II	*First or Second Targum of Esther*	*y.*	Jerusalem Talmud
Tg. Ruth	*Targum of Ruth*	*Yad.*	*Yadayim*
T. Job	*Testament of Job*	*Yebam.*	*Yebamot*
T. Levi	*Testament of Levi*		

Judean Desert Manuscripts

Qumran

1QapGen ar (1Q20)	*1QGenesis Apocryphon*
1QHᵃ	*1QHodayotᵃ*
1QIsaᵃ	*1QIsaiahᵃ*
1QpHab	*1QPesher to Habakkuk*
1QPsᵃ (1Q10)	*1QPsalmsᵃ*
1QPsᵇ (1Q11)	*1QPsalmsᵇ*
1QPsᶜ (1Q12)	*1QPsalmsᶜ*
1QS	*1QRule of the Community*
2Q18 (2QSir)	*2QBen Sira*
2QJob (2Q15)	*2QJob*
2QPs (2Q14)	*2QPsalms*
2QRuthᵃ (2Q16)	*2QRuthᵃ*
2QRuthᵇ (2Q17)	*2QRuthᵇ*
3QLam (3Q3)	*3QLamentations*
3QPs (3Q2)	*3QPsalms*
4Q380	*4QNon-Canonical Psalms A*
4Q381	*4QNon-Canonical Psalms B*
4Q411	*4QSapiential Hymn*
4Q416	*4QInstructionᵇ*
4Q417	*4QInstructionᶜ*
4Q418	*4QInstructionᵈ*
4Q426	*4QSapiential-Hymnic Work A*
4Q498	*4QHymnic or Sapiential Fragments*
4Q525	*4QBeatitudes*
4Q528	*4QHymnic or Sapiential Work B*
4QapocrJosuéᶜ? (4Q522)	*4QProphecy of Joshua*
4QapocrLam A (4Q179)	*4QApocryphal Lamentations A*
4QapocrLam B (4Q501)	*4QApocryphal Lamentations B*
4QBarki Napshiᵃ (4Q434)	*4QBless, Oh My Soulᵃ*
4QBarki Napshiᵇ (4Q435)	*4QBless, Oh My Soulᵇ*
4QBarki Napshiᶜ (4Q436)	*4QBless, Oh My Soulᶜ*
4QBarki Napshiᵈ (4Q437)	*4QBless, Oh My Soulᵈ*
4QBarki Napshiᵉ (4Q438)	*4QBless, Oh My Soulᵉ*
4QCantᵃ (4Q106)	*4QCanticlesᵃ*
4QCantᵇ (4Q107)	*4QCanticlesᵇ*
4QCantᶜ (4Q108)	*4QCanticlesᶜ*
4QIsaᵃ (4Q55)	*4QIsaiahᵃ*
4QJobᵃ (4Q99)	*4QJobᵃ*
4QJobᵇ (4Q100)	*4QJobᵇ*
4QLam (4Q111)	*4QLamentations*
4Qpaleo-Jobᶜ (4Q101)	*4QpaleoJobᶜ*
4QProvᵃ (4Q102)	*4QProverbsᵃ*
4QProvᵇ (4Q103)	*4QProverbsᵇ*
4QPs89 (4Q236)	*4QPsalm89*
4QPsᵃ (4Q83)	*4QPsalmsᵃ*
4QPsᵇ (4Q84)	*4QPsalmsᵇ*
4QPsᶜ (4Q85)	*4QPsalmsᶜ*
4QPsᵈ (4Q86)	*4QPsalmsᵈ*
4QPsᵉ (4Q87)	*4QPsalmsᵉ*
4QPsᶠ (4Q88)	*4QPsalmsᶠ*
4QPsᵍ (4Q89)	*4QPsalmsᵍ*

4QPs^h (4Q90)	*4QPsalms^h*
QPs^j (4Q91)	*4QPsalms^j*
4QPs^k (4Q92)	*4QPsalms^k*
4QPs^l (4Q93)	*4QPsalms^l*
4QPs^m (4Q94)	*4QPsalms^m*
4QPs^n (4Q95)	*4QPsalms^n*
4QPs^o (4Q96)	*4QPsalms^o*
4QPs^p (4Q97)	*4QPsalms^p*
4QPs^q (4Q98)	*4QPsalms^q*
4QPs^r (4Q98a)	*4QPsalms^r*
4QPs^s (4Q98b)	*4QPsalms^s*
4QPs^t (4Q98c)	*4QPsalms^t*
4QPs^u (4Q98d)	*4QPsalms^u*
4QQoh^a (4Q109)	*4QQohelet^a*
4QQoh^b (4Q110)	*4QQohelet^b*
4QRuth^a (4Q104)	*4QRuth^a*
4QRuth^b (4Q105)	*4QRuth^b*
4QtgJob (4Q157)	*4QTargum of Job*
5QLam^a (5Q6)	*5QLamentations^a*
5QLam^b (5Q7)	*5QLamentations^b*
5QPs (5Q5)	*5QPsalms*
6QCant (6Q6)	*6QCanticles*
6QpapPs? (6Q5)	*6QPsalm 78 (?)*
8QPs (8Q2)	*8QPsalms*
11QapocrPs (11Q11)	*11QApocryphal Psalms*
11QPs^a (11Q5)	*11QPsalms^a*
11QPs^b (11Q6)	*11QPsalms^b*
11QPs^c (11Q7)	*11QPsalms^c*
11QPs^d (11Q8)	*11QPsalms^d*
11QPs^e (11Q9)	*11QPsalms^e*
11QT^a (11Q19)	*11QTemple^a*
11QtgJob (11Q10)	*11QTargum of Job*
CD-A	*Damascus Document^a*

Masada

Mas1e	Psalm^a
Mas1f	Psalm^b

Naḥal Ḥever/Seiyal

XḤev/Se 4	Ps (= part of 5/6Ḥev 1b)

Classical and Early Christian Literature

Apos. Con.	*Apostolic Constitutions*	*Rhet.*	*Rhetorica*
1-2 Clem.	*1-2 Clement*	Athanasius	
Did.	*Didache*	*Ep. Marcell.*	*Epistula ad Marcellinum de*
Herm. *Vis.*	Shepherd of Hermas, *Vision*		*interpretatione Psalmorum*
Ign. *Eph.*	Ignatius, *To the Ephesians*	Augustine	
Ign. *Mag.*	Ignatius, *To the Magnesians*	*C. Jul. op. imp.*	*Contra secundam Juliani*
Ambrose			*responsionem imperfectum opus*
Fid.	*De fide*	*Civ.*	*De civitate Dei*
Off.	*De officiis ministrorum*	*Enarrat. Ps.*	*Enarrationes in Psalmos*
Vid.	*De viduis*	*Pat.*	*De patientia*
Aristotle		*Serm.*	*Sermones*
De an.	*De anima*	*Symb.*	*De symbolo ad catechumenos*
Hist. an.	*Historia animalium*	*Tract. Ev. Jo.*	*In Evangelium Johannis*
Metaph.	*Metaphysica*		*tractatus*
Pol.	*Politica*	*Vid.*	*De bono viduitatis*

Eusebius
    Hist. eccl.   *Historia ecclesiastica*
Gregory the Great
    Moral.   *Moralia in Iob*
Herodotus
    Hist.   *Historiae*
Irenaeus
    Haer.   *Adversus haereses*
Jerome
    Comm. Eph.   *Commentariorum in Epistulam*
                ad Ephesios libri III
    Comm. Habac.   *Commentariorum in Habacuc*
                libri II
    Comm. Matt.   *Commentariorum in Matthaeum*
                libri IV
    Epist.   *Epistulae*
    Jo. Hier.   *Adversus Joannem Hierosolymi*
                tanum liber
    Praef. Job   *Praefatio Job*
    Trac. Ps.   *Tractatus sive Homiliae in*
                Psalmos
    Vir. ill.   *De viris illustribus*
John Chrysostom
    Hom. Matt.   *Homiliae in Matthaeum*
Josephus
    Ag. Ap.   *Against Apion*
    Ant.   *Jewish Antiquities*
Justin Martyr
    Dial.   *Dialogus cum Tryphone*
Origen
    Ep. Afr.   *Epistula ad Africanum*
    Fr. Matt.   *Fragmenta ex commentaries in*
                evangelium Matthaei
    Hom. Ezech.   *Homiliae in Ezechielem*
    Or.   *De oratione*
Philo
    Abr.   *De Abrahamo*

    Cher.   *De cherubim*
    Conf.   *De confusione linguarum*
    Contempl.   *De vita contemplativa*
    Det.   *Quod deterius potiori*
                insidari soleat
    Deus   *Quod Deus sit immutabilis*
    Gig.   *De gigantibus*
    Her.   *Quis rerum divinarum heres sit*
    Leg.   *Legum allegoriae*
    Migr.   *De migratione Abrahami*
    Mos.   *De vita Mosis*
    Opif.   *De opificio mundi*
    Plant.   *De plantatione*
    Prov.   *De providential*
    QG   *Quaestiones et soltuiones in*
                Genesin
    Sobr.   *De sobrietate*
    Somn.   *De somniis*
    Spec.   *De specialibus legibus*
Plato
    Crat.   *Cratylus*
    Resp.   *Respublica*
Plutarch
    Art.   *Artaxerxes*
Quintilian
    Inst.   *Institutio oratoria*
Sextus
    Math.   *Adversus mathematicos*
Tertullian
    Adv. Jud.   *Adversus Judaeos*
    Pat.   *De patientia*

Thomas Aquinas
    Expositio   *Expositio in Job ad litteram*
Zeno
    Tract.   *Tractatus*

Periodicals, Reference Works and Serials

ABD	*Anchor Bible Dictionary*, ed. D. N. Freedman (6 vols.; New York: Doubleday, 1992)
ABL	*Assyrian and Babylonian Letters Belonging to the Kouyunjik Collections of the British Museum*, ed. R. F. Harper (14 vols.; Chicago: University of Chicago Press, 1892-1914)
ABR	*Australian Biblical Review*
ACCS	Ancient Christian Commentary on Scripture
ACEBT	Amsterdamse cahiers voor exegese van de Bijbel en zijn tradities
ADPV	Abhandlungen des deutschen Palästina-Vereins
AfO	*Archiv für Orientforschung*
AGJU	Arbeiten zur Geschichte des antiken Judentums und des Urchristentums

AJSLL	*American Journal of Semitic Languages and Literature*
ALASP	Abhandlungen zur Literatur Alt-Syrien-Palästinas und Mesopotamiens
AmUS	American University Studies
AMD	Ancient Magic and Divination
AnBib	Analecta biblica
ANEP	*The Ancient Near East in Pictures Relating to the Old Testament*, ed. J. B. Pritchard (Princeton, NJ: Princeton University Press, 1954)
ANET	*Ancient Near Eastern Texts Relating to the Old Testament*, ed. J. B. Pritchard (3rd ed.; Princeton, NJ: Princeton University Press, 1969)
ANETS	Ancient Near Eastern Texts and Studies
AnOr	Analecta orientalia
AOAT	Alter Orient und Altes Testament

AOS	American Oriental Series	BST	Bible Speaks Today
AOTC	Abingdon Old Testament Commentaries	*BT*	*The Bible Translator*
AR	*Archiv fur Religionsgeschichte*	BTAT	Beiträge zur Theologie des Alten
ASORSVS	American Schools of Oriental Research:		Testaments
	Special Volume Series	BZARB	Beihefte zur Zeitschrift für
ArBib	The Aramaic Bible		altorientalische und biblische
AS	Assyriological Studies		Rechtsgeschichte
ASB	Austin Seminary Bulletin	BZAW	Beihefte zur Zeitschrift für die
ATSAT	Arbeiten zu Text und Sprache im Alten		alttestamentliche Wissenschaft
	Testament	*CAD*	*The Assyrian Dictionary of the Oriental*
AUS	American University Studies		*Institute of the University of Chicago*, ed. E.
AUSS	*Andrews University Seminary Studies*		Reiner et al. (Chicago: Oriental Institute
BA	*Biblical Archaeologist*		of the University of Chicago, 1956-)
BASOR	*Bulletin of the American Schools of Oriental*	*CAH²*	*Cambridge Ancient History*, 2nd ed.
	Research	CahRB	Cahiers de la Revue biblique
BAW	Die Bibliothek der alten Welt	*CAT*	*The Cuneiform Alphabetic Texts from Ugarit,*
BBB	Bonner biblische Beiträge		*Ras Ibn Hani and Other Places*, ed. M.
BBC	Blackwell Bible Commentaries		Dietrich, O. Loretz and J. Sanmartín (2nd
BBR	*Bulletin for Biblical Research*		ed.; ALASP 8; Münster: Ugarit Verlag,
BBRSup	Bulletin for Biblical Research		1995)
	Supplements	CBC	Cambridge Bible Commentary
BCOTWP	Baker Commentary on the Old	*CBQ*	*Catholic Biblical Quarterly*
	Testament Wisdom and Psalms	CBQMS	Catholic Biblical Quarterly Monograph
BDB	F. Brown, S. R. Driver and C. A. Briggs, *A*		Series
	Hebrew and English Lexicon of the Old	CBR	Currents in Biblical Research
	Testament (Oxford: Oxford University	CC	Continental Commentaries
	Press, 1907)	*CCR*	*Coptic Church Review*
BE	Biblische Enzyklopädie	CCSL	Corpus Christianorum: Series latina
BEATAJ	Beiträge zur Erforschung des Alten	*CH*	*Church History*
	Testaments und des antiken Judentum	CHANE	Culture and History of the Ancient Near
BES	Brown Egyptological Studies		East
BETL	Bibliotheca ephemeridum theologicarum	*ChrLit*	*Christianity and Literature*
	lovaniensium	ConBOT	Coniectanea biblica: Old Testament
BETS	*Bulletin of the Evangelical Theological Society*		Series
BH	Bible Handbook	*ConJ*	*Concordia Journal*
BHB	Bibliotheca Hispana Biblica	COP	Cambridge Oriental Publications
BHT	Beiträge zur historischen Theologie	*COS*	*The Context of Scripture*, ed. W. W. Hallo (3
Bib	*Biblica*		vols.; Leiden: E. J. Brill, 2003)
BibInt	*Biblical Interpretation*	CRINT	Compendia rerum iudaicarum ad Novum
BibOr	Biblica et orientalia		Testamentum
BibSem	The Biblical Seminar	CSOLC	Cambridge Studies in Oral and Literate
BIS	Biblical Interpretation Series		Culture
BIW	The Bible in Its World	CSSCA	Cambridge Studies in Social and Cultural
BJRL	*Bulletin of the John Rylands University*		Anthropology
	Library of Manchester	CThM	Calwer theologische Monographien
BJS	Brown Judaic Studies	CTSRR	College Theology Society Resources in
BJSUCSD	Biblical and Judaic Studies from the		Religion
	University of California, San Diego	*CurBS*	*Currents in Research: Biblical Studies*
BKAT	Biblischer Kommentar, Altes Testament	*CurTM*	*Currents in Theology and Mission*
BLS	Bible and Literature Series	*DANE*	*Dictionary of the Ancient Near East*, ed. P.
BMes	Bibliotheca mesopotamica		Bienkowski and A. Millard (Philadelphia:
BMI	The Bible and Its Modern Interpreters		University of Pennsylvania Press, 2000)
BMW	The Bible in the Modern World	*DBI*	*Dictionary of Biblical Imagery*, ed. L. Ryken,
BN	*Biblische Notizen*		J. C. Wilhoit and T. Longman III
BO	*Bibliotheca orientalis*		(Downers Grove, IL: InterVarsity Press,
BR	*Biblical Research*		1998)
BRev	*Bible Review*	*DDD*	*Dictionary of Deities and Demons in the Bible,*
BRS	Biblical Resource Series		ed. K. van der Toorn, B. Becking and
BSac	*Bibliotheca sacra*		P. W. van der Horst (Leiden: E. J. Brill,
BSNELC	Bar-Ilan Studies in Near Eastern		1995)
	Language and Culture	*DDD²*	*Dictionary of Deities and Demons in the Bible,*

	ed. K. van der Toorn, B. Becking and P. W. van der Horst (rev. ed.; Leiden: E. J. Brill, 1999)
DJD	Discoveries in the Judaean Desert
DJG	*Dictionary of Jesus and the Gospels*, ed. J. B. Green and S. McKnight (Downers Grove, IL: InterVarsity Press, 1992)
DLNTD	*Dictionary of the Later New Testament and Its Developments*, ed. R. P. Martin and P. H. Davids (Downers Grove, IL: InterVarsity Press, 1997)
DNTB	*Dictionary of New Testament Background*, ed. C. A. Evans and S. E. Porter (Downers Grove, IL: InterVarsity Press, 2000)
DOTHB	*Dictionary of the Old Testament: Historical Books*, ed. B. T. Arnold and H. G. M. Williamson (Downers Grove, IL: InterVarsity Press, 2005)
DOTP	*Dictionary of the Old Testament: Pentateuch*, ed. T. D. Alexander and D. W. Baker (Downers Grove, IL: InterVarsity Press, 2003)
DPL	*Dictionary of Paul and His Letters*, ed. G. F. Hawthorne and R. P. Martin (Downers Grove, IL: InterVarsity Press, 1993)
DSD	*Dead Sea Discoveries*
DTIB	*Dictionary for Theological Interpretation of the Bible*, ed. K. J. Vanhoozer (Grand Rapids: Baker, 2005)
EBib	Études bibliques
ECC	Eerdmans Critical Commentary
EDSS	*The Encyclopedia of the Dead Sea Scrolls*, ed. L. H. Schiffman and J. C. VanderKam (2 vols.; Oxford: Oxford University Press)
EgT	*Église et théologie*
EH	Europäische Hochschulschriften
EHAT	Exegetisches Handbuch zum Alten Testament
EncJud	*Encyclopaedia Judaica* (16 vols.; Jerusalem: Encyclopaedia Judaica, 1972)
EstBib	*Estudios bíblicos*
ETL	*Ephemerides theologicae lovaniensis*
EuroJTh	*European Journal of Theology*
EvJ	*Evangelical Journal*
EvQ	*Evangelical Quarterly*
FAT	Forschungen zum Alten Testament
FC	Fathers of the Church
FCB	Feminist Companion to the Bible
FCI	Foundations of Contemporary Interpretation
FGH	*Die Fragmente der griechischen Historiker*, ed. F. Jacoby (Leiden: 1954-1964)
FBBS	Facet Books: Biblical Series
GAP	Guides to Apocrypha and Pseudepigrapha
GAT	Grundrisse zum Alten Testament
GBS	Guides to Biblical Scholarship
GD	Gorgias Dissertations
GKC	*Gesenius' Hebrew Grammar*, ed. E. Kautzsch, trans. A. E. Cowley (2nd ed.; Oxford: Clarendon Press, 1910)
GOTR	*Greek Orthodox Theological Review*
GPBS	Global Perspectives on Biblical Scholarship
GTS	Gettysburg Theological Studies
HALOT	*The Hebrew and Aramaic Lexicon of the Old Testament*, L. Koehler, W. Baumgartner and J. J. Stamm (4 vols.; Leiden: E. J. Brill, 1994-1999)
HAR	*Hebrew Annual Review*
HBI	History of Biblical Interpretation
HBS	Herders biblische Studien
HBT	*Horizons in Biblical Theology*
HCOT	Historical Commentary on the Old Testament
HKAT	Handkommentar zum Alten Testament
HO	Handbuch der Orientalistik
HRel	Homo religiosus
HS	*Hebrew Studies*
HSM	Harvard Semitic Monographs
HTKAT	Herders theologischer Kommentar zum Alten Testament
HTR	*Harvard Theological Review*
HTS	Harvard Theological Studies
HUCA	*Hebrew Union College Annual*
HUCASup	Hebrew Union College Annual Supplements
HvTSt	*Hervormde Teologiese Studies*
IBC	Interpretation: A Bible Commentary for Teaching and Preaching
IBT	Interpreting Biblical Texts
ICC	International Critical Commentary
IDB	*The Interpreter's Dictionary of the Bible*, ed. G. A. Buttrick (4 vols.; Nashville: Abingdon, 1962)
IDBSup	*Interpreter's Dictionary of the Bible: Supplementary Volume*, ed. K. Crim (Nashville: Abingdon, 1976)
IEJ	*Israel Exploration Journal*
IJT	*Indian Journal of Theology*
ILBS	Indiana Literary Biblical Series
Int	*Interpretation*
IRT	Issues in Religion and Theology
ISBL	Indiana Studies in Biblical Literature
ISFCJ	University of South Florida International Studies in Formative Christianity and Judaism
JAAR	*Journal of the American Academy of Religion*
JAB	*Journal for the Aramaic Bible*
JANESCU	*Journal of the Ancient Near Eastern Society of Columbia University*
JAOS	*Journal of the American Oriental Society*
JBC	*Journal of Biblical Counseling*
JBL	*Journal of Biblical Literature*
JBLMS	Journal of Biblical Literature Monograph Series
JBQ	*Jewish Bible Quarterly*
JBR	*Journal of Bible and Religion*
JBT	Jahrbuch für biblische Theologie
JCS	*Journal of Cuneiform Studies*
JE	*The Jewish Encyclopedia* (12 vols.; New York: Funk & Wagnalls, 1916)

JEA	Journal of Egyptian Archaeology	NACSBT	New American Commentary Studies in Bible and Theology
JEN	Joint Expedition with the Iraq Museum at Nuzi	NCBC	New Century Bible Commentary
JETS	*Journal of the Evangelical Theological Society*	NEA	*Near Eastern Archaeology*
JHNES	Johns Hopkins Near Eastern Studies	NIB	*The New Interpreter's Bible*, ed. L. E. Keck et al. (12 vols.; Nashville: Abingdon, 1994-2002)
JNES	*Journal of Near Eastern Studies*		
JOTT	*Journal of Translation and Textlinguistics*		
JPSBC	Jewish Publication Society Bible Commentary	NICOT	New International Commentary on the Old Testament
JQR	*Jewish Quarterly Review*	NIDBT	*New International Dictionary of Biblical Theology*, ed. T. D. Alexander and B. S. Rosner (Leicester, UK: Inter-Varsity Press; Downers Grove, IL: InterVarsity Press, 2000)
JR	*Journal of Religion*		
JRAS	*Journal of the Royal Asiatic Society*		
JRT	*Journal of Religious Thought*		
JSJ	*Journal for the Study of Judaism in the Persian, Hellenistic, and Roman Periods*		
		NIDNTT	*New International Dictionary of New Testament Theology*, ed. C. Brown (4 vols.; Grand Rapids: Zondervan, 1975-1985)
JSJSup	Supplements to the Journal for the Study of Judaism		
JSNTSup	Journal for the Study of the New Testament: Supplement Series	NIDOTTE	*New International Dictionary of Old Testament Theology and Exegesis*, ed. W. A. VanGemeren (5 vols.; Grand Rapids: Zondervan, 1997)
JSOT	*Journal for the Study of the Old Testament*		
JSOTSup	Journal for the Study of the Old Testament: Supplement Series		
		NIVAC	NIV Application Commentary
JSPSup	Journal for the Study of the Pseudepigrapha: Supplement Series	NovTSup	Novum Testamentum Supplements
		NSBT	New Studies in Biblical Theology
JSS	*Journal of Semitic Studies*	OBO	Orbis biblicus et orientalis
JTS	*Journal of Theological Studies*	OBS	Oxford Bible Series
JTSA	*Journal of Theology for Southern Africa*	OBT	Overtures to Biblical Theology
JudChr	Judaica et Christiana	OCBC	Oxford Church Bible Commentary
KAI	*Kanaanäische und aramäische Inschriften*, ed. H. Donner and W. Röllig (2nd ed.; 3 vols. in 1; Wiesbaden: Otto Harrasowitz, 1966-1969)	OEAE	*The Oxford Encyclopedia of Ancient Egypt*, ed. D. B. Redford (3 vols.; Oxford: Oxford University Press, 2001)
		OEANE	*The Oxford Encyclopedia of Archaeology in the Near East*, ed. E. M. Meyers (5 vols.; Oxford: Oxford University Press, 1997)
KTU	*Die keilalphabetischen Texte aus Ugarit*, ed. M. Dietrich, O. Loretz and J. Sanmartín (AOAT 24/1; Neukirchen-Vluyn: Neukircherner Verlag, 1976)		
		OF	*Orate Fratres*
		OLA	Orientalia lovaniensia analecta
LACTOR	London Association of Classical Teachers: Original Records	Or	*Orientalia*
		OTE	*Old Testament Essays*
LAI	Library of Ancient Israel	OTG	Old Testament Guides
LAPO	Littératures anciennes du Proche-Orient	OTL	Old Testament Library
LBS	Library of Biblical Studies	OTM	Oxford Theological Monographs
LCBI	Literary Currents in Biblical Interpretation	OTP	*Old Testament Pseudepigrapha*, ed. J. H. Charlesworth (2 vols.; Garden City: NY: Doubleday: 1983)
LCFF	Language, Culture and Female Future		
LCL	Loeb Classical Library	OTR	Old Testament Readings
LDSS	The Literature of the Dead Sea Scrolls	OTS	Old Testament Studies
LHBOTS	Library of Hebrew Bible/Old Testament Studies	OtSt	Oudtestamentische studiën
		PÄ	Probleme der Ägyptologie
LOS	London Oriental Series	PBM	Paternoster Biblical Monographs
LOT	The Literature of the Old Testament	PFES	Publications of the Finnish Exegetical Society
LT	*Literature and Theology*		
LUÅ	Lunds universitets årsskrift	PL	Patrologia Latina [= Patrologiae cursus completus: Series latina], ed. J.-P. Migne (217 vols.; Paris: 1844-1864)
MAD	Materials for the Assyrian Dictionary		
MBPS	Mellen Biblical Press Series		
MDOG	*Mitteilungen der Deutschen Orient-Gesellschaft*	PRSt	*Perspectives in Religious Studies*
		PTR	*Princeton Theological Review*
MGWJ	*Monatschrift für Geschichte und Wissenschaft Judentums*	PTSDSSP	The Princeton Theological Seminary Dead Sea Scrolls Project
MLBS	Mercer Library of Biblical Studies	RA	*Revue d'assyriologie et d'archéologie orientale*
MNTS	McMaster New Testament Studies	RB	*Revue biblique*
NAC	New American Commentary	RD	Religions and Discourse

RelSRev	*Religious Studies Review*			Ancient Near East
RevExp	*Review and Expositor*		SHR	Studies in the History of Religions
RevQ	*Revue de Qumran*			(supplement to *Numen*)
RIA	Reallexikon der Assyriologie, ed. E. Eberling		SHS	Scripture and Hermeneutics Series
	et al. (Berlin: de Gruyter, 1928-)		*SIDIC*	*Journal of the Service internationale de*
RNBC	Readings: A New Biblical Commentary			*documentation judeo-chrétienne*
RS	Ras Shamra		SJCA	Studies in Judaism and Christianity in
RSCT	Rutherford Studies in Contemporary			Antiquity
	Theology		*SJOT*	*Scandinavian Journal of the Old Testament*
RSR	*Recherches de science religieuse*		*SJT*	*Scottish Journal of Theology*
RT	*Religion and Theology*		SOTBT	Studies in Old Testament Biblical
RTP	*Revue de théologie et de philosophie*			Theology
SAA	State Archives of Assyria		SPOT	Studies on Personalities in the Old
SAIS	Studies in the Aramaic Interpretation of			Testament
	Scripture		SPRTS	Scholars Press Reprints and Translations
SANT	Studien zum Alten und Neuen			Series
	Testaments		SPSM	Studia Pohl: Series maior
SAOC	Studies in Ancient Oriental Civilization		*SR*	*Studies in Religion*
SBAW	Sitzungsberichte der bayerischen		SSN	Studia semitica neerlandica
	Akademie der Wissenschaften		SSU	Studia semitica upsaliensis
SBEC	Studies in the Bible and Early Christianity		STDJ	Studies on the Texts of the Desert of
SBET	Scottish Bulletin of Evangelical Theology			Judah
SBL	Studies in Biblical Literature		STL	Studia theologica Lundensia
SBLAB	Society of Biblical Literature Academia		StOR	Studies in Oriental Religions
	Biblica		SubBi	Subsidia biblica
SBLABS	Society of Biblical Literature Archaeology		SUSTU	Studia Universitatis S. Thomae in Urbe
	and Biblical Studies		SWBA	The Social World of Biblical Antiquity
SBLDS	Society of Biblical Literature Dissertation		*SwJT*	*Southwestern Journal of Theology*
	Series		*TA*	*Tel Aviv*
SBLEJL	Society of Biblical Literature Early		TCAAS	Transactions of the Connecticut
	Judaism and Its Literature			Academy of Arts and Sciences
SBLMS	Society of Biblical Literature Monograph		TCS	Texts from Cuneiform Sources
	Series		*TDOT*	*Theological Dictionary of the Old Testament,*
SBLSCS	Society of Biblical Literature Septuagint			ed. G. J. Botterweck and H. Ringgren
	and Cognate Series			(Grand Rapids: Eerdmans, 1974-)
SBLSP	*Society of Biblical Literature Seminar Papers*		*TE*	*Theological Education*
SBLSS	Society of Biblical Literature Semeia		*TGUOS*	*Transactions of the Glasgow University*
	Studies			*Oriental Society*
SBLSymS	Society of Biblical Literature Symposium		*THAT*	*Theologisches Handwörterbuch zum Alten*
	Studies			*Testament, ed. E. Jenni, with C. Westermann*
SBLTT	Society of Biblical Literature Texts and			*(2 vols.; Munich: Kaiser; Zürich:*
	Translations			*Theologischer Verlag, 1971-1976)*
SBLWAW	Society of Biblical Literature Writings		*Them*	*Themelios*
	from the Ancient World		ThSt	Theologische Studien
SBLWGW	Society of Biblical Literature Writings		*ThTo*	*Theology Today*
	from the Greco-Roman World		*ThWAT*	*Theologisches Wörterbuch zum Alten*
SBM	Stuttgarter biblische Monographien			*Testament, ed. G. J. Botterweck and H.*
SBS	Stuttgarter Bibelstudien			Ringgren (Stuttgart: Kohlhammer, 1970-)
SBT	Studies in Biblical Theology		*TLOT*	*Theological Lexicon of the Old Testament, ed.*
ScrCon	Scripture in Context			E. Jenni, with C. Westermann (3 vols.;
SDSSRL	Studies in the Dead Sea Scrolls and			Peabody, MA: Hendrickson, 1997)
	Related Literature		*TLZ*	*Theologische Literaturzeitung*
SEÅ	*Svensk exegetisk årsbok*		TOTC	Tyndale Old Testament Commentaries
SFCT	Series on Formative Contemporary		*TRu*	*Theologische Rundschau*
	Thinkers		*TS*	*Theological Studies*
SGKIO	Studien zur Geschichte und Kultur des		TThSt	Trierer theologische Studien
	islamischen Orients		TW	Theologische Wissenschaft
SHANE	Studies in the History of the Ancient Near		*TynBul*	*Tyndale Bulletin*
	East		UBL	Ugaritisch-biblische Literatur
SHBC	Smith & Helwys Bible Commentary		UBSMS	United Bible Societies Monograph Series
SHCANE	Studies in the History and Culture of the		UCOP	University of Cambridge Oriental

	Publications	WTJ	*Westminster Theological Journal*
UCPSP	University of California Publications in	YNER	Yale Near Eastern Researches
	Semitic Philology	YJS	Yale Judaica Series
UF	*Ugarit-Forschungen*	YOS	Yale Oriental Series, Texts
VC	*Vigiliae christianae*	ZABR	*Zeitschrift für altorientalische und biblische*
VF	*Verkündigung und Forschung*		*Rechtsgeschichte*
VT	*Vetus Testamentum*	ZAH	*Zeitschrift für Althebräistik*
VTSup	Vestus Testamentum Supplements	ZAW	*Zeitschrift für die alttestamentliche*
WBC	Word Biblical Commentary		*Wissenschaft*
WBT	Word Biblical Themes	ZBK	Zürcher Bibelkommentare
WestBC	Westminster Bible Companion	ZDMG	*Zeitschrift der deutschen morgenländischen*
WF	*Wege der Forschung*		*Gesellschaft*
WMANT	Wissenschaftliche Monographien zum	ZDPV	*Zeitschrift des deutschen Palästina-Vereins*
	Alten und Neuen Testament	ZTK	*Zeitschrift für Theologie und Kirche*

Transliteration of Hebrew

Consonants

א	=	ʾ
ב	=	b
ג	=	g
ד	=	d
ה	=	h
ו	=	w
ז	=	z
ח	=	ḥ
ט	=	ṭ
י	=	y
כ, ך	=	k
ל	=	l
מ, ם	=	m
נ, ן	=	n
ס	=	s
ע	=	ʿ
פ, ף	=	p
צ, ץ	=	ṣ
ק	=	q
ר	=	r
שׂ	=	ś
שׁ	=	š
ת	=	t

Short Vowels

_	=	a
ֵ	=	e
ִ	=	i
ָ	=	o
ֻ	=	u

Very Short Vowels

ֲ	=	ă
ֱ	=	ĕ
ְ	=	ĕ (if vocal)
ֳ	=	ŏ

Long Vowels

(ה),	=	â
ֵי	=	ê
ִי	=	î
וֹ	=	ô
וּ	=	û
ָ	=	ā
ֵ	=	ē
ֹ	=	ō

Contributors

Allen, Joel S., PhD. Adjunct Faculty at Union College, Biblical Studies Instructor at Appalachian Local Pastor's School, First United Methodist Church, Barbourville, Kentucky: **Job 3: History of Interpretation.**

Beaton, Richard, PhD. Associate Professor of New Testament, Fuller Theological Seminary, Pasadena, California: **Song of Songs 3: History of Interpretation**.

Belcher, Richard P., Jr., PhD. Professor of Old Testament, Reformed Theological Seminary, Charlotte, North Carolina: **Suffering; Thanksgiving, Psalms of.**

Block, Daniel I., DPhil. Gunther H. Knoedler Professor of Old Testament, Wheaton College, Wheaton, Illinois: **Ruth 1: Book of.**

Boda, Mark J., PhD. Professor of Old Testament, McMaster Divinity College; Professor, Faculty of Theology, McMaster University, Hamilton, Ontario, Canada: **Lamentations 1: Book of.**

Branch, Robin Gallaher, PhD. Professor, Crichton College, Memphis, Tennessee: **Women.**

Brooking, Clark H., ThM. PhD candidate, Hebrew Union College, Cincinnati, Ohio: **Ahasuerus.**

Brown, Walter E., PhD. Professor of Old Testament and Hebrew, New Orleans Baptist Theological Seminary, New Orleans, Louisiana: **Oral Poetry.**

Broyles, Craig C., PhD. Professor of Religious Studies, Trinity Western University, Langley, British Columbia, Canada: **Lament, Psalms of.**

Brueggemann, Dale A., PhD. Director, Eurasia Education Services, Springfield, Missouri: **Protection Imagery; Psalms 4: Titles.**

Bullock, C. Hassell, PhD. Franklin S. Dyrness Chair of Biblical Studies and Professor of Old Testament, Wheaton College, Wheaton, Illinois: **Ethics.**

Cook, John A., PhD. Assistant Professor of Old Testament, Asbury Theological Seminary, Wilmore, Kentucky: **Hebrew Language.**

Creach, Jerome, PhD. Robert C. Holland Professor of Old Testament, Pittsburgh Theological Seminary, Pittsburgh, Pennsylvania: **Cult, Worship: Psalms.**

Davies, John A., PhD. Principal, Presbyterian Theological Centre, Sydney, New South Wales, Australia: **Folly; Theodicy.**

Davies, Peter., BD. Senior Old Testament lecturer, Regents Theological College, Nantwich, United Kingdom: **Animal Imagery**.

deSilva, David A., PhD. Trustees' Distinguished Professor of New Testament and Greek, Ashland Theological Seminary, Ashland, Ohio: **Honor and Shame**.

Dombrowski, Justin, MA. PhD student, Classical Studies, Columbia University, New York, New York: **Esther 3: History of Interpretation.**

Edwards, Timothy M., DPhil. Lector (Biblical Hebrew), Oxford Centre for Hebrew and Jewish Studies, Oxford, United Kingdom: **Targumim.**

Enns, Peter, PhD. Professor of Old Testament and Hermeneutics, Westminster Theological Seminary, Philadelphia, Pennsylvania: **Ecclesiastes 1: Book of; Wisdom of Solomon.**

Estes, Daniel J., PhD. Distinguished Professor of Bible, Cedarville University, Cedarville, Ohio: **Wisdom and Biblical Theology.**

Fantuzzo, Christopher J., MDiv, PhD candidate, University of Gloucestershire, United Kingdom: **Acrostic.**

Ferris, Paul W., Jr., PhD. Professor of Hebrew Bible; Lead Faculty, MDiv & MA (TS) degree programs, Bethel Seminary, St. Paul, Minnesota: **Lamentations 2: Ancient Near Eastern Background.**

Firth, David G., PhD. Lecturer in Old Testament, Cliff College, Calver, Derbyshire, United Kingdom: **Ambiguity; Asaph and Sons of Korah.**

Futato, Mark D., PhD. Robert L. Maclellan Professor of Old Testament, Reformed Theological Seminary, Orlando, Florida: **Confidence, Psalms of; Hymns.**

Garrett, Duane A., PhD. John R. Sampey Professor of Old Testament Interpretation, The Southern Baptist University, Louisville, Kentucky: **Dis-**

course in Proverbs; **Proverbs 3: History of Interpretation.**

Goldingay, John, PhD. David Allan Hubbard Professor of Old Testament, Fuller Theological Seminary, Pasadena, California: **Hermeneutics.**

Grant, Jamie A., PhD. Lecturer in Biblical Studies, Highland Theological College, Dingwall, Scotland: **Editorial Criticism; Kingship Psalms; Royal Court; Wisdom and Covenant; Wisdom Poems.**

Gregory, Bradley C. PhD candidate, University of Notre Dame, Notre Dame, Indiana: **Megillot and Festivals; Purim; Wisdom and Apocalyptic.**

Hamilton, James M., PhD. Assistant Professor of Biblical Studies, Southwestern Baptist Theological Seminary's Houston Park Place Campus, Houston, Texas: **Divine Presence; Theophany.**

Hartley, John E., PhD. Distinguished Professor of Old Testament, Azusa Pacific University, Azusa, California: **Job 2: Ancient Near Eastern Background.**

Heider, George C., PhD. Associate Professor of Theology, Valparaiso University, Valparaiso, Indiana: **Marriage and Sex.**

Heim, Knut M., PhD. Lecturer in Biblical Studies, The Queen's Foundation for Ecumenical Theological Education, Birmingham, West Midlands, United Kingdom: **Wordplay.**

Heiser, Michael S., PhD. Academic Editor, Logos Bible Software, Bellingham, Washington: **Divine Council.**

Hess, Richard S., PhD. Earl S. Kalland Professor of Old Testament and Semitic Languages, Denver Seminary, Littleton, Colorado: **Floral Imagery; Scribes; Wisdom Sources.**

Hildebrandt, Ted A., ThD. Full Professor of Biblical Studies, Gordon College, Wenham, Massachusetts: **Proverb, Genre of.**

Hubbard, Robert L., Jr., PhD. Professor of Biblical Literature, North Park Theological Seminary, Chicago, Illinois: **Kinsman Redeemer and Levirate.**

Irwin, Brian P., PhD. Assistant Professor of Old Testament/Hebrew Scriptures, Knox College, Toronto School of Theology, Toronto, Ontario, Canada: **Ruth 3: History of Interpretation.**

Jackson, David R., PhD. Head of Biblical Studies, William Carey Christian School (and Honorary Associate, Macquarie University), Sydney, New South Wales, Australia: **Solomon.**

Jobes, Karen H., PhD. Gerald F. Hawthorne Professor of New Testament Greek and Exegesis, Wheaton College, Wheaton, Illinois: **Esther 1: Book of; Esther 2: Extrabiblical Background; Esther 4: Additions; Esther 5: Greek Versions.**

Johnston, Philip S., PhD. Tutor in Old Testament and Hebrew, Wycliffe Hall, Oxford, United Kingdom: **Afterlife.**

Kelle, Brad E., PhD. Associate Professor of Old Testament and Hebrew, Point Loma Nazarene University, San Diego, California: **Warfare Imagery.**

Kim, Koowon. PhD candidate, University of Chicago, Chicago, Illinois: **Lemuel and Agur.**

Kitchen, Kenneth A., PhD. Personal and Brunner Professor Emeritus of Egyptology, University of Liverpool, Liverpool, United Kingdom: **Maat; Proverbs 2: Ancient Near Eastern Background.**

Klingbeil, Gerald A., DLitt. Dean of the Theological Seminary, Professor of Hebrew Bible and Ancient Near Eastern Studies, Theological Seminary, Adventist International Institute of Advanced Studies, Silang, Cavite, Philippines: **Ecclesiastes 2: Ancient Near Eastern Background; Wisdom and History.**

Klingbeil, Martin G., DLitt. Professor of Old Testament and Ancient Near Eastern Studies and Vice-President: Academic Administration, Helderberg College, Somerset West, Western Cape, South Africa: **Psalms 5: Iconography.**

Klouda, Sheri L., PhD. Assistant Professor of Biblical Studies, Taylor University, Upland, Indiana: **Zion.**

Koptak, Paul E., PhD. Paul and Bernice Brandel Professor of Communication and Biblical Interpretation, North Park Theological Seminary, Chicago, Illinois: **Intertextuality; Personification.**

Kwakkel, Gert, PhD. Professor of Old Testament, Theologische Universiteit van de Gereformeerde Kerken in Nederland (vrijgemaakt), Kampen, The Netherlands: **Righteousness.**

LeMon, Joel M., PhD. Assistant Professor of Old Testament/Hebrew Bible, Candler School of Theology, Emory University, Atlanta, Georgia: **Parallelism.**

Long, Gary A., PhD. Professor of Hebrew Bible and Ancient Near Eastern Studies, Bethel University, St. Paul, Minnesota: **Song of Songs 2: Ancient Near Eastern Background.**

Longman, Tremper, III, PhD. Robert H. Gundry Professor of Biblical Studies, Westmont College, Santa Barbara, California: **Disputation; Ecclesiastes 3: History of Interpretation; Fear of the Lord; Inclusio; Job 4: Person; Merism; Messiah; Proverbs 1: Book of; Psalms 2: Ancient Near Eastern Background; Refrain; Sound Patterns; Stanza, Strophe; Terseness; Woman Wisdom and Woman Folly.**

Lucas, Ernest C., PhD. Vice-Principal and Tutor in Biblical Studies, Bristol Baptist College, Bristol, England: **Poetics, Terminology of; Wisdom Theology.**

Mabie, Frederick J., PhD. Associate Professor of Hebrew and Old Testament Studies, Multnomah Biblical Seminary, Portland, Oregon: **Chaos and Death; Destruction.**

Magdalene, F. Rachel, JD, PhD. Assistant Professor of Old Testament, Augustana College, Rock Island, IL: **Law.**

Matthews, Victor H., PhD. Professor of Religious Studies and Associate Dean of the College of Humanities and Public Affairs, Missouri State University, Springfield, Missouri: **Social-Scientific Approaches.**

McConnell, Walter L., III, PhD. Previously Lecturer in Old Testament and Hebrew, Singapore Bible College, Singapore: **Meter; Worship.**

McKnight, Scot, PhD. Karl A. Olsson Professor in Religious Studies, North Park University, Chicago, Illinois: **Salvation and Deliverance, Images of.**

Meier, Samuel A., PhD. Associate Professor of Hebrew, Ohio State University, Columbus, Ohio: **Imprisonment Imagery.**

Millard, Alan R., M.Phil. Emeritus Rankin Professor of Hebrew and Ancient Semitic Languages, The University of Liverpool, Liverpool, England: **Sages, Schools, Education.**

Miller, Cynthia L., PhD. Professor, University of Wisconsin, Madison, Wisconsin: **Ellipsis.**

Moore, Erika, PhD. Assistant Professor of Old Testament and Hebrew, Trinity Episcopal School for Ministry, Ambridge, Pennsylvania: **Ruth 2: Ancient Near Eastern Background.**

O'Dowd, Ryan, PhD. Assistant Professor of Old Testament, Briercrest College and Seminary, Ca-

ronport, Saskatchewan, Canada: **Creation Imagery; Frame Narrative.**

Oswalt, John N., PhD. Research Professor of Old Testament, Wesley Biblical Seminary, Jackson, Mississippi: **God.**

Overland, Paul B., PhD. Assistant Professor of Old Testament and Semitic Languages, Ashland Theological Seminary, Ashland, Ohio: **Chiasm; Rhetorical Criticism.**

Perdue, Leo G., PhD. Professor of Hebrew Bible, Brite Divinity School, Texas Christian University, Fort Worth, Texas: **Cult, Worship: Wisdom.**

Phillips, Elaine A., PhD. Professor of Biblical and Theological Studies, Gordon College, Wenham, Massachusetts: **Esther 6: Person; Mordecai; Novella, Story, Narrative.**

Phua, Leong Cheng Michael, PhD. Lecturer, Singapore Bible College: **Architectural Imagery; Sirach, Book of.**

Pickut, William, MA. PhD student, The University of Chicago, Chicago, Illinois: **Lamentations 3: History of Interpretation.**

Pitkänen, Pekka, PhD. Course Leader and Lecturer, Open Theological College, School of Humanities, University of Gloucestershire, Cheltenham, Gloucestershire, United Kingdom: **Historical Criticism.**

Pokrifka, Junia, PhD. Associate Professor of Biblical Studies, School of Theology, Azusa Pacific University, Azusa, California: **Life, Imagery of.**

Pokrifka, Todd, PhD. Lecturer in Theology, School of Theology, Azusa Pacific University, Azusa, California: **Time.**

Rankin, Jeffrey J., PhD. Assistant professor, College of Christian Studies, North Greenville University, Tigerville, South Carolina: **Oral Poetry.**

Rata, Tiberius, PhD., Professor of Old Testament Studies, Grace Theological Seminary, Winona Lake, Indiana: **David.**

Schifferdecker, Kathryn M., ThD. Assistant Professor of Old Testament, Luther Seminary, St. Paul, Minnesota: **Creation Theology.**

Schwab, George M., PhD. Professor of Old Testament, Erskine Theological Seminary, Due West, South Carolina: **Song of Songs 1: Book of; Wasf.**

Seevers, Boyd, PhD. Professor of Old Testament Studies, Northwestern College, St. Paul, Minnesota: **Remembrance.**

Shields, Martin A., PhD. Sydney, Australia: **Autobi-**

ography; Qohelet; Wisdom and Prophecy.

Stallman, Robert C., PhD. Professor of Bible & Hebrew Northwest University, Kirkland, Washington: **Music, Song.**

Strawn, Brent A., PhD. Associate Professor of Old Testament, Candler School of Theology/Emory University, Atlanta, Georgia: **Imagery; Imprecation; Lyric Poetry; Parallelism.**

Swanson, Dwight D., PhD. Senior Lecturer in Biblical Studies, Nazarene Theological College, Manchester, England: **Dead Sea Scrolls.**

Sweeney, Marvin A., PhD. Professor of Hebrew Bible, Claremont School of Theology, and Professor of Religion, Claremont Graduate University, Claremont, California: **Form Criticism.**

Tiemeyer, Lena-Sofia, D.Phil. Lecturer in Old Testament and Hebrew Language, University of Aberdeen, Aberdeen, Scotland, United Kingdom: **Feminist Interpretation.**

Tucker, W. Dennis, Jr., PhD. Associate Professor of Christian Scriptures and Associate Dean for Academic Affairs, George W. Truett Theological Seminary, Baylor University, Waco, Texas: **Psalms 1: Book of.**

Ulrich, Dean R., PhD. Baden, Pennsylvania: **Boaz; Naomi; Ruth 4: Person.**

VanGemeren, Willem A., PhD. Professor of Old Testament and Semitic Languages, Director of the PhD in Theological Studies, Trinity Evangelical Divinity School, Deerfield, Illinois: **Mountain Imagery.**

Wahlen, Clinton L., PhD. Professor of New Testament and Associate Director, Biblical Research Insitute, General Conference of Seventh-day Adventists, Silver Spring, Maryland: **Wisdom, Greek.**

Walton, John H., PhD. Professor of Old Testament, Wheaton College, Wheaton, Illinois: **Job 1: Book of; Retribution; Satan.**

Wegner, Paul D., PhD. Professor of Old Testament, Phoenix Seminary, Phoenix, Arizona: **Text, Textual Criticism.**

Wells, Bruce, PhD. Assistant professor of Hebrew Bible, St. Joseph's University, Philadelphia, Pennsylvania: **Law.**

Williamson, Paul R., PhD. Lecturer in Old Testament, Moore College, Newtown, New South Wales, Australia: **Canon.**

Wray Beal, Lissa M., PhD. Associate Professor of Old Testament, Providence Theological Seminary, Otterburne, Manitoba, Canada: **Psalms 3: History of Interpretation.**

Yamauchi, Edwin M., PhD. Professor of History Emeritus, Miami University, Oxford, Ohio: **Susa; Vashti.**

ACCUSER. *See* SATAN.

ANTHROPOLOGY. *See* WISDOM THEOLOGY.

ACROSTIC

Acrostic is the term commonly applied to a composition in verse in which the initial letters of successive lines or stanzas are intentionally chosen either to outline a deliberate message (e.g., "Jesus Christ, God's Son, Savior" [*ichthys,* "fish"] in *Sib. Or.* 8:218-250) or to observe a traditional downward sequence of letters of the alphabet (e.g., from *ʾālep* to *tāw* in Ps 145). *Acrostic* can also specify the design itself, an artistic technique employed by biblical writers in poems of various genres. As a technique, it demonstrates that biblical Hebrew poetry has its disciplines, accenting the perennial tension in religious expression between freedom and constraint; although *parallelism may be biblical poetry's chief characteristic, in poems that follow this design, acrostic is the chief constraint. Nevertheless, most will agree with Muilenburg (103): "What is notable about this ancient poetry is that such an artificial contrivance does not stand in the way of producing literature of a high order, in which the emotions find full expression and the language bodies forth the intensity and passion of the poet."

Acrostic is both a creative technique of biblical Hebrew poetry and the broad label for a limited number of carefully crafted canonical poems that, in a variety of ways, effectively employ this technique. The acrostic technique provides a precise design for the poet, facilitating a recital of verse capable of captivating the audience and enabling the listener to follow the movement of the poem from beginning to end. In compositions such as Psalm 119 and Lamentations 3 the listener detects the acrostic pattern effortlessly—a definite appeal is made to the ear. But an acrostic composition, which presupposes not only the invention of the Hebrew *alef-bet* but also a literate milieu, was intended for appreciation in written form, whereby appeal is made to the eye.

1. The Hebrew *Alef-Bet*
2. Types and Canonical Examples
3. Function

1. The Hebrew *Alef-Bet*.
Several suggestions have been offered to account for the derivation of this technique. One straightforward explanation is that the form arose indigenously in the literate milieu set off by the alphabetic revolution as creative writers developed techniques consistent with their own form of writing.

Mesopotamian cuneiform and Egyptian hieroglyphics antedate the simplification and reduction of graphemes that took place with the introduction of Semitic alphabets (the earliest nonalphabetic examples are message acrostics; the parade example is The Babylonian Theodicy [*COS* 1.154:492-95]). From writing systems of hundreds of signs, the alphabetic revolution produced systems of less than thirty consonantal signs, easily memorized in a basic order. The Semitic alphabets originated with Proto-Canaanite (eighteenth-seventeenth centuries BC) and continued with Phoenician writing. From the Phoenician system, the Paleo-Hebrew script (c. 800 BC) was developed. Even though the Hebrew language did not adopt the familiar Aramaic script until after the Babylonian exile, the basic Northwest Semitic order is already found in Ugaritic cuneiform (fourteenth century BC).

This revolution affected all aspects of society, affording new opportunities for literary expression in three areas highlighted by A. Demsky

(364): (1) the organization of information and the placing of objects in their proper alphabetic (or numerical) order; (2) the expression of the mysterious and magical or a reference to the divine (cf. Rev 1:8; 22:13); (3) aesthetics as expressed in writing alphabetic acrostic poetry.

Consequently, the earlier view that biblical acrostic technique was imported from the Hellenistic environment no longer prevails. The Greek alphabetic writing system itself developed from the Phoenician system, and in the absence of extensive evidence in Phoenician poetry, it cannot be supposed that alphabetic acrostics came to the Greeks from the Phoenicians (Craigie, 130). Alphabetic acrostic poetry probably developed indigenously in the literatures of both languages. Furthermore, the discoveries of Ugaritic alphabet texts (*KTU* 7.5) and beginner's exercise tablets in Proto-Canaanite script demonstrate that the alphabet was thought of abstractly; that is, scribes familiar with the alphabet taught a basic order of letters to their pupils, leading to the literate milieu in which alphabetic acrostic poetry was composed. That this state of affairs existed in ancient Hebrew society suggests that an early indigenous development provides the broad context within which to appreciate the design and function of canonical acrostic poetry.

2. Types and Canonical Examples.
Canonical examples of alphabetic sequence acrostics are found throughout the OT; there are none in the NT. The canonical examples include Psalms 9; 10; 25; 34; 37; 111; 112; 119; 145; Proverbs 31:10-31; Lamentations 1—4 (cf. 11QPs[a] 21-22, which shows that Sir 51:13-30 [Heb] is an alphabetic acrostic poem; Nah 1:2-8 will not be discussed in this volume). Though limited in number, significant dissimilarities between the canonical acrostics display the considerable versatility of the biblical writers.

2.1. Complete Alphabetic.
2.1.1. One Letter per Line. Psalm 145 is a *hymn of praise to God the king (cf. Ps 111). Apart from a missing *nûn* line, the complete *alef-bet* appears in successive bicola. Without inserting the *nûn* line, forty-four cola (including the final monocolon) make up the poem, suggesting that the omission was intentional. Most manuscripts of the MT do not have it, but one Hebrew manuscript, supported by the LXX, Syriac and 11QPs[a], does offer a *nûn* line nearly identical to

the *ṣādê (ṣdq)* line, except that it begins with *n'mn* ("[The LORD] is faithful," Niphal of *'mn* [cf. Ps 145:17 MT]). This justifies its classification as a complete alphabetic acrostic.

Proverbs 31:10-31, praising the noble wife, is part of the "Sayings of *Lemuel" (Prov 31:1-31). Although renowned for its complete acrostic structure, it is also noteworthy for its arrangement in two halves (Prov 31:10-20 [*'ālep-kāp*]) with thirty-six bicola, two tricola (Prov. 31:15 [*wāw*]; Prov 31:30 [*śîn*]) and a chiastic quatrain (Prov. 31:19-20 [*yôd-kāp*]).

2.1.2. One Letter per Half-line. Psalm 111 is a hymn of *thanksgiving; Psalm 112, a wisdom psalm, is closely modeled after it, elaborating specifically on Psalm 111:10. Vocabulary and expressions are borrowed from it to depict the blessings enjoyed by the one who fears the Lord. Both psalms begin with *halĕlû yāh*, followed by cola each beginning with a new letter of the *alef-bet*. Parallelism of bicola and tricola, *chiasmus, *inclusio and word pairs contribute to the skillful composition.

2.1.3. Stanzaic. Psalm 37 is a *wisdom poem. The alphabetic sequence is followed, but a new acrostic letter begins only the first line of each stanza. The basic unit has two bicola, but *ḥêt* has six (three bicola [Ps 37:14-15]) and *nûn* has five (two lines [Ps 37:25-26]). The sequence is obscured slightly by a preposition at *'ayin* (*lĕ'ôlām* [Ps 37:28b]) and a conjunction at *tāw* (*ûtĕšû'at* [Ps 37:39]).

Psalm 119, a massive didactic wisdom poem, is a repeating stanzaic acrostic. Each of the twenty-two consonants of the *alef-bet* is represented eight times at line-initial position, forming eight-line stanzas. The number of lines corresponds to eight synonyms, distributed throughout the poem, which exalt Torah (cf. Pss 1; 19; 42): *tôrâ* ("Torah" [25x]), *dābār* ("word" [24x]), *mišpāṭîm* ("rulings" [23x]), *'ēdût* ("laws" [23x]), *miṣwâ* ("commandment" [22x]), *ḥuqîm* ("statutes" [21x]), *piqqûdîm* ("charges" [21x]) and *'imrâ* ("sayings" [19x]). These synonyms are distributed throughout 176 lines (with eighteen tricola); in six stanzas all eight terms occur together, and no one stanza contains less than six.

In gravity and literary quality, nothing compares to the artistic achievement of *Lamentations (as a whole, it is larger than Ps 119). Chapters 1 and 2 are stanzaic acrostics; the initial word of each stanza begins with an acrostic letter from *ʾālep* to *tāw* (cf. Ps 37). There are three bicola per stanza, except for *zayin* (chap. 1), a quatrain. Chapter 4 displays the same acrostic pattern, only this time each stanza consists of two bicola. Chapter 3 is the unique central section. Now the initial acrostic consonant appears at the beginning of each line. This intensification in the design of chapter 3 indicates the high point of the book (cf. Lam 3:22-24 MT *[ḥêt]*), fading again in chapter 4 and disappearing entirely in chapter 5 (nonalphabetic). Exploring external parallelism between the five distinct poems, J. Renkema (379) suggests that by the external parallelism of their language and content, identical letter stanzas form song responses enabling the reader to visualize the parallel (responsive) design of the whole.

2.2. Incomplete Alphabetic. Two individual psalms "of David," Psalm 25 (a *lament) and Psalm 34 (a hymn of thanksgiving), unique omit the *wāw* line and, in addition to the *pê* line within the poem, include a second *pê* line after *tāw*. Thus, a total of twenty-two lines is maintained, and each psalm expresses a concluding concern for corporate redemption *(pādâ)*. What is more, this convention makes *lāmed* the middle letter; hence, *ʾālep-lāmed-pê*—the three consonants in the name of the first letter of the *alef-bet*—are found at the beginning, middle and end of the series. The resulting verbal root means "learn" (cf. Prov 22:25 MT). The reader is hereby exhorted to learn the insights that the psalmist passed on (cf. Ps 51:15 MT).

Considered conjointly, Psalms 9 and 10 are individual laments that form an uneven, partially obscured acrostic from *ʾālep* to *tāw*. Psalm 9 ends with *kāp;* however, *dālet* is missing (Ps 9:7 MT). Psalm 10 is less complete, containing a broken sequence from *lāmed* to *tāw: mêm, nûn* and *sāmek* are missing (Ps 10:2-6 MT), as is *ṣādê* (Ps 10:10 MT). Noting the interrelation of the themes, commentators suggest an interpretation on two levels: (1) the level of the initial texts; (2) the unity. There is precedent in a few Hebrew manuscripts and the LXX, which treat them as a literary unity.

2.3. Irregularities of Alphabetic Arrangement. Psalms 9—10 share an irregularity with Lamentations 2—4: *pê* comes before *ʿayin*. In 1962 N. K. Gottwald (24) labeled this "a curious and unexpected disturbance of alphabetic order." Although the evidence weighed against this transposed *pê-ʿayin* order, he prudently refrained from dismissing it as sloppy editing. Instead, he suggested that the thrice-occurring order was the "normal" order; the *ʿayin-pê* order of chapter 1 was the more likely scribal slip. Evidence arrived in 1977 with the discovery of the Izbet Sartah ostracon (c. 1200 BC), a beginner's exercise tablet in Proto-Canaanite script containing an alphabet of twenty-two letters with *ʿay in* and *pê* transposed. Triple abecedaries in Hebrew script from Kuntillet Ajrud (early eighth century BC) provided corroborating evidence. That these are no child's error becomes evident when one considers the biblical acrostics. The *pê-ʿayin* order, then, represents a secondary Israelite scribal tradition of ordering the letters.

2.4. Nonalphabetic Acrostics. In a nonalphabetic acrostic the number of lines matches the number of consonants in the alphabet. Such poems of twenty-two lines do not appear coincidental; rather, they suggest that the alphabetic sequence offered a suitable design numerically as well as linguistically. This has been demonstrated by D. N. Freedman, whose methodology for counting syllables and stress indicates that the range of deviation and abnormality perceived in the canonical examples of biblical acrostic was a deliberate or intended element. Moreover, nonalphabetic acrostics indicate that poets increasingly sought freedom from the constraint of the alphabet by deliberately designing poems with a total number of syllables equal to the total number of lines in half-line, one-line and double-line alphabetic acrostics. The following poems build on this basic foundation of twenty-two lines: Psalms 33; 38; 94; 103; Proverbs 2; 5; 8:1-11, 12-21, 22-31, 32-35; 9:1-18; Lamentations 5.

3. Function.

Following Freedman, we see that the acrostic technique is a poetic constraint analogous to the familiar forms of English versification (couplets, quatrains, stanzas, sonnet, villanelle and sestina). Like these basic forms, the acrostic form provides the poet with a robust design suited to engage an audience attentive to the grouping and spacing of sounds. By means of technique, eye and ear are "charmed by the familiar, yet aroused and captivated by the unexpected" (Watson, 33). Yet acrostic is not merely ornamental; it is part of the communicative process. Put another way, what a poem says is the result of *how* it is said.

The following suggestions have been offered to explain the function of acrostic technique.

3.1. Magic. In his study of Lamentations, Gottwald (25) assessed this explanation sensibly: "By studying the magical ideas associated with language we may undoubtedly learn something about the origin of the alphabet and the acrostic, but any direct transfer to Lamentations is doubtful." Indeed, there is no evidence that any of the biblical acrostics have a magical or occult purpose.

3.2. Pedagogy. The aforementioned poems share a didactic quality; alphabetic acrostics certainly were in use as didactic method, and they are closely associated with the wisdom tradition (cf. Prov 31:10-31; Sir 51:13-30). But the function of each poem must be understood on its own terms. To view Lamentations, for instance, as a device for practice in writing and the imitation of literary technique may miss the point, given the occasion and solemnity of its message. Besides, the more complex canonical acrostics suggest that they did not share the basic function of, say, *The New England Primer,* commended "for the more easy attaining the true reading of English."

3.3. Mnemonic Aid. The mnemonic view also suggests that acrostics had a practical purpose. Again, the complex features of the canonical acrostics militate against it. Incompleteness (missing letters), alternate ordering, irregular patterning, intricacies of style (e.g., the ʾālep-lāmed-pê pattern in Pss 25; 34) and even the sheer length of poems (e.g., Ps 119; Lam 1—5) point in a different direction.

3.4. Display of Skill. Once this design is chosen, poets are forced to use their skill in a special way. Thus, the interplay between structural constraint and creative expression may account for most of the deviations from the standard sequence. The technique displays the poet's prowess; yet, this explanation too fails to explain why acrostic was chosen as a design for communication.

3.5. Completeness. Perhaps the most acceptable view is the one derived from that of Gottwald (28): "If the subject is to be exhausted, the alphabet alone can suffice to suggest and symbolize the totality striven after." This solution, along with display of skill (see 3.4 above), best accounts for the biblical usage. An acrostic is complete, "from A to Z"; yet, an acrostic limits, providing closure, assuring the reader that enough has been said. Incapable of being comprehensive, the poet, by this design, can effectively express the incomprehensible. Religious expression calls for liberty *with* discipline.

What is more, the alphabet belongs to a people, and language is an important aspect of a people's identity. The alphabetic acrostic is the perfect form for expressing corporate praise and lament *coram Deo.* Its semantic import is corporate yet individual, cultural yet theological. F. W. Dobbs-Allsopp (18) writes, "The poet has chosen language as his means of consolation and there is no better symbol of the power and potential of language than the alphabetic acrostic, modeled most likely on the simple abecedaries that were a commonplace in scribal schools. The alphabet stands, as well, as the paradigm symbol of culture and civilization in the ancient Near East, and thus its prominence in these poems profoundly reasserts the values of civilization and culture even in the face of utterly devastating and dehumanizing suffering."

This attractive explanation of the acrostics of Lamentations can be extended profitably to other canonical examples.

See also HEBREW LANGUAGE; LAMENTATIONS 1: BOOK OF; LYRIC POETRY; POETICS, TERMINOLOGY OF; PROVERBS 1: BOOK OF; PSALMS 1: BOOK OF.

BIBLIOGRAPHY. **J. F. Brug,** "Biblical Acrostics and Their Relationship to Other Ancient Near Eastern Acrostics," in *The Bible in the Light of Cuneiform Literature: Scripture in Context III,* ed. W. W. Hallo, B. W. Jones, and G. L. Mattingly (ANETS 8; Lewiston, NY: Edwin Mellen, 1990) 283-304; **A. R. Ceresko,** "The ABCs of Wisdom in Psalm XXXIV," *VT* 35 (1985) 99-104; **P. C. Craigie,** *Psalms 1-50* (WBC 19; Waco, TX: Word, 1983); **A. Demsky,** "Abecedaries," *COS* 1.107:362-65; **F. W. Dobbs-Allsopp,** *Lamentations* (IBC; Louisville: John Knox, 2002); **D. N. Freedman,** "Non-acrostic Alphabetic Psalms," in *The Book of Psalms: Composition and Reception,* ed. P. W. Flint and P. D. Miller (VTSup 99; Leiden: E. J. Brill, 2005) 87-96; **N. K. Gottwald,** *Studies in the Book of Lamentations* (rev. ed.; SBT 14; London: SCM, 1962); **J. Muilenburg,** "A Study in Hebrew Rhetoric: Repetition and Style," in *Congress Volume: Copenhagen, 1953* (VTSup 1; Leiden: E. J. Brill, 1953) 97-111; **J. Renkema,** "The Meaning of the Parallel Acrostics in Lamentations," *VT* 45 (1995) 379-83; **W. Soll,** "Acrostic," *ABD* 1:58-60; **W. G. E. Watson,** *Classical Hebrew Poetry: A Guide to Its Techniques* (repr., London: T & T Clark International, 2004 [1986]). C. J. Fantuzzo

ADDITIONS TO ESTHER. *See* ESTHER 4: ADDITIONS.

AFTERLIFE

The OT books of wisdom, poetry and writings largely reflect the standard Israelite perspective that there is no meaningful existence beyond death. However, a few texts may indicate an emerging hope in some form of continued communion with God, which later developed into a belief in afterlife.

    1. Traditional View of Death
    2. Alternative Views of Afterlife?

1. Traditional View of Death.

For most of the OT, death leads to a shadowy, insubstantial existence in the underworld, called Sheol. There, all are reduced to somnolent inactivity, with no prospect of improvement or escape (Job 3:17-20; 7:9; 17:16 [despite Job's hypothetical wish in Job 14:13]). In particular, the underworld's denizens are cut off from Yahweh and can no longer offer praise or petition: "In death there is no memory of you; in Sheol who will praise you?" (Ps 6:5 [cf. Ps 88:5]). Thus persistence in Sheol is closer to "non-life" than afterlife (so Murphy, 102).

Many psalms assert that this life is the only forum for relationship with Yahweh. Psalm 116:15 boldly asserts that the rupture caused by death even affects Yahweh himself. However, a few texts imply that the underworld is not hidden from Yahweh (Job 26:6; Ps 139:8). Although these do not posit any meaningful contact with the dead, they may hint at alternative views, albeit faintly.

Poetry in psalms and wisdom is by nature evocative and elusive, and their references to death reveal as much about its emotional impact as its conceptualization. Death is portrayed variously—for example, as an enemy that ensnares its prey (Ps 18:6; 116:3) and an insatiable devourer of humans (Prov 1:20; 27:20). The laments often portray the psalmists' anguish when faced with death and are somewhat circumspect in naming Sheol directly, whereas the *thanksgiving psalms convey the joy of deliverance from a no longer threatening underworld.

2. Alternative Views of Afterlife?

Alternative views of destiny after death emerge in other, nonpoetic texts (notably, resurrection in Is 26:19; Dan 12:2). The emergence of these views is often dated well into the postexilic period for many reasons, including the possible influence of Persian dualism and the development of apocalyptic. Even if these views emerged earlier, they had little discernible influence on the postexilic prophetic and historical material.

A few poetic texts discussed below may also point toward alternative views, though scholars assess this variously. First, some argue that all or nearly all of these texts convey the traditional view, and that afterlife interpretations are posterior readings, sometimes discernible in early textual transmission (J. Goldingay on the Psalms [rightly critiquing M. Dahood's speculative approach] and R. E. Murphy on wisdom). Many others accept that at least some of the texts suggest a more positive prospect and must therefore be dated relatively late, in line with other such material. A third approach allows for the positive perspective without necessarily dating the texts late, since theological development is neither linear nor uniform. In any case, much of the poetic literature is very difficult to date accurately. P. S. Johnston, J. D. Levenson and others see a positive perspective in some of theses texts.

2.1. Psalms. A few psalms may suggest some form of positive afterlife, and three in particular are frequently mentioned. Psalm 16 concludes forcefully: "For you will not abandon my life to Sheol. . . . You will show me the path of life . . . at your right hand pleasures endlessly *[neṣaḥ]*" (Ps 16:10-11). Given the psalmist's initial vulnerability, isolation and apparent opponents (vv. 1, 2, 4), this ending could be his defiant affirmation of divine preservation and of blessing in a prolonged earthly life. This would concord with the typical OT perspective, but the psalm may well move beyond it. Its predominantly confident mood might imply that avoiding Sheol is not just escaping immanent danger but is somehow avoiding permanent separation from Yahweh, and that the path of life somehow leads beyond it to continued enjoyment of God. If so, this experience is tantalizingly vague, without name, spatial location or any other details. But present confidence in and communion with God may lead to extended, if imprecise, hope.

Psalm 49 is a wisdom reflection on the themes of piety, riches and death. It ponders the age-old question of the faithful suffering oppression from rich persecutors and offers two responses. The first, in vv. 7-9 (whatever the reading of v. 7a), is that human wealth is powerless to prolong life and to ransom people from the pit, or underworld. This is then developed in vv. 10-14, which underline that these foolish rich end up in Sheol (again, regardless of the exact interpretation of the difficult v. 14). The psalmist's second response, in v. 15, is more succinct and more startling. God will ransom him from Sheol and will receive him. This presents a clear contrast between those whom riches cannot ransom from Sheol and the writer, whom God will ransom. Again, this could assume ransom from immediate, untimely death without asserting anything further. But that is neither stated nor even implied, and the psalm's reflective nature, the contrasting fates and the end of v. 15 together suggest a long-term alternative, however imprecise.

Psalm 73 is another wisdom psalm on the same theme. Here, a sanctuary experience brings insight into the total destruction of the arrogant wicked and the preservation of the upright. However, this contrast is less clearly associated with the psalmist's ultimate fate than in Psalm 49, and the psalm concludes (vv. 27-28) by juxtaposing the end of the godless with the continued present life of the godly. This probably sets the context for interpreting vv. 23-26, which affirm that he is guided continually, will be received "afterward" (*ʾaḥar*) with "honor" (*kābôd*) and despite human weakness will know God's strengthening "for the future" (*lěʿôlām*). All these terms could fit into a this-life perspective; however, their open-endedness could also reflect a nascent hope in some form of survival beyond death and certainly enabled such rereading in later times.

A few psalms contain references to some form of divine record of names, notably "the book of the living" (Ps 69:28; cf. Ex 32:32-33; Is 4:3; Dan 12:2; Mal 3:16). Other books seem to record events (Ps 40:7; 56:8; 139:16; cf. Dan 7:10; 10:21). Some scholars trace the Israelite idea to Babylonian "tablets of destiny" or Persian registers, but the latter are religious and administrative parallels rather than necessary antecedents. The concept of divine records was developed in later Jewish literature and the NT, especially Revelation, in reference to postmortem judgment. Although some interpreters assume a similar understanding in the OT texts, neither their immediate contexts nor wider Israelite beliefs would support this. Given the importance of this life, and the further statements about the wicked

in Psalm 69, its author desires their early death. Other references to divine records can be interpreted similarly. So although the concept lends itself to afterlife reinterpretation, this probably is not its intent in the psalms.

2.2. Job. The book of Job has several references to a spirit world separate from the physical world. The opening chapters present a heavenly court (*see* Divine Council) with Yahweh, "the sons of God" and "the *satan" (Job 1:6-7; 2:1). Job's so-called friends share this worldview, with Eliphaz doubting help for him from "the holy ones" (Job 5:1) and Elihu envisaging a mediating angel who can deliver humans from the pit (Job 33:23-28). Job himself longs for an umpire (*môkîaḥ* [Job 9:33]) who could force God to listen, and believes in a heavenly witness (*ʿēd* [Job 16:19]) who will vouch for him. In this general context, the famous passage of Job 19:25-27 could refer to vindication in the nonmaterial world, and several of its terms could indicate a postmortem experience. In this case, Job has moved beyond traditional views on death to a new perspective.

However, the overall context suggests otherwise. Job still continues his legal argument after chapter 19: he wants to find God, present his case, be acquitted, be tested and emerge like gold (Job 23:3-10). His defiant summation still longs for fair judgment and a divine hearing (Job 31:6, 35). What Job "knows" in Job 19:25 affects neither this subsequent argumentation nor the closing chapters of the book, with Yahweh's creation-centered speeches, Job's humble responses and the this-worldly dénouement of chapter 42.

The immediate context of Job 19:25-27 also fails to support a profound new insight. After lambasting his friends and rehearsing his dilemma, Job longs for a permanent record of his words (Job 19:23-24). This could be a dated record to prove later that he had indeed maintained his innocence (cf. the record in Is 8:1) rather than a monument to survive his death. Further, the chapter concludes with a reference to punishment in this life (Job 19:28-29).

Admittedly, the text of Job 19:25-27 is unclear in its detail; for instance, the NRSV uses several ambiguous terms or phrases ("at the last," "thus," "on my side," "not another") and has five translation-related footnotes. However, three features are clear. First, Job invokes his *gōʾēl*, traditionally the next-of-kin who redeems a family member from slavery, unmortgages property, marries a childless widow and avenges a death (*see* Kinsman-Redeemer and Levirate). It is a fair assumption that the *gōʾēl* can also be legal advocate, despite lack of specific OT reference. Since Job previously longed for an advocate vis-à-vis God (Job 9:33; 16:19), and the outcome here is that he will see God (Job 19:26-27), his *gōʾēl* presumably is this advocate (hardly God himself, still less Job's personified cry, as some argue). Second, this *gōʾēl* will eventually arise to defend Job. The scenario envisaged is probably an earthly court, though the time frame is unclear: both "at the last" and references to skin and flesh are ambiguous. Third, the outcome is that Job sees God. He has longed for this since the onset of his troubles, and at last he will have the opportunity to present his case.

So there is bold faith here: not that Job will survive death, but that he will eventually meet God. This indeed happens at the end of the book, though with an unexpected outcome: instead of defiant self-justification by Job, there is humble contrition, and instead of condemnation by God, there is vindication. Although it interacts with an invisible world, the drama is completed within the visible one. A posited postmortem vindication in Job 19:25-27 does not fit this. Nevertheless, the textual difficulties of these verses could reflect an emergent belief of a positive afterlife among the text's transmitters and translators, and their interpretation of the text accordingly.

2.3. Proverbs. The book of Proverbs has much to say about life and death. This theme pervades chapters 1—9 and occurs in several of the pithy maxims. In particular, the foreign or foolish woman will lead the unwise son to death, Sheol and the *rĕpāʾîm*, or "shades" (Prov 2:18; 5:5; 7:27; 9:18; there are also references to Sheol unrelated to human fate [Prov 1:12; 15:11; 27:20; 30:16]). However, in general the two options envisaged are this present life and the underworld, without the alternative of a blissful afterlife.

A few proverbs might imply an alternative. The snares of death can be averted by wise teaching, and Sheol by physical chastisement (Prov 13:14, 23:14), though the unspoken alternative is presumably this life. "The path of life leads upward to avoid Sheol below" (Prov 15:24), though again this could simply indicate the present life, as in the earlier contrast with the foreign woman's ways (Prov 5:5-6). More intriguing is Proverbs 12:28, where the path of righ-

teousness is life and "no death." But here the second half is awkward, reading literally, "and way of path not death": the nominal phrase *(derek nĕtîbâ)* has redundant repetition, and the negative *ʾal* does not normally precede nouns. Further, many Hebrew manuscripts give this term as *ʾel* ("unto"), while the versions follow this and read the line differently. Thus scholars often reconstruct with an antithetical parallelism as in other life-death proverbs—for example, "but the way of folly *[tôʿēbâ]* leads to death" (see *BHS* note). Similar textual difficulties surround Proverbs 14:32, where "the righteous finds refuge in his death *[bĕmôtô]*." Such refuge is not otherwise an OT concept and is more in line with later eschatology (cf. Wis 4:7-17); further, the LXX and Syriac read a more likely "in his integrity" (Heb *bĕtummô*), implying a simple mistake of metathesis. In summary, the few proverbs that suggest a positive afterlife are uncertain conceptually and/or textually. They hardly indicate a positive perspective, though the textual problems might testify to emerging afterlife beliefs in the early transmission period.

2.4. The Megillot. Ecclesiastes is the only OT book to contain significant reflection on death itself. The Pentateuch prescribes death as a penalty, the Historical Books record it as an event, and the psalms offer prayer against its untimely occurrence, but without significant reflection on the nature of death itself. By contrast, it has been well noted that Ecclesiastes has "the smell of the tomb about it," with three juxtaposed threads.

First, some verses present tranquil pictures of the natural rhythms of birth, old age and death (Eccles 3:2; 12:1-8) or extol the enjoyment of this life for its own sake and not just in reaction to death (e.g., Eccles 3:12-13). This perspective echoes the traditional Israelite approach to death. Second, and more markedly, there is repeated unease over death. Wise and fool, human and animal apparently die alike, without differentiation. This provokes both frustration with the present life and a focus on it alone (Eccles 2:17-18; 3:19-21): neither wealth nor reputation makes any difference at death (Eccles 5:15-16; 6:1-2); life is but a shadow with nothing certain beyond it, and mourning brings more insight than does celebration (Eccles 6:11; 7:2-4). Then, in a key passage, the sage asserts that death awaits all and obliterates all knowledge, passion and activity (Eccles 9:1-10). Third, there are occasional tantalizing glimpses of divine judgment from both *Qohelet and his epilogist (Eccles 3:17; 11:9; 12:14), though without specifying its time frame or providing further detail.

These three strands remain unintegrated. Many scholars stress the negative perspective of death as final, and certainly it is predominant in the book. Others note references to continued existence in Sheol, but this is not meaningful afterlife. Nevertheless, the references to judgment, whatever their origin, may hint at a future reckoning. Like a few psalms discussed above (see 2.1), they may reach beyond the present limits of life and faith toward some undefined further experience.

The other *Megillot have little to add. Ruth and Esther are stories where death is simply recorded as an event. The Song of Songs brushes the theme only with its proverbial assertion that "love is strong [ʿazzâ] as death, passion fierce/hard [qāšâ] as Sheol" (Song 8:6); in other words, love is as irresistible as death is unavoidable. Lamentations is prompted by calamity, destruction and death but focuses on the emotions and faith of the survivor without commenting on the fate of the deceased. Together, these books illustrate well the traditional Hebrew focus on this life and its events and the general disinterest in any individual consciousness beyond death.

See also CHAOS AND DEATH.

BIBLIOGRAPHY. **J. Barr,** *The Garden of Eden and the Hope of Immortality* (London: SCM, 1992); **S. L. Burkes,** *God, Self, and Death: The Shape of Religious Transformation in the Second Temple Period* (JSJSup 79; Leiden: E. J. Brill, 2003); **J. Goldingay,** "Death and Afterlife in the Psalms," in *Judaism in Late Antiquity, Part 4: Death, Life-after-Death, Resurrection and the World-to-Come in the Judaisms of Antiquity,* ed. A. J. Avery-Peck and J. Neusner (HO 1/49; Leiden: E. J. Brill, 2000) 61-85; **P. S. Johnston,** *Shades of Sheol: Death and Afterlife in the Old Testament* (Downers Grove, IL: InterVarsity Press; Leicester: Apollos, 2002); **J. D. Levenson,** *Resurrection and the Restoration of Israel* (New Haven: Yale University Press, 2006); **E. C. Lucas,** "Science, Wisdom, Eschatology and the Cosmic Christ," in *Eschatology in Bible and Theology,* ed. K. E. Brower and M. W. Elliott (Downers Grove, IL: InterVarsity Press, 1997) = *"The Reader Must Understand": Eschatology in Bible and Theology* (Leicester: Apollos) 279-97; **R. E. Murphy,** "Death and Afterlife in the Wisdom Literature," in *Judaism in Late Antiquity, Part 4:*

Death, Life-after-Death, Resurrection and the World-to-Come in the Judaisms of Antiquity, ed. A. J. Avery-Peck and J. Neusner (HO 1/49; Leiden: E. J. Brill, 2000) 101-16. P. S. Johnston

AGUR. *See* LEMUEL AND AGUR.

AHASUERUS

Ahasuerus is the Persian king in the book of *Esther. The name ʾăhašwērôš is the Hebrew equivalent of the Persian Khšayāršan, which, for lack of consonantal equivalents, the Greeks rendered Xerxēs. The son of Darius I, Xerxes ruled the Persian Empire from 485 to 465 BC and was succeeded by his son Artaxerxes I. The LXX erroneously identified the king as Artaxerxes (for a full discussion of the king's identity, see Paton, 51-54).

    1. Xerxes in Classical Sources
    2. Ahasuerus in the Book of Esther
    3. Critical Challenges to the Biblical Depiction

1. Xerxes in Classical Sources.
Inscriptions provide little information about Xerxes, most of them having been heavily influenced by the inscriptions of his father, Darius I (Yamauchi, 188-89). Significant Greek sources include Ctesias's unreliable *History of the Persians,* of which only fragments are preserved, and Aeschylus's *Persians,* produced in 472 BC, just eight years after the defeat of the Persian fleet at Salamis. Since Aeschylus himself fought at Marathon and Salamis, the tragedy provides an eyewitness account presented, of course, with dramatic license. Some information may also be gleaned from Thucydides, but the Greek historian Herodotus is by far the most significant source of extrabiblical information about Xerxes, in terms of both quantity and quality.

Darius, having been defeated by the Greeks at Marathon, was preparing a larger army to continue his policy of expansion. The extreme taxation that these war preparations required incited his Egyptian subjects to revolt. In November of 486 BC Darius died, not yet having put down the rebellion. Xerxes, who had been recognized as the crown prince since 498 BC and had been groomed for the job by a little over a decade of service as the viceroy of Babylon, inherited the Egyptian problem, with the throne, at about the age of thirty-two. He turned his attention first, however, to the completion of his father's palace at Susa. When his brother Ariamenes contested his accession, Xerxes bought him off with gifts and position. By 484 BC Egypt had been recovered, and Xerxes gave his brother Achaemenes charge of that satrapy. With the help of his able brother-in-law Megabyzus, Xerxes was able quickly to put down another rebellion by Babylon. The reprisals against Babylon were severe.

Rebellions out of the way, Xerxes continued building Darius's war machine and, urged on by his cousin Mardonius, planned his northwestern expansion. The attempt proved disastrous for Xerxes. Although Herodotus tends to be untrustworthy with regard to statistics, there is no doubt that Xerxes' capacity for war was considerable. Logistical support for his army was no small burden to the cities along the army's route. A single meal, for example, reportedly cost four hundred talents. Trembling before this mighty foe, the Greeks sent a delegation to Delphi to seek Apollo's prognosis. The oracle gave a dire prediction for Athens. But when the envoys begged for a more favorable answer, Apollo offered a little hope in the "wooden wall." The ensuing debate about the meaning of the wooden wall was settled by Themistocles, who interpreted it as a reference to the Athenian fleet. Xerxes, quite confident himself, sought to further deprive the Greeks of their nerve.

When three spies were caught at Sardis, Xerxes ordered that they be shown the full extent of his forces and released to report what they had seen. The Greeks, with no small difficulty, managed an alliance against the Persian advance. Taking advantage of a local Greek's betrayal, however, Xerxes' forces found an alternate route to the bottleneck at Thermopylae. The news of the failure to hold the pass reached Artemesium, where the Greeks had successfully battled the Persians at sea for two days but had weathered such damage that they were already planning withdrawal when the news arrived. The Greeks withdrew, evacuating Attica. Stationing the Athenian fleet at Salamis in 479 BC, Themistocles led the alliance into a desperate situation. The western exit was blocked by the Egyptian fleet. The allies were trapped. Olmstead (253-355) argues that if Xerxes had waited, the fragile alliance would have disintegrated, and the allied navy would have been forced to come to terms of surrender. Impetuous Xerxes, however, ordered a full attack on the blockaded navy. The narrow passage removed the advantage of Persian numbers. After an initial Persian success against the Spartans, the Athenians came to the rescue and gained the upper hand. The Greeks fought desperately. For every ship that the allies lost, Persia lost five. Xerxes was forced to retreat. Unable to assume the blame for his rash attack, he executed the Phoenician captains for cowardice. In so doing, he lost the support of the Phoenicians and the Egyptians, the core of his naval power. Disappointed, Xerxes traveled to Sardis, leaving the war in the hands of the more able Mardonius. Mardonius's attempts at a diplomatic solution failed, and Mardonius himself was killed in the battle of Plataea. The Ionian Greeks switched sides against their Persian overlords, and the Greeks won liberation.

Pausanias, the Spartan commander at Platea, having been won over by the opulence of the Persian court, then offered to return the Greeks to Persian submission, should he be allowed to marry Xerxes' daughter (Thucydides 1.128). Xerxes gave a favorable reply, but Pausanias's treachery was discovered by the Spartans, and he paid for it with his life.

Herodotus, being a Greek historian, focuses on the battles between Greece and Persia during the late 480s BC He leaves us with a picture of a monarch who, having spent much of his fortune and his ambition, turns instead to sensual conquests. In Herodotus's presentation Xerxes' character is much like that of Cambyses: arrogant, unstable and ineffective. He exhibits poor judgment and often ignores good advice. According to Ctesias (*FGH* 688 F 13), Aristotle (*Pol.* 1211b37-40) and Diodorus Siculus (11.69.1-2), Xerxes was assassinated by the captain of his bodyguard, Artabanus, who hoped to seize the throne but failed. Artaxerxes I Longimanus, Xerxes' son, took the throne instead.

2. Ahasuerus in the Book of Esther.

The author of Esther is uninterested in the Greco-Persian wars. The events of the book begin with a banquet in the third year (483 BC) of Ahasuerus's reign (Esther 1:3), possibly held to drum up support for his military expansion efforts. Ahasuerus, according to M. V. Fox (171), is the only major character in the Esther narrative not presented in the round. He is a flat figure with no private thoughts. His emotions and psychology are all on the surface. He has one obvious character trait: impulsiveness. This manifests itself most notably in his concern for honor. The banquet, whatever its potential political benefit, is aimed at demonstrating the great wealth at his disposal. His attempt to parade his queen, *Vashti, before his guests, "in order to make known to the people and the princes her beauty," was similarly designed to bring him honor. Such impulsiveness fits well with the character of Herodotus's Xerxes, who had the Hellespont whipped, branded and cursed after a storm destroyed part of his fleet (Herodotus *Hist.* 7.35), and who, for the sake of a grand victory, threw caution to the wind and cost Persia the conquest of the Greeks. But Esther's Ahasuerus shows some reserve as well. The Xerxes of the Greek historians spurns the advice of counselors, much to his own chagrin, but the Ahasuerus of Esther is almost completely manipulated by advisors. His advisors take advantage of his fury toward Vashti to urge for an empire-wide decree that women honor their husbands. Haman talks the king into genocide. The king even seeks advice for something so mundane as how he might honor a deserving subject. Ahasuerus hardly fits the role of protagonist or antagonist. Though absolute human power is his, he is easily moved this way and that by his own subjects. Fox (173) suggests that the manipulation is facilitated by Ahasuerus's laziness. Perhaps the respective authors (Greek and biblical) have selected to disclose only those details that fit their own purposes. Or perhaps Xerxes has learned from his mistakes the usefulness of surrounding himself with advisors.

3. Critical Challenges to the Biblical Depiction. Most biblical scholars generally concede a few points of historical connection, without necessarily admitting the historicity of the Esther narrative. L. B. Paton (64), for example, says of Ahasuerus, "The picture of his character given in Est. as a sensual and capricious despot corresponds with the account of Xerxes given by Herodotus vii. ix.; Aesch. Pers. 467 ff.; Juv. x. 174-187." Similarly, Paton (65) acknowledges, "Some of the statements of Est. in regard to Persia and Persian customs are confirmed by classical historians. Thus the arrangement of the banquet (1^{6-8}), the seven princes who formed a council of state (1^{14}), obeisance before the King and his favourites (3^2), belief in lucky and unlucky days (3^7), exclusion of

mourning garb from the palace (4^2), hanging as the death-penalty (5^{14}), dressing a royal benefactor in the King's robes (6^8), [and] the dispatching of couriers with royal messages ($3^{13}\,8^{10}$)." One of the most central objections to taking the narrative as historical, on the other hand, is that the Greek sources are not silent about the queen's name. She is not Vashti (nor Esther) but rather Amestris (Herodotus *Hist.* 7.114; 9.112). Moreover, many point to a problem with Ahasuerus marrying a Jewish woman at all. Herodotus recounts an agreement among seven Persian lords who overthrew the Magians. According to the agreement, the king would be permitted to marry only within the families of the seven (Herodotus *Hist.* 3.84). It should be noted, however, that Herodotus (*Hist.* 7.152) also says, "While it is my duty to record what is reported, I am by no means obligated to believe it. And this, I think, holds for the rest of the book as well." Critics who appeal to this agreement seldom consider the improbability of the tale as a whole. In it, seven lords, debating how to fairly choose a king, leave the choice to the neighing of a horse. If, too, the tale is to be taken seriously, we should consider that the seven also receive the right to enter the king's presence uninvited. The fact that this privilege is granted to this special seven implies that it is denied to most, lending authenticity to Esther's concern. The challenges of reconciling the biblical story with extrabiblical historical sources are many, varied and difficult. Unfortunately, it has not been the custom among many scholars to treat their various sources with equal skepticism. Nothing in the extrabiblical sources provides an insurmountable challenge to the historicity of the biblical narrative.

See also ESTHER 1: BOOK OF; ESTHER 2: EXTRABIBLICAL BACKGROUND; MORDECAI; SUSA; VASHTI

BIBLIOGRAPHY. **J. L. Berquist,** *Judaism in Persia's Shadow: A Social and Historical Approach* (Minneapolis: Fortress, 1995); **P. Briant,** *From Cyrus to Alexander: A History of the Persian Empire* (Winona Lake, IN: Eisenbrauns, 2002); **M. Brosius,** trans. and ed., *The Persian Empire from Cyrus II to Artaxerxes I* (LACTOR 16; London: London Association of Classical Teachers, 2000); **M. A. Dandamaev,** *A Political History of the Achaemenid Empire* (Leiden: E. J. Brill, 1989); **M. V. Fox,** *Character and Ideology in the Book of Esther* (2nd ed.; Grand Rapids: Eerdmans, 2001); **J. D. Levenson,** *Esther* (OTL; Louisville: Westminster John Knox, 1997); **C. A. Moore,** "Archaeology and the Book of Esther," *BA* 38 (1975) 62-79; idem, *Studies in the Book of Esther* (New York: KTAV, 1982); **O. Murray,** "Herodotus and Oral History," in *Achaemenid History, Part 2: The Greek Sources; Proceedings of the Groningen 1984 Achaemenid History Workshop*, ed. H. Sancisi-Weerdenburg and A. Kuhrt (Leiden: Nederlands Instituut voor het Nabije Oosten, 1987) 93-115; **A. T. Olmstead,** *History of the Persian Empire: Achaemenid Period* (Chicago: University of Chicago Press, 1948); **L. B. Paton,** *A Critical and Exegetical Commentary on the Book of Esther* (ICC; New York: Scribner, 1908); **E. M. Yamauchi,** *Persia and the Bible* (repr.; Grand Rapids: Baker, 1996 [1990]).

C. Brooking

ALEF-BET. *See* ACROSTIC.

ALLEGORICAL INTERPRETATION. *See* HERMENEUTICS; SONG OF SONGS 1: BOOK OF.

ALLITERATION. *See* POETICS, TERMINOLOGY OF; SOUND PATTERNS.

ALPHA TEXT OF ESTHER. *See* ESTHER 4: ADDITIONS.

ALPHABET. *See* ACROSTIC.

AMBIGUITY

In *poetics, ambiguity represents the intentional creation of texts that can be understood in multiple ways. Ambiguity is not to be confused with vagueness. A statement is vague when its boundaries are not properly defined. Although undesirable in situations where a closely reasoned argument is developed, ambiguity can add to our appreciation of a text by forcing us to continually reengage with it. It is a tool that writers use to involve readers in the process of creating meaning because of the need to continually reread and recontextualize a text. The classic study of ambiguity remains that of W. Empson as an expression of I. A. Richard's so-called practical criticism. His earlier work focused on short poetic texts, though later studies showed that his approach also worked with longer pieces. He identified seven types of ambiguity, most of which can be seen in the biblical literature. The exceptions are his fifth and seventh types, in which ambi-

guity is either something of which the author was not initially conscious or evidence of an actual contradiction. The presence of these forms is difficult to prove, especially with ancient literature, but as accidents within a text rather than elements of intended art fall out of the realm of poetics. Empson's categories are not completely discrete, but they remain a useful analytic tool. The five that are clearly found in the OT are utilized below. *Qohelet makes most deliberate use of ambiguity, but the technique is employed across the breadth of the OT.

1. Details Effective in Multiple Ways
2. Multiple Possibilities with a Single Resolution
3. Simultaneous Use of Unconnected Meanings
4. Alternative Meanings Combine to Clarify the Author's Intention
5. Apparent Contradictions
6. Conclusion

1. Details Effective in Multiple Ways.
Writers can increase interest by including details that are effective in more ways than one. This occurs when a word or phrase seems to be resolved at one point but is used in a different way later. An effective use of this technique is in the so-called Janus parallelism (*see* Parallelism), in which a word is employed with two completely different meanings. In this way, an author is able to play with the ambiguity of words that either look or sound alike. The classic example of this is Song of Songs 2:12:

> The flowers have appeared in the land;
>> the time of pruning/singing has arrived,
> and the voice of the turtledove is heard in
>> the land.

There is a play on the fact that *zāmîr* can mean both "pruning" and "singing." Thus, the word is resolved in relation to the first line as a reference to the need to prune the plants, but the third line points to the sound of the turtledove, which requires that it is singing that is heard. Both meanings are intended, but the ambiguity inherent in the root enables the author to draw in readers by employing them both. Biblical writers often exploit this richness of ambiguity that exists in a number of Hebrew roots (*see* Hebrew Language).

11

Care must be taken not to confuse ambiguity of this type in translation with those intended within the text. For example, "who does not lift up his soul to what is false/idols" (Ps. 24:4) represents a translational ambiguity. English does not have a word with the semantic breadth to cover both what is generally false and idols in particular, whereas *šāwĕʾ* covers both.

2. Multiple Possibilities with a Single Resolution.

This approach is the opposite of the first. Rather than one detail being made effective in several ways, the detail is allowed only one resolution. The nature of such a resolution should be deferred so that readers are drawn into the text as they seek the meaning that will resolve the ambiguity. Qohelet makes particular use of this technique as he plays with the meaning of certain key terms, most obviously the word *hebel*. The word occurs thirty-eight times in *Ecclesiastes, a little over half the total usage in the OT. The only biblical text in which this word clearly is not being used metaphorically is Isaiah 57:13, which suggests that readers would be accustomed to *hebel* being used outside of its basic meaning of "breath" or "vapor," though nonbiblical texts also use the word in a nonmetaphorical way. Although he makes his opening claim that "all is *hebel* " (Eccles 1:2), Qohelet refrains from providing an exact definition of what he means by it. Rather, by characteristically defining things as *hebel*, he enables readers to gradually build up their interpretation. It is the lack of a direct definition of what is obviously a key term that draws readers in as they seek to resolve the puzzle that is set before them, though it is precisely the fact that Qohelet never provides an exact definition that has led scholars to posit a variety of meanings, such as "vanity," "futility," "meaningless," "ephemeral" and "enigma." That Qohelet intends a single resolution seems probable from his conclusion (Eccles 12:8), though a single resolution does not require that we employ only one word in translation, because that resolution might not conform to the semantic range of a single English word. The pleasure for readers is in seeking to follow all the clues that Qohelet provides as to what he means by *hebel*. Indeed, by refraining from providing an exact resolution, Qohelet continually invites readers to come back and reread the text and to continue the exploration.

3. Simultaneous Use of Unconnected Meanings.

This method of creating ambiguity requires writers to draw on the possibility of multiple meanings inherent in words or phrases, with each meaning being retained within subsequent discourse. Such an approach disorients readers, as they normally seek to retain only one possible meaning. This is distinct from details being used in multiple ways. In that case, ambiguity involves the unexpected move from one meaning to another, with only one employed at any particular point. An example of this is Proverbs 25:15:

> With patience can a ruler be seduced,
> and a soft answer can shatter bones.

One key to the proverb is the semantic range of the word *rak* ("soft"). Elsewhere, it means "weak" (Gen 33:13) or "tender" (Deut 28:54). This proverb draws on and retains those senses but now links them with a verb ("shatter") that elsewhere is associated with battle, with the result that it is the soft answer that is harder even than bones. By making the answer both soft and hard, the proverb employs ambiguity to draw us into the paradox of its world and increase our pleasure in it.

4. Alternative Meanings Combine to Clarify the Author's Intention.

This approach to ambiguity occurs when an author deliberately leaves alternative meanings open as possibilities and only combines them later so as to clarify their intention. It occurs in the use of words and phrases but also can occur in longer texts. This method can be seen in Ecclesiastes 9:11-18. Here, Qohelet shows wisdom as something that is limited (Eccles 9:11-12) but powerful (Eccles 9:13-16), though even when it is effective in achieving its purpose, wisdom does not necessarily achieve anything for the wise. Moreover, the weakness of wisdom is greater than folly among rulers (Eccles 9:17), but wisdom can still be undone by one sinner (Eccles 9:18). Qohelet thus applies a number of different perspectives to wisdom, but his point is precisely that one needs to "ambiguate" the concept of wisdom. Readers are invited to explore this ambiguity because only through this can they recognize what Qohelet holds to be true: one must see wisdom as a polyvalent concept. Once again, it is the use of ambiguity that enables this exploration to occur.

5. Apparent Contradictions.

The use of apparent contradictions is a form of ambiguity that invites the reader to see the way in which statements that seemingly contradict one another actually cohere to create a single meaning. The parade example is Proverbs 26:4-5:

> Do not answer a fool according to his folly,
>   lest you come to resemble him.
> Answer a fool according to his folly,
>   lest he become wise in his own eyes.

On the face of it, these verses are a direct contradiction. However, their placement and close grammatical patterning suggest that they are to be read as a single unit. The effectiveness of a proverb depends upon knowing when to use it, so the placement of these proverbs together suggests not only that both can be true, but also that the wise should know more than just the content of the proverbs: they should also know which one they need to employ in a given situation. Neither proverb on its own teaches this, but through their deliberate juxtaposition and the ambiguity that is created this text now draws in readers to consider their own application of such material.

6. Conclusion.

The book of *Psalms and the Wisdom literature demonstrate a sophisticated appreciation of the role that ambiguity can play. Ambiguity invites readers to enter into dialogue with the text precisely because it resists easy resolution. It enables an author to hold the readers' interest because they cannot be sure where they are being taken. In these ways, the employment of ambiguity provides a mechanism for making these texts points to ponder—surely the aim of any good wisdom teacher.

See also WORDPLAY.

BIBLIOGRAPHY. **W. P. Brown,** "The Didactic Power of Metaphor in the Aphoristic Sayings of Proverbs," *JSOT* 29 (2004) 133-54; **R. J. Clifford,** "Your Attention Please! Heeding the Proverbs," *JSOT* 29 (2004) 155-63; **W. Empson,** *Seven Types of Ambiguity* (3rd ed.; London: Puffin, 1960); **M. V. Fox,** *A Time to Tear Down and a Time to Build Up: A Re-Reading of Ecclesiastes* (Grand Rapids: Eerdmans, 1999); **J. S. Kselman,** "Janus Parallelism in Psalm 75:2," *JBL* 121 (2002) 531-32; **G. Ogden,** *Qoheleth* (RNBC; Sheffield: JSOT Press, 1987); **W. G. E. Watson,** *Classical Hebrew Poetry: A Guide to Its Techniques* (JSOTSup 26; Sheffield: JSOT Press, 1984). D. G. Firth

AMENEMOPE, INSTRUCTION OF. *See* PROVERBS 1: BOOK OF; PROVERBS 2: ANCIENT NEAR EASTERN BACKGROUND.

AMESTRIS. *See* ESTHER 6: PERSON.

ANGEL OF YAHWEH. *See* DIVINE PRESENCE.

ANIMAL IMAGERY

The Wisdom Literature, poetic books and Writings of the OT abound with both literal and metaphorical references to animals. The term *ḥayyāh* (from the root *ḥyh,* "to live, to have life") indicates living creatures in general, especially wild animals (Job 5:23; 28:21; 39:15; 40:20; Ps 148:10). It is usually translated "beast" (Job 5:22; Ps 79:2), and its use is indicative of the great variety of God's creation, portrayed even in their diverse environments, such as signifying animals in dens (Job 37:8), among the reeds (Ps 68:31 [30]), in the field (Ps 104:11), in the forest (Ps 104:20) or even in the sea (Ps 104:25).

All creatures belong to God (Ps 50:10). He gives them life (Job 12:10), satisfying them (Ps 145:16) with food (Ps 136:25, where the term *bāśār,* meaning "flesh," is translated "creature"), and creating and sustaining them by his Spirit (Ps 104:30).

The numerous and varied families and species of animals are categorized into the following main groups:
1. Domesticated Animals
2. Wild Animals
3. Birds
4. Fish and Other Sea Creatures
5. Insects, Reptiles and Other Miscellaneous Creatures
6. Mythological Creatures

1. Domesticated Animals.

1.1. Sheep, Goats. The terms *ʿēder, ṣōn* and *ṣōneh* (Ps 8:7 [8]), often translated as "flock," primarily refer to sheep but may include goats.

The OT's depictions of animals are often directly related to pragmatic concerns, such as the creatures' potential as food, labor or even threat. The ability of flocks to provide milk and clothing (Prov 27:26, 27), plus meat, hides and even musical instruments (the ram's horn or *šôpār,* see Job 39:24; Ps 47:5 [6]; 81:3 [4]; 98:6;

150:3) made them valuable assets. They needed to be carefully looked after (see Prov 27:23) and guarded (Job 24:2). Job's possessions included thousands of sheep (Job 1:3, 16; 42:12), while Qoheleth's flocks surpassed anyone else's in Jerusalem (Eccles 2:7). An abundance of flocks not only designated prosperity but was indicative of God's goodness, so often expressed in natural and agricultural terms in the OT (Ps 107:41; 144:13). Because of such blessing, creation itself responds in praise to God (Ps 65:13), often expressed through figurative language that, for example, sees mountains skipping like lambs (Ps 114:4, 6).

References to sheep are understandably profuse in the Psalms, many of which are attributed to David, who was himself "taken from the sheep pens" (Ps 78:20). In keeping with the representation of God as Shepherd (e.g. Ps 23:1; 80:1 [2]), Israel is often described as his sheep or flock (Ps 79:13; 100:3). This implies God's pastoral care (Ps 95:7) and guidance (Ps 77:20 [21]; 78:52). However, since sheep are also represented as silly creatures, who stray (Ps 119:176, where the term śeh is used), easily scattered and destined for slaughter, they may be representative of God's rebellious people, who have angered God (Ps 74:1) and who deserve chastisement (Ps 44:11 [12], 22 [23]). This metaphor is applied equally to the wicked (Ps 49:14 [15]).

The Song of Songs includes several references to sheep/goats, both literal (Song 1:7, 8, including a reference to gĕdiyyāh—young goats or kids) and figurative (Song 4:2; 6:6, comparing the female lover's teeth to a flock of sheep). Often a knowledge of the local geography informs the similes, such as "Your hair is like a flock of goats [ʿēz, usually a female goat] descending from Mount Gilead" (Song 4:1; 6:5).

Proverbs 30:31 refers to the tayiš, a male goat, among a list of four creatures that strut in a stately manner, while wild male (Ps 104:18) and female goats (Job 39:1) are denoted by the term yāʿēl.

Sheep and goats were basic to the OT sacrificial system. The psalmist promises an offering of rams (ʾayil) in Psalm 66:15 (cf. Job 42:8). However, despite verses such as Psalm 20:3 [4]; 40:6 [7]; 96:8 and 141:2 that employ general terms for sacrifice such as minḥâ or ʿolâ, specific references to the animals to be offered are to be found in the Pentateuch, rather than in poetic or Wisdom literature. For example, the term kebeś, denoting a young lamb, occurs over one hundred times in those first five books, while Wisdom literature contains just two references, neither concerned with sacrifice. Instead, in keeping with the pragmatic concerns of Wisdom literature, the animal is portrayed as the provider of a fleece used for warm clothing (Job 31:20; Prov 27:6). Psalm 50 contains two references to the he-goat (ʿattûd), as the Creator God spurns wrongly motivated sacrifices offered by the wicked in terms similar to those found in Amos 5:21-24 and Micah 6:6-8.

1.2. Cattle, Oxen. There are eight Hebrew words for "cow" found in the OT, signifying the importance of these animals to the Israelite life. Cattle could produce milk, meat and hides, and their additional function as work animals made them a very valuable commodity (Eccles 2:7; Job 1:10). This is implied by the Hebrew term miqneh, denoting livestock, which originates from the root qnh, which is often used of commercial transactions.

This idea of property and possessions is found in Job 1:3; 42:12, where the term bāqār, variously translated "cattle," "herd" or "ox(en)" appears. It denotes larger livestock such as bulls or cows, rather than the sheep and goats indicated by soʾn. Such prized possessions were favored by God in the sacrificial system (Ps 66:15; see Lev 1:3, 10, 14).

Another common term for cattle is bĕhemâ (Ps 148:10). This term sometimes indicates brutish beasts (Job 18:3; Ps 73:22; Prov 30:30). Elsewhere it denotes animals in general (Job 12:7), often in contrast to humankind (Ps 36:6 [7]; 49:12 [13], 20 [21]; 135:8; Eccles 3:18-21, and see Ps 8:7 [8], where humankind's authority over the animals is stated). God owns (Ps 50:10, compare Ps 24:1), preserves (Ps 104:14) and provides for (Ps 147:9, cf. Prov 12:10) such cattle, and their increase is a sign of his blessing (Ps 107:38; cf. Job 21:10). Nevertheless, his wrath and chastisement may affect all his creation, including cattle (bĕʿîr; see Ps 78:48).

Par is a very common term (especially in the Pentateuch) for a young bull, which figured prominently in sacrifices (Ps 50:9; 51:19 [21]; 69:31). It is used metaphorically in Psalm 22:12 [13] to denote the psalmist's enemies, particularly emphasizing their strength. Strength is also the primary meaning of the term ʾabbîr, used in parallel to par in Psalm 22:12 [13], and also translated "bull" in Psalms 50:13; 68:30 NIV.

šôr is usually translated "ox" (Job 6:5). Their hard work ensured good crops (Prov 14:4). They were prized as possessions (Job 24:3), food (Prov 15:17, cf. Prov 7:22) and for sacrifice (Ps 69:31 [32]). Their value and esteem led to their images becoming objects of worship, especially in the fertility religions of the ancient Near East, and at times for apostate Israel (Ps 106:20). Idolatrous images of calves were also made. Psalm 106:19 refers to this use of the term *ʾēgel*, which is used with reference to Lebanon in Psalm 29:6 and the nations in Psalm 68:30 [31].

The term *ʾelep* occurs in Proverbs 14:4, which includes "cattle" among its various translations (Ps 8:7 [8]). This causes some difficulties in translating verses such as Psalm 144:14, where the NIV reads "oxen" with the footnote giving an alternative rendering of "chieftains."

The wild ox *(rěʾēm)* is mentioned in Job 39:9 and Psalms 22:21 [22]; 29:6 and 92:10 [11]. In the last of these references, the psalmist praises God for exalting his horn like that of the wild ox. This symbolism, using the image of a horn to express power and (sometimes arrogant) strength frequently occurs in the poetic literature of the OT (see Ps 18:2 [3]; 75:4, 5, 10 [5, 6, 11]; 69:31 [32]; 89:17, 24 [18, 25]; 112:9; 132:17; 148:14).

1.3. Horses. The horse *(sûs)* was vital to both trade and especially military endeavors in the OT period. Horses often symbolize strength (Job 39:19), especially finite natural power (see Job 39:18), in contrast to Yahweh's unfailing might (Ps 20:7 [8]; 33:17; 76:6 [7]; Prov 21:31). Therefore, Yahweh delights in people fearing him rather than those relying on such natural strength (Ps 147:10).

Horses could imply status (Eccles 10:7), and are linked with royalty and office in the book of Esther (e.g. Esther 6:8-11). There were also the "fast horses especially bred for the king" (Esther 8:10 NIV, where the Hebrew term *rammāk*, possibly meaning "mare," is used. Another term, *rekeš*, meaning "steeds," is used in Esther 8:14).

Sometimes the need to control a horse with bit and bridle (Ps 32:9) or whip (Prov 26:3) is cited as a warning against a lack of self-control or foolishness.

1.4. Donkeys, Asses, Mules. Wild donkeys *(pereʾ*, see Job 6:5; 11:12; 24:5; Ps 104:11) were domesticated in early antiquity, generally to serve as beasts of burden. The wild donkey enjoys its freedom (Job 39:5), while in contrast its domesticated cousin often characterizes stubbornness and ill discipline, at least in Wisdom literature. As such, it becomes a metaphor for the fool, who requires the discipline of a rod as much as a halter is needed for the obstinate male ass *(ḥămôr)* in Proverbs 26:3. A similar warning against imitating the foolish, uncontrollable nature of the mule *(pered)*, the offspring of an ass and mare, is found in Psalm 32:9.

Job 24:3 implies that the he-ass *(ḥămôr)* could be the most basic possession of the disadvantaged, in this case an orphan. However, the she-ass *(ʾātôn)*, possibly due to its breeding potential and milk, is listed as a valuable commodity among Job's possessions (Job 1:3, 14; 42:12).

1.5. Camels. Camels *(gāmāl)* were used for transport and carrying burdens. According to the Bible, this was true from the earliest patriarchal times, although some scholars have disputed this, alleging that the camel was not domesticated until the Iron Age. In addition to their milk, their legendary endurance without water made them valuable resources (e.g., Job 1:3, 17; 42:12).

2. Wild Animals.

2.1. Wild Cats: Lions and Leopards. Seven Hebrew words are used of lions throughout the OT, and it is almost impossible to discern the precise differences between the objects of each term, whether relating to age, prowess or even sex.

It is doubtful that *kěpîr* denotes a young lion, as was once thought. The NIV translates this term as "great lion" in Psalm 17:12 and Psalm 91:13. This creature's roar is compared to a king's rage in Proverbs 19:12 and Proverbs 20:2, while its boldness is an attribute shared by the righteous in Proverbs 28:1.

Often used in parallel with *kěpîr*, the Hebrew term *ʾaryēh* is used to denote lions as fearsome predators, growling (Job 4:10), lying in wait (Ps 10:9; Lam 3:10) and hungry for prey (Job 38:39; Ps 7:2 [3]; 17:12). As such they are often symbolic of the psalmist's enemies (Ps 22:13 [14], 21 [22]; 35:17; 57:4 [5]), or wicked rulers (Prov 28:15, where the term *ʾărî* is used). It should, however, be noted that, while comparisons between wild animals and enemies often occur in the OT's poetic and (generally ahistorical) Wisdom literature, they usually refer to nonspecific or personal foes. This is in contrast to some of the animal imagery found in the prophetic writings, which refer specifically to the threatening world armies of the Assyrian and Babylonian super powers (e.g., Hab 1:6-8).

Šāḥal is another term often used in parallel with *kĕpîr*, (e.g., Job 4:10; Ps 91:13), or with *ʾărî* in Proverbs 22:13 and Proverbs 26:13, where the sluggard invokes the claim of a lion's presence to excuse his indolence. Job 28:8 declares that the stalking *šāḥal* (see Job 10:16) does not inhabit the earth's recesses; instead the *ʾărî* (like the leopards, see below) have dens in the mountains (Song 4:8).

Though the lion *(layiš)* is "mighty among beasts" (Prov 30:30), even lions must look to God for their food (Job 38:39; Ps 104:21). Before God's power the lion's teeth break (cf. Ps 58:6) and its prey disappears, leaving the cubs of the lion/lioness(?) *(lābîʾ)* to disperse (Job 4:10, 11). The psalmist declares that while even mighty lions may decline and deteriorate, those seeking Yahweh will not suffer lack (Ps 34:10).

Song of Songs 4:8 refers to the mountain haunts of the leopard *(nāmēr)*, probably alluding to its habit of surveying the surrounding territory from a high vantage point.

2.2. Wild Dogs, Including Jackals and Foxes. Dogs *(keleb)* are portrayed as wild, snarling, prowling pack members (Ps 59:6 [7], 14 [15]) and so are seen as representative of either the psalmist's enemies (Ps 22:17) or threats to his life (Ps 22:20 [21]). In keeping with the negative connotations of dogs found elsewhere in the OT, the final degradation of having one's body devoured by dogs is alluded to in Psalm 68:23 [24]. Fools are compared to dogs (Prov 26:11) and meddlers to the trouble caused by a provoked dog (Prov 26:17). Ecclesiastes 9:4 demonstrates the vividness and practicality of OT wisdom—in contrast to abstract, speculative reasoning—preferring a live dog to a dead lion. Job 30:1 refers to sheep dogs.

The Hebrew word for jackal only occurs in the plural form *tannîm* in the OT. This howling, desert scavenger of the genus Canis is invariably referred to in contexts of ruin, destruction and desolation, usually due to Yahweh's judgment. It is mentioned in the NIV translations of Job 30:29 and Psalm 44:19, where the KJV reads "dragons," and in Lamentations 4:3, where AV has "sea monsters." The NIV reading is now preferred, as the KJV has read *tannîn* (see the entry on "Dragon" below). The KJV reads "foxes" in Psalm 63:10 [11], while the NIV translates another root, *šûʿāl*, as "jackals" in Lamentations 5:18, but "foxes" in Song of Songs 2:15. This reference sees such creatures as (small) annoying and interfering nuisances that are difficult to prevent.

2.3. Deer, Gazelles etc. The Hebrew term *ʿōper* indicates a male deer or stag. It is used figuratively to describe the male lover in Song of Songs 2:9, 17 and Song of Songs 8:14, paralleling *šĕbî*, meaning gazelle (Prov 6:5), on each occasion. The female form of gazelle *(šĕbiyyâ)*, translated "fawns" by NIV, is used in Song of Songs 4:5 and 7:3 [4] to describe the female lover's breasts.

Another term for stag is *ʾayyāl*. The fleeing leaders/princes of fallen Jerusalem are likened to stags that cannot find pasture in Lamentations 1:16, while the psalmist compares his desire for God to that of a deer panting for water in Psalm 42:1 [2]. (This text is sometimes emended to refer to a female deer, as the opening phrase employs a feminine verb.) The NIV also finds a reference to a deer in Proverbs 7:22, though the Hebrew text is uncertain.

In Job 39:1, God watches the female doe *(ʾayyālâ)* give birth to her fawns, an event also recorded in the NIV footnote of Psalm 29:9 (though the main text reads the Hebrew term *ʾayyālôt* as a plural form of *ʾayil*, meaning "terebinth" or "oak"). The psalmist praises God for his aid in his preparation for battle, including his sure-footedness, which he compares to that of the doe (Ps 18:33 [34]).

Proverbs 5:19 likens the woman married in one's youth to "a loving doe" *(ʾayyālâ)* and "a graceful deer," although the second Hebrew term, *yaʿălâ* more properly describes a female mountain goat. Psalm 22 is set to a tune entitled "The Doe of the Morning."

The injunction employed by the female lover in Song of Songs 2:7; 3:5—"I charge you by the gazelles *(šĕbiyya)* and by the does *(ʾayyālâ)* of the field"—is possibly a play on words, with the animals' nomenclature being very similar to the divine names *šĕbāʾôt* (as in Lord of Hosts/Armies), and *ʾĕlōhîm*.

2.4. Bears. Though omnivorous rather than carnivorous, wild bears *(dōb)* could present a real threat to other animals and to humans, especially if food was scarce or their offspring endangered (compare Prov 17:12). The bear is an image of both danger and power. Wicked rulers are compared to bears attacking in Proverbs 28:15, while God's wrathful judgment on Jerusalem is likened to the mauling of a bear in Lamentations 3:10, 11.

(Job 9:9 and 38:32 refer to the constellation *ʿayiš* as a manifestation of God's creative power. The KJV translates Arcturus, though this is only a star in the constellation Ursa Major. The NIV and NRSV read "Bear.")

2.5. Pigs, Boars. Although prohibited and classified as unclean animals for the Israelites (Lev 11:7), Wisdom and poetic literature does not utilize any "unclean" imagery when referring to pigs. Instead, this prohibition made the pig effectively useless to the Israelite, resulting instead with concern about its "nuisance" value, for example, the wild, ravaging boar *(ḥăzîr)* of Psalm 80:13 [14].

Proverbs 11:22 compares an indiscrete, beautiful woman to a gold ring in a pig's snout.

2.6. Conies, Rock Badgers, Hyraxes. The wisdom and ability of these small creatures, denoted by the Hebrew *šāpān*, to make homes in the crags (Ps 104:18) is admired in Proverbs 30:26.

3. Birds.

3.1. Birds in General. *ʿôp*, from the verb *ʿup*, meaning "to fly," most commonly denotes birds (Job 12:7; 35:11; Ps 104:12), including carrion eaters (Ps 79:2) who were normally shunned as unclean, not only for allegedly hygienic reasons, but perhaps because of their association with the dead. The term may also refer to flying insects.

Another very common term for birds is *ṣippôr* (Ps 8:8 [9]), an allegedly onomatopoeic term, reflecting a bird's chirping cry, often heard in the early morning (Eccles 12:4). This term is used of both wild (Ps 11:1) and pet (Job 41:5 [40:29]) birds. Several verses using this term speak of birds fleeing from attempts to hunt (Lam 3:52) or ensnare them (Prov 6:5). Such imagery is used in various ways, for instance, warning against the hasty action of an unthinking bird (Prov 7:23), or, in contrast, to depict people escaping from their enemies, often through the aid of Yahweh (Ps 124:7).

The Psalmist also compares his solitude to that of a lone bird in Psalm 102:7 [8]. The NIV translates this term as "sparrow" in Proverbs 26:2 and Psalm 84:3 [4], the latter referring to the bird nesting near Yahweh's altar (compare Ps 104:17 and contrast Prov 27:8), so typifying delight, contentment and protection in the presence of God. Psalm 84:3 [4] and Proverbs 26:2 also refer to the swallow *(děrôr)*, in the latter case as an example of ceaseless activity.

3.2. The Eagle and Other Birds of Prey. The

biblical texts demonstrate some keen ornithological knowledge when describing the eagle *(nešer)* that soars and builds high nests (Job 39:27, cf. Prov 30:19), flying quickly into the sky (Lam 4:19) before swooping down on its prey (Job 9:26). This rapidity of movement depicts here, not sudden attacks against an enemy, but the swiftness of time passing. References to the eagle sprouting wings (Prov 23:5) and renewing its youth (Ps 103:5) may reflect its annual molting rather than its longevity, but it is clearly used of the invigorating renewal of strength imparted by Yahweh. However, the term *nešer* may denote other birds of prey as well, such as the vulture (see Prov 30:17 NIV, where the Hebrew reads *běnê nešer*, "son of an eagle"). The reference to a vulture in Job 15:23 involves repointing the Hebrew text on the basis of the Greek Septuagint to read *ʾayyâ*. This term is properly found in Job 28:7, where the subject's exemplary eyesight is reported, and is variously translated "hawk," "kite" or "falcon." It is used in parallel with *ʿayiṭ*, denoting some other unspecified (shrieking?) bird of prey. Job 39:26 uses the term *nēṣ*, probably referring to a hawk or falcon.

3.3. Other Birds. Similar difficulties of translation occur when seeking to identify other birds. The NIV translates *(bat) yaʿănâ* in Job 30:29 as "owl," while other versions prefer "ostrich." (Compare Lam 4:3, though it is difficult to account for the heartlessness of this imagery, perhaps used here as a reprimand against those who treat their offspring badly.) The *rěnānîm* (birds with a ringing cry?) of Job 39:13 are also usually identified as ostriches. Again, there are negative connotations in the following verses, that speak of the bird's lack of care for its eggs, cruelty towards its young and a general lack of wisdom, in what seems to be a caricature of the ostrich's worst possible traits. These are not universally or even generally scientifically observed, but a comparison might be made with the equally inaccurate modern day belief that an ostrich "buries its head in the sand."

Job 39:13 contrasts this bird's wings, that flap joyfully but unproductively, with those of the *ḥăsîdâ*. This bird has impressive pinions and feathers, and nests in pine trees (Ps 104:17), and has been identified as the stork, since it was deemed to be kind to its offspring (the root *hsd* means "kind, steadfast love").

Psalm 102:6 [7] uses the terms *kôs* and *qāʾat*,

which may indicate some kinds of (desert?) owl, although *qāʾat* may refer to the pelican. Whatever the precise identification of these birds, once again the imagery of solitude is invoked.

The dove *(yônâ)* may refer to a variety of birds from pigeons to rock- or turtledoves. The psalmist longs for the beautiful wings (Ps 68:13 [14]) of a dove in Psalm 55:6 [7] to fly from his present troubles, while the following psalm is most probably set to a tune titled "A Dove on Distant Oaks" (see Ps 56:1). Psalm 74:19 also uses *yônâ* in parallel to a reference to God's "afflicted people," for whom the psalmist craves mercy.

The cooing of the dove *(tôr)* is mentioned in Song of Songs 2:12. Song of Songs makes several figurative comparisons between the lovers and birds. The female is called a dove, a bird renowned for its loyalty to its mate (Song 2:14; 5:2; 6:9), a description that is also applied to both her (Song 1:15; 4:1) and her male lover's (Song 5:12) eyes. His hair is "black as a raven" (Song 5:11).

Clean birds could be eaten (Deut 14:11). God's provision of quail *(śĕlāw*, Ps 105:40) is also reported in Psalm 78:27, using the general term, *ʿôp.* Conversely, God—who knows each individual bird (Ps 50:11)—provides food for them, even for the carrion-eating ravens *(ʿōrēb*, Prov 30:17). See Job 38:41 and Psalm 147:9 (and contrast 1 Kings 17:6!).

The notion found even today in common sayings that birds may pass on what they hear (e.g., "a little bird told me") is found in Ecclesiastes 10:20 (contrast Job 28:21).

Birds are literally described as "lords of the wing" *(baʿal kānāp)* in Proverbs 1:17 (cf. Eccles 10:20). God's care and protection is often described figuratively in terms of sheltering his people under his wings (see Ruth 2:12; Ps 17:8; 36:7 [8]; 57:1 [2]; 61:4 [5]; 63:7; 91:4).

4. Fish and Other Sea Creatures.

Fishing has long been an important activity in providing food for humans, although fish without fins or scales were prohibited for Israelites. Fish could be caught with hooks (Job 41:1 [40:25]), spears (41:7 [40:31]) or nets (Eccles 9:12). Due to such constant threats to their existence, fish therefore become representative of the transience and uncertainty of human life (Eccles 9:12). The fish of Egypt died during the first plague when the Nile turned to blood (Ps 105:29).

God has given humankind authority over the natural order, including the fish *(dāg)* of the sea (Ps 8:7, 8 [8, 9]). They are part of God's creation (Ps 146:6) and his general revelation (Job 12:8). The sea, and all its inhabitants ("everything in it," *ûmĕlôʾô*) will rejoice in his kingship (Ps 96:11; 98:7). This includes the innumerable "creeping animals" denoted by the Hebrew *remeś* in Psalms 69:34 [35] and 104:25 (cf. Ps 148:10, where the same word seems to refer to the smaller land animals).

5. Insects, Reptiles and Other Miscellaneous Creatures.

5.1. Grasshoppers/Locusts. Nine words are used of locusts and grasshoppers throughout the entire OT, and it is not always possible to determine their exact meanings and distinctions. This plethora of words for locusts shows both the concern evoked by this creature, and expresses various images and traits associated with it. While a single locust would be no threat (Ps 109:23), their massive grouping in swarms, speedy travel and incredible consumption of crops made them a feared and irresistible terror (Job 39:20) to their victims.

Psalm 78:46 reports the plague of locusts afflicting the Egyptians using the words *ḥāsîl* (derived from a root meaning "to consume") and *ʾarbeh*, the most common term for locust, indicating the vast size of the swarms, as in Psalm 105:34. This verse also uses the term *yeleq*, possibly indicating young locusts. Ecclesiastes 12:5 refers to another form of grasshopper, the *ḥāgāb*, while the locusts' wisdom in their regulated advance despite having no single leader is admired in Proverbs 30:27.

5.2. Frogs, Gnats and Flies. The plagues of flies *(ʿārōb)*, frogs *(ṣĕpardēʿa)* and gnats *(kēn)* that afflicted Egypt are recalled in Psalms 78:45 and 105:30, 31.

The term *zĕbûb* (compare Baal-zebub/Beelzebub, "lord of the flies") is used in Ecclesiastes 10:1 of the dead flies that contaminate ointment.

5.3. Ants, Bees and Spiders. The sluggard is instructed to consider the industrious ways of the ant *(nĕmālâ)* in Proverbs 6:6. Their wisdom in preparing food during the summertime is admired in the only other occurrence of this word, in Proverbs 30:25.

In Psalm 118:12 a swarm of bees *(dĕbôrâ)* becomes a metaphor for the nations that surround the psalmist, but who are defeated with Yahweh's help.

Job 8:14 refers to the flimsy web of the spider (ʿakābîš), which Bildad compares to the fragile hope of the godless. The KJV reference to a spider in Proverbs 30:28 is now rejected, with "lizard" as the preferred meaning of the Hebrew šĕmāmît.

5.4. Moths and Worms. The moth (ʿāš) is connected with ideas of destruction and weakness in the OT. The frailty of human existence is compared to the fragility of the moth in Job 4:19, and to its weakening and ultimate destruction of garments in Job 13:28. This also becomes a picture of God's consumption of the wealth of sinful men (Ps 39:11 [12]), whose endeavours are as flimsy and unstable as a moth's cocoon (Job 27:18).

The term rimmâ for "worm" usually occurs in the context of decay, for example, the description of Job's ailments in Job 7:5. Worms will feed on dead and decaying corpses (Job 21:26), while the associated ideas of suffering, death and decay are the future recompense of the wicked (Job 24:20). The term rimmâ is used in parallel with šaḥat ("the pit, the grave, destruction, corruption") in Job 17:14. It also occurs as a derogatory term in Job 25:6, used in parallel with tôlēʿâ, also translated "worm" (cf. Ps 22:6 [7]).

5.5. Slugs, Snails and Leeches. The slimy trail of the šabĕlûl, translated "snail" (KJV) or "slug" (NIV) is interpreted as the animal "melting away" in Psalm 58:8 [9], to express the psalmist's hope for the eventual demise and disappearance of unjust rulers.

Proverbs 30:15 mentions the ʿălûqâ in the context of four other objects that are never satisfied. Though not entirely certain, the term is usually translated as the blood-sucking leech.

5.6. Lizards and Roosters? The NIV translation of "lizard" is now preferred to the KJV's "spider" for the term šĕmāmît, denoting a creature which, although prone to capture, can be found even in palaces. It occurs only in Proverbs 30:28, among a list of four small but wise animals.

The Hebrew phrase zarzîr motnayim, found in Proverbs 30:31, literally means "girded at the hips/loins." It is clearly intended to denote some animal with stately bearing, although the imagery may be a subtle warning against pride. Modern commentators prefer the NIV's translation "rooster" to the "greyhound" of the KJV.

5.7. Snakes, Serpents. The Hebrew term peten is clearly associated with a venomous snake in Job 20:14, 16, with NIV translating it as "cobra" in Psalm 58:4 [5] and 91:13. In this latter reference, it symbolizes, along with the lion, the threatening enemies against whom Yahweh provides protection and a refuge. Job 20:16 also uses the term ʿepʿeh to indicate another venomous snake, usually translated "adder" or "viper."

The most common word for snake in the OT, found especially in Genesis chapter 3, is nāḥāš (see 2 Kings 18:4). In Psalm 58:4 [5] and in Ecclesiastes 10:11 it implies snake-charming, while the snake's mysterious movement across (smooth?) rocks is marvelled at in Proverbs 30:19. As with peten, the nāḥāš is also a threat to the unwary (Eccles 10:8), while the words of evil men (Ps 140:3 [4]) and the effects of strong drink (Prov 23:32) are compared to its venom. Other terms for snakes, variously translated "asps," "serpents" or "vipers," occur in these verses, specifically ʿakšûb in Psalm 140:3 [4], and sipʿônî in Proverbs 23:32.

Nāḥāš is used in Job 26:13 to refer to the "gliding serpent" pierced by God. It occurs in parallel to Rahab, a name given to the primordial sea monster of chaos, conquered by creator gods in extrabiblical creation myths. For further comment on these myths, see below.

It might also be noted that many of the creatures in this section that are associated with evil (snakes) or decay (worms) show no clear evidence of respiration to the average observer. This possibly suggested that they lacked "the breath of God" and so contributed to the negative imagery of such animals.

6. Mythological Creatures.

6.1. Leviathan. The Hebrew term liwyātān is consistently transliterated as Leviathan in the KJV, RSV and NIV texts of Job 3:8; 41:1; Psalm 74:14 and 104:26. Its description in Job 41:1, and an association with the Egyptian forces resisting the Exodus in Psalm 74:13, 14, has led to suggestions that this is the Nile crocodile. Other suggestions include various species of whale.

However, these contents of these texts have also been compared to certain extrabiblical mythologies that include many-headed (Ps 74:14) and serpentine monsters (the root lwy in Arabic means "to twist"). These can be responsible for eclipses (Job 3:8, 9), or are perhaps representative of chaotic and watery (Ps 74:13) forces that needed to be defeated in primordial history. Comparisons with the Babylonian creation myth involving the slaughter of Tiamat were especially popular in the past, often based on the now discounted link between the Hebrew word *těhôm*, meaning depths (e.g., Ps 77:16 [17]), and the name of the god Tiamat.

It seems churlish to deny that the OT appeals to such myths in its poetic and Wisdom literature, as they are transformed in such a way so as not to lend them any literal credence, but rather to declare Yahweh's creative and conquering power over all other natural and cosmic forces.

6.2. Rahab. The Hebrew term *rahab* literally means "pride," hence the KJV's translation of Job 26:12 as "he smiteth through the proud." Despite this, most modern translations transliterate the term as "Rahab" here and in Job 9:13; Psalm 87:4 and Psalm 89:10 [11]. As with Leviathan, an identification with the Nile crocodile has been postulated, especially as Psalm 87:4 uses the term symbolically of the Egyptian nation. More usually mythological associations are made, as Yahweh triumphs over the sea (*yām*, also the name of a Canaanite god) and crushes the primordial chaos monster, Rahab, in his triumphant creation work (see Ps 89:9-13 [10-14]).

6.3. Dragon, Whale, Sea Monster. The term *tannin* is translated by the NIV as: "monster of the deep"; "monster" (in the waters) and "great sea creatures" in Job 7:12; Psalm 74:13 and Psalm 148:7 respectively. In Psalm 91:13 it is rendered "serpent." Other more specific literal translations have been offered, including whales, sea snakes or dolphins(?). Alternatively, as with Leviathan and Rahab, the term is considered to be symbolic of national forces or mythological monsters opposed to God.

It is noticeable that the three marine creatures above acquired mythical status among the ancient Israelites. This development may be due in part to the Hebrews' general dislike of the sea as the uncanny realm of chaos. Combined with what must have been very limited knowledge of the realm of the sea, the resulting awe and wonder from tales of such creatures almost certainly contributed to the legendary imagery associated with them.

6.4. Behemoth. The single reference to *běhēmôt* in Job 40:15 has provoked much debate. Despite being an apparently plural form of *běhēmâ* ("beast"), it clearly refers to a single animal, probably implying some superlative creature (cf. Job 40:19). Whether it is to be identified with the hippopotamus, elephant or a majestic

but mythical creature remains uncertain, but the emphasis of the passage is clearly on God's creative power. Indeed, the entire imagery of Job 38—41, with its mysterious allusions and grandiose variety of animal imagery, provides a subtle reminder of both humankind's ignorance and its awe before the exuberant and sovereign divine Creator.

See also FLORAL IMAGERY.

BIBLIOGRAPHY. **O. Borowski,** *Every Living Thing: Daily Use of Animals in Ancient Israel* (Walnut Creek, CA: AltaMira, 1998); **E. Firmage,** "Zoology," *ABD* 6.1109-167; **T. L. Forti,** "Animal Images in the Book of Proverbs," *Biblica* 77 (1996) 48-63; idem, *Animal Imagery in the Book of Proverbs* (VTSup 118; Leiden: E. J. Brill, 2008); **P. Riede,** *Im Spiegel der Tiere: Studien zum Verhaltnis von Mensch und Tier im alten Israel* (OBO 187; Göttingen: Vandenhoeck & Ruprecht, 2002); **R. A. Simkins,** *Creator and Creation: Nature in the Worldview of Ancient Israel* (Peabody, MA: Hendrickson, 1994); **B. A. Strawn,** *What Is Stronger Than a Lion? Leonine Image and Metaphor in the Hebrew Bible and the Ancient Near East* (OBO 212; Göttingen: Vandenhoeck & Ruprecht, 2005); **P. Wapnish and B. Hesse,** "Archaeozoology," in *Near Eastern Archaeology: A Reader,* ed. S. Richard (Winona Lake, IN: Eisenbrauns, 2003) 17-26.

P. T. Davies

ANTITHETIC PARALLELISM. *See* PARALLELISM.

APOCALYPTIC. *See* WISDOM AND APOCALYPTIC.

ARCHITECTURAL IMAGERY

A city's buildings provide the essential shelter and protection for its inhabitants. Archaeological excavations in the past century and more have unearthed many important architectural structures of the Bronze Age and Iron Age in all parts of the Near East, albeit fragmentary to some degree. Because there are virtually no ancient buildings that remain above ground, reconstructing the plan and design of any ancient architectural structure depends greatly on the evidence of excavations and archaeological reports (*see DOTHB,* Architecture). Accordingly, the symbolic meanings of ancient architectures have found their reference points in archaeologists' schematic reconstructions as well as from biblical texts. In the Psalter, Wisdom literature and Writings imageries of ancient buildings are numerous, and they can be categorized under residential and military architectures.

1. Residential Architecture
2. Military Architecture

1. Residential Architecture.

1.1. Household and Family. The word *house* denotes a dwelling place, which includes huts, palaces and temples. A typical house *(bayit)* in Iron Age Palestine was basically rectangular with either three or four rooms, normally divided by two rows of monolithic pillars. Entrance to the house was gained through a wooden door from the exterior courtyard, and situated at the back end of the house was a room that archaeologists have called a broadroom, which served as a storage space. The upper level of the house was used for sleeping, dining and entertaining (King and Stager, 28-29). Apart from daily family activities, the basic functions of an Israelite house involved storing items and stabling animals.

The basic symbolism of a house is the household or the family, where the man was the head (Esther 1:22; cf. Ruth 1:9). A house represented one's possessions, such as cattle (Ps 50:9) and offspring (Ruth 4:12; Sir 48:15), and to build a house was to produce a family (Ruth 4:11). One who feared the Lord was blessed with a fruitful family (Ps 128:3) and a house filled with glory, wealth and riches (Ps 49:16 [49:17 MT]; 112:3). Wisdom teachers often contrasted the house of the righteous with the house of the wicked. Whereas the house of the righteous would flourish, the house of the wicked would be destroyed (Prov 14:11; cf. Prov 15:25; 17:13). Unlike the house of the wicked, the house of the righteous gives sustenance and security (Prov 3:33; cf. Prov 7:27). During the Persian era the concept of *honor and shame came to be associated with one house (Herodotus *Hist.* 3.128-129). It was considered an utter shame to lose one's house to another person because it meant the loss of everything, including one's social status (Esther 8:1-2).

"The house of the father" and "The house of the mother" are used to refer to the place of residence of a virgin daughter or a widowed daughter (Ps 45:10; Sir 42:10; cf. Gen 38:11; Lev 22:13; Num 30:16; Deut 22:21; Judg 19:2-3; Ruth 1:8).

1.2. The Temple of Yahweh. Israel believed that God made his dwelling in a house, *bayit* (e.g., Ps 5:7 [5:8 MT]; 23:6; 26:8; 27:4; Lam 2:7; Sir 49:12

Gk; 50:1, 5), which was an assurance of his steadfast love (Ps 5:7 [5:8 MT]; 138:2). The house of Yahweh is also called the temple, which probably resembled the ground plan of a rectangular-house type, although no material remains of the first temple have been uncovered. It was divided into three units: the porch (*'êlām),* the main room *(hêkāl)* and the innermost chamber *(dĕbîr).* Reference to the main room *(hêkāl)* frequently indicated the temple itself (Ps 5:7 [5:8 MT]) and signified a heavenly palace (Ps 18:6 [18:7 MT]; 29:9). Prayers were directed to the heavenly palace (Ps 18:6), the innermost sanctuary *(dĕbîr)* and the chamber of God (Ps 28:2).

Because of God's presence, his house (Ps 26:8; Add Esther 14:9), temple (Ps 11:4; 65:4; 79:1; 138:2; Sir 36:14 [36:19 Gk]; 49:12; 50:7) or sanctuary (Ps 63:2 [63:3 MT]; 68:35 [68:36 MT]; 96:6) is holy, glorious and majestic. It is in the house of Yahweh that his servants offer their service (Ps 134:1; 135:1-2), and the righteous are planted there like plants (Ps 92:13). From the house of Yahweh, God's people receive divine blessings, such as forgiveness of sins, agricultural harvest, economic well-being (Ps 65:4 [65:5 MT]; cf. Ps 92:13) and help (Ps 20:2 [20:3 MT]; cf. Ps 60:6 [60:8 MT]; 108:7). The house of Yahweh also came to mean the created universe, which, like the house of God, is filled with God's holiness (Ps 93:5) and satisfies both humankind and animals with nourishment and provision (Ps 36:8 [36:9 MT]).

The sanctuary, *qōdeš* (Ps 20:2 [20:3 MT]; 74:3; Sir 36:13) or *miqdāš* (Ps 73:17; 74:7; Lam 2:20; Sir 47:13; cf. 1 Kings 8:10-11; 2 Chron 5:11; 29:5, 7; 35:5), is another expression of the house of Yahweh. It refers to God's mighty firmament (Ps 150:1), and it is compared to the earth (Ps 78:69). Important to note, however, is that Israel, God's chosen people, has become the very sanctuary in which God dwells (Ps 114:2; cf. Lam 1:10).

1.3. Royal Palace. Although the term *palace (hêkāl)* refers to God's temple and heavenly palace, it primarily indicates the palace of the king (Ps 45:8, 15 [45:9, 16 MT]; Prov 30:28). There is not enough architectural data to make reconstructions of the palaces in Palestine. The royal palace is a representation of the king 'snation (Ps 144:12) and a symbol of his empire (Esther 7:8; 9:4). The *imagery is set in the context of marriage and justice in the Psalter (Ps 45). As God's viceroy, the king rules from the royal palace, just as God rules from heaven. Contrary to the lavish decoration with ivory that indicates the disparity between the king and his people (cf. Jer 22:13-17), the beauty of the palace is a sign of divine blessing and presence (Ps 45:8 [45:9 MT]).

1.4. Wisdom House. In the wisdom tradition the image of a house is of great significance. It is used to portray the way of life and the character or works of a person. The way of folly is described as a ruined house (Sir 21:4; cf. Sir 21:18 Gk), which incurs the wrath of the deity (Job 15:28) and eventually will be overthrown (Sir 27:1-3 Gk). The house of the wicked woman is considered to be a dangerous place (Prov 7:8), filled with immoral pleasure rather than sustenance and security (Prov 7:27). Thus, young people are exhorted not to go near even its door (Prov 5:8), for it will lead them to death (Prov 2:18; 7:27). To enter the house of folly is to enter into the realm of foolishness, while to enter a house of wisdom is to enter into an intimate union with wisdom (cf. Wis 8:16).

The houses of the wicked and of the righteous are contrasted with, respectively, a spider web (J(Job 8:11-15) and a stone house (Job 8:16-19). The former is marked by its fragility (Job 8:11-15), and the latter is characterized by its strength (Job 8:16-19). The house of those who fear the Lord will be filled with wisdom (Sir 1:17), but disasters will come to the house of sinners (Sir 23:11 Gk; cf. Deut 5:11). The blessings of parents will strengthen the house of their children (Sir 3:9 Gk), but slanderous words will cause damage to the house of the great person (Sir 28:14 Gk).

The most significant description of the house of wisdom is found in Proverbs 9:1. It is built by wisdom with seven pillars (cf. Prov 14:1; 24:3), a design similar to an ancient aristocratic house capable of housing a large number of guests. The wisdom house is understood differently. In light of the fact that wisdom is thought to be a virtuous woman in Proverbs, and the house is set in the context of feasting and celebration (Prov 9:1-6), the house that wisdom built is best seen as a large Israelite house, with the number even symbolizing completeness or perfection (Waltke, 432-33) or the seven poems in Proverbs 2 (Skehan), which signify the abundant blessings of wisdom.

1.5. Human Body. The human body is pictured as a house, characterized by its form as clay and by its origin as dust (Job 4:19) and made up of various parts: arms, legs, teeth, eyes, mouth, ears (Eccles 12:3). Just as a house deteriorates when it gets old, so also does the human body (Eccles 12:3-7). In Song of Songs the word *house* often has sexual connotations. For example, "the house of the mother" *(bêt 'ēm)* depicts both the womb where one is conceived (Song 3:4; cf. Song 8:2) and the genitals of the female who is looking forward to offering her body to her lover (Song 8:2). Furthermore, "house of wine" points to a particular private place where the lovers meet for lovemaking (Song 2:4) rather than a literal "house of drinking wine" (Esther 7:8) or drinking house (Jer 16:8).

One picture that speaks of the beauty of the female body is that of a ower *(migdāl)*. For example, the female's neck is compared to the tower of David (Song 4:4), filled with power and dignity, or an ivory tower (Song 7:4 [7:5 MT]), which suggests a strong and elegant neck. Her nose is likened to the beauty and greatness of the tower of Lebanon (Song 7:4), and her mature breasts are like towers (Song 8:10).

1.6. Death. The place where the dead congregate was thought to be built with houses, each one consisting of a door and windows (Reider, 102-3) and filled with all kinds of treasures (Job 3:15). A death in the family is pictured as "the house of mourning" (Eccles 7:2), and the grave is the house of the dead (Job 3:15). Indeed, death is the meetinghouse for all the living (Job 30:23) and a place of no return for anyone who goes there (Job 7:9-10). Ultimately, humankind would move from this earthly house to the house in another world, Sheol (Job 17:13).

1.7. Israel. The word *house* describes Israel as a community (Ps 114:1) as well as the twelve federation tribes (Ps 98:3; 115:12; 135:19). Rachel and Leah (and their respective maidservants) giving birth to the twelve sons of Israel are seen as building up the house of Israel (Ruth 4:11). When the term is used with a personal name, it bears the duty associated with that person. For example, the house of Aaron (Ps 115:10, 12; 118:3; 135:19) and the house of Levi (Ps 135:20) present Israel as a priestly people (cf. Ex 19:6; Is 61), and the house of David refers to the Davidic court in dispensing justice (Ps 122:5; cf. Ps 101:2, 7).

2. Military Architecture.

2.1. Fortress and Stronghold. To protect itself from the attacks of enemies, a city built on hills needs defense architecture. This defense architecture is a fortress, *mĕṣûdâ* (Ps 31:2 [31:3 MT]), or a stronghold, *miśgāb* (Ps 9:9 [9:10 MT]). The word *fortress* refers to a walled fortification on a high mountain (2 Sam 5:6-7), and the word *stronghold* can indicate any protected place. These two terms are interchangeable, describing an inaccessible, secured building of defense or fortification (Ps 18:2 [18:3 MT]) against enemies (cf. Ps 89:40 [89:41 MT]; 108:10 [108:11 MT]). Although defense architecture does not always provide safety for the city dwellers, it represents the most powerful image of security. In the Psalter primarily, God is portrayed as a fortress in the time of trouble (Ps 31:2-3) and a stronghold in the day of distress (Ps 59:9 [59:10 MT]). Such an image reflects the psalmist's rocklike trust in God's insurmountable power amidst life-threatening dangers (Ps 18:2 [18:3 MT]; 62:6 [62:7 MT]; 31:2 [31:3 MT]). For the psalmist, the ultimate protection is God, in whom alone one finds salvation and deliverance (Ps 18:2 [18:3 MT]; 71:3; 144:2) and steadfast love (Ps 59:17 [59:18 MT]). The presence of the Lord is like an impenetrable stronghold (Ps 46:7, 11 [46:8, 12 MT]), which his people experienced historically (1 Kings 18—20; cf. Is 36—38). This mighty fortress, however, ceases to protect the people when they sin against their rock of refuge (Lam 2:5, 7). Indeed, the state of strength and security is not without condition (Ps 62:1-12).

The word *refuge (māʿ ôz)* is associated with a fortress/stronghold and indicates either a natural or any constructed place of shelter and protection (Ps 28:8; 31:2, 4 [31:3, 5 MT]). The most common use is a figurative one, designating God as the refuge for his people in times of trouble (Ps 27:1; 37:9; cf. Ps 48:3, 13 [48:4, 14 MT]; 122:7) and the "refuge of the head," *māʿ ôz rōʾšî*—that is, the chief fortress (Ps 60:7 [60:9 MT]; 108:8 [108:9 MT]). The righteous take refuge in God (Prov 10:29; Ps 43:2; 52:7 [52:9 MT]), but the wicked take refuge in their riches and wealth (Ps 73:7 [73:9 MT]).

2.2. Wall. Surrounding the fortress, as well as the city, is a huge wall *(ḥēl; ḥômâ; qîr; gādēr)*, which is unlike the stone fence that protects vineyards, orchards or gardens (Eccles 10:8; cf. Prov 24:31). The walls were built of mud brick or stone, enhanced with various features, such as glacis with supporting retaining walls, and dry moat. After the Solomonic era solid walls replaced casemate walls in Palestine. The massive wall, standing between the inhabitants and their enemies, provides the most basic and crucial protection to the city dwellers. The word *wall,* therefore, has become an important portrayal of divine protection and peace (Ps 48:13 [48:14 MT]; 122:7). In the wisdom tradition a wall is said to encircle wisdom's house, and those who encamp near it are wise. Not only are they able to learn wisdom, but also they find protection and security (Sir 14:24; 22:17 Gk).

The wall has negative connotations as well. A wrecked or broken wall expresses the meaning of defeat and God's judgment (Ps 80:12 [80:13 MT]; 89:40 [89:41 MT]; Lam 2:18; cf. Lam 2:7-8), and it is an image of a lazy or ill-disciplined person (Prov 24:31; cf. Prov 25:28). A thick wall of darkness has blinded the adulterers to their sins (Sir 23:18 Gk). The rich see their wealth as a high wall of security (Prov 18:11), but anyone who does not trust in God is in a precarious position like a leaning wall (Ps 62:3 [62:4 MT]). In Song of Songs the imagery of the wall is used in the context of sexuality and contrasted with the "door" *(delet)*. Whereas the door indicates a promiscuous woman, the wall denotes chastity (Song 8:9-10; cf. Song 2:8).

2.3. Gate. The gate *(šaʿ ar)* is the only entrance to the walled city, and its breach implies the fall of the city (cf. Gen 22:17; 24:60). Thus the gate is considered to be the most vulnerable point of defense. The gate could also refer to a public concourse where social and judicial events take place (Job 29:7; 31:21; Ps 9:14 [9:15 MT]; 69:12 [69:13 MT]; 127:5; Prov 22:22; 31:23; cf. Prov 14:19). As a metaphor, it represents the entire city (Ps 24:7, 9; 87:2; cf. Ps 100:4), security (Ps 147:13) and the point of entrance to a certain realm, such as death (Job 38:17; Ps 9:13 [9:14 MT]; 107:18), Hades (Wis 16:13), deep darkness (Job 38:17) and righteousness (Ps 118:19). It is at the gate that the wisdom invitation is made (Wis 6:14), signifying that wisdom instruction is applicable to all people (Prov 1:21; 8:3). Through the gate of wisdom the wise obtain a happy life (Prov 8:34), but for fools it is a dead end (Prov 24:7).

2.4. Tower. A tower *(migdāl)* is part of the defense architecture, usually built at the corners on the wall (cf. 2 Chron 14:7), providing enhancement for the city walls and gates. From the towers the inhabitants could direct arrows and other projectiles at the enemies scaling the walls. The word *tower* renders God's protection against the enemies (Ps 61:3 [61:4 MT]) and indicates his eternal presence (Ps 48:12-14 [48:13-15 MT]). An immovable tower is used to describe the name of the Lord, which gives life to the righteous (Prov 18:10).

In summary, the imagery of architecture has at least two types of representation. With reference to residential building, it represents one's life, death, household, body, a nation or an empire, and the heavenly palace. As an image of military building, it conveys a basic meaning of protection and security.

See also ANIMAL IMAGERY; CREATION IMAGERY; FLORAL IMAGERY; MOUNTAIN IMAGERY; PSALMS 6: ICONOGRAPHY.

BIBLIOGRAPHY. **Z. Herzog,** "Fortifications (Levant)," *ABD* 2:844-52; **J. S. Holladay Jr.,** House, Israelite," *ABD* 3:308-18; **O. Keel,** *The Symbolism of the Biblical World: Ancient Near Eastern Iconography and the Book of Psalms* (Winona Lake, IN: Eisenbrauns, 1997); **P. J. King and L. E. Stager,** *Life in Biblical Israel* (Louisville: Westminster John Knox, 2001); **J. Reider,** "Contributions to the Scriptural Text," *HUCA* 24 (1952-1953) 85-106; **K.-D. Schunck,** "מְצוּדָה," *TDOT* 8:501-5; **K. N. Schoville,** "מָעוֹז," *NIDOTTE* 2:1013-15; **P. W. Skehan,** "The Seven Columns of Wisdom House in Proverbs 1-9, in *Studies in Israelite Poetry and Wisdom,* ed. J. A. Fitzmyer (CBQMS 1; Washington, DC: Catholic Biblical Association of America, 1971) 9-14; **B. K. Waltke,** *The Book of Proverbs: Chapters 1-15* (NICOT; Grand Rapids: Eerdmans, 2004); **G. R. H. Wright,** *Ancient Building in South Syria and Palestine* (2 vols.; HO 7; Leiden: E. J. Brill, 1985); **Y. Yadin,** *The Art of Warfare in Biblical Lands in the Light of Archaeological Discovery* (London: Weidenfeld & Nicolson, 1963); **P. Zimansky,** "Art and Architecture: Ancient Near Eastern Architecture," *ABD* 1:408-19. M. Phua

AROMATICS. *See* FLORAL IMAGERY.

ASAPH AND SONS OF KORAH

In addition to the five books into which the whole is arranged, the book of *Psalms also includes a number of smaller collections, several of which can be identified through their headings. These include the Songs of Ascents and several Davidic collections, as well as those associated with Asaph and the Sons of Korah. Psalms 50; 73—83 are associated with Asaph, while Psalms 42; 44—49; 84—85; 87—88 are associated with the Sons of Korah. Since Psalm 43

is clearly a continuation of Psalm 42, even though the canonical structure has separated it off, it too can be regarded as a Korah psalm. Psalm 88 is unusual in that it appears to have a double title that also associates it with Heman the Ezrahite, though he may have been a leading member of the group (cf. 1 Chron 6:33).

Although the exact function of the titles is disputed, it seems likely that they at least serve to indicate that these psalms are part of identifiable collections, so there is reason to treat them together. It is notable that although most of these psalms occur within the so-called Elohistic Psalter, the last four Korah psalms fall outside of this division. This would suggest some complexity in the canonical process, and that attempts to identify these psalms as northern on the basis of the preference for the name ʾĕlōhîm may confuse a redactional process within the Psalter with evidence for their origin. On the other hand, the peculiar use of "Joseph" as a label for the nation in the Asaph psalms, complete with an unusual Hebrew spelling in Psalm 81:6 (81:5 ET) (uniquely *yĕhôsēp*, suggesting "Jehoseph" as the form of the name), might suggest some northern echoes (Goulder 1996, 24-27).

The book of Chronicles also links both collections to bands of Levitical temple musicians initiated by *David (1 Chron 6:31-48), though internal evidence suggests a later date for the canonical collections, with Ezra-Nehemiah suggesting that both guilds were active after the exile. We are therefore dealing with psalms produced over a period by musical groups rather than by specific individuals whom we can identify. Nevertheless, the Chronicler suggests that these guilds embodied traditions that reached back to the time of David.

1. The Psalms of Asaph
2. The Psalms of the Sons of Korah

1. The Psalms of Asaph.

1.1. Identity of Asaph. Although several figures with the name "Asaph" are mentioned in the OT, the one most likely to be associated with these psalms is mentioned in 1 Chronicles 6:24 as a leader of one of the groups of temple singers established by David. Asaph appears as a worship leader in 1 Chronicles 15:17, 19, while in 1 Chronicles 16:5 he is in charge of *music when the ark was brought into Jerusalem. Subsequently, Asaph was left as a minister of the ark (1 Chron 16:37). 1 Chronicles 25 indicates that

Asaph was involved in leading a musical guild, while 2 Chronicles 5:12 shows him leading a guild of singers when the ark was brought to the temple by Solomon. Chronicles then traces a continuing role for this musical guild through the reigns of Jehoshaphat (2 Chron 20:14), Hezekiah (2 Chron 29:13) and Josiah (2 Chron 35:15). 2 Chronicles 29:30 suggests that a collection of Asaph psalms must have existed at the time of Hezekiah, though we cannot determine the content of this collection, so their relationship to the canonical collection remains unclear. The importance of the reference is that it suggests that a recognizable group of Asaph psalms could be identified in the late eighth century BC. Ezra 2:41 (cf. Neh 7:44) notes that members of the guild returned from the exile, while Ezra 3:10 indicates that they were involved in the dedication of the second temple. Nehemiah 11:17, 22 suggest a continued role for the guild, while Nehemiah 12:46 makes clear that an Asaph collection also existed at the time of Nehemiah. Although we cannot be certain of the content of this collection, it is not unlikely that it bore at least some resemblance to the collection now included in the Psalter. It is clear from internal evidence that the collection includes pieces that originated across the whole of this period. That reference to the Asaph collection extends across such a body of texts renders unlikely the suggestion by Goulder (1996, 28) that Asaph did not exist, and that the name was developed to provide a title for a collection of northern psalms for which a senior musician at the time of David needed to be invented.

1.2. Content of the Psalms of Asaph. Comparatively few psalms contain direct historical references that enable us to date them with certainty, and the Asaph psalms are no exception. Nevertheless, there are enough datable references within the Asaph psalms to indicate that the exile was a significant trigger for the development of the canonical collection. Not all of the psalms necessarily originated with the exile, but the main collection (Pss 73—83) appears to be shaped by concerns generated by the fall of Jerusalem. This is preferable to the suggestion by Goulder (1996, 36) that the Asaph psalms originated at Bethel in the 720s BC, and that the references to Jerusalem derive from editing required to enable their reuse in Judah.

Psalm 50 stands apart from the main Asaph collection and appears to function as a divider between the first collection of the psalms of the Sons of Korah (Pss 42—49) and a collection of Davidic psalms (Pss 51—65) whose titles indicate specific connections with events in David's life recounted in the books of Samuel. This psalm's relationship to the exile is more difficult to determine, but its prophetic rejection of sacrificial worship alone and encouragement toward the offering of thanksgiving certainly would fit with the exile. However, it has a more immediate link with Psalm 51, which likewise downplays the importance of sacrifice as opposed to heartfelt praise. Psalm 50 encourages the nation to see *worship as being more than just the cult, just as Psalm 51 does for the individual. But Psalm 50 also links to the main body of Asaph psalms in that both it and Psalm 81 are "prophetic covenant liturgies" (Craigie, 363) that employ direct address from God within the psalm and call the nation to repentance.

The main body of Asaph psalms occurs in Psalms 73—83. A number of scholars have highlighted the importance of Psalm 73 for the shape of the whole of the Psalter (e.g., Brueggemann and Miller), but we should also understand it as introducing the remainder of the Asaph collection. It is an individual's testimony (Firth, 451-52), telling of a near loss of faith that was averted only through a worship experience in the temple, in which the psalmist realizes that the greatest good is to be found not in who has external prosperity but rather in the presence of God. This individual's testimony could have arisen at any time, but it suggests an answer to a larger issue that would also affect the nation with the fall of Jerusalem. Although a range of dates has been proposed, it seems likely that several of the Asaph psalms reflect quite directly on the destruction of the city and the temple by the Babylonians. Psalm 74:3-8 refers to the damage done to the temple by an unnamed enemy, while Psalms 79—80 refer to events surrounding the city's destruction. The meaning of covenant and the blessings that were supposed to go with it could then be openly discussed, so the placement of Psalm 73 at the head of the collection suggests that this individual's experience is also a paradigm for the nation. Psalms 82—83, which close the collection, can then be read against the experience of the exile as an appeal to God to act against all the nation's enemies, a prayer for the nation to experience what the individual has discovered in Psalm 73. God's justice for a penitent people is announced in Psalm 81, and these prayers look for this justice to be demonstrated.

The Asaph psalms are also marked by an interest in history. Although not unique to this collection (cf. Pss 105—106), it is particularly notable that its heart (Pss 75—80) is shaped by a strong historical consciousness. Thus, Psalm 75 announces that the nation recounts the wondrous deeds of God (Psalm 75:1), before describing God's activity in general terms, a pattern continued in Psalm 76. Against this, Psalm 77 is an individual complaint that sees reflection on history as a way toward resolution of a present crisis (Ps 77:10), a reflection that leads specifically to the exodus. Psalm 78 is the centerpiece of this group, an extended piece that provides instruction on the faithfulness of God through history from the exodus through to David. The psalm insists that God was consistently faithful in the face of national faithlessness, climaxing in the appointment of David as the shepherd of his people. Psalms 79—80 then draw on this historical awareness, while emphasizing that God is the nation's ultimate shepherd, to ask for restoration. Thus, the Asaph psalms are a tightly grouped selection in which covenant, individual testimony and national reflection can be applied to the sense of loss created by the exile.

2. The Psalms of the Sons of Korah.

2.1. Identity of the Sons of Korah. As with Asaph, there are a number of individuals known as Korah in the OT. Again, evidence for the most likely identification of Korah comes from Chronicles. 1 Chronicles 6:22 lists a Korah who was descended from Kohath, one of the three Levite clans responsible for the sanctuary. 1 Chronicles 6:33 includes this group among those organized by David for music in the sanctuary. This Korah is most likely the one who was engaged in a revolt against Moses (Num 16) and was destroyed in the wilderness (Num 16:32). 1 Chronicles 9:19, although in a genealogy of those who returned from exile, contains a telescoped reference back to the same Korah, suggesting that a group that traced its origin back to the time of David was still identifiable in the postexilic period. Chronicles is not consistent in its usage, and at some points it refers only to the Kohathites (2 Chron 29:12; 34:12), and sometimes to the Korahites as a group related to but distinct from the Kohathites (2 Chron 20:19).

The list of gatekeepers in 1 Chronicles 26:1-19 refers to the Korahites in a nonmusical role, but we would expect such a dispersal of tasks across the clan. The MT of 1 Chronicles 26:1-2 links the Korahites to Asaph, but this text probably is corrupt, and we should follow the LXX [cf. REB] and read "Abiasaph," which also conforms to 1 Chronicles 9:19. The Sons of Korah mentioned in the titles of certain psalms are thus to be identified with a Kohathite musical guild that operated across the period of the monarchy and through to the period after the exile. The psalms within this collection could have developed at any point within this period.

2.2. Content of Psalms of the Sons of Korah. The psalms of the Sons of Korah contain even less datable information than do the psalms of Asaph. Given that proposed dates range across several centuries, there is comparatively little value in seeking supposed festal sequences (e.g., Goulder 1982, 1-22) that lie behind them. Rather, their themes are best explored through an examination of their canonical structure. This needs to consider their distribution into two main groups, Psalms 42—49 and Psalms 84—88 (excluding Ps 86, though by its placement it is linked to the Korah psalms), and the strong focus on Jerusalem that is found in all except the closing psalm of each block. Tied in with the theme of Jerusalem is an emphasis on the fact that God is the great king over all the earth, though the place of Israelite kings certainly is acknowledged.

These themes are immediately brought together in Psalms 42—44, which, along with Psalm 88, constitute the only complaint psalms within this collection. Psalm 42 is also closely linked to Psalm 88 in the use of water imagery, not least the comparison of a negative experience of God to a series of waves passing over someone who cannot swim (compare Ps 42:7 and Ps 88:7). The complaint in Psalms 42—43 is somewhat different from Psalm 88 in that it concerns a desire to be in the presence of God, and especially at the sanctuary, when it does not appear that this is possible. As the psalm develops, the psalmist gradually comes to a point of believing that there will be a chance to return to the sanctuary (Ps 43:3-4). This is a source of hope, but the negative experience of God remains. This theme is then expressed in terms of the nation in Psalm 44, which complains of a failure of God to be faithful to the nation even though they had not deviated from the covenant (Ps 44:17-19). As a result, the nation has been defeated in battle. Since it seems that the individual who speaks at some points within this psalm is the king, it is unlikely that the reference is to the exile, so the psalm must have been used at various points where the nation had been defeated in battle. The plaintive cry for deliverance with which it ends insists that the nation should have the same hope as that of the individual in Psalms 42—43.

It is against the background of this negative experience of God that we are to read Psalms 45—48, because they address this concern. Psalm 45 is a royal wedding song that also focuses on the military hope for the nation (Ps 45:2-5). The psalm insists on the close relationship between God and his king and prepares the way for the great affirmations about the reign of God that we find in Psalms 46—48. All these psalms focus on Jerusalem as the city of God. This is less explicit in Psalm 46, which celebrates the nation's ultimate security in God, in which the city remains unnamed but, as the city of God, clearly is Jerusalem. Psalm 47 likewise does not name the city, but it describes the journey of the ark up to the temple in Jerusalem as a celebration of victories achieved by Yahweh (Broyles, 149-50), thus linking back to Psalm 46. The *Zion theme is made explicit in Psalm 48, in which the people are invited to see the strength of the city as a reminder of the greater security offered by God. All of this is to the praise of God, praise that is summoned from all peoples. The opening collection closes with Psalm 49, which is an exploration of the hope of God's people in the face of adversity, a wisdom psalm that explicitly addresses the nations summoned to see the greatness of God in the preceding psalms.

The second Korahite collection follows immediately on from the Asaph psalms. Closely tied to the Asaph psalms (Wilson, 164), this group has less coherence, though themes from the first collection are retained. Thus, Psalm 84 and Psalm 87 celebrate the beauty of Zion with an additional prayer for the Lord's anointed (Ps 84:9). Psalm 85 prays for national restoration, while Psalm 88 is perhaps the bleakest individual complaint in the Psalter, though it also prepares readers for the national complaint of Psalm 89, with which it is paired. Thus, the Korah psalms are bound by dialectic that holds together honest complaint and the hope offered by the presence of God.

See also EDITORIAL CRITICISM; PSALMS 1: BOOK OF.

BIBLIOGRAPHY. **C. C. Broyles,** "The Psalms and Cult-Symbolism: The Case of the Cherubim-Ark," in *Interpreting the Psalms: Issues and Approaches,* ed. P. S. Johnston and D. G. Firth (Leicester: Apollos, 2005) 139-56; **W. Brueggemann,** "Bounded by Obedience and Praise: The Psalms as Canon," *JSOT* 50 (1991) 63-92; **W. Brueggemann and P. D. Miller,** "Psalm 73 as a Canonical Marker," *JSOT* 72 (1996) 45-56; **P. C. Craigie,** *Psalms 1-50* (WBC 19; Waco, TX: Word, 1983); **D. G. Firth,** "Psalms of Testimony," *OTE* 12.3 (1999) 440-54; **M. D. Goulder,** *The Psalms of the Sons of Korah* (JSOTSup 20; Sheffield: JSOT Press, 1982); idem, *The Psalms of Asaph and the Pentateuch* (JSOTSup 233; Sheffield: Sheffield Academic Press, 1996); **H. P. Nasuti,** *Tradition History and the Psalms of Asaph* (Atlanta: SBL, 1988); **G. H. Wilson,** *The Editing of the Hebrew Psalter* (SBLDS 76; Chico, CA: Scholars Press, 1985).   D. G. Firth

ASSONANCE. *See* POETICS, TERMINOLOGY OF; SOUND PATTERNS.

AUTOBIOGRAPHY

The OT contains a small number of texts that may be considered autobiographies, and a larger number of autobiographical texts. An awareness of how these texts function and what literary devices they employ can aid our understanding of their meanings.

    1. Definition
    2. Functions of Autobiography
    3. Autobiographies in Old Testament Wisdom and Poetry
    4. Conclusion

1. Definition.
Modern literary critics have found it difficult to agree on a precise definition of autobiography as a literary genre; indeed, J. Olney (3) described it as "the most elusive of literary documents." Some contend that true autobiographies appeared only following the Enlightenment with the rise of individuality (e.g., Smith and Watson; Weintraub), whereas others argue that such restrictions are culturally biased and unnecessarily reductionistic. J. Sturrock (286), for example, states that "there can be no timeless

definition of autobiography," arguing instead that the "the bounds of the 'autobiographical' will be measured differently from age to age" (see also Howarth, 84).

For the purposes of OT study, autobiography can best be defined as a text in which the author retrospectively relates select events and experiences from his or her own life from the perspective of the author's present. Retrospection is significant because the author evaluates his or her past in light of present knowledge and circumstances—this unlike a diary, which lacks such distanced reflection. Also important is the selectivity of the account, as Sturrock (287) notes: "Whatever an autobiography contains it contains not simply because such has been the writer's experience and he therefore had no option but to include it, but because this is his past as he has chosen to project it. What we are reading is *already* an interpretation and the writer an active, not a passive force." The choice of events recorded in an autobiography is not accidental but deliberate, and all work together to fulfill the author's purpose.

The distinction between an autobiography and an autobiographical text lies in the amount of the author's life that is recorded. A brief reference to a past event from the author's life (as in, e.g., Prov 4:3-9) cannot reasonably be described as an autobiography, but it nonetheless can employ the characteristic traits of the genre and thus be autobiographical.

2. Functions of Autobiography.

Autobiography differs from some other literary genres in that it is defined not by the form of the writing but rather by its content (unlike, e.g., a limerick, which must correspond to a specific pattern but whose subject matter is unconstrained). Consequently, autobiographers may employ a broad range of devices in order to convey their message. Nonetheless, the distinctive features of autobiography can themselves be employed to achieve particular ends, and awareness of these features is important for understanding the means by which authors convey their message as well as the message that they convey, and it may influence the author's choice of autobiography as a means to best communicate the message.

2.1. Authority. The authority of a text is partially bound up with the credentials of the author, and so when autobiographical texts identify their authors, this may function to enhance their authority. This is apparent in the identification of *Solomon as author of wisdom material. It is important to note, however, that the identification of a text's author is not necessarily made in order to enhance the text's authority. D. G. Meade (72), for example, argues that pseudonymous texts could be considered to be authoritative in the ancient world in spite of their pseudonymity, and that the identity of the author could serve ends beyond establishing the text's authority. However, it is also probable that recognition of deliberate deception regarding the author's identity would undermine the authority of a text, particularly when the identification of the author is made specifically to enhance the authority of the text. For this reason it is significant that, although strongly implying identity with Solomon, neither *Qohelet nor the author of the frame (*see* Frame Narrator) of *Ecclesiastes ever makes the identification explicit (see Waltke, 35).

Although autobiography sacrifices the availability of the narrator's omniscient viewpoint for the more limited perspective of an individual who can no longer make authoritative pronouncements on the inner thoughts and motives of others, this can have the effect of enhancing the authority of the text regarding the inner thoughts and motives of the author over that which would otherwise be described by an omniscient narrator by providing firsthand testimony to those thoughts and motives. This immediacy enhances the authority of texts whose authors are otherwise unknown, such as Proverbs 22:17—24:22; 24:23-34.

2.2. Empathy. One distinctive feature of autobiography is the first-person appeal to experiences, feelings and events that the author has personally encountered. An effect of this can be to heighten the link between the author and the audience, for the audience now engages directly with the author's life—there is no intermediate narrator interposed between the two such that the events are further removed from the audience. This can serve to establish an empathic connection between author and audience, between the author's experience and the audience's experience. The first-person nature of autobiographical texts invites audience participation, particularly with forms such as psalms, where it is likely that the texts were recited and used liturgically. Empathy thus can be generated via the immediacy and inherent interiority of the autobiographical form, revealing the inner emotions more directly than in third-person descriptions. The empathic nature of autobiography is frequently exploited in modern autobiographies that, as G. Gusdorf (36-39) has noted, often function as an apologia for the actions of the author's life.

Empathy, however, is not automatically or exclusively generated by autobiographical forms. There must be other elements within the text that allow the reader to identify with the author, and there must be nothing overly offensive about the author's character as depicted in the text. As such, the degree of empathy that a reader feels with an autobiographer may well be culturally determined.

2.3. Distance. In a number of examples of autobiography in the OT, the autobiographical text is embedded within a narrative (such as Qohelet's autobiography in the book of Ecclesiastes, and the Ezra and Nehemiah memoirs within Ezra-Nehemiah). In these instances the autobiography presents an alternative voice to the narrator of the text. As T. C. Eskenazi (126) has observed, this allows the text to present a personal but subjective viewpoint in the first-person voice of the autobiographer as well as a third-person assessment of the autobiographer from the narrator. These distinct viewpoints may allow the narrator to appeal to the autobiography for support of the case being made. Alternatively, however, they may allow the narrator to maintain distance from the autobiographical comments included within the narrative (see 3.3 below).

2.4. Instruction. The reflection on personal experience characteristic of autobiography allows authors to base advice and teaching to others on their past experiences, both to illustrate and to substantiate that teaching. Events are selected, shaped and linked in such a way as to lend support to the author's own purpose in writing. Such an approach is common in Wisdom literature and is employed in a number of other autobiographical texts from throughout the ancient Near East (see Longman 1991, 97-129). This is particularly apparent in Qohelet's autobiography: the events are related in order to substantiate the point that Qohelet ultimately wished to draw, the lesson that he has learned from his experiences (see Eccles 1—2; also Ps 73).

2.5. Achievements. Some West Semitic and Akkadian royal inscriptions served to highlight the personal achievements of the king through recitation of his major accomplishments as well as through comparison with the king's predecessors (Seow, 281-84). The inscription of these autobiographies was intended to stand as eternal testimony to the king and thus "to be the king's assurance of immortality" (Seow, 284). Sometimes these texts also have a didactic element—J. L. Crenshaw (128) highlights Egyptian instructions or royal testaments in which "the pharaohs or viziers collected their insights for the benefit of aspiring young rulers, whom they hoped to steer successfully along paths of wisdom. Such advice appeared in autobiographical form, constituting a king's legacy for his successors."

3. Autobiographies in Old Testament Wisdom and Poetry.

The identification of autobiographical texts in the OT has been less problematic than modern discussions of the genre might suggest. Texts identified as autobiographical are restricted to those that are written in the first-person singular and make reference to events and experiences in the life of the narrator. Although some maintain more subtle distinctions in genre (such as between memoir and autobiography), there is little indication that much is gained in preserving these distinctions (see Longman 1991, 43).

The OT contains a few autobiographies and more examples of autobiographical texts. The focus of the present article is on those found in the Writings, but we should note that the form does exist in other parts of the OT, such as Jeremiah, Ezekiel and Ezra-Nehemiah. Although these texts are not discussed here, their use of autobiographical forms shares some of the general functions of this form outlined above. Examples of autobiographical texts found within the scope of the present volume are discussed below.

Autobiography is particularly suited to Wisdom literature, which often bases its advice in the wisdom garnered by the sage from personal life experiences. This is seen both in the OT and in some of the Egyptian instructions that closely parallel biblical Wisdom literature (e.g., Eccles 1—2; cf. the Egyptian Instruction for Meri-ka-re).

3.1. Psalms. In the book of *Psalms, roughly

two-thirds of the psalms include first-person references, although many of these do not fit the strict definition of autobiography. Psalm 51, for example, while appealing to events in David's life, does so from a perspective contemporaneous with those events rather than retrospectively. Some psalms, such as Psalms 18; 32; 73 and the apocryphal Psalm 151 (an autobiographical account of David's early years) do present reflections on events in the earlier life of the psalmist and so contain true autobiographical elements.

Autobiographical (and other first-person) references in psalms primarily function empathically (see 2.2 above), although in conjunction with the *psalm titles' authorial ascriptions (e.g., "A psalm of David") the association with renowned historical figures also serves to lend a degree of authority to the words of the psalm. When wisdom psalms include autobiographical reflections (e.g., Ps 73), these also function to lend authority to the conclusions drawn on the basis of the author's experiences (see 2.4 above).

3.2. Proverbs. The book of *Proverbs contains a number of autobiographical passages that are too brief to be accurately described as autobiographies (e.g., Prov 4:3-9; 24:30-34; 30:1-9 [see Waltke, 26, 79, 275]). In Proverbs 4:3-9, for example, the writer's only appeal to a life experience is found in v. 3, where he recalls his father's advice to him. The advice itself is then reported, but without autobiographical reflection or appeal to the father's experience. In spite of this, the first-person speech does share some of the aforementioned functions ascribed to autobiography.

The recollections of Proverbs 7:6-20 are closer to true autobiography (Waltke, 81) and are followed by the "autobiography of wisdom" in Proverbs 8, which sufficiently incorporates the characteristics of the genre to qualify as true autobiography. It is written in the first person (Prov 8:4-36), and it relates events in wisdom's past (e.g., Prov 8:22-31). The autobiographical appeal to wisdom's role in creation as an aide to God affirms its divinely endorsed value and authority and underlines the validity of the supposition that at a fundamental level the creation operates in a manner consistent with the presuppositions of the wisdom movement (see Waltke, 407).

3.3. Ecclesiastes. Although the bulk of the book of *Ecclesiastes is phrased in the first-person, spoken by the sage *Qohelet, only the opening chapters (Eccles 1:12—2:26) explicitly relate events from Qohelet's life, and so only these chapters—often designated the "Royal Fiction"—are usually recognized as autobiography. The fact that Qohelet is depicted as a king and relates autobiographical details associates his writing with royal autobiographies (fictional and nonfictional) from the ancient Near East (Seow, 279 [cf. 2.5 above]). Longman (1991, 120-23; 1998, 18-19) has demonstrated formal parallels between Qohelet's words in their entirety (not just the first two chapters) and a subgenre of fictional Akkadian autobiographies, suggesting that the modern tendency to isolate the opening portion of Qohelet's words and identify them as autobiography imposes an anachronistic disjunction into the text as a whole that overlooks the impact that the autobiographical chapters have on the audience's reaction to the remainder of the work.

Scholars differ in their assessment of the significance of Qohelet's autobiography. The fact that Qohelet implies identity with Solomon in part through his autobiographical description of the great Solomonic deeds (Eccles 2:4-7; cf. 1 Chron 27:27-31) grants the words authority and overcomes any tendency of the reader to dismiss the difficult words as those of an erroneous sage (Fox, 153-54; Shields, 111-12; Sharp, 51). C. L. Seow (284) also suggests that Qohelet deliberately employs the royal autobiographical form—used elsewhere in the ancient Near East to exalt rulers and immortalize them through their achievements—to invert the expectation generated by this genre that the ruler had ultimately escaped the constraints of mortality by showing that the greatest of kings is ultimately left with nothing.

Finally, the inclusion of Qohelet's autobiography in the book of Ecclesiastes allows the narrator to maintain distance from the sentiments expressed in Qohelet's words. Qohelet is the *frame narrator's foil—a character presenting authoritative pronouncements as the wisest of the wise but permitting the narrator to avoid fully endorsing those assertions (see Shields 106-9; Longman, 1998, 38-39; *contra* Seow [396] and Fox [371], who claim that the epilogue fully endorses Qohelet's words). Whereas many people today find themselves empathizing with Qohelet, it is not immediately clear that this would have been the response of ancient audiences, who may have been more disturbed by his unorthodox conclusions than are modern readers.

4. Conclusion.

It is clear from both the ancient Near Eastern generic antecedents to OT autobiographies and the specific characteristics of autobiographical texts that the identification of this genre in the OT plays an important role in better understanding the meaning of the texts in which they are embedded. Autobiographical texts can operate in similar ways to other first-person accounts and often employ similar rhetorical devices, but also they offer an enhanced didactic element achieved through their authoritative reflection of past experiences.

See also FORM CRITICISM; FRAME NARRATIVE; QOHELET.

BIBLIOGRAPHY. **J. L. Crenshaw,** *Old Testament Wisdom: An Introduction* (rev. ed.; Louisville: Westminster John Knox, 1998); **T. C. Eskenazi,** *In an Age of Prose: A Literary Approach to Ezra-Nehemiah* (SBLMS 36; Atlanta: Scholars Press, 1988); **M. V. Fox,** *A Time to Tear Down and a Time to Build Up: A Rereading of Ecclesiastes* (Grand Rapids: Eerdmans, 1999); **G. Gusdorf,** "Conditions and Limits of Autobiography" in *Autobiography: Essays Theoretical and Critical*, ed. J. Olney (Princeton, NJ: Princeton University Press, 1980) 28-48; **W. L. Howarth,** "Some Principles of Autobiography" in *Autobiography: Essays Theoretical and Critical*, ed. J. Olney (Princeton, NJ: Princeton University Press, 1980) 84-114; **T. Longman III,** *Fictional Akkadian Autobiography: A Generic and Comparative Study* (Winona Lake, IN: Eisenbrauns, 1991); idem, *The Book of Ecclesiastes* (NICOT; Grand Rapids: Eerdmans, 1998); **D. G. Meade,** *Pseudonymity and Canon: An Investigation into the Relationship of Authorship and Authority in Jewish and Earliest Christian Tradition* (Grand Rapids: Eerdmans, 1987); **J. Olney,** ed., *Autobiography: Essays Theoretical and Critical* (Princeton, NJ: Princeton University Press, 1980); **C. L. Seow,** "Qohelet's Autobiography" in *Fortunate the Eyes That See: Essays in Honor of David Noel Freedman in Celebration of His Seventieth Birthday*, ed. A. B. Beck et al. (Grand Rapids: Eerdmans, 1995) 275-87; **C. J. Sharp,** "Ironic Representation, Authorial Voice, and Meaning in Qohelet," *BibInt* 12 (2004) 37-68; **M. A. Shields,** *The End of Wisdom: A Reappraisal of the Historical and Canonical Function of Ecclesiastes* (Winona Lake, IN: Eisenbrauns, 2006); **S. Smith and J. Watson,** *Reading Autobiography: A Guide for Interpreting Life Narratives* (Minneapolis: University of Minnesota Press, 2001); **J. Sturrock,** *The Language of Autobiography: Studies in the First Person Singular* (Cambridge: Cambridge University Press, 1993); **B. K. Waltke,** *The Book of Proverbs: Chapters 1-15* (NICOT; Grand Rapids: Eerdmans, 2004); **K. J. Weintraub,** *The Value of the Individual: Self and Circumstances in Autobiography* (Chicago: University of Chicago Press, 1978).

M. A. Shields

B

BATTLE IMAGERY. *See* WARFARE IMAGERY.

BEN SIRA. *See* SIRACH, BOOK OF.

BIBLICAL THEOLOGY. *See* WISDOM AND BIBLICAL THEOLOGY.

BICOLON, BICOLA. *See* POETICS, TERMINOLOGY OF.

BOAZ

Boaz is one of the three major characters in the book of *Ruth. His name means "in him is strength," but the book does not exploit the meaning to advance its plot, as it does with *Naomi. According to Ruth 4:21 and 1 Chronicles 2:11, Boaz was the son of Salmon and so a descendant of Judah. Matthew 1:5 adds that his mother (or ancestress) was Rahab, presumably the harlot in Joshua 2. Boaz was a kinsman of Elimelech and, by means of levirate marriage to Ruth, became the great-grandfather of *David. It is unknown whether he was married to someone other than Ruth and had other children.

    1. Boaz's Context
    2. Boaz's Kindness
    3. Boaz's Legacy

1. Boaz's Context.

According to Ruth 1:1, Boaz lived during the days of the judges, a time of apostasy, oppression and upheaval. The judges followed the events of the conquest of Canaan as narrated in the book of Joshua and preceded the rise of monarchy in Israel as described in the books of Samuel. According to the book of Judges, the tribes of Israel repeatedly disregarded Yahweh's covenant with them and came under the dominion of surrounding peoples. Before Boaz is first introduced (Ruth 2:1), Ruth 1:1 further mentions a famine that occurred in Israel at least ten years before Boaz and Ruth met. The book of Ruth does not explicitly interpret the famine as a Deuteronomic curse for covenantal infidelity (cf. Deut 28:15-48).

Although the famine is said to have driven Elimelech and Naomi from Israel to Moab, how the famine affected Boaz lies beyond the book's interest. Ruth 1:6, however, mentions the blessing of Yahweh that ended the famine and presumably provided the climate for Boaz to succeed as a landowner, or at least add to his earlier estate. Ruth 2:1 describes Boaz as *ʾîš gibbôr ḥayîl*, which could be translated "a man of substance and character." Although the expression could have a military connotation (cf. Josh 1:14; 1 Sam 16:18), nothing in the book of Ruth indicates that Boaz was a mighty warrior or a military hero (Block, 651). Rather, he was a godly man in a spiritually dreary era and a well-to-do resident of famine-stricken Bethlehem. The *Targum goes so far as to translate as "a powerful man, strong in the law" (Beattie, 22). Although the introduction of Boaz as a Torah scholar might be an overly expanded reading, the Targum has appreciably conveyed information about Boaz that becomes clearer throughout the remainder of the book: Boaz knew the law and followed it, even at personal cost.

2. Boaz's Kindness.

Ruth 2 begins with Ruth's "chance" wandering into the field of Boaz, about whom she at the time knew nothing. The kindness that Boaz showed Ruth was extraordinary. He told her to stay in his field and allowed her to glean beside the women who were binding cut grain, even though this part of the field normally was off limits to gleaners (Bush, 128). He gave Ruth access to the water supply and even ate with her.

He instructed his workers not to disturb her and so became her protector. Something else to note about Boaz's kindness is the vocabulary used of Ruth in chapter 2. Whereas Ruth called herself a foreigner (*nokriyyâ*) in Ruth 2:10, and said that she was not on the same level as a servant girl (*šipḥâ*) of Boaz in Ruth 2:13, Boaz used "young woman" (*naʿărâ*) in Ruth 2:5 and "my daughter" (*bittî*) in Ruth 2:8. Rather than emphasizing the social distance between him and Ruth and so belittling her, he affirmed her personhood and elevated her standing in the group (Berlin 1983, 89; Block, 659).

Far from being xenophobic, Boaz welcomed a foreigner, even a Moabite, onto his property. Although Deuteronomy 23:3 excluded Moabites from the assembly of Yahweh and prohibited Israelites from making a treaty of friendship with Moab, Boaz recognized Ruth's faith in Yahweh, as evidenced by her loving-kindness to Naomi, and properly regarded her as a member of the covenant community (see Dray, 35). He further invoked God's blessing on her for seeking refuge in the God of Israel. Boaz's own actions indicated his willingness to assist others, but he could not have known at this point how instrumental he would be in the realization of his prayerful blessing of Ruth (Ruth 2:12).

Ruth's initial reaction to Boaz helps the modern reader understand his magnanimity. She was astonished that the landowner would go so much beyond the requirement of the law. Surely Boaz's laborers observed and marveled too (Block, 666). When Ruth returned home at the end of the day, Naomi took note of Boaz's generosity and began to see the hand of God favorably at work in her situation. In Boaz, God's grace had a human face (Sakenfeld, 48). The references to Yahweh in his discussion with his laborers and Ruth indicate that an appreciation of God's grace to him lay behind his kind treatment of others (Block, 655; LaCocque, 65).

His kindness became even more extraordinary on the threshing floor when Ruth approached him to serve as *kinsman-redeemer for Naomi's husband, Elimelech, and her husband, Mahlon. After being awkwardly awakened in the middle of the night, he readily agreed to care for Ruth and Naomi, raise up an heir for their deceased husbands, and hold his deceased kinsmen's property in trust for the heir. When Ruth returned from the threshing floor and reported to Naomi that Boaz did not want her to return empty-handed (Ruth 3:17), Boaz signaled that he would relieve Naomi's earlier complaint about emptiness (Ruth 1:21). The same Hebrew word for "emptily" (*rêqām*) occurs in both verses. Not only would Boaz fill Naomi's stomach with food, but also he would take steps to fill her arms with a son to inherit Elimelech's property.

In essence, Boaz was willing to be the answer to his prayer in Ruth 2:12, but doing so would involve substantial cost to himself. The kinsman-redeemer had to look beyond any personal advantage to the promotion of a disadvantaged relative's full participation in the covenant community (Meyers, 21). The motivation involved belief in the unfailing promise of Yahweh to redeem his fallen creation, which Canaan anticipated, and give an eternal inheritance to his people, even those who had died. In the NT the theme of inheritance made possible by a kinsman-redeemer reaches fulfillment in the person and work of Jesus Christ (see 1 Pet 1:3-5).

Boaz contrasts with the nearer kinsman who was unwilling to put his own assets at risk in order to secure the attachment of Elimelech's name to his property and provide for the temporal needs of Naomi and Ruth. He who would not maintain the name of Elimelech with his patrimony and care for destitute widows remains anonymous (Trible, 190). He seemingly had no appreciation for grace, either received or given, but rather chose what LaCocque (111) calls "the letter of the law." By contrast, Boaz willingly assumed the usufructuary rights to Elimelech's land, married Ruth, and raised Obed, who later inherited Elimelech and Mahlon's patrimony. Boaz answered Ruth's petition on behalf of her deceased father-in-law and husband and thereby demonstrated a living, active and grace-appreciative faith. His name is honorably remembered in the royal and messianic line of David (Mt 1:5).

3. Boaz's Legacy.

Some scholars have concluded that the aristocratic Boaz fell in love with the attractive but socially inferior Ruth. His seemingly kind gestures supposedly had an ulterior and all-too-familiar motive (Fewell and Gunn). Other scholars draw attention to Boaz's alleged perpetuation of androcentrism. Rather than being heroic, Boaz only contributed to the ongoing problem of women's economic dependence on male provision (Sakenfeld, 10, 55-56). There is another way to understand the message of the book.

As seen especially in the closing genealogy, the book of Ruth shares the interest of the book of Judges in kingship as the solution to the woes and ills of the generations after Joshua. Whereas Judges documents the need for a king and indirectly makes an apology for David, Ruth actually names David as the hoped-for king who would put an end to the apostasy and anarchy of the period of the judges. Boaz appears in the genealogy of David and is honorably listed in the seventh position. Why?

The biblical writers associated David's kingdom with the kingdom of God. Aware of David's flaws, they nevertheless believed that Yahweh had made a covenant with David and would work out his plan of redemption through Davidic kingship. What Boaz and Ruth did is instructive for how God builds his kingdom. He uses the faithfulness of godly people in mundane circumstances to advance his purpose. Where there is warm adherence to the covenant, the mundane becomes the scene for the sacred, and otherwise average people contribute, often unknowingly, to a work of God that is much bigger than an individual act of faithfulness and compassion (see Berlin 1994, 259-60). For the biblical writers, Boaz (and Ruth) humbly participated in the establishment of God's reign through David and ultimately, according to the NT, though David's son, Jesus.

See also FEMINIST INTERPRETATION; KINSMAN-REDEEMER AND LEVIRATE; RUTH 1: BOOK OF; RUTH 2: ANCIENT NEAR EASTERN BACKGROUND.

BIBLIOGRAPHY. **D. R. G. Beattie,** trans., *The Targum of Ruth* (ArBib 19; Collegeville, MN: Liturgical Press, 1994); **A. Berlin,** *Poetics and Interpretation of Biblical Narrative* (BLS 9; Sheffield: Almond, 1983); idem, "Ruth and the Continuity of Israel," in *Reading Ruth: Contemporary Women Reclaim a Sacred Story*, ed. J. A. Kates and G. T. Reimer (New York: Ballantine Books, 1994) 255-60; **D. I. Block,** *Judges, Ruth* (NAC 6; Nashville: Broadman & Holman, 2002); **F. Bush,** *Ruth, Esther* (WBC 9; Dallas: Word, 1996); **S. Dray,** "Ruth 3:1-4:22: Living in Grace," *Evangel* 14 (1996) 35-37; **D. N. Fewell and D. M. Gunn,** *Compromising Redemption: Relating Characters in the Book of Ruth* (Louisville: Westminster John Knox, 1990); **A. LaCocque,** *Ruth,* trans. K. C. Hanson (CC; Minneapolis: Fortress, 2004); **C. Meyers,** "The Family in Early Israel," in *Families in Ancient Israel* (Louisville: Westminster John Knox, 1997) 1-47; **K. D. Sakenfeld,** *Ruth* (IBC; Louisville: Westminster John Knox, 1999); **P. Trible,** *God and the Rhetoric of Sexuality* (OBT; Philadelphia: Fortress, 1978).   D. Ulrich

BODY IMAGERY. *See* WASF.

C

CAESURA. *See* POETICS, TERMINOLOGY OF.

CANON

The Greek term *kanōn,* derived from a Semitic root meaning "reed," was first employed in what has become its technical theological sense (i.e., a recognized and fixed collection of authoritative sacred writings) by the church fathers in the fourth century AD However, although the terminology is relatively late, the concept existed much earlier. It is implicit, for example, in the notion of "Scripture(s)" reflected in the NT, and it is generally also inferred from the peculiar talmudic expression "defile the hands" (probably indicating the necessity of ceremonial washing after handling sacred writings), used by Jews from the first century AD. Given the nature of Second Temple Judaism as "a religion of the book," the roots of this concept of canonical Scripture presumably go back still further. To some extent this is confirmed by the testimony of the OT itself to the recognition of some such body of literature (e.g., 2 Kings 22:8—23:25; Neh 8:8—10:36; Dan 9:2; Zech 7:12). Such testimony, however, relates to the Pentateuch and the Prophets (two of the three major canonical sections of the Hebrew OT [Tanak]). With respect to the Writings (the third section of the Hebrew canon, and of particular interest for the present volume), there is no explicit OT testimony to the canonicity of its contents. Evidence for its canonicity must be sought elsewhere. Therefore this article will consider the following:

1. Canonicity and the Formation of the Old Testament Canon
2. Witnesses to the Canonicity of the Writings as a Whole
3. Canonicity of Particular Books within the Writings

1. Canonicity and the Formation of the Old Testament Canon.

The canonical Hebrew OT reflects a threefold division: the Law, the Prophets (subdivided into Former Prophets [Joshua, Judges, Samuel, Kings] and Latter Prophets [Isaiah, Jeremiah, Ezekiel, the Twelve]) and the Writings (*Psalms, *Job, *Proverbs, the Five Scrolls or *Megillot [*Ruth, *Song of Songs, *Ecclesiastes, *Lamentations, *Esther], Daniel, Ezra, Nehemiah, Chronicles). Admittedly, there is considerable variation in Jewish arrangements of the Writings or Hagiographa (see Beckwith, 452-64), but its contents are uniformly agreed upon. While the inclusion of Daniel in this third part of the Hebrew canon (rather than in the Prophets) may be explained (at least in part) by its distinct genre (apocalyptic), the presence of Ezra, Nehemiah, Chronicles, Esther and arguably Daniel may be due to the fact that the second canonical division was already closed. On the basis of this latter premise and the evidence from Qumran, many suggest that the content of the Writings, the final section of the Hebrew canon to be closed, was fixed sometime between the fifth century and the second century BC. The scholarly consensus in the mid-twentieth century suggested a much later terminus (AD 90), but now it is widely agreed that this was based on a faulty understanding of rabbinic discussions that took place at Jamnia (see 2.9 below). Moreover, it fails to give adequate cognizance to the evidence supporting an earlier date, to which we now turn.

2. Witnesses to the Canonicity of the Writings as a Whole.

2.1. Septuagint. The testimony of the Septuagint (LXX) with respect to canonicity is complicated by the fact that extant copies (codices from the fourth and fifth centuries AD) reflect a "larger" canon, interspersing a variety of apocryphal Jewish books among those traditionally recognized by Jews and Protestants as "Scripture." However, there is evidence to suggest that this "larger" canon was not reflected in the original form of the LXX—for example, Philo never cites any of these apocryphal books, and the Jews subsequently replaced the LXX with Aquila's Greek translation (which excluded all apocryphal books).

Besides having additional material, the LXX arranges the canonical books quite differently, appending Ruth to Judges, Lamentations to Jeremiah, including Chronicles, Ezra-Nehemiah and Esther with the Former Prophets, and grouping the poetical and wisdom books (Job, Psalms, Proverbs, Ecclesiastes, Song of Songs) together, along with *Wisdom of Solomon and *Sirach. From this arrangement one may conclude that either the MT's tripartite division was unknown or, more probably, ignored by Christian copyists for polemical reasons.

2.2. Dead Sea Scrolls. Evidence from the *Dead Sea Scrolls (DSS) has raised significant questions with respect to the shape of the Jewish canon by the second century BC. These ancient Jewish scrolls or fragments attest to every book in the Hebrew OT except Esther, but the collections also contain some apocryphal and pseudepigraphal texts, as well as sectarian documents and commentaries. Given the uncertainties over the canonical status of the various materials reflected in these manuscripts, and the fact that it is unclear whether the entire Qumran library has survived, the testimony of the DSS must be handled cautiously. Although it certainly attests to the compilation of and respect for all the canonical OT books (except Esther) by the second century BC, its value for reconstructing the canon of this Jewish sect or of Second Temple Judaism more generally is rather limited.

2.3. Sirach. This apocryphal work, written in Hebrew by Jesus ben Sira around 180 BC (*see* Sirach, Book of), reflects some familiarity with material now found in the third section of the Hebrew canon (e.g., Psalms, Proverbs). Around 132 BC ben Sira's grandson translated the book into Greek, adding a preface in which he refers three times to a tripartite division of the OT. However, while the first two divisions are given their traditional titles ("the law" and "the prophets"), the third is more vaguely described as "the

others that followed them," "the other books of our fathers" and "the rest of the books." This third group is not identified more explicitly, but apparently the author is referring to "a quite specific and venerable block of books" (Miller, 18) known both to himself and to his readers. It is reasonable, therefore, to infer that these "other books" are some or all of the Writings. It is unclear, how-ever, whether this collection was considered "closed" at this point or (*pace* Miller) precisely what status Sirach itself is presented as having vis-à-vis the Scriptures.

2.4. 1-2 Maccabees. The book of 1 Maccabees seems to grant canonical status to at least two books contained in the Writings (i.e., both Daniel and Psalms are cited as authoritative). In 2 Maccabees Nehemiah is said to have founded a library containing, among other things, "the books about the kings and prophets, and the writings of David" (2 Macc 2:13). Presumably, the latter included some or all of the Davidic psalms. In any case, a similar effort to preserve the nation's literary heritage is accredited to Judas Maccabeus in the following verse (2 Macc 2:14). The precise contents of these libraries are unknown, but undoubtedly many were considered to be sacred Scripture (see 1 Macc 1:56).

2.5. Philo. Philo's testimony is again of limited value. He does not sharply distinguish between inspired Scripture and inspired writers, nor does he quote from all the canonical books (Song of Songs, Ruth, Lamentations, Ecclesiastes, Esther, Daniel and Chronicles are never cited). Although it has been inferred from references to "psalms" (*Contempl.* 25) and "the holy writings" (*Contempl.* 28) that the author (most probably Philo [see Beckwith, 115-16]) had in mind the third and closed part of the Hebrew canon (see Leiman, 131-32; Beckwith, 116-17), the evidence is inconclusive; the first could refer simply to the Psalter, and the latter most likely refers to the entire OT.

2.6. The New Testament. While the NT's citations of "Scripture" (Jn 10:35; 19:36; 2 Pet 1:20; cf. Mt 22:29; Acts 18:24; Rom 1:4; 2 Tim 3:15) and its several references to "law" (e.g., Jn 10:34; 15:25) or "the law and the prophets" (e.g., Mt 5:17; Acts 13:15) seem to imply that there was a fixed and recognizable OT canon, the precise contents of this canon are nowhere spelled out. Indeed, the only clear allusion in the NT to the tripartite Hebrew canon is Jesus' reference to "the law, the prophets, and the psalms" (Lk

24:44). The last member of this group is taken by many scholars to refer to what later became known as "the Writings," using one of the most significant books to describe the whole. The plausibility of this theory is enhanced by the traditional location of the Psalter at the head of the Writings (with Ruth serving merely as an introduction in some arrangements) and by the possibility that other first-century writers (e.g., Philo) may have employed similar nomenclature.

Further evidence that the Writings was known in its talmudic arrangement (i.e., bracketed at either end by [Ruth-]Psalms and Chronicles [see Beckwith, 452-64]) by at least the first century AD has been sought in Jesus' statement concerning Zechariah's murder "between the altar and the sanctuary" (Lk 11:51; cf. Mt 23:35). Taking this as an allusion to the incident recorded in 2 Chronicles 24:21, many scholars have detected implicit attestation here to a canon that began with Genesis and ended with Chronicles. In terms of chronology, the martyrdom of Uriah (see Jer 26:23) took place over a century later, making the reference to Zechariah's murder rather anomalous, unless Jesus' statement reflects the canonical shape of the text. However, despite the omission of the qualifying clause in one important ancient manuscript (Sinaiticus), the Matthean text explicitly identifies the victim as the "son of Berakiah," presumably indicating the OT prophet of that lineage (see Zech 1:1), whose martyrdom, though nowhere explicitly recorded, is later attested in Jewish tradition (see the *Targum of Lam 2:20). In any case, unless we dismiss the qualifying phrase as a clumsy historical error (whether editorial or otherwise), we must conclude that too much weight has been placed on this text by those arguing that the OT canon was known in its final form by the early part of the first century AD. Although the NT suggests that some form of tripartite OT canon was recognized by this time, its precise contents, particularly with respect to the Hagiographa, remain uncertain. Some canonical books (e.g., Ezra, Nehemiah, Song of Songs, Esther, Ecclesiastes) are never cited, whereas Jude both cites *1 Enoch* (Jude 14-15) and alludes to *Assumption of Moses* (Jude 9; cf. Heb 11:35b-38). Admittedly, these latter texts are not explicitly cited as authoritative (i.e., as "Scripture"), but their inclusion (as well as the absence of some canonical books) undeniably complicates attempts to use the NT to determine the precise boundaries of the Writings during the first century AD.

2.7. 2 Esdras. This first-century Jewish apocalypse includes an obviously fictitious account of how Ezra dictated to five scribes the contents of ninety-four books over a period of forty days and nights. Of these books, only twenty-four were to be published (2 Esdr 14:45). This is almost certainly a reference to the twenty-four books of the traditional Jewish OT canon. Although obviously not proving that the OT canon was fixed by Ezra, this text clearly intimates that the Hebrew canon was closed not during the first century AD but rather much earlier, and certainly long before AD 90.

2.8. Josephus. In a treatise written around AD 100, the Jewish historian Flavius Josephus draws attention to the fact that Jews, unlike their Greek opponents, have only twenty-two sacred books: "Five belong to Moses . . . the prophets, who were after Moses, wrote down what was done in their times in thirteen books. The remaining four books contain hymns to God and precepts for the conduct of human life" (*Ag. Ap.* 1.8). It is generally believed that the latter four books refer to Psalms, Proverbs, Ecclesiastes and Song of Songs, and that the rest of the Writings have been incorporated in some way with the Prophets (cf. the arrangement in most English versions). Thus the total number that Josephus gives for the Prophets probably reflects a canonical arrangement of these books akin to that of the LXX (e.g., Daniel is counted with the Major Prophets, Ruth is included with either Judges or Psalms, Lamentations is appended to Jeremiah, and each of the following is counted as one book: Samuel, Kings, Chronicles, Ezra-Nehemiah, the Twelve). This seems preferable to the idea that Josephus (cf. also Origen and Jerome) was simply crunching the numbers to make them tie in with the number of letters in the Hebrew alphabet, or that his canon was smaller (so, e.g., Talmon, 68) than that attested to in the contemporary 2 Esdras.

Like 2 Esdras, Josephus traces the fixing of the canon back to the time of Ezra: "the reign of Artaxerxes, king of Persia, who reigned after Xerxes" (*Ag. Ap.* 1.8). Although this undoubtedly reflects popular belief rather than careful historical research, it nevertheless attests to the first-century Jewish conviction that the fixed OT canon could be traced far back into antiquity and certainly was no recent innovation.

2.9. Jamnia. Around the same time that Josephus was working on his treatise *Against Apion,* a group of rabbis gathered at Jamnia (or Jabneh), near Joppa, were debating, among other matters, which books "defiled the hands." Whereas a previous generation of scholarship greatly exaggerated the significance of these discussions, a seminal study by J. P. Lewis in 1964 exposed significant misunderstandings and misreadings of the rabbinic evidence (cf. Beckwith, 276) and thus undermined the reigning critical consensus (i.e., that the Writings [hence, the OT canon] was "officially" closed by the so-called Council of Jamnia about AD 90). However, subsequent scholarship has interpreted the significance of Lewis's findings in two quite different ways. Some scholars, such as R. Beckwith and S. J. Leiman, assume that canonization of the Writings predated Jamnia. For them, the focus of discussion at Jamnia centered more on whether certain books (i.e., Ecclesiastes and possibly Song of Songs) should be "withdrawn" from public use, not whether they should be included in the canon or be given some kind of official imprimatur. In contrast, other scholars, such as J. A. Sanders, insist that the "canonical process" was still ongoing, and that the Writings were not "stabilized" until later.

Thus Jamnia seems to throw little light on the question of the extent of the canon by the end of the first century AD, other than its indirect testimony to the fact that such a canon seems already to have been in existence (*pace* Sanders) that obviously included some or all of the Hagiographa.

2.10. The Talmud. As we noted (see 2.9 above), apparently only two OT books (Ecclesiastes and Song of Songs) came under rabbinic scrutiny at Jamnia. However, it is clear from elsewhere in the talmudic materials that some reservations were subsequently expressed over other books as well (namely, Ezekiel, Proverbs, Esther). However, as Beckwith (274-75) cogently argues, it is untenable to use these later disputes as evidence that the Writings (and hence, the OT canon) were still considered open. One of the five (Ezekiel) belongs to the Prophets, generally considered to have been closed centuries earlier. Moreover, the date of these rabbinic disputes would imply that the OT canon remained open for an incredibly long time (at least two centuries) after Jamnia. It seems safer, therefore, to conclude with Beckwith (275) that this later rabbinic debate "does not show that the canon was open at all." Indeed, if Broyde is correct, a key talmudic expression has been grossly misunderstood; Broyde maintains that "defiling the hands" refers more to keeping such books separate from food (i.e., treated with extra care because they contained the divine name, Yahweh) than to their canonical status per se. It is difficult, nevertheless, to ignore the fact that apparently there were other rabbinic reservations with respect to the books in question (see 3.2, 3.4, 3.5, 3.7, 3.8 below) that prompted the more radical to consider their withdrawal from public use.

2.11. The Church Fathers. As we noted (see 2.8 above), both Origen and Jerome (the latter only in his preface to Samuel and Kings) attest to a twenty-two book OT canon. Others (e.g., Tertullian) give the number as twenty-four, whereas still others (e.g., Augustine) suggest a much higher total (Augustine's "forty-four" most likely includes the OT apocryphal books embraced in the Roman Catholic canon). Thus, while some of the church fathers seem to confirm the traditional Jewish canon, others (particularly in the Western church) adopt the larger canon reflected in extant copies of the LXX. Moreover, some of the patristic testimony raises questions about the canonicity of particular books in the Hagiographa, such as Esther (see 3.8 below).

We may draw some conclusions from the foregoing discussion. A tripartite canon that incorporated some or all of the Hagiographa was certainly in existence by at least the second century BC (see Sirach's prologue), was recognized as authoritative Scripture by first-century AD Judaism (see NT references; Philo; Josephus), had a fixed number of books (depending on how they were counted, twenty-two or twenty-four) by the end of the first century AD (2 Esdras; Josephus; cf. Origen; Jerome), and was traditionally believed to have derived from the Persian era (see 2 Esdras; Josephus). Obviously, some uncertainties over the Writings as a whole remain, but more can be said concerning the canonicity of the individual books. It is to the latter, in particular those that are the immediate focus of the present volume, that we now turn.

3. Canonicity of Particular Books within the Writings.

3.1. Psalms. With respect to the canonicity of the Psalter, the DSS (in particular, 11QPs^a) have introduced a number of issues, not least the mixture of psalms from the biblical Psalter with other, nonbiblical psalms. Moreover, according to Sanders (*ABD* 1.841), over twenty percent of the psalms in the Masoretic canon find no representation in any of the thirty copies of the Psalter at Qumran, even though no block of the Masoretic Psalter is missing. This, along with the additional psalms reflected in the Qumran library, may suggest that the sectarians had a different canon for the Psalter (so Sanders and others) but may just as easily be explained (so Haran) in terms of their liturgical practice (in which both canonical and noncanonical compositions were used, much like a modern hymn book that includes biblical songs or paraphrases).

There are also some minor differences between the Hebrew and the Greek Psalters. The latter combines two consecutive Psalms (Pss 9—10 and Pss 114—115), divides two others (Ps 116 and Ps 147) into separate psalms (Pss 114—115 and Pss 146—147), and includes an additional psalm at the end of the collection (Ps 151, whose Hebrew equivalent is attested to in the DSS). However, the fact that this additional psalm is described as being "outside the number" (i.e., the canonical Psalter) makes it less likely, despite the Qumran evidence, that the Psalter was still in a state of canonical flux in the second century BC Rather, a collection comprising 150 psalms, ostensibly those reflected in the canonical Hebrew Psalter, clearly was recognized prior to its Greek translation for the LXX.

3.2. Proverbs. In the case of Proverbs, the DSS contribute little (together, the two Proverbs fragments attest to some 165 words or portions of words from various chapters, with only minor textual variants), other than corroborating the antiquity of the MT's recensional base. However, there is indirect attestation to the canonical status of Proverbs through usage of the conventional formula for quoting Scripture (i.e., "for it is written" [cf. CD-A 11:20-21, citing Prov 15:8]).

Although there are notable differences between the Hebrew and Greek versions of Proverbs (e.g., as well as having some 130 additional lines, the LXX arranges the latter part of the book quite differently [Prov 22:17—24:22; 30:1-14; 24:23-34; 30:15-33; 31:1-9; 25:1—29:27; 31:10-31], most likely attempting to draw together material of non-Israelite origin), such differences seem to be of minor canonical significance. Admittedly, some additions (and omissions) in the LXX may reflect a different Hebrew *Vorlage,* but other variants apparently reflect either scribal corruption within the LXX itself or the attempt to present an idiomatic and culturally acceptable translation for a Hellenistic audience.

Later rabbinic misgivings expressed over Proverbs and some of the other wisdom books (Ecclesiastes and Song of Songs) relate either to its allegedly "secular" nature (expressing merely Solomon's personal wisdom) or to its apparent internal contradictions (e.g., Prov 26:4, 5), which some rabbis obviously found difficult to harmonize (see Beckwith, 284). Obviously, such reservations were not shared by the majority.

3.3. Job. Although the book of Job's precise location within the Writings has fluctuated (in Hebrew manuscripts generally following either Psalms or Proverbs [see Beckwith, 452-64]), its canonicity has never seriously been questioned. The presence of an Aramaic paraphrase (11QtgJob) at Qumran, as well as the notorious difficulties that even the earliest translators evidently faced (see the LXX), attest both to the book's antiquity and, by implication, its perceived canonical status. Beckwith (73) tentatively suggests that the latter might also be reflected in the Hebrew text of Sirach 49:9 (which possibly associates Job with the prophets but may instead identify him with "strangers"). However, not only are the restored readings in this text uncertain, but also Beckwith's conclusions are not self-evident; one could equally argue that either reading reflects the author's relative ignorance of Job rather than his acquaintance with the canonical book. In any case, the canonicity of the book is amply attested apart from recourse to Beckwith's more speculative arguments.

3.4. Ecclesiastes. Within the Hebrew Bible Ecclesiastes is located among the Megillot, or Five Scrolls, a collection of shorter books (Ruth, Song of Songs, Ecclesiastes, Lamentations, Esther) in the Hagiographa associated with particular festivals. Given the somewhat radical nature of its critique of traditional values (e.g., *wisdom), the canonicity of Ecclesiastes is remarkable. What is not surprising is the fact that it evoked considerable controversy in antiquity. Polarized positions were adopted by the rival schools of Shammai and Hillel in the first century AD. Even though positive, Hillelite assessment of the book's canonicity prevailed, objections (see 2.9,

2.10 above) continued to be raised until at least the fourth century AD. Some have suggested that the inclusion of Ecclesiastes within the canon is due in no small part to the implicit associations of *Qohelet with Solomon, but the fact that other such books (e.g., the apocryphal *Odes of Solomon* and *Wisdom of Solomon*) remained excluded suggests that other factors played a much more significant role in recognizing its status as Scripture.

3.5. Song of Songs. Like Ecclesiastes, this unusual book may partly owe its inclusion within the canon to its associations with Solomon. Once again, however, other significant issues apparently were more decisive. It is also untenable to attribute its inclusion within the canon to the imaginative possibilities afforded by an allegorical interpretation. There does not appear to be much evidence of this among the LXX translators, whose work (c. 100 BC) contains no explicit allegorical tendencies. In any case, such a fanciful hermeneutic undoubtedly was prompted by the underlying premise that this book was already part of sacred Scripture.

As with Ecclesiastes, the status of Song of Songs clearly evoked rabbinic controversy, as is reflected most famously in Rabbi Akiba's strong affirmation recorded in the Mishnah: "No man ever disputed about the Song of Songs that it does not render the hands unclean, for all ages are not worth the day on which the Song of Songs was given to Israel: for all the Writings are holy, and the Song of Songs is the Holy of Holies" (*m. Yad.* 3:5). Whatever the precise nature of such rabbinic disputes (see 2.10 above), without doubt the erotic nature of Song of Songs fueled subsequent opposition in Christian circles, which evidently was met by the allegorical interpretations that lifted the poems above a sensual level.

3.6. Lamentations. The precise location of Lamentations within biblical codices has varied, but its canonicity has never seriously been questioned. This may be due in some measure to its association with Jeremiah in Jewish tradition (Lam 1:1 LXX attributes authorship to Jeremiah), a tradition that explains its location with the Prophets in the LXX and, through the influence of the Vulgate, in most English Bibles.

3.7. Ruth. Like Lamentations, the canonicity of Ruth has been almost universally accepted. Both the NT (Mt 1:5; Lk 3:32) and Josephus (*Ant.* 5.318-37) allude to its contents, and it is in-

cluded in the earliest canonical lists, both Jewish (*b. B. Bat.* 14b) and patristic (e.g., Melito; cf. also Origin and Jerome). Indeed, apart from a mention in the context of the rabbinic dispute over the matter of "defiling the hands" (over which, with respect to Ruth, Song of Songs and Esther, rabbinic opinion allegedly was unanimous), the only direct challenge to the book's status came from an obscure Nestorian commentator in the ninth century AD. One may infer from the Mishnah (*m. Yebam.* 76b-77b) that any rabbinic reservations would have been compounded by difficulties in harmonizing Ruth's portrayal of *levirate marriage and redemption laws with that reflected in the laws and narratives of the Pentateuch, as well as Ruth's more positive approach to marriages between Israelites and Moabites (cf. Deut 23:3-6). Thus, the fact that the canonical status of such a book was never challenged within Judaism clearly attests to the antiquity of that status.

3.8. Esther. Of all the Hagiographa (indeed, of the OT as a whole), the canonicity of Esther undoubtedly evokes the most questions. At least three observations are pertinent: (1) Esther is the only OT book not attested among the DSS; (2) talmudic evidence attests to a long history of debate, going back at least to the second century AD; (3) Esther's canonical status was implicitly or explicitly denied in early patristic writings (e.g., it is absent from Melito's list and rejected by Athanasius, Gregory of Nazianzus and Theodore of Mopsuestia). The book's absence from Qumran may well have been because it clashed with the community's liturgical calendar (so Beckwith, 291-94), but the rejection of this book by others is much more problematic. At least two factors were involved. It seems that it was the apparent secularity of its contents that initially brought the book's canonical status into question. This certainly would explain the more overtly theological and religious content of the noncanonical *Esther Additions reflected in the LXX. The second problem (insofar as the rabbis were concerned) related to the institution of a non-Mosaic festival (cf. *y. Meg.* 1:5; *b. Meg.* 7a) (*see* Purim). It is clear, however, that rabbinic opinions questioning the canonicity of books such as Esther reflect a minority view and are cited primarily to be refuted. Moreover, even though the canonical status of this book has continued to evoke considerable debate, negative evaluations generally have resulted from a failure to appreciate its admittedly more subtle theology.

3.9. Apocryphal Books (Sirach and Wisdom of Solomon). Although these apocryphal books are considered deuterocanonical in the Roman Catholic and Orthodox traditions, they are excluded from Protestant Bibles on the grounds that they were never part of the Jewish canon (for a more detailed discussion, *see* Sirach; Wisdom of Solomon).

4. Conclusion.
According to Beckwith (275), four books of the Hagiographa (Psalms, Job, Proverbs, Daniel) "are among the Old Testament books which, individually, have the fullest attestation to their canonicity in the literature of the last few centuries B.C. and the first century AD." As has been illustrated above, there is also considerable evidence for the canonicity of most of the other books as well. Although it is impossible to say exactly when it attained its final form, it seems fair to conclude that certainly by the second century BC, and possibly even earlier, this collection subsequently known as the Writings was widely recognized as the third and final section of the OT canon.

See also DEAD SEA SCROLLS; EDITORIAL CRITICISM; ESTHER 4: ADDITIONS; INTERTEXTUALITY; MEGILLOT AND FESTIVALS.

BIBLIOGRAPHY. **J.-M. Auwers and H. J. de Jonge,** eds., *The Biblical Canons* (BETL 163; Leuven: Leuven University Press, 2003); **R. Beckwith,** *The Old Testament Canon of the New Testament Church* (Grand Rapids: Eerdmans, 1985); **H. Blocher,** "Helpful or Harmful? The 'Apocrypha' and Evangelical Theology," *EuroJTh* 13.2 (2004) 81-90; **M. J. Broyde,** "Defilement of the Hands, Canonization of the Bible, and the Special Status of Esther, Ecclesiastes, and the Song of Songs," *Judaism* 44 (1995) 65-79; **F. F. Bruce,** *The Canon of Scripture* (Downers Grove, IL: InterVarsity Press, 1988); **S. B. Chapman,** *The Law and the Prophets: A Study in Old Testament Canon Formation* (FAT 27; Tübingen: Mohr Siebeck, 2000); **P. R. Davies,** *Scribes and Schools: The Canonization of the Hebrew Scriptures* (Louisville: Westminster John Knox, 1998); **S. Dempster,** "An 'Extraordinary Fact': Torah and Temple and the Contours of the Hebrew Canon," *TynBul* 48.1 (1977) 23-56; *TynBul* 48.2 (1977) 191-218; **P. W. Flint,** ed., *The Bible at Qumran: Text, Shape, and Interpretation* (Grand Rapids: Eerdmans, 2001); **M. Haran,** "11QPs[a] and

the Canonical Book of Psalms," in *Minhah le-Nahum: Biblical and Other Studies Presented to Nahum M. Sarna in Honour of His Seventieth Birthday,* ed. M. Brettler and M. Fishbane (JSOTSup 154; Sheffield: JSOT Press, 1993) 193-201; **M. Hengel,** *The Septuagint as Christian Scripture: Its Prehistory and the Problem of Its Canon* (Edinburgh: T & T Clark, 2002); **S. Z. Leiman,** *The Canonization of the Hebrew Scriptures: The Talmudic and Midrashic Evidence* (TCAAS 47; Hamden, CT: Archon Books, 1976); **J. P. Lewis,** "What Do We Mean by Jabneh?" *JBR* 32 (1964) 125-32; **L. M. McDonald and J. A. Sanders,** eds., *The Canon Debate: On the Origins and Formation of the Bible* (Peabody, MA: Hendrickson, 2002); **J. W. Miller,** *The Origins of the Bible: Rethinking Canon History* (New York: Paulist, 1994); **H. G. L. Peels,** "The Blood 'from Abel to Zechariah' (Matthew 23,35; Luke 11,50f.) and the Canon of the Old Testament," *ZAW* 113 (2001) 583-601; **J. A. Sanders,** "Canon," *ABD* 1:837-52; idem, "The Stabilization of the Tanak," in *A History of Biblical Interpretation,* 1: *The Persian Period,* ed. A. J. Hauser and D. F. Watson (Grand Rapids: Eerdmans, 2003) 225-52; **A. Stein-mann,** *The Oracles of God: The Old Testament Canon* (St. Louis: Concordia, 1999); **S. Talmon,** "Heiliges Schrifttum und kanonische Bücher aus jüdischer Sicht: Überlegungen zur Ausbildung der Grösse 'Die Schrift' im Judentum," in *Die Mitte der Schrift? Ein jüdisch-christliches Gespräch; Texte des Berner Symposions vom 6.-12. Januar 1985,* ed. M. Klopfenstein et al. (JudChr 11; Bern: Lang, 1987) 45-79; **J. Trebolle Barrera,** *The Jewish Bible and the Christian Bible: An Introduction to the History of the Bible,* trans. W. G. E. Watson (rev. ed.; Leiden: E. J. Brill; Grand Rapids: Eerdmans, 1998); **E. Ulrich,** "The Non-Attestation of a Tripartite Canon in 4Q MMT," *CBQ* 65 (2003) 202-14; **J. C. VanderKam,** "Authoritative Literature in the Dead Sea Scrolls," *DSD* 5.3 (1998) 382-402; idem, "Questions of Canon Viewed through the Dead Sea Scrolls," *BBR* 11.2 (2001) 269-92.

P. R. Williamson

CANONICAL INTERPRETATION. *See* HERMENEUTICS.

CANTO. *See* STANZA, STROPHE.

CHAOS AND DEATH
The *imagery associated with chaos and death in the literature of the ancient world functions

to inform human understanding of the realities of life under the principle of divine activity and design. Such texts are a reflex of cultural etiology—the search to understand and express primary causes and overarching structures in the divine and human realm. As such, these accounts grapple with the dark and difficult realities of human existence and interpret them as a subset of past and present struggles in the divine realm, often including the very process of creation. In the end, the portrayal of a divine act such as the ordering of chaos and the defeat of death acts as a pattern for understanding, preserving and transmitting religious and cultural traditions. Moreover, such stories work to express and codify societal order and codes of conduct as well as to vouchsafe for the efficacy of various religious rituals. Lastly, the study of the imagery of chaos and death in the OT has been both helped and hampered by the discovery of ancient Near Eastern texts having levels of similarity with various texts of the OT (particularly texts in *Job and *Psalms). These ancient Near Eastern texts can provide significant insight into the cognitive context of the biblical writer (and audience) and thus facilitate interpretive clarity and accuracy, but the search is riddled with irrational exuberance on the one hand and irrational avoidance on the other. With these possibilities and pitfalls in view, this article attempts to carefully navigate this search for meaning of chaos and death in the ancient Near East and the OT.

    1. Chaos
    2. Death as the Ultimate Expression of Chaos

1. Chaos.

1.1. Chaos in the Ancient Near East.
The story of divine struggle against chaos *(Chaoskampf)* is commonly symbolized as a battle between a storm god (or a god whose fight is described via storm imagery) and a sea god/goddess (usually denoted via a primordial watery abyss along with a sea serpent/dragon). The narration of this battle between the storm god and the sea god/goddess is frequently found in the context of cosmogonical (stories that focus on the events and mechanics of creation) or cosmological (stories that focus on the meaning of creation) accounts. As with ancient flood accounts, *Chaoskampf* stories are attested in many cultures in the ancient Near East and beyond (e.g., Mesopotamia, Anatolia, Greece, Mari,

Canaan, Syria, India, Egypt, Persia).

In a landmark study, *Schöpfung und Chaos in Urzeit und Endzeit* (1895), H. Gunkel attempted to show that the Babylonian myth *Enuma Elish*, chronicling Marduk's defeat of the sea dragon Tiamat and subsequent creation of the world, was the backdrop for several OT texts involving the imagery of YHWH battling the sea and sea creatures such as Leviathan. This view received widespread support until the discovery and publication of the Ugaritic corpus, after which the OT's references to YHWH's control over the sea, sea monsters and so forth were proposed to actually reflect Syro-Canaanite mythological texts, particularly those concerning Baal's battles with the sea and death. M. K. Wakeman's *God's Battle with the Monster* (1973), J. Day's *God's Conflict with the Dragon and the Sea* (1985) and C. Kloos's *Yhwh's Combat with the Sea* (1986) typify this adjusted approach to the topic of chaos. However, R. S. Watson's recent *Chaos Uncreated* (2005) has challenged this adjusted approach by arguing that chaos imagery is found with too much variation in terminology, context and coordinated motifs to be able to be brought under a single unifying theme.

1.1.1. Mesopotamian Chaos Imagery. Mesopotamia has a long history of stories involving battles against dragon-like creatures of the primordial sea. For example, in a third millennium BC Sumerian text The Feats and Exploits of Ninurta, the Ninurta defeats a seven-headed serpent (as well as other multiheaded adversaries) and contains the (related) primeval waters of Kur before being awarded kingship by the pantheon (Kramer, 76-83). Similarly, Tishpak, the city god of Eshnunna (later associated with the Hurrian storm god Teshup), defeats a monstrous sea dragon in a storm context, a battle likely represented on three Old Akkadian cylinder seals depicting a snake-like dragon with seven heads (Wiggermann, 117-33). Also, an eighteenth-century BC text from Mari notes that the storm god Adad gave the king of Mari (Zimri-Lim) the weapons that he used in his battle against the sea. These noted, the most analyzed Mesopotamian text vis-à-vis the chaos motif is that of *Enuma Elish* (this title is a transliteration of the Akkadian words beginning the text, meaning, "When on high . . ."). This text (*COS* 1.111:390-402) opens with a primeval watery chaos consisting of the male and female procreative powers: the primordial freshwater father, Apsu, and the primordial saltwater mother, Tiamat (also portrayed as a serpentine sea dragon). As these waters mingle, the early generation of gods comes forth representing aspects of the newly differentiated cosmos. This progression, however, engenders conflict as the noise of the newer gods hinders the rest of Apsu. Thus, Apsu determines to destroy the lower gods, but his plan is found out by the "all-knowing" Ea (also known as Nudimmud), who casts a spell on Apsu and slays him. Ea then rests, and his son Marduk is born, while Tiamat plots her revenge along with a host of grotesque demons that she brings forth. With this threat at hand, a new champion is sought, and ultimately Marduk is chosen under the condition that he be granted the highest position in the divine assembly. During the battle, Tiamat opens her mouth to devour Marduk when Marduk uses the wind to prevent Tiamat from closing her mouth and then shoots an arrow into her inward parts, killing her. Afterward, Marduk begins to create the world, using half of Tiamat's body as the firmament (waters) above and fixing a crossbar and posts to hold back these waters of heaven (cf. Gen 1:7-8). Marduk also kills Tiamat's viceroy Kingu (Qingu) and from his blood makes humankind for the purpose of relieving the work of the lower gods. Afterward, the gods construct Esagila (terraced Marduk palace in Babylon) and give Marduk their fifty names (assigning him their authority), formalizing his supremacy.

1.1.2. Egyptian Chaos Imagery. Egyptian texts involving aspects of the chaos motif overlap with the political aspirations of ancient Egyptian political capitals. In addition, Egyptian accounts demonstrate a strong tendency to synthesize and incorporate earlier accounts (and deities) into later stories. From the Old Kingdom Pyramid Texts of Heliopolis (City of the Sun) we learn that an endless ocean of water known as Nun existed in complete darkness before the creation of the cosmos. This watery abyss is often portrayed in temples as a sacred lake and was considered to continue to surround the heavenly lights. From the chaos waters of Nun arises the self-generating sun god Atum, who was understood as being coexistent with the waters of Nun. Atum subsequently differentiated a portion of the waters into the created realm with the balance of the chaos waters understood as an ever-present threat. Atum is often cast standing on a raised pyramid-shaped mound, a pri-

mordial hillock identified as Heliopolis. Atum was considered to be the life spring of all other deities (beginning with the foundational group of deities known as the *Ennead*, or *Pesdjet*) and perpetrator of *Monad* (the notion of totality and order). This *Monad* of Atum had both a constructive aspect, associated with the goddess Isis, and destructive aspect, associated with Seth, the god of chaos. The dynamics of the *Monad* also allowed for the integration of Atum with other aspects of the sun already in view by the time the Pyramid Texts were inscribed, most notably Re (Ra). In conjunction with the move of the capital to Memphis, the Memphite god Ptah was declared to have been the "First Principle," thereby taking precedence over all other recognized gods (*ANET,* 4). Ptah is noted in the Shabaka Stone as having given life to the other gods of Egypt (including Atum of Heliopolis) by means of the desire of his heart together with the creative power of his word. In the cosmogonic account from the city of Hermopolis, the Ogdoad (eight primordial deities [four couples] made by the god Thoth [who was reconfigured to Atum-Re in the New Kingdom period]) represented the conceptualization (and personification) of the elements resident within the primeval chaos preceding creation, including the primordial waters, void, darkness and concealed dynamic force (see Hart, 20-24). These primeval elemental couples interacted with creative efficacy and produced a primeval hillock identified as the city of Hermopolis. Afterward, they create Atum and the Ennead of Heliopolis. Later, priests from Thebes adjusted the Hermopolis account to elevate Amun (the concealed dynamic force of the Ogdoad) as a transcendental deity who is above creation. Like Atum, Amun is later syncretized with Re.

1.1.3. Syro-Canaanite Chaos Imagery. A cache of cuneiform texts discovered on the north Syrian coast at the maritime city-state of Ugarit (Ras Shamra) includes six tablets commonly referred to as the Baal Cycle or Baal Myth (the original title is unknown). The Ugaritic Baal Cycle (*KTU* 1.1-1.6; *COS* 1.86:241-74) has three major sections: (1) the battle between the storm god Baal Hadad (usually referred to simply by his title Baal [lord]) and the sea god Yam(m/mu); (2) the building of a house (palace) for Baal; (3) Baal's battle with Mot (death), ruler of the underworld. The specific sequence of these sections is subject to some dispute (see the summary in Smith,

2-25), partly because of the fragmentary condition of the tablets (Wyatt [1996, 21] estimates that no more than half of the original composition has survived). The Baal Cycle illustrates the drama behind a struggle among the sons of El for power and preeminence within the pantheon, most notably between Yamm and Baal. In addition to sea and river, Baal's adversary Yamm is represented also by monsters associated with the sea, specifically the sea dragon Tunnan (cf. Heb *tannîn* ["dragon"]) and the seven-headed sea creature Lotan (cf. Heb *liwyātān* ["Leviathan"]), probably alternate names for the same creature (note their parallel usage in *KTU* 1.3.III.37-40; 1.83 [see Pitard, 279]). At first, Yamm is given permission from El to build a palace for himself, but as Yamm seeks to exert his authority (including seeking to have Baal handed over so that he could seize his gold), Baal resists and battle ensues. Yamm has the upper hand in battle until the craftsman god Kothar wa-Hasis (or Kothar) intervenes and provides Baal with two clubs, the second of which successfully takes out Yamm. It is in this context that Baal is called the "Rider of the Clouds" and described as having an "everlasting kingdom" and "eternal dominion." After Baal's defeat of the sea god, Astarte exclaims, "Yamm is indeed dead! Baal shall be king!" and work on Baal's palace begins. This noted, in another tablet (*KTU* 1.3), Baal's sister Anat also claims to have defeated the sea and its creatures.

1.2. Old Testament Chaos Imagery. As with the ancient Near Eastern texts noted above, the OT utilizes a variety of images from the realm of nature to portray what is chaotic and seemingly uncontrollable. In further similarity with numerous ancient Near Eastern *Chaoskampf* myths, these inimical forces are drawn from the aquatic realm—the deep powerful sea and its fearsome creatures. Conversely, as also attested in ancient Near Eastern texts, the imagery for the presence and activity of God is often mediated through that which accompanies the battering of the sea—storm imagery.

1.2.1. The Primordial Sea. The image of a raging personified cosmic deep *(tĕhôm)* is perhaps the most pervasive symbol of chaos in ancient mythological texts. The cognate of the Hebrew term *tĕhôm* occurs also in the Ugaritic corpus *(thm/thmt)* and designates the primordial cosmic waters in those texts (cf. *KTU* 1.100.1; 1.3.III.25). There may also be an indirect philological rela-

tionship between *tĕhôm* and the saltwater goddess Tiamat of the *Enuma Elish* account (see Tsumura, 45-52).

In addition to the *tĕhôm*, texts with a mythopoeic (mythopoetic) feel also speak of the waters *(mayim)*, river(s) *(nāhār)* and flood(s) (e.g., *mabbûl, šibbōlet*), as seen in Psalm 93:3; Nahum 1:4; Habakkuk 3:8-9 (cf. *KTU* 1.2). The primeval waters were understood as being located both above the firmament and beneath the earth, with the "windows of heaven" understood as the entry point for water (rain) from above. The understanding of the cosmic deep extends to the realm of God, as YHWH is described as sitting enthroned over the flood as king forever (Ps 29:10) and praised as the one who "lays the beams of his upper chambers in the waters" (Ps 104:3). This is reminiscent of the location of the throne of Ea in the midst of Apsu (the primeval fresh waters) in the Babylonian *Enuma Elish*. Such texts also bring to mind the placement of the palace of the Syro-Canaanite god El, which is described in the Baal Cycle as being located on a cosmic mountain that serves as the source of the primordial oceans/water springs (see *KTU* 1.3.V.6-7; 1.4.IV.21-22; 1.6.I.33-34). In addition, certain poetic texts personify the waters as follows:

The waters saw you, O God; the waters saw you and writhed, even the deeps trembled. (Ps 77:16)
The deep sounded forth its voice; it lifted its hands up high. (Hab 3:10 [cf. Job 28:14; Ps 93:3])
Deep cries out to deep at the sound of your waterfalls. (Ps 42:7)

In addition to these examples, the usage of the deep in the blessings of Jacob and Moses could be construed as personifying the *tĕhôm* (cf. Gen 49:25; Dt 33:13), and the absence of the article with "sea" in Job 9:8 and Psalm 78:13 has been noted as marking *yām* ("sea") as a proper name (although the absence of the article is commonplace in poetry).

On the other hand, YHWH is described as the one who has created the sea and continues to control it, as in Psalm 95: "To him belongs the sea; for he made it as well as the dry land which his hands formed" (Ps 95:5 [cf. Ps 104:6, 9; 146:6]). YHWH is shown to have sovereign mastery over the sea (e.g., "he tramples down the waves of the sea" [Job 9:8]) and everything else in the created realm (see Curtis, 255). In short, "Whatever YHWH pleases, he does—in heaven, in earth, in the seas, and in all deeps" (Ps 135:6 [cf. Jer 31:35]). Waters are described as controlled by God, the boundaries of the sea are noted as specifically set by God (Prov 8:28-29), and the sea is described as kept in place by YHWH (even imprisoned [see Job 38:8-11]). Such descriptions, especially when heard in their cultural context and in light of the details of other ancient Near Eastern texts, underscore YHWH's mastery over the seemingly uncontrollable seas and thus foster trust and faith in YHWH's power. Lastly, it should not be missed that the controlling of the sea and walking on the water demonstrated by Jesus recapitulates the divine mastery over watery forces and consequently shows his divine nature and royal status (Mt 8:23-27; 14:22-34; cf. Job 26:12; Ps 65:7; 89:9 [see Wyatt 1998, 855]).

1.2.2. Chaos Monsters of the Primordial Sea. In addition to the motif of the inimical waters (*těhôm*/deep; *yām*/sea; *mayim*/waters; *nāhār*/river) subjugated by YHWH, other texts intermix YHWH's control over the waters with his mastery over aquatic opponent(s) having serpent- and dragon-like features. These creatures occasionally appear with the term for "snake," providing a serpentine imagery for these monsters of the deep (as also seen in the various sea monsters attested in the various ancient Near Eastern stories noted above). It should be noted that the contextual proximity and interplay of these sea creatures with the oceanic deep makes it clear that they are either closely related to the image of the chaotic waters or perhaps even function as metaphorical synonyms. Attempts have been made to connect these creatures (as well as Behemoth [see Job 40:15-24]) with various animals (such as the crocodile and hippopotamus), but the imagery and descriptions used of these creatures make such identification untenable (if anything, prehistoric fish and dinosaurs would have the closest points of connection). Instead, these aquatic monsters probably are intended to have a mythological tone in line with the poetic intent of a given passage. This is consistent with the fact that a monstrous sea serpent was a common mythological symbol for chaos in the ancient Near East. Lastly, although the frequent parallel usage of these terms in the Bible and elsewhere (such as the Baal Cycle [see *KTU*

1.5.I.1]) implies that only one serpentine sea creature associated with the primordial deep is envisaged, the most common terms found in the OT ("Rahab," "Leviathan," "Tannin") will be surveyed separately below.

The term *Rahab* (Heb *rahab*) appears six times in the OT and has no known cognates in other ancient Near Eastern languages. In two of these occurrences (Ps 87:4; Is 30:7) Rahab refers to Egypt (see 1.5 below). In the other four occurrences, however, Rahab seems to be a serpentine creature associated with the sea. For example, Job notes that God "with his power quieted the sea and with his understanding he crushed Rahab; with his wind ['Spirit'?] the sky became clear; his hand pierced the fleeing serpent" (Job 26:12-13). Also, in a celebration of God's mastery over the created realm Job notes that "the helpers of Rahab crouch down" beneath YHWH (Job 9:13). In like manner, the psalmist notes that God rules the swelling of the sea and stills the rising waves, and that he crushed Rahab "like a corpse" (Ps 89:8-10). Similarly, Isaiah notes that God "cut Rahab in pieces, pierced the dragon . . . the one who caused the sea to dry up, the waters of the great deep [*těhôm*]" (Is 51:9-10). As noted above, the parallel structure of these occurrences indicates a close relationship between Rahab and the sea *(yām)* in Job 26:12; Psalm 89:9-10; Isaiah 51:9-10; Rahab and the deep *(těhôm)* in Isaiah 51:9-10; Rahab and the gliding serpent in Job 26:13; as well as Rahab and the dragon *(tannîn)* in Isaiah 51:9.

Another OT sea creature that evokes much comparative discussion is Leviathan (Heb *liwyātān*). This term occurs six times in the OT (twice in Is 27:1) and has the Ugaritic cognate *ltn* ("Lotan" or "Litan"). As with Rahab, the usage of Leviathan is associated with the sea (see Job 41:1; Ps 104:26), including the image of YHWH dividing the sea and controlling the rivers with his strength (Ps 74:13-15). In addition, Leviathan is used in conjunction with the serpent (*nāḥāš* [Job 26:13; Is 27:1]), as well as the "dragon *[tannîn]* that lives in the sea" (see Is 27:1). The overlap of this imagery can be appreciated from the following texts:

> You divided the sea by your strength; you broke the heads of the sea dragons [pl. of *tannîn*] upon the waters. You crushed the heads of Leviathan; you gave him as food for

the people of the wilderness. You cleaved open springs and brooks; you caused the mighty rivers to dry up. (Ps 74:13-15)

On that day YHWH will punish with his fierce, great and mighty sword Leviathan the gliding serpent, yes, Leviathan the twisting serpent; he will slay the dragon that lives in the sea. (Is 27:1)

In addition, Leviathan's description as a "twisting" and "multiheaded serpent" that is associated with the sea and has been subjugated by God (see Job 41; Ps 73:13-14) is more than reminiscent of the "twisting" serpent with "seven heads" defeated by Baal (and Anat) in conjunction with their battle(s) against the sea god Yamm in the Ugaritic corpus:

Surely I smote Yamm [Sea], beloved of El; surely I made an end of Nahar [River], the mighty god; surely I choked Tunnan [Dragon] . . . I smote the twisting Lotan, the tyrant with seven heads. (KTU 1.3.III.37-40 [cf. KTU 1.5.I.1-4])

Yet, although this sea serpent is associated with the imagery of watery chaos and is subjugated by YHWH, it should not be missed that Leviathan is described as one of the creatures made by YHWH and dependant upon him for life (Ps 104:24-30). Lastly, the likely relationship between Leviathan and the creatures of the book of Revelation should be noted. These creatures—a "great red dragon having seven heads" that spews "water like a river from its mouth" (Rev 12:3, 15) and a beast from the sea having "seven heads" (Rev 13:1 [cf. Rev 17:3])—function as the personification of rebellion against divine order (i.e., chaos) and as such provide an ideal image for *Satan (cf. Rev 12:9; 20:2) in the unfolding of an overarching eschatological schema (see 1.6 below).

In addition to Rahab and Leviathan, another OT creature that seems to be some type of sea serpent or sea dragon is Tannin (Heb *tannin*). This term occurs fourteen times in the OT and has the Ugaritic cognate *tnn* (*tunnan/tannin*). A number of these occurrences are found in OT books outside the focus on the present study, including God creating the "great sea monsters [*tanninim*]" on day five in the Genesis creation account (Gen 1:21), Aaron's staff becoming a Tannin in the midst of Pharaoh and his servants

(Ex 7:9-12 [3x]), as a synonym for "snake" (Deut 32:33; Ps 91:13), and as a symbolic designation for the Babylonian Nebuchadnezzar (Jer 51:34) as well as the Egyptian Pharaoh (Ezek 29:3; 32:2). The inimical nature of the Tannin (and the sea) is implied in Job's question to God, "Am I the sea, or the sea dragon [*tannin*] that you have set a guard over me?" (Job 7:12). Other instances of Tannin tap into the *Chaoskampf* motif, such as God's piercing Tannin and cutting up Rahab in the ancient past (Is 51:9), God's breaking of the heads of Tannin in the waters and dividing the sea (Ps 74:13 [see above]), and God's slaying of the Tannin that lives in the sea on the day Leviathan is vanquished (Is 27:1 [see above]). A similar reference to the deity subduing the "water monster" occurs in the Egyptian Instructions to Merikare (*COS* 1.35:61-66). Similarly, recall that in the Baal Cycle Anat's claims of defeating Yamm included victory against *Tunnan*, cognate to *tannin* (*KTU* 1.3.III.40 [see above]). Given the stress of God's creation of and control over Tannin, the psalmist exhorts the Tannin and the deep (*těhôm*) itself to praise YHWH (Ps 148:7). These examples also show the parallel usage of Tannin with Leviathan, Rahab and the deep (*těhôm*). Lastly, we note that YHWH is portrayed as a fire-breathing dragon in Ps 18:8 in the rescuing of his people, a description similar to the smoke- and fire-snorting Leviathan in Job 41:18-21 (see *ANEP*, 671, 691). A "good dragon" image is also found in the Ugaritic corpus (*KTU* 1.83.5-7), and Baal is described as being enthroned "like the flood dragon" (RS 24.245).

1.2.3. God and Storm Imagery. As noted above, storm imagery is associated with the god that successfully overcomes the chaotic sea and its creature(s) in several ancient *Chaoskampf* myths. In like manner, the OT commonly portrays God's presence in conjunction with storm imagery (often called a "storm theophany"), such as strong winds, lightning and dark clouds. For example, God is noted as one who surrounds himself with clouds (Job 22:14; Ps 97:2), who walks upon the wings of the wind (Ps 18:10; Ps 104:3; cf. Job 22:14), who uses clouds as his chariot (Ps 104:3), who causes clouds to burst with lightning (Job 37:11), who clears up the sky with his wind (Job 26:13), whose voice brings forth abundant rain (Job 38:34; Ps 78:23) and whose thunders shake the earth (Ps 29). With respect to wind imagery, one complicating factor in understanding

YHWH's relationship with the wind is the fact that the common Hebrew word for "wind" is the same as that used for God's "spirit" (as is the case for the Greek term in the NT). This detail aside, a number of these descriptions have points in common with the Syro-Canaanite storm god Baal Hadad, as Baal is understood to have hegemony over storm forces—wind, clouds, rain, thunder, lightning. Thus Baal, like YHWH, is described as riding on the clouds (Ps 68:4) and controlling the release of water via the windows (or floodgates) of heaven (Ps 104:13; cf. Gen 7:11; 8:2). Recall that Baal used the wind against the sea god Yamm in the Canaanite Baal Cycle. Likewise, in the Babylonian *Enuma Elish* account Marduk used the wind in his battle against Tiamat ("He made the flood wave and roused Tiamat . . . he created the four fearful wind . . . he made an evil wind"). Yet YHWH's mastery over such meteorological forces is not portrayed in any sort of battle context but rather stresses his omnipotence over all aspects of the created realm.

Another feature of storm imagery is that of darkness (which can be effected by dark clouds and/or control over the sun and other luminaries). Although the imagery of darkness is not a major part of the Baal Cycle or *Enuma Elish* (although a section near the end of the Baal Cycle seems to imply that the *tnn* [sea dragon] presents a danger to the sun [cf. Job 3:8]), it plays a sizable role in Egyptian accounts, partly due to the Egyptian understanding of a perpetual animosity between the sun disk (in its various divine manifestations) and the chaos serpent. Paintings in the tomb of Ramesses VI (twelfth century BC) indicate that the span of day and night is a cycle of the Egyptian sky goddess Nut swallowing and then birthing the sun god Re, who transverses the sky in the Sun Barge. During this nightly passage, the darkness-dwelling chaos serpent Apep (often known by the Greek name "Apophis") attempts to destroy the sun. In the OT, God's creation and control of light and darkness (Ps 139:12; Is 45:6-8) and control over the domain of both (Ps 104:19-23) mitigates against such a mythological nuance. Instead, God is described as the one who made the constellations of the sky and the one who transforms darkness into morning (and vice versa) on earth (Amos 5:8). This noted, it is striking to see the parallel relationship between God's oversight of light and darkness and his control

of societal order (peace) and disorder (chaos) in the human realm (cf. Is 45:7; see 1.4 below). The NT builds on this imagery of light and darkness by heralding Jesus as the light of the world (Jn 1:4-5; 8:12) and describing believers as children of light (Eph 5:8-14). Lastly, it is striking to recall that in the perfect cosmos of the new creation there is no sea and no night—that is, darkness (Rev 21:1, 25)—both of which characterize the opening scene in Genesis. Instead, God himself will be a perpetual source of light in the new creation.

1.3. Chaos and Creation. OT texts that invoke imagery of YHWH's mastery of the primordial waters and its creatures are frequently found in the context of creation texts. Likewise, in a number of ancient Near Eastern accounts creation is juxtaposed to the subjugation of a cosmic ocean that seems to exist in a dark default eternity. In this schema, the created order arises out of a disordered mass of undetermined matter that is negative or even hostile. The accounts differ at various points, but some type of engagement of a cosmic ocean (and its monsters[s]) functions as a key development in the creation schema. Typically, detail is provided along the lines of a progressive differentiation of matter, such as separating the cosmic waters (e.g., waters above and waters below), separating the heavens from the earth, light from darkness, and land from (primeval) water (Levenson, 122).

For example, in the Mesopotamian *Enuma Elish* the first-generation elemental gods are pictured as undifferentiated and amorphous entities that are progressively differentiated into the ordered created realm. This transformation is underscored by syntax; stative verbs describe the primordial beings while fientive verbs describe the change and progressive differentiation of these primordial elements. The order of this transformation of undifferentiated matter in *Enuma Elish* is quite similar to the order of creation in Genesis 1 as well as poetic summaries of creation such as Job 38—41; Psalm 104. In addition, in the Egyptian Hermopolitan creation account the interaction and differentiation effected by the four primordial elements have points of similarity with the opening scene of Genesis, with the primeval waters *(tĕhôm)* likened to Nun, the darkness with Kek, the formless void (Heb *tōhû wābōhû*) with Heh, and the energic Spirit of God likened to Amun.

Given that the OT begins with the image of a

dark primordial ocean (the *těhôm* of Gen 1:2 [see above]) and unfolds in a comparable manner vis-à-vis incremental differentiation of matter, it is possible to understand the dark *těhôm* (along with the enigmatic and oft-discussed expression *tōhû wābōhû*) as conveying a subtle sense of watery chaos at the onset of creation (cf. Ps 24:2, which notes that YHWH founded the earth upon the seas). Moreover, it has been construed that the structure of Genesis 1 presents the darkness and sea as uncreated (chaotic) realities. Such views are bolstered by the presence of the imagery of a chaotic, unruly sea along with multiheaded sea dragons in poetic texts lauding creation, such as Job 9 (cf. Job 9:8, 13), Job 26 (esp. Job 26:12-13); Job 38—41 (esp. Job 38:8-11; 41), Psalm 74 (esp. Ps 74:12-17), Psalm 89 (esp. Ps 89:9-14), Psalm 104 (esp. Ps. 104:6-9), Proverbs 8 (cf. Prov 8:29) and Isaiah 51 (cf. Is 51:9-10). All told, the process of creation from this perspective would be understood as an outworking of God subjugating, limiting and controlling preexistent chaotic elements into the functioning, ordered cosmos (Levenson, 123, 127).

These points of connection between creation and images of chaos in the OT and points of similarity with ancient Near Eastern cosmogonies causes some to consider the biblical story of creation to be connected (causally or otherwise) with YHWH's conflict with the primordial sea and its monster(s) (see Day, 3). From this perspective, the creation accounts of the Hebrew Bible are understood as presupposing and adopting mythopoeic accounts found elsewhere in the ancient Near East (although it should be stressed that the Baal Cycle does not portray Baal as creator, nor does the Baal Cycle even contain the story of creation). Yet, although the points of connection between the creation details of *Chaoskampf* myths and OT texts with chaos imagery are compelling and informative (especially regarding the cognitive context of the OT), the reality that the creative process delineated in Genesis 1 transforms the unformed and unfilled world into the ordered realm without any sort of cosmic resistance or struggle cannot be overlooked (complex and convoluted attempts at showing various degrees of demythologization notwithstanding [see Levenson, 58-59; Wyatt 1996, 30]). It should also be noted that the path of least resistance is employed in showing "similarities" between the OT and other ancient texts.

For example, references to the created order in the Egyptian hymn to the sun disk Aten find numerous points in common with those of Psalm 104 (esp. Ps 104:1-2, 19-24), including descriptions of the deity and his creative efficacy, creation of seasonal and temporal markers, activities of the created realm, and so forth. Nevertheless, comparison charts for these texts typically omit parts of verses that illustrate important distinctions, such as the statements that portray YHWH not only as creator but also as sustainer of creation, as well as doxological intermezzos (e.g., Ps 104:24). In addition, most of the opening (Ps 104:3-18) and closing (Ps 104:28-30) of the psalm are not included in such comparisons although the cosmological and etiological content of these verses stress the sovereign design and oversight of every detail of the cosmos (Ps 104:3-18) as well as the role of God's Spirit in sustaining the created order (Ps 104:28-30). In light of such details, Psalm 104 could actually be a polemic against the Egyptian ideology of a divine sun! Beyond this, numerous biblical texts stress that God created everything, making the notion of an eternal cosmic sea untenable (Ps 33:6-9; cf. Is 44:24; Col 1:16-17; Heb 11:3). In addition, although YHWH's presence is associated with meteorological and chthonic phenomena (see above), he is not portrayed as *being* these elements but rather as wielding them to accomplish his purposes. Moreover, in sharp distinction to ancient Near Eastern accounts, biblical texts totally lack any sort of theogony (story of the birth of god[s]) or change in God in creation texts (Knight, 141-42). Lastly, it should be pointed out that in Psalm 89 YHWH's ownership of the earth is shown as being rooted in his creation of the world rather than his victory over the symbols of chaos.

1.4. Chaos, Society and Kingship. The motif of bringing order to the undifferentiated (chaotic) aspects of the primordial realm (see above) had a direct bearing on the social structure of ancient societies such as Israel. Put another way, that which begins at the cosmic level with God's defeat (and subsequent control) of chaotic forces extends into the social, political and religious order on earth. Such order is not abstract but rather is purposeful with respect to the realm of humankind. In the same way that boundaries mark the circuits of the heavenly lights and the boundaries of the seas, boundaries (ethical, moral and otherwise) are integral to the realm of humankind (Ps 19; cf. Lev 20:24-26). These boundaries underscore the fact that the subjugation of chaotic forces into an ordered cosmos has a moral as well as a physical dimension. As J. C. L. Gibson (213) notes, "Many of the allusions to Yahweh's defeat of chaos in its various watery or monstrous disguises do carry a connotation of his power over evil." The OT repeatedly affirms that the created realm was founded on YHWH's faithfulness, righteousness and justice (see Ps 33:4-7; 89:8-18), facets of divine nature frequently connected with the notion of *wisdom in texts lauding YHWH's work of creation (Prov 3:19-20; 8:22-31; Jer 10:12 [see Knight, 145]). As J. D. Levenson (118) notes, the issue of holiness "is as fundamental to cosmic order as the separations through which God first brought order out of chaos." Moreover, God's ability to bring order to the created realm via holiness functions as the basis for trust in God's saving power (see Ps 74:12 [see Ollenburger, 56-58, 66; Wyatt 1998, 864]). This connection also underscores the biblical interest in heralding divine-human community within the ordered world, an interest ultimately formalized by covenant (Clifford, 199, 201).

Although the connection between holiness and cosmic ordering is especially pronounced in the OT, the societal dimension to the order of the cosmos is also implicit in other ancient Near Eastern *Chaoskampf* accounts. For example, the principal of moral and cosmic orderliness implicit in YHWH's creation of the world is parallel to the Egyptian concept of *Maʿat (Knight, 149). This notion, commonly translated as "order," "correctness," "truth," "righteousness" and the like, was established at creation and embraced all aspects of reality—from the expanse of the universe to the social and moral aspects of human existence. In the human realm *Maʿat* was especially related to foundational areas of life, including kingship, law, wisdom, agriculture, war and religion (Knight, 139). Moreover, the Pharaoh was understood as having been appointed by the god Re to uphold *Maʿat* (order) and eliminate *Isfet* (disorder) in Egyptian society. Similarly, in the Ugaritic texts Yamm's power in the Baal Cycle is analogous to the chaotic powers of evil that disrupted civilization's existence, and Baal's victory is a victory for peaceful human society. Hence, Baal's victory over Yamm (and Mot [see below]) had great significance for the social world of gods and humans (Clifford,

198). In Babylon the annual recitation of *Enuma Elish* was seen as assuring Marduk's continued mastery over chaos (political, social, natural or otherwise) and his continued oversight of justice and cosmic order for another year. Note that the chaos of social disorder and anarchy in the Babylonian Erra myth implies Marduk's occasional negligence in maintaining an ordered creation.

As we noted, the understanding of social order in the human realm is a reflection of the divine order achieved at the cosmic level. This achievement of cosmic order is typically underscored and celebrated through the motif of divine kingship (enthronement) and subsequently appropriated through the social structure of human *kingship. In ancient Near Eastern *Chaoskampf* accounts the storm god who conquered chaos functions as the "foundation of centralized political power" in human society (Green, 281). In several of these texts, such as the Sumerian Ninurta, the Babylonian *Enuma Elish* and the Syro-Canaanite Baal Cycle, the divine subjugation of chaos is followed by inauguration of divine kingship, celebration and palace building. Thus, Ninurta is awarded kingship after his mastery of the primeval waters and the seven-headed serpent, Marduk receives the names of the gods in becoming their chief after defeating Tiamat, and Astarte declares, "Yamm is indeed dead! Baal shall be king!" following Baal's victory over the sea god. Moreover, as with the palace built for Marduk at Esagila following his victory over the sea goddess Tiamat, the assembly of the gods builds a palace for Baal following his victory over the waters of chaos. Such palaces function as a tangible and spatial expression of divine dominion over chaos and governance of the created realm (Clifford, 192, 197; Fischer, 318-20).

Because some biblical texts (e.g., Pss 29; 93) speak of YHWH's reign and kingship together with imagery of mighty waters, the sea and the flood, it is commonly proposed that the focal point of these texts ultimately pertained to royal ideology, and that the social context of these writings (*Sitz im Leben*) was the enthronement of the king (see Wyatt 1998, 854, 865-67; Levenson, 69; Day, 21). In this approach, the motif of divine control over chaos has been appropriated by the human king, who is understood to have been given the divine mandate to control human chaos. In an OT framework the covenant functionaries of prophet, priest, king and judge are commissioned by God to facilitate social, political and religious order. Nevertheless, it is the king who is the most prominent official charged with preventing societal chaos and upholding order (i.e., righteousness) via divine law. Note that part of God's establishing *David as king (with likely *messianic implications) includes giving him dominion over the sea and the rivers (Ps 89:25). With this in mind, we note that the royal palace functioned as a symbol of stability within human society (Wyatt 1998, 840). In analogy to the Egyptian throne being founded on the cosmic principle of *Monad* (see above), Psalm 89 lauds the Davidic throne as being established upon cosmic righteousness (Ps 89:1-31 [see Anderson, 83]). Yet, although YHWH's mastery of the aquatic realm is indeed connected with his present lordship over creation, the absence of the human king in such texts makes the presumed *Sitz im Leben* of the enthronement of the human king questionable at best. Instead, these texts are heralding the power and sovereignty of God by poetically illustrating his power over the seemingly uncontrollable forces of nature (see 1.7 below).

1.5. The Historicization of Chaos. The imagery of divine conflict with the sea and its dragon is also applied to the historical enemies of Israel in various periods (likewise the Egyptian chaos god Seth was used of Egypt's enemies). For example, texts describing God's deliverance of the Israelites at the Red (Reed) Sea incorporate a considerable amount of storm and water imagery (see Ex 15; Ps 77:17-21; 106:9). In addition, Egypt is referred to by one of the names of the sea dragon, "Rahab," in Isaiah 30:7 (and probably in Ps 87:4), and the Egyptian Pharaoh is referred to as the "great monster that lies in the midst of his rivers" in Ezekiel 29:3 (cf. Ezek 32:2). Similarly, the image of raging waters is applied to the advancing Assyrian army in Isaiah 8:5-8. Storm and chaos imagery is also appropriated to show God's efficacious deliverance at the individual level, as with Psalm 18, where YHWH's rescue of one in the midst of the mighty waters is portrayed through a host of meteorological and chthonic phenomena, including the shaking of the earth, trembling of the mountains, thick darkness, smoke (from God's nostrils), fire (from God's mouth), thunder, hail and lighting (see Ps 18:3-19). Lastly, in light of such imagery, appeals for divine deliverance at both the individual and the national level are frequently rooted in God's victories over the symbols of chaos—Rahab, Tannin (dragon), Tehom (deep), Sea and the like (see Is 51:9-11).

1.6. The Eschatologization of Chaos. In addition to historicizing the motif of divine conflict with the dragon and the sea, other OT texts use this imagery to describe a future eschatological defeat of chaos—a future of hope absent from other ancient Near Eastern myths. This is noteworthy, as the forces of chaos, though subjugated and limited (see Job 38:8-11; Ps 104:5-9), are portrayed not as completely defeated but rather as ever threatening to divine order and human life structures (Levenson, 65). Thus, texts that speak to the final eradication of chaos strike a chord in the human heart. A vivid example of this usage, although found outside the OT books under study here, is worth considering:

> On that day YHWH will punish with his fierce, great and mighty sword Leviathan the gliding serpent, yes, Leviathan the twisting serpent; he will slay the dragon that is in the sea. (Is 27:1)

In this text (found within the so-called Isaianic Apocalypse [Is 24—27]) several of the creatures associated with past divine victory over chaos (cf. Ps 74:12-17) are used to describe a future subjugation of chaos: Leviathan, the gliding serpent and the Tannin (dragon), which lives in the sea. Similarly, in the apocalyptic vision of Daniel 7 God battles four monsters from the sea that stand against his dominion. Such future cosmic struggles against the forces of chaos and evil no doubt factor into NT apocalyptic texts, particularly God's battle with the seven-headed beasts from the sea found in the book of Revelation (e.g., Rev 12:3; 13:1; 17:3) culminating with permanent divine victory over these serpentine beasts (Rev 20; cf. Rom 16:20), a new created order (i.e., a new heavens, a new earth, a new Jerusalem) and everlasting divine reign (Rev 11:17; 19:6). It is in this context that the statement that there will be "no more sea" in this new cosmos (Rev 21:1) should be understood: no longer will there be any residue of seemingly uncontrollable and chaotic forces in God's new creation.

1.7. The Hermeneutics of Chaos (or Vice Versa). As evidenced above, there is a degree of tension between OT texts that mirror ancient Near Eastern myths concerning a primordial battle between the storm god and the sea deity (chaos) and texts that stress that YHWH is the sole, transcendent creator of the cosmos (including the sea and the creatures of the sea). Much biblical scholarship (particularly from segments having a negative or nuanced view of biblical veracity) opts to propose various streams and stages of demythologization used by later writers/redactors on texts with a mythological feel, but this is more a matter of presuppositions than biblical exegesis. Instead, the possibility must be considered that rather than a process of demythologization taking place, the usage of poetic expression included intentional mythologization of various chaos motifs for the purpose of poetic impact and expression. Certainly it seems clear that the "God language" of the Canaanites and Israelites (as well as the Egyptians and Mesopotamians) had numerous points of cultural and linguistic contact (see Smick 1982, 88). Moreover, the brevity and the subtleness of references to ancient Near Eastern *Chaoskampf* accounts suggest a grid of understanding and familiarity with these stories on the part of the biblical writers and the ancient audience. Yet, there is a significant difference between borrowed imagery and borrowed ideology/theology. In short, the ancient Israelite writers may well have used broadly attested mythopoeic imagery and language for poetic purposes (and/or polemical purposes [note the application of Baal's cosmic mountain Zaphon to Mount Zion at Ps 48:2]) without incorporating the thought and ideology attached to such imagery and language.

It is noteworthy that scholars who argue for a biblical adaptation of ancient Near Eastern cosmological and cosmogonical systems of belief freely adjust the biblical text because they find a given poetic colon "overloaded," "intrusive" and the like. Not surprisingly, such adjustments lend even further "support" to their views on the origins of OT mythopoeic language. Similarly, such scholars tend to begin with the a priori assumption that Israel's understanding of God, creation, and so forth is basically the same as that of its neighbors and then proceed (in what amounts to circular reasoning) to read various ancient Near Eastern mythological concepts into the biblical material in a manner that amounts to a hermeneutical and interpretive axiom.

A close look at the literary and contextual usage of chaos terminology suggests that the meaning of this imagery tends to differ based on the genre in which it is found. In narrative literature, for example, the use of such imagery is not attested with clarity (recall the attempt to extract chaos imagery out of Gen 1:2, noted above). In prophetic literature the chaos motif tends to be historicized (e.g., Is 30:7; Jer 51:34), with the figures of chaos applied to Israel's enemies of the time (see above). In apocalyptic literature the chaos imagery functions as a literary medium to express eschatological themes, such as the complete elimination of evil and cosmic strife at the end of time (Is 27:1; Dan 7; Rev 12—13). Lastly, in poetic literature (including wisdom literature written in poetic line) usage of chaos imagery frequently has a mythopoeic feel reminiscent of the various ancient Near Eastern texts surveyed above. Given that the usage of chaos imagery is overwhelmingly attested in the poetic genre, the authorial purpose (*Tendenz*) for such usage must be considered in light of the literary features of this genre. In short, poetic literature utilizes evocative expression in order to create a sensory impact on the hearer or reader as over against other literary types. Such emotive and metaphorical stylistics of poetry can be appreciated by comparing the narrative renderings of the crossing of the Red Sea and the Israelite battle against the army of Sisera with the poetic celebrations of these same events that follow in the biblical text (Ex 14—15; Judg 4—5).

In order to facilitate this emotive quality of poetry, ancient writers (including OT authors) commonly employed the vivid sensory images of nature. In addition to demonstrating models of order and beauty (Ps 19:1-6; Prov 6:6-11; Jer 8:7), the natural realm also provides apt imagery and symbolism for the forces of chaos and disorder. As E. B. Smick (1978, 214-15) notes, "Nature is a theme which frequently evoked mythological language: the storm, fire, the sea, the heavens and the earth and creatures in both spheres." Hence, in poetic descriptions of the crossing of the Red Sea and the Jordan River, aspects of the created realm are commonly personified as combatants for impact (Terrien, 119-20). For example, the waters and the deep are described as "seeing" God and responding in "fear" and "anguish," the sea "looks and flees," the Jordan "retreats," and mountains "skip like rams" (Ps 77:16-20; cf. Ps 114:1-8). Although such poetic imagery personifies elements of the natural realm for literary effect, it is naïve to conclude that these elements were considered living entities. Likewise, although certain poetic passages in the OT personify the sea and present it as an inimical force that YHWH subdues, the purpose of these passages is to show the power and sovereign mastery of YHWH over the seemingly "uncontrollable" elements of nature (see Job 9; 26), not to present the sea as a living foe. Hence, it is not surprising that such texts utilizing mythopoeic images are woven together with confessions of faith and expressions of praise (Longman and Reid, 77). In short, "chaos" terminology is utilized to show comprehensive divine sovereignty and to adjure readers and listeners to have commensurate faith in God for all things large and small (see Ps 77).

2. Death as the Ultimate Expression of Chaos.

Death is the ultimate expression of chaos for the human realm, the final culmination of moral and social disorder (rebellion). Death, like chaos, is a by-product of crossing boundaries established by God. Indeed, the land of death is described as a place "without any order" (Job 10:22). As P. S. Johnston (73) notes, death is "cosmologically opposite to 'heaven.'" Like chaos, death is also connected with images of a tempestuous watery abyss (e.g., Ps 124:2-5; 69:14-15 [see Johnston, 114-24]), partly due to the sense that one sinks down into darkness in both (see Watson, 85-93; Wyatt 1996, 102). Similarly, Job 38:16-17 juxtaposes the gates of the underworld with the depths of the sea, and Job 26:5 places the rĕpā'îm (departed spirits) beneath the waters. In Egyptian images of the netherworld the ka (soul) of the dead sailed through waters of the abyss and its gates and chambers facing various tests and trials (Wright, 16). Similarly, the Mesopotamian understanding of death included a netherworld river journey. The place of death is also associated with the underworld ("belly") of the earth (Tromp, 23-46). In the Syro-Canaanite Baal Cycle the realm of death is controlled by Mot (cognate to the Hebrew word for "death"), who is called "the Beloved of El" (see KTU 1.4.VII.46-47; 1.5.I.6-8). Although Mot is one of the sons of the god El (bn ilm [KTU 1.6.II.13; 1.6.VI.24]) and understood to be the king of the underworld (see KTU 1.6.V.27ff.), Mot is not part of the Ugaritic pantheon and is absent from Ugaritic cultic offering lists, implying that he was not worshiped. Nevertheless, Mot certainly was an inimical force to be appeased and feared (see KTU 1.23). As F. M. Cross (116) notes, Mot "rep-

resents the dark chthonic powers which bring sterility, disease, and death." Mot is depicted in Ugaritic texts as being wide of throat and having an insatiable appetite for gods and people (e.g., KTU 1.6.II.21-23). In the battle between Baal and Mot, Baal is at first swallowed up by Mot (a picture of death) and is brought to the confines of the netherworld, a place of darkness and decay beneath the earth. However, Baal is brought back from the realm of death (a picture of rebirth) with the aid of Anat. The battle between Baal and Mot is sometimes considered to be a metaphor for seasonal changes, with Mot representing the heat and agricultural "death" of the dry season, and Baal representing the moisture and "life" of the rainy season. Although there is a strong connection between seasonal cycles and rituals in ancient cultures (including Israel), there are several problems with this understanding of the Baal Cycle, including the need to change the order of the texts and the concurrent reign of Baal and Mot (see Smith, 60-75; Cassuto, 78-79; Clifford, 195).

In the OT death appears in conjunction with related terms that speak of the realm of the dead, including "destruction," "Abaddon" (place of destruction), "the pit," "Sheol" and "the grave" (Johnston, 83-85; Tromp, 21-98). As with Mot in the Baal Cycle, Sheol/Death enlarges its appetite (Hab 2:5), opens its throat wide (Is 5:14), swallows people (Ps 69:15; Prov 1:12) and is never satisfied (Prov 27:20; 30:15-16; Hab 2:5). In addition to the Baal-like image of an insatiable swallower, death is personified as a hunter of sorts, complete with traps, snares and netting (Job 18:9-13; Ps 18:4; Prov 13:14; 14:27 [see Tromp, 172-75]). As such, death can seize a person suddenly and unexpectedly (Eccles 9:12). Like the realm of Mot, the realm of death in the OT is described with city features, such as gates and bars (see Job 17:16; 38:17; Ps 9:13; 107:18), implying a specific spatial realm of the dead (Johnston, 70-79). This realm of death is a place of darkness (Job 10:21; 38:17), a place of bitterness, terror, distress and sorrow (Ps 116:3; Eccles 7:26), a place of forgetfulness (Ps 88:12), a place of inactivity (Eccles 9:10) and where people are cut off from the Lord and cannot praise him (see Ps 6:5; 30:9; 88:5, 12; 115:17). Death's power over humankind is seen in the fact that all people die (see Ps 89:48), and that those who go to the grave do not return to life (Job 7:9-10; 10:21).

This grim description of death notwithstanding, it is significant to note the biblical emphasis on God's power over death and the grave. By contrast, Baal's battle with Mot does not produce a victor; rather, it ends in a cosmic stalemate (Smith, 105). In short, God's power, sovereignty and omniscience extend into death's realm (Job 26:6; 34:22; Ps 139:8; Prov 15:11; Amos 9:2). Moreover, unlike Baal, God cannot die; his existence is "from everlasting to everlasting" (Ps 90:2). The wayward can "make a covenant with death" and be "in agreement" with Sheol (Is 28:15), but God (demonstrating his power over death) can annul this covenant and cause the agreement not to stand through the messianic cornerstone that he lays in Zion (Is 28:16-18). Thus, God will not abandon his children to Sheol (Ps 16:10) but rather redeems his chosen ones from the power of the grave (Job 19:25-27; Ps 49:5-15) and brings them into (everlasting) life (Ps 16:8-11; 73:24; Dan 12:2). The imagery of death as voracious swallower (see above) meets an ironic reversal when we learn that YHWH will permanently "swallow up death" (Is 25:8; cf. 1 Cor 15:54; Rev 21:4). Since death is the ultimate opponent of divine order, the death of death represents the establishment of the ultimate divine order.

See also AFTERLIFE; CREATION IMAGERY; CREATION THEOLOGY; DESTRUCTION; PSALMS 6: ICONOGRAPHY.

BIBLIOGRAPHY. **W. F. Albright,** *Yahweh and the Gods of Canaan: A Historical Analysis of Two Contrasting Faiths* (Winona Lake, IN: Eisenbrauns, 1990); **B. W. Anderson,** *From Creation to New Creation: Old Testament Perspectives* (Minneapolis: Fortress, 1994); **J. B. Burns,** "The Mythology of Death in the Old Testament," *SJT* 26 (1973) 327-40; **U. Cassuto,** "Baal and Mot in the Ugaritic Texts," *IEJ* 12 (1962) 77-86; **R. J. Clifford,** "Cosmogonies in the Ugaritic Texts and in the Bible," *Or* 53 (1984) 183-201; **P. C. Craigie,** "The Comparison of Hebrew Poetry: Psalm 104 in the Light of Egyptian and Ugaritic Poetry," *Semitics* 4 (1974) 10-21; **F. M. Cross,** *Canaanite Myth and Hebrew Epic: Essays in the History of the Religion of Israel* (Cambridge, MA: Harvard University Press, 1973); **A. H. W. Curtis,** "The 'Subjugation of the Waters' Motif in the Psalms: Imagery or Polemic?" *JSS* 23 (1978) 245-56; **J. Day,** *God's Conflict with the Dragon and the Sea: Echoes of a Canaanite Myth in the Old Testament* (UCOP 35; Cambridge: Cambridge University Press, 1985); **L. R. Fischer,** "Creation at Ugarit and in the Old Testament," *VT* 15 (1965) 313-24; **R. S. Fyall,** *Now My Eyes Have Seen You: Images of Creation and Evil in the Book of Job* (NSBT; Downers Grove, IL: InterVarsity Press, 2002); **W. A. Gage,** *The Gospel of Genesis: Studies in Protology and Eschatology* (Winona Lake, IN: Carpenter Books, 1984); **J. C. L. Gibson,** "The Theology of the Ugaritic Baal Cycle," *Or* 53 (1984) 202-19; **C. H. Gordon,** "Leviathan: Symbol of Evil," in *Biblical Motifs: Origins and Transformations,* ed. A. Altmann (Cambridge, MA: Harvard University Press, 1966) 1-9; **A. R. W. Green,** *The Storm-God in the Ancient Near East* (Winona Lake, IN: Eisenbrauns, 2003); **J. H. Grøbæk,** "Baal's Battle with Yam: A Canaanite Creation Fight," *JSOT* 33 (1985) 27-44; **H. Gunkel,** *Schöpfung und Chaos in Urzeit und Endzeit: Eine religionsgeschichtliche Untersuchung über Gen 1 und Ap Joh 12* (Göttingen: Vandenhoeck & Ruprecht, 1895) = *Creation And Chaos in the Primeval Era And the Eschaton: A Religio-historical Study of Genesis 1 and Revelation 12* (Grand Rapids: Eerdmans, 2006); **G. Hart,** *Egyptian Myths* (Austin: University of Texas Press, 1990); **P. S. Johnston,** *Shades of Sheol: Death and Afterlife in the Old Testament* (Downers Grove, IL: InterVarsity Press, 2002); **O. Keel,** *The Symbolism of the Biblical World: Ancient Near Eastern Iconography and the Book of Psalms* (New York: Seabury Press, 1978); **C. Kloos,** *Yhwh's Combat with the Sea: A Canaanite Tradition in the Religion of Ancient Israel* (Amsterdam: G. A. van Oorschot; Leiden: E. J. Brill, 1986); **D. A. Knight,** "Cosmogony and Order in the Hebrew Tradition," in *Cosmogony and Ethical Order: New Studies in Comparative Ethics,* ed. R. W. Lovin and F. E. Reynolds (Chicago: University of Chicago Press, 1985) 133-57; **S. N. Kramer,** *Sumerian Mythology* (rev. ed.; Philadelphia: University of Pennsylvania Press, 1961); **J. D. Levenson,** *Creation and the Persistence of Evil: The Jewish Drama of Divine Omnipotence* (San Francisco: Harper & Row, 1988); **T. Longman III and D. G. Reid,** *God Is a Warrior* (SOTBT; Grand Rapids: Zondervan, 1995); **D. J. McCarthy,** "'Creation' Motifs in Ancient Hebrew Poetry," *CBQ* 29 (1967) 87-100; **B. C. Ollenburger,** *Zion, City of the Great King: A Theological Symbol of the Jerusalem Cult* (JSOTSup 41; Sheffield: Sheffield Academic Press, 1987); **W. T. Pitard,** "The Binding of Yamm: A New Edition of the Ugaritic Text *KTU* 1.83," *JNES* 57 (1998) 261-80; **E. B. Smick,** "Another Look at the Mythological Elements in the Book of Job," *WTJ* 40 (1978) 213-28; idem, "Mythopoetic Language in the Psalms," *WTJ* 44

(1982) 88-98; **M. S. Smith,** *The Ugaritic Baal Cycle,* 1: *Introduction with Text, Translation and Commentary of KTU 1.1-1.2* (VTSup 55; Leiden: E. J. Brill, 1994); **S. Terrien,** "Creation, Cultus, and Faith in the Psalter," *TE* 2 (1966) 116-28; **N. J. Tromp,** *Primitive Conceptions of Death and the Nether World in the Old Testament* (BibOr 21; Rome: Pontifical Biblical Institute, 1969); **D. T. Tsumura,** *The Earth and the Waters in Genesis 1 and 2* (JSOTSup 83; Sheffield: Sheffield Academic Press, 1989); **M. K. Wakeman,** "The Biblical Earth Monster in the Cosmogonic Combat Myth," *JBL* 88 (1969) 313-20; idem, *God's Battle with the Monster: A Study in Biblical Imagery* (Leiden: E. J. Brill, 1973); **R. S. Watson,** *Chaos Uncreated: A Reassessment of the Theme of "Chaos" in the Hebrew Bible* (BZAW 341; Berlin: de Gruyter, 2005); **F. A. M. Wiggermann,** "Tishpak, His Seal, and the Dragon Mushhushshu," in *To the Euphrates and Beyond: Archaeological Studies in Honour of Maurits N. van Loon,* ed. O. M. C. Haex, H. H. Curvers and P. M. M. G. Akkermans (Rotterdam: Balkema, 1989) 117-33; **J. E. Wright,** *The Early History of Heaven* (Oxford: Oxford University Press, 2000); **N. Wyatt,** *Myths of Power: A Study of Royal Myth and Ideology in Ugaritic and Biblical Tradition* (UBL 13; Münster: Ugarit-Verlag, 1996); idem, "Arms and the King: The Earliest Allusions to the *Chaoskampf* Motif and Their Implications for the Interpretation of the Ugaritic and Biblical Traditions," in *"Und Mose schrieb dieses Lied auf": Studien zum Alten Testament und zum Alten Orient; Festschrift für Oswald Loretz zur Vollendung seines 70. Lebensjahres mit Beiträgen von Freunden, Schülern und Kollegen,* ed. M. Dietrich and I. Kottsieper (AOAT 250; Münster: Ugarit-Verlag, 1998) 833-82.   F. J. Mabie

CHIASM

A sequence of components repeated in inverted order is known as a chiasm (named for the crossover pattern of the Greek letter *chi*: Χ). Repetition may occur at the level of phonemes (similar sounds), lexemes (whether identical or synonymous words), grammatically equivalent components (e.g., subject, verb, object :: object, verb, subject) or conceptually related components (see examples from Prov 1 in 1.2 below). Any number of terms may comprise a chiasm, forming either a fully doubled scheme (e.g., A, B, C :: C', B', A') or a scheme with an isolated center (e.g., A, B, C : D : C', B', A').

Attention to three aspects helps the reader appreciate chiasm in biblical composition: range of use, reliable detection and resulting enrichment.

1. Range of Use
2. Reliable Detection
3. Resulting Enrichment
4. Conclusion

1. Range of Use.

The extent to which authors of wisdom, poetry and writings in the Hebrew Bible employed chiasm may best be grasped by considering varied genres, span of text and frequency with which this device occurs.

1.1. Genre Employing Chiasm. Conceived primarily as a device of poetry, chiasm appears in prose as well (largely at the concept level). D. A. Dorsey (170) recognizes in prose portions of *Job a seven-member prologue sequence that recurs, inverted, in the epilogue. For *Ruth, C. Bovell (178) proposes a chiasm contrasting the two wives of Elkanah, centering in the phrases "the name of the one was Orpah / the name of the second was Ruth" (spanning Ruth 1:1-6).

1.2. Span of Text. A span as compact as one poetic stichos (often comprising a single biblical verse) may contain a chiasm at the grammatical level as the sequence of verb-subject-object reverse order in the second iteration: "shall return, his toil, upon his head :: and upon his pate shall his violence descend" (Ps 7:16 [note that awareness of the underlying Hebrew word order in Ps 7:17 MT is necessary to detect the inversion]). Alternatively, an adjacent pair of verses may be joined by lexical chiasm: "lips, mouth :: mouth, lips" (Prov 18:6-7). Encompassing a still larger span, a concept-level chiasm, or palistrophe (from Gk *palin* ["again"] plus "strophe"), may encompass multiple verses, as in the sophisticated composition "The Appeal of Wealth" (Prov 1:10-19 [palistrophe distinguishes extended chiasms from shorter, stichos-level inversions]).

"The Appeal of Wealth" (Prov 1:10-19)
A. Dual Theme Introduction (v. 10)
  1. Gang's Enticement (v. 10a)
  2. Father's Warning (v. 10b)
B. Enticement by the Gang (vv. 11-14)
  1. A Capital Plan: Inflicting Death on Others (vv. 11-12)
  2. Rationale for Enlistment: Monetary Ends (v. 13)

3. Call to Enlist (v. 14)

B'. Warning by the Father (vv. 15-18)

   3. Call to Withdraw (v. 15)

   2. Rationale for Withdrawing: Violent Means (v. 16)

   1. Capital Consequences: Receiving Death for Oneself (vv. 17-18)

A'. Conclusion (v. 19)

The remainder of Proverbs 1 appears similarly structured, a palistrophe dominating "The Appeal of Wisdom" (Prov 1:20-33, with palistrophe spanning Prov 1:22-33 [a comparable rhetorical analysis was first introduced by Trible]). Following an introduction, unit A (Prov 1:20-21), the palistrophe breaks into fairly balanced halves, B and B' (Prov 1:22-27; 1:28-33). Only a lengthy (tricola) dramatic climax imbalances unit B, portraying the devastating retributive storm to be unleashed against obdurate invitees precisely at the palistrophe's core (Prov 1:27). References to invitees digresses from second-person engage-ment in unit B to third-person reporting in unit B', creating a form-related segmentation endorsing the content-related palistrophic pattern hinging at Proverbs 1:27. Why should Lady Wisdom (*see* Woman Wisdom and Woman Folly) make this digression, recounting the report of "their" hopeless misfortune, if not in hopes that still others— eavesdropping bystanders among the sage's audience—might listen and gain wisdom? The close produces a logical climax as in Proverbs 1:32-33 a palistrophically reprised summary of characters dismisses two met earlier (naïve and fool) while nominating a new, third character: in the place of the scoffer (Prov 1:22), the receptive hearer (Prov 1:33)!

"The Appeal of Wisdom" (Prov 1:20-33)

A. Introduction of Lady Wisdom (vv. 20-21)

B. Wisdom's Speech, Part 1 (vv. 22-27)

   1. Character Survey and Summons (vv. 22-23a)

   2. Wisdom's Proposition: A Choice Offered (v. 23b-c)

   3. Cause for Wisdom's Abandoning the Fools (vv. 24-25)

   4. Response of Wisdom to Fools' Plight (v. 26)

   5. Description of Disaster (v. 27)

B'. Wisdom's Speech, Part 2 (vv. 28-33)

   4. Response of Wisdom to Fools' Plight (v. 28)

   3. Cause for Wisdom's Abandoning the Fools (vv. 29-30)

   2. Wisdom's Principle: A Choice Made (v. 31)

   1. Character Survey and Conclusion (vv. 32-33)

1.3. Frequency of Occurrence. Assured chiasm in poetic material occurs fairly frequently at the levels of grammar and lexeme/synonym, offering a conscious alternative to parallelism so ubiquitous in Hebrew poetry (Kugel, 19). Many prose chiasms similarly have been proposed, often operating at the concept level (see the volume by Dorsey, with its insightful introduction followed by numerous potential chiasms across the OT). However, diligence must be exercised lest the text grow silent beneath the weight of imposed patterns.

2. Reliable Detection.

Two extremes hazard the path of chiasm recognition: underdetection and overdetection. For two reasons, chiasm may go undetected. First, readers accustomed to linear presentations tend to overlook concentric patterns. In this regard, Western readers may be particularly disadvantaged. Second, most grammatical and virtually all phonemic chiasms defy effective translation—for example, the aforementioned grammatical inversion in Psalm 7:16 evident only in Hebrew (Ps 7:17 MT), and similarly the phoneme-level chiasm of Ecclesiastes 7:1: "A good name is better than fine perfume," which limps rather lamely alongside the smoothly pivoting original: *ṭôb šēm miššemen ṭôb.*

Overdetection similarly hazards the path, particularly when concept-level discoveries only invent hopeful chimeras of chiasm. Along a vector of diminishing concern, one should be suspicious of the following scenarios: (1) when segments of the text must be overlooked to achieve chiasm; (2) when form-related markers clearly segmenting the text conflict with chiastic divisions; (3) when titles proposed for chiastic segments seem forced, not reflecting cogently their actual content; (4) when length of chiastically balancing segments is severely lopsided. Criteria such as these may help assess relative merits of conflicting proposals (cf. conflicting palistrophes offered by Shea and by Webster accounting for the whole of *Song of Songs).

3. Resulting Enrichment.

Chiasm may enrich a composition threefold: text-critically, aesthetically and rhetorically.

3.1. Text-Critical Enrichment. Chiasm may alternatively reinforce or raise questions concerning integrity of a given text. Omission of Proverbs 1:16 from two important Greek manuscripts has inclined some to treat it as secondary, an insertion from Isaiah 59:7 to illuminate the fowler saying in Proverbs 1:17 with a second *ki* ("because") clause (so Clifford, 39, with *BHS* notes). However, when viewed against the backdrop of its palistrophic counterpart, the contribution of Proverbs 1:16 grows much more distinct. Whereas Proverbs 1:13 (element B.2.) provides the gang's "Rationale for Enlistment" with a glitter of monetary ends, Proverbs 1:16 (element B'.2.) rebuts with the father's "Rationale for Withdrawing" by turning a spotlight on how reprehensible are the gang's violent means (see 1.2 above). Rather than treating *ki* (which opens both Prov 1:16 and Prov 1:17) as signaling two rather redundant explanatory statements supporting the call to withdraw (Prov 1:15), we now may affirm *ki* of Proverbs 1:16 as explanatory, while the same word in Proverbs 1:17 functions asseveratively ("surely" or "indeed"), adding emphasis to the fowler saying. Thus, detection of a palistrophe enveloping Proverbs 1:16 may reinforce integrity of this verse and may further aid its interpretation (see Welch, 12).

When incomplete, a chiastic pattern may raise the question of whether a balancing member may have been corrupted or lost. Two of three members in Job 17:7a recur chiastically in Job 17:7b ("dimmed with sorrow is my eye :: and my limbs like a shadow—all of them"). Modifying phrases occupy second position ("with sorrow" [B] and "like a shadow" [B']), while body parts dominate the core ("my eye" [C] and "my limbs" [C']). However, the verb "dimmed" (A) finds no balancing verb in "all of them" (A'). By revocalizing the consonants comprising the phrase "all of them" *(klm)*, M. Dahood (124) proposes that stichos B' should read "and my limbs like a shadow are wasted," thereby balancing the verb "dimmed" (A) with "wasted" (A'), thus completing a three-member chiasm.

3.2. Aesthetic Enrichment. At the stichos level chiasm may achieve little more than variety of expression "to break the monotony of persistent direct parallelism" (Watson, 145). Thus the "verb-object :: object-verb" chiasm in both Psalm 26:4 and Psalm 26:5 may signal simply a change-up from parallelism of surrounding lines: "I did not dwell with vain men, and with crafty ones I will not go; I hated [the] assembly of evildoers, and with wicked folk I will not dwell." To appreciate simple chiasms as these, a modern reader need only savor the shuffling of word order, attentively tracking the train of thought as it turns back on itself.

3.3. Rhetorical Enrichment. In a palistrophe, particular attention should be paid to the central member(s). Often the careful reader will find there a climax either of urgency or logic. Palistrophes in full may also serve to reinforce credibility and create reversal (for additional functions of chiasm, see Watson, 145-48).

3.3.1. Climax of Urgency. In "The Appeal of Wealth" (see 1.2 above) it is precisely at the palistrophic core that, back-to-back, both gang and father produce their most urgent pleas (Prov 1:14-15 within Prov 1:10-19 [note that logic swells unabated until Prov 1:19]). Again, in "The Appeal of Wisdom" (see 1.2 above) it is at the core that the storm rages with greatest dramatic ferocity against those who foolishly declined Wisdom's invitation (Prov 1:27 within Prov 1:22-33 [logical climax does not appear until "hearer" of Prov 1:33]).

3.3.2. Climax of Logic. When a logical climax coincides with a palistrophic core, the conjunction unfolds vital insight for the composition as a whole. So, because it is located at a palistrophic core, the heartening hope of Lamentations 3:31-33 should impact the reader more pervasively than do the dismal tones that run toward the end of the chapter (Watson [159], who similarly points out that the theme of divine rescue at the core of Ps 12 should be recognized as overshadowing and dominating the ensuing expansion of wickedness).

3.3.3. Reinforcing Credibility. E. Assis (286-87) observes that narrative advice-giving may be palistrophically structured to convey reasonableness and thereby reinforce credibility. The same impact obtains for poetic advice giving (see 1.2 above, and compare the tightly formed palistrophes in "The Appeal of Wealth" in Prov 1:10-19 and "The Appeal of Wisdom" in Prov 1:22-33 [Trible]).

3.3.4. Creating Reversal. In the palistrophe of "The Appeal of Wealth" (Prov 1:10-19 [see 1.2 above]) the father's statements construct a logical exposé of the gang's deceptive invitation. Point by point he rebuts their claims. Although rebuttal could have been arranged in an A, B, C // A', B', C' parallel pattern, use of the palistrophic A, B, C :: C', B', A' pattern produces structural reversal formally endorsing content reversal contained in the exposé. The result is a remarkably compact and cohesive piece of persuasion, clinching the argument as the logical climax reveals nothing less than witless suicide as the ultimate outcome of the gang's arrogant schemes (Prov 1:19).

4. Conclusion.
Attention to chiastic structures, compact or extended, greatly enriches the reader's grasp both of the literary craft and persuasive impact of biblical compositions, narrative as well as poetic.

See also ACROSTIC; AMBIGUITY; ELLIPSIS; HEBREW LANGUAGE; INCLUSIO; MERISM; METER; PARALLELISM; POETICS, TERMINOLOGY OF; REFRAIN; RHETORICAL CRITICISM; RHYME; SOUND PLAYS; TERSENESS; WORD PLAY.

BIBLIOGRAPHY. **E. Assis,** "Chiasmus in Biblical Narrative: Rhetoric of Characterization," *Prooftexts* 22 (2002) 273-304; **C. Bovell,** "Symmetry, Ruth and Canon," *JSOT* 28 (2003) 175-91; **R. J. Clifford,** *Proverbs* (OTL; Louisville: Westminster John Knox, 1999); **M. Dahood,** "Chiasmus in Job: A Text-Critical and Philological Criterion," in *A Light unto My Path: Old Testament Studies in Honor of Jacob M. Myers,* ed. H. N. Bream, R. D. Heim and C. A. Moore (GTS 4; Philadelphia: Temple University Press, 1974) 119-30; **D. A. Dorsey,** *The Literary Structure of the Old Testament: A Commentary on Genesis-Malachi* (Grand Rapids: Baker Books, 1999); **J. L. Kugel,** *The Idea of Biblical Poetry: Parallelism and Its History* (New Haven: Yale University Press, 1981); **W. H. Shea,** "The Chiastic Structure of the Song of Songs," *ZAW* 92 (1980) 378-96; **P. Trible,** "Wisdom Builds a Poem: The Architecture of Proverbs 1:20-33," *JBL* 94 (1975) 509-18; **W. G. E. Watson,** "Chiastic Patterns in Biblical Hebrew Poetry," in *Chiasmus in Antiquity: Structures, Analyses, Exegesis,* ed. J. W. Welch (Hildesheim: Gerstenberg, 1981) 118-68; **E. C. Webster,** "Pattern in the Song of Songs," *JSOT* 22 (1982) 73-93; **J. W. Welch,** "Introduction," in *Chiasmus in Antiquity: Structures, Analyses, Exeesis,* ed. **J. W. Welch** (Hildesheim: Gerstenberg, 1981) 9-16.

P. Overland

CHRISTOLOGY. *See* HERMENEUTICS; MESSIAH.

COLON, COLA. *See* POETICS, TERMINOLOGY OF.

COMPARATIVE STUDIES. *See* ECCLESIASTES 2: ANCIENT NEAR EASTERN BACKGROUND.

CONFIDENCE, PSALMS OF
Scholars agree that the book of *Psalms contains three clear and primary genres: the *hymn, the *laments and the *thanksgiving psalm. Each of these genres is marked by its own form and content. Other genres have been proposed but have not been universally recognized, mainly because these other genres are said to be united by content only and not by any particular form (*see* Form Criticism). The psalms of confidence are in the latter category. Some scholars (e.g., Collins, Wilson) do not list psalms of confidence in their treatment of genre in the Psalms, while others do (e.g., Clifford, Coogan). This article proceeds on the judgment that there is a group of psalms that can be distinguished from other psalms by their sustained focus on confidence in God in the face of adverse circumstances. Such psalms are called psalms of confidence or psalms of trust.

1. The Place of the Psalms of Confidence
2. The Extent of the Psalms of Confidence
3. The Character of the Psalms of Confidence
4. The Invitation of the Psalms of Confidence
5. The Challenge of the Psalms of Confidence

1. The Place of the Psalms of Confidence.
The psalms of confidence lie somewhere on a continuum between the lament and the thanksgiving psalms. Whereas some scholars see the psalms of confidence as a development of the expressions of confidence that often bring the laments to a close, others associate the psalms of confidence more closely with the thanksgiving psalms (see Lucas). Reasons exist for both of these connections.

The psalms of confidence are like the laments in that both articulate some kind of trouble that the psalmist is experiencing at the moment. This distinguishes the psalms of confidence from the thanksgiving psalms, where trouble clearly is in the past. The trouble in the psalms of confidence is not, however, as painful, as pressing, as is the case in the laments. The trouble seems a bit further away, though it is still felt. In keeping with this, the dominant, negative mood found in the laments is replaced by an overall positive tone in the psalms of confidence. This positive tone is much more like the mood encountered in the thanksgiving psalms, and both express undoubted assurance in God's power to save, whereas the laments are often filled with agonizing questions in this regard.

The psalms of confidence are thus neither laments nor thanksgiving psalms. They lack the deep anguish and the structural elements that characterize the laments. Though confident in God's power to save, the poets who wrote the psalms of confidence had not yet experienced that salvation at the time of composition, as had the authors of the thanksgiving psalms. Although the poets who wrote the psalms of confidence seem to have moved beyond the deep agony of the lament, they are still waiting for the day when a psalm of thanksgiving for salvation gained can be sung (Bullock).

2. The Extent of the Psalms of Confidence.

Given these fuzzy boundaries, it is not surprising that scholars differ to some degree over which psalms belong to this genre. For example, T. Longman includes Psalms 11; 16; 23; 27; 62; 91; 121; 125; 131, whereas C. H. Bullock lists Psalms 4; 16; 23; 27; 62; 73; 90; 115; 123; 124; 125; 126. The present article regards the following as psalms of confidence: Psalms 16; 23; 27; 62; 73; 91; 115; 121; 125; 131.

3. The Character of the Psalms of Confidence.

Although the psalms of confidence have no unifying structural shape, they are united by one distinguishing characteristic: unwavering and sustained confidence or trust in God's ability and willingness to provide deliverance from adverse circumstances.

3.1. The Tone of the Psalms of Confidence. Psalm 27 exemplifies the positive tone of the psalms of confidence.

> The LORD is my light and my salvation—
>   whom shall I fear?
> The LORD is the stronghold of my life—
>   of whom shall I be afraid? (Ps 27:1 NIV)

> Though an army besiege me,
>   my heart will not fear;
> though war break out against me,
>   even then will I be confident. (Ps 27:3 NIV)

> I am still confident of this:
>   I will see the goodness of the LORD

in the land of the living. (Ps 27:13 NIV)

3.2. The Imagery of the Psalms of Confidence. The basis for this confidence is rooted in the character of God and often comes to expression through the *imagery used for God in these psalms. The most frequent image is God as refuge (*see* Protection).

> Keep me safe, O God,
>   for in you I take refuge. (Ps 16:1 NIV)

> The LORD is the stronghold of my life—
>   of whom shall I be afraid? (Ps 27:1b NIV)

> My soul finds rest in God alone;
>   my salvation comes from him.
> He alone is my rock and my salvation;
>   he is my fortress, I will never be shaken.
>   (Ps 62:1-2 NIV)

> I will say of the LORD, "He is my refuge
>   and my fortress,
>   my God, in whom I trust." (Ps 91:2 NIV)

What is arguably the best known and most beloved image for God in the Bible, God as shepherd, occurs in a psalm of confidence.

> The LORD is my shepherd;
>   I have all that I need. (Ps 23:1 NLT)

Implicit in another psalm of confidence is perhaps the tenderest image of God found in the Psalms, God as the mother of a weaned child.

> But I have stilled and quieted my soul;
>   like a weaned child with its mother,
>   like a weaned child is my soul within me.
>   (Ps 131:2 NIV)

Psalm 121 uses the image of guardian for God six times (Ps 121:3, 4, 5, 7 [2x], 8), and Psalm 125 likens God's surrounding presence to that of the mountains that surround Jerusalem.

> Just as the mountains surround and protect
>   Jerusalem,
>   so the LORD surrounds and protects his
>   people,
>   both now and forever. (Ps 125:2 NLT)

3.3. The Nature of Confidence in the Psalms of

Confidence. The expressions of confidence in this genre are "expressions of faith, not cries of victory" (Bullock, 168). These psalms articulate a confidence that has moved the psalmist away from the deep anguish of the lament and toward the joy of the psalm of thanksgiving. Although the psalmist is confident that help is on the way, the help has not yet arrived. This is clear from the oblique allusions and references to present trouble found in these psalms, as well as from the petitions found in the psalms of confidence.

> Keep me safe, O God,
> for in you I take refuge. (Ps 16:1 NIV)

> Hear me as I pray, O LORD.
> Be merciful and answer me! (Ps 27:7 NLT)

> So many enemies against one man—
> all of them trying to kill me.
> To them I'm just a broken-down wall
> or a tottering fence. (Ps 62:3 NLT)

> I lift up my eyes to the hills—
> where does my help come from?
> (Ps 121:1 NIV)

4. The Invitation of the Psalms of Confidence.
In the psalms of confidence the poets not only articulate their own confidence in God but also invite others to share their confidence.

> Wait patiently for the LORD.
> Be brave and courageous.
> Yes, wait patiently for the LORD.
> (Ps 27:14 NLT)

Although it is possible that here the psalmist is addressing himself, or that a priest is addressing the psalmist, it is more likely that the psalmist is addressing another (Wilson). Interpreting this line in the context of similar lines in other psalms in this genre leads to this conclusion, as the following lines demonstrate.

> Trust in him at all times, O people;
> pour out your hearts to him,
> for God is our refuge. (Ps 62:8 NIV)

> O house of Israel, trust in the LORD. . . .
> O house of Aaron, trust in the LORD. . . .
> You who fear him, trust in the LORD. . . .
> (Ps 115:9-11 NIV)

> O Israel, put your hope in the LORD
> both now and forevermore. (Ps 131:3 NIV)

5. The Challenge of the Psalms of Confidence.
While bringing great comfort, the psalms of confidence also bring a great challenge. It is one thing to sing a hymn when all is well, or a lament when trouble is on all sides, or a psalm of thanksgiving when God has delivered us from distress. In each of these cases our psalm and our circumstances match. However, it is quite another thing to express profound confidence in God when help has not yet come. In this case there is a disconnect between our psalm and our situation. As we have seen, however, our confidence is rooted not in our circumstances but in the character of God. God is our refuge, our shepherd, our mother, our guardian, our surrounding mountain. Ultimately in the book of Psalms, God is our king, who reigns over our lives and the world that he has made. So we can sing with the psalmist,

> But as for me, it is good to be near God.
> I have made the Sovereign LORD my refuge.
> (Ps 73:28 NIV)

See also DIVINE PRESENCE; LAMENTS, PSALMS OF; SUFFERING; THANKSGIVING, PSALMS OF; THEODICY; THEOPHANY.

BIBLIOGRAPHY. **B. W. Anderson,** *Out of the Depths: The Psalms Speak for Us Today* (Louisville: Westminster John Knox, 2000); **C. H. Bullock,** *Encountering the Book of Psalms: A Literary and Theological Introduction* (Grand Rapids: Baker, 2001); **R. J. Clifford,** *Psalms 1-72* (AOTC; Nashville: Abingdon, 2002); **J. J. Collins,** *Introduction to the Hebrew Bible* (Minneapolis, MN: Fortress, 2004); **M. D. Coogan,** *The Old Testament: A Historical and Literary Introduction to the Hebrew Scriptures* (Oxford: Oxford University Press, 2006); **H. Gunkel,** *The Psalms: A Form-Critical Introduction,* trans. T. M. Horner (Philadelphia: Fortress, 1967); **T. Longman III,** *How to Read the Psalms* (Downers Grove, IL: InterVarsity Press, 1988); idem, "Psalms," in *A Complete Literary Guide to the Bible,* ed. L. Ryken and T. Longman III (Grand Rapids: Zondervan, 1993) 80-91; **E. C. Lucas,** *Exploring the Old Testament: A Guide to the Psalms & Wisdom Literature* (Downers Grove, IL: InterVarsity Press, 2003); **J. C. McCann,** "Psalms," *NIB* 4.641-1280; **G. H. Wilson,** *Psalms, Volume 1* (NIVAC; Grand Rapids: Zondervan, 2002).

M. D. Futato

CONSONANCE. *See* Sound Patterns.

COSMETICS. *See* Floral Imagery.

COSMIC BATTLE. *See* Creation Imagery.

COSMOGONY. *See* Creation Imagery; Mountain Imagery.

COVENANT. *See* Wisdom and Covenant.

COVENANT FESTIVAL. *See* Cult, Worship; Psalms.

CREATION IMAGERY
Creation imagery describes a group of literary (poetic) activities and pictures that are used throughout the OT to dramatize the Israelite worldview. These include *imagery involving, for example, the heavens, earth, world, seas, mountains, sun, moon, limits and other facets of nature, as well as activities such as forming, creating, making and establishing. Together, these images and their corresponding world-view give way to a deeper *creation theology wherein God has made and ordered the world with primordial purposes in mind. Creation imagery is prominent throughout the Wisdom literature (*Job, *Proverbs, *Ecclesiastes) and *Psalms (see Mays, 75-77). Significantly, the creation images in these books do not directly expound a creation theology; rather, their function is to show and display theological truths in persuasive, unitary, comforting and provocative ways in order to engage the oral and literary traditions of the ancient Near East and thereby display the superiority of the faith, worldview and God of the OT over against the religions, myths and ideologies of surrounding cultures. The poetic tapestry of creation images in these books includes at least seven discernible categories: cosmic battle, *kingship, *theophany, *lament and *theodicy, cosmogony, redemption, *wisdom and order. Although these categories are treated independently here, their role in Israel's worldview makes them inseparable, interdependent, even synthetic images.

1. Cosmic Battle
2. Kingship
3. Theophany
4. Lament and Theodicy
5. Cosmogony
6. Creation and Redemption
7. Wisdom and Creation Order
8. Conclusion

1. Cosmic Battle.
The books of Job and Psalms in particular draw upon imagery of heaven, earth and seas (or waters) in ancient texts such as Genesis and the Egyptian Book of the Dead to depict their own literary and/or theological pictures. These images appear often in Psalms (Ps 8:7-8; 19:1; 33:6-8; 36:5-6; 69:34; 96:11; 104:1-2; 135:6; 146:6) and have at least two related functions. On the one hand, they exalt the goodness of creation. The earth (Ps 104) and the waters (Ps 46:3; 65:7-9; 74:15; 104:6-12; 133:3) are sources of provision and abundance and therefore lead to rejoicing (Ps 19:1-6; 136:2-9; 148:1-14). This supports the second and larger implication, that God has made, established and overcome the powers of the ancient Near Eastern world (Ps 24:1-2; 46:2-4; 65:6-7; 77:16-19; 78:69; 89:11; 93:3-4; 104:5-6; 109:9; 114:5-8; 115:14-18). The earth, waters and chaos are thus transformed from the threatening powers within other ancient worldviews into the one true God's powers of blessing within his creation (*see* Chaos and Death). Psalm 104 uses cosmic imagery in an especially clear way wherein God makes the waters (Ps 104:10), in order for trees to sprout branches, upon which dwell birds, whose singing brings pleasure to humanity (Ps 104:12).

Similarly, the book of Job applies creation imagery to the mystery of Job's suffering. Life on earth for Job and his friends is depicted as an imprisoned condition that gives way to a sense of hopeless toil and ignorance (J(Job 3:23; 7:1-3, 21; 18:17-18; 20:12, 20-22 [cf. Ecclesiastes]). Although wisdom does not promise to solve the ambiguities of life on earth, it does uphold God's good, orderly and powerful control of the creation. For example, God is portrayed as the maker and victor over the cosmic powers of earth, water and Rahab (Job 26:10-14). The divine speeches (Job 38—41) also picture God as the maker and owner of the heavens, earth, seas and all that are in them (Job 38:29-30; 41:11), and as the master of Behemoth and Leviathan (Job 40:15; 41:1). Although Job does not necessarily understand the reason for his suffering, the images of creation (Job 26; 28; 38—41) uphold God's sovereign power and ownership of the world.

2. Kingship.

Yahweh's cosmic battle complements and promotes the images of his kingship over the nations and forces of nature. Psalm 98 proclaims Yahweh's "righteousness," "salvation" and "judgment" before all the nations (Ps 98:1-3, 9) and calls upon Israel (Ps 98:3-6) and the sea, world, rivers and mountains (Ps 98:3-6, 7-9) to rejoice before "the King, Yahweh" (*hammelek yhwh* [Ps 98:6]). Psalm 97 also speaks of Yahweh "reigning" *(mālāk)* and his ownership of clouds, fire and lightning (cf. Ps 95:1-5). As a result, "the earth sees and trembles" (Ps 97:4b), and "the mountains melt like wax before Yahweh, before the Lord of all the earth" (Ps 97:5). There is also an interesting correspondence between the creation imagery in Psalm 24 and Psalm 29, which proclaim God as the "King of glory" (Ps 24:8, 10) and "God of glory" (Ps 29:3) (see Mays, 78-80). God's reign over the nations and the earth are also proclaimed clearly in Psalms 2; 72; 111, often integrating God's kingship with the other seven categories of imagery listed here above.

3. Theophany.

The temple, *mountain and high hill are ancient images that communicate the power, dwelling and presence of deities on earth. O. Keel (113) observes that ancient Egyptian sanctuaries claimed a high hill as the "glorious hill of the primordial beginning." Mesopotamia also understood its "pure hill" *(du-ku)* as a place of primordial beginnings. Furthermore, as Keel notes (113-14), "in the Ugaritic sphere, the conquest of Chaos is also closely related to mountain (hill) and temple."

The Psalter engages this hill imagery through its references to hills, mountains, Sinai, Horeb and *Zion. For the writer in Psalm 121, help comes not from the "hills" but from "Yahweh, the maker of the heavens and earth" (Ps 121:1-2). Furthermore, although Horeb is not the highest mountain, its superiority causes the glorious and many peaked mountain of Bashan to look on it with hatred (Ps 68:8, 14-17). God's victories and mighty acts in Psalm 89 are praised, and the heavens and the earth are ascribed to Yahweh as Tabor and Hermon "shout your name in joy" (Ps 89:5-12). By far, Zion is the predominant choice of mountain or hill imagery in the Psalter, appearing some thirty-nine times in thirty-one psalms. Psalm 48 exalts Zion

most emphatically, making clear that this is the place where Yahweh makes himself known (Ps 48:1-3, 10-11; cf. Ps 84). This imagery not only demonstrates Yahweh's reign over the mountains but even declares that he created them to sing his praises.

Job's appeal to appear before God's divine courts (Job 13:3; cf. Ps 73) also unites creation images with God's presence (see 4 below). N. C. Habel notes the use of the phrase "he who stretches out the heavens" or the "north" (Job 26:7; Ps 104:2) as images of a sanctuary or divine dwelling within creation. We thus find the creation images of theophany and chaos or suffering intersecting with the biblical themes of lament and theodicy.

4. Lament and Theodicy.

As we noted, theophany, or God's presence (*see* Divine Presence), is a creation theme frequently appealed to in suffering, lament and the face of evil. On several occasions Job calls out in his affliction, wishing to stand in God's presence and be vindicated (Job 13:3, 24; 19:15-27; 23:9, 15, 17). When Job finally receives a response in the divine speeches (Job 38—41), God rehearses extensive evidence of the order and purpose built into creation. In the end, Job's comfort and repentance are never said to be on the basis of understanding how his suffering fits into the created design or in having his challenges answered—the text remains conspicuously silent in this regard. He finds satisfaction in that he has finally "seen" God (Job 42:5), referring to the substance of God's speeches about his work in creation (Job 38—41), which represent the personal and intimate presence that Job has longed for.

This same pattern is also apparent in Psalm 73, where the supplicant is perplexed by the prosperity of the wicked until entering the sanctuary of God. Although the sanctuary brings an encouraging reminder of the final destiny of the wicked (Ps 73:17), comfort is emphatically attributed to the presence of God (Ps 73:21-28), who gives *"life" and whose nature is greater than anything in the heavens or the earth (Ps 73:25) (cf. Ps 18:2-5; 42:2; 61:2; 62:1-7). This comfort in the promise of life is a common creation image for both the wisdom sages and the psalmists, whose faith in "life," "the path of life" (Ps 16:11; 27:13; 30:5; 42:2; 52:5; 116:9; 133:3; 142:5; Prov 2:19; 3:2, 16, 18; 4:10, 23; 6:23; 8:35; 9:11) and the "land of the living" (Ps 27:13; 52:5; 116:9; 142:5) brings constant eschatological hope.

5. Cosmogony.

Origins are another major category of images in ancient creation myths and writings as found in the Babylonian Atrahasis epic and the *Enuma Elish*. R. J. Clifford helpfully corrects a modern proclivity to restrict cosmogony to the world and "solar system," which overlooks the ancient concern for the origin of nations and societies in the world (Clifford, 511-12). Although this type of cosmogony is more apparent in the Pentateuch, the Wisdom literature and the Writings also declare that God made (*ʿāśîtā*) the nations (Ps 86:9; cf. Ps 22:27-28) and "made us [Israel]" (*ʿāśānû* [Ps 100:3; cf. Ps 77]). In fact, the use of cosmogony in wisdom and Psalms is as much concerned with the origins of the individual (Job 10; Ps 94:9; 139:13-16) as it is with the heavens and the earth (world) (Job 38:33; Ps 90:2; 95:5; 104:26; 119:90; Prov 3:19-20; 8:22-31; 30:4). With regard to the emphases on the individual, W. P. Brown highlights the concern with human origins in the prayers in Job (Job 10) and Psalm 139. Cosmogonous images therefore have at least two purposes: serving as grounds for comfort and complaint, and testifying to the "craftsmanship" and "reliability" (Keel, 205) of the creator (Ps 8:3; 19:1-6; 24:2; 33:4; 74:16-17; 89:11; 95:5; 102:25; 104:5; 119:73; 144:12).

6. Creation and Redemption.

R. J. Clifford (508) also makes note of the sometimes misleading theological construct of "creation-fall-redemption" as a summary of the OT narrative. Instead, he suggests that creation imagery is always, in a sense, cosmogony and therefore implicitly redemption imagery. Thus it is Yahweh's creative power that brings salvation to Israel (Ps 77:16-19), Zion (Ps 46) and the *king (Ps 18:7-15). Echoing Genesis 1—3, God's creative powers are a saving victory over chaos (Ps 74:13-14; 89:9-18; cf. Ps 142; 144) (see Keel, 215). In this way, we see that creation imagery represents both the context in which Israel will be saved and the paradigm for God's power to do it (Ps 95), such that redemption ultimately is not anthropocentric but rather cosmic. Israel thus understands its salvation as an act of re-creation that includes the redemption of the land (all creation) (Ps 74; cf. Is 48:6-8; 65:17-25; Rom 8:18-25; 2 Cor 5:17).

7. Wisdom and Creation Order.

Finally, most of the creation imagery in wisdom texts attests to the order in God's creative work. R. C. Van Leeuwen describes the effect as one portraying the "carved" nature of the created order wherein God has purposed a fitting place and function for everything that he has made. Job, in his affirmation of this order, feels compelled to understand his suffering in the light of the "boundaries" and "horizons" that God has placed in the world (Job 26:10). This order is apparent also in the metaphor in Proverbs 3:18-20, where wisdom is a "tree of life" and the agent by which God created the world (cf. Ps 104:24). The boundaries and limits within the created order are most emphatic in Proverbs 8:22-31, signified by the repeated use of the Hebrew *ḥōq* ("limit") and *ḥāqaq* ("carve" or "engrave") in Proverbs 8:27, 29. Psalm 104 resonates closely with these images, singing not only of the "place" and "boundary" for the mountains and valleys (Ps 104:8-9) but also ultimately of the wisdom that God used to make all things (Ps 104:24; cf. Job 26:10; Prov 3:19; Col 1:15-29). Even the book of Ecclesiastes, in all its irony and ambiguity, chooses to expresses stability through the rich and orderly images of eating, drinking, working (Eccles 2:24-25; 3:12-13, 22; 5:18-20; 8:15) and marriage (Eccles 9:7-10) as the good "gifts" that God has carved into creation for humanity (see Provan, 38).

8. Conclusion.

Throughout a variety of OT genres creation imagery puts on display an interconnected set of theological truths. In so doing, it illustrates the most basic contours of Israel's worldview, wherein Israel's relationships with God, the earth and the surrounding nations are grounded in God's primordial purpose and design for the whole creation. What emerges is a worldview adorned with pictures of God's kingship, presence and power along with images of Israelite origins, the nature of suffering, the context of redemption and the way to wisdom and knowledge. Over time, this imagery establishes and sustains a corporate memory in Israel with its constant reminders of the order and purpose in God's creation, and, more importantly, the incomparable wisdom, power and glory of the Creator.

See also ANIMAL IMAGERY; ARCHITECTURAL IMAGERY; CREATION THEOLOGY; FLORAL IMAG-

ERY; IMAGERY; MOUNTAIN IMAGERY; PSALMS 6: ICONOGRAPHY.

BIBLIOGRAPHY. **W. P. Brown,** *"Creatio Corporis* and the Rhetoric of Defense in Job 10 and Psalm 139," in *God Who Creates: Essays in Honor of W. Sibley Towner,* ed. W. P. Brown and S. D. McBride (Grand Rapids: Eerdmans, 2000) 107-24; **R. J. Clifford,** "The Hebrew Scriptures and the Theology of Creation," *TS* 46 (1985) 507–23; **N. C. Habel,** "He Who Stretches Out the Heavens," *CBQ* 34 (1972) 417–30; **O. Keel,** *The Symbolism of the Biblical World: Ancient Near Eastern Iconography and The Book of Psalms* (New York: Seabury Press, 1978); **J. L. Mays,** "'Maker of Heaven and Earth': Creation in the Psalms," in *God Who Creates: Essays in Honor of W. Sibley Towner,* ed. W. P. Brown and S. D. McBride (Grand Rapids: Eerdmans, 2000) 75–86; **P. D. Miller,** "The Poetry of Creation: Psalm 104," in *God Who Creates: Essays in Honor of W. Sibley Towner,* ed. W. P. Brown and S. D. McBride (Grand Rapids: Eerdmans, 2000) 87-103; **I. W. Provan,** *Ecclesiastes, Song of Songs* (NIVAC; Grand Rapids: Zondervan, 2001); **R. A. Simkins,** *Creator and Creation: Nature in the Worldview of Ancient Israel* (Peabody, MA: Hendrickson, 1994); **R. C. Van Leeuwen,** "Liminality and Worldview in Proverbs 1–9," *Semeia* 50 (1990) 111–44.

R. O'Dowd

CREATION THEOLOGY

It has long been recognized that "Wisdom thinks resolutely within the framework of a theology of creation" (Zimmerli, 316). Biblical Wisdom literature speaks of God primarily in terms of God's role as creator rather than in terms of God's covenant relationship with Israel or God's involvement in Israel's history. The biblical wisdom books—*Job, *Ecclesiastes, *Proverbs, *Song of Songs—do not speak of history or of God's special revelation to Israel. Rather, they speak of the world as we know it—its pleasures, its hardships, its paradoxes, its beauty—the world of human society and of God's cosmic creation. Given the witness of these texts, virtually all biblical scholars would agree with this assessment by L. Perdue (340): "Each of the wisdom texts finds its theological center in creation."

Creation theology, then, is a vital topic in the study of the biblical Wisdom literature. It also occupies a key place in the study of the book of *Psalms, where concerns for both salvation history and creation theology are expressed (see Pss 8; 19; 24; 74; 89; 104). The Lord, the God of Israel, is acclaimed as the Creator of the world; and Israel, along with the whole creation, is called on to praise its Creator (Pss 148—149).

One cannot speak of a single "creation theology" in the Bible or in the Wisdom literature and Psalms. All the texts proclaim that the God of Israel is the creator of the world, but they differ significantly on other issues, particularly the issue of humanity's place in creation. Despite these differences, however, all the texts address some central questions: What is God's relationship to creation? What is the role and place of humanity in creation? What kind of world is this? How do nonhuman creatures relate to God and to humanity? This article will explore the varied answers to these questions found in the biblical Wisdom literature and in the book of Psalms, using the general categories of creator, creation and humanity to discuss the major emphases of the creation theologies found in these texts.

1. Creator
2. Creation
3. Humanity

1. Creator.

All of biblical tradition, including the Wisdom literature and Psalms, proclaims that God created the world, established order in it, and continues to sustain it. Given this unified biblical witness to God as creator, however, it is interesting to note the different emphases in different texts on God's role in creation. The Wisdom literature and Psalms make various theological claims about God as creator. A few of the more prominent themes are discussed here.

1.1. God and Chaos.
The well-documented ancient Near Eastern motif of the *Chaoskampf*—the battle between the creator god and the forces of *chaos—is referenced in the Wisdom literature and Psalms. In the book of Job, for instance, the myth is referred to a number of times by the character of Job, in reference to God's absolute power (Job 3:8; 7:12; 9:8, 13; 26:12-13). The Sea (a symbol of chaos in the ancient Near East) and the sea monster Leviathan also occupy prominent places in the speeches of God at the end of the book (Job 38:8-11; 41:1-34). In these speeches, however, the Sea and Leviathan are described not as forces of chaos that threaten to overwhelm the world but as wild and beautiful

forces in which God takes delight. In a remarkable image, God attends the birth of the Sea and uses clouds and thick darkness to swaddle the rambunctious newborn infant (Job 38:8-11). The divine speeches describe at great length the sea monster Leviathan, who is called a "king" (Job 41:34). God takes obvious pride in the Sea and Leviathan and gives them a place in creation, even as God also prescribes boundaries for them (Job 38:11; 41:10-11, 33).

Psalm 104 speaks in similar terms of Leviathan, as a creature that God created and in which God takes pleasure (Ps 104:26). In fact, in Psalm 104 God creates Leviathan as something of a bathtub toy, placing the chaos monster in the sea so that God can "play" or "sport" *(śḥq)* with it. In other psalms, however, Leviathan and Rahab (both names for the primordial sea monster) are described in the traditional terms of the *Chaoskampf* myth. In Psalms 74; 89, God's act of crushing or breaking Leviathan/Rahab is recalled as evidence of God's great power over the forces of chaos (Ps 74:13-14; 89:10). In both instances the use of the motif is combined with a lament over the current state of affairs for the psalmist and for Israel: the destruction of the temple and the fall of the Davidic dynasty. God's primordial victory over chaos is held in sharp contrast to the apparent victory of historical forces of chaos over God's chosen people. God is called upon to rise up as of old and defeat the forces of chaos that have overwhelmed his people. As J. Levenson (19) observes, the psalmist "acknowledges the reality of militant, triumphant, and persistent evil, but he steadfastly and resolutely refuses to accept this reality as final and absolute. Instead he challenges YHWH to act like the hero of old, to conform to his magisterial nature." In each instance the theme of God's creating the world through the defeat of chaos monsters is used to urge God to re-create the world in which the psalmist lives in order that it might conform to the good order established at that primordial beginning.

1.2. God and Wisdom. Perhaps the best-known "creation" text in Wisdom literature is the description of creation through the eyes of *Woman Wisdom in Proverbs 8:22-31. The Lord creates (or "begets") Wisdom "the first of his ways" (Prov 8:22). Before God brings forth mountains, hills and springs of water, Wisdom is created. She is beside God as he establishes the heavens and the foundations of the earth, as he gives the sea its limits. In Proverbs 8:30 she is beside God as an *ʾāmôn* ("master worker" [another possible reading is "little child"]). Wisdom delights in creation, rejoicing and playing before God daily, being herself God's "delight," rejoicing in the "inhabited world" and taking delight in humanity (Prov 8:31).

There is debate among scholars over Woman Wisdom's role in creation. Is Wisdom in this text a "created co-creator" (Fretheim, 215), a being who participates in and indeed helps God in God's act of creating? The translation of *ʾāmôn* as "master worker" in Proverbs 8:30 would support such an interpretation (Fretheim, 214), as would the reference in Wisdom of Solomon 7:22 to Wisdom as "the fashioner of everything." On the other hand, if one understands *ʾāmôn* as "little child," the image of Wisdom in Proverbs 8 is that of a child who plays before God and delights in God's creation (Perdue, 91; Fox 2000, 287-89). She is, in this interpretation, more of a fascinated observer than a participant in the act of creating. Such an interpretation is supported by the verbs associated with begetting and birthing at the beginning of this passage (*qnh* ["beget" or "acquire"] in Prov 8:22; *ḥûl* ["give birth"] in Prov 8:24). Both verbs are used in reference to God's activity in creating Woman Wisdom.

Whether Woman Wisdom is a created co-creator or a little child in Proverbs 8, it is important to note that she is neither a full-blown deity in her own right nor simply one creature among many. Woman Wisdom is not depicted as an ancient Near Eastern goddess like Asherah (1 Kings 15:13; 18:19), but neither is she insignificant (Fox 2000, 334-41; Davis 2000, 67). Woman Wisdom is the first of God's ways, created before anything else in the world, and she is God's constant companion during the whole process of creation, from the foundation of the earth to the fashioning of humanity. She is quite possibly God's skilled assistant in the creation of the cosmos, and she is at the least God's "delight," playing before him and rejoicing with him at the exquisite beauty of the created world. Woman Wisdom, as depicted in Proverbs 8, is an integral part of the whole created order.

1.3. God's Delight in Creation. The playfulness of Woman Wisdom in Proverbs 8 points to an important theme in the Wisdom literature and Psalms: God's delight in creation. E. Davis (2000, 68) says of the creation theology of Proverbs 8, "God's decision to create the world was a matter of absolutely free choice. . . . Yet a free choice is not an arbitrary one. God created the world, including and even especially humanity, for the sake of God's own pleasure, as the twofold mention of 'delights' [in Prov 8:30-31] suggests. These two, freedom and delight, belong together, in divine play just as in children's play."

The word used for Woman Wisdom "playing" (śḥq) before God is used also in Psalm 104:26 of God's "playing" or "sporting" with Leviathan. Many English translations of Psalm 104:26 are similar to that of the NRSV: "There go the ships, and Leviathan that you formed to sport in it [the sea]." The verse can also be translated: "There go the ships, and Leviathan that you formed to play with." In order to make the antecedent of "it" the sea, one has to go back to the previous verse. It is more likely that the antecedent of the pronoun is found in the same verse, in the name "Leviathan." God "plays" or "sports" with Leviathan as one would with a bath toy or a pet.

In either translation, of course, the element of play is present in the creation of Leviathan. This element of play and delight is not absent from the rest of the psalm. Psalm 104 as a whole evokes the image of a creator God who delights in what is created. God makes springs gush forth to water the earth abundantly (Ps 104:10-13). God creates not only food to sustain the life of his creatures but also wine "to make joyful [śmḥ] the human heart," and oil "to make the human face shine" (Ps 104:15). What makes God himself joyful (śmḥ) at the end of the psalm is "his works," those things and creatures that God has created (Ps 104:31). Such language describes a God who creates not out of any necessity but rather out of freedom and gratuitousness; a God who values and takes delight in what is created.

This same delight in creation can be seen in the divine speeches of Job (Job 38—41). These speeches are a God's-eye view of creation in all its complexity and beauty. God describes the founding of the earth, "when the morning stars sang together, and all the sons of God shouted with joy" (Job 38:7). God then goes on to describe the birth of the sea, the establishment of the meteorological forces, the stars, the realm of the wild animals, and the two mythological creatures Behemoth and Leviathan. The element of playfulness apparent in Proverbs 8 and Psalm 104 is not lacking in the divine speeches of Job. The same word used in those passages, śḥq ("sport, play, laugh"), is used in Job to describe

the activity of a number of the wild animals: the wild donkey, the ostrich, the warhorse and Leviathan (Job 39:7, 18, 22; 41:29 [MT 41:21]). In most cases the object of these animals' laughter is humanity or humanity's inventions (see 3.2 below). In Job 40:20, however, the verb is also used of the "play" of the wild animals on the hills. Given the attention accorded to laughter and play in the divine speeches, and the exquisite detail with which God describes the creation, God himself seems to take pleasure in that playfulness. All these texts evoke the image of a proud Creator who delights in his beautiful creation.

2. Creation.

Creation—the nonhuman natural world—has a large part to play in the biblical narrative. In earlier biblical interpretation an anthropocentric bias, exemplified in a focus on human "salvation history," can be discerned. In any careful reading of the Wisdom literature and Psalms, such an anthropocentric bias is difficult to maintain. Creation has its own relationship to its Creator, quite apart from human beings. God created the world, cares for it, and in turn receives praise from it. Human beings are, of course, a part of the created order, but they are by no means the only part. Animals, trees, mountains and celestial bodies, along with the rest of creation, have an integral role to play in the biblical story of God's relationship with the world.

2.1. Order in Creation. Any exploration of creation theology has to address the fundamental question "What kind of world is this?" The biblical wisdom writers were interested in that question and offered various answers based largely on observation of the world around them. The *sages of the book of Proverbs, for instance, observed a certain order to the world, an order that could be discerned by human beings seeking wisdom. Many scholars equate the wisdom concept of such an "order" in creation with the Egyptian concept of *maat* (Kayatz, 93-119; Murphy, 161-62). "Ma'at is right order in nature and society, as established by the act of creation, and hence means, according to the context, what is right, what is correct, law, order, justice, and truth" (Morenz, 113). In the biblical Wisdom literature such order was understood as the gift of God and was thought to be discernible at least in part through observation of the natural world.

The ant provides a lesson in hard work and good planning (Prov 6:6-11). Natural elements and creatures provide analogies for human relationships in many passages (e.g., Prov 17:12; 20:2; 25:26; 26:1-2). The ant, the badger, the locust and the lizard are extolled as small but "very wise" (Prov 30:24-28). In all these instances, and many others, the sages of Proverbs discern a certain order in creation, established by God and conducive to the good life, if human beings conform to it. "The LORD by wisdom founded the earth; he established the heavens by understanding" (Prov 3:19). The person who wants to prosper will seek to understand that wisdom, that order, by which the cosmos is established.

The book of Ecclesiastes is, of course, much more skeptical than the book of Proverbs. *Qohelet ("the Teacher"), the primary speaker in Ecclesiastes, spends a lot of time observing the world around him, but mostly what he sees is *hebel:* "All is *hebel*" (Eccles 1:2b). Traditionally translated "vanity," *hebel* is better understood as something like "the absurd" (Fox 1999, 30-33). There is much that is absurd in the world that Qohelet observes: "There is nothing new under the sun" (Eccles 1:9); "For there is no lasting remembrance of the wise man or the fool. For in the days yet to come, all will have been forgotten. Alas! The wise man dies like the fool" (Eccles 2:16); "For the fate of human beings and the fate of animals is one fate. As one dies, so dies the other, and there is one breath for all. Humanity has no advantage over the animals, for all is absurd *[hebel]*" (Eccles 3:19).

To be sure, Qohelet notices a certain order in the world: the sun rises and sets (Eccles 1:5); the wind blows to the north and south (Eccles 1:6); humans and animals are made of dust and return to dust (Eccles 3:20). This order, however, is wearisome to Qohelet. "Locked in an endless cycle of sameness, the cosmos is stripped of all vitality and majesty" (Brown 1996, 124). Even out of his strong sense of the absurd, however, Qohelet is able to affirm certain things: enjoyment is to be found in food, drink and work (Eccles 2:24; 3:13; 8:15); God is to be feared (Eccles 7:18; 8:12-13; 12:13) (*see* Fear of the Lord). In perhaps the most famous passage from the book Qohelet speaks of *time: "For everything there is a time, and a season for every activity under heaven" (Eccles 3:1). What follows is a catalogue of human activities: birth and death, killing and

healing, weeping and laughing, war and peace. Finally, Qohelet speaks of God's activity: "He has made everything beautiful [or 'suitable'] in its time" (Eccles 3:11a). Such an affirmation seems to echo the more traditional wisdom of Proverbs, with its view of a God-ordained order in the world; and yet in the same verse Qohelet denies that humanity is able to understand any such divine activity: "He has also put eternity in their hearts, but humanity cannot find out what God has done from the beginning to the end" (Eccles 3:11b). There may be a certain God-ordained order to the world, but ultimately, according to Qohelet, God's ways are inscrutable.

In the book of Job the question "What kind of world is this?" takes on a certain urgency. The Job of the prologue (Job 1—2) and his companions in the dialogue (Job 3—37) subscribe to a traditional wisdom view: God has ordered the world in such a way that the righteous prosper and the wicked are punished (e.g., Job 1:9-10; 4:7-9; 8:3-7; 11:13-20). Even when he is afflicted unjustly, the patient Job of the prologue accepts his hardships as the traditional wisdom teachers of Proverbs might expect, without complaint: "My son, do not reject the LORD's discipline; and do not loathe his rebuke. For the LORD reproves those he loves, as a father the son with whom he is pleased" (Prov 3:11-12). Though he has done nothing to deserve punishment, the Job of the prologue still seems to believe that God has established a good order in the world: "the LORD gives and the LORD takes away. Blessed be the name of the LORD" (Job 1:21b).

Such a belief system accords well with the world that Job inhabits in the prologue, a world that he describes with longing in Job 29. C. Newsom (187-91) aptly describes this world as a highly structured, hierarchical one in which Job occupies the central position. Surrounding him are family and peers and, on the margins, the poor and powerless, to whom Job offers protection. Outside of this structured world are the wilderness and the wild animals. Job considers this world of wilderness God-forsaken and uses its imagery to speak of his personal desolation: "I have become a brother of jackals, and a companion of ostriches" (Job 30:29). The world of the prologue—the world that Job occupies at the beginning of the book—has no place for wilderness or wild animals. Everything in this world is ordered and structured according to a strict act-and-consequence system: the wicked are punished, and the righteous are protected from anything that might harm them, including dangerous forces of the natural world.

After the *Satan afflicts him, Job descends into chaos. He perceives no particular order to the world. The last word of his first lament names this experience: "What comes is *rōgez* [turmoil, agitation]" (Job 3:26). "*Rōgez* is to the order of lived experience as chaos is to cosmic order" (Newsom, 94). The structured world of the prologue has descended into chaos, as far as Job is concerned. Far from being the creator of order in the world, God is perceived by Job to be the source of the chaos: "The earth has been given into the hand of the wicked.... If it is not he, who then is it?" (Job 9:24). The system of reward and punishment that Job once believed in—the system that his friends still believe in—has been turned upside down, in Job's estimation, so that the wicked prosper, while he, a righteous man, is oppressed by a capricious God (Job 10:1-7; 21:7-13).

In the divine speeches God corrects both visions of the world: that of the friends, in which a strict act-and-consequence pattern governs existence; and that of Job, which sees only chaos and a capricious deity. God proudly puts the world on display: wild animals of every kind, the mythological creatures Behemoth and Leviathan, and the sea, that ancient symbol of chaos. The very structured vision of the friends is incorrect, as God gives a place in the world to wild and dangerous elements; but neither is Job's vision correct, as God places limits on those elements: "Who fenced in Sea with doors when it came bursting out from the womb ... and said, 'Thus far you will come and no further. Here shall your proud waves be stopped'?" (Job 38:8, 11). J. Janzen (235) puts the matter succinctly: "All systematic attempts to read existence ... according to a principle of justice involving strict recompense or retribution break themselves against the fact that the sea is given a place in the cosmos. All attempts to exegete the Book of Job in such a way as to arrive at the conclusion that God there is indifferent to matters of justice overlook the fact that the place of the sea in the cosmos is delimited by divine decree."

The divine speeches describe a world ordered by God; the forces of chaos are not allowed free rein. This world, however, is filled with wild and beautiful creatures that are allowed the freedom to be and become what they were created to be. Job's original vision of a tightly ordered world is broken open to envision creation in its entirety: a place not entirely safe for human beings, but a place in which they too are called to freedom.

2.2. Creation's Praise of God. Creation praises its Creator over and over again in the OT. Most of the references to such praise occur in Psalms and Isaiah (for a list of these occurrences, see Fretheim, 267-68). The morning stars sing together at the dawn of creation (Job 38:7). The heavens tell the glory of God (Ps 19:1). The trees of the forest sing for joy (Ps 96:12). Even the seas and floods, ancient symbols of chaos, clap their hands and rejoice at the coming of the Lord (Ps 98:7-8). In the most exuberant example of this motif the writer of Psalm 148 calls on everyone and everything in creation to sing a "hallelujah" chorus: sun, moon, stars, sea monsters, deeps, fire, snow, wind, mountains, hills, fruit trees, cedars, wild animals, cattle, creeping things, birds and people of every age and station in life. "Let them praise the name of the LORD.... Praise the LORD [halĕlû-yâh])!" (Ps 148:13a, 14b).

Some of these texts that speak of creation's praise of God are oriented to a future, eschatological time. In Psalms 96; 98, for instance, creation bursts into joyful praise because the LORD is coming to judge the earth (Ps 96:13; 98:9). Such an eschatological interpretation is appropriate for many of the prophetic passages in which this motif occurs (Is 35:1-2; 49:13; 66:22-23). Other texts, such as Job 38:7, speak of creation's joy at the beginning of time, at the establishment of the earth. In the majority of occurrences of this motif, however, the orientation is to the present moment, and the creatures of the natural world praise God simply because that is what they are created to do.

Psalm 148 is instructive in this regard. The psalmist calls on all creation to praise the LORD "because he gave the command and they were created. He established them forever; he gave a decree that will not be broken" (Ps 148:5-6). Created things are to praise their Creator because they exist, because God has brought them into being. Praising God is integral to their being. Later the psalmist sings, "Let them praise the name of the LORD, for his name alone is exalted, his majesty is over earth and heaven" (Ps 148:13). Here the concern is for the exaltation of God's name, making God's name known. As T. Fretheim (259) asserts, "These are the two central facets of praise: the honor of God and the witness to others. . . . The one always entails the other." The natural world is made to praise God for who God is and thereby also to witness to humanity of God's goodness and majesty.

Commentators have noted the environmental implications of this motif of creation's praise of God (Fretheim, 257-58, 265; Davis 2001, 35). When humanity damages the earth and its inhabitants, the earth's ability to praise is diminished. A polluted river cannot praise God with full voice. "The heavens declare the glory of God" (Ps 19:1), but not as clearly when they are clouded with smog. In other words, the sin of environmental degradation is sin not only because it endangers or damages the lives of human beings but also because it diminishes creation's ability to praise its Creator. The psalmist writes of the day of judgment, "Let the field exult, and all that is in it. Then all the trees of the forest will shout for joy before the LORD, for he is coming, for he is coming to judge the earth" (Ps 96:12-13a). For the fields, the sea, the forests and all the creatures that inhabit them, the fact that God is coming to judge the earth is very good news indeed. In that day sin, with its pollution and defilement, will be wiped away, and the creation will at last be able to be what it was created to be: a witness to God's glory, singing with full and clear voice in praise of its Creator.

2.3. Paradise Restored. Song of Songs is filled with images of creation: lush and verdant vegetation, flowers, vineyards, wild and domestic animals, fruit, sensual fragrances and, of course, human lovers. The book is in many ways unique in the OT and has engendered many different interpretations over the centuries. Is it a love song? An erotic poem? An extended metaphor about the love between God and Israel, or Christ and the church? However one might read this book, one thing is clear: the created world, with all its abundant fertility and life, is a major part of the story.

Picking up on the imagery of the natural world, both P. Trible and E. Davis argue that the key to understanding Song of Songs is to read it through the lens of Genesis 2—3, the story of the garden of Eden. As Trible (144) says, "the Song of Songs redeems a love story gone awry." Plants and animals, created in Genesis, are named in Song of Songs and used as metaphors for love: the fig tree (Song 2:13), the pomegran-

ate (Song 4:3, 13; 6:7), the cedar (Song 5:15), gazelles (Song 2:9; 4:5), doves (Song 4:1), goats (Song 4:1). The woman herself is called a "garden" (Song 4:12, 16; 5:1; 6:2), like the "garden" of Eden. According to Trible, then, Song of Songs uses the imagery of the natural world to depict the restoration of the original goodness and mutuality of human erotic love, first described in Genesis 2.

Davis, while agreeing with Trible's assessment, argues that Song of Songs restores three relationships damaged in the garden of Eden: not only the relationship between man and woman but also the relationship between humanity and God and the relationship between humanity and the earth (Davis 2000, 232). This last point is of particular interest in delineating the creation theology of Song of Songs.

The world of Song of Songs overflows with lush vegetation, fruit, animals, exotic spices and abundant water. The male lover describes the woman: "Your limbs are a paradise of pomegranates with choice fruit, henna with nard, nard and saffron, calamus and cinnamon, with all trees of frankincense, myrrh and aloes, with all choice perfumes; a garden spring, a well of living water, and flowing waters from Lebanon" (Song 4:13-15). The text describes not so much a person as a land full of the verdant growth and waters of spring. Here there is no serpent; here there are no thorns to curse the earth (Gen 3:1, 18). Instead, the land produces abundant fruit and verdant vegetation for the pleasure of all (Song 2:11-13). "The winter is past; the rains are over and gone. The flowers appear on the earth; the time for singing has come" (Song 2:11-12a). Song of Songs returns us to the garden of Eden, where human love is full and mutual, where the earth is a garden of delights, and where the love between humanity and God is restored (Davis 2000, 251).

This connection with the garden of Eden provides a useful interpretative lens through which to read Song of Songs. It must be noted, however, that the restoration to the garden is not complete. There is an "already and not yet" quality to the vision of Song of Songs. The book describes at length the love of the man and woman for each other, a love expressed in words and actions while the lovers are present with each other (Song 1:2-4; 2:1-13; 4:1-16; 5:1; 7:1-13). It also speaks at various points, however, about the woman seeking her lover and not finding him (Song 3:1-2; 5:2—6:3). Although Song of Songs returns us to the garden of Eden, then, it also acknowledges that the restoration is not yet complete, and it sharpens our desire for that completion, for heaven itself (Davis 2000, 302). Although that desire is not fully satisfied in Song of Songs, the text gives us a taste of what that world will be like, when the shadow of sin cast over the good creation (Gen 3:18; Rom 8:19-22) is lifted, and paradise is restored.

3. Humanity.

Both Job and the writer of Psalm 8 ask God the question "What is humanity?" (Job 7:17; Ps 8:4). The psalmist asks the question in wonder and thankfulness; Job asks it in a parody of the psalmist, out of grief and anguish. The question itself is an important one to raise in any discussion of creation theology. What is humanity? What is humanity's place in creation?

The Wisdom literature and Psalms offer varied answers to this question. For the purposes of this investigation, two of those answers will serve as representative. One is from Psalm 8; the other from the divine speeches in Job (Job 38—41).

3.1. "A Little Less Than God." The psalmist asks, "What is humankind, that you are mindful of them; mortal man, that you take care of him? You have made him a little less than God, and crowned him with glory and honor" (Ps 8:4-5). The psalmist goes on to assert that God has made human beings rulers over the rest of the created order, including domesticated animals and wild animals, birds and fish, and "whatever passes through the paths of the seas" (Ps 8:8).

R. Simkins (221) traces this "lofty" view of humanity to Israelite royal theology and argues that the psalm elevates all human beings to royal status. It might even be said that humanity is understood by the psalmist to participate in divinity, as beings just a little lower than God. A similarly high view of humanity is found also, of course, in the Genesis creation accounts, especially the Priestly creation account of Genesis 1:1—2:3. There, human beings are made in the image of God and, as in Psalm 8, given dominion over the rest of the created order, including animals both domesticated and wild.

In both Psalm 8 and Genesis 1 humanity is the crown of creation. In Genesis God's fashioning of humanity is the culmination of the creation of all the animals, and it is only humanity that is created in the image of God. It is also only

after humanity is fashioned that creation is pronounced not just "good," but "very good" (Gen 1:31). In Psalm 8 humanity rules over creation and occupies a place only a little lower than God himself. In both passages God gives humanity dominion over all the rest of creation. The psalmist asks in wonder, "What is humanity?" (Ps 8:4). The answer that he offers comes out of a very high view of humanity indeed.

3.2. "Look at Behemoth, Which I Made with You." In contrast to Psalm 8 and Genesis 1, the divine speeches of Job 38—41 answer the question "What is humanity?" with a decidedly more humble view. The divine speeches are notable for their detailed description of creation, a description that ranges across the realms of cosmology, meteorology, zoology and mythology. In this whole vision of creation, however, human beings are given little or no attention.

Earlier in the book Job asks the question "What is humanity?" in an apparent parody of Psalm 8 (Job 7:17). Job answers the question by asserting that God is inordinately concerned with human beings, watching and waiting for them to sin. "Will you not look away from me? Will you not leave me alone until I swallow my spittle?" (Job 7:19). Eliphaz asks the same question, and he answers it with a very low view of humanity: "What is humanity, that they can be clean? . . . The heavens are not pure in God's eyes. How much less one who is abominable and corrupt; human beings, who drink perversity like water!" (Job 15:14-16). Bildad, in a similar statement, calls human beings "maggots" and "worms" (Job 25:4-6; cf. Job 4:17-21).

The divine speeches give credence to neither of these views of humanity. In the speeches human beings are not worms, but neither are they the center of God's attention. In fact, the divine speeches answer the question "What is humanity?" with a deafening silence. Human beings appear only as creatures peripheral to the world that God describes: dawn shakes "the wicked" out of the earth; the wild ass mocks the tumult of the city; the eagle drinks up the blood of slain warriors (Job 38:13; 39:7, 30).

The relative insignificance of human beings in the divine speeches is underscored by a question that pointedly implies that humanity is not the center of creation: "Who has made a trench for the flood, and a way for the thunderbolt, to make it rain on an uninhabited land, the wilderness where no person lives?" (Job 38:25-26)

Rain is reserved not just for places of human habitation but also for the wilderness, which is inhospitable, even dangerous, to humanity. God also cares for the wild animals and the mythological creatures Behemoth and Leviathan. These creatures "laugh at" or "mock" (*śḥq*) humanity and humanity's inventions. The wild donkey laughs at the tumult of the city, that quintessential human habitation (Job 39:7); the ostrich laughs at the horse and its human rider (Job 39:18); the sea monster Leviathan laughs at human weapons, which bounce off its impenetrable scales (Job 41:29 [MT 41:21]). These creatures, like the wilderness itself, can be neither controlled nor used by humanity.

Psalm 8 and Genesis 1 speak of humanity's dominion over the animals; the divine speeches of Job subvert this creation theology. God says to Job, "Look at Behemoth, which I made with you" (Job 40:15). Job is equated with a wild creature, albeit one of immense strength. God created them both and does not make one master over the other. Job had earlier claimed to be like a "king" (Job 29:25); however, in the divine speeches it is Leviathan, not Job, who is designated by God as "king over all proud beings" (Job 41:34). In the divine speeches the wild animals serve no human purpose but instead are celebrated as "icons of freedom and dignity" (Brown 1999, 366).

Given the striking absence of humanity from the description of creation in the divine speeches, it must also be noted that the speeches are addressed to a human being. Although designed to put Job "in his place," the speeches at some level acknowledge that he does indeed *have* a place in creation; he is, after all, the sole passenger on this grand tour of the cosmos.

The divine speeches at the end of Job offer a radically nonanthropocentric view of creation. In contrast to the worldview presented in Genesis 1 and Psalm 8, the divine speeches assert that humanity is neither the center nor the crown of creation. The world is not made primarily for the use of human beings. There exist in the world wild and beautiful things not under human control, and God takes delight in those things. God cares for every part of creation, including those places and creatures unused and unusable by human beings. In other words, there is no land or creature that can properly be called "God-forsaken." Wilderness and wild creatures have a value to God (and to humanity)

quite apart from any "use" that humanity can make of them. God takes delight in all creation, not just in human beings.

The creation theologies of the Wisdom literature and Psalms are as rich and varied as the texts themselves. From the cycle of the sun in Ecclesiastes to the lush gardens in Song of Songs, from the singing hills and trees in Psalms to the hard-working ants of Proverbs, from playful Woman Wisdom in Proverbs to the wild beauty of the divine speeches in Job, the natural world plays a vital role in the ongoing story of God's relationship not only with human beings, but with all that God has created.

See also ANIMAL IMAGERY; CHAOS AND DEATH; CREATION IMAGERY; FLORAL IMAGERY; GOD; MAAT; THEODICY; THEOPHANY.

BIBLIOGRAPHY. **W. P. Brown,** *Character in Crisis: A Fresh Approach to the Wisdom Literature of the Old Testament* (Grand Rapids: Eerdmans, 1996); idem, *The Ethos of the Cosmos: The Genesis of Moral Imagination in the Bible* (Grand Rapids: Eerdmans, 1999); **E. F. Davis,** *Proverbs, Ecclesiastes, and the Song of Songs* (WestBC; Louisville: Westminster John Knox, 2000); idem, *Getting Involved With God: Rediscovering the Old Testament* (Cambridge, MA: Cowley, 2001); **M. V. Fox,** *A Time to Tear Down and a Time to Build Up: A Rereading of Ecclesiastes* (Grand Rapids: Eerdmans, 1999); idem, *Proverbs 1-9* (AB 18A; New York: Doubleday, 2000); **T. E. Fretheim,** *God and World in the Old Testament: A Relational Theology of Creation* (Nashville: Abingdon, 2005); **J. G. Janzen,** *Job* (IBC; Atlanta: John Knox, 1985); **C. Kayatz,** *Studien zu Proverbien 1-9: Eine form- und motivgeschichtliche Untersuchung unter Einbeziehung ägyptischen Vergleichsmaterials* (WMANT 22; Neukirchen-Vluyn: Neukirchener Verlag, 1966); **J. D. Levenson,** *Creation and the Persistence of Evil: The Jewish Drama of Divine Omnipotence* (2nd ed.; Princeton, NJ: Princeton University Press, 1994); **S. Morenz,** *Egyptian Religion* (Ithaca, NY: Cornell University Press, 1973); **R. Murphy,** *The Tree of Life: An Exploration of Biblical Wisdom Literature* (3rd ed.; Grand Rapids: Eerdmans, 2002); **C. A. Newsom,** *The Book of Job: A Contest of Moral Imaginations* (Oxford: Oxford University Press, 2003); **L. G. Perdue,** *Wisdom and Creation: The Theology of Wisdom Literature* (Nashville: Abingdon, 1994); **K. M. Schifferdecker,** *Out of the Whirlwind: Creation Theology in the Book of Job* (Cambridge, MA: Harvard University Press, 2008); **H. H. Schmid,** "Creation, Righteousness, and Salvation: 'Creation Theology' as the Broad Horizon of Biblical Theology," in *Creation in the Old Testament*, ed. B. W. Anderson (IRT 6; Philadelphia: Fortress, 1984) 102-17; **R. A. Simkins,** *Creator and Creation: Nature in the Worldview of Ancient Israel* (Peabody, MA: Hendrickson, 1994); **P. Trible,** *God and the Rhetoric of Sexuality* (OBT; Philadelphia: Fortress, 1978); **W. Zimmerli,** "The Place and Limit of the Wisdom in the Framework of the Old Testament Theology," in *Studies in Ancient Israelite Wisdom*, ed. H. M. Orlinsky and J. L. Crenshaw (New York: KTAV, 1976) 314-26.

K. Schifferdecker

CULT, WORSHIP: PSALMS

*Worship is "the attitude and activity designated to recognize and describe the worth" of one to whom homage is paid (Davies, 879). The book of *Psalms contains one of Scripture's most profound and extensive expressions of this "attitude" toward God. Indeed, the psalms praise, laud and give thanks to God for his just and redeeming acts (Ps 75:2-10) and for his incomparable might and grace (Ps 93; 95—99; 118:1-4). The Hebrew title of the book, "Praises" *(těhillîm)*, seems to suggest further that even psalms that complain and petition God represent worship because they are grounded in faith in God's character and actions on behalf of those who seek him.

While the Psalter expresses the attitudinal aspect of worship directly, it also gives witness to the "activity" of worship, albeit indirectly in most cases. The psalms mention performance of songs by singing (Ps 81:1-2; 144:9; 147:7) and playing instruments (Ps 81:2-3; 144:9; 147:7; 149:3; 150:3-5) (*see* Music, Song). They contain references to ritual clapping and shouting (Ps 47:1), dancing (Ps 149:3), processing to the holy place (Ps 132:7) and making sacrifices (Ps 118:27 [although the NRSV renders "bind the festal procession with branches," the word *hag* is perhaps better understood as "festal sacrifice"; see the same term in Mal 2:3]). Biblical scholars often refer to this activity as "cult," which denotes an established set of rituals and the liturgy that accompanies them, in which communion with God is ordered, defined and celebrated. Although the English word *worship* can refer broadly to homage in private and personal forms, the "cult" connotes more narrowly address to God that is regulated and public. In the twentieth century scholars of the psalms focused

much attention on the point that the psalms served originally as the liturgy of Israel's cult, and they attempted to describe the cultic acts that served as the setting for certain psalms. Many such efforts assumed that the particular cult setting was the worship in the Jerusalem temple. Some now believe, however, that many psalms are the products of cult practices that developed in the Diaspora, when Jews were dispersed throughout the ancient Near East after 587 BC.

The purpose of this article is to survey the nature of various psalms that suggests that this material was related to the cult and to summarize some of the leading theories of how psalms specifically were used in cultic practice. Some attention will be paid to the types of questions that remain unanswered in such study.

1. Nature and Centrality of the Cult in Ancient Israel
2. Study of the Relationship of the Psalms to the Cult
3. Signs of Cultic Use of the Psalms
4. Cultic Settings
5. Identity of Cultic Leaders and Participants
6. Current Questions

1. Nature and Centrality of the Cult in Ancient Israel.

For modern Western readers, worship may suggest an activity reserved for one hour of the week that thus is separated from the rest of life. For ancient Israelites, however, all of life was punctuated by sacral activity of a communal and ritualistic character. Hence, the cult permeated life in a way that worship does not in the contemporary community of faith (Buss). Although ancient people certainly practiced prayer and piety apart from the community ("worship" in the more general sense of the word), there was no sense that private expressions of piety would substitute for the cultic. The cult facilitated contact with a "life-creating, order-establishing, and meaning-giving power" (Stolz, 7). Hence, the psalms speak of "seeing God's face" in the holy place (Ps 17:15), or they refer to the temple as the place in which God's justice is made known (Ps 73:15-20). For this reason, the psalmist longed to be among worshipers, because apart from such company, God seemed absent and the enemies more powerful (note that Ps 42—43 is spoken at a distance from the temple and is punctuated by a taunt from opponents, "Where is your God?" [Ps 42:3, 10]). Given the power attributed to participation in the cult, and given the close relationship between the psalms and this established set of rituals, it is understandable that many scholars have been concerned to discern the particular ways and settings in which the psalms were performed.

2. Study of the Relationship of the Psalms to the Cult.

The recognition of the psalms' origins in the cult may be traced to the work of scholars in the "History of Religions" school, whose leading representative was German scholar H. Gunkel (his books and articles appeared between 1904 and 1933 [see Stamm, 34-41; Gerstenberger 1974, 179-88]). When Gunkel began his work, most scholars considered psalms to be artistic pieces that they could interpret in light of the circumstances of their authors, and they spent much effort trying to identify the psalmists and the events that gave rise to particular psalms (Haller, 378-83). But Gunkel thought that the language of these poems was too general and stereotyped to recover any such historical information. He noted that the psalms do not contain personal and historical references, in contrast to a poem such as 2 Samuel 1:19-27, in which "David mentions Saul and Jonathan by name" (Gunkel and Begrich, 7). In fact, Gunkel noted, the psalms contain almost no specific references that allow the scholar to reconstruct the exact circumstances under which a psalm was composed. Gunkel concluded that the generic quality of the psalms was due to their origin in the public and official events of Israelite community life, most notably in the cult. Therefore, he insisted that the main interpretive work was to categorize the psalms according to genre and to identify the social setting (*Sitz im Leben*) that gave rise to each genre (Gunkel and Begrich, 7). That is, he thought that the main task was to recover the *types* of events that lay behind the psalms (not particular historical occurrences). In other words, the main question became, "How were the psalms used in the cult?" (Gunkel thought that the "wisdom psalms" were an exception, being set among "the old men in the gate or in the market" [see Gunkel and Begrich, 21]). It should be noted, however, that Gunkel thought that the psalms in present form were products of personal piety based on cultic originals; so, Gunkel's real question involved

how certain speech forms that appear in the present Psalter were used originally in cultic events. Gunkel's student S. Mowinckel would argue that the psalms as they now appear in the Psalter are the cultic originals. Hence, this difference of opinion shapes the debate in important ways: some scholars assume that the psalms are the actual words used in the cult; others think that the psalms have been influenced by the language of worship but are themselves not "cultic." In any case, all psalms scholars since Gunkel have had to come to terms with the relationship between the psalms and the cult, regardless of the exact view of that relationship.

3. Signs of Cultic Use of the Psalms.

3.1. Implicit Evidence. Although there is little direct information on how the psalms were used in the cult, there is important implicit evidence, some of which is outside the Psalter. For example, psalms that ask God to "arise" (Ps 68:1) or "return" (Ps 132:8) are illuminated by Numbers 10:35-36, which links such language to the procession of the ark to the sanctuary. It reports that when the ark moved from its place, Moses would say, "Arise, O LORD, let your enemies be scattered, and your foes flee before you" (Num 10:35), and likewise when the ark came back to its place, he would say, "Return, O LORD of the ten thousand thousands of Israel" (Num 10:36). Hence, talk of God "arising" or "returning" in the psalms should be heard as part of a ceremony that had as its centerpiece a procession of the ark in celebration of the victory of God over his enemies (see particularly Ps 24:7-10 [Cross, 91-111]).

There is also implicit evidence in the psalms themselves. The antiphonal quality of many psalms suggests cultic use. For example, Psalm 118 opens with an invitation to praise, "O give thanks to the LORD, for he is good" (Ps 118:1a), followed by a statement of God's worthiness to be praised, presumably spoken by the congregation, "His steadfast love endures forever" (Ps 118:1; cf. Ps 118:29). The response in Psalm 118:1 then recurs throughout the next three verses, showing that the psalm is to be spoken publicly, as various groups (Israel [Ps 118:2]; house of Aaron [Ps 118:3]; those who fear the Lord [Ps 118:4]) are called to utter the words "His steadfast love endures forever" (see also Ps 115:9-11; 135:19-20; 136). The alternation of voices appears in some psalms as a shift in voice, from third to first person, perhaps indicating the presence of multiple worship leaders. Psalm 75 begins with a declaration of praise spoken by a worshiper (Ps 75:1). Then Yahweh himself speaks for the rest of the psalm (Ps 75:2-10). Similarly, Psalm 81:1-5a expresses a call to worship and a congregation's response, but Psalm 81:5b introduces "a voice I had not known," the voice of God, who speaks to the end of the psalm (Ps 81:6-16). Such features give these psalms a dramatic character. They probably indicate the participation of a cultic prophet who utters the words of God (see esp. Johnson).

3.2. Explicit Evidence.

3.2.1. Texts Outside the Psalms. There is also some explicit evidence that the psalms were used in the cult. At least two texts outside the Psalter attest directly to this point. According to 1 Chronicles 15:1-16:36, *David led a procession of the ark to Jerusalem. When the ark was in place, David "appointed the singing of praises to the LORD by Asaph and his kindred" (1 Chron 16:7). The content of their praises is reported to be a combination of segments of Psalms 105; 95; 106 (1 Chron 16:8-34). To be sure, the original version of this event in 2 Samuel 6 is less elaborate and does not include these details related to the psalms (it says only that David and company brought up the ark with shouting and the sound of the trumpet [2 Sam 6:15]), but it is significant that the Chronicler, who is supremely interested in worship, connects the psalms and this event.

Jeremiah 33:10-11 likewise associates a particular psalm with a cultic act. The passage reports Jeremiah's prophecy that when the Lord restores good fortune to Judah, once again there will be occasion to bring thank offerings to the temple (see Lev 7:11-18). Such offerings, Jeremiah declares, will be accompanied by the words of Psalm 136:1: "Give thanks to the LORD of hosts, for the LORD is good, for his steadfast love endures forever!" (Jer 33:11). The implications of this passage, however, are not limited to the use of this particular verse or psalm. The common expression "give thanks" comes from the same root word (*yadâ*) as the name of the thanksgiving offering in Hebrew (*tôdâ* [Lev 7:12]). Hence, it is reasonable to assume there is a connection between the thanksgiving offering and words such as "give thanks" and "I give thanks," wherever they appear. The Jeremiah text indicates that the act of making a thanksgiving offering (Ps 116:12-19; cf. Job 33:19-28) ap-

peared in tandem with offering thanks in song (Ps 116:1-11).

3.2.2. Psalm Headings. Perhaps the clearest indicator of the cultic use of psalms within the Psalter itself is psalm superscriptions (*see* Psalms 5: Titles). This information in the headings falls into three main categories. Some psalm titles include notes about an occasion on which a psalm was used or was to be used. For example, the heading of Psalm 30 identifies the psalm as "a song at the dedication of the temple," presumably a reference to the dedication of the second temple in 515 BC; the title of Psalm 38 identifies the work that it introduces as "for the memorial offering," a reference that, though clear enough in content, cannot be identified further; Psalm 92's heading designates the psalm as "a song for the Sabbath." The headings of Psalms 120—134 may also indicate cultic use. They all contain the note "A Song of Ascents" (see the slightly different form of the title in Ps 121). This element of the title likely designates these psalms for use in pilgrimages to Jerusalem (Crow, 1-27).

Psalm titles contain a variety of comments that appear to be musical directives (Gunkel and Begrich, 349-51). Although their meaning is uncertain in most cases, it seems clear that these comments originally involved the manner in which a psalm was performed: "with stringed instruments" (Ps 4:1; 6:1; 54:1; 55:1; 61:1; 67:1; 76:1); "for the flutes" (Ps 5:1); "according to ... " (Heb *ʿal* plus any of a variety of terms—e.g., "the deer of the dawn" [Ps 22:1]; "the Lilies" [Ps 45:1; 69:1]; "the Dove on Far-off Terebinths" [Ps 56:1]). Note the use of this type of direction in relation to musical performance in 1 Chronicles 15:20-21. The elusive term *selâ* may also be classified with information in psalm titles, even though it appears at breaks in the bodies of the psalms (Tate, 33 n. 5a).

These various notes on the performance of psalms almost certainly were added secondarily in a later stage of development when the psalms became written documents. In the case of Psalms 120—134, the grouping as a whole shows signs of having been edited for use in pilgrimage to Jerusalem in the postexilic period (Crow, 159-87). Hence, there is evidence at different levels that some psalms were adapted for a particular cultic use.

4. Cultic Settings.

Space limitations here do not allow a comprehensive survey of theories on the cultic events that lie behind the psalms. The examples that follow are representative of hypotheses put forward.

4.1. Community Psalms and Israel's Festivals. S. Mowinckel was one of the most influential scholars in the study of the relationship between the psalms and the cult, particularly on the matter of what cultic events might lie behind the psalms. Mowinckel proposed certain cultic settings based on what is known of the Babylonian cult, particularly Babylon's New Year festival, or the Akitu. The Babylonian festival featured a declaration of the kingship of Marduk, the chief deity of the Babylonian pantheon. It also included a significant role for the Babylonian king, as actor/leader of cultic activity and as a character in the dramatic celebration. For Mowinckel, this information was essential for understanding the use of psalms in Israel's worship. He proposed a New Year festival in the fall in Israel, at the time identified in later texts with the harvest festival (Ex 23:16; 34:24; Lev 23:23-44). He thought that the center of this celebration was a claim of Yahweh's kingship. The key psalms in his schema were the "enthronement psalms," which have at their center the claim or description of Yahweh as king (Pss 47; 93; 95—99). Mowinckel believed that the final day of the festival was a grand enactment of Yahweh's enthronement, marked by a procession of the ark to the temple. Hence, the words "The LORD is king" (Ps 93:1; 97:1; 99:1) should be rendered "The LORD has become king." He believed that this line constituted a cultic shout at the culmination of the parade to the holy place (Mowinckel, 1.106-92).

Mowinckel thought further that this celebration of Yahweh's kingship was led in large part by the Israelite king, whose rule was also reaffirmed and celebrated in various rituals during the New Year festival, as was the case in Babylon. He rightly saw that the "royal psalms" presented the human king's earthly rule as parallel to the heavenly rule of God, and that these psalms presented the king as God's appointed representative (Ps 2; 89:2-39; 110). Read in light of Babylonian records of the Akitu festival, this delineation of Israel's king indicated to Mowinckel that the king, as God's representative, stood at the center of the New Year celebration and of the cult in general. For Mowinckel, the "I" of the psalms was read in most cases as the voice of the king. The king, speaking as "I," was

not, for the most part, expressing personal complaints; rather, he was representing Israel's "corporate personality." So the king's reign, but also his struggle with enemies, his victories and defeats, was ritually enacted in the festival (see Eaton; Croft).

Reactions to Mowinckel's work reflect the difficulty of the question and the scarcity of direct evidence. Three prominent opinions on Mowinckel's theory are illustrative.

(1) Some scholars reject Mowinckel's notion of a central festival. They note that the OT contains no direct evidence of such a celebration. Moreover, some critics have pointed out that Mowinckel relies too heavily on rabbinical material (which dates to the first two centuries AD) to reconstruct festivals in the monarchical period (Mowinckel, 1.121-25; Stamm, 48-49).

(2) Other scholars not only accept Mowinckel's view that a Babylonian-like event occurred in Israel but also postulate that Israel's cult fit a general pattern in ancient Near Eastern religious expression. Among the more radical proposals was that put forward by scholars in the "Myth and Ritual" school. They held that the Israelite king stood in the place of God in the cult and was himself understood as a semidivine character. Thus the adherents of the Myth and Ritual school pressed Mowinckel's ideas in ways that he did not intend (Gerstenberger 1974, 216).

(3) Perhaps the most common reaction to Mowinckel's work, however, was general agreement, but with suggested modifications. Two such reactions illustrate the nature of the debate. Gunkel agreed with Mowinckel that a New Year festival was celebrated in ancient Israel, and that the ceremony centered on Yahweh's kingship. Gunkel disagreed, however, on the cultic nature of the enthronement psalms as they now appear in the Psalter. Gunkel's objection was based on the fact that the enthronement poems occur in bits and pieces also in Isaiah 40—66, a portion of the book of Isaiah that dates to the Babylonian exile (587-539 BC) or afterward (Is 40:10; 44:23; 49:13; 55:12; 59:19; 60:1; 62:11). For the great prophet of the exile, these poetic lines are eschatological in that they look forward to God's reign, which will be displayed in the return of Judah to its homeland. Gunkel thought it logical that the prophet had reinterpreted the enthronement material for his own historical situation. Since the enthrone-

ment psalms in the Psalter are identical in form and content to what we have in the latest strands of Isaiah, it also seemed to follow that these psalms are not the cultic originals but rather are later eschatological poems influenced by Isaiah 40—66 (Gunkel and Begrich, 80-81).

A. Weiser also shared many of Mowinckel's assumptions but argued that the festival setting for the majority of the psalms was a "covenant festival of Yahweh" in which the Sinai covenant was remembered and renewed. His reconstruction is based on two primary pieces of data. First, the covenant and its renewal predominates in the Hexateuch (Genesis—Joshua) and therefore should be taken as the primary cultic emphasis of early Israel (see Josh 24). Second, Weiser notes that very few psalms (Pss 65; 67; 85; 126) contain emphases that would be at home in the agricultural festivals, which he believes were later developments away from Israel's original emphasis on covenant (Weiser, 27). His theory made sense of the so-called anticultic psalms (Ps 40:6; 50:14; 51:15-17; 69:31), which stand theologically close to the prophets who criticized the practice of ritual without ethics (Amos 5:21-26) (see Szörenyi, 320-33; Clines, 107.). It also accounted for the fact that sacrifice and the agricultural festivals are hardly mentioned in the psalms, a point that some have used to deny the psalms' origin in the cult (Ridderbos, 241). It is interesting to note, however, how Weiser (35) begins his discussion of the liturgy of the covenant festival: "No proper ritual of the Covenant Festival of Yahweh has been handed down to us from Old Testament times, such as has been preserved, for instance, from the Babylonian New Year Festival and the Akitu Festival at Uruk, giving instructions for the execution of the cultic acts and for the recitals of the priests." And yet, Weiser (35) proceeds to say with confidence, "The liturgy which we find in Psalm 50 is part of the order of the feast of the renewal of the Covenant which was celebrated at the Temple of Jerusalem." Weiser's criticism of Mowinckel's theory, that the OT never mentions an enthronement festival, turns back upon his own thesis, for the covenant festival too remains a reconstruction that, however attractive, remains hypothetical (Szörenyi, 213-14).

4.2. Cultic Rituals and the Psalms of the Individual. Just as there are competing theories regarding how the psalms were used in national cultic events, there are also many and various views of how the poems functioned in ceremonies centering on individuals. As we have already seen, some scholars, following Mowinckel, understand the "I" of these psalms to be the king. There are several interrelated theories, however, that attempt to explain how some psalms functioned in the lives of ordinary Israelites. Mowinckel located numerous individual complaint psalms in occasions of sickness and requests for healing (applied to ordinary Israelites but perhaps composed originally for the king). He believed that these psalms should be read against the particular backdrop of sickness caused by curses or "spells" cast by the psalmists' enemies, enemies labeled "evildoers" (Ps 10:15). Mowinckel imagined that healing from such maladies took place in the temple in rituals designed for such circumstances and carried out by priests (Mowinckel, 2.1-8).

H. Schmidt proposed some of these psalms that included a protestation of innocence actually grew out of a judicial process in which an accused person sought vindication through a trial in the temple. The notion that such a procedure was available is supported by numerous texts (Deut 17:8-13; 21:1-8; 1 Kings 8:31-32). Deuteronomy 17:8-13 most clearly identifies the temple and the Levites on duty as the locus of judgment. Psalm 17 is a parade example of a psalm that might be read against this backdrop. It begins with a call for hearing, "Hear a just cause, O LORD" (Ps. 17:1-2), and the rest of the psalm is filled with images of adversaries who falsely accuse the psalmist. The fact that the psalmist asks for God's favorable judgment and for the Lord to confront the accusers (Ps 17:13) lends credence to Schmidt's proposal (see Schmidt). His thesis has continued to maintain adherents. W. Beyerlin supported and expanded the theory, proposing that Psalms 3; 4; 5; 7; 11; 17; 23; 26; 27; 57; 63 have such a judicial process as their setting (see the summary in Gerstenberger 1974, 203-5). L. Delekat proposed a setting similar to that of Schmidt and Beyerlin, but he emphasized the overnight stay in the temple, which is implied in many of the psalms in question. Delekat describes in detail what took place during the night, how the accused received oracles, had dreams, and underwent ordeals. He proposed that the psalms expressing this experience were inscribed on temple or sanctuary walls by the accused (see Delekat). Recently,

K. van der Toorn has revised these theories that focus on a judicial process by focusing on the ordeal that the accused underwent during the night in the temple. He proposes that the psalmist submitted to a drinking ordeal like that described in Numbers 5:11-31, hence the frequent references to a cup in these psalms (Ps 11:6; 16:5; 23:6) (see van der Toorn). This final expression of the thesis in a general way illustrates both the strengths and weaknesses of them all. Van der Toorn is right to emphasize the temple setting of the psalms in question because there are frequent references to seeing God's face (Ps 11:7) or dwelling in the holy place (Ps 23:6). To make the psalms fit the details of his thesis, however, he must apply some of the data in ways that seem contrary to their intention. For example, it is unlikely that the references to a cup in these psalms refer to ordeals, since they connote celebration (Ps 23:5), they symbolize God's protection (Ps 16:5), or they refer to judgment upon the psalmist's enemies (Ps 11:6) (see Johnston).

Particularly important for understanding the cultic background of the psalms is the body of material uncovered in 1929 at Ras Shamra (ancient Ugarit) near the coast of Syria. These works continue to be translated and evaluated for their comparative value. Drawing largely from this material, for example, P. K. McCarter has proposed that psalms using water as a symbol of distress originated in river ordeals meant to determine guilt or innocence (Ps 18:18; 32:6; 66:10-12) (see McCarter). In the end, however, such theories suffer from the same weaknesses as those mentioned above. The proposed ritual (or ordeal in this case) is not mentioned elsewhere in the OT, and the evidence of the psalms must be manipulated too much to fit the pattern of the comparative material.

E. Gerstenberger offers a promising explanation for some psalms that seem to arise from situations of illness. Using sociological models, OT narratives that depict the nature and setting of prayer, and Mesopotamian ritual texts, Gerstenberger proposes that many of these psalms grew out of family ceremonies of healing facilitated by a local cult figure, an "expert" in healing. To support the notion of such a ceremony in the home, he notes, for example, that Hezekiah seeks a "ritual expert" (Isaiah) when he is sick (Is 38). Likewise, 2 Samuel 12 depicts David practicing penitence at home. According to Gersten-

berger, these examples raise the possibility, indeed the likelihood, that many psalms had their setting apart from the temple (Gerstenberger 1980, 165). He proposes that many psalms of sickness reflect a kind of "group therapy" process in which a ritual expert from the clan or tribe restores the infirmed to full communion with the family group (Gerstenberger 1980, 167-69).

5. Identity of Cultic Leaders and Participants.

The question naturally arises of who led cultic events and who participated in the cult. The answers are necessarily hypothetical (as illustrated by Gerstenberger's thesis [see 4 above]), but the types of persons involved in the cult may be sketched out in a general way from explicit evidence in OT texts. As we have already noted, the king was an integral part of the cult. Even if Mowinckel's proposal concerning a New Year festival is off base, the royal psalms evince the monarch's involvement. For example, Psalms 2 and 72 have at least some relationship to coronation ceremonies; Psalm 45 is set in a royal wedding; Psalm 20 is a prayer for the king before battle; Psalm 21 gives thanks to God for protecting and blessing the ruler (see also Pss 18; 89; 101; 110; 132). Also, prophets, Levitical singers and musicians almost certainly had important roles in the cult (see Ps 81:6-16 for evidence of cultic prophets). Psalm headings that associate certain collections with the Korahites (Ps 42—49; 84—89) and *Asaph (Ps 50; 73—83) give witness to the central place that the Levitical guilds had in worship (see 1 Chron 15—16). These groups were exclusively male, but *women also had a formal role in the cult. Psalm 68:25 describes a procession to the sanctuary in which female participants had a recognized place ("the singers in front, the musicians last, between them girls playing tambourines"). Although little more is certain, it is possible that some psalms originally were spoken by women. Psalm 131 is the best example, with Psalm 131:2 seeming to indicate that a woman, a mother, spoke the words "My soul is like the weaned child that is with me" (Miller, 239-43). This should not be a surprise, given the portrait of Hannah making a vow and praying in 1 Samuel 1:9-18.

6. Current Questions.

This survey indicates that the psalms were integrally related to Israel's worship, including the ritual activities that comprised Israel's cult. Despite that rather certain fact, however, numerous questions persist concerning the nature of the psalms and their place in worship. Many of these questions are related in one way or another to the problem of whether the psalms as they now appear in the Psalter are cultic originals, works based on cultic originals, or purely literary works. The number of psalms that originated in the first temple and the question of whether any psalms survived from that period are uncertain. The psalms of *thanksgiving may provide the most certain link to the worship in Solomon's temple (as Jer 33:11 indicates), but they were adapted for a different use in the Second Temple period. For example, Psalm 30 bears the classic signs of the song of thanksgiving (description of being rescued [Ps 30:1-3, 11], inclusion of terminology for giving thanks [Ps 30:12]), but apparently it was used in a very different way in the Second Temple period, according to its superscription ("A song at the dedication of the temple"). Similarly, the language of individual thanksgiving dominates Psalm 129 (Ps 129:1a, 2-4), but the work was adapted for community use, as the phrase, "let Israel say" (Ps 129:1b) attests. The so-called royal psalms also pose problems. Although these works have some relationship to cultic ceremonies related to the monarch (and thus to the first temple), the form in which they now appear in the Psalter indicates they were reshaped for a later theological purpose. Indeed, the fact that they do not contain the names of particular kings, in contrast to practically every such poem from the ancient Near East, indicates that they came to be used as reflections on monarchy or to express hope in a future, idealized ruler (see Starbuck).

The question of how psalms were edited or reshaped for use at a later time has become particularly important because of the current interest in the Psalter as a literary product. Psalm 2:10-12 illustrates the problem. J. J. M. Roberts (132) proposes that the address to the "kings of the earth" had in mind vassals—that is, rulers of Israel's subservient territories—who were present for an Israelite king's coronation. He finds support for this view in records of similar Egyptian ceremonies in which vassals were instructed to pay homage to Pharaoh. The discussion by Roberts is quite helpful for understanding the possible origins of these poetic lines. Nevertheless, the fact that Psalm 2:12a warns the foreign kings with language so similar to Psalm 1:6b raises the possibility that the end of Psalm 2 was brought into its present form in the Psalter to enhance its connection to Psalm 1 as a dual introduction to the book (see Editorial Criticism). Regardless of which perspective is right, it is interesting that this dynamic in current scholarship brings us back, albeit by a different path, to the debates between Gunkel and Mowinckel concerning the enthronement psalms: are the psalms in present form cultic, or do they merely draw from cultic forms and language?

See also CULT, WORSHIP: WISDOM; FORM CRITICISM; KINGSHIP PSALMS; MEGILLOT AND FESTIVALS; MUSIC, SONG; WORSHIP.

BIBLIOGRAPHY. **M. J. Buss,** "The Meaning of 'Cult and the Interpretation of the Old Testament,'" *JBL* 32 (1964) 317-25; **D. J. A. Clines,** "Psalm Research Since 1955: I. The Psalms and the Cult," *TynBul* 18 (1967) 103-26; **S. J. L. Croft,** *The Identity of the Individual in the Psalms* (JSOTSup 44; Sheffield: JSOT Press, 1987); **F. M. Cross,** *Canaanite Myth and Hebrew Epic: Essays in the History of the Religion of Israel* (Cambridge, MA: Harvard University Press, 1974); **L. D. Crow,** *The Songs of Ascents (Psalms 120-134): Their Place in Israelite History and Religion* (SBLDS 148; Atlanta: Scholars Press, 1996); **G. H. Davies,** "Worship in the OT," *IDB* 4.879-83; **L. Delekat,** *Asylie und Schutzorakel an Zionheiligtum: Eine Untersuchung zu den privaten Feindpsalmen* (Leiden: E. J. Brill, 1967); **J. Eaton,** *Kingship and the Psalms* (SBT 32; London: SCM, 1976); **E. S. Gerstenberger,** "Psalms," in *Old Testament Form Criticism,* ed. J. H. Hayes (San Antonio, TX: Trinity University Press, 1974) 179-223; idem, *Der bittende Mensch: Bittritual und Klagelied des Einzelnen im Alten Testament* (WMANT 51; Neukirchen-Vluyn: Neukirchener Verlag, 1980); **H. Gunkel and J. Begrich,** *Introduction to Psalms: The Genres of the Religious Lyric of Israel* (Macon, GA: Mercer University Press, 1998); **M. Haller,** "Ein Jahrzehnt Psalmforschung," *TRu* 1 (1929) 377-402; **A. R. Johnson,** *The Cultic Prophet and Israel's Psalmody* (Cardiff: University of Wales Press, 1979); **P. S. Johnston,** "Ordeals in the Psalms?" in *Temple and Worship in Biblical Israel,* ed. J. Day (LHBOTS 422; London: T & T Clark International, 2005); **B. O. Long,** "Recent Field Studies in Oral Literature and the Question of *Sitz im Leben,*" *Se-*

meia 5 (1976) 35-49; **P. K. McCarter,** "The River Ordeal in Israelite Literature," *HTR* 66 (1973) 403-12; **P. D. Miller,** *They Cried to the Lord: The Form and Theology of Biblical Prayer* (Minneapolis: Fortress, 1994); **S. Mowinckel,** *The Psalms in Israel's Worship* (2 vols.; London: Blackwell, 1962); **N. H. Ridderbos,** "Psalmen und Kult," in *Zur Neueren Psalmenforschung,* ed. P. H. A. Neumann (WF 92; Darmstadt: Wissenschaftliche Buchgesellschaft, 1976) 235-46; **J. J. M. Roberts,** "The Religio-Political Setting of Psalm 47," *BASOR* 221 (1976) 129-32; **H. Schmidt,** *Das Gebet der Angeklagten in Alten Testament* (BZAW 49; Giessen: Töpelmann, 1929); **J. J. Stamm,** "Ein Vierteljahrhundert Psalmenforschung," *TRu* 23 (1955) 1-68; **S. R. A. Starbuck,** *Court Oracles in the Psalms: The So-Called Royal Psalms in Their Ancient Near Eastern Context* (SBLDS 172; Atlanta: Scholars Press, 1999); **F. Stolz,** *Psalmen im nachkultischen Raum* (ThSt 129; Zürich: Theologischer Verlag, 1983); **A. Szörenyi,** *Psalmen und Kult im Alten Testament: Zur Formgeschichte der Psalmen* (Budapest: Sankt Stefans, 1961); **M. E. Tate,** *Psalms 51-100* (WBC 20; Waco, TX: Word, 1991); **K. van der Toorn,** "Ordeal," *ABD* 5.40-42; **A. Weiser,** *The Psalms: A Commentary* (4th ed.; OTL; Philadelphia: Westminster, 1962).

J. F. D. Creach

CULT, WORSHIP: WISDOM

The sages' views of public worship vary over the centuries of sapiential tradition, although it is clear from a careful reading of their writings that they valued this sphere of corporate life, participated in its important rituals and sacred times of divine veneration, and even wrote different psalms in praise of the creator. Some of these even found their way into the Psalter. Their instructions taught their students to inculcate within their character the "fear of Yahweh" and to participate in the worship of God.

1. Wisdom and Worship in Previous Scholarship
2. Identifying Characteristics of Wisdom and Corporate Worship
3. Understandings of Wisdom and Corporate/Public Religion in Israel and the Ancient Near East
4. Motivations for Participation in Cultic Religion
5. Decorum within the Sphere of the Holy
6. The Sages' Criticism of Cultic Religion
7. Did the Sages Compose Cultic Literature?

1. Wisdom and Worship in Previous Scholarship.

Earlier generations of wisdom scholars during the nineteenth century and the first seventy years of the twentieth century usually held, with some exceptions, that the *sages and *scribes of Israel and Judah did not view the religious sphere of public *worship (temple, priesthood, worship, sacred times and space) as an area for their own analysis and teaching. This did not mean that the sages did not believe in the gods or that they refrained from private piety. But the general position in past scholarship was that the sages did not instruct their students to participate in public worship, in particular the cultic expressions of state religion. Indeed, some of these scholars even suggested that the sages rejected cultic religion and offered another approach to the determination of meaning and its import for authentic life. There were three reasons for this. First, the early generations of Christian scholars, under the influence of theological liberalism (e.g., Friedrich Schleiermacher , Adolph von Harnack, Albrecht Ritschl, Ernst Troeltsch), emphasized reason, the fatherhood of God and the moral teachings of Jewish religion while denigrating the Torah and Second Temple religious practice leading to the rise of early Judaism as contributing to a sterile legalism, devoid of the true spirit of religion. Second, this view led some biblical scholars to point to the classical prophets of the eighth through the sixth centuries BC as the apex of Israelite Jewish religion with their emphasis on social justice, individual piety and moral behavior. Thus, sapiential texts, normally dated in the Second Temple era, were generally ignored due to their presumed encrustation with the legalism that developed especially beginning with Ezra and continuing into early rabbinic Judaism. When viewing the canonical wisdom texts, they tended to reach the conclusion that this literature also was rather sterile and lacking in moral and individual piety that was to characterize a person's behavior. Third, under the influence of liberal theology, other biblical scholars tended to portray the sages and scribes as humanists and rationalists who considered the cult to represent a primitive form of religious expression that should be abandoned. Thus, the wise were particularly concerned to steer their students away from participation in the rituals and sacred seasons to a more philosophical and reflective life that sought to capture the major ethical values of human community: love, diligence, patience, proper use of language, and charity. Three examples of these related views of wisdom and the wise are seen in the writings of Johannes Fichtner and, much later, John Priest and William McKane.

1.1. Johannes Fichtner. In his important study of wisdom in 1933 J. Fichtner (36-46) follows the views of liberal theology in arguing that the sages of Israel and the ancient Near East were not concerned with fulfilling the legal requirements of cultic law but rather sought to set forth significant ethical concerns. Thus, for example, sacrifices were to be offered, not as cultic obedience to divine dictate but rather as a means by which the poor are fed. No participant in worship experienced communal acceptance without particular attention to providing for the needs of the poor.

1.2. John Priest. In 1968 J. Priest contended that humanism, in his view, was "the rational analysis of human experience." This was key for Priest's understanding of OT theology because he considered it to result from a humanistic enterprise that sought to determine human interests. Thus, creation is a fundamental theological dogma in the OT and rests on a humanistic enterprise. Yahweh, as creator of the world and maintainer of its continuation, was one of the data of rational investigation. This observation even encompassed divine actions in history. However, in the Second Temple era, due to conquest and Judah as a client state and then colony, the sense of divine action in history became, so Priest contends, increasingly attenuated. The developing view of the law as a static entity contained in a written code led to the "killing of the spirit." However, Priest argues that the intellectual tradition of wisdom continued even then to examine and evaluate religious and moral dimensions of Israelite life. Yet there were also sapiential critics of traditional wisdom. *Job and *Ecclesiastes, in the Second Temple era, moved into a view of skepticism, even pessimism, about the claims of their more conservative colleagues and forebears. These two wisdom texts participated in the humanistic goal to determine meaning in existence and to assess what was true and false, although their conclusions were far more skeptical. This moved beyond law and cult in reaching the height of humanistic analysis. By implication, Priest's argument casts aside the mystery and "magic" of cultic teachings and participation in public religion and leads to a fully humanistic view of theology and human existence in the world.

1.3. William McKane. In his 1970 commentary on *Proverbs W. McKane reorders its materials by following his view of the differentiation between the secular and the moral and religious spheres. He argues that the early sages were in essence humanists not concerned with matters of religion, and that it was only much later in Judah's history that the tradition was theologized and became more focused on religious matters.

The weaknesses of these three illustrations from earlier scholarship become obvious. Indeed, the more extreme argument has been made that the wise saw the realm of the cult to be an order of superstition and magic that should be held in disdain, overtly criticized, and repudiated as a valid way of understanding God and moral behavior. The most glaring defect in this view is the assumption of an ancient dichotomy between the secular and the profane or, stated another way, a contrast between a rational, empirical approach to the determination of meaning and its guidance in moral conduct and a revelatory approach by which the priests receive divine teaching through theophanic teaching, the casting of lots, dreams, and the gift of divine Torah. In my view, the "fear of God/Yahweh" was the foundation of the sapiential worldview from its inception (*see* Fear of the Lord). This means that the sages, from the earliest days of their appearance in the first temple, held that religious faith and piety were the basis upon which their teachings rested.

2. Identifying Characteristics of Wisdom and Corporate Worship.

One of the essential issues to be addressed before we proceed further is the determination of what wisdom means in the sapiential traditions of Israel and the ancient Near East. First, we note the general view that wisdom is a body of knowledge—that is, a tradition that sets forth an understanding of God, the world and nature, humanity and human society. Second, wisdom is understood as discipline—that is, both a curriculum of study and a structured form of behavior designed to lead to the formation of character. Character was shaped through study, reflection and the actualization of virtue in both discourse and action. This embodiment of moral virtue led the sage to live in harmony with the cosmos, society and the Creator. The result of this type of existence was well-being that included both a sense of internal peace and contentment and the external accoutrements of honor, respect, integrity and dignity. Long life, prosperity and joy became the possession of the one who was wise. Third, wisdom is moral discourse and behavior that constructed and legitimated a cosmology in which righteousness, both correct and just behavior as well as proper decorum, ordered the world, society and individual existence. Through the attainment of wisdom the sages were able to enter into and dwell within an aesthesis of beauty, order, justice and life (Schmid 1974).

A second essential issue at the outset involves what the meaning of corporate or public worship implies among the religions of Israel and the ancient Near East in the periods of Israel's and Judah's first and second temples (1200-63 BC). In its broadest terms, corporate/public religion is the ordered response of a community to its belief that a deity has appeared in its midst and has established a relationship with its people, both in terms of their present existence and their future destiny. From this relationship derives a way of life that is understood as living in response to the requirements of this deity and gaining the benefits from this association. To maintain this relationship, the community is expected to worship this divine being as the chief of those gods whom they may recognize and to live in accordance to his or her teachings. On a public level these included rituals and sacred seasons as well as righteous behavior based on the community's public laws believed to have been given by their chief deity. National and regional religions usually include a temple or other sacred space where, the community believes, the deity has appeared and may continue to be encountered; holy seasons in which there were festivals, feast days and other types of times for gathering together to worship and to commune with the high god/goddess; a priesthood that mediates between the deity and the community; and rituals that comprise things such as sacrifices of various types, communal hymns and laments, and prayers, especially of intercession calling for divine aid, forgiveness for sins, and redemption.

3. Understandings of Wisdom and Corporate/Public Religion in Israel and the Ancient Near East.

In approaching the views of the sages and scribes of Israel about cultic religion and to suggest their ways of participating in this aspect of life, we begin with the sages and scribes in the other regions of the ancient Near East: Mesopotamia, Syria and Egypt. One fundamental affirmation to which the sages of the ancient Near East held is that of cosmic order. According to the sages, cosmic order is expressed by numerous terms, among which are *maat* in Egypt, *me* in Sumer, *mešari* in Akkadian cultures and *ṣĕdaqâ* ("righteousness") in Israel and Judah. This order in conceptual or mythological terms was established at creation by the high god who formed and shaped the world. He placed within nature and society a pervasive order that regulated both the structure and the continuation of the world and its various components, ranging from the heavenly bodies, to fertile soil, to the existence and behavior of the species of life on the earth, to anthropological and communal life. The sages taught that the wise were to exist in life-giving harmony with this order in each of its various compartments (Schmid 1968).

3.1. The Sages and Scribes of Egypt. The Egyptian sages sought to observe, understand and then place into their teachings the regulations of *maat* in order to provide guidance to their students who were in quest of knowledge and life. Armed with this knowledge and its incorporation in behavior, the youth were able to begin their journey to obtain well-being in all of its facets, ranging from longevity, to happiness, to honor (see The Instruction for King Meri-ka-Re [*ANET*, 417]). The sages worshiped publicly the high gods of ancient Egypt, but their greatest attention was given to the praise of the various gods of creation (Amon, Re, Amon-Re). The divine creator, or perhaps a god who belonged to his *divine council, observed human behavior both in regard to the responsibilities of the performance of the prescribed duties of worship and individual moral behavior. This god, often called *ntr*, a generic term that avoided the complexities of Egyptian polytheism but did not imply monotheism, was the one who was charged with adjudicating justice, either by himself or through a surrogate, who engaged in rewarding the pious and virtuous wise, and who punished the fool and the recalcitrant sinner. Scholars sometimes have incorrectly argued that this principle of retribution was automatic and gave no room for compassion and forgiveness. This is not the case in Egyptian wisdom. Appeals could be made to the gods for absolution, and it at times was given.

Unique among the sages in the ancient Near East is the belief that the king is divine. Born as Horus, who ruled the world in order and justice, at death the king became Osiris, the ruler of the underworld. Sages were the servants of the king, active in the vast bureaucratic state, although the especially noteworthy ones became honored as teachers whose wisdom was written down and transmitted through the generations, often for many centuries (see "The Instruction of Ptah-hotep" [Lichtheim 1973, 61-80]).

These views did not remain constant throughout the history of Egypt. Certainly they are transparent in the Old Kingdom (c. 2686-2180 BC), but the devastation of the First Intermediate period (c. 2180-2133 BC) led some of the sages to question their essential beliefs (especially the effectiveness of mortuary religion for gaining life in the next world [the West]) (see "A Dispute over Suicide" [*ANET*, 405-7]; "The Admonitions of Ipu-wer" [*ANET*, 441-46]; "In Praise of Learned Scribes" [*ANET*, 431-32]). The wisdom texts of the Middle Kingdom (c. 2133-1670 BC) are decidedly more political in emphasizing loyalty to the king. Still, the king's responsibilities to maintain and participate in the important cults of Egypt are everywhere apparent in the sapiential texts of the time (see "The Instruction for King Meri-ka-Re" [*ANET*, 414-18]). This emphasis on royal and sapiential religious responsibilities continues through the New Kingdom well into the period of Egypt as a Hellenistic kingdom ruled by the Ptolemies (Perdue 1977, 19-64). Texts mentioning public religion in a favorable manner as an important part of sapiential participation include "The Instruction of Ani" (*ANET*, 420-21), in which the sage teaches his young son both the importance of giving prompt consideration to mortuary provisions in order to make the successful transition to the future life and the value of living the life of the "silent man," whose character exudes dispassionate self-control, in contrast to the "heated man," whose passions and garrulous behavior lead to disaster. These two contrasting human types participate in cultic activity, with blessing coming to the former and punishment

to the latter for having disturbed the sanctity of the temple and the god. The young sage is admonished to offer sacrifices and to prostrate himself before the god, thereby pleasing his deity and avoiding divine wrath (see "The Instruction of Amen-em-Opet" [*ANET*, 421–24], a text that instructs a student in cultivating the character of a priestly scribe). In two classical texts from the Late Dynastic and Hellenistic periods, teachers also admonish their hearers to pay attention to cultic responsibilities to their gods ("The Instruction of 'Onsheshonq" [Lichtheim 1980, 159-84]; "The Papyrus Insinger" [Lichtheim, 1983, 93-106]). Thus, corporate religion occurring with the temples of ancient religion was to be practiced by those preparing to become scribes and sages. The only major teaching that fell under criticism was the necessity of mortuary preparations believed in the Old Kingdom to be necessary for eternal life.

3.2. The Sages of Sumer, Assyria and Babylonia. Although the affirmation of cosmic order was more transparent in Egypt, it was also the case that cosmic, social and anthropological compartments of order were significant to the teachings of the wise in these cultures. The myth of "Inanna and Enki: The Transfer of the Arts of Civilization from Eridu to Erech" lists on four occasions more than one hundred elements of creation, each of which has its own *me*, or law regulating its behavior (Kramer, 64-65). These laws originated at creation and continued to bind together and manage the compartments of nature, society and anthropology. In doing so, order and peace were achieved. Wisdom, a gift of the gods to humankind, enabled people both individually and corporately to exist in a relationship of harmony. However, although the high gods (e.g., Anu, Marduk, Assur, Sin) generally were viewed as just and beneficent (see "Advice to a Prince" [Lambert, 112-15]) and thus as maintaining social order, they also were thought to act capriciously and destructively on occasion. This inconsistency, so the Mesopotamians believed, led to periods of tranquility, on one hand, and chaos, on the other (see "The Babylonian Theodicy" [Lambert, 63-91]; "The Dialogue of Pessimism" [Lambert, 107-9]). Even so, the sages rarely advocated the abandonment of worship, in particular of one's personal god, but rather continued to emphasize the importance of religious devotion, all the while hoping for salvation of nation or individual (see "I Will

Praise the Lord of Wisdom" [Lambert, 21-62]). Subsequently, although cultic observance within corporate religion was taught by the sages of Mesopotamia, there was the unsettling belief that the caprice of the gods could even annul faithful and loyal devotion and bring about the destruction of even the pious.

3.3. *The Sages of Israel and Judah.* Israel's and Judah's sages also affirmed the presence of cosmic and social order, which provided the basis for their teachings (Perdue 1990, 457-58). When it came to corporate worship, the traditional, more conservative sages admonish their students to observe religious requirements and to participate in public praise of God (sacrifice, prayer, the making of vows, the priestly casting of lots [Prov 3:9-10; 15:8, 29; 16:33; 17:1; 20:25; 21:3, 27; 28:9; 31:2). Some of the references in these verses could imply private devotion, but the preponderance of the evidence points to corporate worship in most cases. In addition, students were to avoid dalliance with the "Strange Woman" (at times the *personification of *folly, at times Canaanite fertility religion, at times a foreigner [see Prov 7:1-27]). The sages were quick to demarcate the folly of worship brought by the wicked with evil intent and the wise worship of the righteous, whose lives were the basis for their participation in public religion and testimony to others who observed them in life. The narrative Job is also faithful to his cultic responsibilities and adulation of Yahweh, even in the face of great adversity (Job 1—2; 42:10-17). The poetic Job, however, questions the justice of God, who singles out even the righteous and faithful for destruction (Job 9—10). No doubt exists about the emphasis of Job's opponents (Eliphaz, Zophar and Bildad) on faithful obedience to cultic requirements (see esp. Job 5). Indeed, they encourage their suffering friend to seek God in faithful worship, to acknowledge being sinful, and then to wait for forgiveness and restitution to health and well-being. Their assumption is that Job has engaged in some grievous transgression to merit such vile punishment from God. Job denies that he has sinned so egregiously that he should receive such horrible treatment from God. He demonstrates this in the oath of innocence (Job 29—31), when he engages in a judicial means of proving his innocence by means of sacred oath. Among the sins that he forgoes is that of cultic apostasy (Job 31:26-28). Finally, although Job is found innocent of wickedness and disloyalty to God in the concluding narrative and then is restored to his former prominence with the gift of new children, he is required to give a sin offering on behalf of his friends, who became his enemies in the course of the dialogues, in order for them to be forgiven for not "speaking correctly" about Yahweh (Job 42:8-10).

The other sapiential books, including Ecclesiastes, *Sirach and *Wisdom of Solomon, also give an important place to public worship. Although *Qohelet speaks of the transcendent God, who remains hidden to human understanding, he does not reject his worship by sages (Eccles 5:1-7). In issuing four admonitions to his students, he stresses the importance of guarded caution in the realm of the holy, the judicious practice of silence and the uttering of few words, a warning against making hasty vows that go unfulfilled, and the deceitful attempt to pass off a willful sin as an unconscious one. While pointing to the hidden and secretive qualities of God, the teacher still believes that cultic participation is an element of sagacious life. Wise decorum, including especially caution, however, should be practiced in corporate worship. Sirach is filled with emphases on the importance of corporate worship, sacrifices, the temple, festivals and support of the priesthood and singers (e.g., Sir 7:29-31; 39:5-6). Sirach's two most important emphases are the association of *Woman Wisdom with the cult (Sir 24) and the praise of the high priest Simon (II?) in Sirach 50:1-26, which concludes the "Praise of the Pious" (Sir 46—51). Finally, Wisdom of Solomon, composed by a Jewish rhetorician of the first century AD, includes a lengthy "digression" (Wis 13—15) that praises the best of pagan religion, the teachings of philosophy and nature religion, condemns idolatry (the woodcutter, the sailor, the potter), criticizes Egyptian animal worship, and contrasts the faithfulness of Israel with the pagan opponents. The author also assaults the mystery religions, in particular the popular royal Alexandrian cult of Dionysus (disguised as the religion of the Canaanites) for their "detestable practices," "sorcery," "unholy rites," merciless slaughter of children, and the "sacrificial feasting on human flesh and blood" (the last pointing to the Legend of Pentheus and the eating of Dionysus in worship). This text even engages in an assault of the divine status of Ptolemaic kings and the royal cult that worshiped them by contrasting them with *Solomon, the wisest and greatest of the kings, who nevertheless was mortal (Wis 7:1; 9:5). Finally, Wisdom becomes a divine hypostasis and appears to be contrasted to the popular goddess Isis.

3.4. Summary and Conclusions. When one surveys the classical sapiential literature of Israel and the ancient Near East, it is noteworthy to recognize that, save for a few scattered sayings incorporated in various types of texts, only one major piece of this literature completely rejects the value and meaning of cultic religion: "The Dialogue of Pessimism," a Babylonian text from the period of the Cassite rule. Even this is not surprising, however, for this text leads to an emphatic denial of all meaning. If read as a dour or humorous satire, it still denies the possibility of finding the proper course of action that makes life worthwhile. The two dialogue partners in this text, a noble and his wise sage, finally realize that it is impossible to discover anything of value in human existence or to gain any security and sense of well-being in a world that is filled with chaos and domination by the client state's Cassite lords. The contemplated recourse is suicide.

Thus, one necessarily concludes, on the basis of the sapiential traditions in Israel and the ancient Near East, that the sages not only engaged in teaching their students about various topics and practices of cultic religion but also instructed them to participate in its various dimensions of expression. One assumes from these teachings that the sages themselves participated in cultic religion, even though their own approach to life was at times distinctive from that of the priests. However, as one would expect, the traditional sages who supported the state and its rulers as "men and women of the king" in general agreed that the various rituals and teachings of cultic religion were unquestioningly valid and indeed important to observe. This does not mean that the critical traditions in wisdom in the domains of Israel and the ancient Near East refrained from taking to task some of the assumptions and theological understandings of cultic religion and the priests. But this is true of other traditions, including those of the more conventional wise and even, on occasion, the prophets and seers.

4. Motivations for Participation in Cultic Religion.

The traditional sages believed that there were numerous blessings that derived from the deity whose cult, rituals and teachings were honored and practiced. Some among these conservative teachers placed the results in the negative: divine punishment and misfortune in various forms, ranging from dishonor, to poverty, to poor health, to defeat and even death in war, awaited those communities and individuals who neglected their cultic responsibilities. Then too there was the motivation that touched upon the social conscience of the sages, for their gifts and offerings not only honored their deity but also provided for the deity's priests and the community's poor. Finally, it seems that the sages recognized within the human spirit the desire to praise and honor the divine being who presided over their community and at times, on a grander scale, nature, creation and human history.

5. Decorum within the Sphere of the Holy.

The sages instructed their students on how to behave within the sphere of the holy during sacred times. When offering their sacrifices, the students were taught to engage in self-examination in order to insure that they were righteous and were carefully following the guidance of their teachers. Only the worship of the wise, righteous participant in cultic religion was acceptable to the deity. The wicked and the foolish who dared to approach the realm of the holy were, according to the traditional sages, subject to punishment and even destruction for violating the sanctity of the cultic sphere and the righteous deity who was encountered there. Foolish and garrulous behavior placed the worshiper at threat of punishment and even death. And other dimensions of the cultic life—for example, the making of a vow before the deity—were serious matters to be undertaken and then completed. Even Qohelet, the more critically inclined sage, issued this warning (Eccles 5:1-7).

6. The Sages' Criticism of Cultic Religion.

The critical sages pointed to what they considered to be unfounded claims of priests and cultic religion and even regarded this approach to life to be spurious and misleading. Several Sumerian satirical proverbs from the third millennium BC lampoon the pomposity of the *Kalu* priests, while Papyrus Insinger, of the Ptolemaic period (third century BC), warns the chief priest not to ignore his responsibility to engage in intercession on behalf of the worshipers, for this neglect would result in his death. Even Ben Sira gently nudges the priests with whom he served in the temple administration to fulfill their duties responsibly. Thus, sages kept priests under their watchful eye and were quick to point out their shortcomings. One proverb from Israel emphasizes that the decision obtained from the casting of lots (Urim and Thummim) came not from the magic of the chief priest but rather from God (Prov 16:33). Idolatry proved to be a topic for discussion among the sages of the ancient Near East. In Egypt both The Instruction for King Meri-ka-Re (twenty-second century BC) and The Instruction of Ani (1500 BC) wrestled with the difficulty of a transcendent deity who was also present in an idol. Idolatry was mentioned by the sages in Wisdom of Solomon, composed by a Jewish rhetorician likely in Alexandria during the first century BC. This Jewish sophist underscored his view that idolatry arose from the making of an image of a deceased son by a grief-stricken father and was a foolish type of ritual activity practiced by the foolish pagans to their loss (Wis 13—15). He adds that all types of wickedness accrue from this wicked practice, including adultery in lusting after nude and seminude idols of fair goddesses.

During periods of national crisis the sages often blamed the gods and the teaching of their priests. This is apparent in Egyptian wisdom from the strong criticism leveled at mortuary religion and the view that eternal life depended upon it (see "A Dispute over Suicide" [ANET, 405-7]). Elsewhere the creator, Re, along with the divine pharaoh, is blamed by the sage Ipuwer (eighteenth-seventeenth century BC) for the injustice that exists among humans that occasions *chaos, *suffering and death. The author of The Babylonian Theodicy, written during the Cassite dark ages in Babylonia (fifteenth-thirteenth century BC), likewise points the finger of responsibility to the failure of the patron deity of the sage to deliver him from suffering and death. The sufferer in this dialogue asks his friend-turned-opponent of what use is cultic observance offered to such a faithless god. In addition, the Babylonian lord in I Will Praise the Lord of Wisdom (from the Cassite dark ages) comes close to abandoning his patron deity, Marduk, until at the end, when he expresses his faith that his faithful devotion will lead to salvation. From among the biblical wisdom texts, it is especially the character Job in the poetic book who holds God responsible for injustice and at-

tacking to destroy even the righteous. Of course, during the period of the Ptolemaic rule of Judah in the third century BC, Qohelet levels a devastating criticism against cultic religion for assuming that its rituals will lead to redemption. For this sage, God has become a *deus otiosus*—a deity far removed from human knowing and often inactive but not completely. Thus he certainly is to be feared.

7. Did the Sages Compose Cultic Literature?
There is abundant evidence that there were both educated priests and scribes who were members of the temple staffs. They may even have attended the same primary schools that the sages attended. These cultic personnel composed a variety of texts to be used in the instruction of priestly novitiates and in setting forth the esoteric knowledge needed by priests in their ritual activities. This does not mean that the sages were the authors of cultic texts, including lists of omens and signs and ritual procedures, but there were priestly sages and the scribes they employed who were such authors.

In Israel and Judah it is apparent that the sages composed wisdom psalms for private prayers and public devotions in corporate worship. These psalms, bearing the language of instructions, sayings and reflections common to wisdom literature, often are combined with more traditional genres of psalms (*laments, *thanksgiving, *hymns), which spoke of and were used in the worship of God. These include the following: Psalms 1; 19A and 19B; 32; 34; 37; 49; 73; 111; 112; 119; 127. Psalms 1; 19B; 119 express the Torah piety common to traditional wisdom from the period of Ezra into the beginnings of rabbinic Judaism. Within the biblical and deuterocanonical wisdom corpus itself one finds similar psalms: Proverbs 3:19-20 speaks of the harvest, while Proverbs 8 contains three aretalogies of Woman Wisdom (Prov 8:2-11, 12-21, 22-31), which are then concluded by her dissemination of a paraenetic instruction inviting her "children" to follow her teachings in order to discover life and avoid death (Prov 8:32-36). In Sirach one finds numerous wisdom psalms: Sirach 1:1-10; 17:1-24; 18:1-14; 24:1-34; 39:12-35; 42:13—43:33. Ben Sira indicates that his students engaged in the singing of wisdom psalms, and that he himself composed some. Thus, in Sirach 39:15 he admonishes his students, "Ascribe majesty to his name and give thanks to him with praise, with songs on your lips, and with harps; this is what you shall say in thanksgiving." What follows this exhortation is a thanksgiving hymn to God concerning the goodness of creation and the affirmation of divine justice (Sir 39:16-34). He concludes this poem with a synonymous imperative: "So now sing praise with all your heart and voice, and bless the name of the Lord" (Sir 39:35).

Biblical wisdom psalms are similar to those found in the scrolls of the library of Qumran. These include 4Q411, a fragmentary sapiential hymn that praises Yahweh's act of creation; 4Q426; 4Q498, a fragment of which appears to be a wisdom hymn; 4Q528. Another creation hymn is 11QPs^a XXVI (cf. 11QPs^b; 11QPs^c; 11QPs^d; 11QPs^e).

Wisdom psalms are present also in the sapiential literature of ancient Egypt in the forms of hymns, aretalogies and panegyrics. Some of the better-known ones are In Praise of Learned Scribes; The Lament of Khakheperre-sonbe; The Hymn to Refound in the "Instruction of Ptahhotep; The Hymn to Imhotep. Lichtheim also includes in her translation five texts from the Ramesside period that she categorizes as "Prayers Used as School Texts." These include hymns and intercessory prayers.

Wisdom psalms are also present in the Sumero-Akkadian wisdom literature, including what Lambert calls "perceptive hymns." Among these are The Hymn to Shamash; The Blessing of Nisaba by Enki; A Bilingual Hymn to Ninurta. The Shamash hymn sings praise to the god of justice. The Nisaba blessing includes, in a section of the hymn in honor of Enki, a hymnic blessing of this goddess of wisdom as "the all-knowing sage of the gods." In the Ninurta hymn the worshiper sings praise to the deity and provides lists of evil actions of the wicked.

While on occasion the sages mentioned worship in their sayings (Prov 15:8, 29; 21:3, 7; 28:9), important attestations also occur in the instructions (Pss 32; 34; Prov 3:9-10), the dialogues of Job, the reflection on theodicy (Ps 73) and didactic poems (Prov 3:19-20).

See also CULT, WORSHIP: PSALMS; WISDOM THEOLOGY.

BIBLIOGRAPHY. **J. L. Crenshaw,** *Old Testament Wisdom: An Introduction* (Louisville: Westminster John Knox, 1998); **J. Fichtner,** *Die altorientalische Weisheit in ihrer israelitisch-jüdischen Ausprägung* (BZAW 62; Giessen: Töpelmann, 1933); **S. N. Kramer,** *Sumerian Mythology: A Study of Spiritual and Literary Achievement in the Third Millennium B.C.* (Harper: New York, 1961); **W. G. Lambert,** *Babylonian Wisdom Literature* (Oxford: Clarendon Press, 1960); **M. Lichtheim,** *Ancient Egyptian Literature: A Book of Readings,* 1: *The Old and Middle Kingdoms* (Berkeley: University of California Press, 1973); idem, *Ancient Egyptian Literature: A Book of Readings,* 2: *The New Kingdom* (Berkeley: University of California Press, 1976); idem, *Ancient Egyptian Literature: A Book of Readings,* 3: *The Late Period* (Berkeley: University of California Press, 1980); idem, *Egyptian Wisdom Literature in the International Context: A Study of Demotic Instructions* (OBO 52; Göttingen: Vandenhoeck & Ruprecht, 1983); **W. McKane,** *Proverbs: A New Approach* (OTL; Louisville: Westminster, 1970); **L. G. Perdue,** *Wisdom and Cult: A Critical Analysis of the Views of Cult in the Wisdom Literatures of Israel and the Ancient Near East* (SBLDS 30; Missoula, MT: Scholars Press, 1977); idem, "Cosmology and the Social Order," in *The Sage in Israel and the Ancient Near East,* ed. J. G. Gammie and L. G. Perdue (Winona Lake, IN: Eisenbrauns, 1990) 457-78; idem, *The Sword and the Stylus: An Invitation to Wisdom in the Age of Empires* (Grand Rapids: Eerdmans, 2008); **J. Priest,** "Humanism, Skepticism, and Pessimism in Israel," *JAAR* 36 (1968) 311-26; **H. H. Schmid,** *Gerechtigkeit als Weltordnung: Hintergrund und Geschichte der alttestamentlichen Gerechtigkeitsbegriffes* (BHT 40; Tübingen: Mohr Siebeck, 1968); idem, *Altorientalische Welt in der alttestamentlichen Theologie* (6th ed.; Zürich: Theologischer Verlag, 1974); **G. von Rad,** *Wisdom in Israel* (Nashville: Abingdon, 1972).   L. G. Perdue

CURSES. *See* IMPRECATION.

D

DAVID

The Bible is a book about *God. Subsequently, the book of *Psalms communicates a very comprehensive and complex view of God. However, in the process of learning about God in the Psalms, we also discover a view of David, to whom a vast number of psalms has been attributed. The titles or superscriptions provided in the psalms help us understand their historical context and help identify some of their authors (*see* Psalms 5: Titles). One hundred and sixteen psalms have such superscriptions, while thirty-four have no title and thus can be classified as anonymous. Seventy-three of the psalms have *lĕdāwîd* in their superscription. While the preposition *lāmed* (ל) is most often translated "to" or "for," it can also be translated "of," and thus it can be used to denote authorship. Gesenius (GKC 419-20) affirms that "the introduction of the author, poet, etc., by this *lamed auctoris* is the customary idiom also in the other Semitic dialects, especially Arabic." Conceptual parallels, linguistic and thematic analogies between the psalms, and the Samuel/Chronicles parallels make the claim of Davidic authorship most probable. Besides grammatical and linguistic evidence, external evidence from other biblical books points to some Davidic authorship of the psalms. Both Jesus and Peter attest to David's authorship of some psalms (Mark 12:35-37; Luke 20:42; Acts 2:24-36). Furthermore, biblical material supports the fact that David was a prolific writer of sacred poetry. The psalms that bear his name sought to extol and thank God for who he is and what he does, and at the same time they give us a window on one whose soul struggles in an imperfect world. A true reconstruction of David's life, however, must be dependent on the material about him in the historical books of 1-2 Samuel and 1 Kings. Even if one does not accept the Davidic authorship of the psalms attributed to him, a panoramic picture of David emerges from the psalms in their canonical form.

1. Yahweh According to David
2. David's Confessions
3. David's Trust
4. David's Portrait

1. Yahweh According to David.

David's view of God is comprehensive. God is revealed in David's psalms as the creator and sustainer of the universe (Pss 8; 18; 19). He is good (Ps 25:8; 34:8; 145:9), righteous (Ps 7:11; 11:7; 19:9; 145:17), just (Ps 33:5; 37:28; 103:6; 140:12; 146:7), gracious (Ps 103:8; 145:8), faithful (Ps 31:5; 145:13), loving (Ps 25:10; 33:5; 52:8; 62:12; 86:5; 101:1; 103:8; 143:8) and compassionate (Ps 86:15; 103:8; 103:13; 145:8). For David, Yahweh is a personal God. David calls Yahweh "my God" twenty-two times (Ps 3:7; 7:1, 3; 13:3; 18:6, 28; 22:2; 25:2; 30:12; 31:14; 35:23, 24; 38:15, 21; 40:5, 8, 17; 42:6; 43:4; 59:1; 86:2, 12). The Lord is also "my rock" (Ps 18:2, 46; 28:1; 31:3; 42:9; 62:2, 6, 7; 144:1), "my shield" (Ps 3:3; 7:10; 18:2; 28:7; 144:2), "my fortress" (Ps 18:2; 31:3; 59:9, 17; 62:2, 6; 144:2), "my redeemer" (Ps 19:14) and the "God of my salvation" (Ps 18:46; 25:5; 27:9; 51:14). David epitomizes the person who knows that Yahweh is the one who hears and answers prayer. Twenty times David calls or cries out to the Lord (Ps 3:4; 4:1, 3; 17:6; 18:3, 6 [2x]; 22:2; 27:7; 28:1; 30:8; 31:17; 55:16; 56:9; 57:2; 61:2; 86:3, 7; 102:2; 141:1). But David does not pray to some deaf, motionless, distant God; rather, David is confident that Yahweh hears, answers and saves him (Ps 3:5; 4:3; 17:6; 18:3, 6; 55:16; 57:3; 86:7). For David, Yahweh is the sovereign king, who reigns over all creation, and he describes Yahweh's *kingship in mythopoetic language. Yahweh is king, and his kingdom and kingship are superior to any political or mythological ruler. David describes Yahweh as "my king" (Ps 5:2; 44:4; 68:24; 145:1), the king who reigns forever (Ps 10:16; 29:10), the king of glory (Ps 24:7-10), the king over all the earth (Ps 47:2, 7), king over the nations (Ps 22:28; 47:8), the great king (Ps 48:2), king over Jacob (Ps 59:13) and king over all (Ps 103:19).

2. David's Confessions.

The psalms do not present David as one who can do no wrong, and they do not hide his shortcoming and sins. David is portrayed as being aware of his sins and his need to confess them. The psalmist often refers to "my sin" (Ps 32:5; 38:3, 18; 51:2, 3) and "my iniquity" (Ps 31:10; 32:5; 51:2) and acknowledges, "I have sinned" (Ps 41:4; 51:4), even when he has to confess to committing murder (Ps 51:14) (contra Goulder). The sins committed against God and his neighbors produce in David's heart a need for confession (Ps 32:5; 38:18), restoration (Ps 51:12; 60:1), healing (Ps 6:2; 41:4; 147:3) and forgiveness (Ps 25:18; 86:5; 103:3). David is confident in Yahweh's mercy and grace and knows that only God can repair their damaged relationship (Ps 23:6; 25:6; 28:2, 6; 30:8; 31:22; 40:11; 51:1; 55:1; 69:16; 86:6; 103:4; 140:6; 142:1; 143:1; 145:9). David realizes that character, not competence, is the main ingredient for a representative of Yahweh on the throne of Israel.

3. David's Trust.

The psalms portray David as one who experiences anguish at the hands of many foes. David's opponents are defined as enemies (Ps 3:7; 7:4; 9:3, 6; 13:2; 18:17; 25:2; 41:11; 42:9; 54:5; 61:3; 64:1; 143:3), and, showing the personal anguish that David experienced, the expression "my enemy/enemies" appears sixty times in the psalms that name David in their superscript. David's enemies also appear as adversaries (Ps 27:2, 12; 31:11; 42:10; 143:12) and evildoers (Ps 5:5; 6:8; 14:4; 28:3; 36:12; 53:4; 64:2; 101:8; 141:4, 9), and quite frequently David's rivals are described as wicked (Ps 3:7; 7:9; 11:2; 17:13; 36:11; 55:2; 101:8; 139:19; 141:10) (see Tate, 60-64). Their relentless and destructive actions against him cause him sorrow (Ps 13:2; 31:10), grief (Ps 6:7; 31:9) and tears (Ps 6:6; 39:12; 42:3; 56:8; 102:9). Many *laments are David's songs in times of sorrow. Despite the fact that his enemies are trying to destroy him

(Ps 3:1; 56:2; 57:1; 59:1), mock him (Ps 41:6; 102:8), and lie about him (Ps 4:2; 144:8; 11), David trusts in Yahweh. The expression of trust is a key element in the structure of laments (see Longman), and David is portrayed as one who trusts in the Lord. The expression "I have trusted/trust/will trust" occurs eleven times (Ps 13:5; 25:2; 26:1; 31:6; 31:14; 52:8; 55:23; 56:3, 4, 11; 143:8). Besides conveying his trust in God, David expresses his trust in Yahweh's loyal love (Ps 18:50; 25:10; 33:5; 52:3, 8; 62:12; 86:5; 86:15; 101:1; 103:4, 8; 143:8; 145:8).

4. David's Portrait.

The psalms give us a fairly comprehensive image of David. The shepherd-turned-king emerges from the psalms as a spiritual leader who is in constant conversation with the Lord. Besides the verbs employed (qr', pll, z'q), the multitude of jussives employed point to David's intense prayer life (e.g., Ps 5:11; 7:7, 9; 9:19, 20; 10:2; 11:6; 14:7; 16:10; 17:2; 19:13, 14; 25:2, 20; 30:1; 31:1, 17, 18, 24; 32:6; 33:8, 22). David emerges from the psalms as a grateful man who gives thanks to Yahweh for his *protection and provision (Ps 7:17; 9:1; 26:7; 28:7; 30:12; 44:8; 54:6; 57:9; 69:30; 86:12; 108:3; 109:30; 138:1, 2) and exhorts others to join him in expressing gratitude (Ps 30:4; 33:2; 50:14; 100:4; 147:7). Furthermore, David praises God for who God is and what he has done and is doing in his life and in the life of the Israelites. The main verbs depicting David's praises are zmr (Ps 7:17 [7:18 MT]; 9:2 [9:3 MT]; 27:6; 57:7 [57:8 MT]; 59:17 [59:18 MT]; 61:8 [61:9 MT]; 101:1; 108:1 [108:2 MT]; 144:9; 146:2), hll (Ps 22:22 [22:23 MT]; 35:18; 56:4 [56:5 MT]; 69:30 [69:31 MT]; 109:30; 146:2) and ydh (Ps 18:49 [18:50 MT]; 30:12 [30:13 MT]; 35:18; 52:9 [52:11 MT]; 139:14). The imperative halĕlû ("praise") appears fifty times in the three separate Hallel collections, the Egyptian Hallel (Pss 113—118), the Great Hallel (Pss 120—136) and the Concluding Hallel (Pss 146—150) (see Mowinckel). Twenty-eight times halĕlû occurs in the Concluding Hallel, which is attributed to David. Even though David was a great military leader and groundbreaking king, the psalms portray him as a humble man who concerns himself with the interests of the poor. Even though some scholars describe David as a person whom one might want to invite to dinner (see Halpern) or as one who is "wild and greedy in his relationship with women" (Valler, 130), he describes himself as "poor and needy" (Ps 40:17; 86:1; 109:22) and recognizes that the Lord is the one who lifts up the humble (Ps 147:6) and gives them salvation (Ps 149:4). David's humility can be deduced also from his portrayal of himself as a servant (Ps 19:11, 13; 31:16; 35:27; 86:2, 4, 16; 143:2, 12; 144:10). Even though David makes statements such as "How long, O LORD? Will you forget me forever?" (Ps 13:1), the psalms portray David as one who patiently waits for Yahweh's answer and deliverance (Ps 25:5, 21; 27:14; 37:7; 38:15; 39:7; 40:1). But David is also portrayed as very human indeed. When in deep anguish and pain, he invokes curses and judgment on his enemies (Pss 35; 58; 59; 69; 139) (*see* Retribution). David certainly was powerful and talented, but he was not sinless, and he is not meant to be a portrait of morality for us, but rather a mirror for identity.

See also SOLOMON.

BIBLIOGRAPHY. **B. S. Childs,** "Psalm Titles and Midrashic Exegesis," *JSS* 16 (1971) 137-50; **C. Feinberg,** "The Date of the Psalms," *BSac* 104 (1947) 426-40; **M. Goulder,** *The Prayers of David* (JSOTSup 102; Sheffield: Sheffield Academic Press, 1990); **C. Gulston,** *David: Shepherd & King* (Grand Rapids: Zondervan, 1980); **D. M. Gunn,** *The Story of King David: Genre and Interpretation* (JSOTSup 6; Sheffield: Sheffield University Press, 1978); **B. Halpern,** *David's Secret Demons: Messiah, Murderer, Traitor, King* (Grand Rapids: Eerdmans, 2001); **D. M. Howard,** "David," *ABD* 2.41-49; **T. Longman III,** *How to Read the Psalms* (Downers Grove, IL: InterVarsity Press, 1988); **K. P. McCarter,** "The Historical David," *Int* 40 (1986) 117-29; **S. L. McKenzie,** *King David: A Biography* (Oxford: Oxford University Press, 2000); **S. Mowinckel,** *The Psalms in Israel's Worship* (Nashville: Abingdon, 1962); **Y. Natan,** *The Jewish Trinity* (Chula Vista, CA: Aventine, 2003); **M. Reiss,** "Strife in the Household of Kind David," *JBQ* 28 (2000) 227-32; **P. E. Satterthwaite,** "David," *DOTHB* 198-206; **E. Slomovic,** "Toward an Understanding of the Formation of Historical Titles in the Book of Psalms," *ZAW* 91 (1979) 350-81; **E. B. Smick,** "Mythopoetic Language in the Psalms," *WTJ* 44 (1982) 88-98; **M. Tate,** *Psalms 51-100* (WBC 20; Dallas: Word, 1990); **M. Travers,** *Encountering God in the Psalms* (Grand Rapids: Kregel, 2003); **S. Valler,** "King David and 'His' Women: Biblical Stories and Talmudic Discussions," in *A Feminist Companion to Samuel and Kings,* ed. A. Brenner (FCB 5; Sheffield: Sheffield Academic Press, 1994) 129-42.

T. Rata

DEAD SEA SCROLLS

The contribution of the ancient manuscripts found in the vicinity of Khirbet Qumran to the understanding of *Psalms has been a keen focus of study over the past decade and has now reached the stage where the evidence can be summarized with a good measure of clarity. The same cannot be said of the biblical wisdom books, for which the evidence is much more limited and fragmentary and the secondary literature more sparse.

This scarcity needs to be placed in perspective. Of the nine hundred or so manuscripts represented among the DSS, nearly one-third (about 220) are biblical texts. Of the remaining two-thirds, the overwhelming majority are related to the Bible in some manner, as commentary, "rewritten Bible," or development upon biblical topics. It is no overstatement to describe the worldview of the people who wrote, copied, and preserved the manuscripts of the caves as Bible-centered.

That said, the nature of that "Bible" was very different from that of the later canonical listings either of Christian or Jewish Scriptures (*see* Canon). Of the books that become the Hebrew Bible and the Christian OT, priority clearly was given to the Pentateuch—89 of the 220 manuscripts. Beyond this, only two further books of the Bible figure as prominently: Isaiah (21 copies) and Psalms (36 copies [the largest share of all biblical manuscripts]). The "Bible-within-the-Bible" of Qumran can be said to consist of Genesis (20 copies), Deuteronomy (30), Isaiah (21) and Psalms (36). The centrality of these works is emphasized by the recognition that Deuteronomy, Isaiah and Psalms are the books quoted or alluded to most frequently in the rest of the Qumran literature.

The significance of this summary will be seen in this article. On the one hand, the largest section below addresses the psalms and the impact that the DSS of the psalms have for our understanding of their place in the history of the Bible and interpretation. On the other hand, the fact that biblical *wisdom is represented by at most four manuscript copies of any one book means less space is needed to describe them. This imbalance between Torah and the rest of the Bible may be partly due to the accident of preservation; it could be that there were more of some of these books but they were subject to more serious deterioration and destruction. The more likely reason, however, appears to relate to the stage of development in the "canon" during the period of the creation of these manuscripts.

1. The Psalms
2. Biblical Wisdom at Qumran
3. The Rest of the Writings

1. The Psalms.
The evidence of the DSS regarding the psalms touches on a wide variety of topics relating to biblical studies. The significant number of manuscripts and the plurality of texts represented provide important data for *textual criticism and the history of the biblical text for OT studies. The differing order of the psalms in relation to the MT, inclusion of otherwise unknown psalms, and whole manuscripts of noncanonical psalms offer insight into the development of the corpus during the late Second Temple period. The presence of "commentaries" on some of the psalms further adds to our understanding of the interpretation of the psalms in this period and thus, in view of the high degree of citation of psalms in the NT, for NT studies.

1.1. Manuscripts. The manuscript evidence regarding the psalms may be presented in a variety of ways. The first is to count the scrolls. By P. W. Flint's (1997a, 257-64) count, there are thirty-nine psalms scrolls from locations along the Dead Sea: thirty-six from the eleven Qumran caves, one from Naḥal Hever, two from Masada.

The second is to place these numbers in context. We have already noted that the Qumran psalms scrolls represent the largest number of manuscripts of any single biblical book at Qumran. They also come from the widest variety of locations, with copies found in Caves 1, 4, 5, 6, 8 and 11. Two of the Cave 11 manuscripts are among those containing the largest extent of surviving text. Besides these manuscripts containing only psalms, there are seven other texts that include significant citations of the psalms. Together, these psalms scrolls represent nearly twenty percent of biblical manuscripts found.

That said, we need to be cautious with regard to the extent of the original content of these manuscripts. Many of them are too fragmentary to allow any speculation about how many

psalms were in the complete scroll. For example, 4QPs[j] consists of some twenty (MT) verses in eight fragments from Psalms 48, 49 and 51; 4QPs[k] contains a fragmentary column of Psalm 135 and another of Psalm 99 (in that apparent order); 4QPs[n] consists of one fragment of a portion of Psalm 42:5. Altogether, nineteen of the manuscripts are similarly minute, and no conclusions can be drawn as to whether each of these represents the existence of a complete psalms scroll. In light of this count, the evidence for evaluating collections of psalms is limited to no more than twenty manuscripts.

1.2. Collections. There is no scroll that contains all of the biblical psalms, nor are all the biblical psalms extant (only 126). In fact, it appears that none of the manuscripts would ever have contained them all. One reason is that such a scroll would have been very large and unwieldy. Flint points out that 11QPs[a], containing forty-nine psalms, is 5 meters long; a full 150 psalms would mean a scroll 15 meters in length. In comparison, 1QIsa[a] measures just over 7 meters, and 11QT[a] just over 8 meters. It is unlikely any manuscript was ever that long.

Of the longer manuscripts, most appear to have contained psalms only from Psalms 1—89 MT, while others only from beyond Psalm 90. This has given birth to the theory that a corpus of *David psalms reached essentially their canonical shaping prior to this period, with the rest of the Psalter still in process of growth.

This can be highlighted by considering the manuscripts that overlap this division. 1QPs[a], for example, consists of twenty-two fragments containing portions of Psalms 86; 92; 94; 95—96; 119. Little speculation is possible about how extensive this manuscript may have been. Yet, that these fragments come from psalms relatively close to each other makes it conceivable that they represent what is left of the end of a manuscript that concluded with Psalm 119.

In another example, 4QPs[e] contains portions between Psalms 76 and Psalm 130, but without Psalm 119. Psalm 118 is followed immediately by Psalm 104, Psalm 105, then Psalm 120. On the other hand, 11QPs[b], beginning with Psalms 77—78, includes Psalm 119 followed by Psalm 118. What has not commonly been observed of both of these is that although they contain psalms earlier (i.e., in MT numbering) than Psalm 89, none is earlier than Psalm 72, which in the MT contains the note "The prayers of David son of Jesse are ended." Thus, these may represent collections reflecting development beyond the fixed Psalms 1—72.

One manuscript includes a later psalm within a collection of earlier psalms. 11QPs[d] contains fragments from Psalm 6 to Psalm 86 (though not in the MT order), with Psalms 81; 86; 115—116 situated between portions of Psalm 78. Again, there is no way of knowing the original extent of this manuscript. However, if the order of fragments is correctly discerned, the insertion into the account of Israel's faithlessness in Psalm 78 with psalms of supplication and *thanksgiving gives this manuscript an exegetical or liturgical slant that is not seen in other manuscripts. This leaves the question of whether this is a collection of psalms or an exegetical text.

The six fragments of 1QPs[b] include portions of Psalms 126—128, raising the possibility that this manuscript may have contained only the Songs of Ascent. If so, this would mean that we now have manuscript evidence for these as a separate unit prior to inclusion in the larger corpus of the Psalter. However, the point cannot be pressed too far on the basis of such (literally) scant evidence.

The ground is even less stable for pondering what to make of the absence of some psalms from collections. 4QPs[b] contains text of Psalms 91—118 and apparently ended with Psalm 118. In this manuscript Psalm 103 is found at the end of one column, and the next column starts with Psalm 112. The implication may be that the missing psalms, Psalm 104—111, once formed an independent unit. Again, this is an attractive idea for the light that it may shed on the formation of smaller collections, as well as for the question as to why, if these were an existing collection, the MT split them into Book IV and Book V of its Psalter. But these remain speculative questions.

1.3. Excerpted Texts. Whereas some psalms manuscripts were large collections ("Psalters"), others clearly contained only a selection of psalms. We have noted that large scrolls, up to 15 meters in length, would be unlikely as well as cumbersome for either study or quick reference. Undoubtedly, some scrolls were created for more ready access. We speculated above on a possible exegetical purpose for one text, but there are other potential purposes for such scrolls. One suggestion is that some psalms are "excerpted" from a larger collection for particular purposes (Tov 1995a).

Psalm 119 seems to have held a place of importance among the psalms at Qumran. Two manuscripts are likely to have consisted of only this one psalm in a handy "pocket version." The manuscript 4QPs[g] is only 8.4 centimeters high, with no more than eight lines per column; the whole would have been twenty-five columns long. The text is written out in poetic form (stichometrically), with four lines per stanza. 4QPs[h] is taller but shorter, with twenty-one lines per column, extended to nine columns.

It is not difficult to imagine the reason for multiple copies of this psalm existing in a community that lived to contemplate and keep Torah, and that was called to a "perfect walk" (1QS I, 7-9: "in order to welcome into the covenant of kindness all those who freely volunteer to carry out God's decrees; in order to be united in the counsel of God and walk in perfection in his sight, complying with all revealed things" [cf. Ps 119:1]).

Psalm 104 is another that receives this sort of treatment. 4QPs[l] is a single fragment that clearly is a small scroll. The text is presented in stichometric lines little more than 4 centimeters long, which would make for six columns of text, or a handy 35-40 centimeters of leather (Skehan, Ulrich and Flint, 128).

There are other features unique to Psalm 104. In three of the five scrolls that include this psalm the text differs in form from the biblical text. This too seems to have important exegetical significance at Qumran. Additionally, this psalm of thanksgiving begins, "Bless, O my soul, the LORD," the inspiration for another text found at Qumran, *Barki Napshi*, of which five copies survive (4QBarki Napshi[a-e]). This does not appear to be a sectarian text; that is, it does not originate with the Qumran community, but it is considered to be a core sectarian text. The Thanksgiving Hymns, or *Hodayot* (1QH[a]), also show affinity to Psalm 104. These factors point to a common strain of development from this psalm.

A third excerpt of interest, 4QPs89, contains Psalm 89. Interpretation of this manuscript is an illustration of the indistinct territory between what is a "biblical" text and what is "something-else-but-not-quite-biblical" among the DSS. At its first publication this manuscript was described as a source for the canonical Psalter version (Milik 1966, 94). However, P. W. Skehan (1981, 439) argued that this manuscript was based on the canonical psalm, and J. P. M. van der Ploeg (475) viewed it as similar to early Christian *testimonia*, or collections of messianic prooftexts, rather than a psalm. The DJD editors have placed it among the biblical psalms manuscripts

The ambiguity arises from the arrangement of the psalm with a different order to the verses (20-22, 26, 23, 27-28, 31) and possible Aramaic influences. If it is the canonical psalm, it is a different version. The difficulty in deciding how this relates to the canonical Psalm 89 is further complicated by the early date given to this manuscript—dated on palaeography by J. Milik (1966, 95) as having been copied in the period 175-125 BC, making it one of the oldest psalms scrolls. The conclusion that we might draw from the evidence is that on the one hand, Psalm 89 appears to be a firm part of the Davidic collection by this time, and on the other hand, the existence of this version indicates that the text itself was still fluid at least in the second century BC (see Dahmen).

That each of these examples might be viewed as having been excerpted from a collection for reasons of theological importance has implications for our understanding of the role of the psalms in the Second Temple period and in their subsequent canonical shape—the various ways a single psalm is presented may differ from setting to setting, with a different theological function. Interpretation of a psalm cannot be divorced from the purpose of its setting (Brooke, 8).

1.4. "Noncanonical" Psalms. Thus far we have looked at psalms only in comparison to their canonical, "biblical" counterparts. One of the significant aspects of the Qumran psalms scrolls is the inclusion of "noncanonical," or "apocryphal," psalms in a significant number of manuscripts.

The so-called apocryphal psalms are those previously known from Psalters besides the MT. The LXX includes Psalm 151, with a superscription that clarifies it is as supernumerary to the proper Psalm 150, although it is affirmed as having been written by David himself. This psalm and four others also appear in Syriac manuscripts (Sanders 1965, 53). The Syriac translation of the Scriptures is a Christian version, clearly later in provenance than the LXX version, and thus has been regarded as a late witness to the

psalms tradition. As such, the psalms that are extra to the MT have been regarded as of later composition. Now, all of these appear in the most complete Qumran psalms scroll, 11QPs[a]. This factor has forced a reevaluation of their pedigree, so that now the Syriac psalms are seen to be a faithful reflection of the Psalter extant in Palestine at the turn of the era. These apocryphal psalms must be seen as authentically authoritative texts for a significant portion of Second Temple Judaism and early Christianity prior to the fixing of the corpus at some point late in the process of canonization.

The Cave 11 Psalter includes two other previously known compositions, Sirach 51 and the "Last Words of David" from 2 Samuel 23. This scroll begins with MT Psalm 101 and ends with LXX/Syriac Psalm 151, within twenty-eight extant columns. The psalms do not follow the MT order, and they include Psalm 93. The chief divergence is seen following Psalm 145 in column 17: Psalm 154 (Syriac equivalent) → "Prayer for Deliverance" → Psalm 139:8-24 → Psalm 137:1 → Psalm 138:1-8 → Sirach 51 (vv. 13-20, 30) → "Apostrophe to Zion." The final two columns begin with the "Last Words of David," followed by a prose epilogue called "David's Compositions," then Psalm 140:1-5 → Psalm 134:1-3 → Psalm 151.

Besides the "Prayer for Deliverance" and the "Apostrophe to Zion," the Qumran scrolls also include hitherto unknown compositions. 11QPs[a] contains four of the six or seven unique psalms. Two appear here only: the "Hymn to the Creator" and "David's Compositions." The latter serves as the epilogue to this Psalter, to give the total of David's psalms as 4,050. This is broken down into 3,600 psalms, plus other types of songs besides those set for the whole of the liturgical calendar. The purpose of this seems to be to plant the seal of David's authority firmly over all the compositions and thus serves to determine the context for interpreting them.

Two other new psalms, "Apostrophe to Zion" and "Plea for Deliverance," are shared with 11QPs[b], and the latter with 4QPs[f]. 4QPs[f] in turn contains a further two new psalms, one entitled "Eschatological Hymn," and the other "Apostrophe to Judah."

The observation to note here is that new psalms stand alongside texts common to other Psalters, and thus they must be considered of the same importance or validity. They stand as evidence of the breadth of possibilities still open for collections beyond that known in the Masoretic tradition at the time of publication of these texts.

There is another set of manuscripts that need to be taken into consideration but are not normally considered to be "biblical" scrolls. These contain psalms without the inclusion of any material known from the MT or the LXX but are clearly "psalmlike." 4Q380 is a fragmentary collection of compositions: a "Zion Psalm," laments and wisdom psalms (see Schuller, 77). The one complete title reads "Prayer of Obadiah"—whether referring to the prophet or to another person of that name is unclear. 4Q381, similarly, includes ascriptions to "Manasseh," "the man of God" and a "king of Judah" whose name is lost in a lacuna. G. J. Brooke (12) argues that these texts must be included in any theory of the development of the Psalter, not only at Qumran but also in pre-Qumran. This is a valid point that must not be quickly dismissed. It is the nature of scholarship's MT orientation when discussing the psalms that the evidence of manuscripts outside the canonical Psalter is easily disregarded as irrelevant. The implication of the presence of noncanonical psalms *within* manuscripts containing "canonical" psalms for Psalms studies is that the place of noncanonical psalms scrolls such as 4Q380 and 4Q381 must be recognized too. In a period when the collection was not yet fixed, the possibilities for inclusion are broader than has been commonly considered.

1.5. The Growth and Editing of the Psalter.

1.5.1. Growth of the Psalter(s). 11QPs[a], containing some forty-nine psalms, beginning with the canonical Psalm 101, is dated to the middle of the first century AD. The existence of a version so different from the canonical Psalter, and so late in the Second Temple period, has opened a window on the process of the formation of the Psalter.

The official editor of this scroll, J. A. Sanders (1966), argued that this represented a genuine Psalter, establishing that the "canon" of the psalms was not closed at this time. In his view, the process of fixing the text was already virtually complete for Psalms 1—100, but the rest were still capable of rearrangement. S. Talmon (1966) took issue with this thesis, rejecting the idea that these could be considered biblical psalms, because of the inclusion of the prose "David's Compositions." He contended instead that they

are intended for liturgical and homiletical purposes. The liturgical argument was picked up by P. W. Skehan (1978, 169), who further argued that the Cave 11 collection is based on knowledge of the canonical 150 psalms. The fact that eight noncanonical psalms appear among the last eleven canonical psalms indicated for him their late insertion into a fixed order.

These arguments are based on the premise that the MT 150-psalm Psalter was already settled by the time of the translation of the LXX, presumed to have been complete by the second century BC (see Beckwith, 6). On this basis, a much later manuscript such as 11QPs[a] must be seen as a derivative text without canonical pretensions. This could be argued as long as 11QPs[a] was viewed as a one-off text. But the publication of the rest of the Qumran biblical manuscripts, with their evidence of the pluriformity of biblical texts into the first century AD, and particularly the psalms scrolls from Cave 4, has changed the landscape.

P. W. Flint (1997a), who completed the editing of the psalms scrolls begun by P. W. Skehan and E. Ulrich, has put forward the most comprehensive proposal for the relation of the various Psalters and psalms collections to each other. His thesis is that there were three literary Psalter editions: the first consists of Psalms 1/2—89; the second consists of the first edition plus the 11QPs[a] Psalter; the third is the MT Psalter. In other words, the Psalters took form in two parts. First, Psalms 1—89 (the first three books of the MT Psalter) were an established collection at an early date, based on Davidic authorship, most certainly preceding the formation of the Qumran community. Second, the psalms collections continued to develop gradually over the course of one or two centuries, with great flexibility in contents and order of material. We have manuscript evidence of at least three Psalters existing simultaneously in late Second Temple Judaism: an MT type, a Cave 11 type and the LXX type. It is not unreasonable to consider that there could be even more options found within the Qumran scrolls, undetectable, however, due to their fragmentary nature.

Flint's thesis continues by arguing that the Cave 11 Psalter was composed in relation to the solar calendar in use by the Qumran community, among others, representing a 52-piece collection with strong Davidic emphasis. The establishment of organizing principles such as this tends to confirm the nature of the collection as a Psalter, especially when the Psalters are compared as G. Wilson (1997, 463-64) has done. Wilson looks at the shaping of both the MT and the Cave 11 scroll as a whole and sees the Qumran scroll focusing on the need for divine deliverance for Jerusalem. The hope for this deliverance is found in David. The Davidic *messiah's role is prominent, forming the final vision and hope of the Psalter. In contrast, the MT Psalter concludes with the focus on the kingship of Yahweh, with the *yhwh mālāk* psalms (missing from 11QPs[a]) and the closing doxology on his creative power (Pss 145—150). David's role is diminished. The LXX version of Book V, which differs from the MT largely in the addition of more superscriptions of authorship to David plus the added Psalm 151, seems to Wilson to hold a mediating place between the two Psalters.

Looking at the Psalters in this way sheds helpful light on the editorial intentions to be found in the received canonical Psalter. The move away from messianic expectation parallels the downplaying of that element of Judaism following the disaster of the Jewish Revolt, in contrast to the heightened messianism of the pre-Revolt Cave 11 Psalter. When viewed in this way, the MT Psalter increasingly appears to be the latest to be finalized, although it is this Psalter that has the final word.

1.5.2 Editing the Psalter. The questions relating to the nature of the Psalter(s) in the DSS have provoked an awareness and appreciation of editorial purpose in the placing of individual songs and smaller collections in relation to each other. In this respect too, G. Wilson (1985) has helped by drawing attention back to the superscriptions and book divisions of the MT. Psalm 1 provides the clue to how to read the Psalter: it is to be meditated on day and night, as Torah. The Psalter may then be read chronologically, from David himself (Books I-II), to the loss of the kingdom (Book III), exile (Book IV) and expectation of the coming rule of God (Book V). These insights into the shaping of the Psalter are most valuable not for understanding individual psalms on their own but rather for seeing psalms in relation to each other. Ultimately, the insight gained into the purposes of the editor(s) gives insight into the late first century AD, when this Psalter reached its final form. As such, the study of the MT Psalter places us in the very midst of the NT world!

1.6. Conclusion. The Qumran scrolls grant us a view of the psalms that the finished Psalters of the MT and the LXX, being complete and fixed, cannot do. They show us the very process of creation in midpoint of development. We see something of the dynamic that the individual compositions display in their changing relations to each other prior to being cast in the permanency of immovable print. This was a living corpus during the very time that the NT and early Christianity itself were developing. Perhaps some of that dynamic can be seen to continue even beyond the finalization of the canon.

2. Biblical Wisdom at Qumran.

As we noted in the introduction, the evidence for the biblical wisdom books at Qumran is sparse. There are manuscripts of *Job, *Proverbs, *Ecclesiastes and also *Song of Songs (see 3.1 below) among the DSS, but these are among the most fragmentary and least copied at Qumran. None of these appear in more than four copies, and apart from Cave 4, they appear only in the minor cave finds of the Qumran vicinity.

It is not the case that there is no Wisdom literature among the DSS. To the contrary, there is a large corpus of wisdom material preserved in the cave finds, but most of it shows clear development away from the rational, observation-based approach of biblical wisdom toward a wisdom that is based on revelation, particularly a revelation of the *raz nihyeh*, or "mystery that is to be/come." This enigmatic but frequently repeated phrase may be a development of "mystery" as found in the book of Daniel (Harrington, *EDSS* 1.589), an indicator of the eschatological, if not apocalyptic, interests of Qumran wisdom that are in keeping with the preoccupation with the last days found in other genres of literature found among the DSS (*see* Wisdom and Apocalyptic). This development may explain the relative scarcity of biblical wisdom books at Qumran. These new wisdom texts are beyond the scope of this article, and the evidence of the biblical texts can be summarized in relatively brief fashion.

2.1. Job. The evidence for the book of Job is of two types: *Hebrew and Aramaic, or *Targum Job, manuscripts.

2.1.1. The Hebrew Fragments. There are four manuscripts of Job. 2QJob consists of one fragment, dated palaeographically to the Herodian era (c. 50 BC to AD 50), containing portions of five words. These have been confidently identified as coming from Job 33:28-30.

4QJob[a] is dated to the Hasmonean era (c. 100-50 BC). 4QJob[a] is the most extensive of the Job manuscripts, with twenty-six fragments. These preserve text from Job 31:14-19; 32:3-4; 33:10-11, 24-26, 28-30; 35:16; 36:7-11, 13-17, 32-33; 37:1-5, 14-15. Unfortunately, the portion of Job 33:28-30 preserved in this text does not overlap with the Cave 2 fragment. Two fragments (7 I-II; 16 I-II) contain column margins that allow the editors to deduce that there would have been sixteen lines per column, with each column an estimated 10 centimeters high.

4QJob[b] consists of six fragments, containing Job 8:15-17; 9:27; 13:4; 14:4-6; 31:20-21. The editors date it a little later than 4QJob[a], perhaps to the middle or latter part of the first century BC.

4Qpaleo-Job[c] is considered to be the oldest of the Job manuscripts. The fragments contain portions of Job 13:18-20, 23-27; 14:13-18. They are written in the paleo-Hebrew script (sometimes called Phoenician or proto-Hebrew script), one of a small number of biblical manuscripts written this way. These tend also to be among the oldest manuscripts; this one dates somewhere between 225 BC and 150 BC This date means that this was copied prior to the formation of the Qumran community that preserved it, and therefore it was brought to Qumran from elsewhere. Other than Job, almost all of the manuscripts in this script are Torah scrolls. This would seem to indicate the priority given to the Torah from early days, and the inclusion of Job in the number suggests to some that traditional ascription of Mosaic authorship for Job may be the reason (Newsom, 412).

In spite of the fragmentary nature of the manuscripts of Job at Qumran, they provide some important insights into the status of the biblical text of this time. First, two of the Cave 4 texts were written in stichometric, or "poetic," format. Second, whereas the Cave 2 fragment can tell us little about its relation to the MT, 4QJob[a] diverges in several places in terms of orthography and grammatical forms and textual variants, while 4QJob[b] shows no textual variants. 4Qpaleo-Job[c] has only a couple minor variants. The divergences are of minor significance but are evidence of the "fluid" nature of the biblical text in the centuries prior to the Jewish Revolt. The scribal practice in spelling shows

further interesting variety. 4Qpaleo-Job[c] reverts to *plene* spellings (the use of the consonants as vowel signs) less even than does the MT, in comparison to the tendency of the later manuscripts toward fuller spellings. Third, 2QJob, 4QJob[a] and 4QJob[b] contain text from the Elihu speech (Job 32—37); if this portion was a later addition to Job, as some commentators have hypothesized, then the editorial work was done by the first century BC.

2.1.2. The Targum of Job. There are two manuscripts of a Targum of Job among the DSS.

4QtgJob consists of only two fragments, one of which is too small to determine its identity. The other contains text from two separate columns, from Job 3:5-6; 4:7—5:4. Milik (1977) dated this to the second century BC, but A. S. van der Woude places it in the middle of the first century BC The text is virtually identical to the Hebrew of Job.

11QtgJob, on the other hand, preserves about fifteen percent of the text of Job, some ten columns from the end of the book of Job (Job 37:10—42:11). Van der Woude follows M. Sokoloff in suggesting a date for composition of the Targum in the late second century BC, considering the Aramaic to be somewhere between biblical Aramaic and 1QapGen ar. He dates the copy of the manuscript to the early first century AD on the basis of the Herodian script of the *scribe. As to the Aramaic, U. Glessmer (917) follows J. A. Fitzmyer's designation of the Targum of Job, together with the 1QapGen ar and the Targumim Onqelos and Jonathan, as "Middle Aramaic" (200 BC to AD 200). Whatever the dating, this manuscript remains the oldest extant Targum and therefore provides valuable insight into the development of the *Targumim and of the Aramaic language.

As to the translation of Job, it is generally agreed that the underlying Hebrew text is essentially that found in the MT. However, there are a number of places where the translation diverges notably from the Hebrew text, and these are of exegetical interest. Van der Woude perceives a tendency toward rationalism at Job 38:7, where the morning stars shine, rather than sing, together; and embarrassment for Job is avoided by omitting his prayer in Job 31:10 that other men "kneel over" his wife.

Perhaps the most significantly noticeable divergence is found at the end of the book of Job. First, Job does not repent and despise himself but rather maintains his innocence to the very end. Second, God explicitly forgives the sins of Job's friends at his prayer. Third, the text of the Targum ends with Job 42:11, apparently omitting the account of the extravagant restoration of Job's fortune and family. This may be in keeping with the conservatism of the translator found elsewhere, by leaving out mention of the daughters' names.

It is in this history of interpretation of Job, perhaps, that 11QtgJob is of most value.

2.2. Proverbs. Two manuscripts of Proverbs are represented by fragments. 4QProv[a] consists of two adjoining fragments, and 4QProv[b] of seven fragments containing portions of Proverbs 13—15.

4QProv[a] includes the right-hand and bottom margins with the text of Proverbs 1:17—2:1. With this information the editors are able to deduce a column of thirty-six lines at about 27 cm in height. The scribal hand is described as transitional Herodian, from 50 BC to early first century AD, and the text is arranged poetically. The text is the same as the MT, as opposed to the LXX, with only one variant: *mošĕbĕt* ("cord") appears for the MT's *mĕšûbat* ("backsliding") at Proverbs 1:32, rendering the "cords of the simple" in place of "backsliding of the simple." The editors (Skehan and Ulrich) compare this to the "cords of Orion" in Job 38:31. This seems most likely to be a *kāp/bêt* confusion.

4QProv[b] contains Proverbs 13:6-9; 14:5-10, 12-13, 31-35; 15:1-8, 19-31. It is possible that one fragment preserves portions of two words from Proverbs 7:9-11, but this remains open to question. The scribal hand is of a similar dating and script to 4QProv[a], but the poetic arrangement differs both in line division and in consistency. The editors consider it to be copied by an inexpert scribe. There are two variants that draw attention: the *ḥāsēr* at Proverbs 14:34 agrees with the LXX and the Syriac against the MT's *ḥesed;* at Proverbs 15:28 the manuscript omits *yehgeh* ("meditates"). Neither variant is of exegetical interest.

2.3. Ecclesiastes. Two manuscripts of Ecclesiastes were found in Cave 4. 4QQoh[a] is among the oldest of the scrolls, dated paleographically to between 175 BC and 150 BC. The dating is of significance for two reasons. First, it places the origins of the manuscript prior to the Qumran community, having been brought there from somewhere else (the archaeology of Qumran is placed no earlier than 150 BC, and possibly as late as 100 BC). Second, it drives the date of composition of this book back at least to the third century BC. This rules out of contention any theory of the Herodian or even Hasmonean period for the origin of the book. Further, the fact that there are only minor differences from the MT of Ecclesiastes, including the order of the sections and verses, dismisses theories of multiple editions or a confusion of manuscript leaves (see Jarick, 178).

4QQoh[a] is in six fragments, containing Ecclesiastes 5:13-17; 6:1(?), 3-8, 12; 7:1-10, 19-20. The most interesting feature is a space for 15-20 letters between Ecclesiastes 7:6 and Ecclesiastes 7:7. This seems to support previous theories calling for an emendation at this point, such as Proverbs 16:8 (see *BHS* margin).

4QQoh[b] is dated quite generally to the Herodian era, the second half of the first century BC or early first century AD. There are only two fragments, with text from Ecclesiastes 1:10-14.

The fact that the book of Ecclesiastes is not cited anywhere else in Qumran literature raises the question of the importance of this book for the community that preserved these two scrolls. Clearly, the book was being read, but we have no way of knowing to what extent it was used.

3. The Rest of the Writings.
When we turn to look at the remainder of the manuscript evidence in the Ketubim, or Writings, it raises more questions about what is absent than what is present. On the one hand, there are more manuscripts among the scrolls representing *Ruth and *Lamentations than Ecclesiastes or Proverbs. On the other hand, *Esther seems to be wholly absent, and the existence of Ezra through Chronicles (MT order) is a matter of debate. Add to this extremely fragmentary physical evidence the fact that there is no use of or allusion to Ecclesiastes, Song of Songs, or Ruth in the rest of the Qumran corpus, and we have a snapshot of the relative authoritative status of the third category of the Hebrew Bible: it is truly the "miscellaneous" section of the canon, which is still undefined at the time of the copying of the DSS. That is, at the end of the first century BC and the beginning of the first century AD the status of these books is ambiguous as far as the scriptural authority that later becomes canonical is concerned.

3.1. Song of Songs. Song of Songs is sometimes included in the classification of Wisdom literature, so we turn to the evidence of this book first by way of continuity with the previous section. The evidence of the DSS manuscripts introduces variations not seen in any of the texts discussed above but that are shared with some of the others that follow.

There are four copies found at Qumran, three from Cave 4 and one from Cave 6. The notable feature of each is in their size and contents. The height of the scrolls is between 8 centimeters and 10 centimeters, and the column widths between 5 centimeters and 8 centimeters. 6QCant has only seven lines per column and is written with a bold script. These figures can be compared to 4QPs^a, for instance, with thirty-five lines per column of about 12 centimeters in width and 20 centimeters in height, and written in a small script that fits in up to seventy-three letters and spaces. The scrolls of this little book would have been "pocket-sized."

4QCant^c consists of one fragment, with one complete word and two fragmentary words from Song of Songs 3:7-8. 6QCant contains one full column and a portion of a second, with text from the beginning of the book, Song of Songs 1:1-7. It is 4QCant^a and 4QCant^b that present the most information for us. 4QCant^a preserves portions of three columns, Song of Songs 3:4-5; 3:7—4:6; 4:7; 6:11—7:7. 4QCant^b is in three fragments, including text from Song of Songs 2:9—3:2; 3:5, 9—4:1-3, 8-11a; 4:14—5:1.

Both of these manuscripts are described by E. Tov (1995b) as "abbreviated texts," and by J. Jarick as "*Reader's Digest* Song of Songs" because of the clear omission of significant portions of the book as we know it. After Song of Songs 4:7 in 4QCant^a there is a blank line, then the text picks up at Song of Songs 6:11. The editor hypothesizes that similarity of content may be a reason for the omission of the material in between. However, it is useful to note that it is the description of the male body that is passed over (Song 5:10-16). On the other hand, 4QCant^b omits Song of Songs 4:4-7, leaving a closed paragraph space after Song of Songs 4:3 before continuing with Song of Songs 4:8. This time it is the description of key parts of the female body that is omitted. This copy of the book comes to an end at Song of Songs 5:1—the last word of the verse comes at the end of a column, and there is empty manuscript space following.

The reasons for this shortening of the text are a matter of pure speculation, with possible reasons such as censorship or liturgical purposes. What is not speculation, given the differences in omission between the two manuscripts, is that the scribes were shortening a full text of the book that already existed.

3.2. Ruth. The most significant fact regarding the book of Ruth is that there are more manuscripts of Ruth than of either Proverbs or Ecclesiastes, and that there is more of the text extant for this book than any other of the "Festival Scrolls" (*see* Megillot and Festivals). Two manuscripts were found in Cave 2, and two manuscripts in Cave 4. 4QRuth^a, one large fragment of fourteen lines of Ruth 1:1-12, and 2QRuth^a, seven fragments, containing portions of Ruth 2:13—3:8; 4:3-4, are dated to the middle of the first century BC. 4QRuth^b, four fragments from two columns comprising Ruth 1:1-6, 12-16, is possibly as late as the beginning of the first century AD, and 2QRuth^b, one small fragment of seven partial lines of Ruth 3:13-18, is placed middle of the first century AD (Baillet, 71-74; Skehan and Ulrich). There is not enough evidence available in these fragments to make any conclusive observations regarding the development of the text.

3.3. Lamentations. The four manuscripts of Lamentations come from three separate caves. There is no comprehensive theory advanced to suggest why different manuscripts appear in different caves, but it is at least of interest to note that this book is among two of the lesser scroll finds. One comes from Cave 3, notable chiefly as the source of the *Copper Scroll;* the only other biblical manuscripts found were from Ezekiel and Psalm 2. The two small fragments of Lamentations contain only a few words from Lamentations 1:10-12; 3:53-62, one of which is the Divine Name written in Paleo-Hebrew script. Two fragmentary manuscripts come from Cave 5, dating to the first century AD 5QLam^a contains fragments from six separate columns, spanning from Lamentations 4:5 to Lamentations 5:17. 5QLam^b is in one fragment of Lamentations 4:17-20 in four lines. Neither provides enough evidence to offer any suggestions of relationships to either the MT or the Greek versions.

The Cave 4 copy, which preserves substantial portions of three columns containing Lamentations 1:1-18 and a fragment of Lamentations 2:5, in contrast, offers some valuable clues for understanding the development of the text. The text is copied out in prose form (a "careless" semiformal script not meant for a public copy [Cross 2000, 229]), but F. M. Cross (1983, 152) argues that it nevertheless reveals the structure of the meter of the poetry. Further, whereas the text is "badly corrupt" in places, it also has readings considered better than the MT (Cross 1983, 140). These two aspects can be seen together by reference to the *acrostic pattern in which each chapter of Lamentations 1—4 is a complete acrostic. In the MT the poems of Lamentations 2—4 reverse the usual alphabetical order of the letters ʿayin and pê, while Lamentations 1 places the verses in this "normal" order. 4QLam, however, maintains the reverse order (pê then ʿayin) in the first poem. The MT's inconsistency may suggest that there were differences of sequence to the alphabet in some parts of society at the time (Jarick, 175).

There are two further manuscripts that appear to be related to Lamentations, and possibly dependent on it: 4QapocrLam A and 4QapocrLam B. Jarick (175) surmises that the existence of these alongside Lamentations points to a liturgical use with regard to commemoration of the destruction of Jerusalem.

3.4. Esther. Discussion of Esther is an argument from silence. There is no manuscript evidence of the book in the caves by the Dead Sea. In early years the explanations for this absence left open the possibility that some fragments might yet be identified with Esther. Publication in 1992 of an Aramaic text closely related to Esther (Milik 1992), later dubbed 4QProto-Esther, raised hopes that Esther had at last been found. Subsequent analysis is uniquely unanimous (for DSS studies) in the conclusion that this manuscript is not Esther, nor is it a source for the MT or Greek Esther, although it may be related much as are the Greek "additions," or as the *Prayer of Nabonidus* is to the book of Daniel (White Crawford 1996, 325). The new title given for this manuscript is "Tales from the Persian Court."

Given that the book of Esther is longer than the other little scrolls for which multiple copies survive, it now seems certain that no copy was ever present in the Qumran caves. This leaves open the question as to why Esther would be excluded. A common early conjecture was that its relation to *Purim had led to its rejection by the

anti-Hasmonean Qumran sectarians. This explanation still finds adherents (Jarick, 180), while S. Talmon (1995, 266) rejects ideological grounds to argue from rabbinic evidence that it simply had not yet achieved "canonical" status even by the third century AD. This begs the question as to the many other books present at Qumran that never achieved "canonical" status. This question remains open.

3.5. Ezra through 2 Chronicles (MT Order). Three fragments of a single manuscript of Ezra survived in Cave 4, dated to the middle of the first century BC (Ulrich 2000a, 291). Ezra 4:2-6, 9-11; 5:17-6:5 are preserved in extremely fragmentary form, with no more than about fifty words legible. What does survive is virtually identical to the MT, except for the correct forms of two scribal errors that appear in the MT.

A single fragment is all that remains of the books of the Chronicles, from 2 Chronicles 28:27—29:3, which is of a similar date to the Ezra manuscript. Two textual variants disagree with both the MT and the LXX. The fragment contains writing from the last lines of two columns, and the single word identifiable at the end of the first column does not correspond to any of the versions. This discrepancy could be explained as a citation of Chronicles in another work, which would be a strong argument for viewing Chronicles as an authoritative text. Trebolle Barrera finds this unlikely (Trebolle Barrera, 2000), suggesting rather that this text may be a fragment of a psalm or prayer, or is part of another historiographical work (Trebolle Barrera, *EDS* 1.129). Ulrich argues that if this is the case, it is evidence of the "canonical" status of Chronicles.

Missing from the manuscript evidence is any copy of Nehemiah—a fact often forgotten when the assertion is made that only Esther is not found in the Qumran caves. That said, it is reasonable to assume that Ezra and Nehemiah would have been found together in one scroll. The paucity of evidence for these works is worthy of comment. On the one hand, there is considerable evidence of interest in and affinity to Chronicler material in other Qumran manuscripts, such as the *Temple Scroll* (Swanson, 237-39), to indicate that these books were well known at Qumran. On the other hand, the lack of interest in copying the books may suggest that they did not yet have authoritative status, or perhaps had not yet reached their final form, that would put them an a par with other "canonical" books.

Considerations such as this reveal to what extent, when examining the manuscript evidence for each of the books in this section of the Hebrew Bible, we are looking at the formative period of "canon" development, a period that is not complete until well beyond the NT period.

See also CANON; TEXT, TEXTUAL CRITICISM.

BIBLIOGRAPHY. **M. Baillet,** "Textes des Grottes 2Q, 3Q, 6Q, 7Q à 10Q," in *Les "petites grottes" de Qumrân: Exploration de la falaise; les grottes 2Q, 3Q, 5Q, 6Q, 7Q à 10Q; le rouleau de cuivre* (2 vols.; DJD 3; Oxford: Clarendon Press, 1962) 1.45-164; **R. T. Beckwith,** "The Early History of the Psalter," *TynBul* 46 (1995) 1-27; **K. Beyer,** *Die aramäischen Texte vom Toten Meer: Samt den Inschriften aus Palästina, dem Testament Levis aus der Kairoer Genisa, der Fastenrolle und den alten talmudischen Zitaten; aramaistische Einleitung, Text, Übersetzung, Deutung, Grammatik/ Wörterbuch, deutsch-aramäische Wortliste, Register* (3 vols.; Göttingen: Vandenhoeck & Ruprecht, 1984-2004); **J. Blenkinsopp,** "Books of Ezra and Nehemiah," *EDSS* 1.284-85; **G. J. Brooke,** "The Psalms in Early Jewish Literature," in *The Psalms in the New Testament,* ed. S. Moyise and M. J. J. Menken (London and New York: T & T Clark International, 2004) 5-24; **F. M. Cross,** "Studies in the Structure of Hebrew Verse: The Prosody of Lamentations 1:1-22," in *The Word of the Lord Shall Go Forth: Essays in Honor of David Noel Freedman in Celebration of His Sixtieth Birthday,* ed. C. L. Myers and M. O'Connor (ASORSVS 1; Winona Lake, IN: Eisenbrauns, 1983) 129-55; idem, "Lamentations," in *Qumran Cave 4.XI: Psalms to Chronicles* (DJD 16: Oxford, Clarendon Press, 2000) 229-38; **U. Dahmen,** *Psalmen- und Psalter-Rezeption im Frühjudentum: Rekonstruktion, Textbestand, Struktur und Pragmatik der Psalmenrolle 11QPsª aus Qumran* (STDJ 49; Leiden: E. J. Brill, 2003); **R. de Vaux and J. T. Milik,** *Qumrân Grotte 4.II: I. Archéologie; II. Tefillin, Mezuzot et Targums (4Q128-4Q157)* (DJD 6; Oxford: Clarendon Press, 1977); **J. A. Fitzmyer,** "Some Observations on the Targum of Job from Qumran Cave 11," *CBQ* 36 (1974) 503-24 (= "The First-Century Targum of Job from Qumran Cave XI," in *A Wandering Aramean: Collected Aramaic Essays* [SBLMS 25; Missoula, MT: Scholars Press, 1979] 161-82); idem, "The Phases of the Aramaic Language," in *A Wandering Aramean: Collected Aramaic Essays* (SBLMS 25; Missoula, MT: Scholars Press, 1979) 57-84; **P. W. Flint,** *The Dead Sea Psalms Scrolls and the Book of Psalms* (STDJ 17; Leiden: E. J. Brill, 1997a); idem, "Appendix: Psalms Scrolls from the Judaean Desert," in *The Dead Sea Scrolls: Hebrew, Aramaic and Greek Texts with English Translations,* 4A: *Pseudepigraphic and non-Masoretic Psalms and Prayers,* ed. J. H. Charlesworth and H. W. L. Rietz (PTSDSSP; Tübingen: Mohr Siebeck; Louisville: Westminster John Knox, 1997b) 287-90; **U. Glessmer,** "Targumim," *EDSS* 2.915-18; **D. J. Harrington,** *Wisdom Texts from Qumran* (LDSS; London: Routledge, 1996); idem, "Mystery," *EDSS* 1.588-91; **J. Jarick,** "The Bible's 'Festival Scrolls' among the Dead Sea Scrolls," in *The Scrolls and the Scriptures: Qumran Fifty Years After,* ed. S. E. Porter and C. A. Evans (JSPSup 26; Sheffield: Sheffield Academic Press, 1997) 170-82; **N. Jastram,** "Book of Proverbs," *EDSS* 2.701-2; **J. Milik,** "Fragment d'une source du Psautier (4QPs89) et fragments de Jubilés, du Document de Damas, d'un phylactère dans la grotte 4 de Qumrân," *RB* 73 (1966) 93-104; idem, "Les modèles araméens du livre d'Esther dans la grotte 4 de Qumrân," *RevQ* 15 (1992) 321-99; idem, "Targum de Job," in *Qumrân grotte 4.II: I. Archéologie, II. Tefillin, Mezuzot et Targums (4Q 128–4Q157)* (DJD 6; Oxford: Clarendon Press, 1977), 89; **J. Muilenburg,** "A Qoheleth Scroll from Qumran," *BASOR* 135 (1954) 20-28; **C. A. Newsom,** "Book of Job," *EDSS* 1.412-13; **J. A. Sanders,** *The Psalms Scroll of Qumrân Cave 11 (11QPsª)* (DJD 4; Oxford: Clarendon Press, 1965); idem, "Variorum in the Psalms Scroll (11QPsª)," *HTR* 59 (1966) 83-94; idem, *The Dead Sea Psalms Scroll* (Ithaca, NY: Cornell University Press, 1967); **E. Schuller,** "Non-Canonical Psalms," in *Qumran Cave 4.VI: Poetic and Liturgical Texts, Part 1* (DJD 11; Oxford: Clarendon Press, 1998) 75-172; **P. W. Skehan,** "Qumran and Old Testament Textual Criticism," in *Qumrân: Sa piété, sa théologie et son milieu,* ed. M. Delcor (BETL 46; Paris: Duculot; Leuven: Leuven University Press, 1978) 163-82; idem, "Gleanings from Psalm Text from Qûmran," in *Mélanges bibliques et orientaux en l'honneur de M. Henri Cazelles,* ed. A. Caquot and M. Delcor (AOAT 212; Kevelaer: Butzon & Bercker; Neukirchen-Vluyn: Neukirchener Verlag, 1981) 439-52; **P. W. Skehan and E. Ulrich,** "Proverbs," in *Qumran Cave 4.XI: Psalms to Chronicles* (DJD 16; Oxford: Clarendon Press, 2000) 187-94; **P. W. Skehan, E. Ulrich and P. W. Flint,** "Psalms," in *Qumran Cave 4.XI: Psalms to Chronicles* (DJD 16; Oxford: Clarendon Press, 2000); **P. W. Skehan, E. Ulrich and**

J. E. Sanderson, *Qumran Cave 4.IV: Palaeo-Hebrew and Greek Biblical Manuscripts* (DJD 9; Oxford: Clarendon Press, 1992); **M. Sokoloff,** *The Targum to Job from Qumran Cave XI* (BSNELC; Ramat-Gan: Bar Ilan University, 1974); **D. D. Swanson,** *The Temple Scroll and the Bible: The Methodology of 11QT* (STDJ 14; Leiden: E. J. Brill, 1995); **S. Talmon,** "*Pisqeh be'emsa' pasuq* and 11QPs[a]," *Textus* 5 (1966) 11-21; idem, "Was the Book of Esther Known at Qumran?" *DSD* 2 (1995) 249-67; **E. Tov,** "Excerpted and Abbreviated Biblical Texts from Qumran," *RevQ* 16 (1995a) 581-600; idem, "Three Manuscripts (Abbreviated Texts?) of Canticles from Qumran Cave 4," *JJS* 46.1-2 (1995b) 88-111; **J. Trebolle Barrera,** "First and Second Books of Chronicles," *EDSS* 1:129; idem, "Chronicles," in *Qumran Cave 4.XI: Psalms to Chronicles* (DJD 16; Oxford: Clarendon Press, 2000) 295-97; **E. Ulrich,** *The Dead Sea Scrolls and the Origins of the Bible* (SDSSRL; Grand Rapids: Eerdmans; Leiden: E. J. Brill, 1999); idem, "Ezra," in *Qumran Cave 4.XI: Psalms to Chronicles* (DJD 16; Oxford: Clarendon Press, 2000a) 291-94; idem, "Qoheleth," in *Qumran Cave 4.XI: Psalms to Chronicles* (DJD 16; Oxford: Clarendon Press, 2000b) 221-28; **J. P. M. van der Ploeg,** "Le sens et un problème textuel du Ps LXXXIX," in *Mélanges bibliques et orientaux en l'honneur de M. Henri Cazelles,* ed. A. Caquot and M. Delcor (Neukirchen-Vluyn: Neukirchener Verlag, 1981) 471-81; **J. P. M. van der Ploeg and A. S. van der Woude,** *Le targum de Job de la grotte XI de Qumrân* (Leiden: E. J. Brill, 1971); **A. S. van der Woude,** "Targum of Job," *EDSS* 1.413-14; **G. Vermes,** *The Complete Dead Sea Scrolls in English* (London: Penguin, 2004); **S. White Crawford,** "Five Scrolls," *EDSS* 1.295-97; idem, "Has Esther Been Found at Qumran? Proto-Esther and the Esther Corpus," *RevQ* 17 (1996) 307-25; **G. Wilson,** *The Editing of the Hebrew Psalter* (SBLDS 76; Chico, CA: Scholars Press, 1985); idem, "The Qumran *Psalms Scroll* (11QPs[a]) and the Canonical Psalter: Comparison of Editorial Shaping," *CBQ* 59 (1997) 449-64.

D. D. Swanson

DEATH. *See* AFTERLIFE; CHAOS AND DEATH; DESTRUCTION; IMPRISONMENT IMAGERY.

DEBATE. *See* DISPUTATION.

DELIVERANCE. *See* SALVATION AND DELIVERANCE IMAGERY.

DEMOCRATIZATION OF PSALMS. *See* ROYAL COURT.

DESTRUCTION

The concept of destruction is expressed by more than a dozen Hebrew words within the OT books under study within the major Bible translations. For some of these terms, "destruction" is part of the primary semantic domain of the word itself, whereas for other terms (such as *bl[c]*, usually "swallow") the context of the passage suggests a figurative or metaphorical usage of the term signifying destruction. Depending on the term, a word translated as "destruction" in one Bible translation may be rendered in other translations with semantically similar terms such as "doom," "ruin," "desolation" and "annihilation." This semantic overlap can be further appreciated by noting that in the LXX, the Greek translation of the OT, one particular Greek verb is used to translate thirty-eight different Hebrew words related to destroying and destruction.

In addition, the image of destruction may be communicated through nominal or verbal clauses. In the case of nominal clauses, the image of destruction may overlap with that of a place of destruction or even a being of destruction, while in verbal instances, the verbs typically communicate a stative or factitive notion—that is, a (resulting) condition or state of being. This image of destruction usually applies to a physiological entity such as a person or an object, although immaterial notions such as human plans and ambitions may also come to destruction. In the case of individuals, the most common thread throughout the OT books under consideration is that unrighteous behavior (i.e., destructive actions) leads to divinely rendered destruction at the physical or metaphysical level. Lastly, while certain verbal roots such as *'bd* (usually "perish") may be moderately connected to the motif of destruction in certain contexts, they are more clearly related to this image when conjugated in the intensive verbal stems (notably the Piel stem).

1. Destruction in Psalms
2. Destruction in Wisdom Literature (Job, Proverbs, Ecclesiastes)
3. Destruction in Other Texts (Lamentations, Esther, Ruth, Song of Songs)
4. Destruction in Death and Beyond

1. Destruction in Psalms.

In the book of *Psalms the imagery of destruction is most frequently portrayed as the ultimate destiny of the sweeping category of the wicked (Ps 1:6; 9:5; 37:20, 38; 49:5-9; 68:2; 73:18-19; 92:7; 145:20). This presentation of destruction may be in contrast to the ultimate destiny of the righteous (e.g., Ps 1) or as a broader component of God's rebuke of the (unrighteous) nations (e.g., Ps 9). In addition, the appeal for YHWH to bring the wicked to destruction is found in several psalms that have elements of *imprecation (see Ps 35:8; 83:14-18; 143:12) or as part of the theological understanding of the psalmist wherein the wicked are also the afflicters of the righteous (Ps 55:23; 63:9). Destruction is also described in the psalms as the final destiny of liars (Ps 5:6), those who do not submit to God (Ps 2:12), the enemies of the righteous (Ps 9:3), and the enemies of God (Ps 9:6; 21:8-10; 92:9). Even the very names of God's enemies are subject to destruction (see Ps 9:5-6). Destruction is also the ultimate end for the (godless) plans of humankind (Ps 146:4) as well as the (godless) desires of the wicked (Ps 112:10) and the (godless) nations in general (Ps 10:16). The imagery of destruction is likewise employed to speak of the end of those who are far from God (Ps 73:27) and even of God's people who persist in unfaithfulness (Ps 80:3-16; also cf. Ps 106:17-18 with Num 16:30-33), as also reflected in several covenantal texts (e.g., Lev 26:38; Deut 28:20, 63). In addition, destruction is that which the tongue of the deceitful person devises (Ps 52:2), what the enemy of the righteous seeks to do to the righteous (Ps 38:12), and what constitutes the very inward parts of the wicked (Ps 5:9). The image of destruction is also used to describe what will eventually befall the heavens and the earth (Ps 102:25-26)—an aspect of God's righteous judgment precipitating the creation of a new heavens and earth. As such, this destruction of the earth is described as something warranting awe and praise (Ps 46:9). Lastly, destruction in the psalms is also portrayed as something that the faithful will not see (Ps 16:10) and that is mitigated by taking delight in YHWH's instruction, Torah (see Ps 119:92). Nevertheless, the avoidance of destruction by God's people is fundamentally a facet of God's compassion rather than human accomplishment (see Ps 57:1; 78:38; 106:23).

2. Destruction in Wisdom Literature (Job, Proverbs, Ecclesiastes).

In OT Wisdom literature (*Job, *Proverbs, *Ec-clesiastes) the motif of destruction is also frequently used to describe the final end of the wicked (Job 18:12; 21:30; Prov 6:12-15). Similarly, destruction is what will come to the "house" (i.e., posterity) of the wicked (Prov 14:11), the memory and name of the wicked (Job 18:17), the arm (i.e., strength, power, authority) of the wicked (Job 38:15), and the (godless) ambitions and desires of the wicked (Prov 10:28; 11:7). Destruction is also that which awaits liars and deceitful people (Job 6:15-18; Prov 19:9; 21:28), those who forget God (Job 8:11-13), and those who facilitate iniquity (Job 4:7-9; 31:2-3). Destruction is also portrayed as that which the unrighteous brings upon the good (Eccles 9:18), and that which befalls the wealth of the immoral person (Prov 29:3). The image of destruction also portrays the self-inflicted punishment of the adulterer (Prov 6:32). Destruction is also the destination of those who associate with unstable persons (see Prov 24:21-22) and those who do not respond to reproof (Prov 29:1). Moreover, it is the end result of God's judgment against sinful speech (Eccles 5:6). Lastly, note that destruction is commonly described in Wisdom literature as being preceded by pride and human arrogance (e.g., Job 20:4-9; Prov 16:18; 18:12; 29:1)—telltale attributes of the fool in wisdom texts (see also Ps 49, a wisdom psalm). Indeed, in the two-path focus of Wisdom literature (the way of the righteous and the way of the foolish), the path of the fool leads to destruction (see Prov 1:20-33). Similarly, it is the fool whose words destroy self (Eccles 10:12 [cf. Mt 15:18]), neighbor (Prov 11:9) and father (Prov 19:13). Hence, God mocks the looming destruction of fools who scorn his ways (Prov 1:26-27).

3. Destruction in Other Texts (Lamentations, Esther, Ruth, Song of Songs).

In the book of *Lamentations a wide range of terms is used to poetically describe the destruction of Jerusalem by the Babylonians in 586 BC. Such devastation is described as having come not only upon the city of Jerusalem (destruction "as vast as the sea" [Lam 2:13]) but also upon all the inhabitants of the southern kingdom (Lam 2:2), palaces (Lam 2:5), symbols of stability and *protection (Lam 2:9) and even the strength of the prophet Jeremiah (Lam 3:18). Much of this far-reaching image of destruction is summarized in Lamentations 3:47: "Terror and dread have come upon us; devastation and destruction."

Moreover, this imagery of destruction is also reflected in the poetic refrain of Lamentations 2—4: "because of the destruction of the daughter of my people" (Lam 2:11; 3:48; 4:10). Thus, it is not surprising to see that the imprecatory remarks in Lamentations look for the destruction of the enemies of God's people (see Lam 3:66). Yet, it must be emphasized that Lamentations makes it clear that YHWH destroyed Jerusalem's strongholds (Lam 2:5), his appointed meeting place (Lam 2:6) and Jerusalem's wall (Lam 2:8).

In the book of *Esther the image of destruction is used repeatedly in the context of Haman's plot against the Jews and subsequent decree by King *Ahasuerus authorizing the Jews to defend themselves. In both cases the imagery of destruction is commonly presented via a verbal trilogy *(šmd, ʾbd, hrg)* that underscores complete elimination. Thus, after the affront of *Mordecai, Haman's motive in approaching the king is that of bringing such complete destruction to all Jews (Esther 3:6-13). Mordecai's appeals to Esther via Hathach, the royal eunuch, stress this looming elimination of the Jews (Esther 4:7-8), and he reminds Esther that this destruction will be the fate of her father's house if she does not take action (Esther 4:14). Esther's appeal to King Ahasuerus stresses the potential destruction to her and her people as a result of Haman's plot (Esther 7:4), and the king's response (ironically) empowers the Jews (through the verbal triplicate noted above) to destroy their would-be assassins (Esther 8:11). Lastly, the Feast of *Purim relates specifically to Haman casting Pur (lot) with the intended outcome of the destruction of Jews and the implicit divine deliverance rendered via Mordecai and Esther (Esther 9:20-28).

In *Ruth and *Song of Songs attention to "destruction" is scarce, with the book of Ruth using the image to refer to the (first-in-line) *kinsman-redeemer's perception of what he would bring to his own inheritance by marrying Ruth (Ruth 4:6), and Song of Songs using destruction (Song 2:15) to describe what foxes do to vineyards (and hence that the beloved should come and catch these destructive foxes).

4. Destruction in Death and Beyond.

With respect to individuals (or groups such as ungodly nations), destruction is most commonly associated with death—that is, the (physical) destruction of a person's life that ends earthly existence. As such, this portrayal of destruction is found together with various images describing the state of death, such as dust, darkness, shadows and silence. In addition, destruction may also denote the place of the dead and is used in conjunction with notations of the underworld such as the grave, the pit, Sheol and Abaddon. Similarly, in the Talmud "Destruction" is one of the seven names for Gehenna. Moreover, note that Abaddon, Death and Sheol receive *personification in Job 28:22; Proverbs 27:20, giving rise to the sense of a being of destruction (cf. Rev 9:11). These observations aside, the question at hand is whether this physical image of destruction as death in these OT texts is solely the termination of life or whether the imagery of destruction in certain instances transcends beyond the grave and into the *afterlife—in other words, whether the physical portrayal of the destruction of individuals has metaphysical aspects as well that might be understood along the lines of an eschatological destruction. Certainly, the idea of perishing versus eternal life is a clear dichotomy in the NT, but whether this is seen in some sense in the OT texts under consideration is another issue. Moreover, the issue of poetic impact and stylistics cautions against forcing preconceived ideas onto earlier texts. Holding these caveats in mind, we may note that there are a number of texts (especially Davidic psalms) that may be expressing elements of an OT notion of the hereafter and at the very least are consistent with fuller biblical teachings on post-death actualities. For example, *David in Psalm 9 notes that YHWH has blotted out the name of the wicked "forever and ever" (Ps 9:5), and that the ultimate lot of such individuals is "unending ruin" (Ps 9:6; cf. Ps 55:23). In addition, although the iniquity of the wicked seems ever expanding, this reality is explained in light of God's intent to bring them to everlasting destruction (Ps 92:7). Moreover, David in Psalm 22 implies some type of post-death consciousness by noting that all who "go down to the dust" (i.e., die) will bow before the Lord (Ps 22:29). Conversely, David declares in Psalm 103 that YHWH will redeem the life of his people from the pit (Ps 103:4), and in Psalm 16 that YHWH will not abandon their souls to Sheol (Ps 16:10). Similarly, in the book of Job Elihu declares that God not only spares his people from the pit but also enlightens them with the "light of life" through ransom, redemption and acceptance (see Job

33:18-30). This is the same phraseology utilized by the Sons of Korah (*see* Asaph and Sons of Korah) in Psalm 49, which speaks of the impossibility of a person to redeem the soul of another "that he should live forever" but declares that God can do so—the ultimate solution to eternal destruction (see Ps 49:7-15). Lastly, note that the Hebrew expression "he will take me" *(yiqqāḥēnî)* in this psalm (Ps 49:15 [49:16 MT]) uses the same style of expression (i.e., God as subject taking his faithful servant to his presence) as that found when God takes Enoch to his presence in Genesis 5:24, and Elijah to his presence in 2 Kings 2:10-11.

See also AFTERLIFE; CHAOS AND DEATH; FEAR OF THE LORD; LIFE; RETRIBUTION; SUFFERING; WARFARE IMAGERY.

BIBLIOGRAPHY. **H. J. Austel**, "שָׁמַד," *TWOT* 2.935; **R. L. Harrison**, "אָבַד," *TWOT* 1.3-4; **E. Jenni**, "אבד," *TLOT* 1.13-15; **P. S. Johnston**, *Shades of Sheol: Death and Afterlife in the Old Testament* (Downers Grove, IL: InterVarsity Press, 2002); **O. Keel**, *The Symbolism of the Biblical World: Ancient Near Eastern Iconography and the Book of Psalms*, trans. T. J. Hallett (Winona Lake, IN: Eisenbrauns, 1997); **F. Merkel**, "Destroy, Perish, Ruin," *NIDNTT* 1.462-70; **E. H. Merrill**, "שָׁחַת," *NIDOTTE* 4.93-94; **R. E. Murphy**, "Šaḥat in the Qumran Literature," *Bib* 39 (1958) 61-66; **B. Otzen**, "אָבַד," *TDOT* 1.19-23; **J. Schüpphaus**, "בָּלַע," *TDOT* 2.136-39; **N. J. Tromp**, *Primitive Conceptions of Death and the Nether World in the Old Testament* (BibOr 21; Rome: Pontifical Biblical Institute, 1969); **C. Van Dam**, "אֵיד," *NIDOTTE* 1.371; **L. Wächter**, "שָׁחַת," *TDOT* 14.595-99.

F. J. Mabie

DEVOTIONAL INTERPRETATION. *See* HERMENEUTICS.

DIRGE. *See* LAMENTATIONS 1: BOOK OF.

DISCOURSE IN PROVERBS

In contrast to the "sentence" literature of *Proverbs (the two-line aphorisms that make up the bulk of Prov 10–29), the "discourses" are extended texts of more than a single verse that carry forward a sustained argument. A text such as Proverbs 11:2 ("Pride comes and disgrace comes, but with the humble is wisdom") is an individual proverb, but a text such as Proverbs 1:8-19 is a sustained discourse on criminal gangs. The word *discourse* is somewhat misleading in that such texts are always poetry and never prose. But there are *wisdom poems that are not discursive in nature, and thus not every wisdom poem is a discourse.

1. The Two Discourse Types
2. The Great Appeal: Proverbs 1:8—9:18
3. The Young Man as Implied Reader
4. Structure and Interpretation within the Parental Discourses
5. The Date of the Composition of the Discourses

1. The Two Discourse Types.

1.1. Formal Characteristics. Two types of discourse are found in Proverbs. The first and most common is the parental appeal, in which a parent urges a son or sons to be obedient to the precepts of wisdom (e.g., Prov 1:8-19). Proverbs 4:3 indicates that the parent who makes the appeals in Proverbs 1—9 is the father, although the mother is also mentioned (Prov 1:8; 6:20). The second type is the wisdom appeal, in which Woman Wisdom (*see* Woman Wisdom and Woman Folly), a *personification of the ideal of wisdom, calls on the young man to heed her instruction (e.g., Prov 1:20-33). M. Fox (1997) argues that these two—the father with his plain-spoken appeals and Woman Wisdom with her heavenly perspective—speak in counterpoint. The practical advice of the father draws upon and is vindicated by the sublime truth that fills all creation.

Parental appeals usually have several formal features. First, there is an entreaty to listen, which typically has three parts: (1) the implied parent calls out to the implied son (usually calling him "My son"); (2) the parent exhorts the son(s) to listen ("Hear, O sons, a father's instruction" [Prov 4:1]); (3) the parent gives some general reasons that the son should listen ("I give to you good traditional teaching" [Prov 4:2]).

Second, the entreaty to listen is followed by the main body of the appeal. This typically encourages the young man to seek wisdom and to flee from some specific evil (such as criminal behavior or immoral women). The main appeal usually offers the young man an explanation or motivation for doing what is right (such as in Prov 4:6: "Love her [wisdom], and she will guard you"). Although the main body is generally dominated by commands and prohibitions, other types of speech are present. For example, Proverbs 7:6-23 is a lengthy anecdote on a young man's fall into immorality, and Proverbs 2 is essentially a large conditional statement (if the young man embraces wisdom, he will be saved from evil and trouble). Proverbs 4:1-9 includes a retrospective on the teacher's childhood. Two appeals, at Proverbs 5:1-23; 7:1-27, contain a secondary entreaty to listen within the body of the appeal.

Third, parental appeals end with a summarizing conclusion in the form of one or more proverbs (as in Prov 3:35: "The wise will inherit honor, but fools gain disgrace"; Prov 4:19: "The way of the wicked is darkness; they do not know over what they stumble"). The summarizing conclusion is not always present. Proverbs 4:20-27 has as its body (in Prov 4:23-27) a series of exhortations to persevere in the task of achieving virtue; its ending at Proverbs 4:27 is part of that series and is not a summarizing conclusion. Thus, as is common, not every text has all the formal features for its type. Biblical poets did not write according to a template.

It is very important, nevertheless, to distinguish the entreaty to listen from the body of the appeal. Entreaties to listen are not unimportant, but the interpreter who tries to determine the topic of a passage from the entreaty to listen will be confused and probably will focus on the wrong issues. The actual topic—the main thing that the teacher wants to get across—is found in the main body.

The formal pattern of the wisdom appeal is similar to that of the parental appeal. It begins with an introduction to Woman Wisdom, presenting her in a public place calling out to young men who pass by (as in Prov 1:20: "Wisdom cries aloud in the plaza, in the markets she raises her voice"). In the body of the appeal Woman Wisdom speaks in the first person, describing her qualities, promising benefits to those who listen, and issuing warnings to scoffers (as in Prov 1:24-26: "Because I called and you refused to listen . . . I will mock when what you dread comes"). Finally, the wisdom appeal concludes with a series of proverbs (such as Prov 1:32-33).

As indicated above, not every wisdom poem can be called a discourse. There are also wisdom epigrams, which, although more expansive than a single proverb, do not have the discursive features of introduction, sustained argument and appeal, and conclusion. An example of a wisdom epigram is Proverbs 30:11-14, which lists four types of wicked people (cursers of parents,

the unrepentant, the proud, the violent). The epigram, in Proverbs, is essentially a poetic list of virtues or vices.

1.2. The Parental Appeals. Various scholars divide the text somewhat differently (see, e.g., the structural analyses in Murphy; Fox 2000; Waltke; Longman). Based on the criteria described above, however, we can say that the discourses of Proverbs include the following parental appeals:

Proverbs 1:8-19: Avoid the violent life of the criminal gang
Entreaty to listen: 1:8
Body: 1:9-16 (the appeal of the gang in this section forms an inclusion with the appeal of Woman Folly in 9:13-18)
Conclusion: 1:17-19 (a proverb based in fowling at 1:17, with commentary in 1:18, and a second concluding proverb in 1:19: rapacious greed is fatal)

Proverbs 2:1-22: Wisdom protects against temptations from criminal men and immoral women
Entreaty to listen/Body: 2:1-20 (a general call to listen, with the allurements of crime in 2:12-15 and of promiscuity in 2:16-19 representing the two great temptations to the young man)
Conclusion: 2:21-22 (two proverbs: the upright will live, and the wicked will die)

Proverbs 3:1-12: Exhortations to faithfulness, humility and piety
Entreaty to listen: 3:1-4
Body: 3:5-11 (the explicit admonitions to piety here—trusting the Lord in 3:5, making regular offerings in 3:9—are quite unusual in Proverbs)
Conclusion: 3:12 (a proverb: the Lord reproves those whom he loves)

Proverbs 3:21-35: Behaving rightly toward one's neighbors
Entreaty to listen: 3:21-26
Body: 3:27-34 (the exhortations here focus on respecting the rights of others)
Conclusion: 3:35 (a proverb: the wise get honor, and fools get disgrace)

Proverbs 4:1-9: Wisdom is a heritage worth maintaining from generation to generation

Entreaty to listen: 4:1-2

Body: 4:3-6, with a resumption at 4:8-9 (the teacher's recollection of his childhood sets his appeals for the young man to pursue wisdom in the context of a family heritage)

Conclusion: 4:7 (a proverb: the beginning of wisdom is determination to get it, with an exhortation at 4:8-9 that resumes the appeals of the body)

Proverbs 4:10-19: The two ways

Entreaty to listen: 4:10

Body: 4:11-17 (the way of wisdom, full of life, is contrasted with the way of evil, full of restlessness and then death)

Conclusion: 4:18-19 (two proverbs: the wise are in light, but the wicked stumble in darkness)

Proverbs 4:20-27: Persevere in maintaining integrity

Entreaty to listen: 4:20-22

Body: 4:23-27 (the exhortation to moral integrity and clarity of purpose employs metaphors from the body: heart, mouth, eyes, feet)

Conclusion: Not present

Proverbs 5:1-23: Flee the sexual enticements of the immoral woman

Entreaty to listen: 5:1-2, with a secondary entreaty to listen at 5:7 that makes more urgent the appeal to flee from the promiscuous woman

Body: 5:3-6, 8-20 (sexual pleasures—the real but deadly kind from the immoral woman and the wholesome kind from the good wife—are at the heart of this text)

Conclusion: 5:21-23 (three proverbs to the effect that the Lord watches human behavior so that the wicked die in their folly)

Proverbs 6:20-35: Adultery leads to death

Entreaty to listen: 6:20-23

Body: 6:24-33 (the focus is on the suffering that immorality brings)

Conclusion: 6:34-35 (a proverb and comment asserting that a jealous husband has implacable fury)

Proverbs 7:1-27: An example of a young man

destroyed by an immoral woman

Entreaty to listen: 7:1-5, with a secondary entreaty to listen at 7:24, again emphasizing how earnestly the father wants theyoung man to avoid promiscuity

Body: 7:6-23, 25-26 (an anecdote explaining how easily a young man is taken in by the promiscuous woman)

Conclusion: 7:27 (a proverb: the prostitute's house is the way to death)

Proverbs 31:1-9: Warnings on women and wine to King Lemuel from his mother.

Entreaty to listen: 31:2

Body: 31:3-9 (a king should not use his power to indulge in women and wine)

Conclusion: Not present

Proverbs 2:1-22 is unusual in that the entire body of the appeal is one great entreaty to listen. Thus, the formal entreaty to listen and the body are combined here. This is very significant for the macrostructure of Proverbs 1:8–9:18, as described below.

Proverbs 31:1-9 is slightly unusual in that it specifically names the addressee (although we do not actually know who *Lemuel was) and in that it is expressly from the young man's mother rather than his father. Formally, its entreaty to listen (Prov 31:2: "What, my son? And what, O son of my womb? And what, O son of my vows?") is unlike those we see in the other parental appeals (such as "My son, give heed to my wisdom" in Prov 5:1). But the "What?" is rhetorical. It is an implied call for the son to reflect on how he should live and thus is, in effect, an entreaty for him to listen. This text also lacks the proverbial conclusion, but not every parental appeal has that. Even so, the teaching of Lemuel's mother is explicitly a parental appeal, and formally it sufficiently fits the pattern. Clearly, it was not composed with those in Proverbs 1–9 (as Proverbs itself indicates) and is not part of that collection, but it is the same type of text. Proverbs 31:10-31, the poem in praise of the virtuous wife, should not be considered part of the appeal by Lemuel's mother. The "virtuous wife" is a self-contained poem (it is an alphabetic *acrostic) that has nothing in common with Proverbs 31:1-9. It is in fact a large epigram, listing all the virtues and benefits of the good wife. Significantly, Proverbs 31:1-9 is for a king while Proverbs 31:10-31 concerns a middle-class bourgeois household. Apparently, the poem of the virtuous wife was thought to be a fitting conclusion to the whole of Proverbs; it has no specific tie to the teaching of Lemuel's mother.

Proverbs 6:1-19 is not a parental appeal. The passage begins with "My son," but after that it moves into five discrete epigrams (entanglements in loans [Prov 6:1-5]; the lessons of the ant [Prov 6:6-8]; the nature of the sluggard [Prov 6:9-11]; the marks of a schemer [Prov 6:12-15]; aspects of immoral behavior as described by metonymy with the human body [Prov 6:16-19]). The disjointed nature of this passage is unlike what we see elsewhere in the parental appeals, and it appears that the five epigrams have been collected here and given the heading "My son" for the sake of giving the collection a formal parallel to the adjacent parental appeals.

We should observe that there is a good deal of variety in the parental appeals. Proverbs 5:1-23; 6:20-35; 7:1-27 all warn against going to the immoral woman, but each does so in a distinctive manner. In Proverbs 5:1-23 the alluring but deadly enticements of the prostitute are set in contrast to the wholesome sexual pleasures of the good wife. In Proverbs 6:20-35 the focus is on how an affair with another man's wife leads to disgrace and ruin (in particular because of the anger of the cuckolded husband). Proverbs 7:1-27 is a story, almost a morality play, on the fall of the naïve young man to the wiles of the promiscuous woman.

1.3. The Wisdom Appeals. There are three wisdom appeals in Proverbs:

Proverbs 1:20-33: The calamities that befall those who reject Woman Wisdom
Introduction: 1:20-21 (Wisdom cries out in the streets)
Body: 1:22-31 (When calamity strikes, Wisdom mocks those who scorned her)
Conclusion: 1:32-33 (two proverbs: the fools are destroyed by folly, but the prudent are secure)

Proverbs 8:1-36: Woman Wisdom recommends herself by describing her benefits and her origin with Yahweh
Introduction: 8:1-3 (Wisdom calls out at the gates and crossroads)
Entreaty to listen: 8:4-11
Body: 8:12-33 (8:12-21 describes Wisdom's benefits—she gives shrewdness, ability to govern, wealth—and 8:22-31 describes her origin with God)
Secondary entreaty to listen: 8:32-33
Conclusion: 8:34-36 (three proverbs, beginning with a beatitude and followed by two sayings that those who find wisdom live and those who do not die)

Proverbs 9:1-18: A final appeal from Woman Wisdom is set in contrast to an appeal from Woman Folly
Introduction to Woman Wisdom: 9:1-3 (Wisdom has built her house, made a sacrifice, and invites young men to come)
Body of Woman Wisdom's Appeal: 9:4-6
Conclusion: 9:7-12 (six proverbs asserting that scoffers are incorrigible, that the *fear of the Lord is the beginning of wisdom, that wisdom gives life, and that everyone must choose which path to take and bear the results)
Introduction to Woman Folly: 9:13-15 (she is loud, seductive, and calls to passers-by)
Body of Woman Folly's Appeal: 9:16-17
Conclusion: 9:18 (the fool does not know that her way leads to death)

Proverbs 9:1-18, the last appeal of Proverbs 1—9, is striking for setting Woman Wisdom against Woman Folly and for ending Woman Wisdom's appeal with six proverbs, making it the longest conclusion of any appeal. These proverbs reiterate the main theme of the book: the fear of the Lord is the beginning of wisdom. They also segregate humanity into two camps, the scoffers and the wise, forcing the reader to choose between the two. Woman Folly, calling out in the street to men who pass by, clearly is modeled on the street prostitute. By contrast, the good wife who concludes the whole book (at Prov 31:10-31) is in a sense the real counterpart to the personification Woman Wisdom (so also the good wife as lover in Prov 5:18-19 corresponds to "loving" and "embracing" Woman Wisdom at Prov 4:6-8). The implication is that promiscuity and adultery are the quickest way to folly, while marital fidelity to the good wife concretely works out the young man's path to wisdom.

There is also a brief hymn to wisdom in Proverbs 3:13-18. The hymn has an implied but no direct appeal to seek wisdom, and Woman Wisdom herself does not speak. Thus, it cannot be considered a wisdom appeal. It would not appear to be part of the parental appeal of Proverbs 3:1-12, both because the topic of that text is distinct from the topic of the wisdom hymn and because Proverbs 3:12 fulfills the role of a concluding proverb. The wisdom hymn is an interlude, and it anticipates the portrayal of Woman Wisdom with its account of the relationship of wisdom to creation in Proverbs 8:22-31.

2. The Great Appeal: Proverbs 1:8—9:18.
When viewed as a whole, Proverbs 1:8—9:18 has the same structure as the parental appeal, with an entreaty to listen, a main body of teaching and exhortation, and a conclusion. We might call this text the "Great Appeal." The entreaty to listen is in Proverbs 2:1-22, in which, as described above, the entire main body is a call for the young man to give heed. The main body of the Great Appeal (Prov 3:1—8:36) is in three parts, with each part containing one or more parental appeals but each terminating in a text that is not a parental appeal (first in the wisdom hymn [Prov 3:13-20], then in the ethical epigrams [Prov 6:1-19], then in Woman Wisdom's great appeal [Prov 8:1-36]). The three parts progress from a foundational appeal to maintain piety and humility, to the core lessons of the text, then to a reemphasis on the need to avoid promiscuity. The wisdom appeal in Proverbs 9:1-12, with its final series of six proverbs (Prov 9:7-12), fulfills the part of the summarizing conclusion.

The Great Appeal is bounded, moreover, by a two-part prologue (Prov 1:8-33) and, as an epilogue, the appeal of Woman Folly (Prov 9:13-18). The prologue and epilogue are decidedly dark in tone, beginning with the appeal of the criminal gang (Prov 1:8-19) and ending with the appeal of the prostitute-like Woman Folly (Prov 9:13-18). Even Woman Wisdom's prologue speech is dark, focusing on the destruction that befalls those who reject her (Prov 1:20-33). The prologue and epilogue present corruption and death as the stark alternative to the Great Appeal.

Within the Great Appeal, several common elements tie the whole together. These include the aforementioned parallel between the gang's appeal and Woman Folly's appeal, reference to Woman Wisdom at creation in Proverbs 3:19-20; 8:22-31, as well as the presentation of ethical behavior via the metonymy of body parts in Proverbs 4:23-27; 6:16-19. Thus the structure of the Great Appeal is as follows:

1. Prologue (Prov 1:8-33)
The appeal of the gang and the death that it brings (Prov 1:8-19)
Woman Wisdom scorns all who reject her (Prov 1:20-33)
2. Entreaty to Listen: The benefits of heeding wisdom with an implied warning against the temptations of criminal men and immoral women (Prov 2:1-22)
3. Body of Discourse (Prov 3:1—8:36)
First series of ethical and sapiential lessons: foundational matters (Prov 3:1-20)
Maintain humility and piety (Prov 3:1-12)
The hymn to wisdom (Prov 3:13-20)
Second series of ethical and sapiential lessons: core teachings (Prov 3:21—6:19)
Respect for one's neighbors (Prov 3:21-35)
Maintain the family tradition of wisdom (Prov 4:1-9)
Understand the two ways (Prov 4:10-19)
Maintain integrity (Prov 4:20-27)
Flee the immoral woman (Prov 5:1-23)
Ethical epigrams (Prov 6:1-19)
Third series of ethical and sapiential lessons: the special danger of the immoral woman against the glory of Woman Wisdom (Prov 6:20—8:36)
Adultery leads to death (Prov 6:20-35)
An example story of the immoral woman (Prov 7:1-27)
Woman Wisdom's great appeal (Prov 8:1-36)
Conclusion
Woman Wisdom's final appeal with six concluding proverbs (Prov 9:1-12)
Epilogue: the appeal of Woman Folly and the death that she brings (Prov 9:13-18)

Other scholars, of course, have different analyses of the structure of Proverbs 1–9. B. Waltke, for example, argues that it is a *chiasm in eight parts, while other scholars see in these chapters no macrostructure at all.

3. The Young Man as Implied Reader.
The fixation in these appeals on the immoral woman as the source of personal destruction perhaps seems odd to the modern reader. Do these appeals originate in a misogynistic dread of women? Does the text imply that women are

lustful, but that young men, if not corrupted by women, are innocent? We should bear in mind that the addressee in the discourses is the young man (always called "my son" [the NRSV's "my child" in, e.g., Prov 1:8; 2:1; 3:1, is misleading and unfortunate]). The nature of the addressees, that they are young men and not some other group (young women, small children, slaves, elderly people), determines the content of the address. The two principal moral dangers to the young man are the enticement to easy money through crime and the enticement to easy sex through the prostitute. The first temptation that the book actually addresses, in Proverbs 1:8-19, is the appeal to join a violent gang. If the addressees in Proverbs were young women, we may presume, the content of these appeals would be substantially different.

4. Structure and Interpretation within the Parental Discourses.

The interpretation of the parental appeals is generally not difficult. They directly call on the young man to flee immorality, to heed wise teachers, and to fear God. By contrast, the identity and literary origin of the figure of Woman Wisdom is much debated. Suggestions include that she is a personification of divine omniscience, that she is a personification of the wisdom that God built into the world, that she is an Israelite version of *Maat (the Egyptian goddess of justice and order), that she is a literary antagonist to the Canaanite fertility goddess, and that she is a demythologized Israelite goddess (see Whybray). Early Christians uniformly took her to be the Logos, the second person of the Trinity. For all this, the essential message of her appeals—the young man should learn and obey the precepts of wisdom—is not obscure.

5. The Date of the Composition of the Discourses.

The date and *Sitz im Leben* for the composition of the discourses is disputed. Many scholars have argued (or assumed) that the complex discourses are a later, evolutionary development from an earlier stage in which sages taught with pithy aphorisms and proverbs. There is, however, no reason to think that discourses were a later historical development and that the individual proverbs were earlier (as Kitchen has demonstrated, discourses and aphorisms appear together in ancient wisdom texts from the very

beginning). Discursive wisdom certainly antedates the Israelite monarchy (analogous appeals occur in, for example, the teaching of The Eloquent Peasant from the Middle Kingdom of Egypt—a full millennium prior to the reign of *Solomon). W. McKane argues that the discourse genre of Proverbs 1—9 was brought into Israel from Egypt during the reign of Solomon. But, again, the proverb form is found also in early Egyptian wisdom literature. The important point here is that neither the discourse nor the aphorism, as a formal genre, can be said to antedate the other.

On the other hand, Fox (2000) argues that Proverbs 1—9 is later than Proverbs 10—29, not on the grounds of formal genre but on the grounds that in Proverbs the discourses are written as an introduction for the aphorisms. Responding to C. Maier, who argues on the basis of the social conditions evident in Proverbs 1—9 that these chapters come from the Achaemenid period, Fox demonstrates that nothing in these chapters distinctively corresponds to what we know of life in Judea under the Persians. Maier, for example, claims that attacks on the "strange woman" in Proverbs are motivated by the concerns over exogamy in evidence in Nehemiah 13:23-27. But, as Fox remarks, the strange woman of Proverbs is not a foreigner and is not trying to marry the foolish young man. Fox himself argues that Proverbs 1—9 comes from the Hellenistic era, on the grounds that these chapters appear to have come from an intellectually cosmopolitan age. This is indeed the case, but the intellectual environment of Proverbs is decidedly more classical Egyptian than Hellenistic. A. Steinmann argues on linguistic grounds that Proverbs 1—9 is an early text and dates from the Solomonic period. Ultimately, however, the provenance of Proverbs 1—9 must be examined within the framework of a larger discussion of the date and origin of the book of Proverbs as a whole.

See also FORM CRITICISM; RHETORICAL CRITICISM.

BIBLIOGRAPHY. **M. Fox,** "Ideas of Wisdom in Proverbs 1-9," *JBL* 116 (1997) 613-33; idem, *Proverbs 1-9* (AB 18A; New York: Doubleday, 2000); **K. A. Kitchen,** "Proverbs and Wisdom Books of the Ancient Near East," *TynBul* 28 (1977) 69-114; **T. Longman III,** *Proverbs* (BCOTWP; Grand Rapids: Baker, 2006); **C. Maier,** *Die "fremde Frau" in Proverbien 1-9: Eine exegetische und sozialge-*

schichtliche Studie (OBO 144; Göttingen: Vandenhoeck & Ruprecht, 1995); **W. McKane,** *Proverbs: A New Approach* (OTL; Philadelphia: Westminster, 1970); **R. Murphy,** *Proverbs* (WBC 22; Nashville: Thomas Nelson, 1998); **A. Stein-mann,** "Proverbs 1-9 as a Solomonic Composition," *JETS* 43 (2000) 659-74; **B. Waltke,** *The Book of Proverbs: Chapters 1-15* (NICOT; Grand Rapids: Eerdmans, 2004); **R. N. Whybray,** *The Book of Proverbs: A Survey of Modern Study* (HBI 1; Leiden: E. J. Brill, 1995).   D. A. Garrett

DISPUTATION

The term *disputation* indicates an argument between two or more parties (Murphy, 175-76). Another term for this is *debate*. A disputation centers on an issue for which the parties present arguments in favor of their opinion. Disputes can be rational and reasoned, passionate and angry, or a combination of the two. A literary disputation allows for the presentation of two or more sides of an issue. The dispute could end without resolution, but if it does come to a conclusion, then the genre serves the purpose of showing how one position on a matter is better than another.

The disputation form occurs in different parts of biblical literature. The prophets, for example, often used disputation to challenge their audience to confront their betrayal of God and his *law (Graffy). Malachi, in particular, is shaped by six individual disputations (Mal 1:2-5; 1:6—2:9; 2:10-16; 2:17—3:5; 3:6-12; 3:13—4:3). The prophetic corpus, however, is outside the scope of the present volume. Accordingly, this article focuses on the use of disputation in the book of *Job.

The genre of Job as a whole has been variously identified, some even concluding that it is *sui generis*. There is no question, however, that the book heavily depends on the debate form to carry forward its message. Thus, it is important to explore the nature of the genre to understand the book of Job.

1. Disputation in Job
2. The Scope of Disputation in Job
3. Resolution
4. The Rhetorical Function of Disputation
5. Ancient Near Eastern Disputation
6. Summary

1. Disputation in Job.
Job clearly contains disputation in Job 4—27.

Disagreement exists over how extensive the form is in the book. We will consider some other candidates for this literary label after describing the argument between Job and his friends. As we enter the discussion, we should note that the disputation form itself utilizes many different literary forms and devices. R. Alden (35) names the following: "word pictures, metaphors, similes, tightly reasoned logic, prayers, irony, insults, insinuations, protestations, exaggerations, fabrications, and interrogations." In addition, the author of Job makes extensive use of complaints, laments and lawsuits.

1.1. Job and His Three Friends (Job 4—27).
The heart of the book of Job features a disputation between Job and his three friends. The argument begins in Job 4 in the context of Job's *suffering. The prose preface of the book introduces Job as a pious man who enjoys the blessings of God. An accuser ("the *Satan") raises questions about Job's motivation, suggesting to God that his godly behavior is motivated by reward and not by true devotion. God then allows Satan to afflict Job in two phases (Job 1:13-22; 2:7-10) to see if Job would turn against God. Job passes the test, whereupon he is visited by three friends: Eliphaz, Bildad and Zophar. They come to console him and sit with him for seven days in silence (Job 2:11-13).

Finally, the silence is broken by Job, who utters a heartrending lament, bemoaning his condition and wishing he would die, indeed that he had never been born (Job 3). This lament transforms Job's comforters into disputants as they argue over the cause of and solution to his suffering. This debate continues from Job 4 to Job 27 and takes place in three rounds with each of the three friends speaking in turn with Job responding to them individually.

1.1.1. The Issue: Wisdom. It is true that Job's suffering is the trigger of the argument, but a deeper issue emerges as the debate proceeds. As they offer opinions about the cause and solution to Job's suffering, the friends present themselves as wise men. On one level, wisdom is a very practical concept in the ancient Near East, including ancient Israel. Wisdom involved a skill of living, knowing how to maximize success and minimize problems, and how to get out of a problem as quickly and easily as possible. The admonitions, warnings and observations of Proverbs 10—31, for example, serve the purpose of giving principles of living that allow for such success.

The three friends claim to have the wisdom necessary to help Job. They identify Job's problem as sin. They operate with the assumption that sin leads to suffering. They reason, then, that people who sin will suffer, and they go on to state that it follows that if people suffer, then they must be sinners. Thus, to them, the conclusion is obvious. Job suffers; therefore, he is a sinner (Job 4:7-11; 5:5-7; 8:3-4; 11:6; 15:3-5; 18:5-21; 20:4-29; 22:6-11). The solution follows on the diagnosis. If sin is the problem, then repentance is the answer (Job 5:17-27; 8:5-7; 11:13-20; 22:21-30). Thus, they pound away on Job, asserting that he is a sinner in need of repentance.

On the other side of the debate stands Job. He responds angrily to the three friends. He has not sinned so as to deserve his present fate (Job 6:24-30; 10:1-7). He decisively rejects their argument and offers a different perspective. God is unfair (Job 9:21-24); indeed, he reverses proper *retribution (Job 12:4-6; 21:4-16). Interestingly, Job shares the three friends' retribution theology (God punishes the wicked and rewards the righteous) but believes that God has made a mistake (or worse, is unjust) in his case. Job too positions himself as a wise man over against their claim. He believes that he knows the answer to his problem: he must confront God (Job 13:3, 22-27; 22:2-12; 31:35-37), even though at times he says that even this tactic will be futile (Job 9:15-31). Occasionally, he will express the wish for an arbiter—someone who can intercede on his behalf with God—but none ever comes (Job 9:33-35).

The debate has four participants but really only two viewpoints. If there are differences between the arguments of the three friends, they are subtle at best. The three really represent one position, thus raising the question of why the book creates three rather than one debating partner for Job (see 5.2 below). Of course, having three attackers gives the impression of "piling on." It may also register the fact that the friends' viewpoint is the dominant viewpoint of the culture of the day. Further, since Job outlasts the three friends—he keeps talking even after they stop (Job 28—31)—it also is a literary strategy showing the inadequacy of their side of the debate.

Thus, the debate centers on Job's suffering. Deeper down, however, the real issue is the question of the source of wisdom. Where can wisdom be found?

1.1.2. Who Is Wise? At the heart of the debate between Job and his three friends is this question: Who is wise? Who has the correct insight into Job's suffering? Both Job and the friends set themselves up as sources of wisdom and ridicule the wisdom of the other.

Many of the speeches begin with sarcastic dismissals of the perspective of the other disputant: "How long will you say such things? Your words are a blustering wind" (Bildad [Job 8:2]); "Will your idle talk reduce men to silence?" (Zophar [Job 11:2a]); "I have heard many things like these; miserable comforters are you all! Will your long-winded speeches never end?" (Job [Job 16:2]). Often the barbs are directed specifically to the wisdom of the opponent: "But a witless man can no more become wise than a wild donkey's colt can be born a man" (Zophar, directed to Job [Job 11:12]); "Doubtless you are the people, and wisdom will die with you!" (Job to Zophar [Job 12:2]).

Many other examples could be given (Job 12:12; 13:1-2, 12; 18:1-4; 26:2-4), but the most interesting and involved of these insults appears at Job 15:1-13. After stating that Job's mind is filled with "empty notions" and his words are "the hot east wind" (Job 15:2), Eliphaz levels a number of questions at him: "Are you the first man ever born? Were you brought forth before the hills? Do you listen in on God's council? Do you limit wisdom to yourself? What do you know that we do not know? What insights do you have that we do not have?" (Job 15:7-9). These questions imply that Job is claiming great wisdom for himself. The charge that Job thinks that he was the first one ever born not only is associated with the ancient idea that wisdom is connected to old age but also more pointedly suggests that Job is identifying with none other than *Woman Wisdom herself, who was born before the hills (Prov 8:22-31).

Thus, the center of the dispute has to do with who is wise. As they seek to diagnose and remedy Job's problem, they all—Job and his friends—claim wisdom for themselves and deny it to their opponent(s).

1.1.3. The End of the Debate between Job and His Three Friends. The debate ends, unresolved, in Job 27. Neither Job nor the three friends give in to their opponents. The three friends simply go silent. Indeed, the third cycle of the debate (Job 22—27) already indicates that the friends are running out of arguments. In the first two cycles all three friends offered robust speeches that were filled with sometimes angry and always urgent language. The third cycle begins with a strong speech by Eliphaz that questions Job's piety and wisdom, but it is noticeably shorter than the first two (first speech [Job 4—5]: 48 verses; second speech [Job 15]: 35 verses; third speech [Job 22]: 30 verses). Bildad's third speech is a shadow of his earlier self (6 verses [Job 25]; 22 verses [Job 8]; 21 verses [Job 18]. Zophar's speeches in the first two rounds were fiery and substantial (20 verses [Job 11]; 29 verses [Job 20]). In the third cycle he may be completely absent (there is a debate over whether Job 27:13-23 belongs to Zophar rather than Job [see Newsom; Zerafa]). With no further arguments from the friends, Job surprisingly turns to a beautiful meditation on the divine origin of wisdom (Job 28), but then he reverts to a negative view of life in a lamenting protestation of innocence and call for God to hear his case (Job 29—31).

2. The Scope of Disputation in Job.

When one thinks of disputation in Job, the debate between Job and his three friends springs immediately to mind. However, other parts of the book also have qualities of a debate, though they are not as fully developed.

2.1. God versus the Satan (Job 1—2). The prologue introduces the reader to a character who is given not a name but rather a title, "the *Satan." Many English versions give the impression that this figure is the devil (NIV, NLT, NRSV), but there are significant reasons to doubt that this is the proper name for the devil, most notably the fact that the term in question is prefixed with the definite article (*haśśāṭān*, "the satan"), thus precluding it from being a proper name. It is much more likely that this figure is one of God's angelic associates who takes the position of "devil's advocate," so to speak, but is not Satan himself (*see* Divine Council). The title means "the Accuser," which is the role that he takes in reference to Job.

The Accuser has just returned to the heavenly court to give God a report on activities on earth. God asks specifically concerning Job and remarks about his piety. The Accuser gainsays not God's evaluation of Job but rather the motivation for Job's piety. This triggers a debate of sorts between God and the Accuser that results in a test to see who is right. The debate is civil and marked by God's quick willingness to agree

to terms proposed by the Accuser.

The relationship between God and the Accuser is one of a dispute, but it is only important to initiate the plot and lead to the more substantial disputation between Job and the friends and ultimately to the divine responses. After all, somewhat surprisingly, God does not address the Accuser at the end of the book, though what God says in the epilogue (Job 42:6-17) gives the impression that the Accuser lost the debate.

2.2. Elihu (Job 32—37). After the debate between Job and his three friends Elihu steps into the silence (Job 32—37). He is irritated at the inability of the three to convince Job of his error. He is young and therefore had deferred to the older men, but now he appeals not to experience and observation but rather to "the spirit in a man" and "the breath of the Almighty" (Job 32:8) in his argument with Job, thus becoming yet another claimant to wisdom.

Elihu's attempt to enter the disputation, however, ultimately fails. He gives arguments similar to those of the three friends, rehashing the same ideas concerning retribution (Job 33:8-21; 34:5-20). Accordingly, no one, including Job, responds to him. Elihu too has claimed wisdom (Job 32:6-9; 36:4), but his insight does not lead to resolution. At best, this section of the book can be considered an abortive disputation.

2.3. God versus Job (Job 38:1—42:6). During the debate with the three friends Job expressed his wish to enter a disputation with God (see 1.1.1 above). Occasionally, he despaired that it would do any good, but it is interesting that his last words before God speaks to him expressed his desire for an audience with God. However, when God does appear, the audience does not go as he had hoped or thought. The divine speech is essentially a rebuke of Job's pretensions toward wisdom and an assertion of God's power and wisdom. Job does not debate; he repents (Job 40:4-5; 42:1-6).

3. Resolution.

The divine speech (Job 38:1—42:6) and the epilogue (Job 42:7-17) bring the disputation between Job and the three friends to a close. On the surface, the issue had been the cause and solution to Job's suffering, but the deeper question had to do with the source of wisdom. In the final analysis, the human participants in the drama never learn the reason for Job's suffering. Suffering remains a mystery. The question of wisdom, though, has been clearly resolved. None of human characters are wise; they all failed in their analysis of the situation. Only God is wise. Although this was a solution anticipated earlier by Job himself (Job 28), it did not bring him to personal resolution (Job 29—31). God had to intervene and appear to Job in order to set him straight.

4. The Rhetorical Function of Disputation.

The disputation form is one that allows the interaction of more than one perspective on a problem and allows the reader to enter the discussion and consider the strengths and weaknesses of the different perspectives. Some modern interpreters are attracted to the disputation form because it keeps positions in flux (Newsom; Zuckermann). When treated in isolation, the disputes in Job do not mandate a resolution. It is interesting that these recent major treatments of Job often interpret the debate apart from its wider context. However, the canonical book does adjudicate between the characters and judges all human participants as wrong-minded. The book points to God as the one who has the answers and the power.

5. Ancient Near Eastern Disputation.

Perhaps it is not surprising that a vexing issue such as suffering, particularly undeserved suffering, finds treatment in disputation form, allowing for the airing of different perspectives. In the disputation section of Job no resolution emerges, but the book in which it finds its context does resolve at least one aspect of the issue ("Who is wise?") while allowing the question of suffering to remain unanswered.

Ancient Israel is not the only culture that struggled with these questions. Other ancient Near Eastern cultures did so as well, and it is notable that two texts, one Egyptian and one Babylonian, that have been compared to Job are also disputations.

5.1. Egyptian: The Dispute of a Man with His Ba.
In Egyptian we have The Dispute of a Man with His *Ba* (for translation, see Lichtheim, 163-69). According to Egyptian anthropology, the *ba* was a component of the soul, specifically that part which survived into the afterlife. This text is known by one main papyrus (P. Berlin 3024), which comes from the early Middle Kingdom period (Twelfth Dynasty). This is one of a group of pessimistic/speculative texts that were popu-

lar at the time that Egyptian culture emerges from the quagmire of the First Intermediate period (twenty-second century BC). In this case, though, the topic is not so much about political and social confusion as about individual confusion. This text is one of the most difficult to translate and then to understand. It takes the form of a disputation between a man and his *ba*. As noted above, *ba* has been roughly understood as the equivalent of soul and is even translated that way by J. Wilson (*ANET*, 405-7). However, although there is a general similarity between the two concepts, the concept of the *ba* seems more complex than that association allows. Indeed, H. Goedicke discusses the evolution of the idea of the *ba* through Egyptian history and the distinction between an immanent and transcendental *ba*. In any case, what is clear in the text is that both the man and the *ba* express disappointment in life. Life brings trouble. The man spurs the discussion on (as far as we know, since the beginning of this text is broken) by complaining about life and longing for death. It is disputed whether he really contemplates suicide or not, but his *ba* advocates acceptance rather than despondency. At the end, the man continues to praise death in a poem that includes

> Death is before me today
> (Like) a sick man's recovery,
> Like going outdoors after confinement.

He also looks forward to the "other side" of death:

> Truly, he who is yonder will be a living god,
> Punishing the evildoer's crime.

The *ba* and he come to an agreement that the *ba* will stay with him both in this life and the next. According to Goedicke (58), the text is "the promulgation of an idealistic philosophy within which the goal is to master the shortcomings of the mundane world by knowledge of the fleetingness of corporeal existence and of a true eternal home in transcendence."

5.2. Akkadian: The Babylonian Theodicy.
In Akkadian literary tradition two texts in particular are often discussed alongside Job: *Ludlul Bel Nemeqi* and the Babylonian Theodicy (both are most likely composed in the second half of the second millennium BC). The former is a mono-

logue, while the latter is a dialogue that has the form of a disputation. The Babylonian Theodicy is a dialogue between two men who are friends and keep the conversation civil, but they disagree about the relationship between suffering and the gods. The first speaker describes his suffering and his opinion that life, and the gods, are not just. At one point he raises the classic example of injustice:

> Let me [put] but one matter before you:
> Those who seek not after a god can go the
>   road of favor,
> Those who pray to a goddess have grown
>   poor and destitute.
> Indeed, in my youth I tried to find out the
>   will of (my) god,
> With prayer and supplication I besought my
>   goddess.
> I bore a yoke of profitless servitude:
> (My) god decreed (for me) poverty instead of
>   wealth.
> A cripple rises above me, a fool is ahead of
>   me,
> Rogues are in the ascendant, I am demoted.
>   (*COS* 1.154:492-95)

The friend tries to lead him back to the road of orthodoxy by suggesting that his "logic is perverse" and that he "has cast off justice" and "scorned divine design." The text ends, rather unexpectedly, with the friend coming around and at least partially agreeing with the sufferer's assessment. Also, unlike Ludlul, the sufferer ends the text unrestored and requesting such from the gods.

6. Summary.
Disputation is a primary feature of the book of Job. The most heated debate takes place between Job and the three friends, but disputations of sorts, some calm, some abortive, are also seen in the prologue (God versus the Accuser) and in the Elihu monologue. The appearance of God at the end of the book brings the debate to a resolution. The debate centered on the question of the reason for Job's suffering and how he might alleviate his pain, but the deeper issue is the claim to wisdom. All the human parties (Job, the three friends, Elihu) have asserted their wisdom and criticized the others. At the end, however, God comes and definitely states that he is all-wise (and all-powerful), a conclu-

sion anticipated by Job (Job 28) in a temporary moment of clarity. Examination of the literature of the surrounding cultures shows at least two compositions (The Dispute of a Man with His *Ba;* the Babylonian Theodicy) that share the disputation form with Job. Interestingly, all three examine the struggles of human existence.

See also JOB 2: ANCIENT NEAR EASTERN BACKGROUND; SATAN.

BIBLIOGRAPHY. **R. L. Alden,** *Job* (NAC; Nashville: Broadman & Holman, 1993); **H. Goedicke,** *The Report about the Dispute of a Man with His ba: Papyrus Berlin 3024* (JHNES; Baltimore: Johns Hopkins Press, 1970); **A. Graffy,** *A Prophet Confronts His People: The Disputation Speech in the Prophets* (AnBib 104; Rome: Pontifical Biblical Institute, 1984); **J. E. Hartley,** *The Book of Job* (NICOT; Grand Rapids: Eerdmans, 1988); **M. Lichtheim,** *Ancient Egyptian Literature,* vol. 1 (Berkeley: University of California Press, 1973); **R. E. Murphy,** *Wisdom Literature: Job, Proverbs, Ruth, Canticles, Ecclesiastes, and Esther* (FOTL; Grand Rapids: Eerdmans, 1981); **C. Newsom,** *The Book of Job: A Contest of Moral Imaginations* (Oxford: Oxford University Press, 2003); **S. H. Scholnick,** "Poetry in the Courtroom: Job 38-41," in *Directions in Hebrew Poetry,* ed. E. R. Follis (JSOTSup 40; Sheffield: JSOT Press, 1987) 185-204; **K. van der Toorn,** "The Ancient Near Eastern Literary Dialogue as a Vehicle of Critical Reflection," in *Dispute Poems and Dialogues in the Ancient and Medieval Near East: Forms and Types of Literary Debates in Semitic and Related Literatures,* ed. G. J. Reinink and H. L. J. Vanstiphout (OLA 42; Leuven: Departement Oriëntalistiek, 1991) 59-70; **P. P. Zerafa,** *The Wisdom of God in the Book of Job* (SUSTU 8; Rome: Herder, 1978); **B. Zuckermann,** *Job the Silent: A Study in Historical Counterpoint* (New York: Oxford University Press, 1991).

T. Longman III

DIVINE COUNCIL
The term *divine council* is used by Hebrew and Semitics scholars to refer to the heavenly host, the pantheon of divine beings who administer the affairs of the cosmos. All ancient Mediterranean cultures had some conception of a divine council. The divine council of Israelite religion, known primarily through the psalms, was distinct in important ways.

1. Textual Evidence
2. Monotheism in the Hebrew Bible and the
   Divine Council

3. The Divine Council, Jewish Binitarianism and New Testament Christology

1. Textual Evidence.

1.1. The Council of the Gods/God. Comparison of the Hebrew Bible with other ancient religious texts reveals overlaps between the divine councils of the surrounding nations and Israel's version of the heavenly bureaucracy. The parade example is the literature from Ras Shamra (Ugarit). Translated shortly after their discovery in the 1930s, these tablets contain several phrases describing a council of gods that are conceptually and linguistically parallel to the Hebrew Bible. The Ugaritic council was led by "El," the same proper name used in the Hebrew Bible for the God of Israel (e.g., Is 40:18; 43:12). References to the "council of El" include *pḫr ʾilm* ("the assembly of El/ the gods" [*KTU* 1.47:29; 1.118:28; 1.148:9]); *pḫr bn ʾilm* ("the assembly of the sons of El/the gods" [*KTU* 1.4.III:14]); *mpḫrt bn ʾil* ("the assembly of the sons of El" [*KTU* 1.65:3; cf. 1.40:25, 42]); *dr bn ʾil* ("assembly [circle, group] of the sons of El" [*KTU* 1.40:25, 33-34]); *ʿdt ʾilm* ("assembly of El/the gods" [*KTU* 1.15.II:7, 11]). Phoenician texts, such as the Karatepe inscription, also describe a Semitic pantheon: *wkl dr bn ʾlm* ("and all the circle/group of the sons of the gods" [*KAI* 26.III.19; 27.12]).

The *ʿdt ʾilm* ("assembly of El/the gods") of Ugaritic texts represents the most precise parallel to the data of the Hebrew Bible. Psalm 82:1 uses the same expression for the council (*ʿdt ʾilm*), along with an indisputably plural use of the word *ʾĕlōhîm* ("God, gods"): "God [*ʾĕlōhîm*] stands in the council of El/the divine council [*baʿădat ʾēl*]; among the gods [*ʾĕlōhîm*] he passes judgment." The second occurrence of *ʾĕlōhîm* must be plural due to the preposition "in the midst of." The Trinity cannot be the explanation for this divine plurality, since the psalm goes on to detail how Israel's God charges the other *ʾĕlōhîm* with corruption and sentences them to die "like humankind." Psalm 89:5-7 (89:6-8 MT) places the God of Israel "in the assembly of the holy ones" (*biqhal qĕdōšîm*) and then asks, "For who in the clouds can be compared to Yahweh? Who is like Yahweh among the sons of God [*bĕnê ʾēlîm*], a god greatly feared in the council of the holy ones [*bĕsôd qĕdōšîm*]?" Psalm 29:1 commands the same sons of God (*bĕnê ʾēlîm*) to praise Yahweh and give him due obeisance. These heavenly "sons of God" (*bĕnê ʾĕlōhîm* or *bĕnê hāʾĕlōhîm*) appear in other biblical texts (Gen 6:2, 4; Deut 32:8-9, 43 [LXX, Qumran]; Job 1:6; 2:1; 38:7) (Heiser 2001).

Another biblical Hebrew term matching Ugaritic terminology is *dôr*, which often means "generation" but, as with Ugaritic and Phoenician *dr*, may also refer to the "circle" (group) of gods—that is, the divine council (Amos 8:14 [emendation]; Ps 49:19 [49:20 MT]; 84:10 [84:11 MT]).

1.2. The Abode and Meeting Place of the Divine Council. At Ugarit the divine council and its gods met on a cosmic mountain, the place where heaven and earth intersected and where divine decrees were issued. This place was at the "source of the two rivers" (*mbk nhrm*) in the "midst of the fountains of the double-deep" (*qrb ʾapq thmtm*). This well-watered mountain was the place of the "assembled congregation" (*pḫr mʿd*). El dwelt on this mountain and, with his council, issued divine decrees from the "tents of El" (*dd ʾil*) and his "tent shrine" (*qrš* [*KTU* 1.1.III:23; 1.2.III:5; 1.3.V:20-21; 1.4.IV:22-23; 1.6.I:34-35; 1.17.VI:48]). In the Kirta Epic, El and the gods live in "tents" (*ʾahlm*) and "tabernacles" (*mšknt* [*KTU* 1.15.3.18-19]). The Ugaritic god Baal, the deity who oversaw the council for El (see 1.3 below), held meetings in the "heights" (*mrym*) of the mountain Ṣapānu, apparently located in a range of mountains that included El's own abode. In Baal's palace in Ṣapānu there were "paved bricks" (*lbnt*) that made Baal's house "a house of the clearness of lapis lazuli" (*bht ṯhrm ʾiqn ʾum*).

These descriptions are present in the Hebrew Bible with respect to Israel's God and his council. Yahweh dwells on mountains (Sinai or Zion [e.g., Ex 34:26; 1 Kings 8:10; Ps 48:1-2]). The Jerusalem temple is said to be located in the "heights of [*yarkĕtê*] the north [*ṣāpôn*]" (Ps 48:1-2). Zion is the "mount of assembly" (*har môʿēd*), again located in *yarkĕtê ṣāpôn* (Is 14:13). Additionally, Mount Zion is described as a watery habitation (Is 33:20-22; Ezek 47:1-12; Joel 3:18; Zech 14:8). A tradition preserved in Ezekiel 28:13-16 equates the "holy mountain of God" with Eden, the "garden of God." Eden appears in Ezekiel 28:2 as the "seat of the gods" (*môšab ʾĕlōhîm*). The description of Eden in Genesis 2:6-15 refers to the "ground flow" that "watered the entire face of the earth." At Sinai, Moses and others saw Yahweh and feasted with him (Ex 24). The description of this banquet includes the observation that under God's feet was a paved construction of "sapphire stone" (*libnat hassappîr* [Ex 24:10]), just as with Baal's dwelling. Other striking parallels include Yahweh's frequent presence in the tabernacle (*miškan* [Ps 26:8; 74:7] and Zion as Yahweh's tent (*'ōhel* [Is 33:20; cf. 1 Chron 9:23]).

1.3. The Structure and Bureaucracy of the Divine Council. The council at Ugarit apparently had four tiers (Smith 2001, 41-53). The top tier consisted of El and his wife Athirat (Asherah). The second tier was the domain of their royal family ("sons of El"; "princes"). One member of this second tier served as the vicegerent of El and was, despite being under El's authority, given the title "most high" (Wyatt, 419). A third tier was for "craftsman deities," while the lowest tier was reserved for the messengers (*ml'km*), essentially servants or staff. In Ugaritic council scenes lower deities are established or granted spheres of authority and at times are depicted as challenging or confronting El (*KTU* 1.3.V.19-36; 1.6.I.36-55; 1.4.VII.21-25; 1.16.V.26-27) (see Handy 1993).

Evidence for exactly the same structures in the Israelite council is tenuous. Despite the fact that popular Israelite religion may have understood Yahweh as having a wife, Asherah (see Hess), it cannot be sustained that the religion of the prophets and biblical writers contained this element or that the idea was permissible. There is also no real evidence for the craftsman tier. However, the role of the *śāṭān* (*see* Satan), the accuser who openly challenges God on the matter of Job's spiritual resilience, is readily apparent (Job 1:6-12; 2:1-6). In the divine council in Israelite religion Yahweh was the supreme authority over a divine bureaucracy that included a second tier of lesser *'ĕlōhîm* (*bĕnê 'ēlîm; bĕnê 'ĕlōhîm* or *bĕnê hā'ĕlōhîm*) and a third tier of *mal'ākîm* ("angels"). In the book of *Job some members of the council apparently have a mediatory role with respect to human beings (Job 5:1; 15:8; 16:19-21; cf. Heb 1:14).

The vicegerent slot in the Israelite council represents the most significant difference between Israel's council and all others. In Israelite religion this position of authority was filled not by another god but by Yahweh himself in another form. This "hypostasis" of Yahweh was the same essence as Yahweh but a distinct, second person. This is most plainly seen via the Name theology of the Hebrew Bible and the so-called angel of Yahweh (for the angel's connection to the Name, the essence of Yahweh, see Ex 23:20-33; see Heiser 2004, 34-67).

2. Monotheism in the Hebrew Bible and the Divine Council.

2.1. Biblical Polytheism? Many scholars have concluded that the presence of a divine council in the Hebrew Bible means that Israel's religion was at one time polytheistic (there are many gods) or henotheistic (there are many gods, but one is preferred) and only later evolved to monotheism. Polytheism and monolatrous henotheism both presume "species sameness" among the gods. Henotheism in particular assumes the possibility of a power struggle for supremacy in the council, where the supreme authority could be displaced if another god defeats or outwits him. This does not reflect orthodox Israelite religious belief. The biblical data indicate that orthodox Israelite religion never considered Yahweh as one among equals or near equals. The biblical writers refer exclusively to Yahweh as "the God" (*hā'ĕlōhîm* [1 Kings 18:39]) when that term occurs with respect to a singular entity. Yahweh is the "true God" (*'ĕlōhîm 'ĕmet* [Jer 10:10]). The assertion points to the belief that although Yahweh was an *'ĕlōhîm*, he was qualitatively unique among the *'ĕlōhîm*. The primary distinguishing characteristic of Yahweh from any other *'ĕlōhîm* was his preexistence and creation of all things (Is 45:18), including the "host of heaven" (Ps 33:6; 148:1-5; cf. Neh 9:6), language that at times clearly refers to the other divine beings (cf. 1 Kings 22; Job 38:7-8; Is 14:13; cf. Deut 4:19-20; 32:8-9, 43 [LXX, Qumran] with Deut 17:3; 29:25; 32:17). Yahweh's utter uniqueness against all other *'ĕlōhîm* is monotheism on ancient Semitic terms, and orthodox Israelite religion reflects this at all stages.

2.2. Plural 'ĕlōhîm as Human Beings? Many scholars understand the plural *'ĕlōhîm* of Psalms 82; 89 as human rulers, the elders of Israel, no doubt due to the specter of polytheism. This position is highly problematic. If these *'ĕlōhîm* are humans, why are they sentenced to die "like humans"? A clear contrast is intended by both the grammar and structure of the Hebrew text (Prinsloo; Handy 1990). At no time in the Hebrew Bible did Israel's elders ever have jurisdiction over all the nations. There is no scriptural basis for the idea that God presides over a council of humans that governs the nations of the earth. In fact, the situation is exactly the opposite: Israel was *separated* from the nations to be God's own possession, while the other nations were abandoned by Yahweh to the rule of other *ʾĕlōhîm* in the wake of the incident at Babel (Deut 4:19-20; 32:8-9 [LXX, Qumran]; cf. Dan 10:13, 20; see Heiser 2001). It is also difficult to see how the corrupt decisions of a group of humans would shake the foundations of the earth (Ps 82:5). Furthermore, it is clear from Psalm 89:6-7 (89:7-8 MT) that the "sons of God" *(bĕnê ʾēlîm)* in "the council of the holy ones" *(bĕsôd qĕdōšîm)* meet "in the clouds" *(baššahaq)*.

The lesser *ʾĕlōhîm* are not merely idols. Deuteronomy 32:17, when understood against a broad view of Deuteronomy's statements about gods and idols, nullifies this explanation: "They sacrificed to demons *[šēdim]* who are not God *[ĕlōah,* a singular noun], to gods *[ʾĕlōhîm]* they did not know, to new gods that had come along recently, whom your fathers had not reverenced." If the lesser *ʾĕlōhîm* are demons, their existence cannot be denied. One psalmist (Ps 97:7), while mocking the lifeless idols, demands that the lesser *ʾĕlōhîm* *worship Yahweh—a puzzling command if there were no such entities.

2.3. "No Other Gods Beside Me"? How is one to reconcile Israel's divine council with statements in the Hebrew Bible that "there is none beside" Yahweh? Such statements are taken by critical scholars as evidence that Israel had shed its polytheism, and by others as necessitating the strained interpretations noted above. Neither view can be sustained in light of the references to plural *ʾĕlōhîm* and *ʾēlîm* in Second Temple period Jewish texts (roughly 185 in the Qumran material alone [see Heiser 2004, 189-210]) and the Jewish belief in "two powers" in heaven during that same period (Segal). Analysis of the Hebrew text demonstrates that several of the most common phrases in the Hebrew Bible allegedly used for denying the existence of other gods (e.g., Deut 4:35, 39; 32:12, 39) appear in passages that affirm the existence of other gods (Deut 4; 32). The result is that these phrases express the incomparability of Yahweh among the other *ʾĕlōhîm*, not that the biblical writer contradicts himself or is in the process of discovering monotheism. The situation is the same in Isaiah 40—66. Isaiah 40:1-8 is familiar to scholars (via the plural imperatives in Is 40:1-2) as a divine council text (Cross; Seitz). Isaiah 40:22-26 affirms the ancient Israelite worldview that de-

scribed heavenly beings with "heavenly host" terminology (Heiser 2004, 114-18). That Isaiah's "denial statements" should be understood as statements of incomparability, not as rejections of the existence of other gods, is made clear in Isaiah 47:8, 10, where Babylon boldly claims, "I am, and there is none else beside me." The claim is not that Babylon is the only city in the world, but rather that it has no rival.

Some would argue that the descriptions of a divine council are merely metaphoric. Metaphoric language, however, is not based on what a writer's view of reality excludes. Rather, the metaphor is a means of framing and categorizing something that *is* part of a writer's worldview. When in Exodus 15:11 the biblical writer asserts, "Who is like you, O LORD, among the gods *[ʾēlîm]*?" or in Deuteronomy 10:17, "For the LORD your God is God of gods *[ʾĕlōhîm]*," this reflects a sincere belief and is neither dishonest nor hollow. Comparing Yahweh to the ancient equivalent of an imaginary or fictional character cheapens the praise. The psalms contain many exclamations of the incomparability of Yahweh to the other gods (Ps 86:8; 95:3; 96:4; 135:5; 136:2). David (Ps 138:1) proclaims that he will sing the praise of the God of Israel "before the gods" *(neged ʾĕlōhîm)*—a declaration that makes little sense if lesser *ʾĕlōhîm* did not exist.

3. The Divine Council, Jewish Binitarianism and New Testament Christology.

Numerous descriptions and epithets of Ugaritic El and Baal are attributed to Yahweh in the Hebrew Bible (Day, 13-127; Smith 2002, 32-107). This was done for polemic reasons to challenge the authority of El and Baal. For the Israelite, high sovereignty and chief administration of the cosmos was conducted only by Yahweh. Nevertheless, Israel's own divine council had a bureaucratic hierarchy, and that order is consistently described in terms of Yahweh being both the high sovereign and the vicegerent. Orthodox Israelite religion instead had Yahweh as sovereign and a second person who was Yahweh's mediating essence as the vicegerent of the council. This structure reflected Israel's belief in Yahweh's ontological uniqueness as creator of all things, including the other *ʾĕlōhîm* of the council. The notion of two distinct deities at the top of the hierarchy was unthinkable to Israel.

This religious structure is the backdrop to the ancient Jewish acceptance of two powers in heaven (Segal). Since both powers were believed to be good, the belief does not reflect Zoroastrian influence. The belief in two powers in heaven was a contributing factor in the advent of what scholars have termed "binitarian monotheism" in Second Temple period Judaism (Hurtado 1999), which in turn contributes to our understanding of the advent of NT Christology. This contextualizes the description of Jesus as the *monogenēs* ("unique" [see Grudem, 1233-34]) son of God in the NT. Since the Hebrew Bible is clear that there are other sons of God *(běnê [hā]ʾělōhîm),* NT writers clarify that Jesus, as the same essence as the Father, is unique among all heavenly sons of God.

See also CREATION THEOLOGY; DIVINE PRESENCE; GOD; MOUNTAIN IMAGERY; ROYAL COURT; THEOPHANY.

BIBLIOGRAPHY. **R. J. Clifford,** *The Cosmic Mountain in Canaan and the Old Testament* (HSM 4; Cambridge, MA: Harvard University Press, 1972); **F. M. Cross,** "The Council of Yahweh in Second Isaiah," *JNES* 12 (1953) 274-77; **J. Day,** *Yahweh and the Gods and Goddesses of Canaan* (JSOTSup 265; Sheffield: Sheffield Academic Press, 1994); **W. Grudem,** *Systematic Theology* (Leicester: Inter-Varsity Press; Grand Rapids: Zondervan, 1994); **L. K. Handy,** "Sounds, Words, and Meanings in Psalm 82," *JSOT* 47 (1990) 60-73; idem, "The Authorization of Divine Power and the Guilt of God in the Book of Job: Useful Ugaritic Parallels," *JSOT* 60 (1993) 107-18; idem, *Among the Host of Heaven: The Syro-Palestinian Pantheon as Bureaucracy* (Winona Lake, IN: Eisenbrauns, 1994); **M. S. Heiser,** "Deuteronomy 32:8 and the Sons of God," *BSac* 158 (2001) 52-74; idem, "The Divine Council in Second Temple Literature" (Ph.D. diss., University of Wisconsin, 2004); idem, "Monotheism, Polytheism, Monolatry, or Henotheism? Toward an Assessment of Divine Plurality in the Hebrew Bible," *BBR* (forthcoming); **R. S. Hess,** "Yahweh and His Asherah? Epigraphic Evidence for Religious Pluralism in Old Testament Times," in *One God, One Lord in a World of Religious Pluralism,* ed. A. D. Clarke and B. W. Winter (Cambridge: Tyndale House, 1991) 5-33; **L. W. Hurtado,** *One God, One Lord: Early Christian Devotion and Ancient Jewish Monotheism* (Philadelphia: Fortress, 1988); idem, "The Binitarian Shape of Early Christian Worship," in *The Jewish Roots of Christological Monotheism: Papers from the St. Andrews Conference on the Historical Origins of the Worship of Jesus,* ed. C. C. Newman, J. R. Davila and G. S. Lewis (JSJSup 63; Leiden: E. J. Brill, 1999) 187-213; **Min Suc Kee,** "The Heavenly Council and its Type-Scene," JSOT 31:3 (2007): 259-273; **E. T. Mullen Jr.,** *The Divine Council in Canaanite and Early Hebrew Literature* (HSM 24; Chico, CA: Scholars Press, 1980); idem, "Divine Assembly," *ABD* 2.214-17; **S. B. Parker,** "Sons of (the) God(s)," *DDD* 794-98; **W. S. Prinsloo,** "Psalm 82: Once Again, Gods or Men?" *Bib* 76 (1995) 219-28; **A. F. Segal,** *Two Powers in Heaven: Early Rabbinic Reports about Christianity and Gnosticism* (SJLA 25; Leiden: E. J. Brill, 1977); **C. R. Seitz,** "The Divine Council: Temporal Transition and New Prophecy in the Book of Isaiah," *JBL* 109 (1990) 229-47; **M. S. Smith,** *The Origins of Biblical Monotheism: Israel's Polytheistic Background and the Ugaritic Texts* (New York: Oxford University Press, 2001); idem, *The Early History of God: Yahweh and Other Deities in Ancient Israel* (2nd ed.; Grand Rapids: Eerdmans, 2002); **N. Wyatt,** "The Titles of the Ugaritic Storm God," *UF* 24 (1992) 403-24.   M. S. Heiser

DIVINE PRESENCE

The dominant image of divine presence in these OT texts is that of Yahweh dwelling in the temple. The dwelling of *God in the temple is multivalent in that the holy of holies is described as the place where earth and heaven meet. Thus, Yahweh is simultaneously in heaven and in the temple (Ps 11:4), with the ark of the covenant serving as his footstool (Ps 132:7-8). From this vantage point Yahweh observes the whole creation. In tension with Yahweh's covenant presence among his people is the reality that his presence is inescapable because he is everywhere (Ps 139:7-12).

1. Descriptions of Divine Presence
2. Spirit and Angel of Yahweh
3. Blessings of Divine Presence
4. Divine Presence in Biblical Theology

1. Descriptions of Divine Presence.

1.1. Yahweh the Enthroned King. Yahweh is no mere tribal deity with sovereignty over a particular territory, "for to Yahweh is the Kingship, and he rules among the nations" (Ps 22:28). Nevertheless, he has chosen the temple in Jerusalem as the place of his special dwelling among his covenant people Israel (1 Kings 11:13; Ps 79:1). As a corollary to this, other lands are the places of other gods, as reflected in the words of

*Naomi to *Ruth regarding Orpah: "Behold, your sister in law has returned to her people and to her gods" (Ruth 1:15; cf. Deut 4:19). The relationship between land, people and deity can be seen in Ruth's reply as well: "For where you go I will go, and where you lodge I will lodge, your people will be my people, and your God my God" (Ruth 1:16). Orpah goes to her land and her gods; Ruth goes to Israel with Naomi, and there she will serve Yahweh.

The temple in Jerusalem is the place where earth and heaven meet, and God's presence among his people means that he is enthroned in heaven with the ark in the holy of holies as his footstool (see Beale; Wilson). This understanding is seen in the many allusions to Yahweh possessing human characteristics. From these it seems that Yahweh is conceptualized as possessing the human form of a great king on his throne, with the temple as his earthly court and the land of Israel as his domain.

1.1.1. Anthropomorphic Depictions of King Yahweh. Yahweh is characterized as possessing a face, as seeing and hearing, as having a nose and breath, as having a strong arm and hands. All of these physical characteristics communicate the reality of his noncorporal presence. Where English translations refer to the "presence" of God, the direct expression is almost always some variation on the Hebrew root *pnh* ("face"). To be in the presence of God is to be before his face. It is therefore difficult to find a reference to divine presence that is not anthropomorphic, though there are allusions to nonhuman features, such as when Yahweh is described as having wings under which refuge may be found.

In the "presence of Yahweh" *(pĕnēy yhwh)* (Job 1:12) Satan promises that *Job will curse God "to his face" *('al-pāneykā)* (Job 1:11; cf. Job 2:5). Job does not curse, but he does wish to plead his case before the face of God (Job 13:15) and plaintively asks why God has hidden his face (Job 13:24). When God hides his face, he is inaccessible (Job 34:29).

The blessing in Numbers 6:25, "May Yahweh cause his face to shine upon you," is refracted through a number of psalms. For example, "Lift up the light of your face upon us" (Ps 4:6; cf. Ps 11:7; 24:6; 25:16; 27:8-9; 31:16; 36:9; 44:3; 67:1; 80:3, 7, 19; 86:16; 89:15; 118:27; 119:135). Related statements include the question of why Yahweh hides his face, the plea that he not turn his face

away, and the statement that his face is against the wicked (Ps 13:1; 27:9; 34:16; 44:24; 69:19; 88:14; 102:2; 132:10; 143:7). The presence of Yahweh is likewise communicated through the expressions that he sees (e.g., Ps 10:14; 18:24; 19:14; 31:7, 22; 33:13-18; 34:15; 35:17, 22; 37:13; 51:4; Prov 3:4; 5:21) and hears (e.g., Ps 40:1; 69:33; 102:2). Yahweh's word of promise that he will save the righteous and judge the wicked also communicates his nearness to his people (see esp. Ps 73:17-18, 23-28; cf. Deut 32:35).

Yahweh delivered Israel by means of his right hand, his outstretched arm and the light of his presence (Ps 44:3). And having planted them in the land (Ps 44:2), he is now enthroned upon their praises (Ps 22:3). The many references to him sitting on his throne (Ps 45:6; 47:8; 55:19; 97:2; 99:1) and to him being a king (e.g., Ps 10:16; 24:8, 10; 29:10; 47:2; 84:3) substantiate the impression that this stock of images comes from the fund of the conception of Yahweh as the great king in human form. His throne is in heaven, above the cherubim (Ps 80:1; 99:1), and his footstool is the ark in the holy of holies (Ps 99:5; 132:7-8; Lam 2:1).

1.1.2. The Throne Room and Surrounds of Yahweh. The fact that Yahweh is present in the temple, the place where earth and heaven meet, gives rise to a number of figures of speech that bear witness to the presence of God in Israel. By metonymy and synecdoche God's presence is described when allusion is made (moving concentrically inward) to the land of Israel (Ps 78:54; 85:9; Prov 10:30), the land of Judah (Ps 68:16; 76:1-2), the city of Jerusalem (Ps 79:1, 3), the city of God (Ps 48:1), *Zion (Ps 147:12), the holy hill (Ps 149:2) and the holy mountain (Ps 48:1). These references reflect the perspective that this place is important because this is the land and city in which Yahweh dwells. Within the all-important city are the gates and courts of the temple (Ps 92:13; 100:4), the house (Ps 52:8), the dwelling (Ps 43:3; 46:4, 5, 7, 11), and within the temple precincts the altar and its horns (Ps 43:3; 118:27), the cherubim over the ark (Ps 80:1), the throne of Yahweh (Ps 45:6) and his footstool the ark (Ps 99:5). Mention is also made of Yahweh's former dwelling in Shiloh, "where he dwelt among men" (Ps 78:60). These details all reflect the perspective that Yahweh is enthroned among his people with the divine council around him (Ps 82:1; 89:7). By going to the temple in Jerusalem, Israel has unique access to

Yahweh. This reality creates a strong desire to go to (Ps 84:2; 122:1) and remain in Jerusalem (Ps 84:10). These many references also reflect the salvation history of the OT, where Yahweh first inhabited the tabernacle, which after the conquest of the land apparently was pitched at Shiloh, prior to the building of the temple in Jerusalem.

1.2. Other Metaphors and Prepositions.

1.2.1. Metaphors. In addition to describing Yahweh as the enthroned king reigning from Jerusalem, a number of metaphors are employed that describe what Yahweh is for his people. A representative survey of these metaphors will find that God is likened to, for instance, a rock (Ps 62:2), a hiding place (Ps 119:114), a shield (Ps 140:7; Prov 2:7-8), sheltering wings (Ps 57:1; 63:7; 91:4), a strong tower (Ps 61:3; Prov 18:10) and a dwelling place (Ps 90:1; 91:1). Each figure of speech reflects the presence of Yahweh with his people (see 3.1 below).

1.2.2. Prepositions ("With, Near, Around, Upon"). Several statements in *Psalms directly say that Yahweh is with (*'ēt, 'im*) (Ps 14:5; 23:4; 36:9; 91:15; 139:18), before *(lipnēy)* (Ps 16:8, 11; 37:7) and near *(qārôb)* (Ps 34:18; 73:23, 28; 75:1; 119:151) his people. These statements can be understood as anthropomorphic as well, with Yahweh depicted as a companion, such as a shepherd (Ps 23:4). Psalm 33:22 calls for Yahweh's steadfast love to be upon (*'al*) his people, and Psalm 90:17 appeals for his favor to be upon (*'al*) them.

2. Spirit and Angel of Yahweh.

2.1. Spirit.
In Psalm 51:11 David voices a prayer that Yahweh not take his Holy Spirit from him. When read in conjunction with the rest of the OT canon (see esp. 1 Sam 16:13-14; 28:17), this must be interpreted as a prayer from the king who is specially anointed with the Spirit for kingship in Israel. In other words, this statement does not reflect the theology of the NT, where believers are indwelt by the Holy Spirit (e.g., John 7:39; 14:17; Rom 8:9; 1 Cor 3:16; 6:19) (see 4 below). Every OT reference to the Spirit being "upon" or "in" someone in the OT marks that person as distinct. Each time someone is described in this way the Spirit enables that person to do something that no one else in Israel can. An explicit statement that the Spirit of God continually indwells the faithful of Israel on an individual basis is not found in

the OT (Hamilton 2003; 2005). The other references to the Spirit in the Psalms are to his activity in creation (Ps 104:30; cf. Job 33:4), his inescapable presence (Ps 139:7; cf. Job 4:15) and, recalling the imagery of the pillar of cloud leading the people at the exodus, the Spirit leading the supplicant (Ps 143:10). In the OT, as we noted above, Yahweh indwells the temple. This can be contrasted with the NT, where there is no physical temple and God's Spirit indwells the believing remnant.

2.2. Angel of Yahweh.
Two texts in Psalms refer to the "angel of Yahweh" *(mala'k yhwh)*. In Psalm 34:7 we are told that "the angel of Yahweh encamps around those who fear him, and delivers them." The one feared is Yahweh, thus the wording of the text draws a close connection between Yahweh and this angel who represents him. Then in Psalm 35:5-6 the angel of Yahweh drives out the wicked.

3. Blessings of Divine Presence.
The people of Israel enjoy the benefits of Yahweh's presence among them because they are in covenant with him. The corollary is that if the covenant is broken, Yahweh's presence is withdrawn. Since the texts testify to the wicked actually experiencing the angry presence of Yahweh (Ps 68:1-2; 78:66; 83:15; 135:8, 10; 139:19), we must conclude that this withdrawal is relational rather than physical. That is, wicked covenant-breakers do not escape God's presence; rather, instead of his face shining on them, they experience him pursuing them in justice. The righteous psalmists often call on Yahweh to arise against their enemies (*see* Theophany). The blessings of Yahweh's covenant presence with his people are both spiritual and physical, but at points physical blessings cannot be distinguished from spiritual ones.

3.1. Protection.
A common statement in this portion of the OT is that Yahweh is a refuge for his people (e.g., Ruth 2:12; Ps 2:12; 4:8; 5:11; 7:1; 11:1; 12:7; 14:6; 16:1, 8; 17:7; 18:2; 25:20; 28:8; 31:1-4, 20). At one level, taking refuge in Yahweh means trusting in him for protection from one's enemies (Ps 57:1-3; 61:3). At other levels, the refuge that Yahweh provides shields those who seek him from possible shame (Ps 71:1) or keeps the righteous from envying the wicked (Ps 73:3, 17, 28). Entering into the presence of Yahweh and taking refuge in him cause a person to desire righteousness because the reality of Yahweh

exposes the sham of sin's deceitfulness.

There are many terms used to communicate the idea that Yahweh is a refuge. Several of these terms (italicized in the following quotation) are brought together in Psalm 91:1-4:

The one who dwells in the *hiding place* of the Most High, in the *shadow* of Shaddai he lodges. I will say to Yahweh, 'My *refuge* and my *fortress;* my God, I will trust in him.' For he will deliver you from the snare of the trapper, from the pestilence of destruction. With his *pinions* he will *cover* you, and *under his wings* you will seek *refuge;* his faithfulness is a *shield* and *buckler.*

Here the presence of Yahweh is likened to a fortress, which effectively removes one from the fray of combat, and also to a shield and buckler, which are protective in the midst of battle. Further, Yahweh's presence not only protects but also delivers from snares. Yahweh is often referred to as a shield (e.g., Ps 3:3; 5:12; 7:10; 18:2, 30-31; 28:7; 33:20; Prov 2:7; 30:5) and a help(er) (e.g., Ps 46:1; 54:4; 56:9; 115:9-11).

The presence of Yahweh, who sees all and has promised to judge wickedness, is what informs the fear of Yahweh (*see* Fear of the Lord). This healthy fear is protective in that it keeps the righteous from self-destructive behavior. This is clearly expressed in Job 31: "I made a covenant for my eyes, so how could I gaze on a virgin? And what [would be my] portion from God above, or heritage from Shaddai on high? Are not distress for the unrighteous and calamity for those who do iniquity? Does he not see my ways and number all my steps? . . . Because of the dread of the distress from God, and because of his majesty, I was unable [to sin]" (Job 31:1-4, 23).

3.2. Satisfaction. The satisfaction brought by the presence of Yahweh is at times the basic provision of human needs. For instance, in Ruth 1:6 we are told that "Yahweh visited his people to give them food." The sense in which Yahweh satisfies his people, however, is not limited to their physical needs; it also reaches into the arena of satisfaction that pertains to the joy and contentment and pleasure that result from desire realized, purpose fulfilled, emotion made full. Thus we read, "You make known to me the path of life; fullness of joy is your presence. Unending pleasures are in your right hand" (Ps 16:11).

4. Divine Presence in Biblical Theology.

The Israel of the old covenant is a localized people. In other words, the land of promise is central to their religion, and the dwelling of God in the temple constitutes Jerusalem as the focal point of the nation's religious life (for the strong land theme in the OT, see Dempster). In the OT, statements regarding the presence of God reflect the perspective that Yahweh is the king enthroned in heaven and his heavenly throne room is accessed from his earthly dwelling, the temple in Jerusalem (cf. Mt 23:21-22).

This OT perspective is radically altered through the coming of Jesus, the Messiah. Jesus declares that the time for *worship at the temple is over (Jn 4:21-24). The new-covenant people of God have no particular land, and the temple in which God dwells is no longer a physical building but the physical bodies of believers (1 Cor 3:16; 6:19). This reality is reflected in the references to the church's leaders and members being "pillars" (Gal 2:9; Rev 3:12) and "stones" being built into a dwelling of God (1 Pet 2:5; cf. Eph 2:19-22). In the old covenant, God dwells in the temple in Jerusalem, and his people worship him at the temple where he dwells. In the new covenant, God dwells in his people, and they are dispersed throughout the world, worshiping in spirit and in truth (Hamilton 2004). S. Terrien (1978) finds the theme of divine presence to be central for biblical theology.

In addition to the corporate aspect of divine presence there is the reality that God is "with" certain individuals in unique ways (see, e.g., Josh 1:5, 9; 2 Sam 5:10; Ps 23:4; 110:5; Is 7:14; 61:1). God's special presence with Jesus is cited as strong indication that he was indeed the Messiah (e.g., John 3:2; Acts 10:38) (see Alexander).

See also AFTERLIFE; DIVINE COUNCIL; PERSONIFICATION.

BIBLIOGRAPHY. **T. D. Alexander,** *The Servant King: The Bible's Portrait of the Messiah* (Leicester: Inter-Varsity Press, 1998); **A. A. Anderson,** "The Use of 'RUAH' in 1QS, 1QH and 1QM," *JSS* 7 (1962) 293-303; **G. K. Beale,** *The Temple and the Church's Mission: A Biblical Theology of the Dwelling Place of God* (NSBT 17; Downers Grove, IL: InterVarsity Press, 2004); **R. E. Clements,** *God and Temple* (Oxford: Blackwell, 1965); **S. G. Dempster,** *Dominion and Dynasty: A Theology of the Hebrew Bible* (NSBT 15; Downers Grove, IL: InterVarsity Press, 2003); **J. M. Hamilton,** "God with Men in the Torah," *WTJ* 65 (2003) 113-33;

idem, "Were Old Covenant Believers Indwelt by the Holy Spirit?" *Them* 30 (2004) 12-22; idem, "God with Men in the Prophets and the Writings: An Examination of the Nature of God's Presence," *SBET* 23.3 (2005) 166-93l; idem, *God's Indwelling Presence: The Holy Spirit in the Old and New Testaments* (NACSBT; Nashville: Broadman & Holman, 2006); **W. Hildebrandt,** *An Old Testament Theology of the Spirit of God* (Peabody, MA: Hendrickson, 1995); **W. E. March,** "God with Us: A Survey of Jewish Pneumatology," *ASR* 83 (1967) 3-16; **R. J. McKelvey,** *The New Temple: The Church in the New Testament* (OTM; Oxford: Oxford University Press, 1969); **H. D. Preuss,** "Ich will mit dir sein!" *ZAW* 80 (1968) 139-73; **S. Terrien,** *The Elusive Presence: Toward a New Biblical Theology* (San Francisco: Harper & Row, 1978); idem, *The Psalms: Strophic Structure and Theological Commentary* (ECC; Grand Rapids: Eerdmans, 2003); **I. Wilson,** *Out of the Midst of the Fire: Divine Presence in Deuteronomy* (SBLDS 151; Atlanta: Scholars Press, 1995).

J. M. Hamilton

E

ECCLESIASTES 1: BOOK OF

Ecclesiastes poses one of the more interesting hermeneutical challenges in the OT, for two reasons. First, the message of the book seems to be at odds with theological trajectories evident elsewhere in the Hebrew Scriptures. Second, at least on the surface, Ecclesiastes is dotted with noticeable internal inconsistencies.

Discussions reaching back at least to rabbinic times (Beckwith, 274-304; Hirshman) still continue, not only as to the meaning of verses here and there but also in regard to the basic message of the book as a whole. An overview of standard commentaries and introductions will quickly demonstrate that Ecclesiastes is amenable to conflicting interpretations. Is the author incoherent, insightful or confused? Is he a stark realist or merely faithless? Is he orthodox or heterodox? Is he an optimist or a pessimist? Is the final message of the book "Be like Qohelet, the wise man" or "Qohelet is wrong, so do not fall into his trap"?

Discovering the meaning and purpose of Ecclesiastes will likely continue as a back-and-forth journey between overarching concepts and smaller exegetical details, balancing the forest and the trees. But attempting to achieve such a balance seems to involve us in a vicious hermeneutical circle. How one sees the overall purpose of Ecclesiastes will affect how one handles the perplexing details of the book itself, yet that overall purpose cannot be determined apart from those same details. Of course, on one level, this is the case with any biblical book, but the problems are augmented in the case of Ecclesiastes, for it is precisely the details of the book that continue to challenge virtually any statement about its basic purpose. As one reads the book, one begins to draw conclusions about the author's train of thought, only to find a verse or

two later that the author says something that reduces one's conclusions to ashes. This scenario is played out so often in Ecclesiastes that M. V. Fox (1999, 1-26) has argued that rather than trying to impose an internal consistency on the book, we should see that the contradictions in Ecclesiastes are actually the key to discerning its meaning (for a concise review of the issue, see Krüger, 14-19).

1. Authorship and Date
2. Frame Narration and the Message of Ecclesiastes
3. Theological Themes
4. Conclusion

1. Authorship and Date.

The very beginning of the book ascribes the words to follow as those of *Qohelet, which raises three questions: who is Qohelet, when did he live, and who is this other person introducing his words? The first two questions will be addressed here, and the third in §2 below.

1.1. Identifying Qohelet. The meaning and identity of Qohelet has eluded biblical interpreters for centuries and will continue to do so for the foreseeable future. The word is from the Hebrew root *qhl*. The verb means "assemble" or "summon," and the noun *qāhāl* denotes an assembly or convocation. Hence, it is sometimes thought that Qohelet (Qal feminine participle) may denote a speaker in an assembly. The LXX title *(Ekklēsiastēs)* reflects this understanding, and the titles in the Vulgate *(Liber Ecclesiastes)* and in English follow suit. The common English translations of Qohelet as "preacher" or "teacher" further reflect such a secondary understanding. But to attribute this meaning to Qohelet is a matter of tradition and may amount to only a best guess. The word is found nowhere outside of Ecclesiastes, nor is it defined in Ecclesiastes.

Therefore, any attempt to render the word in an English equivalent will remain inconclusive.

One thing can, however, be said with relative certainty: "Qohelet" is not someone's name. The person in question is referred to as "king over Israel in Jerusalem" (Eccles 1:12 [cf. Eccles 1:16; 2:7, 9]). No king is known by that name, so we can safely assume that the name is a pseudonym. This hardly means, however—and it is important to bear this in mind—that the author wishes to deceive the readers. It simply means that the main character of the book is referred to as Qohelet for reasons that still elude interpreters to this day (Provan, 26-31). The more pressing question is whether this person referred to as Qohelet was indeed an actual king of Israel or whether the references to his kingship are likewise, for whatever reason, part of the author's literary output. For many, this is the crux of the matter. To disguise the identity of an actual king by naming him "Qohelet" is one thing, but to refer to him as "son of David, king in Jerusalem" (Eccles 1:1) when he was not is problematic for some interpreters, although it need not be, since there is no reason to assume that adopting a literary persona is an act of deception.

As with any other issue in Ecclesiastes, we must look for an answer by keeping before us the forest as well as the trees. Qohelet is likely a character created by the author to make his point (Fox 1999, 372-73)—that is, a nickname adopted by the writer to maintain a Solomonic connection but distancing himself from the actual person (Longman, 4). The name "Qohelet" is not intended to be a veiled reference to an actual Israelite king, designed either to keep his identity secret or to communicate some cryptic quality. Moreover, the traditional reference to *Solomon specifically would be quite odd, given what we see in Ecclesiastes 1:16: "Look, I have grown and increased in wisdom more than anyone who has ruled over Jerusalem before me." Only *David was before Solomon ruling in Jerusalem. It could be argued that this reference to many kings ruling in Jerusalem should not be restricted to Israelite kings but also include other occupants (e.g., Melchizedek [Gen 14:18], Adoni-zedek [Josh 10:1]). Nevertheless, this argument seems to have an air of desperation about it.

One could adduce, however, 1 Chronicles 29:25 in support of Ecclesiastes 1:16 being compatible with Solomonic authorship: "The LORD highly exalted Solomon in the sight of all Israel and bestowed on him royal splendor such as no king over Israel ever had before." This phrase is similar to what we see in Ecclesiastes 1:16. Since the reference here in Chronicles is clearly to Solomon, it lends a certain weight to reading Ecclesiastes 1:16 as likewise referring to Solomon. But the relevance of 1 Chronicles 29:25 for supporting the Solomonic identity of Ecclesiastes 1:16 is more superficial than substantive. One would first need to explore the theological themes in Chronicles in order to determine how such a designation would have functioned *in Chronicles* (see Japhet 1989; 2000, 43-49). It is not a question, therefore, of refusing to take the Chronicler's words at "face value." It is a question of how this verse functions in the Chronicler's overall purpose, which *is* to take 1 Chronicles 29:25 at face value.

As with Ecclesiastes, a reference to ancient Jerusalemite kings seems wholly out of place for the Chronicler's ideology. One of the clear and central theological foci of Chronicles is all Israel. An isolated (and somewhat cryptic) reference to non-Israelite kings seems a bit of a stretch. The author's purpose for designating Solomon in this way is an exercise not so much in reviewing objectively the history of Solomon as in reviewing Solomon's reign for the benefit of the author's postexilic community. The reference to Solomon in 1 Chronicles 29:25 is meant to evoke in the postexilic community a sense of Israel's strong and ancient royal tradition, which they now are summoned to recapture. In other words, the past is recast in terms of present concerns.

The Chronicler is using the ancient image of Solomon to get across his contemporary theological point that their reconstructed monarchy, their return to Solomonic glory (however inchoate it might be at the time), will likewise be exalted "in the sight of all Israel" like none before. 1 Chronicles 29:25 is part of the Chronicler's theology of Israel's recapture of its glorious past. In fact, in view of 1 Chronicles 29:25, one could just as well, and perhaps more easily, argue precisely the opposite of what a more "plain" reading of Ecclesiastes 1:16 suggests. This verse is not a prooftext for Solomonic authorship but rather an indication that Ecclesiastes likewise participates in a postexilic theological program (on the question of dating, see 1.2 below) similar to what we see in Chronicles. Ecclesiastes too is a book that appeals to Israel's ancient past in order to address contemporary concerns. In other words, reading Ecclesiastes 1:16 in light of 1 Chronicles 29:25 supports the point to be made later (see 2.2 below) concerning Ecclesiastes 12:13: Israel's past provides the context within which to deal with the challenges of Israel's postexilic present.

In *Qohelet Rabbah* (composed sometime after the fifth century AD), appeal is made to 1 Kings 8:1, 22 in support of Solomonic authorship, where the verbal and nominal forms (respectively) of *qhl* are used in reference to Solomon's "assembling" of the leaders of Jerusalem. Hence, it was thought that Qohelet is a cryptic allusion to this episode in Solomon's life, thus identifying Qohelet with Solomon. Such a midrashic solution attests to the mystery surrounding the name, but there is no reason to assume that this oblique allusion is intended to identify Solomon as the author of Ecclesiastes any more than it could be intended simply to anchor the Solomonic persona. In other words, it may simply be that the intention of this allusion (assuming that it is an allusion) is to get the perceptive reader to "think Solomon when you read this."

Or, it is perfectly conceivable that the allusion is not the result of the author's own literary creativity intended only for the most perceptive readers; it may have already become an accepted designation for Solomon by the time Ecclesiastes was written—although we should readily admit that this is highly conjectural and ultimately has no exegetical payoff. Similarly, one could argue that the words of the book are Solomon's, and that the words have been recast in the postexilic period, by which time "Qohelet" had already, for whatever reason, become an accepted nickname for ancient Solomon, and so the author has Solomon referring to himself as such. But at some point an unbiased reader has to appeal to Occam's Razor. Such layered explanations have the ring of desperation, and sooner or later they weaken the point of the argument itself: Solomon authorship.

Ecclesiastes does not claim to be authored by Solomon, and the non-Solomonic authorship of Ecclesiastes is the least problematic position in view of the points made above. This is in harmony with the observation concerning the book's attitude toward kingship. It is often pointed out that the royal persona seems to recede into the background quite quickly (Longman, 4-8). We read of kingly activities from Ecclesiastes 1:12—2:16, but by the time we get to Ecclesiastes 3, the theme of Qohelet's royal explorations is forgotten (Fox 2004, x; for a contrary view, see the full discussion in Christianson, 128-47). In Ecclesiastes 4:13-16 the author seems aloof toward kingship. By the time we get to Ecclesiastes 5:9, he is critical. In Ecclesiastes 8:2-4 and Ecclesiastes 10:20 we see not-so-veiled references to the king being a threat.

1.2. The Hebrew of Ecclesiastes and the Dating of the Book. The language and style of Ecclesiastes have instigated considerable debate among linguists, although it is fair to say that a preexilic date, based on linguistic factors, is the most common position. F. Delitzsch, writing in 1877, is often cited in this regard: "If the Book of Koheleth were of old Solomonic origin, then there is no history of the Hebrew language" (Delitzsch, 190). The point here is that the language of Ecclesiastes is, by all standards of our knowledge of the historical development of *Hebrew, unambiguously of later origin. Likewise, the nineteenth-century Princeton OT scholar W. H. Green, of no mean conservative pedigree, although ambivalent about the matter for some time, conceded later in his career that the language of Ecclesiastes "stands alone in the Bible," and then (a bit reluctantly) he concurred with Delitzsch: "After all that has been said, however, we do not see how the argument from the language can be met. We conclude, therefore, that it is decisive. . . . It is alleged, and the fact seems to be, that the Hebrew of this book is so Aramean [i.e., Aramaic] that it must belong to a period later than Solomon" (Green, 56).

In fact, the similarities between the Hebrew of Ecclesiastes and Aramaic, which did not begin to exert an international influence until the seventh century BC, had led scholars at one time to propose an Aramaic original of Ecclesiastes that was then translated into Hebrew (e.g., Burkitt; Zimmermann; Torrey; for argument against an Aramaic original, see Gordis). Although this theory has not gained scholarly assent, it illustrates the depth of the problem.

Several linguistic indicators in Ecclesiastes suggest a postexilic date (on the following, see more fully Seow, 11-21). (1) The increased use of vowel letters in Ecclesiastes is more consistent with exilic and postexilic developments as seen in their dramatic increase by the time of the

*Dead Sea Scrolls. (2) The Persian words *pardēs* ("garden" [Eccles 2:5]) and *pitgām* ("sentence" [Eccles 8:11]) suggest a time when Persian influenced Hebrew. Although this does not absolutely and necessarily indicate a postexilic setting, it should be pointed out that Persian loanwords occur in the Bible only in books of demonstrably postexilic date (e.g., Chronicles, Ezra, Nehemiah, *Esther). (3) As mentioned above, there is significant Aramaic influence on Ecclesiastes. As with the Persian words, Aramaic influence in isolation does not necessarily prove a late date, but the sheer frequency of these terms suggests more than just a general international "influence"; it suggests an historical setting for the book. (4) Certain grammatical elements are more consistent with an exilic or postexilic date—for example, frequency of the relative pronoun *še-*; exclusive use of the first-person pronoun *ʾănî* instead of *ʾānōkî*; expanded use of *ʾēt/ʾet-* beyond that of direct-object marker; the feminine demonstrative *zōh* rather than *zōʾt;* use of third-person masculine pronominal suffix for feminine plural antecedents; negation formed by *ʾēn* plus the infinitive in Ecclesiastes 3:14 instead of *lōʾ* plus the imperfect. (5) Seow (21-36) also notes that the abundance of economic terms (e.g., "money," "riches," "profit," "account," "salary," "success") bespeaks a Persian-period monetary and commercial economy, since the minting of coins (daric) only began under Darius I in 515 BC (but see Rudman, 15-16, who argues for a Hellenistic date).

Although a postexilic date for Ecclesiastes is the consensus position, arguments to the contrary have been adduced (for a judicious appreciation for these arguments, see Longman, 11-15). One of the more respected, and often cited (by both supporters and detractors), works is the 1988 monograph by D. C. Fredericks. His main observation is that linguistic data place Ecclesiastes no later than the exilic period and possibly preexilic. A general preexilic date, however, still leaves us very far from a demonstration of Solomonic authorship. Fredericks's arguments have not achieved a consensus (see, e.g., Schoors 1992, 221-24). Regardless, his arguments provide a helpful balance to those who would date Ecclesiastes to as late as the second century BC— that is, bearing the marks of the influence of Mishnaic Hebrew (e.g., Whitley; but see the contrary argument by Isaksson). Debate certainly will continue concerning a more precise dating

of Ecclesiastes, but it is unlikely that arguments for authorship in Solomon's time will gain academic support. Any arguments for an early date would gain acceptance only if the linguistic arguments were first met. Until such time, the aforementioned positions of Delitzsch and Green can be employed as a base for subsequent discussion.

2. Frame Narration and the Message of Ecclesiastes.

2.1. The Frame. Understanding the macrostructure of Ecclesiastes is vital for discerning the message of the book as a whole. What strikes the reader is the book begins (Eccles 1:1-11) with the voice of a narrator. Beginning at Ecclesiastes 1:12 and extending to Ecclesiastes 12:7, the narrator gives way to Qohelet's own voice (with the interesting exception of Eccles 7:27). The narrator's voice resumes in the conclusion, Ecclesiastes 12:8-14 (or epilogue, although some commentators refer to Eccles 12:13-14 as the epilogue).

How does this narrator's voice function in the book? After the general introduction of Ecclesiastes 1:1 ("The words of Qohelet, son of David, king in Jerusalem"), we read the narrator's evaluation of Qohelet's words in Ecclesiastes 1:2 (indeed, his summation of Qohelet's teaching). This is repeated virtually verbatim in Ecclesiastes 12:8 (*see* Inclusio).

hăbēl hăbālîm ʾāmar qōhelet hăbēl hăbālîm hakkōl hābel (Eccles 1:2)
hăbēl hăbālîm ʾāmar haqqōhelet hakkōl hābel (Eccles 12:8)

"Meaningless! Meaningless!" says the
Teacher. "Utterly meaningless!
Everything is meaningless." (Eccles 1:2)
"Meaningless! Meaningless!" says the
Teacher. "Everything is meaningless!"
(Eccles 12:8)

Since Ecclesiastes 1:2 and Ecclesiastes 12:8 "frame" the book in this way, the author of the entire book is sometimes referred to as the *frame narrator. Appreciating this structure will help bring a greater understanding of how the book as a whole fits together. Toward that end, any argument that seeks an "original" skeptical book of Qohelet (Eccles 1:12—12:7) to which is clumsily added a later "orthodox" framework is purely conjectural and based on faulty assumptions of what is and is not appropriate for a biblical book to contain. In this regard, the frame narrator's introduction should be taken at face value. There should be no doubt as to what Ecclesiastes is about. We are told explicitly in Ecclesiastes 1:1-2: "The words of Qohelet, son of David, king in Jerusalem. 'Meaningless! Meaningless!' says Qohelet. 'Utterly meaningless! Everything is meaningless.'"

There is no mystery here. The frame narrator is telling the readers what they are about to hear. The problems begin to arise, however, when we presume that the frame narrator's words, even here, represent a negative evaluation rather than simply an attempt to express succinctly the point of Qohelet's words. Yet the remainder of the introduction simply continues in this vein. There is no attempt here to "correct" or sanitize the tone of what will occupy the middle section of the book.

The presence of a third-person frame and a first-person middle raises the question of whether there is one author or two—that is, whether one person is responsible for the first-person discourse and another person for adding on the frame. Some of the motivation for such thinking can be traced to early critical studies, where the search for sources dominated the scholarly landscape. I see no reason not to view the frame narrator as the author of the book, regardless of whatever independent prehistory there might have been for the middle section, although this too is a conjecture (see also Longman, 21). The more active issue, as indicated above, is whether Qohelet is (1) a fictional character created by the frame narrator or (2) the frame narrator's own alter ego, but here too this issue cannot be settled definitively, nor is it vital to do so. Either way, Qohelet represents a point of view about which the frame narrator feels strongly enough to lay out patiently for his readers over 203 of the 221 total verses in the book. There is clearly something here, some lesson that readers are expected to discern. The frame narrator has already given us a fairly explicit map.

2.2. The Epilogue. The epilogue (Eccles 12:8-14) provides a summary and evaluation of Qohelet's words. The basic question is this: Does the narrator give a fundamentally negative or positive evaluation of the content of the book? Or put differently: Is the purpose of the epilogue to correct the errant theology of Qohelet

or to confirm Qohelet's observations? Of course, in reality the matter is more complex than either-or, and the final solution likely contains elements of both. The view taken here is that the epilogue is in fundamental support of Qohelet's observations while at the same time offering a mild corrective (on this, see also Bartholomew, 95-96; Fox 1999, 371, 373; Seow, 38; Provan, 36).

To demonstrate this point, we focus on the last two verses of the epilogue, Ecclesiastes 12:13-14 (for a fuller treatment, see Enns). The book of Ecclesiastes ends thus: "Now all has been heard; here is the conclusion of the matter: Fear God and keep his commandments, for this is the whole duty of man *[kol-hāʾādām]*. For God will bring every deed into judgment, including every hidden thing, whether it is good or evil" (Eccles 12:13-14). Our focus here is the last two words of Ecclesiastes 12:13, *kol-hāʾādām* (lit., "all the man"), translated in the NIV as "the whole duty of man."

It is a widely recognized notion that the epilogue intentionally picks up on the language and themes of Qohelet's discourse (see Shead). The phrase *kol-hāʾādām*, which concludes Ecclesiastes 12:13, is found three other times in the book: Ecclesiastes 3:13; 5:19 (5:18 MT); 7:2 (fourteen times elsewhere in the OT, but these instances are of no consequence for understanding Ecclesiastes). It may be suspected that the author's use of this phrase in Ecclesiastes 12:13 is not meant to be an isolated comment but rather is to be read in light of these previous occurrences. Briefly put, in Ecclesiastes 3:13 and Ecclesiastes 5:19 (5:18 MT), the so-called *carpe diem* passages, Qohelet affirms that *kol-hāʾādām* ("everyone") is to enjoy pleasure in daily existence. In Ecclesiastes 7:2 Qohelet observes that death is the end *(sôp)* of *kol-hāʾādām*. Pleasure and death are two important, indeed, dialectical and pivotal, theological themes in Qohelet's discourse, and the emphatic phrase *ki-zeh kol-hāʾādām* ("Indeed, this is the whole duty of man" [see 2.2.3 below]) in Ecclesiastes 12:13 should be understood as Qohelet's final reflection on these themes.

2.2.1. kol-hāʾādām and Pleasure in Ecclesiastes 3:13; 5:19 (5:18 MT). The first instance of *kol-hāʾādām* is found in Ecclesiastes 3:13, where Qohelet considers the value of pleasure and enjoyment: "I know that there is nothing better for men than to be happy and do good while they live. That everyone *[kol-hāʾādām]* may eat and drink, and find satisfaction in all his toil—this is the gift of God" (Eccles 3:12-13).

The NIV blunts the force of the Hebrew phrase somewhat. Perhaps a better way of translating it here, at least for the purpose of drawing out its theological connections with other passages in Ecclesiastes, is "Moreover, the whole [duty] of man is that he should eat." When we handle this phrase here the way in which it is typically understood in Ecclesiastes 12:13, the contrast between them becomes apparent—which exactly is *kolhāʾādām?* Is it to enjoy the simple pleasures of life, as Ecclesiastes 3:13 has it, or is it to fear God and keep his commandments, as we see in Ecclesiastes 12:13?

The contrast between the two becomes more apparent when we consider the tone of resignation that surrounds Ecclesiastes 3:12-13. Ecclesiastes 3:12 states, "There is nothing better than . . . " (see also Eccles 2:24; 3:22; 8:15). This section follows Ecclesiastes 3:1-9, which likewise (despite Pete Seeger's optimistic interpretation in the song "Turn, Turn, Turn"), reflects Qohelet's resignation to the inevitability of the cycles of life (note the "pessimistic" evaluation of Eccles 3:1-9 given in Eccles 3:9: "What does the worker gain from his toil?" [see Rudman, 89-91]). In fact, Qohelet is revisiting here the theme already introduced by the frame narrator in Ecclesiastes 1:1-11. The recurring cycles of life demonstrate that there is no *yitrôn*, no surplus or profit ("gain" in Eccles 1:3 NIV), and it is this fact that renders all of life *hebel* (NIV: "meaningless"); that is, all human activity is ultimately *hebel* because no human activity produces *yitrôn*. This is the lesson so clearly illustrated in Ecclesiastes 1:5-7. The sun, wind and streams labor, but in the end they are no better off than when they started. No profit or surplus results from their struggles. This drama of nature will be played out on the human stage repeatedly in Ecclesiastes: since death levels the playing field for all, and since "you can't take it with you," it is the inevitability of death that insures that no human activity will provide anyone with a profit or surplus (see, e.g., Eccles 3:19-22). It is this fact that renders life under the sun *hebel*.

It is within this larger context of resignation that *kol-hāʾādām* in Ecclesiastes 3:13 must be understood. Qohelet resigns himself to the fact that eating, drinking and "experiencing what is good" *(rāʾâ tôb)* are what God gives everyone to

do; this is God's "gift" *(mattat)*, not in the sense of a festive present but rather as that which God has assigned for us to do. It is the procurement of mundane benefits, such as eating, drinking and getting some simple pleasures out of life, that, even though there is no "profit" in them, are the very things that everyone can and should do during the days of one's existence. These are the activities that counter, albeit ultimately unsuccessfully, the absurdity of life "under the sun" (understood, I take it, to mean "the land of the living" [i.e., expansively], and not in contrast to a "heavenly" perspective [i.e., restrictively]; for the latter, see Seow, 104-5; Lohfink, 37; for the former, see Longman, 66). And life is absurd in the face of death's inexorable final blow. Finally, Ecclesiastes 3:14-15 continues Qohelet's rather pessimistic appraisal of the human situation. What God has done, the recurring cycle of times and humanity's meager lot in life, are God's doing and cannot be changed. Things will always *(lēʿôlām)* be this way. They cannot be added to *(ysp)* or taken away from *(grʿ)*. The purpose for which God has done it so is "so that they [humanity] will fear *[yrʾ]* him." Precisely what Qohelet means by "fear" can be debated, but certainly it seems to be bound up in the frustrating incomprehensibility of the inevitability that there is nothing new under the sun, a point aptly made in Ecclesiastes 3:15a: "That which is already was, and what will be already was."

The rhythm of life "under the sun" (another recurring theme in Ecclesiastes) does not change, which is the summation of Qohelet's thoughts in Ecclesiastes 1:1-11. In the timing of the circumstances of life, scrutable only to God, the summation of humanity's existence is to accept as God's gift the simple pleasures that come from one's labor. This is what, according to Ecclesiastes 3:13, is for "everyone"; this is what is *kol-hāʾādām*.

As with Ecclesiastes 3:13, so also Ecclesiastes 5:19 (5:18 MT) is a *carpe diem* passage set within a larger context: "Moreover, everyone *[kol-hāʾādām]* to whom God gives wealth and possessions, he gives him the ability to partake of them, to accept his lot and rejoice in his labors. This is a gift from God."

The sentiment expressed here is very similar to that of Ecclesiastes 3:10-15, a point borne out by a number of similarities in wording. Ecclesiastes 5:18 repeats the triad "eat, drink, experience good" of Ecclesiastes 3:13. Moreover, this activity is what Qohelet calls "fitting" (*yāpeh*), thus echoing the notion of God's fitting activity of ordering the rhythms of life (Eccles 3:11). This passage also speaks of what God has given (*mattat*) to humanity (Eccles 5:19), although here it is summed up a bit differently. Whereas Ecclesiastes 3:13 speaks simply of eating, drinking, and experiencing good as humanity's *kol-hā'ādām*, in Ecclesiastes 5:19 the thought is added that God gives humanity wealth (*'ōšer*), possessions (*nĕkāsîm*), and the ability to partake of these things, to accept one's lot (*ḥēleq*), and to rejoice in one's labor (*'āmāl*).

Qohelet's admonition to his readers to content themselves with the pleasures of this life as their portion (*ḥēleq*) is his attempt to construct meaning in a world where meaning, at least for him, has collapsed. But his calls to seize the day, however sincere, are repeatedly relativized by the universal inevitability of death. It is the fact of death that renders all human activity without *yitrôn*, without profit. There is no payoff ultimately to anything we do, since we, like the animals, will die (Eccles 3:19).

2.2.2. kol-hā'ādām and Death in Ecclesiastes 7:2. The juxtaposition of death and *carpe diem* in Ecclesiastes creates a tension that is not resolved until the end of the book. In the meantime, Ecclesiastes 7:2 explicitly ties the theme of death to *kol-hā'ādām:* "It is better to go to the house of mourning than to the house of feasting, because that is the end of everyone [*sôp kol-hā'ādām*]; the living should take this to heart."

Death is a dominant theme in Ecclesiastes (see Burkes). The specter of death routinely nullifies whatever positive conclusions Qohelet might draw. There are a number of explicit references to death in the book (Eccles 2:14-16; 3:2, 19-21; 4:2-3; 5:15-16; 6:3-6; 7:1-2, 4, 17, 26; 8:8; 9:2-12; 11:8; 12:5-6). Although Ecclesiastes 7:2 is the place where Qohelet laments that death is specifically *kol-hā'ādām*, the notion is implied throughout the book. Qohelet's focus on death is disproportionate to what is found elsewhere in the Hebrew Scriptures. As S. Burkes (75) puts it, "With Qohelet . . . death makes its entrance into the Hebrew traditions as a phenomenon to be reckoned with."

Burkes attempts to locate Qohelet's preoccupation with death in the context of larger paradigm shifts in the postexilic world. Specifically, she focuses on Egyptian biographies that share certain themes with Ecclesiastes. Both Ecclesiastes and these Egyptian biographies are part of a larger paradigm shift (Burkes is very careful not to argue for any direct dependence) fueled by "permutations" in the "power structures of the ancient world . . . that were felt far and wide" (Burkes, 6). For the author of Ecclesiastes, who passed his days in such a time of upheaval, death "represents the chief flaw that embraces and subsumes all other problems in the world" (Burkes, 2).

In exile the Israelites began to struggle to come to grips with their lost glory. The status of the group was uncertain, and so the question of the individual's fate began to present itself; the heretofore subdued emphasis on the individual (such as one finds in *Proverbs) comes to the foreground. To put it another way: whatever national hope there might have been for Israel is transferred to the individual (Burkes, 111). God's perpetual covenant fidelity to a nation had been demonstrated (indeed, promised [see 2 Sam 7:5-16]) in the form of possession of land, performance of cult, and an unbroken line of kings. Such things ceased for Israel in the early sixth century BC. But to transfer these promises to the individual is no easy task, for how can an individual experience the perpetual covenant? The reality and finality of death call into question the applicability of God's ancient promises to the individual. Moreover, "The symbolic immortalities offered elsewhere in the Bible, the memory and endurance of a good name, survival through one's children and people, even the qualitative good life that negates the 'death' of folly and unrighteousness, fail utterly in Qohelet's opinion" (Burkes, 111).

Death is that which, for Qohelet, ultimately renders futile humanity's "quest for meaning." All, human and animal alike, come to the same end. Thus, what punctuates Qohelet's theology is that which is the activity of "everyone": to enjoy the pleasures that God has given (Eccles 3:13; 5:19) and then to die (Eccles 7:2).

2.2.3. kol-hā'ādām and Ecclesiastes 12:13. The book as a whole, however, does not let the matter rest there. A solution to the dilemma is provided in Ecclesiastes 12:13. In view of the foregoing discussion, it seems highly unlikely to me that *kol-hā'ādām* in Ecclesiastes 12:13 can be treated in isolation from the theology espoused in the previous uses of the phrase. It seems, rather, that *kol-hā'ādām* contributes to our understanding of the epilogue as a mild corrective to the teachings of Qohelet, by accepting Qohelet's observations as wise (see Eccles 12:9-11) but then going one further.

It seems most unlikely that the epilogist is simply contradicting Qohelet; that is, it is improbable that the teachings of Qohelet, which are expressed very intentionally over the span of roughly twelve chapters, are there merely to be dismissed in the closing verses of the book. Moreover, the epilogue has a decidedly positive tone. Despite legitimate ambiguities in the closing section of the book, it seems clear that the epilogue presents Qohelet as a wise teacher (Eccles 12:9). There is no indication that the epilogue should be seen in fundamental contrast to Qohelet's words. I do suggest, however, that Ecclesiastes 12:13-14 puts Qohelet's observations in a broader perspective. We find a positive evaluation of Qohelet as wise, but with a gentle critique, as can be seen in the use of *kol-hāʾādām* in Ecclesiastes 12:13.

Two things are worth noting concerning the use of *kol-hāʾādām* in Ecclesiastes 12:13. First, this phrase is emphatic: *(kî-zeh kol-hāʾādām)*. Throughout Ecclesiastes the demonstrative pronoun *(zeh/zōh)* is used in a number of climactic statements. In fourteen instances it is used to introduce Qohelet's conclusion *zeh hebel*, "this is meaningless" (Eccles 2:15, 19, 21, 23, 26; 4:4, 8, 16; 5:9; 6:2, 9; 7:6; 8:10, 14). Similarly, it is used as a concluding statement of some sort in twelve other instances (Eccles 1:10, 17; 2:10, 24; 5:15, 18; 7:23, 27, 29; 8:9; 9:3, 13).

When we keep in mind the rather obvious fact that Ecclesiastes 12:13-14 is itself the conclusion of the concluding section of Ecclesiastes, the "concluding" force of *zeh* in Ecclesiastes 12:13 seems self-evident. Further, in light of these observations, it is likely that we should assign likewise an emphatic meaning to *kî*. It is not too much to expect the writer to want to drive home his point emphatically in the closing thought of the book. "Fear God. Keep the commandments. Indeed *[kî]*, this *[zeh]* is *kol-hāʾādām*."

The NIV, as we noted, translates the phrase as "this is the whole duty of man" (NRSV: "that is the whole duty of everyone"). Fox's translation, however, comes closest to reading Ecclesiastes 12:13 as an intentional echo of Ecclesiastes 3:13; 5:19; 7:2: fearing God and keeping the commandments are "the substance, the 'material' of

every person. There should be no alloy" (Fox 1999, 362). If I may put it differently, fearing God and keeping the commandments—this is what truly "summarizes the human experience" or, as the JPS translation puts it, "applies to all mankind." Qohelet is correct in taking to heart the pleasures and rewards of life (Eccles 3:13; 5:19) and facing the stern reality of death (Eccles 7:2). These are central components of the human drama for each Israelite, for "everyone." But more foundational and central is each Israelite's fear of God (*see* Fear of the Lord) and obedience to God's *law.

The conclusion to the book, therefore, does not pit the frame narrator against Qohelet but rather places Qohelet's flesh-and-blood struggles into their larger and theologically ultimate context and perspective. Qohelet was indeed wise in his observations (Eccles 12:9-11), but the frame narrator encourages his readers to view those observations in view of a broader perspective. The epilogist does not encourage his readers to engage further in Qohelet's internal debate. In fact, Ecclesiastes 12:12-13 cuts off debate entirely. And here we may find an indication of why the author adopts a royal persona. The king is the paragon of *wisdom and has at his disposal the necessary resources and time to investigate the meaning of life under the sun. His readers do not. Qohelet's investigation takes him to dark places where his readers cannot, and need not, tread. It is up to the reader, therefore, to heed the epilogist's words, that (1) Qohelet is wise (Eccles 12:9-11); (2) nothing can be added to his words (Eccles 12:12-13a); (3) the proper response is not to dismiss Qohelet's words but rather to move beyond them by acknowledging one's duty to fear God and keep the commandments (Eccles 12:13b), and trust that God is still about the business of setting all thing right (Eccles 12:14). The epilogue acknowledges the true wisdom of Qohelet's observations while at the same time reiterating Israel's central tradition of the fear of God and obedience to Torah. Times have changed, and new challenges may be afoot, but Israel's responsibility remains the same.

In other words, despite the reality of the struggles so eloquently outlined by Qohelet, the answer is still as it always was. Qohelet was indeed wise in his observations of the inconsistencies, even contradictions, of life, as the epilogue points out. But there is something more, and the "more" is not a new twist but rather the tried and true formula of "fear and obedience." Such a solution to the newer problems that beset postexilic Israelites also serves as an appeal to Israel to see their historical vicissitudes from the point of view of traditional categories, thus encouraging a sense of continuity between Israel's past and present, despite the circumstances. The emphatic phrase in Ecclesiastes 12:13 is intended to direct the reader's attention toward a higher goal that sums up Israel's quest for meaning. To paraphrase Ecclesiastes 12:13: "Qohelet is wise, to be sure. As he says, pleasure and death are real and are the portion of everyone *[kol-hāʾādām]*. But there is a deeper, more fundamental obligation upon this earth, which is to fear God and keep his commandments. This is truly for everyone *[kî-zeh kol-hāʾādām]*."

Despite our own theological instincts that might drive us to distance ourselves from Qohelet's blunt observations, the frame narrator spins us around and brings us right up against the words of wisdom that he has so delicately framed. The frame narrator will not allow us to dismiss Qohelet's words as the skeptical ramblings of a fool or unbeliever. We are forced to allow his words to jab us like goads and firmly embedded nails (Eccles 12:11). The frame narrator blocks our escape into the comfort of familiar theological territory, just as he did for his original readers.

3. Theological Themes.

3.1. Dominant Theological Themes in Ecclesiastes.
Ecclesiastes is a difficult book in which to isolate individual themes, as there is a significant amount of interweaving and revisiting of themes and vocabulary. At times it appears that new ideas come almost out of nowhere, and the reader is left to ponder how the pieces of the book connect as a whole. Despite this situation, however, a number of important theological themes present themselves and serve to provide important hooks upon which to hang the various data of the book. These dominant themes are addressed here, although, due to their interconnectedness, they are not presented in isolation from each other.

Perhaps the most recognizable theme is that of "meaninglessness" (NIV), or "vanity" (KJV). These words are attempts to translate the Hebrew *hebel*. Its literal sense is "vapor," which leads to metaphorical uses such as "ephemeral"

(Ps 144:4), "vain," "worthless," "inconsequential" and the like. In Ecclesiastes, however, these meanings rarely fit. Qohelet's main contention is not that life is ephemeral or worthless; rather, his cause of such distress is that there is no payoff in what one does. None of our activities result in any sort of ultimate benefit. Hence, a more apt translation of *hebel* may be, as Fox argues, "absurd." Life as we experience it is "an affront to reason" (Fox 1999, 31; see also Christianson, 83-88). And what sorts of things are absurd? Things such as pleasure, wealth, labor, justice, wisdom—or, to use the summative word of the frame narrator, "everything" *(kōl)*.

Why does Qohelet draw such a conclusion? Because there is no profit *(yitrôn)* in any of our labor *(ʿāmāl)*. The point of the frame narrator's introduction is to illustrate this very point (Eccles 1:3-11). The recurring question "What profit is there?" is rhetorical. The answer is "None at all." No matter how much effort one expends, at the end of the day there is no net surplus. Why is there no net surplus? Because at the end of the day, all die, and so Qohelet laments in Ecclesiastes 3:18-21, "I also thought, 'As for men, God tests them so that they may see that they are like the animals. Man's fate is like that of the animals; the same fate awaits them both: As one dies, so dies the other. All have the same breath; man has no advantage over the animal. Everything is meaningless. All go to the same place; all come from dust, and to dust all return. Who knows if the spirit of man rises upward and if the spirit of the animal goes down into the earth?'"

This is the situation into which all are born. We are all destined to die, and no notion of an *afterlife will change that fact, since we cannot be sure. Since death comes to us all as the final leveler, nothing that we do has any ultimate value, because nothing lasts. So, anything that we might perceive as being meaningful, Qohelet goes to great lengths to point out, is really absurd. Any meaning to be found in these activities or accomplishments is only relative. The best that we can do is to accept our portion *(ḥēleq)*, that which God allows us to do in this life: living day to day—eating, drinking and enjoying the tasks that God has given us.

One may sum up the dominant theological themes in Qohelet thus: Everything is absurd because there is no payoff for anything we do. The main reason why this is so is that death cancels out any such potential profit. What we do have, however, is our lot in life, the day-to-day activities that occupy our time and that, if God pleases, will occupy us to the extent that we do not consider the absurdity of it all.

A plain reading of Ecclesiastes will allow these themes to develop of their own accord, resisting the impulse to align Qohelet's thought with more conventional biblical teaching. As discussed above, the epilogue is somewhat startling in its general support of Qohelet's observations while at the same time taking his thoughts to another level of understanding. The radical nature of the proposed "solution" to Qohelet's struggles can be fully appreciated only when we allow the dominant themes of the book to exert their full force.

3.2. Some Recurring and Important Lexemes for the Theology of Ecclesiastes. In addition to important theological themes, it is helpful to observe dominant lexemes in Ecclesiastes. Providing a list of recurring vocabulary, however, should not be misunderstood as perpetuating a false distinction between words and concepts; rather, it is precisely through the recurring use of vocabulary that the reader is alerted to the author's main concerns. In other words, the importance of these words is in how they are used in Ecclesiastes: they point to concepts. The list of words is simply an indication of specific Hebrew lexemes that recur in Ecclesiastes, thus alerting the reader to conceptual interconnections. The words listed below are not necessarily the most frequent, although some of them certainly are. Some have already been mentioned (see 3.1 above). Only the root is listed if verbal and nominal forms occur.

ʾĕlōhîm ("God") (Eccles 1:13; 2:24, 26; 3:10, 11, 13, 14, 15, 17, 18; 4:17; 5:1, 3, 5, 6, 17, 18, 19; 6:2; 7:13, 14, 18, 26, 29; 8:2, 12, 13, 15, 17; 9:1, 7; 11:5, 9; 12:7, 13, 14)

bqš ("seek") (Eccles 3:6, 15; 7:25, 28, 29; 8:17; 12:10)

ḥokmâ ("wisdom") (Eccles 1:13, 16, 17, 18; 2:3, 9, 12, 13, 14, 15, 16, 19, 21, 26; 4:13; 6:8; 7:4, 5, 7, 10, 11, 12, 16, 19, 23, 25; 8:1, 5, 16, 17; 9:1, 10, 11, 13, 15, 16, 17, 18; 10:1, 2, 10, 12; 12:9, 11)

ḥālak ("walk, go," sometimes a metaphor for death) (Eccles 1:4, 6, 7; 2:1, 14; 3:20; 4:15, 17; 5:14, 15; 6:4, 6, 8, 9; 7:2; 8:3, 10; 9:7, 10; 10:3, 7, 15, 20; 11:9; 12:5)

hebel ("meaningless, absurd") (Eccles 1:14; 2:1, 11, 15, 17, 19, 21, 23, 26; 3:19; 4:4, 7, 8, 16; 5:6, 9; 6:2, 4, 9; 7:6; 8:10, 14; 9:9; 11:8, 10; 12:8)

ḥēpeṣ ("pleasure/delight, matter") (Eccles 3:1, 17; 5:3, 7; 8:3, 6; 12:1, 10)

ḥēleq ("portion") (Eccles 2:10, 21; 3:22; 5:17, 18; 9:6, 9; 11:2)

ṭôb ("good") (Eccles 2:1, 3, 24, 26; 3:12, 13, 22; 4:3, 6, 8, 9, 13; 5:4, 10, 17; 6:3, 6, 9, 12; 7:1, 2, 3, 5, 8, 10, 11, 14, 18, 20, 26; 8:12, 13, 15; 9:2, 4, 7, 16, 18; 11:6, 7; 12:14)

ydʿ ("know, knowledge") (Eccles 1:17; 2:14, 19; 3:12, 14, 21; 4:13, 17; 6:5, 8, 10, 12; 7:22, 25; 8:1, 5, 7, 12, 16, 17; 9:1, 5, 11, 12; 10:14, 15; 11:2, 5, 6, 9)

yitrônyôtēr ("profit, excess") (Eccles 1:3; 2:11, 13, 15; 3:9; 5:8, 15; 6:8, 11; 7:11, 12, 16; 10:10, 11; 12:9, 12)

kōl ("all") (Eccles 1:2, 3, 7, 8, 9, 13, 14, 16; 2:5, 7, 9, 10, 11, 14, 16, 17, 18, 19, 20, 22, 23; 3:1, 11, 13, 14, 17, 19, 20; 4:1, 4, 8, 15, 16; 5:8, 15, 16, 17, 18; 6:2, 6, 7; 7:2, 15, 18, 21, 23, 28; 8:3, 6, 9, 17; 9:1, 2, 3, 4, 6, 8, 9, 10, 11; 10:3, 19; 11:5, 8, 9; 1:4, 8, 13, 14)

kĕsîl ("fool") (Eccles 2:14, 15, 16; 4:5, 13, 17; 5:2, 3; 6:8; 7:4, 5, 6, 9; 9:17; 10:2, 12)

lēb ("heart," intensive referent to one's "inner" self) (Eccles 1:13, 16, 17; 2:1, 2, 10, 15, 20, 22, 23; 3:11, 17, 18; 5:1, 19; 7:2, 3, 4, 7, 21, 22, 25, 26; 8:5, 9, 11, 16; 9:1, 3, 7; 10:2, 3; 11:9, 10)

mišpaṭ ("judgment") (Eccles 3:16; 5:7; 8:5, 6; 11:9; 12:14)

siklût ("fool") (Eccles 1:17 [śiklût]; 2:3, 12, 13; 7:25; 10:1, 13)

ʿôlam ("great expanse of time") (Eccles 1:4, 10; 2:16; 3:11, 14; 9:6; 12:5)

ʿml ("labor") (Eccles 1:3; 2:10, 11, 18, 19, 20, 21, 22, 24; 3:9, 13; 4:4, 6, 8, 9; 5:14, 15, 17, 18; 6:7; 8:15, 17; 9:9; 10:15)

ʿēt ("time") (Eccles 3:1-8 [29x]; 3:11, 17; 7:17; 8:5, 6, 9; 9:8, 11, 12; 10:17)

ṣdq ("righteous") (Eccles 3:17; 7:15, 16, 20; 8:14; 9:1, 2)

qrh ("fate") (Eccles 2:14, 15; 3:19; 9, 3, 11; 10:18)

rʾh ("see, observe, experience") (Eccles 1:8, 10, 14, 16; 2:1, 3, 12, 13, 24; 3:10, 13, 16, 18, 22; 4:1, 3, 4, 7, 15; 5:7, 12, 17; 6:1, 5, 6; 7:11, 13, 14, 15, 27, 29; 8:9, 10, 16, 17; 9:9, 11, 13; 10:5, 7; 11:4, 7; 12:3)

rʿ/rʿh ("evil, unjust" [see ršʿ]) (Eccles 1:13; 2:17; 4:8, 17; 5:12, 13, 15; 6:1, 2; 7:14; 8:3, 5, 11, 12; 9:3, 12; 10:5, 13; 11:2, 10; 12:14)

ršʿ ("evil, unjust" [see rʿ/rʿh]) (Eccles 3:16, 17; 7:15, 17, 25; 8:8, 10, 13, 14; 9:2) *śmh* ("joy") (Eccles 2:1, 2, 10, 26; 3:12, 22; 4:16, 5:18, 19; 7:14; 8:15; 9:7; 10:19; 11:8, 9)

taḥat haššāmeš ("under the sun") (Eccles 1:9, 14; 2:11, 17, 18, 19, 20, 22; 3:16; 4:1, 3, 7, 15; 5:12; 6:1, 12; 8:9, 15, 17; 9:3, 6, 9, 11, 13; 10:5)

Bearing these words in mind—even looking for them—will alert the reader to the interconnectedness of Qohelet's major themes and concepts. And observing such interconnections will force the reader to allow Qohelet himself to set the agenda for how he wishes to be understood. It will also bring to the fore what Fox has so well observed: Qohelet's self-contradictory reflections are not an oddity to be adjusted here and there; rather, they reflect the author's intention for how he wishes to communicates his theological message. Fox sees Qohelet's contradictions as the starting point for interpretation.

> My primary thesis is a simple one: The contradictions in the book of Qohelet are real and intended. We must interpret them, not eliminate them. . . . Qohelet's persistent observation of contradictions is a powerful cohesive force, and an awareness of it brings into focus the book's central concern: the problem of meaning in life. The book of Qohelet is about *meaning:* its loss and its (partial) recovery. . . . Qohelet's contradictions are the starting point but not the message of the book. He marshals them to *tear down* meaning, but he does not stop there. He is not a nihilist. He also *builds up* meaning, discovering ways of creating clarity and gratification in a confusing world. (Fox 1999, 3)

Attention to Qohelet's use of words, which provides a "structure" of sorts to the book, alerts us to the very message that he intends to communicate.

4. Conclusion.
The disjunction with other portions of the OT as well as internal tensions assure that Ecclesiastes will remain one of the more enigmatic and challenging books of the OT. The book's macrostructure—the narrator's words framing the extended dialogues of Qohelet himself—advances its theology, and so it is important to come to resolution of the interplay between them. In the closing verses of the epilogue the author brings the tensions of the book to a resolution, not by

dismissing Qohelet's observations but by acknowledging the wisdom that they contain and then bringing them under the broader (more traditional) umbrella of fearing God and keeping his commandments. The force of this resolution, however, will not be fully appreciated apart from the necessary and challenging work of reading Ecclesiastes patiently and allowing the author to present the case in his time and in his way.

See also AUTOBIOGRAPHY; FOLLY; FRAME NARRATIVE; QOHELET; SOLOMON.

BIBLIOGRAPHY. *Commentaries*: **J. Crenshaw,** *Ecclesiastes* (OTL; Philadelphia: Westminster, 1987); **F. Delitzsch,** *Song of Songs and Ecclesiastes* (repr., Grand Rapids: Eerdmans, 1982 [1877]); **T. Krüger,** *Qoheleth: A Commentary* (Minneapolis: Fortress, 2004); **N. Lohfink,** *Qoheleth* (CC; Minneapolis: Fortress, 2003); **T. Longman III,** *The Book of Ecclesiastes* (NICOT; Grand Rapids: Eerdmans, 1998); **R. E. Murphy,** *Ecclesiastes* (WBC 23A; Dallas: Word, 1992); **I. Provan,** *Ecclesiastes/Song of Songs* (NIVAC; Grand Rapids: Zondervan, 2001); **C. L. Seow,** *Ecclesiastes* (AB 18C; New York: Doubleday, 1997); **R. N. Whybray,** *Ecclesiastes* (NCBC; Grand Rapids: Eerdmans, 1989). *Studies*: **C. Bartholomew,** *Reading Ecclesiastes: Old Testament Exegesis and Hermeneutical Theory* (AnBib 139; Rome: Pontifical Biblical Institute, 1998); **R. Beckwith,** *The Old Testament Canon of the New Testament Church* (Grand Rapids: Eerdmans, 1985); **S. Burkes,** *Death in Qoheleth and Egyptian Biographies of the Late Period* (SBLDS 170; Atlanta: Society of Biblical Literature, 1999); **F. C. Burkitt,** "Is Ecclesiastes a Translation?" *JTS* 23 (1921-1922) 22-26; **E. Christianson,** *A Time to Tell: Narrative Strategies in Ecclesiastes* (JSOTSup 280; Sheffield: Sheffield Academic Press, 1998); **P. Enns,** "כל־האדם and the Evaluation of Qohelet's Wisdom in Eccles 12:13, or The 'A Is So, and What's More, B' Theology of Ecclesiastes," in *The Idea of Biblical Interpretation: Essays in Honor of James L. Kugel*, ed. H. Najman and J. Newman (JSJSup 83; Leiden: E. J. Brill, 2003) 125-37; **M. V. Fox,** *Qohelet and His Contradictions* (JSOTSup 71; Sheffield: Almond, 1989); idem, *A Time to Tear Down and a Time to Build Up: A Rereading of Ecclesiastes* (Grand Rapids: Eerdmans, 1999); idem, *Ecclesiastes* (JPSBC; Philadelphia: Jewish Publication Society, 2004); **D. C. Fredericks,** *Qoheleth's Language: Re-evaluating Its Nature and Date* (ANETS 3; Lewiston, NY: Edwin Mellen, 1988); **R. Gordis,** "The Original Language of Qohelet," *JQR* 37 (1946-1947) 67-84; **W. H. Green,** *Old Testament Literature: Lectures on the Poetical Books of the Old Testament* (Princeton, NJ: Princeton College, 1884); **M. Hirshman,** "Qohelet's Reception and Interpretation in Early Rabbinic Literature," in *Studies in Ancient Midrash,* ed. J. L. Kugel (Cambridge, MA: Harvard University Press, 2001) 87-99; **B. Isaksson,** *Studies in the Language of Qoheleth: With Special Emphasis on the Verbal System* (SSU 10; Stockholm: Almqvist & Wiksell, 1987); **S. Japhet,** *The Ideology of the Book of Chronicles and Its Place in Biblical Thought* (BEATAJ 9; Frankfurt: Peter Lang, 1989); idem, *I and II Chronicles* (OTL; Louisville: Westminster John Knox, 2000); **D. Rudman,** *Determinism in the Book of Ecclesiastes* (JSOTSup 316; Sheffield: Sheffield Academic Press, 2001); **A. Schoors,** *The Preacher Sought to Find Pleasing Words: A Study of the Language of Qohelet* (OLA 41; Leuven: Peeters, 1992); idem, ed., *Qohelet in the Context of Wisdom* (BETL 86; Leuven: Leuven University Press, 1998); **A. G. Shead,** "Reading Ecclesiastes 'Epilogically,'" *TynBul* 48 (1997) 67-91; **C. C. Torrey,** "The Question of the Original Language of Qoheleth," *JQR* 39 (1948-1949) 151-60; **C. F. Whitley,** *Koheleth: His Language and Thought* (BZAW 148; Berlin: de Gruyter, 1979); **F. Zimmermann,** "The Aramaic Provenance of Qohelet," *JQR* 36 (1945-1946) 17-45.

P. Enns

ECCLESIASTES 2: ANCIENT NEAR EASTERN BACKGROUND

No literary text, biblical or extrabiblical, exists in a vacuum. Texts, as well as their authors, are subject to influences from the culture that surrounds them. Many elements, such as language, education, religious persuasion, economic factors and political forces, influence the genesis of any written text and impact the worldview of its author (G. Klingbeil 2007, 5-14). One important element influencing texts is other literary productions, especially from surrounding cultures. This cross-pollination of influence between distinct cultures can easily be appreciated when one considers the present interaction between East and West in the global economy and culture. To be sure, modern cultural interaction cannot be the paradigm for ancient cultural, religious and literary contact. Our communication capabilities are far more advanced than in Iron Age II (or later), the period during which scholars would place the writing of the book of Ecclesiastes. Our educational system is geared toward much broader interaction. Our technical capabilities of cultural and literary exchange (even by means of a translation) are vastly superior to those in existence during the writing of the OT. However, despite technological, geographical and even political limitations, people living in the ancient Near East were aware of their neighbors and surrounding cultures, as can be easily documented from their writings and material cultures (Yannai and Braun; Gestoso; Gural-nick; Hoffner; Hallo 2004).

In the present article a careful look at possible literary and conceptual links between cultures surrounding Palestine at all the four cardinal points will be undertaken. However, prior to discussing the specifics of the ancient Near Eastern background of Ecclesiastes, it will be helpful to examine what comparative studies can and cannot do. This will be followed by a look at the specifics of the comparative data, beginning with Mesopotamia to the east, Syria and Phoenicia to the north, Greece, Anatolia and the Aegean to the west, and Egypt to the south. As will be shown in the section dealing with the nature of comparative data, this article will not primarily strive to establish concrete historical links but rather will look at the intellectual climate of the surrounding cultures. This is not meant to ignore the clearly established historical, political, religious, economical and cultural links between Palestine and these neighboring cultures but will avoid the often contentious issue of who borrowed from whom, which cannot always be resolved satisfactorily. A final important note should be included at the outset here: although the biblical literary creations did not originate in a vacuum, they are definitely not merely the result of literary cross-pollination. According to the self-testimony of Scripture, it was the God of Israel who spoke through them to the ancient Israelites and continues to speak to those looking for divine and practical wisdom.

1. What Comparative Studies Can and Cannot Do
2. Looking to the East: Mesopotamia
3. Looking to the North: Syria
4. Looking to the West: Greece and the Aegean
5. Looking to the South: Egypt
6. Conclusions

1. What Comparative Studies Can and Cannot Do.

Comparative methods in scientific research have a long history. More than a century ago archaeologists of the ancient Near East looked at comparative data of the material culture of surrounding cultures in order to establish dating sequences and understand the typological development of certain pottery forms or architecture. In biblical studies the pendulum has swung from parallelomania (criticized by Sandmel) to parallelophobia (warned against by Ratner and Zuckerman, 51-52) over the past decades. The focus of the comparative method employed to a certain degree has also influenced the outcome and interpretation of the discovered data.

Historical comparison seeks to evaluate the influence of one culture on another and thus to provide a better *Sitz im Leben* for certain cultural, sociological, political or religious phenomena (G. Klingbeil 2007, 63; for further references, see G. Klingbeil 1998, 325-40; M. Klingbeil, 268-82; Malul; Talmon). Generally, historical comparison focuses on data sets that belong to the same historical and geographical context and has been used to demonstrate specific historical links between two cultures. Others use historical comparison to illuminate specific phenomena (literary, historical, religious or cultural) of one culture with phenomena in another culture.

Typological comparison compares societies and cultures that are chronologically and geographically far removed, with little or no possibility of contact. This school of thought presupposes some type of a common religious conscience in humanity and is often employed in anthropological or sociological research. An interesting example of this type of comparison is found in a study by M. Fox (1999, 8-11), who compares Qohelet's sensitivity to the absurd with the thought of Albert Camus. Fox (1999, 9) recognizes that no direct link between Qohelet and existentialism per se is intended, but rather he suggests similar social changes in Judea of the Hellenistic period (which he identifies as the time of origin for the book of Ecclesiastes) and in Europe of the middle of the twentieth century. Other examples of this typological approach are found in works by N. Klaes and by E. Dammann. Obviously, the typological approach lends itself to the proverbial "apples and oranges" comparison and seems to rely heavily on external models (Talmon, 324; Malul, 52-53).

On the other hand, historical comparison does not always provide sufficient data to establish clear lines of development or dependence and can be quite subjective when it comes to evaluating cultural, religious or historical interaction.

A helpful alternative to historical and typological comparisons, and one that shares common ground with both approaches, is the compare-and-contrast approach suggested and practiced by Assyriologist W. W. Hallo (1977; 1990). This method highlights similarities without neglecting possible differences. Furthermore, the focus on cultures belonging to the same historical and cultural stream (such as the Mediterranean basin or the Levant) avoids highly speculative relations available to the modern researcher, who has access to a huge spectrum of data, but unavailable to ancient authors and cultures. In this sense, when looking at the ancient Near Eastern background of Ecclesiastes, one will be able to discover common or dissimilar patterns of ancient wisdom, which, however, should not automatically be construed as indications of historical development with one culture borrowing from another but rather may point to common wisdom traditions or shared sources. In other words, this discussion of ancient Near Eastern background primarily intends to provide data not for a historical exploration of the particular *Sitz im Leben* of the book or its date but rather that bears on the conceptual and literary world of the ancient Near East.

2. Looking to the East: Mesopotamia.

Mesopotamian conceptual similarities to Ecclesiastes have long been recognized. Statements in the Epic of Gilgamesh easily find counterparts in verses from Ecclesiastes. On Tablet III of the Old Babylonian version, Gilgamesh speaks to Enkidu: "Who, my friend, can scale he[aven]? Only the gods [live] forever under the sun. As for mankind, numbered are their days; whatever they achieve is but the wind" (*ANET*, 79). This "wind" metaphor is used frequently in Ecclesiastes (e.g., Eccles 1:14, 17; 2:11; 4:4) to mark the futility of human work and achievement. Another conceptual link can be found in the speech of the alewife Siduri on Tablet X: "When the gods created mankind, death for mankind they set aside, life in their own hands retaining. Thou, Gilgamesh, let full be thy belly, make thou merry by day and by night. Of each day make thou a feast of rejoicing, day and night dance thou and play! Let thy garments be sparkling fresh, thy head be washed; bathe thou in water. Pay heed to the little one that holds on to thy hand, let they spouse delight in thy bosom! For this is the task of [mankind]!" (*ANET*, 90). Similar thoughts to those of Siduri are reflected in Ecclesiastes 9:7-9, pointing to the transient nature of humanity and showing a *carpe diem* motif (see Barton, 162; Longman, 120). J. Y.-S. Pahk (1996) has demonstrated that these conceptual links between Ecclesiastes and Gilgamesh go even beyond the generally cited examples and include Ecclesiastes 8:16—9:10. However, it has been argued that these links are too general and, furthermore, that no specific historical connections can be established (Uehlinger, 196-98).

In terms of structure, T. Longman (120-23) has observed close similarities on the genre level, involving the Akkadian genre of royal (fictional) *autobiography with a didactic ending. Longman makes particular reference to the Cuthaean Legend of Naram-Sin, whose fullest text is a Neo-Assyrian version (English translation in Longman, 228-31). In both cases the text begins with an autobiographical reference "I am" (Eccles 1:12; similar in Adad-guppi Autobiography [*COS* 1.147:477]) and continues to describe the journey of its purported author to discover meaning and happiness (as in the case of Ecclesiastes) or for power and religious guidance (Cuthaean Legend of Naram-Sin). From lines 147-175 the Akkadian text includes instructions given in the first person, which is also similar to the instructions given in the final section of Ecclesiastes (6:10-14). It must be noted that Ecclesiastes also includes instructions in the earlier section dealing with the search for meaning and happiness and cannot be neatly divided as with the Akkadian document. However, the formal and structural similarities, involving royal fiction and self-discourse, suggest conceptual links between the biblical text and the Akkadian counterpart. Particularly the element of self-discourse or internal dialogue is characteristic of Ecclesiastes (Eccles 1:16; 2:1, 15; 3:17, 18; 7:23) and can also be found in Naram-Sin's autobiography: "Speaking to myself, thus I said" (lines 79, 89, 124).

Another possible link to Mesopotamia and its literature is the pessimistic outlook that Ecclesiastes seems to portray. Life is meaningless. Everything is nothingness. Babylonian texts such as Counsels of a Pessimist (Lambert, 107-9) and The Dialogue of Pessimism (Lambert, 139-49) express a pessimistic outlook on life and its futility and express helplessness and bitterness in the face of life's contradictions and realities (Anderson, 63-65; Bottéro; Loretz, 108-10). However, as suggested in current research on Ecclesiastes (Kottsieper, 237; Whybray 1982), the book is not a clear-cut case of a completely pessimistic outlook on life, happiness and human nature (see Zimmer; Schwienhorst-Schönberger 1994). It rather seems to function as a corrective or further development to other biblical Wisdom literature, particularly in its understanding of *ḥokmâ* ("wisdom"). It is highly self-conscious (Fox 1993, 115) and recognizes the limitations of human wisdom, which in turn extends its scope. This recognition of the failure of human *ḥokmâ* (Eccles 7:14) is borne out of personal experience (as indicated by the use of autobiographical information, referring to "I" [Eccles 8:16-17]) and leads finally to the important acknowledgment that as everyone must die, so too wisdom is overwhelmed by death (Fox 1993, 125-26; similarly Crenshaw 1982, 129-37).

The question of the origins of Israelite wisdom represents another possible link to Mesopotamian wisdom. As can be easily perceived in the reading of biblical wisdom texts, there are at least two different loci for the origin of wisdom texts in Israel: scribal schools (*see* Scribes), most probably sponsored by the royal leadership and associated with the court (Whybray 1990), and folk wisdom—that is, wise sayings that were transmitted orally in the context of small villages and the setting of a clan or family (Crenshaw 1995, 2449-50; Garrett, 23-26). Although in Mesopotamian wisdom the scribal tradition is most clearly emphasized, there is evidence of folk wisdom that was orally transmitted (Denning-Bolle, 2-3). Obviously, it is somewhat misleading to speak about Mesopotamian wisdom as a monolithic block, since, even more than in the biblical wisdom tradition, texts originated and were transmitted over several millennia, involving diverse political, cultural and religious contexts. A particular link between the scribal school activity and the nature of folk wisdom can be seen in the Sumerian collections of proverbs, which were widely used as models for scribal exercises in the schools, even though the dominant imagery of the Sumerian proverbs reflects agriculture and animal husbandry and echo the occupations and concerns of shepherds, gardeners, foremen, hired workmen, fowlers, merchants and so on (Alster, 1.xvi-xxiv).

3. Looking to the North: Syria.

Over the past decades the view from the north has become more and more important. While Syria had mostly been ignored during the early days of the rediscovery of the ancient Near East during the late nineteenth and early twentieth centuries (Chavalas 1992, 2), due to the important discoveries of ancient Ugarit, Ebla, Alalakh, Emar, Qatna, Kamid el-Loz, Qadesh, Tel Brak, together with the important Phoenician towns of Sidon and Tyre, the perspective from the north (G. Klingbeil, forthcoming) has become increasingly important. Syrian history and religious practice appear to have reflected more closely Israelite power structures (particularly the important view from the countryside balancing the Mesopotamian focus on major urban centers [Fortin]), and a number of common religious practices (including the importance of prescriptive and descriptive ritual texts, festival calendars, seven-day periods, high priestly anointing rites, etc.) have been described (Fleming 1992; 1996; 1999; Hess; G. Klingbeil 2000; forthcoming).

What possible literary or intellectual influence of background can be posited as having come from the north (see Uehlinger, 160-61)? In the heyday of comparative Semitics, following the discoveries of Ras Shamra in the first half of the twentieth century, M. Dahood (1952; 1966) suggested significant Canaanite-Phoenician influence in the orthography, morphology and syntax of Ecclesiastes—a theory that was challenged later by A. Schoors (1992). Others have suggested that the Phoenician influence on Ecclesiastes could be discovered in later Persian period texts (Azize, 128), including a funerary description from Eshmunazor II of Sidon (c. 465-451 BC): "The words of Eshmunazor, king of the Sidonians: I was snatched away not at *my time*, a child of a few days" (Azize, 128; cf. Gibson 1982, 106-7). The use of ʿ*ty* ("my time") as a reference to death presupposes the important assumption of "appropriate time," a concept found also in Ecclesiastes 3:2. Furthermore, the frequent use of the phrase "under the sun" (e.g., Eccles 1:3, 9, 14; 2:11, 17, 18) has been understood as a hint to Phoenician solar religion (Azize), which may have been used in a polemical sense

against known (non-Israelite) theological concepts—a tendency found in other biblical material as well (see G. Klingbeil 1997 on the references to "sun" and "moon" in Ps 121:6).

Also known from texts of the Persian period (namely, in an Aramaic version found at Elephantine), Ahiqar is another possible candidate for extrabiblical influence on biblical wisdom texts (e.g., for Proverbs [Cazalles]). C. Uehlinger (200-203 [earlier Loretz, 325-27; Küchler, 319-414]) has provided a helpful list of eleven possible parallels. For example, Ahiqar (lines 127-129) emphasizes, similar to Ecclesiastes 2:24, the *carpe diem* motif: "[If] thou [be hungry], my son, take every trouble and do every labor, then wilt thou eat and be satisfied and give to thy children. . . . [If] thou [be needy], my son, borrow corn and wheat that thou mayest eat and be sated and give to thy children with thee" (*ANET*, 429).

While the similarities between Ahiqar and Ecclesiastes require further research (Uehlinger, 201-3), the more recent publication of texts from Late Bronze Age Emar provide further possible links between biblical and Syrian literature (Gianto; Dietrich). Remarkably, Emar VI.4:767 seems to echo a similar text that had been discovered among the texts from Ugarit decades earlier (Dietrich, 9-11). As can be expected, most of the Emarite statements occur in the framework of their polytheistic religious outlook. However, conceptual links can easily be observed: "Destinies have been designed by Ea. Portions have been distributed according to the decree of the god. It has been that way since the days of old. It has been declared from the beginning" (Emar VI.4:767 [Arnaud, 359-65; translation in Gianto, 473]). Ecclesiastes 1:9 seems to reflect a similar observation: "That which has been is what will be, that which is done is what will be done, and there is nothing new under the sun" (NKJV). Similarly, Ecclesiastes 3:14-15 also underlines the important concept that human destinies are controlled by God. It is also interesting to note the "audacious, even iconoclastic" (Gianto, 475) nature of the Emar wisdom text, challenging the traditional belief system and theology manifested in canonical Mesopotamian tradition. *Qoheleth (indicating the sage who refers to himself in the first person singular throughout the volume) also appears to challenge traditional belief systems and is involved in existential (and theological) experiments (Eccles 1:12-14, 17-18; 2:1-23). This search to understand human destiny is further documented in lines 21-24 of the same text from Emar: "Cast off all griefs, ignore troubles. Instead of joy in the heart of a single day, a period of 36,000 [years of silence will come]. May Zirash [the goddess of beer] rejoice in a son like you! This is human destiny" (Emar VI.4:767 [Arnaud, 359-65; translation in Gianto, 476]). Similar ideas are expressed in Ecclesiastes 5:17-19.

As can easily be seen from these brief descriptions of possible Syrian parallels to important concepts contained in the book of Ecclesiastes, the possibility of comparative material from the north should not be overlooked and needs further clarification. The wide chronological frame of reference (beginning in fourteenth/thirteenth-century texts from Ugarit and Emar and extending via Phoenician texts to the Persian period Aramaic *Ahiqar*) underlines two important elements: (1) the look to the north for comparative material is increasingly important and should not be neglected; (2) many of the important (and often unconventional) wisdom concepts found in Ecclesiastes find their echo throughout an extended period of time, suggesting a development of ancient Near Eastern wisdom that provided corrections or alternatives to more typical ancient Near Eastern wisdom concepts.

4. Looking to the West: Greece and the Aegean.
Due to wide-ranging developments in the dating of biblical texts, which generally emphasize an exilic or predominantly postexilic locus for the writing and editing of many (if not most) biblical texts (Finkelstein and Silberman), the view from the west, including Greece and the larger Aegean realm, has become increasingly important in studies dealing with the intellectual background of Ecclesiastes (Braun; Bohlen; Schwienhorst-Schönberger 1994; 2004, 103). To be sure, Greece did not just appear in the Levant after the arrival of Alexander the Great. There is plenty of evidence for an interaction between east and west prior to the Hellenistic period in the material culture (Wenning; Gestoso; Guralnick). Some of the evidence for the Hellenistic influence on Ecclesiastes (and thus a date during the third century BC) includes the reflection of Greek philosophy in the way the book argues its case and has been linked to the Hellenistic diatribe (Schwienhorst-Schönberger 1994). The struc-

tural and argumentative links to Greek philosophy are not necessarily understood as a wholesale adoption of Greek philosophy per se. Clearly, humankind is not an independent entity that can find happiness and fulfillment apart from God or even against God, which in the anthropology and theology of the OT would be unthinkable (Schwienhorst-Schönberger 1994, 296-98). Other studies, however, have particularly marked the difference between Stoic and Epicurean philosophical concepts and Ecclesiastes (Zimmer, 66; Harrison; also Towner, who questions direct Greek influence).

Questioning the existence of direct philosophical and literary links to Greek literature (*see* Wisdom, Greek), some have argued rather for the general reflection of Hellenistic thought in Ecclesiastes (Hengel 1973). N. Lohfink perceives a reflection of governing terminology that seems to evidence the distinction between a central power outside of Jerusalem (Alexandria, considering the fact that the book is dated during the third century BC) and the local power (Jerusalem). Similarly, R. Bohlen (257-59) sees echoes of the consequences of Hellenistic state ideology, administrative structures and the tax system of the Ptolemaic province of Syria and Phoenicia in texts such as Ecclesiastes 4:1 (with particular emphasis on the motif of oppression); 5:8-9 (oppression and perverted justice). However, it seems as if the general motif of oppression is not necessarily a compelling reason to posit a Hellenistic date, as can be easily seen in similar references found in earlier texts of the Hebrew Bible (e.g., Amos 2:6-7; 4:1; Jer 6:6; 7:6; 22:17; Neh 5:1-5). Concerning specific Greek parallel expressions or motifs, O. Kaiser, critically sorting them, still maintains forty-eight parallel motifs, including references to Homer, Theognis, Euripides and Menander. It seems as if even more than two centuries after the first suggestion of Greek influence for Ecclesiastes, no scholarly consensus has emerged, and much of the discussion actually centers on the dating of the book and not necessarily on the intellectual or theological/philosophical background.

5. Looking to the South: Egypt.
Egyptian influence in the conceptual and textual world of Ecclesiastes has been argued re-

peatedly (Shupak; Uehlinger, 207-28; Anderson, 62-63), albeit not unanimously (see Loretz, 89). Examples of Egyptian literature with a strong pessimistic slant include the Middle Kingdom text The Dispute between a Man and His Ba (*COS* 3.146:321-25; *ANET*, 405-7), which relates the conversation of a man with his soul, discussing the futility of life. It has a dialogic style similar to Ecclesiastes (Eccles 1:16; 2:1, 15; 3:17-18). The *carpe diem* motif seems to be reflected in the phrase "follow the happy day and forget worry" (*COS* 3.146:323) and can be compared to similar motifs in Ecclesiastes 2:24; 3:12, 22; 5:17; 8:15; 9:7-9; 11:7-8. However, as has been pointed out before, the time gap between the Middle Kingdom text and biblical Ecclesiastes is considerable and should be noted when positing a particular intellectual or theological Egyptian background. A similar argument could be used for another proposed parallel, The Eloquent Peasant (*COS* 1.43:98-104), likewise composed during the Middle Kingdom period. Similar to Ecclesiastes, this composition contains a *frame narrative, and the body of the work consists of nine complaints that the peasant addresses to the high steward Rensi son of Meru. Part of the second petition is a list of opposites (e.g., the magistrate who shows partiality, a judge who steals what has been stolen, the breath-giver who languishes on the ground). Ecclesiastes contains similar motifs—for example, "Fools are placed in many positions of authority, while wealthy men sit in lowly positions. I have seen slaves on horseback, while princes go on foot like slaves" (Eccles 10:6-7 NIV). Similar ironic inversions (or reversals) are found also in Ecclesiastes 3:16; 7:15; 8:10.

The Song from the Tomb of King Intef (1.30:48-49) belongs to the genre of harper's songs, a small group of lyrics advocating *carpe diem* attitudes (Foster, 317), and should be understood as a genuine Middle Kingdom text, even though the text is preserved only in two New Kingdom copies.

A generation passes, another stays, since the time of the ancestors. The gods who were before rest in their tombs, blessed nobles too are buried in their tombs. . . . Their walls have crumbled, their places are gone, as though they had never been! None comes from there, to tell of their state, to tell of their needs, to calm our hearts, until we go where

they have gone. Hence rejoice in your heart! . . . Follow your heart as long as you live! Put myrrh on your head, dress in fine linen, anoint yourself with oils fit for a god. Heap up your joys, let your heart not sink! (*COS* 1.30:49)

The focus on the present life over against the future life, the latter being an important fundamental belief of Egyptian civilization, is intriguing and seems to reflect similar thoughts in Ecclesiastes (e.g., Eccles 1:11; 3:22; 11:9-10) as well as similar iconoclastic tendencies in the biblical text, which seems to challenge some traditional concepts such as the principle of *retribution, which is well represented in other biblical Wisdom literature.

Another possible parallel in Egyptian literature is found in The Complaints of Khakheperre-sonb (*COS* 1.44:104-6), another Middle Kingdom text. Similar to verses in Ecclesiastes (Eccles 1:13, 17; 8:16; 9:1), the text emphasizes a searching heart as well as the nothingness of memory, also reflected in Ecclesiastes 1:11: "There is no remembrance of former things, Nor will there be any remembrance of things that are to come by those who will come after" (Eccles 1:11 NKJV). The Egyptian text underlines the importance of the past: "I said this in accord with what I have seen: from the first generation, down to those who come after, they imitate that which is past" (lines 6-7 [*COS* 1.44:105]). Learning from the past, including personal experience, is also characteristic of Ecclesiastes (Eccles 1:12—2:26; 7:23-39; 8:16-17).

Another possible link to Egyptian texts, studied by S. Burkes, involves the topic of death in late Egyptian biographies (*see* Chaos and Death). Burkes (235) concludes that in both texts "death is a problem such that each culture's established ways for confronting death's disruptions are, for these authors, no longer effective." Theologically, it appears as if Ecclesiastes is functioning as a counterweight to the concept of divine retribution, which is so clearly promulgated in *Proverbs and *Job. Burkes (236-43) notes that the late Egyptian biographies also seem to present a markedly distinct position on the issue of death as opposed to earlier Egyptian texts; he explains this on the basis of a general shift in religious patterns during the second half of the first millennium.

As we have seen, numerous parallels between Ecclesiastes and Egyptian texts have been suggested. A meaningful comparison should involve comparative data from the same geographic and chronological historic stream, which for Egyptian wisdom literature does not always apply, since many of the aforementioned parallels date to the Middle Kingdom, hundreds of years before the time of Solomon or other loci of the possible origin of the work. In this sense, the emphasis by Uehlinger (207-24) on late Egyptian texts is laudable and helpful and will compel additional future research.

6. Conclusions.

The search for the ancient Near Eastern background of the enigmatic book of Ecclesiastes has provided many surprising links to texts from Mesopotamia, Syria and Egypt. Many of these links referred to texts that originated long before Ecclesiastes was composed. They would not be helpful for a historical comparative approach, but they are relevant for a typological comparative approach, looking at literary and theological motifs that have impacted human beings throughout history. Regarding the possible influence and background from the west, it seems as if the scholarly lines are sharply drawn between those who posit a clear Hellenistic background for the book (including literary structures and rhetorical strategies) and those who reject this thesis. As we noted above, the decision about the Hellenistic influence relies heavily on one's conclusion concerning the dating of the Ecclesiastes.

One important element of a possible ancient Near Eastern background concerns the inner-biblical (or *intertextual) links of Ecclesiastes to other biblical literature. Did Ecclesiastes draw consciously from these texts or even question them or complement them, considering the important theological concept of progressive revelation (Bartholomew, 254-61)?

As already seen in the many references to parallel ideas, terms and structures of Ecclesiastes within the larger framework of the ancient Near East, the notion of the "internationality" of wisdom should be considered (Uehlinger, 157). It is this internationality that may explain some of the links that have been noted throughout this article. This internationality of ancient Near Eastern wisdom may be rooted in humanity's search for answers to questions and situations that go beyond comprehension and are not re-

solved by pat rational or theological answers, and may even require outrageous or radical answers. It is precisely this radicalness that still surprises the modern reader of Ecclesiastes.

See also AUTOBIOGRAPHY; WISDOM, GREEK; WISDOM SOURCES.

BIBLIOGRAPHY. **B. Alster,** *Proverbs of Ancient Sumer* (2 vols.; Bethesda, MD: CDL Press, 1997); **W. H. U. Anderson,** *Qoheleth and Its Pessimistic Theology: Hermeneutical Struggles in Wisdom Literature* (MBPS 54; Lewiston, NY: Mellen Biblical Press, 1997); **D. Arnaud,** *Emar VI.4: Textes de la bibliothèque, transcriptions et traductions* (Paris: Editions Recherche sur les Civilisations, 1987); **J. Azize,** "The Genre of *Qohelet*," *DavarLogos* 2 (2003) 123-38; **C. G. Bartholomew,** *Reading Ecclesiastes: Old Testament Exegesis and Hermeneutical Theory* (AnBib 139; Rome: Pontificio Istituto Biblico, 1998); **G. A. Barton,** *The Book of Ecclesiastes* (ICC; Edinburgh: T & T Clark, 1912); **R. Bohlen,** "Kohelet im Kontext hellenistischer Kultur," in *Das Buch Kohelet: Studien zur Struktur, Geschichte, Rezeption und Theologie*, ed. L. Schwienhorst-Schönberger (BZAW 254; Berlin: de Gruyter, 1997) 249-73; **J. Bottéro,** "Le 'Dialogue Pessimiste' et la transcendance," *RTP* 16 (1966) 4-24; **R. Braun,** *Kohelet und die frühhellenistische Popularphilosophie* (BZAW 130; Berlin: de Gruyter, 1973); **S. Burkes,** *Death in Qoheleth and Egyptian Biographies of the Late Period* (SBLDS 170; Atlanta: Society of Biblical Literature, 1999); **H. Cazalles,** "Ahiqar, *Ummân* and *Amun*, and Biblical Wisdom Texts," in *Solving Riddles and Untying Knots: Biblical, Epigraphical, and Semitic Studies in Honor of Jonas C. Greenfield*, ed. Z. Zevit, S. Gitin and M. Sokoloff (Winona Lake, IN: Eisenbrauns, 1995) 45-55; **M. W. Chavalas,** "Ancient Syria: A Historical Sketch," in *New Horizons in the Study of Ancient Syria*, ed. M. W. Chavalas and J. L. Hayes (BMes 25; Malibu, CA: Undena Publications, 1992) 1-21; **J. L. Crenshaw,** *Old Testament Wisdom: An Introduction* (London: SCM, 1982); idem, "The Contemplative Life in the Ancient Near East," in *Civilizations of the Ancient Near East*, ed. J. M. Sasson (4 vols.; New York: Scribner, 1995) 4.2445-57; **M. Dahood,** "Canaanite-Phoenician Influence in Qoheleth," *Bib* 33 (1952) 30-52; idem, "The Phoenician Background of Qoheleth," *Bib* 47 (1966) 264-82; **E. Dammann,** "Gott und Geister in Sprichwörtern aus Schwarzafrika," in *Biblische und außerbiblische Spruchweisheit: Ergebnisse einer Tagung der Sektion Religionswissenschaft/Missionswis-*

senschaft der Wissenschaftlichen Gesellschaft für Theologie vom 26. bis 29. September 1988 in Basel, ed. H.-J. Klimkeit (StOR 20; Wiesbaden: Harrassowitz, 1991) 105-16; **S. Denning-Bolle,** *Wisdom in Akkadian Literature: Expression, Instruction, Dialogue* (Leiden: Ex Oriente Lux, 1992); **M. Dietrich,** "'Ein Leben ohne Freude . . .': Studie über eine Weisheitskomposition aus den Gelehrtenbibliotheken von Emar und Ugarit," *UF* 24 (1992) 9-29; **I. Finkelstein and N. A. Silberman,** *The Bible Unearthed: Archaeology's New Vision of Ancient Israel and the Origin of Its Sacred Texts* (New York: Simon & Schuster, 2002); **D. E. Fleming,** "The Rituals from Emar: Evolution of an Indigenous Tradition in Second-Millennium Syria," in *New Horizons in the Study of Ancient Syria,* ed. M. W. Chavalas and J. L. Hayes (BMes 25; Malibu, CA: Undena Publications, 1992) 51-61; idem, "The Emar Festivals: City Unity and Syrian Identity under Hittite Hegemony," in *Emar: The History, Religion, and Culture of a Syrian Town in the Late Bronze Age,* ed. M. W. Chavalas (Bethesda, MD: CDL Press, 1996) 81-114; idem, "The Israelite Festival Calendar and Emar's Ritual Archive," *RB* 106 (1999) 8-34; **M. Fortin,** "New Horizon in Ancient Syria: The View from 'Atij," *NEA* 61 (1998) 15-24; **J. L. Foster,** "Lyric," *OEAE* 2.312-17; **M. V. Fox,** "Wisdom in Qoheleth," in *In Search of Wisdom: Essays in Memory of John G. Gammie,* ed. L. G. Perdue, B. B. Scott and W. J. Wiseman (Louisville: Westminster John Knox, 1993) 115-31; idem, *A Time to Tear Down and a Time to Build Up: A Rereading of Ecclesiastes* (Grand Rapids: Eerdmans, 1999); **D. Garrett,** *Proverbs, Ecclesiastes, Song of Songs* (NAC 14; Nashville: Broadman, 1993); **G. N. Gestoso,** "Las relaciones de intercambio entre Egipto y el mundo Egeo durante la época de El Amarna," in *Relaciones de intercambio entre Egipto y el Mediterráneo Oriental (IV-I milenio A.C.),* ed. A. D. Rodrigo (Buenos Aires: Editorial Biblos, 2001) 79-101; **A. Gianto,** "Human Destiny in Emar and Qohelet," in *Qohelet in the Context of Wisdom,* ed. A. Schoors (BETL 86; Leuven: Leuven University Press, 1998) 473-79; **J. C. L. Gibson,** *Textbook of Syrian Semitic Inscriptions, 3: Phoenician Inscriptions* (Oxford: Clarendon Press, 1982); **E. Guralnick,** "Greece and the Near East: Art and Archaeology," in *Daidalikon: Studies in Memory of Raymond V. Schoder, S.J.,* ed. R. F. Sutton (Wauconda, IL: Bolchazy-Carducci Publishers, 1989) 151-76; **W. W. Hallo,** "New Moons and Sabbaths: A Case-Study in the Contrastive Ap-proach," *HUCA* 48 (1977) 1-18; idem, "Compare and Contrast: The Contextual Approach to Biblical Literature," in *The Bible in the Light of Cuneiform Literature,* ed. W. W. Hallo, B. W. Jones and G. L. Mattingly (ANETS 8; Lewiston, NY: Edwin Mellen, 1990) 1-30; idem, "Sumer and the Bible: A Matter of Proportion," in *The Future of Biblical Archaeology: Reassessing Methodologies and Assumptions; The Proceedings of a Symposium August 12-14, 2001, at Trinity International University,* ed. J. K. Hoffmeier and A. Millard (Grand Rapids: Eerdmans, 2004) 163-75; **C. R. Harrison,** "Qoheleth in Social-Historical Perspective" (Ph.D. diss., Duke University, 1991); **M. Hengel,** *Judentum und Hellenismus: Studien zu ihrer Begegnung unter besonderer Berücksichtigung Palästinas bis zur Mitte des 2. Jh.s v. Chr.* (2nd ed.; WUNT 10; Tübingen: Mohr Siebeck, 1973); **R. S. Hess,** "Multiple-Month Ritual Calendars in the West Semitic World: Emar 446 and Leviticus 23," in *The Future of Biblical Archaeology: Reassessing Methodologies and Assumptions; The Proceedings of a Symposium August 12-14, 2001, at Trinity International University,* ed. J. K. Hoffmeier and A. Millard (Grand Rapids: Eerdmans, 2004) 233-53; **H. A. Hoffner Jr.,** "Ancient Israel's Literary Heritage Compared with Hittite Textual Data," in *The Future of Biblical Archaeology: Reassessing Methodologies and Assumptions; The Proceedings of a Symposium August 12-14, 2001, at Trinity International University,* ed. J. K. Hoffmeier and A. Millard (Grand Rapids: Eerdmans, 2004) 176-92; **O. Kaiser,** "Judentum und Hellenismus," *VF* 27 (1982) 68-88; **N. Klaes,** "Indische Spruchweisheit und das Verständnis von *dharma,*" in *Biblische und außerbiblische Spruchweisheit: Ergebnisse einer Tagung der Sektion Religionswissenschaft/Missionswissenschaft der Wissenschaftlichen Gesellschaft für Theologie vom 26. bis 29. September 1988 in Basel,* ed. H.-J. Klimkeit (StOR 20; Wiesbaden: Harrassowitz, 1991) 85-101; **G. A. Klingbeil,** "Sun and Moon in Psalm 121:6: Some Notes on Their Context and Meaning," in *To Understand Scriptures: Essays in Honor of William H. Shea,* ed. D. Merling (Berrien Springs, MI: Andrews University Institute of Archaeology, 1997) 33-43; idem, *A Comparative Study of the Ritual of Ordination as Found in Leviticus 8 and Emar 369* (Lewiston, NY: Edwin Mellen, 1998); idem, "The Anointing of Aaron: A Study of Lev 8:12 in its OT and ANE Contexts," *AUSS* 38 (2000) 231-43; idem, *Bridging the Gap: Ritual and Ritual Texts in the Bible* (BBRSup 1; Winona Lake, IN: Eisenbrauns, 2007); idem, "'Between

North and South': The Archaeology of Religion in LBA Palestine and the Period of the Settlement," in *Critical Issues in Early Israelite History*, ed. R. S. Hess, G. A. Klingbeil and P. Ray (BBR-Sup 3; Winona Lake, IN: Eisenbrauns, forthcoming); **M. G. Klingbeil**, *Yahweh Fighting from Heaven: God as Warrior and as God of Heaven in the Hebrew Psalter and Ancient Near Eastern Iconography* (OBO 169; Fribourg: University Press; Göttingen: Vandenhoeck & Ruprecht, 1999); **I. Kottsieper**, "Alttestamentliche Weisheit: Proverbia und Kohelet (II)," *TRu* 67 (2002) 201-37; **M. Küchler**, *Frühjüdische Weisheitstraditionen: Zum Fortgang weisheitlichen Denkens im Bereich des frühjüdischen Jahweglaubens* (OBO 26; Fribourg: Universitätsverlag; Göttingen: Vandenhoeck & Ruprecht, 1979); **W. G. Lambert**, ed., *Babylonian Wisdom Literature* (Oxford: Clarendon Press, 1960); **N. Lohfink**, "*melek, šallîṭ*, and *môšēl* bei Kohelet und die Abfassungszeit des Buches," *Bib* 62 (1981) 535-43; **T. Longman III**, *Fictional Akkadian Autobiography: A Generic and Comparative Study* (Winona Lake, IN: Eisenbrauns, 1991); **O. Loretz**, *Qohelet und der alte Orient: Untersuchungen zu Stil und theologischer Thematik des Buches Qohelet* (Freiburg: Herder, 1964); **M. Malul**, *The Comparative Method in Ancient Near Eastern and Biblical Legal Studies* (AOAT 227; Neukirchen-Vluyn: Neukirchener Verlag, 1990); **J. Y.-S. Pahk**, *Il canto della gioia in Dio: L'itinerario sapienziale espresso dall'unità letteraria in Qohelet 8,16–9,10 e il parallelo di Gilgameš Me. iii* (Series Minor 52; Naples: Istituto Universitario Orientale, Dipartimento di Studi Asiatici, 1996); idem, "Qohelet e le tradizioni sapienziali del Vicino Oriente Antico," in *Il Libro del Qohelet: Tradizione, redazione, teologia*, ed. G. Bellia and A. Passaro (Milan: Paoline, 2001) 117-43; **R. Ratner and B. Zuckermann**, "'A Kid in Milk'? New Photographs of KTU 1.23, Line 14," *HUCA* 57 (1986) 15-60; **S. Sandmel**, "Parallelomania," *JBL* 81 (1962) 1-13; **A. Schoors**, *The Teacher Sought to Find Pleasant Words: A Study of the Language of Qohelet* (OLA 41; Leuven: Peeters, 1992); **L. Schwienhorst-Schönberger**, *Nicht im Menschen gründet das Glück (Koh 2,24): Kohelet im Spannungsfeld jüdischer Weisheit und hellenistischer Philosophie* (HBS 2; Freiburg: Herder, 1994); idem, *Kohelet* (HT-KAT; Freiburg: Herder, 2004); **N. Shupak**, *Where Can Wisdom Be Found? The Sage's Language in the Bible and in Ancient Egyptian Literature* (OBO 130; Fribourg: University Press; Göttingen: Vandenhoeck & Ruprecht, 1993); **S. Talmon**, "The Comparative Method in Biblical Interpretation: Principles and Problems," in *Congress Volume: Göttingen 1977*, ed. W. Zimmerli et al. (VTSup 29; Leiden: E. J. Brill, 1978) 320-56; **W. S. Towner**, "The Book of Ecclesiastes," *NIB* 5.265-375; **C. Uehlinger**, "Qohelet im Horizont mesopotamischer, levantinischer und ägyptischer Weisheitsliteratur der persischen und hellenistischen Zeit," in *Das Buch Kohelet: Studien zur Struktur, Geschichte, Rezeption und Theologie*, ed. L. Schwienhorst-Schönberger (BZAW 254; Berlin: de Gruyter, 1997) 155-247; **R. Wenning**, "Griechischer Einfluss auf Palästina in vorhellenistischer Zeit," in *Die Griechen und das antike Israel: Interdisziplinäre Studien zur Religions- und Kulturgeschichte des Heiligen Landes*, ed. S. Alkier and M. Witte (OBO 201; Fribourg: Academic Press; Göttingen: Vandenhoeck & Ruprecht, 2004) 29-69; **R. N. Whybray**, "Qoheleth, Preacher of Joy," *JSOT* 23 (1982) 87-98; idem, "The Sage in the Israelite Royal Court," in *The Sage in Israel and the Ancient Near East*, ed. J. G. Gammie and L. G. Perdue (Winona Lake, IN: Eisenbrauns, 1990) 133-39; **E. Yannai and E. Braun**, "Anatolian and Egyptian Imports from Late EB I at Ain Assawir, Israel," *BASOR* 321 (2001) 41-56; **T. Zimmer**, *Zwischen Tod und Lebensglück: Eine Untersuchung zur Anthropologie Kohelets* (BZAW 286; Berlin: de Gruyter, 1999).

G. A. Klingbeil

ECCLESIASTES 3: HISTORY OF INTERPRETATION

Ecclesiastes is a deeply enigmatic but tremendously compelling book. Its interpretation has intrigued generations of readers. Whereas pre-Reformation readings by both Jewish and Christian interpreters shared many assumptions about the book, little consensus exists among readers in the twenty-first century. A survey of the history of interpretation aids interpreters today to situate their own reading and understand more deeply the issues involved in reading the book.

One of the leading problems of interpretation concerns what appear to be tensions or even contradictions within the book. For instance, *Qohelet on numerous occasions concludes that life is "meaningless," but then at crucial points he advocates a lifestyle of joy (Eccles 2:24-26; 3:12-14, 22; 5:18-20; 8:15; 9:7-10). A second example is seen in the apparently conflicted statements about laughter—negative in, for example, Ecclesiastes 2:2; 7:3, but positive in Ecclesiastes 8:15. Are these tensions to be reconciled, and if so, how? Should the tensions be allowed to stand? Are they indications of multiple authors, or at least of more than one voice? Perhaps they are quotations. On the other hand, maybe one theme is subservient to another. All these options have been argued at one point or another in the history of interpretation.

Internal tensions have provoked much discussion and debate, and the same may be said about how the teaching of Ecclesiastes conflicts with the rest of the *canon. For instance, as early as rabbinic times, Ecclesiastes 11:9 ("Be happy, young man, while you are young, and let your heart give you joy in the days of your youth. Follow the ways of your heart and whatever your eyes see") was seen to be in conflict with Numbers 15:39 (where young men were told to "not prostitute yourselves by going after the lusts of your own hearts and eyes").

These features make Ecclesiastes a difficult book to interpret, thus leading to debate among interpreters. The biggest difficulty is to provide the book with a coherent reading that accounts for all the varied emphases and apparent tensions. In this regard, an observation made by C. Newsom (191) is apropos: "It is always interesting to see where the 'interpretive sweat' breaks out in dealing with such an iconoclastic book; moreover, the history of interpretation of Ecclesiastes sheds an important light on contemporary exegesis." C. Bartholomew (forthcoming) suggests that problems arise when these tensions are tamed into what he calls the "heresy of paraphrase," summarizing the book's message to one of its two poles, meaninglessness (Bartholomew prefers "enigmatic") or joy. Of course, many interpreters conclude that a proper reading of the book does see one theme as subservient to the others. All these viewpoints are represented in the history of interpretation.

1. From the Beginning to the New Testament
2. Early and Medieval Interpretation
3. The Modern Period
4. Postmodern Readings
5. Late Twentieth and Early Twenty-First Centuries
6. Conclusion

1. From the Beginning to the New Testament.
Significant consensus exists that Ecclesiastes is postexilic. Debate continues though over whether the book is from the Persian (Seow) or the Hellenistic period (Bartholomew, forthcoming). Some scholars (Fredericks 1988; Kaiser) still argue for a preexilic date for the book, but they are few.

No matter when the book was written, it does not appear to be quoted or even alluded to in other OT texts. Its lack of mention does not necessarily mean that Ecclesiastes was not written during the OT period, but if it were mentioned in later OT books, it would likely inform us how the book was being interpreted in that early period. Ecclesiastes very likely was composed before (though perhaps near) the time of *Sirach (c. 180 BC) and *Wisdom of Solomon (c. first century AD), but, again, has not left an explicit imprint on these generically related books.

The earliest manuscript of the book of Ecclesiastes is from Qumran (4QQoh[a]), published by J. Muilenburg in 1954 and dated to 175-150 BC, while the only other witness to the book at Qumran (4QQoh[b]) is dated sometime between the middle of the first century BC to sometime in the first century AD (Ulrich). 4QQoh[a] thus provides a latest point for the composition of the book, but these texts do not inform us about the book's interpretation.

The NT perhaps quotes Ecclesiastes 7:20 at Romans 3:10 ("There is no one righteous, not even one") along with a collage of other texts predominantly from *Psalms in support of Paul's point that all human beings are sinners. Even more provocatively, Romans 8:20 alludes to the book of Ecclesiastes when Paul pronounces the world as subjected to *mataiotēs*, the Greek equivalent to Hebrew *hebel*, a thematic word in Ecclesiastes variously translated "meaningless, vanity, enigmatic" or even "transient." In this section (Rom 8:18-25) Paul reflects on the effects of the introduction of sin and thus most pointedly on Genesis 3. Here we may see that Paul interprets Qohelet as describing a world of sin ("under the sun") and suffering the effects of God's punishment ("meaningless, meaningless"). If so, then Paul provides the earliest hint at the interpretation of Ecclesiastes on record.

2. Early and Medieval Interpretation.
2.1. Jewish Interpretation. The earliest Jewish traditions about Ecclesiastes and its interpretation are found in the Mishnah, various midrashim and the Talmuds. These sources

reveal differences not only in interpretive strategies but also on the important question of whether the book "makes the hands unclean" or should be "stored away." A book that "makes the hands unclean" is an authoritative book, a holy book, whose use is surrounded by rituals of washing hands and care. To "store away" a book, on the other hand, is to get rid of it, consign it to oblivion.

We noted above that through the ages questions arose concerning the book's fit with the rest of the canon as well as its own internal consistency. We can see this debate in early Jewish sources. In the third chapter of the first tractate of the Mishnah (*Šabbat*), Rabbi Tanhum of Nave is quoted as saying, "O Solomon, where is your wisdom, where is your intelligence? Not only do your words contradict the words of your father, David, they even contradict themselves" (translated from the citation given in Podechard). The Talmud cites the contradiction between Ecclesiastes 2:2; 7:3 and Ecclesiastes 8:15. In the Tosefta (*t. Yad.* 2:14 [fifth century A.D., but quoting earlier sources]), Rabbi Simeon ben Menasia says, "The Song of Songs makes the hands unclean because it was spoken by the Holy Spirit. Ecclesiastes does not make the hands unclean because it is [merely] Solomon's wisdom" (Beckwith, 284). The *Pesiqta of Rab Kahana* (*Pesiq. Rab Kah.* 68b [see also *Lev. Rab.* 28:1]) states, "The sages sought to store away the Book of Ecclesiastes because they found words in it which tended toward heresy" (Beckwith, 287). Jerome picked up and affirmed this sentiment when he noted in the introduction to his commentary, "The Jews say that ... this book seemed fit to be consigned to oblivion, because it asserted the creatures of God to be vain, and preferred eating, drinking, and transitory pleasures to all things; on account of this one section [i.e., Eccl. 12:13-14] [it seemed] to have deserved its authority, that it was included among the divine books" (Beckwith, 287).

Jerome was correct that the majority of Jewish scholars accepted the book in spite of its apparent conflicts with other Scripture. According to *b. Šabb.* 30b, "The sages sought to store away the Book of Ecclesiastes. . . . And why did they not store it away? Because its beginning is words of the Law and its end is words of the Law" (Beckwith, 287). The beginning and end show its orthodoxy, likely referring especially to the last two verses of the book, which encourage the fear of God and obedience to the commandments as well as warn of the coming judgment (Eccles 12:13-14).

Thus, it appears that although Ecclesiastes was questioned, its canonicity was never rejected by the mainstream Jewish community. The question, in other words, was not "Is Ecclesiastes canonical?" but rather, since the book was considered authoritative, "Why is this book canonical?"

The rabbinic sources describe a meeting of important Jewish leaders at the city of Jamnia in AD 90. These leaders discussed a variety of topics, including those books about which there was some debate as to their authority (particularly *Song of Songs and Ecclesiastes). This influential group of scholars concluded that the book did "render the hands unclean," and this has remained the dominant Jewish view on the matter.

In terms of interpretation, the *Targum of Ecclesiastes (c. AD 600) provides an excellent insight into a major early Jewish interpretive approach. First, the Targum makes a strong identification of Qohelet with *Solomon. As we will see, this identification is assumed in both Jewish and Christian interpretation until the Reformation period. Note the importation of an extrabiblical legend about Solomon into the Targum's expansionistic rendering of Ecclesiastes 1:12:

When King Solomon was sitting upon the throne of his kingdom, his heart became very proud of his riches, and he violated the word of God, by gathering many horses, chariots and riders, and amassing much gold and silver. And he married from foreign nations, whereupon the anger of the Lord was kindled against him, and he sent to him Ashmodai, king of the demons, who drove him from his kingdom's throne, and took away the ring from his hand, in order that he should roam and wander about in the world to reprove it. And he roamed about in the outlying towns and the cities of the land of Israel, weeping and lamenting, and saying, "I am Qohelet, whose name was formerly called Solomon, who was king over Israel in Jerusalem." (Levine, 28)

This identification of Qohelet and Solomon may have smoothed the way for many religious communities (Jewish and Christian) to accept the authority of this perplexing book that at times seems out of kilter with the rest of the canon. The Targum goes further and turns the book and Qohelet himself into a statement of the deepest piety. Illustrative is the Targum's transformation of Ecclesiastes 12:12 ("Furthermore, of these, my son, be warned! There is no end to the making of many books, and much study wearies the body") into an exaltation of Torah study: "And more than these, my son, take care, to make many books of wisdom without end; to study much the words of the Law, and to consider the weariness of the body" (Levine, 47). In this way and throughout the Targum interprets the book as a repository of orthodox teaching in perfect harmony with the rest of the canon, particularly the Torah.

Some medieval Jewish manuscripts (e.g., Codex Leningradensis [early eleventh century AD]) list Ecclesiastes among the so-called *Megillot (after *Ruth and Song of Songs and before *Lamentations and *Esther). Jewish tradition associates these five books with five major Jewish festivals. In what is perhaps the most difficult connection to fathom, Ecclesiastes is associated with the Feast of Tabernacles (Sukkot). E. Christianson points out that the Talmud (*b. Ḥag.* 17a) connects Ecclesiastes 3:1, which asserts that there is a time for every activity in heaven, with the "appropriate keeping of the season." Of course, this is a rather superficial connection, and Christianson (31) goes on to speculate "that Ecclesiastes reflects the transient, fragile and joyful mood of Sukkut, which remembers the time in the wilderness of rootless wandering, unstable habitation and the hope of a promised land."

Among later medieval Jewish interpreters, Rashbam (grandson of the illustrious Rashi [c. 1080-1160]) stands out as the first to note that the book has a frame and therefore is a type of edited work (*see* Frame Narrative). His view that Ecclesiastes1:1-2 is an editorial introduction to the words of Qohelet and that Ecclesiastes 12:8 introduces an editorial epilogue, though not immediately embraced, is widely held today. Another medieval work, the thirteenth-century *Zohar* (the most important work of Kabbalah mysticism), asserts another view that is more commonly found in modern commentaries. In order to explain contradictions and tensions within the speech of Qohelet, it posits the idea

that Qohelet is quoting his unbelieving opponents in order to refute them.

2.2. Christian Interpretation. In one sense, Christian interpretation begins as early as the NT (see 1 above). However, we do not have much writing on Ecclesiastes before Origen (third century AD). Still, there seems to be little doubt about the canonical status of the book, at least according to the witness of early canonical lists from the second century AD onwards, including the Bryennios List (2nd century AD), the list of Melito of Sardis (2nd century AD), the three lists of Epiphanius of Salamis (4th century AD) and others (Beckwith, 182-85; Bartholomew, forthcoming). Furthermore, Clement of Alexandria (d. AD 215) cited it in his *Stromata* and introduced it by a formula that indicates its status as Scripture: "It is written." In summary, no evidence exists that Ecclesiastes was ever doubted by the early church, and even Theodore of Mopsuestia, cited by many as an exception to this widespread belief, recognized the book as holy Scripture (Murphy 1992, xxiii).

We do not have a full-fledged commentary from Origen, but besides some comments in his works about the book, we can see his influence in his students, particularly Gregory Thaumaturgos (c. AD 213-270), who wrote an early paraphrase of the book (see Jarick). Similar to the Targum, he explicitly identified Qohelet as King Solomon, as shown by his rendering of Ecclesiastes 1:1: "Solomon (the son of the king and prophet David), a king more honored and a prophet wiser than anyone else, speaks to the whole assembly of God." Also, like the Targum, Gregory turns Qohelet into a spokesperson for theological orthodoxy, in his case Christian orthodoxy.

Although Gregory Thaumaturgos is one of the earliest known interpreters of Ecclesiastes, Jerome (c. AD 347-420 [his commentary was written AD 398-399]) holds pride of place in terms of his massive influence on generations of commentators on the book. Jerome was influenced by rabbinic interpretation but takes it in a decidedly Christian direction. Like all early interpreters, Jewish and Christian, he believes that the book was written by King Solomon. His major influence comes in his view that the book teaches its readers to despise this world and its attractions (the so-called *contemptus mundi* view). In his hands, the book becomes a pamphlet advocating an ascetic perspective and promotes the monastic lifestyle. Indeed, his commentary was written for Blesilla, a daughter of his disciple Paula, to encourage her to maintain an ascetic lifestyle.

The book of Ecclesiastes fit Jerome's purposes well. After all, Qohelet looked extensively under the sun for meaning and concluded that life is meaningless. Specifically, Qohelet examined pleasure, work, wealth, relationships, wisdom and *folly and concluded that such things were not worthy of life. This view can be seen in a letter that he wrote to his disciple Paula, the mother of Blesilla, mentioned above, concerning the course of biblical study that he recommends for her other daughter, Paula. After telling her to begin with Psalms and *Proverbs (for which she can "gather rules of life"), he tells her to proceed to Ecclesiastes third, and this for the reasons that we have been noting. He says, "From the Preacher let her gain the habit of despising the world and its vanities" (for translation, see Pope, 119). Jerome's influence extended beyond his commentary, however, to include his translation of the book into the Latin Vulgate. His translation of *hebel* as *vanitas* led to the traditional English rendering "Vanity of vanities; all is vanity" (see KJV).

J. Wright provides an accessible and helpful survey of quotations from the patristic and early medieval period that demonstrates consistency of interpretation during this period along the lines set down by Jerome. In the eyes of scholars of this period, the book compelled an aesthetic life. These commentators had a tendency to resort to allegory to find deeper meanings of passages. In this regard, one can think of Ambrose's interpretation of the "three strand cord" of Ecclesiastes 4:12 in reference to the Trinity (Jarick, 316).

As we reach the end of the period under discussion in this section, we see some nuance of Jerome's approach in a scholar such as Bonaventura, who wrote his commentary in AD 1253-1257. Bonaventura did not reject the *contemptus mundi* approach, but he did answer the objection that such a view cast aspersions on God, who made the world. He responded that the world is not inherently contemptible, but compared with God, it is nothing. E. S. Christianson (103) cites his "wedding ring" analogy. If a woman loves her ring more than her husband, that is wrong, even adulterous. She should in-stead regard the ring as worthless compared to her husband. Bonaventura also expanded the scope of Ecclesiastes' teaching to make it relevant to the development of the new sciences related to the study of the natural world that were emerging in the thirteenth century AD. (though roots for this approach to the book may be found in Origen, who believed that the teachings of Ecclesiastes related to "natural science" like Proverbs related to "moral science" [Bartholomew 1998, 36]). For this reason, he emphasized a literal approach to the book more than did his predecessors. Recognizing these shifts of emphasis allows us to place Martin Luther, who will begin our next section, in a better context.

3. The Modern Period.

3.1. Luther and the Reformers. Martin Luther (his *Notes on Ecclesiastes* were lectures delivered in 1526) provides a watershed in the interpretation of Ecclesiastes. As noted above, the *contemptus mundi* interpretation of Jerome dominated the scholarly and ecclesiastical approach to the book. Luther vehemently objected to such a view on the basis that it denigrates God, who created the world. Of course, Luther (and other Reformers, such as Melanchthon, who wrote commentaries on Ecclesiastes) had no use for the monastic lifestyle, having rejected it in his revolt against the Catholic Church. Luther did not believe that vanity (*Eitel*) related to the world as much as it did to humanity, or in his (translated) words, "The vanity of the human heart, that is never content with the gifts of God that are present but rather thinks of them as negligible" (Christianson, 107). Bartholomew (forthcoming) well summarizes Luther's constructive approach to Ecclesiastes as "fundamentally positive about civic life even as it wrestles with the difficulties of poor leadership, a problem with which the Reformers were only too familiar. Luther reads Ecclesiastes as a book about politics and the family, about human existence in the context of creation order. Solomon is envisaged not as a solitary but as a political figure deeply concerned about social life." In addition, Luther, like Bonaventura, and others before him also used Ecclesiastes to interact with the new empirical sciences and attendant philosophy. He also found the book to be helpful in his debate with Erasmus over free will.

Of course, Luther did not eradicate the *contemptus mundi* approach to the book. He did, however, provide a robust alternative to it, thus breaking the consensus among interpreters that had persisted for over a thousand years following Jerome. Luther may have been instrumental in breaking yet another matter of agreement in the understanding of Ecclesiastes, that of Solomonic authorship. Indeed, it is commonly taught that Luther, in *Table Talk*, was the first one to question Solomonic authorship. He is cited as saying, "Solomon himself did not write Ecclesiastes, but it was produced by Sirach at the time of the Maccabees. . . . It is a sort of Talmud, compiled from many books, probably from the library of King Ptolemy Euergetes of Egypt." This may have been so, since it is cited in many sources, but there is a problem with the transmission of *Table Talk*, and Christianson (95), in his recent study of the history of interpretation (from which this citation comes), could not find it. If Luther is disqualified, then the view that Solomon was not responsible for the book goes to Grotius (d. 1645), who came to this conclusion based on the appearance of late Hebrew words in the text. From this point on, the consensus on authorship was ended, although Solomonic authorship still has its occasional defenders even today.

3.2. Historical Criticism. The modern period from the late eighteenth century on is marked by the development of historical-critical approaches (*see* Historical Criticism). The tendency in premodern interpretation, which took place mainly in an ecclesiastical setting, was to question neither the scriptural text nor the interpretation of one's tradition. Of course, this is a generalization, but it does explain why certain exegetical ideas could be passed on for hundreds of years. The historical-critical method developed in the modern period questions the text and the tradition to determine the truth of a matter. In this period, we observe intense concerns and questions about issues such as authorship, historical setting, composition history, genre, ancient Near Eastern background, social setting and much more. Descriptions and evaluations and practices of historical criticism vary greatly and cannot be recounted in this article. (For a particularly incisive analysis of historical criticism and a detailed rendition of historical-critical method in regard to Ecclesiastes, see Bartholomew 1998.)

It is often and rightly noted that modern historical criticism first developed in connection with the Pentateuch. J. Wellhausen was not by any stretch of the imagination the originator of historical criticism, but his *Prolegomena to the History of Israel* (1885) is seen as the point where the historical-critical method began its domination of scholarly study of the OT to the present. Wellhausen's focus concentrated on two main objects. The first was the history of the development of the Pentateuch itself (source criticism). Once this was accomplished, the conclusions could be the basis for the history of the development of Israelite religion. In the light of historical criticism, this latter history was different from that presented by the Bible itself (most notably by flipping the order of the Law and the Prophets). The second concern was the reconstruction of the history of Israel and its religion. Such a focus soon had an impact on the Historical Books and the Prophets, but the Wisdom literature, while not completely ignored, was on the periphery of scholarly concern for a while.

Even so, by the end of the nineteenth and early twentieth centuries, historical criticism was used to solve exegetical issues in Ecclesiastes as well as reconstruct its compositional history. One of the more difficult exegetical issues for the book was, as noted earlier, tensions or contradictions within the book. Under the influence of Wellhausian source criticism, commentators "discovered" various sources within the book, partly at least on the basis of these different perspectives. C. Siegfried argued that there were nine hands that contributed to the composition of Ecclesiastes. A decade later, Barton suggested that there were three people behind the book, while Podechard said there were four. Today, few scholars continue in this vein, believing that an appeal to multiple sources is too easy a solution to the issue of the tensions of the book and so are hesitant to appeal to sources or additions to the text. Some would argue that the epilogue is a later addendum. Both M. Fox and T. Longman, among others, argue that someone other than Qohelet is the voice of the epilogue (Eccles 12:8-14). However, neither is certain about nor interested in the question of whether they represent two specific historical individuals or whether Qohelet's speech ever existed as an independent entity. In other words, one can argue for two voices in the book of Ecclesiastes without positing separate sources.

Source criticism developed throughout the nineteenth century, finally influencing the study of Ecclesiastes (for better or worse) at the turn of the century. The next major development in historical-critical method was beginning about that time with the focus on *form criticism. Form criticism is a type of genre analysis with a diachronic dimension. In other words, biblical books and parts thereof are identified in terms of their genre and then are studied to see what their original (usually oral) shape was. In terms of the OT, such study originated in the work of H. Gunkel, who applied it to Genesis and Psalms. Form criticism in the traditional diachronic form, however, has had little impact on the interpretation of Ecclesiastes. Even so, the analysis of the genre as a whole, as well as parts of the book, has become increasingly important (Murphy 1981; Longman 2003; for a description of the present assessment of the genre of the book, see 5.3 below).

Gunkel and his followers also advocated studying the OT in the light of the relatively new ancient Near Eastern sources that were rediscovered beginning in the mid-nineteenth century. Today this type of study is known as the comparative or contextual method. In the early twentieth century, however, most of the comparisons were made to Greek thought (Ranston). This makes sense, since most twentieth- and twenty-first-century interpreters believe that the book was written during the Hellenistic period of the ancient Near East. Today, however, most interest in this area is focused on the generic similarity between Qohelet's speech in Ecclesiastes and ancient Near Eastern autobiographies (Longman; Perdue; Seow). It appears to these scholars that Qohelet's speech within the book (Eccles 1:12—12:7) has the form of an ancient Near Eastern autobiography.

Redaction criticism was introduced to the study of the OT in the middle of the twentieth century. It analyzes the theological impulses at work in the transmission and editing of earlier traditions. Redaction criticism depends on a complex compositional history. For instance, those who divide the Pentateuch into discrete sources that were brought together over the centuries utilize redaction criticism to uncover the theological interests of the collectors of the sources. In the study of Samuel-Kings and Chronicles, redaction criticism examines the theological tendencies of those who drew on the earlier traditions of Israel's past ultimately, it appears, in the exile and the postexilic period respectively. As we have noted,

however, source criticism has had limited or no success in Ecclesiastes, with the possible exception of the epilogue.

The closest that the interpretation of Ecclesiastes has come to a redaction-critical study is the reading by B. Childs and his followers (Sheppard; Longman 2006 [with differences]), though it is probably better to envision these studies as literary analyses of Ecclesiastes in its final form. In these studies, however, the epilogue is seen as a way to conform the book to the rest of the canon.

4. Postmodern Readings.
If premodern approaches to the exegesis of Ecclesiastes were guided by tradition and a respect for authority of the text, and modern approaches guided by a neutral search for the proper interpretation through the use of historical-critical methods, postmodernism casts doubt on determinant meaning of the text. Unlike modern and premodern hermeneutics, postmodernism does not believe that there is a meaning "out there" to be discovered. Such a skeptical approach was anticipated by the existentialist philosophy of the 1960s. Indeed, Ecclesiastes was a favorite of existentialist theologians such as P. Tillich because the ancient book itself often sounded skeptical ("Meaningless, meaningless"). Christianson (257) quotes Tillich as saying, "The spirit of the Preacher is strong today in our minds. His mood fills our philosophy and poetry. The vanity of human existence is described powerfully by those who call themselves philosophers or poets of existence. They are all children of the Preacher, this great existentialist of his period."

Both Tillich's existentialism and J. Derrida's deconstructionism throw a doubtful light on finding meaning in life or in literature. The difference, however, is that existentialism leads to angst, whereas deconstructionism leads to joy. After all, if there is no determinate meaning in the world, then there is no one to tell us what rules to live by. And in terms of literature, there is no one (not even an author) who can tell us what it means. Therefore, we do not interpret the text according to its original meaning but rather we "play" with it or, to use a term current among postmodern biblical interpreters, we "read against the grain." (For a recent example of a postmodern reading of Ecclesiastes, see Koosed.)

5. Late Twentieth and Early Twenty-First Centuries.

It is illuminating to consider the current discussions of the interpretation of Ecclesiastes against the background of the history of interpretation. In this section we will consider different areas of interpretation. The goal here is not to be exhaustive (mostly commentaries from the leading commentary series will be in view), nor is it to give every nuance of interpretation, but instead only broad outlines. The purpose is to describe the "state of the art" rather than resolve the disagreements of interpretation. In the process, we will also be able to give summary of the high points of interpretation over the past two millennia.

5.1. Authorship and Date. With very few exceptions, interpreters up to the time of the Reformation (either Luther or Grotius) accepted the identification of Qohelet with Solomon and dated the book to his time (tenth century BC). Indeed, again with few exceptions (Rashbam in the twelfth century AD), the book was seen to be the product of a single author.

Today, few commentators on Ecclesiastes would identify Qohelet with the historical Solomon. Even conservative commentators (Young; Kidner; Longman 1997 [Kaiser is an exception]) reject the tradition of Solomonic authorship. The connection between Qohelet and Solomon is instead recognized as a literary fiction on the part of the writer of the book. Again, with few exceptions (Fredericks [1988], who argues that the language is preexilic [but see Schoors]), commentators believe that the language and thought date the book to the Persian (Seow) or Greek period (Crenshaw; Lauha; Bartholomew). Even those who remain agnostic believe that the book almost certainly is late (Longman 1997). Accordingly, in the opinion of the majority of scholars, Ecclesiastes is an anonymous book.

5.2. Unity. In terms of unity, after the passing of a period where scholars posited multiple sources (see, on the work of Siegfried, 3.2 above), few scholars today would describe the book as having a complicated redactional history. The debate centers on the relationship between the body of the book (Qohelet's *autobiography) and the frame (Eccles 1:1-3 [or 1:1-11]; 12:8-14). Fox (1977) was the first in the modern period to explore the presence of two voices in the book, one that spoke in the first person as Qohelet and another that spoke about Qohelet (frame narrator).

5.3. Genre and Ancient Near Eastern Backgrounds. Discussions of genres of biblical books and their component parts occupy an important part of contemporary interpretation. Such interest is due in part to the program of form criticism initiated by Gunkel a century ago and more recently to the rise of synchronic literary studies. In any case, a contrast between ancient and modern interpretation may be drawn in the extent and explicitness with which the issue of genre of biblical books is discussed. In the case of Ecclesiastes, it is hard to miss the autobiographical nature of much of the book, particularly Ecclesiastes 1:12—12:7. This is not autobiography of the *res gestae* type, documenting and promoting the great achievements of an individual. *Res gestae* is the type of autobiography normally produced by or for a king. In Ecclesiastes, however, we have a king who searches for the meaning of life and ponders the consequences of his failure to discover any. It is not surprising then that the dominant type of literature within the book is the reflection, although we also find proverbs, anecdotes and more.

A second contrast between ancient and modern exegesis of the book of Ecclesiastes is the use of ancient Near Eastern background. Of course, this is largely due to the fact that the great ancient Near Eastern cultures and literature were only rediscovered in the nineteenth century. Scholars were quick to exploit these new discoveries to enrich their understanding of biblical texts. Until relatively recently, however, scholars have only pointed to similarities in thought between statements by Qohelet and in ancient Near Eastern texts. A case in point is the frequent comparison made between the speech by Siduri, the "barmaid" in the Epic of Gilgamesh, to Qohelet's exhortation to *carpe diem* (see Crenshaw, 51). In the past fifteen years, however, scholars have debated the relevance and significance of a generic similarity between Qohelet's *autobiography and autobiographies from Mesopotamia and Egypt (Longman; Seow; Perdue; Bartholomew).

5.4. Message. The book of Ecclesiastes is a complex book. This article began by citing examples of what appear to be conflicting statements both within the book and also between the book and the broader canon. In contemporary scholarship there is even the added issue of the relationship between the body of the book and the *refrain, especially if one follows Fox's idea that these represent two voices within the book.

As we have seen above, early Jewish and Christian interpretation handled these tensions by simply smoothing them out and ignoring them. The Targum turned Qohelet and the book into a model of rabbinic Judaism, while early Christian interpreters such as Gregory Thaumaturgos and Jerome transformed Qohelet into an orthodox theologian who advocated contempt for this world and a desire for an ascetic lifestyle.

One can still find semblances of such exegetical maneuvers. W. Kaiser, for instance, expends great energy in explaining how all of Qohelet's statements, though on the surface seemingly out of step with the rest of OT tradition, in reality fit in to its overall message. D. Fredericks (1993) is even more ambitious when he argues against the interpretive consensus that *hebel* should be translated consistently as "transient" rather than "meaningless" (Longman), "absurd" (Fox) or "enigmatic" (Bartholomew). Although there are significant differences between the latter three positions, they are all within the same semantic range in contrast to Fredericks's suggestion. To have Qohelet proclaim that everything is "transient" is another attempt to turn him into a consistently orthodox thinker and blunt the radical edge of his message.

Another aspect of discussion concerning the message of the book has to do with the relationship between Qohelet's frequent claim that "everything is meaningless/enigmatic/absurd" with the less frequent but still persistent *carpe diem* statements. Here he urges his hearers to seek whatever joy they can out of life. J. Crenshaw and T. Longman represent one side of the debate, concluding that meaninglessness is Qohelet's final verdict on the world, and that his encouragements to joy come with a tone of resignation. R. Whybray argues the opposite side. He believes that Qohelet's optimism grows with each successive *carpe diem* passage. Bartholomew represents a third view, which cautions against subsuming one of these themes to the other. Bartholomew (forthcoming) believes that both should be held together: "Qohelet's autonomous epistemology, depending on observation, experi-

ence and reason alone, leads him continually to the *hebel* conclusion, which is juxtaposed again and again with his *carpe diem* confessions of the goodness of life. The book is about the struggle to live with and resolve the agonized tension between these two poles."

6. Conclusion.

Coming to the end of this survey of major interpretive paradigms of the book of Ecclesiastes, we are not surprised to see that complete consensus has not yet been reached in its interpretation. Such a complex and profound book will continue to occupy the attention of generations of scholars yet to come. In spite of (or maybe due to) the book's complexity, the presence of Ecclesiastes in the canon serves as a reminder that life itself is complex and not amenable to simple answers.

See also ECCLESIASTES 1: BOOK OF; FEMINIST INTERPRETATION; HERMENEUTICS; MEGILLOT AND FESTIVALS; TARGUMIM.

BIBLIOGRAPHY. **C. G. Bartholomew,** *Reading Ecclesiastes: Old Testament Exegesis and Hermeneutical Theory* (AnBib 139; Rome: Pontifical Biblical Institute, 1998); idem, *Ecclesiastes* (BCOTWP; Grand Rapids: Baker, forthcoming); **G. A. Barton,** *The Book of Ecclesiastes* (ICC; Edinburgh: T & T Clark, 1908); **R. Beckwith,** *The Old Testament Canon of the New Testament Church* (London: SPCK, 1985); **B. S. Childs,** *Introduction to the Old Testament as Scripture* (Philadelphia: Fortress, 1979); **E. S. Christianson,** *Ecclesiastes through the Centuries* (BBC; Oxford: Blackwell, 2007); **J. L. Crenshaw,** *Ecclesiastes* (OTL; Philadelphia: Westminster John Knox, 1987); **K. J. Dell,** "Ecclesiastes as Wisdom: Consulting Early Interpreters," *VT* 44 (1994) 301-29; **M. V. Fox,** "Frame-Narrative and Composition in the Book of Qohelet," *HUCA* 48 (1977) 83-106; idem, "Qohelet," in *Dictionary of Biblical Interpretation*, ed. J. H. Hayes, vol. 2 (Nashville: Abingdon, 1999) 346-54; idem, *Ecclesiastes* (JPSBC; Philadelphia: Jewish Publication Society, 2004); **D. C. Fredericks,** *Qoheleth's Language: Re-evaluating Its Nature and Date* (ANETS 3; Lewiston, NY: Edwin Mellen, 1988); idem, *Coping with Transience: Ecclesiastes on the Brevity of Life* (BibSem 18; Sheffield: JSOT Press, 1993); **C. D. Ginsburg,** *Coheleth: Commonly Called the Book of Ecclesiastes* (London: Longman, 1861); **J. Jarick,** *Gregory Thaumaturgos' Paraphrase of Ecclesiastes* (SBLSCS 29; Atlanta: Scholars Press, 1990); **W. Kaiser,** *Ecclesiastes: To-*

tal Life (Chicago: Moody, 1979); **D. Kidner,** *A Time to Mourn and a Time to Dance: Ecclesiastes and the Way of the World* (BST; Downers Grove, IL: InterVarsity Press, 1976); **J. L. Koosed,** *(Per)mutations of Qoheleth: Reading the Body in the Book* (LHBOTS; London: T & T Clark, 2006); **A. Lauha,** *Kohelet* (BKAT 19; Neukirchen-Vluyn: Neukirchener Verlag, 1978); **É. Levine,** *The Aramaic Version of Qohelet* (New York: Sepher-Hermon Press, 1978); **T. Longman III,** *Ecclesiastes* (NICOT; Eerdmans, 1997); idem, "Israelite Genres in Their Ancient Near Eastern Setting," in *The Changing Face of Form Criticism for the Twenty-First Century,* ed. by M. A. Sweeney and E. Ben Zvi (Grand Rapids: Eerdmans, 2003) 177-95; idem, "Reading Wisdom Canonically," in *Canon and Biblical Interpretation,* ed. C. Bartholomew et al. (SHS 7; Grand Rapids: Zondervan, 2006) 352-73; **J. Muilenburg,** "A Qohelet Scroll from Qumran," *BASOR* 135 (1954) 20-28; **R. E. Murphy,** *Wisdom Literature: Job, Proverbs, Ruth, Canticles, Ecclesiastes, and Esther* (FOTL 13; Grand Rapids: Eerdmans, 1981); idem, "Qohelet Interpreted: The Bearing of the Past on the Present," *VT* 32 (1982) 331-37; idem, *Ecclesiastes* (WBC 23A; Nashville: Thomas Nelson, 1992); **C. A. Newsom,** "Job and Ecclesiastes," in *Old Testament Interpretation: Past, Present, and Future; Essays in Honor of Gene M. Tucker,* ed. J. Mays, D. Petersen and K. Richards (Nashville: Abingdon, 1995) 177-94; **L. G. Perdue,** *Wisdom and Creation: The Theology of Wisdom Literature* (Nashville: Abingdon, 1994); **E. Podechard,** *L'Ecclésiaste* (EBib; Paris: Libraire Victor Lecoffre, 1912); **M. H. Pope,** *Song of Songs* (AB 7C; Garden City, NY: Doubleday, 1977); **H. Ranston,** *Ecclesiastes and Early Greek Wisdom Literature* (London: Epworth, 1925); **A. Schoors,** *The Preacher Sought to Find Pleasing Words: A Study in the Language of Qoheleth* (Leuven: Peeters, 1992); **C. L. Seow,** *Ecclesiastes* (AB 18C; New York: Doubleday, 1997); **G. T. Sheppard,** "The Epilogue of Qoheleth as Theological Commentary," *CBQ* 39 (1977) 182-89; **C. Siegfried,** *Prediger und Hoheslied* (HKAT; Göttingen: Vandenhoeck & Ruprecht, 1898); **E. Ulrich,** "Ezra and Qoheleth Manuscripts from Qumran (4QEzra, 4QQohA,B)," in *Priests, Prophets and Scribes: Essays on the Formation and Heritage of Second Temple Judaism in Honour of Joseph Blenkinsopp,* ed. E. Ulrich et al. (JSOTSup 149; Sheffield: JSOT Press, 1992) 139-57; **R. N. Whybray,** "Qohelet,

Preacher of Joy," *JSOT* 23 (1982) 87-92; idem, *Ecclesiastes* (NCBC; Grand Rapids: Eerdmans, 1989); **J. R. Wright,** ed., *Proverbs, Ecclesiastes, Song of Solomon* (ACCS 9; Downers Grove, IL: InterVarsity Press, 2005); **E. J. Young,** *An Introduction to the Old Testament* (Grand Rapids: Eerdmans, 1949). T. Longman III

ECCLESIASTICUS. *See* SIRACH, BOK OF.

EDITORIAL CRITICISM

Our understanding of the book of *Psalms probably has suffered as a result of its frequent characterization as the "hymnbook of the Old Testament." The Psalter is often considered to be a collection of songs (*see* Music, Song) for *worship, and undoubtedly there is an element of truth in this idea; it is likely that many psalms were sung in public or private worship in their original setting, just as they have been throughout the ages (*see* Cult, Worship: Psalms). However, one thing is certain: the Psalter at some point became a canonical *book* of the OT. It became a book to be read and meditated upon and applied, just like any other book of the OT—not a hymnbook, but a book. The "hymnbook" idea has had a marginalizing effect upon our understanding of the psalms: "The Psalms are poems, and poems intended to be sung: not doctrinal treatises, nor even sermons" (Lewis, 10). This is partly due to contemporary misconceptions concerning the value of the aesthetic. Modernity has tended to assume that anything of real importance and significance should be explained "factually," using propositional ideas. The poetic—with its use of metaphor, imagery and emotive description—is often considered to be insubstantial by comparison. However, nothing could be further from the truth, for the aesthetic and the didactic combine seamlessly in the psalms, and regardless of what the Psalter may have been at various stages of its development, it has become a book of the Christian *canon and as such teaches us theology.

As a book like any other book, Psalms (and the other anthological books of the Writings) has been subject to the same editorial processes that can be observed in the remainder of the canon. Since B. S. Childs's *Introduction to the Old Testament as Scripture* (1979), the general principle that an editorial hand was at work in the formation of the final version of the canon has been broadly accepted with regard to the historical and prophetic books of the OT. However, discussion of the poetic books continued to focus on questions of genre and function within the cult, and scholars generally were skeptical with regard to any notion of editorial shaping of the poetic books. It was widely assumed that nothing other than the random compilation of disparate materials could be observed in Psalms and *Proverbs particularly. So, is it legitimate to speak of editorial criticism with regard to such poetic works?

1. Editorial Shaping of Psalms
2. The Significance of Editorial Shaping in Psalms
3. Editorial Shaping in Proverbs
4. Method in Discerning Editorial Context
5. Conclusion

1. Editorial Shaping in Psalms.
Since the key works of H. Gunkel and S. Mowinckel (*see* Form Criticism), study of Psalms has been dominated by questions of literary genre and usage within Israel's public worship. Consideration of type and cult-function was so preeminent in the secondary literature that questions of editing in the psalms were almost entirely neglected. C. Westermann (251) suggests that "in laying the foundation for his interpretation of the Psalms, Gunkel above all had no interest in how the collection was handed down to us," and this lack of interest in the formation of the Psalter continued through several generations until the 1980s. However, in writing the chapter on the canonical shape of Psalms in *Introduction to the Old Testament as Scripture*, Childs asked a very pertinent question that ultimately led to a sea change in the study of Psalms: "Why is Psalm 1 the first psalm in the Psalter?" (see Childs, 512-14). It is not representative of the major genres of psalms, being neither a *lament nor a *hymn of praise. Equally, it seems unlikely that the first psalm was ever sung by the massed ranks of the covenant community at one of the great festivals, since it is a Torah/Wisdom poem. Psalm 1, therefore, is not significant either with regard to its genre or its function in Israel's cult, so why should it be chosen as the first in the book?

This initial question led naturally to a second: "Why are there so many lexical and structural links between Psalms 1 and 2?" Neither of these two poems is headed by a superscription (which is unusual in Book I of the Psalter), the two psalms are bounded by an *inclusio grounded in the idea of "blessing" (*'ašrê* is used in Ps 1:1; 2:12), the verb *hāgâ* is key to both psalms (used of meditation on the Torah in Ps 1:2 and of the mutterings of rebellion in Ps 2:1), and, among other links, the righteous, the wicked, the law, ideas of judgment and a way that is perishing appear in both poems (see Auffret; Grant, 60-65). Once these observations are made, the reader logically begins to question whether these connections are accidental or are they in fact indications of purposeful editorial activity in the Psalter?

This was the very issue that G. H. Wilson, a student of Childs, sought to address in his *Editing of the Hebrew Psalter* (1985). Having examined editing techniques that were apparent in collections of Sumerian hymns, Wilson went on to ask if such indicators of editorial influence are apparent also in the biblical psalms. The Sumerian hymnic collections contained several explicit indications of editing (e.g., the name of the scribe who gathered a collection), but Wilson also pointed out the presence of "tacit" signs of editing (e.g., grouping hymns according to theme, or the similarity of their first line, called an "incipit"). Although there are no explicit signs of editing in the Psalter, Wilson (1985, 9-10, 182-85) went on to show that there are many tacit indications of the grouping or ordering of psalms in the book.

One of the first and most significant of these signs is seen in the aforementioned placement of Psalms 1—2 at the head of the Psalter. These poems are deliberately linked and seem to have been purposefully placed at the start of the Psalter as an introduction to the wide diversity of material that the reader will encounter within the collection as a whole (McCann, 48-50). It was a common practice in the ancient Near East for the editors of anthologies of hymnic or poetic material to place an introduction at the head of the collection in order to provide the reader with a paradigm for the interpretation of the diverse materials that follow (Van Leeuwen, *NIB* 5.24). The placement of Psalms 1—2 as an introduction to the canonical book as a whole indicates that the biblical Psalter follows this pattern and thus points toward the subtle presence of editorial organization within the psalms.

Once this introduction is observed, it soon becomes clear that there are other obvious indications of deliberate editorial activity throughout the book of Psalms. The division of Psalms into five books separated by doxologies is, arguably, the clearest indication that the order of the psalms is not entirely random (Wilson 2005, 230-31). It is possible that this was a deliberate attempt to echo the Pentateuch within the Writings, and the rabbis compared the "five books of David" with the five books of Moses (Sarna, 18). Whether this was the intent or not, the organization of the psalms into books clearly is not accidental but rather points toward deliberate editorial activity.

Another obvious sign of editing is the incorporation of smaller groupings of psalms into the broader Psalter as collections (e.g., the Songs of Ascent [Pss 120—134]). These psalms, unlike the laments, have not been dispersed throughout the book, but their association with one another is retained by their inclusion as a subcollection within the broader book. Furthermore, we can observe deliberate editorial structuring of these collections retained within Psalms. Perhaps the best example of this is the *chiastic structure of Psalms 15—24. Miller points out that Psalm 15 and Psalm 24 are entrance psalms that focus on questions of access into the temple; Psalm 16 and Psalm 23 are psalms of comfort; Psalm 17 and Psalm 22 are powerful laments; Psalm 18 and the linked Psalms 20—21 are royal psalms; thus leaving Psalm 19, a Torah psalm, as the central pivot of this collection. Other indications of editing include the deliberate juxtaposition of psalms that are apparently "in conversation" with one another. For example, Psalm 90 (and the succeeding psalms in Book IV of the Psalter) seems to provide a response to the depths of despair found in the lament section of Psalm 89 (e.g., cf. Ps 89:39 with Ps 90:14). The lament of Psalm 89 focuses on the demise of the Davidic monarchy and questions whether Yahweh is still in control of the destiny of his people. Psalm 90 responds with the voice of Moses, pointing out that Yahweh was the refuge and dwelling place of the people before king and temple existed, and that he is still their rock even though these institutions have been removed. The ensuing psalms emphasize the continuing reign of Yahweh and also encourage the people with the prospect of the future return of the Davidic king (Mays 1994a, 124-25).

So, although it is impossible to completely remove an element of "randomness" from the Psalter (claims for a logical ordering throughout the whole book go too far), there are many indications of extensive editorial activity within Psalms. Wilson (1985, 199) summarizes the telltale signs of editorial activity in the Psalter:

> I have been able to show (1) that the "book" divisions of the Psalter are real, editorially induced divisions and not accidentally introduced; (2) the "separating" and "binding" functions of author and genre groupings; (3) the lack of a s/s [superscription] as an indication of a tradition of combination; (4) the use of *hllwyh* pss to indicate the conclusion of segments; (5) the use of *hwdw* pss to introduce segments; (6) the existence of thematic correspondences between the beginning and ending pss in some books. All of these findings demonstrate the presence of editorial activity at work in the arrangement of the pss.

2. The Significance of Editorial Shaping in Psalms.

Reading Psalms as a book has important implications for interpretation, primarily in terms of context. Traditionally, each psalm has been treated as an individual unit for interpretation purposes—these were contextless, hermetically sealed units as far as their interpretation was concerned. However, reading Psalms as a book means that, as with every book, passages fall within a context. Why are Psalms 1—2 the only psalms without a superscription in Books I-III of the Psalter? Well, it seems that Psalms 1—2 were meant to be read and understood together as a joint introduction to the book of Psalms, an introduction that focuses on choosing a way of Torah-based devotion to Yahweh and absolute submission to his lordship. However, this double message is clearly heard only when we read these psalms in their canonical context.

Increasingly, scholars are becoming aware of the importance of context even within gathered anthological books such as Psalms and Proverbs. Not that psalms cease to function as individual units for interpretative purposes; it is rather that their context—where the psalm is found in the Psalter—impinges upon the interpretation of that individual unit. It can therefore be argued that individual compositions within the Psalter have limited interpretative autonomy: each psalm is a literary unit in its own right (akin to any pericope within a narrative text), but the meaning found in each unit is often nuanced or influenced by its near neighbors or the collection within which it resides. To read and understand a psalm properly, we must be aware of its setting within any subcollection of which it may be a part, within its book and, indeed, within the whole Psalter. We should pay particular attention to psalms that open or close books or that are central to a book. Psalms are associated—resulting in an interpretative context—by way of their superscriptions (e.g., the Songs of Ascent) or their opening/closing lines (e.g., the "hallelujah" commands found in Pss 111—117; 146—150) or by theme (e.g., the "Yahweh reigns" psalms [Pss 93—99]). So, the position of a psalm within the Psalter impacts how we read that poem (Mays 1993).

For example, Psalm 1 is a literary unit. Despite claims that Psalms 1—2 were once a single composition, Psalm 1 is a composition in its own right. Therefore, it speaks a message to today's reader: the avoidance of evil, the practice of the means of grace, the blessings of being in right relationship with the living God, and the fact that life boils down to a choice between one of two ways. This is Psalm 1's message; however, as we noted, the first two psalms are linked both structurally (through the lack of superscription and the ʾašrê ["blessed"] inclusio in Ps 1:1 and Ps 2:12) and semantically (through the repetition of key terms—e.g., hāgâ ["meditate/plot"] in Ps 1:2 and Ps 2:1; derek ["way"] in Ps 1:6 and Ps 2:12). The editorial association of these two psalms provides each with a context for interpretation. So we should read and understand Psalm 1 in the light of Psalm 2 and vice versa. As J. L. Mays (1994a, 122-23) observes, "The two psalms together call for a piety composed of obedience and trust that is fostered by the entire book. Delight in the torah and taking refuge in the Lord constitute the faith nurtured by the psalms. The psalms offer a 'way' and a 'refuge' in the midst of the wickedness and power of the world."

3. Editorial Shaping in Proverbs.

In many ways, the issues discussed above regarding Psalms apply equally when the Wisdom literature comes under consideration. Although written in poetic form, the book of *Job follows a fairly cohesive narrative structure. Equally, it has been argued that a "narrative" or even "narratives" can be traced through the book of *Ecclesiastes (Christianson). It has generally been thought that the book of Proverbs is also made up of gathered material where questions of context, broadly speaking, were thought not to apply. However, in recent years several works have drawn attention to signs of editorial organization in Proverbs akin to those observable in the Psalter.

The problem of interpreting Proverbs, especially Proverbs 10—29, is well stated by R. C. Van Leeuwen (1988, 2): "In these chapters we find discrete, entirely self-sufficient literary units . . . which are extremely terse in formulation and brief in compass. . . . One is acutely aware that the briefer the literary unit the more difficult the interpretation. The problem is further complicated because the juxtaposed proverbs, to the modern, western mind at least, often appear to have very little to do with one another either formally or materially." Obviously, the individual proverbs of Proverbs 10—29 are even briefer literary units than those found in Psalms. Proverbs 1—9 and Proverbs 30—31 contain longer groupings of proverbial statements, called "instructions," and these provide a much clearer context for the interpretation of the individual proverb. However, Proverbs 10—29 consists of verse after verse of individual proverbial statements without obvious flow, progression of thought or context. The collections appear at first glance to be random, and for many years scholars assumed that there was no purposeful ordering in this section.

The works of Van Leeuwen, K. M. Heim and others go a long way toward dispelling the myth of the random collection of proverbs in the book of Proverbs. Van Leeuwen highlights the editorial organization of proverbs on structural, poetic and semantic levels. In terms of structure, Van Leeuwen points out that although individual sayings and admonitions have a "relative self-sufficiency" in their own right, each proverb is in fact a "paradigmatic building block" used by the author or editor to create larger poetic units. From the perspective of *poetics, it is clear that individual proverbial sayings can be juxtaposed in such a way as to create poems that in turn impact our interpretation of the individual sayings. So contiguous units within a broader poem provide "commentary" on one another; that is, they supply the reader with a context. At the word level, Van Leeuwen points out the frequent repetition of similar words or concepts within juxtaposed proverbial statements, once again indicating continuity and therefore context (see Van Leeuwen 1988, 40-55). Heim develops these observations in more detail, providing thorough criteria for the delimitation of editorial groupings within the book of Proverbs. He suggests that "clusters" of proverbs are to be discerned by observing not primarily the continuation of themes but rather the formal links that associate proverbial sayings. Thus, the reader should look for the repetition of synonyms, word roots, sounds, consonants and so forth in these clusters of proverbs. Heim argues that the movement between clusters is not marked by verses that clearly conclude a particular chain of proverbs; rather, we should watch for a change in the linking device that bonds proverbs into groups (e.g., the movement from a speech-dominated cluster in Prov 11:9-14 to a commerce-focused cluster in Prov 11:15-21) (see Heim, 105-8).

4. Method in Discerning Editorial Context.

Once it is established that editorial hands have in some sense shaped the poetic books, a secondary question must follow: How can we discern the editorial shaping that is apparent in Psalms and Wisdom literature? The basic thesis argued above is that editors have provided us, as readers, with a context for the interpretation of individual poems, proverbs, sayings and instructions. This context inevitably influences our understanding of these individual literary units, so how can we discern these frameworks for interpretation in the poetic books?

With Psalms as our primary example, the basic thesis of a canonical approach to the Psalter is that the ordering and placement of the psalms is not entirely random, but rather the book of Psalms has been shaped by the work of editors in order to impact our understanding of individual poems. In order to legitimately discern editorial activity in the Psalter, some fairly rigorous ground rules must be applied to prevent the misuse of this canonical approach and its decline into rampant subjectivity. G. H. Wilson, as well as being one of the originators of this method, championed correct and clearly defined method. Having highlighted the pitfalls of approaching the Psalter with a preconceived notion of the editorial themes to be found in the book and then "finding" psalms that fit this theory, Wilson (1993, 48) states, "My own preference is to work without a hypothesis . . . and to allow any sense

of the structure that develops to derive from an intensive and thorough analysis of the psalms in question in terms of their linguistic, thematic, literary and theological links and relationships." Wilson suggests that editorial themes can be discerned from "linguistic, thematic, literary and theological links and relationships" observed between psalms. Psalms are linked in order to paint a fuller picture than is seen in their individual parts. Content in context takes on a slightly different meaning. The idea is that the theological concerns of the editors of the Psalter's final form are seen in the way in which they link psalms together and also in their placement of these linked psalms at key junctures throughout the Psalter.

D. M. Howard also provides helpful comment on canonical methodology as it is applied to the book of Psalms. His approach focuses on four areas of linking that show concatenation between individual psalms or groups of psalms: lexical, thematic, structural and genre connections (see Howard, 99-100). He further refines these categories. Regarding lexical links, we should look in particular for "keyword" (*Leitwörter*) links where the same word or phrase is repeated, and for thematic word links where the same concept is expressed using different words. Incidental links, which could be described as nonessential to both psalms, may also appear, so we should be careful not to read too much into the repetition of the commonest of words or phrases. Thematic links are seen via lexical repetition and more generally linked concepts, or even in echoes and responses between psalms. For example, a question asked in one psalm may be answered in the following psalm (e.g., could "The LORD is my shepherd, I shall not want" in Ps 23:1 be a response to "My God, my God, why have you forsaken me?" in Ps 22:1?), or a theme may be expanded upon throughout a chain of psalms (e.g., the "LORD reigns" psalms [Pss 93—99]). Howard sees structural links as particularly helpful when we are dealing with a group of psalms within the larger structure of the Psalter (see 4.1 below). Both Wilson and Howard see genre having only limited importance as a tool for deriving thematic association between psalms; it can highlight interesting indicators (e.g., the possible transition between groups of psalms), but it seems unlikely that the redactors of the Psalter extensively used genre classification as an organizational tool—

content, including the superscriptions, rather than type seems to have directed the editorial placement of the psalms.

Obviously, there may be a certain degree of overlap in these categories. For example, thematic links often become apparent through the observation of lexical concatenation. Or, the use of the same word in consecutive psalms may indicate a structural connection as well as simple lexical linkage (e.g., the repetition of the *ʾašrê* ["blessed"] in Pss 1—2 forms a structural link, an inclusio, that goes beyond the simple repetition of words in successive psalms). However, these ground rules provide a reasonable framework within which the canonical approach can function. Seeking out such indicators of concatenation can help us to define more clearly a context for the interpretation of individual psalms.

4.1. Collections, Superscriptions and Editorial Context. Along with the indications of deliberate editorial association mentioned above, collections and superscriptions are particularly significant for discerning context. Obviously, lexical and thematic repetition is an essential feature indicating the deliberate association of juxtaposed psalms: where there is no repetition of words, ideas and motifs, the reader makes no connection between neighboring psalms. However, an element of subjectivity in charting keyword links remains. Where does concatenation come to an end? Where did it begin? Sometimes linked groups of psalms have a very clear beginning and ending, but often this linking is more difficult to define—for example, Book I is so dominated by Davidic laments that it is difficult to define groupings within that broader collection.

It seems that if a proper definition of psalm groupings is key to the canonical approach to the study of the Psalter, then the method of delimiting groups of psalms needs to be clearly expressed. Concatenation via linking techniques is not always sufficient to define a psalm grouping in and of itself, so the reader should also look for indicators of editorial division. The whole idea of a psalm grouping implies both a conjunctive and a disjunctive literary function. Thus, a group of psalms (or a cluster of proverbs, for that matter) implies a degree of association between the psalms within that grouping, and this in turn implies a degree of separation from neighboring psalms that are not part of this psalm grouping.

Take the Songs of Ascent, for example. How does this grouping impact Book V of the Psalter? Psalms 120—134 clearly comprises a grouping. This is indicated, as is often the case, primarily by their superscription. Each of these fifteen psalms begins with the words *šîr hammaʿălôt* ("a song of ascents"), and there is evidence from both the psalms themselves and extrabiblical material that these psalms were used in the temple during one of the great pilgrimage festivals. So there is good reason to see these psalms as a grouping, and, therefore, the editorial context for the interpretation of any one of these psalms is found within the collection—the emphases of the grouping shapes our understanding of each individual composition. What are the implications for the rest of Book V?

The conjunctive aspect of this collection provides a clear context for the interpretation of these psalms, but the disjunctive aspect of this grouping also gives us indicators as to how we should read the psalms contextually. Psalm 119 and Psalm 135 clearly are not part of the Songs of Ascent, and therefore they fall within a different context. This leads us to question the contextual setting for these compositions. Looking for indicators of other groupings within Book V, we see that Psalms 111—117 form a canonical collection because each of them either begins or ends with the "hallelujah" command (except Ps 114, but it is possible that the "hallelujah" postscript to Ps 113 was originally the superscript for Ps 114). This clearly defined collection leaves Psalms 118—119 as a pairing designed to be read together, as is evidenced by the lexical and thematic overlap that can be observed in these psalms (Grant, 175-80). On the other side of the Songs of Ascent collection we see a group of Davidic psalms from Psalm 138 to Psalm 145, leaving the context for Psalm 135 to be found in relationship with Psalms 136—137 (Mays 1994b, 422).

So we can see that collections are often marked by a common superscription or first line, and that these collections help us to define the context for the interpretation of individual poems. The psalms within the collection are linked, and at the same time they delimit the extent of the association and help us to see connections that may not otherwise have been immediately obvious.

4.2. The Question of Significant Placement. Having examined some principles for establishing context by way of lexical and thematic association, and having looked at the impact of collections on our reading of the text, we will find it helpful to explore some of the principles regarding significant placement within the Psalter. What makes the placement of a psalm or a group of psalms particularly telling from an editorial perspective? At its most basic level, the answer to that question is quite simple: we should pay particular attention to psalms or groups of psalms that are placed at the beginning, middle or end of one of the books of the Psalter.

One of the observations by Wilson (1985, 207-8) on the editorial shaping of the Psalter was the importance of the so-called seam psalms that come at the beginning and the end of the books of the Psalter. These positions within the five books have an obvious significance for understanding the thematic emphases that the editors seek to highlight for the readers of the psalms. The opening thoughts of a book, in a very natural manner, set the tone for what follows, and it has been observed that the psalms that close the book divisions of the Psalter often appear to deliberately echo the initial compositions (deClaissé-Walford, 55-56). Therefore, we should pay particular attention to the beginning and the end of books as we seek to discern editorial emphases. Furthermore, centrality within a book of the Psalter is also considered to be of some significance. E. Zenger (102), referring to the placement of Psalm 119 in Book V, states, "According to the theological perspective of the fifth book of psalms which has the Torah Psalm 119 *intentionally placed in the middle of the composition*, the psalms are a means of opening oneself to the living Torah of YHWH—in accordance with the programme at the beginning of the Psalter, Psalms 1–2, and in accordance with the closing Hallel, Psalms 146–150, which interprets the recitation/singing of psalms as the actualization of the way of life (Torah) instilled in the cosmos" (emphasis added).

Centrality within the respective books of the Psalter also seems to be of importance in defining the emphases that the editors desired to stress. It may be that there is a single, central psalm that clearly lies at the very heart of one of the books (e.g., Ps 119 in Book V), and in other examples it appears to be a collection that is central (e.g., the Pss 15—24 collection in Book I). However, the beginning, middle and end of the five books of Psalms should draw our inter-

est because these in particular seem to be the focus of editorial attention.

Although not all of the aforementioned methodological details apply equally to all of the poetic books of the OT, many of the general principles—especially Wilson's and Howard's suggestions for determining concatenation—may be adopted in our analysis of editorial activity in Proverbs.

5. Conclusion.
All the poetic books of the OT show signs that their final form has somehow been shaped by editors. The task of editorial criticism is to access the themes, concerns and emphases that were key for those who assembled these books as we know them today. Through careful study of the text we see that the poetic texts are not isolated units that stand entirely on their own but rather do in fact have a context that is drawn from the ordering of these collections. These contexts shape our understanding and interpretation of the individual texts found in both Psalms and Proverbs.

See also ASAPH AND SONS OF KORAH; FORM CRITICISM; FRAME NARRATIVE; LEMUEL AND AGUR; PSALMS 1: BOOK OF; RHETORICAL CRITICISM.

BIBLIOGRAPHY. **P. Auffret,** *The Literary Structure of Psalm 2,* trans. D. J. A. Clines (JSOTSup 3; Sheffield: JSOT Press, 1977); **B. S. Childs,** *Introduction to the Old Testament as Scripture* (London: SCM, 1979); **E. S. Christianson,** *A Time to Tell: Narrative Strategies in Ecclesiastes* (JSOTSup 280; Sheffield: Sheffield Academic Press, 1998); **N. L. deClaissé-Walford,** *Reading from the Beginning: The Shaping of the Hebrew Psalter* (Macon, GA: Mercer University Press, 1997); **J. A. Grant,** *The King as Exemplar: The Function of Deuteronomy's Kingship Law in the Shaping of the Book of Psalms* (SBLAB 17; Atlanta: Society of Biblical Literature, 2004); **K. M. Heim,** *Like Grapes of Gold Set in Silver: An Interpretation of Proverbial Clusters in Proverbs 10:1-22:16* (BZAW 273; Berlin: de Gruyter, 2001); **D. M. Howard,** *The Structure of Psalms 93-100* (BJSUCSD 5; Winona Lake, IN: Eisenbrauns, 1997); **C. S. Lewis,** *Reflections on the Psalms* (Glasgow: Collins, 1961); **J. L. Mays,** "The Question of Context in Psalm Interpretation," in *The Shape and Shaping of the Psalter,* ed. J. C. McCann (JSOTSup 159; Sheffield: JSOT Press, 1993) 14-20; idem, *The Lord Reigns: A Theological Handbook to the Psalms* (Louisville: Westminster

John Knox, 1994a); *Psalms* (IBC; Louisville: John Knox, 1994b); **J. C. McCann,** *A Theological Introduction to the Books of Psalms: The Psalms as Torah* (Nashville: Abingdon, 1993); **P. D. Miller,** "Kingship, Torah Obedience and Prayer," in *Neue Wege der Psalmenforschung,* ed. K. Seybold and E. Zenger (HBS 1; Freiburg: Herder, 1994) 127-42; **N. M. Sarna,** *On the Book of Psalms: Exploring the Prayer of Ancient Israel* (New York: Schocken, 1993); **R. C. Van Leeuwen,** "The Book of Proverbs: Introduction, Commentary and Reflections," *NIB* 5.19-264; idem, *Context and Meaning in Proverbs 25-27* (SBLDS 96; Atlanta: Scholars Press, 1988); **C. Westermann,** *Praise and Lament in the Psalms* (Atlanta: John Knox, 1981); **G. H. Wilson,** *The Editing of the Hebrew Psalter* (SBLDS 76; Chico, CA: Scholars Press, 1985); idem, "Understanding the Purposeful Arrangement of the Psalms: Pitfalls and Promise," in *The Shape and Shaping of the Psalter,* ed. J. C. McCann (JSOTSup 159; Sheffield: JSOT Press, 1993) 42-51; idem, "The Structure of the Psalter," in *Interpreting the Psalms: Issues and Approaches,* ed. P. S. Johnston and D. G. Firth (Leicester: Apollos, 2005) 229-46; **E. Zenger,** "The Composition and Theology of the Fifth Book of the Psalter," *JSOT* 80 (1998) 77-102.

J. A. Grant

EDUCATION. *See* SAGES, SCHOOLS, EDUCATION.

ELIHU. *See* JOB 1: BOOK OF.

ELLIPSIS

Ellipsis involves constructions in which a grammatically required element is omitted, thus creating a structural hole or gap.

    1. Introduction
    2. Cross-linguistic Features of Verbal Ellipsis
    3. Distinctive Features of Verbal Ellipsis in Biblical Poetry
    4. Ellipsis in Poetry as Opposed to Prose

1. Introduction.

Ellipsis is the most elusive feature of biblical poetry in that it involves words that are not present but whose existence is understood by speakers and hearers, as well as writers and readers. From a linguistic point of view, ellipsis produces utterances that are *grammatically* incomplete in their surface structure. For example, in Isaiah 1:27 the verb has been elided (or deleted) in the second line: "Zion by justice *shall be redeemed,* /

and her repentant ones by righteousness [   ]." (In the biblical examples of ellipsis in this article, the following conventions are used: the elided material is represented by the blank space within square brackets, the antecedent is in italics, and the two halves of the example are divided by a slash.) The second clause, "and her repentant ones by righteousness," is structurally incomplete without the verb ("shall be redeemed") from the first clause. Some biblical scholars have referred to the verb in examples such as Isaiah 1:27 as a "double-duty" element (e.g., Dahood, §13.44a), thus focusing on the item that is retained in an elliptical construction rather than the item that is deleted.

Less technically, the term "elliptical" is sometimes used to describe utterances that are *contextually* incomplete and require the hearer to supply contextual information (on the distinction, see Lyons, 174-75; Halliday and Hasan, 142-43); this second use of the term will not be considered here.

Verses with elliptical constructions pose two special problems: the necessity of recognizing that ellipsis has occurred, and the need to restore the missing word(s) so that the verse can be read correctly. For native speakers of a language, these challenges are ordinarily met without difficulty and, in fact, unconsciously. We can illustrate these problems using spoken English. Upon hearing the sentence *John ate apples and Sue oranges,* the hearer knows that *Sue oranges* is a sentence fragment that must be resolved as *Sue [ate] oranges.* Native speakers are able to process sentence fragments effortlessly because they have two kinds of innate syntactic knowledge: knowledge of the underlying syntactic structures of their language, and knowledge of the ways in which ellipsis operates upon those structures. Nonetheless, syntax alone is insufficient for interpreting elliptical structures; native speakers also must rely on their knowledge of semantics (the meanings of words), pragmatics (the uses of words within the speech context) and prosody (the sound phrases). Contrast the sentence *John ate the apples slowly and the monkey quickly* with the sentence *John ate the apples slowly and the candy quickly.* The two sentences are identical in surface structure and have the same kind of sentence fragment (a noun phrase [respectively, *the monkey* and *the candy*] and an adverb [*quickly*]), and each allows syntactically for two different interpretations depending upon whether the noun phrase is the subject or the object of the elided verb. On the basis of semantics and pragmatics, however, most English-speakers will interpret *the monkey* as the subject of its fragmented sentence *(the monkey [ate the apples] quickly)* and *the candy* as the object of its fragmented sentence *([John ate] the candy quickly)*. When the two sentences are spoken aloud, the presence or absence of a slight pause provides the hearer with an additional clue to the intended meaning of the speaker (Hartmann), signaling the absence of the implied words from the sentence *(John ate the apples slowly and the monkey* [pause] *quickly)*. Each of these features of language (syntax, semantics, pragmatics, prosody) plays a role in the interpretation of elliptical constructions.

The patterns of ellipsis in biblical *Hebrew must be ascertained through an understanding of the features of ellipsis that are shared among the world's languages (see, e.g., McShane, 136-42) as well as an examination of the features distinctive to biblical Hebrew on the basis of exegetically unremarkable examples. The remainder of this article considers ellipsis of the verb in biblical poetry, since this aspect of ellipsis is most easily illustrated in translation. (For a description of the other kinds of ellipsis in biblical Hebrew, see Geller, 299-312; O'Connor, 124-29, 401-407; Watson, 303-6; Miller 2003; 2005 [on ellipsis of negative words]; forthcoming b [on comparative constructions]; forthcoming a [on prepositions]).

2. Cross-linguistic Features of Verbal Ellipsis.

2.1. Ellipsis Requires Coordinate Clauses. The first feature common to languages concerning verbal ellipsis is that ellipsis is possible only out of coordinate (not subordinate) structures. In English, for example, ellipsis of the verb is possible when two clauses are coordinate (i.e., joined with "and" or "but"), but not when they are subordinate (e.g., joined with "because"). Thus, it is possible to say *Chris cleaned the garage <u>and</u> Lee* [ ] *the car*, but not *Chris cleaned the garage <u>because</u> Lee* [ ] *the car* (see Wilder).

Biblical Hebrew is similar in that verbal ellipsis requires two coordinate clauses, joined with "and" (as in Is 1:27 [see 1 above]), an adversative conjunction (e.g., "but rather" in 1 Sam 30:22), or simply juxtaposed, as in Isaiah 41:7: "The artisan *encourages* the goldsmith, / the one who smoothes with the hammer [ ] the one who strikes the anvil."

In most of the examples in this article the boundaries of the poetic line and the boundaries of the syntactic clause are coterminous, but this is not always the case. Verbal ellipsis occurs out of coordinate structures; the poetic line may or may not provide a suitable environment for ellipsis to take place.

2.2. Ellipsis Requires Correspondence. A second feature of ellipsis is that the two clauses must correspond in some way. In other words, hearers (and readers) are able to determine what belongs in the gap by aligning the two clauses and determining what is missing in one of them.

In biblical Hebrew, verbal ellipsis generally involves a syntactic correspondence of the constituents in the two clauses. This means that the basic building blocks of the clause (e.g., subject, object, prepositional phrases) are identical in both clauses or at least function identically in both clauses. For example, in Isaiah 1:27 the constituents of the two clauses are identical (the Hebrew word order is represented here): "Zion (subject) by justice (prepositional phrase) *will be redeemed* (verb), / and her repentant ones (subject) by righteousness (prepositional phrase) [ ] (deleted verb)." The constituents in both lines have this order: subject, prepositional phrase, verb. The hearer (or reader) knows to restore the verb in the second line because of the syntactic correspondence of the two lines.

It is also possible for corresponding constituents to be slightly different in the two lines if they play the same syntactic role in their respective sentences. Psalm 121:6 illustrates this phenomenon: "Daily the sun *will not strike you*, / and the moon [ ] in the night." The constituents in the two lines match except that the first line has an adverb ("daily") that corresponds to a prepositional phrase ("in the night") in the second line. However, both the adverb and the prepositional phrase function as adverbial modifiers; therefore, ellipsis of the verb and its object is possible from the second line. (The issue of the ways in which the two lines correspond is more complex than is presented here; for additional details, see Miller 2007.)

2.3. Ellipsis Requires Lexical Identity. A third feature of ellipsis involves the identity of the item that is deleted with respect to the corresponding item that is not deleted (i.e., its antecedent). Ellipsis universally requires lexical identity; that is, the item that is deleted must be the same lexical item as the antecedent. In the case of Isaiah 1:27, the only verb that can be understood to have been deleted is a form of *pdh* ("redeem") and not any other verb, not even a synonym. Furthermore, the form of the verb must be understood as passive and as future (technically, the form is imperfective) in both lines ("will be redeemed"). However, ellipsis does not require that the deleted item be identical to its antecedent in every respect.

In biblical Hebrew, the deleted verb need not agree with its antecedent in gender or number (in Is 1:27 "Zion" is fem. sg., whereas "her repentant ones" is masc. pl.). Nor does the deleted verb need to agree with its antecedent in person, as illustrated in Psalm 20:7[8] (the order of deletion is backwards [see 3.1 below]): "Some on chariotry [ ], / and some on horses [ ], / but as for us, on the name of the LORD our God *we will call.*" In the first two clauses the deleted verb must be third-person plural ("they will call"); the antecedent verb in the third line is first-person plural ("we will call").

3. Distinctive Features of Verbal Ellipsis in Biblical Poetry.

In addition to the universal features of verbal ellipsis, biblical Hebrew has several other features.

3.1 Direction of Ellipsis. The first feature relates to the direction of ellipsis, since languages differ in this respect. Biblical Hebrew usually exhibits forwards ellipsis; that is, the verb is present in the first line and is deleted from the second line. However, it is possible for ellipsis to occur in the first line—a situation known as backwards ellipsis. Psalm 20:7[8] (see 2.3 above) provides an example.

Backwards ellipsis is highly constrained in biblical poetry. It occurs only when the antecedent is in final position in the line. The biblical Hebrew patterns are like other languages with respect to backwards ellipsis—languages that allow backwards ellipsis do so only when the constituent to be deleted is in final position (van Oirsouw, 132, 124).

3.2 Position of Verb. The second feature of ellipsis in biblical Hebrew involves the position of the verb in the clause. Ellipsis may occur when the verb is in initial, medial or final position with respect to the other clausal constituents. The most common position is initial position, as illustrated in Isaiah 17:13: "*They will be chased*

like chaff on the mountains before the wind, / and [ ] like whirling dust before the storm."

Medial position is illustrated in Isaiah 60:2: "For behold, darkness *will cover* the earth, / and thick darkness [ ] the peoples."

Ellipsis from final position was illustrated in Isaiah 1:27 (see 1 above) and Psalm 121:6 (see 2.2 above).

3.3. Linear Order. A third unique feature of ellipsis in Hebrew involves the order of constituents. Unlike English, Hebrew allows ellipsis to take place when the order of constituents is in *chiastic (mirror) order, although chiastic order is less common. Psalm 103:7 provides an illustration: "*He made known* (verb) his ways (object) to Moses (prepositional phrase) / to the sons of Israel (prepositional phrase) his deeds (object) [ ] (verb)" (cf. Ps 121:6 [see 2.2 above]) The order of constituents is verb, object, prepositional phrase in the first line, mirrored by prepositional phrase, object, deleted verb in the second line.

3.4 Semantics of Paired Constituents. As we have noted, verbal ellipsis involves a correspondence between the constituents of the two lines. In English, verbal ellipsis results in specific semantic relationships between the pairs of nonverbal constituents. Consider this English sentence: *John writes novels, my brother* [ ] *biographies.*

The paired constituents in the two halves of the elliptical structure are "John"/"my brother" and "novels"/"biographies." The paired words cannot be understood as referring to the same entities; that is, John cannot be the same individual as the speaker's brother, nor can the literary productions be combined to mean "biographical novels." Instead, both sets of paired words are contrastive. As a whole, the construction compares the differing literary outputs (novels as opposed to biographies) of two individuals (John and the brother) (see Prince).

In biblical poetry, however, the semantic relationship between word pairs involving verbal ellipsis is rarely that of contrast (as it is in English). Instead, most commonly the word pairs refer to the same person or entity, as illustrated in Numbers 23:7: "From Aram *brought me* Balaq, / the king of Moab [ ] from the eastern mountains." The constituents in the two lines are in chiastic order: prepositional phrase, verb with object, subject (first line), followed by subject, deleted verb and object, prepositional phrase (second line). The prepositional phrase "from Aram" is paired with "from the eastern mountains," and the subject "Balaq" is paired with "the king of Moab." What is important to note is that in Hebrew the two lines refer to the same action by the same individual rather than to two contrastive actions by two individuals (as English speakers would expect).

Rarely in biblical poetry verbal ellipsis results in truly contrastive word pairs, as in Isaiah 1:21: "Righteousness *was dwelling in her,* / but now murderers [ ]." The verse contrasts "righteousness" as a personified quality with "murderers." By placing these two nouns in an elliptical structure, the poet contrasts the righteous, ethical inhabitants of the past with the wicked, murderous inhabitants of the present.

More commonly, if the word pairs do not refer to precisely the same individual or item, they are nonetheless semantically related in some way, as illustrated in Isaiah 49:23: "Kings *shall be* your foster fathers, / and their queens [ ] your nursing mothers." In this verse the word pairs ("kings"/"queens" and "your foster fathers"/ "your nursing mothers") are not contrastive but complementary. Nonetheless, the two lines describe a single situation, not contrastive actions.

In reading biblical poetry, even in English translation, it is important to remember that word pairs in parallel lines with an elided verb are probably not to be understood as contrastive. This feature of biblical poetry is diametrically opposed to English usage in which verbal ellipsis always produces contrastive word pairs.

Ellipsis of the verb may also result in a longer term in the second half of a word pair. The deleted verb opens up space, so to speak, in the second line, as illustrated in Deuteronomy 32:13: "*He suckled him* with honey from a rock, / and [ ] with oil from a flinty stone" (Alter, 614). The deletion of object plus verb in the first line means that "from a rock" can be paired with the longer descriptive phrase "from a flinty stone" in the second line.

4. Ellipsis in Poetry as Opposed to Prose.
Ellipsis is a prevalent feature of biblical poetry (O'Connor, 128), and undoubtedly it contributes to the perceived *terseness of poetry (Berlin). By contrast, ellipsis of the verb is quite rare, though not completely absent, in biblical prose (Kugel, 321-23). It is not surprising that ellipsis in biblical Hebrew poetry differs from ellipsis in ordi-

nary language; the same is true of English poetry. In ordinary English a verb can only be elided from the second of two syntactically identical clauses: *Leaves adorn the trees, and flowers [ ] the ground.* That is, English routinely elides the verb forwards. But in poetry, backwards ellipsis of the verb may occur, as in the following snippet from Alexander Pope: *Now leaves [ ] the trees, and flowers adorn the ground* (Fabb, 147).

Ellipsis of the verb is rare in biblical prose. It occurs primarily in representations of direct speech rather than in narrative (e.g., Gen 27:12; 28:20, 43:32; Exod 32:27; Lev 26:19; Deut 17:7; but see 1 Kings 20:32 with similar examples in direct speech and narrative). Ordinarily, the verb is in initial position (e.g., 1 Sam 30:22). Rarely, the constituents are in chiastic order (Gen 31:40; Judg 6:37).

Ellipsis of the verb is more highly constrained in prose than it is in poetry. Most importantly, backwards ellipsis of the verb never occurs.

Prose does, however, allow for verbal ellipsis across paired speeches by different characters. For example, in the initial encounter between Joseph and his brothers in Egypt, we have the following exchange in Genesis 42:7: "He spoke with them harshly and he said to them, 'From where *have you come?*' They said, '[ ] from the land of Canaan to buy food.'" The brothers' reply involves verbal ellipsis ("We have come"). Thus, biblical narrative preserves a common feature of conversational style: verbal ellipsis across question/answer pairs.

Biblical prose also allows the word pairs in constructions with elided verbs to be contrastive, as illustrated in Genesis 7:2: "From all the clean animals *take for yourself* seven pairs, a male and its mate, / and from all the animals which are not clean [ ] a pair, the male and its mate." The instructions to Noah involve contrastive word pairs: clean animals as opposed to unclean animals, and seven pairs as opposed to a single pair.

Verbal ellipsis in poetry is far more prevalent than it is in prose. And poetry relaxes several of the syntactic constraints on ellipsis that are found in ordinary language. However, in both poetry and prose, verbal ellipsis in biblical Hebrew can be described as falling within normal cross-linguistic patterns.

See also AMBIGUITY; HEBREW LANGUAGE; MERISM; PARALLELISM; POETICS, TERMINOLOGY OF;

RHYME; TERSENESS; WORDPLAY.

BIBLIOGRAPHY. **R. Alter,** "Characteristics of Ancient Hebrew Poetry," in *Literary Guide to the Bible,* ed. R. Alter and F. Kermode (Cambridge, MA: Belknap Press, 1987) 611-24; **A. Berlin,** *The Dynamics of Biblical Parallelism* (Bloomington: Indiana University Press, 1985); **M. Dahood,** *Ugaritic-Hebrew Philology* (BibOr 17; Rome: Pontifical Biblical Institute, 1967); **N. Fabb,** *Linguistics and Literature: Language in the Verbal Arts of the World* (Blackwell Textbooks in Linguistics; Oxford: Blackwell, 1997); **S. A. Geller,** *Parallelism in Early Biblical Poetry* (HSM 20; Missoula, MT: Scholars Press, 1979); **M. A. K. Halliday and R. Hasan,** *Cohesion in English* (English Language Series 9; London: Longman, 1976); **K. Hartmann,** *Right Node Raising and Gapping: Interface Conditions on Prosodic Deletion* (Amsterdam: Benjamins, 2000); **J. L. Kugel,** *The Idea of Biblical Poetry: Parallelism and Its History* (New Haven: Yale University Press, 1981); **J. Lyons,** *Introduction to Theoretical Linguistics* (Cambridge: Cambridge University Press, 1971); **M. J. McShane,** *A Theory of Ellipsis* (Oxford: Oxford University Press, 2005); **C. L. Miller,** "A Linguistic Approach to Ellipsis in Biblical Poetry: Or, What to Do When Exegesis of What Is There Depends on What Isn't," *BBR* 13 (2003) 251-70; idem, "Ellipsis Involving Negation in Biblical Poetry," in *Seeking Out the Wisdom of the Ancients: Essays Offered to Honor Michael V. Fox on the Occasion of His Sixty-fifth Birthday,* ed. R. L. Troxel, K. G. Friebel and D. R. Magary (Winona Lake, IN: Eisenbrauns, 2005) 37-52; idem, "Constraints on Ellipsis in Biblical Hebrew," in *Studies in Semitic and Afroasiatic Linguistics Presented to Gene B. Gragg* (SAOC 60; Chicago: Oriental Institute of the University of Chicago, 2007) 165-80; idem, "A Reconsideration of 'Double-duty' Prepositions in Biblical Poetry," *JANESCU* (forthcoming a); idem, "The Syntax of Elliptical Comparative Constructions," *ZAH* (forthcoming b); **M. O'Connor,** *Hebrew Verse Structure* (Winona Lake, IN: Eisenbrauns, 1980); **E. F. Prince,** "Discourse Analysis: A Part of the Study of Linguistic Competence," in *Linguistics: The Cambridge Survey,* 2: *Linguistic Theory: Extensions and Implications,* ed. F. J. Newmeyer (Cambridge: Cambridge University Press, 1988) 164-82; **R. R. van Oirsouw,** *The Syntax of Coordination* (Croom Helm Linguistics Series; London: Croom Helm, 1987); **W. G. E. Watson,** *Classical Hebrew Poetry: A Guide to Its Techniques* (JSOTSup 26; Sheffield: JSOT Press, 1984); **C. Wilder,** "Some Properties of Ellipsis in Coordination," in *Studies on Universal Grammar and Typological Variation,* ed. A. Alexiadou and T. A. Hall (Linguistik Aktuell 13; Amsterdam: Benjamins, 1997) 59-107. C. L. Miller

ENEMIES. *See* PSALMS 1: BOOK OF; SUFFERING; WARFARE IMAGERY.

ENTRANCE LITURGIES. *See* PSALMS 1: BOOK OF.

ENVELOPE STRUCTURE/FIGURE. *See* INCLUSIO.

ESTHER 1: BOOK OF

Interpreters throughout history have found the book of Esther to be a troubling presence within the *canon of the OT. It does not read like a religious text, and its only link to the rest of the OT is that the story that it tells involves the Jewish people. It is well known that the book of Esther contains neither the divine name "Yahweh" nor the word *God.* Nevertheless, the Babylonian Talmud finds in the Torah a prophetic allusion to the events chronicled by the book of Esther by observing that the unpointed first-person imperfect verb *ʾstr* ("I will hide") in Deuteronomy 31:18 is identical to the unpointed name *ʾstr* ("Esther") and noting that there God predicts, "I will surely hide [*ʾstr*] my face from them" in response to the rebellion of his people (*b. Ḥul.* 139b). In rabbinic fashion, this allows Esther to be linked directly to the Torah and to be read as a story of God hiding from his people, even though he is not referred to explicitly (Beal, 116-17).

Although the story takes place after Cyrus's decree allows the Jews to return to Jerusalem from exile, there is no mention of Jerusalem, the temple, the law or the covenant as is found in other postexilic books. Unlike the book of Daniel, which also is set in the court of a pagan king, there are no prayers, apocalyptic visions or miracles. Moreover, Esther and *Mordecai do not seem to reflect the character of other great biblical heroes and heroines. Esther shows no concern for the dietary laws when taken into the court of a pagan king, she conceals her Jewish identity, and she pleases the king in one night more than all the other virgins. When she risks her life for her people, she does so only after Mordecai points out that she herself will not escape harm even if she refuses to act. Her request to extend the massacre displays what many interpreters consider to be a surprising attitude of brutality. Similarly, it is Mordecai, Esther's parent figure, who insists that she conceal her Jewish identity. And it is Mordecai's refusal to give Haman the due respect of his office that allows the incident to escalate into a threat to the entire Jewish people. The astute reader sees in Esther and Mordecai a disquieting moral ambiguity at best.

The absence of piety and the presence of sensuality and brutality have posed a perennial problem for interpreters of Esther. John Calvin never preached from the book, nor did he include it among his commentaries. Martin Luther denounced the book of Esther along with the apocryphal 2 Maccabees.

In stark contrast, some Jewish interpreters have held the book in highest esteem. Maimonides (twelfth century AD), for example, ranked it equal to the Pentateuch in his statement that when the Messiah comes, only the Torah and Esther will remain. Its popularity and esteemed value are attested by being the only book outside the Pentateuch to have two *Targumim devoted to it *(Targum Rishon and Targum Sheni)*. Moreover, it is the only biblical book for which the Babylonian Talmud includes a midrashic exposition of the entire book that regulates the liturgical reading of the story and presents haggadic expositions of its text *(Megillah Esther)*.

1. Historical Issues
2. Literary Issues
3. Theology
4. Canon

1. Historical Issues.

1.1. Historical Setting. The events of the story are set during the Persian (Achaemenid) period in the court of the Persian king, who is called *Ahasuerus in the Esther story. The story unfolds while the court is in residence in the winter palace in *Susa, which was located near the modern border of Iran and Iraq. The Achaemenid period begins in 539 BC, when the Persians, under Cyrus the Great, conquered the Babylonians and ends in 330 BC, when the conquest by Alexander the Great inaugurated the Hellenistic Empire. The king of the Esther story, Ahasuerus, is usually identified with Xerxes, who ruled from 486 to 465 BC The name "Ahasuerus" may be an attempt to transliterate either

the Persian (*Khšayāršan*) or Akkadian (*Aḥšiʾaršu*) pronunciation of the king's name into *Hebrew, or it may be a literary appellation given for other reasons, perhaps to mock the Persian monarchy as an institution (Yamauchi, 187). If Ahasuerus is to be identified with Xerxes, then the banquet held in the third year of his reign (Esther 1:3) would correspond with the great war council held in 483 BC to plan for the invasion of Greece. After his queen, *Vashti, was deposed, there is a four-year gap before Esther was chosen to replace her. This would correspond with the time Xerxes was away fighting a disastrous war in Greece (481-479 BC), a war that he lost and that depleted the treasuries of the Persian Empire.

1.2. Author and Date. The author of the book of Esther is unknown. According to the Talmud (*b. Bat.* 15a), the "Men of the Great Assembly" produced the book of Esther, as well as those of Ezekiel, Daniel and the Minor Prophets. Claims that Mordecai himself wrote it are likely a misreading of Esther 9:20. It was, however, likely written by a Jew who lived under Persian rule and who was familiar with Susa and the Persian court, though it need not have been written in Susa (Perrot and Ladiray, 254). Moreover, the story may have been preserved orally for many years before being written down.

The opening of the book of Esther ("This is what happened during the time of Xerxes . . . ") implies that the story is being told well after the fact. An earlier generation of scholars dated Esther to the late Greek era (e.g., Paton, 60-62), but currently most scholars date the writing of the book sometime between 400 BC and 200 BC— that is, late in the Persian period or early in the Greek period. Although there are no fragments of Esther among the Qumran materials, a study of the Hebrew of that period has tended to push the date of Esther back well before 200 BC Those who date the writing of the book of Esther to this earlier period (Baldwin, 48-49; Bechtel, 3; Berlin, xli; Bush, 297; Clines, 291; Levenson, 26; Moore [1995], LVII-LX) do so for a variety of reasons, including these: (1) the author's knowledge of Susa and the palace is consistent with findings by archaeological excavations conducted by the French since 1850 (Perrot and Ladiray, 254); (2) there are many Persian loanwords in the text and few if any Greek loans (Yamauchi, 227); (3) the Hebrew of the text is late biblical Hebrew, similar to that of the books of Ezra, Nehemiah and Chronicles, which are also dated to the two centuries after the exile but before Alexander (539–323 BC). Of special note are approximately thirty proper names in the book that are of Persian or Elamite origin accurately preserved by the MT (Yamauchi, 237). The identification of the names of Haman's sons as *daiva* names found in early Iranian and Hindu texts suggests an early origin for the Esther story, possibly during the reign of Xerxes himself, since a vocalic shift observed in one personal name occurred between the reigns of Xerxes and his son Artaxerxes (Yamauchi, 237-38). (The word *daiva* meant "god" in early Iranian and Hindu texts and was used to designate deity as opposed to human beings or to refer to evil spirits who incited people to violence [Yamauchi, 427]. The latter is particularly fitting in the context of the Esther story.) The Elamite Persepolis tablets have provided many other parallels to the Persian names in Esther (*see* Esther 2: Extrabiblical Background). This suggests that the book was written during the approximately 150 years between the reign of Xerxes and the conquest of Persia by Alexander the Great, and probably earlier in that period rather than later. However, not all scholars agree on this early date, and arguments have been made (e.g., Fox, 139-40) that the language and tenor of the book better fit the social and political world of the Hellenistic period (c. 125 BC).

Although the Greek historian Herodotus confirms much of the historical setting as described by the book of Esther, his history also raises issues about the accuracy of the book of Esther (*see* Esther 2: Extrabiblical Background). Herodotus (*Hist.* 7.114; 9.109) refers to Xerxes' wife by the name "Amestris" and mentions no other wives. Furthermore, he says that Amestris was with Xerxes during his campaign in Greece. Moreover, Amestris was the queen mother during the reign of her son who succeeded Xerxes. Some have suggested that "Amestris" was the Greek name for "Vashti," which was the transliteration of her Persian name into Hebrew. There is no mention of a second wife named "Esther," although this name may have been a literary appellation that played on the name of the Babylonian goddess Ishtar, goddess of love and war. Esther pleases the king more than all the other virgins (Esther 2:17), and she took on warrior-like qualities in the defense of her people (Esther 9:13), possibly making the nickname apt in the view of the author. Moreover, since Persian kings often took more than one wife and had large harems as well, it may be that Herodotus mentions only Amestris, whether or not she was Vashti, because it was she who gave birth to Xerxes' successor, Artaxerxes. All other royal wives and concubines may have been irrelevant to Herodotus if he was concerned with the succession of the Persian dynas

A second problem, concerning Mordecai's age, also calls into question the historicity of the book. Esther 2:5-6 apparently indicates that Mordecai was taken into exile with King Jeconiah in 597 BC. If so, Mordecai would have been 122 years older at the time he served Xerxes. One way to resolve this problem is to read the relative clause in the Hebrew text (*'ăšer hoglâ mîrûšālayim*) as referring not to Mordecai personally but rather to his grandfather Kish, who is also mentioned in the verse. Hence it would have been Mordecai's grandfather Kish who was taken into exile with Jeconiah, and he is mentioned in order to draw a literary affinity with King Saul (see 3.1 below).

Although the names "Vashti" and "Esther" are not mentioned outside of this book, there is extrabiblical evidence that the name "Mordecai" was contemporary. A tablet discovered in 1904 at Persepolis, another of the Persian royal cities, refers to a Persian official during the early years of Xerxes' reign with the name "Marduka" (Yamauchi, 235) Although the name was very common, this occurrence corresponds well in time with the setting of the Esther story.

Despite the literary flourishes, the author of the book apparently intends the Esther story to be read as historically authentic.

2. Literary Issues.

2.1. Genre. Most scholars today consider the story of Esther to be an ancient historical novel (*see* Novella, Story, Narrative), with its historical authenticity a highly debated point. Esther has been labeled variously as a Diaspora novel (Meinhold), a wisdom tale (Talmon), a festal lection (Fox), a festival etiology (Gerleman), a Persian chronicle (Gordis), a historical novel (Levenson), a burlesque comedy (Berlin) and even as carnivalesque (since Esther is read liturgically at the carnival-like festival of *Purim) (Craig). Many scholars affirm the significance and value of the story even though denying that it has any historical authenticity. However, recognizing the story's distinctive literary features does not require discarding its historical value, for the festival of Purim surely arose from some memorable event in the distant past to have become such a universal practice of Judaism for more than two millennia. The story of that event is artfully and memorably told in the book of Esther with irony, satire and even a humor that interprets rather than distorts its message. The mention of 127 satrapies, when Herodotus mentions only twenty, may be an expression of the Persian powers' inflated sense of self-regard as perceived by others (Herodotus *Hist.* 3.89) rather than an egregious historical error that indicates a late date (Fox, 139). The improbable height (seventy-five feet) of the gallows that Haman unwittingly constructs for his own death (Esther 5:14; 7:9) may be taken ironically as the measure of the stature of Haman's own pride and evil. Such "unhistorical" features of the book do not threaten its historical value but rather provide interpretive depth to the story.

Even an understanding of the story as burlesque or carnivalesque recognizes the value of a form of entertainment that vulgarizes a serious topic by treating it with mock dignity, in this case the excesses of the Persian monarchy that led to deliverance from a lethal threat (Berlin, xix). By poking fun at such a serious threat years afterward, the book allows both its pressing power and its ultimate impotence to be recognized and remembered by ordinary people. The carnival-like celebration of Purim teaches each new generation this powerful spiritual lesson.

The story of Esther is not only history artfully told, but also, because it is in the canon of Scripture, it is theology artfully told. There are no statements about God in the book, but because it is in the canon of Scripture of both synagogue and church, in some sense it is a story being told to us by God that offers an opportunity for reflection on his sovereignty with respect to history and with respect to human motives and responsibility.

2.2. The Plot. Esther 1—2 sets the opulent stage in the Persian palace where Vashti defies her husband and king, where all the beautiful virgins of the empire are gathered into the harem, where Esther alone pleases the king with her sensuous beauty, and where Mordecai foils an assassination plot against the king's life. Esther 3—8 recounts how the personal conflict between Mordecai and Haman escalated into the threat of genocide for the Jews, how Esther

dares to seek an uninvited audience with the king at the risk of her life, and how she entertains the king and Haman at two banquets. In a reversal, Mordecai is honored after the king's sleepless night, and Haman's plot is turned against him when the Jews are not only delivered from annihilation but also become an empowered people in the empire. Esther 9—10 explains how from this great deliverance arose the celebration that bears the name "Purim," one of the two Jewish feasts not mandated by the Pentateuch (the other being Hanukkah).

These historical events are artfully woven into a tale of romance and intrigue, with irony, satire and humor. The account is full of irony that parodies the relationship between men and women, beginning with Vashti's disobedience to her husband and king. Furthermore, Ahasuerus, whose word is said to be irrevocable law, never makes one decision of his own in this story. Throughout the story he mindlessly does the bidding of others who skillfully manipulate him for their own ends. The author also parodies the sexual appetite for which the Persian kings were stereotypically known. When the king's advisors propose gathering every beautiful young virgin in the empire for the king to sample, the narrator wryly comments, "This advice appealed to the king" (Esther 2:4). Even the horses used to carry the king's memos were no ordinary horses, but were sired by the royal stud (Esther 8:10). Such topics and comments indicate the author's effort to amuse and entertain as well as inform.

2.3. Characterization. The characterization in the story is masterful. The Persian king, when viewed from the perspective of his Jewish subjects, is a bumbling, inept figure who becomes an object of mocking. Vashti's sensibilities heighten the king's status as a playboy and a dunce. Haman is a demonic villain, characterized by uncontrolled pride and vengeance. Mordecai is the insightful court attendant, conventional in stories of intrigue, who moves the plot by his actions. Esther is a young woman trying to live in two worlds: the Jewish world in which she was raised and the opulent world of the Persian court into which she was thrust. Hers is the only character that develops throughout the book that is aptly named for her. Only she has two names in the story: "Hadassah," a Hebrew name, and "Esther," a Persian name that is perhaps intended as a literary appellation (Esther 2:7). As the story unfolds, Esther develops from a passive young woman who relies on her beauty to get ahead into a powerful leader of the Jewish people on whose authority the customs of Purim still stand (Esther 9:32). Her transformation hinges on that defining moment in her story when she decides to identify with God's covenant people even at the risk of her life. In this specific way Esther serves as an exemplary model for those who would seek after God.

2.4. The Prominent Motif. A prominent literary motif of the book of Esther is the *mišteh* ("feast"), a term most often used to refer to eating and drinking on special occasions (Berg, 31). The word *mišteh* occurs twenty times in the book of Esther and only twenty-six times in the rest of the OT. There are, by some counts, ten feasts that take place in the story. This dominant motif of feasting is apt because the Esther story explains the origin of Purim, a feast still celebrated now by Jews. On the Jewish calendar today, the fourteenth of Adar is called Purim and the fifteenth of Adar is called *Shushan Purim* (i.e., Susa's Purim). The story of Esther explains not only the reason for the Feast of Purim but also why it is celebrated on two different, consecutive days.

The story of Esther both begins and concludes with pairs of feasts that mirror each other (Esther 1:3, 5 [the king gives two feasts]; Esther 9:18-19 [the Jews celebrate two feast days]). Esther also gives not one banquet but two for the king and Haman (Esther 5:4-8, 7:1). Haman's downfall begins between the first and second of Esther's banquets when the king has a sleepless night. Thus there are three pairs of feasts that mark the beginning, climax and conclusion of the story.

2.5. The Structure of Peripety. The literary structure of the book is defined by repetition of the primary motif of feasting (Jobes, 154-58). The three pairs of feasts mark the rise and fall of a plot that is characterized by peripety. The word *peripety* (from Gk *peripeteia*) is a literary term first used by Aristotle (*Rhet.* 1.11.24) to refer to a sudden turn of events in a story that reverses the intended and expected action. The Esther story is structured on reversals that pivot on the king's sleepless night, the one event occurring between the pair of feasts at the book's literary center. By making the pivot point of the peripety an insignificant event rather than the height of dramatic tension, the author is taking the focus away from human action and implies that an unseen force

is controlling the reversal of destiny (see 4.3.1 below). The story provides an example of how form and content mutually interact in a text, for in Esther 9:1 the author explicitly states the theme of reversal that he has subtly built into the very structure of his narrative.

The Esther story is about an event intended to harm the Jews, which, against all expectation, actually results in the opposite. Instead of being destroyed, the Jews are not only delivered but also become empowered through the high rank of Esther and Mordecai. The once powerful destroyer, Haman, not only loses his power but also is himself destroyed. Before Esther's banquets the king promotes Haman, the Agagite, and gives him the signet ring of royal authority (Esther 3:1, 10). After Esther's banquets, the same language is used when we are told that the king promotes Mordecai, the Jew, and gives him the signet ring previously worn by Haman (Esther 10:3; cf. 8:2). On the very day Haman goes to the king seeking permission to kill Mordecai (Esther 6:4), Haman ends up not only failing to kill Mordecai but also publicly honoring him in the king's name (Esther 6:11). Vashti risks her life by defying the king's word and refusing to appear before him when summoned (Esther 1:12); Esther risks her life by defying the king's word and appearing before him unsummoned (Esther 4:11). The story is full of ironic reversals that conspire together to turn Haman's plan to destroy the Jews against him. The Feast of Purim celebrates this grand reversal in the month of Adar because it was a month "when their sorrow was turned into joy and their mourning into a day of celebration" (Esther 9:22 TNIV).

3. Theology.

3.1. Esther in Biblical Theology. This structure of peripety is not simply a literary device that produces an aesthetically pleasing story. The structure of peripety deeply reflects the worldview of the author, and it provides the framework within which to understand the theological implications of the Esther story. The author is suggesting that beneath the surface of human decisions and events there is an unseen and uncontrollable power at work that can be neither explained nor thwarted. Because this story is in the canon of the Jews, and subsequently the Christians, it is proper to construe that unseen power as God. What is the divinely inspired author of Esther trying to say to the original audience about God?

For the Jews who returned to Jerusalem, the postexilic books of Chronicles, Nehemiah, Ezra, Haggai and Zechariah answer in the affirmative these nagging questions: Are we still in covenant relationship with God? Are we still God's chosen people? The author of Esther answers in the affirmative through the reversal of fortune for the Jews living in the Diaspora, where they had no temple or prophet or city. The reversal so prominent in the literary structure of Esther is driven by the conflict between Haman the Agagite and Mordecai the Jew. The identity of Haman as an Agagite is the clue that links the Jews of the Diaspora to the ancient covenant made at Sinai.

Agag was the king of the Amalekites at the time Saul was the first king of Israel (1 Sam 15). The Amalekites were a nomadic people of the southern desert region who frequently raided Israel from the very beginning of its history. They had the dubious distinction of being the first people to attack God's newly formed covenant nation right after the exodus. Because they were the first to attempt to destroy Israel, God promises Moses that he will completely erase the memory of the Amalekites from under heaven and would be at war with them from generation to generation (Ex 17:8-16). In Deuteronomy 25:17-19 God commands Israel, after they settle in the land, to wage war against the Amalekites so as to blot out the memory of Amalek.

In the many years between Moses and King Saul, God gave Israel the land as promised. When Saul came to power, God instructed him through the prophet Samuel to "attack the Amalekites and totally destroy all that belongs to them. Do not spare them; put to death men and women, children and infants, cattle and sheep, camels and donkeys" (1 Sam 15:1-3 TNIV). Saul did attack the Amalekites as he had been commanded, but in direct and willful disobedience to God's command, he took their king, Agag, alive and spared his life along with the best of the sheep and cattle. Because of this disobedience, God rejected Saul's kingship, and eventually Saul was dethroned.

Saul was a Benjaminite whose father was Kish (1 Sam 9:21; 14:51). Mordecai is also identified as a Benjaminite who is also a "son" of a man named Kish (Esther 2:5), depicting Mordecai as a new Saul. This probably explains what has been noted as an historical problem, with Mordecai being 122 years older than the time of the exile of Jeconiah. But the relative clause in the Hebrew text can be read as referring not to Mordecai personally but rather to his grandfather Kish, who is also mentioned in the verse. Hence it would have been Mordecai's grandfather Kish who was taken into exile with Jeconiah, and Mordecai would be his "son" in the sense of a descendant. The mention of Mordecai's relationship to a man named Kish strengthens the literary parallel between Saul and Agag with Mordecai and Haman the Agagite. Over the centuries after Saul spared Agag's life, other perennial enemies of Israel were called Agagites or Amalekites even though they had no ethnic relationship to that ancient people.

The Esther story is another episode of the ancient war between Israel and the Amalekites, and by every indication it looks like Israel will be destroyed. They have no king, no army, no prophet, no land, no temple, no priesthood and no sacrifices. They are but a small minority living at the mercy of a ruthless and powerful pagan monarchy. The reversal that dethrones Haman and empowers Mordecai shows that despite their sin and despite their location away from Jerusalem, God's promise to Israel made at the beginning of their nation still stood. He would still destroy those who would destroy his people, no matter where they were living. In contrast to Saul's covenantal disobedience when he spared the Amalekites and plundered the best of their property, the Jews of Persia struck down all their enemies, but the text is careful to say that they did not lay their hands on the plunder (Esther 9:5-10). In other words, under the leadership of Esther and Mordecai, the Jews of Persia obeyed where Saul had disobeyed. The book of Esther shows that the Jews of the Persian Diaspora were still under God's covenantal care.

The understanding that the conflict documented in the Esther story is another biblical episode of holy war informs modern sensibilities that may be offended, especially by Queen Esther's request that a second day of retaliation be allowed the Jews and that Haman's ten sons be executed and displayed. Throughout its interpretive history this incident has been viewed as morally questionable by many interpreters, both Christian and Jewish (Anderson, 136-37; Baldwin, 106; Bickerman, 215-18; Fox, 220-26; Gordis, 415; Levenson, 121-22; Moore, xxx, 87, 88). When the Lord commanded the conquest of

Canaan, Joshua and the Israelites devoted whole cities to the Lord in destruction, killing every living thing within and burning the buildings to the ground. In this act of holy war the destroyers were acting not on their own behalf but as agents of God's wrath, and thus they were not permitted to profit from the act in any way. In the book of Esther, Haman is portrayed as the leader of destruction against the Jews, but his plan is turned against him by Queen Esther, who not only reveals the plot that leads to Haman's death but also eliminates any of his offspring who might avenge their father in the future. Although this is loathsome to modern sensibilities, clearly Queen Esther came to see herself not only as a monarch of the Persians but also as a leader raised up to protect God's people according to his ancient covenant, and she acted accordingly (Esther 4:14). Ancient Israel's history shows the perennial failure of their greatest leaders to war against moral and spiritual darkness without engaging in it themselves. Scripture shows that no human being is worthy to wage true holy war in God's name. God's strategy against sin and evil awaited the perfect warrior, Jesus Christ, who could execute divine justice with clean hands and a pure heart, thus putting an end to the practice of holy war waged between nations.

Haman the Agagite had cast dice *(pûrîm)* to determine the day on which the Jews of Persia would be destroyed. In this instance, casting dice was not a game of chance but rather a method of pagan divination to determine when Haman's gods would give him victory over the Jews. Haman rolled the dice in the first month of the Jewish year, the month of Nisan (Esther 3:7). The edict of death went out on the thirteenth of Nisan (Esther 3:12), ironically, the very eve of Passover (the fourteenth of Nisan). Passover commemorates the Israelites deliverance from death in Egypt, when the angel of death killed the firstborn of the Egyptians but passed over the homes of the Israelites where the blood of the lamb was smeared on the door. Centuries later in Susa an edict of death went out, but this time the Jewish people are the target. But because of Yahweh's promise to Moses, the rolling of dice would not determine the destiny of God's people. Without a temple or a prophet or a high priest or a burnt offering, without a prayer or a miracle, God providentially worked in a completely pagan world through morally ambiguous

people to fulfill his covenant promise. One clear message of the story is that no enemy can thwart God's electing purpose.

The story of Esther has points of contact with the exodus story beyond the theme of threat and deliverance. Both Esther (Esther 4:10-14) and Moses (Ex 3:11; 4:10, 13; 6:12, 30) are hesitant in their response to step into leadership; both benefit from the wealth of the Gentiles (Esther 8:1-2; Ex 12:36); the success that the Lord grants to both stirs up fear in their enemies (Esther 9:2-3; Ex 15:14-15); and the events centered on Esther and on Moses both result in the institution of a festival, Purim and Passover respectively, that continues to be observed even today. The Esther story also has much in common with the stories of Joseph in Egypt and Daniel in Babylon (Berg, 124, 143), as all three characters are examples of Jews who not only are living in exile but also have been strategically placed in foreign courts of worldly power. The story of Esther, an orphaned female exiled in a foreign culture who rises to a pivotal position of power in a great worldly empire, provides hope to God's people wherever they find themselves to be a marginalized minority, especially in those times and places when God seems frighteningly absent.

Both the name of the feast and the custom practiced on Purim celebrate God's covenantal *protection of his people. The word *pûr* ("die") was a Persian word that occurs in the Bible only in the book of Esther (Hallo, 19, 20, 22). But its Hebrew equivalent, according to Esther 3:7 and 9:24, was *gôral*. The Hebrew word *gôral* occurs frequently in the Hebrew Scriptures to refer not only to the dice-like object but also to the fate or destiny that comes not from the roll of dice but from the Lord—for example, "Lord, you have assigned me my portion and my cup; you have made my lot *[gôral]* secure" (Ps 16:5). Therefore, the name of the feast, "Purim," is a double-entendre that commemorates that the lot, or destiny, of God's people will never be determined by the decision of any foreign power, which at that time was made by the casting of lots.

The custom of sending portions of food to friends and neighbors on Purim also symbolizes the portion that God has destined for his people. In Psalm 16:5 "portion" translates the Hebrew *měnāt*. This Hebrew word, found in the synonymous parallelism of Psalm 16:5, is used to refer to one's destiny, just as *gôral* is used. However, it has a second meaning, referring to choice morsels of food (e.g., 2 Chron 31:4). In Esther 9:19 the Jews send portions (pl., *mānôt*) to one another to celebrate Purim. Because the word has both senses, these portions of food sent as gifts on Purim symbolize the portion, or destiny, allotted by God to his people.

3.2. Esther in Jewish Thought.

3.2.1. The Origin of the Festival. Megillah Esther (the Esther scroll read liturgically at Purim) provides an historical explanation of the origin of Purim, the first Jewish festival not mandated by Torah. Today Purim is still celebrated joyously to commemorate Jewish identity and inviolability. For Jews it is the strongest possible statement against the anti-Semitism that they have repeatedly experienced throughout the ages. The holiday is celebrated by sending gifts of food to friends and loved ones and by extending charity to the poor. The entire book of Esther is read in the synagogue on Purim with a boisterous audience booing Haman and cheering Mordecai with noisemakers. The Talmud prescribes drinking and celebrating on Purim until one cannot tell the difference between "Mordecai be blessed!" and "Haman be cursed!" (*b. Meg.* 7b).

3.2.2. Living as a Religious Minority. The story of Esther is also a tale of how to live as a religious minority in a dominant society where exile has become Diaspora and where issues of *honor and shame and of oppression and affliction are a pressing reality (Beal; Laniak). Unlike other postexilic books, Esther shows no interest in the land of Israel, which has made it for all subsequent generations a story of and for the Jewish people who live outside the land. Esther as a literary character personifies the life of the entire Jewish nation in Diaspora, with its concerns for status, power, security and identity in what has often been a hostile dominant society. Esther exemplifies the virtue of the individual who is willing to self-identify with the Jewish nation in courageous acts of vigilance and wisdom through which God may choose to act (Esther 4:13-14). Thus the story of Esther, repeated annually, helps Jewish communities living in Diaspora to identify with ancient Israel of the Bible.

The traditional prayer recited before the reading of the scroll at the Purim service speaks of the blessings exemplified by the Esther story (Braun, 272):

> Blessed are You, God, our Lord, King of the universe,

Who has sanctified us with His commandments and has commanded us regarding the reading of the Megillah.
Blessed are You, God, our Lord, King of the universe,
Who has wrought miracles for our fathers in those days at this season.
Blessed are You, God, our Lord, King of the universe,
Who has kept us alive, sustained us, and brought us to this season.

3.2.3. Assurance of Deliverance. The book of Esther is still treasured by Jews today and read annually in the synagogues on Purim because they find in it the reassurance that the Jewish race will survive as a people against those who from time to time throughout history have wished to destroy them (Fox, 11-12). The Esther story is a strong statement against anti-Semitism, for in it the unseen God protects his people and destroys those who came against the Jews of Persia. The inmates of Auschwitz, Dachau, Treblinka and Bergen-Belsen wrote out the book of Esther from memory and read it secretly on Purim (Gordis, 13-14). Resistance to annihilation by Jews and their Gentile neighbors was viewed as service to God and devotion to him.

3.3. Esther in Christian Thought.

3.3.1. Divine Providence. Although not an exclusively Christian idea, Christians should see in the book of Esther a demonstration that God's providence works to fulfill God's covenant promise (Jobes, 233-42). God's providence means that in some invisible and inscrutable way he governs all creatures, actions and circumstances through the normal and ordinary course of human life without the intervention of the miraculous. Even in the most pagan corner of the world, God is ruling all things to the benefit of his people and to the glory of his name. And even when his own people, like Esther and Mordecai, make life decisions that come from ambiguous motives at best and outright disobedience at worst, God is still providentially working through those very things for his perfect purposes. The book of Esther is the most true-to-life biblical example of God's providence precisely because God is absent from the story. The story articulates the assumption of the invisible God in human events. The author of Esther had ample opportunity to refer to God, prayer and the covenant. The complete absence of God is the genius of the book from which hope and encouragement flow.

3.3.2. Divine Sovereignty and Human Responsibility. The deliverance of the Jews from destruction in Persia is now a part of redemptive history, but Esther did not know how the story would end when she decided to risk her life and identify herself with God's people. The great reversal that they experienced, which fulfilled God's covenant promise by delivering his people from destruction (Esther 9:1), came about because in her defining moment Esther chose to identify herself with God's covenant people even though at great personal risk. This is perhaps the most striking biblical example of the interplay between God's sovereignty and human responsibility. The defining moment in Esther's own life was at the same time the crucial moment in which God would sovereignly fulfill his promise to his people.

3.3.3. The Necessity of Biblical Revelation. The author of Esther does not interpret the events in the story, and this silence probably is intentional. For instance, in comparison to the book of Daniel, the reader is told neither what Esther was thinking when she was taken into the court of a pagan king nor of her motives in pleasing the king in one night more than all the virgins. The resulting moral and theological ambiguities in the Esther story illustrate the hermeneutical principle that without divine revelation human experience is inherently ambiguous and cannot be rightly understood. The book of Esther is an example where the divinely inspired author refrains from evaluating the motives and behaviors of the characters, leaving a story that bears no marks of a sacred text. Historical narratives without interpretive commentary are inherently ambiguous; events do not carry within them their own interpretation. The construal of the significance of events will depend on the presuppositions of the interpreter. However, when reading in canonical context, interpreters can see in the events of the Esther story the presence of God's hand behind the scenes and can compare the virtues and flaws of Esther and Mordecai to other heroes of the faith only because such matters are made explicit in the interpretive commentary of other biblical historical narratives. Therefore, the explicit, and probably deliberate, absence of God in Esther makes it a canonical illustration that where there is no interpretive revelation, history is inherently morally and theologically ambiguous.

3.3.4. Peripety as the Structure of Redemptive History. The literary structure of peripety found in the book of Esther and its pivot point in an ordinary and insignificant event (the king's sleepless night in Esther 6:1) is an example of the structure of all of redemptive history, where God works through all things to fulfill his covenant promises. Because of sin, we are not living in the Garden of Eden; rather, we live in the Diaspora of history in a world where God is unseen. In such a world only death is expected, but God has worked the ultimate peripety, the ultimate reversal of expected ends, in another seemingly ordinary human event: the birth of a baby in Bethlehem and years later the execution of that man on a Roman cross. The ordinary and the miraculous intersect in Jesus Christ. The cross of Jesus Christ is the pivot point of the great reversal of history, where sorrow has been turned to joy. Through the seemingly insignificant events of the birth of a baby in Bethlehem and the execution of a man on a Roman cross, God has guaranteed us life even though we face certain death. He has reversed our lot. God is working providentially in the completely secular and ungodly course of human events to save those who are his and, against all expectation, to bring all of history to culmination in Christ. There is no plot, no plan that can thwart God's purposes, which stretch from Genesis to Revelation. And Esther lies between the two. The great paradox illustrated so well by the story of Esther is that God is omnipotently present even where God is most conspicuously absent.

3.3.5. The Eschatological Hope of the Esther Story. The resurrection of Jesus Christ has transformed the spiritual heritage of Christians, of which the book of Esther is a part. Christians can face death with the assurance that the grave will not be the victor but that God's people will have victory over the grave against all human expectation. The deliverance of the Jewish nation in Persia foreshadows the redemption of those from all nations who enter into God's covenant promises through Jesus the Messiah.

The story of Esther has been read throughout history as symbolizing the final salvation of God's people in the end. The book of Esther forms a link between the covenant made at Sinai and the eschatological destiny of all whom God will redeem and deliver. The first occurrence of Purim was a spontaneous celebration of the joy of finding oneself still standing on the day after an irrevocable death decree had been executed. The day of death had come and gone, and God's people were still alive! In this sense Purim is a Sabbath, a joyous rest after the battle with death has passed. It symbolizes the eschatological joy of God's people in its most ultimate sense. The final reality of this eschatological hope was realized at the resurrection of Jesus Christ (Rev 1:17-18). Therefore, in Christian thought Purim foreshadows the joyful celebration of one's lot in eternal life secured by God's providence working through the life of Jesus Christ (Acts 4:27-28).

4. Canon.

The canonization of the book of Esther is, of course, closely related to the canonization of the Ketubim (Writings), the third section of the Hebrew Bible, in which it is found. This may have occurred as early as the second century BC, though the date of the closing of the Hebrew canon is debated. However, the celebration of Purim presumably originated independently of the canonization of the text that documented its origin, so the acceptance of Purim as a legitimate festival by mainstream Judaism and the canonization of the book of Esther were no doubt mutually influential. Nevertheless, the canonical status of Esther has been questioned at times. Perhaps one reason is that God and significant elements of Judaism are not mentioned in it. The book of Esther was among a small number of OT books that incited later debate in rabbinic literature over its status (the other books were Ezekiel, *Proverbs, *Song of Songs and *Ecclesiastes). Apparently, both Shammai and Hillel agreed that Esther "makes the hands unclean" (*b. Meg.* 7a), but the precise meaning of that expression with respect to modern concepts of canonicity is not well understood.

One reason that the canonicity of Esther may have been questioned during the Graeco-Roman period, perhaps at the meeting of rabbis at Jamnia about AD 90, is that the Jewish people had not experienced at that time a deliverance from the Romans as their ancestors had from the Persians. After AD 70 Jerusalem once again lay in ruins, which may have challenged a Jewish understanding of the significance of the Esther story. Modern Judaism has similar questions reading Esther on this side of the twentieth-century Holocaust.

The Judean desert materials from Qumran (*Dead Sea Scrolls) offer no relevant evidence since, as is well known, Esther is the only book of the Hebrew Bible not found at Qumran. Fragments from Qumran (*4QProto-Esther*) that allegedly are fragments of Esther bear no direct textual correspondence to the extant book of Esther but rather appear to be fragments of another story also set in the court of a Persian king (de Troyer). None of the sectarian books produced at Qumran quote the book of Esther, nor is the holiday of Purim mentioned in the Qumran documents. This is probably not a happenstance of manuscript fragility, since fragments of smaller books, such as Song of Songs and *Lamentations, have survived. Moreover, fragments of Esther in the Cairo Genizah outnumber the fragments of any other book outside the Pentateuch. It is more likely that the Qumran community did not celebrate Purim as a legitimate holiday because the Torah did not prescribe it. The argument that the Qumran community did not know of the book of Esther because it had not yet been written is unlikely because one of the two Greek versions ends with a colophon that can be dated to either 114 BC or 77 BC, implying that both a Hebrew version and its Greek translation predated the Qumran community (*see* Esther 5: Greek Versions).

Although the NT does not quote the book of Esther, in the early centuries of the Christian church Esther was almost always accepted in the Western canon, although it did not attain universal canonical status until the Councils of Hippo (393 AD) and Carthage (397 AD). As late as the Reformation period, Martin Luther denounced the book and wished that it were not part of the Bible, although it had by that time been canonical for centuries. Like Luther, the rabbis who debated the status of Esther at Jamnia in AD 90 may have been contemplating not whether to add it to the canon but whether it deserved the canonical status that it already enjoyed and perhaps had enjoyed for centuries.

See also AHASUERUS; ESTHER 2: EXTRABIBLICAL BACKGROUND; ESTHER 3: HISTORY OF INTERPRETATION; ESTHER 6: PERSON; FEMINIST INTERPRETATION; MORDECAI; SUSA; VASHTI; WOMEN.

BIBLIOGRAPHY. *Commentaries:* **L. C. Allen and T. S. Laniak,** *Ezra, Nehemiah, Esther* (NIBC; Peabody, MA: Hendrickson, 2003); **J. G. Baldwin,** *Esther* (TOTC: Downers Grove, IL: InterVarsity

Press, 1984); **C. M. Bechtel**, *Esther* (IBC; Louisville: John Knox, 2002); **A. Berlin**, *Esther* (JPSBC; Philadelphia: Jewish Publication Society, 2001); **M. Breneman**, *Ezra, Nehemiah, Esther* (NAC: Nashville: Broadman & Holman, 1993); **F. Bush**, *Ruth, Esther* (WBC 9; Dallas: Word, 1996); **D. J. Clines**, *Ezra, Nehemiah, Esther* (NCBC; Grand Rapids: Eerdmans, 1984); **G. Gerleman**, *Esther* (BKAT 21; Neukirchen-Vluyn: Neukirchener Verlag, 1982); **K. H. Jobes**, *Esther* (NIVAC; Grand Rapids: Zondervan, 1999); **J. D. Levenson**, *Esther* (OTL; Louisville: Westminster John Knox, 1997); **C. A. Moore**, *Esther* (AB 7B; New York: Doubleday, 1995); **L. B. Paton**, *A Critical and Exegetical Commentary on the Book of Esther* (ICC; repr., New York: Scribner, 1976 [1908]). *Studies:* **B. W. Anderson**, "The Place of the Book of Esther in the Christian Bible," in *Studies in the Book of Esther*, ed. C. A. Moore (New York: KTAV, 1982) 130-41; **T. K. Beal**, *The Book of Hiding: Gender, Ethnicity, Annihilation, and Esther* (London: Routledge, 1997); **S. B. Berg**, *The Book of Esther: Motifs, Themes and Structure* (SBLDS 44; Missoula, MT: Scholars Press, 1979); **E. Bickerman**, *Four Strange Books of the Bible* (New York: Schocken, 1967); **M. Braun**, *The Jewish Holy Days: Their Spiritual Significance* (Northvale, NJ: Jason Aronson, 1996); **A. Brenner, ed.**, *A Feminist Companion to Esther, Judith and Susanna* (FCB 7; Sheffield: Sheffield Academic Press, 1995); **K. M. Craig**, *Reading Esther: A Case for the Literary Carnivalesque* (Louisville: Westminster John Knox, 1995); **S. W. Crawford and L. J. Greenspoon**, eds., *The Book of Esther in Modern Research* (New York: T & T Clark, 2003); **L. Day**, *Three Faces of a Queen: Characterization in the Books of Esther* (JSOTSup 186; Sheffield: Sheffield Academic Press, 1995); **K. de Troyer**, "Once More, the So-Called Esther Fragments of Cave 4," *RevQ* 75 (2000) 401-22; **C. V. Dorothy**, *The Books of Esther: Structure, Genre, and Textual Integrity* (JSOTSup 187; Sheffield Academic Press, 1997); **M. V. Fox**, *Character and Ideology in the Book of Esther* (2nd ed.; Grand Rapids: Eerdmans, 2001); **R. Gordis**, "Studies in the Esther Narrative," in *Studies in the Book of Esther*, ed. C. A. Moore (New York: KTAV, 1982) 408-23; **W. W. Hallo**, "The First Purim," *BA* 46.1 (1983) 19-29; **T. S. Laniak**, *Shame and Honor in the Book of Esther* (SBLDS 165: Atlanta: Scholars Press, 1998); **A. Meinhold**, "Die Gattung der Josephgeschichte und des Estherbuches: Diasporanovelle, I," *ZAW* 87 (1975) 306-24; idem; "Die Gattung der Josephgeschichte und des Estherbuches: Diasporanovelle, II," *ZAW* 88 (1976) 72-93; **C. A. Moore**, *Studies in the Book of Esther* (New York: KTAV, 1982); **J. Perrot and D. Ladiray**, "The Palace of Susa," in *Royal Cities of the Biblical World*, ed. J. G. Westenholz (Jerusalem: Biblelands Museum, 1996) 236-54; **R. W. Pierce**, "The Politics of Esther and Mordecai: Courage or Compromise?" *BBR* 2 (1992) 75-89; **S. Talmon**, "'Wisdom' in the Book of Esther," *VT* 13 (1963) 419-55; **M. F. Whitters**, "Some New Observations about Jewish Festal Letters," *JSJ* 32 (2001) 272-88; **H. G. M. Williamson**, *Studies in Persian Period History and Historiography* (FAT 38; Tübingen: Mohr Siebeck, 2004); **E. M. Yamauchi**, *Persia and the Bible* (Grand Rapids: Baker, 1990).   K. H. Jobes

ESTHER 2: EXTRABIBLICAL BACKGROUND

The events of the book of Esther occur in the Achaemenid period (539-330 BC) during the reign of the Persian king Xerxes I (486-465 BC), son of Darius I. The Persian Empire was a superpower in its day that engaged in more than a century of war with the Greeks. Because Alexander the Great finally defeated Persia, that great defeated enemy became the subject of many Greek writings preserved by the victors. Xenophon and Aeschylus wrote about the Persian kings, but the most relevant source with respect to the book of Esther comes from Herodotus, who was reported by Diodorus Siculus (fl. first century BC) to have been a contemporary of Xerxes I (Diodorus 2.32.2). Modern scholarship has identified Xerxes to be the Persian king to whom Esther was married. *Persika*, written by Ctesias, who served as the physician to the king's wife, mother and children in the court of Artaxerxes II (409-355 BC), survives only in references by other Greek writers (e.g., Plutarch, *Art.* 1.2; Diodorus 2.5.4-5), possibly because he was thought to exaggerate to the point of inaccuracy.

Even well into the first century of the Christian era the defeat of the Persians remained a significant event in Greek public memory, and Greek writers continued to produce works about the Persian Empire. Plutarch's *Life of Artaxerxes,* Quintus Curtius Rufus's *History of Alexander,* and Diodorus's history provide general historical and cultural background about the Persians as remembered by their conquerors centuries later, but none are specifically relevant for illuminating the book of Esther.

In addition to Greek sources, archaeologists have excavated from Persia a number of reliefs, friezes and inscriptions written in cuneiform that date from the Persian period.

1. Old Persian, Elamite and Akkadian Inscriptions
2. The Earlier Greek Sources
3. The Later Greek and Latin Sources

1. Old Persian, Elamite and Akkadian Inscriptions.

Although there are twenty-one Old Persian inscriptions that date from Xerxes' reign, they are primarily copies of inscriptions from his predecessor's reign that have merely substituted his name for that of his father, Darius—a practice that was continued by later successors. Of particular note is the Behistun inscription of Darius's rise to power, carved in three languages (Old Persian, Elamite, Babylonian) on a cliff and covering an area fifty-nine feet wide.

The Persepolis Tablets are Elamite inscriptions dating from the reigns of Darius, Xerxes I and Artaxerxes I, found in the ruins of treasury of Persepolis, a major Persian capital destroyed by Alexander the Great. They document payments involved in the construction of Persepolis and the distribution of commodities such as olive oil, grain and food. Although they provide some historical insight into the period, they do not specifically inform the Esther story. However, the Elamite Persepolis tablets do provide ample parallels to the Persian names found in the MT of Esther, suggesting that the story dates from the Persian period. A number of tablets attest the name "Marduka" or "Marduku," from which the name of *Mordecai derives, in reference to possibly as many as four different individuals. A vocalic shift relevant to the spelling of one of the names of Haman's sons in the Esther story is believed to have occurred between the reigns of Xerxes and his son Artaxerxes, providing some evidence that the story originated in the actual period of Xerxes reign.

The Daiva inscriptions of Xerxes found at Persepolis in 1935 are cuneiform tablets written in Old Persian, Akkadian and Elamite, dating from 486-480 BC, during the earlier days of Xerxes' reign. Although they contain much formulaic language common to royal inscriptions, they do confirm that both Xerxes' and his father, Darius, practiced Zoroastrianism, providing some religious background to the world into which the Jewish Esther was thrust. Moreover, the inscription provides historical information about the accession of Xerxes to the throne that confirms material found in the writings of Herodotus, a Greek historian who is perhaps the most important ancient source of greatest relevance to the book of Esther (see 2 below).

2. The Earlier Greek Sources.

Xenophon (c. 430–post 355 BC), an Athenian and a younger associate of Socrates, wrote during the period of war between Athens and Sparta. He was among ten thousand Greek mercenaries whom Cyrus II, the Persian satrap of Lydia, had enlisted in his attempt to usurp the Persian throne from his brother, Artaxerxes II. Both were great-grandsons of Xerxes. Xenophon's *Cyropaedia* (*The Education of Cyrus*) is a narrative written about Cyrus the Great (see 2 Chron 36:23; Ezra 1:1-2; Is 44:28), after whom Xenophon's contemporary Cyrus II had been named. Xenophon presents Cyrus the Great as an idealized leader with the purpose of discussing Greek education, ethics and politics. Thus, *Cyropaedia* offers more insight into Greek thought than into Persian culture.

Aeschylus (525-456 BC) was a Greek playwright of Athens who fought against the invasion of the Persians at Salamis. In 472 BC he wrote the prize-winning play *The Persians*, one of ninety plays that document the triumph of the Greek nationalistic spirit. The play is about Xerxes I, son of Darius, who warred against Athens to avenge his father's defeat by the Greeks at Marathon, and who himself returns to Persia defeated. Xerxes' campaign against Greece took place between the deposal of *Vashti in the third year of his reign (Esther 1:2) and his marriage to Esther four years later (Esther 2:16). Aeschylus writes from the perspective of the Persian council selected by Xerxes to administer the empire while he is away at war, which receives increasingly bad news from messengers reporting back from the front. The play concludes with an appearance of Xerxes lamenting his defeat. In this morality play Aeschylus offers the disastrous defeat of Xerxes as an example of the inevitable fate of a human being whose prideful ambition had exceeded that allowed by the gods to mortals. The Greek playwright's critique of the megalomaniacal ego of the Persian kings resonates with a similar evaluation of the

Persian monarchy found in the book of Esther.

The most extensive and relevant primary source for the Persian period is Herodotus, the "father of history." Herodotus (c. 480-420 BC) was born in Halicarnassus in Asia Minor at the front line of the Greek-Persian Wars at about the time when Xerxes was attacking Greece. He later took up residence in Athens, where he found the Persian attack on the city still recent enough in living memory to provide him an opportunity to discuss a wide range of current interests. The accuracy of the history that he recounts is debated, as Herodotus certainly was not writing history as it is written today. Nor was he writing a treatise on Persia and its culture. The very first line of his writing states his intent: "What Herodotus the Halicarnassian has learnt by inquiry is here set forth: in order that so the memory of the past may not be blotted out from among men by time, and that great and marvelous deeds done by Greeks and foreigners and especially *the reason why* they warred against each other may not lack renown" (Herodotus, *Hist.* 1.1 [italics added]). Like other Greek writers of his time, Herodotus was interested in exploring the relationship and causes of events so that they would not be forgotten by future generations. His reflection on the causes of events led him into areas such as philosophy and moral ethics, which causes modern historians to question his objectivity and accuracy. Furthermore, his worldview assumed an order in which the continents of Asia and Europe were in balance and must remain so for peace and harmony to be sustained. The hubris displayed by the Persians in crossing the Hellespont violated this natural order and caused the gods to intervene, bringing disaster on the Persian kings, whose pride had exceeded that permissible to mere mortals. Herodotus's interest in documenting the reasons for the Greek and Persian wars motivated the arrangement of his material and the association of events in such a way that violates modern principles of historiography. Although the accuracy of what he reports continues to be debated, his work must be recognized as the primary surviving source of information about how the Persians were viewed by their enemy and conqueror.

There is nothing in the writings of Herodotus that could be understood as either a direct reference or an allusion to the events presented by the book of Esther. And because Herodotus was not writing about the Persian culture per se but rather about Persia's attack on the Greek cities in Asia Minor and later on Athens itself, his history provides only background information of a general and incidental nature that informs the book of Esther. Even though Herodotus has often been evaluated by modern historiographers as lacking historical accuracy, differences between Herodotus and the Esther story are often used to argue against the historical accuracy of Esther. It is quite likely that the intents of both Herodotus and the book of Esther have been misunderstood by modern sensibilities; therefore caution is needed in attempts to harmonize them.

Several passages of the Esther story can be compared to the description of the reigns of Xerxes and his father, Darius, as told by Herodotus. Esther 1:1 informs its readers that the Persian king Xerxes ruled over 127 satrapies (provinces), which can be compared to the description by Herodotus (*Hist.* 3.89) of the empire's organization into only twenty satrapies under Darius. If the author of Esther intends his statement to be historical, an expansion or reorganization of the empire under Darius's son Xerxes would have to have occurred. It is also possible that the opening statement in Esther is rhetoric intended to parody the expanse and bureaucracy of the Persian Empire, which would be consistent with the tenor of the story.

Esther 1:1-3 sets the story during the reign of the Persian king referred to in the original Hebrew text as *Ahasuerus but identified by modern scholarship almost certainly as Xerxes. Herodotus (*Hist.* 6.98; 7.34-35; 7.187) describes Xerxes as a tall, handsome and ruthless warrior worthy of the throne. When the incomplete bridge being built to span the Hellespont for his army's assault on Europe was washed away by a great storm, its builders were executed to vent Xerxes' frustration and anger. Esther's plight in approaching this formidable man unbidden is heightened by such knowledge of his character.

The book of Esther knows only two wives of Xerxes: Vashti and Esther. Herodotus (*Hist.* 7.114; 9.109) refers only to one wife of Xerxes by the name "Amestris," who is the mother of Xerxes' successor. Persian kings often took more than wife, but the mother of the heir to the throne held pride of place. Whether Amestris is yet another wife in the harem of the king or represents a different rendering of a Persian name is not known. If, however, the lavish banquets held by Xerxes in *Susa (Esther 1) were part of the great war council where, according to Herodotus (*Hist.* 7.8), Xerxes announced his plan to bridge the Hellespont and lead his army through Europe, then Esther would not yet have been his wife during the campaign that concerned Herodotus. Furthermore, the name "Vashti" may be a literary appellation created by the author, and, since "Vashti" sounds much like the Old Persian for "beautiful woman," it has been argued that Vashti and Amestris are one and the same woman.

Esther 1:14 names seven close advisors to Xer-xes, and Esther 4:11 reports that there was limited access to the king, which was violated on pain of death. Herodotus (*Hist.* 3.84) describes a seven-man counsel associated with Xerxes' predecessor, Darius, who could enter the king's presence at will and unannounced unless the king was with a woman. According to Herodotus (*Hist.* 1.99; 3.77), the practice of the Persian king to be reclusive and to receive no one except through messenger eunuchs began in the reign of Deioces and continued into the reign of Darius. The use of messenger eunuchs in Esther 4 and Esther's worry that the king had not summoned her for thirty days, presumably through a messenger, are true to the custom of the Persian court as described by Herodotus.

In Esther 3:7-14 the plot against the Jews develops as Haman casts lots (*pûr*) to determine an auspicious day for his genocide (*see* Purim). Herodotus (*Hist.* 3.128) also describes the casting of lots to choose a political assassin, which decision was sealed with the king's ring (cf. Esther 3:12).

Herodotus (*Hist.* 3.92-97) describes the specific tribute paid to Darius by the far-flung lands that he had subjugated and explains that the Persians proper paid no tax. The tribute included not only large amounts of silver, gold dust, coins, ore, ebony and elephant tusks but also young boys and girls to serve the court, documenting that the gathering of virgins for the king was not without precedent. From Asia and Libya alone Herodotus calculated a total tribute of 14,560 talents of silver. This figure can be compared to the ten thousand talents of silver that Haman promises to the king's treasury, presumably the silver he would have plundered from the Jews (Esther 3:8-9).

One of the distinctive traits of the Persian Empire was its highly efficient and fast "pony express" system of messengers. Through this system the decrees of Esther 3:13 and Esther 8:10 were sent to all the provinces of the empire. Herodotus explains that a fresh horse and rider would be stationed along the route, one for each day's journey, and they could cover about 250 miles a day. A letter would travel over the Royal Road from Susa (in modern Iran) to Sardis (on the western coast of what is now Turkey) in a week via 111 relay posts. Herodotus (*Hist.* 8.98) praised the efficiency of the riders, saying that "these are stayed neither by snow nor rain nor death nor darkness from accomplishing their appointed course with all speed."

Significant to the Esther story is Esther's invitation to the king and Haman to a banquet at which she invites them to a second banquet. According to Herodotus (*Hist.* 1.133), the Persians delighted in lavish celebrations of birthdays with a festive meal consisting of an ox, horse or camel roasted whole followed by several courses of desserts and abundant wine. The Greek versions of Esther reflect this understanding of the banquet as celebrating Esther's special day of honor, which by Persian custom would be her birthday (though this may have been a ruse that Esther employed to make Xerxes and Haman more inclined to attend).

Herodotus (*Hist.* 1.133) also notes that Persians had the habit of deliberating grave matters while inebriated and confirming their decisions later when sober. This probably reflects the ancient belief that the mental state of drunkenness provides access to the spiritual world and the will of the gods. This custom perhaps informs the statement in Esther 1:7-8 that Xerxes provided such abundant wine that each guest was allowed to drink without restriction. The custom may also be reflected in the statement that after reaching a decision to annihilate the Jews, Xerxes and Haman sat down to drink (Esther 3:15).

The practice of recording the names of benefactors of the king is also confirmed by the report by Herodotus (*Hist.* 8.85) of a Phoenician ship's captain who was recorded among the king's benefactors and given much land for service on the king's behalf. The incident in the Esther story when the king realizes that Mordecai has been recorded as a benefactor in his records but has not received his reward is consistent with Persian practice (Esther 6:1-11).

3. The Later Greek and Latin Sources.

The conquest of Persia by the Greeks remained prominent in national memory such that in the first century of this era four writers continued to include the Persian kings in their writings. The Jewish historian Josephus, of course, includes the Esther story as part of his history of the Jewish nation (*Jewish Antiquities*), but he seems completely dependent on the Greek translation of Esther story, following the LXX text, which identifies the king as "Artaxerxes," the name of Xerxes' son. However, Josephus uses Macedonian month names as found in the Greek Alpha text of Esther but not in the LXX version (*see* Esther 5: Greek Versions). Josephus (*Ant.* 11.277) further makes explicit the connection between the Esther story and the Sinai covenant by identifying Haman as an Amalekite, the appellation for the perennial enemy of the Jews. Josephus (*Ant.* 11.191) attempts to provide an explanation for Vashti's disobedience, explaining that the Persians forbade their wives to be seen by strangers.

Plutarch (c. AD 50–post 119) chose to include Artaxerxes II (404-362 BC), the great-grandson of Xerxes, in his series of *Lives*. The work is primarily concerned with court intrigue during the reign of Artaxerxes II and draws on Xenophon's *Anabasis*. Plutarch (*Art.* 27.2) mentions that Artaxerxes had 360 concubines in addition to a wife whom he loved passionately. Although Artaxerxes lived three generations after Xerxes and Esther, and Plutarch's number may or may not be accurate, this nonetheless suggests that Persian kings were believed to retain large harems, as the Esther story also indicates.

Quintus Curtius Rufus (first century AD) wrote in Latin his *History of Alexander*, in which the history of the Persian kings that led to Alexander's final victory is chronicled. Xerxes is noted for having made "godless war upon Europe" (*History of Alexander* 5.6.1). The luxurious wealth of the Persian royal cities and the deleterious effect of Persian influence on Alexander are noted (*History of Alexander* 5.2.11-12).

Diodorus Siculus (fl. first century BC) was a Greek writer who attempted to write a universal history of events occurring in the same time period throughout the world as he knew it. The prominence of Xerxes in the history of Persia is suggested in that Diodorus defines other people in reference to him. For instance, Diodorus (1.58.4) writes that Egypt fell to the Persians under Darius, "the father of Xerxes." Diodorus (2.32.2) defines the time period of Herodotus, one of his sources, as "at the time of Xerxes," apparently expecting his readers to know when that was. Perhaps the reason the Greeks thought of Xerxes as the paradigmatic king of Persia is that Xerxes led one of the largest armies ever assembled against the Greeks, and yet he failed to defeat them. This event became a defining moment celebrated by Greek writers for half a millennium.

The defeat of Xerxes marked a turning point in the Persian Empire when it began its decline that would lead to Alexander's conquest about 150 years later. Following his disastrous defeat, Xerxes returned to Persia and involved himself in domestic matters, especially the completion of the royal city of Persepolis. It was at this time that the events documented in the book of Esther occur. The opening of the book of Esther 1:1("This is what happened during the time of Xerxes" [TNIV]) would have been read by its original readers in light of their knowledge of Xerxes' disastrous defeat. The description in Esther 1:4-12 of his lavish extravagance during his prolonged war council would have ironically highlighted the hubris of the Persian king before he marched off to his magnificent defeat and returned to Persia having depleted the royal treasury. It is a defeated Xerxes who finds Esther's appeal irresistible and who sees in Haman's plan a huge sum to replenish the royal coffers (Esther 3:9). And so although the ancient sources do not mention Esther or Mordecai or the events they lived out in the court of the Persian king, an understanding of the role of Xerxes in Persian history certainly adds a depth of insight that the author could assume on the part of his original readers.

After returning from his campaign against the Greeks, the remainder of Xerxes' reign was consumed by harem intrigues and the overbearing influence of courtiers and eunuchs—a characterization confirmed and parodied by the author of Esther. Twenty years after ascending the Persian throne, in August 465 BC, Xerxes was assassinated in his bedroom by Artabanus, captain of his bodyguard, about thirteen years after his marriage to Esther (Diodorus 11.69.1).

See also AHASUERUS; HISTORICAL CRITICISM; SOCIAL-SCIENTIFIC APPROACHES; SUSA; VASHTI.

BIBLIOGRAPHY. **Aeschylus**, *The Persians* (2 vols.; LCL; Cambridge, MA: Harvard University Press, 1930 [1922]); **A. Berlin**, *Esther* (JPSBC;

Philadelphia: Jewish Publication Society, 2001); **M. Boyce,** "Persian Religion in the Achaemenid Age," in *Cambridge History of Judaism,* ed. W. Davies and L. Finkelstein (Cambridge: Cambridge University Press, 1984) 279-307; **P. Briant,** *Histoire de l'Empire perse: De Cyrus à Alexandre* (Paris: Fayard, 1996); **Diodorus Siculus** (12 vols.; LCL; Cambridge, MA: Harvard University Press, 1933-1967); **Flavius Josephus,** *The Jewish Antiquities, Books 1-19* (9 vols.; LCL; Cambridge, MA: Harvard University Press, 1930-1965); **J. G. Gammie,** "Herodotus on Kings and Tyrants: Objective Historiography or Conventional Portraiture?" *JNES* 45 (1986) 171-95; **Herodotus** (4 vols.; LCL; New York: G. P. Putnam, 1920-1938); **A. J. Hoerth,** *Archaeology and the Old Testament* (Grand Rapids: Baker, 1998); **R. G. Kent,** "The Daiva-Inscription of Xerxes," *Language* 13 (1937) 292-305; **A. T. Olmstead,** *History of the Persian Empire* (Chicago: University of Chicago Press, 1948); **Plutarch,** *Life of Artaxerxes* (11 vols.; LCL; Cambridge, MA: Harvard University Press, 1916-1928); **Quintus Curtius Rufus,** *History of Alexander* (2 vols.; LCL; Cambridge, MA: Harvard University Press, 1946); **Xenophon,** *Cyropaedia* (2 vols.; LCL; repr., New York: Macmillan, 1925 [1914]); **E. M. Yamauchi,** *Persia and the Bible* (Grand Rapids: Baker, 1990).   K. H. Jobes

ESTHER 3: HISTORY OF INTERPRETATION

The book of Esther has played a considerably larger role in the history of Judaism than in Christianity, largely due to the significance acquired by the festival of *Purim. Understandably, then, the body of Jewish interpretation devoted to Esther is considerably larger and therefore will receive greater attention in what follows here. The history of Esther's interpretation will be treated under the following headings, moving roughly chronologically:

1. Early Jewish Interpretation
2. Patristic Interpretation
3. Rabbinic Interpretation
4. Aramaic Versions of Esther (Targumim)
5. Medieval Jewish Interpretation
6. Protestant Reformation
7. Modern Interpretation

1. Early Jewish Interpretation.

1.1. Versions of Esther. In addition to a number of smaller changes, the major difference between the Greek and Hebrew versions of Esther is the insertion of six lengthy additions to the Greek text (typically designated Additions A-F), which probably date to the second or third century BC (*see* Esther 4: Additions; Esther 5: Greek Versions). These modifications add important theological and ethical dimensions that are entirely absent from the MT. For example, they add Jewish piety to Esther and *Mordecai (not mentioned in the MT), innocence/righteousness to the Jews (again, not mentioned), and God's intimate involvement behind the scenes in rescuing his people (God appears nowhere in the MT Esther).

The presence of the additions implies that the absence of their themes was perceived as a deficiency—but why? It is probably the case that many early Jewish interpreters assumed that Esther, Mordecai and their compatriots were observant Jews, that the prayer and the fasting mentioned in Esther were directed toward the Jewish God, and that God is ultimately responsible for delivering his people from calamity. If so, it makes perfect sense why Esther would be read as a story about God's deliverance of his holy and righteous people from unwarranted persecution at the hands of a foreign power, even though Esther mentions nothing about God or religion. The editors of the additions probably believed that the dimensions that they added were essentially already present in the text and lay embedded beneath the surface, and they were making them explicit. That is, the perceived deficiency was not as much the text itself as the fact that it left much implicit.

On occasion, the Greek additions also interpret Esther directly through interpretive glosses. Thus, for instance, the MT of Esther 3:4 explains that the reason Mordecai refuses to bow (*yistaḥăweh*) before Haman is the fact that he is Jewish (*yĕhûdî*). A priori this should not have prevented him from paying respects to his superiors, especially since there are plenty of OT examples of this practice; therefore it begs for explanation. Addition C, a prayer of Mordecai inserted after Esther 4, puts further elaboration on the lips of Mordecai himself: bowing is an act of worship and an activity reserved for God alone; doing so to Haman would be idolatrous, and therefore Mordecai dutifully refrained.

1.2. Josephus on Esther. The first-century AD Jewish historian Josephus is the only other major extant source to engage Esther. His narrative retelling the story of Esther in *Jewish Antiquities*

(*Ant.* 11.184-296) follows roughly that of the Greek versions of Esther, though it omits the first and final additions (A and F). Thus Josephus recounts the story emphasizing the innocence of the Jews, the Jewishness of the protagonists, the involvement of God, and so on, often augmenting them with additional commentary. This is also not surprising, since it naturally fits into one of *Jewish Antiquities'* larger themes: exaggerating Jewish piety, innocence and utility to foreign governments, which in part seems aimed at combating the contemporaneous treatment of Jews under Roman rule and anti-Semitic stereotypes.

One additional characteristic of Josephus's version of the story is his occasional inclusion of interesting details to explain peculiarities in the text. For example, neither the MT nor the Greek versions of Esther answer the question of why *Vashti refused to come to *Ahasuerus when beckoned. Josephus fills in that detail by explaining that Vashti, "in observance of the Persian customs [*nomoi*], which forbid wives to be seen by other men [*allotrioi*], did not go to the king, even though he repeatedly sent eunuchs to [retrieve] her" (*Ant.* 11.191 [cf. Esther 1:12-15]). This interpretation also explains why Vasthi was holding a separate banquet for "the women of the palace" (Esther 1:9): she and the women celebrated independently because they were not supposed to be seen by the men.

2. Patristic Interpretation.

The book of Esther does not feature prominently in patristic literature, though this should be taken as a direct reflection of its role in the grassroots life of the early church—for example, in devotion, liturgy or homiletics, of which we know little. Nevertheless, where it does appear, it does so with a surprising range of themes. Here we will survey but three.

2.1. The Greek Additions to Esther. One subject of interpretation concerned the canonical status of the additions to Esther (*see* Canon). The early church fathers were aware of the differences between the Greek and Hebrew Bibles, including the absence of Esther's additions from the Hebrew version of Esther. For example, Origen (c. AD 185-254) was intimately aware of the differences because of his work on *textual criticism and dialog with contemporary Jews (Origen *Ep. Afr.* 3). Nevertheless, he was convinced of the authenticity of the additions and regarded them

as inspired and authoritative. His precise rationale for this conclusion is unstated, though perhaps he explained their absence, just as he explained the absence of the Danielic additions (which he also regarded as inspired), as intentional deletions by Jewish scribes. By contrast, Jerome (c. AD 347-420), in his *Prologue to Esther,* regarded the Greek versions of Esther as corrupt and doubted the value of the additions, and therefore he collected them in an appendix to his translation of Esther for the Vulgate. In any case, a majority of the early church eventually came to regard the additions as being rightfully part of God's word.

2.2. Esther as Moral Example. One of the recurring themes in early Christian interpretation of the book of Esther is the use of the character of Esther as an example of piety and Christian virtue. This theme has a relatively consistent purpose and point of departure: God responds to and delights in the faithful, therefore Christians should follow the example of Esther, because of whose piety God delivered her people from the decree of Ahasuerus. Thus, for example, the church father Clement of Rome (late first century) links the deliverance of the Jews to Esther's great faith, humility and fasting in the face of danger to herself and implicitly exhorts his readers to follow her example (*1 Clem.* 50:18-20). Similarly, Athanasius' fourth festal letter (c. AD 332) exhorts his readers to live "silencing their fleshly desires," just as Esther, who through fasting and prayer averted the destruction about to come upon her people (*Festal Letters IV* §2). The church father John Chrysostom (AD 347-407) also exhorts, "Does man frighten you? Hasten to the Lord [in prayer] and you will suffer no evil!" just as Esther, who through prayer delivered her people (*Homilies on the Statues III* §6).

2.3. Esther and Persecution. One of the more unique interpretations belongs to the fourth-century Syrian father Aphrahat, who used Esther as a source of encouragement for the persecuted. In chapter 20 of his *Demonstrations* Aphrahat comforts his followers under duress for their faith and encourages them to persevere. To do so, Aphrahat shows how God's faithful people (in the OT, NT, Apocrypha), like Jesus himself, suffered unjustly at the hands of the wicked so that the readers might follow their examples and press on (resembling Heb 11) even if it requires martyrdom, as it did for Jesus, who for Aphrahat is the archetype of unjust suffering. Among the saints whom Aphrahat uses is Mordecai, of whom he writes, "*Mordecai* was persecuted by the wicked Haman and *Jesus* was persecuted by a rebellious people; *Mordecai* delivered his people from the hands of Haman by his prayer and *Jesus* delivered His people from the hands of Satan by his prayer . . . [and] because *Mordecai* sat and clothed himself with sackcloth he saved Esther and his people from the sword, and because *Jesus* clothed Himself with a body and was illuminated he saved the Church and her children from death . . . [therefore] *Mordecai* received the honor of Haman, his persecutor, and *Jesus* received great glory from his Father instead of his persecutors who were of the foolish people," so as to impel his readers to be like Mordecai, who, like Jesus, endured unjust suffering for God's namesake (*Demonstrations* 20:21 [italics added]).

3. Rabbinic Interpretation.

The rabbinic works that discuss the book of Esther span several centuries. Thus as one might expect, some interpretations, or versions of them, are reproduced in various rabbinic works, although there are numerous differences among them. Nevertheless, the rabbis' general interpretive posture toward Esther is one that they held in common with their Jewish (and to an extent, Christian) predecessors since at least as far back as the composition of the Greek versions: Esther is a religious text about God's deliverance of his holy and righteous people from unjust persecution. In general, what also marks rabbinic interpretation of Esther is its immense exegetical ingenuity.

3.1. Mishnah and Tosefta. The earliest "rabbinic" interpretation of Esther is found in the legal anthologies known as the Mishnah and the Tosefta, compiled in the third century AD. Both devote an entire tractate to Esther, called *Megillah,* short for *Megillat Esther* (= "scroll of Esther"). However, both tractates are devoted mostly to considerations surrounding the proper observance of the holiday of Purim, which Esther both commands and authorizes. A significant portion is devoted to the proper practice of *qĕrîʾat mĕgillâ,* reading the book of Esther on Purim, which is not explicitly commanded in the book but is nevertheless understood as an implied obligation for fulfilling the holiday in Esther 9:28 (*t. Meg.* 1:4, *y. Meg.* 1:5a, *b. Meg.* 2b; cf. *b. Mak.* 23b [see Tabory, 323-

54]). For example, since Esther 9:19-31 authorizes two days for celebrating Purim, the 14th and 15th Adar, tractate *Megillah* opens by discussing their significance for when and where the book of Esther should be read. Both the Mishnah and the Tosefta conclude from the passage that fortified cities that are surrounded by walls that date from the days of Joshua (or Ahasuerus, according to a dissenting rabbi in the *t. Meg.* 1:1) should read the *Megillah* on the 15th of Adar, whereas large villages and cities should read it on the 14th of Adar. From there, both collections explicate various reasons behind this distinction and implications for how it plays out in the lives of Jewish communities.

3.2. Babylonian Talmud. The Babylonian Talmud, assembled probably in the mid-sixth century AD, is a compilation of rabbinic traditions organized according to the Mishnah, similar to a modern commentary to a biblical text. Thus following the Mishnah, the Talmud's tractate *Megillah* is also interested in issues related to Purim observance, though it furthers the discussion by rehearsing numerous debates and vignettes of various rabbis—for example, concerning Esther's place in the canon (*b. Meg.* 7a).

In addition, *b. Megillah* contains a rabbinic commentary on the whole book of Esther, which is the only midrashic commentary on a biblical book to be incorporated into the Talmud (*b. Meg.* 10b-17a). Here the rabbinic dialogs and vignettes serve a variety of purposes—for example, to embellish the villainy of the Ahasuerus, Vashti and Haman (and sometimes Nebu-chadnezzar); to aggrandize the Jewish piety of Esther, Mordecai and their kin; to supply additional contextual information. This is done by appropriating exegetical techniques common to other midrashim. Among the more interesting tendencies of the commentary is that of tying lexical and grammatical peculiarities in the text to a deeper significance rather than a grammatical-historical sense, which is a generic characteristic of midrashic commentary. Thus, for instance, the book's first words, "And it happened in the days of [*wayĕhî bîmê*]," spark a rabbinic discussion about how when these words occur in biblical narrative, they often introduce a period of distress (Heb *sārâ*) (*b. Meg.* 10b; cf. *Tg. Esth. II* 1:1). The commentary also has a penchant for etymologizing names; so, for example, in *b. Megillah* 11a the Talmud discusses various possible derivations of the name "Ahasuerus," such as from the words *ăhîw šel roʾš* ("brother of the head"), on the (incorrect) assumption that he was the brother of Nebuchadnezzar, whom Daniel calls "the head of gold" (Dan 2:38).

3.3. Other Midrashim. There are a number of midrashim that discuss Esther, as well as sections of other midrashim devoted to Esther that have been preserved, the largest being *Megillat Esther Rabbah* (for a list see, Berlin, liii). One of their common themes, following the Talmud and earlier Jewish tradition, is the embellishment of both the villainy of the antagonists and the Jewish piety of the protagonists. Thus, Esther's Jewish devotion is often emphasized by noting that she would not partake of the court's food (cf. Dan 1:8) and did not sleep with Ahasuerus—or if she did, it was after he converted to Judaism. By contrast, the rabbis also denigrate Ahasuerus by identifying him as the king responsible for ceasing the rebuilding of the temple in Ezra-Nehemiah and for using its vessels for his banquets (cf. Dan 1:2), Vashti by identifying her as Nebuchadnezzar's granddaughter, and Haman by portraying him as a bigger fool and miscreant.

4. Aramaic Versions of Esther (*Targumim*).

The Aramaic versions, or *Targumim*, are rabbinic reworkings of Esther that weave their interpretations directly into the text using various strategies such as rewordings and additions of extra narrative sequences, dialogues and exegetical digressions. As such, they probably are better understood as midrashim than as translations. There are two versions of Esther *Targumim*, designated by the names *Targum Rishon* ("first Targum") and *Targum Sheni* ("second Targum"). The interpretive traditions found in the Targumim reflect those found in other rabbinic literature, which has raised the question of how the two corpora relate: was one the source for the other, or were they were both dependent upon a third source, or something else? To date, this is a disputed matter. Attempts to date the composition of the Targumim are based on related considerations in addition to linguistic ones, and therefore they too are disputed. According to B. Grossfeld (1991, 21, 23-25), one of the latest scholars to investigate these issues, both *Targum Rishon* and *Targum Sheni* derive from a lost rabbinic work known as *Esther Rabbati* and were composed in roughly the same period, and no later than the early seventh century AD in Pales-

tine. However, it must be emphasized that these conclusions are still very uncertain.

Like other rabbinic literature and the Greek versions, the *Targumim* approach the text of Esther from the standpoint that Esther is a story about God's deliverance of his faithful people from an undeserved fate. However, unlike the Greek versions, while some of the added material serves the purpose of supplying this perspective, most of it simply assumes it and serves other purposes, such as aggrandizing the Jews, disparaging the Persians/Babylonians, or deriving creative interpretations. The traditions in *Targum Rishon* in general tend to add midrashic material rather than interpret the text directly. So, for instance, when in Esther 1:11 Ahasuerus ordered Vashti to be brought into the banquet, *Targum Rishon* adds that the king ordered her to be brought in "naked, since she used to make Israelite girls work naked and make them beat wool and flax naked, therefore it was decreed that she be brought out naked" (*Tg. Esth. I* 1:11). *Targum Sheni* is similar to *Targum Rishon* in many respects, though it is significantly more expansive and integrates many more fanciful stories and details into its narrative. For example, the first two verses of Esther (Esther 1:1-2) are the catalyst for a long series of midrashic digressions that take up nearly two-thirds of *Targum Sheni*'s first chapter (*Tg. Esth. II* 1:1-3). The majority of this digression seems to stem from a single rabbinic tradition that regards Ahasuerus as one of the ten kings in history who ruled the world (or "will rule" in the case of the tenth—the Messiah in the eschaton), which in turn is the point of departure for a lengthy midrashic recounting of various traditions related to Judaism under Babylonian and Persian rule. It is interesting to note that an appreciable body of these traditions found in the Babylonian Talmud beginning in *b. Meg.* 10b.

5. Medieval Jewish Interpretation.

Medieval Jewish interpreters retain a number of the same assumptions about Esther held by earlier Jewish tradition; however, the questions that they ask of the text and the methods that they appropriate are of a very different character.

5.1. Pěšat Interpretation. The Middle Ages generally saw intense interest in classical literatures of various languages and witnessed important developments in lexicography, grammar, philology and comparative linguistics—including *Hebrew and other Semitic languages. The wake of these developments consequently ushered in a new era in Jewish interpretation of the Bible—not only Esther—whose interests focused largely on understanding the text by explaining difficult words and grammatical forms and interpreting the text in context (not unlike modern commentaries). This new approach, known as *pĕšaṭ* ("simple, literal" interpretation), therefore marked an important departure from the traditional midrashic techniques of earlier rabbinic literature. Moreover, having began in Spain and Northern Africa, it eventually became the dominant method in western Europe throughout the Middle Ages. Famous commentators include Avraham Ibn Ezra (or just Ibn Ezra), Rabbi Shimon ben Yitzhak (= Rashi), and Rabbi Shimon ben Meir (= Rashbam).

5.2. Use of Philosophy. In addition to historical-grammatical concerns, medieval Jewish commentaries were characterized by their creative use of philosophy in exegesis. For example, after the translation of Aristotle's highly influential *Nicomachean Ethics* into Hebrew in the fourteenth century, Jewish exegetes regularly employed its insights in their commentaries. Concerning Esther specifically, Avraham Hadidah, for example, occasionally quoted Aristotle at length to explain and critique Ahasuerus's lavish display of wealth as a sign of personal insecurity. Some commentators also utilized medieval science as an interpretive tool, and the use of astrology was particularly prominent. For instance, many medieval scholars believed that the movement of celestial bodies affected human events. Thus, commentators such as Yitzhak ben Yosef ("the Priest") argued that Haman calculated his plans according to constellation patterns in order to ensure their success, thereby making Israel's deliverance seem all the more miraculous.

5.3. Theological Concerns. Medieval commentators also continued in the footsteps of their forebears by addressing Esther's theological problems, though they charted their own way through them as well. As in the earlier translations and rabbinic exegesis, the absence of God's name from Esther needed explaining. Some commentators (e.g., Ibn Ezra, Saʾadia Gaʾon) offered reasons why God's name was omitted—for example, intentionally for fear that if the book fell into pagan hands, pagan scribes would replace God's name with a pagan god in

order to attribute the miracles to the latter. Others simply explained the absence of God's name as incidental, since obviously he was orchestrating the events of Israel's deliverance. Medieval commentators also had trouble with the book of Esther's lack of Jewish distinctiveness—for example, concerning *kašrût* (kosher law), Sabbath observance and sexual purity. Thus the *Zohar*, a medieval kabbalistic text, realizing that the terms of Ahasuerus's beauty pageant implied that the contestants must sleep with him, explained that God sent down a female spirit disguised as Esther to sleep with the king in order to protect her from sexual sin (*Ki Tēṣē* 3:276a).

5.4. Esther and the Diaspora. Perhaps one of the most historically interesting features of the medieval interpretation of Esther is that it became a paradigm for Jewish communities living in the Diaspora under foreign rule. Jews were treated variously in the medieval period. Under both Christian and Muslim rule Jews enjoyed a recognized, though second-class, status. However, after Christians drove the Muslims from Europe in the thirteenth century, this status slowly degraded. Hatred and persecution of Jews gradually mounted, culminating in the fifteenth century with the Spanish Inquisition and the expulsion of Jews from Spain in 1492 and from Portugal in 1496. The situation of the Persian Jews following Ahasuerus's edict at the hands of Haman therefore had very real, palpable parallels to medieval European Jews. Consequently, medieval commentators frequently interpreted the actions of Ahasuerus and Haman in terms of the contemporary persecutions, as though medieval Jews were recapitulating the events of Esther in their own time. To give one example, Avraham Shalom (fifteenth-century in Spain) explained that the reason Haman encouraged Ahasuerus to exterminate the Jews from his kingdom in Esther 3:8 was that the king believed that it was his duty to unite his kingdom under one religion and to do away with those who disagree, for such could threaten the whole kingdom (*Naveh Shalom* 69b).

6. Protestant Reformation.

A significant number of Esther commentaries were written in the Reformation period, though oddly enough, none by Luther and Calvin, though presumably Calvin intended to write one. However, according to *Table Talk*, a compilation of Luther's statements on various topics collected by his students, Luther did famously remark, "I am so great an enemy to the second book of the Maccabees, and to Esther, that I wish they had not come to us at all, for they have too many heathen unnaturalities. The Jews much more esteemed the book of Esther than any of the prophets; though they were forbidden to read it before they had attained the age of thirty, by reason of the mystic matters it contains" (*Table Talk* §24). *Table Talk* is a notoriously difficult source to interpret, particularly because it is difficult to know to what extent the contents actually reflect Luther's opinions, and because different statements were collected for a range of purposes—for example, didactic and humorous. This challenge no less applies here. Luther apparently did accept Esther as canonical and authoritative, although his unique criteria of justification by faith and whether it urged Christ probably placed it lower in value than other books in his canon. The force of this statement, therefore, probably should not be taken too literally as an indictment against Esther but more so as a cheap shot against contemporaneous Jews.

All Protestant commentators appear to have regarded Esther's genre as literally historical. Protestants used the Hebrew text as the basis for commentary and exhibited a strong interest in the historical, grammatical and lexical aspects of the book of Esther. However, the more prevalent concerns of Protestant commentators appear to have been ethical and religious ones. Thus, for instance, commentators discussed whether Ahasuerus could divorce Vashti, whether Esther had grounds for marrying a pagan, whether Esther was lying by concealing her identity, and numerous other such topics (see Paton, 108).

Roman Catholics also produced a number of commentaries, and although they used the Vulgate text as the basis for commentary and regarded the additions as inspired, they also showed an awareness of issues in the Hebrew text. Many of their interests were similar to those of the Protestants—for instance, historical and linguistic concerns. One interesting feature of Roman Catholic interpretation is its use of typology—in particular, interpreting Esther as a type for which the Virgin Mary is the antitype (see Paton, 108).

7. Modern Interpretation.

Recent interpretation of Esther has swirled around numerous topics ranging from textual history to the *Dead Sea Scrolls. Here we will survey a couple of recent developments concerning Esther's historicity and genre.

7.1. Historical Value. One area that has received much attention is how to situate Esther in relation to ancient Persia. Scholars have increasingly noted that Esther's narrative contains details that are either historically inaccurate or too fanciful to be true (e.g., Fox 2001, 131-39; Berlin, xvii; for literary/thematic problems see Clines, 26-63).

Esther is the only source that records Persia having 127 provinces, which is far too high. The counts from all other extant sources, including Darius's own monuments, indicate there were only twenty to thirty, which is much more realistic (Fox 2001, 132).

Persian society, like others in the ancient Near East, functioned aristocratically, and as a rule kings needed to marry from noble families (Herodotus *Hist.* 3.84). Therefore it would be inconceivable that a Persian king would choose a wife of unknown ancestry and do so by a beauty contest.

Moreover, Esther's portrayal of a Persian dynast, Ahasuerus, as an incompetent ruler dependent on his advisors for recommendations on insignificant matters (e.g., how to honor Mordecai) and unable to discern absurd requests (e.g., to slaughter the Jews) is also hard to believe.

It is also difficult to understand how Persia, which had warmly treated nations previously conquered by Babylonia, including Judah, as Ezra-Nehemiah testifies, would then at a moment's notice and without good reason issue an outlandish edict to exterminate all Jews from everywhere in the empire.

However, scholars have also noted that Esther's portrayal of Persian culture in certain respects seems fairly consonant with the Persian stereotypes found elsewhere in the Mediterranean, particularly in the works of the Greek writers Herodotus, Xenophon and Aristophanes. For instance, these writers describe, often pejoratively, the opulence of the Persian court exhibited in its lavish banquets, its ornate decor, and the king's display of his wealth, all of which are features assumed by Esther's narrative.

The upshot of these observations has led to the affirmation that Esther's assumptions about Persian culture are roughly accurate, if not simply widely held throughout the Mediterranean, but also to the recognition that Esther's overall narrative is not strictly historical.

7.2. Genre Identification. In recent decades a rough consensus seems to have emerged regarding Esther's genre. On the one hand, Esther should be understood as a Diaspora story. Esther was written in a Diaspora context, written for Jews under a foreign power, and reflects a perspective on Jewish life and values in the Diaspora. Moreover, Esther also shares features with other Diaspora stories such as Judith, Tobit, Daniel 1—6 and the additions to Daniel. On the other hand, Esther should be understood in carnivalesque terms. This identification results largely from the recognition of several humorous or ironic episodes, such as Mordecai being honored instead of Haman, and at Haman's unwitting advice; the annals being read to Ahasuerus to cure insomnia; Haman getting the stake instead of Mordecai (Berlin, xv-xxviii; Fox 2001, 141-52).

These observations, in tandem with Esther's historical problems, have raised the question of whether the author of the MT Esther intended the work to be read as fiction or nonfiction—that is, whether he believed it was story or history. The answer largely depends on how one interprets the relationship between the events of Esther to various features of Esther 9—10, though the Purim etiology in particular. For instance, the fancifulness of the narrative coupled with the viability of its background assumptions suggests that the book is something like historical fiction or historical novel (Berlin, xvi-xvii). However, Esther 9—10, which establishes the composition's etiological purpose, gives the impression that the author believed that the events actually happened. This disconnect, in addition to other data, has led scholars to conclude that the practice of Purim and the story of Esther probably were originally independent and became associated at some later point before the writing of the Masoretic Text of Esther (and correlatively that the actual etiology of Purim is lost to us [see Berlin, xlv-xlix; Clines, 31-138]).

See also ESTHER 1: BOOK OF; ESTHER 4: ADDITIONS; FEMINIST INTERPRETATION; MEGILLOT AND FESTIVALS; PURIM; TARGUMIM; WOMEN.

BIBLIOGRAPHY. **A. Berlin,** *Esther* (JPSBC; Philadelphia: Jewish Publication Society, 2001); **D. Börner-Klein and E. Hollender,** *Rabbinische Kommentare zum Buch Ester* (2 vols.; Leiden: E. J. Brill, 2000); **D. J. A. Clines,** *The Esther Scroll: The Story of the Story* (JSOTSup 30; Sheffield: JSOT Press, 1984); **L. Feldman,** *Studies in Josephus' Rewritten Bible* (JSJSup 58; Leiden: E. J. Brill, 1998) 500-538; **M. V. Fox,** *The Redaction of the Books of Esther: On Reading Composite Texts* (SBLMS 40; Atlanta: Scholars Press, 1991); idem, *Character and Ideology in the Book of Esther* (2nd ed.; Grand Rapids: Eerdmans, 2001); **L. Ginzberg,** *The Legends of the Jews,* vols. 4, 6 (Baltimore: Johns Hopkins University Press, 1998); **B. Grossfeld,** *The First Targum to Esther: According to the MS Paris Hebrew 110 of the Bibliothèque Nationale* (New York: Sepher-Hermon Press, 1983); idem, *The Two Targums of Esther, Translated, with Apparatus and Notes* (ArBib 18; Collegeville, MN: Liturgical Press, 1991); idem, *Targum Sheni to the Book of Esther: A Critical Edition Based on MS Sassoon 282 with Critical Apparatus* (New York: Sepher-Hermon Press, 1994); **S. Lieberman,** *Tosefta Ki-Feshutah: A Comprehensive Commentary on the Tosefta,* 5: *Order Mo'ed* (New York: Jewish Theological Seminary of America, 1962); **M. Luther,** *The Table Talk of Martin Luther* (Philadelphia: Lutheran Publication Society, 1997); **C. F. Moore,** *Daniel, Esther, and Jeremiah: The Additions* (AB 44; Garden City, NY: Double Day, 1977); **G. W. E. Nickelsburg,** "Additions to the Book of Esther," in *Jewish Writings of the Second Temple Period,* ed. M. E. Stone (Philadelphia: Fortress, 1984) 135-38; **L. B. Paton,** *A Critical and Exegetical Commentary on the Book of Esther* (ICC; Edinburgh: T & T Clark, 1908); **E. Segal,** *The Babylonian Esther Midrash: A Critical Commentary* (3 vols.; BJS 291-293; Atlanta: Scholars Press, 1994); **Y. Tabory,** *Môʿădē Yiśrāʾel bi-Tĕqûpat ha-Mišnâ wĕ-ha-Talmûd* (= *Festivals of Israel in the Period of the Mishnah and the Talmud*) (Jerusalem: Magnes, 2000) 321-67; **B. D. Walfish,** *Esther In Medieval Garb: Jewish Interpretation of the Book of Esther in the Middle Ages* (Albany: State University of New York Press, 1993). J. Dombrowski

ESTHER 4: ADDITIONS

There are extant six chapter-length additions to the Esther story, designated A-F, which survive only in the two Greek versions (the LXX text and the Alpha text) (*see* Esther 5: Greek Versions). The additions either add explicitly religious language (additions A, C, D, F) or comprise official memos from the Persian king (additions B, E). All but addition D are inserted cleanly into the narrative; addition D is woven into Esther 5 in such a way as to suggest that it may have had a different origin than did the other additions.

1. Origins and Christian Reception
2. Content of the Additions

1. Origins and Christian Reception.

The consensus of scholarship is that additions B and E originated in Greek, but both Semitic and Greek origins have been argued for the other additions. It is apparent that the additions were added subsequent to the original production of both Greek versions. It is uncertain whether the additions were originally introduced to one of the Greek versions all at one time or by different hands at different times. The degree of similarity of the additions in the LXX text (ó-text) compared to the Alpha text (AT) indicates a literary dependence between them. It is not clear if the additions were copied from the ó-text to the AT or vice versa, or if they came from some third source. Although it is unknown when the additions came into the Greek versions, they were present by the late first century AD, as Josephus clearly uses material from additions B, C, D, E in his *Jewish Antiquities*. His omission of apocalyptic material from A and F that reveals Jewish dominance of the Gentile nations may have been due to his sensitivity about war against Gentiles, since Josephus was closely aligned with the Romans.

The additions to the Greek versions as they appear in the LXX (ó-text) are canonical for the Roman Catholic and Eastern Orthodox churches. Protestants place the additions to Esther among the apocryphal writings. When Jerome produced the Latin Vulgate, he knew that these additions were not original even though they were well known to the church because the Old Latin version that had been translated from the Greek included them. He acknowledged their traditional inclusion by excising them from the story and dislocating them into an appendix at the end of the story. Today the English translations produced by the Roman Catholic Church traditionally also include these dislocated chapters, but it is more common to insert them into the narrative where they are found in the Greek versions.

2. Content of the Additions.

When the two Greek versions are compared, the six additions are similar enough to indicate literary dependence between them but they are not identical in wording. This has given rise to complex discussions about to which Greek version they were first added and about the *Tendenz* of the final redactors of each version. Nevertheless, the overall contribution of each addition to the narrative is clear.

2.1. Additions A and F. Additions A and F frame the Esther narrative with an apocalyptic dream and its interpretation that provide a political perspective on the Esther story that would be at home in the Hellenistic era. Addition A introduces the Greek Esther story with Mordecai's dream of two dragons, thunders, earthquake and a tiny fountain that produces a great river of water. *Mordecai understands the dream as revelation from God and ponders it to understand its every detail. The dream is a prelude to Mordecai's discovery of an assassination plot against the king by two eunuchs, which the AT links closely to the interpretation of the dream. Addition A documents that the king then wrote a memo in his book about how Mordecai had foiled this attempt on his life, a detail that later is of great significance to the canonical story (Esther 6:2). Haman's animosity toward Mordecai is explicitly linked to the execution of the two eunuchs upon Mordecai's discovery of their plot, implicating Haman as part of the assassination conspiracy. Haman is identified as an "Agagite" in the Hebrew Masoretic Text (MT) but is introduced in addition A as a "Bugaion" in the ó-text and as a "Macedonian" in the AT.

Addition F ends the Greek Esther story by explaining that the events of the story are a fulfillment of Mordecai's dream that are from God. In the ó-text Esther is identified as the little spring that produces a great river; in the AT she is the little spring, but the river is the nations gathered together against the Jewish people. The two dragons are identified as Mordecai and Haman in both Greek versions. The lots of *Purim are identified as two destinies, one for the people of God and one for the nations, and the events of the Esther story are understood as the moment of decision when these two lots fell. Additions A and F view the Esther story not as an isolated happenstance of history but rather as events divinely orchestrated and prophetically foretold.

Because additions A and F clearly answer to each other, they most likely were introduced into the Greek Esther story at the same time. Because they are apocalyptic, they probably were introduced during the Hellenistic (or Greco-

Roman) era when Hellenistic kings (or later Roman governors) began to oppress the Jews. It seems unlikely that they ever circulated independently of the Esther story as either Greek or Semitic texts. These additions were more carefully redacted into the AT than the ó-text, as evidenced by the omission in Esther 2 of elements that would be redundant following Addition A, whereas the ó-text lets Esther 2 stand unedited in this regard.

The positioning of Mordecai's dream and its interpretation as a frame around the Esther story achieves two literary effects. First, it makes Mordecai the undisputed hero of the story. In the Hebrew MT Mordecai and Esther are introduced at the same point in the story, and their roles in the deliverance of the Jews are so mutually interdependent that it is difficult to judge which should be considered the main character (though it is of note that the book has come down to us with title "Esther" and not "Mordecai"). In the Greek versions addition A introduces both Mordecai and Haman but not Esther, clearly subjugating her role to Mordecai's. This is consistent with the practice of referring to Purim as "Mordecai's Day" and minimizing Esther's role in the Hellenistic period.

Second, additions A and F bring Mordecai into Israel's tradition of great prophetic dreamers such as Joseph and Daniel. The parallels between Mordecai in the court of Persia, Joseph in Egypt, and Daniel in Babylon have long been recognized. In the Hebrew MT Mordecai's spiritual character is left undefined; however, in the Greek versions he becomes an exemplar of faithfulness and the recipient of divine revelation.

2.2. Additions B and E. Esther 3 and Esther 8 of the Hebrew canonical text only state that decrees were written in the king's name, first by Haman and then by Mordecai. In the Greek versions the text of the royal decrees has been cleanly inserted. A very high degree of agreement exists between the ó-text and AT in these additions. Differences amount to only the updating of vocabulary with synonyms, stylistic changes in syntax, and the addition of an occasional pronoun or relative clause for clarity. Although putatively written during the Persian period, additions B and E bear characteristics of documents contemporary in the Ptolemaic period. They are wordy, with a convoluted sentence structure and syntax that achieves flowery rhetoric.

The traits of additions B and E indicate that the same hand composed both. Because both additions include distinctive words that are found elsewhere in the AT but not in the ó-text, it appears that they were first introduced into the AT in a more careful manner and were then simply copied into the ó-text without revision to the rest of the story. This is comparable to what is observed with the introduction of addition A more carefully achieved in the AT than in the ó-text.

2.3. Addition C. Addition C is comprised of the prayers of Esther and Mordecai, thereby introducing the strongest religious element found in the Greek additions. It is often assumed that the fast of Mordecai and Esther in Esther 4:15-17 was accompanied by prayers of supplication; the prayers in addition C document their prayers for deliverance. The overtly religious language of addition C expresses interest in the covenant by alluding to God's previous acts of deliverance, and it specifically mentions the temple, the Jews as God's inheritance, the exodus and circumcision. Such references make explicit what the Hebrew story of Esther only hints: the Jews of the Diaspora are still God's covenant people even though they have chosen not to return to Judah.

The prayers in addition C echo the Greek version of the prayer of Moses in Deuteronomy 9:26-27, where Moses asks God to be merciful because of his covenant with Abraham, Isaac and Jacob. Mordecai bases his plea to God similarly. The deliberate use of the exodus motif by the author of addition C is also seen in the description of the Jewish people as being "in bitter slavery," which draws a close identity of the Jews of Persia with their ancestors in Pharaoh's Egypt, even though historically the Persians did not enslave the Jewish nation.

Addition C exonerates Mordecai and Esther by revealing more of their thoughts and motives. Esther divulges her thoughts about being taken into the harem of the king when she admits that she loathes "the bed of the uncircumcised," casting her relationship with Xerxes (*see* Ahasuerus) in a more virtuous light as measured by Torah. Mordecai explains that it was not from hubris or self-seeking that he refused to bow to "the uncircumcised" Haman but rather out of obedience to the first commandment. Because the Hebrew version of Esther extant in the MT lacks reference to God or the symbols of Judaism, it leaves the events of the Esther story at the periphery of biblical history and theology. The overall effect of addition C is to bring the Esther story into the mainstream of pentateuchal tradition.

The Semitic flavor of addition C has sometimes been used to argue for a Semitic *Vorlage;* however, its style may simply be imitation of the Greek translation of the pentateuchal passages to strengthen its allusion to them.

2.4. Addition D. Addition D stands apart from the other additions with respect to the manner in which it has been introduced into the text. Whereas each of the other additions has been cleanly inserted without integration into the surrounding text, addition D has been woven into the immediately surrounding text, suggesting a different origin for it than for the other five additions. It is also the addition that shows the highest degree of agreement between the ó-text and the AT, suggesting that it was already present in the Hebrew *Vorlage* of the Greek translations.

The outcome of Esther's uninvited approach to the king is summarized succinctly in the Hebrew MT with one verse, Esther 5:2. The first half of this verse is supplemented in the Greek versions by an extensive description that notes the fearsome appearance of the king, the swooning of Esther, and the comment that the king sprang from his throne to take Esther in his arms and comfort her. The second half of Esther 5:2 is included in the Greek versions followed by the several concluding verses of addition D. Because addition D is spliced exactly the same way with the canonical text in exactly the same places in both the AT and the ó-text, it was likely already embedded within the *Vorlage* from which the Greek versions were translated.

Although there is the highest degree of agreement between the ó-text and the AT in addition D, the AT does include the distinctive phrase that the king looked upon Esther when she first approached him uninvited "as a bull in fierce anger." Neither the Hebrew MT nor the LXX of Esther include this phrase, but it is found in the Old Latin version of the Esther story, perhaps suggesting some literary relationship between the AT and the Old Latin.

A second distinctive phrase in addition D as found in the AT is that on Esther's face was "a measure of sweat" as she went uninvited to the king. This Greek phrase may have resulted from misreading the letter *dalet* for a *resh* in a Semitic *Vorlage,* which, if in Aramaic, would change the sense of the word from "good will" to "sweat." This has been proposed as evidence that an Aramaic version of the Esther story that included addition D may once have existed. The collocation of "sweat" and the preparation of a banquet, which was Esther's request when she appeared before the king, is found also in 2 Maccabees 2:26-27, which appears to be an allusion to the Esther story in the form extant in the AT. The book of 2 Maccabees is believed to have been written in Jerusalem to the Hellenized Diaspora Jews in Ptolemaic Egypt during the Hasmonean period, which would imply that addition D, with its distinctive readings as found in the AT, were in circulation before that time.

See also CANON; ESTHER 3: HISTORY OF INTERPRETATION; ESTHER 5: GREEK VERSIONS; TEXT, TEXTUAL CRITICISM.

BIBLIOGRAPHY. **A. Berlin,** *Esther* (JPSBC; Philadelphia: Jewish Publication Society, 2001); **D. J. A. Clines,** *The Esther Scroll: The Story of the Story* (JSOTSup 30; Sheffield: JSOT Press, 1984); **K. de Troyer,** *The End of the Alpha-Text of Esther: Translation and Narrative Techniques in* MT *8.1-7,* LXX *8.1-17 and AT 7.14-41,* trans. B. Doyle (SBLSCS 48; Atlanta: Society of Biblical Literature, 2000); idem, "The End of the Alpha-Text of Esther: An Analysis of MT and LXX 8.9-13 and AT 7.33-38," *Text* 21 (2002) 175-207; **M. V. Fox,** *The Redaction of the Books of Esther: On Reading Composite Texts* (SBLMS 40; Atlanta: Scholars Press, 1991); idem, *Character and Ideology in the Book of Esther* (2nd ed.; Grand Rapids: Eerdmans, 2001); **K. H. Jobes,** *The Alpha-Text of Esther: Its Character and Relationship to the Masoretic Text* (SBLDS 153; Atlanta: Scholars Press, 1996); **C. A. Moore,** *Daniel, Esther and Jeremiah: The Additions* (AB 44; New York: Doubleday, 1977); **C. C. Torrey,** "The Older Book of Esther," *HTR* 37 (1944) 1-40; **E. Tov,** "The 'Lucianic' Text of the Canonical and the Apocryphal Sections of Esther: A Rewritten Biblical Book," *Text* 10 (1982) 1-25; **H. G. M. Williamson,** *Studies in Persian Period History and Historiography* (FAT 38; Tübingen: Mohr Siebeck, 2004). K. H. Jobes

ESTHER 5: GREEK VERSIONS

Modern English translations made within the Protestant and Jewish traditions are translated from the Hebrew Masoretic Text, but all canonical books of the Hebrew Bible survive also in at least one ancient Greek translation. However, the book of Esther is among a few books that survive in two different Greek versions, as do the books of Judges, Daniel, Tobit and 1-2 Esdras. Extant for the book of Esther are manuscripts of the LXX text (ό-text) and the much shorter Alpha text (AT, sometimes referred to as the Lucianic version or *L*-text). Both Greek versions tell the same basic story as found in the Hebrew MT. The ό-text is almost certainly a translation of a Hebrew text that was virtually identical to the MT. The consensus is that the AT also originated as a translation of a Hebrew text, though the relationship of that Hebrew text to the MT is disputed. A significant minority of scholars consider the AT to be not a translation but rather a midrashic retelling of the Esther story that has no direct literary relationship to a *Vorlage*.

1. Characteristics of the Greek Versions
2. Differences between the Greek Texts
3. Relationship of the Three Texts
4. The Manuscripts

1. Characteristics of the Greek Versions.
The most prominent characteristic of the Greek versions is that both contain six additional chapters (A-F) that are not found in any surviving Hebrew version but are so similar in both Greek versions that a common origin is certain (*see* Esther 4: Additions). These six additional chapters contextualize the story for the times in which their Hellenistic readers lived. The Greek versions tone down the mockery of the Persian king, perhaps in respect of the Greek writers' high view of their most powerful enemy. The additions also supply the religious language referring to God, prayer and the covenant that the Hebrew story so notoriously lacks. The first and last additions, A and F, frame the Esther story with an apocalyptic vision of Israel's struggle against, and eventual triumph over, the nations. The effect of this apocalyptic frame reduces the focus on the roles of Esther and Mordecai and makes the story an episode in the age-old struggle of which Hellenistic oppression was yet another incident.

If the colophon found in the manuscripts of the ό-text is accurate, that Greek translation was made in the fourth year of Ptolemy and Cleopatra, which could be dated, depending on which Ptolemy and Cleopatra are intended, to c. 48 BC or c. 77 BC or c. 114 BC. The AT manuscripts includes no such colophon, and the dates of its original production and final redaction re-

main an open question.

The Roman Catholic and Eastern Orthodox churches consider the ό-text, including its six major additions, to be canonical. In the Latin Vulgate the additions were dislocated to an appendix at the end of the story because although they are not found in the Hebrew text, which was the textual base used by Jerome, they did appear in the Old Latin version familiar to the Latin church. Modern English translations of Esther that include the additions tend to place them in their proper sequence within the story.

No current community of faith, either Jewish or Christian, considers the AT of Esther to be canonical. However, the fact that manuscripts of this text were being copied into the thirteenth century suggests that it was valued by some community.

Although both Greek versions tell the same basic story as the Hebrew MT, they do so with different emphases and apparently different purposes. Produced in the Hellenistic era, the Greek versions reflect a Hellenistic political ethos that finds the Jewish people living in a Diaspora ruled by the Hellenistic kings who succeeded Alexander the Great. The role of *Mordecai as a Jew who was loyal to the pagan king is amplified in the Greek versions, perhaps as a message that the Jews were not a political threat and, moreover, that it is good for the king to have Jews in influential positions at court. The mockery of the ruling empire found in the Hebrew text is downplayed or omitted in the translations produced during the Hellenistic period. Two of the six major additions, B and E, are presented as copies of letters from the Persian king, who in the ό-text is named "Artaxerxes," where the AT simply transliterates the Hebrew name, *"Ahasuerus." Although putatively the documents of a Persian king, additions B and E replicate the complicated syntax and vocabulary of court documents known from the Ptolemaic era. Addition E presents the Persian king promoting the Jewish people among his subjects, referring to them as children of the only and true God, who has benevolently directed even the affairs of the Persian Empire. The Persian king describes Jewish practices, though odd by Hellenistic standards, as righteous laws.

Both Greek versions also supply the explicitly religious language needed to make the Esther story more comparable to Ezra, Nehemiah and Daniel, which share the common theme about a

Jewish leader's relationship to a pagan king. Where the Hebrew text mentions that many people became Jews out of fear (Esther 8:17), both Greek versions specify that conversion to Judaism involved circumcision, which had become the notoriously distinctive mark of Jewish identity in the Hellenistic world. The Greek versions make Esther more virtuous by Jewish standards by showing her praying fervently and interceding for the sins of her people, abhorring her marriage to a Gentile, and refusing to eat at the king's table. However, they also downplay her role in the deliverance and describe Esther as fearful. She swoons during her appearance before her husband and king, a stereotypical element found in Hellenistic romance stories of that time.

2. Differences Between the Greek Versions.
Although both Greek versions expand the Hebrew story of Esther in similar ways, there are some notable differences between them. The LXX, or ό-text, more closely follows the Hebrew text extant in the MT when the six major additions are excluded from consideration. The AT is considerably shorter than the ό-text text by frequently lacking the personal names, numbers, dates and repeated elements found in the LXX version. Of the two Greek versions, the AT is less explicitly religious than the ό-text. Because the six additions are secondary to both Greek versions, a comparison of the original emphases of the two texts should exclude them. In the Hebrew text and the ό-text, Mordecai pleads with Esther to intercede for the plight of her people before the king but notes that if she does not, deliverance will be accomplished from elsewhere. The AT states that if Esther does not intercede, their help will come specifically from God, implying a view that God steps in if human beings fail to act. Personal responsibility to act for the well-being of the Jewish nation is implicit in all versions of the story, for punishment is threatened should Esther fail to act on behalf of her people. The AT, however, does not state that Esther's ethnic and religious identity had been hidden, in contrast to the Hebrew story and the ό-text, which underscores the danger of identifying oneself with God's covenant people. The ό-text implies the importance of being an observant Jew if one is to have influence, noting that Esther kept her Jewish way of life even after entering the harem (Esther 2:20). The AT lacks this emphasis, implying that Esther's influence was not directly related to her observance of the *law.

In comparison to the ό-text, the AT magnifies Mordecai's role and minimizes Esther's. This may reflect an emphasis on Mordecai's role as a political hero in the Greek period, as *Purim was referred to at that time as "Mordecai's Day" (2 Macc 15:36). Although the AT states that Purim commemorates this episode of deliverance from the Persian threat (Esther 9:49//Eng. Esther 9:26), it abbreviates the Purim etiology and amplifies the political dynamics of the Jews in relation to a powerful pagan empire. More than the other versions, the AT emphasizes that Jews in positions of political power benefit not only the Jewish nation but also the king and the empire.

In addition to different emphases, there are many differences of detail between the ό-text and the AT. The ό-text explains that Mordecai was raising Esther to be his wife (Esther 2:7), making her marriage to the king more dramatic and poignant, but the AT is silent on that point. All references to cosmetics and the elaborate beauty treatment in Esther 1 are omitted in the AT. The AT also omits reference to the inalterability of Persian law (Esther 8:8), the second day of fighting and then of celebration (Esther 9:13, 19), and the extended Purim etiology (Esther 9:26-32). Esther 1:1 in the AT gives the Macedonian month names "Dystros-Xandikos," which correspond to the Jewish lunar months Adar-Nisan, suggesting that the AT in its present form was read by peoples who used the Macedonian calendar, while the ό-text was read by those familiar with the Jewish lunar calendar. Because of a known intercalating correction to the Macedonian calendar that occurred sometime between AD 15 and AD 46, this particular correspondence existed only from the time of the adjustment through AD 176. This might corroborate the theory of those who would date the production of the AT to the reign of the Roman emperor Claudius, but the month names could easily have been revised at some point in the AT's transmission history.

3. The Relationship of the Three Texts.
Discussion of the relationship of the two Greek texts of Esther to each other and the relationship of each to the Hebrew text has focused on the differences in the endings of the story in each of the three extant texts. The question is whether the Hebrew text(s) from which the

Greek versions were translated ended at a different place than does the MT or whether the endings of the Greek versions represent an intentional redaction by the Greek translators. Some believe that the AT, which is considerably shorter than the ó-text, is a translation of a shorter, earlier Hebrew version that ended at Esther 8:17 and that later received the ending that turns the Hebrew narrative into a Purim etiology. However, even though the three texts begin to diverge even as early as Esther 8:3, there is a substantial core and sequence of material common in the ending of all three versions. To further complicate the issue, the endings of both Greek versions appear to have been redacted extensively but independently when addition E was introduced.

Although the original relationship of each Greek version to the other is debated, the six major additions are almost identical in both (*see* Esther 4: Additions). Examination of the texts shows that their relationship in the additions is quite different than in their canonical sections, indicating that the additions were not original in either version. There is evidence that additions A, B, C, E, F (but not D) were introduced first into the AT and subsequently copied from that version into the ó-text. However, some scholars insist that the additions were originally introduced into the ó-text, if not by the original translator, then in a subsequent redaction, and were later copied into the AT. Addition D has a different relationship to its immediate context than do the other additions, leading some to conclude that it was already in the Hebrew *Vorlage* from which the Greek versions were translated.

The consensus of scholarship holds that the *Vorlage* of the ó-text was an ancestor as it existed in the first century BC of what became the MT several centuries later. Whether that Hebrew *Vorlage* included the ending of the story as found in the extant MT is highly debated. Until the 1960s, the AT was believed to be the Lucianic recension of Esther made by revising the LXX text in the late third century AD and therefore a younger and derivative Greek version. The siglum L in the Göttingen critical edition preserves this understanding of the origin of the AT. Other current theories contend that the AT is a midrashic rewrite of the Esther story, possibly precipitated by the political situation faced especially by the Jews of Alexandria under the reign of Claudius. There is also a weight of scholarship that argues that both Greek versions, exclusive of the six major additions, were translations independently made from respective Hebrew *Vorlagen*. If the AT is the older of the two Greek translations, its Hebrew *Vorlage* may have been an earlier ancestor of the Hebrew text that became the *Vorlage* from which the LXX was later translated and that further developed into the MT. Or it may have been a collateral relative of the MT's ancestor text that was to some extent different from it.

4. The Manuscripts.
The Greek text known as the LXX text (the ó-text, sometimes referred to as the B-text) is widely attested in the four great uncial codices and more than thirty minuscule manuscripts. Apart from the six major additions, it is the Greek version that stands most closely to the extant MT.

The AT is extant in only four manuscripts from the tenth through thirteenth centuries: MS 19 (Chigi R.vi.38), MS 93 (Royal I.D.2), MS 108 (Vat.Gr. 330) and MS 319 (Vatop. 600). MS 392 preserves a text that is a mix of the two Greek versions. The Greek versions formed the textual basis from which the Old Latin, the Sahidic (or Coptic) and the Ethiopic versions were translated.

See also CANON; ESTHER 4: ADDITIONS; TEXT, TEXTUAL CRITICISM.

BIBLIOGRAPHY. **A. Berlin,** *Esther* (JPSBC; Philadelphia: Jewish Publication Society, 2001); **F. W. Bush,** *Ruth, Esther* (WBC 9; Dallas: Word, 1996); **D. J. A. Clines,** *The Esther Scroll: The Story of the Story* (JSOTSup 30; Sheffield: JSOT Press, 1984); **K. de Troyer,** "An Oriental Beauty Parlor: An Analysis of Est. 2.8-18 in the Hebrew, the Septuagint and the Second Greek Text," in *A Feminist Companion to Esther, Judith and Susanna,* ed. A. Brenner (FCB 7; Sheffield: Sheffield Academic Press, 1995) 47-70; idem, *The End of the Alpha-Text of Esther: Translation and Narrative Techniques in MT 8.1-7, LXX 8.1-17 and AT 7.14-41* (SBLSCS 48; Atlanta: Society of Biblical Literature, 2000); idem, "The End of the Alpha-Text of Esther: An Analysis of MT and LXX 8.9-13 and AT 7.33-38," *Text* 21 (2002) 175-207; **M. V. Fox,** *The Redaction of the Books of Esther: On Reading Composite Texts* (SBLMS 40; Atlanta: Scholars Press, 1991); idem, *Character and Ideology in the Book of Esther* (2nd ed.; Grand Rapids: Eerdmans, 2001); **R. Hanhart,** ed., *Septuaginta: Vetus Testamentum Graecum,* 8.3: *Esther* (Göttingen:

Vandenhoeck & Ruprecht, 1966); **K. H. Jobes,** *The Alpha-Text of Esther: Its Character and Relationship to the Masoretic Text* (SBLDS 153; Atlanta: Scholars Press, 1996); **E. Tov,** "The 'Lucianic' Text of the Canonical and the Apocryphal Sections of Esther: A Rewritten Biblical Book," *Text* 10 (1982) 1-25; **H. G. M. Williamson,** *Studies in Persian Period History and Historiography* (FAT 38; Tübingen: Mohr Siebeck, 2004).

K. H. Jobes

ESTHER 6: PERSON

From her inauspicious beginnings as an orphaned young Israelite woman in exile, Esther came precipitously to the throne of Persia, where she acted with courage and determination to deliver her people. Nevertheless, her roles as wife to a pagan king and as activist against those who hated Jews have garnered her considerable criticism.

1. Esther's Identity
2. Assessing the Character and Actions of Esther
3. Lessons from Esther

1. Esther's Identity.

1.1. The Matter of Names. "Hadassah, that is, Esther" (Esther 2:7) is the only character in the book of Esther to have two names, indicative of her two worlds and the two identities that ultimately she would bring together in the power center of the Persian Empire. The Hebrew name "Hadassah" means "myrtle," which carried significant associations of hope (Neh 8:15; Is 55:13). Esther has popularly been identified with Ishtar, the goddess of both love and war. If this was intended as a "literary nickname," it was a good choice, as Esther proved herself in both realms. A seemingly better etymology derives the name from Old Iranian *stara,* meaning "star." In a further close study of the preservation of Old Persian forms, A. S. Yahuda concluded that "Esther" is the Persian equivalent of "Hadassah" and itself means "myrtle." While the Persian for "myrtle" is *as,* the name as it appears in the text preserves an older and longer form, the Medic *astra* via Old Persian. The rabbis pressed *intertextual connections even further, noting that Esther's name was related to the Hebrew word for "hide" *(str).* Citing Deuteronomy 31:18, they drew the parallels of God's being hidden because of the disobedience of the people, Esther's hidden identity, and God's own hiddenness in the book (*b. Hullin* 139b).

1.2. Esther's Two Worlds.

1.2.1. Esther's Jewish Heritage. Esther was a young Israelite woman and an orphan. Esther 2:7 emphasizes the absence of her parents, indicating twice that both had died. But for her cousin *Mordecai, who adopted her as his daughter, she would have been deserted. He cared for her, and she was submissive to his authority.

Although the book of Esther has received sharp criticism for its lack of overt religious language, it is evident that the main characters were infused with their Jewish tradition. When called upon to intervene on behalf of her people, Esther's final words to Mordecai were to enjoin the Jewish community to fast for three days, a most rigorous discipline. It seems that she was entirely familiar with the practice, the circumstances that would prompt such an endeavor, and the God to whom they would appeal.

1.2.2. Into the Persian Court. From that context, Esther was taken with the beautiful young virgins. The doublet describing Esther in 2:7 emphasizes her beauty: "beautiful of form" and "lovely in appearance." In other words, her extraordinary beauty far exceeded the qualifications for being rounded up when the search began for a new queen. Neither she nor Mordecai would have been able to prevent it; the description of the process uses three passive verbs indicating there was little likelihood of opposition (Esther 2:8). No doubt the environment to which she moved seemed a universe away from her Jewish home. Nevertheless, Mordecai made a daily practice of checking on her welfare (Esther 2:11).

Once Esther was in the confines of the court harem, her characteristic deference won her not only the approval of Hegai, the eunuch in charge of the young women, but also ultimately the favor of the king. In the interval, Hegai strategically shepherded her through the year of preparation. The treatment period was "prescribed" with oil massages for six months, no doubt to soften the skin, a significant matter in a hot and dry climate. This was followed by treatment with spices for another six months. The association of myrrh with sexual attraction and love is particularly evident in Song of Songs 1:13; 4:6, 14; 5:1, 5, 13 (see also Prov 7:17) (*see* Song of Songs).

The "rules of the contest" were that each candidate could ask for anything she wished to take with her to the king's palace (Esther 2:13), presumably in order to make herself memorable enough to be summoned again by name. This may also have been their "payment"; the story does not indicate what the items might have been or whether they could keep them. After one night with the king, the woman was a concubine, and if she was not summoned by name, she spent the rest of her life in the harem, essentially reduced to widowhood. It is not entirely clear where a young woman went when she left the king's bedroom in the morning. "Another part of the harem" (Esther 2:14 NIV) is literally "the second house of women," and there was now a different keeper, Shaashgaz, for the used concubines.

1.3. Was There a Historical Esther? Neither *Vashti nor Esther appears in the extrabiblical texts concerning the Persian Empire, raising the question of the historicity of these characters.

1.3.1. Scant Likelihood That Esther Would Become Queen. It has been claimed that the likelihood of Esther becoming queen was slim because the queen was supposed to be chosen from among the seven families whose nobles had participated in the overthrow of the Magi when Darius came to power (Herodotus *Hist.* 3.70-71, 84). The record in Herodotus, however, reflects an agreement among those conspirators just one generation before Xerxes (*see* Ahasuerus). This was not, therefore, a long-standing tradition. Further, it would omit the line of Cyrus itself, and yet the roster of Darius's four wives included two daughters of Cyrus, one of whom was Atossa (Herodotus *Hist.* 3.88), and Xerxes was the son of Atossa. This objection carries little weight.

1.3.2. Absence of Vashti from the Historical Record of Xerxes' Reign. The most challenging problem is the identity of Esther's predecessor, Vashti. Xerxes came to the throne in 486 BC, and ostensibly Vashti was the reigning queen only until her deposition in 483 BC (Esther 1:3). Herodotus (*Hist.* 9.108-112), however, indicates that Xerxes' wife was Amestris and describes her as masterminding a horrifying royal intrigue after the campaign to Greece in 480 BC One possibility is simply to state that neither Esther nor Vashti rose to the surface in Herodotus's records of royal women, of which there may have been quite a number if the lurid circumstances portrayed by Herodotus reflect a pattern for Xerxes. Amestris, after all, was a much more colorful character.

It may be possible, however, that Amestris and Vashti were the same individual. Names are notoriously fluid in transition from one language to another. Although "Vashti" bears little resemblance to "Amestris," it represents the English version of the Hebrew rendition of a Persian name. When Herodotus put the Persian name into Greek, substitutions were necessary because neither the first nor the second consonant had an equivalent in Greek. Amestris not only was Xerxes' wife but also was the daughter of one of his commanders, Otanes, who *was* one of the aforementioned seven (Herodotus *Hist.* 7.61). She had already borne Xerxes two sons, and Artaxerxes, the third, was born in 483 BC. These circumstances may have meant practically that although she could be banished from Xerxes' bedroom and deprived of the crown, there were limits on the banishment and good political reasons for keeping her in the extensive royal household.

Shortly after these events Xerxes headed off to wage war on the western front and was thus occupied for the next three years. It could be that Esther 2:1 ("after these things") refers to this passage of time and that the wholesale roundup of young women did not commence until his return. We do know that Esther's first entrance (after a year of preparation) was in the seventh year of the king, which would have been 479 BC (Esther 2:16). In the meantime, Herodotus (*Hist.* 9.108-112) dishes up the tidbit about Xerxes' dalliance with his niece, Amestris's jealousy, and her cunning and brutal revenge. It may be that after all *these* events Xerxes was more than ready for a new queen! Perhaps his remembering Vashti and what she had done (Esther 2:1) was not entirely with fondness if that memory included her activities in the intervening three years. In any case, the narrative by Herodotus does not explicitly state that Amestris was queen from the seventh to the twelfth years of Xerxes' reign.

2. Assessing the Character and Actions of Esther.

An initial reading of Esther's story leaves one with deep admiration for her courage and resilience in the midst of tragic, trying and extremely dangerous circumstances. As the narrative unfolds, her character develops from what appears to be an initially submissive charge of her cousin to a remarkable authority figure. Her demeanor in the court changed from pleasingly demure to brilliantly strategic. Nevertheless, critics of Esther have arisen in several quarters.

2.1. Esther Deemed a Deficient Role Model.

2.1.1. Feminist Reading of Esther. From a *feminist perspective, Esther's character is anemic in contrast to Vashti, who resolutely refused to be an object in the king's possession. Although the text does not explicitly state why Vashti refused to appear at the king's banquet, it is not difficult to surmise that she was loath to display herself before a large group of men well under the influence of their wine. Her assertiveness eliminated her from the court. Esther, by way of contrast, passively did what the authoritative voice commanded, whether it was Mordecai, Hegai or the king. Once she became queen, she exercised manipulative feminine wiles. All of this has prompted readers from the feminist perspective to view the text as unpleasantly subversive (*see* Feminist Interpretation).

2.1.2. Esther's Lack of Moral Judgment. From another quarter, Esther is deemed an appalling role model because she seems to have had no qualms about entering the harem and participating in a contest the sole focus of which was to satisfy the pagan and lascivious king's sexual appetite. From the outset of Israel's history, intermarriage with the people groups in Canaan was forbidden (Deut 7:1-4) because of the temptation to idolatry. The same motivation was behind the severe measures during the reform activities of Ezra and Nehemiah (Ezra 9:1-2; Neh 13:23-27) when foreign wives were put away. These took place in the mid-fifth century BC, about a generation after the time of Xerxes and Esther. Clearly, her marriage to a pagan king was reprehensible, as was her shameless participation in the royal court activities.

2.1.3. Esther's Abuse of Power. Even worse than her spineless caving in to the comfortable non-kosher life in the palace was her heartless brutality once she got her hands on power. Not only did she devise the banquet scheme so as to bring about the complete humiliation and demise of Haman; she then refused his pitiable plea for his life as he fell at her feet terrified of the king's wrath. After the death of Haman, she and Mordecai joined forces and engineered a counter-edict that sanctioned brutality on the part of the Jews who were defending themselves. Just as damning was Esther's inability to

leave well-enough alone after the first day of fighting between the Jews and their enemies; she had the cruel intent to inflict more violence in Susa for a second day and even asked that the ten sons of Haman be hanged publicly. And finally, the entire text celebrates the establishment of a new festival that commemorates a time of wholesale bloodshed (*see* Purim).

2.2. Restoring the Character of Esther.

2.2.1. Esther "Won Favor" in the Court. The text is emphatic that Esther was "taken" as part of the roundup. In contrast to the potential influence of Queen Vashti, who was fearsome enough to cause the king's chief advisor, Memuchan, to quail, Esther had no such position from which to stage any kind of resistance to the king's men. Nevertheless, contrary to a common presentation of Esther as comprehensively insipid, it is clear that from the moment she set foot in the harem, she was an actor within the wider machinery of the royal household and the court. The hint to this effect lies in the Hebrew idiom translated "she won favor" (which appears repeatedly), a more dynamic expression than the usual "found favor." This says something about her demeanor both in public and in private. Furthermore, she successfully mediated between Mordecai and the king when the first assassination plot was uncovered (Esther 2:22).

2.2.2. Esther's Courageous Choice. When it came time to move into the public arena, Esther courageously faced what appeared to be two equally dismal options. Mordecai's challenge to her was inescapably bleak: "Do not think that because you are in the king's house you alone of all the Jews will escape. For if you remain silent at this time, will relief and deliverance for the Jews arise from another place?" The implicit answer to that question was no. "You and your father's family will perish. And who knows but that you have come to the royal position for such a time as this?" (Esther 4:13-14). Generally, the first part of Esther 4:14 is translated "If you remain silent at this time, relief and deliverance will arise from another place, but you and your father's family will perish." It is possible, however, to read it as a question that is both preceded and followed by threats of her own demise along with all the other Jews. This suggests that Mordecai's words are not posed as a hopeful expectation of deliverance from *somewhere*. Instead, the implication was that once Haman discovered that Esther was both Jewish and related to Mordecai, her fate would be a terrible one. Mordecai did not say how he anticipated that Haman might find out that detail or precisely from what "quarter" this treachery might come. Esther's dilemma was one repeated throughout history; she was hemmed in by circumstances and expected either death as the penalty for breaking the royal law or death at the hands of mob violence. Mordecai's use of "who knows" in this context is a strong statement that Esther was indeed the Jews' only hope and that she was brought to this point for this time.

This was the critical moment for Esther, and she chose publicly to identify with her people even at the likely cost of her life. Her strength of character was manifested in her resolve both to defy the king's law and to confront Haman, the second-most powerful person in the empire. In this pivotal moment she took command, giving orders to Mordecai to mobilize their people. With the knowledge that fasting was an ancient and venerable part of her tradition, Esther called for a corporate and comprehensive fast, thus continuing the communal participation in this crisis that had begun earlier as a response to the edict. This exceeded all mandated fasts for severity: there was to be neither eating nor drinking for three days and nights. It was a radical appeal for God's intervention. Esther further determined that her young women (who may not have been Jewish) would fast in the same manner along with her. Following that, she would enter into the king's presence.

Her closing words to Mordecai are telling. In spite of this dramatic corporate appeal for divine mercy, she may have expected it to fail. It was, after all, contrary to the Persian law, whose effects she knew firsthand! Her statement can equally well be translated "When I perish, I perish," indicating her recognition that death was the likely outcome (Esther 4:16).

2.2.3. Dealing with the "Enemies of the Jews." Finally, what about the apparently wanton bloodletting at the end of the book, beginning with the death of Haman? To address this question, it is necessary to study the nature of Haman's treachery in its wider context. When Haman, whom the narrator repeatedly calls "the enemy of the Jews," initially went to the king to propose their destruction, he kept his charge vague, which was indispensable to gaining the permission that he sought. "There is a certain people dispersed and scattered among the peoples in all the provinces of your kingdom whose customs are different from those of all other people and who do not obey the king's laws; it is not worthwhile for the king to let them rest" (Esther 3:8). "A certain people" made them sound sinister, in that they were unnamed, and yet they are only "one" and therefore insignificant and dispensable. Haman's presentation started with the truth; they were indeed a dispersed people and, in some ways, separated. The accusation then moved to a half truth, that they had different customs from those of all other people, and finally to an outright lie, that they did not keep the laws of the king.

Declaring, "It is not worthwhile for the king to let them rest," Haman proposed a decree as the solution. "If it pleases the king, let a decree be written to annihilate them, and I will put ten thousand talents of silver into the royal treasury for the men who carry out this business" (Esther 3:9). There is a further malevolent facet to Haman's presentation to the king, and here we must presume that the narrator of the Hebrew text was careful to preserve a significant *word play in the dialogue. Haman may have intentionally played on the similar sounds of ʾbd (*lĕʾabbĕdām*, "to annihilate them") and ʿbd (*laʿăbādîm*, "for slaves"). If so, that would explain his appeal to the value of not allowing this unnamed people to "rest." It might also provide an interpretive framework for understanding Esther's reference when she revealed Haman's treachery at the second banquet to the effect that if they had only been sold into slavery, she would have kept silent (Esther 7:4). And finally, it might explain why the king seemed so entirely obtuse about the decree to which Esther referred. Perhaps he had been led to believe that Haman's intent was enslavement, when really it was wholesale murder. At any rate, in speaking to the king, this was the only term that Haman used; when the decree was written, with its triple terminology, there was no mistake as to what he meant. "Dispatches were sent by couriers to all the king's provinces with the order to destroy, kill and annihilate all the Jews—young and old, little children and women—on a single day, the thirteenth day of the twelfth month, the month of Adar, and to plunder their goods" (Esther 3:13). Esther therefore justifiably identified Haman to the king as "this evil Haman" (Esther 7:6).

The specific wording of this original decree is critical for understanding what happened when Mordecai and Esther issued their counter-decree. Once Haman was removed from the scene, the immediate tension subsided, perhaps for several months. Nevertheless, the edict still stood, and it was for that reason that Esther had to make a second and very emotional appeal, falling at the king's feet, weeping (Esther 8:3) and pleading that the original decree of annihilation be revoked. It is important to note that her initial and primary request was the revocation of the decree. When that was refused, other means had to be adopted. In the name of the king, Mordecai issued a decree granting the Jews in every city the right "to assemble and to stand for their lives; to destroy, kill and annihilate any armed force of any nationality or province that might attack them, little children and women, and to plunder their property" (Esther 8:11).

In the prior decree the objects of "to destroy, kill and annihilate" were "all the Jews, from young to old, little children and women." Here, "little children and women" immediately follow "those attacking them," suggesting that the Jews were given permission to kill those in every location who were still intent on carrying out the original decree by attacking them and their families. In light of the irrevocable decree that officially sanctioned their demise, Jewish action was inevitable. The narrative calls the victims of the Jews "enemies" and "those who hated them," noting that they were "men." The verbal pair "to kill" and "to annihilate" recurs in this description of the Jewish attack on their attackers (Esther 9:5, 6, 12) and represents the measured response put precisely in the terms of the decrees. If the five hundred men killed in Susa represented those who had attacked Jews, we might conclude that there was great hostility to Jews right in the capital. Once the bloodshed subsided, the narrative repeatedly emphasizes that the Jews got rest from their enemies (Esther 9:16-18).

Just as the relief is emphasized, so also is the fact that the Jews did not take any plunder from their enemies, even though they were permitted to do so by the measure-for-measure form of the decree. This last detail is stated three times immediately following the number of persons slain (Esther 9:6-10, 15, 16).

3. Lessons from Esther.
Although the central theological notion in Es-

ther is that human devices cannot counteract the sovereign will of God that his chosen people survive, these providential "coincidences," numerous as they are, are lodged in contexts that demand responsible and faithful human choices and action. In the face of apparent divine silence, God's people are compelled to choose between the imperfect alternatives that arise in the real ambiguities of life, just as Esther did. Finally, Esther challenges all readers to consider in what manner God has prepared each of us "for such a time as this."

See also ESTHER 1: BOOK OF; MORDECAI; PURIM; ROYAL COURT; VASHTI; WOMEN.

BIBLIOGRAPHY. **J. Baldwin,** *Esther* (TOTC; Downers Grove, IL: InterVarsity Press, 1984); **T. K. Beal,** *The Book of Hiding: Gender, Ethnicity, Annihilation, and Esther* (London: Routledge, 1997); **S. B. Berg,** *The Book of Esther: Motifs, Themes and Structure* (SBLDS 44; Missoula, MT: Scholars Press, 1979); **A. Berlin,** *Esther* (JPSBC; Philadelphia: Jewish Publication Society, 2001); **J. Berman,** "*Hadassah Bat Abihail*: The Evolution from Object to Subject in the Character of Esther," *JBL* 120 (2001) 647-69; **F. W. Bush,** *Ruth, Esther* (WBC 9; Dallas: Word, 1996); **M. V. Fox,** *Character and Ideology in the Book of Esther* (2nd ed.; Grand Rapids: Eerdmans, 2001); **B. Grossfeld,** *The Two Targums of Esther* (ArBib 18; Collegeville, MN: Liturgical Press, 1991); **L. R. Klein,** "Honor and Shame in Esther," in *A Feminist Companion to Esther, Judith and Susanna,* ed. A. Brenner (FCB 7; Sheffield: Sheffield Academic Press, 1995) 149-75; **T. S. Laniak,** *Shame and Honor in the Book of Esther* (SBLDS 165; Atlanta: Scholars Press, 1998); **J. D. Levenson,** *Esther* (OTL; Louisville: Westminster John Knox, 1997); **M. Simon,** trans., *Midrash Rabbah: Esther* (London: Soncino, 1939); **C. A. Moore,** ed., *Studies in the Book of Esther* (New York: KTAV, 1982); **L. B. Paton,** *A Critical and Exegetical Commentary on the Book of Esther* (ICC; New York: Scribner, 1908); **J. Rosenheim,** "Fate and Freedom in the Scroll of Esther," *Prooftexts* 12 (1992) 125-49; **W. H. Shea,** "Esther and History," *Concordia Journal* 13.3 (1987) 234-48; **B. D. Walfish,** *Esther in Medieval Garb: Jewish Interpretation of the Book of Esther in the Middle Ages* (Albany: State University of New York Press, 1993); **J. M. Wiebe,** "Esther 4:14: 'Will Relief and Deliverance Arise for the Jews from Another Place?'" *CBQ* 53 (1991) 409-15; **J. S. Wright,** "The Historicity of the Book of Esther," in *New Perspectives on the Old*

Testament, ed. J. Barton Payne (Waco, TX: Word, 1970) 37-47; **A. S. Yahuda,** "The Meaning of the Name Esther," *JRAS* (1946) 174-78.

E. A. Phillips

ETHICS

When we speak of ethics, we are speaking of relationship—our relationship to God, to our neighbor, and to the world we live in, and the proper conduct of these relationships. The English word *ethics* is derived from the Greek word *ethos*, which bears the sense of "conduct" or "practice." The OT does not have a synonymous term. Perhaps the closest relative to this word is *mûsār*, which means "discipline" or "teaching" (Kaiser, 2). The term *mûsār* is suggestive of an electric fence that shocks cattle, preventing them wandering into dangers such as the edge of a cliff. So this term is more indicative of the warning system of OT ethics than of the day-to-day principles that regulate human behavior. Although it belongs in the category of ethics, it is only one dimension of this field, thus illustrating the observation that the OT has no single term for *ethics*.

1. Methodology for the Study of Old Testament Ethics
2. Is Old Testament Ethics Normative or Descriptive?
3. The Basis for the Old Testament Ethical System: Creation and Response
4. The Ethics of the Wisdom Literature, Psalms and Writings
5. Social Levels of Wisdom Ethics
6. Conclusion

1. Methodology for the Study of Old Testament Ethics.

Methodology is critical to understanding the Bible, as with any literature. One's approach to the study of OT ethics is crucial, and one method of study will shape the outcome in a way that another might not. The historical-critical method, for example, approaches the biblical text, and thus the study of ethics, through the lens of this methodology. The Wisdom literature, the Prophets and the Pentateuch have their own critical histories, and so their ethics will not look alike. In fact, the historical-critical method has generally viewed the Prophets as representing the highest form of OT ethics. They do not, so the proponents of this method insist, depend so heavily on the Pentateuch, since that portion of the OT was developing only parallel to the Prophets, and only in certain aspects, but did not reach its ethical zenith until the postexilic era. Yet, there is good reason to insist that the Prophets, Wisdom literature and *Psalms, along with much other material of the OT, are premised on the Torah legislation and the "primal events" of Israel's history (Fletcher, 50).

Although B. Childs's canonical method is not ignorant of the results of the historical-critical method, it nevertheless takes more seriously the final form of the literature as we have received it and insists that no study of Scripture is complete until that full dimension of the biblical text has been given its full right to speak. The works of W. C. Kaiser Jr. and C. J. H. Wright fall within this methodology. Generally speaking, this method assumes that there is an underlying unity in the OT that finds its origin in the stories and legislation of the Pentateuch. If we think of the three paradigms of OT faith as Torah, prophecy and wisdom, Torah would form the vertex of the triangle, with prophecy and wisdom being the two flanking sides. That is, the fundamental principles of Israelite religion are laid out in the Torah (*see* Law), with its stories and laws, while the prophets distill the moral essence of the Torah and make that their primary message. At the same time, the wisdom teachers, especially as represented by the book of *Proverbs, draw upon the language and precepts of Torah to commend their ethical position to their students and community of faith. R. E. Murphy (1978, 39) called this a "shared approach to reality," shared by prophets, priests and *sages alike in varying degrees. This writer assumes that the ethics of the Wisdom literature, Psalms and the Writings is essentially a modification of Torah ethics but still identifiable as Torah.

The book of Proverbs presents the sage's instruction as Torah (Prov 3:1; 4:2; 7:2), as it also presents the teaching of parents (Prov 1:8; 6:20). The book of *Ecclesiastes, breathing a different atmosphere than Proverbs, no longer espouses the view that one must believe because the parents did, with *Qohelet taking the liberty to explore the range of wisdom options and life experiences, only to conclude that the whole duty of humankind is to "fear God and keep his commandments" (Eccles 12:13). The book of *Job, in comparison, is concerned with the relationship between the divine and the human, which Job explores in dialogue with his friends, finally submitting himself to the overwhelming power of the Creator, who speaks out of the whirlwind, chiding Job for his presumptuous spirit. *Song of Songs, despite its strongly sexual tone, raises the age-old issue of the relationship between life and death (Song 8:6) and redraws the primal contrast as one between love and death, declaring that love, unlike life, cannot be cancelled out by death (Murphy 1990, 100-105; Webb, 30-32). The book of Psalms is very different from these four books, for it is an anthology of prayers, hymns and meditations collected over hundreds of years. Yet, remarkably, the book preserves the basic ethical system of the wisdom books and indeed, given Psalm 1 as our clue, is set forth by the final editor as a book of wisdom piety.

2. Is Old Testament Ethics Normative or Descriptive?

Before we proceed further, we should consider the question of whether or not OT ethics has a normative force—that is, applies to all ages and societies. This position stands over against the view that the laws of the Torah are descriptive—that is, are essentially historical information whose prescriptive character was binding only on ancient Israel. For Christians, this question is tied to the issue of the place of the OT in the Christian faith. This has been a hotly debated topic through the centuries, and the church's position generally has been to separate the moral and ritual laws and to designate the moral laws as normative and the ritual laws as descriptive. This approach is basically valid, but we do have to answer the question, as R. Wilson (65) has insisted, of why Christians do not accept certain laws, such as the laws that prescribe the execution of heretics (Deut 13) or the annihilation of one's enemies (Deut 20), both of which seem to have a moral rather than a ritual thrust. The distinction that Christians traditionally have made is derived in large part from the NT ethic of love as taught by Jesus: we are to love our enemies and turn the other cheek to our abusers (Luke 6:27-31). Yet this law of love is derived from the OT itself, for Israel was directed to love the Lord with their whole being (Deut 6:5) and to love their neighbors as themselves (Lev 19:18). In fact, OT ethics endorsed a broad range of behavior, extending all the way from "an eye for an eye and a tooth for a tooth" (Exod 21:24 [the law of retaliation]) to the law of loving God with all one's heart and loving one's neighbor as oneself. Although Christians have to some extent embraced the full range of this ethical system, Jesus emphasized the upper end of the OT ethical range (Mk 12:28-31) and de-emphasized the lower range by commanding love for one's enemies (Mt 5:43-46). By that authority, Christians have tended, at least in the modern era, not to execute heretics and not to annihilate their enemies.

3. The Basis for the Old Testament Ethical System: Creation and Response.

The ethical system of the OT is not laid out in systematic form; rather it is found in various dimensions of the Hebrew Bible, beginning with creation itself. Two concepts in the book of Genesis lay the foundation for OT ethics.

3.1. God's Image. The first concept is God's creation of humanity in his own image (Gen 1:26-27). Initially, the Creator put his stamp, his own image and likeness, upon the human person, so that Israel and all humanity to follow could never deny that the creation had a direct relationship to the Creator. Forever God had stamped upon humanity the personal pronoun *mine*, but Adam and Eve tried to erase the divine claim and replace it with their own possessive pronoun, *ours*. OT ethics is the system of human behavior that regulates the human-to-divine and human-to-human relationships, whose object is to reestablish God's claims on his creation.

3.2. God's Goodness. The second concept is the idea of God's goodness. Standing behind the creation story of Genesis 1 is the repeated declaration about creation that "God saw that it was good" (Gen 1:4, 10, 12, 18, 21, 25). This declaration points in the direction of, and climaxes with, the consummate "and behold, it was very good" (Gen 1:31). The idea of "good" in Genesis 1 had not yet flowered into the virtue of "goodness," but the Supreme Good, as W. Bruce (18) calls it, has already become the foundation of OT ethics because the creation narrative reveals the basic character of God, who is good, and who declared his creation to be good, a reflection of his own character.

This idea of "good" occurs in company with that of "evil" in Genesis 2—3, when the Lord God commanded Adam not to eat of the tree of "the knowledge of good and evil." Space here does not permit a discussion of the nature of that knowledge, but we can note that "good" was paired with "evil," drawing out the notion of a contrast between the two. The point is that the "good" of Genesis 1 is not lost as the story of the generic created order opens out into the creation of individuals (Gen 2) and their subsequent fall (Gen 3); rather, the introduction of the "good" in Genesis 1 is followed by its pairing with "evil" in Genesis 2—3, thus setting the stage for an ethic that is distinguished by good and evil. Admittedly, the problem of good and evil is not treated in any systematic way in the OT. The book of Job is the closest that the Hebrew Scriptures come to such a treatment, and it is far from being a systematic one. In fact, the theological thrust of Job is much more in the direction of Job's relationship to God, and thus the human-divine relationship, than of the problem of good and evil.

Deuteronomy sets forth the same set of choices between good and evil, associating good with life, and evil with death, precisely the associations of the Genesis account. When Deuteronomy introduces this dual concept, it is not coincidental that Moses describes the innocence of childhood as an absence of the knowledge of good and evil (Deut 1:34). Nor is it by chance that the land of Canaan is designated the "good" land, just as God called his creation "good" (e.g., Deut 1:25, 35; 3:25). Canaan was, in Deuteronomic terms, a reclaimed Eden.

The assumption of the Genesis text is that God is good, but the first time that the text informs us that God himself knew good and evil is after the fall (Gen 3:22). Yet Adam and Eve, once they had acquired this treasured knowledge, did not know good and evil as God did; rather, theirs was a distorted knowledge acquired from the vantage point of disobedience. From that point on, the OT seeks to introduce a corrective into the divine-human relationship, a corrective that could result only from obedience to God's commandments because the problem arose from the violation of the divine command. God's knowledge of good and evil, perfect and undistorted, set the stage for future revelation of the nature of sin and its corrective, redemption. Obedience becomes the means of implementing the corrective, but the story of redemption is far wider and more complex than the matter of obedience to God's laws. The factor of grace both surrounds the theme of obedience and augments it. That is to say, once human beings have obeyed God's commands, it is only divine grace that puts the stamp of acceptance on their response, and, beyond that, human obedience falls short of meriting the divine blessing, which is nothing more than a gift of grace.

3.3. Obedience as Ethical Response. Actually, the concept of redemption as such does not occur in the Wisdom literature (Job, Proverbs, Ecclesiastes, Song of Songs and some psalms), which is a quandary in itself. Yet, it may very well be that wisdom as a religious paradigm attempted to reclaim creation from the nature religions of Israel's world and, in so doing, shifted creation into the place of redemption. That is not to suggest that redemption as a function of the divine will was lost. In fact, it was preserved in the human function of obedience to the divine laws and in the ethical healing effect that this obedience had on the divine-human relationship. Thus wisdom presents us with a theological paradigm in which creation, rather than redemption (as in the case of the Pentateuch and the Prophets), has become the central feature of God's self-revelation. Yet creation was in itself revelatory, and in the natural order one was to see and again acknowledge God's claims on the world. Although not the same as redemption, it had a redeeming quality.

The idea of a good creation, with the consummate "It was very good," modulates in the Genesis narrative into the idea of obedience. The elemental nature of the fall narrative lies at the base of OT ethics. The first law was God's command not to eat of the tree of the knowledge of good and evil, in which the notion of good begins to take shape and assume its place as the opposite of evil. Even though the meaning of these two terms is not explicated in the narrative, the text implies that "good" was associated with the Creator, who brought a good world into existence and formed humankind in his own image before he distinguished the creation as "very good." From that point on, at least up through the Abraham narrative, the virtue of obedience became the criterion by which the character of the major actors was measured. Childs (204-21) titles his discussion of ethics "The Shape of the Obedient Life." In obedience to God's command, "Noah did this; he did all that God commanded him" (Gen 6:22; cf. Gen 7:5, 9, 16). The narrative about Babel again shows humanity's attempt to erase the divine "mine" and replace it with the human claim "ours" ("Come, let us build ourselves a city, and a tower with its top in the heavens, and let us make a name for ourselves" [Gen 11:4]). Of significance is the recurrence of the divine plural "Let us go down" (cf. "Let us make man in our image" [Gen 1:26]), which signals God in his eternal fullness, whether we understand it as a trinitarian plural or otherwise. In both instances the action that this plural signifies was of monumental importance and, like the Noah account, is followed by another narrative of obedience, the story of Abraham: "So Abram went, as the LORD had told him" (Gen 12:4). The narrative of obedience is further sustained in the covenant of circumcision: "Then Abraham took his son Ishmael and all the slaves born in his house or bought with his money, every male among the men of Abraham's house, and he circumcised the flesh of their foreskins that very day, *as God had said to him* (Gen 17:23 NRSV [italics added])."

In Genesis 18 the Lord introduced a question that divulged the spiritual stature of Abraham: "Shall I hide from Abraham what I am about to do, seeing that Abraham shall become a great and mighty nation, and all the nations of the earth shall be blessed in him?" (Gen 18:17 NRSV). The Lord's answer to the question disclosed the role that Abraham was to play in the ethical life of Israel: "No, for I have chosen him, that he may charge *[ṣwh]* his children and his household after him to keep *[šmr]* the way of the LORD by doing righteousness and justice; so that the LORD may bring about for Abraham what he has promised him" (Gen 18:19 NRSV).

The patriarch was to teach his children and household the ethical ways of life, in the writer's words, "the way of the LORD by doing righteousness and justice." This story naturally continues in the birth of Isaac, with Abraham as the model and the agent of obedience: "And Abraham circumcised his son Isaac when he was eight days old, *as God had commanded him* (Gen 21:4 NRSV [italics added]). The narrator installs the capstone of the theme in Genesis 26:5, when he declares that: "Abraham obeyed *[smᶜ]* my voice and kept *[šmr]* my charge [also from *šmr*], my commandments [from verbal root *ṣwh*, 'command'], my statutes, and my laws" (Gen 26:5 NRSV).

The task of humanity, as the author states it in Genesis 2:15, is "The LORD God took the man and put him in the garden of Eden to till it and keep *[šmr]* it." The verb *šmr* has changed, from "keeping" the garden to "obeying" God, both ideas expressed by the same word. For Abraham, it is no longer maintaining what was committed to mankind—keeping the garden—rather the charge has become communicating the ethical demands of God to future generations. Therefore, before the Lord formally gave the law to Israel on Sinai, Abraham was already the model of the law-keeper in his life of obedience, in contrast to Adam and Eve.

These narratives of obedience lay the foundation for the law that follows in the Torah, law that called for obedience, which was the positive response to the good God, both creator and lawgiver. When Moses set the words of the law before Israel at Sinai in the form of the so-called Covenant Code (Ex 20:22—23:33), the people ratified it with words that resonate with the Noahic and Abrahamic response of obedience: "All that the LORD has spoken we will do and we will be obedient" (Ex 24:7; also Ex 19:8).

Although the Torah narrative does not consciously lay out the foundation of the OT ethical system, the pattern is nevertheless woven into the fabric of the narrative as an intermittent color, and when we look at the narrative landscape, we see the obedience theme as part of the color scheme. Thus the Torah relates the story of Israel's beginnings as a history of obedience to God and his laws.

4. The Ethics of the Wisdom Literature, Psalms and Writings.

The Wisdom literature, Psalms and Writings are a diverse collection of books. The remainder of this article deals largely with the Wisdom literature, under the assumption that wisdom in its preexilic and postexilic forms essentially represented the ethical norm of Israel's faith, stripped of the ritual trappings of Mosaic faith and of the covenantal language of the prophets. Yet the proponents of wisdom did not abandon ritual or covenant. Although those were not the frontispiece of faith, they did not detract from the ethical core of Israel's faith. Wisdom was a religious paradigm that put forth the essential elements of Mosaic religion, not abolishing them altogether but rather setting forth their moral essence. Thus the cultic system became less important than the ethical meaning that stood behind it, in much the same way as the prophets understood the sacrificial system (Mic 6:8). The prophets did not eliminate it but rather put forward its ethical meaning.

4.1. Proverbs as the Ethical Norm. A case can be made for viewing the book of Proverbs as the book that sets forth the ethical norm of Israelite faith, particularly as the wisdom thinkers wanted to present it. Hezekiah's part in one stage of its editing was no accident but rather most likely was an intentional effort to provide an ethical norm for reformation and renewal. Although Proverbs does not parade the covenantal frame of the faith, it is not unaware of it. This is evidenced in the fact that Proverbs overwhelmingly employs the covenant name for God, "YHWH" (87x), suggesting that the thought of Proverbs belongs in the theological category of Mosaic religion (Waltke, 44-45). In addition to this observation, the doctrine of *creation occurs numerous times, distributed quite consistently in the various collections (Waltke, 68):

Collection 1 (Prov 1—9)	3:19-20; 8:22-31
Collection 2 (Prov 10:1—22:16)	14:31; 16:11; 17:5; 20:12; 22:2
Collection 3 (Prov 25—29)	29:13
Collection 4 (Prov 30—31)	30:2-4

In fact, the ethical system of Proverbs cannot be understood without a knowledge of creation: "The LORD by wisdom founded the earth; by understanding he established the heavens; by his knowledge the deeps broke open, and the clouds drop down the dew (Prov 3:19-20 NRSV).

This same theme is played out again in Proverbs 8 when Wisdom revealed that the Lord possessed her at the beginning of his work. The announcement of wisdom in Proverbs 8, however, is more an announcement of her presence at creation—thus implying her authority (Waltke, 69)—than a declaration of instrumental creation. While John refers to the Word rather than wisdom, he combines these two truths in his prologue, the instrumental nature of the Word and its presence in creation: " In the beginning was the Word, and the Word was with God [presence], and the Word was God. He was in the beginning with God [presence]; all things were made through him, and without him was not anything made that was made [instrumental]" (John 1:1 NRSV).

4.2. The Central Moral Virtues: Righteousness, Justice, Equity. The introduction to Proverbs (Prov 1:1-7) lays out for consideration several ethical terms for the moral virtues. W. Brown (25) understands these virtues to fall into systematic categories, giving a *chiastic center with the "moral, communal virtues" as the nuclear focus ("righteousness, justice, and equity" [Prov 1:3b ESV]):

A Intellectual values: wisdom and instruction (v. 2a)
  B Literary wisdom: insight (v. 2b)
    C Instrumental virtue: wise dealing (v. 3a)
    ———————————
      D Communal Virtues: righteousness, justice, equity (v. 3b)
    ———————————
    C' Instrumental virtues: prudence, knowledge, discretion, listening, guidance (vv. 4-5)
  B' Literary wisdom: proverbs, sayings, words of the wise, riddles (v. 6)
A' Intellectual virtue: fear of the Lord (v. 7)

Some may disagree with Brown's categories, but the text does tend to thrust the communal virtues of "righteousness, justice, and equity" to the center of the ethical system. That judgment is verified when the teacher of Proverbs 2, after having instructed his students in the way of wisdom, summarily concludes, "Then you will understand righteousness and justice and equity, every good path" (Prov 2:9 ESV).

4.2.1. Righteousness. The use of the first word, *"righteousness" (ṣedeq), to describe accurate weights (Lev 19:36), suggests that the term, in its most basic meaning, refers to a standard by which other weights were judged to be accurate or inaccurate, a notion that Proverbs affirms (Prov 11:1; 16:11). This primary meaning transfers naturally to moral conduct, both of the individual and the community. Modeled by the Creator himself, this is the standard by which the individual and community are judged (Ps 35:24). It is not an arbitrary standard but rather is one that is foundational to God's own being: "Righteousness and justice are the foundation of your throne." Ethics reflects God's character. This truth is emphasized in the Torah when the Lord instructs the Israelites to conduct their lives in accordance with his character: "Be holy, for I am holy" (e.g., Lev 11:44). Nor is it an impersonal measurement, for "steadfast love and faithfulness go before you" (Ps 89:14). God holds individuals and Israel alike to a standard of conduct, yet that standard is established and maintained by a strong measure of grace, intended for the welfare and betterment of human society and humanity's relationship to the Lord.

Actually, one cannot separate individual and community ethics. The individual ethic feeds into the community and builds its character, while the community ethic supports and undergirds the individual ethic. The OT knows a very delicate balance between individual and corporate identities. They blend into each other, and one validates the other. They do not exist independently.

4.2.2. Justice. The second term, *justice (mišpāṭ),* belongs to the legal vocabulary of the OT, though not exclusively. Both the verb *(špt)* and the noun refer to an action that restores the order of a community (Liedke, 1393). In the relative sense of these terms, justice is what must be done in a given situation to restore and assure conformity to righteousness *(ṣedeq, ṣĕdāqâ).* Although we should not overstate the case, *justice* has an action nuance compared to the more stative nuance of *righteousness* (Wright, 256-57). Thus these two terms often pair up to express the idea of "social justice" (Ps 72:2), even taking the dual concept to its source at the throne of God (Ps 97:5) and attributing to this duality an interactive force in the individual's life: "I put on righteousness *[ṣedeq],* and it put on me; my justice *[mišpāṭ]* was like a robe and a turban" (Job 29:14 [my translation]).

This manner of individual and community conduct produces a state of order in accordance with the Creator's will. Human society, in terms of the Wisdom literature and Psalms, was to reflect the order of creation. In reference to Psalm 146:4, W. Brueggemann (155) comments that God's creation "has a specific ethical commitment and bias, against the 'plans' of the wicked, who attempt to utilize the power of creation for their own destructive ends." The standard of maintenance of this world is righteousness.

4.2.3. Equity. The third major term of the central ethical system set forth in Proverbs is "equity" *(mêšārîm* or *yêšārîm),* a word that bears the sense of "straight" (from *yāšār),* often applied to speech (Prov 8:6), and sometimes used almost synonymously with righteousness (Ps 9:9). God's words and commands are "straight," or they are "upright," characterized by integrity

(Ps 19:9), and the Lord judges the nations with equity (Ps 9:9; 96:10; 98:9). The mode by which God judges the world is the same one that regulates the conduct of the human community (Prov 1:3; 2:9; 8:6, 9).

4.3. The Fear of the Lord Incarnate. The summary statement of ethical behavior is contained in the phrase *"the fear of the LORD" (Prov 1:7; 9:10). Brown (28) calls this the "external contours of ethical character" and observes that "the 'fear' of God deals fundamentally with the heart and center of character, namely the position of the person *in relation* to God."

4.3.1. Job. An "incarnation" of this person who fears the Lord occurs in Job 31, where Job's self-confession contours the spiritual disposition of the righteous individual. The prologue had described Job as a man who was "blameless and upright *[yāšār,* related to *mêšārîm],* one who feared God and turned away from evil" (Job 1:1, 8; 2:3). Then the climactic moment in the dialogue comes when Job announces that God (not humans) knows the way to wisdom, and he is not only the Creator of the world but also the one who defines wisdom itself and, on this occasion, defines it in the same terms that he has used to describe his servant Job in the prologue (Job 1:1): "And [God] said to man, 'Behold, the fear of the Lord, that is wisdom, and to turn away from evil is understanding" (Job 28:28 ESV). By dramatic irony, the reader knows that God is describing his servant Job, to the dismay of Job's friends, and even more important is the fact that this is the only point in the dialogue where we hear the Lord's voice, thus signaling its importance.

The fear of God, then, is a disposition that involves a moral commitment that causes one to shun evil. This divine affirmation of Job's wisdom and thus his character in the poem on wisdom is underscored by Job's own confession in Job 31 of his righteous life. Here, at the end of the dialogue, in order to establish his innocence, Job takes not one oath, but several, to set securely his righteousness before God. The outline of this profile presents the reader with that of the righteous person. Job's relationship to his fellow human beings is largely the subject of this profile: *women (Job 31:1-12), slaves (Job 31:13-15), the poor (Job 31:16-23) and his enemies (Job 31:29-30). Quite significantly, however, he deals with his attitude toward wealth (Job 31:23-24), the power source of much social injustice in ancient times (as well as modern), and the troublesome issue of idolatry (Job 31:26-28), which would have been the most flagrant violation of the OT ethical code, verbalized in the first commandment (Ex 20:3).

Job's oath to establish his innocence toward women—he had not committed adultery (Job 31:1-12)—includes not only the denial of the act itself (Job 31:9) but also of the mental violation of other women (Job 31:1), in keeping with the tenth commandment (Ex 20:17). The ethical principles of Proverbs demand that the patrons of wisdom abstain from adultery (Prov 5; 6:20-35; 7), quite in keeping with Job's understanding of its seriousness, even though Proverbs may be more concerned with the effect of adulterous behavior on society, whereas Job's concern was God's own view of his personal righteousness (Job 31:4).

Job's treatment of his slaves stemmed from his conviction that the same God had made them both (Job 31:15)—a high ethic, to be sure. No less elevated in the ethical system was the view that his treatment of the poor arose from a compassionate conviction that he should treat them as if he were their father or mother (Job 31:18). Not surprisingly, the psalmist, as often was the case, shared the ethics of wisdom and depicted the Lord as the father of the fatherless and the protector of widows (Ps 68:5). This comes close, suggests G. Fohrer (15), to the commandment "You shall love your neighbor as yourself" (Lev 19:18). The proverbs of *Solomon lay out the view that kindness to the poor is equivalent to honoring God (Prov 14:31), and lending to the poor is lending to the Lord (Prov 19:17), an idea also attested by the psalmist (Ps 41:1).

Perhaps most impressive of all is Job's attitude anticipating Jesus' teaching regarding moral posture toward enemies: we should love our enemies and pray for them (Mt 5:43-48). Although Job asserts that he did not rejoice when his enemies fell into trouble (Job 31:29-30), there is still a difference between Job's position and Jesus' teaching, but Job is definitely looking ahead in Jesus' direction.

When we look at this portrait of the righteous man in Job 31, we must confess that, as Fohrer says, Job "stands almost alone upon an ethical summit" (Fohrer, 19). His ethics was cut from the fabric of wisdom teaching, and that teaching was probably more orthodox and normative in the late preexilic and postexilic eras than frequently recognized.

4.3.2. The Excellent Wife. In addition to the general description of those individuals who portray the ethical conduct prescribed by Proverbs, this book also incarnates that person who fears the Lord in the "excellent wife" (Prov 31:10-31). Using the literary form of an *acrostic poem, the poet proceeds through the letters of the Hebrew alphabet, exhausting all twenty-two letters to symbolize a full and complete description of the wise woman, who is synonymous with the "righteous" woman. As such a person, the practical activities of her life verify her spiritual status. Compared to Job 31, hers is a much more practical wisdom, although that is not to be viewed in any disparaging way. This woman is the paragon of "the helper fit for him," the original description of Adam's complement (Gen. 1:18 RSV). She inspires trust in her husband (Prov 31:15), has the best intentions to do good and not harm (Prov 31:12), is diligent in her labor and business dealings (Prov 31:13-18), provides for her maidens (Prov 31:15 [cf. Job 31:13-15]), gives to the poor (Prov 31:20 [cf. Job 31:16-23]), and kindly teaches wisdom (Prov 31:26). Her works praise her in the gate of the city (Prov 31:31). In summary, she turns the commands of wisdom into a beatitude (Prov 31:28) (Brown, 38).

5. The Social Levels of Wisdom Ethics.

Wisdom ethics can be viewed on the level of the individual, the community and the court. Proverbs is a mixture of all three ranks of the social order and the ethical system that regulates them. At one stage of the social ladder, the individual is commanded to keep wisdom's teachings ("My son" [e.g., Prov 2:1; 3:1]), and at another, the community is the object of wisdom's commands ("Hear, sons" [Prov 4:1]). We might say that wisdom sought to change the society from the bottom up, from the individual to the community. The prophets had sought to change it from the top down, from the community/nation to the individual. The two perspectives are complementary. At the higher end of the social spectrum, however, were the king and his *royal court. Despite the power of kings, Wisdom would have them know that they reign only by her authority and sanction (Prov 8:15-16). Their throne, like God's, is established by righteousness (Prov 16:12), and their court is distinguished by right speech (Prov 16:13). Laying aside ethical concerns for a moment, one must pay attention to the sheer authority and power of kings and seek their favor (Prov 16:14-15). In addition to Solomon's imprimatur on Proverbs, Hezekiah added his own contribution (Prov 25:1), exercising his prerogative as king to "search things out" (Prov 25:2). But one cannot expect to turn the searchlight upon the king himself and figure him out, for his heart is not subject to human searching in the same way as one would search out ideas (Prov 25:3). He must be kept at an awesome distance. Yet, the simple principle by which a king secures his court is to remove the undermining elements of evil so that his throne will be established in righteousness (Prov 25:4-5). In view of his power, all the king's subjects should approach him not presumptuously but rather humbly, and if they are worthy, he will elevate them (Prov 25:6-7).

6. Conclusion.

Although the motif of obedience to God's commands is not an explicit theme throughout the Wisdom literature, wisdom's teachings are premised upon it. I have suggested that obedient response to wisdom's instruction is none other than an adaptation of the legal system of the Torah, with its ethical claims in the forefront. This response, laid out in the opening chapters of the Torah, underwrites the entirety of wisdom ethics or any other ethical representations of the OT. It is premised upon the nature of the God whose demands, first revealed in Scripture as putting his imprimatur of goodness on the world that he created. So God's subjects should obey his commandments because he is good.

See also CREATION THEOLOGY; KINSMAN-REDEEMER AND LEVIRATE; LAW; MARRIAGE AND SEX; RIGHTEOUSNESS.

BIBLIOGRAPHY. **J. Barton,** *Understanding Old Testament Ethics* (Louisville: Westminster John Knox, 2003); **W. P. Brown,** *Character in Crisis: A Fresh Approach to the Wisdom Literature of the Old Testament* (Grand Rapids: Eerdmans, 1996); **W. S. Bruce,** *The Ethics of the Old Testament* (Edinburgh: T & T Clark, 1895); **W. Brueggemann,** *Theology of the Old Testament: Testimony, Dispute, Advocacy* (Minneapolis: Fortress, 1997); **B. S. Childs,** *Old Testament Theology in a Canonical Context* (Philadelphia: Fortress, 1989); **V. H. Fletcher,** "The Shape of Old Testament Ethics," *SJT* 24 (1971) 47-73; **G. Fohrer,** "The Righteous Man in Job 31," in *Essays in Old Testament Ethics: J. Philip Hyatt, in Memoriam,* ed. J. L. Crenshaw and J. T. Willis (New York: KTAV, 1974) 1-22; **W. C. Kaiser Jr.,** *Toward Old Testament Ethics* (Grand Rapids: Zondervan, 1983); **G. Liedke,** "שׁפט *špt*, to judge" *TLOT* 3.1392-99; **R. E. Murphy,** *Song of Songs* (Hermeneia; Minneapolis: Fortress, 1990); idem, "Wisdom—Theses and Hypotheses," in *Israelite Wisdom: Theological and Literary Essays in Honor of Samuel Terrien,* ed. J. G. Gammie et al. (Missoula, MT: Scholars Press, 1978) 35-42; **E. Otto,** *Theologische Ethik des Alten Testaments* (TW 3/2; Stuttgart: Kohlhammer, 1994); idem, "Of Aims and Methods in Hebrew Bible Ethics," *Semeia* 66 (2004) 161-72; **B. K. Waltke,** *The Book of Proverbs: Chapters 1—15* (NICOT; Grand Rapids: Eerdmans, 2004); **B. G. Webb,** *Five Festal Garments* (NSBT; Downers Grove, IL: IVP Academic, 2000); **R. R. Wilson,** "Sources and Methods in the Study of Ancient Israelite Ethics," in *Canon, Theology, and Old Testament Interpretation: Essays in Honor of Brevard S. Childs,* ed. G. M. Tucker, D. L. Petersen and R. R. Wilson (Philadelphia: Fortress, 1988) 62-74; **C. J. H. Wright,** *Old Testament Ethics for the People of God* (Downers Grove, IL: InterVarsity Press, 2004).

C. H. Bullock

EVIL. *See* THEODICY.

EXILE. *See* ESTHER 1: BOOK OF.

EXPERIENTIAL INTERPRETATION. *See* HERMENEUTICS.

F

FEAR OF THE LORD

The fear of God/Yahweh is a major theme in the Psalms and Wisdom literature, but it is not found in the other books considered in this volume. It is also found in the Torah (e.g., Ex 9:30; 18:21; Deut 2:25; 5:29), the Historical Books (e.g., 1 Sam 12:14, 24) and the Prophets (e.g., Is 8:13; Jer 5:22, 24; Mic 6:9).

1. Terminology
2. Proverbs
3. Job
4. Ecclesiastes
5. Psalms
6. Conclusion

1. Terminology.

The Hebrew term for fear typically used in the expression "fear of God/Yahweh" is *yir'at,* from the verb *yr'*. W. Van Pelt and W. Kaiser (*NIDOTTE* 2.527-33) indicate that the word has a semantic range that runs from respect to horror. It is difficult to determine the exact English equivalent to this word in the phrase. In most occurrences the "fear of God" is a virtue that is encouraged and leads to right behavior and good results. In some occurrences the "fear of God" is negative (see below on Ecclesiastes as well as reference to the Historical Books there). Thus it is potentially misleading to say that *yir'at* always means "fear" or "respect." But even in its positive use (such as Prov 1:7), there is a debate as to whether it means "respect" or "fear." It may be that the word falls somewhere in between these two English words. "Respect" may not do justice to the gravity of the word, though "fear" may connote an unhealthy dread. Still, the object of fear is the Creator of all, the one who is sovereign over his creation. Those who experience fear in his presence know their rightful place in the universe. An English word that may be a candidate for translation is "awe," understood as veneration of the sacred. With this definition we come close to an understanding of *worship, which van Pelt and Kaiser believe is appropriate for *yir'at* with God or Yahweh as its object.

The verb *pahad* and its nominal form can also be used with God as object. Many translations render both *pahad* and *yr'* as fear, thus obscuring any difference between the two. It is true that *pahad yhwh/'ĕlōhîm* is found more often in negative contexts, particularly referring to the kind of dread that God's enemies experience in holy war or in the context of (potential) judgment on Israelites (1 Sam 11:7; 2 Chron 17:10; 20:29). Even so, it can be used in the sense of a virtue like *yir'at yhwh/'ĕlōhîm* (2 Chron 19:7, and the epithet "Fear of Isaac" [Gen 31:42, 53]). It occurs in this sense in our literature in Psalm 36:2; 119:120 and Proverbs 28:14. In the following discussion we will not differentiate between *pahad* and *yir'at yhwh/'ĕlōhîm* since there is not a significant (or at least discernible) difference in meaning.

2. Proverbs.

"Fear of the Lord" is a fundamental theological idea in the book of Proverbs (Longman 2006, 57-58, 100-104). According to Proverbs 1:2, the purpose of the book is to teach the reader "wisdom and discipline." As one can see in chapters 10—31 (which contains most of the actual proverbs), wisdom is a practical category, a kind of skill in living. The proverbs are pithy observations, admonitions and prohibitions that advocate certain behavior that the book defines as wise, and discourages other behavior (often the opposite) that it calls foolish. For instance, Proverbs 10:4 states: "A slack palm makes poverty; a determined hand makes rich," the former behavior is *folly and the latter is wise. Such proverbs seem devoid of theological content, but this is true only if they are read outside of the context of the entire book.

The preface (Prov 1:1-7) concludes with perhaps the book's most memorable statement:

The fear of Yahweh is the beginning
of knowledge,
but fools despise wisdom and discipline.
(Prov 1:7)

The preface of the book gives way to a series of speeches, mostly of a father to his son, but occasionally of a woman named Wisdom to all the men who are passing by her mountaintop house (see Woman Wisdom and Woman Folly). Chapters 1—9 form a unit that introduces the proverbs of chapters 10—31. As a matter of fact, they provide a kind of lens through which the individual proverbs in those latter chapters should be read. It is interesting that we find the teaching about the "fear of Yahweh" being the "beginning of knowledge" not only at the beginning of this first part of the book but also at the end, thus forming an *inclusio (Prov 9:10, though here "wisdom" [hokmâ] is used rather than "knowledge" [dāʿat]). The phrase is also found in Proverbs 1:29; 2:5; 3:7; 8:13, as well as Proverbs 10:27; 14:2, 26, 27; 15:16, 33; 16:6; 19:23; 22:4; 23:17; 24:21; 28:14; 29:25; 31:30.

But what does it mean that the fear of Yahweh is the beginning of knowledge/wisdom? We have already discussed the difficulty of giving a precise English equivalent to fear in this context, though the basic premise seems to be that to fear Yahweh is to stand in a subservient position to him, to acknowledge one's dependence on him. In this it seems to be the opposite of being "wise in one's own eyes," a point that is made explicitly in Proverbs 3:7. ("Don't be wise in your own eyes. Fear Yahweh and turn away from evil.") Thus it is appropriate to think that proper fear of Yahweh leads to humility and an avoidance of pride, an attitude frequently advocated in Proverbs (Prov 3:5; 6:17; 11:2; 15:25, 33 [in context with "fear of Yahweh"]; Prov 16:5, 18, 19; 18:12; 21:4, 24; 22:4 [again, with "fear of Yahweh"]; Prov 25:5-6, 27; 26:12; 29:23; 30:1-4, 13).

But what does it mean that such an attitude is the "beginning" of wisdom? The word "beginning" (reʾšit) has the sense not only of "first" but also of "foundation" or even "source." It may not be stretching the concept too far to think of

the beginning of wisdom functioning as a presupposition or preunderstanding. It is the first thought that makes all other thoughts fall into place. As M. L. Barre (41) states it, "Fear of Yahweh . . . is the first step—'square one'—in the quest for a meaningful existence." Proverbs does not try to prove the existence of God; it rather presents God's existence as a presupposition that is manifest in its history and nature.

Note that such a claim means that there can be no wisdom/knowledge apart from a relationship with God. Wisdom begins not by accumulating facts, but by having a relationship with God. On one level, from the viewpoint of Proverbs (and the rest of the Bible), this makes perfect sense. How could someone be considered wise if they do not know the most basic and important thing about the universe? Thinking about life begins with the acknowledgment that God is at the center of the universe, not humans ("wise in our own eyes"). Such a perspective also means that one listens to God about how to live life. (For instance, in the words of Proverbs, God's words are presented as coming from the mouth of the father.) One thinks of the Garden of Eden and the choice that Adam and Eve made to reject divine instruction ("Do not eat of the fruit of the tree of the knowledge of good and evil."), but under the influence of the "shrewd" (wisdom gone wrong) serpent to replace the divine instruction with their own assertion of what is right and wrong (Gen 3).

If "the beginning of wisdom is the fear of Yahweh," does that mean that those who do not worship Yahweh have no contribution to make? To judge by the number of times Proverbs seems to utilize the wisdom traditions of other cultures (Egypt and Mesopotamia) (see Proverbs 2: Ancient Near Eastern Background), it seems that the Israelite sages do think they have something to offer, though it is hard to think that they would judge an Egyptian sage, even one from whom they have gained some helpful insight about life, as really wise, since they worshiped false gods. Israelite sages might have chalked up their insight to no more than an ability to express some rhythm of creation into a memorable saying, though they did not discard their insight because of their pagan beliefs. Even so, they adapted it to a Yahwistic framework.

Furthermore, notice that this phrase's insistence that wisdom begins with a relationship with God demonstrates that the very concept is theological and not just practical. In other words, Proverbs 10:4 (quoted above) is giving more than advice about how to avoid poverty. By implying that hard work is wise and laziness is foolish, it is saying that those who work hard are acting like proper worshipers of Yahweh, and those who are lazy are not.

The "fear of the Lord" is thus the beginning of wisdom and sometimes functions as a close synonym of wisdom. Both are connected to ethical behavior. Woman Wisdom herself proclaims: "Those who fear Yahweh hate evil, pride and arrogance, and the path of evil. I hate a perverse mouth" (Prov 8:13; see also Prov 14:2; 16:6; 23:17; 24:21). As such, fear of Yahweh also leads to reward ("The reward of humility, the fear of Yahweh, is wealth, honor, life" [Prov 22:4; see also Prov 10:27; 14:27; 19:23]).

3. Job.

The book of Proverbs advocates the fear of God as the starting point for wisdom, and associates blessings in life with the way of wisdom. The book of Job opens with a description of the protagonist as the epitome of the wise man. The very first verse of the book says: "There was a man in the land of Uz, whose name was Job, and that man was innocent and virtuous, fearing God *[yārē' 'ĕlōhîm]* and turning away from evil." Accordingly, he enjoys the good things of life, wealth and a big, happy family" (Job 1:2-3). This assessment of Job's character is expressed not only here by the narrator but also by God himself (Job 1:8; 2:3). It is even shared by the Accuser *(haśśāṭān)* (*see* Satan). However, the latter wonders about Job's motivation. On the one hand, it leads him to be particularly careful in his piety, offering sacrifices "just in case" (Job 1:5), but the Accuser suspects that he does that out of self-interest. In Job 1:9 he wonders out loud before God: "Is it for no good reason that Job fears God?" Thus God permits the Accuser to remove the blessings to see whether he will remain steadfast in his fear of God. Indeed, Job passes the two tests (Job 1:22; 2:10).

However, as his suffering continues for a period of time beyond the tests, Job grows impatient. After seven days and in the presence of his three friends, Eliphaz, Bildad and Zophar, Job curses the day of his birth in a heart-rending complaint. This complaint propels the three friends into a defense of God based on classic

*retribution theology in a three-cycle debate that extends from Job 4 to Job 27.

The fear of the Lord comes up several times in the context of the debate. In Eliphaz's first speech, he is relatively respectful of Job's previous piety but shocked at this complaining outburst. He thus prods him by saying, "Is not your 'fear' your comfort? Is not the innocence of your ways your hope?" (Job 4:6). Here the comforting fear is the fear of Yahweh, which if he has, so Eliphaz implies, will lead to his ultimate restoration. In his response to this speech, Job counters by charging his friend with treason of their friendship by saying, "A despairing man should have the devotion of his friends, even though he forsakes the fear of the Almighty" (Job 6:14). Job does not admit to so forsaking the fear of Yahweh, but he is saying that even in such a situation friends should stay devoted. They think he has betrayed Yahweh and use that to justify their attack. Job says that even if this were the case, they should remain loyal.

The next time Job refers to fear of God it is in the negative sense of terror (not unprecedented elsewhere, see Ecclesiastes). He wants to talk to God, to set him straight. Job, after all, also holds to the belief that only sinners should suffer. He knows he is innocent, so God must be unjust (Job 9:21-24). He wishes he had an arbitrator or mediator to lessen his "fear of God," so he can stand up to him.

Eliphaz next comes back to the theme of the "fear of God" in his second speech (Job 15:4). Here he castigates Job's wisdom. He suggests that his arguments undermine "fear of God." Next, it is again Eliphaz, this time in his third speech, who raises the issue of the fear of God. He ridicules Job's claim of piety by mockingly asking him, "Is it for your fear that he reproves you?" (Job 22:4).

In the disputations, when "fear of Yahweh" is used positively as a virtue, it is used by one of the three friends, usually Eliphaz, to question Job's proper attitude toward God. Of course, readers of the book know what the characters of the book do not. Job does not suffer because of a lack of fear of God. Ironically, Elihu, the brash young man who comes in after the debate with the three friends, tries to prod Job to a proper fear of God, which he thinks he lacks, by emphasizing God's greatness and power (Job 37:24).

Though the expression "fear of God" does

not appear in the Yahweh speeches or in Job's response to them, we certainly can understand the effect of these speeches as inducing such fear. In Job 38—42 God confronts Job—not because of a sin that led to his suffering but because of his growing impatience with God—with his wisdom and power, and reduces Job to his knees. Here we see Job regain a sense of the fear of God.

In this survey of the theme of the fear of God in the book of Job, we have intentionally passed over its most famous use in Job 28. We have done this because the question of this chapter's place in the book is a serious question. In terms of its content, it is a magnificent assertion of God's wisdom. Human beings can do marvelous things like mine the earth for precious gems and metals. But wisdom is beyond them. The last lines of the poem answer the question of the location of wisdom: "The fear of the Lord—that is wisdom, and to shun evil is understanding" (Job 28:28).

The issue has to do with the location of Job's speech. It occurs at the end of the disputation but is followed by Job's further protestation of innocence and complaint (Job 29—31). Job 28 anticipates the conclusion of the book in its assertion of God's wisdom, but more turmoil follows before the resolution in Job's repentance. Perhaps the best explanation for this is that the book well represents the psychology of a sufferer (see Lo). In the midst of pain, people can have moments of clarity but then fall back into despair.

4. Ecclesiastes.

In Ecclesiastes *yr'* with God (only *'ĕlōhîm*, never Yahweh) as object occurs seven times (Eccles 3:14; 5:6 [English 5:7]; Eccles 7:18; 8:12 [2x], 13; 12:13). Increasingly, commentators have recognized two voices in the book. In Ecclesiastes 1:12—12:7, Qohelet speaks in the first person; in Ecclesiastes 1:1-11;12:8-14 someone else (often called the *frame narrator or second wise teacher) speaks about Qohelet to his son (Eccles 12:12; see Fox, Longman, Bartholomew). Thus, most of the occurrences of "fear God" occur in Qohelet's speech, though it is used once by the second speaker. The frame narrator's exhortation to "fear God" (Eccles 12:13) almost certainly conforms to the positive use of the phrase as found in places like Proverbs 1:7, since in the same context he also urges obedience to God and an expecta-

tion of a future judgment (Eccles 12:13-14).

Commentators, however, are divided over the force of the expression when used by Qohelet himself. Is he advocating a proper pious attitude toward God (so Whybray) or is he suggesting that God acts in the way that he does to frighten people into submission rather than to arouse a sense of respectful awe (Longman, Crenshaw)? In favor of the latter approach is the context of the phrase (so Mavis 216-36), though commentators will continue to disagree over this interpretation as long as they disagree about whether there is tension or agreement between the thought of the body of the book in relationship to the epilogue.

5. Psalms.

The fear of *yhwh/'ĕlōhîm* is a theme encountered over forty times in the book of Psalms, always in the positive sense. W. P. Brown (91-92) tries to establish distance between the use of the phrase in Psalms and Proverbs: "In the psalm [he is speaking specifically of Ps 34, but using this as exemplary], reverence establishes 'refuge' from evildoers; in Proverbs the 'fear of YHWH' provides enlightenment and fosters integrity, the beginning point of moral growth (Prov 1:7; 9:10). For the psalmist, salvation—rather than formation—is paramount." This statement has merit, but the real issue is not so much that the concept is different in the two books but rather the way it is used. In Psalms, as in Proverbs, those who fear Yahweh have put themselves in a properly submissive relationship to God.

Space will not permit an analysis of every use of the phrase "fear Yahweh/God" and its variants in the Psalms, but a few summarizing comments and highlights are in order.

The phrase "those who fear Yahweh/God" in the Psalms is a way of referring to God's people. It is found in connection with "the righteous" (Ps 15:4), "the descendants of Jacob" (Ps 22:23) and those who are obedient to God's law (Ps 112:1; 119:63), God fearers are the ones to whom God reveals his covenant (Ps 25:14), and thus their hope is in his covenant love (Ps 33:18). They are the ones who have taken refuge in God (Ps 31:19) and experience his deliverance (Ps 34:7). Though the expression refers to his people who worship him, the book of Psalms expresses the hope that in the future all people and all nations will fear him (Ps 33:8).

The psalms not only describe God's people

as "God fearers," they also exhort the worshiping community to fear God (Ps 34:10). In Psalm 86:11, the psalmist asks God to give him an "undivided heart" in order to fear him. Indeed, just as the psalms hope for the day the nations will fear God (see reference to Ps 33:8 above; Ps 67:7; 102:15), they also admonish them to fear God as well (Ps 2:11: "You kings. . . . Serve Yahweh with fear and rejoice with trembling").

Those who do fear the Lord experience wonderful blessings. Above, we saw that they are those who know God's deliverance (Ps 85:9) and *protection (refuge, see also Ps 33:18; 60:4). They know God's love and compassion (Ps 103:11, 13, 17). They are also recipients of God's teaching as well as blessed with prosperity and a long family line (Ps 25:12-13), and food (Ps 111:5). They indeed "lack nothing" (Ps 34:10). Those who fear Yahweh are happy (Ps 112:1; 128:1). Accordingly, they are to serve God (Ps 2:11), praise him (Ps 22:23), be humble (Ps 55:19), trust him (Ps 115:11), rejoice (Ps 119:74) and bless Yahweh (Ps 135:20).

Psalm 111:10 is a particularly interesting use of the phrase because here we have the full expression "the fear of Yahweh is the beginning of wisdom" found also in Proverbs and Job. It is paralleled by the expression "all who follow his precepts have good understanding." Psalm 112 then begins with the admonition: "Blessed is the man who fears Yahweh, who finds great delight in his commands." The connection between fearing God and obedience to the commandments and wisdom brings out a connection between wisdom and *law only hinted at in Proverbs. Also of interest are the parallels between Psalm 112, which describes the godly man, and Proverbs 31:10-31, which describes the godly woman (the "noble woman") who is also called a God-fearer (Prov 31:30).

6. Conclusion.

Thus the "fear of *yhwh/ʾĕlōhîm*" is a major theme in Psalms and Wisdom literature. Indeed many, though not all, of the psalms in which "fear of YHWH/ʾĕlōhîm" is found may be categorized as wisdom psalms (e.g., Pss 34; 112) (*see* Wisdom Poetry). Fear is a virtue that leads to piety, praise and humility, since one who fears God recognizes that God, not oneself, is the center of the cosmos.

See also ETHICS; GOD; PROVERBS 1: BOOK OF; WISDOM AND BIBLICAL THEOLOGY; WISDOM AND COVENANT; WISDOM THEOLOGY.

BIBIBLIOGRAPHY. **M. L. Barre,** "Fear of God and the World View of Wisdom," *BTB* 11 (1981) 41-43; **C. Bartholomew,** *Ecclesiastes* (BCOTWP; Grand Rapids: Baker, forthcoming); **W. P. Brown,** "'Come, O Children...I Will Teach You the Fear of the Lord' (Psalm 34:12): Comparing Psalms and Proverbs," in *Seeking Out the Wisdom of the Ancients: Essays Offered in Honor of Michael V. Fox on the Occasion of His Sixty-Fifth Birthday*, ed. R. L. Troxel, K. G. Friebel and D. R. Magary (Winona Lake, IN: Eisenbrauns, 2005) 85-102; **D. Cox,** "Fear or Conscience? *Yirʾat* YHWH in Proverbs 1-9," *Studia Hierosolymitana* 3 (1982) 83-90; **J. L. Crenshaw,** *Ecclesiastes* (Westminster John Knox, 1987); **M. V. Fox,** "Frame-Narrative and Composition in the Book of Qohelet," *HUCA* 48 (1977) 83-106; **A. Lo,** *Job 28 as Rhetoric: An Analysis of Job 28 in the Context of Job 22-31* (VTS 97; Leiden: Brill, 2003); **T. Longman III,** *Ecclesiastes* (NICOT; Grand Rapids: Eerdmans, 1998); idem., *Proverbs* (BCOTWP; Grand Rapids: Baker, 2006); **R. Mavis,** "The Epilogue of Ecclesiastes and the Meaning of the Book" (Ph.D. diss.: Westminster Theological Seminary, 1999); **R. E. Murphy,** "Religious Dimensions of Israelite Wisdom," in *Ancient Israelite Religion: Essays in Honor of Frank Moore Cross*, ed. P. D. Miller Jr. et al. (Philadelphia: Fortress, 1987) 449-58; **W. V. Van Pelt and W. C. Kaiser Jr.,** "*yrʾ*," in *NIDOTTE* 2.533-37; **R. N. Whybray,** *Ecclesiastes* (Grand Rapids: Eerdmans, 1989). T. Longman III

FEMINIST INTERPRETATION

Feminist interpretation is defined as reading the text as a woman and letting a feminist perspective influence one's reading and interpretation. This article provides a survey of feminist interaction with *Psalms, *Proverbs, *Job and the five scrolls: *Song of Songs, *Ruth, *Lamentations, *Ecclesiastes and *Esther.

1. Introduction to Feminist Interpretation
2. Psalms
3. Proverbs
4. Job
5. Song of Songs
6. Ruth
7. Lamentations
8. Ecclesiastes
9. Esther

1. Introduction to Feminist Interpretation.

By its very nature, feminist interpretation is pluralistic; that is, there are no right or wrong readings. Hence, feminist critics may advocate different and often contradictory readings of the same text. Further, the starting point of feminist interpretation of the Bible is not the biblical text in its own right but rather the concerns of feminism. Recognizing that in the history of civilization *women have been marginalized and denied access to positions of authority and influence, feminist scholars seek to expose the strategies by which men have either justified their control over women or encouraged female complicity in their own subordination. In the particular case of the Bible, there is abundant evidence to show that the Bible was produced mainly by men and for men. Most of the characters that appear are male, and in the few cases where women appear, they are mostly presented as someone's wife or daughter, rarely in their own right. When they do appear autonomously, they are famous not for their womanly experience but rather for achievements in roles that received recognition in male domains, such as warrior, prophet or judge (e.g., Deborah). Moreover, even if not all the authors were male, it is the male worldview that is dominant, shared by both men and women at the time. Thus, if the Bible presents us with men's view of women—what men thought women were like, or what they wished them to be—the task of the feminist critic is either to discover traces of female voices within the Bible or to read them into the Bible. Therefore, feminist scholars often find it necessary to step outside the text and raise questions not only about what the Bible says about women but also what its underlying assumptions of gender are. Several methodological approaches are used, most commonly anthropology, sociology and literary criticism (*see* Social-Scientific Approaches; Rhetorical Criticism). The first two seek to learn about women's lives in biblical times, while the third exposes strategies by which women's subordination is inscribed in and justified by texts, focusing on women as characters, on women as readers, or on gender bias in interpretation (see Exum 1995, 65-70).

2. Psalms.

Few attempts have been made to read the Psalter through a woman's eyes, and many of those are *intertextuality studies. For example, U. Bail proposes reading Psalm 55 as a lament by a woman who has been raped. While arguing neither for female authorship nor for rape being the event that triggered the composition in the first place, Bail nevertheless demonstrates how it may serve as a way for woman today to express their suffering as a result of rape. She begins by exploring the *imagery of Psalm 55 and interprets the assaulted city as a metaphor for a woman's body (Heb ʿir ["city"] is a feminine noun), an apt interpretation given the close connection between military defeat of a city and rape of its female inhabitants. The references to the perpetrator being a person close to the victim (Ps 55:12-14) fit the idea of rape as well, since most rapes are carried out by a person known to the victim. Finally, Bail explores the solutions offered by the psalmist. The raped woman wishes for the death of her assaulters (Ps 55:15), and yet, aware that this might not happen, she also disassociates herself from her painful experience using the motif of the desert to symbolize a utopian dream of escape (Ps 55:6-9). Ultimately, she asserts both her own identity and her trust in Yahweh (Ps 55:17-19, 22-23).

A different intertextual reading is offered by B. LaNeel Tanner. Using the Genesis account of Rachel and Leah and their jealousy and competitiveness in the areas of Jacob's love and of childbearing as the starting point (Gen 29—31), LaNeel Tanner reads Psalm 109 as "a prayer for Leah and Rachel when their father forced them to marry Jacob." For example, Psalm 109:1-5 is interpreted as voicing Leah's and Rachel's feelings of hatred of their immediate surroundings, including each other. Of special interest is the idea of the oppressor's children in Psalm 109:9-14. Though these two women are silent in the Genesis account, LaNeel Tanner gives them a voice here in Psalm 109 that reminds us that they too suffered from the antagonism between women, as can be seen later in the Joseph narrative (Gen 37—50), where the sons of Leah turn against the son of Rachel. The psalm ends on a note of praise, read through the statements in Genesis 29:33; 30:6 that Yahweh heard Leah and Rachel.

Another approach, chosen more rarely, is to investigate the symbolism of imagery found in the Psalter. For example, S. Schroer (1998) investigates the biblical metaphor of "Yahweh's wings," found primarily in the Psalter. It is inspired by the behavior of the female goose-vulture, and its use often indicates comfort (parental), *protection and healing. This imagery was often associated with goddesses in ancient Near Eastern and Egyptian images, but there are no traces left of this in Israelite *worship. Instead, the imagery of the protective wings is incorporated by the Israelites into the image of (male) Yahweh, symbolizing not only his protective and nurturing character but also the more dynamic aspects of healing and giving of new strength.

3. Proverbs.

The feminist discussion of Proverbs focuses primarily on the strange/foreign woman in Proverbs 7 and the contrasting picture of Lady Wisdom and Lady Folly in Proverbs 8 (*see* Woman Wisdom and Woman Folly). Feminist scholars are divided in their evaluation of these figures and their interpretation. Other areas of interest are the instruction to King *Lemuel by his mother (Prov 31:1-9) and the *acrostic poem to the "Woman of Worth" (Prov 31:10-31).

3.1. The "Strange" Woman. A negative female character is mentioned throughout the book of Proverbs, variously called "strange" (Prov 2:16; 5:3, 20; 7:5), "foreign" (Prov 2:16; 5:20; 6:24; 7:5; 23:27), "evil" (Prov 6:24), "married" (i.e., unfaithful) (Prov 6:26) and "foolish" (Prov 9:13). The identity and the role of this woman, here treated collectively and named "the strange woman" (see Yee 1995, 111), are much discussed in feminist interpretation. For example, C. V. Camp (2000, 58-66) compares the imagery of the foreign woman in Proverbs 7 with, among other texts, Ezra 9—10; Nehemiah 13; Malachi 2:10-16 and concludes that the key issue with the woman in Proverbs is not so much the fear of idolatry or of intermarriage with women from outside the Judahite community as it is social control of women's and young men's sexual behavior (*see* Marriage and Sex). The strange woman is a cross between an adulterous woman and a prostitute; she is a woman who is sociosexually deviant, alien to the family structure. In this way, she is "strange" or "foreign"; she represents a contrast to what is familiar and "our own." Furthermore, Proverbs 7 describes not the behavior of a particular woman but rather the epitome of deviant sexual behavior outside the control of the patriarchal society. Thus, the strange woman is a symbol of the greatest evil imaginable, portrayed as an improbable combination of sexually deviant activities: she is about to commit adultery against her own husband, but rather than being

a passionate affair, the act is calculated, anonymous sex with a stranger, and an innocent lad at that. Moreover, she is wanton, dressed up but not being a prostitute. She is not controlled by a male and is outside the boundaries of male-controlled sexuality. Lastly, her sexuality is mixed with ritual aspects: she is polluting holy space by engaging in sex during a festival and using the money that she earns to pay her vows (Prov 7:14) and compounding the priestly anointing oil to perfume her illicit sexual encounter (Prov 7:17).

3.1.1. A Male or Female Voice in Proverbs 7? Similarly to the case of Song of Songs, a number of mainly feminist scholars argue in favor of female authorship of Proverbs 1—9 and/or a female identity of the wisdom teacher in the same text. In view of the references to the teaching of the mother (Prov 31:26), the advice to listen to a mother's instruction (e.g., Prov 1:8; 23:22-25), and the teaching of Lemuel's mother (Prov 31:1), male authorship of the entire book of Proverbs need not be taken for granted, even though male authorship may sometimes be implied (e.g., reference to a father's advice in Prov 4:1). One key issue is how to relate to the androcentric values of the text. On the one hand, A. Brenner and F. van Dijk-Hemmes (57-62, 113-30) state that if we see Proverbs as authored by a man, then the text reflects male ideas of women. Alternatively, given that women often internalize the male point of view even when it is not beneficial for them, if Proverbs was (partly) written by a woman, the actual message of the text comes to the same. On the other hand, A. O. Bellis (1998) argues that the sentiments expressed in Proverbs 1—9 could easily have been uttered by a woman who disagrees with the androcentric values, given that the critical issue of the discourse is not so much the restriction of women's freedom as that of men. As such, the advice against "the strange woman" should be regarded not as misogynist but rather as a way of promoting a more egalitarian sexual ethic, expressed within monogamy, from which women stand to gain.

3.1.2. Is the Bad Woman Actually Bad? M. Heijerman outlines three different possible pictures of "the strange woman" that can be derived from the text: "the mother's rival," "the men's scapegoat" and "the needy woman." According to the first portrait, the speaker is the mother of the foolish man, and she sees "the strange woman" as her rival, the one who will break the bond between her and her son. She wants her son to behave sensibly, but most of all she wants to maintain the bond with him and thus her influence over him. Thus the strange woman is a woman who, according to the mother, has not adapted herself to the patriarchal society. As such, she is a threat to the future of the son and therefore also to the happiness of the mother. According to the second portrait, the speaker divides women into two categories, whores and saints, with "the strange woman" clearly belonging to the former. We learn very little about the woman herself from this portrait, only what the man thinks of her, a man who is suspiciously interested in her while at the same time showing disdain for her. The third portrait depicts a helpless woman in a man's society who, left without money due to her husband's absence, turns to prostitution in order to pay her vows. It is also possible that she is turning to adultery due to infertility: suspecting that the fault lies with her husband rather than with her, this is one possible way of getting a son, the crowning glory for a woman in the patriarchal society. Thus, rather than being a rebel against her society, as was the woman of the first portrait, she has adapted herself to the patriarchal society and does everything to uphold its values.

3.1.3. Contrast to Lady Wisdom. Women and/or the female in Proverbs tend to be described as either good (e.g., "Lady Wisdom" in Prov 8) or bad (e.g., "the strange woman" in Prov 7), and this polarization is the subject of much discussion. For example, G. Baumann (76-78) investigates the repercussions of this split for women into "whores" and "saints" then and now. Similarly, C. Newsom discusses the preoccupation with women in Proverbs 1—9. She begins by pointing out that the particular style of discourse—a father giving advice to a son—makes the advice influential and at the same time easy to adopt. Newsom points out that families are not ideologically innocent places, although they give the appearance to be so just because everybody has one. Throughout this advice the danger of the strange woman is polarized by the wholesomeness of Lady Wisdom and a person's own wife. Together, the two women define and secure the boundaries of the symbolic order of patriarchal wisdom. One guards the gateway to hell, the other to heaven. In contrast, as a way of escaping this division of women into whores

and saints, C. V. Camp (2000, 72-89) suggests looking at the strange woman and Lady Wisdom as two aspects of the same identity—an interpretation suggested by the many parallels between the descriptions of the two figures, especially in terms of shared vocabulary. Through this deconstructive reading of the text it is possible to undercut its obvious message of absolute opposition between good and evil and instead to highlight "their paradoxical, but experientially validated, unity" (Camp 2000, 88). Discussing the same interlocking imagery between the strange woman and Lady Wisdom, but reaching less positive conclusions, G. A. Yee (1995) explores how the shared vocabulary and imagery create a picture in which the strange woman functions as the antithesis of Lady Wisdom. The two ostensibly propose the same thing to the son, but the narrator is clear in detailing the outcome of both choices. The result of this for female readers is disturbing. Given the often sexual imagery whereby the son should embrace Lady Wisdom like a lover rather than being enticed by the strange woman, the woman reader is asked to participate in an experience from which she is explicitly excluded. She can identify with the male son and thus translate the female imagery into a male one. Alternatively, the female reader must identify with either Lady Wisdom or the strange woman.

3.2. Lady Wisdom. Personified wisdom (*see* Personification), often called Lady Wisdom, is the subject of the discourse in Proverbs 8. The portrayal of her as a female character is regarded positively by several feminist scholars as opening a way of approaching and worshiping Yahweh in a female yet biblical image. For example, C. V. Camp (1987) discusses how Lady Wisdom can provide women with a feminine aspect of the divine. She states that to acknowledge the goddess of Wisdom "could be an extremely liberating step for reformist Jewish and Christian feminists that would provide further common ground with those women who have opted out of the tradition in favor of contemporary goddess religion." As such, this metaphor can speak powerfully to women claiming either goddess or Judeo-Christian tradition. Along similar lines, G. Baumann (70-76) sees Lady Wisdom as a female mediating figure fully integral to the worship of Yahweh. She is a figure of goddess-like rank at Yahweh's side who, because of her knowledge about the order of the world, is able to give humans advice. She has, however, no cult, and it is doubtful whether she was ever regarded as a character independent of orthodox worship of Yahweh. This may diminish her influence and, indirectly, women's influence as well. She has no direct influence in Yahweh's decision-making, and by not being a goddess in her own right she has less authority and runs the risk of losing her relevance within the context of Israelite theology. Moreover, in her role as a mother who lovingly cares for her children, who nourishes and educates them, and who embodies the authority and will of the father while he is absent, Lady Wisdom is a female role model of the past that serves less well for women today who are active in the political and decision-making realms. Similarly, S. Schroer (1995) argues that the fact that Lady Wisdom, together with authentic feminine experience and identity, was integrated as an aspect of Yahweh offers a possibility for identification for women today. In contrast, Hadley suggests that the references to Lady Wisdom in Proverbs 1; 8; 9; Job 38 constitute a literary compensation for the gradual eradication of the worship of a female goddess and of its assimilation into worship of Yahweh. In particular, J. M. Hadley suggests that the underlying goddess is that of Asherah, known from Canaanite mythology and also as Yahweh's companion in the texts from Kuntillet Ajrud.

3.3. Wisdom and Women's Roles in Society. C. R. Fontaine (1995) discusses the social roles of women in the world of wisdom. She begins by defining the concept of "sage," rejecting the limited definition of a sage as a person with scribal education who has composed a book or piece belonging to the wisdom literature of the ancient world. As such, all but very few women would be excluded. Instead, she suggests a fuller definition, defining the sage as a person who routinely performs one of the following tasks: authorship, scribal duties, counseling, management of economic resources, conflict resolution, teaching and healing. In this wider sense, also a woman could be considered "wise." She then outlines three areas in which female sages function and compares the biblical evidence with that of the rest of the ancient Near East. First, in the private domain, the duties of a capable wife included many "wise" tasks, including teaching and making practical decisions for the running of the houshold (Prov 31). Her opposite is the

woman in Proverbs 7:5-27, who embodies the converse of true, life-giving wisdom. Second, in the public domain, the best example is the queen mother's instruction in Proverbs 31:1-9, with her opposite exemplified by Queen Jezebel, an educated foreign woman who used her intelligence to manipulate her weak husband, Ahab, for her own purposes (see 1 Kings 16:31—21:29). Third is the province of counseling, healers and mourners, where women have left their mark, again both positively as a healer and negatively as a source of death. In this way, the social roles of women are echoed in the two twin figures of Lady Wisdom and Lady Folly. Focusing on the last aspect, Schroer (1995) notes that Lady Wisdom often is described partly as a counseling woman (e.g., Prov 8:12, 14-16). Schroer also highlights the many references to wise counseling women outside the Wisdom literature: the counseling wise woman (e.g., 2 Sam 14), the wise wife (e.g., Sarah in Gen 16; Michal in 1 Sam 19) and the counseling mother of a king (e.g., 1 Kings 2:13-23; 2 Chron 22:3), for better or for worse. In this way, the representation of personified Wisdom as a counseling woman is rooted in sociocultural factors related to Israelite tradition. At the same time, counseling women were respected as the representatives of Lady Wisdom. Schroer concludes with the hope that such a divine image might have exercised influence on women's own position and social reality.

4. Job.

The book of Job is a male-oriented one, containing a few female characters (Job's wife and daughters), whose appearances are limited to the prologue and the epilogue. The bulk of the book is taken up by the speeches of Job, his friends and Yahweh. Nonetheless, several areas of the text invite feminist interpretation (Maier and Schroer). First, Job's daughters seem to have a status within the family that is more prominent than what is typically assumed about the position of daughters in ancient Israel. As such, they can serve as a positive focal point for feminist interpretation. For example, noting that they, in contrast with Job's sons, are named, and drawing attention to the parallels with Zelophehad's daughters (Num 27; 36), who also inherited from their father, C. Maier and S. Schroer portray a Job who, through his own suffering, has come to realize that these women are also entitled to a self-sufficient and financially secure life, independent of men. Second, the divine speech in Job 38—42 provides a platform for a more universal outlook upon life. By rejecting that Job is the center of the universe, the poem points to a less anthropocentric relationship between humans and Yahweh. Similarly, the implicit critical attitude toward the patriarchy expressed in the poem on wisdom (Job 28) can provide a new reading of Job: wisdom, like Yahweh, cannot be bought and is hidden from all. Third, the feminist scholar can look for the suppressed voice of Job's wife. In light of her share of Job's suffering—after all, like Job, she lost her children and her position in the society—she too is a righteous sufferer, a female one who can speak for the many women, past and present, whose suffering is unheard.

Of these three areas, Job's wife has received the most attention, in particular her single statement in Job 2:9 ("Do you still persist in your integrity? Curse God and die"). For example, E. van Wolde (1995, 201-6) treats the statement by Job's wife as pivotal, causing Job to begin questioning Yahweh. By echoing the vocabulary of Yahweh (Job 2:3) and that of the accuser (Job 1:11; 2:5b), adding only one new word ("die"), she urges Job to change from his earlier passivity and to confront Yahweh. She gives her husband a choice, implied in the dual meaning of the Hebrew verb *brk*, ("bless"/"curse"): he can either curse Yahweh, which might cause Yahweh to abandon him, thus resulting in his death, or he can bless Yahweh and die with that blessing on his lips. These words result in a change in Job's relation to Yahweh, from accepting Yahweh's actions (Job 1:21-22; 2:10) to questioning them.

In contrast, L. R. Klein highlights the misogynist aspects of the book of Job. Looking at the use of form and language, Klein compares the male characters' verbosity and the beauty of the poetry of their statements with the mere six Hebrew words spoken by Job's wife. This lack of speech suggests that women are related to the periphery, given only those words that no man can utter. Moreover, it equates women with the wicked (Job 2:10). The daughters born after the calamity are given more of an identity in that they are given names and are described as beautiful (Job 42:14-15). Nonetheless, Klein sees this as yet another example of misogyny: the text discloses that male desire is enjoyed when the ob-

ject is young, beautiful and a virgin/ daughter. The mature and accessible wife is not given any thought. Further, Job sees only his own suffering and desires and spares little thought for those of his wife. His wife is presented as wanting only Job's well-being (Job 2:9), and no word is mentioned about her own loss of children and esteem. In fact, if Job were to lust after a woman, he envisions that his own wife would bear the brunt of the punishment (Job 31:9-10)!

5. Song of Songs.

There is much positive to be said about Song of Songs from a feminist perspective. In no other biblical book are female characters given so much voice, and in no other book is women's sexuality described in such a positive light. Nonetheless, there are of late also more cautious feminist interpreters. One such cautionary voice is J. C. Exum (2000), who lists ten reasons to be alert, including the possibility that the women featured in the text may be the creations of male authors, maybe even representing a male fantasy of the ideal woman rather than representing a female voice, and that even though women are attributed a lot of sexual freedom, the text itself makes clear that "bad things happen to sexually active, forward women" (Exum 30).

5.1. Authorship. One feminist concern is the possible female authorship of at least parts of Song of Songs, depending on each scholar's view of the history of the text. Several matters point in this direction: poetic descriptions of a man's body, feminine aspects of the portrayed ways of life (e.g., mother's house [see Meyers 1993a]) being referred to, the use of the narrative "I" denoting the female lover (Goitein 1993, 58-59), the unusually high ratio for the Bible of female speakers (Brenner and van Dijk-Hemmes, 88-89), women referring to each other as beautiful, lack of inequality of strength between the male and the female characters, and the fact that the woman usually takes the initiative (Bekkenkamp and van Dijk 1993, 79-80).

Looking at the issue from a different direction, J. Bekkenkamp and F. van Dijk (1993, 69) suggest that "what the female texts . . . have in common is their lack of the specific biblical metaphorical language, in which aspects of femininity or male-female relationships are used as symbols for other, 'more important,' realities." In favor of regarding Song of Songs as a female text, Bekkenkamp and van Dijk (1993, 69) point out that the religious nature of Song of Songs is expressed not in "YHWH-talk" but in language and symbolism taken from the daily life in a village and from nature.

5.2. Intertextuality. Female scholars often highlight how a particular text benefits from a comparative reading with other texts, both within and outside the biblical *canon, and how this highlights certain aspects of the given text. One way of reading intertextually is by tracing the development of a given topic throughout the Bible. Notably, intertextuality does not work in one direction only: if a later text draws on the imagery of an earlier one, this later text stays in the mind of the readers when they return to the earlier one and thus influences the reading of the earlier one. Another way of reading intertextually is through juxtaposition: two or more biblical books are brought into conversation with each other. In this way, the order and the hierarchy of the canon are disrupted, and novel ways of looking at a text appear. Lastly, several scholars break free of the biblical canon and read cross-culturally, comparing the biblical text with literature ranging from contemporary Greek novels to modern children's books (see van Wolde 1997b, 427-33).

In the case of Song of Songs, feminist scholars read Song of Songs intertextually primarily with Genesis 2—3; Hosea 1—3; Proverbs 7, mainly focusing on the contrasting picture of female sexuality. For example, P. Trible (144-65) reads Song of Songs as a poem that seeks to rectify the situation recorded in Genesis 2—3. By using primarily literary techniques, Trible highlights the ways in which Song of Songs reuses the imagery of Genesis 2—3 (garden, Yahweh's withdrawal/absence, sexual union, fruit, plants, animals, parents). This reuse creates a contrasting picture: the fruit is no longer forbidden but rather to be savored, and the animals are friends rather than foes later to be crushed. In particular, the punishment is reversed: instead of the woman's desire for the man being part of her punishment, he will desire her. Similarly, J. Bekkenkamp and F. van Dijk (1993, 82-83) argue that Proverbs 7, because of the use of similar wordings, can be interpreted as a reaction to Song of Songs. The area of contrast is primarily that of female sexual initiative: whereas the "I" of Song of Songs is actively looking for her lover as an expression of her love for him, the teacher

in Proverbs warns his young male disciples of the danger of women who make the first move. Sexuality is permitted and can even be enjoyed, but only as the result of male initiative. Lastly, F. van Dijk-Hemmes (1993a) reads Song of Songs alongside Hosea 2, arguing that Hosea 2, by using motifs from Song of Songs, transforms the woman and her seeking for love into a harlot who shamelessly goes after her lover. In this way, Hosea 2 conveys the male point of view while suppressing the female side.

5.3. Allegorical Interpretations. Throughout the history of interpretation Song of Songs has more often than not been allegorized, and one reason for this might be the female character's lack of conformity to the male idea of the female; her initiative and forwardness are unbecoming, and so another interpretation must be more correct (Bekkenkamp and van Dijk 1993, 80-81). In view of this bias, feminist scholars often do not accredit the allegorical readings with any value for today's women. Lately, however, several scholars have looked anew at the allegorical approach to see if anything can be salvaged for the feminist reader. Among them, A. Ostriker suggests that the motif of "love" in Song of Songs can be read to mean both and simultaneously physical and spiritual, profane and sacred love. Furthermore, in view of the comparatively egalitarian view of love in the human sphere, she poses the question of whether such a nonhierarchical love relationship can be possible also with Yahweh.

5.4. The Wasfs. The imagery of especially the last *wasf (Song 7:2-8), often considered bizarre, and its implication for women is much debated. Attempts are made both to redeem the imagery and to problematize it. Positively, M. Falk (1993) compares it with the often equally peculiar metaphors used by past and contemporary poets and suggests that we need, through critical analysis, to bridge the cultural gap between us and Song of Songs. The solution may be found in less precise translations. For example, where an image depends on familiarity with a foreign landscape (e.g., Song 6:5; 7:4-5), it may be preferable to exclude that reference and to substitute something more familiar to the modern, non-Israelite reader. From a different aspect, C. Meyers (1993a) highlights that the imagery has a traditionally male quality, either being military or denoting fierce animals. When, like here, it is applied to a woman, it creates an allusion to female power appropriate to the internal world of Israelite households, where women exercised strong and authoritative positions. Finally, A. Brenner (1993) suggests that rather than redeeming the imagery of the last *wasf*, it should be recognized as a double-edged parody. On one level, it is a male parody of a not-so-beautiful yet sexually attractive woman. On a deeper lever, presuming female authorship, it is a subtle critique of male chauvinism. In contrast, F. C. Black treats the imagery more negatively. In a comparative study, she points out that in many readings, including the ones of Meyers and Brenner, the female body is on display and is described in grotesque terms. Thus, the text compromises her body image and her sexuality, thereby rendering a positive reading doubtful. Instead, Black urges us to accept that the text depicts a woman as ridiculous and thereby reveals a certain unease on the part of the woman's lover and hence on the part of the primarily male audience that gazes upon her, and to begin working from there.

6. Ruth.

The book of Ruth has received mixed reviews by feminist scholars (for a useful overview, see Meyers 1993b, 87). On the one hand, it is deemed positive that a book featuring primarily women and their heroic deeds is given a place in the canon. On the other hand, there is the feeling that Ruth and *Naomi, however pleasant they may be, are but pawns in the patriarchal society, exploited for their biological role in maintaining male lineages. Feminist scholarship focuses mainly on the characters of the book, its possible female authorship and intertextuality.

6.1. The Characters of Ruth, Naomi and Orpah.
P. Trible (166-99) offers a positive evaluation of the character of Ruth. Even though one concern of the book is indeed the need for a male heir to preserve the family patrimony, the book highlights the courage, independence and devotion of Ruth and Naomi, and its focal point is their struggle to survive successfully in a man's world. Throughout the narrative the women take the initiative, thus shaping their own destiny despite living in a patriarchal world. Ruth is the "defier of custom, the maker of decisions, and the worker of salvation" (Trible, 184). When Boaz acts, it is in reaction to Ruth's initiative. As a whole, the book of Ruth suggests a theological interpretation of feminism: "women working out their

own salvation with fear and trembling, for it is YHWH who works in them" (Trible, 196).

More specifically, the issue of Ruth's Moabite nationality is often addressed. What did it mean for Ruth to leave her own nation, culture and religion and to embrace that of her late husband and her mother-in-law? Simultaneously, the character of Orpah has been lifted out of obscurity, suggesting that she, alongside Ruth, can serve as a role model: in contrast to Ruth, she chose to remain in her own culture rather than turning her back on it. For example, B. Honig discusses several aspects of immigrant integration into the adopted culture, asking in particular what Ruth, the alien, provides for the Israelites that an indigenous heroine cannot provide. Honig notes that immigrants have two effects on a society. Positively, immigration reflects the admirable qualities of the adopted country by showing that foreigners are prepared to leave their own land for the benefits of the new one. Negatively, immigrants are feared for the influence that they will have on the receiving nation. In the case of Ruth, Honig suggests that her immigration is the vehicle through which the law comes alive again: "Ruth's choice of the Israelites re-marks them as the Chosen People, a people worthy of being chosen" (Honig, 55). At the same time, Ruth is threatening: she is a foreigner of a hated nation who is dwelling in the midst of the people of Bethlehem. And, as the end of the book alludes, she is never fully incorporated into the Israelite society. Despite her imminent marriage into the society, she is still referred to as Ruth the Moabite (Ruth 4:10). Thus she stays a foreigner. In fact, one way of interpreting Ruth's disappearance after giving birth to Obed at the end of Ruth 4 is to see it as the result of prejudice and lack of integration. Naomi is given the son because Ruth the foreigner cannot be trusted to raise her son properly, in the Israelite way.

From a more personal point of view, L. E. Donaldson discusses the inherent tension between Moab and Israel as displayed by Orpah and Ruth. Donaldson compares the two women with the responses of Native American women to the early European settlers. Dismissing the biblical claim to primacy of the Israelite faith and ensuing culture, Donaldson places Orpah in the center and sees her as a true role model for Native American women. Rather than courting the culture of the dominant power and in the end adopting it, like Pocahontas, Orpah, after her marriage to the Israelite Chilion, returns to her own culture and her own gods. Bringing attention to the ingrained hostility between Israel and Moab, Donaldson describes Ruth indirectly as an indigenous woman who abandons her own background to align herself with those who "break down [the Moabites'] altars etc." (Deut 12:3). Thus, Orpah is the one character who gives hope to Native American women, by choosing the house of her clan and the spirituality of her mother over the desire for another culture.

6.2. A Female Voice. Feminist scholarship is interested in the possibility of female authorship of the book of Ruth. Thus, alongside treating the text as written by a male author and accordingly seeking to expose and evaluate its androcentric values, several scholars read the book as a female text. In this area, F. van Dijk-Hemmes (1993b) discusses the possibility of a female voice in a given text, postulating three main criteria for uncovering such traces: the absence of marked androcentrism, a redefinition of reality from female perspective, and a narrative differentiation of the views attributed to female as against male figures. In addition to these, van Dijk-Hemmes suggests the possibility that although the final literary product was penned by a male author, the underlying oral tradition is the "collective creation of women's culture." She finds that the book of Ruth fulfills all these criteria. For example, the cooperation and mutual respect between Naomi and Ruth stand in sharp contrast to the rivalry of other women couples such as Rachel and Leah, Hannah and Peninnah, and Sarah and Hagar as depicted in other, more androcentric parts of the Bible. Further, the mention of "mother's house" is suggestive of a reality depicted differently from the prevalent male perspective. Moreover, van Dijk-Hemmes follows those scholars who seek Ruth as a book that came into being and was transmitted within circles of professional narrators, and she suggests that the Ruth and Naomi story belongs to the repertory of a female storyteller, "a woman old and wise like one of the heroines of her story, Naomi." A detailed study of one of these aspects, the expression "mother's house" (Gen 24:28; Ruth 1:8; Song 3:4; 8:2) is offered by C. Meyers (1993b). Among other things, Meyers explores how this expression points to a female perspective and thus a female voice within the

book of Ruth. Furthermore, she explores its sociological background and how it testifies to, among other things, women's considerable power within the household. Meyers conclude that when Naomi uses the term "mother's house" in Ruth 1:8, she allows us to hear the language of female experience.

6.3. Intertextuality. Lastly, the book of Ruth has been read intertextually by feminist scholars. For example, E. van Wolde (1997b) highlights the many shared semantic features between the book of Ruth and the narrative of Judah and Tamar in Genesis 38: both women are childless widows, Judah and Boaz are elderly male relatives, both women's actions share the purpose of providing a male heir to the family, both their actions contain elements of concealment and deceit, and both women are neglected at the end of their respective stories. Based on this comparison, van Wolde proceeds by claiming that both Ruth and Tamar are eye-openers. Tamar opens Judah's eyes to the knowledge about his son Er's refusal to provide his brother with an heir and Yahweh's subsequent punitive deed. Similarly, Ruth opens Boaz's eyes to her situation and makes him aware of his possibilities as redeemer and seed supplier. Moreover, Ruth also opens Naomi's eyes, transforming her from a childless widow embittered toward Yahweh to a woman with hope for a future and offspring.

7. Lamentations.

The little that has been written about Lamentations from a feminist perspective focuses largely on the *personification of Jerusalem as a woman and whether or not this image is positive for women then and now. Jerusalem is portrayed as Yahweh's beloved daughter, the spokeswoman for the grieving community, and finally also the victim who confronts Yahweh about his mistreatment of her (Lam 2:20-22).

B. B. Kaiser (166) maintains the positive side, arguing that the adoption of a metaphor of painful female experience was not done in a judgmental way in order to expose the community's sin. On the contrary, by identifying with a suffering woman, the (male) author of Lamentations sought to achieve a more powerful expression of suffering. A contrary position is taken by K. M. O'Connor (188-89). While acknowledging that Jerusalem as Yahweh's daughter appears first to provide contemporary women with a female biblical symbol of high dignity, suggesting that the authors were aware of women's suffering and valued them highly enough to employ them as metaphors of the pain of the community, O'Connor highlights that this imagery can also be harmful for women. Jerusalem is portrayed as a subordinate of the male deity, an object of scorn, the cause of her own suffering (Lam 1:5), and as a woman who collaborates in her own abuse.

Three particular female images have been noted by scholars. The first image is the portrayal of Jerusalem in Lamentations 1 as a woman who is unclean due to her menstruation (Lam 1:9, 17; cf. Lev 15:19-30). Again, Kaiser interprets this imagery positively, regarding the poet's impersonation of a menstruating woman to intensify the expression of anguish as "remarkable in a culture in which attitudes towards menstruation were hardly progressive" (Kaiser, 176). In contrast, O'Connor (189) points out that menstruation, a natural condition of the female body, is used here as a metaphor of shame and humiliation. The same shamefulness of a woman's body is also implied in the picture in Lamentations 1:8, where *Zion is described as naked, symbolizing her degradation and bodily humiliation. The second image is the way in which Jerusalem gives voice to her suffering. According to O'Connor, the reader hears a battered woman, a woman who is beaten and tortured by Yahweh, whom she trusts, and who laments how he inflicted her sorrows in his anger (Lam 1:12-13). Moreover, like contemporary victims of domestic violence, Jerusalem blames herself for her afflictions and acknowledges Yahweh's right to abuse her. Indirectly, this passage "justifies abuse of women by portraying YHWH as the abuser" (O'Connor, 189). The third image is that of motherhood. T. Linafelt (1997) proposes a reading of Lamentations in terms of its concern for children—mother Zion's dying children. This is a reading of a despairing mother who is trying to get Yahweh's attention on behalf of her children, but Yahweh does not respond.

8. Ecclesiastes.

Very little has been written on Ecclesiastes from a feminist perspective. Although there are sections that may testify to a positive view of women (e.g., a positive view of sexuality in Eccles 9:9),

the bulk of the material witnesses to a more negative evaluation (e.g., Eccles 3:5-6). The section that has received most attention is Ecclesiastes 7:25-29. In particular, the statement "more bitter than death is (the) woman" (Eccles 7:26) is the source of much controversy among both translators and exegetes. Was Ecclesiastes a misogynist, the opposite, or something in between? E. S. Christianson provides a useful overview of the variety of interpretations and explores their implication for gender relations. He concludes that a plain reading of the text points to the misogyny of Ecclesiastes, but he also acknowledges that the effort of those scholars who seek to render Ecclesiastes as someone standing outside the views of his own society provides useful confrontation that forces us to reexamine the text again and again. C. R. Fontaine (1998) supports the idea that the plain sense of the text of Ecclesiastes conveys a negative view of women, and she continues by exploring how this negative view was taken up and indeed strengthened by later Jewish and Christian interpreters. In the case of Christianity, she concludes with a discussion of religiously based misogyny, influenced in part by statements such as Ecclesiastes 7:25-29, and its role in the witch hunts in early modern Europe.

Other passages have examined by feminist scholars. Notably, A. Brenner (Brenner and van Dijk-Hemmes, 133-63) counterreads the poem in Ecclesiastes 3:1-9 as a male poem of desire. She focuses on the imagery of the millstone in Ecclesiastes 3:5, which often is given a sexual interpretation in traditional Jewish exegesis (cf. Job 31:9-10): one "casts stones" when one's wife is ritually pure, while one should abstain from doing so when she is unclean—that is, during her menstrual period. This equation of women with stones is troublesome, and Brenner asks what happens to women within the "life" described in the poem? Are they also cast away? In the light of Brenner's counterreading, this verse declares that there exists a (proper?) time for indulging in the sexual act or for getting rid of a woman. In view of the poem as a whole, this interpretation renders it a male love poem exploring the fluidity of love and sexual desire, and how love and sex are dynamic, at times changing and mutating into their opposite.

9. Esther.

The feminist discussion of the book of Esther is

largely centered on the two main female characters, *Vashti and *Esther, and how they are represented. Another area of feminist discussion is the Diaspora background of the narrative and its significance for the portrayal of the characters.

9.1. The Characters of Esther. Feminist scholars are divided in their evaluation of Esther. Characteristics that are regarded as valuable by some scholars, such as her shrewd use of her femininity, charm, pliability and diplomacy, are derided by others who regard Esther as a male fantasy of the ideal woman rather than as a role model that modern women would wish to embrace.

Beginning with a positive evaluation, White portrays Esther as the successful Diaspora Jew. Esther symbolizes the vulnerability and weakness of the Diaspora Jew in two ways: not only is she a Jew in the midst of the Persian Empire and thus marginal, but also she is a woman and thus subordinate to the males surrounding her. As such, her success is doubly remarkable and thus also a model. First, Esther knows to appreciate the advice of more experienced seniors, *Mordecai and Hegai. Thus she is showing herself to be cooperative, an important characteristic for a successful court life. Second, once she becomes queen, she uses her elevated position to enhance the position of her relatives, in this case Mordecai. In contrast, Mordecai, although a sympathetic character, is not equally successful in that he refuses to fit into the situation in which he finds himself. He alienates Haman by refusing to bow down to him. In doing so, Mordecai puts his own community at risk and has to rely on Esther's position to repair the damage. Third, even when taking charge, Esther remains circumspect. Rather than blurting out her request to the king immediately, she wisely takes precautions such as dressing up and asking people to fast on her behalf. This is not cowardice but rather a realistic assessment of the situation. White concludes that Esther, by accepting the reality of a subordinate position and learning to gain power by working within the structure rather than against it, shows how a Jew can build a successful and fulfilling life in the Diaspora (cf. Niditch 1993, 138-40). Along the same lines, S. Niditch (1993) sees Esther as an archetype of a wise woman: "She knows enough to take good advice and to be self-effacing, humble and even-tempered" (135). Esther's cleverness emerges in the way she employs her womanly assets to seduce Haman and *Ahasuerus: she dresses for success, uses flattery, wine and food to reach the king, and is self-effacing in her overall demeanor. Nonetheless, Niditch (1993, 36, 39) points out that Esther, while being "an altogether appealing portrait of women's wisdom for the men of a ruling patriarchate" is "hardly an image meaningful or consoling to modern women." Regarding Esther less enthusiastically, Wyler examines Esther's relationship with Mordecai and points out her compliance with Mordecai's authority throughout her career. Esther is only briefly in command after her confrontation with Mordecai (Esther 4:13-14). Yet as soon as the pogrom against the Jews is past, she slips back into obscurity again, and it is Mordecai, in his new role as vizier, who receives the new power rather than Esther.

9.2. The Character of Vashti. Vashti is in many respects Esther's counterpart. Whereas Esther is portrayed as subdued, obedient, womanly and clever, Vashti comes across as a person with a well-developed sense of (her own) human dignity and the boldness to stand up against royal power that has turned violent. When the king summons her to his drinking party, for the purpose of parading her beauty before his courtiers, she refuses (Esther 1:10-12). It is possible, although not explicitly stated, that Vashti had good reasons, either her modesty or her queenly position, for her refusal to be a spectacle for drunken men. As a result of her disobedience, the king, prompted by his advisors, decides to legally ban a wife's disobedience to her husband, lest all the women of his empire rebel against their husbands. What is needed, according to M. Gendler, is a more balanced picture of the two women. The present condemnation of Vashti's independence and pride, together with the praise of Esther's piety, beauty and obedience, often induces women to choose Esther as the role model. Instead, Gendler suggests reinstating Vashti alongside Esther, in this way combining the attributes of these two women: pride tempered by humility, independence checked by heartfelt loyalties. Such women would be more whole than those who simply seek to emulate Esther.

Vashti's behavior versus that of Mordecai is another topic of feminist discussion. In a sense, Mordecai's refusal to bow to the vizier Haman and the subsequent decision to punish the Jewish population of Persia (Esther 3) is parallel to the episode of Vashti's refusal (Esther 1): because two individuals, out of their own dignity and sense of self, refuse to comply with royal orders, their corporate society suffers (Wyler, 122). Gendler, investigating the estimation of these two characters in traditional exegesis, concludes that similar behavior in men and women is treated differently: whereas Vashti is condemned for her defiance and refusal to submit to Ahasuerus's demands, Mordecai is highly admired for his refusal to debase himself before Haman.

9.3. Comparisons Between the Different Versions. The text of Esther is preserved in three different versions: the MT, the LXX and the Alpha text (*see* Esther 5: Greek Versions). Several scholars, feminist and otherwise, discuss the differences between the different versions. Of special interest to feminist scholars are the different portrayals of the feminine characters as evidenced in the different versions, and how these narratives in general reflect women's status. For example, K. de Troyer compares the limited section Esther 2:8-18, concerning Esther's preparation and selection as Ahasuerus's queen, and concludes that both the MT and the Alpha text are written from a male perspective, the former aiming at an audience of both men and women, and the latter strictly at men. In contrast, a more female perspective, together with a faint note of criticism of the earlier male bias of the MT, can be detected in the version preserved in the LXX. Reaching a different conclusion, T. K. Beal argues that the events narrated in Esther 1 predispose us to view the rest of the book in a certain way. In the case of the MT, the portrayal of Vashti as a heroine in a gender-based conflict against Ahasuerus and his male counselors causes the reader to side with the queen against the king. In contrast, the extended versions found in the LXX and the Alpha text, which include an episode in which Mordecai saves the king from a plot against his life, station the reader in favor of Mordecai and hence also in favor of the king, while Vashti is made to stand in relation with those plotting against the king and later also with Haman. Finally, L. Day (237-41) offers a more extensive analysis of the three versions and of their respective portrayals of the main characters. Although the results of Day's study as a whole go beyond feminist concerns, it has significant implications for feminist hermeneutics.

First, the diversity of the characterizations of Esther allows us to ask new questions with regard to Esther and to utilize her as a model in different ways. Second, the paradigmatic character of the book of Esther is connected with the search of feminist scholars today for a liberating way to claim the Bible as authoritative. In regarding Esther as Scripture, we can find in all three figures of Esther models for faithful living.

See also ESTHER; HERMENEUTICS; NAOMI; RUTH; SOCIAL-SCIENTIFIC INTERPRETATION; VASHTI; WOMAN WISDOM AND WOMAN FOLLY; WOMEN.

BIBLIOGRAPHY. **U. Bail,** "'Vernimm, Gott, mein Gebet': Psalm 55 und Gewalt gegen Frauen," in *Feministische Hermeneutik und Erstes Testament: Analysen und Interpretationen,* ed. H. Jahnow (Stuttgart: Kohlhammer, 1994) 67-84; ET, "'O God, Hear My Prayer': Psalm 55 and Violence against Women," in *Wisdom and Psalms,* ed. A. Brenner and C. R. Fontaine (FCB 2/2; Sheffield: Sheffield Academic Press, 1998) 242-63; **G. Baumann,** "A Figure with Many Facets: The Literary and Theological Functions of Personified Wisdom in Proverbs 1-9," in *Wisdom and Psalms,* ed. A. Brenner and C. R. Fontaine (FCB 2/2; Sheffield: Sheffield Academic Press, 1998) 44-78; **T. K. Beal,** "Tracing Esther's Beginnings," in *A Feminist Companion to Esther, Judith and Susanna,* ed. A. Brenner (FCB 7; Sheffield: Sheffield Academic Press, 1993) 87-110; **J. Bekkenkamp and F. van Dijk,** "The Canon of the Old Testament and Women's Cultural Traditions," in *Historiography of Women's Cultural Traditions,* ed. M. Meijer and J. Schaap (Language, Culture and Female Future 3; Dordrecht: Foris, 1987) 91-108; repr. in *A Feminist Companion to the Song of Songs,* ed. A. Brenner (FCB 1; Sheffield: Sheffield Academic Press, 1993) 67-85; **A. O. Bellis,** "The Gender and Motives of the Wisdom Teacher in Proverbs 7," *BBR* 6 (1996) 15-22; repr. in *Wisdom and Psalms,* ed. A. Brenner and C. R. Fontaine (FCB 2/2; Sheffield: Sheffield Academic Press, 1998) 79-91; **F. C. Black,** "Unlikely Bedfellows: Allegorical and Feminist Reading of Song of Songs 7.1-8," in *The Song of Songs,* ed. A. Brenner and C. R. Fontaine (FCB 2/6; Sheffield: Sheffield Academic Press, 2000) 104-29; **A. Brenner,** "'Come Back, Come Back the Shulammite' (Song of Songs 7.1-10): A Parody of the *wasf* Genre," in *On Humour and the Comic in the Hebrew Bible,* ed. A. Brenner and Y. T. Radday (JSOTSup 92; Sheffield: Almond, 1990) 251-76;

repr. in *A Feminist Companion to the Song of Songs*, ed. A. Brenner (FCB 1; Sheffield: Sheffield Academic Press, 1993) 234-57; **A. Brenner and F. van Dijk-Hemmes,** *On Gendering Texts: Female and Male Voices in the Hebrew Bible* (BIS 1; Leiden: E. J. Brill, 1993); **C. V. Camp,** "Woman Wisdom as Root Metaphor: A Theological Consideration," in *The Listening Heart: Essays in Wisdom and the Psalms in Honour of Roland E. Murphy, O. Carm.,* ed. K. G. Hoglund et al. (JSOTSup 58; Sheffield: JSOT Press, 1987) 45-76; idem, *Wise, Strange, and Holy: The Strange Woman and the Making of the Bible* (JSOTSup 320; Sheffield: JSOT Press, 2000); **E. S. Christianson,** "Qoheleth the 'Old Boy' and Qoheleth the 'New Man': Misogynism, the Womb and a Paradox in Ecclesiastes," in *Wisdom and Psalms,* ed. A. Brenner and C. R. Fontaine (FCB 2/2; Sheffield: Sheffield Academic Press, 1998) 109-36; **L. Day,** *Three Faces of a Queen: Characterization in the Book of Esther* (JSOTSup 186; Sheffield: JSOT Press, 1995). **K. de Troyer,** "An Oriental Beauty Parlour: An Analysis of Esther 2.8-18 in the Hebrew, the Septuagint and the Second Greek Text," in *A Feminist Companion to Esther, Judith and Susannah,* ed. A. Brenner (FCB 7; Sheffield: Sheffield Academic Press, 1993) 47-70; **L. E. Donaldson,** "The Sign of Orpah: Reading Ruth through Native Eyes," in *Ruth and Esther,* ed. A. Brenner (FCB 2/3; Sheffield: Sheffield Academic Press, 1999) 130-44; **J. C. Exum,** "Feminist Criticism: Whose Interests Are Being Served?" in *Judges and Method: New Approaches in Biblical Studies,* ed. G. A. Yee (Minneapolis: Fortress, 1995) 65-90; idem, "Ten Things Every Feminist Should Know about the Song of Songs," in *The Song of Songs,* ed. A. Brenner and C. R. Fontaine (FCB 2/6; Sheffield: Sheffield Academic Press, 2000) 24-35; **M. Falk,** "The *wasfs*," in *Love Lyrics from the Hebrew Bible: A Translation and Literary Study of the Song of Songs* (BLS 4; Sheffield: Almond, 1982), 80-87; repr. in *A Feminist Companion to the Song of Songs,* ed. A. Brenner (FCB 1; Sheffield: Sheffield Academic Press, 1993) 225-33; **C. R. Fontaine,** "The Social Roles of Women in the World of Wisdom," in *A Feminist Companion to Wisdom Literature,* ed. A. Brenner (FCB 9; Sheffield: Sheffield Academic Press, 1995) 24-49; idem, "'Many Devices' (Qoheleth 7.23-8.1): Qoheleth, Misogyny and the *Malleus Maleficarum*," in *Wisdom and Psalms,* ed. A. Brenner and C. R. Fontaine (FCB 2/2; Sheffield: Sheffield Academic Press, 1998) 137-68; **M. Gendler,** "The Restoration of Vashti," in *The Jewish*

Woman: New Perspectives, ed. E. Koltun (New York: Schocken, 1976) 241-47; **S. D. Goitein,** "The Song of Songs: A Female Composition," *Studies in the Bible* (Tel Aviv: Yavneh Press, 1957) 301-7, 316-17; repr. in *A Feminist Companion to the Song of Songs,* ed. A. Brenner (FCB 1; Sheffield: Sheffield Academic Press, 1993) 58-66; **J. M. Hadley,** "Wisdom and the Goddess," in *Wisdom in Ancient Israel: Essays in Honour of J. A. Emerton,* ed. J. Day, R. P. Gordon and H. G. M. Williamson (Cambridge: Cambridge University Press, 1995) 234-43; **M. Heijerman,** "Who Would Blame Her? The 'Strange' Woman of Proverbs 7," in *A Feminist Companion to Wisdom Literature,* ed. A. Brenner (FCB 9; Sheffield: Sheffield Academic Press, 1995) 100-109; **B. Honig,** "Ruth, the Model Emigrée: Mourning and the Symbolic Politics of Immigration," in *Ruth and Esther,* ed. A. Brenner (FCB 2/3; Sheffield: Sheffield Academic Press, 1999) 50-74; **B. B. Kaiser,** "Poet as Female Impersonator: The Image of Daughter Zion as Speaker in Biblical Poems of Suffering," *JR* 67 (1987) 164-82; **L. R. Klein,** "Job and the Womb: Text about Men, Subtext about Women," in *A Feminist Companion to Wisdom Literature,* ed. A. Brenner (FCB 9; Sheffield: Sheffield Academic Press, 1995) 186-200; **B. LaNeel Tanner,** "Hearing the Cries Unspoken: An Intertextual-Feminist Reading of Psalm 109," in *Wisdom and Psalms,* ed. A. Brenner and C. R. Fontaine (FCB 2/2; Sheffield: Sheffield Academic Press, 1998) 283-301; **T. Linafelt,** "Surviving Lamentations," *HBT* 17 (1995) 45-61; repr. in *A Feminist Companion to Reading the Bible: Approaches, Methods and Strategies,* ed. A. Brenner and C. Fontaine (FCB 11; Sheffield: Sheffield Academic Press, 1997) 344-57; **C. Maier and S. Schroer,** "What about Job? Questioning the Book of 'The Righteous Sufferer,'" in *Wisdom and Psalms,* ed. A. Brenner and C. R. Fontaine (FCB 2/2; Sheffield: Sheffield Academic Press, 1998) 175-204; **C. Meyers,** "Gender Imagery in the Song of Songs," *HAR* 10 (1986) 209-23; repr. in *A Feminist Companion to the Song of Songs,* ed. A. Brenner (FCB 1; Sheffield: Sheffield Academic Press, 1993a) 197-212; idem, "Returning Home: Ruth 1.8 and the Gendering of the Book of Ruth," in *A Feminist Companion to Ruth,* ed. A. Brenner (FCB 3; Sheffield: Sheffield Academic Press, 1993b) 85-114; **C. Newsom,** "Woman and the Discourse of Patriarchal Wisdom: A Study of Proverbs 1-9," in *Gender and Difference in Ancient Israel,* ed. P. L. Day (Minneapolis: Fortress, 1989) 142-60; **S. Niditch,**

"Esther: Folklore, Wisdom, Feminism and Authority," in *Underdogs and Tricksters: A Prelude to Folklore* (San Francisco: Harper & Row, 1987) 126-45, 168-70; repr. in *A Feminist Companion to Esther, Judith and Susannah*, ed. A. Brenner (FCB 7; Sheffield: Sheffield Academic Press, 1993) 26-46; **K. M. O'Connor,** "Lamentations," in *The Women's Bible Commentary*, ed. C. A. Newsom and S. H. Ringe (Louisville: Westminster John Knox, 1992) 187-91; **A. Ostriker,** "A Holy of Holies: The Song of Songs as Countertext," in *The Song of Songs*, ed. A. Brenner and C. R. Fontaine (FCB 2/6; Sheffield: Sheffield Academic Press, 2000) 36-54; **S. Schroer,** "Wise and Counselling Women in Ancient Israel: Literary and Historical Ideals of the Personified HOKMA," in *A Feminist Companion to Wisdom Literature*, ed. A. Brenner (FCB 9; Sheffield: Sheffield Academic Press, 1995) 67-84; idem, "'Under the Shadow of Your Wings': The Metaphor of God's Wings in the Psalms, Exodus 19.4, Deuteronomy 32.11 and Malachi 3.20, as Seen through the Perspective of Feminism and the History of Religion," in *Wisdom and Psalms*, ed. A. Brenner and C. R. Fontaine (FCB 2/2; Sheffield: Sheffield Academic Press, 1998) 264-82; **P. Trible,** *God and the Rhetoric of Sexuality* (Philadelphia: Fortress, 1978); **F. van Dijk-Hemmes,** "The Imagination of Power and the Power of Imagination," *JSOT* 44 (1989) 75-88; repr. in *A Feminist Companion to the Song of Songs*, ed. A. Brenner (FCB 1; Sheffield: Sheffield Academic Press, 1993a), 156-70; idem, "Ruth: A Product of Women's Culture," in *A Feminist Companion to Ruth*, ed. A. Brenner (FCB 3; Sheffield: Sheffield Academic Press, 1993b) 134-39; **E. van Wolde,** "The Development of Job: Mrs Job as Catalyst," in *A Feminist Companion to Wisdom Literature*, ed. A. Brenner (FCB 9; Sheffield: Sheffield Academic Press, 1995) 201-21; idem, "Texts in Dialogue with Texts: Intertextuality in the Ruth and Tamar Narratives," *BibInt* 5 (1997a) 1-28; repr. as "Intertextuality: Ruth in Dialogue with Tamar," in *A Feminist Companion to Reading the Bible: Approaches, Methods and Strategies*, ed. A. Brenner and C. R. Fontaine (FCB 11; Sheffield: Sheffield Academic Press, 1997b) 426-51; **S. A. White,** "Esther: A Feminine Model for Jewish Diaspora?" in *Gender and Difference in Ancient Israel*, ed. P. L. Day (Minneapolis: Fortress, 1989) 161-77; **B. Wyler,** "Esther: The Incomplete Emancipation of a Queen," in *A Feminist Companion to Esther, Judith and Susanna*, ed. A. Brenner (FCB 7; Sheffield:

Sheffield Academic Press, 1993) 111-35. **G. A. Yee,** "'I Have Perfumed My Bed with Myrrh': The Foreign Woman (*'iššā zārâ*) in Proverbs 1-9," *JSOT* 43 (1989) 53-68; repr. in *A Feminist Companion to Wisdom Literature*, ed. A. Brenner (FCB 9; Sheffield: Sheffield Academic Press, 1995) 110-26.

L.-S. Tiemeyer

FESTIVALS. *See* CULT, WORSHIP: PSALMS; MEGILLOT AND FESTIVALS; PURIM.

FLORAL IMAGERY

Floral imagery is understood as anything related to plant life that is mentioned in the poetry and Wisdom literature of the OT. Here, this huge subject will be divided in terms of those plants whose products are consumed, those whose products are either applied to the person or used for other human activities, and those plants that are otherwise mentioned in the Wisdom literature. In many cases, various identifications have been proposed for some of the flora described here. This is especially true where the item occurs only once and is therefore subject to a variety of possible referents, given the absence of a more precise description. Designations of various plants are made primarily on the basis of three sources: (1) ancient West Semitic and other Near Eastern sources, including the Hebrew Bible, where the term or its cognate occurs and is described; (2) later sources, including translations of Hebrew terms in the Greek LXX, the Syriac Peshitta, the Latin Vulgate, and the Aramaic *Targumim, as well as the rabbinic literature that comments on the plants mentioned in the Bible; (3) the environment, including both the paleobotanical analyses that recover flora at various archaeological sites throughout the biblical world and what is known of the present ecology in these lands and what kinds of flora the environment supports.

    1. Variety of Flora in Ancient Israel
    2. Edible Flora
    3. Cosmetics and Aromatics
    4. Other Plants

1. Variety of Flora in Ancient Israel.
The wide-ranging topography and numerous ecological zones of Palestine allow for the appearance of numerous and varied types of flora. Beyond that, its neighbors to the north and south were famous for the cedars of Lebanon and the papyrus of Egypt. Finally, the land's role as a crossroads for trade and mercantile activity

brought to it exotic spices and other precious materials from South Arabia and beyond. The poetry of the Bible, with its richness of imagery and expression, found a ready source for inspiration in the beauty and variety of floral sources. One of the earliest Hebrew inscriptions (some would claim that it is closer to Phoenician), dating c. 900 BC and found at the south Palestinian city of Gezer, is itself a poem describing the agricultural year. Beginning with the autumn, it takes the reader through the twelve months of the year and mentions no less than four types of flora, despite its brevity:

Two months of ingathering,
Two months of sowing,
Two months of late sowing,

A month of chopping flax,
A month of barley harvest,
A month of harvest and measuring,

Two months of grape cutting,
A month of summer fruit.

Some seven centuries later, well into the Hellenistic period, the writer of Sirach personifies wisdom in a series of similes drawn from the flora of the region:

I was exalted like a cedar in Libanus,
and as a cypress tree upon the mountains of Hermon.
I was exalted like a palm tree in En-Gaddi,
and as a rose plant in Jericho,
as a fair olive tree in a pleasant field,
and grew up as a plane tree by the water.
I gave a sweet smell like cinnamon and aspalathus,
and I yielded a pleasant odour like the best myrrh,
as galbanum, and onyx, and sweet storax,
and as the fume of frankincense in the tabernacle.
As the turpentine tree I stretched out my branches,
and my branches are the branches of honour and grace.
As the vine brought I forth pleasant savour,
and my flowers are the fruit of honour and riches. (Sir 24:13-17 KJV)

More than a source of life, the flora served as a potent source of poetic imagery for Israel's poets and sages.

2. Edible Flora.

The staple diet in ancient Israel consisted of products made from barley and wheat grains. In addition to the production of bread, the grain could be roasted and eaten as soon as it was gathered (Ruth 2:14). Harvested in March/April, barley was presented as a firstfruits offering at the Feast of Unleavened Bread. *Naomi and her daughter-in-law *Ruth arrived in Bethlehem at the beginning of the barley harvest, and it was during that harvest that she gleaned in the fields of *Boaz (Ruth 1:22; 2:17). She remained until the end of the wheat harvest, which would follow the Feast of Weeks, or Pentecost, in May/June (Ruth 2:23). At that time the firstfruits of the wheat harvest were presented to God. "Barley" and "wheat" can be used as a word pair, as in Job's self-imprecation for briars and weeds instead of wheat and barley (Job 31:40). However, wheat appears more frequently in the poetic literature to describe desirable images. Barley was the food of farm animals and of the poor. Whereas barley never occurs in *Psalms, God's promise to satisfy Israel with the finest of wheat parallels honey (Ps 81:16 [MT 17]) and national peace (Ps 147:14). Sirach 39:26 also refers to wheat, along with salt, honey, milk, wine and oil, when describing what is necessary for a person to live.

The product of the grains most frequently consumed was bread. For *Job, divine instruction is treasured more than his daily bread, which he does not hesitate to share with the poor (Job 23:12; 31:17). In Psalms the dominant imagery for bread includes themes of basic sustenance (Ps 37:25; 104:15), fellowship (Ps 41:9 [MT 10]), evil and evildoers (Ps 14:4; 53:4 [MT 5]; 80:5 [MT 6]), and the manna in the wilderness (Ps 78:25; 105:40; cf. Wis 16:20). In *Proverbs bread imagery is used in connection with the recurring themes of wickedness (Prov 4:17) or idleness (Prov 31:27) and of bread as the essential commodity of life (Prov 6:26; 28:21; 30:8). The well-known proverb of Ecclesiastes 11:1, admonishing the reader to cast bread upon the waters and to find it again much later, also suggests the theme of a basic commodity, as do the occurrences in *Lamentations (e.g., Lam 1:11; 2:12) and in Sirach (e.g., Sir 10:27; 12:5).

Olives and grapes were the other two crops

chiefly cultivated in biblical times. Ideal for the rocky hillside soil of the Mediterranean region, the olive tree does not compete for arable soil with the grains. As a major source of oil and fat in the human diet, it is used in parallel with cream in Job's description of his earlier blessed life (Job 29:6). Its long lifespan, as well as the strength and endurance of such a tree, invites comparison with those who belong forever to the house of God (Ps 52:8 [MT 10]). Perhaps the same characteristics lie behind a blessing of children who will be like olive shoots, not to mention the export of oil as a major source of economic success for Palestine (Ps 128:3). The olive tree is a symbol of fruitfulness (Sir 50:10). The misfortune of the wicked is likened to the loss of olives and grapes, where these occur in parallel (Job 15:33). Grapes are mentioned explicitly elsewhere in the biblical poetic books only in Psalm 80:12 (MT 13), where the lack of protection allows passers by to pick them, just as God allows foreigners to invade Israel. A cluster of grapes represents the female lover's breasts in Song of Songs 7:8 (MT 9), suggesting fecundity and the object of desire. Treading the winepress full of grapes is an image of the labor of learning wisdom (Sir 33:16-17), as the flower before the ripened grape is an image of youth searching for wisdom (Sir 51:15). In addition to one of the necessities of life, the grape's "blood" serves as a libation to God (Sir 39:26; 50:15).

References to wine occur frequently and in many forms. There is the vinegar of wine used for dipping bread (Ruth 2:14), which also appears as an unpleasant drink (Ps 69:21 [MT 22]). There is also the royal wine drunk by the king of Persia and his guests (e.g., Esther 1:7-10) and by the children of Job in their partying (Job 1:13, 18). Elsewhere, wine can be a symbol of joy and blessing (Ps 4:7 [MT 8]; Prov 3:10; Eccles 9:7; 10:19) or of calamity and judgment (Ps 60:3 [MT 9]; Prov 4:17). Wine mixed with (narcotic?) substances provides an image of the worst of divine judgment (Ps 75:8 [MT 9]) and of the seduction that leads to death (Prov 9:2, 5). It is also a symbol of immoderation, and its use in Proverbs brings poverty to those who wish to succeed (Prov 20:1; 21:17; 23:20, 30, 31; 31:4) but relief for those in distress (Prov 31:6). More than any other book, *Song of Songs images the inebriation of wine in kissing (Song 1:2; 7:9 [MT 10]) and in lovemaking (Song 1:4; 4:10; 5:1; 7:2 [MT 3]; 8:2). Nevertheless, in later Jewish Wisdom lit-

erature its dominant image is that of the ungodly (Wis 2:7) and of a source of ruin when drunk to excess (Sir 9:9; 19:2; 31:25-31). Even here, however, wine imbibed in moderation is a joy (Sir 31:28; 32:5-6; 40:20; 49:1).

The date palm appears in Song of Songs 7:7-8 (MT 8-9), where the male likens his lover to such a tree, and her breasts to its cluster of fruit. This echoes an image found on iconography for millennia throughout the ancient Near East (Keel, 240-48). The honey produced from the dates could be a special sweetness and a source of energy. It is sometimes indistinguishable from the honey produced by bees. Date honey may appear as a blessing in Job 20:17 and as a picture of the sweetness of God's law in Psalm 119:103. In Proverbs the lips of the adulteress drip honey (Prov 5:3), and overindulgence in the sweet liquid leads to illness (Prov 25:16, 27; 27:7). The male in the Song of Songs finds milk and honey under his lover's tongue (Song 5:1). In Sirach honey is also paired with milk, including the promise of the land of milk and honey (Sir 39:26; 46:8). It also describes remembrances of saintly figures (Sir 49:1).

The fig tree ripens its fruit several times between June and September, encouraging an image of diligence in order to gain as much fruit as possible (Prov 27:18). Its early harvest produces the sweetest fruit and is the time for the lovers in Song of Songs (Song 2:13). Elsewhere, the loss of fig trees and sycamore figs is a sign of God's judgment against Egypt (Ps 78:47; 105:33). A different tree, the almond tree, produces white blossoms and serves as a metaphor for old age and the coming of white hair (Eccles 12:5).

The pomegranate, a round red fruit filled with seeds, is a symbol of fruitfulness and fertility. Among the psalms and in Wisdom literature it occurs only in Song of Songs. It is used in the pictures of the garden—a metaphor for the female body and its beauty and fruitfulness (Song 4:13; 6:11; 7:12 [MT 13]; 8:2). The pomegranate is also used to describe the female's cheeks or temples hidden behind her veil (Song 4:3; 6:7).

The Hebrew term *tappûah* appears in Proverbs 25:11, where it describes golden representations of this fruit set in silver. Some, however, understand this as grapes of gold rather than a fruit normally associated with the Hebrew term. Elsewhere the term occurs four times in Song of Songs (Song 2:3, 5; 7:8 [7:9 MT]; 8:5), where the tree-grown fruit is sweet and refreshing, producing fragrant breath. The last occurrence in Song of Songs associates the tree with a place of sexual arousal and conception. Although some have identified the fruit as apricot or quince, the most likely designation remains the apple. Despite claims to the contrary, the apple is not limited to more northern areas. It occurs frequently in Greco-Roman literature and appears much earlier in Sumerian texts. The apple in the expression "the apple of one's eye" (Ps 17:8; Prov 7:2; Sir 17:22) is not a reference to a fruit in the original languages; rather, it literally describes the "(little) person" reflected in the pupil of the eye.

3. Cosmetics and Aromatics.

Psalm 45:8 (MT 9) introduces the robes of the royal bride as being perfumed with myrrh, aloes and cassia. Myrrh is a reddish gum resin of some value that would have been imported from southern Arabia. Its value and desirability form a picture of the female's lover (Song 1:13; 5:13), of the perfumed female (Song 3:6; 4:14), of her breasts (Song 4:6) and of the feverish perspiration as she opens to her lover (Song 5:1). Both aloe and cassia derive from India, although the former is also found in eastern Africa and Yemen. It is small with jagged edges to its leaves. The red flowers produce an aromatic juice that was used in embalming processes in Egypt. Like myrrh, aloe describes the female (Song 4:14). In Proverbs 7:17 the bed of the seductress corresponds to the robes of Psalm 45, as it is perfumed with myrrh, aloes and cinnamon. Here cinnamon substitutes for cassia.

Following the MT, spikenard and henna are associated with myrrh in Song of Songs 1:12-14 as perfumes that describe the female and her regard for her lover. Spikenard, or pure nard, comes from the Himalayas. On the other hand, henna occurs as a yellow flower that is native to Palestine. It is commonly used as a reddish dye and can be applied to the body as a deodorant and perfume. With myrrh, spikenard and henna occur in these verses to describe the increasing intimacy that the female envisions for her and her lover.

The greatest concentration of fruits and aromatics occurs in the male's description of his lover's body as a garden that he visits in Song of Songs 4:13-14: greenery, a garden of pomegranates, the best of fruits, henna and spikenard, spikenard and turmeric, spice cane and cinnamon, trees of frankincense, myrrh and aloes,

the best spices. "Turmeric," rather than "saffron," best renders *karkōm* as an aromatic from southeastern Asia. The yellow substance from the flower can be used as a dye and a spice. Spice cane and cinnamon are used with myrrh to produce the holy anointing oil of the tabernacle in Exodus 30:23. If spice cane originated in southeast Arabia, cinnamon came from eastern India, Sri Lanka and China. "Frankincense," rather than "incense," best renders *lĕbônâ* ("whiteness"). Like myrrh, it occurs in southern Arabia and Somaliland (i.e., Djibouti, Somalia and southeastern Ethiopia). Its association with royalty in Song of Songs 3:6 and with myrrh in Song of Songs 4:6 attest to its rarity and value. It was burned to produce a pleasing aroma (Sir 24:15; 39:14; 50:8 [with roses and lilies]). Sirach 24:15 compares the aroma of frankincense with cinnamon and aspalathus, and with myrrh, galbanum, onyx and sweet storax.

If the term *'ezrâ* in Psalm 37:35 is to be so read (and not a metathesis of a form of *'erez* ["cedar"]), then this may designate the bay laurel, a tree accommodated to rocky hillsides whose leaves form wreaths and can be made into a spice. The caper tree is mentioned in Ecclesiastes 12:5. Apparently, it was believed to function as an aphrodisiac (NIV: "desire no longer is stirred"). Ecclesiastes 7:6 identifies the thorny burnet, whose leaves could be used as a potherb.

Flowers whose aroma could be appreciated include the *hăbaṣṣālet*, which is variously rendered as "crocus," "asphodel," "rose" or some other flower bulb. Precise identification is uncertain (cf. the blossoms in Song 2:12), but it serves as a symbol of fertility and beauty in the wilderness (see Is 35:1) and similarly of the female as she describes herself in Song of Songs 2:1. There as well she compares herself to the *šûšan*, sometimes understood as a lily but best interpreted as a water lily or lotus (1 Kings 7:26) and borrowed from the Egyptian term. Although used medicinally in Egypt, lilies appear in the titles (or melodic directions) for four psalms (Ps 45; 60; 69; 80). The flower is mentioned eight times in Song of Songs, whether to describe aspects of the female's beauty (Song 2:2; 7:2 [7:3 MT]), the male's beauty (Song 5:13), or the beautiful setting of the woman's features and the couple's love (Song 2:16; 4:5; 6:2, 3; cf. Sir 39:14). If lotuses can arouse emotions of beauty and love, wormwood or gall can reflect the bitterness of folly or the despair of God's absence (Prov 5:4; Lam 3:15, 19).

If the *ḥallāmût* of Job 6:6 is a vegetable, not an egg or cheese, then it is likely the mallow, a wild plant with a hairy stem and leaves and reddish flowers. Its mucilage is referenced here as being flavorless. The mandrakes, or love fruits, were associated with fertility (Gen 30:14-16). Although their fruit could serve as food and their roots possessed narcotic properties, the focus of Song of Songs 7:13 (MT 14) considers the pleasing and distinctive fragrance that arouses and delights in the context of lovemaking.

4. Other Plants.

Although many of the following plants might be listed under edible flora, their use for human consumption is not described in the Bible.

Identified variously as bramble or buckthorn, the *'āṭād* grows to threaten the pots in Ps 58:9 (58:10 MT). Although its black fruit was used medicinally, this was not the focus of the psalmist's comment. Another plant native to the desert areas of Palestine is the broom bush. This bush grew to be four to twelve feet in height, and the biblical poets focus on its roots, which were used for charcoal. It forms an undesirable fruit in Job 30:4, and its burning coals are the substance of punishment in Psalm 120:4. Elsewhere are other plants of the thorny type. The basic bramble or thorny plant is used to describe the paths of the wicked (Prov 22:5; cf. 2 Esdr 16:32, 77) and the extent to which the hungry will go to gain food (Job 5:5). Nettle occupies the wilderness (Job 30:7) and grows wherever the land is not tended (Prov 24:31). Another type of thorny plant *(ḥēdeq)* blocks the way of the lazy person (Prov 15:19). A final type of thorn bush or thistle *(ḥôaḥ)* occurs as an example of a curse (Job 31:40), a metaphor for the misuse of a proverb (Prov 26:9), and as an image of the friends of a woman in comparison with her surpassing loveliness (Song 2:2). Only in Sirach (Sir 28:24) do thorns became a means of defense for one's possessions.

A poisonous plant *(rō'š)*, possibly related to hemlock, describes the bitter feelings of the author who saw Jerusalem destroyed (Lam 3:19).

The trees found in the poetic and wisdom books include the willow *('ărābâ)*, the pine or cypress *(běrôš)*, and the cedar *('erez)*. The willow or poplar was a tree associated with the exiles in Babylon (Ps 137:2) and with the streams by which they grow (Job 40:22). Found along waterways, the tree is a source of dye, medicines and wood for small objects. The pine is a home for the stork (Ps 104:17). The already noted cedar is one of the most frequently mentioned of all flora. It occurs some seventy-three times in the Bible, nine of which are found in the poetic books. Evidence of its wood appears in biblical-period strata from many ancient sites in and around Palestine, attesting to its use in major (often state-sponsored) projects of the period of the monarchy. The cedars are associated with the cedars of Lebanon (Ps 104:16), often used for building materials (1 Esdr 4:48; 5:55). They are powerful trees (Ps 80:10 [MT 11]) planted by God (Ps 104:16). The might of the behemoth has a tail that is compared to the cedar (Job 40:17), just as others will use it for an image of personal strength and security (Sir 24:13; 50:12). Yet the voice of the Lord is powerful enough to break these mighty trees (Ps 29:5). In Song of Songs cedar wood builds the house of the lovers (Song 1:17) and is the material that the female uses to describe her lover's appearance (Song 5:15). It is also a strong material used to defend the female's sister (Song 8:9). Thus the cedar tree is used to represent strength and power, as well as security and a certain nobility. This is reflected in the cedar of Lebanon, a tree that can reach over one hundred feet in height and half a millennium in lifespan. These facts, combined with the tree's massive size, provide a vivid picture of strength and endurance. At least once, the cedar appears in parallel with the palm tree (Ps 92:12 [MT 13]), where both trees symbolize growth and success. In Song of Songs the female is compared with the palm tree in terms of her height and beauty (Song 7:7-8).

This survey does not exhaust all the flora mentioned in the wisdom and poetic books. General terms for grass *('ēseb, deše'* [Job 5:25; 6:5]), salty and bitter herbs *(mallûaḥ, mārōr* [Job 30:4; Lam 3:15]) and flowers *(ṣiṣ* [Ps 103:15]) all imply the presence of a rich and verdant physical world that could stimulate the imagination of Israel's poets and sages.

See also ANIMAL IMAGERY; ARCHITECTURAL IMAGERY; CREATION IMAGERY; IMAGERY; MOUNTAIN IMAGERY; WASF.

BIBLIOGRAPHY. **O. Borowski,** *Agriculture in Iron Age Israel: The Evidence from Archaeology and the Bible* (Winona Lake, IN: Eisenbrauns, 1987); idem, *Daily Life in Biblical Times* (SBLABS 5; Atlanta: Society of Biblical Literature, 2003); **F. N.**

Hepper, *Illustrated Encyclopedia of Bible Plants: Flowers and Trees, Fruits and Vegetables, Ecology* (Leicester: Inter-Varsity Press, 1992); **R. S. Hess,** *Song of Songs* (BCOTWP; Grand Rapids: Baker, 2005); **D. C. Hopkins,** *The Highlands of Canaan: Agricultural Life in the Early Iron Age* (SWBA 3; Sheffield: Almond, 1985); **I. Jacob and W. Jacob,** "Flora," *ABD* 2.803-17; **O. Keel,** *The Song of Songs* (CC; Minneapolis: Fortress, 1994); **P. J. King,** *Jeremiah: An Archaeological Companion* (Louisville: Westminster John Knox, 1993); **P. J. King and L. E. Stager,** *Life in Biblical Israel* (LAI; Louisville: Westminster John Knox, 2001); **W. D. Suderman,** "Modest or Magnificent? Lotus versus Lily in Canticles," *CBQ* 67 (2005) 42-58.

R. S. Hess

FOLLY

Folly is the antithesis of *wisdom (Prov 15:21; Eccles 2:13, 19), and the fool is one who hates "knowledge" and the *"fear of the LORD" (Prov 1:22, 29). The book of *Proverbs in particular offers an extensive character study of fools and their ways, while the books of *Psalms and *Ecclesiastes further illustrate the nature of folly. *Job will not be considered here because, although it deals with the character of wisdom, it explicitly treats folly only very marginally.

1. Terms for "Fool/Folly" and Some Related Concepts
2. Folly in Proverbs
3. Folly in Ecclesiastes
4. Folly in Psalms
5. The Characteristics of Folly
6. The Consequence of Folly
7. New Testament Development

1. Terms for "Fool/Folly" and Some Related Concepts.

The Hebrew words ʾĕwîl, kĕsîl, sākāl and nābāl are traditionally rendered "fool," and their associated abstract nouns, principally ʾiwwelet, kĕsîlût, siklût and nĕbālâ, "folly." Closely associated terms include petî ("simple, gullible"), ḥăsar-lēb ("mindless"), baʿar ("senseless") and lēṣ ("mocker").

Apart from the "simple" *(petî),* whose manner of life is not yet fixed, the universe of the Wisdom writings, particularly Proverbs, seems, at least on the surface, to be divided into two entrenched camps: the wise and the foolish. The two commonest terms for "fool" in the Wisdom writings are kĕsîl (71x in the OT, all in the Wisdom books)

and ʾĕwîl (22x in the Wisdom writings, 4x elsewhere in the OT). For the kĕsîl ("fool"), folly is a way of life, one not based on revealed knowledge and covenantal *righteousness. If the fear of Yahweh is the fundamental principle of wisdom (Prov 1:7; 9:10), it is the lack of such fear that characterizes the fool (Prov 1:22, 29). The fool is not so much one who inherently lacks intelligence as one who is morally perverse and resistant to the way of the Lord. As such, the fool is contrasted with the "righteous" and closely identified with the "wicked," who delight in doing evil (Prov 10:21, 23; 13:19), just as the "wise" and the "righteous" are coreferential (Prov 9:9; 23:24; Eccles 9:1). The word ʾĕwîl is used with little if any differentiation from kĕsîl, though some detect in ʾĕwîl a slightly stronger term. Fox (41) suggests that the ʾĕwîl is obtuse because of moral perversion, whereas the kĕsîl is or is likely to become morally perverse because of obtuseness, but this subtle distinction is difficult to sustain. Where the two roots are brought into association (and the two terms for "fool" are never found in parallel), it is always the kĕsîl ("fool") who is said to practice ʾiwwelet ("folly"), and in ways suggesting that this folly is both a cause and a result of being a kĕsîl, most notably Proverbs 14:24: "the folly [ʾiwwelet] of fools [kĕsîlîm] yields folly [ʾiwwelet]" (cf. Prov 12:23; 13:16; 14:8; 15:2, 14; 17:12; 26:4-5, 11).

Another word group is derived from the root skl. Sākāl ("fool, foolish") and siklût (śiklût)/sekel ("folly") are restricted in the Wisdom literature to Ecclesiastes (Eccles 1:17; 2:3, 12, 19; 7:17, 25; 10:1, 3, 6, 13, 14). Again, such folly is the result not of a lack of intelligence but rather of a morally perverse stance ("wickedness is folly," or perhaps "folly is wickedness" [Eccles 7:25]), and it is difficult to discern any significant difference in meaning from the other words for "folly" discussed above.

The root nbl is more sparingly used in the Wisdom writings for "fool" and "folly" (9x) and may represent the most hardened of the categories normally glossed as "fool." Through a study of its use elsewhere in the OT, Phillips suggests that a nābāl ("fool") is one who exhibits serious disorderly and unruly conduct leading to the breakup of a relationship. This is borne out by its use in Psalms 14:1; 53:1, where the nābāl ("fool") is the practical atheist whose frame of reference excludes God and the divine revelation. Such fools revile and mock Yahweh's name—that is, God and his revealed character (Ps 74:18, 22). In Proverbs 30:32 such a fool (nābāl) is one who indulges in self-exaltation and plans evil, while in Proverbs 17:7 such fools have "arrogant lips." At the heart of such folly is the quest for human autonomy, the reliance on one's own resources and the failure to acknowledge that true knowledge is derivative from God's—the sin of the garden of Eden. This is not markedly different from the opinionated and self-reliant fool (kĕsîl) of Proverbs 18:2; 28:26 or of the fool ('ewîl) in Proverbs 12:15 whose "way seems right to him."

The petî (related to pātâ ["be open"]) is simpleminded, lacking experience in making moral choices, ready to believe anything (Prov 14:15) (Waltke, 93). Though this word is used without a pejorative tone in Psalms, where it even suggests childlike trust (Ps 19:7; 116:6; 119:130; cf. 1QpHab XII, 4), in Proverbs (15x) it refers to those who are easily led astray (generally the young). It is such impressionable youth who are the target of the competing attentions of *Woman Wisdom and Woman Folly in Proverbs 9. The Wisdom books operate with a doctrine of original sin, for "folly is inherent in a child" (Prov 22:15). The "simple" in Proverbs are not so much morally neutral as morally tainted by the company that they keep ("fools" and "mockers" [Prov 1:22]). Left uncorrected, the innate "perversity" (mĕšûbâ [Prov 1:32]; elsewhere only in the Prophets) of the young will naturally tend to the practice of folly and is in need of the remedy of knowledge and prudence (Prov 1:4; 22; 8:5; 14:18; 21:11).

On the other end of the scale, and closely related to the terms for "fool" discussed above, is baʿar, which refers to a "senseless" person (Ps 49:10; 92:6; 94:8) whose behavior seems less than fully human (Ps 73:22; Prov 30:2). Perhaps the strongest of the words associated with fools is lēṣ ("mocker"), one who behaves with overbearing arrogance and who seems locked into a cynical mindset that allows no room for correction (Ps 1:1; Prov 1:22; 3:34; 9:7, 8, 12; 13:1; 14:6; 15:12 ; 21:24).

2. Folly in Proverbs.

By far the most extended treatment of the nature of folly is to be found in the book of Proverbs. Proverbs 1—9 is devoted to an elaborate depiction of wisdom, though at many points the character of folly and those whose lives are caught up in it is implicit by way of antithesis with the depiction of wisdom, without a word for "folly" necessarily being mentioned (e.g., Prov 1:10-19). Likewise in the sentences that constitute the bulk of the book from Proverbs 10, the nature of folly is revealed explicitly by reference to fools and their behavior and inferentially from its contrast with the character of wisdom. Proverbs 10—15, with its more antithetical style of sentence proverbs, has a greater concentration of explicit statements about folly beginning with the programmatic "A wise son is a joy to his father, but a foolish son is a source of grief to his mother" (Prov 10:1). What follows is a character sketch of a fool, told with touches of humor—for example, the exaggeration in the image of a fool sleeping through harvest (Prov 10:5). The composite portrayal of a fool is designed to reveal the ugliness and ruinous nature of folly. As with all proverbs, one must ponder whether statements about fools are intended as universals or as illustrations of the foolish behavior of some in some situations. Is it always the case that silence is a sign of wisdom, and loquaciousness the mark of a fool (Prov 10:19)? It will sometimes be wise to respond to a fool according to his folly, and sometimes not (Prov 26:4-5).

Just as wisdom is portrayed in the book of Proverbs as a woman inviting the young to her banquet (Prov 9:1-6), so too is folly personified (Prov 9:13-18), and both figures have attracted considerable scholarly interest (see Waltke, 83-87). Both women vie for the attentions of the impressionable, and the appeal of their competing attentions is enhanced by sexual imagery. Each seeks to influence the civic and religious life of the community ("the highest point of the city" [Prov 9:3, 14]); each uses alluring speech and the promise of delectable food as enticements to enter her house. Whereas Wisdom is open and honest in her dealings, casting a watchful eye over her charges (Prov 4:6), Folly is "loudmouthed" and "ignorant" (or "uncaring") (Prov 9:13), thus sharing some characteristics with her targeted clientele (Prov 9:16). She offers her guests illicit fare: "stolen water and food eaten in secret" (Prov 9:17).

Just as suggestions have been made for the origin of the figure of Woman Wisdom in female deities, similar suggestions have been made in the case of Woman Folly. Principal among the deities proposed are Ishtar-Astarte and Anat (Fontaine, 142). Like Anat in the Ugaritic text *Aqhat,* Folly is depicted as a seductive harlot (for the background of prostitution in the ancient world, see Lang, 97-109).

There are similarities in the depiction of Woman Folly and of the "strange woman" *(iššâ zārâ/nokriyyâ)* of Proverbs 2:16; 5:3, 20; 6:24; 7:5; 20:16; 22:14; 23:27; 27:13. Although this figure is sometimes regarded as a foreign seductress, with perhaps overtones of cultic prostitution (cf. 1 Kings 11:9-13; see Blenkinsopp), a better understanding might be that the woman is simply the wife of another man, and thus is an adulterous (presumably Israelite) woman (Whybray, 72-73) whose blandishments embody all that is alluring but off limits to the one who seeks to live by wisdom (Prov 2:16; 5:3; 7:5). While at one level such passages address the literal problem of sexual license, since adultery functions (particularly in the Prophets) as a common image of apostasy (Jer 3:9; Ezek 6:9; Hos 1:2), the figure of the adulterous woman (likened also to a harlot [Prov 23:27]), with the emphasis on her seductive speech (Yee), may serve to suggest other forms of waywardness (Camp, 40-71). The *personification of Folly in Proverbs 9, then, may be simply a creative projection of this image (assisted by the feminine gender of *kĕsîlût* [Prov 9:13]), similar to the personification in Psalm 85:10 of "righteousness and peace." Both the "strange woman" (Prov 2:10-19; 5:1-6) and the personified Folly of Proverbs 9:13-18 are counterposed with Wisdom. The reference to "covenant" in Proverbs 2:17 (its only occurrence in Proverbs) would seem to point beyond the breach of a literal marriage covenant to Israel's covenant unfaithfulness to God. J. Crenshaw (80) notes the prophetic influence on the personified Wisdom. There may similarly be an indication of prophetic language in Proverbs 9:16, with its use of the prophetic term *sûr* ("turn aside, deviate" [cf. Jer 6:28]), thus casting Folly in the role of a false prophet. So it would seem that, with J. Miles (87-101), we should see the figure of the "strange woman" as merging with Woman Folly and filling out the picture. Whereas Wisdom presents as a trustworthy figure, operating in the light, her counterpart is a creature of the night, whose ways are deceptive.

3. Folly in Ecclesiastes.
While also using *kĕsîl* for "fool," Ecclesiastes employs as its characteristic word for "folly" *siklût (śiklût)*, with *sākāl* for "fool" (Eccles 1:17; 2:3, 12, 13, 19; 7:17, 25; 10:1, 3, 6, 13, 14). Such folly is closely associated with "madness" (*hôlēlôt* [Ec-

cles 1:17; 2:12; 7:25; 9:3]; *hôlēlût* [Eccles 10:13]) as a description of the lifestyle that exalts the pursuit of pleasure, and the one whose thoughts are recorded wonders if there is any advantage of wisdom over folly (Eccles 1:17; 2; 6:8; 7:25). In keeping with the tenor of the book, Ecclesiastes portrays folly as a perplexing phenomenon of the real world to be reckoned with, a consequence perhaps of the warped post-fall state of the world (Eccles 7:13). It is frustrating when fools, for example, unsuited to positions of responsibility, are found in high office (Eccles 4:13; 10:6). In other sections of Ecclesiastes are found sentiments reminiscent of the more conventional sentences of the book of Proverbs regarding folly (Eccles 2:13; 5:1, 3-4; 7:4-5, 9, 17, 25; 9:17; 10:1-3, 12-15).

4. Folly in Psalms.
Folly is only an incidental topic in Psalms (Ps 14:1; 38:5; 39:8; 49:10; 53:1; 69:5; 74:18, 22; 85:8; 92:6; 94:8; 107:17), and Psalms presents a somewhat different angle from that of Proverbs. The psalmist seems more ready to acknowledge the ever-present folly or threat of a slide into folly on his own part or of the people of God (Ps 38:5; 69:5; 85:8; 107:17). Psalm 107 is typical of this sentiment in describing the wavering faith of the "redeemed of Yahweh" (Ps 107:2), some of whom "became fools through their rebellious ways" (Ps 107:17) and who then cried out to Yahweh in their distress and were delivered (Ps 107:19). It is also in Psalms that we find the nearest thing in the OT to an expression of atheism or, more accurately, the sin of total disregard for God that characterizes the fool (*nābāl* [Ps 14:1; 53:1]), the universal attitude of those who pit themselves against God and his people. Once, in a passage akin to the mood of Ecclesiastes, the psalmist laments the common fate that befalls the wise and fools (Ps 49:10).

5. The Characteristics of Folly.
From the books of Proverbs, Psalms and Ecclesiastes some common characteristics of folly may be noted. Much of what is said about fools concerns their speech. A fool's mouth is his or her undoing (Prov 18:7) because what is on the tongue and the lips betrays what is in the heart or mind (Prov 10:20-21; 12:23; 15:7, 28; 16:23). The mouth of the fool *(kĕsîl)* both "feeds on" (Prov 15:14) and in turn "spouts" folly (*'iwwelet* [Prov 15:2]). Fools speak too soon and without

listening (Prov 12:23; 18:13). They say too much (Prov 26:7; Eccles 5:3, 10:14). They slander others (Prov 10:18; 11:12; 20:19), are quarrelsome (Prov 20:3), irascible (Eccles 7:9), quick to take offense (Prov 12:16) or verbally aggressive (Prov 29:9). Although fools can at times say valid things such as proverbs, these proverbs, lacking a revelatory frame of reference, are "disabled" (Prov 26:7; cf. Sir 20:20).

More generally, fools are marked by their arrogant and self-confident stance (Prov 14:16) and their complacency (Prov 1:32). They are lazy (Prov 24:30; Eccles 4:5), improvident (Prov 21:20), careless (Prov 26:10) and unreliable (Prov 26:6). They are insincere in their religious commitments (Eccles 5:1, 4) and seek their own pleasure as their highest end (Eccles 7:4). But once they get an idea in their heads, there is nothing stopping them (Prov 17:12). By their behavior, fools are a cause of shame and grief to their parents (Prov 15:20; 17:21, 25; 19:13), a nonentity in the community (Prov 24:7) and held up to public shame (Prov 3:35) (see Honor and Shame).

However, folly is not ultimately about isolated acts of stupidity or waywardness but rather is about a different epistemology, a different orientation to knowledge (Crenshaw, 81). It is succumbing to the allure of this world's godless knowledge as opposed to the knowledge that is based on the "fear of Yahweh" (Prov 1:7, 29). The choice is between autonomy and submission to the Creator. Since "water reflects a face as a person's heart reflects the person" (Prov 27:19), all of the specific outworkings of folly are evidence of a heart-orientation (Ps 14:1; Prov 5:12; 12:23; Eccles 7:4; 10:2) that rejects the revelation of God. The fool is one who literally has a "deficiency of heart" *(ḥăsar-lēb)*—that is, someone who lacks sense (Prov 6:32; 7:7; 9:4, 16; 10:13, 21; 11:12; 12:11; 15:21; 17:18; 24:30) and thus is self-deluding (Prov 14:8).

6. The Consequence of Folly.

What, then, is the outcome of folly? Is there a remedy for folly, or are fools (excluding perhaps the "simple" *[peṯî]* beyond hope? On the one hand, there are absolute statements about the irremediable state of the fool: "Even if you grind a fool *[ʾěwîl]* in a mortar, grinding him like grain with a pestle, you cannot remove his folly *[ʾiwwe let]* from him" (Prov 27:22). The categories of wise and fool seem, at least in Proverbs, to be

largely unalterable categories, and the fate of fools seems to be fixed. At the very least, when left undisciplined and uninstructed, folly persisted in leads to ruin and death (Prov 1:32; 5:23; 8:36; 10:8, 10, 14, 21; 14:12; 15:10; 16:25; 19:3, 18; 23:13; Eccles 4:5; 7:17). The fate of mockers is to be on the receiving end of the awful divine mockery (Prov 3:34).

Such statements need to be read in the context of the purpose of Proverbs as a book of instruction to the young and of warning to them to reflect on their relationship to God and pay attention to the instruction of the book before such attitudes harden, without identifying when that moment comes. Just as the wise need and benefit from reproof, and hence are not above the danger of sliding into folly (Prov 17:10), so also there are indications that enmeshment in folly is not irreversible. The cry "How long will mockers delight in mockery and fools hate knowledge?" (Prov 1:22; cf. Ps 94:8), akin to the anguished laments of Psalms 6:3; 13:1, suggests a hope that folly will not have the last word, and that those who currently deserve the appellation "fools" may not be irredeemable. The experience of the people of God in Psalm 107 rather suggests that mercy may be the hope of those at least of God's people who lapse into foolish behavior but who utter a heartfelt cry for deliverance. Though difficult and of uncertain outcome, since fools tend to despise discipline (Prov 1:7) and ridicule or abuse the means of restoration through sacrifice (Prov 14:9; Eccles 5:1), instruction is urged as the remedy (Prov 8:5), and discipline for fools is encouraged in the hope of a change of orientation (Prov 10:13; 16:22; 19:29; 22:15).

The choice between wisdom and folly is presented as the fundamental and most crucial decision to be made in life, particularly by the young—the choice between life and death—and so, in slightly different language, echoes the covenantal choices of life and death offered to Israel in places such as Deuteronomy 30:15.

7. New Testament Development.

The treatment of folly in the Wisdom writings forms the background to Jesus' strong language concerning the seriousness of calling someone a "fool" in Matthew 5:22. All the more striking, then, is Jesus' illustration of the wise and foolish builders in Matthew 7:26-27, where it is the failure to put Jesus' own words into practice that puts one into the same category as the "fools" of the Wisdom writings, thus implicitly identifying Jesus with Yahweh as the source of knowledge for right living. Similarly, folly characterizes those who are unprepared for the coming of the messianic "bridegroom" (Mt 25:1-13). Paul's characterization of the cross as foolishness in the estimation of the "perishing" is an indictment on them for their failure to acknowledge the true wisdom from God (1 Cor 1:18-25).

See also PROVERBS 1: BOOK OF; WISDOM THEOLOGY; WOMAN WISDOM AND WOMAN FOLLY.

BIBLIOGRAPHY. **J. Blenkinsopp,** "The Social Context of the 'Outsider Woman' in Proverbs 1-9," *Bib* 72 (1991) 457-73; **C. Camp,** *Wise, Strange and Holy: The Strange Woman and the Making of the Bible* (JSOTSup 320; Sheffield: Sheffield Academic Press, 2000); **J. Crenshaw,** *Old Testament Wisdom: An Introduction* (rev. ed.; Louisville: Westminster John Knox, 1998); **C. Fontaine,** *Smooth Words: Women, Proverbs and Performance in Biblical Wisdom* (JSOTSup 356; Sheffield: Sheffield Academic Press, 2002); **M. Fox,** *Proverbs 1-9* (AB 18A; New York: Doubleday, 2000); **B. Lang,** *Wisdom and the Book of Proverbs: An Israelite Goddess Redefined* (New York: Pilgrim Press, 1986); **J. Miles,** *Wise King—Royal Fool: Semiotics, Satire and Proverbs 1-9* (London: T & T Clark International, 2004); **A. Phillips,** "NEBALAH—A Term for Serious Disorderly and Unruly Conduct," *VT* 25 (1975) 237-41; **B. Waltke,** *The Book of Proverbs: Chapters 1-15* (NICOT; Grand Rapids: Eerdmans, 2004); **N. Whybray,** *The Book of Proverbs: A Survey of Modern Study* (HBI 1; Leiden: E. J. Brill, 1995); **G. Yee,** "'I Have Perfumed My Bed with Myrrh': The Foreign Woman (*iššâ zārâ*) in Proverbs 1—9," *JSOT* 43 (1989) 53-68.　　　　J. Davies

FOOL, FOOLISHNESS. *See* FOLLY.

FORM CRITICISM

Form criticism is a foundational exegetical method in the modern critical interpretation of biblical texts. It analyzes the formal features of a text, including its unique syntactical and semantic form or literary structure and its typical linguistic genres that give shape to the text and function within it to facilitate its expression. Form criticism functions both synchronically to analyze the present literary form of the text and diachronically to ascertain and examine its compositional history in relation to its postulated written and oral stages. It works in tandem with other critical methodologies, such as *rhetorical criticism, redaction criticism (*see* Editorial Criticism), tradition-historical criticism (*see* Historical Criticism), *textual criticism, canonical criticism (*see* Canon), newer literary criticisms, the social sciences (*see* Social-Scientific Approaches) and linguistics in the interpretation of biblical texts. Form criticism is intimately concerned with the societal, historical, literary and conceptual settings in which the biblical texts were produced, in which they function, and in which they are read.

1. Form-Critical Theory
2. The Development of Form-critical Methodology
3. Form-Critical Study of Cultic Poetry
4. Form-Critical Study of the Wisdom Literature
5. Didactic Narrative

1. Form-Critical Theory.
A full understanding of the technical terminology employed in the field is essential. "Form" (German, *Form*) refers to the unique formulation of an individual text or communication, whereas "genre" (German, *Gattung*) refers to the typical conventions of expression or language that appear within a text. Genre does not constitute form; it functions within form. Other key terms include *Sitz im Leben* ("setting in life" or "societal setting"), *Sitz im Literatur* ("setting in literature" or "literary setting"), *Formkritik* ("form criticism," or the analytical study of the formal features of a text) and *Formgeschichte* ("the history of form"), which refers to the historical development and function of forms and genres in texts.

Each text is uniquely formulated and constitutes a singular event of communication in relation to the language in which the text is written or translated. Every language, including biblical *Hebrew, Koine Greek and biblical Aramaic, employs a combination of typical semantic, syntactic, and generic linguistic features and elements that are combined to produce its unique textual expressions. Thus, analysis of the formal literary structure of a biblical text requires a full understanding of the semantic and syntactical dimensions of biblical Hebrew, Koine Greek and biblical Aramaic in order to enable the interpreter to grasp the means by which a text organizes and presents its contents. Such formal literary structure appears in the seven-day creation pattern in Genesis 1:1—2:3, in which six days are devoted to creative acts and the seventh day is reserved for the Sabbath as a day of rest and renewal in all creation. It appears in the *acrostic patterns of the book of *Lamentations, in which each verse begins with a successive letter of the Hebrew alphabet as an artistic device that conveys the singer's grief at the downfall of Jerusalem (e.g., Lam 1). Job 10—11 employs the patterns of disputation and forensic speech to convey the demands of *Job for a fair hearing from YHWH.

Analysis of the textual versions of the Hebrew Bible requires a similar understanding of the semantic and syntactical dimensions of the language into which the text is translated or presented, such as Qumran Hebrew, Koine Greek once again, targumic Aramaic, Syriac, Latin and the various dialects of Ethiopic, Coptic, Arabic, Armenian and other relevant languages, in order to facilitate interpretation of the means by which each version reads and conceptualizes the biblical text in question. The versions are not simply translations of biblical texts; they present interpretations of biblical texts based upon the perspectives of their respective translators and the communities in which they were read. The interpreter cannot simply assume that a translated text conveys the same understanding as the parent text. The formal presentation of each text, whether it is a parent or a derivative text, must be evaluated on its own terms. The LXX, for example, reads Psalm 9 and Psalm 10 as a single psalm, so that Psalm 9, which praises G-d for turning back enemies, is combined with Psalm 10, which calls upon G-d to protect the people by punishing the wicked who threaten the people, to produce a text that ultimately demonstrates YHWH's *protection of the righteous. The LXX and targumic versions of *Esther include additional material that refers specifically to G-d in order to address the problem of divine absence in the Masoretic Hebrew form of the text.

Although each text is unique, it employs typical linguistic patterns or genres that function within a specific social, literary or historical context to facilitate the presentation of its contents and ideas. An example of a modern genre is the contemporary novel, which employs typical elements, including a lengthy narration, well-developed plot lines and characterizations, and

some challenge that must be addressed by the fictional or semifictional characters in an effort to entertain, stimulate and influence the reader. Alternatively, the ubiquitous offer of a credit card or loan, which emphasizes favorable interest rates, low monthly payments and easy acceptance, is a well-known standard form or genre in contemporary American society. Biblical texts likewise employ typical genres that were easily recognized by ancient readers. The etiological legend, in which the origins and significance of a contemporary practice, social identity or institutional structure is explained, is well known in biblical narrative (see Gen 28, which explains the origins of the Bethel sanctuary). Likewise, the prophetic judgment speech, in which future or past disaster is explained as a punishment brought upon those who have violated some divine or human expectation or norm of behavior, appears frequently in prophetic and narrative literature (see Amos 2:6-16, in which the prophet threatens northern Israel with divine judgment for failing to observe YHWH's requirements for social justice expressed in Ex 20—24). A typical psalmic genre is the song of complaint, or *lament, in which the psalmist addresses YHWH in an attempt to resolve a threat (see Ps 7, which requests that YHWH defend the singer against unnamed enemies). A typical wisdom genre is the *proverb, a brief saying that may employ *word play, onomatopoeia or other devices to capture the attention of the audience and convey an important teaching derived from experience in life or the observation of nature (note Prov 1:7: "The fear of YHWH is the beginning of knowledge; fools despise wisdom and discipline"). Each of these examples employs typical patterns of linguistic expression, but each is a unique formulation that conveys specific contents in relation to the social, literary and historical settings in which it functions.

Early form critics focused especially on *Sitz im Leben*, but the development of form criticism over the course of the twentieth century has prompted interpreters to recognize a variety of contexts in which a text is produced and in which it functions. Thus, the social, literary and historical settings of a text are key factors in influencing both its composition and its function or interpretation in the contexts in which it is employed and read.

Setting is frequently a very challenging aspect of form-critical research insofar as the early literary as well as the social and historical settings of a text must be reconstructed, and because these settings can change so frequently throughout the lifetime of the text in question. Most interpreters agree that the social setting of the psalms is the liturgy of the Jerusalem temple (*see* Cult, Worship: Psalms), in which the psalms would function individually and perhaps collectively as liturgical expressions of praise for YHWH, lament at misfortune or threat, thanksgiving for divine beneficence, and so forth in relation to the daily and festival calendar of ancient Israel or Judah. Unfortunately, the Bible provides little guidance as to when and how such psalms might function (see, e.g., 1 Chron 16, which portrays the singing of portions of Pss 96; 105; 106 when *David brings the ark of the covenant to Jerusalem), and interpreters are compelled to reconstruct the liturgical occasions in which the psalms would function. Because of the emphasis in Wisdom literature on a father who instructs his son, the roots of wisdom are often identified with family or clan instruction, although the later development of education in ancient Israel and Judah might well call for professional instructors who would take on apprentice students or teach in some sort of school (*see* Sages, Schools, Education).

The literary setting of a text also plays a key role in interpretation. Later interpreters read *Song of Songs as an allegory for the relationship between YHWH and Israel in Judaism or between Christ and the church in Christianity. Song of Songs is also recognized for its wisdom functions, in part because it employs images of creation and human sexuality to depict the relationship between the two lovers, but the original function and social setting of this composition are now lost. Christian versions of the OT also play a role in characterizing Song of Songs as a wisdom book because of its placement together with *Proverbs, *Ecclesiastes and *Wisdom of Solomon due to its purported Solomonic authorship. Song of Songs is recognized for its associations with Passover in Judaism insofar as the Jewish Bible presents Song of Songs as one of the five *Megillot ("Scrolls"), each of which is read as part of the liturgy for a Jewish festival. Such a setting informs the allegorical interpretation of Song of Songs in Judaism as a portrayal of the relationship between YHWH and Israel at the exodus from Egypt.

The historical setting of a text is frequently an important aspect of composition when it is known. Thus, an understanding of the late eighth century BC is key to the interpretation of oracles from Isaiah ben Amoz in Isaiah 1—39. When considered in relation to *Psalms, Wisdom literature, and narratives such as *Ruth and *Esther, however, the historical setting is very problematic. Many interpreters read Ruth or Esther as historical reports that describe with or without some degree of accuracy the events that they report. But when readers recognize the didactic and satirical aspects of these compositions, Ruth emerges as a didactic narrative that emphasizes the legitimacy and importance of conversion to Judaism in the Persian period, and Esther emerges as a Hellenistic period examination of the human responsibility to act in the absence of G-d at a time of threat by a foreign government.

2. The Development of Form-Critical Methodology.

Form criticism emerged in Germany during the late-nineteenth century under the influence of the rationalist perspectives of the European Enlightenment, German philosophical and theological idealism, and the romanticist perspectives of emerging German statehood. It originated in reaction to the dominant literary-critical concern of scholars such as J. Wellhausen with the identification of the original sources that stood behind the present form of the biblical text together with the historical settings and religious perspectives of their authors. H. Gunkel (1862-1932), the originator of form-critical research, was heavily influenced by the folklore studies of Wilhelm and Jakob Grimm and the "history of religions" perspectives that emerged throughout the nineteenth century. He sought to push behind the literary sources identified by scholars to reconstruct the oral stages of tradition, mythology and folklore that would shed light on the life and religious perspectives of the people of ancient Israel and the Near Eastern world.

Gunkel, like many of his time, chauvinistically viewed the ancients as primitive, relatively simple-minded illiterates who were, on the one hand, capable of perceiving the divine at a most basic and ideal level but, on the other hand, incapable of formulating or memorizing lengthy texts. He therefore emphasized the role of short, self-contained literary units in biblical exegesis that represented the ideals of primitive ancient Israelite religiosity. Such short, self-contained and stereotypical texts developed out of a long history of oral transmission among the people until they were assembled into larger narrative cycles, sagas, poetic collections, and so forth, while generally still at the oral stage, and later written down by writers concerned with preserving and editing Israelite tradition.

Gunkel's own research began with a study of the mythological and folkloric background of the NT book of Revelation, which naturally prompted his interest in the mythological and folkloric traditions of the book of Genesis. His groundbreaking commentary on Genesis emphasized the various types or genres of Israelite oral traditions, such as the folktales and myths about the gods and primal human beings, the epic traditions about the lives of the ancestors, or the etiological traditions concerning the origins of tribal and national groups, cultic institutions and practices, geological features, and so on. Because Gunkel was fundamentally interested in the *Sitz im Leben* of texts, such as the family or tribal storytellers of the oral tradition or the cultic performances of narrative or liturgical traditions, his research turned to the psalms. Gunkel's 1933 *Einleitung in die Psalmen*, completed after his death by his student J. Begrich, defined the basic types of psalms, such as the *hymns, individual and communal complaints, royal psalms (*see* Kingship Psalms) and *thanksgiving psalms, as well as their liturgical functions, which continue to stand as the basis for modern research of the psalms.

Gunkel's interest in the *Sitz im Leben* of biblical literature, particularly his interest in the liturgical settings and functions of cultic poetry, continued in the work of his student S. Mowinckel (1884-1965). Because he was Norwegian, Mowinckel was heavily influenced by Scandinavian scholarship, which emphasized a combination of comparative religion and religious anthropology. Such interest was motivated by the study of the oral literature and religious traditions of the Norse peoples of Scandinavia, who were known especially for the composition of the Icelandic sagas concerning the exploits of Norse heroes, as well as those of the Laplander peoples of the north, whose religious traditions resembled those of Asia and the Americas. He was therefore far more interested in the functions of religious traditions and their oral trans-

mission than in their origins or ideal genres, as indicated in his highly influential 1921-1924 six-volume *Psalmenstudien*. The intense interest in Babylonian mythology and liturgical traditions of the time prompted Mowinckel's interest in the liturgical performance of the psalms. His interest and perspectives were particularly influenced by the Babylonian Akitu, or New Festival, in which the *Enuma Elish*, or Babylonian Creation Epic, was performed to commemorate the rule over creation by Marduk, the Babylonian city-god and creator of the world, together with the rule of the Babylonian king. Mowinckel argued that an analogous Israelite New Year was the liturgical *Sitz im Leben* for the performance of many of the psalms that would celebrate YHWH'S kingship over creation (*see* Kingship Psalms), authorization and support for the Davidic monarchy, protection for Jerusalem in particular and Israel in general, and so forth. A particular feature of his research was the recognition that psalms or cultic poetry also appeared in the narrative-historical and the prophetic literature (e.g., Ex 15; Judg 5; Is 12; Hab 3), which suggested that these literatures may also have played a role in Israel's cultic liturgy. Such a phenomenon also highlighted the influence that genres of one type might have on others.

A. Alt (1883-1956), another of Gunkel's students, emphasized the question of institutional setting in his foundational study of the forms of biblical *law. His primary area of expertise was the history, archeology and geography of the land of Israel. He is especially well known for his studies on the origins of Israel in Canaan and the development of the Israelite state as the result of a long process of Israelite settlement among the Canaanites and the efforts of the monarchy to create political and religious unity in an area that had previously been dominated by Canaanite city-states largely controlled by Egypt. His study of Israelite religion emphasized its origins in Canaanite religious practice, particularly the patriarchal or ancestral cults that informed the ancestral traditions of the Pentateuch.

Alt's study of the origins of Israelite law emphasized the formal differences between the two basic types of laws in the Pentateuch. The first was the casuistic law, which included a protasis, or formal statement of the legal case or issue at hand, often introduced by a conditional particle ("if/when a man does such and such"), and the apodosis, or formal decision as to how the case is to be resolved ("then he/you shall do such and such"). The second was the apodictic law (see, e.g., the Decalogue in Ex 20; Deut 5), which categorically commands or prohibits certain behaviors ("you shall/shall not"). Because the casuistic laws corresponded to those found in the Babylonian law codes, such as the Code of Hammurabi, Alt posited that the casuistic laws represented a pre-Israelite Canaanite law form that perhaps developed from Babylonian law that was taken over by the Israelites. The apodictic laws, because of their categorical authoritative formulation, originated among the Israelites in the desert before their settlement in Canaan and were read to the people in the temple or cultic settings of later times as a means of instructing the people in YHWH's laws. Later studies, such as W. Richter's 1966 monograph *Recht und Ethos*, argued that the apodictic laws were not laws at all, because they lacked any means to adjudicate the issue in question, but instead must be recognized as the products of clan or family wisdom and instruction in which a father instructed his children in the expected norms of behavior. Again, such a conclusion points to the interrelationship between generic categories and the influence that one genre might exert on another.

The question of the formation of state continued to influence form-critical work through the first half of the twentieth century, particularly because Germany had only unified as a state in 1870, but the rise of Nazi Germany in the 1930s and 1940s prompted German form critics in particular to focus on the development of history-writing in ancient Israel, particularly because history is such an important means by which modern nations give accounts of themselves, evaluate their actions, and impart identity to their people.

The work of G. von Rad (1900-1971), who was heavily influenced by Alt, is particularly important in relation to the development of OT theology, but his concern with biblical theology begins with a preoccupation of the role that theology plays in the development and conceptualization of historical writing. His 1938 form-critical analysis of the formation of the Hexateuch (Genesis—Joshua) emphasized its role in the development of Israel's self-understanding and religious outlook. Von Rad posited that the J stratum of the Hexateuch,

which established the earliest, basic narrative framework of the Pentateuch and Joshua, had developed out of short, self-contained localized cultic traditions such as the creedal formula in Deuteronomy 26:5b-9 cited by Israelite farmers at sanctuaries when they brought the first fruits of their harvests and flocks to the altar for sacrifice (see also Deut 6:20-24; Josh 24:2b-13). Insofar as this creedal confession articulated YHWH's acts on behalf of the people—that is, how the wandering ancestor Jacob went to Egypt few in number, was enslaved by the Egyptians, and was delivered by YHWH to be brought to this land flowing with milk and honey—they imparted national identity and theological outlook to the people of Israel now settled in the land. They also provided the basis for the expansion of the tradition into the full form of the J stratum of the Hexateuch in the early days of the formation of the Davidic monarchy and ultimately into the final form of the Hexateuch completed by the P stratum in the postexilic era. Insofar as the Hexateuch includes liturgical compositions that instruct the people in the acts of YHWH on behalf of Israel (e.g., Ex 15), von Rad's work opens the way for tracing the influence of liturgical and wisdom concerns in the composition of Israel's narrative historical literature, but his historical interests also determined his view of wisdom, which he understood as Israel's witness to its experience of YHWH in history. Nevertheless, he examined a number of basic wisdom genres, including the proverb, numerical sayings, autobiographical stylization, didactic poetry and narrative, dialogue, fable and allegory, and prayer.

A similar concern emerges in the work of M. Noth (1902-1968), one of Alt's students, who specialized both in the history and archeology of ancient Israel as well as in the tradition-historical composition of Israelite historical narratives. Noth differed from his friend von Rad by positing that the sources or strata of the Pentateuch could not be traced through Joshua and arguing instead that the laws and theological outlook of the book of Deuteronomy provide the historiographical and religious perspectives for the writing of an Israelite historical work that comprised Joshua, Judges, Samuel and Kings. This so-called Deuteronomistic History took up older, localized traditions and incorporated them into a larger historical work that gave account of Israel's history from the time of Israel's entry into the land under Joshua through the Babylonian exile when King Jehoiachin of Judah was finally released from prison by the Babylonian monarch Evil Merodach. The Deuteronomistic History was designed to explain the Babylonian exile as the result of divine punishment for Israel's failure to abide by YHWH's commands as expressed in Deuteronomy. The form-critical basis for Noth's contention appeared in the short, self-contained historical summaries of Israel's history, spoken either by a principal character in the work or simply by the Deuteronomistic History narrator (e.g., Josh 1; 23; 1 Sam 12; 1 Kings 8; 2 Kings 17), that displayed characteristic Deuteronomic language and theological concepts and gave historiographical unity to the composite work. Later studies would point to earlier stages in the composition that were designed to support King Josiah's attempts at national restoration and religious reform, but Noth's work paved the way for understanding the historiographical perspectives and didactic interests inherent in Israelite historical writing. Such concerns would point once again to the influence of wisdom circles in Israelite historical writing.

The aftermath of World War II saw many changes in the field of biblical studies in general and in form-critical theory in particular, as interpreters began to turn away from concern with the formation of state and the organs of central authority to explore a variety of methodological options in the reading of texts. One such impulse came from the work of Swiss theologian K. Barth, whose emphasis on the role of the word of G-d provided an important basis for theological critique of Nazi Germany and acquiescent elements of the church both during and after the war. Such a concern informed the form-critical work of C. Westermann, who throughout his career focused especially on defining the ideal genres of biblical literature as expressions of the word of G-d. He is well known for his studies of the pentateuchal narratives in which he focused especially on defining the ideal or original forms of the divine promises to the ancestors; his studies of prophetic speech, including the generic characters of the prophetic judgment speeches and words of salvation; his study of Job, which isolated genres such as dialogue, lament and disputation prior to announcement of the divine word at the culmination of the book; and his studies of the cultic laments and hymns of praise, which functioned as ideal expressions of the divine word. Westermann's concentration on identifying the ideal genres that stood behind the text proved to be somewhat of a problem in later exegesis, however, insofar as his definition of the generic characteristics behind the text would then serve as the basis for emending the text in question. For Westermann, genre constituted text, but later research demonstrates that genre functions within uniquely formulated texts.

The emerging methodological pluralism of the second half of the twentieth century would further influence form criticism in various ways. French scholars in particular began to explore the fields of linguistics, literature and sociology as concern with central leadership and authority faded in favor of greater interest in the lives of common people in general and the function of language and texts in society. Such work prompted a shift from defining the original oral forms of biblical literature to interpretation of the later and larger written compositions that now appear in the various forms of the Bible and the social contexts in which they functioned. *Rhetorical criticism emerged as both an outgrowth from and complement to form-critical research. As conceived by J. Muilenberg, who began his career as a high school English teacher, biblical interpreters must learn to pay close attention to the rhetorical dimensions of larger literary texts and the rhetorical devices employed to give them literary unity and artistic design. Muilenberg did not propose an abandonment of the traditional form-critical focus on the short, self-contained, original unit but rather saw rhetorical criticism as a means to address a much fuller interpretation of a text. Later rhetorical critics, such a P. Trible, have called for attention to the persuasive aspects of a text—that is, the means by which a text is designed to interact with its audience and to elicit some response, such as the adoption of a particular viewpoint or course of action. Later rhetorical criticism also calls for the study of the *intertextual character of texts, both in terms of the interrelationship among subunits within a text and the interrelationship with other texts by citation or allusion. In this respect, texts may engage with dialogue among themselves, whether deliberately or not. Dialogue and persuasion are key to the didactic character of the Wisdom literature and to the liturgical character of Psalms and

Lamentations, in which people address G-d to express their relationship with the divine or to elicit a response. Such work must be conceived as a fuller realization of form-critical theory insofar as it addresses the forms and functions of texts in relation to social context.

The study of linguistic theory provides important methodological foundations for form criticism's concern with both the literary and linguistic structures and the communicative functions of biblical texts. Early work by F. de Saussure demonstrated that each text constitutes a communicative event in which the basic linguistic elements of *langue*, the common structures of expression in a linguistic system (i.e., grammar, semantics, syntax), and *parole*, the individual forms of expression in which a text appears, combine to generate the communicative event. V. Propp's analysis of Russian folklore further refined this model by distinguishing the communicative roles of the "actant," who sends and defines communication according to his or her own conceptualization of the event, and the "receiver," who receives the communication and interprets it in relation to his or her own linguistic and conceptual context. K. Koch applied these models to biblical exegesis, arguing that *langue* refers to the underlying genres that inform the composition of biblical texts, and that *parole* refers to the individual literary presentation or form of the text. The actant encapsulates the intentions of the author of a text, and the receiver indicates the redactor who interprets and redefines a text by placing it into its later redactional context. Later interpreters influenced by reader-response criticism argue that the receiver would constitute the audience of the text, whether ancient or modern, which plays such an important role in construing the texts and thereby in defining its interpretation. Although the author's or sender's intentions played an important role in formulating the text, reader-response theorists argue that those intentions are not always known or relevant insofar as a text takes on its own life to be construed by its readers once it is written.

W. Richter draws upon linguistic theory to make important contributions to form-critical theory by arguing that exegesis must be understood first and foremost as a literary science. Interpreters must engage the linguistic features and structures of a text, including both its semantic and its syntactical dimensions, in order to interpret its outer literary form or linguistic expression *(parole)* in relation to its inner form or the deep structure of the concepts and contents that it communicates *(langue)*. He therefore differentiates between the *Sitz im Leben*, in which language is generated and in which it functions, and the *Sitz im Literatur*, in which the text appears. Although Richter's model calls for the initial analysis of the synchronic form of a text as literature, his work displays a marked interest in the redaction-critical reconstruction of earlier text forms that purportedly stand behind the present form of the text. His students, such as H. Schweizer, have played important roles in laying the foundation for a linguistic assessment of Hebrew according to its semantic, pragmatic and syntactical dimensions as the basis for assessing the literary forms of biblical texts.

R. Knierim has played an important role in bringing form-critical theory from Germany to the United States and in reflecting upon its theoretical dimensions. He has especially emphasized the formal interpretation of the synchronic dimensions of biblical texts, not because diachronic interpretation is irrelevant, but because synchronic analysis enables the interpreter to engage the text first on its own terms without allowing the presumed diachronic dimensions of texts to control and thereby skew interpretation. Form-critical study of biblical texts necessarily involves redaction criticism at the outset insofar as texts appear in their final redactional forms, and the interpreter is obligated to engage the synchronic form of the text in order first to understand its formulation and conceptualization and then to determine if evidence exists to posit earlier text forms that might be reconstructed from the text at hand. Study of the formulation of a text points to its underlying or infrastructural conceptualizations that drive the composition of the text and play an important role in determining its present form. Knierim's understanding of conceptualization draws heavily on structural anthropology, which examines the deep structures of the human mind based in the structures of language and society and their influence on human communication and worldview. Based in part on Knierim's influence and the emergence of newer literary and text-critical methods, recent form-critical work has focused on the interpretation of larger literary units, particularly entire biblical books, in both their synchronic and diachronic dimensions.

3. Form-Critical Study of Cultic Poetry.

3.1. The Book of Psalms. The book of Psalms has been a primary subject of form-critical research from the beginnings of the discipline through the present. Although the history of form-critical research on Psalms has focused on defining the genres and functions of individual psalms and psalm collections, current form-critical theory calls for initial consideration of the final form of the book of Psalms. The common assertion that the book of Psalms functioned as the hymnbook of the Jerusalem temple may well be true, but the current presentation and arrangement of Psalms provide only a limited indication as to how it would have served in such a role. The account of David bringing the ark to Jerusalem in 1 Chronicles 16, which employs elements from Psalms 96; 105; 106, suggests that the choice of individual psalms for liturgical use was not entirely dependent on their individual placement in the current form of the book (although each appears in the fourth subdivision of the Psalms [see below]).

Most of the psalms have individual superscriptions that characterize them by technical terms indicating type and function, authorship or ascription, setting and so on (*see* Psalms 5: Titles), but the synchronic macrostructure of Psalms comprises five books, each of which concludes with a doxology or formulaic expression of praise of YHWH: *bārûk yhwh* ("Blessed is YHWH") in the case of the first four doxologies, and *halĕlû-yāh* ("Hallelujah") in the fifth. The five books and their concluding doxologies include Psalms 1—41 (Ps 41:13); Psalms 42—72 (Ps 72:18-19); Psalms 73—89 (Ps 89:52); Psalms 90—106 (Ps 106:48); Psalms 107—150 (Ps 150:1-6). Rabbinic tradition maintains that the five-part structure of Psalms deliberately correlates with the five-part structure of the Torah (*Midr. Ps.* 1:2) and reduces the number of Psalms to 147 so that they will correlate with the 147 *sĕdārîm* (sections of the Torah), which would have been read on each Sabbath in the triennial lectionary cycle employed in antiquity (*b. Ber.* 9b-10a). Such a view presupposes rabbinic combinations of Psalm 1 and Psalm 2, and possibly Psalm 114 and Psalm 115, and Psalm 117 and Psalm 118. Indeed, many modern scholars note that Psalm 1 and Psalm 2 together function as an introduction to the book of Psalms insofar as the initial concerns with Torah and *righteousness in Psalm 1 and YHWH's relationship with the David-

ic king in Psalm 2 set basic themes that appear throughout the book. Likewise, Psalm 150, a hallelujah psalm, may serve as a conclusion to the book as a whole as well as to Book 5. Evidence for a correlation of the books of Psalms with the books of the Torah or of the individual psalms with the individual sections of the Torah read in the triennial cycle is lacking thus far. Evidence is also lacking for a correlation with the five-part macrostructure of Lamentations or the five Megillot (Song of Songs, Ruth, Lamentations, Ecclesiastes, Esther), read on Jewish festivals. G. Wilson argues that the current sequence of books in Psalms presupposes a concern with explaining the demise of Davidic kingship by pointing to YHWH's ultimate sovereignty. J. Crenshaw notes a progressive movement from lament in the first book to praise in the fifth. No explanation for the five-part structure of Psalms has yet gained full acceptance. Textual versions must also be considered insofar as the LXX adds Psalm 151, and the Syriac Peshitta adds Psalms 151—155.

Diachronic factors must also be considered in assessing the final form of the book of Psalms, most notably due to the statement in Psalm 72:20: "The prayers of David ben Jesse are completed," which suggests that Books 1 and 2 may once have formed an early version of Psalms. Additional evidence for early collections of psalms include the predominance of psalms ascribed to David in Books 1 and 2; the Elohistic Psalter of Psalms 42—83, so-called because of its preference for the Hebrew term *ʾlhym* ("G-d") in place of the divine name *yhwh* ("L-rd"); the collection of the Psalms of *Asaph (appointed as Levitical singer by David in 1 Chron 6:39) in Psalms 50; 73—83; the Psalms of the Sons of Korah (appointed as temple gatekeepers in 1 Chron 9:19; 26:1, 19, and functioned as temple singers in 2 Chron 20:19; Korah led a failed revolt against Moses in Num 16, but Num 26:9-11 indicates that his sons survived) in Psalms 42; 44—49; 84—85; 87—88; the hallelujah psalms in Psalms 111—112; 106; 133; 135; 146—150; and the Songs of Ascent (Heb *šîr ham maʿalôt*), or pilgrimage psalms, in Psalms 120—134, which celebrate the liturgical ascent or pilgrimage to the Jerusalem temple. The first-century AD Qumran *Psalms Scroll* (11QPs[a]) includes a unique arrangement of thirty-nine psalms from the book of Psalms; 2 Samuel 23:17; Sirach 51:13-30; Psalms 151; 154; 155; and additional material not previously known.

Form-critical research on Psalms has identified a number of basic genres of cultic poetry that stand behind the individual psalms. Each type has its own distinct ideal structure and function that informs the unique form, function and composition of each psalm. At times, multiple genres appear within an individual psalm to serve the purposes for which it was composed and for which it functions. Likewise, typical structural elements of genres may be lacking in individual psalms for similar reasons.

The fundamental genre of cultic poetry is the hymn of praise, which appears in Psalms 8; 19; 29; 33; 47; 65; 66; 78; 93; 95—100; 103—106; 111; 113; 114; 117; 134; 135; 136; 145—150. The hymn of praise is based on a simple two-part structure that includes the call to praise, in which the community is summoned to assemble (presumably in the temple) to praise YHWH, and the basis or reasons for the praise, which include YHWH's might, sovereignty and mercy in delivering the people or the king from threat by enemies or other afflictions and in ensuring the order of creation.

The most prevalent type of cultic poetry in the book of Psalms is the lament or complaint, which constitutes approximately one-third of the Psalter, apparently because the fear of threats of whatever sort is a major motivating factor in liturgical addresses to the divine. These psalms appear as community laments, in which the nation as a whole addresses YHWH at a time of national threat or crisis, and as individual laments, in which an individual addresses YHWH in a time of need. Community laments appear in Psalms 12; 44; 60; 74; 79; 80; 83; 85; 90; 94; 108; 123; 129; 137. Individual laments or complaints appear in Psalms 3—7; 9—10; 13; 14; 17; 22; 25; 26; 28; 31; 35; 36; 38; 39; 40; 41; 42—43; 51; 52; 53; 54—59; 61; 64; 69; 70; 71; 77; 86; 88; 102; 109; 120; 130; 140—143. Typical elements of lament or complaint genre include the address to YHWH, in which YHWH is invoked; the complaint proper, which lays out the situation of crisis that has prompted the nation or the individual to appeal to YHWH; the request for help from YHWH to resolve or alleviate the crisis; the affirmation of trust in YHWH, which confirms the nation's or the individual's confidence in G-d; and a vow to praise YHWH once the crisis has passed.

The thanksgiving psalm genre appears in Psalms 18; 30; 32; 34; 40; 66; 92; 116; 118; 138.

The thanksgiving psalms are designed to express thanks to YHWH for deliverance from some threat or crisis, and they appear to presuppose liturgical processions in the temple (Ps 118:19-29) or a thank offering (Ps 66:13-15; 116:12-19). Typical elements of the thanksgiving psalm include an invitation to give thanks to YHWH, often employing a form of the Hebrew verb *ydh* (e.g., *hôdû lyhwh* ["Give thanks to YHWH"]); an account of the crisis and YHWH's actions of deliverance or relief; praises of YHWH for having acted; offertory formulae to accompany the presentation of a thanksgiving sacrifice; blessings for the participants in the ceremony; and an exhortation to trust in YHWH.

The so-called royal psalms appear in Psalms 2; 18; 20; 21; 45; 72; 89; 101; 110; 132; 144. They were composed, very likely during the monarchic period, to address some event in the life of the king. Royal events might include, for example, a king's coronation, wedding, victory in battle and deliverance from enemies. They comprise a particularly controversial genre because they lack any typical structure and are instead identified by their concern with the monarch. Indeed, they frequently display elements of complaint, thanksgiving and hymns, which suggests that they are not a genre per se but instead thematically define psalms that employ various generic elements to serve their respective purposes.

The Songs of Zion appear in Psalms 46; 48; 76; 84; 87; 122 (cf. Ps 132, which is identified as a royal psalm). These songs have no typical formal structure or elements but instead are identified by their celebration of YHWH's choice of *Zion as the site for the temple or divine presence in the world. Many of the Zion psalms presuppose a liturgical procession, which suggests that they were composed to function as part of celebration of YHWH's sovereignty in the world.

Wisdom and Torah psalms appear in Psalms 1; 19; 37; 49; 73; 112; 119; 127; 128; 133. The wisdom and Torah psalms seem to be designed for meditation or reflection on issues pertaining to G-d, *worship, study of Torah and life in the world. They have no set structure or elements and appear to be defined on thematic grounds. Consequently, their identification as discrete genres is questionable.

Various liturgical psalms appear in Psalms 15; 24; 50; 68; 81; 82; 95; 115; 132. Many presuppose antiphonal dialogue associated with liturgical action, but their identities as distinct genres are often questionable. Entrance liturgies, which express the ideal qualities of one who enters the temple, appear in Psalms 15; 24. Psalm 50 takes up covenant renewal. Psalms 68; 91; 118; 132 take up liturgical processions. Psalm 81 anticipates repentance by the people, and Psalm 82 calls for judgment against the foreign gods for failing to do justice.

3.2. The Book of Lamentations. The book of Lamentations is designed to lament the destruction of the city of Jerusalem by the Babylonians in 587/6 BC. It is traditionally ascribed to the prophet Jeremiah in both Judaism and Christianity due to his penchant for lamentation and to the statement in 2 Chronicles 35:25 that Jeremiah wrote laments over the death of Josiah. Christian Bibles therefore locate Lamentations with the book of Jeremiah in the OT. Jewish tradition, however, places Lamentations among the five Megillot because it is read on the Ninth of Av, the traditional day of mourning in Jewish traditions for the destruction of Solomon's temple by the Babylonians in 587/6 BC and the destruction of the second temple by the Romans in AD 70.

The macrostructure of Lamentations displays a five-part structure that comprises the five chapters of the book. Each part expresses communal mourning or lament over the fate of Jerusalem, generally portrayed metaphorically as the desolate Daughter Zion (Heb *bat-ṣiyyôn*). Lamentations 1 laments Jerusalem's misery; Lamentations 2 focuses on YHWH's actions against Jerusalem; Lamentations 3 focuses on the suffering of an unidentified man who affirms confidence in YHWH and appeals for repentance; Lamentations 4 emphasizes YHWH's anger against the people for their sins; and Lamentations 5 appeals to YHWH to restore the people and temple when the punishment is complete. The rationale and setting for the structure of Lamentations appear to lie in the mourning and appeal for restoration. Such lamentation rituals are mentioned in Jeremiah 41:5; Zechariah 7:3-5; 8:19. Repentance and reconstruction may well constitute the underlying conceptualization of Lamentations.

Lamentations is based especially in the dirge genre, which is generally identified as a funerary genre for mourning the dead. It is characterized by the introductory exclamation *ʾêkâ* ("Alas!") and a characteristic 3/2 poetic *meter

that employs three heavy beats in the first stanza followed by two heavy beats in the second stanza. This characteristic Qinah (Heb *qînâ* ["lament"]) meter may accompany a limping processional walk to symbolize mourning (cf. the limping walk and drawing of blood by the prophets of Baal in 1 Kings 18). The genre appears to draw heavily on the lament or complaint genre found throughout Psalms. It also employs the classic acrostic form, a poetic esthetic device in which each stanza of poetry begins with a successive letter of the Hebrew alphabet from *ʾālep* to *tāw*. City lament genres are also known from ancient Sumer, where they functioned as apologies for the formation of new ruling dynasties in the aftermath of the collapse of the older ruling dynasty and its capital city. They also appear to presuppose mourning rituals for the male fertility gods, Baal of Canaan and Dumuzi or Tammuz of Mesopotamia, who were conceived to have died and entered the underworld during the dry summer season. Mourning rituals for each god were enacted to ensure that their respective consorts or goddess—Anath for Baal, Inanna for the Sumerian Dumuzi, Ishtar for the Babylonian Tammuz—would restore them to the world of the living to inaugurate the rainy season (for Baal, see 1 Kings 18; for Tammuz, see Ezek 8).

4. Form-Critical Study of the Wisdom Literature.

4.1. The Book of Proverbs. The book of Proverbs is the classic example of Wisdom literature in the Hebrew Bible. The introductory superscription identifies the book as "The Proverbs of Solomon ben David, King of Israel" (Prov 1:1). Following superscriptions in Proverbs 10:1; 25:1 likewise attribute the following material to *Solomon, who is lauded in Israelite historical tradition for his wisdom and for his composition of three thousand proverbs (see 1 Kings 5:9-14; cf. 1 Kings 3:4-28; 10:1-13; 2 Chron 1:7-13; 9:1-12). Although Solomon is known for his wisdom, most interpreters are reluctant to conclude that he is indeed the author of Proverbs. Kings in the ancient world tended to be patrons of literary works written by others in the *royal court. The superscription in Proverbs 25:1 states, "These too are the proverbs of Solomon which the men of Hezekiah transmitted," and other superscriptions in the book refer to sections attributed to "the wise" (Prov 24:23), "the words of Agur ben

Jakeh, the Massa; the oracle of the man to Ithiel, to Ithiel and Ucal" (Prov 30:1), and "the words of Lemuel, king of Massa, with which his mother disciplined him" (Prov 31:1).

Proverbs constitutes a form of traditional instruction known throughout the ancient Near East, but especially in Egypt, of a father, a mother, a king, a priest, a wise man or other notable who instructs sons, daughters, disciples, and so forth in the means by which one comes to understand the world and to live productively and responsibly in it. Proverbs is addressed to young men, and it focuses especially on "the fear of YHWH" as the basis for wisdom (*see* Fear of the Lord). It emphasizes proper conduct in relation to other human beings (particularly those in positions of power and authority), proper relations with *women, productive work and personal habits, and the observation of other human beings as well as the natural world as important bases for gaining an understanding of the principles by which the world works. The synchronic formal structure of the book includes six sections, each introduced by a superscription, as indicated above, which identifies the following material by type and authorship. Proverbs 1—9 emphasizes piety and wisdom as paths to success in the world and employs allegorical presentations of wisdom as an ideal wife contrasted with a promiscuous woman (*See* Woman Wisdom and Woman Folly) to illustrate its teachings on proper conduct in the world. Proverbs 10:1—24:22 is a lengthy discourse that seems to comprise a number of earlier collections of proverbs and other didactic forms (*see* Discourse in Proverbs). It emphasizes the problems inherent in pride, sloth, gossip and deceit, and it favors virtues such as faithfulness, self-control, sobriety and industriousness. Many argue that Proverbs 22:17—24:22 is an early collection that resembles the Egyptian Instruction of Amenemopet. Proverbs 24:23-34 emphasizes the practice of justice and the avoidance of laziness. Proverbs 25—29 especially employs comparative statements to emphasize the proper behavior of the king and the importance of perception in the world. Proverbs 30 calls for moderation in one's behavior and consumption. Proverbs 31 presents the instruction of a queen mother to her son concerning overindulgence in drink and with women, and it concludes by extolling the ideal woman.

The basic genre of Proverbs and all Wisdom literature is the didactic speech, which may appear in any oral or written form that conveys instruction to the reading or listening audience. Characteristic genres in Proverbs begin with the *māšāl* ("proverb"), one of the "short sayings" employed in Wisdom literature to convey important teachings. It generally employs a short, *parallel structure and sometimes uses metaphor or allegory to convey its teaching in a form that is easily remembered and quoted at opportune times. It likely derives from popular oral culture, although it now appears in highly sophisticated literary works, such as Proverbs, which presuppose an educated and elite audience. The graduated numerical saying that cites successive numbers of comparable phenomena in the world is an important device for collecting examples to make a point from the comparison, as in Proverbs 30:18-20, which cites three and then four things that the speaker cannot fathom, culminating in the way of a young man with a maiden. Allegories also play a role in Proverbs and in Wisdom literature in general, particularly the comparison of an ideal wife to a cistern from which one drinks for life. Hymns appear in Proverbs as an artistic form that is adopted to pedagogical interests, such as the portrayal of the ideal woman in the acrostic song of Proverbs 31:10-31.

The presentation of royal characters and elite society in the book, together with the sophisticated literary and pedagogical style, points to the royal court as the likely setting for the book of Proverbs. Many speculate that it was produced by a circle of the wise who may have functioned as professional teachers of young students who would aspire for positions of responsibility in the royal court, the temple or elsewhere in ancient Israelite and Judean society.

4.2. The Book of Job. The book of Job differs markedly from the book of Proverbs. Whereas Proverbs envisions a stable social, religious and natural world order that one must observe in order to learn to live successfully in the world, Job presupposes that chaos and absurdity reach to the very highest levels of creation, including even G-d, to undermine any sense of justice and order in the world of human beings or creation at large. In this manner, the book of Job is designed to probe the question of *theodicy—that is, the presumption of G-d's power, justice and righteousness. Although the book of Job ultimately affirms G-d, it points to the human right and responsibility to raise such questions, particularly insofar as life in the world does not always work out in quite the way that a book such as Proverbs might presuppose. Indeed, the wisdom poem of Job 28, which points to the hidden nature of wisdom in the world, alludes to the basic principle of Proverbs that the fear of YHWH is the beginning of wisdom to make its point that only G-d truly understands wisdom. The *suffering of the righteous and attempts to accuse those who suffer of wrongdoing that caused the suffering in the first place are fundamental concerns of the book of Job.

The formal structure of the book of Job is based on a didactic narrative that presents a dialogue involving Job, his wife, his three friends Eliphaz the Temanite, Bildad the Shuhite and Zophar the Naamathite, a fourth figure named Elihu ben Barachel, and finally G-d. The subject of the disputation is Job's suffering and speculation on the part of Job's friends concerning the wrongdoing that he must have committed to deserve such a fate. The narrative begins in Job 1—2 with an account of Job's exemplary piety, righteousness and good fortune in life, Satan's conversation with G-d, in which *Satan states that Job will curse G-d if he is afflicted and G-d acquiesces to the test, and Job's afflictions, including the deaths of his ten children, the loss of all his wealth and property, and his affliction with physical ailments. After he declines his wife's suggestion that he curse G-d and die, Job initiates the dialogue with his three friends by lamenting the day of his birth. Throughout the dialogue in Job 3—27, the three friends articulate a standard theology of reward and punishment in which they contend that Job must have committed some sin that prompted his misfortune. For his own part, Job maintains that he is willing to suffer the consequences if guilty; but also, he cannot understand what he could have done to deserve such suffering and demands an explanation from G-d. Following the wisdom poem in Job 28, which emphasizes that true wisdom is known only to G-d, Elihu continues the *debate with Job in Job 29—37 to no resolution. Finally, G-d appears in Job 38—42 to answer Job. G-d provides no evidence or explanation but demands to know how Job presumes to require an explanation from the creator of the universe. When Job repents, G-d restores Job's fortunes and agrees to Job's request not to punish his friends. The book offers no satisfactory answer to Job's questions but nevertheless speaks to the reality of human life in which people often suffer without apparent cause.

The book of Job clearly employs the didactic narrative as the narrative framework of the book in Job 1—2; 38—42, dialogue between Job and his friends throughout Job 3—27; 29—37, and the hymn extolling the hidden nature of wisdom in Job 28. The most important genre in Job is the disputation speech, which both Job and his friends employ throughout the book to critically examine the arguments offered by each side and to assert their own arguments concerning the nature of suffering, Job's guilt or innocence, and the questions concerning the role of G-d as righteous judge. The disputation speech is characteristic of wisdom, prophetic (Ezek 18:1-20), diplomatic (2 Kings 18—19/Is 36—37) or courtroom (1 Kings 3:16-28) settings. Many interpreters note the forensic style of the argumentation as if the setting were an ancient Israelite courtroom. Basic elements of the genre include a statement of the thesis to be disputed, the counterthesis for which the speaker argues, and the dispute or argumentation proper.

Job is generally recognized as a highly sophisticated and challenging piece of literature that would have found its setting in the highest levels of Israelite and Judean wisdom and educational circles, including the royal court and the temple.

4.3. The Book of Ecclesiastes. Ecclesiastes appears, together with Proverbs and Song of Songs, as a book attributed to Solomon in the Christian OT because its superscription identifies it as "the words of Qohelet ben David, King in Jerusalem." The Tanak includes it as one of the five Megillot insofar as it is read as part of the liturgy for the festival of Sukkot. Sukkot celebrates the completion of the harvest and onset of the rainy season following the New Year in the fall when the people of ancient Israel and Judah lived in temporary dwellings called *sukkôt* ("booths") while gathering the fruit harvest. Sukkot also commemorates the forty years of wilderness wandering at the time of the exodus when Israel lived in temporary dwellings while traveling. Ecclesiastes' focus on the transitory nature of life therefore associates it with the temporary dwellings that symbolize Sukkot.

Ecclesiastes is presented as a first-person discourse on the part of the anonymous *Qohelet, clearly identified as a royal figure and presumed to be Solomon in his old age. Following the book's superscription (Eccles 1:1), the synchronic literary structure of the book includes an introductory motto and poem (Eccles 1:2-3, 4-11) that set the basic concerns of the book as a reflection on the transitory nature and constancy of life insofar as there is nothing new under the sun. The subsequent body of the book (Eccles 1:12—11:6) includes a series of discourses on Qohelet's experience in life, a meditation on the life's experiences and their times, oppression, toil and indolence, companionship, religious duties, wealth, the relations between rulers and subjects, divine action, death, chance, wisdom and *folly, and risk. A concluding poem (Eccles 11:7—12:7) reflects on youth and old age, an *inclusio (Eccles 12:8) reiterates the book's concern with futility, and the epilogue (Eccles 12:9-14) concludes by calling on the reader to fear G-d and observe G-d's commandments as the task of humankind.

The dominant genre of the book of Ecclesiastes is the royal testament, well known from Egyptian examples, in which a king or other figure of authority reflects on life as a legacy for the benefit and instruction of those who someday perhaps would fill similar roles. It therefore employs the *autobiographical form or first-person narration as a type of didactic narrative or discourse for the purpose of instruction. As part of its discourse, Ecclesiastes employs classical wisdom forms, such as proverbs, parables or allegories, numerical sayings, comparative statements and poetry analogous to hymns, as literary devices that facilitate reflection on the concerns of the book. Like Proverbs, Ecclesiastes presupposes an educational setting in the royal court and perhaps in the temple as well.

4.4. Song of Songs. Song of Songs appears together with Proverbs and Ecclesiastes in Protestant versions of the Christian OT because of its attribution to King Solomon ben David. It appears as the first of the five Megillot in the Jewish Tanak because it is read as part of the liturgy for the festival of Passover. Both Christianity and Judaism read the Song of Song's presentation of the relationship between the two lovers as allegory. In Christianity the relationship between the lovers signifies the relationship between Christ and the church. In Judaism the relationship between the lovers signifies the relationship between G-d and Israel, which was especially identified with the exodus from Egypt. Such allegory builds upon the many presentations of the relationship between G-d and Israel as a relationship between husband and wife (e.g., Is 49—54; Jer 2; Ezek 16; Hos 1—3; Zeph 3:14-20).

The superscription of the book identifies it as "The Song of Songs, which was Solomon's" (Song 1:1). The superscription is generally understood to attribute the book to Solomon either as author or as patron. Such attribution is based in part on the statements concerning Solomon's wisdom and composition of poetry in 1 Kings 5:9-14 and his reputation as a lover of women as expressed in 1 Kings 11:1-5 (cf. 1 Kings 10:1-13; 2 Chron 9:1-12). The body of the book, Song of Songs 1:2—8:13, presents a poetic or liturgical dramatization in five major movements or scenes of a love relationship between a woman and a man. Each of the first four movements concludes with a formulaic *refrain addressed to the daughters of Jerusalem. The first movement (Song 1:2—2:7) portrays the woman's expressions of desire for her lover. The second movement (Song 2:8—3:5) describes the approach of the lover and woman's efforts to search for him throughout the city. The third movement (Song 3:6—5:8) portrays the woman's anguish at the loss of her lover. The fourth movement (Song 5:9—8:4) portrays the lovers reunited. The fifth movement (Song 8:5-14) speaks elliptically of the consummation of the relationship.

Song of Songs is especially known for its use of allegory, metaphor and simile—typical wisdom genres—in its portrayal of the lovers in the drama and their interrelationship. *Imagery of the natural world, such as fruit, flowers and animals of various types, are cited to convey their beauty, sweet aromas, strength and ardor and to apply these qualities to the portrayal of the two lovers and their surroundings. The use of the *wasf, a literary device known from Egyptian love poetry of the fourteenth through the twelfth centuries BC, employs metaphorical images of flowers, plants, animals, gold, jewels and so forth to portray the physical form and charms of both lovers as they approach (e.g., Song 4:1-8; 5:10-16; 7:1-10). Critics trace the background of Song of Songs to Egyptian love poetry and to Sumerian love poetry that was sung in conjunction with the sacred marriage rituals of the Sumerian New Year celebration. Similar rites may have been known in ancient Israel, although the portrayal of maiden dancing in the vineyards around the Shiloh sanctuary at the festival of Sukkot is now adapted for polemics against the tribe of Benjamin in Judges 21:19-24. Perhaps Song of Songs functioned in the liturgy of the Jerusalem temple for Passover, Shavuot or Sukkot, each of which marks stages in the agricultural season of ancient Judah. Insofar as the festivals celebrate fertility of the flock and the harvest, they also evoke images of human love. Song of Songs might also have found a place in the royal court of Jerusalem.

5. Didactic Narrative.

5.1. The Book of Ruth. The book of Ruth appears among the Historical Books of the Christian OT following Judges and prior to 1 Samuel due to its portrayal of *Naomi and her Moabite daughter-in-law Ruth during the period of the Judges. Ruth appears as one of the five Megillot in the Jewish Tanak insofar as it is read as part of the liturgy for the celebration of Shavuot ("Weeks"), which celebrates the revelation of the Torah at Mount Sinai. Because of its association with the revelation of Torah at Sinai, Shavuot is also associated with the welcoming of converts into the Jewish community.

Although Ruth is presented as a historical narrative, it is designed as a didactic narrative or *novella, typical in Jewish literature of the Persian and Hellenistic periods (see, e.g., Esther; Dan 1—6; Tobit; Judith; 3 Maccabees) that affirms the acceptance of foreign converts to Judaism. Gunkel classified it among the folktales of the Hebrew Bible, although later interpreters recognize didactic narrative as a derivative form of Wisdom literature. Ruth employs a typical narrative episodic structure to relate the efforts of two women, Naomi and Ruth, to return to the land of Israel to restore their lives following the deaths of their husbands while living in the land of Moab. The narrative focuses especially on Ruth, a Moabite woman, who swears loyalty to Naomi and to her G-d, thereby making her a model for a convert to Judaism. Ultimately, Ruth marries *Boaz, a kinsman of her late husband, in a levirate (*see* Kinsman-Redeemer and Levirate) *marriage intended to preserve the line and legacy of the family (see Deut 25:5-10). Because the family of her late husband is based in Bethlehem, Ruth ultimately becomes the ancestor of King David ben Jesse of Judah and Israel.

The major motifs of the book draw heavily on Genesis 38, which portrays Tamar's efforts to engage her father-in-law, Judah, in a levirate marriage following the deaths of his two sons, who had died after marrying her. Many interpreters see Ruth as a challenge to the expulsion of foreign wives by Ezra and Nehemiah, but such a view fails to note that only those women who continued in their foreign religious practice and customs were expelled; those women who had affirmed G-d and Jewish religious practice are not mentioned (Ezra 9—10; Neh 13:23-28). The book of Ruth likely was written during the early Persian period, but it supports the actions of Ezra and Nehemiah by presenting Ruth as a role model for foreign women married to Jewish men at the time.

5.2. The Book of Esther. The book of Esther appears together with Chronicles and Ezra-Nehemiah among the Historical Books of the Christian OT due to its portrayal of the deliverance of the Jewish people by *Esther and *Mordecai during the reign of the Persian monarch *Ahasuerus (Xerxes I). Esther appears among the five Megillot of the Jewish Tanak because it is read as part of the liturgy for the celebration of *Purim, which celebrates the deliverance portrayed in Esther.

Esther is presented as a historical narrative, but its pronounced use of satire, hyperbole and an impossible historical scenario mark it as an example of the wisdom-oriented didactic narratives or novellas typical of the Second Temple period. The historical Ahasuerus—King Xerxes I of Persia (ruled 486-465 BC)—was barred by Persian law from marrying women outside of a selected circle of Persian noble families, and ultimately he was assassinated by a circle of people that included his own nephew. The Esther narrative, in order to emphasize the potential threat against the Jewish people posed by a negligent foreign government against the background of foreign rule of Judah, portrays him as a drunken fool who pays little attention to the affairs of government and court (unlike the historical Xerxes I). Major characters are modeled on earlier biblical models: Mordecai and Esther are descended from Kish, the father of Saul; Haman, the Persian minister who seeks to destroy the entire Jewish people, is identified with Agag, the Amalekite king who posed a mortal threat to Israel and whom Saul failed to kill (1 Sam 15). The Hebrew version of Esther makes no mention of G-d at all, which is deliberate insofar as the book presents a typical episodic narrative structure designed to examine the human responsibility to act against threat in a time of divine absence. Esther, a Jewish woman intermarried with the Persian king, emerges as the heroine of the narrative to illustrate that everyone, no matter how unlikely, has the responsibility to act in a time of crisis. The LXX form of Esther introduces additional material that introduces references to G-d into the narrative, apparently because its author was troubled by the absence of G-d in the Hebrew version.

See also CULT, WORSHIP: PSALMS; CULT, WORSHIP: WISDOM; EDITORIAL CRITICISM; LAMENT, PSALMS OF; NOVELLA, STORY, NARRATIVE; ORAL POETRY; RHETORICAL CRITICISM; THANKSGIVING, PSALMS OF; WISDOM POEMS.

BIBLIOGRAPHY. **M. J. Buss,** *Biblical Form Criticism in Its Context* (JSOTSup 274; Sheffield: Sheffield Academic Press, 1999); **G. W. Coats,** ed., *Saga, Legend, Tale, Novella, Fable: Narrative Forms in Old Testament Literature* (JSOTSup 35; Sheffield: JSOT Press, 1985); **J. L. Crenshaw,** *Old Testament Wisdom: An Introduction* (Louisville: Westminster John Knox, 1998); idem, *The Psalms: An Introduction* (Grand Rapids: Eerdmans, 2001); **E. S. Gerstenberger,** *Psalms: Part 1, with an Introduction to Cultic Poetry* (FOTL 14; Grand Rapids: Eerdmans, 1988); idem, *Psalms: Part 2, and Lamentations* (FOTL 15; Grand Rapids: Eerdmans, 2001); **H. Gunkel,** *The Folktale in the Old Testament* (Sheffield: Almond, 1987); **H. Gunkel and J. Begrich,** *Einleitung in die Psalmen: Die Gattungen der religiösen Lyrik Israels* (HKAT; Göttingen: Vandenhoeck & Ruprecht, 1933); **J. H. Hayes,** ed., *Old Testament Form Criticism* (San Antonio: Trinity University Press, 1974); **P. G. Kirkpatrick,** *The Old Testament and Folklore Study* (JSOTSup 62; Sheffield: Sheffield Academic Press, 1988); **R. Knierim,** "Old Testament Form Criticism Reconsidered," *Int* 27 (1973) 435-68; idem, "Criticism of Literary Features, Form, Tradition, and Redaction," in *The Hebrew Bible and Its Modern Interpreters,* ed. D. Knight and G. M. Tucker (Chico, CA: Scholars Press, 1985) 123-65; **K Koch,** *The Growth of the Biblical Tradition: The Form-Critical Method* (New York: Scribner, 1969); idem, *Was ist Formgeschichte? Methoden der Bibelexegese* (3rd ed.; Neukirchen-Vluyn: Neukirchener Verlag, 1974); **S. Mowinckel,** *Psalmenstudien* (6 vols.; Kristiania: J. Dybwad, 1921-1924); **R. E. Murphy,** *Wisdom Literature: Job, Proverbs, Ruth, Canticles, Ecclesiastes, Esther* (FOTL 13; Grand Rapids: Eerdmans, 1981); **W. Richter,** *Exegese als Literaturwissenschaft: Entwurf einer alttestamentlichen Literaturtheorie und Methodologie* (Göttingen: Vandenhoeck & Ruprecht, 1971); idem, *Recht und Ethos: Versuch einer Ortung des weisheitlichen Mahnspruches* (SANT 15; Munich: Kösel, 1966); **H. Schweizer,** *Metaphorische Grammatik: Wege zur Integration von Grammatik und Textinterpretation in der Exegese* (ATSAT 15; St. Ottilien: EOS Verlag, 1981); **M. A. Sweeney,** "Form Criticism," in *To Each Its Own Meaning: An Introduction to Biblical Criticisms and Their Applications,* ed. S. L. McKenzie and S. R. Haynes (Louisville: Westminster John Knox, 1999) 58-89; **M. A. Sweeney and E. Ben Zvi,** eds., *The Changing Face of Form Criticism for the Twenty-First Century* (Grand Rapids: Eerdmans, 2003); **P. Trible,** *Rhetorical Criticism: Context, Method and the Book of Jonah* (Minneapolis: Fortress, 1994); **G. M. Tucker,** *Form Criticism of the Old Testament* (Philadelphia: Fortress, 1971); **G. von Rad,** *Wisdom in Israel* (Nashville: Abingdon, 1972); **C. Westermann,** *Praise and Lament in the Psalms* (Atlanta: John Knox, 1981); idem, *The Structure of the Book of Job* (Philadelphia: Fortress, 1981); **G. H. Wilson,** *The Editing of the Hebrew Psalter* (SBLDS 76; Chico, CA: Scholars Press, 1985). M. A. Sweeney

FORTRESS. *See* ARCHITECTURAL IMAGERY; PROTECTION IMAGERY.

FRAME NARRATIVE

A frame narrative is a narrative within another narrative. A common example is found in the book of Deuteronomy, where a narrator begins the book by saying, "These are the words of Moses" (Deut 1:1) and then continues to provide the setting and context for the book (Deut 1:2-5). Moses' first sermon begins in Deuteronomy 1:6, "Yahweh our God spoke to us at Horeb," and he goes on to address Israel in several sermons over the next thirty-three chapters. Throughout the sermons the narrator introduces and even interrupts Moses on several occasions before finally concluding the book with a short memorial and a description of Moses' death in Deuteronomy 34. In this way, the narrator "frames" Moses' sermons and provides a perspective through which Israel can appropriate them in each new generation. The effect of this kind of framed narration both enhances and transforms what would otherwise be a simple narrative. It is only in recent decades that the nature and functions of frame narratives described here have been applied to the interpretation of biblical books. Here we will survey the frame narratives in the wisdom books (*Job, *Proverbs, *Ecclesiastes), making note of the most prominent scholarly contributions.

1. Understanding Frame Narrative
2. Frame Narrative in Job
3. Frame Narrative in Proverbs
4. Frame Narrative in Ecclesiastes
5. Conclusion

1. Understanding Frame Narrative.
To grasp how a frame narrative enhances and transforms an otherwise simple narrative, it is first helpful to understand the general category of the literary frame to which the profound and specialized frame narrative belongs. Nonnarrated frames are quite common in literature and borrow their name from the frames in picture and portrait art because they represent the boundaries or frontiers that arise in texts through changes in voice, genre, scene, language and so on. In classic literature we can compare the neat and careful framing of Jane Austen's character portraits in *Mansfield Park* and *Pride and Prejudice* with the more ambivalent frames that Henry James creates using melodramatic scenes to contrast with the overall pictures in his novels (see Caws). In the OT, *Song of Songs seems to be carefully framed by a woman's voice calling for her lover to meet her in their marriage chambers (Song 1:2; 8:13-14). Still, such simple frames, and their literary and aesthetic effects, are typically perceived subconsciously by the reader.

The frame narrative, however, is an especially explicit type of frame that draws attention to itself in a way that radically transforms a narrative. Such is the effect of the framed narration in *Gulliver's Travels* or in films such as *Citizen Kane, Big Fish* and *Magnolia,* where the occasional voice behind the story guides and directs the audience. The artistic "frontiers" of these frames form an "in-between world" (Traber, 221) that simultaneously gives readers the sense of belonging to and seclusion from the narrated drama. Such narrative voices can be either the main story that frames and is fed by an inner narrative (as in Deuteronomy) or a minor outer voice that orients or qualifies the dominating inner narra-

tive (as in Ecclesiastes). Significantly, frame narratives are much stronger than genre, language or scene frames for their ability to direct the reader toward certain modes of interpretation and to effect intellectual, ethical and spiritual transformation.

That is, the literary form in frame narratives leads to existential levels of transformation such that the act of reading (or hearing or viewing) yields both reflection and understanding (see Caws, 4, 25; Dittmar, 192). For example, using repetition or highlighting in stories, frame narrators become "aids to perception" (Caws, 4) that point to the important or high points in a text. In a similar way, the voice of the frame narrator can also distance itself from the central narrative and create juxtaposition that "engenders interpretation," as in the books of Job and Ecclesiastes (see Dittmar, 191). M. A. Caws (14) observes that frames "call forth the maximum potential in our reading resources" and involve us in ways that a one-dimensional story cannot. In other words, by giving the reader a distanced yet participatory perspective on a story, a frame narrative intentionally creates space for self-examination as the reader moves back and forth between frame and story, between inclusion and exclusion, thereby leading readers to evaluate their own reading methods, values and epistemologies in light of those in the frame and body. In sum, frame narratives add a sophistication to texts that engages the full range of cognitive, spiritual and emotional aspects of human nature and thereby imbue the reading process with countless avenues to entertain, guide, challenge and transform an audience.

2. Frame Narrative in Job.
The book of Job has many frames that arise from changes in scene, voice, language and perspective (see Polzin). The most salient of these is a frame narrator who tells Job's story from a "God's-eye perspective" by prefacing the book in Job 1:1—2:12, introducing most of the speeches in Job 3—42, and providing the conclusion in Job 42:7-17. The perspective of this "omniscient narrator" in the frame is written in prose, and it stands alongside the longer set of human speeches in Job 3—42, written in poetry, and creates a sense of contradictory juxtaposition between the divine and human views of Job's suffering (Habel, 25-35). The juxtaposition is accentuated by the different sides of Job that we

find in the two sections: silent and reverent in the frame, and sporadically reactive in the poetic body (Brenner). Through this juxtaposition the frame and the body draw attention to the "bipolarity" or "dichotomy" that exists between Job's belief and his experience—a tension or conflict common to everyone who trusts in God's sovereignty while living in a fallen world.

Furthermore, the three cycles of speeches between Job and his four friends in the central chapters (Job 3—37) also represent a kind of literary framing that amplifies the tension of the contrary juxtaposition. As the story progresses, the reader obtains at least five perspectives on the relationship between belief and experience: (1) the narrator's (and God's), (2) the friends' in Job 3—25, (3) Elihu's in Job 32—37, (4) Job's in the frame and (5) Job's in the body. These levels of juxtaposition are a part of the book's literary craftedness, which is not written in a way that spews forth universal dogma on the nature of suffering or God's sovereignty. On the contrary, Job's frame-narrative structure demonstrates the natural complexity that arises in communities where tragedy presses in and individuals living in community attempt to cope. The frame narrator thus captures readers in a story that leads them through these many perspectives and thereby simultaneously challenges them to evaluate their own response to the unavoidable tension between belief and experience. In the closing section of the frame the reader is invited to follow Job, as it were, into a higher level of *wisdom—a wisdom highlighted in Job 42:7-8, where God declares his approval of Job's speech. God's approval likely refers not just to Job's confession in Job 42:1-6 but rather to Job's words throughout the book, which, in the face of tragedy, have been able to achieve a balance between God's sovereignty and human experience, thus turning the experiences of suffering into discovery. The frame narrator also effects a second turn, transforming what seems to be a traditional ancient tragedy—with Job as the suffering hero—into a mosaic that displays the wisdom, mystery and faithfulness of the Creator (Job 42:10-17).

3. Frame Narrative in Proverbs.

Although Proverbs is not a narrative with a sustained plot, conflict and resolution, it does have a discernable framing structure and sense of progression that perform the essential roles of a frame narrative. Its frame consists of theological admonitions, interludes and poems in Proverbs 1—9; 30—31, which surround the body of short traditional proverbs in Proverbs 10—29. In the opening frame (Prov 1—9) a series of ten admonitions (Prov 1:1; 1:8-19; 2:1-22; 3:1-12, 21-35; 4:1-9; 4:10-19; 4:20-27; 5:1-23; 6:20-35; 7:1-27) by the father continually appeal to his "son" to follow the way of wisdom, leading readers to identify with the student and embrace the teachings of the book. The frame has two more prominent characteristics. First, "the fear of Yahweh" (*see* Fear of the Lord) as the beginning (and foundation) of wisdom stands at both ends of the book (Prov 1:7; 31:30) in addition to appearing twelve more times throughout Proverbs. Wisdom is thus understood as more than simply a pragmatic enterprise; rather, it is the natural and proper outflow of the life that has been brought into a loving relationship with Israel's redeeming and creating God. Second, the frame is further nuanced by the feminine motifs that increase the urgency of the father's admonitions. In Proverbs 1—9 these motifs are expressed in the five interludes (Prov 1:20-33; 3:13-20; 6:1-19; 8:1-36; 9:1-18) placed between the father's ten admonitions. The feminine motifs return again in the portrait of the "valiant" woman in Proverbs 31:10-31, which closes the book with a remarkable *personification of wisdom centered on the fear of Yahweh (Van Leeuwen; Wolters).

Using the motifs of alluring *women and the fear of Yahweh, the frame embeds wisdom in the fullest imaginable range of human life and culture that can be experienced in God's created order (see Camp). In Proverbs 1—9 the women lure the reader at the levels of sensuality, sustenance and prosperity, inviting the passer-by to turn to their houses and partake of their feasts. Their appeals communicate the urgency of mortal consequences as the paths of wisdom and folly (and the houses of these two women) ultimately lead to life and death (*see* Woman Wisdom and Woman Folly). All the while, fearing the Creator and Redeemer continually depicts the pursuit of wisdom as a relational and religious journey. Finally, the valiant woman in Proverbs 31 appeals to the practical and aesthetic dimensions of life, personifying wisdom as she excels in areas of business, charity, household management, parenting and marriage (Wolters). In this way, the frame shapes reading habits in order to involve readers in God's design for the aesthetic, moral, economic, spiritual and vital nature of life. Wisdom is that most valued treasure (Prov 2:4; 3:13-18; cf. Prov 31:10), which equips God's creatures to walk fittingly within this design.

4. Frame Narrative in Ecclesiastes.

If Ecclesiastes is not the most recognized frame narrative, it certainly is the most controversial, as is evidenced by an increasing number of scholars who variously try to account for the strategic differentiation between the book's main voice (*Qohelet) and the voice of a frame narrator. Most scholars assign Ecclesiastes 1:1-2; 7:27; 12:8-14 to the frame, and the remainder of the book to Qohelet (Longman, however, also attributes Eccles 1:3-11 to the introductory frame). Most also agree that the narrative voice in the first two framing sections maintains a fairly neutral stance in regard to Qohelet's own message. However, both the translation and the interpretation of the narrator's final epilogue (Eccles 12:8-14) are highly disputed, leading to at least three different perspectives on the relationship between Qohelet and the frame.

4.1. Distance and Neutrality. M. V. Fox initiated the turn to frame-narrative analysis some thirty years ago, and despite the anticipated maturation of several decades of research, he has consistently represented the frame as a distancing voice in the book. So, although his translation of the closing epilogue (Eccles 12:8-14) implies that the narrator has fairly strong reservations about Qohelet's wisdom, Fox still sees the narrator in a position of distanced neutrality that affords the reader the space to evaluate both sides of the book (Fox 1977, 103-5) while upholding Qohelet as a sage honestly seeking wisdom in the face of the realities that try his faith. E. S. Christianson also makes a strong case for this "distanced" position and sees the neutrality as a key strategy in leading readers into moral and epistemological self-examination. For both Christianson and Fox, Qohelet's own tendency to observe himself observing is a clue to the multileveled nature of his rhetoric—a rhetoric that demands the reader's self-examination.

4.2. Opposition and Rejection. T. Longman follows Fox's more pessimistic translation of the epilogue yet suggests that this betrays the narrator's reproachful and decided opposition to Qohelet. In this case, Qohelet in the body emerges as a "skeptic" whose theological message can be summarized thus: "Life is full of trouble and then you die" (Longman, 34). According to Longman (274-84), the frame narrator in turn shuns his unproductive musings in favor of a more traditional admonition to fear God and keep his commandments (Eccles 12:13-14). Furthermore, Longman's pessimistic translation of the final epilogue parallels his preference to render Qohelet's thirty-eight uses of *hebel* as "meaningless." In other words, he sees Qohelet's self-centered and skeptical search for wisdom continually leading to a meaningless end, which the orthodox frame narrator rightly denounces.

4.3. Irony and Inclusion. Scholars such C. G. Bartholomew and C. L. Seow take a third perspective on the book in which Qohelet and the frame, through a subtle use of irony, are in fact aligned in the end. As Seow (38) says, "The perspective of the book is one and the same as the framework." In defense of this position, the frame narrator's final epilogue is given a less pessimistic translation (see the arguments in Bartholomew, 158-70). And, besides the translation and role of irony in the book, these scholars prefer to render *hebel* with a more metaphorical sense of "enigma" or "vapor," which assigns to Qohelet a certain awareness of the skepticism that he aims to deconstruct using his polished rhetorical skills and self-involved irony.

As can be seen in the unique intersection of literary, epistemological and linguistic variables in the interpretation of Ecclesiastes, accounting for the role of the frame narrative is an extremely complex task. Nevertheless, whatever the relationship between Qohelet's words and the frame, to one degree or another all the aforementioned scholars agree that the frame-narrative provokes the reader (and reading community) to assess the many perspectives presented in the book and, in doing so, to engage in a self-reflective assessment of personal epistemology and theology. The frame narrative, then, can be seen as a masterful tool in its ability to engage, challenge and shape its reading audience.

5. Conclusion.

The frame narrative provides invaluable insights into understanding the sophisticated literary dynamics of many biblical books. Its presence in Job, Proverbs and Ecclesiastes creates a web of interactions between aesthetic artistry and spiritual and existential transformation. The particular strength of the frame in the Wisdom literature, as we have seen, is to involve readers in self-examination of their morality, epistemology and values and then move them along the path toward a more mature wisdom. And, whereas the frame in Proverbs serves largely to keep wisdom in its proper submission to Yahweh, the frames in Job and Ecclesiastes illumine for readers the many and varied perspectives that are all appropriate to living in the world that God himself has made with wisdom (Prov 3:19-20). Using frames, wisdom thus achieves a unity and foundation amidst the diversity of human experiences.

See also RHETORICAL CRITICISM.

BIBLIOGRAPHY. **C. G. Bartholomew,** *Reading Ecclesiastes: Old Testament Exegesis and Hermeneutical Theory* (AnBib 139; Rome: Pontifical Biblical Institute, 1998); **A. Brenner,** "Job the Pious? The Characterization of Job in the Narrative Framework of the Book," *JSOT* 43 (1989) 37-52; **C. V. Camp,** *Wisdom and the Feminine in the Book of Proverbs* (BLS 1; Sheffield: Almond, 1985); **M. A. Caws,** *Reading Frames in Modern Fiction* (Princeton, NJ: Princeton University Press, 1985); **E. S. Christianson,** *A Time to Tell: Narrative Strategies in Ecclesiastes* (JSOTSup 280; Sheffield: Sheffield Academic Press, 1998); **L. Dittmar,** "Fashioning and Re-Fashioning: Framing Narratives in the Novel and Film," *Mosaic* 16.1-2 (1983) 189-203; **M. V. Fox,** "Frame-Narrative and Composition in the Book of Qohelet," *HUCA* 48 (1977) 83-106; idem, *Ecclesiastes* (JPSBC; Philadelphia: Jewish Publication Society, 2004); **N. C. Habel,** *The Book of Job* (OTL; London: SCM, 1985); **T. Longman III,** *The Book of Ecclesiastes* (NICOT; Grand Rapids: Eerdmans, 1998); **R. Polzin,** "The Framework of the Book of Job," *Int* 28 (1974) 182-200; **C. L. Seow,** *Ecclesiastes* (AB 18C; New York: Doubleday, 1997); **C. Traber,** "In Perfect Harmony? Escaping the Frame in the Early Twentieth Century," in *In Perfect Harmony: Picture and Frame, 1850-1920,* ed. Eva Mendgen et al. (Amsterdam: Van Gogh Museum, 1995) 221-47; **R. C. Van Leeuwen,** "Liminality and Worldview in Proverbs 1–9," *Semeia* 50 (1990) 111-44; **A. Wolters,** *The Song of the Valiant Woman: Studies in the Interpretation of Proverbs 31:10–31* (Carlisle: Paternoster, 2001).

R. O'Dowd

G

GATE. *See* ARCHITECTURE.

GOD

Any attempt to discuss God in a short compass is, in the nature of the case, a daunting task. But it is doubly so in regard to wisdom, poetry and writings. First, there is a wide range of ideas concerning God in this collection of literature. The whole gamut of OT theological concepts is found here, from the intimate and personal Yahweh of the covenant in *Psalms to the distant and almost unknowable God of *Ecclesiastes, and everything in between. Second, that the task is difficult is implied in what was just said: the different genres involved display the multiplicity of ideas in differing constellations. For these reasons, the present article does not attempt to provide an integrated discussion but rather is organized along genre lines.

    1. Divine Titles
    2. Psalms
    3. Wisdom Literature
    4. Writings

1. Divine Titles.

One indication of the diversity of thought in this collection of material is in the distribution of the divine names. "God" (*ʾĕlōhîm*) occurs 404 times in Psalms. The Tetragrammaton (*yhwh*, usually rendered "the LORD") occurs almost twice as often, 731 times. In the Wisdom literature (*Job, *Proverbs, Ecclesiastes) there is a striking reversal of the frequency of the occurrences of these names in Proverbs on the one hand and Job and Ecclesiastes on the other. "God" appears only six times in Proverbs, while "the LORD" occurs eighty-seven times. In Job "God" occurs 118 times and "the LORD" only thirty-three times, and almost all of those in the prologue (Job 1—2) and the epilogue (Job 42:7-17). In Ecclesi-

astes "God" appears forty-one times and "the LORD" not at all. In the remaining literature (*Ruth, *Lamentations, *Esther, *Song of Songs) the variety continues. As is famously known, God does not appear by title in the book of Esther. But it is also true that a divine title occurs only once in Song of Songs: "the LORD" (Song 8:6). In Lamentations and Ruth it is "the LORD" that dominates: forty-three times in Lamentations, twelve times in Ruth. In contrast, "God" appears only once in Lamentations and three times in Ruth. Broadly speaking, these differences can be understood as relating to functional distinctions (as opposed, for instance, to evidence of differing sources). In general, when "God" is used, the writer is referring to the Deity in a more general and abstract way. On the other hand, when "the LORD" is used, the reference is generally to the personal God revealed in the covenant and elsewhere in Israel's experience. This distinction is by no means absolute, but it is broadly useful.

Among other titles used for God in the OT only "the Almighty" (*šadday*) and "the Most High" (*ʿelyôn*) occur with any frequency in these books. "The Almighty" is virtually limited to Job (31x). As with the predominance of "God" in Job, so the frequency of this title speaks of God in more abstract and less personal terms. "The Most High" occurs twenty-two times in Psalms. It is hard to determine any pattern in its usages. It occurs in context with "The LORD" almost exactly as often as it does with "God" (for further discussion, see 2.3.2 below, on God as king in Psalms).

As noted at the opening of this section, the diversity of the ways in which the divine name is used in these parts of the OT is a witness to the richness of the understanding of God that they express.

2. Psalms.

It has been somewhat jocularly said that God is the "center" of OT theology. That is certainly true in regard to Psalms. God is the subject of every psalm. If it is a *lament, it is a lament to God for the situation in which he has allowed his servant to languish. If it is a *hymn, it is in praise of the character and nature of God. If it is a song of *thanksgiving, it is an expression of gratitude for something God has done in the worshiper's life. If it is a *kingship psalm, it is extolling God's monarchy of the world and his establishment of his *messiah on the throne of Israel. If it is a *wisdom psalm, it is admonishing persons to immerse themselves in God's wisdom as it is found in his word. Thus, the psalms are not about the "religion" of Yahweh; rather, they are about Yahweh and Israel in dialogue (so Kraus, 12 [following von Rad]).

2.1. Titles for God in Psalms. We get some sense of this divine centrality when we discover that in the 150 psalms the two main titles for God appear almost 1,200 times, with "the LORD" occurring approximately twice as often (784x; *yhwh* 688x, *yāh* 43x, *ʾădōnāy* as a divine title 53x) as "God" (404x). Given that there are approximately 2,500 verses in Psalms, this works out to an average of one reference to God by name in every other verse throughout the entire corpus. Obviously, such a statement is a broad generalization, since there are many verses where a title may appear twice. However it gives some specificity to the point being made.

When the distribution of the two names is studied, some interesting patterns emerge, for the overall 2:1 ratio is not maintained in specifics. In the first book (Pss 1—41) "the LORD" occurs 290 times as against 68 occurrences of "God," or close to a 4:1 ratio. But in the second book (Pss 42—72) and throughout much of the third (Pss 73—89) the ratio is reversed, with "God" occurring 301 times and "the LORD" occurring 110 times. However, if one limits the consideration to Psalms 42—83, at which point a fairly obvious shift in proportions emerges, the difference is more striking: 281 to 69, or almost exactly the reverse of the first forty-one psalms. Given this fact, it will be obvious that there is a greater preponderance of "the LORD" from Psalm 84 to the end of the collection: 421 to 98, more than 4:1. One should not place undue weight on word counts such as this, but it is still helpful to give some sense of proportion. It also lends support to the emerging consensus that the present collection of the psalms is not in the random order that may appear to be the case at first glance. Clearly, the first forty-one and the last sixty-seven psalms are "Yahwistic," while Psalms 42—83 are "Elohistic." Scholars have debated, and will continue to debate, exactly what these facts mean for the origins of the psalms and for the development of Israelite theology, but those concerns need not detain us here.

Two further points should be made. The first has to do with the most frequent use of *ʾĕlōhîm*, which is as an object of a possessive pronoun or noun, as in "my God," "our God," "God of Jacob/Israel," or "God of truth, salvation, etc." In many of these cases the phrase is used to modify either "the LORD," as in Psalm 18:28, or "God," as in Psalm 67:6. In these cases the line between noun and title begins to become blurred (see also Ps 59:5). The two titles may also appear as a parallel pair (e.g., Ps 18:6, 21; 24:5; 29:3; 55:16; 69:13; 94:22). The second observation has to do with Psalms 14; 53. These two are virtual duplicates except for one thing: Psalm 53 uses "God" exclusively, whereas in Psalm 14 four of the seven occurrences of the divine name appear as "the LORD." Several different explanations for this phenomenon have been put forward, none of them compelling. At a minimum, the two psalms indicate that the two titles were understood to function in an overlapping way.

An additional title of God occurs with some frequency in the psalms. This is "the Most High" (*ʿelyôn*). Of the fifty-three OT occurrences of this title, twenty-two are in Psalms. It occurs equally often as a qualifier of "the LORD" as with "God" and does not seem to be limited to any particular context. The bulk of the occurrences are found in the second and third books, between Psalm 46 and Psalm 97 (18x), with no occurrences after Psalm 107. As might be expected, the title occurs most frequently in contexts related to God's power and sovereignty (e.g., Ps 47:2; 89:27; 97:9). However, it also occurs in the context of praise and *worship (e.g., Ps 7:17; 9:2; 46:4; 50:14), while Psalm 91 speaks of "the Most High" as one's personal hiding place and refuge (Ps 91: 1, 9).

2.2. The Character of God in Psalms. When surveying the psalms, one cannot escape the dominant impression that these poems are above all else concerned to praise, bless and thank God. Even the laments, which struggle over God's apparent absence or inactivity, typically end with a vow of praise to be given not *if* God acts, but *when* he acts. Why is this the case? The simple answer is that the psalmists are overcome with the gracious and dependable character of this God. They cannot say enough good things about him.

This is largely so because of one overriding quality of God expressed in the psalms: *hesed,* a quality that no single English word adequately expresses. The variety of English translations of this term is witness to this fact. Even a partial list includes "goodness," "kindness," "mercy," "grace," "love," "steadfast love," "unfailing love" and "loving-kindness." Interestingly, although the term occurs some 250 times in the Hebrew Bible, there has yet to be found a cognate for it in any other Semitic language. This suggests a situation analogous to *agapē* in NT Greek, where an obscure Greek word was adapted to express an understanding of love not found in classical Greek thought. Be that as it may, *hesed* conveys the idea of the intentional kindness, generosity or loyalty of a superior to an inferior, especially when it is undeserved. Although the term can be used of humans to each other (see 4.4 below), it is primarily used of God from its first occurrence, in Genesis 19:19, onward. This is certainly true of the psalms. More than half of the total occurrences of the word are found in Psalms (130x), and virtually all refer to God. It is a source of praise (136x), a reason for hope of forgiveness and restoration (Ps 51:1), a cause for concern when apparently withheld (Ps 77:8), and a cause for confidence in distress (Ps 59:8). Ultimately, God's *hesed* is the reason why laments typically end in a vow of praise. As Psalm 86:5 says, "You, O Lord, are good and forgiving, full of *hesed* to all those who call upon you." This quality shapes every other quality of God and every other role that he plays. If he becomes angry, it is but for a moment, because his *hesed* endures forever (Ps 103:8-11); if he is the righteous judge, his ordering of his world will always be tempered by his *hesed* (Ps 89:32-33).

Two other qualities are regularly mentioned in the context of *hesed.* They are goodness *(tôb)* and faithfulness *(ʾĕmûnâ).* The classic statement of the first is found in Psalm 136:1 (see also Ps 106:1; 107:1, 118:1, 29). God's goodness is directly related to his nature. That which is good, as Genesis 1 shows, is fully in keeping with the created nature of things. This repeated statement,

"He is good," is a way of saying that God never acts out of keeping with the best interests of the cosmos that he created. Since God is unlimited in power, he certainly could do so, but the psalmists testify in wonder that this God of *hesed* never does.

In that regard, God is utterly reliable. This is the point of the second concept, *ʾĕmûnâ* ("faithfulness"). The consonantal base of the word is *ʾmn* ("be firm, reliable"). The concept occurs no less than seven times in Psalm 89. In the first two verses the singer sets the tone, twice using "faithfulness" as the poetic equivalent and development of *hesed.* Yahweh's grace, compassion and patience are absolutely fixed and dependable. They are so for every generation (Ps 100:5; 119:90), and that truth needs to be made known to each new generation (Ps 40:10; 89:1).

This idea of the Lord's unfailing goodness, dependability and grace is a surprising one in the world of ancient Near Eastern religion, where the gods were thoroughly inconsistent. If they were good on some occasions, they were bad on others. If they were dependable in some instances, they were quite fickle in others. But Yahweh, "the Holy One of Israel" (Ps 71:22; 78:41; 89:18), was not so. His character was the same in all circumstances. This recognition had a profound impact upon the understanding of the concept "holy." It was no longer primarily a description of "otherness," or what Rudolf Otto called "the numinous." Rather, since Israel's God alone was rightly called "holy," and since he was one both in essence and character, then "holy" was no longer limited to the divine essence, but rather its meaning was also to be defined by his unique character. "Holy" occurs in all its forms in Psalms more than 50 times. Most of these are adjectival uses identifying something associated with the Lord, as in "holy temple" (Ps 79:1), "holy oil" (Ps 89:20) and "holy arm" (Ps 98:1). However, this deeper understanding of the unique, "holy" character of God is also apparent, as in Psalm 22:2-5. Because the "Praise of Israel" is "holy," he can be depended upon not to remain silent but rather to faithfully answer prayer. In Psalm 30:5, to joyfully remember the holiness of the Lord is to recall that his anger is but for a moment, while his favor is for a lifetime. To praise the Holy One of Israel is to recount his faithfulness as he acts in *righteousness to redeem his people. In fact, in Psalm

145:17 "holy" and "righteous" are synonyms used to describe the Lord.

All this leads to a characteristic term in Psalms for the nature of God: his "name." It is widely recognized that the "name" of God is not a label or a title but rather a term for his very nature ("what he is in himself" [Kraus, 21]). Thus, when God's "name" is said repeatedly to be "holy" (Ps 33:21; 99:3; 103:1; 105:3; 106:47; 111:9; 145:21), a highly significant point is being made. This is so because God's "name" is not primarily expressed in his otherness. When the psalmists speak of God's holy name, they are thinking of his *hesed*, of his goodness, of his faithfulness, and of his righteousness (Ps 138:2). This is what it means for God to be holy. The fact that the singer is going to extol these "in the face of the gods" is quite significant. He is saying that the "gods" do not even have the right to be called "holy." Yahweh alone is truly other, both in essence and character.

2.3. The Roles of God in Psalms. God's character is revealed in the psalms through several roles that he is said to play in regard to the cosmos and in particular in regard to human beings. Among these are creator, king/judge, covenant Lord, Father, redeemer/deliverer.

2.3.1. Creator. As elsewhere in the OT, so also in Psalms there is no question how the earth came into being. It came into being as a result of the express will of the sole creator, Yahweh, the Lord. He is "the maker of heaven and earth" (Ps 115:15; 124:8; 134:3). All that is the result of his spoken command (Ps 33:6; 148:5); it is the work of his hands (Ps 100:3; 138:8). This latter point is significant in biblical theology because the Bible is at pains to assert that the gods are the work of human hands. This is true not only of the actual idols but also of the theology of idolatry, which is an attempt to make the cosmos amenable to human manipulation and control. So the psalmists can assert that God is high over all the heaven and the earth (Ps 113:4; 148:13), and that he is greater than all the gods (put together?) (Ps 86:8; 96:4; 135:5). The writers are free enough from any mythological outlook that they can playfully call the sea monsters and the deeps—elements that the myth-makers used to express the forces of chaos that constantly threatened the gods—to come and give praise to the true creator of the universe (Ps 148:7).

Because the Lord is the maker of all things, all things are at his beck and call. They join in the song of praise (Ps 103:22), and when they seem to be a threat to God's people, they are no threat to him (Ps 46:2-4); rather, he commands them with calm assurance, and they do his will.

2.3.2. King/Judge. Because God is the maker of the universe, he is its true king (Ps 93:1; 95:3). He rules it with complete sovereignty, and there is nothing to threaten it, most of all not the kings of this earth (Ps 47:1-9). He laughs at their attempts to shake off his sovereignty and to make themselves absolute (Ps 2:4; 59:8). And as king, he is the one who assures that the proper order of things is maintained (Ps 89:14; 98:9; 105:7). This was the task that kings across the ancient Near East took upon themselves. Although it is not incorrect to translate the word for this order as "justice" *(mišpāṭ),* that is only one aspect of a far larger concept. Where there is disorder from the creation plan, there is injustice, oppression, violence and murder. What the psalmists tell us is that where the true king is allowed to rule, there *mišpāṭ* is to be found (Ps 7:11), and they look forward to that great day when the divine order will, through the Lord's messiah, prevail over all the earth (Ps 2:7-12; 89:27-28; 96:10; 110:5-6).

2.3.3. Covenant Lord. Not only is the Lord the king of the universe, but also he is the king who has entered into covenant with his chosen people (Pss 78; 106). But unlike the suzerains of earth who tended to use covenants to bind their subjects while freeing themselves, this covenant Lord has bound himself as well (Ps 106:44-46). And so the psalmists sing the praises of the one who has kept his covenant even when his partners have broken theirs (Ps 78:38-39; 89:33-34). And in that covenant he has revealed the *mišpāṭ* that he has written into his world (Ps 119:149). His instructions are without a blemish, turning a person around (Ps 19:7). To master them and live by them is to come to know wisdom, to inherit the earth (Ps 1:2; 37:30-31; 111:7-10).

2.3.4. Father. But beyond this covenant relationship the psalms depict Yahweh as one who plays an even more personal role in relationship to his people. He is the Father, who will take up his children when their earthly mothers and fathers forsake him (Ps 27:10; 68:5; 89:26). He is the true husband to Israel his beloved (Ps 60:5; 108:6; 127:2). This deeply personal note is sounded again and again as the poets take God's care over them and his intense interest in their concerns as a given. They call upon him in every difficulty, secure in the certainty that he is immediately available to them. This is no "Life Force," no "Unmoved Mover," no "Ultimate Concern." Neither is this the physical father, as the Canaanite god El was said to be the "father of the gods." This is "the lover of my soul" (Ps 31:7; 34:2-22; 84:2) who is the final "refuge" to whom every human can fly (Ps 25:20; 91:2; 141:5).

2.3.5. Redeemer/Deliverer. In the light of all of the aforementioned roles, it is not surprising that the writers of the psalms see the Lord as the one who delivers from every trouble, who redeems from every captivity. The cries of the lamenters are based upon this certainty and grow out of the confusion over why God the deliverer has not yet acted. The hymns extol his nature as redeemer, and the songs of thanksgiving overflow with praise for his deliverance. As the creator, he will accomplish his deliverance, which cannot be deterred or defeated. As the just king, he will not allow the disorder of sin to prevail in his kingdom. As the covenant Lord, he will bring the blessings of the covenant upon any who will put themselves in the position to receive them. As the Father, he is moved with compassion at the plight of his people.

3. Wisdom Literature.
One of the characteristics of ancient Near Eastern wisdom literature is its so-called humanistic bent (see Crenshaw, 55). There is little reference to the divine to be found in it. This wisdom is a thoughtful distillation of the truths of human experience, whether positive or negative. It was not thought to be received from the gods, nor did relations with the gods have much to do with it other than limited counsel about how to conduct oneself in religious settings. This is not at all the case with the Israelite Wisdom literature. Although it does bear unmistakable family resemblance to the other wisdom literature in literary features as well as in its focus on what can be learned from life, God is hardly peripheral to its concerns. Indeed, it might be argued that God is central to the OT Wisdom literature. That is most obviously the case with the book of Job, where the whole focus is on the attempt to justify God's behavior or to call him to account for it. But it is also true with Proverbs and Ecclesiastes, in which the first continually explains the success of good behavior and the failure of bad behavior by reference to Yahweh's desires and

intentions, and the second, while insisting on the unintelligibility of much of God's activity, still maintains that one had better do what God wants!

In all three cases the basis for human choices is not the pragmatic results of human experience but rather "the fear of God/the LORD" (Job 1:1, 8-9; 2:3; 4:6; 28:28; Prov 1:7, 29; 2:5; 3:7; 8:13; 9:10; 10:27; 14:2; 15:6; 16:6; 19:23; 22:4; 23:17; 24:21; 31:30; Eccles 3:14; 5:7; 7:18; 8:12-13; 12:13). The description of the fear of God at the end of Ecclesiastes is as good a one as can be found in short compass: it is to keep the commandments of God, for he will bring every person to judgment for every action. This is very far from the idea that one should decide for or against a behavior on the basis of its proven chances of success. Rather, a behavior's chances of success are (or at least should be) in direct relationship to what the Creator/Judge of the world has determined. And where was the Creator's will for human life to be found? It was to be found in his covenant with Israel. What this means is that while the Israelite Wisdom literature shares many superficial features with that of Israel's surrounding cultures, it is essentially different from them at heart. It also means that the assertion that the Wisdom literature provides an alternative to revelation through salvation history with revelation through ordinary experience (Murphy, 126) is not correct. What it does mean is that Israel's understanding of the significance of ordinary experience was thoroughly conditioned and profoundly altered by what it had learned about God in the arena of salvation history.

3.1. Proverbs. In Proverbs "the LORD" (86x) is far and away the most common title for the Deity, far exceeding "God" (6x). As noted above, this is directly opposite to Job, where "God" (118x) is much more common than "the LORD" (33x), and Ecclesiastes, where "the LORD" does not appear at all. This fact suggests that Proverbs is at pains to assert that it is Yahweh, Israel's God, the God of the covenant, who is in fact the sole fount of wisdom in the earth. This would make sense if *Solomon was indeed the originator of the collection. The empire that his father had bequeathed to him certainly would have suggested that Yahweh was indeed the God of the world, and the insistent monotheism that Solomon had received through the books of Moses would have argued that Yahweh is the *only* God, of the world, the only source of wisdom.

Whatever the explanation of the fact might be, a fact it is. Wisdom is not merely something that humans discover, it being incipient in the world as it is. Rather, wisdom is the creation and possession of God. It exists in the world because it is an expression of the consistent character of things as the Creator made them. He is the source of wisdom and has made the world according to it. Thus, to gain wisdom is to discover the ways of the Lord. That means that acting wisely is not merely a smart thing to do. Rather, it is to fear the Lord. On the other side of the coin, acting foolishly is not merely a stupid thing to do, but is to defy the Lord. Ultimately, in that it denies the verities of existence, *folly is an abomination to God. Thus, in the end we are not speaking merely of the wise person, but about the righteous person. Nor are we speaking about the fool or the scoffer, but about the wicked person. Wisdom has been effectively moved from something primarily pragmatic aimed at achieving success in life to that which is in keeping with the moral reality of things, and foolishness is not merely stupid, but morally wrong (so especially in Psalm 1).

The well-known statement in Proverbs 1:7, "The fear of the LORD is the beginning of knowledge," sets the stage for the Yahwistic understanding of wisdom (see also Prov 9:10, near the end of the opening division of the book, and Prov 15:33). Proverbs 2:5 makes much the same point but goes farther to say that knowledge too is from God. To fear the Lord is to turn away from evil (Prov 3:7). Indeed, it is to hate evil (Prov 8:13; see also Prov 16:6). The *fear of the Lord results in long life (Prov 10:27; 19:23), in confidence (Prov 14:26), and in riches and honor (Prov 22:4). However, if it ever comes to a choice between abundance and the fear of the Lord, the sages urge us to choose the latter every time (Prov 15:16). To fear the Lord is to choose the straight path instead of the crooked (Prov 14:2) and to take the Lord into account in everything that we do (Prov 30:9).

All of this is so because wisdom comes from the Lord (Prov 2:6; 19:21; 21:30; 22:12). Indeed, wisdom was his first creation (Prov 8:22). The verb for "create" used in that statement is not *bārā*ʾ, which speaks of bringing a new thing into existence; rather, it is *qānâ*, which refers to bringing something into existence for oneself, as in "to create wealth." God did not create wisdom as a new thing. It was indeed who he was in himself. But he quantified it, as it were, when he brought the world into existence. Modern attempts to suggest that "wisdom" (the fem. noun *hokmâ*) was once the female consort of God are wrong-headed in the extreme (see Waltke 2004, 83-87). The point is simply to assert in the strongest figurative terms that wisdom is not some principle that exists in tandem with, or even apart from, the Lord but rather is indeed implicit in all that he, the all-wise God, has made (Prov 3:19; see also Prov 20:12; 22:2, 12; 29:13).

This explains the frequent statement that certain behaviors are "an abomination to the LORD." They are not merely stupid, or even wrong; they are a denial of the very way the Lord has made the cosmos. The list of these is instructive. There is the crooked (or perverse) behavior (Prov 3:32; 11:20; 15:9), haughty eyes, a lying tongue, bloody hands, a scheming heart, feet running to evil, a false witness, and one who pits brothers against each other (Prov 6:16; see also Prov 12:22; 15:9, 26; 16:5), a false set of scales (Prov 11:1; 16:11; 20:10, 23), insincere sacrifice (Prov 15:9; 21:3), condemning the innocent and justifying the wicked (Prov 17:5). In his wisdom the Lord has made the world according to certain standards; to deviate from those patterns, even if in the short term the deviation seems to yield good results, is the way of a fool.

On the other hand, the wise choose the Lord's way, entrusting themselves to him (Prov 3:5; 16:20; 22:19; 28:25; 29:25), committing their way and works to him (Prov 16:3), determined to honor him in all things (Prov 3:9), waiting for him rather than attempting to solve their problems without reference to him (Prov 20:22), seeking him and his blessing in all things (Prov 28:5). This is the wise course of action because God stands behind all things. All that is, is because of him (Prov 16:4; 20:24; 21:1; 22:2; 29:13, 26). He understands all things as they really are and evaluates them correctly, things that no human is capable of (Prov 5:21; 15:3, 11; 16:1, 2, 9, 33; 17:3; 20:24, 27; 21:2, 31; 24:17-18). All this is to say that we are not ultimate, and to act as though we are is rankest foolishness. Instead, we ought to try to learn God's ways, commit ourselves to following those ways with all the sincerity that we can muster, and entrust the outcome to him, recognizing that we do not know all things and cannot foresee all outcomes and are almost infinitely capable of self-deception.

When we act in those ways, the book tells us, we will be the beneficiaries of the Lord's elemental goodness and love. One expression of that love will be discipline and reproof (Prov 3:11-12). But if we profit from those and choose the ways of God's righteousness, we will live under his favor (Prov 8:35; 18:22), will have our physical needs supplied (Prov 10:3), will have our posterity secured (Prov 15:25), have access to the Lord in prayer (Prov 15:29), have peace with our enemies (Prov 16:7), have a place of refuge in him (Prov 10:29; 18:10), and have his defense when we are unjustly charged (Prov 29:26).

3.2. Job. As noted above, the majority of the references to the Deity in the book of Job use the title "God" (118x). "The LORD" appears only thirty-three times, almost all in Job 1—2 (the "prologue") and in Job 42:7-12 (the "epilogue"). This fact could be argued to support the conclusion that these two sections of the book are from a different hand, but it must also be considered whether the different titles may relate to the differing views of God prevailing in the sections (on the integrity of the present book, see Janzen, 23-24; contra Pope, xxi-xxv). On this point it is important to note that the long disputation by Elihu, unanswered by Job (Job 32—37), is also thought by many to be a later addition (see Pope, xxvii; but also see Hartley, 28-30). But the title used exclusively there is "God," the one that predominates in the rest of the body of the book (Job 3:1—40:6). Note also that the final section of Ecclesiastes (variously understood as Eccles 12:1-14 or Eccles 12:9-14) is also thought to be from the hand of someone wanting to make the generally pessimistic outlook more palatable. But it continues to use "God" like the rest of the book does. These thoughts are not meant to foreclose discussion on the composition of Job (or Ecclesiastes), but they are meant to say that the conception of God that an author wishes to convey may be at least as important a consideration in the choice of titles as is the assumption of differing authors.

The predominant use of "God" is consistent with the major concern in Job: divine justice considered in broad and general terms. This is not to say that God is thought of in primarily impersonal terms—far from it. Nor is it to say that the God of the covenant is entirely absent from these writings. The occasional appearance of "commandment" in a covenant context, although admittedly rare in Job and Ecclesiastes, still indicates that what is being said is not in ignorance of that whole side of God. Rather, the concern is to deal with broader, even more basic questions. Job, along with Ecclesiastes, is asking the question of whether there is any fundamental consistency at the heart of the Deity. It is for this reason that the term "God" predominates. The location of Job in "the land of Uz" (frequently associated with Edom) and in a patriarchal milieu also reinforces the idea that the concerns addressed in the book are not confined to persons within the Israelite covenant.

This conclusion is furthered when we discover that of the forty-eight OT references to God as "the Almighty" (*šadday*), fully thirty-one of them are found in Job. Of these, sixteen are in the mouths of Job's so-called comforters, including Elihu, and fourteen come from Job. One, in Job 40:2, comes from God himself. As the English translation rightly suggests, this title speaks of the inimitable power of God. In Job it most often appears as the poetic equivalent of "God," and whatever is said of God is also said of the Almighty. However, it should be noted that in almost all cases of such synonymous parallelism in Job, "Almighty" occurs in the second colon. Since the second colon regularly serves to intensify, clarify or specify what the first colon is saying, the point being made is that the God being described is indeed the one whose power is irresistible.

But Job in particular suggests that the understanding of God cannot stop (or begin, for that matter) on that note. Regardless of the ancient Near Eastern wisdom traditions that probably provided the starting point for the Israelite reflections, God is not merely an invisible and irresistible force with which we must, willy-nilly, come to grips. The self-revelation that God had given to Israel precluded that. At the heart of the universe is a divine *person,* and the personal character that God was revealing in Israel's experience had to be factored into any consideration of issues of divine justice. Thus, it is significant that the use of the Tetragrammaton is not restricted in Job to the prologue and the epilogue; it occurs elsewhere, at Job 12:9; 38:1; 40:1, 3, 6; 42:1. The occurrences in Job 38; 40; 42 have to do with Yahweh's personal confrontation of Job. This is no longer an invisible, abstract force providing the hypothetical explanation of things; this is now the transcendent, personal Creator, who stands outside the circle of time and space, having brought it all into existence in his own divine wisdom and power. This is not just "God" or "the Almighty" somewhat abstractly conceived; it is "the Person," and to call that person only "God" would be to do him a grave injustice. In that regard, the lone occurrence in Job 12:9 is interesting. "The LORD" is said by Job to be the sustainer of all life, something that the rest of creation understands very well. In fact, the rest of what is now Job 12, which contains no further titles, may well be understood as a hymn to Yahweh because it develops further the theme of Yahweh's wise sustaining of the earth as an expression of his absolute sovereignty. It is a bit ironic that it was not until the personal revelations recorded in Job 38—42 that the full implications of what he had said in Job 12 became fully real to Job.

In Job 1—2 occurrences of "God" and "the LORD" are fairly evenly distributed. Usually, "the LORD" is used in the dialogue between him and "the Accuser" *(haśśātān)*, and one evidence of the functional distinction mentioned above may be found in the statement that "the sons of God came to present themselves before the LORD" (Job 1:6). "Sons of God" was a technical term identifying the angelic host. Another is the statement "Then Satan answered the LORD, 'Does Job fear God for nothing?'" The "fear of God" is a figure of speech for "living in such a way as to recognize divine authority" (Job 1:1, 8, 9; 2:3; 4:6) (but note the very anomalous "fear of the LORD *[ʾădōnāy]*" in Job 28:28). But it is the personal Yahweh with whom Job and all persons have ultimately to deal. Job expresses this truth when he says, "The LORD gave and the LORD has taken away. Blessed be the name of the LORD" (Job 1:21). Interestingly, the narrator then goes on to say, "Job did not sin or blame God." So although the line between God conceived of as deity and God conceived as personal creator and sustainer of the universe was discernible, it was still fluid.

The explanation for Job's *suffering that is found in Job 1—2 is troublesome. Does God have a right to permit one of his minions to deprive us of the blessings of life and to plunge us into the depths of physical pain as some sort of cosmic test? And even if he does have that right as the Creator, does not the fact that he would do so call into question his fundamental goodness that the psalms so eloquently praise? How could the God of *mišpāṭ*, that right order upon which the functioning of all things depends, willingly allow such disorder to come into existence? These are profound questions, and they receive very profound answers. However, the apparently casual nature of the dialogue in Job 1—2 might cause us to overlook them. That evil in the form of injustice and undeserved suffering is in the world is a given. But why is it in the world? Around the world, thinkers, from the most primitive to the most sophisticated, have been in general agreement. They have concluded that there are two principles inherent in the nature of things, one of order and the other of disorder. It is incorrect to call either one "good" or "evil." That would be like calling the positive pole on a battery "good" and the negative pole "evil." These principles simply are. We humans give them value qualities only because we find order more conducive to our pleasure, comfort and security, concerns to which we tend to give ultimate significance.

To this idea of two eternal coexistent principles, the Bible, and particularly Job, answers with a resounding no. First of all, God is not one of two eternal principles; God is a unique person, incomparable in every degree. "The Accuser" (from which the NT undoubtedly derived the proper noun *"Satan") is no parallel to God. In fact, he has no capacity for independent action; he does nothing except in reaction to God. The LORD, the sole Creator, has invested his creation with certain unchanging behavioral standards against which his human creatures may be evaluated ("blameless and upright, a man who fears God and turns away from evil" [Job 1:8]). There *is* such a thing as evil, therefore, something that is positively contrary to the purposes of the Creator. And why does this exist? It exists not in defiance of the good Creator but rather solely by his permission. Job's statement that both good and evil stem solely from God (Job 2:10) is a remarkable one in the ancient world. Yet, evil is not inherent in God, and as the epilogue makes clear, it does not in any sense qualify his goodness.

But if that is so, why would God permit such things that would contradict his ultimate intentions for the world? The answer is implicit in the prologue. The Accuser insists that Job has chosen to follow God's intentions for humans solely because they have a short-term payoff for Job. He denies that Job has made this choice because these behaviors are intrinsically right, being rooted in the character of the Creator, or even more deeply, because of Job's fundamental commitment to the God who has decreed them. What is being said is that righteousness, as the Bible understands it, is only possible as a relational choice. Righteous behavior is not the thing itself; rather, it is a "symptom," a symptom of something else, that something else being a lifelong choice of God. The Accuser insists that Job has not chosen God but rather has chosen pleasure, comfort and security. If those were taken away, he maintains, that fact would become quite clear. What does become clear is the stunning fact that although Job rants at God and accuses him of cruelty, Job will not deny him. The Accuser's case is so thoroughly discredited that he does not even appear in the book again. As in Genesis 3, the ultimate issue is not between Satan (the Accuser) and God but rather between God and his creatures.

Thus, Job says what the Bible says elsewhere: evil exists in the world for one reason only: relational choice is possible only in the presence of an alternative. God has given his *ḥesed* (Job 10:12) to humans and wishes for a free return. Unless there is a real choice possible, unless humans can choose God in spite of everything, then righteousness, as Satan knows, is meaningless.

In Job 3 we move to the more abstract treatment of divine justice. From here on through the end of Job's speeches (Job 32), God is mentioned explicitly about three times per chapter. A few chapters have as many as seven references, whereas a few have none. But whether there are more references or fewer, God is never far from the center of the discussion, for the whole effort of the comforters is to say that God has done rightly to treat Job as he has, whereas Job is insisting just as vehemently that God has been wrong to do so. Interestingly, Job seems farther from God after the efforts of the comforters than he was before they began.

Interpreters have struggled over how much authority to accord to the assertions of the comforters (see Hartley, 129). Clearly, Job's interlocutors are wrong about him. Are they equally wrong in what they say about God? It seems as though the problem is not so much in the assertions themselves as in the absolutism with which they are asserted. Does God punish the wicked and reward the righteous? Certainly, there are many other places in Scripture that answer yes to that question and do so with vigor, not the

least of which is the other major piece of Wisdom literature in the OT *canon, the book of Proverbs. So what is the problem? Perhaps it is in insisting that these maxims apply to all persons without fail. One of the characteristics of wisdom is that it is "context-specific." Thus, it is possible to find directly contradictory proverbs side by side (Prov 26:4-5). Each has validity in a given circumstance, but neither is absolutely so all the time. The world that Yahweh has created is more complicated and the impact of sin more convoluted than aphoristic wisdom can comprehend. So here, it is not that the comforters are absolutely wrong about God, but rather that they are more in love with the neatness of their own paradigms than they are with either God or his people. The result is that Job, who was willing to resign himself to God's ultimately good care (Job 2:10), though in anguish (Job 3:1-26), is driven by their logic to wonder about the very goodness of God (Job 10:13-22). If it is true, Job says, that the only people who are punished by God are the wicked, and if he, Job, is manifestly being punished even though he has done everything right, then evidently God has found some hidden wickedness that Job does not even know of. But if that is so, why did God even make us? No one can be right before God. Did he make us for destruction (Job 10:18)?

As the exchange goes on, it becomes more strident on both sides. Job is more convinced of his righteousness and the consequent injustice of God, while the comforters become more strident in their assertions that only a truly stupid person could say that God is not just (Job 8:2-3). These attacks move Job even farther: he asserts that God has viciously attacked him without warrant (Job 16:6-14), that God has "wronged" him (Job 19:6). To all of this the comforters can only say that such talk is the true proof that Job has been a wicked man all along (Job 15:5-6; 18:21; 20:29; 22:4-11). Ultimately, Bildad seems reduced to a vicious spluttering (Job 25:1-6), and Zophar is rendered speechless.

Job's final speech (Job 26—32) restates his convictions and his anguish. God is hidden and cannot be reached or understood (Job 26:5-14), but he does punish the wicked (Job 27:13-23). Thus, the whole sum of wisdom is to fear the sovereign (*'ădōnāy*) and to depart from evil (Job 28:28). Yet, that is what Job has done, and what has happened? Not only has God ranged himself against Job, but also he provides no comfort when Job is mocked by the worthless children of people whom he had once graciously helped (Job 29—30). But Job is righteous, and if God would just give him a chance, he would make God admit it (Job 31).

To this point in the book, the argument has basically gone nowhere. It has had two sides, with no meeting point in the middle. Each side is a model of syllogistic reasoning. On the one side, the major premise is that God punishes the wicked with suffering, and the minor premise is that Job is suffering; the conclusion must be that Job is wicked. On the other side, the major premise is that Job is righteous, and the minor premise is the same: Job is suffering; the conclusion is that God is unjust. Given that the conclusion of the one is a denial of the major premise of the other, there can be no resolution. Into all of this comes another voice attempting to break the stalemate. Though still upset at Job's gaucherie in charging God with wrong, Elihu offers some other explanations for suffering. Unfortunately, though all of them are true enough in other contexts, none of them applies to this context. It is true that God uses suffering to reveal himself to people (Job 32—33). It is also true that God uses suffering to discipline and correct people (Job 34). Likewise, God teaches us to hold him in awe through suffering (Job 35—37). But we the readers know that none of them is the correct explanation of Job's suffering.

The failure of Elihu and the other comforters is not much different from Job's. All of them are attempting to force God into the grid of their own rationality. All of them are attempting to explain God's actions on their own terms. The sin of Eliphaz, Bildad and Zophar was to deny the truth about Job in their zeal to make God look good. Job's fault was to say that God had no right to do what he did to him. In the end (Job 38—41) God simply asks, in very graphic terms, who is the cause and who is the effect. Isaiah uses the language of the pottery, asking whether the pot can accuse the potter of going about his work in the wrong way (Is 29:16). The book of Job says that since we cannot even explain the creation, it is foolish for us to demand that the Creator explain himself to us.

3.3. Ecclesiastes. As mentioned above, the only title used for the Deity in Ecclesiastes is "God," even in Ecclesiastes 12, where there seems to be an attempt to put the teachings of *Qohelet into the wider context of Scripture.

This is perhaps as it should be in a book that generally speaks of God in abstract terms. Here the concerns of Job are put into an even wider perspective. "Under the sun," God's ways seem to have no consistency at all. Wise and foolish perish alike. Moreover, the wise often suffer and the foolish often prosper. It would be bad enough if it were that way all the time, but it is not. Sometimes the wise prosper and the foolish suffer. The problem is that one cannot predict when it will happen. Furthermore, it seems that whatever promises ultimate satisfaction in this life always falls short in the end. Nothing quite lives up to its "billing." Life, to Qohelet, seems full of disappointment; all that seems to promise significance ("glory") actually turns out to be empty and worthless ("vanity").

The writer seems to be saying that if we use human experience strictly as our guide, then those who say that life makes sense are talking nonsense. Why he does not allow special revelation (which comes from "beyond the sun") to be brought into the picture more fully is not made clear. It is as though he has set himself an exercise to discover what he can about reality while limiting himself to data from this world. Unlike Proverbs, which celebrates the overwhelming consistencies in God's world, Qohelet ruminates over the troublesome inconsistencies, of which it seems there should be none if there is a good and all-powerful God. One would think that, as in Job, Qohelet would desire to call God to account for this state of things. But that is not the case. The determination to limit the data to this world seems almost absolute. God is not seen as one whom it is possible to confront. He is an inescapable reality, and the world, with its odd set of givens, is unquestionably his work, but he is not presented as a person with whom one could enter into dialogue. In fact, he is all but completely hidden from us. We can discover neither him nor the meaning of what he has done (Eccles 3:11; 7:14; 8:17; 9:1; 11:5).

One might think that in such a case Qohelet would simply dispense with God altogether. If God is beyond our reach and his work is largely unintelligible, then he is of no consequence to us. But that is not the case. There is a God who has made all things (Eccles 11:5), and everything that is, is given from his hand (Eccles 1:13; 2:24; 3:10, 13; 5:19; 6:2; 8:15; 12:7). These are the facts, and there is no way a mere human can rectify them to his or her own liking (Eccles 3:14; 7:13). Still, the question is not merely how to make the best of a bad situation. Things are not as they are merely as a fiat from a hidden Creator. At this point we must observe that if the writer is indeed restricting himself to the data of experience, he is uniquely perceptive. In fact, it is difficult to avoid the conclusion that in spite of his self-imposed restriction, data from special revelation has crept into his thinking. For instance, he declares that he knows that God originally made all men upright (Eccles 7:29), something that certainly does not emerge from human experience. Furthermore, he repeatedly states that God will bring all people into judgment (Eccles 3:17; 5:6; 8:12-13; 11:9; 12:14). Judgment according to what standard? The answer is supplied in Ecclesiastes 12:13: judgment will be according to the commands of God that have been revealed. Given that fact, we are not surprised at the repeated injunction to "fear God" (Eccles 3:14; 5:7; 8:12; 12:13).

It is significant that the observations about life found in Ecclesiastes are very much like those to be found in the so-called existentialist writers from the middle of the twentieth century (see Gordis 1968, 112-21). However, the conclusions of these modern thinkers about the course of action to be taken are dramatically different from those of Ecclesiastes. The existentialists concluded that all events were the result of random chance, with the result that nothing means anything. However, for some unknown reason, humans have to have meaning in order to survive. Thus, we must boldly choose to give ourselves meaning, all the time knowing that there is no such thing. A moment's reflection shows how far Qohelet is from that conclusion. One's situation in life is given by God, and thus there is a possibility of deriving joy from it (Eccles 2:24-25; 5:19-20; 9:7), however temporary and passing that may be. In fact, it is the attempt to invest life "under the sun" with some eternal quality that is doomed to failure, because God has planted eternity in our hearts (Eccles 3:11). Thus, the challenge is to allow each moment to have its own limited value and not to demand of it what could only be true in eternity. Furthermore, we are going to be held accountable for our choices, so we should make them wisely, not giving the temporal a value which the eternal God has withheld for himself (Eccles 8:12-13). The choices in life are not to be made with a kind of

proud absolutism stemming from one's own sovereignty over a meaningless world (note the admonition against foolish vows in Eccles 5:1-7). Rather, they should be made with a quiet humility, recognizing that we have not determined either the parameters of our lives or the standards by which our lives will be judged. And if we cannot explain why everything is as it is, we know enough to make those humble daily choices.

4. Writings.

4.1. Esther. The absence of any explicit reference to God in this book is often attributed to its lateness (the events described would have taken place 483-471 BC) when it is said that the same reverence for God that eventually prevented the speaking of the divine name prevented any overt reference to God at all (see Moore, 636). Thus, it is suggested that the statement by *Mordecai that help will come to the Jews from "another place" (Esther 4:14) is in fact a veiled reference to God. If that is so, it would reflect the same kind of confidence in God that is found elsewhere in these writings. God might not care for his people at the time and in the way the speaker might choose, but there is no doubt that he would respond in his own way and fulfill his ancient promises to his people.

Another possible explanation for the absence of any explicit reference to God in Esther is that it is a deliberate strategy to emphasize the providence of God (Jobes, 43-44). Was God present with his people in exile if there was no explicit word from him about their situation? The answer clearly is yes. He was at work in the "coincidences" that made it possible for what the enemy intended for evil to actually turn out for good for his people (see Gen 50:20). When these coincidences are understood against the backdrop of the rest of the canon, it becomes apparent that even when God seems silent, he is at work on behalf of his people in precisely the same ways as when there was an explicit word.

4.2. Song of Songs. Although Song of Songs has one occurrence of "the LORD" (Song 8:6), the situation is not materially different from Esther, for the reference is of almost no theological significance. Most modern versions actually take it as an adjective of intensity. Thus, the literal "[jealousy is] like a flame of the LORD" is rendered with "like a mighty flame" or something similar. The absence of reference is the more striking because both Jews and Christians have taken this book to be an allegory of the love of God for Israel and/or the church. Persons such as Bernard of Clairveaux have written hundreds of pages about God's love as revealed in the book. It would seem that an appropriate approach to interpretation lies somewhere between a modern skepticism of any "spiritualizing" and the ancient enthusiasm for it. It is hard to believe that the book would have been accorded canonical status (or that the question of canonicity would have even arisen) unless the community had heard the book saying something to them about the God whom the whole Bible reveals (see Longman 2001, 56, 70).

That said, what does the book reveal about the love of God, or, to put it another way, about the nature of the love that God has put into his world? Unquestionably, it speaks of the passion of God's love. God is no "Unmoved Mover," unfeelingly putting processes into motion with calm unconcern for what their outcomes might be. Rather, God desires us with all the consuming desire of a young lover, and we have all the power to wound him that a lover alone has.

The book also tells us that God's love is personal. The love here is between two persons. God does not love us in the same way that he loves his creation. For his love to be known, it must be reciprocated, and reciprocated with the same kind of passion that he has. Being personal, God's love is complex. The relationships described in the book are not simple and straightforward. Reciprocal, personal, passionate relationships are involved. Faith is not merely an intellectual, contractual kind of arrangement. Instead, it involves the deeply affectionate surrender of the soul. It involves "knowing" the other with all the intimacy with which that word is invested in Hebrew (*yādaʿ*).

Song of Songs also conveys to us God's delight in his creation. This is found not only in the way the book expresses the joy of sexuality but also in the references to the goodness of nature and its fecundity. Yet this is by no means a "baptized" fertility myth. No reader would take the book to be hymning the fertility of a divine cosmos, unless led to do so by someone with another agenda. Nature is clearly seen, especially in the light of the rest of the canon, as the product of a good and beneficent Creator. This is an important message for much of the Christian church, which has been infected by a dualism that holds suspect the material world and the desires rooted in it. Song of Songs tells us that in spite of the fall, which has corrupted the way we think we can use the world and its desires to serve our own selfish purposes, God does not see the world and its desires as having become evil (see Barth, 3.1:313-14).

4.3. Lamentations. When reading this book, one is most immediately struck by the pathos of the writer and his situation. However, a study of the references to God in the book reveals a depth of theology that we may overlook in the emotions of sympathy and compassion. Early in the book the references are all to the fact that God has done a terrible thing to his people (Lam 1:5, 12, 14, 15; 2:1, 2, 7, 8, 17). And although the writer freely admits that God was right to do what he did (Lam 1:18) in punishment of his people's rebellion, and that the people had been warned long in advance (Lam 2:17), there is still the sense that the punishment should not have been this severe (Lam 2:20). In this light, it does not seem accidental that the graphic description of God's implacable pursuit of the sufferer in Lamentations 3:1-18 only refers to God with the impersonal third-person pronoun until finally in Lamentations 3:18 the writer says that everything he had hoped for "from the LORD" has perished. God's manner of accomplishing his sovereign purposes (cf. Lam 4:11; 5:19) is beyond human understanding and explanation.

Yet, God is not seen to be implacable. He is always "biddable," to use an archaic but eminently serviceable word. The personified city continually cries out to the Lord to look on its grief in the evident confidence that he will do so and be moved by what he sees (Lam 1:9, 11, 20; 2:18, 20; 5:1, 21). And it is that confidence that perseveres in the darkest hour. After the heart-rending reminiscence of God's actions leading to the death of all hope in Lamentations 3:1-20, the sufferer remembers something else: the Lord's great love (*hesed*) and unfailing compassion. As a result, hope revives (Lam 3:24). This signals a certain change in emphasis in the book. Alongside the continuing lament there is a new emphasis on the positive characteristics of the Lord: his moral rectitude, which will mean that the enemies cannot continue in their ruthlessness indefinitely (Lam 3:36, 64), and his goodness and determination to save (Lam 3:25-26, 50, 58). This means that there is the real possibility of repentance and restoration (Lam 3:40-

41). These, however, are not a foregone conclusion. In the end, Israel must face the terrible reality that unless God lovingly gives them this spirit of repentance, there is no hope whatsoever for them (Lam 5:19-22).

4.4. Ruth. The portrayal of God in the book of Ruth stands in dramatic contrast to that found in Lamentations. Here it is the covenant faithfulness of the Lord that holds center stage. From the report that he had visited his people to lift the famine (Ruth 1:16), until the women's celebration that he had given Naomi "a redeemer" (Ruth 4:14), it is the work of Yahweh on behalf of his people that receives true prominence. Ironically, the accomplishment of that work depends heavily on the faithfulness of the Moabite woman, Ruth, as she chooses to make the "the LORD, the God of Israel" (Ruth 2:12) her "God" (Ruth 1:16). What this says, of course, is that Yahweh is interested not so much in the creation of a people as in covenant faithfulness (cf. Is 56:1-8). That point is quite significant in the context of the genealogy of the Davidic dynasty. The establishment of that dynasty is indeed about the securing of a people's existence. But what is the defining characteristic of that people? Is it racial or behavioral? The apostle Paul insisted, on the basis of Genesis 15, that it was the latter (Rom 4:16-17; Gal 3:6-9), and the book of Ruth seems to bear him out.

The book begins with expressions of *Naomi's implicit faith in the midst of resignation. She invokes the blessings of the Lord on her daughters-in-law (Ruth 1:8-9) while saying that it is because of the Lord that she finds herself destitute (Ruth 1:13, 21). In Ruth 2 the Lord is considered to be the source of blessing and reward (Ruth 2:4, 12, 20; 3:10). He is the one who makes possible conception and birth (Ruth 4:12, 13). He is the one who does the unexpected, giving abundance to the destitute, and children to the widow (Ruth 2:20; 4:14). Underneath all of this is the understanding that was so prominent in Psalms: he is the God of *ḥesed*, the undeserved favor of a superior to an inferior. Naomi invokes it on her daughters-in-law (Ruth 1:8). Ruth demonstrates it to her mother-in-law (Ruth 2:11-12; cf. 3:10). Naomi recognizes it in the providential bringing together of Ruth and Boaz (Ruth 2:20). Boaz generously attributes it to Ruth on the threshing floor (Ruth 3:10). The God of the book of Ruth is at work in history to accomplish his good purposes of redemption from every wrong that troubles his human creatures, from death to destitution to the sins of greed and oppression.

See also CREATION THEOLOGY; DIVINE COUNCIL; DIVINE PRESENCE; FEAR OF THE LORD; FEMINIST INTERPRETATION; LIFE; THEODICY; THEOPHANY; WISDOM THEOLOGY; WORSHIP.

BIBLIOGRAPHY. **L. Allen**, *Psalms* (WBT; Waco, TX: Word, 1987); idem, *Psalms 101-150* (WBC 21; Waco, TX: Word, 1983); **K. Barth**, *Church Dogmatics*, ed. G. Bromiley (4 vols.; Edinburgh: T & T Clark, 1956-1975); **J. Blenkinsopp**, *Wisdom and Law in the Old Testament: The Ordering of Life in Israel and Early Judaism* (rev. ed.; OBS; Oxford: Oxford University Press, 1995); **L. Boström**, *The God of the Sages: The Portrayal of God in the Book of Proverbs* (ConBOT 29; Stockholm: Almqvist & Wiksell, 1990); **W. Brueggemann**, *The Message of the Psalms* (Minneapolis: Augsburg, 1984); **R. E. Clements**, "Wisdom and Old Testament Theology," in *Wisdom in Ancient Israel*, ed. J. Day, R. P. Gordon and H. G. M. Williamson (Cambridge: Cambridge University Press, 1995) 269-86; **P. Craigie**, *Psalms 1-50* (WBC 19; Waco TX: Word, 1983); **J. Crenshaw**, *Old Testament Wisdom: An Introduction* (Atlanta: John Knox, 1981); **R. Gordis**, *The Book of God and Man: A Study of Job* (Chicago: University of Chicago Press, 1965); idem, *Koheleth, the Man and His World: A Study of Ecclesiastes* (New York: Schocken, 1968); **J. Hartley**, *The Book of Job* (NICOT; Grand Rapids: Eerdmans, 1988); **J. G. Janzen**, *Job* (IBC; Atlanta: John Knox, 1985); **K. Jobes**, *Esther* (NIVAC; Grand Rapids: Zondervan, 1999); **W. Kaiser**, "Integrating Wisdom Theology into Old Testament Theology," in *A Tribute to Gleason Archer: Essays on the Old Testament*, ed. W. Kaiser and R. Youngblood (Chicago: Moody, 1986) 197-209; **D. Kidner**, *The Proverbs* (TOTC; Chicago: InterVarsity Press, 1964); idem, *Psalms 1-72* (TOTC; Downers Grove, IL: InterVarsity Press, 1973); idem, *Psalms 73-150* (TOTC; Downers Grove, IL: InterVarsity Press, 1975); **H.-J. Kraus**, *Theology of the Psalms* (Minneapolis: Fortress, 1992); **C. S. Lewis**, *Reflections on the Psalms* (New York: Harcourt Brace, 1958); **T. Longman III**, *The Book of Ecclesiastes* (NICOT; Grand Rapids: Eerdmans, 1998); idem, *Song of Songs* (NICOT; Grand Rapids: Eerdmans, 2001); **J. C. McCann**, *A Theological Introduction to the Book of Psalms: The Psalms as Torah* (Nashville: Abingdon, 1993); **P. Miller**, *Interpreting the Psalms* (Philadelphia: Fortress, 1986); idem, *They Cried to the Lord: The Form and*

Theology of Biblical Prayer (Minneapolis: Fortress, 1994); **C. Moore**, "Esther, Book of," *ABD* 2.633-43; **R. Murphy,** *The Tree of Life: An Exploration of Biblical Wisdom Literature* (2nd ed.; Grand Rapids: Eerdmans, 1996); **L. Perdue**, *Wisdom and Creation: The Theology of Wisdom Literature* (Nashville: Abingdon, 1994); **M. Pope,** *Job* (AB 15; Garden City, NY: Doubleday, 1965); **M. Tate**, *Psalms 51-100* (WBC 20; Waco, TX: Word, 1990); **B. Waltke**, "The Fear of the Lord: The Foundation for a Relationship with God," in *Alive to God: Studies in Spirituality Presented to James Houston*, ed. J. I. Packer and L. Wilkinson (Downers Grove, IL: InterVarsity Press, 1992) 17-33; idem, *The Book of Proverbs: Chapters 1-15* (NICOT; Grand Rapids: Eerdmans, 2004); **E. Zenger**, *A God of Vengeance? Understanding the Psalms of Divine Wrath* (Louisville: Westminster, 1994).

J. N. Oswalt

GODS. *See* DIVINE COUNCIL.

GRAMMAR, HEBREW. *See* HEBREW LANGUAGE.

GREEK VERSIONS OF ESTHER. *See* ESTHER 5: GREEK VERSIONS.

GREEK WISDOM. *See* WISDOM, GREEK.

H

HEBREW LANGUAGE

The Hebrew language of the books of *Psalms, *Job, *Proverbs, *Song of Songs, *Ecclesiastes, *Lamentations, *Ruth and *Esther stands at the margins of Hebrew grammar description. Standard descriptions of biblical Hebrew, especially treatments of its syntax, are based primarily on the prose texts of Genesis through 2 Kings (excluding Ruth in the Hebrew canonical order) because of observed differences between the prose and poetic literature, on the one hand, and between early (preexilic) and late (postexilic) compositions, on the other. These two issues are sometimes interrelated, as observed in Gesenius's Hebrew grammar: "Many of these poetic peculiarities occur in the kindred languages, especially in Aramaic, as the ordinary modes of expression, and probably are to be regarded largely as archaisms which poetry retained" (Kautzsch, 13). The present article surveys, first, prominent characteristics of Hebrew language in the poetic books and, second, the types of language variation that appear in the books treated within this volume and some of the explanations that have been proposed for these variations.

1. Hebrew Poetry
2. Language Variation
3. Conclusion

1. Hebrew Poetry.

Most readers distinguish poetry from prose instinctively, especially when it is arranged in verse. Biblical scholars are likewise well assured that a distinction between poetry and prose can be made within the literature of the Hebrew Bible. The books of Psalms, Job, Proverbs, Lamentations and Song of Songs have long been recognized as poetry, in part in the case of Psalms because of its ubiquitous musical notations and directions (e.g., musical notations such as *selâ* [71x]; directions in the psalm titles such as the title to Ps 4: "To the [music] director on stringed instruments").

However, versification of poetry in the Masoretic Text tradition is extremely rare (e.g., Ex 15; Deut 32) apart from the notable exception of *acrostic poems, in which the lineation is marked by successive letters of the alphabet (e.g., Pss 37; 111; 119; Lam 3). Therefore scholars have had to find other bases for distinguishing poetry from prose. They have proposed various poetic devices that feature prominently in Hebrew poetry as *constitutive* of Hebrew verse, including *meter, *parallelism and *ellipsis (see Cloete, chaps. 2-3). However, several features of the *language* of Hebrew poetry may be identified as partially distinguishing it from prose. These include the relative scarcity of "prose particles" in Hebrew poetry, the prevalence of rare, archaic or archaizing vocabulary and morphology, more loose or free word order, and the meanings and patterns of the verbal forms.

1.1. Prose Particles and Hebrew Poetry.

The term "prose particles" has been applied to several grammatical words that are, statistically speaking, characteristic of Hebrew prose versus Hebrew poetry. D. N. Freedman (6-8) observed that the definite article, relative conjunction and the (untranslatable) marker of definite direct objects are relatively less frequent in poetic texts in the Hebrew Bible than in prose texts. F. I. Andersen and A. D. Forbes (165-83) have substantiated this observation with their statistical analysis of how often each of these grammatical words occurs in each chapter of the Hebrew Bible: chapters with five percent or less frequency for these grammatical words are found in the books of wisdom (Proverbs and Job), lyrical poetry (Psalms and Lamentation) and oracular poetry (mainly Hosea and Isaiah); chapters with five to ten percent occurrence of these grammatical words, while still properly poetic, occur mainly within the prophetic books (Andersen and Forbes, 166); higher percentages of frequency for these prose particles appear in texts classified as prose.

Andersen and Forbes (167) conclude that "the particle frequency is a powerful discriminator between poetry and prose"; however, they decline to elaborate on why these prose particles pattern as they do. A probable explanation for the infrequency of these grammatical words in poetry is the quality of *terseness, characteristic of Hebrew poetry and of poetry generally. A. Berlin (7) identifies terseness with poetic lines "stripped of all but their essential components." Terseness can be explained as the result of the balance between explicitness versus ellipsis and between redundancy versus ambiguity in Hebrew (and most) poetry. This balance entails restricting the use of explicit grammatical words such as the article (indefiniteness versus definiteness), relative conjunction (unmarked versus marked relative clauses) and direct object marker (unambiguous versus ambiguous argument structure) (see Berlin, 16).

This poetic characteristic of terseness is reflected in M. O'Connor's linguistic theory of Hebrew verse structure. O'Connor (138) defines Hebrew verse with a series of syntactic constrictors on poetic line length: poetic lines are limited to 0-3 clause predicators, 1-4 constituents and 2-5 units in length. These syntactic strictures on poetic line length further explain the relative paucity of prose particles in Hebrew verse: their use is partially constricted by the syntactic limitation on line length.

1.2. Vocabulary and Grammar of Hebrew Poetry. Hebrew poetry, especially archaic poetry, is characterized by the feature of rare or archaic vocabulary and word forms. Job and Song of Songs in particular have a high incidence of rare forms and *hapax legomena* (Greenspahn, 199-200). Statistically, rare vocabulary is found predominantly in the poetry rather than the prose portions of the Bible (Greenspahn, 38-39). In addition, words that occur commonly throughout prose and poetry often have more rare counterparts that are limited to poetry (see Sáenz-Badillos, 60). For example, *šm⁽* ("hear") occurs over one thousand times throughout the Hebrew Bible, whereas the denominative verb

ʾzn ("hear") occurs just forty-two times, twenty-two times in the poetry of Psalms, Job, Proverbs and Ecclesiastes, another nine times in the poetic prophetic literature of Isaiah and Hosea (see 1.1 above on "prose particle" frequency in these books), and once each in the archaic poems in Exodus 1; Deuteronomy 32; Judges 5. Similarly, of the fifty-six occurrences of *pʿl* ("do"), the poetic counterpart of *ʿšh* ("do"), forty-one are in Psalms, Job and Proverbs, with most of the remainder occurring in Isaiah, Hosea or the archaic poems of Exodus 15 and Numbers 23.

In addition to rare vocabulary, rare forms, or morphemes, are found in Hebrew poetry. For example, the third-person suffix *-mw* occurs nine and seven times, respectively, in the archaic poems of Exodus 15 and Deuteronomy 32, six times each in Psalm 59 and Psalm 73, five times in Psalm 2, and nineteen times in Job (Young 1993, 125-26). Similarly, the so-called *hiriq compagnis*—a suffixed long-*i* vowel, is mostly confined to poetry, both early and late (e.g., Deut 33:16; Ps 113:5, 6, 7, 9). The asseverative and vocative meanings for the *lāmed* preposition, though paralleled in other Northwest Semitic languages, occurs in the Bible only in poetry—for example, *ky lyhwh* ("for truly Yahweh [is]") in Psalm 89:18 (MT 89:19), and *lrkb* ("O rider") in Psalm 68:34 (MT 68:35).

Although the syntax of biblical Hebrew word order is still not fully understood, it is widely recognized that Hebrew word order is less rigidly fixed in poetry than in prose, as is the case in many other languages (Watson, 49). Conventions of word order are often abandoned in poetry for the sake of verbal artistry, the most commonly noted perhaps being the inverted word order, or *chiasm. Chiastic word order in Hebrew poetry usually involves presenting the units of one line in inverse order from that of the preceding line. For example, compare the following two verses, where the first orders the elements the same way in the two lines (a-b-c / a'-b'-c'), while the second orders the constituents in chiastic order (a-b-c / c'-b'-a').

mnšmt ʾlwh yʾbdw/ wmrwḥ ʾpw yklw
By-the-breath-of God they-perish / and-by-the-blast-of his-anger they-are-consumed (Job 4:9)

yšwb ʿmlw brʾšw/ wʿl qdqdw ḥmsw yrd
Will-return his-own-mischief on-his-own-head

/and-upon his-head his-own-violence will-descend (Ps 7:16 [MT 7:17])

Peculiarities in the use of the verb forms in poetry is perhaps as much overstated as the looseness of word order. Influenced by the apparently radically different meanings for the verbal system in Ugaritic prose and epic poetry, scholars have been unduly swayed towards treating the verbal system of Hebrew poetry as completely distinct from that of prose (e.g., Niccacci, 194). However, one of the hallmarks of poetry is the flouting of language conventions that are well established in prose. Thus it would appear that the meanings/functions of the verb forms in prose are foundational for interpreting the forms in poetry.

Nevertheless, the vicissitudes of the history of the Hebrew language are such as to have created partial homonyms among several prefixed verb conjugations in biblical Hebrew. As a result, some verb forms are ambiguous among the imperfect, jussive and past conjugations. The past conjugation is of special interest because it is the most frequent verb form in prose, where it regularly occurs with a unique, distinguishing *wa-* prefixed conjunction. Not surprisingly, in poetry where particles such as the article and conjunction are often absent, this distinguishing *wa-* prefix is often missing from instances of the past conjugation in poetry—for example, *ybq'* (Ps 78:15); *yšt* (Ps 18:11 [MT 18:12]) (cf. *wayyšt* [2 Sam 22:12]).

Although none of the features of the Hebrew language enumerated here are alone determinative of poetry, together they illustrate general characteristics of Hebrew poetry. J. Kugel (302) observes, "'Prose' and 'poetry' are a matter of degree"; by contrast, it is the closely associated distinction between prose and verse that may be dichotomized (Cloete, 5).

2. Language Variation.

The language of the Hebrew Bible presents numerous grammatical and syntactic peculiarities. Various contributing factors to this state of affairs may be pointed out, including the approximate thousand-year time span in which the literature developed, differences in style among multiple authors and editors, and distinctive grammatical features peculiar to different genres.

Despite widespread regard for the "harmonizing activity of the Masoretes," biblical scholars have long recognized variation in the language of the Hebrew Bible (Kautzsch, vii, 12). The traditional framework for treating these divergences recognizes two or three diachronic divisions and one primary synchronic division in the language of the Hebrew Bible. Diachronically, it is customary to distinguish between the language in those books dated to the postexilic period based on their content (e.g., Esther, Chronicles) and the language of books that have been traditionally seen as largely preexilic in origin (e.g., Ruth, Joshua—Kings). This bipartite division between Late (postexilic) Biblical Hebrew (LBH) and Standard (preexilic) Biblical Hebrew (SBH) is often made into a tripartite division by the additional distinction of Early Biblical Hebrew (EBH), thought to be attested in archaic poems dated to the early preexilic period based on grammar and motifs (e.g., Ex 15; Judg 5; Ps 29). Synchronically, scholars have posited dialectical differences in Hebrew between Northern (Israelite) Hebrew and Southern (Judahite) Hebrew (e.g., Rendsburg). Scholars have held that the majority of SBH compositions are written in the Southern Hebrew dialect and, concomitantly, reflect concerns surrounding the Davidic dynasty and the Jerusalem temple (e.g., the Deuteronomistic History).

The effect of these diachronic and synchronic divisions can be seen in the way biblical scholars have judged compositions that lack clear historical referents as to their provenance and date: those compositions whose language diverges significantly from the norm of SBH (attested in the prose of Genesis through Kings) are identified as either late compositions, thus belonging to the corpus of LBH, or early but northern in origin, having been written or influenced by a Northern Israelite Hebrew dialect. This is exemplified by the remark of S. R. Driver (449) that the linguistic peculiarities in Song of Songs "show either that it must be a late work (post-exilic), or, if early, that it belongs to *North Israel*." A good deal of the material that is the focus of the present article falls within this category of compositions that lack clear historical referents, written in language that often diverges from the language of SBH; this characterization is particularly true of much of the book of Psalms, and the books of Proverbs, Job, Ecclesiastes, and Song of Songs. As a result, scholars and commentators have scrutinized the language in these books in attempts to establish their provenances and dates as well as to in turn use them to establish a coherent picture of the synchronic and diachronic variations in the Hebrew language discernable in the Bible.

However, some scholars have increasingly called into question this standard diachronic-synchronic framework as alternative explanations come to light for the language variation found in these books (e.g., the essays in Young 2003). For example, it has come to be widely held now that the Hebrew language of the post-biblical period developed from colloquial Hebrew of the biblical period, in contrast to the literary language in the Bible itself (Ullendorff, 11). Hence, it has been proposed that many of the linguistic peculiarities traditionally identified as Northern Israelite may simply be colloquialisms that have surfaced in the otherwise literary language of the Bible (Fredericks 1996). It has also been suggested that certain variations in language are intentional and rhetorical, such as dialectic features found in the speech of non-Israelite characters (Kaufman, 55). Finally, one scholar has explained certain language variation in the Bible in terms of an oral or a literary origin for the literature (Polak).

Given these multiple alternative explanations for language variation in the Hebrew Bible, the state of the question is more unsettled now than ever before. The situation is made especially difficult by the constant threat of falling into viciously circular arguments or special pleading with respect to the data. In the remainder of the present article some of the more notable peculiarities in these books are discussed with reference to these alternative explanations.

2.1. Psalms. On one level, *form criticism has isolated formulaic characteristics in the language in the book of Psalms, which has enabled the identification of various psalm types such as psalm of *lament, *hymn, and *thanksgiving psalm. On another level, the language of Psalms is largely resistant to other types of classification (see Driver, 383). Nevertheless, elements of the language (especially vocabulary) of certain psalms along with the much weightier evidence of motifs reminiscent of Canaanite culture (especially as exemplified in Ugaritic literature) have been used to date several psalms to the tenth century BC or earlier (e.g., Pss 18; 29; 68). For example, H. L. Ginsburg argued already in

1935 that Psalm 29 is based on a Phoenician original. Thirty years later M. Dahood (175) noted that "virtually every word in the psalm can now be duplicated in older Canaanite texts." In addition, Dahood observed similar parallelism structures in Psalm 29 as in Ugaritic poetry, as exemplified by the following two examples, which exhibit an a-b-c / a'-b'-d / a'-b'-e pattern.

hbw lyhwh bny ᵓlm / hbw lyhwh kbwd wᶜz / hbw lyhwh kbwd šmw
Give to-the-LORD, sons-of-God / give to-the-LORD honor-and-strength / give to-the-LORD the-honor-of-his-name (Ps 29:1-2)

klb arḫ lᶜglh / klb ṭat limrh / km lb ᶜnt aṯr bᶜl
Like-the-heart-of a-heifer for-her-calf / like-the-heart-of a-ewe for-her-lamb / so-(is) the-heart-of-Anat toward-Baal (*CAT* 1.6 II.28-30; Gibson, 77)

G. A. Rendsburg has sought to show that the language of certain psalms is evidence of dialectic differences between Northern Hebrew and Southern Hebrew. He identified Psalms 9—10; 16; 29; 36; 45; 53; 58; 74; 116; 132—133; 140—141, the Korah collection (Pss 42—49; 84—85; 87—88) and the Asaph collection (Pss 50; 73—83) as having Northern Hebrew features in their language (*see* Asaph and Sons of Korah). Rendsburg identifies rare linguistic characteristics that are cognate with other Northwest Semitic languages as evidence of Northern Hebrew dialectic influence—for example, the second-person feminine -*kî* (versus -*k*) and the third-person masculine -*ôhî* (versus -*āyw*) in Psalm 116: 7, 12, 19, both of which are identical to the Aramaic forms of the suffixes; the use of the relative words *zê/zu* and *še* in Psalms 9:15 (MT 9:16); 10:2; 133:2-3 (versus the prose particle relative *ᵓăšer*), which have cognates in Ugaritic, Phoenician and Aramaic; and the Phoenician plural form *ᵓîšîm* ("men") in Psalm 141:4 (versus the usual *ănāšîm*).

In addition, Rendsburg identifies linguistically conservative features as evidence of Northern Hebrew dialectic influence, including the feminine noun termination -*at* (versus the usual -*â*) in Psalms 16:5-6; 53:1; 74:19; 88:1; 132:4, which is also cognate with the other Northwest Semitic languages, and the retainment of the third *yôd* root letter in verb forms where it generally elides in the biblical Hebrew forms—for example, *yeḥĕsāyûn* versus *yeḥĕsû* in Psalm 36:7 (MT 36:8) (see also Ps 36:9; 73:2; 77:4; 78:44; 83:3; 140:3).

2.2. Proverbs. The international connections of biblical Wisdom literature are well known. They are most clear in the parallel between Proverbs 22:17—24:22 and the Egyptian *Words of Amenemope*. However, Proverbs 30—31 also attests to the international character of wisdom literature. Many commentators translate Proverbs 30:1 as, "The words of Agur, son of Yaqeh, the Massaite," a reading confirmed by "The words of Lemuel, king of Massa" (Prov 31:1) (e.g., Murphy 1998, 225). Elsewhere in the Bible "Massa" refers to a people or tribe from northern Arabia, related to Ishmael (see Gen 25:14; 1 Chron 1:30).

The language in these chapters underscores their international flavor. The Aramaic word for "son," *bar* (versus Heb *bēn*), appears in Proverbs 31:2, and Proverbs 31:3 contains a masculine plural noun ending in the letter *nûn*, as in Aramaic and Moabite, in contrast to Hebrew, in which masculine plural nouns end with the letter *mêm*. The enigmatic phrase *lĕʾîtîʾēl* in Proverbs 30:1 makes sense as an Aramaic palindrome: "I am not God" (see Murphy 1998, 226). The odd use of *mah* ("what") in Proverbs 31:2, it has been suggested, should be understood as cognate to Arabic *mah* (imperative "hear") (see Murphy 1998, 239).

2.3. Job. The book of Job shares the international flavor of wisdom literature found also in Proverbs. A veneer of internationalism is created by the names and locations of the principal characters (Job 1:1; 2:11). However, nowhere is the international character of the book more apparent than in its language, which has been described as a Northern Hebrew dialect, an admixture of Hebrew, and a translation of an Aramaic or Arabic original (see Andersen, 55-61; Gordis, 161, 343 n. 16; Young 1993, 132). In all cases, the book of Job is renowned for the difficulties posed by its rich (e.g., four names for "lion," six words for "trap," four synonyms for "darkness" [Gordis, 160]) and often abstruse vocabulary (over one hundred *hapax legomena* [see Greenspahn, 199]).

Particularly noteworthy are the "Aramaisms" and "Arabisms" in Job—that is, features of grammar and vocabulary that are shared with or explained only by recourse to one or the other of these languages. Job shares grammatical features (e.g., masculine plural noun ending *-în* instead of the customary *-îm*) as well as vocabulary (e.g., *maʿăbād* ["work"] in Job 34:25, versus Heb *maʿăśê*) with Aramaic, and Arabic has been the source of understanding for many of Job's obscure words.

In addition, the book of Job exhibits features characteristic of early (archaic) poetry (e.g., third person suffix *-mô*, preservation of the third root letter *w* or *y*, enclitic *mêm*, relative *zê* [see Saénz-Badillos, 60]) and of late biblical Hebrew compositions (e.g., the verb *qbl* ["receive"]). However, many of these same features can be explained from language contact or as features of a Northern Hebrew dialect, in which case they have no bearing on the dating of the composition (see 2.1 above).

In all, the features of Job have resisted a consensus explanation. Neither the content nor the language of the book points to a definite time or place of composition. Although the theory that the book is a translation of an Aramaic or Arabic original is not seriously entertained anymore, if the international character of wisdom literature is taken seriously, an alternative explanation emerges that the book of Job is a non-Israelite composition, written in a closely related Canaanite dialect, such as Edomite (see Young 1993, 136).

2.4. Ruth. The book of Ruth presents an intriguing mixture of language elements that are associated with SBH and with LBH. This mixture admits of different explanations: some features may be truly archaic, others represent the intentional use of archaic language (i.e., archaizing), and others may be characteristic of a particular Hebrew dialect (Campbell, 25). F. Bush, in his commentary, presents an extensive list of those features that the language of Ruth shares with SBH and those that it shares with LBH, and he concludes that the split in the book should be explained by dating the composition to the exilic period, during the transition from SBH to LBH.

Bush (21), adopting Hurvitz's approach to determining features of LBH, notes that the criteria for identifying a feature as LBH include (1) that it be widely distributed throughout the known postexilic books (e.g., Chronicles, Ezra-Nehemiah, Daniel, Zech 9—14), and (2) that it contrast with an alternative form of expression in SBH. Some of the SBH features that Bush (23-24) isolates in Ruth include the preference for the longer first-person pronoun *ʾănôkî* versus *ʾănî*, the productive use of the past narrative verb form, the defective spelling of "David" (*dwd* versus *dwyd*), and the use of the dual pronominal suffix, which, while rare in SBH, is wholly absent in LBH. Some of the LBH features of Ruth include the greater frequency (versus SBH texts) of objects suffixed directly to verbs, the greater frequency (versus SBH texts) of the preposition *l* rather than *ʾl* following the verb "say," the occurrence of *qwm* in the Piel stem with the meaning "confirm, establish, effect" (Ruth 4:7), and the use of perfect with the *waw* conjunction in a successive chain of events (Ruth 4:7) (Bush, 26-27).

Bush assumes that each datum is characteristic of either SBH or LBH, and that therefore the mixture of features found in Ruth is determinative of a date of composition that lies between these two stages of language. The simplicity of Bush's paradigm is evident when one considers the possibility of alternative explanations for mixtures of features. For example, Bush claims that *wĕnātan* (perfect with *waw* conjunction) in Ruth 4:7 functions like the past narrative verb, which is the expected form here (i.e., *wayyittēn*). However, the verse may not be presenting a past narrative, as Bush assumes, but rather a past hypothetical or habitual situation: "a man *would remove* his sandal and *would give* it to the other party." The use of the past narrative verb is unexpected here; rather, the perfect forms found here express irreal mood, indicated by the verb-subject word order (see Cook, 134-35).

2.5. Esther. Unlike the other books examined here, the setting of the story of Esther provides a decisive *terminus a quo* for the book, in the Persian period. This means that the language of Esther must belong to the later stage of biblical Hebrew. Nevertheless, several different judgments have been rendered on the language in Esther. C. A. Moore (lvii) characterized the language of Esther as being most similar to the LBH of Chronicles and Ezra-Nehemiah. By contrast, R. Polzin (74-75) has argued that Esther is imitative of SBH, in contrast to the LBH of Chronicles and Ezra-Nehemiah, and R. Bergy (followed by Bush, 296-97) has more recently placed the language of Esther between LBH and Mishnaic Hebrew (MH).

Some of the features that Esther shares with MH against LBH compositions include the following: the gerund noun construction (*hštyh*) in

Esther 1:8, which uses a noun pattern typical of MH and would be expressed with an infinitive in SBH and LBH compositions; vocabulary such as *keter* ("crown" [Esther 1:11]), *maʾămar* ("command" [Esther 1:15]), *yšṭ* ("reach out" [Esther 4:11]), *šarbîṭ* ("scepter" [Esther 4:11]) and *illû* ("if" [Esther 7:4a]); idioms such as *gzr ʿl* ("decree" [Esther 2:1], versus SBH *ṣwh ʿl*), *šnh mn* ("be different from" [Esther 3:8], versus SBH *ʾḥr*) and *kāšēr lipnê* ("be acceptable before" [Esther 8:5]).

2.6. Song of Songs. The language of Song of Songs is striking in several ways. Most notable is its use of the relative conjugation *še* to the almost complete exclusion of *ʾăšer* (which occurs only in Song 1:1). Only the book of Ecclesiastes has more occurrences of *še;* however, it employs *ʾăšer* with almost equal frequency. This feature has been taken to be indicative of Aramaic influence or late date, especially in light of the similar, almost exclusive use of *še* in Mishnaic Hebrew. However, such conclusions are problematic in light of the appearance of *še* in archaic Hebrew poetry (Judg 5:7), and the judgment that *še* alternatively may be indicative of a Northern Hebrew dialect (see 2.1 above).

Evidence of foreign influence in Song of Songs is found in its occasional Aramaic spellings and foreign loanwords. The Aramaic spelling of *nṭr* ("keep, guard"), versus Hebrew *nṣr*, is found in several places in the book (Song 1:6; 8:11, 12), and in one passage the Aramaic spelling *bĕrôt* ("juniper"), versus Hebrew *bĕrôš* (Song 1:17), is used. The word *pardēs* (Song 4:13), often translated "park" or "enclosures," is a Persian loanword; *appiryôn* (Song 3:9), variously translated "palanquin" (NRSV) or "chariot" (NIV), is possibly a Greek loanword.

The other striking linguistic feature is the number of *hapax legomena*, thirty-seven in all. Given the size of the book, it contains the highest proportion of such terms of any book in the OT. In addition, F. E. Greenspahn (199) classifies fourteen of these thirty-seven as "absolute *hapax legomena*"—that is, forms built on roots that are not used anywhere else in the Bible (see also Murphy 1990, 75).

2.7. Ecclesiastes. More than any of the other books under discussion here, Ecclesiastes has been at the center of discussions regarding the development of the Hebrew language (note particularly the several monographs from the late 1980s and early 1990s: Isaksson; Fredericks

1988; Schoors). The judgment by F. Delitzsch (190), made in the nineteenth century, on the language of Ecclesiastes is well known: "If the book of Koheleth were of old Solomonic origin, then there is no history of the Hebrew language." Despite the confidence expressed by this assessment of the chronological place of the language of Ecclesiastes, various explanations have been offered regarding the unique features of the book's language. These include that the book was originally composed in Aramaic and translated (poorly) into Hebrew; that it was written by an Israelite living in Phoenicia, and therefore is heavily influenced by Phoenician; that it is written in Northern Israelite Hebrew; and that it is reflective of spoken or colloquial (versus literary) Hebrew (see Seow, 20).

Perhaps a certain degree of truth about the matter may be found in each of these explanations. That it is post-Solomonic seems assured from its use of Persian loanwords—notably *pitgām* ("decision, announcement" [Eccles 8:11]) and *pardēs* ("park" [Eccles 2:5]). Features that have been identified as Phoenician and therefore "early," such as the feminine *-at* ending (versus Hebrew *-â*), are also found in LBH (see Seow, 15). D. M. Gropp (34) has argued that the Aramaic *šlyṭ* ("ruler") is current only during the Persian period, after which *raššay* replaces it, seemingly placing Ecclesiastes firmly in the Persian period. Ecclesiastes shares features such as the frequent use of *še* (136x in the Bible, 68x Ecclesiastes) with other books identified as dialectically Northern, as Song of Songs (Seow, 17).

Several other features of the language of Ecclesiastes are outstanding. First and foremost is the high number of *hapax legomena* and unique expressions in the book. Some of the more notable ones from Delitzsch's long list include the use of the *ănî* form of the first-person pronoun exclusive of the *'ănôkî* form, the use of the direct-object marker *'et* with indefinite objects, the *zô* form of the feminine demonstrative pronoun, and the negation of the infinitive by *'ên* (Delitzsch, 190-98; see also Seow, 17-19).

3. Conclusion.
The peculiarities in the language of the books surveyed here have attracted the greatest attention among the books in the Hebrew Bible from those attempting to untangle the history and varieties of Hebrew in antiquity. The traditional approach ultimately presents itself as a dichoto-

mous model in which SBH is set up as the "norm" with which other varieties of Hebrew language are compared. This is evident from the large group of shared features in EBH, LBH and Northern Israelite Hebrew. This pattern of shared features calls these traditional divisions into question and raises the possibility of alternative explanations for the varieties of Hebrew found in the Bible.

Alternative explanations must take into account variation arising from possible diglossia (i.e., the coexistence of a literary language and a colloquial language) and other differences in registry, the affect of genre and subject matter on language, and the difficulty of distinguishing between archaic language (i.e., the use of older forms of language, often indicative of early compositions) and archaisms (i.e., the intentional use of older forms of language in mimicry of earlier compositions). Similarly, judgments on "loanwords" are notoriously difficult to make, in terms of what sort of influence one language might have had on another and in terms of dating.

These questions are often driven by ideological concerns, such as what are acceptable and unacceptable dates for biblical compositions, an undue pessimism about finding answers to these questions, or an a priori commitment to the lateness of all of biblical culture and writings. Positively, the current debate opens up possibilities of new approaches and answers to these questions.

See also ELLIPSIS; PARALLELISM.

BIBLIOGRAPHY. **F. I. Andersen,** *Job: An Introduction and Commentary* (TOTC; Leicester: InterVarsity Press, 1976); **F. I. Andersen and A. D. Forbes,** "'Prose Particle' Counts in the Hebrew Bible," in *The Word of the Lord Shall Go Forth: Essays in Honor of David Noel Freedman in Celebration of His Sixtieth Birthday,* ed. Carol L. Meyers and M. O'Connor (ASORSVS 1; Winona Lake, IN: Eisenbrauns, 1983) 165-83; **R. Bergy,** "Late Linguistic Features in Esther," *JQR* 75 (1984) 66-78; **A. Berlin,** *The Dynamics of Biblical Parallelism* (Indianapolis: Indiana University Press, 1985); **F. Bush,** *Ruth, Esther* (WBC 9; Dallas: Word, 1996); **H. F. Campbell Jr.,** *Ruth* (AB 7; Garden City, NY: Doubleday, 1975); **W. T. W. Cloete,** *Versification and Syntax in Jeremiah 2-25: Syntactic Constraints in Hebrew Colometry* (SBLDS 117; Atlanta: Scholars Press, 1989); **J. A. Cook,** "The Hebrew Verb: A Grammaticalization Approach,"

ZAH 14 (2001) 117-43; **M. Dahood,** *Psalms 1-50* (AB 16; Garden City, NY: Doubleday, 1965); **F. Delitzsch,** *Commentary on the Old Testament: Ecclesiastes and Song of Solomon,* trans. M. G. Easton (repr.; Peabody, MA: Hendrickson, 1989); **S. R. Driver,** *An Introduction to the Literature of the Old Testament* (New York: Scribner, 1908); **D. C. Fredericks,** *Qoheleth's Language: Re-evaluating Its Nature and Date* (ANETS 3; Lewiston, NY: Mellen, 1988); idem, "A North Israelite Dialect of the Hebrew Bible," *HS* 37 (1996) 7-20; **D. N. Freedman,** "Pottery, Poetry, and Prophecy: An Essay on Biblical Poetry," *JBL* 96 (1977) 5-26; **J. C. L. Gibson,** *Canaanite Myths and Legends* (2nd ed.; Edinburgh: T & T Clark, 1977); **H. L. Ginsburg,** "A Phoenician Hymn in the Psalter," in *Atti del XIX Congresso Internazionale degli Orientalisti: Roma, 23-29 settembre 1935* (Rome: Tipografia del Senato, 1938) 472-76; **R. Gordis,** *The Book of God and Man: A Study of Job* (Chicago: University of Chicago Press, 1965); **F. E. Greenspahn,** *Hapax Legomena in Biblical Hebrew* (SBLDS 74; Chico, CA: Scholars Press, 1984); **D. M. Gropp,** "The Origin and Development of the Aramaic *šallîṭ* Clause," *JNES* 52 (1993) 31-36; **B. Isaksson,** *Studies in the Language of Qoheleth, with Special Emphasis on the Verbal System* (SSU 10; Uppsala: Almqvist & Wiksell, 1987); **S. A. Kaufman,** "The Classification of the North West Semitic Dialects of the Biblical Period and Some Implications Thereof," in *Proceedings of the Ninth World Congress of Jewish Studies: Panel Sessions, Hebrew and Aramaic,* ed. M. Bar-Asher (Jerusalem: Magnes, 1988) 41-57; **E. Kautzsch,** ed., *Gesenius' Hebrew Grammar* (2nd ed.; Oxford: Clarendon Press, 1910); **J. Kugel,** *The Idea of Biblical Poetry: Parallelism and Its History* (New Haven: Yale University Press, 1981); **C. A. Moore,** *Esther* (AB 7B; Garden City, NY: Doubleday, 1971); **R. E. Murphy,** *Proverbs* (WBC 22; Nashville: Thomas Nelson, 1998); idem, *The Song of Songs* (Hermeneia; Minneapolis: Fortress, 1990); **A. Niccacci,** *The Syntax of the Verb in Classical Hebrew Prose,* trans. W. G. E. Watson (JSOTSup 86; Sheffield: JSOT Press, 1990); **M. O'Connor,** *Hebrew Verse Structure* (repr.; Winona Lake, IN: Eisenbrauns, 1997); **F. H. Polak,** "Style Is More Than the Person: Sociolinguistics, Literary Culture and the Distinction between Written and Oral Narrative," in *Biblical Hebrew: Studies in Chronology and Typology,* ed. I. Young (JSOTS 369; London: T & T Clark International, 2003) 38-103; **R. Polzin,** *Late Biblical Hebrew: Toward an Historical Typology of Biblical Hebrew Prose* (HSM 12; Missoula, MT: Scholars Press, 1976); **G. A. Rendsburg,** *Linguistic Evidence for the Northern Origin of Selected Psalms* (SBLMS 43; Atlanta: Scholars Press, 1990); **A. Sáenz-Badillos,** *A History of the Hebrew Language,* trans. J. Elwolde (Cambridge: Cambridge University Press, 1993); **A. Schoors,** *The Preacher Sought to Find Pleasing Words: A Study of the Language of Qoheleth* (OLA 41; Leuven: Peeters, 1992); **C. L. Seow,** *Ecclesiastes* (AB 18C; New York: Doubleday, 1997); **E. Ullendorff,** "Is Biblical Hebrew a Language?" in *Is Biblical Hebrew a Language? Studies in Semitic Languages and Civilizations,* ed. E. Ullendorf (Wiesbaden: Harrassowitz, 1977) 3-17; **W. G. E. Watson,** *Classical Hebrew Poetry: A Guide to Its Techniques* (JSOTSup 26; Sheffield: Sheffield Academic Press, 1986); **I. Young,** *Diversity in Pre-Exilic Hebrew* (FAT 5; Tübingen: Mohr Siebeck, 1993); idem, ed., *Biblical Hebrew: Studies in Chronology and Typology* (JSOTSup 369; London: T & T Clark International, 2003).

J. A. Cook

HEMISTICH. *See* POETICS, TERMINOLOGY OF.

HERMENEUTICS

The word *hermeneutics* is used with varying meanings. This article treats it as a way of looking at the process involved in interpreting texts, the methods that we use, and the approaches that can open up their understanding. In doing exegesis, we seek to understand a text in its original context, in accordance with its own agenda and priorities; we may then move from exegesis to application. When we talk in terms of hermeneutics, we imply a recognition that even our exegetical study is affected by who we are—the questions that occupy us, the culture that we belong to, the way our church has taught us, our personal experience, whether we are wealthy or poor, whether we are male or female, and so on. Further, the process of understanding Scripture is not linear (as the exegesis-application model implies). There is an ongoing both-ways relationship between focusing on a passage's meaning in its own right and focusing on its significance for us in light of questions that concern us. This is as true of historical and critical study as it is of other approaches because the concerns, aims and methods of historical and critical study come from a particular culture, and historical-critical study discovers from the text what its methods allow. All this does not mean (or need not mean) that we find in texts only what we know already. Our perspective and experience do make it possible for us actually to discover aspects of the texts' intrinsic meaning. The trick is to see how we can utilize the positive aspects of the way subjective factors enable us to see objective things in Scripture, and to safeguard against its negative aspects, the way it limits and narrows our perspective or makes us misperceive things. A significant means of making progress in that is looking at Scripture through other people's eyes, so as to perceive and then broaden the narrowness of our own vision.

The printed Hebrew-Aramaic Bible of Jews—the Scriptures that Christians call the Old Testament—comprises the Torah, the Prophets and the Writings. The books covered by this dictionary are the first two-thirds of the Writings; they are followed in the Hebrew-Aramaic order by Daniel, Ezra, Nehemiah and Chronicles. The Torah, the Former Prophets and the Latter Prophets are all broadly coherent collections of books, and one can identify hermeneutical issues that apply to each of them as collections. The Writings do not have a congruity of that kind, and little can be said about interpretation that applies to all of them. But various approaches to interpretation may illumine different subgroups within the Writings.

1. Historical Interpretation
2. Sociological Interpretation
3. Liturgical Interpretation
4. Devotional Interpretation
5. Canonical Interpretation
6. Experiential Interpretation
7. Narrative Interpretation
8. Postmodern Interpretation
9. Feminist Interpretation
10. Typological, Allegorical and Christological Interpretation
11. Post-Holocaust Interpretation
12. Postcolonial Interpretation

1. Historical Interpretation.

1.1. The Writings as a Whole. Scriptural interpretation in the context of modernity emphasized understanding Scripture in light of its historical origin. This illustrates the culture-relative nature of approaches to interpretation, since many scriptural writings give little indication of their specific historical origin; indeed, they can sometimes seem deliberately to conceal

it. Thus the dating of most of the individual books will always be a matter of debate. But compared with the Torah and the Prophets, in the Writings there are more specific references to the Second Temple period. This links with their location at the end of the Hebrew-Aramaic Scriptures; they likely reached their final form as a collection later than the Torah and the Prophets, and therefore they belong distinctively to postexilic times.

We may therefore ask how an understanding of the Second Temple period helps us understand their significance. This involves a circular argument, as the books themselves are our major source for knowledge of the period, though the argument's circularity does not make it wrong.

Ezra and Nehemiah indicate that life was hard for the Judean community in the Persian period, while *Esther and Daniel suggest that the position of Judeans in Persia, too, could be tough. Although Persian control gave Judah more internal freedom than obtained under the Babylonians, it was a province of the Persian Empire, a small community experiencing economic difficulties, partly through the burden of imperial taxation. It existed in uneasy relations or actual conflict with surrounding Persian provinces. And it knew internal tensions related to its economic difficulties and to attitudes to those surrounding peoples. Its experience thus fell far short of the glorious restoration of Israel that prophets had promised, and far short of the glorious events of centuries past related in Exodus, Joshua and 2 Samuel.

The Writings thus function as resources for a community living through tough times. How is it to survive? Continue to *worship Yahweh, cast itself on Yahweh, own its sinfulness, and trust Yahweh (*Psalms, *Lamentations). Reflect on its human experience of life, independently of the agenda or framework set by Yahweh's activity in relation to Israel in events such as the exodus and the making of the covenant (*Proverbs, *Song of Songs). Face the tricky theological questions raised by its experience and think boldly about them (*Job, *Ecclesiastes). See Yahweh's activity behind the scenes of its experience, protecting and using it, and be neither overwhelmed by the power of foreign peoples nor dismissive of them (Esther, *Ruth). Maintain confidence in Yahweh's sovereignty in the political affairs of the empire and over the broad sweep of history (Daniel). Keep telling its story with a recognition of what does get achieved (Ezra, Nehemiah). Do not undervalue the privilege of being able to worship Yahweh in the temple built by *David (Chronicles).

The circumstances of the church in post-Christian parts of the world parallel those of the Second Temple Judean community and thus give it a way in to understanding the Writings, and their varying invitations speak to its situation. If the church in the United States continues to decline, it will share with them in the potential of this parallel.

1.2. Individual Books. Most of the Latter Prophets begin with an introduction offering hermeneutical clues about how to read them. One clue is their reference to a particular human author and a particular historical context, the reign of certain kings. Interpreting them against their specific historical context is then both possible and necessary. Isaiah, Ezekiel and Zechariah, for instance, would not have delivered the same message had they lived in a different century. But in the case of most of the Writings, we do not know their author or what century they belong to. Interpreting them against their specific historical context is impossible and is therefore presumably (if one factors in God's providence) unnecessary.

English translations can give readers the impression that the Psalms begin in a way similar to the Latter Prophets, with the same pointer to understanding them against the background of their author and their author's day, since the expression "psalm of David" looks analogous to the expression "vision of Isaiah." Actually it is not. While "vision of Isaiah" is a construct phrase (the Hebrew equivalent of a genitive), the expression "of David" involves a preposition, *le*, and although it could mean "by David," it could just as easily mean "for David" or "belonging to David." Further, many psalm headings that include the phrase "psalm of David" also describe their psalm as "psalm of the choirmaster" or by means of another such term using the same prepositional construction. This is obscured by English translations, which have phrases such as "for the choirmaster," perhaps to avoid the problem caused by implying that the psalm had two or three authors. Yet further, although "David" can denote David the son of Jesse, the OT can also use the name "David" to refer to a subsequent Davidic king or a Davidic

king to come in the future. So one way or another, there is no strong reason to take the "David" heading as an indication of a psalm's authorship and thus as an invitation to understand a psalm historically. And this fits with the fact that many "David" psalms look later than the time of King David (e.g., speaking as if the temple already exists). For Chronicles, the great significance of David is as the person who under Yahweh set up the arrangements for the temple's building and worship. The heading "of/for/to/belonging to David," alongside headings such as "of/for/to/belonging to the choirmaster," might have similar significance. It affirms that these prayers and praises belong to Israel's proper, David-authorized, divinely authorized worship. The hermeneutical clue that the heading offers is that readers can and should take these psalms as a guide to proper praise and prayer. (We will return to the headings that refer to specific incidents in David's life.)

The actual contents of the psalms also suggest that their date and origin is without hermeneutical significance. Although some psalms refer to circumstances that suggest particular events in someone's life, such as a defeat, an invasion, a wedding or an exile from Jerusalem (see, e.g., Pss 42—46), they never contain concrete information to enable readers to identify which defeat, invasion, wedding or exile. Actually, omitting such information makes it easier to use them; they do not give the impression of being limited in significance to one particular occasion.

Something similar is true about the Wisdom literature. Job is simply anonymous, like narrative works such as Ruth and Esther. As with Psalms, the perennial nature of its subject makes its date and authorship of little significance for its interpretation. It has been seen by some as the oldest book in the OT and by others as one of the most recent. This question affects understanding of the history of Israelite theology and religion; it makes no difference to the book's own meaning.

In some contrast, Proverbs is described as "the proverbs of Solomon," using the genitive, though subsequently, Proverbs 30 begins "the words of Agur," and Proverbs 31 "the words of Lemuel." Ecclesiastes is "the words of Qohelet, the son of David, king in Jerusalem," which suggests an association of its content with *Solomon but also points away from this association by not using the actual name (*qōhelet* might be a pseudonym or a description of a role [*see* Qohelet]). Song of Songs uses the same preposition as Psalms in describing itself as "of/for/by/to Solomon."

Sayings of the kind that dominate Proverbs are usually compositions passed down in tradition; they do not exactly have "authors." But in Middle Eastern nations such as Egypt, the king is responsible for encouraging and propagating learning and education and stands as an embodiment of wisdom. In Israel, Solomon occupies that position, and his relationship with these three books is analogous to David's relationship with the "Davidic" psalms. They are Solomonic in the sense that they count as true wisdom. Like the psalms, they have canonical authority.

In the context of modernity, interpreters emphasized a historical approach to understanding Ruth. Its story is set in the period of the judges, but its last paragraph makes clear that it was written at least as late as David's day, and its location in the Writings suggests that it comes from the postexilic period. That context highlights its emphasis on Ruth's Moabite identity and on its relating how a Moabite comes to be part of David's ancestry; it suggests a different attitude toward marriage with people such as Moabites from the one implied by Ezra 9 (see 5 below). But although a historical approach thus illumines one aspect of Ruth, it takes attention away from many aspects. The story of *Naomi and of Ruth and Naomi's relationship, for instance, becomes insignificant. Historical interpretation both enlightens and obscures.

Among the books in focus in the present volume, Lamentations is the most amenable to historical interpretation, though even here the appropriateness of that approach has been questioned. The LXX provides Lamentations with a preface attributing it to Jeremiah in the aftermath of Jerusalem's fall in 587 BC, and its consequent location after Jeremiah in the Christian Bible encourages the assumption that this is the context for understanding it. With hindsight, one should not be surprised that this consensus assumption has been questioned in our current period, in which every assumption is open to question, though there was a long time lag between scholarly abandonment of the idea of Jeremianic authorship and scholarly questioning of the dating. But Lamentations parallels Psalms in containing no concrete indications of date and authorship. Historical criticism has stuck with the tradition of a date soon after 587 BC because that is the last fall of Jerusalem we know of in OT times. This at least gives us a context against which to imagine the book, and a historical approach thus contributes to its interpretation. But the book's lack of concrete historical reference makes it likely that this is not the only key to it.

2. Sociological Interpretation.

Sociological interpretation of Scripture takes various forms, some closely related to historical interpretation. It may ask about the social location of the authors and readers of the books, even if we cannot identify their identity or historical setting, and of the way the books' content reflects the position of authors and readers in the society and their interests. The material within Proverbs, for instance, may reflect the social contexts of the family (in many of the sayings), of the *royal court (in other sayings) and of the theological school (in the expositions of the significance of wisdom). But no doubt the social background of the actual book of Proverbs (like that of any biblical book and of most books in most contexts) will be that of educated, literary, urban, professional, well-to-do people. This may illumine aspects of its content, such as its attacks on laziness. Ecclesiastes is usually reckoned to have the same background, though its author then expresses disillusion with everything that educated, literary, urban, professional, powerful, well-to-do people have or value. Sociological approaches such as these suffer from the same difficulty as historical approaches: they have to connect a small number of dots on the basis of theories that come from outside the text, and thus they produce conflicting results (on sociological approaches to Proverbs, see Houston; on sociological approaches to Ecclesiastes, see Sneed).

This difficulty becomes clearer when we reconsider the process whereby H. Gunkel introduced sociological interpretation into the study of wisdom, poetry and writings. He sought to redirect study of the psalms from questions about their individual nature and their individual historical background to questions about their recurrent forms of speech and about the social context (*Sitz im Leben*) in which these belonged. This was a potentially fruitful approach, but Gunkel was prevented from realizing more of the potential of a sociological approach by assumptions about the nature of temple worship and about spirituality that he brought to his sociological study. Even the strong internal evidence within the psalms of their intrinsic link with corporate worship did not deflect him from denying that this was their true social context. Sociological approaches to the books have a hard time attending to the content of the books themselves rather than simply reading sociological theories into them. In theory, sociological interpretation should illumine the text; in practice, we would be unwise to rely too much on its alleged results. It may illumine the interpreters more than it does the texts that they interpret.

Asking about the social function of psalms of praise is more illuminating. In Christian worship, declaring that Jesus is Lord creates a world before us. The world and the church do not make it look as if Jesus is Lord; world and church do not live in light of this fact. Yet we know that Jesus *is* Lord, and proclaiming this reality builds up our capacity to continue believing it, even though empirical evidence imperils this conviction, and also builds up our capacity to live on the basis of the statement's truth. Analogously, psalms of praise function to create a world (Brueggemann). Israel knows that Yahweh is the great God and the great King, but the facts of life in Israel often make it look as if Marduk is the great god and Nebuchadnezzar is the great king. In singing the psalms, then, Israel both affirms that the real world is the one in which Yahweh reigns and builds up its capacity to live in light of that fact. Sociological interpretation thus links with liturgical interpretation.

3. Liturgical Interpretation.

Why do the Writings, this miscellaneous collection of books, come together at the end of the Hebrew-Aramaic Bible? There may be a connection with their relationship to worship, which may even explain the puzzling title "the Writings" (this expression, *hakkĕtûbim*, could just as easily be translated "the Scriptures," but the Torah and the Prophets are also part of "the Writings/Scriptures" in this sense). In synagogue worship the weekly Scripture readings come from the Torah and the Prophets. Some of the Writings are used in other ways in worship, but not to provide the regular weekly readings. The Torah and the Prophets are read; the Writings are Scriptures that are written but not read, in this sense (Barton).

The five scrolls of the *Megillot belong together in connection with worship because they came to be used (at least in Ashkenazi communities) at five annual occasions, Passover (Song of Songs), Pentecost (Ruth), the Ninth of Av, in July/August (Lamentations), Sukkot (Ecclesiastes) and *Purim (Esther). The nature of the link with these occasions varies. Song of Songs' association with Passover presupposes the book's interpretation as an allegory of the story of Yahweh's dealings with Israel over the centuries, beginning at the exodus. Ruth's association with Pentecost corresponds to the barley harvest setting of key scenes in the story. Lamentations' association with the Ninth of Av is more intrinsic to the book's nature, as this fast day commemorates the fall of Jerusalem and the destruction of the temple in 587 BC and in AD 70. The link between Ecclesiastes and Sukkot is perhaps that Sukkot is traditionally "the season of our joy," and Ecclesiastes points to false and true places to locate joy. Purim's association with Esther is also intrinsic to the book, which almost ends with Esther establishing this festival to celebrate the deliverance the story tells. A liturgical approach to the Megillot thus illumines aspects of some of them.

The psalm headings also reflect liturgical realities and point to a liturgical interpretation of the Psalter. Paradoxically, the very fact that many of these headings are now unintelligible reflects their liturgical significance; they are the ancient Israelite equivalents to "common meter" or "capo on second fret." For a half-century following on the work of S. Mowinckel, who himself took forward Gunkel's work, much scholarship assumed that the psalms' use in worship was the key to interpreting them, but in the late twentieth century this assumption lost traction. E. S. Gerstenberger attempted to move the focus of interest from the worship of the temple to that of local communities in Judah or in the Diaspora, but this also involves much reading into the texts. The general notion that the psalms were used in Israelite worship is secure enough and significant for their interpretation, but attempts to give more precision to the way they were used founder on the fact that neither their content nor their headings are specific enough in indicating the way they were used, and this focus has drawn attention away from the psalms themselves.

4. Devotional Interpretation.

There is an exception to the rule that the headings of the psalms do not have specific hermeneutical significance. A number of these headings link psalms with specific incidents in David's life. Psalm 51, as well as being "of/for/to the choirmaster," is "of/to/for David"; this heading then adds "when Nathan the prophet came to him after he [David] had gone to Bathsheba." Comparing these long headings with the content of their psalms reveals two features. There is a general fit between heading and psalm, and often there are concrete points of connection with the story that the heading refers to; it would be appropriate for David to cast himself on Yahweh's mercy in the way the psalm expresses it, and appropriate for him to plead that Yahweh's holy spirit not be taken away from him. Yet other specific features stand in tension with its use by David at this point. David could hardly say that he had sinned "only" against Yahweh, and it is odd for him to look for the building up of Jerusalem's walls, with the implication that they have been knocked down.

B. S. Childs (1971) has suggested a plausible understanding of the combination of correspondence and contrast between these long headings and their psalms. In effect, he suggests, they resemble the collocation of passages in a lectionary, which invites congregations to read several passages in relation to one another. The implication is not that these passages were written together or that they exactly correspond but rather that there is sufficient overlap between them to make it fruitful to bring them into mutual association. The analogy suggests that people who use the psalm or who read the relevant David story bring psalm and story together so as to find some indication of the way a person in David's position might pray or some indication of the circumstances in which one might pray this psalm.

The presupposition of these headings may be, then, that David has now become not only the patron of temple worship but also a model for spirituality, as Christians have in fact regularly taken him to be. People read David's story to gain enlightenment on their personal walk with God. The psalms then help them relate David's story to themselves.

Something similar is true about the role of the unnamed king in Ecclesiastes. The book emphasizes the way the things human beings use to bring them fulfillment and happiness cannot actually deliver. This Solomon-like king offers a model test case for this thesis because he was in a position to realize the goals that many people set for themselves. As king, he was able to study all the learning that was available, to indulge himself in pleasure to excess, to bring to completion great achievements in building and creativity, to accumulate great wealth, and to build up a harem. But none of it led anywhere; all of it seemed empty. He could thus testify to that fact for ordinary people who think that these things would give meaning to their lives. So the king becomes instructive for ordinary people's spirituality.

The implication of the way that Psalms and the wisdom books work is that people who bring to the books their own questions about their lives and their relationship with God will discover aspects of the texts' own meaning. On the other hand, like other approaches to interpretation, this has limitations, and it is particularly inclined to narrow down what readers see in stories such as Ruth and Esther, which are about much more than individuals and their lives.

5. Canonical Interpretation.

5.1. Individual Books. As well as drawing attention to their human authorship and their historical origin, the prophetic books describe themselves by means of expressions such as "the word of Yahweh." As well as being of human and historical origin, they are of divine origin.

The Writings do not take this form but rather present themselves as human words. The Christian description of the entire Scriptures as "the Word of God" implies that actually they are divine words just as really as the prophetic books; the difference lies in *how* God was involved in bringing them into being rather than in *whether* God was involved. The way the Writings present themselves suggests that these are works that God came to accept and authenticate rather than works that God initiated. (Theologically, we might still say that God's initiative was prior in bringing them into being; I speak here of the process as the scriptural writings themselves see it.)

When prophets describe something as "the word of Yahweh," they imply the conviction that for better or worse, this prophetic declaration will indeed come about. As Yahweh's word, it demands attention if hearers want to profit from its good news or evade its bad news. Recognizing books such as Psalms or Proverbs or Ruth as "the word of God" will have similar implications. It implies paying attention to them. It implies that churches should read them, whereas in practice churches rather neglect them. Where they do not simply ignore them, Christians may be inclined actively to discount them, implying that they cannot really be divine words. For instance, the psalms say things to God that Christians reckon no one ought to think or feel or say. Ecclesiastes says things to other people that Christians reckon no one ought to think or feel or say. Proverbs makes promises that Christians think cannot be relied on or are otherwise likely to be misleading (e.g., encouraging people to believe in a "prosperity gospel"). It is then Christian practice to ignore these words or reinterpret them so that they fit with what Christians find acceptable.

Although they do not describe themselves as the word of Yahweh, the books implicitly anticipate and counter this attitude by suggesting a claim to something like canonical authority. These are human words that offer authoritative teaching; they are designed to function as canon. The Psalter, for instance, divides into five books, marked by doxologies after Psalms 41; 72; 89; 106. It thus mirrors the Torah, which divides into five books (it is a Pentateuch). The Psalter is a book of teaching about praise and prayer that demands to be heeded in an analogous way to the way the Torah demands to be heeded. It decides what is proper praise and prayer.

The reference to Solomon in the introduction to Proverbs and Song of Songs implicitly ascribes quasi-canonical authority to these books. We have noted that describing them as Solomonic claims for them the kind of authority that attaches to the teaching of someone who is the embodiment of God-given wisdom in the OT story.

Ecclesiastes makes the same point in a slightly different way. It begins by describing its author as *qōhelet,* from the word for the Israelite worshiping congregation, the *qāhāl.* This teacher is thus someone who represents the congregation, not some heretic. The book's closing paragraph nuances the point. It makes specific that Qohelet was indeed a wise man who taught insight to the people, one who taught truth. The description piles up words to underline the book's nature and status in these general terms.

It then comes to comment on its particular nature, observing that in this case the sayings of the wise are like goads or spurs and like nails; it is extremely uncomfortable to have them driven home, but they achieve things as this happens. On the other hand, the conclusion goes on, the reader needs to be wary of them, and it adds the seminarian's favorite verse, stating that of the making of many books there is no end and that much study is wearisome to the flesh. In its context, the point is that one Ecclesiastes is a good idea, but a Bible full of books like it would not be. Ecclesiastes then closes with a safe summary of the orthodox convictions whose difficulties much of the book is concerned to face.

5.2. The Collection as a Whole. The location of the books in the Hebrew-Aramaic canon and in the Greek and English canon also carries implications for their interpretation. In both orders Genesis through Deuteronomy comes first. Then things diverge. The Hebrew-Aramaic division of the canon demarcates the first five books from what follows as "the Torah" over against "the Former Prophets." The Greek canon does not do so and thereby encourages readers to follow the narrative as it continues into Joshua, Judges, Samuel and Kings, with Ruth being inserted into this macronarrative at an appropriate point where it provides a foil to Judges and points forward to the story of David (Jobling). As is the case with a historical interpretation of Ruth, the effect is to highlight certain aspects of the story and to underplay others.

The Hebrew-Aramaic canon follows "the Former Prophets" with "the Latter Prophets": Isaiah, Jeremiah, Ezekiel and Hosea through Malachi. In the Greek canon these come at the end, with Lamentations and Daniel inserted at chronologically appropriate points. We have seen that the effect is to emphasize a historical approach to Lamentations by setting it in the context of Jeremiah's ministry and lifetime. In the Greek canon, further, Chronicles, Ezra, Nehemiah and Esther follow Joshua through Kings, in that chronological order. This again emphasizes a linear, narrative reading of the books, which fits Chronicles, Ezra and Nehemiah (not least given the overlap between the end of Chronicles and the beginning of Ezra). In Esther's case, it has a parallel effect to the one it has on Ruth, making readers see it as part of a larger whole and not simply as a work in its own right, and underplaying other aspects of the story.

The placing of the Writings as a whole at the end of the Hebrew-Aramaic canon is usually reckoned to imply that they have less authority than do the Torah and the Prophets; their absence from the weekly synagogue lectionary fits with that (for other interpretations of the arrangement, see Miles; Dempster). In contrast, the Greek canon's locating of Job, Psalms, Proverbs, Ecclesiastes and Song of Songs in the middle of the collection gives these books more coherence than they have in the Hebrew-Aramaic canon. In the Greek canon they again appear in a quasi-chronological order. Job is traditionally assumed to be a figure from the time of Israel's ancestors, Psalms is associated with David, the last three books with Solomon. At the same time, all five books discuss perennial human issues concerning the nature and basis of human life and of a relationship with God, and they do so with little reference to God's acts in Israel's story, which elsewhere define the meaning of God and the way one would understand those issues. That perhaps reflects the books' historical background in the postexilic period, when the great acts of God belong in the distant past and are hard to relate to.

The Greek canon can be seen as arranged in such a way as to relate to the past (Genesis through Esther), the present (Job through Song of Songs) and the future (Isaiah through Malachi) (Wolff). This understanding parallels the dynamic and suggestive tensions and complementarities within the Writings and between the Writings and the other books. "'Proverbs says, 'These are the rules for life; try them and you will find that they work.' Job and Ecclesiastes say, 'We did, and they don't'" (Hubbard, 6). In Psalms, *suffering usually comes despite people's faithfulness; in Lamentations, it comes because of people's waywardness. Ruth suggests an open stance toward foreign women who identify with Israel; Ezra urges a rigorous stance toward foreign women who do not. In Exodus, God acts in interventionist fashion to bring about Israel's deliverance, and a woman or two make it possible for a man to take the human lead in this process, while in Esther, Israel's deliverance comes about without divine intervention, and a man encourages a woman to take the lead. In Proverbs, right behavior is an expression of insight; in Deuteronomy, it is an expression of obedience to Yahweh. In Genesis 1—2, the relationship between a man and a woman is a practical one; in Song of Songs, it is a romantic one. We learn from the conversation within the Writings and between the Writings and other Scriptures about these questions.

6. Experiential Interpretation.

Although some of the Writings do present themselves as texts designed to function canonically, we have noted that more prominently than the prophetic books they present themselves as human words, and this provides a significant clue for their interpretation. The human experience of readers is a key factor in thinking about hermeneutics, and more systematically than any other parts of Scripture these books appeal to and speak in terms of human experience. Whereas Ruth and Esther relate the experiences of certain ordinary individuals, Psalms, Lamentations, Proverbs, Job, Ecclesiastes and Song of Songs give prominence to first-person expressions of praise, prayer, insight, pain, questioning and enthusiasm. Of course, all human writing reflects human experience, and in the scriptural writings as a whole God speaks through that experience. But these books reflect human experience in a particularly explicit and systematic way.

The experiential aspect to hermeneutics is the focus of a significant nineteenth-century tradition of hermeneutics that saw interpretation as aiming to share or repeat the experience of the writers of a work, our own analogous experience being our way in to being able to do that (Schleiermacher; Dilthey 1976; 1985). Thus we come to these books as people who ourselves praise God, pray, reflect, doubt, suffer and love. If we do not do those things, it is unlikely that we would have a starting point for understanding these books; we would have to put ourselves empathetically into the position of people who indeed do those things. In principle, that is possible because we are human beings like them and have the potential for those experiences if not the experiences themselves. It means that we can understand something of what the books mean when they express their enthusiasm in praise, their pain in prayer, their agonizing about injustice in the world, and the thrill of their love.

At the same time, we then recognize that much of their praise, prayer, agonizing and thrill is quite different from anything that we experience. So our own experience both opens up the possibility of understanding and draws attention to our need to go beyond our own experience if we are to understand the texts. We are thus introduced to the "hermeneutic circle" or, better, "hermeneutic spiral," and the notion of the merging of horizons (Gadamer; Goldingay; Thiselton). It is possible to settle for affirming the features that gel with our own experience and ignoring the rest; the hermeneutic process then becomes a vicious circle. Even the recent renewed appreciation of *lament psalms reflects something about us as readers, in a way analogous to the more traditional Christian emphasis on penitential psalms (Nasuti). Growing in our understanding involves starting from the overlap between our experience and the experience reflected in the text and letting that be a way into appreciating the aspects of the text that we have not experienced.

7. Narrative Interpretation.

Ruth and Esther are short stories. This description does not beg the question of whether they are more factual or more imaginative stories. (My view is that both historical facts and divinely inspired imagination have contributed to them.) But even if they are purely factual stories, they use the techniques of creative writing. Approaches to interpretation that are honed to the nature of creative writing thus contribute to their understanding.

First, character plays a key role in both stories, in the persons of Naomi, Ruth, *Boaz, *Ahasuerus, *Vashti, *Mordecai, Haman and others. Some of these are well-rounded characters with the complexity of human personality—Naomi, for example. Others are simpler characters presented in plain black-and-white fashion—Ahasuerus, for example. This is not to say that the real Ahasuerus was any less complex than Naomi but rather to comment on the role of the character within the story and the questions that are appropriate to understanding their role. Some characters (such as Boaz) are portrayed with sympathy, some (such as Haman) without. Interpreters vary in the way they understand the portrayal of Vashti. People who favor women's subordination are negative about Vashti; people who oppose it are positive about the stance that she takes. The presuppositions that people bring to characters thus influence their interpretation.

Second, there is plot. The framework of Ruth involves the way a family from Bethlehem becomes the ancestors of Israel's greatest king. But events at the beginning of the story threaten to derail this possibility, as the family has to leave Bethlehem for Moab, where all the men in the family die. The plot then has to get the family's mother back to Bethlehem and make it possible for her to have a child who can turn out to be David's grandfather. Like many plots, it involves a series of points where everything could go wrong (e.g., what if Naomi succeeds in persuading Ruth to stay in Moab?) and coincidences (Boaz is a member of Naomi's extended family!). The framework of Esther involves the way the Jewish people in Persia escape a pogrom. In the background is some indulgent and then angry action on the part of the Persian king, interwoven with some assertiveness on the queen's part, which leads to a Jewish girl becoming queen. The more direct background is a Jewish man's resistance to bowing down to one of the king's officials, which provokes the official to manipulate the king into authorizing the pogrom. Again coincidence plays a role (a Jewish girl becoming queen, Mordecai discovering a plot against the king, the king being unable to sleep one night), and again everything could go wrong (what if Esther had not bravely urged the king to reverse his action?). Like Ruth, Esther follows the standard linear plot form: the exposition of a problem, the complexities of events and actions that it leads to, and its eventual resolution.

Third, there is the viewpoint from which the story is told. In Ruth and Esther the story is told in the third person (contrast, in part, Nehemiah). Thus we do not discover as much about the thinking of these lead characters as we might if Ruth or Esther told the story in the first person. But the narrator can tell us things that no individual character in the story can know; the narrator knows things that members of the Persian court say to one another as well as things that ordinary members of the Jewish community say to one another. Indeed, the narrator sometimes knows what people are thinking, though this is only occasionally the case; the narrator does not know everything. It is more characteristic of OT narrative to allow the reader to infer from people's words and actions what was going on inside them. Nor does the narrator know what God is thinking; at least, the story does not tell us. Nor does the narrator offer evaluative comments on people's actions (hence that fact that readers may understand Vashti's actions affirmatively or critically). This makes Ruth and Esther contrast with some other OT narratives. The effect is to tell a story that resonates with regular human experience, in which we regularly do not know what other people are thinking or what God is thinking. We have to work out whether and where and how God is involved in the story. On the other hand, even though told in the third person, the story sometimes adopts the perspective of one of the characters, as if we are looking over their shoulder even though not looking into their mind. Much of Ruth is actually told from Naomi's angle. (The book might more accurately have been called "Naomi and Ruth".) Much of Esther is told from Mordecai's angle, or Haman's.

There are broader aspects to the notion of viewpoint. Together the books imply that any activity of God that people in their context can look for takes place behind the scenes of history and human experience, not in the interventionist fashion of the stories in Exodus and Judges with which in other ways Esther and Ruth have points of contact. Associated with that is their shared conviction that Israelites, and specifically Israelite women, must take responsibility for their destiny and take bold action in relation to the men who hold power in their contexts, using their femininity as they do so.

Fourth, *ambiguity and irony play a part in the stories, related to questions about character, plot and viewpoint. In Genesis, Judges or 2 Samuel we may reckon that narrator and/or author and/or God disapproves of many of the actions that people undertake, though the narrative does not make this explicit. On the basis of information that the story as a whole conveys regarding the narrative's viewpoint, it assumes that readers can make the right inferences, and it leaves them to do so. On the other hand, in some stories there is room for debate about whether the narrator approves of what happens, or whether the author does, or whether God does. Both kinds of ambiguity (resolvable and irresolvable) appear in Ruth and Esther.

Ruth makes no comment on the death of the three men in the story. Is this Yahweh's judgment for the sons' marrying of Moabites? Does Ruth's audacious courting of Boaz relate to Israelite perceptions (or fantasies) of Moabite women? By the end of the story, it is at least clear that the narrator affirms Ruth precisely as a Moabite and believes that Israel should be open to members of other races who come to believe in Yahweh. The story's overall stance in relation to Ruth as a Moabite rules out that pejorative interpretation of the opening events. It is nevertheless an irony that it is a Moabite who provides David with his grandfather. Further, the story leaves ambiguous precisely what happened on the threshing floor, rather in the style of an old-school Hollywood movie; and the question "Was Naomi a scold?" (someone who is always complaining) could become the subject of a scholarly debate (Fewell and Gunn 1988; 1989, Coxon).

In Esther, in light of other parts of the OT, one might wonder whether Jews had any business staying in places such as *Susa and not returning to Jerusalem; the narrator presupposes that it is acceptable for Jews to let exile become dispersion, and that they can expect to find themselves preserved and even successful there. We have noted that the narrator makes no evaluative comment on the Persian men's concern that Vashti's action will encourage other Persian women's insubordination, but its portrayal of the king's general capacity for stupidity and manipulation points to sympathy for Vashti rather than for the king and his fellow husbands. With irony, it is the king's next wife who is the means of reversing his edict. Then with irony, the Jews finally indulge in the pogrom that they had themselves escaped; the narrative at least leaves open the question of whether the Jews had any business killing more than seventy-five thousand people. Indeed, disapproval of the book for this action misses the book's own implicit critique (Goldman): ironically, the Jews end up behaving like Persians at the moment when many Persians have become Jews.

An analogous set of literary approaches studies the nature of Hebrew poetry, with its use of genre, *parallelism and *imagery.

8. Postmodern Interpretation.
Beneath the surface of Ruth and Esther are some more elemental relationships or motifs that also underlie the other books, such as can be examined by structuralism. Further, stories also presuppose antinomies and take sides with regard to them; deconstruction brings these to the surface and questions their easy resolution (for Ruth, see Greenstein; for Esther and Job, see Clines; for both books, see Ruth and Esther, Bush).

Ruth and Esther also have in common that they manifest illuminating links with other OT material. Esther makes for comparison with the Joseph story as well as the exodus story, while Ruth makes for instructive comparison with the story of Tamar as well as other characters in the OT story and other parts of the OT, such as Isaiah 40—55 (Nielsen). The psalms have multiple such intertextual relationships with other parts of the OT (Tanner), such as the retelling of Israel's story in different psalms (*see* Intertextuality). Within the Psalter itself one can often trace the way similar phrases or lines or sequences of lines recur, in varying forms and combinations. Often it may be difficult to know whether such links or similarities are deliberate or coincidental, and if they are deliberate, to know which text came first, but the framework of intertextuality makes it possible to consider their significance without knowing the answer to those questions. Juxtaposing the texts still illumines each of them.

Such awarenesses are an aspect of postmodernity, one of whose features is the recognition that truth is more complicated than it used to be. Christians did once recognize that we actually understand only the hem of God's garments, and some Christian theologians have wondered whether theology best focuses on saying what God is not (e.g., God is not a created being, God is not located in space, God is not within time, God is not human). Postmodernism reminds us about mystery and complexity. Some of the Writings recognize the complexity of who God is and how we relate to God or recognize the limitations in what we can say about these matters.

Job begins from the question why bad things happen to good people, but this question raises more radical ones about God and humanity and their relationship. Using the form of a dramatic dialogue allows the book to look at the problem from a series of different angles and to propound a series of answers to these questions. It does not survey a number of answers and finally declare that one of them is right. All its answers have some truth in them, though they vary in their relevance to Job. Even Yahweh's response does not have the final word, as the end of the story implies a different perspective.

Job may have undergone a process of redaction (e.g., the prose framework of the story may be older than the poetic speeches, and the Elihu speeches may be a later addition). It may also have been subject to some accidental disordering, particularly in the third set of speeches between Job and his friends. But one implication of approaching the book in light of postmodern insights is that we are unwise to try to simplify or tidy the book. Its complexity and untidiness are one way its message is conveyed.

Ecclesiastes' postmodernity is expressed in its reaction to the difficulty of handling those big questions, not by sharing as many partial insights as possible but rather by emphasizing how few things we can say.

9. Feminist Interpretation.
Song of Songs and Ruth were among the first books of the Bible to attract feminist approaches to interpretation (Trible; Brenner 1993a; 1993b; 1995a; 1995b; Bach). *Feminist interpretation asks what happens when *women (or men) attempt to read Scripture in conscious awareness of distinctive features of women's lives (or of men's), such as their bodily experiences and their experience of subordination to men (or subordination of women). Contemporary Western women's insistence on seeing themselves as fully human and standing alongside men rather than as inferior to them opened up the possibility of recognizing the egalitarian aspect to the relationship portrayed in Song of Songs, where the woman speaks first and longest, and the man is not portrayed as the active "lover" and the woman as the acted-upon "beloved." It thus lets Song of Songs speak to subordinationist attitudes in the church. It opened up avenues of analyzing the relationship of Ruth and Naomi and the way they discover how to live as women in a men's world. Similar dynamics were perceived in Esther, the story of the radical feminist Vashti and the liberal feminist Esther (Clines), although they are still, like Ruth and Naomi, finally subordinated to men. In reverse fashion, feminist interpretation raises questions about the aphorisms in Proverbs and their understanding of women and men, and about the figure of the "strange woman," though noting how the aphorisms are set in the context of the different way womanhood features in the book's opening and closing chapters, which form a frame for understanding it (Camp). Feminist interpretation inquires further after the significance of the apparent absence or near absence of women from works such as Psalms and Job (Clines), though also of the potential of reading psalms as women's texts (Rienstra).

10. Typological, Allegorical and Christological Interpretation.

It became customary in Judaism to interpret Song of Songs as a figurative account of Yahweh's relationship with Israel. Successive chapters describe the love relationship between Yahweh and Israel, with its ups and downs, in the exodus period, at Sinai, in the wilderness, in the Promised Land, and so on. Christian interpretation from Origen onward similarly interpreted Song of Songs as a figurative account of Christ's love for the church or of God's love for the Virgin Mary or of Christ's love for the individual believer. Such understandings illustrate the process of interpreting a text in light of convictions that come from outside it.

Premodern reading of the passages in Job about a mediator, an advocate on high and a redeemer (Job 9:33-34; 16:18-20; 19:25-27) referred these passages to Christ. This came decisively to determine popular Christian understanding through the use of the last passage in Handel's *Messiah*. Like much NT reading of the OT, this made use of verbal points of connection that enabled the OT text to help people understand the significance of Christ, but it did not significantly open up the meaning of the OT itself. Indeed, there is a substantial gap between the inherent meaning of the passages and the significance of Christ (e.g., Job wants a mediator who will establish his innocence, not deal with his sin). The intuitive or occasional nature of such interpretation is reflected in the fact that Christian interpretation can also see Job himself as a type of Christ. He is supremely committed to God, profoundly tested by the will of both the Adversary and God, loudly crying out to God in his affliction, let down by his friends, required to sustain devastating suffering because of God's purpose, but finally restored.

Traditional Christian interpretation read the psalms as Christ's praise and prayers. This could take as its starting point the NT's use of some passages from the psalms to interpret the significance of Christ. This was facilitated by a process of reinterpretation of the psalms that had already taken place within Judaism. Some psalms refer explicitly to the king or the anointed one, and when Israel had no anointed king, these could be understood to refer to the king that Israel would surely again have one day, to a coming *Messiah. Given that the psalms in origin are not prophecies but rather declarations relating to Israel's actual kings, we might call the NT's adoption of this approach a typological understanding (Bateman).

We might also think in typological terms about the way Lamentations has been related to Christ's suffering. Lamentations is used in Holy Week in the service of Tenebrae ("Darkness"); Jerusalem's suffering, particularly as expressed in the protest of a male individual in Lamentations 3, can thus illumine Christ's suffering: "Is it nothing to you, all you who pass by?" (Lam 1:12).

The picture of God's wisdom in Proverbs embodied as a person standing alongside God (Prov 8:30) is not explicitly quoted in the NT, but its language and conceptuality underlie the way the NT speaks of Christ as God's Word and God's Wisdom, and it thus facilitates the NT's articulation of the idea that Christ could be divine and preexistent and yet also distinguishable from the Father. The relationship between the OT passage and the significance of Christ again involves overlap rather than identity, and when Christian interpretation sought to read Proverbs 8:22-31 as if it is actually about Christ, it found itself in trouble: reading the OT in Greek, the Arians could make better sense than could the Nicene fathers of the fact that the passage speaks of God's wisdom as being created by God.

11. Post-Holocaust Interpretation.

Christian and Jewish readings of Esther were decisively changed by the Holocaust. For Christians, the key interpretation is that of W. Vischer, who in the 1930s saw the need to read Esther in light of the Nazi persecution of the Jewish people. He attempted but failed to get the church to take seriously Esther's implications for the church's understanding of the Jewish people (and of itself), not least in light of Romans 9—11, and thus to commit itself to the Jewish people's defense. R. Bauckham revisited this reading of Esther when, decades later, Jews and Christians began to face the questions raised by the Holocaust. Among Jewish scholars, S. B. Berg (183-84) comments, "The rampant destruction of European Jewish communities in the recent past is similar to a threat described, but not fulfilled, in Esther. Haman's spiritual descendants proved more successful in attaining their goal of genocide. . . . One message of the Book of Esther, with its emphasis upon Jewish solidarity and human responsibility and action, remained unheard by Mordecai's and Esther's descendants." M. Fox similarly prefaces a study of Esther with an account of how the pogroms of a century ago as well as the Holocaust influence his reading of the book.

In related fashion, M. Kiszner comments that Lamentations comes "hauntingly alive" in light of the Holocaust. T. Linafelt suggests that one reason why Lamentations continues to haunt readers is that the book itself reaches no closure; it is full of protests to God that receive no response. Reading Lamentations in light of the Holocaust illustrates a difficulty that appears in connection with other approaches to interpretation. Either one assimilates Lamentations to the reading context and underplays the emphasis on the way it was Jerusalem's rebellions that led to its fall, or one assimilates Jewish suffering in the Holocaust and elsewhere and implies that it happened through the Jewish people's sins.

12. Postcolonial Interpretation.

The "wind of change" that a British prime minister recognized blowing through Africa in 1960 eventually issued not only in the political independence of former European colonies but also, in the 1990s, in the Two-Thirds World's quest for hermeneutical independence. As happened with feminist interpretation, this involved looking at the Scriptures with different eyes and seeing things that Eurocentric interpretation had not perceived, or seeing how Eurocentric interpretation had skewed things. Eurocentric interpretation thus has the man in Song of Songs addressing the woman as "fair," which rather presupposes that being "lovely" *(yapeh)* involves being white rather than black, while also (paradoxically) it has the woman declaring, "I am dark *but* beautiful." Is she suntanned or is she an African, and is it "but" or "and"? The psalms are illumined by awareness of African culture and traditions rather than simply the assumptions of Western scholarship and by awareness of the experience of exile (see Adamo; Isasi-Díaz [on Ps 137]; more generally, Patte). The traditional negative Christian interpretation of Esther might be seen in colonizing terms (Beal).

The period during which much of the material in these books grew or reached its final form was the time when Judah lived in a quasi-colonial relationship to the Babylonian and Persian Empires (Gottwald). Lamentations is then the hurt prayers of a people living under colo-

nial domination, while Esther is the story of the relationship to the empire of members of a colonized people who live in the imperial capital.

Postcolonial perspectives throw light on Ruth (and vice versa) in paradoxical fashion because of their implications in relation to both Ruth the Moabite and Naomi the Israelite, let alone Elimelech and their sons. Elimelech, Naomi and their sons are forced to become immigrants in a foreign country with which Israel often had a hostile relationship. Ruth in due course commits herself to Naomi in a way that involves her becoming an immigrant in a foreign country and unconsciously challenging its people about what attitude they will take to this foreigner. Or is this people, like a colonizing power, taking away her identity (McKinley)? Women of African descent in the United States or in Europe and black women in South Africa have a way in to appreciating her story and may read it either way, as is also the case with Esther (Dube).

See also EDITORIAL CRITICISM; FEMINIST INTERPRETATION; FORM CRITICISM; HISTORICAL CRITICISM; INTERTEXTUALITY; POETICS, TERMINOLOGY OF; RHETORICAL CRITICISM; SOCIAL-SCIENTIFIC APPROACHES; TEXT, TEXTUAL CRITICISM.

BIBLIOGRAPHY. **D. T. Adamo,** "The Use of the Psalms in African Indigenous Churches in Nigeria," in *The Bible in Africa: Transactions, Trajectories, and Trends,* ed. G. O. West and M. W. Dube (Leiden: E. J. Brill, 2001) 336-49; **A. Bach,** ed., *Women in the Hebrew Bible* (London: Routledge, 1999); **J. Barton,** *Oracles of God: Perceptions of Ancient Prophecy in Israel after the Exile* (London: Darton, Longman & Todd, 1986); **H. W. Bateman,** "Psalm 110:1 and the New Testament," *BSac* 149 (1992) 438-53; **R. Bauckham,** *The Bible in Politics* (London: SPCK; Louisville: Westminster John Knox, 1989); **T. K. Beal,** *The Book of Hiding: Gender, Ethnicity, Annihilation, and Esther* (London: Routledge, 2002); **S. B. Berg,** *The Book of Esther: Motif, Themes, and Structure* (SBLDS 44; Missoula, MT: Scholars Press, 1979); **A. Brenner,** ed., *A Feminist Companion to Ruth* (FCB 3; Sheffield: Sheffield Academic Press, 1993a); idem, ed., *A Feminist Companion to the Song of Songs* (FCB 1; Sheffield: Sheffield Academic Press, 1993b); idem, ed., *A Feminist Companion to Esther, Judith and Susanna* (FCB 7; Sheffield: Sheffield Academic Press, 1995a); idem, ed., *A Feminist Companion to Wisdom Literature* (FCB 9; Sheffield: Sheffield Academic

Press, 1995b); **W. Brueg-gemann,** *Israel's Praise: Doxology against Idolatry and Ideology* (Philadelphia: Fortress, 1988); **F. W. Bush,** *Ruth, Esther* (WBC; Dallas: Word, 1996); **C. V. Camp,** *Wisdom and the Feminine in the Book of Proverbs* (BLS 11; Decatur, GA: Almond, 1985); **B. S. Childs,** "Psalm Titles and Midrashic Exegesis," *JSS* 16 (1971) 137-50; idem, *Introduction to the Old Testament as Scripture* (London: SCM; Philadelphia: Fortress, 1979); **D. J. A. Clines,** *On the Way to the Postmodern: Old Testament Essays, 1968-1998* (2 vols.; JSOTSup 292, 293; Sheffield: Sheffield Academic Press, 1998); **P. W. Coxon,** "Was Naomi a Scold? A Response to Fewell and Gunn," *JSOT* 45 (1989) 25-37; **S. G. Dempster,** *Dominion and Dynasty: A Biblical Theology of the Hebrew Bible* (Downers Grove, IL: InterVarsity Press, 2003); **W. Dilthey,** *Selected Writings,* ed. and trans. H. P. Rickman (Cambridge: Cambridge University Press, 1976); idem, "The Understanding of Other Persons and Their Life-Expressions," in *The Hermeneutics Reader: Texts of the German Tradition from the Enlightenment to the Present,* ed. K. Mueller-Vollmer (New York: Crossroad, 1985) 152-64; **M. W. Dube,** ed., *Other Ways of Reading: African Women and the Bible* (Atlanta: Society of Biblical Literature, 2001); **D. N. Fewell and D. Gunn,** "A Son Is Born to Naomi," *JSOT* 40 (1988) 99-108; idem, "Is Coxon a Scold? On Responding to the Book of Ruth" *JSOT* 45 (1989) 39-43; **M. V. Fox,** *Character and Ideology in the Book of Esther* (2nd ed., Grand Rapids: Eerdmans, 2001); **H.-G. Gadamer,** *Truth and Method* (New York: Crossroad, 1982); **E. S. Gerstenberger,** *Psalms: Part 1, with an Introduction to Cultic Poetry* (FOTL 14; Grand Rapids: Eerdmans, 1988); idem, *Psalms: Part 2, and Lamentations* (FOTL 15; Grand Rapids: Eerdmans, 2001); **J. Goldingay,** *Models for Interpretation of Scripture* (repr., Toronto: Clements, 2004); **S. Goldman,** "Narrative and Ethical Ironies in Esther," *JSOT* 47 (1990) 15-31; **N. K. Gottwald,** *The Politics of Ancient Israel* (Louisville: Westminster John Knox, 2001); E. L. Greenstein, "Reading Strategies and the Story of Ruth," in *Women in the Hebrew Bible,* ed. A. Bach (London: Routledge, 1999) 211-31; **H. Gunkel,** *Introduction to Psalms: The Genres of the Religious Lyric of Israel,* completed by J. Begrich (MLBS; Macon, GA: Mercer University Press, 1998); idem, *The Psalms: A Form-Critical Introduction* (Philadelphia: Fortress, 1967); **W. J. Houston,** "The Role of the Poor in Proverbs," in *Reading from Right to Left: Essays on the Hebrew Bible in Honour of David J. A.*

Clines, ed. J. C. Exum and H. G. M. Williamson (JSOTSup 373; London: Sheffield Academic Press, 2003) 229-40; **D. A. Hubbard,** "The Wisdom Movement and Israel's Covenant Faith," *TynBul* 17 (1966) 3-33; **D. Jobling,** "Ruth Finds a Home," in *The New Literary Criticism and the Hebrew Bible,* ed. J. C. Exum and D. J. A. Clines (JSOTSup 143; Sheffield: Sheffield Academic Press, 1993) 125-39; **A. M. Isasi-Díaz,** "'By the Rivers of Babylon: Exile as a Way of Life," in *Reading from This Place,* 1: *Social Location and Biblical Interpretation in the United States,* ed. F. Segovia and M. Tolbert (Minneapolis: Fortress, 1995) 149-64; **M. Kiszner,** "Holocaust Lamentations," http://www.ais.com /jewishissues/jewishsociety/ Holocaust_Lamen tations.asp; **T. Linafelt,** *Surviving Lamentations: Catastrophe, Lament, and Protest in the Afterlife of a Biblical Book* (Chicago: University of Chicago Press, 2002); **J. McKinley,** "Reframing Her: Biblical Women," in *Postcolonial Focus* (BMW 1; Sheffield: Sheffield Phoenix Press, 2004); **J. Miles,** *God: A Biography* (New York: Simon & Schuster, 1995); **S. Mowinckel,** *The Psalms in Israel's Worship* (2 vols.; Oxford: Blackwell; Nashville: Abingdon, 1962); **H. P. Nasuti,** *Defining the Sacred Songs: Genre, Tradition, and the Post-critical Interpretation of the Psalms* (JSOTSup 218; Sheffield: Sheffield Academic Press, 1999); **K. Nielsen,** *Ruth* (OTL; Louisville: Westminster John Knox, 1997); **D. Patte,** ed., *Global Bible Commentary* (Nashville: Abingdon, 2004); **M. V. Rienstra,** *Swallow's Nest: A Feminine Reading of the Psalms* (Grand Rapids: Eerdmans, 1992); **F. D. E. Schleiermacher,** *Hermeneutics: The Handwritten Manuscripts,* ed. H. Kimmerle (SBLTT 1; Missoula, MT: Scholars Press, 1977); **F. Segovia and M. Tolbert,** eds., *Reading from This Place* (2 vols.; Minneapolis: Fortress, 1995); **M. Sneed,** "The Social Location of the Book of Qoheleth," *HS* 39 (1998) 38-51; **B. L. Tanner,** *The Book of Psalms through the Lens of Intertextuality* (SBL 26; New York: Lang, 2001); **A. C. Thiselton,** *New Horizons in Hermeneutics* (Grand Rapids: Zondervan, 1992); **P. Trible,** *God and the Rhetoric of Sexuality* (Philadelphia: Fortress, 1978); **W. Vischer,** "The Book of Esther," *EvQ* 11 (1939) 3-21; **H. W. Wolff,** *The Old Testament: A Guide to Its Writings* (Philadelphia: Fortress, 1973).

J. Goldingay

HISTORICAL CRITICISM

It is a somewhat difficult task to categorize *Psalms, *Job, *Proverbs, *Ecclesiastes, *Song of Songs, *Esther, *Ruth and *Lamentations together when dealing with historical criticism. In a sense, these books consist of material that is by and large outside the main "fireworks" of biblical criticism, which relates to the Pentateuch and the Historical Books, not to mention the prophetic literature. And yet, a number of interesting questions pertain to this material in this respect. For the purposes of the following discussion, first we will make some general observations about Psalms and the Wisdom literature, as they constitute the bulk of the material in question. After that, we will look at Psalms separately and then at the Wisdom literature, consisting of Job, Proverbs and Ecclesiastes. We will conclude by looking at some issues in relation to Song of Songs, Esther, Ruth and Lamentations, which are fairly disparate from the standpoint of historical criticism, even if Esther and Ruth have overall similarities of genre.

    1. Psalms and the Wisdom Literature
    2. Song of Songs, Esther, Ruth, Lamentations
    3. Conclusion

1. Psalms and the Wisdom Literature.
With Psalms and the Wisdom literature, we are, in a sense, dealing with quite a different set of questions than those associated especially with the Pentateuch and the Historical books and even the prophetic literature. Yet, in another sense, the underlying methods are similar to those applied to the Pentateuch and the Historical Books and the rest of the OT. The Wisdom literature is in many ways timeless, and except for the most conservative readers in the case of Job and Ecclesiastes and perhaps Proverbs, the problem of historical veracity is not a major issue in interpretation. As for Psalms, once the introductory issue of the superscriptions that relate to Davidic (or, for a smaller number of psalms, Mosaic or Asaphite) authorship has been cleared (*see* Psalms 5: Titles), again we can say that we are dealing with material that rather expresses the thoughts and emotions of the writer, not history writing. Even the historical Psalms 78; 105; 106 should be seen more as liturgical reiterations of salvation history than as historiography proper (see Tate, 284; Allen, 40-42, 49-53). In addition, recent advances in text- and reader-centered approaches for reading the OT texts have in themselves lessened interest in historical questions for many (see Longman 1989).

    At the same time, while the focus is on didac-

tic wisdom and on expression of emotion, and granting validity for many nonhistorical approaches to reading, the material does contain references to history. Also, in general, the distinction between history and ideology (or vice versa) is never clear-cut. Thus, while the focus of the historical Psalms 78; 105; 106, and any other psalms that contain historical referents, is not directly on the historical but rather on the didactical and liturgical, it should also be kept in mind that the Historical Books can be seen to have didactical purposes. For example, the book of Joshua can be seen to have been written to exhort the Israelites to remember the great deeds of Yahweh and thereby follow him, and the book of Kings to show the sin of Israel and thus instruct readers to learn from past mistakes. In other words, the difference between the historical psalms and the Historical Books is one of degree and focus rather than of type. Here we can then say that differences, though they exist, are fluid, and certain parts and features of Psalms and the Wisdom literature approach and share with those of the Historical Books. This fluidity between genres can also be extended further. For example, when one says that the prophets were spokespersons of Yahweh, it is impossible to say that none of the prophetic material includes wisdom elements, and, conversely, if wisdom is about knowing Yahweh and following him, such proclamation can easily move toward prophetic elements. In any case, some of the prophetic books and other books of the OT contain wisdom sayings or proverbs that are directly attributable as such (see, e.g., Jer 31:29, and the proverb in 1 Kings 20:11 set within a historical book).

    Having said this and keeping in mind the fluidity between the genres and characteristics of the OT literature, we can move on to some specific features of historical criticism that pertain to Psalms and the Wisdom literature in particular. The history of the criticism until the mid-1970s is well summarized by R. E. Clements. There is sufficient scope to see Psalms and Wisdom literature separately here, and this is what Clements has done and what we will do. We should also note that we restrict our concerns to the canonical OT literature. For example, the late extracanonical works, such as *Wisdom of Solomon* and *Sirach*, could also be drawn in for the considerations of Wisdom literature, as is often done (so, e.g., Murphy 2002; Clifford). If one were to move even a bit further, but without going as far as the NT, wisdom also features in the intertestamental literature (see, e.g., Bennema) and the Qumran documents (see, e.g., Jefferies). However, many of the issues stated here probably can be more or less extended by analogy to the later works, although to do so perhaps would run the risk of making a great oversimplification.

1.1. Psalms. An elementary comment to start with regarding Psalms is that in the precritical time the Psalm titles were seen to refer to authorship. However, it can quickly be pointed out that the Hebrew in the superscription contains the preposition *lě,* which can be translated in a number of different ways and can mean, for example, "dedicated to" instead of "by." Thus, a title such as *těpillâ lěmōšeh ʾîš-hāʾělōhîm* in Psalm 90 could simply mean "A Hymn Dedicated to Moses, Man of God." It has also been pointed out that the titles are likely to have been added to the psalms only later, even though it is not certain when this took place (for further discussion, see Craigie, 31-35).

Here, then, we of course would ask the question of when the psalms themselves were composed. From the titles, except perhaps for Psalm 90, it is clear that by attribution they belong to the time of David and later. As criticism started to exert itself on the materials, estimates varied from the period of the first temple to Maccabean times (see Clements, 77). Typically, clues would be sought from the relation of the references in each psalm to what was known about Israel's history otherwise in order to establish the time when the psalm was composed. Here, of course, the understanding of the history of Israel was based on Wellhausenian (see Wellhausen) reconstruction of that history, founded on the JEDP hypothesis, where J and E were early monarchic, D was Josianic, and P was exilic and postexilic, and on Wellhausen's theory that Israel's *worship developed from simple as attested by JE, to complex as attested by P, with a midpoint as attested by D. Each psalm could be plotted along this continuum, of course incorporating any other information that was known about this history within such a framework. It is worth mentioning here that, though challenged recently, the Wellhausenian framework is still by and large influencing the manner in which the historical background for the psalms is being sought.

In many ways, a decisive development in Psalm studies was brought by H. Gunkel in the beginning of the twentieth century. Gunkel classified the material in the psalms into various forms (*Gattungen*), such as the *hymn, the community *laments, individual laments, songs of *thanksgiving and royal psalms (for a summary, see Clements, 80-81). Looking at the psalms and, for that matter, biblical literature itself based on a classification of such forms or genres is a practice that has been developed further by later scholars and has proved very useful (*see* Form Criticism). At its best, such analysis alerts readers to the question of what kind of literature one is dealing with and thus facilitates better understanding of the biblical texts. As for the psalms, once Gunkel had suggested the differing forms, the next question would naturally be what kind of occasion would have produced the differing psalms that attested such forms, and how and in what occasions the psalms would have been used afterwards.

From here, the focus of attention shifted to the idea that the psalms provided clues that at least some of them were used in the Israelite cult (*see* Cult, Worship: Psalms). In this the work of S. Mowinckel was revolutionary for OT scholarship (for a summary, see Clements, 83-86). For Mowinckel, the psalms were used in Israel's worship, even the individual laments. Then, of course, it would be necessary to think about the exact cultic setting of each psalm. This would then lead into a reconstruction of the cult from the clues provided in the psalms. Here, insights from the already developed discipline of Assyriology also were drawn in. It was surmised that Israel had an equivalent of the Akitu (New Year's) festival, which is well attested in the cuneiform literature from Assyria and Babylonia (for a recent treatment of the festival, see Bidmead). Mowinckel reconstructed an autumnal New Year's festival in Israel based on the Assyro-Babylonian parallels and on evidence in the biblical material that would support a corresponding festival in Israel. Much work was done subsequently on this topic, and even though later scholarship eventually became more cautious about the existence of such a festival in Israel, the matter illustrates how historical reconstruction was and can be done from the psalms. Although there has been scepticism about the exact details, the approach of interpreting the psalms from the standpoint of the cult continues, and rightly so in my view.

On a related note, since the discovery and decipherment of the Late Bronze Age cuneiform alphabetic tablets from Ras Shamra (Ugarit) in the Syrian coast in the mid-twentieth century, scholarship has, after noticing a number of similarities with Ugaritic and Israelite poetry in both form and content, rightly taken this material into account for understanding the Israelite religious outlook (for a summary, see Craigie, 48-56; more generally, see Smith). To this may be added any insights that archaeological finds from the ancient Levant and any other parallels from adjacent cultures of the ancient Near East might be able to offer about Israelite religion. The main concern, as with any historical study, is to use all available material, Israelite and beyond, responsibly in order to reconstruct possible settings for the psalms. When evaluating various possibilities, we must keep in mind that only the logical consistency of the reconstructions can be tested, as we cannot travel to the past to observe. Also, there is no guarantee that only one logically consistent reconstruction is possible (see Pitkänen); and, as for the evidence, no archaeological remains of the first temple have even been found to help make a correlation between the psalms and that temple. In other words, it is likely that no single approach and viewpoint will be sufficient, and we should instead expect a variety of them.

In many ways, Gunkel and Mowinckel stand above others for modern studies of Psalms, as these two scholars have laid the foundations for later study. After them, and in addition to what has been mentioned above, two new related developments in the study of psalms should be noted. First, recently much emphasis has been placed on the development of the Psalter as a collection (see Nogalski, in Ballard and Tucker, 37-54). Again, the primary historical question here has been how and when the psalms started to be grouped together, and how and when such groupings started to form larger collections, then books, and finally the whole Psalter. Numerous theories have been presented, but none has captured the agreement of all scholars. Perhaps the problem is unsolvable. Second, and relating to the formation of the collection, is the matter of how the Psalter itself functions as a single entity, and beyond that, as part of the larger *canon. In this, issues such as develop-

ing themes, link words and so forth are studied across the whole of the Psalter and even beyond (see deClaissé-Walford, in Ballard and Tucker, 93-110). This recent development of focusing on the final form of the text and its interconnectedness was boosted especially by the canonical approach started by B. Childs in the 1970s. It should be noted that even though canonical approaches concentrate on the final form of the texts as part of the canon, they do not necessarily ignore historical criticism as such. A canonical approach can bring helpful insights for interpreting the psalms, and in this area the work of scholars such as J. C. McCann and J. A. Sanders should also be highlighted.

1.2. Wisdom Literature. The first issue here is the question of authorship. As we noted above, the attributions of books, where any exist, generally are not regarded by modern interpreters as indications of authorship. Typically, the book of Job is dated to the latter part of the monarchical period or thereafter (see Hartley, 18), even if the description of Job, the main character, hints toward the patriarchal time as the literary setting of the events. In general, the book is taken as more of a story, even a play (for a summary, see Hartley, 37-38; on Job as drama, see Shelton). As for Ecclesiastes, though the book at first sight seems to refer to *Solomon, even if he is not directly named (see, e.g., Eccles 1:1, 12, 16), most, including the majority of conservative scholars, see the description as an imaginary narrative construction (see Longman 1998, 2-8). With Proverbs, the book itself indicates that it is a collection (cf. Prov 1:1; 10:1; 25:1; 30:1), and the title "The Proverbs of Solomon, Son of David, King of Israel" can simply be seen as ascribing ownership and ultimate derivation of the concept of wisdom in the monarchical period and beyond to Solomon, the king famous for his wisdom. Also, in any case, as we will note below, wisdom existed in the ancient Near East from much earlier times, with documents available from Sumer and Egypt from the late third and the second millennia BC (see *COS*). In any case, wisdom seems to be a universal phenomenon and probably as old as humankind, so Solomon would be a transmitter and promoter of wisdom in addition to perhaps producing some of his own material. Otherwise, even if the attributions do not reflect actual authorship, the dating of the wisdom materials as such is an important concern as part of trying to make sense of the message of each composition or any parts thereof.

Having made these preliminary comments about authorship, we note with Clements (100) that early historical critics, including Wellhausen, paid less attention to Wisdom literature because it did not impinge on the JEDP hypothesis and the accompanying issues. This probably is due to the fact that, granted the genre interlinkages described above, Wisdom literature is characterized by a kind of otherness and timelessness in comparison to the rest of the OT documents. However, in the spirit of the evolutionary nature of the theories of Israel's historical development by the then-contemporary scholarship, it was soon suggested that wisdom was a late phenomenon in Israel (see Clements, 100-101). Against this general backdrop, two important developments can be traced at the beginning of the twentieth century to Gunkel. Gunkel suggested a particular class of men who were associated with wisdom and its promotion. Also, Gunkel recognized the international character of wisdom, and others after him developed parallels from Egypt and Babylon (see Clements, 101-2; for an overview of ancient Near Eastern parallels, see Clifford, 23-41; Smothers, in Ballard and Tucker, 167-80). These two important issues of wisdom schools (*see* Sages, Schools, Education) and the international character of wisdom have continued to the present day (cf. Crenshaw, in Ballard and Tucker, 215-27), and although the idea of evolutionary development has recently been challenged many times over, its legacy of tending to see material as late still hangs over OT scholarship and thus the study of Wisdom literature as well. (This, of course, does not deny that a good amount of material in the OT is late whatever the case. Also, Gunkel did argue that the Wisdom literature had an earlier oral stage [see Clements, 101-2].) As one might guess, in general terms, with lateness may come Greek parallels to the literature (see Clements, 108) and, where possible, Persian ones, even though comparisons with Persian settings are complicated by a relative dearth of contemporary Persian material (see Crenshaw, in Ballard and Tucker, 226). Aramaic features in any of the literature are also generally seen as indications of lateness, even though it is also true that there are references

to the Arameans in Assyrian documents from the late second millennium onward (see *ABD* 1.345-46), and in general there was a lot of cultural interaction in the ancient Near East from very early times, attested by linguistic features such as loanwords (e.g., foreign loanwords in Egyptian in the second millennium).

Once the possible existence of wisdom schools was established, one could start asking questions of how they came into being, what was their remit, how did they relate to the court and to society as a whole, how they developed through the centuries, and so on. These questions have been addressed over the past century; however, no consensus has formed on the answers (see Crenshaw, in Ballard and Tucker, 215-27). Some even deny the existence of such schools, or at least point out that there is no direct evidence in the OT itself, even if the scribal schools in, say, ancient Sumer are well known and used as an analogy to deduce that a similar situation may have existed in Israel (see Whybray, in Dell and Barker, 12-15). But here we may also note that folk wisdom exists everywhere, so a lot of the material may have or even likely originated in this way, in whatever manner it may then have been collected to form the wisdom books now in the canon. The way that Proverbs and, for that matter, any other book within the corpus of the Wisdom literature took shape is an issue on which much ink has been and likely will be spilled (see Murphy 1998). Especially, if there are any stylistic differences or other apparent features attesting unevenness, inconsistencies or separateness of thought, one could attempt to isolate material attesting such features into separate sources and then try to determine a separate setting for each source and trace how these were collected together and edited, in line with an approach more familiar in the context of pentateuchal criticism. At the same time, one could take a different literary approach and explain at least some features in the text that could be taken to indicate sources as having some other reason for their formation that maintains the unity of the text. Or, one could take a canonical approach, perhaps broadly along the lines of the movement initiated by Childs, and, just as with such a canonical approach in relation to Psalms or any other OT literature, look at Wisdom literature as it stands in its final form in the canon even if it was a result of an amalgamation of sources. Be that as it may, it makes sense that, for example, just as with modern sayings such as "Let sleeping dogs lie" and "Don't count your chickens before they hatch," it is likely that proverbs in ancient Israel were floating around on their own and could be brought together only by collecting and presenting them in a single document.

As was hinted above, any consideration of historical settings naturally has a diachronic aspect. As Israel's history moved on, so did its institutions and social structures, whether or not one takes a general Wellhausenian view of development from simple to complex. In this context, and whatever one's view of the general dating of Wisdom literature, one may immediately inquire as to what extent each part of the historical literature represents a particular historical time and setting. In particular, in view of the quite different outlooks of Job, Proverbs and Ecclesiastes, perhaps such differences are not due simply to authorial idiosyncrasies but rather could be anchored further into a *Zeitgeist* of their time. Thus, for example, one might think that it is possible to make historical conclusions based on the fact that Proverbs seems to be fairly optimistic in its outlook whereas Job is questioning and Ecclesiastes rather pessimistic. (This assumes that one can give a crude categorization of the characteristics of these books, an issue that of course has been discussed and debated extensively in academic literature in relation to each book.) And, it is probably fair to say, that it is often thought that as such, Job and Ecclesiastes present correctives to the positive and, in the eyes of many, sometimes even simplistic outlook of Proverbs (see Murphy 2002, 34, 55). However, even if one could independently establish a firm relative dating based on, say, linguistic grounds—for example, the language of Ecclesiastes is often seen to attest late features (see Longman 1998, 11-15)—one may still come back to the question of whether the differences in outlook nevertheless result from differences in the outlooks of the authors as individuals and from a general diversity in Israelite wisdom tradition.

In any case, any reconstruction of Israelite society and its possible historical developments in relation to Wisdom literature proceeds in two directions. On the one hand, one may try to reconstruct any such structures based on the material of the Wisdom literature itself. On the other hand, one may postulate certain structures

based on other Israelite literature and on what is known from archaeology and known similar practices in the ancient Near East, and then see how the Israelite Wisdom literature fits into the picture. In practice, both approaches interact with each other, utilizing insights from each other and at the same time trying to see how any possible discrepancies might be resolved. The overall process is complex and proceeds based on the work of individual scholars and their scholarly communities. The accumulation of knowledge and reconstructions in this academic field, as with OT studies in general, is not always a linear process and can even take some sidetracks and diverse views that may not always be seen as progress in light of later reflection. In general, however, it is probably fair to say that academic study has made some significant achievements in accumulating relevant knowledge and insights over the last two centuries or so of modern study as regards the historical setting and background of the Wisdom literature and, for that matter, other ancient Israelite literature (for two classic sociological analyses of how progress is made in sciences, see Kuhn, Feyerabend).

2. Song of Songs, Esther, Ruth, Lamentations.

These books are, in a sense, "the rest of it" from a canonical perspective and are somewhat hard to look at together from the standpoint of historical criticism. At the same time, it is hard to do justice to them individually in the space of a short article such as this. Therefore, I will mainly draw out some general themes and apply them to these books. The literary setting of Ruth is explicitly premonarchic, Lamentations is clearly about the destruction of Jerusalem and the Babylonian exile, and Esther is about events in the Persian period. As for Song of Songs, the superscription indicates that it is a "song of songs" to Solomon. Here the superscriptive *lĕ* is the same as that for a number of psalms, and therefore, even from the perspective of a straightforward reading of the Hebrew, it may simply be a dedication and need not be taken as a sign of authorship. At the same time, the song makes reference to a king, which would suggest the monarchy as a setting, even though one might plausibly conclude that such references could be created even after the exile when the monarchy ceased to exist.

From the perspective of genre, both Ruth and Esther may perhaps be characterized generally as a kind of historical *novella (see Hubbard, 47; Berlin 2001, xvii). It would probably be correct to say that their genre is, broadly speaking, similar to the Pentateuch and the Historical Books proper. Thus, they can basically be looked into just as any other historical material. However, Ruth and Esther are much shorter than the main Historical Books and do not describe anything on which the main contours of Israel's history hinges. Esther relates the background to the Jewish feast of *Purim, and Ruth narrates the story about the ancestress of David. The information in the books is useful and helpful, but arguably it could be left out without causing any major problems for understanding the history of Israel or the main features of its life. As one might guess, every detail in Ruth and Esther has been subjected to critical scrutiny as regards their historical accuracy, with varying opinions about the matter, even though most would not see more than a historical nucleus in Esther (for some of the issues and problems on Esther, see Levenson, 23-27; for some positive appropriation about the book's historicity, see Baldwin, 16-24). Song of Songs is clearly poetry and can be compared with other Hebrew poetry—for example, the psalms (see Longman 2001, 19, 89, 91). Little direct historical information can probably be gained from Song of Songs, save any general Israelite thinking or customs that it might reflect (see Longman 2001, 19). Lamentations is also poetry, and its specific genre has parallels with lamentations from the ancient Near East, most notably ancient Sumer (see Berlin 2002, 26-30). As such, there is a timeless character to it, even though it clearly expresses the feelings of the poet in the face of an unimaginably terrible catastrophe for him—the conquest of Jerusalem by the Babylonians and its aftermath.

As with any book in the OT, the date of writing has been a topic of discussion for Song of Songs, Esther, Ruth and Lamentations. Apart from the usual questions about sources, redaction and distance of sources, redaction and final form from the events that the books portray, the book of Ruth perhaps could be said to have some distinctiveness in the discussion that relates to it. Here the issue is that although the events portrayed date to the premonarchical period, many commentators would like to date the

book to the postexilic period (see Hubbard, 24-26; for a positive appropriation and a date in the early monarchic period, see Campbell); in any case, the book is often seen to have been written, as R. L. Hubbard (37) summarizes it, to "promote the interests of David and his dynasty." Also, Lamentations perhaps could be equated with the prophetic books in some respect from the perspective of dating, with an idea, as with the prophets, of the possibility or likelihood of an initial version of the book with subsequent redaction to add concerns of a later author or community (see Renkema, 52-53), even though most scholars today see the book essentially as a work that follows closely after the events described (see Miller, 11-12). Esther is, in any case, late and is thus unlikely to capture any controversy even for the most conservative readers as regards the date of its writing. All this said, dating considerations are not always as important as might seem at first, as any early material purporting to be historical might nevertheless not be all that reliable, and any later material might be a result of sources transmitted reliably over a long period of time, as is demonstrated by parallels elsewhere in the ancient Near East (e.g., transmission of Sumerian laments from the early second millennium to late first millennium BC [see Hallo, 224-28]).

3. Conclusion.

After a tour of this diverse collection, we may perhaps say, among other things, that it has illustrated a variegated set of methods and approaches that relate to historical criticism of these literary documents. Perhaps the most prominent that we could list are source, form and redaction criticism, comparison of texts, ancient Near Eastern parallels, linguistic features, and possible societal and cultic settings and structures. On balance, many of these, such as source and redaction criticism, are methods that have been most prominently applied to the Pentateuch and the Historical Books, and some, such as reconstructing wisdom schools and cultic settings of the psalms, are fairly specific to their respective corpus. As regards future research, it is hard to foresee at the moment the probability and extent of any major changes in how the historical issues are approached, but undoubtedly some new perspectives will be brought forward.

See also EDITORIAL CRITICISM; FORM CRITI-

CISM; RHETORICAL CRITICISM; SOCIAL-SCIENTIFIC APPROACHES; SOLOMON; WISDOM AND HISTORY.

BIBLIOGRAPHY. **L. C. Allen,** *Psalms 101-150* (WBC 21; Waco, TX: Word, 1983); **J. Baldwin,** *Esther* (TOTC; Leicester: Inter-Varsity Press, 1984); **H. W. Ballard Jr., and W. D. Tucker Jr.,** eds., *An Introduction to Wisdom Literature and the Psalms: Festschrift Marvin E. Tate* (Macon, GA: Mercer University Press, 2000); **C. Bennema,** "The Strands of Wisdom Tradition in Intertestamental Judaism: Origins, Developments and Characteristics," *TynBul* 52 (2001) 61-82; **A. Berlin,** *Esther* (JPSBC; Philadelphia: Jewish Publication Society, 2001); idem, *Lamentations* (OTL; Louisville: Westminster John Knox, 2002); **J. Bidmead,** *The Akitu Festival: Religious Continuity and Royal Legitimation in Mesopotamia* (GD 2; Piscataway, NJ: Gorgias Press, 2002); **E. F. Campbell Jr.,** *Ruth* (AB 7; New York: Doubleday, 1975); **B. Childs,** *Introduction to the Old Testament as Scripture* (London: SCM, 1979); **R. E. Clements,** *One Hundred Years of Old Testament Interpretation* (Philadelphia: Westminster, 1976); **R. J. Clifford,** *The Wisdom Literature* (Nashville: Abingdon, 1998); **P. C. Craigie,** *Psalms 1-50* (WBC 19; Waco, TX: Word, 1983); **K. J. Dell and M. Barker,** eds., *Wisdom: The Collected Articles of Norman Whybray* (Aldershot: Ashgate, 2005); **P. K. Feyerabend,** *Against Method* (3rd ed.; London and New York: Verso, 1993); **H. Gunkel,** *Einleitung in die Psalmen: Die Gattungen der religiösen Lyrik Israels,* completed by J. Begrich (4th ed.; HKAT; Göttingen: Vandenhoeck & Ruprecht, 1985 [1928-1933]); ET, *Introduction to Psalms: The Genres of the Religious Lyric of Israel,* completed by J. Begrich (Macon, GA: Mercer University Press, 1998); **W. W. Hallo,** *Origins: The Ancient Near Eastern Background of Some Modern Western Institutions* (SHCANE 6; Leiden: E. J. Brill, 1996); **J. Hartley,** *The Book of Job* (NICOT; Grand Rapids: Eerdmans, 1988); **R. L. Hubbard Jr.,** *The Book of Ruth* (NICOT; Grand Rapids: Eerdmans, 1988); **D. F. Jefferies,** *Wisdom at Qumran: A Form-Critical Analysis of the Admonitions in 4Q Instruction* (GD 3; Piscataway, NJ: Gorgias Press, 2002); **T. S. Kuhn,** *The Structure of Scientific Revolutions* (Chicago: University of Chicago Press, 1962); **J. D. Levenson,** *Esther* (OTL; London: SCM, 1997); **T. Longman III,** *Literary Approaches to Biblical Interpretation* (Leicester: Apollos, 1989); idem, *The Book of Ecclesiastes* (NICOT; Grand Rapids: Eerdmans, 1998); idem, *Song of Songs* (NICOT; Grand Rapids: Eerdmans, 2001); **J. C. McCann,** *A Theological Introduction to the Book of Psalms: The Psalms as Torah* (Nashville: Abingdon, 1993); **C. W. Miller,** "The Book of Lamentations in Recent Research," *CBR* 1 (2002) 9-29; **S. Mowinckel,** *The Psalms in Israel's Worship* (Grand Rapids: Eerdmans, 2004 [1962]); original, *Psalmenstudien* (6 vols.; Kristiania: J. Dybwad, 1921-1924); **R. E. Murphy,** *Proverbs* (WBC 22; Nashville: Thomas Nelson, 1998); idem, *The Tree of Life: An Exploration of Biblical Wisdom Literature* (3rd ed.; Grand Rapids: Eerdmans, 2002); **P. Pitkänen,** *Central Sanctuary and Centralization of Worship in Ancient Israel: From the Settlement to the Building of Solomon's Temple* (2nd ed.; GD 4; Piscataway, NJ: Gorgias Press, 2004); **J. Renkema,** *Lamentations* (HCOT; Leuven: Peeters, 1998); **J. A. Sanders,** *From Sacred Story to Sacred Text: Canon as Paradigm* (Philadelphia: Fortress, 1987); **P. Shelton,** "Making a Drama Out of a Crisis? A Consideration of the Book of Job as a Drama," *JSOT* 83 (1999) 69-82; **M. S. Smith,** *Untold Stories: The Bible and Ugaritic Studies in the Twentieth Century* (Peabody, MA: Hendrickson, 2001); **M. E. Tate,** *Psalms 51-100* (WBC 20; Dallas: Word, 1990); **J. Wellhausen,** *Prolegomena zur Geschichte Israel* (6th ed.; Berlin: Reimer, 1905 [1878]); ET, *Prolegomena to the History of Israel* (Edinburgh: A & C Black, 1885). P. Pitkänen

HISTORICAL ALLUSIONS. *See* WISDOM AND HISTORY.

HISTORY. *See* HISTORICAL CRITICISM; WISDOM AND HISTORY.

HONOR AND SHAME

Honor refers to the experience of being esteemed by one's group or other social entities on the basis of embodying that which is deemed desirable, virtuous and socially productive. Shame refers, generally, to the opposite experience of being devalued and belittled on the basis of failing to measure up to or transgressing the same. Concern for one's honor, and for the honor of one's nation, is well attested in the wisdom and poetic texts of the OT and is evidenced in a variety of ways. Individual characters engage in the push and pull of challenges and counterchallenges, trying to gain precedence over one another. The desirability of honor and the undesirability of social disapproval are assumed as a "given" in ethical advice and liturgical petition. Several texts elevate especially the importance of honoring God through observance of the covenant stipulations. *Women risk their reputation to secure an appropriate husband, and they strain against the socially imposed constraints on their expressions of sexual desire. Of special interest is the way in which several of these texts are critical, or at least cautious, about the relative value of the quest for honor and the propriety of several of the means by which honor is attained and protected, and the ways in which the texts challenge stereotypes of the "honor-sensitive Mediterranean person," especially in regard to the behavior of honorable women.

1. Honor, Shame and the Social
   Reinforcement of Group Values
2. Psalms and Lamentations
3. Proverbs and Ecclesiastes
4. Honor Challenges in Esther and Job
5. Song of Songs, Ruth and the Honorable
   Woman
6. Conclusion

1. Honor, Shame and the Social Reinforcement of Group Values.

The interest in honor and shame throughout the OT is amply attested by the incidence of vocabulary pertinent to this realm of human experience (Bechtel, 54-55; Domeris, 94-96; Laniak, 17-23) and corresponds to the widespread acknowledgment of honor and shame as important values in traditional cultures, especially those found around the Mediterranean basin. In these cultures a sense of "belonging" to and being valued by the group is an important component of a stable identity. Individuals are socialized from birth to be concerned about the opinion of significant others (Bechtel, 55). As a result, "the group is capable of exerting great pressure on people, in order to control their behavior" (Bechtel, 51). Honor comes from the affirmation of one's worth by one's peers and society, awarded on the basis of the individual's ability to embody the virtues and attributes that his or her society values. Some of these attributes are ascribed by virtue of one's birth; others are attained as one pursues behaviors and embodies values esteemed by the group (Malina and Neyrey, 28-29). The particular behaviors that are deemed honorable or censurable are specific to each social group, but honor remains an abiding concern. Where a person fails to embody the virtues that are deemed appropriate for

him or her to embody, the group responds by shaming the individual or subgroup, withdrawing acceptance and esteem as a means of pressuring the individual to return to the behaviors valued by the group and as a disincentive to others against following the example of deviants.

This model has been sufficiently rehearsed in greater detail elsewhere, as have substantial criticisms and emendations cautioning against, for example, the imposition of an essentially modern anthropological construction grounded in observation of particular contemporary Mediterranean groups upon the data of ancient texts stemming from other groups and another time (Bechtel; deSilva 1995; 2000a; 2000b; 2002; Domeris; Laniak, 26-32; Malina and Neyrey) (*see* DOTHB, Honor and Shame). Rather than rehearse that material, in this article I will attempt to display what particular texts have to say about the ways in which honor and shame represent concerns of the society represented by the author (and/or characters, in narratives) and how discourse about honor and disgrace functions rhetorically in these texts.

2. Psalms and Lamentations.

The psalms, in many ways the pulse of the prayer and *worship life of ancient Israel, early Judaism and the early church, throb with expressions evidencing concern for the preservation of honor (whether God's, the individual's or the nation's) and the averting of disgrace. Many of the psalms also serve a didactic function, holding up paradigms of honorable behaviors, orientations and commitments for the emulation of those who recite or hear these texts. *Lamentations provides an extended poetical reflection on the experience of national disgrace. Its use of the language of honor and shame is thus very closely related to the use of the same in individual and national laments responding to the experience of contempt or degradation in some form and calling for vindication.

2.1. Psalms. The book of *Psalms is especially rich in the language and conceptual framework of honor and shame. The didactic function of many psalms has often been noted. When this function is combined with the public recitation of the same psalms, we find these texts functioning very much as specimens of epideictic oratory, celebrating honorable patterns of life and behavior, holding these esteemed patterns up before the collective community to be internalized. In Psalm 1 it is the person who walks in line with the Torah, rather than joining with those who think lightly of covenant faithfulness, who is held up as *ʾašrê*, "blessed" or "favored" (Ps 1:1-3), occupying the position that we all would wish for ourselves (on the function of macarisms—statements identifying those who are blessed—in an honor culture, see Hanson). Similarly, Psalm 15 outlines a variety of behaviors that lead to the privilege of being graced with a place in God's tent (Ps 15:1), creating a paradigm that is thus commended to the hearers as worthy of imitation. Interestingly, this involves not only the performance of virtuous behaviors, such as truthful speech, just dealing and fair lending, but also the avoidance of behaviors such as slandering or reproaching one's neighbor. It also entails honoring those who walk in line with the Torah (who "fear the Lord") and despising those who forsake the *law (Ps 15:4), thus being a reliable part of the social mechanism for reinforcing group values (see also Ps 19:7-11; 24:3-5; 32:1-2; 101; 112; 119:1-8; 133).

The psalms also bear abundant witness to an individual's or nation's experience of being shamed and praying for reversal, and thus indirectly to the fact that the avoidance of disgrace and the safeguarding of honor are noteworthy concerns of the communities that produced and used these texts. The psalmists affirm that righteous conduct (walking in line with the covenant) should lead to the secure enjoyment of honor and the other goods of life (Ps 34:5, 8-9; 37:18-19; 127:5). The psalmists pray that they will not be put to shame by their enemies, a request often coupled with the claim that they are counting on God to help them (Ps 25:2; see also Ps 25:20; 31:17; 38:16). Disgrace is deemed inappropriate for "those who wait for" or "trust in" God; rather, it is for those who break faith with the covenant and with their neighbors in the covenant (Ps 25:3), who often pervert the social reinforcement of covenant loyalty by seeking to shame the Torah-observant instead of honoring them (Ps 31:17b-18 [see Bechtel, 71]). It is also appropriate for those who worship idols rather than making the God of Israel their confidence (Ps 97:7).

Experience, however, often runs counter to the expectations of one's moral universe. Despite their innocence, the psalmists encounter taunts from their enemies, including wagging of the head, sneering and verbal abuse (Bechtel [72] lists these as "informal shaming sanctions"), the latter often targeting the psalmists' confidence in God (Ps 22:6-8; 35:15-16; 41:5; 42:10; 69:10-12, 19-20). Whether the psalmists profess uprightness of conduct (Ps 7:5) or pray for God's forgiveness so that they may not fall into disgrace and become "the scorn of the fool" (Ps 39:8), their commitment to continue steadfast in the observance of Torah and in the conviction that God will secure the honor of those who are loyal to God's covenant remains the basis for their prayer and confidence (Ps 119:31, 51, 80).

The same confidence undergirds the psalmists' prayers for dramatic reversal, asking that disgrace and shame befall their enemies (Ps 6:10; 35:4, 26; 40:14-15; 70:2-3; 71:13, 24; 109:29), who are also among the scoffers who do not keep covenant, and that they be put in their proper place below the righteous petitioner (Ps 27:6; 71:21, 24). Indeed, the shaming of the one seems to correspond to the vindication or ascendancy of the other, supporting the view of honor as a "limited good" in the ancient social economy (Laniak, 170-71). Rather than seek to save face through "countershaming" their enemies personally, however, they commit their cause to God (Bechtel, 71). The enemies' shame is complete when God obliterates even the remembrance of their "name" (Ps 9:5-6; 109:13, 15).

This scenario plays out at the national level as well. On the one hand, the tradition leads the psalmists to expect that Israel, or the Davidic king (whose honor God himself establishes [Ps 21:5; 45:7; 110:1]), should experience exaltation over enemies (Ps 72:9-11), rather than being brought low before them (in Ps 89:19, 24, 27, explicitly on the basis of God's own promise), and enjoy a lasting remembrance or "name" (Ps 45:17; 72:17). However, the nation does experience humiliation from enemies and subjection to disgrace (Ps 79:4; 89:41, 45). This can be interpreted as God's action (Ps 44:9, 13-16), no doubt understood within the framework of the covenant blessings and curses, in which case the psalmist might even affirm that God's people have not, in fact, been disloyal and that God should act to restore them (Ps 44:17-26). The psalmists will express the wish, rather, that the nation's enemies be put to shame in a great reversal of present circumstances (Ps 129:5).

It comes as no surprise that God's honor is a major focal point of the psalms, since many of them are explicitly acts of praise, giving honor to God for some combination of character traits and beneficent actions on behalf of the psalmist personally or of the people of God collectively and throughout history. The psalms praise God for these actions and traits: acts of creation, which are an ongoing testimony to God's majesty (Ps 8; 19:1; 24:1-2; 95:3-5; 148); deliverance of the psalmist from his enemies and from disgrace or danger (Pss 9; 18; 30; 34; 118); power to deliver as "the Lord of armies" (Ps 24:7-10; 47); might, majesty and character in general (Pss 29; 100; 145; 150); many mighty deeds on behalf of God's people throughout history (often focusing on some combination of the acts of creation, exodus, giving of the covenant, conquest and the establishment of Jerusalem) and in the present time (Pss 33; 66; 98; 105; 107; 111; 135; 136; 146; 147); bestowal of benefits (Ps 103:1-2; 116:12-19); reigning justly over the cosmos that God has made, including forthcoming judgments (Ps 96:10, 13; 97:1; 98:9; 99:1-5); exaltation over idols or "other" gods (Ps 95:3; 96:3-5; 97:7; 135:5-21).

In this economy of receiving God's gifts and help and returning praise in witness to God's generous character and timely benefits, psalmists use the promise that they will augment recognition of God's honor through their praise and testimony as an incentive to God to act on their behalf. Rescuing the psalmist or granting his petition is in God's own interests in terms of the manifestation of God's honor in the world (see Ps 9:14; 22:21-22; 35:17-19, 27-28; 69:29b-30; 71:14, 16, 18, 23-24; 79:13; 106:47), including among foreigners who worship other gods (Ps 18:49; see also Ps 96:3, 10). In a depiction of the view from the other side, the psalmist portrays God as saying, "Call on me. . . . I will deliver you, and you shall glorify me" (Ps 50:15). Occasionally, the psalmist characterizes his life as one that is full of praise, a reminder to God, as it were, that the psalmist already actively promotes God's honor (Ps 71:6, 8). The implication is, again, that it would be in the best interests of the advancement of God's reputation for God to act to preserve such a person's honor and life, all the more so as the psalmist has proven to be a noble client who returns thanks and praise to his divine benefactor. The death of the psalmist would in fact diminish God's praise and the recognition of God's honor in the world: "Will the dust praise you? Will it tell of your faithfulness?"

(Ps 30:9; see also Ps 88:10-12; 115:17). Many of the psalms can be read as attempts to "make good" on promises made to God in anticipation of deliverance (see esp. Pss 9; 18; 30; 34; 103:1-2; 116:12-19; 118), as the psalmist calls together an audience and calls attention to God's beneficent deeds (Ps 66:16), increasing "reverence" for and "trust" in God (Ps 40:3). Through the ever-widening circles of praise of God's beneficiaries it is hoped that one day all the nations will acknowledge the supreme honor of the God of Israel, worker of wonderful deeds, and the only God (Ps 86:9-10).

God's honor is also presented as being in jeopardy when the honor or safety of the person who has been visibly aligned with God is endangered, not just because the psalmist may be unavailable to praise God in the future, but because those who disregard God will use the downfall of the pious person as a proof of God's weakness or nonexistence. Thus the psalmist can pray for vindication or deliverance "for your name's sake" (Ps 143:11). In vindicating the psalmist, God secures God's own jeopardized reputation before those who look at the psalmist's distress and taunt him, "Where is your God now?" (Ps 42:10). On rare occasion the psalmist can identify his own experience of being dishonored with the dishonor shown God in his community, which is offered as an incentive to God to vindicate both in one fell swoop (Ps 69:7-9; 89:50-51). There is also the danger of dishonor/disgrace befalling those who, being righteous themselves, are associated with the psalmist and bear witness to his disgrace. Here is another incentive to God, from a consideration of the wider honor of God's faithful ones, to act on behalf of the psalmist (Ps 69:6).

Similar dynamics hold true in regard to the fortunes of the nation of Israel, the corporate body of those who are associated with God's name. God's honor is revealed to the nations, who inappropriately give honor to other gods, when Israel is delivered from trouble or is ascendant and its enemies are disgraced (Ps 83:16-18; 98:1-3, esp. 98:2b; 102:13, 15; 115:1-2). Israel's experience of God's blessing results in God's way being "known upon earth, [God's] saving power among all nations" (Ps 67:1-2). This conviction concerning the linkage between God's honor and Israel's standing becomes a source of confidence and trust (Ps 46:10-11).

Conversely, the declining fortune or humiliation of Israel before other nations threatens to call into question God's strength vis-à-vis the gods of the nations. This put God in something of a bind when the requirements of justice necessitated that God punish Israel's disobedience through exile and national calamity (Glatt-Gilad, 65-66). So, again, the psalmists try to rally God to action on behalf of Israel, restoring its honor, by appealing to God to vindicate his own reputation, which is now challenged and slandered by the ascendant nations (Ps 74:10, 18, 22; 79:9-10, 12; 115:1-2). God must respond to the challenges against God's own honor leveled by the nations who have assaulted God's servants and holy temple (Ps 79:1, 10b). Because God is the God of glory, reliance on God and one's connection with God remain the best assurance of one's own honor—over riches, military allies and military power (Ps 20:7-8; 49:5-6, 16-20; 73:20).

The greater power of the psalms is not their testimony to the honor challenges of the various psalmists and the ways in which they sought vindication from God, but rather the effect that they would have upon generations of communities of worshipers who spoke these words again and again in worship and made them "their own," conforming their practices and expectations to those of the psalmists themselves and becoming more like the "honorable person" defined and personified in the psalms, and like that person who is so aligned with God's honor (by honoring God and representing God to the world through his or her obedient conduct) that they can expect God's intervention when their own honor is endangered. The ongoing recitation of the psalms in private and public worship among Jews and, later, Christians continuously keeps alive in those communities these definitions of honor, expectations concerning the relationship of piety and honor, and the dynamics born of the conviction that God's honor and the honor of God's people are intertwined, and no doubt it contributes significantly to the ongoing manifestation of the same in later literature.

2.2. Lamentations. Lamentations gives the reader a close-up view of the experience of shame that accompanies national defeat and disgrace, particularly the experience of conquest (including, here, deportation). Jerusalem's loss of honor is highlighted in the opening of Lamentations (Olyan, 216). The city that once enjoyed the honor of a princess is now diminished to the status of a forced laborer (Lam 1:1 [the NRSV's "vassal" does not capture the degradation of the Heb *mas*]). The former majesty and glorious stature of Jerusalem is gone (Lam 1:6; 3:18). Those who formerly respected the city "now despise her, for they have seen her nakedness" (Lam 1:8). The public exposure of private parts is a typical metaphor for shameful exposure of a city's weakness, grounded in the actual human experience of humiliation in being put on display while naked, whence the practice of leading off the foremost citizens of a conquered city naked and bound, demoralizing them, erasing their former status, and enacting the new, relative status between victors and conquered people (Bechtel, 63-67).

The city is exposed to vicious taunting by (foreign) passers-by and the nation's enemies (Lam 2:15-16; 3:14, 61, 63), who gloat over the city's degradation. Those who ought to have been honored (elites, elders) are especially targeted by the enemy for shaming as a symbol of the degradation of Jerusalem as a whole (Lam 4:16; 5:12). The "national disgrace" is described in greater detail in Lamentations 5:1-14. Jerusalem has gone from being self-sufficient and independent to having to depend on others for bread, water and firewood—indeed, buying back their own resources from their overlords or replenishing what cannot be found in the war zone from the supply of neighboring nations. Low-level Babylonian bureaucrats are now lords over Jerusalem in place of native nobility. Women are vulnerable to sexual assault at the hands of the occupation force.

This political reversal of fortune is interpreted as God's humiliating Jerusalem on account of God's anger, God's response to the provocations of Jerusalem's inhabitants (Lam 2:1; see also Lam 3:45). The people challenged God's honor through their disregard of God's commandments, thus enacting contempt for God (and ingratitude toward their perpetual benefactor); as a result, God has successfully sought satisfaction of God's honor in a staggering riposte. In a sense, however, this relieves some of the cognitive tension of the experience of national defeat. If Jerusalem has been humiliated by God rather than by Nebuchadnezzar, then the basic relationships that define Jerusalem's existence (e.g., as God's chosen city/people, those with whom, out of all peoples of the earth, God is in covenant) and world construction (national defeat does not mean the defeat of Jerusalem's God by

Babylon's gods but rather represents God's punishment of God's own disobedient people) are preserved.

3. Proverbs and Ecclesiastes.

Honor discourse is strongly evidenced in Wisdom literature, chiefly as a motive for the avoidance of certain behaviors deemed to lead to disgrace and for the pursuit of others that lead to honor. It is also here, however, that we find the most direct criticism of contemporary practices related to honor—for example, the response of rebuffing, for the sake of "saving face," some criticism or rebuke that could lead one to follow the way of Torah more closely. *Ecclesiastes, not surprisingly, subjects the entire enterprise of honor-seeking to critical scrutiny along with his enumeration of other "vanities."

3.1. Proverbs. The book of *Proverbs promotes the pursuit of wisdom, that combination of piety and practical savvy that leads to advantage in one's dealings with God and human beings. Many individual proverbs employ sanctions of honor and dishonor (i.e., the promise of being honored or the threat of falling into disgrace) to urge pursuit or avoidance of particular behaviors.

Honor is offered as an incentive for loyalty and faithfulness in dealings with other people (Prov 3:3-4), exhibiting "good sense" (Prov 12:8), pursuing justice and generosity (Prov 21:21), showing diligence and responsibility in one's sphere of duty (Prov 17:2; 27:18), being slow to quarrel or engage in strife (Prov 20:3), and always keeping in view God's superior honor and the need to honor God in all one's dealings (Prov 22:4). The person who does such things enjoys not only honor in this life but also a lasting, praiseworthy remembrance after death (Prov 10:7). Conversely, the threat of being shamed confronts the person who engages in deceitful speech (Prov 13:5), who responds before having heard and understood (Prov 18:13), and who "triangulates" rather than taking up an argument directly with the person involved (Prov 25:9-10). Proverbs 6:30-33 presents an illuminating contrast: shame sanctions are not leveled by the society reflected herein against the thief who steals only to feed himself, though legal sanctions exist to punish the thief who is caught (Prov 6:30-31); however, strong shame sanctions are leveled against the adulterer (Prov 6:32-33; see also Prov 5:8-9), perhaps in the absence of effective legal sanctions.

Throughout Proverbs the title *fool* is itself a term of reproach and disgrace, and thus the construction of the "fool" creates a paradigm for nonimitation throughout Proverbs, whereas the "wise person" presents a paradigm for emulation, insofar as one wishes to be included also under the honorable appellation *wise,* because the "wise person" is esteemed and the "fool" is despised ("The wise will inherit honor, but stubborn fools, disgrace" [Prov 3:35; cf. Prov 26:1; see Laniak, 23]). In addition to the "fool," the "sinner" is also particularly held up as a model not to be emulated, and the author is keenly aware that the visible success that the less Torah-observant enjoy could be a strong incentive to follow their example (Prov 23:17; 24:1-2, 19). The "sinner," who does not live in the *"fear of the Lord," often even receives praise on account of his or her attainment of desirable goods, which can be very misleading to other honor-seeking people (Prov 28:4). Such praise does not here reliably reinforce what is truly honorable, and "those who keep the law" must resist its pull. In this regard, it is questionable whether wisdom and *folly truly represent a different value system than honor and shame (*contra* Domeris) or constitute, rather, a culture-specific manifestation of honor and shame, defining who is esteemed and valued versus who is contemned and devalued in terms of the socially approved behaviors and virtues that each manifests or fails to manifest.

Concern for one's own honor, however, is secondary in Proverbs to the "fear of the Lord." The repeated emphasis on the fear of the Lord "sets before the eyes of the wise person at all times the honor which is due God; 'to fear' in this phrase means to acknowledge the superior worth and power of the Lord, and thus to avoid provoking God's anger and desire for satisfaction through some deed which shows slight regard for God's requirements" (deSilva 1995, 72). God is the ultimate "significant other" before whose eyes one lives at all times, the one whose approval can be gained only by sincerity in righteous living (Prov 5:21; 15:3), and whose disapproval represents grave threat. Thus the tradents of Proverbs urge students to honor God with the appropriate tithes so that their harvests will enjoy God's favor (Prov 3:9-10), to avoid the deviousness in human relationships that shows contempt for God (Prov 14:2; see also Prov 8:13). In particular, those whose social status gives them little "weight" or esteem are to be treated honorably and justly (i.e., according to the commandments), for God's honor is provoked by the person who fails to show love for neighbor, whether rich or poor (Prov 14:31; 17:5). If one encounters adverse circumstances as a result of not walking in line with the commandments, the wise person will respond by repenting, making amends and conforming more fully to God's decrees rather than "despise the LORD's discipline" (Prov 3:11-12), though the book of *Job (among other texts) illustrates that *suffering is not always the result of sin.

As the reflection of God's requirements, respect for the Torah (i.e., observance of its statutes) is essential for honor, both for the individual (Prov 13:13) and for the nation (Prov 14:34). Similarly, and perhaps because instruction in Torah is vitally connected with the instruction received in the household, respect for the instruction of parents marks the honorable person (Prov 15:5; 23:22). The parent-child relationship seems to be especially hemmed in with shame sanctions, protecting parents from injury or insult from those they have benefited either directly (Prov 19:26; 30:17) or indirectly through the shameful actions of their progeny (Prov 10:5; 15:20; 28:7). Where such sanctions are observed, generations become sources of mutual honor to one another (Prov 17:6). Proverbs also exhibits the general elevation of honorable old age as the pinnacle of life to be esteemed by others, a trademark of traditional cultures, rather than as its waning and nadir (Prov 16:31).

Contrary to modern constructions of honor in Mediterranean societies (rightly, Domeris, 96), where humility has a negative value and aggressive self-promotion is presented as the (male) norm (Pitt-Rivers, 43), Proverbs cultivates humility as a core value rather than nurturing a boastful honor/shame culture (Prov 11:2; see also Ps 5:5; 18:27; 113:7-8; 138:6). The wise person exercises restraint in honor-seeking (Prov 25:27), avoids self-promoting speech and behaviors (Prov 25:6-7; 27:2; 30:32), and regards with caution the experience of being praised, seeing it as a test of character (Prov 27:21). However, it is not entirely the case that "humility takes priority over honour" (Domeris, 96), since Proverbs promotes humility (especially in regard to conformity to the group's norms as embodied in To-

rah) as the path toward honor, thus making it valuable precisely because it leads to honor (Prov 15:33; 29:23).

A contemptuous attitude, haughtiness and scoffing (i.e., making light of something and thereby showing a lack of esteem) are traits that alienate a person from God and lead with certainty to a humiliating downfall (Prov 3:34; 8:13; 11:2; 16:5, 18; 18:12; 21:4, 24; see also Ps 10:4; 18:27; 94:2, 4). This stance of scoffing probably includes disregard for the ancestral tradition of Israel, resistance to submitting to Torah and to the instruction of parents, elders and the like. It is the antithesis of delighting in the law of the Lord and submitting to its authority as a pattern for living (as in Ps 1:1-3). Humility, as the antithesis to innovative self-direction, represents a virtue by means of which one finds favor with God and honor before people (Prov 3:34; 15:33; 18:12; 29:23).

Humility is especially required in the face of constructive criticism. The collection gives disproportionate attention to disarming the tendency to regard a rebuke as a verbal honor challenge to be rebuffed (Prov 5:11-12; 6:23; 9:7-8; 10:17; 12:1; 13:1, 18; 15:10, 32). According to the agonistic model of challenge and riposte (Malina and Neyrey), a reproof or word of correction could be viewed as a challenge to honor, evoking a response calculated to deflect the challenge and restore honor in the public eye. In the collection of Proverbs, however, this is only the response of the "scoffer" (Prov 9:7-8; 13:1), who would reject correction from Wisdom's own lips (Prov 1:30). Since honor is essentially derived from obedience to God's Torah, a rebuke from another person "calculated to bring one into closer conformity with the law becomes an opportunity for honor," which is thereby preserved and augmented not by rebuffing a rebuke but rather by embracing it (deSilva 1995, 75). It becomes an opportunity truly to embody the group's norms more fully and thus possess greater and more genuine honor.

By extension, the wise person neither retorts every insult nor engages every challenge to his or her honor (Prov 19:11). That is the strategy of the "fool" (Prov 12:16). Although "one of the most prevalent impulses for people who have been shamed is the need to take revenge for their humiliation," thus to steal back their honor from the person who stole it in the first place (Bechtel, 50), the idea of offering a riposte or counterchallenge to every challenge—part of the paradigm of the "honor-sensitive Mediterranean person" developed in cultural anthropology—was not uniformly regarded as the best defense of one's honor. Or, more precisely, the tradents of Proverbs favored the response of "no response" as the most effective way to deal with verbal assaults on one's honor. Again contrary to the paradigm, Proverbs advises against returning injury for injury as a means of restoring one's affronted honor in the public eye: "Do not say, 'I will do to others as they have done to me; I will pay them back for what they have done'" (Prov 24:29). As a precursor to the Golden Rule, we thus find a progression in the literature of the Jewish culture out of a challenge-riposte system, where one's actions can be provoked, to a posture of beneficence, acting generously toward others as a means of establishing one's nobility and being "above" such challenges (see Mt 5:44-48; Rom 12:17, 21; 1 Pet 3:9).

Proverbs gives scant attention to the particular topic of women in regard to honor and shame when set against, for example, the later collection of wisdom sayings and instructions in *Sirach (see Sir 26:10-16; 42:9-12). A wife can be a source of honor or shame to her husband (Prov 11:4), though we are not told how. A woman who "hates virtue" falls into disgrace (Prov 11:16), but again, "virtue" is left rather unspecified. It might be a mistake to assume from later discussions of female "virtue" (i.e., those available in Sirach or in Greco-Roman ethicists) that these Proverbs have the woman's sexual discretion primarily in view.

The collection has much more to say about the positive side of this equation, namely, how "a gracious woman gets honor" (Prov 11:16), particularly in the renowned description of the good wife in Proverbs 31:10-31. This wife exercises diligence and excellence in household management, providing for the needs of the household (including the neighborhood poor), preserving and extending the wealth and resources of the household and its productivity (e.g., in terms of increasing its arable land). Here, indeed, we do not find the stereotype of a woman "ruled by an acute sense of shame, . . . bounded by the confines of her domestic prison" (Domeris, 97). A woman's circles of praise begin within her family (Prov 31:28-30) but extend to the public spaces presumably reserved for men: "Let her works praise her in the city gates" (Prov 31:31). This stands in stark contrast to the Greek sentiment that she is most honorable "of whom the least is said in public, whether of praise or of blame" (Thucydides *The Peloponnesian War* 2.45.2).

Taken as a whole, Proverbs presents further evidence against taking honor and shame to be the only, or even primary, concern of the circles that produced and read this Wisdom literature. Many of the proverbs rest on the contrast between wealth and want rather than renown and disgrace. Sometimes "a good name is to be chosen rather than great riches" (Prov 22:1), but on the other hand, it is "better to be despised and have a servant than to be self-important and lack food" (Prov 12:9). The latter proverb elevates sufficiency for one's daily needs above (hollow?) pride (Domeris, 96). Purity and pollution sanctions are also at play ("abomination" is as potent a negative value as "shameful" [Prov 16:12; 17:15]), as are considerations of finding what is "pleasant" in life (e.g., Prov 17:1), as well as, quite frequently, considerations of what leads to a safe and secure enjoyment of life's goods as opposed to danger (deSilva 1995, 69-70). In regard to the latter, Proverbs 14:35 provides an interesting example of the topic of safety actually functioning as the sanction for honorable behavior (making "safety" the primary value in that maxim). Although "honor" is prominent among the benefits of attaining wisdom, it stands squarely alongside all of life's other goods (chiefly, sufficiency and security in a long life [Prov 3:13-16; 4:8-9; 8:18]). As Proverbs 25:27 cautions restraint in honor seeking, so too the rhetoric of Proverbs as a whole (i.e., the variety of topics employed to promote particular behaviors) cautions readers to exercise the same restraint when seeking for "honor" in the texts.

3.2. Ecclesiastes. *Qohelet is more directly critical of an overly acute interest in acquiring "honor" or seeking precedence as a driving force in life. He presents himself as a person who had played the honor game well, with the result that he "became great and surpassed all who were before me in Jerusalem." He reports, however, that such claims to precedence over predecessors and contemporaries in terms of the attainment of greater wisdom and knowledge (Eccles 1:16) or greater possessions and visible displays of wealth and "weight" (Eccles 2:7) turned out to be "vanity" and "a chasing after wind" (Eccles 1:17; 2:11), labor without profit.

The highly contested goods of "wealth, possessions and honor" are vulnerable, not lasting. They may carry the promise of (or potential for) happiness, but not happiness itself. Thus, to seek them as one's goal is to miss out on life—the enjoyment of the toil and the fruits at hand (Eccles 6:2). Moreover, "honor" is unreliable. It is often bestowed upon the wicked, who used their precedence to another's hurt (Eccles 8:9-10), such that praise and censure are, again, not consistently granted in line with the values officially espoused by the tradition. Honor is not reliably manifested in social status: fools can be elevated to positions of honor, while the wealthy are abased (Eccles 10:6-7). And the promise of lasting fame also proves to be empty, for "even the remembrance of the dead is lost" (Eccles 9:5; see also Eccles 4:15-16; 9:15). When Qohelet recites the proverb "A good reputation is better than the finest luxuries" (Eccles 7:1), where "reputation" or "name" *(šēm)* refers to the reputation that survives after one's death, he may be doing so to subtly challenge this view by means of a *reductio ad absurdum* (Seow, 234). If one's reputation is really better than enjoying life, then "the day of death is better than the day of birth" (Eccles 7:2) (see Seow, 244). Although he advocates facing death as a means of coming to sober terms with what is worth pursuing in this life, he certainly does not advocate "living" for death and for the vapid fame that is supposed to confer a limited immortality.

The only positive note concerns the pleasure that he found in the toil itself, not the pleasure anticipated in the achievement of precedence (Eccles 2:10). From this he derives the maxim that will become the leitmotif of the whole work: People should "eat and drink, and find enjoyment in their toil" (Eccles 2:24; see also Eccles 3:12-13; 5:18; 8:15; 9:7-10), which is God's gift (Eccles 2:24) and the "lot" of human beings (Eccles 3:22; 5:18), rather than waste life in the pursuit of the "loftier" goals that consume others, just as they previously consumed Qohelet. In light of the unreliability of grants of honor reflecting a person's true character, the fleeting nature of honor and fame, and the hollowness of the attainment of such a vapid "good," honoring God—living in the reverence/fear of God—is the only honor quest that is ultimately affirmed (Eccles 12:13), since God is the only Other who will reliably and unfailingly hold virtue and iniquity accountable (Eccles 12:14).

4. Honor Challenges in Esther and Job.

*Esther and Job relate encounters in which the push and pull of honor challenges and ripostes, the virulent vying for precedence, and visible and physical representations of honor status—all stereotypical feature of constructs of the "ancient Mediterranean person" (Pitt-Rivers; Malina and Neyrey)—are in fact strongly evidenced. Indeed, the honor challenge and riposte/counterchallenge can be seen to drive the plot of both works.

4.1. Esther. Esther is perhaps the most conventional of the "five scrolls" (*see* Megillot and Festivals) in terms of its display of honor-and-shame scripts, and the manifestation and observance of the hierarchy of honor is a consistent theme. The book opens with descriptions of a display by King *Ahasuerus of wealth and largesse in opulent, extended banquets (Esther 1:2-8), a public manifestation of his "weight" and power and honor (Laniak, 167) that reinforces his position at the top of the hierarchy of honor in the kingdom. An act of disobedience to the king by *Vashti—even though his command appears to have threatened to diminish her honor by bringing her out for public display rather than allowing her modestly to remain in the women's chambers with the other female residents of the palace (Klein, 155)—threatens the hierarchy of honor within the household, "causing [all wives] to look with contempt on their husbands" (Esther 1:17). The resulting decree, for which the demotion and banishment of Vashti was to serve as a negative example, commands that "all women will give honor to their husbands, high and low alike" (Esther 1:20). No matter how humble a man might be, he should at least be able to count on being honored, and thus obeyed, by his own wife! Thus the "solution" to Vashti's act of disobedience says far more than is required by the narrative plot, which only necessitates the removal of Vashti to make room for Esther. There is even a hierarchy within the harem, with Esther and her attendants finding favor with the eunuch in charge of the harem and being advanced "to the best place" (Esther 2:9).

The hierarchy that drives the plot forward, however, is the rigid hierarchy among courtiers, embodied in the extreme in the promotion of Haman and the command that all other courtiers do obeisance to Haman by bowing before him, physically representing their relative status upon each encounter (Esther 3:2). *Mordecai refuses to bow down to Haman, thus refusing to acknowledge the status that had been conferred upon Haman by the king, and this constitutes a challenge to Haman's honor. We are not given a reason for Mordecai's resistance other than the fact that Mordecai is a Jew (Esther 3:4). The cause might well be the ancient enmity between Jews and the Amalekites (Klein, 161), which is now rekindled in the action of the story that follows. (The highly theological Greek Esther [see Esther 5: Greek Versions], however, attributes it to Mordecai's piety: he would not bestow on any human being the honors that belong to God alone [Add Esth 13:8-17].) Haman perceives the challenge (Esther 3:5), but his plan for answering it exceeds all bounds. Securing Mordecai's demise alone would be "beneath him" (Esther 3:6). His estimation of the immensity of his honor is such that he believes that only genocide would constitute a sufficient riposte. Here, of course, Haman's sense of honor has crossed the line into the hubris that God opposes, and his downfall is from this point inevitable.

The challenge to Haman's honor is kept ever fresh in his eyes, and in the awareness of the readers, by the presence and behavior of Mordecai. Haman returns from being honored (as he supposes) by the queen's entertainment at a private dinner along with Ahasuerus, but the sight of Mordecai at the king's gate, refusing even to rise to acknowledge Haman, immediately causes him to forget the honors bestowed on him and to stew over not yet being avenged on Mordecai and his people (Esther 5:9-13). Haman's inner mortification is complete when he is selected by Ahasuerus to carry out for Mordecai's benefit the elaborate plan that Haman had devised for the king to show honor to a deserving courtier (thinking that this would be himself). Haman must go on foot, leading Mordecai on horseback and decked in the finest robes, drawing public attention with his own lips to the honor being bestowed on Mordecai (Esther 6:6-10) while he himself is being shamed before his rival (Klein, 167). Haman's wife recognizes this as the beginning of her husband's downfall (Esther 6:13), for instead of putting Mordecai in his place, as it were, he has personally enacted Mordecai's superior status to himself. Haman leaves the second banquet with Esther under quite different circumstances than the first: his face is covered (a shame ritual ac-

cording to Laniak, 168; but note Klein, 169: "Haman's right to sight of forbidden [female] spaces is revoked"), and he is led to be hung out on the gallows that he constructed for Mordecai, there to be publicly displayed and disgraced (Esther 7:8-10). Later, the bodies of his ten sons would be hung up as well, completing the downfall and shaming of the whole household (Esther 9:13-14) (see Klein, 173).

Mordecai's star, on the other hand, continues to rise: he becomes an increasingly powerful person in the king's court and his fame spreads throughout all the provinces (Esther 9:4); he ends the story as "next in rank to King Ahasuerus," with his fame forever recorded "in the annals of the kings of Media and Persia" (Esther 10:2-3). All the honor that was lost by Haman is soaked up, as it were, by his rival Mordecai, confirming the way in which an agonistic culture such as the one displayed in Esther is also one in which honor is regarded as available only in limited quantities (indeed, the latter understanding almost necessitates the competitive orientation to the acquisition of honor).

4.2. Job. Although the cosmic powers and their testing of Job set the stage for the dialogue portions of the book, the speeches themselves are driven by an underlying series of honor challenges and ripostes between Job, his "friends" and the upstart Elihu. It is not just that Bildad, Eliphaz, and Zophar are poor pastoral counselors; they are taking advantage of Job's humiliation to "raise their own status and esteem by 'putting Job down' and treating him as an inferior" (Bechtel, 73). Job's "friends" use shaming to "break" Job (Bechtel, 73), to get him to abandon his position of *righteousness, and to admit that he needs to follow the instruction of his "friends" and confess and repent of the sins that brought him down to the disgraceful condition in which he finds himself (Job 11:3-6). Their attempts at "rehabilitation" are also attempts to gain precedence over Job by establishing themselves as his teachers.

Eliphaz rightly surmises that his speech will be perceived as a challenge that would provoke offense (Job 4:1). He challenges Job with not being able to live up to his own teaching (Job 4:2-5) and thus calls into question his right to have posed as a teacher all these years. He indirectly suggests that Job has been a "fool" (a senseless sinner), for his children have suffered the same fate as the fool's children, who "are crushed in the gate" (Job 5:3-4). He uses a familiar proverb to interpret Job's sufferings as God's "discipline," calling Job to accept it, seek the needed correction of life, and so fall back in line with honorable behavior (Job 5:17; cf. Prov 3:11). Eliphaz concludes with a triumphal declaration that what he has already tested and found to be true, Job has yet to come to learn (and that, from Eliphaz's lips [Job 5:27]).

It is no wonder that Job counterchallenges Eliphaz with a proverb: "Those who withhold kindness from a friend forsake the fear of the Almighty" (Job 6:14). He rejects Eliphaz's rebuke as empty and invites him to try again with more substance next time (Job 6:24-26). Job must defend his status as a man learned in the wisdom of the Jewish tradition in the face of the implied rebukes concerning his lack of wisdom: "What you know, I also know; I am not inferior to you" (Job 13:2). In the push and shove over which person in the circle truly has the right to teach, Eliphaz will return the same defense: "What do you know that we do not know? What do you understand that is not clear to us?" (Job 15:9). None of the characters exhibits the humility before a rebuke that is commended so frequently in Proverbs!

Repeatedly, Job laments the assaults upon his honor that he endures in the speech of his "friends" (Job 12:4-5; 16:4, 20; 17:2, 6; 19:3, 5-6), which amounts simply to ongoing mocking (Job 21:3) on top of the degradation of which he is so intensely aware (Job 9:15; 19:9). He understands that they are engaging him in an attempt to secure their status over him, "magnifying" themselves against him (Job 19:5). This is behavior in which Job himself claims never to have engaged (Job 31:29). His interlocutors, in turn, regard his speech as insulting censure and respond accordingly (Job 20:3).

Job wistfully remembers the honor he used to be shown—notably, symbolized by his juniors withdrawing and the elders rising out of respect and, most of all, by people keeping silent in his presence, waiting for his counsel (Job 29:2-10, 21). His "friends," no doubt, were formerly in that number. Now the situation is reversed. Job's juniors and social inferiors mock him, taunt him, even spit at the sight of him (Job 30:1, 9-10). Job's "honor is pursued as by the wind" (Job 30:15) now that he has suffered a reversal and his status appears to be "up for grabs," to be absorbed by those who successfully challenge him

while he is down. This shaming is all the more painful because it is offered by "people of lower social status who should have honored him simply because of his higher status" (Bechtel, 73-74) (Job 30:1). With the evidence of that status gone (progeny, wealth, physical health, strength), these honor vultures participated in inscribing a new, lower status upon him with their speech and physical affronts.

The reader is unprepared for the voice of the fifth speaker in this dialogue, who has not been hitherto introduced. Elihu's silence up to this point, however, is a manifestation of the same respect-as-silence that Job remembered being shown to him (Job 29:21). Elihu waits to speak until his three elders are finished with their attempts (Job 32:4), but he also sees the failure of the older three friends as his opportunity to gain honor at their expense: "It is not the old that are wise. . . . See, I waited for your words, I listened for your wise sayings, while you searched out what to say" (Job 32:9, 11). Elihu makes explicit the "honor contest" inherent in the dialogue. There will be a winner and a loser in this debate. The one who ends up "teaching" the other establishes his precedence over the other (Job 33:31-33), and Elihu is confident that he will be the one who comes out on top, teaching Job wisdom (Job 33:33), besting the elder three counselors (Job 32:11-12, 15-16), and proving true his haughty claim to be "perfect in knowledge" (Job 36:4).

It is God who resolves this cacophonous clamor of challenges and counterchallenges. God himself puts Elihu in his place (Job 38:2), ironically demonstrating Elihu's closing assertion that God "does not regard any who are wise in their own conceit" (Job 37:24). God also reproves the three counselors, putting them "in their place" once again below Job, on whose mediation they depend for their repentance (Job 42:7-9). But God must also put Job in his place for being willing to presume to put God on the defensive in his attempt to establish his own righteousness (and thus the injustice of his circumstances), the end of which is that Job too understands the humility that mortals must have before God (Job 42:5-6). Job shows God the same respect that princes used to show Job: "I lay my hand on my mouth" (Job 40:4).

5. Song of Songs, Ruth and the Honorable Woman.

Several texts besides Proverbs challenge the stereotypical view of female "shame" (in the positive sense of "modesty"), according to which "honorable" women refrain from all extramarital sexual encounters, remain more or less hidden from the public eye by staying within domestic spaces, and conduct themselves in a manner that shows them to be more concerned with maintaining their sexual purity than attracting a mate (*see* Marriage and Sex).

5.1. Song of Songs. The Shulammite woman, the heroine of *Song of Songs, strains against this stereotype (Bergant), though to what degree is a matter of some dispute. Song of Songs 3:1-4 presents the reader with the astounding scene of a woman looking for her lover in her bed and, not finding him, roaming the streets at night looking for him and leading him back to her mother's bedchamber. In another scene, the woman's lover comes to her chamber at night, provoking both anxiety and desire, and the language drips with sexual double-entendres (Song 5:2-6a). The lover mysteriously disappears by the time she unlatches her bedroom door to admit him, so she roams the streets (again) looking for him, exposing herself to risk and, in fact, this time being abused by the sentinels (Song 5:6b-7). Such behavior would run sensationally counter to the ancient construction of the "honorable" woman (see, e.g., deSilva 2000b), although this "ideal" is based on texts from the Greek and Roman periods. While we observe in Proverbs a far greater degree of engagement with the day-to-day life of the outside world, such engagement with the "night life"—behavior as fitting for a prostitute—is quite unprecedented among descriptions of "honorable" women.

The solution hinges in part on whether one regards the second scene (Song 5:2-7) as the report of the actual nocturnal activity of the woman and her lover (so Bergant, 28, 31) or as a dream, as the introductory sentence would suggest: "I slept, but my heart was awake" (Song 5:1). The latter seems the more likely, given the explicit introduction, the absence of any transitional mention of waking, and the nightmarish transition from rapturous fantasy to being chased and beaten by the sentinels. If this is the case, then Song of Songs does not furnish evidence of a setting in which a young maiden's bedroom is really so easily accessible to a paramour at night, nor in which a woman's amorous desire is really not limited by social expectations (*contra* Bergant, 28, 31). And if

the second scene was but a dream, and nothing more, was she also dreaming the first time, when she was again "upon [her] bed at night" looking for her lover (Song 3:1)? The fact that in this scene the woman is able to lead her lover into her mother's bedchamber (Song 3:4), while later she will lament that social pressures prevent her from doing this very thing (Song 8:1-2a), suggests that we have again a view into the sexual desire of the woman as it would *wish* to be expressed, not as it *could* be expressed in her setting.

Toward the close of Song of Songs one finds several important indications that the "rules" are not really "off" in the world of these lovers. First, the woman expresses a longing to transcend the restrictions of the culture around her, wishing that her lover was her brother so she could kiss him in public (and take him home with her!) without her being despised—that is, regarded as shameless and immodest (Song 8:1-3). This is more than a "reference to public opinion" that nevertheless does not limit the woman's amorous activity (Bergant, 35); it is an admission that "public opinion" really does keep her from doing in the day what she dreams of doing at night.

Second, there is a band of brothers who speak about what they will do to reinforce their sister's honor (Song 8:8-9): whether she proves to be a "wall" or a "door," the brothers are going to be watching out for her virginity and the family honor. In regard to the issue of patriarchal concern with the chastity of women, it is noteworthy that such concern is so diminished here (Bergant, 36), being evidenced only in this passage, as opposed to what one finds in, for example, Sirach centuries later. The woman also indeed rejects her brothers' assessment of her immaturity. They see her as not having blossomed (Song 8:8); she asserts that she is "full-figured" (Song 8:10) (Bergant, 28), though it is impossible to tell whose assessment is closer to the truth ("coming of age" is a complex matter). There is, however, little waking evidence to justify the claim that she "spurns the oversight of her brothers" (Bergant, 34). Her concluding declaration that she was, in fact, a "wall" (Song 8:10) may indicate that despite the fervor of her desire, she preserved her chastity until she was properly married.

Song of Songs gives eloquent expression to the difficulty of social norms and sanctions containing the power of sexual desire and love. In some passages significant boundaries appear to be crossed; in others significant boundaries are obstacles that the woman wishes could be surmounted, but cannot. Even in fantasy or in the world of dreams the crossing of boundaries leads to the suppression of socially disapproved female activity, embodied in the character of the watchmen who beat the woman. Perhaps it is safest to say that Song of Songs shows the interior, passionate life of a lover who wishes that she could live out in the open the desires that she feels burning within her, but who must, like all "honorable" women, learn instead to tame them and conform to the expectations of her society.

5.2. Ruth. In the book of *Ruth the values of honor and shame are not as prominent as in the other texts. Again, we see a woman who challenges both ancient ethical and modern anthropological constructs of the "modest, chaste woman." She goes out by night, unescorted, in her most fetching outfit in order to lie down next to a man who is not her husband, uncovering, most likely, his genitals (Bechtel, 60; Phillips, 14), and then to suggest that they get married (Ruth 3:7-9). Here, it is in fact true that there is no word of reproach for Ruth's behavior (Bergant, 34). Indeed, she receives high praise for her actions from *Boaz, who speaks of her loyalty and her good reputation in the village (Ruth 3:10-13). He takes precautions that no one see her leaving (Ruth 3:14), which would compromise her reputation (and perhaps his own), even as he had earlier that summer sought to protect Ruth from the experience of dishonor from the reproaches of his foremen (Ruth 2:15-16). The village women congratulate *Naomi after Ruth gives birth and express the wish that the child's "name be renowned in Israel" (Ruth 4:14), a wish for lasting honor that comes true, for the child would be known forever as the grandfather of King *David (Ruth 4:17, 22; Mt 1:5-6; Luke 3:32).

In a provocative and persuasive article A. Phillips suggests that the following honor-shame scenarios are operative in the story of Ruth. Naomi uses deceit to spur her slow kinsman Boaz to "do the right thing." By sending Ruth to him at night, after he has consumed adequate amounts of food and drink, Naomi makes Boaz think it possible that he has in fact slept with Ruth. Because he has had sufficient wine, he is not surprised that he cannot remember the details. But the evidence—a woman in whom he has been interested is lying at his ex-

posed genitals—seems clear enough. His own honor is on the line. If he does nothing, and Ruth ends up pregnant, all fingers will be pointing to him, given the special attention and consideration that he has shown to Ruth all summer long. Further, if he jumps now to accept the responsibility of levirate marriage (*see* Kinsman-Redeemer and Levirate), and Ruth ends up pregnant suspiciously soon, all fingers will again be pointing to him. Boaz, therefore, also uses the strategy of deceit to save his own honor. He raises the heretofore unmentioned issue of property redemption to the unnamed next-of-kin, as if that were the primary issue, to throw the community off the scent. Of course, he expected this man to refuse the attractive offer of acquiring land when it was paired with the financially unattractive corollary of performing the duties of levirate marriage. So Boaz is able to save his honor and, indeed, augment it by nobly "doing the right thing" in line with an onerous prescription of Torah, and Naomi has achieved, against all odds, the preservation of her deceased husband's "name" in Israel.

6. Conclusion.

Study of the use of "honor and shame" language in this literature raises many cautions concerning the overly enthusiastic application of models of honor and shame, whether drawn from modern cultural anthropology or even constructed on the basis of ancient texts. Although the social interaction known as the "challenge-riposte" is certainly evidenced in these texts (most notably in Esther and Job), it is also criticized as, in many instances, an inappropriate response to a rebuke from which the recipient ought rather to learn or at least not respond in kind (Proverbs). Although concern for the preservation of honor and avoidance of disgrace is passionately evidenced (Psalms and Proverbs, among others), honor and shame are by no means the only driving considerations in a person's life, standing alongside many other "goods" worth pursuing and possessing (see esp. Proverbs and Ecclesiastes). Most strikingly, perhaps, these texts provide evidence that strongly cautions against the indiscriminate application of later stereotypes of female "shame" and proper female behavior (particularly, being limited to private spaces and embodying passivity in regard to the action of males or the male sphere). Modesty and preservation of sexual purity may not, in the end, be challenged by Song of Songs, but the image of the "honorable" woman keeping to the inside rooms of the house, remaining invisible in an allegedly male sphere, and passively awaiting male initiative is strongly challenged by the behavior of Ruth and of the "good wife" of Proverbs, whose industry and labor is known and celebrated in the places where men sit.

See also FEMINIST INTERPRETATION; SOCIAL-SCIENTIFIC APPROACHES.

BIBLIOGRAPHY. **L. M. Bechtel**, "Shame as a Sanction of Social Control in Biblical Israel: Judicial, Political and Social Shaming," *JSOT* 49 (1991) 47-76; **D. Bergant**, "'My Beloved Is Mine and I Am His' (Song 2:16): The Song of Songs and Honor and Shame," *Semeia* 68 (1994) 23-40; **D. A. deSilva**, "Proverbs," in *Despising Shame: Honor Discourse and Community Maintenance in the Epistle to the Hebrews* (SBLDS 152; Atlanta: Scholars Press, 1995) 69-77; idem, "Honor and Shame," *DNTB* 518-22; idem, *Honor, Patronage, Kinship, and Purity: Unlocking New Testament Culture* (Downers Grove, IL: InterVarsity Press, 2000b); idem, "Honor and Shame," *DOTP* 431-36; **W. R. Domeris**, "Shame and Honour in Proverbs: Wise Women and Foolish Men," *OTE* 8 (1995) 86-102; **T. Frymer-Kensky**, "Virginity in the Bible," in *Gender and Law in the Hebrew Bible and the Ancient Near East*, ed. V. H. Matthews, B. M. Levinson, and T. Frymer-Kensky (JSOTSup 262; Sheffield: Sheffield Academic Press, 1998) 79-96; **D. A. Glatt-Gilad**, "Yahweh's Honor at Stake: A Divine Conundrum," *JSOT* 98 (2002) 63-74; **A. C. Hagedorn**, "Honor and Shame," *DOTHB* 497-501; **K. C. Hanson**, "How Honorable! How Shameful! A Cultural Analysis of Matthew's Makarisms and Reproaches," *Semeia* 68 (1996) 81-111; **L. R. Klein**, "Honor and Shame in Esther," in *A Feminist Companion to Esther, Judith and Susanna*, ed. Athalya Brenner (FCB 7; Sheffield: Sheffield Academic Press, 1995) 149-75; **T. Laniak**, *Shame and Honor in the Book of Esther* (SBLDS 165; Atlanta: Scholars Press, 1998); **B. J. Malina and J. H. Neyrey**, "Honor and Shame in Luke-Acts: Pivotal Values of the Mediterranean World," in *The Social World of Luke-Acts: Models for Interpretation*, ed. J. H. Neyrey (Peabody, MA: Hendrickson, 1991) 25-66; **S. M. Olyan**, "Honor, Shame, and Covenant Relations in Ancient Israel and Its Environment," *JBL* 115 (1996) 201-18; **A. Phillips**, "The Book of Ruth—Deception and Shame," *JJS* 37 (1986) 1-17; **J. Pitt-Rivers**, "Honour and Social Status," in *Honour and Shame: The Values of Mediterranean Society*, ed. John G. Peristiany (London: Weidenfeld & Nicolson, 1965) 21-77; **R. Rabichev**, "The Mediterranean Concepts of Honour and Shame as Seen in the Depiction of the Biblical Women," *RT* 3 (1996) 51-63; **C. L. Seow**, *Ecclesiastes* (AB 18C; New York: Doubleday, 1997). D. A. deSilva

HOUSE. *See* ARCHITECTURE.

HUMANITY. *See* WISDOM THEOLOGY.

HYMNS

The hymn is a song of praise. Even though the hymn is not the most frequent type of psalm in the book of *Psalms, and even though the noun *těhillâ* ("song of praise") occurs in the title of only one psalm (Ps 145), the fact that the ancients named the whole collection of psalms "Praises" *(těhillîm)* indicates the importance of the hymn for the theology of the book of Psalms (Collins). C. Westermann (1981) was the first to note that while the *lament is more frequent than the hymn, lamentation is more characteristic of the earlier portion of the Psalter, while praise dominates the end (note the recurring "Praise *[halělû]* the LORD" at the beginning and end of each of Pss 146—150 and the eleven additional uses of the verb "praise" *[hālal]* in Ps 150). This movement from lamentation to praise articulates the hope of the psalms, a hope that is captured by the language of Psalm 30:5: "Weeping may go on all night, but joy comes in the morning." The hymn is the quintessential song of praise and captures the heart of Psalms: God's glory is our destiny.

1. The Place of the Hymn
2. The Praise of the Hymn
3. The Structure of the Hymn
4. The Content of the Hymn
5. The Use of the Hymn

1. The Place of the Hymn.

Scholars agree that the book of Psalms contains three primary genres: the hymn, the lament, and the *thanksgiving psalm. W. Brueggemann has referred to these three as songs of orientation, disorientation and reorientation. By using these labels, Brueggemann articulates something fundamental about how the three primary genres relate to each other and how they relate to the ebb and flow of life.

Hymns were composed for times when all is well. They are songs for those trouble-free times in life, times when life is well ordered, well oriented. Life is not, however, always experienced as well ordered or well oriented. "Disorientation" better describes life at times. The laments were written for situations such as these. The time eventually comes, however, when one looks back at those troublesome days and says to God, "You have turned my mourning into joyful dancing. You have taken away my clothes of mourning and clothed me with joy" (Ps 30:11 NLT). The songs of thanksgiving were composed to express joy and gratitude to God for such restoration. Over time the memory of the troublesome days grows dim, life is well ordered once again, and the hymn is sung to celebrate the goodness of God in the goodness of life.

2. The Praise of the Hymn.
Although the praise of God is found in a number of genres, the hymn is the primary vehicle of praise in the book of Psalms (Merrill; see also Westermann 1981). The noun *tĕhillâ* ("praise") occurs in the title only of Psalm 145, which is itself a hymn.

2.1. Praise as an Exclamation. The book of Psalms uses "Praise the LORD" on a limited basis as an exclamation. The Hebrew expression *halēlû yāh* ("praise the LORD"), from which the English exclamation "Hallelujah!" is derived, occurs twenty-three times in the book of Psalms and nowhere else in the Hebrew Bible. A number of modern translations rightly render this phrase as an exclamation rather than as a command/imperative (contra Merrill and the NIV; see ESV, NAB, NASB, NLT, NRSV). The exclamatory nature of *halēlû yāh* can be supported by two lines of argument. First, the phrase *halēlû yāh* is consistently used absolutely and only as an opening or closing expression (except in the case of Ps 135:3). This distinguishes *halēlû yāh* from an expression such as *halēlûhû* ("praise him"), which always has some sort of clause or phrase attached (see the multiple examples in Ps 150). Second, the LXX is consistent in not translating *halēlû yāh* but in transliterating it as *allēlouia* (Westermann, *TLOT* 1.371-76). Again, this distinguishes *halēlû yāh* from expressions such as *halēlûhû,* which the LXX regularly translates with the imperative *aineite* ("praise"). The LXX translates the exceptional Psalm 135:3 with the imperative *aineite* ("praise"), showing that it

correctly understood this one instance as a command/imperative and not an exclamation.

2.2. Praise as a Command. Most of the time, however, the imperatives of *hālal* ("praise") and its synonyms, *bārak* ("bless"), *gādal* ("magnify"), *yādâ* ("give thanks"), *kābēd* ("glorify") and *šābaḥ* ("praise"), are commands and not exclamations. As commands, these imperatives require a response. The response looked for is not the use of the exclamation "Praise the Lord!" but is the acknowledging and confessing of God's attributes and actions (Brueggemann; Clifford; Futato 2002). To praise is to acknowledge who God is and what God has done and, in so doing, to render honor and glory to God as the object of praise. Psalm 134:1-3 comes the closest to providing a definition of "praise" when *David says, "I will praise the LORD at all times.... Come, let us tell of the LORD's greatness." To praise the Lord is to tell of his greatness by reciting his attributes and actions. Psalm 103:1-8 is an example, where the psalmist praises *(bārak)* God by confessing God's actions (forgives, heals, redeems, crowns, satisfies) and his attributes (compassionate, gracious, patient, loving).

3. The Structure of the Hymn.
The hymn typically falls into three sections (Estes). The hymn begins by inviting others in the community or beyond to join the psalmist in praising God. The central section delineates the praiseworthy character and actions of God and thereby provides the content or reasons or motivation for praising God. The hymn concludes on a positive note that is usually something like an affirmation of faith or an invitation to continue the praise and *worship of God forever. Psalm 117, the shortest in the Psalter, provides a clear and concise example.

> [1] Praise the LORD, all you nations.
> Praise him, all you people of the earth.
> [2] For he loves us with unfailing love;
> the LORD's faithfulness endures forever.
> [3] Praise the LORD! (NLT)

4. The Content of the Hymn.
In a word, the content of the hymn is praise. This can be unpacked by examining how praise fills each of the three sections of the hymn.

4.1. The Invitation to Praise. The hymns ultimately invite the entire universe to praise the Lord. On the smallest scale, however, David, in

Psalm 103:1-2, invites himself to praise the Lord.

> Praise the LORD, I tell myself;
> with my whole heart, I will praise his holy
>   name.
> Praise the LORD, I tell myself,
> and never forget the good things he does
>   for me. (NLT, 1st ed.)

Sometimes the psalmist broadens the invitation to include the priests and Levites, as Psalm 135:19b-20a.

> O house of Aaron, praise the LORD;
> O house of Levi, praise the LORD. (NIV)

Sometimes the invitation also goes to the entire congregation of Israel, as in Psalm 118:1-2.

> Give thanks to the LORD, for is good!
> His faithful love endures forever.
> Let the congregation of Israel repeat:
> "His faithful love endures forever." (NLT,
>   1st ed.)

At other times the psalmist expands the invitation even further to include all the nations, as in Psalm 117:1.

> Praise the LORD, all you nations.
> Praise him, all you people of the earth. (NLT)

A few times, Psalm 29:1-2 being one (see also Ps 103:20-21), the psalmist transcends the earth to enlist the angels of heaven in the praise of God.

> Give honor to the LORD, you angels;
> give honor to the LORD for his glory and
>   strength. (NLT, 1st ed.)

In unmatched exuberance Psalm 148 calls the whole created realm to join the chorus. Psalm 148:1-6 invites the heavens and its countless hosts to praise the Lord: "Praise the LORD from the heavens" (Ps 148:1). Then Psalm 148:7-14 summons every part of the earth, animate and inanimate, to praise God, who has created and maintains the world: "Praise the LORD from the earth" (Ps 148:7). Psalm 148:13 captures the whole as well as any one verse can.

> Let them all praise the name of the LORD.
> For his name is very great;

his glory towers over the earth and heaven! (NLT)

4.2. The Content of Praise. The central section of the hymn provides the content or reasons or motivation for praising God. Here the psalmist expresses the substance of praise by reciting God's attributes and actions. This section typically takes up most of the space in the hymn and brings a variety of themes into focus. Psalmists often introduce these themes with the Hebrew word *kî*, which can be translated "for" or "because." Recall Psalm 117 as an example: "Praise the LORD. . . . For *[kî]* great is his love toward us" (NIV).

Most of the hymns fall into one of three subgenres: hymns of divine kingship (*see* Kingship Psalms), hymns of creation, or hymns of redemption (Coogan). The hymns of divine kingship celebrate the Lord's rule over heaven and earth. One example is Psalm 29, which ends with this affirmation:

> The LORD sits enthroned over the flood;
> the LORD is enthroned as King forever.
> The LORD gives strength to his people;
> the LORD blesses his people with peace.
>   (Ps 29:10-11 NIV)

This psalm show that God's kingship results in great blessing for his people.

4.2.1. Divine Kingship. Three hymns of divine kingship (Pss 93; 97; 99) begin with the acclamation *yhwh mālāk*, which is customarily translated either "the LORD is king" (NAB, NLT, NRSV, NJPS) or "the LORD reigns" (ESV, NASB, NIV, NKJV). Psalm 96:10 contains this phrase within the psalm, and Psalm 47:8 [MT 47:9] has a similar acclamation, *mālak ʾĕlōhîm* ("God reigns" or "God is king"). Since the days of S. Mowinckel the proper translation of this phrase has been debated. An alternate translation is "the LORD/God has become king." J. Day has presented a compelling defense of this translation. The perfect form of the verb *mālak* can be translated "became king" (1 Kings 16:23a), "reigned" (1 Kings 16:23b) or "has become king" (1 Sam 12:14; 2 Sam 15:10; 1 Kings 1:11, 13, 18; 2 Kings 9:13), but clear examples of "is king" are lacking in the Hebrew Bible. Contrary to common opinion, word order is irrelevant to this discussion, since the inceptive sense ("has become") is found with the order subject/predicate and the order predicate/subject. Compare "But now Adonijah has become king [*ʾădōniyyâ mālak*]" (1 Kings 1:18) with "Have you not heard that Adonijah, the son of Haggith, has become king [*mālak ʾădōniyyāhû*]. . . ?" (1 Kings 1:11). Moreover, the context of *mālak ʾĕlōhîm* in Psalm 47:8 [MT 47:9] provides the best evidence for the inceptive rendering. God has just ascended, having won a great victory (Ps 47:5), and has just taken his seat on his royal throne and begun to reign (Ps 47:8).

Although it is true that from one perspective God has always been king, it is equally true from another perspective that on specific occasions God "became king" in a new sense. G. Vos (342) says, "It will be remembered that the shout 'Absalom is King' was the shout of acclaim at his assumption of the kingship." So even if we stay with the traditional translation "the LORD/God is king/reigns," the parallels with the use of this phrase in reference to human kings indicates that this is an acclamation used at the inception of the king's reign. In reference to the Lord becoming king, Vos goes on to say, "By this is meant a form of statement representing Jehovah as becoming, or revealing himself in the last crisis the victorious King of Israel" (324), and "The simple solution seems to lie in this that 'kingship' is in the O.T. more a concept of action than of status. Jehovah becomes King = Jehovah works acts of deliverance" (342 n. 33), and "The thought is not merely that Jehovah becomes King in order to save, but that through the salvation, as well as in other acts, He arrives at the acme of his royal splendor" (344) (For this same idea of God beginning to reign in the NT, see Rev 11:17, where English translations are agreed in translating the aorist *ebasileusas* with "begun to reign."). There are two key actions through which the Lord "becomes king": creation and redemption.

4.2.2. Creation. The quintessential hymn of creation is Psalm 104, which opens with a portrayal of God as the glorious king.

Let all that I am praise the LORD;
O LORD my God, how great [*gādal*] you are!
You are robed with honor and majesty;
you are dressed in a robe of light.
   (Ps 104:1-2 NLT)

Just as we use the word "majesty" in association with royalty when we refer to a modern queen as "her Majesty," the ancient Hebrews used the word "great" (*gādôl*) in association with royalty. Psalm 47:2 refers to God as "a great [*gādôl*] king." In the same way, Psalm 95:3 refers to the Lord as "a great [*gādôl*] king." In the context of the ancient world at large this expression would be better translated as "the Great King," since it is almost a technical phrase used to refer to the king who reigns supreme over all other kings and kingdoms. This is why the full text of Psalm 95:3 reads,

For the Lord is a great God,
   the great King above all gods. (NIV)

In saying that God is "great," Psalm 104 shouts the praise of the King of kings and Lord of lords. This interpretation is confirmed by the word pair "honor and majesty" (*hôd wĕhādār*). "Honor and majesty" are regularly associated with royalty in the book of Psalms. In Psalm 21:5 God dresses the human king with "splendor and majesty" (*hôd wĕhādār*).

Your victory brings him [the human king]
   great honor,
and you have clothed him with splendor and
   majesty [*hôd wĕhādār*]. (NLT)

In the same way, the divine King is "robed with honor and majesty" in Psalm 104:1. The image is that of God dressed in the magnificent regalia of a reigning monarch. The point is that God's creating and governing of the universe was and is the activity of a king.

4.2.3. Redemption. God also "becomes king" through acts of redemption. Psalm 47, for example, invites the nations to praise the Lord as the "great King over all the earth" (Ps 47:2). He is the God who has just "become king" (Ps 47:9), when he defeated the Canaanite kingdoms and granted the land to Israel (Ps 47:3-4).

Hymns of redemption celebrate "the mighty acts of the LORD," what God has done not in primeval history but rather in Israel's history.

Who can proclaim the mighty acts of the
   LORD
or fully declare his praise? (Ps 106:2 NIV)
We will not hide them from their children;
we will tell the next generation the
   praiseworthy deeds of the LORD,
his power, and the wonders he has done.
   (Ps 78:4 NIV)

Give thanks to the LORD, call on his name;
make known among the nations what he has
done. (Ps 105:1 NIV)

The "mighty acts of the LORD" include his
deliverance of Israel from Egypt (Ps 78:52;
105:26-27; 114:1-2), his dividing of the Red Sea
(Ps 78:13; 106:8-11; 114:3-6), his giving of the law
(Ps 78:5), his care in the wilderness (Ps 78:14-16;
105:39-42; 114:8) and his granting of the land
(Ps 47:4; 78:55).

Psalm 136 combines the themes of creation
and redemption. In this psalm God's "great
wonders (Ps 136:4) include his creation of the
heavens (Ps 136:5-9) and his redemption of Israel from Egypt, through the wilderness, and to
the promised land (Ps 136:10-22). As this and the
foregoing examples show, the subcategories of
hymns of divine kingship, creation and redemption are not rigid but rather are fluid and flexible (Longman).

4.3. The Conclusion of Praise. In keeping with
the positive tone of the first two sections, the
hymns come to a conclusion on an equally positive note. Quite frequently, the conclusion contains a repeated invitation to praise. Thus Psalm
103 ends,

Praise the LORD, you angels,
you mighty ones who carry out his plans,
listening for each of his commands.
Yes, praise the LORD, you armies of angels
who serve him and do his will!
Praise the LORD, everything he has created,
everything in all his kingdom.
Let all that I am praise the Lord.
(Ps 103:20-22 NLT)

The hymn may also come to a close with a
strong affirmation of faith in the Lord, as is the
case in Psalm 29, which affirms that the Lord
rules over the world, and that this rule will result
in great blessing for the Lord's people.

The LORD rules over the floodwaters.
The LORD reigns as king forever.
The LORD gives his people strength.
The LORD blesses them with peace.
(Ps 29:10-11 NLT)

5. The Use of the Hymn.
Brueggemann has well argued that there were
and are at least two ways in which the hymns

functioned and function. One can be called "articulations of order," and the other "affirmations
of faith."

5.1. Articulations of Order. Perhaps no text
better captures the essence of the hymn as an
articulation of a well-ordered life than does
Psalm 16:5-6.

LORD, you have assigned me my portion and
my cup;
you have made my lot secure.
The boundary lines have fallen for me in
pleasant places;
surely I have a delightful inheritance. (NIV)

These are the words of someone who is experiencing life in all of its goodness. The life reflected in the hymn knows no trouble; it is a
happy, blessed life. Fear and anxiety are nowhere to be found, because God in his faithfulness is maintaining the order in life that he
intended from the very beginning. If Genesis 1
reveals anything about God's intention for creation, it is that creation is to be experienced as
well ordered. The rhythm of "and God said" and
"God saw that it was good" and "there was
evening and there was morning" underscores
the orderliness and goodness intended by God
for the world that he made. The hymn is thus
fundamentally a creation psalm—that is, a
psalm that knows the Creator to be reliable in
maintaining a well-ordered world. "Creation
here is not a theory about how the world came
to be.... It is rather an affirmation that God's
faithfulness and goodness are experienced as
generosity, continuity, and regularity" (Brueggemann, 26). The primary use of the hymn was
and is to articulate our praise and gratitude to
God for the good life that he has so generously
granted to us.

5.2. Affirmations of Faith. Life, however, is not
always experienced as well ordered and good,
sometimes for known reasons and at other times
for reasons unknown. Even the great poet who
composed Psalm 104, the quintessential poetic
articulation of a well-ordered world, was aware
of this when he said, "But may sinners vanish
from the earth and the wicked be no more" (Ps
104:35). He knew that the presence of "sinners"
could disrupt the good order of life (Allen). So,
what role can the hymns play in lives characterized by chaos and disorientation? Brueggemann
argues that the hymn can also function as an af-

firmation of faith, as a "great evangelical nevertheless." The hymn expresses the deep desire of the human heart for life as God intends. The human heart knows its origin, life in all of its abundance. The human heart knows the destiny that God desires for all, life in all of its abundance. The human heart longs to experience this life now and not only in the future. This is why the poet who wrote Psalm 27 said,

> Yet I am confident that I will see the LORD's
> goodness
> while I am here in the land of the living.
> (Ps 27:13 NLT)

The hymn can thus be used to express a profound hope that God will show up not in theory but rather in the concrete realities of life and bring order out of chaos. The hymn is an affirmation of faith that Jesus truly came to bring life in all of its abundance (John 10:10).

See also CULT, WORSHIP: PSALMS; FORM CRITICISM; LYRIC POETRY; MUSIC, SONG; PSALMS 1: BOOK OF; REFRAIN; RHYME.

BIBLIOGRAPHY. **L. C. Allen,** *Psalms 101-150* (WBC 21; Waco, TX: Word, 1983); **K. L. Barker,** "Praise," in *Cracking Old Testament Codes: A Guide to Interpreting the Literary Genres of the Old Testament,* ed. D. B. Sandy and R. L. Giese (Nashville: Broadman & Holman, 1995) 217-32; **W. Brueggemann,** *The Message of the Psalms* (Minneapolis: Augsburg, 1984); **R. J. Clifford,** *Psalms 1-72* (AOTC; Nashville: Abingdon, 2002); **J. J. Collins,** *Introduction to the Hebrew Bible* (Minneapolis: Fortress, 2004); **M. D. Coogan,** *The Old Testament: A Historical and Literary Introduction to the Hebrew Scriptures* (Oxford: Oxford University Press, 2006); **L. Coppes,** "הלל," *TWOT* 1.217-18; **J. Day,** *Psalms* (OTG; Sheffield: Sheffield Academic Press, 1995); **D. J. Estes,** *Handbook on the Wisdom Books and Psalms* (Grand Rapids: Baker, 2005); **M. D. Futato,** *Transformed by Praise: The Purpose and Message of the Psalms* (Phillipsburg, NJ: P & R Publishing, 2002); idem, *Interpreting the Psalms: An Exegetical Handbook* (HOTE; Grand Rapids: Kregel, 2007); **E. S. Gerstenberger,** *Psalms* (2 vols.; FOTL; Grand Rapids: Eerdmans, 1988-2001); **H. Gunkel,** *The Psalms: A Form-Critical Introduction* (Philadelphia: Fortress, 1967); **J. H. Hutchinson,** "The Psalms and Praise," in *Interpreting the Psalms: Issues and Approaches,* ed. D. Firth and P. S. Johnston (Downers Grove, IL: InterVarsity Press: 2005) 85-100; **T. Longman III,** *How to Read the Psalms* (Downers Grove, IL: InterVarsity Press, 1988); **E. H. Merrill,** "הלל," *NIDOTTE* 1.1035-37; **S. Mowinckel,** *The Psalms in Israel's Worship* (Nashville: Abingdon, 1962); **H. Ringgren,** "הלל," *TDOT* 3.404-10; **G. Vos,** "The Eschatology of the Psalter," in *Pauline Eschatology* (Grand Rapids: Eerdmans, 1953); **C. West-ermann,** "הלל," *TLOT* 1.371-76; idem, *Praise and Lament in the Psalms* (Atlanta: John Knox, 1981).   M. D. Futato

I

ICONOGRAPHY. *See* IMAGERY; PSALMS 5: ICO-
NOGRAPHY.

IMAGERY

The words *imagery* and *image* are notoriously
slippery ones in the study of literature. When it
comes to poetic theory, they occur in so many
contexts that W. Mitchell (1993b, 556) believes
that "it may well be impossible to provide any rational systematic account of their usage." This is
no counsel of despair, especially coming from
Mitchell, a leading theorist of imagery (see
Mitchell 1986; 1993a; 1994), as much as it is confirmation of the crucial importance and sheer
ubiquity of imagery. A social psychologist has
put it well: "We live on images" (Lifton, 3). And
so does poetry. But much of the difficulty in interpreting poetry revolves precisely around understanding imagery (see Berlin 2004, 2102).
The present article cannot adequately address
such a large and essential topic; instead, it offers
brief overviews of imagery in text and in art, the
latter being an increasingly important arena for
the study of the former (see Mitchell 1986;
1994). Thereafter, the article discusses the problem of correlating textual and artistic images
and then offers a few examples of this type of
image analysis and some concluding reflections
on imagery and theology.

    1. Imagery in Texts
    2. Imagery in Art
    3. Correlating Textual and Artistic Imagery
    4. Case Studies in Text-Art Correlation
    5. Conclusion: Imagery and Theology

1. Imagery in Texts.
To review adequately the study of imagery in
texts would take volumes because *imagery*, as another term for *figurative language*, includes numerous devices such as metaphor, simile,
allegory, *personification, apostrophe and a
host of other figures of speech, not to mention
still other topics (see Watson 2000, 270-73;
J. Black, 51; Mitchell 1993b, 556). Since articles
on specific images found in the OT appear elsewhere in this dictionary, this section treats three
issues: (1) the importance of imagery, (2) how
images work, and (3) interpreting imagery.

    Before we proceed further, a working defini-
tion of *image/imagery* is in order. As Mitchell
(1993b, 556-59) has noted, the terms *image* and
imagery historically have been used in a wide variety of ways (cf. Friedman). Even so, a usable
point of reference is provided by L. Ryken,
J. Wilhoit and T. Longman (xiii) in a recent dictionary devoted to biblical imagery: "An image is
any word that names a concrete thing (such as
tree or house) or action (such as running or
threshing). Any object or action that we can picture is an image." This definition treats the image as a "verbal representation of a concrete
(usually visual) object"; in this view, imagery is
"seen as eliciting mental images in the reader,
evoking a kind of secondary visual representation" (Mitchell 1993a, 553). Though other understandings of *image/imagery* are available, this
"pictorial" or "visual" one is common (see Turco, 55; Oliver, 99; Watson 2001, 251). It should
also be noted that Ryken, Wilhoit and Longman's definition already indicates that imagery
is both "a mode of apprehension" and "a rhetorical device" (Mitchell 1993b, 557; cf. Oliver,
107; Watson 2001, 255); furthermore, it combines elements of text (naming, describing) and
art (image, picturing).

    1.1. The Importance of Imagery to Poetics. Poet-
ry traffics in images. They are "the glory, perhaps the essence of poetry" (Alonso Schökel, 95;
cf. Berlin, *NIB* 4.311; 2004, 2101); imagery, in
turn, is "the central topic of poetics" (Weiss, 140).

The poet William Carlos Williams is famous for saying, "No ideas [in poetry] but in things," to which M. Oliver (19) added, "and . . . no things but in . . . the words representing them." In point of fact, many of the words that poets use are not modifiers (adjectives, adverbs or phrases constructed with either) but rather tropes, figures, imagery (Turco, 55). Good poetry works (*poetics) not by listing "ideas" but rather by discussing ideas via "things" that are described with "words" that are imagistic ("A poem is an artifice of thought . . . and there is no thought except in symbols, in forms" [Turco, 68]).

Scripture operates similarly. As Ryken, Wilhoit and Longman (xiii) note, "The Bible is more than a book of ideas: it is also a book of images and motifs." Nowhere is this truer than at those places where Scripture is, in fact, poetry, including not only Psalms but also major sections of the Wisdom literature and the Prophets. Although many of the images used in the Bible are derived from natural phenomena—in large part, probably, because Israel was a rural, non-industrial and far less urbanized society than our own—they can be highly sophisticated (Watson 2000, 270; Petersen and Richards, 51). This is due in part to the complexity of imagery, imagistic language and image analysis in the first place. Be that as it may, it is true that we miss much "of what the Bible contains if we do not see and understand the literal and symbolic meanings of the Bible's images" (Ryken, Wilhoit and Longman, xiii).

1.2. How Images Work. As we already noted, imagery is a complex phenomenon and can be subdivided into a number of separate categories. Theories abound for understanding how images work and, correlatively, how best to interpret them. For now it can be noted that many scholars believe that imagery functions primarily as a means of comparison (see, e.g., Alonso Schökel, 99, 105-7, 114; Turco, 56-57). W. Watson (2000, 270-71) puts it this way: "The essence of imagery is the juxtaposition of two different levels of meaning" (cf. Watson 2001, 251); Oliver (92, 99) expresses it this way: "*Imagery* means, generally, the representation of one thing by another thing," and poetic language in general is "the language of one thing compared to another thing."

One will recognize similarities between these descriptions of imagery and the way metaphor functions if only because metaphor is a subset of imagery writ large (Alonso Schökel, 99, 108-9; Turco, 57, 61). Study of metaphor, in turn, can provide helpful insight into the interpretation of imagery as a whole (see 1.3 below). Similarities are also seen, however, between imagery as fundamentally comparison—with reference to metaphor especially, including both the *like* and the *unlike* (see Ricoeur)—and how some scholars have characterized the nature of Hebrew *parallelism (see Petersen and Richards, 52, 59; Berlin 1985; Alter). A. Berlin (1997, 27-28), for instance, has argued that parallelism itself is like metaphor (and thus imagery) and vice versa:

> Parallelism juxtaposes lines that are, from a linguistic perspective, equivalent on one level while being different on another. Parallel lines contain grammatical and semantic equivalents but are rarely identical. They are the same and yet different; and it is the productive tension between the sameness and the difference that makes parallelism so effective . . . metaphor and parallelism are two sides of the same coin—counterparts of the same phenomenon in a different dimension. . . . We could say that parallelism operates in the linguistic dimension the way metaphor operates in the conceptual dimension. Parallelism juxtaposes verbal similarities and differences while metaphor juxtaposes non-verbal similarities and differences. It is through the coherent interpretation of both of these types of juxtapositions that meaning is achieved.

Sensitivity to juxtaposition and comparison, and interpreting them coherently, is thus crucial to an adequate understanding of imagery—a point to which we now turn. Before doing so, however, we should note that imagery is used, in no small way, for rhetorical purposes. To be sure, an image enlivens a text in a way that simple informational description does not (see Oliver, 94), but if the text is communicative, then the image is also rhetorical: it creates "an effect in the listener and affects him or her as well" (Turco, 67), at the very least by making demands of its interpreters or readers (Petersen and Richards, 60).

1.3. Interpreting Imagery. As a subset of imagistic language, metaphor is a useful arena in which to discuss interpretation. Like the study of imagery more broadly, the study of metaphor is a large topic of research (Ricouer; briefly, Strawn, 5-16). The old view, which in some ways goes back to Aristotle, is that metaphors simply substitute for the "real" object. As such, they are mostly ornamental and ultimately dispensable. More recent work on metaphors has demonstrated that they are far more than simple decorative devices; instead, they constitute deeply engrained forms of human cognition such that it is impossible either to think or to speak without them (Lakoff and Turner; Lakoff and Johnson; cf. Alonso Schökel, 100-101). Even scientific discourse cannot avoid the metaphorical (e.g., "black hole"), and our everyday speech is saturated with it. Consider, for example, the metaphor "Argument is war," which lies behind statements such as "Your claims are indefensible," "She demolished his point of view," "He shot down all my arguments" and "You attacked every weak point in her talk" (Lakoff and Johnson, 4). Moreover, and as a result, metaphors are highly effective in communicating and therefore are rarely if ever used solely for ornamentation but rather for particular functions (see Watson 2001, 252) and to particular effect, especially because many things could not be said, or said as well, without the image/metaphor (see Weiss, 156).

The influential work on metaphor by M. Black (1962) is useful for biblical studies because it accounts for the different contexts between the one who uses a metaphor and the one who receives it. For ideal communication to take place, the receiver must share the user's "sign-context" (the larger conceptual climate that forms and informs the meaning of the metaphor chosen—e.g., shared language, worldview, literary competence) to adequately understand the metaphor.

If the user and receiver are contemporaries but do not, for some reason, share the same sign-context, questions may be asked and clarification gained through subsequent communication. The situation is quite different and more problematic when the users are long-deceased authors and the metaphors are from ancient texts that attest to a very different sign-context than the modern world. This is the difficult situation facing the one analyzing biblical metaphors. Among other things, it means that a good deal of effort is required to comprehend the meaning of a metaphor in its original (user's sign-) context. As Watson (2000, 270) states, "Particularly in verse, where it is used more intensely and more often, figurative language needs to be understood so that the meaning . . . can be grasped. . . . This entails some knowledge of the background to the Hebrew texts, especially the customs, religion and lifestyle and the geographic and historical setting of Israel and her neighbours."

Watson's point about Israel's neighbors is important because "some [biblical] imagery derives from the mythology of neighbouring civilizations" (Watson 2000, 271). Pragmatically, this means that one must gain some sort of access to what ancient metaphors mean in their ancient settings—biblical, Israelite or otherwise—in no small part because images have histories, some of which can be and clearly are assumed by poets for their audiences (see Turco, 64; Kinzie, 172-73).

Ryken, Wilhoit and Longman (xiv) have stated that to interpret imagery adequately, one must experience the image "as literally and in as fully a sensory way as possible" and subsequently "be sensitive to the connotations or overtones of the image." One must ask, in short, two questions of any image: "What is the literal picture?" and "What does this image evoke?" Both steps—meaning and evocation—necessitate at least some attention to the user's sign-context if widely erring interpretation is to be avoided. (However, for appropriate cautions that such an approach is not foolproof, see J. Black, 56.)

How is access to the ancient sign-context gained? There are at least two ways. The first is careful work with textual instances of the image or metaphor in question. Ancient Near Eastern texts, like biblical ones, abound with imagery (see, e.g., Foster, xviii) such that one may study various occurrences of the image in question, both within Scripture and without. Note one example, from the Epic of Gilgamesh:

> Like a lioness whose cubs are in a pitfall,
> He [Gilgamesh] paced to and fro, back
>   and forth. (Epic of Gilgamesh VIII, 60-61
>   [Foster, 61])

When psalmists cry out with language that is otherwise typically reserved for the vocalization of lions (e.g., the root šʾg in Ps 22:1 [MT 22:2]; 32:3; 38:8 [MT 38:9]), how is this to be understood? Perhaps Gilgamesh's mournful pacing after Enkidu's death sheds some light on the imagistic language utilized (see also Zech 11:3).

But meaning is not made solely in the textual realm, especially in antiquity, where literacy rates were most likely very low. So, the second crucial means of entry into ancient imagery and metaphor is artistic remains. This is a relatively new area of research, which is the subject of the next section. Both means of access, however—the textual and the artistic—help us to interpret imagery. As Ryken, Wilhoit and Longman (xiii) note, whereas some images are universal, or seemingly so, others are "unexpressive until we have been alerted to their significance," and the meaning of still other images "is lost on modern readers unless they are initiated into what the motif meant in other places at other times." The study of image/imagery in text and art is a crucial tool in that initiation.

2. Imagery in Art.

If imagery is a large topic in textual studies, the same is true for art. In fact, a case might be made that the "image-in-text" is dependent upon and generated by the "image-in-art," even if that art is purely mental—the image in the mind. R. Arnheim, for instance, argued that all thinking is dependent on vision. We see things, and that is how we know things (cf. Ramachandran, 24-59; Mitchell 1994, 24). We know them, at least in part, by recreating and reconstructing them, seeing them in or with our mind's eye, as it were. If Arnheim is right, even only partially, then attention to the image in art is imperative, not simply a curiosity. (For an interactionist perspective on images and texts, see Mitchell 1986; 1994.)

The wisdom of such an approach has only recently dawned on biblical scholars. The pioneering work of O. Keel in 1972 (ET, Keel 1997) was the first of its kind to explicitly and extensively investigate biblical literary images with reference to ancient Near Eastern artistic ones. Since that publication, Keel and his students and followers have engaged in wide-ranging research that has cast new and significant light on the Bible. Unfortunately, the method adopted by these scholars has not always been clearly articulated; this has made them vulnerable to attacks from textually myopic scholars who have skeptically asked questions such as "How does one know that an artistic image means this or that?"

In response, it might be said that textual images are certainly no less opaque than artistic ones. Moreover, artistic images, no less than textual ones, have histories (even "grammars") of use that can be investigated as literary images are (see below). Before proceeding further, it must be reiterated that a comprehensive study of image-meaning in art exceeds the space allotted here. Even so, as a first step into this vast area, the classic and instructive work of E. Panofsky in 1939 (reprint, Panofsky 1972) can be considered, especially since it has proven foundational for subsequent thinking.

Panofsky identified three layers of meaning or content in an (artistic) image: (1) primary or natural subject matter, (2) secondary or conventional subject matter, (3) intrinsic meaning or content. As an example, he offered the "image" of meeting an acquaintance (the object) who thereupon removed his hat. The primary subject matter includes the change of visual details marked by the other person's movement and how that movement is done (in good humor or bad, friendly or hostile). But realizing that this movement is a greeting at all depends on secondary subject matter, in this case the conventions that are particular to certain social situations, locales and persons. A larger nexus of action, context and interpretation affords the intrinsic meaning of the image. Panofsky (4-5 [italics added]) explains,

> Besides constituting a natural event in space and time, besides naturally indicating moods or feelings, besides conveying a conventional greeting, the action of my acquaintance can reveal to an experienced observer all that goes to make up his "personality." This personality is conditioned by his being a man of the twentieth century, by his national, social and educational background, by the previous history of his life and by his present surroundings, but it is also distinguished by an individual manner of viewing things and reacting to the world which, if rationalized, would have to be called a philosophy. In the isolated action of a polite greeting all these factors do not manifest themselves comprehensively, but nevertheless symptomatically. We could not construct a mental portrait of the man on the basis of this single action, but only by co-ordinating a large number of similar observations and by interpreting them in connection with our general information as to the gentlemen's period, nationality, class, intellectual traditions and so forth. *Yet all the*

qualities which this mental portrait would show explicitly are implicitly inherent in every single action, so that, conversely, every single action can be interpreted in the light of those qualities.

This three-step system is too neatly differentiated, as Panofsky himself acknowledged; in practice, the three operations "merge with each other into one organic and indivisible process" (Panofsky, 17). Even so, these steps are heuristic in thinking about interpretation of an image, which in his example is not literary or artistic but rather actual, real, performative. Table 1 summarizes Panofsky's steps when applied to the study of artistic imagery proper.

Although scholars have appropriately refined, developed and critiqued Panofsky's schema (see Mitchell 1994, esp. 25-34), his work remains useful. At least three items deserve mention here. First, Panofsky distinguished motifs from images. The latter are motifs with secondary or conventional meaning. This again demonstrates that images have histories and systems of "associated implications" (the characteristics typically connected with the image in question [see M. Black, 41]). Second, Panofsky distinguished between images and combinations of images; these latter are what he called stories or allegories. Iconography in the narrower sense was the identification of these images, stories and allegories; accurate iconographical analysis thus was dependent upon accurate identification of the motifs (Panofsky, 6-7). Third, Panofsky wished to reach a deeper iconographical interpretation or synthesis, what he called "iconology" proper, which is dependent on a correct analysis of the images, stories and allegories (Panofsky, 8). This deeper synthesis may reveal meanings unknown or unintended by the artist insofar as both the artist and the work are products of larger cultural milieus that are formative and operative (see Dikovitskaya, 1-2, 120; Mitchell 1993b, 558), even (and sometimes especially) on unconscious levels. This last observation has two very important implications for the study of imagery, each of which is best dealt with under the rubric of correlation.

3. Correlating Textual and Artistic Imagery.

As we noted previously, the study of ancient artistic imagery with reference to textual imagery is a relatively new development in biblical studies. Scholars have long studied artistic remains (iconography) of various sorts from ancient Israel/Palestine and the ancient Near East, but not always with reference to biblical imagery. J. LeMon has identified three types of iconographic analysis: iconographic-artistic, iconographic-historical and iconographic-biblical. Only the third is concerned with correlating artistic imagery with imagery from the Bible. Once again, Keel is a major pioneer on this point, but his work has spanned all three types (see, e.g., Keel and Uehlinger; Schroer and Keel). Since

Table 1. Panofsky's Method of Image Analysis (Adapted and simplified from Panofsky, 14-15)

Interpretive Object	Interpretive Task	Interpretive Method	Interpretive Control
Primary or natural subject matter: the world of artistic motifs	Pre-iconographical description of motifs	Practical experience: familiarity with objects/motifs and events	History of *style*: insight into why objects and events were expressed by specific forms at certain times
Secondary or conventional subject matter: the world of images and image complexes (stories, allegories)	Iconographical analysis in the *narrow* sense	Knowledge of literary sources: familiarity with themes and concepts at work in an image	History of *types*: insight into why specific themes or concepts were expressed by objects and events at certain times
Intrinsic meaning or content: the world of "symbolical" values reflected/present in the work	Iconographical analysis in the *deeper* sense or, better, what might be called iconographical interpretation/synthesis ("iconology")	"Synthetic intuition": familiarity with tendencies of the human mind	History of cultural "*symbols*": insight into why tendencies of the human mind were expressed by specific themes and concepts at certain times

the iconographical-biblical type of text-art correlation is still in its infancy in biblical studies, methodological clarity is often lacking. Keel and others have provided significant insights, but the methodological question remains: How does one do it?

Returning to Panofsky, we could put the question(s) differently: How does one go about getting the correct interpretation of motifs, then of images and their complexes (stories, allegories), and then, finally, of the intrinsic meaning? For motifs, Panofksy (9) suggested that we rely mostly on *practical experience*. But this goes only so far when it comes to ancient images, about which our practical experience may be irrelevant or inaccurate—a point that Panofsky (9) admitted. So, practical experience must be controlled by the *history of style*—the study of the expression of objects and events in certain forms under various historical conditions (Panofsky, 11 [see Table 1 above]). But how is the history of style known? For Panofsky (11), the student of imagery must have "a familiarity with specific *themes* or *concepts* as transmitted through literary sources, whether acquired by purposeful reading or by oral tradition."

This is the first practical result mentioned at the end of the preceeding section. To get at deeper iconographical meaning/content (i.e., Panofsky's "iconology"), one needs as much purchase on the milieu as possible; literary sources are important, even necessary, tools in that task. "When it comes to representations of *themes* other than" those "which happen to be known to the average 'educated person,' all of us . . . must try to familiarize ourselves with what the authors of those representations had read or otherwise knew" (Panofsky, 11-12). So, even when studying artistic imagery, textual data are a necessity (see Mitchell 1986, 155).

But as important and indispensable as literary sources are, they cannot guarantee a correct iconographical analysis (Panofsky, 12). Knowledge from literary sources must be subjected to the *history of artistic types* (Panofsky, 13 [see Table 1 above]). Moreover, since it is unlikely that we would find a specific text to fit a complex iconographical tableau, "we need a mental faculty comparable to that of a diagnostician" (Panofsky, 14-15). But this intuition too must be chastened, somehow, by the *history of cultural symptoms or symbols.* Panofksy (16) explains,

The art-historian will have to check what he thinks is the *intrinsic meaning* of the work, or group of works, to which he devotes his attention, against what he thinks the *intrinsic meaning* of as many other documents of civilization historically related to that work or group of works, as he can master: of documents bearing witness to the political, poetical, religious, philosophical, and social tendencies of the personality, period or country under investigation. Needless to say that, conversely, the historian of political life, poetry, religion, philosophy, and social situation should make an analogous use of works of art. It is in the search for *intrinsic meanings* or *content* that the various humanistic disciplines meet on a common plane instead of serving as handmaidens to each other.

This is the second practical result: art, no less than text, is a window into the ancient world, including its religion, politics and the like, but, for our purposes, most importantly its poetry and thus its imagery (see Mitchell 1994, 20-21). In the memorable lines from J. Goethe (1.137), "Whoever the poet would understand, must go into the poet's land" (my translation).

4. Case Studies in Text-Art Correlation.

And going into the poet's land really does help one understand the poet(ry). Consider again Panofsky's friend removing his hat. Such a greeting "is peculiar to the western world and is a residue of mediaeval chivalry. . . . Neither an Australian bushman nor an ancient Greek could be expected to realize that the lifting of a hat is . . . a sign of politeness" (Panofsky, 4).

Or consider Amos 1:2: "The LORD from Mount Zion roars [*š'g*] and from Jerusalem utters his voice. The pastures of the shepherds wither, and the top of Mount Carmel dries up" (my translation). The verb *š'g* typically is associated with lions (see, e.g., Judg 14:5; Isa 5:29; Jer 2:15; 51:38; Ezek 22:25; Hos 11:10; Amos 3:4, 8; Zeph 3:3; Ps 22:14; 104:21). A common modern notion of lion imagery associates them with bravery and courage, but that does not match up well with Amos. When one looks to ancient texts and artistic remains (see, e.g., figure 1), however, one sees that these correct the modern misinterpretations, showing that in the ancient world, lions were primary tropes of power and threat (see Strawn). Yahweh's imagistic figuring as a lion in Amos is not because Yahweh is brave or courageous but rather because Yahweh is dangerous and terrifying. No wonder the earth shudders at the sound of the Divine Lion's roar (cf. Amos 3:8).

Figure 1. Late Bronze Age seal from Tell el-Far ah (S.) (Strawn 2005:382 fig. 3.12; Keel and Uehlinger 1998:83 illus. 100).

Or consider Psalm 42:1-2a (MT 42:2-3a): "As a deer longs for flowing streams, so my soul longs for you, O God. My soul thirsts for God, for the living God" (NRSV). There are ancient depictions of the drinking deer (see figure 2), but this particular poetic image is enlightening because the comparison formed by the metaphor of the psalmist and the deer creates a new relationship "such that their qualities become interchanged" (Berlin, *NIB* 4.311). The psalmist becomes deer-like, and the deer becomes human-like. Normally, one does not expect deer to "long" like humans do. But with poetry, all things are possible. Longing seems more characteristic of humans and thirsting for water more characteristic of deer, but the poetic image crisscrosses the two subjects, attributing aspects of the one to the other (Berlin, *NIB* 4.311). In the process God is also affected, imaged as refreshing water (cf. Ps 42:7[MT 42:8]), as necessary and vital as drink to a thirsty animal.

Numerous other examples could be offered (see, e.g., Foster, xviii). Certainly Ryken, Wilhoit and Longman (xv) are correct in saying that "the time is ripe for some bold new commentaries and dictionaries with pictorial accompaniment to make the . . . images come alive." A place to start is with their dictionary, but also with the pioneering work of Keel, the multivol-

ume compendium of images currently in production by Schroer and Keel (cf. also *ANEP*), and the groundbreaking study by W. Brown on psalmic metaphor and "iconic structures."

5. Conclusion: Imagery and Theology.

In conclusion, we may observe that humans are not the only ones who live on images; evidently, God does too. This is true at the literary level where God, who is *sui generis,* must be portrayed and depicted by images and metaphors if God is to be apprehended by humans at all (see Berlin *NIB*, 4.312; Alonso Schökel, 128-38; for "God" metaphors, see Korpel; Gibson, 121-38). This is also true if Genesis 1:26-27 is to be believed, which locates God's image precisely in the image of the human (see Mitchell 1986, 2). God's image lives in the living image of human beings, who in turn live on images, including images of the living God.

Finally, this article has also tried to demonstrate that Scripture itself lives on images (see Ryken, Wilhoit and Longman, xiii. And although images reside in all kinds of literature,

Figure 2. Mid-eighth century seal; unprovenanced, allegedly from Hebron (Keel and Uehlinger 1998:185 illus. 200b; Brown 2002:149 fig. 16).

nowhere are they as dense and as significant as in poetry. Imagery may, then, in the final analysis, be poetry's greatest contribution to theology (see Miller; Wilder 2001; cf. Berlin 2004, 2101-2). As S. Gillingham (278) puts it, "The language of theology needs the poetic medium for much of its expression, for poetry, with its power of allusion, reminds us of the more hidden and mysterious truths which theology seeks to express. . . . Perhaps to learn the art of reading biblical poetry is but a precursor to learning the art of 'doing' theology at all" (cf. Berlin 2004, 2101). Clearly, understanding imagery is a crucial part of both arts.

See also ANIMAL IMAGERY; ARCHITECTURAL IMAGERY; CREATION IMAGERY; FLORAL IMAGERY; IMPRISONMENT IMAGERY; MOUNTAIN IMAGERY; PROTECTION IMAGERY; PSALMS 5: ICONOGRAPHY; SALVATION AND DELIVERANCE IMAGERY; WARFARE IMAGERY; ZION.

BIBLIOGRAPHY. **L. Alonso Schökel,** *A Manual of Hebrew Poetics* (SubBi 11; Rome: Pontifical Biblical Institute, 2000); **R. Alter,** *The Art of Biblical Poetry* (New York: Basic Books, 1985); **R. Arnheim,** *Visual Thinking* (Berkeley: University of California Press, 1969); **A. Berlin,** *The Dynamics of Biblical Parallelism* (Bloomington: Indiana University Press, 1985); idem, "On Reading Biblical Poetry: The Role of Metaphor," in *Congress Volume: Cambridge 1995*, ed. J. A. Emerton (VTSup 66; Leiden: E. J. Brill, 1997) 25-36; idem, "Reading Biblical Poetry," in *The Jewish Study Bible*, ed. A Berlin and M. Z. Brettler (Oxford: Oxford University Press, 2004) 2097-2104; idem, "Introduction to Hebrew Poetry," *NIB* 4.301-15; **J. Black,** *Reading Sumerian Poetry* (Ithaca, NY: Cornell University Press, 1998); **M. Black,** *Models and Metaphors: Studies in Language and Philosophy* (Ithaca, NY: Cornell University Press, 1962); **W. P. Brown,** *Seeing the Psalms: A Theology of Metaphor* (Louisville: Westminster John Knox, 2002); **M. Dikovitskaya,** *Visual Culture: The Study of the Visual after the Cultural Turn* (Cambridge, MA: MIT Press, 2005); **B. R. Foster,** ed., *The Epic of Gilgamesh: A New Translation, Analogues, Criticism* (New York: W. W. Norton, 2001); **N. Friedman,** "Imagery," in *The New Princeton Encyclopedia of Poetry and Poetics*, ed. A. Preminger and T. V. F. Brogan (Princeton, NJ: Princeton University Press, 1993) 559-66; **J. C. L. Gibson,** *Language and Imagery in the Old Testament* (Peabody, MA: Hendrickson, 1998); **S. E. Gillingham,** *The Poems and Psalms of the Hebrew Bible* (Oxford: Oxford University Press, 1994); **J. W. Goethe,** *West-östlicher Divan*, ed. H. Birus (2 vols.; Bibliothek deutscher Klassiker 113; Frankfurt: Deutscher Klassiker Verlag, 1994); **O. Keel,** *The Symbolism of the Biblical World: Ancient Near Eastern Iconography and the Book of Psalms*, (repr., Winona Lake, IN: Eisenbrauns, 1997 [1972]); **O. Keel and C. Uehlinger,** *Gods, Goddesses, and Images of God in Ancient Israel*, (Minneapolis: Fortress, 1998); **M. Kinzie,** *A Poet's Guide to Poetry* (Chicago: University of Chicago Press, 1999);

M. C. A. Korpel, *A Rift in the Clouds: Ugaritic and Hebrew Descriptions of the Divine* (UBL 8; Münster: Ugarit-Verlag, 1990); **G. Lakoff and M. Johnson,** *Metaphors We Live By* (Chicago: University of Chicago Press, 2003); **G. Lakoff and M. Turner,** *More Than Cool Reason: A Field Guide to Poetic Metaphor* (Chicago: University of Chicago Press, 1989); **J. M. LeMon,** "The Iconography of Yahweh's Winged Form in the Psalms" (Ph.D. diss., Emory University, 2007); **R. J. Lifton,** *The Broken Connection: On Death and the Continuity of Life* (New York: Simon & Schuster, 1979); **P. D. Miller,** "The Theological Significance of Biblical Poetry," in *Language, Theology, and the Bible: Essays in Honor of James Barr*, ed. J. Barton and S. E. Balentine (Oxford: Oxford University Press, 1994) 213-30; **W. J. T. Mitchell,** *Iconology: Image, Text, Ideology* (Chicago: University of Chicago Press, 1986); idem, "Iconology," in *The New Princeton Encyclopedia of Poetry and Poetics*, ed. A. Preminger and T. V. F. Brogan (Princeton, NJ: Princeton University Press, 1993a) 552-54; idem, "Image," in *The New Princeton Encyclopedia of Poetry and Poetics*, ed. A. Preminger and T. V. F. Brogan (Princeton, NJ: Princeton University Press, 1993b) 556-59; idem, *Picture Theory: Essays on Verbal and Visual Representation* (Chicago: University of Chicago Press, 1994); **M. Oliver,** *A Poetry Handbook* (San Diego: Harcourt Brace, 1994); **E. Panofsky,** *Studies in Iconology: Humanistic Themes in the Art of the Renaissance* (Icon Editions; Boulder, CO: Westview, 1972 [1939]); **D. L. Petersen and K. H. Richards,** *Interpreting Hebrew Poetry* (GBS; Minneapolis: Fortress, 1992); **V. S. Ramachandran,** *A Brief Tour of Human Consciousness: From Imposter Poodles to Purple Numbers* (New York: Pi Press, 2004); **P. Ricoeur,** *The Rule of Metaphor: Multi-Disciplinary Studies of the Creation of Meaning in Language* (Toronto: University of Toronto Press, 1977); **L. Ryken, J. C. Wilhoit and T. Longman III,** eds., *Dictionary of Biblical Imagery* (Downers Grove, IL: InterVarsity Press, 1998); **S. Schroer and O. Keel,** *Die Ikonographie Palästinas/Israels und der Alte Orient: Eine Religionsgeschichte in Bildern* (4 vols. projected, 1 in print; Fribourg: Academic Press, 2005-); **B. A. Strawn,** *What Is Stronger Than a Lion? Leonine Image and Metaphor in the Hebrew Bible and the Ancient Near East* (OBO 212; Fribourg: Academic Press; Göttingen: Vandenhoeck & Ruprecht, 2005); **L. Turco,** *The Book of Forms: A Handbook of Poetics* (3d ed.; Hanover, NH: University Press of New England, 2000); **W. G. E. Watson,** "Hebrew

Poetry," in *Text in Context: Essays by Members of the Society for Old Testament Study*, ed. A. D. H. Mayes (Oxford: Oxford University Press, 2000) 253-85; idem, *Classical Hebrew Poetry: A Guide to Its Techniques* (2d ed.; JSOTSup 26; Sheffield: Sheffield Academic Press, 2001); **M. Weiss**, *The Bible from Within: The Method of Total Interpretation* (Jerusalem: Magnes, 1984); **A. N. Wilder**, *Theopoetic: Theology and the Religious Imagination* (Lima, OH: Academic Renewal Press, 2001 [1976]).

B. A. Strawn

IMPRECATION

Imprecation pertains to cursing or uttering a curse (i.e., malediction) (Lat *imprecatus*). Most simply, curse may be contrasted with blessing. If blessing "consists of a wish for someone to receive the things considered good in life: land, numerous progeny, sufficient food, clothing, etc.," then curse "is the wish that someone be deprived of these same things" (Crawford, 25; cf. 231; see Stuart, 1218). Numerous examples of malediction or cursing are known from the ancient world and the OT. After an overview of this material, including a discussion of how curses are thought to have worked in antiquity, the present article takes up what is probably the most difficult issue regarding imprecation: the appropriation or contemporary use(fulness) of the imprecatory psalms.

1. Imprecation in the Ancient World
2. How Curses Functioned in Antiquity
3. Imprecation in the Old Testament
4. Appropriating Imprecation: The Case of the Imprecatory Psalms

1. Imprecation in the Ancient World.

1.1. Definitions. Curses are not the same as vows or oaths (see Cartledge, 15-16; Mercer 1912, 1), though the latter are typically promises with curses attached, the curses being the unfortunate results facing those who violated their oaths (Crawford, 109; Brichto, 24-25). In this sense, oaths are self-imprecations (Leick). Curses may appear without oaths, of course, but oaths involve curses. Since the oath is "indirectly referred to and its existence taken for granted in literature of various classes" (Mercer 1912, 1), imprecation is a far-flung phenomenon beyond curse-speech proper. It is not solely an Israelite issue (nor simply an OT one [see 4 below]). According to Leick (217), the most frequent imprecation in the ancient Near East "was that the offender should be without issue and die without leaving a name."

1.2. Attestations. Given the wide range of imprecation in antiquity, a healthy variety of curses are found in ancient Near Eastern literatures. These include, for example, (1) execration texts—objects/texts inscribed with the names of enemies that were subsequently and symbolically destroyed (*COS* 1.32:50-52; *ANET*, 328-29); (2) treaty texts, where the curses specify punishments that face disobedient vassals (*COS* 2.82:213-17; 2.127-29:329-32; *ANET*, 533-34; Walton, 69); (3) magical and mythical texts (Crawford, 25, 207); and (4) inscriptions of various sorts (often royal) from different locales (*COS* 2.21:124-26; 2.30-32:147-152; *ANET*, 653-55; Walton, 65). Indeed, curse formulas are usually found on objects such as monuments, sarcophagi, boundary stones, tombs, treaties and the like, where they typically deter desecration (Keim, 17; for examples, see *COS* 2.54-57:180-83; 2.135:364-68; Dobbs-Allsopp et al., 126-28, 150-51, 507-10; Gevirtz 1961; Crawford, 97-229). These objects were "thus supernaturally 'insured' against theft, breakage, vandalism, and usurpation" (Leick, 217).

The supernatural part of this insurance derives from the fact that the gods were explicitly invoked in these imprecations, thus sanctioning or ensuring the curse (cf. 1 Sam 17:43; see Keim, 17; Leick). Mention of the gods strengthened the force of the statement such that the binding force of an oath or a curse "depended chiefly upon the power and reputation of the divine being invoked" (Mercer 1912, 31-32).

In Babylonia and Assyria, malediction was used in legal and religious ceremonies "of great occasion" but also in the life of everyday people (Mercer 1915, 309). On the one hand, the latter point might be taken as demonstrating that the relationship between the ancients and their gods was of a quite personal sort (Mercer 1912, 32); on the other hand, it makes clear that curses were an "important symbolic tool for ordering human relationships and assuring the proper conduct of social and religious life . . . [and were] crucial for the proper maintenance of social life in the ancient Near East" (Keim, 138). Imprecation, then, at least to some degree, is a primary way ancient societies policed themselves. S. Mercer (1915, 309) put it this way: malediction "seemed to have served almost the same purpose as Common Law does among modern people, for it acted as a restraint, corrective, and stimulant to better deeds."

2. How Curses Functioned in Antiquity.

Among other things, the widespread use of imprecation raises questions regarding how it was thought to function in the ancient mind. Two major issues have occupied scholars, which ultimately are related: (1) the role of the gods in imprecations and (2) whether or not the curse is self-efficacious—that is, if, once uttered, it has a life and power of its own to self-fulfill.

2.1. The Role of the Gods. As we have already noted, the gods are everywhere mentioned in maledictory contexts. In a survey of Iron Age inscriptions, Crawford (132-33) concluded that nearly every one invoked deities by name (the only certain exception is the Ahiram sarcophagus [*COS* 2.55:181]). None of these texts, then, "are vague magical imprecations, rather they are dependent for their fulfillment upon the power of the deities mentioned" (Crawford, 208). This comment reflects and anticipates the debate outlined in the next section. Before turning to that discussion, however, we should note that, among other things, the role played by the gods in cursing demonstrates that imprecation was "reserved for serious issues which were ultimately beyond the retribution of authorities" (Leick, 217 [cf. Mendenhall, 72, 79; see 4 below]).

2.2. The Power of the Curse. Scholarship on imprecation, which often was undertaken by researchers concerned with the role and function of cursing in the OT and ancient Israel, has varied widely over the past hundred years. We might begin with J. Pedersen (1914; 1959, 1.99-181; 2.411-52), who connected the curse to the vitality of a person's *nepeš* ("life" or "soul" [see Keim, 23; Crawford, 17]). This "soul power" makes the curse into something of a magical substance—effective, almost "alive," once uttered. Pedersen's position was followed and developed, with differences, by scholars such as J. Hempel, S. Mowinckel (1961; 1962, 1.236-37) and S. Blank (esp. 82, 95). In a careful monograph published in 1963, however, H. Brichto (210, 215) refuted this "magical interpretation" of curse-speech, at least with regard to the OT: "The biblical text nowhere bears out the identification of every misfortune as an independent, automatic *Ding-an-sich* instrumentality, executing a putative imprecation on the part of the Deity.... Traces of magical thought in the Bible are one thing, the assumption that the operation of curses is magical and independent of the Deity is quite another.... In brief, it is the conclu-

sion here that the evidence for magical concepts underlying the biblical phenomenon of curse (and of blessing) has been grossly overvalued."

2.3. The Gods as the Power(s) of the Curse. Brichto's conclusion is predicated on the fact that the gods—or in the case of the OT, Yahweh—are so often explicitly mentioned or implicitly present in imprecation scenarios. Hence, if the curse has irreversible efficacy, that derives from the divine realm (see Leick). Pragmatically, however, it seems likely that one could be freed from an oath if circumstances so required/permitted, and so, in some cases at least, curses were not irreversible (Mercer 1912, 32-33).

The typical and expected presence of deities in maledictory contexts could even explain differences in curse formulae. S. Gevirtz (1959), for example, drew a contrast between East Semitic curses, with their explicit invocations of the gods, and West Semitic (especially biblical) examples, which often prefer passive constructions (often with *ʾārûr* ["cursed"]). Along the lines of Pedersen and others, Gevirtz took this as evidence that in the West words of imprecation were considered effective within themselves (see Keim, 24). But such a conclusion is neither necessary nor forgone. Lack of explicit reference to deities in certain Western (and biblical) contexts could simply be the result of tabooistic avoidance of the (names of the) gods—a phenomena that is still very much a part of common parlance (cf. "goodbye" from "God be with ye"; or "G-d" or "Ha-Shem" for the divine name; or, more to the point, "Gosh darn" for "God damn").

In the OT, at least, it seems clear that imprecation derives its power solely from God. Three passages, Genesis 27; 32:22-32; and Numbers 22—24, are well-known for possibly attesting to the self-effective power of the word (whether curse or blessing [see Wehmeier]). Such an interpretation can be refuted, however, for each of these passages (e.g., on the Balaam accounts, see Brichto, 208-9; Gordon, 492; more generally, Thiselton; Keim). Even in Genesis 27 it is ultimately Yahweh who determined which son would receive the blessing (Crawford, 25)—a point already made in the prebirth oracle to Rebekah (Gen 25:23). "In the OT, it is Yahweh in every case concerning Israel who determines when blessing or curse will take place" (Crawford, 25 [cf. Brichto, 218]). In fact, the pervasive presence and action of God may explain the passive constructions that Gevirtz worried about. Brichto (213), for example, believed that this syntax was the result of monotheistic theology: "A society which recognized but a single source of power could use passival constructions in its imprecations (and prayers), without there being any question as to the agent who rewards and punishes, vindicates and condemns" (cf., on 1 Sam 11:7, Brichto, 214). That being said, it must be admitted that curses where Yahweh is explicitly invoked by name remain rather rare (for the Bible, see Josh 6:26; 1 Sam 26:19; for inscriptions, see Dobbs-Allsopp et al., 575-76; cf. 126-32, 150-51, 507-10; Crawford, 101, 133, 223).

3. Imprecation in the Old Testament.

As is to be expected, the OT contains imprecations that are related to, if not in fact derived from, those found elsewhere in the ancient Near East. This is no small point, especially for those who struggle with the notion of curse residing in Scripture (see 4 below). It is simply this: malediction was a speech-form in the ancient world. It is present in Scripture because Israel (and the Bible) lived in and was a part of that ancient world and its many speech-forms and other cultural aspects. Although certain curses appear to have been off-limits (see Ex 21:17; Lev 20:9; cf. Deut 27:16), "in such cases it was the *object* of the curse that made it wrong rather than the *process*; pronouncing harm on the innocent was forbidden; pronouncing harm on the evil was appropriate" (Stuart, 1218 [italics added]).

3.1. Imprecation Outside Wisdom Books, Poetry and the Writings.
Outside the special purview of this dictionary (wisdom, poetry, writings), imprecation is found in three primary locales: (1) sanctions for covenantal disobedience (e.g., Lev 26:14-39; Deut 27:11-26; 28:15-68; 30:17-19), (2) prophetic contexts of judgment, and (3) places where individuals declare oaths, which typically involve curses (see 1.1 above). The first two locales can include numerous curse subtypes (Stuart delineates twenty-seven of them), such as the futility curse (Sutherland; Hillers), all of which can be summarized as having to do with "defeat, disease, desolation, deprivation, deportation, and death" (Stuart, 1218). The third locale again indicates that imprecation is more widespread than sometimes thought. Once again, even when it is not explicit, it seems to be the case that prayers for good fortune or imprecations for the opposite "are addressed to the Deity"

(Brichto, 218), the notion of divine involvement being one that Israel shared with its neighbors (Gordon, 492). It would seem, however, that such invocations were never done lightly. Brichto (216) argues that "imprecation is resorted to only when a failure of human resources is acknowledged or anticipated," and that the third commandment may very well be "a prohibition of the use of the name YHWH in unjustifiable imprecations."

3.2. Imprecation in Wisdom Books, Poetry and the Writings Outside the Psalms.
If one brackets oath-taking (e.g., Ruth 1:17), full-blown imprecations outside the Psalter are relatively rare in the wisdom, poetry and writings of the OT. Job utters self-imprecations, including futility curses (Job 31, esp. Job 31:5-8, 16-22, 38-40), and famously curses the day he was born (Job 3:1-26). Personified Wisdom, sounding very much like a prophet, pronounces a futility curse in Proverbs 1:28: "Then they will call upon me, but I will not answer; they will seek me diligently, but will not find me" (NRSV). And personified Zion utters an imprecation on her enemies in Lamentations 1:21-22: "They heard how I was groaning, with no one to comfort me. All my enemies heard of my trouble; they are glad that you have done it. Bring on the day you have announced, and let them be as I am. Let all their evil doing come before you; and deal with them as you have dealt with me because of all my transgressions; for my groans are many and my heart is faint" (NRSV).

Each of these examples, not to mention others, deserves study and discussion; each has a particular function and meaning in its context. With reference to Lamentations 1, for instance, F. Dobbs-Allsopp (73) writes, "The curse serves as a proxy for the community's inability to resist the enemy actively, and as such the poet once again effectively inculcates a compassionate disposition within his readers." Without question, however, it is the imprecatory psalms that are the most (in)famous example of imprecation in the OT. In the final section here they are taken up by means of the question of the ongoing usefulness (or lack thereof) of malediction.

4. Appropriating Imprecation: The Case of the Imprecatory Psalms.

A number of psalms could be identified as imprecatory. A minimum listing would include Psalms 58; 79; 83; 94; 109; 137, but other psalms or portions of psalms could be mentioned (e.g., Ps 5:5-6, 9-10; 12:3-4). This holds true even for the beloved Psalm 139, which ends in a blood-thirsty curse of the wicked, demonstrating the truth that one cannot simply censor imprecation (or judgment) as if that would take care of the problem. As C. S. Lewis (22) wrote, "The bad parts will not 'come away clean'; they may . . . be intertwined with the most exquisite things." This is certainly the case with Psalm 137:1-6 and Psalm 139:1-18, both of which are well-known and well-loved texts of the Psalter that have often made their way into worship, hymnody or lectionaries, but without their imprecatory sections (Ps 137:7-9; 139:19-24). This type of surgery destroys the literary integrity of the compositions. Psalm 137, for example, is heading to vv. 7-9 right from the start; it is not as if the imprecation is an afterthought tacked on to an otherwise beautiful composition (see Miller 2004). Even so, how should we understand violent speech like this in the midst of beautiful prayers to God? Can it be appropriated somehow, or must it be rejected out of hand and without question in light of texts such as Luke 6:28 and Romans 12:14?

Space limitations preclude a full discussion, but the following eight points deserve careful consideration:

(1) One should remember the mechanics of imprecation and the role of the gods therein (see 2 above). "Merely expressing negative wishes had little force. . . . No curse could have effect without Yahweh's superintendence" (Stuart, 1218). "For a curse to be effective it had to have divine authority and to be properly directed" (Gordon, 492). Undeserved curses would not "stick" (see Prov 26:2), and unwarranted curses could backfire on the one who uttered them (see Ps 109:17-20 [see Gordon, 492; and cf. the third commandment]). These points should give one pause when reading Psalm 137. To be sure, v. 7 explicitly calls the Lord to act against Edom, but the constructions in vv. 8-9 are curiously impersonal ("Happy is the one who . . . "). Perhaps the poet knows that Yahweh should not be invoked so directly in an imprecation such as this one; perhaps the sentiment in vv. 8-9 is "merely expressing negative wishes" that thus had little effective force but nevertheless were of benefit to the psalmist (see the third, fourth and fifth points below).

(2) The imprecatory psalms are not alone. As we noted earlier, malediction is a widespread phenomenon in the ancient world and in the OT. In Christian circles it is crucial to point out that cursing is also found in the NT, even in the mouth of Jesus (Mk 11:12-14, 20-25; Mt 21:18-22; [see Brueggemann, 80]), as well as in the mouths of the martyrs under the heavenly altar in Revelation, who ask the Lord to avenge their blood with haste (Rev 6:10 [see the third point below]). Interestingly enough, the *Oxford English Dictionary* gives an early example of the word "damn" from John Wycliffe's 1382 translation of John 8:10. As if these examples were not enough to make the point, it should also be observed that the LXX translates the so-called annihilation formula, whereby people are cut off or forcibly removed from the community (usually Heb *krt* or *ḥrm* [e.g., Ex 31:14]), with the term *anathema* (ἀνάθεμα). This is noteworthy because Paul uses *anathema* in 1 Corinthians 16:22 and Galatians 1:8-9 to similar effect. Even more pointedly, *anathema* is often said against heretics in later Christian creeds and councils (first attested in the council of Elvira [AD 306]). Imprecation is thus not an "Old Testament problem." Said differently, imprecation may be a problem for many Christians, but if so, it is a thoroughly biblical and thoroughly Christian problem (see Colman, 9-10, 21-22). It must be thought through as such.

(3) As E. Zenger (1996) and others (e.g., Firth, 142) have shown, the cry for vengeance that is so striking in the imprecatory psalms is, in reality, a cry for justice. Psalm 79 makes this point well, but so does Revelation 6:10. In Scripture, justice is never a wrong; instead, it is a supreme value. One should recall at this point that the *lex talionis* was actually a way of insuring that punishments were just, that they exactly fit the crime, no more, no less (note the verbs in Ps 137:8; see also Firth, 142). In an extensive study of the root *nqm* ("avenge, take vengeance") in the Bible and beyond, G. Mendenhall (77) argued that this word had to do with the exercise of God's sovereignty; vengeance was never a matter of personal vendetta or "private self-help" (cf. Firth, 141). In fact, actions of self-help "constitute a claim to an imperium on the part of the individual which is incompatible with and actually rebellious against the Imperium of Yahweh" (Mendenhall, 84; cf. 95, 98 [similarly, Firth]). One way this is seen in the imprecatory psalms is that the psalmist's ene-

mies are portrayed as the enemies of God (Miller 1986, 151; Bonhoeffer, 56-60; Davis, 27; Colman, 5, 10-11). Psalm 137, for instance, does not speak of injustices perpetrated against the psalmist—at least not against the psalmist alone—but rather of injustices done to Jerusalem/Zion, the city of God (Ps 137:1, 3, 5-7; cf. Pss 46; 48; 76; 84). In this way, the cry for vengeance is a cry for help, constituting hope for exiles, as well as for "the poor, the brokenhearted, the captives, and the grief-stricken" (Mendenhall, 100 [cf. Miller 1986, 151; Thompson, 68-70; Colman, 12]). In brief, imprecation arises not simply from anger and rage but rather from the complex mixture of those feelings as well as, more deeply, those of grief and sadness, despite and in spite of the rage and anger.

(4) In the case of the imprecatory psalms, the issue is one of violent speech (prayer), not violent acts (see Miller 1986, 153; Brueggemann, 66-67). It is, as P. Miller (2004, 200) notes, "at one and the same time to let it go and to hold it back"—letting the anger and rage go from the one who prays to God, who hears *all* prayers, and holding it back, preventing the rage and brutality from going public. "It is not now a part of our dealing with our neighbor-enemy. It is a part of our life with God" (Miller, 2004). It is far better to pray vengeful thoughts than take vengeful action. Vengeance is left in God's hands (Deut 32:35; Rom 12:19; Heb 10:30), not our own (Miller 1986, 153; 2004, 201; cf. Firth, 141; Brueggemann, 70; Crawford, 22). In this way, imprecatory prayer may end up being prayer *for* our enemies, though certainly in much different fashion than we expected (Davis, 27-28). God's body, evidently, can absorb violence that our enemies' bodies cannot.

(5) The inclusion of curse in prayers to God indicates the full range of emotional honesty and candor that is a hallmark not only of the psalms but also of OT faith writ large (Miller 1986, 150). There is something of psychological wholeness and integrity at work in the imprecatory psalms as opposed to dishonesty, splitting off and denial. To be sure, it is probably the case that prayer is the *only* acceptable place where such thoughts may be entertained or uttered (Miller 1986, 151; 2004, 200); and yet, if and when they are, such prayer can be good, even beneficial, for the soul of the one who prays (Davis, 24-26; cf. 8-9). As W. Brueggemann (64-65) notes, the real problem with vengeance "is

not that vengeance is there in the Psalms, but that it is here in our midst," "in the human heart and the human community" (cf. James 3:9). If we lose the imprecatory psalms, we lose a way to "hold our anger in good faith" and "an opportunity to bring our own anger into the context of our relationship with God ... for our spiritual growth" and healing (Davis, 24-26). The latter do not come through cover-up and denial.

(6) Imprecation can be educative. Even if we have not faced the kind of injustice that produces such prayers, the imprecatory psalms can provide a window onto another's world. We ourselves may not feel such emotion (at the moment), but others do and have (note that Psalm 137 was used as a song by African American slaves). These psalms, then, can instruct our compassion (see Davis, 20) as well as give us words and strategies of containment and coping regarding what to do (and pray) if and when we face similarly dire circumstances.

(7) There is a venerable exegetical tradition that appropriates imprecation by redefining the cursed enemies as more acceptable "targets." The NT sets an example by using Babylon as a cipher or metaphor for all that stands opposed to God (see Miles). This metaphorical Babylon comes to disastrous ruin in Revelation 16:19 (see also Rev 14:8; 18:2, 21). Perhaps, then, the Babylon of Psalm 137 could be similarly ciphered or "metaphorized." The revisioning of the enemies by Lewis (136) is worth quoting in full:

I know things in the inner world which are like babies; the infantile beginnings of small indulgences, small resentments, which may one day become dipsomania or settled hatred, but which woo us and wheedle us with special pleadings and seem so tiny, so helpless that in resisting them we feel we are being cruel to animals. They begin whimpering to us "I don't ask much, but," or "I had at least hoped," or "you owe yourself *some* consideration." Against all such pretty infants (the dears have such winning ways) the advice of the Psalm [137] is the best. Knock the little bastards' brains out. And "blessed" is he who can, for it's easier said than done.

(8) Finally, one could appropriate the imprecatory psalms by following the advice of E. Davis (28), rotating them 180 degrees, so they are no longer pointing at our enemies but rather at us,

and then asking the difficult question "Are there people in the world who would pray such things against me?" This is a sobering thought, and it might well result in a change of our ethic vis-à-vis our enemies, a change that could even lead to praying for them, blessing not cursing them, and turning the other cheek (Mt 5:39-41; Lk 6:28; Rom 12:14), until one day curse will be altogether obsolete and our enemies brought close (cf. Rev 22:3; Ps 83:16; see Colman, 13, 27-28).

These eight considerations are not foolproof (see Crenshaw, 65-68). If we must beware of a simple-minded notion that God has no enemies (Miller 1986, 151; Brueggemann, 72-73), then we must also beware of appropriating the opposite perspective too easily, trusting ourselves too quickly that we can know and accurately identify God's enemies (Miller 1986, 151; Thompson, 68-70; Colman, 11-12). Thoughtful exegetes through Christian history have known this, even if they, in human weakness, often failed to achieve it (for a good example of both, see Colman, esp. 11-12, 26). As J. Thompson (70) observes, "The history of Christian anti-Jewish exegesis—along with other variations that have come and gone, by which the enemies of God or Christ are identified among our contemporaries—ought to stand as an object lesson of what *not* to do with the Psalms. . . . In recovering the imprecatory psalms, we must be skeptical of our ability to know for certain who our real enemies are, when it's enough to know that God is our ally."

Some have thus located God's vengeance and God's allegiance as experienced in the imprecatory psalms in Christ and the cross (see Bonhoeffer, 56-60; Hays, 53-55; cf. Miller 1986, 152; Thompson, 68-70). That may or may not solve all the difficulties, and it will not satisfy all interpreters. Nevertheless, the considerations listed above are sufficient to indicate that there is a way beyond the psalms of vengeance, "but it is a way through them and not around them. And that is so because of what in fact goes on with us. Willy-nilly, we are vengeful creatures. . . . In taking this route through them, we take the route God 'himself' has gone" (Brueggemann, 80-81).

See also DESTRUCTION; HONOR AND SHAME; LAMENT, PSALMS OF; RETRIBUTION; WARFARE IMAGERY.

BIBLIOGRAPHY. S. H. Blank, "The Curse, Blasphemy, the Spell, and the Oath," *HUCA* 23 (1950-1951) 73-95; D. Bonhoeffer, *Psalms: The Prayer Book of the Bible* (Minneapolis: Augsburg, 1970); H. C. Brichto, *The Problem of "Curse" in the Hebrew Bible* (SBLMS 13; Philadelphia: Society of Biblical Literature and Exegesis, 1963); W. Brueggemann, *Praying the Psalms: Engaging Scripture and the Life of the Spirit* (2nd ed.; Eugene, OR: Cascade, 2007); T. W. Cartledge, *Vows in the Hebrew Bible and the Ancient Near East* (JSOTSup 147; Sheffield: Sheffield Academic Press, 1992); B. Colman, *Imprecation against the Enemies of God, Lawful and a Duty: As It Was Deliver'd in a Sermon at the Lecture in Boston, before His Excellency and the General Court, March 20th, 1707* (Boston: B. Green for N. Boone, 1707); T. C. Crawford, *Blessing and Curse in Syro-Palestinian Inscriptions of the Iron Age* (AUS 7/120; New York: Peter Lang, 1992); J. L. Crenshaw, *The Psalms: An Introduction* (Grand Rapids: Eerdmans, 2001); E. F. Davis, *Getting Involved with God: Rediscovering the Old Testament* (Cambridge, MA: Cowley, 2001); F. W. Dobbs-Allsopp, *Lamentations* (IBC; Louisville: Westminster John Knox, 2002); F. W. Dobbs-Allsopp et al., *Hebrew Inscriptions: Texts from the Biblical Period of the Monarchy with Concordance* (New Haven: Yale University Press, 2005); D. G. Firth, *Surrendering Retribution in the Psalms: Responses to Violence in the Individual Complaints* (PBM; Milton Keynes: Paternoster, 2005); S. Gevirtz, "Curse Motifs in the Old Testament and in the Ancient Near East" (Ph.D. diss., University of Chicago, 1959); idem, "West-Semitic Curses and the Problem of the Origins of Hebrew Law," *VT* 11 (1961) 137-58; R. P. Gordon, "Curse, Malediction," *NIDOTTE* 4.491-93; C. B. Hays, "How Shall We Sing? Psalm 137 in Historical and Canonical Context," *HBT* 27 (2005) 35-55; J. Hempel, "Die israelitischen Anschauungen von Segen und Fluch im Lichte altorientalischer Parallelen," *ZDMG* 79 (1925) 20-110; D. R. Hillers, *Treaty-Curses and the Old Testament Prophets* (BibOr 16; Rome: Pontifical Biblical Institute, 1964); P. A. Keim, "When Sanctions Fail: The Social Function of Curse in Ancient Israel" (Ph.D. diss., Harvard University, 1992); G. Leick, "Oaths and Curses," *DANE* 217; C. S. Lewis, *Reflections on the Psalms* (New York: Harcourt, Brace, 1958); G. E. Mendenhall, "The 'Vengeance' of Yahweh," in *The Tenth Generation: The Origins of the Biblical Tradition* (Baltimore: Johns Hopkins University Press, 1973) 69-104; S. A. B. Mercer, *The Oath in Babylonian and Assyrian Lit-*

erature (Paris: P. Guethner, 1912); idem, "The Malediction in Cuneiform Inscriptions," *JAOS* 34 (1915) 282-309; **C. A. Miles**, "'Singing the Songs of Zion' and Other Sermons from the Margins of the Canon," *Koinonia* 6 (1994) 151-73; **P. D. Miller**, *Interpreting the Psalms* (Philadelphia: Fortress, 1986); idem, "The Hermeneutics of Imprecation," in *The Way of the Lord: Essays in Old Testament Theology* (FAT 39; Tübingen: Mohr Siebeck, 2004) 193-202; **S. Mowinckel**, *Psalmenstudien V: Segen und Fluch in Israels Kult und Psalmendichtung* (Amsterdam: P. Schippers, 1961 [1923]); idem, *The Psalms in Israel's Worship* (2 vols.; Nashville: Abingdon, 1962); **J. Pedersen**, *Der Eid bei den Semiten: In seinem Verhältnis zu verwandten Erscheinungen sowie die Stellung des Eides im Islam* (SGKIO 3; Strasburg: K. J. Trübner, 1914); idem, *Israel: Its Life and Culture* (2nd ed.; 4 vols. in 2; London: Oxford University Press, 1959); **D. Stuart**, "Curse," *ABD* 1.1218-19; **K. Q. Sutherland**, "The Futility Curse in the Old Testament" (Ph.D. diss., Southern Baptist Theological Seminary, 1982); **A. C. Thiselton**, "The Supposed Power of Words in the Biblical Writings," *JTS* 25 (1974) 283-99; **J. L. Thompson**, *Reading the Bible with the Dead: What You Can Learn from the History of Exegesis That You Can't Learn from Exegesis Alone* (Grand Rapids: Eerdmans, 2007) 49-70; **J. H. Walton**, *Ancient Near Eastern Thought and the Old Testament: Introducing the Conceptual World of the Hebrew Bible* (Grand Rapids: Baker Academic, 2006); **G. Wehmeier**, "Deliverance and Blessing in the Old and New Testaments," *IJT* 20 (1971) 30-42; **E. Zenger**, *A God of Vengeance? Understanding the Psalms of Divine Wrath* (Louisville: Westminster John Knox, 1996).

B. A. Strawn

IMPRISONMENT IMAGERY

Imagery of imprisonment in the books of wisdom, poetry and writings is used to evoke a variety of responses, from sympathy for those who are prisoners, to an awareness that incarceration may be an appropriate state for some. Other portions of the Bible preserve narrative descriptions of a variety of incarcerations, such as those of Jeremiah (Jer 32—33; 39), the prophet Hanani (2 Chron 16:10) and Joseph (Gen 39—41), with Joseph's becoming the object of attention in the book of *Psalms (Ps 105:17-21). In the books of wisdom, poetry and writings, however, there is a greater emphasis upon employing prison imagery in general for purposes

of instruction or for personal catharsis. Unlike the narrative portions of the Bible that present the fact of imprisonment, the writings are more expansive in describing its dismal features and their affect upon those who are imprisoned: "In dark places he has made me dwell, like those who have long been dead; he has walled me in so that I cannot go out; he has made my chain heavy. . . . He has blocked my ways with hewn stone" (Lam 3:6-9 NASB).

1. Cultural Context
2. God and Imprisonment
3. Kingship and Imprisonment
4. Imprisonment as an Image of Death
5. Imprisonment Imagery and Sin
6. Prison as Prelude
7. Imprisonment Imagery and Self-Discipline

1. Cultural Context.

Prisons in the ancient Near East are, paradoxically, a well-established fact about which little is known. In accord with the fact that prisons are not mentioned as a punishment in the legal material of the Pentateuch—a phenomenon true also of all other law collections from the ancient Near East—the consensus is that prisons generally were not punitive but rather were essentially places of temporary confinement for accused individuals awaiting trial (cf. Lev 24:12; Num 15:34; 1 Kings 22:27) or for convicted offenders or debtors who had to be detained pending the execution of their sentence or payment of their debt (Westbrook 221, 714, 967). Prisoners are poetically juxtaposed with those destined to die (Ps 79:11; 102:20), a perspective that may underscore the primary function of incarceration as temporary detention for a penalty that will be administered later.

The features of prison life that surface as characteristic in the writings are attested in extrabiblical literature (Civil) and include darkness (Lam 3:6 [prisoners are associated with those who cannot see in Ps 146:7-8; cf. Is 42:7]), bronze or iron fetters (Ps 105:18; 149:8; Lam 3:7), confining stone walls (Lam 3:7, 9), and human laments and groans (Ps 79:11; 102:20). Specific parts of the body that are restrained include the feet and perhaps the neck (Ps 105:18). So striking is the imprisonment imagery in the book of Psalms that L. Delekat argued that those psalms in which the psalmist is hounded by people who wish to kill him stem from the experience of individuals seeking asylum in the cities of refuge, where an individual could be confined for protection against personal vengeance by anyone related to the offended party (Ex 21:13; Num 35:9-34; Deut 19:1-3; Josh 20:1-9). Such deprivation of freedom of movement for those who have committed no crime is unattested elsewhere in the ancient Near East, although the royal harem provides a further example of another such institution (Esther 2:3-15; cf. 2 Sam 20:3).

2. God and Imprisonment.

When the rebellious cosmic Sea appeared, God incarcerated it behind bolted doors (Job 38:8-11; cf. Job 26:10; Prov 8:27, 29), a barrier that may include the clouds that at God's behest allow some water to escape (Job 26:8; cf. Gen 1:6-8; 7:11; 8:2). Allusions to other larger-than-life incarcerations of supernatural rebels, this time among the stars, appear in the same chapter where God asks rhetorically if *Job has the ability to put the Sea behind bars: "Can you bind the chains of the Pleiades, or loose the cords of Orion?" (Job 38:31 NASB; cf. Is 14:12-15). Some humans who sense that God is mistreating them can complain of what they see as their similar imprisonment by God: "Am I the sea, or the sea monster, that you imprison me?" (Job 7:12).

As one who is capable of imprisoning the most powerful forces in the cosmos, and being sovereign over all areas of *life, God appears in these texts as the one who is primarily responsible for *suffering and tragedy. God therefore appears either as a jailer or as a monarch whose prerogative it is to incarcerate whomever he will (see Lam 3:6-9, quoted above). But this also means that God is the one who can set free. Thus, when God is portrayed as remedying the ills of human existence (e.g., children without parents, wives who have lost their husbands, individuals without families), among these ills are included prisoners whom God brings out of their confinement (Ps 68:5-6). Such forced confinement can be reminiscent of the Israelite experience in Egypt when Israel served the state as forced labor: the same verb (Hiphil of yṣʾ) that describes the exodus (Ps 105:37, 43; 136:11) is used also to describe God's bringing out to freedom those who are prisoners (Ps 142:7), a phenomenon deliberately juxtaposed with the exodus (Ps 68:6-7). Those who are forcibly removed from human contact by incarceration, so that their groans, laments and cries for help find a limited audience, appeal to God in particular

as the only real source of assistance (Ps 79:11; 88:1, 8; 102:19-20).

3. Kingship and Imprisonment.

When empires extended their authority over neighboring kingdoms in the ancient Near East, those populations who resisted could be treated as prisoners. This same imagery was applied to the extension of the kingdom of God to other nations that do not willingly submit to the God of Israel: Israelites were portrayed as those who have a responsibility "to bind their kings with chains, and their nobles with fetters of iron" (Ps 149:8). Non-Israelite nations may perceive the dominion of God's kingdom and his Davidic king as a confining reality, a prison from which they wish to free themselves when they exclaim, "Let us tear their fetters apart, and cast away their cords from us" (Ps 2:3 NASB).

Imprisonment as a function, indeed duty, of kingship implied that the king had ultimate control over prisoners. The king could delegate this authority, as Pharaoh did with Joseph, a prisoner subsequently freed who was in turn himself given the power "to imprison [Pharaoh's] princes at will" (Ps 105:22 NASB). In the same way that the king could imprison with impunity, he could similarly grant prisoners their freedom. Royal largesse could prompt the release of prisoners when a king came to the throne (e.g., 2 Kings 25:27) or on other special occasions. This notion may be in view when *Ahasuerus celebrated the coronation of his new queen, *Esther, and "made a release to the provinces" (Esther 2:18 KJV). A psalmist recollects that Pharaoh had released Joseph from his imprisonment (Ps 105:20), without noting that Joseph was ever exonerated of the trumped-up charges that led to his imprisonment in the first place. Such amnesty was entirely within the king's authority (Sasson 99-100) and may lie behind the imagery of psalmists who affirm that Yahweh, as the ultimate sovereign, is able to deliver them from their metaphorical or literal bonds (see 2 above).

4. Imprisonment as an Image of Death.

Pits were apparently a characteristic feature of prisons (Gen 40:15; Is 24:22; Jer 38:6). The place to which the dead go is generally portrayed as a dark (Ps 88:6, 12) pit (Ps 28:1; 30:3, 9; 88:4, 6; Prov 1:12), a place to which the wicked go prematurely as a consequence of their evil deeds

(Ps 9:17; 28:1-3), separated from family and friends (Ps 88:8, 18), a place where one is forgotten (Ps 88:5, 12) and from which one's voice no longer falls on listening ears (Ps 30:9). This is imagery that reflects a prison experience, particularly when one hears the psalmist describe his experience at the doorstep of Sheol: "I am shut up and cannot go out" (Ps 88:8). If imprisonment was not primarily a punitive experience but rather a place of confinement pending judgment, then the imagery is even more appropriate when applied to Sheol as a place to which all go, both righteous and unrighteous, and allows for further development in Judaism and Christianity of postmortem perceptions of judgment.

5. Imprisonment Imagery and Sin.

The imagery of imprisonment may portray sin and its consequences: a person's own sins play the role of an arresting officer ("His own iniquities will capture the wicked" [Prov 5:22]) or the binding ropes that immobilize the prisoner ("He will be held with the cords of his sin" [Prov 5:22]). Sinners can expect to find a fate associated with imprisonment in some fashion (Eccles 7:26). The imagery of imprisonment also describes a man deceived by a woman who exploits him for her own purposes. Such a woman plays the role of an arresting officer who seizes the man, her heart being the "snares and nets" that capture him, and her hands being the "chains" that keep him confined once he is captured (Eccles 7:26).

6. Prison as Prelude.

Imprisonment need not be the last word in a person's life, as the psalmist underscores when he retells the story of Joseph with further details not found in the Genesis account (Ps 105:17-21). In fact, Joseph's experience indicates that prison could even be a prelude to an even greater social rank than one had before, for he who was a prisoner became a lord able "to imprison princes" (Ps 105:20-22). Similarly, in Ecclesiastes 4:13-14 prison is not an irrevocable sentence, an assumption that underlies this account of a poor but wise youth who is released from prison to become king—a scenario reminiscent of, but probably not a reference to, the story of Joseph in Egypt. One point of this story in *Ecclesiastes is to establish two social extremes where prison is seen as the complete antithesis of the pinnacle of social life, kingship. Because the writer of Ecclesiastes

contrasts a wise, incarcerated youth with an aged king who is no longer able to heed advice (note that Pharaoh was eager to take good advice from Joseph in contrast to this king), there may even be a suggestion that prison is a place where one is forced to learn some very hard lessons. This would be in accord with the fact that other forms of discipline (e.g., Prov 22:15; 23:13-14; 29:15) are pedagogic as well as punitive in Wisdom literature.

This is the posture that Elihu takes when he reminds Job that incarceration can instruct morally bankrupt individuals. In particular, God is the one who is responsible for confining prisoners, so that those who are bound with fetters (literal or figurative) have the choice of learning from the consequences of their activity and, if they reform, can be set free (Job 36:8-13). When Joseph leaves prison life behind and is given the authority to imprison even the most senior Egyptian officials, this special authority is pictured by the psalmist as a way by which Joseph could instruct Egyptians: "that [Joseph] might teach his elders wisdom" (Ps 105:22). Release from prison results when God decides that it is time or that his purposes have been achieved (Ps 105:19-20).

7. Imprisonment Imagery and Self-Discipline.

Parts of one's body can be metaphorically treated as prisoners who must be immobilized when they jeopardize one's life or do not cooperate with God's wishes. One treats the mouth and tongue as prisoners under guard, restraining them from doing the damage that they would otherwise be free to do (Ps 34:13; 39:1; Prov 13:3). One may even request that God be the jailer in such situations (Ps 141:3). Because desires should not be allowed to roam freely, the language of confinement graphically dramatizes emotional and volitional discipline (Prov 4:23). The notion of the body as a prison for the soul is not present in the Hebrew Bible, but it is not unheard of to witness individuals venting their frustration in seeing life itself as a prison. A desire for death (Job 3:11-23) can include the view that it is God who has made life too confining (Job 3:23).

See also WARFARE IMAGERY.

BIBLIOGRAPHY. **P. Barmash**, *Homicide in the Biblical World* (Cambridge: Cambridge University Press, 2005); **M. Civil,** "On Mesopotamian Jails and Their Lady Warden," in *The Tablet and* *the Scroll: Near Eastern Studies in Honor of William W. Hallo*, ed. M. E. Cohen, D. C. Snell and D. B. Weisberg (Bethesda, MD: CDL Press, 1993) 72-78; **L. Delekat,** *Asylie und Schutzorakel am Zionheiligtum: Eine Untersuchung zu den privaten Feindpsalmen* (Leiden: E. J. Brill, 1967); **M. Foucault,** *Discipline and Punish: The Birth of the Prison* (New York: Vintage Books, 1995; original, *Surveiller et punir: Naissance de la prison* [Paris: Gallimard, 1975]); **J. A. Hoyles,** *Punishment in the Bible* (London: Epworth, 1986); **C. S. Lewis,** "The Humanitarian Theory of Punishment," in *God in the Dock*, ed. W. Hooper (Grand Rapids: Eerdmans, 1970) 287-94; **J. Sasson,** ed., *The Treatment of Criminals in the Ancient Near East* (Leiden: E. J. Brill 1977); **R. Westbrook,** ed., *A History of Ancient Near Eastern Law* (HO 72; Leiden: E. J. Brill, 2003).   S. Meier

INCLUSIO

Hebrew poetry features pervasive repetition. Often the repetition is not exact, but the following occurrences of a word, phrase or poetic line echo its first statement. *Parallelism, one of the most commonly occurring ornaments of Hebrew poetry, is a well-known form of repetition where the second colon repeats yet progresses the thought of the first colon. Parallelism, with its repetition and progression, occurs not only on the semantic level but also on the grammatical and perhaps even the phonological level. Parallelism describes the repetition that exists within a poetic line. Hebrew poems also exhibit repetitions beyond the line. The *refrain is one such example, where a line or part of a line is repeated at various points within the poem. The inclusio is similar to the refrain except that it occurs only twice—at the beginning and at the end of a poetic unit—with the unit being either a stanza or the whole poem. In short, an inclusio is a repeated phrase or whole line that stands at the beginning and end of a poetic unit. Some scholars use the term *inclusio* to include repetition of a mere word or even a similar root at or near the beginning of the poem or unit of a poem, but this extends the concept too far.

    1. Terminology
    2. Function
    3. Examples
    4. Conclusion

1. Terminology.

As is often the case with terminology in Hebrew poetics, the same phenomenon can have more than one name in the scholarly literature. *Inclusio* is the most common term used, but *envelope structure* or *envelope figure* is also found. The latter is the term used by R. G. Moulton (56-58), whom W. G. E. Watson credits with having identified the device in Hebrew poetry (Watson, 282). All three terms point to the function of this device as described in the next section. In classical rhetoric, the same feature is called epanadiplosis (so Moulton, 44).

2. Function.

The function of inclusio is obvious and straightforward. The inclusio delimits a poetic unit, providing a strong sense of beginning and closure. Thus the term *inclusio* indicates that everything that is found between the two occurrences is "included" in the unit. The two related terms that use "envelope" (structure/figure) give us an interesting metaphor. The poetic device of an inclusio delimits a text just like an envelope delimits a text by containing it. By framing the poem or part therein, the device evokes a sense of coherence to the text. In addition to the function of delimitation, the content of the inclusio may point to an important theme of the poem or section of text.

3. Examples.

3.1. Full-Line Inclusio. The following examples are not exhaustive but illustrative. The device is mostly associated with poetry, but at least in one clear case (*Ecclesiastes), it is found in prose as well. The presence of inclusio is most definite when the repetition involves the whole line. We will begin with a look at such examples.

3.1.1. Psalm 8. This is a majestic poem that praises God for his work of creation, including the wonderful status he has bestowed on his human creatures. The poem begins and ends with an expression of awe that extols God's greatness:

> YHWH, our Lord,
>   how resplendent is your name
>   in all the earth! (Ps 8:1, 9)

This inclusio opens and closes the poem and provides the mood throughout. As J. Goldingay (160) puts it, "The repetition of the opening praise underlines the positive wonder and ensures that the worshippers close their praise with thoughts of God, not themselves."

3.1.2. Psalm 103. This psalm opens and closes with a self-admonition to praise God:

Praise YHWH, O my soul;
all my inmost being,
praise his holy name. (Ps 103:1, 22)

Thus, here, besides providing closure, the refrain applies the teaching about God's gracious acts that is found in the body of the psalm. Reflection on God's work leads to thanksgiving and worship. Psalm 104 begins and ends with a similar, but shorter, self-admonition ("Praise YHWH, O my soul," Ps 104:1, 35), but the final statement is followed by one more "Praise YHWH," though in the Septuagint this final phrase is found at the beginning of Psalm 105 (Allen 28). If this textual tradition is correct, then Psalm 105 would have a simple inclusio provided by the opening and closing "Praise YHWH" (similarly Ps 106; also Ps 113).

3.1.3. Psalm 118. This psalm has a military setting and thanks God for rescue from the hand of enemies (Ps 118:5-18). It is a liturgical psalm. A priest presumably calls on Israel, its priests and all the people who fear YHWH to praise him. The opening and closing verses provide an inclusio that summarizes this call to worship:

Give thanks to the LORD, for he is good;
his love endures forever. (Ps 118:1, 29)

3.1.4. Psalms 146—150. These psalms appear to be placed intentionally at the end of the book to provide a doxological conclusion to the psalter. They call on Israel to praise YHWH. Not surprisingly then each psalm begins and ends with the exhortation to "Praise YHWH" (Ps 146:1, 10; 147:1, 20; 148:1, 14; 149:1, 9; 150:1, 6).

3.1.5. Ecclesiastes. Ecclesiastes demonstrates that an inclusio can operate in a prose context. Indeed, there are no literary devices that are exclusive to poetry, though they may find a heightened and intensified use in poetry. After the superscription (Eccles 1:1), the *frame narrator represents the Teacher's (*Qohelet's) thinking with the characteristic phrase: "'Completely meaningless,' Qohelet said, 'Everything is meaningless.'" Qohelet's reflective *autobiography is found in Ecclesiastes 1:12—12:7. When the frame narrator picks up the narrative again in Ecclesiastes 12:8, he begins

with a repetition of Ecclesiastes 1:2. The effect of the repetition is that it leaves the reader in no doubt as to Qohelet's ultimate conclusion that the search for meaning in the world "under the sun" is meaningless. This inclusio and its importance for describing the message of the book of Ecclesiastes is recognized by many interpreters today (Longman, Anderson, Bartholomew).

3.2. Partial-Repetition Inclusio. The above examples are clear and obvious because they appear at the beginning and end of poems and are complete repetitions. The following are perhaps not so clear because they involve more or less repetition. Not all scholars or readers will agree with every other reader's identifications. Sometimes repetitions are incidental and not an intentional echo back to the beginning of a unit. Watson (284), for instance, will suggest an inclusio not only where there is only a single word repetition but also if there are different words derived from a common root. If these are instances of inclusio, they provide a weak sense of closure (i.e., "wicked" in Ps 1:1, 6; "good" in Ps 73:1, 28).

Even so, it does seem fair to recognize instances of inclusio that fall short of full, long repetitions. The following are examples.

3.2.1. Psalm 21 and 29. Psalm 21 is a *kingship psalm that praises the Lord for heeding prayer and granting the king victory and life. God's strength is therefore a major theme in the poem, and the repeated phrase "in your [God's] strength" in the first and last verses (Ps 21:1, 13) seems intentional.

The same might be said for Psalm 29, a hymn that exalts in the "voice of YHWH," The opening line calls on worshippers to ascribe "strength" (ʿōz) to YHWH (Ps 29:10), while the final line calls on God to grant "strength" to his people (Ps 29:11).

3.2.2. Proverbs 1:2-7. The preamble to the book of Proverbs follows the opening verse, which is a superscription. The preamble describes the purpose of the book that follows and then concludes with a statement of the underlying theme of the book (Prov 1:7). The first colon of the purpose statement declares that the "proverbs of Solomon" are "for gaining wisdom [ḥokmâ] and discipline [mûsār]." It does not appear accidental that the climactic thematic statement ends by saying "fools despise wisdom [ḥokmâ] and discipline [mûsār]" (Prov 1:7). The inclusio delimits the preamble and points to a major theme.

3.2.3. Song of Songs 2:8-17. The genre and structure of the Song of Songs is debated. Is it a collection of love poems or a drama? Whatever the answer, the specific outline of the book is difficult to describe, a fact that accounts for the wide variation of outlines among scholars. Song of Songs 2:8-17 appears to constitute a particular unit, defined in part by a partial inclusio provided by the picture of the lover as a gazelle that gambols on the mountains (Song 2:8-9, 17).

4. Conclusion.

The above examples are only illustrative and not exhaustive. Close readers will notice other instances of full and partial repetitions, and it will help them sense units as well as detect major themes.

See also PARALLELISM; POETICS, TERMINOLOGY OF; REFRAIN.

BIBLIOGRAPHY. **L. C. Allen,** *Psalms 101-150* (WBC; Dallas: Thomas Nelson, 2002); **W. H. U. Anderson,** "The Poetic Incusio of Qoheleth in Relation to 1,2 and 12,8," *SJOT* 12 (1998) 203-13; **C. Bartholomew,** *Ecclesiastes* (BCOTWP; Grand Rapids: Baker, forthcoming); **J. Goldingay,** *Psalms: Psalms 1—41* (BCOTWP; Grand Rapids: Baker, 2006); **M. Kessler,** "Inclusio in the Hebrew Bible," *Semitics* 6 (1978) 44-49; **T. Longman III,** *Ecclesiastes* (NICOT; Grand Rapids: Eerdmans, 1998); **R. G. Moulton,** *The Literary Study of the Bible* (London, 1896); **W. G. E. Watson,** *Classical Hebrew Poetry: A Guide to Its Techniques* (2d ed.; T & T Clark, 2005). T. Longman III

INNERBIBLICAL EXEGESIS. *See* INTERTEXTUALITY.

INTERNATIONAL WISDOM. *See* LEMUEL AND AGUR; PROVERBS 2: ANCIENT NEAR EASTERN BACKGROUND.

INTERTEXTUALITY

The word *intertextuality,* broadly defined, refers to the meaningful set of relationships that can be identified between various biblical and extrabiblical texts. The term is also used for methods of interpretation that attempt to go beyond simply tracing a writer's use of earlier sources. Intertextual studies turn attention to ways that later generations of writers and readers interpret and comment on the literary tradition. Some schol-

ars speak of a shift of focus toward the mutual interaction that takes place when texts from the same or different times are read together. In this light, studies of "the Old Testament in the New" show that canonical reading enriches interpretation of the Hebrew Scriptures as it informs a biblical theology of both Testaments.

It is a basic rule of interpretation that context determines meaning, and so in OT Scripture it is the interrelation of parts to the whole that makes meaning and enhances persuasive effect. For example, the meaning of *"fear of the LORD" (Prov 1:7) grows as it is used throughout the book of *Proverbs, especially at the conclusion of the introductory lectures (Prov 9:10) and the conclusion of the entire book (Prov 31:30). Moreover, references to the fear of God at significant points in *Job (Job 28:28), *Ecclesiastes (Eccles 12:13) and certain psalms (Ps 19:9; 34:11; 111:10) point to a wisdom theme. While we may or may not be able to discern whether such common use was meant to point to other texts, what is new in many intertextual studies is the intention to read them together as part of a canonical collection.

1. Theories and Approaches
2. Intertextuality within the Writings
3. Method: Critiques and Proposals

1. Theories and Approaches.

Although there is much debate and some agreement on what is meant by an intertextual approach to biblical interpretation, most of this work can be described in terms of three areas of interest and the related questions that give direction to the method: (1) innerbiblical exegesis; (2) dialogical literary theory; (3) the rhetoric of biblical theology (see Koptak).

1.1. Innerbiblical Exegesis. One area of research examines the use of older Scriptures set in new literary contexts to address new historical situations. Set within the story of *David bringing the ark to Jerusalem to institute *worship there, the song of praise in 1 Chronicles 16:8-36 is constructed from excerpts of three canonical psalms: Psalm 105:1-15, all of Psalm 96 except vv. 10b, 13b, and the first and last two verses of Psalm 106. The new text does not carry over those psalms' references to judgment on Israel and the nations. Instead, the new composite psalm moves in ever widening circles of praise, encompassing Israel (1 Chron 16:8-22), the nations (1 Chron 16:23-30) and all creation

(1 Chron 16:31-34). The new psalm adds "Say also" to introduce the quotation of Psalm 106:47-48 in 1 Chronicles 16:35, inviting its first readers to make the ensuing prayer their own. Exiles could trace this movement of confident praise and then pray in response, "Save us, O God of our salvation, and gather and rescue us from among the nations, that we may give thanks to your holy name, and glory in your praise."

So also, the dedicatory prayer by *Solomon in 2 Chronicles 6:40-42 does not include the conclusion of the source text (1 Kings 8:50-53) but rather inserts a new conclusion fashioned from excerpts of Psalm 132 (vv. 8, 9, 10, 1). The short new psalm puts more attention on the temple and people than on the Davidic king, reversing the message of the original psalm. Thus the Chronicler created two new psalms from the canonical psalms, selecting, deleting and reassembling, all to support the message of renewal promised to a repentant people (Klein).

First to use the term *innerbiblical exegesis* was N. Sarna, in a study of the interpretive variations introduced to the covenant with David in Psalm 89:29-37 (as compared with its narrative source in 2 Sam 7:14-17; cf. 1 Chron 17:3-15). Based on Sarna's work, today there is general agreement on the literary unity of the psalm as an expansion of older core components. The poetry moves between heaven and earth, symbolically linking the divine orders of creation with the Davidic throne, God's representative of order in human affairs. Twelve key words or phrases join the *hymn of Psalm 89:1-18 with the oracle of Psalm 89:19-37, particularly the concluding word of the hymn, "our king," highlighting what is also central to the oracle. Sarna called this the stamp of a single creative editor-psalmist who composed the lament of Psalm 89:38-51 and joined together the components that make up Psalm 89 (see Sarna, 29-33).

Sarna thought that this account of the psalm's composition also explained the variations from the earlier prose oracle. First, the psalm has no word about David's desire to build the temple, thus turning attention to the psalmist's present crisis. Second, 2 Samuel 7:10 promises respite to people of Israel, but because that peace ended with David's reign, the psalmist narrowed it to David personally (Ps 89:22-23). Third, whereas in 2 Samuel 7:14 and 1 Chronicles 17:13 we have "son," Psalm 89:26-27 uses "firstborn," thus limiting the father-son

relationship to David and not his offspring. Fourth, the punishment for sin threatened to the immediate son of David (2 Sam 7:14) was transferred to the entire Davidic dynasty (Ps 89:30). Finally, the psalmist uses *bĕrît* and *šābʿ* in regard to the swearing of a covenant (Ps 89:3, 34-35, 39, 49 [MT 89:4, 35-36, 40, 50]), terms that are not found in the narrative oracle but do appear in David's last words (2 Sam 23:5) and in a psalm commemorating him (Ps 132:11). In this way, Psalm 89 draws attention to the contrast between the earlier promise to the Davidic dynasty and the then present reality of defeat. Whereas previous scholarship had simply tried to establish which of the texts was later and dependent on the other, Sarna argued that the variations were an interpretation, "a pattern of deliberate and original exegesis on the part of the psalmist, who has adapted an ancient oracle to a new situation." Sarna identified that situation as the Aramean-Israelite invasion of Judea in 735-734 BC and the movement to depose Ahaz and replace him with a non-Davidic king (see Sarna, 39-46).

Claiming that interpretation is basic to the work of religious leaders, M. Fishbane added that one can find within the Hebrew Bible the same processes of interpretation that carried over into the writing of the NT and rabbinic Midrash, although each used it in a different way. Fishbane defined *traditum* as the authoritative content, and *traditio* as the complex process of transmission, the reason why the content of the *traditum* is as varied as it is. Revisiting Sarna's work, he spoke of Psalm 89's "transformative exegesis" that brings a sense of closure to prophetic oracles. The nature of the original oracle in 2 Samuel 7 is ambiguous, but that helped keep it alive, even among David's successors (1 Kings 5:5 [MT 5:19]; 8:19-20), and that ambiguity allowed for reshaping of details to address a new historical situation. The psalmist not only reminds the LORD "You spoke" but then actually quotes the LORD's words back to him with modification, applying the vision to the entire Davidic dynasty (see Fishbane 1985, 465-67, 533-35).

Fishbane (2000) recognized that the "intertextuality" of later rabbinic midrash viewed all of Scripture as a coherent whole, and so any part potentially could comment on another. However, his and other studies of innerbiblical interpretation are primarily diachronic in their focus on authors and editors. Buchanan (3) summarizes the approach well: "It makes a great deal of difference in the meaning of a document when it is known to be a literature about a literature."

1.2. Literary Theories. Whereas innerbiblical approaches tend to be grounded in the assumptions and methods of *historical criticism, another group of interpreters draws from developments in literary theory. It was a cultural critic, J. Kristeva, who coined the term *intertextuality*. Her innovations drew inspiration from the anthropological studies of C. Lévi-Strauss and the literary criticism of M. Bakhtin. The former described the mosaic-like design of ancient and "primitive" myths with the term *bricolage*, the work of piecing together a collage of art, mythology or worldview. Here Kristeva found a way to challenge the then-current view that literary texts were autonomous works of individuals and therefore to be valued for their originality. Instead, she argued, if communicators borrow and reuse ideas and their expressions, any work could be understood as part of a network of reference.

Kristeva spoke of a literary work as a "mosaic of quotations; any text is the absorption and transformation of another" (Kristeva, 37). Inspired by Bakhtin's dialogical view of language and literature, she turned her attention from the linguistic unit of the sign to the relation of one sign to another. Words, Bakhtin had observed, live not in dictionaries but in people's mouths. Those words are typically spoken in response or answer to what has gone before. In reaction to structuralist text-centered theory, Kristeva stressed the importance of writers as both creators and respondents, purposefully using citation and reference to achieve persuasive ends (see Clayton and Rothstein; Tanner, 6-10).

Whereas innerbiblical interpretation works within the boundaries of the biblical *canon, the very nature of dialogic theory expands the notion of text to include anything that can be "read," thus revealing an endless network of potential connections with interpretive works of art, music and theater. For some, the dialogic approach implies that there is always more that can be said, leaving interpretation incomplete, tentative and de-centered (Beal). Yet relation to other texts and attention to the multivoiced nature of Scripture need not rule out authorial intention and divine authorship (Phillips, 244).

The dialogic approach in particular offers another starting point for intertextual research within the biblical canon. It assumes that a text enters an environment of varied and even competing speech acts, and that its part in the dialogue is reflected in the text itself as a response. Audiences of readers and hearers also engage texts as active respondents. Therefore, interpreters can do more than identify connections with earlier texts and parse the reuse of well-known words and their associations; they can also explain the function of that reuse, shedding light on its persuasive purpose (Bakhtin; Tull 1999, 166-67). So, for example, the outcry in *Lamentations over the fate of Jerusalem, that "she has no comforter" (Lam 1:2, cf. Lam 1:9, 16, 17, 21), can be read alongside the Lord's answer in Isaiah, "I, I am your comforter" (Is 51:12), the prophet here using what may have been familiar words to declare a new beginning (Tull 2000, 178).

Such interpretive moves need not establish a direct historical relation to a text or the intention to do so by its writers and transmitters. They do look for connections that readers acquainted with the larger body of the canon might make, approaching criticism from a slightly different angle than one that traces reuse, changes and revisions.

So one might look not only at modifications of the promise to David in Psalm 89, but also at dialogical relationships with other psalms and Scriptures. One way to do so is to examine the use of key words both within and outside the psalm. For example, as Sarna noted, the term *hesed* appears in Psalm 89:14, 19, 24, 33, 49 (MT 89:15, 20, 25, 34, 50), linking the Lord's faithfulness with the Davidic covenant and becoming the basis for petition. David is spoken of in Psalm 89:20 as one whom God has "anointed," and that word gives force to the psalmist's charge that the Lord has forsaken this covenant and abandoned the king and people (Ps 89:38-39, 50-51).

Key terms and imagery from Psalm 89 also appear in Psalm 90. A plea for the end of God's punishment argues that life is already too short (Ps 90:10, cf. Ps 89:45), using the words "anger," "fury" and "face" (Ps 90:7-8, 11; cf. Ps 89:46) and the question "How long?" (Ps 90:13; cf. Ps 89:46). The petition made by "your servants" (Ps 90:13, 16; cf. Ps 89:50) makes appeal to the Lord's steadfast love and faithfulness (Ps 90:14; cf. Ps 89:49; see also Ps 89:14, 19, 24, 33). Both laments use images of eternity to recount God's faithfulness, the ancient creation and its orders serving as a sign (Ps 90:1-2; cf. 89:1-14). A lament is made in the hope that God will not reject forever, yet the possibility always exists.

Thus, an examination of verbal links shows that the crisis of Psalm 89—the defeat of the king and apparent failure of the Davidic covenant—is answered by the lament and hopeful confidence in the prayer of Psalm 90. The discovery of terms shared by these neighboring psalms indicates an intention, either by arrangement or composition, to bring the two together in conversation, the petitions of both working together to present an extended sense of lament and, with the addition of the prayers of Psalm 90:13-17, a stronger statement of hope. God, who has been a refuge in every generation, has always been God(Ps 90:1-2). Therefore it is likely that this God will turn in mercy to those who call out to him. If there is sin in the people (as there is in all of humanity [Ps 90:3-12]), God can be petitioned to turn and be gracious (Ps 90:13-17).

Another line of research makes further connection with the biblical narrative. The superscription of Psalm 90, "A Prayer of Moses, the Man of God" (Ps 90:1), was mostly ignored by critical scholars of a previous generation because it appeared to be a later addition not found in early manuscripts. Taking a dialogic view, Tanner finds there a clue of "simultaneous activation of two texts." It has long been recognized that Psalm 90:13 draws its prayer "Turn, O LORD!" and "turn/repent" from Exodus 32:12, and that the wording "man of God" (Ps 90:1) in the superscription also appears as an introduction to prayer in Deuteronomy 33:1, the only use in the entire Pentateuch. But Tanner views the mention of Moses as a "marker," not so much a source as an evocation of another text, wherein the reading of both is mutually enriched by the interaction. So, for example, read against the background of the wilderness wanderings, "You have been our dwelling place" (Ps 90:1) points to God's protection and provision of the children of Israel. The conclusion asks God to "establish the work of our hands," echoing the vocabulary of Exodus 15:17, an earlier poetic reference to God's rule and care for his people. Within this framework the psalm's plea for relief from long-lasting judgment finds its answer in the story of the wilderness generation and God's long-suffering patience with a rebellious people. "Consumed by your anger" (Ps 90:7) points back

to God's response to the golden calf (Ex 32:10; cf. Ex 33:3). The connection to the larger narrative enhances reading of the links. It is only Moses in the entire Hebrew Bible who urges God to "turn" or repent (Ps 90:13; Ex 32:12) and so God does (Ex 32:12). The earlier story inspires the hope of the psalmist's prayer (see Tanner, 90-91).

Finally, research into the canonical shape of the Psalter has shown that the book is composed as a series of psalm pairs and larger groups, ordered within a fivefold structure that may reflect Israel's story of kingdom, conquest and hope for restoration. Interpreters have observed that in Psalm 90, Moses' "answer" to the monarchy's failure leads Israel back to the foundational covenant of Sinai. In this view, the confidence in kingship (Pss 1—72) is modified in light of exile (Pss 73—89), the psalms that follow reminding Israel that the Lord is king (see Kingship Psalms), was refuge before the monarchy, and will be the same even when the monarchy is gone (Wilson 1985; 1986).

Some have described the dialogic approach as having a more synchronic focus, although historical issues of composition and shaping are still at play. Admittedly, there is the possibility of fanciful readings that distort the meaning of text and co-text, but this consideration of the reader's role in making connections and formulating a biblical theology makes an important contribution to preaching and teaching.

1.3. Biblical Theology and Rhetoric. The previous intertextual reading that brought Psalm 89 and Psalm 90 together with the story of Israel's deliverance points toward a third emphasis: the insistence that the Scriptures of Israel be interpreted theologically as canon. The preservation of these books by Jews and Christians (including the earlier work of editing and ordering) is itself testimony that they are of more than historical interest: believers may find there a word of God for contemporary living. The canonical approach brings together a concern for a biblical theology of both Testaments with interest in the rhetorical strategies that invite responses of praise, obedience and trust.

*Rhetorical criticism examines the structure and stylistic techniques of the Bible as a record of an engagement between ancient speakers, discourse and audiences. A rhetorical approach will also look closely at the way a text is shaped as persuasive communication to later generations of readers (Cunningham). Biblical theology is primarily concerned with the function of Scripture as witness to "the God of Israel, who raised Jesus from the dead." Each Testament preserves its distinct witness in mutual engagement. The two tasks for the Christian reader are to interpret the OT *per se* and *in novo receptum*, as received in the NT (Seitz, 3-12).

Relationships within the Hebrew and Christian canon can be identified. Interpreters have recognized the relationship between the prophecies of Isaiah and the *lament psalms, particularly the shared vocabulary "everlasting covenant" and "steadfast love for David" in Isaiah 55:3-5 and Psalm 89:33-35. Some have argued that the royal promises were thereby transferred away from David and to the people in the Isaiah text. Others have come to question this view on canonical grounds, arguing that the promises became a "paradigmatic illustration" for the nations coming to the people (Isa 53:4-5).

A comparison of the canonical shape of the books of *Psalms and Isaiah shows that references to David and/or the monarchy come early in both books but are not as pronounced in the latter parts (Pss 90—150; Isa 40—66). Still, although the promise fades, it does not vanish. The prayer of Moses turns the focus on the sin of the people, not the failure of covenant to David. Isaiah 55:3 calls on that faithful covenant to David as the basis for a new promise to the people. The covenant with David is not revoked but rather becomes the paradigm for a new work of God for Israel. So the kingship of God, sounded throughout the psalms that follow Psalm 90 (Ps 93:1; 95:3; 96:10; 97:1; 98:6; 99:4), is also sounded throughout Deutero-Isaiah (Is 40:10; 41:21; 43:15; 44:6). If at root the question of Israel's laments, particularly that of Psalm 89, is whether the Lord is really king of heaven and earth, it is answered decisively and without change or cancellation of the promise made to David (Seitz, 150-67).

If the question of the Davidic monarchy can be left open, then not only can Isaiah 55:1-5 be read intertextually as a divine answer to Psalm 89, but also the question can remain open with a future orientation, even pointing to a *messiah. Three allusions in Revelation 1:5 identify Jesus the Christ as the answer to the question posed in Psalm 89: Christ is faithful (or enduring) witness (cf. Ps 89:37), firstborn (Ps 89:27a) and ruler over kings of the earth (Ps 89:27b) (see Heim). The covenant with David is not abandoned but rather renewed, and it will be made manifest in Christ's return. Although there is no early Christian citation of Ps 89:49-50, there are numerous NT citations in which Christ takes the Davidic laments as his own or they are attributed to him (Hays). A reading of Revelation 1:5 in light of Psalms and Isaiah presents a strong statement of Christ the king and his call to mission.

2. Intertextuality Within the Writings.

The threefold division of the Hebrew Scriptures as Torah, Prophets and Writings allows for a related canonical question: How is the collection known as the Writings itself a response to the crisis of the end of monarchy and exile, a response to texts that have gone before? Such questions will attend to both the canonically shaped content of the Writings and the needs and dynamics of the community that it addresses. Seen in this light, the various books of the Writings themselves present a variety of possible responses to the crisis of exile, all based in some way on the story of Israel attaining canonical authority as Torah and Prophets.

One proposal envisions the varied genres of the Writings (hymns and laments, wisdom writings, Diaspora stories of heroines, plus the visions of Daniel and historical narrative of Chronicles, Ezra and Nehemiah [not treated in this volume]) as proposals toward what it means to be the people of God after the fall of temple and throne. As strategies for living in a new situation, they offer instruction and inspiration for education, worship and building community (Morgan). Therefore, a brief sketch of intertextual links between the books of the Writings and the OT and NT Scriptures follows.

2.1. Psalms and Lamentations. Psalms of lament, praise, confession and wisdom reflection gave voice to individual and communal relationship with God as centered in Israel's worship. Worship looks back on God's work of salvation with praise and cries out when it appears to be absent. The need for cultic organization may have been important to exiles, particularly in the shift from temple worship to houses of prayer. Worship also provided a source of identity and means of survival, integrating the past, present and future of Israel in song and prayer (Morgan 42-44).

Many of the psalms do contain references to

Torah (Pss 1; 119) (*see* Law), and the prophets' story of the monarchy is reflected in royal psalms and messianic themes (Litwak). Some psalms resemble the literature of wisdom, particularly in questions concerning the prosperity of the wicked (Pss 37; 49). The fivefold structure of the book of Lamentations may reflect the similar structures of Torah and the Psalter, while imagery and phrases shared with Job and lament psalms highlight the mercy of God to righteous and repentant alike (Lam 3:22-24). Such lament is featured center stage at Jesus' crucifixion (Koptak). However, the NT does not remember Job's lament, but only his patience. Job is cited only in the book of James as a model of endurance (James 5:11) and of right speaking and living (see James 3:1-18; cf. Job 9:14-21; 27:1-6; 29:1-17) (see Richardson).

2.2. Wisdom. Living life well as a reflection of creation's order is one concern of the wisdom writings of Proverbs, Ecclesiastes and Job. Later writings such as *Sirach explicitly link wisdom with the Torah, but the emphasis on passing instruction from one generation to the next is found in Proverbs and Deuteronomy. A call to learn wisdom's ways concludes the book of Ecclesiastes (Eccles 12:9-14) and the prophet Hosea (Hos 14:9). Although the wisdom writings make no direct reference to Torah and Prophets (*see* Wisdom and Prophecy), the books of Proverbs, Ecclesiastes and *Song of Songs are set in historical relationship with Israel by association with Solomon. Reading of these books ought not be dehistoricized but rather can be canonically linked to Israel's story (Sheppard).

Readers of the canon in later generations may bring together the opposing perspectives of Isaiah 43:19 ("I make something new") with Ecclesiastes 1:9 ("Nothing new exists under the sun"), examining the way each speaks to the topic of knowledge. *Qohelet helps readers recognize the limits of human knowledge, itself a step forward in wisdom. We do not know if earlier days are better than later days (Eccles 7:10-12), but Isaiah 41:22 claims that good observation of history does produce insight into the Lord's ways: he announces what will come, and it comes. Historical lessons are not enough, however, and a new creation is needed, both in the vision that the suffering servant mediates and a re-creation of the people (Talstra). Wisdom teaching sets a pattern for Jesus, the sage "great-er than Solomon" (Witherington), and NT Christology builds on the personified figure of wisdom (*see* Personification).

2.3. Storytellers for Diaspora Living. *Ruth and *Esther in very different ways depict a heroine's ability to overcome adversity. Both are foreigners to the people among whom they dwell, but the book of Ruth presents an inclusive picture of Israel that receives Ruth, while the book of Esther assumes the need for strong boundaries of national identity as a means to survive in a hostile environment of exile. Common to both is the inescapable sense of divine guidance and aid, everywhere present yet hidden—as the ancient rabbis put it, "gloved." Without divine intervention or prophetic vision, Israel's two concerns for care of the stranger and deliverance from oppression are sustained and held in tension.

The frequent reference to Ruth's Moabite heritage can direct the reader to Moab's origin in the union between Lot and his older daughter (Gen 19:37). This intertextual "marker" links two stories of women facing destitution and the end of their family line, but there is also a contrast. The later story has a happy outcome as Ruth is proved righteous and the question of David's foreign ancestry is put to rest (cf. Deut 23:3, see Nielsen, 20-22). A more obvious marker is the reference that *Naomi makes to Tamar, another woman who acted to insure the future of her wedded family's line. Both Tamar and Ruth appear in the genealogy of Jesus (Matt 1:1-6).

3. Method: Critiques and Proposals.

There is much overlap in the approaches surveyed above, even though they are guided by different sets of questions. Common to each is the search for common vocabulary, images and themes and a shift in focus from identifying sources to looking more closely at the actual theological/rhetorical use. Discussion of methodological issues will continue to include the conscious and unconscious role of authors(s) and editors, as well as the role of later readers in making connections. There will most likely be pressure for greater precision in use of terminology.

But identifying possible connections alone does not make a case for relationship, and various attempts have had their critics. Some claim that larger narrative patterns make intentional links more likely than word links (Noble); others maintain that the idea of canon as an authoritative body of texts sets limits on the multiplicity of meanings and preserves authorial intention (Childs). One proposed solution distinguishes the synchronic study of intertextuality from the diachronic study of allusion and influence. The latter looks at authors and texts, tracing the use and influence of earlier texts; the former looks at the way readers make associations with other texts and an even wider range of "utterances" in their cultural environment (Sommer; Clayton and Rothstein). A similar approach combines Tannen's study of framing-in-discourse with Hollander's theory of echo, thus renewing focus on writers (Litwak). Reader-oriented critics answer that the distinction between allusion and exegesis is too hard to maintain. They recommend another distinction between exegesis as application or actualization of an earlier text, and exegesis as giving new meaning to an earlier text (Weyde). In this way, interpreters can try to honor authorial intention and the possibility of dialogue with later intertexts.

In sum, we begin with the twofold recognition that no text is written without some relation to others, nor is any text read independently of other texts: "No text comes into being or is read as an isolated unit" (Nielsen, 17-18). Therefore, interpretation can and should attempt to trace the marks of intention left in the text, even though the results are often uncertain. But because writing produces a mosaic of references, both conscious and unconscious, texts have their own integrity, "a delicate balance of dependence and independence"; and, because texts are read in particular contexts, intertextuality must attend to readers who respond to both (Phillips, 234).

One helpful proposal distinguishes separate phases in intertextual reading. A first phase tries to identify an author's intentions by means of markers that point to the intertexts by which readers can understand those intentions. A second phase considers the editorial work that can be observed in the formation of the canons of Judaism and Christianity (*see* Editorial Criticism). Although it is much more difficult, if not impossible, to decide whether these intertextual references are intended (or by whom), the reader's work of drawing connections within the canon is brought into play. Finally, a third phase identifies intertexts that are

clearly of a later date and acknowledges the role of a reader in making a connection with postbiblical works of interpretation, including art, music and the interpreter's autobiography (Nielsen). Although the last phase names as intertext what others would simply call an interpretation, it does highlight the dialogical processes at work in the act of reading. At its best, intertextual reading draws its method from the relationships presented by the texts themselves. Perhaps this is its greatest contribution to the effort to hear the message of the OT and the NT as Christian Scripture.

See also Editorial Criticism.

Bibliography. **M. M. Bakhtin,** *The Dialogic Imagination,* ed. M. Holquist (Austin: University of Texas Press, 1981); **T. K. Beal,** "Intertextuality," in *Handbook of Postmodern Biblical Interpretation,* ed. A. K. M. Adam (Saint Louis: Chalice Press, 2000) 128-30; **G. W. Buchanan,** *Introduction to Intertextuality* (Lewiston, NY: Mellen Biblical Press, 1994); **J. H. Charlesworth,** "Intertextuality: Isaiah 40:3 and the *serek ha-yahad,*" in *The Quest for Context and Meaning: Studies in Biblical Intertextuality in Honor of James A. Sanders,* ed. C. A. Evans and S. Talmon (BIS 28; Leiden: E. J. Brill, 1997) 197-224; **B. S. Childs,** "Critique of Recent Intertextual Canonical Interpretation," *ZAW* 115 (2003) 173-84; **J. Clayton and E. Rothstein,** "Figures in the Corpus: Theories of Influence and Intertextuality," in *Influence and Intertextuality in Literary History,* ed. J. Clayton and E. Rothstein (Madison: University of Wisconsin Press, 1991) 3-36; **D. S. Cunningham,** "Rhetoric," in *Handbook of Postmodern Biblical Interpretation,* ed. A. K. M. Adam (Saint Louis: Chalice Press, 2000) 220-26; **M. Fishbane,** *Biblical Interpretation in Ancient Israel* (Oxford: Oxford University Press, 1985); idem, "Types of Biblical Intertextuality," in *Congress Volume: Oslo 1998,* ed. A. Lemaire and M. Saebø (VTSup 80; Leiden: E. J. Brill, 2000) 39-44; **R. B. Hays,** "Christ Prays the Psalms: Israel's Psalter as Matrix of Early Christology," in *The Conversion of the Imagination: Paul as Interpreter of Israel's Scripture* (Grand Rapids: Eerdmans, 2005) 101-18; **K. M. Heim,** "The (God-) Forsaken King of Psalm 89: A Historical and Intertextual Inquiry," in *King and Messiah in Israel and the Ancient Near East: Proceedings of the Oxford Old Testament Seminar,* ed. J. Day (JSOTSup 270; Sheffield: Sheffield Academic Press, 1998) 297-322; **R. W. Klein,** "Psalms in Chronicles," in *CurTM* 32 (2005) 264-

75; **P. E. Koptak,** "Intertextuality," in *Dictionary for the Theological Interpretation of the Bible,* ed. K. J. Vanhoozer (Grand Rapids: Baker Academic, 2005) 332-34; **J. Kristeva,** "Word, Dialogue and Novel," in *The Kristeva Reader,* ed. T. Moi (New York: Columbia University Press) 34-61; **K. D. Litwak,** *Echoes of Scripture in Luke-Acts: Telling the History of God's People Intertextually* (JSNTSup 282; London: T & T Clark, 2005); **R. Mason,** "Inner-Biblical Exegesis," in *A Dictionary of Biblical Interpretation,* ed. R. J. Coggins and J. L. Houlden (London: SCM Press; Philadelphia: Trinity Press International, 1990) 312-14; **D. F. Morgan,** *Between Text and Community: The "Writings" in Canonical Interpretation* (Minneapolis: Fortress, 1990); **K. Nielsen,** "Intertextuality and Hebrew Bible," in *Congress Volume Oslo 1998,* ed. A. Lemaire and M. Saebø (VTSup 80; Leiden: E. J. Brill, 2000) 17-31; **P. R. Noble,** "Esau, Tamar, and Joseph: Criteria for Identifying Inner-Biblical Allusions," *VT* 52 (2002) 219-52; **E. A. Phillips,** "Serpent Intertexts: Tantalizing Twists in the Tales," *BBR* 10 (2000) 233–45; **K. A. Richardson,** "Job as Exemplar in the Epistle of James," in *Hearing the Old Testament in the New Testament,* ed. S. E. Porter (Grand Rapids: Eerdmans, 2006), 213-29; **N. M. Sarna,** "Psalm 89: A Study in Inner Biblical Exegesis," in *Biblical and Other Studies,* ed. A. Altmann, (Cambridge: Harvard University Press, 1963), 29-46; **C. R. Seitz,** *Word Without End: The Old Testament as Abiding Theological Witness* (Grand Rapids: Eerdmans, 1998); **G. T. Sheppard,** "Biblical Wisdom Literature at the End of the Modern Age," in *Congress Volume: Oslo 1998,* ed. A. Lemaire and M. Saebø (VTSup 80; Leiden: E. J. Brill, 2000) 369-98; **B. D. Sommer,** *A Prophet Reads Scripture: Allusion in Isaiah 40-66* (Contraversions; Stanford, CA: Stanford University Press, 1998); **E. Talstra,** "Second Isaiah and Qohelet: Could One Get Them on Speaking Terms?" in *The New Things: Eschatology in Old Testament Prophecy: Festschrift for Henk Leene,* ed. F. Postma, K. Spronk, E. Talstra (ACEBT 3; Maastricht: Shaker, 2002) 225-36; **B. L. Tanner,** *The Book of Psalms through the Lens of Intertextuality* (SBL 26; New York: Peter Lang, 2001); **P. K. Tull,** "Rhetorical Criticism and Intertextuality," in *To Each Its Own Meaning: Biblical Criticisms and Their Applications,* ed. S. L. McKenzie and S. R. Haynes (rev. ed.; Louisville: Westminster John Knox, 1999) 156-79; idem, "The Rhetoric of Recollection," in *Congress Volume: Oslo 1998,* ed. A. Lemaire and M. Saebø (VTSup 80; Leiden: E. J. Brill, 2000) 71-79; **K. W. Weyde,** "Inner Biblical Interepretation: Methodological Reflections on the Relationship between Texts in the Hebrew Bible," *SEÅ* 70 (2005) 287-300; **G. H. Wilson,** *The Editing of the Hebrew Psalter* (SBLDS 76; Chico, CA: Scholars Press, 1985); idem, "The Use of Royal Psalms at the 'Seams' of the Hebrew Psalter," *JSOT* 35 (1986) 84-94; **B. Witherington,** *Jesus the Sage: The Pilgrimage of Wisdom* (Minneapolis: Fortress, 1994).

P. E. Koptak

J

JOB 1: BOOK OF

The place of the book of Job within the Wisdom literature is firmly secured by its themes, content and style. Its literary quality and compelling characters have made it one of the most sublime masterpieces of ancient literature. Yet for all that, it is a book often misunderstood, resulting in the all-too-common belief that it falls short of its goal—thus Bernard Shaw's quip: "If I complain that I am suffering unjustly, it is no answer to say, 'Can you make a hippopotamus?'" (Baker, 17). This cynicism might be appropriate if the book's goal were to give an explanation for human *suffering (as is assumed by existentialist Archibald MacLeish in his play *J.B.*, which is based on the book of Job and won a Pulitzer Prize). Though many have assumed that the purpose of the book is to explain human suffering (observed by Dumbrell, 91), I will propose here that its goal is to guide the reader concerning how to think about God in the face of suffering.

1. Structure and Genre
2. Rhetorical Strategy
3. Message
4. Unity and Composition
5. Date and Context

1. Structure and Genre.

1.1. Structure. A number of views have been proposed regarding the structure of the book, but they focus mainly on the roles of Job 3 and Job 28—31. The question concerning Job 3 is whether it serves as a transition from the narrative frame to the dialogue or as the beginning of the dialogue (see Frame Narrative). The question concerning Job 28—31 revolves around the identification of the speaker in Job 28. On the latter, N. C. Habel (1985, 391) summarizes the diversity of opinions: "Job 28 is a brilliant but em-barrassing poem for many commentators. It has been viewed as an erratic intrusion, an inspired intermezzo, a superfluous prelude, and an orthodox afterthought." Most commentators today consider Job's last speech in the dialogue section to end with Job 27 (e.g., Dhorme, Gordis, Tur-Sinai, Driver-Gray, Hartley, Andersen, Westermann, Rowley, Pope, Habel, Smick). In this scenario Job 28 is usually viewed as the narrator's wisdom *hymn serving as interlude (if not judged simply extraneous or secondarily intrusive), and Job 29—31 is a separate discourse by Job. This modern consensus, against the older traditions that Job's last speech included Job 28 and then continued through Job 31, finds support both structurally (since Job's discourse in Job 29—31 could then be seen as part of a discourse section along with discourses by Elihu and Yahweh) and in terms of content (since the wisdom hymn comes to conclusions that do not reflect Job's thinking as it is represented in his speeches either before or after the hymn [see Habel 1985, 392]). I therefore agree with J. F. A. Sawyer's (255) comparison of Job 28 to the chorus of a Greek tragedy that "looks back to the inadequacy of wisdom as portrayed in the first part of the book and forward to the Yahweh speeches on divine wisdom in the second" (this comparison did not originate with Sawyer [see the variations summarized in Pope, xxx-xxxi], nor does it accept any of the other comparisons to Greek tragedy that have been promulgated). I agree with the commonly proposed structure for the book in Table 1 (in Table 1 a "cycle" involves a sequence of alternating speeches by a number of speakers, while a "series" consists of a number of speeches by the same person).

1.2. Genre: Job as Literature. Above all, Job is a wisdom book of literary complexity, philosophical sophistication, and theological insight and

Table 1. Structure of Job

Narrative Frame: Job 1—3		
	Prologue: Heaven and Earth	1—2
	Job's Opening Lament	3
	Cycle One: Job 4—14	
	Eliphaz	4—5
	Job	6—7
	Bildad	8
	Job	9—10
	Zophar	11
	Job	12—14
	Cycle Two: Job 15—21	
	Eliphaz	15
	Job	16—17
	Bildad	18
	Job	19
	Zophar	20
	Job	*21*
	Cycle Three: Job 22—27	
	Eliphaz	22
	Job	23—24
	Bildad	25
	Job	26—27
Interlude: Wisdom Hymn: Job 28		
	Series One: Job 29—31	
	Job: Reminiscences	29
	Job: Affliction	30
	Job: Oath of Innocence	31
	Series Two: Job 32—37	
	Elihu: Introduction and Theory	32—33
	Elihu: Verdict on Job	34
	Elihu: Offense of Job	35
	Elihu: Summary	36—37
	Series Three: Job 38—41	
	Yahweh: Maintaining Roles/Functions in Cosmic Order	38—39
	Yahweh: Harnessing Threats to Cosmic Order	40:6—41:34
Narrative Frame: Job 42		
	Job's Closing Statements	(40:3-5) 42:1-6
	Epilogue: Heaven and Earth	42:7-17

innovation. No piece of wisdom known from the ancient Near East offers a similar aggregation of the genre classes as is shown by Job. There are other works that feature a sufferer who believes himself to be innocent. Other works exist that use to some extent a dialogue format (as found in the first half of Job) or wisdom discourses (as found in the second half of Job). But the combination of narrative frame, dialogue sequence and discourse sequence is not found elsewhere. Job additionally includes lament (Job 3), wisdom psalm (Job 28) and theophanic speech (Job 38-41) among the types of literature that it weaves into the larger whole (Fyall, 23-24).

1.2.1. Ancient Near Eastern Context. A comparative study of Job in its ancient Near Eastern environment is provided in a separate article (*see* Job 2: Ancient Near Eastern Background), so here only a few comments vis-à-vis genre are needed. The most productive comparison can be made to other pieces of literature that feature the motif of a pious sufferer (Mattingly). These include the Sumerian Man and His God (*COS* 1.179) and the Akkadian Dialogue between a Man and His God (*COS* 1.151), Poem of the Righteous Sufferer (*COS* 1.153), Babylonian Theodicy (COS 1.154) and Dialogue of Pessimism (*COS* 1.155). But these are either dialogues or monologues (not a combination), and they focus on the question of why suffering is experienced by those who are conscientiously observant regarding every religious obligation that they know. Unlike the book of Job, these works truly do try to offer explanations of human suffering, and the typical answers are either that there was an offense that they were unaware of (conveying that human offense is universal, even if some offenses could never be recognized as such) or that deity is inscrutable. Not only are these more simplistic than Job in literary form, but also they seek to penetrate the human dilemma rather than the nature of deity. In both form and substance the book of Job begins where the ancient Near Eastern literature finishes.

1.2.2. Wisdom Literature. On the basis of its themes and literary characteristics, the book of Job can be classified as belonging in the larger category known as Wisdom literature.

1.2.2.1. Themes. The telltale themes include the questions concerning human suffering, the examination of the *retribution principle, the focus on creation, and the exploration and ap-

plication of proverbial sayings to situations in life. The prominent place given to the thoughts and sayings of *sages and the attention paid to traditional teaching reflect the wisdom essence of the book

1.2.2.2. Dialogue and Discourse. Nearly ninety percent of the book is comprised of dialogue or discourse. These are not offered as transcripts preserved from the speeches given at an historic symposium. They proceed from the imagination of the philosopher, not the dictation taken by a stenographer. They are highly literary creations, not records of casual conversation. This is expected in Wisdom literature, and these speeches are no different in that regard from the speeches of *Woman Wisdom and Woman Folly (Prov 8—9).

1.3. Genre: Job as History. Although Wisdom literature can at times include a narrative segment, no example exists in the ancient world of a wisdom book that has been demonstrated to have a historical event as its foundation. That is not to say that historical figures cannot at times be among the characters of the narrative segment. For example, in the Egyptian Instructions literature the pharaohs who are involved in giving or receiving instruction can at times be identified independently in historical records (Amenemhet, Merikare, Ptahhotep). In West Semitic literature most would not hesitate to see a character such as Ahiqar as a historical figure. The Assyrian kings whom he serves are known, and the piece offers description of historical events, although none can be independently verified.

If a historical figure is to be used productively in the narrative frame of Wisdom literature, it is logical to conclude that some generally recognized quality or experience of the figure qualifies him for such a role. For example, the famed Egyptian sage Harjedef, son of Pharaoh Khufu, has a reputation that associates him naturally with wisdom contexts. One could therefore conclude that if Job were to be identified as an historical figure, at least the major outline of his experiences would also find a foundation in history or at least in tradition. Even the possibility of a historical foundation, however, should not lead us to think of this book as a historical book or to look for historical verification of all of its details. It is Wisdom literature, and as such, it has the latitude to freely develop its themes.

None of the foregoing discussion proves that Job is a historical figure, for Wisdom literature can also easily invent characters to represent its protagonists. For example, individuals such as Any or Dua-Khety, both of whom have wisdom pieces attached to their names (respectively, the Instructions of Any, and the so-called Satire on the Trades), may well be fictional. They are portrayed as lower officials and set in realistic settings (known places and, with Any, a known ruler, Ahmose). Even in these cases, however, the characters need not be fictional, and it would be impossible to prove that they were.

That the book of Job places Job in historically known places (e.g., Uz), makes reference to historical parties (however slight—e.g., Sabeans, Chaldeans [Job 1:15, 17]), and reputes him to be a well-known sage suggests that the wisdom piece is based on the life and experiences of a historical person. As in the case of the other wisdom pieces, however, the genre typically operates by means of an author building a wisdom piece around the recognized character. The literature thus retains its status as Wisdom literature, in which we would not go looking for historical verification throughout the various levels of the work. This foundation certainly could be sufficient to account for the references to Job outside of the book (Ezek 14:14, 20; James 5:11) as an actual individual whose experiences have become legendary and taken their place in the traditions of the ancient world. The remainder of the book, including the court scene in heaven, may be better considered as being the literary construct of the wisdom writer, formulated to refocus the discussion in a way that will lead to his innovative resolution of the issues.

2. Rhetorical Strategy.

The rhetorical strategy of the book provides the foundation for identifying its argument and for discussing its unity. The goal of *rhetorical criticism is to identify the function of each major section and the contribution that the rhetorical strategy makes to the whole. As it is unfolded, it also leads to the message of the book—the answers that it offers regarding God's policies in this world and a proposed approach toward dealing with suffering.

2.1. The Scene in Heaven. The scene in heaven serves a number of important functions in setting up the issues in the book. The first point that it makes clearly is that Job is indeed innocent of wrongdoing (Greenberg 1995b, 328; *contra* Brenner). This immediately eliminates the usual answers offered in the ancient Near East, which contended either that there really was an offense that the sufferer was unaware of or that God is simply inscrutable. This cleans the slate of tradition to make room for new explanations. A second point is that by acclaiming Job's *righteousness from the beginning, it is made clear that Job is not on trial. This feature allows the book to focus on God's policy regarding how the righteous are treated. Notice that in the process the book thus tackles the more difficult side of the retribution equation; that is, it is much easier to discuss why the wicked prosper. Finally, the scene in heaven shows that despite the instrumentation of the adversary, God both initiated the discussion and approved the course of action (cf. Job 42:11; see Weiss, 37). This again avoids the easy solution that insulates God by inserting an independently wicked intermediary power. The book would be toothless without this introduction. It would be reduced to philosophical speculation unable to rise above its contemporaries.

2.2. The Role of the Adversary. Christian readers readily identify the adversary as a known character whose profile is provided by the NT. But we cannot be so hasty. "Satan" here is a function, not a personal name (*see* Satan). This is particularly important here, for this *śāṭān* is portrayed neither as an independently volitional being nor as diabolical. He is among the "sons of God," the members of the heavenly council (*see* Divine Council), and he operates only as a subordinate. By permitting this adversary's course of action, God is allowing Job's case to stand as a test case for his policies. One can hardly label this adversary as an embodiment of evil when he simply expresses doubt concerning God's policies, a doubt that God has prompted through his observations concerning Job (Ragaz, in Glatzer, 129).

The role of the adversary is to provide the most important twist in the challenge against God's policies. Any human can contend that it is not a good policy for God to allow righteous people to suffer. This, of course, is Job's challenge. What is an innovation to this discussion is the contention of the adversary that it is not a good policy for God to bring prosperity to righteous people. When the adversary asks the rhetorical question of whether Job serves God for nothing, he in effect questions whether there is such a thing as disinterested righteousness. If righteousness is routinely rewarded, will not people behave righteously just to get the reward? And if that is so, is there really such a thing as true righteousness? Does not the policy of rewarding the righteous actually inhibit true righteousness by turning presumed and even potentially righteous people into ethical mercenaries? One could only answer such questions by taking away the prosperity of someone presumed righteous—the more righteous, the surer the test. The challenge then targets a policy (attributed to God) that is formulated as a principle of retribution: the righteous will prosper and the wicked will suffer. In this way the adversary provides one side of the challenge to God's policy (it is counterproductive for God to prosper righteous people), while Job provides the other side (it is unjust for God to allow righteous people to suffer).

2.3. The Role of Three Friends. All four friends serve as archetypes for the traditional thinking current in the ancient Near East, but Elihu is separated from the other three for a reason. Together, the three main friends function as archetypes that represent the revered wisdom of the ancient Near East at large. In contrast, we would propose that Elihu, with his Hebrew name, serves as an archetype for the contemporary, more recent (therefore, younger) thinking that was current in Israel.

The three friends, like Job himself, believe that Job is on trial, and so they promote the standard perspective and solutions that were the hallmarks of ancient wisdom (*contra* Albertz [245-46], who see the friends as representing Israelite traditional thinking, but supported in general by Gruber [92], who sees the friends as representative of human or Gentile wisdom, and stated outright by Mattingly [333]). Consider this ancient catalogue of symptoms and the assessment offered (for text information and bibliography, see Abusch, 85):

If a man has experienced something untoward and he does not know how it happened to him, he has continually suffered losses: losses of barley and silver, losses of male and female slaves, cattle, horses, and sheep; dogs, pigs and servants dying off altogether; he has heart-break time and again; he constantly gives orders, but no one complies, calls but no one answers; the curse of numerous people; when lying in his bed he is repeatedly apprehensive, he contracts paresis, he is filled with anger against god and king until his epileptic fit, his limbs are hanging down, from time to time he is apprehensive, he does not sleep day or night, he often sees terrifying dreams, he often gets paresis, his appetite for bread and beer is diminished, he forgets the word he spoke: that man has the wrath of the god and/or the goddess on him; his god and his goddess are angry with him.

In the ancient world different courses of action could serve as standard procedure for someone in Job's plight. One method entailed discovery divination to try to gain information concerning either the nature of the offense or, more often, what the deity wanted. A second approach involved incantations to exorcise the source of the evil. One corpus of literature that illustrates such incantations is found in the apotropaic rituals labeled *namburbi*. Third, appeasement could be sought by means of exhaustive lists of offenses to which one confesses, such as those found in the *šurpu* rituals. The latter is most evident in the approach recommended by Job's friends. It was unimportant in this procedure whether Job had actually committed the crimes or whether he was aware of any offenses. Though Eliphaz offers a catalog of Job's sins (Job 22:5-9), it is only hypothetical and suggestive. The friends have no knowledge of any specific offenses of which they can accuse Job. Yet, in accordance with the demands of the retribution principle, they are convinced that he is guilty, and it is on that basis that they urge his response to God. Specifically, they advise him in the first round in general terms to make his plea before God (Job 5:8; 8:5) and put away sin (Job 11:13). They offer no advice in the second round. In the third round Eliphaz makes a lengthy plea for Job to submit to God and return to him (Job 22:21-30). A most telling element is that each of them makes it clear that the principle goal is for Job to regain his favor, status and prosperity (Job 8:5-7; 11:14-20; 22:21-30). Far from representing disinterested righteousness, this promotes a heavily motivated righteousness. In this way, the friends can be seen as those who are advancing the case that the adversary has asserted. Job, in contrast, shows throughout that he is concerned not with restored prosperity (Job 9:21) but rather with clearing up the matter and restoring his reputation as a man who is righteous before God. He wants to contend with God because he has nothing to confess before God (Job 10:7; 13:19, 23; 23:11-12).

Additional evidence that the friends' advice can be understood in appeasement terms is found in Job's responses, particularly his final word to them in Job 27:1-6. He refuses to admit that they are right, and the integrity that he maintains is that he will not simply offer a blanket, blind confession with the hopes that he will appease God's inexplicable wrath and be restored to prosperity. Had he done so in response to the friends' advice, he would have proven that the adversary was right—that he was interested only in his benefits rather than being characterized by true, disinterested righteousness. For all of this to work effectively in the book it is important that Job himself be as ignorant of the scene in heaven as his friends are. If he knows what is truly at stake, the impact of his response would be nullified. Therefore, like his friends, he must believe that he is on trial, and he does. Whatever doubts he harbors and whatever accusations he hurls against the Almighty, as inappropriate and inaccurate as they may be, what is important for the book is that he retains the integrity of believing that righteousness is more important than reward.

2.4. The Role of Wisdom: The Interlude (Job 28). With Job's final refusal to follow the friends' advice in Job 27:1-6, the friends' role is over, as is the role of the adversary whom they represent. Job, who is the prime witness for the defense (of God's policies) rather than the defendant (as he assumed), has demonstrated that his righteousness is truly disinterested. The answers of the friends have been rejected as superficial in that they have misrepresented God (Job 42:7-8) by suggesting that he has only to be appeased for some indiscernible and possibly irrational anger (Mattingly, 332). The adversary need not be mentioned, for he shares in this indictment because the friends were the advocates of his case. The wisdom interlude (Job 28) serves the function of indicating that even though we have heard from the best that the sages of the ancient world had to offer (for discussion of the social location of the friends, see Albertz), we have not yet heard true wisdom. It closes the dialogue section of the book with the promise that there is more to offer (Dumbrell, 92) and so points the direction toward the denouement that is to be first hinted at by the creative position forged by

Elihu, then brought to fruition in the dramatic and revolutionary perspective offered in the speech of Yahweh (Geller, 174).

2.5. The Role of Job's Discourse. Job's three speeches in the discourse section serve an important function as the book proceeds. The reminiscences in Job 29 indicate clearly that what he misses is not the wealth and not even the honor, though both are mentioned in passing. Instead, he focuses on his lost opportunities to do justice, showing that he continues to value righteousness above reward. It may also hint at an implication that he knows how to use power to bring about justice. If he is making such a claim, he is eventually disabused of this delusional conceit by Yahweh's challenge. The theme of justice is continued in Job 30 as he recounts the resulting proliferation of injustice, of which he has now become a victim. The climax of Job's discourses is found in Job 31 as he attempts to turn God's silence, which has been serving as evidence of his guilt, to his advantage. By pronouncing his extended oath of innocence, he has challenged God in such a way that silence would vindicate him. After all, if he has sworn falsely, it is God's obligation to strike him down. If God does not do so, that lack of response stands as Job's exoneration.

2.6. The Role of Elihu. The challenge represented in Job's ostensibly pretentious oath of innocence has created tension in the book (will lightning crackle through the air in response to Job's arrogance?). Elihu's speeches hold the tension in suspense but likewise offer a response to it. This last, desperate resort by Job could easily be interpreted as self-righteousness, and Elihu treats it as such.

As previously suggested, Elihu could be seen as representative of Israelite thinking, suggested by his Hebrew name and his status as newcomer, if by nothing else. In this regard, his newcomer status is reflected in his devaluation of tradition and elevation of revelation (Albertz, 252). Further reason to consider him a suitable representative of Israel is that he is more protective of God's justice than any of the other characters. In that regard, it is important to note that he does not simply rehash the arguments already presented by the other friends. He is more theologically creative as he redefines concepts to try to arrive at a practical synthesis. In fact, he could be considered one of the first true "theologians" (Ehrenberg, in Glatzer, 93-94). He expands the retribution principle so that it not only describes the remedial consequences of past actions (reward for righteousness, punishment or suffering for wickedness) but also now allows that suffering may be disciplinary and thereby preventative as it functions to restrain someone from following an unacceptable course of action. With this redefinition he is now no longer obligated to identify past sins of Job's that would be sufficient to explain the severity of the punishment experienced in his dramatic fall. Instead, he only has to recognize the self-righteousness that Job has demonstrated, so excessive that even God's justice is called into question to defend himself. In Elihu's view, it is this *response* to suffering that provides the explanation, not only for the suffering itself but also for the extent of it. This is far more intricate and nuanced than the friends' simple invocation of the retribution principle. It also puts Elihu in position to actually pin a specific accusation on Job that can be sustained. In this role, he may well see himself as the arbitrator that Job has been requesting throughout the book (Habel 1984). Finally, it should be noticed that Elihu does not buy into the strategy of appeasement, and so he differs from the other friends. His view is more sophisticated than the general ancient Near Eastern one represented by the other friends, but still it is tied too closely to the retribution principle.

2.7. The Nature of Theophany. As Job's friends failed to offer the expected comfort, Yahweh's speeches fail to offer the expected solution. The *theophany has seemed so obtuse to some that it stands as a classic example of obfuscation—changing the subject to avoid the issue, distracting the questioner and inspiring terror all at once. This is a misunderstanding of the very real contribution that the book, through Yahweh's speeches, makes to the discussion, for although Yahweh does not offer the expected solution, what he does offer is, in the end, more honest, more satisfying, more helpful. It is true that Yahweh's speeches from the whirlwind neither explains Job's suffering, defends his own justice, enters into the courtroom for the confrontation that Job requested nor responds to Job's oath of innocence. Instead, the speeches of Yahweh suggest that the entire issue has been misdirected and there can be no right answers when the wrong questions are being asked (on the book's message, see 3 below).

The focus of the theophany is on God's wisdom, not his justice. The initial speech (Job 38:1—39:30) deals with God's wisdom in maintaining order in the cosmos. The questions that identify all the things that Job is incapable of doing carry the implication that they catalogue some of what God does pertaining to roles and functions in the world. These serve as demonstrations of God's wisdom because order is at the heart of wisdom. So, for example, Job 38:4-38 concerns cosmic geography (vv. 4-11, its delimitation; vv. 12-15, its exploitation in doing justice; vv. 16-18, its exploration; vv. 19-24, access to it; vv. 25-38, manipulation of it) and God's maintenance of order in these realms.

At the conclusion of God's first speech Job is ready to confess his lack of wisdom—he has no understanding of the intricate workings of the cosmos and is incapable of maintaining order. But there is more. God's response is to issue a further challenge to Job, now concerning not Job's understanding of the established order but rather his ability to respond to and harness threats to cosmic order. This is the topic of the second speech (Job 40:15—41:34) (based on the conclusion that Behemoth and Leviathan here are not zoological species past or present but rather cosmic creatures [Dumbrell, 94-95; Fyall associates Behemoth with Ugaritic Mot, and Leviathan with Satan]). This task is construed not as doing justice but rather as withholding the forces of disorder. Again this is testimony to God's wisdom and power.

2.8. The Role of the Postscript. Several important elements are addressed in the postscript. Obviously, it is not intended to tie up all the loose ends. It is worthy of notice that Job does not repent of any sin that may be presumed to be the cause of his suffering. Instead, he repents of the accusations that he has cast against God and of his doubts concerning God (Rowley, in Glatzer, 125). This is an indication that the book is more interested in one's view of God than in one's understanding of the causes of suffering. Job never learns of the opening scene in the heavenly court, and he is given no explanation for his suffering. At the same time, however, he indicates that he is satisfied with the information that he does receive—enough so to renounce his self-defense and claims of God's injustice (Clines, xxxix). Job's friends are indicted for their flawed view of God, whereas Job's view of God as one who responds to righteousness and does not need to be appeased is vindicated. Finally, and significantly, God restores Job's prosperity. This does not erase the pain of the initial losses, but it makes an important statement: in the aftermath of this test of God's policies, they remain the same. God will continue to bring prosperity to the righteous because it has been demonstrated that doing so does not inhibit the development of true righteousness.

3. Message.

The book has been described as one big lawsuit (*TDOT* 13.476), with God as plaintiff and Job as the accused, and so it may seem to the characters in the book. But as I have suggested, the author rises above this standard formula to offer the reader a different perspective with greater prospects for progress, whereby God is the accused and Job the unwitting witness for the defense.

3.1. The Indictment. In the heavenly scene (Job 1—2) Job is charged with nothing except *perhaps* questionable motives. His righteousness is affirmed as a given from the beginning, and neither God nor the accuser suggests that Job's behavior is anything short of righteous. The charges are made by the adversary and by Job against God, and it is his policies that are on trial. It would appear that God loses whichever way he goes, for there is no middle ground from which to redeem his policies.

3.2. The "Courtroom." The courtroom that becomes the setting for the drama is philosophical rather than physical—framed by the retribution principle. This setting juxtaposes three claims: (1) God is just; (2) Job is righteous; (3) the retribution principle is true. When the book opens, these three are givens, accepted by all as true. As the book takes shape, however, it becomes logically impossible to maintain all three claims. If we think of the courtroom as a triangle with one of these claims in each corner, we will see that each of the parties makes a choice to defend one corner (see Figure 1). From that vantage point one of the remaining two corners will be accepted, but the third must be forfeited (Tsevat).

The three friends defend the traditional affirmations represented in the retribution principle. They affirm the principle throughout their speeches in many different ways. From that defensive position they also adopt the traditional conviction that God is just. Consequently, they

can only forfeit Job's righteousness, deducing that it has been compromised, though they lack any real knowledge of offense. Given the parameters of the philosophy and the presuppositions that tradition declares, their logic is infallible.

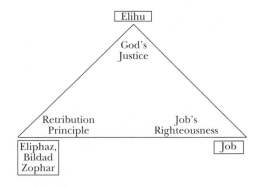

Figure 1. The Triangle of Claims

Job is adamant in his insistence that he has remained as righteous as he ever was. This is not a conclusion born of deduction; rather, it represents his true self-knowledge. Sudden change of fortunes, such as he has experienced, would indicate dramatic failures that represented a significant departure from previous behavior. If his prior behavior had been rewarded, and therefore considered worthy, then there should be no change in his situation, for there has been no variation in his conduct. After he chooses which corner to defend, his vision is too limited to renounce the retribution principle, for he can imagine no viable alternative. But as he affirms its truth, he is left in the unenviable and uncomfortable position of questioning the justice of God (see Job 40:8).

The fourth friend, Elihu (Job 32—37), positions himself firmly in the corner of God's justice. As he adopts this posture, he engages in a philosophical sleight of hand by which he can avoid discarding either the retribution principle or Job's righteousness. As explained in the discussion of the rhetorical strategy, Elihu redefines the parameters, first expanding the retribution principle and then questioning Job's righteousness on the basis of the revised definition. All three human parties (friends, Job, Elihu) accept the triangle as the basis for the discussion and the foundation from which answers must be found. We should also note that it is this setting that is the basis for the indictment against God, since both the accuser and Job assume that God's policy is accurately represented by the retribution principle and on that basis they have pressed their charges.

3.3. The Trial. Two possible responses by Job could result in God's losing the case. The quickest response, and perhaps not contrary to human nature, would have been for Job to succumb to his wife's advice: "Curse God and die." If Job had fallen to that temptation, it would have indicated that only the rewards made life worth living. It would have demonstrated that righteousness did not have a central place in Job's thinking. The second way that God could have lost the case would have been realized if Job had been persuaded by the appeals of his friends and adopted the strategy of appeasement. If Job listened to either his wife or his friends, the adversary would have been declared the victor, and it would have to be concluded that there really was no such thing as disinterested righteousness, thus calling into question the legitimacy of God's policy of rewarding the righteous.

Answering Job's charges against God is more complex. God would lose this part of the case if the retribution principle were allowed to stand unaltered or unnuanced, and given that foundation, he was unable to offer an explanation for the suffering of the righteous in general, and Job in particular. The book makes no attempt to offer the explanation but instead undertakes the task of reformulating the foundation.

The idea that reformulation was an option to be considered first becomes evident in the nuancing commenced by Elihu. Since Job thinks that he is on trial, he is thinking about winning, whereas since it is God's policies that are truly on trial, Job is actually pursuing options that will mean that God loses. God loses if he attempts to explain Job's suffering and cannot adequately do so, and this is precisely the type of explanation that Job is pressing for as he tries to force God into court or manipulate him by oath (Job 31). Of course, another way Job can win the case that he thinks he is involved in (concerning his own righteousness) is if God admits, on the basis of the retribution principle system, that he had acted unjustly and, in effect, apologizes. In this way, Job wins (the retribution principle stands and Job's righteousness is affirmed), but he wins at a terrible cost: God loses not only the case but also

his dignity. He is no longer a God worth serving. Three options are theoretically open to God: (1) give an explanation for righteous suffering, specifically Job's (and thus uphold the retribution principle); (2) admit that Job did not deserve the suffering (and uphold the retribution principle even as he admitted his failure to enforce it); (3) dismantle the retribution principle.

3.4. The Parties and the Case for the Prosecution. These have already been identified. The adversary is one plaintiff, and his case is represented by his team of prosecutors, the three friends. Job has adopted the posture of a second plaintiff in a sort of countersuit to God's allegedly spurious actions against him.

3.5. The Parties and the Case for the Defense. Job, believing that he was on trial, continually requested an advocate to undertake his defense. In the absence of such, he was attempting to press his case in his own defense and feeling inadequate to do so. But since he was not on trial, he needed no such defense. In the real trial, God's defense team has no spokesman. Elihu may be viewed as assuming the role (since he champions the justice of God), but he does not understand the nature of the case. He tries to vouchsafe a victory for God by offering an explanation of Job's suffering by means of adjusting rather than dismantling the retribution principle. Elihu is under the impression that Job is on trial, and he mounts an impressive and irrefutable (because unfalsifiable) accusation against Job, but to no avail. The retribution principle, however manipulated, is incapable of providing the answer.

When Yahweh finally speaks, he does not do so in his own defense. At that stage he has already won the first part of his case (against the adversary) on the strength of his lone witness, Job, who has refused to give up his integrity. Job has served in the role of witness even though he is one of God's prosecutors. In God's response (Job 38—41) the retribution principle system is shown to be simplistic and is dismantled (Dumbrell, 98; Greenberg 1995b, 329). If we go back to the triangle as representing the philosophical courtroom, we could say that God insists on a change of venue—a new setting in which the trial is to be conducted. He discards the triangle as an adequate setting for the discussion. God's wisdom, the direction indicated in the wisdom hymn in Job 28, is a more suitable arena for the discussion of suffering than is God's justice.

Yet it was God's justice, or at least the justice of his policies, that presumably was under investigation. The problem is that for God's justice in running the world to be assessed, someone must have all the information that is involved in God's running of the world (Job 40:8-14; 41:11). God does not try to defend his justice in his discourses, because, as becomes clear, no one is in a position to assess his justice.

3.6. The Verdict. Job demonstrated that his righteousness was not simply a pursuit of blessing and prosperity. Consequently, the adversary's charge against God's policy of blessing righteous people was shown to be false. God demonstrated that his wisdom surpasses the simple equations of the retribution principle, and that the operation of the cosmos is based on wisdom rather than on the premise of the retribution principle. Consequently, Job's charge of injustice, itself premised on the retribution principle, was also shown to be false. God's policies thus were vindicated, and he showed his renewed commitment to them by again heaping blessing on Job.

But how is this not a reiteration of the retribution principle? The difference is that in this new view the retribution principle is not of a system that is the foundation of world order and operation. It does not represent a guarantee or a mechanical cause/effect process. It is God's delight to prosper those who are faithful to him, and it is God's commitment to punish wickedness. That is the nature of God. But this cannot be reduced to a formula (Dumbrell, 102). God has created the natural world and maintains it day by day. But that does not mean that the natural world is endowed with the attributes of God. Rain can be used by God to enforce justice, but the rain is not just (Job 38:25-27). In this way the book refutes the idea of a moral order in the natural world (Kaufmann, in Glatzer, 66). God administers the world in wisdom, and from his sovereign wisdom justice results. We may be lacking sufficient information to be able to affirm that God's justice is being carried out day by day. We do have enough, however, to affirm that he is wise. If we believe that he is wise, then there is good reason to believe that he is just.

If this interpretation is accurate, then the book of Job argues pointedly against the *theodicy philosophies in the ancient world and represents an Israelite modification. This modification, rather than offering a revised theodicy, seeks to reinterpret the justice of God from something that may be debated to something that is a given. In Yahweh's speech it is not his justice that is defended, it is his wisdom.

We have already noted that Job receives no explanation concerning the cause of his suffering, and so we might infer that neither should we expect such explanations for our suffering or for anyone else's. A focus on justice demands explanation of cause and gazes at the past, whereas a focus on wisdom needs only to understand that God in his wisdom has a purpose as it fixes one's gaze on the future. In John 9 when the disciples raise the question about the man born blind, Jesus likewise turns their attention from cause to purpose: "Neither this man nor his parents sinned . . . but this happened so that the work of God might be displayed in his life." Job's friends had considered suffering to be punitive; Elihu had considered it disciplinary; Jesus, following the lead of the book of Job, considers it beyond explanation yet capable of being turned to spiritual profit if it leads to knowledge of God and fellowship with him. This is not a theological or intellectual solution—it is a spiritual insight (Rowley, in Glatzer, 126-28).

It is of interest to note, in conclusion, that the book of Job goes on record to affirm that there is indeed such a thing as the innocent suffering (Hartley, 47; Rowley, in Glatzer, 125), and the NT confirms that assessment. In the end, the book is less interested in why there is innocent suffering than in what is the proper way to think about God when we live in such a world. What satisfied Job in the end was not that he now understood suffering better but rather that he knew God better. As H. H. Rowley (in Glatzer, 125-26) puts it,

In his prosperity he thought that he had known God. Now he realizes that compared with his former knowledge his present knowledge is as the joy of seeing compared with a mere rumor. All his past experience of God was as nothing compared with the experience he had now found. He therefore no longer cries out to be delivered from his suffering. He rests in God even in his pain.

4. Unity and Composition.

Sawyer (253) makes the important observation that the inclusion of a variety of materials in a book is typical of the OT and of Wisdom literature and cannot be taken as prima facie evidence of haphazard redaction. He notes the difference between considering whether the same hand penned each section of the book and considering the extent to which each section is integral to the book. Ancient Near Eastern literature shows a similar propensity to include some variety of materials in a single piece, though not to the same extent as does the OT. For example, there are numerous examples of dispute literature that includes cosmological sections (e.g., Disputation between Ewe and Wheat [*COS* 1.180], Disputation between Bird and Fish [*COS* 1.182], Disputation between Summer and Winter [*COS* 1.183]).

The history of literary criticism of the book of Job has featured many challenges to the literary integrity of the book (see the somewhat cynical summary in Baker, 17-18). A common view of the compositional history of the book sees the narrative frame as having existed independently (as poetic epics [see Sarna]), to be later enlarged with the dialogues and discourses. Furthermore, a general consensus exists that the wisdom hymn in Job 28 and the Elihu speeches in Job 32—37 were later insertions into the book. Some have doubted the originality of the Yahweh speeches, and all have noticed the absence of Zophar's last speech and the abbreviated nature of Bildad's last speech and inferred some corruption in transmission. Some have offered suggestions that Zophar's speech is still there, perhaps in the latter part of Job 27, or even in Job 28.

These views show the common inclination toward atomization in what can at times be presumptuous reconstruction of the history of composition. Recent trends show a greater disposition toward evaluating the final form of the book for its rhetorical coherency, and on this count Job scores well. Given the above analysis of the rhetorical strategy of the book, the Elihu speeches play a pivotal role in the book by offering a more sophisticated view of the retribution principle. The scene in heaven is absolutely essential because only by means of that section is the shift signaled that God's policies are on trial, not Job. Without the scene in heaven, the perception of all of the characters in the book that Job is on trial would also be the only perception available to the reader. It is the scene in heaven that identifies that the real question about Job's suffering does not concern Job's behavior. The real question concerns how God runs the world. The wisdom hymn in Job 28 is essential for the transition from the dialogue section to the discourse section. As we noted in the rhetorical analysis above, it is also essential to indicate the transition from dealing with the adversary's accusation to dealing with Job's much more difficult challenge to God's policies. At every turn the book penetrates the surface issues and the superficial answers to formulate innovative approaches to the age-old question. Regardless of what literary critics can determine or believe that they can determine about the stages of composition and differences in style, the book in its current form coheres magnificently as it builds a sophisticated response to the question of what form faith in the midst of suffering should take.

5. Date and Context.

Some propose a date for the book based on the premise that it offers a metaphor for exilic or postexilic Israel, and we should consider briefly the plausibility of this view. It appears in a variety of permutations, but consider as one example the reasoning expressed by R. Albertz (252), who does not so much attempt to defend the view as to explain how his interpretation would be worked out within this perspective: "It is clear that the purpose of the Book of Job is to provide an increasingly theological foundation for sapiential knowledge. This probably relates to the need to offer the pious segment of the Jewish aristocracy a clear orientation during the period of social crisis in the early postexilic period."

The reluctance of some to proceed in this direction can be summarized in the disappointment evident in the lament of J. J. M. Roberts (111) that for interpreters who go this direction, their "predilection for history reduces Job to a mere cipher for Israel, and his theological problem becomes the problem of understanding Israel's national experience."

On a number of counts this view can be refuted, but I will mention just two. First, it would be difficult to portray Israel in these periods as righteous with no idea of anything that the nation had done wrong. The book would serve very poorly as metaphor if the basic ingredients in the metaphor had no relation to reality. Second, there are no allusions to national calamity (de Moor, 227). To proceed in this direction, then, one is working entirely within the realm of speculation, if not allegory.

As we turn to other options, we need to face the paradox that although the characters are, for the most part, non-Israelite, the book is framed within an Israelite cognitive environment. Therefore, although the plot may well be placed in an early second millennium BC context, the composition of the book must derive from a later period. We will look at each of these issues in turn.

5.1. Setting for the Events. It is common to hear that the chronological setting for the narrative frame is as early as the patriarchal period or even earlier. The actual evidence for this conclusion, however, is slight.

- Wealth measured by cattle and flocks
- Patriarch serving as priest for the family
- Longevity (Job's 140-year lifespan)
- No reference to covenant, Torah, exodus, etc.
- Roving Sabaean and Chaldean tribesmen
- Job 42:11 refers to *qĕśîṭâ*, a unit of money known elsewhere only in Genesis 33:19; Joshua 24:32 (both referring to money paid to the Shechemites for land)

Most of these, however, can be explained by the non-Israelite setting. Job's longevity is striking, but also it could simply be exceptional. The Chaldeans' early history is too little known (they first appear in the first millennium BC), and the Sabeans are not identified with confidence, though as a North Arabian tribe they are more at home in the first millennium BC as well. The unit of money is obscure. None of these provide very convincing evidence, though little circumstantial evidence from the content would offer support of a later setting for the events either. This position is usually maintained by traditional scholars, though it should be noted that J. C. de Moor makes a case for identification of Job with Ayyabu, known from the fourteenth-century BC Amarna texts in the Late Bronze period (de Moor, 242-57).

5.2. Israelite Features. Although unquestionably there are numerous points of contact between Job and Ugaritic language and literature (de Moor), the claim that the book contains more of the religion of Canaan than the monotheism of Israel (so de Moor, 239) cannot be sustained in light of a number of uniquely Israelite

perspectives. With regard to date, the appearance of strictly Israelite features would argue for composition of the book in a period at least post-Sinai (and more likely monarchial), for only then would there be a religious cognitive environment distinctly identifiable as Israelite that can be observed in the book:

- Job's friends attempt to defend the justice of God. Generally in the ancient Near East the gods were considered to be interested in social justice, people prayed to them for justice, and the king was expected to establish justice. But the gods themselves were not necessarily considered just, nor was there any attempt to defend their justice. Furthermore, suffering was not as intimately tied to divine justice (*see* Retribution). Thus this compelling sense that God's justice must be defended is distinctly Israelite.
- Job denies paying homage to the sun or moon, indicating that to do so would be an act of unfaithfulness to God (Job 31:26-28). In the ancient Near East faithfulness to one god above others was not an issue. Only in Israel would homage to celestial deities be considered an offense (Roberts, 113).
- The view of God shows a distinctly Israelite perspective. Even though appeasement is on the table for consideration, the friends never suggest a ritual remedy, which would have been the norm in the ancient Near East (for moral/ethical remedy, see Job 8:6; 11:13-15; for righteousness/blamelessness as criterion, see Job 22:3). Furthermore, in the book of Job God has no needs (Job 22:3) that have to be met by worshipers. This perspective is extremely difficult to document outside of Israel.
- The fact that the appeasement route suggested by the friends is rejected as unsuitable is yet another indication that an Israelite perspective is reflected in the book. Though the Israelites occasionally resort to appeasement, orthodox Israelite theology considered it to presuppose a flawed view of God.

It is interesting that the Israelite view maintained in the book is one that is fully in line with the unsyncretized view that characterized the classical prophets, the Deuteronomist(s) (however identified) and the priestly literature (whenever dated). The book is a product of a fully orthodox perspective at least on these counts.

In conclusion, we should note that early in the second millennium BC a change is evident in how the Mesopotamian texts dealt with the problem of suffering. Previously, one's misfortune was accounted as having angered one's personal god. Increasingly, however, a shift occurred in which the misfortune was not due to one's own offense but rather came about because a third party (e.g., a witch) had provoked the personal god against the individual (thus turning the individual into victim rather than offender). T. Abusch (103-4) suggests that this shift may represent an attempt to solve a theological problem—that is, offering a reason for the god's anger that does not seek for a reason in the behavior of the individual but rather is based on accusations made against that individual by a third party. In the book of Job we see a twist (at several points) to this way of thinking. The third party is not a human practitioner of the occult, but is one of the heavenly council; the personal deity is not aroused to anger, but agrees to a test; and the accusation is not made against the individual, but against the policies of the deity. This is a new level of third-party involvement that fits within an Israelite context, in which witchcraft had no legitimate role in the profile of theology. It is interesting that the friends represent the prior way of Mesopotamian thinking—the personal god is angry—while the narrative frame provides a modified "third party" approach. The friends themselves never hint at the possibility that a third party with power had influenced the situation. This information would lend support to an early date in terms of the presuppositions of the friends, but it might suggest a later date for the third-party involvement, however much diversity the application of it shows. This is interesting in that it is a reversal of the usual suggestion that the narrative frame is original and the dialogue was provided later. Consequently, all of the variety of information available does not offer a clear indication for the dating of either the events or of the book, but here we looked at factors not generally considered in previous treatments that should be part of any future discussion.

See also JOB 2: ANCIENT NEAR EASTERN BACK-GROUND; JOB 3: HISTORY OF INTERPRETATION; JOB 4: PERSON.

BIBLIOGRAPHY. *Commentaries:* F. I. Andersen, *Job* (TOTC; Downers Grove, IL: InterVarsity Press, 1976); **D. J. A. Clines,** *Job 1-20* (WBC 17; Dallas: Word, 1989); **N. C. Habel,** *The Book of Job* (OTL; Philadelphia: Westminster, 1985); **J. E. Hartley,** *The Book of Job* (NICOT; Grand Rapids: Eerdmans, 1988); **M. Pope,** *Job* (3rd ed.; AB 15; Garden City, NY: Doubleday, 1973); *Studies:* **T. Abusch,** "Witchcraft and the Anger of the Personal God," in *Mesopotamian Magic: Textual, Historical, and Interpretative Perspectives,* ed. T. Abusch and K. van der Toorn (AMD 1; Groningen: Styx Publications, 1999); **R. Albertz,** "The Sage and Pious Wisdom in the Book of Job: The Friends' Perspective," in *The Sage in Israel and the Ancient Near East,* ed. J. G. Gammie and L. G. Perdue (Winona Lake: Eisenbrauns, 1990) 243-62; **J. A. Baker,** "The Book of Job: Unity and Meaning," in *Studia Biblica 1978,* ed. E. A. Livingstone (JSOTSup 11; Sheffield: JSOT Press, 1979) 17-26; **A. Brenner,** "Job the Pious? The Characterization of Job in the Narrative Framework of the Book," in *The Poetical Books: A Sheffield Reader,* ed. D. J. A. Clines (BibSem 41; Sheffield: Sheffield Academic Press, 1997) 298-313; **J. C. de Moor,** "Ugarit and the Origin of Job," in *Ugarit and the Bible: Proceedings of the International Symposium on Ugarit and the Bible, Manchester, September 1992,* ed. G. J. Brooke, A. H. W. Curtis, and J. F. Healey (UBL 11; Münster: Ugarit-Verlag, 1994) 225-58; **W. J. Dumbrell,** "The Purpose of the Book of Job," in *The Way of Wisdom: Essays in Honor of Bruce K. Waltke,* ed. J. I. Packer and S. K. Soderlund (Grand Rapids: Zondervan, 2000) 91-105; **R. S. Fyall,** *Now My Eyes Have Seen You: Images of Creation and Evil in the Book of Job* (Downers Grove, IL: InterVarsity Press, 2002); **S. A. Geller,** "'Where Is Wisdom?': A Literary Study of Job 28 in Its Settings," in *Judaic Perspectives on Ancient Israel,* ed. J. Neusner, B. Levine and E. Frerichs (Philadelphia: Fortress, 1987) 155-88; **N. Glatzer,** ed., *The Dimensions of Job: Study and Selected Readings* (New York: Schocken, 1969); **M. Greenberg,** "Job," in *Studies in the Bible and Jewish Thought* (Philadelphia: Jewish Publication Society, 1995a) 335-60; idem, "Reflections on Job's Theology," in *Studies in the Bible and Jewish Thought* (Philadelphia: Jewish Publication Society, 1995b) 327-34; **M. I. Gruber,** "Human and Divine Wisdom in the Book of Job," in *Boundaries of the Ancient Near Eastern World: A Tribute to*

Cyrus H. Gordon, ed. M. Lubetski, C. Gottlieb and S. Keller (JSOTSup 273; Sheffield: Sheffield Academic Press, 1998) 88-102; **N. C. Habel,** "The Role of Elihu in the Design of the Book of Job," in *In the Shelter of Elyon: Essays on Ancient Palestinian Life and Literature in Honour of G. W. Ahlström,* ed. W. B. Barrick and J. R. Spencer (JSOTSup 31; Sheffield: JSOT Press, 1984) 81-98; **G. L. Mattingly,** "The Pious Sufferer: Mesopotamia's Traditional Theodicy and Job's Counselors," in *The Bible in the Light of Cuneiform Literature,* ed. W. W. Hallo, B. W. Jones and G. L. Mattingly (ScrCon 3; Lewiston, NY: Edwin Mellen, 1990) 305-48; **E. W. Nicholson,** "The Limits of Theodicy as a Theme of the Book of Job," in *Wisdom in Ancient Israel: Essays in Honour of J. A. Emerton,* ed. J. Day, R. P. Gordon, H. G. M. Williamson (Cambridge: Cambridge University Press, 1995) 71-82; **J. J. M. Roberts,** "Job and the Israelite Religious Tradition," in *The Bible and the Ancient Near East* (Winona Lake, IN: Eisenbrauns, 2002) 110-16; **N. Sarna,** "Epic Substratum in the Prose of Job," *JBL* 76 (1957) 13-25; **J. F. A. Sawyer,** "The Authorship and Structure of the Book of Job," in *Studia Biblica 1978,* ed. E. A. Livingstone (JSOTSup 11; Sheffield: JSOT Press, 1979) 253-57; **M. Tsevat,** "The Meaning of the Book of Job," in *The Meaning of the Book of Job and Other Biblical Studies* (New York: KTAV, 1980) 1-38; **M. Weiss,** *The Story of Job's Beginning* (Jerusalem: Magnes, 1983); **C. Westermann,** *The Structure of the Book of Job* (Philadelphia: Fortress, 1981); **R. B. Zuck,** ed., *Sitting with Job: Selected Studies on the Book of Job* (Grand Rapids: Baker, 1992).   J. H. Walton

JOB 2: ANCIENT NEAR EASTERN BACKGROUND

Among the wisdom texts of the ancient Middle East the book of Job is an impressive work of erudition. In creating a complex composition that addresses the problem of inexplicable *suffering—the most troubling dimension of human experience—its author drew on a host of genres from the cult, the legal tradition and the wisdom tradition. Furthermore, this author's work, as is characteristic of several works from the wisdom tradition, has an international perspective. The dialogue is set either in Syria or Edom. Edom, famous for its sages (Jer 49:7; Obad 8), is prominent as the home of Eliphaz, the lead comforter, and possibly of the main character, Job. Other peoples and places mentioned include Sabeans, Chaldeans, Tema, Sheba, Cush and Ophir. This poet displays a breadth of knowledge in the wide range of topics found in the speeches—for example, mining (Job 28:1-11), travel of merchants across the desert (Job 6:18-20), a variety of traps (Job 18:8-10), precious metals (Job 22:21-25; 28:1-2), prized jewels and glassware (Job 28:16-19), constellations (Job 9:9; 38:31-32), animal portraits (Job 38:39—39:30), the ideal prototype human (Job 15:7-8) and a sage's report of a revelatory vision (Job 4:12-16). The animal portraits show an interest in scientific categorization such as is attested in documents from Egypt and Mesopotamia. The author of Job was truly an international sage. Thus it is not surprising that documents from Mesopotamia and Egypt that treat the issues of inexplicable suffering and social turmoil offer a variety of parallels in theme, imagery and structure to the book of Job.

1. Mesopotamian Texts
2. Egyptian Texts
3. Conclusion

1. Mesopotamian Texts.

Six texts from Mesopotamia will be considered here. Three are hymns of praise to god for a remarkable recovery from a debilitating illness: the Sumerian Man and His God and two Akkadian texts, A Sufferer's Salvation and I Will Praise the Lord of Wisdom. A fourth text, A Dialogue between a Man and His God, poorly preserved, belongs to this category but differs structurally. Two Akkadian texts use a dialogue format to probe situations that contradict the traditional wisdom teaching on rewards and punishments. In The Babylonian Theodicy a sufferer and a friend discuss the challenges to traditional wisdom that arise from the sufferer's experience. There is also The Obliging Slave, a humorous satire in which a well-to-do master despairs of finding any meaningful activity in this life.

1.2. Hymns of Praise. Some hymns of praise were composed as a liturgical response for recovery from a life-threatening illness (Weinfeld). The recovered person begins and ends the hymn with elaborate praise of his personal god. At the center the supplicant enumerates in detail the ailments from which he was delivered. These texts encouraged ancient Babylonians beset with hardships for no apparent reason to appeal to the god(s) by affirming that the god(s) provide deliverance.

1.2.1. Man and His God (COS 1.179:573-75). The oldest known work in this category, possibly composed around the beginning of the second millennium BC, is the Sumerian poem of some 140 lines entitled Man and His God. An upright young man opens and closes a hymn with exhortations always to exalt one's god. At the core of the poem for some ninety-one lines (28-119), the devotee describes in detail the dreadful illness that he endured even though he was unaware of having committed any specific offense to account for his affliction.

This person, who was severely afflicted, lamented the added suffering caused by the hostility of those with whom he had worked:

> My herdsman maltreats me, who am not
> hostile (toward him),
> My companion says not a true word to me,
> My friend renders my words, truthfully
> spoken, a lie. (36-38)

Not only deeply troubled by his friends' deceiving him, he was especially distressed that they were informing others that his word was a lie (28-29). Their accusations troubled him so deeply that he even accused his god with failing to stop their deceitfulness (37-38). Similarly for Job, a most agonizing aspect of his trial was the fact that God had made his body testify against the truthfulness of his assertions of innocence (Job 16:8). In other words, Job's emaciated body served as irrefutable testimony to his guilt.

Heavy suffering caused this Sumerian to weep bitterly (71). Out of anguish he petitioned his god earnestly for the recovery of strength (98-99). Troubled, he went on to ask,

> How long will you not care for me, will you
> not look after me? (100)

Although he wanted to honor his god and take the right course, his god did not permit him to do so (101-102). He then acknowledged the truth of the wisdom maxim that never had a sinless child been born (104). This saying was strongly affirmed by Job's counselors (e.g., Job 4:17-21; 11:12). By quoting it, the Sumerian sought to move his god to disclose his sins so that he could make confession at the city gate (114-116). In fact, this man's contrite response to affliction is the way that Job's three comforters

wanted him to behave, but he resolutely refused their counsel and affirmed his innocence. Job did not claim that he was sinless but rather that he had never done any wrong that warranted such horrific suffering. The Sumerian's god, assuaged by his devotee's pleas, removed his afflictions, restored his joy, and set a benevolent spirit as his guardian (120-132).

This hymn encourages the devout beset by suffering to lament vigorously and seek god continually, for they will find restoration. However, the Sumerian sufferer never raised the question of divine justice, a major theme of the book of Job. As he lamented, he pondered about several causes for his illness: the decrees of fate (42); Asag, a demon bringing headaches and illness (74); the abandonment of his god (100); and his own sinfulness (104-106), but he did not settle on any one of these as the cause. Clearly, then, this ancient Sumerian understanding of human suffering is opposite to the position presented in the book of Job.

1.2.2. A Sufferer's Salvation (COS 1.152:486). Two Akkadian texts follow a similar structure. Whether or not they were influenced by the preceding Sumerian text, they belong to a common literary tradition. The first, A Sufferer's Salvation (RS 25.460), a text from Ugarit written in Akkadian, is usually dated to the end of the fourteenth century BC (Lambert). This fact serves as evidence that literary pieces treating the theme of the just sufferer were present on Canaanite soil at an early date, thereby adding weight to the possibility that the author of Job was influenced by a wide and varied literary tradition on this subject.

The beginning of this Akkadian text is missing. When the extant text begins, a sufferer, befuddled by his fate, describes how he turned to magicians, soothsayers and augurs for insight into his deplorable condition. However, all means of contacting the spirit world had been shut off (1'-8'). As a result, he had no way of finding out either the cause of his illness or a cure. He was in such a sorry condition that his family had gathered to observe a wake for him (9'-12'). The sufferer then details his many ailments: lack of appetite, insomnia, troubling thoughts. The grateful sufferer renders enthusiastic praise to Marduk, describing this god in antithetical terms (34'-39'):

> [He it] is, Marduk, I entreat(?) him,

I entreat(?) him,
[He it] was who smote me, then was merciful
to me. (33'-34')
. . .
He dashed me down, then grabbed me (as I
fell). (36')

Although the text breaks off, the speaker apparently enumerated the way Marduk brought healing to each part of his devastated body.

1.2.3. The Poem of the Righteous Sufferer (COS *1.153:486-92*). The famous Akkadian text on this theme is The Poem of the Righteous Sufferer, also known as The Babylonian Job or by its opening line, I Will Praise the Lord of Wisdom *(Ludlul bēl nēmeqi)*. The author, a highly learned person, skillfully employed a variety of poetic devices, including alliteration, inclusio, a variety of parallel patterns, and allusion, to compose one of the finest literary documents from ancient Mesopotamia (Foster). The advanced, complex structure of this text attests that its author drew on and advanced a rich literary tradition. Its ancient popularity is attested by the several copies that have been found in several locations from Nineveh to Babylon and by an ancient commentary on it.

A Babylonian sufferer named Subshi-meshre-Shakkan delivered a long monologue of over four hundred lines, opening and closing with a hymn of praise to Marduk, the main god of the Babylonians. At the outset he vividly lauded Marduk's power to bless and to afflict:

I will praise the lord of wisdom, solicitous
god,
[Fur]ious in the night, growing in the day:
Marduk! lord of wisdom, solicitous god
(1.1-3)
. . .
Whose anger is like a raging tempest,
But whose breeze is sweet as the breath of
morn. (1.5-6)
. . .
His scourge is barbed and punctures the
body. (1.21)

Marduk makes humans bear the consequences of their sins, but he also dispels guilt. Here the sufferer affirmed that his goal in composing this text was to encourage people by informing them of Marduk's anger and his kindness:

I, who touched bottom like a fish, will
proclaim his anger,
He quickly granted me favor, as if reviving
the dead.
I will teach the people that his kindness
is nigh,
May his favorable thought take away their
[guilt?]. (1.39-42)

Subshi-meshre-Shakkan went on to complain in detail about the horrific sufferings that befell him when Marduk unexpectedly turned against him. All members of the community, the king, his family, and his god and goddess abandoned him. Those who spoke well of him were punished, while those who defamed him advanced. Everywhere he went people gawked at him as though he were an enemy. His former slaves, male and female, defamed him in public. Others added to his losses. Officials blocked water for irrigation from reaching his fields and took away his prerogatives in the community. Courtiers plotted to do him harm and to gain his wealth:

They parceled my possessions among
the riffraff,
The sources of my watercourses they blocked
with muck,
They chased the harvest song from my fields,
They left my community deathly still, like
that of a (ravaged) foe. (1.100-104)

No one stood up as his helper. Job also mourned his isolation from all, from servants to family members (Job 19:13-19). As part of his avowal of innocence (Job 30), Job bitterly complained that the lowest members of society, those so low that he would not even let their fathers accompany the dogs that watched his flocks, made him their mocking song (Job 30:1-15). However, Job never accused anybody of taking his goods or seeking to do him harm.

In his complaint Subshi-meshre-Shakkan detailed the ailments that troubled his body:

By day sighing, by night lamentation,
Monthly, trepidation, despair the year.
I moaned like a dove all my days,
Like a singer, I moan out my dirge.
My eyes endure(?) constant crying,
My cheeks scald from tears, as if eroded(?).
My face is darkened from the apprehensions
of my heart,

Terror and panic have jaundiced my face.
The wellsprings of my heart quaked for
    unremitting anxiety. (1.105-113)

In several of his speeches Job likewise expressed details of his physical suffering—for example, he said,

I have sewed sackcloth over my skin,
and buried my brow in the dust.
My face is red with weeping,
dark shadows ring my eyes.
    (Job 16:15-16 NIV)

At the end of the first tablet Subshi-meshre-Shakkan expressed the hope that his fortune would change:

Surely in daylight good will come upon me!
The new moon will appear, the sun will
    shine! (1.119-120)

Nevertheless, in the next tablet he continued to describe his suffering in detail, showing that his hope had not been immediately realized. He specifically complained that his sufferings had continued for over a year. By contrast, in the book of Job there are virtually no indicators as to how long Job suffered.

Though not entertaining the question of *theodicy in any depth, this Babylonian acknowledged that his losses troubled his understanding of god:

I wish I knew that these things were pleasing
    to a god!
What seems good to one's self could be an
    offense to a god,
. . .
Who could learn the reasoning of the gods
    in heaven? (2.33-36)

His expression of self-doubt about what a god valued hindered his pursuing a divine explanation for his affliction. Since Job had a stronger sense of the character of divine justice (see Job 29), he was deeply distraught by God's apparent hostility and persistent silence. However, he challenged that hostility. In seeking to hold God accountable, Job longed for an umpire, a friend, or a *kinsman-redeemer, one who would assist him in achieving reconciliation with God. Beyond Job's own quest, the book it-self seeks explanations for unjust suffering in the context of belief in one just God.

Subshi-meshre-Shakkan believed that his fate was such as befell those who had been unfaithful in observing times of prayer and holy days. To contest his apparent infidelity, he recalled that during his prosperity he had been mindful of observing all cultic customs. The character of his self-justification contrasts with Job's declarations of innocence. Subshi-meshre-Shakkan grounded his uprightness on observance of ritual acts, whereas Job grounded his innocence on the moral integrity of his attitudes. Even though at the outset Job is depicted as such a conscientious worshiper that he periodically made sacrifices to atone for any possible curse against God made by his children in their thoughts (Job 1:5), in the dialogue he never recounted any acts of ritual observance in defense of his innocence (see Job 29—31). Rather, Job centered his integrity on the honor he had in the community, his concern for the weak, and the closeness of God in his life.

Affliction reduced Subshi-meshre-Shakkan to constant weeping. His prayers were powerless. Because Marduk had abandoned him, he was convinced that demons tormented his body:

[They (i.e., a spirit and a she-demon) struck
    my he]ad, they closed around my pate,
[My features] were gloomy, my eyes ran
    a flood,
They wrenched my muscles, made my neck
    limp. (2.59-61)
. . .
They churned up my bowels, they tw[isted]
    my entrails(?),
Coughing and hacking infected my lungs,
They infected(?) my limbs, made my flesh
    pasty,
My lofty stature they toppled like a wall.
    (2.65-69)
. . .
A demon has clothed himself in my body for
    a garment,
Drowsiness smothers me like a net. (2.71-72)
. . .
Numbness has spread over my whole body.
    (2.75)
. . .
Signs of death have shrouded my face! (2:81)

To find relief, he turned to diviners and exorcists. But the diviners offered no insight, and the exorcists were unable to drive out these evil spirits. Although there is an enigmatic *Satan, who was Job's adversary in the heavenly counsel, Job never entertained thoughts of demons as the cause of his affliction. Nor did he search out diviners to help discover the cause of his ill fate.

As Subshi-meshre-Shakkan continued to lament, he devoted over sixty lines to detailing his various ailments. In the following words the depth of his humiliation is clearly visible:

> I spent the night in my dung like an ox,
> I wallowed in my excrement like a sheep.
> (2.101-104)

Since he had been confined to bed, his family abandoned any hope of his recovery. So they prepared his grave and performed funeral rites for him.

At the depth of despair, Subshi-meshre-Shakkan suddenly experienced a complete reversal in his fate. In a nightmarish dream he dimly perceived a stately young man clothed in glorious apparel. This visitor told him that a lady had sent him. The lady's words are lost, for the text is broken here. In a second dream he saw one identified as a purifier. That one informed him that he, a citizen of Nippur, had come to perform purification rites on his behalf. While pouring water over Subshi-meshre-Shakkan, he recited an incantation. In a third dream the sufferer beheld a dazzling woman clothed in splendor. She proclaimed release to the sufferer. Then he saw a bearded exorcist, carrying a favorable sign, who had been empowered by Marduk to bring deliverance.

As Subshi-meshre-Shakkan awoke, a serpent that brings healing slithered by, and he recovered immediately. Marduk, having been appeased, accepted Subshi-meshre-Shakkan's prayers and caused his offenses to be borne away by the wind (3.60). It is curious that although Subshi-meshre-Shakkan was unaware of having done any wrong, he expressly stated that his offenses were removed at the time of his healing. By contrast, God never accused Job of any wrongdoing, but only of darkening counsel (Job 38:2). Job withdrew his lament (Job 42:6), but he made no confession of sin. Furthermore, the text never says that God forgave Job any offense.

Subshi-meshre-Shakkan praised Marduk for bringing him full restoration, recounting in detail the return of strength to the various parts of his body (1'-14'). He also mentioned that he survived the river ordeal; unfortunately, more is not known about this ordeal, since the text is fragmented. Subshi-meshre-Shakkan might have sought thereby to prove his worthiness for acceptance back into the community. He then made a procession through the thirteen gates in Esagila, the magnificent temple of Marduk in Babylon. Possibly this was a ritual leading to full reintegration into society. At each gate he received a blessing that corresponded to the gate's name—for example, "Gate of Prosperity," "Gate of Splendid Wonderment," "Gate of Release from Guilt." Arriving inside the temple, he worshiped his god and presented offerings in abundance, causing the gods and spirits to glow with pleasure. Here the text ends, according to Lambert. However, there is a fragment that recounts how the citizens of Babylon, upon seeing that Marduk had restored Subshi-meshre-Shakkan's life, broke out in exuberant praise of their god. Lambert places this fragment before the river ordeal, but Foster places it at the conclusion. In either case, two major purposes of this text are to render high praise to Marduk and to extend hope of recovery for those beset with dreadful illnesses.

Hymnic lines also have an important place in the book of Job. In the first and third cycles of the dialogue Job and the comforters cited hymnic lines. In Job 9:5-13 Job described the absolute power of God over nature and cosmic foes. In Job 12:14-25 he sang of God's power to unsettle the social order. Another time he lamented God's distance (Job 23:8-9, 13-14). The friends praised God's majesty and greatness in hymnic lines, such as the doxology spoken by Eliphaz (Job 5:9-16; cf. Job 11:7-11; 22:12; 25:2-6). Elihu recounted God's glorious power manifested in a mighty storm (Job 36:24—37:13). At the end of the book the Yahweh speeches are essentially a hymn of praise to God's wonders in creating and governing the world.

A few key contrasts between The Poem of the Righteous Sufferer and the book of Job highlight the unique approach to suffering taken in the book of Job. The view of the main god is vastly different. In the Babylonian hymn Marduk is distant and unpredictable, blessing or afflicting at will, whereas Yahweh let his servant Job be afflicted out of high confidence in his ability to maintain his integrity amidst terrible sufferings. At the time of restoration Yahweh did not send an emissary to bring about Job's healing. Instead, he appeared and spoke with his servant about the nature of the created order as he sought to lead Job back to a reconciled relationship. In taking this approach, he treated his follower as an astute thinking person whom he could engage in meaningful conversation about his governance of the universe. Two other marked contrasts are the lack of details given to Job's recovery and the lack of emphasis on Job's reestablishment in society. In fact, in the account of Job it is not even explicitly stated that God healed Job. Rather, the conclusion focuses on the reconciliation of the various parties: Job and God, the friends and God, Job and the friends, and Job and his relatives. Amazingly, in light of the prominence given to honoring god in these Mesopotamia texts, there is no report of Job's rendering praise to God. Clearly, the emphasis in Job's story lies on communion with God, not on performance of rituals.

1.2.4. Dialogue Between a Man and His God (COS 1.151:485). The oldest Akkadian text on this subject, dated to the seventeenth century BC, is entitled "Dialogue between a Man and His God." Its structure—speeches by different parties set in a narrative framework—distinguishes it from the preceding texts (*see* Frame Narrative). Even though large blocks of the text are missing, dialogue does not appear to be an accurate descriptor, for the speeches augment the prose material rather than serving as a response to another's argument.

The text opens with a description of a miserable young man who continually implored his god like a friend (i). While recounting his afflictions, he asserted that he was unaware of having done any wrong (ii). Convinced, however, that retribution produced his ill fate, he acknowledged that even though his god had been kind to him, he had blasphemed the god (iv). Thus he understood his plight to be a revelation of an evil deed, thereby tarnishing his reputation.

After a large break in the text the sufferer recounted the coming of an emissary (viii). That messenger anointed him with oil, gave him food, and ordered his health to return (vii), speaking a powerful word of hope:

Your disease is under control, . . .
the years and days you were filled with
    misery are over. (viii.1-2)

The emissary added that if survival had not

been the destiny of this sufferer, the illness would have taken his life. He exhorted him to remember his god to the end of time (viii.9-10). Next, his personal god delivered a speech telling his devotee that he was to have the confidence that he would live a long life (ix.4). This god promised to provide guardians to protect him and assured him that his strength would return, enabling him to farm his fields again with vigor. The god then exhorted him to feed the hungry from his prospering (ix.6). He was to show compassion with confidence, for "the gate of life and well-being [would be] open" to him (ix.9). These instructions to show benevolence for the deprived based on the assurance of future prosperity are remarkable.

Of the texts from Mesopotamia, only in this one does the personal god, somewhat like Yahweh in the book of Job, directly address the supplicant. Nevertheless, there are significant contrasts in the approaches of the two deities. Whereas the Babylonian god gave his supplicant a variety of instructions and the promise of a blissful future, Yahweh only indirectly asked Job to intercede for the three comforters. He did not give Job any assurance of future prosperity, nor did he exhort Job to carry out deeds of kindness to the weak. This omission indicates that God was confident that Job would continue to live by the highest moral standards (see Job 29; 31). These contrasts underscore the central concern of the book of Job, which is Job's ongoing relationship with God regardless of whether he was prospering or suffering.

1.3. Two Dialogues. Next to be considered are two Mesopotamian texts composed in dialogue format. This format promotes critical reflection and opens up new avenues for thinking about traditional beliefs. It allows a troubled person to search for answers to situations that appear to contradict deeply held beliefs. Although the dialogues in these texts take place between only two parties and the speeches are short, these texts or similar ones surely stood in the lineage of works that influenced the author of Job to develop the expansive format of three interlocutors in debate with the protagonist plus several long speeches from two additional figures.

1.3.1. The Babylonian Theodicy (COS 1.154:492-95). In The Babylonian Theodicy (c. 1000 BC) a sufferer and a friend probe aspects of the issue of unjust suffering that challenge the accepted premise that the established order promotes justice. The work has twenty-seven stanzas, each one having eleven lines that begin with the same syllable. The lines are arranged as an *acrostic to produce the sentence "I am Saggil-kinam-ubbib, an exorcist, an adorant of god and king." The author's name, Saggil-kinam-ubbib, means "May Esagila [Marduk's temple] declare the righteous pure." This sufferer sets forth his own situation as an example of thwarted retribution that challenges the traditional teaching that the upright receive honor while the corrupt receive dishonor. He, the youngest child, having been suddenly orphaned, has had to endure many hardships. An unnamed friend supports the sufferer's search and also diligently defends the perspective of traditional wisdom.

A remarkable trait of this Babylonian dialogue is the polite way that the sufferer and the friend address each other throughout. The sufferer describes his friend as one who really cares for him, and he addresses him with many adulations, such as,

Your mind is a wellspring of depth
    unplumbed,
The upsurging swell of the ocean that brooks
    no inadequacy. (24)
. . .
Your reasoning is a cool breeze, a breath
    of fresh air for mankind. (67)

The friend likewise answers the sufferer in commendatory style:

O date palm, wealth-giving tree, my precious
    brother,
Perfect in all wisdom, O gem of wis[dom].
    (57)

Their politeness stands in sharp contrast to the caustic exchanges between Job and his three interlocutors as they accuse each other of speaking hot, empty words. Bildad says to Job, "Your words are a blustering wind" (Job 8:2). Eliphaz retorts, "Would the wise answer with empty notions or fill their bellies with the hot east wind? Would they argue with useless words, with speeches that have no value?" (Job 15: 2-3). Job likewise castigates the friends, "Will your long-winded speeches never end? What ails you that you keep on arguing?" (Job 16:3). In the climate of the Middle East there is a vast difference between a cool, refreshing breeze from the north

and the harsh, hot winds that blow off the eastern desert, causing tempers to shorten as temperatures rise. Although the parties' "theodicies" are generally cordial, a couple of times they respond in a testy, accusing manner. For example, the friend says,

O just, knowledgeable one, your logic is
    perverse,
You have cast off justice, you have scorned
    divine design.
In your emotional state you have an urge to
    disregard divine ordinances. (78-80)

These words belong to the friend's response to the sufferer's doubting the certainty of retribution in all situations. Another time he says,

Adept scholar, master of erudition,
You blaspheme in the anguish of your
    thoughts. (254-255)

In his tale of woe the sufferer, though very weak, complains that food has become so tasteless that he has no appetite even for beer, which might afford him some relief. He underscores the injustice of his situation by intimating it is lower than that of the onager and the lion, animals that have full stomachs even though they have not presented any offerings to appease a deity (v). The friend's answer is that since the sufferer is only a child, how could he know the purpose of the gods, which is too remote for humans? He further defends traditional belief by stressing that an ill fate awaits these creatures: a piercing arrow awaits the onager, and a pit the lion (vi).

The sufferer discounts this argument with the observation that those unmindful of god prosper. A rich parvenu struts his wealth without making any effort to honor the mother goddess with gifts yet faces no ill consequences. By contrast, even though this sufferer has faithfully sought his god, he now carries a yoke of servitude devoid of profit. Reduced to poverty, he is considered lower than a fool (vii). The friend, in response, charges the sufferer with skewed logic, disregarding divine ordinances. This exchange does have similarities to that between Job and his friends. In the second cycle of the dialogue (Job 15—21) the friends challenged Job's claim that his suffering was unjust by painting vivid portraits of the assured fate of the wicked. Job countered by detailing scenarios of the wicked who were happy and prosperous (Job 21). He particularly challenged the escape clause frequently cited in defense of retribution that maintained that although a wicked person might escape punishment during his life, his children bear the full brunt of the harm that he has done (Job 21:19). In fact, Job argued that a person's fate has little to do with one's devotion (Job 21:22-26).

Another argument of the Babylonian sufferer is that an upright person experiences good, but only partially (xxiii). He supports this position by describing a person with four children: whereas the meager employment of three of them brings the father dishonor, the success of one brings him honor. After judging this illustration to be blasphemy, the friend counters with the claim that the gods compensate with a great reward a righteous person who experiences something bad (xxiv):

> The cow's first calf is inferior,
> Her subsequent offspring is twice as big.
> The first child is born a weakling,
> The second is called a capable warrior.
> (260-264)

Not persuaded, the sufferer enumerates a variety of inequities in society, such as villains becoming rich while the honest are rejected (xxv). He had already lamented the inversion of roles that sometimes takes place in society—for example, a king's son is reduced to wearing rags while a son of a destitute person wears fine clothes (xvii). The friend answers with the ancient Mesopotamian belief that in making humans, the gods gave them perverted speech. Earlier he had argued that any apparent exceptions to just retribution are short lived, noting that a deadly weapon pursues the ungodly swindler (xxii). Therefore, he exhorts his companion to realize that if he seeks after the gods, he will regain in a moment what he had lost in a year (xxii). This instruction echoes the friends' elaborate promises of blessing if Job repented (especially in Job 22:21-30). The Babylonian sufferer concludes by asking the friend to be considerate of his troubles and by praying that his god and goddess might show him mercy (xxvii). The ending is abrupt; apparently, it is to be assumed that the gods answered the sufferer's petition and restored his health.

This Babylonian text defends the precept that the inherent moral order rewards good and punishes evil even though that order does not work precisely in every case. Exceptions to just rewards are only apparent, for the divine purpose is too remote for humans to know. Humans should expect suffering and hardship because they were made with an inclination to perverted words and thoughts. Another answer to incomprehensible suffering is that the wicked who prosper soon experience a contemptible fate. By contrast, Job's story teaches that there are cases of grave suffering caused by a reason that lies outside the behavior or character of the sufferer.

1.3.2. The Dialogue of Pessimism (COS 1.155:495-96). In a humorous Babylonian satire known as The Dialogue of Pessimism or The Obliging Slave, a rich master, deep in despair at finding any meaning in life, converses with his trusted servant about engaging in a variety of activities that might provide him significant pleasure, such as readying his chariot to go for a ride, building a house, or loving a woman. Each time, his valet lauds the pleasure that the contemplated activity offers and encourages his master to pursue that activity. Immediately the master changes his mind, asserting that he will not do what he had just contemplated. At once the servant concurs with his master, pointing out the downside of the spurned activity. Here is an example of their exchange in regard to the master's proposal to make a sacrifice to his personal deity:

> "Slave, oblige me again!"
> "Here, master! Here!"
> "Get a move on and get water for my hands
>   and give it to me so that I can make a
>   sacrifice to my personal god!"
> "Make a sacrifice, master, make a sacrifice! A
>   man who makes a sacrifice to his personal
>   god will be content. On trust he is making
>   loan upon loan."
> "No way, slave. I will not make a sacrifice
>   to my personal god."
> "Don't do it, master, don't do it. Can you
>   teach your personal god to run after you
>   like a dog? He'll just demand of you rites,
>   a votive statue, and many other things."
> (53-61)

At the climax of these exchanges the master asks the servant, "Now, then, what is good?" (60).

353

The servant brazenly proposes that their necks should be broken. The master counters by saying that he will kill the servant first. The servant retorts that should the master do so, he would not be able to survive for even three days—that is, without his servant's help. The extant text stops here. Whether or not this was the original conclusion is unknown.

This text discounts the belief that a human finds meaning either in devotion to a god or the insights of the wise. Consequently, it endorses suicide as an honorable option for the despondent. At the outset Job earnestly wished that God had taken his life even before he was born (Job 3:2-13), but Job never contemplated taking his own life. In his much speaking Job freely disclosed the great agitation that his afflictions caused, but after his first two speeches he steadily moved away from complete despair of life to centering his efforts on finding a resolution to his gloomy condition. He came to place the highest value on a life of personal integrity and on communion with God.

This Babylonian text also illustrates the use of irony and satire in probing the issue of life's meaning. Irony is found throughout the book of Job along with small touches of satire. In a brilliant example of satire Job contemplated the possibility of demonstrating his innocence by performing an ordeal of purification, but he quickly abandoned that thought when he imagined that God would only turn the ordeal inside out by dunking him into a cesspool, thereby making him look not only silly but even more guilty (Job 9:30-31). Satire and irony serve to break through the walls of traditional thought and open up new avenues for viewing difficult issues.

From another perspective this Babylonian text, somewhat like *Ecclesiastes, finds that there are no activities in which humans delight that offer sufficient meaning to keep a depressed person from pursuing suicide (for additional discussion on the topic of suicide, see 2.1 below).

2. Egyptian Texts.

Several Egyptian texts have literary techniques, imagery and concepts comparable to portions of the book of Job. Five texts will be considered here. The first to be considered is A Dispute over Suicide, an account of a man who longs for death as an escape from the hardships of life, since a review of this text complements the preceding discussion about suicide. Next to be treated are three tirades against social disorder, The Admonitions of Ipuwer, The Complaints of Khakheperre-sonb and The Prophecies of Neferti, a genre that the Egyptians prized. The fifth text for consideration is The Protests of the Eloquent Peasant.

2.1. A Dispute over Suicide (COS 3.146:321-25).
A Dispute over Suicide, also called The Dispute of a Man and His Ba, employs a dialogue format to present a person's deep self-reflection on the value of suicide as an escape from depression fed by a corrupt, unresponsive society. In this text a despondent person expresses his troubled thoughts about the worthlessness of life to his ba, the personality that stands over against him. Interpretation of this text is unfortunately hindered by several factors: the loss of the text's beginning, numerous gaps throughout, and obscure language. These factors have led to wide variety in English translations.

The protagonist, weary and disillusioned with life, seeks to persuade his external personality, his ba, to support his longing for death. Ba is often translated "soul," but the Egyptian concept is far more dynamic than what is conveyed by this English term. The ba is a person's life force housed in, but not confined to, the body. Having its own will, it may depart for a time; after a while it longs to return to its physical abode. This characteristic corresponds to the ba's being represented in hieroglyphs as a bird with a human head. At death, the ba wandered about, preferring to return to its bodily home at night. This belief about the ba was a factor in the practice of mummification: the preservation of a corpse was as lifelike as possible so that the ba could recognize its original home.

In order to find bliss in the afterlife this troubled man needs to win his ba's consent to his taking his own life. His ba responds by trying to dissuade him by noting the heartbreak that befalls the dead and by recounting two parables that illustrate the value of life. The master counters with four poems on four subjects, one recited after the other. Each poem prizes death over life. In the first poem the master depicts how woeful his reputation is by comparing it to the worst smells:

> Lo, my name reeks,
> Lo, more than carrion smell

On summer days of burning sky. (87-88)
. . .
Lo, my name reeks,
Lo, more than fishermen smell,
More than the marsh-pools where they fish.
(94-95) [trans. M. Lichtheim 1975]

In the second poem he laments his loneliness, which is virtually incurable because people are so corrupt and self-serving. In the third poem he paints the value of death in several forceful metaphors:

Like the fragrance of myrrh,
Like sitting under sail on a breezy day. (134)
. . .
Like the fragrance of lotus,
Like sitting on the shore of drunkenness. (136)

In the fourth poem he glorifies life in the next world:

Truly, he who is yonder will be a living god,
Punishing the evildoer's crime. (143-144)
. . .
Truly, he who is yonder will be a wise man,
Not barred from appealing to Re when he speaks. (146-147)

The man's arguments move the *ba* to declare that it will stay with its master when he dies.

There are ties between this Egyptian text and the book of Job. Both of these ancient writers used the genre of monologue to present a person's self-reflection. The Egyptian sage uses this genre in the four poems, and the Joban poet casts Job's initial lament in this form (Job 3) as well as the opening of his first response in the dialogue (Job 6:2-13). By contrast, the rest of Job's speeches in the dialogue (Job 5—27) are addressed to specific parties. Another point of contact with the book of Job is the protagonist's intense longing for death as an escape from grave affliction and isolation. At the outset Job too longed for death, wishing that he had been stillborn and gone straight to Sheol, for there the laborer no longer has to listen to the shouts of a taskmaster or feel the whip of the crew chief (Job 3:18). Realizing that this was an impossible wish, he expressed that his longing for death was as great as the longing of those who risk all in search of gold (Job 3:20-22). As he continued to speak, Job

moved away from idealizing life in Sheol to wanting to be brought back to life should God be pleased to hide him for awhile in the grave (Job 14:13-15). Job's agitated, frank lamenting turned his desire from longing for death to proving his innocence so that he might continue to live. By contrast, this Egyptian came to the position that death was welcomed as an escape from loneliness and shame. A primary reason that Job did not contemplate suicide as an avenue of escape from suffering was his view of God. In fact, by the end of the dialogue Job became so confident of his innocence that he swore by God, the giver of life, that he would not compromise his integrity by confessing some contrived wrongdoing so that God might extend his life (Job 27:2-4). In contrast to the Egyptian who yielded to despair at life, Job came to prize a full life, which he believed would return upon his vindication.

2.2. Tirades on Social Chaos. Some Egyptian texts belonging to the genre of wisdom instruction may be more specifically classified as tirades against social disorder. Here a brief outline of Egyptian history from the third millennium BC through the middle of the first millennium BC is useful as an aid in understanding the social motivation underlying these texts. Throughout most of its long history of two and a half millennia, a strong Egypt was ruled by a sovereign pharaoh. But during two periods, known as intermediate periods, rule shifted from a pharaoh to two or three barons of dominant nomes (districts) who vied for control. Thus, ancient Egyptian history is divided into five periods: the Old Kingdom, the First Intermediate Period, the Middle Kingdom, the Second Intermediate Period, the New Kingdom. On the discovery of The Admonitions of Ipuwer in the last century, scholars interpreted this text as a first-hand description of the social turmoil of the First Intermediate Period. Currently this interpretation is under serious challenge. Recent scholars have observed that texts such as this one are verbose, filled with stylized expressions and repetitions that lack any reference to specific times, places and people. Some, such as Lichtheim, argue that scribes wrote these texts during a time of prosperity in order to promote a political agenda. In addition, increased understanding of the First Intermediate Period has shown that during that era Egyptian social order was stable because two dominant monarchs, even though they vied for rule, maintained order. In addition, the evidence is conclusive that two of these texts, The Complaints of Khakheperre-sonb and The Prophecies of Neferti, were composed in the Middle Kingdom, long after the First Intermediate Period.

2.2.1. The Admonitions of Ipuwer (COS 1.42:93-98). The Admonitions of Ipuwer, from either the First Intermediate Period or the late Middle Kingdom, consists of six tirades about disturbed conditions in society. Many scholars conjecture that originally a narrative framework similar to that of the book of Job provided a setting for these speeches. In the first three poems Ipuwer vividly describes the crumbling of social order: servants refuse to do their tasks; gangs dominate the countryside; plowing has ceased in the fields; the cultivated land is giving way to the desert; Asiatics flood the land; women fail to conceive; secure writings of the court are stolen and made public; the writings of scribes are destroyed; laws are thrown out of government buildings and trampled by the rabble; small and great wish that they were dead; some abandon themselves to be consumed by crocodiles; children are killed by being hurled against a wall.

A dominant motif in these texts is the inversion of the social order. As Ipuwer says,

Indeed, poor men have become owners
    of wealth,
He who could not make for himself sandals
    owns riches. (2.4-5)
. . .
Indeed, the noblemen are in mourning
and the poor man is full of joy. (2:7)
. . .
The robber is a possessor of riches and [the
    rich man has become (?)] a plunderer.
    (2.9)
. . .
Indeed, the great council chamber is a public
    resort,
Beggars come and go in the Great Houses.
    (6.12)

Ipuwer was particularly distressed at the complete disregard for the dead; mummification and proper burial were premiere concerns of the nobles. In that day even the deceased who had tombs were laid on high ground, and the art of embalming was becoming lost.

In the fifth poem, on a more positive note, Ipuwer enjoined the people to destroy the ene-my and to remember to perform their standard activities. In doing those activities—for example, bathing those who were ill, fumigating with incense, presenting offerings at the temple, observing regulations—they would give structure to the chaotic situation. Nevertheless, Ipuwer was so bold as to criticize Re, the supreme god, and to charge Pharaoh with not executing the authority of his office:

Authority, Knowledge and Truth are with
    you,
Yet confusion is what you set throughout the
    land,
And the noise of tumult.
Behold, one fights against another,
For men obey what you have commanded.
If three men travel on the road,
They are found to be only two,
For the many kill the few. (12.11-15)

Unfortunately, the Egyptian language in this section is very difficult to interpret. Some scholars take this passage as a criticism of Re, while others find it to be a description of an ideal pharaoh who would restore order and glory to Egypt. In the sixth poem Ipuwer described the joy and beauty of a stable order, a picture of the good times ahead. Overall, this sage, in contrast to the concerns of Job, emphasizes social stability rather than moral justice.

2.2.2. The Complaints of Khakheperrē-sonb (COS 1.44:104-6). Another text belonging to the category of social complaint is The Complaints of Khakheperre-sonb. It was composed in the Middle Kingdom, likely during the reign of Sesostris II. This text is simpler and more personal than the other two in this category. Khakheperre-sonb does not appear to have a compelling political agenda, for he speaks to his own heart about his anguish at the unsettled conditions in society.

Lacking a prose frame, the text begins with these words: "The collection of words, the gathering of maxims . . . by the priest of Heliopolis, the ... Khakheperre-sonb called Ankhu." Troubled by the decaying conditions in society, he enters into an apology for speaking:

I empty my belly of that which is in it,
In loosing all that I have said (before);
For what has been said is repetition.
    (Recto 3)

. . .

One who has spoken should not speak,
But one should speak who has something
    to say. (Recto 5)

. . .

It is hard to keep silent about it. (Recto 13)

This introduction recalls Elihu's apology for taking the floor after Job's three comforters had
turned silent, thereby conceding that Job had
proven his innocence. Elihu defended his
speaking:

I am full of words,
and the spirit within me compels me;
inside I am like bottled-up wine,
. . .
I must speak and find relief;
I must open my lips and reply.
    (Job 32:18-20 NIV)

Desiring to compose a new message free from
trite expressions, Khakheperre-sonb describes
changes that have produced appalling hardships and chaos in society:

Right is cast outside,
Wrong is in the council hall;
The plans of the gods are violated,
Their ordinances neglected,
The land is in turmoil,
Mourning is in everyplace. (Recto 11)

The relaxing of moral constraints encourages all to act crookedly. The resulting gloomy
conditions in society grieve Khakheperre-sonb,
compelling him to vent his feelings and describe
what is going on in order to counter the silence
of the greedy populace.

The Egyptian text ends abruptly. It is unclear
whether or not there was an additional tablet.
Some scholars maintain that the text must have
been longer, arguing that this short complaint is
insufficient to account for this sage's appearance in official lists.

*2.2.3. The Prophecies of Neferti (COS 1.45:106-
10).* A more complex text in the category of social
complaint is The Prophecies of Neferti. The text
itself locates these prophecies in the court of Snef-
ru, a strong, prosperous pharaoh of the Fourth
Dynasty, the Old Kingdom. One day that pharaoh
asked the premier lector-priest and sage of Bastet,
who had a reputation for eloquent speech, to en-

tertain him about the future. The priest painted a
picture of grave natural and social disturbances
that would befall the nation. There would be low
Niles, leading to years of poor harvests. Fish pools
would dry up. Asiatics—foreigners from the area
of Canaan and Syria—would migrate into the
land, driving Egyptians from harvesting the fields
in the delta region and taking cattle from the
plow. Egyptian society would be demoralized. People would be unconcerned if a person nearby became a victim of crime. Family members would
not support each other:

A man sits with his back turned,
While one man kills another.
I show you a son as an enemy,
A brother as a foe,
A man killing his (own) father.
Every mouth is full of "love me,"

Everything good has disappeared. (44-46)

He moved into a description of an upside down
social order:

I show you a lord in worries, the stranger
    satisfied.
He who has never filled up for himself
    is now empty. (47-48)
. . .
I show you the land in turmoil,
The weak of arm is (now) the possessor of
    an arm,
One salutes him who (formerly) saluted.

I show you the lowly as superior. (54-55)

Abruptly, Neferti began to proclaim the redemption that would come to Egypt:

Then a king will come from the south,
Imeny [Ameny], the justified, is his name,
A son is he of a woman of the land of Nubia,
A child is he of Upper Egypt.
He will take the white crown,
He will wear the red crown. (58-60)
. . .
Rejoice, O people of his time,
The son of man will make his name forever
    and ever. (62)

The new pharaoh would restore order. He
would kill troublesome foreigners, Asiatics and

Libyans and bar Asiatics from getting into Egypt. That Pharaoh was Amenemhet, the founder of the Twelfth Dynasty, Middle Kingdom. Mention of this Pharaoh by name leads scholars to classify this text as a political apology for the inauguration of a new dynasty and to assign its composition to that Pharaoh's reign. If that is the case, this text must have been composed in the early days of his reign—that is, before a coup instigated by his own guards and members of the harem, as described in "The Instruction of Amenemhet," turned him into a passive, solitary figure.

Similar to the central theme in these three tirades against social disorder are Job's harangues at injustices in society. His harshest criticism of God's wanton disregard of justice comes in Job 9:22b-24 (NIV):

[God] destroys both the blameless and
   the wicked.
When a scourge brings sudden death,
   he mocks the despair of the innocent.
When a land falls into the hands of
   the wicked,
   he blindfolds its judges.
If it is not he, then who is it?

No wonder God accused Job of darkening counsel (Job 38:2). In a longer piece Job recounted in detail God's robbing officials of their power and position, resulting in social upheavals without any discernible rectitude (Job 12:14-25). In Job 24:1-17 he vividly pictured the strenuous efforts that the weak and the poor must make in order to survive the arrows of cruel, demanding overlords compounded by hostile forces of nature and magnified by their being prey to hardened criminals. Thus Job shares with these Egyptian sages a longing for the rectification of these harsh social injustices.

2.3. The Protests of the Eloquent Peasant (COS 1.43:98-104). The Protests of the Eloquent Peasant comes from the Middle Kingdom, the first half of the second millennium BC. Structurally, this text, like the book of Job, has a prose prologue and an epilogue that envelop a series of speeches. A minor difference is that the speeches of the peasant are a mixture of poetry and prose. The key point of comparison, however, is that the protagonist in both works challenged the administration of justice at the highest level through a sequence of eloquent

speeches: a peasant before a high Egyptian official, and Job before the Israelite God. Interestingly, each plaintiff is cast as a foreigner: an Asiatic peasant in Egypt, and Job, either a Syrian or an Edomite.

In this Egyptian text an Asiatic peasant named Khu-n-Anup was traveling through the delta on his way to Herakleopolis to sell his goods and buy food for his family because hard economic conditions in Canaan threatened their existence. His journey bought him to the property of Nemty-nakht. There the path between the dike and the cultivated fields became very narrow. On seeing the Asiatic approach, Nemty-nakht coveted the goods on his donkeys. To obstruct Khu-n-Anup's travels, he placed a cloth, probably a personal garment, across the path and then ordered Khu-n-Anup not to step on the cloth (the ancients believed that any abuse of one's personal garment shamed its owner and might also cast a spell on the owner). Given that the bank of the dike was steep, Khu-n-Anup decided to pass by carefully stepping through the field. While Nemty-nakht was objecting to this plan, one of Khu-n-Anup's donkeys devoured a clump of barley. Nemty-nakht angrily declared that he would take the donkey and use it to tread out grain in compensation for the offense. Khu-n-Anup replied that the penalty was too high for the small amount of barley consumed. He offered to buy back his donkey for the value of the barley; otherwise he would take his case to the high steward Rensi, an official known for punishing robbers. Outraged, Nemty-nakht severely beat the Asiatic and seized all his donkeys. For ten days the peasant appealed to him for redress, but without success. So he traveled south to Herakleopolis to appeal his case before Rensi. Before taking on this case, Rensi consulted other magistrates. They advised him to have the offender compensate the peasant; by implication they were telling the judge not to disturb the bureaucratic system for a mere peasant. But Rensi decided to hear the case. However, he remained silent throughout the hearings.

In his first petition before Rensi, Khu-n-Anup commended the judge:

If you embark on a lake of justice
May you sail on it with fair breeze. (B1 55-56)
. . .
You are father to the orphan.

Husband to the widow. (B1 63)

. . .

Leader free from covetousness,
A great man free from baseness,
Destroyer of falsehood,
Creator of justice. (B1 66-68)

As seen in these words and in the book of Job (e.g., Job 4:3-5; 29:15-17; 31:13-23), caring for the weak and helping the bereaved served as key evidence that a person was just. Khu-n-Anup concluded this speech with a plea for the judge to decide his case rightly and remove his grief.

After hearing this speech, Rensi informed Pharaoh Nebkaure of the peasant's case and of his great eloquence. Pharaoh, relishing the opportunity to hear such powerful rhetoric, instructed Rensi to detain the peasant for several days without rendering judgment, in order to keep him talking. A court recorder was to transcribe his speeches so that Pharaoh would have an opportunity to hear them. Realizing that usually an Asiatic who was traveling in Egypt was facing duress at home, Pharaoh showed compassion by instructing Rensi to send supplies to the peasant's wife without letting the detainee know. Rensi also supplied daily rations to Khu-n-Anup through a friend. Thus, both in this account and in Job's ordeal the highest official, out of confidence in the protagonist, even though it was unknown to that person, took a major step of benevolence on the sufferer's behalf: Pharaoh provided for Khu-n-Anup's family while he was detained, and God prevented Satan from taking Job's life.

According to plan, Khu-n-Anup returned on each of the following eight days and delivered eloquent pleas. Instead of presenting his own case, the peasant centered on the need for justice to be restored throughout the government's bureaucracy by punishing evildoers and protecting the weak.

At first he addressed the steward politely. But as time lapsed, his rhetoric became more inflammatory, though he employed both commendation and accusation to move the steward to uphold justice:

Punish the robber and protect the miserable.
Be not flood against the pleader!
(B1 143-144)

He lauded the eternal value of upholding justice:

When good is good, it is really good.
For justice is for eternity;
It enters the Necropolis with its doer.
(B1 307-309)

On the other hand, he accused the steward of being a hindrance to justice:

Behold, you are an officer who steals,
A mayor who accepts (bribes). (B1 192)

With these words, Khu-n-Anup warned the steward that he would be held accountable in the afterlife for any injustice in regard to this case.

In the fourth petition the peasant sought to win over the magistrate by describing the unsettled nature of society, a society in which a person of low class could not successfully defend one's own right. Such a charge undercut the magistrate's honor as an administrator and judge committed to justice.

Goodness is destroyed, none adhere to it.
Throwing falsehood's back to the ground
(has also perished). (B1 197-198)
. . .
As a result "gone" is working by night, travel
by day,
and letting a man defend his own right.
(B1 201-202)

Troubled by the steward's persistent silence, Khu-n-Anup pled urgently for him to speak. In the ninth petition he declared that since Rensi had not listened to him, he would appeal to Anibus (the oracle). Job likewise was deeply troubled by God's silence; that silence prodded him to swear a bold oath of innocence (Job 29—31) in an effort to compel God to speak. However, in contrast to a peasant who became increasingly distraught over not winning justice from a high Egyptian official, Job became more confident that in time God would render justice in his case (see Job 23).

After Khu-n-Anup delivered his petition, the high steward had two guards return him to the court. Fearful of punishment, the peasant was surprised to hear his words read from a new papyrus scroll. The scroll was presented to the delighted Pharaoh. Rensi then settled the peasant's complaint by awarding him the property of Nemty-nakht.

This story advocates a proactive execution of justice by high officials in place of prescribing small acts of conciliation design to maintain an entrenched, corrupt bureaucracy. As the peasant argued, justice *(ma'at)* *(see* Maat) was not always congruent with the established order and thus at times must be aggressively advocated and personally established. Job too went against conventional wisdom by refusing to relinquish confidence in his own innocence as he pursued his complaint against God. Clearly, in both texts high value is placed on eloquent speeches as an avenue for achieving social change and theological insight. In both narratives the plaintiffs persevered until a high official took steps to restore justice on behalf of each of them.

3. Conclusion.

As a result of the comparisons made with these texts from Mesopotamia and Egypt, the uniqueness of the book of Job stands out vividly. It is impossible to determine whether the author of Job was directly influenced by one or more of the texts. Nevertheless, the numerous parallels between these texts and the book of Job attest that the author of Job was the recipient of a long literary tradition that reflected on the inexplicable suffering and disruptions in the social and natural orders. In these texts is found the thinking of sages who sought to provide various paradigms for understanding troubling situations that seemed to refute belief in a moral order of just rewards and punishments. In probing these issues, the Joban poet broke ancient literary boundaries by increasing the dialogue partners of the protagonist to five. Yet he skillfully captured the full pathos of the hero's complaints, such as is found in the Mesopotamian hymns of praise for deliverance from affliction, and set them in the context of an intense debate about traditional teachings of retribution. At the same time, he captured Job's great anxiety about his standing with God with the same emotional force as found in those texts in which the protagonist despairs of life. Uniting all these elements in a single work that also offers new perspective on traditional thinking of retribution was a stroke of brilliance.

The book of Job makes a more incisive criticism of traditional beliefs about rewards and punishments than is found in any of the other texts considered. A major difference in Job's stance from that of the other protagonists is that Job never yielded to the heavy pressure of making a contrived confession of sin in order to escape his suffering. As a result, his story now serves as the model of a human who can bear terrible suffering without compromising convictions or honor. Furthermore, his persevering stance supports God's confidence in humans to worship him free from selfish motivations.

In addition, the monotheistic orientation of the book of Job teaches that the one God, unlike the gods of a polytheistic system, is not subject to a controlling impersonal force—fate (Buccellati). Consequently, it denies a variety of beliefs found in these Middle Eastern texts. It rejects the precept that the gods made humans crooked, and it affirms that humans can retain personal integrity even during unjust circumstances. Furthermore, the book of Job does not attribute illness to demons. Thus diviners and exorcists are not sources for relief. The only resolution for such severe affliction is communication with God.

Above all, Job's story establishes the principle that a person's experience of enigmatic suffering or hardship is not to be automatically interpreted as a reproach on one's character. The devout continue to find this teaching very liberating, for Job's story frees them from an oversensitive conscience and gives them confidence with God amidst trials. No longer do believers have to doubt their character or acceptance by God every time they are beset by a misfortune of great magnitude. Nevertheless, the book of Job is in agreement with the view stated in several of these Middle Eastern texts that the ways of the divine world are often hidden from humans.

See also JOB 1: BOOK OF; WISDOM SOURCES.

BIBLIOGRAPHY. **R. Albertson,** "Job and Ancient Near Eastern Wisdom Literature," in *More Essays on the Comparative Method,* ed. W. Hallo, J. C. Moyer and L. G. Perdue (ScrCon 2; Winona Lake, IN: Eisenbrauns, 1983) 213-30; **J. Bottéro,** *Mesopotamia: Writing, Reasoning, and the Gods* (Chicago: University of Chicago Press, 1992); **G. Buccellati,** "Wisdom and Not: The Case of Mesopotamia," *JAOS* 101 (1981) 35-47; **B. R. Foster,** *Before the Muses: An Anthology of Akkadian Literature* (2 vols.; Bethesda, MD: CDL Press, 1993); **J. Gray,** "The Book of Job in the Context of

Near Eastern Literature," *ZAW* 82 (1970) 251-69; **G. E. Kadish,** "British Museum Writing Board 5645: The Complaints of Kha-Kheper-R?'," *JEA* 59 (1973) 77-90; **S. N. Kramer,** " 'Man and His God: A Sumerian Variation on the 'Job' Motif," *SVT* 3 (1969) 170-82; **W. G. Lambert,** *Babylonian Wisdom Literature* (Oxford: Clarendon Press, 1975); **M. Lichtheim,** *Ancient Egyptian Literature: A Book of Readings* (Berkeley: University of California Press, 1975); **G. L. Mattingly,** "The Pious Sufferer: Mesopotamia's Traditional and Job's Counselors," in *The Bible in the Light of Cuneiform Literature,* ed. W. Hallo, B. W. Jones and G. L. Mattingly (ScrCon 3; Lewiston, NY: Edwin Mellen, 1990) 305-48; **C. A. Newsom,** "Critical Curiosity: Genre and Moral Imagination in the Wisdom Dialogue," in *The Book of Job: A Contest of Moral Imagination* (Oxford: Oxford University Press, 2003) 72-89; **B. G. Ockinga,** "The Burden of *Kha'kheperrē'sonbu,*" *JEA* 69 (1983) 88-95; **H. Preuss,** "Jahwes Antwort an Hiob und die sogenannte Hiobliteratur des alten vorderen Orients," in *Beiträge zur alttestamentlichen Theologie: Festschrift für Walther Zimmerli zum 70. Geburtstag,* ed. H. Donner, R. Hanhart and R. Smend (Göttingen: Vandenhoeck & Ruprecht, 1977) 323-43; **J. J. M. Roberts,** "Job and the Israelite Religious Tradition," *ZAW* 89 (1977) 107-14; **N. Shupak,** "A New Source for the Study of the Judiciary and Law of Ancient Egypt: 'The Tale of the Eloquent Peasant,'" *JNES* 51 (1992) 1-18; **E. A. Speiser,** "The Case of the Obliging Servant," *JCS* 8 (1954) 98-105; **W. von Soden,** "Das Fragen nach der Gerechtigkeit Gottes im Alten Orient," *MDOG* 96 (1965) 41-59; **M. Weinfeld,** "Job and Its Mesopotamian Parallels—A Typological Analysis," in *Text and Context: Old Testament and Semitic Studies for F. C. Fensham,* ed. W. Claassen (JSOTSup 48; Sheffield: JSOT Press, 1988) 217-26.

J. E. Hartley

JOB 3: HISTORY OF INTERPRETATION

Traditional interpretations of the book of Job center primarily upon this question: What kind of a person was Job? Was Job a righteous Gentile who patiently endured tragedy upon tragedy with unstinting faith? Or was Job a heathen who challenged God's moral authority and questioned, even blasphemed, divine justice? This wide divergence of opinion stems from tensions within the biblical text itself. The prose framework of the book—prologue (Job 1:1—2:13)

and epilogue (Job 42:7-17)—consists of a narrative concerning Job's undeserved tragedies and final restoration. The poetic body of the work contains dialogues between Job and his friends (Job 3:1—31:40) and between Job and God (Job 38:1—42:6).

In the *frame narrative we encounter an explicitly pious Job. From the opening verse of the book the narrator emphatically insists that Job is above reproach (Job 1:1). Even more, God himself on two occasions affirms the opinion of the narrator concerning Job's righteousness (Job 1:8; 2:3-4). Yet in the poetic body of the text we encounter a Job who appears to many interpreters, particularly later rabbinic interpreters, to be defiant, self-righteous and blasphemous. Job seeks ways to initiate a trial in which he would be able to vindicate himself before God and perhaps receive from God an acknowledgment of God's mistreatment (Job 9:2-35; 13:13-28; 16:18-22; 19:23-27; 23:1-7; 31:35-37).

Not only this, but also Job parodies the Scriptures themselves in fairly shocking ways. In Job 7:17-18 he makes sport of the exalted language of Psalm 8:4, "What are human beings that you are mindful of them?" (NRSV). To the psalmist, these words signify the glorious status that humans enjoy before God. For Job, the words imply that God is unduly fixated upon him in order to bring him into anguish. Job pleads for God to look away for a while so that he can experience some solace: "Will you not look away from me for a while, let me alone until I swallow my spittle?" (Job 7:19 NRSV).

The interpreter of the biblical text must decide which Job trumps the other. Either the claims concerning Job's righteousness found in the narrative structure of the book are emphasized and Job's apparent blasphemies are explained away or Job's impious self-defense found in the poetic body of the text bears interpretive weight so that, in spite of what the frame narrative appears to say, Job has been a sinner all along. What one encounters in traditional interpretations of the book flows from the presuppositions and emphases that each interpreter brings to the text. Although the more pious Job ignited the interpretive imagination more often than not, examples abound, especially among those who interpreted the original Hebrew, that portray the darker side of Job. This view of "Job the blasphemer" became especially predominant in later rabbinic and medieval Jewish interpretation partly as a response to the ubiquitous Christian usurpation of Job as the pious and patient Idumean saint who bore witness to the coming Christ.

1. Job in Scripture
2. Job in Pre-Rabbinic Interpretation
3. Job in Rabbinic Literature
4. Job in Patristic Literature
5. Job in Medieval Literature
6. Job and the Reformers

1. Job in Scripture.

Job's name appears in two biblical passages outside the book itself. Thus, interpretation of the book begins within the biblical *canon. In Ezekiel 14:12-14 Job is aligned with those whose righteousness is commendable. However, in accordance with Ezekiel's general theological perspective, their virtue, great as it was, could not be credited to the account of others in their generation. For Ezekiel, the blessedness of righteousness or the curse of sin cannot be passed on from one generation to another: "The person who sins shall die . . . the righteousness of the righteous shall be his own" (Ezek 18:20 NRSV).

In James 5:7-11 Job comes into the Christian tradition as an example of one whose patience and endurance in adversity ought to be emulated. The Greek term translated "patience" (hypomonē) more precisely means "endurance" or "persistence." Job is hardly patient, but he is persistent. Job also learns that the compassionate mercy of God wins out in the end for those who endure (James 5:11). This passage becomes especially important in the Christian tradition, which consistently finds in Job a saintly moral exemplar.

2. Job in Pre-Rabbinic Interpretation.

2.1. Job in the Septuagint. The LXX provides a glimpse into the earliest postbiblical interpretation of Job. Intense academic disagreement concerning the translational methods and agenda of the Job translator complicate our understanding of how the LXX translator of Job interpreted the book. In the opinion of the majority of scholars the Greek translator of Job rendered the text into a Greek version that transforms the Job of the poetic sections from bombastic doubter into pious and persevering sufferer. This is done by toning down the angry questions that Job poses to God into more palatable affirma-

tions of faith (see Gerleman; Gard). "The translator had not taken the trouble, or had been unable to grasp the thoughts of the Hebrew poet in their whole depth and many facetted richness. . . . The most violent outbursts on the part of Job, where he sees in God a demonic enemy, and where he denies the whole moral order of the world, have been modified in the LXX in several places" (Gerleman, 53).

This opinion has been vigorously rejected by H. Orlinsky in a series of studies in which he contended that the differences between the Greek Job and its Hebrew parent are not due to a broad theological bias but are simply the result of translation technique and concern for good Greek style. Most divergences are due to a Hebrew text differing from the present one (the Masoretic Text) or to the character of the translator's style. This position is followed by H. Heater, who calls the translation style of the Greek Job "anaphoric"—that is, an adaptation of the language of a particular passage from some other part of the LXX, typically from the book of Job itself (Heater, 6).

Orlinsky's work has done much to bring clarity to the subject, but many remain unconvinced and continue to find evidence of a translational bias that seeks to blunt the blasphemies of the Hebrew Job. The process of sanctifying Job is performed not only in the Greek translation but also in the Hebrew textual transmission. The Masoretes, who fixed the standard vocalization of the Hebrew Bible, through a very minor alternation in orthography, transform the written Hebrew text of Job 13:15 from the gloomy and hopeless "He may well slay me; I may have no hope" (NJPS) to a hopeful affirmation to be read in synagogue: "Though He slay me, yet will I trust in Him" (NJPS mg.). The Greek translator garbles the Hebrew completely yet retains Job's piety: "Though the Mighty One lay hand on me, since he has already begun, I will speak and plead before him." Job's counselors are even brought into line by the Greek translator. The Hebrew text has Eliphaz quite certain that Job will discover the justice of God in the end: "And you will know yourself" (Job 5:27). This implies that Job will discover what he has done wrong at some future time. The Greek translation protects Job's honor by adding "if you have done anything." Whereas the Hebrew Job skeptically claims that God wipes out the morally blameless along with the criminals (Job 9:22), the Job of the Greek says, "Anger destroys the great and the powerful."

E. E. Urbach (867) rejects Orlinsky's theory, claiming that Orlinsky either emends the passages that do not fit or explains them away as the result of a Hebrew text differing from the present one. For Urbach, the Greek rendering of Job 14:14 is a key example indicating a translational bias. Whereas the Hebrew Job appears agnostic concerning the corporeal resurrection of the body ("If a man dies, will he live again?"), the LXX Job has no doubt about life in the world to come ("If a man dies, he will live again!"). In an expansion of the Hebrew text of Job 42:17 the Greek version proclaims confidence of Job's participation in the final day of resurrection: "And it has been written concerning [Job] that he will be raised up again with those whom the Lord resurrects." This is in line with the spirit of this Greek translation and is a chief example, for Urbach (867), of the translator's theological bias.

The conclusions of the study by D. Gard continue to have broad approval. First, the LXX translator of Job had a Hebrew parent text not dissimilar to the Masoretic Text of modern printed editions of the Hebrew Bible. Second, many of the deviations of the Greek from the Hebrew are indeed the result of a translation bias. The Greek Job avoids ideas that are theologically offensive, especially passages where humankind is insolent before God. The translator avoids overly anthropomorphic language for God and also tones down passages that describe the destructive forces of God, which may call into question the goodness of God's character (Gard, 92). In these ways the Greek translation of Job downplays the impiety and blasphemies of the Job of the poetic core of the book so that Job is portrayed as more saintly and faithful than the Hebrew Bible strictly allows. Since the LXX was the Bible of the church, Christian exegetes were not, for the most part, exposed to the greater impieties of Job's agnosticism. They interpreted accordingly, as we will see.

2.2. Testament of Job. The sanctification of Job is brought to perfection by the author of *Testament of Job*. Probably writing during the first century BC or AD, this Egyptian Jew clearly was familiar with the LXX version of Job (Spittler, 831). In addition, *Testament of Job* continues in the tradition of the addendum to the LXX that identifies Job with Jobab of Genesis 36 (*T. Job* 2:1). He also parallels the Job of midrash and

identifies Job's second wife as Dinah (*T. Job* 1:6; cf. *b. B. Bat.* 15b; *Gen. Rab.* 57:4). He also bears many similarities with the Abraham of Jewish legend who autonomously discovered the true God of monotheism and abandoned idolatry as a youth (*T. Job* 2—4; cf. *Num. Rab.* 14:2; see Baskin 1983, 30).

Job's generous liberality as a host is vastly exaggerated (*T. Job* 9—11); his house is built with doors in every direction so travelers could enter with minimum hindrance (*T. Job* 9:4). A talmudic legend also bears witness to this tradition: "And why did Job make four doors to his house? So that the poor should not have the trouble of going round the entire house" (*'Abot R. Nat.* 7:1). Job is also an iconoclast like the Abraham of Jewish legend who purges his area of idolatry, throws down idols, and closes idol temples (*T. Job* 2—5). His struggle is entirely against *Satan and not against God (*T. Job* 6—8). This Job suffers not because of a pact between God and Satan but because he has destroyed Satan's idol and has thus raised satanic ire. Yet, he had been forewarned that if he destroyed the idol, this action would bring upon him immeasurable *suffering (*T. Job* 4.5-6). Still, he believed that God would restore him in the end and would raise him up at the day of resurrection (*T. Job* 4:6-8).

The roles of Job and his interlocutors are completely interchanged; they are troubled by Job's present state and lament it bitterly. Job stands up to the temptation to doubt with the words "Shall I sin with my lips against the Lord? It shall surely not come to pass!" (*T. Job* 38:2). By the end, Job is thoroughly transformed into the very incarnation of righteousness and piety, as is evident in the eulogy in which he is called "the strength of the helpless, light of the blind, the father of the orphans.... Who then will not weep for the man of God?" (*T. Job* 53:1-4).

The primary message of *Testament of Job* is that of endurance or patience; Job is the hero of patience and is born to this end (*T. Job* 5:1). While on a dung heap, he invites his first wife, Sitis, to remain resolute in tragedy with him (*T. Job* 26:5). Job remained strong in patience no matter how Satan challenged him. Job could not be enticed away from his long-suffering to contempt (*T. Job* 20:1). Job, like the underdog wrestler, won the match "because he showed endurance and did not grow weary" (*T. Job* 27:4). Satan, in the end, is thoroughly defeated; he breaks into tears and leaves Job as if yielding to a greater wrestler (*T. Job* 27:3-9). "No more fitting summary of the hortatory intent of the testament could be quoted than 27:7: 'Now then, my children, you also must be patient in everything that happens to you. For patience is better than anything'" (Spittler, 836).

3. Job in Rabbinic Literature.

The rabbinic understandings of the book of Job go down very different paths. This is, at least in part, a reflection of the fact that rabbinic interpretation starts with examination of the Hebrew text. The complexities of the Hebrew version of Job have been smoothed out, at least to some degree, by the translator of the LXX. Virtually all Christian interpretation until Jerome's translation of the Hebrew Bible into Latin depended on the LXX translation. A difference of opinion on Job's origins and character dates back to the Tannaitic period: some maintain that Job has no place in the world to come and others maintain the opposite (*b. B. Bat.* 15b). Yet initially, Job's role in rabbinic interpretation was generally positive; Job was a quintessential example of a righteous Gentile who acknowledged and was accepted by God. We will begin by describing this understanding.

3.1. The Righteous Gentile. Although there are numerous Gentiles who acknowledge Israel's God, Job dominates the biblical text in this regard because he occupies an entire canonical book. Nowhere does the biblical text claim that Job is an Israelite, and his mysterious origins from the land of Uz imply that he is not. It is a principle of rabbinic thought, based on the common descent of all humanity as described in the opening chapters of Genesis, that all persons have intrinsic worth and potential righteousness. This is particularly evident in the creed of Rabbi Akiba that all humanity, not only the Jews, are beloved of God as creatures made in the divine image (*m. ʾAbot* 3:15). Even Gentiles were not lacking in legal resources to attain righteousness, since basic laws revealed to Adam and Noah—the Noachide covenant—are self-evident by human perception alone (*Sipre Acharei Mot* 13:10) and are sufficient, for Gentiles, to attain divine favor (*b. Sanh.* 56a; *Gen. Rab.* 16:16; 34:19).

The aforementioned disagreement concerning the moral nature of Job can be seen in the two opinions of Johanan ben Zakkai and Joshua ben Hurqanos (*m. Soṭah* 5:5). Joshua contends (based on Job 13:15 and 27:5) that Job served God out of love and Johanan that Job served God only out of fear (citing Job 1:8). Other rabbis also affirmed Job's righteous status, claiming that Job's generosity with the poor was a model for personal largesse. He provides an example of the principle that one should never gain honor at the cost of bringing dishonor to one's fellows (*b. Meg.* 28a). Job is one of only seven Gentiles who could be called "prophet" (*b. B. Bat.* 15b). Job is lauded for his generosity by one tradition that understands Job 1:10 ("You have blessed the work of his hands") to imply that whoever took the smallest coin from him was blessed (*b. Pesaḥ.* 112a; *b. B. Bat.* 16a; and a similar tradition in *b. Meg.* 28a). Based on Job's prayer for his unhelpful friends (Job 42:10), Job is exemplary as a person who has the generosity of spirit to pray for friends to receive the very things of which he himself has need. It was this virtue that eventuated in the reversal of Job's fortunes toward the end of the story (*b. B. Qam.* 92a).

However, the positive assessment of Job came under increasing scrutiny and criticism as a result of the ubiquitous Christian approbation of Job as a precursor to Christ and a model of pre-Christian piety. This forced rabbinic interpretation to turn toward the darker sides of Job—his defiant self-defense and skepticism of divine beneficence—in order to counter Christian usurpation of their saint. It is to this more negative assessment that we now turn.

3.2. The Not-So-Righteous Gentile. Certain rabbinic texts are ambivalent about Job and portray him as something of an anomaly; he was righteous in one sense but not so righteous in another. In one fascinating interchange Rabbi Meir was asked by his teacher Elisha about Job 42:12, "The Lord blessed the latter days of Job more than his beginning" (NRSV). Rabbi Meir interpreted the passage to mean that the Lord gave Job twice as much as he had before. His teacher chided him for not understanding that the Hebrew could just as easily be translated thus: "The Lord blessed the latter end of Job because of the beginning"—that is, Job is blessed at the end only because of his righteous comportment before his trials began (*b. Ḥag.* 15a; *y. Ḥag.* 2:1, 77a-b; *Eccl. Rab.* 7:8, *Ruth Rab.* 6:4; *b. Qidd.* 39b). The point here is that God found it in his heart to forgive Job's blasphemies and reward him at the end of his life only because of his previous righteousness before his trials began.

Rabbi Hanina understood Job to be the only righteous Gentile whom God deemed worthy of great reward. However, his rewards were temporal, not eternal. God rewarded him lavishly in this life, but his rewards were not to be enjoyed in the world to come (*Gen. Rab.* 57:4). In arguing about the quality of Job's virtue, rabbis disagree on the question of whether or not a Gentile could attain the world to come and its attendant righteousness. In one opinion, Job clearly believed that this present earthly world was all there was, since he cursed God when God brought upon him afflictions. Therefore, the Holy One doubled his wealth in this present world and expelled him from the world to come (*b. B. Bat.* 15b). Job ends up being something of a "best of a bad lot" whose constant complaining and questioning of God proved his inferiority to the Israelites and whose rich earthly rewards were enjoyed in this world only (Baskin 1983, 21).

Many rabbis claim that although Job provided hospitality toward strangers and the poor, he did so only passively because he only helped those who came to him. Job's passivity in this regard explains the tragedies that he undergoes and undercuts Job's case concerning his own righteousness (*'Abot R. Nat.* 7). Many midrashic exegetes could accept that Job was a righteous Gentile, but few could accept that he was more righteous than a father of Israel (Baskin 1983, 18). Rabbis often compared the motives of fear and love for divine service, using Abraham and Job as exemplars for each. The merit of serving God out of fear remains in effect for a thousand generations, but serving God out of love has merit for two thousand generations (*b. Soṭah* 31a). The comment in Job 1:1 that Job "feared God" was proof enough for many that Job served God out of fear alone. Once the rabbis establish that Job served God only out of fear, he loses much of his praise and honor. The problem with serving God out of fear is that it cannot stand the test of adversity (Baskin 1983, 19). The fact that Job contended with God when he was punished (Job 10:2 is cited) is proof that Job served God out of fear, not love (*Midr. Ps.* 26:2). Job is here recognized as a righteous Gentile, one who even is related by marriage to Israel, but he is inferior to descendants of Abraham and to proselytes (Baskin 1983, 18).

3.3. The Unrighteous Gentile. Many different opinions existed among the rabbis as to the date and location of Job's life. These differing opinions were brought about by the lack of specificity in the canonical book itself. Job was believed by some to have lived in Egypt during the period of Moses and, in fact, to have been (along with Jethro and Balaam) one of Pharaoh's advisors. The biblical text describes one of Pharaoh's advisors as "fearing the Lord" (Ex 9:20), which was understood as a subtle reference to Job, who is the only Gentile of whom the Scriptures say that he was a God-fearing man (Job 1:1) (*y. Soṭah* 20c). Although Job was a man who feared God among Pharaoh's counselors, his failure to voice his disapproval over Pharaoh's plan to drown the Israelite children explains Job's legendary sufferings (*b. Soṭah* 11a; *b. Sanh.* 106a; *Exod. Rab.* 27:3). In one tradition, Job is tossed by God to Satan in order to distract Satan long enough for Israel to pass through the Red Sea. Job 2:6 ("Behold he is now in your hands") is intended, according to this interpretation, to distract Satan long enough to provide escape for Israel from Egypt (*Exod. Rab.* 21:7; *Gen. Rab.* 57:4; *y. Soṭah* 20d). This is Job's punishment for his failure to advise Pharaoh against the genocide of Israelite children. Job has been transformed from a righteous Gentile into a despicable criminal.

3.4. The Righteous Israelite. This rabbinic opinion also contradicts the Christian understanding of Job as a Gentile precursor of Jesus without turning to Job's darker aspects: Job was not a Gentile at all, but rather was a righteous Israelite. Job is even believed by some to have been born circumcised. He is described as having been both "blameless and upright" (Job 1:1), and rabbis believed that the use of two adjectives together such as this was no redundancy but had special significance (Baskin 1983, 14). What could be more perfect than to be born circumcised (*'Abot R. Nat.* 2)? Being born circumcised has implications for the continuing Christian and Jewish polemics. Christians claimed that before Moses, just persons lived who did not observe the *law of Moses and who were uncircumcised. Rabbis countered that many righteous persons before Moses had been born circumcised and observed the law in all its details (*Pesiq. Rab.* 28:1, 5; *Gen. Rab.* 11:46; *Num. Rab.* 14:9). The claim that Job was born circumcised, and thus Israelite, makes him off-limits as a Gentile precursor to Jesus (Baskin 1983, 133). Rabbi Jochanan, the head of a *bet midrash* (house of study) in Tiberias of the third century, who is generally believed to have had fairly substantive intellectual interaction with Origen, insisted on Job's Jewishness. Not only did Jochanan insist that Job was a Jew, but also he insisted that Job lived at the time of the return from Babylon (*y. Soṭah* 20c). Here he may well be challenging Origen, who extols Job as a Gentile model of Christian patience and piety from the period between Jacob and Moses (*Or.* 30; *Hom. Ezech.* 4).

Not only did the rabbinic transformation of Job from Gentile into Jew play a role in their anti-Christian polemic, but also it allowed these interpreters to understand Job as a symbol of the sufferings of Israel (Baskin 1983, 25). Job's and Israel's sufferings underwent detailed comparison: both lost sons and daughters, both were robbed of silver and gold, both were cast upon a dung heap (*Pesiq. Rab.* 26:7). The intention of this comparison is clear: just as Job was comforted in his sufferings in the end, so also will be the case for suffering Israel. Israel's destiny is foreseen by the suffering and redemption of Job (*Pesiq. Rab.* 29-30).

It is clear from the foregoing survey that there is no rabbinic consensus on Job. However, the discussion becomes increasingly polemical in that it seeks to counter the Christian appropriation of Job. Yet Job remains an interpretive problem for the rabbis, due in part to their respect for the ambiguities latent in the Hebrew text itself on which they based their interpretations.

4. Job in Patristic Literature.

For numerous reasons that will become clear below, Job occupies an important place in the biblical interpretation of the church fathers. Job takes on several different interpretive roles. In comparison to rabbinic literature, the church fathers are of unified agreement: Job was an Idumean saint. Their opinion is shaped largely by the fact that their sacred texts had already been somewhat sanitized by the translator of the Old Greek translation and by the fact that the NT itself (James 5:11) has already understood Job this way. However, there are still many differing ways in which this Idumean saint can be understood, and many exegetical loads that the biblical text can bear. Several of these will be outlined here.

4.1. Exemplar of Patience and Hospitality. Fol-
lowing the lead of James 5, many Christian exegetes see Job as a quintessential model of patience in the midst of earthly trials. Thus, the *Apostolic Constitutions* demand that the believer accept without complaint any misfortunes, "knowing that reward will be given you by God, as it was given to Job and Lazarus" (*Apos. Con.* 8.8.7). In *1 Clement* (c. 100) Job's humility and piety should be imitated by all the faithful (*1 Clem.* 17). He is placed in the company of Abraham and Moses and other prophets who herald the coming of Christ. Similarly, we are told by Tertullian that Job met every variety of violence of the devil yet was not drawn away from his reverence for God. Because of this, his thorough patience in spirit and flesh is an example and testimony given to us that we might not succumb either to damages of our worldly goods or to losses of those who are dearest, or even to bodily afflictions (*Pat.* 14).

Jerome is unique among the church fathers in that he was fully aware of the difficulties posed by the book of Job in Hebrew and of the differences between the narrative and poetic sections. Because many of these difficulties had been covered up by the LXX (and the Old Latin, which followed it), very few Christians understood the interpretive challenges that the Hebrew text presented. Jerome compares the Hebrew meaning of the biblical poetry to an eel: the more you squeeze it, the sooner it escapes (*Preface to Job*). Although Jerome does challenge many putative Christian beliefs about Job (his equivalence to Jobab, for instance), he admires Job's steadfastness in trial. He recognizes Job as not only a model of patience and hope in adversity (*Comm. Eph.* 3.5) but also as a prophet who foresaw the coming Christ and who comforted himself in his miseries with the hope of resurrection: "The Lord had not yet died, and the athlete of the Church saw his redeemer rising from the grave" (*Jo. Hier.* 30).

4.2. Precursor of Christ. Not only is Job a model of patience in the hope of eternal life, but also his strength in the face of overwhelming tragedy and humiliation and his final vindication prefigure, for many early Christian exegetes, the sufferings and glorification of the Christ. Zeno, the fourth-century bishop of Verona, established a lengthy list of parallels between the sufferings of Job and those of Jesus in his incarnation and passion (*Tract.* 11.15). Since Christianity sought to be a universal religion, the portrayal of saintly pagans became important Gentile witnesses to the incarnation of God in Christ. Just as the Jews had received their revelation of God in Moses and the prophets, so also the Gentiles were seen to have had prophets whose lives and message pointed the way to Jesus Christ. These Gentile prophets opened doors for all peoples to come to their true spiritual home in the church. The coming of God in Christ was not a revelation that discounted all previous divine revelations but rather was one that fulfilled them while it also superseded them. Job's role as an ancient Idumean saint of the pagan world is the ideal expression of righteousness in the sphere of "cosmic religion" (Daniélou, 87).

It was through this theological lens of prevenient grace that Job was interpreted; he provided proof that Christ had come to redeem not just the Jews but all humankind. Augustine approached Job, as was his wont, as an exegete who seeks to motivate piety and devotion to the church. Like many of his predecessors, he understood Job to be a model of both pious living and patience in suffering (*Enarrat. Ps.* 56:18; *Symb.* 10; *Pat.* 9; *Tract. Ev. Jo.* 41.9). Yet, Augustine's interest in Job as a Gentile and as a precursor to Christ stands out. In *City of God* he asks whether there were any outside the race of Israel who belonged to the heavenly city. Anyone who denies that this is possible can be refuted easily by the case of Job, who was neither a native to Israel nor a proselyte but rather an Idumean (clearly following the LXX in its Old Latin translation). Of Job, he says, "He was praised by divine oracle," and "no man of his time is put on a level with him as regards to justice and piety. . . . From this one case we might know that among other nations also there might be men pertaining to the spiritual Jerusalem who lived according to God and have pleased Him" (*Civ.* 18.47). From this, Augustine goes on to affirm that Job must have had some divine prescience of Christ's coming incarnation. Later he claimed that although Job lived before the law of Moses had been given, Job proves that in the hearts of the godly the eternal law had already been inscribed from which the written laws came to be copied (*Serm.* 31.2). Job did not need the written law, for he had personal access to God's law, which preexisted the Levitical priesthood.

4.3. Holy Ascetic. For Ambrose, Job bears a very different interpretive load than for any other patristic writer. Although Ambrose wrote no extended commentary on Job, his scattered comments on Job paint an image peculiar to Ambrose's theological agenda. Ambrose was a student of the Greek fathers and of Philo, yet he proceeded into new territory. His teachers had gone down hermeneutical paths that he had no desire to follow. He has no interest in Job as a righteous Gentile or a prophet to the nations, and he explicitly denies that Job is a type of Christ. The message of Job, to Ambrose, was one of the "insurmountable impediment of wealth to salvation, and the glorious spiritual treasure awaiting the steadfast sufferer" (Baskin 1981, 223). Job exemplifies the blessedness that comes through the endurance of earthly agonies with head unbowed: "What can we think of as more wretched than holy Job, either in the burning of his house, or the instantaneous death of his ten sons, or his bodily pains? Was he less blessed than if he had not endured these things whereby he really showed himself approved?" (*Off.* 2.5.20).

Ambrose links this biblical figure to the pagan virtue of fortitude, so that the pagan virtues exemplified by Pyrrus or Socrates assume a new Christian flavoring. Job exemplifies the spiritual reality of the fact that human beings may attain a life of blessedness only by overcoming bodily agony and by enduring corporeal tribulations with dignity. In the otherworldly philosophical perspective of Ambrose, where riches and bodily comforts impede salvation, the Job of Job 1 had been corrupted by wealth and was purged only by these trials of the soul. Through this interpretive lens, Ambrose justifies Job's denunciation of the day of his birth (Job 3:3)—a feature that strikes many interpreters as blasphemous—as a rejection of life in the flesh that emerges from his desire for eternal life with God (Baskin 1981, 228).

4.4. Model of Human Potentiality. Interpretation of the book of Job significantly shaped the debate that Augustine had with Pelagius and Julian of Ecclanum. Job was of particular theological interest to Pelagian exegetes as an example of a person who was righteous without divine grace. Pelagius laid the groundwork here, arguing in his *Epistula ad Demetriadem* that human nature is basically good because it was created by a good God: "What shall I say of the blessed Job, that most renowned athlete of God, whose wealth was snatched from him, whose estate utterly destroyed, whose sons and daughters died all together, and who, after all this, yet fought against the devil to the very end with his body? ... What a man Job was! A man of the gospel before the gospel was known, a man of the apostles before their commands were uttered!" (PL 30.21-22 [Steinhauser, 303]).

Pelagius extends the notion of divine beneficence to include all creation—a good God can only create good things—such that all humanity can, apart from divine assistance, achieve perfection. Failure to do so is a choice not to manifest what is uniquely one's own nature. All humans are free to choose to do rightly. Job exemplifies a natural capacity that enables all humans to reform themselves even apart from divine succor.

Augustine responds simply by pointing out that Job calls himself a sinner and is clearly aware of his sin, which he humbly confesses (Steinhauser, 304-5). Augustine quotes Job (Job 14:17) as saying, "My misdeeds would be sealed up in a pouch, and you would cover over my guilt" (C. Jul. op. imp. 1.105). Even so, Augustine's comment on Job is spotty at best, for Job only served to weaken his general argument.

While Pelagius wrote commentary on Paul in response to Augustine, Julian realized that Romans was not as good a starting point as Job. Julian focused his biblical comment on Job, writing a full-fledged commentary, *Expositio libri Iob*. For Julian, Job is the quintessential holy human who, apart from heavenly assistance, successfully chose to avoid evil by the force of the human will alone (Steinhauser, 300). For this reason, Julian found in Job a showpiece for human perfectibility that disproves Augustine's notion of inherited sin. Julian extols Job and sees in him the goodness of all human nature: "The life of blessed Job is praised because in him the good of human nature may be known. As established by God even without the teaching of the written law, human nature shows that it can be sufficient in itself for repelling sins and pursuing all virtues" (*Expositio libri Iob* [Steinhauser, 307]). In Job we have a concrete example of a saint who was holy before the birth of Jesus or the giving of the law. "Perhaps Julian's approach may be summarized by his comment on Job 5:9, referring to God who does great and inscrutable things: 'Job recounts the riches of divine providence, which God lavishes upon all generations generally and properly to each and every generation'" (Steinhauser, 307).

The primary bone of contention between Augustine and the Pelagians ends up being this: Did Job sin? If he did not, then he exercised free will and manifests the fundamental goodness of human nature. As Julian argues, Job exemplifies the innate reason that empowers all human beings to determine and perform that which is good. If Job did indeed sin, as Augustine claims, then he does so only because his sinful humanity compares to that of all other humans (Steinhauser, 308).

5. Job in Medieval Literature.

5.1. Gregory the Great. Gregory the Great (d. 604) wrote an extended commentary on the book of Job called *Moralia in Iob,* which intended to explicate the book verse by verse on literal, spiritual and moral levels. However, he wrote not so much a detailed analysis of the text as a doctrinal exposition and exhortation to moral living. Gregory believes, like most other Christian exegetes, that Job was a Gentile who was intended by God to be an example for those who do not know God's laws and to confound the iniquity of those who are under the law (*Moral.* Preface 4). Gregory proclaims the sanctity of the pagan Job and offers him as a model not only of right living but also as one who commands the respect of people (*Moral.* Preface 5). For Gregory, three pagan saints are worthy of mention, each with a particular quality or characteristic unique to them: Abel for his innocence, Enoch for his integrity of morals, Job for his patience in the midst of life's trials (*Moral.* Preface 13). Job was stricken so that his great patience and fortitude might be made known to all, and the excellence of his merit might elevate the patience of others (*Moral.* Preface 12).

Gregory the Great follows Augustine in proclaiming that Job is not only a model of righteousness among the Gentiles but also one who prophesies to the coming Christ (*Moral.* Preface 5). Gregory interprets the Gentile origin of Job as follows: "It is not without cause that the life of a just pagan is set before us as a model side by side with the life of the Israelites. Our Savior, coming for the redemption of Jews and gentiles, willed also to be foretold by the voices of the Jews and gentiles" (*Moral.* Preface, 5). Job's patience in his time of trial made him not only an exemplar of virtue but also a prophet of the coming Christ, whose suffering and vindication he prefigured and foretold. "Christ in this comparison is mankind itself reduced to the nakedness of its tragic condition, of which Job was its most perfect prefiguration" (Daniélou, 99).

5.2. Moses Maimonides. Both Moses Maimonides and Thomas Aquinas, the two greatest medieval Aristotelians, found Job to be of great value in the explication of their philosophical theology. Maimonides devoted two chapters to Job in his famous *Guide of the Perplexed*. He uses his exegesis of Job not only as a platform to expound his philosophical views but also to bring coherence to the book itself. For his solution to the problems that other interpreters found in Job, Maimonides offers his opinion that Job is praised as a righteous individual in the initial chapters but is actually deeply flawed. Job 1:1 praises his moral virtue, but this is a cue to the thoughtful reader that this is the only form of virtue that Job has attained. Job, at the start, has yet to perfect in himself the higher virtues of intellectual perception (Eisen, 72).

Maimonides then is free to interpret the variances in the rest of the book as phases in Job's intellectual ascent and his final attainment of theoretical perfection. Job's angry outbursts at God prove that he lacks a complete understanding of God's ways. The fact that he mourns the loss of his health, wealth and children illustrates that Job, in his inchoate moral state, mistakenly believes that the possession of earthly benefits displays the smile of divine providence (a view that both he and Aristotle reject). Out of his disillusionment, and with divine aid, Job comes to understand (the Aristotelian conception) that divine providence determines not the course of individual lives but only the broader structures of natural law in created order.

This understanding, for Job, leads him to achieve intellectual perfection; physical and material goods bear no significance in comparison to the rewards that come in the contemplation of God. With this general understanding, Maimonides brings coherence to the book by harmonizing the prologue and the final chapters of the book. Job's angry questioning of God proves for Maimonides that Job himself, though perfectly just, remains unwise and in need of intellectual refinement, which his sufferings provide. Maimonides' curious goal here is to critique the shortcomings of his fellow Jews: they, like Job, though just, are in need of philosophical refinement that Aristotle, as mediated by Maimonides, can provide (Yaffee, 112).

5.3. Thomas Aquinas. Thomas Aquinas, Maimonides' Christian counterpart, composed a line-by-line commentary on Job that argues differently from his Jewish contemporary. First, for Aquinas, the story is literally true, while for Maimonides, appealing to some rabbinic authorities, the book is primarily parabolic. Second, for Aquinas, Job is perfectly wise from beginning to end, yet nevertheless he was blameworthy on different grounds (Yaffee, 112).

Aquinas's Job is the ideal student: perfectly wise yet somewhat unformed in practical matters. Although he can refute his antagonists intellectually, he reveals his own faults by the imprudent and misleading manner in which he communicates his wisdom. He even gives his friends the impression that he is blaspheming (*Expositio* 38.1.10-13). In speaking so impulsively, Job gives the false impression that he is prideful and that he actually doubts divine providence and justice (*Expositio* 42.1.1-5). Job's cursing the day of his birth reflects the human sadness that comes from the lower parts of the soul; the upper realms of Job's soul remained rationally convinced that "good must rightly be expected from his misfortunes" (*Expositio* 3.4.98-99 [Clines, 56]). While Job faces external challenges, and even intellectual challenges, internally he remained sure of God's just ways to the end. He thus is an exemplar of a pious soul remaining internally secure while outwardly shaken by personal and intellectual tragedy.

Job his been well instructed in the teachings of the church, but his imprudence has made him insensitive to the negative effects of the manner in which he communicates his teaching. Aquinas's interpretation challenges his readers to, like Job, consider the need for a reduction in the rancor and acerbity ubiquitous in doctrinal disputations. This moderation applies even to those who believe that their opinions reflect the religiously authorized view. In this way, "Aquinas's Job induces the student or professor of Christian wisdom, who is seen to be perfectly wise, to re-examine the practical limitations of the wisdom he professes—and so to communicate that wisdom in a more moderate or considerate way than his training may have suggested to him hitherto" (Yaffee, 118).

For Aquinas, the heart of the controversy between Job and his friends lies in the nature of human perception of cosmic order. Both Job and his interlocutors believed in divine providence and order, but Aquinas's Job, following Aristotle, has doubts about whether providence can be perceived in human events. There is no question that divine order and intentionality shine clearly for all who consider the natural world, but human affairs have no certain perceptible order. In Aquinas, Job's dialogue partners doubt the immortality of the soul, a doctrine that the Thomistic Job heartily affirms. Therefore, his comforters find themselves constrained to perceive the providential plan and purpose in all human affairs because there is no *afterlife to right the wrongs of this life. Human history, for the comforters, must be justly ordered because it does not include the final judgment of immortal souls. Because Job believes in the immortality of all souls, he is not constrained to perceive order in all human affairs; the eternal future world will sort out all historical injustices (Schreiner, 133-34).

6. Job and the Reformers.
6.1. Martin Luther. Martin Luther, who never wrote a complete commentary on Job, everywhere reflects his understanding of Job as a paradigm for spiritual and psychic tension. Job is a pious saint, but at the same time he is a sinner and a doubter. Job plays an important role for Luther as a perfect representative of the paradox that exists between piety and guilt. Luther seeks to bring resolution to the paradox by asking, "How does Job handle this situation?" Importantly, Job does not deny knowledge of the conflict within but admits it openly. It is this open confession of one's sinfulness and lack of self-worth that underlies his very saintliness and piety (Clines, 60). Job has no confidence in his own merit. Luther's understanding of Job 9:28 plays a critical role here. The Vulgate (differently from the Hebrew) reads, "I fear all my works." This, for Luther, is an interpretive key to the book and an expression of Luther's anxiety concerning the dangers of self-justification. He quotes it over and over again.

"For Luther, Job is not someone who is almost perfect, or one who to some degree falls short of true piety; he is, through and through, a saint—who is at the same time also a sinner" (Clines, 61). Job, as a representative believer, even in his bitterness and despair, becomes a model for others to follow. Job's complaints against God are appropriate even for the just. Even his yearning to be dead is, figuratively, only a yearning to be free of human constraints of this world. Luther's Job, while a representative believer, illustrates the paradox that the saintly are particularly conscious of their intractable wickedness and are ever liable to experience the wiles of Satan himself. Yet, in God's mysterious ways, even these temptations serve to prove God's broader purposes.

6.2. John Calvin. Calvin follows Thomas Aquinas in seeing in Job the story of the difficulty of perceiving providence in human affairs. Calvin's Job also insists on the doctrine of the resurrection and of the extension of certainty of divine justice to the last day. As with Aquinas, Job's comforters spoke many true things but were ultimately upbraided for restricting divine justice to human history; they misunderstood earthly events as divine retribution. Calvin, differently from Aquinas, explores more fully the issue of the incomprehensibility of providence and the nature of the hiddenness of God. For Calvin, tension has to be constantly maintained between God's visibility and invisibility; while the God of history must never recede into complete inscrutability, one must never fail to recognize the infinity of God in comparison to human finitude (Schreiner, 134-35).

Calvin's Job does, in the end, find grounds to trust in divine providence in spite of the disorderliness of human affairs. But the affirmation of the unity of God's essential nature binds together Calvin's broader exegesis of Job. One knows that God does not rule arbitrarily or capriciously because God's will remains morally unified and rationally consistent. Natural revelation demonstrates the power of God and his wise control over the cosmos. This contrasts to the mystifying nature of human affairs where the righteous do indeed suffer and the evil often appear blessed. In Calvin's exegesis, Job—as a result of the final whirlwind speeches—came to rightly perceive the difference between God's revelation in nature and in history as the juxtaposition of the comprehensibility and hiddenness of God (Schreiner, 140). "On the basis of the revelation present in nature, Job is to trust that despite appearances, God is still ordering human events with justice and wisdom" (Schreiner, 141). Job's challenge is that which faces all humanity: to lay hold to the promise made clear in creation (the "outskirts of God's ways") with the holy hope that no matter how chaotic human affairs may appear at present, created order points faithfully to the providential goodness of a God who will execute perfect justice on the last day.

See also FEMINIST INTERPRETATION; HERMENEUTICS; JOB 1: BOOK OF.

BIBLIOGRAPHY. **J. R. Baskin**, "Job as Moral Exemplar in Ambrose," *VC* 35.3 (1981) 222-31; idem, *Pharaoh's Counsellors: Job, Jethro, and Balaam in Rabbinic and Patristic Tradition* (BJS 47; Chico, CA: Scholars Press, 1983); **D. J. A. Clines**, "Job and the Spirituality of the Reformation," in *The Bible, the Reformation and the Church: Essays in Honour of James Atkinson*, ed. W. P. Stephens (JSNTSup 105; Sheffield: Sheffield Academic Press, 1995) 49-72; **J. Daniélou**, *Holy Pagans of the Old Testament* (Baltimore: Helicon Press, 1957); **R. Eisen**, *The Book of Job in Medieval Jewish Philosophy* (Oxford: Oxford University Press, 2004); **J. A. Emerton**, "Song of Songs as an 'Answer' to Cline's Book of Job," in *Reading from Right to Left: Essays on the Hebrew Bible in Honour of David J. A. Clines*, ed. J. C. Exum and H. G. M. Williamson (JSOTSup 373; Sheffield: Sheffield Academic Press, 2003); **D. Gard**, The *Exegetical Method of the Greek Translator of the Book of Job* (JBLMS 8; Philadelphia: Society of Biblical Literature, 1952); **G. Gerleman**, *Studies in the Septuagint*, 1: *Book of Job* (LUÅ 43/2; Lund: Gleerup, 1946); **H. Heater Jr.**, *A Septuagint Translation Technique in the Book of Job* (Washington, DC: Catholic Biblical Association, 1982); **W. J. Houston**, "Insights on Job 3, from a Medieval Commentary: Rabbi Samuel Ben Meir (Rashbam) on the Book of Job," in *Reading from Right to Left: Essays on the Hebrew Bible in Honour of David J. A. Clines*, ed. J. C. Exum and H. G. M. Williamson (JSOTSup 373; Sheffield: Sheffield Academic Press, 2003); **J. C. de Moor**, "'Consolations of God': Assessing Job's Friends across a Cultural Abyss," in *Reading from Right to Left: Essays on the Hebrew Bible in Honour of David J. A. Clines*, ed. J. C. Exum and H. G. M. Williamson (JSOTSup 373; Sheffield: Sheffield Academic Press, 2003); **H. Orlinsky**, "Studies in the Septuagint of Job," *HUCA* 28 (1957) 53-57; *HUCA* 29 (1958) 229-71; *HUCA* 30 (1959) 153-67; *HUCA* 32 (1961) 239-68; *HUCA* 33 (1962) 119-51; *HUCA* 35 (1964) 57-78; *HUCA* 36 (1965) 37-47; **J. I. Pfeffer**, *Providence in the Book of Job: The Search for God's Mind* (Brighton: Sussex Academic Press, 2005);

M. H. Pope, *Job* (AB 15: Garden City, NY: Doubleday, 1965); **S. E. Schreiner**, "'Why Do the Wicked Live?' Job and David in Calvin's Sermons on Job," in *The Voice from the Whirlwind: Interpreting the Book of Job*, ed. L. G. Perdue and W. C. Gilpin (Nashville: Abingdon, 1992) 129-43; **R. P. Spittler**, "Testament of Job," *OTP* 1.829-68; **K. Steinhauser**, "Job Exegesis: The Pelagian Controversy," in *Augustine: Biblical Exegete*, ed. F. Van Fletern and J. C. Schnaubelt (New York: Lang, 2001) 299-311; **E. E. Urbach**, *The Sages: Their Concepts and Beliefs* (Cambridge, MA: Harvard University Press, 1987); **N. Whybray**, *Job* (Readings; Sheffield: Sheffield Academic Press, 1998); **M. D. Yaffee**, "Providence in Medieval Aristolianism," in *The Voice from the Whirlwind: Interpreting the Book of Job*, ed. L. G. Perdue and W. C. Gilpin (Nashville: Abingdon, 1992) 111-28.

J. Allen

JOB 4: PERSON

The book of Job is named for its central character. Job is introduced in the first verse of the book (Job 1:1), and the last verse reports his death (Job 42:17). Outside of the book that bears his name, Job is named in only two other contexts in the Bible. In Ezekiel he is cited twice (Ezek 14:14, 20) as a paragon of righteousness, and in the NT James highlights his patience (Jas 5:11). Thus, most of what we know about Job the person comes from Job the book. There are no ancient extrabiblical references to him, and later descriptions of Job (including the references in Ezekiel and James) are more properly the subject of the history of interpretation (*see* Job 3: History of Interpretation).

1. Job's Background
2. Job's Character
3. Job's Story
4. Was Job a Real Person?

1. Job's Background.

Job is from Uz, almost certainly to be associated with the city of that name known to be outside of Israel in an area later known Edom. Although there is a slim possibility that this Uz is to be identified with the Uz in Genesis 10:23 and 1 Chronicles 1:17 associated with Aram, it is much more likely that this Uz is the one in Edom to the east of Israel (Gen 36:28; 1 Chron 1:42; Lam 4:21). After all, some of Job's friends have names associated with an Edomite genealogy (see Eliphaz in Gen 36:10-11) and Edomite locations (Eliphaz the Temanite—Teman is a major Edomite center [Amos 1:12; Obad 9; Jer 49:7, 20; Ezek 25:13]). Furthermore, Edom is renowned for its wisdom (Jer 49:7).

Accordingly, Job is a Gentile, though he worships the true God, much as Melchizedek (Gen 14) and Jethro do. And as with these two other non-Hebrew worshipers of the true God, we do not know how Job came to know and worship him. Although Jethro is an exception, it may be easier to understand Job in the context of a pre-Abrahamic period before the narrowing of the covenant. Certainly the measurement of Job's wealth in terms of numbers of animals (Job 1:2-3) fits better with the (pre)patriarchal period as well. The setting of the story is thus early, although this conclusion says nothing about when the book was written (see Job 1: Book of).

Though Edomite, Job's name is understandable as Hebrew. We do not know much about ancient Edomite language, but what we do know demonstrates its linguistic similarity to *Hebrew. In any case, the names may be given in Hebrew for familiarity's sake. Though understandable as Hebrew or Edomite, the name Job (ʾiyyôb) is of uncertain meaning. It can be translated as an interrogative sentence, "Where is my father?" with "father" being a reference to God. On the other hand, the name has also been connected to a Hebrew verb that means "hate" or "be an enemy" (see Williams). The verb provides the base for the noun "enemy" (ʾôyēb), and if the association is correct, this may be explained by the fact that for a period Job becomes an enemy of God (see Job 13:24 where the verbal form ʾyb is used in this way [so Weiss, 20]).

2. Job's Character.

Job's character is of the utmost importance to his story, and the book wastes no time in describing it. After learning that Job is from Uz, we are told that he is "innocent [tām] and virtuous [yāšār], fearing God and turning away from evil." This language is reminiscent of the description of the "wise" in the book of *Proverbs. The wise are innocent (Prov 2:7, 21; 11:3, 20; 13:6; 19:1; 20:7; 28:6, 10, 18; 29:10) and virtuous (Prov 1:3; 2:7, 21; 8:6, 9; 11:3, 6; 12:6; 14:11; 15:8; 16:13; 20:11; 21:2, 8; 23:16; 29:10). The sage also fears God (Prov 1:7; 9:10; but see also Prov 1:29; 2:5; 3:7; 8:13; 9:10; 10:27; 14:2, 26, 27; 15:16, 33; 16:6; 19:23; 22:4; 23:7; 24:21; 28:14; 29:25; 31:30). In Proverbs 1:7, and elsewhere, the fear

of God (see Fear of the Lord) is coupled with turning from evil (most pointedly, Prov 3:7). In the prologue of the book of Job, Job's character not only is described by the narrator but also is affirmed by God himself (Job 1:8) and is never questioned, even by the Accuser. Thus, in the following sections, when the three friends and Elihu argue that Job's suffering is the result of his sin, we, the readers who have been privy to the dialogue between God and the Accuser, know they are wrong.

Furthermore, Job's piety is exemplary. He even offers sacrifices on behalf of his children just in case they "have sinned and cursed God in their hearts" (Job 1:5). He is careful in his relationship with God, which the narrator of Job finds admirable.

According to the book of Proverbs, such wisdom and godliness should be followed by material blessings, and the reader is not disappointed. The prologue describes Job's enormous wealth (Job 1:3) as well as his large family (Job 1:2). Thus, through a description of his character as well as his blessed life, the reader learns that Job is truly one of the godly wise.

3. Job's Story.

3.1. The Two Tests. Our description of Job thus far applies to him at the beginning of the book. He is godly, wise, pious and rich. He is the epitome of the *sage in Proverbs.

The plot complication begins with an accusation on the part of a figure known in Hebrew as haśśāṭān (Job 1:9-11). The exact identity of haśśāṭān is debated. Christian readers detect the proper name *"Satan" perhaps a bit too quickly here. If it is a proper name, why is the definite article (ha-) prefixed to it? Furthermore, what is the devil doing in heaven convincing God to meddle in the life of his faithful servant Job? The Hebrew root śāṭān means "accuse," thus haśśāṭān means "the Accuser." It appears that this figure is not the devil but rather is one of God's angels. Many questions remain as to why the Accuser takes the role of a prosecuting attorney against Job, but it does resolve the issue of Satan in heaven.

The Accuser in essence accuses Job of self-interested piety. In other words, Job is godly not because he loves God but rather because he loves the gifts of God, the large family, the wealth and his health. Take that away, and Job will turn against God.

At first, God grants the Accuser the right to afflict Job's environment, but not him personally. The consequences are horrible and come in four waves (Job 1:13-19). First, the Sabeans take his oxen and kill his servants. Second, fire comes from the sky (lightning?) and burns up the sheep and the servants watching them. Third, the Chaldeans come and take his camels and kill the servants. Finally, and most horribly, a strong wind blows down the house in which his children are feasting, and all of them are killed. In spite of this, Job demonstrates his disinterested piety by affirming his continued faith in God.

The Accuser, however, is not satisfied and responds to God's satisfaction at Job's behavior with "Skin for skin!" (Job 2:4), a proverb signifying that Job would not really be afflicted until his own health was compromised. God relented again, allowing the Accuser to cause Job physical suffering short of death. Job's affliction is legendary. Covered with painful boils and sitting on a dung heap, Job nonetheless maintained his integrity before God. "Job did not sin in what he said" (Job 2:10).

One might think that this would end the book of Job, but the final paragraph of the prose introduction suggests otherwise as three friends come to console him (Job 2:11-13). Their presence will introduce a second plot complication that will further the story in the chapters to come.

3.2. The Disputation. Job survives two excruciating tests of his piety. He sits in silence for seven days with his equally silent friends, Eliphaz, Bildad and Zophar. Then he snaps. Job 3 records his anguished complaint about God. In many ways, his complaint is formally similar to the type of laments one finds in *Psalms (see Lament, Psalms of), but there are two crucial exceptions. First, the laments complain *to* God, whereas Job complains *about* God. Second, virtually every lament (Ps 88 is the exception) turns to God with prayer or confidence at the end, but Job does not express even a glimmer of hope.

In the final analysis, Job's complaint is closer to the grumbling tradition of the book of Numbers than to the laments of Psalms. The three friends cannot remain silent. Job's complaint energizes them to engage him in a debate.

Job blames God; the three friends blame Job. Both Job and his friends are united, though, in their affirmation of the principle of *retribution: "If people sin, they suffer. Therefore, if people suffer, they are sinners." Such reasoning leads the three friends to diagnose Job as a sinner who needs to repent to restore his relationship with God and regain his blessed life (Job 4:7-11; 11:13-20). Job, on the other hand, denies that he is a sinner, but since only sinners suffer, then God must be unjust (Job 9:21-24). Job wants an audience with God to set him straight (most dramatically, Job 31:35-40).

The debate on one level is about the nature and cure for Job's *suffering. The deeper issue, however, has to do with wisdom (Zerafa). Wisdom is the ability to navigate life. Wisdom helps a person avoid problems or at least get out of problems if they arise. Accordingly, it is not surprising that all four characters assert their own wisdom and denigrate the wisdom of their opponent (see Job 11:12; 12:1-3, 12; 13:12; 15:1-13).

The *disputation achieves no resolution. The three friends run out of arguments and energy and once again become silent. Job, in what appears to be a moment of clarity, powerfully affirms God's superior wisdom (Job 28 [see Lo]) before descending again to complaint, protestation of innocence, and a demand for an audience with God (Job 29-31).

3.3. God Disputes Job. Job will soon get his wish, but with different consequences than he anticipated. Before Yahweh speaks, though, the figure of Elihu asserts himself (Job 32—37). A full accounting of the book of Job would need to analyze this section of the book at some length. However, this article concerns the person of Job, and Elihu in fact has no substantial interaction with Job. Elihu is yet another claimant to wisdom. He represents those who believe that wisdom is connected not necessarily with age but rather with "the spirit in a man" (Job 32:8). Nevertheless, when he makes his case against Job, it is not significantly different from that presented by the three friends (Job 34:11, 25-27, 37). Accordingly, no one, including Job, bothers to respond to him. Job's final interaction is not with Elihu but rather with God himself.

Job had hoped for an audience with God during which he expected to set God straight: "I would give him an account of my every step; like a prince I would approach him" (Job 31:37). In Job 38:1, however, it is God who approaches Job, and this in the form of a whirlwind. God then proceeds to upbraid Job for his prideful assertions of wisdom. God relentlessly barrages Job with question after question, the effect of which is to render Job repentant then silent. Job is not wise; only God is wise.

3.4. Job's Restoration. The prose conclusion to the book (Job 42:7-17) presents the reader with an apparent enigma. Earlier Job had repented (Job 40:2-5; 42:1-5), and now God has restored his blessing. This scenario raises the question of whether the three friends were correct after all. They had argued that Job needed to repent to restore his blessings, and sure enough, that is what happens.

Or is it? Job had already proved, in the first two chapters of the book, that his piety was disinterested. At the end of the book, he was not repenting of the sin that led to his suffering. He was truly an innocent sufferer—at least during the test. However, as time went on, Job had grown increasingly impatient and insistent with God, even, as we have noted, accusing him of injustice. It was this attitude that led to his repentance. Job had "spoken of me [God] what is right," thus becoming an intercessor in behalf of the three friends (Iwanski). The prologue of the book does not undermine the message of the book.

4. Was Job a Real Person?

The book of Job is our main source for knowledge of Job the person. He is not mentioned in any extrabiblical texts. The descriptions of Job in Ezekiel 14:14, 20 as righteous and in James 5:11 as patient (or, probably better, as persevering) are interpretive reflections on the book of Job and do not offer independent information about the man. Indeed, such characterizations are ideal and not nuanced descriptions of Job as we learn about him in the book of Job.

Before leaving the topic of Job as a person, we should ask the question of whether he is a real person or a fictional character. Did Job live and breathe in space and time, or was he a literary construct? This question raises the issue of the genre of the book of Job. Is Job a work of history and thus making historical claims, or is it a didactic text that creates a story in order to reflect on the existential issue of innocent human suffering?

The historical intentionality of Job is difficult to assess. The first lines of a text often are important for genre identification, since they set the tone for what follows. The first verse of Job is similar to the opening verses of Judges 17 and 1 Samuel 1, two passages with an arguable intention to communicate historical events. Some might argue that the reference to Job in Ezekiel 14 as an example of righteousness might support the idea that Job was a real person whose story was known broadly.

On the other hand, large parts of the book of Job are set in poetry, a literary vehicle that betrays artifice. Even if Job was a real person, we are getting something far from a transcript of an actual event. Poetry elevates the book from a specific historical event to a story with universal application. If the book of Job is a historical chronicle, it is also much more. It is wisdom that is to be applied to all who hear it.

In the final analysis, since there are no independent attestations to Job's existence, it is impossible to decide this question dogmatically either way. Indeed, whether or not one understands this book to be historical has little impact on its meaning. Job's story is not a part of redemptive history, where the actual events impact whether or not they have any saving effect. Rather, Job's story serves a didactic purpose. It teaches us that suffering is not always the result of personal sin. Job is the ideal, wise, righteous person, and yet he suffers, teaching those who read his story that they cannot judge the morality of people based on their success or suffering.

See also JOB 1: BOOK OF.

BIBLIOGRAPHY. **D. Iwanski,** *The Dynamics of Job's Intercession* (AnBib 161; Rome: Pontifical Biblical Institute, 2006); **A. Lo,** *Job 28 as Rhetoric: An Analysis of Job 28 in the Context of Job 22—31* (VTSup 97; Leiden: E. J. Brill, 2003); **M. Weiss,** *The Story of Job's Beginning: Job 1—2, a Literary Analysis* (Publications for the Perry Foundation for Biblical Research in the Hebrew University of Jerusalem; Jerusalem: Magnes, 1983); **T. Williams,** "'yb," *NIDOTTE* 1.365-71; **P. Zerafa,** *The Wisdom of God in the Book of Job* (SUSTU 8; Rome: Herder, 1978) T. Longman III

JUSTICE. *See* LAW; RIGHTEOUSNESS; THEODICY.

K

KINGSHIP. *See* CREATION IMAGERY; CULT, WOR-
SHIP: PSALMS; MESSIAH; ROYAL COURT

KINGSHIP PSALMS

For many years the royal, or kingship, psalms have given rise to a great deal of debate. The foci of this debate have changed with the passage of time from discussion of the number of royal psalms to "sacral" and "sacerdotal" kingship, from "the Great Autumn Festival" to the meaning of the "Davidic" superscriptions. The Psalter is liberally laced with indications of kingship involvement, and although these royal themes are not always obvious, they are significant. The kingship background to the psalms is not as visible as praise or lament or *cult, but it is just as important to a right understanding of the theology of the Psalter. The Davidic king is not conspicuous, but there is a sense in which he subtly dominates the book of *Psalms.

1. Genre and the Kingship Psalms
2. Anonymous Kingship
3. Canonical Kingship
4. Continuing Kingship
5. Psalmic Kingship
6. Conclusions

1. Genre and the Kingship Psalms.

Until the 1990s the individual poems of the Psalter tended to be grouped according to their type, and one of H. Gunkel's genre categories was "royal psalms." Gunkel (99) remarked, "The internal unity of [these] psalms stems from the fact that they are *concerned entirely with kings.*" This definition immediately sets some alarm bells ringing. First, this is not a genre classification at all; it is an association based on similarity of content rather than of form. Thus, royal psalms can vary in form between individual complaint songs and individual *thanksgiving songs as long as their focus is on kingship. Second, must a psalm be concerned "entirely" with kings for it to qualify as a royal psalm? Few psalms fit neatly within a single genre category, yet mixed psalms that are dominated by lament, for example, are still categorized as *lament psalms. Should the same discretion not be applied to kingship psalms?

Another potential weakness in Gunkel's definition of royal psalmody is that he focuses on royal nomenclature. He suggests that use of the words *king* and *anointed,* the name "David" and phrases such as "Yahweh's servant" indicate a kingship background. Although this clearly is a logical starting point for any discussion of monarchic psalms, it is questionable whether such naming categories are the only reliable indication of a royal setting. This dubiety is accentuated by the fact that two of the ten psalms that Gunkel highlights as royal (Pss 2; 20; 21; 28; 45; 72; 101; 110; 132; 144:1-11) lack any of these naming characteristics in the psalms themselves (Pss 101; 110). Intuitively, based on their content, Gunkel saw that Psalm 101 and Psalm 110 have a setting in kingship, yet neither of them meets his criteria for declaring them royal. The implications of this subconscious expansion in the royal category are significant, allowing for the possibility that there are in fact many more psalms scattered throughout the Psalter that draw upon kingship themes and ideals. Gunkel allows two anonymous "I" psalms with Davidic superscriptions to be seen as kingship psalms because of their royal content. This being the case, could there not be more such psalms, perhaps even many more?

2. Anonymous Kingship.

J. H. Eaton (1-26) picks up on this ambiguity in

Gunkel's definition of the royal psalms and suggests that there are indeed many more psalms of this type in the Psalter. He argues that Gunkel's treatment of Psalm 101 and Psalm 110 should be applied to all of the anonymous "I" psalms, especially those that bear a Davidic superscription. He highlights several criteria that may indicate a royal background to many of the anonymous psalms. For example, the Chronicler associates *David with psalmody and the preparations for temple *worship, and Eaton suggests that we should understand the psalms' Davidic superscriptions in the light of this association; also, Israel's king had responsibilities with regard to public (temple) worship, where many of the psalms would have been used. Eaton goes on to highlight twenty-four characteristics found in the anonymous psalms of the Psalter that can reasonably be taken to indicate a royal background. For example, the psalmist's enemies are often foreign armies, or the deliverance of this individual has national repercussions, or Yahweh's honor is bound up with the fate of the psalmist. All of these indicators combine to indicate that the king is perhaps the most likely candidate to be the speaker in many of the anonymous psalms. So, when Eaton's theory is applied, a further fifty-four psalms can be added to Gunkel's original ten, thus giving the Psalter a decidedly more "royal" flavor.

3. Canonical Kingship.

The canonical approach to the Psalter further emphasizes the importance of kingship psalms. A canonical reading of the Psalter emphasizes the significance of the psalms that are placed at the beginning and end of its five "books." The argument of G. H. Wilson (85-94) that the seam psalms of Books I-III of the Psalter take on added editorial significance further accentuates the weight of the royal psalms within the book as a whole.

Wilson contends that through charting the progression in the kingship psalms that are placed at the seams of Books I-III, we see a "narrative" that traces the rise and fall of the Davidic monarchy. Psalm 2 describes the inauguration of the Davidic covenant, Psalm 72 reflects the transition of Davidic covenant to successive generations of Israelite kings, and Psalm 89 laments Yahweh's apparent rejection of the Davidic covenant. Questions have been raised about how well this narrative theory works in its detail—especially with regard to the canonical function of Psalm 2 and the suggestion that royal psalms play a less significant role in Books IV-V—but it is now broadly accepted that the kingship psalms have been placed at key junctures throughout the Psalter in order to emphasize royal themes as part of a postexilic, eschatological hope that a Davidic king would reign once again.

4. Continuing Kingship.

This eschatological hope in a restored Davidic kingship sheds some light on a fascinating question: Why are there any kingship psalms in the Psalter at all? The royal psalms originated in the realities of the Davidic monarchy, so why did the editors retain poems that celebrate enthronement ceremonies and royal weddings long after the monarchy ceased to exist?

Democratization and reinterpretation are the keys to understanding the continuing presence of kingship psalms in the Psalter. Apart from occasional superscriptions, the psalms are purposefully unspecific about their historical details and setting. The psalmist pleads his cause before God because of his enemies, but these enemies remain unidentified. Equally, the psalms celebrate great heights of joy, but again, the historical details of these testimonies are never laid out before the reader. This ahistoricity means that psalms are as broadly applicable as possible. The psalms express every emotion conceivable, and the whole point is that this expression of human emotion directed toward God is made available to be adapted to a wide variety of circumstances. The words may have originated on the lips of the king, but the principles are just as valid for the laborer who does not eat if he does not work. The circumstances differ, but the applicability of the spiritual truths of the psalms is the same for each. This is called democratization: the words written by a specific individual grounded in specific circumstances can be appropriated by all people in a wide variety of circumstances where the expression of the psalmist's thoughts and emotions reflect their own (see Miller 1986, 21-24).

Alongside the generalizing effects of democratization, another factor has led to the retention of kingship psalms in the Psalter: reinterpretation. Democratization has shrouded the "royalty" of some of the anonymous psalms; reinterpretation maintains the currency of the more obviously "royal" psalms. Psalm 2, for example, probably was recited at the coronation of each new Davidic king, so why retain such a psalm when there has been no king for many years? Psalm 2 retains its prominent place in the Psalter because its meaning for the covenant community has changed with their change of life setting. This process of reinterpretation seems to have occurred quite naturally throughout the history of the community of faith.

The focus of Psalm 2 on Yahweh's universal rule through his king based in *Zion would have resonated most with Davidic/Solomonic readers when Israel was a (relatively) major player in the ancient Near East and their experience of human kingship was fairly positive. By way of contrast, later preexilic readers, who lived in a period when Judah was politically insignificant and whose experience of kingship was much more negative, would experience a strong degree of cognitive dissonance in the reading of this psalm. The theology of Psalm 2 would be far removed from the reality of their situation. This leads to a process of reinterpretation. If Psalm 2 is not fulfilled in the reality of present kingship, its fulfillment must lie elsewhere—perhaps in a future king of Israel? So a degree of eschatological expectation is added to the reading: "Yahweh reigns, by all means, but surely the king spoken of is not our king. This must be a king who is still to come." This is true all the more for postexilic readers, for whom the king has become a very distant historical memory. Therefore, is it at all surprising that the early Christian community reread and understood Psalm 2 in the light of Jesus the *Messiah (Acts 4:24-28; 13:32-33)?

Such reinterpretation is inherent to psalmody, given the ahistoricity of the psalms. The psalms are *designed* to be appropriated in the way that is most relevant to the community of believers in their particular setting. So the kingship psalms are retained in the Psalter due to processes of democratization and reinterpretation: they point us to the ultimate Davidic king (reinterpretation), who is also the ultimate "everyman" (democratization).

5. Psalmic Kingship.

A theological problem remains, however: Why are the explicitly royal psalms so positive about kingship when much of the OT seems to be a great deal more critical of the office of king? It is often argued that Deuteronomy and its associated historical books are anti-kingship, although this overstates the case. Deuteronomy and the OT Historical Books favor kingship that is exercised in accordance with the kingship law (Deut 17:14-20); the problem was that Israel's kings seldom, if ever, followed that paradigm. Hence, the view of kingship in the rest of the OT is often much more negative than the celebration of kingship found in Psalms.

In response, first, we should remember that psalms are occasional literature; that is, they are meant to teach us something about their given focus, but their intent is not to provide us with a complete picture. This is true of the royal psalms, which celebrate all that is (or can be) good about human kingship practiced alongside the rule of the Great King. They are positive because kingship can be a good thing, but they are not written as a thesis on the relative merits and demerits of kingship. Second, the Psalter is not unaware of the downside of human kingship. Psalm 89:38-52, for example, discusses Yahweh's apparent rejection of the Davidic line, and the prophetic background to these events would be quite clear to readers of this psalm: the house of David fell because the kings of this noble line rejected Yahweh and his ways.

A third element should be borne in mind, however: the whole dynamic of contextual interpretation in the Psalter. Yes, the explicit royal psalms seem to have a very positive view of kingship, but how does their canonical context influence their interpretation? A contextual reading of all of the royal psalms is impossible within the scope of this article, but it does appear that the editors of the Psalter sought to direct their readers to a particular understanding of the future Davidic king by placing some of the kingship psalms in a very specific interpretative context. The Psalter's editors direct our attention to a future king who goes beyond even the best examples of kingship found in Israel's history, to one who will actually fulfill the ideal of kingship, Deuteronomy's kingship law (Deut 17:14-20).

It is interesting that the first and most prominent of the royal psalms (Ps 2) is paired with a psalm that celebrates the *tôrâ* ("instruction") of Yahweh (Ps 1). The themes of *tôrâ* (see Law) and kingship are linked in this introduction to the Psalter, which provides a paradigm for the interpretation of all that follows in the book. Interestingly, the next explicitly royal psalms in the Psalter (Pss 18; 20; 21) also revolve around a Torah psalm (Ps 19). This repeated link between *tôrâ* and kingship primes the reader's curiosity: Are *tôrâ* and kingship poems linked elsewhere in the Psalms? There is one more explicitly *tôrâ*-focused psalm in the book (Ps 119), and, perhaps not surprisingly, we discover that it is linked with Psalm 118, where, it is often argued, the king leads the people in an act of antiphonal worship. Why link the Psalter's three Torah psalms with kingship psalms?

The kingship law (Deut 17:14-20) inseparably links *tôrâ* and monarchy, indicating that, above all else, the king is meant to be the paradigmatic Israelite believer by internalizing Yahweh's *tôrâ* and allowing it to influence every aspect of his life and rule. Each of the historical kings of Israel failed in this task to a greater or lesser degree. So, yes, kingship is celebrated in Psalms 2; 18; 20; 21; 118, but their contextual reading directs our thoughts not toward the best examples of kingship (David or Josiah) but rather to the ideal of kingship. This coming king will be the one who finally keeps the kingship law; he will be the ultimate exemplar of *tôrâ* piety lived out in reality.

6. Conclusions.

There are two main implications to be drawn from these observations regarding the psalms and the king: one theological, one practical. First, on a theological level we are pointed toward a messianism in the Psalter that is subtler than is often portrayed. The expansion of the definition of royal psalms by Eaton leads us to a messianic king who is very deeply human, who experiences the same heights of joy and depths of despair as all humanity.

Second, we are presented with the image of the king as exemplar for the people—grounded in the *tôrâ* of Yahweh and entirely dependent on him. The king has such a prominent role in the Psalter because he fulfilled a representative function within the OT theocracy, representing God to the people and the people to God. The juxtaposition of royal and Torah psalms points the reader to the image of an individual rooted in the torah (Ps 1:2-3) and a king dependent upon Yahweh (Ps 2:12). The anonymous individual in Psalm 1 is to be read as the king, and the king in Psalm 2 is to be understood as the unnamed individual. Psalm 1 "democratizes"

the royalty of Psalm 2, but at the same time Psalm 2 adds a royal flavor to the "everyman" inclusiveness of Psalm 1. The figures of king and anonymous believer merge. This ambiguity presents Christian readers with an example to follow. The true king has set an example for all who would follow him, basing his life in the *tôrâ* (Luke 4:16-21) and living his life in dependence upon his Father (John 5:30). Rereading the kingship psalms christologically, Christians see a picture of Jesus the King as their representative and example.

Seeing the significance of kingship in the Psalter gives us a fuller understanding of the humanity of our Messiah and a greater awareness of the piety that should typify our daily lives. The royal nature of the psalms is both obvious and subtle, but the implications of this kingship theme are significant.

See also EDITORIAL CRITICISM; FORM CRITICISM; MESSIAH; ROYAL COURT.

BIBLIOGRAPHY. **J. H. Eaton,** *Kingship and the Psalms* (2nd ed.; SBT 32; London: SCM Press, 1986); **J. A. Grant,** *The King as Exemplar: The Function of Deuteronomy's Kingship Law in the Shaping of the Book of Psalms* (SBLAB 17; Atlanta: Society of Biblical Literature, 2004); idem, "The Psalms and the King," in *Interpreting the Psalms: Issues and Approaches,* ed. P. S. Johnston and D. G. Firth (Leicester: Apollos, 2005) 101-18; **H. Gunkel,** *Introduction to the Psalms: The Genres of the Religious Lyric of Israel* (MLBS; Macon, GA: Mercer University Press, 1998); **J. L. Mays,** *The Lord Reigns: A Theological Handbook to the Psalms* (Louisville: Westminster John Knox, 1994); **J. C. McCann Jr.,** *A Theological Introduction to the Books of Psalms: The Psalms as Torah* (Nashville: Abingdon, 1993); idem, "The Book of Psalms," *NIB* 4.641-1280; **P. D. Miller,** *Interpreting the Psalms* (Philadelphia: Fortress, 1986); idem, "Kingship, Torah Obedience and Prayer," in *Neue Wege der Psalmenforschung,* ed. K. Seybold and E. Zenger (HBS 1; Freiburg: Herder, 1995) 127-42; **G. H. Wilson,** "The Use of Royal Psalms at the 'Seams' of the Hebrew Psalter," *JSOT* 35 (1986) 85-94.

J. A. Grant

KINSHIP. *See* SOCIAL-SCIENTIFIC APPROACHES.

KINSMAN-REDEEMER AND LEVIRATE

These are two Israelite customs by which a relative removes another relative from great difficulty. Their common goal is to repair family wholeness broken by the trouble, and both aim to continue a childless family line on its land through the *marriage of its widow to a relative. But several features distinguish the kinsman-redeemer from the levirate custom: it involves a close relative (e.g., uncle, cousin, other near kin), not a brother, and also it aims to relieve larger economic woes (e.g., mortgaged family land or kin in debt slavery). The limited biblical data denies us clarity as to how Israel understood their interrelationship, notwithstanding their common concern for preserving family lines.

1. The Levirate
2. The Kinsman-Redeemer

1. The Levirate.

This custom (cf. Lat *levir,* "brother-in-law") obligates the oldest living brother to marry his brother's childless widow in order to provide the deceased an heir to continue his family line (Deut 25:5-10; cf. Gen 38). It also authorizes a legal ceremony whereby the widow may shame her brother-in-law in public if he refuses to do so. Both texts accord the custom high importance, but as Weisberg notes, both also contrast male reluctance to comply (probably concern for clear paternity and property rights) with female advocacy (probably concern for widows' security). Both texts paint uncooperative brothers negatively, but neither requires the custom, unless contextually "brother" in Deuteronomy 25 applies the duty to all Israel (Volgger).

1.1. The Book of Ruth. Echoes of the custom occur primarily in the book of *Ruth. It supports the argument by *Naomi that Ruth and Orpah go home because she is too old to birth them sons to marry (Ruth 1:11). It underlies the purpose that *Boaz voices for marriage to Ruth: "to maintain the dead man's name" (Ruth 4:5 NRSV) so that "the name of the dead may not be cut off from his kindred" (Ruth 4:10 NRSV [cf. Deut 25:6]). On the other hand, despite its similarity to levirate terminology (Deut 25:7, 9), the Hebrew word *yĕbāmâ* (Ruth 1:15) is probably the general kinship term "sister-in-law" (cf. the LXX's *synnymphos* ["co-bride"]; Lat *cognata* ["relative"]), since it describes Ruth's relationship to Orpah (i.e., wife of her husband's brother) rather than to Orpah's husband (cf. Heb *yābām* ["brother-in-law"]).

1.2. Psalm 133. The phrase "brothers dwell together" (Ps 133:1) may refer to one of the conditions of the levirate (Deut 25:1): joint tenancy by male siblings on ancestral property. If so, the psalm originally promoted the practice to foster the prosperity and fertility that result only from caring stewardship of land over generations. But this interpretation hinges on reading the reference to oil on Aaron's beard and collar (Ps 133:2) as a later addition (Ames, 904).

2. The Kinsman-Redeemer.

This custom (*gĕʾullâ* ["redemption"]; *gōʾēl* ["kinsman-redeemer"]) involves a circle of close relatives (*gōʾălîm* [Ruth 2:20; cf. 1 Kings 16:11]) beyond the brother-in-law and concerns needs beyond the provision of an heir. Scattered texts afford it only brief glimpses and limited legal instruction. Local practices and ad hoc innovations probably account for the seeming irreconcilable differences between texts.

2.1. Background. Family *law (Lev 25) tasks the *gōʾēl* with restoring family wholeness from its members' financial losses. He buys (or takes) back mortgaged ancestral land (Lev 25:25-28), relatives' houses sold of necessity (Lev 25:29-31), and kin who sell themselves as slaves (Lev 25:47-49). As clan head, he receives restitution payments for deceased members (Num 5:8), and as *gōʾēl haddām* ("avenger of blood"), he avenges the murder of a relative by killing the killer or a member of his clan (Num 35:19; Deut 19:4-7; Josh 20:1-9; cf. 2 Sam 14:11).

2.2. The Book of Ruth. This lovely story is the only narrative context to feature the kinsman-redeemer as a central motif. The narrative is unique in showing Israelite redemption practices in action in a single case and locale. The limits of Israelite written law and reader ignorance of life "back there" best explain the book's uncertain legal background. However, one may still gain a general sense of the rationale behind the proceedings.

2.2.1. The Debut (Ruth 2:20). It is Naomi who first mentions the kinsman-redeemer (*gōʾēl*) custom, calling Boaz "one of [lit., "from"] our kinsman-redeemers" (NIV [Heb *miggōʾălēnû*]. The plural form points to a small circle of close relatives responsible for caring for needy kin. Her comment interprets Boaz's generosity that day as gracious family loyalty and a possible harbinger of further help. His later mention of a kinsman-redeemer nearer than himself (Ruth 3:12) and deference to the man's rights as the closest living relative (Ruth 4:4) presume a continuum of closeness within the circle of redeemers. However, the specific "help" that the women may expect from the *gōʾēl* remains unstated.

2.2.2. Ruth's Marriage Proposal (Ruth 3:9). Ruth's marriage proposal to Boaz makes the second reference to the custom. Naomi secretly dispatches Ruth at night to the threshing floor near Bethlehem to arrange a marriage (Ruth 3:1-5). Ruth is to dress nicely, lie down beside him, and receive his instructions. Naomi's intent may only be that Boaz match Ruth with someone else, but Ruth proposes marriage to him rather than await his instructions (for the "cloak" metaphor, see Ezek 16:8). She grounds her proposal in the fact that Boaz is a *gōʾēl* (Ruth 3:9)—the only biblical example of marriage to a widow based on *gĕʾūllâ*. How should this be explained? Does she appeal to the *gōʾēl* custom as a broad sense of duty to needy close family or as the application of known laws (e.g., Lev 25; Deut 25)? The broad view reads her proposal in light of Naomi's instructions and comment in Ruth 2:20—that is, an appeal either to the spirit of the redeemer concept (Nielsen) or to Boaz's moral sense of duty to family (Bush). The legal-background view cites the mention of the nearer kinsman's prior rights (Ruth 3:12-13) to argue that some legal principle lies behind her appeal (Hubbard). Further, the contrast between the expectation of Boaz's instructions (Ruth 3:4) and Ruth's unexpected proposal to Boaz as a *gōʾēl* (Ruth 3:9) seems significant. It may imply that Ruth's action exceeds Naomi's purpose by seeking a *gōʾēl* marriage versus an ordinary one (and possibly the provision of a son). If so, it would highlight Ruth's initiative as an admirable act of family loyalty toward Naomi *(ḥesed),* as Boaz later says (Ruth 3:10). But it is unlikely that the levirate plays any role here. Redemption terminology rules (root *gʾl,* not *ybm*), and Boaz is not a brother to Elimelech, nor is Ruth his sister-in-law.

2.2.3. Boaz, Naomi's Land and Ruth (Ruth 4:1-12). The next morning at the city gate (Ruth 4:1-2), Boaz informs the other kinsman of Naomi's wish to transfer a "portion" of Elimelech's land (Ruth 4:3). Boaz asks him either to serve as kinsman-redeemer or to waive the right to Boaz, the *gōʾēl* next in line (Ruth 4:4a). The focus on land, not Ruth, surprises the reader, since the story has said nothing about it. Further, here the *gōʾēl* redeems land from the owner's widow

rather than from an outside mortgage holder (Lev 25:25-28). When the closer kinsman accepts the duty (Ruth 4:4b), Boaz introduces a levirate-like requirement: marriage to Ruth to perpetuate the name of her husband (Mahlon, not Elimelech [cf. Ruth 4:10]) on his ancestral land (Ruth 4:5). This marks the lone OT example where *gĕʾūllâ* combines land and widow, but the author offers no explanation for Boaz's stipulation. No matter, for the closer kinsman cedes to Boaz his prior redemption right *(gĕʾūllâ),* explaining that to serve would damage his own inheritance (Ruth 4:6). Boaz formally exercises his new right, acquiring both land and widow (Ruth 4:9-10), and the town affirms the legality of the deal and blesses the couple (Ruth 4:11-12). Behind this simple scene, however, lurk several vexing legal questions.

2.2.3.1. Naomi's "Sale." When does (or did) the sale occur? In other words, is the *gĕʾūllâ* here preemption (i.e., acquisition from a close relative [cf. Jer 32]) or redemption (i.e., reacquisition from a distant relative or nonrelative [cf. Lev 25])? The perfect verb *mākrâ* (lit., "she sold") in Ruth 4:3 might refer to a past sale, but most scholars and recent translations render it in the present (NRSV: "is selling"; NJPS: "must sell"). Though not problem free, this rendering fits the context better than its alternative. Boaz also uses a perfect of the Hebrew verb *qnh* ("buy, acquire") both for what the kinsman or he is to do now (Ruth 4:5) and what he does at the end (Ruth 4:9-10). These "instantaneous perfects" express an action in the present, especially in solemn statements or legal transactions (cf. 2 Sam 19:30). Further, Boaz twice states that the transaction comes "from the hand of Naomi" and not from someone else (Ruth 4:5, 9). Thus, one need not assume (as some scholars do) that Elimelech "sold" the land before going to Moab, or that Naomi did so while there *(contra* Westbrook, 66-67).

Is this really a sale at all? Unlike typical sales (see Jer 32), here Naomi is absent from the scene, and no money changes hands. The payment may occur later off scene, but a better solution is to render the Hebrew *mākrâ* as "she is surrendering possession of" (see Lipiński), and the root *qnh* as "acquire." The OT attests both renderings in similar contexts, and the object "possession" is probably the land's usufruct, not the land itself (Bush). Thus, the narrative treats the transfer of the *gōʾēl* duty to Boaz (Ruth 4:3-

8) and his formal execution of it (Ruth 4:9-10). But what gives Naomi authority to sell the property? Several biblical examples show that women could control ancestral land. *Job gave both his daughters and sons inheritances (Job 42:15), and the law authorizes daughters of families without sons to inherit the family's lands (Num 26:33; 27:1-11; 36:1-12). In 2 Kings 8:1-6 a widow recently returned from foreign soil appeals to the king to regain her land. That he grants her appeal implies that she herself owned the land before she left, that someone had possessed it in her absence, and that neither her absence nor her gender annulled her right of ownership. The specific background of Ruth 4 is less clear (e.g., did Naomi inherit the land from Elimelech, or did it fall to her as his only survivor?), but the story assumes her right to transfer it. It also reports no objection to the idea from the kinsman or the witnesses.

Does Naomi's ownership of land conflict with her apparent poverty? That is, has Boaz maneuvered the other man through misinformation? Against this, one recalls that Naomi arrived just as the harvest began (Ruth 1:22b), so she had not sown the field. Were it fallow, she would have had no crop to harvest, or if someone else had sown it, the community probably would support that person's right to the fruit of that labor. It seems unlikely that Boaz could fool a small town such as Bethlehem with such an untrue claim.

2.2.3.2. Land Plus Widow: Ploy or Principle? What justifies the requirement that land and widow go together (Ruth 4:5), and why does it cause the closer kinsman to withdraw? A recent consensus avers that the levirate probably aims to ensure that the deceased has an heir to inherit his share of land. But Naomi's postmenopausal age (cf. Ruth 1:12) makes a levirate-like marriage impossible, so the kinsman need only exercise preemption of Elimelech's property (or so he thinks!). Two assumptions probably underlie the land/widow linkage in Ruth 4: a belief that land is inalienable (i.e., it must remain in family hands) and a social expectation (or custom) that close family (e.g., a *gōʾēl*) uphold that value (*contra* Kutsch, 371). By acquiring the field, the nearer kinsman does so and also profits financially from the land. His only "loss" might be the support of Naomi until her death. But why does the unexpected introduction of Ruth—a legal substitute for Naomi as her son

Mahlon's widow (Ruth 4:10)—pose a problem for him? His stated reason is that such a marriage would harm his own inheritance (Ruth 4:6). Certainly, unlike Naomi, Ruth is young enough to produce an heir for Mahlon who would eventually claim the family's land. In Ruth 4:5, Beattie and Sasson support this view by reading the Ketib *qānîtî* ("I will buy") rather than the Qere *qānîtā* ("you will acquire"), but that reading has not found general acceptance, presumes a literal purchase, and is interpretively unnecessary. If the couple had other children (a possible but uncertain assumption), the larger family might do harm by forcing him to divide his inheritance among more children (i.e., into smaller parcels).

But if the case concerns acquisition not purchase (see above), financial motives play less of a role. Thus, more likely his hesitation simply hides his surprise or confusion at the new wrinkle, or perhaps his desire not to be bothered. Perhaps he also found marriage to a non-Israelite (note "Ruth the Moabite" [Ruth 4:5]) distasteful. Whatever the case, a consensus acknowl-edges Boaz's cleverness in maneuvering the proceedings to his liking. The sudden switch from Naomi/Elimelech (and potential profits) to Ruth/Mahlon (and levirate and potential problems) soured the man on the idea. Shrewdly, Boaz began with "a portion of Elimelech's property" (Ruth 4:3) and ends up with "everything" belonging to Elimelech and his two sons as well as Ruth (Ruth 4:9-10). The story remembers him for his great *ḥesed* or "family loyalty" (and as the great-grandfather of *David), while in Ruth 4:1 his reluctant kinsman remains nameless (*pělōnî ʾalmōnî* ["Mr. So-and-So"]).

2.2.3.3. The Newborn. Ruth 4:14 is the only text to identify a newborn as a *gōʾēl*. Naomi's female friends praise Yahweh for providing her Obed, whom Israel will honor for raising Naomi's spirits and for caring for her in old age. The once "empty" Naomi (Ruth 1:21) now has a "son" at last (Ruth 4:17). This example extends the sweep of the kinsman-redeemer's the care of needy relatives into the past and the future. Obed not only perpetuates past family members but also provides for Naomi's own future.

2.3. Yahweh as Redeemer. Some poetical books describe Yahweh, protector of the weak and endangered, as a kinsman-redeemer. Proverbs 23:10-11 warns would-be violators of orphans' property rights that Yahweh is their *gōʾēl* (NJPS:

"a mighty Kinsman"), who will "plead their cause *[rîb]* against you" in court (NRSV), and most certainly will win (cf. Deut 19:14; 27:17; Job 24:2; Prov 22:28; Jer 50:34)! In a broader sense, worshipers in Psalm 19:14 (MT 19:15) and Psalm 78:35 affirm him as their "redeemer" *(gō'ēl)* and "rock" *(sûr)*, their ever reliable protector in danger. Combining *g'l* ("redeem, rescue") and *rîb* ("plead a [legal] cause"), Lamentations 3:58-59 seems to echo the motif of Yahweh as *gō'ēl* (i.e., legal defender). He "took up the cause" *(rîb)* and "saved [the] life" *(g'l)* of an innocent victim of "the wrong" that Yahweh himself witnessed (cf. Ps 72:14 [the king]; 119:154 [Yahweh]). In Psalm 74:2 the language of the "the congregation . . . you acquired *[qnh]*" parallels "you redeemed *[g'l]* as the tribe of your inheritance *[nahălâ]*." The recall of key verbs from Ruth 4 seems to apply the metaphor of Yahweh the redeemer in a new way: at the exodus Yahweh "acquired" through "redemption" not an individual relative but rather a whole tribe as his "inheritance" [njps: "your very own tribe"] for *worship on Mount *Zion (cf. Ex 15:13). Yahweh is to defend not only the poor and needy (Ps 74:21) but also his own cause *(rîb* [Ps 74:22])—his own name defamed by his enemies who destroyed Zion (Ps 74:22; cf. Ps 74:10, 18). Another psalmist pleads with Yahweh to "redeem" him (Ps 69:18) from the public humiliation and scorn of a false accusation (Ps 69:4, 7-12).

2.4. Job 19:25. In this well-known text Job confidently affirms, "I know that my Redeemer *[gō'ălî]* lives, that at the last he will stand upon the earth" (NRSV). Since the context concerns a dispute with God over Job's innocence, "my Redeemer" clearly invokes the kinsman-redeemer motif. Job claims that there is someone who, like a close relative, will finally ("at the end") defend him ("stand" here means "to stand/speak as a witness in court"). However, the identity of that someone and whether the text locates the intervention before or after Job's death remain matters of dispute. One common view identifies God as Job's redeemer and says that his vindication follows his resurrection. That Yahweh bears the title "redeemer" elsewhere commends this view, especially since "living" is a prominent attribute of God (e.g., Ps 42:2; Is 37:17). Indeed, some argue that in view of Job's mortality, a "living redeemer" can refer only to God. But "living" is a common expression not limited to God (e.g., Gen 8:21; Deut 31:27), and the idea of an

earthly resurrection is rare in the OT (only Is 26:19; Dan 12:1-3). Also, elsewhere Job clearly affirms the finality of death (Job 7:9; 10:21) and denies the possibility of resurrection (Job 14:12).

An alternative view interprets the text to indicate that God will intervene, spare Job from death, and restore him to his former health and prosperity. Job 19 would offer his blunt plea: "Vindicate me now; otherwise, don't bother" (Zink, 152). This view certainly fits the book's ending (Job 42:7-17) and requires one to read Job 19:26 as severe *suffering rather than death. Job's hope of emerging the better for his ordeal ("I shall come out like gold" [Job 23:10 NRSV]) might imply vindication in this life, but that Job's suffering and outcry intensify in subsequent chapters casts doubt on this view. Another recent suggestion avers that God vindicates Job after death, but it also presumes a questionable disembodied awareness of that vindication by Job in death and has not won a following. Finally, recent scholars argue for a *gō'ēl* other than God as more consistent with the book's contents and the *gō'ēl* metaphor. Job consistently pictures God as his main adversary (e.g., Job 13:3; 19:6; 31:35). Thus, in their view the book makes better sense if the redeemer defends Job against God rather than if God is both Job's prosecutor and defense attorney. The assumption is that only a third party can properly defend Job against God at the heavenly court.

But who is this nondivine redeemer? N. C. Habel identifies him as a heavenly defense attorney—the heavenly "witness" *('ēd)* who affirms Job's innocence (Job 16:19; cf. Job 33:23; Zech 3:1-5) and counterpart to "the Accuser" *(haśśāṭān [see Satan])* of the prologue (e.g., Job 1:6; 2:1). The OT often portrays God amid a council of heavenly beings, including "the Accuser" and a defender of God's people (perhaps Michael [Dan 10:13, 21]), but elsewhere Job seems actually to deny such a possibility in his case (Job 5:1; 9:33). D. J. A. Clines also equates the *gō'ēl* with the heavenly "witness" *('ēd)* and "advocate" *(śāhēd)* but contextually interprets them as personifications of Job's outcry (Job 16:18-21) (so Ringgren). If so, rather than a person or heavenly being, the redeemer in Job 19 would be a *personification: Job's protestation of innocence directed toward God even in death. Without friends and besieged by God (Job 19:6, 13-19), Job becomes his own *gō'ēl* (the metaphor permits self-redemption), his words comprising his only defense. This view requires one to read Job 19:26-27 as a wish ("If only . . .) rather than an affirmation.

Whatever the case, one thing remains clear: in Job 19:25 Job affirms his confidence in a *gōʾēl* figure who will finally step in to establish his innocence in a decisive lawsuit. Ironically, in the end God does indeed vindicate Job, although no recognizable echoes of the *gōʾēl* motif sound in the book's closing scene (Job 42:7-17).

See also HONOR AND SHAME; RUTH 1: BOOK OF.

BIBLIOGRAPHY. **F. R. Ames,** "Levirate Marriage," *NIDOTTE* 4.902-5; **D. R. G. Beattie,** "The Book of Ruth as Evidence for Israelite Legal Practice," *VT* 24 (1974) 251-67; idem, "Redemption in Ruth and Related Matters: A Response to Jack M. Sasson," *JSOT* 5 (1978a) 65-58; idem, "Ruth III," *JSOT* 5 (1978b) 39-48; **F. W. Bush,** *Ruth, Esther* (WBC 9; Nashville: Thomas Nelson, 1996); **D. J. A. Clines,** *Job 1-20* (WBC 17; Dallas: Word, 1989); **E. W. Davies,** "Inheritance Rights and the Hebrew Levirate Marriage: Part 1," *VT* 31 (1981a) 138-44; idem, "Inheritance Rights and the Hebrew Levirate Marriage: Part 2," *VT* 31 (1981b) 257-68; idem, "Ruth IV 5 and the Duties of the Gōʾēl," *VT* 33 (1983) 231-34; **N. C. Habel,** *The Book of Job* (OTL; Philadelphia: Westminster, 1985); **V. P. Hamilton,** "יבם," *NIDOTTE* 2.392-93; **R. L. Hubbard Jr.,** *The Book of Ruth* (NICOT; Grand Rapids: Eerdmans, 1988); idem, "The *gōʾēl* in Ancient Israel: The Theology of an Israelite Institution," *BBR* 1 (1991) 3-19; idem, "Redemption," *NIDBT* 716-20; idem, "גאל," *NIDOTTE* 1.789-94; **J. E. Hartley,** *Job* (NICOT; Grand Rapids: Eerdmans, 1988); **R. Kessler,** "'Ich weiss, dass mein Erlöser lebet': Sozialgeschichtlicher Hintergrund und theologische Bedeutung der Löser-Vorstellung in Hiob 19,25," *ZTK* 89 (1992) 139-58; **M E. Kutsch,** "יבם," *TDOT* 5.367-73; **A. LaCocque,** *Ruth* (CC; Minneapolis: Fortress, 2004); **E. Lipiński** "מכר," *TDOT* 8.291-96; **J. A. Loader,** "Of Barley, Bulls, and Levirate," in *Studies in Deuteronomy: In Honour of C. J. Labuschagne on the Occasion of His 65th Birthday,* ed. F. García Martínez et al. (VTSup 53; Leiden: E. J. Brill, 1994) 123-38; **J. Morgenstern,** "The Book of the Covenant, Part II," *HUCA* 7 (1930) 159-258; **K. Nielsen,** *Ruth* (OTL; Louisville: Westminster John Knox, 1997); **H. Ringgren,** "גאל," *TDOT* 2.350-55; **J. M. Sasson,** *Ruth: A New Translation with a Philological Commentary and a Formalist-Folklorist Interpretation* (JHNES; Baltimore: Johns Hopkins University Press, 1979); **T. Thompson and D. Thompson,** "Some Legal Problems in the Book of Ruth," *VT* 18 (1968) 79-99; **D. Volgger,** "Dtn 25:5-10: Per Gesetz zur Ehe gezwungen?" *BN* 114-115 (2002) 173-88; **D. E. Weisberg,** "The Widow of Our Discontent: Levirate Marriage in the Bible and Ancient Israel," *JSOT* 28 (2004) 403-29; **R. Westbrook,** *Property and Family in Israelite Law* (JSOTSup 113; Sheffield: JSOT Press, 1991) 57-68, 69-89; **J. K. Zink,** "Impatient Job: An Interpretation of Job 19:25-27," *JBL* 84 (1965) 147-52. R. L. Hubbard Jr.

KORAH, SONS OF. *See* ASAPH AND SONS OF KORAH.

L

LAMENT, PSALMS OF

A lament psalm (also called a psalm of complaint or petition or prayer) is a set poetic prayer aimed to present a need to God so that he may resolve it and further his praise. The corporate laments draw from a variety of national historical traditions and probably were sung at the central sanctuary in times of national crisis. The individual laments likely were intoned in more private, domestic services, and they reflect a simpler piety encapsulated in the phrase "my God." As model prayers, they provide instruction for contemporary spirituality and theology.

1. Genre and Function
2. Individual Laments
3. Corporate Laments: Literary Motifs and Function
4. Traditions of the Individual and Corporate Laments
5. Social Settings of Individual and Corporate Laments
6. Significance for Spirituality and Theology
7. Limits of Lament Psalms and the Biblical Trajectory for Their Reinterpretation

1. Genre and Function.

1.1. What Is a Lament Psalm, and What Is Its Purpose? The psalms of lament form a genre, arguably the most appropriate category by which psalms should be studied (as distinct from topical, chronological or authorial categories). A genre is a shared pattern of communication, usually shaped in particular social contexts, that signals certain expectations of how a text or speech is to be interpreted and used.

The most recurrent and fundamental literary motifs of the lament psalm are lament and petition. Together they make clear that the central aim of this genre is to appeal to God for some-

thing. They endeavor to present the psalmist's case or argument as to why God should intervene. The concluding vows of praise testify that obtaining something from God is not to be viewed as an end in itself. Another aim of lament psalms is to have something to praise God about. Praise should have the last word.

Although each psalm is unique in its own right, the form-critical analysis below should make clear that the individual laments generally follow an established literary pattern (*see* Form Criticism). They are not the free expressions of individual poets. We should also note that the persons and circumstances reflected in these psalms (who? what? where? when?) are generic or nonspecific. The speaking "I" or "we" is not identified, nor is the "they," the enemies. Because these poems make a rich use of *imagery, it is difficult if not impossible to sort out what was originally literal and what was metaphorical. Psalm 35, for example, employs images drawn from various spheres and experiences in life: the battlefield (Ps 35:1-3), agriculture (Ps 35:5), slippery paths (Ps 35:6) and stumbling (Ps 35:15), hunting (Ps 35:7-8), social oppression (Ps 35:10, 20) and personal betrayal (Ps 35:11-16), the law court (Ps 35:11, 23-24), sickness (Ps 35:13) and *animals (Ps 35:17). When the petitioner in Psalm 13 prays, "Give light to my eyes" (Ps 13:3), did this originally denote a physical need, a psychological-emotional one or a spiritual one? Rather than being frustrated by this lack of specificity, we should recognize that this open-ended character of psalms is part of what has made them so popular among God's people throughout the ages. This multivalent language contrasts with the lament by *David in 2 Samuel, which names Saul, Jonathan, the Philistines and the mountains of Gilboa (2 Sam 1:17-27). The individual laments, on the other hand, appear to have been composed to suit recurring, typical occasions—generic times of need—not the particular circumstances of a particular individual in a moment in history. Lament psalms thus present themselves as set prayers written for worshipers to use for typical distresses. Thus, as stated in this article's opening sentence, we may define a lament psalm as a set poetic prayer aimed to present a need to God so that he may resolve it and further his praise.

To use an analogy with the Episcopalian/Anglican *Book of Common Prayer* or *Book of Alternative Services:* while the *hymns and the "liturgies of temple entry" (see 2.1 below) found in the book of *Psalms belong to the regular liturgies in which all worshipers would participate (such as "Morning Prayer" or "The Holy Eucharist" or "The Great Vigil of Easter"), the individual and corporate laments would belong among the "Occasional Prayers," found at the back of the prayer book. The former would be sung at the regular services of the religious calendar; the latter would be sung at special occasions of need.

These observations have important implications. First, understanding lament psalms as set prayers written for worshipers to use for typical distresses helps us moderns come to terms with the many references to enemies and the dire situations portrayed in them. The psalms tend to speak in extremes. Since these model prayers are to be applicable to a wide variety of persons in a wide variety of circumstances, their language must be embracing rather than limiting. Thus, if psalms are to include the full spectrum of human experience, they must speak in the extremes. The Song of Hannah (1 Sam 2:1-10) uses language that is militaristic, universal and even cosmic, yet the specific occasion on which it is sung is simply the birth of a child. "My enemies" (1 Sam 2:1) applies here simply to the rival wife, not to life-threatening militants. In Psalm 127 the "arrows" that people may draw from their quiver to use against "their enemies in the gate" are simply the number of their children (Ps 127:5). Conflict in the psalms, even if military language is used, need not point to physical confrontation. References to enemies may simply be metaphorical imagery for the general notion of threat, whether external danger or psychological dread. A benefit of this line of interpretation is that the psalms become more applicable. One need not actually be on the brink of disaster to

pray a psalm that "cries from the depths." The lament psalms use images that are applicable to a wide range of situations of distress.

In ancient Greek and modern Western cultures people are accustomed to refer to general, abstract notions. The ancient biblical poets, however, typically employed concrete images. Instead of speaking of evil, they spoke more tangibly of "the wicked (people)." To convey the notion of threat they spoke of "enemies." Thus, looking at these poems together provides a wider context for interpreting each psalm individually. It becomes clear that often they do not report the particular social circumstances that occasioned them (as in newspaper reportage), but they paint in familiar strokes scenes that evoke the general psychological and spiritual predicaments that worshipers may face (as in poetic verse). Because the psalms are highly allusive, the circumstances that may have originally occasioned them or the recurring situations for which they were originally composed are highly elusive.

Second, this interpretation helps us to understand how lament psalms relate to personal experience. We should not view a lament psalm as a composition that a psalmist wrote in direct response to his own personal need. Rather, lament psalms are models of prayer composed for the generic needs of God's people. In this respect, a lament psalm is not a mirror reflecting the composer's experience; rather, it provides worshipers a framework to interpret their own experiences and to guide their expressions of prayer. A psalm's development did not necessarily follow the author's changing mood, but it was clearly intended to lead the worshiper's experience. A lament psalm should be read not autobiographically but rather liturgically. We must be cautious, for example, when referring to a "change of mood" in some lament psalms. Instead of supposing, "The psalmist now feels like praising God," we should instead think, "The psalm leads worshipers to praise God."

The psalms were hammered out over generations of living with God. We moderns should not impose upon them our assumptions that individual, private experience is to be valued more highly than the experience of God reflected in a corporate identity. In fact, they are what generations of the believing community have found to be appropriate and effective ways of speaking to God. The worshiper who recites a psalm speaks not with a singular voice but rather with the voice of generations of God's people. This should give greater confidence when speaking to God. In addition, we are invited to read our own personal experience against the wider experience of the community and so see that our experiences are shared by others.

Similarly, the self-descriptions of the speaker as "righteous" or as a "servant" do not reflect the boasting of the composer; rather, they are character profiles to be adopted by worshipers if they wish a psalm to have its desired effect. Though it is not explicit, psalms do have these educative and behavior-modifying functions. In other words, if worshipers want the Lord to answer a given lament psalm, they will need to conform to its claims.

If the individual psalms of lament were composed for the generic needs of God's people, what are we to make of the phrase "a psalm of David" in the psalm superscriptions (*see* Psalms 4: Titles)? This question is particularly acute in those psalms whose superscriptions contain historical references (Pss 3; 7 [?]; 18; 30 [?]; 34; 51; 52; 54; 56; 57; 59; 60; 63; 142), most of which are individual laments. In short, the phrases "a psalm of David" (28x) and "of David, a psalm" (8x) are ambiguous in English and even more so in Hebrew. They probably denoted a Davidic or royal collection of psalms in the preexilic period, as distinct from the Levitical collections of "Asaph" and the "sons of Korah" (*see* Asaph and Sons of Korah). These phrases may have served to honor the chief patron of *worship at the Jerusalem sanctuary and as a kind of imprimatur or certification authorizing the psalms for official, public use.

Later, in the exilic and early postexilic periods, *scribes correlated these "Davidic psalms" with other sacred Scriptures, especially 1-2 Samuel, and added these historical cross-references, thus promoting the reading of these psalms as Davidic prayers. Support for this reconstruction is found in 1 Chronicles. The personal names and the technical musical terms mentioned in the psalm superscriptions are paralleled elsewhere, primarily in 1 Chronicles (esp. 1 Chron 15—16), a postexilic composition. For example, the singers Heman, Asaph and Ethan, mentioned in 1 Chronicles 15:19, are named in the superscriptions of Psalms 50; 73—83; 88; 89. And the musical terms mentioned in 1 Chronicles 15:20-21, "alamoth" (*ʿălāmôt*) and

"sheminith" (*šĕmînît*), appear in the superscripts of Psalms 6; 12; 46. As 1 Chronicles presents David as an exemplar of piety (in contrast to the more historical portrayal of David in 1-2 Samuel) and the one who instituted the singing of psalms (1 Chron 16:7), so these "historical" superscriptions encourage reading these psalms as models of Davidic prayer in the midst of real crises. "David" in 1 Chronicles and the psalm superscriptions thus becomes a symbol of the godly individual before Yahweh. Although it certainly is possible that David authored some psalms, they were preserved not to give us insights into the historical David but rather to show us how to speak to God. (For further discussion on the fit of psalms having historical titles with the events of David narrated in 2 Samuel and elsewhere, see Broyles 1999, 26-31; Childs.)

1.2. Closer Scrutiny of the Genre: Lament, Complaint, Petition or Prayer? "Psalms of lament" is the label most often applied to this genre because the lament motif usually constitutes the psalm's largest section. "Lament" is often used interchangeably with "complaint." Some scholars, such as E. Gerstenberger, label them "psalms of petition," arguing that the goal of such psalms is not simply to bemoan a hardship but also to obtain something from God, a desire that is expressed most directly in the petition section. Both designations, however, suffer the drawback of labeling the genre in terms of one of its constituent motifs, thus exaggerating the importance of the motif and obscuring the value of the others (see the table in 2.1. below). In other words, they are simply subcategories or parts of the larger whole. These labels may also be misleading. A lament may be thought of as mourning an unchangeable crisis, as at a funeral. Labeling the genre as "petition" may give the impression that these psalms are simply a listing of requests to God, which they are not. In addition, the formal petition may not be the clearest expression of a psalm's goal; in some lament psalms the petition is completely absent (Ps 77), and in others the appeal is expressed most clearly by other motifs, such as the lament itself (Pss 88; 89). Perhaps the most appropriate label for the genre is "psalms of prayer" (*tĕpillâ*). This is the term used by the psalms themselves (see Pss 17; 86; 102, and note their respective superscriptions). In the terminology of the Hebrew psalms, "prayer" is the literary form distinguished from "praise" *(těhillâ),* which would include the form-critical categories of "hymn" and "thanksgiving" *(tôdâ).* "Prayer psalm" also has the advantage that, like the label "praise psalm," it makes clear who is the addressee (laments and petitions can be addressed to anyone). Nevertheless, for the sake of continuity and clarity, this article will remain with the more traditional label of "psalms of lament."

Careful observation of the lament psalms reveals a distinction between lament and complaint. Nearly a third of the lament psalms contain a lament against God, most of them corporate laments (on this topic, see Broyles 1989). These "God-laments" complain about God's disposition—his wrath, rejecting, forgetting, hiding his face ("Why, Yahweh, do you reject my soul? Why do you hide your face from me?" [Ps 88:14]). Or they complain about his (non)intervention, whether he is actively hostile ("You have exalted the right hand of his adversaries; you have given all his enemies cause for rejoicing" [Ps 89:42) or passively indifferent ("Why, Yahweh, do you stand afar off; why do you hide in times of trouble?" [Ps 10:1]). The lament psalms containing a God-lament differ not only by the addition of this motif but also by the very character of their appeal. In the lament psalms that lack a God-lament, God is a third party to the distress, and so he is approached as helper and savior. Where the praise of God occurs in these psalms, it appears in its own right as praise. These psalms we may call "psalms of plea." But in the God-lament psalms God is held partly responsible for the distress, and so they also challenge him to restore his favor. Where the praise of God occurs in these psalms, it stands in stark contrast to the lamentable present and thus serves to remind him of the praiseworthy acts that he should renew in the present. We should thus reserve the label "psalms of complaint" for these psalms and not apply it to the lament psalms in general. We must also be careful to observe that the psalms do not make such accusations about God flippantly, since they are reserved for occasions where the distress is either unduly prolonged (e.g., "How long?") or is something near death.

2. Individual Laments.

2.1. Literary Motifs. Lament psalms of the individual generally contain the following literary motifs (see Table 1). H. Gunkel (46) considers Psalm 13 to be "the model of a 'lament of the in-

Table 1. Individual Lament

1. *Address and introductory petition*	"O Yahweh" (Ps 13:1a), "Be gracious to me and hear my prayer" (Ps 4:1c)
2. *Lament*	
a. *I*	"How long must *I* put anxieties in my soul?" (Ps 13:2a)
b. *you (God)*	"How long . . . ? Will *you* forget me forever?" (Ps 13:1a-b)
c. *they (foe)*	"How long will *my enemy* be exalted over me?" (Ps 13:2b)
3. *Confession of trust*	"But I in your loyalty have trusted" (Ps 13:5a)
4. *Petition*	
a. *for favor*	"Look, answer me" (Ps 13:3a)
b. *for intervention*	"Give light to my eyes" (Ps 13:3b)
c. *motive*	"lest my enemy say, 'I have prevailed over him'" (Ps 13:4a)
5. *Vow of praise*	"I will sing to Yahweh" (Ps 13:6)
6. *Thanksgiving in anticipation*	"for he has acted on my behalf" (Ps 13:6)

dividual' . . . in which the individual components of the genre step forth most clearly."

(1) Usually the address is simply God's name ("Yahweh" or "God") or an epithet or title ("my God"). The introductory petition is of a very general nature, aimed at getting God's attention.

(2) The lament may be expressed with three possible grammatical subjects: the speaker, who laments the *suffering; God, who is charged with negligence or hostile action; the enemies, who either cause or exacerbate the affliction. The distress is usually described in such a way as to evoke a response from Yahweh. Generally, the "I-lament" should evoke his pity, the "God-lament" his sense of obligation to help, and the "foe-lament" his anger. Among the psalms of the individual, the I-lament is prominent in those psalms that may be associated with sickness (esp. Pss 38; 41; 88). Mention is also made of emotional turmoil. In the rest, the foe-lament dominates, since the enemies appear to be the primary cause of distress. The enemies' actions usually consist of verbal assaults, either taunting or framing the psalmist with false accusations, or of actual physical assaults, where they seek the psalmist's life. The God-laments tend to be brief and in the form of a rhetorical question (as noted in Ps 13 above). Psalm 88 is a notable exception; seven of its verses are a God-lament in a declarative form.

(3) The confession of trust may predicate an attribute or action about God ("God is/ will . . . "), or it may simply declare the speaker's own trust in God ("I trust/hope . . . "), as in Psalm 31:3, 5a: "For you are my rock and my stronghold; for your name's sake you will lead me and guide me. . . . Into your hand I commit my spirit." The former is very similar to the praise of God expressed in hymnic psalms (e.g., Ps 71:19). At least twenty-seven of the roughly thirty-nine individual laments contain this motif. A few psalms consist solely of this motif in an expanded form and thus are called "psalms of trust" (Pss 11; 16; 23; 62; 63; 91).

(4) The petitions usually first seek God's attention and favor and then request his intervention, whether to save the speaker and/or punish the enemies. The motives, or "motifs to motivate God to intervene," supplement the petitions with reasons and arguments as to why God should act on the speaker's behalf.

(5) In the vow of praise the speaker promises to praise God, presumably at a public offering of a thanksgiving sacrifice, subsequent to the deliv-erance. It is more regularly a part of the individual laments than of corporate laments. According to C. Westermann (1980, 43; 1981, 59-61, 75-78), in the Babylonian psalms the vow of praise "almost always" concludes individual laments but never corporate laments. A vow of praise is evident in twenty-three of the roughly thirty-nine individual laments (Pss 7; 13; 22; 27; 35; 40 = 70 (jussive); 42—43 [counted as one psalm]; 54; 56; 57; 59; 61; 64; 69; 71; 86; 109; 140; 142).

(6) The psalm may close with thanksgiving, which is sung in anticipation of an answer.

A few individual laments contain an assurance of being heard, which acknowledges that God has received the request and thus that deliverance is forthcoming (e.g., Ps 6:8-10). Many scholars believe that after the worshiper had expressed lament and petition, he awaited God's reply from a priestly-prophetic "oracle of salvation." These words were not included perhaps because psalms normally contain only words for the worshiper, and it is also possible that it was considered inappropriate to prescribe words for divine oracles. Traces of "salvation oracles" are found in Psalm 12:5, which compares with Isaiah 33:10-13 (for the pioneering work on this, see Begrich). Other lament psalms contain exhortations (e.g., Ps 27:14; 31:23-24; 55:22), which distinctly point to a congregational setting for their performance. These are comparable to the testimonies offered in thanksgiving (tôdâ) psalms.

The interpreter must be sensitive to the distinctive use of each of these motifs in context. Labeling is not enough. The function of motifs may vary according to context. For example, in terms of their grammatical form, the confessions of trust are very similar to praise: a positive action is predicated of God. But we must discern if the principal function of a confession of trust is simply to affirm the praise of God in the midst of distress (so Ps 54:4) or to remind Yahweh that he has an obligation toward the psalmist (so Ps 22:9-10 in the context of Ps 22:1-10).

In view of the criteria noted above, the following psalms may be classified as individual laments: Psalms 3; 4; 6; 7; 13; 17; 22; 25; 27; 31; 35; 38; 39; 40 (at least vv. 11-17); 41; 42—43; 51; 54; 55; 56; 57; 59; 61; 64; 69; 70; 71; 77; 86; 88; 102; 109; 139; 140; 141; 142; 143. The Psalms of Ascent are a postexilic prayerbook unto themselves, and these generally shorter psalms do not conform as clearly to the standard form-critical models. Among these, Psalm 120 and Psalm 130 can be read as individual laments. According to this reckoning, there are thirty-nine individual laments (counting Pss 42—43 as one psalm). Some commentators consider Psalm 41 to be an individual thanksgiving. Some would add Psalm 63 among the individual laments, but its lack of petition indicates that it shares more in common with the psalms of trust (the expression of longing for God in the opening verses is best characterized as a confession of trust, not a lament). Psalm 139 also has been regarded as an individual thanksgiving and also as a mixture containing wisdom and/or hymnic elements.

Most commentators regard Psalms 5; 26; 28 as individual laments, and some regard Psalms 36; 52 similarly. However, none of these psalms contains a formal lament. They do have clauses where opponents are the grammatical subject, but they do not threaten the speaker directly, nor is there any reference to victims. In fact, they are not identified as the "enemy" (ʾôyēb); instead they are described in the terminology typical of the "wicked" (rāšāʿ), focusing especially on their deceitful speech. They are opponents not because of their direct threat to the speaker but rather on the basis of their moral and religious valuation. Moreover, each of these psalms makes explicit mention of the temple and implies that the speaker is present there, in contrast to the individual laments listed above. They also contain hints that the speaking "I" is not a lone individual in a special need; rather, he is one who speaks on behalf of the general class of worshipers in the regular liturgy. And these psalms contain indications of judgment where there is a parting of the ways: the "righteous," who may enter the temple, and the "wicked," who may not and are to be punished. They actually echo Psalms 15 and 24, which are liturgies of temple entry. In brief, they appear to give voice to a liturgist who represents the congregation and who responds to the priestly temple instruction as found in Psalms 15; 24. In other words, they were composed not for lone individuals in special circumstances of need (e.g., false accusation) but rather for a congregation in the regular liturgies of the temple. The speaking "I" is probably a liturgist speaking on behalf of the individual worshipers (see Broyles 2004).

In some I-lament psalms there is a fine line between the individual and corporate body. It is not clear whether they were originally intended for lone individuals or for an individual who speaks on behalf of fellow worshipers. Some use "we" language (Ps 4:6; 40:3, 5; 59:11). Others contain exhortations (Ps 27:14; 31:23-24; 64:10 [possibly]) or testimony/instruction probably addressed to a group in attendance (Ps 25:8-10, 12-15; cf. Ps 25:22). And some individual laments reflect corporate concerns (Pss 57; 61), such as social unrest (Pss 59; 64).

Laments are not limited to the book of Psalms. Passages such as the following are comparable to individual laments: Jeremiah's so-called confessions (Jer 11:18-20; 12:1-4; 15:15-18; 17:14-18; 18:19-23; 20:7-12 [also note Jer 8:18—9:1; 10:23-25]); Lamentations 3; Habakkuk 1:2-4; 1:12—2:1; the speeches of *Job (for an analysis of prose laments embedded in narrative, see Miller, 337-57).

2.2. Subgroups. The "psalms of the accused" (esp. Pss 7; 17) contain images of one who is falsely accused, seeks "refuge" or asylum, and implores God's vindication. Elsewhere in the OT one thinks of the "cities of refuge" (Ex 21:12-14; Num 35:9-34; Deut 4:41-43; 19:1-13; Josh 20:1-9). Deuteronomy 17:8-13 speaks of legal cases too difficult for the local judges (cf. Deut 16:18). They are to be brought to the temple, so the priests and the judge in office can render the verdict. According to 1 Kings 8:31-32, a person who sins against a neighbor is to take up an oath (perhaps one like Ps 7:3-5) before the temple altar. Yahweh is then implored to pronounce judgment. Yahweh is "to declare wicked/guilty the wicked/guilty" and "bring his way upon his head," and he is "to declare righteous/innocent the righteous/innocent" and "render to him according to his righteousness."

There are also "psalms of sickness." According to K. Seybold, there are those laments with "certain reference to sickness" (Pss 38; 41; 88), those with "probable reference" (Pss 39; 69; 102) and those with "uncertain reference" (Pss 6; 13; 51). In some cases the sickness is perceived by opponents as judgment for sin, and so false accusation and alienation exacerbate the suffering.

In the traditions of the early church the "penitential psalms" include Psalms 6; 32 (a thanksgiving psalm); 38; 51; 102; 130; 143. Upon closer inspection, however, we discover that only Psalms 32; 51; 130 give concerted attention to sin and forgiveness as their chief issue. Psalm

51 is unrivaled in its expression of penitence and the need for inner transformation rather than simply a transformation of circumstances (e.g., enemies, sickness). On the other hand, Psalms 6 and 102 make no explicit mention of sin. Most of Psalm 38 concerns sickness and enemies, and most of Psalm 143 concerns being near death and under enemy attack.

A derivative from the individual lament psalm is the "psalm of trust" or "psalm of confidence," which is simply an isolation and expansion on the motif of the "confession of trust" (*see* Confidence, Psalms of). The most notable example is Psalm 23.

3. Corporate Laments: Literary Motifs and Function.

The motifs found in the corporate lament psalms are similar to those found in the individual laments (see Table 2).

(1) The opening address to God may expand to include several divine titles or epithets (as here in Ps 80:1: "the one who leads Joseph like a flock, the one enthroned on the cherubim").

(2) Generally speaking, the lament sections are longer and more developed in the corporate laments. The "we-laments" are comparatively infrequent, and when they do appear, they usually describe humiliation (e.g., Ps 79:4). Their foe-laments describe the respective distresses: conspiracy to wipe out God's people (Ps 83), the destruction of Jerusalem and its temple (Pss 74; 79), murderous social violence (Pss 9—10) or agricultural dearth (Pss 85; 126). The dominant lament is against God. The God-laments are more frequent among the corporate psalms: nine of the roughly thirty-nine individual laments have them, while ten of the roughly twenty-three corporate laments have them. Each of these contains a verse or two of a God-lament in a question form similar to that found in the individual psalms, but half of them also contain extended sections of God-laments in a declarative form (e.g., "But you have rejected and refused; you have become furious against your anointed. You have repudiated the covenant of your servant; you have defiled his crown to the ground. You have broken down all his walls; you have made his fortifications a ruin" [Ps 89:38-40]). In several corporate psalms that contain a "reference to past saving deeds" (see immediately below) the lament is patterned after this language of praise. In other words, the lament is phrased as a reversal of the praise. In Psalms 9—10; 44; 89 extended sections of praise are recited, along with extended laments that mirror in reverse what is hymned in the praise sections. Psalm 9 recites the praise of God who rescues the oppressed and punishes the wicked, and Psalm 10 shows that for each point of praise there is a cor-

Table 2. Corporate Lament

1. *Address and introductory petition*	"Shepherd of Israel, give ear" (Ps 80:1-3)
2. *Lament*	
a. *we*	"We have been a taunt to our neighbors" (Ps 79:4)
b. *you (God)*	"How long will you burn against the prayer of your people?" (Ps 80:4-6a, 12)
c. *they (foe)*	"and our enemies mock us" (Ps 80:6b, 13)
3. *Reference to past saving deeds*	"A vine from Egypt you uprooted; you drove out nations and planted it" (Ps 80:8-11)
4. *Petition*	
a. *for favor*	"Turn, look from heaven and see!" (Ps 80:14a)
b. *for intervention*	"Attend to this vine" (Ps 80:14b, 17)
c. *motive*	"the shoot that your right hand has planted" (Ps 80:15)
5. *Vow of Praise*	"and on your name we will call" (Ps 80:18)

responding lament that describes the wicked abusing the oppressed with no apparent intervention from Yahweh. Psalm 44 recalls how Yahweh waged war on behalf of Israel's forebears and then laments how Yahweh now simply hands them over to their enemies. Psalm 89 begins singing of Yahweh's kingship and of his promises to exalt the Davidic dynasty but then laments how Yahweh has exalted the king's enemies.

(3) Confessions of trust are virtually absent in the corporate laments. In their place they often recite a reference to past saving deeds, which recalls God's deliverance from an analogous distress known from Israel's history (e.g., Ps 44:1-3). These are drawn from the corporate traditions concerning creation, the ancestors, the exodus, Yahweh, war, *Zion and the temple. When viewed in isolation, these references to past saving deeds are very similar to hymnic praises: God is the grammatical subject, and he performs a saving action. But their juxtaposition with the lament reveals a function very different from that of praise. In Psalm 44, for example, the reference to God's earlier saving deeds (Ps 44:1-3) brings to light the anomaly of God's present destructive action toward his people (Ps 44:9-16, 24-25). The reference to past saving deeds thus functions to remind Yahweh of what he should be doing presently, not to praise him for past actions. These references to earlier saving deeds differ from confessions of trust in the individual laments not only in form and content but also in function. In most cases the confessions of trust function in the psalm to affirm the relationship between Yahweh and the psalmist, but the references to earlier saving deeds function to draw out the contrast between Yahweh's past saving action and his present negligent or hostile action. They serve as historical precedents, arguing that God should now deliver as he had for past generations.

(4) The "hear" type of petition is frequent in individual laments but appears only once in corporate laments (Ps 80:1). Petitions among the latter psalms focus on intervention.

(5) The vow of praise does not stand out as an independent motif as clearly as in the individual lament psalms. Among the corporate laments, only Psalm 79 has the normal form of the vow (Ps 79:13). In other cases God's future praise is echoed in a petition ("Let the afflicted and needy praise your name" [Ps 74:21]) or lies within a result clause attached to a petition ("Re-

vive us, so that we may call on your name" [Ps 80:18]; "Save us, Yahweh our God, and gather us from the nations, to give thanks to your holy name" [Ps 106:47]). (It is interesting to note that virtually all the *"thanksgiving psalms" in the Psalter are for individuals. It is possible that corporate thanksgiving was expressed through the regular hymns, or that for some unknown reason corporate thanksgivings did not make it into the 150 canonical psalms.)

In view of the foregoing criteria, the following psalms may be classified as corporate laments: Psalms 9—10; 12; 14; 44; 53; 58; 60; 67; 74; 79; 80; 82; 83; 85; 89 (also a royal psalm); 90; 94; 106; 108; 137; 144 (with royal adaptations). As noted above, the Psalms of Ascents form a unique collection within book 5 of the Psalter. Among these, Psalms 123; 126 can be read as corporate laments. According to this reckoning, there are twenty-three corporate laments (counting Pss 9—10 as one psalm), thus bringing the total number of lament psalms to sixty-two—by far the largest category of psalms. Some commentators consider Psalms 9—10 as an individual lament, others as an individual thanksgiving. Some commentators interpret Psalms 14 (= Ps 53); 58; 82 also as prophetic psalms. Psalm 67 has been read as a prayer for blessing or as a corporate thanksgiving, depending whether its verbs are seen to express statements (Hebrew imperfects) or wishes (Hebrew jussives).

"I" and "we" language in the psalms does not always clearly indicate whether a psalm originated out of individual or corporate usage. "I" could denote a representative liturgist, speaking on behalf of a congregation (see Mowinckel, chap. 7). And as I will argue later (see 4.3 below), some individual laments appear to have been adopted by the (post)exilic community to voice their corporate lament (see Lam 3). On the other hand, "we" language may not point to corporate usage if the individual speaker is simply voicing corporate solidarity with the people of God.

Outside the book of Psalms, passages such as the following are comparable to corporate laments: Isaiah 59:4-15; Jeremiah 14:2-9; Lamentations 5.

4. Traditions of the Individual and Corporate Laments.

A tradition is any belief or custom passed from

generation to generation. In the OT these beliefs and customs are sacred, normative and generally associated with particular persons, events, places, institutions, symbols or rituals. Little attention has been given to the distinct forms of tradition to which the laments of the individual and the laments of the community appeal (except Albertz).

4.1. Corporate Traditions. The corporate laments draw from a variety of national traditions. First, these psalms appeal to historical traditions concerning the premonarchic period: the exodus (Ps 80:8-11) and Yahweh as warrior during the conquest (Ps 44:1-3) and the judges periods (Ps 83:9-12). In an oracle contained in Psalm 60 Yahweh exults as a victorious warrior, while the opening lament portrays him as now, ironically, waging war against his own people. Psalm 106 rehearses Israel's history from the period of Egyptian slavery to the judges. Occasionally, appeal is made to the "covenant," probably the Sinai covenant (Ps 44:17; 74:20; 106:45). Second, there are echoes of traditions from the early monarchic period: Yahweh's promise of a Davidic dynasty and empire (Ps 89:3-4, 19-37) and his choice of Zion as the location for his temple (Ps 9:11-14; 74:2; 79:1). Third, in the postexilic period, Psalm 85:1-3 appeals to the restoration from exile as an expression of Yahweh's forgiveness. Fourth, the ancient tradition of divine cosmic kingship, the God of the skies, forms the basis for Yahweh's appointment of Davidic kingship in Psalm 89 (Ps 89:1-2, 5-18). In Psalm 74 the reference to God as the "king" who vanquished "the sea" and "Leviathan" (Ps 74:12-17) initially appears to make little sense in a psalm that elsewhere focuses on the destruction of the temple—that is, until we recognize the larger tradition to which the psalm appeals. In this ancient Near Eastern tradition of divine kingship, after the God of the skies subdues the chaotic seas, the construction of his palace-temple is the climactic event. Psalm 74 thus implicitly appeals to God as the cosmic king to restore his earthly temple, his symbol of world order.

4.2. Individual Traditions. With a few possible exceptions that will be discussed below, the individual laments do not draw from the above traditions. They echo a much simpler piety, which may be summarized in their favorite divine title, "my God." Yahweh is hailed as the personal, guardian God, who answers when called upon. Of the fifty-five occurrences of "my God"

(ʾĕlōhay and ʾēlî) in the Psalter, at least forty are clearly used in immediate connection with the psalmist calling, trusting or praising. The worshiper's implicit obligations are to "trust" (e.g., Ps 31:14), to "call" upon God when in distress, and to "praise" God once delivered (e.g., Ps 30:11-12). The divine obligation that surfaces repeatedly is to answer with deliverance (e.g., Ps 13:3; 22:2; 30:2; 38:15). Claims to having a special relationship with "my God" are not unique to Israel. But in the ancient Near East "my God" (i.e., my personal guardian deity) was simply one deity among many and certainly not the chief god (see, e.g., Prayer of Kantuzilis [*ANET,* 400-401] and Man and His God [*ANET,* 589-91]). In this light, we see that the claim to Yahweh/Lord as "my God" is remarkable. The personal, guardian deity of the worshiper is none other than Yahweh, the God of Israel, the Most High, the One incomparable to all spiritual beings.

The significance of this phrase is spelled out most clearly in Psalm 22, where we see the title closely associated with the psalmist's calling and expectation that "my God" should answer (Ps 22:1-2). The next eight verses make evident that the obligations upon worshipers of "my God" are "to trust" and, once delivered, "to praise." The intimacy of the relationship is most evident in Psalm 22:9-10, where Yahweh is described as "the one who drew me forth from the womb, the one who caused me to trust when upon my mother's breast. . . . Since my mother's womb you have been my God."

It is in times of extreme distress that one may best discern the bedrock of one's faith. In these laments that bedrock appears to be this "my God" theology, whereby the worshiper lives to trust, call upon and praise Yahweh. Yahweh is then expected to answer when called upon and especially to preserve his worshiper from premature death. In these laments there is little reference to specifically ethical obligations. This is not to say that *ethics had no role in individual religion, but rather that when one is at the edge of death, the key obligation that was essential to affirm was the relationship with "my God." (On the references to the corporate tradition of "covenant" in Ps 25:10, 14, see 7 below.)

4.3. The Combination of Individual and Corporate Traditions in the Exilic and Postexilic Periods. Surprisingly, the lament psalms show little integration of individual and national traditions.

Psalm 22:3-5 is a notable exception (on Pss 22; 51; 69; 77; 102, see immediately below.) We should expect the individual's experience of crisis and salvation to be related to that of the nation, as we see elsewhere in the OT. According to Deuteronomy 26:1-11, for example, when the farmer was to offer up his firstfruits, his confession consisted of the exodus and conquest traditions. But when the lament psalms of the individual argue for Yahweh to intervene, they do not appeal to the privileges of covenant or of being a citizen of Zion. Those lamenting oppression from enemies do not call on Yahweh to do to them as he did to the Egyptians. Perhaps most surprising is that the individual laments make no mention of Zion or Jerusalem or appeal to the special privileges of praying toward this holy site (see esp. 1 Kings 8:29-30, 35). A few reflect a particular attachment to God's dwelling place (without specifying its location) but give no clear indication that they were actually sung there (Ps 3:4; 27:4-6; probably Ps 57:1; 64:4). Otherwise, allusion to God's dwelling is simply a memory mentioned in the lament (Ps 42:4; 55:14) or a future hope mentioned in the vow of praise (Ps 35:18; 43:3-4; 54:6).

Corporate traditions are found in the individual laments of Psalms 22; 51; 69; 77; 102, but in each case they are found in a discrete section and show a particular affinity to the exilic or early postexilic periods. Both Psalm 51 and Psalm 69 reflect individual distress throughout until their closing verses, where attention turns specifically to Zion and its restoration (Ps 51:18-19; 69:34-36). Psalm 102:1-11 reads like a traditional individual lament, which is resumed in Psalm 102:23-24. But the intervening verses (Ps 102:12-22) affirm that Yahweh "will arise and have compassion on Zion," which now lies in "dust." Nations will fear him "when Yahweh has built Zion." Like these three psalms, Psalm 22 is a lengthy individual lament to which are attached praises or promises that Yahweh's attention to the needy will result in worship from Israel and the nations in generations to come (see Broyles 1999). Psalm 77 also opens with the traditional language of lament, except that it refers to God in the third person, thus sounding more like a brooding meditation than a prayer. God is not addressed directly until the second half, where he is praised for his saving deeds in the exodus. As the psalm develops in its final form, its central issue appears to be the contrast between God's mighty actions in the past and his apparent absence in the present. Although there is nothing in the psalm that ties it to a specific historical period, its appropriateness for the exile is evident. Because the corporate traditions in these individual laments appear to be later insertions, it is likely that earlier preexilic individual laments were used as vehicles of expression for the communities of the exilic period—for the exiles in Babylon and for those who remained in Palestine. Lamentations 3 is a clear example of this phenomenon. Using the literary form of individual lament, it laments the destruction of Jerusalem (see Lamentations 1: Book of).

5. Social Settings of Individual and Corporate Laments.

Most psalms, especially the psalms of temple entry, the hymns, the thanksgivings and the royal psalms (see Kingship Psalms), are replete with liturgical and ritual allusions. They frequently contain plural imperatives addressing a congregation or choir and references to musical accompaniment, to the Jerusalem temple and Mount Zion, and to sacrifices and processions. By contrast, the lament psalms, both individual and corporate, have comparatively few allusions to a congregation, *music or ritual.

The original setting of the corporate lament psalm probably was special crisis services called at the chief sanctuary of the nation in Jerusalem. The prayer by *Solomon at the temple's dedication provides that on occasions of battle defeat or drought, the people may "pray and implore favor . . . in this house" (1 Kings 8:33-36). Jehoshaphat's prayer, on the occasion of foreign invasion, actually invokes Solomon's words (2 Chron 20:5, 9). The prophet Joel, on the occasion of agricultural disasters, calls for the people to "lament" at "a solemn assembly" at "the house of the LORD" (Joel 1:13-16; 2:15-17, whose last verse actually echoes the lament of Ps 79:10). Even when the temple lay in ruins during the exile, there were scheduled services of lamenting and fasting (Zech 7:3-5; 8:18-23; cf. Jer 41:5).

Since the lament psalms of the individual lack allusions to the temple and its rituals and symbols, which is not the norm among the psalms, we probably should not assume that there were any ties to the Jerusalem temple. Given that some individual laments use the language of extreme sickness (Pss 38; 41; 88 [see Seybold]), we should not presume that the sick person must travel all the way to Jerusalem in order to have a lament psalm prayed on his or her behalf. Both E. Gerstenberger and R. Albertz have argued convincingly, both from within the Hebrew Bible itself and from ancient Near Eastern analogies, that the individual laments may have originally been performed in more private ceremonies overseen by a ritual expert, such as a Levite or a clan elder. Given our earlier observations that individual and corporate laments draw from two distinct streams of tradition that are not joined until the exilic period, it is likely that the individual laments were composed outside of official temple circles and probably reflect the piety of the common people, whose trust was in Yahweh "my God." The Deuteronomic centralization of worship under Josiah in 622 BC may have been the factor that later brought the individual laments to Jerusalem and led to their inclusion into corporate worship. Then, after the demise of the temple and its liturgical services in the exile, these two streams of psalmody were merged into new prayers (as in Pss 22; 51; 69; 77; 102 [see 4.3 above]).

6. Significance for Spirituality and Theology.

Lament psalms can be numbered among the most disturbing passages of the Bible, until one actually encounters crisis, and then they can become the most comforting and helpful.

The psalms cannot be regarded as the "word of God" in the same way as the prophetic word, whereby God speaks *to* his people. But in them, Israel hammered out the most appropriate and effective ways of speaking to God. And they have been regarded by generations of God's people as speech that is appropriate to God and thus a fair reflection of who he is. In this respect, they are the "word of God" *for* God's people, as they are models for praying to him. They are thus a legitimate source for constructing an exemplary spirituality for God's people and a theology about God. God is mirrored in these human words. Whereas the hymnic psalms present a theology "from above" (e.g., God's majestic attributes), the lament psalms present a theology "from below"—that is, from a perspective of human need.

To unpack the spirituality of the lament psalms, we should respect not only their contents but also their literary form and function—that is, their genre. In this way, rather than selecting what features seem interesting and help-

ful from our perspective, we should remain truer to the emphases and priorities of the lament psalms themselves.

Their first literary motif is the address of God. Initially, there might seem to be little worthy of comment here because it is obvious that prayer, to be prayer, must be addressed to God. But this fixed convention within the lament genre should make clear that worshipers need to become intentional that in the act of praying they do nothing less than to seek an audience with the Most High. The frequency of the opening address, such as "O Lord," and the introductory petition, such as "hear" *(šĕmaʿ)* (or "give ear" *[haʾăzînâ],* or "give attention" *[haqšîbâ]),* indicates that the words that follow in the prayer are no mere meditation or soliloquy; they are meant to leave an impression on God in heaven. It is an obvious point but also one that makes all the difference: worshipers must consciously fix their minds on the one to whom they address their prayers.

The motif that is most foreign to modern Christian prayer is also the longest: the lament itself. Prayers today usually consist primarily of requests or petitions. But the lament psalms were no mere "business agenda" or "shopping list" telling God what to do. The laments testify to the value of simply telling one's story to God. God is not portrayed simply as "Mr. Fixit"; he is the supreme listener. The image of God reflected in the psalms is one who is interested not only in healing but also in pain. Remarkably, they testify that God can be moved.

One must also be struck by their frankness, especially when complaint is addressed to God himself. The laments are unabashedly told from the worshipers' perspectives. They are a reflection of their perceptions and feelings, not necessarily a synthesis of others' viewpoints. They do not attempt to qualify their rhetoric or consider mitigating circumstances or other explanations. Thus, for example, this classic lament reflects a feeling of God-forsakenness: "My God, my God, why have you forsaken me? Why are you far from my cry for help, the words of my groaning? My God, I cry by day, but you do not answer" (Ps 22:1-2). But a later claim in the psalm shows that this lament is not, in fact, an accurate reflection and evaluation of the state of affairs when viewed in retrospect: "For he has not despised or disdained the affliction of the afflicted; and he has not hidden his face from him and when he cried to him for help he heard" (Ps 22:23). Also, the mere fact that the psalm prays to God at all mitigates the opening lament. These observations have obvious pastoral benefit. The psalms allow for a free vent to one's feelings. Remarkably, believers are not required first to screen them with a methodical "reality check" or to censor expressions not "theologically correct" before voicing them to God. In effect, God allows our feelings to be validated, even if in the final analysis they miss the mark. Reflected in these lament expressions is a deity who is not easily shaken or offended or who needs to be pacified. In other words, this is a God whom we can trust and toward whom worshipers can be vulnerable. The openness and frankness of the laments presuppose a relationship that is direct and personal. Even the complaint "Why do you hide your face?" (Ps 44:24) exhibits the high expectation of a "face-to-face" relationship with God. This invites forthrightness and candor, not averted eyes and politeness for its own sake.

These laments also exhibit a realistic faith, one that is bluntly honest with the realities of life but also takes the promises of God seriously. The faith reflected here does not try to deny reality (mind over matter) or to rationalize the dilemma away, nor does it reject God's word as ineffectual. It recognizes the gap between God's promises and human experience and believes that this dissonance should be presented to God for him to resolve.

In view of the foregoing observations, we must also be struck that these laments were not regarded as aberrations from the faith; they were part of the set prayers for the people of God. Questions and claims of betrayal were not relegated to private counseling sessions with an elder or priest but rather remained a part of authorized prayer services. Lament psalms, and individual laments in particular, compose the largest category of psalms, implying that distress and lament are not the exception to the experience of God's people. Regrettably, lament has been all but censored from most Christian worship services. By always stressing the positive, such worship alienates those suffering pain and depression. And shying away from lament produces unnecessary guilt and, ultimately, a superficial faith.

For us to come to terms with lament language, it is best that we understand its aim as both expressive and evocative, not merely infor-mational. As words given to humans to speak in the midst of pain and distress, they seek to be true to the human perspective in the relationship. In other words, they display genuine feelings whether or not they are rational or theologically correct. They allow for the expression of emotions, not just facts. Since psalms are speech *from* humans *to* God, what is appropriate is determined not solely by who God is but also by who humans are, with all their limitations and weaknesses. These laments are thus true, not in the sense of teaching accurate theological information at every point but rather in the sense of being a true reflection of the divine-human encounter. They are thus the most explicit biblical testimony of the need for authenticity. (In the context of the human heart, the Hebrew term 'ĕmet is more accurately translated "authenticity" than "truth" in the sense of moral perfection: the "doer of righteousness" is defined as the "one who speaks with authenticity in his heart" [Ps 15:2]; and in the context of a confession of sin Ps 51:6 affirms that "authenticity you desire in the inner parts.")

In addition, lament language is evocative. It uses rhetoric to elicit a response of help from God, not necessarily to convey or obtain information. Lamenters asking, "Why do you hide your face?" would not be satisfied with reasons—they want God to stop hiding his face. And lamenters asking, "How long will you hide your face?" (Ps 13:1) would not be satisfied with a period of time—they are complaining that it has gone on long enough. It is not only the rhetorical questions that are evocative. A statement such as "You sold your people for a pittance, gaining nothing from their sale" (Ps 44:12) does not convey theological information but rather seeks to prod God to respond with horror at such an interpretation of events. This lament is similar to that of Moses when he intercedes for the people during the incident of the golden calf: "Why should the Egyptians say, 'With evil intent he brought them out to kill them in the mountains and to finish them off from upon the face of the land'?" (Ex 32:12). The petition and lament of Psalm 44:23 ("Awake! Why do you sleep, O LORD? Rouse yourself! Do not reject forever") is not theologically correct when viewed against the claim of Psalm 121:4 ("Behold, the keeper of Israel does not slumber nor sleep"). But later editors of the Psalter did not go back to censor or soften Psalm 44:23. It remains as legitimate rhetoric that speaks from the appearance of the circumstances.

The presence of petitions in lament psalms shows that lament was not lamentation over unchangeable circumstances, as at a funeral. Lament psalms do invite worshipers to vent their frustrations and pour out their feelings, but there comes a time to seek a way out. The petition motif indicates that these psalms seek change, and that they are based ultimately on promise, not doubt. They acknowledge that something is wrong and affirm that God can put it right. Some readers have characterized the praises as psalms of faith and the laments as psalms of doubt. On the contrary, the lament psalms exhibit faith under the most contrary circumstances.

The motives supporting the petitions and the overall aim of these lament psalms indicate that they "argue" with God. They offer reasons why God should intervene on the speaker's behalf. This is most evident in those corporate laments that set God's promises, echoed in reference to God's earlier saving deeds, side by side with a lament describing the disaster (e.g., Pss 9—10; 44; 89). In this sense, the composing psalmists were theological lawyers arguing the people's case before the Most High. These psalms do not evidence a passive faith that simply accepts circumstances as "God's will"; rather, they show that the promises of God should be taken seriously and affirm that they should become manifest. Assumed here is that God can be moved not only emotionally, as expressed in the laments, but also by reason and by argument. In Psalm 6, for example, the appeal is threefold. First, it pits Yahweh's "loyalty" (ḥesed) against his "wrath." Second, it seeks to move him to pity and to heal by focusing on the intensity (e.g., "my bones shake in horror") and duration ("how long?") of the distress. Third, it seeks rescue from death so that God's worshiper and God's praise may continue.

The confessions of trust and the vows of praise make apparent that the ultimate goal of the lament psalms is the praise of God. Worshipers may vent their feelings and seek to get something from God, but they must also seek to give something back to him.

Finally, we may observe that lament is part of what helps faith grow. This may not be self-evident within the Psalter alone, since all that we have are the prayers themselves. We do not know their final outcome. Although not a formal lament psalm, Psalm 73 testifies to a deeper faith (esp. Ps 73:23-26) following the expression of lament (Ps 73:12-14). But the phenomenon of lament is prevalent elsewhere in the OT. It is evident in Mosaic *law/Torah, the Prophets and the Wisdom literature. Moses (Ex 3:1—4:17; 5:22—6:8; 32:1—34:35), Habakkuk and Job (keeping in mind God's final assessment of Job's speeches in Job 42:7-8) engaged in lament. And remarkably, their words represent some of the most profound breakthroughs in OT faith. Indeed, the plot development around these figures implies that God discloses some of his deepest revelations of himself in response to the frank language of lament (see Westermann 1974).

Several theological implications have already been noted above in connection with the spirituality of the lament psalms. We should also recognize, perhaps most importantly, that these psalms portray Yahweh as deliverer/savior and refuge. Such a proposition is hardly remarkable, except that it implies further that hardships and threats are more the norm to the believer's life, not the exception. We should not presume that God is a guardian who spares his people from all encounters with difficulties and setbacks. The vow of praise that usually concludes lament psalms shows that praise is to be based on deliverance from distress. This notion is confirmed by the flip side of the individual lament psalm—the *thanksgiving of the individual (e.g., Pss 30; 116), which largely consists of a recitation of the earlier lament.

The conception of God as deliverer also impinges on the notion of God's sovereignty. In the "psalms of plea" (i.e., lament psalms without a God-lament) no attempt is made to trace the distress back to God. As savior, he is third party to the distress; he is not portrayed as the controller of all events. Only in the more extreme "psalms of complaint" are questions raised about God's role in the distress, whether that of indifference or hostility (and, surprisingly, rarely that of corrective discipline). In this connection, we should also recognize that the lament psalms presuppose that God can be moved and persuaded to intervene where he might otherwise not do so. These observations reveal remarkable divine condescension, an attribute often overlooked in theological discussions of divine sovereignty. God has the power and right to assert his sovereignty, but the lament psalms testify that he also chooses to condescend to his creatures. In a positive vein, he gives an audience to our prayers. In a vein that is positive but also potentially negative, he grants considerable autonomy or freedom to his creatures, even to the extent that they can become "enemies" and "the wicked," who are the primary causes of distress in the psalms. Circumstances are not a telltale indication of God's posture toward his people. The laments clearly attest that life is not always fair.

As noted above, however, the longest component of the lament psalm—the lament itself—testifies to God as the sympathetic listener. He thereby becomes a partner in our suffering. This divine empathy in some respects prefigures the incarnation, whereby God saves his people first by sharing in their predicament. The lament psalms profoundly disclose the character of God and his way of achieving salvation for his people.

In addition, by looking outside of the book of Psalms, we see that Yahweh not only listens but also answers. In Isaiah 40—55, for example, we hear echoes of laments. In the "trial speeches against Israel" Yahweh explains that the people's lamentable condition is a deserved, deliberate judgment on their sin (Ps 44:10-11 and Is 42:22, 24; Ps 44:12-13 and Is 50:1). And in the "proclamations of salvation" Yahweh responds to their laments with a promise of salvation (Ps 44:12-13 and Is 52:3, 5; Ps 44:24 and Is 49:14; Ps 74:3-8; 79:1, 7 and Is 49:17, 19). By comparing Scripture with Scripture, we clearly perceive that Yahweh is a responsive deity. The many laments and complaints in the psalms, which have no answer there, are answered in the Prophets. He is one who provides reasonable answers to complaints (as in the trial speeches), and he is one who promises hope (as in the proclamations of salvation), lest his people despair.

7. Limits of Lament Psalms and the Biblical Trajectory for Their Reinterpretation.

Few books of the Bible are cherished more deeply than Psalms, especially for how it gives voice to our feelings about God and the experiences that we face. Yet, we must admit that the psalms have their own limitations, especially when we consider God's progressive revelation that extends beyond this OT book. The main roots of psalmody lie in the preexilic period of Israel/Judah's monarchy, where evil was identified primarily in the "enemies" and the "wicked," and the solution was encapsulated in petitions such as "Deliver me," "Crush them," "May they be ashamed." Militaristic images dominate, not only for the worshipers and their situations, but they are also applied to God as warrior (see Warfare Imagery).

It is in God's judgment of the Babylonian exile and thereafter that Israel came to realize more fully that evil lies *among* the people of God. The Prophets had made clear that the human dilemma lies largely within; that is, the problems and tragedies that the people experience are, in part, consequences of their own attitudes and behaviors. Psalm 106, a corporate lament, closes with a postexilic petition: "Save us, Yahweh our God, and gather us from the nations" (Ps 106:47). This concluding verse (Ps 106:48 is actually the doxology closing off book 4 of the Psalter) rounds off a recital of Israel's history of rebellion that begins with this confession of sin: "We have sinned with our forebears; we have committed iniquity; we have acted wickedly" (Ps 106:6). Similarly, Psalm 79, a corporate lament over the decimation of Jerusalem, offers a rare petition that acknowledges "iniquities" among the people of God (Ps 79:8). In Psalm 103:10 and Psalm 130:3-4, both postexilic (see Broyles 1999), the speakers own their "iniquities." Similarly, Psalm 25 confesses "sins" as part of the human condition (Ps 25:7, 11, 18). Its reference to "covenant" (Ps 25:10, 14) is unique among individual laments, but its *acrostic structure and its attention to instruction (Ps 25:4-5, 8-9, 12) and other motifs of the wisdom tradition imply its relatively late date as a literary composition (see Broyles 1999; Craigie).

The final series of lament psalms in book 5, which consists primarily of postexilic psalmody, follows the same trajectory. These psalms recognize evil within the human heart, and some are distinguished by a reference to God's "Spirit" (Ps 139:7; 143:10; also significantly Ps 106:33 MT). Psalm 139, with its lengthy reflections on Yahweh's searching, pursuit and craftsmanship of the individual worshiper, closes with an acknowledgment that the worshiper may possess "disturbing thoughts" and a "hurtful way" within (Ps 139:23-24). Psalm 141 reflects the awareness that a worshiper's heart may be tempted to evil (Ps 141:3-5). Here we also see that the temple symbols of "incense" and "evening sacrifice" are spiritualized, so to speak, as metaphors of prayer and the lifting of hands. Psalm 143:2, in fact, speaks of sin in universal terms: "Do not enter into judgment with your servant, for no one living is righteous before you."

The later psalmody of Psalm 144, a corporate and royal lament, invites us to reinterpret earlier psalmody. Virtually the entirety of Psalm 144:1-11 is drawn from formulas found in earlier psalms, especially Psalm 18. In its original, pre-exilic context of the Davidic monarchy the militaristic imagery of Psalm 18 should be interpreted literally. But Psalm 144 (especially Ps 144:12-15) shows strong affinity to the postexilic period, when the province of Judah had no Davidic king or army under the Persian Empire. Thus, the militaristic language is reinterpreted and reapplied figuratively to point to the aggressive resolve that God's people must maintain against the forces that threaten their security.

Psalm 51, an individual lament, can be read as a "Davidic" prayer against the backdrop of 2 Samuel 11—12, but its main petition section is remarkably unique in the Psalter and shows its strongest affinities to the postexilic penitential prayer found in Isaiah 63:7—64:12 and to the exilic "new covenant" passages of Ezekiel 36:24-32; Jeremiah 24:7; 31:31-34 (contrition of heart is also exceptional among later psalms and the third section of Isaiah: Ps 51:17; 147:3; Is 57:15; 61:1; 66:2). Psalm 51 is unrivaled as a confession of sin, with the inner conscience instructed by God and in its interest in inner transformation rather than a transformation of circumstances (such as sickness or enemies).

It is in these passages that Israel squarely encounters sin and the need for inner transformation. The penitence reflected in the postexilic prayers of Psalm 106; Isaiah 63:7—64:11; Nehemiah 9 contrast sharply with the protests raised in the preexilic laments of Psalms 44 and 89. These later passages also raise expectations about a more immediate encounter with God, particularly through the agency of his "Holy Spirit" (Ps 51:11; 143:10; Is 63:10-11, 14; Ezek 36:27). Such revelations about the Holy Spirit, the universal reality of human sin—among both "the righteous" and "the wicked"—and the possibility of inner transformation are, of course, consummated in the NT. Personal transformation thus becomes a possibility not only for the people of God but also for the "enemies" (Mt 5:44).

See also CULT, WORSHIP: PSALMS; FORM CRITICISM; IMPRECATION; IMPRISONMENT IMAGERY; LAMENTATIONS 1: BOOK OF; SALVATION AND DELIVERANCE IMAGERY; SUFFERING; THANKSGIVING, PSALMS OF; THEODICY.

BIBLIOGRAPHY. **A. A. Aejmelaeus,** *The Traditional Prayer in the Psalms* (BZAW 167; Berlin: de Gruyter, 1986); **R. Albertz,** *Persönliche Frömmigkeit und offizielle Religion: Religionsinterner Pluralismus in Israel und Babylon* (CThM 9; Stuttgart: Calwer, 1978) 23-49; **J. Begrich,** "Das Priesterliche Heilsorakel," *ZAW* 52 (1934) 81-92; **C. C. Broyles,** *The Conflict of Faith and Experience: A Form-Critical and Theological Study of Selected Lament Psalms* (JSOTSup 52; Sheffield: JSOT Press, 1989); idem, *Psalms* (NIBC 11; Peabody, MA: Hendrickson, 1999); idem, "Psalms Concerning the Liturgies of Temple Entry," in *The Book of Psalms: Composition and Reception,* ed. P. W. Flint and P. D. Miller Jr. (VTSup 99; Leiden: E. J. Brill, 2004) 248-87; **W. Brueggemann,** "From Hurt to Joy, from Death to Life," *Int* 28 (1974) 3-19; idem, "The Costly Loss of Lament," *JSOT* 36 (1986) 57-71; **B. S. Childs,** "Psalm Titles and Midrashic Exegesis," *JSS* 16 (1971) 137-50; **P. C. Craigie,** *Psalms 1-50* (WBC 19; Waco, TX: Word, 1983); **E. S. Gerstenberger,** *Der bittende Mensch: Bittritual und Klagelied des Einzelnen im Alten Testament* (WMANT 51; Neukirchen-Vluyn: Neukirchener Verlag, 1980); idem, *Psalms: Part 1, with an Introduction to Cultic Poetry* (FOTL 14; Grand Rapids: Eerdmans, 1988); idem, *Psalms: Part 2; and Lamentations* (FOTL 15; Grand Rapids: Eerdmans, 2001); **H. Gunkel,** *Einleitung in die Psalmen,* completed by J. Begrich (Göttingen: Vandenhoeck & Ruprecht, 1933); **W. W. Hallo,** "Lamentations and Prayers in Sumer and Akkad," in *Civilizations of the Ancient Near East,* ed. J. M. Sasson (4 vols.; Peabody, MA: Hendrickson, 1995) 3.1871-82; **O. Keel,** *Feinde und Gottesleugner: Studium zum Image der Widersacher in den Individualpsalmen* (SBM 7; Stuttgart: Katholisches Bibelwerk, 1969); idem, *The Symbolism of the Biblical World: Ancient Near Eastern Iconography and the Book of Psalms* (London: SPCK; New York: Seabury, 1978) 61-109; **H.-J. Kraus,** *Theology of the Psalms* (Minneapolis: Augsburg, 1986); **P. D. Miller,** *They Cried to the Lord: The Form and Theology of Biblical Prayer* (Minneapolis: Fortress, 1994); **S. Mowinckel,** *The Psalms in Israel's Worship* (2 vols.; Oxford: Blackwell, 1962); **K. Seybold,** *Das Gebet des Kranken im Alten Testament* (BWANT 99; Stuttgart: Kohlhammer, 1973); **C. Westermann,** "The Role of Lament in the Theology of the Old Testament," *Int* 28 (1974) 20-39; idem, *The Psalms: Structure, Content and*

Message (Minneapolis: Augsburg, 1980); idem, *Praise and Lament in the Psalms* (Edinburgh: T & T Clark, 1981); **E. Zenger,** *A God of Vengeance? Understanding the Psalms of Divine Wrath* (Louisville: Westminster/John Knox, 1996).

C. C. Broyles

LAMENTATIONS 1: BOOK OF

The book of Lamentations offers a window into the struggle of the people of God in the wake of the fall of Jerusalem and demise of the kingdom of Judah. The book presents a series of poems that express the grief of the community using language, imagery, forms and theology in line with Hebrew traditions of mourning and *suffering. The struggle expressed in these poems is communicated through contrasting voices: female and male, individual and corporate, bitter and penitent, suppliant and prophetic. The book attempts through the *acrostic style in Lamentations 1—4 to articulate exhaustively the pain of the fall of Jerusalem and provides through the elaborate and copious third poem a way forward through a penitential response to Yahweh's grace. In the end, however, these goals are frustrated by the endurance of suffering, which in the final pericope leads to the abandonment of the acrostic pattern and to the erratic swings between confidence in Yahweh's sovereignty and uncertainty over Yahweh's grace.

1. Authorship and History
2. Genre and Setting
3. Literary Features and Structure
4. Content of Each Poem
5. Theological Traditions and Themes
6. New Testament

1. Authorship and History.

1.1. Authorship. In contrast to the Hebrew Jewish canonical traditions, which placed Lamentations among the Ketubim (Writings) and, as the scribal tradition developed, ultimately among the five *Megillot (scrolls) to be read at the major festivals (*Ruth, *Song of Songs, *Ecclesiastes, Lamentations, *Esther), the Greek Jewish canonical traditions placed Lamentations between Jeremiah and Ezekiel—that is, among the Prophets. This association with the prophets is probably related to the unique superscription that prefaces the book in the Greek tradition, which clearly links the poems to the period immediately after the *destruction of

Jerusalem and identifies Jeremiah as the one responsible: "And it was after Israel had gone into exile and Jerusalem had been laid waste, that Jeremiah sat weeping and composed this lament concerning Jerusalem, saying. . . . "

This connection to Jeremiah may have been suggested by the Chronicler's note in 2 Chronicles 35:25 that Jeremiah composed laments for Josiah, but this note says nothing about the laments related to the fall of Jerusalem. Literary connections have often been identified between Lamentations and Jeremiah (cf. Lam 2:14 with Jer 5:31; Lam 2:22 with Jer 6:25; Lam 3:14 with Jer 20:7; Lam 3:15, 19 with Jer 9:14; 23:15; Lam 3:48-51 with Jer 14:17; Lam 3:53 with Jer 38:6; Lam 4:17 with Jer 2:36), suggesting to some that Jeremiah authored the book. Many have questioned this conclusion, noting that the perspective and ideology of some of the sections of Lamentations stand in tension with the message of a prophet who consistently predicted and justified God's punishment of Judah (cf. Lam 4:17-20 with Jer 2:18; 37:5-10; Lam 1:10 with Jer 26:4-6).

Probably the greatest challenge to Jeremianic authorship for Lamentations is found in the dominant structuring device throughout the book: the acrostic. Similar to Psalms 9—10 and Psalm 119, four of the five chapters in Lamentations are written as an acrostic, which means that each verse (Lam 1—2; 4), or series of verses (Lam 3), begins with a successive letter of the Hebrew alphabet (twenty-two letters). Lamentations 5 contains twenty-two verses but is not written in acrostic. The order of the alphabet in these poems, however, is not identical. Lamentations 1 contains the traditional order of the Hebrew alphabet, where the sixteenth and seventeenth letters are ordered ʿayin/pê. In contrast, Lamentations 2—4 contains the order pê/ʿayin. Evidence from ancient abecedaries reveals that both arrangements of the alphabet were acceptable in Israel, but it is difficult to imagine a single person using two different orders of something as basic as an alphabet. This suggests that that there is not a single genius behind these compositions, but rather that they represent poems used in a common liturgical setting over a period of time.

1.2. Date. This, however, does not mean that the book is unrelated to the prophet Jeremiah and the period in which he lived. Despite the assertion of some (e.g., Provan 1990, 130-43; 1991,

11-12) that the book cannot be set accurately into a particular historical context, most scholars agree that the book reflects the conditions of the final years of the kingdom of Judah in the sixth century BC. In this period Judah experienced the destruction of its city and temple, the exile of its king and upper class, and the massacre of its population. Although the vivid poetry in Lamentations may merely reflect the genius of an imaginative poet and probably shows that these poems were composed by trained liturgists, there is no reason to deny that this vividness arose from the personal observation of the poet(s) or that liturgists could compose authentic expressions of pain for the community (*contra* Westermann, 100-101). F. W. Dobbs-Allsopp (1998) places Lamentations in the period of 586-520 BC based on linguistic evidence as well as intertextual connections to Isaiah 40—55. Additionally, some discern within the book a voice that echoes the voice of Jeremiah or at least the book that bears his name (Lee; Boda 2003), evidence that suggests that the connection of this book to the prophet Jeremiah in the Greek tradition may be legitimate.

Although most scholars place these compositions in the period immediately after the fall of the kingdom of Judah in 587/6 BC (see Westermann, 54-55, 104-5), there has been disagreement over the chronological order of the individual poems that now comprise Lamentations. For instance, S. B. Gurewicz (19-23) argued for the order Lamentations 3, 2, 4, 1, 5; R. Gordis (126-27) for the order Lamentations 2/4, 3, 1/5; and R. Brandscheidt for the order Lamentations 2, 1, 5, 4, 3. Many have argued that Lamentations 5 is the latest of the compositions (see Lee) because of its employment of temporal references such as "forever" *(nēṣaḥ)* and "so long" *(lĕʾōrek yāmîm),* but such evidence is not that helpful because expressions such as these are not only stereotypical in liturgical compositions (see Ps 9:19; 10:11; 23:6; 44:24; 93:5) but also relative to the composer's perspective. Additionally, the reference to the "sins of the ancestors" in Lamentations 5:7, which to some suggests a later generation looking back on the generation at the fall of Jerusalem, is not a secure argument because such appeals are evident in compositions arising in the last decade before the fall of Judah (cf. Jer 31:29; Ezek 18:2). The dominant perspective of the poems is that of life in the land in the wake of the fall of Jerusalem

rather than life in exile, suggesting that it arose among those who had remained in the land after the fall of the city (although there is some interest in the plight of exiles in Lam 4:15 and especially Lam 4:22).

2. Genre and Setting.
The placement of Lamentations among the five Megillot (scrolls) secured its role at the enduring commemoration of the destruction of the Second Temple on the ninth day of Ab in AD 70. This connection to the destruction of the temple probably was seen as appropriate in a later era because of a much earlier precedent in the life of the Jewish community. The link between this book and the demise of the temple and state has informed scholarly discussion over the genre and liturgical setting of the poems in the book (*see* Megillot and Festivals).

2.1. Genre. H. Gunkel saw the various poems as examples of either the funeral dirge (Lam 1; 2; 4), individual lament (Lam 3) or communal lament (Lam 5) (*see* Lament, Psalms of).

2.1.1. Funeral Dirge. After Gunkel, some focused on the funeral dirge as the key form that underlies the poems found in Lamentations (see Jahnow; Lee). Examples of actual funeral dirges are found in 2 Samuel 1:17-27; 3:33-34; Jeremiah 9:16-21; 38:22, with forms modified for poetic use as short prophetic sayings (Is 1:21-23; Jer 9:10, 17-22; Ezek 26:17-18; Amos 5:2) or as popular sayings (Is 14:4-21; 23:1-14; Ezek 19:1-9, 10-14; 27:2-36; 28:11-19; 32:12-16) (see Westermann, 6). The influence of the funeral dirge is usually associated with Lamentations 1; 2; 4.

The employment of female voices and female *personification at various points in Lamentations also suggests the funeral dirge form, since in ancient cultures (including Israel) dirges and laments were often chanted by *women, some of whom engaged in mourning rites as a vocation (2 Chron 35:25; Is 22:12; Jer 7:9; 9:17; Ezek 32:16 [for ancient Near Eastern evidence, see Block, 210, cf. Olyan, Pham]). In ancient societies premature death was most often associated with males, especially in relation to war. Furthermore, males were older than their female marriage partners and, as in modern societies, typically preceded their mates to the grave. This explains why widows and the fatherless were regularly identified as the most vulnerable within ancient cultures and why women were concerned to bear a son to protect their interests later in life (see Ruth 4; 1 Sam 1). Thus the most common occasion for funeral dirges was defeat in war (e.g., 2 Sam 1:17-27). Its counterpart probably was the "call to joy" *(Aufruf zur Freude)*, a form associated with victory in war and usually elicited from women (Is 12:4-6; 54:1; Hos 9:1; Joel 2:21-24; Zeph 3:14; Zech 2:14; 9:9 [see Crüsemann, 55-65]). Interestingly, this form is addressed to "Daughter Zion" in Zephaniah 3:14; Zechariah 2:14; 9:9 and to a female inhabitant of *Zion in Isaiah 12:6, and it is employed in a satirical way in Lamentations 4:21-22.

2.1.2. Lament. Others, however, have questioned the extent of the funeral dirge's influence on Lamentations (see Westermann, 6-11). For these scholars, the lament forms of the Psalter dominate the book, with elements from both individual and communal lament evident throughout Lamentations. As Westermann noted, these forms dominate Lamentations 3; 5, but they are also present throughout the other poems.

2.1.3. Mesopotamian City Dirge. Beginning with the suggestion by S. N. Kramer (see Dobbs-Allsopp 1993, 2-10; Lee, 37 n. 163) that Mesopotamian laments over ruined cities and their sanctuaries were the foundation for the poems in Lamentations, the majority of scholars have highlighted close connections between these two forms (see, e.g., Kraus; Gwaltney; Gottwald 1962; Hillers; Ferris; Westermann; Dobbs-Allsopp 1993; 2002; Bouzard). These Mesopotamian forms were used as part of ceremonies accompanying the refounding and restoration of sanctuaries destroyed by war (see Boda 2006; Boda and Novotny). The Mesopotamian forms link the destruction of a key city and/or its sanctuary to a decision made in the divine assembly and resulting in the abandonment of the sanctuary by its gods. The destruction is carried out by the god Enlil through a human enemy. In the Mesopotamian laments usually the city's patron goddess challenges this decision of the assembly and laments the demise of city and sanctuary (see Dobbs-Allsopp 1993; 2002).

2.1.4. Form. Dobbs-Allsopp (2002, 9) has identified key connections between these Mesopotamian dirges and the book of Lamentations but is careful to note that Lamentations is a "thorough translation and adaptation" of the genre put to a different use. Unlike the Mesopotamian laments, Lamentations employs typical Hebrew poetic devices, clearly identifies the cul-

pability of the people, replaces the destructive god Enlil with Yahweh and the weeping goddess with the personified city of Jerusalem (Daughter Zion), and avoids any mention of the return of Yahweh or restoration of the temple and city (Dobbs-Allsopp 2002). Therefore, in the view of these researchers, the Mesopotamian city dirges may have provided a precedent for some of the elements found in Lamentations, but even so, there is evidence that the form has undergone significant changes and may only echo a general tradition of lamenting over the destruction of a city and sanctuary. This evidence, along with the fact that the Mesopotamian city dirges typically incorporated lament prayers, could explain why other traditional Hebrew forms, including the funeral dirge (cf. 2 Sam 1:17-27 with Lam 1:1-11, 17; 2:1-12; 3:48-51; 4:1-6) and the individual (Lam 1:12-16, 18-22; 2:20-22) and communal (Lam 3:40-47; 5) lament can also be identified within Lamentations (see Gunkel; Westermann). Of the five poems, only Lamentations 1; 2; 4 are usually seen as reflecting strongly the genre of the city dirge, with Lamentations 3 dominated by individual lament with some communal lament, and Lamentations 5 comprising a communal lament.

Although it is possible that all three form traditions (funeral dirge, individual lament, communal lament) have informed the book of Lamentations (see O'Connor, 10-11), there may be another way to explain the connections at least to the Mesopotamian city-dirge tradition. The use of a goddess to express the predicament of the city and sanctuary within the Mesopotamian city-dirge tradition suggests that it has been influenced by the ubiquitous phenomenon of female mourning rites in ancient societies. Therefore, it is likely that the ancient Mesopotamian liturgists envisioned a *divine council akin to human society, with a female figure crying out against the merciless acts of a male-dominated divine council as she mourned the loss of the city and sanctuary. Motifs shared by the city dirges in Mesopotamia and the poems in Lamentations, therefore, can be attributed to female mourning rituals that ancient societies shared in common.

2.2. Setting. Even if a link can be established between the Mesopotamian city dirges and the poems in the book of Lamentations, the absence of any reference to the rebuilding of the sanctuary and the return of the deity shows clearly that the setting in which the poems in Lamentations arose is different from the ceremonies related to temple refoundation that gave rise to the Mesopotamian city dirges (see Dobbs-Allsopp 2002; *contra* Gwaltney). The fixation with the events surrounding the fall and destruction of the city and its aftermath in Lamentations suggests that the setting of the poems is most likely the series of days of fasting that arose immediately after the fall of Jerusalem. Evidence for mourning rites associated with the destroyed sanctuary and possibly also the fallen state is found in Jeremiah 41:4-9. There, eighty men from Shechem, Shiloh and Samaria, displaying rites associated with mourning (shaved beards, torn clothes, self-inflicted wounds, weeping), are depicted in the seventh month as on their way to "the house of Yahweh" with grain offerings and incense. While this evidence comes from the beginning of the Babylonian exilic period, Zechariah 7—8 speaks of the practice of four fasts during the "seventy years" of the exile, fasts that took place in the fourth, fifth, seventh and tenth months (Zech 7:5; 8:19). That these fasts were related at least to the temple in Jerusalem (as Jer 41) is suggested by the fact that a delegation from Bethel approaches the priests and prophets of "the house of the LORD Almighty" (Zech 7:3) to determine whether they should now come to an end with the second temple nearing completion. Some have suggested that the four fasts were related to a complex of four key events related to the fall of the Judean kingdom (Wellhausen, 103-7; Ackroyd, 207 n. 122): tenth month (588 BC), the siege of Jerusalem began (2 Kings 25:1; Jer 39:1); fourth month (587 BC), Jerusalem's walls were breached, and leadership fled (2 Kings 25:3-7; Jer 39:1-10; 52:6-11); fifth month, Jerusalem was destroyed (2 Kings 25:8-12; Jer 52:12-16); seventh month, Gedaliah was assassinated (2 Kings 25:25-26; Jer 41:1-3). Since the delegation from Bethel in Zechariah 7 originally only asked about one fast (fifth month [Zech 7:3]), which was expanded first to two fasts (fifth, seventh months) in Zechariah 7:5 and later to four fasts (fourth, fifth, seventh, tenth months) in Zechariah 8:19, it is possible that these fasts reflect a diversity of rites observed by different communities within the land and possibly also in exile.

Other compositions that may have arisen in this liturgical setting are now found in the Psalter (Pss 44; 60; 74; 79; 83; 106; 123; 137) as well as in narrative books describing the practice of penitential prayer in the Persian period (Ezra 9; Neh 1; 9; Dan 9). That the same context is suggested for both laments and penitential prayers, the latter coming to dominate the liturgical expression of the Persian period community, is bolstered by close literary and ideological connections that have been established between the book of Lamentations and this tradition of penitential prayer (see Boda 2003). Close associations also between Lamentations 3 and the prophetic lament liturgy found in Jeremiah 14:1—15:4 (which most likely occurred during the reign of Zedekiah, last king of Judah) suggests a common liturgical setting for prayers of lament and penitence throughout the sixth century BC.

3. Literary Features and Structure.
Observations on the original setting of the individual compositions provide some insights into the historical circumstances that gave rise to these compositions as well as the basic building blocks of the individual poems. However, such insights need to be supplemented by analysis of the final canonical shape of these originally independent prayers. This involves paying attention to key rhetorical features employed throughout the collection (*see* Rhetorical Criticism).

3.1. Personification. One regular rhetorical feature is personification, usually related to the city of Jerusalem, but also to its gates, walls, roads and surrounding kingdom. By personifying these physical structures and regions, the composers were able to vividly describe the pain and express the heart cry of the people. There is a sense that the poets send out God's "precious" Zion to intercede for them, hoping that she may have greater success to gain Yahweh's ear (see Lanahan, 43-45; Heim).

3.2. Voice. Another rhetorical feature has been highlighted especially in the work of N. Lee, who analyzes the modulating voices throughout the book (although see Westermann, 65, 139-40). Lee identifies the two dominant voices in Lamentations with two voices that can be discerned in the book of Jeremiah: Jeremiah the prophet and a female poet voicing personified Jerusalem's pain (called "Jerusalem's poet"). This dialogue, which Lee (42) traces back to "different poetic singers who performed their composed songs in response to one another," is prominent in Lamentations 1; 2; 4. The female perspective of Lamentations 5 (cf. Lam 5:14b with Lam 5:15a) and links to the earlier cries of personified Jerusalem (cf. Lam 5:17 with Lam 1:13, 22; Lam 5:17 with Lam 4:17) suggest that the communal lament of Lamentations 5 has taken over the role of the personified Jerusalem (Lee, 196).

Lee's study, building off of the earlier work of W. F. Lanahan on Lamentations and especially C. Mandolfo on biblical laments, highlights the importance of sensitivity to the various voices that appear throughout the book (cf. Boase). No two poems are alike in the structuring of the voices. One needs to be alert to the impact that employing various voices has on the reading of the poem. W. C. Kaiser (44) picks this up in his analysis of Lamentations 1 when he notes, "It would appear that emotional and psychological progress is realized in this poem as it moves from a more distant, descriptive 3rd-person reporting in verses 1-11 to a more personal, private 1st-person speech in verses 12-22." The poem begins with an external point of view, observing the pain of the personified city, only to give voice to the suffering woman who discloses her inner turmoil. In Lamentations 3 this inner turmoil is presented from the outset and is expressed not by the city personified as a woman but rather by a suffering man (warrior?). The interplay of various voices provides more opportunities to express and experience the pain of the crisis.

3.3. Acrostic. A third key rhetorical feature in Lamentations is the acrostic that structures four of the five poems (Lam 1—4). This literary device appears at several points in the OT (Pss 9—10; 25; 34; 119; 145; Prov 31:10-31; Nah 1) as well as in other Semitic literature, including Akkadian, Ugaritic, Paleo-Canaanite (see Westermann, 98-100; O'Connor, 12). Several purposes have been offered to explain the use of acrostics, including fulfilling magical rites, aiding memorization of poems, emphasizing completeness, or producing aesthetically pleasing literature (Westermann, 98-100; O'Connor). Although there may be multiple purposes behind the use of acrostics, most likely they communicate that the poem expresses totality, and in the case of Lamentations both the total devastating effect of the destruction and the total expression of the pain of those who experienced it.

3.4. Structure. The uniqueness of each po-

em's acrostic pattern in Lamentations 1—4 shows that each poem in the book has its own integrity. Nevertheless, some have questioned whether the book merely represents an anthology of poems or instead was designed as an integrated collection. Although recognizing independence for each poem, J. Renkema (1988; 1998), for instance, argues for a collection united by connections between equivalent letter stanzas in the four poems (e.g., elements in stanza ʾālep in Lam 1 may be found in stanza ʾālep in Lam 2, 3 or 4). Although some examples seem to support his view, the evidence is not consistent across all stanzas in all poems. D. J. Reimer draws on modern grief theory in order to trace the thematic structure of Lamentations, concluding that the book moves through the stages of isolation (Lam 1), anger (Lam 2), bargaining (Lam 3), depression (Lam 4) and acceptance (Lam 5). Reimer is careful to admit that these themes are only "dominant" in their respective poems, but these various stages appear at various points in all the poems—a point that led earlier scholars to abandon such psychological theory as a basis for structural analysis (see Moore; Joyce). Especially difficult to this structure is Reimer's identification of the final poem with its conclusion vacillating between confident hope and embittered lament.

The fact that Lamentations 3 has not only the longest poem but also the most complicated acrostic brings rhetorical focus onto this poem within the collection. The reader should take note of the message of this central poem, which represents the height of rhetorical artistry and so also, as O'Connor (13) has said, functions as "the book's most important chapter, the book's theological heart." This central poem points to a theological solution to the present suffering, one that accentuates Yahweh's grace and justice (Lam 3:1-40). This solution, however, is seriously challenged in the remainder of the book, first in the central poem itself (Lam 3:41-66) and then in the two poems in Lamentations 4—5. This latter is emphasized recently by I. W. Provan (1991), Dobbs-Allsopp (1997) and T. Linafelt, who remind readers that the book does not end with Lamentations 3:40. The final two chapters contain poems shorter than Lamentations 1—3, with Lamentations 5, although containing twenty-two verse units as the first four poems, abandoning the acrostic pattern. This suggests that Lamentations 5 signals the end of this completeness—something made clear in its painful and dialectal conclusion. As O'Connor (13-14) has argued, Lamentations 4—5 "move back to themes of grief, anger, and despair, and smother hope like a blanket over fire." Therefore, overall flow of the book of Lamentations suggests an honest struggle in the midst of the darkness of the exile, even if it foreshadows the dominant solution that will be adopted within the community in the wake of the exile (cf. Ezra 9; Neh 1; 9, Dan 9; see Boda 2003).

4. Content of Each Poem.

4.1. Lamentations 1.

1:1-11	Third-person description of Zion's suffering
1:12-16	First-person singular cry of Zion to onlookers (the nations?)
1:17	Third-person description of Zion's suffering and its cause
1:18-19	First-person singular cry of Zion to the nations about Yahweh's innocence and Zion's rebellion
1:20-22	First-person singular cry of Zion to Yahweh about the nations' guilt (malediction)

The first poem in the collection draws the reader in to view the pain of personified Zion from an external vantage point through third-person speech (Lam 1:1-11). At the outset no attribution of guilt is given; the reader is allowed to experience the shocking pain before realizing in Lamentations 1:5 and again in Lamentations 1:8-9 that Zion's sins lie behind this suffering. This first section introduces a key emphasis of this poem: the solitude of the city—first seen in the opening declaration that she is "deserted' (Lam 1:1) and then in the refrain in Lamentations 1:2, 10: "There is none to comfort her." At two points in this opening section the poet uses the device of apostrophe to give voice to the suffering city, both consisting of cries for Yahweh to look upon her affliction (Lam 1:9, 11). The detachment of the first half of the poem is soon lost in the second half as Lamentations 1:12-16 shifts to the first-person voice of the city as she pleads with those who pass by. Zion echoes the themes already introduced in the third-person section, admitting her sins and repeating the refrain of solitude in Lamentations 1:6, "no one is near to comfort me," al-

ready encountered in Lamentations 1:2, 10. For a moment in Lamentations 1:17 the perspective shifts to the external with a short third-person description of Zion that again reminds the reader "There is no one to comfort her." But then the poem plunges back into the bitter first-person pain of Zion that carries the poem to its conclusion (Lam 1:18-22). In this concluding section Zion first speaks to the nations about Yahweh ("Listen all you peoples" [Lam 1:18-19]), admitting that her suffering was caused by her rebellion; Yahweh was innocent. Her speech then engages Yahweh directly, expressing her distress, admitting her culpability, but also highlighting the pain that the nations have inflicted upon her (Lam 1:20-22). Here again the refrain emerges in Lamentations 1:21: "There is no one to comfort me." This section calls for vengeance upon those who have treated Zion so brutally, suggesting that although the discipline was deserved, the nations have violated God's justice in their actions.

4.2. Lamentations 2.

2:1-10	Third-person description of the suffering of Zion and Judah
2:11-12	First-person singular lament over Zion's suffering
2:13-19	First-person singular address to Zion
2:20-22	First-person singular lament of Zion to Yahweh

The second poem begins, as did the first poem, with a detached third-person description of the pain (Lam 2:1-10) focusing on the city (Daughter Zion) and kingdom (Daughter Judah) as women. The final verse in this section (Lam 2:10) describes rites connected to mourning and lament (sit on ground in silence, sprinkle dust on heads, put on sackcloth, bow heads to the ground), and this introduces the first-person voice that emerges in Lamentations 2:11-12, the voice of one who weeps while observing the pain of the people. In Lamentations 2:13-19 this or another first-person voice turns and addresses Daughter Zion directly, highlighting the city's suffering, attacking the false prophets, and identifying the defeat of the enemy as the planned judgment of Yahweh. As in Lamentations 2:10, so Lamentations 2:18-19 depicts the rites of mourning and lament of the people and even encourages such rites from the "walls of Daughter Zion"

(Lam 2:18-19). In response to this invitation a voice of prayer addresses Yahweh directly to conclude the poem in Lamentations 2:20-22. In the first poem Daughter Zion asked onlookers this searching question: "Is any suffering like my suffering that was inflicted on me, that the LORD brought on me in the day of his fierce anger?" (Lam 1:12). In this second poem Daughter Zion addresses this to God directly: "Whom have you ever treated like this?" (Lam 2:20).

4.3. Lamentations 3.

3:1-20	First-person singular lament over God's judgment on the male poet
3:21-24	First-person singular transition to hope
3:25-39	Application of the poet's experience to all people
3:40	First-person plural cohortative invitation
3:41-47	First-person plural communal response
3:48-51	First-person singular lament over God's judgment on the people
3:52-66	First-person singular thanksgiving and request (malediction)

The third poem begins with the expression of a "man" (*geber* [Lam 3:1]) who has experienced suffering at the hand of God (Lam 3:1-17) and explains to the reader how he moved from despair (Lam 3:18-20) to hope (Lam 3:21-24). This situation is then applied universally to anyone who experiences similar circumstances (Lam 3:25-39)—a presentation that prompts an invitation to the entire community to examine their ways and return to God (Lam 3:40). A response to this invitation by the people comes in Lamentations 3:41-47, and this response appears to reject the observation in Lamentations 3:39 that no one has a right to complain against God. This communal complaint argues that although they have admitted their sin, God has not responded to them (Lam 3:41-47). Furthermore, a first-person common singular voice follows in Lamentations 3:48-51, weeping over the despicable state of the city-community, and functions as a transition to a closing individual prayer in Lamentations 3:52-66, which contains both thanksgiving and request.

The source of hope for the afflicted man (Lam 3:1-20) in Lamentations 3 is clearly his consideration of the gracious character of God

in Lamentations 3:21-33. Here the composer uses the breadth of Hebrew lexical stock of "grace," including "covenant loyalty" (*ḥesed* [Lam 3:22, 32]), "compassions" (*raḥămîm* [Lam 3:22, 32]), "faithfulness" (*'ĕmûnâ* [Lam 3:23]), "goodness" (*ṭôb* [Lam 3:25, 26, 27]) and "salvation" (*tĕšû'â* [Lam 3:26]). In light of such grace, the poet encourages the people to wait (*qwh* [Lam 3:25]), seek (*drš* [Lam 3:25]), wait silently (*yḥl* Hiphil + *dûmām* [Lam 3:26]), bear the yoke (*nś'* + *'ōl* [Lam 3:27]), sit alone (*yšb* + *bādād* [Lam 3:28]), be silent (*dāmam* [Lam 3:28]), put the mouth in the dust (*ntn* + *be'āpār pîhû* [Lam 3:29]), give the cheek to the smiter (*ntn* + *lĕmakkēhû leḥî* [Lam 3:30]), and be filled with reproach (*śb'* + *bĕḥerpâ* [Lam 3:30]). Such actions describe the posture of passively accepting the discipline of God but also of awaiting God's deliverance.

This all leads to a presentation of the justice of God in Lamentations 3:33-38, teaching that God "does not afflict with delight" (Lam 3:33) but rather disciplines because of sin (Lam 3:37-38). In light of this, there is no room for complaint when being punished for one's sins (Lam 3:39). Thus in this central poem it is a consideration of the grace of God that is to prompt an acceptance of the discipline of God and a refusal to complain in light of one's culpability. It is this that leads to the key penitential invitation in Lamentations 3:40. Nevertheless, the frustration of the people comes out in Lamentations 3:41-47 as they declare that they admit their sins (Lam 3:41), and yet God has not pardoned, and they continue to live in their suffering. The repetition of the term "destruction" (*šeber*) in Lamentations 3:47-48 shows that the first-person common singular voice (possibly the same one that began the poem in Lam 3:1-20) feels this frustration of the people (Lam 3:48, 51) and is committed to interceding for the people (Lam 3:49) until Yahweh looks upon their suffering (Lam 3:50). This same voice closes off the poem with a prayer of request for himself as well. In this closing prayer the poet calls for God's justice and vengeance on his enemies (Lam 3:59-66) based on his own past experience of God's salvation (Lam 3:52-58).

4.4. Lamentations 4.

4:1-10	First-person singular description of the need of the people
4:11-16	Third-person description of the

need of the people

4:17-20   First-person plural lament over
disaster

4:21-22 Second-person prophetic announcement of judgment and salvation

The fourth poem begins in Lamentations
4:1-10 with a first-person description of the need
of the people (see "my" in Lam 4:3, 6, 10), focusing especially on the common fate of those considered most (children) and least (princes)
vulnerable. In this section the focus is on the deplorable circumstances rather than on the cause
of the crisis. With Lamentations 4:11-16 the
poem shifts into a third-person description of
the need, now identifying the cause as Yahweh's
fierce anger against the sins of prophets and
priests (Lam 4:13). In Lamentations 4:17-20 a
first-person plural voice, possibly the voice of
the prophets and priests who now "grope
through the streets as if they were blind" (see
Lam 4:14), emerges. This voice articulates the
failure of both international allies (Lam 4:17)
and national leadership (Lam 4:20) to rescue
them in their time of need. The poem ends
(Lam 4:21-22) with what appears to be a prophetic announcement of judgment and salvation, declaring a curse against the rival Daughter
Edom, who takes pleasure in their demise, and
promising Daughter Zion that her punishment
will one day end.

4.5. Lamentations 5.

5:1   Request: call for Yahweh's attention

5:2-18   Lamenting the predicament, admitting guilt

5:19   Motivation for God to act

5:20   Questions (borderline accusations)

5:21   Request: call for Yahweh's action

5:22   Motivation for God to act

What is immediately noticeable about the final poem in the book is that even though it consists of twenty-two units, it is not an alphabetic
acrostic, as are the other four. There are other
points of divergence. It is the shortest of all the
poems and the most consistent, employing a
first-person plural voice throughout. The poem
contains the elements typical of the communal
laments of the Psalter, with the depiction of the
predicament (Lam 5:2-5, 8a, 9-16a, 17-18), the assignment of the cause of the predicament (Lam
5:6-7, 8b, 16b, 20, 22), the motivations for help

(Lam 5:19, 21) and the request for help (Lam
5:1, 21). In the prayer of Lamentations 5 there is
no denying that the cause of the predicament is
traced to the sin of the people: both in the previous generation (Lam 5:6-7) and (most likely) in
the present generation (Lam 5:16b). However,
the questions of Lamentations 5:20 ("Why do
you always forget us? Why do you forsake us so
long?") and the suggestion of Lamentations 5:22
("unless you have utterly rejected us and are
angry with us beyond measure") imply that the
endurance of the predicament is God's responsibility. What is missing is blame directed at the
enemies that dominates much of the earlier poems in Lamentations. The request forms a
bracket around the entire poem with three imperatives for God's attention in Lamentations
5:1 ("remember . . . look . . . see") and two imperatives for God's action in Lamentations 5:21.
The community longs for God to cause them to
return to God in covenant relationship, a return
that has both physical and spiritual dimensions,
and to renew their community's experience to
the glory days of the past. The final stanza of
Lamentations 5 brings the book as a whole to an
awkward end, vacillating as it does back and
forth between the postures of hope (Lam 5:19,
21) and frustration (Lam 5:20, 22). It is not surprising in the darkness of the exile that the book
ends without acrostic style and with the declaration of frustration. As Linafelt (60) has argued,
"The book is left opening out into the emptiness
of God's nonresponse. By leaving a conditional
statement dangling, the final verse leaves open
the future of the ones lamenting."

5. Theological Traditions and Themes.

5.1. Suffering and Redemption. Taken as a
whole, these diverse poems provide theological
resources for suffering and salvation (see Kaiser). The present pain is identified as a loss of
rest (Lam 1:3) and inheritance (Lam 5:2), an absence of comfort (Lam 1:2, 9, 16b, 17a, 21) and
especially a loss of covenant relationship with
Yahweh through the loss of the religious structures that sustained this relationship (Lam 2:1, 6,
7, 9c). This pain has affected all levels of society,
whether rich/poor, male/female, young/old, all
aspects of society (physical, social, spiritual) and
even ongoing generations of society (past and
present).

The poems express the reason for pain in
various ways. At times the frustrated voice of the

poets suggest that this pain, or at least its enduring quality, is purposeless, the result of an angry God whose wrath will never be satisfied (Lam 5:20, 22). At many places it is clearly seen as discipline for sin (Lam 1:5, 8-9, 14, 18, 20; 2:14; 3:39-42), even though the amount of suffering seems to be out of proportion to the sin of the people, pain at a level unknown to humanity (Lam 1:12; 2:20). Lamentations 3:40 suggests that there is a purifying role as the people speak of examining and testing their ways. Of course, the cause of the pain is often linked to the wiles of enemies taking advantage of the people's plight (Lam 1:21-22; 2:16; 3:52-66; 4:21-22; 5:2, 8), even if this opportunity was provided by Yahweh's legitimate judgment (Lam 1:15, 17; 2:17; 4:13).

The cause of the suffering is linked to the three classic reasons found in the biblical lament tradition: self, enemy, Yahweh. The various poems consistently identify the supplicants as responsible for their own pain due to their rebellion against God. The enemies often become the subject of the lament. Yahweh is regularly identified as playing an active role in the suffering that has been experienced, but this is carefully nuanced with the qualification that this action was justified because of the sins of the community.

The request in the various prayers is dominated by calls for Yahweh (e.g., Lam 1:11, 20; 2:20-21) or passing nations (e.g., Lam 1:12, 18, 21) to give attention to the need of the people, for God to uphold their cause (Lam 3:59), and for God to wreak vengeance on their enemies (Lam 1:22; 3:64-66; 4:21-22). At times voices describe or exhort the people or city to cry out to Yahweh (Lam 2:18, 19), to call for relief (Lam 3:55-56), to confess and repent from their sin (Lam 3:40-42), to wait upon Yahweh by submitting to the suffering (Lam 3:19-30), even though at other times such cries are considered rejected by Yahweh (Lam 3:8). In Lamentations 5 the request becomes far more explicit and practical, calling at the outset (Lam 5:1) for Yahweh to give attention to their past circumstances and their present disgrace, and at the end (Lam 5:21) for Yahweh to restore their relationship with him and renew their life as in "days of old."

Strategies for surviving the present pain appear at various places in the poems. Key is accepting culpability for this suffering—that is, admitting one's sins and even the sins of former generations (Lam 5:7, 16) and absolving Yahweh of any wrongdoing (Lam 1:16). At a couple of places Yahweh's character is highlighted as essential for living through the pain. In Lamentations 3:19-39 the poet encourages a submissive posture toward the suffering, one demanded by the culpability of the sufferer. In this section the poet clings to the gracious character of Yahweh, and it is this that gives him hope. Additionally, it is Yahweh's sovereignty over the affairs of the world that infuses meaning into the present discipline (Lam 3:34-38). In Lamentations 5:19 the community clings to the eternal and sovereign character of Yahweh. Surviving the pain, however, will mean not just a theological reorientation but also a spiritual reorientation, one that involves crying out to God (Lam 2:18-19), a cry that ultimately involves not complaint (Lam 3:39) but self-examination, repentance and confession (Lam 3:40-42).

5.2. Zion, Retribution and the Character of Yahweh. One cannot miss the central role that *Zion theology plays in the book of Lamentations (see Albrektson, 219-30; Ackroyd, 46; Renkema 1998, 44-45). This theology was foundational to Judah's kingdom and thus emphasized by royal circles and the priestly groups that the monarchy supported. The first move that *David made as king of the united tribes was to shift his capital from Hebron, which lay in the heart of Judah's tribal territory, to Jerusalem, which lay on the northern border Judah shared with Benjamin and was a city without traditional attachment to any tribe. This shift helped David control the northern tribes, uniting the nation geographically at Jerusalem and personally in the Judahite king. The connection between the name "Zion" and Jerusalem is uncertain, but it appears that it predates David's arrival in the city, a part of which was called "the fortress of Zion" (2 Sam 5:7; 1 Chron 11:5). Another dimension of Davidic kingship also appears to be associated with the pre-Davidic Jerusalemite tradition, that of Melchizedek's priestly kingship (cf. Gen 14:18-19 with Ps 110). As various psalms reveal (Pss 2; 46; 48; 76; 84; 87; 122; 137), the Zion tradition depicted Jerusalem as the place of God's dwelling and seat of his rule over all the earth, replacing and exceeding the Canaanite seat of divine rule on Mount Zaphon. So exalted was this city that it is seen as invincible, secure from any attack of the enemy—a belief that led to an emphasis on the inviolability of Zion, lulling the people into a false confidence based on God's past choice of Jerusalem and its sanctuary. The prophets will confront this royal ideology, predicting that Zion would be destroyed (Jer 26:18-19; cf. Jer 7:1-15; Mic 3:12) and its sanctuary abandoned by Yahweh (Ezek 10) because of the rebellious behavior of the people. It is understandable, then, why the Zion tradition is expressed so strongly in the book of Lamentations as the people struggle with the promises related to the city of Jerusalem and its sanctuary. In the book it is the Zion tradition that is associated with the most bitter elements of lament and pain.

Combined with this Zion theology, however, is a strong *retribution theology that has been informed by the Deuteronomistic and prophetic traditions and accepts that the fall of Jerusalem has been caused by the covenantal rebellion of the people against Yahweh (see Brandscheidt; Gottwald 1962, 66, 70; Albrektson, 230-37; Ackroyd, 46; Hawtrey, 78). Thus, even when the lament is most bitter, there is always an admission of the culpability of the people.

However, the greatest hope in the book is not related to either the election theology of Zion or the retribution theology of Deuteronomism or prophetism; rather, it is only with the abandonment of Zion theology in the central chapter that one is shown the way forward for the community. In place of Zion theology is the key grace tradition (Lam 3:21-33), linked especially to the ancient rehearsal of Yahweh's "name" found in Exodus 34:6-7 (cf. Num 14:18; Ps 86). This fixation on the "character creed" is followed immediately in Lamentations 3:33-39 with a theology of divine discipline closely allied with Deuteronomic and possibly *wisdom theology (see Gottwald 1962, 71-72), which reminds the people that God does not "afflict with delight" (Lam 3:33) or approve of injustice (Lam 3:34-36) but rather dispenses discipline because of sin (Lam 3:37-38). Instead of complaint (Lam 3:39), the people are encouraged to examine their ways and turn back to God and confess their sins (Lam 3:40). This solution is informed by the agenda set out in several key earlier texts: Leviticus 26:40-41; Deuteronomy 30:1-4; 1 Kings 8:46-51, even though these texts look to the exilic community and Lamentations to the community left behind in the land (see Boda 2003).

The book of Lamentations showcases the theological struggle of a people living in the wake of the greatest crisis in their history. In it we observe the intersection of several key theological streams that rose to prominence in the closing moments of the kingdom of Judah. As the central poem and conclusion to the book make clear, the theological struggle would remain unresolved in the short run.

6. New Testament.

Lamentations is not the final word on the Jewish community in Jerusalem. The fasts with their laments and penitential prayers at the temple site would be replaced by the renewal of the festal calendar with the reconstruction of the second temple in the late sixth century BC. But Zion would never regain the glory of the preexilic era, and the dominance of the penitential prayer tradition after the exile is testimony to the fact that the people longed for more. This longing can be discerned among that cast of faithful characters who appear in the temple courts early in the gospel of Luke (Zechariah and Elizabeth, Simeon and Anna, Joseph and Mary) as they await the *messiah and identify him in Jesus. This Jesus would enter into his people's suffering in a land still under foreign occupation. He would express his pain over and compassion for Jerusalem and yet predict its downfall (Luke 13:34-35). Like Lamentations 3, his message would be focused on God's gracious invitation to repentance. He would even cry out in lament to God ("My God, my God, why have you forsaken me?" [Mt 27:46; Mk 15:34]) on that hill outside of Zion as he hung dying for the sins of his people and those of the whole world. It is interesting to see how the Zion traditions are resurrected in the NT to describe the new experience of grace for the people of God in Jesus Christ, who functions in the order of Melchizedek, as these traditions are transferred to the "heavenly Jerusalem," which is both a present reality (Heb 7:1-9:28; 12:22-23) and a future hope (Rev 21).

See also FEMINIST INTERPRETATION; LAMENTATIONS 2: ANCIENT NEAR EASTERN BACKGROUND; LAMENTATIONS 3: HISTORY OF INTERPRETATION; ZION.

BIBLIOGRAPHY. *Commentaries*: A. Berlin, *Lamentations* (OTL; Louisville: Westminster John Knox, 2002); F. W. Dobbs-Allsopp, *Lamentations* (IBC; Louisville: Westminster John Knox, 2002); R. Gordis, *The Song of Songs and Lamentations: A*

Study, Modern Translation and Commentary (rev. ed.; New York: KTAV, 1974); **D. R. Hillers,** *Lamentations* (2nd ed.; AB 7A; Garden City, NY: Doubleday, 1992); **H. J. Kraus,** *Klagelieder (Threni)* (3rd ed.; BKAT 20; Neukirchen-Vluyn: Neukirchener Verlag, 1968); **I. W. Provan,** *Lamentations* (NCB; Grand Rapids: Eerdmans, 1991); **J. Renkema,** *Lamentations* (HCOT; Leuven: Peeters, 1998). **Studies: P. R. Ackroyd,** *Exile and Restoration: A Study of Hebrew Thought of the Sixth Century B.C.* (OTL; Philadelphia: Westminster, 1968); **B. Albrektson,** *Studies in the Text and Theology of the Book of Lamentations, with a Critical Edition of the Peshitta Text* (STL 21; Lund: Gleerup, 1963); **D. I. Block,** *The Book of Ezekiel: Chapters 25-48* (NICOT; Grand Rapids: Eerdmans, 1998); **E. Boase,** *The Fulfilment of Doom? The Dialogic Interaction between the Book of Lamentations and the Pre-Exilic/Early Exilic Prophetic Literature* (LHB/OT 437; New York: T&T Clark, 2006); **M. J. Boda,** "The Priceless Gain of Penitence: From Communal Lament to Penitential Prayer in the 'Exilic' Liturgy of Israel," *HBT* 25 (2003) 51-75; idem, "From Dystopia to Myopia: Utopian (Re)visions in Haggai and Zechariah 1-8," in *Utopia and Dystopia in Prophetic Literature,* ed. E. Ben Zvi (PFES 92; Helsinki: Finnish Exegetical Society; Göttingen: Vandenhoeck & Ruprecht, 2006) 211-49; **M. J. Boda and J. R. Novotny, eds.,** *From the Foundations to the Crenellations: Essays on Temple Building in the Ancient Near East and Hebrew Bible* (AOAT; Münster: Ugarit-Verlag, forthcoming); **W. C. Bouzard,** *We Have Heard with Our Ears, O God: Sources of the Communal Laments in the Psalms* (SBLDS 159; Atlanta: Scholars Press, 1997); **R. Brandscheidt,** *Gotteszorn und Menschenleid: Die Gerichtsklage des leidenden Gerechten in Klgl 3* (TThSt 41; Trier: Paulinus-Verlag, 1983); **F. Crüsemann,** *Studien zur Formgeschichte von Hymnus und Danklied in Israel* (WMANT 32; Neukirchen-Vluyn: Neukirchener Verlag, 1969); **F. W. Dobbs-Allsopp,** *Weep, O Daughter of Zion: A Study of the City-Lament Genre in the Hebrew Bible* (BibOr 44; Roma: Editrice Pontificio Istituto Biblico, 1993); idem, "Tragedy, Tradition, and Theology in the Book of Lamentations," *JSOT* 74 (1997) 29-60; idem, "Linguistic Evidence for the Date of Lamentations," *JANESCU* 26 (1998) 1-36; **P. W. Ferris,** *The Genre of Communal Lament in the Bible and the Ancient Near East* (SBLDS 127; Atlanta: Scholars Press, 1992); **N. K. Gottwald,** "Lamentations," *Int* 9 (1955) 320-38; idem, *Studies in the Book of Lamentations* (rev. ed.; SBT 14; London: SCM Press, 1962); **H. Gunkel,** *Einleitung in die Psalmen: Die Gattungen der religiösen Lyrik Israels* (HKAT; Göttingen: Vandenhoeck & Ruprecht, 1933); **S. B. Gure-wicz,** "The Problem of Lamentations 3," *ABR* 8 (1960) 19-23; **W. C. Gwaltney Jr.,** "The Biblical Book of Lamentations in the Context of Near Eastern Lament Literature," *Scripture in Context II: More Essays on the Comparative Method,* ed. W. W. Hallo, J. C. Moyer and L. G. Perdue (Winona Lake, IN: Eisenbrauns, 1983) 191-211; **K. Hawtrey,** "The Exile as a Crisis for Cultic Religion: Lamentations and Ezekiel," *RTR* 52 (1993) 74-83; **H. Heater,** "Structure and Meaning in Lamentations," *BSac* 149 (1992) 304-15; **K. M. Heim,** "The Personification of Jerusalem and the Drama of Her Bereavement in Lamentations," in *Zion, City of Our God,* ed. R. S. Hess and G. J. Wenham (Grand Rapids: Eerdmans, 1999) 129-69; **H. Jahnow,** *Das hebräische Leichenlied im Rahmen der Völkerdichtung* (BZAW 36; Giessen: Töpelmann, 1923); **P. Joyce,** "Lamentations and the Grief Process: A Psychological Reading," *BibInt* 1 (1993) 304-20; **W. C. Kaiser,** *A Biblical Approach to Personal Suffering* (Chicago: Moody, 1982); **S. N. Kramer,** *Lamentation over the Destruction of Ur* (AS 12; Chicago: University of Chicago Press, 1940); **W. F. Lanahan,** "The Speaking Voice in the Book of Lamentations," *JBL* 93 (1974) 41-49; **N. Lee,** *The Singers of Lamentations: Communities under Siege, from Ur to Jerusalem to Sarajevo* (BIS 60; Leiden: E. J. Brill, 2002); **T. Linafelt,** *Surviving Lamentations: Catastrophe, Lament, and Protest in the Afterlife of a Biblical Book* (Chicago: University of Chicago Press, 2000); **C. Mandolfo,** *God in the Dock: Dialogic Tension in the Psalms of Lament* (JSOTSup 357; London: Sheffield Academic Press, 2002); **C. W. Miller,** "The Book of Lamentations in Recent Research," *CBR* 1 (2002) 9-29; **M. S. Moore,** "Human Suffering in Lamentations," *RB* 90 (1983) 534-55; **K. M. O'Connor,** *Lamentations and the Tears of the World* (Maryknoll, NY: Orbis, 2002); **S. M. Olyan,** *Biblical Mourning: Ritual and Social Dimensions* (Oxford: Oxford University Press, 2004); **X. H. T. Pham,** *Mourning in the Ancient Near East and the Hebrew Bible* (JSOTSup 302; Sheffield: Sheffield Academic Press, 1999); **I. W. Provan,** "Reading Texts against an Historical Background: The Case of Lamentations 1," *SJOT* 1 (1990) 130-43; **D. J. Reimer,** "Good Grief? A Psychological Reading of Lamentations," *ZAW* 114 (2002) 542-59; **J. Renkema,** "The Literary Structure of Lamentations (I-IV)," in *The Structural Analysis of Biblical and Canaanite Poetry*, ed. W. van der Meer and J. C. de Moor (JSOTSup 74; Sheffield: Sheffield Academic Press, 1988) 294-396; **J. Wellhausen,** *Prolegomena zur Geschichte Israels* (6th ed.; Berlin: Reimer, 1905); **C. Westermann,** *Lamentations: Issues and Interpretation* (Minneapolis: Fortress, 1994).

M. J. Boda

LAMENTATIONS 2: ANCIENT NEAR EASTERN BACKGROUND

Although communal mourning is relatively uncommon in the modern West, we do experience it from time to time. For example, the surprise attacks in 2001 on New York and Washington and the aborted attack that ended in Shanksville, Pennsylvania, made the date "9/11" notorious. That calamity shook the American people, and nations around the world publicly expressed their grief over it.

Public, communal grieving was common in the ancient Near East (Morgenstern, 164-66). When an individual died, the community would gather to grieve, and "professional" keeners were engaged to lead the funereal expressions. Similarly, when a calamity befell an entire community, they would join in public mourning and engage members of a guild of professional mourners to lead the community in lamentation. The guild was responsible for composing and performing dirges that expressed the grief of the entire community. In the Ugaritic "Poem of Aqhat," for example, these professional mourners are referred to as *bkyt* ("weeping women"), *mšspdt* ("women who lead in mourning") and and *pzġm ġr* ("men with mutilated skin").

The Hebrew Bible reports that Israel shared these public expressions of grieving. Israel also had its professional keeners (J(Jer 9:17), both male and female (2 Chron 35:25). At times, some in Israel even engaged in self-mutilation, common in the ancient Near East (Jer 16:6; 41:5). However, this was proscribed by Torah (Deut 14:1), as a countercultural measure to set Israel apart from its neighbors. The best examples of ancient Near Eastern lament literature are Sumerian.

1. Sumerian Context
2. Sumerian City Laments
3. The *Eršemma, Balag* and *Šuilla* Laments
4. Summary

1. Sumerian Context.

Although a significant volume of Sumerian literature has survived from the mid-third millennium BC, the classic communal laments emerge after the demise of the neo-Sumerian Empire (c. 2000 BC). The earliest copies of lamentations over the destruction of a city are several Sumerian poems preserved from the Old Babylonian period (c. 2000-1600 BC) as part of a scribal curriculum until the last quarter of the eighteenth century BC

At its most basic, the content of a communal lament expresses complaint as well as sorrow and grief over some perceived calamity and an appeal for deliverance to deity. From the perspective of their worldview, the destruction of a city(-state) could be explained only as the result of the arbitrary, often capricious anger of one or more of the great gods. And against that assumption, it seemed that the city's patron deity had consequently abandoned its domain. It is apparent that such a composition was intended to be used by or on behalf of a community as they reflected on and commemorated a socially and religiously devastating event.

2. Sumerian City Laments.

2.1. Introduction. To date, six distinctive Sumerian city laments have been discovered and published. Three of these are considered major compositions: the Lamentation over the Destruction of Ur, the Lamentation over the Destruction of Sumer and Ur, and the Lamentation over the Destruction of Nippur. Two others are the Lamentation over the Destruction of Sumer and Uruk and the Lamentation over the Destruction of Eridu. The sixth, very poorly preserved, is a lament for Ekimar.

The classic city laments were written primarily in the main Sumerian dialect, *emegir*. However, the *emesal* dialect is also used in the laments over Nippur, Eridu and Uruk. Because some texts use *emesal* when a woman is speaking, it is sometimes referred to as women's language. However, *emesal* also appears to have been the language of the *gala*-priesthood. The *gala*-priests included both males and females. They chanted laments and so were associated in the literature with female keeners and mourners. One Old Babylonian text claims that the *gala*-priesthood was established by the god Enki to chant "heart-soothing laments for Inanna."

S. Kramer was the first to publish a critical

edition of a city lament. Given points of similarity with the biblical book of Lamentations over Jerusalem, he titled it the Lamentation over the Destruction of Ur. However, it is important to remember the observation by S. Tinney (19) that "the nature of genres and texts is highly culturally specific . . . and it would be fallacious to assume that the significance of texts in such divergent cultures as ancient Israel and ancient Mesopotamia can be mapped onto the other by the semantic trick of using the same modern term to denote both." The point is that, as far as we know, none of these compositions are formally designated as a "lamentation" by their composers. M. Green (1975, 283) concludes, "The city-lament could be another body of literature like myth or epic, which was not viewed by the Sumerians as a single genre."

2.2. The Ur Lament. The Lamentation over the Destruction of Ur (*ANET,* 455-63; *COS* 1.166:535-39) is a 436-line literary masterpiece. It commemorates the fall of Ur to the Elamite and Sua people during the reign of Ibbi-Sin (c. 2006 BC). The opening *kirugu* (musical notation for a section) consists of a long list of gods who have abandoned their respective cities. Then the goddess Ningal, Ur's patron deity, laments the ruination of her city when the god Enlil did not hold back his devastating "storm." She cries out, "My city has been destroyed; my house too has been destroyed; O Nanna, Ur has been destroyed, its people have been dispersed" (lines 249-50). The god Nanna is pled with to restore the city. He is implored to protect the city and keep its citizens "pure."

It is evident that the lament was composed within one generation or so of the event. Characteristic of the neo-Sumerian city laments, it is written primarily in *emegir,* the main Sumerian dialect. However, the first two of its eleven *kirugu*s are in the *emesal* dialect, which seems to have been reserved in Sumerian literary texts for female subjects.

2.3. The Sumer and Ur Lament. The reconstituted text of the Lamentation over the Destruction of Sumer and Ur is 519 lines long, making it longer than the Lamentation over the Destruction of Ur. In this composition the gods have decreed that the divine powers of Sumer be overturned and the city and temple be destroyed. Then, in the aftermath of its destruction, Enlil decrees that Ur be rebuilt and flourish.

Analysis of more than thirty tablets and fragments indicates that the five *kirugu*s of this lament have fairly well preserved roughly eighty percent of the original composition. Mention of the capture of Ibbi-Sin (lines 35-37) suggests that this lament is roughly contemporary with the Lamentation over the Destruction of Ur.

2.4. The Nippur Lament. The lament over Nippur is a 323-line composition divided into twelve *kigurus.* The Nippur lament stands out because there is a shift in theme and tone between the two parts of the composition. The first part is descriptive of destruction and the *suffering that accompanied it; the second part is a hymn of praise to the king and the god Enlil for restoring Nippur.

This lament was composed at Nippur or Isin during the reign of Išme-Dagon (c. 1953-1934 BC), written to be performed in Enlil's temple by the *gala*-priest and the king.

2.5. The Uruk Lament. The lament over the destruction of the city of Uruk and its temple consists of some 251 lines divided into twelve *kirugu*s, half of which are badly damaged or missing. It begins by describing the gods' decision to destroy the city, whose population has become too numerous and a nuisance to the gods. So the gods created a monstrosity that terrorized the city and destroyed it. In the final *kirugu* Išme-Dagon pays obeisance to the goddess Inanna, "Lady whose greatness is vaster that the mountains." He offers to serve her as her steward and prepare a great sacrifice to her. He pleads with her to intercede with the great Anunna-gods on behalf of him and the city.

2.6. The Eridu Lament. The lament over the destruction of the city of Eridu and its temple presently consists of approximately163 lines divided into eight *kirugu*s. The gods Enlil and Damgalnuna (Enlil's consort) grieve over their destroyed temples.

Typical of the Neo-Sumerian city laments, it is written predominantly in the *emegir* dialect. The lament seems to have been composed perhaps either during the reign of Išme-Dagon of Isin (1953-1934 BC) or during the reign Nur-Adad of Larsa (1865-1849 BC), who (re)built a temple at Eridu for the god Enki.

2.7. Structure of the City Laments. Formally, each of the classic city laments is structured as extended stanzas that are marked off by the musical notation *kirugu.* Within these stanzas, thematic elements are developed (see Table 1).

2.8. Use of City Laments. There is some indication that the city laments may have been used

Table 1. Structure of Sumerian City Laments

Lament over Ur	Lament over Sumer and Ur	Lament over Nippur
I. Complaint of abandonment (*kirugu* 1; lines 1-39) II. Call to lament (*kirugu* 2; lines 40-76) III. Ningal's supplication to Nanna about "Storm" and its effects (*kirugu* 3-4; lines 77-172) IV. Description of devastation caused by "Storm" (*kirugu* 5-6; lines 173-253) V. Ningal's lament soliloquy (*kirugu* 7; lines 254-330) VI. Lament for Ningal (*kirugu* 8; lines 331-387) VII. Supplication to Nanna about "Storm" (*kirugu* 9-10; lines 388-417) VIII. Appeal to Nanna for restoration (*kirugu* 11; lines 418-436)	I. Detailed complaint about "Storm" and its effects (*kirugu* 1; lines 1-118) II. Complaint and lament of Sumerian cities (*kirugu* 2; lines 119-282) III. Complaint of Ur (*kirugu* 3; lines 283-339) IV. Complaint and supplication of Sin to Enlil (*kirugu* 4; lines 340-489) V. Appeal for restoration and imprecation (*kirugu* 5; lines 490-500+x+1)	I. Complaint of abandonment of city and temple (*kirugu* 1-3; lines 1-116) II. Call to lament (*kirugu* 4; lines 117-38) III. Appeal to Enlil to restore city (*kirugu* 5-7; lines 139-213) IV. Appeal to Enlil to restore Sumer and Akkad (*kirugu* 8; lines 214-46) V. Litany of restoration (*kirugu* 9; lines 247-62) VI. Description of restoration (*kirugu* 10-12; lines 263-323)

liturgically for a time. For example, in the Curse of Agade, an oracle of the gods against the city because it had been defiled, we read,

> The old women who survived those days,
> The old men who survived those days,
> The chief lamentation singer *[gala]* who
>   survived those days,
> For seven days and seven nights,
> Put in place seven *balag*-drums, as if they
>   stood at heaven's base, and
> Played *ub*, *meze* and *lilis*-drums for him
>   [Enlil] among them [the *balags*].
> The old women did not restrain [the cry]
>   "Alas my city!"
> The old men did not restrain [the cry] "Alas
>   its people!"
> The lamentation singer *[gala]* did not
>   restrain [the cry]
> "Alas the *Ekur* [the god Enlil's 'House like a
>   mountain']!"
> Its young women did not restrain from tearing their hair,
> Its young men did not restrain their sharp
>   knives. (lines 196-206)

Another clue to liturgical use is the division of these compositions into liturgical or musical sections, each designated *ki-ru-gu₂*.

In some cases, it appears that lament played a liturgical role in the aftermath of destruction. It was a means of coping with grief. However, there is reason to believe that, for at least some of these city laments, the occasion of their observance was the dedication of the rebuilt city and temple. The lament was a cry for the deity to return home and prosper its subject city. There is no indication that these city laments were used in annual rites of commemoration.

3. The *Eršemma, Balag* and *Šuilla* Laments.

3.1. **Eršemma.** In the aftermath of the fall of the third dynasty of Ur, the center of power shifted roughly seventy-five miles to the northwest to the city-state of Isin, now controlled by Išbi-Irra. Thus the Isin dynasty was established. It flourished c. 2000-1800 BC Eventually the Isin dynasty collapsed under pressure from a developing dynasty at Larsa, just twenty-two miles northwest of Ur. This development was the subject of several *eršemma* lamentations.

The *eršemma*, which is supposed to mean "crying" of the *šem*-drum or tambourine, apparently receives its name from the practice of reciting this type of composition to the accompaniment of that instrument. It does not make reference to any specific disaster; rather, it seems suited for liturgical use.

3.2. Balag. During the first millennium BC, the *eršemma* laments are found alongside another type of composition, the *balag*. The *balag* apparently took its name from the fact that it was chanted to the accompaniment of a harp or lyre-type instrument called *balag*. The *balag* compositions tended to be rather general in their descriptions of the troubles. Rather than memorializing a disaster, they seem to be intended to assuage the wrath of the gods, as they were used liturgically. These first-millennium laments were bilingual Sumerian/Akkadian, but they lacked the literary flourish of the classical city laments.

3.3. Šuilla. The *šuilla* prayers represent another lament subgenre. They took their name from the gesture of "lifting the hands" when these laments were recited or prayed. Most of the extant *šuilla* laments are bilingual Sumerian/Akkadian as well.

3.4. Structure of Eršemma *and* Balag *Laments.* The structure of *eršemma*s that have been discovered from the Old Babylonian period appear to be indicated by the use of a repetend rather than the *kirugu* notation. First-millennium *eršemma*s may have two or three components. These were marked not by the *kirugu* notation but rather by a heavy line in the clay tablet that separated one section from another.

First-millennium *eršemma*s were commonly associated with the *balag* compositions in the liturgy. But the *balag*s used the *kirugu* notations common to the city laments. There seem to be two main forms of *balag* laments. One type expresses a complaint and an appeal for restoration; the other type adds praise.

4. Summary.

The expression of pain and grief is formalized in the ancient Near Eastern laments, and the gods are confronted over their role in the calamity. The laments may speak of a divine decree that stands behind the calamity. The decree is described as a tremendous storm surge that cannot be stopped or deflected but rather devastates everything in its path.

Secondarily, the antagonist of the lamentation may be a foreign enemy whose attacks are decried. But even here, the gods may be taken to task for merely standing by as the catastrophe occurred, in essence abandoning their city and people to the foe. The laments recount the re-

sulting devastation to the material culture as well as to the society. Families are torn apart. Justice is lost. And the laments complain that religious institutions are devastated as well, and that "light in darkness is overwhelmed." It is typical of the Mesopotamian laments to protest that the calamity was undeserved: the people are likened to an innocent ewe, at least as compared with the rapacious enemy.

Apart from the classical city laments, an element of praise is found in many of the lamentations, especially the *eršemma*. The expressed desire of the community is that the gods will hear the lament, be pacified and reconciled to their people, and restore the city to its former glory.

See also LAMENT, PSALMS OF; LAMENTATIONS 1: BOOK OF.

BIBLIOGRAPHY. **M. Cohen,** *Balag-Compositions: Sumerian Lamentation Liturgies of the Second and First Millennium B.C.* (SANE 1/2; Malibu, CA: Undena, 1974); idem, *Sumerian Hymnology: the Eršemma* (HUCASup 2; Cincinnati: Hebrew Union College, 1981); idem, *The Canonical Lamentations of Ancient Mesopotamia* (2 vols.; Potomac, MD: Capital Decisions, 1988); **J. Cooper,** *The Curse of Agade* (JHNES; Baltimore: Johns Hopkins University Press, 1983); **F. Dobbs-Allsopp,** *Weep, O Daughter of Zion: A Study of the City-Lament Genre in the Hebrew Bible* (BibOr 44; Rome: Pontifical Biblical Institute, 1993); **P. Ferris,** *The Genre of Communal Lament in the Bible and the Ancient Near East* (SBLDS 127; Atlanta: Scholars Press, 1992); **M. Green,** "Eridu in Sumerian Literature," Ph.D. diss., University of Chicago, 1975; idem, "The Eridu Lament," *JCS* 30 (1978) 127-67; idem, "The Uruk Lament," *JAOS* 104 (1984) 253-79; **S. Kramer,** *Lamentation over the Destruction of Ur* (AS12; Chicago: University of Chicago Press, 1940); **R. Kutscher,** *Oh Angry Sea (a-ab-ba- hu-luh-ha): The History of a Sumerian Congregational Lament* (YNER 6; New Haven: Yale University Press, 1975); **P. Michalowski,** *The Lamentation over the Destruction of Sumer and Ur* (Winona Lake, IN: Eisenbrauns, 1989); **J. Morgenstern,** *Rites of Birth, Marriage, Death and Kindred Occasions among the Semites* (Cincinnati: Hebrew Union College, 1966); **S. Tinney,** *The Nippur Lament: Royal Rhetoric and Divine Legitimation in the Reign of Išme-Dagon of Isin (1953-1935 B.C.)* (Occasional Publications of the Samuel Noah Kramer Fund 16; Philadelphia: University of Pennsylvania Museum, 1996).

P. Ferris

LAMENTATIONS 3: HISTORY OF INTERPRETATION

Jewish interpretive traditions regarding the book of Lamentations connect the book loosely with the prophet Jeremiah. Both the Aramaic version (*Targum) of Lamentations (*Tg. Lam.*) and the rabbinic midrash (*Lamentations Rabbah*) are concerned to demonstrate Yahweh's justice in dealing with Jerusalem and to establish the extrabiblical significance of Jeremiah's prophecies in their exegesis of the canonical book. Although no commentary on the book of Lamentations as extensive as those derived from Jewish traditions has survived from before the ninth century AD, Christian interpretive traditions regarding the book seem to have associated it with the prophet Jeremiah from a very early time, possibly as a result of earlier Jewish exegesis. The tradition is by no means monolithic, but the major interpretive shift introduced by the rise of Christianity has been to understand the extrabiblical significance of Lamentations primarily in regard to Jesus, and only as a function of those correspondences to ask after the book's significance in other areas. Critical scholarship treats the book of Lamentations as an essentially human text and is primarily concerned with questions of provenance and literary analysis. On theological matters, the critical interpretive tradition has very little to say about the extrabiblical significance of Lamentations and focuses instead on attempts to describe the historical and theological developments with Judah during the sixth century BC that might have given rise to the work.

1. Jewish Interpretive Traditions
2. Christian Interpretive Traditions
3. Critical Interpretation

1. Jewish Interpretive Traditions.

As stated above, Jewish interpretive traditions regarding the book of Lamentations connect it closely with the prophet Jeremiah. Both *Targum Lamentations* and *Lamentations Rabbah* are concerned to demonstrate Yahweh's justice in dealing with Jerusalem and to establish the extrabiblical significance of Jeremiah's prophecies in their exegesis of the canonical book. (Gwaltney refers to the latter impulse as "the prophecy-fufillment mode of interpretation.") Although the entire body of Jewish reflection on the book of Lamentations is too extensive to treat in this article, much of what will be left unsaid about the topic in what follows could be shown to fit under one or both of these principles.

1.1. Targum. No settled date has been established for the completion *Targum Lamentations*. Based on the late date of extant manuscripts and the mixed linguistic character of the texts that have been preserved, it is likely that no precise dating is possible, although historical references in the work suggest that the Targum cannot have been compiled in its final form before the beginning of the Hasmonean period.

In many respects, *Targum Lamentations* is less a translation of the Hebrew text than a new presentation of its content in explicitly Deuteronomistic terms. In particular, *Targum Lamentations* is at pains to justify Jerusalem's destruction as a result of God's righteous judgment against sin. The author shows no real evidence of being troubled by a need to provide direct, one-to-one linguistic parallels for the MT of Lamentations, as long as the larger objective is met. Examples of this element within the work might easily be multiplied, but *Targum Lamentations* 1:1 is perhaps as clear an indication of the work's general theological character as any:

Jeremiah the prophet and high priest told how it was decreed against Jerusalem and against her people that they were to be judged by exile and that they were to be mourned over—ʾēykâ!—just as Adam and Eve were judged, who were driven from the Garden of Eden, and the Lord of Eternity mourned over them—ʾēykâ! The divine attribute of justice testified, and spoke about the enormity of her sinfulness, and she was sent away. And because of (the sinfulness) that is in her midst, she will dwell by herself just as a man whose flesh is afflicted with a leprous plague (also) dwells alone. In this way, *the city that was full of crowds and many people has been emptied* of them, and *she has become like a widow*, and *the one who was exalted among the nations*, and *the ruler over provinces* that used to pay her tribute, *has come to lowliness* and (even) to (the point of) paying them a head-tax. (my translation)

Although the immediate justification for Yahweh's judgment against Jerusalem is expressed in relation to Israel's faithlessness upon entering the promised land (*Tg. Lam.* 1:2), *Targum Lamentations'* description of Israel's guilt is not limited to specific episodes from the biblical period. Other sins named as justifications for God's wrath include oppression of orphans and widows as well as excessive taxation of the children of Israel (*Tg. Lam.* 1:2), failure to keep the festivals prescribed by Yahweh (*Tg. Lam.* 1:4), transgressing the word of Yahweh (*Tg. Lam.* 1:20), ceremonial impurity and failure to keep Yahweh's commandments (*Tg. Lam.* 2:9, 17), killing priests and prophets (*Tg. Lam.* 2:20), and false prophecy (*Tg. Lam.* 3:13), many of which extend well outside the realm of biblical history. Similarly, the destruction of Jerusalem described in MT Lamentations is also presented in terms of both biblical and extrabiblical historical events. Thus, both Nebuchadnezzar's destruction of Jerusalem (*Tg. Lam.* 1:2) and the conquest of the land by Titus and Vespasian (*Tg. Lam.* 1:9) are presented as the subject matter actually under consideration in the biblical text. In this way, the author of *Targum Lamentations* uses the basic hermeneutical principles that we have noted to express what he perceives as the broader historical and theological significance of the Hebrew *Vorlage*: God's righteous anger over sin justifies the destruction of Jerusalem described in Lamentations, as well as the various struggles experienced by Yahweh's people throughout all of recorded history, for entirely interchangeable reasons.

1.2. Rabbinic Midrash. Lamentations Rabbah is an exegetical compilation of interpretive statements made by various Jewish scholars of the Tannaitic and Amoraic periods (a time span of AD 200 to 600). It expounds the MT of Lamentations verse by verse, and sometimes word by word. The teachings included in the work have been culled from other sources, including the Jerusalem Talmud, *Genesis Rabbah* and *Leviticus Rabbah*, and do not include a mention of any *sage known to have been alive after the fourth century AD. Formally, the book is divided into thirty-six *petiḥaʾot* (corresponding to the numerical value of the first word of the Hebrew text) and five *parashiyyot* (corresponding to the five chapters of MT Lamentations).

Although it is true that *Lamentations Rabbah* does not present a smooth propositional explication of the biblical text, J. Neusner has shown that it is possible to discern some interpretive structure within the collection and to identify several key points in its overall theology. As with

Targum Lamentations, rabbinic midrash relating to the MT of Lamentations reflects a deep desire to show the justice of God's judgment against Jerusalem and to portray God's wrath against sin as an ongoing reality in the experience of his people. In the rabbinic exegesis of Lamentations, however, this agenda is accompanied by an increased emphasis on God's corresponding compassion and mercy, as well as the opportunity for repentance and reconciliation in the aftermath of divine chastisement. Thus, in its approach to Lamentations 1:22 (MT: "Let all their evil doing come before you, and deal with them as you have dealt with me because of all my transgressions, for my groans are many and my heart is faint."), Parashah 1 of *Lamentations Rabbah* records the following statements:

> When they sinned in double measure, they were smitten in double measure, but they were comforted in double measure.
>
> When they sinned in double measure: "Jerusalem has committed a sin," (Lam 1:8)
>
> . . . they were smitten in double measure: "that she has received from Yahweh's hand double for all her sins," (Is 40:2)
>
> . . . but they were comforted in double measure: "Comfort, comfort, my people." says your God. ("Speak tenderly to the heart of Jerusalem and cry to her that her warfare is ended, that her iniquity is pardoned, that she has received from Yahweh double for all her sins"). (Is 40:1-2)

As this quotation suggests, the interpretive program of *Lamentations Rabbah* is carried out by means of extensive reference to other portions of the Hebrew Bible. In this respect, the rabbinic midrash on Lamentations is more narrowly exegetical than *Targum Lamentations*, although the interpretive assumptions and objectives remain very much the same. What this quotation does not make clear is the frequency with which the rabbinic exegetes use extrabiblical historical references to help make sense of the judgments pronounced against Jerusalem in the book of Lamentations. For example, Parashah 2 of *Lamentations Rabbah* specifically identifies numerous postbiblical events related to the Bar Kokhba rebellion as having some direct bearing on the text of Lamentations and its ongoing historical significance.

1.3. Jewish Liturgical Use of Lamentations.

Largely as a function of the interpretive traditions that we have just observed, selections from Lamentations are read on the Ninth of Av (July-August, according to the modern calendar), on which date Judaism commemorates not only the destruction of the temple described in Lamentations but also the destruction of the second temple, the end of the Bar Kokhba rebellion and the plowing over of Jerusalem by the Romans.

2. Christian Interpretive Traditions.

AS stated above, although no commentary on the book of Lamentations as extensive as those derived from Jewish traditions has survived from before the ninth century AD, Christian interpretive traditions regarding the book seem to have associated it with the prophet Jeremiah from a very early time, possibly as a result of earlier Jewish exegesis. The tradition is by no means monolithic, but the major interpretive shift introduced by the rise of Christianity has been to understand the extrabiblical significance of Lamentations primarily in regard to Jesus, and only as a function of those correspondences to ask after the book's significance in other areas. Practically speaking, this new approach to Scripture seems to have deemphasized sustained interaction with the text in all of its particulars, particularly in the early church, in favor of a more selective search for specific data points that could be used to support a particular line of reasoning or address a single, specific set of circumstances.

2.1. Early Church. Among the surviving documents produced by the early church, various passages from the book of Lamentations are quoted, although no commentaries on the complete text are now known to be extant. Taken together, the early church's uses of Lamentations are remarkably limited, both with respect to the variety of passages that seem to have attracted attention and in terms of the specific purposes for which the book of Lamentations appears to have been considered appropriate. By far the most popular verse of Lamentations used in these writings is the LXX version of Lamentations 4:20:

Pneuma prosōpou hēmōn, christos kyriou, synelēmphthē en tais diaphthorais autōn hou eipamen, En tē skia autou zēsometha en tois ethnesin

The breath of our nostrils, the Lord's anointed

one, was caught in their destructions, of whom we said, "In his shadow we shall live among the Gentiles."

Given the presence of the Greek word *christos* (= *māšîaḥ* ["anointed one"] in the MT), this passage was explicitly identified as a reference to Jesus Christ by the church fathers and was put to considerable use, especially in apologetic discussions. Use of the Greek word *pneuma* (= *rûaḥ* ["breath, wind, spirit"] in the MT) also seems to have been highly suggestive for the church fathers. Given the prevalence of LXX Lamentations 4:20 in patristic exegesis of the book, a few representative citations will be useful in demonstrating the distinctly Christian turn in the history of interpretation during this time (translations are from *Ante-Nicene Fathers* and series 1 and 2 of *Nicene and Post-Nicene Fathers*).

(1) Irenaeus, *Demonstration of the Apostolic Preaching* (71): "And in another place, Jeremiah says: '*The Spirit of our face, the Lord Christ*'; and '*he was taken in their snares, of whom we said under His shadow we shall live among the Gentiles.*' That, being the Spirit of God, Christ was to become a suffering man the Scripture declares, and is, as it were, amazed and astonished at His sufferings, that in such manner, He was to endure sufferings '*under whose shadow we said that we should live.*' And by 'shadow,' he means His body. For just as a shadow is made by a body, so also Christ's body was made by His Spirit."

(2) Rufinus, *A Commentary on the Apostles' Creed*, in the context of defending Christ's death and resurrection: "But they who boast themselves of the knowledge of the Law will say to us, 'You blaspheme in saying that the Lord was subjected to the corruption of death and to the suffering of the cross.' Read therefore what you find written in the Lamentations of Jeremiah: '*The Spirit of our countenance, Christ the Lord, was taken in our corruptions, of whom we said, we shall live under His shadow among the nations.*' Thou hearest how the prophet says that Christ the Lord was taken, and for us, that is for our sins, was delivered to corruption. Under whose shadow, since the people of the Jews have continued in unbelief, he says the gentiles lie, because we live not in Israel but among the gentiles."

(3) Basil, *On the Spirit*, in the context of asserting the divinity of the Holy Spirit: "It is at all events possible for us to arrive to a certain ex-

tent at an intelligent apprehension of the sublimity of His nature and of His unapproachable power by looking at the meaning of His title, and at the magnitude of His operations, and by His good gifts bestowed on us, or rather on all creation. He is called Spirit, as 'God is a Spirit,' and *'the breath of our nostrils, the anointed of the Lord.'"*

Other passages from Lamentations attested among the writings of the early church include Lamentations 1:1; 1:2; 1:4; 1:8; 1:16; 1:20; 2:1-2; 3:28; 3:31-32, 34; 3:53. Among these, Lamentations 3:34 ("To crush under his feet all the prisoners of the land") and Lamentations 3:53 ("They have cut off my life in the pit and have laid a stone upon me") have also been put to explicitly christocentric use by Mehodius (seven times) and Rufinus *(A Commentary on the Apostles' Creed)*. The rest are generally employed in various reflections on individual *suffering and repentance (Lam 1:2, 4, 16, 20; Ambrose *Concerning Repentance* [book 2, chap. 6]; Lam 1:8: Clement of Alexandria *The Teacher* [book 1, chap. 9]; Lam 3:31-32, 34: Ambrose *Concerning Repentance* [book 1, chap. 5]) or are used to comment on events from the history of the early church in some way (Lam 1:1: Gregory of Nazianzus *On Athanasius;* Lam 1:4: Gregory of Nyssa *Funeral Oration on Meletius*; Lam 2:1-2: Eusebius *Church History* [book 8, chap. 1]; Lam 3:28: Gregory of Nazianzus *Second Oration*).

2.2. Medieval and Reformation Commentaries. This period in the history of interpretation for the book of Lamentations covers an enormous body of literature that cannot be examined in detail here. For the most part, these exegetes seem to have been concerned with citing and maintaining the general trajectories of interpretation drawn by the early church. Early versions of complete commentaries on the book by Hrbanus Maurus and Paschius Radbertus are still extant and will give some idea of the character of medieval exegesis (see Matter), while Calvin's commentary is indicative of the shift toward something closer to modern historical-critical interpretation that came about during the late Middle Ages and the Reformation.

2.2.1. Hrbanus Maurus. As with previous exegetes in both the Christian and Jewish traditions, Maurus comments on Lamentations in direct connection with the prophecy of Jeremiah. He draws from the few patristic commentaries available to him, although the bulk of the

work appears to have been the product of his own reflection on the book. Maurus tends to downplay the historical significance of the text in favor of a reading that can be applied in much broader terms, so that the city of Jerusalem represents the individual soul, while the overall narrative of Lamentations portrays the soul's confrontation with sin.

2.2.2. Paschasius Radbertus. Radbertus is responsible for the first standalone treatment of the book in the Latin tradition. The preface is an excursus on the theological significance of mourning. In Radbertus's interpretation the book Lamentations is presented as the theological and devotional counterpart to Song of Songs. The former is a description of the suffering brought about by God's abandonment, while the latter expresses the blessed state of those who enjoy God's care and protection. Drawing heavily from Hrbanus, as well as numerous biblical passages that he understands as relevant to the text of Lamentations, Radbertus explicates the book in terms of the past, present and future destruction of Jerusalem, the church and the individual soul.

2.2.3. John Calvin. Later in the Middle Ages, historical and grammatical analysis came to be viewed as the proper foundation for biblical interpretation, upon which all legitimate readings must necessarily be based. Aquinas, in particular, was instrumental in thus separating literal and historical exegesis from spiritual and theological interpretation (see Smalley, 10-42). With respect to the history of interpretation for the book of Lamentations, John Calvin's commentary is emblematic of this shift toward historical and philological inquiry as the primary focus of exegesis. Note, for example, the tone of the work's opening paragraph:

I undertake now to explain the Lamentations of Jeremiah. We must inquire when the book was composed by the Prophet, and also what was the object of the author. Grossly mistaken was Jerome, who thought that it is the elegy which Jeremiah composed on the death of Josiah; for we see nothing here that is suitable to that event. There is indeed mention made in one place of a king, but what is said there cannot be applied to Josiah; for he was never driven into exile, but was buried at Jerusalem with his fathers. From the whole contents of the book, we may justly conclude that it was written after the city was destroyed and the people taken into exile. (Calvin, 299)

It would be misleading to suggest that Calvin takes no interest in the spiritual and theological significance of the book of Lamentations, although these introductory statements are of a piece with the rest of his commentary. For confirmation of this, perhaps the best evidence is to observe his commentary on Lamentations 4:20, which was put to extensive christological use by earlier exegetes. In his commentary Calvin does not draw any explicit link from Lamentations 4:20 to the NT but rather is content to focus on the significance of that verse in relation to the historical fall of Jerusalem in 587 BC.

2.3. Christian Liturgical Use of Lamentations. In some liturgical traditions selections from the book of Lamentations are read during the Lenten season, on Maundy Thursday, Good Friday and Holy Saturday. As with Jewish liturgical uses of the book, this points out what is clearly a perception of the book's intimate connection with both corporate and personal penitence and reflection.

3. Critical Interpretation.

As stated above, critical scholarship treats the book of Lamentations as an essentially human text and is primarily concerned with questions of provenance and literary analysis. On theological matters, the critical interpretive tradition has very little to say about the extrabiblical significance of Lamentations and focuses instead on attempts to describe the historical and theological developments with Judah during the sixth century BC that might have given rise to the work. In some sense, it may seem artificial to lump all commentaries produced since the Reformation together under the heading "critical commentaries." This is particularly true when the heading has been explicitly distinguished from "Christian interpretation," since many of the exegetes who have written during this time period perhaps considered themselves to fall within the Christian religious tradition. Nevertheless, it is true that much of the methodology employed in recent times has been shaped by critical assumptions about Scripture, and, as P. House has suggested (Garrett and House, 278-81), this has led to a sharp decline in explicitly Christian reflection on the significance of Lam-

entations, either in theological or devotional terms.

3.1. Criticism and the Fragmentation of Lamentations. The basic assumptions of critical studies include a suspicion about the authority of religious tradition as a guide to interpretation and a commitment to the idea that any work of Scripture is essentially the same as any other humanly produced work of literature. This approach to the book of Lamentations has brought with it a number of changes in the interpretation of the book. To begin with, the book's close association with the prophet Jeremiah has been almost universally set aside in favor of more agnostic approach to the question of authorship (the book itself does not actually ascribe authorship to Jeremiah). Along with this, questions of literary genre and observations about literary style have led to a reexamination of the book's basic literary unity as well as its possible connection with other similar literary texts from elsewhere in the ancient Near East. At the present time, the weight of critical scholarly opinion seems to be that the book of Lamentations is a work of mixed literary genre, probably written by several authors, with close affinities to both the *lament psalms of the Hebrew Bible and the city laments produced in both Babylonian and Assyrian cultures.

3.2. Expressions of Suffering and the Theology of Lamentations. As a purely literary text, the themes that dominate the text of Lamentations are plain enough. Among the most obvious are suffering and loss, the desire for some kind of meaning in the face of Jerusalem's destruction, and hope for future deliverance. Particularly since the second half of the twentieth century, interpreters have tried to establish what set of historical circumstances and theological vision best accounts for the various themes of Lamentations.

3.2.1. Gottwald. N. Gottwald has argued that the theological vision driving the book of Lamentations was the expectation of God's blessings in response to covenant keeping, an idea that he described as central to Deuteronomistic theology. For Gottwald, this Deuteronomistic expectation of blessing would have been operative in Jerusalem around 587 BC as a result of the Josianic reforms, only to be directly contradicted by the historical reality of Jerusalem's destruction at the hands of foreign invaders. This conflict between faith and experience, he suggested, would have given rise to the kind of religious questioning depicted in Lamentations. There is much to be commended in Gottwald's work, but his view of the theological foundation for the book of Lamentations has been subject to a number of criticisms, many of which were first articulated by B. Albrektson in 1963.

3.2.2. Albrektson. In response to Gottwald's view of the theology of Lamentations, B. Albrektson makes two central arguments. First, judging from the text of Lamentations, Albrektson argues that the reforms of King Josiah do not appear to have created among Judah's inhabitants anything like the expectation of blessing that Gottwald has in mind. Instead, he points out that there is another aspect of Deuteronomistic theology—the expectation of judgment against covenant-breakers—already on display in the text itself (see Lam 1:5, 8, 18). Second, Albrektson argues that the expectation of divine protection, which he agrees is present in Lamentations, is better understood as a function of *Zion theology, first developed by earlier authors in the Psalter (see Ps 46:6-8; 48:2-9; 76:2-7, 13). Thus Albrektson sees not a single central point but rather two foci: the Deuteronomistic assurance of judgment against covenant-breakers and the psalmists' confidence in the inviolability of Zion as the theological principles that hold the themes and content of the book of Lamentations together.

3.2.3. Commentaries after Albrektson. Since 1963, the theological analysis of Lamentations presented by Albrektson seems generally to have been accepted, even if it has been objected that he tends to overstate the retributive element of Deuteronomistic theology in Lamentations (inasmuch as he ignores the author's sympathy for the inhabitants of Jerusalem) and to question whether the inviolability of Zion and the impregnability of Jerusalem are actually identical concepts in the Hebrew Bible. One important development after Albrektson has been the tendency to place renewed emphasis on the importance of the expression of radical suffering as a legitimate and necessary aspect of sincere religious experience. This move is perhaps most extensively reflected in the work of C. Westermann, although F. Dobbs-Allsopp, J. Renkema, I. Provan, P. House and others also have advocated a similar focus of attention in recent years. From the perspective of discussions about the theological vision presented by the book of Lamentations, this move is particularly helpful because it focuses attention on the point at which the various strands of OT theology presented by the book of Lamentations actually come into contact with one another.

See also FEMINIST INTERPRETATION; HERMENEUTICS; LAMENTATIONS 1: BOOK OF; MEGILLOT AND FESTIVALS; TARGUMIM.

BIBLIOGRAPHY. **B. Albrektson,** *Studies in the Text and Theology of the Book of Lamentations, with a Critical Edition of the Peshitta Text* (STL 21; Lund: Gleerup, 1963); **A. Berlin,** *Lamentations* (OTL; Louisville: Westminster John Knox, 2002); **C. M. M. Brady,** *The Rabbinic Targum of Lamentations: Vindicating God* (SAIS 3; Leiden: E. J. Brill, 2003); **J. Calvin,** *Commentaries on the Prophet Jeremiah and Lamentations,* (Grand Rapids: Eerdmans, 1950); **F. W. Dobbs-Allsopp,** *Lamentations* (IBC; Louisville: Westminster John Knox, 2002); **D. A. Garret and P. R. House,** *Song of Songs, Lamentations* (WBC 23B; Nashville: Thomas Nelson, 2004); **N. K. Gottwald,** *Studies in the Book of Lamentations* (Chicago: Allenson, 1954); **W. C. Gwaltney Jr.,** "The Biblical Book of Lamentations in the Context of Ancient Near Eastern Lament Literature," in *Scripture in Context II: More Essays on the Comparative Method,* ed. W. W. Hallo, J. C. Moyer and L. G. Perdue (Winona Lake, IN: Eisenbrauns, 1983) 191-211; idem, "Lamentations, Book of," in *Dictionary of Biblical Interpretation,* ed. J. H. Hayes (2 vols.; Nashville: Abingdon, 1999) 2.44-48; **D. Hillers,** *Lamentations* (2nd ed.; AB 7A; Garden City, NY: Doubleday, 1992); **S. N. Kramer,** "Sumerian Literature and the Bible," in *Studia biblica et orientalia,* 3: *Oriens antiquus* (AnBib 12; Rome: Pontifical Biblical Institute, 1959) 198-225; **É. Levine,** *The Aramaic Version of Lamentations* (New York: Hermon Press, 1976); **E. A. Matter,** "The Lamentations Commentaries of Hrbanus Maurus and Paschius Radbertus," *Traditio* 38 (1982) 137-63; **T. F. McDaniel,** "Alleged Sumerian Influence on Lamentations," *VT* 18 (1968) 198-209; **J. Neusner,** *A Theological Commentary to the Midrash,* 5: *Lamentations Rabbati* (Lanham, MD: University Press of America, 2001); **I. Provan,** *Lamentations* (NCBC; Grand Rapids: Eerdmans, 1991); **J. Renkema,** *Lamentations,* (HCOT; Leuven: Peeters, 1998); **B. Smalley,** *The Study of the Bible in the Middle Ages* (Oxford: Blackwell, 1983); **C. Westermann,** *Lamentations: Issues and Interpretation* (Edinburgh: T & T Clark, 1994).

B. Pickut

LAW

Legal analysis of the poetic books and other writings under consideration confronts a diverse set of genres, data and perspectives. Only a few common themes emerge. Of these, the most important may be law's relationship to the divine administration of justice in the world. Other issues to be addressed include allusions to law in poetic *imagery and the depiction of legal practice in narrative. These matters will be considered by means of examining each book's legal content and import.

In referring to "the law," the discussion below does not distinguish between biblical law, whether referred to in the Writings or in the Pentateuch, and the law of ancient Israel and Judah. No conclusive evidence exists, however, to show that the two were the same (Wells 2004, 11-15). There may have been significant overlap between the laws in the Bible and those in force in Israelite and Judahite society, especially in the postexilic period, but this is not certain. The law referred to in the poetic and narrative texts examined here, therefore, reveals what was considered right behavior from particular religious perspectives. It may or may not reveal information regarding operative societal law.

1. Divine Justice and Law
2. Poetic Imagery and Law
3. Narrative and Law
4. Summary

1. Divine Justice and Law.

Many of the psalms and numerous wisdom passages consider the justice, or injustice, of Yahweh's actions and his intervention in the affairs of life. The books of *Psalms and *Proverbs tend to present what was likely the traditional understanding of this issue in ancient Judah. Yahweh is just and is consistently so. The books of *Job and *Ecclesiastes raise critical questions regarding this understanding. All four books share, however, the assumptions that Yahweh is the final judge of human behavior, may put humans on trial, and gives blessings to those found righteous and punishment to those found guilty of sin (Avalos, 242-44). They view relationship with Yahweh through the eyes of law. Thus, much of the language used in the prayers, instructions and discourses of these writings also

has legal meaning (Magdalene 2007a).

1.1. Psalms. At least two questions are pertinent to a legal analysis of the psalms. First, what was the "law" for the authors of the psalms? Their prayers, *laments, songs of *thanksgiving and other poetic expressions contain references to law in general and also to specific commandments. The latter include a number of prohibitions well known from the Pentateuch, including those against false oaths (Ps 10:7; 24:4), lending money at interest or accepting bribes (Ps 15:5), false accusation (Ps 27:12), robbery and economic abuse (Ps 62:10), the worship of foreign gods (Ps 81:9) and the mistreatment of widows and orphans (Ps 94:6). As implied above, though, this question is different from asking what was the law of the society in which the psalmists lived. Second, how did the authors of the psalms understand the function of what they called law with respect to their own and their community's relationship with Yahweh? In other words, why was it important or how was it beneficial for them to "keep" the law (e.g., Ps 119:34)? The answer to both questions could well lie in the psalms' connection to legal issues and perspectives that are found primarily, although not exclusively, in the book of Deuteronomy. It appears that the psalmists' law either is or is very much like Deuteronomic law (Miller). Moreover, a strongly Deuteronomic point of view underlies the psalmists' emphasis on adherence to the law. This connection to Deuteronomy manifests itself both in the psalms' legal vocabulary and in their view of divine retributive justice.

First, it is Deuteronomic terminology for law that pervades the psalms (e.g., Ps 7:6), especially the three so-called Torah psalms (Pss 1; 19; 119). The six key terms used are *tôrâ* ("law, teaching"), *ʿēdût* ("decrees"), *piqqûdîm* ("precepts"), *ḥōq* ("statute, law"), *miṣwâ* ("commandment") and *mišpaṭ* ("judgment, ruling"). Due to the poetic *parallelism in which these words occur, it is difficult to identify precise distinctions in meaning among them. They probably function in the psalms as various ways to refer to a particular body of law, which appears to derive, in large measure, from Deuteronomy. The "law [*tôrâ*] of Yahweh" in Psalm 1 points to Deuteronomy, since the specific statement about meditating on the *tôrâ* day and night occurs only in Psalm 1:2; Joshua 1:8. The latter clearly has the law of Deuteronomy in view, and this increases the likelihood that the former does as well. Furthermore, the authors of Psalm 19 and Psalm 119, as well as other passages (e.g., Ps 78:5), have clustered their key legal terms to place greater emphasis on the law. Similar clusters of these very terms occur almost exclusively in Deuteronomy and the Deuteronomistic History (Deut 5:31; 6:1; 7:11; 11:1; 26:16-17; 1 Kings 8:58; 2 Kings 17:37).

Second, the psalms and Deuteronomy share the same pronounced view of retributive justice. For Deuteronomy, it is obedience to Yahweh's commandments that will bring health, prosperity and success (Deut 15:4-6; 28:1-14). He requites disobedience with sickness, poverty and defeat (Deut 28:15-68). The psalmists' view is remarkably similar. For them, Yahweh is the supreme and righteous judge of the cosmos (e.g., Ps 7:8-11; 82:1). As such, he makes covenants (e.g., Ps 25:10; 89:3), investigates *(bāḥan; ḥāqar; nāśâ; pāqad; ṣārap)* possible covenantal breaches (e.g., Ps 7:9; 17:3; 26:2; 44:21), and enforces the covenants with lawsuits *(rîb; mišpāṭ* [e.g., Ps 82; 143:2]). Yahweh evaluates the degree to which an individual or a society adheres to covenantal law (Ps 78:10; 103:18) and blesses or punishes accordingly (Ps 1:5-6; 5:12; 9:17; 33:12; 37:17). At times, though, the psalmists believed that this system of justice had malfunctioned, and that the misfortune that they were experiencing was unfair. This was when they would petition Yahweh for assistance (e.g., Ps 4:1; 5:2; 17:1; 55:1-2; 119:154; 130:2-3), appealing to his own rules of justice and couching their prayers in terms that simultaneously carried religious and legal significance: "call" *(qārā᾽)*, "hear" *(šamaᶜ)*, "listen" *(he᾽ĕzin)*, "answer" *(ᶜānâ)*, "redeem" *(gā᾽al)*, "cry" *(šāwaᶜ)*, "prayer, supplication, petition" *(tĕpillâ)*, "complaint" *(śiaḥ)* and numerous others (Bovati). The psalmists believed that Yahweh could be persuaded of the merit of their petitions and would then act on their behalf (Morrow, 47-48). The petitioners thus felt that they were justified in pleading for vindication for themselves (e.g., Ps 26:1) and ruin for their adversaries (e.g., Ps 143:11-12). Additionally, if the oppression resulted from a seemingly unfair divine judgment against the psalmist, he or she could petition Yahweh to rehear the case and could submit additional evidence of *righteousness to Yahweh (e.g., Ps 88).

1.2. Proverbs. The Wisdom literature in Proverbs reiterates in many respects the view of justice and much of the vocabulary contained in

Psalms (e.g., Prov 18:17; 19:28; 23:11). It is "righteousness" that Yahweh will reward with economic prosperity, good fortune and long life; those who displease Yahweh, conversely, are punished (Prov 3:33; 10:24-25; 12:21). For these wisdom texts, being in the right includes behavior that accords with the law: accurate weights and measures (Prov 11:1; 20:23), justice in the judicial system (Prov 12:17; 14:25) and general obedience to the "commandments" (Prov 10:8; 13:13). When Proverbs addresses matters of law at length, it generally reveals an understanding that coincides with long-standing legal tradition. For instance, the discussion in Proverbs 6 about adultery fits well with what is known regarding laws governing adultery throughout the ancient Near East (Wells 2005). The text is addressed to men, and it contrasts prostitution (paying for sex with an unmarried woman) with adultery (having sex with a married woman, not simply any woman other than one's wife). The former will cost money or goods, but the latter can be lethal (Prov 6:26). Moreover, if a man commits adultery, his life is now in the hands of the offended husband, who has the legal right to decide the adulterer's fate (Prov 6:34-35) (*see* Marriage and Sex).

A righteous life includes, however, more than strict adherence to the law. Mere obedience no longer equals the blessing of Yahweh. The equation requires the addition of wisdom—that is, the range of virtues considered to accompany a life governed by wisdom: diligence (Prov 6:6-11; 10:4), generosity (Prov 14:31; 22:9), judicious speech (Prov 17:28; 21:23), humility (Prov 18:12; 22:4) and sexual fidelity (Prov 5:18-20), among others. If the psalmists' views on what would merit the blessing of Yahweh tend toward a "law alone" approach, those in Proverbs favor one that is "law plus."

This raises the question of the relationship between wisdom and law. Recent scholarship has adopted a variety of viewpoints on this issue. One position holds that wisdom, in a sense, gave birth to law. According to this view, early Israel, as revealed in portions of the Pentateuch, functioned more or less as a loose collection of households and kinship groups and had no binding law that transcended the authority of family and clan leaders. Disputes would have been resolved, therefore, not by means of established rules but rather by appeal to the collective wisdom and experience of the groups and leaders involved in the dispute. Over time, as legal thinking evolved, many of the rules that were concretized in pentateuchal law originated in the accumulated store of this tribal wisdom from an earlier era (Blenkinsopp). The importance of this type of wisdom may have led not only to legal traditions that later took written form but also to the practice of recording wisdom instructions in writing. This might explain the similar statements found in both legal and wisdom texts on topics such as treatment of one's parents (Ex 21:17; Prov 20:20), deceptive business practices (Deut 25:15; Prov 11:1; 16:11) and respect for property boundaries (Deut 19:14; Prov 22:28; 23:10). Thus, proponents of this position maintain that much of pentateuchal law likely developed within an intellectual environment steeped in wisdom rather than within a forensic setting (Jackson, 45-59).

Another point of view finds the idea that wisdom birthed law highly questionable. It can be argued that if one derives from the other, then wisdom derives from law and that the evolutionary understanding of Israelite society assumed by the first view may not be accurate. In fact, it seems equally legitimate to conclude that pentateuchal texts intend to portray early Israel as being governed by a substantial body of formal legal rules (Barmash, 20-27). The rise of wisdom may well have come later as an attempt to move from a strictly rules-based system that operated only within rigid boundaries to an advice-based way of living that had implications for areas of life outside the bounds of law. The range of advice and topics that arise in Wisdom literature, consequently, can be seen as grounded in but reaching well beyond the law (Krüger 1997). Ultimately, though, the book of Proverbs itself provides insufficient data to determine with any degree of certainty wisdom's precise relationship with law. Assertions about an organic relationship between law and wisdom must remain tentative (Crenshaw 1995, 419-25). There is some textual evidence for the view that wisdom is based in law, but this comes only in later Jewish Wisdom literature, particularly *Sirach, which proclaims the student of wisdom to be primarily a student of *tôrâ* (Sir 24:23; 38:34b; 39:8).

1.3. Job. With the book of Job a different perspective on law and justice begins to appear. Scholarship on Job has revealed that the book is replete with legal content. Most notably, the book tends to follow the format and procedures of a trial (Scholnick). It seems that the author's purpose for this elaborate trial story is to explore a common conception in his day that those who undergo suffering are the subject of a divine trial and of retributive punishment if found guilty. The characters of the book generally agree on how justice should operate: the wicked should experience suffering as punishment for their wickedness, while the righteous should be blessed. They disagree, however, regarding whether or not justice actually does work this way and, if it does not, whether Yahweh or God (hereafter "God" because the Joban text alternates terminology) should be held responsible (Newsom, 336).

Much disagreement exists among scholars regarding who brings the legal action in Job, the nature of the action, the bases of the charge, when the charge is brought, who is the trial's judge, and so forth. From a legal comparative perspective, whereby the book's legal metaphors are examined in light of ancient Near Eastern trial procedure, the book may be described as follows. The trial is complex but seems to begin when the *Satan brings a formal legal accusation against Job in the *divine council that Job possesses a blasphemous mind (Job 1:11; 2:5). God must permit the trial to proceed in order not to corrupt or circumvent the existing divine legal system. Thus, Job endures a torturous legal investigation. The Satan's hope is to hear Job blaspheme God to his face, an act that would serve as the best evidence on the charge before the council (Magdalene 2007b, chap. 5). Job assumes, though, that God is the accusing party and decides to countersue God (Habel, 38; Westbrook 1988, 35 n. 134). He claims that God is guilty of abuse of authority (Job 10:2-7; 19:6-7), primarily for bringing a suit that lacks sufficient justification.

The book's law reflects important aspects of the legal system in force during the Neo-Babylonian and early Persian periods. During those periods, for instance, Mesopotamian trial courts often required the accusing party to produce a second accuser or corroborating witness before finding the defendant guilty (Magdalene 2004). This practice may reveal why Job seeks to find someone to join his claim as a second accuser against God (Job 19:25), but no one is willing. Instead of taking Job's position, the three friends seek to impeach Job, impugn his integrity, and defend God. Adopting the Deuteronomic view of retributive justice, they believe that Job's punishment is an appropriate divine response to a sin that he surely must have committed (Job 22:4-11). The friends insist that Job plead guilty and seek God's mercy.

Elihu's appearance on the scene in Job 32 has been the cause of no little debate. Most scholars see him and his speeches as an editorial insertion subsequent to the original composition of the book. Within the legal framework described above, though, his appearance is not necessarily intrusive. Elihu contends that Job's speeches do indeed constitute blasphemy. He goes on to accuse Job directly and offers a prosecutorial speech (Job 34). In this way, Elihu becomes the Satan's second accuser in the trial before the divine council. He thereby picks up where the Satan left off and completes the case against Job (Magdalene 2007b, chap. 9).

What happens at the end of the book can reasonably be characterized as an out-of-court settlement (Magdalene 2007b, chap. 10). Job, perhaps intimidated by the forcefulness of God's defense and certainly without a second accuser, concedes in his countersuit. God, though having defended himself vigorously, seems forced to admit that allowing the suit against Job to go forward was unfair (Job 42:8; cf. Job 42:11). There is no decisive legal victory for either party, opening up the possibility for settlement. The existence of the settlement is apparent from God's restoration of Job's children, property and honor. Such restoration, particularly doubling Job's previous property, strongly resembles—given evidence from ancient Near Eastern trial records—the penalty that might have been imposed on God had Job's countersuit been successful. Settlements often mirrored, at least in part, damage payments that a court might award, but they avoided the humiliation of a formal finding of guilt. In the end, the book falls short of refuting the claim that God justly controls the suffering of humankind, but it opens the door for critical assessment of that proposition.

1.4. Ecclesiastes. Understanding the treatment of law in Ecclesiastes requires a decision regarding the book's literary integrity and purpose because it seems to contain conflicting ideologies and approaches to the law. At times, the book appears dismissive of any sure reliance on the law (e.g., Eccles 7:15; 8:14-17). At other times, the book speaks as if it embraces a traditional understanding of the import of following the law (e.g., Eccles 11:9). This is particularly true of the epilogue, which advocates, albeit briefly, a very high view of the law or the "commandments" *(miṣwôt)* and maintains that the law is "the whole duty of man because God will bring every deed into judgment *(mišpāṭ)*" (Eccles 12:13-14).

As a result, scholars hold profoundly different views of the literary integrity and purpose of the book. One view argues that a single author wrote the whole of the book. The question confronting those who hold this position is whether the author sought ultimately to refute traditional wisdom, theology and law (Crenshaw 1987) or held a more conflicted attitude toward these ideas (Fox). A second view contends that one author wrote most portions of the book, but a later editor inserted glosses of a more traditional nature to soften the radical views of the text (Murphy 1990b, 49-63). A third view maintains that the composer of the book's prologue and epilogue used the speeches of *Qohelet as a foil to demonstrate the weaknesses in Qohelet's arguments; the point of the book comes in the epilogue (Longman). Deciding between these views may depend on how one understands the purpose of the epilogue. Is it attempting to correct the ideas of Qohelet? Or does the epilogue reflect a genuine endorsement of Qohelet's critical, even skeptical, approach? The debate continues, but most recent scholarship tends to see the epilogue as congruent with Qohelet's speeches (Krüger 2004, 207-15).

If Qohelet's speeches do indeed convey much of the book's message, it can be said that the book's reception of law, wisdom and the traditional view of divine *retribution is significantly less enthusiastic than that in much of Proverbs. Instead of regarding a priori the traditional understanding of law and justice as normative, the book measures that understanding against lived experience and finds it wanting, much like Job (Eccles 4:1-3). To be sure, the book does not entirely abandon the concept of divine retribution, nor does it omit references to matters of law; however, it affords neither one a prominent place in its discourses. One of its key points may be that a monolithic view of life and the workings of divine justice is shortsighted or even naïve.

The explicitly legal issues raised by the text are few. It laments injustice in the judicial system (Eccles 3:16); its call for the fulfillment of vows

(Eccles 5:4-6) may hark back to pentateuchal statements regarding promissory oaths (Lev 5:4); and it values timely enforcement of the law (Eccles 8:11). Yet, in its discussion of each of these and other issues (e.g., Eccles 10:20) the text's overriding concern is to keep in proper perspective aspects of life that lie outside the scope of law. A legalistic approach to life, as found in some other Second Temple texts (e.g., Bar 3:9; 4:1), is rejected.

2. Poetic Imagery and Law.

The poetic texts of the *Song of Songs and *Lamentations attempt to capture emotions and experiences that are difficult to put into words. The language is often figurative and highly evocative. At first glance, the books seem to say little about law, though certain passages do have legal concerns in view.

2.1. Song of Songs. The poems collected here utilize sexual imagery, and most sexual relations were governed by law. Early in the book the principal female refers to an argument with her brothers over the guarding of her "vineyard" (Song 1:6). This word can have sexual connotations, and the woman's failure to guard her vineyard may refer to the loss of her virginity. At the end of the book, the brothers reenter the picture and claim that they will "build upon" or "enclose" (Song 8:9) their sister as a way to protect her and, presumably, her sexuality. These texts raise legal issues, though there is a fair amount of uncertainty regarding their interpretation (Murphy 1990a).

The book likely refers to a premarital tryst or, at the very least, the potentiality of such. Premarital sex can be defined as taking place before the woman is betrothed. The betrothal period was a type of inchoate marriage, and it commenced upon the payment of the bride price by the groom's family to the bride's. Like adultery, premarital sex was defined in terms only of the marital status of the woman involved. The marital status of the man was irrelevant. If the woman was either inchoately or fully married, for any man to have sex with her constituted adultery. If she was not yet betrothed, and a married man had sex with her, their relations would not be considered adulterous (Wells 2005).

Though not nearly as serious as adultery, premarital sex did have legal consequences. For example, the law in Exodus 22:16-17 requires a man who has sex with an unbetrothed virgin to pay her father an amount equivalent to a standard bride price, even if the father refuses to let his daughter marry the man (cf. Deut 22:28-29). The law's concern centers on the father's economic well-being. It is unlikely that the father would be able to obtain a full bride price (or even one at all) once his daughter has already had sexual relations with a man. Correspondingly, the brothers in Song of Songs probably are concerned about their economic welfare rather than their sister's safety or virtue. Although fathers typically were the ones to negotiate with their daughter's potential suitors and to make the final arrangements for the marriage, it was not uncommon for brothers to assume this role (Roth, 5-6).

2.2. Lamentations. This collection of poems mourns the destruction of Jerusalem at the hands of the Babylonians (587/586 BC) and grieves bitterly over the resulting hardships and horrors for the city's people. Although each poem may come from a different author, all of them share an interpretive framework as they attempt to understand what has happened and why. This framework comes in large part from the traditional view of divine justice reflected in Psalms and Proverbs. Punishment and disaster come from Yahweh because of sin and disobedience (Lam 1:8-9, 18; 4:13; 5:7); marauding armies are simply tools in his hand. In fact, not one of the poems explicitly mentions the direct cause of the devastation, the Babylonians. Nevertheless, some texts appear to question the fairness of how Yahweh has dealt with Jerusalem (e.g., Lam 2:20; 5:20). This questioning is not the same as that of the author of Job, whose protagonist is innocent and sees no justice whatsoever in his suffering. Instead, Lamentations reflects an attitude that admits to wrongdoing but disputes whether the severity of the punishment fits the severity of the crime (Dobbs-Allsopp). Several lines refer to Yahweh's refusal to show mercy or have pity (*ḥāmāl* [Lam 2:2, 17, 21; 3:43]), and the two most hopeful of the poems end with an angry, demanding tone (Lam 3; 5).

This interpretive framework also possesses judicial overtones. As in Psalms, the poets here are bringing their case before Yahweh. The language of litigation comes through strongly in Lamentations 3, where the metaphor likely is one of legal appeal. The poet begins with reference to his "crying" (*zāʿaq*) and "pleading" (*šāwaʾ*) to Yahweh but fears that his "petition/

prayer" *(těpillâ)* has been ignored (Lam 3:8; cf. Lam 3:44). He characterizes his cause as a "lawsuit" *(mišpāṭ* [Lam 3:35]; *rîb* [Lam 3:36]), and in Lamentations 3:58-59 he uses specific language appropriate to appeals: "You have litigated *[rîb]* the litigations of my life *[rîbê napšî]*. . . . May you now judge my judgment *[šāpěṭâ mišpāṭi]*." To initiate this appeal, the poet has "summoned" or "called" *(qārā'* [Lam 3:55, 57]) Yahweh to "draw nigh" *(qārab* [Lam 3:57]) so that his "cry for relief" *(rěwāḥâ, šaw'â* [Lam 3:56]) will not go unheard *(šāma'* [Lam 3:56]). Thus, the poet feels as if he and his people have already been convicted and sentenced and must now ask Yahweh to reconsider their cause. In the end, though, the poets of Lamentations seem uncertain of what the future will hold. The tragedy that they have experienced stunts their confidence that Yahweh will mitigate their sentence and award them vindication.

3. Narrative and Law.

The books of *Ruth and *Esther diverge significantly in their treatments of law. The author of Ruth seems to have stayed close to known legal traditions and practices and to have modified them little for the sake of the story. Esther, in contrast, plays with law and appears to misrepresent standard legal practice at several points in the narrative.

3.1. Ruth. The legal content of the book of Ruth relates primarily to matters of redemption and levirate marriage *(see* Kinsman-Redeemer and Levirate). With respect to both issues, however, the book assumes a fair amount of knowledge on the part of the reader. Thus, difficulties confront a thorough legal analysis. The major crux comes in Ruth 4:1-6, when the rules governing redemption and levirate marriage intersect.

Redemption of a plot of land would have occurred only after that land had been sold. In Ruth 4:3 *Boaz speaks of the sale of land belonging to *Naomi. A number of English translations (KJV, RSV, NRSV, NIV) render the Hebrew verb *mākěrâ* (from the root *mkr,* "sell") in the present tense to say that Naomi "is selling" the land. This understanding is problematic (Zevit). First, the verb *mākěrâ* is a perfect and is most naturally translated in the past tense. Second, the text would not refer to the act of "redeeming" *(gā'al)* the land (Ruth 4:4) were Naomi still in possession of it and looking to sell it. Redemption was, in essence, the act of buying

back. At times, those who were facing destitution sold their land to another for less than the land's fair market value. Although this practice was allowed, it was deemed vital that each family retain the right to regain ownership of its inheritable land (e.g., Lev 25:23-28). Property sold in this way, therefore, could be repurchased (redeemed) by the sellers themselves or by a relative, typically for the same low price at which it had been sold (Westbrook 1991, 90-117). This seems to be the situation envisioned in Ruth. It can be inferred that Naomi and her husband sold their land out of desperation before moving to Moab. In Ruth 4 it is now time for that land to be redeemed—bought back—not by Naomi, who is without sufficient resources, but rather by her nearest male relative.

The unnamed relative in question is happy to redeem the land until Boaz raises the specter of levirate marriage. As Naomi's nearest male relative, this man is first in line to act as redeemer, to inherit the land upon Naomi's passing, and to fulfill the requirements of levirate marriage. In his initial willingness to help Naomi, he appears focused only on the first two and has overlooked the third until Boaz reminds him (Ruth 4:5). He then changes his mind. Why? The law of levirate marriage, as described in Deuteronomy 25:5-10, required that a deceased husband's brother marry the widow, but only if the deceased had no sons. The purpose was to give the widow an opportunity to bear a son who would keep alive the "name" of the deceased— that is, the deceased's title or right to his portion of inheritable land (Westbrook 1991, 71-77). The brother who married the widow would be fathering a son who would receive the deceased's portion of the estate, a portion to which the brother might otherwise be entitled. The author of Ruth, though, assumes that in the absence of brothers, the responsibility for marrying the widow—here, Ruth—falls to the nearest male relative. This is essentially what Boaz makes clear to the unnamed relative and what changes the latter's mind. He does not wish to be encumbered with this responsibility if, in the end, Ruth should bear a son who would then inherit the redeemed land and likely be entitled, as a son, to a share of this man's property as well (Davies). He states that he does not want to "endanger my own estate" (Ruth 4:6 NIV).

On more minor points of law, the book is somewhat obscure. Naomi is said to have sold the land (Ruth 4:3), but whether women always had the right to buy and sell land in the ancient Near East is doubtful. Evidence for this right comes mostly from later periods. Some argue that Naomi's role as seller thus points to an exilic or postexilic dating of Ruth (Zevit). That may be so, but it is not unreasonable to imagine Naomi acting as a joint seller with her husband or even as his agent. The book also describes the transaction between Boaz and the relative as taking place at the city gate and before a group of city elders. This is not a trial, as some have concluded, but rather a negotiation at which the elders serve as observing witnesses (Wells 2004, 28-29). That negotiations and transactions of this sort were required to take place in such a high-profile venue in ancient Judah is, however, unlikely. Finally, when Naomi takes the child to her bosom and becomes his nurse (Ruth 4:16), the neighborhood women declare, "A son has been born to Naomi" (Ruth 4:17). This is unusual from a legal perspective. We would have expected the text to say that a child was born to Ruth's first husband by operation of the levirate. If, on the other hand, this were an instance of surrogacy parenthood, Naomi would have taken the child "upon her knee" and accepted the child as her own (Gen 30:3). Since the book of Ruth follows neither of these traditions, it appears to present in this instance a deviation from traditional biblical law.

3.2. Esther. The law in Esther is difficult to analyze. Recent scholarship has emphasized the satirical and even comedic nature of the book (Berlin). A number of passages may thus contain exaggerations, distortions or outright fabrications for dramatic effect (Craig). Examples include the inordinate feasting and carousing (Esther 1:4-5), the year-long pampering of each would-be queen before the king has sex with her (Esther 2:12-14), and the huge number of killings carried out by the Jews (Esther 9:16-17).

One particular difficulty arises with the book's use of the Persian loanword *dāt* ("law, decree, edict"). The word occurs frequently, but several of its uses appear to reflect the author's literary concerns rather than actual legal practice. The decree, for instance, that each husband "should be ruler over his own household" (Esther 1:22 NIV) is unlike any known royal edict. The same is true of the other decrees in the book, especially as they are articulated in the Additions to Esther. The rule that individuals who appear unsummoned before the king are put to death (Esther 4:11) sounds more like legend than law. The idea that any decree "written in the laws of Persia and Media . . . cannot be repealed" (Esther 1:19 NIV) may also fit this category. That this same idea appears in Daniel (e.g., Dan 6:8) confirms its renown in Jewish lore but not necessarily its historicity (Valeta). The basic purpose of these legal pronouncements is to depict a petty, paranoid and grandiose Persian administration.

On the other hand, several elements in the book may relate to operative law known to the author through experience or tradition. First, the language used to describe the adoption of Esther by *Mordecai (Esther 2:7) matches standard ancient Near Eastern language for this type of legal transaction. Second, Haman's accusation against the Jews (Esther 3:8-9) is couched in terms of treason. The text may be attempting to place Haman in the role of an official, known in Persian times as the "eye of the king," whose duty it was to guard against sedition and to denounce those suspected of such activity (Magdalene 2007b, chap. 5 n. 17). Third, the reference in Addition A to the interrogation of those plotting to assassinate the king (Add Esth 12:3) is striking. Interrogation of suspects in southern Mesopotamia during the Neo-Babylonian, Persian and Hellenistic periods often involved torture and was designed to extract confessions (Magdalene 2007b, chap. 4). This is precisely what the text describes. Other parts of the story, such as the method for publishing new laws (e.g., Esther 3:12-14) and execution by hanging (Esther 7:10), are legally plausible, though they cannot be directly confirmed by historical evidence. This is not to say that these elements confirm the narrative's historical nature; rather, they may reflect instances when the author incorporated matters of law that required no substantial modification for literary purposes.

4. Summary.

What these books reveal about law is important in at least two respects. First, apart from the book of Esther, the texts tend to treat the actual practice of law in keeping with pentateuchal legal traditions. Esther seems to parody certain non-Judahite legal traditions in order to satirize imperial structures. Second, this material, when taken together, reveals conflicting assessments of divine justice. The books of Psalms, Proverbs and, to a large degree, Lamentations side mainly with the traditional understanding that Yahweh's justice system is fair. Other texts, primarily Job and Ecclesiastes, begin to raise questions regarding this standard view of divine justice. They challenge whether obedience to the law or even a life guided by both law and wisdom will inevitably be rewarded with the hallmark features of Yahweh's blessing: good health, prosperity, social respect, long life. This unorthodox perspective must have competed with the more official stance that became ensconced in some later Second Temple literature such as Sirach. In the end, both the early Jewish and Christian communities welcomed both points of view into their sacred canon.

See also ETHICS; KINSMAN-REDEEMER AND LEVIRATE; WISDOM THEOLOGY.

BIBLIOGRAPHY. **H. Avalos,** *Illness and Health Care in the Ancient Near East: The Role of the Temple in Greece, Mesopotamia, and Israel* (HSM 54; Atlanta: Scholars Press, 1995); **P. Barmash,** *Homicide in the Biblical World* (Cambridge: Cambridge University Press, 2005); **A. Berlin,** *Esther* (JPSBC; Philadelphia: Jewish Publication Society, 2001); **J. Blenkinsopp,** *Wisdom and Law in the Old Testament: The Ordering of Life in Israel and Early Judaism* (rev. ed.; Oxford: Oxford University Press, 1995); **P. Bovati,** *Re-Establishing Justice: Legal Terms, Concepts and Procedures in the Hebrew Bible* (JSOTSup 105; Sheffield: Sheffield Academic Press, 1994); **K. M. Craig Jr.,** *Reading Esther: A Case for the Literary Carnivalesque* (LCBI; Louisville: Westminster John Knox, 1995); **J. L. Crenshaw,** *Ecclesiastes* (OTL; Philadelphia: Westminster, 1987); idem, *Urgent Advice and Probing Questions: Collected Writings on Old Testament Wisdom* (Macon, GA: Mercer University Press, 1995); **E. W. Davies,** "Inheritance Rights and the Hebrew Levirate Marriage, Part 2." *VT* 31 (1981) 257-68; **F. W. Dobbs-Allsopp,** "Tragedy, Tradition, and Theology in the Book of Lamentations," *JSOT* 74 (1997) 29-60; **M. V. Fox,** *A Time to Tear Down and a Time to Build Up: A Rereading of Ecclesiastes* (Grand Rapids: Eerdmans, 1999); **N. C. Habel,** *The Book of Job* (OTL; Philadelphia: Westminster, 1985); **B. S. Jackson,** *Wisdom-Laws: A Study of the Mishpatim of Exodus 21:1-22:16* (Oxford: Oxford University Press, 2006); **T. Krüger,** "Die Rezeption der Tora im Buch Kohelet," in *Das Buch Kohelet: Studien zur Struktur, Geschichte, Rezeption und Theologie,* ed. L. Schwienhorst-Schönberger (BZAW 254; Berlin: de Gruyter, 1997) 303-25; idem, *Qohelet* (Hermeneia; Minneapolis: Fortress, 2004); **T. Longman III,** *The Book of Ecclesiastes* (NICOT; Grand Rapids: Eerdmans, 1998); **F. R. Magdalene,** "Who Is Job's Redeemer? Job 19:25 in Light of Neo-Babylonian Law," *ZABR* 10 (2004) 292-316; idem, "The ANE Legal Origins of Impairment as Theological Disability and the Book of Job," *PRSt* 34 (2007a) 23-60; idem, *On the Scales of Righteousness: Neo-Babylonian Trial Law and the Book of Job* (BJS 348; Providence, RI: Brown Judaic Studies, 2007b); **P. D. Miller,** "Deuteronomy and Psalms: Evoking a Biblical Conversation," *JBL* 118 (1999) 3-18; **W. S. Morrow,** *Protest against God: The Eclipse of a Biblical Tradition* (Sheffield: Sheffield Phoenix Press, 2006); **R. E. Murphy,** *The Song of Songs: A Commentary on the Book of Canticles or the Song of Songs* (Hermeneia; Minneapolis: Fortress, 1990a); idem, *The Tree of Life: An Exploration of Biblical Wisdom Literature* (ABRL; New York: Doubleday, 1990b); **C. Newsom,** "The Book of Job," *NIB* 4.319-637; **M. T. Roth,** *Babylonian Marriage Agreements, 7th-3rd Centuries B.C.* (AOAT 222; Kevelaer: Butzon & Bercker; Neukirchen-Vluyn: Neukirchener Verlag, 1989); **S. H. Scholnick,** "The Meaning of *Mišpaṭ* in the Book of Job," *JBL* 101 (1982) 521-29; **D. Valeta,** "Court or Jester Tales? Resistance and Social Reality in Daniel 1-6," *PRSt* 32 (2005) 309-24; **B. Wells,** *The Law of Testimony in the Pentateuchal Codes* (BZABR 4; Wiesbaden: Harrassowitz, 2004); idem, "Sex, Lies, and Virginal Rape: The Slandered Bride and False Accusation in Deuteronomy," *JBL* 124 (2005) 41-72; **R. Westbrook,** *Studies in Biblical and Cuneiform Law* (CahRB 26; Paris: Gabalda, 1988); idem, *Property and Family in Biblical Law* (JSOTSup 113; Sheffield: Sheffield Academic Press, 1991); **Z. Zevit,** "Dating Ruth: Legal, Linguistic and Historical Observations," *ZAW* 117 (2005) 574-600.

B. Wells and F. R. Magdalene

LEMUEL AND AGUR

The dearth of data inhibits us from saying anything definite about Agur and Lemuel except that they are non-Israelite *sages to whom a part or the whole of Proverbs 30—31 is attributed. The LXX and the Vulgate do not recognize the words as names. Early rabbis discovered epithets for *Solomon in *ʾāgûr* and *lĕmûʾēl* rather than two names of sages. Now, however, it is generally accepted that "Agur" and "Lemuel" are the names of two foreign sages, not *noms de plume* for Solomon. If *maśśāʾ*, traditionally rendered "burden" or "prophetic oracle," is to be taken as a place name "Massa," then Agur and Lemuel can be considered sages of the East whose wisdom is recognized and admired in ancient Israel. Both the style and the content of the proverbs collated in Proverbs 30—31 seem to provide additional confirmation of their foreign origin.

1. Early Jewish Interpretation
2. Sages of the East
3. Agur's Proverbs
4. Lemuel's Proverbs

1. Early Jewish Interpretation.

The rabbis discovered allegorical designations for Solomon in *ʾāgûr* and *lĕmûʾēl* instead of personal names. According to *Midrash Exodus* 6:1 (also see *Midr. Num.* 10:4; *Midr. Song* 1:10; *Midr. Eccles.* 1:2), Solomon was called Agur, son of Jakeh, because he collected (*ʾāgar*) the words of Torah but then spat them out (*hēkî*) by ignoring the warning against multiplying wives. The Vulgate is reminiscent of this Jewish tradition: *verba congregantis filii vomentis* ("words of the collector, the son of the vomiter"). *Midrash Proverbs,* however, provides a different interpretation, although it also regards "Agur" and "Lemuel" as epithets for Solomon. Solomon was so called because he girded (*hāgar*) his loins for wisdom and freed himself (*nāqî*) from sin (*Midr. Prov.* 30:1). In either way, *bēn,* the Hebrew word for "son," is taken metaphorically as a designation of the bearer of the quality rather than literally. "Lemuel" is another appellative for Solomon in that he spoke "to or against God" (*lĕmô ʾēl*) and said, "I can multiply wives without sinning" (*Midr. Eccles.* 1:2). In Proverbs 31:1 the LXX, which does not recognize a Hebrew proper name in "Lemuel," echoes this rabbinic interpretation: *hoi emoi logoi eirēntai hypo theou* ("my words spoken by God"). A story in *Midrash Numbers* 10:4 provides another interpretation of the name. It relates that Solomon married Pharaoh's daughter on the eve of the dedication of the temple. She kept him awake with music until late at night and made him sleep late into morning by covering his bed with a canopy. The next morning, the dedication service could not be performed until his mother, Bathsheba, intervened. According to this story, Solomon is called "Lemuel" because he belittled the temple of God, as if to say, "What use is God to him *[lammâ lôʾēl]*."

These midrashic interpretations, for which there is no palpable evidence, originate in the assumption that the entire book of *Proverbs is the work of Solomon. This assumption is in turn based on a literal understanding of the title in Proverbs 1:1 as meaning that Solomon himself wrote all of Proverbs. The book of Proverbs, however, constitutes a collection of materials whose authors and backgrounds are varied. This has led modern scholars to argue that the words are in fact two proper names, not *noms de plume* for Solomon.

2. Sages of the East.

Scholarly consensus is that Agur and Lemuel are non-Israelite sages. In support of this consensus is the recognition of *maśśāʾ* (Prov 30:1; 31:1) as a place name rather than as a reference to a "prophetic oracle." Although taking *maśśāʾ* as a toponym necessitates an emendation of the Masoretic *hammaśśāʾ* ("oracle") to *hammaśśāʾî* ("the Massaite") or to *mimmaśśāʾ* ("from Massa") in Proverbs 30:1 and relocation of *athnach* under *maśśāʾ* in Proverbs 31:1, many scholars see more problems in keeping the MT as it stands. For instance, it is impossible to translate *lĕmûʾēl melek* as "King Lemuel" because *melek* ("king") should be marked for definiteness (*hammelek* ["the king"]), as rendered by the *Targum (lmʾl mlkʾ). Moreover, an understanding of *hammaśśāʾ* as a "prophetic oracle" in Proverbs 30:1 does not fit well with the individual and reflexive tone of what follows (cf. Prov 30:2-9). Likewise, the use of *maśśāʾ* as a prophetic oracle in Proverbs 31:1 does not harmonize with the admonitions (cf. *yissĕrattû* ["she instructed him"]) that follow. The interpretation of *maśśāʾ* as a place name is attested in the medieval version *Graecus Venetus,* in the Arabic Van Dyke version, and by many modern English translations (RSV, JB, NAB, NEB, NJPS).

If *maśśāʾ* is to be taken as a proper name, its approximate location can be inferred from its other attestations in biblical and extrabiblical sources. Massa in Genesis 25:14 and 1 Chronicles 1:30 (cf. Gen 10:23) may refer to either an area or a people northwest of the desert of North Arabia, since Dumah and Teima, which precede and follow *maśśāʾ* respectively in the ethnonymic list, are located in the Arabic desert. First-millennium cuneiform sources also attest to the biblical Massa. Two of them are worth noting here. First, the Summary Inscriptions of Tiglath-Pileser III (744-727 BC) lists Massa among a nomadic group that paid tribute to him on the borders of Palestine (see *COS* 2.117B:288). There, Massa is listed along with peoples such as Tema (cf. Gen 25:14), Saba (cf. Job 1:15) and *Hayappâ* (biblical Ephah [cf. Is 60:6]), which are located in North Arabia. Second, one of the *Nabû-šum-liṣir* letters (*ABL* 260) reports an assault by Ayakabaru, chieftain of Massa. Since *Nabû-šum-liṣir* served as an officer under Assurbanipal (688-627 BC) in the southwestern border region of Babylonia, the land of Massa may have been located anywhere in North Arabia. In summary, the textual evidence suggests North Arabia as the location of Massa.

Additional historical support for Agur and Lemuel as being non-Israelite sages comes from North and South Arabian inscriptions. The consonantal name ʾ*gr* is attested in one of the Nabatean inscriptions: "Agur, the avenger (?), has been removed" (van den Branden, 495). Similarly, the consonantal name *yqh* appears as an element of composite names, such as *yqhmlk* in a Sabaean inscription (Ryckmans, 1.81). Considering that the names are not known elsewhere in biblical or epigraphic Hebrew, their attestations in Arabian inscriptions, along with the identification of Massa as a North Arabian tribe, is suggestive of the identity of Agur and Jakeh. Although it is historically improbable to identity the biblical Agur and Jakeh with any of these figures in the inscriptions, the existence of namesakes in Arabia adds cogency to the assertion that Agur son of Jakeh belonged to one of the nomadic tribes in North Arabia. Lemuel has no other biblical or extrabiblical attestation. However the name might be analyzed, it is generally accepted that "Lemuel" is a non-Israelite name (cf. *lāʾēl* ["belonging to God"]; *lšmš* ["belong to Shamash"]; *ištar-ilšu* ["Ishtar is his God?"]; *ymʾil* ["Yammu is God?"]).

Taking Agur and Lemuel as foreign sages, particularly sages of the East, and their proverbs as Eastern wisdom goes well with the biblical attitude toward foreign wisdom, particularly the wisdom of the people of the East. It is well known from biblical sources that foreign wisdom was recognized and admired by ancient Hebrews. In 1 Kings 5:10 Solomon's wisdom is compared with that of both Egypt and the people of the East, assuming the excellence of the latter. *David quotes an "eastern" proverb (*mĕšal haqqadmōnî*) as he spares Saul's life (1 Sam 24:13 [MT 24:14]). We read in Jeremiah 49:7

and Obadiah 8 of wise men of Teman and Edom and of their wisdom. Finally, *Job was a sage from the peoples of the East, as his residence in Uz may suggest. It may not be a coincidence that Job's three friends also come from the same general geographic area. It may even be said that Proverbs constitutes an international anthology of wisdom literature. In it, we have not only Israelite wisdom but also foreign wisdom that has been borrowed as authentic wisdom and adapted to Israelite use (cf. Prov 22:17—24:22).

3. Agur's Proverbs.

3.1. Extent of Agur's Proverbs. The extent of Agur's words has been the subject of much scholarly debate. The question concerns not only their end point but also where they begin. The latter question is posed precisely due to the enigmatic *lĕʾîtîʾēl lĕʾîtîʾēl wĕʾukāl* (Prov 30:1), which, as it stands, gives two hearers of the words: "to Ithiel, to Ithiel and Ucal." The infelicitous repetition of "Ithiel" and the improbability of "Ucal" as a name have led modern scholars to emend or repoint vowels so as to make a sentence out of the phrase (for various proposals, see textual notes in the MT or Clifford, 260). The NEB, for instance, translates it as "I am weary, O God, I am weary and worn out" (cf. ESV, NRSV, NLT). The NAB renders it as "I am not God; I am not God that I should prevail." There is no solid linguistic or historical evidence that would tip the scales in favor of one emendation or another. One's overall understanding of Agur's theology seems to be the major factor in any decision. Those who regard Agur's words as atheistic tend to emend it to say, "There is no God, there is no God" (*lāʾ ʾîtay ēl lāʾ ʾîtay ēl*).

The question of where Agur's proverbs end is equally difficult to answer. The decision is often made on the basis of one's understanding of Agur's proverbs. Those who see Agur as agnostic or atheistic, for example, do not want Agur's words to go beyond Proverbs 30:4, for Proverbs 30:5-9 appears fairly orthodox. Apart from the fact that Proverbs 30:2-4 does not necessarily project Agur as a cynic, however, semantic disjunction does not evidence a different voice in the Wisdom literature where juxtaposition of discrete themes is the norm. Since the text does not clearly break the sayings by introducing any sage or title, it may be assumed that the entirety of Proverbs 30 belongs to Agur's proverbs.

3.2. Agur's Proverbs as International Wisdom.

Agur's proverbs reveal many cross-cultural characteristics both in style and content. Rhetorical questions in Proverbs 30:4, for example, are reminiscent of divine questions posed to Job, an eastern sage (cf. Job 38). Recently, van Leeuwen has shown that the first question in Proverbs 30:4 is found in variant form in Mesopotamian texts (cf. Dialogue of Pessimism; Gilgamesh). High respect for God's words and their strict preservation in Proverbs 30:5-6 find parallels in ancient *scribes' conservative attitude to traditional wisdom; Ptahhotep cautions with reference to his own work, "Don't take a word and then add nothing thereto, Don't put one thing in place of another" (cf. Lichtheim, 75). Merikare was told, "Copy your fathers and your ancestors. . . . See, their words endure in writing" (cf. Lichtheim, 99). Even the prayer in Proverbs 30:7-9 is without parallel in ancient wisdom; avoiding extremes and keeping to the middle way is considered characteristic of a wise man in Egyptian wisdom (cf. The Instructions of Ptahhotep). Numerical sayings, such as in Proverbs 30:15-30, are also widely employed in ancient Near Eastern literatures (cf. Ahiqar, lines 92-93 [*KTU* 1.4 III:17-21]). These cross-cultural features, however, are redacted to accommodate Yahwistic piety in Proverbs 30. Although Agur's prayer in Proverbs 30:7-9, for instance, counsels the golden mean by denying both riches and poverty, Agur's desire to remain faithful to Yahweh informs the entire prayer. The concern for the golden mean here is not an end in itself as in Egyptian wisdom but rather serves as a means for expressing Yahwistic piety. Some scholars aver that Proverbs 30:5-9, which are religious in tone, must be a later addition to the original words of Agur in Proverbs 30:2-4. From the earliest date, however, religious piety has been an important part of Wisdom literature, not only of Israel but also of its ancient neighbors. It would be fairer to say that a Jewish editor appropriated cross-cultural topoi, including religious piety, to advance Israelite Yahwism in Proverbs 30.

4. Lemuel's Proverbs.

The proverbs attributed to Lemuel also reveal international features. They take the form of royal instructions, widely attested in the Ancient Near East (cf. *Merikare* [Lichtheim, 97-112]; *Amenemhet I* [Lichtheim, 135-38]; *Advice to a Prince* [Lambert, 110-15]). Although it is extremely rare that such instructions are attributed to the queen mother, she was often referred to as the source of wisdom. She had a role in the education of her children and was often instrumental in selecting a wife for her son. Moreover, the instructions of Lemuel's mother reflect an ancient Near Eastern royal ideology. The instructions addressed to Merikare, for instance, emphasize justice and compassion for the widow, the orphan, the poor and the needy. Hammurabi, a Babylonian sage-king, presents himself as king of justice and as a shepherd who speaks for the orphan and the widow. Thus, the instructions of Lemuel's mother are firmly at home in this ancient Near Eastern royal ideology. These cross-cultural topoi, along with such Aramaisms as *bar* ("son") and *mĕlakin* ("kings") dovetail with the non-Israelite origin of Lemuel's proverbs. Just as in Agur's proverbs, however, Lemuel's proverbs have been adapted to accommodate Israel's religion. Lemuel is not only her biological son, *bĕrî* ("my son"), but also a son given in answer to a vow made to Yahweh by her, *bar-nĕdārāy* ("son of my vows" [cf. 1 Sam 1:11]). This son of her vows should seek *ēšet ḥayil* ("a virtuous wife") who fears Yahweh.

See also PROVERBS 1: BOOK OF; WISDOM SOURCES.

BIBLIOGRAPHY. **R. J. Clifford,** *Proverbs* (OTL; Louisville: Westminster John Knox, 1999); **J. L. Crenshaw,** "A Mother's Instruction to Her Son (Proverbs 31:1-9)," in *Urgent Advice and Probing Questions: Collected Writings on Old Testament Wisdom* (Macon, GA: Mercer University Press, 1995) 382-95; **J. Day,** "Foreign Semitic Influence on the Wisdom of Israel," in *Wisdom in Ancient Israel: Essays in Honour of J. A. Emerton,* ed. J. Day (Cambridge: Cambridge University Press, 1995) 55-70; **I. Eph'al,** *The Ancient Arabs: Nomads on the Borders of the Fertile Crescent, 9th-5th Centuries B.C.* (Jerusalem: Magnes, 1982); **C. Gottlieb,** "Words of the Exceedingly Wise: Proverbs 30:31," in *The Biblical Canon in Comparative Perspective,* ed. K. L. Younger (ScrCon; Lewiston, NY: Edwin Mellen, 1991); **W. G. Lambert,** *Babylonian Wisdom Literature* (Winona Lake, IN: Eisenbrauns, 1996); **M. Lichtheim,** *The Old and Middle Kingdoms,* vol. 1 of *Ancient Egyptian Literature* (Berkeley: University of California Press, 1975); **R. D. Moore,** "A Home for the Alien: Worldly Wisdom and Covenantal Confession in Proverbs 30,1-9," *ZAW* 106 (1994) 96-107; **G. Ryckmans,** *Les noms* *propres sud-sémitiques* (3 vols.; Bibliothèque du Muséon 2; Louvain: Bureaux du Muséon, 1934); **K. Spanier,** "The Queen Mother in the Judaean Royal Court: Maacah—A Case Study," in *A Feminist Companion to Samuel and Kings,* ed. A. Brenner (FCB 5; Sheffield: Sheffield Academic Press, 1994) 186-95; **A. van den Branden,** *Les inscriptions thamoudéennes* (Bibliothèque du Muséon 25; Louvain-Heverlé: Bureaux du Muséon, 1950); **J. D. van Leeuwen,** "The Background to Proverbs 30:4aa," in *Wisdom, You Are My Sister: Studies in Honor of Roland E. Murphy, O. Carm., on the Occasion of His Eightieth Birthday,* ed. M. L. Barré (CBQMS 28; Washington, DC: Catholic Biblical Association of America, 1997) 102-21.

K. Kim

LEVIATHAN. *See* CHAOS AND DEATH; CREATION THEOLOGY.

LEVIRATE. *See* KINSMAN-REDEEMER AND LEVIRATE.

LITURGICAL READINGS, JEWISH. *See* MEGILLOT AND FESTIVALS.

LIFE, IMAGERY OF

"Life" is a virtually all-encompassing concept; thus, the imagery for life in these books is abundant and diverse. Yet certain theologically significant patterns centered on the God of Israel emerge amidst the complex plethora of imageries for life. The various imageries of life are informed by the scriptural metanarrative of creation, fall, salvation and consummation. In light of this fourfold redemptive scheme, the diverse and even apparently contradictory ways in which life is portrayed can be meaningfully united and ordered. Although the following presentation of the imagery of life does not directly follow this fourfold narrative scheme, it is informed by and consistent with this scheme. The format of presentation in the present article follows thematic categories that emerge more directly from the biblical books that are treated.

1. Life as Created, Earthly Existence
2. Fruitful Life versus Futile Life
3. Afterlife
4. Summary

1. Life as Created, Earthly Existence.

The imagery of breath/soul/spirit, light, and clay connects all life to God as the Lord of life.

God is the creator and sustainer of life, and at death God is the taker of life.

The Hebrew word *ḥayyîm* ("life") denotes the earthly existence that begins when the breath, soul or spirit of God is breathed into the nostrils of creatures, both humans and animals (Job 27:3; Eccles 3:19-21; cf. Gen 1:20, 2:7; 9:4). The imagery of God breathing into creatures divine *nĕšāmâ* ("breath" [Job 4:9; 27:3; 32:8; 33:4; Ps 18:15]), divine *nepeš* ("soul" or "life" [Job 41:21; Ps 11:5; Prov 6:16]) and/or divine *rûaḥ* ("spirit" or "breath" [Job 4:9; 27:3; 34:14; Ps 18:15; 33:6; Eccles 3:19]) identify God as the source of life.

In addition to breath of God, the metaphor of light points to God as the life-giver. As light dispels darkness, generates energy, and causes growth and life, light is a powerful symbol of life. Light is often equated with life (Esther 8:16; Job 3:4, 20, 23; 33:28-30) and, indirectly, with God (Job 24:13; 25:3; 29:3). Where God and God's light are, there is life (Ps 36:9). Conversely, where there is only darkness—a metaphor for life away from God—there is misery, horror and death (Job 3:4; 17:12-13; 18:18-21).

God is depicted not only as imparting life but also as fashioning each human in the womb like a potter molding clay (Job 10:8-11; 31:15; Ps 139:13). God mysteriously creates distinctive forms of life, human or animal. The uniqueness of each human is the result not only of a particular genetic makeup but also of God's spirit and hand distinctively fashioning each human. The supernatural and the natural world are seen as seamlessly woven together.

God's involvement in creaturely life continues through the entire lifespan. God is depicted as drawing the babes out of the womb like a midwife (Ps 71:6) and continuing to sustain life like a mother (Job 10:18; Ps 22:9-10; 71:6). Only as long as the breath of God is in creatures' nostrils can creaturely life continue (Job 27:3; cf. Gen 2:7; Ps 104:29). Psalm 104 provides other images for God's ongoing providential care for all living things (see also Ps 136:25; 145:15-16). God provides springs of water for the wild beasts to drink (Ps 104:10-11), causes the grass to grow for the cattle and vegetation for humanity (Ps 104:14), and grants food for the lions and creatures of the sea (Ps 104:21, 27-28). God is even said to respond to the cries of the young raven and prepare its food (Job 38:41). Bread, food, drink and water provide powerful images of life sustained by God. By contrast, images of draught and starvation depict the denial of life as a form of judgment (Ps 107:33-34; Lam 1:11).

The life that God breathes into creatures is portrayed as fleeting. Life and everything in it is *hebel* (Eccles 1:2), which literally means "vapor" (Ps 144:4; Prov 13:11; 21:6) and is often translated as "breath" (RSV, NRSV, NJPS). "Vapor" figuratively speaks of the ephemeral nature of life (Fredericks, 11-32) and its absurdity (Fox, 27-42). The translation "vapor" is preferred over against the traditional rendering "vanity" (KJV), especially given the plethora of images for the brevity and transience of life used in close connection with *hebel*. Human life is portrayed as breath, as a runner quickly passing by, as a swift eagle, a flower, a shadow, a cloud, a dream (Job 7:7-9; 9:25-26; 14:1-2; 20:8; Ps 90:10). Life possesses goodness (see 2.1 below), but that too is passing.

Not only is life fleeting, it is fragile, as is powerfully captured by the imagery of clay. Unlike rock, clay is malleable in consistency and brittle when dry. When powdered, it blows away like dust. Clay and dust provide powerful metaphors for the insignificant and fragile human existence marred by sin and under divine judgment: "For dust you are and to dust you will return" (Gen 3:19). Humans are "formed out of the clay" (Job 33:6) and are made "as clay" (Job 10:9). They are "like a broken vessel" (Ps 31:12) or like refuse, "broken in pieces between morning and evening; unobserved, they perish forever" (Job 4:19-20). They die a sudden, unpredictable death only to "return to dust" (Job 10:9; 34:15; cf. Ps 104:29).

God gives and takes life (Job 9:22; 12:10). When God determines to "gather to himself his spirit and his breath" of life (Job 34:14; cf. "the breath-spirit of life" *[nišmat-rûah hayyîm]* in Gen 7:22), earthly existence comes to an end, and dust returns to dust (Job 21:26; 34:14; Ps 104:29; Eccles 3:20; 12:7). As physical life is given indiscriminately as a gift, so it is taken indiscriminately without apologies. The righteous and the wicked alike face death, and its timing is unpredictable. Thus *Qohelet bemoans the fact that there are righteous who die prematurely and wicked who live long (Eccles 7:15), and that "there are righteous people to whom it happens according to the deeds of the wicked" or vice versa (Eccles 8:14; cf. Ps 73). Before physical death the righteous one has no advantage over the beast or the wicked; all suffer a common fate

(Eccles 3:19). Once God takes back "his spirit and his breath," it is irreversible. Unlike a cut tree that sprouts again, the dead do not come back (Job 14:7-10). "As water evaporates from the sea, and a river becomes parched and dried up, so man lies down and does not rise" (Job 14:11-12). From conception to death, God the potter has absolute mastery over his creatures.

2. Fruitful Life versus Futile Life.

The term *hayyîm* ("life") also refers to the fullness of redeemed life found in God and in God's *wisdom. The personified character *Woman Wisdom (Ps 21:4-7; Prov 3-4; 8:1-9:12) offers life and is even identified as "life" (Prov 4:13, 22; 8:35). She is also called "a tree of life" (Prov 3:18), "the spring of life" (Prov 4:23), "the path of life" (Prov 5:6) and "the way of life" (Prov 6:23). Woman Wisdom is the source and giver of life. Those who find her find "the good life, longevity, a large family, prestige, joy, and (inherit the) land" here and now (Murphy 29, 104). This usage of "life" stands differentiated from the life that is breathed into every living thing, human or animal, which may be lived apart from conscious allegiance to God or wisdom. Imbedded in this usage of "life" is the recognition that unless a person embraces Woman Wisdom of the living God, one faces not only the physical death that is universal but also the cursed way of existence or "death" (including poor quality of life, dishonor, premature physical death) that *folly dishes out to those who reject wisdom (Prov 2:19; 9:10).

There are two paths of life, characterized by wisdom or folly, and two corresponding categories of people: the righteous who fear God, and the foolish who do not. Psalm 1 provides the paradigmatic outlook and outcome of the two ways of life. The good life of the righteous is portrayed as a fruitful tree of life, and the condemned life of the wicked is portrayed as empty chaff.

2.1. Imagery for the Fruitful Life of Wisdom.

2.1.1. A Fruitful Tree by Streams of Waters. The ideal life of the righteous is likened to "a tree firmly planted by streams of water" (Ps 1:3). As a tree drinks up the water day and night, so do the righteous delight in, meditate on, and feast upon the word of God on any given day (Ps 1:2; cf. Ps 119). The *law of God produces obedience and *fear of the Lord, which is the beginning, substance and end of wisdom (Ps 19:7-11; 34:11-22; 111:10; Prov 1:7; 9:10; 15:33). In the fear of the Lord the righteous do not walk, go, sit, stand or assemble with the deceitful, wicked, sinners or evildoers (Ps 1:1; 26:1, 4-6). Instead, they walk in innocence, integrity and truth. The true nourishment for righteous life, then, is wisdom and obedience to the word of God.

A fruitful and prosperous tree is a symbol of a righteous life that is both blessed and a blessing to others: they "yield fruit in their season . . . whatever they do, they prosper" (Ps 1:3). The righteous enjoy divine favor and blessings of security, safety, health, longevity, peace, pleasure, happiness, prosperity, riches and honor (Prov 1:33; 3:2-4, 8, 16-18, 25-26; 8:35; 9:11; 10:27). Such manifold blessings are manifested in, for example, the "woman of strength" of Proverbs 31. The life under divine favor and blessings "in season" take on the divine identity and characteristics of wisdom. They become a "wellspring of life" or a "tree of life" to others, instructing others in the way of life (Ps 112:2-5, 9; Prov 10:11; 13:14; 15:4; 18:4; 31:26; cf. Job 11:17). Life, wisdom and *righteousness spring forth and bless others.

The life of *Job is an image of the fruitful tree of Psalm 1. Job is a man of faithfulness, impeccable justice and righteousness. Job enjoys *divine presence, favor, friendship, guidance, protection and blessings on his family (Job 29). He possesses unsurpassable wisdom and understanding, and both young and old pay their respect and listen to his wisdom. He is affluent; his "steps bathe in cream," even as "boulders pour out streams of oil" (Job 29:6). He is exceedingly compassionate and generous to the poor, "making the widow's heart sing for joy" (Job 29:13; cf. Prov 31:20). He lives like a king, and his life is glorious (Job 29; 31). When he is severely tried, he stands the test and becomes even more prosperous than ever before.

*Song of Songs is a description and celebration of a good life of love, pleasure and joy. Although God is mentioned only once in this book (Song 8:6), it portrays life as redeemed from the curses of Genesis 3; it is life under divine blessings beyond the hostility of nature and male domination (Trible). Not only is there mutuality and equality between the woman and the man, but also the female lover is "the most prominent" (Trible, 102). A similar pattern is observed in the book of *Proverbs, where Woman Wisdom and the "woman of strength" are highly active, visible and influential in the public sphere

as well as in the private. In the garden of love the lovers find each other, praise each other, and become one flesh. Unlike the situation in Genesis 3, conception and birthing are considered positive and are celebrated (Song 6:9; 8:5). Likewise, good marriage and having children are archetypes of the good life in the book of *Ruth and in Proverbs 31. In the garden of love there is life abundant, filled with "every tree that is pleasant to the sight and good for food" (Gen 2:9 RSV), and animals for human joy and love songs. "All nature extols the love of female and male" (Trible, 114). The life of love in the redeemed garden is one of delight as in the garden of Eden before disobedience.

The life of an individual is inextricably tied to that of the corporate life of the family (typically made up of three to four generations in ancient Israel) and the nation. Thus, Proverbs lays a strong emphasis on parents passing down a godly heritage and on children receiving parental instructions regarding divine law and wisdom (Prov 1:8; 6:20; 13:1). The happy, blessed lover in the garden of love is a product of her mother's godly instructions (Song 8:2). The woman of strength of Proverbs 31 teaches the law, and her entire household respects her: "She opens her mouth in wisdom, and the law of covenant faithfulness [hesed] is on her tongue. . . . Her children rise up and call her blessed; her husband praises her" (Prov 31:26, 28). Children who receive a godly heritage can be compared to a seed from a tree planted by the streams of water that falls by the same streams and then grows and prospers. A fruitful tree fosters other fruitful trees.

Some texts in the book of *Psalms see the transgenerational transfer of inheritance as taking place even before birth; they portray prenatal human existence as already having a moral character, which is described either as sinful and estranged from God (Ps 51:5; 58:3) or as having "conscience" (kilyâ [Ps 139:13 NJPS]) and being cherished by God (Ps 71:6, 139:13-16). For the righteous, divine favor begins in the womb: "Your eyes saw my embryo; and in your book were all written the days that were ordained for me, when as yet there was not one of them." (Ps 139:16). In contrast, "The wicked go astray from the womb, they err from their birth, speaking lies" (Ps 58:3). Rather than being eyebrow-raising statements about "predestination unto reprobation," these poetic depictions are best understood as vivid illustrations of the concept of transgenerational reward or *retribution found in Exodus 20:5-6; 34:6-7, which is carried forward into Psalms. The image of God forming the "conscience" of the babe in the womb (Ps 139:13) poignantly captures the motif of divine *ḥesed* ("covenant faithfulness") reaching to children's children of those who love God (Ps 103:17-18). The unborn child going astray is a disturbing picture of the parents' "hatred" of God, poisoning their children from the womb, putting the children in danger of being "cut off" along with their iniquitous parents (Ps 109:12-14).

2.1.2. "Does Not Wither." The tree firmly planted by the streams of water "does not wither" in drought or disaster (Ps 1:3; cf. Ps 37:19). The biblical writings are not without the realism that life is full of temptations and trials, threats and dangers: "Many are the afflictions of the righteous" (Ps 34:19). A fruitful and wise life is not free of painful or less-than-ideal experiences. Conversely, even the futile or cursed life is not necessarily entirely lacking in ideal experiences (e.g., wealth and longevity). Thus, the good life is not necessarily measured by the extent of pleasant experiences or absence of pain but rather by other criteria, such as the fear of the Lord and, as necessary, sustained faithfulness through harsh trials in life. The godly face torments, misfortune, oppression, injustice and persecution in the very context of the covenant faithfulness of God. They bring their painful experiences and explosion of emotions in a form of lament, complaint, petition, hope and trust, and they are not disappointed.

Ruth, Job and *Ecclesiastes agree that both good and adversity ultimately come from God (Ruth 1:20-21; Job 1:21; 2:10; Eccles 7:14). There are three main categories of trial or adversity that the righteous face in life: (1) natural disasters and tragedies; (2) persecution by enemies; (3) divine testing. These three categories are grippingly illustrated by the stories of reversal of Ruth, *Esther and Job respectively. Each one endures and overcomes severe trials in life by maintaining love for God and receives the blessings of life in an even greater measure.

Through famine and the death of her husband and sons, *Naomi experiences complete "emptiness" (Ruth 1:3-5, 20-21). Ruth, who is also deprived of her husband, selflessly devotes herself to her desolate mother-in-law, Naomi,

and to the God of Israel. Ruth then navigates successfully through androcentric Israelite society under Naomi's shrewd instructions and reverses their situation, from emptiness to fullness, from despair to happiness, from destitution to riches. Out of her comes the greatest king of Israel. Unaware, her life takes on historic significance as she carries on her acts of covenant faithfulness *(ḥesed)*, the price of which is heavy (Larkin, 52). Unaware, in her life divine *ḥesed* and providence converge with human *ḥesed* and initiative (Larkin, 50-52). The virtues of self-sacrifice, conformity to an imperfect social system, and seeking common good over against the personal good are not typically coveted or promoted by contemporary feminists, but these are the very virtues that turned around these women's lives and eventually the life of a whole nation.

In a different context, Esther also chooses a selfless path for the good of many. Though an empress, she remembers God, identifies with the powerless and endangered, and puts her life on the line. In this way, Esther brings about the salvation of her people, the people of God. The story of Esther illustrates the perennial persecution that the righteous people of God (in this case, the Jewish people as a whole) face among the ungodly. Similarly, many psalms describe the situation in which unsuspecting righteous people are persecuted or oppressed by the wicked. The wicked "desire," "seek," "watch for," "band together against," "plot against," and "gnash their teeth at" the poor, humble, meek and "those whose ways are upright" in order to "lay snare," "set an ambush," "take away," "trample," "crush," "slay" and "destroy" their very life (Ps 7:5; 10:1-11; 31:13; 35:4; 37:12, 14, 32; 38:12; 40:14; 54:3; 56:6; 59:3; 63:9; 70:2; 71:10; 94:21; 143:3). But the righteous turn to God to "defend," "deliver," "save," "rescue" "hide," "preserve," "sustain" and "prolong" their life (Ps 21:4; 22:20; 27:1; 35:17; 54:4; 61:6; 64:1). And the righteous are confident that the Lord delivers them out of all afflictions (Ps 34:19) and executes vengeance on their behalf (Ps 18:47; 27:14; 33:18). Whether for the corporate people of God (as in Esther) or the righteous individual (as in some of the psalms), then, divine justice and reversal of evil will come sooner or later. The wicked will come to an end. There is a relief in life, either in this life or in the next.

Then there is Job, whose main adversary was

God. God's testing of the human heart is not an anomaly that exists only in the book of Job. Several of the books unapologetically assert that it is a normal part of life. "The LORD is in His holy temple; the LORD's throne is in heaven; . . . His eyelids test the sons of men. The LORD tests the righteous and the wicked" (Ps 11:4-5 NASB [cf. Prov 17:3; Eccles 3:17]). God tests "them in order for them to see that they are but beasts" (Eccles 3:18), to refine them "as silver is refined" (Ps 66:10), and to expose and condemn the wicked and to confirm and vindicate the righteous: "When he has tried me, I will come out as pure gold" (Job 23:10 [cf. Ps 11:6-7; 17:3]). Job is a righteous man, thus he expects good life experiences, but evil is given to him instead (Job 30:26). When God hands Job over to *Satan, Job's torment is excruciating. Job curses the day he was born, "despises" and "loathes" his life (Job 3; 9:21; 10:1). Life is wretched and detestable, comparable to the "maggot" and "worm" of rotting food or decaying corpse (Job 25:6). But through it all Job does not curse God. In the end God declares the afflicted Job righteous and the undiscerning friends guilty. Job is vindicated, and his family and fortune are restored (Job 42:11-17). The book of Job paints a picture of life that evades human expectations of fairness and strict retribution. Apparently, *suffering is not proportionate to wickedness, nor is blessing proportionate to righteousness. In fact, Job was tried precisely because he was righteous, so that when Job endured the test without turning against God, God's estimation of Job's unsurpassed righteousness is proven correct, and Satan's accusation of Job's righteousness as only skin deep is proven wrong.

2.2. Images of the Futile Life.

2.2.1. "Like Chaff." The life of the wicked or the foolish is "like chaff" (Ps 1:4; 83:13), which lacks substance and value. The wicked live an existence that denies the true and proper nature of life, which is oriented to the word of God and obedience to it. The foolish despise God's word and wisdom and the wise instruction given through their parents (Prov 1:7-8).

Since the foolish lack understanding and discernment, their life is precarious like "chaff that the wind blows away" (Ps 1:4; 83:13). With no word or fear of God to hold them down or direct them, they "walk in darkness" and "stumble" (Eccles 2:14; Prov 4:19). But ironically, when "the foolishness of man ruins his way, his heart

rages against the LORD" (Prov 19:3). The foolish acknowledge God only to blame God. Fools let seducers capture them with their eyelids (Prov 6:25) and follow seducers "as an ox goes to the slaughter" (Prov 7:22), and thereby they are "reduced to a loaf of bread" (Prov 6:26 NASB). Fools have no power to resist the temptation and are easily led astray. Fools are humorously identified as sluggards for their laziness: "As the door turns on its hinges, so does the sluggard on his bed" (Prov 26:14 [cf. Prov 13:4; 20:4; 24:33-34; 26:15]). They are compared to swine for their lack of discretion: "Like a ring of gold in a swine's snout is a beautiful woman who lacks discretion" (Prov 11:22).

Qohelet lived a life of folly (to use the language of Proverbs) because he did not have the fear of the Lord or wisdom: "I have seen everything during my lifetime of futility" (Eccles 7:15). He pursued wisdom and knowledge, but because he lacked the fear of the Lord and obedience, they were either unattainable or useless to him. After great accomplishments, acquisition of a measure of wisdom and knowledge, and chasing of pleasure and wealth, he declares them annoyingly pointless, painful and grievous, utterly unsatisfying and evil (Eccles 1:3-16; 2:1-23; 4:4, 8; 5:10; 6:3). Often the accomplishments and wealth of the fool are given to others to enjoy (Eccles 2:18, 26; 6:2; cf. Prov 13:22). "This is absurd and an evil torment" (Eccles 6:2). Indeed, the life of folly is filled with great irritation and suffering and divine wrath (Eccles 5:17).

2.2.2. Judged and Destroyed. While these books uphold the principle of retribution or of sowing and reaping (emphasized by Proverbs), they also testify to the exasperating reality that the wicked can succeed and prosper (Ps 37:1, 7; 73:3-9; Prov 24:19). Ultimately, however, "the way of the wicked will perish" (Ps 1:5-6). Sooner or later the wicked will be judged, condemned and destroyed by God (Ps 1:4-5; 73:17-20; Job 27:8), for folly will lead to death (Prov 2:18-19; 5:5), and "those who hate [wisdom] love death" (Prov 8:36).

In Psalms we see that divine judgment can be presented either as a temporary discipline for the righteous person who needs correction or as a permanent and more serious state of judgment on the unrepentant sinner. Insofar as people are unrepentant, their life can be spent in sorrow under divine chastisement for iniquity, sin and rebellion (Ps 31:10; but see Ps 31:14-24). Divine retribution can come in various forms: illnesses, calamities, rejection, emotional pain, withdrawal of divine presence, abandonment by family and friends, financial loss, personal enemies, premature death.

Whereas the psalms often portray an individual under judgment, the book of *Lamentations is replete with the imagery of brutal corporate suffering under the judgment of God. Jerusalem experiences the excruciating pains and overwhelming hardship of exile and *destruction as a consequence of abandoning God's covenant. Instead of life, death is everywhere: "In the street the sword bereaves; in the house it is like death" (Lam 1:20). Because of hunger and thirst, those that were once "whiter than milk" are "blacker than soot," with "their skin shriveled on their bones" (Lam 4:7-8). "Babes and suckling languish in the squares of the city," and "their life runs out in their mothers' bosoms" (Lam 2:11-13 NJPS [cf. Lam 2:19; 4:4]). The greatest horror comes when parents cannibalize their own children (Lam 2:20; 4:10). Indeed, "Better were those pierced with the sword than those pierced with hunger" (Lam 4:9). Life under judgment is cursed and brutal. As Qohelet would say, the dead are better off than the living, and one who has never existed is better off than both of them (Eccles 4:3; 6:3; but see Eccles 11:7-8).

Yet, there is room for mercy in the most severe judgment, both for individuals and nations. When humility and repentance are forthcoming, God can be moved to forgive and save those who fear him (Pss 31; 32), for God maintains his covenant love (Ps 32:10-11). From the depth of oppressive pain the writer of Lamentations recalls the true nature of God: "But this I call to mind, and therefore I have hope: Truly, the LORD's covenant faithfulness is not spent, and his compassion never come to an end" (Lam 3:21-22). God does not delight in punishing the wicked, and his punishment is but temporary (Lam 3:31-33). After affirming the just nature of divine punishment and upholding divine goodness, the writer calls the remnant to an honest admission of sin and to a return to the Lord (Lam 3:40-41). Further, the writer prays to God in several ways, offering an all-out supplication for the forgiveness and restoration of Jerusalem, a complaint about the people's massive suffering, and a petition for vengeance on the city's enemies (Lam 3:42—5:22).

3. Afterlife.

Ultimately, the "life" that the Woman Wisdom offers refers to an *afterlife with God (see 1 above), the path to which is paved by Woman Wisdom herself (Prov 5:6; 6:23). Although some might interpret the Wisdom literature and Psalms as being concerned only with life here and now, there is no clear dichotomy between the material/temporal and spiritual/eternal in these writings. Furthermore, given the brevity and limited nature of life, the biblical writers often reflect on delayed divine reward or retribution and extend their hopes for divine justice and a fully redeemed life beyond the grave. Biblical writers affirm that God will judge the whole earth (Job 9:15; 23:7; Ps 9:8; 50:6; 75:2; 96:13; Eccles 3:17) and find hope and consolation in God's eventual justice (Eccles 12:14) and in the related thought of life after death (Fredericks, 86). Accordingly, Job and Psalms present the contrasting motifs of the destruction of the wicked in Sheol and the enduring life of the righteous in divine presence. Against the view that Sheol in these writings is simply a place where all the dead are confined, its usage pressures us toward the interpretation that Sheol is a place for the wicked, from which the righteous are redeemed. An ancient sage reflects, "The path of life leads upward for the wise, that he may keep away from Sheol below" (Prov 15:24 NASB). The "life" that wisdom offers and the "death" that folly guarantees, then, ultimately point to immortality and everlasting destruction respectively. Proverbs' presentation of life and death, blessings and curses, as binary opposites is best seen partly as a pedagogical strategy expected of its genre and intended to encourage in a young pupil righteous choice and obedient living in a world of double reality (Ngwa, 141) and partly as a realistic description of the ultimate outcome of one's life on earth.

The eventual fate of the wicked is compared to "the beasts that perish" and is contrasted from the righteous, who will be received by God and will "see the light" beyond this life (Ps 49:15, 19-20; 73:16-27). Having been cut off from the presence of God (Job 27:8), the souls of the wicked are abandoned to Sheol, their names are forever "blotted out of the book of life," and they are destroyed (Ps 9:5; 16:10; 69:28). Unlike what happens to the wicked, God writes the names of the righteous in the book of life and redeems their life *(nepeš)* from Sheol (Ps 16:10;

69:28; cf. Job 19:25-26; 30:23). After reflecting on how the life of the wicked is limited to this world only, the psalmist declares his confidence in his final destiny in God's presence: "For You will not abandon my soul to Sheol; nor will You allow Your Holy One to undergo decay. You will make known to me the path of life; in Your presence is fullness of joy; in Your right hand there are pleasures forever" (Ps 16:10-11 NASB [cf. Ps 49:14-20; Job 19:25-26; 30:23]). Even if the righteous are not vindicated in this life, they have the hope and consolation of the afterlife with God. Accordingly, as Qohelet might say, "Even if everything is absurd, *nevertheless* we must fear God and keep commandments" (Fox, 144).

4. Summary.
Life in a fallen world is brief and transient, and often it is empty and unbearable. Yet, in obedience and right relationship with God the life that humanity once had in paradise can be partly recovered. This redemptive quality of life is measured not by the extent to which pain and suffering are eliminated from life but rather by character and relationships. Those who maintain covenant faithfulness to God and integrity with people (both neighbors and enemies) will experience the fullness of life in God. But the possibility of tasting the goodness of life in the fallen world is often limited by the apparent absence of justice in this world (Job and Ecclesiastes). Such frustration is partly resolved by divine judgment of both the wicked and the righteous. Whether in this world or in the next, the divine Judge ultimately will grant justice. The true content and end of life, then, consists of fear of, obedience to, and love of the Lord.

See also AFTERLIFE; CREATION THEOLOGY; WISDOM THEOLOGY.

BIBLIOGRAPHY. **W. Brueggemann**, *The Psalms and the Life of Faith* (Minneapolis: Fortress, 1995); **F. W. Dobbs-Allsopp**, *Lamentations* (IBC; Louisville: John Knox, 2002); **M. V. Fox**, *A Time to Tear Down and a Time to Build Up: A Reading of Ecclesiastes* (Grand Rapids: Eerdmans, 1999); **D. C. Fredericks**, *Coping with Transience: Ecclesiastes on Brevity in Life* (BibSem 18; Sheffield: JSOT Press, 1993); **K. J. A. Larkin**, *Ruth and Esther* (OTG; Sheffield: Sheffield Academic Press, 1996); **R. E. Murphy**, *The Tree of Life: An Exploration of Biblical Wisdom Literature* (Grand Rapids: Eerdmans, 1990); **K. N. Ngwa**, *The Hermeneutics of the "Happy" Ending in Job 42:7-17* (BZAW 354; Berlin: de Gruyter, 2005); **P. Trible**, "Love's Lyrics Redeemed," in *A Feminist Companion to the Song of Songs*, ed. A. Brenner (FCB 1; Sheffield: JSOT Press, 1993) 100-120.   J. Pokrifka

LITURGICAL INTERPRETATION. *See* HERMENEUTICS.

LOVE POETRY. *See* SONG OF SONGS 2: ANCIENT NEAR EASTERN BACKGROUND; WASF.

LYRIC POETRY

The word *lyric* comes from Greek *lyra* ("lyre"), a stringed instrument. In time, the term came to be used not only of the harp but also for the sung words that accompanied the *music (cf. the English word *lyrics*). In poetic theory, lyric, along with narrative (or epic) and dramatic poetries, comprises one of the three categories of poetic literature (J. Johnson, 713). Rigid distinctions among these types are not always possible, as there is of necessity some overlap: the three share certain characteristics and devices. Even so, the classification of poetry into these three main kinds is sufficient indication that lyric can be distinguished from the other two, at least to some degree (see 1.2). As a first, very preliminary, statement, it should be said that lyric poetry retains "most prominently the elements which evidence its origins in musical expression—singing, chanting, and recitation to musical accompaniment" (J. Johnson, 713). Of course, narrative/epic and dramatic poetries can also evidence deep connections to music (see Lord). But with lyric, the "musical element is intrinsic to the work intellectually as well as aesthetically" (J. Johnson, 713). Musicality or, more broadly, auditoriness/aurality again is not limited to lyric, being the general possession of all poetries (Berlin 2004, 2101). Even so, for various reasons discussed in further detail below, lyric must depend even more than other types on the "naked properties of language"—the intrinsic "music" of the poetic word itself, as it were—"as its basic resource for making meaning" (Dobbs-Allsopp 2002, 12; cf. 2006, 348, 356, 358; Langer, 259). The present article discusses lyric and lyric sequences in poetic theory more generally before tracing both within the OT. Finally, the macrogenre of Scripture as a whole is considered in light of the lyric.

1. Lyric Poetry
2. Lyric Poetry in the Old Testament

3. The Lyric Sequence
4. Lyric Sequences in the Old Testament
5. The Bible as Lyric Poetry/Lyric Sequence

1. Lyric Poetry.

1.1. Lyric and/as Music. Although lyric's association with music is intrinsic, encoded in the etymology of the term itself, this does not hold true for its subsequent history. Indeed, beyond the ancient Greek world, "the *literal* use of music ceases to be a meaningful genre criteria" (Dobbs-Allsopp 2006, 348). Hence, despite the fact that lyric was originally sung (cf. Greek *melikos* ["member, song"] poetry; see Turco, 120; Race), early on even classical poets such as Horace ceased composing poetry exclusively for musical settings (Dobbs-Allsopp 2006, 348; cf. J. Johnson, 713, 717). Eventually, that is, lyric "found itself bereft of the very element which had been the foundation of its lyricism—music" (J. Johnson, 714). Definitions of lyric must move, therefore, from modal (or performative) understandings, having to do with music, to generic ones (Dobbs-Allsopp 2006, 349).

1.2. The Lyric Beyond Music. Identifying the standard or essential characteristics of the lyric genre is difficult, however, given the interplay of devices that are present therein but also at work in other types of poetry or in literature more generally (Dobbs-Allsopp 2006, 349). It is the case, then, that no one element characterizes lyric to the extent that said element is found in no other genre of literature. Instead, lyric contains several key elements in high density and in particular combination (Dobbs-Allsopp 2006, 378). But even here one must beware of essentialism, as there are dozens of lyric genres with particular aspects and emphases (see J. Johnson, 715; Turco).

A useful starting point is offered by the definition of lyric as "*chiefly* . . . a nonnarrative, nondramatic, nonrepresentational kind of poetry" (Dobbs-Allsopp 2006, 350). This definition immediately distinguishes lyric from narrative/epic and dramatic poetries. The definition should not, however, be taken as indicating that lyric never contains narratival or dramatic elements. It can and frequently does (see 3-4 below). But these are not pronounced or pre-dominant. In fact, the "aspiration toward something other than narrative may well be the most tractable lyric characteristic of Hebrew verse more generally" (Dobbs-Allsopp 2006, 351).

Lack of narrative interest or execution is, in no small measure, a reflex of the fact that lyric poetry is typically brief (Lindley, 4). Said differently, lyric poetry is "a discontinuous form. . . . we normally do not expect the kind of linear unfolding of events that produces a plot" (Exum, 42). The brief and poetic (i.e., lyrical) nature of the lyric precludes extensive character development, emplottment, and so forth that one finds in prose narrative. Instead, there are sudden shifts of topic, speaker and theme (Exum, 42); even when characters are present, the portrait thereof is synchronic, not diachronic. So, although it may be true that "behind every lyric, sometimes vaguely sketched, sometimes clearly defined, is a story that explains the present moment of discourse . . . in lyric poems . . . the story exists for the song," not the song for the poetry (W. Johnson, 35; see also Dobbs-Allsopp 2006, 357-58).

F. Dobbs-Allsopp points out that in the absence of cohesion-aiding devices such as plot or argumentation, lyric is cast upon other resources to do its work. One such resource is form, another the power of language itself, still another the heightened use of emotions, yet another tropological density—the use of many poetic features and figures of thought in close combination (see Dobbs-Allsopp 2006, 363, 364 n. 81, 378; cf. Fisch, 118-19; Alter, 133; J. Johnson, 714). Instead of plot, form; instead of argument, metaphor; instead of story, marked use of heightened language—all in tight formation. These are among the hallmarks of lyric. D. Lindley (4) summarizes matters well: "We may then accept that many lyrics are short, many speak of heightened feeling in a poetic present and are uttered by a voice in the first person, and a significant number are written for music or out of a musical impulse."

But Lindley (4) is quick to point out that "many . . . poems we might wish to call 'lyrics' have few or none of these qualities." This again warns against "essentializing" any one (or more) aspects (or combination); it also indicates that lyric shares even its most central qualities with other kinds of literature, just as lyric often can employ devices found primarily or extensively in those other genres. It is the density of brief scale, lack of plot or argumentation, prominence of the speaking voice over developed characterization, radical dependence on language—especially expressive language—and the like that distinguish lyric (Dobbs-Allsopp, forthcoming).

Two comments should be added before turning to lyric poetry in the Bible. First, the brief scale of lyric poems "means, as a purely practical matter, that . . . [they] will be limited in the scope of their subject matter" (Dobbs-Allsopp 2006, 365). They are too small to speak *in extenso* about a topic; they are, by definition (and scale) episodic. Second, the lyric's reliance on language alone, along with the way it employs that language, shares certain properties with the music that originally inspired this type of poetry. Such properties would include "rhythm, meter, a pervasive heightening of sonority through alliteration, assonance, and the like" (Dobbs-Allsopp 2006, 377). The sound patterns of lyric itself, that is, are representative of music (J. Johnson, 715). But even when they are not sung, "*literary lyrics* carry their own music . . . no extraneous musical accompaniment is required" (Turco, 120).

2. Lyric Poetry in the Old Testament.

Regarding the item last mentioned, J. Johnson (726) writes,

> From its primordial form, the song as embodiment of emotion, the l[yric] has been expanded and altered through the centuries until it has become one of the chief literary instruments which focus and evaluate the human condition. In flexibility, variety, and polish, it is perhaps the most proficient of the poetic genres. In the immediacy and keenness of its expression, it is certainly the most effective. These qualities have caused the 19th and 20th c[enturies] to look upon the l[yric] as largely their own, but l[yric] poetry has belonged to all ages.

As proof of the latter point, Johnson (715-16) states that lyric is "as old as recorded lit[erature], and its history is that of human experience at its most animated," and he goes on to note lyric exemplars in Sumerian, Assyro-Babylonian, Hittite and Egyptian.

Certainly the same situation obtains for Hebrew examples (J. Johnson, 716). In fact, S. Driver (360) stated rather categorically that "Hebrew poetry is almost exclusively *lyric*." More recently, H. Fisch (118-19) has remarked that the definition of poetry (especially lyric) as "the maximum foregrounding of the utterance . . . is truer of the Psalms probably than of any other poetry"

(cf. Alter, 133). Indeed, it could be argued that there is no narrative or dramatic poetry in the Bible at all. Even the so-called historical psalms (e.g., Pss 78; 105; 106) are not of sufficient scale to approximate narrative/epic poetry. With its "hodge-podge collection of traditions," which "are not sequenced or otherwise developed logically," a composition such as Psalm 114 only further exemplifies the distance from narrative/epic poetry that Hebrew poetry typically evidences (see Dobbs-Allsopp 2006, 353). This could be profitably contrasted with the long narrative/epic poems known from Ugarit (Baal, Kirta, Aqhat) or Mesopotamia (Gilgamesh, Erra) (see Dobbs-Allsopp 2006, 365). The OT has no manifest equivalent. The closest approximation—a poetic substratum that underlay the Old Epic (J/E) or certain parts of the Pentateuch—is completely speculative and thoroughly reconstructive in nature (Cross; Damrosch).

Further evidence of the lyric nature of most (all?) Hebrew poetry comes from its connections to music. It is often said that Hebrew knows no word for "poetry." The closest approximation appears to be *šîr* ("song" [e.g., Ps 45:1; 46:1; 76:1; 120:1; Song 1:1]). Other terms used are also related to music: *mizmôr* (NRSV: "psalm"; derived from the root *zmr*, "sing praise") or *qînâ* ("lament, dirge") (see Dobbs-Allsopp 2006, 374-77). To these linguistic data one might add the large number of artifacts recovered from ancient Israel/Palestine that have to do with music (Braun). Or, to return to *Psalms, the number of terms appearing to have something to do with music, whether that is reference to instruments (e.g., Ps 33:1-3; 93:4; 150:3-5), rhythmic patterns or tunes (e.g., Ps 6:1; 12:1; 57:1), or even groups of singers and musicians (Ps 68:26; cf. Ps 150:3-5), is noteworthy (see further Dobbs-Allsopp 2006, 374-77). Admittedly, not all of these data or their precise relationship to music are transparent, but at many points in the psalms the connection is explicit. Consider Psalm 98:5: "Sing praise *[zammĕrû]* to Yahweh with the lyre *[bĕkinnôr]*, with the lyre *[bĕkinnôr]* and the sound of a praise-song *[zimrâ]*" (my translation).

Taken cumulatively, then, this kind of terminology—not to mention other musicological data such as the *refrains present in Psalm 136—betrays "at least an originary concern for music for the compositions so named" (Dobbs-Allsopp 2006, 375; cf. Fisch, 119; J. Johnson, 716), a point reinforced by the artifacts and iconography from ancient Israel/Palestine (Strawn and LeMon; Braun).

Some scholars have gone further, arguing that the psalms are full-blown lyric, regardless of musicality—that is, poetry that is "reflexively conscious of the importance of poetry" (Fisch, 119; cf. further 104-35; see also Driver, 359-91; Lowth, 278-315; Berlin, *NIB* 4.303; Dobbs-Allsopp 2006). Fisch (108) believes that Psalm 49:3 is an "announcement of lyrical intent" (see also Ps 5:1; 19:14; 104:34), while Dobbs-Allsopp (2006, 359 n. 59) states that the reference to "my work" *(maʿăśay)* in Psalm 45:1 (MT 45:2) is "one of the rare instances in which a biblical writer shows some conscious awareness of craft. . . . 'my work' . . . would be the precise equivalent to the Greek notion of poesy." In sum, it would seem that the psalms are predominantly and preeminently lyric (Dobbs-Allsopp 2006), a point reinforced by the history of their reception because the psalms inspired many of the great lyricists and lyric collections (see 3-4 below).

*Song of Songs also fits the description of lyric poetry (Exum, 1; Fisch, 104). Though some scholars have argued that Song of Songs is dramatic poetry and have ascribed various parts to different *dramatis personae,* the work is not overtly or explicitly dramatic: the different "actors" are never so identified, nor is a plot of any sort given (Fisch, 104; Exum, 78-79). This situation contrasts rather markedly with the one that obtains in the book of *Job, where the speakers are regularly introduced and the poetic sections are emplotted by the prose framework (see Dobbs-Allsopp, forthcoming). "To turn [Song of Songs] into a drama, too much has to be read between the lines" (Exum, 78). It is better to treat it as lyric (see 3-4 below).

The book of *Lamentations is another example of lyric poetry in the OT. Dobbs-Allsopp (2002, 14-20) highlights the high-density use of metaphor; poetic diction; the play of syntax and lineation, including enjambment; *wordplay; pun; euphony; *personification; and the extended use of the alphabetic *acrostic as a formal constraint.

One additional aspect of lyric poetry not mentioned earlier seems especially suitable to biblical examples of the genre. It is what R. Greene (1991, 5-6) discusses as the capacity of lyric to impose "the subjectivity of the scripted speaker on the reader"; or, to put it in Dobbs-Allsopp's (2006, 367-68) terms, lyric's ability to be reuttered. Fisch (118) puts it slightly differently, that, in the process of reading and rereading, the words of the lyric become "their [the readers'/speakers'] words, the expression of their individuality on each and every occasion of reading or singing." To be sure, there is a sense in which all literature can be "road tested" for a while (see Booth), but the brevity of scale and scope, the episodicity, and the property of the speaking voice (see J. Johnson, 726; Fisch, 104; Turco, 120) make poetry, especially the lyric, particularly well suited for reutterability, or what might just as easily be termed (re)appropriation (see Fisch, 127; Miller 1986; 2000, 248-49). We are able to "try on this [lyric] voice and what it says because we have been explicitly included in that voice" (Dobbs-Allsopp, forthcoming). The history of reading the Bible is, in no small measure, the history of (re)uttering and (re)appropriating the words of Scripture. Nowhere is this truer than in the case of the psalms, the Hebrew lyric par excellence.

3. The Lyric Sequence.

Despite the fact that the lyric contains no extended logical argumentation or developed progression of plot and character, poets have long strung together independent and self-contained poems into larger collections or lyric sequences. Well-known examples include Petrarch's 366-poem sequence *Canzoniere,* George Herbert's *The Temple,* John Donne's *Holy Sonnets,* Walt Whitman's *Leaves of Grass* and T. S. Eliot's *The Wasteland.* The practice of lyric sequencing is an ancient one, however, to judge from the evidence from the ancient Near East (J. Johnson, 715, 724; Dobbs-Allsopp 2006, 366). There are, first, various literary catalogs that have survived, suggesting the practice of poetic collecting (Dobbs-Allsopp 2006, 366 n. 85; for an attempt to find a catalog of lyric poems in Ps 68, see Albright). There is also the very early collection of forty-two Sumerian temple hymns (Sjöberg and Bergman 1969), all of which share the same basic form, appear to proceed in an orderly geographical sequence, and which were compiled by Enheduanna, the daughter of Sargon of Akkad, who claims authorial responsibility for the collection (see Dobbs-Allsopp 2006, 366 n. 85). From Egypt there are various collections of love lyrics (Fox), and, from later periods, one might add to this listing the pseudepigraphical *Psalms of Solomon* (Dobbs-Allsopp 2006, 366

n. 85). The practice of placing lyrics in larger collections is, therefore, an ancient and widespread phenomenon.

At its simplest, the lyric sequence is a "collocation of lyrics" (Greene 1993, 727) that can be structured by any number of devices—formal, fictional, calendrical and so on (Greene 1993, 727)—such that they "tend to interact as an organic whole" (Rosenthal and Gall 1982, 9). After Petrarch, the lyric sequence became "not merely a 'form' but a complex of generic capacities" (Greene 1993, 727). Within this complex a balance must be struck between the overall "unity" of the collection and the integrity of the individual lyric poems themselves (Greene 1993, 728). The latter are often "heterogeneous in form," but nevertheless they interact holistically by means of the sequence (Rosenthal and Gall 1993, 728). In effect, then, the modern lyric sequence is "a single poem" (Greene 1993, 728) or "a modern lyric poem writ large, its several parts providing the same sort of emotive or apperceptive thrusts of affective lang[uage] in relation to the whole as do the shifts of tonal coloration and intensity in a single lyric" (Rosenthal and Gall 1993, 728). These comments are evocative when applied to Scripture (see 4 below). Before doing so, however, we will find it instructive to ask how lyric sequences work.

First, since the lyric sequence is writing in the lyric mode but on a larger scale, it helps to counteract the limitations inherent in the brief scale that is a hallmark of lyric poetry (see above). So, one way that lyric poetry can and does manifest larger development, progression, argument, even plot or narrative-like devices, is by lyric sequencing. The dynamics of the sequence itself are varied. On the one hand, they are "primarily emotive and associative" (Rosenthal and Gall 1993, 728), like lyric poetry generally; on the other hand, there is a plethora of structuring characteristics that can be delineated for lyric sequences. While their form is "unusually protean" (Rosenthal and Gall 1993, 728), one might nevertheless highlight the fact that lyric sequences (1) employ lyric as the mode of discourse; (2) consist of multiple, discrete poems; and (3) exhibit perceivable coherence and integrity (Dobbs-Allsopp, forthcoming). Moreover, the overarching structures present in the sequence are themselves lyrical in that they defy reduction to simplistic thematic, logical or narratalogical explication/paraphrase.

Much more could be said, but it must suffice here to say that the lyric sequence contains both centripetal and centrifugal movements (see Grossberg; Greene 1991, 20; Dobbs-Allsopp 2006, 372, 374; Rosenthal and Gall 1993, 729). In the former, the larger sequence keeps the poems together, though it does so in the open way characteristic of lyric. In the latter, the individual poems making up the sequence press outward, given their lyric episodicity, even while the various strategies of linkage (e.g., repetition; echoing key words; variation on themes, diction, imagery and topic; development of "plot" [see Miner, 222; Dobbs-Allsopp 2006, 357]) apparent in the sequence hold them together. Both movements, that is, contain within themselves elements of the opposite. Whatever the case, it should be stressed that the disjunction or discontinuity that is present alongside obvious moments of continuity is not a defect but rather is a sign of the specifically *lyric* structure of the sequence (Dobbs-Allsopp, forthcoming). In analyzing a sequence, then, one must attend to both the individual poem and the larger sequence, while simultaneously considering the thrusts toward both fragmentation and unification that mark lyric sequences.

It must be admitted, of course, that strategies of connection, structuring and unity are, to some degree at least, constructed by the reader. J. Exum (42) for example, speaking specifically of Song of Songs, notes that there is a strong "readerly tendency to read sequentially and to make sense of a literary work as a whole; in other words, to read for plot.... We create connections as we read, revising them, abandoning them and adopting others when necessary.... [In so doing] we have begun to create a 'story.'" However, said "story" may not *actually* be present—not in *lyric* contexts—despite the fact that certain details "tease and tantalize us to find connections [even] where they are lacking" (Exum, 42). One conclusion here is that we must remember that even when unity, development or progression is found, the overall context is lyrical. Even if the lyric sequence gestures at "encompassment," that is, it is only a gesture, because in lyric the poetic subject(s) "can never be fully and satisfactorily contained" (Dobbs-Allsopp, forthcoming).

4. Lyric Sequences in the Old Testament.

Writing about recent research on poetic collections like the lyric sequence, E. Miner (222) has stated that "because discovery of the unifying principles of such collections has come only relatively recently, it seems very likely that further study will reveal numerous other p[oetic] c[ollections]."

And so it has, and does, when applied to the Bible, though such an endeavor is still very much in its infancy (see Dobbs-Allsopp 2002; 2006; forthcoming).

The place to look for lyric sequences in the OT is precisely where lyric poems reside: Psalms, Song of Songs and Lamentations. In the light of lyric sequences, it becomes possible that these books are not (especially in the case of Psalms) solely or only (random) collections of poems but are instead lyric sequences or at least comprised of such. Indeed, maybe these "books" are not books at all but rather lyric poems "writ large."

The conclusion drawn by M. Rosenthal and S. Gall (1993, 729) on lyric sequences is an instructive entrée into the issues:

> The m[odern] p[oetic] s[equence] frees us to look at poems of all periods, long and short, in a new way, for its dynamics are those of lyrical structure itself, defined as the *overall directive energy of movement*—the progression, juxtaposition, and interrelation of all the lyric centers, dynamic shifts, and tonal notes—in a poem or s[equence]. The object of lyrical structure is neither to resolve a problem nor to conclude an action but to achieve the keenest, most open realization possible. The best s[equences] depend for their life on *the interrelation of lyric centers*—units that present specific qualities and intensities of emotional and sensuously charged awareness in the *lang[uage]* of a passage, not in the supposed feelings of the author or of any implied "speaker." (first two sets of italics added)

The psalms come immediately to mind in light of Rosenthal and Gall's comment, in part because, historically, the authors of more recent lyric sequences (e.g., Petrarch) took the psalms as their model (see Greene 1993, 727). The psalms are also a natural location to look for poetic sequencing insofar as scholars have recently paid increased attention to the "shape and shaping" of the Psalter as a whole—an endeavor that is sometimes called reading the psalms

"as a book" (see, e.g., Wilson; McCann) (*see* Editorial Criticism). Some of this research has focused on clearly demarcated units (whether by title or genre) in the Psalter, such as the Songs of Ascents (Pss 120-134 [see Grossberg]). At other times, the connections have been less transparent but no less evident—for example, the way Psalms 1—2 coinhere to introduce the Psalter (Miller 1993), or the chiastically formal structure of Psalms 15—24 (Miller 1994; see also, on Pss 51—100, Hossfeld and Zenger). Such readings are fascinating and typically quite insightful; it remains to be seen how "intentional" they are (if intent matters) or if they are primarily constructed by the reader/scholar.

Working in a somewhat different vein, W. Brueggemann has offered a reading of "the entire directive energy of movement" (Rosenthal and Gall 1993, 729) in the Psalter, treating it as a lyric sequence of sorts (though he does not use this language) that moves from Torah obedience to unbounded praise. In a recent work on metaphor in the Psalter, W. Brown has demonstrated the pervasive generativity of two dominant metaphors, that of "refuge" (theology) and "pathway" (ethics); this is certainly what Rosenthall and Gall (1993, 729) would call "the interrelation of lyric centers."

At the very least, such scholarship suggests the viable presence of lyric sequences in the psalms and the benefit that will result from further study. But research on lyric sequences also indicates that "reading the psalms as a book" is at best a misnomer for this type of approach and represents a fundamental misunderstanding of the nature of the Psalter's unity (and disunity) as "storied" or "narrative" instead of what it clearly is: a collection (sequence or even collection of sequences) of lyric poems. This is no matter of splitting hairs over scholarly nomenclature; it is a crucial distinction that impacts readerly expectation, analysis and interpretation (see 5 below).

The lyrical nature of Song of Songs has already been discussed above. It can be repeated here that Exum and Fisch, among others, have critiqued interpretations of the work that impose a structural unity upon it but in nonlyrical mode—namely, as a drama—primarily because the plot for such unity and drama must be provided "from outside the textual world" (Exum, 42; see further 42-44, 78-79). It appears that Exum (33-37) herself prefers to think of Song of Songs as a long lyric poem rather than a lyric sequence, but insofar as the lyric sequence is in many ways just another way to write a long lyric poem (see 3 above), this distinction may be interpretively negligible. Regardless, Exum (44) certainly is correct that "we should be wary of looking for narrative progression in a lyric poem that meanders the way the Song does." This makes any search for plot development or progression or drama in Song of Songs a desperate move, even though "there is, of course, poetic development" (Exum, 44), which is precisely what one would expect in a lyric sequence.

Finally, Dobbs-Allsopp (forthcoming) has made a compelling case that Lamentations is a lyric sequence on the basis of numerous observations, including the work's "varied and countervailing fragmenting and cohering practices; the sense of development manifested among the several poems, and the strong sense of closure projected by the whole." Still other lyric sequences might exist in the OT. One thinks, perhaps, of Proverbs 1—9 + 31 or of other subcollections in the Psalter or even in prophetic books. This remark by Miner (222) holds true, then, for Hebrew lyric as well as much later types: "it seems very likely that further study will reveal numerous other p[oetic] c[ollections]."

5. The Bible as Lyric Poetry/Lyric Sequence.
A final possible contribution of lyric poetry to the Bible can be profitably entertained. Not only can it be said that parts of the Bible are lyric poetry and that the Bible contains lyric; also, insofar as the Bible, at a macrolevel, is not easily reduced to a linear plot line or "narrative," no matter how generously construed, perhaps it is worth thinking about Scripture as a grand poem or sequence of poems, perhaps even as a lyric sequence. Of course, it can be said that if one defines *narrative* broadly, then the Bible can, in fact, be read as "the great story of God." Biblical scholars, theologians and laity make this move all the time. However, defining narrative in such great breadth stretches the category almost beyond recognition and thus somewhat trivializes the claim (see Strawson, 438-40). At the very least, it could be asserted in reply that "poetry" too can be similarly stretched and broadened (with concern over subsequent trivialization duly noted). If so, and if one does in fact think of the Bible more like a great poem or lyric sequence than a grand story, what difference would it make? What benefits accrue?

First, one might consider possible detriments that are present in readings that are insufficiently poetic—that is, overly narrative. This is a large topic that cannot be treated here; it must suffice to say that, generically, the Bible includes much that is not narrative. Fully one-third of the OT is poetic, and this certainly is among its great contributions to Scripture. To be sure, parts of the OT and of the NT can be read in narrative succession (e.g., Genesis through Ezra-Nehemiah or the Gospels and Acts), but in both Testaments this "plot" breaks down when one encounters material either that is out of narrative (or chronological) order and must then be placed back within the plotted story (e.g., the Prophets or the Epistles) or that seems largely uninterested in that story in the first place (e.g., much of the wisdom and poetic writings and the book of Revelation). Even within the main "plot-books/blocks," a simple, straightforwardly narrative reading breaks down. Chronicles repeats material from Genesis, Samuel and Kings; it does not simply "continue the story." For their part, the Gospels are more like repetitive refrains than continuations of the same version (contrast the Syriac Diatessaron). And, although Luke and Acts appear to comprise a narrative unity that continues the story of Jesus into the early church, virtually all editions of the NT stubbornly separate the two by imposing John as another, perhaps climactic, Gospel refrain.

There is, in short, a price to be paid for "narrativization"—this imposing of order and linearity on what is, in fact, in many ways disorderly or episodic (see Taylor, 491; Aichele, 95; Strawson), dare one even say lyrical? Despite the wide (even hegemonic) influence that "narrative" currently enjoys, it must be asserted that a closer look at specific parts of Scripture as well as Scripture as a whole indicates that narrative should not hold a monopoly on ways of construing the Bible (and its macrogenre). As its best, narrative theology (inadvertently?) leaves too much out and lets important things slip through; at its worst, it is constructed (advertently?) to avoid things that Scripture itself deems it important for us to have (see Taylor, 490).

To be sure, it is somewhat natural to assume or "find" narratival structuring in what we read (see 3 above). It is natural because so much of what presently counts as literature or written material is narratival in basic and fundamental ways (see Dobbs-Allsopp 2006, 350 n. 14; Exum,

42). We should realize, however, that our present context, which favors narrative so much, is also exerting pressure upon us to read in precisely those sorts of ways; this pressure, moreover, is exacerbated by various hermeneutical, psychological and theological movements that seek to find (empirically) or recommend/impose (ethically) a "narrative structure of reality" on the entirety of our lives. But the existence of poetry, in general, and of lyric and lyric sequences, specifically, suggests that this need not be so (see, more generally, Strawson). Reading for plot and expecting to find such is, in short, a constructed phenomenon, imposed *ad extra,* neither necessary nor implicit—at least not always. There are, after all, other ways of writing and reading (see Landow), other ways of finding form and meaning in our lives. Meaning need not be the result of or the sole purview of narrative; it could just as easily be an "osmotic, systemic, not staged in consciousness" kind of product (Strawson, 448). Or, it could be lyrical. Even our life "stories," when we tell them, are often little more than a pastiche (sequence?) of moments, episodes, snapshots, altogether comparable to a lyric poem or lyric sequence. The connections holding these together may be linear and progressive, but they need not be always and only narratival (see Strawson). One's "story" could just as easily be one's grand "lyric poem."

The same points could be argued for Scripture. The Bible can indeed be read as a story, but such a move is a readerly construct, one that is not widely self-evident and that carries with it obvious benefits but also certain detriments. For one example of the latter, the Scripture-as-Story approach may (in)advertenly function to privilege only or primarily the NT as the "climax of the covenant." The OT becomes, in such a scenario, "mere background," of little use even if it is granted putative import. A narrative approach may also create unrealistic expectations: all elements of the plot will be (or are) tied up nicely, eventually, at the end.

Thinking Scripture-as-Lyric/Lyric Sequence offers different results. For one, poetry in general and lyric in particular frequently complicate and ambiguate the reading experience. Not all loose ends are tied up nicely. More pointedly, it is unnecessary that they be so. Life is not like that; why should Scripture be? Study of lyric sequences has shown that both centrifugal and centripetal tendencies are important and de-serve attention (see 3 above). Hence, not only what binds the Testaments together (internally or between the two) is important, but also what resists such unification. Readerly consternation over the Bible's "tensions" or "contradictions" becomes a largely moot problem in the face of lyric's tendency to fragmentation and disjuncture. This is, in a word, what one expects of lyric poetry. In this way, poetry (and Scripture) again imitates life.

Even so, there are points of connection, overlap and structure in Scripture-as-Lyric/Lyric Sequence, but these are not simplistically or primarily diachronic, related to plot and recounted in story mode, linearly, with causation (see Forster, esp. 25-42, 83-103; Strawson, 439). Instead, the unity of a Testament (or of the Christian Bible) is complex and chainlike "wherein each of the poems is joined to some subset of the other poems in the sequence in a multiplicity of overlapping ways" (Dobbs-Allsopp, forthcoming). Gone is the "climax of the covenant." In its place is the thick and difficult beauty of the poetry that is (the entirety of) Scripture.

Here, too, much more could be said; regardless, it should be stressed that these sorts of considerations do not indicate that lyric is necessarily better (or worse) than other kinds of discourse, only that it is *different* from other kinds of discourse (Dobbs-Allsopp, forthcoming) and its benefits deserve to be weighed and measured, especially as they often seem to answer the weaknesses of narratival modes. In this way, what Dobbs-Allsopp (2006, 379) says of the psalms could hold equally true for Scripture as a whole: "Psalmic poetry through its very lyricism may even inspire us to new ways of seeing and imagining, even to new ways of thinking. . . . Lyric thinking . . . is most assuredly a different kind of thinking, a thinking otherwise." This different kind of thinking, present in the lyric poems of the Bible itself, is one that "thrive[s] in ambiguity and complexity, that emerge[s] rhythmically and through the play of syntax, that [is] implicit in a poem's tone and get[s] argued through the precision of an image"; if we recovered such thinking, it would move us and our interpretation decidedly "beyond a commentary tradition that in the main has relegated its estimation of the intellective capacities of psalms to that which can be translated into conceptual paraphrase alone" (Dobbs-Allsopp 2006, 378; cf.

374). Gone will be the paraphrase or the proposition; in its place, the poetry.

Thought of in this way, lyric, with all its accompanying benefits and particularities, clearly takes its place (perhaps pride of place) among the seminal contributions that poetry makes to study of Scripture, theology and biblical theology. Historically and cross-culturally, lyric is widely associated with religion and ritual activity, where it is especially "expressive of mystical experience" (J. Johnson, 715), perhaps because it, like poetry more generally, "is open . . . [it] articulates the mystery [of God] but leaves it there" (Miller 2000, 247; see also 245, 249).

See also ORAL POETRY; PARALLELISM; POETICS, TERMINOLOGY OF.

BIBLIOGRAPHY. **G. Aichele Jr.,** *The Limits of Story* (SemeiaSt; Philadelphia: Fortress; Chico, CA: Scholars Press, 1985); **W. F. Albright,** "A Catalogue of Early Hebrew Lyric Poems (Psalms LXVIII)," *HUCA* 23 (1950-1951) 1-39; **R. Alter,** *The Art of Biblical Poetry* (New York: Basic Books, 1985); **A. Berlin,** "Introduction to Hebrew Poetry," *NIB* 4.301-15; idem, "Reading Biblical Poetry," in *The Jewish Study Bible*, ed. A Berlin and M. Z. Brettler (Oxford: Oxford University Press, 2004) 2097-104; **W. C. Booth,** *The Company We Keep: An Ethics of Fiction* (Berkeley: University of California Press, 1988); **J. Braun,** *Music in Ancient Israel/Palestine*, trans. D. W. Stott (Grand Rapids: Eerdmans, 2002); **W. P. Brown,** *Seeing the Psalms: A Theology of Metaphor* (Louisville: Westminster John Knox, 2002); **W. Brueggemann,** "Bounded by Obedience and Praise: The Psalms as Canon," in *The Psalms and the Life of Faith*, ed. P. D. Miller (Minneapolis: Fortress, 1995) 189-213; **F. M. Cross,** *Canaanite Myth and Hebrew Epic: Essays in the History of the Religion of Israel* (Cambridge, MA: Harvard University Press, 1973); **D. Damrosch,** *The Narrative Covenant: Transformations of Genre in the Growth of Biblical Literature* (San Francisco: Harper & Row, 1987); **F. W. Dobbs-Allsopp,** *Lamentations* (IBC; Louisville: Westminster John Knox, 2002); idem, "The Psalms and Lyric Verse," in *The Evolution of Rationality: Interdisciplinary Essays in Honor of J. Wentzel van Huyssteen*, ed. F. L. Shultz (Grand Rapids: Eerdmans, 2006) 346-79; idem, "Lamentations as a Lyric Sequence" (forthcoming); **S. R. Driver,** *An Introduction to the Literature of the Old Testament* (New York: Meridian, 1956 [1897]); **J. C. Exum,** *Song of Songs: A Commentary* (OTL; Louisville: Westminster John Knox, 2005); **H. Fisch,** *Poetry with a Purpose: Biblical Poetics and Interpretation* (ISBL; Bloomington: Indiana University Press, 1988); **E. M. Forster,** *Aspects of the Novel* (New York: Harcourt, Brace & World, 1955); **M. V. Fox,** *The Song of Songs and the Ancient Egyptian Love Songs* (Madison: University of Wisconsin Press, 1985); **R. Greene,** *Post-Petrarchism: Origins and Innovations of the Western Lyric Sequence* (Princeton, NJ: Princeton University Press, 1991); idem, "Lyric Sequence: I. Renaissance to Romanticism," in *The New Princeton Encyclopedia of Poetry and Poetics*, ed. A. Preminger and T. V. F. Brogan (Princeton, NJ: Princeton University Press, 1993) 727-28; **D. Grossberg,** *Centripetal and Centrifugal Structures in Biblical Poetry* (SBLMS 39; Atlanta: Scholars Press, 1989); **F.-L. Hossfeld and E. Zenger,** *Psalms 2: A Commentary on Psalms 51-100*, ed. K. Baltzer (Hermeneia; Minneapolis: Fortress, 2005); **J. W. Johnson,** "Lyric," in *The New Princeton Encyclopedia of Poetry and Poetics*, ed. A. Preminger and T. V. F. Brogan (Princeton, NJ: Princeton University Press, 1993) 713-27; **W. R. Johnson,** *The Idea of Lyric: Lyric Modes in Ancient and Modern Poetry* (Los Angeles: University of California Press, 1983); **G. P. Landow,** *Hypertext 3.0: Critical Theory and New Media in an Era of Globalization* (3rd ed.; Baltimore: Johns Hopkins University Press, 2006); **S. Langer,** *Feeling and Form: A Theory of Art* (New York: Scribner, 1953); **D. Lindley,** *Lyric* (Critical Idiom 44; London: Methuen, 1985); **A. B. Lord,** *The Singer of Tales*, ed. S. Mitchell and G. Nagy (2nd ed.; Harvard Studies in Comparative Literature 24; Cambridge, MA: Harvard University Press, 2000); **R. Lowth,** *Lectures on the Sacred Poetry of the Hebrews* (4th ed.; London: Tomas Tegg, 1839 [1753]); **J. C. McCann,** ed., *The Shape and Shaping of the Psalter* (JSOTSup 159; Sheffield: JSOT Press, 1993); **P. D. Miller,** *Interpreting the Psalms* (Philadelphia: Fortress, 1986); idem, "The Beginning of the Psalter," in *The Shape and Shaping of the Psalter*, ed. J. C. McCann (JSOTSup 159; Sheffield: JSOT Press, 1993) 83-92; idem, "Kingship, Torah Obedience, and Prayer: The Theology of Psalms 15-24," in *Neue Wege der Psalmenforschung: Für Walter Beyerlin*, ed. K. Seybold and E. Zenger (HBS 1; Freiburg: Herder, 1994) 127-42; idem, "The Theological Significance of Biblical Poetry," in *Israelite Religion and Biblical Theology: Collected Essays* (JSOTSup 267; Sheffield: Sheffield Academic Press, 2000) 233-49; **E. Miner,** "Collections, Poetic," in *The New*

Princeton Encyclopedia of Poetry and Poetics, ed. A. Preminger and T. V. F. Brogan (Princeton, NJ: Princeton University Press, 1993) 222-23; **W. H. Race,** "Melic Poetry," in *The New Princeton Encyclopedia of Poetry and Poetics,* ed. A. Preminger and T. V. F. Brogan (Princeton, NJ: Princeton University Press, 1993) 755; **M. L. Rosenthal and S. M. Gall,** *The Modern Poetic Sequence* (New York: Oxford University Press, 1982); idem, "Lyric Sequence: II. Modern British and American," in *The New Princeton Encyclopedia of Poetry and Poetics,* ed. A. Preminger and T. V. F. Brogan (Princeton, NJ: Princeton University Press, 1993) 728-29; **A. Sjöberg and E. Bergman,** *The Collection of Sumerian Temple Hymns* (TCS 3; Locust Valley, NY: J. J. Augustin, 1969); **B. A. Strawn and J. M. LeMon,** "'Everything That Has Breath': Animal Praise in Psalm 150:6 in the Light of Ancient Near Eastern Iconography" in *Bilder als Quellen / Images as Sources: Studies in ancient Near Eastern artifacts and the Bible inspired by the work of Othmar Keel,* ed. S. Bickel, S. Schroer, and C. Uehlinger (OBO; Fribourg: Academic Press; Göttingen: Vanden-hoeck & Ruprecht, forthcoming) 451-85 and Pls. xxxiii-iv; **G. Strawson,** "Against Narrativity," *Ratio* 17 (2004) 428-52; **M. C. Taylor,** "Impossible Story," *Cross Currents* 36 (1986-1987) 489-92 [review of Aichele 1985]; **L. Turco,** *The Book of Forms: A Handbook of Poetics* (3rd ed.; Hanover, NH: University Press of New England, 2000); **G. H. Wilson,** *The Editing of the Hebrew Psalter* (SBLDS 76; Chico, CA: Scholars Press, 1985).

B. A. Strawn

M

MAAT

This is an Egyptian word conventionally transcribed as *maat* or *maet,* containing central ʾ*ālep* and ʿ*ayin* left unexpressed in the popular-usage transcriptions cited. It is from a root *maa,* basically meaning "be straight" (literally), then "be straight in conduct," "be true, just, right(eous)." Hence, the abstract noun *maat* includes truth, justice, rightness, right order in the universe within its orbit. It was the fundamental concept undergirding the values of ancient Egyptian culture, governing relations between deity and humans and within human society in that culture. It was thus in some measure analogous with Hebrew *ṣedeq, ṣědāqâ, ṣādaq* ("right," "righteousness/justice," "be right/just"). Like Hebrew *ḥokmâ* ("wisdom"), Egyptian *maat* was personified, and in its case right from the beginning (as a fem. word) in the form of a goddess, Maat, to whom even temples and cult were later assigned.

    1. Oldest Occurrences, the *Maat* Hieroglyph, Basic Range of Meaning
    2. Historical Development in the Concept of *Maat*
    3. *Maat* and Old Testament Terms and Concepts

1. Oldest Occurrences, the *Maat* Hieroglyph, Basic Range of Meaning.

1.1. Oldest Occurrences. This Egyptian term probably was pronounced originally as **muʾʿat,* becoming *muʾʿa* (attested in cuneiform transcriptions) in the third and second millennia BC. Going down into the first millennium BC, it was reduced to *ma(ʿ),* attested through Greek transcripts, and by Roman times it appeared as *me* (as preserved in Coptic). As both verbal stem *mu ʿa* (conventionally *maa*) and derived feminine noun *muʾʿat* (conventionally *maat*), this word is clearly attested from the very beginnings of pharaonic history, from the First and Second Dynasties onwards (third millennium BC, particularly in personal names of kings and officials and then ever more widely throughout the rest of Egyptian history down to Roman times.

1.2. The Maat *Hieroglyph and Basic Meanings.* Its significance is multifold and is illustrated by the main hieroglyph used to write the term: a straight piece of wood, usually completely rectangular, or with one end cut at a slant, and wide enough to be a level base (as for a seat or throne). In some early cases it is tapered, as if to be a wedge, such as might be used to achieve a straight, even level where this was lacking. As in English, "straight" can be a synonym for regular and generally accepted behavior, not simply for straight-shaped objects. Thus *maat* for "straight" conduct came to embrace all that was right in life, including justice and truth(fulness).

1.3. The Fields of Meaning. Leaving aside literal, physical straightness (as of objects), meanings include the following. (1) "Be true" (adjective-verb *maa*) and "truth" (derived fem. noun *maat*), as contrasted in context with nonfactual situations, lies or deceit. (2) What is "real, genuine," by contrast with artificial products (e.g., real/natural versus artificially manufactured gemstones), and authentic in quality (even in negative use—e.g., "a real coward") as opposed to mere (and unreal) appearance. (3) Ethically, what is "just, justice," by contrast with wrongdoing and crimes. Thus, for example, in a two-party contest in a law court the vindicated party was declared to be "(in the) right" *(maa)* and the guilty one condemned as "(in the) wrong" *(ʿadja).* (4) Generally, *maa(t)* is the term applied to describe "right action/practice, rightness, righteous(ness)" in daily personal conduct at all levels and in public life to the highest level from the pharaoh (its official upholder) downwards. (5) Less pragmatically, *maat* was essential (in Egyptian eyes) for the right functioning of their universe, so that it not lapse into chaos. (6) The special term *maa(t)-kheru* (lit., "true of voice") applied both to the dead who passed the last judgment "justified" by their good life and deeds and, at times (by anticipation), to the living. In this-worldly contexts gods, kings and other mortals could be described by this term when "triumphant" over ill-intentioned foes or "vindicated" against them. (7) From earliest times *maat* ("right, justice") was also personified as a deity, and (being a feminine word) as a goddess, Maat. The Egyptians took this so seriously that by the New Kingdom (later second millennium BC) they built temples to her, with all appropriate cult, as at Karnak (in the North precinct) probably under Amenophis III and certainly from Ramesses II onward. The literary practice of *personification of concepts and so on was always common in Egypt at all periods (third millennium BC onward) and likewise in the ancient Near East; neither there nor in the Hebrew Bible did it owe anything whatsoever to classical or Hellenistic Greek usage, despite false statements to the contrary from the later nineteenth century AD down to the present. As the sun blazing with light in the sky was deemed to see everything on earth, the Egyptians vested justice in their preeminent sun-god, Re (or Ra). Thus, in texts and temple wall-scenes Maat (treated as a goddess) personified justice and was unendingly associated very closely with Re (even as his daughter) and repeatedly entitled the "Eye of Re," his organ for seeing injustice, to apply justice *(maat)* to it.

2. Historical Development in the Concept of *Maat.*

2.1. Archaic Period (c. 3000-2700 BC). The sole inscriptions that we have for this period are on administrative wooden or bone/ivory labels, personal and institutional seal-impressions and modest-sized monuments, with very restricted subject matter. Personal names could include *maat*. So with an official named Nefer-qed-maat, "good is the character of [either] right/justice [or] (the goddess) Maat," while the Second Dynasty pharaoh Sekhem-ib was surnamed Per-en-maat (for this period, see Kahl 2003, 2.169-73).

2.2. The Old Kingdom or "Pyramid Age" (c. 2700-2150 BC). In this age of Egypt's first great-

ness data for *maat* begin to multiply, and at more than one level. Two pharaohs incorporated *maat* into their official titles. As Horus-King, Snofru (Fourth Dynasty) called himself Neb-maat ("possessor [and activator] of right/justice"), while, in heading up the Fifth Dynasty, Userkaf entitled himself Iri-maat ("doer of right/justice"). Later such kings included in their pyramid tombs the royal funerary rituals, spells and hymns that make up the vast corpus of the Pyramid Texts. Already these illustrate the various applications of the term *maat* set out above (see 1.3 above). Already we find Maat personified as a goddess closely linked with the sun-god Re (§§1582, 1768, 1774 [translated in Faulkner, 238, 259, 260]). And likewise so it is with most of the attested meanings of *maat* the term. So too for what was true, real, on the right way (§1142 [Faulkner, 186]), and used of righteous folk (needing a boat, §1188 [Faulkner, 191]). Archetypally we find, "I have set Right *[maat]* in place of wrong" (§265 [Faulkner, 61]), or "that I may bring justice" (§323 [Faulkner, 69]), and so on.

Much more informative, beginning in the Old Kingdom, are the formal autobiographical inscriptions of the high officials, found in their tomb-chapels. On such texts (right through to the Late Period) an indispensable representative survey (with translations of typical and key texts) is that given by M. Lichtheim. In the Old Kingdom officials speak of "speaking" and "doing" right *(maat)* and exemplify it by their just deeds—for example, speaking for the people's good and not evil against others; paying for work done from one's own resources (not those of others); not using force against people; pleasing his god and his king alike by both speaking truth and doing right. From the wisdom texts, Ptahhotep cites *maat* as the basic principle that overcomes all wrongs.

2.3. The First Intermediate Period (c. 2150-2100 BC). After the Old Kingdom, during the later part of this period and on into the Middle Kingdom, many of the Pyramid Texts passed into a new funerary corpus—the Coffin Texts—used by high and middle ranking officials, and mention of *maat* continued here also.

However, in this period of reduced royal authority local provincial governors and officers speak out for themselves from their tomb-texts and stelae. They continued to invoke *maat*, but also increasingly they presupposed it as the basis of their enlightened treatment of their people and elaborated on their show of personal good character in that context.

2.4. The Middle Kingdom and Second Intermediate Period (Eleventh-Seventeenth Dynasties) (c. 2100-1550 BC). In this period the great officials continued to stress justice increasingly, with personally righteous conduct, as their ideal. At this time right behavior in this life began to be linked with hope for a blessed hereafter and one's attitude toward the gods. Both for kings and commoners, the need to live justly and mercifully with one's people (whether family, local community or the nation) is also stressed in the royal wisdom-works (Merikare, Amenemhat I) and other literature. But now the possibility of wrong overcoming right is also glimpsed, even if only in moments of deep pessimism (as in The Man Tired of Life, and the Discourse of Khakheperre-sonb).

2.5. The New Kingdom (Eighteenth-Twentieth Dynasties) (c. 1550-1070 BC). In the Middle Kingdom the concept of doing right *(maat)* had three foci: king, society and the individual. But in the Eighteenth Dynasty scribal thinkers added a fourth dimension: the active presence and role of the gods (see Lichtheim, 54). Personal piety grows apace in the record, linked with doing right.

Then suddenly Akhenaten imposed his regime of directing all official worship exclusively to the sun-god, as embodied in the visible sun-disc (the Aten) and mediated through himself as prophet and son of Aten. No other deity was openly recognized on Akhenaten's monuments; hence it was a true monotheism, cult of one single deity, except insofar as Akhenaten also proceeded to identify himself in some measure with the sun-god. There was no room for goddesses; Maat was now solely *maat* ("truth, right, justice"), but not in traditional terms. The king himself was the one who "lives on/by *maat*" ("truth, right"); his officials imbibed his "Teaching" and followed his rulings (from Ay, her No. 62 [see Lichtheim, 61]) to attain a state of *maat*—that is, rightness in the king's sight. And that was all; the old moral and ethical imperatives of over a thousand years' standing simply disappear from view; Akhenaten is himself the norm on Aten's behalf. Thus, this remarkable pharaoh appears briefly as the world's only monotheistic postmodernist: only one god, and no explicitly endorsed values outside of himself.

After Akhenaten's fall Egypt simply resumed the old ways and the traditional values, especially *maat*, whose praises were sung once more and with emphasis (see Lichtheim, 63-65, esp. 65). Doubtless shaken by the seeming absence of their gods under Akhenaten's audacious experiment, for a time the more theological scribes experimented with squaring the circle by trying to reckon all deities as forms of Amun the supreme, and hence ultimately but one. However, this was too risqué beyond educated circles, and almost two thousand years of tradition soon engulfed such speculation in oblivion.

Instead, under the Ramesses-kings of the Nineteenth and Twentieth Dynasties, right-doing, just and merciful behavior, speaking and doing *maat* are not only owed to the king but are seen increasingly as the will of the gods and in hopes of a blessed afterlife. One did right, *maat*, god-fearingly. Much interest has always focused on a small group of texts (mainly thirteenth century BC) among the many inscriptions left by members of the community of royal workmen (of the Kings' and Queens' Valleys) in their village chapels at Deir el-Medina in western Thebes. These are the stelae that show a penitential side to Egyptian religion. Someone does wrong; ill fortune follows and is viewed as divine punishment. Then the afflicted person is contrite, confessing the wrong and seeking forgiveness and restoration. And when healing follows, thanksgiving may follow. In Egyptian theology the rule of *maat* was broken, consequences followed, the cause was admitted, and *maat* was restored. In the Hebrew Bible this same sequence (e.g., as in the structure of the book of Judges) is inevitably labeled by scholars as "Deuteronomic" and is assigned arbitrarily to six centuries later. But such concepts were not new even in the thirteenth century (let alone the seventh) and go back to at least the early second millennium BC (as in the Mari archive). We have parallel theologies in which obedience to a norm or norms is paramount. In Egypt it was *maat;* in the Hebrew community it was Yahweh's covenants (Abram, Moses); in Aleppo (Mari text) it was the command of the local deities. The "critical scholarship" over a century ago had no inkling of any of this and fails to fit the vastly enlarged field of known facts.

On the royal level, especially in Ramesside times, the pharaohs are commonly shown offering *maat* ("truth, right") to the gods, shown as a tiny figure of the goddess in their outstretched hand. Interpretations of this vary. It basically may symbolize the whole duty and acts of the king as executor of *maat* through his support of justice, proper order and right standards of conduct throughout his realm, as well as maintaining faithfully the cults of the gods—there are words *maa* ("make offering," "offerings"), which by punning would permit a reading of these concepts also into his act of "offering *maat*" and exhibiting his legitimacy of rule (see Teeter). In funerary religion the concept of *maat* also appears in the compilation of spells for the afterlife known to moderns as the Book of the Dead. Here the most famous passage is Spell 125, the so-called "Negative Confession," wherein the deceased person at the Hall of (Final) Judgment denies having committed a long series of antisocial and impious actions against the truth/right *(maat)* (for the text, see Allen, 97-101; for *maat* elsewhere in the Book of the Dead, see the list of references [under "right," "righteous," "truth"] in Allen, 274, 280). Already in the Middle Kingdom denials of committing various wrongs feature in autobiographies of officials, which continues into the New Kingdom, when this practice becomes associated with hopes for bliss (or otherwise) in the afterlife; it was from this rich and long-established repertoire of what was *maat* and non-*maat* that the composer(s) of Spell 125 of the Book of the Dead could draw their own great series of do's and don't's (on this, see Lichtheim 103-44, and the illuminating "moral indexes" in Lichtheim 145-55).

2.6. The Later Periods (Hellenistic and Roman) (c. 1070-300 BC). In the Third Intermediate Period our sources are fewer, but the statues of the priests of Amun in Thebes in the Libyan Twenty-Second/Twenty-Third Dynasties give a lively conspectus of their devotion to deity, this being exemplified in their righteous conduct in everyday life (helpful and generous to others especially in need). During the Nubian Twenty-Fifth Dynasty, and the revival of culture and power in the Twenty-Sixth Dynasty, then during Persian rule ("Twenty-Seventh Dynasty"), and under the "resistance" (Twenty-Eighth to Thirtieth Dynasties), and after Alexander's takeover, into Greco-Roman times, the *maat* tradition of right behavior in obedience to deity, and to the ruler as upholder of *maat*, continued through to the end of Egypt's ancient civilization. It was a high ideal, nobly set forth, and (as in any human society) often "honored" in the breach as well (and as much?) as in the observance.

3. *Maat* and Old Testament Terms and Concepts.

Both in the OT and elsewhere in the biblical world the Semitic languages had terms by which their users could express the same range of meaning as did *maat* for the Egyptians. Thus, in biblical Hebrew terms such as *ṣedeq* and *yāšār* and their derivatives (and in part *kēn* and *ʾēmet*) well covered all the concepts represented by *maat*. The *ṣedeq* group of words expresses "right(ness)," "righteous(ness)" and sometimes "vindication"; note the derivatives *ṣĕdāqâ* ("righteousness, just[ice], what is right"), *ṣadeq* ("be just, justify, vindicate, declare just"), *ṣaddîq/ ṣadôq* ("just, righteous"). The root *ṣdq* is old, and words from it go back to at least the early second millennium BC (in Amorite, *ṣidqum*) as well as the fourteenth century (Amarna letters, *ṣaduq* ["right, just"]) and in thirteenth-century Ugaritic, *ṣdq* ("just, lawful, legitimate"). The other major Hebrew word, *yāšār*, with its basic meaning of "straight, level," also, like *maat*, applies that physical concept in good metaphorical fashion to straight conduct and, by extension, to upright behavior; derivatives *mēšārîm* and *mîšôr* cover "even(ness)" and "equity" as well as literal (geographical) plains. Like *ṣdq*, *yšr* has its ancient cognates: in Akkadian (Assyro-Babylonian) *ešēru* ("go straight, be/become alright, set to rights") is well attested from the third millennium BC onwards, along with corresponding derivatives *mišaru* and *mišartu* ("render justice" and "justice"). In Ugaritic too we have *y(a)š(a)r* ("upright") and *m(i)š(a)r* ("justice").

More modestly, *kēn* (from *kwn*) can cover "right/honest, true," while its Akkadian relative *kittu* (from *kintu*) expresses "truth, justice, faithfulness" and so on. Just like Maat in Egypt (and also third millennium BC onwards), Kittu was personified as a goddess and as daughter of the sun-god, but here, of course, daughter of Shamash, not Re. Other personifications among the Mesopotamians took a darker hue: fate/death (as Namtaru) were personified, even as vizier at the court of the queen of their netherworld, and death itself (Irkallu) was personified as a goddess. In the Hittite world sincerity, law, justice and seemingly good and bad were also personified (late second millennium BC). Neither justice nor right(eousness) was personified in Hebrew; they were simply qualities coming from God and to be implemented by humans. The one significant personification in Hebrew is of wisdom (ḥokmâ), simply as a vivid literary device (see Proverbs 2: Ancient Near Eastern Background; and briefly on range of personifications, Kitchen, 5-6). Another Hebrew term, 'ĕmet, covers "faithfulness" and "reliability" and thus "truth"; the root may possibly recur at Ugarit.

In all these fields Egyptian maat and Semitic ṣedeq, yāšār, kēn/kittu and 'ĕmet together give expression to concepts that to the present day are the indispensable basis for the conduct of human life and affairs both within human society and to deity, creator of peoples and concepts alike. Egyptian maat and its spread of usages is a valuable conceptual and social parallel running alongside the biblical terms ṣedeq, yāšār and so forth and their relatives in that world. Such concepts were familiar in societies over a thousand years before Abraham; he and his world lived by such basics toward deity and their contemporaries, as did (almost five centuries later) Moses and his brethren, and the Hebrew nation and its many neighbors then and down to Greco-Roman times. These values were always cherished constants, even though (in a sinful world, then as now), of course, they were always open to abuse by the unscrupulous, who were in turn judged by these standards.

See also ETHICS; RIGHTEOUSNESS.

BIBLIOGRAPHY. **T. G. Allen,** trans., *The Book of the Dead, or, Going Forth Day by Day: Ideas of the Ancient Egyptians Concerning the Hereafter as Expressed in Their Own Terms* (SAOC 37; Chicago: University of Chicago Press, 1974); **R. O. Faulkner,** *The Ancient Egyptian Pyramid Texts, with Supplement* (Oxford: Clarendon Press, 1969); **J. Kahl,** ed., *Frühägyptisches Wörterbuch* (6 vols.; Wiesbaden: Harrassowitz, 2002-); **K. A. Kitchen,** "Some Egyptian Background to the Old Testament," *TynBul* 5-6 (1960) 4-18; **M. Lichtheim,** *Maat in Egyptian Autobiographies and Related Stdies* (OBO 120; Freiburg: Universitätsverlag; Göttingen: Vandenhoeck & Ruprecht, 1992); **E. Teeter,** *The Presentation of Matt: Ritual and Legitimacy in Ancient Egypt* (SAOC 57; Chicago: Oriental Institute of the University of Chicago, 1997). K. A. Kitchen

MARRIAGE AND SEX

The Bible's books of *Psalms and Wisdom literature (*Job, *Proverbs, *Ecclesiastes) deal frequently with panhistorical, human issues. It is therefore somewhat surprising that, with the exception of Proverbs, relatively few references to marriage or sex are found therein. The "historical" books that are treated in this volume (*Ruth, *Esther, *Lamentations) display a similar unevenness of coverage (i.e., relatively frequent in Ruth, less so in the other two books). It is, of course, in Song of Songs, which does not easily fit in either of the foregoing groups, that we find the Bible's most explicit and extensive discourses on sex (if not marriage, too, as we will see).

1. Psalms and Wisdom Literature
2. Ruth, Esther, Lamentations
3. Song of Songs
4. Conclusion

1. Psalms and Wisdom Literature.
1.1. Marriage and Sex in Psalms. Since the focus of the psalms is, by and large, on either individual or communal expression, particularly in relationship to God (as opposed to interpersonal relationships), there are relatively few references to marriage or sex. Nevertheless, there are two of note: the royal wedding psalm (Ps 45) and a pair of psalms on the role of God in family life (Pss 127—128).

1.1.1. Psalm 45. This psalm is categorized by form critics as a "royal psalm" (see Kingship Psalms), and yet it is unique in a number of respects. First, while royal weddings were hardly personal or private affairs (in Israel or elsewhere), the psalmist does address both groom and then bride individually (to be sure, the king is addressed individually elsewhere in royal psalms, such as the coronation psalm [Ps 2:7-9], albeit not at such length). Second, while the particularities of the envisioned wedding are doubtlessly affected by the social standing of the parties, it is notable that the psalm explicitly envisions the bride's departure from her people and her father's house (Ps 45:11), quite the opposite direction of movement from that envisioned in Genesis 2:24. Third, the superscription (which may indeed, as most scholars believe, amount to an early commentary on the original poem) states that the psalm is ʿal-šōšannîm. While the meaning and usage of the term are uncertain (for full discussion, see *HALOT,* 1455), and the same term is found also in the superscription to an individual *lament (Ps

69:1), the noun (or its singular, *šôšannâ*) occurs eight times in Song of Songs meaning "lily," including an erotic description of the male lover in Song of Songs 5:13. The same superscription calls the psalm a *šîr yĕdîdōt* ("love song"). With due caution, we note that the Ugaritic root *ydd* meant "love (sexually)," although its usage in classical Hebrew appears to be broader, "favorite" or "friend" (so Zobel, 445). Of special interest, however, is the contention by H.-J. Zobel (446) that the psalm entered the *canon thanks only to "its having been reinterpreted as referring to the relationship between Yahweh and his people"—a theological move that we will re-encounter in spades when we come to Song of Songs. In sum, however unusual this psalm may be within the Psalter, it does represent the book's one explicit mention of the act of marriage, assumes procreative acts to follow ("your [masc. sg.] sons" [Ps 45:16]), and at least its superscription hints at erotic overtones withal.

1.1.2. Psalms 127—128. Psalms 127—128 appear in the midst of the "Songs of Ascents" (Pss 120—134). At first glance, Psalm 127 seems to address itself to architectural construction (house/city [Ps 127:1]), but the swift transition to a discussion of the blessing of sons in Psalm 127:3-5 inevitably recalls the multiple meanings of "house" (including progeny) in 2 Samuel 7. Psalm 127:5, then, and Psalm 128:1 speak from a thoroughly male perspective of the happiness of the man *(geber)* whose marriage ("wife" [Ps 128:3]) the Lord blesses with multiple children (Ps 127:5; 128:3) and even grandchildren (Ps 128:6). Given our earlier observations about the nature of the book (and what we will see are the far more frequent treatments of our subject in Proverbs), it is notable that both psalms use a word typical of Wisdom literature, *ʾašrê* ("happy" [cf. Ps 1:1]).

In sum, to this point the discussion of sexuality has been within marriage, from a male perspective, and for the explicit (if not exclusive) purpose of procreation.

1.2. Marriage and Sex in Proverbs. If Psalms deals almost entirely with vertical (God-human) relationships, Proverbs represents the opposite extreme: while a theological umbrella is set over the whole in Proverbs 1:7 ("The fear of the LORD is the beginning of knowledge"), much of the book is taken up with more earthly, everyday matters, most famously in the parts of Proverbs 22—23 that overlap with the far older Egyptian

"Instruction of Amenemope." It is therefore to be expected that horizontal (human-human) issues, including marriage and sex, will find far more prominence in Proverbs than in Psalms, and it is so.

1.2.1. Lectures Against the Nokriyâ (Loose/ Strange Woman) and Praise of Sex Within Marriage. With the exception of an *acrostic poem at the close of the book (Prov 31:10-31), the book's focus with respect to our topic is on the guidance of men, especially young men. Most often, this is done through the *via negativa,* with repeated warnings against liaisons with a *nokriyâ* (NRSV: "loose woman"; NJPS: "strange woman"; lit., "foreign woman"). The most extensive presentation is in three lectures in Proverbs 5:1-23; 6:20-35; 7:1-17 (see also Prov 2:16-17; 20:16 [= 27:13]; 22:14; 23:27-28). The lectures presume that the primary temptation is to adultery in the sense of relations with another man's wife, and they warn against the husband's unmitigatable wrath (Prov 6:29-35), against public humiliation (Prov 5:14 [in an *"honor and shame" culture!]) and apparently against sexually transmitted diseases (Prov 5:11), and they certainly threaten death as the inevitable outcome (Prov 5:5, 23; 7:27; cf. 9:18). Notably, given the visual nature of modern pornography and sex-based marketing, throughout the book's cautions it is not the woman's looks but rather her smooth speech that is of greatest concern (Prov 2:16; 5:3; 6:24; 7:21; cf. 9:15-18). Finally, the lectures present an extended portrayal in Proverbs 7 of the *nokriyâ* as seductress unto death (traditionally, "Woman Folly"), who is then juxtaposed with the sublime *"Woman Wisdom" in Proverbs 8 (but who in turn is described neither as wife nor as sexual partner and will therefore not be further discussed here).

Right in the midst of these dire warnings is a more positive statement—in fact, the OT's sole explicit tribute to sex within marriage (with the arguable exception of Gen 2:24): Proverbs 5:15-19. Interestingly, several of the metaphors are the same as those featured in Song of Songs: drinking water; a well; a doe (cf. Song 4:12, 15; 2:7; 3:5).

Still, in all, arguably the most intriguing moment occurs in one of the early warnings: "You will be saved from the loose woman, from the adulteress with her smooth words, who forsakes the partner of her youth and forgets her sacred covenant [lit., 'covenant of her God']" (Prov

2:16-17 NRSV). Although "covenant" surely refers in the first instance to literal marriage, its mention in the context of "the partner of her youth" and of God inevitably brings to mind the common prophetic use of marriage as a metaphor for God's covenant with Israel and of adultery/prostitution for Israel's idolatry and apostasy (cf. Jer 2:1-2; Ezek 16; 20; 23; Hos 1—2). Such a linkage to Israel's historical experience and thereby more generally to a figurative level of meaning will prove most significant when we take up the difficulties of other, less easily interpreted passages, above all in Song of Songs.

1.2.2. Proverbs on Women as Wives: Ambiguity to Modern Ears. As is well known, Proverbs is a collection of collections, and those in Proverbs 10 and following are more epigrammatic than what precedes. In terms of our topic, the male-centeredness of the book comes obviously (indeed, to modern ears, obnoxiously) to the fore: Proverbs 18:22 speaks glowingly of the blessings of a wife (cf. Prov 19:14), and Proverbs 12:4 speaks similarly of a "good wife" ('ēšet-ḥayil [developed at length in the aforementioned concluding acrostic in Prov 31]), but Proverbs 19:13; 21:9 (= 25:24); 21:19; 27:15-16 all comment invidiously on life with a "nagging" or "contentious" woman. Further, Proverbs 30:23 states that the earth shudders at the marriage of a "loathsome" (so NJPS; lit., "hated") woman, and the mother of King *Lemuel advises him against the distractions of wine and *women in the pursuit of justice for the poor (Prov 31:3).

Finally, and in some ways surprisingly, the book concludes with a paean to the 'ēšet-ḥayil (NRSV: "good wife"; NJPS: "capable wife"; lit., "woman/wife of might"), depicting her as a woman of independence and vigor, entrusted by her husband with the management of the household. To be sure, she is these things, in part at least, to provide leisure for her husband to be "prominent in the gates" (Prov 31:23), so that there is some debate over how liberated she truly is (see Davis, 154-55). Nevertheless, by contrast with what we hear otherwise of women's standing in ancient times (the Bible often included), the husband's words in Proverbs 31:29 ring true: "You surpass them all."

1.3. Marriage and Sex in Job.

1.3.1. The Narrative Framework. Job was married, and he and his wife obviously had sexual relations: he has seven sons and three daughters at the beginning of the book, loses them, has another seven sons and three daughters at the end of the book (presumably by the same wife), and finally lives to see the fourth generation (Job 1:2, 19; 42:13, 16). Beyond that, his wife serves early on as a foil to Job's *righteousness, advising him, "Curse God [MT: 'Bless God'], and die," which he refuses to do, comparing her words to those of "foolish women" (Job 2:9-10). She then disappears for the rest of the book (but for a rhetorical reference in Job 31:10, see 1.3.2 below).

1.3.2. The Poetic Dialogues. Otherwise, the references to marriage and sex in the book are few and fleeting. Two of Job's "friends" raise the subject briefly: Eliphaz tells Job to accept God's reproof because one who does so will not fail in bed (so NJPS) and will have many children (Job 5:24-25); Bildad warns that the wicked (including, by implication, Job) will be bereft of children (Job 18:19). For his own part, Job complains that adulterers get away with it (Job 24:15). He longs for the days when he was confident of lifelong vigor and potency (Job 29:20). And the concluding set of self-curses by which he seeks to force God's personal appearance begins with a protestation that he has not even lusted with his eyes (Job 31:1) and continues later with an extension of the *lex talionis* to himself and his wife, in the event that he has committed anything approaching adultery (Job 31:9-12)—an extrapolation otherwise unknown in Scripture or ancient Near Eastern law. In short, while sexual purity at least has pride of place in Job's self-defense, marriage and sex play a minor role in this literary and theological *magnum opus*, essentially reinforcing what we have already heard from Psalms 127—128: potency and offspring are a blessing from God and a sign of faithfulness.

1.4. Marriage and Sex in Ecclesiastes.
Of all the biblical books covered in this volume, Ecclesiastes probably has the least to say explicitly on our topic. One could, to be sure, argue that the observations in Ecclesiastes 1 that "nothing ever really changes" in human existence apply: millennia come and go, but essential human issues like these perdure with only outward alteration.

Otherwise, one is left with a negative warning against female entanglements (Eccles 7:26) and, by way of counterpoint, a more positive word (Eccles 9:9). But even the latter places the joys of marriage *sub specie aeternitatis*: "Enjoy life with the wife whom you love, all the days of your vain life that are given you under the sun, because that is your portion in life and in your toil at which you toil under the sun" (NRSV). This sentiment certainly is in keeping with the most famous passage of the book (Eccles 3:1-8), including the observation that there is "a time to embrace, and a time to refrain from embracing" (Eccles 3:5).

Finally, we take brief note of a text that some Jewish interpreters have seen as an allusion to sexual profligacy versus restraint: "a time for throwing stones, and a time for gathering stones" (Eccles 3:5 [see Machinist, 1609]), as well as one beloved by Christian preachers at weddings (Eccles 4:9-12 [esp. "Two are better than one. . . . A threefold cord is not quickly broken"]). Neither one clearly or necessarily has to do with our topic.

2. Ruth, Esther, Lamentations.

2.1. Marriage and Sex in Ruth.

2.1.1. Levirate Marriage. The most distinctive feature of our topic within the book of Ruth is, of course, its exemplar of levirate marriage (*see* Kinsman-Redeemer and Levirate). The practice is commanded in Deuteronomy 25:5-10 and is known elsewhere in the ancient Near East (for references, see Hamilton, 567). The law itself forces a certain penultimacy upon marriage, as it commands what is elsewhere forbidden— marriage and sexual relations between a man and his brother's wife (cf. Lev 18:16)—thereby stipulating a higher value on the preservation of the dead brother's "name in Israel." However, while the principle behind the Deuteronomic law certainly is present in Ruth (Ruth 4:5), there are notable differences in the details. Deuteronomy 25:5-10 provides for the refusal to perform levirate marriage, but it is a matter of public shaming, complete with removal of the sandal and spitting in the face, both performed by the widow. In Ruth 4 the refusal is portrayed as a straightforward business decision, with no necessary shame involved (and Ruth not even present). Further, according to Ruth 4, the Deuteronomic interest in the preservation of the dead man's name is merged with the need to keep allotted portions of the promised land in the family, as provided by Leviticus 25:25. These discrepancies have provoked much scholarly discussion, especially of the variety of genres and the dating of the relevant portions of Leviticus, Deuteronomy and Ruth (for summary discussion and references, see Niditch, 452-53). In the end, whether one reads Ruth as history or later historical fiction, the author clearly expects that the reader will recognize verisimilitude in the book's narration of the practice.

2.1.2. Marriage, Sex and Interpersonal Relationships Beyond Both. Levirate marriage is not the only source of tension in Ruth surrounding the ultimacy of the marriage relationship within the social order. Already in Ruth 1, both Ruth and Orpah must wrestle with reality (their precarious situation as widows, soon to be in a foreign land) versus their love for *Naomi as a concomitant of her status as mother to their late husbands. Many scholars have noted that, in fact, quite apart from husbands, the relationship between Naomi and Ruth is the key one in the book (some even speculating that a lesbian relationship developed between them [see Haffner, 34], although there seems little evidence beyond the use of "cleave" in Ruth 1:14 [cf. Gen 2:24]).

What is without question is that it is Naomi whose canny sense of the male psyche leads to Ruth's union with *Boaz and relief for both women from their untenable economic situation. Ruth's first encounter with Boaz may be by "chance" (Ruth 2:4 [about as close as the book comes to overt divine intervention]), but Naomi is quick to see the possibilities, and it is she who arranges for Ruth to be alone with Boaz on the threshing floor. There has been much debate over whether or not Naomi's plan entails overt seduction (the issue largely depends on how one interprets "feet" in Ruth 3:4, 7-8 [see Campbell, 121, 131-32]). Most likely, the narrator is being deliberately opaque on the point (or "suggestive," in the neutral sense of the term). In any event, the early-morning encounter leads quickly enough to a literal gift of seed (Ruth 3:15), to be followed as soon as legally possible by human seed and pregnancy (Ruth 4:13).

The book of Ruth, then, adds a distinctive historical twist to the biblical discussion of marriage and sex (via levirate marriage), but it also features timeless reminders of the inevitable interweaving of both into a social fabric with strings attached to far more than the two individuals involved. (In fact, some scholars believe that the book was a postexilic composition directed against the exclusivist movement that included the dissolution of exogamous marriages under the leadership of Ezra and Nehemiah [cf. Ezra 9—10; Neh 13:1-3] by placing a Moabite woman clearly in the lineage of the revered King *David.)

2.2. Marriage and Sex in Esther. With the book of Esther we face many of the same issues as in Psalm 45, only more so: the marriages in the book are not merely royal, but Persian. In fact, in the view of many scholars the nature of the book as a "comic farce for a carnivalesque holiday [*Purim] . . . with its bawdiness and slap-stick humor," such that "nothing about the events of the story is realistic," calls into question the historical value of any details of significance with regard to our topic (so Berlin, 1623). (Thus, for example, the process for selection of the Persian queen is utterly contrary to what is otherwise known, both as to eligibility and as to process.) Even so, the book ranked only with Song of Songs as the subject of rabbinic debate as to its canonicity: in addition to the failure of the book even to mention God, the Jewish heroine is married to a non-Jew in the very period of Ezra and Nehemiah (see the concluding paragraph in 2.1.2 above).

However, in many ways the most interesting treatment of marriage and sex in the book has nothing to do with Queen Esther. Rather, it is the events leading up to her selection: the refusal of Queen *Vashti to appear on command before the inebriated king and his nobles (Esther 1:10-12). Some have speculated that the king's command was for the queen to appear "wearing a royal diadem [and nothing else]" (so the *Targumim and Talmud), so that the queen's refusal is really protecting him from his own worst expression of sexuality. But the real problem, at least within the narrative world of the book, is that "the queen's behavior will make all wives despise their husbands" (Esther 1:17). Thus, at very least the book illustrates the fine line between gender roles and, as it were, naked abuse of power (cf. the far more egregious example of Amnon and Tamar [2 Sam 13]). Queen Vashti may lose her crown, but it is King *Ahasuerus who emerges as an emasculated pawn in an inflexible social matrix.

2.3. Marriage and Sex in Lamentations. Given its subject matter, it is no surprise that, with one exception, any mention of marriage or sex in Lamentations is figurative. Whether by simile ("like a widow" [Lam 1:1]) or by metaphor ("Jerusalem has become among them a thing unclean [lit., 'a menstruating woman']" [Lam 1:17]), the fallen city is described as bereft of husband (for the "great reversal" of this image, see Is 62:4) and as one ritually impure—a symbol of her moral depravity (cf. the prophetic usage of adultery as a metaphor for apostasy/idolatry [see 1.2.1 above]). The one literal reference is to the multiple rapes that occurred during the conquest of Jerusalem and Judah (Lam 5:11). Yet even here, one suspects that the author is simply expanding on the prophetic metaphor: just as Israel was guilty of adultery both literally (as in the incidents of the golden calf [Ex 32:6] and Baal-Peor [Num 25:1, 8]) and figuratively (by violating her "marriage" covenant with God), so also is she raped, literally, in the horrible experiences of women during the fall of city and land, and figuratively, as the integrity of the land and its people are violated at will by their enemies (for what some have termed a "pornographic" pursuit of a similar line of thinking, cf. Ezek 16:35-42). (A final note: Lam 4:6 also compares the guilt of God's people to that of Sodom, but despite the assumptions inherent in the English legal term "sodomy," this text does not specify the nature of the city's wickedness.)

3. Song of Songs.

3.1. What Is Clear About Song of Songs. With respect to our topic, Song of Songs provides half a loaf, but that in abundance: it is difficult to find anything that is not in some way related to sex, but marriage is mentioned, at most, obliquely, as the man addresses the woman as *kallâ* ("bride") in Song of Songs 4:8-12; 5:1 (and some would argue that "bride" is to be taken no more literally than the oft-accompanying "sister"; see Murphy, 156). The scant mention of marriage is a serious question with which we must deal, but from the outset we may affirm two points on the basis of this book. First, Song of Songs is the Bible's ultimate refutation of any Platonic or gnostic depreciation of the material body in general or sexuality in particular; otherwise put, there is no sin inherent in sex. Second, Song of Songs affirms (yea, celebrates) sexual expression as an expression of love and joy in its own right and not merely as an instrumental means to the end of procreation (*pace* numerous church fathers). Beyond these two points, there is little that is self-evident.

3.2. Song of Songs as "Locks to Which the Key Has Been Lost" (Saadia Gaon). Part of the problem is that the book is notoriously difficult to follow. Efforts to read it as a drama or liturgy have waxed and waned among scholars; most scholarly commentary now leans toward seeing the book as a collection of love poems. (The last thirty years have seen a veritable explosion in commentaries on Song of Songs. The history of scholarship is well summarized by Pope, and more recently by Longman and by Hess.)

But what is one to make of this chunk of undigested erotica in the midst of the canon? As is well known, both Jews and Christians have often sought refuge in allegory, even when otherwise adamantly opposed to the practice. Mystics of both faiths, in particular, have meditated on Song of Songs as an entrée into insight about the communion of the individual soul with God or of the community of the chosen, whether Israel or the church, with God (or, for Christians, with Christ the bridegroom). As is the case with some contemporary Christian music, if one is unaware of the context, one might often take their words as boldly erotic, even sensuous.

More recently, scholars both within and without communities of faith have sought to make sense of Song of Songs on a literal level. Often cited is the resemblance of the physical descriptions that the lovers provide of one another to the Arabic *wasf. *Feminist scholars have emphasized the proactive role of the woman, whose words do indeed predominate (Brenner, 185-88). By contrast with Psalms and the Wisdom literature examined above, this book is anything but androcentric (although see Exum, 27-29). But the overall *Sitz im Leben* of the work remains elusive, with proposals advanced for everything from weddings (Origen) to funerals (Pope) to drinking bouts (*b. Sanh.* 101a) to the simple celebration of human love (Falk; Murphy; Davis; Longman; Hess).

3.3. A Canonical Key to Song of Songs. Regardless of its origins, those who read from within a Jewish or Christian community of faith must deal with Song of Songs as Scripture. To this end, a particularly promising trajectory is that suggested by P. Trible, who holds that Song of Songs serves, at least in its canonical context, as a commentary on Genesis 2—3, describing how God wanted sex to be before the fall (Trible, 47). Read in this way, Song of Songs is particularly explicative of Genesis 2:18-25, climaxing, as it were, with "The two of them were naked, the man and his wife, yet they felt no shame" (NJPS).

As is true generally in exegesis, context is everything. If accepted, Trible's reading trumps the (at most) scanty mention of marriage in Song of Songs by placing the entire work within the umbra cast by its referent text in Genesis. Further, one may argue that such a reading solves the eternal debate between the literal and figurative readings of the book with a resounding "yes" or "both/and": just as the prophets' description of Israel's idolatry as adultery worked on both the literal and figurative levels (see 1.2.1 and 2.3 above), so also Song of Songs provides the obverse, positive picture, both of literal, human love and the love of, with, and within the divine that one may hold by faith as the source of human love, but which humans can understand only by figure and extrapolation from the love that they may know intimately between themselves. Christians of at least some traditions will see here a sacramental dimension in marriage and sex; Jews and Christians together can hold that Song of Songs describes a garden that, like Eden, has bounds. (For an independently developed and formulated exposition along these same lines, see Longman, 58-70.)

4. Conclusion.

Neither the Bible in general nor the eight books at the focus of this volume are a systematic manual for teaching or life, nor do they provide a "marriage manual" or a guidebook to sanctified sexuality. What does come forth from their necessarily culturally conditioned (usually monarchical, often androcentric) pages is a vision of both marriage and sexuality as a sign of God's blessing. Moreover, there are at very least strong hints of a canonically sanctioned figurative level of application to God's relationship with his chosen people.

As is often the case in turning from exegesis of the ancient text to modern life, there are ambiguities and lacunae. For instance, although the books that we have examined (with the possible exception of Esther) uniformly envision monogamy as the norm, the two books that have provided the most material (Proverbs and Song of Songs) are explicitly attributed to King *Solomon—he of the seven hundred wives and three hundred concubines (1 Kings 11:3). However unlikely Solomon's authorship may be as a matter of history, the attributions illustrate the theological challenge. Similarly, present controversialists on subjects such as same-sex marriage find themselves mounting arguments almost entirely from silence with respect to these books.

The fact is that the Bible does not explicitly address every conceivable question, at least not in every one of its subsections. One can adduce examples and infer principles and still be hard pressed to assert, "Thus saith the LORD."

In the end, biblical books such as these eight serve best when heard where they choose to speak: however much human perversity may have twisted our experience of them, marriage and sex are gifts of God, not merely for the fulfillment of the divine command "Be fruitful and multiply" (Gen 1:28), but for the joy, even the "completion" (Gen 2:18), of those united in them.

See also CREATION THEOLOGY; FEMINIST INTERPRETATION; LAW; SOCIAL-SCIENTIFIC APPROACHES; SONG OF SONGS 1: BOOK OF; WOMEN.

BIBLIOGRAPHY. **A. Berlin**, "Introduction to Esther," in *The Jewish Study Bible*, ed. A. Berlin and M. Z. Brettler (Oxford: Oxford University Press, 2004) 1623-1625; **A. Brenner**, "Love Me Tender, Love Me True . . . : I Am an Anonymous Woman from the Song of Songs," in *I Am . . . : Biblical Women Tell Their Own Stories* (Minneapolis: Augsburg Fortress, 2004) 163-90; **E. F. Campbell Jr.**, *Ruth* (2nd ed.; AB 7; Garden City, NY: Doubleday, 1975); **E. F. Davis**, *Proverbs, Ecclesiastes, and the Song of Songs* (WestBC; Atlanta: Westminster John Knox, 2000); **J. C. Exum**, "Ten Things Every Feminist Should Know about the Song of Songs," in *The Song of Songs: A Feminist Companion to the Bible*, ed. A. Brenner and C. R. Fontaine (FCB 2/6; Sheffield: Sheffield Academic Press, 2000) 24-35; **M. Falk**, *Song of Songs: A New Translation and Interpretation* (San Francisco: HarperSanFrancisco, 1990); **D. W. Haffner**, "Sexuality and Scripture: What *Else* Does the Bible Have to Say?" *Reflections* 92.1 (2006) 32-35; **V. P. Hamilton**, "Marriage (OT and ANE)," *ABD* 4.559-69; **R. S. Hess**, *Song of Songs* (BCOTWP; Grand Rapids: Baker, 2005); **T. Longman**, *Song of Songs* (NICOT; Grand Rapids: Eerdmans, 2001); **P. Machinist**, "Notes to Ecclesiastes," in *The Jewish Study Bible*, ed. A. Berlin and M. Z. Brettler (Oxford: Oxford University Press, 2004) 1603-1622; **R. E. Murphy**, *The Song of Songs* (Hermeneia; Minneapolis: Fortress, 1990); **S. Niditch**, "Legends of Wise Heroes and Heroines," in *The Hebrew Bible and Its Modern Interpreters*, ed. D. A. Knight and G. M. Tucker (Philadelphia: Fortress, 1985) 445-63; **M. H. Pope**, *Song of Songs* (AB 7C; Garden City, NY: Doubleday, 1977); **P. Trible**, "Depatriarchalizing in Biblical Interpretation," *JAAR* 41 (1973) 30-48; **H.-J. Zobel**, "יָדִיד," *TDOT* 5.444-48.

G. C. Heider

MEANINGLESSNESS. *See* ECCLESIASTES 1: BOOK OF.

MEGILLOT AND FESTIVALS

The word *Megillot*, which simply means "scrolls" in Hebrew, is used in a more specific sense to refer to the collection of the five smallest books of the "Writings" (Ketubim) of the OT. The concept of the Megillot as a group developed over a long period and was closely tied to the emerging usage of these five books during the festivals of the Jewish liturgical year. The Megillot is comprised of the *Song of Songs, *Ruth, *Lamentations, *Ecclesiastes and *Esther. The Jewish festivals in which they are read in their entirety are, respectively, Passover, Pentecost, the Ninth of Av, Tabernacles and *Purim.

1. The Megillot
2. The Festival of Passover
3. The Festival of Pentecost (or Weeks)
4. The Fast of the Ninth of Av
5. The Festival of Tabernacles (or Booths)
6. The Festival of Purim
7. Conclusion

1. The Megillot.

1.1. The Emergence of the Megillot. The concept of the Megillot as a unique group within the Writings section of the OT is not attested in either the Second Temple period or the Talmudic period. In fact, during the talmudic era the term *megillah* was applied only to the book of Esther, as evidenced by the tractate of that name. The talmudic listing of the books of the *canon does not have the five books of the Megillot together but rather follows the chronological order of their presumed authors (*b. B. Bat.* 14b). The earliest textual witness that groups the Megillot together is the Leningrad manuscript (upon which the *BHS* is based), which dates from the early eleventh century. The order found there is Ruth, Song of Songs, Ecclesiastes, Lamentations, Esther. There are manuscripts from the thirteenth century that still reflect both arrangements, and by the fifteenth century there are Bibles that include the Megillot in the order of the Ashkenazic liturgy: Song of Songs, Ruth, Lamentations, Ecclesiastes, Esther.

Although there is some evidence that these

five books were viewed as somehow distinct as early as the Second Temple and Tannaitic periods (cf. *b. Ber.* 57b; see Tov, 205), the textual witnesses of the OT demonstrate that the concept of "the Megillot" did not coalesce enough to make an impact on canonical arrangements until the medieval period. It is largely unclear as to the degree to which the grouping of these five books was understood as a well-defined unit in the intervening centuries.

As a further clue toward this end, one might look to the compilation of the *Midrash Rabbah,* which is a body of work containing rabbinic exegeses and midrashim on the five books of the Pentateuch and the five books of the Megillot. Although the midrashic literature is notoriously difficult to date, *Lamentations Rabbah* and *Esther Rabbah (I)* likely date from the fifth century, while *Song of Songs Rabbah* and *Ruth Rabbah* probably date from the sixth century. *Ecclesiastes Rabbah* is often dated from sometime between the mid-seventh century and the end of the eighth century. Because all of them contain earlier material, it is evident that even before these dates there was a large amount of exegetical work being done on these books. Whether they represent a response to an already existing liturgical need or merely reflect a parallel process to that of associating the books of the Megillot with the festivals is uncertain. All that can be deduced from the evidence of the *Midrash Rabbah* is that prior to the first clear evidence of their public liturgical use these five books were especially prominent in the study of the Bible in Jewish communities. The most likely explanation for the emergence of the concept of the Megillot is that the five books were viewed as distinctly special and were a particular focus of exegesis even before the talmudic period. This situation, along with the results of rabbinic exegesis (see below), contributed to their incorporation into the Jewish liturgy. This in turn contributed significantly to the canonical grouping of the books as "the Megillot," culminating in the Ashkenazic arrangement of the books according to the order of their liturgical use.

1.2. Liturgical Contours and Connections Among the Books of the Megillot. As a unified collection, the books of the Megillot have several interconnections in the sphere of their liturgical use. The specific cantillations for each of the five books varies among Jewish communities, with respect both to melodies and to whether the text is read by one person or by the congregation. As a general rule, the cantillations are derivative from those for other parts of the Bible, especially from those used in the Pentateuch. Depending on the Jewish community, there is often one melody for multiple books of the Megillot, especially among Song of Songs, Ruth and Ecclesiastes (the three pilgrimage festivals). Though the cantillation of Esther is often unique, in some communities it shares motifs with Song of Songs or Ruth. Furthermore, due to the nature of the material, the cantillation of Lamentations is unique not only among the Megillot but also in Jewish liturgy in general.

The festivals generally share a common liturgical pattern. For example, at the end of every festival (and Sabbath) service the priestly benediction from Numbers 6:22-26 is recited. Among Sephardic groups both the biblical book and its *Targum are read during each of the festival services.

1.3. The Megillot and Christian Liturgy. The reading of each book of the Megillot in its entirety on certain festival days in Judaism has no corresponding phenomenon in Christianity. Other than various selections from these biblical books that appear in the normal lectionary cycles, only a few thematic connections occur between the books and Christian liturgy. For instance, in the Roman Catholic, Lutheran and Methodist (but not the Anglican) lectionaries, Lamentations 3:1-24 is read the day before Easter on Holy Saturday, which is the most significant fast day in the Christian liturgical calendar (cf. Jn 2:19-21). It is also notable that in the medieval Western church selections from Song of Songs figured prominently in the celebration of various Marian feasts (e.g., the Feast of the Annunciation and the Purification of the Blessed Virgin Mary).

2. The Festival of Passover.

2.1. The Festival. The festival of Passover is one of the three pilgrimage feasts and is celebrated from the fifteenth through the twenty-first of Nisan (March-April). According to Exodus 12, Passover was instituted when God instructed the Hebrews to smear the blood of a slaughtered lamb on their doorframes in order to be exempt from the tenth plague, the death of the Egyptian firstborn. Subsequently, the celebration of Passover commemorated this event and the exodus of the Hebrews from their bondage in Egypt. Its most notable characteristic was the slaughter and consumption of the paschal lamb, and it is also closely associated with the festival of Unleavened Bread (Ex 13). Evidently, it was rarely celebrated during the biblical period, two exceptions being the lavish celebrations of Hezekiah and Josiah (2 Kings 23:21-22; 2 Chron 30:13-27; 35:1-19). However, upon the Jews' return from exile, it was kept much more regularly and with added regulations (Segal, 231-69). Its observance in the Second Temple period is attested in Palestine (Ezra 6:19-22; *Jub.* 49) as well as at Qumran (11QT^a XVII) and Elephantine. After the destruction of the temple in AD 70 the ritual slaughter of the Passover lamb was no longer kept among those within rabbinic Judaism (the practice remained among the Samaritans), and its celebration became increasingly characterized by the Seder meal and the Passover haggadah (cf. *b. Pesaḥ.* 116a).

2.2. The Association of Song of Songs with Passover. It is quite likely that the tradition of reading Song of Songs as an allegory of God's history with Israel was already common during the Second Temple period. These allegorical interpretations that were set forth by rabbinic scholars became important for laying the groundwork for the association of Song of Songs with Passover.

The exegetical traditions that connect Song of Songs with the events surrounding the exodus from Egypt are first attested in the third century AD. Primary among these traditions was the interpretation of Song of Songs 1:9, "To a mare of the chariots of Pharaoh I compare you, my beloved," as referring to the crossing of the Red Sea (Ex 14). Once Song of Songs was understood as referring allegorically to the narrative of Israel's salvation history, other connections with the Passover and the exodus emerged. For example, Song of Songs 2:9, which refers to looking through windows and lattices, often was placed in the context of the Destroyer passing through on the night of the tenth plague (e.g., Targum of Song 2:9). Other themes probably reinforced the association of Song of Songs with the season of Passover. Both are set in the springtime, and the prophets' characterization of Israel as God's bride provided a strong parallel as well (e.g., Isa 62:5; Jer 2:2). Because the liturgical use of Song of Songs depends upon these exegetical developments, it could not have been used during Passover prior to the third

century AD and probably was not used consistently until the sixth century AD (Alexander, 53-56).

2.3. The Liturgical Use of Song of Songs During Passover. Song of Songs is read on the intermediate Sabbath of Passover. If the first and eighth days of the festival fall on a Sabbath, then Song of Songs is read on the first day in Israel and on the eighth day elsewhere. Some Jewish communities have divided the reading of the book over the last two days of the festival. It is also customary among Sephardic Jews to read it on the eve of each Sabbath between Passover and Pentecost, a practice that arose in the sixteenth century under the influence of strands of Jewish mysticism.

Song of Songs is read before the Torah scroll is removed from the ark for the assigned Torah reading. On an intermediate Sabbath the Torah reading is taken from Exodus 33:12—34:26 and Numbers 28:19-25, and the haftarah text is Ezekiel 37:1-14. On the first day of the festival the Torah readings consist of Exodus 12:21-51 and Numbers 28:16-25, and the haftarah is Joshua 5:2—6:1; 6:27. If Song of Songs is being read on the final day of the festival, then it precedes the Torah reading of Deuteronomy 14:22—16:17 and Numbers 28:19-25 and the haftarah reading of Isaiah 10:32—12:6.

3. The Festival of Pentecost (or Weeks).

3.1. The Festival. Pentecost was also one of the three pilgrimage feasts and was celebrated on the sixth of Sivan and also on the seventh for those in the Diaspora (May-June), fifty days after Passover (hence the name, Pentecost). Because of their alternate calendar, those at Qumran celebrated the festival on the fifteenth of Sivan. The festival marks the end of the barley harvest and the beginning of the harvest of wheat and fruit (cf. Ex 23:14-19; Lev 23:9-22; Deut 16:9-12). Since this was a major festival, no work was permitted during the festival (Num 28:26).

3.2. The Association of Ruth with Pentecost. During the Second Temple period the celebration of Pentecost was still centered on its agricultural roots and provided an opportunity for Israel to rejoice over God's provisions. The central feature for the pilgrims was the presentation of two offerings to the temple: an offering of firstfruits and an offering of two leavened loaves.

However, unlike Tabernacles and Passover, the rituals surrounding Pentecost were exclusively tied to the temple. Therefore, after the fall of the temple in AD 70 and the corresponding dislocation of the Jews from the land of Israel, the festival could not continue to be celebrated as before. The result was that the festival underwent a transformation that shifted the focus of Pentecost from its agricultural character to a commemoration of a redemptive historical event in the life of Israel. It was not long before this link emerged. If Passover commemorated the exodus from Egypt and Pentecost was held fifty days after Passover, then on the basis of Exodus 19:1 rabbinic interpreters sought to demonstrate that Pentecost coincided with the giving of the Torah on Sinai. The first correlation of these two events is found in a statement by Rabbi Meir (mid-second century AD) recorded in *Exodus Rabbah* 31. This connection between Pentecost and the reception of the Torah is important because it laid some of the groundwork for the association of the festival with the book of Ruth.

Ultimately, the historical circumstances that resulted in the reading of Ruth on Pentecost are only partially clear. It must have begun after the mid-second century AD, when the connection between the reception of the Torah and Pentecost first appeared, but before the fourth century AD, when explanations for the reading of Ruth during the festival are found (Bloch 1980, 249). It is not until much later, in the eighth century, that there is an explicit reference to the public, liturgical reading of Ruth as part of the festival (*Sop.* 14:3 [see Beattie, 9]). A number of explanations have been offered for this practice, but it is difficult to discern the respective weights that should be assigned to each one. Some rabbis explained the connection by pointing out a narrative similarity between Ruth and the exodus generation. Both had undergone ordeals of suffering before expressing loyalty to God and his *law (cf. Ex 19:7-8; Ruth 1:16-17). This parallel was subsequently reinforced by other interpreters. Ruth's loyalty to *Naomi was used homiletically to illustrate the loyalty that Israel should have for the Torah, and the tendency among some rabbinic interpreters to characterize the exodus generation as "converts" offered a parallel to Ruth's Moabite background.

Some rabbis also pointed to the fact that both Pentecost and the book of Ruth are set at harvest time (Ruth 1:22), although, to be precise, Ruth is set at the beginning of the barley harvest, which is earlier than the wheat harvest of Pentecost. A final connection between Ruth and Pentecost is the talmudic tradition that *David, a descendent of Ruth, had been born and had died on Pentecost (cf. *Ruth Rab.* 3:2; *y. Beṣah* 2:4, 61b). However, it is important to remember that these thematic connections between Ruth and the festival do not necessarily imply any historical causality. It is always possible that a particular explanation was conceived after the fact to explain an already existing relationship.

3.3. The Liturgical Use of Ruth During Pentecost. The book of Ruth is read during the morning service of Pentecost. For those who celebrate the festival on both the sixth and seventh of Sivan, it is read on the morning of the second day. A notable exception to this is the practice among Sephardic Jews of reading half of Ruth on the first day and the other half on the second day. Typically, Ruth is read prior to the morning Torah reading, which consists of the account of the revelation at Sinai in Exodus 19—20 and the sacrificial laws for the festival in Numbers 28:26-31. The haftarah reading is taken from Ezekiel 1:1-28; 3:12. None of the benedictions that appear among other Megillot festival readings are recited before or after the reading of Ruth other than the priestly benediction from Numbers 6:22-26. Due to the connections between Pentecost and David, many Jewish communities also read selections from *Psalms during the festival service.

4. The Fast of the Ninth of Av.

4.1. The Fast. The Ninth of Av has as its primary reference point the remembrance of the destruction of the first temple in Jerusalem by Nebuchadnezzar in 586 BC. According to the biblical records, Nebuzaradan entered Jerusalem and burned the temple on or after either the seventh of Av (2 Kings 25:8-9) or the tenth of Av (Jer 52:12-13). Various explanations have been offered to harmonize the two accounts (e.g., *b. Taʿan.* 29a), but eventually rabbinic scholars concluded that the date given in Jeremiah was the most precise for the burning of the temple. However, the fast was observed on the ninth of Av, marking the beginning of the destruction of the temple, rather than on the tenth, when the majority of the destruction was done.

The only biblical mention of the fast of the Ninth of Av is a possible allusion in Zechariah 7:5, which states that the fast "of the fifth month

[Av]" had been in observance for "these seventy years." This would imply that the fast was instituted very soon after the fall of the temple, possibly even on the first anniversary (the news had reached Babylon within six months [see Ezek 33:21]). Scholars are divided over whether the Ninth of Av was observed after the construction of the second temple. Certain mishnaic passages seem to imply that it was being observed (Ydit, 937), but most scholars doubt that it continued after the exile (Bloch 1978, 248).

Nevertheless, it certainly was being observed soon after the fall of the second temple, which Josephus says also happened on the tenth of Av (J.W. 6.249-250). The fact that the destruction of the two temples culminated on the same day, accompanied by the fact that the last stronghold of the Bar Kokhba revolt, Bethar, fell on the ninth of Av in AD 135, led to the conclusion that the ninth of Av functioned as the day of disaster par excellence. According to the rabbinic literature, two other disasters happened on this date. Both the decree that the exodus generation would be prohibited from entering the promised land and the construction of a pagan temple on the temple mount of Jerusalem in AD 136 were said to have occurred on the ninth of Av (b. Taʿan. 26b, 29a). For many Jews, it is more than mere coincidence that the expulsion of Jewish communities from England (1290) and Spain (1492), as well as the beginning of World War I (1914) and the deportation of Jews in Warsaw to Treblinka (1942), all fell on the Ninth of Av.

4.2. The Association of Lamentations with the Ninth of Av. Because both are reflections on the fall of the temple, the association of Lamentations with the fast of the Ninth of Av is easily understandable (as with Esther and Purim). Yet, the liturgical use of Lamentations took significantly longer to develop than did Esther (see 6.2 below). Whereas Lamentations was being read privately in talmudic times (b. Taʿan. 30a), the first mention of its public liturgical use dates from the post-talmudic era, in Soperim 14:3 (eighth century).

4.3. The Liturgical Use of Lamentations During the Ninth of Av. The book of Lamentations is usually read during both the evening and morning services of the Ninth of Av, though some congregations read it at only one of the services (Sop. 18:4). It is the only book of the Megillot that is recited without a blessing either before or after the reading. Several changes in the synagogue service reflect the somber mood of the day, including the dimming of the lights and sitting on low benches or on the floor (see Sop. 18:4-8). Though there are Torah readings during both the morning and the evening services, the study of the Torah, because it is considered a source of joy, is forbidden only on the Ninth of Av. The texts that are permitted to be read during the fast are Lamentations (and *Lamentations Rabbah*), *Job, Leviticus 26, the more somber chapters of Jeremiah, and the talmudic passages concerning the destruction of Jerusalem.

Since the time of Rashi (AD 1040-1105), and probably earlier, there has been a custom in some communities not to end with the final verse of Lamentations. Instead, in order to end the liturgical reading on a hopeful note, the congregation follows the reading of Lamentations 5:22 with a recitation of Lamentations 5:21 again: "Bring us back to you, O LORD, that we may be restored. Renew our days as of old." This verse is then echoed by the reader of the scroll. This liturgical practice, along with the rabbinic tradition that the Messiah would be born on the ninth of Av (*Lam. Rab.* 1:51; *y. Ber.* 2:3), reflect the theological principle that it is often at the nadir of human experience, in the midst of suffering and mourning, that God chooses to begin his work of redemption.

5. The Festival of Tabernacles (or Booths).

5.1. The Festival. The festival of Tabernacles is the third of the three pilgrimage festivals and begins on the fifteenth of Tishri (September-October) and lasts for eight days, though the final day is often treated as a separate festival called Shemini Azeret. Coming at the end of the autumn harvest and commemorating the wilderness journey following the exodus, Tabernacles was equally an agricultural and redemptive-historical festival. In the Bible it is also called "the feast of ingathering" (e.g., Ex 23:16), "the feast of the LORD" (e.g., Lev 23:39) and, as an indication of its importance, even simply "the feast," during which *Solomon consecrated the temple (1 Kings 8:2). Before the destruction of the second temple in AD 70 the main feature of the festival was the large number of sacrifices that were offered (Num 29). However, after the destruction of the temple the central feature became the practice of dwelling in temporary, but carefully constructed, booths throughout the week in order to remember the experience of the Hebrews of the exodus generation while they were in the desert (Lev 23:42-43 [see Rubenstein, 320]). This practice stresses both the providential care of God and the ultimate impermanence of human life. In biblical times it also functioned as the occasion for the public reading of the Torah every seven years (Deut 31:10-13).

5.2. The Association of Ecclesiastes with the Festival of Tabernacles. Within the relationship between the Megillot and the five festivals, the connection between Ecclesiastes and the festival of Tabernacles is the least obvious and the last to be attested. There are only a few connections between them that are offered to explain the association of the two.

First, the recurring theme of "Eat, drink, and be merry" (e.g., Eccles 2:24-25; 3:13; 5:18; 8:15; 9:7) is thought to correspond to the joyful mood and agricultural context of the festival (cf. Eccles 3:2). Paradoxically, another basis for association that is often cited is the somber, pessimistic outlook of much of Ecclesiastes. This outlook is seen as a complement to the onset of the rainy winter season that begins around the time of the festival of Tabernacles (Stemberger, 274). The pessimism toward earthly pleasures that is portrayed in Ecclesiastes is also thought to evoke a sobriety that directs one's attention to the ultimate questions in life, which is particularly appropriate because the celebration of Tabernacles has a decidedly future, eschatological orientation (Zech 14:16). Furthermore, the statement concerning the payment of vows (Eccles 5:4-5) is considered poignant because the yearly cycle of reading through the Torah ends on Simhat Torah, which closes the festival of Tabernacles. Finally, rabbinic interpreters saw an allusion to the festival in Ecclesiastes 11:2, which reads, "Give a portion to seven and even to eight, for you do not know what calamity may occur on earth." The festival of Tabernacles lasts for eight days, but since post-talmudic times the final day has been treated as an independent festival called Shemini Azeret, based on Numbers 29:35 (in Israel this day corresponds to Simhat Torah; elsewhere it is the day before Simhat Torah). With the institution of Shemini Azeret, the festival of Tabernacles took on a 7/8 structure, which was understood to recall Ecclesiastes 11:2.

Scholars have noted that these intersections between Ecclesiastes and the festival have the character of ad hoc explanations and lack the specificity that is present among other cases, such as Esther with Purim and Lamentations with Ninth of Av. This all contributes to the thesis that the association of the two was secondary and took place under the influence of the larger movement of associating the Megillot and the festivals. If this is the case, then only a broad window for the introduction of the practice of reading Ecclesiastes during the festival can be postulated. The fact that its mention in *Soperim* 14:3 is almost certainly not original and appears to be a later insertion implies that the formal association was made after the eighth century (Stemberger, 263). The *terminus ad quem* for the introduction of Ecclesiastes into the liturgy for the festival of Tabernacles is the eleventh century, when it appears in the services of Ashkenazic Jews (Knobel, 4). Determining at what point between the eighth and the eleventh centuries Ecclesiastes came into public use during the festival is unclear because its liturgical emergence among Ashkenazic communities was likely gradual.

5.3. The Liturgical Use of Ecclesiastes During the Festival of Tabernacles. The reading of Ecclesiastes during the festival of Tabernacles is not a uniform practice throughout Judaism and is most closely associated with Ashkenazic Jews. Notably, in Sephardic Judaism Ecclesiastes plays no role in the celebration of Tabernacles. For those communities that do incorporate it into the liturgy, the book of Ecclesiastes, like Song of Songs on Passover, is read only on the intermediate Sabbath. If the first and eighth days fall on the Sabbath, then it is read on the eighth day, Shemini Azeret.

Ecclesiastes is read only during the morning service on its appropriate day, and it precedes the Torah reading. It is interesting in this regard that one of the earliest references to the liturgical reading of Ecclesiastes, *Mahzor Vitry* (thirteenth century), states that the entire congregation reads it while seated, in distinction from having the book read to them. There are four sets of readings for the festival. On the first day the Torah reading is Leviticus 22:26—23:44 and Numbers 29:12-16, and the haftarah reading is Zechariah 14:1-21. For the second day the reading from the Torah is the same as the first day, but the haftarah reading is 1 Kings 8:2-21. The intermediate Sabbath has Exodus 33:12—34:26 and a portion of Numbers 29 for the Torah reading and Ezekiel 38:18—39:16 is the haftarah. The Torah reading for the final day is Deuteronomy 14:22—16:17 and Numbers 29:35—30:1, which is accompanied by the haftarah reading from 1 Kings 8:54-66.

6. The Festival of Purim.

6.1. The Festival. In conformity with Esther 9:21-22, Purim originally was celebrated on the fourteenth and fifteenth of Adar (February-March) in order to commemorate the rest that the Jews received from their enemies in the wake of the victory of Esther and *Mordecai over Haman. After the fall of the second temple, Purim began to be celebrated only on the fourteenth of Adar. It is marked by intensely jubilant celebration and is often viewed as the mirror opposite of the Ninth of Av.

6.2. The Association of Esther with the Festival of Purim. Among the Megillot, the relationship of Purim to Esther is the most obvious and natural, and by the first century AD the Esther scroll was being read during the festival. By the second century AD a confluence of events, including the fall of the second temple (AD 70), the failure of the Bar Kokhba revolt (AD 135), and the confirmation of Esther's canonical status, resulted in the more systematic observance of Purim. From the second century AD to the present day the reading of the Esther scroll has functioned as the central feature of the celebration of Purim.

6.3. The Liturgical Use of Esther During the Festival of Purim. The central feature of the evening and morning services of Purim is the reading of the Esther scroll. The Torah reading that is read alongside Esther during the morning service is Exodus 17:8-16, which describes the war of Moses and Joshua with Amalek. At the end of the passage is the promise by God that he "will utterly blot out the memory of Amalek from under heaven (Ex 17:14). This is particularly poignant on Purim because Haman was a descendent of Amalek (cf. Esther 3:1; 1 Sam 15:8-9).

The reading of the Esther scroll is introduced with a series of three blessings, to which the congregation responds with "Amen." The vocalization of the scroll is done with a cantillation whose tempo and style reflect the nature of the events being narrated, whether joyous or gloomy. Since the third century it has been the practice that when the reader reaches the list

of the ten sons of Haman (Esther 9:7-10), the names (and the word "ten") are uttered quickly in one breath to reflect the fact that they were executed together (*b. Meg.* 16b). A similar custom, based on a midrashic interpretation of Proverbs 10:7 (*Gen. Rab.* 49), involves the adults in the congregation whispering "The memory of the righteous shall be for a blessing" after Mordecai's name and "The name of the wicked shall rot" after Haman's name. This is mirrored by the practice of children using rattles or stones to drown out the mention of Haman's name. Conversely, there is a custom, dating from at least the tenth century, that when the reader reaches the "four verses of redemption" (Esther 2:5; 8:15-16; 10:3), he raises his voice and is accompanied by the chorus of the congregation.

At the conclusion of the reading of the Esther scroll another blessing is pronounced: "Blessed are you, O Lord our God, the King of the Universe, who pleads our cause, who renders judgment on our behalf, who avenges us, who fulfills retribution on the enemies of our life, and exacts recompense for us from our foes. Blessed are you, O Lord, who exacts recompense for his people Israel from all their foes, the God who saves" (*b. Meg.* 21b).

7. Conclusion.

The most likely scenario for the emerging use of the Megillot may now be sketched. The evidence of Ruth, Lamentations and Esther suggests that the private reading of each book on the corresponding festival preceded the formal incorporation of the books of the Megillot into the public festival liturgy, even by centuries. Already in the Second Temple period Esther, or parts of it, were read during the festival of Purim. Though previously read privately, by the close of the talmudic period (eighth century) the books of Ruth, Lamentations and Song of Songs had been incorporated into the liturgy of the synagogue. Following these developments, sometime between the eighth and the eleventh centuries, the book of Ecclesiastes was linked with the festival of Tabernacles. This final connection was likely made in order to match the final book of the Megillot with the only pilgrimage festival without a corresponding book. Yet, the associations of these books with their respective festivals did not occur in isolation but rather developed alongside one another. Once Esther began to be read on Purim, the basic paradigm of using books liturgically was set in motion. The evidence suggests that the unfolding process of incorporating the rest of the books of the Megillot into the other Jewish festival liturgies was long and gradual, spanning almost a millennium.

See also CANON; ECCLESIASTES 3: HISTORY OF INTERPRETATION; ESTHER 3: HISTORY OF INTERPRETATION; LAMENTATIONS 3: HISTORY OF INTERPRETATION; PURIM; RUTH 3: HISTORY OF INTERPRETATION; SONG OF SONGS 3: HISTORY OF INTERPRETATION.

BIBLIOGRAPHY. **P. S. Alexander,** *The Targum of Canticles* (ArBib 17A; Collegeville, MN: Liturgical Press, 2003); **D. R. G. Beattie,** *The Targum of Ruth* (ArBib 19; Collegeville, MN: Liturgical Press, 1994); **L. Blau,** "Megillot, The Five," *JE* 8.429-31; **L. Blau and N. Schmidt,** "Bible Canon," *JE* 3.140-54; **A. Bloch,** *The Biblical and Historical Background of the Jewish Holy Days* (New York: KTAV, 1978); idem, *The Biblical and Historical Background of Jewish Customs and Ceremonies* (New York: KTAV, 1980); **A. Herzog,** "Scrolls, The Five," *EncJud* 14.1057-59; **L. Hoffman,** *The Canonization of the Synagogue Service* (SJCA 4; Notre Dame, IN: University of Notre Dame Press, 1979); **A. Z. Idelsohn,** *Jewish Liturgy and Its Development* (New York: Schocken, 1967); **L. Jacobs,** "Shavuot," *EncJud* 14.1319-22; **P. S. Knobel,** *The Targum of Qohelet* (ArBib 15; Collegeville, MN: Liturgical Press, 1991); **R. Posner, U. Kaploun and S. Cohen,** eds., *Jewish Liturgy: Prayer and Synagogue Service through the Ages* (Jerusalem: Keter, 1975); **J. L. Rubenstein,** *The History of Sukkot in the Second Temple Period* (BJS 302; Atlanta: Scholars Press, 1995); **N. Scherman and M. Zlotowitz,** חמש מגילות / *The Book of Megillos* (New York: Mesorah Publications, 1986); **J. B. Segal,** *The Hebrew Passover from the Earliest Times to A.D. 70* (LOS 12; London: Oxford University Press, 1963); **G. Stem-berger,** "Die Megillot als Festlesungen der jüdischen Liturgie," in *Das Fest: Jenseits des Alltags,* ed. M. Ebner et al. (JBT 18; Neukirchen-Vluyn: Neukirchener Verlag, 2003) 261-76; **M. Strassfeld,** *The Jewish Holidays: A Guide and Commentary* (New York: Harper & Row, 1985); **E. Tov,** *Textual Criticism of the Hebrew Bible* (2nd ed.; Minneapolis: Fortress, 1992); **M. Ydit,** "Av, The Ninth of," *EncJud* 3.936-40.

B. C. Gregory

MEMORY. *See* REMEMBRANCE.

MERISM

Merism is a literary device that uses an abbreviated list to suggest the whole. The most common type of merism cites the poles of a list to suggest everything in between, though the term *merism* is also used to refer to more extensive, but not exhaustive, lists (see 3 below). Since a merism is a part for a whole, it is an example of synecdoche, which itself is subspecies of metonymy (a trope of association in which one term stands for another, typically broader, term) rather than metaphor (a trope of comparison). The English word *merism* derives through Latin *merismus* from Greek *merismos* ("dividing, partition") and Greek *meros* ("part").

1. The Scope of Merism
2. The Function of Merism
3. Examples of Merism
4. Conclusion

1. The Scope of Merism.

In the OT merism occurs most frequently in poetry, but it is also found in prose. Indeed, scholars often see the first appearance of merism to be in Genesis 1:1, "In the beginning, God created the heavens and the earth," where "heavens" and "earth" are taken as two poles of a list that suggest the whole. In other words, it is another way of saying that God created everything. It must be admitted, however, that in this case "heaven" and "earth" might simply identify the whole; that is, there are no other parts, similar to saying "mother" and "father" to refer to parents. Another example from a prose context is seen in 1 Kings 4:25: "During Solomon's lifetime Judah and Israel, from Dan to Beersheba, lived in safety, each man under his own vine and fig tree." Dan, the northernmost significant settlement in the land, and Beersheba, the southernmost, represent all the cities and land between them.

As we noted, however, merism occurs more frequently in poetry. Indeed, there is only one literary feature that is distinctive to poetry in Hebrew, *terseness (see 2). The most pervasive features (*parallelism and *imagery) also occur in prose (the existence of *meter is debatable at best). Merism is an example of a secondary poetical device—that is, one, like the *acrostic, that occurs only sporadically in Hebrew poetry. Examples, however, may be seen in the psalms and all the wisdom books (not to mention the poetical parts of the prophets).

2. The Function of Merism.

In the preceding section we noted that most of the conventions of Hebrew poetry, including merism, are also found in prose. If one can speak of a distinctive difference between poetry and prose, it would have to do with length. Poetry is terse, saying a lot using few words. Poetry is compact language. Hebrew poetry is composed of typically short cola that form parallel lines (and at least occasionally *stanzas/strophes), while prose is made up of longer sentences grouped into paragraphs.

The brevity of the poetic line is achieved in a number of ways. Metaphor, simile, *ellipsis and the suppression of conjunctions all contribute to the shortness of the line. Merism, as a device that uses abbreviated lists to suggest the whole, does this as well. Thus, the major function of merism is to enhance the terseness of the line, thereby producing a dramatic effect as well as necessitating a more active involvement of the interpreter/reader.

Song of Songs 7:13 provides an example: "The mandrakes give forth their scent, and on our entrance is every precious gift; the new as well as the old I have treasured for you, my love." This verse concludes one of the woman's passionate speeches to her lover (Song 7:11-13 [see Longman, 199-202]). The second poetic line of this verse is quite vague. She has saved up or treasured "the new" and "the old" for her lover. This begs the question "New or old *what?*" Readers must engage their imagination to consider the matter. The immediately preceding context might suggest new and old sweet-smelling plants, but why old plants? It is likely that here "new" and "old" are used as a merism defined by "polar word-pairs" (Watson, 321). Thus, "new" and "old" might refer to all things. She has stored up or treasured everything near and dear to her for her lover. So from this example we see how the reader's involvement is evoked by the merism. In addition, merism imparts more interest to the line. To say "new" and "old" is much more vivid, concrete and interesting than simply saying "everything."

Some merisms, particularly those of the "polar word-pair" type, appear together with some frequency. The pair "young" and "old" is an example. Lamentations 2:21a bemoans the destruction of Jerusalem with this statement: "Young and old lie together in the dust of the street." We may confidently recognize "young" and "old" as a polar word-pair merism. The poet certainly did not believe that the middle-aged were immune to the disaster. This text is not the only place where this word pair is used as a merism. Restricting our scope to the books covered in this dictionary, we can cite Job 29:8; Psalm 148:12. If we look beyond these books, we will find a number of other examples (e.g., Is 20:4; Ezek 9:6).

These examples supplement the evidence provided by other frequently occurring pairs of words in poetry to bolster a theory that ancient Hebrew poetry was originally *oral poetry, and, on the basis of analogies with ancient Greek (Homer) and modern Yugoslavian poetry, that ancient Hebrew poets constructed their work using a set metrical pattern and certain stereotyped word pairs (Watters; Gevirtz). Due to recent persuasive arguments against the presence of meter in Hebrew poetry, among other factors, this theory has declined, though not totally disappeared, in recent years.

3. Examples of Merism.

An exhaustive list of examples of merism is impossible here. The following examples are just a sampling from the poetical books covered in this dictionary (*Job, *Psalms, *Proverbs, *Ecclesiastes, *Song of Songs, *Lamentations). In the process of examining these examples, we will also discern some variations between different types of merism.

We have already referenced the use of the "young" and "old" merism in Job 29:8. In a prose context, Job 2:7 describes how the Accuser afflicted Job "from the soles of his feet to the top of his head." The implication, of course, is that no part of his body escaped the disease. In the context of Job's lament, as he expresses his desire to be among the dead, he says that "the small and the great" are there (Job 3:19). Understood rightly as merism, this means that everyone, regardless of social status, is there.

The psalms provide a number of examples of merism, though only a few will be cited here. Psalm 139:2-3 expresses awareness of God's all-encompassing knowledge with two meristic statements:

> You know when I sit and when I rise;
>   you discern my thoughts from afar.
> You discern my going out and my lying down;
>   you are familiar with all my ways.

Through the use of the polar opposites of sitting and rising as well as going out and lying down, the psalmist says that God is fully aware of his inner life as well as his actions.

W. Watson (322) categorizes Psalm 148:7-12 as a list merism:

> Praise the LORD, from the earth,
>> you great sea creatures and all ocean
>>> depths,
>> lightning and hail, snow and clouds,
>>> stormy winds that do his bidding,
> you mountains and all hills,
>> fruit trees and all cedars,
> wild animals and all cattle,
>> small creatures and flying birds,
> kings of the earth and all nations,
>> you princes and all rulers on earth,
> young men and women,
>> old men and children.

Whereas a polar word-pair merism simply names two items that are on opposite ends of a spectrum, intending to refer to everything in between, a list merism is more extensive, though not exhaustive. In this example, the first colon calls on "the earth" to praise the Lord. The following verses list a number of things from the earth that are to praise the Lord. It is not an exhaustive list; rather, it is a partial list suggestive of a full list.

In Psalm 74:12-17 God's creative sovereignty is established by a series of merisms (G. Wilson [in a personal communication]) including day and night (all time), sun and moon (all the celestial bodies), summer and winter (all the seasons).

Proverbs 6:1, warning the wise person to avoid guaranteeing loans to everyone, speaks of the opposites "neighbor" and "stranger." Proverbs 14:10 admits that no one can fully understand the emotions of another. The mention of "bitterness" and "joy" indicates the poles of the emotional spectrum and is a meristic way of referring to all the emotions.

One of the most memorable uses of merism occurs in the famous poem of Ecclesiastes 3:1-8. The poem lists fourteen areas of activity by citing their polar opposites. For instance, there is a time to be born and a time to die, citing, of course, the beginning and the end of one's earthly existence. By citing the two extremes of life, it assumes that life as a whole has its appointed time.

A final example comes from the Song of Songs 4:16. Here the woman responds to the man's loving admiration of her "garden," which he described as locked, by opening it up for him with these words:

> Wake up, north wind,
>> And come, south wind!
> Blow on my garden,
>> and let its spices flow forth.
> Let my lover come into his garden
>> and eat its choice fruit.

Here the words *north* and *south* stand here for all the winds. The woman thus is saying that she opens herself up completely to the man.

4. Conclusion.
Merism is a device that contributes to the brevity of the poetic line. Rather than citing all the parts, it evokes the thought of a whole by citing just a few (most typically two and typically the opposite poles) of a list.

See also CHIASM; INCLUSIO; PARALLELISM; POETICS, TERMINOLOGY OF; TERSENESS.

BIBLIOGRAPHY. **H. A. Brongers,** "Merismus, Synekdoche und Hendiadys in der bibel-hebräischen Sprache," *OTS* 14 (1965) 100-114; **S. Gevirtz,** *Patterns in the Early Poetry of Israel* (SAOC 32; Chicago; University of Chicago Press, 1963); **A. M. Honeyman,** "Merismus in Biblical Hebrew," *JBL* 71 (1952) 11-18; **J. Krašovec,** *Der Merismus im Biblisch-Hebräischen und Nordwestsemitischen* (BibOr 33; Rome: Biblical Institute Press, 1977); **T. Longman III,** *Song of Songs* (NICOT; Grand Rapids: Eerdmans, 2001); **M. O'Connor,** *Hebrew Verse Structure* (Winona Lake, IN: Eisenbrauns, 1980); **W. G. E. Watson,** *Classical Hebrew Poetry: A Guide to Its Techniques* (2nd ed.; London: T & T Clark, 2005); **W. Watters,** *Formula Criticism and the Poetry of the Old Testament* (BZAW 138; Berlin: de Gruyter, 1976).

T. Longman III

MESSIAH

The English word *messiah* derives from Hebrew *māšîaḥ* through the Greek *Messias* (John 1:41; 4:25). The Hebrew word is a noun, "anointed one," formed from the verb *māšaḥ* ("anoint"). In the Torah anointing (and the root *māšaḥ*) is mostly connected to consecration rituals, and when it comes to people, it is the priests who are anointed for special service to God (Ex 28:41; 29:7; 30:30; 40:15). Exodus 25:6 describes the anointing oil kept on hand at the tabernacle presumably for use in consecration rituals. Outside of the Torah anointing refers to the ritual used to consecrate a king (2 Chron 6:42; 23:11; Ps 2:2; 18:50; 20:6; 28:8; 45:7; 84:9; 89:20, 38; 132:10, 17). Nearly all these references are associated with the king's role as protector and vanquisher of Israel's enemies.

This article is not concerned simply with the concept of anointed king or anointed priest in the biblical books under study here; rather, we are interested to explore the question of whether there is an eschatological messianic expectation in these books. To what extent do these books manifest an expectation of a future messiah?

Christian interest in this question is fueled by the eschatological use in the NT of certain texts from the corpus of OT poetical books. To be clear, we are not talking simply of an anticipation of the coming of Christ in a general sense; we have a more narrow focus. Some studies of the messianic idea are framed too broadly in that they incorporate any kind of christological expectation (Kaiser; van Groningen). We are concerned only with the expectation of a future royal or priestly deliverer because that is more in keeping with the OT concept.

1. Hermeneutical Considerations
2. The Messiah in the Book of Psalms
3. The Messiah in Wisdom Literature?
4. The Messiah in Song of Songs
5. The Messiah in the Books of Ruth and Esther

1. Hermeneutical Considerations.

Significant differences exist among scholars when it comes to the question of messianic expectation in the OT. Part of the problem has to do with the question of the location of meaning in the biblical text. Thus, it is important for the present study to acknowledge its viewpoint as to the meaning of a biblical text. When messianic import is attributed to a text, what does that mean?

This question is relevant because the NT discovers messianic significance in texts that very clearly were not so understood during the OT period. Not only is it likely that the original audience did not recognize the eschatological import of relevant texts, but also it is uncertain at best whether the authors of these texts would have been conscious of eschatological messian-

ic meaning. However, such an idea would not have shaken the confidence of NT authors or have caused them to apply these texts in another way. After all, they understood that the human author's intention did not exhaust the meaning of the text. They believed that God was the ultimate author of Scripture (2 Tim 3:14-17; 1 Pet 1:10-11). And in the light of the work of Christ, they read the OT in a way that brought out its deeper significance. Such considerations are clearly important as we study the messianic significance of the Psalter.

2. The Messiah in the Book of Psalms.

The background to the use of "anointed" in reference to the king in the book of *Psalms may be found in the Former Prophets, particularly in the book of Samuel. Although the Torah anticipated kingship (Gen 49:8-12; Num 24:17), there were no kings of Israel during this time period. However, when Saul became the first king, he was known as God's anointed (1 Sam 10:1; 12:3, 5; 15:7 [overall he is called "anointed" some fifteen times]). Of even more significance for our topic, as we will see, is that the anointing of *David is mentioned a number of times, sixteen in all, and the ritual of his anointing is narrated in 1 Samuel 16. As we read on in the history, *Solomon, Jehu and other kings are also specifically connected with anointing. The historical practice of anointing kings, thus indicating God's choice and empowerment, provides the background to the anointed king of Psalms. In other words, the most immediate and primary reference to the anointed in Psalms refers to the historical kings of Israel and Judah.

2.1. Psalms of the Anointed King: Psalm 2. We begin with an examination of a selection of psalms that refer to the anointed king. Psalm 2:1-2, for instance, says,

Why do the nations rage,
    and the peoples plot in vain?
The kings of the earth take their stand,
    and the rulers take counsel with each other,
against Yahweh,
    and his anointed.

Later we will see that this psalm receives extensive attention in the NT in reference to Jesus, but in its OT setting there is no obvious indication that the psalm looked far beyond its immediate historical setting. Notable, for instance, is its relationship to the Davidic covenant—for instance, in Psalm 2:7, which echoes 2 Samuel 7:14, describing the fatherlike relationship that God had with the king. Many scholars, perhaps rightly, identify this psalm as a coronation *hymn, though that is certainly not the only possible understanding of the contemporary use of this text.

The first stanza expresses bewilderment at the attempt of the nations to throw off the bondage of Yahweh and his anointed king. We are somewhat at a loss to understand exactly what kind of historical background generated such a thought. There were few time periods when Israel or Judah under the Davidides had vassals who would contemplate throwing off their shackles. Even those times, like that of David himself when Israel did exercise sovereignty over nearby states, do not exactly fit the rather grandiose claims implied by this first stanza. In its ancient setting, however, this may simply be the type of hyperbole generated by the beginning of a new reign.

The line that most closely associates this psalm with coronation is Psalm 2:6: "I have appointed my king on Zion, my holy mountain." But the text does not clearly indicate that this is an act presently taking place. An alternative explanation of the psalm could be that of a pre–holy war hymn wherein God's words become a note of assurance to the king before a battle. No matter what the precise setting, there is no doubt that Psalm 2 can be fully explained on the background of its OT context. It is not a predictive text per se.

What is true of Psalm 2 is true of the other psalms that mention the "anointed"; that is, they refer to the human monarch. Psalm 18:50, for instance, is a tricolon that puts "king," "anointed" and "David and his descendants" in parallel:

He gives great victories to his king;
    he shows covenant love to his anointed,
      to David and his descendants forever.

Psalm 20 speaks of God rescuing his anointed king, Psalm 28 of his being a safe fortress for his anointed, and so forth (see Ps 45:7; 84:9; 89:20; 132, 10, 17).

It is true that on occasion the language used to describe the anointed king surpasses that which can comfortably be applied to any of the human kings who ruled in Jerusalem during the OT time period. For instance, in Psalm 2 God grants the king "the whole earth" as his inheritance and the ability to smash the kings of the earth like clay pots. Even the most powerful kings of Israel did not actually possess such tremendous power, but even so, the language does not obviously point to the far-distant future but rather may be ascribed to the rhetoric of the court or an ideal picture. As we will observe, though, such language does lend itself to further development.

Indeed, the further development may have begun during the monarchical period. It is true that Psalm 2 does not have an authorship ascription. Interestingly, though, Acts 4:25-26 cites the psalm as Davidic. This may be part of the general tendency (observed in the LXX and the Peshitta) to associate all the psalms with David, but one would be hard-pressed to find a period other than David's that would be better suited for the composition and first use of this poem.

David was the recipient of the promises of the covenant of kingship (2 Sam 7). Although his relationship with God and his reign were anything but undisturbed, one can imagine Psalm 2 being used during his time and certainly afterward during the coronation of Solomon. But if it was a coronation psalm or a pre–holy war song, it would be available for use in later reigns. Surveying the history of the monarchy from Solomon through Zedekiah makes one realize that the psalm, if used at all, would have rung hollow. After all, this time period was known for apostasy, syncretistic worship that was rampant among later Davidic rulers. Even syncretistic kings may have sung Psalm 2 at their coronation (after all, they must have been aware that their kingship was contingent on their descent from David, whose dynasty was established by their God Yahweh), but to the pious the song would have rung hollow.

Indeed, it was likely the dissonance between the content and tone of Psalm 2 and the reality of Judah's kings and their political subordination to other great world powers that set their minds wondering whether the psalm had repercussions beyond that which may be read from a minimal reading of the poem. This dissonance would have reached its ultimate crisis point at the time Zedekiah was removed from the throne by Nebuchadnezzar and in his place a relatively weak Babylonian governor came to manage Judah.

When the monarchy disappeared, the faithful had to grapple with the significance of the Davidic covenant, in which God promised not to "take my steadfast love from him as I took it from Saul, whom I put away from before you. Your house and your kingdom shall be made sure forever before me; your throne shall be established forever" (2 Sam 7:15-16). And along with the question of the continuing significance of the Davidic covenant, the faithful would also wonder about the abiding relevance of psalms that speak of God's anointed king, and further, psalms that speak of the king (without specific reference to the ritual of anointing).

Of course, one option was to give up on the promise, to dash the hope that Yahweh cared for them. Probably many took that route. But for those who were convinced that God would not lie or deceive, they would come to believe that the psalm did more than describe present realities. They would look to the future for a king who would fit the picture of the anointed as described in Psalm 2.

Of course, due to the paucity of textual material in antiquity, much of the foregoing description of the discovery of the deeper significance of *kingship psalms such as Psalm 2 is speculative. What is clear is that the authors of the NT read the psalms in the light of Jesus' life and ministry and identified him as the anointed one. This may be well established by the frequent use of Psalm 2 in the NT in reference to Christ (e.g., Mk 1:11 par.; 9:7 par.; Acts 4:23-31; 13:33; Rom 1:4; Heb 1:5; 5:5; 2 Pet 1:17; Rev 11:18; 19:19).

2.2. Royal Psalms: Psalm 110. Not every royal psalm uses the word *anointed*. However, the very concept of "king" implies anointing because this was the ritual that demonstrated God's choice and empowerment. Thus, many of the other royal psalms were pressed into service to extol that Jesus was the Christ, the anointed one. Preeminent among these is Psalm 110, distinguished by the multiplicity of citations in the NT (Matt 22:41-45 par.; 1 Cor 15:25; Heb 1:3; 5:6; 7:17, 21) as well as by its unique combination of the royal and priestly roles, both anointed offices (see 2.1 above). Psalm 110 is certainly the most enigmatic song in the Psalter. One of the main reasons why this psalm is so difficult has to do with the divine declaration that the king is "a

priest forever according to the order of Melchizedek" (Ps 110:4). With this reference, we have a difficult psalm citing an obscure event in Genesis 14.

First, though, it is important to establish the fact that this psalm does have a meaning in its OT context before it takes on the eschatological significance recognized in the NT. Like Psalm 2, Psalm 110 has a contemporary setting either as a coronation psalm or, more likely, a pre–holy war battle song. It begins with a divine oracle to the effect that God tells the king to take a position of honor at his right hand, while God, the divine warrior, subdues his enemies. Much of the rest of the psalm assures the king of his ultimate victory, thanks to his intervention. It is the Lord who will see to the expansion of the human king's power.

In this context the psalmist proclaims to the king that God has promised on oath: "You are a priest forever in the order of Melchizedek" (Ps 110:4). This statement is doubly surprising. In the first place, there are other texts that express concern that kings not assume priestly prerogatives (1 Sam 13:8-15; 2 Kings 15:3-5). And second, the king is connected not to the native Israelite priestly line of Aaron but rather to the patriarchal-period priest Melichizedek, whose story is told in Genesis 14.

It is possible, if not likely, that these two actually go together. For one thing, Melchizedek provides a precedent for a priest-king, since he was both, being the king of Salem. He was the one who greets Abraham after successful holy war and receives a portion of the plunder. Melchizedek does provide a pretext for attributing to the king priestly functions without blurring the distinction between the kingship and Aaronic priesthood.

The point is that Psalm 110, like the other royal psalms, has a setting within the world in which it was composed. However, like them as well, as the monarchy falters and ultimately fails, the faithful come to grasp a deeper significance of this psalm. After all, the psalm combines royal, priestly and warrior language, and the authors of the NT understand Jesus as their king, priest and the warrior who saves them from their spiritual enemies.

2.3. David Psalms: Psalm 16. Besides psalms that specifically refer to the "anointed king" and those that are explicitly royal, the NT recognizes the messianic significance of psalms that are labeled Davidic. Psalm 16 is a case in point. The psalm itself nowhere uses the term *māšaḥ* or its cognates, nor does the content of the psalm in any way betray a royal origin. However, the title identifies it as a psalm of David, and so it would have been natural for the early church to read it as such. In this way, the psalm becomes the utterance of David, who is the anointed king of Israel.

Thus, as Psalm 16 is reread in the light of the death and resurrection of Christ, it would have been quite natural to read it as if uttered by Christ. In this context the message would take on a deeper significance that is implicit in the psalm itself. Psalm 16:10, for instance, could easily be understood in relationship to the historical David as the expression of his confidence that God would save him from some present threat to his life or, better, from a fate reserved only for the wicked (for the argument that Sheol was reserved for the wicked alone, see Johnston).

> For you will not abandon my soul to Sheol;
>   you will not allow your faithful follower
>   to see the Pit.

But as the NT recognized (Acts 2:27; 13:35), it was not David who experienced this protection in the ultimate sense—a point proven by pointing to David's grave—but only Christ, who had been raised from the dead.

2.4. A Messianic Editing of the Book of Psalms?

We examined Psalm 2 simply as a leading example of a psalm that over time came to have important messianic significance in the eyes of the church. However, the choice of this example also leads to a discussion of the possible messianic significance of the structure of the book of Psalms.

Most people read the book of Psalms as a relatively unordered collection of hymns. The book is not systematically structured in obvious ways such as chronology or topic or genre. However, a recent school of thought influenced by the work of G. H. Wilson has suggested a more subtle kind of editorial organization, and recently Wilson has argued that the final order of the book has messianic significance.

Wilson did his early work (1985) under the influence of his mentor, B. S. Childs, who is best known for advocating the canonical approach that looks for meaning in the final form of a text. Childs (511-13) had suggested that Psalter's

structure might have a rationale, and Wilson took up the challenge. He argued that a structure could be found by examining the psalms at the so-called seams of the book—that is, the psalms that open and close the five "Books" of the Psalter. Wilson notes that a number (but not all) of these psalms have to do explicitly with the Davidic covenant, and that some of the others could be read in a way to make them relevant.

Psalm 2 is the first such, which, though not mentioning David even in the title or referring to the covenant, is connected to the covenant because of the language that alludes to the Davidic covenant in 2 Samuel 7 (see 2.1 above). Wilson believes, therefore, that Psalm 2 announces the Davidic covenant. Psalm 41, which closes Book I, is taken as a statement of confidence in the Davidic covenant—this in spite of the fact that the covenant is not mentioned or alluded to in the body of the psalm.

Wilson does not comment on the opening composition of Book II (Ps 42) as relevant, but he does believe that the closing psalm, Psalm 72, is. This psalm, according to its title, is a psalm of Solomon, but Wilson treats it as a psalm of David and a prayer for Solomon. He believes that this psalm provides for the passing on of the covenant promises from David to his son.

At the end of Book III the concern with the Davidic covenant becomes explicit for the first time. Wilson (1985, 213) believes that Psalm 89 is about "a covenant remembered but a covenant failed. The Davidic covenant introduced in Ps 2 has come to nothing and the combination of three books concludes with the anguished cry of the Davidic descendants."

Book IV is then supposedly the answer to the dilemma expressed by Psalm 89 at the end of Book III. It asserts that Yahweh is king and particularly is a refuge (a theme picked up and developed by Creach). So it is a call to trust Yahweh now that the monarchy is gone.

As for Book V, Wilson does not believe that this section could be as ingeniously edited, for there are a number of psalms that came into the collection via preexistent groups. In conclusion, Wilson (1985, 227) states that this fifth book is an answer to the "plea of the exiles to be gathered from the diaspora." The answer is to trust and depend on Yahweh.

Thus, Wilson sees a development within the structure of the Psalter from a confident assertion of Davidic covenant to its failure and the reassertion of hope in Yahweh's kingship in the absence of the monarchy. In other words, the shape of the Psalter takes on messianic proportions, since he also describes a connection with David here.

This ingenious reading certainly is appealing, but there are reasons to be hesitant about accepting it. First, Wilson's reading is based on a selective view of the psalms at the seams. Not all the "seam psalms" are relevant (e.g., Pss 42; 71; 90). Second, some of the psalms fit only if interpreted in a certain way. This is true of Psalm 41, which is not explicitly about the covenant, but also Psalm 89, which is not obviously about the failure of the Davidic covenant. The hope implied in the appeal to God makes it clear that the psalmist does not think that the covenant has failed; God just needs to be goaded into action by this extreme language. Third, there are psalms that clearly are concerned with the Davidic covenant that are left out of the schema— for example, Psalm 132, which is positive about the Davidic covenant in a way that Wilson's interpretation would not lead us to expect. Finally, one has to seriously question any new insight like this that has not been recognized over the millennia of previous interpretation. Of course, a new insight could be gained, but the burden of proof must be quite heavy.

3. The Messiah in Wisdom Literature?

To explore whether or not it is appropriate to speak of the messiah in Wisdom literature, it is important to be reminded of a crucial distinction. Although Jesus states that the "the law of Moses and the prophets and the psalms" (Lk 24:44)—in essence, the entirety of what we would call the OT—anticipated his coming, he does not mean that all the books engendered a specifically messianic expectation. The messianic expectation has to do with royal, priestly and prophetic roles because these were the people who were anointed in the OT.

Undoubtedly, Jesus was viewed as the wisdom teacher par excellence in the NT (*see* Proverbs 1: Book of; Woman Wisdom and Woman Folly). However, the question is whether or not this should be defined as a messianic expectation. We will address this question book-by-book, but we will see that these books add little if anything to the discussion, and attempts to see "messiah" in these books are belabored.

3.1. Proverbs. A good ruler was one who was endowed with great wisdom from God. Indeed, Solomon, named in the superscription of the book of Proverbs, was well known for his great, divinely bestowed wisdom. However, even within the book of Proverbs wisdom is not restricted to the royal office, so it is too far an extension to argue that the wisdom of Proverbs is a messianic type of wisdom, and in any case the book of Proverbs does not strike an eschatological tone and thus did not raise messianic expectations (*contra* Laato, 252-55; Perrin, 57-59).

3.2. Ecclesiastes. In a recent article R. Perrin argues that the reference to "the son of David" (Eccles 1:1) and the "one shepherd" (Eccles 12:11) form a narrative frame (*see* Frame Narrative) that reveals the messianic intention of the book of *Ecclesiastes, or at least of its final third- or second-century BC redaction. Perrin believes that here we have the combination of messianic and wisdom themes that is known during the intertestamental and NT period. He believes that the combination of "son of David," wise "words" and "king of Jerusalem" (not "Israel") indicates a transcending of past reference and has eschatological significance. He draws parallels that are explicitly messianic in *Sirach (Sir 24:9-12) and *Psalms of Solomon* (*Pss. Sol.* 17:21-24, 30, 32). In this interpretation *Qohelet/Solomon is the messianic sage.

Perrin makes some interesting and provocative points, but it is hard to come away with any other impression than that he is overly subtle in his connections. One need only review the many different ideas of what "one/a S/shepherd" means in Ecclesiastes 2:11 to understand the speculative nature of his suggestion (Longman 1998, 278-80).

3.3. Job. W. Kaiser (61-64) devotes a whole section of *The Messiah in the Old Testament* to the book of *Job. He argues that four texts in Job are relevant to the development of the messianic idea in the book: Job 9:33; 16:19-21; 19:23-27; 33:23-28. After surveying these passages, Kaiser (64) concludes that the book of Job anticipates a messiah who will be "an arbitrator, a mediator, a heavenly advocate and witness, a redeemer, and an interpreter of the enigmas of his life."

These texts are among the most difficult to interpret in a difficult book. But even granting that Kaiser is correct in his interpretation, he is not identifying a specifically messianic expectation in Job in the sense that we are using "messiah" here, since none of the expected traits of

Job's arbitrator in heaven have anything to do with an "anointed" office.

4. The Messiah in Song of Songs.

*Song of Songs has a storied history of interpretation (*see* Song of Songs 3: History of Interpretation). Until the mid-nineteenth century the book was interpreted as an allegory of the history of redemption. In Jewish circles the man in Song of Songs was identified with God, and the woman with Israel. The *Targum then interpreted Song of Songs as allegorically describing the history of Israel from the exodus to the future messianic age. For instance, it takes Song of Songs 8:2 as a reference to the messianic banquet. Christian interpretation, in its historical allegories, simply substituted Christ for Yahweh, and the church for Israel. Few today, however, would read Song of Songs in this way, and so messianic interpretation of the book has also diminished.

5. The Messiah in the Books of Ruth and Esther.

These books too are only indirectly relevant to an expectation of the messiah. One of the functions of *Ruth, however, is that it tells the story connected to the genealogy of David, the future anointed king of Israel, and in Matthew 1 Ruth is cited as part of the line that includes the kings of Israel and culminates with Jesus, David's greater son. *Esther narrates the escape of the people of God from total destruction, which means the preservation of the line that eventually would produce Jesus, the Messiah. Such is the argument of K. Jobes (45): "The New Testament teaches that the Old Testament promises of future salvation were ultimately secured by the death and resurrection of Jesus Christ. The deliverance of God's people from Haman's death decree assured that the continuance of the Jewish nation from which their *Messiah* would come. The Messiah brought a deliverance from death not limited to escaping the holocausts of history, but a deliverance from the grave that inevitably awaits each of us, both Jew and Gentile alike."

See also KINGSHIP PSALMS.

BIBLIOGRAPHY. **B. S. Childs,** *Introduction to the Old Testament as Scripture* (Philadelphia: Fortress, 1979); **J. Creach,** *Yahweh as Refuge and the Editing of the Hebrew Psalter* (JSOTSup 217; Sheffield: Sheffield Academic Press, 1996); **K. Heim,** "The Perfect King of Psalm 72: An 'Intertextual Inqui-

ry,'" in *The Lord's Anointed: Interpretation of Old Testament Messianic Texts,* ed. P. E. Satterthwaite, R. S. Hess and G. J. Wenham (Grand Rapids: Baker, 1995) 223-48; **K. Jobes,** *Esther* (NIVAC; Grand Rapids: Zondervan, 1999); **P. S. Johnston,** "'Left in Hell'?: Psalm 16, Sheol and the Holy One," in *The Lord's Anointed: Interpretation of Old Testament Messianic Texts,* ed. P. E. Satterthwaite, R. S. Hess and G. J. Wenham (Grand Rapids: Baker, 1995) 213-22; **W. Kaiser,** *The Messiah in the Old Testament* (Grand Rapids: Zondervan, 1995); **A. Laato,** *A Star Is Rising: The Historical Development of the Old Testament Royal Ideology and the Rise of the Jewish Messianic Expectation* (ISFCJ 5; Atlanta: Scholars Press, 1997); **T. Longman III,** *Ecclesiastes* (NICOT; Grand Rapids: Eerdmans, 1998); idem, "The Messiah: Explorations in the Law and Writings," in *Messiah in the Old and New Testaments,* ed. S. E. Porter (MNTS; Grand Rapids: Eerdmans, 2007); **R. Perrin,** "Messianism in the Narrative Frame of Ecclesiastes?" *RB* 108 (2001) 37-60; **C. Rosel,** *Die messianische Redaktion des Psalters: Studien zu Entstehung und Theologie der Sammlung Psalm 2-89* (CThM 19; Stuttgart: Calwer, 1999); **G. van Groningen,** *Messianic Revelation in the Old Testament* (Grand Rapids: Baker, 1990); **G. H. Wilson,** *The Editing of the Hebrew Psalter* (SBLDS 76; Chico, CA: Scholars Press, 1985); idem, *Psalms,* vol. 1 (NIVAC; Grand Rapids: Zondervan, 2002a); idem, "Psalms and Psalter: Paradigm for Biblical Theology," in *Biblical Theology: Retrospect and Prospect,* ed. S. Hafemann (Downers Grove, IL: InterVarsity Press, 2002b).

T. Longman III

METAPHOR. *See* IMAGERY; POETICS, TERMINOLOGY OF.

METER

Over the past two centuries considerable conversation has arisen about the nature of or the existence of meter in biblical Hebrew poetry, so that, next to *parallelism, it has been the most actively discussed issue with regard to biblical poetics. The nature of the debate and conclusions proffered are closely tied to one's understanding of the term *meter.* As we will see, "Those who advocate meter in Biblical poetry define meter in a much looser manner than scholars who deny meter in the Biblical text" (Vance, 11). Indeed, it is a strict understanding of meter as used by scholars of nonbiblical poetry that leads many to insist that it plays no significant role in biblical literature. However, since meter is one of the major characteristics of many types of poetry, other scholars assume that biblical poetry is metrical and that identifying the type of meter used by the ancient Israelites will aid the exegetical process.

This article introduces the four main types of poetic meter, each of which has at some time been identified as being present in Hebrew poetry. In addition, it examines arguments against meter being found in biblical poetry to any significant extent if at all. A brief introduction to what is often called *qinah* meter is also given.

1. Proposed Types of Poetic Meter
2. Arguments Against Meter
3. *Qinah* Meter

1. Proposed Types of Poetic Meter.

Poetic meter is related to rhythm, the natural flow of a language whether in poetry or prose. As compared to rhythm, meter is characterized by being regularized and systematized in a manner that is easily recognizable. Students of poetry identify four common types of meter, each with its own distinctive characteristics: quantitative, accentual, syllabic, accentual-syllabic. At different times in history each of these meters has been said to appear in biblical poetry. Today, however, only the accentual and syllabic meters are given serious consideration.

1.1. Quantitative Meter. Quantitative meter, the meter of classical Greek and Latin poetry, is based upon the length of the syllables (the quantity or duration of sound in utterance) found in a poetic line. In classical poetry syllables are classified as long or short, depending upon the length of time required to pronounce them (a long syllable is said to take twice as long to pronounce as a short one). Quantitative meter is measured by counting a combination of syllables that are referred to as feet. The five main types of metrical feet are (1) iamb (short-long); (2) trochee (long-short); (3) spondee (long-long); (4) dactyl (long-short-short); (5) anapest (short-short-long). A line of poetry is scanned according to the number of feet used. Thus a line with one foot is monometer, two feet is dimeter, three feet is trimeter, four feet is tetrameter, five feet is pentameter, six feet is hexameter, and seven feet is septameter. The line can be further described by combining the type with the number of feet found in a line. Thus a

poem might be written in dactylic hexameter (which frequently substitutes a spondee for a dactyl, as in Homer and Virgil), iambic pentameter or some other.

From very early Christian times claims were made that biblical authors made use of this type of meter when they wrote poetry. Thus Josephus wrote that "Moses also composed a song unto God, containing his praises, and a thanksgiving for his kindness, in hexameter verse" (Josephus *Ant.* 2.346), even though he gave no examples of how he determined this. Similarly, other writers, including Origen, Jerome, Augustine and perhaps Philo, made similar claims without explaining how they scanned the biblical verses to support their conclusions. It is generally assumed that these early authors used this terminology to convince people of their day that biblical poetry was not inferior to classical poetry. Although a few scholars during the modern period attempted to describe Hebrew poetics according to a quantitative scheme, their work has been deemed unsuccessful. To a great extent this is because the *Hebrew language places a greater emphasis on stress than on the length of vowel sounds. Since no serious proponent has appeared since the early nineteenth century, discussion of this approach with regard to biblical Hebrew is mainly of historical interest.

1.2. Accentual Meter. Accentual meter focuses strictly on the accented or stressed syllables of a line of poetry so that only the accented syllables are counted. Since unaccented syllables are considered irrelevant for counting accentual meter, feet are not normally taken into account. This approach was developed in the nineteenth century by J. Ley, K. Budde and E. Sievers (thus often called the Ley-Budde-Sievers method) and quickly became the predominant way to scan biblical poetry. Although practitioners vary in the exact procedure used, meter is generally determined by counting the major stresses denoted by the Masoretic accents in each of the bicola, tricola and so on of a poetic line. The meter of a particular line could thus scanned as 3:3, 3:2, 2:2:2 (alternately $3 + 3, 3 + 2, 2 + 2 + 2$) and so forth, indicating the number of stresses in each colon as they relate to the stresses in the adjoining colon/cola of a line.

Although not strictly an accentual approach, G. Gray, followed by T. Robinson, based meter upon units of Hebrew words (combinations of nouns, pronouns, prepositions, etc.) that are semantically related to other word units found in parallel colon/cola. This method of identifying poetic meter clearly was a development of R. Lowth's description of parallelism, as both Gray and Robinson understood parallelism as the primary aspect of Hebrew poetry. Even though word groups rather than accents are counted, the patterns identified frequently coincide with the accentual meter assigned to a line. A similar approach is practiced by J. Kurylowicz and A. Cooper, who focus on word complexes that are identified not on the basis of semantic parallelism but rather from grammatical criteria. What has been referred to as syntactic-accentual meter finds one significant accent on a word complex that may include a word with its proclitics and conjunctions, nouns in a construct relationship, words linked by a *maqqēp,* or other words closely related syntactically (Longman, 238-41). A secondary stress in a word complex is considered metrically irrelevant. The basic metrical pattern for this approach appears to be 2:2, though alternate forms are identified.

Another variation on the accentual approach is found in S. Mowinckel, who, by taking the unaccented syllables into account, determined that biblical meter was principally iambic and occasionally anapestic, although he admitted that there are many exceptions. Mowinckel's scansion generally adds one more stress to the meter of a colon, thus yielding 4:4, 4:3, 3:3 and so forth.

The accentual approach suffers from several weaknesses. As the foregoing description demonstrates, those who practice the method do not fully agree on how to identify or count accents. A related problem is that the method usually relies upon the accentuation and vocalization found in the Masoretic Text, even though the exact pronunciation of Hebrew when the Bible was written is unknown and inaccessible. In many instances, practitioners resort to emending the Masoretic Text apparently to ensure that the text conforms to their metric theory. A further negative concerns the macrostructure of a poem. Although it can be argued that most cola contain two or three accents, it is impossible to demonstrate that any metrical pattern is replicated in multiple poems in the Bible or even within the strophic structure of a given poem. It is thus almost essential to speak of biblical poetry as always exhibiting mixed meter. This lack of a real metric pattern gives reason to question whether poetry in the Bible can be said to display accentual meter at all.

1.3. Syllabic Meter. Beginning with F. Cross and D. Freedman, Hebrew poetry has been identified as exhibiting syllabic meter. This approach determines meter by counting the syllables of a poetic line. As distinct from the scansion derived by the accentual approach, which usually yields two or three accents, syllable counting recognizes each colon as having anywhere between three and thirteen syllables and notes that corresponding cola have roughly an equal number of syllables. In most cases, corresponding cola are either long (between eight and thirteen syllables) or short (between three and five syllables) and will be scanned accordingly (e.g., 4:4; 8:8:7; 11:11). Lines that deviate from expected patterns, rather than being seen as a reason to question this approach, are considered part of the larger pattern that may have been deliberately composed for effect. The balance in syllables expected between matched cola is not found in the so-called *qinah* verses, in which the second colon is consistently shorter than the first colon.

As with the accentual method, this approach exhibits several weaknesses. Although there is significant correspondence between the number of syllables in corresponding cola, there does not appear to be any relation between the number of syllables in a poetic line and those adjacent to it. This distinguishes what is found in biblical poetry from recognized forms of syllabic poetry in which every line contains exactly the same number of syllables (as in French Alexandrine poetry) or in which consecutive lines follow a rigid pattern and the poem has a limited number of lines (as in Japanese haiku). If Hebrew poets used syllabic meter, they apparently did not intend to follow a rigorous pattern within a given poem, much less the entire genre. It is therefore not uncommon for supporters of this approach to admit finding a "thoroughly mixed meter" in which one can find "the free variation of couplets and triplets without discernable pattern" (Stuart, 215). That Hebrew poets might be so free in their compositions as to leave no discernable patterns greatly diminishes the possibility that they used syllabic meter.

Discussions of syllabic meter frequently make reference to anacrusis, a unit of speech that is found at the beginning of a line but not counted as part of the metrical structure of the line. Words in this position often are identified as interjections, conjunctions or pronouns that provide the reader with reason to pause and consider the words that follow. In many cases, however, it appears that anacrusis is invoked simply as a means of balancing the meter in corresponding cola, as the same parts of speech that are evaluated as anacrusis in one colon may not be in another colon.

Other problems arise with regard to the textual basis for counting syllables. Whereas Freedman and others usually base syllable counts upon the Masoretic Text, they recognize that it may not reproduce the original syllables accurately. As a result, their scansion of biblical poems according to syllables can be considered tentative at best. Others, such as Cross and Stuart, who emend the text so that it more closely resembles a hypothetical original reading, risk the accusation of shaping the text to fit their metrical theory, as that appears to motivate changes in readings above textual or even literary concerns.

1.4. Accentual Syllabic Meter. Accentual syllabic meter takes over the nomenclature used in the discussion of quantitative meter, giving it a different meaning. Instead of basing meter on long and short vowels, this approach focuses on stressed and unstressed syllables, which are grouped into feet. An iamb is therefore understood to be composed of an unstressed-stressed syllable unit rather than a short-long vowel unit. Other types of feet can be similarly redefined. Although common in English poetry, this complex meter has rarely been identified as a basis for Hebrew poetry. Although supported by F. Hare and J. Saalschütz, in the seventeenth and nineteenth centuries respectively, it has had no serious followers in more than a century (though J. Kugel [296] states that W. Albright, despite his unclear descriptions and inconsistent practice, followed this approach).

2. Arguments Against Meter.
In contrast to these attempts to identify meter in Hebrew poetry, a number of scholars have concluded that it simply does not exist, at least not in the sense that the term is used to describe other forms of poetry. Meter in poetry is generally understood to be so regular that it is like "a contract between the poet and the reader wherein the poet declares what he or she is going to do" and readers can readily recognize whether they have succeeded or not

(Vance, 15). The best that supporters of various types of meter in biblical poetry can claim is that there is some kind of correspondence between the number of accents or syllables within the parallel structure of a poetic line, and that the number of accents or syllables in the various lines of a poem is roughly the same. That Hebrew poets are said to have had enormous freedom within these parameters in how they constructed their poems does nothing to support the presence of meter as normally understood. Furthermore, the lack of agreement between scholars as to the kind of meter used or how it can be scanned indicates that Hebrew poetry is far from regular; and without regularity, it is not strictly metrical. That many have recognized these problems lends credence to the claim that "it is possible to discern an emerging scholarly consensus that denies the existence of meter in classical Hebrew poetry" (Petersen and Richards, 42).

From an exegetical point of view, it appears that identifying meter in a biblical poem accomplishes little. Its use as a means to distinguish poetry from prose is problematic in that many prose sentences exhibit similar syllabic and accentual patterns. The comparative presence or absence of parallelism, degree of terseness, and use of figures of speech serve as a better guide for identifying poetry than does meter. In the same way, a focus on parallelism will likely produce a better understanding of the similarities in length of complementary cola within a line of poetry. Finally, the use of metric arguments for emending the text (when there is little or no textual support for the change) is suspect because arguments in its support are circular by nature.

3. *Qinah* Meter.
Beginning with Budde's studies on the book of *Lamentations, scholars have referred to a special type of Hebrew meter that is said to be found in lament poems and is thus characteristic of a dirge (see Lament, Psalms of). Named after the Hebrew word for a lament or dirge, *qinah* meter is scanned 3:2 following accentual meter (Hölscher and Mowinckel scan it 4:3 by including secondary accents) and usually 8:5 following syllabic meter. The second colon is described as being shorter in order to display a "limping" or "falling" rhythm to express the unfulfilled hopes of the singer. An example can be given from

Lamentations 2:5:

> *hayâ ʾădōnáy kĕʾôyéb* [three accents; eight syllables]
> The-Loŕd has-becóme like-an-eńemy
> [in the Hebrew phrase the verb comes first]
> *billáʿ yiśrāʾél* [two accents; five syllables]
> he-has-swállowed-up Iśrael

It is clear that this pattern is reproduced in many lines in biblical laments. Even so, it would be incorrect to conclude that biblical poets uniformly made use of the 3:2 form in their composition of dirges. First, this syllabic pattern is common in many types of Hebrew poetry, not just in laments. Second, within a given lament one may find lines that exhibit a number of different "metrical patterns." Third, some biblical laments (e.g., 2 Sam 1:19-27; Lam 5) consistently make use of other accentual and syllabic patterns. The best that can be said of the *qinah* meter is that some but not all Hebrew poets may have followed such a pattern as they wrote laments. Even so, the lack of this pattern in many laments and its presence in other genres indicates that one must exert great caution in assuming that this pattern was characteristic of Hebrew dirges.

See also PARALLELISM; POETICS, TERMINOLOGY OF; SOUND PATTERNS.

BIBLIOGRAPHY. **K. Budde,** "Das hebräische Klaglied," *ZAW* 2 (1882) 1-52; idem, "The Forms of Hebrew Poetry," in *Dictionary of the Bible,* ed. James Hastings (4 vols.; New York: Scribner, 1902) 4.3-9; **F. M. Cross and D. N. Freedman,** *Studies in Ancient Yahwistic Poetry* (SBLDS 21; Missoula, MT: Scholars Press, 1975; 2nd ed., BRS; Grand Rapids: Eerdmans, 1997); **D. N. Freedman,** *Pottery, Poetry, and Prophecy: Studies in Early Hebrew Poetry* (Winona Lake, IN: Eisenbrauns, 1980); **W. R. Garr,** "The Qinah: A Study of Poetic Meter, Syntax and Style," *ZAW* 95 (1983) 54-75; **G. B. Gray,** *The Forms of Hebrew Poetry: Considered with Special Reference to the Criticism and Interpretation of the Old Testament* (New York: KTAV, 1915; repr., Eugene, OR: Wipf & Stock, 2002); **J. L. Kugel,** *The Idea of Biblical Poetry: Parallelism and Its History* (New Haven: Yale University Press, 1981); **J. Kurylowicz,** *Studies in Semitic Grammar and Metrics* (London: Curzon Press, 1973); **J. Ley,** *Grundzüge des Rhythmus, des Vers- und Strophenbaus in der hebräischen Poesie* (Halle: Waisenhauses, 1875); idem, *Leitfaden der Metrik der hebräischen Poesie* (Halle: Waisenhauses, 1887); **T. Longman III,** "A Critique of Two Recent Metrical Systems," *Bib* 63 (1982) 230-54; **S. Mowinckel,** *The Psalms in Israel's Worship,* (Grand Rapids: Eerdmans, 2004); **D. L. Petersen and K. H. Richards,** *Interpreting Hebrew Poetry* (GBS; Minneapolis: Fortress, 1992); **T. H. Robinson,** *The Poetry of the Old Testament* (London: Duckworth, 1947); **D. K. Stuart,** *Studies in Early Hebrew Meter* (HSM 13; Missoula, MT: Scholars Press, 1976); **D. R. Vance,** *The Question of Meter in Biblical Hebrew Poetry* (SBEC 46; Lewiston, NY; Edwin Mellen, 2001). W. McConnell

MOAB. *See* RUTH 2: ANCIENT NEAR EASTERN BACKGROUND.

MONSTERS. *See* CHAOS AND DEATH; CREATION THEOLOGY.

MORDECAI

After experiencing injustice and facing the threatened annihilation of his people in the Persian Empire, Mordecai rose to become second only to King Xerxes (*Ahasuerus). His roles in the *Esther narrative, however, have raised questions as to whether he was a godly Jew living in exile or had succumbed to the allure of the Diaspora culture.

1. Mordecai's Jewish Identity
2. Mordecai's Identity in the Context of the Persian Empire
3. Was Mordecai a Faithful or a Fundamentally Disobedient Jew?
4. The Ugly Specter of Anti-Semitism
5. Mordecai Becomes a Public Figure

1. Mordecai's Jewish Identity.

1.1. Living in Exile. The Hebrew word order of Esther 2:5 is significant. The verse begins with "a Jewish man, who was in the citadel of Susa." These identifying marks appear even before Mordecai's name, and they hint at the conflict that follows, setting up the Jewish counterpoint to the Persian court. Mordecai is repeatedly called "Mordecai the Jew," distinguishing him in the Diaspora context. His status as an exile is emphasized in Esther 2:6, which literally reads, "who was exiled from Jerusalem with the group of exiles which was exiled with Jeconiah, king of Judah, whom Nebuchadnezzar, king of Babylon, took into exile." The exile of Mordecai's forebears in 597 BC along with Jeconiah indicates that it was an upper-class family (2 Kings 24:8-16; Jer 29:1-2). The eunuchs, nobles and officials of the king were taken in that wave.

1.2. Mordecai's Genealogy.

1.2.1. Who Was Taken into Exile? The author speaks of "Mordecai, son of Jair, son of Shimei, son of Kish, a Benjamite, who was taken into exile from Jerusalem" (Esther 2:5b-6a). The primary question regarding the genealogy is the impossible age of Mordecai if the relative clause that commences Esther 2:6 refers to him being taken into exile rather than the last individual in the list, Kish. That is the customary way to read such Hebrew constructions. However, because that is unlikely for a narrator seemingly so careful about detail, it is more probable that Kish was indeed the individual taken into exile. In that case, he and these other immediate forebears of Mordecai had names that reflected earlier generations of the family tree.

1.2.2. The Amalekite Connection. Mordecai's tribal affiliation with Benjamin and the ancestor named Kish were clear connections to King Saul, whose father was Kish (1 Sam 9:1; 1 Chron 8:33). Haman is also explicitly linked to a venerable line, that of Agag. The astute audience would recognize some significant unfinished business from the early period of the Israelite monarchy when Saul was commanded by the Lord to obliterate the Amalekites, whose king was Agag (1 Sam 15). This was not capricious; the judgment upon the Amalekites was a fulfillment of God's declaration in Exodus 17:14 that he would erase the memory of the Amalekites because of their attack on Israel as described earlier in the chapter. That assault was a brutal one, as they attacked those who were weak and straggling behind (Deut 25:17-19). Saul, however, disobeyed the Lord and left Agag alive. The confrontation between Mordecai and Haman revisited that old ethnic tension, this time shot through with the injustice of Haman's rise to power while Mordecai remained unrecognized.

1.3. Practicing the Disciplines of Judaism.
When Mordecai learned of the deadly decree issued by Haman in the name of the king, he donned the garb of mourning along with Jews in every province to which the edict had come (Esther 4:1-3). After challenging Esther to intervene with the king on behalf of the people, he carried out her instructions to fast along with the Jews of *Susa

(Esther 4:17). In the interval his challenge to her is memorable: "Do not think that because you are in the king's house you alone of all the Jews will escape. For if you remain silent at this time, will relief and deliverance for the Jews arise from another place?" The implicit answer to that question was no. "You and your father's family will perish. And who knows but that you have come to the royal position for such a time as this?" (Esther 4:13-14). Generally, the second part of Esther 4:13 is translated "if you remain silent at this time, relief and deliverance will arise from another place, but you and your father's family will perish." It is possible, however, and more logical to read it as a question that is preceded and followed by threats of her own demise along with all the other Jews. This suggests that Mordecai's words were not posed as a hopeful but indefinite expectation of deliverance from some unnamed quarter. Instead, his message was comprehensively grim. Once Haman had discovered that she was both Jewish and related to Mordecai, her fate would be a terrible one regardless of her position as queen. Thus, she needed to act in the knowledge that she was the only hope.

2. Mordecai's Identity in the Context of the Persian Empire.

Although "Mordecai" reflects a common Persian name *(Mardukâ)*, there is no solid external corroboration of this particular Mordecai's position as second in the empire. There is an undated cuneiform document from the Persian period that refers to *Mardukâ*, who was thought to be in high office either late in the reign of Darius I or at the beginning of Xerxes' rule. First published by A. Ungnad in 1940-1941 and repeatedly referenced by subsequent scholars, it was hailed as evidence of the well-positioned Mordecai whom the biblical text represents. Nevertheless, more recent appraisals of the document question whether the *Mardukâ* of this text was really as prominent as initially thought and whether he was in office after 502 BC.

An equally challenging question is why Mordecai would bear the name of Babylon's chief deity, Marduk. In the genealogy of Hebrew names the appearance of "Mordecai" is notable. It is possible that he, like his cousin Esther, had a Hebrew name that simply does not appear because his narrative roles unfolded primarily in the Persian court. On the other hand, this may also be a hint that Mordecai had adopted, to a troubling degree, more than merely superficial trappings of Persian culture.

3. Was Mordecai a Faithful or a Fundamentally Disobedient Jew?

In contrast to Haman, Mordecai's emotions, thoughts and motives are hidden. As a result, there are readers who claim that both Mordecai and Esther suffered severe moral lapses that resulted in the silent disapproval of God. Others see them as courageous and devoted Jews living in the tenuous circumstances of a threatened minority population.

3.1. Mordecai's Choice to Remain in the Diaspora.

3.1.1. Evidence of Accommodation. That Mordecai was living in Susa—to say nothing of using the name "Mordecai" and serving in some capacity in the Persian court—is posited as evidence of disobedience and lack of loyalty to God and his covenant people. With the Babylonian exile, the Jews' religious identity had been undermined by loss of connection to the land and by the seductive appeal of the dominant culture. When the Persians replaced the Babylonians, and Cyrus issued his edict (539 BC) sending the exiles back to Judah to rebuild the temple, only a remnant did indeed return. The rest remained comfortably established throughout the Diaspora. By the time Xerxes took over the realm of Persia in 486 BC, these people likely had assimilated to a significant degree, and Mordecai was among them.

3.1.2. Mordecai's Residence in Susa Was Evidence of God's Providence. It is, however, significant in this regard that both Ezra and Nehemiah at the outset of their individual stories were likewise in high-profile positions in Susa. Neither of them is sanctioned for disobedience. In fact, it is telling that those events took place just about a generation after the crisis narrated in the book of Esther. Perhaps the wave of pro-Jewish sentiment as evidenced at the end of Esther and the pattern set by Mordecai's position paved the way for the prominent roles that both Ezra and Nehemiah held in the Persian court prior to their respective returns to Judea.

3.2. Mordecai's Role vis-à-vis Esther.

3.2.1. An Exploitative "Guardian"? A further charge against Mordecai centers on his willingness to send Esther into the "den of iniquity" that was the Persian court. Perhaps he was motivated by concern for his own advancement and was ready to exploit her evident beauty toward that end. Once Esther moved into the king's palace, Mordecai took his place in the gate, a position of significant power. Moreover, Mordecai forbade Esther, once she found herself in that context, to reveal her identity with God's covenant people, for that would entirely compromise his growing power.

3.2.2. A Faithful Guardian. Contrary to the picture of a worldly and callous Mordecai, however, there are hints early in the text that he was anything but that. The Hebrew word order of Esther 2:7 is significant. It begins with "He was caring for," emphasizing Mordecai's role as guardian of Esther. The verse emphasizes the absence of Esther's parents, indicating twice that both had died and intimating that, apart from Mordecai, she would have been deserted. Even though Esther was Mordecai's cousin, she was sufficiently younger that he adopted her as his daughter.

The description of Esther emphasizes her beauty—literally, "beautiful of form" and "lovely in appearance." In other words, her extraordinary beauty far exceeded the criteria for being rounded up in the net; there were "young woman," "virgin" and "lovely in appearance" (Esther 2:3). In Esther's case, being taken was unavoidable. Once she was trapped in the harem, Mordecai's concern for her was evident in his daily walk outside the palace (Esther 2:11).

3.3. Mordecai's Refusal to Bow to Haman. Haman had been appointed to a position of honor higher than any other nobles in the realm, and all were commanded to prostrate themselves in his presence (Esther 3:2). Mordecai was consistent in his adamant refusal to bow to Haman. This event was taking place in the gate complex, which was sufficiently expansive that Haman did not notice the noncompliance of Mordecai until he was informed. Once the court functionaries knew that Mordecai was Jewish, they not only ceased to try to persuade him to bow as they had been doing, but also they turned the matter over to Haman (Esther 3:4).

3.3.1. Personal and Nationalistic Pride? This incident that touched off Haman's fury might have been a matter of Mordecai's own wounded pride and his strong sense of ethnic identity. Having to prostrate himself before Haman would have been a difficult blow to Mordecai, whose faithfulness to the king in exposing the assassination plot had gone unrecognized for about five years (cf. Esther 2:16 with Esther 3:7). Further, these personal tensions may have reflected the long-standing hostility between Israelites and Amalekites. Thus, rather than evidencing strong religious convictions in his refusal to bow, perhaps Mordecai simply responded with pride and nationalistic fervor that was, in the end, extremely reckless, given the consequences. Even though the expressions "kneeling down" and "falling on one's face" (Esther 3:2, 5) are often used in conjunction with *worship of God, verbal pairs are a prominent stylistic touch throughout Esther. These two terms may simply be another one of these many rhetorical flourishes and lack any overtones of worship or idolatry.

3.3.2. Deep-Rooted Conviction Regarding the Worship of God. There are instances in the biblical text where Israelites bowed to human kings (1 Sam 24:8; 2 Sam 14:4; 18:28; 1 Kings 1:16) and to other superiors (Gen 23:7; 27:29; 33:3), but those Hebrew expressions are not the same as the verbs used in this context, *ḥāwâ* and *kāraʿ*. Instead, when these two verbs are used elsewhere together in the biblical text, they always describe an individual doing obeisance in the presence of God (2 Chron 7:3; 29:29; Ps 22:29 [MT 22:30]; 95:6). Contrary to the suggestions that Mordecai's refusal to bow was merely a sense of personal and ethnic honor, to be ordered to do this must have offended Mordecai's most fundamental convictions.

4. The Ugly Specter of Anti-Semitism.

For reasons that are not articulated, Mordecai commanded Esther not to reveal her ethnic identity. It is further evident from the events at the king's gate (Esther 3:2-4) that being Jewish jeopardized Mordecai's security. There seems to have been a strong subcurrent of anti-Semitism brewing in the court, in Susa, and in the realm at large. This widespread antipathy toward the Jews would serve as fertile ground in which to sow Haman's decree. Haman clearly expected extensive public participation in his plan to annihilate the Jews. The populace of Susa was thrown into an uproar by the decree of the king and Haman (Esther 3:15), but the nature of that confusion is unclear, and there was a significant part of the empire that decided to attack the Jews, even in the face of the second decree, which allowed the Jews to defend themselves.

5. Mordecai Becomes a Public Figure.

5.1. Honored in the Public Square. Neither the king nor Haman had slept during the pivotal night described in Esther 5:10—6:3, and both had Mordecai in mind, although with entirely different objectives. Xerxes was agitated because his failure to reward Mordecai reflected badly on him. Haman was vexed because again Mordecai obviously had refused to pay him honor. Thinking that the king's phrase "the man whom the king delights to honor" applied to him, Haman described the honors that he so ardently desired, continuing to interweave "the man whom the king delights to honor." This was a practice session; he would announce it repeatedly and publicly with reference to Mordecai.

Both the royal horse and the regal garment were to be ones that the king himself had used. A crest (lit., "crown") on the horse's head was not an unusual ornamentation in ancient Near Eastern art; such equine headpieces appear regularly in Assyrian reliefs. Most likely, this was not to be a parade through the streets but rather a stationery demonstration in the city square. The verbs that are translated "has ridden" and "led through" are better understood as "mount," implying the symbolic position to which Haman would be required to raise Mordecai as a public act of honor.

After Haman's extended description, the actual event in the city square is sparingly narrated. Although the king seemingly was unaware of the antipathy between Haman and Mordecai, those who watched the spectacle would have known the preceding incidents. It must have felt like a cruel irony to Mordecai because the inevitable and deadly decree was still in effect. Perhaps, not knowing any of the precipitating events, he construed it as a scene of mockery in which he was forced to be the passive recipient.

5.2. Long Overdue Promotion. After Haman's death on the gallows the king gave Mordecai the signet ring that had been worn by Haman, and Queen Esther appointed him guardian over Haman's estate (Esther 8:2). He was attired in regal garments and a gold crown (Esther 8:15). Finally, he wielded significant power such that even those in high positions in the empire feared him (Esther 9:3-4).

5.3. Mordecai's Countermeasures.

5.3.1. The Original Decree. The specific wording of the original decree to annihilate the Jews is critical in order to understand what happened when Mordecai and Esther issued their counter-decree: "Official letters were sent by couriers to all the king's provinces to destroy, kill and annihilate all the Jews—young and old, little children and women—on one day, the thirteenth day of the twelfth month, the month of Adar, and to plunder their goods" (Esther 3:13).

5.3.2. The Decree of Mordecai. In the name of the king, Mordecai issued a decree. The king's edict granted the Jews in every city the right "to assemble and to stand for their lives; to destroy, kill and annihilate every armed force of any people or province attacking them, little children and women, and to plunder their property" (Esther 8:11). The syntax of the phrase "little children and women" is ambiguous and has often been interpreted as giving the Jews the right to destroy women and children. Nevertheless, in the prior decree the objects of "to destroy, kill, and annihilate" were "all the Jews, from young to old, little children and women." Here, "little children and women" immediately follow "those attacking them," suggesting that the Jews were given permission to kill those in every location who were still intent on carrying out the original decree by attacking them *and their families.* Because the direct focus of the Jewish self-defense was armed adversaries, it is illogical to think that Mordecai's government mandate was issued against the women and children of the enemies. A further direct quotation of the previous edict comes at the very end with the permission to take plunder. Given the fact that the following narrative is emphatic that the Jews did not take plunder even though permitted to do so, it seems that if there had been a legal allowance to slaughter women and children, some comment would have been made regarding that outcome as well. Instead, the casualty report is presented in terms of numbers of *men* killed (Esther 9:12, 15). In sum, Mordecai cited specific phrases from the previous decree to emphasize that this was specifically a countermeasure. Because of the irrevocability of these laws, the terms of the second edict had to reflect those of the first as protection for the Jews. Just as the relief is emphasized, so also is the fact that the Jews did not take any plunder from their enemies, even though they were permitted to do so by the measure-for-measure form of the decree.

5.4. Instituting the Festival of Purim with Esther. In Esther 9 the focus of the text moves from the narrative of deliverance to the means for perpet-

uating the memory of that tremendous occasion. Toward that end, Mordecai wrote more than once to establish, confirm and impose the observance of *Purim. The repetitious elements in this description and the general tangle of language come together in a remarkably apt form to convey the monumental effort needed to confirm the new festival.

5.5. Mordecai's Ongoing Political Presence. Mordecai was second to the king, a fact echoing Joseph's role, and he was a benefactor to the Jews, serving as an advocate and spokesperson in the government for the Jewish community (Esther 10:3). His prominent position set the stage for the historical roles of Ezra and Nehemiah. The text closes with "speaking *shalom* for all his descendants," a poignant reminder of the necessity for Jews throughout the succeeding centuries to have someone positioned to intercede for their well-being.

See also ESTHER 1: BOOK OF.

BIBLIOGRAPHY. **O. T. Allis,** "The Reward of the King's Favorite (Esther vi.8)," *PTR* 21 (1923) 621-32; **W. B. Barrick,** "The Meaning and Usage of RKB in Biblical Hebrew," *JBL* 101 (1982) 481-503; **D. J. A. Clines,** "In Quest of the Historical Mordecai," *VT* 41 (1991) 129-36; **A. D. Cohen,** "'Hu Ha-goral': The Religious Significance of Esther," *Judaism* 23 (1974) 87-94; **M. V. Fox,** *Character and Ideology in the Book of Esther* (2nd ed.; Grand Rapids: Eerdmans, 2001); **W. Horbury,** "The Name Mardochaeus in a Ptolemaic Inscription," *VT* 41 (1991) 220-26; **S. H. Horn,** "Mordecai, a Historical Problem," *BR* 9 (1964) 14-25; **F. B. Huey Jr.,** "Irony as the Key to Understanding the Book of Esther," *SJT* 32 (1990) 36-39; **T. S. Laniak,** *Shame and Honor in the Book of Esther* (SBLDS 165; Atlanta: Scholars Press, 1998); **J. D. Levenson,** *Esther* (OTL; Louisville: Westminster John Knox, 1997); **C. A. Moore,** "Archaeology and the Book of Esther," *BA* 38 (1975) 62-79; idem, ed., *Studies in the Book of Esther* (New York: KTAV, 1982); **L. B. Paton,** *A Critical and Exegetical Commentary on the Book of Esther* (ICC; New York: Scribner, 1908); **W. H. Shea,** "Esther and History," *ConJ* 13.3 (1987) 234-48; **M. Simon,** trans., *Esther and Song of Songs,* vol. 9 of *Midrash Rabbah* (London: Soncino, 1939); **F. S. Weiland,** "Literary Clues to God's Providence in the Book of Esther," *BSac* 160 (2003) 34-47; **J. M. Wiebe,** "Esther 4:14: 'Will Relief and Deliverance Arise for the Jews from Another Place?'" *CBQ* 53 (1991) 409-15; **E. Yamauchi,**

"Mordecai, the Persepolis Tablets, and the Susa Excavations," *VT* 42 (1992) 272-75.

E. Phillips

MOT. *See* CHAOS AND DEATH.

MOUNT ZION. *See* MOUNTAIN IMAGERY; ZION.

MOUNTAIN IMAGERY

Mountain imagery occurs with regularity in the poetry of the OT, frequently sharing mythic features familiar from the literature of the broader ancient Near Eastern world. Broadly speaking, we can group the imagery around the general cosmogonic and cosmic images associated with Yahweh's kingship and the specifically Israelite imagery of Mount Zion.

1. Hebrew Words
2. The Mountains and Yahweh's Kingship in Creation
3. Mount Zion

1. Hebrew Words.

The basic Hebrew word for "mountain" is *har*, a word of unknown derivation and without cognates in other Semitic languages. It is found some 550 times in the Hebrew Bible but does not occur in Ruth, Esther, Ezra or Ecclesiastes. A close synonym, *gibʿâ* ("hill"), is found in *parallelism with *har* (37 out of 59x; see Prov 8:25; Song 2:8; also esp. in Isaiah).

The Hebrew for "rock" (*ṣûr* [74x]) is cognate to the common word for "mountain" in Aramaic *(ûr).* "Rock" and "mountain" occur in parallel expression in Job 28:9-10. "Rock" and its synonym *selaʿ* (66x) also occur in parallelism. Yahweh is *ṣûr* and *selaʿ* for the godly (Ps 18:2 [MT 18:3]; 31:2-3 [MT 31:3-4]; 71:3).

"Field" (*śādeh* [333x]) is a cognate of the Akkadian word *šadû* ("mountain"). The fields of Moab (Ruth 1:2 [simply "Moab" in the NIV]) are better understood as the mountains—that is, the elevated plateau of Moab (see also Ps 132:6: "the fields of Jaar"). The words *mountain* and *field* are in parallel expression in Ps 50:11; 104:10-11. The "gazelles [does] of the field" (Song 2:7; 3:5) were likely living in mountainous areas (cf. Ps 104:18).

The word *gĕbûl* ("territory, border") is etymologically connected to the Arabic word for "mountain" *(jabal)* and occurs in parallelism with "mountain" in Ps 78:54. The overlap in meaning of *gĕbûl* with "mountain" may be occa-sioned by the international custom of marking political and tribal areas by mountains.

2. The Mountains and Yahweh's Kingship in Creation.

2.1. Mountains: Cosmogony, Cosmos, Chaos and Yahweh's Kingship.

2.1.1. Mountains and Cosmogony. The assumption of connections between mountains in Mesopotamian cosmogonies and the OT has given rise to several critical interpretations: a cosmic mountain as the center of the world and, related to this, the mountain as the navel of the world (Butterworth; Clifford; Talmon; Terrien). It is preferable to view the literary associations with mountains in the OT as mythopoeic, as Israel's poets employ standardized images. They all agree that Yahweh is absolutely independent of and prior to creation, and that mountains are contingent on him. Though not thinking in categories of *creatio ex nihilo,* one psalmist speaks of the birth of mountains (Ps 90:2) in relationship to Yahweh's eternality (cf. Ps 65:6).

2.1.2. Mountains and Yahweh's Kingship. By employing the language of myth, biblical authors invite readers to envision God's strength in creating the cosmos. They speak of a primeval chaos, but under Yahweh's control, that he shaped into a cosmos. The resulting order is reflective of his wisdom and kingship.

2.1.2.1. Yahweh's Wisdom. The cosmos reveals the wisdom of the Creator. In Proverbs 8 the sage envisions *Woman Wisdom as a witness to Yahweh's creative work, including the mountains (Prov 8:24-29). Rather than speculate on the age of the earth, Israel's poets celebrate the antiquity and stability of creation, as represented by the mountains and hills (Job 15:7; Ps 90:2; Prov 8:25). They write lyrically about the order of creation, revealing Yahweh's wisdom, righteousness, and justice (Ps 36:6). His creation (mountains and the deep [Ps 36:6]) reveals cosmic order that is characterized by righteousness and justice. Everything in creation reveals Yahweh's royal splendor and wisdom (Ps 104:24).

2.1.2.2. Yahweh's Kingship over Chaos. In mythopoeic imagery water opposes cosmos. Psalm 104 pictures the primeval chaos as the power of water over the mountains (Ps 104:6-10; cf. Ps 65:5-11). Yahweh's rebuke of the water forever changed its power. Instead of water being a destructive force, it is largely a beneficent force. It comes down in the form of precipitation on mountains, runs down, waters the earth, enables vegetative growth, and thereby it makes human and animal life possible (Ps 104:10-18).

Mountains provide refuge and provision. They form the framework of creation together with the ocean depths, over which Yahweh rules (Ps 95:4; 148:8-9). All creatures of the air, the land and the sea inhabit this space. They receive plentiful rains (Ps 104:13; cf. Ps 148:8) that permit an abundance of vegetation to cover the rocks (Ps 65:12; 72:16; 147:8). Trees provide shade on the mountains (Ps 80:10). Birds find refuge (Ps 11:1; cf. Ps 50:11), and game and small animals roam wild in the mountains (Job 39:5-8; 40:20; Ps 50:10-11; 76:4; 104:18; Song 4:8). Humans explore the mountains in search of precious metals and stones (Job 28).

Psalm 104 closes with a prayer that the Creator God will restore order into this world that has again turned into chaos by the wicked (Ps 104:35). At his coming to judge the wicked the mountains will quake and smoke (Ps 104:32). The opening and closure of the psalm link the world of creation (cosmos) with the world as redemption (a new creation), as the psalmist inspires the godly with the hope that in the end Yahweh's subjugation of the wicked will be like the subjugation of the water in the beginning.

2.1.3. Mountains: Coexistence of Cosmos and Chaos. The ambivalence connected with mountains maintains the tension between creation and redemption. On the one hand, mountains evoke an image of primeval order, the garden of Eden. It is in this idealized setting that we find the two lovers in *Song of Songs (Longman). The lover is likened to a gazelle coming from the mountains (Song 2:8-9, 17; 8:14) but also to a dove hiding in the mountains (Song 2:14). The beloved too is imagined as living in the mountains (Song 4:8). The mountains are laden with spices and smells (Song 4:6; 8:14).

On the other hand, mountains are also associated with danger (chaos). The destructive force of mountain fires endangers the habitat of animals (Ps 83:14; cf. Ps 144:5). Mountains also erode over a long period of time. The stalwart *Job likens his troubles to the erosion of mountains into grit (Job 14:18-20). His orderly life has turned into chaos.

The quaking of mountains is an evocative image of the Day of the Lord (Ps 18:7; 104:32; 144:5). Mountains representative of the stability of creation serve as an image of the great power

of God over against the chaotic forces on earth. In the images associated with *theophany the poets speak of the disestablishment of creation at Yahweh's coming. When he turns against the cosmos in judgment and wrath, mountains are leveled to plains (Job 9:5-7) or melt away like wax (Ps 97:5).

The quaking of the mountains as part of the theophanic imagery may signify redemption. The poet of Psalm 114 imagines the mountains, together with the waters of the sea and the Jordan, as thrown in convulsion at Yahweh's deliverance of Israel from Egypt (Ps 114:1-4).

2.1.4. Mountains and the Renewal of the Cosmos. The majesty of the mountains, covered with luxuriant vegetation, serves as an image of redemption in Psalm 80:7-11. Yahweh has made this world to be a cosmos, maintains it, and guarantees that it is a blessed and safe place for his creatures (Ps 72:3). Yet, this world is in need of redemption. The cosmos is continually at risk because of evil. Israel's poets realistically portray the chaotic forces in the world. Psalm 46 envisions a city surrounded by pounding waves that reduce the mighty mountains to mere objects that slide into the sea (Ps 46:2-3). The psalmist encourages the godly not to fear, for even though the mountains may disappear, the city of the Lord will not succumb to these forces (Ps 46:4-5).

Psalm 72 celebrates a world at peace under the agency of the messianic agent. The mountains and hills in such a world are symbols of peace and righteousness (Ps 72:3). The chaotic forces of the present world structures are seen as being transformed into conformity to God's will, expressive of his kingdom on earth. Then everything (people and mountains) praises him (Ps 98:8; 148:7-10; cf. Ps 144:9). The harmonious functioning of the cosmos may be likened to a restoration to the primeval bliss of the garden of Eden.

2.2. Yahweh as the Rock. The metaphor of Yahweh as the Rock is a rich image of redemption. As Yahweh provided water for his people from a rock in the wilderness for Israel (Ps 78:15-16; 105:41; 114:8), so he continues to be the Rock for all who call on him in faith. The image of Yahweh as the Rock is as rich as the many words connected with it: "Yahweh is my rock [selaʿ], my mountain fortress [mĕṣûdâ] and my deliverer; my God is my rock [ṣûr], in whom I find refuge. He is my shield and the horn of my salvation, my high place of refuge *[miśgāb]*" (Ps 18:2; cf. Ps 9:9; 31:2).

The Rock of Israel is both the hope of *David (Ps 18:2, 31; 19:14; 27:5; 28:1; 31:2-3; 62:2, 6, 7; 89:26; 144:1-2 [messianic agents]) and of all the godly (Ps 78:35; 92:15; 94:22; 95:1; cf. Ps 37:39; 43:2).

3. Mount Zion.

3.1. Mount Zion as a Microcosm.

3.1.1. Cosmos. Yahweh's rule over creation finds its particular focus in Mount Zion (Ps 76:2). It is Yahweh's holy mountain and also his city (Ps 48:1). The dual images of mountain and city figure prominently in the language of *Zion in the Psalter. Zion is a peaceful place where God's people find rest and shelter (Ps 46:4-5, 11). It is a beautiful and joyful place (Ps 48:2). Located on the highest mountain (Ps 48:2; 78:69), it is an image of security and victory. The language of Zion has mythopoeic allusions to Baal's victory over Yam and to his exaltation on Mount Zaphon. The choice of Zion over against Sinai or Bashan spatially defines Yahweh's kingship on earth and symbolically marks his presence (*see* Divine Presence) with his people (Ps 68). It also is a mark of his love for his people (Ps 87:1-2; cf. Ps 78:68).

3.1.2. Cosmos and Chaos. In a Zion psalm the psalmist likens Zion to a city of peace (cosmos) surrounded by forces of water (Ps 46:3) or chaos. As a microcosm, Mount Zion reflects a world of order in a world of opposing forces, and the godly find refuge in Zion. In many psalms the lamenters turn to Mount Zion in prayer, awaiting Yahweh's response and redress (Ps 3:4).

3.2. The Holiness of Mount Zion.
The mountain of the Lord is holy (Ps 43:3; 48:1; 87:1; 99:9). The mountain image signifies Yahweh's exclusion, exaltation and otherness, but it also marks his inclusion and embrace of people who conform to his expectations (Pss 15; 24). Mount Zion is truly a microcosm of the cosmos, as it represents a world of God's presence and order (Levenson).

3.3. Mount Zion and the Messianic Agency.
Hope in the efficacy of the messianic agent is a concrete expression of Yahweh's kingdom (Ps 2:6). Psalm 72 opens up the grand expectation that the messianic agent will bring peace and righteousness in the mountains and hills (Ps 72:3). He too is engaged in the removal of chaos with the hope of a righteous cosmos.

3.4. Mount Zion as a Symbol.
3.4.1. The Location of Zion. The city of Jerusalem (Mount Zion) was a localized symbol of Yahweh's kingdom. It is symbolic of the presence of the Great King. But the structures of Jerusalem, the temple, and the Davidic dynasty are contingent on the reality of Yahweh's presence. In the book of *Lamentations the poet reflects on Yahweh's angry abandonment of Mount Zion (Lam 2:2, 5). It has become a wasteland, a haunt of jackals (Lam 5:18).

3.4.2. The Universality of Zion. The poets and prophets transform the image of Zion beyond the local expressions to a symbolic expression. Zion is a symbol of the reality of Yahweh's rule, however or wherever his kingship is manifest on earth. Yahweh's gracious sustenance of all of life, especially the godly, and his judgment of the wicked are manifest expressions of his kingship (Pss 146—149; cf. Lam 5:19). As such, Mount Zion is a universal symbol. Wherever and however the reality of Yahweh's presence and kingship are evident, Mount Zion as the city of God is real. It is the mother city of all the people of God, whether Jews or Gentiles (Ps 87:4; cf. Gal 4:26; Heb 12:22-25).

See also Creation Imagery; Imagery; Kingship Psalms; Psalms 6: Iconography; Zion.

Bibliography. **E. A. S. Butterworth,** *The Tree at the Navel of the Earth* (Berlin: de Gruyter, 1970); **R. J. Clifford,** *The Cosmic Mountain in Canaan and the Old Testament* (HSM 4; Cambridge, MA: Harvard University Press, 1972); **J. D. Levenson,** *Creation and the Persistence of Evil: The Jewish Drama of Divine Omnipotence* (Princeton, NJ: Princeton University Press, 1994); **T. Longman III,** *The Song of Songs* (NICOT; Grand Rapids: Eerdmans, 2001); **M. Selman,** "הַר," *NIDOTTE* 1:1051-55; **S. Talmon,** "הַר," *TDOT* 3:42-47; **S. Terrien,** "The Omphalos Myth and Hebrew Religion," *VT* 20 (1970) 315-38.

W. A. VanGemeren

MUSIC, SONG

Music is the patterned use of sound-producing tools in a relevant cultural context (Braun, *OEANE* 4.70), and singing is the musical use of voice. The Bible frequently refers to music and song in the context of its grand narration of God's redemption, but nowhere does it consciously consider the nature or fitting uses of music. The ubiquity of music in modern times and its high level of development can lead to unwarranted assumptions about music in the biblical period. It is therefore wise to keep in mind one's chronological, social and religious distance from the biblical world.

From antiquity, music has been a part of everyday life, particularly at occasions of birth, celebration, battle and mourning. But in the wisdom and poetic books of the OT most of the references to music and song are in the context of prayer, lament, thanks and praise (*see* Lament, Psalms of; Thanksgiving, Psalms of). According to J. Begbie (*DTIB*, 522), about three-fourths of the musical references in the OT are to song, probably because of associations of musical instruments with surrounding pagan cultures as well as the strong emphasis placed by God's covenant people on the word. The present article considers the nature of sources for studying biblical music and then focuses on music and singing in *Psalms and *Song of Songs. It concludes with some thoughts intended to foster appreciation of the inherent benefits of construing portions of the Bible as music.

1. Sources of Information
2. Music and the Psalter
3. Music and Song of Songs
4. Suggestions for Further Consideration

1. Sources of Information.
Studies of music and song in the OT have tended to draw almost exclusively from textual references in the Bible itself. These data are significant, especially when considered in light of their highly developed literary contexts. Given that the OT developed as part of a wider world of literature and culture, research on this topic must be broadened. To this aim, J. Braun (2002) crafted his study of music in ancient Israel to include the non-Israelite cultures of Palestine. Furthermore, Braun (2002, 5) redirected his focus of research from textual to archaeological evidence that he considered primary. This expansion of research helps not only to identify many of the musical instruments mentioned in the Bible but also to illuminate the technical, social and religious or symbolic dimensions of music. This section thus provides the broad context for the following treatment of music and song in Psalms and Song of Songs.

1.1. Textual Evidence. As a collection of documents developed and preserved by living communities, the Bible contains texts that were finalized long after the events that they depict

actually took place. The books of Chronicles, for instance, employed descriptions of First Temple music and Levitical personnel as established by *David to encourage the postexilic community to carry on that heritage. The study of choral music in these books by J. W. Kleinig pays close attention to the Chronicler's literary use of earlier traditions in this new postexilic setting. This is also the period in which the Psalter took final shape, so it is appropriate to study how earlier psalms have been organized and incorporated into the final five-book structure that now exists. The judgment about whether or not David and *Solomon actually achieved the level of musical or liturgical sophistication described in Chronicles is linked in part to one's views about authorial creativity and textual development, but it is unlikely that the Chronicler could have successfully fashioned a literary memory of the past without some basis in reality. It is therefore important that all textual evidence from the Bible be considered in light of the best practices of biblical exegesis. In general, this means that texts must be read within their own literary contexts with attention to semantics, flow of thought, and genre. Texts should also be understood in relation to the wider historical, religious, geographical and social realities of the ancient world and the specific situation in life from which these texts arose. In particular, the musical terminology of the Bible reflects the function of music in ancient societies. Where this is forgotten, the spiritual affinity that some modern readers have with the devotional thrust of the Psalter may have quite little to do with the musical life of these songs in ancient Israelite liturgical practice. To be helpful, contemporary applications and lessons drawn from the Psalter must relate to our own times, but not at the expense of being mindful of the former situations in which believers used these texts to express meaning and significance.

Outside the Bible, literary sources are sparse, but occasionally helpful in the identification of some instruments such as redefining the *kinnôr* as a type of lyre with very wide range of uses. From the city of Ugarit around 1400 BC comes a Hurrian cult song with text and some indications of musical performance. Philo, Josephus, the Mishnah, plus the Babylonian and Jerusalem Talmuds and other rabbinic literature also shed light on the topic, but their relatively late date must be taken into account. Though chronologically closer to the biblical world, ancient translations of the Bible such as the LXX, Peshitta and Vulgate often provide less illumination than expected. Many of the biblical terms for music were technical and had already fallen out of use even in the Second Temple period, so LXX translators had to make educated guesses when handling some terms (such as the Gk *diapsalma* for the Heb *selā* in Ps 3:2 and elsewhere). Sometimes they could do no better than simply transliterate (rendering the Heb *māḥălat* in Ps 53:1 as *maeleth*).

The NT and writings of the church fathers provide Christian perspectives. Aside from the christological and eschatological importance of the Psalter in the NT, this evidence supports the claim that the psalms were not merely poems to be read and interpreted but rather were songs to be sung in corporate *worship (Eph 5:19). It is generally held that except for the *šôpār* (a goat or ram's horn), Levitical instrumental worship music was absent from the synagogue after the destruction of the Second Temple in AD 70. This may be the main reason why the NT does not mention instruments in the context of worship, though it should be noted that it does not prohibit or criticize such use (Begbie *DTIB*, 523). Many music historians hold that the reason for the paucity of examples of Roman music is its destruction by the early church. Regarding Greek music, merely remnants can be deduced from documents detailing the development of music theory by Pythagoras and continued by Boethius. This material would have been difficult to eradicate because of its inclusion in the larger philosophical systems of thought. For example, it was part of the Quadrivium (Acoustics).

The practice of musically intoning the text of the Bible is ancient. The system of accents found in the MT was codified in writing around the middle of the first millennium AD. But E. J. Revell has found evidence in the LXX of an early pre-Christian accent system. This setting of the Bible to chant, though somewhat musical, was not a mere aesthetic ornament; it helped to fix the interpretation of the text by punctuating it into syntactic units. For example, Rabbi Akiba (c. AD 50-135) believed that chanting the text aided in its interpretation. He thus taught that the study of the *law was equivalent to singing (*b. Sanh.* 99a).

1.2. Archaeological and Iconographic Evidence.
Because the Bible does not adequately describe the instruments that it mentions or the music that they made, archaeological evidence is essential. For example, the traditional identification of the *nēbel* as a harp is probably wrong because the harp is unattested in the biblical period; the instrument probably is a lyre (Braun 2002, 22-24). With few exceptions, the actual sounds of ancient instruments cannot be reproduced. Archaeological evidence of musical instruments themselves is strongest for durable items such as cymbals, bells and objects made from pottery or bone, such as rattles, flutes and conch trumpets. Wood, strings and membranes are more prone to decay.

Iconographic evidence of music comes from metal and terracotta figurines, rock etchings, drawings on pottery, ivory tablets, alabaster reliefs, murals, seals, coins and mosaic floors.

2. Music and the Psalter.
In their current form, psalms are typically understood as Scriptures to be read and sometimes prayed rather than as songs to be sung. Following S. Mowinckel, scholars generally now agree that most of the psalms first came to life in the context of public liturgical worship at the temple. Private or familial singing certainly took place (cf. the use of Psalms 113—118 [the Hallel] at Passover), but the musical use of the psalms was adopted from their role in the temple service itself (Mowinckel, 2.88; *see* Psalms 3: History of Interpretation). The destruction of the temple in AD 70 put an end to this liturgical use and effectively silenced the Psalter, which now is studied mostly for its theological contribution. The task of appreciating the connection between music and the Psalter raises two fundamental questions. First, how do we know that the psalms were music? Second, what difference does this make?

2.1. The Musical Nature of the Psalter.
2.1.1. Superscriptions. At least ninety-five of the 116 superscriptions mention musical terms (*see* Psalms 5: Titles). The word *mizmôr* ("psalm") in superscriptions is extremely common (57x). It is related to the verb *zmr*, which basically means "play an instrument" or "sing a song according to musical accompaniment" and thus refers to a musical piece (Allen, 116). The word *šîr* ("song") appears to be more specific, referring to a vocal composition. Each of Psalms 120—134 bears the heading *šîr hammaʿălôt* ("song of ascents"), and they probably were used in the context of pilgrimages to the temple. The Psalter includes

other types of compositions, but since the meaning of these words is uncertain, they usually are not translated but rather are simply transliterated as *maskil, miktam, shiggaion*. We do not know if they are musical, though it appears that, in light of Nehemiah 12:46, the word *tĕhillâ* in Psalm 145:1 means "song of praise."

Some psalms have technical indications about their performance, perhaps tunes to which they were to be sung, though as far back as the LXX their meanings were in doubt. The Hebrew prepositions *ʿal, bĕ* and *ʾel* preface these terms and in these contexts probably refer to how the psalm was to be performed in the sense of "according to" or "with." For example, *ʿal-ʾayyelet haššaḥar* in Psalm 22:1 would mean "according to the doe of the dawn," and *ʿal-yônat ʾēlem rĕḥōqîm* in Psalm 56:1 would mean "according to the dove of the distant terebinth trees." Immediately following the initial word *lamnaṣṣēaḥ* ("to the director") in Psalms 57:1; 58:1; 59:1; 75:1 there is simply *ʾal-tašḥēt*, which means "do not destroy." It is very likely that most of these kinds of expressions in psalm headings are musical, but available data do not equip scholars to be conclusive in every instance.

For the following items, the summary of options by Braun (2002, 39-41) is well informed. The expression *ʿal-ʿălāmôt* (Ps 46:1) is variously understood as the high soprano tuning of an instrument, a reference to a female musician, or perhaps some connection to the octave or eighth tone. The expression *ʿal-haggittît* (Ps 8:1; 81:1; 84:1) could be an instrument or style of music from the city of Gath or some reference to a song related to the practice of pressing wine grapes. The phrase *ʿal-māḥălat* (Ps 53:1; 88:1) probably is a musical reference to dance (*maḥôl*), some kind of pipe or wind instrument (from the root *ḥll*), or some indication that the psalm should be performed in a quiet or depressed manner. The expressions *binginôt* and *ʿal-nĕgînat* derive from the root *ngn*, which has to do with the playing of instruments, but there is insufficient evidence to be more specific (see Ps 4:1; 6:1; 54:1; 55:1; 61:1; 67:1; 76:1). The heading of Psalm 5 contains *ʾel-hannĕḥîlôt*, which modern translations tend to understand as a reference to flutes, although the LXX, Vulgate and other early versions did not treat it as a musical term at all. In Psalm 6:1; 12:1 we see *ʿal-haššĕmînît*, which is related to the number "eight." Although it may refer to an eight-

stringed instrument, the fact that the heptatonic scale was commonly known in Ugarit strengthens the claim that it has to do with octaves. A few psalms have forms of the word *šûšan* ("lily") in their headings (Ps 45:1; 60:1; 69:1; 80:1). Even though early versions do not take these as musical indications, most today read them as references to lyrics of some kind.

The word *lamnaṣṣēaḥ* is common in psalm superscriptions (55x [also in Hab 3:19]). The verb *nṣḥ* has to do with supervision, and most modern translations understand *lamnaṣṣēaḥ* to function as a dedication of the psalm to a musical director or perhaps choirmaster. This certainly is possible, though in light of the LXX and Vulgate, Braun (2002, 38) maintains that it does not possess any particular musical meaning. Since the word appears at the end of the lone psalm in Habakkuk 3 rather than at its heading, the suggestion by B. K. Waltke that it was originally a colophon at the end of one psalm that eventually became appended to the beginning of the ensuing psalm is attractive. If this were so, the number of psalms for the director would remain the same, but the identity of most of them would change. For example, Psalm 3 would be reclassified as a *lamnaṣṣēaḥ* psalm.

The Bible contains about twenty words for musical instruments, most of them appearing in the book of Psalms. Archaeological and iconographic evidence has greatly helped to clarify their identification, though questions remain. They may be classified according to the sounds that they produced as idiophones (bells, cymbals, rattles), membranophones (drums, tambourines), chordophones (strings) and aerophones (pipes, trumpets, horns).

Finally, twenty-four psalm superscriptions make reference to temple singers: *Asaph, the sons of Korah, Heman, Ethan and Jeduthun. David's installation of these Levitical musicians and their role in the Solomonic temple (according to many references in 1-2 Chronicles) supports the claim that these particular psalms were publicly sung, as were most of the psalms.

2.1.2. Content of the Psalms. The book of Psalms is replete with references to the temple and its courts. This testifies to the use of psalms in that setting which was full of music. Psalm 68 is a prime example. Not only is it dedicated to the director of music and classified as a "psalm" and "song," but also it exhorts the righteous and the earth's kingdoms to rejoice with singing (Ps

68:3-4, 32). Psalm 68:24-27 describes a procession with music and song into the temple sanctuary itself.

In addition to frequent commands to sing, shout and play music, there are indications that the psalms called for vocal responses from worshipers. The expression *halĕlû-yāh* ("praise Yah") is more than a interjection with semantic value; it has a performative liturgical function whereby worshipers signaled their participation and approval. It would have been a fitting response to the singing of psalms. Psalm 136 is antiphonal in that it punctuates each line with "His love endures forever!" Psalm 129, a song *(šîr)* of ascents, uses the phrase "let Israel say" to call for the covenant community to participate in the liturgy, and Psalm 24 (a *mizmôr*) seems to describe a gathering at the temple when the people sing an answer the question "Who is this king of glory?" with affirmations of the Lord as a mighty and victorious warrior.

2.2. The Musical Significance of the Psalter.

The dynamic of the Psalter is its movement between the two poles of revelation and response. This is clearly evident in Psalm 136, which praises God for who he is (Ps 136:1-3), followed by his works in creation (Ps 136:4-9) and redemption (Ps 136:10-24). The worshiper's response is a series of refrains in every verse that thoroughly saturate the psalm. This dynamic comes to musical expression when the psalmist claims that his song is from the Lord himself (Ps 40:3) and thus is offered back God as something even more pleasing than the sacrificial offering of animals (Ps 69:30-31). The musical ministry of the Levites appointed by David is described as prophetic and thus of divine impetus (1 Chron 25:1-8). Even in lament the psalmist can identify his own prayer as God's "song" that is with him through the night (Ps 42:8; cf. Job 35:10). Even the Lord's statutes become the psalmist's "song" (Ps 119:54). According to J. H. Eaton (104), "Music is from the Lord and for the Lord."

The music of the Psalter is not simply an aesthetic adornment; it is participation in the ongoing musical praise in the universe. The psalms describe this praise in the widest possible terms. Not only are Israel and the nations called to praise God (Ps 99:1-5), but also heavenly beings (the "sons of God" and "angels") take part (Ps 29:1; 103:20; 148:2; cf. Job 38:7). Most striking, however, is the praise that arises from creation itself. The phrase "the heavens declare the glory of God" (Ps 19:1) could be taken as a metonymy for the inhabitants of the heavens were it not for the poetic parallel line that adds specificity: "the sky [*rāqîaʿ*, lit., 'firmament'] proclaims the works of his hand" but without words (Ps 19:4). In Psalm 57:8 the psalmist says that he will use stringed instruments to awaken the dawn, presumably so that it too may join him in praise. In Psalm 65:12-13 the pastures, hills, meadows and valleys sing praises to God because he has lavishly blessed them with rain and abundance. The seas, world, rivers and hills join with God's people in a psalm that calls for praise to the Lord with singing and musical instruments in a "new song" (Ps 98:1), which probably is a technical term for a victory song (Longman and Reid, 45). The crescendo of this universal symphony rises from Psalm 148, which calls on practically every conceivable member of creation to praise the Lord: not only people of all ages and status but also angelic beings, celestial bodies, both wild and domestic animals that move on land and in the sea and air, trees of the field and forest, plus the inanimate elements of nature, lightning, hail, snow, clouds and fierce wind. The lyrical music of the Psalter is thus not only a fitting way for the faithful to respond to the Lord's creative and redemptive acts but also an integrated part of the perpetual *hymn of praise generated from the entirety of heaven and earth.

3. Music and Song of Songs.

Apart from the book's title, there is no explicit connection between Song of Songs and actual music in ancient Israel. Unlike the psalms, here there are no musical or liturgical notations. The book never mentions any musical instruments, nor does it suggest any particular social setting for its performance. The phrase "season of singing" (Song 2:12) is the only reference to music within the book, and it yields no knowledge of whether or not Song of Songs itself was ever performed, let alone by whom or for what reasons. The book is clearly poetic and presents dialogue between two (or possibly three) persons as well as refrains from a group, which interpreters sometimes refer to as a "chorus."

The history of interpretation of Song of Songs shows extreme variety but with a clear interest in the meanings of the poems themselves rather than the book's social location or function as a musical song. For example, Rabbi Akiba (c. AD 50-135) strongly rejected the singing of this text with literal reference to its sexuality. He preferred to construe the book in terms of God's loving relationship to Israel. In early Christian interpretation Origen (AD 185-253/54) understood the book as a wedding song in dramatic form but was far more interested in its allegorical, "spiritual meaning." To call Song of Songs a drama, however, is not to equate it with performance in the theater. The text has been performed as an oratorio in modern times, but this says nothing of its ancient genre. Its classification as a cantata or operetta is not only highly questionable on literary grounds but also is anachronistic. Some of the poems are similar to songs sung at Arab weddings (*see* Wasf), but the lasting insight from this observation is that most likely the primary sense of Song of Songs has to do with human love. The poems have been compared with the "sacred marriage" texts of Mesopotamia, but of all the lyrical literature of the ancient Near East, Song of Songs bears greatest similarity to love songs from Ramesside Egypt (1305-1150 BC). The strength of this connection makes it probable that the book is a structured anthology of love songs that were originally performed in nonreligious settings as musical entertainment.

The eventual canonical status of the book testifies to its great theological value. In summary, regardless of how and on what occasions Song of Songs may have been sung in antiquity, the book lyrically celebrates the nature and physical expression of romantic love between a man and a woman who are together made in the image of God, the ultimate focus of true praise.

4. Suggestions for Further Consideration.
We can read and interpret the musical texts of the Bible, understanding them as best we can within their literary and cultural contexts, but there is a dimension of music that is more evident in personal experience than description. Certainly, we must be careful to avoid projecting our modern knowledge of music and the social settings in which it occurs back into the biblical world, but we must also eschew a minimalist approach that entertains only what can be affirmed. By its nature, music is creative and depends on imagination in order to thrive. The present article therefore concludes with some thoughts about music and song in relation to composers, performers and audiences. They are offered not as verified conclusions but rather as suggestions for further consideration.

Music itself is a type of language. The practice of pairing the mood, style and other characteristics of music to lyrics is known as "text painting." Composers tend to do this, whether formally or informally. We cannot know for certain how or by what principles biblical composers set their worship texts to music, but we do know that their subject was lofty and worthy of their best efforts, and praise of God's nature and redemptive acts on their behalf gave ultimate meaning to their existence as God's covenant people. Whether in the roles of composers or performers, accomplished musicians do not slavishly receive or repeat a tradition. They participate and contribute with skill, energy and imagination. Perhaps in their own human way, biblical musicians sought to tap into ever-running hymns of praise, offered to God in the heavenly court or even by nature itself.

Music is often noted for its emotional affect, but the use of music in praise also tends to focus attention away from oneself to the nature and acts of God, thus functioning to transport one's thoughts to another realm. The act of singing lends artistic expression to truth and thus has a cognitive function that promotes personal appreciation, approval, assent and adoration. Music activates the powers of memory and thus endures not only through the day and night but also into times of crisis and trial as well as celebration and thanksgiving. Texts set to music often come to life when they are needed most, seemingly pressed into service by life's circumstances.

Music is a vehicle that unites elements within a person, simultaneously activating the eye, ear, body, breath and voice in addition to the verbal aspects of memory and language. The performance of music by groups, either instrumentally or in choral style, affirms the members' essential contributions, connectedness and interdependence. Musicians and singers understand that their musical achievement is synergistic and thus far greater than the sum of its parts.

Those who listen to the music and songs of others may participate mentally through concurrence and perhaps even materially through patronage. Thus they may align themselves with the affirmations of the texts and personal values of the performers, especially when these are deeply held and shared beliefs about God, human nature and the world. Members of an audience may include persons who themselves were once musicians or singers who by choice or necessity no longer perform with a group. Hearing familiar or otherwise classic compositions can have powerful effects on one's sense of memory, relation to God, and cohesion to family and other social networks. Listening to music can be both therapeutic and edifying.

The acts of composition, singing and playing musical instruments are more demanding of time and resources than plain writing and reading. They are highly appropriate expressions of divine service that by proper definition encompasses one's whole being—in short, loving God with the full strength of one's very heart and soul.

See also CULT, WORSHIP: PSALMS; FORM CRITICISM; LYRIC POETRY; ORAL POETRY; PSALMS 5: TITLES; REFRAIN; SOUND PATTERNS.

BIBLIOGRAPHY. **L. C. Allen,** "זמר," *NIDOTTE* 1.1116-17; **J. Begbie,** "Music, the Bible and," *DTIB* 521-24; idem, *Theology, Music and Time* (Cambridge Studies in Christian Doctrine; Cambridge: Cambridge University Press, 2000); **J. Braun,** *Music in Ancient Israel/Palestine: Archaeological, Written, and Comparative Sources* (BIW; Grand Rapids: Eerdmans, 2002); idem, "Musical Instruments," *OEANE* 4.70-79; **J. H. Eaton,** "Music's Place in Worship: A Contribution from the Psalms," in *Prophets, Worship and Theodicy: Studies in Prophetism, Biblical Theology, and Structural and Rhetorical Analysis, and on the Place of Music in Worship; Papers Read at the Joint British-Dutch Old Testament Conference Held at Woudschoten, 1982,* ed. A. S. Van der Woude (OtSt 23; Leiden: E. J. Brill, 1984) 85-107; **M. V. Fox,** *The Song of Songs and the Ancient Egyptian Love Songs* (Madison: University of Wisconsin Press, 1985); **T. Longman III,** *Song of Songs* (NICOT; Grand Rapids: Eerdmans, 2001); **T. Longman III and D. Reid,** *God Is a Warrior* (SOTBT; Grand Rapids: Zondervan, 1995); **J. W. Kleinig,** *The Lord's Song: The Basis, Function and Significance of Choral Music in Chronicles* (JSOTSup 156; Sheffield: JSOT Press, 1993); **S. Mowinckel,** *The Psalms in Israel's Worship,* trans. D. R. Ap-Thomas (2 vols.; New York: Abingdon, 1962); **E. J. Revell,** "The Oldest Evidence for the Hebrew Accent System," *BJRL* 54 (1971-1972) 214-22; **B. K. Waltke,** "Superscripts, Postscripts, or Both," *JBL* 110 (1991) 583-96; **G. H. Wilson,** *Psalms,* vol. 1 (NIVAC; Grand Rapids: Zondervan, 2002). R. C. Stallman

N

NAOMI

Naomi is one of three major characters in the book of *Ruth. She was the wife of Elimelech, mother of Mahlon and Chilion, mother-in-law of Ruth and Orpah, and grandmother of Obed. According to the genealogy of Ruth 4:18-22, Naomi was the great-great-grandmother of *David. She is mentioned only in the book of Ruth.

Naomi's name is derived from the Hebrew verb *nāʿēm*, which means "to be pleasant." The meaning of her name contrasts with Naomi's state of mind at the end of Ruth 1. After the death of her husband and sons in Moab, Naomi returned to Bethlehem and asked to be called *mārāʾ*, which means "bitter." The book of Ruth, though, always refers to her as Naomi.

1. Naomi's Context
2. Naomi's Emptiness
3. Naomi's Scheme
4. Naomi's Fullness

1. Naomi's Context.

The book of Ruth opens with a reference to the days when the judges ruled. The judges followed the events of the conquest as narrated in the book of Joshua and preceded the rise of monarchy in Israel as described in the books of Samuel. The recollection in Ruth 1:1 of the people and events described in the book of Judges sets Naomi in a time of apostasy, injustice and tumult.

Ruth 1:1 additionally says that there was a famine in Israel. Elimelech and Naomi left Bethlehem, which means "house of bread" in Hebrew, and moved to Moab, which had refused to offer bread to the Israelites during the wilderness years (Deut 23:4). What Elimelech's move to Moab signaled about his relationship with Yahweh and the gods of Moab is uncertain.

The meaning of Elimelech's name ("My God is king") stands out in the period of the judges, when there was no king and just about everyone (perhaps even Elimelech) ignored the commands of the divine king (Judg 21:25).

2. Naomi's Emptiness.

Modern readers of Ruth cannot know for sure if Naomi approved of the move to Moab or of her sons' marriages to Moabite women. The Pentateuch warns generally against intermarriage with Gentiles because of the threat of syncretism (e.g., Deut 7) and specifically against friendship with Moab because of its earlier antagonism toward the tribes (Num 22:1-6; 25:1; Deut 23:3-6). The text does not say if Naomi went with her husband reluctantly or favored the move and the marriages. It merely reports that Elimelech, Mahlon and Chilion died in Moab. The reader can infer that Naomi was devastated on several fronts (see Rauber, 29). She grieved the loss of her husband and children. She had no male protector or provider in a male-dominated world. She was an alien in Moab. These circumstances influenced her to respond in an ambiguous way.

On the one hand, Naomi prayed for Yahweh's kindness upon Orpah and Ruth (Ruth 1:8), but such a prayer may have been more formulaic and polite in contexts of departure (Sakenfeld, 24). As far as Naomi could tell, there was nothing more that she could do to secure their present and future. The text does not indicate if she ever considered the possibility of levirate marriage for herself, Orpah, and/or Ruth with *Boaz or the nearer kinsman (see Kinsman-Redeemer and Levirate). What the text explicitly conveys is that Naomi felt unable to repay the kindness of her daughters-in-law and so bade Yahweh's favor upon them (Hubbard, 103).

On the other hand, Naomi wanted to send her daughters-in-law away because she thought that the hand of God was against her, and that they would experience disfavor because of their association with a spiritual pariah. She acknowledged their kindness (ḥesed) to her (Ruth 1:8-9) but said nothing of Yahweh's kindness to her (Freedman, 29; Trible, 169). In fact, upon returning to Bethlehem, Naomi alleged that God Almighty had made her life bitter and empty. God supposedly had brought misfortune (lit., "done evil" [Ruth 1:21]) upon her and witnessed against her through the loss of her loved ones. Even more troubling is her instruction to Ruth to return with Orpah to her people and her gods (Block, 639). This piece of maternal advice does not fit well with the earlier blessing in Yahweh's name, and it is unthinkable that a daughter of Abraham would discourage willing Gentiles from being exposed to the means of grace in the covenant community. Naomi's theology may have become eclectic in Moab or perhaps, in the theologically aberrant climate of the judges period, was never well informed.

It is evident that Naomi's circumstances (her grief and predicament) influenced her to develop a hardened view of divine sovereignty (Grant, 432-33). Although the text does not say that God was angry with Naomi or that the famine and deaths were forms of judgment (Freedman, 35; Hubbard, 127), Naomi measured God's goodness by what was happening to her and by how many of her desires were met. Consequently, she did not view her situation as an opportunity to minister to her Gentile daughters-in-law. Ruth 1 also never says that Naomi prayed; instead, she resorted to conventional wisdom and tried to impose it on Orpah and Ruth.

Naomi's situation was not as empty as she thought. Ruth 1:6 says that Yahweh visited his people to provide food, and Ruth 1:22 mentions Naomi's return during the barley harvest. Of course, Ruth's commitment to her eventually brought fullness in the form of gleanings and an heir.

3. Naomi's Scheme.

At the end of Ruth 1 Naomi had no hope for the future and seemingly considered Ruth an inconsequential part of her life. Yahweh allegedly had brought her back empty. By the end of Ruth 2 Naomi had plenty of food for the short term because of Ruth's industriousness and Boaz's generosity. More significantly, Naomi's attitude began to change as she considered the more permanent help that might come from Boaz's interest in Ruth (Ruth 2:19-20).

Still, as many as seven months elapsed between the initial encounter of Ruth and Boaz in Ruth 2 and the meeting on the threshing floor in Ruth 3 (Block, 677). The meeting was Naomi's idea, and she should receive credit for wanting to find a husband for Ruth. Her scheme, though, was fraught with potential disaster.

Naomi told Ruth to bathe, dress, and go to the threshing floor where Boaz was spending the night winnowing his grain. Approaching Boaz on the threshing floor was not a prudent idea. Naomi put Ruth in real danger (Block, 687; LaCocque, 83). Because threshing floors lay outside the town, Ruth could have been abducted on the way and never reached Boaz. Boaz could have taken offense at Ruth's forwardness and refused to have anything more to do with her. Though a man of standing in the community, he could have taken advantage of Ruth and, if necessary, lied about what happened. It seems unlikely that anyone would have believed Ruth's side of the story or even that Naomi would have publicly defended her Moabite daughter-in-law. There was simply no guarantee that Boaz would respond favorably or honorably. Also, someone could have awakened and seen Ruth at Boaz's feet. In the unsavory days of the judges, prostitutes would offer their services at such places (cf. Hos 9:1). Naomi did no one any favor that night. She put both Ruth and Boaz at risk of yielding to temptation or being unjustly accused.

Nevertheless, the providence of God working through the faithfulness of Ruth and Boaz in an awkward setting produced a favorable outcome for the meeting (see Hubbard, 69-70, 195-96). After Ruth 3 Naomi does not speak anymore. She who tried to arrange a marriage and secure her future waited for others to realize her hope.

4. Naomi's Fullness.

The end of Ruth 3 brings the unwelcome news of a kinsman nearer than Boaz. Naomi did not mention him after Ruth returned from her first day of gleaning in Boaz's field. What his relationship to Naomi and Elimelech was is unknown.

On the threshing floor Boaz had indicated his willingness, even desire, to perform the role of kinsman-redeemer. When the nearer kinsman declined, Boaz and Ruth married with the approbation and blessing of the townspeople. Yahweh blessed their union with the birth of a son, Obed. The book of Ruth ends with Naomi holding her grandson, who, by virtue of levirate marriage, was also counted as Elimelech's son and heir. Obed, whose name in Hebrew means "servant," served Naomi by inheriting her husband's property and caring for her in her latter years. He embodied the assurance of God's faithfulness to keep his promises and give his people an inheritance.

The book of Ruth ends with a moving final scene. Naomi, back home in Bethlehem (the house of bread), had enough food to eat and held in her arms a grandson who was also her legal son. She who had accused Yahweh of bringing her back empty now enjoyed life to the full.

See also BOAZ; FEMINIST INTERPRETATION; RUTH 1: BOOK OF; RUTH 4: PERSON; WOMEN.

BIBLIOGRAPHY. **D. R. G. Beattie,** trans., *The Targum of Ruth* (ArBib 19; Collegeville, MN: Liturgical Press, 1994); **D. I. Block,** *Judges, Ruth* (NAC 6; Nashville: Broadman & Holman, 2002); **D. N. Fewell and D. M. Gunn,** *Compromising Redemption: Relating Characters in the Book of Ruth* (Louisville: Westminster John Knox, 1990); **A. D. Freedman,** "Naomi's Experience of God and Its Treatment in the Book of Ruth," *Proceedings of the Eastern Great Lakes and Midwest Biblical Society* 23 (2003) 29-38; **R. Grant,** "Literary Structure in the Book of Ruth," *BSac* 148 (1991) 424-41; **R. L. Hubbard Jr.,** *The Book of Ruth* (NICOT; Grand Rapids: Eerdmans, 1988); **A. LaCocque,** *Ruth* (CC; Minneapolis: Fortress, 2004); **D. F. Rauber,** "Literary Values in the Bible: The Book of Ruth," *JBL* 89 (1970) 27-37; **K. D. Sakenfeld,** *Ruth* (IBC; Louisville: Westminster John Knox, 1999); **P. Trible,** *God and the Rhetoric of Sexuality* (Philadelphia: Fortress, 1978).

D. Ulrich

NARRATIVE. *See* NOVELLA, STORY, NARRATIVE.

NARRATIVE INTERPRETATION. *See* HERMENEUTICS.

NEW YEAR FESTIVAL. *See* CULT, WORSHIP: PSALMS.

NINTH OF AV, FESTIVAL OF. *See* MEGILLOT AND FESTIVALS.

NONCANONICAL PSALMS. *See* DEAD SEA SCROLLS.

NOVELLA, STORY, NARRATIVE

*Ruth and *Esther are captivating narratives, as uncertainty and potential danger turn into redemption and deliverance. Although each story is its own self-contained unit, the *intertextual connections to other biblical characters and events are rich. These narratives also raise distinct challenges in regard to language, unity of text, genre, historicity and purpose.

1. Characteristics of Narrative
2. The Question of Genre
3. Function and Purpose of Narrative

1. Characteristics of Narrative.
Good narrative is a complex interweaving of characters, plot and setting presented by the narrator, who speaks from outside the plot, moving it forward by reporting activities, descriptions and dialogue. In most cases the narrator in the biblical text is omniscient, knowing the inner lives of the characters and selectively reporting their thoughts, feelings and intentions. The narrator often is omnipresent, moving easily from one location to another, omnipotent in the domain of the story, and is rarely neutral but instead conveys a moral and ethical tone, passing judgment on characters and events (Sternberg, 84-128).

1.1. Narrative Technique. Narrative technique indicates the way the language is used to convey meaning (Gunn and Fewell, 147-57). Important features include sentence structure, word order, word choice, verbal forms and repetition. When Esther informed the king of Haman's treachery, the narrator introduces his response with "Then King Ahasuerus said, and he said to Queen Esther . . ." (Esther 7:5). The awkward repetition of "said" works very well to indicate the "sputtering" of the king. He was so shocked that he had to catch his breath and start all over again.

The dominant word in Ruth 1 is *return*, as it is the essence of *Naomi's charge to Orpah and Ruth, her own homeward-bound intention, and Ruth's choice to return with her. These initial events shape the rest of the book. Throughout Esther there is an overabundance of word pairs, sets of statements and requests, and indications of parallel events. These commence with excessive doublets in the description of the opulent and officious Persian court (Esther 1). At several key points dyads are replaced by triplets, most notably in the context of the decrees sanctioning and effecting violence (Esther 3:13; 7:4; 8:11). They in turn give way to fourfold verbal "strings" of jubilation (Esther 8:16; 9:19, 22). Parallel events shape the comprehensive *chiastic structure that ties together the entire book, emphasizes the theme of reversal from the threat of annihilation to the festive joy and rest (Esther 9:1), and finds its center in the insomnia of the king (Esther 6:1), a development entirely outside the scheming of the human characters.

A second notable linguistic feature of Esther is the predominance of passive verb forms in critical contexts. Esther's early appearances are almost exclusively described in this manner; she is acted upon by larger, nameless forces. This same anonymity has a wider circle than just Esther and the young women. It pervades the court scenes of the narrative, divesting the bureaucracy of accountability. The passive forms allow for ambiguity in regard to who is responsible for what transpires.

Narrators often use irony to introduce complications that destabilize traditional perceptions (Gunn and Fewell, 55). Famine in the land around Bethlehem ("house of bread") hints at the disobedience of the covenant people that had brought them to such a state, even though the idyllic narrative in Ruth is a distinct contrast to the spiritual darkness in the book of Judges. Esther, an orphan and an alien with no voice in regard to her presence in the overindulgent Persian court, effected sweeping empire-wide changes.

1.2. Characterization. S. Bar-Efrat (93) has called character and plot the soul and body of narrative. Major characters may be round, flat or functionary (Berlin, 23). Round characters are dynamic and evidence fullness, change and complexity. Readers are given windows into their thoughts and emotions. By way of contrast, we know much less of the inner lives of flat characters. Both Esther and Haman represent round characters. Esther's personality is complicated, as she appears to develop from acquiescent to boldly challenging and yet from the outset demonstrates a courage that defies passivity. The character of Haman centers on his alternately inflated and wounded ego, which is fully on display. *Mordecai, on the other hand, is opaque, and the reader is left to guess as to his motives for the determinative action of defying

the king's order to prostrate himself before Haman.

Minor functionary characters, also called agents or helpers, contribute significantly to narrative movement. Their configuration at the beginning often creates absence. The deaths of Elimelech, Mahlon and Chilion necessitated the eventual appearance of the *kinsman-redeemer in the person of *Boaz. It was essential that *Vashti be banished from the Persian court before Esther could even enter the narrative scene. Minor characters are present agents as well. The people of Bethlehem represented the social context in which *hesed* was practiced by Boaz and Ruth. In Esther the functionaries in the Persian court played a key role in making up the mind of the king.

Naming is definitive. In Esther Mordecai is repeatedly called "the Jew," while Haman is "the Agagite," both designated as outsiders in the Persian court and both representative of parties to a long-standing ethnic conflict. Likewise, the text emphasizes that Ruth was a Moabite woman, one not welcome in the congregation of Israel (Deut 23:3). This affected how the Bethlehem community would perceive and receive her and adds to the tension regarding the genealogy of *David (Gunn and Fewell, 58; Berlin, 86-88).

The outward appearances of biblical characters are rarely described in detail (Berlin, 34). Therefore, Esther's extraordinary beauty, described with a pair of doublets, signifies that she had no chance of escaping the roundup of young virgins. Likewise, specific references to donning attire or changing clothing carried messages. Ruth not only put on her best clothes in accordance with Naomi's instructions (Ruth 3:3) but also, on her own, requested that Boaz spread the "wing" of his garment over her (Ruth 3:9), indicating the protection of the redeemer. Although the narrative does not directly reveal Mordecai's thoughts, his refusal to abandon his mourning clothes (Esther 4:4) and his later assumption of royal dress (Esther 8:15) are indirect windows into his intentions.

By way of contrast, the moral nature of biblical narrative is evident in the concern to represent characters as righteous and good, or evil and disobedient. Mordecai's actions in his role as Esther's guardian indicated his steadfast nature (Esther 2:11). The reader is introduced to Boaz as a worthy man even before his name is given (Ruth 2:1). Boaz in turn affirmed Ruth's strength of character in dialogue with her, describing her self-sacrifice in returning to Bethlehem with Naomi (Ruth 2:11-12) and declaring that her actions were guided by *hesed* (Ruth 3:10).

Dialogue in biblical narratives is an essential mechanism for both characterization and for moving the plot along. Out of the eighty-five verses in Ruth, more than fifty are dialogue. Naomi's forthright declaration of her own bitterness of soul in her utter bereavement (Ruth 1:13, 20-21) was the backdrop for Ruth's extraordinary devotion. It is significant that the first words that Ruth uttered were her declaration of allegiance (Ruth 1:16-17). Dialogue may be interior, as exemplified in the inner workings of Haman's ego as he presumed to identify himself as the "man the king wishes to honor" (Esther 6:6-9). It appears in mediated speech as the eunuch Hathach assisted in the "conversation" between Mordecai and Esther once the decree of annihilation had been published (Esther 4:5-16). The mediation slows the exchange, giving ample narrative time to establish Esther's determination and resolve.

1.3. Plot Development. The events that make up a narrative are linked in terms of both time and causality, providing a meaningful structure for what otherwise might seem to be random occurrences (Gunn and Fewell, 101-5). There is a starting point, a series of complicating relationships and events, and a resolution to the conflict or problem. The exposition sets up the situation and reveals in a microcosm what is important. That Bethlehem in Judah and Moab are mentioned twice in Ruth 1:1-2 indicates that a major theme of this story is foreignness. The name "Elimelech" ("My God is king"), likewise mentioned twice (Ruth 1:1-3), is equally important, as his name had to be carried on after his death. In Esther the extravagant Persian court was the setting from which Vashti was dismissed. What might appear in the early stages of a narrative to be extraneous is found later to be essential. It was Mordecai's unacknowledged discovery of the assassination plot (Esther 2:21-23) that later turned the whole tide of events around.

Each of the events is selected and shaped to contribute to the unity and coherence of the story; in good narrative they crescendo toward the complication and its resolution. Individual biblical narratives combine to form "salvation histo-

ry" (Gunn and Fewell, 48). In Ruth provision of someone to carry on the name of the house of Elimelech has a greater meaning in the line of Judah, David and Jesus. After the crisis of the exile the people of God in the Diaspora were spared annihilation as a result of the courage of Esther and Mordecai.

1.4. Setting. In regard to the setting of a narrative, both temporal and spatial issues are significant. Bar-Efrat (141-58) distinguished between external and internal time. The former indicates the period in which a narrative occurred. For Ruth this would be the period of the Judges, while for Esther it was the Persian Empire. In each case the story establishes those connections with the outside temporal world at the outset. Within the narrative, however, there are also chronological indicators that pace the story. Internal time is flexible, moving rapidly in some cases and slowing down in others. Specific time indicators, such as "when they had lived there about ten years" (Ruth 1:4), move the narrative quickly. Flashbacks and abrupt movements compress it. In contrast, conversation and description slow down narrated time. Most of Ruth 2 is devoted to Boaz and Ruth becoming acquainted as she was gleaning in his field.

The biblical text is replete with geographical references, and these narratives are no exception. The country of Moab, located east of the Dead Sea, was not as drastically affected by famine as was the country of Judah. Esther opens in the citadel of *Susa, where Xerxes was showing off his power and wealth to representatives from the large number of provinces under Persian control. Generally in biblical narrative specific places are not extensively described. That makes the first chapter of Esther especially dramatic.

2. The Question of Genre.

The nature of the narratives of Ruth and Esther as they have been briefly described is a necessary starting point for exploring the wide range of opinions about their genre. Unfortunately, the designations that have been applied to these texts are brought to the study from outside the literary context of the Semitic world and are often not accurately applied (Bush, 33). Terms such as *novella, folktale, idyll* and *romance* for Ruth, and *novella, festival etiology, legend, wisdom tale, farce* and *burlesque* for Esther come from European literary contexts. There are reasons for suggesting each, but all of them imply that the works are primarily fiction, driving a wedge between literary art and historical veracity. Strikingly absent from most attempts to assign genre to these texts is the designation *historical narrative*. Nevertheless, it is important to entertain that possibility.

2.1. Novella, Short Story, Historical Narrative. Fully lodged in the category of fiction, a novella is a prose composition intended to entertain and edify. Shorter than a novel, it focuses on dramatic action, development of characters with personality, and dialogue. There are differences of opinion in regard to the form and content boundaries between novella, short narrative tale and historical narrative. According to W. L. Humphreys (82), a novella is a crafted literary work that is too short to be a novel and too long to be a short story. It is fiction, telling not what happened but rather "what happens." Further, whereas the novella develops character, the short story simply reveals it. The short-story form in Israel had its own conventions and style, focusing on the normal concerns of life and demonstrating that the sphere where human activity took place was also where God was at work (Campbell, 90-93). There is an unmistakable emphasis on the sovereignty of God as the story unfolds.

2.2. Reliable Narrative Historiography. The style of the Esther narrative, with its concern for dates, numbers, names and procedures, indicates that it was intended to be read as history. In many details the correspondence between Esther and extrabiblical sources is remarkable, a point conceded by most scholars. Given the careful representations in Ruth and Esther of their geographical and historical contexts, the best label, especially for Esther, might simply be "historical narrative." Although this runs counter to the presumption on the part of much of scholarship that literary artistry and historical reliability cannot coexist (see Provan, Long and Longman, 75-97), the essence of these narratives is the provision by God for the deepest needs of individuals and whole communities when they were in dire straits. That message of hope is severely diminished if the providential interventions of God are merely inspirational fiction. In that case, God has turned from "the lord of history into a creature of the imagination, with the most disastrous results" (Sternberg, 32).

3. Function and Purpose of Narrative.
Narratives provide structures for articulating worldviews and giving meaning to reality. They are didactic, often designed to convey information (Provan, Long and Longman, 81). The story of Esther authenticated the annual celebration of *Purim commemorating the deliverance of Jews across the empire from annihilation. Esther was to be read annually so that Israelites would relive blotting out the memory of their archenemy. This emphasis was particularly important because Purim, unlike the major Jewish festivals, had not been instituted at Sinai (*see* Megillot and Festivals).

Storytelling is a discipline that brings order to human experience, teaches morality, and offers criticism (Gunn and Fewell, 1-2). Reading Ruth and Esther means probing the cultural and ethnic conflicts and potential injustices that are embedded in the stories. In spite of ambiguity regarding whether or not Ruth is an example of levirate marriage, the related issues of redemption of land and restoration of family name are central. The Esther narrative is the one biblical text focused solely on life in the Diaspora. Unlike the rest of the postexilic literature that emphasizes return to the land, this narrative presents the complexities involved with the choice to remain in the dispersion and the vulnerability of those Diaspora communities. The ubiquitous verbal dualities also may reinforce the theme of dual loyalty with which Jews in the Diaspora context have always wrestled.

At the same time, all biblical narrative is designed to bring the reader to a further understanding of the sovereign and covenant God, even though this main character is planted behind the scenes of these particular narratives as they deal with the concerns of life in Bethlehem and Susa. Numerous providential coincidences are lodged in contexts that demanded responsible and faithful human choices and action. Ruth clearly teaches about *hesed,* the role of the kinsman-redeemer, and the larger socio-theological matter of redemption. The divine silence in Esther compels God's people to choose between the imperfect alternatives that arise in the real ambiguities of life, just as Esther and Mordecai did. At the same time, people of faith are confident that God will address injustice and suffering and will preserve his people in his wisdom and in his time.

See also ESTHER 1: BOOK OF; FORM CRITICISM;

FRAME NARRATIVE; HISTORICAL CRITICISM; RHETORICAL CRITICISM; RUTH 1: BOOK OF.

BIBLIOGRAPHY. **R. Alter,** *The Art of Biblical Narrative* (New York: Basic Books, 1981); **S. Bar-Efrat,** *Narrative Art in the Bible* (JSOTSup 70; Sheffield: Almond, 1989); **A. Berlin,** *Poetics and Interpretation of Biblical Narrative* (BLS 9; Sheffield: Almond, 1983); **F. Bush,** *Ruth, Esther* (WBC 9; Dallas: Word, 1996); **E. F. Campbell Jr.,** "The Hebrew Short Story: A Study of Ruth," in *A Light unto My Path: Old Testament Studies in Honor of Jacob M. Myers,* ed. H. Bream, R. Heim and C. Moore (GTS 4; Philadelphia: Temple University Press, 1974) 83-101; **D. M. Gunn and D. N. Fewell,** *Narrative in the Hebrew Bible* (OBS; Oxford: Oxford University Press, 1993); **W. L. Humphreys,** "Novella," in *Saga, Legend, Tale, Novella, Fable: Narrative Forms in Old Testament Literature,* ed. G. Coats (JSOTSup 35; Sheffield: JSOT Press, 1985) 82-96; **J. D. Levenson,** *Esther* (OTL; Louisville: Westminster John Knox, 1997); **S. Niditch,** "Legends of Wise Heroes and Heroines: I. Esther, II. Ruth," in *The Hebrew Bible and Its Modern Interpreters,* ed. D. Knight and G. Tucker (Philadelphia: Fortress, 1985) 445-56; **I. Provan, V. P. Long and T. Longman III,** *A Biblical History of Israel* (Louisville: Westminster John Knox, 2003) 75-93; **M. D. Simon,** "'Many Thoughts in the Heart of Man . . .': Irony and Theology in the Book of Esther," *Tradition* 31 (1997) 5-27; **M. Sternberg,** *The Poetics of Biblical Narrative: Ideological Literature and the Drama of Reading* (ILBS; Bloomington: Indiana University Press, 1987); **F. S. Weiland,** "Historicity, Genre, and Narrative Design in the Book of Esther," *BSac* 159 (2002a) 151-65; idem, "Plot Structure in the Book of Esther," *BSac* 159 (2002b) 277-87; idem, "Literary Conventions in the Book of Esther," *BSac* 159 (2002c) 425-35; idem, "Literary Clues to God's Providence in the Book of Esther," *BSac* 160 (2003) 34-47.   E. Phillips

O

ONOMATOPOEIA. *See* SOUND PATTERNS.

ORAL POETRY

Oral poetry may be defined as poetry composed in a nonliterate setting without the aid of the resources for writing, despite the potential availability of such resources. Obviously, however, stating a definition is problematic. Although the definition above focuses on composition, assessing oral quality or nature may involve consideration not only of composition but also of transmission and preservation, as well as a multitude of scenarios involving the possible intersection of oral and literate activity in all three of these areas. In short, any understanding of oral poetry must contend with at least two nagging questions. First, if the material originally was oral, why, and how, did it eventually become written? Second, what indicators in this written material give evidence that it once was oral? (For an early, broad-based treatment, see Finnegan, 7-24; for a later, summary treatment focused on the Hebrew Bible, see Niditch, 5-6.) The second question has been the focus of the vast majority of research in the area, and the short answer to that question has been that formulaic language in the written form reflects an oral heritage; however, although scholarship as a whole affirms that biblical poetry is formulaic in some sense, no such consensus exists that formulaic nature equals orality.

    1. Oral Poetry and Oral Culture
    2. Oral Formulaic Theory
    3. Hebrew Word Pairs and Orality
    4. Hebrew Poetry and Orality
    5. Current State
    6. Future Prospects

1. Oral Poetry and Oral Culture.

The common assumption is that the ancient world out of which biblical poetry would have come reflected primarily an oral culture. Certainly, writing was developed very early, but that activity apparently was limited to a select few so that the vast majority of the populations would not have been able to write or read. Scholarly work as early as the eighteenth century reflects the idea that the Hebrew Bible either includes epic pieces or that at least some of those materials are based on older, underlying poetic epic materials (Conroy, 2-15). Even though this particular theory is supported by little hard evidence, the idea that Hebrew poetic materials were oral in nature, at least at their beginnings, is not hard to imagine. Much research has focused on the subject of possible oral antecedents of the biblical materials, with the work of Hermann Gunkel being perhaps the best-known and most influential example (Gunkel, 3-9). The problem arises in trying to make more specific statements about the nature of those materials, the nature of the production of those materials, or about the nature of the evidence for such materials and their production.

2. Oral Formulaic Theory.

Although consideration of the possible oral nature of biblical materials does not owe its origins to the area of study called "oral-formulaic theory" (more recently, "oral theory"), the area of study has been influenced greatly by it. The theory, in brief, is that consistent formulaic style in written documents from ancient times signals that the material in the documents originally was oral in nature. This theory historically is credited primarily to two scholars, M. Parry and his student and protégée A. Lord (Foley, 11-17).

    Parry's analysis of the works of Homer led him to the conclusion that the majority of the material was formulaic; that is, it consisted primarily of ready-made phrases used to express typical themes that in combination with other themes constituted the larger stories. This conclusion, in turn, led him to theorize that the nature and style of the material indicated that it had been composed orally, by itinerant poets/singers, in spontaneous performances before live audiences. In addition, although the poets/singers could display creativity and innovation, the vast majority of their material's content was traditional in nature, drawn from a widely known stock of formulas and themes passed on orally from person to person, from generation to generation, in these acts of performance.

Parry was not content to simply posit a reasonable theory; he wanted to validate it, if possible. So beginning in 1933 he did field studies in Yugoslavia among traditional Serbo-Croatian storytellers, resulting in the discovery of remarkable parallels between the more modern stories and storytellers and their characteristics and those of the Homeric works, so much so that he considered his earlier theory validated. However, Parry's life and work were cut short by a tragic accident, and Albert Lord continued his work, culminating in his monumental *The Singer of Tales* (1960), which set forth the theory and its evidence in a clear and compelling fashion.

Although oral-formulaic theory was a revolutionary development in the field, from the beginning the theory has had detractors, and its form has evolved over the years. Even Lord himself has been open to adjusting some definitions, understandings and applications. Nevertheless, its influence has been constant not only in the field of Homeric studies but also in comparative literature studies and, to a more limited extent, biblical studies.

3. Hebrew Word Pairs and Orality.

Perhaps the most fruitful area in biblical poetics for an application of the distinctive nature of oral theory developed in connection with the long-standing recognition of ubiquitous *parallelism in Hebrew verse. Although Parry's work in Homeric epic, with its emphasis on the metrical utility of narrative orality, received its just share of critique, the assumption of orality continued to garner support from ongoing textual work in a variety of ancient literary settings.

Taking R. Lowth's classic formulation of parallelism as a starting point, a number of biblical scholars during the first quarter of the twentieth century noted the presence of poetic convention much like that of the Hebrew Bible in diverse writings of the ancient Near East. Perhaps the most significant find was the discovery of fixed word pairs extant in the parallel lines of both biblical Hebrew and Ugaritic literature. H. L. Ginsberg first documented various examples of these "standing pairs" in several articles published in the 1930s (Ginsberg and Maisler, 248 n. 15; Ginsberg 1935, 327; 1936, 172). An expansion of the work undertaken in the 1940s and 1950s by M. Cassuto and M. Held led to the suggestion by the latter of a hypothetical "dictionary of parallel words" available to Semitic poets for use in the composition of traditional hymnic materials (Cassuto 1943; 1947; Held).

A brief example of these word pairs should suffice. Particular words for "mountains" and "hills" or "silver" and "gold" were observed repeatedly in successive lines of Hebrew and Ugaritic verse. Without regard to content or context, the presence of the first appeared to guarantee essentially the positioning of the second. With a rhythmic regularity, an evocation of the "mountains" brought about an echo of the "hills," or for "silver" the companion mention of "gold," in the highly stylized structure of poetic parallelism. The prevalence of such phenomena led to a certain expectation of the word pair as a fixed expression. Such fixed pairs abound throughout the Hebrew and Ugaritic corpora.

An increasing interest in orality and the use of formulaic language eventually intersected with the compositional convention of word pairs in the study of Hebrew poetry. In the 1960s two scholars attempted to establish a foundational connection between oral theory and parallel word pairs in positing a biblical "oral poetry." S. Gevirtz (10) suggested that traditional language such as the fixed pair or, in his words, "cliché" served a mnemonic function in furthering the compositional utility of an essentially oral art. W. Whallon (153-54) surmised that rather than aiding the poet's memory in performance, traditional word pairs facilitated the oral poet's spontaneous creation of parallelism with its own brand of "impressive elegance." A third scholar, R. Culley (32), expanded the concept of formulaic language beyond the limitation of the "word pair" proper to include a catalog of repeated phrases "a line long" in the poet's oral arsenal. Each of these studies in some unique way evoked the work of Parry and his assumption of orality as the driving force behind ancient epic literature.

With the importance of word pairs firmly established in the burgeoning lexicon of oral poetry, the decade of the 1970s witnessed both the broadening of a philosophical basis for the supposed orality of biblical Hebrew poetics and a growing consensus toward caution in light of the highly speculative nature of such pursuits. P. Yoder (480-81) sought to equate "A-B pairs" with Parry's definition of formula, exchanging the formal requirement of *meter for parallelism, and thereby to identify the use of traditional word pairs as the common stock of the oral poet. M. Dahood (78-86) aimed to recover the "Canaanite thesaurus" underlying the Ugaritic and Hebrew texts as a tool for textual criticism and exegesis. R. Coote (60), while affirming parallel pairs as a "conventional resource" of the oral poet, challenged the fixed nature of the word pair in its fundamental formulation. W. Watters (142-47) demonstrated that the word pair not only was the dominant formulaic expression in Hebrew poetry but also was characteristic of both oral and written literature and implied that as such it should not be styled the champion of orality in the biblical corpus. Such caution also was echoed during the latter half of the decade in the works of D. Freedman (12-13) and P. Craigie (56). The rise of linguistic research, which emphasizes the grammatical aspects of parallelism, and the recognition of limitations within the inherently theoretical framework for assumed orality contributed to a stagnation of exploration into the nature of fixed word pairs during the 1980s (Berlin, 157). In light of the erudite dismantling of Lowth's basic premise of parallelism by J. Kugel in *The Idea of Biblical Poetry*, prospects for a revival of interest in word pairs and orality appear unlikely.

4. Hebrew Poetry and Orality.

Efforts to sift through the poetic materials of the Hebrew Bible in hopes of finding hard evidence of orality have failed to produce a convincing case for the existence of an expressly oral residue. As noted above, the presence of formulaic language in Hebrew verse, whether at the line or phrase level, offers only a hint of oral convention, particularly in light of the use of formulas in undoubtedly written compositions (i.e., *acrostic psalms). Even fixed word pairs, which appear as a logical extension of the oral poet's craft, may be simply the result of a colloquial characteristic of human communication, as likely to occur in the conventional creation of literature as the spontaneous tradition of oral performance. Perhaps most troubling for an estimation of biblical orality is the nature of the materials themselves, ranging from collections of *wisdom in various forms to a limited corpus of short, anonymous *hymns betraying an uncertain provenance.

One example of the difficulty associated with the application of oral theory to the poetics of the Hebrew Bible may be discerned in a cursory examination of the several compositions in the Psalter (Pss 47; 93; 96—99) identified by S. Mowinckel as enthronement psalms (Mowinckel, 1.106-92). Since the vast majority of work in oral poetry has focused on *Psalms, this grouping of related songs (*see* Music, Song) may be understood as representative not only of other poetic materials in the broader context of the Hebrew *canon but also of the suggested oral history that stands behind such literary activity. On the surface, notable features of the enthronement psalms recommend recourse to orality as an explanation for a shared sensibility of divine sovereignty. The form-critical category itself is based on the presence of formulaic language, "the Lord reigns." Similarity in vocabulary ("king," "throne," "holy"), stock phrases ("all the earth"), use of repetition ("sing praises" in Ps 47, "the floods" in Ps 93, "ascribe" in Ps 96) and the presence of fixed word pairs ("peoples/nations") at the surface level all point to an oral origin. One might suggest that psalms of this sort could have been composed extemporaneously by skilled oral artisans for an ancient annual festival of reaffirmation exalting the kingship of Yahweh (*see* Kingship Psalms). Further, one may suppose that this group of psalms circulated orally for years among the traditions of ancient Israel, eventually becoming encoded at the hand of the poet or some scribal assistant to preserve their artistry or even prevent their loss. Yet despite the compelling attraction of such speculation, these psalms are extant only as members of a literary collection that allows no easy access to its compositional roots or to the history of its individual components, save an occasional attribution (sons of Korah in Ps 47 [*see* Asaph and Sons of Korah]) or parallel presentation (1 Chron 16 in Ps 96). Thus, regardless of the role of orality in the composition or preservation of these particular psalms, their substantial contribution to the canon of Hebrew Scriptures remains as a *written* witness to the majesty of Israel's God and King.

5. Current State.
Despite the fact that the subject of orality is commonly broached in the larger field of biblical studies, recent studies in Hebrew poetry show little focus on the issue of orality, apparently reflecting the perspective that considering the possible oral nature either is unimportant to reading and interpreting the material or at least is not essential to doing so. One may propose a number of reasons for this fact. (1) Notwithstanding an early flourish of work on biblical poetry and orality, no sustained trend in this direction ever materialized, and such study seems to have developed little since the assessment by R. Coote in 1976. (2) Oral poetry is ethereal in nature, and so identifying "oral poetry" via written material with confidence is quite difficult because of the challenge of establishing truly objective criteria for identifying it and of determining any objective method for isolating and interpreting it. (3) There has been a growing focus on the Bible as literature with a concomitant focus on appreciation of the final form of the material along with its "inherent" qualities and style. With this approach to poetry, the study begins with an assumption of all-encompassing artistry, proceeds with close reading that exposes key words and devices, patterns and structures, and concludes with suggestions of meaning evident in the texture, form and content of given texts.

6. Future Prospects.
The scenario described above seems to require this question: What value would consideration of a proposed oral nature add to the study of Hebrew poetry? Perhaps the best answer is to refer to the proposal by S. Niditch (6, 24) that an oral aesthetic or mentality permeates the biblical material as a whole. Although establishing a clear and firm methodology for recognizing and analyzing the oral aspects of biblical poetry seems impossible at present, embracing an assumption of remnant orality will allow readers to approach the texts with a healthy sensitivity to all characteristics of the material, including possible oral aspects. That sensitivity has potential to help inform current literary, linguistic approaches to biblical poetry. Perhaps it can also precipitate some continuing innovative attempts to clarify the nature and value of the oral qualities of those materials that in turn could lead to better reading and deeper understanding. Given the common assumption of the oral background for many if not most biblical materials, such an approach would seem only logical.

See also CULT, WORSHIP: PSALMS; FORM CRITICISM; LYRIC POETRY; METER; PARALLELISM; POETICS, TERMINOLOGY OF; SOUND PATTERNS; WISDOM POEMS; WORDPLAY.

BIBLIOGRAPHY. **A. Berlin,** "Parallelism," *ABD* 5.155-62; **M. Cassuto,** "Biblical Literature and Ugaritic Literature," *Tarbiz* 14 (1943) 1; idem, "Parallel Words in Hebrew and Ugaritic," *LeÜonénu* 15 (1947) 97-102; **C. Conroy,** "Hebrew Epic: Historical Notes and Critical Reflections," *Bib* 61 (1980) 1-30; **R. Coote,** "The Application of Oral Theory to Biblical Hebrew Literature," *Semeia* 5 (1976) 51-64; **P. Craigie,** "The Problem of Parallel Word Pairs in Ugaritic and Hebrew Poetry," *Semitics* 5 (1977) 48-58; **R. Culley,** *Oral Formulaic Language in the Biblical Psalms* (Toronto: University of Toronto Press, 1967); **M. Dahood, with T. Penar,** "Ugaritic-Hebrew Parallel Pairs," in *Ras Shamra Parallels: The Texts from Ugarit and the Hebrew Bible,* ed. L. Fisher (3 vols.; AnOr 49; Rome: Pontificum Institutum Biblicum, 1972) 1.71-387; **R. Finnegan,** *Oral Poetry: Its Nature, Significance and Social Context* (Cambridge: Cambridge University Press, 1977); **J. Foley,** *Oral-Formulaic Theory and Research: An Introduction and Annotated Bibliography* (New York: Garland, 1985); **D. Freedman,** "Pottery, Poetry, and Prophecy: An Essay on Biblical Poetry," *JBL* 96 (1977) 5-26; **S. Gevirtz,** *Patterns in the Early Poetry of Israel* (SAOC 32; Chicago: University of Chicago Press, 1963); **H. L. Ginsberg,** "The Victory of the Land-God over the Sea God," *JPOS* 15 (1935) 327-33; idem, "The Rebellion and Death of Ba'lu," *Or* 5 (1936) 172-80; **H. L. Ginsberg and B. Maisler,** "Semitized Hurrians in Syria and Palestine," *JPOS* 14 (1934) 248-60; **H. Gunkel,** *Genesis,* trans. Mark E. Biddle (Mercer Library of Biblical Studies; Macon, GA: Mercer University Press, 1997); **M. Held,** "More Parallel Word Pairs in the Bible and in the Ugaritic Documents," *Leshonénu* 18/19 (1952-1954) 144-60; **J. Kugel,** *The Idea of Biblical Poetry: Parallelism and Its History* (New Haven: Yale University Press, 1981); **A. Lord,** *The Singer of Tales*

(New York: Atheneum, 1973); **S. Mowinckel,** *The Psalms in Israel's Worship,* trans. D. R. Ap-Thomas (2 vols.; Nashville: Abingdon, 1962); **S. Niditch,** *Oral World and Written Word: Ancient Israelite Literature* (LAI; Louisville: Westminster John Knox, 1996); **M. Parry,** *The Making of Homeric Verse: the Collected Papers of Milman Parry,* ed. A. Parry (New York: Oxford University Press, 1987); **W. Watson,** *Classical Hebrew Poetry: A Guide to Its Techniques* (JSOTSup 26; Sheffield: JSOT Press, 1984); **W. Watters,** *Formula Criticism and the Poet-ry of the Old Testament* (BZAW 138; Berlin: de Gruyter, 1976); **W. Whallon,** *Formula, Character, and Context: Studies in Homeric, Old English, and Old Testament Poetry* (Cambridge: Harvard University Press, 1969); **P. Yoder,** "A-B Pairs and Oral Composition in Hebrew Poetry," *VT* 21 (1971) 470-89.

W. E. Brown and J. J. Rankin

ORALITY. *See* ORAL POETRY.

P

PALACE. *See* ARCHITECTURE.

PARADISE. *See* CREATION THEOLOGY.

PARALLELISM

Generally speaking, *parallelism* is the term used by scholars to describe the congruence (or lack thereof) of comparable elements in corresponding lines of Hebrew poetry. Many believe that this binary-like phenomenon, including the relationship that it creates or maintains between poetic lines, is a defining, if not the definitive, characteristic of biblical poetry. Vigorous debate continues, however, regarding the precise nature of parallelism, its structures and types, how best to describe it, and how (or even if) it communicates meaning within a poem.

1. Two Points of Entry
2. Parallelism: A Brief History of a Biblical Idea
3. "Theological Parallelism"
4. Parallelism and the Canon of Scripture
5. Conclusion

1. Two Points of Entry.

Two recent definitions of parallelism offer instructive starting points into the discussion. The first is by G. Wilson (39):

The sense of . . . [parallelism] is that after the statement of an initial line, a second (and sometimes a third) line is generated that shares some obvious grammatical-structural similarities with the first and yet redirects the focus of the first through alternate words and expression. The close grammatical-structural similarity between lines provides continuity that emphasizes the *parallel* character of the two lines, while the distinctive phraseology of each phrase lifts the phenomenon beyond

mere repetition and offers the opportunity for expansion or advancement on the original line's meaning.

The basic aspects of this definition might be exemplified by a vast number of poetic lines in the OT. Consider, as one example, Psalm 19:1 [MT 19:2]:

> The heavens are recounting the glory of
>   God,
> and the firmament proclaims his deed.
>   (our translation)

The nomenclature differs among scholars, but the first clause can be designated line (or colon or verset) A, and the second clause line (or colon or verset) B. Together, A and B comprise a bicolon. The specific content of the two lines of this bicolon are tightly related: the subjects of the two clauses, "the heavens" and "the firmament," obviously correspond; the verbal roots utilized, "recount" and "proclaim," both speak of communication; and the direct objects, "the glory of God" and "his deed," also relate to one another. This is "the parallel character of the two lines" of which Wilson speaks. But the phraseology is distinctive, as his definition also notes. "The firmament" is a specific aspect of the "heavens" (see Gen 1:1, 6-7); the verbal roots are different; and the movement from God's glory to God's deed may suggest that the former is somehow manifested or revealed in the latter. There is indeed parallelism in Psalm 19:1, and clearly this is not "mere repetition." Instead, when analyzed closely, these two fairly simple lines contribute to a rather dense, though terse, poetic sentiment: the sky, part of God's creation, testifies to God's incomparable nature.

Wilson's definition emphasizes that parallelism must not be misconstrued to mean that all of the elements of one line find exact correspondence in the second. The following definition of parallelism by A. Berlin (2004, 2098-99 [italics added]) is a second useful entry point, clarifying the nature of the lines' relationship:

Parallelism is the pairing of a line (or part of a line) with one or more lines that are in some way *linguistically equivalent*. The equivalence is often *grammatical* . . . both parts of the parallelism may have the same syntactic structure. . . . Another form of equivalence is *semantic* . . . the meaning of the lines is somehow related. . . . [But] equivalence does not imply identity. The second line of parallelism rarely repeats exactly the same words or exactly the same thought as the first; it is more likely to echo, expand, or intensify the idea of the first line in any one of a number of ways.

There are obvious similarities between Wilson's definition and Berlin's, though the latter's notion of linguistic equivalence, encompassing both grammar and semantics, not to mention nonidentity, is more inclusive than Wilson's. This broader and, at the same time, more specific definition of parallelism—it includes grammatical-syntactical correspondence, not simply that of semantics (meaning)—is indicative of much of the current state of research on parallelism. To understand why this is the case and how things have arrived at this point, one needs a sense of how the study of parallelism has changed over the past 250 years.

2. Parallelism: A Brief History of a Biblical Idea.

2.1. R. Lowth and **Parallelismus Membrorum.** The modern study of parallelism began in the eighteenth century with the lectures of R. Lowth (1710-1787) (see Jarick). Prior to Lowth, scholars considered *meter to be the hallmark of Hebrew verse, as it is in ancient Greek and Latin poetry, both of which clearly influenced their perspective. But in his *Lectures on the Sacred Poetry of the Hebrews* (first published in 1753), Lowth (1839, 33-34) argued to the contrary, asserting that the laws governing Hebrew meter were largely unrecoverable, and turned his focus to the relationship of poetic lines. Others before him had described this relationship, especially in the psalms, but

Lowth (1839, 204) argued that *parallelismus membrorum* ("parallelism of members")—the way poetic lines respond to one another (note that for Lowth, *membrum* ["member"] translates Gk *kōlon* ["line"] [see Kugel 1981, 2-3 n. 4; Baker 1973])—was "the origin and progress of that poetical and artificial conformation of the sentences which we observe in the poetry of the Hebrews." In his work on Isaiah, Lowth (1834, ix) described his understanding of the phenomenon: "The correspondence of one verse, or line, with another, I call parallelism. When a proposition is delivered, and a second is subjoined to it, or drawn under it, equivalent, or contrasted with it, in sense; or similar to it in the form of grammatical construction, these I call parallel lines; and the words or phrases, answering one to another in the corresponding lines, parallel terms."

While admitting that the "certain equality, resemblance, or parallelism" between lines or elements of the line "has much variety and many gradations; it is sometimes more accurate and manifest, sometimes more vague and obscure," Lowth (1839, 205) nevertheless asserted that "it may . . . on the whole, be said to consist of three species." These three species or types of parallelism are synonymous parallelism, antithetic parallelism and synthetic (or constructive) parallelism (Lowth 1839, 205-14).

2.1.1. Synonymous Parallelism. The first type occurs when poetic lines repeat "the same sentiment . . . in different, but equivalent terms" (Lowth 1839, 205). Psalm 24:1 provides an excellent example:

The earth and its fullness are the LORD's,
the world, and those who dwell in it. (our
   translation)

Both lines echo the same thought: everything in the world belongs to God. They do so with parallel elements: "the earth" corresponds to "the world"; "its fullness" matches "those who dwell in it." The only element from the first line that goes unparalleled is "the LORD," but this habit of deletion, gapping or *ellipsis from line A to line B is frequent in Hebrew poetry (Lowth 1839, 208 [see 2.5.4 below]) and normally does not complicate comprehension.

2.1.2. Antithetic Parallelism. The second type occurs "when a thing is illustrated by its contrary being opposed to it" (Lowth 1839, 210). Note Psalm 1:6:

For the LORD knows the way of the righteous
(ones),
but the way of the wicked (ones) will perish.
(our translation)

Here the two lines establish a contrasting
(i.e., antithetical) relationship between two types
of "ways," asserting that those who walk therein
reach very different outcomes. The careful reader will note that the elements are not as balanced or parallel in Psalm 1:6. The Lord actively
knows (NRSV: "watches over") the way of the
righteous, but the way of the wicked is said to
perish on its own, as it were, without any indication of God's agency. Even so, the broad contrast between the parallel ways is clear.

2.1.3. Synthetic (or Constructive) Parallelism. The
third type occurs when "the sentences answer to
each other, not by the iteration of the same image or sentiment, or the opposition of their con-
traries, but merely by the form of construction"
(Lowth 1839, 211). Lowth (1839, 212) provides this
example from Psalm 77:17 [MT 77:18]:

The clouds overflowed with water;
The atmosphere resounded;
Thine arrows also issued forth.

The relationship of these lines is much looser than in the previous examples. Indeed, they
are parallel only insofar as some of the elements
seem to match one another: "the clouds," "the atmosphere" and "thine arrows" (presumably a
metaphor for lightning) all play a role in the poet's description of a violent rainstorm. Also, the
grammatical construction of each line is comparable. However, the elements are not obviously
synonymous, nor do they provide strong contrasts (antitheses) for one another. Lowth (1839,
211-12) considered synthetic parallelism to consist of "all such [parallelisms] as do not come
within the two former classes." Synthetic parallelism is thus a kind of catchall category; when
poetic lines are neither synonymous nor antithetical, Lowth placed them in this third type.
Lowth (1839, 213) admitted that the category was
thus very loose and difficult to delineate with
precision: "The variety in the form of this synthetic parallelism is very great, and the degrees
of resemblance almost infinite: so that sometimes the scheme of parallelism is very subtle
and obscure, and must be developed by art and
ability in distinguishing the different members

of the sentences, and in distributing the points,
rather than by depending upon the obvious
construction."

These comments prefigure the work of subsequent generations of scholars who have
sought to mitigate the ambiguity of synthetic
parallelism by refining Lowth's basic tripartite
schema. Otherwise, a very real problem arises:
what keeps mundane prose from being just another kind of synthetic parallelism (see 2.4.2
below)?

2.2. "The Laws of Parallelism." Despite the
problems with synthetic parallelism that were apparent from the beginning, Lowth's argument
that all Hebrew poetry exhibited *parallelismus
membrorum* won the day and went virtually un-
challenged for well over a century. One of the
most important results of his work was the determination of the genre of prophetic literature:
since it exhibits extensive use of parallelism, it
must be interpreted and analyzed as poetry rather than prose. In fact, some of the most thoroughgoing utilizations of Lowth's schema were
executed in work on the prophets—for example,
L. Newman and W. Popper's studies of Amos and
Isaiah, published in 1918. Indeed, by this time,
Hebrew poetry was thought to function so strictly
according to the "laws of parallelism" that if the
text did not adhere to these laws, then textual
emendation was in order (Newman and Popper,
449); thus, "Defect in parallelism is due to defect
in text, and conversely . . . once the right of emendation is admitted, the emendation must be on
the basis of parallelism" (Newman and Popper,
448). Parallelism thus moved from being a description of Hebrew poetry, to a tool in genre
analysis, and, in the work of Newman and Popper, to a lawlike factor useful for, among other
things, textual criticism and emendation.

It is somewhat ironic that the flaws in
Lowth's third category actually helped to propa-
gate his theory by encouraging subsequent
scholars to develop new ideas, all the time working within his tripartite schema. So, for example,
Newman and Popper (136) attempted to shore
up Lowth's legacy by classifying new varieties of
parallelism that would better explain the unac-
ceptably vague category of synthetic parallelism.
Such was not the case with G. Gray, who saw the
flawed third type of parallelism as an opportunity to refine Lowth's system. In 1915, arguing that
synthetic parallelism was no category at all, Gray
(reprint 1972, 49-50) introduced the categories

of "complete parallelism" and "incomplete parallelism," which together are "not distinct from, but mere subdivisions of synonymous and antithetic parallelism."

In his description of complete and incomplete parallelism Gray introduced a system of describing parallelism, referring to a Hebrew word in any given line by a letter (e.g., a, b, c) which could be mapped to its parallel in the second line (e.g., a', b', c'). Complete parallelism occurs when every term in the first line is parallel to a term in the second, whether the lines relate to one another synonymously or antithetically. The complete—in this case, synonymous—parallelism of Job 4:9 provides one such example (in the following, hyphenated words translate one Hebrew word):

```
a              b           c
By-the-breath of-God they-perish,
   a'              b'            c'
and-by-the-blast of-his-anger are-they-
          consumed. (Gray 1972, 61)
```

The antithetic parallelism of Proverbs 15:1 provides another:

```
a    b        c           d
A-soft answer turneth-away wrath,
   a'      b'      c'     d'
but-a-grievous word stirreth-up anger.
     (Gray 1972, 62)
```

Incomplete parallelism occurs when some of the terms from the first line occur in the second line, while others do not. An example is Song of Songs 2:1:

```
a    b      c
I-am a-rose-of Sharon,
        b'       c'
   a-lily-of the-valleys. (our translation)
```

This example demonstrates incomplete parallelism "without compensation"; that is, the second line is shorter than the first (Gray 1972, 74). Gray noted that Hebrew poetry also exhibits incomplete parallelism "with compensation," which means that although some elements in the lines go unparalleled, they are roughly the same length. In this scenario, the second line omits an element from the first but compensates by introducing a new element to balance the

line length. Consider Psalm 58:6 [MT 58:7]:

```
a       b         c          d
O-God, rip-out their-teeth from-their-mouth,
   b'          c'            e          a'
break the-fangs-of      the-young-lions, O-
LORD! (our translation)
```

In this verse, element d from the first line goes unparalleled, but to compensate, the second line adds element e (which can be seen as "backward" or "reverse gapped" [see 2.5.4 below]), providing the proper noun to which the personal pronouns refer.

According to Gray, countless other permutations can be found in biblical poetry that mix complete, incomplete, synonymous and antithetic parallelism in various ways. In general, though, he found incomplete parallelism to be much more common than complete parallelism. Indeed, in some poetic lines the parallelism is so incomplete that it is functionally nonexistent. Thus, if one were to chart biblical poetry with regard to parallelism, "the graph would run from zero (no parallelism) through all the gradations of incomplete parallelism to 100 (complete parallelism)" (Freedman 1972, xxv-xxvi). The vast, vast majority of poetic lines, however, would fall in the 1-99 range.

Gray's work preceded the discovery of the ancient city of Ugarit by nearly fifteen years; once Ugaritic was deciphered and its poetic texts translated, his categories of complete and incomplete parallelism took on new significance. It was quickly observed that Ugaritic poetry, like Hebrew, was also marked by parallelism, but often with a higher degree of identical (Gray's "complete") parallelism. This led W. Albright and a generation of his students, especially F. Cross and D. Freedman (see Albright; Cross and Freedman; also Freedman 1980; Cross) to two important conclusions: (1) Hebrew poetry (especially early Hebrew poetry as they defined it) stands in the same tradition of "Canaanite" poetry to which Ugaritic literature also belonged, and of which it was a primary repository (see also Gevirtz); (2) the formality or, at least, the higher incidence of "complete" parallelism that marked Ugaritic poetry vis-à-vis Hebrew poetry facilitated the establishment of a relative typology between the two literatures with results for the dating of each (see Robertson). Thus, Albright et al. suggested that examples of looser, incomplete types of parallelism were *later* than examples of very tight, synonymous, even identical types of parallelism. In this way, they were able to delineate a corpus of "ancient Yahwistic poetry," including texts such as Genesis 49, Exodus 15, Numbers 23—24, Deuteronomy 32—33 and Judges 5 (Freedman 1980, 14), and thereafter construct broad theories of Israelite religion and history on the basis of this early corpus (see, e.g., Freedman 1980, 77-178).

It should not be missed that these historical-religious reconstructions and the relative typology and chronology were all predicated, in no small way, on an understanding of parallelism. Cross and Freedman (5) explicitly state that Ugaritic and Hebrew poetry shared one "dominating principle . . . that of balance or symmetry: *parallelismus membrorum.*" Using the typology of early, tight regularity ("repetitive parallelism") to later, looser (ir)regularity, Cross and Freedman (71 n. 1) concluded that "the early poetry of Israel, like that of Ugarit, was quite regular in structure, and susceptible to quantitative analysis" (cf. Freedman 1980, 2-11).

At this point, things have come somewhat full circle: from pre-Lowthian meter, to parallelism *instead* of meter (see 2.1 above on Lowth), to parallelism *as* meter. Not only does this "historical" use of the "laws of parallelism" strike one as contrary to the spirit of Lowth's original insights, it is also not far removed from Newman and Popper's work, because instances or characteristics of "later" Hebrew poetry that were found in the corpus of "early" Hebrew poetry were often emended—with or without textual support from other ancient versions (see Cross and Freedman, esp. 5; Goodwin; Kugel 1984, 114)—often with an accompanying note: *metri causa* ("on account of the meter" [note: not on account of the *parallelism,* though the two are confused and identified at this point in the scholarship]). Alternatively, high incidence of nonrepetitive parallelism was irrefutable evidence that a poetic text was late. The "laws of parallelism" seem to have become even more reified in the historical-grammatical work of the Albright school. And, despite the very real and important gains that were made thereby, especially for historical and history-of-religion pursuits, one cannot help but wonder if the laws of parallelism had not killed the spirit of Hebrew poetry. There are, after all, other things at work beyond diachrony that can explain difference in poetry (see Berlin 2004, 2101-2).

2.3. The "Spirit" of Parallelism.

Soon after Lowth asserted that parallelism was the essential element of Hebrew poetry, scholars began to comment on the function of parallelism, arguing for its unique suitability as the "spirit" of poetry. Toward the end of the eighteenth century, J. Herder (1.41) described the expressive power of parallelism this way:

> Poetry is not addressed to the understanding alone but primarily and chiefly to the feelings. And are these not friendly to . . . parallelism? So soon as the heart gives way to its emotions, wave follows upon wave, and that is parallelism. The heart is never exhausted, it has forever something new to say. So soon as the first wave has passed away, or broken itself upon the rocks, the second swells again and returns as before. This pulsation of nature, this breathing of emotion, appears in all the language of passion, and would you not have that in poetry, which is most peculiarly the offspring of emotion[?]

Herder's (admittedly Romantic) understanding of parallelism is much broader than Lowth's, extending to encompass different types and styles of nonbiblical poetry. For example, Herder (1.42) saw parallelism as the common element of Alexandrine verse (a German metrical form, common in the seventeenth and eighteenth centuries, consisting of lines of twelve syllables with the caesura between the sixth and the seventh syllables):

> That is parallelism altogether. Examine carefully why it so powerfully enforces instruction, and you will find it to be simply on account of its parallelism. All simple songs and church hymns are full of it, and rhyme, the great delight of Northern [European] ears, is a continued parallelism. . . . To this same Oriental [i.e., Hebrew] source we are indebted both for rhyme, and the uniform movement of our church musick [sic].

Herder's work demonstrates that when one (considerably) expands the definition of parallelism, it "appears" in a vast number of cultures and their poetic forms. Indeed, Herder believed Hebrew parallelism to be the origin of all poetic parallelism writ large the world over. This position is not accurate, of course, because Ugaritic poetry (see Pardee; LeMon), as well as other ancient Semitic poetries, contain parallelism (Foster, xvi-xvii; Reiner, 298; Buccellati, 119-20) and antedate the OT, sometimes by centuries. Note one example from the Epic of Gilgamesh II.43-44:

> He anointed himself with oil, turned into
> a man,
> He put on clothing, became like a warrior.
> (Foster, xvii)

Nevertheless, ever since Lowth's breakthrough lectures, scholars of poetries as varied and disparate as Finnish, Chinese, Mongolian, Indic and Turkic (to name but a few) have identified parallel structures in their respective poetries, describing them on analogy with the poetry of the Hebrews (see O'Connor 1993; Gentz) (the same is true for ancient Near Eastern parallelism [see Watson 2007, 130]). Consider, for example, the following lines from *Beowulf*, which exhibit later propensities toward parallelism:

> The leader of the troop unlocked his
> word-hoard;
> The distinguished one delivered this answer.
> (Heaney, 19)

Then there is the great English poet Gerard Manley Hopkins (1844-1889). Writing thousands of years after *Beowulf* or the Epic of Gilgamesh, Hopkins adopted biblical parallelism as a model for the foundational structural device of his poetry and claimed that it was fundamental to all poetic speech. From Lowth, via Herder, to Hopkins—among the many others who could be mentioned—parallelism had morphed from a characteristic of Hebrew verse to a universal poetic principle.

No one has done more to promote this expansive understanding of parallelism than the Russian-born linguist R. Jakobson. Jakobson cited and accepted Hopkins's notion that parallelism was foundational to poetry, subsequently delineating extensive parallel structures in Russian folk songs. Significantly, Jakobson argued that parallelism is not simply an intracolonic phenomenon. Instead, he saw parallelism at work everywhere in a poem: in its microstructures, including the repetition of individual letters, syllables and words (according to Jakobson, rhyme is just another form [phonological] of parallelism), as well as in macrostructures such

as *inclusios, *refrains and the repetition of images or ideas throughout a poem. So, for Jakobson, *any coupling or repetition at any distance* within a poem constituted parallelism, and he claimed that parallelism (understood in this very broad way) was the essential means by which all poets structure discourse.

Jakobson's seminal work inspired a generation of linguistic anthropologists to study parallelism in this broad sense, going deep into poetry, especially its syntax, in the process. These efforts have prompted some to suggest that parallelistic poetry has similar rhetorical and psychological effects across cultures. P. Boodberg wrote in 1954 that "parallelism . . . is intended to achieve a result reminiscent of binocular vision, the superimposition of two syntactical images in order to endow them with solidity and depth, the repetition of the pattern having the effect of binding together syntagms that appear at first rather loosely aligned" (cited in Fox, 27). Building off of Boodberg's suggestion, J. Fox (28) speculated that "if . . . the brain's processing of verbal information is of the same order as its processing of visual information, then there may well be a neuro-physiological underpinning for the almost hypnotic appeal of [parallelistic] ritual language performances." When linguistic anthropological research like this is taken into account, one emerges with a kind of common (even universal?) poetic parallelism that is not simply a parochial (Hebrew) poetic device but rather a structure of human thought—at the very least, a structure of the poetic mind (see Wagner, 1-26; Kinzie, 57).

If there is any truth to this, then parallelism is not simply a device or form of Hebrew poetry but rather is a primary avenue by which meaning is conveyed within the poems of the OT (see Alter, 205; Berlin 1985, 17, 140-41)—and not just there, but in many different kinds of poetry, from many different parts of the world, in many different languages. In this perspective, parallelism is very much the spirit of poetry, but that spirit has come a long way from Herder's day. It is no longer a romanticized spirit that blows wherever the spirit will; instead it is a ubiquitous, even robotic, spirit that moves with bewildering linguistic, grammatical and syntactical precision.

2.4. Reassessing Parallelism.

2.4.1. Linguistic Approaches. Although it is true that "repetition of sound, syllable, word, phrase, line, strophe, metrical pattern, or syntactic structure lies at the core of any definition of poetry" (Shapiro, 1035), one might well ask Jakobson et al. if their broad definition of parallelism, rooted as it is in repetition, is the same thing as *biblical* parallelism. Has parallelism, in its broad and ever-varied linguistic construal(s), largely outgrown its usefulness as an analytical category? Two important writers on Hebrew poetry would answer this question in the affirmative, at least to some degree. But before turning to the work of J. Kugel and R. Alter, we should note that a number of biblical scholars have followed Jakobson, approaching biblical parallelism largely as a grammatical-syntactical phenomenon; indeed, Lowth (1834, ix) himself spoke of parallelism "in the form of grammatical construction." Included here is the work of M. O'Connor, which offers an understanding of Hebrew line structure as governed by a highly complex system of syntactical "constraints" (see O'Connor 1997, esp. 65; 1993; see also Holladay). This syntactical constriction, not parallelism, O'Connor argues, is the fundamental feature of Hebrew poetry. Even so, O'Connor (1993, 877) believes that the "core of . . . p[arallelism] is [also] syntactic; when syntactic frames are set in equivalence by p[arallelism], the elements filling those frames are brought into alignment as well, esp[ecially] on the lexical level (thus the term 'semantic p[arallelism]')." This is to say that syntactical parallelism precedes semantic parallelism, and similar sentiment undergirds the important linguistic work of E. Greenstein among others (cf., e.g., Berlin 1985; *ABD* 5.135-62; Collins; Geller). Greenstein pursues the deep structure of parallel lines, observing that oftentimes this deep structure is precisely parallel even though the surface structure seems patently not. The problem here, however, is twofold: (1) it is probably safe to say that many, if not most, readers (at least those who are not linguists) rarely, if ever, are consciously aware of deep structure; (2) more importantly, the deep structure is often defined so generically (e.g., a sentence comprising a noun phrase and verb phrase, the latter of which consists of a verb and another noun phrase as the object) as to be of little interpretive value. However, Greenstein's attention to psycholinguistics—that is, how parallelism affects audience perception—is a welcome and significant development (see also Berlin 1985, 9-10). Briefly, Greenstein

(54) argued that the more difficult (or incomplete) the parallelism, the more it demanded "effort" or "audience participation": "Gaps in surface stimuli place a higher level of involvement on the perceiver. . . . The audience is engaged by having to form the complete image in its mind. . . . [Incomplete parallelism] involves greater processing by the audience and is therefore engaging; [complete parallelism] represents a full stimulus and tends to disengage" (cf. Berlin 1985, 134).

Building upon the work of Greenstein, but especially on that of Jakobson, Berlin has offered what is probably the most robust treatment of biblical parallelism from a linguistic perspective (but see also Pardee), treating it in its grammatical (morphological and syntactical), lexical and semantic (including word pairs and patterning), and phonological (sound pairs) aspects. Her treatment is especially noteworthy for its balance, taking care not to privilege syntax over semantics (or vice versa): "both are important aspects of parallelism, along with . . . other aspects" (Berlin 1985, 23). Employing the broad view of Jakobson and tracing parallelism in so many different facets and on so many levels of the poem, Berlin (1985, 4) is able to conclude that "in a certain sense parallelism *is* the essence of poetry." Like Greenstein, she pays attention to literary effect (psycholinguistics), pointing out, among other things, that parallelistic contexts influence one's expectation of parallelism. Writ large, such an observation could explain Lowth's creation of "synthetic parallelism" in the first place: equivalences in close proximity, the similarity of surface structures, and the number of linguistic equivalences in so much of Hebrew poetry encourages one to read other verses, also, as binary sentences (see Berlin 1985, 134).

As Berlin's work makes clear (see also Geller), many who write from a linguistic perspective recognize that the meaning of a poem is not exhausted by discussion of its syntax (see Howard, 346-47, 350, 367; Alter, 215 n. 11). The same is true for parallelism. To repeat an earlier sentiment: if parallelism is the spirit of Hebrew poetry, one wonders if the heaping up of rules—typological or, in the linguistic case, syntactical—has not killed that spirit. And, again, is parallelism ultimately and in some sense finally or only repetition? The works of Kugel and Alter speak to both these issues of poetic meaning and how parallelism is both more and less than repetition. Though differing in many ways (see, e.g., Alter, 18-19), they are united on several fronts, especially in their basic agreement that the Lowthian system misunderstands parallelism (and thus Hebrew poetry), and that parallelism can be spoken of in fairly straightforward, even simple, terms rather than only through exceedingly complex syntactical or semantic analyses.

2.4.2. J. Kugel. Kugel's work appeared before Alter's. His contribution is twofold. First, he challenged the notion that parallelism was the defining mark of Hebrew poetry. He pointed out that there are a number of prose texts and, still more basically, certain features of Hebrew prose that reflect supposedly poetic aspects, most notably parallel terms and structures (e.g., Num 5:12-15 [see Kugel 1981, 64]). Conversely, there are some poetic texts that are difficult to define as parallel in any meaningful sense of the term (e.g., Ps 119:54). Hence, one "can no longer equate parallelism and Hebrew poetry" (Petersen and Richards, 27) but instead must reckon with a prose-poetry continuum. (Contrary to some opinion, however, Kugel did not give up on distinguishing poetry and prose completely but rather felt that a simplistic, hard-and-fast distinction between the two was unhelpful to interpreting both [see Kugel 1984, esp. 110, 115].) This observation has far-reaching consequences that cannot be dealt with here, but it suffices to note that it strikes yet another blow against Lowth's (or, at least, the Lowthians') equation of parallelism and poetry (see O'Connor 1997). Second, Kugel leveled a withering critique on Lowth's three categories of synonymous, antithetical and synthetic parallelism. Kugel (1984, 107) thinks that "the taxonomic approach to parallelism has in the past proven largely futile, and that the multiplication of categories of semantic or other parallelism has had a particularly diverting, and therefore negative, effect on an overall understanding." The taxonomic approach is obviously that of Lowth and followers such as Newman and Popper, Gray, and others. In its place, Kugel has offered something that is simpler: a focus on what he calls the "pause sequence." Kugel represents this schematically as follows:

_____ / _____ //

Here, the first dash is the A "clause" (remem-

ber that Kugel does not think of poetic lines or cola proper), which is followed by a brief pause, then by the B "clause" and a longer pause (Kugel 1981, 51). Kugel (1984, 107) understands this pause sequence as "seconding," and believes it to be the characteristic mode of parallelism. In seconding, "B typically reinforces A by backing it up, going it one better, amplifying, embellishing, and so forth" (Kugel 1984, 108). So, in his now famous definition, Kugel (1981, 1, 23, 42, 58) defines biblical parallelism as "A is so, and what's more, B" or "A, and as a matter of fact, B." In point of practice, there is a virtually infinite number of ways that B seconds A—for example:

- true addition ("'A is so, and what's more B,' that is, both A and B are so")
- equation ("'A is so, yes, B is so,' that is, A *or* B is so, it does not matter which")
- "going one better" ("'A is so, nay, B is so,' that is, in fact B is so") (Kugel 1981, 43)

Even so, "taxonomy and re-tropification" are dangers that must be avoided because the delineation and multiplication of categories "risks departing from that basic, 'seconding' sentence which underlies their particulars and whose nature has determined the quality of the medial and final pauses in the sentence" (Kugel 1984, 108). As Kugel (1981, 58) puts it, "Biblical parallelism is of one sort, 'A, and what's more, B,' or a hundred sorts; but it is not three." Taxonomic approaches to parallelism are "a hundred" (or more); Lowth's are three. Both numbers do not add up to the "one sort" (seconding) that Kugel has identified. The end of Lowthian categories could hardly be put any more strongly.

2.4.3. R. Alter. Building on the insights of B. Hrushovski, Alter came to similar conclusions as Kugel, but independently (see Alter, xi). Alter (1985, 10) understands the poetic line as marked by "dynamic movement from one verset [or line/colon] to the next," not by synonymous stasis. In fact, "literary expression abhors complete parallelism, just as language resists true synonymity, usage always introducing small wedges of difference between closely akin terms" (Alter 1985, 10). Alter (10-11) traces the understanding of "semantic modifications" or "disharmony in a harmonious [parallelistic] context" back to Herder, who observed that "the two [parallel members] . . . confirm, elevate and strengthen each other in their convictions or their rejoicings" (Herder, 1.40). So, in a memorable phrase not unlike Kugel's, Alter (11) epitomizes the relationship between parallelistic lines as "how much more so," stating that "this impulse to intensification is . . . the motor force in thousands of lines of biblical poetry." Alter (12) does admit that it is not "obligatory that every paired set of terms in parallel versets reflect development or intensification," but in most cases, at least according to Alter's perceptive readings, most do. This development or intensification happens in larger poetic structures and movements but also in words set in parallel where the "predominant pattern of biblical poetry is to move from a standard term in the first verset to a more literary or highfalutin term in the second verset" (Alter 1985, 13). A good example is in Genesis 49:11b:

> He washes his garment in *wine,*
> and his robe in *the blood of grapes.* (our
> translation)

The effect of such "heightening or intensification . . . of focusing, specification, concretization, even what could be called dramatization" (Alter 1985, 19)—the "how much more so" in semantically paired lines (and there are numerous types)—"is clearly to introduce a 'new perception' through the device of parallelism" (Alter 1985, 16).

Again, though Kugel and Alter have points of difference, they are united in asserting the wrong-headedness of the Lowthian tripartite schema for understanding (let alone exhausting) the possibilities of relationships in the parallelistic line. Still further, they concur that the emphasis in Lowth's system (and in those who follow him overmuch) has been too strongly (and wrongly) placed on synonymity (see also Clines). Linguistic approaches to parallelism would say much the same. But it is safe to say that Kugel and Alter go further, laying the accent in their understanding of parallelism heavily and clearly on difference—the differentiation between parallel lines (see Kuntz 1993, 325-26; Berlin, *NIB* 4.304). As Alter (18 [italics added]) puts it, "The evidence of line after line of biblical verse suggests that we are too quick to infer [the] automatic and formulaic rhetorical gesture of repetition when *more than that is going on.*" Adjudicating the role of sameness versus difference in rep-

etition is, in fact, a large issue of debate in both literature and hermeneutics (see, e.g., Strawn). It cannot be solved here. Even so, it should be noted that some theorists (especially those depending on Jakobson) continue to speak extensively of modes of recurrence, of which repetition, equivalence, similarity, symmetry and congruence are part (e.g., Nel), and that others maintain that, in many ways, Lowth was right in seeing that parallelism is largely "a matter of correspondence" (Petersen and Richards, 34; cf. Berlin 1985, 2), even if that correspondence is diverse and pluriform. We would want to assert, in some distinction from Alter and Kugel, that the repetition at work, at least in some "parallel" or congruent constructions, indicates that *sameness* is every bit as important as *difference.* This assertion is, in no small way, the result of learning from the insights of both linguistic and literary approaches to parallelism. *Both* sameness *and* difference matter. To neglect one and favor another is to mistake something crucial about the nature of Hebrew prosody (see similarly Berlin 1985, 11, 154 n. 2).

2.5. Main Types of Parallelism. The history of research on parallelism indicates that one must navigate between the Scylla of Lowth's overly simplistic tripartite schema, on the one hand, and the Charybdis of falling prey to an ever-expanding taxonomy of subtypes that delivers diminishing returns, on the other. Even so, as Alter (10) asserts, parallelism offers a framework wherein disharmony functions within a larger harmonious context. Or, as Berlin (*NIB* 4.307) puts it, "The effect [of parallelism] is to advance the thought, while at the same time creating a close relationship between the parallelism's constituent parts." So, with all due respect to Kugel's critique of the taxonomic approach, and despite the fact that Lowth's categories are flawed, it is still possible, perhaps even necessary, to speak of different types of parallelism. Indeed, a number of scholars have offered such typologies (see Berlin 1985; Pardee; Watson 1994; 2001; Alonso Schökel), and a handful of types are selectively summarized below. Most, but not all, of these have been chosen due to their perceptibility—that is, how readily apparent and available they are to the reader (see Berlin 1985, 10, 130-35). In addition to the fact that the listing below is not comprehensive (and a comprehensive listing would miss much of the point [see Kugel 1981; cf. Berlin 1985, 2]), one must always remember that skillful poets work both within and against conventions. So, although the types given below are important, this listing neglects numerous examples of mixed types.

2.5.1. Parallelism of Morphological Elements. This category includes such things as the repetition of the same (or a semantically related) verbal root but in different aspects. For example, in Psalm 29:10 the Hebrew root *yšb* ("sit") appears in both the perfective and imperfective aspects:

YHWH sat enthroned *[yāšāb]* at the flood;
YHWH sits enthroned *[wayyēšeb]*, king
    forever. (Berlin 1985, 35)

Another example comes from Psalm 24:7, where the same verbs appear in different conjugations:

Lift up *[śĕʾû; Qal of nsʾ]* your head, O gates;
and be lifted up *[wĕhinnāśʾû; Niphal of nsʾ]*,
    O ancient doors.

2.5.2. Parallelism of Number. This appears when consecutive lines contain cardinal or ordinal numbers, with the number usually increasing from the first line to the second, often in an "x // x+1" pattern (e.g., Job 5:19; 33:24; Ps 62:11 [MT 62:12]; Prov 6:16; 30:15, 18, 21, 29; Eccles 11:2). The prevalence of this type of parallelism confirms that numbers in Hebrew poetry typically convey relative plurality rather than exact specificity, as in, for example, Micah 5:5 [MT 5:4]:

Then we will raise against him SEVEN
    shepherds,
EIGHT chiefs of men. (Watson 2001, 144)

2.5.3. Staircase Parallelism. This occurs when a thought is interrupted by an epithet or other element, only to have the thought resumed from the beginning and completed in the next line (Watson 2001, 151). Note the tricola in Psalm 77:16 [MT 77:17]:

When the waters saw you, O God,
when the waters saw you, they were afraid;
the very deep trembled. (NRSV)

Also Proverbs 31:4:

It is not for kings, O Lemuel,
It is not for kings to drink wine,
or for rulers to desire strong drink. (NRSV)

2.5.4. Ballast Variant Parallelism. Here, the second line exhibits ellipsis. Ellipsis (also called "gapping") is one of the most common features of Hebrew poetry (see O'Connor 1997, 122-29). It is when one element from the first line is left out in the next (reverse ellipsis is when an element from the second is left out of the first). In ballast variant parallelism the second line is expanded, despite the ellipsis, so that the lines roughly correspond in length (cf. Gray's "incomplete parallelism with compensation" [see 2.2 above]). Take, for example, Proverbs 7:16:

I have decked my couch with coverings,
colored spreads of Egyptian linen. (NRSV)

The second line contains no verb clause describing the action. The poet balances the length of the two lines by presenting an expanded description of the bed coverings, which were introduced only cursorily in the first line.

2.5.5. Positive-negative Parallelism. This occurs when the same or similar idea(s) is expressed first positively and then negatively (Berlin 1985, 56). Consider Proverbs 6:20:

My child, keep your father's commandment,
and do not forsake your mother's teaching.
(NRSV)

2.5.6. Gender-matched Parallelism. Proverbs 6:20 also evidences gender-matched parallelism, where "father," a masculine noun in the first line, is balanced in the second by a feminine noun, "mother." Despite the frequency of this pattern in Hebrew verse, most gender-matched parallelism is difficult to identify in English translation (see Watson 1994, 192-239). Psalm 85:11 [MT 85:12] offers a further example, in which two grammatically feminine terms in the first line correspond to masculine terms in the second.

Truth [*ʾĕmet*, fem.] will spring up from the
    earth [*ʾereṣ*, fem.],
and justice [*ṣedeq*, masc.] will look down
    from the heavens [*šāmayim*, masc.]. (our
    translation)

2.5.7. Nominal-pronominal Parallelism. This is a frequently occurring pattern in which one line contains a proper noun and the second line replaces the noun with a pronoun. Psalm 33:2 is a well-balanced example:

> Praise the LORD *[yhwh]* with the lyre;
> make melody to him *[lô]* with the harp of ten strings. (NRSV)

2.5.8. Half-line or *Internal Parallelism.* This type demonstrates that parallelism is not limited to bicola or tricola (see Watson 1994, 104-91). Rather, parallel elements may appear within a single line of poetry, as in Job 1:21:

> The LORD gave, and the LORD has taken away. (NRSV)

Internal parallelism often appears in a line that does not correspond explicitly to the lines surrounding it. In such cases it seems that internal parallelism provides these (mono)cola with balance and symmetry so that they can stand on their own among other, more tightly parallel lines. It functions, in other words, "to strengthen a structure otherwise lacking in cohesiveness" (Pardee, 188).

2.5.9. Macro- and Microparallelisms. As noted earlier, linguistic approaches to parallelism in the tradition of Jakobson have expanded the concept to such a degree that it may be traced not only between two or three lines but also across large sections of poetry or poems as a whole (see Pardee; LeMon). In this way, *inclusios, *chiasms, *refrains and other types of repetition (imagistic or ideational) become examples of macrostructural parallelism. Many types of macroparallelism are perceptible to readers of the Bible in English; unfortunately, many linguistic forms of parallelism are lost in translation, especially when they are of the microstructural variety. Such is the case with phonological parallelism, otherwise known as assonance (and consonance), alliteration and rhyme.

Given the plethora of forms and types of parallelism, some of which are discernable in translation and many of which are not, it is easy to lose sight of what it means to interpret Hebrew poetry. Interpreting a poem is not coterminous with simply identifying the various types of parallelism at work, even though the latter task can help with the former. Instead, the task of interpretation entails discerning how these parallelisms function, how they provide structure to the poem, and how that structure and those parallelisms contribute to the poem's meaning, much of which is not contingent solely upon parallelism. Finally, when facing the daunting task of interpreting poetry, biblical or otherwise, one must remember that poems resist easy analysis, categorization and paraphrase (see Longenbach; Kinzie). They elude interpretation even as they invite and require it. A poem is a poem and means as a poem, creating meaning through its poetry. This is no tautology but rather the nature of poetic language, what Jakobson called "the poetic function"—the way poetic language functions to draw attention to itself and focuses on the message for its own sake (see Berlin 1985, 7, 9, 17, 140-41). The meaning of the parallel line is, then, at a profound poetic level, irreducibly the parallel line itself.

3. "Theological Parallelism."

It remains to speak of further meanings created by Hebrew parallelism and the scholarly work done on it. To take the former issue first, an interesting case is found in the work of Augustine. Like other authors of the time, Augustine practiced a kind of prosopological exegesis "wherein the reader of the psalm identifies what person *[prosopon]* is speaking in a given verse or to what character a verse refers" (McCarthy, 31). At the same time, especially in his early work on the psalms, Augustine believed that all Scripture spoke of Christ and the church, the head and his body (*de domino et corpore eius*). It was the task of the exegete, then, to discern when the verse's referent shifted from head to body or vice versa. In practice, however, Augustine tended to mix the distinct voices of Christ and the church into the one voice of the whole Christ (McCarthy, 31-32). This singular voice of Christ comprises all his members (*Enarrat. Ps.* 17.51) and "comes to express, if not actually effect, the union of God and humanity, the one true mediator" (McCarthy, 32). This means that Christ spoke human words and humans can speak Christ's, or, in Augustine's own words, "Let Christ speak, because the Church speaks in Christ, and Christ speaks in the Church, both body in the head and head in the body" (*Enarrat. Ps.* 30[2] s.1.4).

This exchange of words, which is "rooted in the divine Word's appropriation of human flesh, allows Augustine to emphasize the singularity of the psalms' subject" (McCarthy, 32).

Augustine's approach to the psalms does not manifest a technical appreciation of the types and forms of parallelistic poetry. Even so, it is important to observe that in many ways his interpretation is only possible with, and is in fact facilitated by, parallelism. Moreover, in his ultimate emphasis on the unity of the "one voice," Augustine prefigures, in his own way, theorists who also stress the ultimately unified nature of parallel Hebrew bicola. What is important in Augustine's reading is how he applies these insights to produce a kind of "theological parallelism" whereby oneness is forged out of twoness (cf. Berlin 1985, 16): Christ and the members of his body (the church) are combined in the one voice of the whole, incarnate Christ.

4. Parallelism and the Canon of Scripture.
A second additional meaning created by parallelism or, in this case, by the scholarly work on parallelism is found in the work of C. Miles, who has employed research on parallelism to profitably (and somewhat metaphorically) understand the relationship of the two Testaments of the Christian Bible (see Miles, 179-95). Miles (179) suggests that "we consider the canon of Scripture on analogy with a . . . [bicolon] of Hebrew verse." Depending on Kugel's work in particular, Miles posits that the OT and NT are like the A and B lines of a Hebrew bicolon. Just as the relationship between the two lines is variable and elastic, so too the relationship between the Testaments cannot be construed simplistically or monodirectionally, as is done in, for instance, many of the law-gospel, promise-fulfillment, and narrative schemata that are familiar from homiletical treatments of the OT or from various OT or biblical theologies. Many (certainly not all) of these schemata treat the OT as little more than background, introduction or premise—oftentimes flawed or erroneous in some way—for the "climax" that comes in the NT. But, as Miles (186) points out, "The function of parallelism is not to focus our attention [only] on the second [line]. The 'true addition' represented in the 'what's more' of B is not an end in itself, for, as Kugel makes clear, A + B is a *single statement*. . . . What is heightened or intensified, therefore, is

not the meaning of one *part* of the poetic line (namely, part B), but the meaning of the poetic . . . [bicolon] *as a whole.*"

Pragmatically, this means that a virtually infinite number of approaches to the OT's relationship to the NT (and, correlatively, the homiletical use of the OT) are authorized and recommended—indeed, as many as the number of ways two lines of a bicolon can be related (Miles, 190-91; cf. Berlin 1985, 127; *NIB* 4.308). At times, the relationship between the Testaments is one of virtual synonymy; they say virtually the same thing, with the OT's witness sufficient, to some degree at least, in and of itself. But at other times the relationship is otherwise. Whatever the case, there is always a sense of seconding, "what's more," and "afterwardness" in the B line of the NT (Miles, 188). Even so, understanding the Testaments per Hebrew parallelism will permit no simple supersessionism(s): "there is never a sense in the dynamic of Hebrew parallelism in which A is devalued or made obsolete" (Miles, 188-89). Instead, just as "A + B is a single statement" (Miles 2000:186 [cf. 189 on the whole being different than the sum of its parts "because the parts influence or contaminate each other," Clines, 95]), so too the Christian Bible, comprised of two Testaments, is a single statement—"the gospel of God," to use Miles's (190) terms.

> In this approach, we will still find it necessary to attend to the things that the Testaments equate and the things that they contrast, but we will do so with the understanding that it is through the relationship their parallelism creates that we are shown the message of Scripture as a whole. Or, to state the claim even more strongly, it is through the dynamic interplay of the Old and New Testaments, that is, through the various expressions of their parallelism, that the meaning of the gospel of God is realized. (Miles, 189)

Such a position has ramifications for the individual treatment of both Testaments as well. So, on the one hand, "the New Testament witness is never simply privileged *a priori*" (Miles, 192), and, on the other, "the rhetorical effect achieved when the Testaments are formally adjoined . . . is not a diminishing of the significance of the Old Testament, but a heightening or intensification of the meaning of the canon of Scripture as a whole" (Miles, 191).

5. Conclusion.
In conclusion, the study of parallelism not only casts essential light on the meaning of a large corpus of the biblical text (approximately one-third of the OT is poetry) but also may raise one's sensitivities toward the theological interpretation of some of the poetic passages therein, while at the same time affording unique insight into the structure and interpretation of the *canon of Scripture itself. Parallelism might also help to explain the function of poetic metaphor, the two being "two sides of the same coin—counterparts of the same phenomenon in a different dimension . . . parallelism operat[ing] in the linguistic dimension the way metaphor operates in the conceptual dimension" (Berlin 1997, 27-28). Although parallelism may not contain meaning within itself as a poetic device or linguistic structure (Berlin 1985, 135, 138), "by controlling the ways by which words reach their destination parallelism always has meaning" (Greenstein, 70); and by structuring the text, parallelism "has an impact on how its meaning is arrived at" (Berlin 1985, 135). Since "the poetic function—the 'focus on the message for its own sake'—is achieved through parallelism . . . [then] parallelism becomes our entrée into the message" (Berlin 1985, 17 [see further, 138-41]). If even a portion of the above sentiments are true, then despite the very real and perduring difficulties associated with analyzing parallelism, the attempt is clearly worth the effort.

See also ACROSTIC; AMBIGUITY; ELLIPSIS; HEBREW LANGUAGE; LYRIC POETRY; ORAL POETRY; POETICS, TERMINOLOGY OF; SOUND PATTERNS; TERSENESS; TEXT, TEXTUAL CRITICISM; WORDPLAY.

BIBLIOGRAPHY. **W. F. Albright,** *Yahweh and the Gods of Canaan: A Historical Analysis of Two Contrasting Faiths* (repr., Winona Lake, IN: Eisenbrauns, 1990 [1968]); **L. Alonso Schökel,** *A Manual of Hebrew Poetics* (SubBi 11; Rome: Pontifical Biblical Institute, 2000); **R. Alter,** *The Art of Biblical Poetry* (New York: Basic Books, 1985); **A. Baker,** "Parallelism: England's Contribution to Biblical Studies," *CBQ* 35 (1973) 429-40; **A. Berlin,** *The Dynamics of Biblical Parallelism* (Bloomington: Indiana University Press, 1985); idem, "On Reading Biblical Poetry: The Role of Metaphor," in *Congress Volume: Cambridge, 1995,* ed. J. A. Emerton (VTSup 66; Leiden: E. J. Brill, 1997) 25-36; idem, "Reading Biblical Poetry," in *The Jewish Study Bible,* ed. A. Berlin and M. Z. Brettler (Oxford: Oxford University Press, 2004) 2097-104; idem, "Introduction to Hebrew Poetry," *NIB* 4.301-15; idem, "Parallelism," *ABD* 5.135-62; **G. Buccellati,** "On Poetry—Theirs and Ours," in *Lingering Over Words: Studies in Ancient Near Eastern Literature in Honor of William L. Moran,* ed. T. Absuch, J. Huehnergard and P. Steinkeller (HSS 37; Atlanta: Scholars Press, 1990) 105-34; **D. J. A. Clines,** "The Parallelism of Greater Precision," in *Directions in Biblical Hebrew Poetry,* ed. E. Follis (JSOTSup 40; Sheffield: JSOT Press, 1987) 77-100; **T. Collins,** *Line-Forms in Hebrew Poetry: A Grammatical Approach to the Stylistic Study of the Hebrew Prophets* (SPSM 7; Rome: Pontifical Biblical Institute, 1978); **F. M. Cross,** "Toward a History of Hebrew Prosody," in *From Epic to Canon: History and Literature in Ancient Israel* (Baltimore: Johns Hopkins University Press, 1998) 135-50; **F. M. Cross and D. N. Freedman,** *Studies in Ancient Yahwistic Poetry* (2nd ed.; Grand Rapids: Eerdmans, 1997 [1975]); **B. R. Foster,** ed., *The Epic of Gilgamesh: A New Translation, Analogues, Criticism* (New York: W. W. Norton, 2001); **J. J. Fox,** ed., *To Speak in Pairs: Essays on the Ritual Languages of Eastern Indonesia* (CSOLC 15; Cambridge: Cambridge University Press, 1988); **D. N. Freedman,** "Prolegomenon," in *The Forms of Hebrew Poetry: Considered with Special Reference to the Criticism and Interpretation of the Old Testament,* by G. B. Gray (repr. New York: KTAV, 1972 [1915]) xxxvi-xxxvii; idem, *Pottery, Poetry, and Prophecy: Studies in Early Hebrew Poetry* (Winona Lake, IN: Eisenbrauns, 1980); **S. A. Geller,** *Parallelism in Early Biblical Poetry* (HSM 20; Missoula, MT: Scholars Press, 1979); **J. Gentz,** "Zum Parallelismus in der chinesischen Literatur," in *Parallelismus membrorum,* ed. A. Wagner (OBO 224; Fribourg: Academic Press; Göttingen: Vandenhoeck & Ruprecht, 2007) 241-69; **S. Gevirtz,** *Patterns in the Early Poetry of Israel* (2nd ed.; Chicago: University of Chicago Press, 1973); **D. W. Goodwin,** *Text-Restoration Methods in Contemporary U.S.A. Biblical Scholarship* (Naples: Istituto Orientale di Napoli, 1969); **G. B. Gray,** *The Forms of Hebrew Poetry: Considered with Special Reference to the Criticism and Interpretation of the Old Testament* (repr., New York: KTAV, 1972 [1915]); **E. L. Greenstein,** "How Does Parallelism Mean?" in *A Sense of Text: The Art of Language* *in the Study of Biblical Literature; Papers from a Symposium*, ed. E. L. Greenstein (Winona Lake, IN: Eisenbrauns, for Dropsie College, 1983) 41-70; **S. Heaney,** *Beowulf: A New Verse Translation* (New York: W. W. Norton, 2000); **J. G. Herder,** *The Spirit of Hebrew Poetry*, trans. J. Marsh (2 vols.; Burlington, VT: Edward Smith, 1833 [1782-1783]); **W. L. Holladay,** "*Hebrew Verse Structure Revisited (I-II): Which Words 'Count'? Conjoint Cola, and Further Suggestions,*" *JBL* 118 (1999) 19-32, 401-16; **G. M. Hopkins,** "Poetic Diction [1865]," in *The Collected Works of Gerard Manley Hopkins*, 4: *Oxford Essays and Notes*, ed. L. Higgens (Oxford: Oxford University Press, 2006) 120-22; **D. M. Howard Jr.,** "Recent Trends in Psalms Study," in *The Face of Old Testament Studies*, ed. D. W. Baker and B. T. Arnold (Grand Rapids: Baker and Apollos, 1999) 329-68; **B. Hrushovski,** "Prosody, Hebrew," *EncJud* 13.1195-240; **R. Jakobson,** "Grammatical Parallelism and Its Russian Facet," *Language* 42 (1966) 399-429; **J. Jarick,** ed., *Sacred Conjectures: The Context and Legacy of Robert Lowth and Jean Astruc* (LHBOTS 457; London: T & T Clark, 2007); **M. Kinzie,** *A Poet's Guide to Poetry* (Chicago: University of Chicago Press, 1999); **J. L. Kugel,** *The Idea of Biblical Poetry: Parallelism and Its History* (New Haven: Yale University Press, 1981); idem, "Some Thoughts on Future Research into Biblical Style: Addenda to *The Idea of Biblical Poetry*," *JSOT* 28 (1984) 107-17; **J. K. Kuntz,** "Recent Perspectives on Biblical Poetry," *RSR* 19 (1993) 321-27; idem, "Biblical Hebrew Poetry in Recent Research, Part I," *CurBS* 6 (1998) 31-64; idem, "Biblical Hebrew Poetry in Recent Research, Part II," *CurBS* 7 (1999) 35-79; **J. M. LeMon,** "The Power of Parallelism in KTU^2 1.119: Another 'Trial Cut,'" *UF* 37 (2005) 375-94; **J. Longenbach,** *The Resistance to Poetry* (Chicago: University of Chicago Press, 2004); **R. Lowth,** *Lectures on the Sacred Poetry of the Hebrews*, trans. G. Gregory (4th ed.; London: Thomas Tegg, 1839 [1753]); idem, *Isaiah: A New Translation with a Preliminary Dissertation, and Notes, Critical, Philological, and Explanatory* (10th ed.; Boston: William Hilliard, 1834); **M. C. McCarthy,** "An Ecclesiology of Groaning: Augustine, the Psalms, and the Making of Church," *TS* 66 (2005) 23-48; **C. A. Miles,** "Proclaiming the Gospel of God: The Promise of a Literary-Theological Hermeneutical Approach to Christian Preaching of the Old Testament" (Ph.D. diss., Princeton Theological Seminary, 2000); **P. J. Nel,** "Parallelism and Recurrence in Biblical Hebrew Poetry," *JNSL* 18 (1992) 135-42; **L. I. Newman and W. Popper,** *Studies in Biblical Parallelism: Pt. I, Parallelism in Amos; Pt. II, Parallelism in Isaiah, Chapters 1-10* (UCPSP 1/2-3; Berkeley: University of California Press, 1918); **M. O'Connor,** "Parallelism," in *The New Princeton Encyclopedia of Poetry and Poetics*, ed. A. Preminger and T. V. F. Brogan (Princeton, NJ: Princeton University Press, 1993) 877-79; idem, *Hebrew Verse Structure* (repr., Winona Lake, IN: Eisenbrauns, 1997 [1980]); **D. Pardee,** *Ugaritic and Hebrew Poetic Parallelism: A Trial Cut ('nt I and Proverbs 2)* (VTSup 39; Leiden: E. J. Brill, 1988); **D. L. Petersen and K. H. Richards,** *Interpreting Hebrew Poetry* (GBS; Minneapolis: Fortress, 1992); **E. Reiner,** "First-Millennium Babylonian Literature," *CAH*^{2} 3/2 (1992) 293-321; **D. A. Robertson,** *Linguistic Evidence in Dating Early Hebrew Poetry* (SBLDS 3; Missoula, MT: Society of Biblical Literature, 1972); **M. Shapiro,** "Repetition," in *The New Princeton Encyclopedia of Poetry and Poetics*, ed. A. Preminger and T. V. F. Brogan (Princeton, NJ: Princeton University Press, 1993) 1035-37; **B. A. Strawn,** "Keep/Observe/Do—Carefully—Today! The Rhetoric of Repetition in Deuteronomy," in *A God So Near: Essays on Old Testament Theology in Honor of Patrick D. Miller*, ed. B. A. Strawn and N. R. Bowen (Winona Lake, IN: Eisenbrauns, 2003) 215-40; **A. Wagner,** ed., *Parallelismus membrorum* (OBO 224; Fribourg: Academic Press; Göttingen: Vandenhoeck & Ruprecht, 2007); **W. G. E. Watson,** *Traditional Techniques in Classical Hebrew Verse* (JSOTSup 170; Sheffield: Sheffield Academic Press, 1994); idem, *Classical Hebrew Poetry: A Guide to Its Techniques* (2nd ed.; JSOTSup 26; Sheffield: Sheffield Academic Press, 2001); idem, "The Study of Hebrew Poetry: Past—Present—Future," in *Sacred Conjectures: The Context and Legacy of Robert Lowth and Jean Astruc*, ed. J. Jarick (LHBOTS 457; London: T & T Clark, 2007) 124-54; **G. H. Wilson,** *Psalms*, vol. 1 (NIVAC; Grand Rapids: Zondervan, 2002).

J. M. LeMon and B. A. Strawn

PARALLELISMUS MEMBRORUM. See PARALLELISM.

PARANOMASIA. See POETICS, TERMINOLOGY OF; WORDPLAY.

PASSOVER, FESTIVAL OF. See MEGILLOT AND FESTIVALS.

PENTECOST, FESTIVAL OF. *See* MEGILLOT AND FESTIVALS.

PERIPETY. *See* ESTHER 1: BOOK OF.

PERSIA. *See* SUSA.

PERSONIFICATION

Personification is a figure of speech that attributes human characteristics to plants, animals, objects or abstractions. A nearly universal feature of writing and speaking in every age, this device was given the name *prosōpopoeia* (from Gk *prosōpon* ["face"] and *poiein* ["to make"]) by classical rhetoricians. Aristotle (*Rhet.* 3.10.6; 3.11.1-4) praised Homer for speaking of inanimate things as though they were living, making them vivid, and Quintilian (*Inst.* 9.3.89) saw the figure in common sayings such as "Avarice is the mother of cruelty" (see Arthos and Brogan). One contemporary literary approach finds it wherever nonhuman entities are endowed with intelligence and/or speech (Paxson).

If literary works and their symbols are "verbal patterns of experience" (Burke, 152-53), personification is a special form of symbolic action, one that uses depictions of human speaking and acting to convey an emotion, an idea or a strategy for coming to terms with a situation in life. Biblical examples range from the simple metaphor in "Let all the trees of the forest sing for joy" (Ps 96:12) to the extended monologues of *Woman Wisdom (Prov 1:20-33; 8:4-36). In these personifications metaphor and characterization are combined in varying proportions to depict typical patterns of personal interaction, inviting readers to engage them with their own responses. As used throughout Scripture, personification highlights that which characterizes the human person, the ability to use language to enter into relationship with God; it is one of many ways that biblical rhetoric inspires and calls forth obedient love of God.

1. Inchoate (Basic) Personification
2. Synecdochic Personification
3. Collective Personification
4. Characterized Personification

1. Inchoate (Basic) Personification.

Brief and simple attributions of human qualities are scattered throughout *Psalms and, to a lesser extent, the other writings. All creation responds to the work of God with praise, demonstrating the extent of God's majesty and setting an example for human *worship. The seas lift their voice (Ps 93:3-4), joined by the heavens, fields and trees (Ps 96:11-12), the distant shores and all the earth (Ps 97:1), mixing their voices with those of God's people (Ps 98:1-9; 100:1-5; 148:1-14). Mountains are born and sing praise (Ps 90:2; 89:12), but they also look with envy at *Zion, where God resides (Ps 68:15-16). An extended metaphor in Psalm 19:1-6 reflects on the capacity of the heavens to praise and teach, even though "there is no speech, nor are there words." In answer to the protests of *Job, the Lord asks if Job was present at creation when the morning stars sang and heaven shouted for joy (Job 38:7): "Can you send the lightnings . . . so they say to you, 'Here we are'?" (Job 38:35).

Common objects, animals and locales all take on human characteristics. The shepherd's rod and staff offer comfort as a sign of God's care (Ps 23:4), but wine the mocker and beer the brawler will lead the unsuspecting astray (Prov 20:1). The swift ostrich laughs at the horse and rider, while the brave horse laughs at fear (Job 39:18, 22). Earth and Sheol are addressed as though they could hear and respond (Job 16:18; 17:14). Sheol, the barren womb, thirsty earth and hungry fire never say "Enough!" (Prov 30:15-16). The depths of the sea and Abaddon confess that they do not know where *wisdom is to be found (Job 28:14, 22). The land itself cries out when defrauded (Job 31:38), and the deserted roads of conquered Jerusalem mourn (Lam 1:4).

These basic personifications make poetic descriptions vivid and interesting, but they are more than mere ornamentation. What is true of metaphor in general also applies here: personification communicates truth in a unique and compelling way for which there is no substitute.

2. Synecdochic Personification.

A synecdoche is a figure in which a part stands for the whole, or the whole for a part (from Gk *synekdechesthai* ["to take up or understand with another"]). Biblical personifications sometimes attribute an action to the character quality that it reveals. The exclamation by *Naomi in Ruth 2:20 provides an example: "May he be blessed by the LORD, whose kindness has not abandoned the living or the dead." Whether the kindness belongs to the Lord or *Boaz (the grammar allows either), clearly it is this person's kindness (*hesed*) that has not forsaken the two women. Because the act of kindness is given indirect attribution, the quality of the action itself takes center stage. So also the word spoken by God represents divine action and purpose: "By the word of the LORD the heavens were made" (Ps 33:6), a word that runs swiftly like a messenger to carry out the divine will (Ps 147:15-18).

Human emotions and virtues also become actors, sharpening the focus on their role in human motivation and interaction. Two lodgers are contrasted in "Weeping may linger for a night, but joy comes with the morning" (Ps 30:5). Love sleeps and can be awakened (Song 2:7; 8:4), but when stirred, it is stronger than death (Song 8:6-7). Hunger can drive a worker like a taskmaster (Prov 16:26), but a lazy person's appetite just craves and stays hungry (Prov 13:4). Love and faithfulness meet; righteousness and peace kiss (Ps 85:10).

Representative parts of the body can stand for human thoughts, feelings and actions. The psalms speak of the steadfast heart that leaps for joy (Ps 28:7; 51:7), the crushed bones that rejoice (Ps 51:8), and the yearning flesh that faints (Ps 63:1; 84:2), all in answer to the divine call. The heart knows its own bitterness, and the foolish heart rages against the Lord (Prov 14:10; 19:3); in this way the intentions of a person are shown to be private and, at times, even deceptive. The psalmist rebukes the powerful for the evil done with a razor-sharp tongue and then turns to address the deceitful tongue itself: "You love all words that devour" (Ps 52:1-4; cf. Ps 73:8-9; 120:1-4). So also discontent and covetous eyes instigate the mouth that leads to sin (Eccles 4:8; 5:6; cf. Job 15:5-6). A series of proverbs on the mouth and lips imagine that they act according to their own purposes, choosing that which finds favor or is perverse (Prov 10:11, 14, 18, 21, 32).

In sum, the synecdochic personification of actions, emotions, virtues and body members invites readers to deepen their understanding of relationships with God, neighbor and creation by offering a fresh angle of vision and sharpening focus on the positive or negative quality of an interaction.

3. Collective Personification.

Collective personifications place special focus on God's relation with people groups. In some cases they portray rejection of God and the resulting judgment. Nations can conspire against the Lord's anointed (Ps 2:1-2), and a rebellious country can suffer a series of unstable and short-lived rulers (Prov 28:2).

The most developed of these personifications appears in the book of *Lamentations, where conquered Jerusalem is described, named and quoted (some interpreters also believe that the "man of affliction" in Lam 3 is the personified voice of the exiles [see Berlin, 84-85]). Although it is not possible to determine the degree to which it draws from Mesopotamian city laments (Biddle), prophetic imagery (Hillers, 32-41) or the psalms of *lament, the personification of Jerusalem in a variety of female roles startles the imagination and evokes an emotional response. In short, "Jerusalem, personified as a woman, suffers only as a woman can suffer" (Berlin, 8-9).

In the first two chapters of the book the plight of Jerusalem is reported by a grief-stricken observer who periodically turns to address her directly: "To what can I liken you that I may comfort you, Virgin Daughter Zion?" (Lam 2:13b). Abandonment links the various descriptions of *suffering. Jerusalem is empty, left alone like a war widow (Lam 1:1); the image brings together the traditional Deuteronomic sense of widows' vulnerability with the immediate sense of grief. She who was noble and surrounded with servants is now set to forced labor like a slave, weeping bitterly at night with tears on her cheeks (Lam 1:1-2). None of her illicit lovers is there to lend comfort; her friends have betrayed her, even becoming her enemies (Lam 1:16-17), and the plunder and destruction of the temple is described as an act of rape (Lam 1:10).

Personifications of the suffering city name "Zion" (Lam 1:17; 2:6) as "Daughter Zion" (Lam 1:6; 2:1, 4, 8, 10, 13, 18; 4:22), "Virgin Daughter Zion" (Lam 1:15; 2:13), "Daughter Judah" (Lam 2:2; 2:5) and "Daughter Jerusalem" (Lam 2:13; 2:15). The final word to "Daughter Zion" promises an end to punishment, directing it instead on her enemy "Daughter Edom" (Lam 4:21-22). "Daughter" may be poetic speech for any young female, perhaps a diminutive term of endearment for someone of marriageable age (Berlin, 10-12). It may also carry some connotation of home and stability, a counterbalance to the males who go out to make war. In any case, "Daughter" reminds readers that this warfare has battered, violated and deserted one both beloved and vulnerable (Follis, 1103).

The observer's reports are periodically interrupted by the words of Woman Jerusalem herself. Combined use of description and the very words of the distressed, says Aristotle (*Rhet.* 2.8.8-16), are especially effective in calling forth pity. Woman Jerusalem herself asks onlookers, "Is it nothing to you, all you who pass by? . . . Is any suffering like my suffering?" (Lam 1:12). She grieves over her lost and destitute children with words that may have been inspired by the real mothers of Jerusalem who could not feed their children (Lam 1:16; cf. Lam 2:11-12, 19-20; 4:2-4, 9-10). The observer calls her to lament and repent (Lam 2:13-19), and she does, directing her contrition, grief and even her anger to God: "Look, LORD!" (Lam 1:9b, 11b, 20-22; 2:20-22). Although there are other laments in the book spoken by a single male exile (Lam 3) and the collective voice of the people (Lam 5), it is Daughter Zion who turns lament into accusation, asking God, "Whom have you ever treated like this?" (Lam 2:20).

Jerusalem's outcry calls upon the reader to look and see, to come alongside and comfort. Her lament asks God to do the same and break the divine silence that pervades the book. The female experience of suffering becomes the lead metaphor of the book, compelling the poet to speak in a woman's voice (Kaiser, 182). It becomes one among a chorus of voices struggling to find meaning, offering the community of exiles a means to deal with its pain, to express the inexpressible (Heim, 141, 146).

Jerusalem suffers for her sins, but that suffering is nearly unspeakable, especially that of her children. Contemporary readers are thereby encouraged to raise their questions about innocent and inexplicable suffering, particularly in the face of human genocides (as the twentieth century witnessed in Germany, Cambodia, Yugoslavia and Rwanda). At the same time, they are challenged to deepen their theology of sin and judgment, rejecting facile explanations of current events.

In sum, the descriptions and quotations of Woman Jerusalem offer readers and hearers visual image and voice by which they too may situate themselves in relation to God. Some will join with her in lamenting, repenting and contending with God. Others will make stronger identification with those who suffer, increasing their capacity for compassion and service. Ultimately, the personification helps Bible readers engage life at its most raw and profound moments.

4. Characterized Personification.

Compared to Woman Jerusalem, the female figures of Woman Wisdom and Woman Folly in the book of *Proverbs have more highly developed characterizations of personality and purpose. The two are set in contrast: one speaks for the good of her hearers, while the other speaks to their pleasures and ultimately brings about their demise. The opposing life ways of wisdom and *folly lead their followers to life or death, thus setting the stage for a dramatized debate in which each voice vies for attention and allegiance.

The drama reaches its high point in Proverbs 9 as the two become competing hosts, each beckoning passers-by with an invitation to a meal. Woman Wisdom has built her own house, slaughtered meat, and mixed wine with spices to prepare a sumptuous feast. A woman of means, she sends her servants to call out an invitation to the table, a symbol of her teaching: "Leave your simple ways and live, walk in the way of insight" (Prov 9:6). An example of that teaching follows, drawing a contrast between the wise and mockers and urging the listener to choose one way or the other (Prov 9:7-12).

Woman Folly asks no such thing, for she has not left those simple ways herself. She sits idly at the door of her house, without servants, calling out with her own voice a parody of Woman Wisdom's invitation, even repeating her words: "Let all who are simple come to my house!" (Prov 9:16; cf. Prov 9:4). Yet Woman Folly offers no teaching except her claim that stolen water is sweet and bread eaten in secret is delicious. She makes no offer of life as Woman Wisdom does, nor does she disclose that her house is the home of the dead (Prov 9:18). Coming at the end of the series of instructions and lectures that form the introduction to the book (Prov 1:1—9:18), the juxtaposed invitations underline the repeated charge to "get wisdom" (Prov 2:1-6; 3:13-18; 4:5-7; 5:1; 8:10-11). The choice between wisdom and folly is unavoidable; to ignore the charge is to decide for folly.

Moreover, both figures and the words of their debate serve as primary symbols for the many characterizations of wise and foolish living presented throughout the book: "The wise woman builds her house, but the foolish one tears it down with her own hands" (Prov 14:1).

Folly becomes the primary symbol for both the smooth words of the strange or "other" woman (Prov 2:16-19; 5:1-6; 6:23-29) and the deceitful words of evil men (Prov 2:12-15; 4:14-17; 6:12-15). Both forms of seduction illustrate the misuse of speech and its potential to persuade. Woman Folly's "teaching" about stolen water (Prov 9:17) calls to mind the warnings against extramarital relationships (Prov 5:1-23; 7:6-27), and her promises sound remarkably similar to those made by the violent gang (Prov 1:10-19).

Similarly, Woman Wisdom brings together the images of a wise and good wife and associates them with the instruction that the wise parents offer to their son. Wisdom will enter a person's heart and protect it from seduction to evil, just like the parent's teaching (Prov 2:10-16; 6:20-24). Wisdom can be "found" like a wife who brings good things to her husband (Prov 3:13-18; 18:22; 31:10-31) (see Camp). Therefore, the young man is told to love and cherish wisdom, calling her "my sister," a term of marital endearment (Prov 4:6-9; 7:4-5; cf. Song 5:1-2) (see Murphy). As an example of ancient Near Eastern instruction that was typically directed to young men, these personifications must be interpreted and taught in a way that includes men and *women, the young and the old. Moreover, preachers and teachers will remember that both men and women are made examples of wisdom and folly, avoiding gender stereotypes.

But Woman Wisdom is more than a good wife: she is a counselor of kings. Her script is enriched by a monologue that proclaims her love of truthful speech and inspiration of righteous rulers (Prov 8:1-16); the authority that she claims is grounded in her presence at creation. Because she was witness as God established the orders of the cosmos, she can advise human authorities on right social order (Prov 3:19-20; 8:22-36). As personified in Proverbs and Job 28 (and as further developed in the apocryphal books *Sirach, Baruch, *Wisdom of Solomon), wisdom represents a way of life and a mediation of divine instruction that NT writers used to describe Jesus Christ, the wisdom of God (1 Cor 1:24; Col 1:15-17; 2:2-3).

The rich and varied use of personification encourages the biblical interpreter to identify examples of the figure and, more importantly, to discover their rhetorical strategies as expressions of God's desire for relationship. Personification as a kind of symbolic action gives a face and a voice to the broad range of life experiences, skillfully crafted to shape a response of faithfulness.

See also ANIMAL IMAGERY; CREATION IMAGERY; FEMINIST INTERPRETATION; FLORAL IMAGERY; IMAGERY; MOUNTAIN IMAGERY; POETICS, TERMINOLOGY OF; WOMAN WISDOM AND WOMAN FOLLY; ZION.

BIBLIOGRAPHY. **J. Arthos and T. V. F. Brogan,** "Personification," in *The New Princeton Encyclopedia of Poetry and Poetics,* ed. A. Preminger and T. V. F. Brogan (Princeton, NJ: Princeton University Press, 1993) 994; **A. Berlin,** *Lamentations* (OTL; Louisville: Westminster John Knox, 2002); **M. E. Biddle,** "The Figure of Lady Jerusalem: Identification, Deification and Personification of Cities in the Ancient Near East," in *The Biblical Canon in Comparative Perspective,* ed. K. L. Younger Jr., W. W. Hallo and B. Batto (ANETS 11; Lewiston, NY: Edwin Mellen, 1991) 173-94; **T. V. F. Brogan and A. W. Halsall,** "Prosopopoeia," in *The New Princeton Encyclopedia of Poetry and Poetics,* ed. A. Preminger and T. V. F. Brogan (Princeton, NJ: Princeton University Press, 1993) 994; **E. W. Bullinger,** *Figures of Speech Used in the Bible* (Grand Rapids: Baker, 1975) 861-69; **K. Burke,** *Counter-Statement* (2nd ed.; Berkeley: University of California Press, 1968); **C. V. Camp,** *Wisdom and the Feminine in the Book of Proverbs* (BLS 11; Sheffield: Almond, 1985); **E. R. Follis,** "Zion, Daughter of," *ABD* 6.1103; **K. M. Heim,** "The Personification of Jerusalem and the Drama of Her Bereavement in Lamentations," in *Zion, City of Our God,* ed. R. S. Hess and G. J. Wenham (Grand Rapids: Eerdmans, 1999) 129-69; **D. Hillers,** *Lamentations* (rev. ed.; AB 7A; Garden City, NY: Doubleday, 1972); **B. B. Kaiser,** "Poet as 'Female Impersonator': The Imagery of Daughter Zion as Speaker in Biblical Poems of Suffering," *JR* 67 (1987) 164-82; **P. E. Koptak,** "Reading Scripture with Kenneth Burke: Genesis 38," in *To Hear and Obey: Essays in Honor of Fredrick Carlson Holmgren,* ed. P. E. Koptak and B. J. Bergfalk (Chicago: Covenant Publications, 1997) 84-94; idem, *Proverbs* (NIVAC 15; Grand Rapids: Zondervan, 2003); **R. E. Murphy,** "The Personification of Wisdom," in *Wisdom in Ancient Israel: Essays in Honour of J. A. Emerton,* ed. J. Day, R. P. Gordon and H. G. M. Williamson (Cambridge: Cambridge University Press, 1995) 222-33; **J. J. Paxson,** *The Poetics of Personification* (Cambridge: Cambridge University Press, 1994).

P. E. Koptak

PLOT DEVELOPMENT. SEE NOVELLA, STORY, NARRATIVE; RUTH 1: BOOK OF.

POETICS, TERMINOLOGY OF

The terminology used by scholars when discussing Hebrew literature, and especially poetry, can be confusing. This is not just because they use unfamiliar technical terms that the nonspecialist cannot understand; it is also because sometimes different terms are used to refer to the same thing, and occasionally the same term is used with different meanings. The present article concentrates on the more common terms used in discussion of Hebrew poetry. The terms are divided into three groups: (1) those used in discussion of the basic unit of Hebrew poetry; (2) those used to refer to specific features or characteristics of Hebrew poetry; (3) those used to refer to units of poetry larger than the basic unit.

1. The Basic Unit of Hebrew Poetry
2. Features Characteristic of Hebrew Poetry
3. The Structure of a Hebrew Poem

1. The Basic Unit of Hebrew Poetry.

1.1. Definition of Terms. The most common feature of Hebrew poetry is a **sentence**, which is divided into two parts by a pause or break in sense, for which the technical term is **caesura**. This break is marked in modern editions of the Bible by a punctuation mark, a comma or semicolon in English translations and an accent mark in the Hebrew text. In scholarly papers it is sometimes marked by a single or repeated slash—for example, Psalm 33:6-7:

> By the word of the LORD the heavens were made //
> and by the breath of his mouth all their host.
> He gathers the waters of the sea as a heap //
> he puts the deeps in storehouses.

The original Hebrew text did not have punctuation marks, and so the caesura has to be recognized on the grounds of the meaning of the two parts of the sentence and, sometimes, the grammar (the use of "and" in the Hebrew in Ps 33:6 clearly marks a break in the sentence).

Some scholars use the term **line** to refer to the whole sentence (Alter, 9), while others use it of the subunits that make up the sentence (O'Connor, 52; Watson, 12). J. P. Fokkelman (38) uses "line" of the whole sentence and describes it as "the verse in the literary sense." Unfortunately the use of the term **verse** to refer to a unit of Hebrew poetry can cause confusion because these literary verses do not always coincide with the numbered verses in the Bible, a point that Fokkelman (13-14) recognizes. Less common now than it used to be is the use of the term **stich** (sometimes **stichos**) of either the whole sentence (O'Connor, 52) or its subunits (Watson, 12).

A variety of terms are used for the subunits of the sentence. The one now used most commonly is **colon** (pl., **cola**). R. Alter (9) prefers to use the term **verset**, as does Fokkelman (30, 46), though he sometimes uses "colon" as an alternative. M. O'Connor (52) prefers to use the term **line** to refer to the subunits, a term that Watson (12) uses interchangeably with "colon." Although most of the scholars who use the term **hemistich** use it as an alternative to "colon," W. G. E. Watson (12) uses it of "a subdivision of the colon, generally equal to half the length of the colon."

Watson (12) comments, "The two-colon unit can almost be taken as standard in Hebrew poetry." A sentence of this type is called a **bicolon**. Sentences can be made up of three cola (a **tricolon** [e.g., Ps 18:8]), four cola (a **tetracolon**, sometimes called a **quatrain** [e.g., Jer 2:13]) or, rarely, more.

1.2. The Debate. There is a debate about what constitutes the "basic unit" of Hebrew poetry (Gottwald, 831). O'Connor (52-54) argues that it is "the smallest apparent unit," what he calls the line, and others call the colon. D. Clines (95) argues that in a bicolon the meanings of the two cola have to be taken together so that the understanding of one modifies the understanding of the other; as a result, the meaning of the whole is more than the sum of its parts. The same would, of course, apply to a tricolon or tetracolon. Fokkelman (45-47) too recognizes what he calls the verse (a bicolon, tricolon, etc.) as the basic unit of meaning in Hebrew poetry; however, he points out that its meaning must be understood in the context of the whole poem of which it is part.

2. Features Characteristic of Hebrew Poetry.

2.1. Introduction. Scholars differ in their lists of the features that are characteristic of Hebrew poetry. Most agree that *parallelism, *terseness (including *ellipsis) and the use of *imagery are important characteristics. Some, like O'Connor, have gone below the "surface" of the text to look for characteristics at the level of the underlying grammar. There is considerable disagreement about the importance of *meter or rhythm, with most doubtful of their importance. Other features that depend on the sound of words— rhyme, paronomasia, alliteration, assonance— are lost when the Hebrew is translated into another language.

2.2. Parallelism. This term is used to describe the occurrence of a bicolon in which the words in the second colon correspond in some way to those in the first colon. It is generally recognized as *the* characteristic feature of Hebrew poetry. R. Lowth, in the mid-eighteenth century, was the first person to attempt a systematic analysis of parallelism in Hebrew poetry. He identified three main types of parallelism: synonymous, antithetic and synthetic.

In synonymous parallelism the second colon repeats the sense of the first, though with some variation. For example, Psalm 77:11:

I will remember the deeds of the LORD;
yes, I will remember your wonders of old.

An antithetic parallelism occurs when what is said in the second colon contrasts what is said in the first. For example, Psalm 30:5:

For his anger is for a moment;
his favor is for a lifetime.

The third category, synthetic parallelism, included all those bicola in which the second colon did not either repeat or contrast the first. This third category is a rather vague and unsatisfactory one, and so some scholars have proposed ways of understanding the nature of parallelism in Hebrew poetry other than Lowth's three categories. Alter argues that the second colon focuses, heightens or specifies what is expressed in the *first colon. In Psalm 77:11 the "deeds" mentioned in the first colon are specified as "wonders of old" in the second. The second colon of Psalm 30:5 is a heightening of what is said because the brevity of God's anger is contrasted with the long-lasting nature of God's favor. J. Kugel sums up what he sees to be the essence of parallelism in the formula: "A, and what's more, B." B in some way "seconds" the thought of A.

Lowth's approach emphasizes semantic par-

allelism—that is, correspondence between the meanings of the two cola. Berlin draws attention to the importance of grammatical parallelism in Hebrew poetry. This can take various forms. Parallelism can be produced by replacing one word with another that has the same grammatical function: a noun in the first colon may be replaced by a pronoun in the second, as in Psalm 33:8:

Let all the earth fear <u>the LORD</u>,
let all the inhabitants of the world stand in awe of <u>him</u>.

A feminine word may be replaced by a masculine one, or vice versa. A perfect form of a verb can be replaced by an imperfect form. There can also be more extensive grammatical "transformations" to produce parallelism. A noun clause may replace a verbal one, as in Psalm 34:1:

<u>I will bless</u> the LORD at all times,
<u>This praise</u> shall continually be in my mouth.

There can be a change in the mood of the verb. In Psalm 6:5 a statement is put in parallel with a question:

For in death there is no remembrance of you;
in Sheol who can give you praise?

Berlin also puts some emphasis on lexical parallelism. A major aspect of this is the use of traditional "word pairs" such as "man/woman," "earth/heaven" and "loyalty/truth."

2.3. Terseness. Hebrew poetry says what it has to say in as few words as possible. It is rare for a colon to contain more than four words. According to Berlin (5), "It is not parallelism per se, but the predominance of parallelism, combined with terseness, which marks the poetic expression of the Bible." One feature of this terseness is that certain words and particles that are commonly used in prose either are not used at all or are used much less often in poetry. These are the conjunction "and," the definite article (both of which are prefixes in Hebrew), the relative pronoun and the definite-object marker. D. N. Freedman (1987, 16-17) suggests that the frequency with which these occur in a piece of Hebrew text is an excellent indicator of whether that text is poetry or prose.

2.4. Ellipsis. This is the omission of a word within a poetic or grammatical unit where it would be expected to be present. The most common form of ellipsis in Hebrew poetry is the omission of a verb from the second colon of a bicolon. The reader is expected to supply the verb from the first colon. An example is Psalm 114:4:

> The mountains skipped like rams,
> the hills like lambs.

This contributes to the terseness of Hebrew poetry. O'Connor (401) uses the term **gapping** to refer to ellipsis, and he asserts that it is a basic feature of Hebrew poetry and does not occur in Hebrew prose.

2.5. O'Connor's "Constraints." O'Connor has tried to describe Hebrew poetry in terms of the way in which lines (what others call colons) are structured grammatically. The study of grammatical structure is called "syntax." O'Connor argues that Hebrew poetry can be defined in terms of "syntactical patterns," the various ways in which lines are structured. In his view, it is the existence of limitations on the kinds of patterns that occur, what he calls "syntactical constriction," that is the fundamental feature of Hebrew poetry that distinguishes it from prose. In order to understand his "constraints," it is necessary to understand his terminology. He uses three terms to refer to various constituents of a line or colon.

> **Unit.** Most words count as individual units. However, there are some words in Hebrew, called particles, that O'Connor does not count as units. They usually depend on other words.
>
> **Constituent.** This is a word or phrase that has a specific grammatical function in a line or colon. The first line of Psalm 106:7 can be divided into four constituents (each is indicated by the words joined by hyphens): "Our-fathers, when-in-Egypt, did-not-consider your-wonderful-works." The first constituent is the grammatical subject of the line, the third is the action carried out by the subject, and the fourth is the grammatical object of the line. The second is a phrase that defines when the action took place.
>
> **Clause predicators.** The most common of these is the verb. In the example given from

Psalm 106:7, it is the verb "consider."

O'Connor gives a list of "constraints." The first four are fairly straightforward, while the other two more complex.

> A line contains from zero to no more than three clause predicators.
> A line contains at least one and no more than four constituents.
> A line contains at least two and no more than five units.
> A constituent may contain no more than four units.
> If a line contains three clause predicators, it cannot contain a dependent noun or noun phrase, and if it contains two clause predicators, only one of them may have a dependent noun or noun phrase.
>
> If a line contains one or more clause predicators, it cannot contain a noun or noun phrase that is not dependent on one of them.

2.6. Imagery. A characteristic of poetry in many cultures is that it makes more frequent and more intense use of *imagery than is found in prose. This is so with Hebrew poetry. A common way of making a verbal image, a "word picture," is by comparison. The two commonest types of comparison are **simile** and **metaphor**.

A **simile** is an explicit comparison. In English it is often expressed by using the words "like" or "as." For example, "They are like trees planted by rivers of water" (Ps 1:3).

In a **metaphor** the two things being compared are simply equated with one another without using "like" or "as." For example, "The LORD is my shepherd" (Ps 23:1). This can be quite arresting when the similarity between the elements of the metaphor is not immediately obvious, forcing the reader to stop and think about it.

There are several reasons why a poet might want to make use of imagery. First, an image often makes an emotional impact that a straightforward statement would not. Saying, "God looks after me" does not have the impact of "The LORD is my shepherd." Second, images can carry more than one meaning. An ancient Hebrew reader of Psalm 23 would see connotations of royalty in the shepherd image because ancient Near Eastern rulers were often spoken of as shepherds of their people. This brings out a third reason for the use of imagery: it aids the terseness of Hebrew poetry, saying a great deal in just a few words.

2.7. Meter. One feature of poetry in many cultures is the presence of a regular rhythmic sound pattern, called meter (sometimes spelled "metre"). Because biblical Hebrew stopped being a living language over two thousand years ago there are inevitable uncertainties about how it was spoken, and about intonation and stress (*see* Hebrew Language). This is one reason why there is considerable debate about whether meter is a feature of Hebrew poetry and, if it is, what form it takes.

S. Mowinckel, for example, argued that poetry is often connected with singing, and singing implies a rhythm. Thus, it was likely that Hebrew poetry, especially the psalms, would be characterized by meter. Mowinckel (163) argued that "the Hebrew poetic rhythm is in principle iambic." An **iambic meter** is one in which there is an alternation of stressed and unstressed syllables. Mowinckel (172-74) recognized that the meter within a psalm is sometimes irregular and suggested that this might be due to textual errors or later revision and rewriting of the poem.

This irregularity of meter in many Hebrew poems leads some scholars to deny that meter is an important feature of Hebrew poetry (Kugel, 297-98; O'Connor, 138). Kugel argues that whatever approximate regularity there may be in the meter of a poem arises from the balancing of ideas that is a feature of parallelism. Watson (100), however, points to instances of unusual word order in poetry as evidence that the poet was trying to produce a specific pattern of stress. Watson (92) accepts, though, that the meter is not consistent throughout a Hebrew poem. This inconsistency or variability leads S. E. Gillingham (68) to prefer to speak of rhythm rather than meter because "'rhythm' implies discernible patterns, used with fluidity and flexibility throughout a poem."

2.8. Rhyme. Two words rhyme when they sound alike. Rhyme does not play an important role in Hebrew poetry. **End-rhyme**, the correspondence in the sound of words, or the final syllable of words, at the end of the lines in poem is a well-known device in English poetry. It is very rare in Hebrew poetry. When it does occur, usually it is the result of using the same suffix or ending in successive cola (Watson, 231).

2.9. Paranomasia. This is the deliberate use of two or more different words that sound alike. Song of Songs 1:3 provides an example. Here the

words for "your anointing oils" *(šĕmānêkā)* and "your name" *(šĕmekā)* sound alike. This reinforces the idea of the man's reputation ("name") having a good "aroma" like that of anointing oil.

2.10. Alliteration. This is the result of the repetition of the same consonant. Alliteration usually occurs within a colon or bicolon, and it can be seen as a way of giving a kind of cohesion to the unit. In Psalm 127:1 the two words at the end of each colon in the first bicolon contain the Hebrew consonant *bêt* (English transliteration *b*).

> Unless the LORD builds the house / / those who build it labour in vain
> *'im-yhwh lō'-yibneh bayit / / šāw' 'āmlû bônāyw bô*

The Hebrew consonant *šin* (English transliteration *sh*) is prominent in the second bicolon. The second half is three words in Hebrew, each beginning with *šin*.

> Unless the LORD watches over the city / / the watchman stays awake in vain
> *'im-yhwh lō'-yišmor-'îr / / šāw' šāqad šômēr*

2.11. Assonance. This occurs when a series of words contains a distinctive vowel sound or certain vowel sounds in a specific sequence. As with alliteration, it gives cohesion to a colon or bicolon. In Psalm 102:6 the first word in each colon has the same sequence of three vowels.

> I am like a desert owl / / I am like an owl of the waste places
> *dāmîtî . . . / / hāyîtî . . .*

3. The Structure of a Hebrew Poem.

3.1. Introduction. Most studies of Hebrew poetry have concentrated on the level of the colon or bicolon. Relatively little study has been made of the rhetorical patterns that might encompass the whole poem (*see* Rhetorical Criticism). Part of the reason for this is uncertainty about how to set about analysis at this level. It is rare to find explicit markers of structure in the text, though there are two that do occur: the *refrain and the *acrostic. Although some scholars use the terms **strophe** and *stanza more or less interchangeably (Gillingham, 64, 196), more often they are distinguished, with the stanza being the larger unit, composed of two or more strophes.

3.2. Refrain. This is a repeated sentence, or sentences, which divides the poem into sections. In Psalm 67 the sentence "Let the peoples praise you, O God; let all the peoples praise you" (Ps 67:3, 5) divides the psalm into three sections. In this case the refrain is a fixed formula. Psalm 80 has a refrain that varies slightly. The way God is referred to is heightened in each repetition: "O God" (Ps 80:3), "O God of hosts" (Ps 80:7), "O LORD God of hosts" (Ps 80:19). The variation is greater in Psalm 56:4, 10-11. The repetition of an identical refrain in Psalm 42:5, 11; 43:5 suggests that originally these two psalms were a single poem.

3.3. Acrostic. An acrostic is a poem in which the first letters of successive lines form a recognizable pattern. The examples in the OT follow the order of the letters in the Hebrew alphabet. The best-known examples are Psalm 119; Proverbs 31:10-31; Lamentations 1—4. In Proverbs 31:10-31 and Lamentations 1; 2; 4 each verse begins with a successive letter of the Hebrew alphabet. In Lamentations 3 the verses are grouped into threes, with each verse in the group beginning with the same letter. Psalm 119 has groups of eight verses beginning with the same letter.

3.4. Strophe. A strophe consists of a group of bicola that are linked in some way. Most strophes contain two or three bicola, though they can be longer, and in a few cases a single bicolon can be regarded as a strophe. There are various ways in which a group of bicola can be linked. The following are some possibilities (Fokkelman, 89).

A compound sentence may extend over two or more bicola.

The group of bicola may formulate or explain a single thought.

The bicola may form a clear series of some kind.

The group of bicola may form an embedded speech, such as a quotation.

The group of bicola may present or work out a metaphor or simile.

The group may be bound together by *inclusio (the use of the same word or phrase at the beginning and at the end).

Psalm 13 provides an example of how strophes may be recognized. The first strophe (Ps 13:1-2) is clearly marked out by a series of four questions, each beginning "How long . . . ?" The second strophe (Ps 13:3-4) is a single compound sentence, and it is also marked out by a change from question to command or plea: "Consider and answer me. . . ." The third and final strophe (Ps 13:5-6) is marked by a change from plea to an expression of trust in God: "But I trusted in your steadfast love. . . ." Psalm 2:7-9 is an example of a strophe that is an embedded quotation. In Job 14 there are two strophes that develop a metaphor or simile. In Job 14:7-9 it is the image of a felled tree regenerating from its rots, and in Job 14:10-12 human death is compared to the drying up of a lake. There is an inclusio marking out the strophe of Psalm 69:8-10 (ET 69:7-9), though it is not clearly seen in most English translations.

Upon you [for your sake] I have been abused
. . .

your abuses [abuses aimed at you] have
fallen upon me.

3.5. Stanza. Longer poems can often be divided into stanzas consisting of two or three (occasionally more) strophes. No fixed rules can be given for recognizing stanzas (Fokkelman, 117; Watson, 162). Stanza division is usually based on content, so that new stanzas are marked by changes in subject matter. For example, Psalm 19 can be divided into three stanzas: Psalm 19:1-6, 7-10, 11-14. Occasionally there are markers, most obviously refrains.

See also ACROSTIC; CHIASM; ELLIPSIS; FORM CRITICISM; FRAME NARRATIVE; IMAGERY; INCLUSIO; LYRIC POETRY; MERISM; METER; MUSIC, SONG; ORAL POETRY; PARALLELISM; PERSONIFICATION; REFRAIN; SOUND PATTERN; STANZA, STROPHE; TERSENESS; WORDPLAY.

BIBLIOGRAPHY. **R. Alter,** *The Art of Biblical Poetry* (New York: Basic Books, 1985); **A. Berlin,** *The Dynamics of Biblical Parallelism* (Bloomington: Indiana University Press, 1985); **D. Clines,** "The Parallelism of Greater Precision: Notes from Isaiah 40 for a Theory of Hebrew Poetry," in *Directions in Hebrew Poetry,* ed. E. R. Follis (JSOTSup 40; Sheffield: JSOT Press, 1987) 77-100; **T. Collins,** *Line-Forms in Hebrew Poetry: A Grammatical Approach to the Stylistic Study of the Hebrew Prophets* (Rome: Biblical Institute Press, 1978); **J. P. Fokkelman,** *Reading Biblical Poetry: An Introductory Guide* (Louisville: Westminster John Knox, 2001); **D. N. Freedman,** "Pottery, Poetry and Prophecy," *JBL* 96 (1977) 5-26; idem, "Another Look at Biblical Hebrew Poetry," in *Directions in Hebrew Poetry,* ed. E. R. Follis (JSOT-

Sup 40; Sheffield: JSOT Press, 1987) 11-28; **S. A. Geller,** *Parallelism in Early Hebrew Poetry* (HSM 20; Missoula, MT: Scholars Press, 1979); **S. E. Gillingham,** *The Poems and Psalms of the Hebrew Bible* (Oxford: Oxford University Press, 1994); **N. K. Gottwald,** "Hebrew Poetry," *IDB* 3.829-38; **W. L. Holladay,** "*Hebrew Verse Structure* Revisited (I): Which Words 'Count,'" *JBL* 118 (1999a) 19-32; idem, "*Hebrew Verse Structure* Revisited (II): Conjoint Cola, and Further Considerations," *JBL* 118 (1999b) 401-16; **J. Kugel,** *The Idea of Biblical Poetry* (New Haven: Yale University Press, 1981); **R. Lowth,** *Lectures on the Sacred Poetry of the Hebrews* (London: T. Tegg & Son, 1835); **S. Mowinckel,** *The Psalms in Israel's Worship,* vol. 2 (Oxford: Blackwell, 1962); **M. O'Connor,** *Hebrew Verse Structure* (Winona Lake, IN: Eisenbrauns, 1980); **T. H. Robinson,** *The Poetry of the Old Testament* (London: Duckworth, 1947); **L. A. Schökel,** *A Manual of Hebrew Poetics* (SubBi 11; Rome: Pontificio Istituto Biblico, 1988); **W. G. E. Watson,** *Classical Hebrew Poetry: A Guide to Its Techniques* (JSOTSup 26; Sheffield: JSOT Press, 1986). E. C. Lucas

POETRY, HEBREW. *See* PSALMS 1: BOOK OF.

POLYTHEISM. *See* DIVINE COUNCIL.

POSTCOLONIAL INTERPRETATION. *See* HERMENEUTICS.

POSTHOLOCAUST INTERPRETATION. *See* HERMENEUTICS.

POSTMODERN INTERPRETATION. *See* HERMENEUTICS.

POVERTY, PROVISIONS FOR. *See* RUTH 2: ANCIENT NEAR EASTERN BACKGROUND.

PRAISE. *See* HYMNS; WORSHIP.

PRISON. *See* IMPRISONMENT IMAGERY.

PROPHECY. *See* WISDOM AND PROPHECY.

PROPHETS. *See* WISDOM AND PROPHECY.

PROTECTION IMAGERY

The psalmist's praise for the protector-Lord resonates with military tones: "I love you, O LORD, my strength, O LORD, my crag, my fortress, my deliverer, my God, my rock in whom I seek refuge, my shield, and the horn of my salvation, my stronghold" (Ps 18:1-2). We also hear cultic, judicial, pastoral, medical, wisdom and family echoes in protection imagery. And the "root metaphor" behind most of this is kingship, whether divine or divinely ordained (Mettinger, 92).

1. Military Protection Imagery
2. Nonmilitary Protection Imagery

1. Military Protection Imagery.

1.1. Refuge. Refuge serves as the key biblical protection image. The ancient Near Eastern ideas of finding refuge in cult and king occur frequently, often alongside related imagery having to do with fortifications and good defensive terrain.

1.1.1. Ancient Near Eastern Background of the Metaphor. J. Creach (61-62) posits three sources of Israel's metaphor of divine refuge: (1) *Zion, whose ramparts signaled security (citing Keel, 179-80; Ps 31:1-4; 61:2b-4; 71:1-3; see also 1 Chron 11:5b, 7-8; Prov 18:10), and whose temple functioned as "the place of refuge *par excellence*" (citing Keel, 181; 1 Kings 1:50-53; cf. 1 Kings 2:28-34; see also Ex 21:13-14; Num 35:10-34); (2) Palestine's rugged topography, which had provided literal refuge to *David (citing Keel, 180-81; 1 Sam 22—24; 2 Sam 23:14; (3) the mother bird, whose outstretched wings symbolized protection (citing Keel, 191-92; Ps 17:8; 36:7; 57:1; 61:4; 63:7; 91:4; Ruth 2:12; see also Deut 32:10-12; Mt 23:37b).

Contrary to some claims (noted by Keel, 180-81), this royal/divine protection imagery is not unique to Israel. Various ancient Near Eastern confessions acknowledge dependence upon their king as protector (Creach, 56-58), and they incorporate protection metaphors into divine titles—for example, *Anu-du-di* ("Anu is my bulwark"), *Ištar-dūrī* ("Ishtar is my wall"), *Ellil-kidīnī* ("Ellil is my protection") (Widengren, 82). Similar metaphorical titles apply to Marduk, Adad, Ashur, Nebo, Shamash, Ea and Dagan (Widengren, 324-25).

1.1.2. Royal Connections of the Metaphor. Generally, the Lord provides this refuge, either as a king protecting his realm and subjects or as a host sheltering his guests (e.g., Ps 23:5-6; 27:4; 65:4; 84) (see Keel, 198). Zion gives refuge because, according to Psalm 48:2, it is "the city of the great king" (Creach, 55). By analogy, Israel's king (Ps 84:9; 89:18) or even other rulers (Ps 47:8-9) can serve as a "shield" (*māgēn* [cf. Rom 13:1-7; 1 Tim 2:1-2; 1 Pet 2:13-17]). The book of *Lamentations rued the failure of the ideal of the protective royal "shadow" (Lam 4:20; cf. Jer 39:5-7).

1.1.3. Stronghold or Fortress. The Hebrew text frequently uses *ṣûr* ("rock") or *selaʿ* ("stone" or "cliff, crag") as a figure for the protector God. The LXX of *Psalms avoids the metaphorical *petra* for God, tending towards literal explanations, either an outright *theos* (Ps 18:31, 46; 28:1; 31:2; 62:2, 6-7; 71:3; 73:26; 92:15; 95:1 [LXX: 17:32, 47; 27:1; 30:3; 61:3, 7-8; 70:3; 72:26; 91:16; 94:1]) or other literal explanations of the metaphor, such as "strength" *(krataiōmai)*, "help" *(boēthos)*, "protector" *(antilēmptōr)* or "firm support" *(stereōma)* (Olofsson, 35-37). The praise "my rock" (e.g., Ps 62:2, 6-7) frequently parallels either similar figures such as "strength . . . stronghold" (Ps 31:2) and "fortress" (Ps 71:3) or more literal language such as "salvation" (Ps 18:46) or "redeemer" (Ps 19:14).

A range of related terms express the same idea of metaphorical refuge in God: "mountain stronghold" *(mĕṣûdâ, māʿōz)* or "strength" *(ʿōz)*. With three exceptions in our literature (Job 39:28; Ps 66:11; Eccles 9:12), *mĕṣûdâ* serves as a divine title that symbolizes Yahweh's protection (Ps 18:2; 31:2-3; 71:3; 91:2; 144:2). And the two nominal derivatives of the verb *ʿzz* ("be strong") define Yahweh as a powerful ally (e.g., Ps 28:7; 59:17; 81:1; 118:14) or as an excellent defensive position (e.g., Ps 27:1; 28:8; 31:2; 37:39; 43:2; 52:7; Prov 10:29). A "mountain refuge" *(miśgāb,* from *śāgab,* "be set on high") implies a secure height. As with the "stone" terms, the LXX often eliminates this metaphor as a title for God, using "protector" *(antilēmptōr)* instead (e.g., Ps 18:2; 59:9, 16-17 [LXX: 17:3; 58:10, 17-18]).

1.1.4. Cover or Shelter. Various terms describe divine cover or shelter. With one exception (Ps 104:18), the psalms always describe finding "refuge" *(ḥāsâ, maḥseh)* as divine protection in this life (Ruth 2:12b; Ps 91:2, 9; Prov 30:5) or even after death (Prov 14:32). The LXX can use the equally metaphorical *kataphygē* ("refuge") (Ps 46:1 [LXX 45:1]), but it generally abandons the metaphor in favor of the literal sense, using terms such as "hope" *(elpis),* "help" *(boēthos)* or "protector" *(antilēmptōr).* The mention of "hiding" *(sātar)* can imply that there will be no protection when, for example, God hides his face (e.g., Job 13:24; Ps 13:1; 27:9; cf. Num 6:24-26), and it can even imply deceit (Job 24:15; 34:22).

But the "hiding place" *(sēter)* may also be protective (e.g., Job 14:13; Ps 17:8; 27:5). The protection by a king can be described as "shade, shadow" *(ṣēl)* (Song 2:3; Lam 4:20), as can the more figurative protection of either wisdom or money (Eccl 7:12). And it is especially useful to describe protection found in God's shade (Ps 121:5), especially under the shadow of God's wings (Ps 17:8; 36:7; 57:1; 63:7; 91:1). God provides "cover" *(sākak)* for his people (Ps 5:11; 91:4), perhaps even functioning like a helmet to cover the head (Ps 140:7) just as he does as a shield to protect the body.

1.1.5. Den or Dwelling. The word *māʿōn* has its background as the animal's den or lair (Job 37:8; 38:40; Ps 104:22; Song 4:8). Sometimes the remoteness of the lair symbolizes the transcendence of God's habitation, which is then applied metaphorically to God's abode in the temple (Wilson, 1015-16). Above all, this can refer to the temple as a place of escape, literally, but perhaps also figuratively (Ps 84:3). Nonetheless, O. Keel (181) notes that even this symbolism of refuge avoids images associated with death: "Yahweh is never called 'my cave' or 'my crevice,' though *in concreto* these were resorted to for refuge as frequently as rocks and mountaintops. . . . From the perspective of cosmic 'geography,' however, they belong to the realm of the netherworld and are not suited for description of Yahweh, who is a God of life."

1.2. Armaments. One armament is defensive, the "shield" *(māgēn, ṣinnâ).* Sometimes God provides the shield in the person of his anointed king (Ps 84:9; 89:18), but more often God himself takes up the shield and comes to the rescue (Ps 35:2). Sometimes a divine characteristic such as salvation (Ps 18:35), favor (Ps 5:12) or faithfulness (Ps 91:4) is the shield, and sometimes God himself is the shield (e.g., Ps 3:3; 18:30; 33:20; Prov 2:7; 30:5). So a common divine appellation is "my shield" (Ps 7:10; 18:2; 28:7; 119:114; 144:2) or "our shield" (Ps 33:20; 59:11). J. F. D. Creach (29) wonders if "shield" eventually became a dead metaphor meaning little more than "helper" or "protector," because *māgēn* is never used of Yahweh as a shield against enemy arrows, though that figurative expression would sometimes have been appropriate (e.g., Ps 11:2; cf. Eph 6:16). Indeed, the LXX of Psalms translates it as *hyperapistēs* ("protector") most of the time.

Other armaments incorporated into the protection imagery are offensive, though used for protection. The Lord can take to his wind-driven "cloud-chariot" (*rĕkûb* [Ps 104:3]), sometimes described as "cherubim" (*kĕrûb* [Ps 18:10]), and his hosts can command thousands of them (Ps 68:17) in defense of his people. "Lightning" (*'ôr;* i.e., God's "arrows" [*hēṣ*]) provides protection by scattering or piercing the heart of the psalmist's enemies (Ps 18:14; 45:5; 144:6). Sometimes God protects by stringing his "bow" (*qešet*) to fight the psalmist's enemies (Ps 7:12), other times by breaking their bows (Ps 46:9) so they cannot employ them against "the upright" (Ps 11:2; 37:14). And the same dual dynamic applies to other weapons that God may wield himself (Ps 18:14; 144:6) or remove from enemy hands (Ps 76:3), such as the "sword" (*ḥereb* [Ps 45:3]) and "spear" (*ḥănît* [Ps 35:3; 46:9]).

1.3. Other Military Protection. The psalmist frequently asks God to "guard" (*šāmar*) or "watch over" (*nāṣar*) him. In a metaphorical sense, wisdom, instruction, discretion, a parent's instruction, and so forth are said to guard and watch over the disciple (Prov 2:11; 4:4-6; 6:20-24). In turn, those who adhere to those principles guard and watch over their own lives (Prov 13:3; 16:17; 19:16; 21:23).

Although "shade" or a "shadow" (*ṣēl*) is often associated with things ephemeral (e.g., Ps 102:11; Eccles 6:12) or even with death (e.g., Ps 44:19; 107:10, 14), God's "shade" is consistently construed as positive. In this case, its background is like shade that protects from sunstroke. The shade is God himself (Ps 91:1; 121:5), but sometimes it is mediated, whether through his appointed kings (Is 32:1-2; Lam 4:20; cf. Judg 9:15; see also Song 2:3) or through his gift of "wisdom" (*hokmâ* [Eccles 7:12]).

The "wing" (*kanap*) also symbolizes protection, either by the phrase "shadow of your wings" (Ps 17:8; 36:7; 57:1; 63:7) or by "wings" used with a verb for finding shelter/refuge (*ḥāsâ* [Ruth 2:12; Ps 61:4; 91:4]). The image of a bird spreading her wings over her hatchlings is at the root of this image (cf. Mt 23:37). Some also suggest that this could also be connected to the cultic image of the cherubim, whose wings extended protectively over the ark (Keel, 190, citing Ps 36:7; 63:7; see also Kraus, 2.248-49). Note also the parallel between "wings of the wind" and the "cherubim" (Ps 18:10/2 Sam 22:11) or the "cloud-chariot" (Ps 104:3).

The "horn" (*qeren*) may symbolize protec-

tion. O. Keel (146) connects the "horn of my salvation" (Ps 18:2/2 Sam 22:3) "with the power of protection offered by the horns of the altar," where the blood of atonement was applied (Keel, 146; citing Lev 8:15; 16:18; 1 Kings 1:50; 2:28; Amos 3:14). Indeed, most plurals of *qeren* refer to the altar's horns. On the other hand, M. Brown (991) connects the phrase with the use of *qeren* to refer to a hillside "promontory" or "peak" (Is 5:1) and says that it may mean something more like "peak of safety," a notion paralleled by calling God a "rock," "fortress" or the like. However, the singulars and duals refer either to literal animal horns or to the power that they symbolize, and the lifted horn often symbolizes oppressive power. So the psalmist looks forward to a time when the horn of the wicked will be cut off (Ps 75:4-5, 10) in favor of the divine "horn of salvation" (Ps 18:2), who is in turn represented by the Davidic king whose horn God exalts (Ps 89:17, 24; 92:10; 112:9; 132:17; 148:14).

2. Nonmilitary Protection Imagery.

2.1. Medical. When facing death, the psalmist cries out, "Heal me" (*rāpā'* [Ps 6:2b]), and later he is thankful for God's healing (Ps 30:2; 103:3). Sometimes it is difficult to determine whether this is literal healing from deathly sickness (Ps 6:2), psychological or spiritual healing (Ps 147:3), or more a matter of rescue from a generally unhealthy situation (Ps 41, esp. v. 4; 107, esp. v. 20). Perhaps these would have been inconsequential distinctions for Israel, who would have understood healing in a more holistic way that linked physical healing, forgiveness and wellness of the "soul" (Chan, Song and Brown, 1165-68).

2.2. Cultic. Here we have first to do with the image of Mount Zion as a mountain redoubt, and particularly the representation of the temple as a fortress (see 1.1.3 above), which may reflect the common ancient Near Eastern motif of the mountaintop as the abode of the gods. But we also hear of the temple as a sanctuary from blood vengeance and of the altar as the symbol of that sanctuary. In fact, as previously noted (see 1.3 above), the symbol "horn" does frequently refer to the altar's horns, where one might find refuge (e.g., 1 Kings 1:50-51; 2:28). Even the birds find sanctuary in God's presence at the temple (Ps 84:3), so how much more so do God's own people.

2.3. Judicial. Sometimes protection comes by

judicial intervention against an oppressor (Job 5:4; 6:23; Ps 10:18; 72:4, 12, 14; 82:3) or as the result of judicial vindication in the face of unjust accusations (e.g., Ps 7:6, 8, 11; 35:23). So the psalmist cries out, "Argue my case" (Ps 119:154), and he expresses confidence that "the LORD will champion their cause" and get justice for the poor (Ps 140:12).

2.4. Pastoral. We hear of the protective shepherd (Ps 23) or of his "arm(s)" (Ps 28:9). Since "shepherd" is a royal metaphor, it can involve enthronement (Ps 80:1) and with protecting a dynastic inheritance (Ps 28:9). And perhaps the talk of "hedging" *(sûk/śûk)* is a pastoral image of using a thorny hedge to protecting the flock (cf. 1 Sam 25:16) or crop field (Ps 80:12; cf. Is 5:5). It would be the background for the complaint by *Satan that God overprotects *Job (Job 1:10) or Job's complaint that God unfairly restricts him (Job 3:23; cf. Hos 2:6).

2.5. Light. If the threat is ominous darkness of death (Ps 38:10), the protection may come from God either as "light" *('ôr)* or a "lamp" *(nēr)* (e.g., Job 29:3; 33:28; Ps 13:3; 18:28; 112:4; 132:17). Or God may snuff out the light of the enemy (Prov 13:9; 20:20; 24:20). M. Selman notes the covenantal aspect of God's promise of light, which featured in the Aaronic blessing (Selman, *NIDOTTE* 1.324-25, 327, citing Num 6:24-26; Ps 27:1; 31:16; 67:1; 80:3, 7, 19; 89:15). When God gives light, he is doing one of two things: he may be answering the problem of the darkness of death by sustaining the light of life (Selman, *NIDOTTE* 1.325, citing Ps 13:3), giving of his own light to keep alight a person's flickering lamp of life (Selman, *NIDOTTE* 3.159, citing Ps 18:28); or he may be giving spiritual understanding (Selman, *NIDOTTE* 1.325, citing Ps 19:8; 119:130), which is paralleled by the life-sustaining function of "law/teaching" *(tôrâ),* and with "wisdom" *(hokmâ)* and other terms in that semantic range (e.g., Ps 119:105; Prov 6:23; 20:27).

2.6. Parental or Nursing. Protective actions can be described figuratively as those of a "father" (Job 29:16; Ps 68:5; 89:26) or of a "mother" at whose breasts children find not only nourishment but also protection (Ps 22:9b; Lam 4:3). Or God can be even described as a "midwife" who safely brought the psalmist into the world (Ps 22:9a; 71:6). So Lamentations describes exile as the loss of parental protection suffered by orphans (Lam 5:3).

2.7. Miscellaneous. Protection metaphors are as diverse as the many threat metaphors to which they respond. Protection from a fatal slip might come in the form of a helping hand from the Lord (Ps 145:14), from his strong right hand (Ps 18:35-36) or even from his *ḥesed* ("steadfast love" [Ps 94:18]). This might also be accompanied by better trail maintenance (Ps 18:35-36). The fear of disappearance into the depths or into the pit of Sheol provokes the cry "Do not let the depths engulf me, do not let the pit swallow me" (Ps 69:14-15), although, ironically, Job seeks temporary asylum in Sheol (Job 14:13). If the lion, feral dog or wild ox—or people who are equally rapacious—threaten the psalmist's soul, then the protector breaks jaw, fang, claw and horn (Job 29:17; Ps 3:7; 22:21; 58:6; 75:10; 124:6).

See also CHAOS AND DEATH; CONFIDENCE, PSALMS OF; KINGSHIP PSALMS; LIFE; SUFFERING; THEODICY; WARFARE.

BIBLIOGRAPHY. **M. L. Brown,** "קָרַן," *NIDOTTE* 3.990-92; **A. K.-Y. Chan, T. B. Song and M. L. Brown,** "רָפָא," *NIDOTTE* 3.1162-73; **J. F. D. Creach,** *Yahweh as Refuge and the Editing of the Hebrew Psalter* (JSOTSup 217; Sheffield: Sheffield Academic Press, 1996); **O. Keel,** *The Symbolism of the Biblical World: Ancient Near Eastern Iconography and the Book of Psalms* (New York: Seabury, 1978); **H.-J. Kraus,** *Psalms* (2 vols.; Minneapolis: Augsburg, 1989); **T. N. D. Mettinger,** *In Search of God: The Meaning and Message of the Everlasting Names* (Philadelphia: Fortress, 1988); **S. Olofsson,** *God Is My Rock: A Study of Translation Technique and Theological Exegesis in the Septuagint* (ConBOT 31; Stockholm: Almqvist & Wiksell, 1990); **M. J. Selman,** "אוֹר," *NIDOTTE* 1.324-29; idem, "נֵר," *NIDOTTE* 3.159-60; **G. Widengren,** *The Accadian and Hebrew Psalms of Lamentation as Religious Documents: A Comparative Study* (Stockholm: Thule, 1937); **G. H. Wilson,** "מָעוֹן," *NIDOTTE* 2.1015-16.

D. A. Brueggemann

PROVERB, GENRE OF

What is a proverb? How is a single proverb changed when pulled out of its original story and resituated in a collection? How does a proverb's meaning shift when it is recontextualized after being taken from a collection and merged back into a new and often diverse story? Do all proverbs move with and invoke the same level of authority? What literary forms occur in the biblical text of *Proverbs (better-than, abomination, numerical sayings, etc.)? Do larger units of pairs, strings/clusters, mini-collections and whole collections actually exist and reflect editorial intent? The goal of the present article is to crack open the core nature of the pithy proverbial sayings by wrestling with these and related questions.

1. Historical and Cultural Universality of the Proverb Genre
2. Toward a Definition of the Proverb
3. The Virtual Potential of Collected Proverbs
4. Proverbial Usage
5. Proverbial Authority
6. Proverbial Orality
7. Hebrew Proverbs
8. Proverbial Forms
9. Editorial Compositional Units
10. Future Directions and Reflections

1. Historical and Cultural Universality of the Proverb Genre.

From the ancient clay tablets of Sumer (c. 2500 BC) to postmodern Internet pop-ups, the proverb has crossed all cultural, linguistic and literary boundaries. It appears embedded in epics, poems, songs, plays, novels and modern advertising, and stands solo in a myriad of international and regional proverbial collections. The human urge to classify, generalize and codify experience, filtered through a culture's ideals and values, helps explain the universality of the proverb. One might say that proverbs are an encoding compression schema of the mind (Honeck).

The detachable and collectable proverbial form was early bound into Sumerian proverb collections, including the Shuruppak Instructions, dating back to 2600-1800 BC, shortly after the invention of writing itself (Alster). Old Babylonian proverbial clusters were copied from Sumerian unilingual collections into bilingual lists, even maintaining the same sequence and thereby reflecting the international movement of early proverbial wisdom (Lambert). Later, Ahiqar, who served as a sage in the Assyrian courts (c. 700 BC), recorded proverbs that were widely transmitted across the ancient Near East and Ahiqar was even translated into Arabic.

Egypt also has a long tradition of proverbial instructions, often in a parent-to-child format, extending from the Old Kingdom (c. 2600-2100 BC [e.g., Hardjedef, Kagemeni]), Middle Kingdom (c.

2000-1600 BC [e.g., Ptahhotep]) and New Kingdom (c. 1500-1080 BC [e.g., Amenemope, Ani]) down to demotic and the Ptolemaic times (c. 300 BC [e.g., Ankhsheshonq]) (Lichtheim; Pritchard).

Adages from classical Greek and Roman times have been compiled, and English, Chinese, European and Russian collections are also voluminous (Mieder 1986). Oral proverbial production is still very much alive in the folklore of numerous groups on the African continent. The proverbial form is an ancient, universal and culturally fluid form.

2. Toward a Definition of the Proverb.

Cervantes defines proverbs as "short sentences drawn from long experience." Ibn Ezra describes the proverb as having "three characteristics: few words, good sense, and a fine image." The world's leading paremiologist (from *paroimia*, Gk for "proverb"), W. Mieder, defines the proverb as "a short, generally known sentence of the folk which contains wisdom, truth, morals, and traditional views in a metaphorical, fixed and memorizable form and which is handed down from generation to generation" (Mieder 2004, 3). While the Hebrew term *māšāl*, often translated "proverb," can include longer units such as instructions (Prov 1:10-19), numerical sayings (Prov 30:29-31) and *acrostics (Prov 31:10-31), it is often used for short proverbial sentences (Prov 10-22). Even in the longer wisdom forms there is a compression of thought and expression.

Mieder's definition fits well with the biblical proverbs: (1) proverbs are short (in Prov 10—29 usually self-contained short sentences); (2) proverbs are used among the folks ("As the proverb of the ancients says" in 1 Sam 24:13, as opposed to the prophetic "Thus says the LORD"); (3) proverbs are metaphorical (e.g., "tongue is choice silver" in Prov 10:20); (4) proverbial forms are fixed (e.g., "better than" proverbs [Prov 19:1], yet open to variation [cf. Prov 10:1 with Prov 17:25]); (5) proverbs proffer wise and moralistic advice (e.g., righteous/wicked contrast [Prov 10:3]; wise/foolish contrast [Prov 10:8]); (6) proverbs are transmitted intergenerationally (in Prov 4:3-4 the father tells his son to listen to the advice that his father gave him; see also Prov 31:1-9).

The structural paremiologists A. Dundes, A. L. Kuusi and G. B. Milner have noted that binary (+/-) oppositions between the topic and comment often characterize proverbial sentences. Milner's doubled binary opposition, which he labels "quadripartite structure," though not absolutely universal, is frequently seen in the biblical proverbial formulations. For example, Proverbs 10:4:

Topic	Comment
Lazy hands [-]	make a person poor [-]
but diligent hands [+]	bring wealth [+]

Paremiological studies have shown how modern proverbs are translated from one culture to another (see 1 Kings 4:31-34; Prov 30:1; 31:1). Such intercultural modern proverbial transitions may shed light on connections between Proverbs 22 and the Egyptian Amenemope (see Washington; Ruffle). In addition, they have offered ways of conceptualizing and analyzing proverbs. Paremiologists have also developed models for tracing a proverb and its variants historically through a thousand years and across numerous cultures. C. Westermann and F. W. Golka have explored the use of African proverbs, which provide great profit for understanding biblical proverb formation and contexts in which they functioned.

In short, as modern literary studies (see Longman and Ryken; Alter) have enriched the exegesis of the biblical text, so too paremiological studies are able to give perspectives that shed light on how biblical proverbs work. The enriching dialogue between scholars of biblical proverbs and paremiologists is in its infancy (see Fontaine).

3. The Virtual Potential of Collected Proverbs.

A proverb is created from a singular situation (1 Sam 10:12). An observed pattern is isolated and a general inference formulated. This inductively, deductively or analogically derived inference is then distilled into a concise, poetically crafted statement. The proverb is then detached from that original setting to be used as an intergenerationally traditional saying among the folk in a thousand diverse contexts. Often it is transformed and twisted with use (e.g., "Different strokes for different folks" to "Different hopes for different folks"; cf. Prov 13:14 with 14:27). Traditional sayings are then gathered by editors into collections. These collections are taught to children, students, *scribes and royal officials in

homes, schools and royal courts (see Gammie and Perdue). An individual proverb learned in the collection is later recontextualized or instantiated in a hundred different contexts, unleashing its potential in specific new situations (see Jas 5:20; cf. Prov 10:12).

Some conclude that proverbs that have been detached from their original situations into sterile collections are dead (Mieder 1974). However, once detached or decontextualized into a collection, the collected proverb becomes much more flexible and gains multisemantic possibilities and polysituational adaptability in terms of its future use. Its potential is virtual in the collection and realized when it is reattached and recontextualized.

How the proverb is understood changes when it is taken from a collection and put into diverse and new interactional situations (see Fontaine, 57-58). Thus one may cite "A wise child brings joy to a father" (Prov 10:1a) to encourage a child to make a wise decision, to challenge a parent to show emotion, to thank a faithful adult child or to critique a parent's response. The virtual potential of this collected proverb may be realized in a multitude of ways when it is recontextualized in each new interactional situation.

4. Proverbial Usage.

Proverbs are detachable units designed for conversational reattachment in new situations. The importance of proverbial usage is clearly acknowledged in the book of Proverbs itself: "Like a lame man's legs that hang limp is a proverb in the mouth of a fool" (Prov 26:7, 9).

Not only should the content of what is said be understood, but also the actual impact of the statement on the listener should be carefully noted. This may be seen in the use of Proverbs 14:15: "A simple person believes anything." One can easily imagine recontextualizing this same proverb in a wide range of speech-act contexts in order to expose, humiliate, rebuke, mock, warn, guide, encourage, evaluate, humor, cause reflection or instruct, among others. Thus the situation of use is as important in shaping its current meaning as an analysis of the semantic/syntactic content of the proverb and its original *Sitz im Leben*.

Culture also plays a role in determining how a proverb is to be understood. In Scotland, "A rolling stone gathers no moss" indicates the need to keep up with modern trends lest undesirable moss grow and reveal a lack of mental vitality. In England, on the other hand, the same proverb means that if things are continually in flux, desirable traits (moss) will not have sufficient stability to thrive (Kirshenblatt-Gimblett). Culture impacts how proverbs are interpreted, and one must make an effort to understand both the culture of origin and the current culture of usage.

When the proverb is instantiated, it is cited as coming from a wider community rather than as originating from a specific author ("As they say" [cf. 1 Sam 10:11-12; 19:24]). Hence the locus of authority is moved from the speaker using the proverb to a collective indirect tradition. Proverbs also function phatically to establish, maintain and restore social relationships and to reinforce solidarity and accepted norms that bond a community together (cf. the "friends" of *Job).

In Proverbs 1:17, "How useless to spread a net in full view of all the birds!" is used as a concluding argument to turn a young person away from the lure of violent companions. The proverb is easily identified. There is a shift from a literal description of hoodlums shedding innocent blood to a proverbial metaphor in the image of a bird and a snare (see also Prov 5:15; Eccles 1:18; 4:5-6; 9:12-13). Here, as often, the proverb is used to close or concisely summarize an argument.

5. Proverbial Authority.

It should be clear at this point that it is difficult to discuss the independent veracity of a collected proverb and its authority, especially when the proverbs in collections are so polyvalent and decontextualized. Genre does not determine whether the Scriptures are true; it merely shapes how that truth is formulated into text. The historical narratives face a similar difficulty in authority when moving from a historical particular to a generalized application. Proverbs are not meant to be dogmatized into universal propositional truths. That was one of the mistakes made by Job's "friends."

How is the authority of Proverbs to be understood? Is Proverbs 10:4, "Poverty comes from a lazy hand, but a diligent hand makes wealth," a promise? It is easy to cite examples of people who have been diligent but remained poor and of others who have been lazy yet live in the lap of luxury. Furthermore, the book of Proverbs itself indicates that although working hard leads

to profit, evil companions (Prov 1:18) or another's greed may quickly negate or pillage the benefits of hard work and leave one ultimately impoverished. A proverb is not a promise.

The proverb may be commenting on only one aspect of a situation rather than encompassing the whole. Because of its unitary, pithy nature, a proverb cannot be taken as a guarantee of complex outcomes. In order to describe a multifaceted situation comprehensively, multiple proverbial vectors may be needed. In short, proverbs are true but are encapsulated and focused on just one aspect of a diverse reality.

The manner in which the proverbial genre engages authority is nuanced and multidimensional. At least five categories may be observed in exposing the contours of proverbial authority: (1) a universal mandate (Prov 3:5), (2) an ideal-confirming exhortation (Prov 10:4), (3) a simple nonmoral observation (Prov 14:10), (4) an ideal-disconfirming warning (Prov 11:13), (5) an absolute prohibition (Prov 6:16-17). These five categories are proffered to demonstrate that the authority of the genre is not uniform and flat but rather variegated and contoured. A wise interpreter must avoid universalizing and dogmatizing a particular proverbial saying.

Furthermore, when proverbial usage is added into the mix, the scope of authority may have nothing to do with the reason for citation. Perhaps the proverb is cited simply for pointed humor, such as the sluggard who is too lazy to raise his hand up to his mouth (Prov 19:24; 22:13).

6. Proverbial Orality.

Another underlying aspect of the proverbial genre that should not be overlooked is the oral nature of proverbs in terms of their original creation, transmission and use. It is no accident that the theme of speech and oral communication is central in Egyptian wisdom literature as well as in Israelite proverbs (Prov 11:9; 12:14, 18; 16:24, 27). The oral implications of the frequently repeated phrase "Listen, my son" should not be neglected.

Orality may help explain the variations found in duplicate proverbs (Prov 9:4, 16; 14:12; 15:25 [see Snell]). Sometimes half-verses are repeated but linked to different matching cola (Prov 10:6, 11). Often variants are introduced in whole verse repetitions with one-word (Prov 19:5, 9), two-word (Prov 10:1; 15:20) or three-word differences (Prov 10:2; 11;4; 15:13; 17:22). Numerous modern collections cite the same proverb with multiple variations (e.g., "Don't change horses in midstream" and its alternative, "Don't swap horses while crossing a stream"). At other times proverbial phrases are purposefully "twisted" by the user to make counter-proverbs (e.g., "Spare the rod and spoil the child" becomes "Spoil the rod and spare the child").

7. Hebrew Proverbs.

7.1. māšāl. The term translated "proverbs" in the title of the book of Proverbs, *māšāl,* means "likeness" or "similitude." There is a diversity of genres tagged by the label of *māšāl:* popular sayings (Jer 23:28; 31:29), literary aphorisms (Prov 10:1-22:16), taunt songs (Is 14:4; Mic 2:4; Hab 2:6-8), bywords (Deut 28:37; 1 Kings 9:7) and allegories (Ezek 17:1-10; 20:45-49). The *māšāl* calls for one to reflect and make connections mapping the ideals expressed in the text onto the current situations.

7.2. Sound Techniques. The proverbs of the book of Proverbs were crafted in poetic form. Modern examples showing the significance of sound can be seen in sayings such as "Practice makes perfect" and "Forgive and forget."

It is clear that the *sages who originally crafted proverbs were keenly sensitive to the sounds of their sayings. For example, Proverbs 10:9a:

hōlēk battōm yēlek betah
One who <u>walks</u> honestly <u>walks</u> securely.

Note the symmetrical (final *-ek* followed by initial *b + t*), a sound repetition that reinforces the "walk" *(hōlēk/yēlek)* word/root repetition. It is no surprise that those who edited the collections also used sound to link the proverbial sentences into longer clusters (see Prov 11:9-10, where each line begins with the preposition *bĕ* ["by"]).

7.3. Semantic Parallelism. *Parallelism is the most significant and frequent poetic device used in Hebrew proverbs. The following categories provide basic handles on how the two parallel lines are related (Kugel; Alter; Berlin; Watson). G. H. Wilson has developed the first three categories after taking into account Kugel's "A, and what's more, B" critique of Lowth's "Standard description" (synonymous, antithetical, synthetic) approach. The proverbial sentences of Proverbs 10—29 most frequently have opposing parallel lines.

7.3.1. Affirming Parallelism. Proverbs 16:28 (ABC/A'B'C'):

A perverse person stirs up dissension;
a gossip separates close friends.

7.3.2. Opposing Parallelism. Proverbs 10:1 (ABC/A'B'C'):

| A wise son | brings joy | to a father; |
| a foolish son | is a grief | to his mother. |

7.3.3. Advancing Parallelism. Proverbs 16:7 (ABC/DEF):

When a person's ways are pleasing to the LORD,
he makes even his enemies live at peace with him.

7.3.4. Metaphoric Parallelism. Proverbs 16:15 (ABC/A'B'C'):

In the light of the king's face is life,
and his favor is like a cloud of the spring rain.

7.4. Syntactic Parallelism. The ordering and paralleling of syntactic units (S = subject, V = verb, O = object, M = modifier) are carefully examined in the major works on Hebrew poetic structures (O'Connor; Collins). The book of Proverbs manifests these carefully crafted features that are often covered over in translation. So the NIV hides the *chiasm in the translation of Proverbs 10:12:

Hatred [S] stirs up [V] dissension [O],
but love [S] covers [V] all wrongs [O].

The Hebrew ordering is SVO/OVS, which highlights a chiastic structure with a "hate/love" *inclusio linking the beginning and ending of the bicolon.

7.5. Proverbial Figurative Features. The proverbial literary genre is often poetically and rhetorically crafted with a diverse range of figures of speech.

7.5.1. Metonymy. This is a figure in which one word or phrase is substituted for another with which it is closely associated. So Proverbs 27:24b states, "And a crown [i.e., the king] is not secure for all generations."

7.5.2. Simile. This is a statement that makes a comparison between two diverse realms using the markers "like" or "as." Proverbs includes numerous similes (Prov 10:26; 18:8; 19:12). Proverbs 12:18a illustrates this trope when it makes this point: "Reckless words pierce like a sword."

7.5.3. Metaphor. This is a comparison of two diverse realms without the explicit use of "like" or "as" (see Prov 18:4; 20:15b; 21:6b). In Proverbs 18:10, "The name of the LORD is a strong tower" metaphorically likens the name of the Lord to the security and protection of a strongly fortified tower.

7.5.4. Hyperbole. This is an overstatement that helps the proverb to focus attention on the aspect of the situation that is being encapsulated. Thus, the sages recommend that when dining with a ruler, it is best to "put a knife to your throat if you are given to gluttony (Prov 23:2).

7.5.5. Synecdoche. This is a figure in which a part is used for the whole, or the general for the specific (see Prov. 17:7a, 22a; 18:6a, 7a). Proverbs 10:20a mixes a "silver" metaphor and a "tongue" synecdoche: "The tongue of the righteous is choice silver."

7.5.6. Personification. This is a major figurative trope in Proverbs 1—9; 31. *Personification occurs when an inanimate object or abstraction is given human qualities. Thus "Wisdom" calls out in the streets (Prov 1:20), laughs (Prov 1:26), was born and aided God in the creation of the world (Prov 8:22). Indeed, how to understand this feminine personification or hypostasis is one of the most debated aspects of the book of Proverbs (see Camp).

7.6. Proverbial Themes and Vocabulary. Besides sound patterning, parallelism and heightened use of figures of speech, the biblical proverb genre is also characterized by certain themes and vocabulary that help mark out its conceptual space. Although certain vocabulary sets do not necessarily prove a wisdom tradition origin, the lists given by R. N. Whybray are the most useful. Some characteristic wisdom words are "lacking sense" *(ḥăsar-lēb)*, "fool" *(kĕsîl, nābāl, ʾĕwîl)*, "counsel" *(ʿēṣâ)*, "simple" *(petî)*, "mocker" *(lēṣ)*, "discerning" *(nābôn, mēbîn)*, "discipline" *(mûsār)*, "way" *(derek)*, "knowledge" *(daʿat)*, "understanding" *(tĕbûnâ)*, "blessed" *(ʾašrê)* and various forms of "wisdom" *(ḥkm, ḥokmâ)*, to name a few (Whybray 1974). There is often a heavy use of antithetical word pairs (e.g., "wise/foolish" *[ḥākām/kĕsîl]*; "righteous/wicked" *[ṣedeq/rāšāʿ]*; "diligent/

sluggard" *[ḥārûṣ/rĕmiyyâ]*).

Major themes that the proverbial genre addresses are diverse. However, categories such as wise/foolish, righteous/wicked, diligent/sluggard, rich/poor and topics of friendship, speech, wicked/virtuous woman, Yahweh and the king are commonly reflected in this genre, as well as the avoidance of topics such as the temple, priesthood, prophets and events of redemptive history and the covenant.

7.7. Motivational Structures. The motivational structures are clear in admonitions that are often accompanied by an explicit motive clause. Often, however, motivations are not found in explicit motive clauses but are revealed only after one looks below the surface syntax to the motivational level.

Character/Consequence (Prov 10:1a, 2b, 3a, 6a):
A wise son [+ Character] makes a father glad [+ Consequence]. (Prov 10:1a:)

Character/Act (Prov 10:12a, 14a):
The wise [+ Character] store up knowledge [+ Act]. (Prov 10:14a)

Character/Evaluation (10:20a; 11:1a):
A righteous tongue [+ Character] is choice silver [+ Evaluation]. (Prov 10:20a)

Act/Consequence (Prov 10:17a, 19a):
When many words are spoken [-Act], there is no no lack of sin [- Consequence]. (Prov 10:19a)

Appearance/Reality (Prov 13:7; 14:13):
There is one who pretends to be rich [+ Appearance] yet has nothing [- Reality] (Prov 13:7a)

These structures reveal an "approach/avoidance" motivational structure with didactic intent. The most frequent underlying structure is "character to consequence" and not "act to consequence," as promulgated in early wisdom studies (von Rad).

8. Proverbial Forms.
The proverbial form is easily identified not just from the poetic techniques of sound, syntax, parallelism, figures, themes and vocabulary involved but also because the proverbial state-

ments often conform to architectonic proverbial literary structures. The proverbial forms recorded in the historical sections of the Bible are one-line traditional sayings or folk proverbs (e.g., Gen 10:9: "Therefore it is said, 'Like Nimrod a mighty hunter before the LORD'"; see also Judg 8:2, 21; 1 Sam 10:12; 24:13; Ezek 9:9; 18:2, 25, 29; see Fontaine). In the past many thought that the two-line poetically parallel wisdom sayings found in the book of Proverbs were a later development from one-line proverbs. With the discovery of proverbial collections in the ancient Near East, such a simplistic unilinear literary evolution—from simple one-line sayings to complex poetic bicola—must be rejected.

Within the book of Proverbs there are clearly two types of literary forms: the instructions, which are characterized by the imperative and second-person form of direct address (Prov 1—9; 22:17—24:22; 31:1-9 [instructions, admonitions]), and the sentence sayings, which are generally in the third person and nonimperative (Prov 10:1—22:16; 24:23-34; 25—29 [numerical, better-than, comparative, abomination, beatitude, Yahweh, contrary sayings]).

8.1. Instructions: "Listen, my son" (Prov 1—9; 22—24). M. Fox divides the instructions of Proverbs 1—9 into ten father-son lectures (Prov 1:8-19; 2:1-22; 3:1-12; 3:21-35; 4:1-9; 4:10-19; 4:20-27; 5:1-23; 6:20-35; 7:1-27) and five interludes (Prov 1:20-33; 3:13-20; 6:1-19; 8:1-36; 9:1-18) that feature *Woman Wisdom speaking. The lectures/instructions usually have the format of a direct address or "call to hear" ("Listen, my son" [Prov 1:8; 2:1; 3:1; 4:1; 5:1]) followed by an exhortation ("Listen . . . do not forsake your mother's teaching" [Prov 1:8; 2:1b-5; 3:1; 4:1; 5:1]) and an explicit motivation ("for they will be a garland" [Prov 1:9; 2:6; 3:2; 5:3]). This introduction is followed by a lesson proper ("If violent hoodlums allure you . . ." [Prov 1:10-16]), a conclusion that may include a proverb (Prov 1:17: "How useless to spread the net in full view of the birds") and a concluding apothegm ("and so these prowl for their own blood" [Prov 1:18-19]) to reinforce the teaching (Fox, 45). The ten lectures can be divided into three subsets: (1) call to apprenticeship (Prov 1:8-19; 2:1-22; 4:1-9; 4:10-19), (2) call to remember and obey (Prov 3:1-12, 21-35; 4:20-27), (3) warnings against illicit sexual relations (Prov 5:1-23; 6:20-35; 7:1-27). The interludes are addresses given by Woman Wisdom, extolling her instruction (Prov 1:20-33), virtues (Prov 9:1-18;

31:10-31), benefits (Prov 3:13-20) and skills (Prov 8:1-36).

8.2. Admonitions: "Guard your heart, for it is . . ." (Prov 4:23). The admonitions are found in both Mesopotamian and Egyptian wisdom literature. The highest concentrations are in the instruction sections of Proverbs 1—9; 22:17—24:22. The admonition architectonic formula is as follows (a ± means the item is optional, i.e., it may or may not be present): ± call to listen ± condition ("if") + imperative + motivation ± summary instruction. Proverbs 3:5 provides a well-known example: "Trust in the LORD with all your heart" (imperative) + "he will make your paths straight" (motive) (see also Prov 3:3-4, 9-10; 4:21-22, 23; 23:10-11; 31:8-9). Prohibitions employ the same form, but in the negative—for example, Proverbs 3:11-12: "Do not despise the LORD's discipline" (negative jussive) . . . + "because the LORD disciplines those he loves" (motive) (see also Prov 5:8-14; 4:14-16; 6:25-26) (see Nel; cf. the discussion of prohibitions in Crenshaw 1995).

8.3. Numerical Sayings: "Three things are too amazing . . . four that I . . ." (Prov 30:18). The numerical saying is based on careful observation of some feature(s) collected and classified using a numerical pattern: "There are X . . . and X+1 . . ." (Prov 30:15b-16, 18-17, 21-23, 24-28, 29-31; 6:16-19; 26:24-25; cf. Job 5:19-22; Eccles 7:16-17; Amos 1—2; Sir 23:16-17). Numerical sayings are derived from nature (Prov 30:15-16, 18-19), society (Prov 30:21-23), ethics (Prov 6:16-19; 30:7-9) and theology (Job 5:19-22; 33:14-15). Often the last line (X+1) contains the point being highlighted and uses the numerical pattern for heightening. Some view the numerical patterning as a mnemonic device. G. S. Ogden notes that this form was utilized by the prophets (Amos 1—2). Confucius even used it for sexual topics (cf. Prov 30:19) (Ogden; Roth). Others tie this form back to a listing type phenomena found in the early onomastica.

8.4. "Better Than" Sayings: "Better poor . . . than rich . . . " (Prov 19:1). In modern times we use this form, as in "Better late than never." This form connects Israelite wisdom with Egypt, where, interestingly, it frequently refers to economic evaluations as it does in Israelite proverbs. So Amenemope says, "Better is bread with a happy heart than wealth with vexation" (Lichtheim 2.152). The simple form "Better A than B" is most often extended into a quadripartite structure: "Better A + x than B + y." An example of this is seen in Proverbs 16:8: "Better a little with righteousness than great wealth without justice" (e.g., Prov 12:9; 15:16-17; Eccles 4:3, 6; Sir 40:19-26). A variation of this form is the "not good" proverb (Prov 17:26; 18:5; cf. Eccles 3:12, 22) (Bryce; Ogden).

8.5. Comparative Sayings: "For as churning milk produces butter . . . " (Prov 30:33). The comparative proverb manifests the essential nature of the proverb that makes an analogical comparison of one realm with another. Thus, the biblical sage writes, "Like a city with broken walls is a person who lacks self-control" (Prov 25:28; cf. Prov 26:11, 21, 23; 30:33). There is a high concentration of the simile pairs/clusters in Proverbs 25—26. The comparative cluster Proverbs 25:28—26:2 indicates that the chapter break for Proverbs 26 was misplaced.

8.6. Abomination Sayings: "The way of the wicked is an abomination to the LORD" (Prov 15:9). Some of the earliest Sumerian collections also have this form, which references their deities: "Debts not cleared . . . are an abomination to Utu" (Alster 1.196). The biblical sage writes, "A false balance is an abomination to the LORD, but an accurate weight is his delight" (Prov 11:1; cf. Prov 11:20, 15:8-9). In antithetical parallelisms the "abomination" is often balanced by "his delight" (Clements). Some have proposed that proverbs that mention "the LORD" ("YHWH") were later additions inserted into an early more secular proverb collection (McKane). The lengthy history of the abomination sayings calls such a proposal into question.

8.7. Beatitudes: "Blessed is one who is kind to the poor" (Prov 22:9). The beatitude, or macarism, is best known from the Sermon on the Mount (Mt 5:3-11), but this form is also found in the wisdom psalms (Ps 1:1; 32:1-2; 112:1-2). The use of "blessings" in the covenant (Lev 26; Deut 27—28) should not be confused with their use in wisdom texts, as they function quite differently in the two genres. The beatitude form appears in Egyptian instructions as well as biblical proverbs (Prov 8:32, 34; 29:18; cf. Sir 14:1-2). Proverbs 28:14a states, "Blessed is the one who always fears the LORD" (Nel).

8.8. Yahweh Sayings: "The Lord [YHWH] is far from the wicked" (Prov 15:29). Whybray (1979) notes that of the 375 sayings (interestingly, the gematria for the name *"Solomon" equals 375), fifty-five (fifteen percent) are Yahweh sayings (contra McKane, who believes the Yahweh say-

ings were later additions to a secular proverbial core). Proverbs 15—16 contains a marked increase in the number of Yahweh sayings and is positioned at the center of the book of Proverbs. An inclusio begins and ends the book with "the fear of the LORD" (Prov 1:7; 31:30; cf. Eccles 12:13). The section Proverbs 15:33—16:9 is a concentrated collection of Yahweh sayings followed by a series of king sayings (Prov 16:10-15).

Generally, the Yahweh sayings are used at the collection level. K. M. Heim (288) notes that the following chiastic pattern has a Yahweh-saying inclusio bonding Proverbs 21:1-31 together.

[A] Yahweh sayings (vv. 1-3)
    [B] diligence (v. 5)
        [C] nagging wife (v. 9)
        [C'] nagging wife (v. 19)
    [B'] laziness (v. 25)
[A'] Yahweh sayings (vv. 30-31)

8.9. Contrary Proverbs: "Answer not a fool . . . Answer a fool . . . " (Prov 26:4-5). Contrary or paradoxical proverbs have been common fare from ancient proverbs collections of many cultures (e.g., Sumerian: "From 3,600 oxen there is no dung") to modern English sayings. Does "absence make the heart go fonder"? Or is it "out of sight, out of mind"? Perhaps the twisted proverb has it right in "absence makes the heart to wander." This antonymity between proverbial sayings looks like a contradiction if one understands proverbs in a dogmatic or absolutist manner. Yet, in almost every proverb collection, opposites are recorded and often juxtaposed, with the "contradiction" purposefully used to break the bands of an isolated dogmatic approach and to necessitate the importance of coming to grips with the polysituational use of proverbs.

Thus the biblical proverb pair in Proverbs 26:4-5—one advising, "Do not answer a fool according to his folly," and the next one just as clearly advising, "Answer a fool according to his folly"—is common fare in proverb collections from around the world. The editors deliberately placed these contrary proverbs back to back. This dissonance leads one away from simplistic dualistic dogmatism to a situationally nuanced wisdom.

9. Editorial Compositional Units.

To what extent does divine guidance extend to

the anonymous authors of these diverse sentences or to the editors who determined the canonical shape of the text in Hezekiah's day (Prov 25:1) and others who later assembled the whole book of Proverbs? The LXX reordering of collections reinforces the idea that the order was still fluid even into the Hellenistic period of the LXX (after 200 BC) (see Cook). How did the editors compile the proverbs into collections? What techniques and ethos do their work of collecting and editing reveal? Is it possible to interpret above the sentence level on the plane of the pair, string/cluster and collection?

9.1. Pairs. Many have noted the apparent randomness of the sentence sayings in Proverbs 10—29. However, literary and linguistic techniques have revealed over sixty proverbial pairs in the sentence sayings (Hildebrandt). Several identifiable techniques were used to bind individual proverbs into pairs.

First, repeated catchwords may semantically link two proverbs into a pair. Proverbs 13:21-22 provides an interesting example, where the first proverb begins with "sinners" and the second ends with "sin," thereby forming an inclusio that bonds the two sayings together. This is further enhanced by the first proverb's ending with the word *ṭôb* ("good") and the second proverb's beginning with that same word. Thus, a chiasm spans the pair and links them in an ABBA pattern: sinners/good/good/sin. Clearly, the juxtaposing of these two was not random.

Second, the linking between the pairs is often thematic (Prov 21:25-26; 13:2-3). Thus both verses of Proverbs 12:18-19 address issues of speech without the presence of a single catchword. Sometimes this thematic pairing may be antithetic, as in Proverbs 16:12-13, where one saying references that which the king detests, while the next identifies that in which the king delights (see also Prov 18:10-11).

Sometimes two proverbs with a metaphor or simile are juxtaposed (Prov 10:25-26; 14:26-27; 27:15-16). In these cases the shared figure of speech provides the sense of cohesion.

When proverbs are paired, each sentence should first be interpreted as an isolated unit, then the relationship to its pair explored as a second layer of interpretation and interaction.

9.2. Acrostic: Proverbs 31:10-31. An acrostic begins each line with consecutive letters of the alphabet, although some variations are allowed. The acrostic form has proven impossible to translate without overt paraphrasing. To construct such a piece demands careful planning and textual crafting and manifests clear authorial intent. The book of *Psalms exhibits the acrostic format (Pss 9—10 [taken together]; 25; 34; 111; 112; 119; 145). The poem of the virtuous woman in Proverbs 31:10-31 is a concluding acrostic to the book of Proverbs. Many have made suggestions as to the function of the acrostic form, from mnemonic/pedagogical to giving a sense of completeness or exhaustiveness—the "A to Z" on the virtuous woman. The acrostic form may present an underlying sense of "order" *(*maat)* that wisdom or this virtuous woman brings to the life of her family. Besides its use as superlative highlighting for the themes of Psalm 119 and Proverbs 31, the acrostic form is often used in lament contexts (see *Lamentations) where the acrostic may be referencing the notion of deep providential "order" prevailing in the face of overwhelming chaos.

T. P. McCreesh (1985) has suggested that the poem in Proverbs 31 is an inclusio, as the book begins with Woman Wisdom's invitation (Prov 1) and concludes with a description of the many ways that this virtuous woman (Woman Wisdom) will serve those who embrace her. Others, such as A. Wolters, see this poem as a panegyric to the valiant wife (cf. Ps 112), parallel to Israel's heroic poetry (cf. the Song of Deborah in Judg 5). While B. K. Waltke (2.518) rejects McCreesh's identification of the valiant wife with Woman Wisdom as allegorical and unreal, he contrasts such an allegorical figure to someone like *Ruth, who was a real model. I would like to reinvigorate McCreesh's case. Woman Wisdom is contextually relevant to Proverbs, whereas the heroic Ruth, Deborah and Psalm 112 are contextually distant. Perhaps the relationship between Woman Wisdom in Proverbs 1—9 and real Israelite women, as understood by C. V. Camp (285-86), can be adapted to fit Proverbs 31. For the sage, what is more valuable than "rubies" (Prov 3:15; 8:11; 31:10)? It is Woman Wisdom, not an allegorical, mythical wise woman, but perhaps modeled on the real wise women of Israel (see 2 Sam 14:2). Woman Wisdom as an inclusio between Proverbs 1—9 and Proverbs 31 is convincing to me, although most prefer a "heroic wife" motif (e.g., Wolters; Waltke).

9.3. Strings/Clusters. Many recent studies have focused on collectional aspects of Proverbs, as seen in the works of Skehan, Heim, Van Leeuwen and Whybray, along with extensive work done by Germans from the days of G. Boström and Skladny, to Plöger, Scherer, Scoralick and Krispen. The recent bounty of commentaries (Plöger; Meinhold; Murphy; Whybray 1994; Garrett; Perdue; Fox; Koptak; Longman; and esp. Waltke) also reflects this rich collectional approach to proverb interpretation.

Heim sees Proverbs 10:6-11 as a cluster being delimited by the inclusio repetition of "but violence overwhelms the mouth of the wicked" in Proverbs 10:6b and Proverbs 10:11b. Waltke notes the alternating AB/AB pattern in Proverbs 20:8-11 introduced with a janus (Prov 20:8) that points back in an inclusio to Proverbs 20:2 and forward to the next cluster that it begins.

[A]   the king's justice (v. 8)
    [B]   universal human depravity (v. 9)
[A']   the Lord's justice (v. 10)
    [B']   human depravity from youth (v. 11)

These chiastic, alternating and inclusio structures are helpful in isolating such clusters. These brief examples show the importance of reading the sentence sayings in light of the pairing and the clustering strategies by which the editors built up their collections.

9.4. Larger Units and Collections. The book of Proverbs is explicitly composed of seven collections as designated by the superscriptions:

1:1—9:17	Instructions about Woman Wisdom and Woman Folly
10:1—22:16	Sentence sayings of Solomon
22:17—24:22	Sayings of the wise
24:23-34	More sayings of the wise
25:1—29:27	More proverbs of Solomon collected by the men of Hezekiah
30:1-33	Sayings of Agur
31:1-31	Sayings of King Lemuel that his mother taught him

Although many critics view the "Solomonic enlightenment" historically linking these collections to Solomon as a literary fiction, this is not supported by the superscriptions themselves (Prov 1:1; 10:1; 25:1), the literary form (see Kitchen) or the historical descriptions of the period (1 Kings 3:5-6; 4:29-34; 2 Chron 1—9), where even international connections are uniquely highlighted, particularly with Egypt (1 Kings 3:1; 9:16).

R. C. Van Leeuwen isolates a subcollection in Proverbs 25-27. Similarly, B. V. Malchow demonstrates that Proverbs 28—29 is a subcollection that he labels a "manual for future monarchs." Heim (288) provides an encapsulation of the whole of Proverbs 21 as a subcollection.

10. Future Directions and Reflections.
Many have used proverbs in defense of pedagogical techniques (memorizing, use of the rod, etc.), to offer advice on how to make money (diligence/wealth motifs [cf. Benjamin Franklin's "Way of Wealth"]), and to reinforce a black/white cognitive-ethical framework that actually subterfuges the use of proverbs for attaining higher-order thinking and more advanced aspects of spiritual formation. Although it is clear that proverbial familiarity can be beneficially inculcated at a young age, the wisdom potential of these sayings needs to be explored within the framework of adult cognitive-ethical development, emotional intelligence and wisdom/spiritual formation (see Sternberg and Jordan).

The power and potential of the well-crafted collected proverbs are designed to be unleashed and recontextualized in the particular story of each individual. Proverbs deny helplessness by encouraging those pursuing Woman Wisdom to make responsible choices that matter and have real consequences, all the while realizing that although a person may plan a course, one's steps are ultimately determined by the Almighty (Prov 16:9). Hence, a humbling, reverential *fear of the Lord is the only valid foundation, or *pou sto*, to begin one's pursuit of wisdom (Prov 9:10).

See also CHIASM; DISCOURSE IN PROVERBS; FORM CRITICISM; INCLUSIO; PARALLELISM; POETICS, TERMINOLOGY OF; PROVERBS 1: BOOK OF.

BIBLIOGRAPHY. **B. Alster,** *Proverbs of Ancient Sumer: The World's Earliest Proverb Collections* (2 vols.; Bethesda, MD: CDL Press, 1997); **R. Alter,** *The Art of Biblical Poetry* (New York: Basic Books, 1987); **A. Berlin,** *The Dynamics of Biblical Parallelism* (Bloomington: Indiana University Press, 1985); **G. Boström,** *Paronomasi i den äldre hebreiska maschallitteraturen med särskild hänsyn till proverbia* (LUÅ 1; Lund: Gleerup, 1928); **L. Boström,** *The God of the Sages: The Portrayal of God in the Book of Proverbs* (Stockholm: Almqvist & Wiksell, 1990); **G. E. Bryce,** "Better-Proverbs: An

Historical and Structural Study," in *Book of Seminar Papers: The Society of Biblical Literature, One Hundred Eighth Annual Meeting, Friday-Tuesday, 1-5 September 1972*, ed. L. C. McGaughy (2 vols.; Missoula, MT: Society of Biblical Literature, 1972) 2.343-54; **C. V. Camp**, *Wisdom and the Feminine in the Book of Proverbs* (BLS; Sheffield: JSOT Press, 1985); **R. E. Clements**, "The Concept of the Abomination in Proverbs," in *Texts, Temples and Traditions: A Tribute to Menahem Haran*, ed. M. Fox et al. (Winona Lake, IN: Eisenbrauns, 1996); **T. Collins**, *Line-Forms in Hebrew Poetry: A Grammatical Approach to the Stylistic Study of Hebrew Prophets* (Rome: Biblical Institute Press, 1978); **J. Cook**, *The Septuagint of Proverbs: Jewish and/or Hellenistic Proverbs? Concerning the Hellenistic Colouring of LXX Proverbs* (VTSup 69; Leiden: E. J. Brill, 1997); **J. L. Crenshaw**, *Studies in Ancient Israelite Wisdom* (New York: KTAV, 1976); idem, *Urgent Advice and Probing Questions: Collected Writings on Old Testament Wisdom* (Macon, GA: Mercer University Press, 1995); **J. Day, R. P. Gordon and H. G. M. Williamson**, eds., *Wisdom in Ancient Israel: Essays in Honour of J. A. Emerton* (Cambridge: Cambridge University Press, 1995); **A. Dundes**, "On the Structure of the Proverb," in *The Wisdom of Many: Essays on the Proverb*, ed. W. Mieder and A. Dundes (Madison: University of Wisconsin Press, 1981) 43-64; **C. R. Fontaine**, *Traditional Sayings in the Old Testament* (BLS; Sheffield: Almond, 1982); **M. Fox**, *Proverbs 1-9* (AB 18A; New York: Doubleday, 2000); **J. G. Gammie and L. G. Perdue**, *The Sage in Israel and the Ancient Near East* (Winona Lake, IN: Eisenbrauns, 1990); **D. A. Garrett**, *Proverbs, Ecclesiastes, Song of Songs* (NAC; Nashville: Broadman, 1993); **F. W. Golka**, *The Leopard's Spots: Biblical and African Wisdom in Proverbs* (Edinburgh: T & T Clark, 1993); **K. M. Heim**, *Like Grapes of Gold Set in Silver: An Interpretation of Proverbial Clusters in Proverbs 10:1-22:16* (BZAW 273; Berlin: de Gruyter, 2001); **T. Hildebrandt**, "Proverbial Pairs: Compositional Units in Proverbs 10-29," *JBL* 107 (1988) 207-24; **R. P. Honeck**, *A Proverb in Mind: The Cognitive Science of Proverbial Wit and Wisdom* (Mahwah, NJ: Lawrence Erlbaum, 1997); **B. Kirshenblatt-Gimblett**, "Toward a Theory of Proverb Meaning," in *The Wisdom of Many: Essays on the Proverb*, ed. W. Mieder and A. Dundes (Madison: University of Wisconsin Press, 1981) 111-22; **K. A. Kitchen**, "Proverbs and Wisdom Books of the Ancient Near East: The Factual History of a Literary Form," *TynBul* 28 (1977) 69-114; **P. E. Koptak**, *Proverbs* (NIVAC; Grand Rapids: Zondervan, 2003); **J. Krispen**, *Spruchkompositionen im Buch Proverbia* (EH 349/23; Frankfurt: Bern; New York; Peter Lang, 1989); **J. L. Kugel**, *The Idea of Biblical Poetry* (New Haven: Yale University Press, 1981); **A.-L. Kuusi**, "Towards an International Type-System of Proverbs," *Proverbium* 19 (1972) 698-736; **W. G. Lambert**, *Babylonian Wisdom Literature* (London: Oxford University Press, 1960); **M. Lichtheim**, *Ancient Egyptian Literature* (3 vols.; Berkeley: University of California Press, 1975); **T. Longman III**, *Proverbs* (Grand Rapids: Baker, 2006); **T. Longman III and L. Ryken**, *A Complete Literary Guide to the Bible* (Grand Rapids: Zondervan, 1993); **B. V. Malchow**, "A Manual for Future Monarchs," *CBQ* 47 (1985) 238-45; **T. P. McCreesh**, "Wisdom as a Wife: Proverbs 31:10-31,"*RB* 92 (1985) 25-46; idem, *Biblical Sound and Sense: Poetic Sound Patterns in Proverbs 10-29* (JSOTSup 128; Sheffield: JSOT Press, 1991); **W. McKane**, *Proverbs: A New Approach* (OTL; Philadelphia: Westminster, 1970); **A. Meinhold**, *Die Sprüche* (2 vols.; ZBK 16; Zürich: Theologischer Verlag, 1991); **W. Mieder**, "The Essence of Literary Proverb Study," *Proverbium* 23 (1974) 888-94; idem, *Proverbs: A Handbook* (Westport, CT: Greenwood Press, 2004); idem, *The Prentice-Hall Encyclopedia of World Proverbs* (New York: Prentice-Hall, 1986); idem, *Wise Words: Essays on the Proverb* (New York: Garland, 1994); **W. Mieder and A. Dundes**, eds., *The Wisdom of Many: Essays on the Proverb* (Madison: University of Wisconsin Press, 1981); **G. B. Milner**, "Quadripartite Structures," *Proverbium* 14 (1969) 379-83; **R. E. Murphy**, *Proverbs* (WBC 22; Nashville: Thomas Nelson, 1998); **P. J. Nel**, *The Structure and Ethos of the Wisdom Admonitions in Proverbs* (Berlin: de Gruyter, 1982); **M. O'Connor**, *Hebrew Verse Structure* (Winona Lake, IN: Eisenbrauns, 1980); **G. S. Ogden**, "Better Proverb (Tob-Spruch), Rhetorical Criticism, and Qoheleth," *JBL* 96 (1977) 489-505; **L. G. Perdue**, *Proverbs* (IBC; Louisville: John Knox, 2000); **O. Plöger**, *Sprüche Salomos (Proverbia)* (BKAT 17; Neukirchen-Vluyn: Neukirchener Verlag, 1984); **J. P. Pritchard**, *Ancient Near Eastern Texts Relating to the Old Testament* (Princeton, NJ: Princeton University Press, 1969); **W. Roth**, *Numerical Sayings in the Old Testament* (VTSup 13; Leiden: E. J. Brill, 1965); **J. Ruffle**, "The Teaching of Amenemope and Its Connection with the Book of Proverbs," *TynBul* 28 (1977) 29-68; **A. Scherer**,

Das weise Wort und seine Wirkung: Eine Untersuchung zur Komposition und Redaktion von Proverbia 10, 1-22, 16 (WMANT 83; Neukirchen-Vluyn: Neukirchener Verlag, 1999); **R. Scoralick,** *Einzelspruch und Sammlung: Komposition im Buch der Sprichwörter Kapitel 10-15* (BZAW 232; Berlin: de Gruyter, 1995); **P. W. Skehan,** "A Single Editor for the Whole Book of Proverbs," in *Studies in Ancient Israelite Wisdom,* ed. J. L. Crenshaw (New York: KTAV, 1976) 329-40; **U. Skladny,** *Die altesten Spruchsammlungen in Israel* (Gottingen: Vandenhoeck & Ruprecht, 1962); **D. C. Snell,** *Twice-Told Proverbs and the Composition of the Book of Proverbs* (Winona Lake, IN: Eisenbrauns, 1993); **R. J. Sternberg and J. Jordan,** eds., *A Handbook of Wisdom: Psychological Perspectives* (New York: Cambridge University Press, 2005); **R. C. Van Leeuwen,** "The Book of Proverbs," *NIB* 5.17-264; **G. von Rad,** *Wisdom in Israel* (Nashville: Abingdon, 1981); **B. K. Waltke,** *The Book of Proverbs* (2 vols.; Grand Rapids: Eerdmans, 2005); **H. C. Washington,** *Wealth and Poverty in the Instruction of Amenemope and the Hebrew Bible* (SBLDS 142; Atlanta: Scholars Press, 1994); **W. G. E. Watson,** *Classical Hebrew Poetry: A Guide to Its Techniques* (JSOTSup 26; Sheffield: JSOT Press, 1984); **C. Westermann,** *Roots of Wisdom: The Oldest Proverbs of Israel and Other Peoples* (Louisville: Westminster John Knox, 1995); **R. N. Whybray,** *The Intellectual Tradition in the Old Testament* (BZAW 135; Berlin: de Gruyter, 1974); idem, "Yahweh-Sayings and Their Context in Proverbs 10:1-22,16," in *La sagesse de L'Ancien Testament: Travaux présentés au Colloquium Biblicum Lovaniense XXIX tenu du 29 au 31 août 1978,* ed. M. Gilbert (BETL 51; Gembloux: Duculot; Leuven: Leuven University Press, 1979) 153-65; idem, *The Composition of the Book of Proverbs* (JSOTSup 168; Sheffield: Sheffield Academic Press, 1994); **G. H. Wilson,** *Psalms,* vol. 1 (NIVAC; Grand Rapids: Zondervan, 2002); **A. Wolters,** *The Song of the Valiant Woman: Studies in the Interpretation of Proverbs 31:10-31* (Waynesboro, GA: Paternoster, 2001).

T. Hildebrandt

PROVERBS 1: BOOK OF

The book of Proverbs is the preeminent collection of wisdom in the Hebrew Bible. *Ecclesiastes and *Job are also wisdom literature, but they contest optimistic views concerning the rewards of wisdom rather than defining the nature of wisdom per se. In order to define wisdom in the light of the teaching of the book of Proverbs, one might be deceived into thinking that it is no more than the skill of living. Certainly, Proverbs guides its ancient and modern readers on the right path and warns against the evil path, but Proverbs is more than a collection of observations, prohibitions and admonitions. At its foundation, Proverbs describes wisdom as a relationship; it begins with the "fear of the LORD" (Prov 1:7). No wonder Proverbs, along with Genesis and *Psalms, remains one of the most popular books of the OT among modern readers.

1. History of Composition
2. Genre
3. Ancient Near Eastern Background
4. Structure
5. Theological Message

1. History of Composition.

1.1. Author and Date. The book begins with the following superscription: "The proverbs of Solomon, the son of David, king of Israel." Traditionally, the book has been closely connected with *Solomon (c. 970-930 BC), described in the book of Kings as the paragon of wisdom, a gift that was granted to Solomon upon his request (1 Kings 3:1-15). Solomon often is pictured as demonstrating extraordinary wisdom (1 Kings 4:29-34), a wisdom with which he achieved international fame. He is also said to have "composed three thousand proverbs, and his songs number a thousand and five" (1 Kings 4:32). Furthermore, Solomon is mentioned in the superscription of the two other major OT wisdom books, Ecclesiastes and *Song of Songs. The rabbis *(Midrash Rabbah)* describe these three books as coming from the three phases of his life by stating, "When a man is young, he composes songs; when he grows older, he makes sententious remarks; and when he becomes an old man, he speaks of the vanity of things."

However, though a first reading of the superscription might lead one to assume that Solomon was the author of the entirety of the book, internal evidence throws that idea into doubt. In short, the book occasionally mentions others who have contributed to the making of the final product. First mention should be made of an anonymous group of *sages referred to simply as "the wise" (Prov 22:17; 24:23). The wise are connected with the proverbs found in Proverbs 22:17—24:34. Later we will refer to the ancient Near Eastern, particularly Egyptian, background to the material in this section. While the reference to "the wise" is nonspecific, material in the last two chapters of the book are ascribed to individuals who are specifically named, Agur (Prov 30:1) and Lemuel (Prov 31:1), although they remain enigmatic because they are not named elsewhere in the Bible (*see* Lemuel and Agur). Finally, another anonymous group is said to have contributed to the final form of the book: "men of Hezekiah" (Prov 25:1). Hezekiah was king of Judah in the late eighth and early seventh centuries BC, over two centuries after Solomon ruled a united Israel. These men were likely *scribes or sages who worked in his court. However, the exact nature of their contribution is not absolutely clear, since the verb used to describe their work could indicate that they simply added additional Solomonic proverbs, though it might also intend to say that they redacted them.

Thus, at best, Solomon was responsible for only part of the book, not the whole composition. Indeed, the mention of Solomon in Proverbs 1:1 might be taken as simply citing the most well-known or perhaps the source of the wisdom tradition that constituted the book of Proverbs. The fact that he is mentioned in the superscription, which is the first verse of the preamble (Prov 1:1-7), and then again in Proverbs 10:1, may well indicate that the material from Proverbs 1:8—9:18 is anonymous. The material that the book itself ascribes to Solomon is Proverbs 10:1—22:16; 25:1—29:27.

In conclusion, if one regards the indications within the book, the origins of the book of Proverbs might be associated with Solomon, but its redaction continued for centuries afterward. Like the composition of Psalms, so also the composition of Proverbs may have taken place over a long period of time before it finally came to a close and no more proverbs were added. Indeed, the considerably different structure of LXX Proverbs as well as a number of additions may indicate that this process continued even beyond the time that the Hebrew text tradition adapted by the Masoretes came to a close.

Before concluding this discussion of authorship, we should note the fact of repeated proverbs throughout the book. D. C. Snell has cataloged the evidence for repeated verses according to the following categories (of which only representative examples are given in the parentheses):

> Whole verses repeated with spelling variations (Prov 14:12/16:25; 18:8; 26:22)
> Whole verses repeated with one dissimilar word (Prov 6:10-11/24:33-34)
> Whole verses repeated with two dissimilar words (Prov 10:1/15:20; 11:1/20:23)
> Whole verses repeated with three dissimilar words (Prov 10:2/11:4)

Thus, it appears that individual proverbs were added over time. According to Snell (74), "Scholars generally agree that there are few indications of the absolute dates when the composers and editors worked." The situation may be like that in Psalms (compare duplicate psalms such as Pss 14; 53), where similar and near similar psalms were added because different groups of psalms came into the collection at different times, and while there would be a majority of new psalms in a new group, it may contain one or more that already existed in the collection. Even so, their presence may indicate something to the reader: the importance of such a theme. In other words, repetition, resulting from whatever reason, leads to emphasis.

But none of this information helps us date any individual proverb with great confidence. And in any case, proverbs are like jokes and riddles. It is hard to recover the date of their composition. They often emerge in an oral context and eventually find their way into a written collection such as the book we know as Proverbs. Perhaps Solomon did compose some proverbs, but he might also have been a collector.

We cannot say much for certain about the date of individual proverbs or the date of the final form of the book. However, perhaps we can say something about their social origins. Are they from the upper levels of society or the lower? Are the proverbs derived from the court, the farm, the school, the temple or some other place within Israelite society? To that subject we now turn.

1.2. Social Setting. In the modern period, G. von Rad was a pioneer in this discussion, arguing that proverbs found their social setting among royal scribes working in the service of the king. Evidence for this includes the connection with Solomon and the men of Hezekiah, noted in Proverbs 25:1 (see 1.1 above). In addition, we will soon observe that Proverbs has analogues from the ancient Near East, especially ancient Egypt. Many of these texts have a court origin, as is illustrated by the most famous related Egyptian text, the Instruction of Amenemope. Amenemope was a lower-level bureaucrat who was instructing his son.

More recently this question has been concerned with the issue of whether or not there were scribal schools in ancient Israel that might have fed graduates into the royal bureaucracy (*see* Sages, Schools, Education). The first mention of such a school is from the later book, *Sirach, which refers to the *bet midrash.* Of course, schools could have predated their first attested reference, and probably did so, but the evidence in favor is then inferential.

A. Lemaire has put forward the best arguments in favor of the existence of schools during the OT time period. He points to the discovery of a handful of extrabiblical texts that appear to come from a school setting. Tablets that contain lists of the alphabet provide a good example. Other scholars, including F. Golka, argue that these documents support literacy, not schools. While the fact that Egypt, Mesopotamia and even Canaan provide evidence of schools may strongly support the idea, we have nothing like concrete proof that will establish the existence of schools. And in addition, the explicit comments of the OT (Deut 4:10; 5:31; 11:19) as well as the dynamics of Proverbs 1—9 suggest that learning came about when a father instructed his son in a family setting.

Golka and his teacher C. Westermann took a different tack to the question. Rather than looking at ancient analogies such as Egypt, they observed living societies that they felt were socially similar to ancient Israel. That led them to tribal Africa, where they examined the production of proverbs in those societies. The similarities led them to argue that biblical proverbs originated with small farmers of Israel.

This proposed setting might explain proverbs such as Proverbs 10:5, "An insightful son harvests in the summer; a disgraceful son sleeps during harvest," but not ones such as Proverbs 23:1-3, which more likely comes from a court setting: "When you sit down to dine with a ruler, carefully consider what is in front of you. Place a knife at your gullet to control your appetite. Do not long for his delicacies, for they are false food." The best conclusion recognizes that the proverbs of the biblical book do not come from a single social setting. The book is a collection from a variety of settings.

1.3. Textual Transmission. A comparison of the structure of the book of Proverbs in the Massoretic tradition (as represented by the Codex Leningradensis) and the Greek tradition (LXX), dated to around 200 BC, reveals a significant difference (Cook). The order matches through Proverbs 24:22, then it diverges in the following way:

Masoretic Text	Septuagint
24:23-34 (Further Sayings of the Wise)	30:1-14 (Agur)
25:1—29:27 (Hezekiah's Men)	24:23-34 (Further Sayings of the Wise)
30:1-14 (Agur)	30:15-33 (Numerical Parallelisms)
30:15-33 (Numerical Parallelisms)	31:1-9 (Lemuel's Mother)
31:1-9 (Lemuel's Mother)	25:1—29:27 (Hezekiah's Men)
31:10-31 (Poem to the Noble Wife)	31:10-31 (Poem to the Noble Wife)

Besides a difference in order of passages in the last part of Proverbs, there are also a number of texts that we find in the MT that are not found in the LXX (Prov 4:7; 8:33; 16:1, 3; 20:14-19), as well as many additions in the LXX that are not in the MT (Tov 1990; 1992, 337).

The difference between the MT and the LXX is the most important variant to consider, since the other versions (Syriac, Vulgate, Targum) are of no additional significance because they reflect one of those two traditions. The Dead Sea materials only include a minimal witness to the book of Proverbs (*see* Dead Sea Scrolls).

But why is there a difference between the MT and the LXX, and, further, what is the significance of the variance? Two views have been put forward. E. Tov believes that there are two different editions of the book. However, B. Waltke (2004, 6-9) more recently has shown the Greek text to be a rather free translation of the Hebrew, heavily influenced by Stoic philosophy and Jewish midrashic thinking. Such a conclusion, while minimizing the importance of the Greek version as a textual witness to the original text, does not preclude its importance on occasion.

2. Genre.

2.1. Superscription: **māšāl.** The superscription

of the book contains a genre label when it begins "The proverbs [*mišlê*, the construct form of *māšāl*] of Solomon." Unfortunately, one does not get very far trying to define the genre through etymology or even through a study of the word itself, since the semantic field seems rather broad. In Proverbs 1:6 the term is parallel with "words of the wise," so perhaps the word *māšāl* simply refers to the fact that this literary vehicle is part of the wisdom teacher's pedagogical repertoire. The Greek equivalents are *paroimia* and *parabolē*, which supports this idea. It also points to the fact that the underlying verb may be *māšāl* I, "be like," implying a comparison or teaching by metaphor, rather than *māšāl* II, "rule" or "dominate." It is possible but not likely that the noun "proverb" plays on both words. If so, it would point to the fact that the proverb intends to draw comparisons so that the recipient can stay in control of a situation. But ultimately we will not understand the genre of proverb or of the book and its parts through etymology. It is best to turn to the contents.

The first observation that we can make is that there seems to be a difference between Proverbs 1—9 and Proverbs 10—31. The bulk of the former is extended speeches or discourses (*see* Discourse in Proverbs), while the latter is shorter, briefer observations, warnings, prohibitions and encouragements. The latter, as we will see, is much closer to what we call proverbs in English.

2.2. Discourses: Proverbs 1—9. First we take a closer look at the discourses. Most of the discourses are speeches of a father (sometimes speaking also on behalf of his wife [see Prov 1:8]) to his son. However, on a few occasions the speaker is a woman named "Wisdom," who addresses all the young men who are walking by her (Prov 1:20-33; 8:1-36; 9:1-6), and on one occasion, another woman, named "Folly," speaks to the young men (Prov 9:13-18) (*see* Woman Wisdom and Woman Folly).

M. Fox (45-46) has correctly described the components of a discourse as typically containing an exordium, a lesson and a conclusion, though there is considerable variety in the amount of space devoted to these three elements. The exordium includes a call for the recipient to pay attention, which is accompanied by motivation to do so. The lesson is the object of teaching, and the conclusion brings the

teaching to a close, sometimes by describing the consequences of listening or not listening to the lesson.

Proverbs 2 is an example of a discourse that has a major emphasis on the exordium, which essentially takes up the first half of the chapter. It invokes the son ("My son" [Prov 2:1]), calling on him to pay attention. Motivations are given, notably the fact that if the son seeks wisdom, God will grant it to him. The lesson includes admonition to avoid evil women and men (Prov 2:12-19), and the conclusion is stated in the last three verses (Prov 2:20-22).

Proverbs 7 is a discourse of father to son that begins with an exordium in Proverbs 7:1-5. The exordium anticipates the lesson as concerned with avoidance of promiscuous women. Even so, the lesson proper is found in Proverbs 7:6-23 and is in the form of an anecdote of a seduction. Proverbs 7:24-27 drives home the point to the son: he needs to avoid the approach of the seductress, or he will be ruined.

2.3. The Proverb (Proverbs 10—31). The bulk of Proverbs 10—31 is composed of short, pithy sayings that offer observations, warnings, prohibitions and encouragements. Typically these are bicola, but tricola and even longer proverbs also occur. There are longer speeches resembling discourses in Proverbs 30—31, but these are the exceptions.

We will examine the proverb first by looking at a typical bicolon and use as our illustrative example the very first proverb of the section: "A wise son makes a father glad, and a foolish son is the sorrow of his mother" (Prov 10:1).

2.3.1. Poetic Style. The first observation to make is that the proverb is poetic in style (as is the discourse). Thus, it demonstrates some of the characteristics of poetry, including *terseness and *parallelism. Poetry is compact language, and proverbs are no exception. This adds punch to the statement, helping to make it memorable. Often a proverb furthers its memorability by the use of a *sound play of one type or another. This aspect of the proverb is often lost on the non-Hebrew reader but can be illustrated by reference to proverbs in English: "Haste makes waste"; "Look before you leap"; "A stitch in time saves nine."

Rhyme is never used in Hebrew poetry; the nature of the language makes it too easy to do and therefore not interesting poetically. However, there are examples of other types of language manipulation, such as alliteration. For instance, Proverbs 30:20 has a sound play:

This is the way of the adulterous woman:
   she eats and wipes her mouth,
   and she says, "I have done nothing wrong!"

kēn derek ʾiššâ mĕnāʾāpet
* ʾāklâ ûmāḥătâ pîhā*
* wĕʾāmrâ lōʾ-pāʿaltî ʾāwen*

The content of this verse focuses on the woman's mouth, and this message is underlined by the fact that a high proportion of the letters are labials, signifying sounds formed by the lips (particularly the letters *m* and *p*).

Although Proverbs 10:1 does not have a really striking sound play, it is terse and has a tight parallel structure. Specifically, it is a parallelism built on antonyms (often called antithetic parallelism), very common in Proverbs. Thus, "wise" parallels "foolish," "joy" parallels "grief," and "father" parallels "mother." The constant is the son. An antithetical parallelism looks at the same truth from opposite perspectives; it is not making opposite points.

Another common feature of parallelism is not present in this example: *imagery. However, imagery is a common feature of proverbs, as in, for instance, Proverbs 10:11: "The mouth of the righteous is the fountain of life, but violence overwhelms the mouth of the wicked."

The use of metaphors such as "the fountain of life" adds interest and memorability as well as emotional impact to a proverb. Most proverbs articulate fairly obvious points, and the poetic quality of the proverb adds greatly to its overall impression.

2.3.2. Time-Sensitive. Another characteristic of the proverb genre is that its validity is dependent on circumstance; the proverb does not necessarily express a timeless truth. Proverbs are right only if they are stated to the right person at the right time.

This helps explain the presence of contradictory proverbs. In English, both "Too many cooks spoil the broth" and "Many hands make light work" are true if applied to the correct situation. So too in Proverbs there are clearly contradictory verses, most famously Proverbs 26:4-5: "Don't answer fools according to their stupidity; otherwise you will become like them yourself. Answer fools according to their stupidity; otherwise they will become wise in their own eyes." It takes a sage who is able to read people and situations to know which of these two is rightly applied.

A number of proverbs reflect this time-sensitive quality. For example, "It is a joy to a person to give an answer! How good a word at the right time!" (Prov 15:23). Apparently, giving a cheerful greeting is unwise if done at the wrong time of day: "Those who bless their neighbors with a loud voice in the early morning—it will be considered a curse to them" (Prov 27:15).

According to *Qohelet, in the book of *Ecclesiastes, there is a right time for everything: "For everything there is a season, and a time for every activity under heaven: a time to be born and a time to die; a time to plant and a time to uproot what has been planted; a time to kill and a time to heal; a time to tear down and a time to build" (Eccles 3:1-3). What frustrates Qohelet is that though God knows these times and human beings do not, not knowing ruins the whole wisdom enterprise. After all, if one applies a proverb at the wrong time, it is useless: "The legs of a lame person hang limp, and so does a proverb in the mouth of fools" (Prov 26:7). It can even be dangerous: "Like a thorn bush in the hand of a drunk, so is a proverb in the mouth of fools" (Prov 26:9).

Returning to the proverbial observation in Proverbs 10:1, we should ask, Is it always true, and if not, under what conditions is it true? Clearly, it is not always wise to bring joy to parents. Some parents are abusive and derive joy from harming their sons and daughters. The proverb presupposes wise parents, those whose happiness would derive from their child moving in a godly direction.

The point is clear: the conditions for the truth of a proverb must be explored before or as it is being applied. Although all this is true and important in the proper understanding of proverbs, we must admit that certain proverbs are always true. For instance, Proverbs 11:1 states, "Fraudulent scales are an abomination of Yahweh, but an accurate weight brings his favor." If there are exceptions to this proverb, they are so rare as to be unimportant.

2.3.3. Rewards and Punishments. Proverbs often describe a wise, righteous, godly action and contrast it with a foolish, wicked, ungodly one. Sometimes a proverb will focus on one or the other. Some of these proverbs associate such behaviors with consequences. This is true not just of the proverb form per se; consequences are connected to wisdom and *folly in the discourses as well.

For instance, notice the reward that Woman Wisdom offers those who become intimate with her: "With me are riches and honor, enduring wealth and prosperity. My fruit is better than fine gold; what I yield surpasses choice silver" (Prov 8:18-19). On the other hand, the ultimate result of following Woman Folly is death (Prov 9:18).

Two issues need to be addressed regarding the teaching concerning *retribution in Proverbs. The first concerns the agency of the punishment, and the second is whether or not the teachings on reward and punishment are promises.

2.3.3.1. The Agent of Reward and Punishment. In regard to the first question, while in Proverbs good things happen to good people and bad things happen to bad people, rarely is the agent of the blessing and punishment named. Sometimes the connection between act and consequence is simply stated, with no mention of how it will happen. In the case of a text such as Proverbs 21:7 ("The violence of the wicked will sweep them away, for they refuse to act with justice"), it seems as if the evil acts themselves will rebound onto the evildoer. They reap the consequences of their reward. In Proverbs 18:6 ("The lips of fools lead to accusation; his mouth invites blows") the very words of fools will result in their pain. Interestingly, a text such as Proverbs 24:16 ("For the righteous may fall seven times but get up, but the wicked will stumble in evil") reveals that the sages understood that bad things will happen to good people—after all, the righteous are said to stumble and more than once. However, the righteous, as opposed to the evil, will get up again. In other words, the bad things that happen to good people are simply temporary setbacks. They are, after all, on a road that ends in life. K. Koch famously described this as "the act-consequence relationship"—that is, an act that leads inexorably to a certain consequence. L. Bostrom and others have qualified this to "the character-consequence relationship," noting that acts arise out of character and are more like a symptom than the reason for the consequence.

On the other hand, Proverbs 16:5, "All the haughty are an abomination to Yahweh; they surely will not go unpunished," although it does not make a direct connection, certainly leaves the impression that Yahweh has something to do with the punishment. After all, it is the fact that the act is an abomination to Yahweh that leads to the punishment. Finally, there are texts that do make a connection between Yahweh and reward and punishment: "For the one whom Yahweh loves he will correct, even the father who treats a son favorably" (Prov 3:12); "The curse of Yahweh is in the house of the wicked, but he blesses the home of the righteous" (Prov 3:33); "Yahweh will not let the righteous starve, but he will push away the desire of the wicked" (Prov 10:3).

So, in conclusion, some texts lead us to think that the acts of the wicked will come back to haunt them, and other texts imply or directly connect Yahweh to the rewards and punishments that come on people. However, the two are really not different. The former may imply that Yahweh will see that people get what they deserve. Perhaps the best way to think of it is that Yahweh built the world in a way that punishments are inherent to bad actions and rewards to good actions. Yahweh is ultimately behind all consequences. As Bostrom (139) puts it, "Our investigation . . . has led us to the conclusion that the world view of the sages was neither built upon a concept of an impersonal order nor of actions with 'automatic,' built-in consequences, but on the active participation of the Lord in the affairs of men in conjunction with man's own responsibility" (see also Waltke 2004, 73-76).

2.3.3.2. Are Proverbs Promises? This raises the question of whether proverbs present the rewards and punishments of wise and foolish behavior as promises or guarantees, and if not, then what are the proverbs? Two a priori considerations might give one pause. The first has to do with common experience. The theme of undeserved affliction is taken up even in popular writing in our own culture (e.g., Rabbi Harold Kushner's *When Bad Things Happen to Good People*), and the Bible, in narrative texts such as the Joseph story, shows that such misfortune does indeed occur. Joseph, when approached by Potiphar's wife, behaves in accordance with the extensive teaching on resisting the advances of a seductress (compare Prov 5—7 with Gen 39). However, rather than incurring blessing, Joseph's upright behavior gets him thrown in jail.

A proverb does not give guarantees; rather, it indicates the best route to a desired end. That end will be achieved, all other things being equal. An illustration is provided by Proverbs 22:6, a proverb often cited by young parents as a promise: "Train up youth in his path, then when they age, they will not depart from it." The proverb has an ambiguity that often is overlooked. Whose path is it talking about? The translation given above shows its interpretive prejudice by taking "youth" as a plural and "his" as a singular. This indicates the translators' position that the path is God's rather than, as some take it, the path or "bent" of the child. This interpretive decision does not bear on the topic under discussion, so we will bracket it and go on.

If one treats this proverb as a promise, then it indicates that godly training assures a parent that the child will not depart from the path. As a dark consequence of this, however, if a child goes bad, this proverb can become a reason for guilt: the parent must have done something wrong. However, it is wrong to consider the proverb as advancing a promise. Instead, it is saying that if one trains up a child in a godly way, it is more likely that the child will end up godly than if there is no such training. However, all things might not be equal. It may be that the child comes under the influence of a bad peer group, and even though the parents have been diligent, the child has gone the wrong way. This latter situation is the cause of parental worry in the first discourse of the book (Prov 1:8-19).

Thus, it is wrong to treat proverbs as guaranteeing health, wealth and prosperity for wise behavior and failure and ultimately death for foolish behavior (Waltke 1996). Even so, the book lays out a strategy to optimize the joys of life and minimize the frustrations.

As a final comment on the subject of retribution in the book of Proverbs, we note R. C. van Leeuwen's observation that the book itself shows an implicit awareness that the wise do not always get material rewards, as is evidenced by the "better than" proverbs that pepper the book. Proverbs 19:1 is illustrative: "Better to be poor and walking in innocence than to have crooked lips and be a fool."

"Better than" proverbs show relative values. Riches are good, but innocence is better; therefore, if a choice must be made, the latter must be taken over the former. This statement demonstrates awareness that not all the innocent become wealthy. Returning to the example of Joseph resisting the advances of Potiphar's wife and going to jail, we would have to say that he chose wisely when he acted with integrity and gave up his freedom. As the story continues, we see that even though the short-term consequences of his actions were not good, the very fact that he was in jail was what ultimately brought him in contact with the chief cupbearer, who ultimately introduced him to Pharaoh, which meeting led to the survival of the Jacob's family.

3. Ancient Near Eastern Background.

Since the early twentieth century, any treatment of the book of Proverbs must take account of its ancient Near Eastern background. Here I present a summary from my perspective (for a more extensive treatment, *see* Proverbs 2: Ancient Near Eastern Background).

Even within the Bible itself there seems to be a great openness and appreciation of the wisdom of the surrounding nations. When Solomon's wisdom is praised, he is said to supersede the wisdom of the people of the east and of Egypt (1 Kings 4:29-30). For this to be a true compliment, some value must be ascribed to these foreign traditions. Such relative valuation would have been inconceivable in other areas of Israelite thought, such as prophecy.

3.1. Egyptian Instructions. Of all the surrounding nations, it is Egypt that has yielded the most evidence of wisdom literature similar to Proverbs. Indeed, it was the translation of one particular instruction text in the early twentieth century, Amenemope (see 3.1.1 below), that initiated the modern comparative study of the book of Proverbs.

The primary genre of Egyptian wisdom had the native term *sby3t* attached to it. This word is often translated as "instruction" or "teaching," though J. D. Ray suggests that "enlightenment" may be closer to its true meaning. These texts appear as early as the Old Kingdom (2715-2170 BC) and down to the demotic period (seventh century BC and after). Indeed, it was one of the most popular genres in Egyptian literature. These instructions come from the upper levels of Egyptian society and are composed in large part of advice about how to get along in that society and perhaps even move upward. As in Proverbs, a father instructs his son in these texts.

In some examples the father is the king. These compositions begin with a preamble (often similar to Prov 1:1-7) that introduces the speaker as well as the addressee. We will refer to one specific text and an important concept to shed light on this genre.

3.1.1. Amenemope. I have chosen Amenemope for special treatment because of the role that it has played in the interpretation of Proverbs. The main papyrus (now in the British Museum and dated between the tenth and sixth centuries BC) was first discovered in 1888 but not translated until 1923, at which time its relevance for the study of Proverbs was immediately recognized.

The text contains the instructions of Amenemope, identified as the "Overseer of Grains," to his son, Hor-em-maa-Kheru. Similar to other instructions, the text has a preamble that gives not only lengthy descriptions of the speaker and a shorter one of his son but also a statement of purpose that includes "the teaching of life, the testimony for prosperity, all precepts for intercourse with elders, the rules for courtiers, to know how to return an answer to him who said it, and to direct a report to one who has sent him . . . to rescue him from the mouth of the rabble, revered in the mouth of the people" (translations from Amenemope are those of J. A. Wilson in *ANET,* 421-25). Unique to Amenemope among the Egyptian Instructions and relevant to the interpretation of Proverbs, as we will see, is the division of the following text into thirty chapters. The content of the advice contrasts the "heated man" over against the "silent man," reminiscent of the contrast of the foolish person and the wise.

Scholars have noted specific correspondence between select passages from Amenemope and Proverbs as follows:

> Do not rob the poor because they are poor,
> or crush the afflicted in the gate. (Prov 22:22)

> Guard yourself from robbing the poor
> From being violent to the weak.
>   (Amenemope iv, 4-5)

> Do you see those who are skillful in their
>   work?
> They will serve kings;
> they will not serve common people.
>   (Prov 22:29)

> As for the scribe who is experienced in
>   his office
> He will find himself worthy to be a courtier.
>   (Amenemope xxii, 16-17)

> Do not wear yourself out to get rich;
> be wise enough to desist.
> When your eyes light upon it, it is gone;
> for suddenly it takes wings to itself,
> flying like an eagle toward heaven.
>   (Prov 23:4-5)

> Do not strain to seek excess
> When your possessions are secure
> If riches are brought to you by robbery
> They will not stay the night in your
>   possession.
> When the day dawns they are no longer
>   in your house.
> Their place can be seen but they are
>   no longer there.
> The earth opened its mouth to crush
>   and swallow them
> And plunged them in Dust.
> They make themselves a great hole, as
>   large as they are.
> And sink themselves in the underworld.
> They make themselves wings like geese,
> And fly to heaven. (Amenemope ix, 14-x, 5)

> Do not remove an ancient landmark
> or encroach on the fields of an orphan,
> for their redeemer is strong;
> he will plead their cause against you.
>   (Prov 23:10-11)

> Do not remove the boundary stone on
>   the boundaries of the cultivated land.
> Nor throw down the boundary of the widow.
>   (Amenemope vii, 12)

Note that these parallels are particularly intense in the section that is identified as "the words of the wise," leading to speculation that there is a particularly close relationship in this section with ancient Near Eastern material, and maybe even a special influence from Amenemope. For this reason, the preamble (Prov 22:17-21) to this section is typically emended (slightly) to refer to the "thirty" sayings of the wise, paralleling the thirty chapters of Amenemope.

But this raises the difficult question of influence. Which came first, the Hebrew or the Egyptian, or was the influence more indirect than that? Advocates are found on the side of Egyptian priority (Emerton), Israelite priority or a third, common source. A recent viewpoint argues that although there are similarities between Amenemope and Proverbs, the parallels are not unique to those two texts (Ruffle; Kitchen). In other words, the more we learn about Egyptian instruction, the more parallels we observe with a number of different Egyptian instructions. Not only that, but also we see similarities of both with other cultures' wisdom, most notably the Aramaic Ahiqar (see 3.3 below). Perhaps the best conclusion is that there is not a specific relationship between Proverbs and Amenemope, but rather that both texts are part of an international tradition of wisdom that shares many similarities. In the light of the similarities, the differences, particularly the role of Yahweh in the wisdom of Proverbs, stands out even more.

3.1.2. Maat. The concept of **maat* is frequently expressed in Egyptian Instructions. *Maat* refers to the order and harmony of creation; its associated ideas are truth and justice. A rupture in the harmony, truth and justice of the creation is an assault against *maat*. Although *maat* often is presented as an impersonal concept, it is also represented on occasion as a goddess. *Maat* determines what is right and wrong. The Instruction genre informs a person how to live in conformity with *maat*. In line 64 of Merikare (and Instruction from Middle Kingdom) we find this admonishment of the addressee: "Do justice [*maat*] whilst thou endurest upon earth" (*ANET,* 415).

The idea of *maat* as the order of creation is similar in concept to wisdom's role in creation (Prov 3:19-20; 8:22-31). To live well in this world, it is important for a person to be wise and live in conformity with wisdom. Indeed, some scholars have detected *maat* behind the figure of Woman Wisdom.

3.2. Sumerian Wisdom. Sumerian proverb collections are extremely old, very likely going back to the Early Dynastic III period (2600-2550 BC). They continued in use for a very long period of time. Indeed, most of the tablets come from the Old Babylonian period in the early second millennium. Although there is not the same specific connection between Proverbs and comparable Sumerian texts, they do share many similar themes, as we can see from the following summary provided by B. Alster (1.xviii): "a woman's daily routine, family relationships, the good man, the liar, legal proceedings, Fate, the palace, the temple and their gods, as well as historical and ethnic allusions." Besides the early proverb collections there is also a Sumerian text known as the Instructions of Shuruppak, which has the same father-son dynamic found in Proverbs 1—9 and the Egyptian Instruction texts.

3.3. Aramaic Wisdom. The Ahiqar text has some striking similarities with Proverbs. The story was first known through the apocryphal book of Tobit as well as in Syriac, Armenian, Arabic and other languages (Lindenberger). However, in the early twentieth century an Aramaic version was discovered in Egypt that dates to the fifth century BC but may well reflect a composition that was written soon after the setting a hundred years earlier. The story is set in the sixth century BC during the reigns of the Assyrian kings Sennacherib and his son Esarhaddon. However, there is no independent evidence of the existence of a historical Ahiqar from this time period.

The first part of the text tells the story of Ahiqar, a wise man in the Assyrian court. He is raising his nephew Nadin to succeed him, but the latter betrays him by casting the suspicion of the king on him. The latter decrees his death and dispatches one of his generals to execute him. Fortunately for Ahiqar, he had saved this general's life earlier, so the general returns the favor by faking the wise man's execution.

Later the Egyptians approach Esarhaddon to ask for an adviser to help with a building project, and the king bemoans the fact that the brilliant Ahiqar is not available. The general uses this as an occasion to bring Ahiqar back to public attention. The king greets him warmly and then Ahiqar beats Nadin for his traitorous activities. He then launches into a lengthy instruction setting. Teachings similar to those found in Proverbs can be seen in two examples: "The son who is instructed and restrained, and on whose foot the bar is placed [will prosper in life]" (Saying 2); "Spare not your son from the rod; otherwise can you save him [from wickedness]?" (Saying 3). Compare this teaching with Proverbs 23:13-14.

4. Structure.

The structure of the book of Proverbs may first

be outlined according to its extensive authorship rubrics (see 1.1 above):

1:1	Superscription
1:2-7	Preamble (stating the purpose)
1:8—9:18	Extended Discourses on Wisdom
10:1—22:16; 25:1—29:27	Solomonic Proverbs
22:17—24:34	Sayings of the Wise
30	Sayings of Agur
31:1-9	Sayings of Lemuel
31:10-31	Poem to the Virtuous Woman

However, it is also possible to outline the book in another way. Indeed, as we will see in §5 below, the most important observation to make on the structure is the difference between Proverbs 1—9 and Proverbs 10—31. The division here is one that follows a genre distinction between extended discourses and proverbs per se (see 2 above).

4.1. Structure of Proverbs 1—9. This section is composed of discourses or speeches of a father to a son or Woman Wisdom to young men in general, with occasional proverbs. Upon analysis, this section may be outlined as follows:

1:1-7	The Purpose of the Book
1:8-19	Avoid Evil Associations
1:20-33	Do Not Resist Woman Wisdom
2:1-22	The Benefits of the Way of Wisdom
3:1-12	Trust in Yahweh
3:13-20	Praising Yahweh
3:21-35	The Integrity of Wisdom
4:1-9	Embrace Wisdom!
4:10-19	Stay on the Right Path
4:20-27	Guard Your Heart
5:1-23	Avoid Promiscuous Women; Love Your Wife
6:1-19	Wisdom Admonitions: Loans, Laziness, Lying and Other Topics
6:20-35	The Danger of Adultery
7:1-27	Avoid Promiscuous Women: Part II
8:1-36	Wisdom's Autobiography
9:1-6, 13-18	The Ultimate Encounter: Wisdom or Folly
9:7-12	Miscellaneous Wisdom Sayings

4.2. Structure of Proverbs 10—31. Casual readers of Proverbs 10—31 come away with the impression that these chapters are relatively randomly organized. Although there is some clustering of proverbs with similar themes (e.g., the Yahweh proverbs of Prov 15:33—16:9 followed by kingship proverbs in Prov 16:10-15), there is no systematic ordering of proverbs by topic.

Recent work on Proverbs, however, has raised the issue of whether there might be order that hitherto has gone undetected. A number of scholars have made the argument that there is an intentional and subtle structure that permeates Proverbs 10—31. The most recent sustained argument for this position is that of K. M. Heim, who critiques and incorporates earlier insights. Heim (106) argues for a coherent organization of proverbs based on phonological, semantic, syntactic and thematic repetition. He believes that this organization has gone unrecognized because only one of these strategies has been the object of study. Armed with the preunderstanding that there is coherence, and with many ways of seeing it, it is not surprising that Heim concludes that proverbs fall into clusters like the twigs of a grape vine. Once he delineates the units, he then interprets individual proverbs within the cluster. This last point is the interpretive payoff of his ideas, and unfortunately, if he is wrong, it means that he is imposing meaning on these proverbs.

The problem with Heim's approach is that the criteria of association that he allows are so broad and varied that one is bound to see connections, but more than one possible set of connections could be seen. Creative minds can create subtle associations between proverbs and then also "recognize" subtle associations between proverbs in a cluster. The human mind, after all, can associate the most disparate facts.

Instead, the best conclusion is that proverbs are indeed arranged in more or less random fashion, especially in regard to their subject matter. Von Rad (6) is correct: "Basically each sentence, each didactic poem, stands on its own." For example, proverbs on anger are not gathered together but rather are scattered throughout the book (Prov 6:19; 16:14; 19:11, 12, 19; 21:19; 25:23; 27:3-4; 29:8, 22). An explanation for such randomness may be found in the history of composition. Since, as Snell has pointed out, there are many near and completely identical proverbs in the book, it seems logical to think that individual proverbs were added over time, individually and/or in groups. It might also be pointed out that randomness is a characteristic of ancient Near Eastern wisdom collections. In Egyptian tradition, for instance, there is very clear arrangement along thematic lines only with the Papyrus Insinger, the copy that we have dating to the first century AD, though its composition may go back to Ptolomaic times (fourth to first century BC), still very late in comparison to biblical proverbs.

5. Theological Message.

5.1. Old Testament Context.
It is a common misconception that the book of Proverbs is secular or downplays theological themes. O. Eissfeldt (47) says, "The basis for the commendation of wisdom and piety is on the one hand purely secular and rational." Although there is no denying that Yahweh is sometimes explicitly mentioned in the book, some scholars (Whybray, 72; McKane, 1-22) have gone so far as to say that when Yahweh's name is found in the text, it is an indication of a late redaction of an earlier consistently secular book.

It is true that Proverbs is different from other books of the Bible in regard to theology. The book lacks connection to redemptive history or expansive references to important ideas such as the covenant (*see* Wisdom and Biblical Theology). Elements of *worship, such as sacrifice, prayer and temple, if mentioned at all, are not a central part of the teaching of the book. However, the final form of the book is deeply and pervasively theological. Indeed, the concept of wisdom is not simply a practical skill but is a theological idea (*see* Wisdom Theology). This perspective may be argued from the book in two main ways.

5.1.1. Fear of the Lord.
Throughout the book (at least 21x) wisdom/knowledge is characterized as *"fear of the Lord," perhaps nowhere more famously than as the conclusion to the preamble that introduces the book: "Fear of the LORD [Yahweh] is the beginning of knowledge; fools despise wisdom and discipline" (Prov 1:7).

This defines wisdom, and conversely folly, in a theological manner. Indeed, it characterizes wisdom as a relationship. To be wise, one must fear God. The idea of fear is probably not best understood as terror, on the one hand, or mere respect, on the other; rather, to fear God means to acknowledge one's subordinate and dependent place in the universe. It is more like knee-knocking awe.

5.1.2. Woman Wisdom.
It is more than the teaching on the fear of Yahweh that leads to this conclusion. It also has to do with the role of Woman Wisdom in the book. Woman Wisdom is found only in Proverbs 1—9, but on the background of foregoing discussions of the structure of the book, we will see that the individual proverbs found in Proverbs 10—31 should be read only against the background of the hermeneutical lens provided by Proverbs 1—9. But first, who is Woman Wisdom?

Proverbs 1—9 has two types of discourse: (1) a father instructs his son; (2) Woman Wisdom speaks to all the young men who go by. The implicit reader of the book is a young male. This man is often described as walking on a path. The "path" is an extensively used metaphor throughout the first part of Proverbs, culminating in Proverbs 9. Everyone is walking on a path, or, perhaps better said, on one of two types of path: a straight path or a crooked path. The path refers to one's life. In the book there are two types of path, two types of *life. One is "crooked" (Prov 2:15) and "dark" (Prov 2:13). Danger lurks on this path (Prov 1:10-15; 2:12-15). These dangers include traps and snares that can foul up one's walk on the proper path of life. The dark path represents one's behavior in this life, but it culminates not in life but in death. On the other hand, there is the right path, the path that leads to life. This path is straight and well lit. The person who stays on this path will not stumble.

Later readers, both during the OT period and after, are to imagine themselves as that young man walking the path and listening to the instruction of the father and the admonitions of Woman Wisdom. This is particularly true when we reach Proverbs 9, which is a climactic point in the book where the reader is called upon to make a decision before encountering the individual proverbs that follow in the second part of the book.

In Proverbs 9 the young man/reader is walking the path and hears a voice coming from a magnificent house "from the pinnacle of the heights of the city" (Prov 9:3). It is Woman Wisdom, who issues an invitation: "Whoever is simpleminded turn aside here.... Come, eat my food, and drink the wine I have mixed. Abandon simplemindedness and live. March on the path of understanding" (Prov 9:4-6). But there is another voice, also coming from a house "at the heights of the city," who is identified as Woman Folly. She too issues the young man/reader an invitation: "Whoever is simpleminded turn aside here.... Stolen water is sweet; food eaten in secret is pleasant" (Prov 9:16-17). The reader now must make a choice. With whom will he dine? But who are these women, and what is the significance of the choice?

The main key to interpreting the symbolic value of Woman Wisdom is the location of her house on the highest point of the city. In ancient Near Eastern cities the temple, representative of the presence of deity on earth, was the building on the highest point. Thus, it is clear that Woman Wisdom is a *personification of Yahweh's wisdom and ultimately of Yahweh himself. On the other hand though, Woman Folly's location is also on the heights of the city. This also indicates the divine status of this figure. Woman Folly represents the false gods and goddesses that seek to lure the Israelite away from the true God. Thus the choice between Woman Wisdom and Woman Folly is no less than a fundamental religious choice between the true God and false gods.

A possible objection to this interpretive approach may be raised. In Proverbs 8 Woman Wisdom is described in some detail, and part of the description involves her role in observing the creation of the world (*see* Creation Theology). She is also described as the firstborn of creation (Prov 8:22-31). How can she be God *and* the firstborn of creation? But for that matter, what would it mean in regard to God's attribute of wisdom to press the language in detail as a literal description? Like all poetic metaphors (and personification is a type of metaphor), the language is not meant to be understood in that way. Part of the art of interpretation is the uncertain process of coming to grips with how far the comparison may be taken. The major point of these verses seems to be that creation and wisdom are inextricably bound. Thus, if one wants to know how the world works and thus to successfully navigate life, one had better know

this woman, Yahweh's wisdom—that is, Yahweh himself.

However, whether Woman Wisdom stands for God or for God's wisdom, the choice remains a religious one and one that colors wisdom and folly with theological significance. Proverbs 10:1 provides an illustration: "A wise son makes a father glad, and a foolish son is the sorrow of his mother." Reading this proverb through the lens of the choice between Woman Wisdom and Woman Folly would lead to the conclusion that this is more than just a wise observation. More deeply, it says that a son who makes a parent glad is showing wisdom, which means that he is acting like someone who has aligned himself with Yahweh, the true God. On the other hand, a son who makes his parents sad is showing himself to be a fool and therefore is acting like one who worships idols. The point is that the very ideas of wisdom and folly are religious concepts. Though the terms "wisdom" and "folly" are not used in every verse in the second part, every verse does use associated vocabulary or simply positive or negative language to indicate whether a behavior is wise or foolish. Thus, the whole book is theological to its core.

5.2. New Testament Perspective. The NT reveals an interesting association between Woman Wisdom and Jesus Christ. But first we note the pervasive NT teaching that Jesus was characterized by divine wisdom. In the Lukan narratives concerning Jesus' infancy and youth we see a strong emphasis on Jesus' wisdom. The narrator makes a point of noting the young Jesus' growth in wisdom (Lk 2:40, 52). Furthermore, when Jesus is old enough to go to the temple, he amazes the teachers of the law and other witnesses of his astonishing wisdom (Lk 2:41-51). When Jesus began his teaching ministry, all the people who heard him were astounded by his profound wisdom (Mk 1:21-22; 6:2). He even utilized the parable (Heb *māšāl*) as his main teaching vehicle. He was the sage par excellence.

Whereas the Gospels demonstrate that Jesus was wise—indeed, wiser than Solomon—Paul asserts that Jesus is not simply wise, but that he is the very incarnation of God's wisdom. Twice Paul identifies with God's wisdom. In 1 Corinthians 1:30 Paul says, "God made Christ to be wisdom itself," and in Colossians 2:3 he proclaims that in Christ "lie hidden all the treasures of wisdom and knowledge." Given this background, it is not surprising that the NT subtly associates Jesus with Woman Wisdom, particularly as presented in Proverbs 8.

But there is more than a general association between Jesus and wisdom. He is also associated with the figure of Woman Wisdom. We can see this in his response to his opponents in Matthew 11:19, where he defends himself against their attacks by saying, "Wisdom is proved right by her actions" (TNIV).

Elsewhere in the NT Jesus is described in language that is reminiscent of Proverbs 8. We look first at Colossians 1:15-17: "Christ is the visible image of the invisible God. He existed before anything was created and is supreme over all creation, for through him God created everything in the heavenly realms and on earth. He made the things we can see and the things we can't see—such as thrones, kingdoms, rulers, and authorities in the unseen world. Everything was created through him and for him. He existed before anything else, and he holds all creation together" (NLT).

Though clearly not a quotation from Proverbs, this text would be recognized by someone well versed in the OT, as Paul was, as saying that Jesus occupies the place of Wisdom. Indeed, the literal rendition of the Greek of the sentence that ends "is supreme over all creation" is "He is the firstborn of all creation." Paul is inviting a comparison: Wisdom was firstborn in Proverbs 8; Jesus is firstborn in Colossians. Wisdom is the agent of divine creation in Proverbs; Christ is the agent in Colossians. In Proverbs 8 we read, "By me kings reign, and nobles issue just decrees. By me rulers rule, and princes, all righteous judgments" (Prov 8:15-16). And in Colossians 1:16 Paul says that Christ made "kings, kingdoms, rulers, and authorities." The message is clear: Jesus is Wisdom herself.

The author of Revelation is a further witness to the connection between Wisdom and Jesus. In the introduction to the letter to the church at Laodicea we read, "This is the message from the one who is the Amen—the faithful and true witness, the ruler of God's new creation" (Rev 3:14). The last phrase (he archē tēs ktiseōs tou theou) resonates with the ideas behind Proverbs 8:22-30. In particular, the phrase may represent the meaning of that difficult word in Proverbs 8:30, the "architect" ('āmôn) of creation. The allusion is subtle but clear: Jesus stands in the

place of Woman Wisdom.

Even more subtly, we might note that the great preface to the Gospel of John echoes with language reminiscent of the poem about Woman Wisdom in Proverbs 8. The Word of God (the Logos), who is God himself, was "in the beginning ... with God. ... He created everything there is" (Jn 1:1-3); indeed, the "world was made through him" (Jn 1:10). Jesus, of course, is the Word, and the association is with language reminiscent of Woman Wisdom.

Seeing the connection between Jesus and Woman Wisdom has important implications for how Christians read the book of Proverbs. We have already noted that the ancient Israelite reader would read the metaphors of Woman Wisdom and Woman Folly as a choice between Yahweh and the false gods of the nations. This decision would have little relevance to modern readers, who are not trying to make a choice between God and Baal; the latter is not a live option, and the NT claims to reveal the nature of the Godhead more carefully. That is, the NT presents Jesus as the mediator of our relationship with God. The gospel choice is a decision whether or not to follow Jesus. Thus, to understand the invitation of Woman Wisdom as the invitation of Christ to relationship with God makes the book contemporary to Christian readers.

As for Woman Folly, she may be taken as anything or anyone who seeks to divert our primary attention away from our relationship with Jesus. Idols today typically are subtler than in ancient times. Rather than being lured by deities and their images, we are captivated by more abstract and conceptual idols: power, wealth, relationship, status, and the like.

See also DISCOURSE IN PROVERBS; FEMINIST INTERPRETATION; FORM CRITICISM; PROVERB, GENRE OF; PROVERBS 2: ANCIENT NEAR EASTERN BACKGROUND; PROVERBS 3: HISTORY OF INTERPRETATION; WOMAN WISDOM AND WOMAN FOLLY.

BIBLIOGRAPHY. *Commentaries:* R. J. Clifford, *Proverbs* (OTL; Louisville: Westminster John Knox, 1999); M. V. Fox, *Proverbs 1-9* (AB 18A; Garden City, NY: Doubleday, 2000); T. Longman III, *Proverbs* (BCOTWP; Grand Rapids: Baker, 2006); W. McKane, *Proverbs* (OTL; Philadelphia: Westminster, 1970); R. E. Murphy, *Proverbs* (WBC; Nashville: Thomas Nelson, 1998); L. G. Perdue, *Proverbs* (Interp; Louisville: Westminster John Knox, 2000); **R. C. Van Leeuwen,** "Proverbs," in *The New Interpreter's Bible, Vol. 5* (Abingdon, 1997), 19-264; **B. Waltke,** *Proverbs: Chapters 1-15* (NICOT; Grand Rapids: Eerdmans: 2004); idem, *Proverbs: Chapters 15-31* (NICOT; Grand Rapids, Eerdmans, 2005). *Studies:* **B. Alster,** *Proverbs of Ancient Sumer* (2 vols.; Bethesda, MD: CDL Press, 1997); **L. Bostrom,** *The God of the Sages: The Portrayal of God in the Book of Proverbs* (ConBOT 29; Stockholm: Almqvist & Wiksell, 1990); **J. Cook,** *The Septuagint of Proverbs: Jewish and/or Hellenistic Proverbs? Concerning the Hellenistic Colouring of LXX Proverbs* (VTSup 69; Leiden: E. J. Brill, 1997); **O. Eissfeldt,** *The Old Testament: An Introduction, including the Apocrypha and Pseudepigrapha, and Also the Works of Similar Type from Qumran; The History of the Formation of the Old Testament* (New York: Harper & Row, 1965); **J. A. Emerton,** "The Teaching of Amenemope and Proverbs xxii 17-xxiv 22: Further Reflections on a Long-Standing Problem," *VT* 41 (2001) 431-52; **F. Golka,** "Die israelitische Weisheitsschule oder 'des Kaisers neue Kleider,'" *VT* 33 (1983) 257-71; **K. M. Heim,** *Grapes of Gold Set in Silver: An Interpretation of Proverbial Clusters in Proverbs 10:1—22:16* (BZAW 273; Berlin: de Gruyter, 2001); **K. Kitchen,** "Proverbs and Wisdom Books of the Ancient Near East," *TynBul* 28 (1977) 69-114; **K. Koch,** "Gibt es ein Vergeltungsdogma im Alten Testament?" *ZTK* 52 (1955) 1-42; **A. Lemaire,** "The Sage in School and Temple," in *The Sage in Israel and the Ancient Near East,* ed. J. G. Gammie and L. G. Perdue (Winona Lake, IN: Eisenbrauns, 1990) 165-83; **J. Lindenberger,** *The Aramaic Proverbs of Ahiqar* (Baltimore: Johns Hopkins University Press, 1983); **T. Longman III,** "Proverbs," in *Zondervan Illustrated Bible Backgrounds Commentary,* ed. J. Walton (4 vols.; Grand Rapids: Zondervan, forthcoming); **J. D. Ray,** "Egyptian Wisdom Literature," in *Wisdom in Ancient Israel,* ed. J. Day et al. (Cambridge: Cambridge University Press, 1995) 17-29; **J. Ruffle,** "The Teaching of Amenemope and Its Connection with the Book of Proverbs," *TynBul* 28 (1977) 39-68; **D. C. Snell,** *Twice-Told Proverbs and the Composition of the Book of Proverbs* (Winona Lake, IN: Eisenbrauns, 1993); **E. Tov,** "Recensional Differences between the Massoretic Text and the Septuagint of Proverbs," in *Of Scribes and Scrolls: Studies on the Hebrew Bible, Intertestamental Judaism, and Christian Origins Presented to J. Strugnell on the Occasion of His Sixtieth Birthday,* ed. H. W. Attridge, J. J. Collins and T. H. Tobin (CTSRR 5; Lanham, MD: University Press of America, 1990) 43-56; idem, *Textual Criticism of the Hebrew Bible* (Minneapolis: Fortress; Assen: Van Gorcum, 1992); **R. C. Van Leeuwen,** "Wealth and Poverty: System and Contradiction in Proverbs," *HS* 33 (1992) 25-36; **G. von Rad,** *Wisdom in Ancient Israel* (London: SCM, 1972); **B. K. Waltke,** "Does Proverbs Promise Too Much?" *AUSS* 34 (1996) 319-36; **C. Westermann,** *Wurzeln der Weisheit: Die altesten Spruche Israels und anderer Volker* (Gottingen: Vanderhoeck & Ruprecht, 1990); **R. N. Whybray,** *The Concept of Wisdom in Proverbs 1-9* (London: SCM, 1965); **B. Witherington III,** *Jesus the Sage: The Pilgrimage of Wisdom* (Minneapolis: Fortress, 1994).

T. Longman III

PROVERBS 2: ANCIENT NEAR EASTERN BACKGROUND

The existing biblical book of Proverbs is not just one book, but rather four: Proverbs of *Solomon son of *David (Prov 1—24 [hereafter "Solomon I"]), Proverbs of Solomon copied out by Hezekiah's men (Prov 25—29 [hereafter "Solomon II"]); Words of Agur (Prov 30); Words of Lemuel from his mother (Prov 31) (*see* Lemuel and Agur). The last three are shortest and simplest, each having an identifying authorial title followed directly by the main text (Type A). The first is the longest and more complex (Type B), having a similar title (with preamble, Prov 1:1-7) but followed by a long prologue (Prov 1:8—9:18) and a subtitle (Prov 10:1) to introduce the main text (Prov 10—24). Ending the latter are two segments, cited as "Words of the Wise" (Prov 22:17; 24:23a). Thus, broadly, Solomon I would date to c. 950 BC, Solomon II (in final form) to c. 700 BC (under Hezekiah), and Agur and Lemuel hardly much later.

The wisdom in Proverbs is specifically instructional wisdom, framed as from an instructor (e.g., a parent) to a junior (e.g., a son or sons). This is distinct from observational wisdom (as in the Sumerian proverb collections of the third to early second millennia BC [for which, see Alster 1991-1992; 1997]) and from wisdom by debate (third to first millennia BC), closer to *Job and *Ecclesiastes.

Traditionally, for the last 130 years or so, not a few OT scholars have regarded most (if not all) of Proverbs to be of postexilic origin, and Proverbs 1—9 as the latest segment of it. However, such views remain purely theoretical, without adequate reference to most of the real and relevant data now available from the biblical world itself—that is, the ancient Near East. Such data cast a very different light on the books of Proverbs.

1. Scope of Ancient Near Eastern Background
2. Near Eastern and Biblical Structures and Formats
3. Near Eastern Evidence on Concepts and Linguistic Indicators in Proverbs
4. The Subject Matter of Proverbs in Its Near Eastern Context
5. Concluding Perspective on Proverbs in Its Ancient Near Eastern Context

1. Scope of Ancient Near Eastern Background.

1.1. Geography and General Date of Near Eastern Instructional Wisdom Books. Most of such works are found in ancient Egypt through the third to first millennia BC, some twenty-seven in all, plus five "letter-writing" instructional books and the onomastica (word lists), all for training *scribes, taking us to at least thirty-three works overall. Some are known complete, some by mere allusion, and the rest in varying states of (incomplete) preservation. The next largest series is from Mesopotamia (Sumer, Assyria and Babylonia), again through the third to first millennia BC, with the oldest work (Shuruppak) in two Sumerian "editions" and one Akkadian [Assyro-Babylonian] version, four more damaged such works, plus three minor fragments (one, the beginning of one of the other works?)—a total of about nine works so far. Then, in the Syro-Anatolian realm are two items: part of a Babylonian/Hurrian bilingual text from Ugarit, and a Hittite translation of another Akkadian text likewise (both thirteenth century BC). Finally, outside the Bible, one West Semitic text, the Proverbs of Ahiqar (Aramean officer of Esarhaddon of Assyria) in Aramaic, in a fifth-century copy from Egypt. So, here are three more works. Thus, we have a grand total of about forty to forty-five items in six languages, plus the four books within our Hebrew book of Proverbs, for almost fifty items in seven languages altogether. Older bibliographical summaries are included in Kitchen 1977; 1979; these can be supplemented in part from more recent collected translations such as those by W. K. Simpson; Hallo and Younger.

1.2. Specific Distribution by Date and Type of Ancient Near Eastern Books. Direct examination shows that all of these instructional wisdom writings correspond in overall format to either Type A (like Solomon II; Agur and Lemuel) or Type B (like Solomon I), insofar as they are sufficiently preserved to determine.

1.2.1. Third Millennium BC. For Type A (title and main text only) we have (so far) the Instructions of Hardjedef (Old Kingdom, in New Kingdom copies) and the Instructions for Merikare (First Intermediate Period, in later copies). Given the individual styles and contents of both, they should be assigned to their attributed periods; they are wholly different from Middle Kingdom works. For Type B (title, prologue, subtitle [optional], main text) we possess the complete and splendid Ptahhotep from Egypt (proper to the Old Kingdom, including from later allusions) and the Old Sumerian version of Shuruppak from third-millennium contexts at Abu Salabikh and Adab in Mesopotamia. For translations of Egyptian texts, see, for example, Lichtheim, vol. 1; W. K. Simpson (sometimes partial only); for Shuruppak, see Alster 1974.

1.2.2. Early Second Millennium BC. Within c. 2000-1600 BC, Type A works are absent so far, but for Type B our sources increase. From Twelfth Dynasty Egypt (Middle Kingdom) we have a cluster of four works: one by Khety son of Duauf (exalting the scribal career over all others); two loyalist works, Sehetepibre (named from an excerptor [author's name not yet recovered]) and A Man for His Son (deliberately anonymous, for general usage); and one of royal origin, ostensibly by Amenemhat I on his dynasty's behalf (for translations, see Lichtheim, vol. 1; W. K. Simpson [at times incomplete]). From Mesopotamia, so far, we have only the Classical Sumerian and Akkadian versions of Shuruppak (Alster 1974 [Sumerian]; Lambert [Akkadian]).

1.2.3. Late Second Millennium BC. Here, with ever increasing source materials, Type A comes back into view. From Egypt come the Instruction from Ancient Writings (anonymous, because it purports to collect just older sayings) and the brief Instruction by Hori (early Twentieth Dynasty), plus the clutch of "letter-writing" instructions (of Qagabu; for Pentaweret; of Nebmarenakht; of Piay [in Caminos]; "Setekhmose" is only [so far] a title line). These belong to the Nineteenth-Twentieth Dynasties. To the latter (by origin) belongs also the Onomasticon of Amenemope (Gardiner). Of this class (Type A), Mesopotamia and the Hittites offer (so far) only an Akkadian original and a Hittite version of Shube-awilim.

Type B flourished as ever. From Egypt in this group come the works by the vizier Amatju (Ahmose), the high priest Amenemhat (Eighteenth Dynasty) and the scribes Aniy (Nineteenth Dynasty?), Amennakht and the famous Amenemope, of the early Twentieth Dynasty (c. 1170 BC) (the last three are in Lichtheim, vol. 2; W. K. Simpson). From Mesopotamia we have currently just the Counsels of Wisdom (Lambert).

1.2.4. First Millennium BC. Here, in Egypt a Theban priest Nebneteru (c. 860 BC) presents a short set of admonitions but without any formal title within another text. Definitely of Type A are the demotic-language instructions of Papyrus Louvre D.2414 (Ptolemaic [third-first centuries BC]), but the beginning of the Insinger texts (Ptolemaic period, first century BC? [Lichtheim, vol. 3]) is lost. In Greek is the beginning of Amenothes (Greco-Roman period). From Mesopotamia the Akkadian Advice to a Prince falls probably within c. 1000-700 BC (Lambert, 110-15). From the Levant we have the three final compositions from the Hebrew book of Proverbs: Solomon II, Agur and Lemuel (c. 700 BC).

For Type B we have the Saite Instruction from within c. 570-400 BC (full publication in Jasnow) and Ankh-Sheshonqy (Lichtheim, vol. 3; W. K. Simpson) from the late Ptolemaic period (within the third to first centuries BC?) from Egypt. From Mesopotamia, but based on a West Semitic character, we have an instruction of the Aramean Ahiqar, official of Esarhaddon of Assyria (c. 670 BC) in a fifth-century Aramaic copy (Porten and Yardeni, 22-53). All three of these have narrative prologues. To this epoch (c. 950 BC) would belong, by its title, Solomon I, being the first twenty-four chapters of the Hebrew book of Proverbs. (For the data bearing on this, see 2 below.)

2. Near Eastern and Biblical Structures and Formats.

2.1. Review of the Structural Features of the Books Within Proverbs in Near Eastern Context. Thus, the four constituent books in Proverbs are in literary terms part of a long-lived and extensive family of some fifty compositions through most of three thousand years. This corpus offers us very clear guidance over the constants and changing norms to be found in this category of literature and thereby on the format, dating and so forth of the Hebrew works. This can best be

seen by examining each main feature in turn. This was previously done on a strictly factual basis in three papers by K. A. Kitchen (1977; 1979; 1998), which remain fundamental; complementary to these is the 1977 work by J. Ruffle.

2.1.1. Form and Use of Titles and Subtitles. Use of an initial formal title is practically universal in this class of writings; only when (very rarely) the body of instruction is incorporated into another text does this not happen, as in the case of Nebneteru (see 1.2.4 above). Again, almost all these formal titles name an author or compiler, always in the third person, usually with a title or epithet(s); exceptions are rare—for example, the Man for His Son (an "everyman" text) and According to Ancient Writings (collection of old sayings) from Egypt. In Egypt a noun-based formulation was used: "(Beginning of) the Instruction by ... (NN)." This usage is followed by Levantine writers—so by Ahiqar ("[These are the W]ords of Ahiqar...") outside the OT, and by Solomon I/II ("The Proverbs of Solomon...") and by Agur and Lemuel ("the Words of Agur/ Lemuel...") inside it. By contrast, Mesopotamian writers preferred a verbal construction, be it narrative ("NN gave instruction...") or imperative ("Hear the counsel of NN..."). In all cultures further features could be added at will. Commonly, an author might address his son (sometimes named) or sons, or else an apprentice or other younger person. Title lines could be extended by inclusion of numerous personal titles and epithets of the author, or by claims for the work's aims or value (cf. Ptahhotep, subtitle), or by other literary embellishments (so the Classical Sumerian version of Shuruppak, initial time clauses). The title and preamble in Solomon I (Prov 1:1-7) is longer than the title lines in Solomon II (Prov 25:1), and both are longer than with Agur and Lemuel. In turn, going back in time, the subtitle in Ptahhotep and the initial titles of Amenemope and of the Onomasticon of the other Amenemope are all longer than that of Solomon I. Long, medium and short titles occur at all periods; in short, there is no total "evolution" from short to medium to long in the case of main titles or subtitles to these instructional works—quite the opposite! The more complex title/preamble of Solomon I is strictly in keeping with its greater complexity and length as compared with Solomon II, Agur and Lemuel, just as is the case with other Near Eastern works of varying length and complexity, regardless of date.

Subtitles and interjected cross-headings deserve notice. Thus, Khety son of Duauf divides his main text into two, with a commendation of the scribal career worth the toil of schooling (e.g., Lichtheim, 1.189-90; W. K. Simpson, 435 §22). In Solomon I a minimally simple subtitle divides between the prologue and main text (Prov 10:1), and at Proverbs 22:17; 24:23 we have, respectively, an interjection and another brief subtitle. Long before all these, alongside the Egyptian Ptahhotep with his complex subtitle between prologue and main text, the Old Sumerian versions of Shuruppak (third millennium BC) use a remarkable alternating twin series of standard longer and shorter subtitles (longer ones each having a subprologue). Then, in the early second millennium, the Classical Sumerian version has only two numbered, standard subtitles, and then the fragmentary Akkadian one shows no trace of any at all. In other words, subtitles begin complex and then shrink in size and importance during the third, second and early first millennia BC. Only Ankh-Sheshonqy (third-first centuries BC) has a long one between the prologue and main parts of his text (Lichtheim, 3.164, at 5:14-19; Jastrow in W. K. Simpson, 504, at 4/x+15ff.), an archaic throwback stylistically to the ancient usage of Ptahhotep.

The use of numerical headings to mark off sets of numbered teachings begins (at present) with Amenemope (c. 1170 BC) and is found almost a millennium thereafter more elaborately in the Insinger demotic wisdom book (see Lichtheim, 3.184-217). The repeated attempts to foist a reference to unnumbered "thirty (sayings)" upon Solomon I (Prov 22:20) are unjustified (see 3.2.3 below).

2.1.2. Formats and Nature of Prologues. The presence or absence of a prologue is the marker between the two types of instructional wisdom text. Inspection of the entire corpus reveals the following clear facts. (1) Before c. 1000 BC all the known prologues (bar one) are exhortatory. The prologue of Solomon I (Prov 1—9) falls into this category. All these call upon the reader to heed the admonitions given and extol their aims. The sole exception is Ptahhotep, who uses his prologue to state his old age and failing health to the king to ask him to appoint his son to his office in his stead, which the king grants; so this borders on narrative instead. (2) During the first millennium BC (sometime after c. 1000 BC) the known prologues are narrative. They tell of events and do not exhort. This is seen in the Saite Wisdom, Ahiqar and Ankh-Sheshonqy. (3) Before c. 1000 BC the exhortatory prologues are all short to medium in length; the oldest exhortatory prologues are short, while both short- and medium-length examples are found in the second millennium. The post-1000 BC narrative prologues, however, are usually long, as befits a story-narrative. So somewhere around the second-first millennium change, prologues change their content (exhortation to narrative) and become regularly much longer. The attempt to dismiss prologues as merely anything that precedes the main text, without specific or datable usage (Weeks 1994, 6, 13), is thus wholly mistaken on visible and self-existent evidence from an entire corpus (see Kitchen 1998, esp. 351-53, 359-63 [giving translations of most of the existing prologues]). (4) In our external corpus, in every case, the prologue is always an integral part of the original text; it is not, and contextually cannot be, something added in ages afterward.

This fourfold situation puts Solomon I in a very interesting position. He is exhortatory (both in person and through Wisdom personified) and so belongs firmly to the traditions of the third to second millennia, pre-1000 BC. Yet he goes on at some length (Prov 1—9), as the later and narrative books do. In other words, Solomon I is at a literary hinge, a point of transition from the second to first millennia BC, which, at his traditional date line (c. 950 BC), can only be described as precisely right and, for independent factual reasons, not simply tradition. Furthermore, Proverbs 1—9 has to be part of the original text of Proverbs 1—24, exactly as with all other instructional books here; it cannot have been added on in front of Proverbs 10—24 at some very late date. Nor are these four lines of data the only evidence to indicate such a result (see 2.1.3 below).

2.1.3. The Nature and Authenticity of Ascribed "Authorships." Over the last century and more, the attribution of the authorship of the various segments of Proverbs to Solomon, Agur and Lemuel (and the role of Hezekiah's copyists) has frequently been dismissed, and likewise attempts have been made to discredit the named authorships of Egyptian and other texts to serve the same aim. Two points require attention: (1) What does "authorship" of an instructional wisdom text actually imply? (2) How far (and why) should the ascribed "authorships" (whatever their nature) be granted credence, if at all?

First, there is the nature of such "authorship." That a text claims to be by Solomon or Amenemope does not imply that they should be considered to have personally first invented every admonition, phrase or concept now found in the books ascribed to them. This is already clear in Solomon I, where, in Proverbs 22:17, he publicly equates what he now writes ("what I teach") with "Words of the Wise," clearly from others who have preceded him. And again explicitly in the subtitle at Proverbs 24:23, he declares, "These also are Words of the Wise." We are not told who these earlier *sages were, nor does it intrinsically matter; and often, older wisdom had passed from its first formulators through many other minds and lips to lose its original identity. For us today, "A stitch in time saves nine" has now no known author, but the truth of its embedded principle is universally evident. This is also the case in antiquity. This is true not only for Proverbs but also, and demonstrably so, in the other Near Eastern instructional books. Thus, sayings of Hardjedef (Fourth Dynasty) reappeared later in Ptahhotep (Fifth Dynasty), in a Koptos decree (:G) of Pepi II (Sixth Dynasty), and then in Merikare (Tenth Dynasty), while Ptahhotep's work probably was cited by Merikare and then more definitely in a loyalist instruction early in the Twelfth Dynasty and under Sesostris III of the later Twelfth Dynasty (for references, see Kitchen 1998, 349 nn. 7-9). The later citations are not marked out by named author any more than in Proverbs. They also constitute serious evidence for the genuinely Old Kingdom date of composition for the works of Hardjedef and Ptahhotep. Thus, it is perfectly possible for Solomon (or anyone else) to have searched out older sources of wisdom, mulled over them, and used them directly or duly modified in his own work. Hardjedef is modified by his excerptors, for example. So Amenemope might have been among the Wise used or modified by Solomon (or whoever), but there is no explicit proof (on this, see 4.1-2 below).

Second, there is the authenticity of these ascribed authors/compilers. In several cases there can be no doubt about the reality of the "authorships" mentioned. Thus, in his tomb chapel in Western Thebes, under Amenophis II (c. 1420

BC), the high priest of Amun, Amenemhat, caused to be inscribed in stone a "monumental" copy of his own instruction for his children and for posterity; he uses his own career as a shining example for his offspring to follow (Cumming, 114-15, no. 425). Regrettably, this text is now lost after the opening section, but of its authorial origin there can be no doubt. Already, over half a century earlier (under Hatshepsut or Tuthmosis III [early fifteenth century BC]), the Instruction by the vizier Amatju/Ahmose for his son and vizierial successor User was deliberately inscribed by User in his West Theban tomb (Tomb no. 131) in honor of succeeding his father as vizier. At Deir el-Medina (the workmen's village for the Valley of the Kings) the authors Amennakht and Hori of the late Nineteenth/early Twentieth Dynasties (c. 1200 BC or soon after) actually seem to have dedicated their respective works not to their own sons (as normal) but rather to each other's sons as a compliment (Bickel and Mathieu)—no doubt of their reality either. Again, Aniy was a middle-rank scribe of the West Theban temple of either Queen Ahmose-Nefertari (mother of Amenophis I, but cult flourishing throughout the New Kingdom [c. 1520-1070 BC]) or Queen Nefertari wife of Ramesses II (hence, c. 1280/1260 BC); his reality we have no reason to doubt.

Likewise, the "famous" Amenemope, whose work is so often compared to Proverbs; he was a temple administration official in Akhmim with a tomb at neighboring Abydos, a wholly realistic situation. In earlier times, as in the Twelfth Dynasty, Khety son of Duauf (or "Dua-Khety") was evidently an East Delta official and in New Kingdom tradition had been a "ghost writer" serving King Amenemhat I (whose resultant Instruction we possess); neither king nor amanuensis can be dismissed, the king's reign being monumentally well attested. Merikare is a monumentally attested king of the Ninth/Tenth Dynasty, and the wisdom text laid down for him reflects well the conditions at that dynasty's end before the Eleventh Dynasty took over. It has no relevance at any later date. Finally, there is the Old Kingdom. Imhotep (text not yet recovered) is a monumentally attested chief officer of King Djoser (Third Dynasty), while Hardjedef is one of several well-attested sons of Kheops, builder of the Great Pyramid (Fourth Dynasty [c. 2600 BC]). His text appears to be quoted by later writers, setting him back in the Old Kingdom. The oft-cited lack of literary manuscripts from that period means absolutely nothing, but simply reflects the vast losses (c. 98 percent) of all ancient Egyptian papyri and could be reversed by chance finds anytime. There are good specimens of Egyptian literature (hymnology) in the huge Pyramid Texts corpus (engraved in stone in some pyramids) and of literary biographical narratives in private tomb chapels of the period; these hint at what is lost or yet unrecovered. So we have no reason to reject an Old Kingdom date for writers attributed to that epoch. The content and style of Kagemni, Hardjedef and Ptahhotep do not suit any later period. Hence, most Egyptian authorial attributions are to be treated as real. In the Late Period, Ankh-Sheshonqy may be the author of the work in whose prologue and subtitle he appears (if it dated by origin to the Thirtieth Dynasty [fourth century BC]), but it may otherwise be drafted by his son or be pseudepigraphic; we have no evidence to go on. The author (name lost) of Pap. Louvre D.2414 may have been real, but we have nothing to go on. Thus, most Egyptian attributions should be taken seriously.

As for the Levant and Mesopotamia, omitting Proverbs for the present, we have only Ahiqar in West Semitic; such a man did live under Esarhaddon, in Mesopotamian tradition, as a high counsellor (ummanu) bearing also the good Akkadian name "Aba-ninnu-dari." He is therefore historical. That he wrote the Ahiqar text is not provable; the introductory narrative prologue is in the first person (like Ptahhotep), which would favor it being historical rather than fiction. Going much further back, our two remaining early Mesopotamian authorial figures are much more shadowy. The oldest, the Sumerian Shuruppak, is presented as instructing his son Ziusudra—the name of the Sumerian equivalent to Noah. Shuruppak may then be equivalent to Ubar-tutu, king of the city Shuruppak, hence a "Shuruppak(ite)." If so, these are two figures of very distant tradition indeed (long before, e.g., Gilgamesh), and their direct authorship of any existing work will seem a priori unlikely. The remaining pair, Shube-awilim and his son Zur(?)ranku, are wholly shadowy figures, of whom nothing tangible is known, and could even conceivably be just literary reflexes of Shuruppak and Ziusudra; so no clear judgment is possible in their case. So for Mesopotamia, one pair of figures comes from before the flood and is incommensurable, while another pair remains totally obscure at present. Alone, Ahiqar should stand out as a real person of high official rank and as possible author of what is attributed to him. Arameans were numerous in the Neo-Assyrian royal courts and appear in reliefs of Tiglath-pileser III [c. 740 BC], writing in Aramaic upon scrolls, alongside cuneiform scribes with clay tablets. So, Ahiqar, if author, would have written in Aramaic that was very close to the standard Aramaic of the copy that we have now.

What, then, about Solomon, Agur and Lemuel? On this showing, in the shadow of Egypt and Assyria, and reputed to have lived c. 950 BC (Solomon) and perhaps two centuries or so later (Agur, Lemuel [their land Massa attested eighth century BC]), there is no reason so far to doubt the ascriptions in Proverbs (see above on titles, prologues, etc.). But other points invite comment to round off any such inquiry. An authorship compilatory at least in part raises no problems so far.

2.1.4. Direct Personal Address in Book Titles and Texts Proper.

2.1.4.1. To Son(s) in Book Titles. In Egypt, wherever the introductory book title is preserved, at least twelve have the author addressing a son, apprentice (sometimes by name) or children (anonymous plural). In Mesopotamia all the six preserved book title lines address the son (three by name). In contrast to both Egypt and Mesopotamia, our Hebrew books never name the son or sons addressed, and these are never included in the book titles. Lemuel, of course, acknowledges himself as his mother's son, but it is he, not she, who is reporting the instruction given, so she is not named instead.

2.1.4.2. To Son(s) in the Main Text of Books. Here, Egypt and Mesopotamia differ completely. All over the place—in prologues, subprologues and throughout the text—the Mesopotamian works address "my son," all the way from Old Sumerian Shuruppak down to the Counsels of Wisdom and five times in Ahiqar's main text. But in the whole run of Egyptian main texts never once do we find any second-person address to "my son" anywhere. Here, the three shorter Hebrew books stand closer to Egypt than to Mesopotamia. "My son" occurs but once each in Solomon II (Prov 27:11) and in Lemuel (Prov

31:2). By contrast, Solomon I has "my son" thirteen times and "my sons" three times, all in the prologue (Prov 1—9), but only twice ("my son") in the whole of the main text (Prov 19:27; 24:13). The frequency in the prologue goes with earliest Mesopotamian usage, by contrast with Egypt and later-period texts. The rarity of "my son" in the main text compares well with mid-to-late second-millennium Mesopotamian texts; less so with Ahiqar (who does it more). In summary, Solomon I goes with earliest Mesopotamian usage in its prologue and with second-millennium usage in its main text; first-millennium texts there go further than Solomon I. Again, Solomon I holds a hinge position between the second and first millennia BC in this department.

2.1.4.3. Personal Address: Command versus No Command. The Egyptian works very often tell the reader to listen, pay heed, and so forth, but without saying "my son." In Mesopotamia usage is divided. Their writers say "listen, my son" (hearkening context) in their prologues, but occurrences of "my son" in their main texts do not have "listen." As in Mesopotamia, this is also true in Solomon I (main text, no "listen" [Prov 19:27; 24:13]) and in Solomon II (Prov 27:1) and Lemuel (Prov 31:2 and *parallelism). The prologue of Solomon I (all of Prov 1—9) is another matter. Here, we have twelve cases of "listen, my son" to four cases of "my son" without "listen" (a 3:1 ratio). Thus, Proverbs 1—9 is a true prologue, and it corresponds to Near Eastern usage (especially early Mesopotamian)—no question of late first-millennium usage.

2.1.5. The Nature and Types of Main Texts of Books. To the casual eye, the main texts of most of these works look like merely unconnected series of injunctions and aphorisms. However, a threefold distinction occurs. First is a unitary (or continuous) main text, from beginning to end. Examples of this crop up at all periods—for example, for Type A texts we have in Egypt Hardjedef, Ancient Writings, Hori, the "letter-writing" instructions, the Onomasticon and Pap. Louvre D.2414 and Amenothes; Mesopotamia offers Shube-awilim and the Advice to a Prince; in Hebrew we have Solomon II and Agur. Type B texts from Egypt of this type include Ptahhotep, Man for His Son, Amenemhat I and Ankh-Sheshonqy; from Mesopotamia come the Akkadian Shuruppak, Counsels of Wisdom and Ahiqar. In all these works author-compilers may flit back and forth freely between topics.

The second group comprises works with a two- or three-sectioned text. In such cases, each section is commonly devoted to a particular theme, but the division(s) left unmarked; such are Egyptian Merikare and biblical Lemuel. Others mark the sections off with cross-heads/subtitles or interjections—for example, Egyptian Aniy, Old-Sumerian Shuruppak and biblical Solomon I.

Third, there are the multisegmented texts, the use of explicitly numbered sections. This is as old as Sumerian Shuruppak (third/early second millennia BC [sections of miscellaneous content]) and halfway through preclassical antiquity with Amenemope's thirty chapters on topics, but in part repetitive (c. 1170 BC), as well as in late Hellenistic times (the Insinger demotic text, with twenty-five sections on specific topics). The main point to note here is that all three usages coexist through three millennia; there is no "development" from one to another.

2.1.6. Poetic Conventions in Main Texts. Here the picture is varied but quite clear. Throughout the third and second millenia BC, into the opening centuries of the first millennium, poetic parallelism (like that found in, e.g., *Psalms) is the dominant form of expression, and the two-line couplet or bicolon is the dominating "building block." This is true equally of the nonbiblical and biblical texts alike. But alongside the ubiquitous couplet, three-line, four-line and even longer line groupings were quite widely used as needed at all periods (for references, see Kitchen 1977, 88-89 nn. 45-52).

However, from about the sixth/fifth centuries BC onward a new trend sets in: the use of individual one-line precepts, often gathered together in larger blocks. This first properly appears in Amenemope (twelfth century), is clearly evident in the Saite Wisdom (within c. late sixth to early fourth centuries), and is rampant in Ahiqar (fifth century at latest) and in Ankh-Sheshonqy and Insinger (Hellenistic period). These facts have been noticed by others in Egyptology (e.g., J. F. Quack and R. Jasnow). Likewise, verbal reiteration (using a word or phrase in several successive one-line sayings) abounds in these late works but has modest forerunners all the way back to the third-millennium Shuruppak. What is noteworthy is the absolute dominance of the traditional third/ second millennium parallelistic couplet (in all its subforms) in all four of the constituent books that make up the biblical book of Proverbs—no great runs of single-liners here, or hardly at all. In this particular matter of the objective history of Near Eastern poetics specifically in wisdom literature, the tenth to early seventh centuries are just about the minimum dates possible for Solomon I and the group Solomon II/Agur/Lemuel, respectively. The matter was different in, for example, hymnody or prophetical works, outside the Bible or within it. Again, one may find both "atomistic" usage of runs of pithy sayings (whether couplets or longer) and also "organic" paragraphs or miniature essays, including side by side in one and the same work, and at all periods. (For listing with references, see Kitchen 1977, 90-91.)

3. Near Eastern Evidence on Concepts and Linguistic Indicators in Proverbs.

3.1. Use of "Non-wisdom" Concepts in Near East and Proverbs.

3.1.1. Personification. For well over a century attention has been given to the role of personified Wisdom in Proverbs 8—9. For much of that time, down to the early 1950s, not only was Proverbs 1—9 regarded as the latest part of Proverbs, but also, latest of all, this section personifying wisdom was even attributed to Greek influence (so, e.g., O. Eissfeldt as late as 1965). That extreme view is less evident today, following more recent comparisons with Egyptian *maat* both as the principle of "right, justice, right order of life" and as a *personification of these qualities, and in fact to the extent of being treated even as a full goddess, eventually with her own temples and cult, as at Karnak in Thebes, from at least the Ramesside period (Nineteenth-Twentieth Dynasties [c. 1295-1070 BC]), if not already under Amenophis III (Eighteenth Dynasty [c. 1390-1352 BC])—in biblical terms, broadly since Moses' time. However, OT scholars still illogically assign a late (postexilic) date to Proverbs 8—9, even though the theory of Greek influence is (in effect) exploded.

Personification in OT times had nothing whatsoever to do with Greeks of the fifth to second centuries; it was endemic to the entire biblical world of the ancient Near East, and already from the third millennium BC onward. In Egypt, Hike ("Magic") appears as a male deity in the funerary temple of Sahure (c. 2500 BC), in the Pyramid Texts (copies of a century later) and even in a priestly title. Concepts such as Hu ("Authoritative Command") and Sia ("Understanding")

were personified throughout the third and second millennia BC; from the Middle Kingdom (c. 1900 BC) we have the double-barreled Iir-Sedjmy ("Sight-and-Hearing"), similar in concept to other double-named entities at Ugarit (see below).

Early and late, Mesopotamians also personified diverse entities such as Egyptian Maat or Hebrew Wisdom. From at least the early second millennium the god Enki's wife Damgalnunna was assigned two personified ministers: "Hearing" (Uznu) and "Intelligence" (Khasisu). The underworldly messenger Namtaru was but a personification of Sumerian Namtar ("Destiny" [fourteenth century BC]). From the second millennium, Kettu as "Justice" and Mesharu as "Law" were likewise personified, by Hittites and Hurrians as well as by Babylonians. In North Syrian Ugarit, in the thirteenth century BC, the local religious myths include the personified Kothar-wa-Khasis ("Skill-and-Understanding" [cf. Uznu/Khasisu above]). And so on, a myriad of other examples from a variety of spheres (not only religion, *ethics and abilities) might be called upon (for detailed references, see Kitchen 1960). All of the data cited there and here long predate Solomon or any other date for Proverbs 1—9 or Proverbs 8—9.

Thus, there is no reason whatsoever to speculate about a "theologized wisdom" of supposedly postexilic date; Proverbs 1—9 (and in fact Prov 8—9) are no more "theologized" than the rest of Proverbs 1—24 (in which mentions of Yahweh crop up in not a few passages). Deities appear or are respected in the third- and second-millennium instructional wisdom books of Egypt and the Near East also, for which our well-dated manuscript evidence firmly excludes any attempt to banish them to a "postexilic period"; so, this non sequitur must be abandoned for Proverbs too.

3.1.2. Covenant. The term běrit ("covenant") appears just once in Proverbs (Prov 2:17). It certainly cannot be used to support any date for that verse or its context later than the tenth century BC. Outside of the OT, the concepts of covenant, contract and treaty are well attested. Thus, in tablets from Qatna (central Syria) in the fifteenth/fourteenth centuries BC, a *biritu* is "cut." Then in the thirteenth century BC at Ugarit we find in a Hurrian hymn El-*brt* and El-*dn* ("El of the Covenant" and "El of Judgement") in a good religious context. In contemporary Egypt Nineteenth Dynasty mentions occur (reigns of Sety I and Merenptah) of hired labor, male and female respectively. And then clear usage in the Year 11 victory text of Ramesses III (Twentieth Dynasty [c. 1170 BC]) shows us the defeated Libyans seeming to plan making a covenant amongst themselves and certainly seeking a (vassal) treaty with the pharaoh. Thus, *běrît* is well-attested in religious, commercial and political contexts during c. 1400-1170 BC, long before Solomon's day (and long before the often later dates wrongly assigned to Hebrew *běrît* in much OT scholarship).

3.2. Linguistic Points in Proverbs.

3.2.1. Aramaisms. A common excuse sometimes offered in the past for assigning a late (exilic/postexilic) date to most of Proverbs has been the alleged presence of Aramaisms. The error here comprises two assumptions: (1) an Aramaism in itself must always be "late" (c. 600 BC and thereafter); (2) specific supposed Aramaisms are themselves of late date. The first assumption is no longer tenable because the presence of a land of Aram and of Arameans is not late but rather comfortably precedes any realistic date for Solomon's reign (c. 971 BC at earliest). Aram as an entity is firmly vouched for by its presence in a topographical list of Near Eastern names in the funerary temple of Amenophis III (c. 1370 BC) in Western Thebes (at Kom el-Hetan); this is fully accepted by all who know the Egyptian data of this particular type. In turn, this extinguishes the question mark that used to be set against the presence of the term "Aram" ("Pa-Aram") in a Late Egyptian Miscellany under Merenptah (Year 3 [c. 1211/10 BC]; the "Pirem" of Caminos [109, 113], who did not recognize it). After that, during the twelfth century, the Arameans grew in number and power in Syria and eventually endangered the very existence of Assyria in the east, under Tiglath-pileser I (1115-1076 BC), who ceaselessly fought against them. These people groups would have spoken one form or another of Old Aramaic, as would Hadadezer of Aram-Zobah (c. 1025-990 BC) in David's time. Thus, early Aramaic would be current already down to the northern borders of Israel before Solomon ever ascended his throne.

The second assumption is limited to very few words indeed; four in particular in Solomon I are (1) *qabbēl*, "receive, accept" (once, in Prov 19:20), (2) *naḥat*, "to go/bring down" (once, in

Prov 17:10), (3) *rᶜ*, of uncertain meaning (Prov 18:24), (4) *ḥesed* (II), "reproach" (Prov 14:34). The first word perhaps is not Aramaic at all, being scarcely attested in Standard Aramaic ("complain," not "receive," in P. Cowley 37:3) or until the *Dead Sea Scrolls, too late to be of significance (the supposed example in Amarna Letter 252 has been eliminated: it is *qbl*, "to fight back"). As Common West Semitic, the second word is firmly attested in Ugaritic, then only in poetic usage in later Hebrew, and going on in prose in later Aramaic. The third word is open to too many possibilities even not Aramaic, and it may simply be Hebrew (for various alternatives, see Kitchen 1977, 106). And as a rare West Semitic term, the fourth word simply does not occur at all in any external Aramaic or other source in the pre-Hellenistic period. Anything later is irrelevant. By contrast, we have (5) *bar* for "son" and (6) the plural *mělākîn* for "kings" in Proverbs 31:2-3—in the text of the easterner Agur! In his case, early Aramaic connections were likely; the Old-Aramaic *br* for "son" is attested from at least the later ninth century (Zakkur of Hamath), and compare the Moabite plurals (Mesha Stela [ninth century BC]) in *-in*. Thus, appeal to Aramaic on dating is essentially a delusion.

3.2.2. Other Linguistic Items. The Hebrew of Proverbs is well-linked to wider Semitic usage, including specifically West Semitic (*see* Hebrew Language). Thus, the term *marbaddîm* ("coverlets") in Proverbs 7:16 again links up with Ugaritic (thirteenth century BC). Likewise, the words for "pledge": *ᶜărubbâ* goes away back to Old Assyrian *erubbatum*, almost a thousand years before Solomon, while *ᶜarrabon* is attested from thirteenth-century Ugaritic. Staying with finance, we find offerings or vows expressed as being "due" from somebody by using the preposition *ᶜal* (Prov 7:14), again at Ugarit. In another direction (returning to Prov 7:16), the otherwise unattested word *ᵓēṭûn* ("yarn" [meaning "cloth"]), once linked by some to Greek *othonē*, would on context be better linked with Egypt, and that might include an Egyptian origin for this word (cf. Egyptian *idmy* ["linen"], third millennium onwards; *idn*, late second millennium). Thus, when adequate background is available, the plea for late origins fails; when we have no data or scarcely any, then for the time being no strong conclusions can be drawn anyway.

3.2.3. The Conundrum of Proverbs 22:20: "Al-

ready" or "Excellent Things" or "Thirty (Sayings)"? A rather special case concerns Proverbs 22:20. The word *šilšôm* here has often raised a question mark in the minds of Hebraists. In Hebrew this word is usually part of a bound expression, *ʾetmôl šilšôm*, meaning "already, previously" and the like, which made good sense. The expression is literally "yesterday-and-the-day-before." In the Hebrew of the OT *ʾtěmôl/ʾetmôl* ("yesterday") is found several times on its own (2 Sam 15:20; Job 8:9; Ps 90:4; Is 30:33; Mic 2:8). And from a thousand years before these, in early Akkadian (*CAD* 18, 2006, 416). So one similar occurrence of *šilšôm* should not be rejected a priori. One alternative of long-standing is based on the Qere reading *šālîšim*, understood as "excellent things" or something similar. However, a close examination of the data on the text indicates that such a word (with such a meaning) strictly does not exist, however good it might sound (see Emerton, 435-38). The full publication of an Egyptian text, the Instructions of Amenemope, in the early 1920s with its "Thirty Chapters" of imparted wisdom led A. Erman to suggest in 1924 that the Hebrew *šilšôm* should be revocalized as *šělôšim* ("thirty"), making the verse Proverbs 22:20 read along the lines of "Have I not written for you thirty (things) of counsel and knowledge?" Then E. Sellin endeavored to find just thirty admonitions in Proverbs 22:22b—24:22 to fit in with this suggested reading. Both Erman and Sellin sought to establish similarities linking the two texts and to have the text of Proverbs more or less directly dependent on Amenemope. Many have followed them since. Here, we reexamine the matter of *šilšôm*. (For wider comparisons, see the next section.)

That *šilšôm*, understood as "already, previously," makes good sense has been noted by a variety of scholars, such as J. Ruffle and R. N. Whybray, both discussed at length by Emerton. He favors the "thirty" reading but is unconvincing in trying to dispose of *šilšôm* as "already" or something similar. His only positive suggestions against it are two. First, he misinterprets the phrase "written for you" as "written to you," and then he misunderstands his mistranslated dative as referring to the author writing a letter to the person addressed (Emerton, 439). As he remarks, no other such reference exists elsewhere in the Wisdom literature—but neither does it exist here, for it is merely his own mistranslation. The text of Proverbs 22:20 remains quite simply

"Have I not written for you already, with counsels and knowledge?" and this merely refers to the immediately preceding text of Proverbs 1:1—22:19. Second, he overvalues the usage of the versions and later commentators from the LXX into medieval times. But the LXX's "triply" (*trissōs*) is nothing more than a guess by the Hebrew-to-Greek translator of the consonants *š-l-š-m*, whether with *w* or *y* before the final *m* (main text or margin). All the subsequent interpretations (other than "already"), from the Latin Vulgate to F. Delitzsch, are unsoundly based guesswork and should be dismissed.

Thus, the only two interpretations to be considered are either *šilšôm*—with ellipse of *ʾetmôl*—("already") or the emended vocalization *šělôšim* ("thirty"). The latter solution has led to repeated attempts to find (or to force) just thirty admonitions in the Hebrew text of Proverbs 22:22—24:22. However, the most natural understanding of the text finds thirty-three items, not thirty, unless (with some) one treats four verses as "introductions" to immediately following proverbs/admonitions; such would be Proverbs 23:12 with vv. 13-14; Proverbs 23:19 with vv. 20-21; Proverbs 23:26 with vv. 27-28; and, less certainly allowed, Proverbs 23:15-16 with vv. 17-18 (see Emerton, 448). This would give us twenty-nine items plus the introduction in Proverbs 22:17-21, as "first" saying, to make up thirty (for other guesses, see Emerton, 451-52). However, the omission of *ʾetmôl* in the locution *ʾetmôl šilšôm* for "already, previously," if (accidentally) unique in Hebrew, is clearly attested elsewhere—a matter that has escaped the notice of biblical scholars.

Back in the early second millennium BC the Old Babylonian lexical word lists set out equivalences between Sumerian and Babylonian words and expressions for the convenience of scribes. In one such list we have Babylonian *shalshumi* ("day before" [i.e., "yesterday"]) given on its own three times with various Sumerian equivalents; the Babylonian form of *ʾetmôl*, which is *timali* ("yesterday"), is then similarly given with its equivalents, separately, *after* the *shalshumi* entries. Thus each part of the full expression *timali shalshumi*, "the day before yesterday" (precursor of Heb *ʾetmôl šilšôm*), could be treated on its own. Nor is this restricted to mere lists. It also clearly occurs in current written documents of the same period, up to one thousand years before Solomon or Proverbs. An Old

Babylonian letter uses *shalshumi* in "the day-before-(yesterday), over (someone's) health I kept watch," while in another such letter from Mari a man writes "the day-before, I reached Terqa," or "already I have reached Terqa," again using *shalshumi* on its own (no *timali*). At Nuzi, c. 1500 BC or just later, a case records witnesses to a man's thefts of sheep: "by force, Peshkilishu took (it) three-days-past/previously" (*shalushmu*, for *shalshumu*, with metathesis, *ush* for *shu*?), and "he did not return it already/three-days-back." In the Amarna Letters (fourteenth century BC), in the full form *tumal shalshami*, our expression occurs meaning "previously, already, recently," and so too in later periods (for references, see *CAD* 17.1.268b [cf. 262b]; Moran, 360 top). Thus, an isolated *šilšôm* (no *ʾetmôl*) in Proverbs 22:20 is not an isolated phenomenon but rather has ancient precedents going back for a millennium, and in part also the meaning "already, previously." In Proverbs 22:20 it is an archaism as befits poetic style, and as required by the format of this verse. Thus, Hebrew *hă-lōʾ* (twin particles) + first main word *(kātabtî)*, then *lĕ-kâ* (twin particle/pronoun) + second main word *(šilšôm)* is balanced in the second half of the verse by *bĕ* (preposition) + first main word *(môʿēṣōt)*, then *wā* (conjunction) + second main word *(dāʿat)*.

So, we have *hă-lōʾ* + *kātabtî*, *lĕ-kâ* + *šilšôm* ("have-not + I-written, to-you + already"), then *bĕ* + *môʿēṣōt*, *wā* + *dāʿat* ("with + counsels, and + knowledge").

In this very tight poetical format there is simply no room for an additional word, *ʾetmôl*, which would wreck the balance of the whole verse. Therefore, we should see here the plain fact of historic archaism (a feature of poetry in any case), using a term that fits excellently, and in a short form to fit the format of the whole verse. The interpretive acrobatics performed here to find thirty sayings are superfluous.

4. The Subject Matter of Proverbs in Its Near Eastern Context.

4.1. The Debate over Amenemope and Proverbs 22—24.
In the 1920s the "thirty sayings" issue led to intense interest not only in finding numerically thirty sayings in (or imposing them upon) Proverbs 22:22—24:22 but also in close comparisons between the subject matter to be found in Amenemope and Proverbs 22—24. It has to be said that in the excitement of the chase to find the greatest possible number of

parallels, some did not scruple recklessly to emend either (or both) of the Hebrew and Egyptian texts to force a "relationship" artificially (see, e.g., D. C. Simpson, 236-39, left-hand columns and notes, citing also Erman, Gressman, etc.; cf. Ruffle, 52-54), and most did not bother to check how far the topics and ancient attitudes in question were actually unique to these two books (possibly significant) or in fact shared by them with other such writings through the centuries (giving insignificant parallels). Solomon makes it clear, twice over, that he is teaching from sources that included "Words of the Wise" (Prov 22:17; 24:23), and he does not specify that these men were all Hebrews; indeed, Agur and Lemuel were not (being probably from Massa, on the northwest Arabian fringe), and Job quite possibly not. And, as we noted (see 1.2.3), Amenemope in the twelfth century BC (and ostracon, c. 1000 BC) was earlier than Solomon.

One thing is certain: Proverbs 22:22—24:22 is not remotely a straight, consecutive translation from Amenemope. As long since compactly pointed out by J. A. Wilson (in *ANET*, 424 n. 46), the supposed citations in Proverbs from, or allusions to, Amenemope never occur in the same order in the two books, except for two consecutive "links" each in Amenemope chapters 9 and 11. Otherwise, if we follow the sequence of passages in Proverbs claimed as linked to Amenemope, we find that our supposed biblical copyist has jumped backwards and forwards all over the place in a most bizarre fashion. The links (in biblical order) go as follows:

To A(menemope)'s chapter 1 (for Prov 22:17-18), then back to A's introduction (for Prov 22:19), then wildly forward to A's concluding chapter 30 (Prov 22:20), then back to A's introduction (Prov 22:21), and on to A's chapter 2 (Prov 22:22). Nothing for Proverbs 22:23. But away up to A's chapter 9 (two separate passages: Prov 11:13-14; 13:8-9) for Proverbs 22:24, 25. Another gap (nothing for Prov 22:26-27), but down back to A's chapter 6 for Proverbs 22:28; then all the way on to A's chapter 30 again (Prov 22:29). Then back to A's chapter 23 (Prov 23:1-3), still further back to A's chapter 7 (Prov 23:4-5), followed by another jump forward to A's chapter 11, in two separated passages (Prov 14:5-10; 14:17-18) and with chapter 9 (cf. Prov 23:6-7, 8). Then on again to A's chapter 21 (Prov 23:9), then all the way back to A's chapter 6 again, but in two separated passages, Proverbs 7:12-15; 8:9-

10 (for Prov 23:10-11). Then a clear gap, with nothing in Amenemope for Proverbs 23:12—24:10. Finally, A's chapter 8 (for Prov 24:11), but nothing more at all in Amenemope for Proverbs 24:12-22.

In short, absolute chaos, if one really wishes to assume that Proverbs had here been derived directly from the text of Amenemope. This situation disproves misleading statements such as that by D. C. Simpson (235) that "the passages quoted from the latter [Amenemope] often appear in the same context, and mostly, though by no means invariably, stand in the same relative order in it as the corresponding Hebrew proverbs do in the Hebrew Book of Proverbs." The facts are clearly otherwise: apart from the separated pairings in Amenemope chapters 9 and 11, the tabulation given above shows with crystal clarity that there is no overall corresponding order between the two books. And any suggestion of recopying through some unknown and wholly theoretical intermediate text would be a counsel of despair.

A second qualifying factor is that, on careful scrutiny, the supposed Hebrew borrowing from Amenemope often turns out to be shorter than the assumed Egyptian original. In other words, if Solomon, or anyone else in Jerusalem, had made use of Amenemope (or any other such text from among Words of the Wise), then they did so critically, using only what seemed to be a suitable expression of what they had approved of, and reset in a Yahwistic mental context.

Third, one cannot neglect the wider context of both Amenemope and Proverbs (see 4.2 below). They both belong to a millennial-long tradition of international wisdom, both instructional and otherwise. A good example of the misleading result of failure to compare right across the board can be illustrated by one classic example involving both works and the wider context. Thus, in Proverbs 23:4-5, "(wealth) takes wing like an eagle flying off into the heavens," while Amenemope (10:4-5, after a longer screed) observed that "(riches) make themselves wings, like geese, and fly off to heaven"—at first glance, a striking resemblance, varied only by a change of bird. However, neither is wholly "original"; some eight hundred years before, a Sumerian proverbialist wrote, "(Like) migratory birds, wealth finds no place to settle" (Sumerian Proverb Collection 1, no. 18 [Alster 1997, 10]). In other words, once this concept—wealth all too easily flies off like the birds—had been formulated, it too flew from mouth to mouth and mind to mind (and text to text) just like the birds.

4.2. Wider Relationships. Various themes common to Proverbs (esp. Prov 22:20—24:22) and Amenemope are by no means exclusive to these two works; such cases thus cease to constitute any evidence for the supposed special relationship between Amenemope and Proverbs. One may add other cases to join that of wealth and fugitive birds just cited. (1) Not too surprisingly, both Amenemope (chap. 1) and Proverbs, both at its real beginning (Prov 1:1-6 and passim) and in this section's beginning (Prov 22:17-21), loudly advertise their wares: true wisdom with good consequences. But so also did several others. From the third millennium so too do Ptahhotep (Egypt) and Shuruppak (Mesopotamia [all three editions]). From the early second millennium (cited mainly in Kitchen 1998, 359-63) so too do Sehetepibre, Man to His Son, Khety son of Duauf, and Amenemhat I (all from Egypt), and in the late second millennium the Vizier Amatju, the High Priest Amenemhat, and Amennakht (all from Egypt). Such usage was customary wherever this kind of literature flourished, and no case can be made for assuming any specific relationship between any of these works (or with and between Amenemope and Proverbs) on this matter. (2) Respect for one's mother occupies Aniy (7:19) as also Proverbs (Prov 23:22). (3) By contrast, a responsible man should beware of sexual affairs and women of uncertain status, with not only Aniy (3:13) and Proverbs (Prov 2:16; 23:27) but also Ptahhotep (§18) well over a thousand years earlier. (4) By all such authors, oppressing the poor stood condemned, not only in Proverbs (Prov 22:22-23; see also Prov 18:5) and Amenemope (chap. 2) but also by Khety son of Duauf (verso 4 [c. 1970 BC]) and in Mesopotamia the Counsels of Wisdom (lines 57-60 [c. fourteenth-twelfth century BC]) (Lambert, 101). (5) In contrast, one should care for the poor with not only Proverbs (Prov 3:27) and Amenemope (chap. 11) but also with Aniy (5:10) and Counsels of Wisdom (61-65). (6) Table manners engaged the attention of the ancients. Again, not only in Proverbs (Prov 23:1-3, 6-8) and Amenemope (chap. 23) but also over a millennium earlier in Egypt's Pyramid Age, with Kagemni (§§3-4) and Ptahhotep (§7). (7) To be a diligent man with chance of high office is reflected not only in Proverbs (Prov 22:29) and Amenemope (chap. 30) but also in Khety son of Duauf. (8) The bad-tempered person of Proverbs 22:24-25 is comparable not solely with the "hothead" or passionate person of Amenemope chapter 9. The Egyptian term also recurs in Papyrus Sallier I, 8:6 (incomplete context), in contrast to the quiet man: desert waters are opened to the latter but are sealed against the former, "who finds his mouth"—that is, the loud-mouthed (c. 1210 BC [see Caminos, 321]). For the term *shemem* ("hothead"), and older *taa* in Egyptian, see Shupak 1993, 117-18:1-2. Thus similarly, over a thousand years before, Ptahhotep (§§23, 25 [Lichtheim, 1.70]) warned against hotheads, as did both Man to His Son (§§19-20) and, closer in time to Amenemope, Aniy (5:3; 6:15 [Lichtheim, 2.138, 140]), among other texts. In Mesopotamia early on, the early and classical versions of Sumerian Shuruppak also deal with the quarrelsome (Alster 1974, 15, 37: 31). So there is no exclusive link here for Amenemope and Proverbs. (9) As for removing (= violating) field boundaries, the claim of relationship with Proverbs 22:28; 23:10-11 and Amenemope chapter 6 holds water only if the theme is otherwise known nowhere else. It is not easily found in other wisdom instructions but certainly is found in other texts, and it was severely punishable. These include many references in Mesopotamia, as in the Middle-Assyrian Laws and on so-called *kudurru*-stelae (*RlA* 3.8.639; see Slanski), and in Egypt in such as the Instructions to the Vizier (§10 [c. 1530 BC]) and the Nauri Decree by Sethos I (§§12A/B [c. 1290 BC]) (Kitchen 1993, 46). Thus, the topic is, in effect, probably too banal to be used to plead any special relationship.

In other words, almost all topics found in the Words of the Wise in Proverbs are in fact shared not only with Amenemope but also with other instructional wisdom all the way from Mesopotamia to Egypt, and through two millennia (third and second), besides in other types of documents. No "special relationship" can be safely established in such cases. It should be added that the same phenomenon of parallels in varying degrees between the rest of Proverbs, Amenemope and other Egyptian and Near Eastern wisdom books can also be amply documented (see, e.g., in some detail, Ruffle, 37-52). Thus, there is no adequate material reason to prefer "links" with any special part of Proverbs in such a situation.

5. Concluding Perspective on Proverbs in Its Ancient Near Eastern Context.

The foregoing critical survey has utilized compactly not solely the biblical text of Proverbs in isolation (as favored in the later nineteenth century and by too many since then) but rather the entire available corpus of instructional wisdom writings from the whole biblical world through three millennia in order to provide a clearly objective (because independent) framework of the history of the features of this group of writings at all periods, in sequence. Measured against that independent sequence and range of data, the results are clear. There is no evidence of any kind in favor of the later nineteenth-century purely theoretical presentation, but there is considerable independent evidence (given above) that clearly favors the datings implied by the biblical text's explicit headings and inherent features (literary, linguistic, conceptual, etc.). It may be helpful to summarize here, as follows, in ten points.

(1) All titles are expressed in the third person, with an author/compiler's name, except for two anonymous compilations, of traditional material or for universal application. In the vast majority of cases the ascriptions are to be taken seriously, and in several cases we know that these ascriptions are factual. Only a "pre-flood" ascription is unlikely to be literally true, while Shube-awilim is obscure. Subtitles and interjected cross-headings (before or within main texts) are optional.

(2) Two classes of such writings exist: Type A (simply title plus main text) and Type B (title, prologue, sometimes subtitle, then main text). Half the corpus (including Solomon II, Agur and Lemuel) is of Type A, and the other half of Type B (including Solomon I). Occurrence of both types throughout the third, second and first millennia proves that there is no "evolution" from simpler Type A to more complex Type B, unless it happened before c. 2600 BC (on which, of course, we have no evidence). Thus, all four documents within Proverbs come well inside long-established customary usage either way.

(3) Prologues themselves show change through time. Other than Ptahhotep (the oldest in Egypt), they are without further exception used by authors to state their aims and/or proclaim the worth and importance of what they are writing, so throughout the third and second millennia. In the first millennium (when preserved

at all), from the sixth century onward, they are narrative, sometimes biographical. In the third/second millennia they are short going on to medium in length; in the first millennium they run up to considerable length, when present. Thus, being exhortatory (like third/second millennia) and yet of some length (first millennium), Solomon I's prologue (Prov 1—9) is clearly "transitional," sharing one feature with the past and having one looking toward the future.

(4) Use of addresses to "my son(s)" in prologues and main texts and of personal commands varies in place and time; here, Solomon I is again transitional, between east (Mesopotamia) and West (Egypt), and between the second and first millennia.

(5) The "main text" in all these works can fall into one of three formats: unitary throughout, quite a number (including Solomon II, Agur), or segmented into two or three sections, with or without subheadings (so also Solomon I), or explicitly numbered off in "chapters" or sayings (from Sumerian to Amenemope and demotic; not in the OT).

(6) During the third, second and early first millennia all such works are expressed in poetic parallelism, commonly in two-line couplets, but as needed using more complex units; so in all four books in Proverbs. By clear contrast, from the sixth/fifth centuries onward this format was largely superseded by use of one-line sayings, often in large blocks, sometimes with repetition of part of the wording in a series. This is almost totally absent from Proverbs, which belongs before c. 600 BC in its entirety on these grounds alone, besides the other data.

(7) Regarding the occurrence of certain concepts, use of personification (e.g., of Wisdom in Prov 8—9) has nothing whatsoever to do with Greek influence at any time. Personification was a commonplace usage throughout the ancient and biblical Near East during the third and second, as well the first, millennia BC. Compare Maat in Egypt ("Righteousness/Justice"), who early on became a full goddess, unlike Hebrew Hokmat ("Wisdom"), at least in Proverbs. Also, *bĕrît* ("covenant") as both a concept and a word is solidly attested from at least the mid-to-late second millennium BC, before any Hebrew monarch, priest or prophet ever used it.

(8) In regard to linguistic matters: (1) Arameans had been around in a limited way since the fourteenth/thirteenth centuries BC

and expanded in much of the Near East during the twelfth-ninth centuries BC. Their language inevitably went with them; so, Aramaisms must be expected from twelfth/eleventh centuries at least. (2) Four supposed items in Proverbs are absent, or nearly so, in Old/Standard Aramaic, while two clear items reflect the eastside links of Agur (Massa) northwards (and cf. ninth-century Moabite). Much of the regular vocabulary of Proverbs is of Common Semitic/Common West Semitic origin, much of that going back into the second millennium BC and even beyond. What was alleged to be Greek (*'ēṭûn*) is most likely long-established Egyptian, for example.

(9) The much-disputed *šilšôm* on its own, meaning "previously, already," has precisely the same form (no prefixed *'etmôl*) already back in the early (and probably middle) second millennium BC (lexical lists, letters, court case); from then and/or the fourteenth century the meaning "already, previously" is attested (not just original "day-before-[yesterday]"). In Proverbs 22:20 it is simply an archaism used to fit into a restricted poetical context. It has nothing to do with the "thirty (sayings)" of Amenemope, nor are there necessarily exactly thirty sayings in Proverbs 22:22—24:22. So this supposed link with Amenemope falls away.

(10) None of the topics treated in common in both Amenemope and Proverbs are unique to them alone within the Wisdom literature corpus, except for the condemnation of shifting land boundaries, and this recurs amply in other, non-wisdom contexts. Also, the order of treatment of topics in Proverbs and Amenenope differs very drastically indeed, and the Hebrew aphorisms are often shorter than the Egyptian ones. Neither work can be taken as simply a straight translation of the other, nor can any irrefutable direct relationship between the two texts be established. On the other hand, Amenemope was written well before Solomon reigned or wrote. And Solomon twice says explicitly that he has drawn upon "words of wise men"; there is nothing to exclude his drawing upon and even reformulating topics from Amenemope any more or less than any other source, but nothing can be proved either way. Even today, "A stitch in time saves nine" remains a true observation for all of us, regardless of anyone's theology or beliefs.

In summary, the ancient Near East offers an independent network of firm, factual controls over what opinions may be valid or invalid regarding the origins, formats and literary history of the four constituent books of Proverbs. It is regrettable that what was simply speculative "no facts" theory in the later nineteenth century has been in effect canonized into (hyper)critical dogma during the twentieth century. It is the duty of the twenty-first century to peel away these untenable accretions and replace them with clear factual data and clear rational results that derive directly from impartial and tangible data.

See also ASAPH AND SONS OF KORAH; DISCOURSE IN PROVERBS; FORM CRITICISM; HISTORICAL CRITICISM; MAAT; PROVERB, GENRE OF; PROVERBS 1: BOOK OF; WISDOM SOURCES.

BIBLIOGRAPHY. **B. Alster,** *The Instructions of Shuruppak: A Sumerian Proverb Collection* (Mesopotamia 2; Copenhagen: Akademisk Forlag, 1974); idem, "Early Dynastic Proverbs and Other Contributions to the Study of Literary Texts from Abu Salabikh," *AfO* 38-39 (1991-1992) 1-51; idem, *Proverbs of Ancient Sumer: The World's Earliest Proverb Collection* (2 vols.; Bethesda, MD: CDL Press, 1997); **S. Bickel and B. Mathieu,** "L'écrivain Amennakht et son enseignement," *Bulletin de l'Institut français d'archéologie orientale au Caire* 93 (1993) 31-51 and plates 1-8; **R. A. Caminos,** *Late-Egyptian Miscellanies* (BES 1; London: Oxford University Press, 1954); **B. Cumming,** *Egyptian Historical Records of the Later Eighteenth Dynasty, Fasc. II* (Warminster: Aris & Phillips, 1984); **J. A. Emerton,** "The Teaching of Amenemope and Proverbs xxii 17-xxiv 22: Further Reflections on a Long-standing Problem," *VT* 51 (2001) 431-65; **A. H. Gardiner,** *Ancient Egyptian Onomastica* (3 vols.; London: Oxford University Press, 1947); **W. W. Hallo and K. L. Younger,** eds., *The Context of Scripture,* vol. 1 (Leiden: E. J. Brill, 1997); **R. Jasnow,** *A Late Period Hieratic Wisdom Text (P. Brooklyn 47.218.135)* (SAOC 52; Chicago: Oriental Institute of the University of Chicago, 1992); **K. A. Kitchen,** "Some Egyptian Background to the Old Testament," *TynBul* 5-6 (1960) 4-18; idem, "Proverbs and Wisdom Books of the Ancient Near East," *TynBul* 28 (1977) 69-114; idem, "The Basic Literary Forms and Formulations of Ancient Instructional Writings in Egypt and Western Asia," in *Studien zu altägyptischen Lebenslehren,* ed. E. Hornung and O. Keel (OBO 28; Freiberg: Universitätsverlag; Göttingen: Vandenhoeck & Ruprecht, 1979) 235-82; idem, *Ramesside Inscriptions Translated and Annotated: Translations,* vol. 1 (Oxford: Blackwell, 1993); idem, "Biblical Instructional Wisdom: The Decisive Voice of the Ancient Near East," in *Boundaries of the Ancient Near Eastern World: A Tribute to Cyrus H. Gordon,* ed. M. Lubetski, C. Gottlieb and S. Keller (JSOTSup 273; Sheffield: JSOT Press, 1998) 346-63; **W. G. Lambert,** *Babylonian Wisdom Literature* (Oxford: Clarendon Press, 1960); **M. Lichtheim,** *Ancient Egyptian Literature: A Book of Readings* (3 vols.; Berkeley: University of California Press, 1973-1980); **W. L. Moran,** *The Armarna Letters* (Baltimore: Johns Hopkins University Press, 1992); **B. Porten and A. Yardeni,** eds., *Textbook of Aramaic Documents from Ancient Egypt,* 3: *Literature, Accounts, Lists* (Jerusalem: Hebrew University, 1993); **J. Ruffle,** "The Teaching of Amenemope and Its Connection with the Book of Proverbs," *TynBul* 28 (1977) 29-68; **N. Shupak,** *Where Can Wisdom Be Found? The Sage's Language in the Bible and in Ancient Egyptian Literature* (OBO 130; Fribourg: Universitätsverlag; Göttingen: Vandenhoeck & Ruprecht, 1993); **D. C. Simpson,** "The Hebrew Book of Proverbs and the Teaching of Amenophis," *JEA* (1926) 232-39; **W. K. Simpson,** ed., *The Literature of Ancient Egypt* (3rd ed.; New Haven: Yale University Press, 2003); **K. E. Slanski,** *The Babylonian Entitlement narûs (kudurrus): A Study in Their Form and Function* (Boston: American Schools of Oriental Research, 2003); **S. Weeks,** *Early Israelite Wisdom* (OTM; Oxford: Clarendon Press, 1994). K. A. Kitchen

PROVERBS 3: HISTORY OF INTERPRETATION

The history of the interpretation of Proverbs begins with the early translations of the book and reaches to scholarly analyses of the text in current commentaries, monographs and essays.

    1. The Septuagint and the Targum
    2. Early and Medieval Jewish and Christian Interpretation
    3. English Protestant Interpretation: Jonathan Edwards
    4. Proverbs in Modern Study

1. The Septuagint and the Targum.

1.1. The Septuagint of Proverbs. The starting point for our investigation of the history of the interpretation of Proverbs—that is, the earliest point at which we have a sustained interpretation of the text—is the LXX translation of the book. There is a serious problem, of course, in using an ancient translation to determine the interpretive methodology and presuppositions of its translator: the tendencies of the translation are most apparent where that translation differs from the Hebrew text, but in many cases the LXX is not appreciably different in meaning from the received Hebrew of the MT. Also, there are reasons why the LXX might differ from the MT that have nothing to do with the translator's hermeneutics (e.g., textual corruptions in either the LXX or the MT; an LXX translation based in postbiblical meanings for a Hebrew word; simple translation error). Sometimes, however, differences in the LXX can be attributed to the translator's hermeneutic. For Proverbs, the following tendencies in the LXX translation can be observed:

- Using abstractions to replace the vivid, metaphorical language of the MT, as in Proverbs 12:6—MT: "The words of the wicked are for an ambush of blood, but the mouth of the upright delivers them"; LXX: "The words of the wicked are deceitful, but the mouth of the upright delivers them."
- Giving proverbs a moralizing or spiritual tone that goes beyond what the MT states, as in Proverbs 13:11—MT: "Wealth from nothing [i.e., wealth acquired quickly and with little effort] shrinks, but he who gathers it by hand [i.e., who acquires wealth over time and with effort] increases it"; LXX: "Property hastily gained with lawlessness becomes small, but the one who gathers to himself with piety becomes abundant—a just man shows compassion and lends."
- A preference for antithetical proverbs with their underlying duality of good versus evil. Many proverbs of the MT are antithetical in nature, but the LXX sometimes has antitheses where the MT does not, as in Proverbs 11:7—MT: "When a wicked man dies, [his] hope will perish, and the expectation of power perishes"; LXX: "When a righteous man dies his hope will not perish, but the boast of the ungodly perishes."
- Occasional recasting of theological language in a manner more suited to Second Temple Judaism, as in Proverbs 29:18—MT: "In the absence of [prophetic] vision, a people is left unrestrained, but blessed is he who keeps law"; LXX: "There should be no interpreter for a lawless people, but the one who keeps the law is blessed." The MT

speaks of the charismatic role of the prophet where the LXX has the exegete or interpreter; this may be a deliberate reflection of the religious sensibilities of Hellenistic era Judaism. The LXX also contrasts a lawless (paranomos) people with the one who keeps the *law (nomos)—a rendition that reflects the importance of Torah in this community.

- Avoidance of blatantly sexual language, as in Proverbs 5:19—MT: "A lovely deer, a graceful doe. Let her breasts saturate you at all times; be intoxicated always in her love"; LXX: "A deer of companionship, a colt of your favor, so let her associate with you. Let her very self be regarded as yours and you stay with her at all times. For in going about in the companionship of this woman you shall come forth enriched."
- A recasting of proverbs on laziness and diligence, so that they deal with other moral or spiritual issues, as in Proverbs 20:13a—MT: "Do not love sleep, lest you lose your property"; LXX: "Do not love to malign, so that you not be cut off."

What are we to make of such differences? Sometimes, of course, the translator's *Vorlage* may have contained a reading different from that found in the MT, but some scholars, most notably J. E. Cook, argue that the translator of Proverbs had a Hebrew *Vorlage* not significantly different from the MT. This translator was capable, but he was also willing to take some liberties with the text, so that the LXX renditions are driven more by his theological and exegetical purposes than by variant readings in the underlying Hebrew. The translator at times diverged significantly from his parent Hebrew text in order to make clearer what he believed to be the actual meaning of the book.

However, the precise orientation of the translator's presuppositions are debated. Suggestions include that he engaged in Jewish midrashic exegesis or, conversely, that he was heavily influence by Hellenistic thought. G. Gerleman, for example, has argued that the tendency to recast proverbs on laziness reflects Stoic philosophy in that Stoicism did not consider laziness a vice. On the other hand, Cook claims that the LXX of Proverbs is fundamentally Jewish in outlook (even that it was translated in Jerusalem rather than in Alexandria), but that it does incorporate non-Jewish ideas to reinforce what is already present in the Hebrew text. For example, Proverbs 6:6-8 in Hebrew uses the analogy of the ant to demonstrate the value of being industrious, but the LXX is greatly expanded by the inclusion of a discussion of the wise labor of the bee. Cook argues that this expansion is demonstrably derived from the portrait of the bee in Aristotle's *Historia Animalium,* and that the LXX translator used it because he believed that it enhanced the point being made in the Hebrew.

Some scholars, such as E. Tov, are not persuaded that the translator of the LXX would have been willing to render the Hebrew so freely, and they say that some of the differences must be due to its having a different parent text (an argument for this is the fact that the LXX places Prov 30:1-14 after Prov 24:22 and sets Prov 30:15–31:9 after Prov 24:34). Even so, one should not ascribe all differences in the LXX of Proverbs to a *Vorlage* different from that of the MT. For example, as P. Gentry points out, sometimes the LXX translator gave a different reading to a parent text that, in its Hebrew consonants, was identical to that behind the MT. An example is in Proverbs 23:7, where the MT has "as he thinks *[šā'ar]* in his soul," and the LXX has "like a hair *[śē'ār]* in the throat," but both readings are based in the same *Vorlage,* with the consonant שׂ *(śin or šin)* in שער being unpointed. Thus, not every variant reading is theologically motivated, but many of the tendencies of the LXX—a moralizing and theologizing tone, avoidance of potentially offensive language, a fixation on the "good versus evil" antithesis—must be reckoned as examples of the religious outlook of the translator.

1.2. The Targum of Proverbs. The Aramaic *Targumim, with their free and expansive paraphrases of biblical texts, also give us insight into early Jewish interpretation. The date of the Targum of Proverbs is uncertain; it may be from as early as the second century AD or as late as the ninth century AD. It strongly resembles the Syriac Peshitta, so that many scholars believe that it is actually based on the Syriac rather than the Hebrew, although others believe this to be prima facie unlikely and argue that the Syriac is dependent on the Targum. Be that as it may, the Targum of Proverbs is noteworthy for lacking the kind of expansive, haggadic paraphrase that one often sees in the Targumim. It may be that Proverbs, by nature a plain and practical book, did not attract the kind of exegetical extravagance seen elsewhere in the Targumim.

The Targum does have a few of the same traits as the LXX. For example, it avoids the explicit sexuality of Proverbs 5:19, rendering it as, "a hind of love and a gazelle of grace. *Learn good conduct* at all times and in love of her *you will grow ever stronger*" (emphasis original in Healy translation, indicating where the Targum is different from the MT). Also, the Targum recasts the theological language of Proverbs 29:18, rendering it as "*When the evil are many* the people are *broken*, but happy is he who keeps the law" (emphasis original in Healy). In the main, however, the Targum is a fairly straightforward rendering of Proverbs; its interpretations are often identical to what one sees in the MT.

2. Early and Medieval Jewish and Christian Interpretation.

2.1. Premodern Rabbinic Interpretation. Midrash Mishle (Midrash on Proverbs) is an invaluable source of lore and teaching on Proverbs in the rabbinic tradition. Although compiled in about the ninth or tenth century AD by an unknown redactor at an unknown location, it contains rabbinical teachings based in Proverbs from much earlier, using both Palestinian and Babylonian rabbinic sources and citing the Mishnah, Tosefta, Mekilta, Babylonian Talmud and Genesis Rabbah, among others. It almost invariably uses texts from Proverbs as launching pads for extended discussions in rabbinical doctrines and controversies of its time; it rarely expounds on the contextual or literal meaning of a verse.

A marvelous example of such exposition is in the comments on Proverbs 10:3, "The LORD does not let the righteous go hungry, but the desire of the wicked he thwarts." This leads into rabbinic comments on the basis of divine judgment in the last day, and in particular to assertions that one finds life and vindication through the study of Torah. This in turn leads to an explication, by means of a fictitious drama of divine judgment, of the entire rabbinic program of righteousness through study. Interrogating a "disciple of the sages," God first asks if he had meditated on Torah. If the answer is affirmative, God then examines him to see if he knows the Mishnah. If he knows that, he must show that he has recited the Midrash on Leviticus, and then he is examined on his knowledge of the midrashim on all of the Pentateuch. If he accomplishes that, he must demonstrate that he has recited haggadah and, passing that, demonstrate knowledge of the Talmud. Finally, he must show that he had engaged in the mystical meditation on the nature of God's chariot (Ezek 1).

Torah has all but supplanted the role of Wisdom in *Midrash Mishle*. In its exposition of Proverbs 8, it regularly in effect reads "Torah" for Wisdom. Thus, discussing Proverbs 8:30, it simply comments, "At first Torah was in heaven." At Proverbs 22:1, "A good name is preferable to great riches, and favor is better than silver or gold," it comments that a person who has silver and gold without Torah has nothing, and that the "favor" that excels riches in value is surely Torah. Training a child in the proper way to go (Prov 22:6) likewise refers to teaching Torah.

At times *Midrash Mishle* relates Proverbs to biblical or legendary stories. Proverbs 27:17 ("Iron sharpens iron, and one man sharpens another") is taken to refer to the conflict between Moses and Pharaoh. But "Good news puts fat on the bones" (Prov 15:30) leads into a lengthy anecdote on how Rabbi Johanan ben Zakkai warned the Jews that their rebellion against Rome (in the war of AD 66-70) would bring down the temple. He then by trickery escaped Jerusalem and made his way to the camp of Vespasian, to whom he predicted that Nero would die and Vespasian would replace him as emperor. When the report of his election to the imperial throne arrived, Vespasian was perplexed that he could not put on his boot, but Rabbi Johanan was able to explain that the good news had put fat on his bones.

Other rabbinical texts handle Proverbs in much the same way as does *Midrash Mishle*. The *Leviticus Rabbah*, for example, in establishing the point that Israel alone has true prophets, cites Proverbs 15:29 ("The LORD is far from the wicked, but he will hear the prayer of the righteous"), explaining that the "wicked" are the prophets of the nations and the "righteous" are the prophets of Israel.

It should not be supposed, however, that all early Jewish interpretation of Proverbs was midrashic. Jewish scholars also produced commentaries that gave a more literal and contextually based interpretation of the biblical texts (the *peshat*, "plain sense" commentaries). Commentaries on Proverbs in this mode include those by

Shlomo ben Isaac (d. 1105), Moses Kimhi (d. c. 1190) and Levi ben Gershom (Gersonides [d. 1344]). Even *Midrash Mishle* can exegete the text in a fairly literal manner, as at Proverbs 26:18-22, where it explains that these verses refer to slander and gossip.

2.2. Proverbs in the New Testament. Two NT allusions to Proverbs reflect a general biblical literacy more than any specific manner of interpreting the text. When both Jesus in Matthew 16:27 and Paul in Romans 2:6 apparently cite part of Proverbs 24:12 ("Will not [God] repay a man according to his work?"), it is doubtful that either was reflecting on the context of these words in Proverbs. Rather, the language of Proverbs has influenced the rhetoric of Jesus and Paul. That is, both speak in the idiom of the OT. We should note that similar language also appears in Psalm 62:12.

Usually, the NT interprets a text from Proverbs quite literally and applies it in a manner in keeping with its original usage. A good example is the citation of Proverbs 3:11-12 in Hebrews 12:5-6 (see also the citations of Prov 3:34 in 1 Pet 5:5; Prov 10:12 in 1 Pet 4:8; Prov 11:31 in 1 Pet 4:18). The citation of Proverbs 25:21-22 in Romans 12:20 could be added to this list, although admittedly the intended meaning of the Proverbs text is difficult. 2 Peter 2:22 cites Proverbs 26:11 ("A dog returns to its vomit") in its original sense but adds to that a citation from the Aramaic wisdom text Ahikar 7.27 to the effect that a pig, after a bath, wallows in mire. In short, the NT generally cites aphorisms in Proverbs in accordance with their most obvious moral meanings.

A much more controversial question is whether Paul in 1 Corinthians 1:24, where he calls Christ the "wisdom of God," is alluding to Proverbs 8. That is, does Paul imply that *Woman Wisdom is in fact the Logos? The universal conclusion of the patristic authors is that he does (see 2.3 below). There is good reason for believing, however, that this is not the case.

The "wisdom of God" in 1 Corinthians 1:17-31 is paradoxical. It is a wisdom that appears to be *folly in that it asserts that God redeemed humanity via a condemned and crucified criminal. In this, it is incomprehensible to the wisdom-seeking Greeks, just as it is offensive to the Jews who look for a Messiah coming in power. The divine folly of 1 Corinthians 1 is focused on the cross and calls upon people to seek grace. By contrast, there is no paradoxical divine folly in Woman Wisdom of Proverbs 8. Her appeals are based upon her relationship to creation, suggesting that prudence and moral rectitude are in harmony with the order that is built into the world (*see* Creation Theology). Such harmony is the polar opposite of the paradoxical tension— the divine wisdom as a stumbling block—found in Paul's thought. Woman Wisdom calls upon her hearers to sound judgment and rational behavior rather than to a counterintuitive work of grace. In short, apart from the word *wisdom*, it is difficult to see any connection between Proverbs 8 and 1 Corinthians 1. The citations listed above, moreover, suggest that the NT writers read Proverbs in a straightforward manner for practical exhortation.

2.3. Patristic and Medieval Christian Interpretation: Christ the Wisdom of God. Samples of post-NT Christian reflections on Proverbs can be given (see Wright), but early and medieval Christian exegetes actually gave relatively little attention to Proverbs. Their basic understanding of the nature of the Solomonic books was from Origen via Jerome: Proverbs is wisdom for beginners; *Ecclesiastes is for the more proficient and is meant to keep them from the vanity of the world; *Song of Songs is a mystical introduction to the love of God for the advanced reader. Thus, interpreters gave far more attention to Song of Songs than to Proverbs.

In addition, early Christian interpretation of the OT was driven first by the conviction that it testified to Christ and second by the conviction that the saving truths of the gospel could be found everywhere in its pages. The first major hermeneutical conflict that Christianity faced was with the Jews, who contended that Jesus Christ was not to be found in their Scriptures. It is not surprising, therefore, that early Christian reading of Proverbs quickly gravitated to its portrayal of Wisdom (especially in Prov 8). Citations of Proverbs 8 are found in the writings of the great theologians of the early church (such as Irenaeus, Clement of Alexandria, Origen, Augustine), as well as in the lesser lights of early Christian scholarship. Their unanimous viewpoint, following the early apologists Justin Martyr and Athenagoras (both second century AD), was that the Logos was the Wisdom of Proverbs 8. The identification of Christ with Woman Wisdom, however, carried with it a grave problem: Wisdom herself declares that the Lord created her at the beginning of his work (Prov 8:22). This gave an enormous opening to the heretic Arius (c. AD 256-336), who readily conceded that Christ could be identified as the Wisdom of Proverbs, and from that argued that only God the Father was truly and innately eternal.

Athanasius (AD 293-373) responded to Arius with *Contra Arianos,* which contains perhaps the most important piece of patristic exegesis of a text from Proverbs. According to C. Kannengiesser, Athanasius responded by pointing out that Proverbs 8:22 is "proverbial" in nature; that is, it is set within a literary figure and cannot be applied directly to Christ without first working through its figurative elements. Furthermore, Athanasius asserted that with this, as with any text, one must inquire into its "time" *(kairos),* "person" *(prosōpon)* and "point" *(pragma).* The point of Proverbs 8:22, he claimed, is that Wisdom makes a self-disclosure that can be identified only with the person of Christ and with the time of the incarnation. And it is at the incarnation, not as the eternal Word, that Wisdom says, "You created me."

Another text of great significance to early Christian interpreters was Proverbs 22:20-21, which in the LXX begins, "And you, write these things for yourself in a threefold manner." Origen took this to refer to the threefold meaning behind each text of Scripture (the literal, moral and spiritual, analogous to the human body, soul and spirit). Jerome transmitted this hermeneutical canon to the Western church, and it became a pillar supporting the medieval program of allegorical exegesis.

Elsewhere, just as the rabbis related Proverbs to traditional rabbinical teaching on Torah, the church fathers frequently related texts from Proverbs to the incarnation or to other NT teachings. In Proverbs 9:2-5, where Wisdom slaughters her beasts and sets her table with bread and wine, Hippolytus in his fragments on Proverbs sees the Eucharist (so also Cyprian *Letter* 63.5; Bede *Commentary on Proverbs* 1.9.5). John Cassian (*Conference* 24.24.6) relates Proverbs 15:19 ("The way of a sluggard is like a hedge of thorns, but the path of the upright is a built-up highway") to our pilgrimage to the heavenly Jerusalem. Evagrius of Pontus (*Scholia on Proverbs* 304.25.10) used Proverbs 25:8-10, an exhortation against taking one's neighbors to court without first trying to settle a matter quietly, as an appropriate text for discussing our freedom and friendship with God in Christ.

A good example of this tendency is in Bede's comments on Proverbs 22:29, which in context teaches that skillful and diligent workers will be duly recognized (the Vulgate version can be rendered, "Have you seen a man quick in his work? He will stand in the presence of kings; he will not be before lowly men"). Bede, however, takes the proverb to refer to the final judgment and uses it to allude to heretical teachings: "Whomever you see quick in his work, that is, both vigorous and anxious in a good work which is his to do, understand that in the day of the last judgment, that one will be standing in the presence of the Apostles, who will sit with Christ to judge the world. For clearly that one will have kept their commands and will not be counted among the company of lowly teachers—whose errors he avoided—that is to be set on the left hand of the judge" (*Commentary on Proverbs* 2.22.29).

It would be wrong, however, to suppose that the early and medieval expositors always jumped from the text of Proverbs to distinctively Christian doctrine. Frequently their comments directly expound on the practicalities of virtuous living described in the text. Ambrose (*Duties of the Clergy* 1.3.10-11) uses Proverbs 4:23 as a basis for an exhortation to keep close watch over one's thoughts and speech. Augustine, in *Sermon* 36, uses Proverbs 13:7 for a discourse on wealth and on the dangerous pride that it engenders. A favorite passage for early and medieval Christians was Proverbs 31:10-31, the portrait of the valiant woman. This could be allegorized as a portrait of the church maintaining pure doctrine, but it could also be read more literally as a song in praise of flesh-and-blood women (as did Gregory of Nazianzus in praising his parents and his sister). Augustine, in drawing out distinctively Christian or "spiritual" lessons from this text, never lost sight of the fact that it was first concerned with a virtuous woman.

3. English Protestant Interpretation: Jonathan Edwards.

By its very nature, Proverbs is not a focal point for theological controversy. Most of its teachings are practical, and notwithstanding the difficulty of translating a number of individual proverbs, the essential meaning of any specific discourse or proverb is self-evident. Thus, it was not a bone of contention in the theological battles of Christians and Jews (there are exceptions to this

rule: Peter the Chanter of Paris, writing in the late twelfth century, indicates that Jews and Christians wrestled over Prov 30:4, a text that a Christian naturally would read in a trinitarian manner ["What is his name, and what is the name of his son, if you know?"]). As we have seen, the figure of Wisdom was heavily employed in Jewish and Christian theological rumination, and any tradition could take an individual proverb and apply it to that tradition's ideals, albeit often in an arbitrary manner. Despite all this, the bulk of Proverbs was simply too plain and straightforward for it to attract a great deal of this kind of theological attention.

But it is this very quality of plainness and practicality about righteousness that made Proverbs especially attractive to one Christian tradition. Protestant Reformed theology, especially that of the English variety, looked upon Proverbs as a treasure. Both Matthew Poole (1624-1679) and Matthew Henry (1662-1714) extolled Proverbs as a practical guide to devout and upright living, and both gave it considerable attention. The most expansive meditation on Proverbs in this tradition is the massive commentary by Charles Bridges (1794-1869). But perhaps the greatest theologian to read Proverbs in this manner was Jonathan Edwards (1703-1758).

At the very beginning of his career, in 1722, Edwards resolved that "A righteous man who can find?" (Prov 20:6) would be fulfilled in himself. Edwards believed that *Solomon had written Proverbs for young men who sought to bring all the habits of mind and body into subjection. As S. J. Stein demonstrates, throughout his life Edwards used it as a basis for self-examination and meditation. He took "Be not wise in thine own eyes" (Prov 3:7) as a prohibition of pride about one's own holiness, judgment or virtue. He preached from Proverbs, believing, with Matthew Henry, that the counsels of Wisdom were a counteragent to the counsels of *Satan.

But Stein points out that Edwards did not merely engage in pious moralizing. Edwards's theory of metaphor and imagination played an important role in his analysis of Proverbs. Reflecting on Proverbs 25:11 ("A word fitly spoken is like apples of gold in pictures of silver"), Edwards stated, "The words are silver and the sense and fruit is gold." That is, the core teachings—the actual meaning—of the text, like apples of gold, obviously have great value. But the very words—the language and metaphor by which the meaning is conveyed—are also to be prized. These are the "pictures of silver." In doing its work of edification, the text addresses intellect as well as imagination both through that which is signified (the meaning of the text) and its signifier (the poetics of the text). Thus the text ultimately leads us to Christ, who is both the true wisdom and the beauty of holiness. The poetics are not merely ornamentation, making the truth somewhat more pleasing, but rather are the very means into the truth. Therefore, when Edwards commented on Proverbs, he was not content merely to leap to the essential meaning of the text; he also wrestled with the implications of its form and metaphor. For example, Edwards noted how often Proverbs described the qualities of the righteous and the wicked under metaphors of physical anatomy (their eyes, hands, feet and so forth, as in Prov 10:10; 15:30; 23:26; 25:17), and he followed suit, using similar language in his sermons.

As Edwards matured, he came more and more to recognize that his youthful attempts to discipline himself into godliness were doomed to fail, and so also came to recognize the need for grace. Thus, for him, the wisdom of Proverbs was not merely instruction in righteousness but was ultimately Christ himself, who draws us into holiness by his grace and beauty. We should note in passing, however, that the Puritan divines were not the only theologians who regarded biblical wisdom as a guide to sanctification; this was a favorite theme of the Franciscan Bonaventure (1221-1274) also.

4. Proverbs in Modern Study.

4.1. The Abandonment of the Solomonic Authorship of Proverbs in the Nineteenth Century. At the beginning of the nineteenth century Proverbs was widely regarded as a very ancient work and possibly of Solomonic origin. By the end of the century most scholars had abandoned that view. The story of how scholarly opinions were transformed has been documented by R. Smend.

In 1835 W. Vatke advocated a fifth-century BC date for Proverbs, primarily on the grounds that the ethical and moral spirit of the book was incompatible with an earlier date. By 1873 even the relatively conservative F. Delitzsch would dismiss the notion of Solomonic authorship as implausible. Like many of his contemporaries and much of subsequent scholarship, he believed

that different parts of Proverbs had come from different eras. Most scholars believed that the sentence proverbs of Proverbs 10:1—22:16 were for the most part older, and conversely they believed that the wisdom discourses of Proverbs 1—9 were later, although there were some exceptions (*see* Discourse in Proverbs). E Bertheau, writing in 1883, listed three reasons for rejecting a preexilic date for the material of Proverbs: (1) there was no reference to Proverbs in the prophetic books; (2) Proverbs implies that Yahwism has triumphed over paganism in Israel; (3) Proverbs appears to be similar to *Sirach. When T. K. Cheyne addressed the issue in 1893, the consensus was that the present book of Proverbs is a postexilic production. C. Toy, writing for the International Critical Commentary series in 1899, came to similar conclusions.

As scholars entered the twentieth century fairly confident that Proverbs was postexilic, the question of the book's date was no longer the center of attention (although interest in that issue has never disappeared). And although some of the questions raised in the twentieth century were already raised in the nineteenth, such as the matter of whether there were wisdom "schools" in ancient Israel, these were much more thoroughly examined in the twentieth century. In addition, the flood of ancient Egyptian and Mesopotamian wisdom texts made available in the twentieth century provoked great interest in setting Israelite wisdom in its context. The story of twentieth-century investigations into Proverbs has been documented by R. N. Whybray (1995).

4.2. The Roots of Israelite Wisdom and of Proverbs.

4.2.1. The Sitz im Leben *of Proverbial Wisdom.* In seeking the *Sitz im Leben* of Proverbs, scholars have debated whether the teachings of the book are derived primarily from Israelite folk sayings or from formal schools. On the one side is the view that Proverbs primarily represents an institutional endeavor, created by formal schools of "wisdom" that were centrally located, perhaps royally sponsored, and that drew heavily upon international wisdom and perhaps also upon traditional Jewish religious instruction, such as the Torah. On the other side is the view that proverbs by nature are folk sayings, and that they were passed down as tribal wisdom and family exhortation until they were at last codified in an editorial process that ended in the postexilic era. There is, of course, a wide variety of distinctive positions within the spectrum of these two models.

G. von Rad is a champion of the view that Israelite wisdom was heavily dependent upon the international wisdom of Egypt and Mesopotamia. For him, the Israelite Wisdom literature was primarily a work of formal schools that, beginning in the united monarchy, encountered and formally studied the older, international wisdom. Frequent reference to kings in Proverbs (such as at Prov 25:2) suggests a royal sponsorship of wisdom schools. A number of influential scholars substantially agree with this, but others differ, arguing that most of Proverbs seems derived from ordinary life rather than from the court, and that even in Egypt wisdom literature is not always from high officials. Whybray (1974) argues that in the OT *wise* and *wisdom* have no particular association with the royal court, and that there is little reason to assume that there was a school of the wise at the center of power.

A related question was whether schools as formal institutions of learning for the young existed in Israel (*see* Sages, Schools, Education). Analogies from Egypt and Mesopotamia suggest that Israel, like those cultures, must have developed formal teaching institutions for families above the status of the yeoman peasants. Some scholars, such as B. Lang (1979) and A. Lemaire, claim that the existence of such schools is demonstrable archaeologically due to the discovery of abecedaries and other such inscriptions. Others, however, argue that the evidence is in fact very slim, noting the complete lack of reference to any such schools in the OT itself.

On the other side of this issue are scholars who argue that Israelite wisdom was a native development from family and tribal teachings. In particular, a number of scholars, following O. Eissfeldt, argue that the shorter, pithy sayings of Proverbs 10—29 are similar to folk proverbs found in every culture. H. W. Wolff and E. Gerstenberger argue independently for the existence of a *Sippenweisheit*, or "folk wisdom," behind biblical wisdom. Many other scholars, however, are unconvinced. There is, at present, little consensus on this issue beyond awareness that the background of Israelite wisdom is complex and probably not explicable on the basis of a single source.

4.2.2. Secular Wisdom and Yahwistic Wisdom Redactors. Another, related issue concerns whether Proverbs contains an older layer of "secular" wisdom upon which a later layer of Yahwistic piety has been superimposed. The essential idea is that Proverbs contains evidence of an older wisdom that was concerned primarily with prudent behavior, much like the common aphorisms of many cultures, but that this material, in a Yahwistic redaction, was supplemented with sayings that were explicitly religious and focused on Yahweh. No one exploited this concept so fully as did W. McKane, who argues that there are in fact three layers or categories of material in the sentence literature of Proverbs 10—29. "Class A" is the older wisdom and teaches the individual how to have a successful and harmonious life. Examples from Proverbs 13 include Proverbs 13:1, 3, 4, 7, 8, 10, 11, 12, 13, 14, 15, 16, 18, 19a, 20, 24. "Class B" is like Class A in that it is also secular, but it is primarily concerned with the well-being of the community and points out types of antisocial behavior that damage the community. Examples from Proverbs 13 include Proverbs 13:2, 5, 17, 19b. "Class C" proverbs are a later reworking of Class A proverbs to give them a theological message and are identified by the presence of "God language." Examples from Proverbs 13 include Proverbs 13:6, 9, 21, 22, and 25.

Scholars have not been persuaded by McKane's schema, and in general the consensus is that there was no Yahwistic edition of Proverbs. It is obvious to many interpreters that some of the proverbs are distinctive for explicitly naming Yahweh, but it is not clear that this indicates that a separate redaction took place. The explicit mention or nonmention of Yahweh is in fact just one of the variables that one can see in Proverbs (other variables being, for example, the mention or nonmention of the king, different types of *parallelism, and the presence or absence of various kinds of metaphor). Reviewers point out also that a distinction between "secular" and "religious" teachings in the manner described above is anachronistic for early Israel and the ancient Near East.

4.2.3. Egyptian and Mesopotamian Connections. The discovery of wisdom texts from Egypt and the ancient Near East in the late nineteenth and early twentieth centuries provoked an enormous wave of research into the background of biblical wisdom literature. Egyptian wisdom material predating its biblical counterparts—in some cases by more than a millennium—included from the Old Kingdom *The Maxims of Ptah-hotep;* from the First Intermediate Period *The Teaching for Merikare;* from the Middle Kingdom *The Teaching of King Amenemhet I for His Son Senwosret; The Admonitions of Ipuwer; The Eloquent Peasant; The Man Who Was Weary of Life;* and from the New Kingdom *The Instructions of Any; The Instruction of Amenemope.* In addition, Sumerian and Akkadian proverbs from Mesopotamia were discovered, as well as the Akkadian *Counsels of Wisdom.* A later wisdom text of significance is the *Story of Ahikar,* known from an Aramaic text dating to about 500 BC.

Henceforth, Israelite wisdom could never be studied in isolation from its international context, and it became *de rigueur* for every modern commentary on Proverbs to contain a discussion of ancient Near Eastern wisdom. The Egyptian *Instruction of Amenemope* provoked an enormous amount of discussion because of its similarity to Proverbs 22:17—24:22. Parallel to the thirty chapters of Amenemope, the enigmatic Hebrew of Proverbs 22:20a is widely emended to read, "Have I not written thirty sayings for you" (NIV), and the text of Proverbs 22:17—24:22 fairly easily divides into an introduction and thirty teachings. Although there are many differences between the two works, analogous teachings are undeniable (such as the warnings about how to behave when dining with a high official in Prov 23:1-3 and in Amenemope chap. 23). Scholars argue over how these similarities might be explained, suggesting either that one of the two texts influenced the other, or that both looked back to an earlier source, or that they had no direct connection but both drew on common wisdom ideas. No clear consensus exists beyond the conclusion that Amenemope is from the New Kingdom and so predates Proverbs.

Ancient Near Eastern wisdom also provided grounds for reopening the question of the date of the composition of Proverbs. K. A. Kitchen (1977) examines all the extant literature and on formal grounds concludes that there is little reason to date Proverbs late, contrary to what nineteenth-century scholars had concluded. In particular, Kitchen demonstrates that there is no evidence that the complex "discourse" wisdom of Proverbs 1—9 constitutes a later development, with the "sentence" wisdom being earlier. The assertion that Proverbs could not have

come from the early first millennium is undermined by the ancient parallels. In particular, both D. Garrett and B. Waltke argue that the Egyptian and Mesopotamian wisdom indicates an early date for the composition of Proverbs (*see* Proverbs 2: Ancient Near Eastern Background).

4.2.4. The Origin and Significance of the Proverbial Bicolon. Examining individual proverbs, scholars wondered if they saw evidence for the historical development of the formal proverbial bicolon. O. Eissfeldt, W. O. E. Oesterley and J. Hempel argued that in many cases the *sages took an original one-line folk saying and added to it a second line in antithetical or synonymous *parallelism. But B. Gemser pointed out that the demotic wisdom literature, appearing as the latest of the Egyptian wisdom texts, uses one-line sentences with no parallelism, and he effectively undercut the evolutionary theory. Although some more recent scholars continue to believe that traces of folk wisdom may be evident in Proverbs, few think that these are identifiable or that a history of the development of the bicolon can be traced.

Scholars also noticed that some bicola were indicative statements (the *Aussagewort,* such as Prov 17:18: "A man without sense shakes hands and puts up security for his neighbor") and others were admonitions (the *Mahnwort,* such as Prov 24:28: "Do not testify against your neighbor for no good reason, or use your lips to deceive"). Hempel, noting that the *Mahnwort* was more common in the later chapters of Proverbs, argued that this represents a later stage in evolution of the proverb form. Subsequent scholars debated the issue, some asserting that one could not demonstrate chronological development using this formal device, and others simply asserting that the distinction between *Aussagewort* and *Mahnwort* was overdrawn and of little significance.

4.3. The Personification of Wisdom. Scholars have focused a great deal of attention on the relationship between Wisdom personified as a woman (Prov 1:20-33; 8) and Maat, the Egyptian goddess of justice and order. Although few today would deny that the Egyptian notion of *maat* could have had any influence on Israelite thinking, equally few would assert that Maat is either the counterpart to or the origin of Proverbs' Woman Wisdom. The differences between the two are at least as significant as the similarities. Unlike Woman Wisdom, Maat in the Egyptian texts does not make exhortations recommending herself to young men. Maat is a goddess, but Woman Wisdom is a *personification. The Egyptian word for "wisdom" is not personified in the manner that the Hebrew word is. Lang (1986) argues that Proverbs 8 was originally a song of self-praise sung by an Israelite goddess that was redacted and demythologized to give it its current form.

4.4. The Editorial Grouping of Proverbs. Scholars have debated whether there is any order to the sentence aphorisms of Proverbs 10—29. Many scholars treat the individual sayings as being, in effect, without context or structural order. R. N. Whybray (1979) suggests that "Yahweh sayings" have been inserted among the proverbs to provide some order or to make comments on proverbs in the immediate context. For example, he argues that Proverbs 15:16 reinterprets Proverbs 15:17. O. Plöger observes that sometimes individual proverbs are set together in pairs or in small groups. A. Meinhold groups the proverbs into small collections or paragraphs. D. Garrett similarly argues that proverbs are set in groups identified through parallel structuring, catchwords or common themes and metaphors.

4.5. Repetition in Proverbs and Its Significance. On the basis of a linguistic analysis of the text, J. Grintz (1968; 1993) argues that the major collections in Proverbs 1:1—24:34 were created in the age of Solomon (arguing, e.g., that there are clear linguistic ties between Prov 1—9 and Prov 22:17—24:22). He contends that the collections of Proverbs 25:1—31:31 were added in the reign of Hezekiah, in keeping with the biblical claims. Thus, he maintains that the editorial history of Proverbs is reflected in the order of the book in the MT. D. C. Snell, however, on the basis of an analysis of repetition within Proverbs, takes issue with Grintz's claim that Proverbs 1—9 is closely related to Proverbs 22:17—24:22. He argues that the redaction of the book had a more complex history, beginning with Proverbs 25—29 in the reign of Hezekiah and with other collections added thereafter in three subsequent stages. Snell has also given subsequent scholars a valuable database of repetition in Proverbs to explore.

4.6. The Virtuous Woman of Proverbs 31:10-31. The poem of the virtuous woman at the end of Proverbs has attracted a good deal of attention. A number of scholars have made proposals regarding the structure of the poem. Some take its alphabetic *acrostic layout to be a mnemonic device (e.g., Toy), but others have found that explanation insufficient and look for other explanations. W. G. E. Watson argues that the acrostic is meant to persuade the reader that the poem has exhaustively treated its subject. Interpreters are divided as to what structure the poem may have beyond its obvious acrostic pattern. Garrett suggests that the poem has a chiastic structure (see Chiasm), with Proverbs 31:23 at its center and pivot, implying that the poem is a last word of advice to the young man, telling him that this is the kind of woman he ought to seek for a wife.

Many scholars naturally interpret this passage as being concerned primarily with the ideal of the wife, mother and homemaker. M. B. Crook argues that this poem was the memorandum of a lesson on home economics for aristocratic young women in a formal school setting. Others interpreters, such as T. McCreesh, maintain that the woman of Proverbs 31 is neither a real nor even an ideal wife, but that the subject of this text is Woman Wisdom, analogous to what we see in Proverbs 1—9. C. Camp argues that by basing the abstraction of wisdom in the actual wise women of Israel, Proverbs 1—9 and 31 "recontextualizes" wisdom under the theological metaphor of the prudent woman. A. Wolters, on the other hand, suggests that Proverbs 31:27 contains in the Hebrew word ṣôpiyyâ ("[she is] watching") a deliberate *wordplay on sophia, the Greek word for "wisdom."

4.7. The Theology of Proverbs. Whybray (1995) has laid out ten broad areas of consensus about the theology of Proverbs in modern scholarship.

1. It does not focus on Israel.
2. It has some historical ties to ancient Near Eastern wisdom literature.
3. It focuses on practical ethics for the individual.
4. It is generally optimistic in outlook, in contrast to Ecclesiastes.
5. It does not lay out a complete systematic theology.
6. It teaches that one's behavior determines whether one prospers or suffers.
7. At least some of its teachings are religiously motivated.
8. It is thoroughly monotheistic.
9. Gaining "wisdom" is the key to a good life.
10. Wisdom is the gift of God.

Whybray also lays out ten disputed areas, which we can best describe as ten questions.

1. Does Proverbs have a unified message?
2. Is Proverbs an alien corpus within the OT, having more in common with international wisdom than with Israel's covenant theology? H. D. Preuss asserts that in Proverbs Yahweh is not so much the God of the law, of Israel's cult, and of the Genesis creation narrative; he is rather the deity who upholds the moral world order of wisdom.
3. Is Proverbs essentially practical, or does it have a theology? J. C. Rylaarsdam, for example, argues that it is a religious work, and he seeks to show that Wisdom is parallel to the Old Testament concept of the divine Spirit.
4. Is Proverbs more anthropocentric than theocentric? W. Zimmerli argues that the anthropocentric nature of Proverbs is evident in how it admonishes the reader but does not base its legitimacy in an appeal to divine authority.
5. According to Proverbs, is *suffering imposed by God on evildoers, or is suffering simply the natural outcome of evil behavior? In divine *retribution the evildoer suffers because God directly punishes that person for evil acts, but in an "act-consequence" theory of retribution, each evil action carries within it its own reprisal, so that suffering, personal ruin, disgrace and death are intrinsic to evil behavior. God, in effect, does not need to intervene with punishment because the evildoer brings down destruction on his or her own head. An act-consequence interpretation of Proverbs sets it apart from a book such as Deuteronomy, in which retribution is always a direct judgment from God.
6. In contrast to Torah, should Proverbs be regarded as sage advice instead of authoritative doctrine? Zimmerli's anthropocentric understanding of Proverbs suggests that it is more properly advice than it is revelation.
7. Is Proverbs rooted in a theology of creation? This is highly disputed, with some scholars asserting that the orderliness of creation is behind the moral world order espoused in Proverbs, and others saying that there is virtually no reflection on creation in Proverbs.
8. Does Proverbs teach that there is a pervasive ordering of the world (analogous to Egyptian *maat*)? R. E. Murphy argues that although there are impressive parallels between goddess Maat and Woman Wisdom in Proverbs 1—9, claiming to see a world order in Proverbs 10—15 is a transposing of Egyptian ideals upon Proverbs.
9. Has Yahwistic theology been imposed by a later redactor upon proverbs that originally were either secular or more generically religious? Against McKane, who argues that the earliest layer of Proverbs is secular, M. Fox maintains that the teachings of Proverbs are essentially a religious system, but that an explicitly Yahwistic book of Proverbs is a second stage of development. Even at this later stage, Fox says, the harmonization is somewhat superficial in that Israel's history and covenants are not brought into wisdom teaching until Sirach.
10. How is Woman Wisdom to be interpreted? That is, what is she? Is she a personified attribute of God (divine wisdom)? Against this, von Rad distinctively argues that Wisdom is an attribute not of God but rather of creation. Wisdom is thus present in the world and available to people at large. But, as we have seen, many other interpretations of Woman Wisdom have been offered.

In general, the interpretation of Proverbs has moved toward both greater unity and greater fracturing. Against the earlier sectarian interpretations of the text (whether distinctively Jewish or Christian), most today see it as a book of practical virtue in a monotheistic framework. On the other hand, critical assessments of the origins of its formal patterns of discourse and aphorism, of its relationship to other ancient Near Eastern wisdom, and of the meaning of its portrayal of Woman Wisdom have led to a wide diversity of opinions and to no consensus.

See also FEMINIST INTERPRETATION; PROVERBS 1: BOOK OF; PROVERBS 2: ANCIENT NEAR EASTERN BACKGROUND; SOCIAL-SCIENTIFIC APPROACHES.

BIBLIOGRAPHY. **Bede,** *In Tobiam; In Proverbia;*

In Cantica Canticorum; In Habacuc, ed. D. Hurst (CCSL 119; Turnhout: Brepols, 1983); **C. Camp**, *Wisdom and the Feminine in the Book of Proverbs* (Decatur: Almond Press, 1985); **J. E. Cook,** *The Septuagint of Proverbs: Jewish and/or Hellenistic Proverbs? Concerning the Hellenistic Colouring of LXX Proverbs* (VTSup 69; Leiden: E. J. Brill, 1997); **M. B. Crook**, "The Marriageable Maiden of Prov. 31:10-31," *JNES* 13 (1954) 137-40; **O. Eissfeldt**, *Der Maschal im Alten Testament: eine wortgeschichtliche Untersuchung nebst einer literargeschichtlichen Untersuchung der* משל *genannten Gattungen "Volkssprichwort" und "Spottlied"* (BZAW 24; Giessen: A. Töpelmann, 1913); **M. V. Fox,** "Aspects of the Religion of the Book of Proverbs," *HUCA* 39 (1968) 55-69; **D. Garrett,** *Proverbs, Ecclesiastes, and Song of Songs* (NAC; Nashville: Broadman, 1993); **B. Gemser**, "The Instructions of 'Onchsheshonqy and Biblical Wisdom Literature," in *Studies in Ancient Israelite Wisdom*, ed. James L. Crenshaw (New York: Ktav, 1976), 134-60; **P. J. Gentry**, "The Septuagint and the Text of the Old Testament," *BBR* 16 (2006) 193-218; **G. Gerleman,** *Studies in the Septuagint, III: Proverbs* (LUÅ 52/3; Lund: Gleerup, 1956); **E. Gerstenberger**, *Wesen und Herkunft des sogenannten apodiktischen Rechts im Alten Testament* (Bonn: Rheinischen Friedrich-Wilhelms-Universität, 1961); **J. M. Grintz,** "משלי שלמה" *Leshonenu* 33 (1968), 243-69; ET in D. Snell, *Twice-Told Proverbs and the Composition of the Book of Proverbs* (Winona Lake, IN: Eisenbrauns, 1993) 87-114; **J. F. Healy**, "The Targum of Proverbs," in *The Aramaic Bible*, vol. 15, ed. M. McNamara (Collegeville, MN: Liturgical Press, 1991); **J. Hempel**, "The Forms of Oral Tradition," in *Record and Revelation*, ed. H. Wheeler Robinson (Oxford: Clarendon Press, 1938), 28-44; **C. Kannengiesser**, "Lady Wisdom's Final Call: The Patristic Recovery of Proverbs 8," in *Nova doctrina vetusque: Essays on Early Christianity in Honor of Fredric W. Schlatter, S.J.*, ed. D. Kries and C. B. Tkacz (AmUS; New York: Peter Lang, 1999) 65-77; **K. A. Kitchen,** "Proverbs and Wisdom Books of the Ancient Near East," *TynBul* 28 (1977) 69-114; idem, "The Basic Literary Forms and Formulations of Ancients Instructional Writings in Egypt and Western Asia," in *Studien zu altägyptischen Lebenslehren*, ed. E. Hornung and O. Keel (OBO 28; Freiburg: Universitätsverlag; Göttingen: Vandenhoeck & Ruprecht, 1979) 235-82; **B. Lang**, "Schule und Unterricht im alten Israel," in *La Sagesse de l'Ancien Testament*, ed. M. Gilbert (BETL

51; Gembloux: Duculot, 1979), 186-201; idem, *Wisdom and the Book of Proverbs: An Israelite Goddess Redefined* (New York: Pilgrim Press, 1986); **A. Lemaire**, *Les écoles et la formation de la Bible dans l'ancien Israël* (Göttingen: Vandenhoeck & Ruprecht, 1981); **T. McCreesh**, "Wisdom as Wife: Proverbs 31:10-31," *RB* 92: 25-46; **W. McKane**, *Proverbs: A New Approach* (OTL; Philadelphia: Westminster, 1970); **A. Meinhold**, *Die Sprüche* (Zürich: Theologischer Verlag, 1991); **R. E. Murphy**, "Assumptions and Problems in Old Testament Wisdom Research," *CBQ* 29: 407-418; **W. O. E. Oesterley**, *The Book of Proverbs* (London: Methuen & co., 1929); O. Plöger, "Zur Auslegung der Sentenzensammlungen des Proverbienbuches," in *Probleme biblischer Theologie: Gerhard von Rad zum 70. Geburtstag*, ed. Hans Walter Wolff (München: C. Kaiser, 1971), 402-16; **H. D. Preuss**, *Old Testament Theology* (Louisville: Westminster John Knox Press, 1995); **J. C. Rylaarsdam**, *Revelation in Jewish Wisdom Literature* (Chicago: University of Chicago, 1946); **B. Smalley,** *Medieval Exegesis of Wisdom Literature*, ed. R. E. Murphy (SPRTS; Atlanta: Scholars Press, 1986); **R. Smend**, "The Interpretation of Wisdom in Nineteenth-Century Scholarship," in *Wisdom in Ancient Israel: Essays in Honour of J. A. Emerton*, ed. J. Day, R. P. Gordon and H. G. M. Williamson (Cambridge: Cambridge University Press, 1995) 257-68; **D. C. Snell,** *Twice-Told Proverbs and the Composition of the Book of Proverbs* (Winona Lake, IN: Eisenbrauns, 1993); **S. J. Stein**, "'Like Apples of Gold in Pictures of Silver': The Portrait of Wisdom in Jonathan Edwards's Commentary on the Book of Proverbs," *CH* 54 (1985) 324-37; **E. Tov**, *Textual Criticism of the Hebrew Bible* (Minneapolis: Fortress, 1992); **C. Toy**, *Proverbs* (ICC; Edinburgh: T & T Clark, 1899); **B. L. Visotzky,** *The Midrash on Proverbs* (New Haven: Yale University Press, 1992); **G. von Rad**, *Wisdom in Israel* (London: SCM Press, 1972); **B. Waltke**, *The Book of Proverbs: Chapters 1-15* (NICOT; Grand Rapids: Eerdmans, 2004); **W. G. E. Watson**, *Classical Hebrew Poetry: A Guide to its Techniques* (New York: T & T Clark, 2005); **R. N. Whybray**, *The Intellectual Tradition in the Old Testament* (BZAW 135; Berlin: de Gruyter, 1974); idem, "Yahweh-Sayings and their Contexts in Proverbs, 10,1–22,16," in *La Sagesse de l'Ancien Testament*, ed. M. Gilbert (BETL 51; Gembloux: Duculot, 1979), 153-65; idem, *The Book of Proverbs: A Survey of Modern Study* (HBI 1; Leiden: E. J. Brill, 1995); **H. W. Wolff**, *Amos' Geistige Heimat* (Neukirchen-Vluyn: Neukirchener

Verlag, 1964); **A. Wolters,** "*Ṣôpiyyâ* (Prov. 31:27) as Hymnic Participle and Play on *sophia*," *JBL* 104 (1985) 577-87; **J. R. Wright,** *Proverbs, Ecclesiastes, Song of Solomon* (ACCS 9; Downers Grove, IL: InterVarsity Press, 2005); **W. Zimmerli,** "Concerning the Structure of Old Testament Wisdom," in *Studies in Ancient Israelite Wisdom*, ed. James L. Crenshaw (New York: Ktav, 1976), 175-207.   D. Garrett

PROVIDENCE, DIVINE. *See* ESTHER 1: BOOK OF; RUTH 1: BOOK OF.

PSALMS, NONCANONICAL. *See* DEAD SEA SCROLLS.

PSALMS 1: BOOK OF

The psalms have remained a central fixture for corporate worship and private devotion over the centuries. Readers have been enamored by their poetic language, rich *imagery and stark honesty. In addition, the psalms provide readers with a glimpse into the cultic life of ancient Israel and offer a primer on OT theology. As with all poetic texts, interpretation comes with slow and thoughtful reflection. Form and meaning are mingled together carefully, requiring interpreters to be attentive to all matters simultaneously. In learning to appreciate the poetic and literary quality of the Psalter, contemporary readers will find its theological voice intensified and sharpened. And like generations before, they will find the Psalter to be God's Word to them even as they make it their word to God.

    1. Title and Titles
    2. Approaches to the Psalter
    3. Genre
    4. Hebrew Poetry
    5. The Psalter as a Book
    6. Theological Themes in the Psalter
    7. The Psalms and the New Testament

1. Title and Titles.

1.1. The Name of the Book. The words *psalm* and *psalter* are of Greek origin. The word *psalm* derives from the Greek *psalmos*, which refers to the playing of a stringed instrument. This term appears in the LXX as a translation for the Hebrew word *mizmôr*, which appears fifty-seven times in the psalm titles and refers to a song that is accompanied by *music. The association of *psalmos* with the biblical book appears relatively early. In Luke 24:44 Jesus speaks of the "Law of

Moses, the Prophets and the Psalms *[psalmoi]*" (NIV), although this probably does not indicate the full collection of psalms as it appears today. Later, in Codex Vaticanus (fourth century AD), the plural *psalmoi* appears as a title for the entire collection, and roughly a century later, in Codex Alexandrinus, the term *psalterion* ("Psalter") stands as the title to the biblical book.

Still, the common Hebrew designation for the collection of psalms is *tĕhillîm*, from the verbal root *hll*, meaning "praise." In rabbinic literature the book is frequently referred to as *Sefer Tehillim* ("Book of Praises"). Yet in the earliest Hebrew manuscripts (Codex Aleppo and Codex Leningradensis) no title appears. This is evident in Codex Aleppo. After the closing Masorah in the book of Chronicles, one line has been left vacant, followed by Psalm 1.

1.2. The Attribution to David. Despite the absence of his name in the "title" of the book, *David has long been associated with the book of Psalms and with Israelite psalmody in general. There is little doubt that the frequent appearance of David's name in the psalm titles contributed to such an association. In the Hebrew Psalter there are seventy-three psalms that include the phrase *lĕdāwīd* in the psalm title. Although the precise meaning of the preposition *lĕ* remains uncertain, ancient readers of the psalms apparently interpreted it as indicative of David's close association with Israelite psalmody. Within the group of seventy-three psalms that mention David in the title, thirteen have an extended note that not only mentions David but also attempts to locate the psalm within the life of David himself (Pss 3; 7; 18; 34; 51; 52; 54; 56; 57; 59; 60; 63; 142). As B. Childs (1971, 149-50) has suggested, such titles are best understood as midrashic or protomidrashic exegesis, in which later scribes attempted to connect the poetic language of the psalm with the narrative of David's life. For example, in Psalm 51 the psalmist prays, "Wash me thoroughly from my iniquity, and cleanse me from my sin. For I know my transgressions, and my sin is ever before me. Against you, you alone, have I sinned and done what is evil in your sight. . . . Purge me with hyssop, and I shall be clean; wash me, and I shall be whiter than snow" (Ps 51:2-4a, 7 NRSV).

In reflecting on the life of David, the scribes added this superscription to the psalm: "A psalm of David, when the prophet Nathan came to him after he had gone into Bathsheba." The superscription thus functions to meld poetry with prose, uniting the language of the psalm with the life of King David.

The association of David with psalmody is not without biblical warrant. The books of Samuel recount David's association with music, particularly his skillful playing on the lyre (1 Sam 16:14-23). In 2 Samuel 1 David appears as psalm composer, issuing forth a lament (*qînâ*) over the fallen Saul and Jonathan, and later, in 2 Samuel 6, he appears as cultic leader, ushering the ark of the covenant into Jerusalem.

Beginning in the postexilic period, however, the relationship between David and the cultic life of Israel received a vigorous reappraisal. In the rehearsing of Israel's history, the book of Chronicles moves beyond the claim that David was a king who was also musically skilled (as indicated in the book of Samuel) and instead presents David as the founder of Israel's cultic life—music, song and occasion. Indicative of the Chronicler's assessment of David as central to Israel's cultic life, the Chronicler records not only that David could make music and musical instruments but also that he made the instruments for four thousand Levites. The Chronicler also records that it was David who gave specific directives related to the appointed festivals.

Later Jewish writers adopted a similar perspective on the relationship between David and psalmody. In Sirach 47 the writer extols, "He sang praise with all his heart, and he loved his Maker. He placed singers before the altar, to make sweet melody with their voices. He gave beauty to the festivals, and arranged their times throughout the year" (Sir 47:8b-10a NRSV).

In the LXX version of the Psalter the compilers associated David with eighty-five psalms (as opposed to the seventy-three in the Hebrew text). Those who composed the *Dead Sea Scrolls may have been the most gratuitous in their comments. David is lauded for his musical productivity and is credited with having composed 3,600 psalms, 446 songs and four additional songs for the sick. Later, David's association with Israelite psalmody extended to the point where David not only was associated with the psalmody but also was credited as the author of the Psalter itself. In the Babylonian Talmud tractate *Baba Batra* it says, "Moses wrote his own book, the Balaam pericope, and Job. Joshua wrote his own book and eight verses of the Torah [Deut 34:5-12]. Samuel wrote his own book, the book of Judges, and Ruth. David wrote

the book of Psalms" (*B. Bat.* 14b).

Although the titles were not part of the original psalms and thus provide little evidence as to authorship, they do prove invaluable in understanding the history of interpretation. They suggest the continued attempt at locating the poetic voice of psalmody within the storied life of Israel.

1.3. Textual Transmission. The MT Psalter, based upon Codex Leningradensis, differs in varying fashion from two other significant textual traditions, the Greek Psalter and the Dead Sea Psalms scroll.

1.3.1. The Greek Psalter. Although translation of the Hebrew Psalter into Greek presumably began some time after 200 BC, the oldest textual witnesses to the Greek Psalter are Codex Vaticanus, Codex Sinaiticus and Codex Alexandrinus. Codex Vaticanus is a fourth-century AD manuscript that includes the entire Psalter except for Psalms 105:27—137:6. Codex Sinaiticus, also a fourth-century AD manuscript, contains the entire Psalter. Codex Alexandrinus is a fifth-century AD manuscript in which Psalms 49:20—79:11 are absent, but the remainder is intact.

The numbering of the psalms in the Greek Psalter deviates from that in the Hebrew tradition. Some psalms that stand separately in the Hebrew tradition (Pss 9—10; 114—115) appear as a single psalm in the Greek Psalter. The following chart shows the variations in numbering.

MT	LXX
1—8	1—8
9—10	9
11—113	10—112
114—115	113
116:1-9	114
116:10-19	115
117—146	116—145
147:1-11	146
147:12-20	147
148—150	148—150
(none)	151

Each of the Greek traditions mentioned above includes an additional psalm, Psalm 151. The superscription to the psalm reads, "This psalm is ascribed to David as his own composition (though it is outside the number), after he had fought in single combat with Goliath" (NRSV). In this psalm David's abilities on the lyre and the harp are extolled, as well as his victory over the Philistine warrior. The super-scription appears to acknowledge the 150 psalms as a fixed or established entity, to which Psalm 151 was added subsequently. The attribution of the psalm to David, coupled with the fact that this psalm appears as the conclud-ing psalm of the Greek collection, suggests the continued close association of David with Isra-elite psalmody in general and the Psalter in particular.

1.3.2. The Dead Sea Psalms Scroll. Of all the biblical books represented among the Dead Sea Scrolls, the book of Psalms appears most fre-quently, with at least thirty-nine psalm scrolls or manuscripts having been discovered (thirty-six at Qumran, two at Masada, and one at Nahal Hever). The most significant find was 11QPs[a]. Found in 1961, and published later (1965, 1967) by James Sanders, 11QPs[a] contains parts of forty-one canonical psalms from book 4 and book 5 of the Psalter, providing the most exten-sive psalms scroll.

The contents of 11QPs[a] have generated much debate concerning the nature of the col-lection found at Qumran. Although the scroll begins with Psalm 101, it quickly diverges from the traditional ordering of the last one-third of the Psalter as found in the MT. In addition, non-biblical material is present in this portion, in-cluding, among others, "Plea for Deliverance," "Apostrophe to Zion" and "Hymn to the Cre-ator" (for the entirety of the collection, see Flint, 174). The contrast between the two collections led Sanders to propose the "Qumran Psalms Hy-pothesis." Perhaps most influential from his hy-pothesis was the suggestion that whereas Psalms 1—89 appear to have been stabilized earlier, the final section of the Psalter exhibited consider-able fluidity. The later work of G. Wilson (1985) and P. Flint have confirmed Sanders's earlier suggestion concerning the stabilization of the Psalter and also his contention that 11QPs[a] was a true Psalter for the Qumran community. Such findings have led to a renewed discussion per-taining to the formation, both date and theolog-ical intention, of the MT Psalter.

2. Approaches to the Psalter.
Numerous methodological approaches have been employed in studying the Psalter, at least three of which deserve particular mention be-cause they have been formative in shaping the direction and scope of subsequent work on the text: (1) the form-critical approach; (2) the cult-functional approach; (3) the canonical ap-proach.

2.1. Hermann Gunkel and the Form-Critical Ap-proach. Prior to H. Gunkel (1862-1932), and con-sonant with historical-critical approaches of that era, scholars such as J. Wellhausen, B. Duhm and A. Ralhfs had attempted to locate individual psalms within specific historical contexts. More particularly, these scholars, and others, ascribed most of the psalms to the Maccabean period (sec-ond century BC). Driving such a late date was their aversion to the cultic institutions and rites of ancient Israel, as well as their insistence that the conflict between the enemies and the psalmists probably was indicative of the societal turmoil and class struggle present during this period.

Gunkel, however, moved in a different direc-tion, rejecting attempts at the historical specificity of individual psalms, and instead sought "to bring some kind of order to this material, which takes such diverse forms . . . and is spread out over so many centuries" (Gunkel, 5). To this end, Gunkel analyzed the structure of the psalms, noting also the forms of expression that appeared conven-tional to different structures. Each psalm could be classified based on its setting in life *(Sitz im Leb-en)*, its thought and mood, and its literary form *(Formensprache)*. From this analysis, Gunkel sought to categorize all psalms according to their respective types or forms *(Gattungen)*.

Gunkel identified four major types of psalms (see also 3 below): *hymns, community *la-ments, individual laments and songs of *thanks-giving. Gunkel noted that there are other forms in the Psalter, but these are found in lesser num-ber. They include royal psalms, songs of *Zion, songs of Yahweh's enthronement, entrance lit-urgies and wisdom psalms.

Gunkel contended that although Israelite psalmography originated in the preexilic period (contrary to many of his contemporaries) and was transmitted orally, many of the psalms present in the Psalter are "spiritualized" replicas of the earlier "types." Any mention of cultic mat-ters in the psalms was meant as metaphorical.

2.2. Sigmund Mowinckel and the Cult-Functional Approach. A number of Gunkel's students adopt-ed and adapted his approach to *form criticism. Foremost among Gunkel's students was a Scan-dinavian student, S. Mowinckel (1884-1965). Al-though Mowinckel was influenced by Gunkel's work, he was equally influenced by Danish anthropologist V. Gronbeck, whose work focused on the structure and behavior of primitive societies, with particular interest in the function of cult within those societies.

While acknowledging his debt to Gunkel, Mowinckel charted a new course in psalms study. He sought to relate each psalm more directly to the events within the cultic life of the community itself. Whereas Gunkel had maintained that the extant psalm compositions were in fact only replicas of earlier oral traditions, Mowinckel argued that these compositions were originally composed for actual use in the cult. As a result, Mowinckel sought to determine the function of the psalm within the cult itself.

The most influential (and controversial) theory espoused by Mowinckel was the notion of a New Year's festival in ancient Israel meant to celebrate the enthronement of Yahweh as king. Although specific indication of such a festival is absent in the biblical literature, Mowinckel contended that the autumnal festival mentioned in the text (Ex 23; 34; Lev 23) suggests an earlier festival meant to celebrate the enthronement of Yahweh. In an effort to reconstruct such a festival, Mowinckel was forced to draw on the yearly Mesopotamian Akitu festival. He surmised that Psalms 93—99, which celebrate the kingship of Yahweh, would have been central to the liturgy of the festival. In addition, and similar to the Akitu festival, Mowinckel argued that the Israelite king was meant to play the role of Yahweh in the festival. Modified forms of Mowinckel's thesis appear later in the works of Artur Weiser (a "covenant renewal" ceremony) and Hans-Joachim Kraus (a "Royal Zion festival"). Such theories, though intriguing, have failed to sway contemporary scholarship.

2.3. The Canonical Approach. Since the 1980s the focus in Psalms scholarship has shifted away from the reading and interpretation of individual psalms as with the methodologies proposed by Gunkel and Mowinckel. Beginning with B. Childs's *Introduction to the Old Testament as Scripture* (1979), the question of the canonical shape of the Psalter has received significant attention, opening up another methodology for exploring the world of the text. Questions related to both the shape of the Psalter and the processes behind that shaping have moved to the fore.

G. Wilson, a student of Childs, explored the various editorial techniques employed in the collecting of the psalms. Wilson (1985, 199) concluded that such was "the result of a purposeful, editorial activity which sought to impart a meaningful arrangement which encompassed the whole" (*see* Editorial Criticism). Among the many contributions of Wilson (and others) was the insistence on recognizing that several units appear to have been edited together in the final collection of the Psalter, and further, the insistence on taking the position of those units seriously in interpreting the text. Thus, the Psalter could be understood as a "book" with the following components:

Introduction	Psalms 1—2
Book 1	Psalms 3—41
Book 2	Psalms 42—72
Book 3	Psalms 73—89
Book 4	Psalms 90—106
Book 5	Psalms 107—145
Conclusion	Psalms 146—150

Such a reading of the Psalter led Wilson to conclude that the book divisions of the Psalter were real, editorially induced structures. Furthermore, Wilson noted that the shaping of the Psalter appears most evident at the "seams" of the various books, where royal psalms appear to have been strategically positioned. Finally, such an approach argues that the introductory and concluding psalms are critical to reading the remainder of the Psalter (see 5 below).

3. Genre.

In his form-critical approach Gunkel identified various types, or genres, of psalms. Although the poetic nature of the texts themselves allows for much fluidity and flexibility within each genre, there are identifying features of each form worth noting. Some types, or genres, are easily identifiable because they share common literary conventions. Other psalms are associated by type predicated upon the subject matter of the psalm itself. Because many of the psalm types overlap in language and imagery, the precise categorizations of psalms according to types tend to deviate from each other.

3.1. Individual Lament. The most frequent type of psalm is the individual *lament, with nearly one-third of the psalms falling into this category. The structure of the lament psalm generally follows this pattern: (1) opening address, often in the form of a vocative ("My God"); (2) description of the distress or crisis; (3) plea for help (from God), often followed by reason for God to hear or act; (4) profession of trust; (5) promise to praise God or to offer a sacrifice. Although the precise order of these components may vary somewhat from psalm to psalm, most laments will contain all five elements.

3.1.1. The Prayers of the Accused. There is a large subgroup of lament psalms often called "The Prayers of the Accused" (Pss 3; 4; 5; 7; 11; 17; 25—27; 31; 35; 41—42/43; 52; 54—59; 77; 86; 94; 102; 109; 139—140; 142). False allegations have been levied against the psalmist, and in return the psalmist pleads for vindication from these unjust accusations: "Vindicate me, O God, and defend my cause against an ungodly people; from those who are deceitful and unjust deliver me!" (Ps 43:1 NRSV).

Earlier interpreters (H. Schmidt, W. Beyerlin, L. Delekat) suggested that these psalms had their origins in a sacral trial that took place within the temple court—a type of asylum. There the psalmist would issue forth his complaint and await a judgment from God concerning the lament. Although more recent scholars retain some sense of an "asylum ritual" (K. Seybold) in the psalms or at least acknowledge some type of "divine jurisdiction" (H.-J. Kraus) in the psalms, others have questioned such reconstructions and, moreover, whether there is adequate evidence to suggest such a ritual (Day, 29).

3.1.2. The Psalms of Illness. Another significant subgroup of the lament psalms contains language pertaining to the illness of the psalmist (Pss 6; 13; 38; 39; 69; 88; 102). In these psalms the psalmist prays for healing (Ps 6:2) from illness, often lamenting about his physical condition (Ps 102:3). E. Gerstenberger (1988, 62) has proposed that these psalms may have been used by local "ritual experts" who prepared a service for the ailing person in which the individual offered a sacrifice and then recited the psalm from the sickbed.

A dominant image in these psalms is that of Sheol (*see* Afterlife). Whether speaking of Sheol specifically (Ps 88:3) or using more metaphorical language such as the "pit" (Ps 69:15) or "deep waters" (Ps 69:2), the psalmist's frequent use of such images suggests an understanding of illness as an intrusion of Sheol into this life.

3.2. Communal Lament. The communal laments were psalms uttered during times of national crisis (Pss 12; 44; 60; 74; 79; 80; 83; 85; 89; 94:1-11; 126; 137). The *Sitz im Leben* for such

psalms probably was some type of special festival set aside for lamentation. A possible example of such an occasion is found in Judith 4:9-15. A central feature of the communal lament is the rehearsal of the history between God and his people, often citing God's mighty deeds performed on the behalf of his people as motivation for God to "arouse" from his sleep and deliver his people. Although not every circumstance surrounding these psalms can be identified (Ps 44), the destruction of the temple in 587 BC appears to have been the subject matter of a number of communal laments (Pss 74; 79; 137). For example, in Psalm 74, the community laments, "And then, with hatchets and hammers, they smashed all its carved work. They set your sanctuary on fire; they desecrated the dwelling place of you your name" (Ps 74:6-7 NRSV).

As J. C. McCann (647) has suggested, although not all of the communal laments may have been written in response to the events of 587 BC, it seems likely that all of them were "eventually read and heard in view of this crisis."

3.3. Hymn. *Hymns, sometimes referred to as songs of praise, make up over one-fifth of the Psalter (Pss 8; 19A; 29; 33; 46—48; 65; 66A; 68; 76; 84; 87; 93; 95—100; 103—104; 111; 113—114; 117; 122; 134—136; 145—150). Their format is rather simple, having only three elements: (1) opening invitation to praise; (2) rationale for praise, often introduced by the Hebrew particle meaning "for" *(kî);* (3) renewed call to praise.

The shortest psalm, Psalm 117, is a song of praise and provides a helpful example of this form: "Praise the LORD all you nations! Extol him, all you peoples! For *[kî]* great is his steadfast love toward us, and the faithfulness of the LORD endures forever. Praise the LORD!" (Ps 117 NRSV).

Although the command "Praise the LORD" frequently stands at the beginning of such psalms (see Pss 146—150), other introductory words may appear as well, including "Bless the LORD" (Ps 134), "Shout to the LORD" (Ps 100) and "Rejoice in the LORD" (Ps 33).

The hymns often are grouped together and are found more readily in the second half of the Psalter, whereas the lament psalms appear to dominate the first half. Therefore, one could say that the Psalter moves from lament to praise, reaching a crescendo of praise in Psalms 146—

150. This might explain, in part, why the rabbis and later Jewish writers tended to refer to the Psalter as the *Sefer Tehillim* ("Book of Praises").

There are some subgroups to this type that appear throughout the Psalter, each with a distinctive focus: psalms to the Creator, Zion psalms and enthronement psalms.

3.3.1. Psalms to the Creator. There are at least five psalms that invoke *creation imagery: Psalms 8; 19A; 33; 104; 136. Although these psalms refer to elements of nature, they are not "psalms of creation." Instead, and perhaps more precisely, these psalms invoke images of creation with the goal of praising the Creator. Thus, the psalmist proclaims, "By the word of the LORD the heavens were made, and all their host by the breath of his mouth" (Ps 33:6 NRSV).

Perhaps the most thorough praise to the Creator occurs in Psalm 104. There the psalmist extols God, praising him for stretching out the heavens as a tent (Ps 104:2), setting up the foundations of the earth (Ps 104:5), and filling the creation with water, grass and animals, and even Leviathan (Ps 104:26).

Some of the creation imagery employed in these psalms reflects the larger ancient Near Eastern context in which the psalmist lived. For example, Psalm 104:19-24 appears to resemble, in some form, a hymn to the sun-disc (Aten) by Pharaoh Akhenaten. Although the exact nature of the dependence remains a matter of dispute, the psalmist does appear to have employed "stock phrases" from Egyptian poetry (Kraus 1993, 302). Similarly, Psalm 29 characterizes God as a storm-god, drawing from images typically associated with Baal and Canaanite poetry (Day, 42-43; Wilson 2002, 509-10). In both cases it would be a gross oversimplification to assert that the psalmist merely inserted the name of Yahweh where the previous god's name appeared. More likely, the psalmist's use of stock images from other ancient Near Eastern cultures suggests a high level of poetic sophistication, manifested in the ability to draw from a larger "bank" of images while also articulating with specificity the psalmist's own tradition.

3.3.2. Zion Psalms. Reference to *Zion and the temple appears throughout the Psalter. Six psalms, however, appear to focus on Zion in particular: Psalms 46; 48; 76; 84; 87; 122. Within these psalms the psalmist also makes use of traditions associated with Zion theology. Yet it is not the city itself that is the object of praise but

rather the presence of God (*see* Divine Presence). In Psalm 46 the psalmist proclaims, "There is a river whose streams make glad the city of God, the holy habitation of the Most High. God is in the midst of the city; it shall not be moved" (Ps 46:4-5 NRSV). In some ways, Zion serves as a cipher for the active and protective presence of God among his people. It is this presence that demands the celebration and praise of the psalmist.

A frequent theme in several Zion psalms is the inviolability of Zion (cf. Pss 46; 48; 76). The nations appear set to destroy Zion, yet the psalmist confidently asserts that "within its citadels, God has shown himself a sure defense" (Ps 48:3 NRSV), able to destroy the weapons of war (Ps 46:9; 76:3). These psalms also suggest that despite the uproar of nations and the challenge of foreign kings, Zion is a city that will not be moved (Ps 46:5), for it is the city of the Great King (Ps 48:2). These psalms seek to rebuff the apparent threats from other nations by suggesting that the presence of the city of God guarantees the work of God on their behalf (Ps 46:6-7; 76:5-6). As McCann (668) has noted, while these psalms celebrate the reign of the Great King, they also acknowledge that this reign is "constantly and pervasively opposed." Although the language regarding Zion appears extravagant at times—even calling it the center of the earth (Ps 48:2)—such psalms should be understood as bold statements of trust that dare to counter the claims of the larger and more powerful enemies that surrounded it.

3.3.3. Enthronement (or "Yahweh Reigns") Psalms. There are six hymns referred to as enthronement psalms (or "Yahweh reigns" psalms, from Heb *yhwh mālak*). As previously indicated (see 2.2 above), these psalms were central to Mowinckel's thesis regarding an autumnal festival that presumably celebrated the coronation of Yahweh as king. Mowinckel suggested that the phrase *yhwh mālak* would have been understood to mean "the LORD has become king," reflecting the people's enthronement of Yahweh as king for another year. Others have asserted that the phrase is more durative in sense, and thus would be rendered "Yahweh is king" (Kraus 1988, 86-89). The particular points arguing for or against a *Sitz im Leben* associated with an autumnal festival need not be rehearsed here (see Day, 67-87).

The chief theme, in any case, is the declaration of the reign of God. In these psalms the reign of God is frequently coupled with other central theological themes found throughout the OT. For example, in Psalm 93 the psalmist alludes to Yahweh's role as Creator, and in so doing, reinforces Yahweh's rightful position as king (Ps 93:1-2). His victory over the floods confirms his capacity as cosmic king to hold *chaos at bay and retain order (Ps 93:3-4). Twice (Ps 93:1; 96:10) Yahweh is praised for having established the world and ensuring that it will not be moved.

Another frequently invoked theme in the enthronement psalms is that of the nations. Yahweh subdues the nations (Ps 47:3), and it is through his victory over the nations that he has demonstrated his rule (Ps 98:1-2). Yet the nations are also said to be the location where the reign of God is to be proclaimed. The psalmist exhorts, "Declare his glory among the nations, his marvelous works among all the peoples" (Ps 96:3 NRSV).

In Psalm 97 the recognition of Yahweh as king will extend to all the coastlands, calling "all peoples to behold his glory" (Ps 97:6). Because of the reign of Yahweh, those who worship idols will be put to shame (*see* Honor and Shame), and ultimately they will recognize that Yahweh stands as king above all other gods (Ps 97:9).

3.4. Psalms of Thanksgiving. In the psalms of *thanksgiving the psalmist offers thanks to Yahweh for deliverance from some form of distress. Often the psalm of thanksgiving is understood as a complement to the individual lament. Many individual laments conclude with a vow by the psalmist that if he is delivered from his distress, he will offer praise and sacrifice to Yahweh. The psalm of thanksgiving, on the other hand, presupposes that such distress has been remedied, thus leading the psalmist to fulfill some vow or sacrifice of thanksgiving. Strikingly, though, psalms of thanksgiving occur with much less frequency than the laments. Although a few scholars, most notably C. Westermann, have argued that there are no individual psalms of thanksgiving, the majority conclude that the following psalms fall within this type: Psalms 18; 30; 32; 40A; 52; 66B; 92; 116; 118; 138. Only one communal psalm of thanksgiving is readily identifiable: Psalm 124. To this psalm Gunkel added Psalms 66B; 67; 129, although his assignments have not met with universal agreement.

The structure of the psalms of thanksgiving exhibits considerable variation. In principle, however, there are three major sections to the psalm: (1) introduction, in which the psalmist states his desire to offer thanks to Yahweh; (2) narrative body, in which the psalmist recounts his distress and cry to Yahweh for deliverance, with the final section noting how Yahweh delivered the psalmist; (3) conclusion. Of the three sections, the conclusion exhibits the greatest variation, perhaps raising the question as to its usefulness in defining the type itself.

The psalms of thanksgiving apparently arose from various circumstances. The psalmist gives thanks for being delivered from illness (Pss 30; 41). In other psalms the psalmist rejoices in his victory over enemies (Pss 52; 92). And in others the psalmist gives thanks for forgiveness (Ps 32). In several psalms the psalmist expresses his desire to give "testimony" of his deliverance. In Psalm 116 the psalmist extols, "I will pay my vows to the LORD in the presence of all his people, in the courts of the house of the LORD, in your midst, O Jerusalem" (Ps 116:18-19 NRSV). The desire to give testimony of deliverance suggests that these psalms may have had their original *Sitz im Leben* in the cult and, more specifically, within the great worship festivals of ancient Israel (Kraus 1988; Seybold).

3.5. Royal Psalms. The psalms within this group are unified more around a particular theme than formal literary features. Although the psalms represent a variety of literary forms, they are characterized by their explicit reference to the king (*see* Kingship Psalms). Gunkel initially identified a modest number of psalms that fell within this type: Psalms 2; 18; 20; 21; 45; 72; 89; 101; 110; 132; 144:1-11. These psalms appear to refer to particular incidents within the life of a king. Psalm 2 and Psalm 110 are coronation psalms, invoking language of investiture ("You are my son; today I have begotten you" [Ps 2:7b]). Psalm 45 was composed probably for the wedding of a king, and several psalms are related to events associated with battle (Ps 18; 20; 144:1-11).

Subsequent to the work of Gunkel, the number of royal psalms was expanded, particularly by Scandinavian and British scholars, with some suggesting as many as forty psalms to be assigned to this type (S. Croft; J. Eaton). The heavy emphasis on the role of the king within the cult of ancient Israel has led many of the same scholars to postulate that within the autumnal festival the king played an important role. The theory suggests that the king undergoes a ritual of humiliation. In this cultic event the king symbolically suffers defeat at the hands of the enemies but is vindicated by the deliverance of Yahweh. Although proponents of this and similar theories have tried to base their reconstruction on several royal psalms (Pss 2; 18; 89; 101; 110; 118), they have failed to persuade the majority of scholars. The lack of explicit reference to such a ritual, both within the psalms and in the historical narratives, has resulted in skepticism toward its existence.

3.6. Wisdom and Torah Psalms. Beginning with Gunkel, scholars have suggested that there is "wisdom poetry" within the Psalter. As evidence, Gunkel noted that the psalmist frequently referred to his speech as "wisdom" (Ps 37:30; 49:3), "instruction" (*tôrâ* [Ps 78:1; 94:12]), "riddle" (Ps 49:4; 78:2) and often spoke of the "fear of Yahweh" (*see* Fear of the Lord). As with the royal psalms, the wisdom psalms do not exhibit a strict literary form; instead, they are identified based on thematic and linguistic usage. Among those frequently identified as wisdom psalms are Psalms 1; 37; 49; 73; 112; 128. Although the precise number of wisdom psalms differs, depending on the interpreter, most acknowledge the existence of such a classification.

In recent years, however, some scholars (most notably J. Crenshaw) have vigorously questioned the category "wisdom psalms." Given the paucity of information regarding the life and work of the *sages in ancient Israel, it is only speculation that they participated in "learned psalmography" (*contra* Mowinckel). J. Crenshaw (94) has suggested that the most we should affirm is that "some psalms resemble wisdom literature in stressing the importance of learning, struggling to ascertain life's meaning, and employing proverbial lore." Rather than limiting the language of "wisdom" only to the sages, Crenshaw suggests that such language and ideas would have been of concern to all "thoughtful people."

The Torah psalms, which are frequently listed as a subset of the wisdom psalms, receive such a designation, of course, because of their heavy emphasis on the *tôrâ* of Yahweh. There are only three such psalms in the Psalter: Psalms 1; 19; 119. Psalm 119 is the Torah psalm par excellence. Ten different terms are em-ployed in reference to the *tôrâ* of Yahweh, and they appear throughout the 176-verse *acrostic poem. Psalm 1 stands at the beginning of the Psalter (see 5.1 below) and contrasts the way of the righteous with the way of the wicked. The *tôrâ* of Yahweh functions as the fundamental guide that leads one into the way of the righteous.

3.7. Entrance Liturgies. Within the Psalter there are at least two psalms that fall within this category, Psalm 15 and Psalm 24, while others, such as Psalms 92; 100; 118, have similar characteristics. The structures of Psalm 15 and Psalms 24 are nearly identical. The psalm opens with a question concerning who may enter the temple, followed by an answer (from a priest?) stipulating the particular requirements for entrance. The psalm concludes with a blessing or an affirmation of those qualified to enter the temple. Gerstenberger (1988) has suggested that while such psalms may have been intended originally to designate who could enter the temple, later use of the psalm probably was meant to reflect "nonsacrificial, 'ethical,' worship of early Jewish communities." In this sense, these psalms possess a catechetical function, as suggested by Galling and Seybold.

4. Hebrew Poetry.

Reading Hebrew poetry demands that the interpreter pay as much attention to the literary and aesthetic nature of the text as to the semantic range of individual words. The defining features of Hebrew poetry include *parallelism and *terse (Berlin) or compressed (Wilson 2002) speech. Parallelism and the various poetic devices that contribute to the meaning of the overall work deserve careful consideration by those reading such material.

*Meter (i.e., iambic pentameter) is another element frequently found in poetic texts of differing cultures. A number of proposals related to the meter of Hebrew poetry have been offered, but none appear to have gained consensus, leading some scholars (Kugel; Berlin) to argue that there is no meter in Hebrew poetry.

4.1. Parallelism. Although not the first to note the parallel structure of Hebrew poetry, R. Lowth, in 1753, articulated a view of parallelism that has remained central to the study of poetry for nearly two centuries. In his view, parallelism can be defined as the correspondence of one line with a subsequent line. For example,

For he spoke, and it came to be;
he commanded, and it stood firm.
  (Ps 33:9 NRSV)

The difficulty comes, however, in attempting to understand the relationship between the lines. Due to the various relationships that can be expressed between the two lines, Lowth forwarded the notion that parallelism could be found in one of three basic forms: synonymous, antithetic and synthetic (or constructive). Although Lowth's tripartite division of parallelism has been challenged by more recent studies of Hebrew poetry, it has remained central to any discussion of Hebrew poetry. As a result, brief examples of the three types of parallelism identified by Lowth are provided here, followed by a brief treatment of more contemporary approaches.

4.1.1. Synonymous Parallelism. In synonymous parallelism the second line, or line B, repeats the sentiment of line A. Although repetition of specific terms may not occur, Lowth observed the presence of equivalent terms. For example, in Psalm 59 the psalmist prays,

Deliver me from my enemies, O my God;
protect me from those who rise up against
  me.
Deliver me from those who work evil;
from the bloodthirsty save me.
  (Ps 59:1-2 NRSV)

In each line an imperative requesting divine assistance appears, with the repetition of the same verb twice. In addition, the "enemies" are described in varying terms but referring to the same entity, and in each case the object of the verb is the first-person singular pronoun ("me"). Such repetition heightens the intensity of the request and of the psalm in general, causing the reader to ponder the plight of the psalmist not once, but repeatedly.

4.1.2. Antithetic Parallelism. In this form of parallelism line B stands in contrast to line A. As Lowth noted, not only are sentiments contrasted, but also even specific words stand in stark contrast. In Psalm 1 the psalmist provides a comparison of the righteous and the wicked:

For the LORD watches over the way of the
  righteous,

but the way of the wicked will perish.
  (Ps 1:6 NRSV)

The contrast presented in such parallel lines provides the reader instruction concerning the fate of those who choose wrongly. Rather than simply stating that one should choose the way of the righteous, such a construction affords the reader the rationale concerning that choice.

4.1.3. Synthetic or Advancing Parallelism. Lowth suggested a third category of parallelism, which he termed "synthetic parallelism." More recently, Wilson (2002, 43) has noted the inadequacy of that term and suggested that this form of parallelism is better represented by the term "advancing parallelism." What makes the category distinct from synonymous or antithetic parallelism is that line B does not exhibit similarities with line A in regard to syntax, structure or semantics. Line B advances the theme presented in line A. For example, in Psalm 53 the psalmist says,

Fools say in their hearts, "There is no God,"
They are corrupt, they commit abominable
  acts;
there is no one who does good.
  (Ps 53:1 NRSV)

Although all three lines share a similar theme, that of the "fool," they lack the type of formal parallel structure seen in synonymous and antithetic parallelism. Line A indicates what the fool says, line B indicates what the fool does, and line C offers a summative evaluation. As Wilson (2002, 45) suggests, advancing parallelism offers the psalmist "maximum flexibility in creating lines that develop, direct, and advance" the movement of the psalm.

4.1.4. Additional Forms of Parallelism. Most work on the Psalms in the twentieth century adopted Lowth's tripartite categorization of parallelism, offering occasional modification, particularly to the third type. In an effort to clarify, additional forms of parallelism have been suggested (see Watson, 114-59). A number of lines exhibit what is often referred to as "staircase parallelism." In such a pattern elements from line A are repeated in line B with additional comments added to complete the thought. Such a feature is exhibited in Psalm 9:

The LORD is a stronghold for the oppressed,
  a stronghold in times of trouble. (Ps 9:9 NRSV)

Due to the large number of metaphors present in Hebrew poetry, and especially in the Psalter, a number of scholars have noted what they call "emblematic parallelism." A simile or a metaphor appears in one line and is meant to stand in relationship to an element in the other line. A familiar example comes from Psalm 42:

As a deer longs for flowing streams,
so my soul longs for you, O God.
(Ps 42:1 NRSV)

Additional types, such as incomplete parallelism, Janus parallelism, climactic parallelism, advancing parallelism and metathetic parallelism, have been noted (Wilson 2002, 39-48).

4.1.5. Post-Lowthian Studies in Parallelism. Recent studies in Hebrew poetry have attempted to move beyond Lowth's initial thesis, challenging the prevailing notion of parallelism. Many have lamented that Lowth's tripartite division is too limiting and actually forces the text into preconceived categories rather than recognizing the diverse nature of parallelism within Hebrew poetry. Drawing from modern linguistic studies, research on parallelism has expanded, offering new categories for understanding the phenomenon of parallelism: semantic aspect, grammatical aspect, lexical aspect and phonological aspect.

4.1.5.1. Semantic Aspect. The semantic aspect refers to the relationship in meaning between the two lines and best represents Lowth's form of categorization. The 1981 work of J. Kugel, however, offered one of the first sustained challenges to Lowth's view of parallelism, particularly as it related to the semantic aspect of parallelism. Kugel observed that the majority of parallelism present in the Hebrew poetry is neither synonymous (as presupposed by Lowth) nor antithetical. To the contrary, Kugel (57) avers that "all parallelism is really 'synthetic,'" which prompted him to reassess the manner in which one spoke of the relationship between lines. From this, Kugel developed his well-known formula: "A is so, and what's more, B is so." Thus, in a typical verse line B has what Kugel calls a "seconding" or "afterwardness" function. Yet this is much more than the Lowthian idea of synonymous or antithetical restatement. As Kugel (52) explains, "B typically supports A, carries it further, backs it up, completes it, goes beyond it." In short, line B is connected with line A to construct a single, complex statement.

The following verse appears to reflect Kugel's observations:

But I call upon God,
And the LORD will save me. (Ps 55:16 NRSV)

In this verse line B is not synonymous with line A, nor is it antithetical; rather, it appears to "complete" the thought from line A, even going beyond it.

Similarly, R. Alter has attempted to delineate the features of parallelism. Alter prefers to speak of line B having a focusing or intensifying function within the parallel structure. Although the explanations of semantic paral-lelism by Kugel and Alter appear similar, the two scholars should not be thought of as identical in approach to Hebrew poetry. Alter suggests that there are specific literary indicators within a text that suggest that it is poetic. Kugel, however, believes that while there is both prose and poetry in the Hebrew Bible, much of the prose can be understood as poetic. Hence for Kugel even poetic prose should be read in light of his thesis "A is so, and what's more, B is so." Alter, a literary critic, however, prefers to limit his analysis only to those texts that exhibit indicators of poetry.

4.1.5.2. Grammatical Aspect. The grammatical aspect of parallelism considers the syntax of poetic lines and the equivalent nature of that syntax. Generally, Hebrew poetry exhibits what can be called "grammatical equivalence: the second line substitutes something grammatically different, but equivalent, for a grammatical feature in the first line" (Berlin, 32). For example,

God has taken his place in the divine
council;
in the midst of the gods he holds judgment.
(Ps 82:1 NRSV)

In line B the pronoun "he" is parallel to the noun "God" in line A. Although parallel terms may come from different word classes (noun // pronoun; noun // relative clause; substantive [noun, adjective, participle] // verb), the syntax of the line remains equivalent.

A number of parallel lines are crafted so that semantically parallel terms serve a different syntactic function in their respective lines. The psalmist states,

I will observe your statutes;

do not utterly forsake me. (Ps 119:8 NRSV)

The first-person pronoun is used in both lines, which thus are semantically parallel, but in line A the pronoun is the subject, whereas in line B it is the direct object of the verb. Consideration of the grammatical aspect suggests that parallelism involves not only the meaning of the entire line but also the relationship between the individual grammatical components.

4.1.5.3. Lexical Aspect. The lexical aspect of parallelism relates to the pairing of terms in parallel lines. Considerable work has been done in identifying word pairs (both in Hebrew and Ugaritic poetry) that appear in parallel lines. Certain sets of terms appear regularly such as "day/night" and "heaven/earth." When words from the same class are paired together, it is known as "paradigmatic pairing." The most common form of paradigmatic pairing suggests contrast, resulting in oppositional terms ("righteous/wicked"; "good/bad"; "woman/man").

Another form of pairing is known as syntagmatic pairing. A frequent type of syntagmatic pairing is known as conventionalized coordinates. Often two terms will appear in parallel lines forming a hendiadys ("loyalty/truth") or a *merism ("heavens/earth"). An example of a merism appears in Psalm 8:

How majestic is your name in all the earth!
You have set your glory above the heavens.
(Ps 8:1 NRSV)

The individual terms are not employed separately to indicate location; rather, they appear together in an effort to generate a meaning that exceeds their individual usage. In the case of Psalm 8, the psalmist announces that all of creation is filled with the majesty and glory of God.

4.1.5.4. The Phonological Aspect. The phonological aspect refers to the presence of sound pairs within parallel lines. Sound pairs are identified as "word or lines of the same or similar consonants in any order within close proximity" (Berlin, 104). In addition to grammatical and semantic equivalence, Psalm 122:7 exhibits phonological equivalence:

Let there be peace *[šlwm]* within your walls,
security *[šlwh]* in your towers. (Ps 122:7)

There are a large number of other instances

where the sound pair is not lexically equivalent (as in Ps 122:7), yet the similarity of the consonants serves to suggest that the "equivalence of sound signifies equivalence of sense" (Berlin, 112).

4.2. Poetic Devices. In addition to parallelism, the psalms employ a number of stylistic and literary devices. Not only do these devices exhibit the technical nature of Hebrew poetry in general, but also they reinforce the notion that, as with most all poetry, meaning and aesthetics are inseparable. Unfortunately, some of these devices are lost in the translation process (i.e., assonance, alliteration, onomatopoeia, paronomasia). Although these are treated in depth elsewhere in the present volume, a brief explanation of selected poetic devices is given here.

4.2.1. Chiasm. *Chiasm is related to parallelism in that it involves the relationship between two lines. The second line reverses the order of the sentence elements presented in the first line. In Psalm 63 the psalmist states

My soul clings to you;
your right hand upholds me. (Ps 63:8 NRSV)

Although the wording is altered slightly in the second line, the repetition is evident, yielding the following pattern (characteristic of chiasm in general):

A   B   C
C'   B'   A'

Chiasm may be found in larger textual units (Ps 36:6-7; 72:1-2; 101:3-7) as well as in entire psalms (Ps 86).

4.2.2. Inclusio. *Inclusio is the repetition of lines or phrases at the beginning and end of a composition, thus forming a type of literary envelope. For example, Psalm 8 opens and concludes with the line "O LORD, our Sovereign, how majestic is your name in all the earth" (Ps 8:1, 9 NRSV). Frequently, the framing statements identify an important theological concept related to the meaning of the entire psalm. Psalm 118 opens and concludes with the line "O give thanks to the LORD, for he is good; his steadfast love endures forever" (Ps 118:1, 29 NRSV). The remainder of the psalm offers a song of thanksgiving for deliverance from enemies, reinforcing the nature of Yahweh's steadfast love.

4.2.3. Simile. A simile is a figurative device

meant to compare a topic with an image. Markers such as "like" or "as" appear in such language to indicate the nonliteral nature of the expression. In speaking of the king, the psalmist writes, "May he be like rain that falls on the mown grass, like showers that water the earth" (Ps 72:6 NRSV).

4.2.4. Metaphor. Metaphors are another example of figurative language meant to offer a comparison. Unlike a simile, however, there are no markers present to indicate a comparison. Instead, the topic is immediately associated with the image, drawing a more forceful comparison between the two. Metaphors are invoked repeatedly in the psalmist's language about God. Since God is *sui generis*, the psalmist must resort to metaphorical language ("rock," "refuge," "fortress," "king") in characterizing God. Unlike the simile, however, the basis of the comparison is left unstated, forcing the interpreter to consider the ramifications of the implied connection.

4.2.5. Metonymy. Metonymy is a figure of speech in which the name or designation of one thing is substituted for that of another object that is closely associated. There is no intended comparison between the two terms; it is simply a case of lexical substitution. In Psalm 73:9 the psalmist announces, "They set their mouths against heaven." In this verse "mouths" has been inserted, or substituted, for "words."

4.2.6. Synedoche. Synedoche is another type of figurative substitution. In this figure of speech the whole is represented by a part (or vice versa), or a particular is used to refer to the whole (or vice versa). In Psalm 93:2 the psalmist says that Yahweh's "throne is established from of old." The psalmist is not speaking of a literal throne but rather has employed the word "throne" in reference to the dominion and rule of Yahweh as king.

4.2.7. Apostrophe. An apostrophe is a figure of speech in which the psalmist speaks directly to an absent person(s) or thing(s) as though actually present. Frequently in the psalms the psalmist will speak to kings or even foreign nations, often employing apostrophe. For example, in Psalm 137 the psalmist speaks directly to Babylon: "O daughter Babylon, you devastator! Happy shall they be who pay you back what you have done to us!" (Ps 137:8 NRSV). Typically, the use of an apostrophe involves some form of direct address (note the use of "you" throughout) marked by a vocative ("O daughter Babylon").

5. The Psalter as a Book.

Following recent trends in biblical studies, psalms study has considered the final shape of the Psalter. Although the book of Psalms does represent 150 discrete units, scholarship has moved to consider how, and in what ways, these units function together. Focus has shifted from the individual psalms to larger units and even the entire Psalter itself. Psalms 1—2 have been recognized as providing the introduction to the collection, while Psalms 146—150 offer a concluding run of psalms. Book 4 (Pss 90—106) has been recognized as the editorial center of the Psalter, and as such it provides a central theme to the reading of the entire corpus.

5.1. Psalms 1—2 as Introduction. The connections between the two introductory psalms have been well-rehearsed in a number of studies: neither psalm has a title; the two psalms are framed by an inclusio using the word ʾašrê ("happy" [Ps 1:1; 2:12]); both psalms include hāgâ in their opening lines (Ps 1:2: "meditate"; Ps 2:1: "plot"); the wicked mentioned in Psalm 1 are juxtaposed with the unruly nations and leaders in Psalm 2. Although some have suggested that Psalm 1 and Psalm 2 were added to the Psalter at roughly the same time (deClaissé-Walford, 41), others have contended that Psalm 2 was part of a larger collection (most likely Pss 2—89), and that Psalm 1 may have been added at a later, redactional stage (Rösel, 95; Zenger, 41). Rather than attempting to weigh the merits of either position here, we will focus on the function of the two psalms as an introduction to the Psalter.

The opening psalm, reminiscent of the wisdom tradition, presents the reader with two fundamentally different options for life. Although the psalm opens with reference to the "happy" or "blessed" person, the identity of that individual is established based on a comparison with the "wicked," "sinners" and "scoffers." Unlike these, however, the righteous individual delights in the "law [tôrâ] of the LORD" and will be rooted by "streams of water." And unlike the wicked, whose path will perish (Ps 1:6), the righteous will prosper in all that they do, and the Lord will watch over their way (Ps 1:3, 6). Thus the opening psalm presents two ways of life, but the way of the righteous is one predicated upon tôrâ obedience. In this instance tôrâ probably is meant not only in its narrower sense (i.e., the *law) but also in its broader sense, meaning "instruction." Psalm 1, then, exhorts the readers to root their lives in the law of the Lord while also recognizing the instructive nature of the Psalter as Scripture (Childs 1979, 513-14).

The second psalm, no doubt, reflects a coronation ceremony during the preexilic period, yet its position at the beginning of the Psalter raises questions as to its function in the corpus. Wilson (2002, 114) has suggested that this psalm possesses at least three levels of meaning: (1) its original use for ideological authorization of the Davidic kings; (2) its later reuse in an early collection of the Psalter (Pss 2—89); (3) its use with Psalm 1 as an introduction. It is the last level of meaning that is of interest here.

The royal psalms (particularly Ps 2) appear to have been reinterpreted by subsequent generations, especially following the exile (see Starbuck, 205-12). As Childs (1979, 516) has observed, and others after him have confirmed, the location of Psalm 2 appears to emphasize "the kingship of God as a major theme of the whole Psalter." The notion of a human king was appropriated in messianic fashion, leaving room for the possibility of a new king or a new understanding of kingship (Tucker). Until then, however, the community is called to assert that the true King, Yahweh, reigns. As McCann (665) has concluded, "The perspective of the Psalter from the beginning is eschatological—that is, God's reign is proclaimed as a present reality, but it is always experienced by the faithful amid opposition."

Together, Psalm 1 and Psalm 2 call the reader to heed the instruction of Yahweh and acknowledge that despite circumstances that appear to the contrary, the Lord reigns. The remaining psalms serve as variations on these themes, highlighting the instruction of Yahweh and wrestling with the notion of the reign of Yahweh.

5.2. Book 4 as Editorial Center. If Psalms 1—2 provide an editorial introduction to the Psalter, Psalms 90—106 may stand as the editorial center of the entire corpus. Wilson (2002, 123-24) has noted that the royal psalms in the first half of the Psalter (Pss 1—89) appear to rehearse the story of the Davidic monarchy. Psalm 2 celebrates the covenant between Yahweh and the human king. Psalm 72, a prayer for the king, represents the passing of kingship to subsequent generations, and Psalm 89 laments Yahweh's apparent rejection of the Davidic covenant and the subsequent destruction of the nation.

Psalms 90—106 reorient the theological message of the Psalter. The first of the group, Psalm 90, lists Moses in the superscription. Although probably not a psalm of Moses, the mention of Moses returns the reader to a time in Israel's history when the nation was led by only one king, Yahweh. This theme is reinforced with the appearance of the enthronement psalms in the middle of this collection. Of the seventeen psalms in this collection, six are enthronement psalms (Pss 93; 95—99), celebrating the kingship of Yahweh. The final two psalms are historical psalms, recounting the faithfulness of Yahweh in the deliverance of his people out of Egypt and into the promised land. These psalms are meant to counter the crisis of exile, reasserting belief in the reign of Yahweh, even with the apparent absence of a human king.

5.3. Psalms 146—150 as Conclusion to the Psalter. The final five psalms in the Psalter provide an emphatic conclusion to the entire work. Overall, the five psalms offer a sustained call to "praise the LORD." Each of the five psalms contains an inclusio, opening and closing with *hallelû-yâ* ("praise the LORD"). This sustained call to praise God reaches a crescendo in Psalm 150. In this psalm the call to praise Yahweh appears twelve times throughout the psalm, followed by one last *hallelû-yâ* in Psalm 150:6, operating as a concluding imperative for the entire Psalter. Thus, whereas the earlier psalms (particularly Pss 3—89) were filled with lament, most notably lamenting the loss of kingship in Psalm 89, the final run of psalms suggests that lament does not have the last word in the lives of those who take seriously the *tôrâ* of the Lord and confess his reign. Psalm 150:6 appears as the final invitation: "Let everything that has breath praise the LORD."

6. Theological Themes in the Psalter.

In addition to careful attention to the literary structure of individual psalms and the editorial shape of the entire corpus, the interpreter must also be sensitive to the range of theological themes throughout the Psalter. Although the following themes are by no means exhaustive, they are suggestive of the theological range present in the psalms (for a comprehensive treatment, see Kraus 1992).

6.1. Yahweh as King. As suggested previously (see 5.1-2 above), the reign of Yahweh is central to the message of the Psalter, and the rehearsal of this theme appears frequently throughout the work. The kingship of Yahweh may be considered the "root metaphor" of the entire Psalter. All subsequent affirmations about the work and activity of Yahweh are predicated upon the assumption that Yahweh reigns as king. The references to Yahweh as divine warrior (Ps 18:7-15; 24:7-10) and judge (Ps 9:7; 105:7) are extensions of the central affirmation that Yahweh reigns as king. As J. Mays (30) has noted, "When viewed as limbs and branches dependent on the substance of this root metaphor, the psalms are the poetry of the reign of the LORD." Thus, whether explicitly announced (Ps 97:1) or more subtly claimed (Ps 82), the reign of Yahweh stands as the central theological claim of the Psalter.

6.2. Yahweh as Refuge. The theme of Yahweh as refuge (*ḥāsâ*) appears frequently, especially in the psalms of lament and encompasses a significant number of familiar metaphors within the Psalter, including "rock," "wings" and "holy mountain" (Creach; Brown). Not only does the final line of Psalm 2 remind the reader that "Happy are all who take refuge *[ḥāsâ]* in him," but also the verb often appears in the opening line of individual psalms (e.g., Ps 7:1; 11:1; 16:1; 71:1), thus establishing it as one of the operative themes of that psalm.

The psalmist also makes reference to being "in the shadow of your wings." Although this metaphor emerges from the constellation of images associated with animal metaphors (*see* Animal Imagery), particularly those from the ornithological world, the metaphor of wings is connected with the notion of refuge, connoting the protective and nurturing capacity of God. Other images such as "shield" and "fortress" (Ps 144:1-2) are employed similarly.

6.3. Yahweh as Creator. In attempting to portray the power of God, the psalms often resort to creation imagery. Several psalms (Pss 29; 93; 104) invoke ancient Near Eastern images of a cosmic combat with primeval chaos. For the psalmist, however, these images of a primeval battle reassert the claim that Yahweh reigns, and further that the reigning King has the capacity to create order out of chaos anew. In essence, these images not only celebrate what God has done but also celebrate and anticipate what God may yet do through his continued creative care.

Creation also plays a critical role in the Psalter in testifying to the reign of Yahweh. In Psalm 19 the psalmist explains, "The heavens are telling the glory of God; and the firmament proclaims his handiwork" (Ps 19:1 NRSV). Similarly, Psalm 97 announces that "the heavens proclaim his righteousness" (Ps 97:6 NRSV). The voices of creation join with the voices of God's people in announcing the one true God, who reigns over all creation.

6.4. Enemies. Repeatedly throughout the Psalter come allusions to the threats and taunts of enemies. In the psalms of the individual those who offer such threats are identified by various terms: "enemies" (*ʾōyēb* [Ps 3:7; 6:10; 7:5; 41:5]), "foes" (*sar* [Ps 3:1; 13:4; 23:5]), "evildoers" (*mĕrēʿîm* [Ps 26:5; 27:2]) and "wicked ones" (*rĕšaʿîm* [Ps 3:7; 12:8; 26:5]). In addition to excessive hubris (Ps 10:6; 14:1), the enemies appear to have turned their attention upon the psalmist, persecuting the poet in both word and deed. To highlight the nature of such attacks, the psalmist resorts to three metaphors in an effort to relay the nature of the threat: the enemies are compared to (1) a hostile army that attacks a helpless people (Ps 27:3; 55:18); (2) hunters who seek their prey (Ps 9:15; 35:7-8); (3) wild beasts that attack unsuspecting victims (Ps 22:12-13; 27:2) (Kraus 1992, 130-31).

In other psalms, particularly communal laments and royal psalms, the enemies are those nations hostile to Israel and Judah. These enemies appear stronger in number, often coming in chariots and on horses (Ps 20:7), thus forcing the king (or the community) to turn to Yahweh for deliverance from the invaders. These nations are the ones that do not know Yahweh and do not call on his name (Ps 79:6). Thus the threat of the enemies is also a challenge to the honor and the name of Yahweh. The community implores Yahweh to act, not simply to redeem them, but more critically to restore "the glory of your name" (Ps 79:9).

In addition to individual enemies and national foes, the psalmist also speaks more figuratively, referring to the primeval foes as a force to be reckoned with. In Psalm 74 the psalmist alludes to several primeval foes: "You divided the sea by your might; you broke the heads of the dragons in the waters. You crushed the heads of Leviathan" (Ps 74:13-14a NRSV). The primeval foes are meant to illustrate the disorder, destruction and chaos that threaten the ordered world in which Yahweh reigns as king. Yet, as Kraus (1992, 129) has observed, "the primeval powers are used to show by comparison how great Yahweh's power is."

7. The Psalms and the New Testament.

The early church made extensive use of the Psalter, quoting or alluding to it more than any other OT work. Apparently, the early Christian community continued the Jewish practice of making the psalms part of their liturgical materials. Paul encourages the community at Colossae to "sing psalms, hymns, and spiritual songs" (Col 3:16 NRSV) to God. Paul expresses similar sentiments in Ephesians 5:19-20.

In addition to the psalms functioning as a resource in early Christian worship, they served as a theological resource for the Christian community in its attempt to interpret the Christ event. To this end, a number of psalms were employed repeatedly in the NT, most notably Psalms 2; 22; 69; 110; 118.

The NT writers, particularly the Synoptic writers, cited Psalm 2 in their presentation of Jesus as God's anointed. At the baptism of Jesus, Psalm 2:7 ("You are my son; today I have begotten you" [NRSV]) is remembered, attesting to the divine sonship of Jesus while also formally announcing his rule as king. This same verse is quoted elsewhere (Acts 13:33; Heb 1:5; 5:5) in celebrating the exaltation of Christ. In addition, other themes from Psalm 2 appear, particularly the notion of the threat against God's anointed and his triumph over the nations (see Ps 2:8-9). In the book of Acts, Luke makes frequent use of these themes as he reflects upon the community's struggle for identity and survival. Upon the release of Peter and John, the community gathered together and "raised their voices" (in song?): "Sovereign Lord, who made the heaven and the earth, the sea, and everything in them, it is you who said by the Holy Spirit through our ancestor David, your servant: 'Why did the Gentiles rage, and the peoples imagine vain things? The kings of the earth took their stand, and the rulers have gathered together against the Lord and against his Messiah'" (Acts 4:24-26 NRSV). The community interpreted, through the lens of the Psalter, not only the hostile reception of Jesus by the world but also their own hostile reception.

Three of the longest laments, Psalms 22; 31; 69, are used extensively by the Synoptic writers in their accounts of Jesus' suffering and death. In addition to the cry of dereliction uttered from the cross (Ps 22:1 [Mt 27:46; Mk 15:34]), other el-

ements of the passion narrative have their parallels in Psalm 22 in particular. The Synoptic writers note the derision heaped on the one suffering, with those passing by shaking their heads in shame (Ps 22:7 [Mt 27:39; Mk 15:29; Lk 23:35]). Matthew also showed how those who passed by hurled insults at the suffering one (Ps 22:8 [Mt 27:43]), and all three Synoptic writers, plus John, drew attention to the dividing of the clothes and the casting of lots (Ps 22:18 [Mt 27:35; Mk 15:24; Lk 23:34; John 19:24]). Yet the methodology of the NT writers was far more complex than mere "proof-texting" from the OT in an effort to add credence to their narratives. Rather, the language of lament proved to be fertile ground for expressing the depths (and riches) of Christ's passion. As H.-J. Kraus (1992, 189) has suggested, Christ "not only identifies himself with all the suffering that finds expression in the Psalms . . . but also he alone is the servant of God, in whose life and death are fulfilled all the sufferings of all those who cry out in prayer."

Although explicit citations of the psalms appear absent in Revelation, idioms, phrases and concepts from the Psalter are readily present. The central affirmation of the Psalter, the rule of God over the world (see 6.1 above), functions as the dominant theme throughout Revelation (Rev 4:2, 9; 5:1, 7, 13; 6:16; 7:10, 17; 19:4; 21:5). In the enthronement psalms the psalmist announces, "the LORD reigns" *(yhwh mālak);* likewise, in Revelation 19:6 the author proclaims, "the Lord God reigns" *(ebasileusen kyrios ho theos).* In addition to the celebration of God's kingship in Revelation there is frequent mention of songs and the singing of a new song (Rev 5:9; 14:3). And toward the end of the Revelation, not only is the image of Zion reappropriated (Rev 21:9—22:5), but also the author recounts a vision of a heavenly multitude offering praise. Three times they begin their praise with "Hallelujah" (Rev 19:1, 3, 6), drawing the reader back to the conclusion of the Psalter. In so doing, the author reaffirms the continued reign of God and urges the reader to wait with the same hopeful expectation articulated in the book of Psalms.

See also ASAPH AND SONS OF KORAH; CONFIDENCE, PSALMS OF; CULT, WORSHIP: PSALMS; DAVID; DEAD SEA SCROLLS; EDITORIAL CRITICISM; FORM CRITICISM; HYMNS; LAMENT, PSALMS OF; LYRIC POETRY; POETICS, TERMINOLOGY OF; PROTECTION IMAGERY; THANKSGIVING, PSALMS

OF; WORSHIP.

BIBLIOGRAPHY. *Commentaries:* **L. Allen,** *Psalms 101-150* (WBC; Rev. ed.; Nashville: Thomas Nelson, 2002); **W. Brueggemann,** *The Message of the Psalms: A Theological Commentary* (Minneapolis: Augsburg, 1984); **P. Craigie,** *Psalms 1-50* (WBC; Rev. ed.; Nashville: Thomas Nelson, 2004); **E. Gerstenberger,** *Psalms: Part 1, with an Introduction to Cultic Poetry* (FOTL; Grand Rapids: Eerdmans, 1988); idem, *Psalms, Part 2 and Lamentations* (FOTL; Grand Rapids: Eerdmans, 2001); **F.-L. Hossfeld and E. Zenger,** *Psalms 2* (Hermeneia; Minneapolis: Fortress, 2005); **H.-J. Kraus,** *Psalms 1-59* (Minneapolis: Fortress, 1988); idem, *Psalms 60-150* (Minneapolis: Fortress, 1993); **J. L. Mays,** *Psalms* (IBC; Louisville: Westminster John Knox, 1994); **J. C. McCann Jr.,** "Psalms," NIB 4.641-1280; **M. Tate,** *Psalms 51-100* (WBC; Dallas: Word, 1990); **G. Wilson,** Psalms, vol. 1 (NIVAC; Grand Rapids: Zondervan, 2002). *Studies:* **R. Alter,** *The Art of Biblical Poetry* (New York: Basic Books, 1985); **W. H. Bellinger Jr.,** *Psalms: Reading and Studying the Book of Praises* (Peabody, MA: Hendrickson, 1990); **A. Berlin,** *The Dynamics of Biblical Parallelism* (Bloomington: Indiana University Press, 1985); **W. P. Brown,** *Seeing the Psalms: A Theology of Metaphor* (Louisville: Westminster John Knox, 2002); **B. S. Childs,** "Psalm Titles and Midrashic Exegesis," *JSS* 16 (1971) 137-50; idem, *Introduction to the Old Testament as Scripture* (Philadelphia: Fortress, 1979); **J. Creach,** *Yahweh as Refuge and the Editing of the Hebrew Psalter* (JSOTSup 217; Sheffield: Sheffield Academic Press, 1996); **J. Crenshaw,** *The Psalms* (Grand Rapids: Eerdmans, 2001); **J. Day,** *Psalms* (OTG; Sheffield: Sheffield Academic Press, 1992); **N. deClaissé-Walford,** *Reading from the Beginning: The Shaping of the Hebrew Psalter* (Macon, GA: Mercer University Press, 1997); **P. W. Flint,** *The Dead Sea Psalms Scrolls and the Book of Psalms* (STDJ 17; Leiden: E. J. Brill, 1997); **K. Galling,** "Der Beichtspiegel," *ZAW* 47 (1929): 125-30; **E. S. Gerstenberger,** *Psalms: Part 1, with an Introduction to Cultic Poetry* (FOTL 14; Grand Rapids: Eerdmans, 1988); idem, *Psalms: Part 2, and Lamentations* (FOTL 15; Grand Rapids: Eerdmans, 2001); **H. Gunkel,** *The Psalms: A Form-Critical Introduction* (FBBS 19; Philadelphia: Fortress, 1967); **J. Kugel,** *The Idea of Biblical Poetry: Parallelism and Its History* (New Haven: Yale University Press, 1981); **C. Rösel,** *Die messianische Redaktion des Psalters: Studien zu Entstehung und Theologie der Sammlung Psalm 2-89* (CthM 19; Stuttgart: Calwer, 1999); **K. Seybold,** *Introducing the Psalms* (Edinburgh: T & T Clark, 1990); **S. R. A. Starbuck,** *Court Oracles in the Psalms: The So-Called Royal Psalms in Their Ancient Near Eastern Context* (SBLDS 172; Atlanta: Society of Biblical Literature, 1999); **W. D. Tucker Jr.,** "Democratization and the Language of the Poor in Psalms 2-89," *HBT* 25 (2003) 161-78; **W. G. E. Watson,** *Classical Hebrew Poetry: A Guide to Its Techniques* (JSOTSup 26; Sheffield: Sheffield Academic Press, 1984); **G. Wilson,** *The Editing of the Hebrew Psalter* (SBLDS 76; Chico, CA: Scholars Press, 1985); **E. Zenger,** "Der Psalter als Wegweiser und Wegbeleiter: Ps 1-2 als Proömium des Psalmenbuchs," in *Sie wandern von Kraft zu Kraft: Aufbrüche, Wege, Begegnungen; Festgabe für Bischof Reinhard Lettmann,* ed. A. Angenendt and H. Vorgrimler (Kevelear: Butzon & Bercker, 1993) 29-47. W. D. Tucker Jr.

PSALMS 2: ANCIENT NEAR EASTERN BACKGROUND

The psalms may be described as song and as poetry, but foremost they are the prayers of ancient Israel. Of course, they are not the only prayers that Israel ever uttered. The Bible is filled with prayers in both prose and poetic format, some of which, like the psalms, were sung, and of course there were countless prayers that were spoken and never recorded. The book of Psalms is unique in being the official collection of Israel's corporate prayers. These were the prayers spoken during formal *worship. S. Mowinckel rightly called the book of Psalms the hymnbook of the temple. So it is correct also to regard Psalms as Israel's prayer book.

Not surprisingly, the religions of the ancient Near East also had their prayers, a number of which have been recovered in the modern period. Prayer is communication with one's God/gods, presupposing that the deity was thought to be a person. The people of Mesopotamia, Egypt, Hatti and Syro-Palestine thought of their gods in a personal way, and so they engaged them in conversation. Prayer is one side of that conversation.

Scholars have found it illuminating to read the psalms in the light of other ancient prayers. The best approach to studying the psalms in the light of their cultural analogues is not simply to draw on parallels but also to take note of the differences that exist between these various prayer traditions. But before any type of comparison can be made, the data must first be described. We thus begin with a survey of the prayers of ancient Mesopotamia, Egypt, Hatti and Syro-Palestine. Knowledge of the psalms is here presupposed and will not be described in any detail (see various articles on Psalms in the dictionary). While proceeding culture by culture, this survey will be structured according to the literary form of the prayers. These forms (*hymn, *lament, etc.) will be compared with their analogues in Psalms. Afterward, we will observe the similarities and differences in terms of style (*terseness, *parallelism, *imagery, etc.) as well as content.

1. Formal Analysis
2. Poetic Analysis
3. Content Analysis
4. Promise and Pitfalls
5. Conclusion

1. Formal Analysis.

1.1. Sumerian Prayers. Sumerian is the oldest known written language. The earliest Sumerian writing comes from about 3000 BC and is mostly economic in nature. Literary texts are known from closer to the middle of the third millennium BC, and the first hymns came from the period when the earliest Semitic rulers dominated the area of southern Mesopotamia, and are also well attested. Both hymns and laments are found in Sumerian.

1.1.2. Sumerian Hymns. Three types of hymns are attested in Sumerian: (1) hymns to various deities; (2) temple hymns; (3) hymns to kings. After a brief introduction to all three types, we will note the special importance of an author of a number of Sumerian hymns, Enheduanna.

1.1.2.1. Hymns to Deities. Not surprisingly, the bulk of hymns in the Sumerian corpus are hymns to various deities. We have well over one hundred such hymns through the Old Babylonian period that offer worship to many of the main gods of the pantheon. As an example, we note a portion of a hymn to the god Ninurta that draws particular attention to this god's function as a god of war. Throughout the hymn each stanza is repetitive, the first part lauding "my king," and the second specifically naming Ninurta:

[My king], of the house of the contentious
(and) disobedient, you are its adversary,
Of their city, you are its enemy.

Lord Ninurta, of the house of the
contentious (and) disobedient, you
are its adversary,
Of their city, you are its enemy.
(*ANET*, 577)

1.1.2.2. Temple Hymns. Numerous examples exist of hymns that celebrate not the deity per se but rather the god's dwelling place. A prime example of such a hymn is one dedicated to Ekur, which was the name of the temple of Enlil found in the city of Nippur. This hymn begins by praising the house as a whole and its parts as a "great mountain," the actual meaning of the Sumerian term "Ekur."

The great house, it is a mountain great,
The house of Enlil, it is a mountain great,
The house of Ninlil, it is a mountain great,
The house of darkness, it is a mountain
great,
The house which knows no light, it is
a mountain great,
The house of the Lofty Gate, it is a mountain
great. (*ANET*, 582)

One can surmise that the exaltation of the god's house is a way of exalting the god. After all, the temple would represent sacred space made holy by the presence of the god represented by his image.

1.1.2.3. Royal Hymns. We have a number of hymns in which it is the king himself who worships the deity and/or is himself the object of celebration (*see* Kingship Psalms). Twenty-four of the royal hymns are connected with the neo-Sumerian king Shulgi (twenty-first century BC). These hymns, particularly those that extol the king himself, are part of a program where Shulgi and his theologians promoted him as a divine figure—a rare practice in ancient Mesopotamia. Scholars speculate that the purpose was to give Shulgi the religious backing to create an empire in southern Mesopotamia. In the following example Shulgi worships Enlil. The hymn begins thus:

Enlil, the eminent one, the sovereign (god),
whose utterance is trustworthy,
Nunamnir, the eternal shepherd of the Land,
who hails from the Great Mountain,
The great counselor, the leader of heaven
and earth,

who is in control of all the divine offices. (*COS* 1.57:552)

The hymn also praises Enlil for choosing Shulgi to rule in the land. He is described as "a lion's seed," "the shepherd" and "the protective spirit of the land." J. Klein has argued that this and other Shulgi hymns were composed for use during his coronation. All told, there are well over one hundred attested examples of this genre in Sumerian, reaching into the early Old Babylonian period, where the rulers of cities such as Isin, Larsa and even Babylon allowed themselves to be praised, though they did not consider themselves gods.

1.1.2.4. Enheduanna. Special mention should be made of Enheduanna, the daughter of Sargon, the founder of the Akkadian dynasty, the first Semitic dynasty in Mesopotamia. These Akkadian speakers adopted Sumerian as their literary language, and Enheduanna, the high priestess of the moon god Nanna, was the first named author. She is known for her hymns. She functioned as priestess for forty years during the twenty-third century BC. Interestingly, the cycle of hymns that we have from her are concerned not with Nanna but with Inanna, the goddess of love and war (Hallo and van Dijk; De Shong Meador). In the opening of one such hymn Enheduanna praises the goddess as the one who controls the *me*, a Sumerian word and concept that denotes what Farber (*COS* 1.161:522) calls "the cultural norms which are the basis of Sumerian civilization and all aspects of life."

> Queen of all the *me*, radiant light,
> Life-giving woman, beloved of An
>   (and) Urash,
> Hierodule of An, much bejewelled,
> Who loves the life-giving tiara, fit for en-ship,
>   who grasps in (her) hand, the seven *me*,
> My queen, you who are the guardian of
>   all the great *me*,
> You have lifted the *me*, have tied the *me*
>   to your hands,
> Have gathered the *me*, pressed the *me* to your
>   breast.

Among other works attributed to her are forty-two hymns addressed to temples from the southern city of Eridu to the northern city of Sippar and the eastern city of Eshnunna (Sjoberg, Bergmann and Gragg).

1.1.3. Sumerian Laments. Sumerian was a language rich in lament literature, both corporate and individual. We know a number of different types by their native designations, but in the following we will survey only the most discussed types and those most relevant for comparison with the biblical genre.

1.1.3.1. Corporate Laments: The Balag *and the* Ershemma. Perhaps the most famous of all Sumerian laments are the so-called city laments that were composed in response to the destruction of Ur at the end of the Third Dynasty of that city. However, those texts are more relevant to the study of the book of *Lamentations rather than Psalms because they are historically specific laments (see Dobbs-Allsopp). Related to these city laments connected to the fall of Ur is the *balag* genre, which are also communal laments concerning the downfall of a city. The significant difference of the *balag*s is that they lack the historical specificity of the earlier texts. In this they may be compared in subject matter to the biblical communal laments bemoaning such destruction (Pss 44; 74; 79; 89; 137). The *balag* was an instrument, probably a harp, and thus probably accompanied the singing of these laments. These texts were written in a dialectical form of Sumerian called *emesal,* which was the language of the *gala*-priests who performed ritual lamentations (Kutscher).

The late (first millennium BC) congregation laments *(balag)* often had an *ershemma* connected to them. The word *ershemma* means something like the "lament of the *shem*-drum" and indicates the instrument that accompanied the singing or chanting of the lament by the *gala*-priest. The rituals of the *gala*-priests were usually recited in *emesal* (see above), and this includes the *ershemma.* The *ershemma* is a lamentation connected to the cult (Cohen). Indeed, from the cultic calendars of Uruk and Ashur we see that the *ershemma* concluded the liturgy. It was a song of intercession. In the description of E. R. Dalglish, they are "generally very formal, filled with epithetic and laudatory invocations, often with repetitious formula to induce the deities to repent" (Dalglish, 20). He divides the extant *ershemmas* into early ones from the First Dynasty of Isin (Old Babylonian period, the first half of the second millennium BC) and late ones from the first millennium BC. A number of the former are connected with the actual fall of the Dynasty of Isin, wherein the goddess of that city (Nin-Isina) laments the destruction of the city. But others are not connected with an actual destruction and therefore probably were reused in ritual contexts. The late *ershemma*s, on the other hand, were the ones, mentioned above, that were connected to the late congregational *balag*s.

1.1.3.2. The Private Lament: The Letter Prayer and the Ershahunga. Whereas the *balag* and the *ershemma* were communal laments, individuals could also petition the gods for help with their own troubles. Sumerian worshipers considered suffering to emanate from the anger of their gods. When suffering came in the form of illness or some other misfortune, they approached their gods in their sanctuaries in order to attempt to appease them.

An early form of delivering a prayer to a deity was accomplished by inscribing the message on a votive object. However, this method proved too costly for most. One interesting more economical strategy was the letter prayer, of which we have some examples (*COS* 1.164-65:532-34). The gods were represented by statues, and worshipers would write prayers in the form of letters and deposit them in the presence of a god. In this way the prayer would be constantly in the presence of the god. We have examples of both royal and nonroyal letter prayers. An even later form of Sumerian private petition is the *ershahunga*, meaning "lament that calms the heart" (of the deity), which explains its purpose. We know of at least 130 examples of this genre, mostly from the first millennium BC, from actual examples or from the citation of first lines in literary catalogs. These prayers were uttered to request healing from sickness, protection from and the destruction of enemies, or deliverance from the punishment of sin.

1.2. Akkadian Prayers. Although the Babylonians and Assyrians spoke and typically wrote in Akkadian, a Semitic language written in cuneiform, they often composed their prayers in Sumerian, usually the *emesal* dialect, and thus the prayers described above were often uttered by Akkadians (cf. the *ershahunga*s of the first millennium). However, there is also a tradition of bilingual and unilingual Akkadian prayers, predominantly hymns, but also one significant lament genre, the *shuilla*.

1.2.1. Akkadian Hymns. Numerous hymns of praise to various deities are attested, and a number are easily accessible in English translation (*ANET*, 383-91; *COS* 1.114-17:416-19; B. R. Fos-

ter, 1.65-74; 2.491-544). Perhaps the most famous is the great hymn to Shamash, the god of the sun. Shamash is praised as the one who physically illumines the world and, as the one who exposes the darkness, is also known as a protector of justice. A short citation from the song illustrates:

> At the brightness of your light, humankind's
> footprints become vis[ible].
> You blunt the horns of a scheming villain,
> The perpetrator of a cunning deal is
> undermined,
> You show the roguish judge the (inside of)
> a jail. (*COS* 1.117:418)

Hymns are directed to other deities (Marduk, Ishtar, etc.), who are extolled by their specific attributes and epithets. P. D. Miller (26) notes that there are relatively few thanksgivings, mostly general descriptions of praise.

1.2.2. Akkadian Laments: The Shuilla. The term *shuilla* is a Sumerian one meaning "to lift the hand" and likely refers to some kind of ritual gesture that accompanied the uttering of this prayer. Though the name is Sumerian, and there was a corporate lament in Sumerian by this name, there also is a well-attested Akkadian genre. Besides language, another difference between the Sumerian and Akkadian genres is that the latter are individual laments. According to W. W. Hallo (1878), they "combine the form of an incantation with the function of a prayer." These prayers begin with a hymn that specifies attributes of the deity that are relevant for the second section, which is a petition. The petitions concern things such as illness, the effects of witchcraft and the fear of death. The petitioners often recognize their own fault as a condition of their present dire situation, as is illustrated in the following example from a *shuilla* addressed to Marduk:

> Because of my misdeed, known or unknown,
> [I have been found neglectful], have
> trespassed, slighted, and sinned;
> [As against] my father, my begetter, against
> your great divinity,
> [I have been neglectful], have trespassed,
> slighted, and sinned. (Hunt, 156)

The third and final section of a *shuilla* is a renewed call to praise the deity.

1.3. Egyptian Prayers. Prayers are attested in the Egyptian language from the earliest period of the literature (Old Kingdom) down to the very latest periods (for collections, see J. L. Foster; Assmann; Barucq and Daumas). D. B. Redford has indicated that hymns and poetry comprise much of Egyptian literature. Also, Redford (2237) notes, hymns were sung, and they were sung in such a fashion that "the singing of the priests in the temple was likened to the rhythmic clatter of baboons at the rising of the sun." The reference to the priests is a reminder that many of these hymns were part of the formal worship liturgy of Egypt. In terms of their content, J. L. Foster (1995b, 2) points out that Egyptian prayers express "the entire gamut of religious emotions and attitudes seen in the hymn and prayers of later religions—classical or Judaeo-Christian." The earliest hymns are found in the Pyramid Texts, which are from the Old Kingdom (particularly the Fifth Dynasty and the Sixth Dynasty [2428-2250 BC]). These are writings from the pyramid walls and include a collection of spells, incantations and hymns. These texts assisted the dead pharaoh in his transition to the divine sphere. The Old Kingdom Pyramid Texts were produced for royalty. These are replaced by the Middle Kingdom Coffin Texts and then by the New Kingdom Book of the Dead. These latter two contain prayers, hymns and spells that enable common people to make the journey to the afterlife.

1.3.1. Hymns to Various Deities. The only significant difference between Egyptian hymns and other ancient Near Eastern hymns is the name of the deity who is the object of praise. Many Egyptian deities are the focus of attention in the numerous Egyptian hymns, including Osiris, Horus, Thoth, the divine pharaoh and even the divinized Nile, as the following excerpt illustrates: "Hail to thee, O Nile, that issues from the earth and comes to keep Egypt alive! Hidden in his form of appearance, a darkness by day, to whom minstrels have sung. He that waters the meadows which Re created in order to keep every kid alive" (*ANET*, 372).

1.3.2. The Great Hymn to Aten. Certainly the most famous and striking of all Egyptian hymns is the one dedicated to the Aten (sun-disc). The Aten was worshiped as early as the Twelfth Dynasty (c. 1900 BC), but devotion to him was intensified during the Amarna period (Eighteenth Dynasty), specifically during the rule of Akhenaton (fourteenth century BC). For reasons presently being debated, this king elevated Aten to the level of exclusive worship. Because of this, Akhenaton is frequently compared to Moses as promoting a monotheistic religion. Thus, this hymn takes on a special importance as purportedly expressing the theological ideas associated with this religious innovation.

Though discovered on the tomb wall of the pharaoh's minister Ay, the hymn speaks in Akhenaton's voice. It expresses the pharaoh's unique religious ideas with a powerful and beautiful style. It begins with a request to Aten that also praises the deity in his function as providing light to the world.

> Let your holy light shine from the height
>   of heaven,
>   O living Aten,
>   source of all life!
> From eastern horizon risen and streaming,
>   you have flooded the world with your
>   beauty.
> You are majestic, awesome, bedazzling,
>   exalted, overlord of all the earth,
>   yet your rays, they touch lightly, compass
>   the lands
>   to the limits of all your creation.

Reading on, one is struck by the intensely intimate language by which Akhenaton addresses his god:

> And you are in my heart;
>   there is no other who truly knows you
>   but for your son, Akhenaton.
> May you make him wise with your inmost
>   counsels,
>   wise with your power,
>   that earth may aspire to your godhead,
>   its creatures fine as the day you made
>   them. (J. L. Foster 1995a, 1751-53)

This hymn expresses the religious devotion of only a moment in the history of Egyptian religion. After Akhenaton's death his exclusive devotion to the sun-disc was rejected, and religion reverted to what was normal in Egypt.

1.4. Hittite Prayers. The Hittite empire that flourished in Asia Minor during the mid-second millennium BC left behind records of a significant number of prayers that have since been recovered, translated and published (Lebrun).

These prayers show that the Hittites approached their gods and goddesses for many of the same reasons as their neighbors did (de Roos). Hittite prayers may be characterized by three elements that may either be independent of each other or combined into a single prayer: *arkuwar, mugawar, walliyatar.*

The *arkuwar* is a defensive prayer in which the supplicant mounts a self-defense against the gods in the context of suffering of some sort that is understood as a punishment for sin. The best-known prayer from Hatti, the Plague Prayer of Murshili (latter fourteenth century BC), is a prayer of the *arkuwar* type. King Murshili's prayers are set in the twentieth year of a plague that has ripped through his country. It began during the reign of his father, Suppiluliuma I, and also claimed the life of his brother, Arnuwanda II. Murshili, though admitting that the son can inherit the sins of his father, defends himself and pleads with the gods on the basis of the fact that retribution has been made, in large part, by the plague itself: "What is [this]? Hattusa has made restitution through the plague. It [has made restitution] twenty-fold. So it happens. And the souls of the Storm-god of Hatti, my lord, [and of] the gods, my lords, are simply not appeased" [from the second plague prayer] (*COS* 1.60:156). The defense is legal, using language from the law court. Indeed, as de Roos (2000) states, "The Hittites expressed their relations with their gods not in terms of grateful sentiments, but in terms of justice and juridical judgment."

The *mugawar* is an invocation, an appeal to the god to pay attention. Kantuzili, a prince from around the time of Suppiluliuma I, uttered such a prayer to the Hittite sun-god, asking that god to intercede with his personal god, an underworld deity, on behalf of his sickness, when the sun-god descends at night into the underworld: "O Sun-god, when thou goest down to the netherworld (to be) with him, forget not to speak with that patron-god of mine and apprise him of Kantuzilis' plight!" (*ANET,* 400).

Finally, the *walliyatar* is a song of praise. An example of such a song may be given from a hymn to Telepinus, the Hattian storm-god, whose beginning gives the tenor of the whole: "Thou, Telepinus, art a noble god; thy name is noble among all gods; among the gods art thou noble, O Telepinus. Great art thou, O Telepinus; there is no other deity more noble and mighty

than thou" (*ANET,* 397).

Thus the Hittites praised their deities and turned to them in times of trouble and suffering. Hymn and lament are both found among their extant prayers.

1.5. Northwest Semitic Prayers. So far no separate hymns or laments written in a Northwest Semitic language (Eblaite, Ugaritic, Aramaic, etc.) have been discovered outside of the Bible. Even so, because of references within other texts, we know that such likely existed. Two examples may be presented. The largest collection of Northwest Semitic texts outside the Bible comes from the digs at Ras Shamra, or Ugarit. The best-known texts from this group are narrative myths. In these myths the main characters are often depicted as appealing to the gods for help. For instance, at the beginning of the Kirtu text the king of that name bemoans the loss of his family in a way that draws the attention of the gods. Similarly, the opening of the Aqhat epic features King Danel implicitly requesting that the gods give him a son. The dominance of narrative myth and lack of hymnic literature leads K. van der Toorn (1995, 2053) to say that "it should perhaps be assumed that in places such as Ugarit priests sung the texts of myths instead of psalms of praise."

Nonetheless, we do have an example of a petition to Baal in *KTU* 1.119:28-34:

> O Baal, drive away the mighty one from
>   our gates,
> the warrior from our walls!
> Bulls, O Baal, we will offer up,
> vows, Baal, we will pay!
> Male animals, Baal, we will offer up,
> *hitpu* sacrifices, Baal, we will perform:
> A banquet, Baal, we will go up,
> the paths to the temple, Baal, we will walk!

Outside of the Ugaritic texts, not much can qualify as prayer. In this context, however, the Aramaic inscription of Zakir, king of Hamat and Lu'ash, is commonly mentioned. It is not a prayer, but it alludes to a prayer that the king offered in the midst of battle ("I lifted up my hand [in a gesture of prayer] to Be'elshamayn, and Be'elshamayn heard me").

1.6. The Forms of the Psalms in the Context of the Ancient Near East. Communication with the divine is an integral part of all major ancient Near Eastern religions. Looking at it from an Israelite perspective, Miller (5) rightly notes that "when Israel began to pray to the Lord, it did so in the midst of peoples whose arms had long been raised and whose heads had been bowed to the gods that directed their lives and delivered them from disaster." Indeed, the literature of Egypt, Sumer, Babylon, Assyria, Egypt and, to a lesser extent, Canaan gives ample evidence of hymns of joy and songs of grief and disappointment.

One must conclude that there is great formal similarity between the prayers of these different cultures. In general, the hymns heap praise on the deities for who they are, what they provide for the world, and what they have done for the community and for the individual. Epithets are used as well as descriptive phrases to extol the deity. Furthermore, the laments of the region share similar concerns. Van der Toorn (1985, 62-67) highlights four major areas that recur in the laments of the ancient Near East: physical ailments, social strife, mental problems and disagreement with the divine realm.

Besides these general similarities, there are some specific ones as well. For instance, like Sumerian temple hymns, Israel knows of songs that celebrate their God by virtue of extolling the place where he chose to make his presence known. These are the so-called *Zion hymns (Pss 46; 48) as well as other hymns that reflect on the beauty of the sanctuary (Ps 84). In addition, there are extensive prayers that celebrate or provide petitions for the king (Pss 20; 21), a phenomenon that we noted throughout the ancient Near East. This, of course, is hardly surprising, considering the importance of the king, whether divine or not, throughout the Near East.

Attempts to find differences between the prayers of Israel and those of the rest of the Near East are often unpersuasive because they are based on degree rather than kind, and, in any case, we have only a selection of prayers. Even so the following differences may be noted.

(1) Israelite hymns often praise Yahweh for his acts in history (Pss 77; 78; 114; 137). Near Eastern hymns tend to praise their gods by means of reference to their function within the pantheon and by reference to their attributes and epithets. Of course, Yahweh, as sole God, incorporates all functions, attributes and epithets, and, as we will note later, he often is described in terms that are used in ancient Near Eastern literature for their gods. The lack of sustained attention to the gods' acts in history in the hymns is not absolute (see texts such as the Lamentation over the Destruction of Ur [not discussed in this article]), and it does not mean that ancient Near Eastern people did not conceive of their gods as active in the historical process (see Albrektson).

(2) The laments of Israel typically open with invocation, petition and complaint; the laments of Mesopotamia start with praise before moving on to petition. It is easier to describe this difference than to give an explanation of its significance. Could it be that Israelites felt freer to complain to God because they were in a covenant relationship with him? Could it be an indication of a more intimate relationship with God? It does seem inappropriate to propose, as some do, that the fact that Mesopotamian prayer opens with praise suggests that the worshipers who use them are whining or trying to extort an answer to their prayer.

(3) Evidence indicates that a number of the subgenres of prayer in the ancient Near East Akkadian *shuillas,* for instance, were connected to incantation rituals. Since divination was largely prohibited in Israel, we have nothing quite comparable.

2. Poetic Analysis.

Besides form, Hebrew poetry shares certain literary conventions with other ancient Near Eastern texts. Although this can be seen just by reading the texts side by side, there has not been a major comparative study in this area. The present article will offer only a few comments concerning major aspects of poetic language (terseness, parallelism, imagery). Focus will be on Akkadian and Ugaritic poetry because these are the only other major corpora of ancient Semitic poetry. Nonetheless, we should note that Akkadian poetic tradition shows signs of being influenced by Sumerian conventions, particularly in being, at times, highly repetitive. The study of Israelite poetic style has been helped by reference to these parallel literatures (Watson, 4-10), although it has been notoriously overused by M. Dahood and his students (see 4 below).

2.1. Terseness. Most, if not all, poetry is terse, using few words to communicate its message. In Hebrew poetry this terseness is achieved by *ellipsis, relative nonuse of prose particles and conjunctions, and imagery. The brevity of the poetic line may be observed on a printed page of the Hebrew Bible by all the white space. Virtually any line of Akkadian or Ugaritic poetry could be quoted to make this point.

Even in English the opening line of Psalm 23 is terse: "The LORD is my shepherd, I will lack nothing." In Hebrew, however, it is even briefer: *yhwh rōʿî lōʾ ʾehsār.* In the description of Baal's feast in *CTA* 3 i 8-17, we observe the same short, staccato-like lines:

> He arises, serves,
>> and gives him drink:
> He puts a cup in his hand,
>> a goblet in his two hands,
> A large vessel, mighty to look upon,
>> belonging to the furnishing of the
>> heavens,
> A holy cup women may not see,
>> a goblet 'Athiratu may not eye;
> One thousand *kd*-measures he takes from the
>> new wine,
>> ten thousand he mixes into his mixture.
>> (*COS* 1.86:250)

2.2. Parallelism. A second characteristic of Hebrew poetry shared with Akkadian and Ugaritic poetry is parallelism. Not every line of Hebrew poetry exhibits parallelism, but it is pervasive. "Parallelism" is the term to describe the echoing effect of poetry:

> Blessed are those who do not walk in the counsel of the wicked,
>> And in the way of sinners do not stand,
>> And in the seat of mockers do not sit.
>> (Ps 1:1)

This is a tricolon that illustrates the nature of parallelism well. Parallelism does not merely repeat the same thought two or three times; it always expands, intensifies, and sharpens the idea with each new colon (see Kugel). In this case, the three parts of the verse intensify the relationship with evil as it moves from walking (a casual acquaintance) to standing (more settled) to sitting (firmly ensconced) with it.

Although the level of parallelism most obvious to a reader of an English translation is on the level of meaning, as illustrated here (semantic parallelism), the feature also operates on a grammatical level. The three cola of Psalm 1:1 also cohere through grammatical parallelism, as

the three parallel subordinate clauses have the following pattern:

> *Blessed are those …*
>> negated verb / prepositional phrase
>> prepositional phrase / negated verb
>> prepositional phrase / negated verb

Parallelism is found extensively in Ugaritic poetry, as is illustrated by the following examples from the Baal myth:

> In a dream of the Gracious One, the kindly
>> god,
>> in a vision of the Creator of creatures,
> The heavens rain down oil,
>> the wadis run with honey.
>> (*COS* 1.86:271)

This example contains two bicola. In the first, "dream" parallels "vision" both in construct with an epithet of the god El. In the second, "heavens" parallels "wadis," both of which are effusive with luxurious liquid (oil and honey). However, although this example is a bicolon, it has long been noted that Ugaritic poetry exhibits a higher proportion of longer parallel lines, as this example from earlier in the myth illustrates:

> She seizes Motu, son of 'Ilu:
>> with a knife she splits him,
>> with a winnowing-fork she winnows him,
>> with fire she burns him,
>> with grindstones she pulverizes him,
>> in the field she sows him. (*COS* 1.86:270)

Here we have a parallelism of five parts, each describing a means by which Anat decimates Mot, the god of death, who has just consumed Baal.

2.3. Imagery. The third major identifying feature of poetry is an extensive use of figurative language. *Imagery seems to be a staple of poetry across cultures, so it is not surprising to discover that all ancient Near Eastern poetry utilizes imagery. It is therefore unnecessary to cite numerous examples of poems to make the point, but later we will observe not only that there is a similar use of imagery but also that specific ancient Near Eastern images are consciously appropriated by Israelite psalmists (see 3.1 below). However, for the present we will note the opening of a hymn for Shamash, the sun god, from the time of Assurbanipal:

Light of the great gods, resplendent
illuminator of the universe,
Lofty judge, shepherd of the celestial
and earthly regions. (*COS* 1.143:474)

In these opening lines we have the metaphors of judge and shepherd applied to the sun-god, who is literally the illuminator of the universe.

2.4. Secondary Poetical Devices. Along with the extensive use of terseness, parallelism and imagery throughout the psalms, there is a host of secondary poetical devices occasionally used in these poems. The list of such devices is too long to be discussed here (*see* Inclusio; Merism; Personification; Refrain; Rhyme; Sound Play; Wordplay; see also Watson). One example will have to suffice. The *acrostic form is used in a few psalms (e.g., Pss 9; 10; 111; 112; 119). These psalms begin each unit (whether a colon, a parallel line or a whole stanza) with successive letters of the Hebrew alphabet. Both Akkadian and Ugaritic poetry also have examples of poems or parts of poems where attention is given to some kind of pattern at the beginning of the lines. Interestingly, Akkadian also has examples of what are called sentence acrostics—for instance, the Babylonian Theodicy, where the twenty-seven stanzas each have lines that begin with the same syllabic sign that when taken together may be translated "I, Saggil-kinam-ubbub the incantation priest, fear god and king." The study of similar or nearly similar poetic devices enriches our understanding of their significance in Hebrew poetry.

3. Content Analysis.

Perhaps most interesting to readers of Psalms are the similarities and differences when it comes to the content of the psalms. There are comparisons to be made not only in terms of form and style but also in terms of content. Similar themes and images will be discussed in this section, as well as two psalms that have been recognized to have particularly close connections with ancient Near Eastern ideas. Many specific differences in content can also be pointed to, but we will focus on one obvious major one: the object of petition and praise.

3.1. Shared Imagery. Many, many images are shared between the Bible and its ancient Near Eastern parallels (see Keel). Here we will focus on a few striking illustrative examples (*see*

Psalms 6: Iconography).

3.1.1. Conflict with the Waters. Throughout the psalms God is pictured as dominating or defeating the waters (Day; Kloos; Wakeman; Curtis). For example, in Psalm 24:1-2 we read,

The earth is the LORD's, and everything in it,
the world, and all its inhabitants,
for he founded it on the seas
and established it on the rivers.

The conflict motif is stronger in the description found in Psalm 18:14-15:

He shot his arrows and scattered them
[the enemy],
with great bolts of lightning he routed
them.
The valleys of the waters were exposed
and the foundations of the earth laid bare
at your rebuke, LORD,
at the blast of breath from your nostrils.

The theme of conflict against the waters may also be found in reference to the exodus, specifically the crossing of Sea of Reeds. For instance, we read in Psalm 77:16 (see also Ps 114),

The waters saw you, God,
the waters saw you and writhed;
the very depths quaked.

Scholars are rightly convinced that passages such as these have as their background the ancient Near Eastern creation conflict motif as found in the Babylonian text known as the *Enuma Elish* and in the Ugaritic Baal myth (*see* Creation Theology). T. Jacobsen has argued that the latter came first and influenced the development of the former.

Nonetheless, we begin with a summary of the plot of the former, since the latter is broken. The *Enuma Elish* begins with a theogony. The two primordial gods, Apsu (the salt water) and Tiamat (fresh water), give birth to the younger gods. These are more active, and they disturb the sleep of their parents. As a result, Apsu, over Tiamat's objections, decides to kill the children. However, Ea, the god of wisdom, discovers the plot and through a preemptive strike kills Apsu and is enthroned on the floodwaters (see comment on Ps 29:10 in 3.2.2 below). The unintended consequence of this action was to anger Tiamat, who now turns her anger on the younger gods. She is a more formidable enemy than her husband, and Ea knows that he is no match for her. After Ea issues a challenge to the rest of the gods, it is his own son Marduk who steps forward to take on the challenge. He will battle Tiamat on condition that if he wins, he will be proclaimed the king of the pantheon.

He does defeat her, and afterwards he splits her body in half "like a shellfish" (she is a sea monster). He uses the top half to create the heavens and the lower half to create the earth (by pushing back and bounding her waters).

It is Marduk's defeat of Tiamat that is of interest to us. Although Genesis 1 does not use the conflict myth to describe creation, the psalms use it to describe the dominance of Yahweh and his ability to establish and maintain order out of chaos.

The Canaanite analogy to the *Enuma Elish* makes the biblical connection seem even closer. The relevant episode begins when the messengers of Yamm (the Sea) show up at the divine assembly to proclaim him king. He also demands that Baal become his servant. The other gods acquiesce, but Baal does not, and he requests that the craftsman god Kothar-wa-Hasis make him two clubs. With these clubs he fights and defeats Yamm. At this point the text breaks off, but most scholars think that it continued by describing creation. Also relevant is that later texts describe Leviathan (Lotan) as an associate of Yamm (see 3.1.2 below).

3.1.2. Leviathan. Connected to the previous topic but deserving of special comment is the Canaanite background to the creature known as Leviathan in the Bible. Most interesting is the reference to Leviathan in Psalm 74:13-17, which praises God by saying,

You split open the sea by your strength;
   you broke the heads of the monsters in
     the waters.
You crushed the heads of Leviathan
   and gave it as food to the creatures of
     the desert.
You opened up springs and streams;
   you dried up the ever-flowing rivers.
The day is yours, and yours also the night;
   you established the sun and moon.
You set all the boundaries of the earth;
   you made both summer and winter.

In Ugaritic literature, Leviathan *(Ltn)* is a seven-headed sea monster that is defeated by Baal (*KTU* 5.1.28). The picture in Psalm 74 is intentionally describing Yahweh in language that is reminiscent of the false gods who seduced Israelites away from proper worship of Yahweh.

3.1.3. Rider on the Clouds. The image of Yahweh riding the clouds is not infrequent in the book of Psalms (and in the prophets). Psalms 18; 68; 104 picture God as riding the cloud. This is storm-god imagery again. Thus, we are not surprised to hear that Baal is so described in Ugaritic literature. As a matter of fact, one of the most common epithets applied to Baal is "the one who rides the clouds." This storm cloud is the divine war chariot.

3.1.4. Zion and Zaphon. For many years Psalm 48:2 was thought to praise *Zion, God's holy place, on "the sides of the north." Since the discovery of the Ugaritic materials, scholars and translators have come to a different conclusion. As the TNIV renders the verse,

Beautiful in its loftiness,
   the joy of the whole earth,
like the heights of Zaphon is Mount Zion,
the city of the Great King.

The Hebrew word *ṣāpôn* is now recognized not to be "north," but rather the name of Baal's sacred mountain, Mount Zaphon (identified with Mount Casius in modern Syria) (*see* Mountain Imagery).

3.2. Specific Psalms.

3.2.1. Psalm 104 and the Hymn to Aten. Previously, we noted an extraordinary and unique Egyptian hymn that was dedicated to the sole worship of the sun-disc, Aten (see 1.3.1.2 above). Many scholars have commented that this psalm bears some kind of definite relationship to Psalm 104. J. L. Foster (1995a, 1759) focused on three elements of similarity: tone, some shared general ideas and one very specific parallel. The tone of both is celebratory of nature created by God and therefore leads to the worship of the deity. Both poems open with praise of God's glory and brilliance. Indeed, the opening of Psalm 104:2 sounds like the worship of a sun deity, "The LORD wraps himself in light as with a garment," while the Egyptian poem begins "Let your holy light shine from the height of heaven." In addition stanzas 9 and 10 of the hymn describe how Aten supplies the water, similar to

Yahweh's actions in how Psalm 104:10-13. Further, both Aten and Yahweh are named as source of life, and their absence is associated with death.

> Once you rose into shining, they lived;
>> when you sink to rest, they shall die.
> For it is you who are Time itself,
>> the span of the world;
>>> life is by means of you. (Hymn to Aten,
>>> stanza 12)

> All creatures look to you
>> to give them their food at the right time.
> When you give it to them,
>> they gather it up;
> when you open your hand,
>> they are well satisfied.
> When you hide your face,
>> they are terrified;
> when you take away their breath,
>> they die and return to the dust.
>> (Ps 104:27-29)

However, the most striking connection is in a passage that could be so close only if the psalmist (writing later) was aware of the Egyptian hymn.

> You set the darkness, it becomes night,
>> when all the beasts of the forest prowl.
> The young lions roar for their prey
>> and seek their food from God.
> The sun rises, and they withdraw;
>> they lie down in their dens.
> Then people go out to their work,
>> to their labor until evening.
> How many are your words, LORD!
>> In wisdom you made all of them;
>> the earth is full of your creatures.
> There is the sea, big and wide,
>> teeming with creatures without number—
>> living things both large and small.
> There the ships go back and forth,
>> and Leviathan, which you formed to play
>> there. (Ps 104:20-26)

Undoubtedly there is some connection between these two songs, with the Egyptian exercising some kind of influence on the construction of the Hebrew, but there are also indications of other influences on the psalm. For instance, the reference to Leviathan could only come from Canaan. We turn now to a look at a psalm that is filled with Canaanite-like language, Psalm 29.

3.2.2. Psalm 29 as Transformed Baal Hymn. It is well known that the Canaanite god Baal was a storm-god. He was the one who dispensed rain, flashed lightning, and created thunder. Psalm 29 pictures Yahweh as a storm-god in language reminiscent of Baal (Ginsberg; Cross; Craigie). The repeated reference to Yahweh's voice, for instance, certainly connotes thunder. After all, lightning accompanies his destructive "voice" (Ps 29:7).

Indeed, there are other features of this psalm that further tie Psalm 29 to Canaanite theology. For instance, the opening verse appeals to the "heavenly beings" *(bĕnê ʾēlîm)*, the Ugaritic cognate being a reference to the pantheon, the "sons of El." Poetically, the psalm has a high percentage of repetitive parallel lines and tricola, characteristics of Ugaritic poetry. Furthermore, the geographical references (Lebanon, Sirion, Desert of Kadesh) point to a location north of Israel per se. Finally, mention should be made of Psalm 29:10, where the theme of Yahweh's enthronement over the flood is connected to the creation conflict theme (see 3.1.1 above) and perhaps specifically associated with the picture of Ea building his throne on the body of Apsu in the opening of the Enuma Elish.

All in all, the evidence indicates that the psalm may be a Baal poem transformed to become a poem to worship Yahweh. This might have taken place by simply substituting the name "Yahweh" for "Baal." However, the fact that we have no Ugaritic hymns should give our confidence pause here. We can see the connection by virtue of themes in the epics and poems, and we do have good reason to suspect that there were Canaanite poems in spite of the lack of evidence. Nonetheless, because of a lack of direct evidence, we must allow for the possibility that an Israelite poet created this poem. However, if so, then that poet must have intentionally composed it using Canaanite ideas and poetic conventions.

3.3. Rationale. Why would Israelite poets utilize ancient Near Eastern religious ideas in their compositions, particularly to describe their unique God in the language of pagan gods? It is doubtful that this was done unconsciously or as a means of affirming these foreign gods. The best explanation is that the poets were demonstrating that Yahweh was the one and only true God. In Psalm 29 it is not Baal, but rather Yahweh, who provides storm and rain. In this way, the psalmists appeal to those Israelites who were tempted to worship false gods to get what they wanted.

4. Promise and Pitfalls.

Familiarity with ancient Near Eastern materials can indeed lead to new insights and a richer reading of the psalms. Indeed, in the cases of Psalm 29 and Psalm 104, recognition of their connection to Near Eastern poems with similar imagery allows an identification of an apologetic function of these poems. Thus, we have noted the benefit of such study. However, there are also potential pitfalls that can result from an overzealous and uncontrolled reading of the psalms in relationship to ancient Near Eastern literature. Two examples may be cited in this regard.

S. Mowinckel commands respect for his many contributions to the study of the OT and the psalms. He is the scholar who more than anyone else reminded readers of the cultic setting of the psalms, for instance (*see* Cult, Worship: Psalms). However, he overused ancient Near Eastern analogies in order to propose a single *Sitz im Leben* for the psalms in an annual enthronement ceremony that purportedly took place on New Year. He argued this not so much on innerbiblical evidence but rather by positing an analogue with the Babylonian Akitu (New Year) festival. Though his views held sway and dominated discussion for years (and even today comprise a required episode in any narrative history of modern psalm interpretation), no scholar working in the area today would affirm his conclusions in this matter. The connection between the psalms and this particular ancient Near Eastern background was much too tenuous, and thus scholars recognize that Mowinckel's ideas were an imposition of ancient Near Eastern religious ideas on the OT.

A second cautionary tale may be told in connection with the work of M. Dahood. The central thesis of Dahood's approach to the book of Psalms is that the Hebrew needs to be rewritten in the light of discoveries in Northwest Semitic language (in particular Ugaritic, but toward the end of his career also Eblaite), including poetic devices and imagery. He maintained extremely high regard for the Hebrew consonants but low regard for the vocalization and word separation done by the Masoretes (AD 400-1000). He believed that through the rediscovery of ancient literature modern scholars now knew how to read the psalms better than the Massoretes did. Thanks to the critical work of J. Barr and others, it is now clear that Dahood overreached in his use of Near Eastern texts in interpreting the psalms, and so his conclusions do not enjoy significant support today.

Fortunately, today it appears that most modern academic commentaries on the psalms use the ancient Near Eastern material in a more judicious manner. Even so, it is necessary to evaluate each case on its own merits.

5. Conclusion.

We have observed a significant similarity in the form and style of the psalms and their ancient Near Eastern analogues. Even in the area of content, especially when measured by imagery, there is substantial connection. However, it is appropriate to conclude by highlighting the difference between the two traditions that must be borne in mind when comparing the two. The object of petition and worship is completely different. That is, psalms utilize the forms, style and imagery to worship Yahweh, whom they proclaim as the only legitimate deity in the universe.

See also Cult, Worship: Psalms; Form Criticism; Hymns; Kingship Psalms; Lament, Psalms of; Lyric Poetry; Oral Poetry; Psalms 1: Book of; Thanksgiving, Psalms of.

Bibliography. **B. Albrektson,** *History and the Gods: An Essay on the Idea of Historical Events as Divine Manifestations in the Ancient Near East and in Israel* (ConBOT 1; Lund: Gleerup, 1967); **J. Assmann,** *Ägyptische Hymnen und Gebete* (BAW; Zürich: Artemis, 1975); **J. Barr,** *Comparative Philology and the Text of the Old Testament* (Winona Lake, IN: Eisenbrauns, 1987); **A. Barucq and F. Daumas,** *Hymnes et prières de l'Égypte ancienne* (LAPO 10; Paris: Cerf, 1980); **M. E. Cohen,** *The Canonical Lamentations of Ancient Mesopotamia* (2 vols.; Potomac, MD: CDL Press, 1988); **P. C. Craigie,** "Psalm XXIX in the Hebrew Poetic Tradition," *VT* 22 (1972) 143-53; **F. M. Cross,** "Notes on a Canaanite Psalm in the Old Testament," *BASOR* 117 (1950) 19-23; **A. H. W. Curtis,** "The 'Subjugation of the Waters' Motif in the Psalms: Imagery or Polemic?" *JSS* 23 (1978) 244-56; **M. Dahood,** *Psalms* (3 vols.; AB 16, 17, 17A: Garden City, NY: Doubleday, 1966-1970); **E. R. Dalglish,** *Psalm Fifty-One in the Light of Ancient Near Eastern Patternism* (Leiden: E. J. Brill, 1962); **J. Day,** *God's Conflict with the Dragon and the Sea: Echoes of a Canaanite Myth in the Old Testament* (COP 35; Cambridge: Cambridge University Press, 1985); **J. de Roos,** "Hittite Prayers," in *Civilizations of the Ancient Near East,* vol. 3, ed. J. M. Sasson (New York: Scribner, 1995) 1997-2005; **B. De Shong Meador,** *Inanna, Lady of Largest Heart: Poems of the Sumerian High Priestess Enheduanna* (Austin: University of Texas Press, 2000); **F. W. Dobbs-Allsopp,** *Weep, O Daughter of Zion: A Study of the City-Lament Genre in the Hebrew Bible* (BibOr 44; Rome: Editrice Pontificio Istituto Biblico, 1993); **A. Falkenstein and W. von Soden,** *Sumerische und akkadische Hymnen und Gebete* (BAW; Zürich: Artemis, 1953); **P. W. Ferris Jr.,** *The Genre of Communal Lament in the Bible and the Ancient Near East* (SBLDS 127; Atlanta: Scholars Press, 1992); **B. R. Foster,** *Before the Muses: An Anthology of Akkadian Literature* (3rd ed.; 2 vols.; Bethesda, MD: CDL Press, 2005); **J. L. Foster,** "The Hymn to Aten: Akhenaten Worships the Sole God," in *Civilizations of the Ancient Near East,* vol. 3, ed. J. M. Sasson (New York: Scribner, 1995a) 1751-61; idem, *Hymns, Prayers, and Songs: An Anthology of Ancient Egyptian Lyric Poetry,* ed. S. T. Hollis (SBLWAW 8; Atlanta: Scholars Press, 1995b); **H. L. Ginsberg,** "A Phoenician Hymn in the Psalter," in *Atti del XIX Congresso Internazionale degli Orientalisti: Roma, 23-29 settembre 1935* (Rome: Tipografia del Senato, 1938) 472-76; **W. W. Hallo,** "Lamentations and Prayers in Sumer and Akkad," in *Civilizations of the Ancient Near East,* vol. 3, edited by J. Sasson (New York: Scribner, 1995) 1871-81; **W. W. Hallo and J.-J. van Dijk,** *The Exaltation of Inanna* (YNER 3; New Haven: Yale University Press, 1868); **J. Hunt,** "The Hymnic Introduction of Selected 'Suilla' Prayers Directed to Ea, Marduk, and Nabu" (Ph.D. diss.; Brandeis University, 1994); **T. Jacobsen,** "The Battle between Marduk and Tiamat," *JAOS* 88 (1968) 104-8; **O. Keel,** *The Symbolism of the Biblical World: Ancient Near Eastern Iconography and the Book of Psalms* (New York: Seabury Press, 1978); **J. Klein,** *Three èulgi Hymns: Sumerian Hymns Glorifying King èulgi of Ur* (BSNELC; Ramat-Gan: Bar-Ilan University Press, 1981); **C. Kloos,** *Yhwh's Combat with the Sea: A Canaanite Tradition in the Religion of Ancient Israel* (Leiden: E. J. Brill, 1986); **J. L. Kugel,** *The Idea of Biblical Poetry* (New Haven: Yale University Press, 1981); **R. Kutscher,** *Oh Angry Sea (a-ab-ba hu-luh-ha): The History of a Sumerian Congregational Lament* (YNER 6; New Haven: Yale University Press, 1975); **R. Lebrun,** *Hymnes et prières hittites* (HRel 4; Louvain-la-Neuve: Centre d'Histoire des Religions, 1980); **T. Longman III,** "The Psalms and Ancient Near Eastern Prayer Genres," in *Interpreting the Psalms,* ed. P. John-ston and D. Firth (Leicester: Inter-Varsity Press, 2005); **P. D. Miller Jr.,** *They Cried to the Lord: The Form and Theology of Biblical Prayer* (Minneapolis: Fortress, 1994); **S. Mowinckel,** *The Psalms in Israel's Worship* (Nashville: Abingdon, 1962); **D. B. Redford,** "Ancient Egyptian Literature: An Overview," in *Civilizations of the Ancient Near East,* vol. 3, ed. J. M. Sasson (New York: Scribner, 1995) 2223-41; **A. W. Sjoberg, E. Bergmann and G. B. Gragg,** *The Collection of Sumerian Temple Hymns* (TCS 3; Locust Valley, NY: J. J. Augustin, 1969); **K. van der Toorn,** *Sin and Sanction in Israel and Mesopotamia: A Comparative Study* (SSN 22; Assen: Van Gorcum, 1985); idem, "Theology, Priests, and Worship in Canaan and Ancient Israel," in *Civilizations of the Ancient Near East,* vol. 3, ed. J. M. Sasson (New York: Scribner, 1995) 2043-58; **M. Wakeman,** *God's Battle with the Monster: A Study in Biblical Imagery* (Leiden: E. J. Brill, 1973); **J. H. Walton,** "Hymns, Prayers, and Incantations," in *Ancient Israelite Literature in Its Cultural Context* (Grand Rapids: Zondervan, 1989); **W. G. E. Watson,** *Classical Hebrew Poetry: A Guide to Its Techniques* (London: T & T Clark, 2005).

T. Longman III

PSALMS 3: HISTORY OF INTERPRETATION

Through the ages of the church the psalms have lived in its liturgy, praises and scholarship. They give evidence of God's kingship and his messiah's reign and enable the church to reflect upon its own response to that reign. This article explores the history of the interpretation of the psalms. Given the multitude of ways the psalms have been used, this article traces the history of interpretation as reflected in the scholarship of the church and leaves to other studies the exploration of the rich use of the psalms in liturgy and prayer, in literature and art.

1. Psalms in the New Testament
2. Psalms in Patristic Literature
3. Psalms in the Medieval Period
4. Psalms in the Reformation

5. Psalms in the Modern Period

6. Directions for the Future

1. Psalms in the New Testament.

The NT quotes extensively from the LXX text of Psalms, using the psalms in a variety of ways. One discovers the psalms used apologetically (e.g., Rom 3:4, 10-18; 4:7-8; 11:9-10) and as a basis for extended commentary (Heb 3:7-4:13). However, employing hermeneutical practices common to first-century Judaism, the early church uses the psalms primarily in a messianic sense, showing that the life, death and resurrection of Jesus fulfilled the predictions of the psalms for the coming *messiah.

This messianic, Christological reading occurs several ways. First, *David is presented in the NT as a prophet (Mt 22:43; Mk 12:36; Acts 2:30; 4:25), and Davidic psalms are presented as foretelling messianic events (Mt 22:43-45; Acts 2:25, 31; 4:11). Second, in the Gospel accounts Jesus quotes from the psalms (e.g., Mt 21:16 [Ps 8:2]; Mt 21:42; Mk 12:10; Lk 20:17 [Ps 118:22-23]; Mt 22:44-45; Mk 12:36-37; Lk 20:42-44 [Ps 110:1]), as do the Gospel writers (Mt 4:6; Lk 4:10-11 [Ps 91:11-12]; Mt 21:9; 23:39; Mk 11:9; Lk 13:35; 19:38; Jn 12:13 [Ps 118:25-26]). These quotations are given as evidence of the messiahship of Jesus. Third, the book of Acts uses the psalms to provide proof of Jesus' messiahship (Acts 2:25-28, 34-35 [Ps 16:8-11; 110:1]) and connects the continuing events of the early church to messianic psalms (Acts 4:10-11 [Ps 118:22-23]). Fourth, the presentation of Jesus as messiah is achieved by stringing together several psalms used as proof texts (e.g., Heb 1:5-13 [Ps 2:7; 104:4; 45:6-7; 102:25-27; 110:1]). In all of these ways the NT writers attest their conviction that Jesus is the messiah, and that this is predicted in the psalms.

2. Psalms in Patristic Literature.

2.1. Psalms in the Apostolic Fathers. The apostolic fathers continue the NT emphasis on the prophetic nature of the psalms. *Barnabas* 5:12 (citing Ps 22:21) names the psalmist as a prophet who foretells the death of Christ, and *1 Clement* 16:15-16 (citing Ps 22:6-8) foretells his humble life. In *1 Clement* 36:4-5 the author uses Psalm 22:7-8; 110:1 to make messianic claims in the same way the NT does.

The apostolic fathers also cite the psalms pastorally, exhorting ethical conduct and Christian service. For instance, *Didache* 3:7 (citing Ps 37:11) urges meekness of life, while Polycarp, *To the Philippians* 6:3 (citing Ps 2:11), urges fearful service of God.

In *Barnabas* 10—11 we discover allegorical interpretation of Psalm 1 similar to that found in the later fathers. First, the righteous man as a tree of life planted by streams of water is allegorical of a Christian's hope in the cross and descent into the waters of baptism. Second, the three types of wicked people to be avoided are given as the explanation of three types of foods to be avoided in the Mosaic *law—the law is the allegory now rightly explained in the key given in Psalm 1:1.

The apostolic fathers, in reading the psalms as prophecies foretelling Christ and as a resource for pastoral care and exhortation, reflect the interpretation of the NT and provide a hermeneutical bridge to the church fathers. Their allegorical reading is not found in the NT's interpretation of the psalms. This hermeneutic is, however, taken up in the later church fathers and subsequent interpretation until the modern period. In interpreting the psalms for the church, this becomes the indispensable method for over one thousand years.

2.2. Psalms in the Church Fathers. The church fathers refer to the psalms frequently in their apologetic, ethical and pastoral works as well as in commentaries. The fathers continue to read the psalms as prophecy, finding proof of Christ. Especially for the early church fathers, this often occurs in the context of apologetic argumentation with Jews and gnostics. Justin Martyr (*Dial.* 32—33) argues that Psalm 110 prophesied Christ's ascension and exaltation, and Psalm 22 is used by Justin Martyr (*Dial.* 98—106), Irenaeus (*Haer.* 4.20, 33) and Tertullian (*Adv. Jud.* 10) as prophetic proof of Christ's passion. Text-critical awareness formed a part of such argumentation. For instance, Tertullian and Justin Martyr, using a text of Psalm 96:10 that states that the Lord reigns "from the tree" (which was likely a Christian interpolation), argue that the Jews had altered the text for apologetic purposes.

In interpreting the psalms, the church fathers reflect the developing interpretive traditions of Alexandrian and Antiochene hermeneutics. Alexandrian exegesis, going beyond the text's literal meaning to its spiritual meaning, dominates patristic writing and later medieval work. Thus, in *Enarrationes in Psalmos*, in a homily on Psalm 120 (the first Psalm of Ascent), Augustine argues that these psalms speak of one who ascends upward in spiritual life, away from the "earthly, fragile, temporal objects" and toward God alone. Likewise, his homily on Psalm 114 reads the historical recital of the Israelites' removal from Egypt as the Christian's own movement out of the bondage of sin, or depicting the church's doctrine of baptism. Jerome, although engaged with historical and grammatical questions (his Psalms translation from Hebrew to Latin provides the basic text for the Roman Catholic Church), moves beyond them to the spiritual meaning of the psalms, leaving behind what was considered the letter that kills for the true spiritual food of the Psalter.

Patristic interpretation includes the superscriptions of the Psalms (*see* Psalms 5: Titles), which are treated as part of the inspired psalm text. Authorship is not questioned but generally is ascribed to David as a prophet. Considered key to a correct interpretation of the psalm, these titles are given mystical, allegorical interpretations enabling the psalms of David to refer to Christ. The obscure musical notations, interpreted through an etymological and allegorical approach, are also given christological import. By this method, Jerome (*Tract. Ps.* 61) interprets the title phrase in Psalm 16, "A Miktam of David," etymologically as indicative of the humility (from *mākak*, "be humiliated") and perfection (*tām*) of Christ. This mystical interpretation of the titles was the norm until the modern era.

The church fathers are not unconcerned with psalm types and the shape of the book of Psalms. Athanasius (*Ep. Marcell.* 14) categorized the psalms as narrative, prayer, petition, thanksgiving, confession, prophecy, praise and exhortation, and Jerome (*Tract. Ps.* 1) reflects a tradition of reading Psalm 1 as introductory to the Psalter as a whole. These questions, which become paramount in modern interpretive methods, never gained a place of primary importance in this era; rather, the focus is on reading the psalms for their spiritual meaning, finding in them Christ and his church.

Some work of the Antiochene fathers on the psalms remains extant. Theodore of Mopsuestia produced a commentary on Psalms 1—81, using an approach similar to a modern grammatico-historical approach. Ascribing authorship to David, he argues that David spoke prophetically, but only of events concerning the nation of Israel, and only up to the Maccabean period; in other words, no psalm prophesied Christ, and psalms could apply to him only through analogous circumstances. Yet, despite his rejection of the allegorical method of the Alexandrians, Theodore was not totally free of it. His exegetical work on Psalm 45, which he deemed messianic (along with only Pss 2; 8; 110), is really an allegorical approach in which the king is Christ, and the bride is the church.

3. Psalms in the Medieval Period.

Medieval scholars are not noted for moving Psalms interpretation into fresh arenas. Instead, they reproduce the tradition of the fathers, amassing collections (called glosses) of nonannotated patristic comments that surround and interleave each psalm. Psalms exegesis in the medieval period follows the allegorical and spiritual readings of the church fathers, now fully expanded to fourfold interpretation (literal, allegorical, tropological, anagogical). Reading psalm titles as part of the inspired text, and applying to both titles and text the fourfold interpretive methods, these scholars saw the psalms everywhere speaking prophetically of the life, death and resurrection of the Christ. Additionally, the church is hermeneutically retrojected into the OT people of God, and the psalms are robbed of any historical placement in the life of the Israelites. For instance, in Psalm 52 the given historical setting is allegorically interpreted by the Venerable Bede (cited in Neal and Littledale 2.211), so that David becomes Christ, Saul becomes the persecuting Jew, and Doeg becomes Judas the traitor or the antichrist, while Ahimelech the priest stands as the elect church.

During the later medieval period fruitful interaction between some Christian and Jewish commentators (such as Nicholas of Lyra and Rashi in the twelfth century) refined knowledge of the Hebrew text. Text-critical issues in the Vulgate were addressed, with some interpreters questioning or rejecting the accepted Vulgate version. This interaction was at times married to a more Antiochene, literal method (as in Hugh and Andrew of St. Victor). However, neither the Antiochene influence, nor attention paid to the original text, was able to offset the centuries-long interpretive traditions of the fathers. It did, however, demonstrate the advantage to psalms study of the original languages and the results of a more literal hermeneutic, both of which were of great importance to the Reformers' interpretation.

4. Psalms in the Reformation.

New interpretive methods of the Protestant Reformation reflect the atmosphere of learning contemporaneous to it. A retrieval of the original language of the psalms text, a concern for the historical setting of the psalms, and an effort to interpret the psalms by the biblical text alone, apart from the dogmas of the Roman Catholic Church, characterize this period. The two great Reformers, Luther and Calvin, are indicative of these efforts.

Luther's introduction to his first lecture series on the psalms and his lectures and homilies on selected psalms reveal his interpretive strategies; Calvin's work is contained in his commentary on the book of Psalms. Luther still interprets to discover the fourfold meaning of the text, allowing (theoretically, at least) for spiritual readings only if the same truth is elsewhere stated historically. When Psalm 17:7 speaks of "those who withstand Thy right hand," the passage is first allegorical, for Christ is the right hand and power of God (as also noted in Ps 118:16), second tropological, for the right hand is the merit of Christians experienced in life through the gracious work of God, and third anagogical, for the right hand is the awarding of glory in the future (as argued from Mt 25:33-34) (Luther 10.111). Yet the overriding interpretive principal is that every psalm speaks prophetically of Christ and, by extension, the church conformed to Christ in all things. By this method the righteous man of Psalm 1 is both Christ and the church, which righteously rejects the ways of all the ungodly. Calvin, on the other hand, rejected allegorical interpretation, seeking the literal meaning of the text through grammatical and historical analysis. However, he moves beyond the text's literal meaning by finding in the psalms types of Christ and the church. In this way, Psalm 2 is interpreted according to David's historical reign but is interpreted typically as true prediction of Christ (Calvin 1.11).

The Reformers affirm the prophetic nature of the psalms and the traditional authorship ascriptions. Yet Calvin (3.159) can consider Psalm 74 (an Asaphite psalm [*see* Asaph and Sons of Korah]) possibly originating in the exilic or Antiochene period. However, he does not argue vehemently for such possibilities; his interests lie instead in interpreting the psalms for pastoral application. Both Reformers reject the etymological and allegorical interpretation of the psalm titles, allowing that many of the terms are obscure and likely are musical notations.

Calvin (1.xxxvii-xxxix) exhibits the deep pastoral sense of the Reformers in their work with the psalms. He gives the several pastoral purposes of the psalms in the preface to his commentary: inner contemplation, instruction in prayer, praise, holy living and the knowledge of eternal salvation. Both Luther and Calvin use the psalms to exhort believers in practical living.

5. Psalms in the Modern Period.

5.1. The Eighteenth Century: Hebrew Poetry. Up to the eighteenth century, psalms interpretation continued in the medieval and Reformation interpretive traditions, but increasingly in the eighteenth century the application of historical assumptions and approaches moved scholarly interpretation away from the dominant model of spiritual interpretation. In 1753 R. Lowth, professor of poetry at Oxford University, published his lectures on the psalms as *De sacra poesi Hebraeorum*. His concerns are not theological but rather literary and historical, and they express themselves in two interpretive claims. First, as ancient poetry, the psalms must be read in light of their historical and cultural setting—a hermeneutic that became increasingly important in psalms interpretation throughout the modern period. Second, he explores the form of Hebrew poetry, most particularly the *parallelism of poetic lines. His formulation of synonymous, antithetic and synthetic parallelisms delineates the discussion of Hebrew poetry for the modern period, with little major advance until J. Kugel's *The Idea of Biblical Poetry* in 1981.

Lowth still holds to Davidic authorship of the psalms but moves away from the allegorical interpretation of the fathers. Instead, he speaks of a "mystical allegory" that allows the literal meaning to remain alongside a typological reading that, as prophecy, points forward to the Christ.

5.2. The Nineteenth Century: Historical-Critical Interpretation. Historical concerns dominate this century's psalms study. Consequently, authorship, occasion, date, Psalter formation, and Hebrew linguistics and grammar form the discussion (*see* Historical Criticism). The superscriptions' historical value is generally discounted, and new historical settings are considered as Davidic authorship is relinquished in whole or in part. W. de Wette's 1811 commentary rejects Davidic authorship and an early date for the psalms, and most critical scholars in the century follow suit to one degree or another. F. Delitzsch (1867), G. H. A. von Ewald (1880) and J. J. S. Perowne (1882) each credit some of the psalms to Davidic authorship (Delitzsch allows for fifty psalms, von Ewald that some of the *lĕdāwīd* psalms [Pss 3—41] could be Davidic, Perowne that the majority of these psalms were Davidic). Most discount the historical settings in the superscriptions and place many psalms in the exilic and postexilic eras. The Maccabean era is considered a locus of composition because an evolutionary idea of religion posited that such individual expressions of faith must stem from a later, developed, internalized religion. T. K. Cheyne (1888), a most extreme expression of this idea, denies in toto the reliability of the superscriptions and their authorial designations, placing the Psalter's composition almost totally in the Maccabean era. By the late nineteenth century, however, commentators such as C. A. Briggs and S. R. Driver question the reasonableness of such wholesale late composition, and though Maccabean psalms are not discounted a priori, the claim is increasingly considered unjustifiable.

Not all commentators move from the precritical stance toward authorship and the reliability of the superscriptions. M. A. Schimmelpenninck, in her work of 1821 and 1825, is aware of the new historical-critical theories but rejects them, as does E. W. Hengstenberg in 1842. In these few authors the historical-critical wave is resisted but not stemmed.

The process of the Psalter's composition is commonly discussed in the commentaries of this period. Most recognize the discrete collections in the Psalter (such as the Davidic Psalms [Pss 3—41; 51—72], the Asaphite collection [Pss 78—83], Psalms of Ascent [Pss 120—134]) and posit an expanding Psalter from the early (and possibly Davidic) period to the postexilic period and even the Maccabean period. Widespread recognition of the fivefold book pattern continues in this era, but little attention is given to the themes and theologies of each collection; this is left to a later period.

Psalms interpretation also benefits in this era from advances in Hebrew grammar and philology, and text-critical studies. Commentators such as von Ewald, Briggs and Delitzsch bring these advances to their commentaries in an attempt to more fully illuminate the original setting and meaning of the psalms. This pursuit also evidences itself in strictly grammatical studies of the Psalter, such as J. J. Greswell's 1873 *Grammatical Analysis of the Hebrew Psalter,* produced for use by students preparing for entry to Oxford's divinity school. This work demonstrates a prevailing mood in scholarship that historical and cultural understanding was basic to a correct interpretation of the psalms.

Finally, the allegorical method was largely eschewed in this period. With the loosening or relinquishment of Davidic authorship and the concomitant prophetic nature of the Psalter, many psalms that had been interpreted christologically and messianically throughout church history were no longer so interpreted. Although the church generally had read the messianic psalms (identified variously as Pss 2; 45; 72; 110, etc.) prophetically and christologically, many historical-critical commentators did not. Rather, they argued, these psalms spoke of an earthly king such as David or another earthly king. For some interpreters, however, these messianic psalms could also form an ideal of a king, which ideal Christ subsequently realizes (Driver, Briggs and Briggs), or present a type with a promised antitype (Perowne, Kirkpatrick, Delitzsch), or a messianic hope settled on the Davidic line, which hope was gradually transferred to the future (Delitzsch on Pss 110; 45; 72; 132).

5.3. The Twentieth Century: Form-Critical Interpretation. The historical-critical approaches of the nineteenth century continue into the twentieth century and to the present day. However, in the 1920s and 1930s a new interpretive approach to the psalms revolutionized psalms interpretation. H. Gunkel's form-critical approach (*see* Form Criticism) moves the locus of interpretation from the historic questions of authorship and occasion to questions of psalm forms and the life setting (*Sitz im Leben*) of the various forms. Grouping the psalms in form typologies (*Gattungen*), Gunkel demonstrates the uniformity and variance within these forms. Each form is given a life setting in the cult (*see* Cult, Worship: Psalms) as both individuals and community participate in ritual acts in response to life experiences. The forms were as ancient as the cult itself, but later, imitative psalms were also composed by pious poets for individual use outside of the cult setting. Originating in the seventh century, before the collapse of the state of Judah, these private spiritual songs became especially popular in the postexilic period. So influential was Gunkel's form-critical approach that virtually all subsequent critical commentaries take up his psalm-form typology, although not without modification (most notably, C. Westermann's *Praise and Lament in the Psalms* redesignates Gunkel's four main categories of psalm types).

Of note in Gunkel's study is his treatment of royal psalms (which, he argued, were Pss 2; 18; 20; 21; 45; 72; 101; 110; 132; 144:1-11) (*see* Kingship Psalms). Belonging to the monarchic period, these royal psalms arose out of specific historical situations (such as a royal wedding, or praise for a military victory). The most frequent life setting of these psalms, however, is a royal enthronement festival, which, he posited, took place annually during the fall of the year. The psalms that were sung at the festival (Pss 2; 21; 72; 110) evolved into an eschatological interpretation once the monarchy failed.

Gunkel's theory of the cultic *Sitz im Leben* and an annual royal enthronement festival is furthered by his student S. Mowinckel. Using the New Year's enthronement festival of Mesopotamian and Canaanite literature as a model, he argues for a similar festival in Israel. The cult participants used the *yhwh mālāk* psalms (Pss 93; 96—99 [Mowinckel translates *yhwh mālāk* as "YHWH is become king"]) to reenact the cosmic, mythic enthronement of Yahweh. Mowinckel argues that much of the Psalter was used in this hypothetical festival. Although Mowinckel's thesis is largely discounted today as overly speculative and without support in the Historical Books, some commentators have followed a similar line by situating psalms in a cultic festival. A. Weiser's 1962 commentary situates Psalms in an autumnal festival of covenant renewal, and H.-J. Kraus's 1978 (ET 1988) commentary situates them in an autumnal royal *Zion festival celebrating the divine founding of the Davidic dynasty and God's choice of Jerusalem.

5.4. The Twentieth Century: Continuing Historical-Critical Interpretation. Despite Gunkel's emphasis on the study of the form and life setting of the psalms, not all scholars since then have made these concerns their focus. Some continue the historical-critical questions of author, date, occasion, language and Psalter formation. For instance, M. Buttenwieser's 1938 commentary (ET 1969) arranges the Psalter chronologically, dating the psalms from the period of Joshua until the Persian period and allowing for a few

psalms authored by David. He questions the validity of form criticism's findings, as well as the theory of a cultic festival of enthronement. M. Goulder, in a series of studies from 1982 to 1998, also works within a historical-critical paradigm but with an awareness and use of form-critical categories. He argues that the psalm headings, though late and often erroneous, did contain some authentic historical record. By these, Goulder argues that the Psalter as it stands proceeds chronologically from the Davidic era to the postexilic era and, for the *lĕdāwīd* psalms, speaks of historical moments in the life of David. Defending his return to a largely traditional reading of the psalms' date and setting, he urges that his claim is not due to fundamentalist biblicism but rather is supported by the internal evidence in the Psalter itself. Some conservative psalms commentators, such as H. C. Leupold (1959) and D. Kidner (1973; 1975), continue to hold to traditional ascriptions of authorship. For each, the superscriptions are later editorial interpolations yet contain authentic memories of historical setting and authorship. However, even these more traditional stances on the historical-critical questions are not conducted without attention to the influence of Gunkel's form-critical approach.

Another interpretive method that merits notice in this era is the comparative philology spurred by the mythic and poetic texts found at Ugarit. M. Dahood's *Anchor Bible* commentaries (1965-1970) give a fresh translation of the psalms, together with a philological commentary that seeks to resolve many of the textual anomalies and difficult Hebrew words and phrases by comparison to Ugaritic. On the strength of the epigraphic evidence, Dahood argues that the psalms are preexilic, and that some (Pss 2; 16; 18; 29; 60; 68; 72; 108; 110) may have been composed in the Davidic era; none date from the Maccabean era. Dahood's commentary has been criticized for too enthusiastically attempting to solve all the difficult passages in Psalms with supposed Ugaritic phrases and parallels, but his methodology has not been totally rejected, as is evidenced by P. Craigie's more moderate application of this method in 1983.

5.5. The Twentieth Century: Reading the Psalms as a Whole. Over the last thirty years the trend in the study of Psalms has shifted once again. Rather than focusing interpretive efforts on the history behind the psalms (of author and occasion, or of cultic setting or form), the trend has moved to consider the psalms not as disparate units but rather as comprising a whole book shaped intentionally and theologically by its editors, often in the postexilic period and later (*see* Editorial Criticism).

Awareness of the book as a whole is not a new enterprise. Throughout the history of interpretation attention has been given to the collections within Psalms (such as the Korah, Asaph or Ascents collections), the Psalter's five-book structure with its doxological conclusions to each book, as well as the introductory nature of Psalms 1—2 and the conclusive nature of Psalm 150. Driver, in the nineteenth century, traced concatenations of words in some contiguous psalms as evidence of redactional activity in shaping the collection. But these piecemeal observations had little sense of the book's overall structure, much less a theology that informed that structuring.

The seedbed of this method was prepared by several scholars (such as B. Childs [1979], who argued that Ps 1 was a Torah-focused introduction to the collection, intentionally directing the individual to read the collection for the purpose of personal reading, study and meditation), but it was G. H. Wilson's *The Editing of the Hebrew Psalter* (1985) and subsequent work that particularly spurred this approach. Wilson argued that the Psalter was shaped by the presence of both explicit and nonexplicit editorial markings, such as the doxologies, the terminology found in the superscriptions, and markings at the "seams" of the five books. Theologically, the Psalter's structure recognized the apparent failure of the Davidic covenant (books 1-3), and in light of that failure books 4-5 held this Davidic hope in tension with the call of wisdom to dependent trust in Yahweh alone as king.

Wilson's efforts to read the shape of the Psalter under the twin themes of royal covenant and Torah wisdom are taken up by many scholars. For instance, both J. L. Mays (1987; 1994) and J. C. McCann (1993a) work with the canonical Psalter, discerning its shape by these twin themes. For Mays, the royal and wisdom themes are introduced in the dual introduction of Psalms 1—2 to the whole Psalter, and each psalm must be read in the dual light of God's sovereign reign and the instruction of the Torah. McCann also reads the whole Psalter through this dual theme introduced in Psalms

1—2. He also takes into consideration form-critical interpretation, reading Psalms as presenting three types of instruction for life under God's sovereignty: psalms of instruction for praise, prayer and profession.

Each of these scholars attempts to read the "story" or "theme" of the Psalter, just as one would do for other biblical books. This "story" arises out of the redactor's own social and historical setting and can be exegeted accordingly. One recent study that attempts such an exegesis is N. L. deClaissé Walford's *Reading from the Beginning* (1997). Her study takes up the shape presented by Wilson but focuses additionally on the purpose of such shaping in the postexilic community, positing the book as a rationale for continued existence of the surviving postexilic community. Answering the questions of "Who are we?" (books 1-3) and "What are we to do?" (books 4-5), the Psalter charges the community to remember their identification as the people of Yahweh and his Torah. It is this sense of identity that imparts hope for continued existence in difficult circumstances, enabling, finally, the praise in Psalm 150.

Other attempts to read the "story" of the Psalter proceed without deClaissé Walford's exegesis of the redactional community. W. Brueggemann (1984; 1991) reads the psalms canonically and rhetorically for a contemporary audience, without concern for the Psalter's message to the redactor's community. Discerning broad movement in the psalms from obedience to Torah in the midst of suffering (the focus of Pss 1—72) to praise (the focus of Pss 73—150), he asks how the message speaks to those experiencing contemporary crises of experience with God. The pivot point in which the movement from obedience to praise is accomplished is Psalm 73, where the doubting sufferer encounters Yahweh in his temple and reawakens hope and the reality of trustful communion with God.

Finally, another example, from D. C. Mitchell (1997), demonstrates continuing work on the canonical shape of the Psalter. Rather than seeing a Psalter shaped by Davidic covenant and Torah, Mitchell argues that it bears an eschatological shape. Comparing the Psalter to the eschatological program in Zechariah 9—14 and other prophets, he discerns the same program in the Psalter. This program proceeds through the whole Psalter and includes such eschatological events as the bridegroom-king who comes to

Zion (Ps 45), the gathering of scattered Israel to Jerusalem (Ps 50), the gathering of hostile nations against Jerusalem (Pss 73—83) and the final rescue of Israel by their king-messiah (Ps 110).

6. Directions for the Future.

The exploration of the redactional shape and theology of the Psalter remains a fruitful field of inquiry. Although the historical reconstruction of the redactional setting could become overly speculative, and some critical self-assessment must be maintained in the observation of the marks of redactional activity, R. N. Whybray's (1996) negative assessment of the attempts may be premature because the method does continue to refine its approach, determining means of critical self-assessment. Certainly, its theological and canonical appeal remains an exciting resource for churchly interpretation.

Historical-critical and form-critical approaches, though no longer enjoying the focused attention of the twentieth century, will remain means by which the text is examined. The persistence of the historical component throughout the history of interpretation of the psalms makes it unlikely that such questions will be neglected. Positivistic conclusions regarding authorship, occasion, date and the superscriptions' reliability have long been set aside, but the fact of the inclusion of the superscriptions in the canonical Psalter will continue to legitimately bring these questions into the interpretive process, particularly as interpreters question in what way these superscriptions should shape the reading of the text.

As the questions of modernity are succeeded by the questions of postmodernity and the multiplicity of interpretive perspectives currently undertaken, one of the effects upon Psalms study is to reengage the precritical interpreters. Can the interpretive approaches of the church fathers and the medieval era be taken up again? Can these methods be reincorporated as new attention is paid to the theological shape of the Psalter and a more nonhistorical, reader-oriented interpretive process is explored—especially since theological and reader-oriented readings were hallmarks of the precritical interpreters? How might (or should) precritical concerns and methods be shaped by interpreters who have themselves been shaped by the critical traditions? What theological insights of these interpreters should mark current interpretive efforts? These are questions being engaged by scholars such as B. E. Daley (2003) and may see a new respect for the concerns of the precritical interpreters and perhaps also a nuanced reincorporation of their theological approach.

Finally, the history of interpretation of the psalms will continue to engage the crucial element of the interpreter as one addressed by these very personal poems of encounter with God. As has been the question of the interpretive work through the centuries, How do these words addressed to God become God's word to people? The psalms continue to speak, and the interpreter must wrestle with them to correctly hear and respond to that message.

See also DEAD SEA SCROLLS; FEMINIST INTERPRETATION; FORM CRITICISM; HERMENEUTICS; HISTORICAL CRITICISM; MEGILLOT AND FESTIVALS; PSALMS 1: BOOK OF; PSALMS 2: ANCIENT NEAR EASTERN BACKGROUND; SOCIAL-SCIENTIFIC APPROACHES; TARGUMIM.

BIBLIOGRAPHY. *Apostolic Fathers,* (2 vols.; LCL; Cambridge, MA: Harvard University Press, 1976-1977); **C. A. Briggs and E. G. Briggs,** *A Critical and Exegetical Commentary on the Book of Psalms* (2 vols.; Edinburgh: T & T Clark, 1906); **W. Brueggemann,** *The Message of the Psalms* (Minneapolis: Augsburg, 1984); idem, "Bounded by Obedience and Praise: The Psalms as Canon," *JSOT* 50 (1991) 63-92; **M. Buttenwieser,** *Psalms Chronologically Treated, with a New Translation* (New York: KTAV, 1969); **J. Calvin,** *Calvin's Commentaries,* 4-6: *Commentary on the Book of Psalms,* 1-5 (repr., Grand Rapids: Baker, 1979); **T. K. Cheyne,** *The Book of Psalms or The Praises of Israel: A New Translation, with Commentary* (London: Kegan Paul, Trench, 1888); idem, *The Origin and Religious Contents of The Psalter in the Light of Old Testament Criticism and the History of Religions* (London: Kegan Paul, Trench, Trübner, 1891); **B. S. Childs,** "Reflections on the Modern Study of the Psalms," in *Magnalia Dei: The Mighty Acts of God; Essays on the Bible and Archaeology in Memory of G. Ernest Wright,* ed. F. M. Cross (Garden City, NY: Doubleday, 1976) 377-88; idem, *Introduction to the Old Testament as Scripture* (Philadelphia: Fortress, 1979); **P. C. Craigie,** *Psalms 1-50* (WBC 19; Waco: Word, 1983); **M. Dahood,** *Psalms* (3 vols.; AB 16, 17, 17A; Garden City, NY: Doubleday, 1965-1970); **B. E. Daley,** "Is Patristic Exegesis Still Usable? Some Reflections on Early Christian Interpretation of the Psalms," in *The*

Art of Reading Scripture, ed. E. F. Davis and R. B. Hays (Grand Rapids: Eerdmans, 2003) 69-88; **N. L. deClaissé-Walford,** *Reading from the Beginning: The Shaping of the Hebrew Psalter* (Macon, GA: Mercer University Press, 1997); **R. J. Deferrari,** ed., *The Fathers of the Church: A New Translation*, vols. 48, 57 (Washington, DC: Catholic University of America Press, 1963, 1965); **F. Delitzsch,** *Biblical Commentary on the Psalms*, vol. 1. (Grand Rapids: Eerdmans, 1949); **W. de Wette,** *Commentar über die Psalmen* (Heidelberg: Mohr & Zimmer, 1811); **S. R. Driver,** *Studies in the Psalms*, ed. C. F. Burney (London: Hodder & Stoughton, 1915); idem, *An Introduction to the Literature of the Old Testament* (repr., Cleveland: World Publishing Company, 1963 [1891]; **J. Eaton,** *Kingship and the Psalms* (Naperville, IL: Allenson, 1976); **M. Goulder,** *The Prayers of David (Psalms 51-72): Studies in the Psalter, II* (JSOTSup 102; Sheffield: Sheffield Academic Press, 1990); **J. J. Greswell,** *Grammatical Analysis of the Hebrew Psalter* (Oxford: J. Parker, 1873); **H. Gunkel,** *The Psalms: A Form-Critical Introduction* (Philadelphia: Fortress, 1967 [1930]); **E. W. Hengstenberg,** *Commentary on the Psalms* (3 vols.; Edinburgh: T & T Clark, 1846); **R. C. Hill,** *Theodore of Mopsuestia: Commentary on Psalms 1-81; Translated with an Introduction and Notes* (SBLWGW 5; Atlanta: Society of Biblical Literature, 2006); **W. L. Holladay,** *The Psalms Through Three Thousand Years: Prayerbook of a Cloud of Witnesses* (Minneapolis: Fortress, 1996); **D. Kidner,** *Psalms 1-72: An Introduction and Commentary on Books I & II of the Psalms* (TOTC; London: Inter-Varsity Press, 1973); idem, *Psalms 73-150: A Commentary on Books III-V of the Psalms* (TOTC; London: Inter-Varsity Press, 1975); **A. F. Kirkpatrick,** *The Book of Psalms* (Cambridge: Cambridge University Press, 1902); **H.-J. Kraus,** *Psalms 1-59: A Commentary* (Minneapolis: Augsburg, 1988 [1978]); idem, *Psalms 60-150: A Commentary* (Minneapolis: Augsburg, 1989 [1978]); **J. L. Kugel,** *The Idea of Biblical Poetry: Parallelism and Its History* (New Haven: Yale University Press, 1981); **H. C. Leupold,** *Exposition of the Psalms* (Grand Rapids: Baker, 1959); **R. Lowth,** *Lectures on the Sacred Poetry of the Hebrews (1787)* (2 vols.; Anglistica & Americana 43; repr., Hildesheim: G. Olms, 1969); **M. Luther,** *Luther's Works*, vols. 10-11, ed. H. C. Oswald; vols. 12-14, ed. J. Pelikan (St. Louis: Concordia, 1955-1976); **J. L. Mays,** "The Place of the Torah-Psalms in the Psalter," *JBL* 106 (1987) 3-12; idem, *The Lord Reigns: A Theological Handbook to the Psalms* (Louisville: Westminster John Knox, 1994); **J. C. McCann,** *A Theological Introduction the Book of Psalms* (Nashville: Abingdon, 1993a); idem, ed., *The Shape and Shaping of the Psalter* (JSOTSup 159; Sheffield: JSOT Press, 1993b); **D. C. Mitchell,** *The Message of the Psalter: An Eschatological Programme in the Book of Psalms* (JSOTSup 252; Sheffield: Sheffield Academic Press, 1997); **S. Mowinckel,** *The Psalms in Israel's Worship* (2 vols.; New York: Abingdon, 1967); **J. M. Neale and R. F. Littledale,** eds., *A Commentary on the Psalms: From Primitive and Mediaeval Writers; And from the Various Office-books and Hymns of the Roman, Mozarabic, Ambrosian, Gallican, Greek, Coptic, Armenian, and Syriac Rites* (4 vols.; New York: AMS Press, 1976); **R. J. Payne,** *Athanasius: The Life of Antony and the Letter to Marcellinus* (Classics of Western Spirituality; New York: Paulist, 1980); **J. J. S. Perowne,** *The Book of Psalms: A New Translation with Introductions and Notes Explanatory and Critical* (2 vols.; Andover, MA: W. F. Draper, 1882); **A. Roberts and J. Donaldson,** eds., *The Ante-Nicene Fathers: Translations of the Writings of the Fathers Down to A.D. 325* (10 vols.; Grand Rapids: Eerdmans, 1979-1986); **P. Schaff,** ed., *A Select Library of the Nicene and Post-Nicene Fathers of the Christian Church* (repr., Grand Rapids: Eerdmans, 1956); **M. A. Schimmelpenninck,** *Psalms According to the Authorized Version; With Prefatory Titles and Tabular Index of Scriptural References from the Port Royal Authors, Marking the Circumstances and Chronologic Order of Their Composition; To Which Is Added, an Essay upon the Psalms, and Their Spiritual Application* (London: J. & A. Arch, 1825); **B. Smalley,** *The Study of the Bible in the Middle Ages* (Notre Dame, IN: University of Notre Dame Press, 1964); **G. H. A. von Ewald,** *Commentary on the Psalms* (2 vols.; London: Williams & Norgate, 1880-1881); **A. Weiser,** *The Psalms* (Philadelphia: Westminster, 1962); **C. Westermann,** *Praise and Lament in the Psalms*, (Atlanta: John Knox, 1981); **R. N. Whybray,** *Reading the Psalms as a Book* (JSOTSup 222; Sheffield: Sheffield Academic Press, 1996); **G. H. Wilson,** *The Editing of the Hebrew Psalter* (SBLDS 76; Chico, CA: Scholars Press, 1985). L. Wray Beal

PSALMS 4: TITLES

The titling of the psalms provides notes about composition and performance, often using untranslatable technical terms. Scholars divide over whether the titles are authentic, especially in regard to authorship and the historical notes attached to fourteen of the Davidic psalms.

1. Problems
2. Title Information

1. Problems.

1.1. Meaning of Technical Terms. Many technical terms remain untranslatable, as frequent recourse to transliteration indicates. Some seek a universal key. For example, J. Thirtle linked *gittît* with the *gat* ("wine press") and thus to the harvest festival of Tabernacles and then tried to link other unidentified terms to particular festivals. H. Gunkel (350) identified *gittît* as a gentilic and then reasoned, "Other substantives ending with *t* should also be conceived as *nomen gentilica.*" Gunkel (349) also noted "commonalities" in the terms; so after translating *binginôt* as "with stringed instruments" and noting the proximity of references to musical instruments, he generalized that terms such as this "relate to musical performance."

1.2. Authenticity of Titles.

1.2.1. Different Views of Authenticity. S. Mowinckel (2.100-101) calls the historical notes "midrash ... unhistorical, speculative exegesis of disconnected details." B. Childs (521-22) sees them as an authoritative, though secondary, setting for the psalms, a community act of reinterpretation, universalizing each individual psalm by "relating it to the history of David as a representative man." But if these titles were midrashic additions, we would expect them to match something obvious in the psalm itself. And if these titles were to "Davidify" the Psalter, we would have expected far more of them to be titled "by David," as we see in the LXX, and we would have expected far more mention of instances from the life of *David. Evangelical scholarship generally attributes significant authority to the titles. D. Kidner (1973, 33) even appears to treat them as inspired, canonical Scripture, noting that the NT even builds arguments on authorship notes (e.g., Mk 12:35-37; Acts 2:29-36 [using Ps 110:1]; Acts 13:35-37 [using Ps 16:10]).

1.2.2. Problems for Authenticity. Various problems cast a shadow over the authenticity of the historical and authorial notes. First, some doubt that composing psalms is what one might expect of David when he was hiding in caves and fighting Philistines (Ps 57:1; 142:1). The reply to this is that those hardships were the occasioning incidents for these psalms, like the

World War 1 trenches that provoked the poetry of soldiers such as Robert Graves, Wilfred Owen and Siegfried Sassoon and their French and German counterparts. Second, some see historical tension with OT and broader ancient Near Eastern history. Psalm 56 says that David composed it "when the Philistines seized him in Gath"; however, the historical record says that David took himself to the king of Gath to escape Saul (1 Sam 21:10; 27:1-3). But note that David began to fear the king of Gath, feigned insanity, and "escaped to the cave of Adullam" (1 Sam 21:12—23:1). Several Davidic psalms mention the temple, before his son *Solomon built it; however, the tabernacle could be called "the LORD's house" (Josh 6:24) or "the LORD's temple" (1 Sam 1:9). Supposedly late Aramaisms in the Psalter no longer seem such a problem: "Aramaic" loan words appear in Ugaritic texts from hundreds of years before David's time, and liturgical materials may have been updated lexically from time to time. Third, some say that the third-person reference in the psalm titles seems incongruent with the first-person reference in the psalm itself. That would not necessarily even undermine Davidic authorship of these titles, since the psalm text itself sometimes refers to David in the third person, probably dealing with his official position as "the king" (Pss 21; 61; 63; 110). And it does even less to undermine the titles' authenticity if we accept that the titles were authentic canonical editorial activity like we see elsewhere in the OT (e.g., Num 12:3; Deut 34).

1.2.3. Support for Authenticity. As to the issue of Davidic authorship, we do well to note that the normal ancient Near Eastern practice acknowledged the king as patron of the cultus; indeed, the OT knows David as Israel's poet-singer par excellence (e.g., 1 Sam 16:14-23; 2 Sam 23:1-7; 1 Chron 6:31; 15:16; 16:7; 25:1; 29:30; Ps 18 = 2 Sam 22; Ezra 3:10; Neh 12:24-47).

Intertestamental material continued this line of thought (Sir 47:8-10), and the LXX expanded the list of Davidic titles by fourteen (Pss 33; 43; 71; 91; 93—99; 104; 137; 151), with Ps 151 being a "supernumerary" *(exōthen tou arithmou)* but still the genuine article *(idiographos)* (Ps 151:1). Josephus states that David "composed songs and hymns to God in varied meters" (Josephus *Ant.* 7:305-306), and Philo reports that David "sang/ wrote hymns *[hymneō]* to God" (Philo *Conf.* 149).

This continued into the NT. Jesus himself

built arguments that hinged upon Davidic authorship (Mt 22:41-46 [using Ps 110:1]), as did Peter (Acts 2:25-29 [using Ps 16:8-11]). Finally, two psalms are called Davidic even though their titles did not show it in the Hebrew (Heb 4:7 [using Ps 95:7-8]) or even in the LXX (Acts 4:25-26 [using Ps 2:1-2]).

One final note supporting authenticity is the LXX's confusion over many of the titles' technical terms. It appears that the titles were already old enough that various archaic technical terms had already fallen out of use when the LXX translators saw them.

1.3. Superscript or Postscript? Thirtle (4-5, 10-16) first developed the idea that anything preceding the literary genre and author was actually a postscript for the previous psalm, like the pattern observed in Habakkuk's prayer (Hab 3:1, 19). B. Waltke (586) defined it similarly, saying that the superscript contained information about composition, and the postscript about performance. Waltke (589-95) compiled evidence:

1. Egyptian hymns incorporate colophons (see *ANET,* 365, 367, 370, 371).
2. Hymns outside the Psalter use that pattern (Hab 3:1, 19; Is 38:9-10, 20b).
3. Psalm 3/4 could match the superscript-subscript pattern of Habakkuk 3; Isaiah 38.
4. The narrative equivalent of Psalm 18:1 lacks the "putative postscript" (2 Sam 22:1).
5. The identification of *lamnaṣṣēaḥ* ("for the choir master") as a subscript of Psalm 41, rather than the start of the superscript for Psalm 42, retains the sharp change from "psalm of David" that occurs throughout all of book 1 (Pss 3—41) to the Korahite psalms of book 2.
6. Identifying everything up to "A maskil of Heman the Ezrahite" as the postscript for Psalm 87 solves the apparent double titling for Psalm 88.
7. Potential subscripts match language in their own psalm (e.g., Ps 56:1, cf. Ps 55:7, 8).
8. The LXX differed from the MT in its handling of this information in some psalms (Pss 104—106; 111—117).
9. 11QPs[a] has a postscript for Psalm 145.
10. Psalm 148b-c may have introduced Psalm 149.
11. With the exception of the textually corrupt superscript of Psalm 88, "for the choir master" always appears as the first element in superscripts in the present Psalter's arrangement, which would allow for consistent assignment of this and what follows as postscripts for their preceding psalm.

Kidner (1973, 42) made cautious use of the postscript idea. For example, he noted that the LXX *alloiōthēsomenōn* of Psalms 45; 69; 80 vocalized the Hebrew not as "lilies" *(šôšannîm)* but rather as "those who change" *(šeššōnîm);* so he said that L. Delekat was on track with his reference to "those whose situation changes for the worse," which he referred back to Psalm 44 (citing Delekat, 294-95 on Pss 44—45). Kidner (1973, 43) wondered if "doves" (Ps 56:1) might be a postscript for the previous psalm, which mentions doves (Ps 55:6-7). Kidner (1973, 181 n. 1) also noted that the final word of Psalm 48:14 is *ʿal-mût,* which, if joined, as many Hebrew manuscripts do, "can be revocalized as *ʿōlāmôt,* 'evermore,' as in the LXX, Vulg." If so, that would be an example of an intact postscript retained in Psalms. As did Waltke, Kidner (1975, 317) noted that this could solve the double-titling of Psalm 88. All in all, these arguments make a case for suggesting that everything up to the note of literary genre or authorship may be postscript for the previous psalm.

2. Title Information.
2.1. Postscripts: Performance Directions.
2.1.1. General Directions. (1) *lamnaṣṣēaḥ,* "for the choir master," occurs fifty-five times in psalm titles (Pss 4—6; 8; 9; 11—14; 18—22; 31; 36; 39—42; 44—47; 49; 51—62; 64—70; 75—77; 80; 81; 84; 85; 88; 109; 139; 140 [or postscript for the psalm preceding each of those]) and once in Habakkuk 3:19. Translations tend toward "for the leader" or "choir master," understanding this Piel participle of *nāṣaḥ* to refer to "supervision" (e.g., Ezra 3:8-9), in this case supervising musicians (e.g., 1 Chron 15:21). The LXX has *eis to telos* ("to the end"), from its Niphal or its nominal form *nēṣaḥ* ("duration" [e.g., Jer 8:5]). The rabbis translated it either way: "to the Eternal" (*Midr. Ps.* 139) or "for the leader" (*Midr. Ps.* 140).

(2) *selâ,* generally transliterated, is not a title, but it falls in the class of performance directions like those given in psalm titles. It occurs seventy-one times in Psalms, and three

times in Habakkuk's prayer (Hab 3:3, 9, 13). The LXX rendered this *diapsalma*, referring to an interlude with musical instruments (cf. the Persian *sala* ["song, sound of string"]). Since Thirtle, it has been common to treat it as a stanza marker serving "the purpose of the modern" (Thirtle, 145); however, it sometimes interrupts the flow of thought (e.g., Ps 55:19-20; 68:7-8, 32-33; 85:2-3; Hab 3:3, 9). Some suggest that the term comes from *sālal* ("raise")—for example, to raise the pitch or volume of the singing. For example, B. Edwards (72, 77) says that it indicates "the expression of very strong, earnest feeling" in "an urgent appeal to God," and Edwards (73-79) suggests that it called for singing at full force with trumpet accompaniment, like the priestly "reminder" trumpets that accompanied some sacrifices (e.g., Lev 23:24; Num 10:9-10). Its omission never impairs the meaning of the passage, so it is common to remove it typographically from the flow of the text, often to the right margin, whether transliterated as usual or translated (e.g., "pause" [NJB] or "interlude" [NLT]).

(3) *higgāyôn*, generally transliterated, does not occur in the psalm titles, but it appears to be a musical performance direction, and in Psalm 9:16 it immediately precedes *selâ*. If we see it as a way of playing a string instrument (Ps 92:3), we might arrive at something like Mowinckel's "musical flourish" (Mowinckel, 2.211; so also BDB); however, if we connect it with the use of the term *higgāyôn* for "whispers" (Lam 3:62) or "meditation" (Ps 19:14), we might arrive at something like a psalm sung *sotto voce*, which we see in various translations such as "muted music" (NJB), "meditation" (NKJV) or "quiet interlude" (NLT).

2.1.2. Melodies or Styles. (1) *bingînôt/binginōt*, "with stringed instruments" (Pss 4; 6; 54; 55; 67; 76 [or postscript for Pss 3; 5; 53; 54; 66; 75]); and *ʿal-nĕginat*, "on stringed instruments" (Ps 61 [or postscript for Ps 60]). This comes from *nāgan*, "play a stringed instrument," like David's *kinôr* (e.g., 1 Sam 16:16-23; 18:10; 19:9).

(2) *ʾel-hannĕḥilôt*, "with the flutes" (Ps 5:1 [or postscript for Ps 4]). The rabbis connected this with *naḥălâ* ("inheritance"), as does the LXX *klēronomousēs* ("inherit") and the Vulgate (*hereditatem*), perhaps as a tune name about their tribal inheritance (see Ps 4:8). Mowinckel (2.210) connects this with *ḥālâ* ("grow weak, tired, ill") and says that it is a song to be sung against disease.

However, most connect this with *ḥālîl* ("flute"), one of the instruments played in royal and religious processions (1 Kings 1:40; Is 30:29), by bands of ecstatic prophets (1 Sam 10:5), or for mourning (Jer 48:36).

(3) *ʿal-haggittît*, "according to [the tune or style] 'Gittith'" (Pss 8; 81; 84 [or postscript for Pss 7; 80; 83]). The LXX *(lēnos)* and Vulgate *(torcularibus)* derive it from *gat* ("wine press"), identifying it as a vintage song, perhaps for the Feast of Tabernacles (Thirtle, 55-66; Delekat, 292-93). The rabbis linked the wine press with divine wrath against the wicked nations (Joel 3:13), which meant redemption for Israel (*Midr. Ps.* 8; 84). This might work well with its use as postscript for Psalm 7 (see Ps 7:6-16). However, Gunkel (349-50) is probably right in understanding this as *nomen gentilicum*, "according to the Gathites," which could refer to an instrument (Targum: "*kinôrāʾ* from Gath"), style or tune originating in Gath, where David had parked the ark of the covenant, and where it blessed the house of Obed-Edom "the Gittite" (2 Sam 6:10-12).

(4) *ʿal-ʿălāmôt*, "according to [the tune or style] 'Alamoth'" (Ps 46 [or postscript for Ps 45]; cf. 1 Chron 15:20). If this is related to *ʿalmâ* ("young woman"), it could be "to [the voice of] *young women*, either lit, or of soprano or falsetto of boys" (BDB) or perhaps of high-pitched musical instruments (*HALOT*, citing Delekat, 292-93). The LXX *kryphiōn* ("hidden things") presupposes *ʿal-ʿălūmôt*, which the rabbis described as the "hidden things," unfathomable wonders of God (*Midr. Ps.* 46, citing Job 5:9), and which Mowinckel (2.215-16) relates to cultic mysteries.

(5) *ʿal-haššĕmînît* clearly means "on 'the eighth'" (Pss 6; 12 [or postscript for Pss 5; 11]; cf. 1 Chron 15:21), but its reference is ambiguous. Rabbinic midrash referred it to *worship above and beyond the general practice of seven times a day (Ps 119:164), to circumcision on the eighth day (Lev 12:3), or even to Israel's dispersion into eight kingdoms derived from the pairs of limbs on Daniel's statue: Babylon/Chaldea, Media/Persia, Greece/Macedonia, Ishmal/Edom (*Midr. Ps.* 5, citing Dan 2:31-33). Some infer the lower "octave" of men's voices, especially in contrast to the *ʿălāmôt* ("soprano" [1 Chron 15:20-21]); however, that is anachronistic and gender-bending to boot, because the octaval "eighth" is a musical concept more modern than ancient Near Eastern musical notation, and "the eighth" is

feminine. J. Glueck (33) retains the "bass" range by a connection with *šmn* ("fat"), implying a low tone because "the larger the vibrating body the deeper the pitch." It is more common to associate this note with an unidentified eight-stringed instrument (cf. 1 Chron 15:21; see Kraus, 1.31; Eerdmans, 60), like the Targum's *kinora*, perhaps a "harp" or "lyre of eight strings" (Ps 6:1; 12:1). Most English translations transliterate it as an unexplained style or tune.

(6) ʿ*al-tašḥēt*, "to [the tune] 'Do Not Destroy'" (Pss 57—59; 75 [or postscript for Pss 56—58; 74]; cf. Deut 9:26). This is likely the catchword for a tune name (Mowinckel, 2.214-15). The cry fits the content of all four psalms as well, whether construed as postscripts or superscripts.

(7) ʿ*al-māḥălat*, "according to [the style or tune] 'Makhalath'" (Ps 53 [or postscript for Ps 52]); and ʿ*al-māḥălat lĕ*ʿ*annôt*, "according to [the tune or style] 'Makhalath Leanoth'" (Ps 88 [or postscript for Ps 87]). This may be a catchword for a tune name (e.g., "set to 'Makhalath'"); however, other options are possible: a reference to style linking it with *mĕḥôlâ* ("for a dance"), a performance note linking it with *ḥālîlâ* ("on a flute"), or a note about occasion linking it with *maḥăleh* ("for an illness" [cf. NJB: "in sickness"]). The last suggestion fits well with the title of Psalm 88, where it combines with *lĕ*ʿ*annôt*, which could be from ʿ*nh* and mean either (a) "'humiliate,' namely, one's soul" (Mowinckel, 2.212) or "accompany penance" (Sawyer, 34); or (b) "for responding," as the LXX *apokrithēnai* ("answer") understood it.

(8) ʿ*al-šôšannîm*, "according to [the tune] 'Lilies'" (Pss 45; 69 [or postscript for Pss 44; 68]); ʿ*al-šûšan* ʿ*ēdût*, "according to 'The Lily of Testimony'" (Ps 60 [or postscript for Ps 59]); and ʿ*el-šôšannîm* ʿ*ēdût*, "with/according to 'The Lilies of Testimony'" (Ps 80 [or postscript for Ps 79]). "Lilies" probably served as a catchword for a tune name, whether by popular connection with poetry about love and fertility (Song 2:1-2, 16; 4:5; 5:13; 6:2-3; 7:2; cf. Ps 45) and by extension with blossoming Israel (Hos 14:5; cf. Mt 6:28; Lk 12:27), or by connection with temple imagery (1 Kings 7:19, 22, 26; 2 Chron 4:5). The fuller expression's link with covenantal testimony (ʿ*ēdût*) could even hint at some connection with the ark of the covenant that viewed Aaron's budding rod as "lilies of revelation" (Mowinckel, 2.214).

(9) ʿ*al-yônat* ʾ*ēlem rĕḥōqîm*, perhaps "to [the tune] 'Dove of the Distant Oaks'" (Ps 56 [or postscript for Ps 55]; cf. Ps 55:6). The term ʾ*lm* makes for uncertainty in this title. The LXX interpreted it as ʾ*ēlîm* ("gods" or "holy ones"), rendering it *tou laou apo tōn hagiōn memakrymmenou* ("the people far from the saints" or "the people far from the holies"—i.e., in exile), which the Vulgate followed with *populo qui a santis longe*. That fit David's "exile" in Gath, which the title mentions. Mowinckel (2.214) approves the change to ʾ*ēlîm* ("gods"), but he says that it refers to "the doves to the distant gods," alluding to a cultic act like that of a scapegoat but using a dove instead (linking Lev 16:8 with Lev 14:2-7, esp. v. 7). The Geneva Bible of 1599 kept the ʾ*ēlem* ("silent") in its rendering, "dumme doue in a farre countrey" (so also NKJV, HSCB). Translations that opt for "oaks" or "terebinths" (RSV, NIV, NRSV, ESV, NLT, NET) understand ʾ*ēlem* to be an alternate form of ʾ*ēlîm* from ʾ*ayil*. Gunkel's bias toward gentilics for any vague term that ends with -*t* leads him to change *yônat* to *yawānît* ("Greeks") and render it "according to the Greek manner of the distant Islands" (Gunkel, 350). The cautious approach of transliterating it as a tune name or style called "Jonath Elem Rekhoqim" may be wise (e.g., KJV, NASB, JPS, NJPS).

(10) ʿ*al-*ʾ*ayyelet haššaḥar*, "to [the tune] 'Doe of the Dawn'" (Ps 22 [or postscript for Ps 21]), probably is a tune named by its catchword. Mowinckel (2.21) says that it refers to an animal sacrificed at dawn; however, Israel's cultus sacrificed only domesticated animals. Nonetheless, morning sacrifice may originally have been in view, perhaps understanding the leaping doe as figurative of the dawn. The LXX *antilēmpseōs* ("help") must have read ʾ*ĕyālût* ("help" [see Ps. 22:19]) instead of ʾ*ayyelet*, as did the Targum, ʿ*l tqwp qwrbn tdyr*ʾ *dqryst*ʾ ("on the strength of the regular morning sacrifice"). We may safely dismiss Gunkel's modification of ʾ*ēyyelet* to the gentilic ʾ*ēlatît* ("Elathites"—i.e., from Elath in the Gulf of Aqabah).

(11) ʿ*almût labbēn*, "to [the tune] 'Death of the Son'" (Ps 9 [or postscript for Ps 8]; cf. Ps 48:14) or perhaps "according to [the tune or style] 'Alamoth'" (cf. Ps 46:1). As it stands [ʿ*almût*], this expression is uncertain; however, many manuscripts have ʿ*al-mût* ("concerning death"), which this note follows. Indeed, Psalm 9 refers to death by three common terms: *māwet* ("death" [Ps 9:14]; cf. *mût* and the ancient Near Eastern deity *Môt*), *šaḥat* ("pit" [Ps 9:16]) and *šĕ*ʾ*ôl* ("grave, un-

617

derworld" [Ps 9:18]), though those links would mean little if this is actually a postscript for Psalm 8. The *ʿal-mût* at the end of Psalm 48 may actually be a fragment of the title of Psalm 49. If so, it could read like the directions here in Psalm 9. However, it could just as well be read like the title of Psalm 46, as some Hebrew manuscripts have it (Ps 48:14 [MT 48:15]); indeed, the LXX *hyper tōn kryphiōn* ("concerning things hidden") here in Psalm 9 assumes the same *ʿal-ʿălūmôt* that it assumed in the title of Psalm 46.

2.2. Superscripts: Composition.

2.2.1. Types of Composition. (1) *šîr*, "a Song," is a general term for any type of song (e.g., Gen 31:27; Ex 15:1, 21; Judg 5:12), but it may have a more technical meaning in the psalm titles, where it appears to refer to vocal performance with cantillation (Delekat; Kaiser, 352). It is most often accompanied by musical instruments, which might be called *kĕlê šîr*, or "instruments of song" (Kraus, 1.21, citing 1 Chron 15:16; 16:42; 2 Chron 7:6; 34:12; Neh 12:36; Amos 6:5). "A psalm can be at once a *šîr* and a *mizmôr*" (Mowinckel, 2.207); other than when combined as "song of ascents" (*šîr hammaʿălôt* [Pss 121—134]), *šîr* occurs without *mizmôr* ("psalm") only three times in psalm titles (Pss 18; 45; 46).

(2) *mizmôr*, "a Psalm," occurs fifty-seven times in the Psalter and nowhere else; therefore, we might consider it a technical term for temple music. The verb *zāmar* may mean "pick," whether referring to pruning fruit (Lev 25:3-4; Is 5:6) or to plucking a string instrument. By steps of extension, it refers to strumming a kithara, or harp, then to a song sung to string accompaniment (Pss 4; 6; 67; 76), and finally to temple music in general, such as a "psalm" for a flute (Ps 5:1). The English word *psalm* goes back to the LXX use of *psalmos*, a term for twanging a bowstring.

(3) *miktām*, generally transliterated, is always as "a Miktam of David" (Pss 16; 56—60; cf. Is 13:12). The LXX's *stēlographia* ("pillar inscription"), the Targum's *glîpāʾ tĕrîṣā* ("engraving/ writing that is straight/upright/perfect"), and the Vulgate's *tituli inscriptio* read the Hebrew as *miktāb* ("writing"). C. T. Hodge (1.636-41) notes that medieval Jewish writers took it variously: some saw it as a musical term to denote melody and rhythm (Rashi), the melody (Ibn Ezra) or a musical style or instrument (Kimhi); some (followed by von Ewald, 1.39-41) separated *miktām* into the preposition *mīn* and *ketem* ("from

gold"), taking it figuratively as "a precious or golden song" (*Midr. Ps.* 16); and some thought that the separation should be *māk* and *tām* ("humble" and "perfect" [e.g., *Midr. Ps.* 16]; cf. Aquila: *tapeinou teliou*, "humble and perfect"; Jerome: *humilis et simplex*]). Some now connect *miktām* with *katama* ("hide, conceal"), deriving various senses from that, such as a mystery psalm, one with hidden meaning; something hidden like a treasure; something hidden until now and thus "a new song"; a psalm sung with covered lips—that is, for personal or private prayer or meditation (note NJB: "in a quiet voice"). Mowinckel (2.209) derives it from the Akkadian *katāmu*, speaking of either "a song of hiding" (i.e., under God's protection) or "a song of covering" (i.e., atoning). Hodge (637) objects, "Akk. *katāmu* is not recorded as having the meaning 'cover' in the sense of 'atone for,' as does Heb. *kāpar*." Glueck (35) suggests that it derives from *kātam* ("stain, or be stained" [e.g., Jer 2:22]) and is linked to "blood, bloodstain, or a place of bloodshed" that may be paralleled with *šaḥat* ("pit"), *šĕʾôl* ("underworld, grave") and *môt* ("death"), terms that "are present in all the Miktam Psalms." This diverse uncertainty makes the best choice the transliteration "Miktam," which almost all English translations adopt unless they are translating or are influenced by the Vulgate (e.g., Douay-Rheims, NJB).

(4) *maśkîl*, "a Maskil" or possibly "an efficacious (psalm)," is used in the heading for a variety of psalm types: wisdom (Pss 45; 89), royal (Pss 32; 78) and especially petition (Pss 42/43; 44; 52—55; 74; 88; 142). The term occurs a few other places, generally associated with wisdom and its attendant success (Ps 14:2; 47:7; 1 Sam 18:14-15; Job 22:2; Prov 10:5, 19; 14:35; 16:20; 17:2; 21:12). It derives from *śākal*, which is most often translated "succeed, or prosper"; however, it is an intellectual term too, meaning "comprehend, discern, perceive." H. Kosmala (237) notes that the majority of the passages where *śkl* forms are used reflect on knowledge of God, and that the term eventually came to refer to "a person who pleases God," such as the Qumran teacher, or to a way of life that pleases God, like that laid down in the Qumran *Manual of Discipline* (see Kosmala, 238-40). So also the rabbis connected it with the principle that "the path of life leads upward for the intelligent/wise person *[maśkîl]*" (Prov 15:24) and to the hopeful upward look to God for deliverance (*Midr. Ps.* 32); or they could just

call it a "meditation" (*Midr. Ps.* 142). From the connection with wisdom, Kraus (1.25) talks of "presenting songs and poems in a skilled, intelligent, and artistic way" (see esp. Ps 47:7). Mowinckel (2.209) very possibly is on track when he notes the connection with petitions and then says that this should be understood as a successful, that is, "efficacious," song.

(5) *šiggāyôn*, "a Shiggaion" (Ps 7 [cf. *ʿal šigyōnôt* in Hab 3:1]). The term's etymology and meaning are unclear; therefore, the LXX just has *psalmos*, as does the Vulgate *(psalmus)*, and the Peshitta simply omits anything to represent it. Contemporary treatments tend to derive it either from the Hebrew *šāgâ* ("go astray, wander" [BDB] or "stagger" *[HALOT]*) or from the Akkadian *šigû* ("howl, lament, dirge"). If they follow the Hebrew *šāgâ*, they speak of "staggering verse" or "dithyrambic poetry," perhaps resulting from or provoking ecstatic experience (Eerdmans, 76-77; Dahood, 1.41); if they follow the Akkadian *šigû*, they speak of a dirge (Mowinckel, 2.209) or of an "agitated lament" (Kraus, 1.26). The rabbis went for "impulsive speech," like David's *imprecation against his enemies (*Midr. Ps.* 7, citing 1 Sam 26:10; Ps 6:10; cf. Eccl 10:20).

(6) *těhillâ*, "a Praise [song]" (Ps 145; cf. Ps 147:1; *šîr těhillâ* in Neh 12:46) designates this hymn as a "cultic doxology" (Mowinckel, 2.204).

(7) *těpillâ*, "a Prayer," which may be "of David" (Pss 17; 86; 142), "of Moses" (Ps 90) or "of someone who is humble, poor, afflicted" (Ps 102). Indeed, these psalms are all petition psalms.

(8) *hallělû yâ* or *halělû ʾet-yhwh*, "praise the LORD." This Piel imperative may serve as the superscript for several psalms (Pss 106; 111; 112; 113; 135; 146—50), and of those, it is a *chiastic subscript for all except Psalm 111 and Psalm 112. For some, it is a subscript only (Ps 35; 105; 115—117).

2.2.2. Association with Individual or Group. (1) Nearly half of the psalms (73 of 150) have titles ascribing them to David, using either the simple *lědāwīd*, "by David" (Pss 3—9/10; 11—17; 19—32; 34—35; 37—41; 51—65; 68—70; 86; 89; 101; 103; 108—110; 122; 124; 131—133; 138—145), or the fuller note *lěʾebed yhwh lědāwīd*, "by the servant of the LORD, David" (Pss 18; 36). The nature of that association is not immediately clear because the ascription is *lědāwīd*, and the preposition *l-* could indicate a psalm written "by," "for," or even "about." So it could mean "be-

longing to" a Davidic collection, which is paralleled by the Ugaritic expression *lbʿl*, or "[tablet belonging] to [the/a] Baal [cycle]" (Pardee, 301). However, when linked with a personal name in the psalm titles, this seems best taken as the *lamed auctoris* (Waltke and O'Conner, 206), thus "*a psalm of David* (properly belonging to David as the author)," for which "*of David* is used alone elliptically" (Kautzsch 1910, §129c). Certainly the expansive title of Psalm 18 indicates authorship: "By David *[lědāwīd]*, who addressed to the LORD the words of this song in the day when the LORD delivered him from the grip of all his enemies and from the hand of Saul" (Ps 18:1). Fourteen titles include historical notes, all of them about David (Pss 3; 7; 18; 30; 34; 51; 52; 54; 56; 57; 59; 60; 63; 142). Except for two (Pss 7; 18), all share the same syntax, which hints at an editorial regularity: infinitive construct introduced by *b-* and a subordinate clause using finite verbs. This may indicate a later editor's attempt to "Davidify" the Psalter; it may, on the other hand, preserve reliable tradition identifying the Davidic psalms.

(2) *lišlōmô*, "by Solomon," associates two psalms with David's son Solomon (Pss 72; 127), who is said to have composed 1,005 songs (1 Kings 4:32).

(3) *lěhêmān haʾezrāḥî*, "by Heman the Ezrahite" (Ps 88). The chronicler lists Heman as a leader of Levitical singers (1 Chron 6:33; 15:16-17, 22; 16:41-42; 25:1-6) who prophesied with musical accompaniment by Levitical instrumentalists and by priests blowing their trumpets (2 Chron 5:12-13; 7:6; 29:25-28). "Ezrahite" may be derived from "Zerah" instead of "Ezrah" (1 Chron 4:17), seeing that an Ethan and a Heman descended from Zerah (1 Chron 2:6). Since Heman is listed among the sages (1 Kings 4:31), perhaps it is fitting that this psalm is a *maśkîl* (see 3.2.1.4 above).

(4) *lěʾêtān hāʾezrāḥî*, "by Ethan the Ezrahite" (Ps 89). A descendant of the Mararite division of Levites (1 Chron 6:44), Ethan joined Heman and Asaph in leading temple music (1 Chron 15:17, 19). Like Heman, Ethan (or Jeduthun) is listed among the sages (1 Kings 4:31), and like Psalm 88, this psalm is a *maśkîl* (see *maśkîl* under 2.2.1. above).

(5) *lěmōšeh ʾîš-hāʾělōhîm*, "by Moses, the man of God" (Ps 90). Before David, Moses himself was known as a composer of song (Ex 15:1-18; Deut 31:19, 30; 32:1-44; 33:1-29).

(6) Psalm 39 attributes authorship to Jeduthun, using the expression *lidûtûn* ("by Jeduthun"), which is following the Qere in replacing the Kethib *lîdîtûn* ("by Idithun"). Psalm 62 and Psalm 77 probably direct that these psalms be sung by the Jeduthun choir, or according to a Jeduthun style or tune, using the expression *ʿal-yĕdûtûn* ("concerning Jeduthun" [Ps 62:1]), and also replacing *ʿal-yĕdîtûn* with *ʿal-yĕdûtûn* (Ps 77:1) (cf. 1 Chron 25:1-2; 2 Chron 5:12). Along with Asaph and Heman, Jeduthun (= Ethan [1 Chron 15:17, 19]) was one of David's chief prophets/musicians (1 Chron 16:41-42; 25:1, 3, 6; 2 Chron 5:12; 35:15). His descendants apparently formed a choir that continued into the postexilic period, as did the Korahites (see below).

(7) *libnê-qōraḥ*, "by/for the sons of Korah" (Pss 42; 44—49; 84; 85; 87; 88). This could refer to something authored/commissioned by the Korahite choir; however, it probably directs that the psalm be sung by the Korahite choir. Among David's followers in the wilderness (1 Chron 12:1, 6), the descendants of the rebel Korah survived into the postexilic period to serve as temple guards and servants (1 Chron 9:19, 31-32; 26:1, 19) and worship leaders (2 Chron 20:19). By an irony of grace these descendants of priestly usurpers are included among the Psalter's authors or performers—and not the priests.

2.2.3. Directions for Using the Psalm. (1) *šir-ḥănukkat habbayit*, "song for the dedication of the house" (Ps 30). David gathered the temple building material and organized its musicians and guards, so we should not be surprised to see that he wrote a psalm for its eventual dedication, even though not he, but rather his son Solomon, would build and dedicate it. This psalm may also have played a key role in the Hanukkah rededication of the temple (1 Macc 4:36-61; 2 Macc 10:1-9; Jn 10:22).

(2) *lĕhazkîr*, "bring to remembrance" or "get God's attention" (Pss 38; 70 [NET]). Mowinckel (2.212) helpfully links this with the memorial sacrifices, suggesting that it might have been sung to accompany such an offering (see Lev 2:2, 9, 16; 5:12; 24:7 [cf. Acts 10:4]). It might also be useful to note that both of these psalms are petitions.

(3) *lĕlammēd*, "for instruction" (Ps 60). J. Sawyer (34-35) notes two other poetic compositions described with this term and suggests that they may have been used to accompany the teaching of the *law (see Deut 31:19, 22; 2 Sam 1:19-27, esp. v. 18).

(4) *lĕtôdâ*, "for thanksgiving," aptly titles a thanksgiving hymn (Ps 100).

(5) *lĕyôm haššabbāt*, "for the day of Sabbath" (Ps 92). Interestingly, elsewhere the LXX adds labels for other days of the week: *tēs mias sabbatōn*, "for Sunday" or "for the first [day] of the week" (Ps 24 [LXX 23]); *tetradi sabbatōn*, "for Wednesday" or "for the fourth [day] of the week" (Ps 94 [LXX 93]); *eis tēn hēmeran tou prosabbatou*, "for Friday" or "for the day before the Sabbath" (Ps 93 [LXX 92]).

(6) *hammaʿălôt*, "of ascents" (Pss 120; 122—134), or *lammaʿălôt* (Ps 121). The early translation "song of degrees" (GNB, KJV) gave way to "song of ascents" (RSV, NIV); however, either translation requires explanation. Kraus suggests the possibility that it indicates "a wayfaring psalm" for postexilic returnees "going up *[hāʿōlîm]* out of captivity" (Ezra 2:1), for those who made an "ascent *[hammaʿălâ]* from Babylon" (Ezra 7:9). The rabbis also could link these psalms with deliverance, from the Egyptians or from any oppressor (*Midr. Ps.* 120); however, they could also link them with ascending in pilgrimage to the Jerusalem temple (*Midr. Ps.* 122). Kraus (1.23) thinks it useful to combine two ideas: a "song of steps *[hammaʿălôt]*" up to the throne, temple levels or altar (citing Ex 20:26; 1 Kings 10:19-20; 2 Chron 9:18-20; Ezek 40:6, 22, 26, 31, 34, 37, 49; 43:17), and a "pilgrimage song" or "processional song," understanding the "ascents" *[mʿlh]* as a technical term for "pilgrimage" (Ps 24:3; 122:4; cf., e.g., Mk 10:33; Lk 2:4) or for procession to a shrine (2 Sam 6; 1 Kings 12:32-33; 2 Kings 23:1-2) or to the city of David (Neh 3:15; 12:37; Lk 2:4). Kraus (1.24) admits, "Only Psalm 122 is applied to a pilgrimage, and only Psalm 132 to a procession" but still thinks of Psalms 120—134 as a pilgrimage songbook that includes various kinds of songs.

See also ASAPH AND SONS OF KORAH; DAVID; PSALMS 1: BOOK OF.

BIBLIOGRAPHY. **B. S. Childs,** *Introduction to the Old Testament as Scripture* (Philadelphia: Fortress, 1979); **M. Dahood,** *Psalms* (3 vols.; AB 16, 17, 17A; Garden City, NY: Doubleday, 1966-1970); **L. Delekat,** "Probleme der Psalmenuberschriften," *ZAW* 76 (1964) 280-97; **B. B. Edwards,** "Studies in Hebrew Poetry," *Bibliotheca Sacra & Theological Review* 5 (February 1848) 58-79; **B. D. Eerdmans,** *The Hebrew Book of Psalms* (OtSt 4;

Leiden: E. J. Brill, 1947); **J. J. Glueck,** "Some Remarks on the Introductory Notes of the Psalms," in *Studies on the Psalms: Papers Read at Sixth Meeting Held at the Potchefstroom University for C.H.E., 29-31 Jan. 1963* (Potchefstroom: Pro Rege, 1963) 30-39; **H. Gunkel,** *Introduction to Psalms: The Genres of the Religious Lyric of Israel* (Macon, GA: Mercer University Press, 1998); **C. T. Hodge,** "Miktam," in *Semitic Studies in Honor of Wolf Leslau on the Occasion of His Eighty-Fifth Birthday, November 14, 1991,* ed. A. S. Kaye (2 vols.; Wiesbaden: Harrassowitz, 1991) 1.634-44; **O. Kaiser,** *Introduction to the Old Testament: A Presentation of Its Results and Problems* (Minneapolis: Augsburg, 1975 [1970]); **E. Kautzsch,** ed., *Gesenius' Hebrew Grammar* (2nd ed.; Oxford: Clarendon, 1910 [1909]); **D. Kidner,** *Psalms 1-72* (TOTC; Downers Grove, IL: InterVarsity Press, 1973); idem, *Psalms 73-150* (TOTC; Downers Grove, IL: InterVarsity Press, 1975); **H. Kosmala,** "Maśkil," *JANESCU* 5 (1973) 235-41; **H.-J. Kraus,** *Psalms* (2 vols.; Minneapolis: Augsburg, 1989); **S. Mowinckel,** *The Psalms in Israel's Worship* (2 vols. in 1; BRS; Grand Rapids: Eerdmans, 2004 [1951]). **D. G. Pardee,** "The Preposition in Ugaritic," *UF* 8 (1976) 215-322; **J. F. A. Sawyer,** "An Analysis of the Context and Meaning of the Psalm-Headings," *TGUOS* 22 (1967-1968) 26-38; **J. W. Thirtle,** *The Titles of the Psalms: Their Nature and Meaning* (London: Henry Frowde, 1904); **H. von Ewald,** *Commentary on the Psalms* (2 vols.; Theological Translation Fund Library 23-24; London: Williams & Norgae, 1880-1881); **B. K. Waltke,** "Superscripts, Postscripts, or Both," *JBL* 110 (1991) 538-96; **B. K. Waltke** and **M. O'Conner,** *An Introduction to Biblical Hebrew Syntax* (Winona Lake, IN: Eisenbrauns, 1990).

D. A. Brueggeman

PSALMS 5: ICONOGRAPHY

*Imagery is the essence of biblical poetry. However, studies on biblical imagery are mostly focused on the semantic value of words in their contexts and only rarely on the actual images that may lie behind the words. Ancient Near Eastern iconography as a growing field in biblical studies provides a tool through which the thought world of the biblical authors may be accessed not only via the literary poetic device but also through a visual artifact that can be related to the text. The psalms need to be seen and not just read, as W. Brown suggests in his extensively reviewed work on the relationship between metaphor and icon.

1. Image and Text
2. Ancient Near Eastern Iconography
3. Iconography and the Psalms

1. Image and Text.

The relationship between image and text can be manifold and complex. Traditionally, Judeo-Christian sources have given preference to the text over the image, but at least since H. Gressmann's *Altorientalische Bilder zum Alten Testament* (1927) and J. Pritchard's *The Ancient Near East in Pictures Relating to the Old Testament* (1954) there is an awareness that the OT was written in a sociocultural context that abounded with images, and that these images have had an impact on the biblical text. A simple example is found in Psalm 65:9 (MT 65:10) where a somewhat enigmatic reference is made to the *peleg ʾĕlōhîm* ("canal of God"), which can be interpreted as a conduit of water flowing downward from the heavenly realm to the earth, an iconographic motif known from Middle-Assyrian and Middle-Babylonian times. Figure 1 shows a Kassite cylinder-seal with an inscription dating it to the fourteenth century BC. On it there is the water-god Ea surrounded by lush vegetation and holding in each hand a vase from which streams of water flow downward into receptacles on the ground.

The predominance of text over image in biblical scholarship has been criticized repeatedly, and the argument usually adduced is that this has its roots in an aniconic Judeo-Christian tradition. However, archaeology and the study of imagery in the Bible point to the fact that the biblical authors were aware of and accustomed to the images around them. Iconographic studies, especially those from the University of Fribourg in Switzerland, have recently taken this notion to its furthest conclusion in attempting a reconstruction of the religious history of Palestine/Israel based on images without any explicit reference to the Hebrew Bible. Preference in this case is given to the image over the text, based on the minimalist assumption that the text of the OT is of limited value for historical reconstructions. A more differentiated approach would recognize text and image as two independent media, each of which has strengths or weaknesses and needs to be interpreted in its own right within relevant hermeneutic parameters. Furthermore, each source has to interact with the other through comparison, whereas the point of departure for the comparative process within the context of OT studies needs to be the biblical text.

1.1. Imagery in the Psalms. It is impossible to talk about imagery in the psalms without touching on the realm of metaphor. Metaphor, as suggested by A. Berlin in *The Dynamics of Biblical Parallelism*, is almost intrinsic to *parallelism as the strongest expression of Hebrew poetry, which indicates that imagery in the psalms usually is transmitted via this literary device. Although most scholars recognize the importance of metaphor in the Psalter, there is little material that discusses the subject in a systematic manner, taking into consideration modern metaphor theory and cognitive linguistics. Most of the literature available on the subject is following in the footsteps of P. Macky's

Figure 1. Kassite cylinder-seal

interactive metaphor theory, and the recent discussion of metaphor criticism in the psalms can be summarized under three emerging angles. (1) Semantics and pragmatics: The study of metaphor in the palms has to be done in reference to both semantics and pragmatics, taking into consideration both meaning and usage. This implies a closer look at the cultural and social context of the metaphor, including the iconographic ancient Near Eastern image as discussed in this article. (2) Cognitive linguistics: Metaphors transmit content but also no content, drawing at the same time on different domains of knowledge and combining

them in a new and creative way; they structure our thinking theologically through what they tell us and what they do not. Metaphors in the psalms can be cognitively categorized and represent universal truths that cannot be expressed otherwise. Therefore, metaphors in the psalms have a rhetorical or ideological force that should not be underestimated. (3) *Intertextuality: Metaphors have a chronological aspect and appear on a timeline; they should be studied with reference to their usage and reusage in biblical texts, which through intertextual markers indicate that they refer to the same metaphor, possibly shifting or creating its meaning along the way. In this way, imagery in the psalms can help us to gain a clearer understanding of the religious history of the OT and to understand our own modern and personal religious histories.

1.2. Literary and Literal Image. Athanasius (c. AD 293-373), in his letter to Marcellinus, states that the reader of the psalms "is enabled to possess the image deriving from the words," referring to expressions that can be realized in both image and language. Cognitive linguistics has demonstrated the level of understanding (cognition) that a metaphor is able to evoke, as the most prominent trope of biblical imagery, through the incongruity between different domains of knowledge. The resulting new meaning is based on the reader/hearer's ability to map from the known toward the unknown. Although modern metaphor theory deals adequately with the issues of semantics and pragmatics, the question of the origin of the metaphor in the poet's mind is rarely addressed. Images are derived from imagination, and the imagery actually opens a window into the poet's mind. We often look through this window to discern the meaning of the imagery, but frequently we overlook the image behind the imagery. The iconoclastic debate of church history has warned against the icon becoming the idol, which happens when the deity's power is harnessed within the physical structure of the image. However, the fear of idolatry has impoverished the hermeneutical endeavor to discover the image behind the imagery.

Mostly, pictorial remains from the ancient Near East have been treated as illustrations of texts or described under art-historical perspectives, but seldom are they taken into consideration when it comes to the reconstruction of religio-cultural history. A stela from a clearly Iron Age I archaeological context near the gate at Bethsaida (figure 2) showing a semiabstract image of an anthropomorphic figure with a sword and a bovine head, which has been identified as a moon-deity, may actually tell us a great deal about problematic cultic practices of OT times at the city gate that motivated religious reforms like the one mentioned in the short information provided in 2 Kings 23:8, which says that King Josiah "broke down the shrines at the gates." O. Goldwasser goes further in establishing the cognitive relationship between the image and imagery on the basis of Egyptian hieroglyphs, where the relationship between text and picture is probably the most intricate, stating that in this pictorial form of

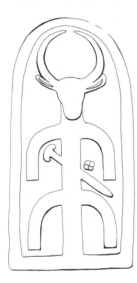

Figure 2. Bethsaida stela

writing the "intellectual leap" between icon and phonetic metaphor has been accomplished. Thus, the biblical poets drew from a conceptual stock of imagery that can and needs to be related to the images of the ancient Near East within the parameters of a balanced comparative methodology. The question that follows is, "What caused the biblical writers to use an iconographic motif and translate it into the medium of language and create thus a new context influenced by their particular set of hermeneutical criteria?" In order to answer this question, one has to look at the often-neglected methodological issues underlying ancient Near Eastern iconography.

2. Ancient Near Eastern Iconography.

As a separate discipline within biblical studies, ancient Near Eastern iconography describes and interprets the pictorial remains of ancient cultures. It focuses on the development of themes and motifs throughout the material culture of the ancient Near East and tries to establish possible relationships with the cultural and religious history of the ancient world.

2.1. Studies in Ancient Near Eastern Iconography.
The results and advantages of an iconographic approach to the biblical text have been demonstrated through a number of publications associated with the Biblical Institute at the University of Fribourg, Switzerland, so one can speak of the "Fribourg school" of ancient Near Eastern iconography. O. Keel's widely cited *The Symbolism of the Biblical World: Ancient Near-ern Iconography and the Book of Psalms* (the original German edition was published in 1972) focused on the Psalter with the intention of surveying the conceptual similarities between the biblical text and the ancient Near Eastern image, drawing mainly on Mesopotamian and Egyptian monumental art. A number of exegetical studies followed that recognized the abundance of archaeological remains in the realm of miniature art from Syro-Palestine (e.g., seals and amulets). Methodologically, they approached the evidence more systematically, taking into consideration chronological and geographical delimitations. More recent publications have moved from mere biblical theme-oriented studies toward a primary concern with the iconographic evidence as such and its consequential bearing on the religious history of ancient Israel. In the same way, the focus has shifted from exegetical issues to the synthesizing and integration of iconographic evidence into an overall picture of religious belief in ancient Israel. Thus the attempt is to contribute to the reconstruction of the religious conceptual world *(Vorstellungswelt)* of Israel through pictorial material. The Fribourg school has produced a number of important reference works such as the *Corpus der Stempelsiegelamulette aus Palästina/Israel,* of which two volumes have been published so far. The most ambitious and recent project has been the writing of a religious history of Palestine/Israel and the ancient Near East based solely on pictorial evidence, with a deliberate avoidance of referring to the biblical text *(Die Ikonographie Palästinas/Israels und der Alte Orient: Eine Religions-*

geschichte in Bildern). However, while it appears that in its publication the Fribourg school has moved progressively away from the biblical text, most recently critique has been voiced from within that this lack of reference actually constitutes a methodological weakness.

2.2. Methodology in Ancient Near Eastern Iconography. The interpretation of an iconographic object needs to be informed by methodological guidelines comparable to the hermeneutic process that guides the process of biblical interpretation. Keel's methodological study *Das Recht der Bilder gesehen zu werden* (1992) draws on but moves beyond E. Panofsky's iconographic interpretation scheme, which divides the interpretative process up into three steps:

> Preiconographic description: based on the practical experience of the describer; aimed at the primary object
>
> Iconographic analysis: based on the knowledge of literary sources for comparative purposes, focuses on type-history; the secondary or conventional subject is the objective
>
> Iconological analysis/interpretation: based on synthetic intuition and a knowledge of cultural symptoms and symbols, aimed at the establishing of meaning

Keel has especially criticized Panofsky's second methodological step because it reverts to an interpretation of images on the basis of textual sources and arrives at the following conclusions: (1) each picture has to be evaluated in its own right without the reception bias of Judeo-Christian exegesis before it can be linked exegetically to a text; (2) image and word are not dichotic but rather should be complementary to each other, mutually enhancing; (3) pictures can be interpreted with the help of other pictorial material without necessarily resorting to textual sources. Within the interpretation process each image has to be divided into components that together, and in a contextual relationship, constitute the image and its meaning. The important compositional elements of an image are the motif, the scene and the decoration, while their relationship has to be understood within an architectural hierarchy that is comparable to the hermeneutical circle of exegesis on a linguistic level that works within the sequence of word, phrase, sentence, unit, section and so on.

Figure 3 shows the iconographic interpretation scheme in a graphic way. The circular depiction demonstrates the reciprocal relationship between the individual components of the image. While it is important to understand the smallest units, the overall meaning of the image can be derived only from an integrated interpretation of all the elements.

Only after the image has been understood in its own right can an attempt be made to compare it to a literary text—that is, to the biblical word. According to Keel, such a comparison

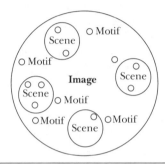

Figure 3. Hermeneutical circle of image interpretation

may yield a variety of relationships between the biblical text and the ancient Near Eastern thought world as expressed by the iconographic image: (1) a text can directly refer to an ancient Near Eastern image, such as the description of Chaldean soldiers in Ezekiel 23:14-15; (2) a text can be implicitly influenced by pictorial representations, such as the description of the four living creatures in Ezekiel 1; (3) a text and an image can independently refer to a common subject matter, such as the rewarding of an official (Gen 41:37-45) and several New Kingdom Egyptian tomb paintings.

2.3. Comparative Method: Time and Place. The conceptual relationship between imagery and image in the psalms as outlined in this article necessitates some reference to the comparative method and its ramifications for biblical studies.

Comparative method involves the comparison of biblical phenomena with other phenomena that occur in the whole realm of the ancient Near Eastern setting in general. The comparisons have to work on the level of cultural systems without isolating individual phenomena from their respective cultural context. The underlying principles of the comparative method are based on the assumption that there are common characteristics between societies and cultures, which allow the researcher to make valid comparisons. Early iconographic studies took place on a grand scale (typological comparison) assuming a general cultural uniformity in the ancient Near East—for example, liberally comparing a text from the Psalter with an Assyrian palace relief. A more contextual approach focuses on both differences and similarities, trying to strike a balance between contrasts and parallels, and needs to be informed by the two governing principles of the comparative method: place (geography) and time (chronology). Without entering the discussion of dating the psalms, there seems to be sufficient evidence to propose a chronological framework from the Iron Age I down to the Persian period for the Psalter from which comparative material could be drawn. Geographically, the period outlined above comprises such a number of historical situations and locations that it seems advisable to advance the geographical limitations beyond the immediate Palestinian/Israelite borders (e.g., Ps 68 presupposes a Trans-Jordanian locale, possibly, even reaching into Syria, while Ps 137 is set against the backdrop of the Babylonian exile) but give preference to objects from Syro-Palestine.

3. Iconography and the Psalms.

Already in the early twentieth century H. Gunkel, in his commentary on Psalms, recognizes the contribution of iconography to the study of the psalms. In his interpretation of Psalm 17:8 he makes reference to objects, especially from Egypt, that show divine beings with wings spread protectively over humans. The purpose was to illustrate the integration of Israelite belief into ancient Near Eastern culture and the evolution of OT religious history out of it. As shown above, the metaphorical character of Hebrew poetry as the principle vehicle of communication in the psalms necessitates an iconographic approach to the Psalter.

3.1. Iconography and Illustration. Figures 1 and 2 draw examples from ancient Near Eastern iconography to illustrate specific biblical texts without paying attention to the methodological issues. While this approach needs to be benchmarked with the parameters of the comparative method mentioned earlier (see 2.2 above), there is a wide interest in this usage of iconography for biblical studies because it can provide a snapshot of ancient cultures, peoples or objects

that helps us to visualize and in turn contextualize the biblical text. Keel's foundational work on iconography in the psalms followed this approach and still represents the most important reference work in this area.

The following illustrations show the possibilities of this approach to iconography. The expression in Psalm 68:21, "Surely God will crush the heads of his enemies, the hairy crowns of those who go on in their sins" (NIV), is compatible with the familiar smiting-god motif from ancient Near Eastern iconography. The motif usually depicts weather and war gods with different geographical and chronological characteristics, but it is clear that the gesture always indicates the supremacy of the god versus the subjugation of the enemy or animal respectively. We may take as an example an ivory silhouette inlay from Samaria, dating from the eighth century BC (see figure 4), which shows a male figure standing in a striding position, wearing the double crown of Upper and Lower Egypt. With his right hand raised above his head, he is holding a club ready to strike, while with his left hand he is grasping the hair of an enemy who is kneel-

Figure 4. Ivory from Samaria

ing in front of him with his hands raised toward the standing figure. The detail of the "hairy skull" mentioned in Psalm 68:21 is not a by-product of the psalmist's vivid imagination or an exercise in *parallelismus membrorum* (*see* Parallelism) but rather serves as an important part of the imagery, indicating the animal-like character of the enemy. Thus the subjugation of the enemy is closely associated with the triumph over the chaotic forces, represented by the hairy skull. However, a closer look reveals that there are no distinct divine attributes present, so the figure could also be identified with the pharaoh in his typical posture, denoting his dominion over the enemies. Nevertheless, the king often was depicted in postures normally associated with the iconography of deities, and divine attributes frequently were associated with him

Figure 5 shows a typical and rather unambiguous depiction of Baʿal-Seth, the amalgamation of a Semitic deity and an Egyptian one. It is found on a steatite scarab from Lachish (Tell ed-Duweir) and comes from a Late Bronze grave that was reused until the Iron Age IIC (720/700-600 BC). Stylistically, it belongs to the Nineteenth

Figure 5. Steatite scarab from Lachish

to Twenty-Second Dynasty (1295-900 BC). Although the god is often found in a more passive stance, here he is depicted as fighting the horned snake representing the Apophis-snake in Egyptian mythology, and the chaos-waters in Canaanite myth. It is interesting to note that the enemy has been substituted by an animal that nevertheless exemplifies the equivalent threat. A further modification of the smiting-god motif that may shed light on Psalm 68:21 is found in a number of objects that show the smiting-god without any immediate context; that is, the smiting-god motif has been isolated from a concrete war situation, reducing the gesture of the raised arm holding the weapon to strike at an enemy to a mere emblem, a symbol of victory and dominion. Thus the smiting god becomes the menacing god without active involvement in the battle,

portrayed in an almost canonized position.

Figure 6 shows a cylinder-seal (dated around 1750 BC) on which the Syrian weather-god Baʿal Zaphon is depicted in a smiting-god posture in the middle of a holy wedding ceremony with a banquet scene attached to it, but no enemy at all is present.

Thus the author of Psalm 68:21 is referring not to a literal depiction of Yahweh's intervention in human warfare but rather to God's subjugation of any type of adverse forces that the psalmist may encounter.

3.2. Iconography and Exegesis. The foregoing examples have been employed as illustrations for a text in the psalms more or less along the lines of Keel's popular book (1978), which provided a limited number of categories (conceptions of the cosmos, destructive forces, temple, conceptions of God, king, man before God) for which iconographic illustrations were presented. In comparison, a more systematic approach to the usage of iconography in the exegetical process of a particular passage is demonstrated in the following.

Figure 6. Hermatite cylinder-seal with unknown provenance

Since the discovery of Ugaritic literature and its comparison with the biblical text, Psalm 29 has been linked to a Canaanite background. From this perspective it has served as a paradigm for the examination of Hebrew-Canaanite literary interdependence and thus has been the subject of numerous studies. H. Ginsberg in 1935 suggested a Phoenician origin for this psalm, although a closer look at the text reveals that the Ugaritic parallels viewed from the perspective of recent biblical scholarship may not present such a strong case for a Phoenician origin of the psalm as when Ginsberg, as a precursor of the Pan-Ugaritic school, originally formulated this hypothesis. The geography of the divine thunderstorm described in Psalm 29:3-9 of the poem describes the movement of a thunderstorm from the Mediterranean toward the coast and further inland. The first two toponomies represent few problems (Ps 29:3-6). However, the identification of Kadesh, or the "semi-desert Kadesh," has been the subject of wide discussion because it could refer to a desert area close to Kadesh on the Orontes, as well as to the arid region in the southern Negev, close to Kadesh Barnea. Although one cannot rule out an underlying figurative meaning for the geographic allusions, it seems clear that in the poet's description of the thunderstorm they follow a geographical progressive pattern and do not serve as a mythological depiction of the Yahwistic thunderstorm in general. It would then seem thinkable that the author used imagery commonly known from its general Syro-Palestinian background, but that he reworked it according to his rhetorical intentions and filled it with a new content. This line of interpretation, which can be motivated on exegetical grounds (see Klingbeil, 84-99), can also be approached from an iconographic-comparative perspective, as will be demonstrated in the following.

"The voice of Yahweh is upon the waters, the God of glory thunders" (Ps 29:3a-b). The main motif of Psalm 29, the *qôl yhwh* ("voice of the LORD"), has been identified as referring to the approaching sound of a thunderstorm moving inland from the Mediterranean. It depicts Yahweh as a storm and weather god, to which the iconographic motif of the god in the winged sun-disk probably comes closest. The audible sound of thunder, obviously, cannot be easily reproduced by an iconographic image, but the densely feathered wings of the god in the winged sun-disk motif from ancient Near Eastern iconography have been identified as symbolizing the dark clouds and stormy heavens associated with a thunderstorm. Figure 7 shows part of a glazed tile from Assur dating to the time of Tukulti-Ninurta II (890-884 BC). The sun-disk is depicted as encompassing the winged god completely, while there are rays or flames of fire depicted within the sun nimbus. The bearded god has a large feathered tail and a pair of large wings that go beyond the border of the sun-disk. He is wearing a beard and a rounded crown. With his hand, the god is holding a bow that he has stretched to its limits, pointing at an imaginary or at least not visible enemy (the scene has been broken off on the right side). Below (not shown), a chariot scene is visible of which only the head of the charioteer and the upper part of the horse's head are visible. Around the winged sun-disk are stylized clouds (not shown) with raindrops suspended from the upper border. The association of the god with rain clouds demon-strates his identification with a storm and weather deity, while the wide wings symbolize the dark, thundering heaven. The atmospheric phenomena are directed against the enemies of the Assyrian king,

Figure 7. Glazed tile from Assur

thus creating a complex image of the god fighting from heaven with meteorological weapons. The winged god in the sun-disk can be identified with the Assyrian sun and weather god Šamaš.

With regard to the thunder, the club that the smiting weather god often holds in his hand has been associated with the sound of thunder in the way of Baʿal beating the heavens like a drum with his club, but the club rather should be understood as a weapon in the fight against an enemy and not be confused with the thunderbolt (lightning). Figure 8 shows a stela from Ras Shamra (Ugarit), dated on the basis of comparative material to the Late Bronze Age. The relief shows a barefoot male god in a passant position facing to the right. The figure is wearing a short kilt ornamented with horizontal stripes and held together by a broad belt. A curved dagger or sword is attached to the belt. The figure is wearing a helmet with a high point from which a pair of bull's horns protrudes from the front. He has a long beard reaching to his chest, and his hair ends in long curls. The god has his right hand raised above his head, holding a club ready to strike, while the other hand is holding a spear in a vertical position with the broad blade pointing to the ground. The shaft of the spear spreads out into a plant, not into a shaft of lightning as proposed elsewhere, since the iconography of the weather-god with the bundle of lightning is completely different from this depiction. The identification of the figure does not present major problems, and we are confronted with a depiction of the weather-god Baʿal in his normal posture as the smiting-god, but holding a vegetation spear in his hand, thus establishing his close affinity to fertility and vegetation. In Ugaritic texts Baʿal is described as a god who possesses lightning and thunder (*KTU* 1.3 III 23, 1.101 obv 3-4) and he is the bringer of rain and fertility (*KTU* 1.4 VII 29-31 and 1.16 III 5ff.).

"Yahweh is over mighty waters" (Ps 29:3c). The *mayim rabbîm* ("mighty waters") have repeatedly been associated with the chaotic forces repre-

nance housed in the Musées Royaux, Brussels (see figure 9). Stylistically, it has been assigned to the Ramessidian dynasties corresponding to the period 1300-1150 BC (Late Bronze Age IIB). Depicted on it is a winged figure wearing a short kilt with tassels. Although the body is anthropomorphic, the top part depicts the head of the Seth animal with long ears and a protruding snout. The figure has a pair of wings attached to its back that are typical of Baʿal and Seth and their combination during the Late Bronze Age. With his one hand raised above his head, he is holding a long lance or javelin, thrusting it down into a horned snake that he is grasping with the other hand. The tail of the snake is curved upward behind the god. Although the depiction is clearly Egyptian in style, and the streamers that often betray the Egyptian-Canaanite combination of Baʿal-Seth are missing, the figure should be identified with this god.

Figure 8. Stela from Ras Shamra

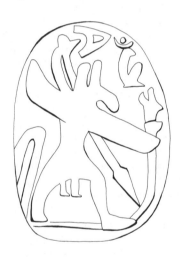

Figure 9. Steatite scarab of unknown provenance

sented by the horned snake of Canaanite mythology. Various motifs of ancient Near Eastern iconography show the struggle of the Canaanite-Egyptian god Baʿal-Seth with the spear against the horned snake. The depictions show him thrusting his weapon in a downward movement into the body of the snake. Most of the images depicting this motif originated during the Late Bronze Age and the Iron Age I, and a good example is a steatite scarab of unknown prove-

However, in Psalm 29 no direct struggle is reflected between Yahweh and the chaotic waters—a fact that necessitates caution toward an interpretation of the biblical text along mythological lines.

"And he makes Lebanon skip like a calf, and Sirion like the young of an aurochs" (Ps 29:6a-b). The association of the weather-god with mountains has been noticed in figure 6. The god is standing on three mountaintops, although there is no indication of a destructive earthquake-like event on the seal from northern Syria representing this motif. Whereas in the iconographic depic-

tions of gods striding over mountains the mountains are portrayed as a constant and stabile factor supporting the mountain god, almost as a cultic pedestal, the psalmist describes them as fragile objects subjected to Yahweh's earthquake, which causes them to skip uncontrollably. Although the author of the psalm takes up the familiar mountain motif, he does not use the imagery in the expected manner but rather injects a new content that appears to be rather polemical for the ancient Near Eastern cultural context.

"The voice of Yahweh hews out lightning" (Ps 29:7a). In similar fashion to Psalm 18:15, Yahweh's appearance, in this case, Yahweh's voice, is associated with lightning. Although the imagery is that of the effect of Yahweh's voice on the rocky surface of the mountains, images showing the weather god using the bundle of lightning as a weapon may serve as comparative material. Figure 10 is a basalt stela, 135 cm in height, found at Arslan-Tash. It was found in the temple constructed by Tiglath-pileser III (744-727 BC), which dates it with some accuracy to the second half of the eighth century BC. The image shows a god in a striding position facing to the right. He is standing on top of a bull, one foot on the animal's horns, the other foot resting on its back. The posture is indicating a running motion, whereas the bull is depicted in a similar stance. The god is dressed with a short kilt, over which he is wearing a long robe. On his head the god is wearing the high rectangular horned crown customary to depictions of Neo-Assyrian gods. Above the crown a disk is visible with rays depicted in it. The god is armed with a long sword attached to his belt, pointing toward the back. On his shoulder he is carrying a bow and a quiver. One arm is raised above his head in a striking or throwing position, while the other arm is extended diagonally downward toward the front. In both hands he is holding a double three-forked bundle of lightning. From a Neo-Assyrian perspective, the god can be identified with the weather god Adad, whereas the three-forked bundle of lightning in the striking hand has replaced the weapon that one normally would expect. He is now completely equipped with meteorological weapons, and the character of the lightning as an attacking weapon becomes increasingly evident. It is no longer held in a passive gesture in front of the god as in other depictions; rather, it is raised above his head

with the intention to strike down on the imaginary enemy. The single most important element in the identification of the weather god remains the bundle of lightning, although a bull and other elements often also serve as indicators that a depiction of the weather-god is intended.

The famous "Ba⁽al au foudre" (figure 8) with the vegetation spear may be an indicator of the combination of the imagery of lightning with fertility. However, whereas the iconographic depictions may picture the lightning as a complementing factor to fertility, Psalm 29 portrays its effects on fauna and flora in a rather destructive way, evoking rather an imagery of warfare: "The voice of Yahweh breaks cedars; yes, Yahweh, shatters the cedars of Lebanon" (Ps 29:5a-b), and "The voice of Yahweh causes the desert to writhe; Yahweh causes the desert Kadesh to writhe. The voice of Yahweh makes the hinds to

Figure 10. Basalt stela from Arslan-Tash

bring forth and lays bare the forests" (Ps 29:8a-9b).

The overall picture that emerges from a comparison of Psalm 29:3-9 with the iconographic evidence shows a tendency toward using the prevalent iconographic motifs of particularly the northern Syrian and Mesopotamian repertoire but reapplying them polemically and subjecting them to the force of Yahweh's voice as the ultimate controlling factor in the upheaval of nature. The northern geography of the psalm furthermore contributes to such an understanding, while the imagery employed in the psalm has been utilized in such a way that it leads from the known to the surprising—that is, reinterpreting the imagery from the perspective and under the dominion of Yahweh's voice.

3.3. Contribution of Iconography to the Study of the Psalms. Although iconography can supply us with an illustration of the typical and institutional, it cannot provide "historical photographs" on the basis of which history can be reconstructed. Nevertheless, the study of ancient Near Eastern iconography can be used to reconstruct the religious concept world in which the OT was written. However, image and text have to be placed alongside each other continuously in order to create a more complete picture of the Psalter that represents a cross-section of OT religious thought. In comparing the biblical texts with the iconographic images, a number of parallels as well as contrasts can be established. On the whole, it appears that the authors of the psalms utilized imagery that was familiar to them from their general Syro-Palestinian environment and that can be related to iconographic sources reflecting such imagery. However, one can by no means talk of a one-to-one relationship, establishing a simple line of dependency. There are distinct contrasts and variations of motif on such a scale that one is compelled to assume a certain adaptation of the iconographic material in accordance with the intentions of the respective psalmist. In interpreting such a state of affairs, we would assume that the biblical author utilized imagery familiar to the ancient Near Eastern cultural background and applied it to Yahweh. During this process, a number of adaptations took place, and familiar iconographic motifs were filled with new content as they appeared in literary form in the psalms. The motivation for such a practice would be the demonstration of the superiority of Yahweh over against the ancient Near Eastern pantheon, a notion that is clearly monotheistic in orientation. Yahweh sometimes takes on attributes familiar from other gods of the ancient Near East, but he never does so in a static way; he is not restricted by them, and they do not become his emblems, designating him as weather god, war god or any other type of god per se. Rather, he fills them with a new or slightly different content and goes beyond them, which serves to create the dichotomy between the one God and the many gods. Thus Yahweh

always remains the *totaliter aliter.*

An iconographic approach to the study of the psalms is opening new and unexpected vistas onto the Bible, which, although in literary form, often communicates its eternal truths through a variety of imagery that probably is the most appropriate way to speak about God. As a final observation, it is interesting to note that most of the relevant comparative iconographic material that can be related to the Psalter stems from Late Bronze and Iron Age archaeological contexts, a fact that may reopen the long-debated question of dating of the psalms.

See also ANIMAL IMAGERY; ARCHITECTURAL IMAGERY; CHAOS AND DEATH; CREATION IMAGERY; FLORAL IMAGERY; IMAGERY; IMPRISONMENT IMAGERY; LIFE, IMAGERY OF; MOUNTAIN IMAGERY; PROTECTION IMAGERY; THEOPHANY; WARFARE IMAGERY.

BIBLIOGRAPHY. **M. Barasch,** "The Idol in the Icon: Some Ambiguities," in *Representation in Religion: Studies in Honor of Moshe Barasch,* ed. J. Assmann and A. I. Baumgarten (SHR 89; Leiden: E. J. Brill, 2001) 1-26; **A. Basson,** *Divine Metaphors in Selected Hebrew Psalms of Lamentation* (FAT 15; Tübingen: Mohr Siebeck, 2006); **A. Berlin,** *The Dynamics of Biblical Parallelism* (Bloomington: Indiana University Press, 1985); **W. P. Brown,** *Seeing the Psalms: A Theology of Metaphor* (Louisville: Westminster John Knox, 2002); **I. Cornelius,** *The Iconography of the Canaanite Gods Reshef and Ba'al: Late Bronze and Iron Age I Periods (c. 1500-1000 BCE)* (OBO 140; Fribourg: University Press; Göttingen: Vandenhoeck & Ruprecht, 1994); **O. Goldwasser,** *From Icon to Metaphor: Studies in the Semiotics of the Hieroglyphs* (OBO 142; Fribourg: University Press; Göttingen: Vandenhoeck & Ruprecht, 1995); **O. Jäkel,** "How Can Mortal Man Understand the Road He Travels? Prospects and Problems of the Cognitive Approach to Religious Metaphor," in *The Bible through Metaphor and Translation: A Cognitive Semantic Perspective,* ed. K. Feyaerts (RD 15; Oxford: Peter Lang, 2003) 55-86; **O. Keel,** *Jahwe-Visionen und Siegelkunst: Eine neue Deutung der Majestätsschilderungen in Jes 6, Ez 1 und 10 und Sach 4* (SBS 84/85; Stuttgart: Katholisches Bibelwerk, 1977); idem, *The Symbolism of the Biblical World: Ancient Near Eastern Iconography and the Book of Psalms* (New York: Seabury, 1978); idem, "Iconography and the Bible," *ABD* 3.358-74; **O. Keel and C. Uehlinger,** *Gods, Goddesses, and Images of God in Ancient Israel* (Minneapolis: Fortress, 1998); **M. G. Klingbeil,** *Yahweh Fighting from Heaven: God as a Warrior and as God of Heaven in the Hebrew Psalter and Ancient Near Eastern Iconography* (OBO 169; Fribourg: University Press; Göttingen: Vandenhoeck & Ruprecht, 1999); **D. Kroneman,** "The LORD Is My Shepherd: An Exploration into the Theory and Practice of Translating Biblical Metaphor" (Ph.D. diss., Free University of Amsterdam, 2004); **P. W. Macky,** *The Centrality of Metaphors to Biblical Thought: A Method for Interpreting the Bible* (SBEC 19; Lewiston, NY: Edwin Mellen, 1990); **M. Malul,** *The Comparative Method in Ancient Near Eastern and Biblical Legal Studies* (AOAT 227; Neukirchen-Vluyn: Neukirchener Verlag, 1990); **E. Panofsky,** "Ikonographie und Ikonologie," in *Ikonographie und Ikonologie: Theorien, Entwicklung, Probleme,* ed. E. Kaemmerling (Bildende Kunst als Zeichensystem 1; Cologne: Du Mont, 1979) 207-25; **L. Ryken,** "Metaphor in the Psalms," *ChrLit* 31.3 (1982) 9-29; **S. Schroer and O. Keel,** *Die Ikonographie Palästinas/Israels und der Alte Orient: Eine Religionsgeschichte in Bildern,* 1: *Vom ausgehenden Mesolithikum bis zur Frühbronzezeit* (Fribourg: Academic Press, 2005).

M. G. Klingbeil

PSALTER, GROWTH OF. *See* DEAD SEA SCROLLS; PSALMS 1: BOOK OF.

PSALTER, SHAPE OF. *See* EDITORIAL CRITICISM; PSALMS 1: BOOK OF.

PSEUDO-SOLOMON. *See* WISDOM OF SOLOMON.

PUNS. *See* WORDPLAY.

PURIM

Purim is a Jewish festival dating from pre-Christian times that originally was celebrated on the fourteenth and fifteenth of Adar (February-March), though it came to entail certain practices on the thirteenth as well. The celebration of Purim commemorates the victory of *Esther and *Mordecai over Haman and the resulting conquest of the Jews over their enemies. It is a minor festival within the Jewish liturgical year, meaning that work is permitted during the festival

1. Purim in the Bible and in Early Jewish and Christian Literature
2. Origins
3. History of Celebration

1. Purim in the Bible and in Early Jewish and Christian Literature.

1.1. Esther. The book of Esther presents itself as providing the story of the origins of the festival of Purim, and its rationale is detailed in Esther 9. Haman had orchestrated a plot to exterminate the Jews on Adar 13, but Mordecai and Esther succeeded in having the decree reversed, thus allowing the Jews to defeat their enemies. However, due to the request of Esther, the Jews in *Susa were permitted to continue killing their enemies on the next day as well, the fourteenth of Adar (Esther 9:13-15). Therefore, although Purim is based on the events of Adar 13-14, it actually commemorates the respite that the Jews obtained from their enemies (Esther 9:21-22) and thus is celebrated on Adar 14-15 (see Levenson, 126). It seems clear, then, not only that the author sought to explain the origin of Purim but also why there may have been discrepancies over the date(s) on which it was to be celebrated.

In addition to giving an account of the origin of the festival, the book of Esther offers an explanation as to the origin of the festival's name. In Esther 9:24-26 the author anchors the name "Purim" in the word *pûr,* and in both places where *pûr* occurs in Esther (Esther 3:7; 9:24-26) the author translates it with the Hebrew word for "lot," *gôrāl.* This implies that the composition of Esther had sufficient historical and/or cultural distance from the institution of the festival to require an etymological explanation for its name. The word *pûr* evidently entered the Hebrew language as a loanword from the East Semitic languages, the possible candidates being either the Assyrian or the Babylonian word *pūrū,* meaning "lot" (see Bosman and Van Dam, 590).

It is notable that in the LXX of Esther 9:26, 28, 29 the festival is called not Purim but *Phrourai* ("days of protection"). In fact, the name is omitted altogether in the LXX of Esther 9:31, 32. This is particularly striking because in the LXX Additions to Esther the explanation of the festival is linked specifically to the casting of lots. In fact, the author seems to be answering the question of why the name of the holiday, Purim, is plural. These Additions to Esther were likely composed at a time when it was necessary to defend the validity of the celebration of Purim.

1.2. Early References outside the Old Testament. The earliest extant reference to the festival of

Purim outside of Esther is found at the end of 2 Maccabees, where the fourteenth of Adar is called "the Day of Mordecai" (2 Macc 15:36). It is interesting to note in this respect that the author shows no awareness of the Fast of Esther, later held on the thirteenth of Adar as a preliminary event to Purim (see Goodman, 7). The other major early attestation of Purim is found in the work of Josephus (*Ant.* 11.291-296), who states that *Phrourai* (following the LXX) was still in regular observance among his contemporaries. Some scholars have also speculated that Purim may underlie the festival reference in John 5:1. However, the content of John 5 does not necessarily make the identification with Purim any more likely than with other festivals such as Tabernacles or Weeks. In any case, the fact that the festival is left unspecified is probably intentional, since that chapter of John focuses on the issue of the Sabbath.

2. Origins.

One of the most debated aspects of the book of Esther remains the origins of the festival of Purim. As one would expect, the conclusion of a particular scholar regarding this issue is largely dependent on that scholar's view of the historicity of Esther. Those who ascribe a high degree of historicity to the book are more inclined to accept the claims of the author regarding the institution of Purim. While the festival's Babylonian name could be explained from the Persian setting of the Esther story (contra Moore, 637), one of the primary problems not related to the historicity of Esther for these scholars is the absence of religious motifs that one would expect in a Jewish festival. In fact, there are a number of elements that found their way into the celebration of the festival that run counter to Jewish norms (see 3 below).

Those who regard Esther as primarily a secondary, fictional story that was written in order to provide an etiology for the festival itself have naturally searched for the origins of the festival in other ancient Near Eastern cultures. On the basis of the Babylonian origin of the name and the similarity of the names "Esther," "Mordecai," "Haman," and *"Vashti" to the Babylonian gods Ishtar and Marduk and the Elamite gods Humman and Mashti, the most common hypotheses over the past century and a half have centered on a Persian or a Babylonian provenance for Purim. Indeed, scholars have pointed out a number of similarities between Purim and various pagan festivals such as Farvardigan, the Zoroastrian Festival of the Dead (see Moore, 637) and the Babylonian New Year festival (Polish). However, given the combative nature of the story of Esther, the parallels with Babylonian or Persian cultures could indicate not dependence but rather polemical engagement. A smaller number of scholars (e.g., Herst) have also postulated a Palestinian origin for Purim, arguing that it is an adaptation of the festival held on the thirteenth of Adar to celebrate Judas Maccabaeus's victory over Nicanor in 161 BC (cf. 1 Macc 7:26-50).

Yet in the final analysis it must be admitted that the alleged external origins of Purim are largely dependent on the assumption that Esther lacks historicity. On balance, the number of proposals for the festival's origin, none of which has come close to commanding a consensus, indicates that our knowledge of this aspect of early Judaism is insufficient to move us beyond mere conjecture. Consequently, at this point the search for the historical origins of Purim has lost much of its fervor, and it seems unlikely that any theory of the origins of Purim, including that found in the book of Esther, will gain scholarly consensus in the near future.

3. History of Celebration.

3.1. The Second Temple Period and Late Antiquity. As mentioned above, the evidence concerning the celebration of Purim in early Judaism is sparse. Just as there have been no copies of Esther discovered among the *Dead Sea Scrolls, so also there is no evidence that Purim was observed at Qumran. Scholars have offered a number of explanations for this phenomenon, but the precise reason for its absence is still not clear. It is possible, though not certain, that Purim was recognized in Jerusalem as early as the third century BC when the LXX began to be produced (Bloch 1980, 281). From what can be deduced from mishnaic sources, it seems that the earliest celebrations in the land of Palestine did not contain the exuberant customs that would appear later (see 3.2 below). In fact, in *Esther Rabbah* there are numerous exhortations on the virtues of temperance. Rather, Purim probably was marked by a certain degree of solemnity, with informal retellings of the story of the festival's origins among families and possibly also the exchange of gifts. By the first century AD the scroll of Esther, or at least parts of it, began to be read publicly in Jerusalem and the surrounding areas. Apparently in conformity with Esther 9:17-18, the feasting and the reading of the Esther scroll took place on different days, on the fourteenth for open cities and on the fifteenth for walled cities. Further allowances were made for the schedules of farmers, who came to market only on Mondays and Thursdays and would therefore have the scroll read to them at that time (*b. Meg.* 4a). Likewise, if either the fourteenth or the fifteenth of Adar fell on a Sabbath, the reading of the scroll was moved to the thirteenth or the fourteenth respectively.

With the fall of the second temple in AD 70 and the resulting dislocation of the Jews from the land of Israel, the celebration of Purim took on a uniform character, and the allowances for farmers and the divergent dates for celebration were eliminated in favor of one celebration to be held on the fourteenth of Adar (see *b. Meg.* 2a; cf. *b. B. Bat.* 25b). The historical reasons for this phenomenon are not completely clear, and several explanations have been offered throughout Jewish history, ranging from Rabbi Yochanan (third century) through medieval times (Bloch 1980, 282-83). Although there were a few who objected to the institutionalization of Purim (*b. Meg.* 7a), the events of the second century AD made the formal acceptance of Purim relatively easy.

In light of the devastating effect of the destruction of the temple in 70 AD, one can see how the story behind Purim, detailing the deliverance of the Jews from those who were persecuting them, took on added significance. This development was strengthened by the nearly contemporary recognition of Esther's canonicity and helped to elevate the significance of Purim and the corresponding public reading of Esther in the Jewish liturgical calendar. From the second century AD forward, the public reading of the scroll of Esther became the central feature of the celebration of Purim, and typically it was performed in both the morning and the evening (*b. Meg.* 4a) and with a special cantillation (*see* Megillot and Festivals). By this time, another major feature of Purim, the collecting of funds for the poor (based on Esther 9:22), was also well established.

3.2. The Post-Talmudic and Medieval Periods.
In subsequent centuries the celebration of Purim began to take on an increasingly jubilant character, most likely from the influence of Babylonian Jews (Segal, 116). Already by the fourth century, the sage Raba had famously declared that on Purim people should become so intoxicated that they could not distinguish between cursing Haman and blessing Mordecai (*b. Meg.* 7b). In approaching the medieval period, Purim began to take on several customs that added to the drama and pageantry of the festival. Among the most enduring practices is the custom, dating from the twelfth century in Italy and southern France, of producing parodies of everything from the Talmud to popular Jewish culture. The typical method of these parodies was inversion and satire of religious and social structures. Talmud students were permitted to mock their teachers, and in Eastern Europe the practice began of electing a "Purim Rabbi" who would deride and make fun of those in religious and social authority. This motif of inversion and parody also manifested itself in other aspects of Jewish life. Gambling and intoxication were permitted only on Purim. Furthermore, the tradition of masquerading, dating from sometime in the medieval period, eventually developed to the point of cross-dressing, which, though strictly prohibited by the Torah (Deut 22:5), in the fifteenth century was ruled permissible during Purim by Rabbi Moses Mintz (Bloch 1980, 292). Of course, there were some who objected to these practices as being excessive, but on the whole they became widely accepted throughout Judaism.

3.3. The Modern Period.
Just as Purim was particularly poignant after the fall of the second temple, it has again taken on special significance in post-Holocaust Judaism due to the manifest parallels between Haman and Hitler. Although some Reform congregations have abolished the observance of the festival, it is still widely observed and enjoyed in modern Judaism and is particularly revered among both Hasidic and Kabbalistic groups. The most visible celebration of Purim since the 1920s, especially in Israel, is the yearly *Adloyada* (meaning "until one does not know," from Raba's statement) carnival in Tel Aviv, which involves food and drink, a parade, and even a beauty pageant to select a "Queen Esther."

See also MEGILLOT AND FESTIVALS.

BIBLIOGRAPHY. **A. Bloch,** *The Biblical and Historical Background of the Jewish Holy Days* (New York: KTAV, 1978); idem, *The Biblical and Histori-*

cal Background of Jewish Customs and Ceremonies (New York: KTAV, 1980); **H. Bosman and C. Van Dam,** "פורים," *NIDOTTE* 3.590-91; **P. Goodman,** *The Purim Anthology* (Philadelphia: Jewish Publication Society, 1964); **R. E. Herst,** "The Purim Connection," *USQR* 28 (1973) 139-45; **L. Jacobs,** "Purim," *EncJud* 13.1390-95; **K. Jobes,** *Esther* (NIVAC; Grand Rapids: Zondervan, 1999); **J. D. Levenson,** *Esther* (OTL; Louisville: Westminster John Knox, 1997); **C. A. Moore,** "Esther, Book of," *ABD* 2.633-43; **D. Polish,** "Aspects of Esther: A Phenomenological Exploration of the *Megillah* of Esther and the Origins of Purim," *JSOT* 85 (1999) 85-106; **E. Segal,** *Holidays, History, and Halakhah* (Northvale, NJ: Jason Aronson, 2000).

B. C. Gregory

Q

QINAH METER. *See* METER.

QOHELET

"Qohelet" is the title of the character to whom the words recorded in Ecclesiastes 1:2—12:8 are attributed, the remainder of the book being the work of an anonymous "frame narrator" (*see* Frame Narrative). Although Qohelet's words form the bulk of the book of *Ecclesiastes, it does not necessarily follow that the messages of the book and of Qohelet coincide. Indeed, the fact that the narrator presents what is effectively an extended quotation from Qohelet allows for some distance to be maintained between the two (see Longman 1998; Shields). Consequently, both the book as a whole and the character Qohelet deserve separate examination. This article focuses on the latter.

    1. The Meaning of "Qohelet"
    2. The Identity of Qohelet
    3. The Teaching of Qohelet
    4. Summary

1. The Meaning of "Qohelet."

The designation "Qohelet" is an English transliteration of the Hebrew word *qōhelet*, used to describe the otherwise anonymous speaker of the words recorded in the first-person voice throughout the body of the book of Ecclesiastes. That the word *qōhelet* probably is a title rather than a name is suggested by the fact that the morphologically feminine word *qōhelet* is formally similar to other words describing occupations (e.g., Ezra 2:55, 57; Neh 7:57, 59), that elsewhere substantive participles are used to designate a profession (see Fox, 161), and by the appearance of the definite article on the term in Ecclesiastes 12:8 and probably also in Ecclesiastes 7:27. The translation rather than transliteration of the term in the LXX also suggests that it

was likely understood as a title at the time Ecclesiastes was translated into Greek.

Many modern translations render "Qohelet" with "Preacher," implying a religious context to the activity of Qohelet. This reflects an understanding of the significance of the term *qōhelet* at least partly influenced by the shift in meaning of the Greek *ekklēsia* from secular to religious, so that the Greek *Ekklēsiastēs* came also to be associated with a religious context (Whybray 1989, 18). The fact that Qohelet is said to teach the people (Eccles 12:9) and his activities are compared to a shepherd pastoring a flock (Eccles 12:11) is cited as evidence that the religious overtones of "preacher" are appropriate (Seow 2001, 249).

This, however, is probably not the best understanding of the term *qōhelet*. The epilogue specifies that Qohelet taught knowledge (*daʿat* [Eccles 12:9]), and although the content of that knowledge is not spelled out, within the context of Wisdom literature such knowledge is parallel with wisdom, which, for Qohelet, offers little information about God. The title *qōhelet* is nowhere used with reference to any religious functionary elsewhere in the Bible. The identification of Qohelet as a *sage more likely implies that Qohelet taught wisdom to the people, and the content of the wisdom recorded in Ecclesiastes is marked by the absence of references to the major religious tenets of ancient Israel. These considerations highlight the inappropriateness of a religious interpretation for the title.

The root meaning of the term *qōhelet* lies in "gather," and most commentators agree that Qohelet is so designated for his work in gathering, whether gathering of wealth, of people for instruction in wisdom, or of wisdom sayings in his guise as a sage. Linguistically, it is perhaps the second of these options that is to be pre-

635

ferred, since the verb *qāhal* is elsewhere always used in reference to gathering people, and the nominal forms always elsewhere refer to gatherings of people.

2. The Identity of Qohelet.

2.1. Qohelet as King Solomon. Traditionally, Qohelet has been identified with *Solomon, and there are good grounds for concluding that we are meant to associate the two. Qohelet claims to have been a son of *David (Eccles 1:1), who was king over Israel—not just Judah—in Jerusalem (Eccles 1:1, 12). Both Solomon and Qohelet were wise men par excellence (1 Kings 4:29-34; Eccles 1:13-17; 12:9), extremely rich (1 Kings 4:21-28; Eccles 2:7-10), the owners of cattle and gardens (1 Chron 27:27-31; Eccles 2:4-7), masters of many slaves (1 Kings 10:5; Eccles 2:7) and concubines (1 Kings 11:3; Eccles 2:8, although see Seow 1997, 131; Shields, 131-32), and had many musicians (1 Chron 25; 2 Chron 5:12-13; Eccles 2:8). Attempts to associate Qohelet with other historical figures do not share these numerous parallels.

D. G. Meade (57-58) notes the reason for the identification with Solomon: "The choice of Solomon by Qoheleth is also a deliberate attempt to place his work firmly in the context of the Solomonic wisdom tradition." In addition to this, however, Qohelet's identification with the foremost sage in ancient Israel puts his wisdom beyond dispute, in spite of his many disturbing conclusions.

There are, however, a few difficulties with identifying Qohelet with Solomon, aside from the failure of the text to make the identification explicit. First, it has long been held that Ecclesiastes 1:12 implies that Qohelet had been king but was, at the time of writing, no longer king. This understanding is reflected in the LXX as well as in Jewish tradition but does not correspond to what is recorded about Solomon's reign elsewhere in the Bible. C.-L. Seow (1997, 119), however, argues that the verb form here can be understood to indicate an existing state, not necessarily a past state, although elsewhere in Ecclesiastes the perfect form of the verb *hyh* ("be") frequently refers to the past (e.g., Eccles 1:9; 3:15; 7:10).

Another oft-cited problem is found in Ecclesiastes 1:16, which extols Qohelet's wisdom as greater than that of any of his predecessors in Jerusalem. Such a claim sounds a little hollow

for Solomon, whose only predecessor was David. Against this, however, is the fact that similar language is explicitly used of Solomon in 1 Chronicles 29:25, suggesting that the assertion may be formulaic and should merely be understood as a superlative reference to his wisdom (see Seow 1995, 282).

Finally, most scholars also believe that Qohelet's guise as king is a pretense that is dropped after Ecclesiastes 2, where royal status no longer plays any significant part in the argument. This claim is enhanced by the presence of a number of passages thought not to reflect the perspective of a king because they complain about injustices that the king presumably could have redressed (e.g., Eccles 4:1-3; 5:8-9 [see Meade, 56; Kaiser, 84]). Seow (1997, 48) argues that this pretense is a deliberate adoption by the author of the genre of royal autobiography precisely in order to subvert it and demonstrate that even the greatest and wisest kings share the same senseless fate as the rest of us. However, M. V. Fox (153) notes that although Qohelet's royal status disappears from view after Ecclesiastes 2, it is never "cancelled." Furthermore, the identification by Longman (1991, 120-23) of generic parallels with fictional Akkadian autobiographies with didactic endings suggests that any disjunction between the "royal fiction" of Ecclesiastes 1—2 and the remainder of the work is ill founded (*see* Autobiography).

The failure of the text explicitly to identify Solomon as Qohelet, however, should not be overlooked. No other OT text makes such allusions in ascribing authorship, nor is there any reticence in ascribing Solomon as author of substantial portions of *Proverbs as well as of some nonbiblical texts such as *Psalms of Solomon*. B. K. Waltke (35) notes that the failure of the text to explicitly identify Solomon as the author allows Qohelet to be associated with Solomon while avoiding the "morally questionable practice of pseudonymity." The fact that Qohelet is never explicitly identified with Solomon suggests that the association exists to serve a purpose other than outright identification, and the most widely recognized reason for the association is to establish the authority and integrity of Qohelet's wisdom (see Fox, 159-60).

2.2. Qohelet the Sage. Less controversial is the identification of Qohelet as a wise man, a sage. We are told in the epilogue that Qohelet not only was wise but also taught and even corrected the wisdom of others (Eccles 12:9-10 [see Shields, 62-63]). Qohelet also proclaims his own prowess as a sage (Eccles 1:16). He frequently adopts common wisdom forms in his writing (e.g., Eccles 10:1-15). He claims to use his wisdom in search of answers to the problems of life (e.g., Eccles 1:13), and his primary question, "What gain is there for a person in all his toil at which he toils under the sun?" (Eccles 1:3 [see Ogden, 22-26]) essentially underpins the entire wisdom enterprise (see Crenshaw, 10; Shields, 125).

Furthermore, Qohelet is not merely identified as a sage; he is identified as the preeminent sage. This is apparent from his implied identification with Solomon (see 2.1 above), his own testimony (Eccles 1:16), as well as the description in the epilogue (Eccles 12:9-10). He corrected wisdom and taught the people, suggesting that wisdom was more than a hobby—it was his profession. The effect of all this is to assure the reader that Qohelet's qualifications as a sage were beyond reproach.

2.3. Qohelet the Old Man. Few other things can be said about Qohelet's identity. Most conclude that he was an older man—an impression built upon the retrospectivity of his autobiographical reflections in Ecclesiastes 1—2 (as well as the time it would have taken to accomplish all that is recorded in those chapters), on his concern over the status of his legacy, on his preoccupation with death, and on the inference that his advice to the young must be made from the perspective of one who can look back on his own youth (Eccles 11:9; 12:1). Although R. N. Whybray (1989, 21-22) notes that these arguments cannot conclusively prove Qohelet's advanced age, he agrees that he is at least "mature."

2.4. Was Qohelet a Real Person? The difficulty in identifying Qohelet with any known historical figure, together with the text's failure to explicitly identify him, do lend some credence to the notion that Qohelet may have been a construct of the frame narrator, a foil through whom the narrator makes plain his meaning (see Fox, 159-60). Furthermore, the fact that most scholars do identify Qohelet as a real person may in part be attributable to the influence of *historical criticism that relegated the frame narrator's words to a later editor and thus afforded them little significance in understanding

the words of Qohelet that they enclose. If the frame is treated as original—and there is no evidence that it is not—then the frame narrator is responsible for the final form of the work and the shape and form of Qohelet's words.

Ultimately, there is insufficient data to decide whether Qohelet existed or was merely a creation of the frame narrator. Furthermore, the "reality" of Qohelet has little bearing on the ultimate interpretation of Ecclesiastes, for even if he did exist, the material attributed to him in the book of Ecclesiastes has been selected and arranged by the frame narrator for his own ends.

3. The Teaching of Qohelet.
The teaching of Qohelet recorded in Ecclesiastes provides us with insight into Qohelet's beliefs. The diversity of interpretations of Qohelet's words indicates that there is consensus neither on their meaning nor on the aim of Qohelet's teaching or even on much of its substance.

3.1. Qohelet's Contradictions. One prominent feature of Qohelet's words that complicates any systematic attempt to understand his thinking on many topics is the apparent contradictions with both the remainder of the OT (such as the advice of Eccles 7:16; 9:2-3; 11:9 [cf. Num 15:39]) and among his own sayings (e.g., on life and death [Eccles 9:4-6 versus Eccles 2:17; 4:2]; regarding wisdom [Eccles 1:17-18; 2:13-16 versus Eccles 7:11, 19; 9:16-18]).

A number of schemes have been devised for handling these inconsistencies. It is widely acknowledged that Qohelet occasionally quotes from another source in order to respond to it, and this understanding has been employed most extensively by T. A. Perry. This allows contradictory passages to be assigned to different voices, not to Qohelet's one voice. Perry's approach offers a neat solution to the problem, but is itself improbable because in the vast majority of instances that Perry identifies, the text lacks sufficiently clear indicators that the speaker is changing (Shields, 3-4), and the introductory description of the work as the "words of Qohelet" (Eccles 1:1) conditions the reader to treat the subsequent material as being from Qohelet alone unless there are unambiguous signs to the contrary.

Another solution is the idea that Qohelet's contradictions reflect the reality of life: not everything can be reconciled, and there are inevitable paradoxes—a notion reflected also in Proverbs 26:4-5 (Fox, 3). Similar is the suggestion that Qohelet's words were designed to present not a unified perspective but rather Qohelet's own developing understanding of the world in which he lived, although the idea of progress in Qohelet's thought is undermined by the narrator's failure to acknowledge it by closing Qohelet's words with the same summary with which they were opened.

In the end, the contradictions may reflect a number of these factors. Within the context of the work as a whole they can be seen as just one expression of the failure of Qohelet to make sense of the world in which he lived, a failure ultimately expressed by the narrator in the summary statement found at the beginning and end of Qohelet's words: "Everything is senseless."

3.2. Everything Is Senseless. There has been some debate about what, if anything, constitutes Qohelet's main thesis. G. S. Ogden (14-15), for example, sees the question of advantage (Eccles 1:3; 2:22; 3:9; 5:16; 6:11) as fundamental to Qohelet's point. Others suggest that Qohelet's main point is to commend joy in life (see 3.6 below). These approaches, however, overlook the fact that the frame narrator has explicitly identified the point he most wants to highlight from Qohelet's teaching: "Everything is senseless [hebel])" (Eccles 1:2; 12:8).

The Hebrew term *hebel* has been interpreted in a number of different ways, although almost everyone agrees that it is negative. The term has traditionally been rendered in English with the word "vanity," although this word is no longer in favor because it has undergone a decisive semantic shift away from meaning "empty" to meaning "self-pride." Other suggestions include "fleeting" or "transitory," "futile," "senseless," "incomprehensible," "mystery" or "enigma," "meaningless" and "absurd." Although it is both difficult and inappropriate to attempt to equate the Hebrew term with any single English gloss, it is perhaps the idea that everything is senseless that most closely corresponds with Qohelet's awareness that the sage cannot comprehend the world—it makes no sense, and so wisdom's worth is severely constrained (e.g., Eccles 8:17 [see Shields, 112-21; Fox, 31 n. 5]).

3.3. God. There are a number of aspects to Qohelet's theology that are difficult to reconcile with the remainder of the OT. Qohelet gives no indication that he is aware of any form of divine

revelation. *God is distant, mysterious and inaccessible (see Dumbrell, 242-43). Qohelet's words, quite unlike those of the psalmists, reflect no personal relationship with God, but only a reluctant admission that life is subject to his unpredictable whims. Knowledge of God, for Qohelet, is based not on revelation but rather on observation and analysis.

Yet in spite of this, for Qohelet, God is absolutely sovereign. In accord with the fundamental presuppositions of wisdom in ancient Israel, he acknowledges that God is in control of all that takes place, and that he appropriately orders all events (Eccles 3:1-8, 11). However, whereas the task of the sage was to learn to benefit from an awareness of the inner workings of God's world, Qohelet discovered that God had not revealed this information, and thus the sages were incapable of fulfilling this task (Eccles 3:11; 8:17). Any chance to enjoy one's toil, according to Qohelet, is entirely contingent upon God (Eccles 2:24-26). J. L. Crenshaw (124) notes that Qohelet "speaks as if God were indifferent power before which we must cower in fear," and "in Qoheleth's mind it was impossible to tell whether God looked on humans with interest or with disdain."

Qohelet's doubts about God's goodness thus are clear: he believes that God is in control and that there are appropriate times for all things, yet the world does not operate according to any discernible principle of justice that was essentially foundational to the thinking of the sages. The logic of the sages and the logic of God are irreconcilable, and so the world makes no sense—all is *hebel*.

3.4. Wisdom. Qohelet's attitude toward wisdom is not clear-cut. In a number of places he appears to extol wisdom's virtues (Eccles 2:13-14; 4:13; 7:5, 11-12, 19; 8:1, 5; 9:15; 10:10), but elsewhere he urges caution in embracing wisdom (Eccles 7:16), affirms its frailty and its unattainability (Eccles 7:23; 8:16-17; 9:11, 18; 10:1), and warns that it brings only trouble (Eccles 1:18). Although some attribute this apparent ambivalence toward wisdom to Qohelet's quotation of traditional wisdom in order to refute it (see George, 284), it is not clear that *all* these passages can simply be written off as quotations. Whatever merits wisdom may have, however, are only relative, since both fool and sage share the same fate—death—and so wisdom clearly offers no solution to the ultimate problem facing everyone (Eccles 2:15-16; 9:3). The sage, according to Qohelet, cannot understand the workings of God's world and so is unable to use wisdom to secure good outcomes in life. As such, wisdom is of only relative merit and is sometimes more trouble than it is worth (Eccles 1:18; 7:16). In reaching this conclusion, Qohelet is in agreement with the negative attitude toward human wisdom presented in the bulk of the remainder of the OT (Shields, 7-20; Spina, 271). On the other hand, Qohelet's assessment of wisdom seems at odds with any reading of Proverbs that understands that book as teaching that the attaining of wisdom affords the wise the ability to steer their way through life avoiding strife and gaining wealth and long life, or as teaching that God predictably operates in this world according to principles of retributive justice wherein the good are rewarded and the bad punished (see Sneed, 48-49; Dumbrell, 246).

3.5. Death. A number of scholars have highlighted the centrality and severity of death in Qohelet's thought (see, e.g., Burkes, 35-80). Death is fundamental to all of Qohelet's thought, for it is the inevitability of death that undermines every attempt to make sense of life and so forces him to conclude that everything is senseless *(hebel)*. For Qohelet, wisdom's benefit over *folly is only relative because death comes to both sage and fool (Eccles 2:12-17). Likewise, any benefit gained from hard work is lost because of death (Eccles 2:18-23). W. P. Brown (139-40) summarizes Qohelet's thoughts on death: "Death ultimately undermines all distinctions between the righteous and the wicked, even between humans and animals. It topples all lofty aspirations and thus inspires a profound acceptance of life on its own terms. Instead of espousing suicide as the final solution, Qoheleth commends the fleeting, yet redemptive, nature of enjoyment (9:7-10)" (cf. Burkes, 74).

3.6. Joy. Another repeated theme of Qohelet's is the exhortation to enjoy life (e.g., Eccles 2:10, 24; 3:12, 22; 5:17-18). A few scholars have picked up on this and suggested that it ought to be considered the final message that Qohelet wishes to convey to his readers (see Whybray 1982; Kaiser, 93; Kline, 32-36). Ogden (48) also finds Qohelet's exhortations to enjoy life supersede his despair: "Qoheleth is life-affirming because he envisages human life in all its mystery as a gift of God. He may at times feel despair,

and on occasion 'hate' life both for what he sees and experiences in it, but these are only passing responses. His final and decisive response, and thus his advice to all, is 'take and eat,' for God has given you life."

Although it cannot be denied that Qohelet affirms the enjoyment of life, the significance of his affirmation can be (and frequently has been) overstated. Qohelet affirms joy not because it is the goal of life but rather because life itself is empty and senseless—he does not say that joy is good, but only that there's nothing better (see Eccles 2:24). If there is no ultimate purpose, then the best that Qohelet can suggest in his wisdom is that his students enjoy what they can when they can. Yet even this is not the whole story for Qohelet, who also recognizes that enjoyment is contingent upon God's will (Eccles 2:24-25; 6:2 [see Seow 1997, 48]), and since God's ways are inscrutable, joy is sporadic and unpredictable and should be seized when it presents itself. However, it cannot reliably be secured by the sage, because the world makes no sense (see Sneed, 49-50).

4. Summary.

Qohelet is a complex character whose depiction in the text is sometimes difficult to assemble into a consistent figure. Two points stand out. First, the narrator of Ecclesiastes presents Qohelet as a real person with the highest credentials as sage and king and expects us as readers to take his words and his experiences seriously so that we may learn from him as well as from the few words that the narrator appends to Qohelet's teachings. Qohelet's autobiographical speech and first-person reflections, his appeals to his status and experience, and the affirmations of the epilogue all serve to present Qohelet as the ultimate sage, whose reflections on wisdom are both accurate and trustworthy. Qohelet's message was that although wisdom could provide some benefits, in the end it could not solve the great problems of life and death.

Second, much of what Qohelet says is disturbing and difficult to reconcile with the remainder of the OT. Scholars have made numerous attempts to address this problem, and the diversity in approaches highlights the depth of the problem. In the end, however, the frame narrator calls us to recognize that Qohelet is right: the speculative wisdom of Qohelet cannot make sense of the world. The narrator points to another answer: obedience to God (Eccles 12:13).

See also AUTOBIOGRAPHY; ECCLESIASTES 1: BOOK OF; SOLOMON.

BIBLIOGRAPHY. **W. P. Brown,** *Character in Crisis: A Fresh Approach to the Wisdom Literature of the Old Testament* (Grand Rapids: Eerdmans, 1996); **S. Burkes,** *Death in Qoheleth and Egyptian Biographies of the Late Period* (SBLDS 170; Atlanta: Society of Biblical Literature, 1999); **J. L. Crenshaw,** *Old Testament Wisdom: An Introduction* (rev. ed.; Louisville: Westminster John Knox, 1998); **W. J. Dumbrell,** *The Faith of Israel* (Leicester: Apollos, 1988); **M. V. Fox,** *A Time to Tear Down and a Time to Build Up: A Rereading of Ecclesiastes* (Grand Rapids: Eerdmans, 1999); **M. K. George,** "Death as the Beginning of Life in the Book of Ecclesiastes," in *Strange Fire: Reading the Bible after the Holocaust,* ed. T. Linafelt (New York: New York University Press, 2000) 280-93; **O. Kaiser,** "Qoheleth," in *Wisdom in Ancient Israel: Essays in Honour of J. A. Emerton,* ed. J. Day, R. P. Gordon and H. G. M. Williamson (Cambridge: Cambridge University Press, 1995) 83-93; **M. M. Kline,** "Is Qoheleth Unorthodox? A Review Article," *Kerux* 13 (1998) 16-39; **T. Longman III,** *Fictional Akkadian Autobiography: A Generic and Comparative Study* (Winona Lake, IN: Eisenbrauns, 1991); idem, *The Book of Ecclesiastes* (NICOT; Grand Rapids: Eerdmans, 1998); **D. G. Meade,** *Pseudonymity and Canon: An Investigation into the Relationship of Authorship and Authority in Jewish and Earliest Christian Tradition* (WUNT 39; Tübingen: Mohr Siebeck, 1986); **G. S. Ogden,** *Qoheleth* (Readings; Sheffield: JSOT Press, 1987); **T. A. Perry,** *Dialogues with Kohelet: The Book of Ecclesiastes* (University Park: Pennsylvania State University Press, 1993); **C.-L. Seow,** "Qohelet's Autobiography" in *Fortunate the Eyes That See: Essays in Honor of David Noel Freedman in Celebration of His Seventieth Birthday,* ed. A. B. Beck et al. (Grand Rapids: Eerdmans, 1995) 275-87; idem, *Ecclesiastes* (AB 18C; New York: Doubleday, 1997). idem, "Theology When Everything Is Out of Control," *Interpretation* 55 (2001) 237-49. **M. A. Shields,** *The End of Wisdom: A Reappraisal of the Historical and Canonical Function of Ecclesiastes* (Winona Lake, IN: Eisenbrauns, 2006); **M. Sneed,** "The Social Location of the Book of Qoheleth," *HS* 39 (1998) 41-51; **F. A. Spina,** "Qoheleth and the Reformation of Wisdom," in *The Quest for the Kingdom of God: Studies in Honor of George E. Mendenhall,* ed. H. B. Huffman, F. A. Spina and A. R. W. Green (Winona Lake, IN: Eisenbrauns, 1983) 267-79; **B. K. Waltke,** *The Book of Proverbs: Chapters 1-15* (NICOT; Grand Rapids: Eerdmans, 2004); **R. N. Whybray,** "Qoheleth, Preacher of Joy," *JSOT* 23 (1982) 87-98; idem, *Ecclesiastes* (OTG; Sheffield: Sheffield Academic Press, 1989). M. A. Shields

QUMRAN. *See* DEAD SEA SCROLLS.

R

REFRAIN

Hebrew poetry features repetitions on many levels, from the phoneme to whole verses. A refrain is a repetition on the macrolevel (i.e., the verse) and is easily observed even in translation. The English word *refrain* (there is no known ancient Hebrew equivalent) derives from an Old French verb, *refraindre* ("repeat"), which itself may come from Vulgar Latin *refringere*. What distinguishes the refrain from other forms of repetition is that it occurs on the verse level and serves to end a section. Refrains occur in songs and poems (and *Psalms and *Song of Songs are both). Refrains may be distinguished from an envelope structure (i.e., *inclusio), which refers to a poetic unit (sometimes the whole poem [see Ps 8]), which begins and ends with the same verse, the repetition occurring only in these two places.

W. Watson (295-99) helpfully distinguishes three types of refrain: strict refrain, variant refrain and chorus. The first type is verbatim, and the second reveal variations, but only enough that they are still recognizable as related. The chorus is differentiated from the other two by frequency of occurrence in the poem (see on Ps 136 below).

1. The Function of the Refrain
2. Refrain in Psalms
3. Refrain in Song of Songs
4. Refrain in Ecclesiastes
5. Refrain in Job 28

1. The Function of the Refrain.

Refrains serve a variety of functions in songs and poems (or even narrative). First, it is a structural device segmenting a composition into different sections, often referred to as a strophe or stanza (Watson, 32, 34; van der Lugt). In this regard, if the refrain ends the poem, it can also give the poem a sense of closure (Pss 42—43). Second, since a refrain is repeated at least twice in a poem, it gives the thought expressed in the refrain a certain importance by means of emphasis. One comes away from a song or a poem with the thought or idea expressed by the refrain reverberating in one's mind. Third, the refrain, at times at least, invites the participation of the audience. Indications are (see on Pss 24; 136 below) that the performance of some poems involved the leader (a priest?) who would recite or sing parts of the psalm while the audience (congregation?) would respond with the words of the refrain.

2. Refrain in Psalms.

Since the psalms are poems as well as songs, one might expect to find the use of refrains. This is indeed the case, although one might be surprised at their infrequency. The following psalms contain repetitions that seem to be some form of refrain.

2.1. Psalms 24; 46. Psalm 24 has a liturgical feel to its use of the refrain. After a kind of entrance liturgy asking and answering the question of who can enter the holy place, the final verses are an interchange between two parties that are best understood as the priest or priests who are serving as gatekeepers to the city or temple and the priests who are accompanying the ark of the covenant back after successful holy war. The latter call on the former to open the gates to allow entry (Ps 24:7, 9). The gatekeepers then ask, "Who is the king of glory?" (Ps 24:8, 10), followed by the response from the first group that it is the Lord in his appearance as warrior (there is some variety in this refrain).

Psalm 46 is another psalm that celebrates God's power to protect his people as their warrior in the context of holy war. The psalm's twice-repeated refrain, "The LORD of heaven's armies is here among us; the God of Jacob is our fortress" (Ps 46:7, 11), emphasizes this theme and brings both the poem's first part and the poem as a whole to a close. Some commentators suggest or at least wonder whether there might have been originally a refrain between v. 3 and v. 4, since that would lead to the formation of three equal length stanzas. There is, however, no textual evidence for this (Terrien, 370-71).

2.2. Psalms 42—43. These psalms are united by a common refrain (Ps 42:5, 11; 43:5) and thus are often considered an original unity, though no convincing reason has been suggested for why they were eventually divided. Treating the two psalms as one, we can recognize the composition as a lament bemoaning the psalmist's separation from the presence of God and the mocking that he receives from other people (*see* Lament, Psalms of). The psalmist's grief is intensified by memory of intimate fellowship with God (Ps 42:4). The thrice-repeated refrain then expresses the psalmist's grief, but it also includes an attempt to transform grief into hope: "Why are you downcast, O my soul? Why so disturbed within me? Put your hope in God, for I will yet praise him, my help and my God."

The emphasis in the psalm, then, is the psalmist's present state of mind as well as his hope for transformation from sadness to hope. Besides adding emphasis, the refrain structures the poem into three stanzas (Ps 42:1-5, 6-11; 43:1-5) and provides a sense of closure, since the third repetition ends the poem.

2.3. Psalm 49. This psalm is well known for sharing similar theological and ethical concerns as the book of *Ecclesiastes. The psalmist, however, has a sense, not shared by *Qohelet, that there is a difference between the death of the godly and that of the foolish (Eccles 3:16-22; 9:1-12; 12:1-7). A twice-recurring refrain emphasizes the negative end of the latter: "A man who has riches without understanding is like the beasts that perish" (Ps 49:12, 20).

2.4. Psalm 56. According to the strophic analysis by S. Terrien, the refrain of this psalm, professing trust in God, occurs in the middle of the strophe. The second occurrence (Ps 56:10-11) is longer than the first (Ps 56:4), and both express the kind of confidence that the godly person has even in the presence of dangerous enemies.

2.5. Psalm 57. This psalm begins like a lament, asking God to protect the psalmist from dangerous enemies, and concludes, not atypically for a lament, with a statement of confidence. The twice-repeated refrain, "Be exalted, O God, above the heavens. Let your glory be over all the earth" (Ps 57:5, 11), seeks the exaltation of God.

2.6. Psalm 67. This short psalm has a twice-repeated refrain (Ps 67:3, 5 [in this case, not ending the poem]). The poem expresses the desire that God be praised throughout the world, and that is the hope expressed in the refrain: "May the nations praise you, O God. Yes, may all the nations praise you."

2.7. Psalm 80. This psalm is meant for a time when God seems absent from his people and they feel pressed by their enemies. The refrain captures the intention of the psalm, which is to persuade God to return his protective presence to them: "Restore us . . . and let your face shine upon us, that we may be saved." It is repeated three times (Ps 80:3, 7, 19), the second and third occurrences varying from the first in that rather than simply referring to God as "God" (*'ĕlōhîm*), they use God's battle name, "God of heaven's armies" (*'ĕlōhîm ṣĕbā'ôt*).

2.8. Psalm 99. This psalm is a kingship *hymn that praises God as king (*see* Kingship Psalms). The refrain, which varies in its three occurrences, calls on Israel to praise God because of his holy nature (Ps 99:3, 5, 9).

2.9. Psalm 107. This psalm demonstrates an unusual use of two refrains: the one seems to answer the other. Four times the psalmist talks about a specific problem and uses the refrain "Then they cried out to the LORD in their trouble, and he delivered them from their distress" (Ps 107:6, 13, 19, 28), and four times, after describing God's response to their cry for help, the psalmist says, "Let them give thanks to the LORD for his unfailing love and his wonderful deeds for men" (Ps 107:8, 15, 21, 31).

2.10. Psalm 136. This psalm contains a stellar example of what Watson calls a chorus, which is a refrain that permeates a passage. In this case, all twenty-six verses conclude with the statement "for his covenant love is forever" (*kî lĕ'ôlām ḥasdô*). The first part of the verses typically recounts some great act of Yahweh. The psalm is a remembrance psalm that, after thanking God for who he is (Ps 136:1-3), continues by praising God for what he has done, beginning with the creation and then continuing with the exodus from Egypt and settling his people in the Promised Land. The psalm is traditionally understood to have a liturgical setting, with the priest speaking the first colon of the verses and the congregation responding with the refrain.

3. Refrain in Song of Songs.

Most modern interpreters agree that Song of Songs is love poetry, but differences still exist between those who see it is a drama and those who see it is an anthology, a collection of love poems. Among those who adopt the anthological view of the book, the next question concerns how to divide the poems and whether there is any cohesiveness to the collection as a whole (Longman 2001, 54-56). The appearance of two refrains throughout the book provides strong evidence, along with other verbal echoes, consistency of characters and repetition of scenes, in favor of affirming some level of cohesiveness to the question, though attempts to work out a tight and definite overall structure of the book may be overreaching (Dorsey, 199-213).

The refrains also serve to emphasize certain major ideas in Song of Songs. The first refrain, "His left hand is under my head, and his right hand embraces me" (Song 2:6; 8:3), binds the beginning and end of Songs of Songs and highlights the intimacy of the relationship between the man and the woman in this book, which celebrates human love. The second refrain, "I adjure you, daughters of Jerusalem, by the gazelles or the deer of the field, not to awaken or arouse love until it desires" (Song 1:7; and, with some variation, Song 3:5; 8:4), warns against stepping too quickly into such an intimate relationship (see Schwab)

4. Refrain in Ecclesiastes.

Scholars and translations differ over whether Ecclesiastes is predominantly prose or poetry. No doubt exists, however, about the recurrence of various refrains throughout the book. These refrains include a rhetorical question, "What profit is there . . . ? (Eccles 1:3; 3:9; 5:16), as well as the statement that pursuing purpose in life is "like chasing the wind" (Eccles 1:14; 2:11, 17, 26; 4:4, 6; 6:9). These and other refrains occur often, but nowhere near as frequently as does "Meaningless, meaningless, everything is meaningless" (Eccles 1:2; 2:1, 15, 19; 3:19; 5:10; 6:11; 7:6; 8:10, 14; 9:9; 11:8; 12:8). The pervasiveness of its use, and the occurrence at the beginning and end of Qohelet's speech, give the reader the impression that this is the teacher's bottom line.

A second refrain (with variation occurring at Eccles 2:24-26; 3:12-14, 22; 5:18-20; 8:15; 9:7-10), however, speaks of finding joy in life. Whether this is spoken with a note of resignation (Longman 1998) or more confidently (Bartholomew) is a matter of debate.

5. Refrain in Job 28.

Job 28 has been a point of intense debate in research on *Job in terms of how it fits with the plot of the book. No question, however, attends the theme of the chapter: it powerfully affirms God's exclusive claim as the source of all wisdom. Twice Job asks expecting a negative answer: "But do people know where to find wisdom? Where can they find understanding?" (Job 28:12, 20). This refrain then points to this assertion: "God alone understands the way to wisdom; he knows where it can be found" (Job 28:23).

See also FORM CRITICISM; LYRIC POETRY; PARALLELISM; POETICS, TERMINOLOGY OF; STANZA, STROPHE.

BIBLIOGRAPHY. **C. G. Bartholomew**, *Ecclesiastes* (BCOTWP; Grand Rapids: Baker, 2008); **D. A. Dorsey**, *The Literary Structure of the Old Testament* (Grand Rapids: Baker, 1999); **T. Longman III**, *Ecclesiastes* (NICOT; Grand Rapids: Eerdmans, 1998); idem, *Song of Songs* (NICOT; Grand Rapids: Eerdmans, 2001); **T. Muraoka**, *Emphatic Words and Structures: A Study of Psalms with Refrains (Psalms 42-59)* (JSOTSup 104; Sheffield: JSOT Press, 1990); **G. Schwab**, *The Song of Songs' Cautionary Message Concerning Human Love* (SBL 41; New York: Peter Lang, 2002); **S. Terrien**, *The Psalms: Strophic Structure and Theological Commentary* (Grand Rapids: Eerdmans, 2003); **P. van der Lugt**, *Cantos and Strophes in Biblical Hebrew Poetry: With Special Reference to the First Book of the Psalter* (OtSt 53; Leiden: E. J. Brill, 2006); **W. G. E. Watson**, *Classical Hebrew Poetry: A Guide to Its Techniques* (2d ed.; T & T Clark, 2005).

T. Longman III

RELIGION. *See* CULT, WORSHIP: WISDOM

REMEMBRANCE

In the OT books of wisdom and poetry the concept of remembrance typically means more than simply recalling some thought; it also includes acting in accordance with that thought. This is true regardless of whether a person or God does the remembering. The present article explores this concept of remembrance by first defining the basic Hebrew words used to describe remembering and surveying their occurrence in the books of poetry and wisdom as well as the rest of the OT. It then discusses the basic meanings covered by the verb "remember" and its synonyms and describes how the concept varies when used of human or divine subjects. Finally, it treats the less common nouns used for "remembrance" to see if their meanings vary from that of the verbs and thus add to the general field of meaning.

1. Attestation
2. Basic Meanings
3. Humans Remembering
4. God Remembering
5. Remembrance as a Noun
6. Conclusion

1. Attestation.

Hebrew has a basic root *zkr*, which appears in various forms, used with a range of meanings centered on remembering. The root *zkr* appears in the wisdom and poetic books most often as a verb (79x) but also as a noun (20x). When used as a verb, *zkr* appears in three common Hebrew verbal stems, usually with the basic meanings associated with those stems: Qal (simple active, "remember" [66x]), Niphal (passive, "be remembered" [5x]) and Hiphil (causative, "bring to remembrance" [8x]). The nouns *zēker* ("remembrance, memory" [15x]) and *zikkārôn* ("memorial, reminder" [5x]) also include the same basic idea of something remembered.

The various Hebrew words derived from *zkr* appear frequently throughout the OT but are found most often in *Psalms and the other books of wisdom and poetry (99 of 344 total occurrences). This coincides with the occurrences of the word *lēb* ("heart"), also found most often in Wisdom literature. In Hebrew, the heart is the organ of perceiving and storing knowledge, as the mind is in English. Having something in one's heart means to be conscious of it or to remember (Wolff, 46-47). Because of this connection in Hebrew thought and language, both "heart" and "remember" occur frequently in the books of wisdom and poetry.

Nearly all of the forms of *zkr* mentioned above can also be found in the Pentateuch (68x), as well as in the historical (92x) and prophetic (90x) sections of the OT, but typically less often than in the books of poetry and wisdom. By contrast, four nominal forms from the root

zkr—*ʾazkārâ* ("memorial offering"), *mazkîr* ("recorder") and the proper names *zĕkaryâ* and its variant *zĕkaryāhû* ("Zechariah, Zecharyahu") as well as *zikrî* ("Zicri" or "Zichri")—occur in the other sections of the OT but do not appear in the books of wisdom and poetry. Most of these occurrences of *zkr* and its related forms relate to the general idea that the Israelites' God had acted on their behalf as recorded in their historical books, and thus they should remember his deeds and act faithfully toward him. The poetic books describe how the Israelites often celebrated and drew on this historic, vital relationship with their God. When they did not, the prophets called them to account.

2. Basic Meanings.

2.1. "Recall Some Fact." The Hebrew verb *zkr* may simply refer to recalling some fact that someone was not currently bearing in mind. For example, one of the accusers of *Job challenges him to act righteously and escape his current troubles, at which time he would remember his former troubles as merely fleeting (Job 11:16). The Judean exiles taken to Babylon recall with fondness their homeland and capital, Jerusalem (Ps 137:1, 6). Similarly, a destroyed Jerusalem (a figure for the city's inhabitants) recalls the good times before its destruction, in contrast to its current misery (Lam 1:7). These occurrences include the idea most closely associated with the common English idea of remembering: simply thinking again about something that the person had been aware of in the past.

2.2. "Consider, Keep in Mind." A stronger use of *zkr* goes beyond just recalling something to considering or keeping something in mind. For this idea, the biblical authors also sometimes used the synonymous roots *hgh* or *śyh* ("meditate, consider") or the negative *lōʾ škḥ* ("not forget"). The matter being considered could be positive or negative. Job's accusers challenge him to consider the positive truth that God protects the innocent (Job 4:7); Job, likewise, also keeps in mind the unpleasant truth that the wicked sometimes prosper (Job 21:6). The matter being considered can also be something physical or nonphysical. The Persian king *Ahasuerus considers his former queen, *Vashti, after he had deposed her (Esther 2:1). Later *Mordecai, the cousin of the new queen, *Esther, commanded his fellow Jews to keep their recent deliverance in mind by making it a perpetual holiday (Esther 9:28). Whatever the item, the person doing the remembering was supposed to bring it to mind and keep it there.

Occasionally, a negated idea of considering had a very different meaning. Not to remember or consider a deceased person meant the end of that person's existence entirely. In common OT thought life ended at the grave. Thus, if one's name or reputation did not live beyond the grave in someone's memory, that person's existence had ceased entirely. Such a fate might happen as a natural part of history (Eccles 1:11), but it might also have moral overtones. The enemies of Israel (and Israel's God) set out to "destroy [Israel] as a nation, so that their name will no longer be remembered" (Ps 83:4). More often, Israel's God brought about this fate on Israel's enemies or on evil people as punishment for their sins (Job 24:20; Ps 109:14-15). With this concept, not being remembered after death was usually a terrible fate that God imposed on those who deserved it.

2.3. "Think About and Act Accordingly." Probably the most common aspect of remembering goes beyond simply considering some truth to thinking about and acting in accordance with that truth. "Recollection concerns not only past events, but also the consequences their memory entails" (Eising, 67). For example, when the author of *Ecclesiastes says to his learner, "Remember your Creator in the days of your youth" (Eccles 12:1), he is urging him to bear in mind that he lives before the one who created (and will ultimately judge) him, and thus he should act as one who will some day face that creator and judge. Sinners do not remember God; rather, they forget God and betray the covenant that they have made with him or perhaps even pursue other Gods (Ps 44:17, 20). Such evil people even think that God has forgotten their actions and will not hold them accountable (Ps 10:11). These illustrations help show that both humans and God remember and forget, as the following discussion will explain more fully

3. Humans Remembering.

When the authors of poetry and wisdom refer to humans "remembering," they might use any of three shades of meaning already discussed. Humans may recall, consider, or think about and act accordingly in regard to places, events or other people, but the passages usually refer to people remembering God. In addition, human remembrance most often includes the idea of appropriate behavior toward God. Even when humans simply recall some matter, they often recall something connected to God—perhaps their past relationship with God, God's sovereignty, or his miracles on behalf of his people (Ps 22:27; 42:4; 77:11).

Remembering God and his deeds often leads to positive action. "So closely is remembering associated with action that at times it functions as a synonym for action of various kinds" (Allen, 1103). This response might be *worship (Ps 103:18; 105:5) or obedience (Ps 103:18). In addition, despondent psalmists often draw courage and hope from considering God's past works and gain strength to persevere during times when danger lurks but God seems distant and silent (Ps 63:6; 77:3; 143:5).

On the other hand, not thinking about God's gracious character and deeds may lead his people to acts of unfaithfulness or rebellion against him (Ps 78:42; 106:7). "The failure to remember was not mere absentmindness; it was covenant(al) unfaithfulness" (Verhey, 668). This usage provides another example of how God's people need to think often about their God and what he has done for them in order to maintain a proper relationship with him.

A somewhat different nuance of remembering is found in the use of the Hebrew root *zkr* in the causative Hiphil stem, meaning "cause to remember" or "proclaim." In these relatively rare occurrences a person draws something praiseworthy to the attention of others that they may consider and appreciate it. The praiseworthy item might be something as simple as a laudable relationship between two lovers (Song 1:4), but again, it usually refers to something connected to God. The psalmists praise God by proclaiming how he has helped his people with his mighty deeds. With this proclamation the psalmist expects that his audience will respond with celebration and trust in their God (Ps 20:7 [see Driver]; 45:17; 71:16). Proclaiming, like the other nuances of recalling, considering and thinking about to act accordingly, typically tries to keep the people of God connected to him, the one who helps them. If they do, they can better respond to him as they should.

4. God Remembering.

As described above, humans can remember or

proclaim various things. Likewise, God remembers, but the categories of meaning for God's remembering differ somewhat from those used with humans. The texts do not speak of God recalling anything, but they do say that he considers things. Frequently, God acts on what he considers, and this action often is based on his own character or on earlier promises made to his people.

Like humans, God considers or takes notice of things. His consideration often involves his care for or sustenance of the person or thing. To communicate this idea, the Hebrew authors also use the synonym *pqd* ("care for, come to aid"). God considers or cares for humanity in general and endows us with great significance (Ps 8:4). In a different sense, the psalmist needs God's care to sustain his life lest he perish (Ps 88:5). God's understanding and help are particularly important in light of human nature with its physical weakness and inclination to sin. God indeed does understand and remember these human tendencies, and this leads him to forget or forgive even repeated sin (Job 7:7; 10:9; Ps 78:39; 89:47).

God's sustenance and forgiveness are two examples of how God's consideration or remembrance leads him to act for the benefit of his people, to whom he is committed. "The essence of God's remembering lies in his acting toward someone because of a previous commitment" (Childs, 34). He acts on behalf of his people when he delivers or restores them after judgment (Ps 74:2; 79:8; 106:4). Such restoration can happen only because God also considers aspects of his own character—his mercy and faithfulness (Ps 25:6) and his fidelity in keeping his promises and his covenant with his people (Ps 106:45; 111:5). "The covenant is not just something from the past, and [God] remembering it is not merely the neutral apprehension of an image from the past.... God ... is faithful to it ... and acts in accordance with it" (Verhey, 667). The greatest example of God keeping his covenant and fulfilling his promises is his deliverance of Israel from Egypt, as he had promised to Abraham long before (Ps 105:8, 42-43; cf. Ex 2:24-25). God's faithful acts of deliverance and aid should produce joy and praise in his people, and they should bear witness to others about his marvelous character (Ps 98:3; 106:4-5). A corollary of God acting for his people is that he also acts against their enemies. He protects the af-

flicted from their oppressors and takes vengeance when necessary (Ps 9:12; 89:50; 137:7).

Thus, the ways that God remembers coincide with the ways that humans remember except that God need not recall anything. Usually, one finds God remembering by acting appropriately for his people based on his gracious character and his faithfulness to his commitments.

5. Remembrance as a Noun.
The preceding discussion of the verbal uses of *zkr* ("remember") show the major nuances of meaning implied in the verb and how those fit when used of humans and of God. The discussion now turns to the less frequent nominal forms that appear in the poetic and wisdom literature: *zēker* ("remembrance, memory") and *zikkārôn* ("memorial, reminder"). The more limited range of meanings found with the nouns overlaps with some of the ideas found with the verbs.

The noun *zēker* is used largely of some remembrance carried out by humans, in which they may or may not remember other humans or God. If humans maintain a remembrance of other humans after death, it is because the dead were righteous, and their memory is a blessing that continues perpetually (Ps 112:6; Prov 10:7). By contrast, the memory of those who are wicked or oppose Israel does not continue; it "rots" and ends with them (Job 18:17; Ps 9:6; 34:16), sometimes because of God's judgment (Ps 109:15). For the author of Ecclesiastes, such an end of memory will be the fate of all regardless of their character (Eccles 9:5). When *zēker* describes human remembrance of God, it usually refers to humans considering God's deeds or character—his holiness, goodness or righteousness (Ps 97:12; 111:4; 145:7). Such consideration leads to praise and thanksgiving in each generation (Ps 6:5; 30:4; 102:12), much like with the verbal ideas already discussed.

The noun *zikkārôn* refers simply to the memory of people or things. This memory may exist in the past or future or refer to wise or foolish people (Eccles 1:11). The word is also used of a royal annal ("book of remembrances" [Esther 6:1]) and the maxims (sayings remembered) of Job's friends (Job 13:12). Apart from these final, rarer uses, the nominal uses of the root *zkr* fit well within the field of meaning established by the verbs, though the usage is more limited.

6. Conclusion.

In conclusion, remembering is something that both humans and God do. Humans recall, consider and act with some truth in mind. That truth is often a benevolent act of God or some aspect of the person's relationship with God. That relationship exists because God remembers people. He considers and acts graciously toward them, often because he is committed to them. In response, his people should offer him their praise, loyalty and obedience.

See also THANKSGIVING, PSALMS OF; WORSHIP.

BIBLIOGRAPHY. **L. C. Allen,** *"zkr," NIDOTTE* 1.1100-1106; **J. Blau,** "Reste des I-Imperfekts von *ZKR,* Qal," *VT* 11 (1961) 81-86; **H. J. Boecker,** *Redeformen des Rechtslebens im Alten Testament* (2nd ed; WMANT 14; Neukirchen-Vluyn: Neukirchener Verlag, 1970) 106-11; **P. A. H. de Boer,** *Gedenken und Gedächtnis in der Welt des Alten Testaments* (Franz Delitzsch-Vorlesungen 1960; Stuttgart: Kohlhammer, 1962); **B. S. Childs,** *Memory and Tradition in Israel* (SBT 37; Naperville, IL: Allenson, 1962); **G. R. Driver,** "Hebrew Homonyms," *VT* 16 (1967) 53-54; **H. Eising,** "זָכַר, זֵכֶר, אַזְכָּרָה, זִכָּרוֹן" *TDOT* 4.64-82; **T. E. McComiskey,** *"zākar, zēker, zikkārôn, zekaryâ, zekaryāhu, ʾazkārâ,"* *TWOT* 1.551-53; **W. Schottroff,** *"Gedenken" im Alten Orient und im Alten Testament: Die Wurzel ZAKAR im Semitischen Sprachkreis* (WMANT 15; Neukirchen-Vluyn: Neukirchener Verlag, 1964); **A. Verhey,** "Remember, Remembrance," *ABD* 5.667-69; **H. W. Wolff,** *Anthropology of the Old Testament* (Philadelphia: Fortress, 1974).
B. Seevers

RETRIBUTION

The "retribution principle" is the conviction that the righteous will prosper and the wicked will suffer, both in proportion to their respective *righteousness and wickedness. In Israelite theology the principle is integral to the belief in God's justice. Since God is just, the Israelites held that it was incumbent on him to uphold the retribution principle.

Having a worldview in which God was absolutely just and compelled to maintain the retribution principle, the Israelites developed the inevitable converse corollary: those who prosper must be righteous (i.e., favored by God), and those who suffer must be wicked (i.e., experiencing the judgment of God).

Thus, the retribution principle was an attempt to understand, articulate, justify and systematize the logic of God's interaction in the world. The fact that human experience often seemed to deny the tenets of the retribution principle required that the retribution principle be qualified or nuanced in order to be employed realistically in the philosophical/theological discussion. How can God be just if he does not punish the wicked? In order to answer this question, the retribution principle frequently was under discussion in Israelite *theodicy (defense of God's justice in a world where *suffering exists, though in more modern terms the conversation has grown into a philosophical discussion concerning the origin of evil), driven particularly by the context of ethical monotheism. The retribution principle does not of necessity operate in the context of theodicy, but because of Israel's theological commitments this tendency can be observed in the OT. After examining the status of the retribution principle in the ancient Near East, this discussion will return to a consideration of the relationship between the retribution principle and theodicy.

1. Retribution Principle in the Ancient Near East
2. Retribution Principle and Theodicy
3. Resolving Tensions between the Retribution Principle and Experience
4. Underlying Retribution Theology
5. Retribution Principle in the Wisdom Literature
6. Retribution Principle: Israelite Theology versus Biblical Theology
7. Pragmatic Postscript

1. Retribution Principle in the Ancient Near East.

The literature of the ancient Near East continually demonstrates that people believed that the administration of justice in the human world was a concern and responsibility of the gods. It was, for example, considered the principal jurisdiction of the Babylonian god Shamash to administer justice (thus he is the god to whom Hammurapi reports with his legal collection). However, administering justice is not the same thing as being just. If the gods are not truly just by character but rather are simply duty-bound or interested in justice from a heuristic standpoint, then the retribution principle plays a different role. The questions that swirl around the retribution principle lose their philosophical urgency in the ancient world due to the fact that injustice in the world often is not blamed on the gods but rather on demons and humans. In Mesopotamian thinking evil was built into the cosmos by means of the "control attributes" (Sumerian *me*) that are woven into the fabric of the cosmos, but even those had not been established by the gods. Since evil existed outside of the jurisdiction of the gods, divine administration of justice did not necessarily eliminate suffering. Some misfortune came about simply because of how the world was. In both Egyptian and Mesopotamian thinking the gods were not considered responsible for evil in the world, and therefore the presence or experience of evil did not have to be resolved in reference to the justice of the gods (this in contrast to Israel, where nothing existed outside the jurisdiction of God's sovereignty). In the Sumerian "Lament over the Destruction of Ur," the city is destroyed not as an act of justice or injustice but rather because it was time for kingship to be passed on. Likewise with regard to individuals, suffering can sometimes just be one's lot in life for the present. It is also clear that personal misfortune could be considered to be the result of offending the gods, even if the offense were committed innocently. In such cases it is not that the gods were unjust; they simply were not very forthcoming about communicating their expectations.

The so-called theodicy texts from Mesopotamia consistently fail to affirm or defend the justice of deity. Instead, they affirm pervasive and often ignorant offense by humans and the general inscrutability of the gods.

> I wish I knew that these things were pleasing to one's god!
> What is proper to oneself is an offence to one's god;
> What in one's own heart seems despicable is proper to one's god.
> Who knows the will of the gods in heaven?
> Who understands the plans of the underworld gods?
> Where have mortals learnt the way of a god?
> (Lambert, *Ludlul bel Nemeqi*, 41:33-38)

A sense and expectation of the retribution principle at a basic level remains evident here, though the gods were relieved of responsibility because of the way the function of the cosmos was perceived. Even in the areas where the gods could be held responsible, they, like human judges, may be doing their best to administer justice, but do so imperfectly.

Although Mesopotamians did not seek to defend the justice of the gods, they still believed in the retribution principle. Since they lack revelation of what the deities required, the people believed that offense to the gods was unavoidable, and thus sin was pervasive. Consequently, no one could claim to be innocent (van der Toorn 2003, 62). But if worshipers had been ritually conscientious, the expectation was that the god whom they worshiped would protect them. This expectation is based on the belief not that the god is just, but rather that the god is sensible. The gods need what humans provide, and the gods in return are capable in most circumstances of providing protection. The offenses committed against the gods in a large majority of cases constituted failure to provide what the gods needed or violation of that which was sacred. The deity naturally responds with anger, disdain or neglect, leaving the individual vulnerable. The system works this way not because the gods are just, but rather because they are needy, and the retribution principle remains intact.

In this sense, though people of Mesopotamia might believe that the gods do indeed punish those who earn their wrath, this conviction cannot offer an explanation for all suffering. The explanation that those who suffer must be wicked could not work because in the ancient Near Eastern worldview much of the suffering that people experienced was not orchestrated by the gods; rather, it was possible because of the inattention of the gods or simply by a course of circumstances or the nature of the world. Even if the gods abandoned a person because of some offense, they were not responsible for the ensuing evil; it is just that they did nothing to prevent it. They had withdrawn their favor and protection.

The gods in the ancient world did not care about defending their character. They were concerned about preserving their prerogatives and their executive perquisites. When a god did not receive the cultic rites to which he was entitled, his status was threatened and his wrath and/or abandonment was predictable. The gods wished for the king and society to be characterized by justice because a stable and prosperous community most effectively provided for the needs of the gods.

In Egyptian thinking the retribution principle represents one aspect involved in the establishment of *maat, which is the ultimate goal of the gods and therefore of those who exercise authority on behalf of the gods in the human realm. This connection between the retribution principle and maat is inherent in this definition of maat: "the principle that forms individuals into communities and that gives their actions meaning and direction by ensuring that good is rewarded and evil punished" (Assmann, 128). So defined, J. Assmann considers maat to represent the totality of all social norms. If maat is to be preserved and attained, positive behavior should be recognized and recompensed while negative behavior should be punished. This is rooted not in divine attributes (e.g., justice) but rather in divine goals (pursuit of maat).

In conclusion, in the ancient Near East the gods have a level of responsibility to see that good and right prevail not because they are compelled by their character or attributes but rather because they have the power to exercise such influence, and it works to their advantage to do so. The retribution principle is understood as a logical syllogism in a context where gods expect their needs to be met and have the power to punish or recompense accordingly. In Mesopotamia the most natural matrix for retribution principle thinking is in the realm of ritual, whereas in Egypt it is one of the primary mechanisms in the establishment of maat.

2. Retribution Principle and Theodicy.

Theodicy in its modern philosophical and existential guise concerns the origin and nature of suffering and evil. In theology proper (whether mythological, broadly metaphysical, or in ethical monotheism) the philosophical question naturally focuses its attention on the divine role in suffering and relationship to evil. The retribution principle progresses from philosophy to pragmatism in trying to understand and formulate how deity acts in the world. The extent to which deity can theoretically be considered responsible for evil is what draws theodicy and the retribution principle together in theological conundrum. In the preceding section of this discussion we noted that the gods in the ancient Near East were somewhat relieved of responsibility because their role in the origin of evil was limited, and because they were often only indirectly considered the cause of suffering. This understanding of the role of deity, along with

ambivalence regarding whether the gods were inherently just, nearly eliminates theodicy from the discussion. Although people continued to have deep concerns over how deity acted in the world and therefore their interests in the retribution principle remained robust and vital, the retribution principle could not be employed in theodicy. Given the aforementioned considerations, it is fair to conclude that "theodicy" is a misnomer when applied to the ancient Near East: the origins of evil were impersonal, and the gods were neither just nor took ethical responsibility for suffering.

In Israel the absence of any source of divine authority other than Yahweh limited the philosophical possibilities regarding the origin of evil and the source of suffering (1 Sam 2:6; Job 2:10; Eccles 7:14; Is 45:7). No supernatural power alongside Yahweh or outside of Yahweh's sphere of power existed. At the same time, Yahweh was considered powerful, good and just. Thus one might say that the theodicy question bloomed in Israel, and in this hothouse of theological tension the retribution principle provided the traditional explanation despite its obvious inconsistencies in accounting for human experience. As we tour the Wisdom literature's treatment of the retribution principle below, we will see the tension between the retribution principle as theodicy and the retribution principle as theology. The affirmations of the retribution principle in the text are intended to be theological in nature and serve well in that capacity. In contrast, the Israelites were inclined to try to wield that theology in service to theodicy, a role for which it was singularly unsuitable. The role of the book of *Job is to perform the radical surgery that separates theology from theodicy, contending that in the end Yahweh's justice must be taken on faith rather than worked out philosophically. He does not need to be defended; he wants to be trusted. The entire constellation of God's attributes is at work in a complex coordinated manner. Justice is part of that constellation, but it does not trump all other attributes. Thus, the retribution principle cannot serve the purposes of theodicy.

3. Resolving Tensions between the Retribution Principle and Experience.

Having addressed the relationship between the retribution principle and the character and activities of deity, we now turn to the relationship between the retribution principle and human experience. The general belief in the retribution principle created certain tensions that needed to be resolved in the face of experiences that did not conform to the retribution principle. Resolution of these tensions could potentially assume a number of different configurations.

3.1. *Qualification Regarding the Nature of Deity*. In this approach deity is not just, or the quality of divine justice differs from human perception, or deity has simply not given enough information to allow individuals to know what earns divine favor or wrath. We have already encountered this latter option in the ancient Near East where revelation was scant and obligations to deity were often seen in cultic terms. When such was the case, a ritual resolution of suffering was sought by trying to appease a deity who was angry for unknown reasons. This general inclination is observable in the argument of Job's three friends in the dialogue section of the book . The qualification is that sometimes people suffer not because they are wicked, because they are ignorant of their offense, but the retribution principle is retained.

3.2. *Qualification Regarding the Purpose of Suffering*. Suffering in this approach is not simply punishment from a just God; it may have an educational purpose (the explanation preferred by Elihu in Job 32—37) or may be focused on some spiritual benefit (the position adopted in the NT as Christian suffering is seen as sharing in the suffering of Christ). The qualification is that sometimes people suffer because, as uncomfortable as it is, they stand to benefit from it. This may represent a departure from the retribution principle formula as in the Christian context but can still include an aspect of the retribution principle, as it does in Elihu's position. He maintained that Job's suffering was punishment from God, but it operated in the sphere of prevention rather than remediation (i.e., for sinful inclinations detected rather than past sins being judged).

3.3. *Qualification Regarding the Timing of the Execution of the Principle*. All agreed that divine reaction to righteousness or wickedness was generally not immediate, but how much time lapse could there be without compromising the integrity of the formula? In societies where varying destinies after death are considered possible, true justice may be deferred when not experienced in this life. In the ancient world (Israel included, Egypt excepted) reward and punishment in the *afterlife was not part of the belief system, so the timing issue deepened the mystery rather than providing a resolution. In Christian thinking, however, this is often a basis for theodicy. The qualification is that people sometimes suffer for now, but that justice must be viewed over the scope of time. The retribution principle is retained, but its scope is extended into the afterlife.

3.4. *Qualification Regarding the Role of Justice in the World*. This approach suggests that justice is complex and cannot be reduced to a formula like the retribution principle. It recognizes that justice is rarely transparent and requires one to have more information than is readily available. It gives God the benefit of the doubt as it accepts by faith that God is just regardless of how any given individual is faring. As such, it adopts the main statement of the retribution principle ("The righteous prosper, the wicked suffer") as proverbially and theologically accurate. However, it denies the corollary that suggests that a person's prosperity or suffering can serve as the basis for discerning whether a person is righteous or wicked. The qualification is that justice is not the sole foundation of how God works in our world, because given a fallen world, perfect justice is not attainable, and that the basis for God's operation of the world is his character, not just one attribute or another. God, in his wisdom, is concerned with provisional justice, given the parameters of an imperfect world.

4. Underlying Retribution Theology.
In Israelite theology God is just and administers justice in the world. God employs the retribution principle to give insight into his character and to articulate the general parameters of his administration. This activity can be traced on both a corporate and an individual level. The unique shape of the retribution principle within Israelite thought is heavily influenced by two philosophical preconceptions: the existence of only one God, and the absence of a belief in reward and punishment in the afterlife.

4.1. *Corporate Level, Covenant Theme*. On a corporate level this theology is evident as it is expressed in the covenant blessings and curses. Consequently, it is also evident in the judgment oracles of the prophets, since they pronounce the doom that the Israelites have brought upon themselves by their covenant violations. The corporate aspects of the retribution principle are worked out literarily by the Chronicler as he traces its effects through the history of the monarchy. On the corporate level the retribution principle provided for occasional tension (e.g., Ps 44; Esther), but since it could be worked out over the long span of history, it carried less immediacy, urgency or poignancy. Corporate retribution principle in Israel is a covenant theme, and since covenant violation was rampant, the claim of innocence was difficult to maintain.

4.2. Individual Wisdom Theme. In contrast, the retribution principle on the individual level is a wisdom theme. This connection is laid out plainly in Psalm 1 and is confirmed repeatedly in the central role of the retribution principle in the Wisdom literature. It is important to note, however, that the biblical text offers affirmation only of the main proposition ("The righteous prosper, the wicked suffer"), not of the deduced converse corollary ("The one who prospers is righteous, the one who suffers is wicked"). Logically, the corollary could be asserted only if the main proposition is true universally and consistently. Nevertheless, it appears that the Israelites did tend to extend their expectations to include the corollary, as the book of Job, and the need for a book such as Job, imply. The tension of the book is created by the corollary as both Job and his friends conclude that his suffering can only be explained as punishment from God. We will return to this below.

4.3. Connection to Monotheism and Afterlife. Since Israel was to believe in only one God, who was responsible for every aspect of the cosmos, it was very difficult to absolve him from responsibility for suffering. If he were to be considered just, then they believed that he must maintain the retribution principle. If there were no chance to achieve final justice in the afterlife, then he was obliged to do so within the lifetime of the individual; note Psalm 27:13: "I am still confident of this: I will see the goodness of the LORD in the land of the living." These factors combined to pose the conundrum of the retribution principle and human experience and led to the retribution principle being used for theodicy. It is in Israel, therefore, that we see the formulation of the inherent connection between the retribution principle and theodicy that becomes commonplace in the history of theological discourse.

5. Retribution Principle in the Wisdom Literature.

5.1. Psalms. The psalmist expects the retribution principle to work (Ps 37; 55:22). He considers himself innocent and therefore expects God to relieve his suffering or trials and thus vindicate him from "corollary inferences" (Pss 26; 35). The problem that is most frequently the premise for the psalmist's complaints and his invocation of the retribution principle is the perception that God has abandoned him or is hiding his face from him (e.g., Ps 13; 22:1; 38:21; 44:24). God is not viewed as the cause of his suffering, but God has not come to his aid to relieve his suffering. Yahweh's absence makes one vulnerable to suffering at the hands of the enemies of God and perhaps even to death. What the psalmist longs for is not prosperity per se but rather the presence of Yahweh, which brings life and deliverance (Ps 31:14-24; 84; 102:28). In this sense, the retribution principle in *Psalms could be reformulated more specifically as "The righteous will enjoy God's presence and its accompanying benefits; the wicked will forfeit the presence of God and will suffer the consequences of abandonment."

In contrast to the *lament psalms in which the psalmists' circumstances are under discussion, some of the wisdom psalms turn greater attention on the circumstances of others, specifically, the wicked. Now instead of trying to understand the suffering of the righteous and the apparent abandonment by God, the psalmists seek to understand the prosperity of the wicked and God's apparent failure to judge those whose actions deserve punishment (e.g., Pss 37; 49). The retribution principle thus serves as a backdrop to the psalms of *imprecation in which the psalmist lists specifics of the sorts of things that would have to come upon the wicked in order for the proportionality of the retribution principle to be maintained (see Ps 109). If God is administering justice through the retribution principle, then a slap on the wrist will not suffice.

In Psalms, then, we see the expectation that the retribution principle will govern human experience and the repeated affirmation that the retribution principle gives adequate expression to theologically sound expectations. The experiences, however, of inexplicable suffering by the righteous and the observation of apparent prosperity and success of the wicked lead to questions and confusion about God's stance. These testify to their deep-seated misunderstanding of God's commitment to the retribution principle and the resulting misapplication of it.

5.2. Proverbs. The book of *Proverbs actually has some relief to offer in that it clearly positions the retribution principle in the category of proverbial saying, most notably in a variety of permutations in Proverbs 10—12 (see Prov 10:3, 9, 16, 24, 25, 27, 30; 11:5, 6, 18, 19, 21; 12:2, 7, 21). The significance of this cannot be overstated. Proverbial sayings, by definition, are generalizations, which therefore find their truth in the fact that they stand as probabilities, not as guarantees for what must be true without exception (Van Leeuwen, 25-31). They are to be interpreted existentially (reflecting a possibility that is observed with some degree of regularity; descriptive of tendencies) rather than universally (reflecting necessity on every occasion). Such statements indicate that there is a higher probability of the stated action than of any of the possible alternatives (for an extensive treatment of genre and grammatical issues, see Cook).

5.3. Ecclesiastes. In the book of *Ecclesiastes *Qohelet holds the retribution principle at arm's length, but he does hold it. He advises his readers to fulfill ritual obligations to avoid inciting divine wrath (Eccles 5:1-7), but his most direct discussion of the retribution principle is in Ecclesiastes 8:12—9:4. He labels the experiences that contradict the retribution principle as meaningless (Eccles 8:14), but despite those contradictions he advises that it will go better for those who fear God (Eccles 8:12-13). His teaching can be summarized in the advice that people should live as if the retribution principle were true, but that they should not expect it to be reflected in their personal circumstances. He refuses to employ the retribution principle in theodicy because "No one can comprehend what goes on under the sun" (Eccles 8:17). A further caveat, however, is that the retribution principle itself is ultimately meaningless because "all share a common destiny" (Eccles 9:2): death overtakes them all.

5.4. Job. The book of Job is all about God's policies and what role the retribution principle has in those policies. It is not the retribution principle that is on trial, nor is it Job who is on trial, despite the fact that both he and his friends assume that he is (although from the beginning the book declares him righteous, from

God's mouth). The scene in heaven, to which none of the human characters is privy, provides the information that it is God's policies, and particularly his use of and commitment to the retribution principle, that are on trial. The tension of the book is established in the two competing charges offered by *Satan and Job respectively. The former claims that God's policies should be called into question because rewarding the righteous inhibits the development of true, disinterested righteousness ("Does Job fear God for nothing?" [Job 1:9]). Thus the retribution principle is called into question by suggesting that it is counterproductive for the righteous to be rewarded. The latter (Job) claims that God's policies should be called into question because they inexplicably allow for righteous people to suffer, contrary to his stated preferences (i.e., the retribution principle). If God is just, then it is contrary to his character for the righteous to suffer. These two charges set the stage for the book and provide a context for exploration of solutions. The way the book works this out is traced in detail in the article on the book of Job; here we must focus attention specifically on the retribution principle.

M. Tsevat has proposed that the tension in the book can be diagrammed by a triangle depicting the three elements to be defended by various proponents: God's justice, Job's righteousness and the retribution principle. Given the situation that develops in the book, the proponents make choices as to which element must be defended above all, and in the process they must decide which of the three elements is expendable, for all three cannot be maintained.

Job's three friends defend the retribution principle and show themselves willing to deny Job's righteousness to support their defense. In the first round of speeches the focus is on God's protection of the righteous (Job 4:6-7; 5:18-27; 8:5-7). The destruction of the wicked is stated in brief principle (Job 11:11) and alluded to as the problem of Job's sons (Job 8:4). In the second round the emphasis is entirely on the punishment that comes to the wicked (Job 15:20-35; 18:5-21; 20:4-29), and this same theme is picked up from a different perspective in the third round (Job 22:15-20). All of this is defense of the retribution principle, not defense of God or his justice, though Bildad gets the closest in his contention that God does not pervert justice (Job 8:3). At occasional junctures other affirmations are made concerning God: he is more righteous than human beings (Job 4:17); he exercises his power in the world to accomplish his will (Job 5:8-16; confirmed by Job in Job 12:13-25); he effects the retribution principle (Job 8:20-22); as judge, he sees and knows (Job 22:12-14); he establishes order in the cosmos (Job 25:2).

As in the ancient Near Eastern literature, the friends fully believe in the retribution principle but do not employ it for theodicy, though their view of God has more of an Israelite shape than an ancient Near Eastern one (specifically in that they do not treat God as having needs, nor do they see the solution in ritual terms). Nevertheless, they agree with the two basic tenets of ancient Near Eastern thinking regarding suffering: (1) they affirm human ignorance of what God demands, thereby affirming innate human sinfulness (Job 4:18-21; 22:5-9; 25:4-6); (2) they affirm the inscrutability of deity (Job 11:7-9; 15:7-16).

Job chooses to defend his own righteousness and, since he sees no possibility of neutralizing the retribution principle, is left with suspicions about God. In Job's speeches we find an anti-theodicy (e.g., Job 19:6; 24:12) as he refuses to defend God or make excuses for him. Indeed, this is what God reprimands Job for (Job 40:8). By his oath in Job 31, Job attempts to pressure God into providing his own theodicy (Nicholson, 79).

In contrast, Elihu is distinct as the participant who actually offers a theodicy. His defense of God's justice is in the category of "educative theodicy"; that is, suffering serves to bring potential problems to our attention so that they can be remedied. Elihu still believes in the retribution principle and defends it, but he builds a case that suffering is not just God's response to past sin. It can also preempt future or potential sin. In choosing to defend God's corner of the triangle, he also calls Job's righteousness into question, but in a more nuanced way than do the other friends. He does so by redefining the retribution principle (preventive not remedial), and on the basis of that redefinition he finds fault in Job (his self-righteous response to suffering).

It is in God's speeches that the true solution is found in a revised perspective on God's policies and priorities, and in a revised vision of the retribution principle. The triangle is too simplistic and reduces God's policies to a narrow system in which justice is the trumping attribute and the retribution principle is law. God does not choose one of the three elements of the triangle to defend; rather, he discards the triangle model as artificial and inadequate.

The book thus offers a modified view of the retribution principle that construes it in proverbial and theological terms; that is, it is useful to describe what God is like and therefore can serve as a basis for identifying general trends in human experience. But the retribution principle offers no guarantees. The book in effect takes a contra-theodicy position: rather than defending God's justice, it defends his wisdom. Though it is not a theodicy, it is very interested in the retribution principle and its legitimacy. In the end, the retribution principle is rejected as a foundation for divine activity in the human realm, but it is reclaimed on the proverbial and anecdotal levels as representative of the character of deity. God delights in bringing prosperity to the righteous, and he takes seriously the responsibility of punishing the wicked. It is therefore of some importance that at the end of the book God restores Job, thus reemphasizing his commitment to the retribution principle properly understood as a theological principle that cannot be employed for either assessment of God's character (theodicy) or of any person's character. Thus the basic premise of the retribution principle is retained ("The righteous prosper, the wicked suffer"), but since it does not represent a strict formula that always maintains, the corollary fails: it cannot be assumed that a suffering person is wicked, or that a prosperous person is righteous.

6. Retribution Principle: Israelite Theology versus Biblical Theology.

Did the Israelites believe the retribution principle and its converse? A sufficient number of texts demonstrate that they were aware that it was not enforced moment by moment (e.g., Ps 37:7, 25). That is, they realized that on certain occasions there might be a time lag before the books are balanced. With that caveat, they largely accepted the truth of the proposition but often were inclined to treat it as the main determining factor for God's activity. Consequently, they show a clear inclination to also accept the converse corollary as true and use it to shape their expectations and to formulate their theodicy.

In contrast to this Israelite theology, the biblical theology of the Wisdom literature is more cautious and nuanced. The text never affirms the converse corollary, so it cannot be framed as a biblical teaching. Furthermore, Proverbs couches the retribution principle in proverbial language, Ecclesiastes casts suspicion on it, and the book of Job details its limitations. Thus biblical theology rejects the retribution principle as providing a theodicy yet embraces it in its theology.

The issue continues to factor in theological discussion into the NT. Jesus confronts it explicitly on two occasions. In John 9:1-3 the disciples ask the retribution principle question, inquiring about the cause of the malady of the man born blind. Jesus' answer turns them away from the issue of theodicy (indicated by the question of cause) and toward an expanded theology: suffering should be evaluated not with regard to cause (actions in the past) but rather with regard to purpose (God's ongoing plan). Thus his reply: "That the work of God might be displayed in his life." As in the book of Job, no explanation for the suffering is forthcoming, possible or necessary. What is important is to trust God's wisdom and to seek out his purpose.

In Luke 13:1-5 the question is asked concerning whether those who had died in recent tragedies deserved their death. Again Jesus answers in a way that turns the attention away from cause, and he even states that a one-to-one correspondence between sin and punishment should not be made. The alternative that he offers is that they should view the incident as a warning. Consistent with John 9, he refuses to engage the question of cause and directs the attention of his audience to purpose.

Paul weighs in on the retribution principle question in Galatians 6:7: "A man reaps what he sows." Here he states the retribution principle proverbially without neutralizing its theological impact. That he adopts this nuancing is clear in that his teaching regarding suffering does not embrace the converse corollary.

7. Pragmatic Postscript.
Based on the foregoing assessment, it is fair to conclude that the retribution principle, properly nuanced and applied, is a biblical teaching about the nature of God and, as such, is true. Still, we must be careful to understand it as theology, not theodicy; as proverbial rather than propositional; as operating within the realm of God's wisdom,

not just his justice; and as investigated in relation to purpose rather than to cause.

Given this nuancing, we can see that a proper understanding of the retribution principle offers yet another argument concerning the bankruptcy of certain popular evangelical movements such as "the health-and-wealth gospel." The Scripture passages used as proof texts for such movements are invariably based on an unnuanced propositional reading of the retribution principle that views it as propositional truth that offers promises to be claimed. Simply put, proverbs are not promises, and the retribution principle offers no guarantees.

See also IMPRECATION; JOB 1: BOOK OF; MAAT; PROVERBS 1: BOOK OF; RIGHTEOUSNESS; THEODICY.

BIBLIOGRAPHY. **J. Assmann,** *Mind of Egypt: History and Meaning in the Time of the Pharaohs* (New York: Metropolitan Books, 2002); **J. A. Cook,** "Genericity, Tense, and Verbal Patterns in the Sentence Literature of Proverbs," in *Seeking Out the Wisdom of the Ancients: Essays Offered to Honor Michael V. Fox on the Occasion of His Sixty-fifth Birthday,* ed. R. Troxel, K. Friebel and D. Magary (Winona Lake, IN: Eisenbrauns, 2005) 117-33; **J. L. Crenshaw,** *Theodicy in the Old Testament* (Philadelphia: Fortress, 1983); **J. C. de Moor,** "Theodicy in the Texts of Ugarit," in *Theodicy in the World of the Bible,* ed. A. Laato and J. C. de Moor (Leiden: E. J. Brill, 2003) 108-50; **H. A. Hoffner,** "Theodicy in Hittite Texts," in *Theodicy in the World of the Bible,* ed. A. Laato and J. C. de Moor (Leiden: E. J. Brill, 2003) 90-107; **A. Laato and J. C. de Moor,** eds., *Theodicy in the World of the Bible* (Leiden: E. J. Brill, 2003); **W. G. Lambert,** *Babylonian Wisdom Literature* (Oxford: Clarendon Press, 1960); **F. Lindström,** "Theodicy in the Psalms," in *Theodicy in the World of the Bible,* ed. A. Laato and J. C. de Moor (Leiden: E. J. Brill, 2003) 256-303; **A. Loprieno,** "Theodicy in Ancient Egyptian Texts," in *Theodicy in the World of the Bible,* ed. A. Laato and J. C. de Moor (Leiden: E. J. Brill, 2003) 27-56; **E. W. Nicholson,** "The Limits of Theodicy as a Theme of the Book of Job," in *Wisdom in Ancient Israel,* ed. J. Day, R. P. Gordon and H. G. M. Williamson (Cambridge: Cambridge University Press, 1995) 71-82; **M. Tsevat,** "The Meaning of the Book of Job," in *The Meaning of the Book of Job and Other Biblical Studies* (New York: KTAV, 1980) 1-38; **K. van der Toorn,** *Sin and Sanction in Israel and Mesopotamia: A Comparative Study* (SSN 22; Assen:

Van Gorcum, 1985); idem, "Theodicy in Akkadian Literature," in *Theodicy in the World of the Bible,* ed. A. Laato and J. C. de Moor (Leiden: E. J. Brill, 2003) 57-89; **R. C. Van Leeuwen,** "Wealth and Poverty: System and Contradiction in Proverbs," *HS* 33 (1992) 25-36; **W. von Soden,** "Das Fragen nach der Gerechtigkeit Gottes im Alten Orient," *MDOG* 96 (1965) 41-59.   J. H. Walton

REWARDS. *See* PROVERBS 1:BOOK OF.

RHETORICAL CRITICISM

Rhetorical criticism may be defined as the analysis of a text's compositional artistry with an eye to audience impact (Watson and Hauser, 14; Fox 1981, 54). Despite Origen's claim in *On First Principles* that the Bible was rhetoric-free (lest faith should "rest in the skillful use of words . . . and not in the power of God" [quoted in Patrick and Scult, 30]), recent readers have detected rhetoric emerging widespread from genres as varied as sermon, wisdom and narrative accounts. Even a poem of "thanksgiving serve[s] as testimony . . . which lends persuasive influence to the weighing, waiting human listener for whom the verdict concerning the trustworthiness of Israel's God has not yet been decided" (Brueggemann, 126).

1. Origins
2. Varieties
3. Axioms
4. Method
5. Assets
6. Liabilities
7. Illustrations
8. Conclusion

1. Origins.

Although documented study of rhetoric dates to Aristotle with his three genres (deliberative, judicial, ceremonial), three modes of proof (*ethos, pathos, logos*)—later expanded under Cicero with his five arts (invention, structure, style, memory, delivery)—the field of biblical research did not engage analysis of rhetoric until the latter half of the twentieth century. After H. Gunkel's *form criticism had invited consideration of those life situations where biblical passages may have originated and operated by attending to any conventions signaling such settings, there grew a discontent among certain readers who heard the text extending a further invitation: to

recover the very dynamic of its message by exploring how its arrangement of thought and deployment of literary devices produced distinct effects within the audience. One such discontented reader was J. Muilenburg, whose 1968 SBL presidential address, "Form Criticism and Beyond," launched the movement christened by him as "rhetorical criticism." An avowed debtor to Gunkel, Muilenburg issued a twofold charge for emerging rhetorical critics. Operating from the premise that a literary composition typically is fashioned as a unity capable of careful craftsmanship rather than an unbounded collage, of first importance is "to recognize precisely where and how it begins and where and how it ends" (Muilenburg, 9). Then, second, one may "recognize the structure . . . discern the configuration of its component parts . . . note the various rhetorical devices . . . the sequence and movement" (Muilenburg, 10).

Despite the title "rhetorical criticism" and his determined search for "rhetorical devices," Muilenburg was accused of resurrecting mere stylistic analysis, what G. Kennedy terms "secondary rhetoric"—thoughtfully arranged communication irrespective of persuasive impact (so W. Wuellner, see Trible, 48; Robbins 1997, 26; Patrick and Scult, 29). The years since have seen the pairing of persuasion with stylistics to redefine the nature of rhetorical criticism, reviving the Aristotelian notion that by definition rhetoric involves attempting to influence one's audience (Kennedy's "primary rhetoric").

2. Varieties.

The rhetorical movement has been influenced by an array of other criticisms, including modernism and formalism (C. Brooks, T. S. Eliot), reader-response (K. Burke, W. J. Ong, S. Fish), structuralism and semiotics (F. de Saussure, R. Barthes), deconstruction (J. Derrida, P. de Man), psychological and psychoanalytic (M. Foucault, P. Brooks), Marxism and New Historicism (R. Williams), feminism (E. Showalter, H. Cixous), African-American (H. L. Gates Jr.) and ethical/canonical (N. Frye, J. H. Miller) (see Olbricht, 101). Inevitably, rhetorical criticism responded with various perspectives. P. Trible, who trained under Muilenburg, chronicles five (Trible, 57-67). First, "traditional" rhetorical criticism follows classical patterns as evidenced by the neo-Aristotelian criticism of University of Chicago in the 1940s (Lundbom 1997, xxiv). Second, "experiential" emphasizes the impact of text upon the critic, who proceeds to make judgments and experience insights. Third, "dramaturgical" draws attention to symbol as the core of rhetoric, endeavoring to detect motive behind any persuasive presentation. Fourth, "sociological" considers within the communicative exchange the relative status of composer, characters and audience (including critic) as well as social cues implied by setting so as to tease out dynamics of power and potential employ of text as a persuasive force alternatively to conserve or destabilize one's position (see E. Schüssler Fiorenza's 1987 SBL presidential address, a marked divergence from Muilenburg's) (Schüssler Fiorenza, 19, 46; Robbins 1996, 3). This perspective recalls Plato's objection lest rhetoric "exploit the resources of language to make the 'weaker cause appear stronger' and to promote the acquisition of power as an end in itself without consideration for the well-being of the soul" (Gaonkar, 151). Fifth, "postmodern" envisions the original rhetorical "work" emerging as an ever-new "text" through each event of reading. What follows here traces the traditional perspective outlined by Watson and Hauser (see definition above).

3. Axioms.

A cluster of axioms scaffolds rhetorical criticism, sketching its rest and reach. First, a text (oral or written) may evidence sufficient coherence to impact an audience demonstrably—for example, 1 Kings 19:2-3; Esther 4:13-5:2; Job 1:13-21 (Lundbom 1997, xxiii-xxiv). Second, careful examination (close reading) of that text, scrutiny of figures with their function, may illumine means of impact (Campbell, 503, 508; Weiss). Third, to allow for potential coherence, extant form of the text should be studied as a synchronic whole (Watson and Hauser, 5). Fourth, with legal philosopher R. Dworkin, the text merits interpretation as the best text it can be—an interpretation marked by comprehensiveness, consistency, cogency, plentitude and profundity (Patrick and Scult, 21, 85-87). Finally, in the interest of OT studies it is axiomatic that rhetors were capable of tailoring text long before the art donned classifications supplied by Aristotle, Cicero and Quintilian (Lundbom 2001, 325).

4. Method.

How, then, does a rhetorical critic engage the task? If a text may possess coherence, the task begins with detecting outer boundaries (Muilenburg, 8-10). Then one may proceed to map the rhetorical topography within, alert for literary devices marking inner boundaries of constituent units, attentive to form- and content-indications of cohesion, transition, progression or climax (Muilenburg, 10; Amit, 9, 17-18). For literary devices are no mere ornamentation but rather collectively signify the text's very meaning (Berlin, 17-18). Once isolated, the nature of textual terrain contributed by each unit may be distilled. Such distilled concepts may surface after probing, "What unspoken question may this unit answer, contributing to a comprehensive scheme?" Synthesis follows analysis, mapping the arrangement of unit concepts in hopes of exposing latent logical structure. If structure should emerge, one then may consider the text's purpose—how it may have impacted the audience (Andrews, 7). All the while the critic must self-monitor, remaining attentive to personal filters that may skew one's view of the textual landscape.

Fundamental to the entire process is recognition of literary/rhetorical devices and sensitivity to the roles that they play in the text (Lundbom 1997, xxiv). Many instances will illustrate devices not formally catalogued until some three centuries later: accumulation, alliteration, analogy, aphorism, asyndeton, authority, *chiasm, comparison, epithet, euphemism, hyperbole, *inclusio, irony, metaphor, palistrophe, paradox, paronomasia, progression, reason, repetition (esp. anaphora and epiphora), rhetorical question, simile and, occasionally, *pathos* and *ethos* (drawn principally from Lundbom 2001, 325-37). But other devices may be uniquely Hebraic, eluding detection by the untrained eye. Features such as extensive repetition, meter variation or abrupt shift of person must not be dismissed prematurely as indicative of inferior composition or careless editorial work. At times these may be shown to serve calculated rhetorical goals (Lundbom 2001, 325-26; Watson and Hauser, 6-7; Berlin, 20-21).

5. Assets.

Two principal assets spring from rhetorical criticism. First, if one allows as axiomatic that an extant text may preserve effectual, audience-impacting meaning, then rhetorical criticism may offer the best avenue for reviving that meaning with its dynamism (Muilenburg, 9; cf.

Berlin, 17-18). This approach excavates the literary unknowing that accumulates inescapably over millennia, so as to expose communicative structures and imagine how they served hearers gone by. It seeks "to move beyond the mere identification of forms and genres toward reconstituting the text as a piece of living discourse" (Patrick and Scult, 13). This asset holds value for all modern readers, not least those persuaded of normative currency in these texts.

Second, discovery of rhetorical coherence in a text otherwise divided along source- and form-critical lines has invited reconsideration of textual integrity (Patrick and Scult, 17; Watson and Hauser, 9; Lee, 8). One may need to reconsider whether at times our ability to detect such fault lines may not exceed the ancients' ability to produce them.

6. Liabilities.

Along with the assets come two liabilities: underdetection and overdetection of rhetorical devices. Lacking any ancient manual of Hebrew rhetoric, one risks detecting only those later attested in Greek or modern notions of the art. Only careful, sustained exposure to texts of the OT and cognate cultures will accumulate observations yielding confident assertions (Watson and Hauser, 7; Patrick and Scult, 30; Lundbom 1997, xxix).

Conversely, overdetection may posit persuasive impact when none is warranted. Single devices supported by multiple attestation, boundaries reinforced by form-plus-content intersection, logical arrangements that are redundant and without lacunae—all subjected to peer critique—these disciplines guard against wishful subjectivity (see Course, 12; Allen, 577).

7. Illustrations.

The worth of any critical approach may best be assayed by sampling its wares. Just as varied perspectives catalogued by Trible (see 2 above) mapped an array of potential rhetorical trajectories, so also varied literary terrain of individual Bible books will produce yet another array of varied insights (bound, with occasional exception, by a common thread of the neo-Aristotelian perspective). Illustrations below range from isolated poems (*Psalms) to connected poems (Proverbs 1—9), from spiraling disputations (*Job) to gemlike apothegms (Proverbs 10—29), from philosophical reflections (*Ecclesiastes) to explicit love poems (*Song of Songs), from poetic expressions of communal anguish (*Lamentations) to narratives celebrating family or ethnic survival (*Ruth, *Esther). They place a premium on searching for secondary rhetoric and sometimes detect primary rhetoric as well.

The following illustrations present first a sample analysis of a select passage ("The Appeal of Wealth" [Prov 1:8-19]). Then follow briefer examples arranged by book, attesting rhetoric across writings, poetry and wisdom of the OT.

7.1. Sample Analysis of Proverbs 1:8-19. The analysis of "The Appeal of Wealth" moves from consideration of outer boundaries to inner structures. Rhetorical strategies potentially impacting the audience conclude the study.

7.1.1. Outer Boundaries. A vocative summons, "Listen, my son" (Prov 1:8a), appears to mark the upper boundary of this passage, as attested in other passages where a comparable expression calls for attention to an ensuing body of teaching (Prov 2:1; 3:1; 4:1, 10; 5:1; 6:1). This formal boundary marker is endorsed by a content marker as the book introduction plus hallmark apothegm (Prov 1:1-7) gives way to teaching concerning wise associations: company not to keep (Prov 1:10-19) and company to keep (Prov 1:20-33).

The lower boundary appears signaled formally by the particle "such" opening Proverbs 1:19, serving a summary function. Content again intersects form as the theme of wealth-by-violence gives way to Woman Wisdom's overture in Proverbs 1:20-33 (*see* Woman Wisdom and Woman Folly).

7.1.2. Inner Structures. Five structures bind units within the poem. First, an imperative-plus-incentive structure lends coherence to the opening quatrain (Prov 1:8-9). Second, the vocative "my son" opens the second unit (Prov. 1:10-19) and a subunit within it as well (Prov 1:15-18). Third, a conditional statement dominates the second unit. Both protasis and apodosis prefigure in Proverbs 1:10 as a dual-theme introduction. An extended protasis unfolds in Proverbs 1:11-14 followed by an extended apodosis (flagged by the vocative "my son") in Proverbs 1:15-18.

Further sophistication emerges with the fourth structure, a palistrophe (extended chiasm), as protasis components are compared with apodosis counterparts (*see* Chiasm). Balanced pairing provides strikingly contrastive options for the following implicit questions: (1) Who is about to come to a demise, and how (Prov 1:11-12 :: Prov 1:17-18)? That is, will it be the innocent victim at the hands of the gang, or will it be the gang itself, self-destructing? (2) Why should one take the challenge, whether the gang's challenge to enlist or the father's to withdraw (Prov 1:13 :: Prov 1:16)? That is, should monetary ends move one to enlist, or should violent means move one to withdraw? (3) How must one respond (Prov 1:14 :: Prov 1:15)? Enlist or withdraw? Consideration of these implicit questions yields the outline below. The structure is rife with reversals. With point-for-point rebuttal the father deftly turns the gang's argument inside out, both in terms of form (palistrophe) and content.

The fifth device, dense conclusion, provides maximal closure as terms or concepts earlier encountered recur in a concluding segment. Based on the Hebrew reading, only one word of Proverbs 1:19 fails to recall earlier terms or themes. It is the opening term, "such," a word marking consequence or recapitulation, out of place except in a conclusion: "Such are the ways of one who specializes in violence: the life of its handler will it seize" (my translation).

7.1.3. Rhetorical Strategies. Five rhetorical strategies may be observed in this brief poem. First, an implicit appeal to authority emerges from the father-son/speaker-audience relationship. Second, exposure that the claim to arrogant gain is a mere masquerade erupts from the palistrophic sequence of rebuttal reversals, seriously undercutting the gang's rhetoric. Use of palistrophe enabled the father immediately to counter the apex of the gang's appeal ("Pitch your lot in with us!" [Prov 1:14]) with the most energetic line of his counterappeal ("My son, do not walk along the way with them—withdraw your foot from their path!" [Prov 1:15]). Third, an apothegm of the foolish fowler subjects the gang to rhetoric of ridicule: they display less brains than do birds, tumbling into the net that they themselves have spread (Prov 1:17-18). Fourth, a dense conclusion leaves no prior thought or theme idle, as a lens focusing all earlier shafts of light to a brilliant closural beam. Finally, the prospect of certain, disastrous consequences reverberates through the poem's apodosis, cresting a logical crescendo in its last line—sufficient, it would be hoped, to deter the youth through fear and instill receptivity for Woman Wisdom's appeal about to be disclosed (Prov 1:20-33).

"The Appeal of Wealth" (Prov 1:8-19)

A. Parental Summons (vv. 8-9)
  1. Admonition (v. 8)
  2. Incentive (v. 9)
B. Parental Warning (vv. 10-19)
  1. Dual Theme Introduction (v. 10)
    a. Gang's Enticement (v. 10a)
    b. Father's Warning (v. 10b)
  2. Enticement by the Gang (vv. 11-14)
    a. Capital Plan: Inflicting Death on Others (vv. 11-12)
    b. Rationale for Enlistment: Monetary Ends (v. 13)
    c. Call to Enlist (v. 14)
  2'. Warning by the Father (vv. 15-18)
    c. Call to Withdraw (v. 15)
    b. Rationale for Withdrawing: Violent Means (v. 16)
    a. Capital Consequences: Receiving Death for Oneself (vv. 17-18)
  1'. Dense Conclusion (v. 19)

7.2. Further Illustrations from Proverbs. G. D. Pemberton pays particular attention to *ethos, pathos* and *logos* within ten "father" speeches of Proverbs 1—9. Pemberton (80) concludes, "These chapters constitute a striking rhetorical anthology that seems less likely to be the fortuitous result of haphazard collecting than the product of careful rhetorical discernment and selection." Not only does the father employ rhetoric, but also persuasive ploys arise from the alien woman (Pemberton, 65). These ten speeches may have served as rhetorical models for training young logicians (Pemberton, 80). M. V. Fox (1997, 621-23) notes in the father's speeches the persuasive traits of authority, promise and warning, intimacy, vividness, irony. *Personification of sapience through the character of Woman Wisdom creates yet another rhetorical ploy, clothing abstract with concrete, and this in a gender most winsome for the *sage's audience (principally, young men).

Among the aphorisms dominating Proverbs 10—29 Fox recognizes enthymemic rhetoric, where an intentionally incomplete syllogism requires the audience to supply omitted premises or conclusions. Thus in Proverbs 13:5 the saying "The righteous man hates a deceitful word, but the wicked will be ashamed and disgraced" implies omitted segments (supplied here in italics): "The righteous man hates a deceitful word *and will gain honor,* but the wicked *loves a deceitful word and* will be ashamed and disgraced" (see Fox 2004, 172). By engaging the audience to supply missing portions, the sage effectively enlists their aid in persuading themselves, simultaneously "train[ing] the reader to think like the sage" (Fox 2004, 176).

Full-length commentaries suggesting structural links in *Proverbs are rare. The work of B. K. Waltke (2004, 9-28) in this regard offers a particularly valuable contribution. For Proverbs 10:1—22:16 one should also consult K. M. Heim.

7.3. Illustrations from Psalms. Rhetorical study of Psalms may be distinguished based on orientation to Kennedy's primary rhetoric (persuasive art) or secondary rhetoric (compositional art irrespective of persuasion) (see 1 above). Attention to primary rhetoric is most helpfully illustrated in a treatment of Psalm 61 by W. H. Bellinger. Investigation of structure, intensification and poetics fuels the observation that "each section builds on the preceding one and is somewhat distinct; the psalm moves through a clear sequence," contributing to a persuasive whole (Bellinger, 385, 388).

A study of Psalm 103 by T. Willis provides another instructive model, illuminating not only content-based themes but also stylistic devices. These observations combine to clarify the poem's meaning with its persuasive dimension, calling the audience to imitate the poet's confidence in God during difficult times.

J. H. Coetzee examines politeness strategies in so-called enemy psalms (Pss 2; 3; 13; 41; 42/43). Through this lens he discovers the suppliant at times employing the argumentation strategy of positive politeness (endorsing the divine auditor's positive self-claims) or at other times that of negative politeness (subversively affirming superior traits of the auditor in such a way that he may feel obliged to behave in a corresponding fashion—just as the suppliant hopes) (Coetzee, 212-13).

In metaphors of tree and chaff Y. Gitay detects a persuasive ploy (Ps 1). By wrapping in fresh language a familiar principle (God supports the righteous but undermines the wicked), the sage increases odds of capturing the audience's attention (Gitay, 143).

Studies such as the following sharpen one's grasp of secondary rhetoric. Sensitivity to structure amplifies meaning in a study of Psalm 1 by C. J. Collins. A close reading of Psalm 23 by M. S.

Smith highlights its repeated terms, sounds and concepts, endorsing cohesion across metaphor boundaries of shepherd/host. In an examination of Psalm 69 L. C. Allen surfaces structure, solves ambiguous forms, and strengthens a symmetry-based claim of textual integrity. Attention to *acrostic, first-last verse inclusio, and key words characterize a study of Psalm 145 by A. Berlin, yielding a deeper impact for the poem's message. Again in Psalm 145 R. Kimelman uses close reading techniques to tease out still more inclusios at the subunit level, overturning premature notions that acrostic alone dominates the poem's structure and meaning.

7.4. Illustrations from Job. Unlike relatively independent compositions within Psalms, disputative dialogue spanning most of Job invites exploration of primary rhetoric across multiple chapters. Such is the focus of J. E. Course, who examines recurring words to trace whether successive speeches genuinely respond or merely speak past prior statements. He posits that "windy words" of Job 16:3a responds to "windy knowledge" of Job 15:2a; "indignation" of Job 6:2a responds to the same in Job 5:2a; credentials as a "wise man" in Job 15:2a respond to Job's dismissal of so-called wisdom in Job 12:2b; "mocking" attributed to God in Job 9:23b is turned to an accusation against Job as mocker in Job 11:3b (Course, 145-46).

D. J. A. Clines (1982) similarly traces speeches but clusters together all speeches of a single character. By listening to tone (an admittedly subjective gauge) and topoi (themes), he probes degrees of coherence. Avoiding subjective measures such as tone, P. van der Lugt (486-503) concentrates on transition markers and how they may provide more objective indicators of thought groupings. Nevertheless, some may question whether all fifty-five formal features listed by van der Lugt should be so classed.

Questions capture the attention of M. V. Fox, particularly those posed by God to Job. With characteristic insight, Fox (1981, 57-58) observes that part the a rhetorical question's power lies in its ability to identify knowledge common to speaker and auditor, thus establishing a degree of intimacy between the two parties. D. R. Magary (292, 296-97) studies questions as well, not in closing chapters but in all preceding poetry (Job 3—37). Interrogatives often open these speeches, a device whose function is to produce rapid engagement between speaker and auditor. Further, they generate emphasis by clustering and contribute both coherence and progression.

H. Viviers tries the persuasive effectiveness of Elihu's speech according to classical categories of rhetoric and finds it wanting. "No matter how hard Elihu tries to be the fitting champion of the doctrine of retribution, he becomes the embarrassing devastator thereof, even to the convinced proponents of traditional wisdom" (Viviers 1997, 151). Viviers concludes that he was a novice rhetor, the antimodel. Was this a ploy to amplify God's ensuing speeches by contrast? M. J. Lynch similarly examines Elihu's powers of persuasion. He concludes that Elihu's negative rhetorical *ethos* (in the Aristotelian sense of a speaker's credibility) supplants his *logos* (line of reasoning) so that even truthful allegations within Elihu's speech fail to persuade (Lynch, 363).

D. Patrick and A. Scult take a different tack. When considering portions thought to have been confused, they make recourse to textual reconstruction. When contemplating God's responses from the whirlwind, they weigh each interpretation against Dworkin's canon: "Does this produce the 'best Job' reading?" An interpretation presenting a God who would appear capricious, bullying, irrelevant they dismiss as less than the best reading. They do not work at establishing patterns throughout the book but rather seek to make sense of the larger messages contained therein. Fittingly, their chapter devoted to Job is entitled "Finding the Best Job" (Patrick and Scult, 81-102).

7.5. Illustrations from Ecclesiastes. Ecclesiastes may provide the best terrain for detecting rhetorical strategies less common in classical categories. D. B. Miller (163-67) offers a remarkably illuminating examination of *ethos*, destabilization and restablization to achieve persuasive aims. Competence, status and moral character of the speaker (*Qohelet) apparent from the text contribute to his *ethos*, while rhetorical questions supply the primary force eroding the audience's sense of stasis. Rhetorical questions together with wisdom sentences serve the restabilization process as Qohelet helps the audience to escape the trap of "viewing every part of their lives, even their religious practice, as a means of manipulating their own success and security" (Miller, 163).

E. P. Lee (26) discovers a "rhetoric of subversion" operating through miscues and "indirection," cleverly vectoring the reader to unexpected conclusions. As an example, according to Lee (27-28), the aim of the poem concerning times (Eccles 3:1-8) is not so much to describe suitable times for human activity on a temporal plane as to lay subversive groundwork for the sudden introduction of a strikingly untimely dimension: eternity (Eccles 3:11).

G. D. Salyer focuses on first-person statements coloring much of Ecclesiastes, noting their inherent subjectivity. This speaker-voice undermines credibility (*ethos*), combining with pendulum swings of dissonantal illogic to generate a "rhetoric of ambiguity" or "vain rhetoric" (Salyer, 11-17, 388). Such autocentric ambiguity is not ambivalent rather but strategic, intentionally frustrating the reader since "the 'whole truth' is never disclosed in any satisfactory way" (Salyer, 126). This in turn invites the reader to conclude that if autocentric reasoning is so fatally flawed, perhaps one ought explore a transcendental point of view, remembering one's creator before the daylight of temporal life finally dwindles away (Salyer, 238, 398).

Both T. Forti and N. Kamano also explore rhetorical dimensions of Ecclesiastes. Forti closely considers fauna imagery in two verses (Eccles 9:4; 10:1). Kamano appeals to deconstruction as a king transitions to a sage capable of skilled rhetoric. Kamano (420) also proposes a palistrophe (Eccles 1:3—3:9).

7.6. Illustrations from Song of Songs. Even the erotic composition of Song of Songs may display thoughtful arrangement enhancing audience impact. D. A. Dorsey (1990, 94-96) detects seven chiastically arranged segments encompassing the entire book, five of which further subdivide into sevenfold structures. Structure endorses content, producing a message of "egalitarianism and mutuality in romantic love that is virtually unparalleled in ancient Near Eastern literature" (Dorsey 1999, 213). H. Viviers (2002) similarly notes freedom of mutual physical enjoyment as an indication that gender power has been leveled, likely a calculated message contrasting patriarchal orientation of the source culture.

7.7. Illustrations from Esther. Narrative terrain presents rhetorical options often distinct from poetry. Nevertheless, secondary rhetoric's attention to boundaries, subunits, logical interrelation of parts, and scrutiny of grammar and syntax still may drive studies of narratives such as Esther, as evident in work by C. V. Dorothy and by S. B. Berg. Berg (185, 108-9) detects "a carefully structured, unified composition" including reversal and a book-length palistrophe. D. J. A. Clines (1984, 35, 39) accords the speech by *Mordecai in Esther 4 "rhetorical brilliance" while sensing logical weakness in Esther 9.

G. Snyman adopts a different perspective, highlighting how people employ text to influence and justify actions, especially when people in power use the Bible to justify oppression. Ideologies and motives are examined, whether motives of interpreter or motives of actors in texts. Fundamentalism is important to Snyman because persons holding texts in a fundamental grasp seem more likely to identify with (and so appropriate the stories of) biblical characters (such as black South Africans under apartheid identifying with Esther and the Jews when counteracting the Persian pogrom).

7.8. Illustrations from Ruth. The priorities of cohesiveness and intentional structure consistent with secondary rhetoric characterize studies in Ruth. B. Rebera (123, 148) traces three key Hebrew lexical items (*šûb, mût, ben*) through two modes of telling (narrative and dialogic structures) to show integration of the story. E. R. Wendland finds the clarity of Ruth's message enhanced by two simultaneous structures. First is a four-segment linear structure typical for narrative plot: setting–conflict–complication–climax–resolution–coda (Wendland, 31-39). Second is a concentric or palistrophic structure wherein the first six of seven segments encompassing the book contain concentric patterns (Wendland, 39-46). Furthermore, "two distinct compositional frameworks, the linear and the concentric, converge at key points in the discourse, particularly at the structural core of each Act [*sic*], to develop and highlight the central theme of '*hesed* in action'—on both the divine and human levels of participant interaction" (Wendland, 55). Due to frequent occurrence of concentric structures, Wendland (40) suspects that "recognition and interpretation of such chiastic structures were an important part of every mature person's 'literary' competence, whether a text were received aurally or in writing."

According to D. F. Rauber (165), sensitivity to pattern provides the key to reading Hebrew literature. With singular esteem for Ruth's subtle artistry, Rauber traces emptiness-fullness along a vector of escalating anguish from agricultural barrenness to the emptiness of a child-bereaved widow. Fullness then returns to the land, followed by Obed's birth, which restores hope to the family.

7.9. Illustrations from Lamentations. D. A. Dorsey and J. Renkema both sense a high degree of cohesion spanning the five poems of Lamentations. Dorsey uncovers the Qinah lament pattern (three-plus-two meter) operating not only at verse level but also at chapter level. The three chapters of Lamentations 1—3 form a triad typified by three lines per acrostic designation, while the two chapters of Lamentations 4—5 supply the following pair, devoting only two lines per acrostic step (Lam 4) or none at all (twenty-two verses of Lam 5 are not acrostic). Thus the acrostic scheme provides an index over the five chapters displaying a vector of escalating weakness or dissolution, paralleling Budde's description of Qinah as "rhythm that always dies away" (quoted in Dorsey 1988, 84). Form endorses content to convey exquisite grief in a Hebrew modality.

Renkema concentrates on concentric patterns lending unity to the entire book. These lead to the isolation of Lamentations 3:17 and Lamentations 3:50 as a structurally related pair, comprising the book's central theme (Renkema 1988b, 333; 1998, 337).

8. Conclusion.
Since its beginnings in 1968, rhetorical criticism has expanded both in depth and breadth. Introduction of multiple perspectives calls for care in reading and precision in writing of secondary literature lest confusion cancel insight. Depth of analysis in turn calls for careful critique lest the "best text" turn out to be little more than a figment of the critic's imagination. Given these cautions, many remain convinced that rhetorical criticism offers the best avenue enabling the modern reader "to think the thoughts of the biblical writer after him" (or her, in the case of the mother of King *Lemuel in Prov 31) (Muilenburg, 9). To the degree that those thoughts delivered persuasive impact, such an empathetic reading is of particular worth for "our postmodern situation, which refuses to acknowledge a settled essence behind our pluralistic claims, [and which] must make a major and intentional investment in the practice of rhetoric, for the shape of reality finally depends on the power of speech" (Brueggemann, 71).

See also ACROSTIC; CHIASM; DISCOURSE IN PROVERBS; EDITORIAL CRITICISM; FORM CRITI-

CISM; FRAME NARRATIVE; HERMENEUTICS; INCLUSIO; MERISM; PERSONIFICATION; POETICS, TERMINOLOGY OF; TERSENESS; WORDPLAY.

BIBLIOGRAPHY. **L. C. Allen,** "The Value of Rhetorical Criticism in Psalm 69," *JBL* 105 (1986) 577-98; **Y. Amit,** "Progression as a Rhetorical Device in Biblical Literature, *JSOT* 28 (2003) 3-32; **J. R. Andrews,** *The Practice of Rhetorical Criticism* (New York: Macmillan, 1983); **W. H. Bellinger,** "Psalm 61: A Rhetorical Analysis," *PRSt* 26.4 (1999) 379-88; **S. B. Berg,** *The Book of Esther: Motifs, Themes and Structure* (SBLDS 44; Missoula, MT: Scholars Press, 1979); **A. Berlin,** "The Rhetoric of Psalm 145," in *Biblical and Related Studies Presented to Samuel Iwry,* ed. A. Kort and S. Morschauser (Winona Lake, IN: Eisenbrauns, 1985) 17-22; **W. Brueggemann,** *Theology of the Old Testament: Testimony, Dispute, Advocacy* (Minneapolis: Fortress, 1997); **K .K. Campbell,** "Modern Rhetoric," in *Encyclopedia of Rhetoric,* ed. T. O. Sloane (Oxford: Oxford University Press, 2001) 498-509; **D. J. A. Clines,** "The Arguments of Job's Three Friends," in *Art and Meaning: Rhetoric in Biblical Literature,* ed. D. J. A. Clines, D. M. Gunn and A. J. Hauser (JSOTSup 19; Sheffield: JSOT Press, 1982) 199-214; idem, *The Esther Scroll: The Story of the Story* (JSOTSup 30; Sheffield: JSOT Press, 1984); **J. H. Coetzee,** "Politeness Strategies in the So-Called 'Enemy Psalms': An Inquiry into Israelite Prayer Rhetoric," in *Rhetorical Criticism and the Bible,* ed. S. E. Porter and D. L. Stamps (JSOTSup 195; Sheffield: JSOT Press, 2002) 209-36; **C. J. Collins,** "Psalm 1: Structure and Rhetoric," *Presbyterion* 31.1 (2005) 37-48; **J. E. Course,** *Speech and Response: A Rhetorical Analysis of the Introductions to the Speeches of the Book of Job (Chaps. 4-24)* (CBQMS 25; Washington, DC: Catholic Biblical Association of America, 1994); **C. V. Dorothy,** *The Books of Esther: Structure, Genre and Textual Integrity* (JSOTSup 187; Sheffield: JSOT Press, 1997); **D. A. Dorsey,** "Lamentations: Communicating Meaning through Structure," *EvJ* 6 (1988) 83-90; idem, "Literary Structuring in the Song of Songs," *JSOT* 46 (1990) 81-96; idem, *The Literary Structure of the Old Testament: A Commentary on Genesis-Malachi* (Grand Rapids: Baker, 1999); **T. Forti,** "The Fly and the Dog: Observations on Ideational Polarity in the Book of Qoheleth," in *Seeking Out the Wisdom of the Ancients: Essays Offered to Honor Michael V. Fox on the Occasion of His Sixty-Fifth Birthday,* ed. R. L. Troxel, K. G. Friebel and D. R. Magary (Winona Lake, IN: Eisen-

brauns, 2005) 235-55; **M. V. Fox,** "Job 38 and God's Rhetoric," *Semeia* 19 (1981) 53-81; idem, "Ideas of Wisdom in Proverbs 1-9," *JBL* 116 (1997) 613-33; idem, "The Rhetoric of Disjointed Proverbs," *JSOT* 29 (2004) 165-77; **D. P. Gaonkar,** "Contingency and Probability," in *Encyclopedia of Rhetoric,* ed. T. O. Sloane (Oxford: Oxford University Press, 2001) 151-66; **Y. Gitay,** "Rhetorical Criticism," in *To Each Its Own Meaning: An Introduction to Biblical Criticisms and Their Application,* ed. S. L. McKenzie and S. R. Haynes (Louisville: Westminster John Knox, 1993) 135-49; **R. G. Hall,** "Ancient Historical Method and the Training of an Orator," in *The Rhetorical Analysis of Scripture: Essays from the 1995 London Conference,* ed. S. E. Porter and T. H. Olbricht (JSNTSup 146; Sheffield: Sheffield Academic Press, 1997) 103-18; **K. M. Heim,** *Like Grapes of Gold Set in Silver: An Interpretation of Proverbial Clusters in Proverbs 10:1-22:16* (BZAW 273; Berlin: de Gruyter, 2001); **N. Kamano,** "Character and Cosmology: Rhetoric of Qoh 1,3-3,9," in *Qohelet in the Context of Wisdom,* ed. A. Schoors (BETL 136; Leuven: Leuven University Press, 1998) 419-24; **R. Kimelman,** "Theme, Structure, and Impact," *JBL* 113 (1994) 37-58; **E. P. Lee,** *The Vitality of Enjoyment in Qohelet's Theological Rhetoric* (BZAW 353; Berlin: de Gruyter, 2005); **J. R. Lundbom,** *Jeremiah: A Study in Ancient Hebrew Rhetoric* (2nd ed.; Winona Lake, IN: Eisenbrauns, 1997); idem, "Hebrew Rhetoric," in *Encyclopedia of Rhetoric,* ed. T. O. Sloane (Oxford: Oxford University Press, 2001) 325-28; **M. J. Lynch,** "Bursting at the Seams: Phonetic Rhetoric in the Speeches of Elihu," *JSOT* 30 (2006) 345-64; **D. R. Magary,** "Answering Questions, Questioning Answers: the Rhetoric of Interrogatives in the Speeches of Job and His Friends," in *Seeking Out the Wisdom of the Ancients: Essays Offered to Honor Michael V. Fox on the Occasion of His Sixty-Fifth Birthday,* ed. R. L. Troxel, K. G. Friebel and D. R. Magary (Winona Lake, IN: Eisenbrauns, 2005) 283-98; **D. B. Miller,** *Symbol and Rhetoric in Ecclesiastes: The Place of Hebel in Qohelet's Work* (SBLAB 2; Atlanta: Society of Biblical Literature, 2002); **J. Muilenburg,** "Form Criticism and Beyond," *JBL* 88 (1969) 1-18; **T. H. Olbricht,** "The Flowering of Rhetorical Criticism in America," in *The Rhetorical Analysis of Scripture: Essays from the 1995 London Conference,* ed. S. E. Porter and T. H. Olbricht (JSNTSup 146; Sheffield: Sheffield Academic Press, 1997) 79-102; **D. Patrick and A. Scult,**

Rhetoric and Biblical Interpretation (JSOTSup 82; Sheffield: Almond, 1990); **G. D. Pemberton,** "The Rhetoric of the Father in Proverbs 1-9," *JSOT* 30 (2005) 63-82; **D. F. Rauber,** "Literary Values in the Bible: The Book of Ruth," *JBL* 89 (1970) 27-37; repr. as "The Book of Ruth," in *Literary Interpretations of Biblical Narratives,* ed. K. R. R. Gros Louis (Nashville: Abingdon, 1974) 163-76; **B. Rebera,** "Lexical Cohesion in Ruth: A Sample," in *Perspectives on Language and Text: Essays and Poems in Honour of Francis I. Andersen's Sixtieth Birthday,* ed. E. W. Conrad and E. G. Newing (Winona Lake, IN: Eisenbrauns, 1987) 123-49; **J. Renkema,** "The Literary Structure of Lamentations (I)," in *The Structural Analysis of Biblical and Canaanite Poetry,* ed. W. van der Meer and J. C. de Moor (JSOTSup 74; Sheffield: JSOT Press, 1988a) 294-320; idem, "The Literary Structure of Lamentations (II)," in *The Structural Analysis of Biblical and Canaanite Poetry,* ed. W. van der Meer and J. C. de Moor (JSOTSup 74; Sheffield: JSOT Press, 1988b), 321-46; idem, "The Literary Structure of Lamentations (III)," in *The Structural Analysis of Biblical and Canaanite Poetry,* ed. W. van der Meer and J. C. de Moor (JSOTSup 74; Sheffield: JSOT Press, 1988c) 347-60; idem, "The Literary Structure of Lamentations (IV)," in *The Structural Analysis of Biblical and Canaanite Poetry,* ed. W. van der Meer and J. C. de Moor (JSOTSup 74; Sheffield: JSOT Press, 1988d) 361-96; idem, *Lamentations,* trans. B. Doyle (HCOT; Leuven: Peeters, 1998); **V. K. Robbins,** *Exploring the Texture of Texts: A Guide to Socio-Rhetorical Interpretation* (Valley Forge, PA: Trinity Press International, 1996); idem, "The Present and Future of Rhetorical Analysis," in *The Rhetorical Analysis of Scripture: Essays from the 1995 London Conference,* ed. S. E. Porter and T. H. Olbricht (JSNTSup 146; Sheffield: Sheffield Academic Press, 1997) 24-52; **G. D. Salyer,** *Vain Rhetoric: Private Insight and Public Debate in Ecclesiastes* (JSOTSup 327; Sheffield: JSOT Press, 2001); **E. Schüssler Fiorenza,** *Rhetoric and Ethic: the Politics of Biblical Studies* (Minneapolis: Fortress, 1999); **M. S. Smith,** "Setting and Rhetoric in Psalm 23," *JSOT* 41 (1988) 61-66; **G. Snyman,** "Identification and the Discourse of Fundamentalism: Reflections on a Reading of the Book of Esther," in *Rhetorical Criticism and the Bible,* ed. S. E. Porter and D. L. Stamps (JSOTSup 195; Sheffield: JSOT Press, 2002) 160-208; **P. Trible,** *Rhetorical Criticism: Context, Method, and the Book of Jonah* (Min-

neapolis: Fortress, 1994); **P. van der Lugt,** *Rhetorical Criticism and the Poetry of the Book of Job* (OtSt 32; Leiden: Brill, 1995); **H. Viviers,** "Elihu (Job 32-37), Garrulous but Poor Rhetor? Why Is He Ignored?" in *The Rhetorical Analysis of Scripture: Essays from the 1995 London Conference,* ed. S. E. Porter and T. H. Olbricht (JSNTSup 146; Sheffield: Sheffield Academic Press, 1997) 137-53; idem, "The Rhetoricity of the 'Body' in the Song of Songs," in *Rhetorical Criticism and the Bible,* ed. S. E. Porter and D. L. Stamps (JSOTSup 195; Sheffield: JSOT Press, 2002) 237-55; **B. K. Waltke,** *The Book of Proverbs* (2 vols.; NICOT; Grand Rapids: Eerdmans, 2004-2005); **D. F. Watson and A. J. Hauser,** *Rhetorical Criticism of the Bible: A Comprehensive Bibliography with Notes on History and Method* (BIS 4; Leiden: E. J. Brill, 1994); **M. Weiss,** *The Bible from Within: the Method of Total Interpretation* (Jerusalem: Magnes, 1984); **E. R. Wendland,** "Structural Symmetry and Its Significance in the Book of Ruth," in *Issues in Bible Translation,* ed. P. C. Stine (UBSMS 3; London: United Bible Societies, 1988) 30-63; **T. Willis,** "'So Great Is His Steadfast Love': A Rhetorical Analysis of Psalm 103," *Bib* 72 (1991) 525-37.

P. Overland

RHYME. *See* POETICS, TERMINOLOGY OF; SOUND PATTERNS.

RHYTHM. *See* POETICS, TERMINOLOGY OF.

RIGHTEOUSNESS

In English Bible translations the word *righteousness* is used as the equivalent of the Hebrew nouns *ṣedeq* and *ṣĕdāqâ*. According to some scholars, the basic meaning of these nouns and their cognates *ṣdq* ("be righteous") and *ṣaddîq* ("righteous") denotes conformity with a norm or standard (Reimer, 746). Others define the basic meaning as denoting community loyalty (Koch, *THAT* 2.515 = *TLOT* 1051-52; von Rad 1957, 368-72 = 1962, 370-74) or underscore the notion of proper order (Scullion).

These various suggestions need not be mutually exclusive, as the words involved can have different meanings in different contexts. Generally speaking, however, one could maintain that when these words are attributed to persons or things, the nature or acts of these persons or things accord with what may be expected from them (cf. e.g., "sacrifices of righteousness" in Ps 4:5 and "paths of righteousness" in Ps 23:3; see

Kwakkel, 42-44, 156, 244).

This article mainly deals with texts in *Job, *Psalms, *Proverbs, *Ecclesiastes and *Lamentations, in which most English versions have "righteousness" or "righteous." In addition, some texts will be discussed in which one of the Hebrew words just mentioned usually is translated differently—for instance, by "right" or "innocent." Admittedly, the idea of righteousness is not totally absent in *Ruth, *Esther and *Song of Songs. However, these books are not included here because they lack the Hebrew words in question.

1. Psalms and Lamentations
2. Proverbs
3. Ecclesiastes
4. Job

1. Psalms and Lamentations.

1.1. The Righteousness of God.

1.1.1. A Virtue of God as Judge and King. In several psalms God is praised or invoked because of his righteousness. Righteousness is one of the most outstanding virtues of his being the judge of his people and of the whole world.

Psalms 96—99 are *hymns in which God is glorified as king of all the earth. As such, he will judge all the peoples in righteousness (Ps 96:13; 98:9). Righteousness and justice are the foundation of his throne (Ps 97:2). Psalm 50 announces God's coming as the judge of his people Israel; at his coming, the heavens proclaim his righteousness (Ps 50:6).

As a judge, God also makes use of his righteousness to settle personal conflicts in which his servants are involved. Accordingly, Psalm 35:24 says, "Vindicate me, O LORD my God, according to your righteousness." If God indeed vindicates his servants, they will praise him because of the righteousness that he shows in dealing with their situation (Ps 7:17; 35:28).

The beneficial results of God's righteousness are stressed in all psalms in which it is referred to. God's righteousness brings about the deliverance of those who are in distress because of unjust charges or persecution by enemies (Ps 31:1; 71:2). "The LORD works righteousness and justice for all the oppressed" (Ps 103:6 NIV). God's right hand, filled with righteousness, protects Zion against hostile kings who attack the city of the Lord (Ps 48:10).

By virtue of God's intervention as a righteous judge, order is restored among his people and all over the world. This implies, first of all, that

the wicked are checked and that the righteous can live safely and freely (Ps 7:9; 9). However, the results of God's righteousness extend much further than that. Psalm 65:9-13 describes what will happen when God answers his people with awesome deeds of righteousness (Ps 65:5): their land will abound in water, crops and flocks, and the valleys will shout for joy and sing (see also Ps 72:16; 85:12). In a similar vein, the hymns about God's kingship proclaim the gladness of the heavens, earth, sea, fields, forests, rivers and mountains when he will have come to judge the world (Ps 96:10-13; 98:4-9).

Of course, God's righteousness as a judge implies that he judges honestly. His verdicts are in accordance with the facts and the norms of justice (see, e.g., Ps 98:9, where *ṣedeq* ["righteousness"] is paralleled by *mēšārîm* ["equity"]). Such righteous judgment is clearly a blessing for society. But as a righteous judge, God does not limit himself to the strict administration of justice, as if he were a judge who is interested not in the people before him but only in the application of the *law. This is evident particularly in those texts in which God's righteousness is mentioned as a synonymous parallel to his salvation (Ps 71:15; 98:2) or in which it is bracketed with words such as "love," "truth," "faithfulness," "peace," "goodness" and "compassion" (Ps 40:10; 89:14; 145:7-9). Psalm 51 even refers to God's righteousness as grounds for the remission of terrible sins, for the psalmist says that his tongue will sing of God's righteousness if God saves him from bloodguilt (Ps 51:14; see also Ps 103:3, 6, 10, 12, 17; 143:1-2).

All this could be summarized by saying that God's righteousness stands for his dealing with his people and the world in a way that accords with what could be expected from him in view of his promises. These promises are part and parcel of his covenants with Abraham, Israel and *David. It may strike us, then, that God's righteousness is only rarely associated with his *běrît* (the Hebrew word usually translated "covenant") in the psalms (the exceptions are Ps 50:5, 16; 89:3, 28, 34; 103:18; 111:5, 9; 132:12). In a larger sense, however, God's particular relationship with Israel is presupposed in many psalms that proclaim his righteousness, as can be inferred from expressions such as "my God" (Ps 7:1, 3; 22:1), "our God" (Ps 48:1, 8; 99:5) and "his faithfulness to the house of Israel" (Ps 98:3).

Given the positive nature of God's righteousness, it need not surprise us that some scholars have stated that the idea of a punitive righteousness of God is lacking in the OT (von Rad 1957, 389 = 1962, 377). The correct element in this view is that the aim of God's righteousness clearly is the redemption of his people or the salvation of the world. Punishment never figures as the main or the only purpose of God's intervention as a righteous judge (perhaps with the exception of Ps 50, which is dominated by God's accusations against the wicked). Yet redemption and salvation cannot be achieved if God does not proceed against the wicked. Accordingly, their fall is mentioned in several psalms as the indispensable corollary of God's intervention by virtue of his righteousness (e.g., Ps 7:11-16; 9:3, 5-6, 15-17, 20; 11:6). Therefore, one can claim that punishment is not the main goal of God's righteousness but is, nevertheless, part of it.

It might also be punitive righteousness that is alluded to in Lamentations 1:18 (Renkema, 179-81). Strictly speaking, however, the text simply says that in executing his judgments (described in the context) God is in the right; *Zion herself is the only one to blame, for she has rebelled against God's word.

1.1.2. God's Gift to People. Apart from being a virtue of God, righteousness is also mentioned in the psalms as a gift that he bestows on people. Thus, Psalm 72:1 prays to God for righteousness and justice for the Davidic king. The effect of this will be that the king will act as a righteous judge who defends the afflicted and helps the needy. Moreover, his country will be mighty and prosperous.

Similarly, Psalm 132:9 asks God to clothe his priests with righteousness. This is linked to God's promise to clothe the priests of Zion with salvation (Ps 132:16), which is associated with abundance of food (Ps 132:15). According to Psalm 24:5, God gives righteousness to those who come to the temple hill with clean hands and a pure heart, and who look forward to his favor (NIV and NRSV: "vindication" instead of "righteousness"). As the parallel in Psalm 24:5a makes clear, this righteousness is conceived of as a blessing to those who receive it. Both Psalm 24 and Psalm 132 show that righteousness is a gift of God that he distributes in the temple cult. This could also be the reason why the temple gates were called "the gates of righteousness," as may be inferred from Psalm 118:19-20.

1.2. The Righteousness of the People.

1.2.1. In Upholding the Law. Just like God as the judge of all the earth, people who have to act as judges should do so in righteousness. This applies most of all to the king (Ps 45:4, 7; 72:2), but also to other rulers (Ps 58:1; 82:2-3). If they refuse to rule in righteousness, the weak and the poor will fall prey to the injustice and the violence of the wicked (Ps 58:2-5; 82:2-4). In that case, the rulers must fear that God will come to the aid of the righteous by depriving the rulers of their high positions (Ps 58:6-11; 82:6-7).

1.2.2. In Daily Life. In many psalms the righteous are contrasted with the wicked. Unlike the wicked, the righteous fear God (Ps 31:19). They trust in him and take refuge in him (Ps 5:11-12; 37:3, 5). They love his commandments (Ps 37:31; 112:1). They turn from evil and steer clear of the wicked and their schemes (Ps 1:1; 34:14). They seek peace and further other people's well-being by sharing their goods with them (Ps 34:14; 37:21, 26). They do not use their tongues so as to harm other people; rather, they speak truth and wisdom (Ps 15; 37:30).

Quite often the righteous are to be found among the poor and needy (Ps 140:12-13; 146:7-9), while the wicked are rich and powerful (Ps 49:16-20; 73:3-5, 12). But even if they are in need for some time, the righteous are better off, for in the end they will surely prosper (Ps 34:8-10, 19-20; 37; 92:12-14). In Psalm 112:3, 9 the psalmist is so sure about this that "righteousness" is made almost synonymous with "prosperity," describing the blessings of the righteous by means of the phrase "their righteousness endures forever" (see also Ps 37:6).

1.2.3. In Conflicts. Many individual laments, but also psalms belonging to other genres, refer to conflicts between the righteous and the wicked (see also Lam 4:13, where the prophets and the priests are accused of killing the righteous). When appealing to God because of such threats, the psalmists clearly were convinced that they themselves belonged to the righteous. However, when praying to God, they never explicitly say that they are one of the righteous (i.e., a ṣaddiq). In Psalm 143:2 the psalmist even confesses that no one living is righteous before God.

Nevertheless, they do refer to their own righteousness (ṣedeq [Ps 7:8; 18:20, 24]). In some cases this primarily means that they claim innocence versus the accusations of their persecutors (Pss 7; 17). Yet their claims have a wider scope. The psalmists also claim to be loyal to

665

God in a more general sense. They demonstrate this loyalty by their very appeal to God (Ps 7:1; 17:1-2; 18:6) but also by being obedient to his commandments (Ps 17:5; 18:22).

None of this implies that they consider themselves to be free from sin. The issue at stake in the psalms in which people point to their own righteousness is not whether people can be totally free from sin or not; rather, what is at stake is that those who are loyal to God may expect him to deal with their case in a righteous way. That is, God will keep his promises by saving those who are faithful to him from the lethal attacks of those who rebel against him (Kwakkel, 291-304).

2. Proverbs.

2.1. A Gift of Wisdom. Right at the beginning of the book of Proverbs righteousness is mentioned next to wisdom, discipline, insight, justice, equity, knowledge and the like as one of the virtues that will be acquired by those who are willing to listen to the proverbs of *Solomon (Prov 1:2-6). At least some of the younger people who are addressed by these words may be expected to work as officials or rulers in the future (cf. Prov 1:8, 10; see Lemaire). Proverbs 8:15 says that kings and rulers can make righteous laws and decisions only if they get insight from wisdom, which is, in that chapter, presented as a lady who was brought forth by the Lord before the creation of the world (Prov 8:22-29). In Proverbs 31:8-9 the mother of King *Lemuel points to an important element of ruling in righteousness in that she associates righteous judgment with defending the rights of the poor and helpless.

2.2. A Fountain of Life. The collection of proverbs that opens in Proverbs 10:1 abounds with maxims in which the righteous are contrasted with the wicked. Yet it does not spend many words defining righteousness and righteous behavior. It says, for instance, that righteousness in speech implies that one speaks the truth, and that the mouth of the righteous brings forth wisdom (Prov 10:31; 12:17; 16:13). The righteous hate falsehood (Prov 13:5), they think seriously before they answer (Prov 15:28), and they make just plans (Prov 12:5). They are good and generous to their neighbors, especially the poor, as well as their animals (Prov 12:10; 21:26; 29:7). In times of need they take refuge in the name of the Lord (Prov 18:10). They do not trust in their riches (Prov 11:28). In short, they lead a blameless life (Prov 20:7). Most of these things could be linked with the instructions of God as these can be found in, for instance, the Pentateuch, but Proverbs refrains from doing so; it does not define righteousness in terms of obedience to the laws of Moses.

Many more words are devoted to the beneficial effects of righteousness for the righteous themselves. Righteousness delivers people from death, trouble and punishment (Prov 10:2; 11:8, 21; 12:21). The lives of the righteous are secure, fruitful and prosperous (Prov 12:12, 28; 13:21; 16:31). Their desires will be granted (Prov 10:24). They will receive joy and honor (Prov 10:28; 14:19; 21:21). And although righteousness itself is better than wealth (Prov 11:4; 16:8), the righteous may be sure that they will also receive riches (Prov 13:22; 15:6). In short, "He who sows righteousness reaps a sure reward" (Prov 11:18 NIV).

In most cases these effects are not explicitly ascribed to the intervention of God. One often gets the impression that righteousness rewards itself, while the wicked are punished by their own wickedness. Note, for instance, Proverbs 10:2b, "Righteousness delivers from death," and Proverbs 11:5b, "The wicked falls by his own wickedness" (see also Prov 11:6; 12:13; 13:6; 29:6). According to K. Koch, the concept behind these texts is that good and bad actions create a sphere of influence in which the built-in consequences of an action (i.e., well-being or mischief respectively) take effect. This does not imply that God is not involved at all. He surely is, but not as a judge who distributes rewards and punishments that have no inherent relationship to the human actions themselves. His role rather is to set the built-in consequences of human actions in motion and bring them to fulfillment (Koch 1972, 134-38, 150-52, 166-67 = 1983, 60-62, 70-72, 74, 78; *THAT* 2.517 = *TLOT* 1053).

Several texts in Proverbs indeed refer to the active involvement of the Lord (e.g., Prov 10:3; 15:3, 9, 29). These texts should not be contrasted to others that do not explicitly mention God's activities. Instead, it can be maintained that when the latter texts are read in the context of the book of Proverbs as a whole, they presuppose in some way or another the involvement of God. However, the way in which God is involved (i.e., as a judge or otherwise) does not seem to be the main point of interest of the proverbs. What they are claiming is that righteousness certainly will be rewarded, and wickedness surely will lead to disaster (even if one may have to wait some time before these effects are realized [Prov 28:28; 29:16]). The pointed form of the maxims contributes considerably to the powerful expression of this firm conviction (see Janowski, 181-83).

3. Ecclesiastes.
It is precisely this conviction in Proverbs that is challenged in Ecclesiastes. *Qohelet knows that God will judge both the righteous and the wicked, and that it will not go well with the wicked (Eccles 3:17; 8:13). Yet he observes that the righteous and the wicked share the same fate (Eccles 9:2). Sometimes righteous people even get what the wicked deserve, whereas wicked people get what should be reserved for the righteous (Eccles 8:14).

The idea that what one sees need not agree with what should be might also be found in Ecclesiastes 7:15—that is, if the text is read as follows: "(I saw) a righteous person perishing despite his righteousness and a wicked person prolonging his life despite his wickedness." One could, however, also read "through" instead of "despite." This interpretation fits the next verse (Eccles 7:16) quite well, as it warns against excessiveness in pursuing righteousness and wisdom. Such zealotry ends in bewilderment or self-destruction because it does not take into account that no one on earth is so righteous as to do good without ever sinning (Eccles 7:20). Moreover, it gives evidence of too high a view of what people can achieve, which contrasts with the humility of those who fear God (Eccles 7:18).

It is clear, then, that in its discussion of righteousness and its effects, Ecclesiastes differs considerably from Proverbs. Nevertheless, they firmly agree with each other in that both point to the *fear of the Lord as the only attitude that befits people and that leads to well being (Prov 1:7; 14:27; 22:4; Eccles 8:13; 12:13-14).

4. Job.
The dialogues of Job and his friends can well be interpreted as a debate about righteousness. Can Job be charged with unrighteousness? If not, how does his fate accord with God's righteousness?

Job's friends hold on to the traditional conviction that the upright will not perish, and that those who plow evil will reap trouble (e.g., Job 4:7-9). This must also apply to Job's case; otherwise, God would pervert justice and righteousness, which he does not (Job 8:3). The friends then account for Job's plight, first, by pointing to the fact that humans cannot be righteous in the sight of God; in other words, God detects shortcomings that deserve to be punished even in those who are as pious as Job (Job 4:17-19; 15:14; 25:4) (see Clines, 112, 132; Reimer, 754). Second, they do not refrain from also accusing him of great wickedness (Job 22:5-9).

In Job 9:2 Job claims that a mortal cannot be righteous in the sight of God. Further on in this chapter, however, it turns out that he does not mean this in the same sense as do his friends. What Job is pointing out is that even if he is innocent, God will declare him guilty. If Job wants to dispute that, God is so powerful that he will always win.

As for himself, Job maintains his righteousness and refuses to deny his integrity (Job 27:5-6). This position is fleshed out in several passages in Job's speeches, most prominently in his oath of innocence in Job 31. In this chapter Job denies, among other things, having committed adultery, falsehood and idolatry. In Job 29:12-17 he defines his righteousness, which surrounded him as his clothing, in terms of help for the poor and needy, which corresponds with Job 31:16-23. He affirms that he has not departed from God's commandments (Job 23:10-12). As long as he lives, his conscience will not reproach him about anything (Job 27:6; see also Job 33:9).

All this agrees with the eulogies on Job's virtues by the narrator and by God himself in Job 1:1, 8; 2:3. If, then, the traditional view on *retribution held by Job's friends is true, Job feels urged to conclude that he is suffering wrongs at the hand of God (Job 16:6-14; 19:6-7; 27:2). The only way out of all this is for God himself to intervene as a judge so as to vindicate Job versus his friends and versus God himself. In spite of his skepticism uttered in Job 9—10, this is what Job asks at the end of his defense in Job 31:35-37 (see also Job 16:19-21; 19:25-27; 23). In this connection, *ṣdq* ("be righteous") should be given legal rather than moral connotations. In other words, it refers in a more concrete way to innocence or being right in a specific case.

Then *ṣdq* can be translated as "be right," "be vindicated" or "be innocent" (thus, e.g., Job 9:15, 20; 11:2; 13:18).

Finally, God fulfills Job's wish and begins to speak. He fires many critical questions at Job. Yet he never disputes what Job has said about his own upright behavior, nor does he endorse the view of Job's friends (contrast Job 42:7-8).

What God is reproaching Job with is the latter maintaining his own righteousness at the expense of God's righteousness (Job 40:8; in this God agrees with Elihu [see Job 32:2; 34:17]). On this point Job must renounce what he has so boldly declared (Job 40:1-5; 42:1-6). Consequently, the purport of God's speeches is that he, as God, is so great that people must trust that he is behaving righteously, even if they are puzzled by his dealings with them, and even if he does not reveal to them the grounds of his unusual behavior.

See also HONOR AND SHAME; MAAT; SUFFERING; THEODICY; WISDOM THEOLOGY.

BIBLIOGRAPHY. **D. J. A. Clines,** *Job 1-20* (WBC 17; Dallas: Word, 1989); **B. Janowski,** *Die Rettende Gerechtigkeit* (BTAT 2; Neukirchen-Vluyn: Neukirchener Verlag, 1999); **B. Johnson and H. Ringgren,** "*ṣādaq*," *ThWAT* 6.898-924 = *TDOT* 12.239-264; **K. Koch,** "Gibt es ein Vergeltungsdogma im Alten Testament?" in *Um das Prinzip der Vergeltung in Religion und Recht des Alten Testaments*, ed. K. Koch (WF 125; Darmstadt: Wissenschaftliche Buchgesellschaft, 1972) 130-80; ET (abridged), "Is There a Doctrine of Retribution in the Old Testament?" in *Theodicy in the Old Testament*, ed. J. L. Crenshaw (IRT 4; Philadelphia: Fortress, 1983) 57-87; idem, "*ṣdq* gemeinschaftstreu/heilvoll sein," *THAT* 2.507-30 = *TLOT* 1046-62; **G. Kwakkel,** "*According to My Righteousness*": *Upright Behaviour as Grounds for Deliverance in Psalms 7, 17, 18, 26 and 44* (OtSt 46; Leiden: E. J. Brill, 2002); **A. Lemaire,** "The Sage in School and Temple," in *The Sage in Israel and the Ancient Near East*, ed. J. G. Gammie and L. G. Perdue (Winona Lake, IN: Eisenbrauns, 1990) 165-81; **D. J. Reimer,** "צדק," *NIDOTTE* 3.744-69; **J. Renkema,** *Lamentations* (HCOT; Leuven: Peeters, 1998 [1993]); **H. G. Reventlow and Y. Hoffman,** eds., *Justice and Righteousness: Biblical Themes and Their Influence* (JSOTSup 137; Sheffield: JSOT Press, 1992); **J. J. Scullion,** "Righteousness," *ABD* 5.724-36; **G. von Rad,** *Theologie des Alten Testaments*, 1: *Die Theologie der geschichtlichen Überlieferung Israels* (Munich: Kaiser, 1957); ET, *Theology of the Old Testament*, 1: *The Theology of Israel's Historical Traditions* (New York: Harper & Row, 1962).   G. Kwakkel

ROCK, YAHWEH AS. *See* MOUNTAIN IMAGERY.

ROYAL IDEOLOGY. *See* ROYAL COURT.

ROYAL PSALMS. *See* KINGSHIP PSALMS.

ROYAL COURT

The royal court lies in the background of much that we read in the psalms and Wisdom literature. It is highly likely that both psalmody and wisdom were, to one degree or another, court-sponsored enterprises. That is not to say, of course, that there was no writing of psalms or practice of wisdom outside the royal courts, but there are many indications that the court of the kings of Israel, and later Judah, provided the backdrop to the authorship and use of certain psalms and also the context for the development of at least some of the Israelite wisdom traditions.

It is likely that several of the royal psalms were written to celebrate the major events of court life. For example, Psalm 2 probably was written to celebrate the enthronement of a new king in the line of *David, whereas a royal wedding is the likely *Sitz im Leben* for the penning of Psalm 45. In other psalms the king appears to lead the people in public worship, celebrating Yahweh's goodness to the covenant community (e.g., Ps 118), whereas yet others extol the significance of *Zion as the home of both temple and court, Yahweh and David (e.g., Ps 78:67-72; 122).

Throughout the ancient Near East wisdom traditions often were focused around the activities of the royal court. Kings were famed for their wisdom, and courtiers were schooled in the ways of wisdom so that they would be able to advise well. The Historical Books of the OT indicate that such associations between the royal court and wisdom applied every bit as much in Israel as with their neighbours. King *Solomon, for example, is seen as the archetypal wisdom ruler, and the historical narratives frequently point out the influence (for good or for evil) of counselors associated with the court. The psalms and wisdom writings are firmly set in the context of the royal court, a context that provides important background information for the interpretation of many of the poetic texts.

1. The Royal Court and the Psalms

2. The Royal Court and Wisdom
3. Conclusion

1. The Royal Court and the Psalms.

The book of *Psalms is ingrained with indications of court background and ideology. Kingship themes are played out, not only in the specifically royal psalms but also in many others where there are subtle indications of kingly origins (*see* Kingship Psalms). This should not take us by surprise, for there were many hymnic collections from the ancient Near East in which celebration of the achievements of kings plays a prominent role (see Starbuck, 80-83). There are three elements of the court background to the Psalter that particularly deserve our attention: (1) the Davidic superscriptions; (2) the democratization of psalms; (3) the royal ideology found in the psalms.

1.1. The Davidic Superscriptions. One of the key indications of court influence in the Psalter is the frequent occurrence of the *lĕdāwīd* ("of David") superscription (e.g., Ps 3:1; 4:1; 5:1). Some seventy-three psalms bear a Davidic title, and in many ways the figure of David dominates the book of Psalms. The meaning of the Davidic superscriptions is discussed elsewhere in the present volume (*see* Psalms 5: Titles); however, for our purposes, the psalms' repeated titular references to David serve, at the very least, to illustrate the strong ties between the kingly line and Israel's *hymns. So strong is this association that the *Midrash Tehillim* describes the five books of the Psalter as a Torah given by David akin to the Pentateuch given by Moses, and Rabbi Meir (*b. Pesah.* 117a) attributes the praises of all the psalms to David. The thoroughly Davidic flavor of the Psalter reflects a long-standing connection between court and psalmody. This association appears to have begun with David himself, but it continues throughout the generations of the Davidic line of kings. Speaking of the kingship psalms in particular, J. I. Durham (428) writes,

> Each of these psalms was very probably composed within the circle of the royal court of the Davidic dynasty and for purposes even more specific . . . than the canonical form of the psalm-texts may suggest. The psalms in general have undergone a process of democratisation by which psalms bound to quite specific contexts . . . have been universalised to make them applicable in Israel's

worship on a continuing basis. The royal psalms were subject to this process even more than . . . other psalm texts because they were applicable by design to all the Davidic kings, each David in succession. Even the psalms dealing with so specific an occasion as a royal wedding or a national disaster had repeated use. Otherwise, they would not have found place in the canonical Psalter.

It is difficult to say for sure how the link between the royal court and Israel's psalmody worked in reality. The origins of the association are most likely found in the Historical Books' presentation of King David as musician, author of psalms and sponsor of the musical setting of the Jerusalem temple (see 1 Sam 16:14-23; 2 Sam 1:17-27; 1 Chron 25). David certainly wrote psalms, but there are indications that this link went further than kingly authorship of the psalms. Other than Solomon, who is described as having written "one thousand and five songs" (1 Kings 4:32), and to whom two of the canonical psalms are dedicated (Pss 72; 127), the Historical Books do not point to David's descendants being prominent *writers* of psalms. So the royal court link with psalmody must be broader than simply the fact that David wrote psalms.

This, in turn, speaks to the question of the meaning of the *lĕdāwīd* superscriptions. Clearly, David wrote psalms, but probably this is not the root of all of the Davidic superscriptions (see Nogalski, 42-48; Wilson, 78-79). It seems likely that the *lĕdāwīd* superscription also indicates that psalms were written *about* one or other of the kings in David's line (all of Israel's and, later, Judah's kings from the time of Solomon onwards were "sons of David").

Take, for example, Psalm 20. This psalm has a *lĕdāwīd* superscription, yet it appears to be a prayer *for* the king and tribute to Yahweh for his deliverance *of* the king. The psalm itself is written in the third person, so the author is not speaking about himself, and it ends with the words "O Yahweh, save the king!"—an acclamation often used in support of the king but not usually voiced by the king himself. Therefore it seems that the psalms are influenced more broadly by the royal court. It is very likely that Psalm 20 and many of the other psalms with Davidic and other superscriptions were actually written by representative figures of the court circle and dedicated to the king of the day. These anonymous figures most likely were priests (Wilson, 386), prophets (Mays, 350) or *sages (Terrien, 303) who served within the royal sphere. Their participation in the writing and use of psalms underlines the strong association that existed between the royal court and psalmody.

1.2. Democratization. The Davidic superscriptions indicate something of the broad influence of the royal court on psalmody: certain kings penned psalms, but there were also psalms written in their honor, probably by a range of figures who served a variety of functions within the court (Croft, 179-81). What difference does court origin make to our understanding and interpretation of the psalms? In one sense, royal milieu makes very little difference for today's reader, yet there is a fairly profound significance to be drawn from the psalmic *Sitz im Leben.*

As we saw above, Durham points to "a process of democratisation by which psalms bound to quite specific contexts . . . have been universalised to make them applicable in Israel's worship on a continuing basis." This was a feature common to much of the hymnody of the ancient Near East, where hymns and poems originally intended for use in a specific context (often some event in life of the court) are later generalized for adoption in a wider context by a broad range of individuals. The net effect of this process of democratization is that many of the specifically royal aspects deriving from the court origins of the psalms have been diluted by their application to the whole of the covenant community. However, if we look closely we can see that indications of this royal background are still discernible.

The significance of the psalms' court setting is found in an interpretive invitation for readers of the psalms throughout all generations to see themselves as part the court of the king. There is a real sense in which the process of democratization is a two-way street. It takes the particular and generalizes it for application to many, but it also particularizes the many by inviting them to see themselves standing in the shoes of the king and his courtiers. A clear example of this is found in the association of the "blessed person" of Psalm 1 with the "king/son/anointed one" of Psalm 2. There are many lexical and thematic links that tie these two psalms together (McCann, 41-43), and the net effect of this close as-

sociation is to democratize the king of Psalm 2, but also to "royalize" the individual believer of Psalm 1. P. D. Miller (91-92) observes,

The dual introduction [Pss 1—2] creates a certain ambiguity for the reading of the psalms. The subject of the introduction is clearly the king against his enemies. But it is also the *ʾîš* [man] against the wicked, that is *anyone* who lives by the Torah of the Lord and thus belongs to the righteous innocent who cry out in these psalms. So one may not read these psalms as exclusively concerning rulers. . . . The ruler is the *ʾîš* of Psalm 1, but to no greater extent than any member of the community who delights in the law of the Lord and walks in the way of the righteous. . . . The *ʾîš* of Psalm 1 is as much a ruler as the ruler of Psalm 2 is an *ʾîš.*

So there is a sense in which democratization invites all subsequent readers of the psalms to see themselves in the court of the king. There is a very rich biblical imagery of access implied by the democratization of court imagery. We are invited to sing hymns of praise, to offer prayers of complaint, to meditate on word and world and wondrous works, all in the presence of the King. The human king, as representative of God to the people and the people to God, was assumed to have in some sense "special" rights of access to Yahweh. The democratization of the court-based psalms means that we, as readers, can see ourselves as having these same "privileged" rights of access before the throne of the High King—a rich image indeed.

1.3. Royal Ideology. The similarities between the court setting of the psalms and the court setting of other ancient Near Eastern hymnic collections gives rise to another question that should be addressed. To what extent does the expression found in the royal psalms reflect the inflated royalist ideology found in collections of royal hymns outside Israel? This is often referred to as *Hofstil* ("court style"). Many of the royal hymns of the ancient world presented a highly exaggerated view of the king: he is described in almost superhuman terms, his feats are elevated to epic status, and every conceivable superlative is adopted. From the time of H. Gunkel, some scholars have argued that the royal psalms, finding their root in the deferential practices of the court, actually express no more than this standard Near Eastern *Hofstil* in their celebration of the Davidic kingship.

Although the royal psalms definitely display deference towards the king, it would be a giant leap to equate this with the excesses of hyperbole found in some non-Israelite hymnic collections. The universal rule of the Davidic king, celebrated in poems such as Psalms 2; 110, is never attributed to the incredible abilities of the particular king but rather is firmly rooted in the fact that the king is Yahweh's chosen servant and it is Yahweh who rules the whole earth. The royal psalms of the Psalter are, in many ways, more about the kingship of Yahweh than they are about the rule of the human king, because human rule is never more than vice-regency. The rule of the king is one of derived authority; therefore it would be inaccurate to describe the psalms rooted in the royal court as displaying the *Hofstil* of Israel's neighbors (Waltke, 1111).

2. The Royal Court and Wisdom.

The OT Wisdom literature is also deeply ingrained with background themes and imagery derived from the court. Ancient Near Eastern wisdom schools normally were based around the royal court and served to prepare young men for service at court (the book of Daniel gives insight into this practice in the Babylonian royal court). Equally, many examples of ancient Egyptian wisdom texts that have been discovered seem to be geared around the preparation of young men for service at court (e.g., The Instruction of Amenemope). So it is right to ask whether the royal court is the natural didactic setting for Israel's Wisdom literature as well.

The evidence from the wisdom books themselves seems ambiguous. There is some mention, scattered throughout *Proverbs and *Ecclesiastes (e.g., Prov 14:35; 16:10-15; Eccles 8:1-4), of how one should behave before kings, but this could hardly be described as a major focus of the canonical wisdom books. In terms of content, taking the OT wisdom books at face value, we clearly see that their aim is not specifically to prepare young men for life at court but rather to prepare every reader to live life well. Nevertheless, although the Wisdom literature is not specifically aimed at equipping the next generation of the civil service, there are aspects of the royal background to wisdom that deserve further attention.

2.1. The Sage in the Royal Court. Although Isra-

el's wisdom practice seems to have extended far beyond the royal court to the family, the marketplace and every aspect of daily life, the Historical Books frequently point to the importance of royal counselors or sages. These figures would advise king and court in a wide variety of situations from legal matters to international diplomacy to military tactics, although there was never any guarantee that the king would follow wise counsel (Whybray, 133-37). The sages are key background players in many of the OT narratives, and their advice often had a climactic impact on the course of Israel's history. For example, 2 Samuel 15—17 points to the significance of good advice from royal advisers from the perspective of King David. He was well aware that a good adviser was a powerful force within the court and prayed for Ahithophel's advice to be thwarted (2 Sam 15:31). Another example of the significance of the sages within the royal court is found in 2 Kings 12, where King Rehoboam follows the wrong advice, and this leads to the division of the kingdom. So we see that the advisers to the court played a significant role in Israel and Judah's political and religious history.

2.2. King Solomon as Sage. Another key link between the royal court and the Wisdom literature is the presentation of King Solomon as the archetypal wise ruler and sage in 1 Kings 1—11. This passage is quite honest in its assessment of Solomon's many failings, and these are presented as an ironic denial of the wisdom with which he was gifted. However, 1 Kings 4:29-34; 10:1-13 present Solomon as practitioner of wisdom par excellence: the author of thousands of proverbs (reflected in the titles of the book of Proverbs), an expert on the natural world and a "big hitter" on the international stage of wisdom schools. There is a real sense in which Solomon becomes conceptually associated with the wisdom books, just as David is associated with psalmody and the Psalter. So we see that wisdom is not just the remit of the royal adviser but also is the purview of the king. However, as with psalmody once again, the extent to which this link between the king and wisdom continues throughout the Davidic line is far from clear. It appears that after the flowering of wisdom in the Israelite court during the reign of Solomon, there are only sporadic examples of wise kings (e.g., Hezekiah [Prov 25:1]).

The image of Solomon as sage is influential more broadly within Israel's wisdom tradition.

Perhaps the classic example of this is seen in the presentation of a "Solomonic" royal persona as the central character of Ecclesiastes. Traditionally, Solomon has been seen as the author of Ecclesiastes, even though the title of the book does not make this explicit claim and Solomonic authorship is difficult to reconcile with several elements of the text (see Longman, 2-9). However, the figure of *Qohelet in Ecclesiastes is consciously presented in the light of Solomon as kingly practitioner of wisdom (see Fox, 159-60; Longman, 57-58). This choice of persona for Qohelet (whether a real person or a literary creation) further indicates the pervasive influence of King Solomon as sage, and therefore of the royal court, within Israel's wisdom tradition.

3. Conclusion.

Although it is not often an explicit subject of debate in and of itself, Israel's royal court is a significant background motif within the Psalter and the OT Wisdom literature. King, kingship and the royal court provide the milieu for many of the psalms and for much of the books of Proverbs and Ecclesiastes. In many ways, the significance of the court background to these poetic texts is lost in the passage of time through the democratization of royal texts. However, it is still important for the reader to bear in mind that these texts find their roots in a royal setting. As we noted, it was often thought in the ancient world that the king had special rights of access to God and that courtiers had special access to the king; the democratization of these texts indicates that everyone who fears God has the same access to the divine court as any chosen representative throughout Israel's history. Another rich image derived from court background is found in one of the wisdom psalms, Psalm 73. We have noted the significance of the sage or royal adviser within the court, but the prayer of *Asaph to God in Psalm 73:24 turns that common image on its head to emphasize once again the access that every believer has into the court of the High King: "You guide me with your counsel, and afterwards you will take me into glory." The Writings are rife with images of advisers guiding the king with counsel, for good or for evil, but here we are reminded that all those who walk in the ways of Yahweh are guided by the counsel of the King himself.

See also DAVID; KINGSHIP PSALMS; SAGES, SCHOOLS, EDUCATION; SOLOMON.

BIBLIOGRAPHY. **S. J. L. Croft,** *The Identity of the Individual in the Psalms* (JSOTSup 44; Sheffield: JSOT Press, 1987); **J. I. Durham,** "The King as 'Messiah' in the Psalms," *RevExp* 81 (1984) 425-35; **M. V. Fox,** *A Time to Tear Down and a Time to Build Up: A Rereading of Ecclesiastes* (Grand Rapids: Eerdmans, 1999); **T. Longman III,** *The Book of Ecclesiastes* (NICOT; Grand Rapids: Eerdmans, 1998); **J. L. Mays,** *Psalms* (IBC; Louisville: John Knox, 1994); **J. C. McCann,** *A Theological Introduction to the Books of Psalms: The Psalms as Torah* (Nashville: Abingdon, 1993); **P. D. Miller,** "The Beginning of the Psalter," in *The Shape and Shaping of the Psalter,* ed. J. C. Mc-Cann (JSOTSup 159; Sheffield: JSOT Press, 1993) 83-92; **J. D. Nogalski,** "From Psalm to Psalms to Psalter," in *An Introduction to Wisdom Literature and the Psalms: Festschrift Marvin E. Tate,* ed. H. W. Ballard and W. D. Tucker (Macon, GA: Mercer University Press, 2000) 37-54; **S. R. A. Starbuck,** *Court Oracles in the Psalms: The So-Called Royal Psalms in Their Ancient Near Eastern Context* (SBLDS 172; Atlanta: Scholars Press, 1999); **S. Terrien,** *The Psalms: Strophic Structure and Theological Commentary* (ECC; Grand Rapids: Eerdmans, 2003); **B. K. Waltke,** "Theology of the Psalms," *NIDOTTE* 4.1100-1115; **R. N. Why-bray,** "The Sage in the Israelite Royal Court," in *The Sage in Israel and the Ancient Near East,* ed. J. G. Gammie and L. G. Perdue (Winona Lake, IN: Eisenbrauns, 1990) 133-39; **G. H. Wilson,** *Psalms,* vol. 1 (NIVAC; Grand Rapids: Zondervan, 2002).

J. A. Grant

RUTH 1: BOOK OF

The book of Ruth is widely recognized as a superlative literary achievement of ancient Israel. With its sensitive portrayal of *women in crisis, its admiration for a righteous man, and its profound theology it offers readers in every age not only a window into life in the ancient Near East but also inspiration for good and godly living.

1. Title
2. Date and Authorship
3. Genre and Intention
4. Literary Style
5. Canonical Position
6. Theological Message
7. Outline

1. Title.

The biblical book of Ruth derives its name from

one of its three main characters, the Moabite daughter-in-law of *Naomi and eventual husband of *Boaz. Ruth is named twelve times in the book but elsewhere in the Bible only in Matthew's genealogy of Jesus (Mt 1:5). That the book should be named after Ruth is remarkable for several reasons. First, Ruth was not an Israelite. She was a Moabite—a fact that the narrator and Boaz emphasize by their repeated references to her as "Ruth the Moabite" (Ruth 1:22; 2:2, 21; 4:5, 10; see also Ruth 2:6). This is the only book in the OT *canon named after a non-Israelite. Second, it is not clear that Ruth is the main character of the book. Admittedly, she appears as a significant character in more episodes than does either Naomi or Boaz, but the book opens by describing the crisis in Naomi's family, highlighting her own emptiness, and concludes with the resolution of her crisis and the declaration of her fullness in the birth of Obed. Indeed in all of Ruth 4 the narrator appears intent on drawing readers' attention away from Ruth. This impression of the secondary role of Ruth is reinforced by the manner in which the characters relate in the account. Scholars have recognized the importance of direct speech in this book. Of the 1,294 words in the book, 678 occur on the lips of the characters. However, of the three main actors in the drama, Ruth speaks least often, and her speeches are the shortest (Block 1999, 588). Based on the plot, the book could be titled "The Book of Naomi," but on the basis of the dialogue, the concluding episode and the final genealogy, "The Book of Boaz," also would be appropriate.

2. Date and Authorship.

Although the Talmud attributed the authorship of both Judges and Ruth to Samuel (b. B. Bat. 14b-15a), like the rest of the books in the OT and most literary texts from the ancient Near East, the book offers no hint of interest in the identity of its author. Efforts to date the book must be deduced from the internal evidence—language and style, historical allusions, themes. However, the frustratingly inconsistent nature of the evidence has led to a wide range of dates, from the time of *David to the postexilic period. Since J. Wellhausen, critical scholars have tended to date Ruth in the postexilic period. This conclusion is based upon five principal arguments: (1) the language of the book, particularly its alleged Aramaisms and late Hebrew

forms of expression (Bush, 22-30; Fischer, 86-88); (2) the legal customs reflected, specifically the need to explain the ceremony of the sandal in Ruth 4:7, which presupposes a time when the practice was no longer understood; (3) the interest in genealogies expressed in Ruth 4:18-22, recalling the "priestly" genealogies in the Pentateuch and Chronicles, especially 1 Chronicles 2:3-15; (4) the extremely favorable portrayal of Ruth the Moabite, which, along with Jonah, balances the narrow ethnocentrism of Ezra and Nehemiah (Ezra 10; Neh 13:23-27); (5) the allusions to the allegedly postexilic "Deuteronomic" work of Judges, especially Ruth 1:1; (6) The canonical placement of Ruth among the Writings (Hagiographa), rather than the (Former) Prophets, suggesting that the latter section had been closed (Nash, 350-51).

In the face of the problem of subjectivity of some of these arguments, F. Bush has attempted to base discussions of the date and provenance of the book of Ruth on more objective footings by focusing particularly on the language of the book. Taking advantage of the work of several recent diachronic analyses of biblical texts, Bush observes that the author employed at least ten linguistic features that are characteristic of standard biblical Hebrew (SBH), which is preexilic by definition (see Hebrew Language). These features tempt one to affirm the assertion by E. F. Campbell (26) that "no linguistic datum points unerringly toward a later date."

But how early should we date the book? Some contend that the book was composed during David's lifetime as an apology for his kingship. The narratives in the books of Samuel suggest that resistance to David's rule persisted throughout his reign. Such opposition came most naturally from the Saulide party, particularly Benjaminites and others from the northern tribes who resented the favoritism with which they perceived David to be treating Judah (2 Sam 19:40—20:2). One can imagine the opposition demeaning David by pointing to his lowly origins in Bethlehem (Mic 5:2) and the contemptuous Moabite connection in his genealogy. Against this backdrop the author intentionally highlights Bethlehem, as an oasis of tranquility and honor in the troubled period of the judges, and Ruth, David's Moabite ancestress, as a paragon of virtue. Noting the narrator's rare literary talent, sensitive disposition toward women, access to the family traditions, devout Yahwistic faith and the literary integrity of the book (it is not simply cheap propaganda), M. Gow (207-10) speculates that Nathan may have been the author.

Others who find in Ruth a pro-Davidic polemic date its composition in the reign of *Solomon (Nielsen, 21-29; cf. Hubbard 1988, 46). On the one hand, some of his subjects may have questioned his character and his right to rule, since he achieved the throne through intrigue and violent elimination of other contenders (1 Kings 1—2). This opposition increased toward the end of his reign (1 Kings 12). On the other hand, the long and relatively peaceful reign of Solomon provided an ideal context for the flourishing of culture, which finds one of its fullest blooms in the book of Ruth. Literarily, the book of Ruth bears a closer resemblance to the so-called Yahwist narratives of Genesis and the stories in Samuel than the accounts in Chronicles and the book of *Esther. Recognizing that the book tells a woman's story, A. Bledstein argues that the book is the work of a female author, perhaps Tamar, the daughter of David, and great-great-granddaughter of Ruth [and namesake of another Tamar involved in the same issues as are dealt with in Ruth], who had herself experienced the tragedies that befell even royal women in a patriarchal culture.

Citing a series of clichés and phrases that have affinities with early Israelite literature but are not found after the period of Elisha, and interpreting the alleged Aramaisms (see below) as evidences of a Northern Hebrew dialect, M. Weinfeld suggests that the book may have been composed in northern Israel during the time of Elisha (*EncJud* 14.518-22). Although he does not explain why this idyllic account of David's origins would have been an issue for a northern author, one might speculate that a century after the northern kingdom had split off from the Davidic house the book may have been written to convince northerners to abandon their kings and reunite with Judah. However, the book lacks any hint of polemics against the kings of northern Israel. The renaissance of the Davidic house under Hezekiah (716-687 BC) also could have inspired the book of Ruth. In the opening thesis statement of the account of Hezekiah's reign the historian observes that Hezekiah did right in the sight of Yahweh according to all that his ancestor David had done (2 Kings 18:3), and that Yahweh was with him (2 Kings 18:7), which

recalls two similar comments concerning David in 1 Samuel 16:18; 18:14. Even the note that Hezekiah defeated the Philistines (2 Kings 18:8) may be intended to link him with David (cf. 2 Sam 5:17-25).

Earlier we noted that the book of Ruth shares a series of linguistic features with standard biblical Hebrew (SBH), which seemed to suggest that the book derives from preexilic times. However, the situation is complicated by an equally impressive series of features that push it in the direction of late biblical Hebrew (LBH), perhaps as late as the Persian period (Sperling, 594). Bush (24-30) concludes that the author of Ruth cannot have lived earlier than Ezekiel, whose work reflects the linguistic transition between SBH and LBH. At the earliest, the work could have been composed in the late preexilic or early exilic period, though the cluster of late and Aramaic features in Ruth 4:7 suggests an early postexilic date, perhaps shortly after 538 BC. Recognizing that languages do indeed evolve from generation to generation, Bush has attempted to put the dating of the book on more objective grounds than the subjective ideological or thematic bases that have been appealed to in earlier studies. The faithful in Israel, particularly those associated with the Davidic house, and perhaps women in general, will have delighted in this story of a resourceful Naomi and her courageous foreign-born daughter-in-law and passed it on from generation to generation by word of mouth. In fact, although the language of narrative (in contrast to poetry) tends to be updated with the retelling in each generation, some of the archaic features may represent linguistic fossils from earlier times. Bush suggests that the author's aim was to present Naomi, Ruth and Boaz as models of *hesed* for his readers to emulate. However, as secondary objectives, the book also affirms God's absolute control over the affairs of this world and his providential involvement in the lives of individuals. The link with David in the dénouement and conclusion/coda (Ruth 4:17-22) elevates both the story and David by focusing the reader's attention on developments beyond the events of the account, and by reflecting David's worth "through the quality of life of his forbears" (Bush, 53). Whereas a previous generation of scholars dismissed Ruth 4:17-22 (exclusive of Ruth 4:17c) as a postexilic "priestly" addition to the story, Bush highlights its role as the capstone of the book.

On the surface, Bush appears to have adduced strong arguments for a late exilic provenance. However, since the entire OT represents but a linguistic fragment of the full Hebrew language spoken in ancient Israel, we do well to hold loosely to our reconstructions of the history of language. If the book of Ruth derives from late exilic or early postexilic times, the fact that scholars have found only eight clearly late features in a composition of 1,294 words is remarkable. But if the Aramaisms and supposedly late features are evidences of a dialect spoken and written some distance from Jerusalem/Judah, then other possibilities emerge.

Beyond the linguistic considerations, the reference to "the days when judges governed" in the opening verse suggests that the author was familiar with the record of the premonarchic period as a distinct era found in the book of Judges. The ignoble qualities of most of the characters in the book of Judges cast into even sharper relief the nobility and integrity of the characters in Ruth. If the book of Judges was composed to alert what remained of the nation of Israel to the people's spiritual declension during the reign of wicked Manasseh (Block 1999, 64-67), it is unlikely that Ruth was composed before the latter half of the seventh century BC.

The book's interest in the Davidic house may be best interpreted against the backdrop of the renaissance of the dynasty under the reign of Josiah (540-609 BC) (Sasson, 230-32). Not only is the tender-heartedness of Boaz explicitly attributed to Josiah (2 Kings 22:19), but also Josiah is the only king whose fidelity to the covenant as outlined in Deuteronomy is characterized as "turning to Yahweh with all his heart/mind *[lēbāb]*, and with all his being *[nepheš]*, and with all his resources *[mē'ōd]*" (2 Kings 23:25 [on this as a quality of Boaz, see further discussion below]). Furthermore, the Moabite connection surfaces in the observation that Josiah removed the high place in Jerusalem that Solomon had built for Chemosh, "the abomination of Moab" (2 Kings 23:13). By highlighting the personal and spiritual integrity of "Ruth the Moabite," the author may be diffusing charges by Josiah's detractors that blood of the despicable Moabites flowed through the veins of the king. This date is late enough to accommodate the cultural and chronological distance required between the composition of Ruth 4:7 and the events described in this chapter. Apparently, the original readership was no longer familiar with the custom of the sandal. It may also account for some of the book's LBH and Aramaic features. Although Bush (30) opts for an early postexilic period for the book of Ruth, he acknowledges the possibility of a date in the late preexilic period.

Like all other proposals for the date of composition for the book of Ruth, my suggestion is provisional and subject to critique. Even if it is correct, the identity of the author remains unresolved. If the book was written by a resident of the territory once part of the northern kingdom, that person could either be a Judean who had moved north or a survivor of the Assyrian conquest and occupation. But why would a resident of the north have composed a literary piece involving a Judahite family from Bethlehem from half a millennium earlier? Perhaps some in the north had objected to Josiah's political ambitions and denigrated his character by highlighting the ethnic blemish in the royal family. This tractate responds by demonstrating that nobility is more than an issue of blood; it is a matter of character. Both Boaz and Ruth represent all that was virtuous and authentically pious *(hesed)* in Israel's own covenantal tradition. Furthermore, the fact that a foreigner such as Ruth could be so thoroughly integrated into the life and faith of Israel opened the door to non-Israelites living in the Assyrian province. With her immortal declaration in Ruth 1:16-17, this Moabite serves as a model for all aliens: if they will cast their lot in with the people of Israel and commit themselves to Yahweh their God, they too may find a home in the covenant community.

Perhaps more important than silencing Josiah's detractors, with this book the author celebrated the return of his own region to the only legitimate dynasty the Israelites had ever known. The narrator undoubtedly drew on traditions based in Bethlehem, but the story of the rise of the house of David from the chaos of the premonarchic period must have been rehearsed with delight throughout the nation's history. The linguistic features that link this work with early biblical Hebrew may represent echoes of earlier versions of the story, but in retelling the story for the present generation, the author sought to inspire his fellow northerners to cast their lot with the revived Davidic house. Perhaps in the story he found grounds for hope for his own time. Just as Yahweh had preserved the lineage of David through the dark days of the judges, so also he had preserved the residents of the north through the night of Assyrian domination. The book of Ruth is a testimony to the blessing that comes to those who will live in faithful covenant relationship with God (*hesed*) and to God's providential hand upon the house of David. In claiming Ruth as an ancestor, the Davidic dynasty has nothing to be ashamed of. On the contrary, she symbolizes the universal scope of the Davidic covenant implied by the enigmatic but profound affirmation in 2 Samuel 7:19: "This is the instruction/revelation for humanity *[tôrat hāʾādam]*."

In view of the composition's obvious interest in women and its sympathetic portrayal of events from a female point of view, some have proposed a female author (Bledstein; cf. Fischer, 93-94). However, the narrator's obvious sympathy toward women does not mean that a man could not have authored it, any more than that an optimist could not have been responsible for the final form of *Ecclesiastes. Analogous to Ecclesiastes, which consists largely of *Qohelet's personal account of life (cast in *autobiographical form) but is framed by the perspectives of a third person (Eccles 1:1-11; 12:8-14), the book of Ruth incorporates stories told from a woman's perspective. However, the opening paragraph (Ruth 1:1-5) and most of the final chapter (Ruth 4:1-13), but especially the concluding genealogy (Ruth 4:17b-22), obviously represent traditional male perspectives (see Bauckham). We cannot a priori rule out the possibility of a woman having authored the book. However, given the paucity of evidence for female literary activity in Israel and in the world around, the theory seems strained. It is better to focus on the gender perspective of the book than on the gender of its author (so also Meyers, 89) (*see* Feminist Interpretation).

3. Genre and Intention.
Generically, the book of Ruth divides into two unequal parts: (1) a complex narrative account constructed with a typical plot leading from problem/crisis (Ruth 1:1-5 [cf. Ruth 1:21]) to resolution (Ruth 4:13-17); (2) a short genealogy (Ruth 4:18-22). We begin by considering the latter first because the issues are simpler.

3.1. The Concluding Genealogy. Structurally, the genealogy consists of a formal heading, *wĕʾēlleh tôlĕdôt pāreṣ* ("Now these are the generations of Perez"), followed by nine entries constructed after the pattern, "A sired B," yielding a total of ten names/generations. The form of the title is familiar from Genesis, where it occurs nine times, and Numbers 3:1. Except perhaps for Genesis 2:4, elsewhere the formula always precedes the lists of generations. The linear (as opposed to segmented) form of the genealogy and the pattern of the entries, with ten generations climaxing in the seventh (Boaz; cf. Enoch in Gen 5:21-24; Peleg in Gen 11:18-19 [cf. Gen 10:25]), suggest an artificial construction modeled after Genesis 5; 11:10-26. In 1 Chronicles 2:3-15 is preserved an official version of the present genealogy. The Chronicler repeats all of the information found here but recasts the genealogy in three significant ways: (1) the form is segmented, rather than linear, including the names of brothers and sisters of the persons named in Ruth; (2) the scope is extended by beginning with Judah, the tribal ancestor, and ending with the names of David's sisters; (3) the style is changed from the present consistently formulaic presentation of each entry to a variety of forms of expression. Linear genealogies represent an economic form of historiography by which an author asserts the legitimacy of the last person named to certain rights, privileges, roles and power that come with membership in this direct line. By attaching this genealogy to the story of Naomi and Ruth, the author emphasizes that the significance of the birth of Obed goes far beyond satisfying Ruth's maternal instincts or filling the emptiness that Naomi had experienced at the beginning. The birth of Obed represents a critical link in the sequence of historical events that began with Perez and climax in the (divine) election of David as king over Israel. Although the experiences of Ruth and Naomi and Boaz are of great interest to the reader, and in their responses they serve as models of *hesed* for all who claim membership in the covenant community, the lives of these women have primary significance for the part that they play in the eventual emergence of David.

3.2. The Narrative. Identifying the genre of the preceding narrative is a more difficult task. Scholars have characterized Ruth as an "idyllic" narrative, "a poetic popular sage" (Gunkel, 82), comparable to an ancient nursery tale in poetic form (Myers). While J. Myers's analysis relies too much on a simplistic distinction between poetry and prose that is no longer accepted, the notion that the book is composed in an elevated poetic style has recently been revived (Korpel). Some have applied the conclusions of the folklorist V. Propp regarding the characteristics of personae found in Russian fairy tales and have concluded that Ruth has the form of a folk tale (Sasson). Others suggest that the present account is a combination of two distinct orally transmitted tales portraying the reversal of feminine fortunes—a Naomi story and a Ruth story—which originally represented separate, although parallel, folk tales. Recent commentators have tended to apply three literary categories to the book of Ruth: tale, *novella, short story. Because biblical scholars sometimes use such expressions slightly differently than do students of other literary traditions, and because their meanings overlap, definitions of these categories are needed (see Block 1999, 601-2; Coats, 63-70).

A "tale" may be defined as a short narrative written or spoken in prose or verse. Typically, the plot of a tale is simple, moving quickly from problem to resolution without complication or subplots. Presentation of the event is more important than developing the characters of the principal participants. In common literary usage a *"novella" is a fictional narrative often restricted to a single suspenseful situation or event that leads to a surprising though logically consistent conclusion (Cuddon, 954-55). Novellas involve the evolution of characters as well as the evolution of an event (plot). The definition of the "short story" is most elusive. How long is "short"? For some, the difference between a novella and a short story is one of length. If a novella is viewed as a middle-distance race, then the short story is a one- or two-hundred-meter sprint (Cuddon, 865-66). According to others, the short story typically has a simpler plot and fewer characters than the novella has. However, whereas a novella develops its characters, a short story reveals them. In the latter, the issue is not how characters evolve with changing circumstances but rather how different events and situations reveal the true characters of the participants (Humphreys, 84-85).

Given these definitions, it is easier to classify the book of Ruth. With respect to length and complexity, the book falls between the tale and the novella—that is, within the range of the short story. This classification is confirmed by the manner in which the characters are treated: although one may detect some development in the character of Naomi, the author's primary purpose is to expose the characters of Naomi and Ruth and Boaz. Reflecting great literary skill, all the scenes contribute to the revelation of their *hesed,* their genuine goodness and loyalty that expresses itself in "loving their neighbors more than they love themselves."

Furthermore, the book's fundamentally historical character reinforces its classification as a short story rather than a tale or a novella. Although some treat the book of Ruth as ideological fiction, both the opening clause, "In the days when judges judged Israel" (Ruth 1:1) and the concluding genealogy anchor the events described in a specific historical period. Between these frames the narrative contains no literary or linguistic features that push it in the direction of fiction or invite the reader to interpret this account as a *māšāl* ("proverb, figure of speech, parable,") or a *šîr* ("song, poem"). Furthermore, the book records no miracles, no supernatural visits, no revelations of extrahistorical and extraterrestrial realities. The picture of the lives of the characters is entirely realistic and in keeping with what is known of life in Palestine in the late second millennium BC: the famine and consequent migration of Elimelech and his family (Ruth 1:1); the allusions to methods of burial (Ruth 1:17); the geographic portrayal of Bethlehem as a walled town with gates, and the location of the threshing floor outside the town; the scenes of workers harvesting the grain (Ruth 2); emotions of the characters in the face of grief, anxiety, joy; the nature of the social relationships between mother-in-law and daughter-in-law, landowner and workers, citizen and the citizenry, husband and wife, grandmother and grandson; the legal process (Ruth 4:1-12). Indeed, to ensure that readers grasp the historical and cultural significance of events, in Ruth 4:7 the narrator adds a parenthetical explanation for their benefit. In any case, it seems unlikely that the author of a story whose aim was to honor David would have invented a plot in which the great-grandmother of Israel's greatest king was a despised Moabite (Hubbard, 48). Finally, in the NT Matthew apparently understood the story to recount real events. In his genealogy of Jesus (Mt 1:1-17), the aim of which was to affirm Jesus' right to the messianic title, he deliberately inserts the name of Ruth (along with Tamar, Rahab and the wife of Uriah [Bathsheba]), even though her name was missing from the genealogy at the end of Ruth and her presence here does nothing to enhance Jesus' royal claims. Without the book of Ruth, Matthew would have had no basis for even knowing Ruth's name.

Like the book of Judges, the book of Ruth should be interpreted as a historiographical document. It describes real experiences of real people in real time at real places. The storyteller does indeed exhibit great literary skill and promote a particular ideology, but to classify the story as fiction is to miss the primary point of the book: to honor David by remembering the noble characters in his family history. Accordingly, the book of Ruth is best classified as an independent historiographical short story. The story of Joseph in Genesis 37—50 or the Gideon cycle in Judges 6—9 may be seen as analogues, except that these have been adapted and integrated into larger compositions.

4. Literary Style.

4.1. Plot. As a piece of literature, the book of Ruth is one of the most delightful ever produced. The narrator is a master at painting word pictures, skillfully employing the techniques of suspense, dialogue, characterization, repetition, reticence, *ambiguity, *word play and *inclusio and creatively adapting ancient traditions to produce this moving work of art. The book of Ruth is constructed as a lively literary piece intended to be read orally and heard at one sitting (see Nielsen, 4). It exhibits a tightly knit and carefully controlled plot (Berlin, 83-110), whose structure may be portrayed graphically as in figure 1.

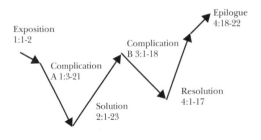

Figure 1. The Plot Structure of the Book of Ruth

4.1.1. Exposition (Ruth 1:1-2). The opening verses set the stage, introducing what we expect to be the main characters: Elimelech; his wife, Naomi; and their two sons, Mahlon and Chilion. Because of a famine in their hometown of Bethlehem in Judah, they move to Moab.

4.1.2. First Complication (1:3-22). The lives of this family are complicated when first Naomi's husband and then their two sons die, leaving three widows with no men to provide security for them. As the primary character in Ruth 1, Naomi describes her situation: she claims that she went away full and has come back empty (Ruth 1:19-21). This is both incorrect and correct, depending upon how one understands "fullness." If by "fullness" we mean having food and enjoying life, she was wrong, for the family had moved to save their lives from starvation. But if by "fullness" we mean family, she was correct. She had left with a husband and two sons; she returned as a widow, without husband or progeny. Between these verses the narrator introduces Ruth, a second principal character in the plot, who insists on casting her lot with her mother-in-law. In the meantime, Naomi has introduced a fundamental issue in the book: because she is too old to remarry and bear sons, it looks as if the second emptiness will never be resolved. And this creates the real crisis: the line of Elimelech is in danger of dying out. Unless one has read the book to the end, this may not seem of great consequence, beyond the personal grief of Naomi, but for the narrator, this introduces the key issue in the book: how can the line be rescued so that Yahweh's chosen king, David, may appear in due course? Ruth 1:22 is transitional, summarizing the response of Naomi and setting the stage for the next phase.

4.1.3. Solution (2:1-23). The chapter opens with an expositional introduction of a third principal, Boaz (Ruth 2:1), and concludes again with Naomi's interpretation of the intervening events, particularly the contact with Boaz (Ruth 2:20-22). The intervening narrative links Boaz and Ruth in an economic relationship and introduces them to each other in ways that reveal the finest aspects of both characters. Naomi's concluding statement heightens the readers' interest and expectation of a quick resolution of the crisis.

4.1.4. Second Complication (3:1-18). Naomi's speech in Ruth 2:20 had raised the prospect of an early resolution of the second form of emptiness, Naomi's lack of progeny and Ruth's lack of security in the house of a husband. Framed by two speeches by Naomi (Ruth 3:1-4, 18), Ruth 3 introduces a complication to this hope. Faithfully following her mother-in-law's instructions and brazenly calling upon Boaz to marry her, Ruth discovers that Boaz is not in a position to do so. Because Boaz is not the first in line to claim the property of Elimelech and, with it, the widowed Ruth, he must decline her proposal. But he offers hope by suggesting that one way or another Ruth will be "redeemed," though both obviously hope that Boaz will be the man to do it (*see* Kinsman-Redeemer and Levirate).

4.1.5. Resolution (4:1-17). The final act in the drama commences with Boaz taking the initiative to resolve the legal question and concludes with the narrator's announcement that the son born to Naomi is the grandfather of David. Between these borders three groups comment on what has happened, and in so doing they provide important clues to the significance of these events: (1) having won the right to Elimelech's land and Ruth's hand, Boaz declares his intention of preserving the name of the deceased (Mahlon and Elimelech) (Ruth 4:9-10); (2) the men of Bethlehem pronounce a blessing upon Ruth, praying that she will join the ranks of Rachel and Leah and Tamar, who built the house of Israel/Judah (Ruth 4:11-12); (3) the women of Bethlehem announce Naomi's complete fulfillment in her daughter-in-law and her grandson and pray that the son's name will become famous in Israel (Ruth 4:14-15). None of these parties realizes the long-range significance of their pronouncements. But the narrator does, declaring first Yahweh's auspicious role in the birth of the boy (Ruth 4:13), and then on the heels of the naming of Obed, announcing that he was the grandfather of David (Ruth 4:17).

4.1.6. Genealogical Epilogue (4:18-22). The concluding genealogy reminds the readers that the story just told is more than an inspiring tale of a family of genuinely good people. The author has described the critical role played by the seventh link in this chain. Like Enoch in Genesis 5:22, 24, righteous Boaz shows us what it means to walk with God. Furthermore, far from disqualifying David from the kingship of Israel because Moabite blood flows in his veins, it is precisely the Moabite connection that raises his genealogy above the ordinary.

4.2. Intertextual Issues. While the plot of the book of Ruth is intriguing in its own right,

through the effective use of echoes and allusions, the narrator seems to betray a familiarity with a wide range of other biblical texts or traditions (Zakovitch, 49-59; Fischer, 47-48). Perhaps the most striking *intertextual link is found in Boaz's characterization of Ruth as an *ʾēšet ḥayil* ("woman of nobility") in Ruth 3:11. The only other occurrence of this phrase in the Hebrew Bible is found in Proverbs 31:10, in the heading of an *acrostic portrayal of an honorable woman. Some have also interpreted Naomi as a female *Job. The book begins with her struggles over having lost everything, including her family, and ends with the birth of a "son" and the pronouncement that one daughter-in-law like Ruth is to be treasured more than seven sons (Ruth 4:15; cf. Job 42:13).

Reference has already been made to the opening clause, "In the days when judges judged" (Ruth 1:1). This comment does more than fix the events chronologically. As is reflected in the Old Greek's placement of Ruth after Judges, it invites the reader to interpret what follows in the light of the book of Judges as a whole. Judges had ended on a negative note, lamenting the absence of a king in Israel. In Ruth the royal motif surfaces in the first person identified by name, "Elimelech," which means either "El is Milku" or "(my) God is king." Perhaps because of a failure to recognize Yahweh's kingship, when famine strikes, Elimelech and his wife move out to the land where Chemosh reigns. However, throughout history people have read the last statement of Judges as a signal that the solution to the problems represented in the book is to be found in the (coming) king David. The placement of Ruth after Judges appears to reflect this interpretation.

The link to Judges is reinforced by locating Elimelech in "Bethlehem of Judah," an expression that occurs elsewhere only in Judges (Judg 17:7-8; 19:1, 18) and in 1 Samuel 17:12, where David is introduced as "the son of the Ephrathite of Bethlehem of Judah." The former name has not been heard since Genesis 35:19; 48:7, where the place of Rachel's burial was identified as "Ephrathah—that is, Bethelehem." Since this event links Ephrathah/Bethlehem with Ephraim (Rachel was the mother of Joseph; in the book of Judges Bethlehem of Judah is linked with Ephraim through two Levites [cf. Judg 17:1, 7-9; 19:1]), part of the agenda of the book of Ruth may be to highlight Bethlehem as a Judahite/Davidic town rather than an Ephraimite one.

In the book we hear numerous echoes from and allusions to the narratives of Genesis (Gen 2:24; 12:1 in Ruth 2:11; Gen 12:10; 26:1 in Ruth 1:1; Gen 19:30-38 in Ruth 3:1-9; Gen 24:27 in Ruth 2:20). Many have noted that the only two occasions in which the narrator attributes specific actions to Yahweh are Ruth 1:6; 4:13. Remarkably, both references allude to Yahweh's first oracular pronouncements in the Bible (Gen 3:14-19) The reference to Yahweh giving "bread" *(leḥem)* in Ruth 1:6 recalls Genesis 3:16, where Adam is promised "bread" *(leḥem)* as a reward for hard work in a fallen world. Ruth 4:13 and Genesis 3:16 are linked by rare nominal forms of the root *hārâ* ("conceive, be pregnant"), *hērāyôn* and *hērôn*, respectively. It appears from the use of the *ʾelleh tôlĕdôt* formula in Ruth 4:18 that the book of Ruth is to be interpreted as a continuation of the narratives of Genesis, where the formula occurs eleven times. Specifically, by reducing the genealogy to ten entries, the author presents the lineage of David as the third phase of history, preceded by phases that extend from Adam to Noah (Gen 5), and Noah to Terah (Gen 11:10-26). Remarkably, the four patriarchal generations are omitted from this scheme. Furthermore, by identifying Boaz as the seventh link in this chain, the author recognizes in him a watershed of human history, analogous to the periods represented by Enoch (Gen 5:21-24) and Peleg (Gen 10:25).

However, the most important intertextual studies involve the application and adaptation of specific laws found in the Holiness Code and the Deuteronomic Torah (Zakovitch, 42-48): (1) leaving the edges of fields of grain for the poor to glean (Ruth 2:1-7, 15-16; cf. Lev 19:9-10; Deut 24:19); (2) levirate marriage (Ruth 1:15; 4:7-10; cf. Deut 25:5-10; also Gen 38:8); the root *ybm* ("consummate a marriage with one's brother-in-law") occurs only in these three contexts (cf. van Wolde, 8-24); (3) redemption *(gāʾal)*, though the present text involves the redemption of a widow in addition to land that had fallen out of the family (Ruth 3:9, 12-13; 4:3-6, 9-10; cf. Lev 25:25-28, 47-50 [an indentured slave]); the closest analogues to the present redemption of a widow occur in Isaiah (Is 54:5, 8); (4) marriage to a Moabite; the identification of Chilion's and Mahlon's wives as Moabite (Ruth 1:4) and the six references to Ruth as a Moabite (Ruth 1:22;

2:2, 6, 21; 4:5, 10) invite the reader to interpret these events in the light of Deuteronomy 7:3-4, which prohibits Israelites from marrying pagans, and Deuteronomy 23:3-5, which excludes Moabites from the assembly of Yahweh for ten generations. The liberality with which each of the antecedent laws is interpreted in this book is remarkable.

5. Canonical Position.
The Babylonian Talmud observes that Ruth, like Esther and *Song of Songs, does indeed "make the hands unclean" *(b. Meg.* 7a), suggesting early recognition of the book's canonical status. The four fragments of the book found in the caves of Qumran attest to its importance in this community (Campbell, 40-41). However, the place of the book of Ruth within the canon of the Hebrew Scriptures was quite fluid (Beckwith, 452-68; Fischer, 95-112; Brandt, 121-39). The Ben Hayyim textual tradition (used in Jewish worship today and followed in the NJPS) has Ruth in the second place among the five *Megillot, after Song of Songs and before Lamentations, Ecclesiastes and Esther. This arrangement is determined by the chronological sequence of the five annual festivals at which these books were read: Passover, Shavuot (Weeks, Pentecost), Ninth of Ab, Sukkot (Tabernacles) and *Purim, respectively. The most obvious explanation for linking Ruth with Shavuot is the timing of the events in the book. Since they occur at the beginning of the barley harvest (Ruth 1:22), late April or early May, it is appropriate to read this book during the festival in which the offering of new grain was an important part of the ritual, Shavuot, celebrated fifty days after Passover (Lev 23:15-21). However, according to tradition, this festival also celebrated Yahweh's establishment of his covenant with Israel at Sinai *(Midrash Zuta* on Ruth 1:1). Some traditions suggest that the book was read at this festival as an allegorical portrayal of Yahweh's relationship with Israel: just as Ruth sought refuge under the wings of Boaz, so also Israel sought refuge under the wings of God when they received the Torah (see Zakovitch, 70). But it may also have been read for the moral examples that its characters provide inasmuch as they all live according to the will of Yahweh (Fischer, 101). However, a rabbinic tradition links the reading of the book on Shavuot with David by noting that he died on Shavuot, on the Sabbath

(*Ruth Rab.* 3:3; cf. *b. Šabb.* 30b; *y. Beṣah* 2:4).

The other three canonical locations highlight the Davidic significance of the book of Ruth even more. Deemed by some to be the earliest arrangement, the Talmudic *b. B. Bat.* 14b has Ruth at the head of the Ketubim (Hagiographa), before *Psalms. This means that David's genealogy is read immediately before Psalms 1—2, and that the book functions as the prologue not only to the book of Psalms, but also to the following books, Ecclesiastes and Song of Songs, which are linked to Solomon, and even Job, which has a clear royal flavor.

In the Ben Asher family of manuscripts (represented by Codex Leningradensis, the basis of *BHS*) Ruth is sandwiched between *Proverbs and Ecclesiastes. This location between two Solomonic works not only affirms the Davidic nature of Ruth but also places the story of Ruth immediately after the acrostic celebration of wifely nobility in Proverbs 31:10-31. This location and the fact that the expression ʾēšet hayil occurs only in Proverbs 31:10 and Ruth 3:11 suggests that the *scribes responsible for this arrangement viewed Ruth as the supreme example of the nobility described in Proverbs 31.

The placement of the book of Ruth between Judges and 1 Samuel in Christian Bibles follows the arrangement of the Old Greek version. This position seems to have been recognized by Josephus (*Ag. Ap.* 1.7-8), whose tally of twenty-two books for the OT suggests that Ruth was attached to Judges, just as Lamentations was combined with Jeremiah. This arrangement of the canon provides the reader with welcome relief after the depressing book of Judges. Whereas Judges develops the theme of the increasing spiritual infidelity and its effects in Israel in the premonarchic period, Ruth highlights the nature of genuine covenantal piety during this same period. Perhaps even more important, according to this arrangement, the book of Ruth presents the solution to the fundamental problem in the premonarchic period as reflected in the closing refrain of Judges: Israel has no king (Judg 21:25). Furthermore, in this location the book also prepares the way for the books of Samuel, whose opening sequence of events climaxes in Hannah's oracle predicting a coming king/Messiah (1 Sam 2:10).

It is difficult to determine which of these arrangements is original. Each offers insight into the thinking of the respective "caniclers," and each contributes to the reading of Ruth as a Davidic book in its own distinctive way.

6. Theological Message.

Like the narratives of Genesis, the Deuteronomic Historians and the Chronicler, the book of Ruth communicates a profound theological and ideological message.

6.1. The Portrayal of God in the Book of Ruth.

6.1.1. Names and Epithets for God. Ruth expresses a theological awareness only in her first speech, where, as a Moabite, she refers to *God by the generic designation ʾĕlōhîm ("deity"). All the other characters in the book identify God by his personal covenant name, "Yahweh." Indeed, in Boaz's first reference to God when addressing Ruth he expressly identifies Yahweh as "the God of Israel" (Ruth 2:12). Of special interest is Naomi's twofold reference to God as šadday (Ruth 1:20-21), apparently an abbreviation of ʾēl šadday, an ancient epithet of God reflecting his role as chief of the heavenly council that met on top of the sacred mountain (Block 1999, 605). In the Hebrew Bible it is as šadday that God creates and rules the world and supervises the moral order, punishing evil and rewarding good (Hubbard, *NIDOTTE* 4.1155).

6.1.2. The Sovereign Rule of God. Apart from Ruth 1:6; 4:13, the narrator never refers directly to God, leading some to devalue the theological significance of the book (Sasson, 249). However, others have rightly spoken of "the hidden hand of God" quietly at work behind the scene (Hals). The narrator may not speak directly of God's involvement, but reading between the lines, we may recognize his hand in at least five ways.

First, God's hand is present in apparently natural events. Any Israelite familiar with the stipulations of Yahweh's covenant with Israel, particularly the "blessings and curses," will have seen in the famine referred to in Ruth 1:1 the fulfillment of Leviticus 26:19-20 and Deuteronomy 28:23-24. One may also surmise that in the mind of the narrator the deaths of Elimelech, Chilion and Mahlon in Moab were further consequences of the spiritual crisis in the land. Naomi certainly recognized the hand of God behind her personal misery (Ruth 1:20-21).

Second, God's hand is present in apparently chance events. In context, *wayyiqer miqrehā* in Ruth 2:3 means "her chance chanced upon," or in colloquial English, "by a stroke of luck" (cf. 1 Sam 6:9). The narrator's choice of phrase forces the reader to sit up and ask how it was that Ruth "happened" to land in the field of a man who was not only gracious but also a potential gōʾēl ("redeemer") Ruth's arrival at Boaz's field was one more evidence of the providential hand of God, who is directing the personal affairs of the characters toward the goal announced in Ruth 4:17c. The same could be said for the arrival of the gōʾēl just as Boaz sat down at the gate in Ruth 4:1-2.

Third, God's hand is present in the delicate and daring schemes of humans. Whatever the meaning of margĕlōt ("feet") in Ruth 3:4-14, the scheme to provide security (mānôaḥ) for Ruth concocted by Naomi and implemented by her daughter is suspicious from the standpoint of custom and morality and is fraught with danger. And Ruth's demand that Boaz marry her is highly irregular from the perspective of custom: a foreigner proposing to an Israelite; a woman proposing to a man; a young person proposing to an older person; a destitute field worker proposing to the landowner. But instead of taking offense at Ruth's forwardness, Boaz blesses her, praises her for her hesed, calls her "my daughter," reassures her by telling her not to fear, promises to do whatever she asks, and pronounces her a noble woman (ʾēšet ḥayil). This extraordinary reaction is best attributed to the hand of God controlling Boaz's heart and tongue when he awakes.

Fourth, God's hand is present in the legal process. In Ruth 4 Boaz submits the issue raised by his and Ruth's desire to marry to the normal legal process. But just then, "Mr. So-and-So" happens to pass by the gate where Boaz had sat down (Ruth 4:1). This unnamed man's lame excuse for not wanting to take the land and Ruth (Ruth 4:6) leads directly to the desired outcome. The case could easily have gone the other way, but in the mind of the narrator, God seems to have determined the result from the beginning.

Fifth, God's hand is present in biological and reproductive matters. In Ruth 4:13 the narrator finally attributes a specific action to God: he granted Ruth conception. The statement would not be that significant were it not for Ruth 1:4, which suggests that despite being married to Mahlon for ten years, Ruth had been unable to bear children. Her previous barrenness was another expression of Yahweh's curse for Israel's rebellion in this period, and perhaps for Elimelech and Naomi's move to Moab. But now,

in the climactic event, Yahweh enables her to conceive.

Underlying every episode in the book is God's providential hand, orchestrating events so that David could emerge from the depressing and chaotic Israelite environment during the days of the Judges. Whereas in the book of Judges God's hand is involved directly punishing Israel for sin, raising up deliverers, and then rescuing his people, in this book he acts quietly through the lives of ordinary people. The seeds of the future dynasty were sown in this private family of Bethlehem. That the greatest king of Israel should trace his roots to a destitute widow, her Moabite daughter-in-law and an aging bachelor from the humble town of Bethlehem is hereby portrayed as a supreme divine accomplishment.

6.1.3. The Gracious Acts of God. Theologically, the most significant statement in the book may be Naomi's response to Ruth's first visit to Boaz's field: "Blessed be he by Yahweh, whose hesed has not forsaken the living or the dead" (Ruth 2:20). Hebrew hesed cannot be translated with one English word. This is a covenant term, wrapping up in itself all the positive attributes of God: love, covenant faithfulness, mercy, grace, kindness, loyalty—in short, acts of devotion and loving-kindness that go beyond the requirements of duty (see Sakenfeld 1978; 1985; 1999, 11-12). Yahweh's special relationship with Israel is expressed in the phrase "his people" (Ruth 1:6) and in the obverse, "Yahweh, the God of Israel" (Ruth 2:12). How does Yahweh express this commitment in the book? According to the narrator, it is by intervening on behalf of his people (pāqad) and giving them food (Ruth 1:6), and by causing Ruth to conceive (Ruth 4:13). Although Naomi seems for a time to have lost sight of Yahweh's hesed (Ruth 1:13, 20-21), she tells her daughters that they may expect him to show his kindness by granting rest (mĕnûḥâ) in the house of a husband (Ruth 1:9). Later she sees his hesed clearly in leading Ruth to the field of a man who is not only gracious but also a gōʾēl (Ruth 2:20). Boaz declares his awareness of Yahweh's hesed when he blesses his workers with a plea for Yahweh's presence (Ruth 2:4), when he prays that Yahweh will reward Ruth's diligence (Ruth 2:12), when he characterizes Yahweh as one under whose wings the poor and the alien find refuge (Ruth 2:12), and when he invokes Yahweh as the guarantor of his good will toward Ruth (Ruth

3:13). The witnesses to the legal proceedings whereby Boaz gains the right to marry Ruth invoke Yahweh's *hesed* when they bless Ruth and pray that this Moabite woman might join the ranks of the matriarchs Leah and Rachel (Ruth 4:11) and that he will give Boaz progeny *(zera')* through Ruth (Ruth 4:12). The women acknowledge Yahweh's *hesed* by praising him for having provided Naomi with a *gō'ēl* (Ruth 4:14). Despite the hardships and frustrations that the characters experience, the tone of the book of Ruth is set and maintained by the blessings that punctuate the narrative from beginning to end (Ruth 1:8-9; 2:4a, 4b, 12, 19 [without naming the Lord], 20; 3:10; 4:11-12, 14a, 14b-15). These benedictions are grounded in the assumption that Yahweh is a gracious, covenant-keeping God.

6.2. The Portrayal of the People of God in the Book of Ruth.

6.2.1. The Personal Fulfillment of Torah Righteousness. Perhaps more than any other book in the Hebrew Bible, in Ruth the participants in the events not only reflect the character of the God behind those events but also, for the most part, embody the best of Torah *righteousness. To be sure, the book opens with a compromising picture of a family headed into exile because of a famine, and the image of Naomi in her bitterness is less than ideal (Ruth 1:13, 20-21), but these are the expressions of a woman deeply wounded by her calamities. Ironically, the divine quality of *hesed* is expressly attributed only to the character who begins outside the covenant community, Ruth (Ruth 3:10). In this context the expression refers to Ruth's covenantal commitment to the family, especially to Naomi, her mother-in-law. For the most part Naomi is cast in the role of Ruth's matron (Ruth 1:1-13; 2:2; 3:1, 16, 18), with a keen sense of responsibility for securing Ruth's security *(mānôah)* and well-being *(yîtab-lāk)* (Ruth 3:1). In so doing, she demonstrates *hesed*. However, those who observe this relationship in action express their particular admiration for Ruth. Boaz commends her for repeated acts of *hesed* performed out of commitment to her mother-in-law (Ruth 3:10); and the people of Bethlehem attach an epithet to her that no other woman in the Hebrew Bible bears, *'ēšet hayil* ("woman of standing, noble woman" [Ruth 3:11]); and in the end her devotion to Naomi is described as "love" (*'āheb* [Ruth 4:15])—that is, covenant commitment that actively seeks the well-being of the next person.

The roots of this reputation are found in Ruth's immortal verbal commitment to Naomi in Ruth 1:16-17. On the surface, it is possible to interpret these words cynically, as an expression of Ruth's parasitic dependence on her mother-in-law, but the echo of Genesis 31:13 in Boaz's interpretation of Ruth's action (Ruth 2:11) places her actions on par with the migrations of the patriarchs, who also stepped out in faith, leaving the lands of their birth. Within the ancient Near Eastern context, Ruth's claim of Naomi's people as her people and of Naomi's God as her God represents a repudiation of her Moabite status and her initiation into the covenant people of Yahweh. With this commitment, her every act is one of loyalty to her mother-in-law and of faith in Yahweh, even her morally ambiguous actions at the threshing floor (Ruth 3:1-7) and her rather forward proposal to Boaz (Ruth 3:9). As a Moabite, she had lost her father-in-law and her husband and had been unable to conceive a child (Ruth 1:4-4), but as an Israelite, she gained a mother-in-law, a husband, a son and a place in the nation's history alongside Rachel and Leah. In the perspective of the NT, specifically in Matthew's genealogy of Jesus the *Messiah, from which the names of Sarah and Rebekah and Leah and Rachel are missing, we find Tamar and Rahab and Ruth and Bathsheba (Mt 1:3-6).

In terms of covenantal piety, Boaz casts an equally impressive figure. The closest that the narrator comes—or anyone else for that matter—to defining his character is the former's attribution of the epithet *'îš gibbôr hayil* (Ruth 2:1). This expression is often interpreted socio-economically as a reference to his economic or political standing in the community (NRSV). However, in the light of his actions, and in view of the portrayal of Ruth the *'ēšet hayil* as his female counterpart (Ruth 3:11), the narrator, with the expression *'îš gibbôr hayil*, introduces us to "a prominent man of noble character" (TNIV). Ruth's request for permission to glean in the field of one in whose sight she might find favor *(hēn* [Ruth 2:2]) adds to the reader's anticipation. Judging by the manner in which men treat women in Judges, these qualities are in short supply in Israel at this time. But when Boaz appears, he embodies both nobility and grace. The way that he and his harvesters greet each other expresses a remarkably wholesome relationship with economic inferiors (Ruth 2:4). The kindness that he shows to Ruth in his first encounter with her is anything by patronizing. In commending her for seeking refuge under the wings of Yahweh, the God of Israel, he reveals a profound ethical principle—he represents the wings of God (Ruth 2:12). When he is informed of his potential role as a *gōʾēl*, he seizes the opportunity to preserve his kinsman's line and his patrimony.

6.2.2. The Corporate Fulfillment of Torah Righteousness. The preceding discussion has focused on individual expression of Torah piety, but the narrative of Ruth also provides a window into the experience of covenantal righteousness in everyday social structures. Some have cynically interpreted the story of Ruth as a "pernicious, exploitative tract" because it supports a patriarchal culture in which women's primary role is to bear children and in which Gentile women are dangerous because they are sexually manipulative (Levine, 79). However, it is preferable to see in its portrayal of domestic and communal relationships a normative patricentrism in which male figures, the heads of the household *(bêt ʾāb)* perceive their roles not as positions of power but rather as positions of responsibility. This is a peaceable community in which the temptation for those with authority to lord it over those in their charge is restrained, a community in which men seek the interest of women, and in which the weak and marginalized are invited to full participation (see Sakenfeld 1999, 9-11).

The narrative itself reflects this commitment. Many have noted the distinctively feminine perspective from which events are described in the book of Ruth (see Bauckham). The narrator paints some of the key scenes, especially those involving female characters, with a sensitive and sympathetic feminine brush: Naomi's encouragement of her daughter-in-law to return to their homes, since Naomi is returning to her homeland, and Ruth's determination to stay with her (Ruth 1:6-18); the women of Bethlehem's reaction to Naomi's return, and Naomi's response (Ruth 1:19-21); Ruth's request for permission to go and scavenge for grain (Ruth 2:2-3); Ruth's return to Naomi with the fruit of her labor, and Boaz's kindness (Ruth 2:18-23); Naomi's instructions for "snagging" Boaz, and Ruth's response (Ruth 3:1-6); the report of the conversation between the two women upon Ruth's return (Ruth 3:16-18); the response of the village women to the birth of Obed (Ruth 4:14-17). This sensitivity is maintained in the other scenes where men control the action: Boaz's treatment of Ruth in the field (Ruth 2:4-16); his response to her proposal on the threshing floor (Ruth 3:6-15); his handling of the legal proceedings in the gate, especially his interpretation of the honorific role she will play in the ongoing life of the clan (Ruth 4:1-10); the blessing of the elders and witnesses, which, though addressed to Boaz, is effusive in its exaltation of Ruth (Ruth 4:11-12). Even Yahweh's blessing of the sexual consummation of the marriage is presented as a gift to Ruth (Ruth 4:13).

The picture of gender realities in Ruth is a far cry from that which is portrayed in the narratives not only in Judges but also in many scenes in the patriarchal narratives of Genesis and the narratives of David's family life in 2 Samuel. However, it is in keeping with the ideals presented in Deuteronomy. The Deuteronomic Torah calls for a society that is unapologetically patricentric (see Block 2003, 40-48). However, the trajectory for the kind of patricentrism called for is set in the Decalogue. With subtle modifications, the Deuteronomic version reinforces the responsibility of the heads of households to ensure the well-being of all in their charge. The particular interest in women's well-being is evident in the invitation to all to join in *worship at the central sanctuary (Deut 12:12, 18), the instructions for the treatment of a captive woman who is claimed as a wife (Deut 21:10-14), the inclusion of the wife in cases involving rebellious children (Deut 21:18-21), the protection of women in cases of divorce (Deut 24:1-5), the regulations regarding levirate marriage (Deut 25:5-10), and elsewhere. Deuteronomy 25:5-10 is especially significant, not only because it has a direct bearing on the interpretation of the legal process in Ruth 4 but also because of the sympathy that it expresses for a woman who has been wronged in such cases. In his responses to the issues that the female characters in the narrative present, Boaz proves that he is governed not merely by the letter of the law but rather by its spirit. This is covenant righteousness (cf. Deut 16:20) at its best.

The same applies to other aspects of the narrative that are linked to the regulations of Leviticus and Deuteronomy. On the surface, Boaz's marriage to Ruth looks like a violation of Deuteronomy 23:3-6, which prohibits admission of a Moabite to the assembly of Yahweh for ten generations. The rabbis rationalized Boaz's action by distinguishing between male and female Moabites. According to *m. Yebam.* 8:3, the prohibition concerning Ammonites and Moabites is eternal; nevertheless, today their women are permitted. However, within the overall spirit of the Deuteronomic Torah, after Ruth's conversion to the people and God of Naomi, and in view of the Torah righteousness that she demonstrated, it is preferable to look upon Ruth as an Israelite. Given the presence of Rahab in Boaz's own genealogy (Mt 1:5), Boaz, looking at Ruth's faith, may have been blind to her race. If the book of Judges shows that not all who claim descent from Abraham are in covenant relationship with Yahweh, then, just as Caleb had demonstrated in an earlier generation, the book of Ruth establishes that outsiders to this physical lineage may represent the true community of faith. In so doing, the book confirms Paul's adage in Romans 2:28-29: "For a person is not a true Israelite from the outside in, nor is true circumcision an external and physical reality. Rather, a person is an Israelite from the inside out, for real circumcision is a heart issue—it is spiritual, rather than literal. This person does not receive the praise of others but of God." Beyond this, nowhere do the laws of Israel associate the *gōʾēl* with the redemption of widows or aliens; rather, the institution of *gĕʾullâ* applies to lost property and lost freedom (slaves [Lev 25:25-28, 47-50]). The application of the notion to Ruth demonstrates again that the persons in the narrative are driven by the underlying spirit of Torah rather than by its letter. Accordingly, the instructions in Deuteronomy should not be viewed as providing final boundaries for covenant righteousness (Moses could not possibly provide legislation for every eventuality); rather, they present minimal requirements, presenting a moral compass and an ethical trajectory for the community of faith.

6.3. The Messianic Significance of the Book of Ruth. Although in the past many have linked the messianic significance of the book of Ruth to Boaz the *gōʾēl* as a typological foreshadowing of Jesus the Christ our redeemer, neither the OT nor the NT makes this connection. Indeed, Boaz is never mentioned again outside genealogies (1 Chron 2:11-12; 2 Chron 3:17; Mt 1:5; Lk 3:32). If any character in the book functions typologically of the Messiah, it would be Obed, and this for four reasons: (1) the special circumstances of his birth from a previously barren woman (cf. Isaac in Gen 21); (2) the content of

the blessing invoked upon him by the women of Bethlehem—he is identified as a *gōʾēl* and one who restores life *(mēšîb nepeš);* (3) the superlative elevation of his mother at his birth; (4) the name given to him by the community: *ʿôbēd* ("Servant"), which anticipates David, the anointed servant of Yahweh (2 Sam 7), and ultimately the Isaianic servant.

In the providence and grace of God, five hundred years after the writing of this delightful narrative, the NT opens with an announcement of the fulfillment of this promise to another young woman who displayed all the marks of *hesed* and had found favor with God (Luke 1:26-38). Mary would be most blessed among women, for she too would bear a son. But this son would be greater than Ruth's child and even greater than her great-grandchild. His name will be "Jesus," and he will be called "the Son of the Most High" (LXX: *hypsistos;* Heb *ʿelyôn*), and Yahweh will give him the throne of his father David.

According to the genealogy that concludes the book of Ruth and to the NT genealogies, Boaz's significance lies in his representing a critical link (the seventh) in the chain that leads from Perez to David, and ultimately from Abraham and Adam to the Christ. At a time in history when the light of divine revelation was in danger of being extinguished (1 Sam 3:1-3), Boaz appeared, exhibiting true faith and demonstrating Torah righteousness. In lavishing his grace on Ruth and eventually marrying her, he not only served as the wings of Yahweh in the immediate circumstance but also, in long-range terms, secured the identification of the Messiah with all of humanity, Jew and Gentile.

7. Outline.

The preponderance of dialogue in the book of Ruth encourages us to interpret the composition as a drama in four main acts, followed by a genealogical postlude (see Zenger, 15-18; Grant, 424-41). Although each act is set in its own time and place, together they contribute to the artful presentation of the narrator's central theme: the providential hand of God in the preservation of Israel's royal line during the dark days of the judges. For purposes of exposition, the following outline reflects the dramatic manner in which this theme is developed.

Theme: The Preservation of Israel's Royal Line

Outline

Act 1: The Crisis for the Line (Ruth 1:1-21)
  1. The Setting for the Crisis
    (Ruth 1:1-2)
  2. The Nature of the Crisis (Ruth 1:3-5)
  3. The Response to the Crisis
    (Ruth 1:6-18)
  4. The Interpretation of the Crisis
    (Ruth 1:19-21)
Act 2: The Ray of Hope for the Line
  (Ruth 1:22—2:23)
  1. The New Setting (Ruth 1:22—2:1)
  2. The Initiative of Ruth (Ruth 2:2-3)
  3. The Grace of Boaz (Ruth 2:4-16)
  4. The Results (Ruth 2:17-23)
Act 3: The Complication for the Line
  (Ruth 3:1-18)
  1. The Scheme of Naomi (Ruth 3:1-5)
  2. The Implementation of the Scheme
    (Ruth 3:6-15)
  3. The Results of the Scheme
    (Ruth 3:16-18)
Act 4: The Rescue of the Line (Ruth 4:1-17)
  1. The Legal Resolution (Ruth 4:1-12)
  2. The Genealogical Resolution
    (Ruth 4:13-17)
Epilogue: The Royal Genealogy
  (Ruth 4:18-22)

See also BOAZ; FEMINIST INTERPRETATION; KINSMAN-REDEEMER AND LEVIRATE; NAOMI; RUTH 2: ANCIENT NEAR EASTERN BACKGROUND; RUTH 3: HISTORY OF INTERPRETATION; RUTH 4: PERSON; SOCIAL-SCIENTIFIC APPROACHES; WOMEN.

BIBLIOGRAPHY. *Commentaries:* **D. I. Block,** *Judges, Ruth* (NAC 6; Nashville: Broadman & Holman, 1999); **F. Bush,** *Ruth, Esther* (WBC 9; Dallas: Word, 1996); **E. F. Campbell Jr.,** *Ruth* (AB 7; Garden City, NY: Doubleday, 1975); **I. Fischer,** *Rut* (HTKAT; Freiburg: Herder, 2001); **R. L. Hub-bard Jr.,** *The Book of Ruth* (NICOT; Grand Rapids: Eerdmans, 1988); **A.-J. Levine,** "Ruth," in *The Women's Bible Commentary,* ed. C. A. Newsome and S. H. Ringe (Louisville: Westminster John Knox, 1992) 78-84; **K. Nielsen,** *Ruth* (OTL; Louisville: Westminster John Knox, 1997); **K. D. Sakenfeld,** *Ruth* (IBC; Louisville: Westminster John Knox, 1999); **Y. Zakovitch,** *Das Buch Rut: Ein jüdischer Kommentar* (SBS 177; Stuttgart: Katholisches Bibelwerk, 1999); **E. Zenger,** *Das Buch Ruth* (ZBK 8; Zürich: Theologischer Verlag, 1986). *Studies:* **R. Bauckham,** "The Book of Ruth and the Possibility of a Feminist Canonical Interpretation," *BibInt* 5 (1997) 29-45; **R. Beckwith,** *The Old Testament Canon of the New Testament Church and Its Background in Judaism* (Grand Rapids: Eerdmans, 1985); **A. Berlin,** *Poetics and Interpretation of Biblical Narrative* (BLS 9; Sheffield: Almond, 1983). **A. J. Bledstein,** "Female Companionships: If the Book of Ruth Were Written by a Woman . . . ," in *A Feminist Companion to Ruth,* ed. A. Brenner (FCB 3; Sheffield: Sheffield Academic Press, 1993) 116-35; **D. I. Block,** "Marriage and Family in Ancient Israel," in *Marriage and Family in the Biblical World,* ed. K. M. Campbell (Downers Grove, IL: InterVarsity Press, 2003) 33-102; **P. Brandt,** *Endgestalten des Kanons: Das Arrangement der Schriften Israels in der jüdischen und christlichen Bibel* (BBB 131; Berlin: Philo, 2001); **A. Brenner,** ed., *A Feminist Companion to Ruth* (FCB 3; Sheffield: Sheffield Academic Press, 1993); **G. W. Coats,** "Tale," in *Saga, Legend, Tale, Novella, Fable: Narrative Forms in Old Testament Literature,* ed. G. W. Coats (JSOTSup 35; Sheffield: JSOT Press, 1985) 63-70; **J. A. Cuddon,** *A Dictionary of Literary Terms and Literary Theory* (3rd ed.; Oxford: Basil Blackwood, 1991); **M. D. Gow,** *The Book of Ruth: Its Structure, Theme and Purpose* (Leicester: Apollos, 1992); **R. Grant,** "Literary Structure in the Book of Ruth," *BSac* 148 (1991) 424-41; **H. Gunkel,** "Ruth," in *Reden und Aufsätze* (Göttingen: Vandenhoeck & Ruprecht, 1913) 69-92; **R. M. Hals,** *The Theology of the Book of Ruth* (Minneapolis: Fortress, 1969); **R. L. Hubbard Jr.,** "Ruth, Theology of," *NIDOTTE* 4.1153-57; **W. Humphreys,** "Novella," in *Saga, Legend, Tale, Novella, Fable: Narrative Forms in Old Testament Literature,* ed. G. W. Coats (JSOTSup 35; Sheffield: JSOT Press, 1985) 82-96; **M. Korpel,** *The Structure of the Book of Ruth* (Pericope 2; Assen: Van Gorcum, 2001); **D. A. Leggett,** *The Levirate and Goel Institutions in the Old Testament, with Special Attention to the Book of Ruth* (Cherry Hill, NJ: Mack, 1974); **C. M. Meyers,** "Returning Home: Ruth 1:8 and the Gendering of the Book of Ruth," in *A Feminist Companion to Ruth,* ed. A. Brenner (FCB 3; Sheffield: Sheffield Academic Press, 1993) 85-114; **J. Myers,** *The Linguistic and Literary Form of the Book of Ruth* (Leiden: E. J. Brill, 1955); **P. T. Nash,** "Ruth: An Exercise in Israelite Political Correctness or a Call to Proper Conversion?" in *The Pitcher Is Broken: Memorial Essays for Gösta W. Åhlström,* ed. H. G. Åhlström and L. K. Handy (JSOTSup 190; Sheffield: Sheffield Academic Press, 1995) 347-54; **K. D. Sakenfeld,** *The Mean-*

ing of Hesed *in the Hebrew Bible: A New Inquiry* (HSM 17; Missoula, MT: Scholars Press, 1978); idem, *Faithfulness in Action: Loyalty in Biblical Perspective* (OBT; Philadelphia: Fortress, 1985); **J. M. Sasson,** *Ruth: A New Translation with a Philological Commentary and a Formalist-Folklorist Interpretation* (2nd ed; Sheffield: Sheffield Academic Press, 1989); **S. D. Sperling,** "Ruth, Book of," in *Encyclopaedia Judaica* (2nd ed.; Jerusalem: Keter, 2007) 17.592-95; **E. van Wolde,** "Texts in Dialogue with Texts: Intertextuality in the Ruth and Tamar Narratives," *BibInt* 5 (1997) 1-28; **B. G. Webb,** *Five Festal Garments: Christian Reflections on the Song of Songs, Ruth, Lamentations, Ecclesiastes and Esther* (NSBT 10; Leicester: Apollos, 2000); **M. Weinfeld,** "Ruth, Book of," in *Encyclopaedia Judaica* (Jerusalem/New York: Keter/Macmillan, 1971-2) 14.518-24.

D. I. Block

RUTH 2: ANCIENT NEAR EASTERN BACKGROUND

The book of Ruth opens, "Now it happened in the days when the judges ruled" (Ruth 1:1). This reference places the events of the book between the death of Joshua after the initial conquest of Canaan (Josh 11:23; Judg 1:1) and the establishment of the monarchy during the time of Samuel the prophet (1 Sam 10:1-2). The exact dates of this period are difficult to determine because of unresolved questions about how to interpret the textual and archaeological data concerning the exodus from Egypt and the conquest. Scholars are divided between the so-called early date (c. 1450 BC) and late date (c. 1250 BC).

Migrations in southeastern Europe and southwestern Asia during the latter half of the second millennium BC led to the disruption of long-established populations in these regions. The disintegration of many cultures (i.e., the Hittite Empire and the Ugarit kingdom) has been attributed to the invasion of the southeastern Mediterranean coast by the mysterious Sea Peoples from the west. Egypt's initial success in repelling these western invaders was not matched in Canaan, where the Sea Peoples established five strongholds in southwestern Canaan. During this period of upheaval the larger international powers of the day (Egypt in the southwest, Mitanni in northern Mesopotamia, the Hittites in western Asia Minor) were preoccupied either with domestic issues or foreign issues that did not concern directly the land of Canaan. Their formidable, though occasional, presence in the area (i.e., Egypt's battles with the Hittites over control of the coastal highway leading to Syria) would provide a strong inducement toward peaceful coexistence among the smaller nations of the Levant. When the pressures from international powers waned, the Israelites often were engaged in warfare with local, hostile neighbors (Moabites, Canaanites, Midianites, Ammonites, Philistines, with the enigmatic Cushan-Rishathaim, king of Mesopotamia, perhaps being a notable exception [see Judg 3:7-11]). The Merneptah Stela (*ANET,* 320), unearthed by Flinders Petrie in 1896 in Thebes, eulogizes Pharaoh Merneptah, who ruled Egypt c. 1236-1223 BC. In a poem recounting Merneptah's campaign into Canaan, one line reads, "Israel is laid waste, its seed is not." This earliest known reference to Israel outside the Bible places Israel in a grouping with other defeated Canaanite states and coincides with the general time frame of the events related in the book of Ruth.

1. Moab
2. Status of Widows
3. Widowhood and Remarriage
4. Provisions for the Poor and Disenfranchised
5. The Court Scene
6. Genealogy

1. Moab.

In 1868, at the ancient site of Diblon (near the town of Dhiban in modern Jordan), the Moabite Stone was discovered. It is an inscription of the Moabite king Mesha, describing Moab's successful revolt against an unnamed Israelite ruler, presumably Ahab (874-853 BC) or possibly Jehoram his son (852-841 BC) (*ANET,* 209-10; see also 2 Kings 1:1; 3:4-27). What is important for our purposes is that the language attested by the Moabite Stone is closely related to the *Hebrew language, suggesting that at least the linguistic barriers to social intercourse between Israelites and Moabites were low.

2. Status of Widows.

Life expectancy rates in the ancient Near East were low due to factors such as famine, war, poverty and illness. The odds of surviving many of these disasters favored *women, leading to a proportionally large number of widows. Throughout the ancient Near East the family was the primary source of support for widows. Support could come from a dowry provided by the woman's family to the couple at time of *marriage that remained in the wife's possession after the death of her husband, specific provisions for her in her husband's will, incorporation into the household of one of her surviving male relatives, or remarriage. Most of these remedies and the prevailing patriarchal system of property ownership and inheritance rights in ancient Near Eastern societies made a widow dependent on her surviving male family members for sustenance. This could leave her vulnerable, particularly if, as in the case of *Naomi, she had no surviving male family members, if her sons, father, brothers, father-in-law or brothers-in-law proved negligent in caring for her, or if her husband had not made provision for her in his will. In the worst case, a widow could be left to choose between slavery, prostitution or destitution.

The customary provisions and legal protections for widows varied, but it was widely held that a mark of a good ruler was his care for widows. In the Ugaritic Tale of Aqhat (fourteenth century BC or earlier), a story about a childless ruler named Dan'el, who is blessed with a son, Aqhat, Dan'el's ruling activity is described as "judging the cause of the widow, adjudicating the case of the fatherless" (A.v. 4-7). In another Ugaritic tale about a ruler, "The Legend of King Kirtu" (fourteenth century BC or earlier), the king's son, who desires to seize the throne, constructs an accusation against his father's rule. The accusation begins, "Thou hast let thy hand fall into mischief. Thou judgest not the cause of the widow, nor adjudicatest the case of the wretched" (C.vi. 33-34, 46-50). In the Egyptian text Instructions for King Meri-Ka-Re (copied in the fifteenth century BC but purporting to be written for a pharaoh who ruled in the twenty-second century BC) the ruler is advised, "Do justice whilst thou endurest upon earth. Quiet the weeper; do not oppress the widow" (§45).

In addition to the role of the monarch as insurer of justice, preserved ancient Near Eastern laws dealing with widows give us a varied and incomplete but instructive picture of the extent of legal protection provided for widows. Eshnunna, a city in northern Mesopotamia west of Babylon, was a prominent military power at the end of the nineteenth and early eighteenth centuries BC under King Naram-Sin. The Laws of Eshnunna (LE), the earliest extant law collection written in Akkadian, have been preserved in three school exercise texts in which both the prologue and epilogue are missing. LE §17, while not speaking directly to the situation described in the book of Ruth, offers insight into the historical period: "Should the son of a man bring bride-money to the house of (his) father-in-law, if one of the two deceases, the money shall revert to its owner." In the case of the husband's death, the widow's father is prohibited from using the bride-price for, among any number of other things, maintenance of his widowed daughter.

The Code of Hammurabi (CH [c. 1792-1750 BC]), attributed to the sixth ruler of the Old Babylonian (Amorite) dynasty, is the most comprehensive extant legal code surviving from the ancient Near East. Hammurabi had monumental stelae inscribed with his law code erected throughout major cities of his kingdom as testimony to his repeated claims: "Hammurabi, the devout, god-fearing prince, to cause justice to prevail in the land, to destroy the wicked and evil, that the strong might not oppress the weak" (CH §30). His laws have survived in some fifty manuscripts dating from the reign of Hammurabi to the middle of the first millennium BC. The most impressive artifact is a diorite stela, about 2.3 m tall, depicting the sun-god Shamash's commissioning of Hammurabi to write the law code. The stela was carried off to Susa by Elamite raiders some five hundred years after Hammurabi's death and was discovered by the French archaeologist J. deMorgan in 1901-1902. CH §171-172 provide for a widow to retain possession of her dowry, retain any documented marriage gift given to her by her husband or, in its absence, receive a share of the estate equal to that of the other heirs, and remain in her husband's house until she decides to remarry. If she does remarry, she may take her dowry with her but must leave the marriage gift to her children. CH §177 requires a widow whose children are still minors to get the consent of the court and to sign an affidavit with her new husband that they will protect her deceased husband's estate and raise his children until they come into their inheritance. Implied in these provisions is the widow's control as a trustee over her deceased husband's estate while her children are still minors.

In the Middle Assyrian Laws (MAL), a series of clay tablets discovered in ancient Ashur and dated to the twelfth century BC, MAL §46 deals in some detail with the case of a widow who "does not wish to leave her house on her husband's death." This clause most likely refers to the woman's desire not to remarry outside her husband's family, since most of the provisions that follow have her moving somewhere else anyway. The law illustrates the wide variety of ways in which a widow might be provided for by her family. First, the husband could have specifically made a bequest for her in his will. If not, she could move in with one of her sons, and the sons of her husband by all his wives would help pay for her support. If she had no sons of her own, she could move in with one of her husband's sons by another wife. If the sons of another of her husband's wives are unwilling to support her, her own sons must take on the burden and "she shall do their work." Finally, one of her husband's sons (from another wife) could marry her and take full responsibility for her support.

The Neo-Babylonian Laws (NBL), written in Akkadian and commonly attributed to the Neo-Babylonian period (c. seventh-sixth century BC), were discovered in the British Museum by F. E. Peiser, who translated and published them in 1899. Although these are the latest of the extant ancient law codes, they have been poorly preserved, with only nine out of an original sixteen paragraphs being legible. These laws include two provisions relating to widows. NBL §12 stipulates that a widow with no children will receive from the estate only her dowry and any marriage gift given to her by her husband. If she had no dowry, "the judges shall appraise her husband's property and something commensurate with her husband's property shall be given her." NBL §13 grants the widow who remarries the right not only to her dowry but also to any marriage gift from her deceased husband.

These laws assume and attempt to enforce, channel, delimit or supplement the customary family-oriented practices used in ancient Near Eastern cultures to provide for widows. They present not a systematic, comprehensive overview but rather a sampling of solutions to specific problems encountered by courts when parties to customary practices were sufficiently unhappy with the outcome to bring a complaint. They hint at possible alternate solutions to the predicament of Naomi and Ruth. They also point indirectly to the importance of the one remedy that we have largely overlooked in our survey so far: remarriage.

3. Widowhood and Remarriage.

Typically, the father or eldest son in the household made the contractual arrangements with the prospective bride's parents. A male could negotiate for himself if his father was deceased or if he was an adult. The fact that there is no mention of a father-in-law in BE 6/1.101 (Babylonian Expedition of the University of Pennsylvania, Series A: Cuneiform Texts) and CT 8.2a (Cuneiform Texts from Babylonian Tablets in the British Museum) is interpreted as indicating that the groom was responsible for his own negotiations (Campbell). Depending on local traditions and circumstances, a widow could also negotiate a marriage contract on her own behalf. The Code of Hammurabi speaks of a widow's remarriage as a free decision. "If that woman has made up her mind to leave [the deceased husband's house], she shall leave to her children the marriage-gift which her husband gave her (but) take the dowry from her father's house in order that the man of her choice may marry her" (CH §173). Likewise, in CH §177, when "a widow, whose children are minors, has made up her mind to enter the house of another," she is legally restricted only to protect the rights of her deceased husband's heirs.

Another example of this freedom is found with "war widows," cases in which a woman facing hardship because her husband is away from home for a long period of time remarries. The Laws of Eshnunna (LE §29-30) frame the issue in a way that leaves the woman's autonomy in doubt: "another man takes his wife." In other texts, however, the wife clearly seeks remarriage. CH §134 states, "If the seignior was taken captive and there was not sufficient to live on in his house, his wife may enter the house of another, with that woman incurring no blame at all." MAL §36 and §45 address similar situations by basing the wife's freedom to remarry on the absence of a father-in-law or sons to support her. A woman without a father-in-law or sons whose husband is missing for a number of years is free to marry the husband "of her own choice."

The relative freedom of a widow to choose a new marriage partner varied with location and circumstances. In some cases, endogamous remarriage was encouraged due to her deceased husband's family's vested interest in the dowry.

In 1929 excavations in modern Iraq unearthed some four thousand clay tablets written in Akkadian cuneiform from the ancient Hurrian city of Nuzi (or Nuzu), which flourished c. 1500-1350 BC. Evidence from Nuzi demonstrates that a widow was penalized for remarrying due to the financial hardship that the loss of her dowry inflicted on her deceased husband's family (JEN 4.444:19-23; see Campbell). Similarly, there appears to have been a tendency toward forced endogamy as a way of providing for the widow and at the same time protecting the deceased husband's family from financial loss. The underlying cultural value is continued ownership of ancestral property.

Variations of the levirate marriage are attested in some ancient Near Eastern law codes, including an Akkadian text from Ugarit, MAL §30, §33, §43, and Hittite Laws §193. MAL §30 addresses the relatively unlikely situation in which a married son dies, his father has only one other son, and that son is already betrothed to another woman. The ruling is that the father will give the widow of his dead son to the other son regardless, the relationship of his remaining son to the betrothed to be determined by other factors. The ruling suggests that marrying a widow to one of her husband's brothers was a common practice. MAL §43 refers specifically to a situation in which the bride had been promised but the relationship had not yet been consummated. It presents a long list of alternate spouses for the betrothed, including any of the deceased's brothers and sons, with the proviso that if the deceased's sons are under ten years of age, the betrothed's father has the option of returning the bride-price instead. MAL §33 deals with the case of a woman whose husband dies while she is still living with her father. The text is damaged, but it appears to give the father the choice of how to provide for his daughter: "If he wishes, he may give her in marriage to her father-in-law. If her husband and her father-in-law are both dead and she has no son, she becomes a widow; she may go where she wishes." Another interesting feature of this law is that the woman is not considered a "widow" (almattu) unless other domestic arrangements cannot be found.

The Hittite Laws (HL) were discovered on two clay tablets at Boğazköy (also known as Hattusas), in modern day Turkey in 1893. They were written in Hittite with cuneiform script some-

time near 1200 BC. Several copies written in Old Hittite have turned up since, putting the original composition back at least as far as 1600 BC. HL §193 reads, "If a man has a wife, and then the man dies, his brother shall take his wife, then his father shall take her. If in turn his father dies, one of his brother's sons shall take the woman whom he had." Translators differ over the exact identification of the "man," the "brother," the "father" and the "brother's sons." In any case, there is a clear succession of potential spouses for the widow as in MAL §43.

These laws indicate that in many parts of the ancient Near East it was common practice for a widow to marry a near relative of her deceased husband. In most cases the laws do not explain the purpose of the practice, making it difficult to relate them to the biblical practice of levirate marriage. We can at least say that the practice of a woman marrying a near relative of her deceased husband was part of Israel's cultural milieu and may be reflected in the understanding of the responsibilities of the *kinsman-redeemer (gōʾēl) found in the book of Ruth.

4. Provisions for the Poor and Disenfranchised. In the Egyptian "Tale of the Eloquent Peasant" (c. 1800 BC) an unscrupulous official named Thutenakht devises a plan by which to seize the donkeys of an unsuspecting peasant named Khun-Anup, who happens to be journeying through on his way to securing food for his hungry family. Thutenakht has a servant block the road with linen sheets, thus forcing the unsuspecting Khun-Anup to steer his donkeys onto the grain field. When one donkey enjoys a mouthful of the tempting grain, Thutenakht beats the man and seizes his donkeys. The persistent Khun-Anup eloquently pleads his case before the courts and finally wins the hearing of a sympathetic official after being rebuffed by lower court officials. He delivers nine elaborate and impressive speeches, and his rhetorical skill moves the court to grant him justice and punish the offending Thutenakht. The court decision demonstrates the importance of extending justice to the lower classes, in this case hospitality to travelers in Egypt.

Ruth's determination to glean in the fields (Ruth 2:2) reflects her understanding (inferred perhaps from Naomi's teachings) of one of the prescribed rights of the disenfranchised. Mosaic legislation required that the harvesters deliberately leave grain around the edges and in the corners of the field for the economically vulnerable, which included widows, the fatherless and aliens (Lev 19:9-10; 23:22; Deut 24:19). Her words "in whose eyes I may find favor" (Ruth 2:2) reflect the reality that not all were careful to fulfill their obligations to the destitute as prescribed in the Torah.

Ration lists from Mesopotamia reflecting the dietary intake of average citizens may shed light on the significance of the amount of barley that Ruth gleaned on her first day in the fields (Ruth 2:17). Once calculations have been adjusted for variations in time and measurement, it appears that one liter (usually of barley) was the average food ration throughout Mesopotamia. Assuming the preexilic measurement equivalent of an ephah (ten to twenty liters of barley), it appears that Ruth gleaned enough barley on her first day (an ephah) to sustain Naomi and herself for about one week. If one assumes that Ruth continued to glean this much each day (Ruth 2:23), by the end of the harvest season she would have gleaned enough provisions for almost a year. Certainly the abundant generosity of *Boaz would have not been lost on the initial audience, familiar with daily rations (Younger).

A recently published document, "Widow's Plea," a fifteen-line Hebrew inscription from Iron Age Israelite society discovered in 1960, recounts a childless widow pleading her case before the king, requesting usufruct privileges of a part of her deceased husband's fields. Lack of information regarding issues such as the age of the widow, prior inheritance arrangements, and the marital status of the deceased husband's brother render the inscription of limited value. However, "Widow's Plea" may shed light on Ruth's choice of words in her self-descriptions to Boaz. When the startled Boaz awoke from his sleep and inquired as to who was at his feet, Ruth responded by identifying herself as "your servant Ruth" (Ruth 3:9). English translations obscure what are most likely subtle but important distinctions between the various Hebrew words used for servant in the book. Although the words šipḥâ and ʾāmâ can be used interchangeably (Gen 30:3-4), some scholars suggest that semantic distinctions are discernible. In their first encounter Ruth identified herself as Boaz's šipḥâ (Ruth 2:13), a term used to refer to a female slave who found herself at the bottom of the social ladder, one who performed menial

service and thus was not considered as a potential candidate for marriage or concubinage by a freeman. But in the scene at the threshing floor Ruth chose a different Hebrew word, this time identifying herself as Boaz's ʾāmâ, a word never used to refer to menial service, which leads some scholars to suggest that it denotes a female occupying a higher position on the social ladder, one who in particular was an eligible candidate for marriage (or concubinage) to a freeman. The translation "handmaid" or "maidservant" might bring out this nuance better. Ruth delicately nuanced her self-designation in order to emphasize her social proximity to Boaz and thus establish her potential as a wife. The usage of ʾāmâ twice in "Widow's Plea" appears to support this nuanced understanding of the word as an appropriate discretionary term used by a woman in her pleas to a recognized individual of higher social status and authority (so also Younger).

Furthermore, Ruth went beyond Naomi's directives and asked Boaz to "spread the corner of your cloak over me, for you are a near kinsman" (Ruth 3:9). Ruth's request reflected an ancient Near Eastern marriage custom (still practiced among some Arab cultures) whereby a man symbolically secured a wife by placing the corner of his garment about her. Such action indicates his willingness to protect the woman as well as his readiness to consummate the marriage with sexual activity. It has been suggested that the symbolic action further pointed to marriage as an event that covers a woman's nakedness, as opposed to adultery, which was viewed as the uncovering of a woman's nakedness.

Ancient Near Eastern towns usually were walled and built on top of a hill for purposes of defense. The town gate was extremely important for the life of the community. In addition to controlling access into the town, it served as an assembly place where judicial, social, religious, business and political matters were discussed and resolved. It contained both inner and outer rooms for conducting business, as well as lookout towers where watchmen would be stationed to alert the inhabitants of an approaching threat. Thus, it is appropriate to think of a gate complex rather than a single structure. Threshing floors are often associated with city gates (2 Aqht 5:6-7; 1 Kings 22:10), although in the book of Ruth the threshing floor is located outside of the town (Ruth 3:15).

5. The Court Scene.

Ruth 4 opens with Boaz going up to the town gate and sitting down with some of the elders of the town, eagerly waiting for the unnamed kinsman to come by so that the legal issue could be resolved. Boaz explained to the relative that Naomi wanted to sell some property belonging to her deceased husband, Elimelech. The designation of the property as the deceased Elimelech's allotment (Ruth 4:3) highlights the Mosaic emphasis on the land as an inheritance from the Lord that was to remain within the family (Lev 25:23). The precise nature of Naomi's situation is unclear. It is possible that her current destitute situation was forcing her to temporarily forfeit the usage of the land. The reference does not seem to refer to her outright selling of the land, since the patricentric nature of property transference did not allow for a widow to claim the land (Num 27:1-11). Here we have an example of divergence between Mosaic legislation and ancient Near Eastern law. According to CH §171, a man could grant, by a sealed and witnessed document, property to his wife, who was then free to dispose of the land as she saw fit, as long as the property remained with one of the man's children. She could not assign the property to her own family or to children by a later husband. Additionally, whereas the Code of Hammurabi acknowledged three classes of society (the *amelu*, the *mushkenu*, the *wardu*), distinguishing them in legislation, the Mosaic law, *as written*, applied to all Israelites regardless of social or economic status. As may be expected, corruption, especially favoritism toward those in power and mistreatment of the disenfranchised, was found in the Israelite courts (see Is 5:8-10; Mic 2:1-2). However, whereas in the Mosaic legislation, for example, all widows, regardless of social or economic status, were to be treated the same way, in Babylon these recognized distinctives were built into the law itself.

After the relative ceded his responsibilities, he removed his sandal, gave it to Boaz in the presence of the town elders, and publicly rejected the offer (Ruth 4:7-8). The sandal gesture served as a symbolic pointer to the man's waiver of his own rights and transferal of them to another and thus is to be distinguished from the prescription cited in Deuteronomy 25:8-10, where the spurned widow was to disgrace him publicly and spit in his face. A number of legal texts from Nuzi describe transfers of land ownership in terms of the current owner "lifting his foot" off the property and placing the new owner's foot on the property (JEN 59, 9-10). The verbal similarity with Ruth 4:7-8 suggests at least a shared legal tradition.

Boaz then invokes all the assembled elders and other parties at the trial as witnesses to his purchase of the land and acquisition of Ruth as his wife, to which they all agree orally. Numerous legal documents from various sites in the ancient Near East attest to the practice of recording the resolution of a civil case in writing, with the presiding officials and all the parties to the case present at the trial acting as witnesses by having their names affixed to the written record, often accompanied by an identifying mark, such as a thumbnail impression or a seal pressed onto the document using the type of seal cylinders commonly recovered from ancient Near Eastern excavations. Although nothing in the text of Ruth indicates that the decision was documented, Boaz's summary statement and the invocation of witnesses bears a strong resemblance to the procedures followed in these documents.

There is no indication in Ruth 4 that either Naomi or Ruth was present at the proceedings. It appears that Boaz took care of the entire matter. Boaz won the right to purchase the land and marry Ruth. Boaz's marriage to Ruth was followed by the birth of their son Obed, who is called Naomi's kinsman-redeemer by the women of the town (Ruth 4:13-17). The production of an heir was the primary focus of marriage in the ancient Near East. Failure to do so disrupted the generational inheritance system and left the parents in a vulnerable situation with no one to care for them in their later years.

6. Genealogy.

The book of Ruth ends with a linear genealogy (Heb *tôlĕdôt*) that traces Boaz's ancestral line from Perez to the future king *David. The genealogical epilogue attests to God's *ḥesed* in providing a king that emerged from the tumultuous period of the judges. Furthermore, David's Judean pedigree is emphasized. The ten-member genealogy finds parallels in the king lists of surrounding ancient Near Eastern cultures, suggesting that the book of Ruth functioned as a royal birth narrative. Both in Babylon (The Genealogy of Hammurabi's Dynasty) and in Assyria (The Assyrian King List) ideal genealogies were constructed to establish the pedigree of the royal lineage. Scholars have also noted that the ten-member construct parallels other biblical genealogies (Adam to Noah [Gen 5:1-32]; Shem to Abraham [Gen 11:10-26]). The impulse to organize important periods of time around the number *ten* may explain the position of Perez (whose ignoble beginnings would hardly be considered a desirable focal point for a royal genealogy) at the beginning of the list in Ruth 4 rather than the more desirable name (if not character) of Judah, Perez's father, whose name was more readily associated in ancient Israel (Gen 49:8-10) with royal legitimacy. Commencing the genealogy with Perez also assigns Boaz the honorable seventh position and provides a link between Perez's own levirate history (Gen 38) and that of Obed, the child born to Boaz and Ruth through the levirate relationship (Ruth 4:12).

See also KINSMAN-REDEEMER AND LEVIRATE; MARRIAGE AND SEX; SOCIAL-SCIENTIFIC APPROACHES.

BIBLIOGRAPHY. **D. Block,** *Judges, Ruth* (NAC 6; Nashville: Broadman & Holman, 1999). **K. M. Campbell**, *Marriage and Family in the Biblical World* (Downers Grove, IL: InterVarsity Press, 2003); **M. W. Chavalas and K. L. Younger Jr.,** *Mesopotamia and the Bible: Comparative Explorations* (Grand Rapids: Baker Academic, 2002). **P. R. Davies and J. Rogerson,** *The Old Testament World* (2nd ed.; Louisville: Westminster John Knox, 2005). **J. de Waard and E. A. Nida,** *A Translator's Handbook on the Book of Ruth* (London: United Bible Societies, 1973); **E. Lacheman,** "Note on Ruth 4:7-8," *JBL* 56 (1937) 53-56; **M. D. Matlock,** "Obeying the First Part of the Tenth Commandment: Application from the Levirate Marriage Law," *JSOT* 31 (2007) 295-310; **V. H. Matthews**, *Studying the Ancient Israelites: A Guide to Sources and Methods* (Grand Rapids: Baker Academic, 2007); **V. H. Matthews and D. C. Benjamin,** *Old Testament Parallels: Laws and Stories from the Ancient Near East* (3rd ed.; New York: Paulist, 2006); **K. R. Nemet-Nejat,** *Daily Life in Ancient Mesopotamia* (Peabody, MA: Hendrickson, 1998); **E. Neufeld**, *The Hittite Laws* (London: Luzac, 1951); **J. M. Sasson, ed.,** *Civilizations of the Ancient Near East* (4 vols.; Peabody, MA: Hendrickson, 2006); idem, *Ruth: A New Translation with a Philological Commentary and a Formalist-Folklorist Interpretation* (Baltimore: Johns Hopkins University Press, 1979); **E. A. Speiser**, "Of Shoes and Shekels," *BASOR* 77 (1940) 15-20; **W. von Soden,** *The Ancient Orient: An Introduction to the Study of the Ancient Near East* (Grand Rapids: Eerdmans, 1985). **J. H. Walton,** *Ancient Israelite Literature in Its Cultural Context: A Survey of Parallels between Biblical and Ancient Near Eastern Texts* (Grand Rapids: Zondervan, 1989); idem, *Ancient Near Eastern Thought and the Old Testament: Introducing the Conceptual World of the Hebrew Bible* (Grand Rapids: Baker Academic, 2006); **K. L. Younger Jr.,** "Two Comparative Notes on the Book of Ruth," <http://www.jtsa.edu/Documents/pagedocs/JANES/1998%2026/Younger26.pdf>.

E. Moore

RUTH 3: HISTORY OF INTERPRETATION

For over two millennia the book of Ruth has been valued for its literary charm and elegance. From generation to generation Jewish and Christian interpreters of Ruth have found in its pages material relevant for spiritual nurture, preaching, apologetics and everyday living. The wide and varied uses of Ruth reflect the many communities within which Ruth has been read and the challenges faced by those communities as they have applied Ruth in their own social and historical contexts.

    1. Place in the Canon
    2. Jewish Exegesis
    3. New Testament
    4. Early Church
    5. Medieval Jewish and Christian Exegesis
    6. Reformation
    7. Modern Era

1. Place in the Canon.

In Hebrew manuscripts the book of Ruth appears among the Writings (Ketubim). The commonly found order of *Proverbs, Ruth, *Song of Songs is reflected in the Leningrad Codex and may be inspired by an understanding of Ruth as an illustration of the virtuous woman (*ʾēšet-ḥayil* [Prov 31:10; also Ruth 3:11]) described in Proverbs 31:10-31. The arrangement of Ruth before Song of Songs connects it to another book in which love and *marriage are dominant interests. Where Ruth follows Song of Songs as the second of the five *Megillot, the intent seems to have been to follow the order of the Jewish festivals at which the books were read. The Talmud

(*B. Bat.* 14b) offers a list of books in which Ruth appears ahead of *Psalms as the first book of the Writings. This arrangement may arise from the association both books have with *David. For its part, the LXX counts Ruth among the Historical Books, placing it between Judges and Samuel. This arrangement seems inspired by the reference to the Judges period in Ruth 1:1 and may also reflect the rabbinic belief that all three books were authored by Samuel. The Talmud, by virtue of its discussion of authorship (*B. Bat.* 14b) and by introducing quotations from Ruth with the phrase "As it is written" (e.g., *b. Soṭah* 42b), shows the book to have been accepted as inspired at an early date within Judaism.

2. Jewish Exegesis.

2.1. Josephus. In his *Jewish Antiquities* the Jewish historian Josephus provided a retelling of Ruth (Josephus *Ant.* 5.318-337) designed to present the Jewish people favorably to a Greco-Roman audience and demonstrate that God rewards the virtuous (Josephus *Ant.* 1.20) (see Sterling, 105). Josephus significantly condenses and alters the biblical account by his omission of most instances of direct speech and references to God. The latter tendency is curious because it pushes the activity of God into the background and seems at odds with Josephus's stated desire to show how God can elevate anyone regardless of humble origin (Josephus *Ant.* 5.337). At several points Josephus alters the text of Ruth in keeping with the sensitivities and expectations of his Gentile readership. Most notable among these is the way in which he glosses over the episode of Ruth's conversion, proselytism being a sensitive issue in first-century Roman society where traditional religion and values were in decline. Elsewhere, Josephus shows deference to those same Roman values in the scene in which Ruth visits *Boaz at the threshing floor. Although Josephus is not reluctant to imply that the intention of *Naomi was for Ruth to have intercourse with Boaz (Josephus *Ant.* 5.328), he makes it clear that no intercourse took place, going so far as to state that Obed was born a full ten months after the marriage of Boaz and Ruth (Josephus *Ant.* 5.330, 335). Further on, Josephus presumably anticipates the sensitivities of his audience when he departs from the biblical text and explains the nearest relative's reluctance to redeem as being rooted in the fact that he was already married (Josephus *Ant.* 5.334), thus avoiding a portrayal of polygamy. The insertion at the end of his account of the statement that God had decreed a twenty-one-generation lifespan for David's house (Josephus *Ant.* 5.336) allows Josephus at once to reassure his audience and register his own tacit disapproval of the Davidic messianism that flourished in first-century Roman Palestine. Despite his interest in virtue, it is the case that Josephus exhibits less of the pietistic and didactic interests that characterize the work of his rabbinic contemporaries.

2.2. Talmud and Targum. Within the Talmud Ruth is revered for her place in the ancestry of David (*b. Ber.* 7b; *b. B. Bat.* 14b). In *b. Šabbat* 113b the manner in which Ruth prepares for her meeting with Boaz is interpreted spiritually in order to provide a model for the observance of the Sabbath.

Like other texts of the same genre, the *Targum to Ruth is an Aramaic paraphrase of the Hebrew text that adds background, addresses interpretive problems, and explains the meaning of the original. The Targum adds background information by identifying Boaz with the judge Ibzan (*Tg. Ruth* 4:21; cf. Judg 12:8-10) and Ruth as a daughter of the Moabite king Eglon (*Tg. Ruth* 1:4; cf. Judg 3:12-30). It also seeks to situate the book liturgically by connecting the reference to the barley harvest in Ruth 1 with the fact that Naomi and Ruth arrive in Bethlehem at Passover (*Tg. Ruth* 1:22). The logical problem of how Ruth is able to transport the large amount of grain given to her after her nocturnal encounter with Boaz is addressed by the remark that she was given miraculous strength for the task (*Tg. Ruth* 3:15).

Throughout the Targum observance of Torah is emphasized and celebrated. For example, the sons Mahlon and Chilion die because they violated the Torah's ban on intermarriage with Moabites (*Tg. Ruth* 1:4; cf. Deut 23:4). Occasionally, Torah is expounded by the creation of expanded conversations that move from the biblical story line to legal instruction. Elaborating on the conversation that Ruth and Naomi have on the road to Judah, the author places in the mouth of Naomi specific details regarding the number of commandments and the length of a Sabbath day's walk (*Tg. Ruth* 1:16-17). The legal problem of Ruth's foreign status is addressed when Ruth first encounters Boaz and quotes to him the Deuteronomic injunction against Moabites entering the congregation of Israel (Deut 23:4). In response, Boaz remarks that this edict was intended to apply only to males, and that he himself had received prophetic knowledge that from Ruth there would arise both kings and prophets (*Tg. Ruth* 2:10-11). Although the moral and spiritual admonitions of the Targum on Ruth are generally unremarkable, at times the treatment of specific points of halakah follows a view that is at odds with that espoused in the Mishnah—a fact that may suggest an early origin for at least parts of the Targum (É. Levine, 6-8; Beattie, 11).

2.3. Midrash. The Midrash *Ruth Rabbah* contains a wide range of rabbinic teaching inspired by, or at least structured around, the book of Ruth. Throughout, slight or imagined oddities in the text inspire questions or comments that become catalysts for densely packed rabbinic speculation or instruction on a wide range of topics. After this manner, even the first verse of the book gives rise to teaching on topics so diverse as leadership, rejection of wisdom, weights and measures, and global famines (*Ruth Rab.* 1.1-5 [Neusner V]). At Ruth 1:14, the similarity in sound between the name "Orpah" and the number "four" in Hebrew gives rise to the opinion that Orpah traveled only four miles (Aram *my lyn*) with Naomi, and that four heroes would descend from her (*Ruth Rab.* 2.20 [Neusner XVIII:i1.A-2.B]). At many points the text of Ruth leads to the exegesis of an entirely different biblical book. The death of Mahlon and Chilion (Ruth 1:5), for example, prompts a note about the warnings that God gives prior to exercising judgment, which in turn leads to a treatment of the first chapter of *Job and the death of Job's children (*Ruth Rab.* 2.10 [Neusner IX:i.1]).

The Midrash interprets the names in Ruth as having narrative and spiritual significance. "Elimelech," for example, is understood (erroneously) to mean "To me belongs kingship" (*Ruth Rab.* 2.5 [Neusner VI:ii.1.A-D]), while the name "Orpah" is related to the word for "back," signifying the manner in which she turned her "back" on her mother-in-law and returned to her gods (*Ruth Rab.* 2.9, 21 [Neusner VIII:i.2.A-D; XIX:i.1]). The death of Elimelech is viewed as divine punishment brought on because he had abandoned the people of Bethlehem in their time of need (*Ruth Rab.* 1.4 [Neusner V:iii.1.B-I]). The conversion of Ruth in Ruth 1:16 pro-

vides impetus for a discussion of what is proper behavior for a good Israelite woman. Consequently, Naomi is described as instructing Ruth to avoid the theater and the circus, but to ensure that her house has a mezuzah (*Ruth Rab.* 2.21-22 [Neusner XX:i.2.A-3.I]). Both Ruth and Boaz are celebrated for their virtue, with Ruth being praised for her modesty (*Ruth Rab.* 4.6 [Neusner XXXI:i.2]) and Boaz for his love of Torah (*Ruth Rab.* 5.15 [Neusner LVI:i.1-3]). The emphasis on Torah is evident elsewhere in the way in which the closer relative is derided for being unaware of it (*Ruth Rab.* 7.7, 10 [Neusner LXVIII:i.3; LXXII:i.1]).

The theme of social justice emerges quite naturally in rabbinic comments on the book of Ruth. The episode in which Ruth gleans in Boaz's field, for example, provides an opportunity to discuss the importance of caring for the needy, with the rabbis going so far as to say that when God judges the world, it will be for Israel's failure to care for the poor (*Ruth Rab.* 5.9 [Neusner XLV:i.1-9]). The midrashic treatment of Ruth sounds strange to modern ears, but it is a testimony to the value that the rabbis placed in the book as Scripture and to the effort that they made to ensure that it remained relevant for Jewish life and learning.

3. New Testament.

Ruth is mentioned in the NT only once, appearing alongside Tamar and Rahab in the genealogy of Jesus provided by Matthew (Mt 1:1-18). The fact that this list makes no attempt at thoroughness in its mention of *women shows that those who are included are in some way exceptional. Although interpreters going back to Jerome (*Comm. Matt.* 1.1.15-20) have emphasized the allegedly scandalous aspect of each woman's story, it is better to see each figure as an example of one who demonstrated a remarkable faithfulness and strength of character that allowed her to overcome serious disadvantage to contribute to the messianic line. That this is the case is suggested by the fact that Bathsheba is alluded to only as "Uriah's wife," placing the emphasis not on her adultery but rather on Uriah the Hittite's faithfulness to David. Thus, Matthew presumably includes Ruth as one who, despite her foreign origin, demonstrated profound covenant faithfulness in the manner in which she supported Naomi and entered into a marriage primarily intended to benefit her mother-in-law.

4. Early Church.

The earliest references to the book of Ruth among the writings of the church fathers are to its place in the *canon. Where Ruth is treated theologically, the person of Ruth is often understood to represent the church. Origen (c. 185-251/254), for example, views the story of how a Moabite came to be counted among Israel to represent the manner in which pagans enter the church (Origen *Fr. Matt.* 7 [1:5]). Ambrose of Milan (c. 333-397) regards the removal of the relative's sandal in Ruth 4:8 to mystically prefigure John the Baptist's claim to be unworthy to remove Christ's sandals (Mark 1:7; Luke 3:16; John 1:27; Acts 13:25) and to be symbolic of the marriage between Christ and the church (Ambrose *Fid.* 10.69-70). Similarly, Jerome (c. 347-419) sees Ruth as a type who fulfilled the prophecy of Isaiah 16:1 that a ruler would come out of the "rock of the wilderness" (i.e., Moab) (Jerome *Epist.* 53.8). Occasionally, Ruth is also identified with Israel. John Chrysostom (344/354-407), regards Ruth's appearance in the genealogy of Christ as a reminder that God espoused himself to those who would be unfaithful (i.e., Israel) and shows that a person is not limited by the unworthiness of their ancestors (Chrysostom *Hom. Matt.* 3.5; also *Hom. Matt.* 1.14).

Other patristic use of Ruth is didactic, pietistic and pastoral. For Augustine (354-430), Ruth teaches that widows could remarry (Augustine *de bono Viduitatis* 5) but also suggests that the most blessed women were those who married out of obedience rather than lust (Augustine *de bono Viduitatis* 10). Ambrose regards Ruth as an example of the benefits that accrue to those widows who invest in the spiritual development of younger women (Ambrose *De viduis* 6.33-34). Jerome often uses the book pastorally. When writing to a grieving friend, he once likens himself to Ruth, who had comforted a similarly bereaved Naomi (Jerome *Epist.* 39.5). More daring in his use of Ruth is Ephrem the Syrian (b. c. 306), who sees in Ruth's nocturnal encounter with Boaz a sexual advance symbolic of the boldness with which penitents should approach Christ (Ephrem the Syrian *Hymns on the Nativity* 7).

5. Medieval Jewish and Christian Exegesis.

Medieval Jewish exegesis builds upon the interest and content found in the Targum and the Talmud. In keeping with his predecessors, Rashi frequently employs the rabbinic technique of using a detail of the text to raise a question that in turn introduces a point of teaching. Rashi moves beyond earlier interpreters, however, by his use of grammatical observations in his exegesis.

For Rashi, the text can be a source of practical wisdom ranging from the sensitivity required when dealing with proselytes (Ruth 1:8) to the benefits of vinegar in hot weather (Ruth 2:14). More significant, however, is the way in which Rashi consistently interprets details of the text in conformity to talmudic teaching and ethics, even if this means overlooking the plain meaning of the Hebrew text. When Ruth and Naomi arrive at Bethlehem, the city is stirred up, not on account of the return of Elimelech's widow, but rather because of the sudden death of Boaz's wife (Ruth 1:19)—a detail made necessary by the fact that the Talmud required a potential *levir* to be unmarried. Likewise, the indication in the biblical text that Boaz was in a good mood while at the threshing floor is, according to Rashi, attributable to the fact that he was meditating on Torah (Ruth 3:7).

Medieval Christian interpretation of Ruth shows indebtedness to both Jewish and patristic exegesis. Treatments of Ruth from this era reflect a range of interpretive approaches, from the historical to the literal to the allegorical. Isidore of Seville (c. 560-636) provides a short allegorical treatment that continues the patristic tradition of seeing Ruth as a type of the church, pledging to follow Naomi in the same way that the church is committed to suffer for Christ (*On Ruth* [in Smith, 7-8]). A widely used medieval reference tool was the twelfth-century *Ordinary Gloss (Glossa Ordinaria)*. This work arranged primarily allegorical comments around the framework of Jerome's translation. Its presentation of multiple lines of allegorical interpretation demonstrates the range of opinions then current in the medieval church. According to the *Ordinary Gloss*, the famine that struck Bethlehem represents a scarcity of men learned in spiritual things, and the sojourn of Elimelech ("my God is king") in Moab represents the manner in which Christ sojourned in this world with his bride the church (Naomi). Naomi's two sons stand for the prophets and the apostles. The death of Elimelech in Moab is identified with Christ's ascension, after which the church/

Naomi is left on her own in the world. Boaz represents Christ at his second advent, intervening to rescue the church from the powers of the world. According to another view, however, Elimelech and Naomi stand for the Ten Commandments and synagogue respectively, and the death of Elimelech stands for the manner in which the Ten Commandments gave way to the Beatitudes (Smith, xiv-xv, 11-30). The later *Additions to the Ordinary Gloss* adds material that is less allegorical and reflects the enduring influence of Jewish and patristic traditions, culled as it is from sources including the Targum, Josephus, Jerome, Theodoret, Chrysostom and Ambrose (Smith, 31-36).

A short, largely historical, treatment of Ruth formed part of the *Scholastic History* produced by the French scholar Peter Comestor (d. c. 1179). This distillation of the biblical text, supplemented with material from Josephus and Comestor's own comments, has a decidedly historical slant, being generally limited to a straight explanation of the text with little allegorical embellishment. Reflective of this interest is the disproportionate attention given to the problem of the ritual involving the exchange of the sandal in Ruth 4 (*Scholastic History* 23: *On the Book of Ruth* [in Smith, 37-39]).

The two later works by Hugh of St. Cher (c. 1200-1263) and Nicholas of Lyra (c. 1270-1340) treat the book of Ruth from literal and allegorical perspectives and incorporate material from earlier Jewish and Christian exegesis. Hugh anticipates later canonical interests in his discussion of the reasons for the placement of Ruth between Judges and Kings, arguing that the beginning and the end of the book show it to be a bridge between the eras of the Judges and David. Although occasionally straying into the symbolic, Hugh's treatment of the literal sense is generally limited to offering clarification of the text and highlighting items of devotional interest.

In his comments on the allegorical aspect of the text Hugh shows an overarching interest in contrasting the church with the errors of Judaism and so reflects something of the anti-Semitism that was common in medieval Christian Europe. Thus, the famine that struck Bethlehem was an era of spiritual want in which the *law had become corrupted by Judaic traditions. In keeping with this tendency, Orpah is presented as the synagogue, which remained in unbelief,

and Ruth as the Gentile church, which clung firmly to Christ. The manner in which Ruth washes, anoints, and dresses prior to her nocturnal meeting with Boaz is taken as reflecting the way in which the believer receives baptism, the anointing of the Holy Spirit, and virtue respectively. Naomi's barrenness represents the synagogue and its inability to bear spiritual descendants except through the church. In a similar vein, the rejoicing of the neighborhood women is understood as symbolic of the virtuous inhabitants of heaven who praise the fertility of the church (*Postills on Ruth* [in Smith, 41-55]).

Nicholas of Lyra was a scholar of such stature that his commentaries were among the first to be printed. More than most medieval commentators, he incorporates a significant amount of Jewish interpretation, drawing heavily on the work of Rashi. Nicholas emphasizes the literal aspect of the text, showing a keen interest in placing the events of Ruth chronologically within the era of the Judges, noting particularly the difficulty in identifying Boaz as the judge Ibzan (Judg 12:8-10) and Ruth as the daughter of Eglon, king of Moab (Judg 3:12-30). Elsewhere, Nicholas draws upon the OT and Jewish exegesis to explain customs such as betrothal and levirate marriage (*see* Kinsman-Redeemer and Levirate). On occasion, Nicholas works to draw spiritual lessons even from a straightforward reading of the book. Typical of this is the manner in which he holds up Ruth's obedience to her mother-in-law, Naomi, as an example of humility and virtue.

Most of the spiritual teaching in Nicholas's work appears in his treatment of the moral sense of the text. Here Nicholas sometimes goes beyond the biblical text itself and founds his interpretation on Jewish tradition. For example, the belief that Elimelech's death was punishment for his miserly character is presented as a warning to the wealthy that they should not ignore the pleas of the less fortunate. Here too, Nicholas uses the allegorical method to provide instruction. The way, for example, that Ruth gleans in Boaz's field is seen as illustrative of the manner in which the humble and devout believer should listen to sermons and draw from them precepts that will provide guidance in life (*Postills on Ruth* [in Smith, 57-67]). The work of Nicholas of Lyra betrays a general awareness and admiration of Jewish learning. He sees the story of Ruth as a picture of one who converts to

Christianity, but he does so without the anti-Jewish undertone that colors the work of many of his predecessors, including Hugh of St. Cher.

6. Reformation.

When the Reformer Martin Luther (1483-1546) broke with the Roman Church, he did so not only over theological and ecclesiological issues but also by his eventual abandonment of the fourfold interpretative method that had long dominated Christian hermeneutics. For Luther, this involved a new emphasis on the literal sense of the text at the expense of the allegorical. This did not mean, however, that Luther ceased to read the OT christologically. For example, Luther describes the redemption of the foreigner Ruth as demonstrating how the divine word attracts and blesses not only members of the church but also outsiders (*Lectures on Genesis* 12.4 [Luther 2.276]; 35.2 [Luther 6.227-28]). Similarly, the manner in which Ruth lays down before Boaz is taken to be a picture of the way in which the soul lays down at the humanity of Christ and is covered by his righteousness (*Lectures on Romans* 4.7 [Luther 25.265]). Animosity toward the Jewish people sometimes found in medieval Christian exegesis surfaces in Luther's belief that Ruth's incorporation within Israel demonstrates that Jews and Gentiles are one flesh and shows Jewish arrogance to be without warrant (*Lectures on Genesis* 38.1-5 [Luther 7.14]; 41:45 [Luther 7.200-201]).

During this era of turmoil and persecution many Protestants strongly identified with the characters of Ruth and took comfort from the book's theme of deliverance. The Geneva Bible of 1560—the preferred translation of the English Reformers and Plymouth Colony—reflects this situation in its introduction to Ruth: "Wherein also figuratively is set forth the state of the Church which is subject to manifold afflictions, and yet at length God giveth good and joyful issue, teaching us to abide with patience till God deliver us out of troubles." During this period and subsequently the homiletical and devotional use of Ruth flourished. Ludwig Lavater (1527-1586), the Swiss reformer and son-in-law of Heinrich Bullinger, published no fewer than twenty-eight sermons on the book of Ruth. In the following century homiletically derived commentaries on Ruth were produced by the English preachers Richard Bernard (c. 1567-1641) and Thomas Fuller (1608-1661).

Around this same time John Bunyan (1628-1688) rendered the entire book of Ruth as poetry.

7. Modern Era.

Late nineteenth- and early twentieth-century interpretation of Ruth reflects the higher-critical interests then dominating the academy. During this period an awareness of Ruth's placement among the Writings, the alleged presence of Aramaisms, and the need to explain the rite involving the sandal (Ruth 4:7) moved discussion of dating beyond the rabbinic view and convinced many of the likelihood of a postexilic date of composition. Details such as the fact that Ruth's son is proclaimed as belonging to Naomi (Ruth 4:17) suggested to some the presence of distinct literary sources (Volz)—an approach that continues to have adherents (Brenner 1983). This era also witnessed the rise of an appreciation of the book's aesthetic qualities, anticipating the trend toward literary analysis that would emerge in the late twentieth century. Hermann Gunkel is representative of this era in seeing the book of Ruth as a poetic, popular legend that preserves nothing historical. Gunkel regarded the original story as featuring only Naomi as a destitute Judaean widow restored through the institution of levirate marriage. Only at a later stage was the character of Ruth incorporated into the narrative in a way that enhanced its overall poignancy. Gunkel broke new ground in the study of Ruth by describing it as a *novella—a short work of fiction featuring modest character development and a single, dominating event (Gunkel 1913; 1930).

Throughout the twentieth century much scholarly interest in Ruth focused on the character of the legal proceedings depicted in Ruth 4 and their possible relationship to the Israelite custom of custom levirate marriage (Gordis; Leggett; Anderson). Also of interest was the dating of the book, with much attention paid to the 1975 work of E. F. Campbell, who expressed doubt about both the benefits of attempting to reconstruct the oral and literary history of Ruth and the criteria used to argue for a late date for the book's composition. In the wake of the latter, more recent studies have tended to argue for the possibility of a preexilic, or early postexilic, origin for the book (Bush, 18-30). At present, however, no consensus on dating exists. Continuing the aesthetic interest initiated by Gunkel, many recent studies have focused on literary aspects of Ruth. Significant among such treatments have been analyses of the shape of the work (Bertman; Gow), its inner biblical allusions (Fewell and Gunn; Black) as well as its plot (Green) and theme (Bush, 47-53). Appreciation of the book's sophisticated literary structure has rendered earlier source-critical analyses of the book outmoded. Likewise, recognition of covenant loyalty (ḥesed) as a dominant theme has won many away from the earlier view that saw the book solely as a polemic against racial intolerance in the postexilic era of Ezra and Nehemiah.

Treatments of the book by feminist writers have often explored issues left unaddressed by the text but that are increasingly relevant given the distance between the patriarchal culture of ancient Israel and the very different social landscape of the industrialized West (see Feminist Interpretation). For example, the nineteenth-century struggle to open a wider range of career opportunities to women provided a context for the retelling of Ruth by pioneering feminist Elizabeth Cady Stanton, who described the Moabite widow as one who "believed in the dignity of labor and of self-support" (Stanton, 39). Among feminist authors perceptions of the book's message and value have varied widely, with some seeing the story as a model for lesbian relationships (Alpert), and others as a celebration of the relationship between two strong and resourceful women (Brenner 1983). For many, the patriarchy underlying the book renders it potentially exploitative, teaching that a woman's worth can be fully realized only through marriage and childbearing (A.-J. Levine; Masenya). Those who fall into this category sometimes find the emphasis on male inheritance in Ruth 4 to be in tension with the female interests in Ruth 1—3. For P. Trible (192-96), this tension is resolved by the women of Bethlehem who do not allow the story to be subverted by patriarchy, but who transform it into a "story of women making a new beginning with men." A few writers, however, have addressed this inner tension by examining the function of patriarchy within an ancient social context of female vulnerability and in so doing have been able to focus on the book's theme of covenant loyalty (Rowell).

Increasingly, Ruth is read from different social locations (see Social-Scientific Approaches). Some who have written from the perspective of

a visible minority have seen in Ruth the story of an outcast who challenges negative stereotypes (Masenya) or a tale that speaks to the plight of foreign workers (Brenner 1999). Still others have sought to interpret the story against the background of the Native American experience (Donaldson 1999).

For many interpreters, the literary beauty of Ruth remains its most compelling feature. It is a remarkable achievement that in just eighty-five verses, an unknown author has woven a tale of covenant loyalty, the hidden work of God, and the ancestry of the Davidic line that has taught, comforted, and challenged readers for over two millennia.

See also HERMENEUTICS; MEGILLOT AND FESTIVALS; RUTH 1: BOOK OF; RUTH 2: ANCIENT NEAR EASTERN BACKGROUND; SOCIAL-SCIENTIFIC APPROACHES; TARGUMIM.

BIBLIOGRAPHY. R. T. Alpert, "Finding Our Past: A Lesbian Interpretation of the Book of Ruth," in *Reading Ruth: Contemporary Women Reclaim a Sacred Story*, ed. J. A. Kates and G. T. Reimer (New York: Ballantine, 1994) 91-96; A. A. Anderson, "The Marriage of Ruth," *JSS* 23 (1978) 171-83; D. R. G. Beattie, ed. and trans., *The Targum of Ruth* (ArBib 19; Collegeville, MN: Liturgical Press, 1994); S. Bertman, "Symmetrical Design in the Book of Ruth," *JBL* 84 (1965) 165-68; J. Black, "Ruth in the Dark: Folktale, Law and Creative Ambiguity in the Old Testament," *LT* 5 (1991) 20-36; A. Brenner, "Naomi and Ruth," *VT* 33 (1983) 385-97; idem, "Ruth as a Foreign Worker and the Politics of Exogamy," in *Ruth and Esther*, ed. A. Brenner (FCB 2/3; Sheffield: Sheffield Academic Press, 1999) 158-62; F. W. Bush, *Ruth, Esther* (WBC 9; Dallas: Word, 1996); E. F. Campbell Jr., *Ruth* (AB 7; Garden City, NY: Doubleday, 1975); L. E. Donaldson, "The Sign of Orpah: Reading Ruth Through Native Eyes," in *Ruth and Esther*, ed. A. Brenner (FCB 2/3; Sheffield: Sheffield Academic Press, 1999) 130-44; D. A. Fewell and D. M. Gunn, "'A Son Is Born to Naomi!': Literary Allusions and Interpretation in the Book of Ruth," *JSOT* 40 (1989) 99-108; E. Giannarelli, "Ruth and the Church Fathers," *SIDIC* 23.2 (1990) 12-15; R. Gordis, "Love, Marriage and Business in the Book of Ruth: A Chapter in Hebrew Customary Law," in *A Light unto My Path: Old Testament Studies in Honor of Jacob M. Meyers*, ed. H. N. Bream et al. (GTS 4; Philadelphia: Temple University Press, 1974) 241-64; M. D. Gow, *The Book* of *Ruth: Its Structure, Theme and Purpose* (Leicester: Apollos, 1992); **B. Green,** "The Plot of the Biblical Story of Ruth," *JSOT* (1982) 55-68; **H. Gunkel,** "Ruth," in *Reden und Aufsätze* (Göttingen: Vandenhoeck & Ruprecht, 1913) 65-92; idem, "Ruthbuch," in *Die Religion in Geschichte und Gegenwart,* vol. 4, ed. H. Gunkel and L. Zscharnack (2nd ed.; Tübingen: Mohr Siebeck, 1930) 2180-82; **D. A. Leggett,** *The Levirate and Goel Institutions in the Old Testament, with Special Attention to the Book of Ruth* (Cherry Hill, NJ: Mack, 1974); **A.-J. Levine,** "Ruth," in *The Women's Bible Commentary,* ed. C. A. Newsom and S. H. Ringe (2nd ed.; Louisville: Westminster John Knox, 1998) 84-90; **É. Levine,** *The Aramaic Version of Ruth* (AnBib 58; Rome: Biblical Institute Press, 1973); **M. Luther,** *Luther's Works* (55 vols.; St. Louis: Concordia; Philadelphia: Fortress, 1955-1986); **M. Masenya,** "Ruth," in *Global Bible Commentary,* ed. D. Patte (Nashville: Abingdon, 2004) 86-91; **G. M. Rowell,** "Ruth," in *The IVP Women's Bible Commentary,* ed. C. Clark Kroeger and M. J. Evans (Downers Grove, IL: InterVarsity Press, 2002) 146-53; **L. Smith,** ed. and trans., *Medieval Exegesis in Translation: Commentaries on the Book of Ruth* (TEAMS Commentary Series; Kalamazoo, MI: Medieval Institute Publications, 1996); **E. C. Stanton,** ed., *The Woman's Bible* (2 vols. in 1; repr., Salem, NH: Ayer, 1988); **G. E. Sterling,** "The Invisible Presence: Josephus's Retelling of Ruth," in *Understanding Josephus: Seven Perspectives,* ed. S. Mason (JSPSup 32; Sheffield: Sheffield Academic Press, 1998) 104-71; **P. Trible,** *God and the Rhetoric in Sexuality* (OBT; Philadelphia: Fortress, 1978); **P. Volz,** "Review of D. W. Nowack, *Richter-Ruth übersetzt und erklärt* (HKAT I.4)," *TLZ* 26.13 (1901) 345-49.

B. P. Irwin

RUTH 4: PERSON

Ruth is one of three major characters in the book of Ruth. Although *Naomi is "brought on stage" before Ruth and "taken off" after Ruth, Ruth is the heroine, and the book that bears her name is suitably titled. The etymology and meaning of Ruth's name are uncertain and so do not figure into the message of the book. Outside of the book of Ruth, Ruth is mentioned only in Matthew 1:5 as the mother of Obed.

1. Ruth's Context
2. Ruth's Commitment to Yahweh
3. Ruth's Faith in Action
4. Ruth's Legacy

1. Ruth's Context.

The opening verse of the book of Ruth sets the context of Ruth's life in the period of the judges. The judges followed the conquest, as narrated in the book of Joshua, and preceded the rise of the monarchy in Israel, as described in the books of Samuel. Ruth, however, spent her early years in Moab. Because of Ruth's *marriage to an Israelite man, and because of extensive interaction between Israel and Moab, Ruth must have had some awareness of the political and social chaos described in the book of Judges, as well as of the tense relations between her homeland and that of her husband (Num 21—25; Judg 3:12-30). She would have known both the Moabite and Israelite perspectives on these events.

As suggested by Ruth 1:1, this background came into play for Ruth at the time of Mahlon's death and Naomi's decision to return to Bethlehem. Naomi advised her daughters-in-law to go back to their mothers. She undoubtedly knew that Orpah and Ruth would not be accepted in Bethlehem (Block, 632; Sakenfeld, 32), but Moabite women who were formerly married to Israelite men may also not have been accepted back into their Moabite circle of relations. The Moabites were hardly sympathetic with the Israelites' conquest of Canaan or the theological justification of it. Although it is hard to say how religious Elimelech, Naomi, Mahlon and Chilion were, even a nominal commitment of Ruth's in-laws to Yahweh could have led to her being ostracized from her family and friends.

If Naomi's future was uncertain because of losing a husband and two sons and living in an alien land, Ruth's future (and Orpah's) was equally uncertain. Nevertheless, Ruth committed herself to a disillusioned older woman who apparently had nothing and departed with her to a land where she would hardly be welcome. Why would Ruth not follow Orpah's example and remain in Moab?

2. Ruth's Commitment to Yahweh.

Ruth stayed with Naomi because she knew that the God of Israel accepted people regardless of background. How Ruth knew this about Yahweh is uncertain. Ruth 1 does not give the impression that Naomi was an energetic evangelist. According to J. C. Howell (283), "Naomi is hardly the kind of winsome witness sometimes paraded in church life today." Still, Ruth's faith apparently owed something to her in-laws, through whom she must have learned about Yahweh's acts and promises. Naomi's blessing of Orpah and Ruth in Yahweh's name (Ruth 1:8-9) would have made no sense if neither Orpah nor Ruth knew who Yahweh was.

The text is clear about why Ruth stuck with Naomi. Certainly Ruth cared for her mother-in-law, but Ruth clung to Naomi because of her devotion to the God of Naomi's people. In Ruth 1:16 Ruth exhibited the essence of clinging by her modification of the covenant motto. Instead of "I will be your God, and you will be my people" (cf. Ex 6:7), Ruth affirmed that God and God's people would be hers. Although the extent of Ruth's conversion is a debated issue (see Berlin, 48; Block, 641; Hubbard, 120; Sakenfeld, 32-33), Ruth left her homeland and entrusted her destiny to Naomi's God.

The Targum captures the sense of Ruth 1:16 with the following expansion: "Ruth said, 'Do not urge me to leave you, to go back from after you for I desire to be a proselyte'" (Beattie, 20). What God had done through the descendants of Abraham had accomplished its intended purpose of drawing this Gentile to faith (cf. Gen 12:2-3). "Proselyte," however, may be too weak a term. Ruth underwent more than a religious conversion. Perhaps more accurately stated, Ruth's religious conversion included a willingness to forsake all other ties—familial, ethnic, national (Block, 641). Did she understand even more than many of the Israelites what it meant to be a daughter of Abraham and part of the people of God? A person's blood descent from Abraham did not guarantee a relationship with Abraham's God (Grant, 439); rather, one had Abraham as spiritual father through sharing Abraham's faith in Yahweh and observing Yahweh's commands.

*Boaz recognized Ruth's commitment from what he had heard about her and also observed. When they first met, he was not disturbed by her nationality. Ruth had given up everything and had cast herself completely on the God of Israel. Although she was not a blood descendant of Abraham, her faith had the same object as his. As Abraham had left his family behind in Haran, so also Ruth had recently separated herself from the Moabites and identified with God's people (Sakenfeld, 33). Here was the essence of holiness to which God's people were called. Moreover, Ruth upheld the *law by showing

kindness to disadvantaged Naomi. She had done all this because of her trust in the God of Israel. Boaz properly regarded Ruth as a member of the covenant community. She was no foreigner barred from the assembly of God's people. The OT never called for ethnic or racial separation per se. Its standard for separation was theological (Atkinson, 67). God's people could not mix the tenets and practices of incompatible worldviews, and Ruth was not trying to do so. She had committed herself unreservedly to the content of Israel's faith, and her actions indicated her continuation in a true profession.

Ruth's devotion to this God who saved irrespective of nationality led her to make unusual decisions. Rather than take the seemingly safer option of staying in Moab, Ruth threw herself on the mercy and care of the God of Israel. Her trust in a covenant-making God caused her to abandon all other sources of security. If Orpah followed the sensible advice of Naomi, Ruth, it would seem, threw caution to the wind and made a foolish decision. She cast her lot with a destitute mother-in-law in an alien land. This decision occurred in the context of personal upheaval and emotional distress. When Ruth declared that her mother-in-law's God would be her God, there was nothing calm and ideal about her circumstances. Along with Naomi, Ruth had suffered a devastating loss that made her future insecure. Nevertheless, she, a Moabite, affirmed the essence of the Abrahamic covenant. Indeed, her faith surpassed Abraham's because she had no personal command or promise from Yahweh (Nielsen, 49; Sakenfeld, 33); rather, she acted on what God had promised to Abraham, and this in devastating and dire circumstances. She surely knew the risks from a human perspective, but the God of Israel (her God by faith) was, to her way of thinking, bigger than her predicament.

3. Ruth's Faith in Action.

The first chapter of Ruth ends with the return of Naomi to Bethlehem. Although Ruth was with her, Naomi did not seem eager to introduce her daughter-in-law to the people of Bethlehem and, in fact, brushed her off indirectly with references to emptiness and misfortune. Perhaps Naomi was embarrassed in front of the homefolks by a Moabite daughter-in-law. Still, they had returned because there was food in Bethlehem. They were now dependent on each other for survival.

The availability of food, however, did not automatically alleviate hunger. Whatever the status of Elimelech's property, Naomi and Ruth did not have a crop to harvest or money to buy food from someone else. Moreover, Naomi gave no indication that the nearer kinsman, Boaz, or anyone else was available to help. The immediate situation for these two widows was nothing short of desperate.

It was at this point that Ruth showed initiative and went out to the fields to glean. The law allowed for poor people and aliens to do this (Lev 19:9-10; Deut 24:19-22). Landowners could harvest their crops by passing through their field or orchard once. Any fruit or vegetable that was missed or dropped was to be left for the less fortunate to gather. Landowners were also not to reap the corners of their fields. It was, then, the responsibility of the disadvantaged person to pick up what remained. The landowner did not have to expend time and energy to make the ripe produce more readily available to the needy. Although the text is silent about how Ruth learned these details and provisions of the law, Ruth continued to evidence an active faith that trusted God and God's people to care for the needy.

Oppression, of course, was always a possibility, especially during times of spiritual coldness. It was one thing to have laws, another to keep them. Other passages from later periods of apostasy and apathy indicted God's people for taking advantage of widows (Ps 94:6; Is 1:23, 10:1-2; Mal 3:5). Ruth hoped to find a landowner who would allow her on his property, but there were no guarantees. The law told God's people how to live as such, but it could not coerce godly conduct. As events turned out, Ruth met not the owner of the field but rather his foreman, who, in keeping with the law, allowed Ruth to glean in the field that had already been harvested. When Boaz came later in the day, he exceeded the provision of the law by granting Ruth permission to pick grain alongside of his servant girls (Bush, 128).

Ruth 2:3 offers insight into the book's theology. The sentence literally reads, "Her chance chanced the portion of the field belonging to Boaz." A more idiomatic translation would capture the sense of the Hebrew: "It just so happened that she found herself in a portion of the field that belonged to Boaz." The reference to

blind chance is a brilliant rhetorical device that makes for good storytelling and theologizing. The writer did not believe in luck (Ruth 1:6, 4:13) but rather used this expression to get the reader thinking about the providential activity of God in the lives of Naomi and Ruth (Hals, 11-12; Sakenfeld, 47). Ruth's good fortune strained any belief in chance. From a human perspective, Ruth happened to glean in Boaz's field. She wandered into his field without intention or even knowledge. She could have just as unknowingly entered the field of the nearer kinsman or someone else. From the author's perspective, though, Ruth was on Boaz's property by design, and something significant was about to happen.

The "chance" wandering of Ruth onto Boaz's property is reinforced by what Naomi did not say in Ruth 2:2. When Ruth indicated her intention to glean in the field of "anyone in whose eyes I find favor," Naomi offered no suggestion as to where to inquire first. If Naomi had said nothing about kinsmen and levirate marriage while she, Orpah and Ruth were still in Moab, she again remained silent about advantageous possibilities (see Kinsman-Redeemer and Levirate). Being back home in Bethlehem had apparently not raised her hope for any familial solution to her (and Ruth's) destitution. The reader, therefore, cannot assign any credit to Naomi for Ruth's success in Boaz's field. Naomi's seemingly half-hearted consent to Ruth's initiative at the start of the day heightens the providential intervention of Yahweh later in the day. It also accentuates the faith and hope of Ruth.

Ruth continued to display faith during the nocturnal meeting on the threshing floor. The text does not report what she thought about Naomi's scheme and why she went ahead with it. It merely records her assent and compliance. Ruth went to the threshing floor, waited for the right moment, uncovered Boaz's legs, and lay down. In the context of a nocturnal meeting of a man and woman, the suggestive language—uncovering feet (or legs) and lying down—charges this encounter with sexual innuendo. Still, Ruth and Boaz did not commit fornication. If the double entendre indicates how awkward and tempting the situation was for both, the dialogue reveals their mutually godly intentions (Bernstein, 19-20; Campbell, 138). Ruth put Naomi's plan into action so as to ask Boaz to be the answer to his earlier prayer (Ruth 2:12) by redeeming Elimelech's land and fathering a child for Naomi. Ruth went to the threshing floor for more than herself (Sakenfeld, 61-62). Boaz's praise of Ruth demonstrated his understanding of her true intentions. By referring to her as a woman of noble character, he applied the same term to her that was used of him in Ruth 2:1. Ruth became his equal. She went from being a Moabite, a foreigner, and one less than Boaz's servant girls to being "my daughter" and now a woman of noble character.

Her background meant little now, for she had confessed her faith in Yahweh and demonstrated what was arguably the highest act of regard for the perpetuity of God's covenant with his people: pursuing levirate marriage. If the townspeople already knew that Ruth was a woman of noble character, all that would remain for them to say is that she was worth more than a son, even seven sons. This they did after Ruth and Boaz married and had a son (Ruth 4:15).

4. Ruth's Legacy.

In the first half of the twentieth century scholars typically considered the book of Ruth a charming and idyllic tale about humans who persevered against great odds in a bleak time and survived (Hals, 1). Ruth, of course, modeled industry, sacrifice and risk-taking. It is common today for feminist scholars to deny that the book of Ruth is charming and instead denounce the book's patriarchy (Linafelt and Beal, 81; Sakenfeld, 10). The intimate scene with a more domestic flavor in Ruth 3 regrettably gives way both to the legal proceedings at the gate between Boaz and the nearer kinsman and later to the genealogy of David. Still, feminist scholars salvage the book by lauding Naomi and Ruth for taking the initiative for their well-being and securing their place in society without male patronage (see Feminist Interpretation).

One cannot help but notice that Ruth acted with other interests in mind. Ruth approached Boaz on the threshing floor in order to invoke the law of levirate marriage for her and Naomi's situation. Ruth had earlier made use of the law that allowed needy people to glean in another person's field. Ruth understood that these laws were given to benefit her, not oppress her as a woman (Bauckham, 35). Rather than think that the male proceedings at the gate reduced her to a piece of merchandise, she would have considered them a necessary part of the solution to her and Naomi's plight. In a seemingly hopeless situation the law provided a way forward to prevent scandal and produce a happy outcome. Ruth wanted the scene at the gate to occur in order to legitimize what she and Boaz had agreed to do earlier on the threshing floor. Together, they were humbly and unselfishly acting on behalf of deceased relatives and surviving Naomi.

Ruth's legacy is not securing her future in reaction to patriarchy; rather, it is unconventionally but covenantally responding to God's grace by ministering to others in mundane yet extraordinary circumstances. Ruth could have never anticipated how Yahweh would take care of her and Naomi, but her commitment to Yahweh became the stage for him to act mightily and redemptively. Ultimately, her son became an ancestor of King David (Ruth 4:17) and of Jesus the *Messiah (Matt 1:5).

See also BOAZ; NAOMI; RUTH 1: BOOK OF; WOMEN.

BIBLIOGRAPHY. **D. Atkinson,** *The Message of Ruth* (Downers Grove, IL: InterVarsity Press, 1991); **R. Bauckham,** "The Book of Ruth and the Possibility of a Feminist Canonical Hermeneutic," *BibInt* 5 (1997) 29-45; **D. R. G. Beattie,** trans., *The Targum of Ruth* (ArBib 19; Collegeville, MN: Liturgical Press, 1994); **A. Berlin,** "Ruth: Big Theme, Little Book," *BRev* 12 (1996) 40-43, 47-48; **M. J. Bernstein,** "Two Multivalent Readings in the Ruth Narrative," *JSOT* 50 (1991) 15-26; **D. I. Block,** *Judges, Ruth* (NAC 6; Nashville: Broadman & Holman, 2002); **F. Bush,** *Ruth, Esther* (WBC 9; Dallas: Word, 1996); **E. F. Campbell Jr.,** *Ruth* (AB 7; Garden City, NY: Doubleday, 1975); **R. Grant,** "Literary Structure in the Book of Ruth," *BSac* 148 (1991) 424-41; **R. M. Hals,** *The Theology of the Book of Ruth* (Philadelphia: Fortress, 1969); **J. C. Howell,** "Ruth 1:1-18," *Int* 51 (1997) 281-84; **R. L. Hubbard Jr.,** *The Book of Ruth* (NICOT; Grand Rapids: Eerdmans, 1988); **T. Linafelt and T. K. Beal,** *Ruth and Esther* (Berit Olam; Collegeville, MN: Liturgical Press, 1999); **K. Nielsen,** *Ruth* (OTL; Louisville: Westminster John Knox, 1997); **K. D. Sakenfeld,** *Ruth* (IBC; Louisville: Westminster John Knox, 1999).

D. Ulrich

S

SAGES, SCHOOLS, EDUCATION

The place of the sage, or wise person, in Israelite society is not clear, although some attended kings. Although presumably they were responsible for "wisdom writings," which inculcate good and godly behavior in the young, there is no evidence for them running schools. *Scribes probably taught apprentices to read and write in the OT world. Traces of basic education survive in ancient Hebrew epigraphs, but, while the range of school texts known from Babylonia and Egypt is lacking, the biblical texts themselves may have served as standard works for training scribes.

1. The Sage
2. Schools in the Ancient Near East
3. Schools in Ancient Israel
4. Wisdom Books and Schools
5. Education in Ancient Israel

1. The Sage.

The sage, or wise person, is mentioned more often in the books of biblical wisdom, poetry and writings than in other books. The Hebrew ḥākām (fem. ḥākāmâ) signifies not merely one with knowledge or skill but rather one with the ability to apply that experience advantageously, as the illustration of the small animals in Proverbs 30:24-28 shows. The Aramaic cognate is comparable in meaning (see. e.g., *Ahiqar* 1, 12, 178), as is the Akkadian *emqu*. In these biblical books knowledge of the world and its ways as God's creation is almost always in view, even if not stated explicitly, so the sage is one who acknowledges and reveres God. That knowledge of God derives from his revelation, so the sage's wisdom is based upon the principles of God's *law and the ways they can be applied in the varied situations of life. Not unnaturally, the wisdom books extol the wise as finding greater joy in life (Prov 3:35; 14:24; 21:20; 24:5; Eccles 8:1),

but they recognize that not all the wise enjoyed prosperity (Eccles 4:13), for even when their advice led to success, they might gain little or no credit (Eccles 9:14-15).

There was no profession of being a sage, but it is likely that once a person's wisdom had been recognized, a group of followers might gather to benefit in whatever way they could, to learn and develop their own abilities, for the wise share knowledge (Prov 15:7), and their sayings were passed on orally or in writing (Prov 1:6; 22:17; Eccles 12:9-10). There is no evidence that there were schools where the wise taught in a formal way, although their services may have been employed to educate youngsters in the *royal court in order to prepare them for political and diplomatic service or to advise the king. Certainly, the wise were expected to counsel kings in their decisions (Esther 1:13; 6:13), and so a king such as *Solomon or Hezekiah might make or have made collections of the sayings of the wise (Prov 1:1; 25:1).

2. Schools in the Ancient Near East.

Wherever writing was established, scribal education followed. Reading and writing held a distinctive place in life, but they should not be understood as being entirely apart from other crafts; they were skills that could be learned like any other (e.g., potting, weaving, metal-casting), although the training may have taken longer. However, because only scribes could give precise permanence to events and open records of the past, their skill gave them a privileged position, access to information that could affect others deeply, as, for example, determining who sold a property to whom or when a loan was to be repaid. A major element in scribal training, therefore, was clarity and accuracy in writing and copying, vital for administration, for legal contracts and for surveying, either for construction projects or for estimating yields and so taxes. These aspects are particularly evident in the relics of scribal training from Babylonia and Egypt versus those from the Levant, where the materials used have mostly perished.

2.1. Babylonia. The most extensive remains of ancient Near Eastern scribal education come from Babylonia. Among the oldest cuneiform tablets, written slightly before 3000 BC, are numerous copies of lists of words arranged by category (e.g., names of fish, pottery vessels, human occupations), the start of a tradition that continued to be maintained in various forms over the next three millennia (Nissen, Damerow, and Englund, 105-9)—enduring tradition is a feature of Babylonian culture. By the middle of the third millennium BC, Sumerian hymns and prayers, magical spells, myths and wisdom literature were being written down, some by pupil scribes, and many continued to be copied for several centuries. Scribes also began to compose "royal" inscriptions, celebrating the achievements or piety of their rulers. Although few school tablets—that is, lists of signs with their values, lists of words, mathematical tables—are available from the next half millennium, the enormous clerical activity of the Third Dynasty of Ur (c. 2112-2004 BC), visible in tens of thousands of clay tablets, attests a centralized training system, with the names of over 1,500 scribes being recorded.

Schooling is best known from the eighteenth and seventeenth centuries BC, by which time Sumerian had ceased to be a widely spoken language; so, although many Sumerian texts were copied, increasingly texts were written in Semitic Babylonian. Excavations at houses in Nippur, Ur, Uruk and other towns have yielded hundreds of clay tablets produced by pupil scribes. They reveal a curriculum running from elementary writing exercises, learning individual signs, through copying the teacher's text of a few lines, often a proverb, then word lists, mathematical tables and model contracts to extensive literary compositions. Some of the literary works probably were written versions of traditional *oral poems, some may have been composed in writing for particular purposes (e.g., hymns honoring individual kings), some may have been compiled for didactic purposes (e.g., collections of proverbs, debates), and the students themselves may have made up accounts of school life. Often only the first few dozen lines of long compositions were copied.

Babylonian scribes did not learn their craft in large classrooms; the houses where the school texts have been found were not big. In some cases canceled or discarded exercises survive. Teaching most probably was in the hands of individual scribes, with small numbers of pupils attending them in their homes, learning their trade as apprentices, but all followed a similar syllabus. Within the highly organized administration of the kingdom of Ur, King Shulgi (c. 2094-2047 BC) may have prescribed this curriculum, following older practices and setting the pattern for subsequent generations (on Babylonian schooling, see Black et al., xl-l, 275-352). Scribal exercises exist from later periods showing a similar syllabus continued in use, with some of the same compositions continuing to be copied, but evidence for teaching arrangements is meager. Pupils learned in private houses in the first millennium BC, but there were also "schools" attached to temples (Wiseman, 86-92; Gesche). At that time, scribes belonged to "families" who traced their professional ancestry back to renowned scribes of earlier centuries. Very successful or ambitious scribes could rise high in royal service, but the majority were employed in administrative tasks or sold their services to any who required them. Through each period of Babylonian history there is a remarkable uniformity in the script, which implies interchange of scribal activities between major centers, despite the training of scribes in most towns.

2.2. The Levant. Beyond the boundaries of Babylonia and Assyria, training in the cuneiform system followed the same basic syllabus, so that tablets from sites in Syria or Anatolia or Elam may be used to fill gaps in broken tablets found in Babylonia. However, the distance and lack of central control meant that, at the same time, local variations arose, and the influence of local languages is visible, as seen clearly in the texts of Ebla, c. 2300 BC (Biggs).

At Ugarit, on the coast of Syria in the Late Bronze Age, scribes learned the Babylonian cuneiform script and language and, beside it, a cuneiform alphabet created for their local West Semitic language. Clay tablets inscribed with traditional Babylonian school texts and others bearing the characters of the thirty-letter "Ugaritic alphabet" in order are witnesses to educational processes, but no school building has been identified. The Babylonian school texts and the tablets bearing the Ugaritic alphabet shared the same provenances as administrative and religious compositions, implying that scribes taught pupils alongside their regular work (see Pedersén, 68-80).

Throughout the Levant in the Late Bronze Age there were scribes in quite small towns who could read and write Babylonian cuneiform and so had received training somewhere. The recovery of school texts at such sites as Hazor, Megiddo (a fragment of the Epic of Gilgamesh) and Aphek shows that the training was not confined to the major centers (Horowitz, Oshima and Sanders).

Pharaohs had monumental inscriptions in Egyptian erected along the paths of their marches through the Levant, and where they established garrisons and administrative centers they left scribes who would have written in Egyptian and possibly trained local youths. Regrettably, their work, written on perishable materials, is lost, apart from a few brief ostraca concerning taxes (see, e.g., Goldwasser).

2.3. Egypt. Information from Egypt is less extensive because few town sites have been excavated, and papyrus, the common writing material, perishes in all but the driest environments. Inscriptions refer to a "room of writing" attached to some temples where boys of upper-class families could learn the scribal skills for about four years. Letter writing, grammar, foreign languages, onomastics, geography, mathematics and geometry, and ethics and morals are listed as the subjects covered (Fischer-Elfert; Williams 1972; *ABD* 2.395-99). The majority went on to work in the administration and could rise to very high positions in palaces and temples, but most would be occupied with daily routines of administration and accountancy.

School exercises survive in the form of extracts from literary works written on stone flakes, wooden boards and potsherds, some with a teacher's corrections, and, when more advanced, on papyrus. The onomastics, or lexical lists, are similar to Babylonian ones and have been seen to underlie the enumerations of creation in Job 38—39; Psalm 148; Proverbs 30:24-31 (von Rad), but dependency of the Hebrew texts on these Egyptian lists is far from certain, for the areas that they cover and their order are not so particular (*see* Proverbs 2: Ancient Near Eastern Background). Frequently copied compositions include The Satire on the Trades, which lauds the scribal profession above all others, and Satirical Letter, in which one scribe chafes another, principally about his ignorance of the geography of the Levant, evidently a part of the curriculum (*ANET,* 432-34, 475-79; *COS* 1.48:122-25; 3.2:9-14). Noteworthy is the apparent "syllabus" of three "wisdom" texts in the early second millennium BC: the Satire on the Trades, the Instruction of a Man for his Son and the Loyalist Instruction (Simpson, 329-36, 337-39, 198-200). The word rendered "instruction" is *sboyet,* which corresponds to Hebrew *tôrâ* ("teaching, instruction, guidance") and *mûsar* ("teaching"), although it does not share the element of the fear of God so clearly. Egyptian "instruction" was concerned primarily with the maintenance of good order, inculcating moral and cultural values. As in Babylonia, a uniformity of script prevailed, which suggests that a single authority had ultimate control of scribal training.

3. Schools in Ancient Israel.

Evidence for schools in ancient Israel is slight. The word "school" does not occur in the Hebrew Bible, making its first appearance in Sirach 51:23: "Turn to me, you unlearned, and stay in my house of instruction" *(bêt midraš).* Some scholars think that a few biblical passages hint at the existence of schools, Proverbs 22:17-21 among them, but their interpretation is dubious (Weeks, 132-36; Davies, 199-201). The expectation that schools in antiquity were comparable with European schools has given rise to the concept of buildings organized with classrooms having desks or benches. The Babylonian and Egyptian contexts make that most unlikely, so no physical schools would be discovered in Israel. Pupils sat on the floor around their teacher, in his house or street, who probably wrote on the ground initially. The discovery of monumental inscriptions in adjacent kingdoms of the Ammonites, Moabites, Phoenicians and Aramaeans dating from the tenth to the sixth centuries BC points to a high level of scribal training in the major centers in those countries, which makes it improbable that the same did not hold in Israel and Judah. The uncertainty of the biblical references to schools has to be set beside the epigraphic evidence.

Greater impetus to adopt the concept of schools in Israel came from A. Lemaire, who set that beside the biblical texts and the situation in

Babylonia and Egypt (Lemaire 1981; 1992; cf. Puech 1988). In opposition, in 1991 D. W. Jamieson-Drake mounted a theoretical argument against the existence of schools in "Monarchic Judah." He asserted that a socio-archaeological model of Judean society did not allow for "formalized scribal training" to exist outside Jerusalem, and Jerusalem only became sufficiently powerful to sustain such training in the eighth and seventh centuries BC. The weak archaeological indications for settlement, public works and luxury objects that he collected were his proof of that (see Jamieson-Drake; cf. Weeks, 132-56). Although some writers cite his work favorably, Jamieson-Drake's mishandling of the archaeological remains and his failure to take proper account of all the epigraphic material seriously undermine his case (see Lemaire 1992; Millard 1992). Even if "formalized scribal training" in the sense of a "school" did not exist outside Jerusalem, the existence of Hebrew inscriptions from the tenth century BC onward is proof that teaching of some sort occurred, and the wide distribution of Hebrew writing in the eighth and seventh centuries BC, scribal exercises included (see 3.1 below), implies that instruction in the rudiments of writing and accountancy took place far from the capital (*see DOTHB*, Hebrew Inscriptions).

3.1. Writing Exercises and Basic Education. The basic task of learning the script was far lighter for Israelite pupils than for Babylonian or Egyptian. The Hebrew alphabet, adopted from the Canaanites, of only twenty-two letters could be mastered quite rapidly, unlike the complicated scripts of those other cultures, which needed some years of study. Unhappily, little of the Hebrew pupils' work is visible, for in ancient Israel most writing was done on leather or papyrus sheets and rolls or on wooden tablets coated with wax, all of which decay when buried in the damp soil of most of the land. Occasionally people scratched on stone, and one specimen is generally agreed to be the oldest piece of Hebrew writing and to be a scholar's exercise. That is the Gezer Calendar, a small stone tablet roughly engraved with seven lines listing farming activities through the year. It is dated to the late tenth century BC (Renz, 1.30-37). The discovery in 2005 at Tel Zayit in the Shephelah of the letters of the alphabet incised on a boulder built into a wall brings a significant new witness to the spread of writing in the tenth century BC (Tappy).

Recovery of potsherds used as writing materials (ostraca) has attested the skill of Hebrew scribes and some aspects of their training. Scores of ostraca result from official or commercial accounting; others preserve brief messages and lists of names. In several places alphabets have been found, whole or partial (see Renz, 2.1.22), which are practice pieces or idle scribbles or examples of bragging. The last may be seen at Kuntilet ʿAjrud, on the desert road to Elath, where, on two large jars, graffiti were written about 800 BC. They include three incomplete alphabets and the opening phrases of letters, some overlapping, as if one man was trying to outdo another in displaying the extent of his education (Renz, 1.59-64). At Kadesh Barnea, in the far south, ostraca include two lists of numbers, in the form borrowed from Egyptian hieratic, on one followed by the weight unit "gerah," on the other perhaps by "homer" and the sign for "shekel" (Renz, 1.339-43). These appear to be pupils' exercises. At Arad one ostracon (88) carries three lines of a narrative, each incomplete, which may have been copied from a royal inscription as writing exercise. It begins, "I was king in . . ." and refers to the king of Egypt (Millard 1978, 26; Renz, 1.302-5).

The uniformity of the Hebrew script and language (*see* Hebrew Language) in texts from the preexilic period indicates some kind of central authority ensuring that all communications were intelligible (Rollston, 68), although the use of vowel letters remained optional (Millard 1991). The rare examples of formal inscriptions on stone (Siloam Tunnel Inscription, Siloam Tomb and two fragments found in Jerusalem; a crumb of a stela from Samaria [Renz, 1.178-89, 261-65, 190-91, 266-67, 135]) reveal the ability to create longer texts, like those from the Moabite and Aramaean kingdoms. Almost all of the ostraca, graffiti and inscriptions display authorial ability to write the script rapidly and the language fluently—signs of efficient teaching producing the "skillful writer" (Ps 45:1).

3.2. Further Education. The epigraphic remains demonstrate the initial stages of scribal education but are too meager to inform us about any broader syllabus that pupil scribes in Israel may have followed. However, the texts from Babylonia and Egypt suggest a wide range of subjects, and the biblical books themselves are witnesses to more advanced levels of education. The authors of the poetic and wisdom books had learned how to narrate history (*Esther), to write philosophical treatises (*Ecclesiastes), to create a dialogue dealing with the problem of theodicy (*Job), write hymns and compose lyric poetry (*Psalms, Song of Songs), and gather and arrange good advice (Proverbs). The wide-ranging knowledge of the world that Job and Proverbs display attests good general knowledge and detailed observation (e.g., mining [Job 28:1-11]; "Leviathan" [Job 41]; the "four small things" [Prov 30: 24-28]). The "wise" are the most likely authors of the "wisdom" books. The book of Proverbs has Solomon's name both in the initial sentence (Prov 1:1) and at the head of Proverbs 25, where additions were made in Hezekiah's reign. Nothing is known of Agur and Lemuel (Prov 30:1; 31:1) (see Lemuel and Agur). Here the name need not denote the originator of every sentence but rather that the collecting was done at his behest or in his honor. This does not mean that he had no part at all in the composition. A similar situation obtains with Egyptian instructional works (Millard 2006).

Babylonian pupils learned Sumerian and Akkadian, and some learned other languages so that they could interpret for mercantile or diplomatic purposes, either orally or in writing. In the third and second millennia BC some Levantine scribes had to learn Babylonian, and some Egyptian. At least six languages were read at Ugarit in the thirteenth century BC, with interpreters rendering messages from foreign rulers into the local tongue. Scribes in other small independent principalities in Syria-Palestine wrote to the pharaohs in Babylonian, occasionally adding notes in their own, Canaanite, language, and the pharaoh's scribes responded in Akkadian. In the Egyptian Instruction of Any there is mention of teaching Nubians, Levantines and others to speak Egyptian (COS 1.46:114). In Israel during the monarchy, besides traders who acquired a working knowledge of languages relevant to their businesses, there were officials who learned Aramaic, and in the Persian Empire, while Aramaic had come to be widely used for administrative purposes, local languages also were written (Esther 3:12; 8:9).

4. Wisdom Books and Schools.

It is widely maintained that "Wisdom literature" may have been one element in the education of more advanced Babylonian and Egyptian students in preparation for careers at court or in the temples. The address to "my son" and the instructions in good behavior, etiquette and morals are common to them and to Proverbs. The terms "father" and "son" in these compositions often are taken to mean "teacher" and "pupil." However, there are no references to students or schools, so the intimate family setting is the preferable context for the composition of these pieces. In the Egyptian texts a father addresses his son—for example, "The maxims of good speech spoken by ... Ptahhotep.... Thus he said to his son ... " and "Written by ... Amenemope ... for his son" (ANET 413, 421; COS 1.47:116). Likewise, in the oldest Sumerian "wisdom" book, copied already c. 2500 BC, "Shuruppak gave instructions to his son Ziusudra" (Black et al., 284-92).

There is no good reason to suppose that these books, once written, were confined to schools or that established scribes may not have copied them, either for their own delectation or for other educated professionals, priests among them. Kings too might enjoy these and similar books. The Egyptian Prophecies of Neferti claim that a pharaoh called for his counselors to send a "wise" son of theirs to entertain him with his eloquence. When Neferti spoke, the king wrote his words on a scroll (COS 1.45:107). Nevertheless, where texts from scribal training are found, copies of "wisdom books" are often among them, both in the areas where the cuneiform script was current and in Egypt. Literature and "school texts" lay together in libraries in a Late Bronze Age temple at Emar on the middle Euphrates, and at Ugarit the same was true (Pedersén, 61-80). In the old Assyrian capital city, Assur, a family of scribes active in the eighth and seventh centuries BC owned a large collection of tablets, with "wisdom" texts among them that may have served as textbooks. However, a family of exorcist priests flourishing in the seventh century BC in Assur owned a large library of about six hundred clay tablets bearing literary works. Their technical texts predominate, beside copies of hymns, prayers and epics; they do not appear to have been teaching the scribal art or literary skills. In another small library, beside incantation texts for curing the sick was, perhaps appropriately, a copy of part of the Poem of the Righteous Sufferer (ANET, 434-37; COS 1.152:486-92). To the northwest, a family of priests living at Huzirina (modern Sultantepe), near Haran, in the seventh century also owned many books, including "wisdom" works (for these libraries, see Pedersén, 134-36, 178-79). Wisdom books from Egypt apparently were deposited in tombs or tomb chapels, but most texts on ostraca were produced in teaching the workers who decorated the tombs in the Valley of the Kings and elsewhere (Quirke 1996).

5. Education in Ancient Israel.

In Israel everyone who practiced a craft or profession would have been in a position to train younger people to follow them. The apprentice system is the simplest and most likely means of education in all societies, especially in villages and small towns, and reading and writing are skills readily acquired in that way. Norms of behavior are learned in the family circle, parents and older relations teaching children. For higher levels of education, youngsters might go to recognized teachers, whether for advanced scribal skills or other subjects in which there may have been an involvement for the wise. Observing that modern knowledge of Sumerian, Babylonian and Egyptian literature depends to a large degree on the discovery of texts copied by pupil scribes, Lemaire (1981) offered the hypothesis that the biblical texts survive because they were selected for use in schools. Here a distinction has to be made between the texts from those areas and those from Greece and Rome, for none of the former survive because they are religious works that other circles may have wished to preserve. The circumstances of the fall of Jerusalem to Nebuchadnezzar perhaps make it easier to suppose that priests and prophets, rather than schoolteachers, saved books (see Barr 1983). Whatever the means by which the biblical books were collected and transmitted, it is to the training and education of ancient Israelites that they are owed.

See also DEAD SEA SCROLLS; HEBREW LANGUAGE; SCRIBES.

BIBLIOGRAPHY. **J. Barr,** review of *Les écoles et la formation de la Bible dans l'ancien Israël,* by A. Lemaire, *BO* 40 (1983) 137-42; **R. D. Biggs,** "Ebla Texts," *ABD* 2.263-70; **J. Black et al.,** eds., *The Literature of Ancient Sumer* (Oxford: Oxford University Press, 2004); **H. Brunner,** *Altägyptische Erziehung* (Wiesbaden: Harrassowitz, 1992); **M. Civil,** "Education (Mesopotamia)," *ABD* 2.301-5; **J. L. Crenshaw,** *Education in Ancient Israel* (New York: Doubleday, 1998); **G. I. Davies,** "Were There Schools in Ancient Israel?" in *Wisdom in Ancient Israel: Essays in Honour of J. A. Emerton,* ed. J. Day, R. P. Gordon and H. G. M. Williamson (Cambridge: Cambridge University Press, 1995) 199-211; **H.-W. Fischer-Elfert,** "Education," *OEAE* 1.438-42; **P. D. Gesche,** *Schulunterricht in Babylonien im ersten Jahrtausend v. Chr.* (AOAT 275; Münster: Ugarit-Verlag, 2001); **O. Goldwasser,** "Hieratic Inscriptions from Tel Sera' in Southern Canaan," *TA* 11 (1984) 77-93; **W. Horowitz, T. Oshima and S. Sanders,** *Cuneiform in Canaan: Cuneiform Sources from the Land of Israel* (Jerusalem: Israel Exploration Society, 2006); **D. W. Jamieson-Drake,** *Scribes and Schools in Monarchic Judah: A Socio-Archaeological Approach* (JSOTSup 109; Sheffield: Almond Press, 1991); **K. A. Kitchen,** *Poetry of Ancient Egypt* (Documenta mundi 1; Jonsered: Paul Åströms, 1999); **A. Lemaire,** *Les écoles et la formation de la Bible dans l'ancien Israël* (OBO 39; Fribourg: Editions Universitaires; Göttingen: Vandenhoeck & Ruprecht, 1981); idem, review of *Scribes and Schools in Monarchic Judah: A Socio-Archaeological Approach,* by D. W. Jamieson-Drake, *JAOS* 112 (1992) 707-8; idem, "Education (Israel)," *ABD* 2.305-12; **A. R. Millard,** "Epigraphic Notes, Aramaic and Hebrew," *PEQ* 110 (1978) 23-26; idem, "Variable Spelling in Hebrew and Other Ancient Texts," *JTS* 42 (1991) 106-15; idem, review of *Scribes and Schools in Monarchic Judah: A Socio-Archaeological Approach,* by D. W. Jamieson-Drake, *Society for Old Testament Study Book List* (1992) 34-35; idem, "Authors, Books and Readers" in, *Oxford Handbook of Biblical Studies,* ed. J. W. Rogerson and J. Lieu (Oxford: Oxford University Press, 2006) 641-57; **H. J. Nissen, P. Damerow and R. K. Englund,** *Archaic Bookkeeping: Writing and Techniques of Economic Administration in the Ancient Near East* (Chicago: University of Chicago Press, 1993); **O. Pedersén,** *Archives and Libraries of the Ancient Near East 1500-300 B.C.* (Bethesda, MD: CDL Press, 1998); **P. Piacentini,** "Scribes," *OEAE* 3.187-92; **E. Puech,** "Les écoles dans l'Israël préexilique: Données épigraphiques," *Congress Volume: Jerusalem 1986* (VTSup 40; Leiden: E. J. Brill, 1988) 189-203; **S. G. Quirke,** "Archive" in *Ancient Egyptian Literature: History and Forms,* ed. A. Loprieno (PÄ 10; Leiden: E. J. Brill, 1996) 379-401; **J. Renz,** *Handbuch der althebräischen Epigraphik* (3 vols. in 4; Darmstadt: Wissenschaftliche Buchgesellschaft, 1995); **E. Robson,** "The Tablet House: A Scribal School in Old Babylonian Nippur," *RA* 95 (2001) 39-66; **C. Rollston,** "Scribal Education in Ancient Israel: The Old Hebrew Epigraphic Evidence," *BASOR* 344 (2006) 47-74; **M.-J. Seux**, *Hymnes et prières aux Dieux de Babylonie et d'Assyrie* (Paris: Cerf, 1976); **W. K. Simpson**, *The Literature of Ancient Egypt* (new ed.; New Haven: Yale University Press, 1973); **R. E. Tappy et al.**, "An Abecedary of the Mid-Tenth Century B.C.E. from the Judaean Shephelah," *BASOR* 344 (2006) 5-46; **G. von Rad**, "Job XXXVIII and Egyptian Wisdom," in *The Problem of the Hexateuch, and Other Essays* (Edinburgh: Oliver & Boyd, 1966 [1955]) 280-91; **S. Weeks**, *Early Israelite Wisdom* (Oxford: Clarendon Press, 1994); **R. J. Williams**, "Scribal Training in Ancient Egypt," *JAOS* 92 (1972) 214-21; idem, "Egyptian Literature (Wisdom)," *ABD* 2.395-99; **D. J. Wiseman**, *Nebuchadnezzar and Babylon* (Oxford: Oxford University Press, for the British Academy, 1985).

A. R. Millard

SALVATION AND DELIVERANCE IMAGERY

By far the greatest concentration of salvation and deliverance imagery in our literature is found in the psalms, which are the focus of this article. As the ordinary Israelite appealed to the king for deliverance (*hôšî'â hammelek* [2 Sam 14:4]), so too the psalmist, who by tradition frequently was King *David, appealed to God for deliverance (*hôšî'â yhwh* [Ps 12:1]) from his personal, tribal and national enemies (see Fabry and Sawyer, 445-46). Images of salvation and deliverance abound in the book of *Psalms, with the root for "save" (*yš'*) appearing in almost half the psalms. And God, who is present in the temple, is therefore praised and exalted for his salvation. Indeed, the act of praise is a multifaceted act of faith, protest and hope (Brueggemann, 112-32). The God of Israel is the God of salvation.

    1. General Features
    2. Images of Salvation
    3. God, My Savior
    4. Salvation from What?
    5. Arguments for Salvation
    6. Benefits of Salvation

1. General Features.

The focus of the various images for salvation and deliverance in the psalms is on personal deliverance from enemies and life's real troubles rather than, as is often the case in Christian theology, on images of salvation in the *afterlife for

the individual (see Holladay). It is this focus on real-life problems, such as being surrounded by enemies intent on killing the psalmist, that gives to the psalms a potent vision not only of salvation but also of a life of faith, a life of prayer, and a life of petitioning God for deliverance from physical dangers. Thus, Psalm 54:4-5: "But surely, God is my helper [*'ōzēr*]; the Lord is the upholder of my life [*napši*]. He will repay my enemies for their evil. In your faithfulness [*ba'ămittĕkā*], put an end to them." Here God's redemptive help emerges from his faithfulness into preservation of the petitioner's life and judgment on those who work evil. If the major focus of redemption is rescue from one's personal enemies, it remains true that the Psalter is primarily a public book of the cultus rather than of private piety (Kraus 1988, 77; 1986, 138-43). The formerly individual cry has become the cry of the cultic-shaped community.

Sometimes the psalmist extends this earthly form of salvation to become national: return to the land and the return of God's favor on his people are perceived as forgiveness and pardon and the withdrawal of wrath (Ps 85:1-3). National confession leads to national salvation and deliverance, as history shows: "Both we," the psalmist says, "and our ancestors have sinned. . . . Yet he saved them for his name's sake. . . . So he saved them from the hand of the foe. . . . They forgot God, their Savior. . . . Many times he delivered them. . . . Save us, O LORD our God" (Ps 106:6, 8, 10, 21, 43, 47 NRSV throughout article). A common expression for this is that of God restoring the fortunes of Israel (e.g., Ps 53:6).

However, even if the focus in the psalms is on the psalmists' more physical dangers and national condition, one psalm stands tall as a focus on personal forgiveness and redemption from sin: Psalm 51. David has committed murder, and he pleads with the "God of my salvation" for forgiveness from "bloodshed" (Ps 51:14).

Formally, the appeal to deliverance (*yēša', yĕšû'â, tĕšû'â,* as well as the roots *mlt* and *nṣl*) in the book of Psalms takes on the form of a legal or a heart-rending plea (Ps 7:6-8; 22:19-21) and lament (Miller, 55-134). Fundamentally, the deliverance expected is earthy, physical and lifesaving. At the personal level, the cries for deliverance in the psalms are graphically real and express an individual pleading with God in the most demanding of situations, when life seems to be in danger (Ps 6:4-5). The theme of redemption in the psalms emerges from the world of military violence and victory, suggesting that some of the psalms may have been written on the night of celebrating a battle victory (see, e.g., Ps 18).

A paradigmatic expression of the psalmist's understanding of salvation and deliverance as the act of God is found in Psalm 74:12: "Yet God my King is from of old, working salvation in the earth." A paradigmatic psalm expressing the theology of salvation and deliverance is Psalm 3. After rehearsing his case before Yahweh that his foes are many and are making accusations not only against him but also against the reputation of God (Ps 3:1-2), the psalmist (traditionally, David) says, "But you, O LORD, are a shield around me, my glory, and the one who lifts up my head" (Ps 3:3). In confidence, the psalmist then speaks of crying aloud to Yahweh, who hears from "his holy hill" (Ps 3:4). So confident is he in Yahweh's saving powers that he is able to sleep, unafraid of "ten thousands of people who have set themselves against me all around" (Ps 3:5-6). Suddenly, as if the enemies have arrived, the psalmist utters, "Rise up, O LORD! Deliver me, O my God!" (Ps 3:7a). God's deliverance, the psalmist testifies, is characterized by striking the psalmist's enemies on the cheek to shatter their teeth (Ps 3:7b-c). Finally, the psalmist utters a theological statement in parallelistic fashion: "Deliverance *[hayĕšûʿâ]* belongs to the LORD; may your blessing *[birkātekā]* be on your people" (Ps 3:8).

2. Images of Salvation.

A central notion of salvation is seen in Psalm 31:1: "In your righteousness deliver me." God's *righteousness is God's saving faithfulness that results in deliverance, surely evoking God's covenant faithfulness from the days of Abraham. Notice how each of these terms fills the others with meaning: "Your *steadfast love*, O LORD, extends to the heavens, your *faithfulness* to the clouds. Your *righteousness* is like the mighty mountains, your *judgments* are like the great deep; you *save* humans and animals alike, O LORD" (Ps 36:6, NRSV, italics added). God's steadfast love, faithfulness, righteousness and judgments lead to the psalmist's salvation.

God's salvation can be expressed in a number of ways, each of which is deserving of separate treatment (see Fabry and Sawyer; Stolz). Thus, salvation can be seen as a form of protec-

tion from an immoral generation (Ps 12:7-8; 17:8-9; 31:6-8; 69:29) and from those who seek death (Ps 17:11-12; 71:1-6). Thus, "preserve my life" is in parallel with "save" in Psalm 86:2, and "steadfast love" with "delivered" in Psalm 86:13. God can "answer" (*ʿnh* [Ps 20:6; 60:5]) and "deliver" (*nṣl* [Ps 59:2; 71:2]); God's deliverance is at the same time "blessing" (*brk* [Ps 28:9]). Another word for this is "save" (*plṭ* [Ps 37:40; 71:2]) because God has "rendered and established justice" (*dyn* [Ps 54:1]) and "vindicated" (*špṭ* [Ps 72:4]) his own. This occurs because God can "preserve the life" (*šāmrâ napšî* [Ps 86:2]) of his chosen ones.

Yet another expression is "redeem" (*gāʾal* [Ps 19:14; 106:10]). God saves as the shepherd who will guide his people through life (Ps 28:9). God's shining face of blessing expresses the presence of salvation and restoration to the land (Ps 31:16; 80:3, 7, 19). Salvation from sin implies being washed (Ps 51:2, 7) and God hiding his face from one's sins (Ps 51:9) in addition to God creating a clean, new heart (Ps 51:10). Naturally, salvation implies forgiveness (Ps 79:9; 85:2). All of these expressions echo "save" or "deliver" in the psalms.

At times the images for deliverance can be cosmic, extravagantly so if not even apocalyptic in tone. After the psalmist of Psalm 18 prays, "the earth reeled and rocked," and then the psalm lays out a poetic litany of the cosmic echo as God delivers (Ps 18:7-15; cf. Ps 74:12-17).

3. God, My Savior.

If the psalms are shaped by earthly concerns, the psalmists know that there is only one Savior, the one and only God of Israel (Ps 62:1-2 [see Kraus 1986, 17-49]). "The LORD looks down from heaven; he sees all humankind"; therefore, "A king is not saved by his great army; a warrior is not delivered by his great strength. The war horse is a vain hope for victory, and by its great might it cannot save" (Ps 33:13-17 [cf. Ps 44:6-7; 118]). Why? God alone is the Savior, and he is steadfast in his love and in his righteousness to save (Ps 145:13-21). This Savior God is faithful (Ps 36:6, 10). "Why are you cast down?" the psalmists ask, urging instead, "Hope in God" (Ps 42:5, 11; 43:5).

God is exalted above the heavens and therefore can act mightily to rescue his own (Ps 57:5, 11). Thus, "For God alone my soul waits in silence; from him comes my salvation" (Ps 62:1).

And thus victory is salvation and deliverance: "O sing to the LORD a new song, for he has done marvelous things. His right hand and his holy arm have gotten him victory" (Ps 98:1).

God is the "shield around me" and "my glory" and the "one who lifts up my head"; God is on "his holy hill" and will "strike all my enemies" to whom "deliverance" belongs—all from Psalm 3 as expressions of God as Savior. God is a fortress-like and walled "refuge" (Ps 7:1; 18:30), one whose right hand provides salvation (Ps 17:7). God's saving work leads to praise of God as "rock," "fortress," "deliverer," "shield," "horn of salvation" and "stronghold" (Ps 18:2). God is invoked to rise up in anger and fury to exact "judgment" (*mišpaṭ* [Ps 7:6-7]). A thematic statement is found in Psalm 20:7: "Some take pride in chariots, and some in horses, but our pride is in the name of the LORD our God."

This God is partial to the brokenhearted, the crushed in spirit, and the oppressed and poor and needy (Ps 34:18; 76:9), and so someone prays that King *Solomon (according to the superscription) may have the same discernment and justice-establishing ways (Ps 72:1-4, 13 [see Kraus 1986, 150-54]). God is also partial to his righteous people who serve and take refuge in him (Ps 34:19-22). But there is a universal dimension to salvation in the psalms, one that is cosmic (Ps 65:5-8). God's saving act, expressed as forgiveness, is also an act of judgment against oppressors (Ps 79:8-13), showing that forgiveness at times is God's social and earthly vindication and restoration of Israel. Because he knows God's victories intimately, David the king cries out, "You are my Father, my God, and the rock of my salvation!" (Ps 89:26)

At times the psalmist expresses the ultimate longing as the *visio Dei*, as in Psalm 17:15: "As for me, I shall behold your face in righteousness; when I awake I shall be satisfied, beholding your likeness." One thinks of Moses (Num 12:8; Deut 4:12, 15) or the archetypal benediction (Num 6:4-5), but one would be hard-pressed to demonstrate that the psalmist here is thinking of the afterlife. Instead, we are to envision the psalmist knowing that he has been vindicated because the face of God is upon him (Ps 17:2 [see Goldingay, 245]).

Because God is Savior, the psalmist loves God and turns toward him in praise and exaltation (Ps 18:1). Because God alone is Savior, the psalmist appeals repeatedly to faithfulness and

obedience to the God who will save and deliver those who are faithful and obedient (Pss 37; 119).

4. Salvation from What?

Salvation in the psalms is intensely partisan, political and personal. It is panoramic as well: "For he has delivered me from every trouble, and my eye has looked in triumph on my enemies" (Ps 54:7). Familiarity with the psalms of Israel leads one to see in Psalm 27:1 the heart of salvation: "The LORD is my light and my salvation [*'ôrî wĕyiš'î]*; whom shall I fear? The LORD is the stronghold of my life; of whom shall I be afraid?" Here we are not to think so much of eternal life as of earthly enemies and situations that fail to buckle the knees of the psalmist because he knows God is the Savior who can protect, deliver and exalt over all of one's foes. The psalmist proceeds to offer evidence of why he ought to be afraid but continues to express confidence in God because he can say "O God of my salvation!" (Ps 27:9). So he exhorts others (and himself) to "wait for the LORD" (Ps 27:14 [cf. Ps 109:31]).

Deliverance, then, is most often from enemies, and salvation is a social experience in this world (Ps 31:14-16; 109; 119:94, 117, 146 [on the enemies in the psalms, see Tate, 60-64]). Thus, in the context of complaining about enemies, which psalms of David are in the habit of doing, David can say, "But I call upon God, and the LORD will save me." How often will he complain? "Evening and morning and at noon I utter my complaint and moan, and he will hear my voice" (Ps 55:17; see also Ps 57:1-6; 59:2). David has plenty of capacity to speak extravagantly of how many enemies he has: "More in number than the hairs of my head are those who hate me without cause" (Ps 69:4), so he calls on God to save him (Ps 69:1, 13, 18) and his people (Ps 69:35). Sometimes the psalmist pleads to be saved from the immoral condition of those around them, characterized by dishonest words and oppression of the poor (Ps 12).

The psalmist seeks deliverance from foes who are personally accusing the psalmist (Ps 3:1-2); from intense pain and weeping over his expectation of imminent death (Ps 6:5-7; 31:9-10; 69:19-21) at the hands of his "foes," who are "workers of evil" (Ps 6:7-8); from pursuers who are like a lion that "will tear me apart" and "drag me away" (Ps 7:2); from adversaries (Ps 17:7; 25:2); from "my strong enemy" who was too mighty for him to defeat and who had confronted him (Ps 18:16-19 [cf. Ps 22:12-13]). We are told repeatedly that the psalmist was spared death by conquering the military enemy (Ps 18:31-42; cf. Ps 69:22-28). Indeed, he "beat them fine, like dust before the wind; I cast them out like the mire of the streets" (Ps 18:42). The helpless psalmist is helped by the mighty God from the "day of trouble" (Ps 20:1, 6). The psalmist is at times depressed and scorned and mocked (Ps 22:7-8, 14-18). At times he is fearful, and God saves him from those fears (Ps 34:4-10). Often his life is on the line (Ps 116:1-4, 12-13). Most often the psalmists seek to be delivered from death in order to preserve life (Ps 6:4-5; 31:13). "The cords of death encompassed me; the torrents of perdition assailed me; the cords of Sheol entangled me; the snares of death confronted me" (Ps 18:4-5).

A classic formation of this is found in Psalm 18, a victory song for "salvation" from one's enemies (see also Ps 20:9). Because of the Deuteronomistic view of history, captivity or defeat was perceived as discipline, and that meant that restoration in the land or victory was expressed as salvation and forgiveness (Ps 60:5; cf. Ps 69:35-36; 80; 85). Salvation at times means return to the land or restoration of divine favor toward those in the land (Ps 85:4, 7). "Surely his salvation is at hand for those who fear him, that his glory may dwell in our land" (Ps 85:9). This statement precedes a few lines where redemption is nearly synonymous with springs and rain for the land and crops of abundance.

Common human experiences give rise to God's saving acts. Psalm 107 perhaps best puts this all into one grand display: some wandered hungry and thirsty in deserts, some lived as prisoners in darkness and gloom because of their rebellion against God, some were deathly ill because of their sinful ways, some experienced the terror of storms at sea (Ps 107:4, 10-11, 17-18, 25-27), but then "they cried to the LORD in their trouble, and he saved them from their distress" (Ps 107:6, 13, 19, 28).

David's classic confessional psalm, Psalm 51, clearly states that salvation is from one's sins and sinful state (Ps 51:5), and that salvation creates newness and joy (Ps 51:10-12).

5. Arguments for Salvation.

The psalmists plead with God for deliverance for a variety of reasons (Miller, 114-26), not the least of which is the reputation of God, which can be enhanced by the psalmist who seeks to remember God in praise (Ps 6:5). The psalmist expects and hopes for deliverance from his enemies because he trusts in God (Ps 28:7). The arguments for God to answer the plea that one finds on the lips of the psalmist often evolve as the psalmist moves from disorientation to orientation (Brueggemann, 3-32, 67-83).

David, at least, pleads with God not on the basis of his own merits but rather on the basis of his brokenness (Ps 51:17). However, the psalmist routinely appeals to his own virtues of goodness, righteousness (Ps 7:8), integrity (Ps 7:8), uprightness of heart (Ps 7:10), godliness/piety and faithfulness (Ps 12:1). He can state that his deliverance is the reward of his righteousness, cleanness of hands, obedience, blamelessness and guiltlessness (Ps 18:20-24). God's judgments correspond to human behaviors (Ps 18:25-27). Those who know the mighty warrior God of salvation is the creator, who sits on the top of the hill (Zion), who dwells in a holy place, who dispenses blessings and who vindicates his people are also they who live properly: clean hands, pure hearts, honesty, and those who seek God (Ps 24:1-6, 7-10). A psalm of *Asaph says much the same: "Those who bring thanksgiving as their sacrifice honor me; to those who go the right way I will show the salvation of God [běyēšaʿ ʾělōhîm]" (Ps 50:23).

What Israel is to "remember" shapes the identity of Israel, and so appeal to the past shapes how the psalmists petition God for salvation. Thus, "In you our ancestors trusted; they trusted, and you delivered them [wattĕpallĕṭēmô]. To you they cried, and were saved [wĕnimlāṭû]" (Ps 22:4-5 [cf. Ps 44:1-8]).

The psalmist is willing to be put to the test: "If you try my heart, if you visit me by night, if you test me, you will find no wickedness in me; my mouth does not transgress" (Ps 17:3).

At times the psalmist offers a concession and suggests that if he has sinned, he does not deserve salvation but instead whatever consequences he gets: "If I have done this, if there is wrong in my hands, if I have repaid my ally with harm or plundered my foe without cause, then let the enemy pursue and overtake me, trample my life to the ground, and lay my soul in the dust" (Ps 7:3-5). The psalmist can even remember his former sins and appeal to God to lead him in the way of salvation, a salvation (Ps 25:5) that means deliverance from enemies (Ps 25:20).

6. Benefits of Salvation.

God's act of delivering, rescuing or granting victory over one's enemies or foes is simultaneously an act of righteousness or justice, suggesting that righteousness is not simply a moral attribute but is a saving action (*ṣĕdāqâ* [Ps 7:17; 31:1; 71:15]). The psalmists know that God can bring them their desires by lifting up the head (*ûmērîm rōʾšî* [Ps 3:3]) and turning back in shame their opponents (Ps 6:10), even cutting off their lips for their dishonest words (Ps 12:3-4). The psalmist is "made the head of the nations" (Ps 18:43) by the saving act of God. Those who are delivered are spared shame (Ps 22:5; 31:1).

God's might (*ʿōz* [Ps 21:1; 28:7-8; 140:7]) empowers the psalmist to "crush a troop" and "leap over a wall" (Ps 18:29) and to use war weapons with agility and success (Ps 18:34-42); God's might leads to enemies cowering before the conquering commander (Ps 18:43-45). That might leads to the exaltation of the king (Ps 18:46-50) and to exultant song (Ps 98). God's deliverance brings light (Ps 18:28; 27:1) and sets the psalmist on "the heights" (Ps 18:33).

The psalmist knows of the benefit of blessing both for himself (*bĕrākâ* [Ps 3:8]) and, not unusually, for others within his ambit of influence (Ps 22:21-31). He makes promises of what he will do because of God's salvation (Ps 71:14-24).

Finally, the psalmist's evocation of the incident at Meribah and Massah (Ex 17:7) in Psalm 95 makes one think that the "rock" of our salvation speaks of God's provision of living water (Ps 95:1, 8-11).

See also CHAOS AND DEATH; CONFIDENCE, PSALMS OF; DIVINE PRESENCE; FEAR OF THE LORD; LAMENT, PSALMS OF; PROTECTION IMAGERY; SUFFERING; THANKSGIVING, PSALMS OF; THEODICY; WARFARE IMAGERY.

BIBLIOGRAPHY. **W. Brueggemann,** *The Psalms and the Life of Faith* (Minneapolis: Fortress, 1995); **H.-J. Fabry and J. F. Sawyer,** "יֵשַׁע," *TDOT* 6.441-63; **J. Goldingay,** *Psalms 1-41* (BCOTWP; Grand Rapids: Baker Academic, 2006); **W. L. Holladay,** *The Psalms through Three Thousand Years: Prayerbook of a Cloud of Witnesses* (Minneapolis: Fortress, 1996); **H.-J. Kraus,** *Theology of the Psalms* (Minneapolis: Augsburg, 1986 [1979]); idem, *Psalms 1-59* (Minneapolis: Augsburg, 1988 [1978]); **P. D. Miller,** *They Cried to the Lord: The Form and Theology of Biblical Prayer* (Minneapolis: Fortress, 1994); **F. Stolz,** "*Yšʿ hi.* To Help," *TLOT* 2.584-87; **M. H. Tate,** *Psalms 51-100* (WBC 20; Dallas: Word, 1990).

S. McKnight

SATAN

Although the Israelites undoubtedly believed in the reality of a demon world, demonology is little attested in the OT. In fact, there is no agreed upon term for demons. What can be gathered from the data from the ancient Near East and the OT in general would place demons in the terrestrial realm, generally in waste places, having little contact with the legitimate divine realm, aside from occasionally being used as instruments for punishment. Nothing here matches the information offered about the character identified by the term *śāṭān* in the OT.

1. Lexical Profile
2. The Profile of Satan in Job
3. Socioreligious Profile

1. Lexical Profile.

"Satan" is one of the few words that English has borrowed from Hebrew. In the OT it finds usage both as a verb (*śāṭan*) and a noun (*śāṭān*). As a verb, it means "oppose as an adversary" or "accuse" (Ps 38:20; 71:13; 109:4, 20, 29; Zech 3:1). As a noun, it can be applied to a human being, thus designating an adversary (1 Sam 29:4; 2 Sam 19:23; 1 Kings 5:4; 11:14, 23, 25; Ps 109:6). Finally, in the category of most interest to this study, the noun is applied to celestial beings (Num 22:22, 32; 1 Chron 21:1; Job 1—2 [14x]; Zech 3:1-2 [3x]).

There are no cognates to the Hebrew term in Semitic languages, so they offer no help in unraveling the history of the term. If the technical usage (noun applied to supernatural being) were original and the other usages developed from it, we would have to conclude, judging from the nuances of those derived terms, that there was little of a sinister nature in the being, for these other usages evidence none of that element. In contrast, however, the broadly generic sense of the common noun and verb usage suggests that the technical usage is a secondary development (Day, 17-23).

If this were indeed the case, it would be logical to assume that a supernatural being would have been given this designation as a description of his function—that is, a heavenly adversary. This finds confirmation in the fact that in most of the cases where the noun is applied to a supernatural being, the definite article is attached to it. In English, when we refer to someone by means of a proper name, we do not use a definite article (e.g., "Sarah," not "the Sarah"). In this practice Hebrew behaves identically. Therefore we must conclude that the individual in Job 1—2 and Zechariah 3:1-2 should be identified as "the accuser" (description of function) rather than as "Satan" (proper name) (for a discussion of whether 1 Chronicles 21:1 evidences the word as a proper name or an indefinite accuser, see Japhet, 374-75). P. Day (128-29) suggests that the shift to using "satan" as a proper name does not occur until the second century BC:

> The earliest datable evidence for שטן used as a proper name comes from *Jub.* 23:29 and *As. Mos.* 10:1, both of which can be dated to the persecutions of Antiochus IV ca. 168 B. C. E. The deuterocanonical texts that antedate 168 B. C. E. speak of evil demons and corrupt angels, but no text uses the name Satan. In Tobit, for instance, the evil demon who had to be restrained before Tobit could marry Sarah is named Asmodeus (Tob 3:8, 17). In the earliest level of 1 Enoch 6—11, the leader of the angels who were punished as a consequence of their intercourse with the daughters of men is Shemihazah; in a later addition to these chapters, he is called Asael. In short, whereas the deuterocanonical literature prior to 168 B. C. E. speaks of specific names for evil demons and corrupt angels, no extant tradition employs the proper name Satan. The available evidence, therefore, points to the second century B. C. E. for the earliest occurrences of the proper name Satan.

Another assumption that we have often carried blindly into the OT is that the technical term always applies to the same supernatural being, a single satan. This is easily refuted by the fact that Numbers 22:22, 32 refer to the angel of the Lord as being a satan. Not only can we identify "satan" here as a functional designation, but also we can now consider the possibility that as a function it is not intrinsically evil (Weiss, 35-41). Furthermore, since we would not assume that the angel of the Lord is the accuser in every

context, it follows that the accuser is not necessarily always the same supernatural being.

Job 1:6 would lead us to understand that a certain divine being whose precise identity is unimportant and who has the current and temporary status of accuser is being introduced into the narrative. The advantage of this interpretation is that it is consistent with known Israelite (and Mesopotamian) legal practice in that "accuser" was a legal status that various people temporarily acquired in the appropriate circum-stances, and not a post or office. (*DDD*[2] 728)

Consequently, it is possible that the individual designated the accuser in *Job is not the same individual designated as the accuser in Zechariah or Chronicles. Though they may be the same individual, we cannot simply assume that they must be, or that the Israelites would have considered them to be the same individual. Pseudepigraphic literature refers to many satans (e.g., the list of five satans in *1 En.* 69:4-12, first century BC at the earliest [see D. Russell, 254-55]).

2. The Profile of Satan in Job.

If we had no name for this individual and had to build his profile from the text of Job, what conclusions could we draw? First, we would observe that the satan comes among "the sons of God" (Job 1:6). It is clear, therefore, that he has access to the heavenly throne and likely that he is counted among the members of this *divine council (cf. Ps 89:5-8; see Mullen, 190-244; Weiss, 31-33), though some have identified him as an intruder (see discussion in Page, 25-26). Secondly, the satan does not initiate the discussion of Job; he merely offers an alternative explanation of his righteous behavior. Though it is common for the satan's job to be portrayed as seeking out human failings (Page, 26), it is God's policies that are the true focus of the challenge (Day, 80-81). Job's character is only the test case. In that vein, the existence of disinterested *righteousness and the effect of a reward system on a person's motives are both legitimate issues. God neither scoffs at the challenge nor discounts the legitimacy of the question.

What the satan is in fact challenging is God's blueprint for divine-human relations. In other words, the satan is questioning the validity of a moral order in which the pious unfailingly prosper. The test of true righteousness would be worship without the promise of reward. (*DDD*², 728)

The common view that the role of the satan should be compared to the Persian "secret service," the eyes and ears of the king (e.g, Forsyth, 114), would be unacceptable if he serves to question the policies of God rather than the behavior of humans. In this sense we might consider a loose analogy to someone designated as "parliamentarian" in a group organized by Roberts Rule of Order. His/her job is to identify procedures that are out of order. The role is intended to serve, not disrupt.

Another question introduced by whether the satan targets God or Job concerns his demeanor toward Job. Some have inferred that the satan relished the opportunity to strike at Job. The text does not attribute to God or to the satan any personal emotional response to Job's tragedy. God has struck Job as much as the satan has (implied in Job 1:12; 2:3; see Weiss, 37), and both lack any sympathetic response. It would be arbitrary, then, to assume that the satan enjoyed it while God sadly endured it. There is no expression of glee; there is no diabolical chuckle. "Nothing personal, Job—there is a major philosophical issue on the line that supersedes individual circumstances."

M. Weiss concludes that nothing intrinsically evil emerges in the author's portrayal of the satan in Job. Certainly what he does has negative consequences for Job, a righteous man, but the text makes it clear that God is at least equally responsible for what happens to Job, thus freeing the actions from being implicitly evil (Weiss, 37 [*contra* Page, 27-28]). There is no tempting, corrupting, depraving or possessing.

The result of this profile is that we are not in a position to claim that the satan in the book of Job should be identified with Satan as we know him in the NT on the premise that they act the same way. In fact, there is little if any overlap between their two profiles. This does not prove that they are not the same individual; it merely reduces (if not eliminates) the basis for claiming that they must be equated. The profile of the Hebrew satan in the book of Job does not answer to the same description as the Christian view of Satan in the NT. The pictures are not contradictory, and they may even be complementary, but we could not consider them homogeneous.

3. Socioreligious Profile.

The profile of the satan in Zechariah 3:1 shows a great deal of similarity to that in Job, so it is important to take a brief look there to see what it contributes to formulating a larger profile. When Joshua the high priest stands before the presence of God, he is confronted by the satan and opposed because he is covered with the stains of his and his people's guilt. Is the satan wrong to oppose him on this count? Weiss (36-37 [see also Meyers and Meyers, 185-86]) says no:

True, he "opposes," though not in a spirit of malice, but rather because he meticulously clings to justice, on the principle "Let justice be done though the heavens fall." After all, Joshua the high priest was in fact guilty: he was dressed in garments covered with excrement, and he himself donned them in his guilt. Satan did not garb him in foul clothes through an unjust accusation. The garments are removed when God forgives his sin: he is acquitted not through justice, but through mercy, through pardon.

On the other hand, one significant difference between the scenarios in Job and Zechariah is that in the latter the satan is rebuked, while in the former he is not (Weiss, 37). C. Meyers and E. Meyers (186) contend that this rebuke is not directed against the satan performing his function but rather concerns the evidence that he brings. Here again we find the satan raising issues concerning God's policies. In Job it was the policy of rewarding the righteous that was being questioned; in Zechariah it is the policy of forgiveness and restoration (Day, 118-21). Rather than a lengthy test to confirm the legitimacy of God's policy as we had in Job, in Zechariah the satan is rebuked on the grounds that punishment had been appropriately accomplished (Joshua is a smoldering brand drawn from the fire; Zech 3:2).

A different profile emerges in other passages. In Numbers 22; 1 Kings 11; 1 Chronicles 21 the satan is viewed as a quasi-independent agent by means of whom punishment is initiated. How does this compare to the profiles in Job and Zechariah? There, his function was one directed toward God, in the sense that he initiated challenges concerning God's policies. In these other books, however, his function is directed toward humans. Are we dealing in the OT with two separate profiles or simply two aspects of a single profile? Only speculation could provide answers to these questions. But again, we must note how different the profile(s) is from that which is later provided by the NT, where Satan is linked directly to a principle of evil (J. Russell, 189). The NT profile reflects the development of thought that took place throughout the intertestamental period, traceable through literature that evidences some of the progression in theological thinking that is later affirmed by the NT (see Ringgren, 313-16). By the time of the NT much of this thinking has been accumulated into the profile of the one called "Satan," the diabolical enemy leading the forces of evil.

If the profile shows no features of demon, fallen angel or tempter, what alternatives remain? A glance into the cognitive environment of the ancient Near East may provide another possibility. In comparative literature it must be observed first that there is no parallel to the satan character in the pieces from Mesopotamia that explore the case of the pious sufferer. Likewise, there is no concept of a chief of demons or a being who is the source and cause of all evil (DDD^2 236). Since the heavenly court at times features legal proceedings among the members of the court, another place to look for parallels is in the roles within the legal system. A number of different terms refer to individuals (divine or human) who can bring a variety of formal accusations, serve as litigants or informants, or call for accountability (*amkil karsdi* [*CAD* K, 222]; *beml dabambi* [*CAD* D 3-4]; *beml dimni* [*CAD* D 155]; *batiqu* [*CAD* B 166]). None of these offer precise parallels to the role of the satan, but they have the most potential. A final note: in the court system, whether human or divine, no evidence is extant that suggests that a single being was assigned any of these roles permanently (see discussion in Magdalene).

The role of the satan in the book of Job would be seen as one who acts as a court functionary challenging the policies of God, specifically, his policy of blessing the righteous, though it is unclear whether he should be seen as legal opponent, litigant or informant. His challenge strikes right to the heart of the *retribution principle, a tenet for which the book seeks to provide a corrective. The satan's case is pressed unwittingly by the three friends, for if Job listens to them and confesses to sin simply to appease deity and be restored to favor, then the satan wins his case.

When the role of the friends ends in Job 27, the satan's case also is shown to be groundless, and there is no need to mention him again.

See also DIVINE COUNCIL; JOB 1: BOOK OF.

BIBLIOGRAPHY. **P. L. Day,** *An Adversary in Heaven: Śāṭān in the Hebrew Bible* (HSM 43; Atlanta: Scholars Press, 1988); **N. Forsyth,** *The Old Enemy: Satan and the Combat Myth* (Princeton, NJ: Princeton University Press, 1987); **L. K. Handy,** "The Authorization of Divine Power and the Guilt of God in the Book of Job: Useful Ugaritic Parallels," *JSOT* 60 (1993) 107-18; **S. Japhet,** *1 & 2 Chronicles* (OTL; Louisville: Westminster John Knox, 1993); **K. R. Joines,** *Serpent Symbolism in the Old Testament* (Haddonfield, NJ: Haddonfield House, 1974); **F. R. Magdalene,** *On the Scales of righteousness: Neo-Babylonian Trial Law and the Book of Job* (Brown Judaic Studies 348; Providence, RI: Brown University, 2007); **C. L. and E. M. Meyers,** *Zechariah 1-8* (AB 25B; Garden City, NY: Doubleday, 1987); **E. T. Mullen,** *The Assembly of the Gods: The Divine Council in Canaanite and Hebrew Literature* (HSM 24: Missoula, MT: Scholars Press, 1980); **H. Ringgren,** *Israelite Religion* (Philadelphia: Fortress, 1966 [1963]); **D. S. Russell,** *The Method and Message of Jewish Apocalyptic* (Philadelphia: Westminster, 1964); **J. B. Russell,** *The Devil: Perceptions of Evil from Antiquity to Primitive Christianity* (Ithaca, NY: Cornell University Press, 1977); **S. H. T. Page,** *Powers of Evil: A Biblical Study of Satan and Demons* (Grand Rapids: Baker, 1995); **M. Weiss,** *The Story of Job's Beginning* (Jerusalem: Magnes, 1983).
J. H. Walton

SCHOOLS. *See* SAGES, SCHOOLS, EDUCATION.

SCRIBES

The role of scribes in the poetic and wisdom writings is significant. This article surveys the ancient Near Eastern and specifically the West Semitic background of the scribe and its influence upon the scribe in ancient Israel. The article then turns to consider the occurrences of the scribe and the art of writing in the poetry and writings of the OT.

    1. Background
    2. Scribes in the Poetry and Writings of the
       Bible

1. Background.

In the ancient Near East scribes often used these same types of literature to practice their skills in writing. This is true in the major civilizations of Babylon, Assyria, Egypt, the Hittites and their scribal centers. Similar literature is found in the second-millennium BC archives of the West Semitic world, including Alalakh, Emar, Mari and Ugarit. All preserve evidence of wisdom literature and its various forms. The great mythological stories, including the Epic of Gilgamesh, the Enuma Elish and many others, were recorded in poetic form. The scribes used difficult and challenging compositions to develop their skills. Writing in syllabic and ideographic scripts, they could exhibit their abilities with the use of esoteric signs. Thus the scribal art was a difficult occupation to learn and one that meant there were few who could skillfully read and write their scripts.

This was not the case in ancient Israel. There, the written script was alphabetic and included only about twenty-two different signs versus the hundreds found in the cuneiform and hieroglyphic scripts of many of the surrounding civilizations. The result was that reading and writing were more accessible. It may well have been the case that more people could acquire scribal training more easily. Already in the eleventh-century BC village of Izbet Sartah (biblical Ebenezer) there existed an alphabetic text on which a student was practicing the writing of letters of the alphabet. Judges 8:14 bears witness as to how a young man, caught at random from the Jordan Valley town of Succoth, could write out the names seventy-seven local officers. Another alphabetic practice text was discovered in 2006 at tenth-century Tel Zayit southwest of Jerusalem (Hess 2006). Although the degree of literacy might not be clear, it is evident from these and other examples, throughout the land and in every century (Hess 2002), that from early in Israel's settlement the ability to write was not so limited as in the neighboring civilizations (*see* DOTHB, Hebrew Inscriptions).

In other matters, however, the scribes of Israel did resemble their counterparts elsewhere. Royal officials employed scribes to record the events of their reign. The priests also preserved written records for purposes of maintaining precise instructions regarding their rituals, and for tax and other records of income and expense. Even more direct is the relationship between the scribal traditions of those who wrote the psalms and other poetry of Israel, and the West Semitic scribes of the Late Bronze Age (Day). Thus

there is a continuity of specific expressions as well as parallelisms and forms between the poetry of thirteenth-century BC Ugarit and that of the psalms. The style of expression of the fourteenth-century BC Hymn to the Sun by the Egyptian pharaoh Akhenaten has some remarkable similarities of phrasing and structure with parts of Psalm 104. Further, the Amarna letters from the same period, with their expressions of worshipful loyalty and their pleas for assistance from Canaanite city leaders to the pharaoh in Egypt, bear resemblances on many levels to many of the psalms where there is a writer who, as a leader of Jerusalem and its land, expresses worshipful loyalty and requests assistance from his overlord in the heavens. Further, specific expressions such as "the strong arm of pharaoh" and "set his name on Jerusalem" parallel "the hand of the LORD" (Job 12:9; Ps 75:8) and "the dwelling of your name" (Ps 74:7) in biblical poetry. This, along with the *chiasm, synonymous *parallelism and other poetic structures bear witness to the continuation of a scribal tradition from Canaanite antecedents to David and the poets of the Hebrew Bible (Hess 1989).

2. Scribes in the Poetry and Writings of the Bible.
The role of the scribe in ancient Israel could and did take on components of creativity and composition. Thus Psalm 45:1 records how the psalmist's tongue is that of a skilled writer who is able to compose the wedding song that follows. This statement itself indicates something of the manner in which the scribe displaced the oral tradition of storytelling and oral composition (*see* Oral Poetry). The root for the word *scribe* and *scroll*, *spr*, can also be used to describe the oral recitation of a story, a song or any matter. This is only one example of the transition from oral to written of which the Bible is aware and in which the scribes of Israel played an important role (Goody; Niditch; Millard; Schniedewind 2004; van der Toorn). In the wisdom corpus it may find a reflection in the observation about the making of scrolls and the weariness that work with scrolls produces (Eccles 12:12 [note that the word translated "study" here is a good guess, but it occurs only here and perhaps in a related form in Ugaritic, where it appears in parallel with the word for "document"]).

Elsewhere in the psalms the use of the root *spr* for "scribe" and "scroll" envisions compositions that have a divine origin. This includes the enigmatic reference to a scroll that contains writing about the psalmist (Ps 40:7), and the written decree regarding the fate of the enemies of God's people (Ps 149:9). It is clearer in the description of the psalmist's enemies as blotted out of the book of life (Ps 69:28) and the observation that the days of the psalmist are written in God's book (Ps 139:16). Elsewhere Yahweh writes in a document about nations (Ps 87:6), and writing takes place in anticipation of a future generation (Ps 102:18).

In *Job as well, God functions as a scribe who writes against Job (Job 13:26) and to whom Job makes a request that the indictment against him be placed in writing (Job 31:35). Elsewhere Job longs for his words to be written on a scroll (Job 19:23), although it is not clear who is writing the words.

In *Proverbs the student is commanded to write the instruction. However, the place of the writing is on the "tablet of your heart" (Prov 3:3; 7:3). Thus the writing is not literal but rather a metaphor for the memorization and internalization of the material that the student learns. In Proverbs 22:20 the teacher refers to writing some thirty proverbs for the student. Compare this with Ecclesiastes 12:10, where the teacher also writes good words for the student. Proverbs 25:1 refers to the proverbs of *Solomon that the men of Hezekiah, presumably *sages of that era, passed along. Given that the material is now in written form, it is reasonable to assume that they were scribes who wrote this material. However, the verb describing what was done with the proverbs carries the basic sense of "transmit" or "pass along." Therefore it could define something that was orally transmitted. Nevertheless, the presence of extrabiblical seal impressions and other texts (such as the Siloam Tunnel inscription), as well as indications from the editorial notes in the books of Kings and the work of the prophet Isaiah (and Micah), combine with the archaeological and geopolitical evidence of the period to suggest that Hezekiah's reign at the end of the eighth century BC was a time of relatively prolific production of biblical literature (Schniedewind 2004), and thus a time of significant scribal activity.

Of all the books in the corpus under consideration, the one that contains the greatest number of references to scribal activity is *Esther. Set in the Persian period, it is also one of the latest of the books. Here the use of writing is connected with authoritative decrees to be enacted. Royal decrees are often so described (Esther 1:19, 22; 3:9; 8:5, 8-10, 13; see also the apocryphal Add Esth 13:1), as well as the decree of Haman (Esther 3:12-14; 4:8). Royal annalistic records are also mentioned (Esther 2:23; 6:1-2; 10:2). *Mordecai conducts his own correspondence with the provinces (Esther 9:20-32).

Thus the scribe and the scribal arts of Job and *Psalms (and perhaps *Ecclesiastes as well) focus on the role of God and the divine authority of decisions that are made in heaven regarding mortals on earth. In the Second Temple period the scribes may have been responsible for collection of the psalms into the work as we now have it. However, this role in *canon formation is disputed insofar as the evidence from Qumran does not necessarily support an agreed-upon canonical book before the first century AD. Scribes continued to read and interpret the poetic and wisdom texts of the Bible as suggested by the Wisdom literature of the intertestamental period. The figure of the scribe in Proverbs is largely one concerned with the preservation and instruction of wisdom to the next generation of students. In Esther the scribe is tied with authoritative decrees that are often royal and make decisions of life and death for the people of the Persian empire, both Jews and Gentiles.

The important role given to scribes would continue in Judaism in the context of poetic and wisdom writings. In the second-century BC wisdom scroll of *Sirach there is this statement: "One's prosperity comes by the hand of the Lord, and he gives his glory to (the face of) a scribe" (Sir 10:5). Thus, even though the NT would place a negative evaluation on various scribes, both it (Mt 13:52) and Judaism's heritage in the Mishnah and later Jewish literature would remember the key role of scribes in the continuity of God's word, including the wisdom traditions of instruction and authority.

See also EDITORIAL CRITICISM; HEBREW LANGUAGE; ROYAL COURT; SAGES, SCHOOLS, EDUCATION; TEXT, TEXTUAL CRITICISM.

BIBLIOGRAPHY. **J. L. Crenshaw,** *Education in Ancient Israel: Across the Deadening Silence* (ABRL; New York: Doubleday, 1998); **J. Day,** *Psalms* (OTG; Sheffield: Sheffield Academic Press, 1990); **J. Goody,** *The Logic of Writing and the Organization of Society* (Cambridge: Cambridge University Press, 1986); **R. S. Hess,** "Hebrew Psalms and Amarna Correspondence from Jerusalem: Some Comparisons and Implications," *ZAW* 101 (1989) 249-65; idem, "Literacy in Iron Age Israel," in *Windows into Old Testament History: Evidence, Argument, and the Crisis of "Biblical Israel,"* ed. V. P. Long, D. W. Baker and G. J. Wenham (Grand Rapids: Eerdmans, 2002) 82-102; idem, "Writing About Writing: Abecedaries and Evidence for Literacy in Ancient Israel," *Vetus Testamentum* 56 (2006) 342-46; **A. R. Millard,** review of *Oral World and Written Word: Ancient Israelite Literature,* by S. Niditch, *JTS* 49 (1998) 699-705; **S. Niditch,** *Oral World and Written Word: Ancient Israelite Literature* (LAI; Louisville: Westminster John Knox, 1996); **W. M. Schniedewind,** "Orality and Literacy in Ancient Israel," *RelSRev* 26 (2000) 327-2l; idem, *How the Bible Became a Book: The Textualization of Ancient Israel* (Cambridge: Cambridge University Press, 2004); **K. van der Toorn,** *Scribal Culture and the Making of the Hebrew Bible* (Cambridge: Harvard University Press, 2007). R. S. Hess

SEA, PRIMORDIAL. *See* CHAOS AND DEATH.

SEX. *See* MARRIAGE AND SEX; SONG OF SONGS 1: BOOK OF.

SHAME. *See* HONOR AND SHAME; SOCIAL-SCIENTIFIC APPROACHES.

SHEOL. *See* CHAOS AND DEATH.

SIMILE. *See* POETICS, TERMINOLOGY OF.

SIRACH, BOOK OF

Sirach, one of the books of the OT Apocrypha, was written originally in Hebrew in Jerusalem during the first quarter of the second century BC and translated into Greek by Ben Sira's grandson in Egypt around 132 BC. It is similar to the book of *Proverbs in form and content, but it contains unique features atypical of the traditional Wisdom literature. As part of the Second Temple Jewish Wisdom literature, the book sheds light on the intellectual and social situation of Judaism during the Hellenistic era. The author demonstrates the superiority of Jewish wisdom and encourages his readers to keep their traditions. For him, Jewish wisdom finds its ultimate expression in the Mosaic Torah, and it is by subscribing to this Torah that one can be wise.

1. Historical Background
2. Literary Analysis
3. Wisdom Teaching
4. Sirach and the New Testament

1. Historical Background.

1.1. Authorship, Title, Date. The author of Sirach is identified as "Yeshua ben Eleazar ben Sira" (*yēšûaʿ bēn ʾelʿāzār ben sîrāʾ* [Sir 50:27; 51:30 MS B]) or "Jesus" (*Iēsou* [Sir Prologue 7]), also known as Ben Sira. The book is known under several names: "Sirach" (NRSV), "The Wisdom of Jesus Son of Sirach" (*Sophia Iēsou huiou Seirach* [LXX]), "The Wisdom of Joshua Son of Sira" (*ḥokmat yēšûaʿ ben sîrāʾ* [Hebrew]), "Ecclesiasticus" (Vulgate), "The Book of Ben Sira" (*sēper ben sîrāʾ* [*b. Ḥag.* 13a; *b. Nid.* 16b]) and "The Books of Ben Sira" (*sipri ben sîrāʾ* [*t. Yad.* 2:13]). In short, "Sirach" is the Greek name, "Ben Sira" the Hebrew, and "Ecclesiasticus" the Latin. Following the NRSV, "Sirach" is adopted here for the title of the book, and the name "Ben Sira" is used in reference to the author.

It is generally believed that Sirach was written in the period 200-175 BC, and that the Greek translation was made in the period 132-116 BC (but see Hengel 1974, 1.131; Peters, xxxiv-xxxvii). The dating of the book is extrapolated from its prologue, which speaks of Ben Sira's grandson's time of arrival in Egypt in 132 BC (i.e., the thirty-eighth year of King Euergetes' reign). It is further established in conjunction with the fact that the book does not mention the persecution of Antiochus IV (176-164 BC), and with the reference in Sirach 50 to Simon II (219-196 BC), who presumably is dead by then.

1.2. Text and Canon. The watershed studies of Sirach began in 1896, when the first Hebrew fragment (Sir 39:15—40:8) from the Cairo Geniza was identified by S. Schechter (see Reif). The textual history of the book is, nevertheless, notoriously complex. There are at least two forms of Sirach in the Greek version (G I and G II), numerous Hebrew manuscripts (A, B, C, D, E, F, M, 2Q18, 11QPs[a]), several manuscripts in the Syriac version and an Old Latin translation. There exist two Hebrew versions, a shorter Hebrew original (H I) and a longer text of more than one Hebrew recension (H II). Whereas H I (200-175 BC) is the basis for G I, the grandson's Greek translation, H II (mid-first century BC-AD 150) is the basis for G II (MS 248 [AD 150-200]), on which the Old Latin is based (Kearns). The combination of H I and H II serves as the *Vorlage* of the present Peshitta (Winter). Despite the complexity of the textual history, the Greek translation, particularly J. Ziegler's critical edition, constitutes the standard text for the study of Sirach. Recently, P. Beentjes arranged all the extant Hebrew MSS and compiled a somewhat user-friendly Hebrew text edition (without the critical apparatus), which, although not without problems, provides a valuable tool for Ben Sira research in years to come.

The status of the book is debated among the Jews. Some excluded it from their *canon (*y. Sanh.* 28a; *b. Sanh.* 100b; *t. Yad.* 2:13), while others, such as the Qumran community (2Q18; 11QPs[a]; Mas1h), the Jews in the Diaspora (LXX) and some rabbis (citing the book with the standard formula for scripture citation: "it is written" [*b. Ḥag.* 13a; *b. Nid.* 16b, *y. Ber.* 11c]), considered it authoritative. By the end of the first century AD the book was officially excluded from the Jewish canon. One of the main reasons for this exclusion was the belief during the time of Ben Sira that the Jewish canon had been set, according to the Greek prologue of Sirach (cf. Sir 39:1), which speaks of the existence of a tripartite Scripture (Beckwith, 80-93, 111; but see VanderKam).

The early Christian church adopted the Jewish canon (i.e., the so-called Palestinian Canon) as its OT and assigned Sirach to the Apocrypha (Beckwith, 386-95). However, together with the other books of the Apocrypha, the book has been accepted as part of the deuterocanonical writings in the Catholic tradition (Council of Trent [1546]). The Reformers consistently excluded the Apocrypha from their canon (Belgic Confession, Article 6 [1562]; Westminster Confession of Faith 1.3 [1647]), although among Protestant churches today, the Anglican Church continues to use the Apocrypha in its lectionary (Articles of Religion, Article 6).

Despite the noncanonical status of the books of the Apocrypha, Protestants have begun to recognize their importance, along with the other Second Temple Jewish writings, because of their value in the study of Second Temple Judaism, biblical interpretation and early Christianity (Carson, xliv-xlvii). Today virtually all of the Apocrypha is included in the NRSV.

1.3. Ben Sira and His Time.

1.3.1. The Profile of Ben Sira. Ben Sira saw himself as a *scribe (Heb *sôpēr;* Gk *gramma-*

teus), as well as a wisdom teacher, and his book as a source of wisdom (Sir 38:24; 50:27). He also considered himself a latecomer in the long sapiential tradition (Sir 33:16-18), when he may have started his career at a relatively young age (Sir 51:23-30; cf. Sir 39:1-5). Ben Sira devoted himself to the diligent study of the Torah, the Prophets and other writings (Sir Prologue 7-10), and he acquired much wisdom through the study of "the wisdom of the men of old" (Sir 39:1) and from his travels (Sir 34:9-12). Judging from his conviction that only those who are free from manual labor could pursue wisdom (Sir 38:24-25), it is likely that he never was engaged in such work. He is also thought to be a priest, given his familiarity with and high regard for the priesthood (e.g., Stadelmann). He was considered to be a rich Jewish intellectual, a landowner and a slave owner (Blenkinsopp 1995a, 15-20), a judge, counselor and member of the assembly or a temple scribe (Hengel 1974, 1.133). All these are, at most, only conjectures. What is clear is that Ben Sira was a "transitional" *sage. He is, on the one hand, a traditional wisdom teacher, and on the other hand, an interpreter of Scriptures. As a transitional figure, he was doing more than what the traditional wisdom teachers were doing. He interpreted Scriptures, making it part of the subject of his inquiry (Kugel, 10-11).

1.3.2. Judaism and Hellenism. The older view (e.g., Smend) that there appeared a direct antipathy between Judaism and Hellenism no longer holds true (Hengel 1974, 1.104-5). The relationship between Judaism and Hellenism is a complex and multifaceted one. Hellenism infiltrated subtly into the political, religious, economical, intellectual and social aspects of the ancient Near East. Although the Greek language, as well as the Greek way of life, had dominated all strata of the population, the traditional Jewish religious heritage remained uncompromised among the vast majority of the Jews. Initially, the Jews in Palestine considered the Greeks their "eschatological enemies" and experienced a polemical, rather than a cultural, confrontation. It was at the beginning of the third century BC, with the political stability and the return of the Diaspora Jews, that an intellectual milieu began to flourish. In particular, Jewish wisdom and apocalypticism began to directly encounter Greek ideas (Hengel 1980, 110-12), and Sirach is one book that shows direct Greek influence

(Sanders, 27-59). It is appropriate to see Judaism during the Second Temple period as "Hellenistic Judaism" (Hengel 1974, 1.104).

1.3.3. Purpose of the Book. Set within Palestine of the Second Temple period, Ben Sira was, without doubt, faced with the challenge of Hellenism. His struggle was immediately noticeable: to fight the liberal aristocracy and at the same time to keep a low profile before the powerful (e.g., Sir 4:7; 7:14a; 8:11, 14; 9:13). The attitude that Ben Sira had toward Hellenization, however, is a matter of debate. M. Hengel (1974, 1.138-53) sees an "apologetic-polemical" character against Hellenistic liberalism in Ben Sira's teaching (Sir 41:8-9), while B. Mack (101-2) argues that Ben Sira was sympathetic to the Hellenistic culture (Sir 38:24—39:35), and J. Collins (41, 54-56) contends that Ben Sira's intention was constructive rather than apologetic. For T. Middendorp (173-74), Ben Sira was holding a mediating position, seeking to bridge Greek civilization and ancient Jewish tradition. Indeed, nowhere in Sirach do we find any explicit polemic against, or advocacy of, Greek civilization. Nevertheless, it is impossible to rule out the apologetic tone when Ben Sira seeks to convince his readers to acquire wisdom (e.g., Sir 2:7-17; 14:20-15:10; 19:20-30; 32:18-33:3; 42:2). P. Skehan and A. Di Lella (16) maintain that Ben Sira's purpose "was not to engage in a systematic polemic against Hellenism but rather to convince Jews and even well-disposed Gentiles that true wisdom is to be found primarily in Jerusalem and not in Athens, more in the inspired books of Israel than the clever writings of Hellenistic humanism."

2. Literary Analysis.

In the past, Ben Sira was often seen as a "successor" (*Nachfolger* [Middendorp, 78]) and a "conscious imitator" (Schechter, 12) of Proverbs. Compared to the other earlier wisdom writers, he was less of a "creative thinker," "master stylist" or even an "innovator in literary genres" (Skehan and Di Lella, 21, 43). Recently, however, scholars have come to believe that Ben Sira made distinct contributions (Coggins, 62-68). His style of writing reflects wisdom poetry of his time, and his thinking is greatly influenced by earlier nonsapiential biblical writings as well as by Greek and Egyptian literature (Sanders, 27-59).

2.1. Literary Genres. Like Proverbs, the poetry of Sirach is generally marked by *parallelism, either in single or multiple couplets. But the sayings of Ben Sira consist of both long and short teachings made up from various genres, such as "proverbs," "hymns of praise," "songs of thanksgiving," "laments," "prophetic speeches" and "wisdom personified speeches" (see Baumgartner, 165-92), with the genres of *māšāl* (Sir 1—43) and rewritten Bible (Sir 44—49) being the most prominent ones.

2.1.1. māšāl. The basic meaning of *māšāl* is "likeness/comparison," and it is generally used to describe a popular aphoristic saying (*TDOT* 9.67). Like Proverbs, Sirach contains "better" sayings, with the standard formula *ṭôb min* (Heb) or *kreissōn* (Gk) (e.g., Sir 20:31; 40:28). Numerical sayings usually take the form "x/x plus one" and have their emphasis on the second, larger number (e.g., Sir 23:16-18; 25:1-2, 7-11; 26:5-6, 28; 50:25-26). Ben Sira's numerical sayings stretch from 2/3 (Sir 23:16-18) to 9/10 (Sir 25:7-11). Other types of *māšāl* include, among others, "happy" sayings (e.g., Sir 14:1-2, 20; 25:8-9; 26:1) and "woe" sayings (Sir 2:12-14; 41:8).

2.1.2. Rewritten Bible. The section known as the Praise of the Fathers (Sir 44—49) has been understood differently: for example, a hymn in praise of men (Baumgartner), encomium of Simon (Lee), encomium of Israel's heroes (Collins) and epic historiography (Mack). Since the tales of the heroes were told in an "augmented" manner (Enns, 17), and in accordance with the biblical order, the best designation is "rewritten Bible" (Hayward). Although the form of rewritten Bible is entirely lacking in the biblical Wisdom literature, it is present in the OT (e.g., Ps 78; 105; 106; 135; 136; Neh 9:6-37) and in the NT (e.g., Acts 7; Heb 11). Similar to the OT, the history of Israel is retold in poetic form, and selected characters, from Enoch to Nehemiah, are singled out as ideal figures.

2.1.3. Others. Other than *māšāl* and rewritten Bible, there are two unique genres worth mentioning: the autobiographical saying and the hymn of praise. Although the autobiographical saying is also found in the biblical Wisdom literature (Prov 4:3-9; 24:30-34), Ben Sira, like *Qohelet before him, regularly uses his personal experience (e.g., Sir 33:16-17; 51:13-16) as a basis for his teaching (cf., e.g., Eccles 2:17-26). A hymn of praise is an expression of one's gratitude to God. But in Sirach several hymns appear in which Ben Sira extols both divine wisdom and human wisdom (e.g., Sir 39:12-35; 42:15-43:33; 44:1—50:24; 51:1-12).

2.2. Structure and Content. Sirach is not merely a collection of collections, for it has a clearly set out structure and organized content. It begins with an introductory poem (Sir 1:1-10) and an alphabetic *acrostic (Sir 1:11-30) and ends with another alphabetic acrostic (Sir 51:13-20), which forms a literary *inclusio for the book (Skehan and Di Lella, 74). The book may be structured thematically as follows:

Greek Prologue
Wisdom Sayings (Sir 1:1—43:33)
The Praise of the Fathers (Sir 44:1—49:16)
Conclusion (Sir 50:1—51:30)

2.2.1. Greek Prologue. The value of the prologue is not limited to the understanding of the development of the biblical canon. It provides important information regarding the Greek translation. The grandson not only explains his purpose and the issues involved in the process of translation but also provides reading strategies and insists that his work is comparable to the Jewish-Greek Scriptures. Thus, the prologue, written a couple of generations later, is to be seen as an integral part of the book (Wright).

2.2.2. Wisdom Sayings (Sir 1:1—43:33). Wisdom sayings in proverbial form permeate Sirach, leading many to think of Sirach as being patterned after Proverbs. The content of Sirach (fifty-one chapters!), however, is more diverse and covers a wide range of topics. No less than thirty-one topics have been identified in Sirach 1—43 (Murphy, 73). Although they are not arranged in any systematic order (Skehan and Di Lella, 4-5), they are made up of two major collections: Sirach 1:1—23:28; 24:1—43:33.

Both collections have similar structure. They start out with a wisdom poem that speaks of the source of wisdom, which is the Lord (Sir 1:1-10; 24:1-34), and the application of wisdom, which is the *fear of the Lord (Sir 1:11—2:17; 25:1-11). Notably, in the introductions to both collections similar language, such as "the depth of the abyss" (Sir 1:3; 24:5), wisdom as a tree spreading its branches (Sir 1:20; 24:16), wisdom as coming from the Lord (Sir 1:1; 24:3), and wisdom being created first by God (Sir 1:4; 24:9), is employed.

In Sirach there are various types of wisdom sayings—for example, on friendship (Sir 6:5-17; 22:19-27; 37:1-6), wealth and poverty (Sir 13:15-

24; 13:25—14:10; 31:1-11), speech and tongue (Sir 19:4-17; 20:1-8, 18-26; 23:7-15; 27:11-21; 28:12-26; 32:3-13), death and life (Sir 14:11-19; 38:16-23; 41:1-4), relationship with *women (Sir 9:1-9), relationship with parents (Sir 3:1-16), relationship with the needy (Sir 3:30—4:10), pride and humility (Sir 3:17-29; 9:12-13; 10:26—11:6), generosity (Sir 18:15-18), leadership (Sir 9:17—10:18), food (Sir 30:18-25; 31:12—32:2; 37:27-31), slaves (Sir 33:24-31), sacrifice and offering (Sir 34:21—35:13), prayers (Sir 35:14-20), children (Sir 30:1-17; 42:9-14), sickness and health (Sir 38:1-15), character (Sir 27:4-10; 27:30—28:11), dreams and divination (Sir 34:1-11), giving (Sir 29:1-28) and hard work (Sir 40:28-30). They are placed in the context of the fear of the Lord. This means that these sayings can no longer be treated as traditional teachings but rather must be applied in light of this new context.

It is characteristic of wisdom teachers to compare and contrast wisdom and foolishness (Sir 19:20-30; 21:11—22:2, 7-18; 37:16-26). Ben Sira also gives readers the option to choose between wisdom and *folly (Sir 15:11-20). With the intention of encouraging readers to embrace wisdom, on the one hand, he lays out the consequences of foolishness: death (Sir 21:1-10), disgrace (Sir 23:16-27), divine wrath (Sir 27:22-29), shame (Sir 33:20-24; cf. Sir 41:15—42:8) and judgment (Sir 16:5-14; 40:10); on the other hand, he insists that a wise person will have a good name (Sir 41:11-14), glory (Sir 1:11, 19; 4:13) and honor (Sir 10:19-20), will find favor with God (Sir 32:14-17), and is promised a life of peace and security (Sir 34:14-20).

There are several topics in Sirach that are rare for Wisdom literature, the first of which is prayer. In Proverbs there is only one brief prayer (Prov 30:7-9). In Sirach there are two extended prayers, one in each of the two wisdom collections. The prayer for self-discipline (Sir 22:27—23:6) reveals Ben Sira's piety, and the prayer for God's people (Sir 36:1-22) shows Ben Sira's love for his country. Another topic is that of women, comprising about 7 percent of Sirach (Trenchard, 1). Ben Sira appears to be extremely negative toward women. For example, he attributes the origin of sin and its resultant death to Eve (Sir 25:24) and criticizes women of improper conduct. His forthright comments on women (Sir 9:1-9; 19:2; 23:22-26; 25:16-26; 42:13-14), however, do not necessarily make him a misogynist (so Trenchard, 172-73); rather, this biased attitude toward women may be a reflection of the view of women current in his male-dominated society (Camp).

2.2.3. The Praise of the Fathers (Sir 44:1—49:16). This hymn, a continuation of Sirach 1—43 (Mack, 189-93), is entitled "Praise of the Fathers of Old" (Heb) or "Praise of the Fathers" (Gk). It begins with a prelude (Sir 44:1-15), which provides a hermeneutical key to the reading of the Praise of the Fathers. Several key words, notably *ḥesed* ("piety"), *kābôd* ("glory") and *šēm* ("name, reputation"), are listed as wisdom criteria by which the fathers are evaluated. A list of twelve categories of offices is given (Sir 44:3-6), but without mentioning the individual office holders. This shows Ben Sira's lack of favoritism toward any office and his emphasis on wisdom over status. For example, rulers are praised not because they are rulers per se but rather because of their wise dominion (Sir 44:3a).

Immediately after the prelude, a catalogue of historical personas from Enoch to Nehemiah is introduced (Sir 44:16—49:16). Enoch, the ideal wisdom figure, is the first and the last person mentioned (Sir 44:16; 49:16), creating an inclusio to situate all the fathers in the wisdom perimeter (cf. Sir 45:2, 7, 12, 23; 46:2; 50:5, 11). These ancient fathers are presented in accordance with the canonical division from Enoch to Phinehas (Pentateuch: Sir 44:16—45:26) and from Joshua to Nehemiah (Prophets: Sir 46:1—49:16).

What is unique is that certain characteristics of these figures are nowhere to be found in the OT. For example, Enoch is seen as a sign of knowledge (Sir 44:16 MS B), and Abraham as a keeper of the *law (Sir 44:20). Most strikingly, Aaron receives a great amount of attention (Sir 45:6-22) compared to Moses (Sir 45:1-5).

Ben Sira regards Joshua a prophet after Moses (Sir 46:1), and the judges, whose bones returned to life, as being free from idolatry (Sir 46:11-12). As for the kings, Ben Sira speaks of *David as playing with the lions, and his "horn" as being exalted by God forever (Sir 47:3, 11). *Solomon is indicted not on the basis of his accumulation of wealth and of having had many wives but rather because of his submission to women (Sir 47:19), which is the cause of the schism (Sir 47:21). With reference to the defeat of the Assyrian army, he gives credit to the people's prayer (Sir 48:20), which brought down a deadly plague (Sir 48:21 Heb). It has nothing to do with the angel's work (cf. 2 Kings 19:35-37) or the prayer of Hezekiah (cf. 2 Kings 19:14-19). He compares Josiah with a threefold quality that relates to the senses (Sir 49:1): incense (smell), honey (taste) and music (hearing). Ben Sira speaks highly of the prophets. He sees in the return of Elijah (Sir 48:10) the fulfillment of Malachi 4:5-6. Elisha was a great prophet filled with the spirit. After he died, his body continued to prophesy (Sir 48:13 [cf. 2 Kings 13:21]). For Ben Sira, it was Isaiah, not God, who prolonged Hezekiah's life (Sir 48:23). He believes that the bones of the twelve (minor) prophets, like the bones of the judges, had returned to life and given strength and hope to Jacob (Sir 49:10).

2.2.4. Conclusion (Sir 50:1—51:30). The Praise of the Fathers is culminated in the person of Simon II (Sir 50:1-24), who was an ideal priest and a wise person. Like the fathers, he demonstrated his wisdom in his building activities (Sir 50:1-4; cf. Sir 48:17-22) as well as in his priestly duties during the Day of Atonement or the daily whole-offering (Sir 50:5-21; cf. Sir 45:6-22). The praise of Simon is followed by a numerical saying (Sir 50:25-26) and an epilogue (50:27-28 [50:29 Gk]), which summarizes the blessing of wisdom. The last chapter contains a prayer of thanksgiving for deliverance (Sir 51:1-12), a hymn of praise (Sir 51:12 i-xvi MS B [cf. Ps 136]) and an acrostic wisdom poem in the form of autobiography (Sir 51:1-30).

3. Wisdom Teaching.

Sirach is about wisdom. It is constructed with a wisdom frame: a wisdom poem at the beginning (Sir 1:1-10), at the end (Sir 51:13-30) and in the middle (Sir 24:1-34). Ben Sira deals extensively with interpersonal relationships, such as those among family members (e.g., parents, children, slaves), friends, women, rulers and the poor. He also touches on various aspects of social ethics—for example, speech, table etiquette and discrimination. He takes seriously matters of life and death, religious obligations, the problem of evil and the justice of God. As a wise teacher, Ben Sira not only learns wisdom but also contributes to it (see Sir 21:15). Compared to the teachings of the earlier wisdom teachers, his is more comprehensive (von Rad, 241-42). Two areas of his teaching will suffice to illustrate this.

3.1. Wisdom and the Fear of the Lord. According to his grandson in the prologue, Ben Sira's purpose is to write something pertaining to instruction and wisdom, in order that "those who love learning might make even greater progress in living according to the law" (Sir Prologue 12-14 NRSV).

This purpose is also stated at the end of the book: "Instruction in understanding and knowledge I have written in this book. . . . Happy are those who engage in these things; and those who take them to heart will become wise. For those who do them will be strong for all things, for the light of the Lord is their path" (Sir 50:27-29 Gk). In Ben Sira's words, this wisdom, first and foremost, is to be found in the Lord: "All wisdom is from the Lord, and it is with him forever" (Sir 1:1 Gk). He affirms that only the Lord is wise (Sir 1:8-9), and that wisdom was first created by God (Sir 1:4, 9; cf. Sir 24:8-9).

To obtain this wisdom, however, is not impossible. Ben Sira follows the traditional understanding: "To fear the Lord is the beginning of wisdom" (Sir 1:14a Gk). The expression "fear God" occurs some sixty times in Sirach. Together with wisdom, it depicts the central concern of Ben Sira. Traditional wisdom teachers affirmed that the fear of God is the beginning of wisdom (e.g., Prov 1:7), but Ben Sira had more to say. The fear of the Lord is not only the beginning of wisdom (Sir 1:14); it is also the fullness of wisdom (Sir 1:16), the crown of wisdom (Sir 1:18), the root of wisdom (Sir 1:20) and, above all, life (Sir 50:28c Heb). For Ben Sira, fearing God is a covenantal concept equal to loving God, keeping his commandment, and walking in his ways (cf. Deut 6:4-6; 10:12-13; 30:11-20). He maintains, "Those who fear the Lord will not disobey his words, and those who love him will keep his ways. Those who fear the Lord will seek to please him, and those who love him will be filled with his law" (Sir 2:15-16 Gk), and "The one who fears the Lord will do this, and the one who holds to the law will obtain her [wisdom]" (Sirach 15:1 Gk). Indeed, "The whole of wisdom is the fear of the Lord, and in all wisdom is the performance of the law" (Sirach 19:20 Gk).

The relationship between wisdom and Torah is not entirely new in earlier biblical texts (e.g., Deut 4:6-7; 30:11-16). The idea permeates Sirach (e.g., Sir 1:26; 2:16; 6:37; 10:19; 15:1, 14-15; 19:20; 21:11; 23:27; 31:8-10; 32:15-16, 23-24; 33:1-3; 34:8, 22-23; 35:1, 8; 39:1-2; 41:8; 42:2) and comes to a sharper focus in the great wisdom poem in Sirach 24:1-34. Closely resembling

Proverbs 8 in form, with seven stanzas of five lines (Skehan and Di Lella, 331), Sirach 24 portrays wisdom in greater detail. Wisdom personified, which is a contextualization of the aretalogy of Egyptian Isis (Marböck, 47-54), disclosed her origin (Sir 24:3-17), identified herself with the law (Sir 24:23-29) and likened herself to a channel of instruction (Sir 24:30-34) (see Woman Wisdom). She journeyed from the mouth of the Most High (Sir 24:2) to "the heights" and a "pillar of cloud" (Sir 24:4), to heaven, the abysses, the sea, and to all the world (Sir 24:5-6 [cf. Job 22:14]) in search of a resting place (Sir 24:7). Eventually, she found her abode in the "holy tabernacle" in Jerusalem (Sir 24:8, 10). It is in this context that Ben Sira equates wisdom with the book of the covenant of the Most High God (Sir 24:23). For the first time in Jewish tradition the correlation of wisdom and Torah is explicitly pronounced. Whereas the focus on Deuteronomy is on corporate covenantal obligation, in Sirach the emphasis is on the individual quest for wisdom (Blenkinsopp 1995b, 86-87, 152-53). Through this identification of wisdom with the law, Ben Sira is able to combat Hellenism more effectively (Hengel 1974, 1.157-62). Wisdom is not found in Greek culture; rather, it is located in the temple of Jerusalem (Sir 24:7-8, 23-27). In essence, the way to wisdom is through obedience to the Mosaic law.

The relationship between wisdom and Torah is demonstrated in the lives of the ancient fathers (Sir 44—49). For example, Enoch pleased the Lord (Sir 44:16; cf. Sir 2:16); Noah was found perfect (Sir 44:17; cf. Sir 31:10); Abraham kept the commandments (Sir 44:20; cf. Sir 6:37; 23:27); Moses demonstrated humility (Sir 45:4; cf. Sir 10:26-11:6); Aaron offered acceptable sacrifices (Sir 45:14; cf. Sir 35:1-13); Phinehas feared the Lord (Sir 45:23; cf. Sir 1:11-20); Joshua and Caleb trusted the Lord (Sir 46:4-6; cf. Sir 2:1-6); the judges did not fall into idolatry (Sir 46:11; cf. Sir 30:19); David loved the Lord (Sir 47:8; cf. Sir 2:15-16); Hezekiah pleased the Lord with his work (Sir 48:22; cf. Sir 35:20); Josiah had a lasting name (Sir 49:1; cf. Sir 41:11-14). These ancient fathers are praised not merely because of the role they played in the history of salvation; rather, they are praised because wisdom is not hidden in them (Sir 41:14).

3.2. Wisdom and the History of Israel. The most distinctive contribution of Ben Sira in his sapiential instruction, however, is not in his association of wisdom with the Mosaic law but rather in his attention to the history of Israel. This historical data is highly selective; certain individuals are highlighted and emphasized (e.g., the priestly figures Moses, Aaron, Phinehas, prophets as miracle workers), while other characters (e.g., Ezra, famous women such as Ruth and Deborah) are omitted. Even some significant historical events (e.g., the exodus and the crossing of the Red Sea) are absent.

Ben Sira's retelling of history shared with, and, to a certain extent, was guided by, certain exegetical traditions circulating during his time. For example, Sirach 44:16 Heb (Cowley and Neubauer, 20) reads, "Enoch was found perfect and walked with the Lord, and he was taken, a sign of knowledge to all generations." The language "a sign of knowledge" is found in *1 Enoch* 92:1, a retelling of Genesis 5:24. According to Jewish tradition, Enoch was taken up to heaven and returned from heaven with revelation. It is in this regard that he has become a sign of knowledge (Kugel, 174-78). The Greek translation has Enoch as an example of repentance rather than as a sign of knowledge, which reflects a different tradition that speaks of Enoch repenting of his sinful life, walking with the Lord, and thus pleasing the Lord and being taken up (cf. Wis 4:10-14; Philo, *QG* 1.82; *Abr.* 17 [see Kugel, 193-94]).

Israelite history is retold from a wisdom perspective, as was expected of a wisdom teacher (Sheppard, 13, 117-19). Thus, even the fathers, who were not seen as wise in the Pentateuch or the Prophets, are now viewed from the perspective of wisdom (cf. Wis 10). They are portrayed strictly as either good or evil, or as men of wisdom or men of folly (Kugel, 22), just like the wisdom sayings which are given in two opposites— for example, good and evil, life and death, the godly and the sinner (Sir 33:14-15), *honor and shame (Sir 10:19). Specifically, they are measured against three wisdom criteria: piety, glory and reputation (Sir 44:1-15). For example, Solomon (Sir 47:12-21), a wise king par excellence according to the popular standard, is not wise according to Ben Sira's measure. Ben Sira questions Solomon's piety by exposing his motive and priority in his building activities (Sir 47:13), points out that Solomon ceased to be wise in his old age (Sir 47:14a), and indicts Solomon for subjecting himself to women (Sir 47:19). As a result, Solomon failed to be a wise king.

4. Sirach and the New Testament.

Although Sirach is not explicitly cited in the NT, A. Sundberg (54-55) has compiled at least forty-one references of Sirach in the NT, with the majority found in the Gospels and the Epistle of James. In the Gospels many of Jesus' teachings parallel Ben Sira's. For example, with reference to prayer, both of them warn against unnecessary repetition in prayer (Mt 6:7; Sir 7:14) and insist on perseverance in prayer (Lk 18:1; Sir 7:10). They agree that forgiveness of others is the prerequisite of God's forgiveness (Mt 6:12; Sir 28:2). But Jesus went beyond Ben Sira and stressed the need to pray even for one's enemies (Mt 5:44)—an example that he himself set for his followers (Lk 23:34; cf. Sir 50:25-26). In the area of almsgiving, Jesus and Ben Sira emphasize generosity (Mt 5:42; Sir 4:4-5), for it is a sign of God's children and reflects God's generous love (Mt 5:45; Sir 4:10). Ben Sira, however, limits his generosity to the godly person and to one's friend (Sir 12:4-7; 14:13). For Jesus, one's generosity should be extended to all, without any bias, and it must be done in secret (Mt 5:42; 6:23). The most prominent parallel between Jesus and Ben Sira is their wisdom invitation (Mt 11:28-30; Sir 51:23-27; cf. Sir 6:24-28; 24:19). Both invitations entreat listeners to take up their yoke and are given in the context of wisdom learning. Whereas Ben Sira's invitation is extended to the youth, Jesus' invitation is directed to all the weary. Moreover, in Sirach, it is Wisdom who utters the invitation, but in Matthew, it is Jesus, wisdom personified, who offers the invitation.

Although the Epistle of James does not fit into the genre of wisdom literature, James's teachings are sapiential and have several contacts with Sirach. They have the same basic understanding of wisdom, which is from God (Jas 1:5; Sir 1:1) and allows one to face testing and trials (Jas 1:2-4; Sir 2:1-6). They speak of two kinds of wisdom, a true one and a false one (Jas 3:15-17; Sir 19:20-30). For Ben Sira, the difference between the two lies in the fear of God and in the keeping of his commandments. James, on the other hand, is more specific in showing the difference. For him, true wisdom is manifested in one's character, humility and good deeds, while false wisdom belongs to the devil and is reflected in one's bitter envy and selfish ambition.

James and Ben Sira deal extensively with speech and the tongue. The evil of the tongue is portrayed in pictorial language, and the readers are encouraged to properly handle it (Jas 3:1-12; Sir 28:12-26)—for example, to be slow to speak but quick to hear (Jas 1:19; Sir 5:11-12). Interestingly, with reference to sickness, both authors believe that prayer is vital. Prayer not only brings physical recovery but also deliverance from sin (Jas 5:14-16; Sir 38:9-15). Whereas Ben Sira advises the ill to seek the help of physicians as well as to offer sacrifices, James advises the assistance of church elders. For him, the sick person is to be anointed with oil, but for Ben Sira, it is the offering, rather than the sick person, that is anointed with oil.

These similarities do not necessarily mean that NT authors are dependent on Sirach, but they are a reflection of a shared worldview in a similar milieu. Despite all the similarities, there is a radical difference between Sirach and the NT. Ben Sira has correctly highlighted the origin of wisdom and the relationship between wisdom and the law, but the NT authors have come to a deeper understanding of wisdom. For them, traditional wisdom has a trajectory. Wisdom finds its fulfillment in Jesus, and the cross has become the ultimate expression of God's wisdom for human kind (1 Cor 1:18-31).

See also WISDOM OF SOLOMON.

BIBLIOGRAPHY. **W. Baumgartner,** "Die literarischen Gattungen in der Weisheit des Jesus Sirach," *ZAW* 34 (1914) 161-98; **R. Beckwith,** *The Old Testament Canon of the New Testament Church* (Grand Rapids: Eerdmans, 1985); **P. C. Beentjes,** *The Book of Ben Sira in Hebrew: A Text Edition of All Extant Hebrew Manuscripts and a Synopsis of All Parallel Hebrew Ben Sira Texts* (VTSup 68; Leiden: E. J. Brill, 1997); **J. Blenkinsopp,** *Sage, Priest, Prophet: Religious and Intellectual Leadership in Ancient Israel* (LAI; Louisville, Westminster John Knox, 1995a); idem, *Wisdom and Law in the Old Testament: The Ordering of Life in Israel and Early Judaism* (rev. ed.; Oxford: Oxford University Press, 1995b); **G. H. Box and W. O. E. Oesterley,** "The Book of Sirach," in *The Apocrypha and Pseudepigrapha of the Old Testament in English,* ed. R. H. Charles (2 vols.; Oxford: Clarendon Press, 1913) 1.268-517; **C. V. Camp,** "Understanding a Patriarchy: Women in Second Century Jerusalem through the Eyes of Ben Sira," in *"Women Like This": New Perspectives on Jewish Women in the Greco-Roman World,* ed. A.-J. Levine (SBLEJL 1; Atlanta: Scholars Press, 1991) 1-39; **D. A. Carson,** "The Apocrypha/Deuterocanonicals: An Evangelical View," in *The Parallel Apocrypha,* ed. J. R. Kohlenberger III (New York: Oxford University Press, 1997) xliv-xlvii; **R. J. Coggins,** *Sirach* (GAP; Sheffield: Sheffield Academic Press, 1998); **J. J. Collins,** *Jewish Wisdom in the Hellenistic Age* (OTL; Louisville: Westminster John Knox, 1997); **A. E. Cowley and A. Neubauer,** eds., *The Original Hebrew of a Portion of Ecclesiasticus, XXXIX.15 to XLIX.11, Together with the Early Versions and an English Translation, Followed by the Quotations from Ben Sira in Rabbinical Literature* (Oxford: Clarendon Press, 1897); **P. Enns,** *Exodus Retold: Ancient Exegesis of the Departure from Egypt in Wis 10:15-21 and 19:1-9* (HSM 57; Atlanta: Scholars Press, 1997); **C. T. R. Hayward,** "Rewritten Bible," in *A Dictionary of Biblical Interpretation,* ed. R. J. Coggins and J. L. Houlden (London: SCM, 1990) 595-98; **M. Hengel,** *Judaism and Hellenism: Studies in Their Encounter in Palestine during the Early Hellenistic Period* (2 vols.; Philadelphia: Fortress, 1974); idem, *Jews, Greeks and Barbarians: Aspects of the Hellenization of Judaism in the Pre-Christian Period* (Philadelphia: Fortress, 1980); **C. Kearns,** "Ecclesiasticus, or the Wisdom of Jesus the Son of Sirach," in *A New Catholic Commentary on Holy Scripture,* ed. R. C. Fuller et al. (London; Nelson, 1969) 541-62; **J. L. Kugel,** *Traditions of the Bible: A Guide to the Bible as It Was at the Start of the Common Era* (Cambridge, MA: Harvard University Press, 1998); **T. R. Lee,** *Studies in the Form of Sirach 44-50* (SBLDS 75; Atlanta: Scholar Press, 1986); **B. L. Mack,** *Wisdom and the Hebrew Epic: Ben Sira's Hymn in Praise of the Father* (Chicago: University of Chicago Press, 1985); **J. T. Maertens,** *L'Éloge des pères: Ecclésiastique XLIV-L* (Bruges: Abbaye de Saint-André, 1956); **J. Marböck,** *Weisheit im Wandel: Untersuchungen zur Weisheitstheologie bei Ben Sira* (BZAW 272; Berlin: de Gruyter, 1999); **T. Middendorp,** *Die Stellung Jesu ben Siras zwischen Judentum und Hellenismus* (Leiden: E. J. Brill, 1973); **R. E. Murphy,** *The Tree of Life: An Exploration of Biblical Wisdom Literature* (3rd ed.; Grand Rapids: Eerdmans, 2002); **N. Peters,** *Das Buch Jesus Sirach oder Ecclesiasticus* (EHAT 25; Münster: Aschendorff, 1913); **S. C. Reif,** "The Discovery of the Cambridge Ben Sira MSS," in *The Book of Ben Sira in Modern Research: Proceedings of the First International Ben Sira Conference, 28-31 July 1996, Soesterberg, Netherlands,* ed. P. C. Beentjes (BZAW 255; Berlin: de Gruyter, 1997) 1-22; **J. T. Sanders,** *Ben Sira and Demotic Wisdom* (SBLMS 28; Chico, CA: Scholars Press,

1983); **S. Schechter,** "A Fragment of the Original Text of Ecclesiasticus," *Expositor* 4 (1896) 1-15; **G. T. Sheppard,** *Wisdom as a Hermeneutical Construct: A Study in the Sapientializing of the Old Testament* (BZAW 151. Berlin: de Gruyter, 1980); **P. W. Skehan and A. Di Lella,** *The Wisdom of Ben Sira* (AB 39; Garden City, NY: Doubleday, 1987); **R. Smend,** *Die Weisheit des Jesus Sirach* (Berlin: Reimer, 1906); **H. Stadelmann,** *Ben Sira als Schriftgelehrter: Eine Untersuchung zum vormakkabäischen Sofer unter Berücksichtigung seines Verhältnisses zu Priester-, Propheten- und Weisheitslehrertum* (WUNT 2/6; Tübingen: Mohr Siebeck, 1980); **A. C. Sundberg,** *The Old Testament of the Early Church* (HTS 20; repr., New York: Kraus, 1969); **W. C. Trenchard,** *Ben Sira's View of Women: A Literary Analysis* (BJS 38; Chico, CA: Scholars Press, 1982); **J. C. VanderKam,** "Revealed Literature in the Second Temple Period," in *From Revelation to Canon: Studies in the Hebrew Bible and Second Temple Literature* (JSJSup 62; Leiden: E. J. Brill, 2000) 1-30; **G. von Rad,** *Wisdom in Israel* (London: SCM, 1970); **M. M. Winter,** "The Origin of Ben Sira in Syriac," *VT* 27 (1977) 237-53, 494-507; **B. G. Wright,** "Why a Prologue? Ben Sira's Grandson and His Greek Translation," in *Emanuel: Studies in Hebrew Bible, Septuagint, and Dead Sea Scrolls,* ed. S. M. Paul et al. (VTSup 94; Leiden: E. J. Brill, 2003) 633-44; **J. Ziegler,** ed., *Sapientia Iesu Filii Sirach* (Septuaginta: Vetus Testamentum graecum 12/2; (Göttingen: Vendenhoeck & Ruprecht, 1965).

M. Phua

SOCIAL-SCIENTIFIC APPROACHES

The body of literature in the OT that has been identified as wisdom, poetry and writings is an interesting collection because in many ways these books stand outside the historical framework that exists in much of the Pentateuch, the chronicle of nation-building in Joshua—2 Kings, and the prophetic corpus. Instead, the emphasis here is on the basic values of Israelite society and on the ways in which individuals and groups learn to cope with their world in good times and bad. Of course, Israelite society is exemplified in *law, royal annals and prophetic speech, but often it is deeply embedded in what is referred to as *emic* (= insider) perspective, and little explanation is provided for the benefit of the audience. The text in fact contains presuppositions about social situations that were quite understandable to the original audience but have now lost some of their meaning for modern readers. However, in a piece of wisdom literature or a short story like that of *Ruth, a basic assumption about their society's understanding of both human and divine actions represented by the principles of reciprocity or social identity can be examined in greater detail and thus may provide a more thoughtful approach to biblical interpretation. In other words, these works do not simply affirm a particular value or position; they also provide intellectual data that can in turn be analyzed in the light of life experience or a sequence of events that test the measure of the ancient society's views on patience and perseverance, as well as group identity and self-identity.

One particularly helpful method of biblical criticism that addresses the fabric of society evidenced in these books of wisdom and poetry is the social-scientific approach. It outlines a set of established social protocols and identifies theories and methods with which to analyze the basic social values and understandings in ancient Israel (Elliott, 50; Jonker, 3-5). In this way, it becomes a somewhat easier task to recognize how the social world of ancient Israel operated. Of course, no one social-science model can be touted as the most reliable or most useful for the reconstruction of the ancient world. Although some scholars may favor a particular method or theory, most choose to take a more eclectic approach, applying a variety of social theories to what is revealed by the ancient textual material and the exposed archaeological data (see Esler and Hagedorn). Most also recognize that building a social model of an ancient culture based on information drawn from the study of modern cultures has its dangers (Sneed). Presuppositions or the desire to make the data fit the chosen model simply discredit the process (Herion; Carter, 23-28). However, a careful application of these models can be useful in tying data together. By taking a more objective stance on the relative value of these models, the researcher and the reader can engage in continuous self-evaluation and a restructuring of the interpretative approach as needed. To demonstrate this, this article examines several basic social settings, situations and mechanisms that draw on examples from the biblical text.

1. Honor and Shame
2. Kinship and Identity
3. Reciprocity
4. Spatiality

1. Honor and Shame.

The concepts of *honor and shame are two sides to the same cultural coin, and they function within a Mediterranean culture like that of ancient Israel as incentives for "correct" behavior as defined by their community and as disincentives to "incorrect" behavior. Striving to be honorable or to acquire honor is status-building for both the individual and the household. Shame attaches to every member of a household if any member engages in speech or action that threatens their honorable state or endangers the existence of the household. In this way, wisdom serves as a guide to behavior in ancient Israelite society, and it is used to determine what is considered to be "right thought," "right speech" and "right action." Beyond actual behavior patterns, what also occurs is the labeling of individuals as either honorable or shameful as an indication of how the village reacts to a particular household in their community (Goode, 60-61). Thus what can be termed as life-giving behavior was labeled "wise" or "cool-headed" (= honorable) in wisdom tradition, and clearly destructive or antisocial behavior was identified as "foolish" or "hot-headed" (= shameful). Wisdom therefore is an expression of both the common sense and the moral tone of a society. Aphorisms, laws and the official chronicle of events in a king's reign all reflect the basic attitudes about correct behavior and speech. In this regard, it is possible to take note of the string of evildoers found in *Proverbs: "sinners" (Prov 1:10-19) whose greed leads them to rapacious acts, ambushing the innocent, but losing their lives in the end; and the "loose woman" whose adulteries entice fools to their death (Prov 2:16-19; 5:3-6; 7:6-27; 9:13-18). A similar contrast is found in admonitions praising hard work as the key to success and prosperity (Eccles 5:12). The wise are called on to take note of the industriousness of the ant (Prov 6:6-11), and they are cautioned that a "child who sleeps in harvest brings shame" (Prov 10:4-5). In fact, the lazy are "like vinegar to the teeth and smoke to the eyes" to their employers (Prov 10:26).

1.1. Honorable and Dishonorable Behavior. Ultimately, honor was the true measure of a household's ability to care for its members and to provide assistance to the weak in society (widows, orphans, strangers) who for whatever reason could not care for all of their own needs.

Thus, *Job models honorable behavior in caring for strangers, not allowing them to "spend the night in the street" (Job 31:32). It could be said that Job is imitating God, who guarantees under the covenant to "watch over the alien and sustain the fatherless" (Ps 146:9). A household was labeled as dysfunctional or without honor when it refused to meet these social obligations (Ps 94:6) or worked actively to "bring down the poor" (Ps 37:12, 14). The disrepute that they obtained from their antisocial behavior endangered the entire community and justified the curtailment or restriction of their license to make a living in the village, to buy, sell, trade, marry, arrange marriages, serve in assemblies and send warriors to the tribe (Matthews and Benjamin 1993, 143). An exemplar of this is found in the "x + 1" sequence detailed in Proverbs 6:16-19, where we are told that the Lord hates "haughty eyes, a lying tongue, and hands that shed innocent blood, a heart that devises wicked plans, feet that hurry to run to evil, a lying witness who testifies falsely, and one who sows discord in the family" (compare similar sentiments in Ps 18:27; 27:12; 120:2; Prov 1:6).

1.2. Dispute Resolution. To deal with potential and actual disputes within society and to maintain a measure of social stability, certain controls (laws as well as customs) are established to set standards of acceptable/honorable behavior. This explains the continual reaffirmation of trust in and obedience to the law as a measure of honorable behavior and wisdom that becomes a hallmark of the biblical *sage and psalmist (Esther 1:13; Ps 1:2; 19:7-10; Prov 28:7; 29:18). One method that assists with the interpretation of the social character of legal pronouncements is the sociology of law, which is capable of tracing (1) the evolution of social controls and the causes behind their development; (2) forms of legal reasoning and discourse; (3) "the degree of freedom and coercion existing in the form of law" coupled with the connection between economics and politics (Milovanovic, 3-4). Of course, not all social controls can be defined as law. Customary behavior, adherence to rules, or social norms may or may not be dependent upon physical coercion by a deputized group or be based on a written set of laws (Hoebel). This seems clear when we note the role of village elders who worked toward consensus to make a judgment or settlement on the legal disputes involving the legal status of

Ruth and *Naomi and the disposition of Elimelech's property near Bethlehem (Ruth 4:1-12). There is also a cohesion attached to actively shaming individuals who may have engaged in incorrect behavior or who have harmed the community by their actions. Psalm 129 details the blessings that will be obtained by those who "fear the LORD" and "walk in his ways" (Ps 129:1-5) and calls on God to "put to shame" those who hate *Zion. In cursing Israel's enemies, the psalmist expresses a national identity and political resolve and uses shaming as a weapon to increase Israel's honor at the expense of "out-groups" that have caused great harm (Boda, 1407-11).

2. Kinship and Identity.

Every person has a network of associations based on blood relations, commercial ties, political alliances or membership within a particular village, community or tribe (Coote, 40-47). All of these can be defined in kinship terms, although the strongest are blood ties. There may be some confusion in reading ancient literature because social labels such as father, son, mother, daughter and sister (see Song 5:1) may refer to blood kinship, marital relationship, political status or economic alliances. For instance, in the Egyptian teachings of Ptah-hotep (c. 2500 BC) the protégé or apprentice is referred to as "son." Similarly, in Proverbs the relationship of father and child or of son to father and mother can be construed either as a blood tie or as a broader association based on common interests (Prov 4:1-5; 23:22-25).

2.1. Social Dislocation. Because no culture lives entirely in a social vacuum, kinship ties become even more complicated when they are expanded to include temporary or long-term relationships with neighboring peoples in the form of economic or political agreements. When that occurs, family-based values and relationships inherent to both cultures come to the fore in the social mixing, requiring that each maintain its singular identity amidst a larger society comprised of crisscrossing social differences (Bahloul, 27). Persons deprived of these relationships due to a natural disaster or war or as a result of immigration become liminal, persons who do not belong to the society in which they find themselves (see the depiction of the ruined Jerusalem as a displaced widow in Lam 1:1-7). Sometimes they attempt to associate themselves with other persons who are in a similar social condition, or they simply accept the label of resident alien *(gēr)* that marks them as outsiders (Judg 19:16). Those who do not choose to accept this type of dislocation may seek a form of social repositioning. For instance, Ruth attempts to redefine herself in Naomi's eyes from Moabite widow into the widow of an Israelite (Ruth 1:16-18), someone who wishes to transfer her identity to that of an Israelite culture and community (see Matthews 2006). Once Naomi accepts Ruth's resolution, the narrative then hinges on the uncertainty of the reaction by her audience in Bethlehem and is not resolved until she marries Boaz (Ruth 4:11-12).

2.2. Social Obligation. Each social tie is also associated with recognized social obligations that govern behavior. For instance, Job's concern for his children extends to making sacrifices in their name in order to insure that their obligations are met (Job 1:5). In the complex realm of kinship ties, encompassing both blood and socially constructed relationships, those that are termed righteous are recognized as persons "who deal generously and lend, who conduct their affairs with justice," and their name "will be remembered forever" (Ps 112:5-9). It is therefore understood that "those who are greedy for unjust gain make trouble for their households" (Prov 15:27), and in so doing they damage the ability of the household to establish honorable ties with other households.

3. Reciprocity.

In all of its forms, reciprocity functions as a balancing principle insuring that every act has a social and/or legal consequence (Stansell, 69). As a result, gift-giving (both kin-based and not kin-based), hospitality, social welfare systems and patron-client associations operate according to a recognized protocol within ancient Israelite culture. The questions asked by social scientists focus on the "why" or the logic of the gift, incorporating an economic analysis as well as an examination of social rank and status of the exchange involved (Sahlins, 185-210; Bourdieu). Of course, imbalances can occur if one party chooses to abuse the practice or disregards standards of behavior (i.e., commits a crime or abuses a weaker individual [note Abraham's hard dealings with Ephron in Gen 23]). Forms of generalized reciprocity include charity, gifts given to kin or one's circle of friends, and in no instance requires or expects immediate return or service in exchange. Charity is a form of gift-giving, but it does not carry with it an expectation of return and instead serves as a form of honorable, moral behavior (note Boaz's gift of additional grain to Ruth when she is gleaning in Ruth 2:15-16). In the third century *Sirach goes so far as to state that a person should "show a cheerful face" when giving a gift because the Lord "will repay you sevenfold" (Sir 35:11-13 [cf. Prov 11:25]).

3.1. Symmetrical Exchange. One of the most common forms of reciprocity is a balanced or symmetrical exchange of gifts with little or no delay in the process of exchange (Cook, 81-82). This usually serves as part of the process of building social or political relationships or as a commercial transaction (see the injunctions on fair practices in Prov 20:10-23). The assumption here is that an unbalanced exchange can create measurable tensions and is therefore to be avoided (see the admonitions to maintain honest balances and scales in Prov 11:11; 16:11; Ezek 45:10). In a fair exchange, an enterprising individual like the "capable wife" of Proverbs 31:10-31 can engage in a cottage industry such as the production of linen garments and sashes that she can sell to merchants, thereby strengthening the financial standing of her household and adding honor to its members through her diligence (Prov 31:24-27). The value of honest exchange benefiting both parties is also chronicled in Sirach's list of items that bring no shame, which includes making a profit "from dealing with merchants" (Sir 42:1-5).

3.2. Asymmetrical Exchange. When an imbalanced exchange does occur, this may be the result of asymmetrical reciprocity in which the participants are of unequal social status. Their dealings, like those in symmetrical reciprocity, generally include an exchange of goods and services with the intent of benefiting both parties (patron and client), but they maintain a clear sense that the weaker party is expected to make payment in terms of "homage and loyalty or political support or information" (Stegemann and Stegemann, 36 [see Prov 19:22; 20:6]). There are also situations in which an imbalanced exchange occurs that represents an aggressive tactic to gain favor (Prov 19:6). It also may be designed to shame someone by giving a gift that cannot be financially or socially balanced and thus is used to intimidate or bribe (Ps 26:10) an

opponent (Matthews 1999). With this in mind, the wise are cautioned against becoming a borrower and thus a slave to the lender (Prov 22:7; see also *Ahiqar*, Saying 41.ix:127 in Matthews and Benjamin 2006, 307). Sirach points out the charitable aspects of providing a loan to a neighbor in need but also is clear that repayment may lead to "empty promises" and curses (Sir 29:1-7).

4. Spatiality.

Spatiality examines "lived space" (those places in which human occupations and activities occur) as a means of determining group identity and social boundaries (McNutt, 37). For it is "by acting in space in a particular way [that] the actor is inserted into a particular relation with [his/her society's] ideology" (Cresswell, 17). However, physical space is continuously redefined by human presence and individual interpretation of the ideology of place (Matthews 2003, 12). In dealing with this phenomenon, cultural geographers use the term "landscape" when referring to "the relation between the natural environment and human society" (Rose, 86). In order to decipher the spatial understanding of the ancient Israelites as they viewed or lived in particular places, we can identify the physical places where the Israelites work, worship, transact business, practice and execute legal decisions. These mundane social practices take on different meanings, purposes or intentions depending on where in space and time that they occur and who is performing the action in question. Thus the content or substance of the act (farming, speech, ritual, transaction) derives meaning from the rank, authority or status of the person involved and from the physical and symbolic "space" (including time, place, occasion, setting) involved. It should also be noted, however, that the meanings that can be derived from place often "have more to do with everyday living and doing than with thinking" (Buttimer, 171).

4.1. Rural Social Space. One graphic example of how recurrent patterns of behavior lead to an expansion in the understanding of spatial usage is found in the agricultural practices of ancient Israel. Farmers brought their harvested stalks of grain to a centrally located communal threshing floor (Deut 16:13; Job 5:26). They processed the grain there using a threshing sled to separate the stalks or chaff from the grain (2 Sam 24:22;

Job 41:30). This was followed, when the wind was just right (Sir 5:9), by a winnowing and sieving process that eventually resulted in piles of grain arranged around the facility (Ruth 3:2-3). At that point, the threshing floor took on an enhanced social character. Instead of being just a communal place of work, processing grain, it became a place associated with the future plans of the community, embodied in the distribution of their harvest (Borowski, 59-62). And, because of its complex social character, it provides the perfect setting for the negotiation between Ruth and Boaz over her identity and presence in the Bethlehem community (Ruth 3).

4.2. Urban Social Space. Within ancient cities and towns zones of influence, both economic and political, were established based on proximity to market space, entry gates and physical and social elevation within the boundaries (city walls) of the community as a whole (Soja, 65-66). The ability to fill or use particular "social space," therefore, is based on communal expectations that are attached to that "place" (Cresswell, 21-27). This is sometimes based on law (Lev 12:1-4) and sometimes is enforced by tradition or common understanding. For example, there is no law that says that the elders must spend their time sitting in the gate waiting to see if a legal case would be brought before them. Instead, it is clear that they often chose to sit in the gate because it was a place to transact business, share gossip, and demonstrate their status as men of property and influence (note Lot in Gen 19:1, and the "well-served" husband who is "known in the city gates" in Prov 31:23). On a more formal basis, the demonstration of bravery by *Esther in placing herself "in the inner court" of the palace in a spot where the king, "sitting on his royal throne . . . opposite the entrance to the palace" would see her plays on the concentric zones of priority attached to private spaces (Esther 5:1). These are magnified in palaces and temples, where restrictions on entrance magnify as a person passes through these zones to the heart of power.

This article does not, of course, contain a full list of social-scientific concepts and the methods used to analyze them, but it does suggest some avenues for research into the world of ancient Israel. They demonstrate that the examination of social values, customs and "lived experiences" as exemplified in the biblical text are indeed avenues worth exploring.

See also HERMENEUTICS; HONOR AND SHAME; KINSMAN-0REDEEMER AND LEVIRATE; MARRIAGE AND SEX; WOMEN.

BIBLIOGRAPHY. **J. Bahloul,** *The Architecture of Memory: A Jewish-Muslim Household in Colonial Algeria, 1937-1962,* trans. C. du Peloux Ménagé (CSSCA 99; Cambridge: Cambridge University Press, 1996); **P. J. Boda,** "A Social-Scientific Reading of Psalm 129," *HvTSt* 58 (2002) 1401-14; **O. Borowski,** *Agriculture in Iron Age Israel* (Winona Lake, IN: Eisenbrauns, 1987); **P. Bourdieu,** "Marginalia—Some Additional Notes on the Gift," in *The Logic of the Gift: Toward an Ethic of Generosity,* ed. A. D. Schrift (New York: Routledge, 1997) 231-41; **A. Buttimer,** "Home, Research, and the Sense of Place," in *The Human Experience of Place and Space,* ed. A. Buttimer and D. Seamon (London: Croom Helm, 1980) 166-96; **C. E. Carter,** "A Discipline in Transition: The Contributions of the Social Sciences to the Study of the Hebrew Bible," in *Community, Identity, and Ideology: Social Science Approaches to the Hebrew Bible,* ed. C. E. Carter and C. L. Meyers (Winona Lake, IN: Eisenbrauns, 1996) 3-36; **Z. A. Cook,** "Reciprocity—Covenantal Exchange as a Test Case," in *Ancient Israel: The Old Testament in Its Social Context,* ed. P. F. Esler (Minneapolis: Fortress, 2006) 78-91; **R. B. Coote,** "Tribalism: Social Organization in the Biblical Israels," in *Ancient Israel: The Old Testament in Its Social Context,* ed. P. F. Esler (Minneapolis: Fortress, 2006) 35-49; **T. Cresswell,** *In Place, Out of Place: Geography, Ideology, and Transgression* (Minneapolis: University of Minnesota Press, 1996); **J. H. Elliott,** *What Is Social-Scientific Criticism?* (Minneapolis: Fortress, 1993); **P. F. Esler and A. C. Hagedorn,** "Social-Scientific Analysis of the Old Testament: A Brief History and Overview," in *Ancient Israel: The Old Testament in Its Social Context,* ed. P. F. Esler (Minneapolis: Fortress, 2006) 15-32; **E. Goode,** *Deviant Behavior* (3rd ed.; Englewood Cliffs, NJ: Prentice-Hall, 1990); **G. A. Herion,** "The Impact of Modern and Social Scientific Assumptions on the Reconstruction of Israelite History," *JSOT* 34 (1986) 3-33; **A. A. Hoebel,** *The Law of Primitive Man: A Study in Comparative Legal Dynamics* (New York: Atheneum, 1974); **L. Jonker,** "The Influence of Social Transformation on the Interpretation of the Bible: A Methodological Reflection," *Scriptura* 72 (2000) 1-15; **P. M. McNutt,** "'Fathers of the Empty Spaces' and 'Strangers Forever': Social Marginality and the Construction of Space," in *Imagining Biblical Worlds: Studies in Spatial, So-*

cial, and Historical Constructs in Honor of James W. Flanagan, ed. D. M. Gunn and P. M. McNutt (JSOTSup 359; Sheffield: Sheffield Academic Press, 2002) 30-50; **V. H. Matthews**, "The Unwanted Gift: Implications of Obligatory Gift Giving in Ancient Israel," *Semeia* 87 (1999) 91-104; idem, "Physical Space, Imagined Space, and 'Lived Space' in Ancient Israel," *BTB* 33 (2003) 12-20; idem, "The Determination of Social Identity in the Story of Ruth," *BTB* 36 (2006) 49-54; **V. H. Matthews and D. C. Benjamin**, *Social World of Ancient Israel, 1250-587 BCE* (Peabody, MA: Hendrickson, 1993); idem, *Old Testament Parallels: Laws and Stories from the Ancient Near East* (3rd ed.; Mahwah, NJ: Paulist, 2006); **D. A. Milovanovic**, *A Primer in the Sociology of Law* (2nd ed.; New York: Harrow & Heston, 1994); **G. Rose**, *Feminism and Geography: The Limits of Geographical Knowledge* (Minneapolis: University of Minnesota Press, 1993); **M. Sahlins**, *Stone Age Economics* (Chicago: Aldine-Atherton, 1972); **M. Sneed**, "Wisdom and Class: A Review and Critique," *JAAR* 62 (1994) 651-72; **E. W. Soja**, *Postmodern Geographies: The Reassertion of Space in Critical Social Theory* (Chicago: University of Chicago Press, 1987); **G. Stansell**, "The Gift in Ancient Israel," *Semeia* 87 (1999) 65-90; **E. W. Stegemann and W. Stegemann**, *The Jesus Movement: A Social History of Its First Century* (Minneapolis: Fortress, 1999). V. H. Matthews

SOCIOLOGICAL INTERPRETATION. *See* HERMENEUTICS; SOCIAL-SCIENTIFIC APPROACHES.

SOLOMON

In the OT and in later traditions Solomon is understood to have been the personal exemplar of wisdom within the framework of Israel's covenant with the Lord. Solomon is to wisdom much as Moses is to Torah, and *David to the psalms (Moberly).

1. Solomon's Wisdom
2. Solomon's Folly
3. Conclusion

1. Solomon's Wisdom.

Solomon is established as the exemplar of wisdom in 1 Kings 1—11; 1 Chronicles 28— 2 Chronicles 9. Within OT Wisdom literature his name is connected with *Psalms (Pss 72; 127), *Proverbs, *Ecclesiastes and *Song of Songs. Jesus is said to have identified Solomon as an exemplar of wisdom (Mt 12:42; Lk 11:31). Apart from these texts, most references to Solomon in both Testaments speak either of his wealth (1 Kings 14:26; Mt 6:29; Lk 12:27) or his oversight of the construction of the temple (2 Kings 21:7; 24:13; 25:16; 1 Chron 6:10, 32; 18:8; 22:5-7, 17-19; 23:1; 2 Chron 12:9; 33:7; 35:3; Ezra 2:58; Neh 7:60; Acts 7:47). In spite of his introduction of pagan shrines and worship (2 Kings 23:13; Neh 13:26), his reign is depicted as something of a golden age in Israel's history (1 Chron 22:9; 2 Chron 11:17; 30:26; 35:4; Neh 12:45). During the Second Temple period and beyond, works and stories associating Solomon with wisdom multiplied (Duling).

According to 1 Kings, Solomon's wisdom covered, specifically, the domains of politics (1 Kings 1:52-53; 2:6, 9), building (1 Kings 3:1-3; 5—7; 9:10; 10:14-22), dreams and visions (1 Kings 3:5-15; 6:11-13; 9:1-9; 11:9, 11-13), judicial decisions (1 Kings 3:16-28; 5:7, 12), academic and scientific research and literary composition (1 Kings 4:29-34), as well as the ability to solve the most difficult questions. It was his wisdom that attracted the attention of the Queen of Sheba (1 Kings 10:1-22) and others (1 Kings 10:24). Significantly, the final summary of Solomon's life in 1 Kings 11:41-43 makes no mention of his wealth or temple building but rather mentions only his wisdom.

Chronicles, while framing the account of Solomon within an *inclusio that refers to his wisdom, omits what is not relevant to the temple and cult (Dillard; Selman 1994a; 1994b).

1.1. Solomon in the Wisdom Literature. When we turn to the works within the OT wisdom literature that are linked to Solomon's name, we are immediately confronted with some significant changes in focus. Here the wisdom of Solomon is predominantly set in the context of family life—a picture that not only departs significantly from the domains mentioned in Kings and Chronicles but also raises questions, given the picture presented of Solomon's domestic life (1 Kings 3:1; 11:3-8; Neh 13:26). Indeed, his son Rehoboam could be seen as the epitome of the fool of the book of Proverbs, being the son who rejected wisdom (1 Kings 12).

References to Solomon in Psalms 72:1; 127:1; Proverbs 1:1; 10:1; 25:1; Song of Songs 1:1 are most easily understood as ascriptions of authorship. According to 1 Kings 4:32, Solomon wrote 1,005 songs (LXX: five thousand) and "coined" three thousand proverbs. Similarly, 2 Samuel

23:1 links *David with the writing of songs (*see* Music, Song). Occasionally, titles of this type are used within Psalms in contexts that give additional specific information concerning the circumstances under which the song was composed (e.g., Pss 3; 18; 51 [see also 2 Sam 22:1]). We also have instances of this form used outside the book of Psalms where authorship is clearly ascribed (Hab 3). Critical questions concerning the veracity of such ascriptions turn on matters of historicity, proposed sources, editorial activity and so forth rather than on the nature of the conventional meaning of the idiom (*see* Psalms 4: Titles).

1.2. A Solomonic "Golden Age." G. von Rad spoke of Solomon's reign as a high point in Israelite culture as well as commerce. Less helpful was his attempt to draw a parallel between the Solomonic era and the European "Enlightenment." Solomon did import into Jerusalem the cults and ideas of the Gentiles, but this did not represent a step into a rationalistic, secular worldview or the product of a naturalistic conception of "wisdom" (Alt; Whybray; Fox). The wisdom associated with Solomon in the OT is consistently one rooted in the *fear and knowledge of the Lord (Prov 1:7), accessed by divine revelation (Prov 2:6; cf. 30:1-6), and maintained by the discipline of the Lord (Prov 3:11-12). It is therefore not merely secular, or the rational product of "the power of the human mind" (*contra* Fox). It is made manifest in a righteous lifestyle that is faithful to the Lord (Provan; Waltke) in a corrupt and dangerous world.

R. Whybray (133) points out, "No Israelite king other than David (2 Sam 14:20) and Solomon is specifically credited with wisdom in the Old Testament," nor is any group identified as "the wise" to be found at the court of any Israelite king (noting the lack of the Hebrew definite article in Prov 22:17; 24:23).

Apart from Moses and David, the only named authors of psalms included in the collection are men who, like Solomon, were appointed to office by David (*Asaph, the sons of Korah, Jeduthun). Thus the wisdom of this "golden age" is closely tied to the temple and cult, in keeping with the selective presentation of Solomon's regime in 1—2 Chronicles.

This correlation can further be seen in the references that connect Solomon to the book of Ecclesiastes (Eccles 1:1, 12-17; 2:12; 12:9-10) and other references in Song of Songs (Song 1:5; 3:9,

11; 8:11-12). The nature of Solomon's connection with these works, however, is difficult to determine.

1.3. Psalms.

1.3.1. Psalm 72. This psalm title most naturally would be taken to attribute authorship to Solomon, but the location of Psalm 72 immediately before the closing statement to Book 2 of the collection implies that this psalm was understood to be one of "the prayers of David the son of Jesse" (Ps 72:20). Most scholars therefore understand it to be a prayer of David *"for* Solomon" as Solomon was about to assume the throne. Certain elements in the psalm reflect the concerns of the historical narratives of Solomon's reign. Although there is no mention of wisdom in either of the psalms bearing his name, there is concern for his ability to make just decisions and specifically to rescue the children of the poor (Ps 72:1-4 [cf. 1 Kings 3:9, 6-28)], for *righteousness and peace to be maintained, and for his rule to extend beyond the bounds of God's covenant promise to Abraham (cf. 1 Kings 4:21, 24). The kingdom of Sheba is mentioned twice, firstly to call for the king of Sheba to present gifts and bow down to him (Ps 72:10-11) and then specifically for the gold of Sheba to be given to him (Ps 72:15). The language of the psalm recalls the covenants with both Abraham and David (Ps 72:17 [cf. Gen 12:3; 2 Sam 7:9, 13, 16]).

1.3.2. Psalm 127. Psalm 127, in contrast to Psalm 72, is clearly attributed to Solomon and links the building of the temple (Ps 127:1-2) with the building of a family (Ps 127:3-5). These two things being placed in parallel under the ascription to Solomon serves to tie together the two dominant aspects of his place: first, as head of the dynasty that was the house God promised to build for David (2 Sam 7:11), second, as the one who would build the house for the Lord's name (2 Sam 7:13) in Jerusalem. These two themes are then intricately woven together throughout the writings of the NT both with respect to the person and work of Jesus and in the foundation and growth of the new-covenant church as both bride and temple.

1.4. Proverbs. The heading to the book of Proverbs clearly was intended to ascribe the entire work to Solomon, if not as the originator of every saying, at least as the one who gathered them together. Further notices throughout the book (Prov 10:1; 25:1; 24:23; 30:1; 31:1) indicate that the work is a collection. Part of this collection was "copied" (not "collected" [NLT]) by "the men of Hezekiah" (Prov 25:1). It is widely recognized that much of this teaching in similar content and form can be found in the extant literature of the ancient Near East dating more than a millennium before Solomon's era. The extensive assertion of wisdom's origins as being with the Lord God of Israel, the creator and judge of all humankind, serves both to domesticate the wisdom of the nations to him and to give the work a polemical function. In this the work also exemplifies the principle advanced in the prologue depicting "the wise" as men who will "listen and add to their learning . . . for understanding proverbs and parables, the sayings and riddles of the wise" (Prov 1:5-6) and so complements the accounts of Solomon's throne as the place to which foreign rulers would come who seek wisdom.

Proverbs and Ecclesiastes share the setting of a father teaching wisdom to his son (Prov 1—9; 31:2; Eccles 12:12). T. Longman (2001) notes that the sequence of books in the Hebrew order of the Kethubim, locating the book of *Ruth between Proverbs and Song of Songs, appears to be an intentional linking of texts that focus on the ideal wife, this theme forming an inclusio in Proverbs. The reference to the wisdom of King *Lemuel as coming from his mother (Prov 31:1) forms its own inclusio with *Woman Wisdom (Prov 1:20).

Proverbs is concerned to equip one to deal with the realities of an unrighteous and corrupt world. It therefore seeks to ensure that the faithful are not also the naïve. Jesus' instruction to his disciples to "be as crafty as the snakes and as pure as the doves" (Mt 10:16, my translation) well summarizes the concerns of the book. Thus Solomon's apostasy would be seen, in the categories of the Proverbs, as foolishness, not just weakness or wickedness.

1.5. Song of Songs. The title of "Song of Songs" (Song 1:1) indicates that this, the "Best Song," was written by Solomon. As in the case of Proverbs 1:1, we might understand authorship here to include editorial collection of other people's work into an anthology. There is nothing in the text to support, and much that would militate against, understanding the bridegroom of these songs to be Solomon himself (see discussion in Murphy; Longman 2001). As songs, these do not purport to be historical accounts and could best be described as inspired and didactic fantasy.

The most significant difficulty with respect to Solomonic authorship comes from the picture of Solomon's marital situation as presented in the Historical Books. Certainly, given the description and evaluation of Solomon's marriages and family life as presented in 1 Kings 3:1; 11:1-8; Nehemiah 13:26, one would not expect Solomon to be the source of any sound wisdom pertaining to the kind of marital relationship that had the sanction of Israel's covenant Lord (*see* Marriage and Sex).

The erotic nature of this work has produced its own challenges for interpreters. At the most challenging point, the unpleasant reality must be faced that a man reputed to have had a thousand *women in his harem is here credited with composing a song or collection of songs depicting erotic love and making no mention of God. Any understanding of wisdom as "skill" independent of covenant faithfulness and piety is then at liberty to take what may fairly be called a cynical approach to this work (see Clines, cited in Longman 2001, 8). Such an understanding requires that the work first be considered apart from its canonical context, and then the question is raised, with greater intensity, as to how it could have found and maintained a place in that context. Thus the reader, depending on his or her underlying assumptions and values, could either take a cynical view of the work or could imagine Solomon as a man who, by the reality of his errors, both understood the ideal and was able to describe and commend its virtues to others. The reader is left to speculate and to imagine the various possibilities that may connect Solomon with such a work.

It is appropriate at this point to make the connection between this question and the inherent dilemma presented by "wisdom" literature, particularly in its common expression in the form of the *māšāl* (proverb, riddle, parable). Solomon was renowned for his ability to solve problems. It is in the nature of such literature to set forth problems but not always to solve them, except by implication. T. Polk (573) notes, with respect to the function of the *māšāl*, "Telling a parable is a matter of presenting to others an imaginatively shaped paradigm (a model of reality, a description of experience) and asking that they recognize it as somehow true. From the point of view of the parable, the readers' determination toward it, whatever their responses, identifies their place in the parable's world, and hence their relation to its truth. In our judgements toward the parable, the parable judges us." One wonders, then, whether "the Song of Songs that is Solomon's" was not intended to have such a function.

1.6. Ecclesiastes. Ecclesiastes similarly poses some interesting difficulties in its connection with the name and person of Solomon. Although Solomon is not named either as the author or as one of the characters in the narrative, the frame author does indulge in a very deliberate presentation of clues that are most easily recognized as identifying Solomon as the source of the wisdom under consideration (*see* Frame Narrative).

The main figure in the book is identified by a coded title: *"Qohelet." The word means literally "the one who calls or assembles." Longman (1998, 2) notes a possible connection with Solomon's role in assembling Israel as recorded in 1 Kings 8:1-2, 14, 22, 55. The title may be used here as something of a nickname such as critics might use of a head of state, although the NIV's translation, "teacher," seems to import meaning beyond the semantic range of the term.

He is "son of David, king in Jerusalem" (Eccles 1:1). Certainly, the subsequent descriptions make specific connections with the account of Solomon in 1 Kings (Eccles 1:12-13, 16; 2:4-16; 12:9-10). Although none of these references need refer only to Solomon, and the reference to kings (plural) "who ruled in Jerusalem before me" seems strange, the specific links to Qohelet's devotion to wisdom are sufficient to make Solomon the most obvious candidate.

Use of the title "Son of David" (Eccles 1:1) makes this identification far stronger than might first appear. Except for the references to Amnon and Absalom in 2 Samuel 13:1, this title is found elsewhere in the OT only to refer to Solomon (1 Chron 29:22; 2 Chron 1:1; 13:6; 30:26; 35:3; Prov 1:1). The title is not used of anyone past the first generation of David's sons, and of these, only Solomon was king in Jerusalem. In the context of a book that seems to be deliberately hinting at the identity of Qohelet, it is difficult to see this reference as the only exception. Any other possibility would place these hints in the domain of the insoluble, and one would then wonder at the purpose of the author in offering them.

The connection between Qohelet and Sol-

omon does not imply Solomonic authorship of the material attributed to Qohelet. Clearly, the frame author is reflecting on the life and work of Qohelet and drawing from this material his own conclusions that are then conveyed to his son (Eccles 12:9-14). In framing the work as a father-son wisdom lesson, the frame author may have been deliberately mimicking the father-son scenario of Proverbs 1—9 as a polemical device.

While affirming the value of the many proverbs and sayings, the frame author is ultimately highly critical of Qohelet/Solomon as a wisdom figure. Pointedly, he reminds his son that real wisdom is a gift of "one Shepherd," and that, unlike Qohelet, one needs to "fear God and keep his commandments" because ultimately everything, including one's wisdom, must be brought before the judgment of God.

2. Solomon's Folly.

In the light of the criticism of Solomon found in Ecclesiastes, 1 Kings and Nehemiah, we must face the question as to how the man so closely identified with wisdom could have ended his days in such *folly.

Here we are confronted with one of the very remarkable characteristics of the OT portrayal of significant figures in the history of redemption. Across a range of centuries, sources, authors and works, a consistent pattern in the OT canonical documents may be observed. Nearly all of the people who play significant parts in the accomplishment of God's redemptive and revelatory purposes—for example, Noah, Abraham, Isaac, Jacob, Judah, David, Solomon, Gideon, Samson or even a figure such as *Esther— are presented as people who are, by the standards of the OT *law, seriously, if not fatally, flawed in their life and character. There is almost a contrived inconsistency between their positive contribution to God's plans and purposes and their failures in their personal lives. Significantly, the flaws in their characters are usually or most prominently located in the domain of family life.

In this tradition, while Solomon stands out most brightly as the one who serves to bring Israel to the climax of their national history as the chosen people of God, he is also the most prominent example of personal and public unfaithfulness. The fact that this is such a consistent pattern throughout the OT must be taken into account in any attempt to interpret both the man and the texts associated with his name.

It may be helpful to draw a parallel between our understanding of Samson and Solomon in this regard. Given the accounts of his feats of physical strength, Samson is commonly depicted as a figure that one might associate with Hercules, and yet the point of the narrative is that his strength was a manifestation of the Spirit of God working in and through him. When he chose to be unfaithful with Delilah, the Spirit of God left him, and he was as weak as any other person. Given the extensive role that Solomon plays as a person of wisdom across a range of OT texts, we might be excused for treating his words in 1 Kings 3:7, "I am only a little child and do not know how to carry out my duties" (NIV), as a conventional expression of false modesty. Nevertheless, the author of the Kings narrative stresses the fact that Solomon's wisdom was a gift of God. This reality is also a theme in Proverbs and forms the conclusion of the polemic of Ecclesiastes (Eccles 12:13-14).

3. Conclusion.

The overall impression of Solomon's wisdom is that it is a gift of grace given by God to an inadequate and naturally foolish and dysfunctional man, a man raised in privilege who lived without restraints, and who ultimately failed to live up to his calling. He, along with the rest of the persons who are used as teaching models in the OT (see 1 Cor 10:6, 11), leaves the reader longing for something and someone better. The juxtaposition in OT texts of Solomon's wisdom with Torah, throne and temple was a stimulus for later and varied eschatological developments within Judaism. In such a context, the NT writers presented Jesus as that man who is "greater" than Solomon (Mt 12:42; Lk 11:31) and such other exemplars (Mt 12:41; John 4:12-14; 8:53-58; Heb 3:3), precisely because there was no such discontinuity between his nature and conduct as a man and his endowment by the Holy Spirit.

See also ECCLESIASTES 1: BOOK OF; PROVERBS 1: BOOK OF; QOHELET; SONG OF SONGS 1: BOOK OF; WISDOM OF SOLOMON.

BIBLIOGRAPHY. **A. Alt,** "Die Weisheit Salomos," *TLZ* 76 (1951) 139-44; ET, "Solomonic Wisdom," in *Studies in Ancient Israelite Wisdom,* ed. J. L. Crenshaw (New York: KTAV, 1976) 102-12; **R. B. Dillard,** *2 Chronicles* (WBC 15; Waco, TX: Word, 1987); **D. C. Duling,** "Solomon, Exorcism, and the Son of David," *HTR* 68 (1975) 235-52; **M. V. Fox,** *Proverbs 1-9* (AB 18A; New York: Doubleday, 2000); **A. Lemaire,** "Wisdom in Solomonic Historiography," in *Wisdom in Ancient Israel: Essays in Honour of J. A. Emerton,* ed. J. Day, R. P. Gordon and H. G. M. Williamson (Cambridge: Cambridge University Press, 1995) 106-18; **T. Longman III,** *The Book of Ecclesiastes* (NICOT; Grand Rapids: Eerdmans, 1998); idem, *Song of Songs* (NICOT; Grand Rapids: Eerdmans, 2001); **R. W. L. Moberly,** "Solomon and Job: Divine Wisdom in Human Life," in *Where Shall Wisdom Be Found? Wisdom in the Bible, the Church and the Contemporary World,* ed. S. C. Barton (Edinburgh: T & T Clark, 1999) 3-17; **R. E. Murphy,** *The Song of Songs* (Hermeneia; Minneapolis: Fortress, 1990); **K. I. Parker,** "Solomon as Philosopher King? The Nexus of Law and Wisdom in 1 Kings 1-11" *JSOT* 53 (1992) 75-91; **T. Polk,** "Paradigms, Parables, and Meshalim: On Reading the Mashal in Scripture," *CBQ* 45 (1983) 564-83; **I. W. Provan,** "On 'Seeing' the Trees While Missing the Forest: The Wisdom of Characters and Readers in 2 Samuel and 1 Kings," in *In Search of True Wisdom: Essays in Old Testament Interpretation in Honor of Ronald E. Clements,* ed. E. Ball (JSOTSup 300; Sheffield: Sheffield Academic Press, 1999) 153-73; **M. J. Selman,** *1 Chronicles* (TOTC; Downers Grove, IL: InterVarsity Press, 1994a); idem, *2 Chronicles* (TOTC; Downers Grove, IL: InterVarsity Press, 1994b); **G. von Rad,** "The Beginnings of Historical Writing in Ancient Israel," in *The Problem of the Hexateuch, and Other Essays* (Edinburgh: Oliver & Boyd, 1966 [1944]) 166-204; **B. K. Waltke,** *The Book of Proverbs* (2 vols.; NICOT; Grand Rapids: Eerdmans, 2004); **R. N. Whybray,** "The Sage in the Israelite Court," in *The Sage in Israel and the Ancient Near East,* ed. J. G. Gammie and L. G. Perdue (Winona Lake, IN: Eisenbrauns, 1990) 133-39; **G. H. Wilson,** "The Use of Royal Psalms at the 'Seams' of the Hebrew Psalter," *JSOT* 35 (1986) 85-94. D. R. Jackson

SONG. *See* MUSIC, SONG.

SONG OF SONGS 1: BOOK OF

Song of Songs is one of a number of wisdom (or sapiential) books of the OT. It is meant to be read along with *Proverbs, *Job and *Ecclesiastes. Each of these three books explores God's wisdom in various ways, as does Song of Song. Song of Songs presents to the reader the highs and lows of the experience of love—everything from lovesickness and warnings to the revelry of marital bliss. Read canonically, this love points away from itself to its Creator, who is intimately at issue in matters sexual (for a canonical reading, see 4 below).

1. Introduction
2. Authorship and Date
3. History of Interpretation
4. Why the Song of Songs Is in the Bible
5. Outline

1. Introduction.

1.1. Interpretative Issues. S. Freehof suggests that the whole book is a dream. M. Sadgrove reads it as a wisdom book, finding in it an exploration of the mystery of love comparable to *Job exploring the mystery of suffering, and *Ecclesiastes the mystery of existence. P. Trible uses the garden of Eden as the key to understanding Song of Songs—a celebration of humanity created male and female. But a new reader to Song of Songs immediately experiences an onslaught of images that blur and reel from one to the next without an obvious organizing principle. It leaves one's head spinning. One wonders if there is any order to it all, or if a story is being told with identifiable scenes, characters, plot or story line. To the novice reader, the book is a confusing riddle.

In addition, the imagery is enigmatic. Why is the girl's nose compared to a tall tower (Song 7:4)? Is this meant to be funny? Much of the material in the book is blatantly sexual and erotic, as, for example, "Your stature is like that of the palm, and your breasts like clusters of fruit. I said, 'I will climb the palm tree; I will take hold of its fruit.' May your breasts be like the clusters of the vine, the fragrance of your breath like apples" (Song 7:7-8 NIV).

Here the reader is treated in poetic form to the thoughts and intentions of the boy who is sexually interested in the girl. He desires to "climb" her and "lay hold of" her breasts. Why is material of this sort in the Bible? And if it is intended to arouse interest in sexual matters, why are many of the images (such as the girl's nose compared with a tower) seemingly so uncomplimentary? To many, Song of Songs remains hopelessly inaccessible.

1.2. Where Is God? In addition to the questions already raised, the reader may also expect the text to reveal something about the character and mighty works of God. After all, the Bible is a religious book, treating sacred matters of faith. But Song of Songs seems uninterested in God, his covenant with Israel or any of the usual critical issues in the OT. This book of the Bible seemingly defies Paul's assertion that "all Scripture is profitable for reproof, correction and training in righteousness" (2 Tim 3:16-17). Instead, it treats human sexuality and passion, but without noting children or clearly requiring *marriage as a prerequisite. And the girl's father is not even mentioned.

This absence of what one naturally expects from a biblical book creates tension for the reader. Since Song of Songs is included in the *canon, it "lives" in a context seemingly at odds with its own unique message and viewpoint. This tension (a heavenly book that celebrates quite earthly material) forces the reader to look for meaning beyond the obvious. In a word, this calls for interpretation.

1.3. The Need for Interpretation. Christians often approach the Bible expecting every part to be about salvation and Christ, as NT books assert (Mt 5:17; Lk 24:27; 2 Cor 1:20). But Song of Songs seems completely uninterested in salvation. How, then, can it point to the Savior? Is it an allegory of the covenanted love relationship between God and Israel? It does not read like such an allegory. For example, the girl is usually more aggressive in her pursuit than the boy, running out into the streets to seek him. Does this imply that the girl represents the Lord, and the boy represents Israel? Although this conclusion may seem bizarre, it is the kind of unavoidable confusion entailed when Song of Songs is read allegorically. After all, modern-day churches sing the hymn "Rose of Sharon" about Jesus, whereas in Song of Songs the flower celebrates the girl. If the boy allegorically represents God, then who is his mother (Song 8:5)? Does Song of Songs 5:10-16 really describe the *Messiah, or even God, from head to foot (Loewe)? If not, then where will the reader find God in Song of Songs; why is this book in the Bible (on this issue, see 4 below)?

After examining issues of authorship and date for Song of Songs, we will take a brief overview of the history of interpretation—how Jewish and Christian interpreters have sought to resolve these tensions and bring clarity to its many images and poems. This is followed by a discussion of the theological implications of the modern-day scholarly consensus of answers, such as it is.

2. Authorship and Date.

The dating of Song of Songs is complex because the book has some features that appear late and others that seem early or Solomonic. Scholars have argued for completion dates ranging from the time of *Solomon to the third century BC.

2.1. Solomon. The title associates Song of Songs with the name of Solomon and literally reads, "The Song of Songs which is to Solomon." But in the book the institution of the harem is critiqued. This calls into question Solomon's reputation and casts him in a bad light. For example, Song of Songs 6:8-10 unfavorably compares the bloated harem with the singular charms of one unique young woman. Hers is an undiminished glory, celestial in proportions, outshining his many wives and concubines. Another example is near the close of the book, where the harem is a "vineyard" that has become a bureaucratic business, again unenviable to those enjoying a single woman (Song 8:11-12). Solomon is not an active character anywhere in the book but rather a foil against which the true characters (the boy and girl) interact and pursue love. Thus Solomon may not have personally penned any of the actual poems of Song of Songs. Surely he did not create the book to undermine his own interests and reputation.

On the other hand, love lyrics that predate Solomon and have very similar features to Song of Songs have been discovered in various locales, most notably Egypt (Fox). Song of Songs in some ways seems cut from the same cloth as these. Thus it is patent that Solomon could have produced much of the book, and that songs like Song of Songs (in many ways) did in fact exist in his time. In addition to the Egyptian materials, there are Mesopotamian, Tamil and Canaanite texts that bear some affinity with Song of Songs and reach as far back as the Bronze Age (Pope; Meek 1922-1923; Rabin). A Solomonic date is generally consistent with ancient Near Eastern evidence.

2.2. Evidence from Hebrew. It is precarious to try to date a biblical book from its particular brand of Hebrew and select vocabulary (*see* Hebrew Language). An example of this is seen in how Song of Song's use of the prefix *še*- to denote the relative pronoun has been used to ar-

gue both for a late date (Harman; Pope) and for an early date (Rabin). It is possible that what might be mistaken for a "datable" characteristic is actually an idiosyncratic dialect, the byproduct of a place, not a time. However, there are some words that do in fact suggest a late date. For example, in Song of Songs 4:13 the Persian word *pardes* ("paradise") is found, which suggests a date from the Persian period. Yet there are few of these, and no Greek loan words.

2.3. Conclusion. As usual with biblical books, Song of Songs exhibits some features that appear to be early and others that appear to be late. We must keep in mind that even if one adopts the traditional view that Solomon authored all or part of the book, it was the property of literate *scribes who copied and transmitted it from generation to generation. Very late was the stage when their task was merely to make commentary and reproduce as accurately as possible the "original." Before then, they enjoyed freedom to be creative in reworking and formatting their texts. These copyists lived through very different times, faced various spiritual struggles over the years, were immersed in cultures of great diversity, and even spoke in different languages. Although the essential core of Song of Songs originally was intended to answer a spiritual need at some point in time (perhaps the time of Solomon), as the centuries passed, these needs changed, and perhaps so did Song of Songs to some extent, until it finally solidified into the form known today in the MT.

3. History of Interpretation.

It has been common in the history of interpretation to imagine that Song of Songs is about the covenanted love between God and Israel (*see* Song of Songs 3: History of Interpretation). After all, the prophets conceptualized this covenant as a marriage. Hosea was told to marry Gomer, and the dysfunctional couple became a picture of what it was like for the Lord to love his wayward people (Hos 1—3). In the light of these other texts, it is easy to follow an argument that allegorically reads Song of Songs as speaking of God and his people.

Yet if Song of Songs were found in any other forum than the biblical canon, it would be universally recognized as a collection of love poems that revel in a man and woman's physical passion and lovemaking. Many such lyrics have been discovered that date from about the time of Solomon, and no one reads them as allegories of anything. They are simply love songs, akin to romantic music that one might hear in modern culture today.

Thus a tension exists between what Song of Songs is and how it functions in a religious book. We now turn to various ways of resolving this tension in the history of interpretation (on why the book is in the Bible at all, see 4 below).

3.1. Earliest Hints. The Old Greek translation of Song of Songs presents a more or less uninterpreted and untampered rendering. Some difficult words, such as the place name "Amana" (*'amānâ*) in Song of Songs 4:8, are rendered in terms that reveal spiritual values—in this case, "faith." But the almost complete absence of this sort of interpretation is evidence that the translators did not read the text in general as a repository of these same spiritual virtues. In other words, "faith" is unabashedly found in the text where the Hebrew word seems to warrant it, yet this kind of warrant occurs quite infrequently. The great bulk of the text is woodenly glossed without being transformed into a series of allegorical or metaphorical expressions of theology. Thus, Song of Songs seems to have been understood in its literal sense by the Old Greek translators in the centuries following the close of the Hebrew canon.

The Talmud records an ancient tradition (perhaps c. AD 100) that depicts Rabbi Aqiba distressed and angry because the Jews of his day were singing Song of Songs for entertainment while wining and dining (*b. Sanh.* 101a). Of course, in these cases the revelers would be singing not about the relationship between God and Israel but rather of much earthier subject matter. The tension felt by Aqiba and later Christians between Song of Song's sexual content and its placement in the Bible was not an issue for these revelers. The talmudic notation also demonstrates that early medieval rabbis already were interpreting the book as being about something other than human sexuality.

Of course, if Song of Songs had been discovered written on a pottery shard in an excavated mound by an archeologist, it would have been immediately and universally recognized as an erotic love song treating sexuality between human paramours. This observation alone goes a long way toward establishing the genre of the book and thus how to read it. A number of ancient love songs of just this sort have been dis-

covered, dating to about the time of Solomon. One must conclude that Song of Songs as originally understood was regarded as a celebration of love and sex, and the propensity to read it as an allegory of spiritual things was a late innovation in its history. The tension between its sexual content and religious setting simply was not felt in earliest times. The book was not about God and Israel, or about Christ and the church; rather, it was about any man and woman in love, without God being explicitly in view. It is this fact that prompted the later rereadings of the book.

3.2. Allegory: Read in Context of Scripture.

3.2.1. Why Allegory? Long before the conversion of pagans throughout the ancient world to Christianity, many of them had already learned to read their own scriptures (e.g., the *Iliad* and the *Odyssey*) in an allegorical sense. Much in the Greek poets was deemed unworthy of high philosophical ideals and demeaning to true religion. The poets wrote of humans causing injury to gods in earthly battles, of the cannibalistic Cyclopes (beloved son of blue-maned Poseidon), of crooked-minded Kronos emasculating his father, of Ares (bane of all humankind, crusted with blood, breacher of walls), and so on. These stories were embarrassing in the face of philosophical ideals and religious scruples. Thus, a technique of reinterpreting the old stories as allegories with a higher meaning was developed to help alleviate the cognitive dissonance that such unworthy descriptions of the gods produced.

The Christians of antiquity inherited the philosophical technique of interpreting difficult passages as pointing away from themselves to a profound and virtuous meaning. One example of this is seen in the ancient Christian interpreter Origen. When he approached any text, he looked for misrepresentations of reality, unbelievable events, distortions or mistakes, heresy, immorality, contradictions, absurdities and statements about biblical figures that he felt should apply only to Christ. He understood these and other observations to be unerring clues from God that the text was not meant to be taken at face value, but rather that a "spiritual" reading was intended. Thus, problems in the Bible would in fact be considered mistakes or errors if left to be understood merely in the literal sense. But the tension between the Bible being God's word and what the text actually says was resolved through allegorizing it, thereby bringing it into line with the rest of Scripture. This method also characterized Jewish interpretation.

3.2.2. The Context of Scripture. Any part of the Bible was read in the context of the whole, and the whole counsel of God in Scripture was the context in which any one part was read. For example, Song of Songs does not explicitly speak of God, the worshiping soul, salvation, the history of Israel or any religious matters. This is a problem because the Bible as a whole is a holy book. Within this book various observations may be made. First, Hosea and other prophets used the metaphor of marriage to describe the relationship between God and Israel; in fact, at times in Hosea this metaphor is explored in a quite earthy fashion. Second, the one other love song in the Bible (Ps 45) is cited in Hebrews 1:8 and read there as speaking of Christ. This naturally would lead a reader with a penchant for allegory to Song of Songs. Third, the Old Greek version of Song of Songs often translated the Hebrew term for sexual love as *agapē*. This word had a sexual use in the Old Greek, but not so in the NT. When Amnon raped his sister Tamar, the word used for his feelings of "love" for her is *agapē* in the Old Greek (2 Sam 13:1). But in the NT *agapē* is almost a technical word that denotes a selfless, sacrificial love. It is not hard to imagine that when a reader with the eyes of an allegorist encountered *agapē* in Song of Songs, nonsexual meanings suggested themselves. This is how allegorists handle every text of the Bible, not only the Song of Songs.

The allegorical approach more or less typified how Song of Songs was handled throughout the patristic and medieval eras (c. AD 500-1500), and this continued through the Reformation and post-Reformation periods. Some who read it in a literal fashion questioned why it was part of the Bible at all. After all, removing it from the Bible is one way of resolving the tension. O. Keel (7) argues along these lines to conclude that Song of Songs must have "achieved canonical status in its 'profane' sense."

"Tell me, O thou whom my soul loveth, where thou feedest, where thou makest thy flock to rest at noon" (Song 1:7 KJV). As a typical Puritan allegorist, H. Aisworth (c. 1612) sees here the church's request to Christ for instruction in the administration of his kingdom on earth; "As he formerly made her partaker of his heavenly calling, so he would direct her further in to the place where, and manner how, he feedeth his flock." Two centuries later, J. Gill (83) preserved this interpretation of Song of Songs 2:7: "The Church says not to stir up my love, which is applicable to Christ, the charge that this love should not be stirred up but with pleasure agrees with Christ, who is endued with sovereignty, and ought to be at his own liberty to stay with or remove from his people when he pleases." In modern times the allegorical method persists (e.g., Daniélou; Leahy; Tournay; Fountain).

"Historical allegories" read Song of Songs as if it were about the love between God and Israel (or Christ and the church); "philosophical/mystical allegories" read the book as being "about the communion between God and the individual soul" (Longman, 26). For example, note what some interpreters have done with Song of Songs 1:6: "Do not stare at me because I am dark, because I am darkened by the sun. My mother's sons were angry with me and made me take care of the vineyards; my own vineyard I have neglected" (NIV).

B. Kamel notes that the girl thinks of herself as "very dark" due to her sin, but God sees only beauty. "The beauty of human nature captivates the heart of God, it is all black in its nature and character but God has washed it in baptism, thus the beauty in us is God's work, 'We will make for you ornaments of gold studded with silver' " (Kamel, 14). Contrast this with the comment on the same verse by J. Sizoo (150), who calls her cry "I tended other's vineyards, but not my own!" a "devastating criticism of those who in seeking to minister to others neglect to keep alive in their own souls the fires of faith." Sizoo also notes that Song of Songs features a garden, and the girl calls the north and south winds to blow upon it (Song 4:16). The southern wind is spring, and this makes the garden flourish; the northern is winter, representing loneliness and disillusionment. Sizoo then references philosophers and poets who have benefited by hardship. The elements in Song of Songs thus interpreted represent not God's relationship with his people, but ideals, principles to live by, philosophical concepts.

All of these allegorical approaches generally can be found echoed in ancient Christian and Jewish apologists (Longman, 26-30). Both communities of faith needed to explain the presence of Song of Songs in their holy book. They did not invent allegory; they simply used it as an interpretative technique perfectly acceptable in their day. And until recently allegory was the traditional method of treating Song of Songs.

3.2.3. The Ultimate Failure of Allegory. "Allegory involves so much interpretative ambition that it can create the impression that the real source of meaning is in the reader's imagination and not in the text itself" (O'Keefe and Reno, 90), being revelatory of the interpreter's genius rather than the Scripture. With allegory, the text becomes whatever the interpreter wants it to become, and no two allegorists agree on an interpretation (note the readings of Song 1:6 in 3.2.2). Allegory does not elucidate the text's meaning but rather obscures it. Origen argued thus: one of the midwives whom Pharaoh commanded to kill the Hebrew infants was named Puah; "Puah" means "modest" or "blushing"; blushing is the color red; red is the shed blood of Christ. Allegorization was one technique that Christian interpreters used to make the text point to Christ (Fairbairn). But each step leads further and further from the text itself, the end result having virtually no connection with it. M. Silva (74) likens allegory with arbitrariness: "The most powerful argument against the allegorical method is that it seems to allow for no controls. In effect, anyone can see any meaning he or she wishes to see in any passage."

The Protestant Reformers, trying to test church traditions against Scripture, were suspicious of impromptu interpretations such as this and abandoned allegorical interpretation for most texts. Without controls, it is impossible to determine the relative worth of variant interpretations. Illuminating the text thus necessitates staying as close as possible to what it actually says and not launching off into flights of theological fancy. Song of Songs was perhaps the last bastion of allegorical reading, until the discovery of ancient love lyrics put to rest any remaining doubts as to its subject matter.

But to reject allegory is to reject a long-standing technique that tried to resolve tension between Song of Song's literal sense and the Bible's religious character. If not allegory, then what? How else might the book be read so that it produces a meaning consonant with the expectations of a reader of Scripture? What, then, does Song of Songs have to say to a community of faith?

3.3. Seeking to Identify Song of Song's Genre.

Various alternative ways of reading Song of Songs were employed in the nineteenth and twentieth centuries. Here we briefly recount some of them.

3.3.1. Drama. One nonallegoral way of regarding Song of Songs is to read it as an ancient sample of performance art, a drama meant for the stage. Hypotheses were advanced to discover a plot, identify the characters, reverse-engineer scenes and acts and chorus lines, and so on. The context for this reading was not the Bible (which has no other plays) but rather a generic context of the love story.

F. Delitzsch popularized the two-character romance, having discerned six acts, each with two scenes. The two characters were the man and woman. Here is a literalistic reading of Song of Songs (Delitzsch was not looking for a higher, spiritual meaning) that put on display certain moral virtues, such as single-minded devotion to one's lover. The book becomes, then, a sort of parable whereby the overall virtue can be deftly transferred into the sphere of the religious, without every detail being pressed into artificial service as in allegory.

The dramatic approach spawned many permutations. Delitzsch argued against other dramatists such as G. H. A. von Ewald, who envisioned a three-character drama. Von Ewald found five acts, and the overall storyline treats the lecherous King Solomon attempting to woo the simple but beautiful shepherdess away from her true love. S. R. Driver later popularized the three-character approach, finding a serious exploration of the moral issues of fidelity in the face of great temptation there, which again easily dovetails as a metaphor for the Israelite's call to be faithful to God in the face of idols. I. Provan (246) reads Song of Songs as a "stirring tale of fidelity to first love in the face of power, coercion, and all the temptations of the royal court."

Although the dramatic approach has some more recent proponents (e.g., Seerveld; Glickman; Dillow; Provan), it is doomed to be unpersuasive. This is so because the dramatic approach depends upon the correct identification of the storyline for its meaning. As with allegory, no two dramatists agree on the cues for the performance. Every scholar has a different set of scenes, acts, and so on. They cannot even agree on the number of characters or on what the overall plot is. The various theories cancel each other out. In addition, it is doubtful that a story such as a romantic novel or morality play existed in antiquity.

3.3.2. Syrian Weddings. In addition to reading Song of Songs in the generic context as a drama, Delitzsch suggested a traditional wedding ceremony as an alternative provenance. Parts of the book are similar to practices today in Arabic villages that might preserve ancient forms. The placement of Song of Songs in this context was influential in the early part of the twentieth century, but modern-day scholarship has moved away from this stance because of ancient Near Eastern cognate materials deemed more relevant. A number of ancient poetical forms have been identified as possible original settings for Song of Songs. Three will be presented here (3.3.3-5 below).

3.3.3. Tamil Love Poetry. C. Rabin suggests that Song of Songs reflects the high point of Israelite trade with South Arabia and South India and is cut from the same cloth as Tamil (Akam) poetry. The atmosphere of expensive spices and perfumes finds its provenance not among shepherds but rather among merchants who travel between the source of these and Jerusalem. Nard, myrrh and cinnamon are Indian products. This incense created the "pillars of smoke" seen on the caravan from afar (Song 3:6). This trade did not necessarily flourish only in Solomon's era but perhaps also in the days of Hezekiah or Josiah (Brenner 1983).

Although there are many parallels between Song of Songs and Tamil love poetry, there are also many differences. For example, the dialogues in Song of Songs between the boy and girl are lacking in the comparable literature. Song of Songs does not follow many of the poetic conventions of the Tamil poetry. In the Tamil poems the girl is not described in detail in linear fashion, a form important in Song of Songs (the *"wasf"). Perhaps most importantly, the Tamil poems clearly and expressly have marriage in view as the culmination of love, while for the most part Song of Songs avoids making this explicit (Mariaselvam). Comparing Song of Songs with Egyptian and Tamil poetry, H. Fisch (85) notes, "But when all the parallels have been noted, the Song really stands out as unique. It touches heights and depths that are unknown in love poetry of the ancient Middle East, indeed the love poetry of any time."

The comparison with Tamil poetry has not generated nearly as much interest as two other generic contexts: the ancient fertility cult and Egyptian love lyrics, to which we now turn.

3.3.4. Ancient Fertility Cult. Like other nations, ancient Israel worshiped many gods and participated in the cultic rites of the Canaanites and the Babylonians. For example, the prophets condemned the observance of the *marzēah* feast (Jer 16:5; Amos 6:7). This was a feast of drunkenness meant to affirm life over death (Wittenberg). Although this feast was condemned by the prophets, M. Pope read Song of Songs in light of it and other cultic acts. The key verse is Song of Songs 8:6, which sets love over against death. According to this theory, Song of Songs is what remains (having been purged and rewritten by Yahwist scribes in later years) of an originally religious text, part of a liturgy used in pagan worship. He cites as examples the wine house where the feast was held (Song 2:4), the spices used for burial (Song 5:1), the black maiden who originally was the moon goddess (Song 1:5), and the recounting of Ishtar's search through the underworld for her lover (Song 5:5-7). Pope concludes that Song of Songs once was a religious text that celebrated divine love between god and goddess. Of course, having a religious provenance would help to explain its inclusion with other religious texts—the Bible. Thus, the present context of Song of Songs as religious literature is actually offered as evidence that it was once used as part of a fertility ritual.

The major difficulty with this is that the extant Song of Songs does not treat divine love at all but rather treats love that is quite earthly. The liturgical theory postulates that the sacred elements have been edited out. In the words of T. Meek (95), "The transforming influence of later Yahwism has almost completely obliterated the elements of the dying and rising god, the sacred marriage, and the place of the king in the rites."

The tension between the present Song of Songs and its place in sacred Scripture is quite similar to the tension between Song of Songs and its placement among ancient religious texts: it just does not seem to fit. One final generic context has been proposed that has the advantage of not being in tension with the Song: ancient Egyptian love lyrics.

3.3.5. Egyptian Love Lyrics. Lyrics dating from one hundred to three hundred years before

Solomon are the most similar literature discovered so far to the present Song of Songs. They treat love between humans, not gods. They are more or less secular. In addition, they are small and do not add up to an overall narrative. They are not meant to be performed on stage. Song of Songs seems cut from the same cloth as these, without having to hypothesize a past where Song of Songs was more religious in character. For example, compare M. Fox's translation of selected lyrics with Song of Songs (RSV) in Table 1.

As can be readily observed in these examples, the Egyptian material seems consonant with Song of Songs. In fact, it is more so than any of the other contexts thus far explored by modern scholarship. Thus there is extant material that bears remarkable likeness to Song of Songs, that is secular, and that even can be dated to the Solomonic era, from which a number of conclusions can be drawn regarding the nature of the biblical Song of Songs. In light of this, a consensus regarding Song of Songs has emerged, although it is not universally held.

3.3.6. Consensus. The most recent and best commentaries approach Song of Songs as an anthology of individual love lyrics that do not comprise an overall storyline with plot and so forth, but that instead explore one or another aspect of love as in the Egyptian model (e.g., Fox; Murphy; Exum; Longman; Schwab 1997; 2002; Forthcoming; Keel). Thus Song of Songs is like the book of *Psalms, wherein each individual psalm stands on its own, and the psalms do not form an ongoing narrative beyond very general observations. "There is no 'story' or plot to speak of, but a series of encounters (or encounters sought) expressed through the sighs and wishes of lyrical language. And threaded throughout, there is vibrant, perplexing imagery" (Black, 303).

Song of Songs is about human, not divine, love. Thus, its placement in Scripture is not due to any explicitly cultic setting. It seems as though the way in which the book is regarded by most today has returned to the perspective of the audience in the Second Temple period. In addition, the appropriate method of interpretation is a literalistic one that highlights the book's explicit subject matter—passionate sex—not one that allegorizes this topic away. Each scene explores human love and passion, which are timeless and dynamic human realities. But this leaves unresolved the tension of why such material was ever included in the Bible. This question we explore next.

4. Why Song of Songs Is in the Bible.
"It was its allegorical interpretation that indubitably made possible its canonization as part of Holy Scripture" (Waterman, 1). Alternatively, a cultic past is suggested by both Pope and Meek. But Song of Songs has more affinity with secular love songs than with religious texts, and the allegorical approach *followed* its inclusion in Scripture, as a way of resolving the tension brought about by the presence of an erotic work in a holy book. So the question remains: Why is it there?

The secular character of Song of Songs suggests that it was not used as a religious text per se, but its perspective does suggest a particular

Table 1. Comparison with Egyptian Love Lyrics.

Egyptian Lyrics	Song of Songs
I am yours like the field planted with flowers and with all sorts of fragrant plants.	My beloved is to me a cluster of henna blossoms in the vineyards . . . I am a rose of Sharon, a lily of the valleys.
To hear your voice is pomegranate wine (to me): I draw life from hearing it.	Your cheeks are like halves of a pomegranate behind your veil.
Come spend the day in pleasure, (one) morning, then another—two days, sitting in (my) shade.	With great delight I sat in his shadow, and his fruit was sweet to my taste.
Her friend is at her right as she gets him intoxicated and does whatever he says.	O that his left hand were under my head, and that his right hand embraced me!
The beer hut is disarrayed from drink.	He brought me to the banqueting house, and his banner over me was love.
But she has remained with her brother.	How sweet is your love, my sister, my bride! How much better is your love than wine.

cultural and religious setting. God is not the explicit subject of the book, but religious matters are at issue in its treatment of sexuality, to which we now turn.

4.1. History of Israel. As noted by liturgical theorists, ancient Israel was a religious plurality (see 3.3.4 above). This was true under Solomon as well, who built temples to many gods for his wives. In the Hebrew Bible there were predominantly two philosophies of life at issue, two principal ways of thinking that were contending for the hearts and minds of the people. One contestant was Yahweh, the God of Abraham, Isaac and Jacob, who delivered his people from Egypt and gave righteous laws through Moses; the other was represented by Baal, the fertility god, who was worshiped through ritual prostitution and sex. The fertility cult offered to Israel a radically different understanding of human sexuality. As C. J. Whitesell (93-94) observes, they believed that "sexual intercourse releases divine power into the world to refresh the reproductive forces of nature, to renew the power of the king, and to stimulate fertility in domestic animals and in women. Even sex occurring privately and spontaneously between individuals recalls this primary religious archetype; as a result, where the goddess reigns, the personal aspect of sexual interplay does not fully emerge." In order to break the hold of Baalism on the people, a very different interpretation of sexuality had to be asserted and taught and embraced.

Israel's unique tradition was of one God, the Creator of heaven and earth, who made his people to serve and honor him. This faith necessitated a very different view of sex: it has no magical properties; it is part of the creation rather than being divine and transcendent; it is for private enjoyment rather than public exhibition. Song of Songs portrays this monotheistic view of sex, which stands over against the alternative view of Baal worship. According to J. Snaith (5), "The Song is unashamedly sexual, and . . . is also quite free of any specific references to the fertility cults of Israel's neighbors. Since no cultic-mythological significance is apparent, we should acknowledge the Song's free and open attitude to human sexuality as opposed to the sexual religious practices of Canaanite fertility religion. Perhaps the Song was included in the canon because it was a non-mythological, non-cultic, non-idolatrous, outright, open celebration of God-given sexual love." The contest between Yahweh and Baal included a contest between two different viewpoints about sexuality. It is to this that Song of Songs eloquently speaks.

4.2. Monotheistic Interpretation of Sex. Song of Songs seems to be a sampling of a Yahwistic understanding of human sexuality, seen against the backdrop of the polytheistic fertility cult. It presents a viewpoint that may have helped to wrest Israel away from its infatuation with Baal.

One's view of sex has in it a theology, a view of God. Sex is intrinsically religious and points to this. For example, Genesis begins with God alone speaking, until Eve is brought to Adam. Then Adam blurts out his joy at the sight of her, "Bone of my bones, flesh of my flesh," because "The two shall become one flesh." God is being worshiped in Adam's rejoicing over his wife, because sex is inherently religious. In the Bible there are three things in which a person can be utterly lost. One is negative: alcohol. The person who drinks too much loses control and behaves foolishly. But alcohol is used as a metaphor for two positive ways to lose oneself. First, being "drunk in the Spirit" and losing oneself in worship and devotion to God; second, to lose oneself with one's beloved. Note Proverbs 5:19, "Let her [your wife] . . . satiate you always," and Song of Songs 5:1, "Eat, O friends, and drink; drink your fill, O lovers." Passion between lovers also images God's passion for his people and his people's for him. In the NT Paul uses this viewpoint to describe how Christ loves his church (Eph 5:24-33).

This monotheistic vision of sexuality—it is a part of creation meant for private enjoyment, governed by God's laws, which images his love for his people—has won the day. Since the perspective offered in Song of Songs has so decisively triumphed and become formative for the Judeo-Christian civilization, students of the Bible today read it and wonder why it is there at all. Song of Songs seems simply to be stating the trivially obvious. But when it is remembered that this vision has not always been accepted, and that ancient Israel flirted with a very different understanding of sex, then Song of Songs, with its tacit polemic against Baal, makes perfect sense. Sex and God go together—tamper with one's view of either, and the other is also affected. The liturgists and allegorists are right in that Song of Songs speaks to religious matters, but those matters concern human sexuality as understood by Yahwist traditionalists over against the fertility cult.

5. Outline.

5.1. Overview. The traditional chapter divisions do not help one to read Songs of Song with understanding. As we noted earlier, a novice reader experiences an onslaught of images that blur and reel from one to the next without an obvious organizing principle, a confusing riddle (see 1.1 above). Various ways of parsing up the book into manageable and meaningful portions have been proposed in order to help bring some order to the chaos. Note the nine columns in Table 2. The first is the standard chapter divisions of Song of Songs. The second is Schwab's divisions into fourteen units, followed by Goulder's different division into fourteen units. This is followed by the fourth and fifth (Delitzsch; von Ewald), two-character and three-character dramatist divisions. The latter tried to divide up the book into acts and scenes, but no such attempt was ultimately successful.

Other approaches to parsing the Song of Songs are represented in the next columns. The sixth is that of M. Falk, who found thirty-one different units. Dividing a book into chapters or units is done so that order may be brought to what would otherwise be an undifferentiated mass of verses. When a small book such as Song of Songs is broken up into thirty-one tiny units (although some units are longer), the goal of finding a meaningful order is lost. In other words, Falk has more or less brought the book full circle to having no divisions at all. Of all the books of the Bible, Song of Songs is perhaps the most fluid and least amenable to organizational analysis. Like love itself, the structure that one discovers is the structure one brings to it. But in the human mind there is a need for chapter-level divisions. If Song of Songs were merely verses strung together, there would be no sense of order or control. A meaningful structure should actually help the reader to read the book.

The ninth column is a summation of these various approaches. Dashed lines are subdivisions of major sections. The division points that almost all have in common are shown. This clearly reveals the artificiality of those who impose a chiastic structure on the text, for only the supposed *chiasms fail to show a division where all other approaches have one. The points of agreement between the others are the strongly typed poems (the "dream" poems in Song 3:1; 5:2, Solomon's procession in Song 3:6; the break at Song 6:4) and the three adjurations of Song of Songs 2:7; 3:5; 8:4. The drama theorists sometimes also fail to recognize an otherwise universally acknowledged break.

5.2. Identifying the Outline. Various clues are suggested by the text of Song of Songs to help us decide how to parse it into manageable portions. A sampling of these is given here.

5.2.1. Inclusio. The phenomenon of *inclusio occurs where the opening line of a poem is repeated in the closing line, thus forming an identifiable boundary. For example, Song of Songs 2:8-9 begins a scene with "The voice of my beloved! Behold, he comes, leaping upon the mountains, bounding over the hills. My beloved is like a gazelle, or a young stag" and ends in Song of Songs 2:17 with "Until the day breathes and the shadows flee, turn, my beloved, be like a gazelle, or a young stag upon rugged mountains" (RSV). The opening and closing lines relate to one another and contain the material between them as a unit. Thus, ideally the reader may expect the material of Song of Songs 2:8-17 to be a literary unit of text, a single poem, that treats an identifiable subject. In the case of Song of Songs the subject always has something to do with love.

Another poem begins in Song of Songs 6:4 with "You are beautiful as Tirzah, my love, comely as Jerusalem, terrible as an army with banners" and ends in Song of Songs 6:10 with "Who is this that looks forth like the dawn, fair as the moon, bright as the sun, terrible as an army with banners?" (RSV). It is contingent on translators whether or not such possible inclusios are made visible to the reader. Unfortunately, this is not always done, as in the NIV. Compare the two verses below.

Song of Songs 6:4	Song of Songs 6:10
You are beautiful, my darling, as Tirzah,	Who is this that appears like the dawn,
lovely as Jerusalem,	fair as the moon, bright as the sun,
majestic as troops with banners.	majestic as the stars in procession?

In Hebrew the last line is identical, but can be read various ways. The NIV supplies two dif-

Table 2. Comparison of Proposed Divisions of Song of Songs

Standard chapters	Schwab	Goulder	Delitzsch	Ewald	Falk	Webster	Dorsey	Summaryy
1	1	1		Act 1	1			
					2			
					3			
					4	A1	A	
					5			
	2	2			6			
					7			
					8			
2				Act 2	9		B	
	3	3			10	A2		
					11			
					12			
3	4	4			13		C	
	5	5		Act 3	14	xxxx		
4	6	6			15	B1	D	
					16			
	7	7			17	B2		
					18			
5	8	8			19	C		
	9	9						
6	10			Act 4	20	B'1	C'	
		10			21			
	11				22	B'2		
		11			23			
7		12			24			
	12				25		B'	
	13	13			26	A'1		
					27			
8				Act 5	28		A'	
					29			
	14	14			30	A'2		
					31			

ferent ways, thus completely obscuring the possible inclusio. When seeking to discover the organization of a work of poetry, the reader should stick with a more literal translation so as to recognize when the original language is conveying significant repetitions.

5.2.2. Strongly Typed Scenes. Some scenes are obviously a unit. For example, the wedding procession in Song of Songs 3:6-11 is an integral poem that everyone recognizes. The dream sequences also read as single poems and have no need of other devices (such as inclusio) to identify them.

No two scholars agree on where every section begins and ends, but if Song of Songs is read as an anthology of poems with no overall plot or story to tell, the overall meaning of the book is not compromised by this failure of consensus.

5.3. Results of This Analysis. The analysis in the outline below assumes that the four calls to the daughters of Jerusalem not to stir up love, or what to tell her lover, are endings of sections (Song 2:7; 3:5; 5:8; 8:4). Sometimes the ending is obvious, as in scene 7. After the man has relished his bride, tasted every titillating fruit, the erotic scene closes with "Eat, O friends, and drink: drink deeply, O lovers!" (Song 5:1 RSV).

Song of Songs may be divided into fourteen separate scenes. Each scene should be read in the way we read the psalms—somewhat independently of the others. This analysis is from Schwab (forthcoming).

The Title (Song 1:1)
The Anthology of Songs (Song 1:2—8:12)
  Scene 1: Daydreams and Perfume in the Presence of the King (Song 1:2-12)
    A. In the Presence of the King (Song 1:2-4)
    B. Reminiscences (Song 1:5-8)
    C. In the Presence of the King (Song 1:9-12)
  Scene 2: An Outdoor Fantasy (Song 1:13—2:7)
    A. Love in the Glade (Song 1:13—2:3a)
    B. Love in the Wine House (Song 2:3b-6)
    C. Adjuration to Beware of Love (Song 2:7)
  Scene 3: Turn, My Beloved, Be Like a Gazelle! (Song 2:8-17)
    A. My Lover Arrives (Song 2:8-9)
    B. My Lover Calls (Song 2:10-15)
    C. My Response (Song 2:16-17)
  Scene 4: Upon My Bed I Sought Him, but I Did Not Find Him (Song 3:1-5)
    A. My Disturbing Dream (Song 3:1-4)
    B. Adjuration to Beware of Love (Song 3:5)
  Scene 5: Who Is This Coming Up from the Desert? (Song 3:6-11)
  Scene 6: You Are All Beautiful; There Is No Flaw in You (Song 4:1-7)
  Scene 7: I Have Come into My Garden, My Sister, My Bride! (Song 4:8—5:1)
    A. Lebanon (Song 4:8-11)
    B. Paradise (Song 4:12—5:1a)
    C. Drink Deeply, O Lovers! (Song 5:1b)
  Scene 8: I Opened To My Lover, but He Had Turned and Gone (Song 5:2-8)
    A. My Disturbing Dream (Song 5:2-7)
    B. Adjuration: What to Say (Song 5:8)
  Scene 9: Tell Us about This Lover! (Song 5:9—6:3)
    A. What Kind of Lover Is He? (Song 5:9-16)
    B. Where has he Gone? (Song 6:1-3)
  Scene 10: Who Is This, as Awesome as an Army with Banners? (Song 6:4-10)
  Scene 11: Let Us See If the Vine Had Budded (There I Will Give you My Love) (Song 6:11—7:12)
    A. Looking for Signs of Spring (Song 6:11-13)
    B. How Fair You Are (Song 7:1-6)
    C. I Am My Lover's, and His Desire Is for Me (Song 7:7-10)
    D. Let Us Look for Signs of Spring (Song 7:11-12)
  Scene 12: O, That You Were Like a Brother to Me! (Song 7:13—8:4)
    A. If Only You Were Mine (Song 7:13—8:3)
    B. Adjuration to Beware of Love (Song 8:4)
  Scene 13: Who Is This Coming Up from the Desert? (Song 8:5-7)
    A. Love and Death (Song 8:5-7a)
    B. Love and Pauperization (Song 8:7b)
  Scene 14: Solomon, You Can Keep Your Silver (Song 8:8-12)
    A. Reminiscence (Song 8:8-9)
    B. Assessment of Her Youth (Song 8:10)
    C. Parable of Solomon's Vineyard (Song 8:11-12)
Final Thought, Conclusion to the Whole Song (Song 8:13-14)

5.4. Conclusion. As was noted earlier, no two critics parse Song of Songs in the same way. Many subjective decisions must be made to analyze the book in the way it is presented above. For example, each adjuration is read as a closing line (e.g., Song 2:7; 3:5). But it is possible that these form an inclusio that contains the material between. The *inclusios discovered by Schwab (see 5.2.1 above) to bound material may not in fact be inclusios at all but rather may demarcate common beginnings or endings of units, or may be simply accidentally placed with no structural significance whatsoever.

In the end, there is no scientific or objective way to determine with certainty where one scene ends and another begins. It is poetry, and it is not intended to be easy. The reader must slow down, carefully imbibe the imagery, the highs and lows of emotion, the shifting settings and perspectives of the "Greatest Song," and let it have its way.

See also FEMINIST INTERPRETATION; LYRIC POETRY; MARRIAGE AND SEX; ORAL POETRY; POETICS, TERMINOLOGY OF; SONG OF SONGS 2: ANCIENT NEAR EASTERN BACKGROUND; SONG OF SONGS 3: HISTORY OF INTERPRETATION; WASF; WOMEN.

BIBLIOGRAPHY. *Commentaries:* **F. Delitzsch,** *Commentary on the Song of Songs and Ecclesiastes* (Edinburgh: T & T Clark, 1877); **C. Exum,** *Song of Songs* (OTL; Louisville: Westminster John Knox, 2005); **D. Garrett,** *Proverbs, Ecclesiastes, Song of Songs* (NAC 14; Nashville: Broadman, 1993); **J. Gill,** *An Exposition of the Song of Solomon* (Puritan Classics; Grand Rapids: Sovereign Grace Publishers, 1971 [1854]); **S. C. Glickman,** *A Song for Lovers: Including a New Paraphrase and a New Translation of the Song of Solomon* (Downers Grove, IL: InterVarsity Press, 1976); **O. Keel,** *The Song of Songs* (CC; Minneapolis: Fortress, 1994); **T. Longman III,** *Song of Songs* (NICOT; Grand Rapids: Eerdmans, 2001); **R. E. Murphy,** *The Song of Songs* (Hermeneia; Minneapolis: Fortress, 1990); **M. H. Pope,** *Song of Songs* (AB 7C; Garden City, NY: Doubleday, 1977); **I. Provan,** *Ecclesiastes, Song of Songs* (NIVAC; Grand Rapids: Zondervan, 2001); **G. Schwab,** "Song of Songs" in *Expositor's Biblical Commentary* (rev. ed.; Grand Rapids: Zondervan, forthcoming); **J. G. Snaith,** *Song of Songs* (NCBC; Grand Rapids: Eerdmans, 1993). *Studies:* **H. Ainsworth,** *Annotations on the Pentateuch, the Psalms, and the Song of Solomon,* vol. 2 (Ligonier, PA: Soli Deo Publications, 1991 [1612]); **F. Black,** "Beauty or the Beast? The Grotesque Body in the Song of Songs," *BibInt* 8 (2000) 302-23; **A. Brenner,** "Aromatics and Perfumes in the Song of Songs," *JSOT* 25 (1983) 75-81; idem, "To See Is to Assume: Whose Love Is Celebrated in the Song of Songs?" *BibInt* 1 (1993) 265-84; **J. Daniélou,** "The Canticle: A Song of Sacraments," *OF* 25 (1950-1951) 97-103, 161-65; **S. J. Dillow,** *Solomon on Sex* (New York: Thomas Nelson, 1977); **D. A. Dorsey,** "Literary Structuring in the Song of Songs," *JSOT* 46 (1990) 81-96; **S. R. Driver,** *Introduction to the Literature of the Old Testament* (Edinburgh: T & T Clark, 1909); **D. Fairbairn,** "Patristic Exegesis and Theology: The Cart and the Horse," *WTJ* 69 (2007) 1-19; **M. Falk,** *Love Lyrics from the Bible: A Translation and Literary Study of the Song of Songs* (BLS 4; Sheffield: Almond, 1982); **H. Fisch,** *Poetry with a Purpose: Biblical Poetics and Interpretation* (ISBL; Indianapolis: Indiana University Press, 1988); **T. E. Fountain,** "A Parabolic View of the Song of Solomon," *BETS* 9 (1966) 97-101; **M. Fox,** *The Song of Songs and the Ancient Egyptian Love Songs* (Madison: University of Wisconsin Press, 1985); **S. B. Freehof,** "Song of Songs," *JQR* 39 (1949) 397-402; **M. D. Goulder,** *The Song of Fourteen Songs* (JSOTSup 36; Sheffield: JSOT Press, 1986); **A. M. Harman,** "Modern Discussion on the Song of Solomon" [review of *Song of Songs,* by M. H. Pope], *RTR* 37 (1978) 65-72; **B. Kamel,** "Repentance in the Song of Solomon," *CCR* 6.1 (1985) 13-16; **R. Kimelman,** "Rabbi Yohanan and Origen on the Song of Songs: A Third Century Jewish-Christian Disputation," *HTR* 73 (1980) 567-95; **F. S. Leahy,** "Song of Solomon in Pastoral Teaching," *EvQ* 27 (1955) 205-13; **R. Loewe,** "The Divine Garment and Shi'ur Qomah," *HTR* 58 (1965) 153-60; **A. Mariaselvam,** *The Song of Songs and Ancient Tamil Love Poems" Poetry and Symbolism* (AnBib 118; Rome: Editrice Pontificio Istituto Biblico, 1988); **T. J. Meek,** "Canticles and the Tammuz Cult," *AJSLL* 39 (1922-1923) 1-14; idem, "The Song of Songs: Introduction," in *The Interpreter's Bible,* ed. S. Terrien (New York: Abingdon, 1956) 5.91-98; **F. Meleka,** "A Review of Origen's Commentary on the Song of Songs," *CCR* 1 (1980) 125-29; **J. O'Keefe and R. R. Reno,** *Sanctified Vision: An Introduction to Early Christian Interpretation of the Bible* (Baltimore: Johns Hopkins University Press, 2005); **Origen,** *Homilies on Genesis and Exodus* (FC; Washington, DC: Catholic University of America Press, 1981); **W. E. Phipps,** "Plight of the Song of Songs," *JAAR* 42 (1974) 82-100; **C. Rabin,** "Song of Songs and Tamil Poetry," *SR* (1973-1974) 205-19; **S. J. Riekert,** "A Few Notes on the Tannaitic Interpretation of Canticles," in *Aspects of the Exegetical Process,* ed. W. Wyk (Pretoria West: NHW Press, 1977) 130-48; **H. H. Rowley,** "The Interpretation of the Song of Songs," in *The Servant of the Lord and Other Essays on the Old Testament,* ed. H. H. Rowley (London: Lutterworth, 1952) 189-234; **M. Sadgrove,** "The Song of Songs as Wisdom Literature," in *Studia Biblica 1978: Sixth International Congress on Biblical Studies, Oxford, 3-7 April 1978,* 1: *Papers on Old Testament and Related Themes,* ed. E. A. Livingstone (JSOTSup 11; Sheffield: JSOT Press, 1979) 245-48; **C. J. Scalise,** "Allegorical Flights of Fancy: The Problem of Origen's Exegesis," *GOTR* 32 (1987) 84-88; **G. Schwab,** "Cultivating the Vineyard: Solomon's Counsel for Lovers," *JBC* 15.3 (1997) 8-20; idem, *The Song of Songs' Cautionary Message Concerning Human Love* (SBL 41; New York: Peter Lang, 2002); **C. Seerveld,** *The Greatest Song: In Critique of Solomon* (Palos Heights, IL: Trinity Pennyasheet Press: 1963); **M. Silva,** *Has the Church Misread the Bible? The History of Interpretation in the Light of Current Issues* (FCI 1; Grand Rapids: Academie Books, 1987); **H. Simke,** "Cant 1:7f in Altchristlicher Auslegung," *TZ* 18 (1962) 256-67; **J. R. Sizoo,** "Winds of God [Song of Solomon 4:16]," *JRT* 10.2 (1953) 149-54; **R. J. Tournay,** "Les Chariots d'Aminadab (Cant 6:12): Israël, peuple théophore," *VT* 9 (1959) 288-309; **P. Trible,** *God and the Rhetoric of Sexuality* (Philadelphia: Fortress, 1978); **G. H. A. von Ewald,** *Das Hohelied Salolmo's: Übersetzt mit Einleitung, Anmerkungen und einem Anhang über den Prediger* (Göttingen: Rudolph Deuerlich, 1826); **L. Waterman,** *The Song of Songs: Translated and Interpreted as a Dramatic Poem* (Ann Arbor: University of Michigan Press, 1948); **E. C. Webster,** "Pattern in the Song of Songs," *JSOT* 22 (1982) 73-93; **C. J. Whitesell,** "Behold, Thou Art Fair, My Beloved," *Parabola* 20 (1995) 92-99; **G. H. Wittenberg,** "Amos 6:1-7: 'They Dismiss the Day of Disaster but You Bring Near the Rule of Violence,'" *JTSA* 58 (1987) 57-69.   G. Schwab

SONG OF SONGS 2: ANCIENT NEAR EASTERN BACKGROUND

Song of Songs—can one find another work so fascinating, so splendid? The title "Song of Songs" is a nearly literal translation of the Hebrew *šîr haššîrîm,* which is that language's way, among others, of saying "the most sublime of all songs."

While love enriches the human as oak en-

hances Cabernet, one must appreciate no less the diversity of its expression. No single culture has the market on love. No one group experiences love to the exclusion of others. Love has found expression in the hands of gifted writers throughout the world, throughout time. Joy, ecstasy, yearnings, puzzlement and, yes, pain and sorrow find voice within love.

Song of Songs, while certainly "most sublime" for those who placed it within the *canon of Hebrew Scriptures, was but one literary expression of love among the cultures of the ancient Near East. We turn to consider these other ancient cultures and the literature that they have left behind.

 1. Egyptian Literature
 2. Sumerian Literature
 3. Akkadian Literature
 4. (North)west Semitic Literature
 5. Song of Songs within the Ancient Near East

1. Egyptian Literature.

What we have of Egypt's ancient love songs come, primarily and interestingly, from one particular era: the Ramessides of the Nineteenth and Twentieth Dynasties (c. 1300-1150 BC). This is not to say that Egypt had no love songs before the Ramessides, but only that we possess nothing earlier.

Among the first scholars to notice similarities between Egypt's love poetry and Song of Songs was A. Erman. The fête of love in these Egyptian lyrics, when compared with the Mesopotamian inventory, as we will see below, is distinctly more human-oriented. Unlike Sumerian love songs, very little in Egypt suggests cultic settings and rituals, divine sex acts, acted out by royals and surrogates, in part, to promote well-being and fertility in the land. Deities are mentioned (e.g., Hathor and Sothis in Chester Beatty I #35, #31, respectively), but Egyptian poetry warmly portrays rapturous *human* sexual attraction and emotion. Here, however, we must be cautious. Although Egyptian love poetry is more "secular" than its Mesopotamian counterpart, the distinction between religious and nonreligious is likely nowhere near as sharp as it would be to modern readers, who should not lose sight of the ancients' fusion of religion with their conceptual understandings. For example, the star Sirius, after about a seventy-day disappearance from the night sky, would reappear at dawn around June

21, coinciding generally with the start of the Nile's life-infusing inundation (Davis, 112). To the Egyptians, Sirius was the goddess Sothis. This is an underpinning to the simile about the female lover in Chester Beatty I #31: she is "like Sothis rising at the beginning of a good year." A fine simile, to be sure, to the modern reader, it is deeply intertwined with the divinized conceptual outlook of those ancient writers.

The language in Egypt is far less sexually explicit than in Mesopotamia. In the latter, the goddess Inanna, for example, speaks explicitly of her "vulva" (Sum gal$_4$) as a "well-watered, rising mound," asking Dumuzi, her lover, to "plow" it (Inanna-Dumuzi P ii). The same anatomical region might be in mind in Egypt in the more coyly expressed "double doors" open in the "middle of her house" (Papyrus Harris 500 #7) (Fecht, 76). (On a nonfigurative level, the latter song comprises the words of a male outside his lover's home, much like Romeo outside Juliet's window.) Here, in its subtlety and its focus on human lovers, is where Egypt's literature, not Mesopotamia's, is arguably more similar to Song of Songs.

The Egyptians may well have composed love songs before the Ramessides, but their emergence within this era reflects cultural developments of the day (Fox 1985, 183; White, 74-79). The poetry's roots likely belong to the Amarna age, roughly half a century before the occurrence of the first extant love songs. Out of Pharaoh Akhenaton's heretical devotion to Aton (rather than to long-standing Amon) blossomed a revolution in art and literature, a prominent characteristic being the open depiction of intimacy between royal family members. Pharaoh eats with his family, plays with his daughters, embraces and kisses his wife. A. Hermann (62) has argued that such depictions of intimacy programmatically reinforced Akhenaton's ideology that Aton's influence should permeate personal emotions (see also Fox 1985, 183). Though worship of Aton would die shortly after Akhenaton's own death, intimate portrayals would continue without their fusion to Aton. Enter the Ramessides.

The Egyptian inventory of love songs is systematically numbered, thanks to the initial work of Hermann (1959). Though M. Fox's later seminal work on Egyptian love songs needed to adjust the numeration (1985), Hermann, by and large, is still followed, as is the case here.

1.1. Papyrus Harris 500. This papyrus from Egypt's Nineteenth Dynasty (thirteenth century BC) was discovered in a casket within Ramesses II's mortuary temple, the Ramesseum. Likely an anthology, the papyrus's verso holds two fictional tales. The love songs are found on the recto.

Badly damaged in parts, the songs are placed within three groupings (A, B, C). Pause marks divide each of the songs, and many have titles in red ink. Group A (#1-8) and B (#9-16) contain sixteen songs, while Group C (#17-19) comprises a single, three-stanza song. The papyrus holds an additional two songs, badly fragmented.

The literary voice in Group A switches between female and male, but not consecutively. The lovers express their affection both in second and third person. Though at least one scholar has tried to weave these songs into one storyline (Suys), such attempts have been met with skepticism. Couched within a variety of settings, the songs seem to be not a true dialogue between two lovers but rather an anthology of eight autonomous songs (Fox 1985, 196). The female is lying with her lover in song #1; the male is sailing to Memphis in #5; in #7 the male, at least on a nonfigurative level, is a frustrated lover outside the female's house. Group B, which begins with the phrase "The Beginning of the Entertainment Song," is a collection of eight independent songs written only in female voice. Here is a sampling from these two groups (translations are from Fox 1985, 7-25):

#2 (Female)
Your love is mixed in my body,
   like . . . ,
[like honey(?)] mixed with water,
      like mandragoras in which gum
         is mixed,
         like the blending of dough with. . . .
Hasten to see your sister, . . .

#3 (Male)
The vegetation(?) of the marsh(?) is bewildering.
[The mouth of] my sister is a lotus,
   her breasts are mandragoras,
[her] arms are [branches]. . . .

#4 (Female)
My heart is not yet done with your

lovemaking,
my (little) wolf cub!
Your liquor is (your) lovemaking. . . .

#9 (Female)
The beauty of your sister,
the beloved of your heart,
when she has come back from
the meadows!
My brother, my beloved,
my heart longs for your love,
. . .
All the birds of (the land of) Punt—
they have descended on Egypt,
anointed with myrrh.
The first to come
takes the bait.
His fragrance is brought from Punt;
his claws are full of balm.
My heart desires you,
Let us release it together. . . .

#12 (Female)
I have departed [from my brother].
[Now when I think of] your love,
my heart stands still within me.
When I behold sw[eet] cakes,
[they seem like] salt . . .
The scent of your nose alone
is what revives my heart. . . .

Group C (songs #17-19) is a single poem with three stanzas, each one beginning with a *word-play on a type of flower. Appropriately titled "The Flower Song," the three flower types offer a conceptual coherence throughout each respective stanza. The *mḫmḫ*-flower, for example, plays on the Egyptian word *mḫ3* ("balance"): "*mḫmḫ*-flowers: my heart is in balance with yours. For you I'll do what it wills, when I am in your embrace" (Fox 1985, 26, 197).

1.2. Cairo Love Songs. Written on a now fragmented vase from either the Nineteenth or the Twentieth Dynasty are two songs (Davis [111] has argued for one, cyclical song) known as the Cairo Love Songs. In one of the songs, which Fox (1980, 102, 104; 1985, 31, 36) has entitled "The Crossing," the female thinks only of her absent lover, his voice, his form. She desires to bathe in his presence at river's bank in a diaphanous linen tunic. There, along the river, we discover that the male is present, but on the *other* side, separated from her by crocodile and current. Strengthened by her spell-like love, he finds the crocodile to be "a mouse," and the current "dry land." Rapturously they embrace, and he kisses her parted lips. Passion building, he orders the preparation of a bed for their lovemaking. On her bed, linen tucked between her legs, fragrance on her body, the lovers leave us—the poem ends.

In the song "Wishes," or perhaps "If only," after the opening phrase in each stanza, a man opines for the woman he desires. His is the only voice we hear. Each stanza develops his particular wish. He wishes that he were his lover's private attendant, able, as she, to be close and to envisage her unclothed body. He yearns to be her laundryman, rubbing himself with her clothes. He desires to be her seal ring, with her every day. He imagines himself spending mornings throughout his lifetime as her mirror. He longs for her to be close to him, like flowers on a wreath. He wishes that she would come to him, promising a festival to the god capable of granting this.

1.3. Papyrus Chester Beatty I. This long papyrus from Thebes, dated to the Twentieth Dynasty (twelfth century BC), has three groups of love songs (A, B, C), all intact. Additionally, the papyrus holds a myth about Horus and Seth, two royal hymns (one certainly related to Ramesses V) and several short business documents.

Though the papyrus itself reads, "The Beginning of the Sayings of the Great Entertainer," Fox (1985, 51) has labeled Group A (songs #31-37) "The Stroll," after the central event that underpins the drama of this grouping. Alternating through each of the seven stanzas, the voices of a young man and woman ponder their passion for each other, without, sadly, the other knowing fully the obsession that they share. The stanzas do not appear to follow a chronological storyline, but they do seem to rehearse events that bind these two lovers together. In #31 the lad, as the young lady walks by, reflects on her physical beauty, in rhetoric similar to the *wasfs, or physique descriptions in Song of Songs (e.g., Song 4:1-7). He speaks of her skin, eyes, lips, neck, breasts, hair, arms, fingers, waist, derrière and thighs. In #32 the girl, in her voice, says that "love of him has captured me." The boy has come close to her house, but the girl's mother prevents her from going to him. In song #33 the boy describes how he set out one day to go to the girl's house.

He meets a "Mehi in his chariot, together with the lovers." The lad becomes confused, afraid to join Mehi lest he become involved with him. The meaning of all this remains unclear to us, but the boy's hesitation prevents him from reaching the girl. In #34 the girl's heart "jumps" after him, but she wrestles to keep it within her, and she does. As the male's hesitation in #33 prevented his meeting her, her struggle to contain her heart keeps her from meeting him. In the remaining three stanzas (#35-37) their mutual hesitancy restrains them from meeting one another. The boy, we read, finally becomes ill with love, declaring how only a visit from his lover would cure him. The song ends without the two ever being together.

Group B (#38-40) represents a poem of three stanzas, all from the female's voice. Each stanza follows a structure. (1) The girl invites the boy to hurry to his "sister"—the girl herself. (2) The wishful hastening is couched in three images of swiftness: a royal messenger, a horse, a gazelle. (3) Each is then developed in rhetoric that draws from the stanza's "speed" image. The third stanza (#40) is illustrative of the structure and imagery that hastens toward love, perhaps complete with the faintness that may come from high passion. The swift gazelle, at times shaky, is to arrive at the lover's "cave"—by most all accounts, a metaphor for the female's most private part (Fox 1985, 68; Hermann, 152; White, 101).

If only you would come to (your) sister
        swiftly,
    like a gazelle bounding over the desert,
whose legs are shaky, whose body is weary,
    for fear has entered his body.
    . . .
(Then) ere (you) kiss your hand four times,
    you will arrive at her cave. (Fox 1985, 66-67)

Group C (#41-47) begins with the rubric "The beginning of the sweet saying, which was found in a book container, and which the scribe Nakhtsobek from the necropolis wrote." These seven songs appear to be an anthology, though common imagery and themes perhaps make them appear to be more unified than they really are (Fox 1985, 200).

1.4. The Turin Love Song. This love song, three stanzas (#28-30), comes from a Twentieth Dynasty papyrus, whose present home is Turin, Italy. The copyist wrote the first line of each stanza

in red, helping us to recognize its three-unit composition. Two lovers, probably not the same two in each stanza (Fox 1985, 50), hiding away, concealing their sexual intimacy among branches and leaves, underpin the song. The true characters are three trees, one in each stanza, personified with thought as they gaze upon the couple's sexual frolic beneath them. The first two, proud of their splendor, decry the couple's self-absorption, threatening to call them out and expose them. The third tree, however, pledges shelter and secrecy. Forbidden love and stealing away to a secretive tryst among luxuriant foliage has its echo in Song of Songs 1:16-17.

1.5. "Love Song" Memorial Inscriptions. Although not precisely love songs in the sense as those above, some memorial inscriptions seem, in effect, love songs to departed ones. We look at two examples.

1.5.1. Inscription for Mutirdis. From the Twenty-Second Dynasty (tenth-eighth centuries BC) comes a sixteen-lined inscription praising the life and physical attributes of Mutirdis, priestess of Hathor. "Sweet, sweet of love, says King Menkheperre. Sweet, say men. Mistress of love, say women." Praise for her physical features follow: "Blacker her hair than the black of night . . . [whiter] her teeth than bits of plaster . . . her breasts are set firm on her bosom" (Fox 1985, 349; White, 189-90).

1.5.2. Petosiris's Song to His Wife, Renpet-nefret. This Ptolemaic tomb inscription extols the virtue of Renpet-nefret. "Sweet in speech, excellent in counsel . . . great of praise in her city, . . . who speaks good things . . . greatly loved by all." The rhetoric is not unlike the "Noble Woman" in Proverbs 31.

2. Sumerian Literature.

Sumerian love poems abound. In Egypt, though, where the love and lovemaking appear to be among commoners, most Sumerian love songs, but not all, are divine lyrics expressing divine lovemaking—deities fill the roles of lovers. These arguably cultic texts likely played their most prominent role in an annual rite known as "sacred marriage." Indeed, S. Kramer (1962, 25), building on the work of T. Meek, adamantly suggested that portions of Song of Songs, too, were "cultic in origin, and were sung in the course of the *hieros gamos*, or 'sacred marriage,' . . . [which] has Mesopotamian roots . . . back to . . . the Sumerian Dumuzi-Inanna cult." Precisely what the "sacred marriage" entailed is not obvious. Indeed, for some, the rite's arguably scanty, less-than-clear evidence casts a shadow on whether it existed at all (Rubio, 269; Sweet). Some rite, however, appears to call out through the texts. Related to celebrations surrounding the New Year, between the second half of the third millennium to the beginning of the second millennium BC, the king, representing Dumuzi, would have sexual intercourse (real or otherwise) with a woman, probably a priestess, representing the goddess Inanna (Rubio, 269). Echoes of this apparent ritual survive into the first millennium in the poems of the new characters of Nabu and Tashmetu (see 3.8. below). A "blessing" motif, present in most all of these cuneiform songs, attests to an important purpose: securing good fate for the ruler and country. The king's union with the (surrogate) goddess secured fertility and abundance for the land and its population (Sefati, 48-49).

The poems focus on more than a mere sex act. They, like their Egyptian and biblical counterparts, express a wide range of love's emotions. In contrast, though, to the subtle, even coy eroticism in Song of Songs and Egyptian love poems, sexual explicitness, as we noted above, is vivid in Sumerian compositions:

[Inanna = female:]
My own vulva [Sum *gal₄*], *a well-watered, rising
    mound—*
I, the maiden—who will plow it?
My vulva, the wet and well-watered ground—
I, the young lady—who will station there
    an ox?
[Dumuzi = male:]
Young lady, may the king plow it for you,
May Dumuzi, the king, plow it for you!
    (Inanna-Dumuzi P ii, lines 25-30
    [adapted from Sefati, 91])
The king goes with lifted head to the holy
    lap,
Goes with lifted head to the lap of Inanna,
Ama-*ušumgalanna* beds with her,
He delights in her pure lap. (Iddindagan
    A, lines 185-88 [Sefati, 105])
Your right hand you have placed on
    my vulva,
Your left, stroked my head,
You have touched your mouth to mine.
    (from Inanna-Dumuzi [Kramer 1969, 105;
    see also *COS* 1.169A:541])

Although these Sumerian poems and Song of Songs share similar nature and garden imagery along with brother-sister address, though only "sister" appears in the latter, most scholars find that the differences undermine any theory suggesting that Song of Songs was derived from a cultic liturgy. Song of Songs is disinterested in fertility and lacks (1) blessings, (2) the ritual rhetoric of the cuneiform, (3) nature's reinvigoration in imagery of resurrection.

The ancient scribes commonly would add to a composition a subscript, which apparently categorized the work according to genre. The subscript could also name the deity or hero to whom the song was dedicated. Among those with a subscript, the classification *balbale* dominates. Though somewhat unclear, these *balbale* songs perhaps are a special category of declamation (Sefati, 25), connected in one way or another to the "theme of love, courtship, sacred marriage and the fertility of fields and flocks" (Sefati, 28). The majority have no narrative to set the background or to introduce the characters' voices; nearly all of them are dialogues or monologues (Sefati, 24)—a similarity with Song of Songs. An interesting feature, with character voice in mind, is the use of *emesal* (Sum *eme-sal*), a dialect, likely a "genderlect," not uncommonly used when women speak in these and other Sumerian texts. Pronunciation and specific words, in part, distinguish *emesal* from standard Sumerian, *emegir*.

2.1. Inanna and Dumuzi Love Poems. A divine couple, Inanna (prominent goddess associated, in part, with love, fertility, rain, storm and war) and Dumuzi (deified primeval shepherd-king), appears extensively in Sumerian literature. The literary works focus principally on (1) the couple's love affair and marriage, (2) Dumuzi's death, (3) his fate in the netherworld (Sefati, 17).

The love poems exploring their love affair and marriage—at present some thirty-eight songs involving roughly 1,700 lines (Sefati, 18)—are our primary focus here. They vividly describe their love and marriage. The lyrical descriptions on the lips of those who speak have fewer parallels with Song of Songs when compared with those associated with Shu-Suen and Ludingirra (see 2.2 below). This is not to say, though, that one finds no similarities. The epithet of "sister" for the female is a connection. Dumuzi's vocational epithet of "shepherd" accords with shepherd imagery in Song of Songs (Song 1:7). The female voice, both in the Inanna-Dumuzi poems and in Song of Songs, speaks of the male's left arm by her head while his right arm caresses her body. In Song of Songs, though, the male (coyly) "embraces," while in Inanna-Dumuzi his right arm is (explicitly) "placed on [her] vulva." And, as we noted earlier, nature and garden imagery abound in both.

Looking at one poem, Love by the Light of the Moon (title in *COS* 1.169C:542-43; see also *ANET,* 639-40), will give us a brief yet meaningful glimpse. Inanna, innocently singing and dancing under a night sky, is met by Dumuzi (here named Ama-ushumgalanna [a by-name]), who embraces her. Inanna pleads with him to let her go home, apparently fearing her mother's wrath should she discover Inanna's absence from home in the presence of a stranger. Dumuzi talks of women's "false words," suggesting the idea of deceit, allowing the two to spend the night making love. Because of a fragmentary text, we do not know their actions that night. The story, however, continues with the two arriving at Inanna's home. The poem ends with praise, likely by Ningal, Inanna's mother, for Dumuzi, who, she claims, makes plants grow abundantly and thus is worthy of Inanna's "pure lap."

2.2. Message of Ludingirra to His Mother. A beloved son, Ludingirra, commissions a royal courier to journey to the city of Nippur with greetings to his mother, Shat-Ishtar. Should the messenger not know her, Ludingirra says, "I shall give you some signs" (line 9 [Civil, who offers a full translation]). Ludingirra follows with five such signs, poetic descriptions of his mother's charms and beauty. The first sign focuses on her diligent lifestyle in rhetoric somewhat similar to the Noble Woman (= a *personification of wisdom) in Proverbs 31:10-31.

The remaining signs appear more personal, focusing on the lady's person in rich, metaphoric imagery. Although sensual language seems appropriate for Song of Songs, such talk about one's mother, if indeed present in this poem, strikes a modern reader as less than seemly. The language, unlike Inanna-Dumuzi's, is, to be sure, subtle—the courier (and the modern reader) is spared explicit reflections on the mother's intimate anatomy. J. Cooper (161-62), however, argues that sensuality permeates the poem. Cooper compares the third sign with Song of Songs 4:12-15:

> My mother is a heavenly rain, water for the best seeds,
> A bountiful harvest, which grows a second crop:
> A garden of delight, full of joy,
> An irrigated fir-tree, covered with fir-cones;
> An early fruit, the yield of the first month;
> A canal which brings luxuriant waters to the irrigation ditches,
> *A sweet Dilmun date, sought in its prime.*
> (lines 33-39 [Civil, 4-5])

The male lover in Song of Songs says the following about the woman:

> An enclosed garden is my sister, my betrothed,
> An enclosed pool, a sealed spring is my sister.
> Your irrigated fields are an orchard:
> Pomegranates along with the choicest fruit,
> Henna along with nard, nard and saffron, cane and cinnamon,
> Along with all scented woods, myrrh and aloes,
> Along with all the finest spices.
> *You are a garden spring, an artesian well, streaming from Lebanon.* (Song 4:12-15)

2.3. Royal Love Songs. Sumerians composed royal love songs about their kings and their consorts. The king often filled the role of Dumuzi, while the female, often a priestess, played Inanna. Such songs appear to be closely linked with the so-called sacred marriage rite.

2.3.1. Shulgi of Ur. In a text known as Shulgi X we read of King Shulgi of Ur (c. 2050 BC) traveling on his royal boat, stopping at several cities (Klein, 124-66). In four episodes Shulgi enters the local deity's temple bearing gifts. The deity responds by blessing him.

In the first episode—the longest—Shulgi docks at the quay of Uruk-Kullaba amid the adulation of his people. As he enters the Eanna temple complex, the goddess Inanna, seeing him, spontaneously chants a sensuous poem in the *emesal* dialect, recollecting the sexual pleasure in, most likely, her annual sacred consummation with Shulgi. She then blesses him. It is this episode, with its erotic language, that most closely resembles Song of Songs. Shulgi then travels on, the poem taking us along his journey.

We are uncertain whether this text depicts Shulgi's journey during the New Year festival, celebrating the sacred marriage rite. Such a thought has been the most common interpretation. Shulgi X, however, may simply be the end of another text (Shulgi D). If so, Shulgi, after a triumphal return from battle, visits major Sumerian temples, bestowing gifts to the various deities (Klein, 129).

2.3.2. Shu-Suen of Ur. Associated with King Shu-Suen, who reigned after Shulgi in the Ur III dynasty, are three *balbale* songs worth our attention. The first, Shu-Suen A, is a text difficult to understand fully, and Y. Sefati (344-50) rehearses the history of interpretation. In a *balbale* pertaining to the goddess Baba, a female lover praises the queen mother for bearing Shu-Suen. The lover beckons Shu-Suen, who has brought much pleasure, to pay her attention and invites him to her genitals, which are "sweet like her beer." In Shu-Suen B and C, both *balbale*s pertaining to Inanna, the female lovers draw heavily on imagery related to honey and sweetness. In Shu-Suen B the woman wishes to run after him to the bed, beckoning him to "sleep in our house till dawn," and opining, "If only you would do to me your sweet things." In Shu-Suen C the female lover, whose "hair is lettuce, well-watered," describes Shu-Suen as a "handsome man," a "farmer who brings superb grain," and "honey to my eyes . . . charm of my heart."

2.3.3. Iddin-Dagan of Isin. A love poem focuses on Iddin-Dagan, third ruler of Isin. It offers a clear expression of a New Year's sexual liaison between Inanna (actually, her human surrogate) and Iddin-Dagan. In imagery reminiscent of Song of Songs 6:10, Inanna first is praised for

> . . . her coming forth radiantly at evening,
> . . . the holy torch which fills the heaven,
> . . . her stance in heaven, like the moon and
>   the sun.
> *From above and below, all the lands know*
>   *(of these things).* (lines 11-14 [Reisman, 186])

Later, after lengthy accounts of processions and praise for Inanna, on "New Year's day, the day of ritual" (line 174):

> My lady bathes (her) pure lap,
> She bathes for the lap of the king.
> She bathes for the lap of Iddin-Dagan,
> The pure Inanna washes with soap,
> She sprinkles cedar oil on the ground,
> The king approaches (her) lap proudly,

He approaches the lap of Inanna proudly,
Ama'ušumgalanna lies down beside her,
He caresses her pure lap.
. . .
She makes love with him on her bed,
(She says) to Iddin-Dagan: "You are surely my
   beloved." (lines 180-188, 191-192
         [Reisman, 191])

2.3.4. Anonymous King of Uruk. This text (D1 in Sefati, 301-11), about seventy extant lines over three columns, is set within a sacred marriage ceremony between an unnamed king and the goddess Inanna. The king talks of his "good house," likely later identified as the Erigal temple (line 9), which is in Uruk. Here, preparations are made for a sexual liaison. Inanna, over the course of some twenty lines, longs for the bed. Spreading it out, she beckons the king. Ninshubur, faithful majordomo, escorts the king to Inanna's lap. Blessing are then spoken for the king: "Grant him a propitious and renowned reign . . . may there be carp-floods under him in the river . . . may wild sheep and goats multiply under him in the forests . . . may lettuce and cress grow under him in the garden-beds." The king, in the following lines, as the extant text ends, consummates the union, going "with lifted head to the holy lap [of Inanna]."

3. Akkadian Literature.

The Akkadian corpus embraces cultic, like Sumerian, and secular love lyrics. The texts range from early to late in respective dialects. Old Akkadian is the dialect of the last half of the third millennium BC. At millennium's turn, the language is classified according to two regional dialects: Babylonian and Assyrian. Each of these regional dialects has chronological classifications. Love lyrics occur in Old Akkadian, Old Babylonian (first half of the second millennium), Middle Babylonian (second half of the second millennium), Neo-Babylonian and Neo-Assyrian (both in the first half of the first millennium).

3.1. Old Akkadian Magical Love Charm. Discovered at Kish, this thirty-eight-lined tablet, written in the Old Akkadian dialect, is a "love magic" incantation invoked by a man to enable him to gain a woman's favor (Foster, 1.56; Gelb, 7). The language is not easy to understand; one only need compare the rather different translations offered by I. Gelb (7-12) and B. Foster

(1.56-57). Foster (1.56-57) proposes the following events. The chanter invokes Ea, the god of wisdom and incantations, and mentions that a love charm sits in the lap of Ishtar surrounded by "sap." Two "demonic" maidens fetch the charm. With it in hand, the man casts the spell upon the woman whom he desires. The woman's imagined response of erotic desire for him is offered, with the text then suggesting that the spell has done its work.

3.2. Old Babylonian Love Lyrics of Rim-Sin of Larsa. Associated with Rim-Sin, King of Larsa in the Old Babylonian period, this dialogue celebrates his cultic sacred marriage rite with a priestess during the New Year festivities (Foster, 1.98; van Dijk, Goetze and Hussey, 28). The voices of Rim-Sin and his anonymous lover speak. A third voice, a chorus of cultic singers, interjects into the dialogue.

3.3. Old Babylonian Love Song Discovered at Kish, Text 1063. This fragmentary love song expresses the desire for lovemaking. The language is quite erotic and passionate and appears devoid of cultic overtones, appearing "secular." In the first column a female addresses a man, encouraging him to make love to her. She refers to herself in the plural, not uncommon in amatory texts expressing the words of Ishtar and Inanna (Westenholz, 417): "Reach forth with your left hand and stroke our vulva, play with our breasts." Later we read, "I will make [love] and do your pleasure, lusty one" (Westenholz, 423).

3.4. Old Babylonian Love Song of Nanay and Muati. Understanding this text is complicated by the uncertainty of which side is the obverse, which side the reverse (Foster, 1.96-97). What is certain is that the poem celebrates the love of Nanay, a goddess of love, for Muati, a god about whom we know little. Nanay looks favorably upon Babylon and its king, Abieshuh, mentioned in the text. Attracted to Muati, Nanay apparently brings him to the city. The lyrics extol the pleasure of their lovemaking. If the tablet's sides are correctly comprehended, the song ends with a prayer for King Abieshuh's longevity.

3.5. Old Babylonian Love Poem of a Faithful Lover. The faithful lover is a young lady, deserted by her man for another woman. Despite the young man's harsh words to her, she is restrained and persistent in her view that she will recapture his affection. Only when she speaks of her rival does her tone grow harsh. Her patient, quiet love, in the end, wins. Shunning the

rival, the man declares, "May the other woman be our enemy, Ishtar being witness!" Humor peppers the dialogue, and lyrics rarely if ever focus on sex or anatomical descriptions. An embrace and a kiss are as far as the lyrics take us. Gossipy women intrude into the text, reminding one, somewhat, of the "Daughters of Jerusalem" in Song of Songs. The poem appears to be "secular," lacking cultic overtones (Held, 4).

3.6. Middle Babylonian Love "Ballad" of Ishtar and Dumuzi. A tablet, residing today in the British Museum (BM 47507), uniquely inscribed with a "monumental" script, is a love song, according to its editor, "not quite like anything else in Akkadian" (Black, 25). An intent to be sung, a brisk narrative style, secular rhetoric (despite the presence of the two deities) and lack of poetic dialogue inspire J. Black (25) to describe this love song as a "ballad."

The ballad, according to Black, has two storylines: a fantasy in the mind of Ishtar, followed by reality. Ishtar, cast as an infatuated but restrained young girl, fantasizes that she invites Dumuzi to spend the night with her in her parents' house. She envisions the door and bolt (an image found in Song 5:5) rejoicing as he enters, and she contemplates his "lusty" presence. She, still in her fantasy, expresses how she would ask him to remove his sandals and eat, forgetting for the moment his shepherding duties. Damage to the tablet prevents us from reading more of her reverie. The balance of the tablet appears to narrate what Ishtar actually did. The bathos is heartrending. She finds Dumuzi at his sheepfold (compare Song 1:7-8) and can only utter small talk about how pleasant the waters are for the sheep. The ballad ends.

3.7. Neo-Babylonian "Love Lyrics." In this badly fragmented text Marduk and Ishtar speak amorously to each other. Devoid of clear context, "bed chamber" and the cleansing of female genitalia nevertheless set an erotic tone. Ishtar here is Marduk's concubine, with the text apparently reciting angry words from Marduk's wife, Ṣarpanitum. Originally interpreted as a sacred marriage rite between Marduk and Ishtar (Lambert), another view sees it as a jealousy ritual addressing Ṣarpanitum's anguish over her husband's love of Ishtar (Edzard).

3.8. Neo-Assyrian Love Lyrics of Nabu and Tashmetu. These lyrics are the dialogue between the deities Nabu (Marduk and Ṣarpanitum's son) and Tashmetu, encouraged by a chorus. A brief introductory entreaty offers devotion to the two gods. The dialogue, with choral interjection, intimately describes the lovers' physiques and richly uses garden imagery, much like Song of Songs: Tashmetu's thighs are "a gazelle in the steppe . . . ankles are a springtime apple . . . she washes herself, she climbs into bed . . . Why are you so adorned, Tashmetu? So I can go to the garden with you, my Nabu" (Foster, 2.903; see also Livingstone, 35-37). Most commentators see this poem as evidence for the practice of the sacred rite marriage continuing into the first millennium.

3.9. Miscellaneous Late Magical Love Charms. From the first millennium we have a number of "love magic" incantations, similar in genre to the Old Akkadian love charm (see 3.1 above). Potency is a recurring concern. Foster (1.884-85) provides convenient translations. One, entitled "Harpstring," incants, "Let my potency be (steady as) running river water, Let my penis be a (taut) harpstring, Let it not slip out of her." Another, "I Have Made a Bed," chants, "Potency! . . . What Ishtar does for Dumuzi, What Nanay does for her lover . . . Let me do for my lover!"

4. (North)west Semitic Literature.

From the Late Bronze Age, the ancient city of Ugarit (near the Mediterranean coast in modern Syria) affords us a couple worthwhile texts.

4.1. Descriptive Love Lyrics in the King Kirta/ Keret Epic. Within the epic of King Kirta (*KTU* 1.14-16) we encounter the repetition of physique description. Job-like King Kirta loses his family—wife and heirs are gone. The god El, however, notices his plight and in a dream shows Kirta how to find a wife, keeping him from ruin. Kirta is to wage a war campaign against King Pabil of Udum, taking his daughter, Hurriy, for his wife. The epic continues, developing a story of intrigue, illness and jealousy. The brief descriptions of Hurriy, however, are our focus here. Refusing wealth and other spoils of war, Kirta asks for Hurriy, expressing that "her beauty is Anat's beauty, Athirat's loveliness is her loveliness, her eyebrows are lapis lazuli, her eyes are alabaster bowls . . . I rest in the gaze of her eyes" (*KTU* 1.14 iii 41-45 // vi 26-30 [author's translation]; see also Wyatt, 196-98, 204).

4.2. The Gracious Gods (KTU 1.23 = RS 2.002). This myth, interspersed with liturgy, depicts the sexual liaison of El with two divine females, Athirat and Rahmay. The sexual

encounter, explicitly told, produces two divine offspring, Shahar (Dawn) and Shalim (Dusk). Either they are the "gracious gods" or they and other born gods comprise the "gracious." Ironically, these gracious gods begin to devour birds of the sky and fish of the sea. El banishes them and their mothers into the desert to hunt for their food. During a seven-year trek they come upon a "watchman" of irrigated fields who provides for them. The function of this myth is unknown. A sacred marriage rite (de Moor, 117), a famine-relief liturgy (D. Pardee in *COS* 1.87:274-83) and a royal marriage liturgy (Wyatt, 324-25) have been suggested.

The sexual union is lengthy and vivid. Double-entendre teases out the imagery. We read of El's "hand" (Ugar *yd*), a well-known "penis" euphemism, growing "as long as the sea." He grabs, raises up, and aims his "staff" and "walking stick" (real and figurative?). He kisses the women's lips, "sweet as pomegranate," and "from kissing came conception, from embracing, 'heat' [impregnation?]."

5. Song of Songs within the Ancient Near East.

What insight might our look at ancient Near Eastern love songs offer in understanding Song of Songs? Love poetry served cult; it also expressed rapturous secular passion among royals and commoners. If Song of Songs served a cultic function among the Israelites, it does not show that purpose as translucently as do Mesopotamian and Ugaritic texts. If the book expresses secular obsession, as Egypt's culture demonstrates, should we look for a storyline or classify the contents as little more than an anthology? The ancient Near East clearly shows us the possibility for both. That no distinct storyline has won the day among scholars might tip the balance that Song of Songs is, at the end of the day, an anthology of sensuous lyrics.

Song of Songs, however, appears to be more than a hodgepodge, and, in the end, I am persuaded that it is best understood as a collection of love lyrics unified through associative links: (1) repetends, (2) portrayal of characters, (3) a loose narrative frame (Fox 1985, 209-22).

Words ("lily," "blooming-vine," "dear"), phrases ("my dove," "my perfect one"), clauses ("My beloved is mine, and I am his"), adjurations (Song 2:7; 3:5; 5:8; 8:4), themes of searching and finding (Song 3:1-4; 5:2-8) and imagery through metaphor and simile recur throughout the book. Such repetends bolster Song of Song's unity.

Two personae—two lovers—express their passion throughout the book. Egyptian love poetry clearly "role plays." The same lovers, through literary fiction, can be royalty, servants or shepherds. Escaping their true circumstances, Egyptian lovers assume these various roles or disguises. Dumuzi, in the Inanna-Dumuzi love poems, is often a shepherd. Had we only Song of Songs, we could easily insist on three distinct main characters: a king (no less than *Solomon himself), a shepherd, a woman. Ancient Near Eastern parallels, however, push one to consider the plausibility that Song of Songs expresses the words of a single couple, who, at times, use royal and shepherd imagery.

Springtime is the only season behind Song of Songs. Leaving the city to steal away to the countryside is a theme that runs throughout. The female lover and her brothers quietly develop in their relationship. These, in part, embolden Fox (1985, 222) to talk of the book's loose narrative framework.

Through the lens of the wider context of love lyrics among ancient Near Eastern cultures, we perhaps ought to see Song of Songs as a woven anthology of secular lyrics that celebrate passion between two young lovers.

See also MARRIAGE AND SEX; SONG OF SONGS 1: BOOK OF; SONG OF SONGS 3: HISTORY OF INTERPRETATION; WASF; WOMEN.

BIBLIOGRAPHY. **J. A. Black,** "Babylonian Ballads: A New Genre," in *Studies in Literature from the Ancient Near East by Members of the American Oriental Society Dedicated to Samuel Noah Kramer,* ed. J. M. Sasson (AOS 65; New Haven: American Oriental Society, 1984) 25-34; **M. Civil,** "The 'Message of Lú-Dingir-Ra to His Mother' and a Group of Akkado-Hittite 'Proverbs,'" *JNES* 23 (1964) 1-11; **J. S. Cooper,** "New Cuneiform Parallels to the Song of Songs," *JNES* 90 (1971) 157-62; **V. L. Davis,** "Remarks on Michael V. Fox's 'The Cairo Love Songs,'" *JAOS* 100 (1980) 111-14; **J. C. de Moor,** *An Anthology of Religious Texts from Ugarit* (Nisaba 16; Leiden: E. J. Brill, 1987); **D. O. Edzard,** "Zur Ritualtafel der sog: 'Love Lyrics,'" in *Language, Literature, and History: Philological and Historical Studies Presented to Erica Reiner,* ed. F. Rochberg-Halton (AOS 67; New Haven: American Oriental Society, 1987) 57-69; **A. Erman,** *The Literature of the Ancient Egyptians: Poems, Narratives, and Manuals of Instruction, from the Third and Second Millennia B.C.,* trans. A. M. Blackman (London: Methuen, 1927); **G. Fecht,** "Die Wiedergewinnung der altägyptischen Verskunst," *Mitteilungen des deutschen archäologischen Instituts, Abteilung Kairo* 19 (1963) 54-70; **B. R. Foster,** *Before the Muses: An Anthology of Akkadian Literature* (2 vols.; Bethesda, MD: CDL Press, 1993); **M. V. Fox,** "The Cairo Love Songs," *JAOS* 100 (1980) 101-9; idem, *The Song of Songs and the Ancient Egyptian Love Songs* (Madison: University of Wisconsin Press, 1985); **I. J. Gelb,** *Sargonic Texts in the Ashmolean Museum, Oxford* (MAD 5; Chicago: University of Chicago Press, 1970); **M. Held,** "A Faithful Lover in an Old Babylonian Dialogue," *JCS* 15 (1961) 1-26; **A. Hermann,** *Altägyptische Liebesdichtung* (Wiesbaden: Harrassowitz, 1959); **J. Klein,** *Three Shulgi Hymns: Sumerian Royal Hymns Glorifying King Shulgi of Ur* (BSNELC; Ramat Gan: Bar-Ilan University Press, 1981); **S. N. Kramer,** "The Biblical 'Song of Songs' and the Sumerian Love Songs," *Expedition* 5 (1962) 25-31; idem, "The Sacred Marriage and Solomon's Song of Songs," in *The Sacred Marriage Rite: Aspects of Faith, Myth, and Ritual in Ancient Sumer* (Bloomington: Indiana University Press, 1969) 85-106; **W. G. Lambert,** "Divine Love Lyrics from Babylon," *JSS* 4 (1959) 1-15; **A. Livingstone,** ed., *Court Poetry and Literary Miscellanea* (SAA 3; Helsinki: Helsinki University Press, 1989); **T. J. Meek,** "Babylonian Parallels to the Song of Songs," *JBL* 43 (1924) 245-52; **D. Reisman,** "Iddin-Dagan's Sacred Marriage Hymn," *JCS* 25 (1973) 185-202; **G. Rubio,** "Inanna and Dumuzi: A Sumerian Love Story," *JAOS* 121 (2001) 268-74; **Y. Sefati,** *Love Songs in Sumerian Literature: Critical Edition of the Dumuzi-Inanna Songs* (BSNELC; Ramat Gan: Bar-Ilan University Press, 1998); **É. Suys,** "Le genre dramatique dans l'Égypte ancienne," *Revue de questions scientifiques* 105 (1934) 437-63; **R. F. G. Sweet,** "A New Look at the 'Sacred Marriage' in Ancient Mesopotamia," in *Corolla Torontonensis: Studies in Honour of R. M. Smith* (Toronto: University of Toronto Press, 1994) 85-104; **J. van Dijk, A. Goetze and M. I. Hussey,** *Early Mesopotamian Incantations and Rituals* (YOS 11; New Haven: Yale University Press, 1985); **J. G. Westenholz,** "A Forgotton Love Song," in *Language, Literature, and History: Philological and Historical Studies Presented to Erica Reiner,* ed. F. Rochberg-Halton (AOS 67; New Haven: American Oriental Society, 1987) 415-25; **J. B. White,** *A Study of the Language of Love in the Song of Songs and Ancient Egyptian Poetry,*

(SBLDS 38; Missoula, MT: Scholars Press, 1978); **N. Wyatt**, *Religious Texts from Ugarit* (BibSem 53; Sheffield: Sheffield Academic Press, 2002).

G. A. Long

SONG OF SONGS 3: HISTORY OF INTERPRETATION

The Song of Songs, or Canticle of Canticles from *canticum canticorum* in the Latin tradition, has long held a prominent place in both Jewish and Christian communities. It has not only contributed to the formation of their corporate understandings of their relationship to God, spirituality, and notions of love and human sexuality but also played a significant role in individualistic expressions of spirituality and engagement of God. As a result, the history of interpretation as well as the hermeneutical issues posed by the book reveal to us the challenges of reading and interpreting the biblical documents, and demonstrate the degree to which culture and the social location of the readers impact their interpretation of Scripture. And in the case of the Song, important insights into the ties that bind humanity's physical existence with experience of God are made evident.

While it may be somewhat surprising to find such a sensual, erotic text within the canon, the Song's popularity has resulted in a complex interpretive history. Furthermore, the Song presents unique hermeneutical challenges; it has been read both corporately and individualistically, allegorically and profanely. To illustrate its impact, one need only note the commentaries written on it. By the sixteenth century over a hundred commentaries had been composed on the Song, whereas texts like Romans and Galatians, central in today's Christian imagination, could muster only a handful. Deemed inappropriate for the immature, who might be lured into pursuing sensual pleasures outside the ethical boundaries of the text and community, the Song was understood for many generations as a vault that contained treasures solely for the mature, and its meaning was thought to be encrypted within imagery that could only be unlocked by the key of allegorical interpretation.

With the rise of scientific models of historical biblical exegesis, it has become fashionable to discard the seemingly subjective heritage of Jewish and Christian allegory in favor of an "objective" analysis and interpretation that clear the way for the recovery of the text's "original mean-ing" in a proposed historical context. While such investigation can be elucidating, an unfortunate repercussion of this venture has deprived modern readers of certain theologically rich elements that an allegorical approach afforded. In this article we will explore issues that arise in its complicated interpretive history.

1. Canonization
2. Jewish Interpretation
3. Early Christian and Medieval Interpretation
4. Reformation Interpretation
5. Sixteenth- and Seventeenth-Century Roman Catholic Interpretation
6. Modern Interpretation
7. Hermeneutical Issues and Implications

1. Canonization.

The public reading of passages like Song of Songs 7:8-9, "I said, 'I will climb your palm tree, I will take hold of its branches, let your breasts be like the clusters of the vine, and the fragrance of your breath like apples, Your mouth is like the best wine,'" causes a degree of discomfort in most multigenerational faith settings today. This is not surprising given that the Song is one of the most profane texts included in the Hebrew *canon. In addition to its erotic language and themes, the name of God is nowhere mentioned or alluded to. The Song neither possesses a notion of salvation history or divine *law nor offers explicit moral guidelines.

So why is the Song included in the canon? The answer remains elusive, in part because there are few early traditions that discuss the topic, and there is a decided lack of information concerning introductory matters. It is often implied that if one could only unravel the reason for its inclusion into the canon, we would have an early witness to how the text was read and understood. But it may in fact be just the opposite: understanding its interpretive tradition may lead to reasons for its inclusion. Furthermore, one might also argue that the manner of reading that gave rise to its canonical status provides a hermeneutical key for the faith communities that read it today. Thus, the interpretive issues related to the Song have existed since its inclusion into the canon. The struggle today over whether the Song ought to be read simply as humanistic love poetry or an allegory is not a new question.

One position holds that the Song acquired its

revered status because of its association with Solomon (Song 1:1). Early Jewish traditions seem to suggest as much. A difficult text in Josephus *Contra Apion* 1.8 observes that twenty-two agreed upon books constitute the canon. Of these, four are Solomonic "hymns to God and precepts for the conduct for life." Unfortunately, these books are never named. The "hymns to God" are most likely the book of Psalms and the three remaining are Proverbs, Ecclesiastes and one other. Most argue that Josephus was referring to the Song, but we cannot be sure. An even less convincing allusion possibly occurs in a statement by Ben Sirah in Sirach 47:17, "Your [Solomon's] songs, proverbs and parables." What these two citations may indicate is that the Song was associated with Solomon early on, which could in part account for its inclusion. It is not clear how the Song was read, whether as Wisdom literature (and thus a collection of poems/songs extolling human love) or as an allegory.

The traditional position, if one exists, maintains that the Song achieved canonical status in the OT because it was read symbolically/allegorically, depicting Israel's relationship to the LORD. There are a few early traditions that may affix a symbolic, though not necessarily allegorical in the strict sense, reading by the first century and early second century AD.

That the well-known Rabbi Aqiba (d. AD 135) thoroughly knew and highly esteemed the Song suggests that it had already been considered Scripture for some time. Several quotes attributed to Aqiba are important for this discussion. In the first, Aqiba disputes about the use of the Song in settings deemed inappropriate for Scripture. In *t. Sanhedrin* 12:10 he is quoted as saying, "Whoever sings the Song of Songs with a tremulous voice in a banquet hall and so treats it as a sort of ditty will not participate in the world to come." In *ʾAggadat šir hašširim* Aqiba reputedly said, "Had not the Torah been given, Canticles would have sufficed to guide the world." And perhaps the most important tradition related to the issue of canonicity is another saying attributed to Aqiba in dialogue with Rabbi Yose in the Mishnah (*m. Yad.* 3:5): "God forbid!—no man in Israel ever disputed about the Song of Songs that it does not render the hands unclean, for all the ages are not worth the day on which the Songs of Songs was given to Israel; for all the Writings are holy, but the Song of Songs is the Holy of Holies." The phrase "render the hands unclean" affirmed the

canonicity of a document. This final tradition suggests that there was still some debate in the first century regarding the canonicity of the Song and Ecclesiastes. From Aqiba's perspective, not to include the Song in the canon was unthinkable. These quotes provide evidence that a respected rabbi deemed the Song worthy of its canonical status and indicate that there was probable broad acceptance of the Song's inclusion into the canon early, at the latest by AD 100, and likely much earlier, since Aqiba's death is dated to AD 135. Further, Aqiba's outspoken disapproval of the frivolous public use of the Song implies there is an appropriate sacred use. Thus, some have concluded that the Song, although associated with Solomon and love poetry, was read symbolically. and it was this reading that led to its inclusion into the canon.

In an odd twist, four manuscripts of the Song were found among the Dead Sea Scrolls. One might wonder what a monastic group of celibate males was doing with four copies of this mildly erotic text. One of the scrolls is diminutive in size, leading to speculation that it was reduced for travel and possibly served as a devotional text. Another has a significant lacuna in which a major section of chapters 5—7 was removed. Regardless of the peculiarities of the text, it is reasonable to conclude that the Song was read as Scripture at Qumran, over a century prior to Aqiba. And while it is impossible to know exactly how it was read, given the theology and practices of that community there is good reason to believe that it was read symbolically.

The reason for the inclusion of the Song is another point that is not especially clear. Its association with Solomon may be an important contributing factor. Whether it was read as Wisdom literature alongside Proverbs and Ecclesiastes is doubtful. But having said this, it is difficult to establish what genre it was considered. The argument goes that because of its Solomonic connection, it had to be Wisdom literature and thus was initially understood as depicting love between a man and a woman. The difficulty is that this seemingly goes against the earliest readings of the Song. This broader cultural and linguistic context, when added to the Jewish narrative of God's marriage with Israel, might add a further implicit influence upon how the Song was read within Jewish communities. It is perhaps significant to mention that the earliest Christian canonical lists include the Song (as early as the end of the first century AD).

2. Jewish Interpretation.

The Song was widely read and valued throughout the history of Judaism, but it was not for the faint of heart. It was included on the short list of passages that the young and immature were forbidden to read. The power of the Song could not exist were it not for the authentic voice derived from human experience, and such explicit passion, as beautiful as it is, could lead the young astray. As noted above, the earliest attested interpretation of the Canticles is found in a few provocative appellations attributed to Rabbi Aqiba. Aqiba lived during the later part of the first and early second centuries AD. One of the most respected rabbis of his period, he died during the Bar Kochba Revolt, supporting Bar Kochba as messiah. Other traditions also suggest that Aqiba read the Song symbolically as a love song between Israel and the LORD (*m. Ta'anit* 4:8). The most substantial occurrence is found in the *Mekilta de Rabbi Ishmael*, Shirata 3:49-63, which comments on Exodus 15:2. In this text an explicit symbolic reading of parts of the Song is developed to express the intimacy between God as the Beloved and Israel (e.g., Song 5:9). The section concludes, "But Israel reply to the Nations of the World: You have no part of Him; on the contrary, 'My Beloved is mine, and I am His' (Cant 2:16), 'I am my Beloved's and Beloved is mine' (Cant 6:3)." This does not necessarily represent an allegorical interpretation, but it does suggest that the Song was read symbolically very early. Nevertheless, Aqiba's aforementioned comment about people misusing the Song in wedding banquets, etc., indicates that some regarded the text as a profane document.

A symbolic reading of the Song would not have spontaneously erupted. There existed popular notions of *hieros gamos* in the surrounding Hellenistic culture known mostly through the initiation rites and rituals of the mystery cults. These cults date back to as far as 600 BC and many promoted notions of a relationship/experience of a god within the context of human sexuality. There was already a potent, well established metaphor within Jewish traditions from which it could even more naturally develop. Within Israel's earliest history, the Torah recounts the unique, monogamous relationship expected of Israel by the LORD. As M. Weinfeld

has observed, "I will be your God, and you will be my people" (Lev 26:12) may also echo marital language. In fact, the intimate language of marriage—of love, loss, desire, yearning, separation, divorce and renewal—composes one of the dominant metaphors of the OT and is used to describe the relationship between the LORD and his people Israel. As this relationship degenerated, the prophets used marital language to address Israel's unfaithfulness to the LORD, often describing Israel's behavior pejoratively as "harlotry" (Jer 3:1-5; Ezek 16:25). We find similar motifs throughout the prophets, such as Hosea 1—3 and Isaiah 62:3-5.

The Song, however, makes no mention of past infidelities and unfaithfulness; rather, it extols a relationship in full bloom. It is in this context that Isaiah 62:3-5 may offer insight. The language of Isaiah, while acknowledging prior indiscretions, points to a new beginning and betrothal:

> You shall no more be termed Forsaken, and your land shall no more be termed Desolate; but you shall be called My Delight Is in Her, and your land Married; for the LORD delights in you, and your land shall be married. For as a young man marries a young woman, so shall your builder marry you, and as the bridegroom rejoices over the bride, so shall your God rejoice over you. (NRSV)

The Song captures in glorious detail the feelings both bridegroom and bride share for each other. E. Davis and others have argued that this vision of Isaiah for a broken Jerusalem prompted the composition of the Song, which imaginatively expanded on the theme. Certainly the symbolic world of betrothal, of the bridegroom rejoicing over the bride, provides a rich resource for Israel's theological imagination of its relationship to God. What is fascinating is that the Song includes no hint of past indiscretions or pain. If it is a composition reflecting upon the future hope for a broken Jerusalem, it is thoroughgoing in its application.

The motivation for the composition of the Song may thus be more complicated than it first appears. Whether or not the text is a loose collection of love songs or composed as an allegory from the outset, there existed within the imagination of the Jewish people the constructs that would form the basis for a symbolic and, eventually, an allegorical reading. It is impossible to know if this notion lies at the heart of the reading in the Dead Sea Scrolls or Aqiba; however, a symbolic reading of the Song does represent a shift in the use of marriage imagery from its "plain sense" meaning to understanding the relationship of the Jewish people and their God.

Although a later development, the inclusion of the Song with the other four scrolls in the *Megillot provides further information regarding how it was interpreted within Judaism. Each scroll was read during one of the feasts in the Jewish calendar. The Song comprises the first scroll and was read during Passover. Reasons for this relationship between the Song and Passover are not entirely clear; however, it most probably is because of the linkage of the exodus with the interpretation of Song of Songs 1:9 (see also the tannaitic *Mekilta de Rabbi Ishmael*) and possibly the reference to spring in Song of Songs 2:11-13. Although it is doubtful that the Megillot provides evidence for an early allegorical reading of the Song, since it is difficult to determine when this connection first occurred, it is another important piece of evidence in reconstructing the traditional reading of this book. From the point of Aqiba on, the majority of texts support an allegorical model.

The allegorical interpretation is most developed in the Targum on the Song (*see* Targumim). The Targum, an Aramaic translation/interpretation of the Song, is dated to the seventh century AD. But this is the closing date of the work. It may, and many would argue it does, contain ancient material within it, since the Targum is not simply a translation but also the received interpretation of the book throughout the ages. It presents a carefully constructed allegory of Israel's relationship with the LORD that moves from the Exodus to the coming of messiah. P. Alexander observes that in the language and various states in which the bride and bridegroom are described, the Targumist locates the communion, estrangement and reconciliation of Israel and its God. The structure and development of the Targum reflects this rhythm:

1:1—3:6   the exodus and wilderness wandering

3:7—5:1   the temple, God's presence and reception of beautiful, chaste Israel

5:2—6:1   exile and estrangement

6:2—7:9   release from exile, reconciliation, renewal

7:10—8:14   exile, renewal and coming of messiah

The allegory is both complex and thoroughgoing. The young, chaste bride represents Israel and Jerusalem, and the bridegroom is the LORD. Song of Songs 1:2 opens with the exodus, and the giving of revelation is likened to "the kisses of his mouth." In Song of Songs 1:8 the assembly of Israel is the beautiful young woman whom the bridegroom loves. And Song of Songs 1:17, which extols the beauty of the first temple, anticipates the temple to be built by the *messiah out of cedar from the Garden of Eden. Many of the details of the text are woven into the history of salvation understood in Israel's metanarrative. That it culminates with the coming of messiah offers an eschatological tone, which provides both a hopeful future and expresses the joys and sorrows of human existence.

During the medieval period an allegorical reading was dominant throughout most of the Jewish tradition, the differences occurring in the referents of the terms and phrases within the Song. However, the Jewish interpretive history did expand beyond this allegorical model. Maimonides (d. 1204), the great rabbi of the thirteenth century AD, explores a spiritual, individualized interpretation. He suggested that the Song also expressed the desire of the human soul for God. The voice of the woman captures the soul's longing for God. As with many of his positions, Maimonides's views on the Song were adopted by rabbis that followed him. Another view that had some prominence understood the virgin/bride to be personified Wisdom (Don Isaac Abrabanel). The impact of the ideas and cultural change of the Renaissance and Enlightenment would also impact the synagogue and their interpretation of the Song, but not as radically as that of Christianity. The Jewish model of interpretation was adopted from the beginning in the early Christian community, and the two communities in many ways parallel each other throughout history. This is not surprising given the interchange between the synagogue and church in many regions.

3. Early Christian and Medieval Interpretation.
The Song first becomes explicitly visible in the

Christian tradition in the work of Hippolytus, whose commentary on the Song is the earliest known. Allusions to the Song may have appeared much earlier, however, even in the NT documents themselves. As is well documented, the NT contains certain elements of the *hieros gamos* (sacred marriage) traditions. For example, Jesus employs the metaphor of the bride and bridegroom to describe his relationship to his disciples (Mt 9:15; 25:1, 5; Jn 3:29). This vivid metaphor is infused with eschatological implications and expresses metaphorically his relationship to the people of God. Although the background for nuptial imagery in the NT is much disputed and many point to its possible similarities with the Hellenistic mystery cults, there are good reasons to believe that the Song forms the basis for the tradition. The most obvious is that the theological imagination of the early Christian population was shaped primarily by the OT and the theological world of Judaism. Thus the manner in which the Song was read in early Judaism is foundational for understanding how the text was read in early Christianity. As such, it is probable that the Song lies behind Jesus' use of this concept since when read symbolically it remains one of the few positive, eschatological portrayals of nuptial imagery within the Bible. This is especially so if the Song was read symbolically during his life. The Song and the Jesus material may also lie behind the theologically rich notion of the church as the Bride of Christ (Eph 5), texts like 2 John and the image of the new Jerusalem in Revelation 21. Regardless of how one decides on this issue, there is within the pages of the NT a world of reference that includes an eschatological, even mystical relationship between God and his people.

Hippolytus of Rome (d. 235) is the first of the early Christian authors we know of who produced an actual written work on the Song, although it has only survived in pieces (Song 1:1—3:8) that are difficult to access. One of the most prolific authors of the Roman church in the early centuries, Hippolytus is important for many reasons. His work is the first extant commentary that explicitly addresses the Song in early Christianity. It seems that Origen, a younger colleague, may have visited him in Rome. Thus, it is possible that Origen's work on the Song was influenced by Hippolytus, whose views on the Song clearly support a broadly allegorical reading of it. He read it as a love song between Christ and the church. This corporate reading is important, especially in light of the more individualistic reading that would appear later. Further, in keeping with this corporate notion, he was interested in the broad salvation-historical movement of the text. Israel is replaced by the church. He is the first to interpret the male breasts of Song of Songs 1:2 (so LXX) as the two testaments. Further, his is a generally soteriological reading of the Song. Since so little of his work survives, it is difficult to be more comprehensive in one's comments; however, Hippolytus clearly establishes a symbolic/allegorical reading of the Song very early and lays the foundation for Origen's work, which would become the most influential commentary for later authors.

Origen's commentary and homilies on the Song (c. 244) are perhaps the most crucial for understanding the interpretation of the Song in the medieval period, an era in which the Song was the most loved and commented upon text of all. There are, for example, over one hundred extant commentaries and homilies on the Song from the sixth to the fifteenth centuries. This focused literary output is to a large extent reliant on the early work of Origen. Origen was born in Alexandria and moved later to Palestine, and his writings betray an awareness of Hellenistic thought while simultaneously demonstrating a profoundly Jewish influence. It is too simplistic to describe his reading of the text as allegorical, which would lead to a repressed sexuality and mystical introspection. His method is more complex than that. Careful with literary issues, he affirms that it is a marriage song composed by Solomon in the form of a drama, and he comments extensively on the literary conventions used, making reference to Greek literature. Key to understanding Origen is his prologue to the Song, in which he makes clear that his use of the allegorical method is an attempt to get at the theological relevance of the text for his audience. In his opinion, the literary character of the Song essentially demands such a reading. With regard to Origen's understanding of humanity, his work does betray an affinity to the Neo-Platonism of his day. The human person possesses an outer shell and an inner soul, and this dualism shapes his understanding of the physical and of love. He parallels the concern of the Jewish rabbis for the immature who might read the Song, suggesting that they may be led into pursuit of fleshly lust. Instead, the mature learn to listen to the Song, which speaks to the needs of the inner soul; love in the Song refers to love directed toward God. It is Origen's concern for both the plain sense of the text and the symbolic readings that shape the spiritual meaning of the text that lays the framework for the subsequent medieval commentaries. Perhaps most importantly, Origen offers both an ecclesiological, corporate reading of the Song and an individualistic one. The bridegroom is Christ and the bride the church, and what is true for the church is true for each individual. Origen opened the door to the notions of the inward spiritual journey of the individual and the marriage of the soul to God.

There are few commentators through the medieval period who interpret the Song in a literal fashion. Theodore of Mopsuestia, bishop from 392 to 428, deemed the Song a secular love song not suited for the canon and strenuously resisted Origen's approach to the text. Another, Julian of Eclanum, a Pelagian, produced a non-allegorical commentary that was subsequently challenged by Bede.

On the other hand, Jerome, in spite of his cautions against Origen, had great respect for his commentary on the Song and adopted the approach in his own work. Gregory the Great did likewise in his work on the Song, and its popularity reinforced the allegorical reading of the Song throughout the empire. The Song for Gregory may literally be a collection of erotic love poems and speeches between two lovers, but it is through this medium that God calls the soul of the believer to a more passionate embrace of his love.

A thoroughgoing Marian exegesis was first expounded by Rupert of Deutz at the beginning of the twelfth century. Deutz was a prolific author and theologian from the period. His study on the Song sought to explore the idea of the incarnation. When he considered more fully the role of Mary as the one through whom the incarnation occurred, he developed a reading of the Song with those sensitivities. Bernard of Clairvaux's commentary on the Song is perhaps the pinnacle of the medieval period, both for its literary and spiritual quality. It is powerful both in its spiritual insight and the evocative language that urges devotion and the experience of unification with God. But Bernard is clear that such passion and devotion is reserved for the monastery and that the union of the person, both body and soul, will not occur until the veil of death is crossed.

The motivation for and use of allegory in medieval texts is often represented by modern scholars as resulting from an ascetic push within the church due to a rejection of physicality and sexuality and a pursuit of spirituality. Such a negative caricature misunderstands the medieval situation and allegory. Notions of the body, human sexuality, spirituality and the pursuit of God were much more nuanced even amongst the ascetics. Medieval commentators on the Song do not betray this repulsion with the physical nor the repression that is so often attributed to them. Instead, there is more often than not an appreciation for the physical. Recent studies of this issue suggest that it is more of a projection of erotic obsession from the modern period. Rather the hermeneutic that underlies allegory marks an attempt to demonstrate the love of God through Christ in the OT documents. Nuptial imagery, the intimate love between Christ and the church and the individual soul, is perhaps the most intimate form. Further, the language from the commentators is marked by purity, and a chaste, even innocent devotion to Christ. As E. A. Matter argues, the modern mind seems fundamentally to misunderstand the medieval mind with regard to this topic.

4. Reformation Interpretation.

The Renaissance and the Reformation initiated a shift in how the Song was interpreted. Luther's work on the Song, while not thoroughgoing in its execution, is an important marker for this change in the exegesis of the book. As noted earlier, there were already in the history of interpretation those who emphasized a more literal reading that viewed it as a piece of profane literature. But these were marginal voices. In Luther we discover an important voice in the shaping of exegesis for the Reformation. He produced one of the few extended expositions on the Song, which is itself an important observation given the Song's prominence up until this time. He rejects, at least in part, the emphasis upon the individual, a mystical reading, and even the historical notion that it is a collection of love songs by Solomon for Pharoah's daughter. Instead, he intentionally attempts to chart a new course in interpretation that is historically located. His method is perhaps more important than his actual position. He suggests that the Song was written as a political encomium that addressed issues relating to the political state of Israel. Solomon's composition gives thanks to God for the love God has given to Israel. Even with his historical method, however, allegory remains a part of his practice. God is the male figure throughout the Song and the bride is the people of Israel. The woman can also represent the church and, occasionally, even the individual's soul. Luther may be less than consistent in his application of his hermeneutical model, but his work does represent a sustained attempt to break from the previous centuries of interpretation.

Calvin and many of his followers, however, maintained a more traditional, ecclesial reading of the Song. Some went so far as to argue, in a manner similar to the historical reading of the Talmud, that it detailed the history of the Protestant church, culminating with the victory over the Catholic Church. Given the hostility toward Catholicism at this time, it should not surprise us that Protestant scholars held a similar disdain for a Marian reading of the Song. Nevertheless, a renewed concern for philology, historical analysis and a critical engagement with hermeneutical assumptions that lie behind the interpretation of the text begin to emerge during this period, and would radically alter how the Song was interpreted within the community of faith. The rise of the historical-critical approach sought to establish controls or boundaries for the meaning of the text through an increasing emphasis on its historical and literary character.

5. Sixteenth- and Seventeenth-Century Roman Catholic Interpretation.

Roman Catholic interpretation of the Song remained within the broad stream of approaches that developed during the medieval period. The primary interpretation viewed the Song as an allegory depicting Christ and the church (ecclesial), but in some quarters, particularly the monasteries, there was also further exploration of the individual, inward spirituality that began with Origen. The well-known Spanish Carmelite mystics St. Teresa of Avila (1515-1582) and St. John of the Cross (1542-1591) continued with the notion of the "spiritual marriage" of the soul with Christ. The Marian interpretation also flourished. But alongside these approaches, there was also an emphasis upon the Hebrew text and philology, and an engagement of Jew-ish scholarship on the Song.

The work of Erasmus represents a progressive voice in Roman Catholicism during this period. Although he enjoyed only limited influence during his lifetime, he had a substantial impact upon the scholarship of the subsequent seventeenth century and beyond. His emphasis upon the plain sense of the text and an exegetical model that focused upon the grammatical-historical countered the mystical, individual and Marian readings that had become so deeply embedded in the medieval imagination. Several important works followed those of Erasmus that explored in greater detail the historical background for the Song. For example, H. Grotius (1583-1645) called attention to potential Hellenistic parallels for the Song. He argued that a Hellenistic provenance would mark the Song as a collection of humanistic love songs. Another influential work was that of Bishop Bossuet (1627-1704), who was one of the earliest to argue that the Song was composed as a Solomonic nuptial liturgy. These are only a few examples from a rich diversity that arose within Catholic circles. The struggle between the scholars and the monasteries was beneficial in that it helped preserve the strengths of both the allegorical and historical approaches to this complex text. It is unfortunate that this period marked the shift in the theological imagination of both Protestants and Catholics. The Song, and much that it stood for, was sidelined, and theological texts like Romans and Galatians moved to the forefront.

6. Modern Interpretation.

The transition to the modern period and the impact of the Enlightenment is writ large in the scholarly literature on the Song. The intellectual energy and curiosity of this period and its interdisciplinary engagement has led to many thoughtful analyses of the Song. It has become, however, one of the lesser studied books of Bible due to its esoteric and seemingly nontheological content. During the eighteenth and nineteenth centuries there was a decided move away from medieval allegorical interpretations to a more historically grounded model after Theodore of Mopsuestia, Origen, Luther and Erasmus. The focus shifted from ecclesial and individual spirituality to a critical investigation of its origins, language, context and the potential sources that may have influenced its composition. Perhaps as importantly, the discussion turned from how the text was read in the church or synagogue to more academic matters. If the medieval interest was almost solely in the rich allegorical interpretation of the Song that had christological, ecclesial and soteriological themes in view, the shift that began with the Reformers, Erasmus and others was marked by a concern to understand its history. Whether this latter view is as scientific as it assumes is currently being questioned, but the emphasis upon philology, the Hebrew text, archeology and literary elements has served to provide a wealth of information that would frame the context for the present-day interpreters of the Song.

There are three general approaches to the Song in modern scholarship, each with their own variations. They include: (1) The Song celebrates Israel's marriage to God through the use of cultic nuptial imagery derived from the cultures surrounding ancient Israel; (2) The song is a collection of love songs that extols the virtues of human love and nothing more; (3) The Song is an allegory that depicts the lavish love affair between God and Israel. Each of these assumes that the original compositional history provides the hermeneutical key to unlock the Song's meaning and in turn shapes how it should be read within a community of faith. From these, two further issues emerge. First, its compositional history is important since its genre, date, authorship, style, conceptual world and so forth tell us much about what the text means, but because it is poetry, this is a much more complicated issue than first appears. Second, for communities of faith that read the Song as sacred text, the relationship between its historical origins and how the text ought to be interpreted is not immediately clear.

The publication of the Akkadian and Sumerian texts opened a new world for interpreters who were looking for comparisons for the Song in the surrounding ancient Near Eastern cultures. Scholars focused upon the ancient texts and assumed that the belief systems, practices and rituals that may have existed in these cultures necessarily also existed in Israel and shaped the writing of the Song. These ancient religious rites explored and celebrated their relationship to their god in ways that are reflected in the erotic nuptial imagery. Given the difficulty in demonstrating beyond a surface level that the Song reflects such cultic rituals within Israel's cultus, the supposed similarities have not proved overly convincing for most scholars.

A more promising model that now commands the majority opinion among scholars suggests that the origin of the Song is best explained through parallels with Egyptian love poetry (thirteenth to eleventh centuries BC). The Song bears striking similarities with the Egyptian love songs (Fox), which are not tied to an experience of the divine but are simply short poems/songs that celebrate human love and affection. Similarities in language, motifs, metaphors and content may suggest that the Song derives from this period in history in Israel's history. If this is the case, then the Song is a loose collection of love songs/poetry that extols human love and probably fits well within the broader category of wisdom literature. With this identification, the interpretation of the Song and its role within a community of faith differs from that conjured by the medieval imagination. The Song now becomes a beautiful erotic poem that lauds human sexuality between a man and woman within a monogamous relationship. Some sex therapists go so far as to use it as a handbook of sorts for helping couples with difficulties in their sexual relationship.

Given the popularity of understanding the Song as a collection of humanistic love songs, one might be forgiven for disregarding other trends in scholarship which have brought to light fascinating dimensions of the Song. Rather than viewing the Song as merely a loose collection of love songs, recent interests in literary criticism have pointed out the development of themes, characters and certain dramatic elements. And although it is difficult to trace a single unifying plot, as one might expect to find in a narrative or drama, there is something of a unified whole. The inclusion of dialogue, for example, serves to assist in the creation of this unity. If there is a unity, however, an important question emerges regarding whether it is an edited collection of mildly erotic poetry, or whether the author sought to create a poetic drama. Another school of interpretation argues that the book is a drama (F. Delitzsch, C. D. Ginsberg, S. R. Driver, I. Provan). In fact, a century ago this was the dominant position. The difficulty remains, however, in determining whether there are two or three characters in addition to the chorus, and in understanding the exact nature of the plot of the drama.

Other scholarly investigations have caused

some to posit female authorship for the Song based on the voice of the woman and her behavior throughout. The woman's openness regarding her desires and pursuit of the groom is remarkable given the likely cultural constraints of the time. Others have pointed to possible theological reflection as a subtext through allusion to important biblical texts, Genesis 2—3 in particular (Trible). Although less dominant, there remains a strong voice that continues to support an allegorical reading. Much depends on the definitions of a symbolic or allegorical reading. Positions vary from a broad symbolic poetic model that does not seek to press details to a more engaged allegory. Intriguing are the allusions to the OT that are seemingly present in the Song (Is 62:3-5) that perhaps shape the message and content of the allegory (Davis), infusing it with theological content that makes a statement about Israel and its relations with God. Whether allegorical, or psychological and mystical, or simply exploring an amorous, freely expressed relationship between a male and female, the Song evokes a beauty and Edenic quality (Gen 2—3) that transcends culturally embedded notions of love and desire. The haunting question of whether the meaning of the text necessarily resides in this social and historical context of human love and passion or whether it points to another dimension has not been resolved. The twists and turns of interpretive models and their societal and cultural parallels suggest that the answer may not be easily found, but they certainly raise a host of hermeneutical issues that are fascinating to explore.

7. Hermeneutical Issues and Implications.

As mentioned above, the Song, which was once one of the most esteemed books in the canon, has fallen from its exalted position to become largely marginalized. Such a demotion is unfortunate, and modern readers are deprived as a result. The Song is one of those texts in which we encounter beauty and learn about true humanity and love, emotional and physical attraction in all its human complexity and power. When compared to expressions of human passion in the surrounding cultures of that time and ours today, however, the Song presents a different portrait of human sexuality than might be expected. While honest and authentic, it remains discrete, innocent, even naïve in some

ways. Such innocence and authenticity are evident in both the bride and groom. As is frequently noted, the bride speaks openly and without embarrassment about her desires, her passions, her sexuality and interests. She refers to his body and her desire for him without self-consciousness. This is a picture we perhaps least expect given common misconceptions about the traditional culture from which it arose. And the groom expresses himself similarly. Theologically, these observations are important for understanding the Song. Regardless of how it is read, the "plain sense" or surface reading of the text offers a robust physicality embodied in two people who extol with their community the free expression of their love, sexuality and desire for fulfillment within the confines of a monogamous relationship.

But how is a person or community in our time to read and interpret such a document? Is it a book solely about sex and love, a biblical text for sex-education classes or counselors? Or is there another level of meaning that explores the relationship between the human and the divine? Very often the historical-critical and allegorical interpretations are treated as polar opposites, apparently irreconcilable. But is this cleavage necessary? As the early and later allegorists well understood, the plain sense of the text is a crucial first step in the interpretation process.

The historical-critical approach that has characterized much of biblical scholarship over the past few centuries has contributed greatly to understanding the Song and provided some interpretive controls that limit the inherent subjectivity of other approaches. The judicious philological, cultural and historical analyses helped frame the context of the content and message of the Song. This is particularly the case with the metaphors and imagery, which demand an awareness of the cultural and linguistic context to unlock their meaning. The authority that is conferred upon the Song as a result of its reception into the canon renders the Song's exploration and expression of passion as exemplary for the community of faith. But lest one think that it be read simply on its own, the canonical location of the Song within the canon suggests further boundaries for meaning. For example, the woman who pursues her beloved in the Song is starkly contrasted with the loose, adulterous woman of

Proverbs 2:16-19. Here the canon places constraints upon the meaning of the Song and further develops the motifs of faithfulness, trust, monogamy, covenant and so forth that are implicit in the Song but explicit in the surrounding books. Regardless of whether one considers the text fundamentally as allegory, the expression of love between the man and woman within the text must itself cohere with God's view of an appropriate expression of human love and sexuality as expressed through the cultural medium of that period. Thus the Song provides a poetic expression of love and passion for the people of God in which physicality is an important element in the experience of life's beauty. And this too is a gift of God.

The overwhelming tendency of both Jewish and Christian communities has been to read the Song either symbolically or allegorically. Apart from a few disparate voices, it was not until the development of the historical-critical method that there was a noticeable shift concerning how the text was read. While there has been a need to arrive at agreed-upon controls for meaning in order to limit the almost limitless possibilities that an allegorical model offers the reader, perhaps too frequently the challenge to the allegorical reading is based on the misconception that it diminishes the import of the physical in its quest for a spiritual engagement of God. This rejection of the plain sense meaning, it is assumed, derives from a decided distrust of and distaste for physical matters, the result of a gnostic or neo-Platonic influence. While no doubt true in some cases, the better allegorical treatments devoted much energy and care to investigating the plain sense of the text. It was clear that the physical provided an authentic portrait of the human relationship with God. The Song loses its symbolic power if it lacks coherence. The use of such intimate, physical, emotive language itself validates the physical, and validates the lovers as paradigmatic.

Several questions emerge for the reader of this text. To what degree should the historical-critical method and its assumptions and conclusions, in this case unknowable conclusions regarding date, authorship, genre and historical situation, shape the reading of the text? To this one might further inquire about the role that the history of interpretation ought to play in interpreting the text. Rejection of a minority or aberrant reading is one thing, but to dismiss many centuries of a particular method may not be entirely appropriate. Further, if the Song was received into the canon based on a symbolic/allegorical reading, it seems legitimate to ask whether this does not itself provide a hermeneutical key for interpreting the book. It is perhaps the poetic nature of the Song that allows for a level of meaning beyond the literal. The poetic opens windows to worlds unknown and unexplored, inviting us to love openly and passionately, with all our being. It moves us beyond the rational, to engage all that it means to be human. It may also be that it expresses in poetic form what it means to love the Lord your God with all your heart, soul and might.

See also FEMINIST INTERPRETATION; SONG OF SONGS 1: BOOK OF; SONG OF SONGS 2: ANCIENT NEAR EASTERN BACKGROUND; TARGUMIM; WASF.

BIBLIOGRAPHY. **P. S. Alexander,** *The Targum of Canticles: Translated, with a Critical Introduction, Apparatus, and Notes* (ArBib 17A; Collegeville, MN: Liturgical Press, 2003); **A. Brenner,** "Women Poets and Authors," in *A Feminine Companion to the Song of Songs,* ed. A. Brenner (Sheffield: JSOT Press, 1993); **E. F. Davis,** *Proverbs, Ecclesiastes, and the Song of Songs* (WestBC; Louisville: Westminster John Knox, 2000); **M. V. Fox,** *The Song of Songs and the Ancient Egyptian Love Songs* (Madison, WI: University of Wisconsin, 1985); **T. Longman III,** *Song of Songs* (NICOT; Grand Rapids: Eerdmans, 2001); **E. A. Matter,** *The Voice of My Beloved: The Song of Songs in Western Medieval Christianity* (Philadelphia: University of Pennsylvania Press, 1990); **R. E. Murphy,** "History of Exegesis as Hermeneutical Tool: The Song of Songs," *BTB* 16 (1986) 87-91; idem, *The Song of Songs: A Commentary on the Book of Canticles or the Song of Songs* (Hermeneia; Minneapolis: Fortress, 1990); **R. A. Norris,** trans. and ed., *The Song of Songs: Interpreted by Early Christian and Medieval Commentaries* (The Church's Bible; Grand Rapids: Eerdmans, 2003); **M. Pope,** *Song of Songs: A New Translation with Introduction and Commentary* (AB 7C; Garden City, NY: Doubleday, 1977); **A. Robert, R. Tournay with A. Feuillet,** *Le Cantique des Cantiques: traduction et commentaire* (EBib; Paris: Librairie Lecoffre, 1963); **W. H. Schoff,** ed., *The Song of Songs: A Symposium* (Philadelphia: The Commercial Museum, 1924); **P. Trible,** *God and the Rhetoric of Sexuality* (OBT 2; Philadelphia: Fortress, 1978).

R. Beaton

SONS OF KORAH. *See* ASAPH AND SONS OF KORAH.

SOUND PATTERNS

Careful readers of Hebrew poetry, even in translation, are well aware of patterns formed by repeated thought (semantic *parallelism and occasionally *stanzas/strophes), grammar and syntax (grammatical parallelism), and even words (*wordplays). Patterns are also formed on the level of the sound of words (sound play or phonological parallelism). Sound plays are less pervasive in Hebrew poetry than semantic parallelism, and of course they may be detected only by readers of the original language. They do not carry over easily or elegantly into translation in another language.

As an occasional trope, sound patterns may be considered a secondary poetical device, though they function in both a structural and an aesthetic way. Rarely, sound plays demonstrably support the thought of a poetic line (see 2 below). Studies of Hebrew poetry often recognize four types of sound patterns: rhyme, consonance, assonance, onomatopoeia. In this article, alliteration refers to a combination of consonance and assonance.

1. Definitions
2. Functions
3. Types
4. Conclusion

1. Definitions.

In general, a sound pattern is based on the "sound-identity of words" or the "echoing of words" in near vicinity to each other (Goldsmith, 15). An obvious example of a sound pattern comes from the children's verse "Peter Piper picked a pair of pickled peppers." The constant repetition of the consonant *p* links these words together, but so does the predominance of *i* and *e* vowels.

The repetition of consonants is consonance, while assonance indicates the near identity of the vowel sounds. When both assonance and consonance occur in a poetic line, it is referred to as alliteration. Some interpreters, however, use *alliteration* and *consonance* as synonyms in reference to consonantal sound patterns (see Watson, 225-26; *contra* McCreesh, 27; Goldsmith, 15-16). Whereas alliteration and assonance permeate a poetic unit, rhyme exists between two or more whole words. Take the English proverb "A

stitch in time saves nine," where "time" and "nine" create a jingle. Onomatopoeia is also on the level of the word, in this case the single word, whose meaning and sound are related. A snake's "hiss" and an owl's "hoot" provide helpful examples.

It is often difficult to determine when these sound patterns occur in Hebrew poetry. After all, language has a limited number of consonants and, especially, of vowels, so accidental congruence is a genuine possibility. From the given examples below, however, it is hard to escape the idea that the ancient poets were conscious of these devices and used them to enhance their poems.

2. Functions.

Why do poets bother to create sound plays? Specifically, why do ancient Hebrew poets expend creative energy forming patterns of sounds? Looking at the same question from a different perspective, we can ask, "What effects do alliteration, assonance, rhyme and onomatopoeia have on the hearer/reader of poetry?"

In the first place, we recognize sounds patterns as part of a panoply of artistic devices available to the poet to draw attention not only to the message of the poem but also to its beauty. In other words, sound plays serve an aesthetic function. Poets are concerned about how they present their message as well as the thought content of their poetry. Poetry is artificial language, which is distanced from everyday speech. Indeed, literary prose is also artificial, but less so. Alliteration draws attention to itself. Of course, in everyday conversation someone might very occasionally voice an alliterative statement. If too much alliteration is used, however, the speaker is considered affective (a negative assessment). On the other hand, multiple sound plays often enhance the beauty of the poem. Sound plays also indicate that even if the poems were not composed orally, which they may have been, they were certainly to be heard, since that is the realm in which sound plays have their effect.

Sound plays do more than beautify language, though that is important enough. They often create cohesion in a literary unit. In Hebrew poetry that unit is most often the verse or poetic line. In this way, sound patterns, which might be considered a type of phonological parallelism (Cooper, 86-93), support the cohesion provided by semantic and grammatical parallelism.

Though the phenomenon is rarely attested, sound plays can support the meaning of a passage. One of the most developed discussions of this phenomenon, however, is found in the study of Nahum 1:10 by A. Cooper (86-88).

> kî ʿad-sîrîm sĕbūkîm ûkĕsobʾām šebûʾîm
> ʾukkĕlû kĕqaš yābēš mālēʾ
> Like thorns they are entangled,
>   like drunkards stinking of drink;
> they will be fully consumed like dry stubble.

In a context that speaks of drunkards, the verse uses a superabundance of sibilants that produce a kind of slurry effect that mimics drunken speech. (Note also the use of many sibilants in Job 12:25, a verse that refers to the staggering of drunkards.)

3. Types.

3.1. Rhyme.
Rhyme occurs when two or more words sound the same. A rhyme is not dependent on identical or nearly identical consonantal or vowel sounds. Although critics suggest a number of different categories of rhymes based on whether the rhyme exists in the last syllable, the second-to-last stressed syllable and so forth, the scarcity of rhyme in Hebrew does not invite further development here.

This is not to deny the existence of some rhyme in Hebrew. After all, in Genesis 1:2 the primordial heavens and earth are described in what is certainly an intentional rhyme as tōhû wābōhû ("formless and void")

Though present, rhyme does not appear to be a significant interest of ancient poets (or of prose writers, as the Genesis passage reminds us). At least that is the persuasive position of W. Watson (232), who says that "some cases of rhyme may be fortuitous, due to the limited number of word-endings available." In other words, rhyming may be purely accidental in a language such as Hebrew, which forms words in predictable ways. Even so, M. O'Connor represents scholars who defend the idea that Hebrew poets had a larger appreciation and more frequent use of rhyme. His arguments have some persuasive power to them. Among other things, he points to Arabic poetry (a Semitic language like Hebrew), which clearly utilizes rhyme, and to C. Krahmalkov's study of neo-Punic poetry.

Based on the evidence that we have, it is probably best not to deny that poetry has rhyme, but we should not expect widespread use. We should be hesitant to ascribe rhyme to a passage if the connection is drawn through common grammatical features. Even more, any attempt to emend a text to reconstruct rhyme should be abandoned.

3.2. Consonance.
Consonance occurs when a particular consonantal sound dominates a poetic unit. This may be a single consonant, but more often it is a group of related consonants. Consonants may be grouped according to how they are formed by the mouth, throat and lips. In the example from Nahum 1:10, the consonance is formed by sibilants (produced by a stream of air directed through a narrow passage in the mouth toward the teeth: ṣādê, sāmek, šîn, śin, zayin). Proverbs 30:20 has a predominance of labials (articulated with both lips or the lower lip and the upper teeth). They include bêt, mêm, pê:

> kēn derek ʾiššâ mĕnāʾāpet
> ʾāklâ ûmāhātâ pîhā
> wĕʾāmrâ lōʾ-pāʿaltî ʾāwen
> This is the way of an adulterous woman:
> she eats and wipes her mouth,
> and she says, "I have done nothing wrong!"

The use of labials likely suggested itself to the poet because of the intent of the verse, which draws attention to the mouth of the adulterous woman.

Nahum 1:10 and Proverbs 30:20 demonstrate consonance supporting the meaning of the passages, but it is more often the case that consonance is not directly related to the meaning but rather serves a cohesive function, helping to bind the poetic line. Proverbs 13:17 uses labials in a proverb on messengers:

> malʾāk rāšāʿ yippōl bĕrāʿ
> wĕṣîr ʾĕmûnîm marpēʾ
> A wicked messenger will fall into evil,
> but a reliable envoy brings healing.

3.3. Assonance.
To repeat, assonance refers to the "sound-identity" of vowels and is thus the flip side of consonance. Semitic language has three classes of vowels (a, e/i, o/u). With only three classes of vowels, the possibility of accidental assonance is likely, though it is also likely that poets on some occasions exploited vocalic

sounds to produce an effect that they thought pleasing and also perhaps produced cohesion.

Ecclesiastes 7:2 provides an example. The transliteration demonstrates the frequency of *i/e* vowels that does not seem coincidental:

> *ṭôb lāleket ʾel-bêt-ʾēbel*
> *milleket ʾel-bêt mišteh*
> Better to go to a house of mourning
> than to go to a house of drinking.

3.4. Alliteration. Alliteration refers to those occasions where both assonance and consonance are found. An example that borders on rhyme is seen in Song of Songs 1:3:

> *šemen tûraq šĕmekā*
> Your name is poured-out oil.

3.5. Onomatopoeia. Here the sound play has to do with the origins of the word itself. The word's sound is related to its meaning. Watson (235) provides an excellent example from Song of Songs 1:2, where the word Hebrew word for *kiss* is formed from a sound that resembles a kiss:

> *yiššāqēnî minnĕšiqōt pîhû*
> Let him kiss me with the kisses of his mouth.

4. Conclusion.
Sound patterns such as rhyme, consonance, assonance, alliteration and onomatopoeia are part of the Hebrew poets' strategy for ornamenting their language and occasionally supporting their message or, even more frequently, imposing cohesion on a poetic unit, particularly the line. On many occasions we are left to guess whether the "sound-identity" of a poem is accidental or occasional. On virtually all occasions it is impossible to replicate the sound pattern in English or other languages without sounding stilted. Even so, the careful reader of Hebrew poetry will be sensitive to the potential presence of such patterns.

See also HEBREW LANGUAGE; POETICS, TERMINOLOGY OF; WORDPLAY.

BIBLIOGRAPHY. **A. Cooper,** "Biblical Poetics: A Linguistic Approach" (Ph.D. diss., Yale University, 1976); **U. R. Goldsmith,** "Alliteration," in *Princeton Encyclopedia of Poetry and Poetics*, ed. A. Preminger (Princeton, NJ: Princeton University Press, 1965) 15-16; **C. R. Krahmalkov,** "Two New-Punic Poems in Rhymed Verse," *Revista di studi fenici* 2 (1975) 169-205; **T. P. McCreesh,** *Biblical Sound and Sense: Poetic Sound Patterns in Proverbs 10-29* (JSOTSup 128; Sheffield: JSOT Press, 1991); **M. O'Connor,** *Hebrew Verse Structure* (Winona Lake, IN; Eisenbrauns, 1980); **W. G. E. Watson,** *Classical Hebrew Poetry: A Guide to Its Techniques* (2nd ed.; London: T & T Clark, 2005); **J. P. van der Westhuizen,** "Assonance in Biblical and Babylonian Hymns of Praise," *Semitics* 7 (1980) 81-101.   T. Longman III

SPACIALITY. *See* SOCIAL-SCIENTIFIC APPROACHES.

SPIRIT, DIVINE. *See* DIVINE PRESENCE.

STANDARD BIBLICAL HEBREW. *See* HEBREW LANGUAGE.

STANZA, STROPHE

The terms *canto, stanza* and *strophe* refer to structural divisions within a poem. Scholars use these terms with different meanings, and so confusion often accompanies their use. Further, disagreement exists whether such terminology is appropriate for Hebrew poetry. This article describes the issues and debate.

The study of these larger structural units takes a practical turn in the formatting of modern translations. Stanza/strophe divisions typically are marked by an additional space. Thus, translators must make determinations of structure in order to format the psalm.

1. Definitions
2. Do Hebrew Poems Have Stanzas/ Strophes?
3. Examples
4. Conclusion

1. Definitions.
Canto, stanza and *strophe* are the most popular terms for verse formations in Hebrew poetry above the level of the individual poetic line (although van der Lugt [522-35] and Watson [168-200] use *strophe* in reference to the line). The language derives from the analysis of classical poetry. Indeed, the word *strophe* comes from the Greek word for "turn" and refers to the fact that the Greek chorus would walk in a certain direction on stage when delivering a speech and then turn to deliver the next unit (the antistrophe). In classical poetry these poetical units normally were of the same length.

Unfortunately, the terminology has not been used consistently in the study of Hebrew poetry. For instance, most scholars use *strophe* and *stanza* interchangeably in reference to any grouping of verses above the poetic line. Others, such as W. Watson (160-63), argue that stanzas are composed of strophes. He notes that a possible etymology of *stanza* is from the Italian for "room," and that the stanzas are like the rooms of a house, while the strophes are the furniture that composes the room. Although it is unlikely that *stanza* has this etymology, the picture image clarifies Watson's understanding of the relationship of the parts of a poem. P. van der Lugt (72) now prefers the term *canto* to *stanza*.

The rest of this article focuses on the question of the existence of larger structures in Hebrew poems. Rather than using *strophe* to refer to the elements that compose a stanza (alternately canto), I will use *stanza* and *strophe* interchangeably (and avoid *canto*) to refer to macrostructures within a poem.

2. Do Hebrew Poems Have Stanzas/Strophes?
Van der Lugt (1-68) has performed an important service by narrating the history of the discussion of macrostructure of Hebrew poems from the early nineteenth century to the early twenty-first century. The first scholar to use strophe as a category in the study of Hebrew poetry was J. L. Saalschütz in 1825. He delineated four marks that help distinguish the strophes of a poem: (1) *acrostic; (2) *refrain; (3) the Hebrew term *selâ;* (4) content (see van der Lugt, 4). As we will see, these markers are still considered significant.

Since the time of Saalschütz to the present day (see van der Lugt; Watson; de Moor) a minority of scholars have focused on the analysis of strophic structures. Indeed, in his commentary on the Psalms, S. Terrien constructed his outline of each psalm on an investigation of strophic structure. On the other hand, from soon after Saalschütz to the present day there have also been naysayers. Although it is hard to deny that certain psalms fall into sections larger than the poetic line, these are rarely regular, uniform divisions. Also, as we can already see from Saalschütz's four markers of strophes, some (acrostic, refrain, *selâ*) do not occur widely in Hebrew poetry and do not always coincide with the fourth category, content.

For instance, in Psalm 67 a refrain appears: "May the peoples praise you, God; may all the peoples praise you" (Ps 67: 3, 5). But does it separate stanzas? A close look suggests that it does not. It is more likely that it serves as a kind of *inclusio in the middle of the poem, surrounding Psalm 67:4, which also has the form of a wish.

The term *selâ* may, indeed may often, separate units within a poem. The use of *selâ* in Psalm 3 roughly divides logical units in the poem (though one might expect a *selâ* after Ps 3:6) and also brings the psalm to closure. But *selâ* also occurs in contexts where there is no obvious major break between sections (i.e., Ps 4:4; 68:32).

When all is said and done, it should be recognized that most poems divide nicely into larger units based on content, sometimes bolstered by rhetorical devices such as acrostic, refrain and *selâ*. Watson (163), in my view, gets it right when he states, "It is generally agreed that (a) stanza division tends to be based on content; (b) there are certain stanza-markers showing where stanzas begin and/or end and (c) there are no hard and fast rules. It is a matter of feel." As we will observe in the examples below, these stanza markers include a judicious use of acrostic, refrain, *selâ* and content.

3. Examples.
3.1. Marked by Acrostic. Acrostics are clear and undisputed markers of structure within psalms, and examiners of strophic structure have devoted a lot of attention to them. That said, in most cases, acrostics are really better indicators of structure on the level of the poetic line, since most acrostics have a new letter every line and do not form larger structures (see Pss 111; 112). There are two exceptions to this rule. The first and the most impressive is Psalm 119. This psalm changes successive letters in eight-verse blocks. These eight-verse blocks also utilize eight different Hebrew words that are in the semantic domain of "law." These two features produce a magnificent poem of twenty-two strophes. Lamentations 3 is a second example. While Lamentations 1; 2; 4 are verse-by-verse acrostics, Lamentations 3 moves to a successive letter in three-verse blocks (see Longman).

3.2. Marked by Refrain. Previously, we noted that refrains do not always indicate strophes; sometimes they provide emphasis on a theme within the psalm or serve some other purpose. They rarely divide the psalm into even or nearly even sections. Even so, it is hard to deny that at least occasionally refrains provide closure to a major unit within a psalm that could be called a strophe. Psalms 42—43 are good examples. It is commonly recognized that these two psalms were originally one psalm, as is indicated by the thrice-repeated refrain "Why are you cast down, O my soul, and why are you disquieted within me? Hope in God; for I shall again praise him, my help and my God" (Ps 42:5, 11; 43:5). The refrain neatly divides the poem into three units, with the refrain serving to close the strophes (Ps 42:1-5, 6-11; 43:1-5). For a full discussion of this topic, see Raabe.

3.3. Marked by Content. Here is where Watson's assertion that structural analysis is a "matter of feel" comes most into play, although typically appeal can be made to rhetorical features of the psalm. Psalm 98 can serve as an example. A close reading indicates that this psalm falls into three equal strophes (Ps 98:1-3, 4-6, 7-9). Each strophe calls on its hearers to praise God. The dynamism of the psalm is in part that the group of hearers expands from strophe 1 (Israel) to strophe 2 (all the inhabitants of the earth) to strophe 3 (all creation, animate and inanimate). Further, each strophe praises God for different reasons. The first praises God as Israel's Savior, the second as the earth's King, and the third as the Judge of all creation. Finally, there is also movement in terms of the time frame. Strophe 1 looks to the past, strophe 2 considers the present, and strophe 3 looks to the future.

3.4. Marked by Generic Components. Modern scholars recognize typical components of the major genres of the psalms. A lament, for instance, often contains an invocation, pleas to God for help, complaints, a confession of sin or assertion of innocence, *imprecations, a statement of confidence in God's response and/or a *hymn (*see* Lament, Psalms of). Not every lament has all these elements, but whatever elements a particular psalm contains may indicate stanza/strophe breaks. An outline of Psalm 69 looks like this:

Invocation and Initial Plea to God for Help (v. 1a)
First Complaint (vv. 1b-4)
Confession of Sin (vv. 5-6)
Second Complaint (vv. 7-12)
Second Plea to God for Help (vv. 13-18)
Third Complaint (vv. 19-21)
Imprecation (vv. 22-28)
Third Plea to God for Help (v. 29)

Hymn of Praise (vv. 30-36)

3.5. Marked by šelâ. Among the more intriguing features of certain psalms (and Hab 3) is the appearance of the Hebrew word šelâ. This word occurs within the body of the psalm but not in the verse itself. It appears to be some kind of direction for the performance of the psalm. Much uncertainty surrounds its meaning and translation (see Craigie, 76-77). The problem is that more than one possible philological argument can be made, and since the word does not appear in a sentence, context gives no guidance to the lexicographer. This problem goes back to ancient times, since the versions translate the word in different directions.

Our present interest in šelâ does not require that we define its meaning; rather, we are interested in whether it might mark stanza/strophe divisions in those psalms in which it appears. In some cases (such as Psalm 3) it seems to appear in places of major division in the thought of the psalm, but in some psalms (see Ps 68:7) šelâ appears in the middle of a sentence. The best that can be said is that šelâ occasionally may help modern interpreters confirm stanza divisions that they would likely recognize through close attention to the transitions (whether content or generic) of the psalm.

4. Conclusion.

Attention to the issue of stanzas/strophes within a poem reminds readers of Hebrew poetry that there are larger units within a poem than the poetic line. The line is where most scholarly attention is directed. However, attempts to develop scientific-type criteria for the determination of boundaries are likely to fail. Although the markers discussed above (acrostic, refrain, šelâ, content, genre components) will often aid the interpreter, in the final analysis the delineation of the structure of a poem is, to repeat the words of Watson, a "matter of feel."

See also ACROSTIC; LYRIC POETRY; MUSIC, SONG; PARALLELISM; POETICS, TERMINOLOGY OF; REFRAIN.

BIBLIOGRAPHY. **P. C. Craigie,** *Psalms 1-50* (WBC 19; Waco, TX: Word, 1983); **J. C. de Moor,** "The Art of Versification in Ugarit and Israel II: The Formal Structure," *UF* 10 (1978) 187-217; **T. Longman III,** *Jeremiah and Lamentations* (NIBC; Peabody, MA: Hendrickson, 2008); **P. R. Raabe,** *Psalm Structures: A Study of Psalms with Refrains* (JSOTSup 104; Sheffield; JSOT Press,

1990); **J. L. Saalschütz**, *Von der Form der hebräis-chen Poesie, nebst einer Abhandlung über die Musik der Hebräer* (Königsburg: A. W. Unzer, 1825); **P. W. Skehan,** "Strophic Patterns in the Book of Job," *CBQ* 23 (1961) 125-42; **S. Terrien,** *The Psalms: Strophic Structure and Theological Commentary* (Grand Rapids: Eerdmans, 2003); **P. van der Lugt,** *Cantos and Strophes in Biblical Hebrew Poetry: With Special Reference to the First Book of the Psalter* (OtSt 53; Leiden: E. J. Brill, 2006); **W. G. E. Watson,** *Classical Hebrew Poetry: A Guide to Its Techniques* (2d ed.; London: T & T Clark, 2005).   T. Longman III

STORM IMAGERY. *See* CHAOS AND DEATH.

STORY. *See* NOVELLA, STORY, NARRATIVE.

STRONGHOLD. *See* ARCHITECTURE; PROTECTION IMAGERY.

STROPHE. *See* STANZA, STROPHE.

SUFFERING

Suffering is evidence that something is terribly wrong with the world. The pain, loss, distress and affliction connected to suffering are problematic in a world created and ruled over by God. At times it appears that suffering trumps the goodness of God. However, there is more emphasis in Scripture on how people respond to suffering than on explaining the origin of suffering. This article takes a thematic approach to suffering in *Psalms, *Lamentations, *Proverbs, *Job and *Ecclesiastes and examines the causes of suffering, the responses to suffering, God's relationship to suffering and, finally, the resolution of suffering. Although the agony of suffering is fully expressed in the laments, there are clear affirmations that God's justice will ultimately prevail.

1. The Causes of Suffering
2. Responses to Suffering
3. God's Relationship to Suffering
4. The Resolution of Suffering

1. The Causes of Suffering.
1.1. Sin, Wickedness, Foolishness. The psalms express the wide range of human experience and emotion, from the praise of the *hymns to the pain of the *laments. The laments are a response to suffering and can be used to explore some of the causes of suffering. The source of

trouble in the laments is either God, or the enemy, or the self, which threatens one's relationship with God, one's social standing in the community or the meaning of life (Westermann 1981a, 169-71). Psalm 13:1-2 seems to have all three in view. Sandwiched between God and enemies, the psalmist engages in self-examination over the experience of sorrow (Ps 13:2). Such despair over the affect of suffering is not sinful, but there are times when suffering is caused by one's own sin. For example, sin brings alienation from God and the possibility of his judgment (Ps 6:1; 51:11; 102:2). Sin causes inner spiritual turmoil, disrupts a person's well-being (Ps 6), and may cause physical distress (Ps 32:3-4). Alienation from God because of sin brings misery, and the only way to gain relief is to confess the sin to God and receive cleansing and restoration (Ps 51).

According to the book of Proverbs, a person's own foolishness and wickedness can cause suffering. Part of the purpose of Proverbs is to demonstrate the negative consequences of foolishness and wickedness so that people will walk in the way of wisdom and *righteousness in order to experience the benefits that come from wisdom. A rejection of wisdom may lead to calamity, terror, distress and anguish (Prov 1:24-27). People who reject wisdom will eat the fruit of their way (Prov 1:31), which ultimately includes ruin and death (Prov 1:32; 2:22; 9:18). Although it is clear that sin and *folly may lead to suffering, not all suffering can be related in a mechanical way to foolishness and sin.

1.2. The Actions of Enemies/Others. A lament psalm might focus on the enemies as the cause of the suffering. They are hard to identify because of the typical and metaphorical language used to describe them. Such language allows the enemies to be broadly defined as those who are troubling anyone who uses the psalms (Miller). The enemy can be personal, such as a close companion who becomes a traitor (Ps 41:9; 55:13), or a national enemy, like Babylon, which conquered Israel and destroyed Jerusalem and the temple (Ps 137). Such nations were instruments of God's judgment against the sinfulness of Israel (Lam 1:5). Yet, there is hope expressed in the pleas for the renewal of Israel (Ps 79:9; Lam 5:21) and judgment for the nations (Ps 79:6-7; Lam 1:22). Others, though not necessarily termed enemies, can be the cause of suffering. The wicked display antisocial behavior that is disruptive of the community, which may lead to injustice (Prov 14:31). The kings and the judges were supposed to uphold justice, but wicked kings and unjust judges could also be the source of oppression (Prov 13:23). Thus many times suffering is the result of external causes brought about by the actions of others.

1.3. Unfulfilled Expectations of Life. When life does not turn out as it should for the wise and the righteous, the result can be inner turmoil, despair and struggle with the meaning of life. Psalm 73 struggles with the prosperity of the wicked—a struggle that almost led to the conclusion that it was vain to live for God (Ps 73:13). The psalmist wrestled with this question so much that it became a wearisome task (Ps 73:16) and almost resulted in stumbling (Ps 73:1). *Qohelet had the same struggle with the apparent unfulfilled expectations of a life lived by wisdom. Not only does wisdom not deliver on its promises, but also the righteous experience what the wicked deserve while the wicked experience what the righteous deserve (Eccles 8:14). Although there is reward *(ḥēleq)* to labor that should be enjoyed (Eccles 2:10; 9:9), there is no profit *(yitrôn)* to labor (Eccles 1:2; 2:11). It does not really matter if one is wise or a fool, for the wise die just like the foolish (Eccles 2:13-14). Qohelet wonders why he was so wise (Eccles 2:15), and he asserts, "I hated life" and "I hated all my toil" (Eccles 2:17-18). The benefits of wisdom fall short for the righteous and the wise, which is a source of Qohelet's struggle with the meaninglessness of life.

1.4. Frustration with God.

1.4.1. Lament Psalms. Unfulfilled expectations cannot be separated from one's relationship with God, for God has promised certain things to his people. The lament psalms give voice to suffering and are a legitimate way to express frustration with God when he is perceived as part of the problem (Ps 13:1). Psalm 22 moves back and forth between the psalmist's horrible situation and what is known to be true about God. How does one reconcile being abandoned by God (Ps 22:1-2) with God's deliverance of his people in the past (Ps 22:3-5)? How does one reconcile the mocking treatment of the psalmist by others (Ps 22:6-8) with the psalmist's own close relationship to God from the womb (Ps 22:9-11)? Although W. Brueggemann may be too venturesome when he says that the supremacy of God, the greater party in the relationship, is

called into question in the laments, and that all power relations are under review, he is correct to affirm that the speech of the petitioner is heard, and that it is appropriate to raise justice questions before the throne. There are times when the psalmist struggles with God's lack of response to suffering. In Psalm 88 the psalmist is facing a crisis situation, and three times prayer goes out to God for help (Ps 88:2, 9b, 13), but each time there is no response from God. The situation is not resolved, and the psalm ends in darkness (Ps 88:18).

1.4.2. Job. God also becomes a problem from Job's perspective. Whereas *Satan complained that God had hedged Job in and protected him (Job 1:10), Job complains that God has confined him (hedged him in) to his situation of suffering (Job 3:23). Job perceives God as a hunter who pursues the prey so that he experiences "the terrors of God" (Job 6:4 NASB). Job wishes that God would leave him alone and quit harassing him (Job 7:17-19). He sees himself in contention with God without any possibility of winning because God destroys the blameless and the wicked (Job 9:17-19, 22). In fact, it seems that God has given Job over to the wicked (Job 16:11), and that God is Job's enemy (Job 30:20-21). In the midst of his struggle Job states that he loathes his life (Job 10:1). G. von Rad points out that suffering is not the real problem of the book, but rather God's role in the suffering. God himself has become the enemy (Westermann 1981b, 45), expressed in accusations against God (Job 16:9, 19:7-12).

1.4.3. Lamentations. The book of Lamentations, which contains five laments related to the fall of Jerusalem, also wrestles with God in a situation of grievous suffering. God is the one who has brought this calamity against his people because of their sin (Lam 1:13-14). God is a divine warrior who has fought against his people like an enemy (Lam 2:4-5). He has abandoned his people, leaving them without hope (Lam 2:7; 3:18). God is challenged to see the horrible suffering of the people (Lam 2:20). The book ends with a focus on God's anger without resolution of the problem (Lam 5:21-22). Although E. Gerstenberger refers to God as scornful, it may be better to understand God as faithful to his covenant promises of judgment, for as Gerstenberger notes, there is confession of sin but no protestations of innocence in Lamentations.

1.4.4. Ecclesiastes. Whereas Job addressed

God directly and pursued him with passion, Qohelet does not address God directly. God is always called Elohim, never Yahweh, which is the more personal covenant name of God. The first time God is mentioned (Eccles 1:13) is to assert that he has given to human beings "a grievous task" (NASB), which is a negative statement no matter how one understands *ra*ʿ ("evil, grievous"). Although God is within the horizon of Qohelet's view, he is never brought in as a solution to the problems with which Qohelet is struggling. Part of the reason is that it is impossible for anyone, including the wise, to figure out what God is doing in the world (Eccles 3:11; 8:16-17). The unfulfilled expectations of life are related to a breakdown of the deed-consequence relationship, with the result that the righteous and the wicked do not get their due rewards (Eccles 2:15-17). Qohelet should be comforted that the deeds of the righteous and the wise are in the hand of God, but that makes little difference. One cannot be sure what lies ahead, because in the end it does not really matter if one is righteous or wicked (Eccles 9:1-2). Overall, God is distant and is to be approached carefully (Eccles 5:1-3, 7), which has implications for how one understands the "fear of God" in sections of Qohelet's struggle (see Longman). Although some (e.g., Whybray) argue for a joyous Qohelet, others (e.g., Crenshaw 1987, 73) argue that there is not the warmth of a trusting relationship with God in Qohelet. The confusing nature of the ways of God in the world is a source of despair. The key word of the book is *hebel,* used in the refrain "Utterly meaningless! Everything is meaningless" (Eccles 1:2 NIV).

2. Responses to Suffering.

A key term that describes a sufferer is ʿ*ānî,* with ʿ*ŏnî* describing the situation of suffering, both physical and mental. These terms occur regularly in Psalms, Lamentations and Job where suffering and responses to suffering are described. Many times ʿ*ānî* describes the spiritual condition of the sufferer as one who belongs to the people of Israel (Ps 72:2), who cries out to Yahweh (Ps 34:6), and who is delivered (Ps 35:10). The affliction itself can cause the sufferer to turn to God (Ps 25:16).

2.1. Submission and Worship. Just as there are a variety of causes to suffering, so there are a variety of responses to suffering. Job's initial response to suffering is submission. After losing his

children, his wealth (Job 1:13-19) and his health (Job 2:7-8), he responds with *worship. He acknowledges God's sovereignty (Job 1:20-21), refuses to curse God, and is willing to accept both good and calamity from God (Job 2:9-10). Although Job does not know what has gone on between Satan and God in the heavenly council and thus does not understand his suffering, he worships God. The challenge by Satan, that God is worthy of being worshiped only because he is the dispenser of blessings (Job 1:9-10; 2:4-5), is shown to be false by Job's initial response to his suffering.

2.2. Questions. Worship and submission are the right way to respond to suffering, but many times such a response comes at the end of a process of wrestling with God, which is described in the laments. Whenever God seems distant and unresponsive, it is natural for questions to arise. Many times these questions wrestle with what appears to be the ineffectiveness of God's own covenant promises. The questions in Psalm 89:46-48 come in the context of the troubles of the monarchy. Has God renounced his covenant promises to *David (Ps 89:38-39)? Questions also arise because the lack of response from God is not in character with the way God has acted in the past (Ps 22:3-5) and in the psalmist's own life (Ps 22:9-11). The questions in Psalm 88:10-12 are a way for the psalmist to continue to appeal to God to act in the situation of suffering. They show the desperate nature of the crisis and plead with God to do something before death takes over and the opportunity for God to demonstrate his covenant faithfulness is gone. Psalm 88 ends in darkness and leaves the psalmist in an unresolved situation.

The book of Lamentations also describes an unresolved situation. The high point of the book comes in the middle poem, where the steadfast love and faithfulness of God are affirmed (Lam 3:22-27). The rest of the book continues to lament the suffering. The book ends with a "why" question addressed to God, a plea for God to restore the people, and a reminder of the cause of the suffering (Lam 5:20-22).

The questions in the lament psalms and Lamentations are not arrogant, challenging questions but rather are questions that arise out of a covenant relationship with God. Not only do they call on God to be faithful to his covenant promises, but also they are a way to express the deep anguish of soul in the midst of suffering. Life does not always turn out the way people expect, and there are times when God seems absent and his covenant promises unfulfilled. But these questions are ultimately the response of faith in God. They do not express mere resignation to the situation of suffering but rather demonstrate the hope that God will act in faithfulness to the covenant promises. Ultimately, they are an acknowledgment of the goodness and faithfulness of God.

2.3. Perseverance. A key question in the midst of suffering is whether the sufferer will persevere in faith. The lament psalms move beyond the questions toward the praise of God. There must come a time when the sufferer worships God even if the situation does not appear to have a resolution. Otherwise, the questions might turn into challenges to God's sovereignty and justice. Such a scenario happens to Job, whose response of submission changes in Job 3 with his curse (Job 3:1-10) and his lament (Job 3:11-26). Job moves from a compliant, submissive response to a challenging, questioning one. The stark reality of this change is seen when one compares Job 1:11; 2:5, 9, where the issue is whether Job will curse God, with Job 3:1, where Job "cursed the day of his birth" (NIV). Although Job curses something that is in the past and cannot be altered, it shows the change in Job. He moves from a God-centered emphasis to a human-centered focus. The lament ends with a barrage of "I" and "my" pronouns (Job 3:24-26). Instead of waiting on God, Job waits on death (Job 3:21) because he has lost the purpose for living (Job 3:23). God is now seen as a problem. Instead of protecting Job by putting a hedge around him (Job 1:10), God has confined him to this situation of suffering so that he cannot escape (Job 3:23). God seems to be on trial as Job questions God's justice in asserting that God destroys both the blameless and the wicked, and that God mocks the calamity of the innocent (Job 9:20-23). It is apparent that unrelieved suffering of the kind Job experienced may produce shifts in attitudes toward God and toward the suffering itself. One now wonders whether Job has gone too far, whether he will persevere, and whether true wisdom will be found to help Job in his struggles.

3. God's Relationship to Suffering.
One of the key issues of suffering is the relationship of suffering to God. Israel affirms the goodness and faithfulness of God, who pours out covenant blessings upon his people. God is the sovereign Creator, who has the power to implement his justice in the world. God is also near to his people and is their shield and defender. Thus it is a problem when justice is not evident and blessings are not experienced by God's people.

3.1. The Sovereignty of God. Although suffering may at times appear to call into question God's justice, the Wisdom literature clearly affirms that God is sovereign and is in control of the events of this life. Every event falls under the sovereign control of God, even the casting of the lot into the lap (Prov 16:33). People can make all kinds of plans, but the purposes of Yahweh will stand (Prov 19:21). Instead of seeing God as sovereign, N. Habel argues that in Job 1—2 God is presented as a capricious, arbitrary deity, more like a Canaanite god, who destroys a human being to win a wager with Satan. However, J. Hartley points out that the discussion is not a wager, for no sum was set to be handed over to the winner. Rather, God is sovereign over Satan and the tragedies that come into Job's life, as each time God places limits on what Satan can do (Job 1:12, 2:6). Job's initial responses to his suffering focus on God as the ultimate source of all things, including blessing and tragedy (Job 1:21-22; 2:9-10).

3.2. The Mystery of God's Ways.

3.2.1. The Deed-Consequence Relationship Is Not Mechanical. J. Crenshaw (1995, 396-97) argues that the book of Proverbs is a didactic obstacle to biblical salvation faith because the emphasis on wealth goes against other Scriptures that focus on the plight of the poor, eventually leading to a collapse of the view of *retribution. However, an understanding of the nature of the genre of a proverb as not giving the whole picture (Waltke), along with a more nuanced view of the structure of Proverbs (Van Leeuwen 1992), leads to much different conclusions. Many of the proverbs in Proverbs 10—15 are antithetical sayings that set forth the contrast between the wise and the foolish, or the righteous and the wicked. On the one hand, the wicked will be cut off (Prov 2:22; 10:27) and come to ruin (Prov 3:25); on the other hand, the righteous will experience God's blessings, which include security (Prov 1:33), favor with God and people (Prov 3:4; 12:2), healing (Prov 3:8), wealth (Prov 3:16; 10:22) and long life (Prov 3:16; 10:27). The blessings of wisdom are rooted in the fear of Yahweh (*see* Fear of the Lord), so that the blessings of wisdom ultimately come from God. Thus, it is a mistake to draw a mechanical connection between righteousness and these blessings. There is mystery in the way life works out. Proverbs itself recognizes the possibility of the suffering of the wise and the prosperity of the wicked. The blessings of wisdom, such as health, wealth and long life, are not absolute goods in this life. This is clearly set forth in the "better than" sayings, such as, "Better is a little with righteousness than great income with injustice" (Prov 16:8 NASB). Having less wealth with righteousness is better than having more wealth with injustice. Wealth is a relative good, subordinated to righteousness. Thus, to be poor does not necessarily indicate that one is not wise or righteous: "Better the poor walking in integrity than one perverse of speech who is a fool" (Prov 19:1 NRSV). The implication of these proverbs is that suffering is not always a sign of foolishness or wickedness, and wealth is not always a sign of righteousness or wisdom.

3.2.2. False Conclusions Based on Suffering. It is a mistake for people to draw conclusions related to God's justice or another person's righteousness based solely on suffering. Qohelet does the former, and Job's friends do the latter. Qohelet operates on the basis of observation (note the many uses of the verb *rāʾâ* ["see"]). Based on his own observations, he comes to the conclusion that wisdom does not deliver on its promises, and justice is not accomplished in this world. These concerns lead to the assertion "All is vanity *[hebel]* and a striving after wind" (Eccles 1:14 ESV). Even though it is clear to the reader from Job 1—2 that Job is blameless (Job 1:1) and is not suffering for sin (Job 1:8-12), Job's friends argue that he is suffering because of sin that he has committed (Job 4:8; 8:4; 11:13-14). They are operating with a mechanical concept of the deed-consequence relationship. They cannot affirm at the same time both God's justice and Job's integrity, because of Job's suffering. When Job continues to proclaim his innocence, the debate deteriorates into meaningless talk (Job 27:12) and false accusations (Job 22:5-11). Job dramatically asserts his integrity in a series of self-imprecations in Job 31, which calls upon God to activate the curses or clear him (Hartley). Thus, it is the integrity of Job that unites the submissive Job of the pro-

logue and the questioning Job of the dialogues (Brown).

It seems clear that an answer to Job's dilemma cannot be found on a human level, since such wisdom resides only with God (Job 28:23), who finally responds in Job 38. He accuses Job of darkening counsel by speaking of things that he does not understand (Job 38:2). In the first speech (Job 38:1—40:2) God asserts his power to maintain the universe as the Creator and Lord. Job is shown the power and glory of God in contrast to his own limited understanding and power. The panorama of creation in the first speech stands in contrast to the self-centered perspective of Job's world (compare Job 3:23-26). Job has no answer for God's questions, admits his own insignificance, and no longer calls for vindication (Job 40:3-5). God's second speech (Job 40:6—41:34) accuses Job of discrediting his justice in trying to justify himself while he condemns God. God challenges Job to govern the world, and it becomes clear that only God has the power to govern the world. Job ultimately submits to the mystery of God's sovereignty in suffering. Although Job is correct, over against the friends, that he is not suffering because of sin, he is wrong in calling into question God's justice. Job's second response is confession and repentance (Job 42:1-6). Although there is some debate concerning the meaning of *nāham* (for the options, see Newell), a common view is that it means "repent" or "recant" in the sense of changing one's mind or course of direction (Habel; Hartley; Newell). Brown sees a double entendre with the added meaning that Job found "comfort" (another nuance of *nāham*) over his state of utter destitution. In the end, Job is vindicated over against his friends on the major issue of whether Job is suffering because of sin (Job 42:7). God tells Job to pray for his friends, and he does so before his suffering ends (Job 42:8).

Although Crenshaw (1995, 467) wonders if the exaltation of God in Job comes at the expense of human beings, it is better to acknowledge that human beings must come to terms with the greatness of God and the mystery of his governing the world. God feels no compulsion to tell Job about the events of Job 1—2 or to explain to Job the reason for his suffering. A simplistic reason for suffering does not suffice, especially one that operates with a mechanical connection between deed and consequence.

There is always a temptation to give a simplistic answer or to allow the experience of suffering to call into question the justice of God.

4. The Resolution of Suffering.

4.1. The Faithfulness of God. There is great mystery connected to suffering. Sometimes suffering comes as a result of sin, and only confession and repentance will bring relief. However, there is not always a clear explanation for the purpose of suffering. Whatever the cause of suffering, the resolution of suffering is rooted in God's faithfulness. God's justice will prevail, and God's people will be delivered. This is the underlying hope in every situation of suffering. Even in seemingly unresolved situations there is hope. In the psalm that ends in darkness there is a glimpse of light in the appeal to "the God of my salvation" (Ps 88:1). Although still stinging from the anger of God and the destruction of Jerusalem, the writer of Lamentations affirms God's faithfulness (Lam 3:22-23). The use of *acrostic poems in Lamentations points to a belief in the order and stability of life even in the chaos of suffering.

4.2. God's Justice Will Prevail.

4.2.1. Affirmation of God's Justice in Job and Ecclesiastes. The resolution of suffering in Job comes when Job is willing to submit to the mysterious ways of God's sovereignty and abandon the claim that God is unjust. God never explains to Job the reasons for his suffering, but he is concerned about Job's response to his suffering. Although Job questions God's justice, there are times when he is confident that justice will prevail. He affirms a witness in heaven who will testify on his behalf (Job 16:19) and a redeemer (*gōʾēl*) who will come to his defense (Job 19:25). Whether Job 19:25-26 expresses the prospect of vindication in this life or after his death (see discussions in Hartley; Habel), it is a strong confirmation that he will receive justice in the debate concerning his integrity, which occurs in Job 42:7 and in Job's restoration. Qohelet may at times doubt whether God's justice is at work in this world (Eccles 7:15), but the book ends by affirming God's justice (Eccles 12:13-14). The important thing is to fear God and keep his commands because God will bring every work into judgment, including the secret things of life. Both Job and Ecclesiastes struggle with issues of justice but end by affirming God's justice.

4.2.2. The Final Destination of the Righteous in the Psalms. The lament psalms have a movement from despair to confidence in God's response and the praise of God (Ps 13:5-6; 22:22-31) (*see* Confidence, Psalms of). There are more laments in the Psalter than there are hymns because the psalms recognize the suffering of life and allow for its full expression. And yet suffering does not have the last word. Psalm 1 lays out the destiny of the righteous and of the wicked. As one moves through the Psalter, one experiences all the joys and trials of life, including the dark night of the soul experienced in suffering. However, just as the laments move toward the praise of God, so the Psalter moves toward the final destination of the righteous, which is the all-out praise of God (Ps 146—150).

4.2.3. Trusting in Yahweh (the Lord). The call to trust Yahweh in Proverbs is a call to commit the experiences, outcomes and suffering of life into God's sovereign hands (Prov 3:5-6). The connection between wisdom and blessing and between wickedness and ruin is not part of an impersonal world order, nor is there just an inner connection between deed and consequence with Yahweh acting like a midwife (Koch), but the world order is created and sustained by the Lord (Waltke). God will ensure that justice is done, and that ultimately the righteous and the wise are rewarded. If humans fail each other, and even if the earthly system of justice fails, Yahweh will not fail, even though the method or the process of justice is left unspecified. Ultimately, the wicked will receive what they deserve, and the desire of the righteous will be granted (Prov 10:24). Hope perishes with the death of the wicked (Prov 11:7), and wealth makes no difference in the day of death (Prov 11:4). However, the suffering of the righteous will give way to life, represented by the tree of life (Prov 3:18).

4.2.4. The Hope of Life. The horrible nature of suffering and the expressions of grief in suffering need to be given their full due. People may need to work through their suffering, and God is able to handle all their questions. If lament is lost, we are left with anxiety, despair and a God of the status quo (Brueggemann). But lament gives hope that God will respond, that God's justice will ultimately prevail, and that the righteous and the wise will receive all the blessings that are promised to them. Job's honor and wealth are restored when he receives twice as much as he had before (Job 42:10-17). There is hope that the blessings of God will be experienced in this life, but there is also a recognition that these blessings encompass more than this earthly life. Although H.-J. Kraus is hesitant to affirm life after death in Psalm 16:9-11, arguing that life on earth and deliverance from death are in view, he does recognize that the direction of such verses is toward life beyond death because Yahweh's liberating power knows no limits (the same can be said for Ps 49:15). The reward of life in Proverbs includes all the blessings for which one would hope, such as health and prosperity, but it also includes no death (Prov 12:28). Although in the Wisdom literature death can refer to an early, premature death (von Rad), it seems clear that there is more at stake than just a long life on this earth. R. Van Leeuwen (*NIB* 5.17-264) understands the tree of life (Prov 3:18; 11:30) to be a metaphor for the good life offered by wisdom, without the connotations of everlasting life in the garden of Eden. However, it is hard to limit the blessings of wisdom to this life alone. Life associated with the tree of life would include eternal life because of its connection with the garden (Waltke). Although the OT is not as clear as the NT on *afterlife, the fact that God's justice will prevail and God's people will experience life give hope for the one who fears the Lord to persevere in the face of suffering.

See also CHAOS AND DEATH; DIVINE PRESENCE; JOB 1: BOOK OF; THEODICY.

BIBLIOGRAPHY. **W. P. Brown,** *Character in Crisis: A Fresh Approach to the Wisdom Literature of the Old Testament* (Grand Rapids: Eerdmans, 1996); **W. Brueggemann,** "The Costly Loss of Lament," *JSOT* 55 (1986) 57-71; **J. L. Crenshaw,** *Ecclesiastes* (OTL; Philadelphia: Westminster, 1987); idem, *Urgent Advice and Probing Questions: Collected Writings on Old Testament Wisdom* (Macon, GA: Mercer University Press, 1995); **F. W. Dobbs-Allsopp,** *Lamentations* (IBC; Louisville: Westminster John Knox, 2002); **E. S. Gerstenberger,** *Psalms, Part 2, and Lamentations* (FOTL 15; Grand Rapids: Eerdmans, 2001); **N. C. Habel,** *The Book of Job* (OTL; Philadelphia: Westminster, 1985); **J. E. Hartley,** *The Book of Job* (NICOT; Grand Rapids: Eerdmans, 1988); **K. Koch,** "Is There a Doctrine of Retribution in the Old Testament? (1955)," in *Theodicy in the Old Testament*, ed. J. L. Crenshaw (Philadelphia: Fortress, 1983) 57-87; **H.-J. Kraus,** *Psalms 1-150* (2 vols; CC; Philadephia: Fortress, 1993); **T. Longman III,** *The Book of Ecclesiastes* (NICOT; Grand Rapids: Eerdmans, 1998); **P. D. Miller Jr.,** *Interpreting the Psalms*

(Philadelphia: Fortress, 1986); **B. L. Newell,** "Job, Repentant or Rebellious?" *WTJ* 46 (1984) 398-416; **R. C. Van Leeuwen,** "Wealth and Poverty: System and Contradiction in Proverbs," *HS* 33 (1992) 25-36; idem, "The Book of Proverbs," *NIB* 5.17-264; **G. von Rad,** *Wisdom in Israel,* trans. J. D. Martin (Valley Forge, PA: Trinity Press International, 1972); **B. K. Waltke,** *The Book of Proverbs* (2 vols.; NICOT; Grand Rapids: Eerdmans, 2004); **C. Westermann,** *Praise and Lament in the Psalms* (Atlanta: John Knox, 1981a); idem, *The Structure of the Book of Job: A Form-Critical Analysis* (Philadelphia: Fortress, 1981b); **R. N. Whybray,** "Qoheleth, Preacher of Joy?" *JSOT* 23 (1982) 87-98.   R. P. Belcher Jr.

SUMERIAN CITY LAMENTS. *See* LAMENTATIONS 2: ANCIENT NEAR EASTERN BACKGROUND.

SUPERSCRIPTIONS. *See* PSALMS 4: TITLES

SUSA

Susa was the major city of Elam, the area of southwestern Iran. Susa was located in a fertile alluvial plain 150 miles north of the Persian Gulf and at the base of the Zagros Mountains. Since the area is intolerably hot in the summer, the Achaemenid kings spent only the spring in Susa, spending the summer in the palace at Ecbatana and several months of the winter in Babylon. C. Tuplin (73) comments, "All the calendar dates in Nehemiah and Esther make Susa a winter or early spring location." Susa was the site of the story of *Esther in the days of *Ahasuerus (Xerxes). Esther contains numerous references to the (citadel) of Susa (Esther 1:2, 5; 2:3, 5, 8; 3:15; 8:14; 9:6, 11, 12). Daniel saw himself in a vision in the citadel at Susa by the Ulai Canal (Dan 8:2); he also heard a man's voice from the Ulai (Dan 8:16). Nehemiah was at Susa when he received news of the desolate state of Jerusalem's walls (Neh 1:1).

    1. Classical References
    2. Archaeological Discoveries
    3. The History of Susa

1. Classical References.

Because Susa was the eastern terminus of the Royal Road from Sardis (Herodotus *Hist.* 5.52-53; 8.98), established by Darius I, many notable Greeks appeared at the royal court of Susa, including Histiaeus of Miletus (Herodotus *Hist.* 5.30), Demaratus of Sparta (Herodotus *Hist.* 7.3) and Callias of Athens (Herodotus *Hist.* 7.151).

2. Archaeological Discoveries.

2.1. The Mounds. There are four major mounds at Susa, which the French excavators call (1) Acropolis, (2) Apadana, (3) Ville Royale, (4) Ville des Artisans. The first three form a diamond-shaped area with sides about 1,000 m (3,280 ft.) long. The Acropolis is the most important of the mounds for the earlier Elamite eras. It was settled at the earliest date and has been the most extensively excavated. The Acropolis rises steeply at its highest point 38 m above the waters of the Shaur River. A castle built by French excavators, using bricks from the site, now stands on the northern point of the Acropolis. Susa was occupied continuously from 3500 BC to the thirteenth century AD. Today the modern village of Shush lies on the Shaur below the slopes of the Acropolis.

2.2. The Excavations. The famous Jewish traveler Benjamin of Tudela (Spain) visited the site in AD 1165 and observed the Jewish community of Shush, noting that there were seven thousand Jews and fourteen synagogues there. W. K. Loftus, a Scot, visited the site in 1850 and correctly identified the site as ancient Susa. The French have sponsored annual excavations at Susa from 1897 to the present except for the periods of the World Wars. The first director, from 1897 to 1912, was J. de Morgan, who during the 1901/1902 season found the stela of Hammurabi's Code. R. de Mcquenem cleared the palace on the Apadana from 1909 to 1923. From 1946 to 1966 the expedition was directed by R. Ghirshman, who uncovered an Achaemenid village in the Ville des Artisans. In the 1960s M.-J. Steve and H. Gasche conducted extensive work on the Acropolis. From 1969 to 1979 J. Perrot and D. Ladiray excavated the Achaemenid palace.

3. The History of Susa.

3.1. The Third and Second Millennia BC. The earliest pottery from Susa comes from a depth of 11 m from a cemetery and is dated to 3500 BC. In the third millennium BC Susa was closely connected with Sumer in southern Mesopotamia. Sargon of Agade (2371-2316 BC) conquered Susa. The rulers of the Ur III period married Elamite princesses from Susa. This did not prevent the sack of Ur by the Elamites in the reign of Ibbi Sin (2029-2006 BC).

3.2. The Middle Elamite Era. The apogee of

Elamite culture was reached in the Middle Elamite period (1300-1100 BC), when Elamite kings from Susa attacked Mesopotamia, bringing an end to the Kassite Dynasty (c. 1160 BC). But then the Elamites disappeared from history for three centuries.

3.3. The Neo-Elamite Era and Ashurbanipal's Destruction of Susa. The Elamites supported various Chaldean rebels, such as Merodachbaladan, in their struggles against the dominant Assyrians. Ashurbanipal (668-627 BC) utterly destroyed Susa in 646 BC and deported some of its peoples to Samaria (Ezra 4:9-10).

3.4. Achaemenid Susa. When the Persian king Cyrus (see Ezra 1:1-4) conquered Babylon in 539 BC, he returned Elamite gods that had been taken back to Susa. Darius I made Susa his capital in 521 BC. The city covered about 300 acres. He built a great defensive wall about the palace, surrounded by a moat filled with water. He erected his palace on an artificial terrace 49 ft. high.

3.4.1. The Apadana. The Apadana was a hypostyle audience hall, which had six rows of six columns each, covered 12,000 m^2. The fluted stone columns were topped with capitals decorated with bulls' heads. Although none of the columns remain standing, they were probably 65 ft. high.

3.4.2. The Palace. There was a series of public courts connected by passageways to the inner residential rooms and to storerooms. The palatial complex covered an area of 38,000 m^2. The palace and the Apadana were decorated with molded glazed brick panels colorfully depicting griffins, winged bulls and lions.

In 1970 two foundation inscriptions in Elamite and Akkadian were discovered *in situ* in the palace. A trilingual (Elamite, Old Persian, Akkadian) inscription of Darius, known as the "Charter of Foundation," boasted that Darius employed materials and workers from every part of the vast Persian Empire (cf. Esther 1:1-6). It reads in part, "The cedar timber, this a mountain by name Lebanon from there was brought.... The gold was brought from Sardis and from Bactria, which here was wrought.... The silver and the ebony were brought from Egypt.... The stonecutters who wrought the stone, those were Ionians and Sardians."

3.4.3. The Gate House. In the 1970s the French discovered a monumental gatehouse 80 m to the east of the palace. The gate was 40 x 28 m, covering about 1,200 m^2. Its central room was a square, 21 m per side. This would have been the gate where *Mordecai sat (Esther 2:19, 21; 5:9,13; 6:10). The discovery of the gate has convinced the French excavators that the author of Esther had an accurate knowledge of Susa. Also, by the gate an oversized statue of Darius, missing its head, was discovered. It was engraved with four languages, including hieroglyphics, indicating that it was made in Egypt. At the Ville Royale another monumental gate, a propylaeum, measuring 24 x 24 m was discovered.

3.4.4. Xerxes and the Later Achaemenids. Xerxes made Susa his principal winter residence. In 1973 the excavators discovered two column bases with trilingual inscriptions of Xerxes. It was to Susa that Xerxes retired from Sardis after his disastrous campaign in Greece in 480/479 BC (Herodotus *Hist.* 9.108). Inscriptions from the gate indicate that Xerxes completed his father's work at Susa. During the reign of Artaxerxes I (464-424 BC), under whom Nehemiah served, the Apadana burned to the ground. No inscription attests to the building activities of Artaxerxes I at Susa. The Apadana was reconstructed by Artaxerxes II (404-359 BC), who faithfully reproduced Darius's structure. In 1969 bulldozers accidentally uncovered a new hypostyle hall, measuring 123 x 114 ft., with eight rows of eight columns, on the plain west of the Shaur. Inscriptions indicate that this was the provisional palace of Artaxerxes II while he proceeded with the reconstruction on the Apadana. The central area was free of buildings and perhaps was used for military parades.

3.5. Alexander and His Successors. In 331 BC Alexander captured Susa and its enormous treasure without resistance. Alexander then proceeded to Persepolis, which he burned down. In 324 BC, after his return from campaigns in the east, Alexander celebrated the symbolic marriage of himself and eighty Macedonian officers to native brides at Susa. Under the Seleucids Susa was renamed Seleucia-on-the-Eulaios. The area later fell under the Parthians, who gave the Greek inhabitants of Susa considerable freedom.

3.6. Parthian Sasanian and Islamic Eras. Ghirshman excavated in the Ville des Artisans a necropolis of the Partho-Seleucid period (300 BC to AD 200). From about AD 250 Susa began to flourish under the Zoroastrian Sasanids. A revolt by Christian Nestorians was suppressed by Shapur II (AD 309-379) with the destruction of Susa. The Arabs captured Susa in AD 638. A mosque, with a striking conical tower, at the edge of the Shaur has been venerated as the tomb of Daniel, a tradition that may go back to the eighth or even seventh centuries AD.

See also AHASUERUS; ESTHER 2: EXTRABIBLICAL BACKGROUND; VASHTI.

BIBLIOGRAPHY. **P. Amiet,** *Suse: 6,000 ans d'histoire* (Monographies des musées de France; Paris: Ministère de la culture et de la communication, Editions de la Réunion des musées nationaux, 1988); **R. Boucharlat,** "The Palace and the Royal Achaemenid City: Two Case Studies—Pasargadae and Susa," in *The Royal Palace Institution in the First Millennium BC: Regional Development and Cultural Interchange between East and West,* ed. I. Nielsen (Monographs of the Danish Institute at Athens 4; Aarhus: Aarhus University Press, 2001) 113-22; **P. O. Harper,** J. Aruz and F. Tallon, eds., *The Royal City of Susa: Ancient Near Eastern Treasures in the Louvre* (New York: Metropolitan Museum of Art, 1992); **J. Perrot and D. Ladiray,** "La porte de Darius à Suse," *Cahiers de la délégation archéologique française en Iran* 4 (1974) 43-56; idem, "Susa—City of Splendour," in *Royal Cities of the Biblical World,* ed. J. G. Westenholz (Jerusalem: Bible Lands Museum, 1996) 237-53; **J. Tricher et al.,** "Suse, les dernières découvertes," *Dossiers d'archéologie* 138 (May 1989) 8-90; **C. Tuplin,** "The Seasonal Migration of Achaemenid Kings: A Report on Old and New Evidence," in *Studies in Persian History: Essays in Memory of David M. Lewis,* ed. M. Brosius and A. Kuhrt (Achaemenid History 11; Leiden: Nederlands Instituut voor het Nabije Oosten, 1998) 63-114; **F. Vallat,** "L'inscription trilingue de Xerxes à la porte de Darius," *Cahiers de la délégation archéologique française en Iran* 4 (1974) 171-80; idem, *Suse et l'Elam* (Recherche sur les grandes civilisations 1; Paris; ADPF, 1980); **E. Yamauchi,** *Persia and the Bible* (Grand Rapids: Baker, 1990), chap. 7. E. Yamauchi

SYLLABIC METER. *See* METER.

SYNONYMOUS PARALLELISM. *See* PARALLELISM.

SYNTHETIC PARALLELISM. *See* PARALLELISM.

T, U, V

TABERNACLES, FESTIVAL OF. *See* MEGILLOT AND FESTIVALS.

TARGUMIM

The quadriliteral root *trgm* is used in rabbinic literature to refer to any translation of the Scriptures, as well as an individual who mediates the teaching of an important *sage to the gathered audience. It has come, however, to refer specifically to the numerous Aramaic translations of the Hebrew Bible made by Jews in late antiquity. Despite the multiplicity of Aramaic translations, only two of the Targumim became "authorized" (*Targum Onqelos* to the Torah and *Targum Jonathan* to the Prophets) by the Babylonian Jewish community, despite originating in the Palestinian Jewish community. In Palestine, however, numerous Targumim for all portions of the Bible flourished during the first centuries of the Common Era (second-ninth centuries AD).

The Targumim to the Writings fall into two categories. First, there are the five scrolls (*mĕgillôt*): *Lamentations, *Song of Songs, *Ruth, *Ecclesiastes and *Esther, which were read on the Ninth of Av, Passover, Shavuot, Sukkot and *Purim respectively (*see* Megillot and Festivals). The date at which each book became associated with a particular festival and thus incorporated into the liturgy is unclear, although we know that Esther was read, and translated, at Purim from Tannaitic times (see *t. Meg.* 3:20-21 [*mĕgillâ* literally means "scroll" and refers specifically to the book of Esther]). For the other books, it appears that their incorporation into the liturgical celebrations, with their respective Targum, occurred much later.

The second group comprises *Psalms, *Job and *Proverbs (Chronicles is also part of the Writings in Jewish tradition [*see* DOTHB, Chroni-

cles, Books of]), none of which were read publicly in the synagogue.

1. The Origin and Purpose of the Targumim
2. *Targum Psalms* (*Tg. Ps.*)
3. *Targum Job* (*Tg. Job*)
4. *Targum Proverbs* (*Tg. Pr.*)
5. *Targum Canticles* (*Tg. Cant.*)
6. *Targum Lamentations* (*Tg. Lam.*)
7. *Targum Qohelet* (*Tg. Q.*)
8. *Targum Ruth* (*Tg. Ruth*)
9. *Targum Esther* (*Tg. Est.*)
10. Conclusion

1. The Origin and Purpose of the Targumim.

The Babylonian Talmud (*b. Meg.* 3a) records divine displeasure at the prospect of a Targum to the Writings of the Hebrew Bible being revealed by Jonathan ben Uzziel. This tradition in reality represents an attempt at censorship of those Targumim that were not authorized by the Babylonian Jewish community (i.e., all Targumim other than *Targum Onqelos* for the Torah and *Targum Jonathan* for the prophets). Such an attempt at censorship actually serves as testimony to the very presence of those forbidden Targumim, and today we have Targumim to every book of the Writings except for Daniel and Ezra-Nehemiah. The questionable status of such Targumim remained into the late tenth/early eleventh century AD, where we find Rabbi Hai Gaon, in response to a question on the Targum of Esther, describing the Targumim of the Hagiographa as the translation of "common folk" because God had forbidden Jonathan ben Uzziel from translating the Writings.

Scholars have always asserted that the Targumim arose within a liturgical setting and were designed for the uneducated masses that no longer understood *Hebrew (Shinan). However, we now know that Hebrew was still a living language in the first centuries AD (Fraade). This, combined with the fact that we have Targumim to books that were not read publicly in the synagogue (see *m. Šabb.* 16:1; *b. Šabb.* 115a; 116b), raises the question of the original function/intention of all the Targumim. Recent scholarship, therefore, has stressed the importance of their educational function, both in the school *(bêt hasēper)* and in the study house *(bêt hamidrās)* (Fraade; Van der Kooij). Scholarship has also shown that the Targumim themselves assume knowledge of the Hebrew from their readers (Fraade). It would seem, therefore, that they did not necessarily originate among a populace that needed a translation, or that the synagogue was necessarily their place of origin. In other words, the Targumim seek to bring their readers to the Hebrew text, as opposed to bringing the Hebrew text to the readers (Fraade). In this respect, the Targumim are unique among early Bible translations (except, perhaps, for the very initial stages of the LXX), all of which seek to bring the Hebrew text to a populace that does not understand it. Such a view is particularly important for those Targumim that have no liturgical function, as it provides a *Sitz im Leben* in which they can be placed and studied.

Despite some (disputed) suggestions that the Targumim (in general) arose within a priestly community, the Targumim of the Writings belong firmly within rabbinic tradition (except, perhaps, for *Targum Proverbs*), and as such, they "rabbinize" the Scriptures. Thus we find that the unspecified day on which *Satan appeared before God in Job 1:6 is identified in the Targum as Rosh Hashanah, the day of judgment; the "divine assembly" in Psalm 82:1 the Targum identifies as Torah scholars; and the "kisses of his mouth" in Song of Songs 1:2 are specified as the "Torah, six orders of the Mishnah and the Talmud." The Targumim therefore hold a unique mediating position between the written Torah and the oral Torah of rabbinic tradition; dependent upon the written Scripture, the Targumim, however, lead their readers/hearers to a rabbinic understanding of those Scriptures. In other words, they combine the text with tradition and make sure that the text leads to tradition and not away from it (see *Sipre Devarim* 161).

Before proceeding to a description of the individual Targumim, we must note that all the Targumim to the Writings are anonymous, undated and have undergone a process of trans-

mission that has added to the text in such a way as to make it impossible to uncover an original *Urtext.* (At what point "oral" Targumim were committed to writing and then the "text" was stabilized is extremely difficult, if not impossible, to ascertain.) Such a situation should not lead to the conclusion that the Targumim are simply collections of disparate traditions. The extant versions are not; rather, they are carefully crafted texts that evince creativity from within the broader context of rabbinic tradition. As such, they record for us how particular books (not simply verses, as is often found in the various midrash collections) were read, as books, in (rabbinic) Jewish late antiquity.

2. *Targum Psalms (Tg. Ps.).*

As yet, there is no critical edition of *Targum Psalms,* although various individual manuscripts have been published (Diez Merino 1982; Cohen; de Lagarde). The manuscript tradition has been grouped into three distinct families with various differences between them. Until the publication of a critical edition, a complete picture of their relationship cannot be painted, although the similarities between the traditions far outweigh in number and significance the differences and point to an original Targum of Psalms that has undergone textual revision over time, as opposed to numerous versions gradually conforming to one another.

Targum Psalms, along with *Targum Job,* is written in Late Jewish Literary Aramaic, a dialect that contains both eastern and western forms as well as numerous Hebraisms. Numerous Greek and Latin loan words are also present in the Targum, which derived from Palestinian Judaism not before the fifth century AD, and quite probably later. The manuscript tradition is medieval, and it is clear that later copyists/editors added to the text during its transmission.

Targum Psalms contains a mixture of styles, translating some psalms literally with no expansions, whereas others, while remaining close to the Hebrew, will use two or three Aramaic words to translate the various nuances found within the one Hebrew root (e.g., Ps 2:6). Yet again there are some psalms (e.g., Pss 68; 110; 137) that contain numerous midrashic expansions to the text, with more than one translation for some verses incorporated into the text, marked by the phrases *tārgûm ʾaḥēr* or *lāšôn ʾaḥēr* (e.g.,

Ps 110:1). It is important to note, however, that even in the most expansive of "translations" it is possible to see the connections to the Hebrew text that lie behind them.

Targum Psalms clearly belongs within the rubric of rabbinic Judaism and incorporates themes such as Torah study, prayer, the final judgment with reward for the righteous and *retribution for the wicked, and the patriarchs and their merit. Therefore, God's "dwelling places" in Psalm 43:3 are changed in *Targum Psalms* to "study halls," and "commune with your own heart upon your bed" in Psalm 4:4 becomes "say prayers with your mouth and petitions in your heart; pray upon your couch." It should not be viewed, however, as simply a pastiche of rabbinic ideas, as there is ample evidence of creativity. Such creativity was exercised from within rabbinic tradition and utilized rabbinic methods of study. Its aim was to marry the written Scriptures with the oral tradition and thus make the biblical psalms relevant in a different age and in different circumstances.

3. Targum Job (Tg. Job).
The translation of Job into Aramaic began in Second Temple times, as is evidenced by the finds at Qumran (4QtgJob; 11QtgJob) and by the tradition in the Talmud (*t. Šabb.* 13:2-3), where we find Rabban Gamliel the elder enclosing an Aramaic Targum of Job in bricks on the Temple Mount. The Qumran "Targum" is literal, in contrast to parts of *Targum Job,* and although there appears to be no direct relationship between the two texts, some similarity in method has been uncovered (Gold), which suggests that further research in this area would be fruitful. However, caution is required, as similarity in method on its own cannot demonstrate any specific relationship between the two texts.

Targum Job, grouped linguistically alongside *Targum Psalms,* also contains numerous (over forty) multiple translations for single verses indicated by the rubric *tārgûm ʾaḥēr* or *lāšôn ʾaḥēr.* The number of these multiple translations varies according to each manuscript, and for some verses there are three translations given. The origin of these multiple translations is disputed. W. Bacher suggested that a late glossator added a more literal translation of verses that he viewed as too midrashic and then placed the literal translation into the text and relegated the expansive one. P. Churgin, however, saw the mi-

drashic translations as being added later. The consensus now views *Targum Job* as a creation of a copyist who utilized numerous manuscripts that differed from one another. The differences from each manuscript were first placed in the margin, and then later copyists added them into the text marked with *tārgûm ʾaḥēr* or *lāšôn ʾaḥēr.* Such a solution is yet to account for the origins of these multiple traditions, and thus more research is needed before the complete picture can be painted. Such research is possible since the publication of a critical edition by D. Stec (1994). The similarity in style and language between *Targum Job* and *Targum Psalms* has led some to suggest a common author. Such a conclusion is premature and is based on insufficient evidence, and therefore much research remains to be done on both texts before issues of common authorship are addressed comprehensively.

Throughout *Targum Job* there are numerous midrashic additions. The *law and its study are commonly added to the text (see *Tg. Job* 3:17; 24:13), as is the reward for meritorious works (*Tg. Job* 2:11; 3:17). Heaven, angels and life in the world to come are also added on various occasions. Many of these additions are less overtly rabbinic than in other Targumim to the Writings, which may suggest that its origins are earlier. Scholars have cited various reasons for an early date, including phrases such as "Father in Heaven" (*Tg. Job* 34:36) and "fire of Gehenna" (*Tg. Job* 3:17), alongside the pronominal use of *memra* for humans (e.g., *Tg. Job* 7:8; 19:18). Such evidence points to a possible early date and suggests that it is possible to find early traditions within the text; yet, as we have it today, the aforementioned conclusion stands: as a whole, *Targum Job* is a creation of a later copyist.

4. Targum Proverbs (Tg. Pr.).
There is no critical edition of *Targum Proverbs,* and only one manuscript has been published (Diez Merino 1984), alongside de Lagarde's publication of the text of *Targum Proverbs* from the *Biblia Rabbinica.* J. Healey has published an English translation, using de Lagarde's text as the source.

Targum Proverbs is unique among the Targumim of the Hagiographa on many levels. First, it evinces an extremely close relationship to the Peshitta (around thirty percent of the verses in the Targum agree with the Peshitta against the Hebrew). Some scholars have suggested that this relationship came about because the Peshitta was dependent upon an earlier version of *Targum Proverbs*. The Targum was then reworked at a later date by a copyist/translator into the form we have today (M. Z. Segal). However, other scholars have claimed that the Targum is dependent upon the Syriac version, with the translator consulting the Hebrew and thus translating some verses independently, this latter point being used to explain the differences (Weitzman; Diez Merino 1984). The problem, expressed by some, for this latter solution is that of Jews relying on a Christian translation. However, Rabbi Hai Gaon (AD 939-1038) is known to have dispatched someone to consult with the Nestorian Catholicos on an obscure verse in Psalms (Ps 141:5)—a fact that goes some way to allaying this problem (Weitzman).

Second, compared to the other Targumim of the Hagiographa, *Targum Proverbs* is unusual also in that it has no midrashic or haggadic expansions, despite various midrashim on verses from Proverbs, particularly connecting the Torah with wisdom and assigning it a role in the creation of the world, as well as those that pick up on *Solomon as author and relate it to his request for wisdom in 1 Kings 3. There is also no particular avoidance of anthropomorphisms within *Targum Proverbs*, with some actually being inserted by the Targum itself (see *Tg. Pr.* 22:11).

Many issues remain open with *Targum Proverbs* and will remain so until the publication of a critical edition of the text allows further research to proceed on a more solid footing.

5. *Targum Canticles (Tg. Cant.)*.

Linguistically, *Targum Canticles* is written in Late Jewish Literary Aramaic (along with *Tg. Ps.* and *Tg. Job*), probably in Palestine sometime in the eighth or ninth century AD. There is as yet no critical edition, although numerous texts have been published (e.g., Melamed; Fontela), reflecting both the eastern and western recensions of the manuscript tradition.

Targum Canticles opens with the Midrash of the Ten Songs, beginning with Psalm 92, which, according to Jewish tradition, was sung by Adam when he repented and the Sabbath came and protected him from punishment, and ending with the song that is spoken of in Isaiah 30:29 and sung by the returning exiles at the dawn of the messianic age. This last song provides a smooth link into *Targum Canticles* in that it is sung at the time of Passover, and Song of Songs was read during the Passover celebrations. The Midrash of the Ten Songs as a whole also serves both to explain the name of the book and to set the stage for the historical sweep that the Targum gives to the book, beginning with the exodus, "When the people of the house of Israel went out from Egypt" (*Tg. Cant.* 1:4), and ending with the Messianic age, "And at that time the King Messiah will be revealed" (*Tg. Cant.* 8:1). As such, there is clearly an attempt to read the book as a book and to provide it with a coherent unity. In this reading God is the "beloved" and Israel is the "bride," in keeping with rabbinic interpretations of the book. Such a unified structure suggests a single author; however, there remain differences between the eastern and western recensions of the text, but these are not so significant as to deflect from the essential unity of the Targum. A full treatment of this issue, however, depends upon the publication of a full critical edition.

The author clearly was learned in and committed to rabbinic tradition and held the rabbinic academy in great esteem. Thus we find that the world is sustained by the merit of the "head of the college" (*Tg. Cant.* 7:3). The merit of the righteous is a theme throughout the Targum and not only secures protection and sustenance for them in the years of exile (*Tg. Cant.* 1:8) but also results in the coming of the *Messiah (*Tg. Cant.* 7:13-14). The righteous are also portrayed as those who study the law and the words of the sages, and who rise early to go to the house of study.

The lateness of its composition is also signified by its messianism. Although we find in *Tg. Cant.* 4:5 mention of two Messiahs—"Messiah son of David and the Messiah son of Ephraim"—the final "messianic" section of the book (beginning at *Tg. Cant.* 7:13) refers only to the King Messiah (Son of David), who is described in *Tg. Cant.* 8:1 as a Torah scholar. The Targum's positive attitude to the Hasmoneans also suggests a late date, as it is in contrast to the decidedly indifferent attitude toward them in the Talmud.

The Targum ends with an exhortation to the house of Israel, through the mouth of Solomon, to commit themselves to Torah study and to pray for the coming of the Messiah.

6. *Targum Lamentations (Tg. Lam.)*.

The Ninth of Av is the preeminent day of mourning in Jewish tradition, remembering five events in Jewish history: the decree that the generation of the desert would die in the wilderness, the destruction of the first temple and of the second temple, the fall of Bethar in the Bar Kokhba rebellion, and the plowing up of Jerusalem by the Romans (see *m. Taʿan.* 4:6). The reading of the book of Lamentations accompanied this fast, first privately and then publicly, and its accompaniment with the Targum is first recorded in *Soperim* 42b. This late reference (seventh century AD) suggests that *Targum Lamentations* must have originated sufficiently before this date in order for it to be accepted and incorporated into the liturgy. It should also be borne in mind that a text's reception into the liturgy does not preclude its earlier use in private or public study. The dating of this text therefore remains, as with many of the Targumim to the Writings, an open question.

Targum Lamentations begins in a very expansive style (especially chap. 1), with many expansions designed to justify the destruction in terms of Israel's sin, so immediately in *Targum Lamentations* 1:1 the exile of Jerusalem, described as a punishment, is likened to that of Adam and Eve, and the "attribute of Justice" declares, "Because of the greatness of her rebellious sin that was within her, thus she shall dwell alone." The Targum continues in *Targum Lamentations* 1:2-4 by describing the bad report brought by the spies and then the destruction of the temple by Nebuchadnezzar and subsequent exile of Judah because of their treatment of orphans and widows, the hard labor inflicted upon fellow Israelites and their failure to observe the three pilgrimage festivals. Thus the Targum is rightly seen to be a rabbinic response to the book of Lamentations, in which God is vindicated for the destruction of Jerusalem (Brady). As well as this "vindication," it is also designed to encourage its readers to respond appropriately to their present situation—that is, in repentance, study, prayer and synagogue attendance:

> Arise, O Congregation of Israel dwelling in exile. Busy yourself with Mishnah in the night, for the Shekinah of the Lord is dwelling before you, and with the words of Torah at the beginning of the Morning watch. Pour out like water the crookedness of your heart and turn in repentance. And pray in the synagogue before the face of the Lord. Raise your hands to him in prayer for the life of your children who thirst with hunger at the head of every open market. (*Tg. Lam.* 2:19)

The Targum is not without hope, for the Lord will see the repentance of Israel and their change in behavior, and thus *Targum Lamentations* transforms a bleak verse in the Hebrew into one of hope: "You [God] will declare freedom to your people, the House of Israel, by the King Messiah, just as you did by Moses and Aaron" (*Tg. Lam.* 2:22). Many of these exegetical traditions have parallels in rabbinic midrashim and particularly in *Lamentations Rabbah*.

There is as yet no critical edition of *Targum Lamentations*, although the textual tradition has been discussed at length (Alexander 1986). There are two recensions: one Yemenite and one western, with the western recension being more expansive and possibly influencing the later Yemenite manuscripts.

7. *Targum Qohelet (Tg. Q.)*.

The custom of reading the book of Ecclesiastes on the intermediate Sabbath of Sukkot is late and therefore has no influence on *Targum Qohelet* whatsoever, which can be dated (approximately) to the seventh-ninth centuries AD. *Targum Qohelet* provides a systematic, rabbinic reading of the biblical book that once struggled both for acceptance and for its place in the *canon (see *m. Yad.* 3:5). Therefore the book is described as "words of prophecy" from "Solomon, the son of David" (*Tg. Q.* 1:1 [see also *Tg. Q.* 1:4; 3:11; 4:15]). The prophetic nature of Solomon's work was a significant factor in its acceptance by some as "inspired"; thus we find him prophesying in *Targum Qohelet* 1:1-2 of both the future division of the kingdom under Rehoboam and the destruction of Jerusalem and the temple by the Babylonians. It is this vision of the future that causes him to utter, "Vanity of vanities"; however, the universal vanity of life in this world has been transformed by the Targum into a specific cause and effect, with the addition "Vanity of vanities of everything for which I and David my father labored."

Targum Qohelet also seeks to smooth out any theological difficulties that the book raises and to explain within the confines of rabbinic ideology some of the more elliptical passages. Therefore, the conclusion in Ecclesiastes 2:24, "There is no good thing for a man but that he should eat and drink and let himself experience pleasure in all his toil," is transformed in *Targum Qohelet:* "There is nothing worthwhile for a man except that he eat and drink and enjoy himself before the people, to obey the commandments of the Lord and to walk in straight paths before Him so that He will do good to him for his labor." On numerous occasions the Targum simply adds ideas to the text that transform its general, universal nature to a very specific rabbinic context. Therefore we find the "time to be born and a time to die" (Eccles 3:1) transformed into "a time chosen to bear sons and a time chosen to kill rebellious and blaspheming sons, to kill them with stones," and the "time to embrace and a time to refrain from embracing" (Eccles 3:5) changed to "a time chosen to embrace a wife and a time chosen to refrain from embracing a wife during the seven days of mourning." Many of these "additions" are similar to interpretations found in *Qohelet Rabbah,* and it seems likely that both were dependent upon the same source(s).

A. Levy prepared a critical edition of *Targum Qohelet* in 1905, and a new edition is needed. There is a translation in the Aramaic Bible series (vol. 15); it is based, however, upon an eclectic text using both western and eastern manuscripts.

8. Targum Ruth (Tg. Ruth).

Targum Ruth contains many additions to the biblical text that have parallels in rabbinic literature, and in particular *Ruth Rabbah.* Thus we find the Targum beginning with a list of ten famines decreed to be on the earth from creation until the coming of the Messiah (cf., the Ten Songs in *Tg. Cant.*), and *Boaz in *Targum Ruth* 2:11 declaring, "It has been told to me on the authority of the sages, that when the Lord decreed [against intermarriage with Moab], He did not decree against the women, but against the men." We also find that Jesse was considered sinless and died only because the sin of Adam and Eve brought about the decree of death on all (*Tg. Ruth* 4:22). These and other interpretations are explicitly rabbinic and evince a close relationship with the rabbinic world. *Targum Ruth,* however, is unusual in that there are passages that have prompted some to suggest a sectarian origin for this Targum. In *Targum Ruth* 1:17 four types of death penalty are listed: ston-

ing, burning with fire, being put to the sword and hanging on the gallows. Rabbinic law has a similar list but does not permit hanging, but rather strangulation (see *m. Sanh.* 7:1; *Ruth Rab.* 2:24). However, 11QT^a LXIV, 6-11 permits "hanging" as a form of punishment, and thus some have suggested that *Targum Ruth* reflects premishnaic, sectarian (even Sadducean) law. To suggest a sectarian origin for the whole Targum from this text seems exaggerated (other texts cited by those in favor of a sectarian origin, *Tg. Ruth* 1:22; 4:7, lack any reason to be considered sectarian), yet the conflict with mishnaic law remains, and therefore some have proposed a pre-rabbinic/mishnaic origin for *Targum Ruth.* Such an early dating is bold and sometimes relies on an assumption that material that contradicts the Mishnah must be premishnaic, which clearly is unsustainable. It is possible that there is some Karaite influence, which would clearly rule out a premishnaic date. Those suggesting an early date, however, also point to the pronominal use of *memra* (*Tg. Ruth* 3:8; 1:17 in some manuscripts), which is assumed must belong to a period before the word took on any theological import. Suffice to say the exact origins of *Targum Ruth* remain unclear, and as with the other Targumim to the Writings it may well contain some traditions that are early and some that are much later.

Further research into *Targum Ruth* can now proceed on a firmer footing after the publication of a critical text (Beattie).

9. Targum Esther (Tg. Est.).

There is some debate over the number of Targumim there are to the book of Esther. There is a scholarly consensus over the two Targumim to the book that appear in Bomberg's *Biblia Rabbinica* (Venice, 1517), *Targum Esther 1* and *Targum Esther 2;* however, there is debate over the authenticity of the third Targum that is found in the Antwerp Polyglot of 1569-1572. The presence of more that one Targum to Esther has been acknowledged for a millennium or more. Rabbi Hai Gaon, writing at the end of the tenth century AD states, "Furthermore, we have here in Babylonia several versions of Targum Esther, differing from each other; and one has many additions and midrashim in it, while another does not." *Targum Esther 1* and *Targum Esther 2* are expansive, with the latter being the more expansive of the two, whereas the disputed third

Targum is very literal. M. Goshen-Gottstein (and later B. Grossfeld) does not accept the authenticity of the third Targum, viewing it rather as a product of a sixteenth-century humanistic editing policy that purged the expansive texts of their many additions. P. Grelot, however, views it as an authentic Targum that represents the oldest recension of *Targum Esther*.

These complexities cannot be easily resolved, and, as the foregoing quotation from Rabbi Hai Gaon indicates, the multiplicity of Targum texts to the book of Esther is a historical phenomenon, and one that precludes definite conclusions in identifying the earliest strata or even an *Urtext*. Both Targumim are very expansive, with *Targum Esther 2* being twice as expansive as *Targum Esther 1*. Many of these additions serve to rabbinize a book that, like Ecclesiastes, struggled to be accepted. Thus, although the Hebrew does not contain any explicit reference to God, both Targumim to Esther have numerous references and epithets for him (e.g., "Father in Heaven" [*Tg. Est. 2* 1:1; 3:8]; "the Holy One" [*Tg. Est. 1.* 5:1]); the biblical book of Esther has no mention of the law, dietary regulations, covenant, and so on, whereas both *Targum Esther 1* and *Targum Esther 2* have Esther observe the commandments: "Sabbath and festivals she would observe; during the days of separation she watched herself, cooked dishes and wine of the nations she did not taste, and all the religious precepts which the women of the house of Israel were commanded, she observed" (*Tg. Est. 1* 2:20).

Within *Targum Esther 1* and *Targum Esther 2* numerous legends appear that have parallels only in the late Midrash collection *Esther Rabbah*, and thus it seems that these Targumim did not reach their final form until the early Middle Ages. There are parallels to other rabbinic midrashim, and by far the majority from Amoraic collections. This late date should not, however, deflect the fact that the book of Esther was read during the feast of Purim from Tannaitic times, and as such, there may well have been a Targum read alongside it from an early date (see *t. Meg.* 3:20-21).

Targum Esther 1 and *Targum Esther 2* contain much parallel material, yet there are numerous differences between them, which suggests that both are dependent upon the same source but were created independently of one another. Such a situation accounts for both the similarities and the differences.

10. Conclusion.

Despite troubled beginnings and, in particular, their questionable status within the Babylonian Jewish community, the Targumim of the Writings eventually became established within rabbinic Judaism, with Rabbi Nathan ben Jehiel of Rome (AD 1102) quoting freely from them in his *Aruch*, and all of them included in the Rabbinic Bible, published in the sixteenth century. Today, among the remaining Yeminite Jewish communities in Israel, the Targumim to the five *mĕgillôt* are still recited (if not understood by many) in the synagogues during their respective feasts. These Targumim, with their long history, remain an important witness to how Jews read these books in antiquity (and still read them today). They were seen, however, as more than "translations"; they became part of the revelation (oral Torah) that was handed to Moses on Mount Sinai and passed on through the generations (*m. ʾAbot* 1), and as such, they were viewed as "revelation," not merely human ingenuity.

The Jews, as with their Christian counterparts, viewed the entire Hebrew Scriptures as divine revelation, whose component parts could not be confined to a single meaning, but whose contents had to be "turned, turned and turned again" in order to unearth the treasures contained therein. The Targumim of the Writings, as we have them today, provide a glimpse of some of the treasures that were unearthed.

See also MEGILLOT AND FESTIVALS; PURIM.

BIBLIOGRAPHY. **P. S. Alexander**, "The Textual Tradition of Targum Lamentations," *Abr-Nahrain* 24 (1986) 1-26; idem, *The Targum of Canticles* (ArBib 17A; Edinburgh: T & T Clark, 2003); **W. Bacher**, "Das Targum zu Hiob," *MGWJ* 20 (1871) 208-23, 283-84; **D. R. G. Beattie**, "The Targum of Ruth: A Preliminary Edition," in *Targum and Scripture: Studies in Aramaic Translation and Interpretation in Memory of Ernest G. Clarke*, ed. P. V. M. Flesher (SAIS 2; Leiden: E. J. Brill, 2002); **C. M. Brady**, *The Rabbinic Targum of Lamentations: Vindicating God* (SAIS 3; Leiden: E. J. Brill, 2003); **P. Churgin**, *Tārgûm Kĕtûbîm* (New York: Horeb, 1945); **M. Cohen**, ed., *Miqrāʾôt Gĕdôlôt Hāketer* (2 vols.; Ramat-Gan: Bar Ilan University Press, 2003); **P. de Lagarde**, ed., *Hagiographa Chaldaice* (Leipzig: Teubner, 1873); **L. Diez Merino**, *Targum de Salmos: Edición príncipe del Ms. Villa-Amil n.5 de Alfonso de Zamora* (BHB 1; Madrid: Consejo Superior de Investigaciones Científicas, Instituto Francisco Suárez, 1982); idem, *Targum de Proverbios: Edición príncipe del Ms. Villa-Amil n.5 de Alfonso de Zamora* (BHB 6; Madrid: Consejo Superior de Investigaciones Científicas, Instituto Francisco Suárez, 1984); **T. M. Edwards,** "The Targum of Psalms," in *Interpreting the Psalms: Issues and Approaches,* ed. P. J. Johnston and D. G. Firth (Leicester: Apollos, 2005) 279-94; **C. H. Fontela,** *El Targum al Cantar de los Cantares (Edición Crítica)* (Colección Tesis Doctorales 92/87; Madrid: Editorial de la Universidad Complutense de Madrid, 1987); **S. Fraade,** "Rabbinic Views on the Practice of Targum and Multilingualism in Jewish Galilee of the Third-Sixth Centuries," in *The Galilee in Late Antiquity,* ed. L. I. Levine (New York: Jewish Theological Seminary of America, 1992) 253-86; **S. L. Gold,** "Targum or Translation: New Light on the Character of Qumran Job (11Q10) from a Synoptic Approach," *JAB* 3.1/2 (2001) 101-20; **M. Goshen-Gottstein,** "'The Third Targum' on Esther and MS Neofiti 1," *Bib* 56 (1975) 301-29; **P. Grelot,** "Observations sur les targums I et III d'Esther," *Bib* 56 (1975) 53-73; **B. Grossfeld,** *The Two Targums of Esther* (ArBib 18; Edinburgh: T & T Clark, 1991); **J. F. Healey,** *The Targum of Job* (ArBib 15; Edinburgh: T & T Clark, 1991); **E. Levine,** *The Aramaic Version of Qohelet* (New York: Sepher-Hermon Press, 1978); **R. H. Melamed,** *The Targum to Canticles: According to Six Yemen MSS, compared with the "Textus Receptus" as Contained in de Lagarde's "Hagiographa chaldaice"* (Philadephia: Dropsie College for Hebrew and Cognate Learning, 1921); reprinted from *JQR* 10 (1919-1920) 377-410; *JQR* 11 (1920-1921) 1-20; *JQR* 12 (1921-1922) 57-117; **A. Shinan,** "The Aramaic Targum as a Mirror of Galilean Jewry," in *The Galilee in Late Antiquity,* ed. L. I. Levine (New York: Jewish Theological Seminary of America, 1992) 241-51; **D. M. Stec,** *The Text of the Targum of Job: An Introduction and a Critical Edition* (A GJU 20; Leiden: E. J. Brill, 1994); idem, *The Targum of Psalms* (ArBib17; Minnesota: Liturgical Press, 2004); **A. Van der Kooij,** "The Origin and Purpose of Bible Translation in Ancient Judaism: Some Comments," *AR* 1.2 (1999) 204-14; **R. Weiss,** *The Aramaic Targum of Job* [in Hebrew] (Tel Aviv: Chaim Rosenberg School for Jewish Studies, Tel Aviv University, 1979; **M. Weitzman,** *The Syriac Version of the Old Testament: An Introduction* (UCOP 56; Cambridge: Cambridge University Press, 1999).

T. M. Edwards

TEMPLE. *See* ARCHITECTURAL IMAGERY.

TERSENESS

Literary specialists make a broad genre distinction in written language between poetry and prose. In spite of J. Kugel's otherwise probing analysis, most scholars believe that there is a distinction between poetry and prose in ancient biblical Hebrew literature. The vast majority of modern English versions recognize this by their formatting of the printed page. Even the casual reader of Hebrew poetry can differentiate poetry from prose in the OT at a mere glance, since a page of poetry is distinguished by lots of white space. This feature is a result of one of the key traits that distinguish poetry from prose: terseness. The term is borrowed from Kugel (87-94), who, though denying the poetry-prose distinction, does see terseness as a feature that "heightens" biblical style. Kugel (87) says that "it amounts to far more than the concision and compression of expression that one associates with poetry. It is more reminiscent of 'telegraph style' ('Urge support tax reform package for increase housing starts 1980') or the elliptical language of some popular sayings ('Red sky at morning, sailor take warning'), in which some of the signposts of ordinary discourse have been stripped away."

1. The Features of Poetry
2. The Definition of Terseness
3. The Production of Terseness
4. Ambiguity

1. The Features of Poetry.

The reader of English translations of the Bible can easily tell whether a page of text is poetry or prose, but the Hebrew scholar has more difficulty. It is true that three books—*Job, *Psalms, *Proverbs—have a distinctive accentuation *(te'amîm),* but these were added by the Masoretes (AD 400-1000).

Part of the problem of definitively distinguishing poetry from prose in the Bible is that there does not appear to be a single trait or even a group of traits exclusive to poetry and absent in prose. For many years it was thought that *meter might fulfill that function as it does in other poetic traditions, but meter remains undiscovered and may not even exist in Hebrew poetry (Longman). Even so, there are three features that are pervasive in poetry: *parallelism, *imagery, terseness. Of these three, terseness is arguably the most distinctive to poetry (though we will see that it is partly a function of the other two). Terseness, of course, is the focus of the present article.

2. The Definition of Terseness.

"Terseness" simply refers to the brevity of the poetic line. Whereas prose is built on sentences that form paragraphs, poetry is built on cola that form parallel lines. The cola typically are short, with the first line often longer than the second. Although it is not uncommon that the two cola are of equal length, it is rare indeed when the second colon is longer than the first. A colon typically contains two to four words. The first two verses of Psalm 3 can be used to illustrate (hyphens connect English words that constitute a single word in Hebrew, and parentheses indicate words that are not in Hebrew):

> Yahweh, how many (are) my-foes;
>> many are-those-who-rise against-me.
> Many say to-me:
>> "(There is) no victory for-him in-God."

> *yhwh mâ-rabbû ṣārāy*
>> *rabbîm qāmîm ʿālāy*
> *rabbîm ʾōmrîm lĕnapšî*
>> *ʾēn yĕšûʿātâ lô bēʾlōhîm*

Terseness adds punch to poetry. Poetry says a lot using a few words. As a result of this feature, poetry is not easily skimmed; rather, the compactness of poetry requires the interpreter to slow down and reflect or meditate. As we will also observe later, this feature raises the level of *ambiguity of the poetic line as well.

3. The Production of Terseness.

3.1. General Economy of Words. In the first place, the poet is conscious of the number of words that he or she uses. Literature in general is a self-conscious use of language. Poets are just as conscious of *how* they say something as they are of *what* they say. The brevity of the poetic line is noticeable in English translation, but it is even more obvious in the Hebrew original. For instance, the NIV renders Psalm 70:2a with the following twelve words:

> May those who seek my life
> be put to shame and confusion.

In Hebrew, however, there are two words per colon:

> *yēbōšû wĕyaḥpĕrû*
> *mĕbaqšê napšî*

This can be literally rendered with hyphens showing single words in the Hebrew (notice that the NIV transposes the cola):

> May-they-be-shamed and-may-they-be-confused
> those-who-seek my-life.

But besides what appears to be a general self-consciousness on the part of the poet as to the number of words used, the terseness of Hebrew poetry is achieved in some other recognizable ways.

3.2. Parallelism and Imagery. Parallelism is the echoing effect in Hebrew poetry. Within a poetic line most elements in the first part are echoed in some fashion in the second part. However, typically the poet finds a way to use fewer words in the second colon. Parallelism is one way in which linguistic concision is achieved.

A second poetic convention that contributes to terseness is *imagery. Imagery is often achieved through association (metonymy) or, more often at least in Hebrew poetry, through comparison (metaphor). Metaphor brings together two things that are essentially different from each other, though they are similar in some fashion that merits the comparison. When Psalm 23:1a states, "The LORD is my shepherd," we are invited to unpack the comparison. This unpacking reveals how metaphor contributes to terseness. First, in keeping with the point in 3.1 above, it is important to point out that the five words of the English translation are really only two in Hebrew: "The-LORD [is] my-shepherd." Second, the metaphor packs a lot of meaning. When the interpreter asks what it means, the answer can only come by means of a lengthy prose statement: "It means that the Lord guides, protects and comforts his people, who are the sheep." And this prose description can go on, especially if one tries to represent the emotional impact of the metaphor. Indeed, it is almost certainly impossible to translate everything that the metaphor intends to communicate by transposing the metaphor into prose.

3.3. Prose Particles. An attentive reading of obviously poetic texts reveals a radically diminished use of the definite article *ha,* the relative pronoun *ʾăšer* and the direct object marker *ʾēt.* Often they are missing where one would expect to find them in a standard piece of prose. F. Andersen and D. Freedman (1980) have followed up on this intuition and have run statistical analyses showing that in a typical prose text these "prose particles," as they call them, constitute fifteen percent or more of all words, while in typical poetic text they constitute five percent or less. Furthermore, Andersen and Freedman (60-61) claim that the "gap is a fairly wide one and while some pieces fall between the two categories, most cluster at the high and low ends of the scale." These scholars use this data to differentiate prose from poetry in questionable instances, such as Hosea, but their insight is also a further contribution to a proper understanding of how terseness is produced by Hebrew poets.

3.4. Lack of Conjunctions. Poets restrict the use of conjunctions. Conjunctions are words that join clauses and sentences and often guide the reader as to the relationship between these semantic units. It is not that there are absolutely no conjunctions in poetry, but they are used more sparingly. Notice the relationship between the first and second lines of Psalm 23:1: "The LORD is my shepherd; I will lack nothing." There is no conjunction between v. 1a and v. 1b. One can easily imagine a prose verse saying something like "The LORD is my shepherd; therefore, I will lack nothing" or "Since the LORD is my shepherd, I will lack nothing." But such conjunctions are rare. Indeed, though it does occasionally appear, the simple *waw* conjunction is more rare in poetry than in prose. Although this observation is a fair one based on extensive reading of the literature, it must be admitted that the same kind of careful statistical study has not been done on this aspect as it has on the prose particles.

One notable exception to the lack of conjunctions in Hebrew poetry is the use of the conjunction *kî* in the causal ("because") sense. It is often used in a *hymn to indicate the reasons for praise: "Sing to Yahweh a new song, for *[kî]* he has done marvelous acts" (Ps 98:1a). In psalms of *lament the *kî* marks the reasons for grief or complaint: "By the rivers of Babylon, there we sat and wept, as we remembered Zion. In the midst of the poplars we hung our harps, for *[ki]* there those who captured us asked us for songs" (Ps 137:1-3).

So again, although poets employ conjunc-

tions on occasion, there is a significantly diminished usage. One result is the heightening of an intentional ambiguity, and a second result, germane to the present article, is a further reduction in line length.

3.5. Ellipsis. A final major way by which Hebrew poets produce terseness in their lines is through the use of ellipsis. *Ellipsis is the omission from the second colon of a major element found in the first colon (e.g., verb or noun or prepositional phrase), though the missing element is understood in the second.

It is true that completely parallel lines may be found in Hebrew where each element in the first colon is echoed in the second:

> Let them exalt him in the assembly of the
> people,
> and praise him in the meeting of the elders.
> (Ps 107:32)

Frequently, however, the second phrase will omit a part (usually the first element) of the first clause with the understanding that the omitted part of the first clause is to be read into the second clause. Usually it is the verb that is omitted:

> You have put me in the lowest pit,
> in deep and dark places. (Ps 88:6)

The verb is missing in the second phrase, but of course we are to understand the sense of the second phrase as "(You have put me) in deep and dark places."

The effect of ellipsis is to bind two phrases more closely together. There is no question as to whether the two phrases go together in a single line. A further effect, however, is economy of expression. In other words, ellipsis promotes terseness.

Proverbs 31:4 is a good example of a nonverbal ellipsis:

> Not for kings, Lemuel, not for kings to drink
> wine,
> and for rulers to desire strong drink.

In this case it is the negative that is elided.

4. Ambiguity.

Poets say a lot using a few words. Thus, poetry packs rich meaning in few words. This feature requires readers to slow down and meditate as they interpret a poem. Many of the features that contribute to terseness also heighten *ambiguity. Poetry does not speak as directly as prose, but on the other hand, it involves readers as whole people, not just an intellect, as they engage a poem.

Here is a fairly literal translation of Psalm 131:

Yahweh, my-heart (is) not exalted;
　my-eyes not lifted up.
And-I-do-not-concern-myself with-great-things,
　and-things-too-wonderful for-me.
But I-have-stilled
　and-quieted my-soul.
Like-a-weaned-child with its-mother,
　like-a-weaned-child (is) my-soul to-me.
Israel, hope in-Yahweh,
　from-now until-forever.

Although some conjunctions appear in this psalm, some are missing between cola, and this requires the interpreter to supply them, thus creating ambiguity. For instance, what is the connection between v. 1a and v. 1b? Though not lending to the ambiguity, the ellipsis of v. 2b ("I do not concern") helps create the terseness. The imagery of v. 2 (in what way my soul's relationship to God is like that of a weaned child to a mother) is also ambiguous.

All in all, terseness, with its often attendant ambiguity, lends interest to the poem and requires the reader/interpreter to be deeply engaged with the material.

See also AMBIGUITY; ELLIPSIS; PARALLELISM; POETICS, TERMINOLOGY OF.

BIBLIOGRAPHY. **F. I. Andersen and A. D. Forbes,** "'Prose Particle' Counts of the Hebrew Bible," in *The Word of the Lord Shall Go Forth: Essays in Honor of David Noel Freedman in Celebration of His Sixtieth Birthday,* ed. C. L. Meyers and M. O'Connor (Winona Lake, IN: Eisenbrauns, 1983) 165-83; **F. I. Andersen and D. N. Freedman,** *Hosea* (AB 24; Garden City, NY: Doubleday, 1980); **D. N. Freedman,** "Pottery, Poetry, and Prophecy," *JBL* 96 (1977) 5-26; idem, "Another Look at Hebrew Poetry," in *Directions in Biblical Hebrew Poetry,* ed. E. R. Follis (JSOTSup 40; Sheffield: JSOT Press, 1987) 11-28; **J. L. Kugel,** *The Idea of Biblical Poetry: Parallelism and Its History* (New Haven: Yale University Press, 1981); **T. Longman III,** "A Critique of Two Recent Metrical Sys-

tems," *Bib* 63 (1982) 230-54.

T. Longman III

TEXT, TEXTUAL CRITICISM

The term *text* refers to the precise wording of an extant manuscript (handwritten copy) of a literary composition. The term *textual criticism* is used of the science and art that seeks to determine the most reliable wording of a text (see McCarter, 18; Tov 1992, 1). It is a science because specific rules govern the evaluation of various types of copyist errors and readings, but it is also an art because these rules cannot be rigidly applied in every situation. The goal of OT textual criticism is to work back as closely as possible to the final form of the text that was maintained by early *scribes and was later canonized.

This article provides a brief overview of OT textual evidence in general and then, more specifically, for each of the poetic books. It then describes textual critical principles used to determine the best reading of the text. Finally, two examples give an idea of the issues encountered in the poetic books during the process of textual criticism.

1. Textual Evidence
2. Textual Critical Principles
3. Textual Critical Examples

1. Textual Evidence.

1.1. General Overview. Little is known about the earliest stages of the transmission of the biblical texts. Divine revelation was most likely initially handed down orally from generation to generation, but at some point it was committed to writing to ensure its accuracy. These original manuscripts, or autographs, of the OT no longer exist, but we have copies of copies made by scribes, whose primary job was to retain God's revelation. The autographs probably were written on scrolls made from papyrus or leather (see Jer 36). When biblical scrolls began to show signs of wear from everyday use, they were copied and then reverently buried (since they contained the sacred name of God). There was little reason to retain these worn copies, since scribes were meticulous in copying them. Sometimes worn copies were placed in a genizah ("hidden" place) until there were enough to bury. One of these genizahs was found in the late nineteenth century when an old synagogue in Cairo was being renovated.

Initially, priests (or a special group of priests)

maintained the sacred traditions. Then, from about 500 BC to about AD 100, there arose an influential group of teachers and interpreters of the *law called the *soferim* ("scribes"). The Babylonian Talmud states, "The older men were called *soferim* because they counted [*sfr*: "count, recount, declare"] all the letters in the Torah" (*b. Qidd.* 30a). Scholars often discuss the difficult question of what this early text may have looked like and how closely it corresponds to the modern Masoretic Text (MT), the common form of today's Hebrew Bible. Evidence from about the mid-third century BC on indicates that for several centuries a variety of Hebrew texts coexisted (e.g., proto-MT, LXX, Samaritan Pentateuch and possibly others suggested by some of the Dead Sea manuscripts). The Hebrew manuscripts copied before the first century AD show two tendencies: they preserved the accuracy of the text, while at the same time the text was revised or updated within certain boundaries. The scribes assigned to Scriptures a high degree of authority and upheld them with great reverence, but they desired to have their readers understand them. When the scribes came across something that they felt was inappropriate or objectionable, they would modify the text but place notes in the margin so that the reader would be aware of the change (e.g., a superlinear *nûn* was added in Judges 18:30 along with the scribal note indicating that the *nûn* was added because Jonathan's actions better resembled those of a son of the wicked Manasseh [מנשה] than a son of Moses [משה]). Scribal notations may also have been used to indicate a question or reservation about a specific reading of a text (e.g., Kethib/Qere readings; inverted *nuns*, *sebirin*). From about AD 100 to AD 300 a group of scribes called the *tannaim* ("repeaters") maintained the sacred traditions and developed meticulous rules that were to be followed when copying biblical scrolls (e.g., no word or letter was to be written from memory; if more than three mistakes were found on any page, it had to be destroyed and redone). These rules helped maintain an accurate text, but the scribes also allowed certain types of revisions: (1) *matres lectionis* were added (certain consonants included as precursors to vowel points) and the modernization of archaic spellings; (2) corrections were made (see 4QIsa[a] where words are crossed out or consonants written above the text); (3) about 350 BC texts began to be written in Assyrian (square) script instead

of paleo-Hebrew (paleo-Hebrew manuscripts were eventually looked down upon).

W. F. Albright (1957, 79) describes a practice common throughout the ancient Near East: "Instead of leaving obvious archaisms in spelling and grammar, as later became the fashion in Greece and Rome, the scribes generally revised ancient literature and other documents periodically." However, sometime shortly after the turn of the century the scribes no longer allowed the text to be modified, and their job narrowed to preserving the accuracy of Scripture, which they did with amazing precision. There is very little variation in any of the extant manuscripts dated to the first and second centuries AD (e.g., from Masada, Naḥal Ḥever, Wadi Murabbaʿat and Naḥal Ṣeʾelim), each reflecting the proto-MT. There is still debate over how and why the text became so unified following the first century AD. Some argue that the group that maintained the proto-MT was the only one to survive the destruction of the second temple (Tov 1992, 195; Albrektson 1978). Others suggest that there was a purposeful standardization of the text (Waltke 1978, 57; Würthwein, 15-16). The latter seems most likely for two reasons: (1) there was a desire to provide a consistent standard for debates between Christians and Jews in the first century AD (cf. Justin Martyr, *Dial.* 68); (2) Hillel the Elder needed a standardized text on which to base his seven rules of biblical hermeneutics (ʾ*Abot R. Nat.* 37A). Both the sheer number of manuscripts and the quotations in the rabbinic literature suggest that the proto-MT was maintained by the authoritative center of Judaism. Thus sometime during the first century AD the proto-MT apparently became the dominant textual tradition.

Evidence for the OT text comes primarily from two major sources: (1) Hebrew manuscripts, and (2) recensions, translations or versions. Some of the most important in each category are as follows.

1.1.1. Hebrew Manuscript Evidence. In the middle of the twentieth century the number of early OT manuscripts increased significantly, largely due to the discovery of the manuscripts popularly known as the *Dead Sea Scrolls. The discovery of the Dead Sea Scrolls revolutionized the field of OT textual criticism because for the first time Hebrew manuscripts (or at least fragments) from at least as early as the first century AD were available for most of the OT. Nonetheless, most of the earliest extant Hebrew manuscripts are still a significant distance from the autographs of the OT.

The extant Hebrew manuscripts of the biblical books include approximately 222 manuscripts from the Dead Sea area, a few other early Hebrew manuscripts and about two thousand Hebrew manuscripts from medieval times or later.

1.1.1.1. Dead Sea Scrolls. The Dead Sea Scrolls provided texts of the OT from approximately one thousand years earlier (i.e., from about 250 BC to AD 135) than what had been available prior to their discovery. Currently, manuscripts or fragments (usually several copies) of all the biblical books (except *Esther and possibly Nehemiah) have been found in eleven caves surrounding Qumran (about seven miles south of Jericho) and in several other caves around the Dead Sea.

1.1.1.2. Silver Amulets. Currently the oldest extant fragment of any of the OT is written on two silver amulets dated to the mid-seventh century BC. They contain part of the priestly benediction of Numbers 6:22-27 and are similar to the MT, though there are some omissions. However, these omissions may be due to the limited size of the amulets.

1.1.1.3. Later Hebrew Manuscripts. From the second half of the eighth century AD to the mid-tenth century AD the Ben Asher family played a leading role in recording and maintaining the MT at Tiberias. Two manuscripts are the earliest and most complete copies of the MT. First, there is the Aleppo Codex. According to its colophon, the consonantal text was attributed to Shelomo ben Buyaʿa, and Aaron ben Moses ben Asher added the pointing and the Masorah about AD 930. This is the earliest manuscript of the MT, but in the early twentieth century a fire destroyed one quarter of it (Gen 1:1—Deut 28:16; Song 3:12 to the end of the OT, including *Ecclesiastes, *Lamentations and *Esther). Second, there is Codex Leningradensis (Leningrad Ms. B19^A, L). This manuscript was the base text for the most recent critical editions of the Hebrew OT (*BHK, BHS, BHQ*), since it is the oldest and most complete manuscript of the OT presently accessible. A colophon dates this important witness of the Ben Asher family to AD 1008.

1.1.2. Evidence from Recensions, Translations and Versions. There are three important concepts to remember in dealing with secondary sources. First, the process of translating a text from one language to another involves a distinct set of problems, such as the grammatical/syntactical differences between languages and the difficulties of finding equivalent words. Second, it is not always possible to tell if divergences reconstructed from the various versions arose from discrepancies in the Hebrew text or from idiosyncrasies of the translators who may have modified the text, either intentionally or unintentionally. Third, it is important to know which translations are related so that particular readings are not given too much weight. For example, the LXX was the basis for the Old Latin, Sahidic, Ethiopic, Syro-Hexapla and Georgian versions. In addition, works such as the Vulgate claim to be translations of an original Hebrew text and yet were heavily influenced by Greek and Old Latin versions.

1.1.2.1. Septuagint (LXX). Historically, the LXX had an important influence on both Jews and Christians. Jewish immigrants living in the cosmopolitan city of Alexandria were compelled to abandon their native language, but the translation of their laws into Greek was one way for them to maintain their faith. This Greek translation became so popular, however, that it was increasingly seen as the standard form of the OT and was subsequently adopted by Christians. About seventy percent of the NT's quotations of the OT appear to come from the LXX. The more Christians embraced the LXX and used it to argue their beliefs (e.g., Is 7:14), the further the Jewish community distanced themselves from it. As a result, other Greek translations were made by Jewish scholars (e.g., Aquila, Symmachus, Theodotion) to meet their needs.

1.1.2.2. Aquila. Aquila, from Sinope (in Pontus on the Black Sea), converted to Judaism and became a disciple of Rabbi Akiba. About AD 130 he produced a literal Greek translation that closely followed the Hebrew text—even the Hebrew definite direct object marker (ʾet), usually left untranslated, is indicated by the article or by the Greek word *syn* ("so, with, together with") followed by the accusative case (i.e., grammatical case marking the direct object).

1.1.2.3. Theodotion. Early church tradition says that Theodotion was a Jewish proselyte who lived in Ephesus during the second century AD (Irenaeus *Haer.* 3.21.1, according to Eusebius *Hist. eccl.* 5.8, 10). His Greek translation was midway between the strictly literal translation of Aquila and the literary elegance of Symmachus. Theodotion succeeded in producing a translation that retained much of its Semitic flavor and yet was readily understandable to his Greek-speaking audience. One peculiarity of his work is that he often transliterated rather than translated words, even fairly common ones.

1.1.2.4. Symmachus. This translation probably dates to the early mid-third century AD. According to Eusebius and Jerome, Symmachus was an Ebionite (an early Christian sect considered heretical by the early Christian fathers for observing some form of the Jewish law) (Jerome *Vir. ill.* 54; *Comm. Habac.* 3.13; *Praef. Job;* Eusebius *Hist. eccl.* 6.17). Symmachus's elegant Greek style enabled him to prepare an idiomatic translation of the MT that occasionally manifests significant independence and originality.

1.1.2.5. Aramaic Targumim. Aramaic translations and explanations regarding the interpretation of the text arose, and these are known as *Targumim. Some Targumim contain a fairly literal translation of the MT (e.g., Targum of Job, Targum of Proverbs), whereas others are paraphrastic, adding interpretive and explanatory material (e.g., Targum of Song of Songs). Only a fraction of these Targumim have survived; nevertheless, they are important to textual criticism for at least three reasons: (1) some include translations of the text *(lemmata);* (2) they mention early Jewish traditions regarding the interpretation of the biblical texts; and (3) they are written in Aramaic (*see DOTHB*, Aramaic Language), which is closely related to biblical Hebrew (*see* Hebrew Language). The quality of the translations varies greatly among the Targumim, but on the whole they reflect the MT.

1.1.2.6. Latin Versions. "Old Latin" is a collective term for the Latin versions in existence before the Latin Vulgate. Fragments in Old Latin exist from the Pentateuch, *Psalms and the Major and Minor Prophets; more can be gleaned from works of the church fathers. The fragments most likely were translated from a copy of the LXX, though some passages seem to reflect a reading closer to the Hebrew text. Jerome (c. AD 345-420) was commissioned to revise and standardize the many differences in the Old Latin texts. At first he began by translating the psalms from Old Latin texts based primarily on the LXX *(Psalterium Romanum),* and then from the LXX *(Gallican Psalter),* but these proved unsatisfactory, so eventually he learned Hebrew in order to translate them from the original language. Even though his proficiency was limited, it was better

than any other previous church father. His Latin version of the OT (AD 390-405), translated from the original Hebrew text, became the standard edition of the Bible for over one thousand years.

1.1.2.7. Syriac Versions. There are two major translations of the OT into Classical Syriac (Eastern Aramaic). The first and most important is the Syriac Peshitta (*peshitta* probably means "simple or common"), translated from the Hebrew, and the second is the Syro-Hexapla, translated from the Greek. Around the fifth century AD the Syriac Peshitta emerged over other Syriac translations. The OT text of the Peshitta appears to have been translated quite literally from a Hebrew text fairly close to the MT but was subsequently revised with the aid of the LXX (Würthwein, 81).

1.2. Specific Evidence for the Poetic Books. There are relatively few early Hebrew manuscripts pertinent to the poetic books, but they are largely in agreement with the text of the MT. The texts of some of the poetic books appear to be fairly well preserved in the MT (e.g., Ecclesiastes, Song of Songs), while others are not as well preserved (e.g., *Job, Psalms, *Proverbs). Due to the nature of the books and their rare vocabulary, these latter works raise a number of difficulties.

1.2.1. Psalms. Comparison of parallel passages of the MT of Psalms indicates a number of divergences. For example, there are over one hundred differences between the parallel psalms in Psalm 18 and 2 Samuel 22 (cf. also Ps 14 and Ps 53; Ps 40 and Ps 70). However, on the positive side, there are more early manuscripts for comparison than for any other poetic book. Thirty-nine scrolls or fragments of Psalms (i.e., thirty-six from Qumran; two from Masada; one from Naḥal Ḥever) and four commentary texts containing portions of psalms texts were found in the area of the Dead Sea. Most are fragmentary, and some do not appear to have ever been part of complete psalters (e.g., 4Q89 [4QPs^g]; 4Q90 [4QPs^h]; 5Q5 [5QPs]). Of the 150 canonical psalms, only 126 appear in the thirty-nine psalm scrolls or in the pesherim from the Dead Sea area, and there are at least fifteen apocryphal psalms (Flint, 703). At least ten of these psalm compositions are arranged stichometrically, reflecting a poetic format (1Q10 [1QPs^a]; 3Q2 [3QPs]; 4Q84 [4QPs^b]; 4Q85 [4QPs^c]; 4Q89 [4QPs^g]; 4Q90 [4QPs^h]; 4Q93 [4QPs^l]; 5Q5 [5QPs]; 8Q2 [8QPs]; Mas1e), while twenty-one are arranged in prose format (1Q11 [1QPs^b]; 1Q12 [1QPs^c]; 2Q14 [2QPs]; 3Q2 [3QPs]; 4Q83 [4QPs^a]; 4Q87 [4QPs^e]; 4Q88 [4QPs^f]; 4Q91 [4QPs^j]; 4Q92 [4QPs^k]; 4Q94 [4QPs^m]; 4Q95 [4QPs^n]; 4Q96 [4QPs^o]; 4Q97 [4QPs^p]; 4Q98 [4QPs^q]; 4Q98a [4QPs^r]; 4Q98f [4QPs^w]; 4Q522 [4QapocrJosh^c?]; 6Q5 [6QpapPs?]; 11Q6 [11QPs^b]; 11Q7 [11QPs^c]; 11Q8 [11QPs^d]), and at least one is mixed (11Q5 [11QPs^a]). They are dated as shown in Table 1.

The order of the psalms often differs from the MT (e.g., 4Q83 [4QPs^a]; 4Q84 [4QPs^b]; 4Q86 [4QPs^d]), but the superscriptions are generally very similar (e.g., Ps 123, "A Song of Ascents. [Of David]" [MT: simply "A Song of Ascents"]; Ps 145, "A Prayer. Of David" [MT: "A Song of Praise. Of David"]).

One of the most important of these is *Psalms Scroll^a* (11Q5 [11QPs^a]) from Qumran cave 11, found in February 1956. This scroll dates to the first half of the first century AD. It is in very good condition at the top, but the bottom third is in an advanced state of decomposition. It contains forty-one canonical psalms from the last third of the Psalter (though not in canonical order), seven apocryphal psalms, Psalm 151 (which is recorded in the LXX), and a psalm from Sirach 51:13-20. The name "Yahweh" (יהוה, *yhwh*) is also written in paleo-Hebrew script. Its text basically follows the MT, though it contains hun-

dreds of relatively minor textual differences—a small number are more substantial (e.g., inclusion of the *nûn* verse in Ps 145:13, which does not appear in the MT [11Q5 (11QPs^a) XVII, 2-3]). Excavations at Masada in 1963-1965 uncovered the remains of fourteen scrolls, including biblical, sectarian and apocryphal texts. They date to sometime before AD 73, when the Romans stormed the fortress, and provide further evidence that the Hebrew text was unified during the first century AD. Some of the more interesting biblical texts for our purposes are fragments from Psalms (Psalm^a [Mas1e], containing Ps 81:2b to Ps 85:6a) and Psalm 150 (Psalm^b [Mas1f]). The Masada manuscripts are written in Hebrew square script and are very similar to the MT (e.g., one variant: *'ohelê 'dwm*, "the tents of Edom" [MT Ps 83:7], reads *'lhy 'dwm*, "the gods of Edom" [Mas1e II, 19]). In 1952 a fragmentary Hebrew manuscript of Psalms (5/6Hev1b) was discovered at Naḥal Ḥever (Wadi Habra), located about one mile south of Ein Gedi on the western shore of the Dead Sea. In 1960 a larger portion of the same manuscript was found (XHev/SE4). All the biblical texts from these caves are dated to about AD 130, and their translations are virtually identical to the MT.

The Qumran texts are by far the most helpful for textual critical purposes on the book of

Table 1. Qumran Psalm Mnuscripts

DATE	MANUSCRIPT
Second century BC	4Q83 [4QPs^a]; 4Q98f [4QPs^w]
First century BC	1Q10 [1QPs^a]; 4Q84 [4QPs^b]; 4Q86 [4QPs^d]; 4Q88 [4QPs^f]; 4Q92 [4QPs^k]; 4Q93 [4QPs^l]; 4Q95 [4QPs^n]; 4Q96 [4QPs^o]; 4Q98d [4QPs^u]; 4Q522 [4QapocrJosh^c?]; Mas1f
Herodian (early first century BC)	1Q12 [1QPs^c]; 2Q14 [2QPs]; 4Q90 [4QPs^h]; 4Q94 [4QPs^m]; 4Q97 [4QPs^p]; 4Q98a [4QPs^r]
First century AD	1Q11 [1QPs^b]; 3Q2 [3QPs]; 4Q85 [4QPs^c]; 4Q87 [4QPs^e]; 4Q89 [4QPs^g]; 4Q91 [4QPs^j]; 4Q98 [4QPs^q]; 4QPs^s; 4Q98b [4QPs^s]; 4Q98c [4QPs^t]; 5Q5 [5QPs]; 6Q5 [6QpapPs?]; 8Q2 [8QPs]; 11Q5 [11QPs^a]; 11Q6 [11QPs^b]; 11Q7 [11QPs^c]; 11Q8 [11QPs^d]; 11Q11 [11QapocrPs]; Mas1e; XHev/Se 4

Psalms. The LXX version is probably even more corrupt than the Hebrew text. The Latin Vulgate version of Psalms comes from the *Gallican Psalter*, which is a translation from the LXX, not a Hebrew text like the rest of the Latin Vulgate. The Syriac Peshitta apparently was translated from a Hebrew text but subsequently was revised in light of the LXX. Therefore the versions are often of little help for textual criticism in the book of Psalms.

1.2.2. Job. The Hebrew text of the book of Job appears to have suffered more corruption in the course of transmission than any other book of the OT, forcing commentators and textual critics to regularly suggest emendations. Even when the text does not appear to be corrupt, the meaning is often uncertain, as is testified in several of the ancient translations. Qumran yielded only four fragments of this book, dated between about 225 and 150 BC (4Q101 [4Qpaleo-Job^c]) and AD 50 (2Q15 [2QJob]; 4Q99 [4QJob^a]; 4Q100 [4QJob^b]). These last three manuscripts are written in Herodian script and are quite fragmentary. 4Q99 (4QJob^a) is the largest manuscript and contains Job 31:14-19; 32:3-4; 33:10-11, 24-26, 28-30; 35:16; 36:7-11, 13-27, 32-33; 37:1-5, 14-15. 4Q100 (4QJob^b) is the next largest and contains Job 8:15-17; 9:27; 13:4; 14:4-6; 31:20-21. 2Q15 (2QJob) contains only five words from Job 33:28-30. These manuscripts mainly follow the text of the MT with only a few orthographic differences and variant readings (Newsom, 412). The last manuscript of Job (4Q101 [4Qpaleo-Job^c]), dated between 225 and 150 BC, contains portions of Job 13:18-20, 23-27; 14:13-18 and is written in paleo-Hebrew script. Its text is written stichometrically, has dots or strokes between words, contains very few *matres lectionis*, and is very close to the MT. There are also two Targumim of Job (4Q157 [4QtgJob]; 11Q10 [11QtgJob]), both of which are dated by their script to the early first century AD, though several scholars have dated 11Q10 (11QtgJob) much earlier, to the second century BC. 4Q157 (4QtgJob) contains an Aramaic translation of Job 3:5-9; 4:16-5:4, and 11Q10 (11QtgJob) includes most of Job 17—42. Both appear to closely follow the text of the MT, but the ending of 11Q10 (11QtgJob) differs significantly from the MT, and in a few cases this manuscript agrees with the LXX against the MT.

The LXX text of the book of Job is sometimes a very literal translation and at other times is closer to a paraphrase than a translation. This may be due to the obscurity of the *Vorlage*. The text of the LXX is about 350-400 lines shorter than the MT. There is little reason to favor the shorter text, since the passages omitted do not seem to have a different characteristic form or style, and their absence often destroys the parallel structure seen in the MT. Origen added the missing lines from the later Greek text of Theodotion, but subsequent copyists often were not careful to distinguish between the two texts and combined them as if they were the original LXX text. The Greek versions seldom resolve the difficulties of the MT due to paraphrasing and occasional theological bias (e.g., revocalizing the negative particle in Job 13:15 to affirm trust in God [Pope 1973, xliv-xlv; see also Orlinsky 1935-1936; 1957; Wevers, 187-90). G. Gerleman (18) has argued that the LXX translator(s) of the book of Job used a *Vorlage* very similar to the proto-MT but had limited understanding of the language (see also Waltke 1979, 221-22). The ancient versions in general seem to follow the MT quite literally (e.g., Syriac, Latin Vulgate, Aramaic Targumim), but they need to be examined carefully in passages where the MT is questioned. The Syriac Peshitta sometimes clarifies the meaning of an obscure Hebrew word, and the Aramaic Targum contains some interesting interpretations but offers little help in resolving difficulties. There is a curious situation in the Latin Vulgate of the book of Job. Jerome appears to have translated very literally in some places but quite freely in others. This work also appears to have been influenced by the Greek translations of Aquila, Theodotion and Symmachus.

1.2.3. Proverbs. The text of the book of Proverbs also has significant difficulties, but some of the alleged corruptions may merely be questions regarding grammar and the rare vocabulary of this book (e.g., in Prov 26:23 *kesep sigim* ["silver dross"] perhaps should be revocalized as *kěsapsāgîm* ["like glaze"] [Albright 1955, 12]). The Qumran manuscripts contain only two fragments from the book of Proverbs, dated between 50 BC and AD 50. 4Q102 (4QProv^a) has thirty-nine verses (Prov 1:27—2:1), and 4Q103 (4QProv^b) has 125 verses (Prov 9:16 [possibly Prov 9:4]; 13:6-9; 14:6-13; 14:27-28[?]; 14:31-15:8; 15:19-31). Together they yield only four minor and two more significant variants from the MT (in Prov 15:28 the omission of *yehgeh* ["meditate"], and in Prov 1:32 *môškôt* ["cord"] instead of *měšûbat* ["apostasy"]) (Jastram, 702).

There are some interesting differences between the text of the LXX in the book of Proverbs and the MT. First, several texts are in the MT but not in the LXX (e.g., Prov 4:7; 8:33; 16:1, 3; 20:14-19) or are in the LXX but not in the MT (about thirty partial verses, according to Fox, 363). Second, there are notable differences in the order of the latter parts of these two texts (see Table 2). H. Washington (194-97) is probably

Table 2. Differences in Order in Proverbs

Masoretic Text	Septuagint
24:23-34 "Further Sayings of the Wise"	30:1-14 "Agur"
25:1—29:27 "Hezekiah's Men"	24:23-34 "Further Sayings of the Wise"
30:1-14 "Agur"	30:15-33 "Numerical Parallelisms"
30:15-33 "Numerical Parallelisms"	31:1-9 "Lemuel's Mother"
31:1-9 "Lemuel's Mother"	25:1—29:27 "Hezekiah's Men"
31:10-31 "Virtuous Wife"	31:10-31 "Virtuous Wife"

correct in suggesting that this rearrangement is due to the author's attempt to strengthen the Solomonic authorship of the book of Proverbs.

There are also other considerable differences between the text of the MT and that of the LXX. E. Tov argues that they come from different editions of the book, but J. Barr and B. Waltke probably are more correct in understanding them as a free translation of the Hebrew text influenced strongly by Stoic philosophy and Jewish midrashic thinking. Barr (1975, 158) says that the LXX text of Proverbs often starts out with a very literal translation of the text but then breaks loose "from literality and completes the sentence with a composition so loosely related to the original that it might equally be considered as an original composition rather than a rendering."

The Targum of Proverbs is a fairly literal translation, but it is unique in that when the Hebrew text is unclear, it sometimes follows the Peshitta (it is identical to the Peshitta in 300 out of 915 verses) and sometimes the LXX (in 85 places it is closer to the LXX than the Hebrew). The Latin Vulgate and Syriac Peshitta seem to reproduce the Hebrew fairly literally, but both show significant dependence upon the LXX.

1.2.4. Ruth. The text of the book of Ruth is relatively free from significant problems; according to R. Hubbard (2) only one text (Ruth 2:7) "resists satisfactory solution." There are just eight fragments from four different Qumran manuscripts of the book of Ruth. The largest fragment, 2Q16 (2QRuth[a]), is dated by paleography to the first century AD and contains Ruth 2:13-23; 3:1-8; 4:3-4. It is the only Ruth manuscript with enough surviving text to assure that it follows the MT fairly closely. The next largest, 2Q17 (2QRuth[b]), dated to about 50 BC, contains Ruth 3:13-18 and does not appear to follow the MT as closely. The smallest fragments, 4Q104 (4QRuth[a]), containing Ruth 1:1-12, and 4Q105 (4QRuth[b]), containing Ruth 1:1-6, 12-15, are dated by paleography to the first century AD and are not complete enough to assess their textual nature. The Targum of Ruth follows the MT quite closely, except for a few paraphrastic departures. The LXX text of Ruth is a fairly literal (occasionally even slavishly literal) translation of the MT; paraphrases that are included demonstrate a good understanding of the Hebrew language (e.g., Ruth 1:9; 4:1, 7). The Syriac Peshitta is a much freer translation and seldom has preferred readings to the MT (possible exceptions are Ruth 1:9; 4:1, 7). There are only about twelve places where the texts of the versions differ from the MT, and these generally do not significantly help resolve textual critical issues in the book of Ruth.

1.2.5. Song of Songs. The text of Song of Songs is fairly well preserved, but its unique vocabulary (it has many *hapax legomena*) and terse style still make it one of the most difficult to interpret in the OT. There are only four minor fragments of this book from Qumran. The largest, 4Q107 (4QCant[b]), is dated to the end of the first century BC and includes Song of Songs 2:9-17; 3:1-2, 5, 9-10; 4:1-3, 8-11, 14-16; 5:1. The next largest, 4Q106 (4QCant[a]), is dated to the early first century AD and contains Song of Songs 3:7-11; 4:1-7; 6:11(?)-12; 7:1-7. 6Q6 (6QCant) is dated later than the other fragments to the early first century AD but contains only Song of Songs 1:1-7. The smallest fragment, 4Q108 (4QCant[c]), is dated to the end of the first century BC and has only Song of Songs 3:7-8. The texts of all of these manuscripts deviate only slightly from the MT. For example, in Song of Songs 3:11 the text of 4Q106 (4QCant[a]) has "daughters of Jerusalem" instead of the MT's "daughters of Zion." It is interesting that in 4Q106 (4QCant[a]) and 4Q107 (4QCant[b]) some passages appear to have been intentionally left out, suggesting that they may have been liturgical manuscripts, not biblical scrolls.

There are very few places were the text of the versions appears preferable to the MT (e.g., Song 4:8, אֲתִי ["come"] instead of the MT's אִתִּי ["with me"]; Song 7:10, שְׂפָתַי וְשִׁנָּי ["my lips and my teeth"] instead of the MT's שִׂפְתֵי יְשֵׁנִים ["lips of sleepers"]). Yet there are still places where the MT is uncertain (e.g., Song 6:12). The LXX provides a very literal Greek translation of the Hebrew text in Song of Songs; however, there are a few harmonistic readings and expansions. The translator of the Targum of Song of Songs frequently used the Hebrew text as a launching pad to soar into interpretational expositions that are not always obviously connected to the original Hebrew text (Pope 1977, 21). Both the Latin Vulgate and the Syriac Peshitta are fairly literal renderings of the MT, with only minor variations.

1.2.6. Ecclesiastes. The text of Ecclesiastes is largely free from textual corruptions. The main difficulties relate to the unusual vocabulary and the message of the book. Only two fragmentary manuscripts of Ecclesiastes were found, in cave 4 at Qumran. The first and larger one, 4Q109 (4QQoh[a]), is dated by paleographic evidence to 175-150 BC. It contains Ecclesiastes 5:14-18 [MT 13-17]; 6:1, 3-8, 12; 7:1-10, 19-20. The second one, 4Q110 (4QQoh[b]), is dated to about 50 BC and has Ecclesiastes 1:10-14(15?). Both manuscripts follow the MT very closely, with only slight variants. The versions are of some help to textual criticism, for the text of the LXX of Ecclesiastes is so literal that some of the idioms do not make sense in Greek (e.g., Heb definite direct object marker indicated by Gk *syn* + accusative [similar to Aquila's version]). Some have even argued that Aquila translated it (Barthélemy, 21-33) or edited it (Hyvärinen, 88-99), but this probably is unnecessary. T. Longman (25) argues that the majority of the differences between the LXX and the MT are mistranslations of the Hebrew text. The Targum of Ecclesiastes contains parts that are paraphrastic and inter-

pretive, as well as parts that offer a literal translation of the Hebrew text. The Latin Vulgate is fairly close to the MT, as is the Peshitta, though the latter occasionally departs from the MT and appears to be dependent upon the LXX.

1.2.7. Lamentations. The text of Lamentations is in a relatively good state of preservation, possibly due to the structure of the poems. In general, the ancient translations are of little help in determining the original text in difficult passages, since they arise from a text essentially the same as the Hebrew text. Four manuscripts of the book of Lamentations from Qumran are all quite fragmentary and probably date to the first century AD. The largest text, 5Q6 (5QLam[a]), contains Lamentations 4:5-8, 11-16, 19-22; 5:1-13, 16-17, but according to J. Milik (175), the character of its text is uncertain. The next largest text, 4Q111 (4QLam), contains Lamentations 1:1-16 and a fragment of Lamentations 2:5. It is written in a vulgar, semiformal script that mainly follows the MT but makes a significant number of changes to it. In some places its readings may improve the MT (White Crawford, 296). The last two texts are quite fragmentary. 5Q7 (5QLam[b]) contains Lamentations 4:17-20 and has handwriting different from that of 5Q6 (5QLam[a]). 3Q3 (3QLam) includes Lamentations 1:10-12; 3:53-62 and appears to follow the MT. This latter text has the divine name "Yahweh" written in paleo-Hebrew script.

The LXX seems to be a literal translation of a Hebrew text that is very similar to the MT (at times extremely literal) (see Albrektson 1963, 208). Differences may be attributed more to transmissional corruptions within the LXX than to a difference in Hebrew *Vorlage*. The Greek text of Lamentations appears to come from the *Kaige* recension, which is a Greek text that has been brought into line with the MT by its ancient editors (Hillers, 41). The Targum of Lamentations, the Latin Vulgate and the Syriac Peshitta likewise come from a Hebrew text very similar to the MT. The Targum of Lamentations seems to have entirely rewritten the book and is more helpful for polemic reasons than for textual evidence.

1.2.8. Esther. Even though there are no significant problems with the MT of the book of Esther, J. Baldwin (42) notes, "No other book of the OT has come down to us in so many variant forms." Presently, the oldest extant Hebrew text of the book of Esther is dated to the eleventh century AD (Codex Leningradensis, 1009); there are no manuscripts from Qumran. The traditional LXX text is similar to the MT, but the Lucianic text differs significantly from the MT at certain points and appears to derive from a considerably different Hebrew text. There are 107 verses (the Hebrew text has 167 verses) that have become known as the Greek additions to the text of Esther. Jerome knew that these were not part of the Hebrew text and placed them in his section of deuterocanonical works. A colophon at the end of the additions dates the book to the "fourth year of the reign of Ptolomy and Cleopatra," suggesting a date of 114 BC, and some of the details in these additions even contradict the Hebrew text. When Jerome translated the Latin Vulgate, he found the Old Latin texts of the book of Esther to be extremely corrupted; he therefore claims to have rendered a literal translation of the Hebrew text. It still contains numerous minor variants from the MT that may reflect another version of the Hebrew text. The Syriac Peshitta appears to follow closely, and at times almost rigidly, a Hebrew text very similar to the MT. Both Aramaic Targumim of Esther use a Hebrew text very similar to the MT and then add explanations and embellishments. The first Targum is twice as long as the MT, and the second one is four times longer.

2. Textual Critical Principles.

Since the texts were transmitted over such a long period of time, it is understandable that minor errors crept into various manuscripts. Therefore the job of the OT textual critic is to work back as closely as possible to the original reading of the text by comparing the external evidence (other Hebrew manuscripts and ancient versions) and internal evidence (hints from grammar, style, vocabulary, etc.). Intuition and common sense must guide this process. Informed judgments about a text depend upon one's familiarity with copyist errors, manuscripts, versions and their authors.

2.1. Types of Errors. Even though the scribes copying the manuscripts had a strong desire to maintain an authoritative, standardized text, common copyist errors still appear, including confusion of similar letters, homophony (substitution of similar-sounding letters or words), haplography (omission of a letter or word), dittography (doubling a letter or word), metathesis (reversal in the order of two letters or words),

fusion (two words being joined as one) and fission (one word separated into two). These types of mistakes are unintentional but still are introduced into the text through the copying process. However, as we noted above, there are also intentional changes that are introduced into the text, including updating spelling or grammar, euphemistic changes and theological changes.

2.2. The Process. One of the best ways to locate possible corruptions in the Hebrew text is to search for difficulties in translation, faulty or awkward grammar, apparent textual corruptions or variants in the various versions of the OT. Modern critical editions of the MT (e.g., *BHS, BHQ*, the Hebrew University Bible Project) have already done much of this work in their textual apparatuses. They note the pertinent external evidence from the various Hebrew sources (e.g., Hebrew manuscripts [Dead Sea Scrolls, medieval manuscripts]) and versions (e.g., LXX, Samaritan Pentateuch, Syriac Peshitta, Latin Vulgate) to help determine the most plausible original reading of the text. The next step is to examine internal evidence to see if there are any hints to help determine the original reading (e.g., grammatical structures, similar vocabulary, stylistic features). Four questions will help determine the most plausible original reading. (1) Which reading could most likely give rise to the others? (2) Which reading is most appropriate in its context? (3) Which reading is favored by the weight of the manuscript evidence? (4) Does the passage contain a secondary reading or gloss? This is where skill, knowledge and balance on the part of the textual critic are needed to help determine the most plausible reading of the text. In general, only about ten percent of the Hebrew text has any question regarding the original reading of the text, and of these, only a small portion make any significant difference in meaning.

3. Textual Critical Examples.

We will first illustrate an easy textual variant and then a more difficult as examples of the types of textual issues encountered in the poetic books.

3.1. Song of Songs 4:8. Here there is merely a change in vowel points, which were added much later by the Masoretes between AD 500 and 800. The first word in the verse is אִתִּי (*'ittî*), which, as pointed in the MT, means "with me." The editors of *BHS* suggest reading this text as אֵתִי (*'ētî*), meaning "come," which is supported by the LXX (δεῦρο), Syriac Peshitta and Latin Vulgate. This reading also corresponds well with the parallel unit, which uses בּוֹא (bô'), meaning "come, go." It is easy to see why the Masoretes would have vocalized this word as "with me," since the second unit also contains this word. If אֹתִי is not pointed as a verb, then one needs to be supplied by the readers. Given the grammar and the external evidence, it seems reasonable to argue that the pointing of the passage is incorrect in the MT and should instead read אֱתִי ('ĕtî), meaning "come."

3.2. Psalm 2:11-12a. Here we find one of the most difficult textual corruptions. Read literally, the text says, "Serve the LORD with fear and rejoice with trembling. Kiss the son, lest he become angry and you perish in the way." If this translation is correct, בַּר (bar) is translated as the Aramaic, not the Hebrew, word for "son" (the Hebrew word for "son" appears in Ps 2:7). Using the Aramaic word for "son" is plausible because the psalm appears to be addressing the nations that would most likely speak Aramaic (cf. וְרוֹזְנִים ["and rulers"] in Ps 2:2). But why use the Hebrew word for "son" just a few verses earlier? The editors of *BHS* suggest a variety of other options for reading this text. First, they, along with the collections of variants from Kennicott, De Rossi and Ginsburg, suggest the reading בְּשִׂמְחָה ("in joy") instead of בְּיִרְאָה ("in fear"). Second, the *BHS* editors prefer reading the phrase גִילוּ בִּרְעָדָה: נַשְּׁקוּ־בַר ("rejoice with trembling. Kiss the son") as: בִּרְעָדָה נַשְּׁקוּ לְרַגְלָיו (בְרַגְלָיו) ("in trembling. Kiss his feet"). The supposition is that the word וְגִילוּ was misplaced and should appear at the end of the phrase (in addition to metathesis of the *yôd* and *lāmed*). A final suggestion is to read the text as וְגִדְלוּ שְׁמוֹ בְרעדה ("and magnify his name in trembling") and delete the "kiss the son" as dittography. The versions are of little help here because they either read something very similar (Syriac Peshitta) or seem to entirely misunderstand the passage (e.g., the LXX has the curious reading δράξασθε παιδείας ["accept correction"], and the Latin Vulgate reads similarly). It is also possible that בַּר could be translated as "field," so that kissing the ground is a sign of submission (Ringgren, 12). At this point there does not seem to be a clearly superior resolution to what appears to be a corruption of this text.

See also CANON; DEAD SEA SCROLLS; ESTHER 4: ADDITIONS; ESTHER 5: GREEK VERSIONS.

BIBLIOGRAPHY. **B. Albrektson,** *Studies in the Text and Theology of the Book of Lamentations, with a Critical Edition of the Peshitta Text* (STL 21; Lund: Gleerup, 1963); idem, "Textual Criticism and the Textual Basis of a Translation of the Old Testament," *BT* 26 (1975) 314-24; idem, "Reflections on the Emergence of a Standard Text of the Hebrew Bible," in *Congress Volume: Göttingen, 1977* (VTSup 29; Leiden: E. J. Brill, 1978) 49-65; **W. F. Albright,** "Canaanite-Phoenician Sources of Hebrew Wisdom," in *Wisdom in Israel and in the Ancient Near East: Presented to Harold Henry Rowley in Celebration of His Sixty-fifth Birthday, 24 March 1955*, ed. M. Noth and D. W. Thomas (VTSup 3; Leiden: E. J. Brill, 1955) 1-15; idem, *From Stone Age to Christianity: Monotheism and the Historical Process* (2nd ed.; Baltimore: John Hopkins Press, 1957); **J. G. Baldwin,** *Esther* (TOTC; Downers Grove, IL: InterVarsity Press, 1984); **J. Barr,** "B'RS-MOLIS: Prov XI.31, 1 Pet IV.18," *JSS* 20 (1975) 149-64; idem, *Comparative Philology and the Text of the Old Testament: With Additions and Corrections* (Winona Lake, IN: Eisenbrauns, 1987); **W. D. Barrick,** "Current Trends and Tensions in Old Testament Textual Criticism," *BT* 35 (1984) 301-8; **D. Barthélemy,** *Les devanciers d'Aquila: Première publication intégrale du texte des fragments du Dodécaprophéton trouvés dans le désert de Juda, précédée d'une étude sur les traductions et recensions grecques de la Bible réalisées au premier siècle de notre ère sous l'influence du rabbinat palestinien* (VTSup 10; Leiden: E. J. Brill, 1963); **E. R. Brotzman,** *Old Testament Textual Criticism: A Practical Introduction* (Grand Rapids: Baker, 1994); **J. Cook,** "The Dating of Septuagint Proverbs," *ETL* 69 (1993) 383-99; **F. E. Deist,** *Towards the Text of the Old Testament* (2nd ed.; Pretoria: Kerkboekhandel Transvaal, 1981); idem, *Witnesses to the Old Testament: Introducing Old Testament Textual Criticism* (LOT 5; Pretoria: Kerkboekhandel Transvaal, 1988); **P. W. Flint,** "Psalms, Book of," *EDSS* 2.702-7; **M. V. Fox,** *Proverbs 1-9* (AB 18A; New York: Doubleday, 2000); **G. Gerleman,** *Studies in the Septuagint I: The Book of Job* (LUÅ 1/43.2; Lund: Gleerup, 1946); **C. D. Ginsburg,** *The Old Testament, Diligently Revised According to the Massorah and the Early Editions with the Various Readings from MSS and the Ancient Versions* (4 vols.; London; Trinitarian Bible Society, 1926); **M. H. Goshen-Gottstein,** "The Textual Criticism of the Old Testament: Rise, Decline, Rebirth," *JBL* 102 (1983) 365-99; **L. J. Greenspoon,** "Symmachus," *ABD* 6.251; idem, "Theodotion," *ABD*

6.447-48; **D. R. Hillers,** *Lamentations* (2nd ed.; AB 7A; New York: Doubleday, 1992); **R. L. Hubbard,** *The Book of Ruth* (NICOT; Grand Rapids: Eerdmans, 1988); **K. Hyvärinen,** *Die Übersetzung von Aquila* (ConBOT 10; Lund: Gleerup, 1977); **N. Jastram,** "Proverbs, Book of," *EDSS* 2.701-2; **S. Jellicoe,** *The Septuagint and Modern Study* (Oxford: Clarendon Press, 1968); **P. Kahle,** *The Cairo Geniza* (2nd ed.; Oxford: Clarendon Press, 1959); idem, *Der hebräische Bibeltext seit Franz Delitzsch* (Stuttgart: Kohlhammer, 1961); **P. Katz,** *Philo's Bible: The Aberrant Text of the Bible Quotations in Some Philonic Writings and Its Place in the Textual History of the Greek Bible* (Cambridge: Cambridge University Press, 1950); **B. Kennicott,** *Vetus Testamentum Hebraicum cum variis lectionibus,* (2 vols.; Oxford: Clarendon, 1776-80); **R. W. Klein,** *Textual Criticism of the Old Testament: The Septuagint after Qumran* (GBS; Philadelphia: Fortress, 1974); **E. Levine,** *The Aramaic Version of Lamentations* (New York: Hermon, 1976); **T. Longman III,** *The Book of Ecclesiastes* (NICOT; Grand Rapids: Eerdmans, 1998); **P. K. McCarter,** *Textual Criticism: Recovering the Text of the Hebrew Bible* (GBS; Philadelphia: Fortress, 1986); **B. M. Metzger,** *The Text of the New Testament: Its Transmission, Corruption, and Restoration* (3rd ed.; Oxford: Oxford University Press, 1992); **J. T. Milik,** "Textes des Grotte 5Q," in *Les "petites grottes" de Qumrân* (DJD 3; Oxford: Clarendon Press, 1962); **C. M. Moore,** *Esther* (AB 7B; Garden City, NY: Doubleday, 1988); **C. A. Newsom,** "Job, Book of," *EDSS* 1.412-13; **H. M. Orlinsky,** "Some Corruptions in the Greek Text of Job," *JQR* 26 (1935-1936) 133-45; idem, "Studies in the Septuagint of the Book of Job," *HUCA* 28 (1957) 53-74; *HUCA* 29 (1958) 229-71; *HUCA* 30 (1959) 153-67; idem, "The Textual Criticism of the Old Testament," in *The Bible and the Ancient Near East: Essays in Honor of William Foxwell Albright,* ed. G. E. Wright (London: Routledge & Kegan Paul, 1961) 113-32; **D. F. Payne,** "Old Testament Textual Criticism: Its Principles and Practice," *TynBul* 25 (1974) 99-112; **M. H. Pope,** *Job* (3rd ed.; AB15; Garden City, NY: Doubleday, 1973); idem, *Song of Songs* (AB 7C; Garden City, NY: Doubleday, 1977); **H. Ringgren,** *The Messiah in the Old Testament* (SBT 18; London: SCM, 1956); **B. J. Roberts,** *The Old Testament Text and Versions: The Hebrew Text in Transmission and the History of the Ancient Versions* (Cardiff: University of Wales Press, 1951); idem, "The Textual Transmission of the Old Testament," in *Tradition and Interpretation: Essays by Members of the Society for Old Testament Study,* ed. G. W. Anderson (Oxford: Clarendon Press, 1979) 1-30; **G. B. De Rossi,** *Variae Lectiones Veteris Testamenti . . .* (4 vols.; Parmae: Ex Regio typographeo, 1784-88); **S. Talmon,** "The Old Testament Text," in *The Cambridge History of the Bible,* vol. 1, ed. P. R. Ackroyd and C. F. Evans (Cambridge: Cambridge University Press, 1970) 159-99; repr. in F. M. Cross and S. Talmon, eds., *Qumran and the History of the Biblical Text* (Cambridge, MA: Harvard University Press, 1975) 1-41; **J. A. Thompson,** "Textual Criticism, OT," *IDBSup* 886-91; **E. Tov,** "The Text of the Old Testament," in *The World of the Bible,* ed. A. S. van der Woude, trans. S. Woudstra (BH 1; Grand Rapids: Eerdmans, 1986) 156-86; idem, "Recensional Differences between the Massoretic Text and the Septuagint of Proverbs," in *Of Scribes and Scrolls: Studies on the Hebrew Bible, Intertestamental Judaism, and Christian Origins Presented to John Strugnell on the Occasion of His Sixtieth Birthday,* ed. H. W. Attridge, J. J. Collins and T. H. Tobin (CTSRR 5; Lanham, MD: University Press of America, 1990) 43-56; idem, *Textual Criticism of the Hebrew Bible* (Minneapolis: Fortress, 1992); idem, "Textual Criticism, Old Testament," *ABD* 6.393-412; **B. K. Waltke,** "The Textual Criticism of the Old Testament," in *Biblical Criticism: Historical, Literary and Textual,* by R. K. Harrison et al. (Grand Rapids: Zondervan, 1978) 47-65; also in *Expositor's Bible Commentary,* vol. 1, ed. F. E. Gaebelein (Grand Rapids: Zondervan, 1979) 211-28; idem, "Aims of Old Testament Textual Criticism," *WTJ* 1 (1989) 93-108; idem, "Old Testament Textual Criticism," in *Foundations for Biblical Interpretation: A Complete Library of Tools and Resources,* ed. D. S. Dockery, K. A. Matthews and R. B. Sloan (Nashville: Broadman, 1994) 156-86; idem, "How We Got the Hebrew Bible: The Text and Canon of the Old Testament," in *The Bible at Qumran: Text, Shape, and Interpretation,* ed. P. W. Flint (Grand Rapids: Eerdmans, 2001) 27-50; **H. C. Washington,** "Wealth and Poverty in the Instruction of Amenemope and the Hebrew Proverbs: A Comparative Study in the Social Location and Function of Ancient Near Eastern Wisdom Literature" (Ph.D. diss., Princeton Theological Seminary, 1992); **J. Weingreen,** *Introduction to the Critical Study of the Text of the Hebrew Bible* (New York: Oxford University Press, 1982); **J. W. Wevers,** "Septuaginta-Forschungen," *TRu* 22 (1954) 85-138, 171-90; **S. White Crawford,** "Five Scrolls," *EDSS*

1.295-97; **T. D. Winton,** "The Textual Criticism of the Old Testament," in *The Old Testament and Modern Study: A Generation of Discovery and Research; Essays by the Members of the Society,* ed. H. H. Rowley (Oxford: Clarendon Press, 1951) 238-59; **A. Wolters,** "The Text of the Old Testament," in *The Face of Old Testament Studies: A Survey of Contemporary Approaches,* ed. D. W. Baker and B. T. Arnold (Grand Rapids: Baker, 1999) 19-37; **E. Würthwein,** *The Text of the Old Testament: An Introduction to the Biblia Hebraica,* trans. E. F. Rhodes (Grand Rapids: Eerdmans, 1979) 12-100; **J. Ziegler,** *Antike und moderne lateinische Psalmenübersetzungen* (SBAW 3; Munich: Verlag der Bayerischen Akademie der Wissenschaften, in Kommission bei Beck, 1960).

P. D. Wegner

THANKSGIVING, PSALMS OF

Psalms of thanksgiving give thanks to God because he has responded to a specific request for help, which leads to offering a sacrifice of thanksgiving at the temple to celebrate God's deliverance. Although there is much agreement among scholars concerning these psalms, genre assumptions do affect how they are understood. This article discusses how the psalms of thanksgiving have been understood in light of the different approaches to the history and development of genre. A fluid concept of genre and more flexibility in regard to the *Sitz im Leben* (setting in life) greatly enhance our understanding of the psalms of thanksgiving.

1. Individual Psalms of Thanksgiving
2. Community Psalms of Thanksgiving
3. The Importance of Thanksgiving

1. Individual Psalms of Thanksgiving.

1.1. Identification. The list of individual psalms of thanksgiving varies from scholar to scholar. For example, H. Gunkel includes Psalms 18; 30; 32; 40:2-12; 41; 66; 92; (100); (107); 116; 118; 138; S. Mowinckel lists Psalms 30; 32; 34; 73; 92; 103; 116; and C. Westermann includes Psalms 9; 18; 30; 31:7-8, 19-24; 32; 40:1-12; 66:13-20; 92; (107); 116; (118); 138. Such variety is due in part to different assumptions concerning the history and development of genres (see 1.2 below).

1.2. Genre Analysis.

1.2.1. Sitz im Leben. Genre analysis usually focuses on mood, content, structure and *Sitz im Leben.* Most scholars affirm that the *Sitz im Leben*

of the psalms of thanksgiving is a *worship service at the temple in connection with the thanksgiving offering (tôdâ).* Such an offering might be brought in response to a vow made by the worshiper in a difficult situation (Ps 50:14-15; 66:13-14). The bringing of a sacrifice in the payment of a vow is an opportunity to praise God in the presence of the people (Ps 116:14) by declaring how God had answered prayer and brought deliverance (Ps 66:16). A thanksgiving song (*hôdâ*) sung by temple servants in the sanctuary would also be part of the service (*see* Music, Song).

1.2.2. Mood and Structure. The dominant mood of the thanksgiving psalms is thanksgiving for deliverance, which is emphasized in the structure of these psalms. A declaration of intent to give thanks usually comes near the beginning, followed by the account of the distress and the change that has come to the psalmist's life because of the deliverance. Gunkel calls this account the identifying mark of the genre, which consists of the report of the distress, a summons to Yahweh and the deliverance. The second main part is a confession directed to others that Yahweh was the one who delivered from the distress (Ps 18:27-28; 34:6-9). The third main part consists of the thanksgiving sacrifice brought by the worshiper (Ps 66:13-15). The psalm might end with further affirmations of thanksgiving or exhortations for others to give thanks (Ps 118:28-29). It is recognized that the aforementioned order is flexible (Gunkel), and that the third part may be lacking (Mowinckel). Such a general structure is recognized by others (e.g., Westermann 1981; Weiser; Gerstenberger 1988).

1.2.3. Relationship to the Hymn. The mood of a thanksgiving psalm is similar to the *hymn. Gunkel distinguishes the hymn from the psalm of thanksgiving in that the latter gives thanks to God for a specific act of deliverance in the life of the worshiper, while the former gives general praise for God's great being and deeds. The distinction between the thanksgiving psalm and the hymn has been generally followed by scholars. Westermann, however, has argued that there is not a separate concept of "thanks" in Hebrew. The verb *yādâ,* many times discussed under the imperative form *hôdâ,* is never used in the OT as an expression of thanks between people. And in relationship to God, our concept of thanks is too centered upon ourselves to communicate the meaning of this verb. Rather, Westermann argues, the expression of thanks to God should be seen as a way of praising God. Thus, instead of the separate categories "psalm of thanksgiving" and "hymn," he places both under the category "psalms of praise." He calls hymns "descriptive psalms of praise" because they praise God for his actions and for his being. He calls psalms of thanksgiving "declarative psalms of praise" because they praise God for a specific act of deliverance, which is then reported, or declared, in the song of thanksgiving (see Westermann 1981, 25-32).

Although Westermann shows that the concepts associated with the psalms of thanksgiving and the hymns can at times be placed under the general idea of praise, the original categories are still followed by most scholars—E. Gerstenberger (1988) being a more recent example—because there is a legitimate distinction between hymns and psalms of thanksgiving. Westermann himself recognizes the basic distinction between general praise of God for his actions and being, which is the focus of hymns, and specific praise for a specific act of deliverance, which is the focus of psalms of thanksgiving. There are enough distinctions between these two ideas to justify the separate concept of thanksgiving. Linguistically, there is a distinction between the imperative call to praise of the hymn, which uses *hillēl*, and the expression of thanksgiving arising out of a particular situation, which uses *yādâ* (Westermann, *TLOT* 2.504). Although there is overlap between the two verbs, so that *yādâ* may at times be translated "praise," there is also an independent use of *yādâ* in the Psalter, where it is appropriate to translate it "give thanks." Such a translation is particularly appropriate when the psalm reflects a response of the psalmist to God's deliverance from a particular situation of distress. Psalms of thanksgiving may also mention vows and a thanksgiving offering *(tôdâ)*. When a psalm gives evidence of such a setting, the best translation of *yādâ* is "give thanks."

1.3. Different Approaches to Genre Affects Interpretation: Psalm 32. Significant differences among scholars concerning the history and development of the genres affect the interpretation of the psalms of thanksgiving. These differences can be seen in an examination of Psalm 32, where the passion of the psalmist raises questions concerning genre and the relationship of the psalm to the *cult.

1.3.1. Mixed Genres and Passion Evidence of

Lateness. H. Gunkel argued that the oldest genres were pure and simple, and that mixed genres occurred later when the genres influenced each other. In earlier times the individual was less forthcoming, but in later times the individual was empowered to express something personal, which is where the power and religion of the individual poet came to prominence. The prophetic era, with its negative evaluation of external worship, was key to the development of pious spiritual songs, which were sung apart from the temple ceremonies. However, these later spiritual poets continued to use the form of the different genres, breathing new life into them. Psalm 32 has been influenced by the prophetic movement. It probably was sung by the psalmist outside the sanctuary, perhaps even in the home. Earlier psalms of thanksgiving would have been composed by temple personnel, which explains their uniformity and impersonal tone, but Psalm 32 is full of passion because the poet speaks from his own experience of forgiveness. The influence from other genres is seen in that wisdom has penetrated this psalm in the use of the beatitude (Ps 32:1), the similitude (Ps 32:9) and the instruction (Ps 32:6-8).

1.3.2. Cult Emphasis. S. Mowinckel turns Gunkel's scenario on its head by arguing that the unmixed simple forms are later than the composite forms. The great poets were not late in history but early. Mowinckel placed most psalms in the period of the monarchy in the context of a New Year festival. The psalms were composed for the cult, so they use indefinite wording. The personal element is not omitted, because the temple personnel may have written the psalms on the basis of their own personal experience, even if they wrote for cultic purposes. Thus in Psalm 32 the traditional basic type is hidden behind the personal and didactic.

A. Weiser connects the psalms to a yearly covenant festival that reenacts the *theophany of God at Sinai. This provides the external framework in which most preexilic psalms, such as Psalm 32, had their setting. Psalm 32:6 speaks of offering prayer at the right time, which refers to the moment when God appears in a theophany at the festival cult.

1.3.3. Native Genre Designations. H.-J. Kraus develops genre categories that are derived from the terminology in the psalms themselves in order to avoid foreign categories. Psalm 32 is placed among the "songs of prayer" *(tĕpillâ),* which includes prayer songs of the individual, community prayer songs and thanksgiving songs. Although Kraus eliminates some of Gunkel's categories, he shares the latter's assumptions concerning the influence of wisdom. Psalm 32 is a thanksgiving psalm and is to be dated late, perhaps even used apart from the temple.

1.3.4. Small-Group, Postexilic, Synagogue Use. E. Gerstenberger (1988) calls into question the priority of the cult and emphasizes that there were rituals throughout Israel's history that served the needs of the common people in their small-group settings. These personal structures persisted even when secondary organizations, such as tribal, monarchical and temple structures, arose. Small-group settings became prominent in the form of local community worship in the final phase of OT history. The Psalter became a hymnbook for the synagogue communities of the Persian and Hellenistic periods. As older prayers were set in the postexilic context, a new emphasis on individual guilt and personal salvation arose. Psalm 32 reflects this changed social structure. It is used by the community of the faithful in a synagogue setting. No references are made to sacrifices, and the wisdom element is dominant. Such individual forms of exhortation seem to be indicative of postexilic religion.

1.4. A Better Understanding of Genre.

1.4.1. A Fluid Concept of Genre. While acknowledging the contributions that the aforementioned scholars have made to form-critical analysis of the psalms, we nonetheless should note problems with some of their assumptions (*see* Form Criticism). Gunkel operated with a rigid view of genre that limited each genre to one social setting and made any "mixture" of genres late. Based on more recent theories of genre, T. Longman argues for a fluid concept of genre that pays attention to the similarities of a text with other texts but also attends to the peculiarities of a text. Psalm 32, in a broad sense, could be classified as poetry, but more narrowly it could be classified as a thanksgiving psalm, or a thanksgiving psalm concerning forgiveness, or a thanksgiving psalm with wisdom elements for the instruction of God's people. Such an analysis does not solve all problems related to the role of wisdom in the psalms, but it recognizes that the poets had some freedom in the composition of their poems in order to accomplish their purposes. The passion expressed in Psalm 32 is not

necessarily a sign of lateness. Kraus's category "songs of prayer" covers too broad a range of psalms to be useful (see Day). Although there may be some benefit to genre designations that are intrinsic to the psalms, Longman shows the benefit of using genre terms that are not native to the time of the literature.

1.4.2. A More Flexible Concept of the Sitz im Leben. A rigid view of the setting of the psalms is also problematic. Mowinckel argued that the psalms were composed by temple personnel using basic types for temple use, but then it is difficult to explain the passion of the poets. He recognized that they may have written out of their own experience even when composing for the temple. However, although many psalms were written for temple use, the origin of the psalms should not be forced into one festival setting. Gerstenberger called into question the connection of the psalms to the cult, but he also understood the psalms to be liturgical in origin and placed them in a small-group setting of the synagogue in the postexilic period. He contends that Psalm 32 is not a private meditation but rather is meant to be witnessed by the congregation. However, little is known of the existence of synagogues in the Persian period, and many psalms are accepted by scholars as preexilic. Westermann (1981) also calls into question a close relationship of the psalms to the cult and sees the setting of the psalms related to life situations. This gives more flexibility to their origin. The psalms of thanksgiving arise out of everyday experience, which is prior to the worship service in the temple. The passion of Psalm 32 thus comes from the life experience of someone who has been forgiven. Perhaps a dichotomy between being written by temple personnel for temple use and being written by an individual and adapted to temple use is a false one. Flexibility in the concept of genre and life setting better explains the evidence that one finds in the psalms.

2. Community Psalms of Thanksgiving.

2.1. Identification Debated. There is much overlap between the individual psalms of thanksgiving and the community psalms of thanksgiving, including the mood of thanksgiving, the central structural element of deliverance from distress, and the connection to a service in the temple. However, the number of community psalms of thanksgiving is debated.

807

Weiser lists only Psalm 124, but Gerstenberger (1988) and Gunkel list Psalms 66; 67; 124; 129. Perhaps there are few community psalms of thanksgiving because of the influence of a later style (Gunkel) or the influence of other genres, such as the hymn (Gerstenberger; Weiser). Westermann (1981) connects the community psalms of thanksgiving to songs of victory in Israel's history (Judg 5), which do not make it into the Psalter because after the Babylonian exile Israel did not experience any victories.

2.2. Focus on Main Elements. If one takes into account the main elements that make up a psalm of thanksgiving in the context of a community response, a few more psalms would seem to fit this genre. For example, although Psalm 107 does not make Weiser's list, he later identifies it as a community thanksgiving offered at the festival. Gerstenberger (2001) also recognizes strong thanksgiving elements in the psalm, although he identifies it as a "reflection on praising," perhaps because of the hymnic elements in Psalm 107:33-41. Gunkel and Mowinckel list Psalm 107 as an individual psalm of thanksgiving, perhaps because different groups of individuals give thanks, but the psalm is directed to the community of the redeemed, evidenced by the use of the plural (Ps 107:1-2). Psalm 107 expresses the mood of thanksgiving (Ps 107:1, 8, 15, 21, 31), includes an account of four different situations of danger from which the people were delivered (Ps 107:4, 10, 17, 23), and calls for those delivered to offer sacrifices of thanksgiving (Ps 107:22). A more flexible view of genre allows Psalm 107 to be classified as a community psalm of thanksgiving. Other psalms, such as Psalms 65; 75, could also be included.

3. The Importance of Thanksgiving.

The psalms of thanksgiving show the importance of giving thanks to God. They also demonstrate the active involvement of God in the life of the people. It is no surprise that thanksgiving dominates the NT in light of God's greatest act of deliverance in the death, burial and resurrection of Jesus Christ. As the Israelites offered up sacrifices in thanksgiving to God, so believers today give thanks to God always and in every situation (Eph 5:18; 1 Thess 5:13).

See also HYMNS; LAMENT, PSALMS OF; PSALMS 1: BOOK OF.

BIBLIOGRAPHY. **J. Day,** *Psalms* (OTG; Sheffield: Sheffield Academic Press, 1992); **E. S. Ger-**stenberger, *Psalms: Part 1, with an Introduction to Cultic Poetry* (FOTL 14; Grand Rapids: Eerdmans, 1988); idem, *Psalms: Part 2; and Lamentations* (FOTL 15; Grand Rapids: Eerdmans, 2001); **H. Gunkel,** *Introduction to Psalms: The Genre of the Religious Lyric of Israel* (Macon, GA: Mercer University Press, 1998); **H.-J. Kraus,** *Psalms 1-59* (CC; Minneapolis: Fortress, 1988); idem, *Psalms 60-150* (CC; Minneapolis: Fortress, 1989); **T. Longman III,** "Form Criticism, Recent Developments in Genre Theory, and the Evangelical," *WTJ* 47 (1985) 46-67; **S. Mowinckel,** *The Psalms in Israel's Worship* (2 vols.; Grand Rapids: Eerdmans, 2004); **A. Weiser,** *The Psalms* (OTL; Philadelphia: Westminster, 1962); **C. Westermann,** *Praise and Lament in the Psalms* (rev. ed.; Atlanta: John Knox, 1981); idem, "ידה", *yhd hi.* To praise," *TLOT* 2.502-8. R. P. Belcher Jr.

THEODICY

Theodicy is discourse about the justice of *God in the face of indications to the contrary—the presence in the world of evil in all its forms. How can God allow evil to exist in his world if he is capable and desirous of removing it? Must we limit either the omnipotence or the benevolence of God because of the reality and prevalence of injustice or calamity? Stated thus, the problem is a "trilemma": God must not be good, or God cannot be in control, or evil is an illusion. Further, if God is not to be thought of as lacking knowledge of all the consequences of his well-intentioned actions, then omniscience is also at least a tacit assumption of classical theodicean discussion. The issue, as formulated in Western philosophical and theological enquiry, thus has to do with the coherence of the Christian portrayal of God. It deals with the core of theology: what is God like, and how does he relate to the world? Did the writers of the OT wisdom books and their contemporaries perceive the issue in these terms, and if so, did they attempt to write theodicies in an endeavor to mount a coherent defense of God against the charge of negligence or willful injustice?

1. Theodicy in the Ancient World
2. Theodicy in the Old Testament Wisdom Books
3. A Synthesis of Theodicy in Old Testament Wisdom Books
4. Conclusion

1. Theodicy in the Ancient World.

Israel was not the only nation of the ancient world to have cause to reflect on issues of divine justice. The wisdom literatures of Egypt and Mesopotamia in particular include some material analogous to that contained in the OT, and theodicy, as a central wisdom issue, is no exception.

The texts from Egypt that treat issues broadly concerned with theodicy cover a range of genres, from mythological texts to philosophical discourse, and there is no single approach to the problem of evil in relation to the activity of the gods. Generally considered central to the discussion is the concept of *maat, the divine order or harmony in the world, to be upheld by the gods and the pharaoh. Within that framework there are texts such as The Story of Sinuhe, which reflects a predestinarian stance, and the Instruction for Merikare, with its optimistic outlook on the punishment of evil and the power of magic. There are the Coffin Texts, which see evil as an inevitable aspect of the world order, brought to expression through gods or humankind. The Admonitions of Ipuwer struggles with questions of divine justice. Why does the "herdsman of all men" allow confusion and death to go unchecked? The Wisdom of Amenemope sets out a view of maat that relates the upholding of order to the unpredictable free will of the gods.

In the Sumerian poem A Man and His God a man protests his righteousness and blames his *suffering on the neglect of his god, though the poet acknowledges universal human sinfulness. The Babylonian text I Will Praise the Lord of Wisdom presents the complaint of a righteous sufferer that the divine will is incomprehensible. The Dialogue of Pessimism adopts a nihilistic stance with regard to life, and the Babylonian Theodicy, like the book of *Job, is in the form of a dialogue (see Disputation) between a sufferer and his "friend" as a means of exploring the god's dealings with humanity.

This is not the place for a full treatment of the relationship of any of these texts to the OT wisdom texts (in this dictionary, one could explore the entries on ancient Near Eastern background for each of the OT Wisdom books). There are no compelling reasons to regard any of the biblical discussions of theodicy as being direct borrowings of non-Israelite material, although some influence from Wisdom of Amenemope on Proverbs 22:17—24:22 is considered likely (see Washington). Much of the similarity

frequently observed may be due to the fact that the texts deal with universal questions in a culturally cognate milieu.

2. Theodicy in the Old Testament Wisdom Books.

All sections of Scripture have material relevant to the discussion of theodicy. The Historical Books from Joshua to 2 Kings, for example, may be viewed as an extended theodicy designed to provide an explanation as to why God was justified in punishing Israel for covenant unfaithfulness. It is principally the Wisdom literature, however, notably *Proverbs, *Psalms, Job and *Ecclesiastes, that deals in greater depth with the issues of evil and human suffering in relation to the character and purposes of God.

There is a widespread understanding that Israelite wisdom can be divided into two fundamentally different outlooks on the world: a conventional wisdom that sees right conduct bringing rewards and evil having dire consequences, and a more pessimistic and skeptical wisdom that questions the assumptions of conventional wisdom and undermines the basis of covenantal obedience. Thus D. Clines (lxi) can speak of the "determinism" of the book of Proverbs, with its "rather rigid notion of cause and effect," whereas the books of Job and Ecclesiastes "introduce that needed element of sophistication and realism into the philosophy of Wisdom, calling into question as they do so the universal validity of the tenets of Proverbs." These more skeptical works, it is believed, dare to question the naive outlook that held to an ultimately coherent and moral universe. For W. Brueggemann (317-403), all of Israel's wisdom tradition, but particularly those elements that stress the hiddenness, ambiguity or negativity of God, constitute Israel's "countertestimony," which must be held in tension with the "core testimony" set forth elsewhere in the OT.

The view adopted here (cf. Provan, 31-39) is that although there are different emphases and perspectives among the OT writers and within the wisdom tradition, there is no simple antithesis of conventional and skeptical wisdom on issues relating to the moral order, nor any incompatibility with Israel's covenant faith. Not every writer will adopt the same stance or foreground the same truths of a complex theological conundrum. Statements on the outworking of the "retributive principle" (the righteous are rewarded and the wicked punished) (*see* Retribution) may stand alone or be juxtaposed with laments and probing discussions on injustice. Given that their observations were astute in numerous other ways, if the biblical wisdom writers are to be worthy of the name *"sage," we should be slow to think them obtuse in their reflections on the moral order of the universe simply because counterexamples to their expressions of confidence in retributive justice can be cited. When the psalmist makes use of a proverbial sentence in noting that he has "not seen the righteous forsaken or their children begging food" (Ps 37:25 [cf. Prov 13:25]), we wonder, Did he walk around with his eyes closed? Or are his words in context designed to make us look beyond the hardship that we do observe? Why would we be tempted to "fret" (Ps 37:1) if evildoers did not sometimes flourish while the innocent suffer?

In an influential essay first published in German in 1955, K. Koch argues for the operation of an impersonal "action-consequence relation" rather than any notion of the retribution of God against behavior that is contrary to a fixed norm. L. Boström (90) refines this relationship to character-consequence, where, he observes, promises of reward and threats of punishment are characteristically linked with lifestyle. As indicated below, both character and actions are best regarded as outworkings of a covenantal relationship—the "fear of Yahweh"—that is at the core of the wisdom writers' concern as the fundamental and determinative principle for living in God's world (*see* Fear of the Lord). Each of the major OT Wisdom books will be considered in turn for its contribution to the theodicy discussion.

2.1. Theodicy in Proverbs. The book of Proverbs contains numerous formulations of the retributive principle, many of which, it is true, make no reference to God—for example, "The wages of the righteous lead to life, but the income of the wicked leads to punishment" (Prov 10:16). Hence some, following Koch, assume that Proverbs portrays a mechanistic outlook in which consequences follow inevitably upon actions (see discussion in Murphy). Aiding this perception is the observation that Hebrew words for "evil" can refer both to moral evil and to its consequences in judgment.

Some pairings of action and consequence are inherently logical associations (Prov 10:4;

24:33-34). In other proverbs the consequence is expressed in the passive voice (Prov 10:9, 24, 31; 14:11, 14; 20:20; 21:28), as the writer seems unconcerned to identify the source of the punishment. Whatever the origin of the individual sentences of the book of Proverbs (and it may be that many of them had an independent life as popular maxims before their incorporation into the canonical book), their adoption into the literary and theological matrix of Proverbs entails a transformation of meaning. Proverbs 1—9, an extended encomium on the benefits of wisdom, sets the book in a theological context where it is the fear of Yahweh that is to undergird the instruction and one's reflection on and response to the principles of morality (Prov 1:7; 2:5; 9:10). Behavior and its consequences grow out of a covenant relationship (Prov 1:29-33). It is Yahweh who dispenses justice (Prov 3:31-35; 16:4-5; 22:22-23; 23:10-11). Some proverbs indicate God's displeasure at certain behavior, with no explicit reference to its consequence (Prov 12:22; 15:8-9, 26; 17:15), while the personal involvement of God in judgment is given as a motive for not taking revenge (Prov 20:22).

Counterproverbs such as Proverbs 26:4-5 suggest that each is to be approached thoughtfully, not treated as absolute and universal in its application. They encourage reflection on the circumstances and the sense in which every proverb, not least those of the action-consequence type, is true. So a statement such as "The fool will be servant to the wise" (Prov 11:29) is there to be pondered, whether or not Proverbs gives any counterexamples of fools rising to positions of prominence (Prov 30:22; cf. Eccles 10:6). Moreover, Yahweh will not be bound with respect to the manner and timing of his responses. He is sovereign in all that he does (Prov 16:4, 9, 33; 19:21; 20:24; 21:1).

The realistic perspective on evil presented in Proverbs gives us pause to reflect on the character of the seemingly simple formulae of *righteousness and reward. The world of Proverbs abounds with those "who delight in doing wrong and celebrate the perversity of evil" (Prov 2:14). Regrettably, the guilty are sometimes acquitted, and the innocent condemned (Prov 17:15). The "better" proverbs offer the reader a value judgment on the options that may present themselves in a world that is far from ideal (Prov 15:16-17; 16:8). There is something enviable in the condition of the wicked (Prov 3:31; 23:17;

24:1, 19). The "how long?" sayings of the psalms of *lament find their counterpart in Proverbs 1:22; 6:9. While these two instances are addressed to the "simple" and the "lazy," since God is viewed as in control, there is an implicit appeal, as in the lament genre, for God to bring an end to the perversity.

Retribution may be delayed, but the reader is urged to wait for God to bring justice (Prov 20:22). There will be a settling of accounts, for nothing escapes God's scrutiny (Prov 24:12). How and when God will intervene to reward the righteous and punish the wicked is left unclear, but the life that Proverbs holds out for the wise righteous ones may hint at something beyond the temporal (Prov 3:2; 4:10; 9:11; 14:32; 15:24; cf. Is 53:10 [see Waltke, 104-5]). The life on offer is relationship with God (which, as Jesus notes in Mt 22:32, does not allow death to have the final word).

In the end, though, there is much about the world that is not clearly understood. The process of reflection is encouraged (Prov 25:2), but with no expectation that it will yield simple and satisfying answers. The path of wisdom lies in trust in Yahweh, not reliance on human understanding (Prov 3:5).

2.2. Theodicy in Psalms. The book of Psalms presents many moods in dealing with aspects of the justice of God. A dominant note of the Psalter is the celebration of Yahweh's kingship over creation (*see* Kingship Psalms), and his exercise of justice is acclaimed in association with this sovereignty (Ps 9:7-8; 10:16-18; 89:11-14; 96:10-13). The focus is on personal and sovereign divine agency in reward and punishment (Ps 75:7). God's righteousness is seen by the nations but is exercised particularly on behalf of the elect (Ps 37:28; 50:1-6; 67:4; 98:1-9) and the more defenseless members of society (Ps 10:18; 68:5; 72:2; 76:9; 103:6; 146:7).

Psalm 1 is generally thought to have been consciously composed as a preface to the completed collection. This opening psalm speaks confidently of the two ways: the righteous flourish, while the wicked are blown away like chaff. This is due not to impersonal retributive forces but rather to the providential "knowledge" of Yahweh (Ps 1:6). On any view that understands the compilation of the Psalter as an intentional theological activity, it must be apparent that the compilers did not see any incompatibility between such overarching statements and those psalms in the corpus that cry out in anguish at the injustice in the world. Hence we should be slow to dismiss Psalm 1 and the many expressions of the retributive principle in the Psalter as naive.

Another characteristic of the Psalter is its reflection on God's covenant promise to *David as the one through whom his just rule is to be mediated to the world (Pss 2; 110). The failure of the Judean monarchy prompts agonizing heartsearching over God's apparently failed promises (Pss 89; 132).

Many psalms appeal to God to act in judgment—that is, in salvation (Ps 5:11-12; 7:6; 26:1; 35:23-24; 43:1; 54:1; 71:2; 94:2). The appeal for God to intervene can be on the basis of one's righteousness (Ps 7:8; 35:24; 58:11), while there can also be a recognition of sin (Ps 32:5; 51:4) or of the fact that before God no one can claim to be in the right (Ps 14:3; 143:2). The psalmist's affliction can be acknowledged to be consistent with God's righteousness (Ps 119:75), and the ultimate recourse is an appeal to his love and mercy (Ps 4:1; 6:4; 25:16; 27:7; 31:9; 40:11; 51:1; 90:13; 109:21). The "how long?" cries of anguish are among the most poignant of the many expressions of lament that echo through the Psalter (Ps 6:3; 62:3; 82:2; 89:46; 90:13; 94:3; 119:84). As I. Fløysvik (135-77) demonstrates, the heart of the distress expressed in the psalms lies in the wrath of God, his passionately aroused hostility, and sometimes for no apparent reason (Pss 22; 44; 88), not in the impersonal operation of a retributive principle. What is most troubling is when God fails to heed the cry of his suffering people, when he "hides his face" in time of trouble and hence justice is delayed (Ps 10:1; 18:41; 22:1-2; 43:2; 44:9-16; 74:1; 143:7) (see Balentine).

Three psalms that deal at some length with issues of theodicy are Psalms 37; 49; 73 (see Ross). Psalm 73:1-16 laments the prosperity and the carefree arrogance of the wicked. There is seemingly no point to the psalmist's own integrity. At Psalm 73:17, however, a shift of mood occurs. The poet's proximity to God in the (earthly? heavenly?) "sanctuaries of God" gives him access to a divine perspective on things. He sees beyond present appearances to the "end" that God has in store for the psalmist's opponents. His previous anguish over the situation of those who live in defiance of God, relative to his own, is admitted to be lacking in depth (Ps 73:21-22). God will set the wicked on a slippery slope to ruin, while "glory" awaits the one whose highest good is to be near God (Ps 73:23-28). Had the poet stopped short at v. 16 (cf. Ps 88, which ends on a gloomy note), we might have been inclined to categorize the psalm as an example of the "skeptical" wisdom that calls into question God's active "knowledge" and mastery of the moral order of the universe, whereas the latter verses, with their affirmation of confidence in God, make the psalm a conventional expression of Israel's covenant faith, albeit one that gives expression to the perplexity of life's present circumstances. Not every reference to the circumstances of the wicked and the righteous should be expected to cover both perspectives—present anguish and ultimate reasurance—within a given compass. The psalms of *confidence sit comfortably alongside the psalms of lament in the same collection. There is nothing in the laments that contradicts the theology of God's commitment to his covenant. The laments presuppose this theology but agonize over the apparent conflict between their theology and their experience of God. Their "solution" is prayer; that is, the lament is directed to God himself, a personal and relational God who has it in his power to "wake up" (Ps 35:23) and act on behalf of his people.

There is an eschatological dimension to the justice of God when the psalmists express confidence that God will come to establish justice and turn tears into joy (Ps 96:13; 98:9; 110:6; 126:5; 135:14). Some psalms lament the finality of death (Ps 6:5; 30:9), but there are, as recognized by L. Greenspoon, glimpses of resurrection in Psalm 22:29; 23:6; 49:15; 73:23-28.

2.3. Theodicy in Job.

The bulk of the book of Job is a poetic dialogue involving the suffering Job and his "comforters" (Job 3:3—40:6). Readers (but not the characters of the dialogue) are given a glimpse of a heavenly perspective in Job 1—2, where we overhear the divine evaluation of Job ("blameless and upright" [Job 1:8]). We learn that it is "the satan," the heavenly prosecutor and agent of disruption, who inflicts on Job an escalating series of disasters. There can be no resort to dualism as a response to evil, however, as the satan clearly acts only as permitted by God (see Satan).

The premise of the book is that suffering is under God's control. Job asks, "Are we to accept good from God and not trouble?" (Job 2:10). While protesting his innocence, Job seems to have feared just such calamity as befalls him

(Job 3:25), and he laments the fact that God treats both good and bad the same way (Job 9:22). Hence, from the outset, the character of Job is portrayed as having a nuanced view of the application of the retributive principle.

Eliphaz is typical of the response of the interlocutors: "What innocent person ever perished; where were the upright ever destroyed?" (Job 4:7). These comforters are often taken as representatives of conventional Israelite wisdom, spokesmen for the principle of retributive justice as elsewhere expressed in biblical wisdom (e.g., Clines, 123). They are more accurately seen as caricatures, guilty of a simplistic overstatement and inappropriate application of these principles. With the advice of Job's comforters, and even Job himself, as the foil, the writer challenges the view that there is a simple correlation of wrongdoing and suffering. While at one level the work may be seen as an encouragement to patient perseverance in the event of unexplained suffering (cf. Jas 5:11), the suffering of Job is a backdrop against which to portray something of the nature of God's government of the world and to raise the question of how humankind is to relate to such a God. Is it on a transactional basis of reward for loyal service, or one of love and trust despite personal hardship (Job 1:9; 2:10)?

The voice of God from the whirlwind (Job 38—41) highlights the disparity of creator and creature. God is the source and measure of wisdom and does not owe Job an explanation. Job ought not to have condemned God in pursuing his own vindication. The outcome is Job's "repentance" (Job 42:6), not in the sense that Job assents to his comforters' charge of hidden sins that merit his suffering, but rather in acknowledging his woefully limited horizons (Dumbrell).

The epilogue, in which Job is vindicated and restored to health, wealth and good standing in society, demonstrates that the work is not antithetical to the retributive principle as such. The experience of suffering is always made more unbearable by the sense of abandonment by family, friends or God, with "none to comfort" (Ps 18:41; 22:1; 69:20; Eccles 4:1; Lam 1:2, 9). In the end, in a very "conventional" wisdom outcome, Job receives not only the approbation of God for having spoken what was right (Job 42:7) but also the genuine and tangible support of family and friends (Job 42:11).

2.4. Theodicy in Ecclesiastes. Ecclesiastes operates for much of the work on the level of empirical observation, a perspective on life "under the sun" (Eccles 1:3 [and 25x]), with perhaps only a hint of an ultimately revelatory perspective (Eccles 12:11). Whether from two or more hands—the voice identified as *Qohelet, responsible for the bulk of the material, and a *frame narrator/epilogist(s), responsible for the opening and closing sections (so Longman)—or (more traditionally) from the one hand who adopts a persona and a limited perspective, which may not be the author's ultimate perspective, is not important for our purposes. The perspective of Qohelet is that "all is *hebel*" (Eccles 1:2 [and 29x]). Although *hebel* is often translated as "meaningless" (which may be encompassed within the semantic domain of the word), there is good reason to see in this thematic statement not so much a philosophical comment as a psychological one—"bewildering, frustrating" (cf. the LXX's *mataiotēs* and its echo in Rom 8:20). Frustration, compared to "chasing the wind" (Eccles 1:14), a hatred of life (Eccles 2:17) bordering on despair (Eccles 2:20), anger (Eccles 5:17) and perhaps a resigned acceptance of one's lot (Eccles 2:24; 3:12, 22) are some of the varying moods of this sage.

What Qohelet observes is troubling. Things are not as they ought to be (though he does not clearly tell us how he knows what ought to be). There is an unfairness in life's vicissitudes (Eccles 2:21-23; 3:16-21; 7:15-18; 8:10-14; 9:1-6). Qohelet is a realist, observing the injustice, oppression and evil that plague the world (Eccles 3:15-17; 4:1, 3; 5:8; 9:11). This is a fallen world, and D. Clemens has drawn attention to the echoes in Ecclesiastes of language from the narrative of the fall (Gen 3). The righteous do perish, while the wicked live long (Eccles 7:15; 8:14). From all observation, death offers no solution in terms of rewards and punishments, for a common fate awaits humans and animals, the wise and the foolish, the righteous and the wicked (Eccles 2:15-16; 3:18-21; 9:2). It might not be so troublesome but for the fact that humanity seems destined for higher things. We long to understand things from an eternal perspective (Eccles 3:10-11) but find ourselves exasperatingly incapable (Eccles 7:24; 8:17; 11:5). Everything happens in its time in ways that are beyond human control (Eccles 3:1-8). The "heavy burden" that people endure is one that God has laid on them (Eccles 1:13). We must learn to accept that there are things we cannot alter (Eccles 1:15). Life's circumstances are not some hand dealt by an impersonal fate; they are attributable to divine providence (Eccles 5:19-20; 6:2; 7:13-14; 9:1).

Taking all of this on board, for Ecclesiastes, what should characterize the human experience is to "fear God and keep his commandments" (Eccles 12:13) (see Enns). Perplexities may remain, but it is not our place to resolve them, but rather to abide in a relationship of trust in our maker (Eccles 12:1). The work concludes with an intimation of final judgment (Eccles 12:14).

In Ecclesiastes we certainly have no theodicy in the sense of a solution to the problem of evil. As with any issue, however, perhaps the first step toward a solution is a clear and honest statement of the problem—"Life is frustrating, and then there's death"—and Ecclesiastes has at least provided this. The world that we experience is not ultimately as God designed it.

2.5. Theodicy in Lamentations. The book of Lamentations is an emotional outpouring in response to Jerusalem's downfall. In genre it is similar to the communal laments of the book of Psalms. Even more distressing than the physical devastation at the hands of enemies is the sense of shame and disgrace that this engenders as Jerusalem's conquerors gloat over the city's fate (Lam 1:7, 8, 21; 2:17; 3:45; 5:1). The city feels abandoned by God (Lam 2:3, 7; 3:44; 5:20). Worse, God was actively responsible for the disaster and is the real enemy (Lam 1:12, 14, 15, 17; 2:4, 5, 21; 3:43; 4:11). Yet, while the individual of Lamentations 3 (probably corporate Jerusalem) laments the calamity (Lam 3:59-66), there is no charge of injustice against God or any doubting of his power to intervene. God is still sovereign (Lam 5:19) and is in the right (Lam 1:18). The cause of Jerusalem's rejection is rebellion (Lam 1:5; 4:13). What has happened is not a whim on God's part; it has been planned (Lam 1:17; 2:17; 3:37-38)—an outworking, it would seem, of the covenant curse (see Deut 28—29). God does not enjoy the affliction of his people and will not reject them forever (Lam 3:31-33). If the calamity is due to covenant unfaithfulness on Israel's part, then that same covenant, and the character and purposes of the God who initiated it, give rise to a longing that once again God might bring about a restoration in the spirit of Deuteronomy 30 (Lam 1:21; 4:22).

The vision of hope positioned centrally to the book is founded on the divine character (Lam 3:22-33). Although almost certainly the events in mind are those surrounding the destruction of Jerusalem by the Babylonians in 587 BC, the lack of specific historical reference facilitates the book's service as an expression of the bewilderment of the people of God to distressing circumstances in any age and an encouragement to renewed confidence in the rightness of God's actions.

3. A Synthesis of Theodicy in Old Testament Wisdom Books.

Rather than a confusion of competing theodicies (or anti-theodicies), the biblical wisdom writers present a coherent, though multifaceted, approach to the issue. The following sections present a synoptic approach to the central issues canvassed by the OT wisdom books as they relate to theodicy.

3.1. The Reality of Evil. The biblical wisdom writers affirm and bemoan the reality of evil as a part of the makeup of this present world. Nowhere do they assume it to be inherent or necessary in a material universe. The ideal of the created order is represented in, for example, Psalm 8, where we see a marvelous world originally placed under the dominion of humankind (Ps 8:5-8; cf. Gen 1:26). Yet humanity exercises that dominion neither within God-given constraints nor for God-honoring purposes.

Although evil is often divided by philosophers and theologians into physical (natural calamities), moral (intentional harm perpetrated by responsible agents) and religious (rebellion against the revealed will of God), the OT writers regard all evil as a perversion of God's intended order for his creation and a manifestation or consequence of universal human sin (Ps 14:3; Prov 20:9; Eccles 7:29). There is no effort to probe beyond human sin to ascertain its ultimate origins or to ponder why God allowed such a state of affairs to come into being. The result is a universe that has become subject to frustration (Eccles 1:2; cf. Rom 8:20). The created order is warped as a consequence of sin and God's response (Eccles 1:15; 7:13).

3.2. The Sovereignty of God. Although the fool may disregard God and his sovereignty ("practical atheism" [Ps 14:1; cf. Prov 30:2-3]), theoretical atheism is never considered a viable option by the voices that we hear in the biblical texts.

The biblical writers portray the God of Israel as the unrivaled sovereign over the universe.

3.2.1. The Sovereignty of God over Natural Forces. A number of wisdom passages celebrate God as the creator and maintainer of all (Job 38—39; Pss 104; 139; Prov 8:22-31; Eccles 3:14; 12:1). The outcome of all that happens in God's world, even the casting of a lot, is dependent on his decision (Prov 16:33). The physical elements, even as agents of destruction, are under his command (Ps 18:7; 29:9-10; 65:6-7; 74:15; 78:47; 104:4, 7; 107:29, 33; 148:8). There is no attempt by the biblical writers to hide behind some notion of limited sovereignty when it comes to "natural" evil (Ruth 1:21; Ps 104:9; Prov 8:29).

3.2.2. The Sovereignty of God over Human Actions. God is also said to be in control of human activities (Ps 66:12; Prov 16:9; 20:24; 21:1, 30-31; Eccles 9:1). Even evil people and evil actions are not beyond the reach of God's power (Prov 16:4, 7; 29:13). Unless, with J. Crenshaw (2005, 75-86), we assume that human freedom is incompatible with divine omnipotence, and that by creating humans as free agents God circumscribed his own sovereignty (and the biblical writers nowhere do this), the problem as it affects the justice of God encompasses the human cruelty and oppression that are rife in our world.

3.3. The Omniscience and Wisdom of God. There is no recourse to a notion of limited knowledge or wisdom on God's part. In wisdom God brought into being all that is (Ps 104:24; Prov 8:22-31), and his watchful eye is upon all (Prov 15:3). Psalm 139 is an exposition of God's complete knowledge of human nature. God is the source of all wisdom and knowledge (Prov 2:6). It is on the basis of his complete knowledge that God can be relied on to execute justice (Prov 15:11; 22:12; 24:11-12; cf. Job 11:11).

3.4. The Incomprehensibility of God. A consequence of all of the above is that God's plans and procedures in dealing with humanity and the world are beyond our understanding. The wisdom poem of Job 28 is, in context, designed to remind the reader of the limitations of human understanding on the deep issues that are the theme of the book (see also Job 12:13; 36:29; 37:5; 42:3; Ps 92:5; 127:1-2; 131:1; 139:6, 17; 147:5; Prov 30:18-19; Eccles 8:17; 11:5).

3.5. The Benevolence of God. God is acclaimed as benevolent toward his creation (Ps 145:9). More commonly, God is represented as committed to doing good to or blessing his elect people

(Ps 5:12; 29:11; 34:8; 84:11; 86:5; 100:5; 103:8; 106:1; 135:3; Lam 3:25). This does not lead the OT writers to take such benevolence for granted, and it is a constant prayer on their lips that God act in accordance with his revealed character (Ps 25:6; 28:9; 40:11; 51:1; 67:1; 69:16; 119:132; 125:4; 134:3; Lam 5:1, 21-22). It is this clear understanding of God's love and goodness that makes his occasional apparent failure to act all the harder to bear (Job 7:21; 13:24; Ps 42:9; 77:9; Lam 5:20). Partial answers may be found in God's loving but painful discipline designed to bring about repentance and instill character in his people (Ps 118:18; Prov 3:11-12). Elsewhere, suffering is presented as that which fosters a closer trust in God and delight in his word (Ps 119:50, 143), and the covenant promise "I will be with you" (Gen 26:24) finds its most comforting application in the darkest times (Ps 23:4).

God is himself portrayed as sharing in the sufferings of his people. T. Fretheim (138-48) notes how God's restraint of his anger (e.g., Ps 78:38) is not without pain to himself, and God risks his reputation in subjecting his people to judgment (Ps 74:10-11; 78:61).

3.6. The Justice of God. Creation and the maintenance of order in the universe belong closely together. It is the task of the sovereign to uphold justice in his realm; how much more should we expect God, who made the world, to establish and uphold righteousness and punish wrongdoing. Many instances can be found where God's role is not stressed, but contextual considerations leave no room for an impersonal operation of an action-consequence relation.

3.6.1. Present Justice. The biblical writers portray God as a righteous judge to whom the oppressed may turn in the expectation of finding the justice they seek. However, God is sovereign also in his manner of dispensing justice. It is this sovereignty that gives rise to so much of the perplexity expressed. If God is able to withhold punishment and show mercy, then God's exercise of justice does not proceed according to a formula (Ps 30:5; 85:1-3; 103:10). M. Seifrid (416) observes that there are more than four times as many references to a "saving righteousness" in the OT than to punitive divine justice; thus, there has been significant discussion as to whether God's righteousness is to be seen as primarily relational, consistent with his saving purposes toward the elect, or norm-based and retributive. This question cannot be

explored in the present article, but it may be the case that a resolution is to be found in an understanding of the character of the new covenant (Jer 31:31-33), with its congruence of covenantal relationship and heart-inscribed righteousness.

Sometimes the involvement of God in the administration of justice is not in the foreground (*Esther), which might lead us to assume that the writer accepted with equanimity the fact that God seems inactive, remote or hidden. More commonly, the distance of God compounds the distress factor, all the more perplexing because it seems out of character for God to be silent to his people's pleas, or worse, actively hostile toward them (Job 13:24; 24:1; 34:29; Ps 10:1; 13:1; 44:24; 69:17; 88:14; 102:2).

The OT wisdom writers believed they lived in an ordered and moral universe in which virtue is rewarded and wickedness is punished, or, to be more precise, in which relationship with God ("the fear of Yahweh") and the lifestyle consistent with that relationship lead to blessing. All biblical writers are aware of the problems in maintaining such a notion, feeling the tensions intensely at times but maintaining it nonetheless.

3.6.2. Future Justice. The nations around Israel had notions of life beyond death and it would be strange if Israel did not do so also (*see* Afterlife). Although final judgment, resurrection and re-creation customarily have been regarded as at best peripheral to OT theology, some recent study suggests that the resurrection hope is more central to the OT, including the psalms and wisdom books (Greenspoon). The teaching of Jesus would suggest a hermeneutic of the OT that sees resurrection as built into the fabric of Israel's covenant faith (Lk 24:44-46). It is this faith, rather than some older notion of "international wisdom," that undergirds the OT Wisdom literature. Whether, with Y. Hoffman, we see the idea of retribution as a major factor in shaping Israel's eschatology, life beyond the grave offers another arena for retribution and restitution.

Although there is no easy recourse to a theodicy of ultimate retribution, Proverbs may hint at a balancing of the books beyond the grave (Prov 24:16, 19-20). Ecclesiastes, despite its prevailing empirical stance, looks to a time when "God will summon up the past" (Eccles 3:15) and ends on a note of confidence in ultimate justice (Eccles 12:14). Though of uncertain meaning, Job 19:26 may be an indicator of Job's faith in his ultimate vindication in the resurrection, a hope also held out in some psalms (see 2.2 above).

4. Conclusion.

The OT wisdom writers were well aware of the real tensions and perplexities raised by their covenant faith and their experience of the world. They were realists who struggled to comprehend the ways of God. They provide material, sometimes intensely felt, pertinent to the theodicy discussion, but it does not appear that they ever saw themselves as metaphysical theologians setting out to solve a logical conundrum. Their statements on the moral order, though often cast in the form of overgeneralizations and hyperboles so far as present experience indicates, are affirmations of faith, grounded in the character of God and statements of the principle on which he ultimately operates, though his ways are beyond discovery. If Job (and the reader of Job) cannot have access to the answers for the barrage of questions in Job 38—41, why should Job (or we) expect to be given the answer to inexplicable suffering? We are put in our place by such challenges as God utters in Job 40:8: "Would you discredit my justice? Would you put me in the wrong to put yourself in the right?" Thus the wisdom writers, while rhetorically seeking answers, were actually content to leave some questions unanswered in the spirit of Deuteronomy 29:29. Their "answer" lay in acknowledging that God is God. They might attempt to put God in the dock as a literary device to give vent to their bewilderment and pain, but ultimately they reject the notion that God is subject to human scrutiny. Rather than attempt to offer a rational explanation, to resolve the tensions by limiting God's power or denying his goodness, they (even the so-called skeptical writers) seek to instill in their readers the fear of Yahweh (Job 28:28; Ps 111:10; Prov 1:7; 9:10; Eccles 12:13). We may not understand God's ways, but God knows what he is doing, and the OT wisdom writers inspire confidence that the tensions will receive their ultimate resolution. A Christian perspective is that the OT is not God's ultimate word, and although the NT will continue to leave many questions unanswered (1 Cor 13:12; 1 Jn 3:2), the confidence that Christians have in the justice and wisdom of God finds its confirmation in Christ (1 Cor 1:30).

See also CHAOS AND DEATH; DIVINE PRESENCE; GOD; PROTECTION IMAGERY; RIGHTEOUSNESS; SUFFERING; THEOPHANY.

BIBLIOGRAPHY. **S. E. Balentine,** *The Hidden God: The Hiding of the Face of God in the Old Testament* (Oxford: Oxford University Press, 1983); **L. Boström,** *The God of the Sages: The Portrayal of God in the Book of Proverbs* (ConBOT 29; Stockholm: Almqvist & Wiksell, 1990); **W. Brueggemann,** *Theology of the Old Testament: Testimony, Dispute, Advocacy* (Minneapolis: Fortress, 1997); **D. A. Carson,** *How Long, O Lord? Reflections on Suffering and Evil* (Leicester: Inter-Varsity Press, 1990); **D. M. Clemens,** "The Law of Sin and Death: Ecclesiastes and Genesis 1-3," *Them* 19.3 (1994) 5-8; **D. J. A. Clines,** *Job 1-20* (WBC 17; Dallas: Word, 1989); **J. L. Crenshaw,** *Urgent Advice and Probing Questions: Collected Writings on Old Testament Wisdom* (Macon, GA: Mercer University Press, 1995); idem, *Defending God: Biblical Responses to the Problem of Evil* (Oxford: Oxford University Press, 2005); idem, ed., *Theodicy in the Old Testament* (London: SPCK, 1983); **W. J. Dumbrell,** "The Purpose of the Book of Job," in *The Way of Wisdom: Essays in Honor of Bruce K. Waltke,* ed. J. I. Packer and S. K. Soderlund (Grand Rapids: Zondervan, 2000) 91-105; **P. Enns,** "*kl-h'dm* and the Evaluation of Qohelet's Wisdom in Qoh 12:13 or 'The 'A is So, and What's More, B' Theology of Ecclesiastes,'" in *The Idea of Biblical Interpretation: Essays in Honor of James L. Kugel,* ed. H. Najman and J. H. Newman (JSJSup 83; Leiden: E. J. Brill, 2004) 125-37; **I. Fløysvik,** *When God Becomes My Enemy: The Theology of the Complaint Psalms* (Saint Louis: Concordia Academic Press, 1997); **T. E. Fretheim,** *The Suffering of God: An Old Testament Perspective* (OBT; Philadelphia: Fortress, 1984); **L. J. Greenspoon,** "The Origin of the Idea of Resurrection," in *Traditions in Transformation: Turning Points in Biblical Faith,* ed. B. Halpern and J. D. Levenson (Winona Lake, IN: Eisenbrauns, 1981) 247-321; **Y. Hoffman,** "The Creativity of Theodicy," in *Justice and Righteousness: Biblical Themes and Their Infuences,* ed. H. G. Reventlow and Y. Hoffman (JSOTSup 137; Sheffield: Sheffield Academic Press, 1992) 117-30; **K. Koch,** "Is There a Doctrine of Retribution in the Old Testament?" in *Theodicy in the Old Testament,* ed. J. L. Crenshaw (IRT 4; Philadelphia: Fortress, 1983) 57-87; **A. Laato and J. C. de Moor,** eds., *Theodicy in the World of the Bible* (Leiden: E. J. Brill, 2003); **T. Linafelt and T. K. Beal,** eds., *God in the Fray: A Tribute to Walter Brueggemann* (Minneapolis: Fortress, 1998); **T. Longman III,** *The Book of Ecclesi-*

astes (NICOT; Grand Rapids: Eerdmans, 1998); **R. E. Murphy,** "Wisdom—Theses and Hypotheses," in *Israelite Wisdom: Theological and Literary Essays in Honor of Samuel Terrien,* ed. J. Gammie et al. (Missoula, MT: Scholars Press, 1978) 35-42; **L. G. Perdue and W. C. Gilpin,** eds., *The Voice from the Whirlwind: Interpreting the Book of Job* (Nashville: Abingdon, 1992); **L. G. Perdue, B. B. Scott and W. J. Wiseman,** eds., *In Search of Wisdom: Essays in Memory of John G. Gammie* (Louisville: Westminster John Knox Press, 1993); **I. Provan,** *Ecclesiastes, Song of Songs* (NIVAC; Grand Rapids: Zondervan, 2001); **J. F. Ross,** "Psalm 73," in *Israelite Wisdom: Theological and Literary Essays in Honor of Samuel Terrien,* ed. J. Gammie et al. (Missoula, MT: Scholars Press, 1978) 161-75; **M. Seifrid,** "Righteousness Language in the Hebrew Scriptures and Early Judaism," in *Justification and Variegated Nomism, 1: The Complexities of Second Temple Judaism,* ed. D. A. Carson, P. T. O'Brien and M. Seifrid (WUNT 2/140; Tübingen: Mohr Siebeck, 2001) 415-42; **B. K. Waltke,** *The Book of Proverbs: Chapters 1-15* (NICOT; Grand Rapids: Eerdmans, 2004); **H. C. Washington,** *Wealth and Poverty in the Instruction of Amenemope and the Hebrew Proverbs* (SBLDS 142; Atlanta: Scholars Press, 1994); **J. W. Wenham,** *The Enigma of Evil: Can We Believe in the Goodness of God?* (Grand Rapids: Academie Books, 1985).

J. Davies

THEOPHANY

A theophany is a manifestation of God. The English word *theophany* is formed from two Greek words, *theos* ("God") and *phainō* ("appear"). Descriptions of theophanies are prominent in *Job and *Psalms, and this article focuses on these texts (for more general treatments, see the entries in *DOTP* and *NIDOTTE;* for theophany in narrative, see Savran). In Job and Psalms the appearance of Yahweh is accompanied by cosmic disturbances that shake the earth, bring mighty winds, deep clouds, coals of fire, lightning and smoke. When God reveals himself in these ways, his absolute uniqueness is communicated. This revelation of God results in vindication and right thinking among his people, while his enemies are thrown down and confounded. In some ways, theophanies capture the whole point of biblical theology in that they show the incomparability of Yahweh as he reveals himself to save his people through the judgment of their enemies (see Hamilton

2006a). In this he is showing mercy to those who fear him and justice to those who disregard his claim on their allegiance (see Ex 34:6-7).

1. Characteristics of a Theophany
2. Content of a Theophany
3. Consequences of a Theophany
4. Theophany in Biblical Theology

1. Characteristics of a Theophany.

In Job 38:1; 40:6 Yahweh speaks to Job out of the tempest, or storm wind *(sĕʿārâ).* In Psalm 18:7-15 the appearance of Yahweh is marked by the reeling and rocking of the earth and the trembling and quaking of the foundations of the mountains at the anger of Yahweh (Ps 18:7). Yahweh is depicted in anthropomorphic terms as smoke goes up from his nostrils and fire from his mouth (Ps 18:8). He descends from his heavenly dwelling place by bending the heavens, and there is thick darkness under his feet (Ps 18:9). Yahweh is depicted as riding on a cherub, and the cherub is poetically synonymous with "the wings of the wind *[rûaḥ]*" (Ps 18:10) (see Craigie, 174). The darkness of thick water clouds serves as his canopy and cover (Ps 18:11), and there is brightness before him as hail and hot coals of fire burst forth (Ps 18:12). His voice is the thunder (Ps 18:13), and the lightning is his arrow with which he routs the enemy (Ps 18:14). The great wind of the blast of his nostrils moves the waters so that the sea floor is revealed (Ps 18:15). As T. Hiebert (510) has observed, theophanies such as this combine the imagery of a mighty thunderstorm with anthropomorphic depictions of God as a conquering deliverer.

The theophany in Psalm 18 is particularly full in that it describes elements of thunderstorms and earthquakes accompanying the manifestation of Yahweh (see Eichrodt, 2.17-18). As the fullest description of a theophany in the Psalter, Psalm 18 also informs the earlier calls in Psalms for God to arise and help (or statements that he will do so [e.g., Ps 2:5; 3:7; 6:8-10; 10:12; 17:13]) as well as the shorter descriptions of God appearing to judge his enemies and save his people that come later in the collection (e.g., Ps 50:1-3; 77:16-20; 83:15; 94:1-2; 97:2-5; 104:1-3; 144:5-8). These features of the biblical texts also influence later extrabiblical literature, as J. VanderKam has shown.

2. Content of a Theophany.

2.1. Communicating Theological Truth.

2.1.1 To Answer Job's Questions about the Problem of Evil. In the theophany at the end of the book of Job the overpowering manifestation of Yahweh in the whirlwind arrests attention so that the matchless knowledge, power and authority of Yahweh can be declared. This is accomplished through a salvo of queries that the Lord directs at Job. The questions start with the created realm in Job 38 and move to living beings in Job 39 (for the suggestion that the material is arranged in both a linear and *chiastic fashion, see Miller). In Job 40 Job is questioned as to his audacity to contend with Yahweh, before having his attention directed to Behemoth, and then in Job 41 he is questioned about his ability to control Leviathan. All of this is intended to reveal the unique wisdom and power of God, vindicating God's righteousness in the face of the evidence from Job's life that God has not been fair to Job or that God might not be able to ensure that cosmic justice is upheld.

Beginning with the cosmos, Yahweh questions Job regarding his knowledge of the scope and results of the laying of the earth's foundation (Job 38:4-7). Next come questions regarding the shutting in of the sea so that it does not escape its set boundaries (Job 38:8-11). Job is asked if he has commanded the day, with all the morning light brings, to dawn (Job 38:12-15). Yahweh next challenges Job to declare his experiential knowledge (which Job obviously does not have) of the springs of the sea (Job 38:16), the gates of death (Job 38:17), the expanse of the earth (Job 38:18), the dwelling places of light and darkness (Job 38:19-21), the storehouses of the snow and hail (Job 38:22-23) and the point from which light and wind are distributed (Job 38:24). Yahweh next asks Job to explain to him the physics of rain, lightning and ice (Job 38:25-30), before asking if he can control the stars (Job 38:31-33), summon the clouds (Job 38:34) or send out the lightnings (Job 38:35).

Questions regarding living beings are introduced in Job 38:36, when God asks Job who gave wisdom to the inner parts of humanity and understanding to the mind. This is followed by a final question about the clouds and the waterskins of heaven (Job 38:37-38), before all the questions in Job 39 focus on living beings. With the overlap of these topics, the questions regarding the created realm and those who inhabit it are interlocked.

In Job 39 Yahweh asks Job about mountain goats and does (Job 39:1-4), wild donkeys (Job 39:5-8), the wild ox (Job 39:9-12), the ostrich (Job 39:13-18), the horse (Job 39:19-25), the hawk (Job 39:26) and the eagle (Job 39:27-30). As Job is asked to explain the mysteries of the cosmos and the ways of its living beings, the deluge of questions makes the point stated clearly elsewhere in the Wisdom literature: "Just as you do not know what is the way of the spirit as the bones are in the full womb, so you do not know the work of God who has made the whole" (Eccles 11:5).

This becomes explicit in Job 40:1-2, as Yahweh says, "Shall the one who contends with Shaddai be one who finds fault? The one who reproves God, let him answer it!" Throughout the book Job has been insisting on the merits of his case and calling for justice (e.g., Job 6:2, 24, 30; 10:1-22; 19:7; 23:1-10; 27:2), and the theophanic manifestation of Yahweh forces Job to recognize that if he does not fully comprehend the way of Yahweh in the created realm and in the animal kingdom, he cannot expect to fully comprehend the way of Yahweh in his dealings with human beings. Job recognizes this and pledges silence in Job 40:3-5.

Yahweh, however, is pleased to give Job more to think on concerning his sovereign power, so he continues to question Job out of the whirlwind (Job 40:6-7). Having dared Job to show himself equal to God in splendor (Job 40:8-14), Yahweh directs Job's attention to Behemoth (Job 40:15-24). Job is then asked if he can control Leviathan (Job 41:1-10), and this is concluded with a piercing question from Yahweh in Job 41:11: "Who has given to me that I should repay? Everything under heaven is mine!" From this climactic statement of his own absolute freedom from obligation, Yahweh goes on to extol the might of Leviathan (Job 41:12-34). The implication of Yahweh's questions as to whether Job can conquer and control Leviathan is that Yahweh has such power. Leviathan is the great beast of the sea, the place whence evil comes. As the lord of the evil sea, Yahweh's ability to bait (Job 41:1) and employ (Job 41:4) Leviathan for his own purposes corresponds to Yahweh's ability to entice *Satan to accomplish his will at the outset of the book of Job (Job 1:7-12; 2:3-6). Thus, the theophany at the end of Job communicates that Yahweh is the irreducible, incomprehensible, unconquerable Lord of all, including the evil that seems to prevail in events such as those that happen to Job (see Fyall).

2.1.2 Encouragement for the Faithful. It appears that these descriptions of the appearance of Yahweh are intended encourage those who trust him. So, for instance, the celebration of Yahweh's glory in Psalm 29 communicates that in whatever circumstances faithful Israelites may be, the reality is that the sons of God should ascribe glory to Yahweh (Ps 29:1-2). Yahweh, in majestic power, speaks with authority over the waters (Ps 29:3-4), over Lebanon and Sirion (Ps 29:5-6), over the wilderness of Kadesh (Ps 29:7-8), with the result that all who behold him gasp, "Glory!" (Ps 29:9). Yahweh's sovereignty is announced (Ps 29:10), and the psalm closes with a prayer that Yahweh give strength to his people and bless them with peace (Ps 29:11). The rhetorical effect of the exultant announcement of Yahweh's powerful word in Psalm 29:3-9 is to encourage the fainthearted and bring the awareness of Yahweh's greatness to bear on difficult circumstances. This is also apparent in Psalm 10:17: "The desire of the afflicted you hear, O Yahweh, you will establish their hearts."

2.2. Calling for and Celebrating Deliverance. The theophanies in Psalms are unlike the one in Job in that the beneficiaries of the theophany are not engaged in a propaedeutic dialogue with Yahweh. Instead, the superscription to Psalm 18 speaks of the day Yahweh rescued *David from all his enemies and from Saul. The Psalms theophanies are about the deliverance of God's people and the defeat of his and their enemies (see 3 below).

Psalm 18 opens with a statement of love for Yahweh because of what Yahweh is for the psalmist: strength, rock, fortress, deliverer, refuge, shield, horn of salvation, stronghold (Ps 18:1-2). In the next verse the psalmist states that he calls upon Yahweh, who is worthy of praise, and Yahweh responds by saving him (Ps 18:3). After this introduction the distress that the psalmist faced is described (Ps 18:4-5), followed by an illustration of the cry for help described in Psalm 18:3. The cry comes to Yahweh in his temple, and it reaches his ears (Ps 18:6). The cry coming to Yahweh's ears is part of the anthropomorphism of the imagery, the full picture of which has Yahweh enthroned in the heavens with the ark of the covenant in the holy of holies as his footstool. Yahweh sits as king, and his temple in Jerusalem is the place on earth from

which he is accessed. This understanding informs the theophany of Psalm 18:7-15 summarized earlier (see 1 above; *see* Divine Presence).

Yahweh is depicted in these theophanies in Psalms as rising from his throne in heaven (Ps 17:13), bending the heavens (Ps 18:9), and riding a cherubim as a chariot (Ps 18:10) to rescue his servant (Ps 18, superscription).

3. Consequences of a Theophany.
After God confronts Job, Job despises himself and repents in dust and ashes (Job 42:5-6), but then Job is vindicated, and those who tormented him are rebuked (Job 42:7-9). Similarly, the coming of the Mighty One in Psalm 50 is first a call for his faithful ones (Ps 50:5) to *worship him correctly (Ps 50:1-15), followed by a rebuke of the wicked (Ps 50:16-23). When Yahweh appears in conquering glory, his enemies are terrified (Ps 2:5). The enemies of God's people have their teeth shattered from Yahweh's blow to their cheek (Ps 3:7). These enemies are warned that they will be ashamed (Ps 6:10). The shameful defeat of the enemies of God's people results in the vindication of those who trust him, and this dual aspect of God's appearance on behalf of his people is expressed in Psalm 9. There we read that enemies perish before the presence of Yahweh (Ps 9:3), while the psalmist is lifted up from the gates of death (Ps 9:13). When Yahweh is urged to rise up and remember the afflicted (Ps 10:12), he is simultaneously called upon to break the arm of the wicked (Ps 10:17). The psalmist exhorts Yahweh to arise and confront and subdue the wicked, which is also the deliverance of the psalmist's soul (Ps 17:13). When Yahweh appears, he will utterly destroy his enemies (Ps 21:8-13). The cumulative teaching of these representative indications (many similar texts could be cited) of what happens when Yahweh appears on behalf of his people is that nothing and no one can stand against Yahweh. Neither the sea (Ps 74:13) nor Leviathan (Ps 74:14) nor foes of Israel (Ps 74:10) have any hope of overcoming Yahweh when he arises to defend his cause and stretch forth his mighty right arm to save (Ps 74:11, 22).

4. Theophany in Biblical Theology.
In Psalm 2 Yahweh terrifies his enemies (Ps 2:5), but then the executor of his wrath is his anointed king, who breaks enemy nations with a rod of iron (Ps 2:9). Obeisance to Yahweh takes

the form of kissing God's "son" (Ps 2:10-12). When the king rides out victoriously in Psalm 45:4, his throne is identified with the throne of God (Ps 45:6). Psalm 110 speaks of Yahweh shattering heads on the day of his wrath (Ps 110:6 [*rō'š* here typically is rendered "chiefs"]), and there is a close connection between the day of Yahweh's wrath in Psalm 110:6-7 and the day of the king's power (Ps 110:3; see Hamilton 2006b). These texts, and there are others, seem to bring together the day of victory for Israel's king and the day on which Yahweh rises to save his people and judge their enemies (*see* Kingship Psalms).

The Gospels present Jesus in theophanic glory at the transfiguration (Mk 9:2-8 par.), and the mountain setting, the radiant glory and the human response—a desire to worship—provide points of contact with the theophanies of Psalms. The pleas in Psalms for God to rise and defeat his enemies and save his people find their ultimate answer in what is described in the book of Revelation. There the risen and glorified Jesus promises comfort for his battered people (Rev 1—3) before unsealing the scroll (Rev 5—8), which results in the seven trumpet blasts (Rev 8—11), which in turn give way to the seven bowls of God's wrath (Rev 15—16). The outpouring of God's wrath results on the final overthrow of Babylon, God's great enemy (Rev 17—18), and the appearing of the messianic warrior king, Jesus, to save and judge (Rev 19—20). T. Glasson (259) contends, "The importance of the OT theophanies in relation to NT conceptions of the End has never been sufficiently realized." Once all this is accomplished, God dwells with his people in the new heavens and new earth (Rev 21—22).

See also GOD; SALVATION AND DELIVERANCE IMAGERY; THEODICY; WARFARE IMAGERY.

BIBLIOGRAPHY. **G. K. Beale,** *The Temple and the Church's Mission: A Biblical Theology of the Dwelling Place of God* (NSBT; Downers Grove, IL: InterVarsity Press, 2004); **P. C. Craigie,** *Psalms 1-50* (WBC 19; Nashville: Thomas Nelson, 1983); **W. Eichrodt,** *Theology of the Old Testament,* trans. J. A. Baker (2 vols.; OTL; Philadelphia: Westminster, 1961-1967); **R. S. Fyall,** *Now My Eyes Have Seen You: Images of Creation and Evil in the Book of Job* (NSBT; Downers Grove, IL: InterVarsity Press, 2002); **T. F. Glasson,** "Theophany and Parousia," *NTS* 34 (1988) 259-70; **J. Hamilton,** "The Center of Biblical Theology: The Glory of God in Salvation through Judgment?" *TynBul* 57 (2006a) 57-84; idem, "The Skull Crushing Seed of the Woman: Inner-Biblical Interpretation of Genesis 3:15," *The Southern Baptist Journal of Theology* 10.2 (2006b) 30-54; **T. Hiebert,** "Theophany in the OT," *ABD* 6.505-11; **T. Longman III and D. G. Reid,** *God Is a Warrior* (SOTBT; Grand Rapids: Zondervan, 1995); **J. E. Miller,** "Structure and Meaning of the Animal Discourse in the Theophany of Job (38,39-39,30)," *ZAW* (1991) 418-21; **J. J. Niehaus,** *God at Sinai: Covenant and Theophany in the Bible and the Ancient Near East* (SOTBT; Grand Rapids: Zondervan, 1995); idem, "Theophany, Theology of," *NIDOTTE* 4.1247-50; **M. F. Rooker,** "Theophany," *DOTP* 859-64; **G. W. Savran,** *Encountering the Divine: Theophany in Biblical Narrative* (JSOTSup 420; London: T & T Clark International, 2005); **J. VanderKam,** "The Theophany of Enoch I 3b-7, 9," *VT* 23 (1973) 130-50.   J. Hamilton

TIME

Time is a manifold aspect of the created order in which both God and humanity act. Rather than using one main term or concept for time, the OT uses diverse terminology for time or temporal realities. The materials relevant to time can be fruitfully organized and explained by using the categories of natural time, historical time and eschatological time. The theology of time also involves reflection on eternity and its relationship to temporal realities and experiences.

    1. Terms Related to Time
    2. Different Kinds of Time
    3. Time and Eternity

1. Terms Related to Time.
Although Hebrew terminology and syntax are capable of expressing an abstract concept of "time in general" (Barr, 96-104; see Eccles 9:11), the OT does not emphasize such an abstract concept of time (de Vries, 343-50; Tomasino, *NIDOTTE* 3.564; von Rad, 99-100). Instead, its writers usually use terms and phrases that refer to specific, concrete temporal moments, periods, cycles or experiences of time. For the purposes of this article, the following two Hebrew terms are the most important.

1.1. "Day" (yôm). The most frequently used temporal term in the OT is *yôm,* usually translated "day." Its primary meaning is the period of light as opposed to night (Esther 4:16; Job 17:12

[used figuratively]; 24:16; Ps 1:2; 139:12). Yet it is an exceptionally flexible term, often used in various prepositional phrases. It is frequently used to refer to the whole cycle of night and day, a "twenty-four hour" day (e.g., Ruth 4:5; Esther 1:10; Job 3:1, 6), or a more general time period (Job 15:23; 21:13; 38:23; Ps 102:2; Prov 11:4; Lam 2:16, 21). It also has many specific uses either by itself or in idioms, such as "lifetime" (Job 14:6; Eccles 7:15), "every day" (Ps 140:2), "holiday" (Esther 8:17) or a previously announced special "day" (Lam 1:21). The plural, *yāmîm*, often refers to an extended period, either indefinite (Prov 3:2; 9:11; Eccles 2:16; 7:10) or set within certain parameters, such as a person's or people's lifetime ("my days" [Job 17:11; Ps 39:4-5; 102:11]; "all the days of my life" [Ps 23:6; 27:4]; cf. "our days" [Ps 90:9-15]). In the phrase "all the days" it means "forever" or "always" (similar to a use of *ʿôlām*). We can learn much about the OT temporal perspectives from a contextual analysis of various adverbial expressions containing *yôm*, whether they relate to the past ("the day past" or "yesterday"), the present ("present day" or "today") or the future ("the day future" or "tomorrow") (see de Vries).

1.2. "Time" (ʿēt). The Hebrew term most commonly translated "time" is *ʿēt*, which is used some forty times in *Ecclesiastes and twenty-two times in *Psalms. The term *ʿēt* can usually be translated as "a time" and usually expresses "a point in time" or "a period of time" when an event or set of events occur (Tomasino, *NIDOTTE* 3.563-64). It can also express the "appropriate time" or "right time" for an event (Prov 15:23; Eccles 8:5; cf. Eccles 3:2-8, 11; see Kronholm, 447). Occasionally, *ʿēt* seems to refer to time in general, as when *Qohelet states, "The race is not to the swift, nor the battle to the mighty . . . but time [ʿēt] and chance befall them all" (Eccles 9:11) (see Barr, 98; Kronholm, 449).

2. Different Kinds of Time.

Time may be discussed in terms of three interrelated but distinguishable types: natural time, historical time and eschatological time (see Preuss). Each of these three aspects of time has both negative elements arising from human sin and divine judgment upon it and positive aspects arising from the goodness of creation and God's redemptive work within it. Natural, historical and eschatological time correspond loosely to God's works of creation, redemption and con-

summation respectively. Biblical writers urge humans to relate to time's varied faces with wisdom and appropriate ethical and liturgical behavior.

Much debate has taken place as to the extent to which various biblical writers have a "cyclical" conception of time or a "linear" conception of time. This way of construing the debate can be critiqued for problematically imposing concepts upon the OT writings that do not fit its patterns of thinking (Childs, 76-84). The OT includes both the cyclical understanding of time and linear concepts of time (Kronholm, 446-47; Tomasino, *NIDOTTE* 3.564), with cyclical (natural) time constituting the "building blocks" of linear (historical and eschatological) time.

2.1. Natural Time.

2.1.1. Natural Cycles of Time. There are several cycles of time rooted in nature through the heavenly bodies—sun, moon and stars (see Ps 104:19-23). Thus, natural time refers to the daily, monthly, seasonal and yearly rhythms that mark everyday experience in what Qohelet calls life "under the sun" (see Preuss). The most basic natural marker of time is the day *(yôm)*, which can be subdivided into evening and morning or into evening, morning and noonday (Ps 55:17), and which forms a seven-day week that culminates in the Sabbath. Although the week is established by direct divine ordination without the mediation of the heavenly bodies, we may consider it to be part of the natural cycles of time.

In addition, there are cycles of time set by the natural life cycles and developmental stages of human beings. There are the generational cycles of about forty years (Ps 78:5-8; Eccles 1:4) and the natural life cycle of about seventy years (Ps 90:11). Exceptions to the typical human lifespan are understood as signs of divine action. Such exceptions could be a sign of divine judgment, as in the case of premature death, which some writers understand as dying before one's time (Job 15:32; Eccles 7:17). Alternatively, such exceptions could indicate extraordinary divine favor, as in cases of unusually "long life" (Ps 21:4). Developmental stages mark human lives: prenatal (Ps 58:3; 139:13-16), birth, infancy (the period of breastfeeding), childhood (after weaning [Ps 131:2]), youth (Eccles 12:1; Lam 3:27), adulthood (child-rearing age) and old age (Ps 71:9).

Much about natural time is predictable and orderly, but it also involves a measure of unpredictability because human beings cannot foresee the temporal unfolding of life with precision. For example, one cannot determine whether or exactly when a child will be born. Or one cannot predict the precise timing of death, though surely will it come (Eccles 9:11).

The predictable cycles of natural time and the unpredictability within it speak volumes about the finite, time-bound and uncontrollable character of human creaturely life. The order and limits of natural time largely organize and determine human life and activity. People are not free simply to ignore natural temporal cycles by going without sleep when it is nighttime or trying to grow crops in the winter. One cannot simply choose to live as few or as many years as one wants to.

All human beings are subject to the order, limits, predictability and unpredictability of natural time. But depending on the beholder, such characteristics can be experienced in different ways. For some, natural time is experienced as frustrating and stultifying in its constraints on human freedom and disruptive hindrances upon human efforts. Viewing the temporal cycles apart from God's good purposes, Qohelet declares the natural cycle of time to be meaningless, wearisome and frustrating—along with everything else (Eccles 1:4-5). "There is nothing new under the sun," and this is depressing (Eccles 1:9; cf. Eccles 1:9-10; 3:1-15; 9:11; see Kronholm, 448-49). Yet, for the godly, the stability and predictability of the natural cycles of time provide a reassuring reminder that, under divine providence, there is meaningful order in created life (Pss 104; 139). The limitations and unpredictability function as reminders to submit to the eternal God, who transcends human limitations (as in Pss 90; 102).

2.1.2. Natural Time and Divine Providence. Indeed, through the eyes of faith and wisdom biblical writers (including Qohelet) generally understand all of life in time as sustained, ordered and governed by the wise and good hand of God (Ps 104:19-23; 145:15). *Job points to the existence of specific, divinely ordered times even for the animals to give birth (Job 39:1-2).

At the heart of God's providence is God's sustenance and governance of humanity, of whom God is particularly "mindful" (Ps 8:4). The psalms often express a deep sense of God's sovereign and providential care: "My times are in your hands" (Ps 31:15; cf. Ps 39:5-7; 90:9-10, 12, 14; 139:1-18; also Job 7:6; 8:9; see Sæbø, 27). De-

spite the generally pessimistic tone of his writing, Qohelet, in Ecclesiastes 3, confirms the reality of divine providence. He declares, "There is an appointed time [zĕmān] for everything, and there is a time [ʿēt] for every event under heaven" (Eccles 3:1 NASB). There is a time for each one of a whole variety of activities, events and emotions (Eccles 3:2-8). God's providential order even includes the time of distress or of trouble (Eccles 3:2-8; cf. Job 38:23; Ps 37:19, 39; Prov 25:19). Qohelet concludes with the conviction that God "has made everything appropriate [yāpeh; 'fair, beautiful'] in its time [ʿēt]" (Eccles 3:11 NASB).

2.2. Historical Time. Besides the kind of time that runs in repetitive natural cycles, there is historical time, the meaningful unfolding of distinctive events under divine providence. Although one may speak of historical time as "linear," some texts point to the linear history itself as being marked by cyclical patterns in which "nothing is new under the sun" (Eccles 1:9 [cf. the cyclical patterns in Judges]). The concept of historical time is more important for narrative books such as *Ruth and *Esther, but wherever an awareness of God's providence over human life is evident, the concept of historical time typically is close at hand. Historical time includes several different ideas within it.

2.2.1. Chronology. Historical time includes the basic idea of chronology, understood as the neutral notion of one event following another in a countable, measurable manner. The books of Ruth and Esther work with this aspect of time whenever they record when something happened (using the language of "in the *nth* year, the *nth* month"). Ruth opens with a time reference, "in the days when the judges ruled" (Ruth 1:1 NASB), and offers temporal markers at key seams within the book (e.g., Ruth 1:4, 22; 2:23). Ruth also concludes with a genealogy (Ruth 4:17-22), a paradigmatic biblical way of patterning historical time in relation to God's purposes, especially God's promise to bless Abraham's descendents. Esther is full of temporal markers, including some twenty-four uses of the term for "month" *(ḥōdeš)*. "Temporal sequence is of great importance in the development of the book of Esther" (de Vries, 114), especially to highlight key junctures in the narrative's plot.

2.2.2. Divine and Human Action in History. Historical time transcends mere uniform, quantitative chronology to tell the story of the qualitative history-shaping actions of God and humans (on the quantitative-qualitative distinction, see de Vries, 343-46). Historical time is marked by times and seasons that tell a dramatic story with stretches of "flatland" (periods of everyday time that may be cyclical or repetitive) interspersed with "peaks and valleys" (positive and negative epoch-shaping actions). The most important peaks and valleys of history are constituted by purposeful divine acts of salvation and judgment, with or without the active participation of humanity. As some psalms testify, God's redemptive work in human history includes judgment for the sin of both Israel (e.g., Ps 44:9-16; 60:1-5; 81:11-12; 137:7) and the nations (e.g., Ps 60:6-12; 105:23-45; 108:9-13). The book of *Lamentations emphasizes the judgment that comes on God's own people, speaking of the "day of the LORD's wrath" (Lam 1:12; 2:1, 21-22) (see Sæbø, 31). Yet when God's wrath comes on the enemies of Israel, the day of God's wrath is often also portrayed as the day of God's salvation for his people (e.g., Ps 108:9-13).

Although God is the primary actor in and sovereign over historical time, godly people can become redemptive agents who participate in shaping the historical course of Israel and the nations. As the books of Ruth and Esther suggest, these agents can include *women. In the book of Esther implicit divine providence meets individual responsibility and risk-taking. God's good purposes for individuals and groups are fulfilled in a paradoxical interweaving of divine and human action. This mysterious conjunction is evident in the well-known question that *Mordecai poses to Esther: "And who knows whether you have not attained royalty for such a time as this?" (Esther 4:14 NASB).

Despite the significance of individual persons and their actions, the view of time and history is often marked by communal and transgenerational ways of thinking that stand in contrast to (post)modern Western individualism. For example, the psalms understand retribution for the good or evil actions of individuals in intergenerational terms (Ps 37:28-29; 112:2). More obviously, God's election and love for Israel extend from generation to generation (Ps 103:17; Lam 3:22-23).

Remembering and celebrating the past redemptive events form an important part of historical time and the life of the righteous. A corporate liturgical celebration in the book of Esther includes the inauguration of the festival of *Purim (Esther 9:24-28). As is true of all annual liturgical feasts and festivals (see Megillot and Festivals), Purim integrates remembrance of a once-for-all event of corporate deliverance (historical time) into the yearly seasonal calendar (natural time). The psalms include a multitude of personal and corporate declarations of thanksgiving based on God's past deliverance of the psalmist. *Worship that celebrates God's past actions also involves hope and trust that God can and will act in a similar way in the near and distant future.

A proper response to God as the Lord of history also includes remembering God's past acts of judgment or discipline as an incentive to live obediently in the present and the future: "Today, if you would hear his voice, do not harden your hearts, as at Meribah, as in the day of Massah in the wilderness" (Ps 95:7-8 NASB). The liturgical "today" in Psalm 95:7 refers to any day in which God's people can hear and respond to God, showing the capacity of liturgical time to bring past, present and future together under God's everlasting lordship (cf. Heb 3:7, 13, 15; 4:7).

2.3. Eschatological Time. The appointed time for final salvation and judgment is not now but rather in the future, in what can be called an eschatological future. Eschatological time is the final consummation of God's purposes for creation (including the final destiny of nations and individuals).

Eschatological time exists in both continuity and discontinuity with the time that precedes it, including natural and historical time. On the one hand, the final state of history or human existence is qualitatively different from life in time as we know it; on the other hand, eschatological time also stands in continuity with the time that precedes it, for two main reasons. First, eschatological time involves a restoration or recovery of the uncorrupted time of the original created order—an order that is partly reflected in natural and historical time. As such, there is truth to the notion that "beginning time" (German *Urzeit*) corresponds to "end time" (German *Endzeit*), although the biblical writers overcome the mythical idea of a complete and ahistorical repetition of the beginning at the end (Childs, 73-84). Second, there is also continuity between time as humans know and experience it (i.e., time as fallen and redeemed) and eschatological time. The merciful and judging actions of God in natural and historical time point to a future in which God's redemptive purposes will be consummated or perfected.

The general description of "eschatological time" given so far awaits further concretization through the testimony of the texts considered below. These texts can be divided into those that are primarily concerned with the future of collective bodies (like Israel and the nations) and those that concern the future of individuals respectively. Whether corporate or individual in focus, texts on eschatological time have important functions in the life of the righteous (see 2.3.3 below).

2.3.1. Corporate Eschatological Time. Many psalms address the corporate eschatological destiny of Israel and the nations. Consider these words from Psalm 22: "All the ends of the earth will remember and turn to the LORD, and all the families of the nations will bow down before him, for dominion belongs to the LORD and he rules over the nations.... Posterity will serve him; future generations will be told about the LORD" (Ps 22:27-28, 30 NASB). This future global victory rests upon God's universal, everlasting and ultimately unrivaled reign (Ps 45:6; 103:19), manifested in both wrathful judgment and merciful salvation. Some texts highlight the distinctiveness of Israel in God's unchanging covenant purposes (Ps 102:13, 16; 147:19-20; cf. the promise to *David in Ps 89), but not in a way that is incompatible with the ultimate blessing and worship of the nations (Ps 47:1-2; 66:4, 8; 67:1-7; 86:7; 102:15-16, 21-22). Although these texts are open to differing levels of fulfillment (historical, eschatological or both), they do indicate what the final end of history will be like under the rule of God.

2.3.2. Individual Eschatological Time. Some scholars would significantly restrict the theme of life after death in the OT (which some see only in the book of Daniel), but contrary to that view, a few texts clearly speak of final destiny of individuals as transcending this earthly life. Although some texts speak in an agnostic or pessimistic manner about what happens at or after death (e.g., Ps 39:13; Eccles 3:19-21), many others speak differently. God has not yet carried out all the divine plans in history. There is a future that awaits both the righteous and the unrighteous that is qualitatively different than the present order of existence. The wicked will per-

ish and be cut off from the presence of God (Job 27:8; Ps 22:29; 49:19-20; 73:17-20, 27; Prov 5:11). The wicked have no future (*ʾaḥărît*), and their "lamp will be put out" (Prov 24:20 [cf. Prov 13:9; 20:20]). In contrast, the righteous will be received by God after death and delivered from *šĕʾôl* (Ps 16:10-11; 49:15; 73:24; Prov 15:24; 23:14). So then, even the book of *Proverbs, known for its emphasis on this-worldly, temporal retribution, seems to speak of a future for the righteous beyond this life: "Do not let your heart envy sinners, but live in the fear of the LORD always. Surely there is a future [*ʾaḥărît;* lit., "latter end"], and your hope will not be cut off" (Prov 23:17-18 NASB [cf. Prov 24:14]). Such texts point to a future in which, through the eternal God, people can participate in abundant and everlasting life.

2.3.3. Functions of Eschatological Time. A biblical perspective on eschatological time has several divinely ordained functions in the life of the righteous. First, it produces in the righteous, individually and corporately, hope in what God can and will do in the future. The author of Lamentations testifies to the power of remembering the faithfulness of God, as proven in past actions, to fuel hope for the future in the midst of present darkness and adversity (Lam 3:20-26, 31-33). The future hope of the righteous is not one of a Hellenistic dualism, which downgrades the goodness of life in time and materiality. Accordingly, the godly are invited to enter into the blessings of everlasting life with God even during this life.

Second, the proper hope in a coming eschatological time also produces patience and the ability to persevere through *suffering. Job manifests these qualities in an exemplary fashion, and the blessed end of his story points indirectly to the final eschatological blessings that await righteous sufferers (Job 42:11-17; cf. Jas 5:11). Accordingly, diverse writers provide ample attestation of the need to "wait on God" (or "hope in God") for his future action (Job 14:14; Ps 25:3, 5, 21; 27:14; 37:7, 9, 34; 39:9; 69:3, 7; 130:5; 147:11; Prov 20:22; Lam 3:26; cf. Ruth 3:18). Patience and endurance are crucial especially when suffering elongates time in our subjective experience (the converse of the popular notion "Time flies when you are having fun").

Third, eschatological time produces an awareness of eventual moral justice of life. Human actions will be judged and rewarded. Besides rewards and punishments in the earthly life, the outworking of retribution can be extended into future generations and into the *afterlife (see the texts cited in 2.3.1-2 above).

3. Time and Eternity.

The foregoing discussion of aspects of a biblical theology of time has left several questions unanswered. Perhaps the most important is the question of the relationship between time and eternity. Insofar as it is possible to determine, how do these writers understand eternity, and how does it relate to time in all its complexity?

3.1. "Eternity" (ʿôlām). The term ʿôlām, used no less than 440 times in the OT, is sometimes translated "eternity" or "everlasting" (there are similar terms, but ʿôlām is by far the most frequent and important). Its most basic meaning is "far" or "distant time," which allows the word to be used (sometimes within construct forms) in the sense of "ancient" or "long ago" and, more commonly (over 260x in the OT), in the sense of the (distant) "future" or "forever" (Preuss, 533-36; Tomasino, *NIDOTTE* 3.346-50). The term cannot be used as equivalent for philosophical notions about God, such as purely timeless eternity or even unbounded time ("everlasting"). That said, some texts do use the term ʿôlām to refer to all time, stretching backward and forward. For example, the psalms use the phrase "from everlasting to everlasting" for praise (Ps 41:13) for God's *ḥesed* (Ps 103:17) and for God's own existence (Ps 90:2). Whereas the first two references may be restricted to the range of human history or existence, the last reference (Ps 90:2) refers to God as everlasting or eternal in a more complete sense. Although ʿôlām and related terms are used to refer to God and God's activities, they also are frequently applied to human activities.

3.2. God's Eternality and Time. There are certain question about the nature of time and eternity that the Bible does not answer for us with precision, yet certain themes remain clear. God, as creator of heavens and earth, transcends the limitations of time that humans experience; God exists forever from the past to the future (Ps 90:2; 102:12, 26-27; 135:13). Yet as a redeemer and Lord of the heavens and earth, God is immanent in natural, historical and eschatological time. Accordingly, God's covenant faithfulness *(ḥesed)* "endures forever" (Ps 89:2; 100:5; 106:1; 107:1; 118 [passim]; 136 [passim]), and God

rules as a king forever (Ps 9:7; 10:16; 29:10; 66:7; 145:13; 146:10; Lam 5:19).

In this conjunction of transcendence and immanence, God is eternal yet closely related to time. K. Barth (621-40) describes God's multifaceted transcendent and immanent relation to time in terms of three categories that are helpful for our thematic analysis here: the eternal God is pretemporal, supratemporal and posttemporal.

God is pretemporal as the creator of heavens and earth (Ps 90:2; 102:25; 121:2; 124:8; Prov 8:23-26). As the creator of the world and its time, God is not bound or limited by time. God does not need time to accomplish creative miracles: "For he spoke, and it was done; he commanded, and it stood fast" (Ps 33:9 NASB). After the initial act of creation, God's ongoing relation to time is quantitatively and qualitatively different from humankind's relation to it. God exists everlastingly, without a beginning or an end, and exists outside of time in some sense (Barth, 608-40). God is "from everlasting to everlasting" (Ps 90:2).

God is supratemporal as the sustainer, sovereign and redeemer of time. God, who transcends time and is in that respect "timeless," is also immanent in time and positively related to time. God continually acts in time to providentially sustain the temporal structures of nature and to bring about the divine redemptive purposes, becoming voluntarily subject to the certain limits and constraints of time in the process. Yet, in other respects, God is not bound to the limits of time. It is precisely God's transcendent eternality and constancy that prompt the psalmist to reach out to God in prayer as a trustworthy and ever-present help (e.g., Ps 90:1-2). God's eternity enables God to be present to people in all times. Again, God experiences time differently than do human beings: "For a thousand years in your sight are like yesterday when it passes by, or as a watch in the night" (Ps 90:4 NASB [cf. Job 10:5]). The God who acts in natural and historical time is therefore neither purely timeless nor purely time-bound. (For the view that God everlastingly exists inside of the "unending duration" of the linear time that God providentially directs, see Cullmann, 62, and passim. This view stands in some contrast to the view presented here and represented by Barth.)

God is posttemporal as the consummator of all things in eschatological time (see 2.3 above).

The heavens and earth and their time will perish; "But you [God] are the same, and your years will not come to an end" (Ps 102:27 NASB). Natural time will perish along with the created heavenly bodies, but the eternal God remains fundamentally the same in and beyond creation, redemption and consummation.

3.3. Humanity and Eternity. Although human beings are emphatically limited by time, they can also participate in eternity through God's gracious action and the proper human response to it. This is clear in several ways.

First, human life derives from eternal God, and human beings have "eternity" within them, although their final destiny may or may not be with God and his blessings. "He has also set eternity [ʿōlām] in their heart" (Eccles 3:11 NASB). Although it is impossible for human beings to comprehend eternity fully, their hearts long for it.

Second, although human life on earth is fleeting, human beings are called to enter a meaningful relationship with the Eternal One, who has entered into human life and human time to act and to save. Through a covenant relationship with the eternal God, human beings can enter into God's constancy and eternity, for God's covenant faithfulness and love "endures forever." Such human participation in everlasting covenant relationship involves the enduring corporate existence of God's people on the earth. Those who do good will "abide forever [ʿôlām]," be "preserved forever [ʿôlām]" by God, and "dwell forever [ʿôlām]" in the land (Ps 37:27-29 NASB).

Third, covenant relationship with God on earth, individual or corporate, issues in an everlasting relationship with God after this life. The godly are invited into the presence of the eternal God (see 2.3.2 above). The psalmist confesses that God upholds him and sets him in the divine presence forever (ʿôlām) (Ps 41:12-13). God therefore will be praised forever, and his redeemed and perfected people surely will participate in this. The Lord is to be blessed by his people "from this time forth and forever" (Ps 113:2; 115:18; 121:8; 131:3). The godly, therefore, have derivative eternity or everlastingness. Human eternity in the eternal God's presence, then, is not an unaided, natural quality or capacity; rather, it is a divine gift that can be forfeited through an ungodly life or confirmed through right relationship with God.

See also ECCLESIASTES 1: BOOK OF; GOD.

BIBLIOGRAPHY. **J. Barr,** *Biblical Words for Time* (SBT 33; London: SCM, 1962); **K. Barth,** *Church Dogmatics,* vol. 2.1 (Edinburgh: T & T Clark, 1957); **B. S. Childs,** *Myth and Reality in the Old Testament* (2nd ed.; SBT 27; London: SCM, 1962); **O. Cullmann,** *Christ and Time: The Primitive Christian Conception of Time and History* (rev. ed.; London: SCM, 1962); **S. J. de Vries,** *Yesterday, Today, and Tomorrow: Time and History in the Old Testament* (Grand Rapids: Eerdmans, 1975); **T. Kronholm,** " עֵת " *TDOT* 11.434-51; **H. D. Preuss,** "עוֹלָם," *TDOT* 10.530-545; **M. Sæbø,** "יוֹם," *TDOT* 6.12-32; **A. Tomasino,** "ʿolām," *NIDOTTE* 3.345-50; idem, "ʿēt," *NIDOTTE* 3.53-67; **P. A. Verhoef,** "yôm," *NIDOTTE* 2.419-424; idem, "Time and Eternity" *NIDOTTE* 4.1252-55; **G. von Rad,** *Old Testament Theology,* vol. 2 (New York: Harper & Row, 1965).

T. Prokrifka

TORAH PSALMS. *See* PSALMS 1: BOOK OF.

TOWER. *See* ARCHITECTURE.

TWO WAYS. *See* WISDOM THEOLOGY

TYPOLOGICAL INTERPRETATION. *See* HERMENEUTICS.

VANITY. *See* ECCLESIASTES 1: BOOK OF.

VASHTI

Vashti was the queen of King *Ahasuerus (Xerxes), whom he deposed for her refusal to appear at his request before a banquet. Her deposition opened the door for the choice of a new queen, the Jewish *Esther (Esther 2:17), who would then be in a position to avert the genocide of her people.

1. Vashti, the Deposed Queen of King Ahasuerus
2. Amestris, the Wife of Xerxes
3. Vashti in Later Jewish Tradition
4. Vashti, a Heroine against Patriarchy?

1. Vashti, the Deposed Queen of King Ahasuerus.

According to Esther 1:4, the great Persian king Ahasuerus held a banquet at *Susa for four months. He then prepared a feast for a select group in his opulently decorated palace, with an abundance of drinking taking place. Vashti, the queen, also gave a feast for the *women in the palace. But when Ahasuerus, who wanted to show off the queen's beauty to his guests, commanded her appearance, she refused (Esther 1:11-12). J. Baldwin (60) comments, "Her impertinence in refusing to appear, so humiliating the king in front of all the leaders of the realm, was predictably dangerous on her part." D. J. A. Clines (11) draws the contrast between the king's "power over his empire and his impotence to bend his wife's will."

The king's seven counselors were alarmed that her example might incite all the wives to be similarly disobedient, and they counseled the king to ban Vashti from his presence (Esther 1:19) and issue a proclamation throughout the empire that every man should be the ruler of his own house (Esther 1:22). Several commentators note the irony that the dissemination of this decree serves to publicize Vashti's disobedience throughout the empire.

T. Laniak (43 n. 26) observes, "Interestingly, Vashti is referred to as 'Queen Vashti' six times (vv. 9, 11, 12, 15, 16, 17), once as 'the queen' (v. 18) and then, in the context of the edict to banish her, she is simply 'Vashti' (v. 19). When her title is removed, she exits the plot." C. Moore (14), commenting on Esther 1, observes, "But above it all looms the fascinating figure of Xerxes, the might king, mastered by wine, defied by his queen, and ill-advised by his friends. Xerxes stands desperately in need of a good consort."

2. Amestris, the Wife of Xerxes.

Many scholars consider the depiction of Vashti as Xerxes' queen to be one of several factors that point against the historicity of Esther (e.g., Moore, xlvi). According to Herodotus (*Hist.* 7.61) Xerxes' queen was Amestris, a very vengeful, powerful and influential woman. She was the daughter of Otanes, one of the supporters of Darius's bid for power after the usurpation of the magos Gaumata (Smerdis). After the Greeks repulsed his invasion in 479 BC, Xerxes, while staying at Sardis, was attracted first to the wife of his brother Masistes, then to their daughter Artaynte. The king gave his niece a robe, which Amestris herself had woven. When Amestris discovered this affair, she was furious but bided her time until the king's birthday. At that time Amestris made a request that the king could not refuse, which allowed her to kill Masistes' entire family (Herodotus *Hist.* 9.108-113). Also, in old age Amestris sacrificed seven young men and

seven girls to the god of the underworld as a substitute for herself (Herodotus *Hist.* 7:114).

Some scholars (Wright; Shea) have suggested that by assuming certain phonetic modifications, one can identify Vashti with Amestris. W. Shea has worked out a detailed synchronism to show how the events in Esther, which has a gap between the third year (Esther 1:3) and the seventh year (Esther 2:16), can be harmonized with Xerxes' absence in Greece from 480 to 479 BC.

As to the objection that Amestris wielded power when her son Artaxerxes I came to the throne in 464 BC, Shea (240) points out that we have no surviving evidence that "Amestris was Xerxes' queen between his 7th and 12th year." Shea further suggests that if Amestris/Vashti's brutality had occurred in Susa just after Xerxes' return from the west, it would have provided the king with a further reason to find another chief wife.

Hubbard's reexamination of the passages in Herodotus concludes that Her. 7.61 actually refers to a male, that Her. 7.114 offers nothing certain regarding Amestris (c. 480 BC), and that the novelistic genre of Her. 9.108-13 casts doubt on this passage's historical reliability. He rejects the identification of Vashti with Amestris, but allows the possibility of the identification of Esther with Amestris.

3. Vashti in Later Jewish Tradition.

One talmudic rabbi maintained that Vashti refused to come because she had been smitten with leprosy (*b. Meg.* 12b). According to the Talmud, the wicked Vashti was the granddaughter of Nebuchadnezzar (*b. Meg.* 10b). The rabbis thought that she was unclad, as if "wearing the royal crown" (Esther 1:11) meant that that was all she wore. "The king ordered these seven princes to bring Queen Vashti unclad. Since she used to make Israelite girls work unclad and made them beat wood and flax for her on the Sabbath day, therefore, it was decreed upon her to be brought unclad" (Grossfeld, 35). Since Vashti also prevented the rebuilding of the temple, she was executed unclad (Grossfeld, 128).

4. Vashti, a Heroine Against Patriarchy?

F. Bush (354) comments, "Vashti's refusal to be shown off like a common concubine . . . before the tipsy hoi polloi of the Citadel of Susa reveals a sense of decorum and self-respect that places her outside of the mocking characterization that the narrator has given the rest of the royal court. She is evaluated positively."

With the emergence of *feminist interpretation in the last generation, whatever Vashti's reason for not complying with the king's command, she has become a heroine to be admired for her refusal to yield to the unreasonable demands of patriarchy. According to A. Laffey (57), "In my own interpretation, and in contrast to Esther, Vashti is truly the heroine. She risks almost certain yet unknown punishment to do what: to disobey her *ba'al,* her master and lord, her husband; to assert her own identity and decision-making potential; to preserve her dignity and self-respect." Clines (32) believes that the book of Esther is satire: "The emperor himself, who lives in unparalleled wealth and exercises well-nigh universal dominion, is shown up to be, at bottom, an utterly unselfconscious male chauvinist who is astonished to be worsted in the battle of the sexes when on every other front he is masterfully supreme."

See also AHASUERUS; ESTHER 2: EXTRABIBLICAL BACKGROUND; ESTHER 6: PERSON.

BIBLIOGRAPHY. **J. G. Baldwin,** *Esther* (TOTC; Leicester: Inter-Varsity Press, 1984); **A. Berlin,** *Esther* (The JPS Bible Commentary; Philadelphia: Jewish Publication Society, 2001); idem, "The Book of Esther and Ancient Storytelling," *JBL* 120 (2001) 3-14; **F. Bush,** *Ruth, Esther* (WBC 9; Waco, TX: Word, 1996); **D. J. A. Clines,** *The Esther Scroll: The Story of the Story* (JSOTSup 30; Sheffield: JSOT Press, 1984); **A. C. Florence,** "The Woman Who Just Said 'No,'" *Journal for Preachers* 22 (1998) 37-40; **M. V. Fox,** *Character and Ideology in the Book of Esther* (SPOT; Columbia: University of South Carolina Press, 1991); **B. Grossfeld,** *The Two Targums of Esther* (The Aramaic Bible 18; Collegeville, MN: Liturgical Press, 1991); **R. L. Hubbard Jr.,** "Vashti, Amestris and Esther 1,9," *ZAW* 119 (2007) 259-71; **A. L. Laffey,** "The Influence of Feminism on Christianity," in *Daughters of Abraham: Feminist Thought in Judaism, Christianity, and Islam,* ed. Y. Y. Haddad and J. L. Esposito (Gainesville: University Press of Florida, 2001) 50-64; **T. S. Laniak,** *Shame and Honor in the Book of Esther* (SBLDS 165; Atlanta: Scholars Press); **C. A. Moore,** *Esther* (AB 7B; Garden City, NY: Doubleday, 1971); **E. Segal,** *The Babylonian Esther Midrash* (3 vols.; Brown Judaic Studies 291; Atlanta: Scholars Press, 1994); **W. H. Shea,** "Esther and History," *AUSS* 14 (1976) 227-46; **J. S. Wright,** "The Historicity of the Book of Esther," in *New Perspectives on the Old Testament,* ed. J. B. Payne (Waco, TX: Word, 1970) 37-47. E. Yamauchi

VIOLENCE. *See* WARFARE IMAGERY.

VIRTUOUS WOMAN. *See* PROVERBS 1: BOOK OF; WOMEN.

VOCABULARY, HEBREW. *See* HEBREW LANGUAGE.

W

WALL. *See* ARCHITECTURAL IMAGERY.

WARFARE IMAGERY

Warfare imagery within the OT wisdom, poetry and writings draws upon both practical elements of ancient warfare, such as implements of weaponry and armor, and ideological aspects of warring, such as conceptions of enemies, victory and defeat. Some of these books contain narratives that relate battle stories reminiscent of those found in the Historical Books (e.g., Esther 9:1-17), but warfare most often appears in metaphors and symbols. The images used in these metaphors and symbols can be grouped into three major clusters: (1) implements of warfare; (2) warriors and enemies (human and divine); (3) experiences of warfare (individual and communal). For contemporary readers, especially those who consider these texts to be sacred Scripture, the warfare imagery within these clusters raises additional interpretive issues.

1. Warfare Imagery
2. Interpretive Issues

1. Warfare Imagery.

1.1. Implements of Warfare. References to specific implements of war (e.g., weapons, vehicles, equipment) constitute the most basic kind of warfare imagery in the biblical texts and can function in literal and metaphorical ways. For ancient Israel, as for the ancient Near East more broadly, the weapons mentioned fall into the two main categories of offensive and defensive. Furthermore, many weapons used by humans have metaphorical counterparts that can be used by God for either assistance or punishment.

1.1.1. Offensive Weapons. Both short- and long-range offensive weapons figure regularly in the OT wisdom, poetry and writings. A list of the major weapons appears in Job 41:26-29: sword, spear, dart, javelin, arrow and club (all named as ineffective against Leviathan). Especially in the psalms offensive weapons often denote those tools of war that are surpassed by the power of trusting in God or that God has broken in order to provide victory over enemies (Ps 44:6; 76:3; 144:11). More regularly, however, weapons such as swords (the most frequently mentioned short-range weapon [see Fretz, 893]) function as metaphors for all kinds of evil perpetrated by the wicked, especially hurtful words that have the power to wound like a blade (Job 5:15; Ps 37:14; 57:4; 64:3; Prov 12:18).

The most frequent long-range weapon that appears in both literal and metaphorical capacities is the bow. In the psalms the bow occurs variously as the weapon of a hunter and a warrior, and it is often unclear which image is operative in a given text (cf. Ps 37:14; 64:3-4; see Keel, 94). Arrows often are symbols related to the destructive power of the speech of the wicked and thus appear as metaphors for the tongue (Ps 120:4) and false speech (Ps 57:4; 64:3; Prov 25:18). Because of their nature as long-range weapons, the bow and arrow function especially well as symbols of quick, unexpected and even random *destruction. Perhaps for this reason, they are primary examples of divine weapons that Yahweh is envisioned as using against individual Israelites, the nation and its enemies (Lam 2:4; 3:13; cf. Job 20:24; Ps 18:14; 21:12; 64:7; 77:17). Additionally, the bow appears in ancient Near Eastern texts such as the SA.ZI.GA incantations as a sexual innuendo connoting masculinity and virility, with a broken or loose bow used to represent the loss of these traits. This comparative background perhaps shows the claims that Yahweh has broken the bow of enemies to be a case of double-entendre asserting their failed virility and establishing Yahweh's power (see Chapman).

1.1.2. Defensive Weapons. The imagery of defense and protection abounds in the OT poetic literature. While many texts contain general protection language, some utilize specific images of fortresses, towers and citadels. Drawing on the structures used to fortify ancient cities against sieges, these images are occasionally of fortifications that Yahweh is said to have placed around *Zion (Ps 48:3, 12-13; 122:7). On most occasions, however, they are metaphors for Yahweh or his name that represent divine protection from a variety of literal and symbolic enemies (Ps 61:3; 62:2; 91:1-2; Prov 18:10).

The shield, which was the primary piece of protective equipment for the ancient warrior, is one of the most frequently used metaphors in the psalms to represent Yahweh's protection from enemies (e.g., Ps 3:3; 33:20; 115:9-11; cf. Prov 30:5). Usually made of a frame of wood or metal covered with leather, shields came in two major kinds: a smaller, normally round, shield to defend against hand-to-hand weapons, and an upright shield extending from the feet to the chin used to block projectiles such as arrows. The use of shield imagery for Yahweh also connotes a sense of intimacy as Yahweh serves as a shield-bearer who marches into battle with the individual (cf. Ps 35:1-2; see Keel, 222; Brown). Thus, the image of a shield often occurs in contexts that contain other protective images such as "rock" (Ps 18:2), as well as images that communicate Yahweh's active involvement in the conflict (Ps 7:6-13; 33:18-22). By extension, some psalms apply the image of a shield to the human king, who then stands as the symbol of protection for the people (Ps 84:9; 89:18).

1.2. Warriors and Enemies.

1.2.1. Humans as Warriors and Enemies. The OT wisdom, poetry and writings make frequent references to the actions and characteristics of ancient warriors. The ideal warrior possesses the highest levels of wisdom, strength and courage and thus is able to deliver those who are oppressed (see Ps 45:1-5; Prov 24:5). In contrast to the Historical Books, virtually all of the human warriors in the texts under discussion here are conventional or ideal figures rather than particular historical individuals. Further, these books do not normally apply warrior imagery to average Israelites. Even in the psalms that are prayers for deliverance that employ the language of being in a battle (see 1.3.1 below), the warriors are typically the nation as a whole (Ps 44; 60:9-12; 91; 149:5-9). The royal psalms portray the king (*see* Kingship, Psalms of), who is not identified by name, as the ideal warrior, a portrayal that is similar to the depictions of warring kings in Egyptian iconography (cf. Ps 45:3-4; 72:1-10; 110:5-6; see Sherlock, 121; Keel, 291).

Similarly, human enemies in these books are rarely identified as specific individuals. Enemies of God, persons or the nation, designated with a variety of terms (e.g., "foe," "wicked"), are sometimes mythic powers of evil and *chaos but usually take the form of a private enemy in a personal situation, a corporate enemy such as a foreign nation, or a symbolic enemy such as disease or foolishness (Keel, 78). On many occasions the psalms depict these enemies taking general actions such as lying about or oppressing the worshiper or community (Ps 13:3-4; 25:19; 31:7-8; 142:6). At other times, however, the enemies take specifically warlike actions against God's people with literal and metaphorical weapons such as swords and bows (Ps 7:1-5; 37:14-15; 120:5-7).

To add to the rhetorical force of the enemy imagery, the psalms frequently use *animal metaphors, especially of lions, to depict various enemies (Ps 7:2; 17:12; 22:13; 91:13). These metaphors draw upon ancient Near Eastern pictures in which lions are often shown crushing human prey, and they represent the psalmist's enemies as those who lie in ambush and pounce unexpectedly (Keel, 85). The use of animal metaphors may function to dehumanize the enemies and thus more easily subject them to the impersonal destruction rendered in battle (see Hobbs, 191-92). On the other hand, the use of lion imagery in particular may serve to present the enemy with the highest degree of strength and power and thus may constitute a rhetorical move that serves to invoke the deity's help (see Strawn).

1.2.2. God as Warrior and Enemy. Depictions of Yahweh as a warrior constitute the most prevalent subset of warfare imagery in the OT wisdom, poetry and writings. The nature, variety and significance of this imagery have received much scholarly attention (see Schwally; Fredriksson; von Rad; Longman and Reid; Miller; Craigie; Sherlock; Lind). The most relevant texts to consider are those that go beyond simply describing Yahweh as giving victory or possessing weapons and assert that he is actually involved in the fighting in some way. Such imagery finds its roots in some of the earliest poetry connected with the exodus from Egypt, which envisions Yahweh as a warrior on Israel's behalf (e.g., Ex 15:3; cf. Ps 106:10-11; 135:10-12; see Miller). This general imagery is also connected with the practices that have come to be called "holy war," especially as reflected in Deuteronomy and Joshua (see von Rad; Schwally; Longman and Reid, 32-47). Although its exact nature and origins remain debated, "holy war" denotes a bundle of diverse practices that center on the idea of warfare as a sacred event, enacted by God alone through miracle or by human armies on behalf of God, and often involving the complete slaughter of enemy peoples as an act of devotion to the deity. Both the imagery of a god who fights as a warrior and the various conceptions of holy war are ancient ideas shared by Israel's neighbors throughout the ancient Near East (see Weippert). A ninth-century BC inscription from King Mesha of Moab (cf. 2 Kings 3:4-5), for example, describes the slaughter of Israelites at Nebo undertaken as an act of devotion to the Moabite god (see COS 2.23:138).

Within the OT wisdom, poetry and writings the primary manifestation of the divine warrior is Yahweh fighting against Israel's enemies. This imagery takes several forms (see von Rad, 11; Niditch, 1): (1) Yahweh fighting alone, sometimes by miracle without any physical means and other times by using weapons (Ps 7:12-13; 17:13-14; 35:1-3; 59:11-12; 64:7); (2) Yahweh using elements of nature such as fire, lightning and hail as weapons to fight Israel's battles (Ps 18:12-19; 68:8-10; 83:13-18; 97:3-5); (3) Yahweh leading a divine army of heavenly beings to fight Israel's battles (Ps 34:7; cf. 2 Kings 6:8-23), an image represented by the divine title *yhwh ṣĕbāʾôt* ("LORD of Hosts"), which literally translates "LORD of armies" (e.g., Ps 24:10); (4) Yahweh serving explicitly or implicitly as the commander of Israel's army as it goes into war (Ps 18:34; 44:9; 60:10; 124:2-3).

The image of the divine warrior is, however, a two-sided one: Yahweh also appears as an enemy who fights against Israel (see Sherlock; Longman and Reid). Such imagery often relates particularly to the exile of 586 BC. The book of *Lamentations, for example, uses explicit military language to describe Yahweh's role in Jerusalem's destruction: "The LORD has become like an enemy; he

has destroyed Israel . . . he has made the enemy rejoice over you" (Lam 2:5, 17 NRSV). Likewise, the communal *lament psalms give expression to this imagery following defeat in battle (Ps 60:1, 10; 80; 89), and the speeches of *Job personalize the imagery of Yahweh as enemy (Job 9:17-18; 16:12-14; 19:11-12; cf. Ps 38:1-8).

By using the imagery of Yahweh as a divine warrior, these texts recast the community's military victories as gifts rather than accomplishments achieved by its own might. Yet this imagery also proclaims that Yahweh's character may manifest itself in judgment against Israel. Thus, the imagery redefines the conflicts of individuals and the nation as larger conflicts in which Yahweh is involved, and some psalms can assert that Yahweh's destructive actions have the goal of bringing an end to war (Ps 46:9; 76:1-3).

1.3. Experiences of Warfare. The third cluster of warfare imagery draws upon diverse experiences of war known to individuals and communities, experiences that include different types of battle situations, the realities of triumph and defeat, and communal practices in and theological reflections upon conflict.

1.3.1. Battle Imagery. Both the psalms and the Wisdom literature use imagery of battles in literal depictions of historical conflicts and metaphorical representations of various kinds of personal, psychological and theological struggles. For example, the language of several psalms calls for God to "arise" (*qûm* [e.g., Ps 3:7; 7:6; 9:19; 68:1]), a term that commonly appears with military connotations throughout the OT (cf. Josh 7:13; Judg 4:14; see Sherlock, 128-29). Battle imagery depicting historical conflicts can describe the participation of the nation, the king or an individual. Psalm 149:6-7, for instance, offers a prayer for Israel's warriors in preparation for battle: "Let the high praises of God be in their throats and two-edged swords in their hands" (NRSV [cf. Ps 48:3-8; 76:1-6; 91:1-7]). Especially in the Wisdom literature, however, battle imagery functions metaphorically to describe struggles with hostile neighbors and wicked actions (Prov 1:10-19; 11:11-14; 12:6). Battle imagery also provides a ready comparison to assert the superiority of wisdom. Ecclesiastes 9:13-18, for example, offers the parable of a small city able to withstand the onslaught of a mighty king because of one wise individual (cf. Prov 21:22).

The imagery used in these texts draws upon various kinds of battles. Job 1 attributes the death of Job's servants and family to plundering raids by groups of Sabeans and Chaldeans. Other texts use the imagery of open-terrain battles in which rows of spearmen and archers engaged in hand-to-hand combat (Ps 35:1-3; 91:7). Most regularly, however, the texts use the imagery of siege warfare. Siege warfare was brutal; it involved the building of a siege wall and siege ramps around a city, the cutting off of food and water for the inhabitants, and the subsequent impaling and mutilation of captured citizens. Assyrian reliefs frequently depict siege warfare, which was a common practice in the ancient Near East (see Keel). The lament psalms in particular often use the imagery of a siege to describe the actions of national and personal enemies (Ps 22:12-22; 27:3-9; 74:1-8; 79:1-3), and Lamentations 3—4 employs the horrors of siege warfare to depict what Zion has suffered at the hands of Yahweh.

1.3.2. Triumph and Defeat. Individual, royal and communal psalms employ the language of triumph to celebrate both military victories over corporate enemies and personal deliverance from metaphorical enemies such as neighbors and illnesses (Ps 92:10-11; 118:10-18). The most characteristic images of triumph in these texts are references to seizing, subduing, striking or crushing enemies (e.g., Ps 47:3; 68:21), references paralleled in ancient Near Eastern texts and iconography from Assyria and Egypt that represent kings striking down enemies and placing them under their feet (Keel, 9).

The imagery of defeat also functions on both the national and personal level. This imagery especially employs the language of victimization, presenting individuals and the nation as victims, innocent or otherwise, of war-like actions (Ps 59; 74; 143:3). The most explicit examples of defeat imagery are in the communal lament psalms and the book of Lamentations, both of which emphasize the aspect of Israel *suffering at the hands of Yahweh (see 1.2.2 above), a notion echoed in other ancient Near Eastern texts in which a deity fights against his or her own people. More specifically, the major types of defeat envisioned in these texts include Yahweh refusing to go out with Israel's armies and thus ensuring their defeat (Ps 44:9; 60:10), Yahweh delivering individuals or the nation into the hands of an enemy as punishment (Ps 78:62-64; 79:1-5; Lam 1:5), and Yahweh himself striking Israel (Ps 89:38-45; Lam 2) (see Lind, 110).

Just as some "divine warrior" texts attribute Israel's victories to Yahweh, by involving Yahweh directly in every defeat, these poetic texts assert that Israel's negative experiences do not represent a failure or defeat of Yahweh himself. Against an ancient Near Eastern background that often interpreted a nation's military defeat as the conquering of its deity by a stronger deity, these texts daringly assert that Yahweh remains sovereign over everything that befalls his people (but see, e.g., Is 40:27). Even while Yahweh remains sovereign, however, the same communal lament psalms that describe Israel's suffering often emphasize that Yahweh suffers the effects of the nation's defeat through violence and ridicule, since the destruction has befallen his temple, his people and his name (cf. Ps 74:7, 18; 79:10; see Keel, 100; Fretheim).

1.3.3. Communal Practices and Reflections. The language of many of the communal and royal psalms fits well with the community's experiences during different stages of military conflict. These psalms find parallels in ancient Near Eastern texts that describe religious rituals such as the seeking of oracles from priests and sacrifices to various gods connected with the preparation, conduct and aftermath of war (Craigie, 117). For example, the calls for Yahweh to "arise" and the admonitions for warriors to carry the praises of God into battle (e.g., Ps 7:6; 149:6-7) may have served as liturgical preparations before a military campaign. Psalms that emphasize the dangers faced by warriors and pray for their protection (e.g., Ps 91) may have functioned liturgically during the course of military campaigns.

The conclusion and aftermath of battles especially seem to have occasioned liturgies that reflected upon the experiences of warfare. Probably because of the conviction that Yahweh participated in battle on Israel's behalf, the experience of success in war generated praise. Psalm 124, for instance, is a communal psalm of *thanksgiving that attributes national victory over enemies to Yahweh's presence with Israel, and Psalm 18 is a lengthy royal thanksgiving in which the king praises Yahweh for granting him victory and vengeance (cf. Ps 21). Conversely, several psalms represent national laments after the experience of failure in battle, compositions likely employed in communal rituals of repentance and supplication (Pss 44; 60; 80). The book of Lamentations, with its references to symbols of mourning such as dust and sackcloth (Lam 2:10), may likewise have functioned in rituals reflecting upon the destruction of Jerusalem.

The so-called *imprecatory psalms also give expression to and reflect upon the experiences of warfare, especially the suffering and humiliation associated with defeat at the hands of historical enemies. The major psalms of this genre (Pss 7; 35; 58; 59; 69; 83; 109; 137; 140) are prayers to God that call for divine violence against enemies and give expression to the human longing for revenge. Although the language and imagery of these psalms may raise moral and theological problems for modern readers (see 2.2-3 below), they serve a rhetorical function similar to that of the texts that attribute Israel's military defeats to Yahweh. By calling upon Yahweh to exact revenge, the imprecatory psalms effectively assert that Yahweh has not been conquered and remains sovereign. Additionally, the brutality and revenge in these psalms remain at the level of prayer and do not become actions carried out by the supplicants. Hence, they represent a theological response to war that expresses yet transfers the vengeance and violence to the divine prerogative.

The overall form and imagery of the book of Lamentations also represent an expression of and theological reflection upon the experiences of defeat and suffering in war. The book's poems share the characteristic of a personalized, weeping voice, at times the voice of the city of Zion personified as a widowed female (Lam 1:1, 16). This tone and content are similar to the ancient Near Eastern "city laments," Mesopotamian texts that depict and lament, often through the words of a weeping goddess, the destruction of major cities and their shrines (see Dobbs-Allsopp, 1-10) (see Lamentations 2: Ancient Near Eastern Background). Such city laments make the theological assertion that the city's defeat is the result of divine decision and thereby resist the conclusion that the city's god has been defeated. Thus, this theological response leaves Yahweh's sovereignty in place but gives sheer expression to the grief associated with destruction, a grief that even leads the poet to question whether Yahweh has gone overboard in a punishment that exceeded what was warranted (cf. Lam 4:6; see Fretheim).

2. Interpretive Issues.

The imagery clusters described above, especially the ways that they embed conceptions of warfare and violence within theological reflections upon God and humanity, raise some interpretive issues for contemporary readers, particularly those who see these texts as sacred, authoritative Scripture. Although a full analysis cannot be offered here, we may identify some lingering questions.

2.1. The Uniqueness of the Old Testament. The similarities between Israel's warring rhetoric and actions described in the OT and those of their ancient Near Eastern neighbors depicted in extrabiblical texts and reliefs may raise the question of the special status of the OT. As we noted earlier, military imagery in the OT consistently appears with similar theological aspects and claims to the imagery in ancient Near Eastern texts and art (see Weippert). Interpreters thus are left to wrestle with the question of whether and how Israel's warring activities were different from those of their neighbors, and how, if at all, the OT's similarity to its environment affects its special status for Jewish and Christian communities (see Craigie; Hobbs; Longman and Reid). For some, the OT's uniqueness is directly tied to its authority and thus is something to be established. For others, the very lack of uniqueness, which demonstrates that the OT writers used warfare imagery because of their own cultural context, aids in explaining the texts' violent portrayals of God and humans that may raise ethical difficulties.

2.2. The Ethics of Divine and Human Violence. Beyond the question of comparison, warfare imagery in which God demonstrates and sanctions the most violent types of activities raises some general ethical difficulties for modern interpreters. Biblical texts clearly attest the devastating effects of God's actions on women, children and the environment (e.g., Lam 2:19-21; 4:4; 5:11), and these depictions have been used to justify human violence (Fretheim, 366). Even though contemporary readers can place the OT's warfare imagery into its historical and comparative context, the canonized rhetoric of war can have destructive, even if subconscious, effects on peoples and cultures. Christian readers may also find it difficult to reconcile the OT images of God as warrior with some characterizations of God in the NT and may be tempted to dismiss the OT as less revelatory for Christian faith and practice. It is sometimes equally difficult, however, to reconcile the war imagery with some other traditions within the OT itself, traditions that emphasize peace and peacemaking (Sherlock, x) or express discomfort with and offer limitations on war (see Niditch).

Options abound for dealing with the *ethics of divine and human violence in the OT (see Collins). Perhaps one should "spiritualize" or allegorize the imagery into spiritual warfare against evil or sin (Stone). Perhaps interpreters should emphasize that the imagery establishes divine sovereignty and evokes human dependence by asserting that human armies achieve victory or suffer defeat only as allowed by God (Miller). Perhaps readers should see the imagery as a gracious sign that God condescends to participate in human, albeit sinful, historical experiences for the sake of redemption, even as one wishes that the chosen experiences were poetry or beauty rather than war (Craigie; cf. Hobbs). Maybe such imagery is necessary for communities such as ancient Israel that are marginal and incapable of fending off powerful forces to achieve liberation (Brueggemann; Sherlock).

Whatever the eventual outcome, any consideration of the warfare imagery should probably begin by emphasizing the diversity within the OT that in some way relativizes the emphasis on war and violence, a diversity that includes concern for foreigners and slaves in Deuteronomy and the notion of vicarious suffering in Isaiah. Even within the OT's multiple war ideologies there is a significant tradition that stresses warfare through miracle only, and this may have given rise to an ideology of nonparticipation (Niditch; Lind). This type of diversity likely demands a variety of ethical approaches by readers in various contexts.

2.3. The Sexualization of Warfare Imagery.

Along with devastating effects on combatants, children and the environment, warfare imagery in biblical and nonbiblical texts particularly involves portrayals of *women and language of female sexuality (see Chapman). Victory is associated with masculine imagery, and defeat with feminine imagery. Assyrian inscriptions and reliefs, for example, consistently depict Assyrian kings with masculine titles and images but symbolize defeated peoples as vulnerable women and prostitutes (Chapman). The OT maintains this same connection between warfare imagery and gendered language by applying royal and masculine imagery to God and by using feminine metaphors (virgin, harlot, adulteress) to symbolize capital cities such as Samaria and Jerusalem (Kelle). Further, particularly in contexts of warfare, texts such as Lamentations use metaphors of physical and sexual violence against women, especially rape and dismemberment, to describe the destruction of cities (see Lam 1:9-10; Ezek 16; 23; Hos 2; Nah 3:5-7). Such imagery functions theologically in these texts to preserve Yahweh's *honor even when his capital was destroyed, by fixing the blame not upon a failure of the deity's power but rather upon the unfaithfulness of the personified woman/city (Chapman, 65).

At its most basic level, the OT's use of such imagery is a cultural phenomenon. In Israel's environment war itself was a gendered activity in which men primarily did the fighting. Even so, such gendered imagery can shape the way contemporary readers conceive of gender and power and has the potential to solidify gender biases and justify male domination. Interpreters thus are left to seek ways to appreciate the power of such imagery for biblical writers and ancient contexts while considering its broader implications. Perhaps an initial move of approaching such feminine metaphors through ancient rhetorical contexts and conventions can simultaneously illuminate the origins of the imagery, demonstrate how particular metaphors function within rhetorical discourses, and expose less apparent assumptions upon which such imagery rests (see Kelle). Various approaches to this initial task may unlock the transcendent power of the gendered metaphors without ignoring their inherent dangers (*see* Feminist Interpretation).

See also CHAOS AND DEATH; DESTRUCTION; IMPRISONMENT; GOD; SALVATION AND DELIVERANCE IMAGERY; THEOPHANY.

BIBLIOGRAPHY. **W. P. Brown,** *Seeing the Psalms: A Theology of Metaphor* (Louisville: Westminster John Knox, 2002); **W. Brueggemann,** *Theology of the Old Testament: Testimony, Dispute, Advocacy* (Minneapolis: Fortress, 1997); **C. R. Chapman,** *The Gendered Language of Warfare in the Israelite-Assyrian Encounter* (HSM 62; Winona Lake, IN: Eisenbrauns, 2004); **J. J. Collins,** "The Zeal of Phinehas: The Bible and the Legitimation of Violence," *JBL* 122 (2003) 3-21; **P. C. Craigie,** *The Problem of War in the Old Testament* (Grand Rapids: Eerdmans, 1978); **F. W. Dobbs-Allsopp,** *Weep, O Daughter of Zion: A Study of the City-Lament Genre in the Hebrew Bible* (BibOr 44;

Rome: Pontifical Biblical Institute, 1993); **H. Fredriksson**, *Jahwe als Krieger: Studien zum alttestamentlichen Gottesbild* (Lund: Gleerup, 1945); **T. E. Fretheim**, "'I Was Only a Little Angry': Divine Violence in the Prophets," *Int* 58 (2004) 365-75; **M. J. Fretz**, "Weapons and Implements of War," *ABD* 6.893-95; **T. R. Hobbs**, *A Time for War: A Study of Warfare in the Old Testament* (OTS 3; Wilmington, DE: Michael Glazier, 1989); **O. Keel**, *The Symbolism of the Biblical World: Ancient Near Eastern Iconography and the Book of Psalms* (Winona Lake, IN: Eisenbrauns, 1997); **B. E. Kelle**, *Hosea 2: Metaphor and Rhetoric in Historical Perspective* (SBLAB 20; Atlanta: Society of Biblical Literature Press, 2005); **M. C. Lind**, *Yahweh Is a Warrior: The Theology of Warfare in Ancient Israel* (Scottdale, PA: Herald, 1980); **T. Longman III and D. G. Reid**, *God Is a Warrior* (SOTBT; Grand Rapids: Zondervan, 1995); **P. D. Miller Jr.**, *The Divine Warrior in Early Israel* (HSM 5; Cambridge, MA: Harvard University Press, 1973); **S. Niditch**, *War in the Hebrew Bible: A Study in the Ethics of Violence* (New York: Oxford University Press, 1993); **F. Schwally**, *Der heilige Krieg im alten Israel* (Leipzig: Dietrich, 1901); **C. Sherlock**, *The God Who Fights: The War Tradition in Holy Scripture* (RSCT 6; Lewiston, NY: Edwin Mellen, 1993); **L. G. Stone**, "Ethical and Apologetic Tendencies in the Redaction of the Book of Joshua," *CBQ* 53 (1991) 25-35; **B. A. Strawn**, *What Is Stronger Than a Lion? Leonine Image and Metaphor in the Hebrew Bible and the Ancient Near East* (OBO 212; Göttingen: Vandenhoeck & Ruprecht, 2005); **G. von Rad**, *Holy War in Ancient Israel* (Eugene, OR: Wipf & Stock, 2000); **M. Weippert**, "'Heiligerkrieg' in Israel und Assyrian," *ZAW* 84 (1972) 460-93.   B. E. Kelle

WASF

The wasf is a poetic form that is found in a number of places in the Bible, but most notably in the Song of Songs. Using the wasf form, the boy and girl both express their love by describing how the other's body affects them.

1. Description of the Wasf Genre
2. How to Read a Wasf
3. Specific Examples of the Wasf
4. Biblical Wasfs Outside Song of Songs
5. Extrabiblical Descriptions

1. Description of the Wasf Genre.

***1.1. Introduction to the Term* Wasf.** Recounting the memoirs of J. G. Wetzstein, F. Delitzsch describes in his commentary on *Song of Songs the marriage rituals of the *Nawâ* people, a town in the Batanian plain, which he recorded in 1860. Part of the wedding ceremony is a memorized description of the bride. This detailed recitation is called in Arabic a *wasf.* Delitzsch (175) includes a sample of the genre:

> Her nose is like the date of *Irâk*, the edge of the Indian sword;
> Her face is like the full moon, and heartbreaking are her cheeks.
> Her mouth is a little crystal ring, and her teeth are rows of pearls,
> And her tongue scatters pearls; and, ah me, how beautiful her lips!
>   . . .
> Her neck is like the neck of the roe which drinks out of the fountain of *Kanawât.*
> Her breast like polished marble tablets, as ships bring them to Sidon.
> Thereon like apples of the pomegranate two glittering piles of jewels.
> Her arms are drawn swords, peeled cucumbers—oh that I had such!
> And incomparably beautiful her hands in the rose-red of the *Hinnâ*-leaf;
> Her smooth, fine fingers are like the writing reed not yet cut;
> The glance of her nails like the Dura-seeds which have lain overnight in milk;
> Her body is a mass of cotton wool which a master's hand has shaken into down,
> And her legs marble pillars in the sacred house of the Omajads.

The similarity between this example of traditional poetry and some portions of the Bible are striking. Due to this generic affinity, since the mid-nineteenth century such poems in the Bible have been called wasfs. Other terms are also used for the genre, such as simply a "descriptive song" (Murphy, 418).

1.2. Song of Songs. There are four wasfs in Song of Songs, three describing the young lady (Song 4:1-7; 6:4-7; 7:1-10), and one her spectacular man (Song 5:10-16). Two of the wasfs in Song of Songs are full-body descriptions (one of the man, one of the woman), and the other two are partial descriptions that invoke the whole body. A wasf may be observed also in Ezekiel 16:10-13, where Yahweh describes the ornamentation of his beloved Israel in leather and silk, expecting passion in return. There the description proceeds from toe to head as in Song of Songs 7:1-10. As there, it is also sexually charged (Ezek 16:15-34).

Because modern-day Middle Eastern weddings use the wasf form, older scholarship tended to read Song of Songs as exemplary of traditional nuptials. But R. Murphy (419) nicely summarizes a later consensus: "There is no one life-setting for this kind of description; all that is necessary is love and admiration on the part of a lover." Since it is unclear how ancient the modern wedding elements really are, and since some ancient texts have been discovered with close affinity to Song of Songs—some as old as *Solomon—scholarship has tended to move away from reading Song of Songs as comprising material drawn from matrimony.

2. How to Read a Wasf.

The repetition of various portions of wasfs are labeled "beauty refrains" by M. Deckers (178)—refrains sung by one lover in praise of the other. Partly on the basis of these refrains, critics have attempted to prioritize the wasfs in Song of Songs, seeking to determine which came first, and which are derived from the others. This kind of analysis results in labeling some portions of wasfs "authentic" and considering others derivative (Angénieux, 587). This approach does not aid the interpreter in reading the material at hand. What follows below is a discussion of more helpful approaches to discern meaning in the wasf genre.

2.1. Statement of the Problem.
If the wasf were easy to understand, it would not have attracted so much scholarly attention. But the genre has proven to be a conundrum. This is because the points of comparison made in the poems seem bizarre and absurd. In the biblical wasf each body part is sequentially compared with something from daily life that reminds the lover of the beloved. The features actually being compared are often difficult to identify, and at first glance the comparisons seem grotesque or comedic. For example, Song of Songs 7:4 compares the Shulamite's nose to the "tower of Lebanon." Immediately, the reader imagines a Pinocchio-like nose, making the girl a fitting consort for Cyrano de Bergerac. However, this is found in an erotic celebration of the lady, and one must seek to find other points of comparison (in this case, perhaps her nose, or her face,

is likened to a military outpost, the point being that this damsel is formidable and not to be approached lightly).

Various methods have been employed to explicate the dense barrage of confounding imagery one encounters in Song of Songs. In the mid-twentieth century a literalistic hermeneutic was attempted, the results being rather unsatisfactory. Some interpreters have continued to seek meaning in the admittedly disturbing connotations and have drawn negative conclusions. A more refined interpretative scheme is reviewed below in counterpoint to the literalistic/negative one.

2.2. The Literalistic/Negative Method.
One approach to the wasf is to read it with the sensibilities and poetic appreciation of the modern audience. In other words, modern readers find the associations funny or monstrous, and, therefore, so did the ancient audience. "That the girl's neck is like an armed fortress . . . is a plainly ludicrous image, and the author's contemporaries would scarcely have had any other impression of it" (Waterman, 38).

L. Waterman, for example, reads Song of Songs as motivated by hatred for Solomon among those in the northern tribes that suffered much under his poor administration. Thus, for example, in Song of Songs 4:2 "not a tooth is lacking" means no more than "you have good teeth," hardly a "remark for a suitor to make to a young woman who is his prospective bride" (Waterman, 37). "The first requirement of Song of Songs was the humiliation of Solomon, which was accomplished in the rebuff administered by a humble peasant girl from the North" (Waterman, 38-39). J. Whedbee (267) calls Song of Songs 3:7-11 "a parody of a royal processional . . . whose rhetoric is designed to satirize an ostentatious display of royal pomp."

M. Segal likewise takes a literalistic approach to the wasf: "Only as playful banter can be rationally explained the grotesque description by the lover to the damsel. . . . Pure fun is also the lover's offer to take the damsel to the high mountain tops of the Lebanon in order to frighten the little girl with the horrid lions in their dens and the tigers" (Segal, 480).

F. Black experiments with using the "grotesque" as a hermeneutical grid, and she remarks, "Three of the detailed body descriptions pertain to the woman, and these may be conflated to create a fuller picture of a creature who is ill-proportioned, odd-looking and impossible. A giant, her head is as massive as Mt. Carmel. Her hair is described as a flock of goats, and, alternately, as purple threads. Her neck, a mere tower built by human hands, should snap under Carmel's weight. And the tower which is her nose juts out awkwardly and unbalances" (Black 2000, 311).

In Black's reading of Song of Songs the wasf genre serves both to attract and to repulse, to throw the reader off balance and disorient. She demonstrates one way that a literalistic reading strategy leads to a negative reaction. The wasf's imagery has also been understood as casting aspersions or mockery. For example, A. Brenner (1992, 115) reads the final wasf of Song of Songs as "a parody of the *wasf* genre, a humorously critical and sometimes ambiguous appraisal of the dancing woman." Brenner argues that the wasf moves from foot to head (reverse order from others in Song of Songs), and she emends the text to compare the girl in Song of Songs 7:5 to the Ammonite capital, concluding that the association would have evoked ambivalent or negative feelings. She also notes the poem's immodesty. (Of course, the wasf of Ezekiel 16:10-13 also moves upwards and is surely not meant to disparage Israel's beauty, and the man's description is just as immodest.)

Scholars also take issue with the lone description of the man in Song of Songs 5:10-16. F. Landy calls this wasf "stiff and tense," and, except for the face, it is "coldly metallic and disjointed" (Landy 71, 80). However, the lady concludes the poem, "He is altogether desirable" (Song 5:16 RSV).

2.3. Toward a Better Hermeneutic. The opposite extreme from Waterman is represented by R. Soulen, who suggests that the image presented in the wasf has nothing to do with what the girl looks like and associates emotions rather than appearances: "Interpretation is most correct which sees the imagery of the wasf as a means of arousing emotions consonant with those experienced by the suitor as he beholds the fullness of his beloved's attributes" (189). Thus, the positive feelings that the poet experiences while looking at, for example, a mountain range, are consonant with the good sensations felt while gazing upon her head (Song 7:5).

The difficulty with this approach is that the associations in the wasf are then arbitrary. Instead of comparing eyes with doves and hair with a flock of goats (Song 4:1), the poet might just as well have compared hair with doves and eyes with goats (Murphy, 420). Often, the images in the wasf do in fact seem to be particularly associated with their referents: "The poet does lead us to expect some sensory correspondence between the images and their referents" (Fox 1983, 226).

A better approach is to recognize that the associations often are not about what the beloved looks like but rather treat senses and qualities other than sight. For example, C. Meyers (217-19) finds a group of militaristic and architectural images employed to describe Song of Songs; these images convey not how the woman appears to the eye but rather attributes such as power, danger, strength, might and aggression. Comparing lips to lilies might highlight the sense of smell (Falk 1982, 81).

Because the associations are not obvious, the reader is forced to slow down, read carefully and closely, savoring each bodily characteristic while searching for the often-odd point of comparison. Often in the wasf equivalences are not obvious and thus necessitate careful meditation. One is forced to relish the details of the beloved, thus engaging and entering into the experience of erotic love espoused in the lyric.

2.4. Gendered Descriptions. C. Exum observes differences between how the girl describes the boy and how he describes her. Her description of him (Song 5:10-16) "is more relational than his" (Exum, 21). "An important difference between the woman's description of the man and his descriptions of her is that she speaks of him as 'he,' whereas he addresses her as 'you.' She describes him to the women of Jerusalem, the audience within the poem, rather than addressing him directly" (Exum, 203).

It is only in the context of the company of Jerusalem's women that the girl "conjures" her man in the description. She describes him from memory in answer to a question—it is a way to deal with his absence. On the other hand, when the boy speaks, he is spontaneously moved when gazing upon her to cry out her glorious description—it is a way "to cope with her devastating presence" (Exum, 21). Exum (22) analyzes the phenomenon as follows:

A cultural notion of woman as other may have some bearing on the different status the

837

woman and the man have with respect to the gaze. On the basis of what we can construct from the rest of the Bible, in ancient Israel the male body was considered the norm. It is not therefore an occasion for anxiety. The female body is the other, mysterious, and thus provokes a more complex response. What is often described as the more static nature of the woman's description of the man may be due to a reticence to describe the male body any more explicitly. Thus the man's descriptions are more visual, whereas hers are relational.

Exum's analysis is mitigated somewhat in the woman's self-description of lovesickness when in his presence (Song 2:4-6). Her description of the man is larger than life; he is "dazzling" or "radiant" in Song of Songs 5:10. She chooses "blood red" rather than "ruddy" in that verse, a bright, golden, spectacular and almost theophanic image (see Rev 1:13-16). In her mind, his body is anything but ordinary.

3. Specific Examples of the Wasf.

3.1. Song of Songs 4:1-5. As an example of the difficulty of interpreting the wasf genre, five verses are analyzed below, in a loose translation of Song of Songs 4:1-5 (Schwab 1997, 10).

> You are beautiful, my love, you are beautiful!
> Your eyes are doves behind your veil.
> Your hair—a flock of goats, sauntering down the valley.
> Your teeth—a flock of sheep rising from their washing, each with its twin.
> Your lips—ruby red, and your mouth is delightful.
> Your open mouth—a succulent pomegranate behind your veil.
> Your neck—the tower of David, hung about with a thousand warriors' shields.
> Your two breasts—two fawns, twins of a gazelle, that graze among the lilies.

The reader is at once confronted with this odd equation: her eyes are doves. The first impulse of the modern reader is to imagine that her eyes look like doves—a literalistic interpretation. Doves are white, eyes are white. It has been suggested that birds and eyes in Egyptian hieroglyphs have a similar shape (see Soulen, 187). However, the comparison probably includes

elements other than how they look; in fact, their appearance may not be the equivalence at all. Perhaps a dove's flapping wings remind him of her eyelashes. If the dove is a symbol for innocence or purity, then the association invokes her sexual fidelity (Dillow, 29). The text is not simply describing her appearance but rather, more importantly, how the man sees her. It may be called "imputed beauty"—beauty in the eye of the beholder, seen not only when he gazes upon her but also in her reflection throughout all of creation.

The next image compares her hair to goats "sauntering down the valley." One may imagine a flock of jet-black goats, streaming down a hillside. They might appear as one large composite, a covering of thick hair all in motion, rippling and appearing to toss about in the wind. Such a sight causes the shepherd to think of his beloved.

"Your teeth—a flock of sheep rising from their washing, each with its twin." Again from the vantage point of the slope, another sight graces the shepherd's senses, causing him to see his beloved's smile reflected in the countryside. Below, down the hill, is a pond from which a flock of white sheep is drinking. Each animal is reflected in the water ("each with its twin"), creating the illusion of a double row of white curved into a smile (Falk 1993, 230).

Everywhere the man goes, and throughout his day, he is reminded of the beautiful face of the one he loves. Yet not all of the images in the wasf necessarily reflect how she appears. The next verses seem to invoke more the senses than sight. Her mouth is a "succulent pomegranate." This probably is a reference to its taste and juiciness. His enjoyment of her mouth is not simply in the looking; it involves the sense organs of tongue, lips and palate.

Her neck is compared with the tower of David, bristling with military defenses. Although the lady might be wearing a necklace, the leading metaphor is warlike—she is intimidating and dangerous, and is best approached with caution. This imagery is similar to Song of Songs 8:10: "I was a wall, and my breasts were like towers" (RSV). There, her breasts being like towers equals herself being a wall: she was impregnable, closed to all suitors, until the day she was spoken for (Song 8:8). This formidable lady's breasts were off-limits, as was her neck and the rest of her.

Perhaps the oddest image found in the wasf genre is this: "Your two breasts—two fawns, twins of a gazelle, that graze among the lilies." Obviously, her breasts do not appear as gazelles. What, then, is the point of comparison? Surely not smell or taste. Maybe the association is their softness, or perhaps light brown color. Might their distinctive stotting motion bring her to mind when the shepherd observed gazelles gracefully bounding?

3.2. Song of Songs 7:1-5. Note that Song of Songs 4:1-5 traced the girl's figure from the head downwards in a straight line. This is important to keep in mind when the Hebrew is obscure and the reader must guess what body part is being highlighted. For example, consider another five verses, Song of Songs 7:1-5 (Schwab 1997, 12):

> O princess, your steps are elegant in your
>   dancing shoes,
> Your curved thighs are like hand crafted
>   jewels.
> Your "navel"—a rounded vessel full of wine.
> Your pubes—a mound of wheat, encircled
>   with lilies.
> Your breasts—two fawns, twins of a gazelle.
> Your neck—an ivory tower.
> Your eyes—pools by the city gate.
> Your nose—a pinnacle overlooking the
>   frontier.
> Your head—a glorious mountain.
> Your hair—deepest purple, captivating the
>   king in its locks.

This wasf (like Ezek 16:10-13) vectors from feet to head, the opposite direction from the other three wasfs in Song of Songs. Her sculpted legs are anatomically perfect, like the perfect work of an artist. Working upward, the translator is challenged by two terms. First, there is the so-called navel. The Hebrew word in question occurs once in the Bible, and although its meaning may be inferred from similar words found elsewhere, the primary method to determine its meaning is its immediate context here: a body part in a straight line, something between the thighs and the "belly" that is a moist vessel. The belly button is not in line and thus should be disqualified. It is probably her vulva; her intoxicating and pungent vaginal moisture is her "wine."

Continuing in a straight line, we encounter the next item, often translated "belly," "a mound of wheat, encircled with lilies." But the Hebrew word behind it (*beten*) usually depicts internal organs, such as "womb." The only "mound" that sports soft feathery ornamentation ("lilies") is the pubes or mons veneris ("Mount of Venus"). It is interesting that the man is called a gazelle that "grazes among the lilies" (Song 6:3). Of course, her two breasts also do the same (Song 4:5), suggesting that the image of lilies has multiple referents. The gazelle also has multiple referents, depicting both his sexual enthusiasm for her and the aspect of her appearance that so arouses him.

4. Biblical Wasfs Outside Song of Songs.
Full-body descriptions of a man or woman are rarely found outside Songs of Songs. Nebuchadnezzar's dream (Dan 2) is one, and it includes elements similar to Song of Songs 5:10-16.

Another is Ezekiel 16:10-13:

> I clothed you also with embroidered cloth
>   and shod you with leather,
> I swathed you in fine linen and covered
>   you with silk.
> And I decked you with ornaments,
>   and put bracelets on your arms,
>   and a chain on your neck.
> And I put a ring on your nose,
>   and earrings in your ears,
>   and a beautiful crown upon your head.
> Thus you were decked with gold and silver;
>   and your raiment was of fine linen, and
>   silk, and embroidered cloth;
>   you ate fine flour and honey and oil.
> You grew exceedingly beautiful,
>   and came to regal estate. (RSV)

"Shod" with leather is a reference to her feet. From this, the wasf quickly ascends upwards to her face, where most of the description occurs (like Song 5:10-16). The point again is to highlight the beauty and desirability of the lady. In this description, however, rather than presenting the reader with objects of comparison, the writer puts forward her fine clothing. The symbolism is just as acutely present, however. This is so because unlike Song of Songs, the woman in Ezekiel is not an actual flesh-and-blood female but rather is a representation of the nation Israel. Her marriage covenant is the Mosaic covenant. The flour, honey and oil were Israel's

Table 1: Chester Beatty I A, 31 and Song of Songs

Chester Beatty I A, 31	Song of Songs	
One alone is (my) sister, having no peer	6:9	My dove, my perfect one, is only one
Behold her, like Sothis rising At the beginning of a good year: Shining, precious, white of skin	6:10	Who is this that looks forth like the dawn, fair as the moon, bright as the sun
Lovely of eyes when gazing	6:5	Turn away your eyes from me, for they disturb me
Long of neck	7:4	Your neck is like an ivory tower
Her hair true lapis lazuli	7:5	Your flowing locks are like purple
Full (her) derrière, narrow (her) waist, Her thighs carry on her beauties	7:1	Your rounded thighs are like jewels, the work of a master hand
Lovely of (walk) when she strides on the ground	7:1	How graceful are your feet in sandals
She has captured my heart in her embrace	4:9	You have ravished my heart with a glance of your eyes
She makes the heads of all (the) men Turn about when seeing her	6:13	Turn, turn, that we may look upon you
Her coming forth appears Like (that of) her (yonder)—the (Unique) One	6:10	Who is this that looks forth like the dawn

homegrown products. The silver and gold that ornament her represent the economic prosperity of the nation. Thus, one must decode the imagery in a similar fashion as in any wasf of Song of Songs.

Other descriptions have been identified with the wasf genre, some of which are in biblical wisdom material. For example, D. Bernat (334) labels the descriptions of Behemoth and Leviathan in Job 40—41 as examples of the genre "enemy-wasf." Behemoth's body parts are systematically listed and sometimes compared with metal or wood. The sexual element is highlighted there, such as in Job 40:17, where the creature "delights in" his "tail" as if it were a cedar tree (Wolfers, 370-71). Leviathan also is described in mostly human-sounding terms, and sometimes parallels may be found between his poem and verses in Song of Songs. In company with these monstrous descriptions Bernat includes Goliath of 1 Samuel 17. Goliath's description begins with his bronze helmet, continues down his bronze coat of chain mail, to the leggings of bronze. Then his great weapons are detailed, and finally his challenge and threat.

Bernat (341) also analyzes the description of the Woman of Virtue that concludes the book of *Proverbs (Prov 31:10-31) as an "anti-wasf" because it ignores her physical appearance completely. However, her description roughly corresponds with the male wasf in Song of Songs 5:8—6:1, which begins with finding ("if you find my beloved" and "a woman of virtue who can find?"). The woman is compared with jewels (Prov 31:10). Both Song of Songs' man and Proverbs' Woman of Virtue have laudable arms (Song 5:14; Prov 31:19-20), and both descriptions end by referencing speech (Song 5:16; Prov 31:26). The Proverbs 31 woman also mentions beauty (Prov 31:30), as in Song of Songs 6:1. So, the so-called anti-wasf actually bears some affinity with Song of Songs' full-body wasf of the man. Her description is often couched in masculine terms, such as her loins in Proverbs 31:17 (which parallel his "tusk" of Song 5:14).

5. Extrabiblical Descriptions.

As we noted earlier (see 1.1 above), the name *wasf* is an Arabic word meaning "description"; when applied to the poetry of Song of Songs, the term links it with a culture outside the Bible. However unchanged over the years, the wedding practices observed by Wetzstein have uncertain provenance. But there are also examples of love literature from antiquity also comparable to Song of Songs.

The closest analogues to Song of Songs are found in Egyptian love lyrics. These predate Solomon by centuries; Song of Songs shares with them many motifs and imagery usage. One example from the Chester Beatty collection (group A, no. 31) is called "The Stroll," and it reads as follows (Fox 1985, 52):

One alone is (my) sister, having no peer:
    More gracious than all other women.
Behold her, like Sothis rising
    At the beginning of a good year:
Shining, precious, white of skin,
    Lovely of eyes when gazing.
Sweet her lips (when) speaking:
    She has no excess of words.
Long of neck, white of breast,
    Her hair true lapis lazuli.
Her arms surpass gold,
    Her fingers are like lotuses.
Full (her) derrière, narrow (her) waist,
    Her thighs carry on her beauties.
Lovely of (walk) when she strides on the
    ground,
    she has captured my heart in her embrace.
She makes the heads of all (the) men
    Turn about when seeing her.
Fortunate is whoever embraces her—
    He is like the foremost of lovers.
Her coming forth appears
    Like (that of) her (yonder)—the (Unique)
    One.

This sample includes a number of elements discoverable in biblical wasfs. J. White (149) notes that jewels (lapis lazuli) and metals (gold) have affinity with Song of Songs 5:11-15. Table 1 illustrates the similarity between this material and Song of Songs (modified RSV).

Despite the close similarity of poetic device and manner of expression, Fox (1983) notes differences between the Egyptian love lyrics and Song of Songs: Song of Songs is a literary unit, not a collection of individual lyrics not originally bound together; in it can be found actual dialogue between lovers rather than mere monologues; the wasf is more literalistic in the Egyptian songs rather than metaphorical as in Song of Songs. In Songs of Songs' wasfs, "A lover looks at his beloved and through the prism of her beauty sees an ever-present Arcady. In fact, the imagery shows us a world *created* by love, for it comes into being and is unified only through the lovers' vision of each other" (Fox 1983, 227). "Egyptian love poems are introspective, depicting people analyzing their own feelings, 'Oh, if

only I were her hairbrush, then I could be close to her!' Song of Songs is not like that at all. The only navels that the young couple gaze upon are each other's" (Schwab 1997, 15). W. Watson (260) contrasts the Egyptian description of her skin color as "white" with Song of Songs 1:6, which has "very dark."

Other ancient love songs are further removed from Song of Songs. Sumerian, Akkadian and Ugaritic love poems mostly treat the exploits of the gods. Poems in which one human describes another in amorous terms are rare. One example of this is the Message of Ludingira to His Mother, "in which the beloved mother's anatomy is described in highly erotic language" (Westenholz, 2474). This text describes Ludingira's mother using four "signs" to recognize her: "My mother is brilliant in the heavens, a doe in the mountains, a morning star abroad in noon, precious carnelian, a topaz" (Cooper). This resembles Song of Songs 5:9—6:1, where the woman describes her man and her friends express the desire to search for him.

See also AMBIGUITY; ANIMAL IMAGERY; FEMINIST INTERPRETATION; FLORAL IMAGERY; LYRIC POETRY; MARRIAGE AND SEX; SONG OF SONGS 2: ANCIENT NEAR EASTERN BACKGROUND.

BIBLIOGRAPHY. **J. Angénieux,** "Les trois portraits du Cantiques: Étude de critique littéraire," *ETL* 42 (1966) 582-96; **D. Bergant,** "My Beloved Is Mine and I Am His (Song 2:16): The Song of Songs and Honor and Shame," *Semeia* 68 (1994) 23-40; **D. Bernat,** "Biblical Wasfs beyond the Song of Songs," *JSOT* 28 (2004) 327-49; **F. Black,** "What Is My Beloved? On Erotic Reading and the Song of Songs," in *The Labour of Reading: Desire, Alienation, and Biblical Interpretation,* ed. F. C. Black, R. Boer and E. Runions (SBLSS; Atlanta: Society of Biblical Literature, 1999) 35-52; idem, "Beauty or the Beast? The Grotesque Body in the Song of Songs," *BibInt* 8 (2000) 302-23; **A. Brenner,** "A Note on bat-rabbîm (Song of Songs VII 5)," *VT* 42 (1992) 113-15; idem, "To See Is to Assume: Whose Love Is Celebrated in the Song of Songs?" *BibInt* 1 (1993a) 265-84; idem, "Women Poets and Authors," in *A Feminist Companion to the Song of Songs,* ed. A. Brenner (FCB 1; Sheffield: JSOT Press, 1993b) 58-66; **G. B. Caird,** *The Language and Imagery of the Bible* (Grand Rapids: Eerdmans, 1980); **D. J. A. Clines,** "Why Is There a Song of Songs and What Does It Do to You If You Read It?" in *Interested Parties: The Theology of Writers and Readers of the Hebrew*

Bible, ed. D. J. A. Clines and P. R. Davies (JSOTSup 205; Sheffield: Sheffield Academic Press, 1995) 94-121; **J. Cooper,** "New Cuneiform Parallels to the Song of Songs," *JBL* 90 (1971) 157-62; **M. Deckers,** "The Structure of the Song of Songs and the Centrality of *nepes*," in *A Feminist Companion to the Song of Songs*, ed. A. Brenner (FCB 1; Sheffield: JSOT Press, 1993) 172-96; **F. Delitzsch,** "Remarks on the Song by Dr. J. G. Wetzstein," in *Commentary on the Song of Songs and Ecclesiastes* (Edinburgh: T & T Clark, 1877) 162-76; **S. J. Dillow,** *Solomon on Sex* (New York: Thomas Nelson, 1977); **L. M. Eslinger,** "The Case of an Immodest Lady Wrestler in Deuteronomy 25:11-12," *VT* 31 (1981) 269-81; **C. Exum,** *Song of Songs* (OTL; Louisville: Westminster John Knox, 2005); **M. Falk,** *Love Lyrics from the Bible: A Translation and Literary Study of the Song of Songs* (BLS 4; Sheffield: Almond, 1982); idem, "The *Wasf*," in *A Feminist Companion to the Song of Songs*, ed. A. Brenner (FCB 1; Sheffield: JSOT Press, 1993) 225-33; **M. V. Fox,** "Love, Passion, and Perception in Israelite and Egyptian Love Poetry," *JBL* 102 (1983) 219-228; idem, *The Song of Songs and the Ancient Egyptian Love Lyrics* (Madison: University of Wisconsin Press, 1985); **F. Landy,** *Paradoxes of Paradise: Identity and Difference in the Song of Songs* (BLS 7; Sheffield: Almond, 1983); **T. Longman III,** *Song of Songs* (NICOT; Grand Rapids: Eerdmans, 2001); **A. Mariaselvam,** *The Song of Songs and Ancient Tamil Love Poems* (AnBib 118; Rome: Editrice Pontifico Istituto Biblico, 1988); **D. Merkin,** "The Woman on the Balcony: On Reading the Song of Songs," *Tikkun* 9.3 (1994) 59-64, 89; **C. Meyers,** "Gender Imagery in the Song of Songs," *HAR* 10 (1987) 209-23; **R. E. Murphy,** "Form Critical Studies in the Song of Songs," *Int* 27 (1973) 413-22; **M. H. Pope,** *Song of Songs* (AB 7C; Garden City, NY: Doubleday, 1977); **M. Rozelaar,** "An Unrecognized Part of the Human Anatomy," *Judaism* 37 (1988) 97-101; **J. C. Rylaarsdam,** "Song of Songs and Biblical Faith," *BR* 10 (1965) 7-18; **G. Schwab,** "Cultivating the Vineyard: Solomon's Counsel for Lovers," *JBC* 15.3 (1997) 8-20; idem, *The Song of Songs' Cautionary Message Concerning Human Love* (SBL 41; New York: Peter Lang, 2002); idem, "Song of Songs," in *Expositor's Biblical Commentary* (rev. ed.; Grand Rapids: Zondervan, forthcoming); **M. H. Segal,** "Song of Songs," *VT* 12 (1962) 470-90; **R. N. Soulen,** "*Wasfs* of the Song of Songs and Hermeneutic," *JBL* 86 (1967) 183-90; **L. Waterman,** *The Song of Songs: Translated and Interpreted as a Dramatic Poem* (Ann Arbor: University of Michigan Press, 1948); **W. G. E. Watson,** "Some Ancient Near Eastern Parallels to the Song of Songs," in *Words Remembered, Texts Renewed: Essays in Honour of John F. A. Sawyer*, ed. J. Davies, G. Harvey and W. G. E. Watson (JSOTSup 195: Sheffield: Sheffield Academic Press, 1995) 253-71; **E. R. Wendland,** "Seeking the Path through a Forest of Symbols: A Figurative and Structural Survey of the Song of Songs," *JOTT* 7.2 (1995) 13-59; **J. Westenholz,** "Love Lyrics from the Ancient Near East," in *Civilizations of the Ancient Near East*, vol. 4, ed. J. Sasson (New York: Scribner, 1995) 2471-84; **J. W. Whedbee,** "Paradox and Parody in the Song of Solomon: Towards a Comic Reading of the Most Sublime Song," in *The Bible and the Comic Vision* (Cambridge: Cambridge University Press, 1998) 263-77; **J. B. White,** *A Study of the Language of Love in the Song of Songs and Ancient Egyptian Love Poetry* (SBLDS 38; Missoula, MT: Scholars Press, 1975); **C. J. Whitesell,** "Behold, Thou Art Fair, My Beloved," *Parabola* 20 (1995) 92-99; **D. Wolfers,** *Deep Things Out of Darkness: The Book of Job, Essays and a New English Translation* (Grand Rapids: Eerdmans, 1995).
G. Schwab

WEAPONS. *See* PROTECTION IMAGERY; WARFARE IMAGERY.

WIDOWS, WIDOWHOOD. *See* RUTH 2: ANCIENT NEAR EASTERN BACKGROUND.

WISDOM, GREEK

Greek wisdom exerted a profound influence on Jewish thinking throughout Hellenistic times and into the Roman period. Ethics permeate OT wisdom literature, which considers human beings "creatures of one God, without regard to ethnic origin or cultic affiliation" (Collins 1997, 10). Generally included in this category are *Proverbs, *Ecclesiastes and *Job (sometimes also *Song of Solomon and certain "wisdom psalms" [e.g., Pss 1; 32; 34; 37; 49; 73; 78; 91; 112; 127; 128]). Although the biblical Wisdom literature is indebted more to ancient Near Eastern influence than to Greek philosophy, later works manifest a greater awareness of and dialogue with Greek ideas. The LXX translation (*DNTB* 1099-1107) of the biblical wisdom books already evidences some movement in this direction—a tendency carried further in Pseudo-Phocylides (*DNTB* 868-69), *Wisdom of Solomon (*DNTB*

1268-76) and the writings of Philo of Alexandria (*DNTB* 789-93).

1. Hellenistic Context
2. Terminology
3. Relation of Wisdom to God and Torah
4. Relation of Wisdom to Jewish Apocalyptic
5. Conclusion

1. Hellenistic Context.

1.1. Historical Factors. All wisdom writings require context for understanding. Though timeless in one sense (and thus difficult to place on a trajectory of "early" to "late" wisdom material), some Jewish wisdom writings show familiarity with Greek ideas and interacted with them. Jews settled widely throughout the ancient world, but Diaspora literary output was centered in Alexandria. The best explanation for this phenomenon is that Alexandrian Jews who could afford education in the gymnasia had access to it (until the privilege was severely restricted by Claudius in AD 41) and were thus better able to interact with Hellenistic ideas than were others such as Ben Sira of Jerusalem (Collins 1997, 149-50) (*see* Sirach, Book of).

Somewhat paradoxically, the Hebrew wisdom books exhibit a more universal outlook than do their Hellenistic counterparts, which are more ethnocentric (see Murphy 1990, 114). Perhaps for this reason, Jewish literature written in Greek has often been considered mission-oriented (e.g., Hengel, 1.168) and instrumental in producing a large class of God-fearers sympathetic to the Jewish faith (Feldman, 321-22). Others (e.g., Tcherikover; Goodman, 57) maintain that this literature was primarily meant for the edification of Hellenistic Jews. Most likely, the actual situation lay somewhere in between: Jews sought to articulate their faith in "educated" terms for the benefit of their fellow Jews as well as to present their faith in the most attractive light for their Greek counterparts.

1.2. Impact on the Septuagint. The impact of Hellenistic thinking on the LXX is widely recognized not only by the translators' reformulation of Hebrew concepts into Greek and the utilization of the metrical conventions of Greek poetry (Thackeray) but also by their evident familiarity with the ideas of Plato, Aristotle and other Greek philosophers (Gerleman 1956, 15, 29-31). An example is seen in the positive attitude toward the bee in LXX Proverbs 6:8a-c (alluded to in Ps.-Phoc. 171-174; cf. Aristotle, *Hist. an.* 622B;

627A), which contrasts sharply with the Hebrew notion that the bee was evil and dangerous (Deut 1:44; Ps 118:12; Is 7:18). Differences of opinion exist as to whether LXX Proverbs inclines toward Greek ideas (Gerleman 1950; 1956; Hengel 1.162-63) or opposes them (Cook 1995; 2001). Possible evidence for anti-Hellenistic rhetoric includes LXX Proverbs 2:16, where the seductive woman is already understood metaphorically as "foreign wisdom" (Hengel, 1.155), which makes a person wander "far from the straight way" and become a stranger to "righteous judgment" (cf. Prov 7:5). Similar is the warning in Proverbs 9 against intercourse with the foolish woman. LXX Proverbs 9:18 has lengthy "pluses" (i.e., readings not found in the MT—many would call them "additions") that warn against foreign water (twice), a foreign river and a foreign fountain. There may even be a pejorative allusion to the mythical river Styx, which the dead supposedly cross en route to Hades (see Cook 1995, 358). In any case, there does seem to be in these verses a negative evaluation of foreign (i.e., non-Israelite) wisdom. By contrast, true wisdom is personified as a sister in Proverbs 7:4 and as a virtuous woman in Proverbs 8:1—9:6 (*see* Personification).

Later Jewish wisdom literature continues the tendency begun with the LXX, drawing still more heavily on Greek philosophy and ethics. Pseudo-Phocylides, although making no overt reference to Judaism, stands closest to traditional Hebrew Wisdom literature. Philo's closely reasoned philosophical works are the most Hellenistic of the extant Jewish writings. Situated between these extremes are the writings of Aristobulus (*DNTB* 118-21) and *Wisdom of Solomon.

2. Terminology.

The LXX translation of the OT wisdom books articulated Greek equivalents for the basic Hebrew wisdom terminology. Although the style of translation is generally freer for the wisdom books than for other OT books, the effort to convey the meaning of the original Hebrew text in clear, idiomatic Greek is apparent (see Clifford). Still, it remains an open question to what extent the LXX in general and the wisdom books in particular can be considered a reliable witness to its Hebrew parent text. Stylistic considerations and cultural sensitivity have sometimes led the translator(s) to replace synonymous *parallelisms with antitheses as well as to soften or even eliminate metaphorical or potentially offensive language (Gerleman 1956, 18-27), including some anthropomorphisms (Gerleman 1946, 58-59).

The basic Hebrew wisdom vocabulary exemplified in Proverbs 1:1-7 can be classified into three discrete categories (see Horne, 25) that the LXX translates with a fair degree of consistency. Cognitive terminology includes "wisdom" (*sophia* [Heb *ḥokmâ*]), "instruction" (*paideia* [Heb *mûsār*]), "understanding" (*phronēsis* [Heb *bînâ*]), "shrewdness" (*panourgia* [Heb *ʿormâ*]), "knowledge" (*aisthēsis* [Heb *daʿat*]), "skill" (*kybernēsis* [Heb *taḥbūlôt*]), "prudence" (*ennoia* [Heb *mĕzimmâ*]) and *"fear of the Lord" (*phobos theou* [Heb *yirʾat yhwh*]). Rhetorical terminology includes "saying" (*paroimia* or *parabolē* [Heb *māšāl*]), "figure" (*skoteinos logos* [Heb *mĕlîṣâ*]) and "riddle" (*ainigma* [Heb *ḥîdâ*]). Moral terminology includes *"righteousness" (*dikaiosynē* [Heb *ṣedeq*]), "justice" (*krima* [Heb *mišpāṭ*]) and "equity" (*orthos* [Heb *mêšārîm*]). Some Greek terms such as "virtue" (*aretē* [Wis 4:1; 5:13; 8:7; Ps.-Phoc. 67]) and "technical skill" (*technē* [Wis 13:10; 14:4; 17:7; Sir 38:34]) are restricted to later Jewish writings. Other important terms are absent or are used in a nontechnical sense (e.g., *ei dos* ["form"], *eudaimonia* ["tranquility"], *apatheia* ["indifference"], *epochē* ["suspension of belief"]).

3. Relation of Wisdom to God and Torah.

3.1. Wisdom in Jewish and Greek Conceptions. Wisdom in the Jewish conception comes from God and hence focuses on the capacity for moral discernment issuing in wise choices: "The fear of the LORD is the beginning of wisdom and there is good understanding to all who practice it. And piety toward God is the beginning of discernment, but the impious regard wisdom and instruction as worthless" (LXX Prov 1:7). Virtue *(aretē)* is central also in Greek philosophy, but generally this wisdom is understood more in terms of innate ability. The early Greek writers equated wisdom with expertise in a particular skill or vocation (e.g., Homer *Iliad* 15.411-412 [the term here is *sophiē*]). However, by the sixth century BC, *sophia* refers to a more theoretical knowledge, one's learning, judgment and *aretē* (Wilckens). For the philosophers of this pre-Socratic period, wisdom involved an enquiry into the nature and origin of things. Heraclitus insisted that the only constant in our universe is change, that all things are in con-

stant flux (cf. Plato *Crat.* 402A; see Kirk, Raven and Schofield, 195-97). Parmenides countered that what we call reality is an illusion and that the true reality is eternal, unchanging and unknowable (frgs. 6-8). Such a position was disputed by the pluralists, most notably Leucippus and Democritus, who described the universe in purely material terms as consisting of particles or atoms (for the relevant texts, see Kirk, Raven and Schofield, 413-27). Such a materialist view of things proved even less appealing to the Greeks than the ideas of Parmenides and only added to the climate of skepticism regarding the possibility of knowing anything with certainty, which in turn encouraged viewing ethical issues in more relative terms.

More pragmatic were the Sophists, who stressed both that virtue can be taught and the usefulness of developing rhetorical skill. Prominent among them was Protagoras, who articulated the maxim "Man is the measure of all things" (frg. 1, quoted in Sextus *Math.* 7.60), thus recognizing the limits of what can be known but without denying the value of the quest. The Sophists, however, were incisively criticized by Socrates and his student Plato. Virtue cannot be taught, according to Socrates, but rather must be discovered for oneself—wisdom being the greatest of all virtues. Plato (427-347 BC) systematized our knowledge of reality in terms of unchanging, ideal "forms" *(eidoi)* or ideas (esp. "the good") in the intelligible world and their constantly changing counterparts in the visible world ("images" *[eikones]*). The human *psychē* ("soul"), as the seat of reason, already belongs partly to this transcendent, eternal realm of ideas (e.g., Plato *Resp.* 6.508-511). Therefore, knowledge of virtue is innate and not, as the Sophists had maintained, taught. Plato's conception of the intelligible world reconciled the earlier views of Heraclitus and Paremenides and comported also to some extent with the Hebrew view of wisdom as originating with God prior to creation (Prov 8:22-25 [on which, see Hengel, 1.162-63]) and as knowable (Prov 8:17).

Aristotle (384-322 BC), on the other hand, began more concretely with the observable, denying the Platonic conception that forms exist apart from being or that the soul exists apart from the body, asserting rather that every substance is defined by certain essential properties (Aristotle *De an.* 2.2.414a). He differentiated being from becoming as well as the corresponding principles of rest and motion, identifying God as the eternal, "unmoved mover." He also distinguished *sophia*, the most complete kind of knowledge, from *philosophia*, which is the human quest for understanding (Aristotle *Metaph.* 12.8.1073a; 1.2.982a-983a). He taught also that since virtue operates in accordance with reason, virtue can be defined by reason. The four cardinal virtues of self-control, prudence, justice and courage, so prized by the Greeks, were important also for Jewish writers, as is clear from Wisdom 8:7, which singles out precisely these. The context also makes clear, however, that these qualities come not from human reason but rather from divinely personified wisdom.

3.2. Reconciling Jewish and Greek Conceptions. Philo (c. 25 BC to AD 50), a well-educated Jew of Alexandria, used an allegorical method to show, without invalidating the literal sense (Philo *Migr.* 91-93), the harmony between traditional Jewish faith and Greek philosophy. Following Plato, he identified God as the utterly transcendent One and pure Being *(ōn)*. At the same time, he insisted on God's immanence in our world through the Logos, which he identified with divine wisdom (Philo *Op.* 16-25; *Prov.* 1; *Det.* 115-118). The Logos as impersonal being *(ti)* is both transcendent and immanent, God's instrument in creation, and thus able to bridge the intelligible (i.e., real) and material worlds (Berchman, 28-31). With his notion of the Logos, Philo made his most important contribution (heavily influencing later Christian readings of the OT, as the writings of Clement of Alexandria and Origen show [see Chadwick]). Formulations similar to Philo's conception of the Logos are used of Jesus *mutatis mutandis* by NT writers (Jn 1:1-18; Col 1:15-17). Like the sapiential books of the LXX, Philo emphasizes moral virtues as characteristic of the religious person (see Wahlen, 13-14). In harmony with his Platonist outlook, anything perceptible by the senses is considered inferior because it belongs to the physical realm rather than to the pure realm of ideas (Philo *Opif.* 31). So, although observance of the ritual laws is everywhere assumed, notions of impurity tend to be couched in moral terms in relation to the person's conscience and intention (Philo *Spec.* 3.209; *Deus* 128). Bodily purifications are meaningless if the mind is not cleansed (Philo *Det.* 21; *Cher.* 95; *Spec.* 1.277).

3.3. Relation of Wisdom to Torah. The extent to which the Septuagintal wisdom literature identifies wisdom with Torah is disputed. Some find no clear equation between the two (e.g., Gerleman 1956, 42). More recently, J. Cook (1999) has argued vigorously for their identification, at least in LXX Proverbs. There is general agreement that the Greek text of Proverbs has a stronger religious coloring than does its Hebrew counterpart (Gerleman 1956, 38). Industriousness is often translated into moral terms (e.g., "good speech" replaces "manual labor" in LXX Prov 12:14, while LXX Prov 12:24, 27 contrast not the lazy with the diligent but rather the deceitful with the elect or the pure respectively). According to Proverbs 10:22, the rich owe their prosperity to "the blessing of the LORD," but the LXX limits this blessing of wealth to the "righteous" *(dikaios)*, and in LXX Proverbs 10:15 poverty is associated with the "impious" or "ungodly" *(asebēs* [cf. Heb *dal]*). Interestingly, most of the occurrences of *asebēs* in the LXX are in the wisdom books, over one-third in Proverbs alone, frequently as a translation for the "wicked" (Heb *rasaʿ* [e.g., Prov 10:6-7; 15:8-9; 21:27; 24:24]). There are also pluses in LXX Proverbs that exalt obedience and condemn the violation of ritual prescriptions (Prov 21:27; 29:27). It is a very small step from these admonitions to understanding the Jewish Torah as the epitomization of these religious ideals. According to LXX Proverbs 9:10, "To know the law is the indication of a sound mind" (cf. LXX Job 34:27). More vivid still is LXX Proverbs 28:4 (cf. *Let. Aris.* 139): "Those who forsake the law praise impiety, but those who love the law build a wall around themselves" (on which, see Cook 2001, 474-79).

Later Jewish writings (developing earlier hints [e.g., Deut 4:6; Ezra 7:14, 25]) advance this tendency toward identifying wisdom with Torah: "He who fears the Lord will act thus, and he who has the law will attain wisdom" (Sir 15:1 [cf. 4 Macc 1:16-17]). Bringing God and his ways still closer to humans is *Wisdom of Solomon (Crenshaw, 168-69), which describes wisdom as "a breath of the power of God, and a pure emanation of the glory of the Almighty" and as "a reflection of eternal light, a spotless mirror of the working of God, and an image of his goodness" (Wis 7:25-26). Though not explicitly identified with the law, wisdom is here closely associated with God's "goodness" *(agathotētos)*, and, like wisdom, the law is called an "imperishable light" (Wis 18:4). The latter reference, part of a lengthy section detailing God's providential care of Israel during the exodus (Wis 11—19), is typical of references in Second Temple period wisdom literature to the distinctive history, traditions and cult of Israel (see also Wis 9:8; 10:1-21; cf. Sir 24). Wisdom reflection was gradually moving away from its universalist roots toward a more particularist and apologetic stance. It is not surprising, then, that we find barely disguised references to Egypt (Wis 16:16; 19:1) and Babylon (Wis 16:18) in polemic against the idolatry of the "impious." At the same time, this polemic is not anti-Gentile per se but rather seeks to align itself with the attitude of enlightened Greeks who opposed extreme forms of idolatry (Collins 2005, 122).

4. Relation of Wisdom to Jewish Apocalyptic.

Wisdom literature, it would seem, should have little in common with the apocalyptic mindset. After all, the former stresses the immanence of wisdom as part of the natural order for the present life, while the latter stresses the transcendence of wisdom as accessible only through the revelation of "mysteries" and spotlights life in the eschaton. Although the proposal that wisdom gave birth to apocalypticism (von Rad, 277-78) is no longer seriously entertained (see Stone, 388-89), there are a number of ideas common to both genres, such as just *retribution, ethical dualism and the importance of wise teachers. Indeed, the earlier apocalypses, such as Daniel and *1 Enoch,* have been classified as "mantic wisdom" (Müller). Distinguishing these from the wisdom books is their emphatic historical determinism, the hiding of wisdom in mysterious metaphors, and the reliance on supernatural revelation. Rabbinic Judaism tended more toward the traditional forms of Hebrew wisdom, while apocalyptic wisdom resonated more with early Christianity (Collins 1990, 354).

The hope of an *afterlife, more characteristic of apocalyptic writings, is present also to a certain extent in the wisdom books of the LXX. Job, for example, affirms, "For if a person should die, having finished the days of his life, he will live; I would endure until I shall be again" (LXX Job 14:14). Clearer still is the Septuagintal addition in Job 42:17: "Yet it is written of him [Job] that he will arise with those whom the Lord resurrects" (see Gerleman 1946, 60-63). Therefore, it comes as no surprise that later wisdom books express a similar hope (Wis 3:1-8; 5:15-16; Ps.-Phoc. 103-104 [on which, see Collins 1997, 165-66; van der Horst, 93-97]). At times, this results in nice, if not

always coherent, distinctions between soul, spirit and the body: "The educated hellenistic Jew had to steer between two erroneous courses: *a)* the dualism of Platonistic philosophies which looked upon matter as evil and upon immortality as an intrinsic quality of the soul to be achieved by escape from the body; *b)* the pantheism of contemporary philosophy, especially Stoicism, which identified man and his destiny with the universe in some fashion" (Reese, 161-62). Some Jewish *sages were influenced by Platonic notions of an immortal soul, which explains occasional reference to the soul's preexistence (Wis 8:19-20; Philo, *Somn.* 1.133-143; *Gig.* 6-9; *Plant.* 11-14 [see Wahlen, 52-53]).

5. Conclusion.

The expression of Jewish wisdom in Greek facilitated dialogue between Greeks and Hellenized Jews, particularly in Alexandria. The LXX provided the essential terminology and, in the wisdom books at least, already shows signs of Greek influence. Jewish religious values and concepts are increasingly expressed in Hellenistic terms—a tendency epitomized by the works of Philo. A persistent difference between Greek and Jewish perspectives is the foundational Hebrew insistence that "the fear of the LORD is the beginning of wisdom." Also more specifically Jewish concerns exemplified by the Torah were given more prominence in wisdom instruction. A growing speculation about the afterlife also appears, shifting the genre closer toward Jewish apocalyptic. This fertile discussion of wisdom significantly advanced Jewish philosophical thought from its OT roots and provides the indispensable context for understanding the rise of Christianity, for it is within this context that its ideas were first forged.

See also ECCLESIASTES 2: ANCIENT NEAR EASTERN BACKGROUND; SIRACH, BOOK OF; WISDOM AND APOCALYPTIC; WISDOM OF SOLOMON.

BIBLIOGRAPHY. **M. L. Barré**, "'Fear of God' and the World View of Wisdom," *BTB* 11 (1981) 41-43; **F. W. Beare**, "Greek Religion and Philosophy," *IDB* 2.487-500; **R. M. Berchman**, *From Philo to Origen: Middle Platonism in Transition* (BJS 69; Chico, CA: Scholars Press, 1984); **H. Chadwick**, "Philo and the Beginnings of Christian Thought," in *The Cambridge History of Later Greek and Early Medieval Philosophy*, ed. A. H. Armstrong (Cambridge: Cambridge University Press, 1967) 133-92; **R. Clifford**, "Observations on the

Texts and Versions of Proverbs," in *Wisdom, You Are My Sister: Studies in Honor of Roland E. Murphy, O. Carm., on the Occasion of His Eightieth Birthday*, ed. M. L. Barré (Washington, DC: Catholic Biblical Association of America, 1997) 47-61; **J. J. Collins**, "The Sage in the Apocalyptic and Pseudepigraphic Literature," in *The Sage in Israel and the Ancient Near East*, ed. J. G. Gammie and L. G. Perdue (Winona Lake, IN: Eisenbrauns, 1990) 343-54; idem, *Jewish Wisdom in the Hellenistic Age* (OTL; Louisville: John Knox, 1997); idem, *Encounters with Biblical Theology* (Minneapolis: Fortress, 2005); **J. Cook**, "The Septuagint as a Jewish-Hellenistic Document," in *VIII Congress of the International Organization for Septuagint and Cognate Studies, Paris 1992*, ed. L. Greenspoon and O. Munnich (SBLSCS 41; Atlanta: Scholars Press, 1995) 349-65; idem, "The Law of Moses in Septuagint Proverbs," *VT* 49 (1999) 48-61; idem, "The Ideology of Septuagint Proverbs," in *X Congress of the International Organization for Septuagint and Cognate Studies, Oslo 1998*, ed. B. Taylor (SBLSCS 51; Atlanta: Scholars Press, 2001) 463-79; **J. L. Crenshaw**, *Old Testament Wisdom: An Introduction* (Louisville: Westminster John Knox, 1998); **L. H. Feldman**, *Jew and Gentile in the Ancient World* (Princeton, NJ: Princeton University Press, 1993); **G. Gerleman**, *Studies in the Septuagint: I. Book of Job* (LUÅ 52/2; Lund: Gleerup, 1946); idem, "The Septuagint Proverbs as a Hellenistic Document" *OTS* 8 (1950) 15-27; idem, *Studies in the Septuagint: III. Proverbs* (LUÅ 52/3; Lund: Gleerup, 1956); **M. Goodman**, "Jewish Proselytizing in the First Century," in *The Jews among Pagans and Christians in the Roman Empire*, ed. J. Lieu, J. North and T. Rajak (London: Routledge, 1992) 53-78; **M. Hengel**, *Judaism and Hellenism: Studies in Their Encounter in Palestine during the Early Hellenistic Period*, trans. J. Bowden (2 vols.; London: SCM, 1974); **M. P. Horne**, *Proverbs, Ecclesiastes* (SHBC; Macon, GA: Smyth & Helwys, 2003); **G. S. Kirk, J. E. Raven and M. Schofield**, *The Presocratic Philosophers* (2nd ed.; Cambridge: Cambridge University Press, 1983); **M. Lichtheim**, *Ancient Egyptian Literature* (3 vols.; Berkeley: University of California Press, 1975-1980); **A. A. Long and D. N. Sedley**, *The Hellenistic Philosophers* (2 vols.; Cambridge: Cambridge University Press, 1987); **P. Merlan**, "Greek Philosophy from Plato to Plotinus," in *The Cambridge History of Later Greek and Early Medieval Philosophy*, ed. A. H. Armstrong (Cambridge: Cambridge University Press, 1967) 12-

132; **H.-P. Müller**, "Mantische Weisheit und Apokalyptik," in *Congress Volume: Uppsala 1971* (VTSup 22; Leiden: E. J. Brill, 1972) 268-93; **R. Murphy**, "A Consideration of the Classification 'Wisdom Psalms,'" in *Studies in Ancient Israelite Wisdom: Selected, with a Prolegomenon*, ed. J. L. Crenshaw (LBS; New York: KTAV, 1976) 456-67 (originally published in *VTSup* 9 [1962] 156-67); idem, *The Tree of Life: An Exploration of Biblical Wisdom Literature* (2nd ed.; ABRL; Grand Rapids: Eerdmans, 1990); **O. S. Rankin**, *Israel's Wisdom Literature: Its Bearing on Theology and the History of Religion* (Edinburgh: T & T Clark, 1954); **J. M. Reese**, *Hellenistic Influence on the Book of Wisdom and Its Consequences* (AnBib 41; Rome: Biblical Institute Press, 1970); **E. J. Schnabel**, *Law and Wisdom from Ben Sira to Paul* (WUNT 2/16; Tübingen: Mohr Siebeck, 1985); **R. C. Solomon and K. M. Higgins**, *A Short History of Philosophy* (New York: Oxford University Press, 1996); **M. E. Stone**, "Apocalyptic Literature," in *Jewish Writings of the Second Temple Period*, ed. M. E. Stone (CRINT 2/2; Philadelphia: Fortress, 1984) 383-441; **V. Tcherikover**, "Jewish Apologetic Literature Reconsidered," *Eos* 48 (1956) 169-93; **H. St. J. Thackeray**, "The Poetry of the Greek Book of Proverbs," *JTS* 13 (1912) 46-66; **P. W. van der Horst**, *Jews and Christians in Their Graeco-Roman Context: Selected Essays on Early Judaism, Samaritanism, Hellenism, and Christianity* (WUNT 1/196; Tübingen: Mohr Siebeck, 2006); **G. von Rad**, *Wisdom in Israel* (London: SCM, 1972); **C. Wahlen**, *Jesus and the Impurity of Spirits in the Synoptic Gospels* (WUNT 2/185; Tübingen: Mohr Siebeck, 2004); **U. Wilckens**, "σοφία, κτλ," *TDNT* 7.465-76.

C. Wahlen

WISDOM AND APOCALYPTIC

Scholars have long debated the nature of the relationship between wisdom and apocalyptic in the world of the ancient Near East. Because it is likely that apocalyptic emerged at least in part from wisdom traditions, it shares certain convictions and perspectives with sapiential thought. Yet it is also indebted to other theological streams, such as biblical prophecy, and thus stands apart as a new and distinct phenomenon.

1. Preliminary Issues
2. The Problem of the Origins of Jewish Apocalyptic
3. Wisdom and Apocalyptic in Early Jewish Literature

4. Wisdom and Apocalyptic: Compatibility and Distinctions

1. Preliminary Issues.

1.1. Terminology. In considering the topic of apocalyptic, one of the central problems and causes of confusion is the imprecision that has often attended the use of the terms involved. As a corrective to this problem, the work of P. Hanson and J. Collins has provided scholars with some basic terminological distinctions. The word *apocalypse* refers to a literary "genre of revelatory literature with a narrative framework, in which a revelation is mediated by an otherwordly being to a human recipient, disclosing a transcendent reality which is both temporal, insofar as it envisages eschatological salvation, and spatial insofar as it involves another, supernatural world" (Collins 1979, 9). The expression *apocalyptic eschatology* indicates a religious outlook that stands in continuity with biblical eschatology but with the significant difference that divine intervention is largely transferred from the realm of ordinary history and human agency to a cosmic, cataclysmic end to the present world and the establishment of a new order (Hanson 1975, 11-12). Finally, the term *apocalypticism* refers to a "symbolic universe" where apocalyptic eschatology has escalated to the status of an ideology, usually as the sociological response to the communal feeling of alienation and/or persecution (Hanson 1976, 30). In this article these conventions will be followed, and the word *apocalyptic* will be used to refer to the patterns of thought characteristic of both apocalyptic eschatology and apocalypticism without necessarily specifying one to the exclusion of the other. Furthermore, it must be recognized that none of these three are homogeneous entities but rather are modern attempts to classify diverse but related literatures, worldviews and sociological phenomena from the Second Temple period.

1.2. Relating Wisdom and Apocalyptic. In order to assess the relationship between wisdom and apocalyptic, it is helpful to distinguish three modes in which they may be related. The first is the diachronic relationship between the two: what role, if any, does wisdom play in the emergence of apocalyptic? The second concerns the interaction of wisdom and apocalyptic thought in literary works and genres. The third mode is a synthetic assessment of the degree to which wisdom and apocalyptic thought are compatible and to which they are in conflict.

2. The Problem of the Origins of Jewish Apocalyptic.

2.1. Initial Theories. Apocalypses began appearing throughout the Near East during the Hellenistic period as a response to Greek oppression. They are attested in both Egypt and Persia, but the greatest concentration of extant apocalypses come from Jewish authors, whether in Palestine or in the Diaspora. In the case of Jewish apocalypses, the persecutions of the second century BC, probably exacerbated by nostalgia for Israel's former monarchy, initiated a flourishing of apocalyptic thought that continued for several centuries. However, although certain historical circumstances may be shown to be instrumental causes of apocalyptic compositions, the rise of apocalyptic as a phenomenon has enough unique qualities that it is impossible to trace its origins solely as the organic outgrowth of any one tradition or circumstance. Rather, it must be viewed as both a new phenomenon and one that draws upon a confluence of other theologies and literary domains.

Throughout the first half of the twentieth century there were two main theories as to what provided the primary source for apocalyptic thought. First, a number of scholars held that apocalyptic was a derivative of Persian dualism and thus constituted a departure from the monotheism of the biblical prophets. The other major view, especially among British scholars such as H. H. Rowley and D. S. Russell, was that apocalyptic developed out of Israelite prophecy. This latter view was based on the understanding that eschatology was a central component of both biblical prophecy and the later apocalypses, not to mention the fact that several apocalypses refer to themselves as prophecies (e.g., Rev 1:3; *4 Ezra* 1:1). This discussion about origins underwent something of a revolution in the 1960s and 1970s due to the publication of some significant works with the result that prophecy and wisdom became the two leading proposals.

2.2. Biblical Prophecy as the Primary Source (P. Hanson). In his seminal work, *The Dawn of Apocalyptic,* P. Hanson argued that there is no reason to seek the source of apocalypticism in a foreign religion such as Zoroastrianism, since it is explainable as a development from postexilic prophecy, as exemplified by Isaiah 56—66 and Zechariah 9—14, amid the sociological context of warring factions and widespread pessimism in postexilic Palestine. Although Hanson certainly does not presume that all the features of apocalyptic may be explained from postexilic prophecy, and although most scholars have seen Hanson's work as a helpful and needed corrective, he has been challenged by others for neglecting to note the features of apocalyptic thought that intersect with wisdom literature (see Wilson, 81-83).

2.3. Wisdom as the Only Source (G. von Rad). Although there were earlier scholars who advocated viewing sapiential thought as the primary source of apocalyptic, G. von Rad is both the most well known and the most extreme in his views. For von Rad, biblical prophecy could not have played any part in the emergence of apocalyptic because the two have mutually exclusive views of history. He argued that the message of the prophets operates within the framework of "election traditions" and redemptive history. Over against this, apocalyptic literature has lost this historical sensitivity by conceptually objectifying the whole historical process, resulting in a transcendental and eschatological dualism that dichotomizes history into two aeons, the present one and the one to come. This led von Rad (1962-1965, 2.301-8) to conclude that the heart of apocalyptic literature is the revelation of knowledge that is ahistorical and based on a "universal Jahwism." From this vantage point, the sapiential worldview provides the essential matrix for the rise of apocalypticism, a position that finds additional support in the apocalyptic books of *1 Enoch* and Daniel, wherein these two characters are portrayed as having sagelike qualities. Von Rad (1972, 279) explained the incorporation of dualistic and eschatological ideas as the growth and "branching out" of wisdom in the postexilic period.

2.4. Toward a Synthetic Approach. Though the vast majority of scholars have not adopted von Rad's position without serious qualifications, most have recognized that sapiential thought played an important role in the emergence of apocalyptic. There are three principal problems with von Rad's thesis. One is that he drew too sharp a distinction between prophecy and apocalyptic without recognizing the undeniable continuities between the two. Second, and related to the first, is that he did not adequately account for the fact that wisdom literature generally lacks the kind of eschatology found in apocalyptic. Third, he failed to distinguish properly between different types of wisdom. With regard to the third problem, subsequent studies have provided the appropriate nuance for understanding how wisdom serves as a background for apocalypticism.

In a landmark essay H.-P. Müller made the crucial observation that the kind of wisdom that is the source of apocalypticism is neither the "courtly-pedagogical" kind (e.g., Prov 20:26; cf. 1 Kings 3:4-28) nor the more democratic kind (e.g., Prov 3:27-35), both well known from Israelite traditions, but rather the mantic kind of wisdom that is characterized by divination and dream interpretation. Given the prevalence of mantic wisdom in Mesopotamia, it becomes immediately clear why its influence in Jewish literature only appears in the postexilic period. The strength of Müller's thesis is that mantic wisdom, unlike other types of wisdom, is better able to account for some of the central features of apocalyptic thought than is classical prophecy: the nature of its eschatology, its determinism, its emphasis on the authority of special enlightenment, and its method of encoding reality in symbolic images.

Further refining the framework of Müller's thesis, J. Collins has delineated five types of wisdom: (1) wisdom sayings (e.g., Prov 10—31); (2) theological wisdom (e.g., Prov 8; Job); (3) nature wisdom (e.g., Job 28; 38—41); (4) mantic wisdom; (5) revelatory wisdom. Collins (1997, 388) observes that whereas the biblical wisdom books fall primarily in the first three categories, apocalyptic comes from the fifth category and is influenced by the fourth. The significance of this taxonomy is that it highlights the fact that what qualifies as Near Eastern wisdom is broader than what is characteristic of classical biblical wisdom, and this fact must be taken into account in understanding how apocalyptic draws on wisdom elements.

The observation by Müller and Collins that the discussion of sapiential origins of apocalyptic must be broader than the central paradigm of wisdom in the OT has been mirrored by J. VanderKam in his analysis of the prophetic influence on apocalyptic. Although the OT is sharply critical of the type of divination found throughout Mesopotamia, there are some types of divination that are viewed favorably, such as the Urim and Thummim (cf. Num 27:21; 1 Sam 28:6; Ezra 2:63) and the ephod (1 Sam 23). Furthermore, there is a considerable conceptual and formal overlap between prophecy and divination. Formally, their relationship is evident from the fact that biblical writers both juxtapose the function of the two (cf. Deut 18; Isa 44; 47; 48) and the methods of the two (Jer 27; Ezek 13; Mic 3). Therefore, prophecy considered from a broader perspective than what is primarily exemplified by biblical prophecy shows some overlap with Near Eastern divination, and this helps to explain how postexilic strands of thought that developed out of biblical prophecy could accommodate some of the divinatory aspects of mantic wisdom. Conceptually, postexilic prophecy and divination emphasize divine revelation, are concerned with the future, and are interested in interpreting/decoding previous messages (VanderKam 2000b, 241-54).

While Collins has pointed to a definition of wisdom that is broader than what is normally considered to be OT Wisdom literature, VanderKam has pointed to a broader definition of prophecy that includes divinatory elements. Therefore, it is somewhat of a false dichotomy to maintain that apocalyptic is derived primarily from either prophecy or mantic wisdom. The overlap of the two worlds, particularly in the domains of divination and dream interpretation, seems to be the most likely candidate for the primary matrix from which apocalyptic thought emerged. It should be noted that the kind of fluidity found between wisdom, prophecy and apocalyptic is not unique in Second Temple Judaism. The distinctions between priestly, prophetic, didactic and scribal schools are much less clear in the Second Temple period than in the First Temple period (*see* Sages, Schools, Education).

While it seems evident that sapiential thought was a significant source of apocalyptic thought, it is much less clear whether apocalyptic communities developed out of sapiential communities. The lack of sociological data for certain groups within Second Temple Judaism makes the latter question very difficult to answer. J. Smith has argued that both wisdom and apocalyptic are scribal phenomena. If so, then apocalyptic communities likely would have emerged from within the sociological context of scribal schools.

In addition to the sapiential, prophetic and divinatory influences on the emergence of apoc-

alyptic, several scholars have pointed out the number of similarities between Jewish apocalyptic literature and the Akkadian Prophecies (sometimes called the Akkadian Apocalypses), which denote five texts: Text A, the Uruk Prophecy, the Dynastic Prophecy, the Marduk Prophetic Speech and the Shulgi Prophetic Speech. Given the emphasis on predicting the future through the means of revelation or divination, these prophecies bear greater resemblance to historically oriented Jewish apocalypses (e.g., Dan 7—12; the "Apocalypse of Weeks" in *1 En.* 85—90) than to those that focus more on heavenly journeys (e.g., *T. Levi* 2—5). Other similarities with Jewish apocalypses found in the Akkadian Prophecies are predictions by pseudonymous characters and the tendency to predict the future in cryptic language. Although there are eschatological elements in the Uruk Prophecy, the other four texts betray less of an eschatological focus than do the later Jewish apocalypses. This has led some scholars to question the possible influence of the Akkadian literature on the emergence of Jewish apocalyptic, but the number of key similarities indicates that, at the least, the streams of tradition and modes of thought that contributed to the rise of apocalyptic were varied and present throughout the ancient Near East.

3. Wisdom and Apocalyptic in Early Jewish Literature.

Because apocalypticism drew from wisdom thought and literature, there was a resultant intermingling of the two. The authors of Jewish apocalypses were heirs to Israel's religious and literary heritage and thus easily drew upon sapiential concepts in the composition of their works. Conversely, the production of wisdom literature could not help but be influenced and sometimes even framed by apocalyptic thought. Therefore, as one moves through the Second Temple period, the nexus between genre and content begins to break down as apocalyptic and sapiential thought each begins to interpenetrate their corresponding genres (Nickelsburg 2005, 20). Although a comprehensive discussion of this phenomenon is not possible here, a few examples will serve to highlight the interaction between wisdom and apocalyptic in early Jewish literature.

3.1. 1 Enoch. During the Second Temple period apocalyptic thought began to crystallize predominantly around two figures: Enoch and Daniel. Correspondingly, the books of Daniel and *1 Enoch* (the earliest extant Jewish apocalypses) provide the best examples of the incorporation of mantic wisdom into apocalyptic thought and literature. Because *1 Enoch* likely has apocalyptic material extending back into the third century BC, it is now customary to view this work, rather than Daniel, as the starting point for the discussion of the rise of Jewish apocalyptic (see VanderKam 2000a, 266).

Although *1 Enoch* is usually classified as an apocalypse, it seems to present itself as a collection of wisdom in the form of a testament (cf. *1 En.* 98:9; 99:10; see Argall, 17). In fact, *1 Enoch* is more accurately viewed as a composite of several generic forms, including, among others, testament, apocalypse, oracle and epistle. However, despite the variety of generic forms, it is clear that the book as a whole reflects the "apocalyptic construction of reality" (Nickelsburg 2001, 120). What is most striking in this respect is that the central figure within this apocalyptic reality, Enoch, is portrayed as a mantic *sage who receives his wisdom directly from heavenly revelation (Collins 1997, 347).

The precise interaction of wisdom and apocalyptic in *1 Enoch* is complex and debated. This is especially true when a certain literary form is attested in both the prophetic and sapiential literature (e.g., the "woe" form in *1 En.* 96:8). Nevertheless, there are some clear examples where wisdom instruction has been integrated into an apocalyptic passage. For example, throughout the Epistle of Enoch (*1 En.* 91—107) there are numerous uses of wisdom forms and vocabulary (e.g., *1 En.* 91:3; 94:1), including a reference within the Apocalypse of Weeks (*1 En.* 93:3-10; 91:11-17) to the reception of sevenfold instruction by the righteous (*1 En.* 93:10). Beyond the incorporation of sapiential elements into specific apocalypses within *1 Enoch*, the general apocalyptic outlook of the book is thoroughly interwoven with references to wisdom and its corresponding themes (e.g., *1 En.* 5:8; 37:1; 81:1—82:4; 99:10; 105:1-2).

3.2. Daniel. Although the book of Daniel lacks sapiential literary forms (as in *1 Enoch*), its content provides the clearest example of the incorporation of mantic wisdom into an apocalyptic text. In fact, according to Müller, the redactional history of Daniel parallels the transition from mantic wisdom to apocalypticism. The court narratives in Daniel 2—6, widely held to be the earliest portions of the book, present

Daniel as a mantic sage who is gifted at interpreting the king's dreams, far exceeding the abilities of his Babylonian counterparts. His commitment to prayer, abstention from idol worship, and devotion to the *law (Dan 1) set his mantic wisdom in a distinctively Jewish context.

However, the characterization of Daniel as a mantic sage becomes transformed through the addition of Daniel 7—12. Now, rather than interpreting the dreams and visions of the foreign king, the sagely Daniel is himself the recipient of divine revelation in the form of apocalyptic visions. Similarly, the content of the king's dreams provides thematic continuity with the apocalyptic section of the book (compare Dan 2 and Dan 7). The blending of mantic wisdom and apocalyptic in the book of Daniel is further demonstrated by the similar role played by revelation in the two halves of the book. In both sections revelation comes through the medium of encoded dreams/visions (compare Dan 2; 4 with Dan 7; 8) or through the ability to interpret divine writings (compare Dan 5 with Dan 9). It appears that the theme in Daniel 2—6, that revealed wisdom enables the sage to make future predictions, has been appropriated by the author(s) of Daniel 7—12 as the model for the apocalyptic predictions of the future found there. These predictions go well beyond the near future of one kingdom as in Daniel 2—6 and encompass all of history in an eschatological program.

3.3. 4QInstruction (1Q26, 4Q415-18, 423). Among the collection of wisdom texts found among the *Dead Sea Scrolls, one that is of particular interest is 4QInstruction (= Sapiential Work A), which is often dated to the last century BC because the fragments are written in the Herodian script. The work is characterized by instructional material and exhortations that recall the traditional Israelite wisdom found in *Proverbs and *Sirach. The themes of virtues and vices, wealth and poverty, and social and familial relationships recur throughout the document. Furthermore, there are similar formal structures, such as the tendency to address the author's instructions to "the understanding son/pupil" (e.g., 4Q417 2 I, 18 [cf. Prov 1:8]).

However, 4QInstruction is especially important because it is perhaps the earliest witness to the expression of an apocalyptic worldview through a composition that is thoroughly sapiential in form and content. Near the beginning of the document the motivation for living righteously is set in the dual contexts of God's ordering of the world and of final judgment and cosmic upheaval (4Q416 1 1-18). Righteousness and iniquity are often addressed within the framework of apocalyptic eschatology (e.g., 4Q418 126 1-10). This blending of sapiential ethics and apocalyptic eschatology is captured by the frequent use throughout the work of the enigmatic phrase *raz niḥěyeh*, which may be translated as "the mystery that is to be" (Aitken, 186). It seems to refer to the comprehensive scope of the divine plan/will in all its creational, ethical and eschatological aspects and demonstrates the way in which the genre of wisdom could contain traditional sapiential material that had been reconceptualized into an apocalyptic worldview.

3.4. Wisdom of Solomon. Wisdom of Solomon is typically placed within the category of wisdom literature. This designation suggests itself by the pseudepigraphical attribution to *Solomon, the numerous references to wisdom, the use of didactic exhortation, and its inclusion of proverbs with formal similarities to those found in the books of Proverbs and Sirach. Yet perhaps more than any other Second Temple work, Wisdom of Solomon blurs the generic categories of wisdom and apocalyptic.

In Wisdom of Solomon 1—5 the exhortation to a life of wisdom, virtue and faithfulness occurs in the context of cosmology and eschatology and is grounded in the final judgment of the wicked and the vindication of the righteous. Wisdom is understood as salvific, the fail-proof guide to immortality (Wis 1:4-5; cf. Wis 8:17; 9:18). The apocalyptic tenor of these first five chapters has led some commentators to designate this section of Wisdom of Solomon as "the book of eschatology." Furthermore, these chapters contain some striking parallels to *1 Enoch*. The final judgment in Wisdom of Solomon 5 is similar to *1 Enoch* 62—63, and the method of reasoning in Wisdom of Solomon 2—5 resembles that in *1 Enoch* 102—104. Even throughout the rest of the book wisdom is portrayed in cosmic and universalistic terms. These connections have led many to conclude that the author has adopted the apocalyptic tradition and presented it through the lens of Hellenistic Jewish philosophy (Nickelsburg 2005, 28).

4. Wisdom and Apocalyptic: Compatibility and Distinctions.

From the perspective of the origins of apocalyptic and a survey of the apocalyptic literature it becomes clear that apocalyptic thought is best considered to be a particular kind of wisdom. This historical relationship implies that there is a certain amount of compatibility between the two.

Throughout the apocalypses revelation and hidden knowledge are characterized as wisdom, and the central figures themselves are portrayed more as sages than as prophets (e.g., Daniel and Enoch). The wisdom and apocalyptic worldviews thus share certain core convictions. Both see themselves as rooted in Israel's religious traditions and evidence an interest in both the Torah and the Prophets as authoritative. Both lay great emphasis on righteous living and the need for ethical exhortation. Both claim that revelation is ultimately from the God of Israel, and that Israel, as God's people, has certain covenantal obligations and privileges. Finally, both wisdom (especially Hellenistic wisdom) and apocalypticism share an interest in the structure of the universe as a medium of God's will and as inextricably linked to history, salvation and eschatology.

However, as the thought and literature of apocalyptic began to flourish, it developed characteristics and emphases that distinguished it from more traditional forms of Jewish wisdom. First, although especially similar to Hellenistic wisdom in some ways, Jewish apocalypticism lacked the philosophical orientation present in many of these texts. Rather, the apocalyptic texts tended to be oriented toward mythological/cosmic imagery. Second, in sapiential texts wisdom is generally available to all who pursue it and/or pray for it, but in apocalyptic texts wisdom is often encoded and mediated through dreams, visions or celestial patterns. Third, in wisdom literature revelation is often related to the Mosaic Torah, whereas in apocalyptic literature new revelation is presented, though it is viewed as compatible with the Mosaic Torah. Finally, as apocalypticism developed, it increasingly reflected both a spatial and a temporal dualism that generally was absent from sapiential thought. The spatial dualism concerns the dichotomy between heaven and earth, a barrier that only the specially gifted may traverse (e.g. *1 En.* 17—19). Often what occurs in the heavenly realm has decisive implications for the earthly realm (e.g., Dan 10:10-21; Rev 6). The temporal dualism views all of history as divisible into two main epochs: the present age and the age to come (e.g., *1 En.* 71:15; cf. Heb 1:1-2). The former is typically viewed as containing much evil and suffering, whereas the latter is characterized by the restoration of the good and the vindication of God's people. The transition point of these two ages is the direct and cataclysmic intervention of God.

The complexity of wisdom and apocalyptic in early Judaism resists their compartmentalization into two completely distinct phenomena. Rather, within the diverse spectrum of Second Temple Judaism the designations *wisdom* and *apocalyptic* reflect patterns of thought that, while not coextensive, have significant overlap.

See also WISDOM THEOLOGY; WISDOM AND PROPHECY.

BIBLIOGRAPHY. **J. K. Aitken,** "Apocalyptic, Revelation and Early Jewish Wisdom Literature," in *New Heaven and New Earth: Prophecy and the Millennium; Essays in Honour of Anthony Gelston,* ed. P. Harland and C. Hayward (VTSup 77; Leiden: E. J. Brill, 1999) 181-93; **R. A. Argall,** *1 Enoch and Sirach: A Comparative Literary and Conceptual Analysis of the Themes of Revelation, Creation and Judgment* (SBLEJL 8; Atlanta: Scholars Press, 1995); **J. J. Collins, ed.,** *Apocalyptic: Towards the Morphology of a Genre* (SBLSS 14; Missoula, MT: Scholars Press, 1979); idem, *Seers, Sybils and Sages in Hellenistic-Roman Judaism* (JSJSup 54; Leiden: E. J. Brill, 1997); idem, *The Apocalyptic Imagination: An Introduction to Jewish Apocalyptic Literature* (2nd ed.; Grand Rapids: Eerdmans, 1998); **J. G. Gammie,** "Spatial and Ethical Dualism in Jewish Wisdom and Apocalyptic Literature," *JBL* 93 (1974) 356-85; **P. Hanson,** "Apocalypticism," *IDBSup* 29-34; idem, *The Dawn of Apocalyptic: The Historical and Sociological Roots of Jewish Apocalyptic Eschatology* (Philadelphia: Fortress, 1975); idem, "Jewish Apocalypticism against Its Near Eastern Environment," *RB* 78 (1971) 31-58; **H.-P. Müller,** "Mantische Weisheit und Apokalyptik," in *Congress Volume: Uppsala, 1971* (VTSup 22; Leiden: E. J. Brill, 1972) 268-93; **H.-P. Müller and M. Krause,** "חכם," *TDOT* 4.364-85; **G. W. E. Nickelsburg,** *1 Enoch 1: A Commentary on the Book of 1 Enoch, Chapters 1-36; 81-108* (Hermeneia; Minneapolis: Fortress, 2001); idem, "Wisdom and Apocalypticism in Early Judaism: Some Points for Discussion," in *Conflicted Boundaries in Wisdom and Apocalypticism,* ed. B. G. Wright III and L. M. Wills (SBLSymS 35; Atlanta: Society of Biblical Literature, 2005) 17-37; **C. Rowland,** *The Open Heaven: A Study of Apocalyptic in Judaism and Early Christianity* (New York: Crossroad, 1982); **D. S. Russell,** *The Method and Message of Jewish Apocalyptic, 200 BC–AD 100* (Philadelphia: Westminster, 1964); **J. Z. Smith,** "Wisdom and Apocalyptic," in *Religious Syncretism in Antiquity: Essays in Conversation with Geo Widengren,* ed. B. A. Pearson (SFCT 1; Missoula, MT: Scholars Press, 1975) 131-56; **M. Stone,** "Lists of Revealed Things in the Apocalyptic Literature," in *Magnalia Dei: The Mighty Acts of God; Essays on the Bible and Archaeology in Memory of G. Ernest Wright,* ed. F. M. Cross, W. E. Lemke and P. D. Miller (Garden City, NY: Doubleday, 1976) 414-54; **J. C. VanderKam,** *Enoch and the Growth of an Apocalyptic Tradition* (CBQMS 16; Washington, DC: Catholic Biblical Association of America, 1984); idem, "Prophecy and Apocalyptics in the Ancient Near East," in *From Revelation to Canon: Studies in the Hebrew Bible and Second Temple Literature* (JSJSup 62; Leiden: E. J. Brill, 2000a), 255-75; idem, "The Prophetic-Sapiential Origins of Apocalyptic Thought," in *From Revelation to Canon: Studies in the Hebrew Bible and Second Temple Literature* (JSJSup 62; Leiden: E. J. Brill, 2000b) 241-54; **G. von Rad,** *Old Testament Theology* (2 vols.; New York: Harper, 1962-1965); idem, *Wisdom in Israel* (Nashville: Abingdon, 1972); **R. R. Wilson,** "From Prophecy to Apocalyptic: Reflections on the Shape of Israelite Religion," *Semeia* 21 (1981) 79-95. B. C. Gregory

WISDOM AND BIBLICAL THEOLOGY

The OT Wisdom literature is marked by several prominent emphases. For this reason, until recent times most OT theologies tended to neglect or discount wisdom because it did not seem to fit well into theological syntheses that were derived from the major tenets of salvation history. Since the latter part of the twentieth century, however, wisdom increasingly and rightfully has come to be recognized as having a vital place not only in OT theology, but also in the theology of the entire biblical *canon.

1. Emphases of Old Testament Wisdom
2. Neglect of Wisdom in Biblical Theology
3. Connections between Wisdom and Other Old Testament Texts
4. Place of Wisdom in Old Testament Theology
5. Place of Wisdom in Biblical Theology

1. Emphases of Old Testament Wisdom.

Because OT wisdom bears many similarities to the wisdom texts of other ancient Near Eastern civilizations, it has often been dismissed as secular. Nevertheless, a careful reading of the wisdom books evidences that wisdom functions within the same theistic worldview that permeates the rest of the OT. Although R. Murphy and L. Perdue likely overstate the case when they follow W. Zimmerli in describing wisdom theology as creation theology, it is undeniable that wisdom speaks of the world that has been shaped and is now being governed by the all-wise Creator (Clements 1995, 271). Proverbs 3:19 states that Yahweh by wisdom founded the earth. He has imbedded wisdom in the world, and humans are challenged to seek diligently for it (Prov 4:7).

Wisdom uses an inductive approach as it observes carefully the natural and human world. As it detects general patterns of cause and effect, it derives from them lessons that can be applied to other situations. C. Grizzard (214) notes that the wisdom sages "learned about God by studying God's creation, including humanity. They found evidence of God's power and purposes in the rhythms of nature and urged their followers to incorporate that order into their own lives even as they also acknowledged that there would always be matters they could not understand." An example of this procedure of wisdom can be seen in Proverbs 6:6-11, in which the observation of the ant (Prov 6:6) yields a pattern of industrious work (Prov 6:7-8) that is taught as a warning to the sluggard (Prov 6:9-11).

The underlying sense of wisdom in the Hebrew Bible is skill in a variety of contexts. In the OT wisdom books wisdom is defined especially in the moral sense of skill in living. More specifically, wisdom is skill in living according to Yahweh's moral order. The beginning of wisdom is the fear of Yahweh (Prov 9:10)—that is, deep respect and reverence for Yahweh that prompts one to follow his way (see Fear of the Lord). As B. Waltke (1979, 389) observes, biblical wisdom places its trust not merely in the order observable in Yahweh's world, but rather in Yahweh himself, who ordered the world (Prov 3:5). OT wisdom, and in particular the book of *Proverbs, distinguishes between two divergent paths of behavior. On the one hand, wisdom reveres Yahweh's word and character, and thus follows the path characterized by righteous behavior that results in life in all of its dimensions; on the other hand, *folly values autonomy rather than revering Yahweh's word and character, so it chooses to follow the path characterized by wicked behavior that results in death in all of its manifestations (see Chaos and Death).

The linkage between a person's acts and the resulting consequences has often been called *"retribution," and its classic expression can be seen in Proverbs 26:28 (NASB): "He who digs a pit will fall into it, and he who rolls a stone, it will come back on him." In the book of *Job this general cause-and-effect pattern is elevated into a rigid dogma of retribution theology in which Job's experience of calamity is assessed by his three friends as proof positive of his personal sin. Job himself also assumes the validity of the retribution formula, but he cannot reconcile his confidence in his own innocence with the calamity that he is experiencing. What Job and his comforters learn from Yahweh is that there are aspects of experience that transcend human understanding, and that cannot be forced into the retribution formula. Indeed, Proverbs itself teaches this truth: "Man's steps are ordained by the LORD. How then can man understand his way?" (Prov 20:24 NASB). This element of divine mystery prompted in OT wisdom the consideration of *theodicy, the attempt to understand why bad things happen to good people in the world governed by the sovereign God who is both all-powerful and completely good.

Contemporary education typically focuses on what the learner is to know or what the student is to do. By contrast, the predominant concern of OT wisdom is what the human is to be. Character formation is at the heart of true wisdom; as M. Fox (620) states, "Wisdom is a configuration of soul; it is *moral character*. And fostering moral character, it is no understatement to say, is at all times the greatest goal of education."

2. Neglect of Wisdom in Biblical Theology.

Many of the distinctive emphases of OT wisdom have been viewed as though they are unique to the wisdom books, with the result that early OT theologies scarcely mention wisdom at all. R. Whybray (116) concludes from this omission that "Proverbs seems in fact to have been generally regarded as a rather commonplace and pedestrian moral handbook with little theological content." This neglect of wisdom continued throughout the heyday of the biblical theology movement during the middle of the twentieth century, as the various major proposed centers of OT theology tended to marginalize the wisdom texts (for examples, see Ollenburger). For example, both W. Eichrodt's focus on covenant and G. von Rad's emphasis on salvation history had the effect of pushing wisdom to the periphery. Although subsequently von Rad did indeed write a seminal volume on wisdom in Israel, he viewed wisdom as Israel's response to God rather than as an integral part of the divine revelation.

It is undeniable that wisdom has a set of emphases different from those that are prominent in the OT *law, history and prophecy. K. Farmer (30) summarizes the data well:

> The "mighty acts of God" in Israel's history (the exodus, the giving of the law at Sinai, the crossing of the Jordan, etc.) are neither celebrated nor remembered in Proverbs, Ecclesiastes, and Job. Unlike Israel's salvation history, which sees evidence of God's activity in extraordinary events, the wisdom writings are primarily concerned with the regularities of ordinary life. The covenant between God and Israel, which plays such an important part in the religion of Israel, is seldom if ever mentioned by the wisdom writers. The only statements they make about God's actions in the past concern the creation of the world, not the creation of Israel.

When biblical theology is defined in terms of the events of salvation history, as has been typical in most of the prominent OT theologies, then wisdom is necessarily relegated to the margins.

In some cases, rather than being treated with benign neglect, wisdom has suffered outright rejection by biblical theologians. For instance, H. Preuss fixes his attention on the similarities between biblical wisdom and the wisdom texts from Egypt and Mesopotamia. He concludes from these parallels that biblical wisdom has borrowed material that is essentially pagan, and consequently the wisdom corpus is totally alien to the faith of Israel. From a different direction, but with the same effect, many biblical scholars seem to evidence an implicit prejudice in favor of special revelation and against general revelation. As a result, the Law and Prophets, with their frequent "Thus saith the LORD" statements, are regarded more favorably than the divine truth mediated through human observation that predominates in the Wisdom literature. Wisdom, then, often comes to be regarded as secular and inferior and therefore is presumed to have little of significance to contribute to biblical theology.

3. Connections between Wisdom and Other Old Testament Texts.

It is evident that the wisdom books have distinctive emphases that are not found as frequently in other OT texts. Nevertheless, that should not obscure the fact that there are many significant parallels between wisdom and the other portions of the OT. In contrast to the ancient Near Eastern wisdom texts, biblical wisdom bears the marks of monotheistic Yahwism. When Yahweh speaks to Job from the whirlwind, he is the same deity who is revealed in the Law, the Prophets and *Psalms. Similarly, the God of wisdom is the sole creator of heaven and earth (see Prov 8:22-31), just as in the narratives in Genesis 1—2. Furthermore, the God presented in wisdom has the same attributes as the God who is described in the prophets, and to whom the psalmists address their praise and prayer.

Even a casual reading of the wisdom books reveals that the actions and attitudes that are condemned as folly and wickedness are the same kind as those that are prohibited in the law and denounced by the prophets. In the study of a specific passage, P. Overland (440) demonstrates that Proverbs 3:1-12 is rooted in the Shema of Deuteronomy 6:4-9 to such an extent that "the product was a sapiential rendition of classic covenantal piety." Throughout the prophetic texts the themes, literary features and images of wisdom are employed frequently, and the link between acts and consequences found in wisdom is so pronounced in prophecy that some scholars have regarded wisdom as the application of the prophetic theme of divine justice to the mundane experiences of everyday life (Clements 1976, 100-101). Assessing the substantial similarities between the Wisdom literature and the legal and prophetic literature, Waltke (2004, 67) concludes, "Moses, the prophets, and the sages were true spiritual yokefellows sharing the same Lord, cultus, faith, hope, anthropology, and epistemology, speaking with the same authority, and making similar religious and ethical demands on their hearers. In short, they drank from the same spiritual well."

The presumption that wisdom is secular runs aground on the fact that the Psalter, which embodies the *worship and piety of ancient Israel, makes ample use of wisdom features (*see* Cult, Worship: Wisdom). Nearly thirty psalms have been categorized by various scholars as wisdom psalms due to the parallels between their language and themes and those that are prominent in the wisdom books. What qualifies a psalm to be considered a wisdom psalm is still much in question, but at very least it must be acknowledged that about a dozen psalms have a sufficient concentration of wisdom language that they can be read side by side with the traditional wisdom of Proverbs (e.g., Pss 1; 37; 119) or the speculative wisdom of Job and *Ecclesiastes (e.g., Pss 39; 49; 73).

It should also be noted that theodicy, which is such a prominent theme in the Wisdom literature, finds expression in other parts of the OT as well. The prophets Jeremiah and Habakkuk cry out about evil that has afflicted those who are innocent, and Psalm 49 and Psalm 73 consider the obverse side of the issue, when those who are evil seem to enjoy undiluted good. The challenges to retribution theology that permeate Job and Ecclesiastes, then, find similar expression in the psalmic and prophetic traditions as well.

It is clear that OT wisdom tends to have emphases that are in large part different from the major concerns of the rest of the OT. At the same time, however, the substantial connections between the wisdom books and the other OT texts demonstrate an underlying unity of thought. OT theology, then, must recognize the differences without making wisdom foreign to the biblical corpus, and it also must highlight the similarities without subsuming wisdom under a central theme, such as covenant, salvation history or the acts of Yahweh, that is too specific to allow wisdom to speak with its own distinctive voice. D. Hubbard (16) points in the right direction as he considers the proper place for wisdom in OT theology: "Prophets, sages, psalmists, court historians—all had access to the same resources in the history, worship, and folk ethos of the people. They differed in emphasis but not in basic orientation. They all saw their God, Yahweh, as Lord of nature, history, and personal experience; but they chose different ways of making this lordship known." At many places wisdom reinforces themes expressed in the Law, the Prophets and Psalms, but even in its distinctive differences wisdom does not contradict the rest of the OT but rather it supplements what is taught elsewhere.

4. Place of Wisdom in Old Testament Theology.
In contrast to von Rad, who speaks of multiple theologies in the OT, it is better to step back to consider the broader worldview that encompasses the entire OT canon. Although the various OT texts clearly have their own distinctive emphases, they share a common understanding of reality. Wisdom has much to contribute to this perceptual framework that pervades the OT. Murphy (1978, 39-40) notes well, "The average Israelite shared to some extent in the sapiential understanding of reality (which was, without doubt, not alien to Yahwism for them). Such an understanding was not a mode of thinking cultivated exclusively by one class; it was shared at all levels of society that interpreted daily experience. It came to be crystallized in a recognizable body of 'wisdom literature,' but the mentality itself was much broader than the literary remains that have come down to us."

Every worldview provides answers to several basic questions. The answers that wisdom gives to the worldview questions correlate well with the answers given in the rest of the OT texts. In answering the question "What is real?" wisdom regards Yahweh as the creator of all of the universe and of all humans. Because he has created all humans, he is concerned for both the rich and the poor, the Jews and the Gentiles. Yahweh's interests, then, include but transcend the covenant nation of Israel to address humanity as a whole.

Wisdom does not speak directly to the worldview issue of what it means to be human, but implicitly it views humans as created in the image of God (cf. Gen 1:26-27). Being made in the image of God, humans are enjoined to imitate their Creator in their behavior. Humans are called to become like Yahweh so that they can live in fellowship with him and thus live up to the unique purpose for which he created them. The prominent wisdom motif of the path of wisdom fits well with the descriptions of godly individuals such as Enoch and Noah walking with God (Gen 5:22, 24; 6:9) and the divine call to Abram to walk before God and be blameless (Gen 17:1).

It is evident that the most prominent theological contribution of wisdom is in the area of *ethics, as it answers the worldview question "What has value?" All human behavior is evaluated by Yahweh (Prov 17:3). Because Yahweh is inherently holy, what he commands is right. The legal stipulations in the Pentateuch, and the prophetic challenges drawn from them, express the standard that God has established for humans. These divine legal demands are clear, but they do not cover all areas of human experience, and it is at this point that the Wisdom literature forms a supplement to the legal literature of the OT. D. Kidner (13) explains, "There are details of character small enough to escape the mesh of the law and the broadsides of the prophets, and yet decisive in personal dealings. Proverbs moves in this realm, asking what a person is like to live with, or to employ; how he manages his affairs, his time and himself."

When wisdom sayings recommend human behaviors that correspond to what Yahweh does elsewhere in the OT, it is evident that wisdom views behavior that imitates God as good. C. Wright (41) observes that "many of the little details of behavior commended in the book [of Proverbs] do indeed reflect the character of God himself. There is emphasis on the virtues of faithfulness, kindness, work, compassion, social justice, especially for the poor and oppressed, generosity, impartiality, truthfulness and integrity. All of these reflect the character and concerns of the LORD God." This ethical standard of *imitatio Dei*, which can be found in explicit form in Leviticus 19:2, "You shall be holy, for I, the LORD your God, am holy," anticipates the more familiar NT standard of the imitation of Christ, which is really just a specification of *imitatio Dei*, because Christ is God incarnate.

The contrasting paths of wisdom (which equals *righteousness) and folly (which equals wickedness) produce an abundance of antithetical sayings in the wisdom texts. The Wisdom literature, then, teaches that what is wrong is what deviates from God's righteous path. Folly is the failure or refusal to reverence Yahweh (Prov 1:7). Departing from the fear of Yahweh is to take the path of folly, which leads to destruction in all of its forms. Proverbs 3:5 contrasts trust in Yahweh (the path of wisdom) with leaning on one's own understanding, an insistence upon human autonomy that is at the root of folly and wickedness (cf. Gen 3:6; Jer 17:9).

Although the wisdom books do not speak specifically of the history of the covenant nation of Israel, they do answer some aspects of the worldview question "Where is history going?" The OT speaks more broadly than just the election and history of Israel, because Genesis 1—11 traces God's dealings with humanity as a single unity. Even when Yahweh calls Abram, he says that in Abram all the families of the earth would receive divine blessing (Gen 12:3). Perdue (343) is correct, then, when he says, "For the sages, divine activity and providence cannot be limited to Israel's election and history. Election may be properly understood only within the larger theological parameters of divine creation and providential rule over cosmos and history." OT wisdom presents Yahweh as sovereignly directing history to his own ends, which may well be inscrutable to humans (Job 42:2; Prov 16:9; 20:24; 21:1).

The final worldview question is "What can be known, and how can it be known?" Much of the OT features God speaking directly to humans in special revelation, so that, for example, the prophets frequently preface their oracles with the expression "Thus saith the LORD." In the wisdom books, for the most part God communicates to humans through general revelation. Humans are challenged to observe Yahweh's world and reflect upon his imbedded moral order in his creation so that they can derive lessons for life (e.g., Prov 6:6-11; 24:30-34). This proper approach of natural theology yields divine truth that supplements the truth that God elsewhere reveals through Moses and the prophets.

As wisdom answers the basic worldview questions, it reflects a theological understanding that corresponds with teaching found in the rest of the OT. Wisdom, then, though it has emphases that in many cases are different from the Law, the Prophets and Psalms, does not constitute a disparate worldview. Rather, its contributions complement and supplement what is taught elsewhere in the OT texts.

5. Place of Wisdom in Biblical Theology.

For Christian readers, it is evident that the OT narrates a story that is completed only in the NT. The creation that has been marred by sin early in the OT finds its restoration only at the end of the NT. The two Testaments fit together like a two-volume novel or a two-reel film, with the OT anticipating the NT, and the NT referring back to the OT. Therefore, it seems misguided to read the OT in isolation and to construe its meaning as though it were a complete story in itself.

It may well be that the various attempts by OT theologians to ascertain the center of the OT have failed at this very point. Just as an exclusive focus on covenant, salvation history or the mighty acts of Yahweh has obscured the contributions of wisdom to OT theology, so too viewing the OT in isolation from the NT could well lead to theological distortions. J. Barr correctly champions the agenda of biblical theology, and he rightfully urges that in this effort NT texts be seriously engaged rather than treated superficially.

The contributions of the OT wisdom books to this agenda of biblical theology have only been sketched to date, and much important work remains to be done by scholars. H. Blocher (25-26) has identified numerous links between the teaching ministry of Jesus and OT wisdom, as Jesus in his preaching and in his controversies with the scribes often employs wisdom language and techniques. In passages such as 1 Corinthians 1:18-31 and Colossians 2:1-8 Paul teaches that Christ is the wisdom of God, in contrast to the false human reasoning that permeated the Roman world of the first-century AD. These references suggest that there are likely many significant connections between wisdom and the NT that remain to be explicated and integrated by biblical theologians.

See also CREATION THEOLOGY; WISDOM THEOLOGY; WISDOM AND COVENANT; WISDOM AND PROPHECY.

BIBLIOGRAPHY. **J. Barr,** *The Concept of Biblical Theology: An Old Testament Perspective* (Minneapolis: Fortress, 1999); **H. Blocher,** "The Fear of the Lord as the 'Principle' of Wisdom," *TynBul* 28 (1977) 3-28; **R. E. Clements,** *One Hundred Years of Old Testament Interpretation* (Philadelphia: Westminster, 1976); idem, "Wisdom and Old Testament Theology," in *Wisdom in Ancient Israel,* ed. J. Day, R. P. Gordon and H. G. M. Williamson (Cambridge: Cambridge University Press, 1995) 269-86; **J. L. Crenshaw,** *Old Testament Wisdom: An Introduction* (rev. ed.; Louisville: Westminster John Knox, 1998); **W. Eichrodt,** *Theology of the Old Testament* (2 vols.; OTL; Philadelphia: Westminster, 1961-1967 [1933-1939]); **K. A. Farmer,** "The Wisdom Books: Job, Proverbs, Ecclesiastes," in *The Hebrew Bible Today: An Introduction to the Critical Issues,* ed. S. L. McKenzie and M. P. Graham (Louisville: Westminster John Knox,

1998) 129-51; **M. V. Fox,** "Ideas of Wisdom in Proverbs 1-9," *JBL* 116 (1997) 613-33; **J. Goldingay,** "The 'Salvation History' Perspective and the 'Wisdom' Perspective within the Context of Biblical Theology," *EvQ* 51 (1979) 194-207; **C. S. Grizzard,** "The Scope of Theology in Wisdom Literature," in *An Introduction to Wisdom Literature and the Psalms: Festschrift Marvin E. Tate,* ed. H. W. Ballard Jr. and W. D. Tucker Jr. (Macon, GA: Mercer University Press, 2000) 195-214; **D. A. Hubbard,** "The Wisdom Movement and Israel's Covenant Faith," *TynBul* 17 (1966) 3-33; **D. Kidner,** *Proverbs* (TOTC 15; Downers Grove, IL: InterVarsity Press, 1964); **R. E. Murphy,** "Wisdom—Theses and Hypotheses," in *Israelite Wisdom: Theological and Literary Essays in Honor of Samuel Terrien,* ed. J. G. Gammie et al. (Homage 3; Missoula, MT: Scholars Press, 1978) 35-42; idem, *Proverbs* (WBC 22; Nashville: Thomas Nelson, 1998); idem, "Can the Book of Proverbs Be a Player in 'Biblical Theology'?" *BTB* 31 (2001) 4-9; **B. C. Ollenburger, ed.,** *Old Testament Theology: Flowering and Future* (rev. ed.; SBTS 1; Winona Lake, IN: Eisenbrauns, 2004); **P. Overland,** "Did the Sage Draw from the Shema? A Study of Proverbs 3:1-12," *CBQ* 62 (2000) 424-40; **L. G. Perdue,** *Wisdom Literature: A Theological History* (Louisville: Westminster John Knox, 2007); **H. D. Preuss,** *Old Testament Theology* (2 vols.; OTL; Louisville: Westminster John Knox, 1995-1996 [1991-1992]); **C. H. H. Scobie,** "The Place of Wisdom in Biblical Theology," *BTB* 14 (1984) 43-48; **G. V. Smith,** "Is There a Place for Job's Wisdom in Old Testament Theology?" *TJ* 13 (1992) 3-20; **G. von Rad,** *Old Testament Theology* (2 vols.; New York: Harper & Row, 1962-1965 [1957-1960]); idem, *Wisdom in Israel* (Nashville: Abingdon, 1972 [1970]); **B. K. Waltke,** "The Book of Proverbs and Old Testament Theology," *BSac* 136 (1979) 302-17; idem, *The Book of Proverbs: Chapters 1-15* (NICOT; Grand Rapids: Eerdmans, 2004); **R. N. Whybray,** *The Book of Proverbs: A Survey of Modern Study* (HBI 1; Leiden: E. J. Brill, 1995); **C. J. H. Wright,** *Old Testament Ethics for the People of God* (Downers Grove, IL: InterVarsity Press, 2004); **W. Zimmerli,** *Old Testament Theology in Outline* (Atlanta: John Knox, 1978 [1972]). D. J. Estes

WISDOM AND COVENANT

It is often argued that the OT Wisdom literature rejects the key themes that are emphasized in the other books of the Hebrew Bible. Whereas the Pentateuch and the Prophets—and, for that matter, many of the other books found in the Writings—focus on the key themes of exodus and salvation history, temple and cultus, and the covenant between Yahweh and his people, none of these are prominent themes in the Wisdom literature. R. Murphy (36) has described the Wisdom literature as being "strangely silent" about God's interventions in Israel's history (exodus, covenant, cult, etc.). It is commonly suggested that the reason for this silence is that wisdom is a secular, humanistic discipline that is simply not interested in such religious matters. Clearly, covenant runs as a thread throughout the OT. Arguably present in the Creator's relationship with Adam and Eve, it certainly is the backbone of all God's dealings with his community in history—from Noah to Abraham to Moses and Israel to *David to Christ and beyond. If covenant is absent from the books of *Job, *Proverbs and *Ecclesiastes, it would indeed be a remarkable fact that sets these writings apart from the rest of the Bible, perhaps even indicating a competing ideology, as some have suggested.

We must remember, however, that the Wisdom literature communicates with the reader using contemplative techniques. The type of material that we read in the Wisdom literature is specifically designed to make us pause to give serious thought to the subject matter at hand. Wisdom communication is always subtle and skilful, and so a lack of conspicuous reference does not necessarily indicate the absence of a theme. Although the *sages are not preoccupied with explicit discussion of covenant as an overt theme (the word *covenant* occurs only twice in Job, once in Proverbs, not at all in Ecclesiastes), several features found in these books draw our attention to this type of relationship with God. These factors indicate that a proper understanding of covenant is essential if we are to attain the goal of wisdom: a life well lived.

1. The Fear of Yahweh
2. Proverbs and Deuteronomy
3. Shared Concerns of the Wisdom Literature and the Rest of the Old Testament
4. Covenant as Background to the Wisdom Literature
5. Conclusion

1. The Fear of Yahweh.
The first and major link between OT covenant theology and the Wisdom literature is found in the concept *"the fear of the Lord." Israelite wisdom and the fear of Yahweh and are inseparably linked in the OT. We are told that the fear of the Lord is the beginning (Prov 1:7) and the end (Eccles 12:13) of wisdom, and all true Hebraic wisdom is saturated in this idea.

The importance of the fear of the Lord in the Wisdom literature is not difficult to spot. The prologue to the book of Proverbs (Prov 1:1-7) concludes with a summary statement for the reader to remember while reading the rest of the book: "Fear of Yahweh is the beginning of knowledge; wisdom and instruction fools despise." This prologue to Proverbs emphasizes the vital importance of wisdom in the life of the reader, and the final verse of this packed exhortation stresses that there is no such thing as true wisdom apart from the fear of the Lord. The centrality of the fear of the Lord is further emphasized by the structural significance of this idea within the book. Proverbs divides into two major sections, with Proverbs 1—9 being dominated by lengthy instructions, whereas Proverbs 10—31 is shaped in the main by the pithy two-line sayings that we traditionally associate with proverbial wisdom. It is significant that "the fear of the Lord" brackets both of these major sections. Proverbs 9:10 reminds the reader, "The beginning of wisdom is fear of Yahweh; and knowledge of the Holy One is understanding," whereas Proverbs 31:30 says that "a woman who fears Yahweh is to be praised." This bracketing method informs the reader that the whole book should be read through the lens of the "fear of the Lord." The image engendered by enveloping the major sections and the complete book with "fear of Yahweh" is one of true wisdom being inextricably linked to right relationship with the covenant God.

Similarly, the fear of God is integral to the framework of the book of Job. Job 1:1 relates that Job a man who "feared God and shunned evil," and the key wisdom poem lying at the heart of the book reminds the reader in the thick of the debate that the essence of wisdom is remarkably simple: "To fear the Lord is wisdom; and to turn from evil is understanding" (Job 28:28). So the idea of the "fear of God" brackets the whole of the central debate about innocent *suffering. The message for the reader is the same as we see in Proverbs: there may be much in life that we struggle to understand, but in order to be "wise" we must fear God.

Equally, "the fear of God" provides thematic stepping stones through the complexities and contradictions of Ecclesiastes. Many aspects of life (e.g., labor, wealth, pleasure and even wisdom itself) are both endorsed and decried in the meandering deliberations of *Qohelet. The fear of God is not a prominent theme throughout the book, but it is never presented as having a negative flip side. All other aspects of life that come under Qohelet's consideration may be both "good" and "bad." However, the four occurrences of the fear of God in the book (Eccles 3:14; 5:7; 8:12-13; 12:13) are always without a down side. These orthodox statements in the midst of the complexity of Qohelet's thought serve as beacons for the reader to chart a way through the text. Ecclesiastes' epilogue concludes with a wonderful expression of the essential symmetry of the "fear of the Lord" in our quest for wisdom. Proverbs 1:7 tells us that the fear of the Lord is the beginning of wisdom, and Ecclesiastes 12:13 declares, "The end of the matter; all has been heard. Fear God and keep his commandments, for this is the whole duty of man." The fear of Yahweh is essential to wisdom. It is wisdom's beginning and end, and true wisdom is impossible to attain apart from this type of relationship with Yahweh. As we will see below, the idea of the fear of Yahweh is inexorably linked with the concept of covenant relationship between God and his people.

By way of aside, there is much discussion as to whether there is a difference between the "fear of Yahweh" and the "fear of God" or of "the Lord" (*'adōnāy*). Does one indicate covenantal relationship with Israel's God, and the other a more general religious affiliation? R. Whybray (27) points out, "This God, whom [Qohelet] calls *(ha-)Elohim* but who is in fact identical with the Yahweh of the OT, is the sole creator of the world and holds the fate of every human being in his hands." There can be little doubt that the original readers of the Wisdom books would have understood the "fear of Yahweh" and the "fear of God" as one and the same thing.

2. Proverbs and Deuteronomy.

How is it that the "fear of Yahweh" indicates the presence of covenant theology within the Wisdom books? There are two answers to this question: (1) Proverbs' focus on the fear of Yahweh points us specifically to relationship with Israel's covenant God as being key to true wisdom; (2) fear of Yahweh takes the reader deep into Israel's covenant theology because of its intertextual links with the book of Deuteronomy.

To deal with the first (and most obvious) of these points very briefly, it is significant that Proverbs almost exclusively talks about the "fear of Yahweh," the covenant God of Israel, rather than using the more generic terms for "god" or "the gods" that were shared by other nations. Wisdom had a very international flavor in the ancient Near East, and proverbial statements similar to ones found in Proverbs are found also in the ancient literature of many of the nations that were Israel's neighbors. The fact that the authors and editors of Proverbs focus on the necessity to fear Yahweh if one is to be wise indicates that this is Israel's own brand of wisdom. They did not simply adopt other ancient wisdom ideas but rather adapted them to conform to Israel's own worldview. Therefore, they make it clear that true wisdom apart from relationship with Israel's covenant God is a non sequitur—there can be no wisdom apart from covenant relationship. R. Van Leeuwen (33) points out the significance of the fear of Yahweh concept in terms of Israel's covenant status:

With very few exceptions, Proverbs refers to God as 'the LORD' (Yahweh), the God who made covenant with Israel and led the people throughout history (cf. Gen 20:11; Eccl 12:13). Proverbs never uses אֵל (*'ēl*, 'god') and uses אֱלֹהִים (*'ĕlōhîm*, the most common word for 'god' or 'gods') only three times: 2:5, parallel to 'fear of the LORD'; 3:4; 25:2. The editors of Proverbs are very consistent in avoiding the suggestion that the God of the sages is any other than Israel's covenant God, Yahweh (see Exod 3:15; 33:18-20; 34:6-7; John 1:14-18). Proverbs has profound similarities to ancient Near Eastern wisdom. Perhaps the consistent use of 'Yahweh' was meant to forestall the idea that the God of Proverbs was not Israel's covenant God.

Second, it is Deuteronomy, a book structured according to the pattern of ancient Near Eastern covenantal treaties, that defines for us what it means to fear Yahweh. The "fear of Yahweh" concept is, of course, rooted in the biblical account of the Sinai covenant. When this covenant was forged between Yahweh and Israel, the people literally trembled with fear (Ex 20:18-21). However, we can see a movement in the biblical text whereby the reality of the Sinai experience comes to be used metaphorically to describe one's life response to God; it becomes a type of shorthand form of expressing total commitment to God. "The great phrase "the fear of the LORD" grounds human knowledge and wisdom (cf. 9:10) in humble service of Yahweh.... Although this phrase has its origin in the experience of God's numinous majesty (as at Sinai, Deut 4:9-10), it eventually has come to express the total claim of God upon humans and the total life-response of humans to God" (Van Leeuwen, 33).

It is Deuteronomy 10:12-13 that provides the "dictionary definition" of the fear of Yahweh as it functions throughout the rest of the Scriptures: "And now, Israel, what does the LORD your God require of you, but to fear the LORD your God, to walk in all his ways, to love him, to serve the LORD your God with all your heart and with all your soul, and to keep the commandments and statutes of the LORD, which I am commanding you today for your good?" These verses should be understood as an epexegetical statement (see Christensen, 204). The main question ("What does the LORD your God require of you?") is answered by the initial central statement ("fear the LORD your God"), and each of the following statements explains what it actually means in reality to fear Yahweh ("walk in his ways, love him, serve him and keep his commandments"). In this definition a bridge is built between Israel's salvation history and their Wisdom literature. These are not separate entities, one focused on covenant and the other rejecting it; rather, they share the same concern: how does one live life well before the living God? Both sets of literature come to the conclusion that it is impossible to do so apart from real, and therefore inevitably covenant, relationship with God.

There are many other links between Deuteronomy and the OT Wisdom literature that show a common grounding in Israel's covenant-steeped worldview. Take, for example, the exhortation found in both sets of literature to "walk in the ways of Yahweh" (Deut 8:6; 11:22; cf. Prov 5:21; 11:20) or to choose between the ways of the Lord and the ways of the wicked, between life and death (Deut 30:15-20; cf. Prov 1—9, which is dominated by discussion of the two

ways and the effect of choosing one over the other). Also, some commentators point out that the legal stipulations of Deuteronomy are expanded upon in the maxims of the Wisdom literature. The *law provides a bare minimum standard, a line that we must not cross. Proverbial wisdom, on the other hand, sets related goals that we should aspire to fulfill (Kline, 64-67).

Thus we can see that there is a very strong tie between the literature that focuses on covenant and salvation history (Exodus; Deuteronomy) and the OT Wisdom literature.

3. Shared Concerns of the Wisdom Literature and the Rest of the Old Testament.

It would be unwise to draw too sharp a distinction between the Wisdom literature and the rest of the OT, as some scholars are tempted to do. As well as the conceptual connection via the fear of Yahweh, the Wisdom literature shares many of the same concerns expressed in the OT books that are commonly considered to be "covenantal." A prime example of these common concerns is the importance of social justice and concern for the poor.

The Prophets often pointed out Israel's and Judah's breach of the covenant because of their failure to care for the weak and the voiceless in their societies (e.g., Is 1; Jer 7; Mal 3). Failure to care for widows, orphans and sojourners was one of the key factors that led to the fall of Israel and the exile of Judah. They broke covenant with Yahweh because they did not protect the weak in their society from exploitation. Similar concerns are endorsed in the Wisdom literature. Job, for example, defends himself by pointing out his care for widow, orphan and stranger (Job 31:16-23), thus setting the reader a high ethical example to follow. The observation of oppression is one of the most vexatious issues for Qohelet (Eccles 4:1-3; 5:8-9). Resolution of this problem can only be found in the book's summary statement that the whole duty of humankind is to "fear God and keep his commandments" (Eccles 12:13). Only in this way can society be transformed. Equally, the book of Proverbs says, "Blessed is he who is generous to the poor" (Prov 14:21), and "Whoever oppresses the poor insults his Maker" (Prov 14:31). Care for the vulnerable is just one of many possible examples that illustrate that the concerns of the Wisdom literature, though perhaps expressed in very different terms, often reflect the same themes found in the "classically covenantal" texts of the OT. Other examples include the prohibition of idolatry in the Torah and Prophets, which finds metaphorical expression in many texts in the Wisdom literature that speak against adultery, or the *creation theology of the Wisdom literature that strongly resonates with Genesis, or the common themes of family, vocation and ethics shared by both the Wisdom literature and the rest of the OT. The form of expression and some of the subject matter is indeed different in the Wisdom literature, but this does not mean that it speaks with an entirely different voice from the rest of the OT. As B. Waltke (64) points out, "The apparent lack of integration between Proverbs and the rest of the Old Testament . . . is more superficial than real."

4. Covenant as Background to the Wisdom Literature.

As well as the many thematic similarities found in the Wisdom literature and the covenantal passages of the OT, we can also observe that the idea of covenant is vital if we are to understand what we read in Job, Proverbs and Ecclesiastes. Take Job, for example: what, exactly, is his problem? Clearly, he has suffered much, but then, the capricious gods of the ancient Near East could turn nasty at the drop of a hat. It is covenant relationship that lies at the heart of Job's lament. Why does he take things so hard? Why does he not resort to the fatalism commonly found in ancient Near Eastern wisdom materials—"It was the will of the gods"? Job cries out because precisely he has a different expectation of his God. He speaks of the days when "the friendship of God was upon my tent; when the Almighty was yet with me" (Job 29:4-5). The close presence and benevolence of God are the very essence of covenant relationship. The gods are bound by nothing, but Job expected God to relate to him in a particular way. The essence of his complaint is based in the understanding that God had not kept his side of "the covenant deal." If we remove covenant from Job, we cannot understand the central message of the book.

Similarly with Ecclesiastes, would Qohelet have experienced such a profound existential crisis if he did not have an expectation of justice and meaning in the ordering of daily reality? Why does Qohelet expect to find meaning and order "under the sun"? Because he has been led to this expectation by the history of Israel's dealings with Yahweh. As M. Fox (51-70) points out, Qohelet believes in *"righteousness" and "justice," and it is the observed lack of these characteristics in the surrounding reality of life that leads to his crisis of perspectives. Righteousness and justice are key aspects of the OT's presentation of covenant and are characteristics to be expected of both parties to the covenant, both God and people. It is this lack of expected relationship between Creator and his creation that leads to Qohelet's view that everything is meaningless. Once again, reading Ecclesiastes apart from covenant makes no sense.

Throughout all of the books of the Wisdom literature we can observe a very basic expectation of order or structure. We see this in the creation theology that is common to each of the three books (e.g., Job 37—39; Prov 8; Eccles 1). Due to this expression of an ordered reality, Proverbs is often misrepresented as presenting a mechanistic worldview: "If you do A, then you can expect B." Both Job and Qohelet are disturbed by what they see to be a lack of order either in their lives or in the world round about them. This expectation of order is grounded in their belief in the existence of a divine-human contract.

In essence, Yahweh has promised to relate to his people in a certain way. Hence, the authors and editors of Proverbs are able to say, "If you follow a lifestyle that pleases God, you can expect positive consequences." Equally, Job and Qohelet expect a certain stability and structure in the lives that they lead. Their crises arise in the discovery that life is often not like that. Their expectations are the logical consequence of their belief that there is a Creator God who orders all things, and that he is *their* God. "It is in the context of this conviction, that God is making the world work out, that wisdom's practical teaching about life may be seen. Its content is similar to what we call ethics or what the salvation-history calls keeping the covenant, but its context . . . is very different" (Goldingay, 203). Wisdom material is very different in style and focus from the rest of the OT, but we should not let these differences lead us to the conclusion that covenant is absent. Covenantal ideas provide the backbone to the presuppositions of Israel's wisdom worldview, and the three books of the Wisdom literature cannot be understood apart from covenant.

5. Conclusion.

Although the OT Wisdom literature is in many ways unique within the *canon of Scripture, it does not remove itself from the key theological concepts of that broader canon. The theme of covenant is not an explicit focus in Proverbs, Job and Ecclesiastes, but it does provide essential background for a proper understanding of these books. The authors/editors of these works are steeped in the Hebrew worldview, and the covenantal basis of that worldview shines through clearly in the Wisdom literature, even though its focus often is elsewhere.

See also FEAR OF THE LORD; GOD; WISDOM THEOLOGY; WISDOM AND PROPHECY.

BIBLIOGRAPHY. **D. L. Christensen,** *Deuteronomy 1:1–21:9* (rev. ed.; WBC 6A; Nashville: Thomas Nelson, 2001); **M. V. Fox,** *A Time to Tear Down and a Time to Build Up: A Rereading of Ecclesiastes* (Grand Rapids: Eerdmans, 1999); **J. Goldingay,** "The 'Salvation History' Perspective and the 'Wisdom' Perspective within the Context of Biblical Theology," *EvQ* 51 (1979) 194-207; **J. A. Grant,** "Wisdom and Covenant: Revisiting Zimmerli," *EuroJTh* 12.2 (2003) 103-13; **D. A. Hubbard,** "The Wisdom Movement and Israel's Covenant Faith," *TynBul* 17 (1966) 3-33; **M. G. Kline,** *The Structure of Biblical Authority* (Eugene, OR: Wipf & Stock, 1989); **R. E. Murphy,** "Wisdom—Theses and Hypotheses," in *Israelite Wisdom: Theological and Literary Essays in Honor of Samuel Terrien,* ed. J. G. Gammie et al. (Missoula, MT: Scholars Press, 1978) 35-42; **R. L. Schultz,** "Unity or Diversity in Wisdom Theology? A Canonical and Covenantal Perspective," *TynBul* 48 (1997) 271-306; **R. C. Van Leeuwen,** "The Book of Proverbs," *NIB* 5.19-264; **B. K. Waltke,** *The Book of Proverbs: Chapters 1-15* (NICOT; Grand Rapids, Eerdmans, 2004); **R. N. Whybray,** *Ecclesiastes* (NCBC; Grand Rapids: Eerdmans, 1989).

J. A. Grant

WISDOM AND HISTORY

Introductions to biblical wisdom do not usually include a section on wisdom and history (Berry; Dell 2002, 107; Estes; a notable exception is Rendtorff 1977). It is often assumed that biblical Wisdom literature as a genre was not concerned with history per se but rather emphasized other elements of human existence, such as the training of leaders and children, or functioned as a corrective to Torah that at times challenged theological or ethical traditions (Berry, 6-9). The emphasis on the human condition in general and relationships between individuals is sometimes used to underline Israel's dependence on extrabiblical wisdom literature, since there is apparently no space to see Yahweh's saving acts in history in biblical Wisdom literature (Dell 2002, 107). In view of these issues, the first section of this article reviews the basic characteristics of OT history and historiography, and then follows a discussion of specific historical references found in biblical Wisdom literature. The question of how major themes of OT Wisdom literature interact with history and historiography is the subject of the next section. Particular attention is given to the motifs of "God is in control," "A godly life is a happy life," "building of God's house" and "paradise regained." Some scholars have argued for the inclusion of the books of Daniel and *Esther among the corpus of biblical Wisdom literature. Thus, the following section looks at these two books and highlights their perspective on history, as well as selected included historical references, and compares their perspective with the one of classical Wisdom literature already described. Finally, a conclusion summarizes the findings of this article and points to further research in this particular field.

1. The Nature of Old Testament History and Historiography
2. Historical References in Wisdom Literature
3. Important Themes in Wisdom Literature and Their Links to History
4. History in Borderline Books: Daniel and Esther
5. Conclusions

1. The Nature of Old Testament History and Historiography.

The past thirty years have witnessed an ongoing debate concerning the historicity and historiography of the texts of the Hebrew Bible. Scholars such as J. van Seters (1975; 1983; more synthesized, 1995), T. Thompson (1974; 1987; 1992), P. Davies (1992; 2002), N. Lemche (1985; 1988; 1996 [1998]) and others have challenged the notion of the basic historicity of the biblical texts. In fact, their challenge went beyond the mere question of historical references and reliability and focused upon the genre of history writing per se. This is not the place to rehash the heated debate between those scholars who ascribe minimal historical intention and historicity to the biblical texts and those who perceive the biblical authors as intentional (hi)story tellers, attributing an underlying historicity to the biblical text (see *DOTP*, Historical Criticism, 404-6; Kofoed). Biblical historiography is characterized by its specificity and is often marked by its theological, selective, interpretive, biographical and intentional nature (see *DOTP*, Historical Criticism, 401-20; Long 1994; 2002; Provan, Long and Longman, 3-97). One of the underlying issues in which modern scholarship often seems to misread biblical history writing involves the matter of successful communication. After all, every author, regardless of his or her intentions, convictions and presuppositions, wants to communicate effectively. In this sense, sociolinguistic pragmatics provides a helpful window, reminding us that language is generally used to communicate intentionally. Although this is not the ultimate proof of the historicity of biblical texts, it highlights a sense of the interaction reported in biblical narrative and the suggested contexts that resemble the realities of natural, everyday communicative action (Winther-Nielsen, 76-78).

Up to this point, most observations concerning the historicity of biblical historiographical writing presupposed narrative texts. In other words, the discussion concerning biblical historiography deals generally and often exclusively with narrative texts. Stories seem to be the arena of history, and much ink has been used to define the relationship between the two (Millard; Chisholm). As has been pointed out by J. Kofoed (190-247), this issue boils down to the question of the genre of history writing. Due to rigid genre distinctions, some scholars discount any nonnarrative texts as ahistorical and irrelevant for the historical endeavor, pointing to their underlying intentions, theology, ideology or focal point as arguments for their nonhistorical nature. A case in point for this phenomenon is seen in the poetics of biblical narrative, which have been studied over the past decades (Sternberg; Berlin) and have provided useful categories for describing the artistry of biblical narrative along the lines of poetic discourse. Three relevant elements of biblical narrative poetics involve the scenicness, the subtleness and the succinctness of the narratives of the Hebrew Bible (Provan, Long and Longman, 91-93). In other words, biblical narratives seem to share a particular "canon" of characteristics that echo components associated generally with poetry.

If so, would it be possible to posit the possibility of other genres (including wisdom) being relevant for the historiographical endeavor? Obviously, biblical Wisdom literature is set in a specific cultural, political and religious context and thus reflects and, to a certain degree, communicates these realities. Although this historiographical interest is not the main focus of biblical wisdom, it seems to be latently present, emphasizing particularly the life conditions and life choices of individuals. As with any ancient text, perspective, literary style, theology (or ideology) as well as authorial intention need to be taken into consideration if one is to responsibly understand ancient history writing (see Veenhof, 28-34). It was the art of story telling (narrative), of proclaiming Yahweh's will for his covenant people or the nations (prophetic texts), of teaching important life lessons (wisdom), or of producing legal or ritual texts that was done by the biblical authors, and this art needs to be recognized. In this context it is particularly interesting to look at the neighbors of ancient Israelites and their perception of the interaction between the individual, the community (be it family, clan, tribe, or people) and *time.

In Egypt the preferred historiographical method was not the sort of interpretive history that had its beginnings in the Western tradition with Herodotus and Thucydides, but the past was seen as a repository of knowledge and wisdom (Kadish, 110) that did not emphasize long chronological lines but often employed biographical inscriptions or localized annals that were more often than not disconnected (Simpson, 191) and lacked the broad sequential perspective so typical of Western historiography. Mesopotamian history writing was distinct and often employed the genres of annals, synchronistic histories and king lists (Veenhof, 42-48). Fictional *autobiography has also been described as an important Mesopotamian genre that is not automatically devoid of historical value due to its fictional or intentionally imaginative nature (Longman 1991, 209-10). Interestingly, the didactic nature (or at least ending) of many of the Akkadian fictional autobiographies suggests a fascinating link to biblical Wisdom literature that also combines the individual perspective with the didactic concern of communicating valuable experiences to a new generation (Longman 1991, 127). Furthermore, as has been shown by A. Cohen in his study of dehistoricizing strategies in third-millennium BC cuneiform royal inscriptions and rituals, it was often the unlinking of a text from a particular historical context that gave it authority and even pointed to the divine realm, where the passage of time is a nonissue. All these considerations of literary strategies, genres and historiographic perspective are indeed helpful in our quest to locate the nexus between history and wisdom in the context of the OT. However, biblical wisdom is also different from other ancient Near Eastern literature inasmuch as it is part of the Bible, with its authority claim based on divine inspiration and revelation. If Scripture's own claim of divine origin is indeed true and valid (2 Tim 3:16), its authority is not exclusively based on historicity but rather points beyond to issues of hermeneutical presuppositions and personal faith commitments. The following section looks at some of the historical references that appear in biblical Wisdom literature.

2. Historical References in Wisdom Literature.

History requires three essential elements: time, space and (mostly) action. Whatever we do happens in time and space. In this section particular attention is given to the embedded historical references in biblical Wisdom literature, including place names, personal names and clear or possible historical allusions. The main focus of this section is on the classical biblical wisdom texts, including *Job, *Proverbs, *Ecclesiastes and *Song of Songs, as well as relevant wisdom psalms. The books of Esther and Daniel, which at times have been associated with wisdom literature (Talmon; Collins, 48-50, 69-70 [see also further bibliographical references there]), are treated separately in a subsequent section.

2.1. Space and Geography in Old Testament Wisdom Literature. Historical references generally involve references to places, people and particular historical events or situations. In reviewing the available data, one is surprised to see different patterns emerging when one considers the core of biblical wisdom texts. Whereas Job, Proverbs and Ecclesiastes include few references to specific places, the pictorial language of Song of Songs is full of geographical references. Some specific examples should suffice to illustrate this

surprising trend, which suggests that biblical Wisdom literature does not seem to follow a "standard" pattern, particularly when it comes to the use of place references. Job 1:1 open the book with a reference to *ʾereṣ ʿûṣ* ("the land of Uz") a geographical reference that only occurs twice more in the Hebrew Bible (Jer 25:20-21; Lam 4:21) in regard to a location. Based on the biblical data, two possible locations can be inferred: a southern location in the vicinity of Edom (see Lam 4:21) and a northern site northeast of Palestine in the Hauran (see Hartley, 65-66). Other place references in the book of Job include Tema and Sheba (Job 6:19), which most probably refer to locations in Arabia and are associated with caravan routes (Liverani; Ricks, 1171; Yamauchi, 90-91). The last concrete geographical location mentioned in Job is Cush (Job 28:19), and this is associated with Hebrew *piṭdâ*, a semiprecious stone that has been identified as "topaz" (NIV, NKJV) or "peridot/chrysolite" (NLT), which refers to a silicate mineral found at various locations in the eastern and western desert of Egypt as well as the island of Zabargad in the Red Sea (Aston, Harrell and Shaw, 47). Apart from this limited number of specific geographical references, the book of Job includes quite a number of generic references, such as the city gate (Job 29:7 [of which city?]), the *ʿărābâ* ("wilderness" [JPS, NASB, NIV], "wasteland" [NIV, NJB], "steppe" [NRSV; Revidierte Elberfelder Bibel]) and *mělēḥâ* ("salt land" [JPS, NASB], "salt plains/flats" [NIV, NJB]) found in Job 39:6, as well as the Jordan River (Job 40:23).

Even fewer references to locations are found in Proverbs, which does not include any specific reference to any known place and only generic references to streets (Prov 1:20, 21), "public squares" (*rěḥōbôt* [Prov 1:20; 5:16; 7:12; 22:13; 26:13]) and city gates (Prov 1:21; 8:3; 14:19; 22:22; 24:7; 31:23, 31). The situation is similar in Ecclesiastes, where Jerusalem is mentioned five times (Eccles 1:1, 12, 16; 2:7, 9), in contexts that seem to make reference to the personal experience of the author. In Ecclesiastes 2:8; 5:8 [MT 5:7] the technical term *mědînâ* ("province, satrapy") appears, a term that occurs often in postexilic literature from the Persian period, though surprisingly it can also be found several times in the Ahab narrative in 1 Kings 20, which describes life during the ninth century BC.

The situation changes dramatically in Song of Songs. Places and geography seem to play a major role in the literary design and communication strategy of the book, and which may represent a conscious effort to reflect the importance of the spice trade in Iron Age Israel (Malena, 171-75). Places inside Palestine include En-Gedi (Song 1:14), the Sharon (Song 2:1), Mount Gilead (Song 4:1; 6:5), Tirzah (Song 6:4), Jerusalem (Song 1:5; 2:7; 3:5, 10; 5:8, 16; 6:4; 8:4), Mount Carmel (Song 7:5) and Baal Hamon (Song 8:11), whose exact location is not easily established (Schmitz). Outside Palestine proper, a significant number of locations are also referred to, often in the metaphorical language so characteristic of Song of Songs (Hess, 29-35). These geographical references include Kedar (Song 1:5), which in this context and due to the reference to the (black) tents of Kedar may point to nomadic tribes in Arabia (Knauf, *ABD* 4.9). Seven times a reference to Lebanon is found (Song 3:9. 4:8 [2x], 11, 15; 5:15; 7:5), often connected with the mountain range or specific characteristics associated with the mountain range (e.g., smells, wood, height, water). This particular geographical reference seems to play a very important role in the structural design of Song of Songs and highlights the broad dimension of the poet's love song (see Japhet; Müller).

The fact that the book includes so many references to locations outside the core land of Israel could be interpreted as a conscious literary strategy to go beyond the local realms. In other words, geography informs the literary and narrative perspective (see G. Klingbeil 2002b; Malina 2007). This love story is so big that the whole (known) world is just big enough to hold it (or compare it to). Other references outside of Israel include the crest of Amana, standing in parallelism to the top of Senir and the summit of Hermon (Song 4:8) and associated with the heights of the Lebanon. Further to the north, the city of Damascus is mentioned (Song 7:4). Transjordanian towns are also referred to several times. The location of Mahanaim (Song 6:13) is not entirely clear (Edelman [473] identifies Telul ed-Dhahab el Garbi as the biblical Mahanaim, while others identify the site as Penuel [Gaß, 447-48]), but Heshbon (Song 7:4) has been identified without a doubt. Similar to the other biblical Wisdom literature, Song of Songs also contains a significant number of nonspecific geographical indications, including references to "the city" (Song 3:2-3; 5:7 [possibly Jerusalem]), streets and squares (Song 3:2), a

banqueting house (Song 2:4), the house of the mother (Song 8:2), the tower of David (Song 4:4), "the wilderness" (Song 8:5) and city walls and towers [of silver] (Song 8:9-10).

In view of all these geographical references, the interplay between the specific and the non-specific becomes immediately visible. One wonders why any author would mix both categories, particularly considering the overall purpose and intent of wisdom literature, which is to teach important ethical standards and reflect about profound life choices. One possible explanation of this intriguing phenomenon may be the conscious effort by the author(s) to make the observations, metaphors, comparisons or proverbs more abstract and thus more applicable to every place and situation. A similar observation has already been suggested for ritual appearing in narrative texts, where often (though not always) "specific" nonspecific location markers are employed in an effort to avoid shrine mentality without falling into the opposite danger of spiritualization of something very concrete (G. Klingbeil 2004, 509-11). In other words, this may be a conscious communication strategy by the author/editor that recognizes that human existence is located in space but is not limited to a particular space. Interestingly enough, in the case of Song of Songs it appears that the location references involving intra-Palestine, Transjordanian and Syrian places can be connected to the description of the extension of the kingdom of Israel during the time of united monarchy under *Solomon (cf. 1 Kings 4:21).

2.2. People in Old Testmanent Wisdom Literature. When it comes to people that are mentioned in the classical biblical Wisdom literature, a similar interplay between specific and generic persons can be noted. Job 1:1 introduces one of the protagonists of the book but does not supply the patronymic information so prevalent in the historical literature of the OT. What is supplied, however, is the place of habitation ("Uz"), a pattern that reoccurs in connection to Job's friends (Eliphaz the Temanite [Job 2:11], Bildad the Shuhite [Job 2:11], Zophar the Naamathite [Job 2:11]), although an exception to the rule should be noted when Elihu, the son of Barachel, the Buzite of the family of Ram (Job 32:2) is introduced. J. Hartley (429) considers the full patronymic formula an indication of Elihu's youth and lack of personal accomplishment. This is a possibility, but one should consider the literary conventions of the book. Would it be possible that by including full patronymic information (including tribal and clan information), the nameless author makes Elihu more real than the other three friends of Job? Many possible historical links for the pedigree of Elihu have been suggested (see Hartley, 428-29; Knauf, *ABD* 2.463), but it seems clear that by differentiating Elihu from all the other members of the cast, the author wants to emphasize his "rootedness" in history.

Besides the four friends and Job himself, no other clearly identifiable person appears in the book. However, numerous faceless people emerge onto the stage, suggesting again the pattern of a mix between the specific and the generic. The people of the east (Job 1:3) appear in a summary statement describing the incredible riches and blessings of Job prior to his afflictions as a fixed point for comparison. Representatives of distinct social strata appear in the speeches of both Job and his friends: day laborers (Job 7:1), slaves or servants (Job 7:2; 31:13), maidservants (Job 31:13), widows (Job 22:9; 24:3; 29:13; 31:16; 30:25; 31:19), "counselors" (*yôʿăṣim* [Job 12:17]), judges (Job 12:17) and kings (e.g., Job 3:14; 12:18; 15:24; 29:25). In the final narrative section Job's brothers and sisters (Job 42:11) are mentioned, who seem to combine both the specific and the generic, given that the reader knows nothing about them except that they are related to Job. The final mention is reserved for three daughters of Job, who are specifically identified (Jemima, Keziah and Keren-Happuch [Job 42:14]), together with seven sons (unnamed [Job 42:13]) and a final reference to the last 140 years (historical time!) of Job's life (Job 42:16).

One particular personage who appears in Job has not yet been described but requires further considerations. In Job 16:9-14 God is described as a divine warrior, employing military techniques involving siege techniques and archery (Hartley, 261). The metaphor of the divine warrior is well known in poetic and narrative literature of the OT (including Deuteronomy [Nelson], *Psalms [M. Klingbeil], Isaiah [Brettler] and Daniel [Anderson]) and may function as a link between Wisdom literature and historical and prophetic texts. In other words, the important concept of Yahweh fighting in time and space for his people Israel, which is linked to important events in the OT that are clearly un-

derstood by its authors to be historical (such as the exodus, the conquest, and the delivery of Jerusalem from the hands of the Neo-Assyrian assault), makes the appearance of this motif in Wisdom literature conspicuous and suggests a similar notion of historicity of these events as in other biblical books.

Proverbs contains a considerable number of references to different persons or groups. However, with the exception of the threefold reference to Solomon, son of *David, king of Israel (Prov 1:1; abbreviated version in Prov 10:1; 25:1) and the men of Hezekiah, the king of Judah (Prov 25:1), no clearly identifiable personality is referred to. To be sure, when Proverbs refers to Agur, it includes the patronymic reference "son of Jakeh" (Prov 30:1). Furthermore, this Agur is associated with Ithiel (Prov 30:1) and Ucal (Prov 30:1), but so far neither of these has been identified in a particular historical context. T. Longman (2006, 517-18) interprets the Hebrew noun *hammaśśāʾ* as a gentilic reference to the Massaite, emending the Hebrew to *hammaśśāʾî*, which may be an indication of a tribe in Arabia related to the Ishmaelites (Gen 25:14; 1 Chron 1:30). By an allegorization of the name and its patronymic addition, the midrash on Proverbs tried to retain Solomonic authorship (Visotzky, 117), while others have understood this name as a riddle whereby "Agur" means "I am a sojourner" and "Jakeh" represents an acronym for *yhwh qādôšhû* = "YHWH is holy" (Skehan, 27-45). However, the clear formulaic expression that appears over 1,500 times in the OT suggests a proper name of an unknown person who was considered to be the author or collector of the following sayings (Waltke, 465). Some scholars have interpreted the references to Ithiel and Ucal in Proverbs 30:1 not as personal names but rather as verbal forms, resulting in the translation "I am weary, O God, I am weary, O God, and I am exhausted" (Clifford, 259; also NLT, Redivierte Elberfelder Bibel). Although the syntax of this clause is slightly awkward, the pattern of the preposition *lĕ* + personal name is widely used in biblical Hebrew as an indication of an audience (e.g., Ex 14:5; *lĕmelek miṣrayim* ["to the king of Egypt"]). Furthermore, the name "Ithiel" appears also in Nehemiah 11:7 in a list of Benjamite returnees who lived in Jerusalem. The final specific reference to a particular person in Proverbs is King Lemuel (Prov 31:1, 4 [along with his mother!]), who likewise has not been satisfactorily identified. It is interesting to note that in Proverbs 31:1 the appositive "king" does not include a definite article, and so the complete phrase should be translated as "The sayings of Lemuel, a king" (see Waltke, 501), which would further make him less specific.

Besides these limited references to specific individuals (who remain obscure to the modern reader anyway), Proverbs also includes numerous generic references, involving again all social strata and economic classes. The following list is incomplete but does provide a glance at the wide variety of people/groups mentioned: "prostitute" (*ʾiššâ zônâ* or simply *zônâ* [Prov 6:26; 7:10-18; 23:27; 29:3]), "adulteress" (*zārôt* = "strange [women]" [Prov 22:14] and *ʾiššâ měnāʾāpet* = "adulterous woman" [Prov 30:20]), maids serving at a table (Prov 9:3), kings and princes (e.g., Prov 14:28; 14:35; 19:10, 12), the poor (e.g., Prov 14:31; 19:4-5, 17; 22:2, 7, 16, 22), widow (Prov 15:25), the "laborer" (*ʿāmēl* [Prov 16:26]), the stranger (Prov 20:16) and orphans (Prov 23:10).

It could be argued that this impressive mix of people from all walks of life suggests the general applicability of the included proverbs, thus making biblical Wisdom literature a more democratic enterprise and combining royal, scribal and folk (or family) wisdom sayings. As already seen in the observations concerning places, the biblical author(s) of Proverbs combine some more specific references with generic references, which would have a twofold effect on the immediate audience: first, similar to modern brand names, it would raise the recognition value ("Ah, this comes from King Solomon or from King Agur or King Lemuel"); second, it would not be limiting itself to royal wisdom or any particular socioeconomic context.

Ecclesiastes seems to be designed along similar lines. The only possible recognizable figure in the book appears in the superscription (Eccles 1:1) and is described as *qōhelet ben-dāwīd melek bîrûšālāim* ("[the] preacher, the son of David, king in Jerusalem"). No exact name is given, although the canonical context (i.e., Proverbs and Song of Songs) as well as the wisdom tradition associated with Solomon (1 Kings 3—11 [see Brueggemann, 104-23]) would make Solomon the obvious choice for the identity of the preacher. Besides this hint at a particular (historical) person, the book contains quite a number of autobiographical references to the supposed author (e.g., Eccles 1:16-17; 2:1, 12; 4:13) that are always marked by the use of the first-person singular. Similar to Proverbs, other figures mentioned in Ecclesiastes are more of a generic type, such as the oppressed (Eccles 4:1), the poor (Eccles 4:13; 5:8; 6:8), whose reoccurring presence underlines the importance of this figure in biblical Wisdom literature (see Sticher, 304-15 discussing the importance and theology of the poor in wisdom psalms), princes (Eccles 10:15-16), the haughty one (Eccles 5:8) and "the laborer" (*hāʿōbēd* [Eccles 5:12]). Again the figures come from all walks of life, which may once more underline the generalizing intention of the author.

The situation in Song of Songs is slightly different. Solomon is mentioned several times (Song 1:1, 5; 3:7, 9, 11; 8:11, 12), often in a descriptive (or comparative) context that employs verbal third-person masculine singular forms. A more generic reference that has been interpreted as a reference to Solomon is the reference to "the king" (Song 1:4, 12). Other generic references in the book include the "daughters of Jerusalem" (Song 1:5; 2:7; 3:5, 10; 5:8, 16; 8:4) or the parallel expression "daughters of Zion" (Song 3:11), sixty warriors of Israel (Song 3:7) or the more undefined "warriors" (Song 4:4), lover (e.g., Song 4:1; 7:9, 10), watchmen (Song 5:7), maidens (Song 6:9), sixty queens and eighty concubines (Song 6:8, 9), the Shulammite (Song 6:13) and the prince's daughter (Song 7:1). As can be easily seen when compared to the use of specific and nonspecific persons (or protagonists) in the earlier examples of biblical Wisdom literature, the use of persons in Song of Songs is indeed quite limited, most probably due to the particular purpose of the love poem. All protagonists mentioned in the text seem to be associated with the court, and there is no space, for example, for the poor or the widow and orphan who have been so prevalent in the Wisdom literature discussed earlier. Does that mean that the book was irrelevant to other socioeconomic groups outside the court? Definitely not, particularly when one considers the more abstract (or, rather, nonspecific) nature of the protagonists, which over the centuries caused so much discussion about the author and the historical *Sitz im Leben* of the book (see Tanner). Similar to modernity's often absurd fascination with royal love stories, the choice of this nonspecific description may have been a way to increase interest and applicability of the main points of the poem. After all, love stories seem to run along similar lines throughout history.

2.3. Historical Allusions in Old Testament Wisdom Literature. As already observed in the discussion of the use of space and protagonists in biblical Wisdom literature, the historical allusions are generally nonspecific. At the same time, however, real life is described, but typically without providing specific time indications, which are quite common in the historical narrative literature of the OT. Job is described as a major stockman in Job 1:3. Seven thousand sheep, three thousand camels, five hundred yoke of oxen and five hundred donkeys represented considerable assets in the real world of the ancient Near East, and in cultic contexts seven thousand sheep indicated an immense collective offering for Yahweh that could be taken from booty (2 Chron 15:11) or given by leadership for particular celebrations (2 Chron 30:24). At the end of Job's ordeal, as part of his public restoration, Job receives twice as many sheep, camels, yoke of oxen and donkeys as he previously owned (Job 42:12). Although the data is tentative, it appears from the way the loss of his herds is communicated (Job 1:14-17) and based on the size of Job's herds that Job practiced transhumant herding, whereby shepherds led their animals on seasonal grazing expeditions (Borowski, 29-30). Other elements marking a regular life in the book of Job include the references to feasts, sacrifices and ritual (Job 1:4-5, 13; 42:8), the different raids by known tribal groups (Job 1:15, 17), weather phenomena such as lightning and tornados (Job 1:16, 18-19), disease (Job 2:7; 7:5), as well as the mourning rites (Job 1—2) that have been recognized as clearly matching other mourning rites in the OT (Thi Pham, 24-27).

Up to this point, all historical allusions in Job have been associated with the narrative prologue or epilogue. What about the actual wisdom texts sandwiched in between these narrative brackets? The natural world is ever present (Riede, 120-52), as seen in references to lion (Job 4:10-11; 38:39), moth (Job 4:19), wild donkey (Job 6:5; 11:12; 24:5; 39:5), ox (Job 6:5; 40:15), spider (Job 8:14), the "stupid" cattle (Job 18:3), dog (Job 18:11; 30:1), jackal (Job 30:29), owl (Job 30:29), raven (Job 38:41), mountain goat (Job 39:1), doe (Job 39:1), wild ox (Job

39:13), ostrich and stork (Job 39:13), horse (Job 39:18, 19-25), locust (Job 39:29), hawk (Job 39:26) and eagle (Job 39:27-30). Interestingly, this use of *animals for comparisons is known from other wisdom literature from the ancient Near East, particularly Sumerian proverbs (Alster 1997, esp. collection II). At a minimum, the author of Job was a keen observer of nature around him. It has been shown that animal comparison appears also repeatedly in the Historical Books (e.g., 1-2 Samuel [see Riede, 65-106]) together with other functions (see *DOTHB*, Agriculture and Animal Husbandry, 1-20), and their presence aims at providing fixed points of comparisons that resulted in making the text more real.

Famine (Job 5:20, 22; 30:3) and war (Job 5:20) appear as well as references to the mining business (Job 28:1-11) and "male shrine prostitutes" (qĕdēšîm [Job 36:14]), thus covering a wide spectrum of life experiences. Interestingly, the motif of the God who controls the weather repeatedly occurs in Job (Job 37:3-13; 38:22-30, 34-35) and squarely positions the book in the OT conflict between Yahweh and Baal (e.g., 1 Kings 17—18), which so is often played out in the history of Israel.

Similar to other ancient Near Eastern cultures, divine creation is one of the mainstays of Israel's worldview and appears readily in biblical Wisdom literature (Job 9:5-9; 14:15; 28:24-26; 33:4-6; 38; Prov 3:19-20; 8:22-31; 22:2; Eccles 11:5; 12:1 [see Crenshaw; Yee; Hermission]). References to creation appear in any text type or genre of the OT, and many studies have focused on this important theological motif (*see* Creation Theology). For the ancient Israelite, God's involvement in human history during the creation of the world (and thereafter as well) was a given (see Fanwar; Mulzac; Simkins) and stands in stark contrast to the disengagement of God from history in Western thought (Rae, 268). Outside of Wisdom literature, creation is often associated with covenant (Miller), which, however, does not appear to be the case here. What does creation have to do with history, one may wonder, especially living in an age where the origin of humanity is being explained by the theory of evolution? First, creation was not merely a theological dictum but rather was understood as a "real," historical event. In this sense, the scholarly emphasis on creation theology does not reflect the understanding of the ancient Israelite.

The OT talking about creation is phenomenological and does not always fit easily into modernity's scientific worldview. Second, by linking wisdom to creation, the biblical authors underline their concern for history. Wisdom develops in history and is also concerned with historical realities.

As already seen in the discussion of the historical allusions in Job, the author(s) of Proverbs anchor the sayings and proverbs in real life. Adultery, a sad reality in all historical periods, appears repeatedly (Prov 5:3-20; 6:24-35; 7:5-23) and is an important issue in the book. Parallel to the use of animals in Job, animals (both domesticated and wild) are repeatedly used in the comparative language of Proverbs (e.g., doe and deer [Prov 5:19], gazelle [Prov 6:5], bird [Prov 6:5], ant [Prov 6:6; 30:26], ox [Prov 7:22], deer [Prov 7:22], bear [Prov 17:12; 28:15], war horse [Prov 21:31], eagle [Prov 23:5], lamb and goat [Prov 27:26-27], lion [Prov 28:15; 30:30], rock badger [Prov 30:26], locust [Prov 30:27], lizard [Prov 30:28], cock [Prov 30:31]). All these animals are employed as particular examples of specific characteristics ("fast as," "roaring like," "busy as," etc.), and again careful observation of animal behavior in real life forms the basis of the comparison.

Other historical allusions involve references to different types of "sacrifices" (šĕlāmîm in Prov 7:14, and the more generic zebaḥ in Prov 15:8; 21:27), which sometimes are set in contrast to heartfelt prayer and seem to echo (or prefigure, depending on how one dates biblical Wisdom literature) the prophetic critique of cult practice separated from a true change of heart and action in favor of the needy and oppressed. (1 Sam 15:22; Hos 6:6; Is 1:15-18; Jer 7 [see Zenger; Boecker; Callaway; Lange]). In this sense, Wisdom literature, with all its sayings, reflection and teachings, aims squarely at real life and critiques conditions that are not in harmony with the divine principles of right living. Another reference to the practical implications of right living is found in Proverbs 23:10, where the reader is commanded not to move ancient borders. Similarly, the lack of protection that the fatherless experience should not be used to enlarge one's own fields.

Proverbs 22:2 contains an important reference to divine creation (which is taken for granted) and emphasizes that both rich and poor are created by the same God and in this sense share a similar standing before God. Interestingly, the "tree of life" motif associated with creation appears in Proverbs 15:4, where its life-giving qualities are compared to soothing language ("gentle words" [NLT]). This is also connected to the "paradise regained" motif discussed below.

Ecclesiastes includes also quite a number of historical allusions, which are presented in a generic way. There are universal realities of life, such as the course of the sun, the wind and the journey of rivers, which are governed by eternal principles and do not change (Eccles 1:5-7). Seasons come and go, life cycles repeat themselves continuously (Eccles 3:1-8), including also the inevitable (historical) fact of death (Eccles 7:2; 9:2-6), and in the middle of it is God as the Creator and Sustainer (Eccles 3:11; 11:5; 12:1). Ecclesiastes is also full of things that happen in the real life. Building projects (Eccles 2:4-6), the purchasing of slaves (Eccles 2:7), the amassing of riches (Eccles 2:8), religious activity (Eccles 5:1-7) and warfare (Eccles 8:8) are among these historical allusions. Can one put a date or a place on these events? No, but their presence suggests the particular perspective of the author/editor of the volume, who seems to have come from the upper strata of society. The fact that the author ("preacher") writes in the first-person singular throughout most of the book suggests the communication of important information (including also historical hints). Although this is definitely not a conclusive argument for Solomonic authorship of the work (see Longman 1998, 2-9), in the overall design of the work it serves an important purpose, which, I think, is associated with a tendency to anchor the "wise" saying of *Qohelet in real life. This is a unique feature of Ecclesiastes that distinguishes the book from the rest of biblical Wisdom literature.

In contrast to the more numerous allusions to generic historical events in Job, Proverbs and Ecclesiastes, Song of Songs includes very few relevant references, which is most probably due to the particular nature of its content. As is already familiar from the other wisdom texts, there is description of the natural world, including animals (sheep [Song 1:8; 4:2], goats [Song 1:8; 4:1], mare [Song 1:9], gazelle [Song 2:7, 9, 17; 4:5; 7:3; 8:14], dove [Song 2:14; 5:2, 12; 6:9], fox [Song 2:15], stag [Song 2:9, 17; 8:14], lion [Song 4:8], leopard [Song 4:8], raven

[Song 5:11]), plants and other beautifying products (Song 4:12-14) and precious stones (Song 5:13-16). In Song of Songs 8:6, reference is made to a seal, an important socioeconomic status marker that also was often an expression of the religious worldview and identity of its bearer (Hallo). The biblical author applies the characteristics and the way that this well-known everyday object was worn to the covenant relationship between the two lovers.

To summarize this section, it is clear that similar to the use of places and protagonists, one encounters the close interaction between specific and generic historical allusions whereby the generic (or nonspecific) allusions represent the vast majority. Often, "personal" histories are sought to be shaped by ethical statements that require choices by the individual. This character development is an important topic of biblical Wisdom literature (Brown) and focuses on "personal" history instead of the political history so dear to modern historiographical definitions and perspectives. The sum of these personal histories and choices will make up the "future" history of a people responsible to God because of the relationship between Creator and creation. In other words, the all-encompassing focus on creation that is so obvious in Wisdom literature goes beyond the theological realm and points to an understanding of history where Yahweh not only is the Creator (and thus in charge) but also requires obedience and ethical choices from his creation. In this sense, the emphasis is not so much on the collective choices and action that characterizes political and cultural history as on the individual (= social) history, a concept that can be seen also in other ancient Near Eastern cultures. One wonders why the natural world consistently appears in biblical Wisdom literature. Obviously, there is an important link to creation, but beyond this it seems to be a reflection of the close observation by the biblical authors that looked at the world around them as one that could teach valuable lessons for the human inhabitants of creation.

3. Important Themes in Wisdom Literature and Their Links to History.

In the following analysis several important themes of Wisdom literature and their importance for an appropriate understanding of biblical history and especially historiography are treated in summary fashion.

3.1. "God Is in Control" Motif. The motif of God's control in human affairs represents a mainstay of biblical thinking. God not only is the Creator and originator of life but also is in control of human history and installs or deposes kings and princes (Dan 1:2; 2:21) and controls the lives of poor and rich, powerless and powerful (1 Sam 2:6-10). Although this particular concept has been connected to the so-called Deuteronomistic History (Collins, 160), it seems to be pervasive, including classical biblical wisdom literature. A good example is found in the prologue of Job, which provides a glimpse behind the veil separating heavenly and earthly realities (Job 1—2). As already mentioned, the creation focus in Wisdom literature seems to underscore this motif of God being in control. Sinners are consumed by the breath of God and perish at his anger (Job 4:9). God controls wisdom and "might" (*gĕbûrâ* [Job 12:13]), an interesting combination because "might" occurs regularly in the biblical historical literature as a marker of military or political prowess (e.g., Ex 32:18; 1 Kings 15:23; 16:5, 27; 22:46). Due to his might, God can tear down, and it will not be rebuilt; he can shut out, and it will not be opened (Job 12:14). God is the giver of wealth and possessions and honor (Eccles 6:2) and gives and maintains life (Eccles 8:15). Above all, he is the judge of everyone, and he evaluates every deed (Job 21:22; Eccles 3:17; 11:9; 12:14)—truly a central characteristic of the motif of God's control.

3.2. "A Godly Life Is a Happy Life" Motif. Biblical wisdom literature is full of practical advice that is to guarantee a happy life. The focus of this particular motif is not the big picture of kings, empires and multinational companies but rather the life of the individual. The accent on the personal over against the corporate or collective provides an interesting reflection of the thinking (or ideology) prevalent at the time of writing the biblical wisdom books. As with the motif of God being in control (see 3.1 above), the bigger picture is not completely out of focus. Kings, empires, peoples, the world and cosmic space appear and are interacted with, even though this appears not to be the main focus. As in other biblical texts, a delicate balance between the individual and the corporate perspective is being kept, since both perspectives occur together in many different genres (G. Klingbeil

2002a; Freund; Kaminsky), which seems to be a reflection of the basic anthropology of the Hebrew Bible (Janowski).

The emphasis of personal choices and personal piety and their direct bearing on one's life should also be connected to the important motif of "character development," which represents a major topic of wisdom literature (Brown). The development of the character is personal history and occurs in the reality of daily life. The emphasis on a personal history has already been mentioned in the discussion of ancient historiography and is quite distinct from modernity's infatuation with "objective historical data," which generally is mostly concerned with the history of the elite that affects the whole.

3.3. "Building of God's House" Motif. As has been pointed out by R. van Leeuwen, another important motif connecting biblical Wisdom literature to historical literature and thus suggesting an important link for the discussion of wisdom and history is the motif of the building of God's house (Prov 3:19-20), which in turn is linguistically and conceptually connected with God's work in creation (as already associated in Ps 78:69), the construction of the tabernacle (Ex 31:1-3; 35:30-31) and the building of Solomon's temple (1 Kings 4—6). More general house-description wisdom passages are found in Proverbs 9:1-6; 14:1; 24:3-4. It is particularly the building-of-God's-house motif that links Solomon with biblical wisdom, as can be seen in 1 Kings 4:29-30, 34; 5:12; 10:7. While many have questioned the direct link between Solomon and the origin and development of wisdom literature (e.g., Scott; Brueggemann, 116), others have argued for the existence of important wisdom schools (*see* Sages, Schools, Education) in the urban centers of the Late Bronze Age and the Iron Age as well as the existence of tribal or family wisdom traditions that may have fused in Israel in royal schools and, similar to other West Semitic wisdom texts, can be found in extrabiblical texts from the ninth and eighth centuries BC (Lemaire, 110-13), and a preexilic date for biblical Wisdom literature is not only possible but even more probable than its wholesale location in the postexilic or Persian period (Dell 2004). The absence of clear references to the exile in biblical Wisdom literature seems to also point in the direction of a preexilic date for the composition of the larger portion of biblical wisdom texts, considering the fact that exile represents

an important motif in later historical literature (McConville). After all, why would such an all-encompassing issue not be mentioned in texts that seek to guide in practical life issues?

3.4. "Paradise Regained" Motif. As has been shown by V. Hurowitz, references to motifs associated with the paradise narrative of Genesis 2 are found quite regularly in biblical Wisdom literature, beyond the general references to creation per se already discussed above. Proverbs 3:18 compares the obtaining of wisdom to "*a tree of life*" *(ʿēṣ-ḥayyim),* which corresponds to the phrase found in Genesis 2:9, minus the definite article connected to the noun *ḥayyim* ("life"). Given the fact that most critical scholars would include Genesis 2:9 in the Jahwist source (Westermann, 186-90), dated to the tenth or ninth century BC (Emerton, 126-28), the appearance of the motif, which does not appear elsewhere in the Hebrew Bible, seems to add more weight for a preexilic date of Proverbs. Proverbs 11:30 associates the "tree of life" motif with righteous acts, while Proverbs 13:12 compares a fulfilled hope with a tree of life. Finally, Proverbs 15:4 suggests that a gentle tongue is like a tree of life. Although the last three references clearly are metaphors used to communicate more effectively, the mere fact of the presence of this motif seems to provide a link to the important story of origins found in Genesis 1—3. As shown by Hurowitz (57-61), this is not the only link between Proverbs 3 and the story of paradise. "Prov 3:13-20 offers a solution to Man's eternal quest for return to Paradise and the Tree of Life. Wisdom will restore Humankind to the Paradise from which he was driven" (Hurowitz, 61). Connecting this important theological concept (which in the OT went beyond the mere theological perspective and represented an important historical outlook) with the *personification of wisdom in Proverbs 8 and its role in creation, the motif of paradise regained represents a clear link to the narrative texts describing Israel's origins.

4. History in Borderline Books: Daniel and Esther.

Although Daniel and Esther contain ideas that are also present in biblical Wisdom literature, their overall design, content and particular formulaic expressions point to their rootedness in history. Given that a full-fledged discussion of the history and historicity of both biblical books cannot be attempted here, some relevant data will serve as convincing evidence to exclude these books from the general corpus of biblical Wisdom literature and to underline their intrinsic history perspective. The literature discussing the historicity of Daniel is immense. Scholars have clearly marked the Babylonian ambience of the book, in terminology and linguistics (e.g., Paul 2005a; 2005b; Avalos; Stefanovic) as well as in specific historical references. References to the Neo-Babylonian king Nebuchadnezzar II, the administrative realities of the Neo-Babylonian Empire, the subsequent Persian Empire, together with the historical narratives of Daniel 1—6 clearly underline the importance of history in the book. Crucial to this discussion is, obviously, the dating of the book of Daniel—that is, whether it should be dated to the sixth century BC (as its internal trappings suggest) or whether it should be read as a second-century BC anonymous document that was written after the events described or prefigured in the book had taken place (see Hasel; Ferch). Imitating historical narrative literature of the OT, Daniel contains many references to dates that use the synchronistic method (e.g., "in the third year of King Jehoiakim" [Dan 1:1]; "during the second year of his [Nebuchadnezzar's] reign" [Dan 2:1]). Even the apocalyptic chapters are generally anchored in history and mention precise historical references (e.g., "early during the first year of King Belshazzar's reign" [Dan 7:1]; "during the third year of King Belshazzar's reign [Dan 8:1]; "first year of the reign of Darius the Mede" [Dan 9:1]; "in the third year of King Cyrus of Persia" [Dan 10:1]). Clearly, history is not only important in terms of future prophetic predictions but also is part and parcel of the book's inherent historiographical perspective, shared with most of the OT literature, that God is in control of history.

The situation is similar in the case of the book of Esther. The volume shares many trappings of historical narrative, including an internal dating scheme closely associated with the Persian king Xerxes (Weiland). Places and people are carefully named. The text also employs very rare terminology that appears also in Persian period Aramaic inscriptions (G. Klingbeil 1995) and that seems to be associated with a specialized high-speed postal system. To be sure, the protagonists of the narrative are not easily identified in the extrabiblical texts from the period (Firth), and the current scholarly consensus

seems to favor categorizing the book as fiction or novel (*see* Novella, Story, Narrative). However, from a formal perspective, the text of Esther resembles more closely historical narrative texts than classical biblical Wisdom literature. And it is here that the circle closes and brings us back to the discussion of biblical historiography, so distinct from modern Western notions about historicity and historiography.

5. Conclusions.

The present journey into wisdom and history has been tricky but at the same time rewarding. Although biblical Wisdom literature does not share many of the formal characteristics of biblical historical narrative, it indeed contains numerous references to people, places and actions, the three key elements of historical writing. It seems as if most of these references are purposefully kept more general or indefinite in order to make the content more abstract and thus easily adaptable for general application, disassociated from a particular historical *Sitz im Leben*. This tendency has also been observed in earlier Mesopotamian literature and should not necessarily be construed as a particular (negative) stance toward history. Many shared motifs and themes link biblical Wisdom literature with historical narrative, foremost among them the important concept that God is the creator of the earth and of human beings and thus controls the destiny of humanity. Other motifs, such as the important ones of "God is in control," the "building of God's house" and "paradise regained," have been shown to represent important elements of biblical Wisdom literature. It seems that more relevant links can be discovered between biblical Wisdom literature and historical narrative once our fairly biased and schematic understanding of the nature of historiography has been recognized.

See also HISTORICAL CRITICISM.

BIBLIOGRAPHY. **B. Alster,** *Proverbs of Ancient Sumer,* vol. 1 (Bethesda, MD: CDL Press, 1997); **L. O. Anderson Jr.,** "The Michael Figure in the Book of Daniel" (Th.D. diss., Andrews University Theological Seminary, 1997); **B. G. Aston, J. A. Harrell, and I. Shaw,** "Stone," in *Ancient Egyptian Materials and Technology,* ed. P. T. Nicholson and I. Shaw (Cambridge: Cambridge University Press, 2000) 5-77; **H. Avalos,** "Daniel 9:24-25 and Mesopotamian Temple Rededications," *JBL* 117 (1998) 507-11; **A. Berlin,** *Poetics* *and Interpretation of Biblical Narrative* (BLS 9; Sheffield: Almond, 1983); **D. K. Berry,** *An Introduction to Wisdom and Poetry of the Old Testament* (Nashville: Broadman & Holman, 1995); **H. J. Boecker,** "Überlegungen zur Kultpolemik der vorexilischen Propheten," in *Die Botschaft und die Boten: Festschrift für Hans Walter Wolff zum 70. Geburtstag,* ed. J. Jeremias and L. Perlitt (Neukirchen-Vluyn: Neukirchener Verlag, 1981) 169-80; **O. Borowski,** *Daily Life in Biblical Times* (SBLABS 5; Atlanta: Scholars Press, 2003); **M. Z. Brettler,** "Incompatible Metaphors for YHWH in Isaiah 40-66," *JSOT* 78 (1998) 97-120; **W. P. Brown,** *Character in Crisis: A Fresh Approach to the Wisdom Literature of the Old Testament* (Grand Rapids: Eerdmans, 1996); **W. Brueggemann,** *Solomon: Israel's Ironic Icon of Human Achievement* (SPOT; Columbia: University of South Carolina Press, 2005); **M. C. Callaway,** "A Hammer That Breaks Rock in Pieces: Prophetic Critique in the Hebrew Bible," in *Anti-Semitism and Early Christianity: Issues of Polemic and Faith,* ed. C. A. Evans and D. A. Hagner (Minneapolis: Fortress, 1993) 21-38; **R. B. Chisholm Jr.,** "History or Story? The Literary Dimension in Narrative Texts," in *Giving the Sense: Understanding and Using Old Testament Texts,* ed. D. M Howard Jr. and M. A. Grisanti (Grand Rapids: Kregel, 2003) 54-73; **R. J. Clifford,** *Proverbs* (OTL; Louisville: Westminster John Knox, 1999); **A. C. Cohen,** "Dehistoricizing Strategies in Third-Millennium B.C.E. Royal Inscriptions and Rituals," in *Proceedings of the XLV Recontre Assyriologique Internationale,* Pt. 1: *Harvard University: Historiography in the Cuneiform World,* ed. T. Abusch et al. (Bethesda, MD: CDL Press, 2001) 99-112; **J. J. Collins,** *Daniel* (Hermeneia; Minneapolis: Fortress, 1993); **J. L. Crenshaw,** "When Form and Content Clash: The Theology of Job 38:1-40:5," in *Creation in the Biblical Traditions,* ed. R. J. Clifford and J. J. Collins (CBQMS 24; Washington, DC: Catholic Biblical Association of America, 1992) 70-84; **P. R. Davies,** *In Search of "Ancient Israel"* (JSOTSup 148; Sheffield: JSOT Press, 1992); idem, *Whose Bible Is It Anyway?* (2nd ed.; London: T & T Clark International, 2002); **K. J. Dell,** "Wisdom," in *The Biblical World,* vol. 1, ed. J. Barton (London: Routledge, 2002) 107-28; idem, "How Much Wisdom Literature Has Its Roots in the Pre-Exilic Period," in *In Search of Pre-Exilic Israel: Proceedings of the Oxford Old Testament Seminar,* ed. J. Day (JSOTSup 406; London: T & T Clark International, 2004) 251-71; **D. V. Edelman,** "Maha-

naim," *ABD* 4.472-73; **J. A. Emerton,** "The Date of the Yahwist," in *In Search of Pre-Exilic Israel: Proceedings of the Oxford Old Testament Seminary,* ed. J. Day (JSOTSup 406; London: T & T Clark International, 2004) 107-29; **D. J. Estes,** *Handbook on the Wisdom Books and Psalms* (Grand Rapids: Baker, 2005); **W. M. Fanwar,** "Creation in Isaiah" (Ph.D. diss., Andrews University Theological Seminary, 2001); **A. Ferch,** "The Book of Daniel and the 'Maccabean Thesis,'" *AUSS* 21 (1983) 129-41; **D. G. Firth,** "The Third Quest for the Historical Mordecai and the Genre of the Book of Esther," *OTE* 16 (2003) 233-43; **R. A. Freund,** "Individual vs. Collective Responsibility: From the Ancient Near East and the Bible to the Greco-Roman World," *SJOT* 11 (1997) 279-304; **E. Gaß,** *Die Ortsnamen des Richterbuchs in historischer und redaktioneller Perspektive* (ADPV 35; Wiesbaden: Harrassowitz, 2005); **W. W. Hallo,** "For Love Is Strong as Death," *JANES* 22 (1993) 45-50; **J. E. Hartley,** *The Book of Job* (NICOT; Grand Rapids: Eerdmans, 1988); **G. F. Hasel,** "Establishing a Date for the Book of Daniel," in *Symposium on Daniel,* ed. F. B. Holbrook (Daniel and Revelation Committee Series 2; Washington, DC: Biblical Research Institute, 1986) 84-164; **H.-J. Hermission,** "Observations on the Creation Theology in Wisdom," in *Creation in the Old Testament,* ed. B. W. Anderson (IRT 6; Philadelphia: Fortress, 1984) 118-34; **R. S. Hess,** *Song of Songs* (BCOTWP; Grand Rapids: Baker, 2005); **V. A. Hurowitz,** "Paradise Regained: Proverbs 3:13-20 Reconsidered," in *Sefer Moshe: The Moshe Weinfeld Jubilee Volume. Studies in the Bible and the Ancient Near East, Qumran, and Post-Biblical Judaism,* ed. C. Cohen, A. Hurvitz and S. M. Paul (Winona Lake, IN: Eisenbrauns, 2004) 49-62; **B. Janowski,** "Der Mensch im alten Israel: Grundfragen alttestamentlicher Anthropologie," *ZTK* 102 (2005) 143-75; **S. Japhet,** "'Lebanon' in the Transition from Derash to Peshat: Sources, Etymology and Meaning (with Special Attention to the Song of Songs)," in *Emanuel: Studies in Hebrew Bible, Septuagint and Dead Sea Scrolls in Honor of Emanuel Tov,* ed. S. M. Paul et al. (VTSup 94; Leiden: E. J. Brill, 2003) 707-24; **G. E. Kadish,** "Historiography," *OEAE* 2.108-11; **J. S. Kaminsky,** *Corporate Responsibility in the Hebrew Bible* (JSOTSup 196; Sheffield: Sheffield Academic Press, 1995); **G. A. Klingbeil,** "רכש and Esther 8, 10.14: A Semantic Note," *ZAW* 107 (1995) 301-3; idem, "Entre individualismo y colectivismo: Hacia una perspectiva bíblica de la naturaleza de la iglesia," in *Pensar la iglesia hoy: Hacia una eclesiología adventista; Estudios teológicos presentados durante el IV Simposio Bíblico-Teológico Sudamericano en honor a Raoul Dederen*, ed. G. A. Klingbeil et al. (Libertador San Martín: Editorial Universidad Adventista del Plata, 2002a) 3-22; idem, "'Up, Down, In, Out, Through and Back': Space and Movement in Old Testament Narrative, Ritual and Legal Texts and Their Application for the Study of Mark 1:1-3:12," *EstBib* 60 (2002b) 283-309; idem, "Altars, Ritual and Theology—Preliminary Thoughts on the Importance of Cult and Ritual for a Theology of the Hebrew Scriptures," *VT* 54 (2004) 495-515; **M. G. Klingbeil**, *Yahweh Fighting from Heaven: God as Warrior and as God of Heaven in the Hebrew Psalter and Ancient Near Eastern Iconography* (OBO 169; Fribourg: Universitätsverlag; Göttingen: Vandenhoeck & Ruprecht, 1999); **E. A. Knauf**, "Elihu," *ABD* 2.462; idem, "Kedar," *ABD* 4.9-10; **J. B. Kofoed**, *Text and History: Historiography and the Study of the Biblical Text* (Winona Lake, IN: Eisenbrauns, 2005); **A. Lange**, "Gebotsobservanz statt Opferkult: Zur Kultpolemik in Jer 7,1–8,3," in *Gemeinde ohne Tempel/Community without Temple: Zur Substituierung und Transformation des Jerusalemer Tempels und seines Kults im Alten Testament, antiken Judentum und frühen Christentums*, ed. B. Ego, A. Lange and P. Pilhofer (WUNT 118; Tübingen: Mohr Siebeck, 1999) 19-35; **A. Lemaire**, "Wisdom in Solomonic Historiography," in *Wisdom in Ancient Israel: Essays in Honour of J. A. Emerton*, ed. J. Day, R. P. Gordon and H. G. M. Williamson (Cambridge: Cambridge University Press, 1995) 106-18; **N. P. Lemche**, *Early Israel: Anthropological and Historical Studies on the Israelite Society before the Monarchy* (VTSup 37; Leiden: E. J. Brill, 1985); idem, *Ancient Israel: A New History of Israelite Society* (BibSem 5; Sheffield: JSOT Press, 1988); idem, *Die Vorgeschichte Israels: Von den Anfängen bis zum Ausgang des 13. Jahrhunderts v. Chr.* (BE 1; Stuttgart: Kohlhammer, 1996); ET, *Prelude to Israel's Past: Background and Beginnings of Israelite History and Identity* (Peabody, MA: Hendrickson, 1998); **M. Liverani**, "Early Caravan Trade between South-Arabia and Mesopotamia," *Yemen* 1 (1992) 111-15; **V. P. Long**, *The Art of Biblical History* (FCI 5; Grand Rapids: Zondervan, 1994); idem, "How Reliable Are Biblical Reports? Repeating Lester Grabbe's Comparative Experiment," *VT* 52 (2002) 367-84; **T. Longman III**, *Fictional Akkadian Autobiography: A Generic and Comparative Study* (Winona Lake, IN:

Eisenbrauns, 1991); idem, *The Book of Ecclesiastes* (NICOT; Grand Rapids: Eerdmans, 1998); idem, *Proverbs* (BCOTWP; Grand Rapids: Baker, 2006); **S. Malena**, "Spice Roots in the Song of Songs," in *Milk and Honey: Essays on Ancient Israel and the Bible in Appreciation of the Judaic Studies Program at the University of California, San Diego*, ed. S. Malena and D. Miano (Winona Lake, IN: Eisenbrauns, 2007) 165-84; **J. G. McConville**, "Faces of Exile in Old Testament Historiography," in *After the Exile: Essays in Honour of Rex Mason*, ed. J. Barton and D. J. Reimer (Macon, GA: Mercer University Press, 1996) 27-44; **A. R. Millard**, "Story, History, and Theology," in *Faith, Tradition and History*, ed. A. R. Millard, J. K. Hoffmeier and D. W. Baker (Winona Lake, IN: Eisenbrauns, 1994) 37-64; **P. D. Miller Jr.**, "Creation and Covenant," in *Biblical Theology: Problems and Perspectives; In Honor of J. Christiaan Beker*, ed. S. J. Kraftchick, C. D. Meyers Jr. and B. C. Ollenburger (Nashville: Abingdon, 1995) 155-68; **H.-P. Müller**, "Der Libanon in altorientalischen Quellen und im Hohenlied," *ZDPV* 117 (2001) 116-27; **K. D. Mulzac**, "'Creation' in the Book of Jeremiah," in *Creation, Life, and Hope: Essays in Honor of Jacques B. Doukhan*, ed. J. Moskala (Berrien Springs, MI: Old Testament Department, Seventh-day Adventist Theological Seminary, Andrews University, 2000) 29-44; **R. D. Nelson**, "Divine Warrior Theology in Deuteronomy," in *A God So Near: Essays in Old Testament Theology in Honor of Patrick D. Miller*, ed. B. A. Strawn and N. R. Bowen (Winona Lake, IN: Eisenbrauns, 2003) 241-59; **S. M. Paul**, "Dan 6:8: An Aramaic Reflex of Assyrian Legal Terminology," in *Divrei Shalom: Collected Studies of Shalom M. Paul on the Bible and the Ancient Near East 1967-2005*, ed. S. M. Paul (CHANE 23; Leiden: E. J. Brill, 2005a) 139-44; idem, "Daniel 6:20: An Aramaic Calque on an Akkadian Expression," in *Divrei Shalom: Collected Studies of Shalom M. Paul on the Bible and the Ancient Near East 1967-2005*, ed. S. M. Paul (CHANE 23; Leiden: E. J. Brill, 2005b) 329-31; **I. Provan, V. P. Long and T. Longman III**, *A Biblical History of Israel* (Louisville: Westminster John Knox, 2003); **M. A. Rae**, "Creation and Promise: Towards a Theology of History," in *"Behind" the Text: History and Biblical Interpretation*, ed. C. G. Bartholomew et al. (SHS 4; Grand Rapids: Zondervan, 2003) 267-99; **R. Rendtorff**, "Geschichtliches und weisheitliches Denken im Alten Testament," in *Beiträge zur alttestamentli-*

chen Theologie. Festschrift für Walter Zimmerli zum 70. Geburtstag, ed. H. Donner, R. Hanhart and R. Smend (Göttingen: Vandenhoeck & Ruprecht, 1977) 344-53; **S. D. Ricks,** "Sheba, Queen of," *ABD* 5.1170-71; **P. Riede,** *Im Spiegel der Tiere: Studien zum Verhältnis von Mensch und Tier im Alten Israel* (OBO 187; Fribourg: Universitätsverlag; Göttingen: Vandenhoeck & Ruprecht, 2002); **P. C. Schmitz,** "Baal-Hamon," *ABD* 1.551; **R. B. Y. Scott,** "Solomon and the Beginnings of Wisdom in Israel," in *Wisdom in Israel and in the Ancient Near East: Presented to Professor Harold Henry Rowley in Celebration of His Sixty-fifth Birthday, 24 March 1955,* ed. M. Noth and D. W. Thomas (VTSup 3; Leiden: E. J. Brill, 1955) 262-79; **R. A. Simkins,** *Creator and Creation: Nature in the Worldview of Ancient Israel* (Peabody, MA: Hendrickson, 1994); **W. K. Simpson,** "Egypt," in *The Ancient Near East: A History,* ed. W. W. Hallo and W. K. Simpson (New York: Harcourt Brace Jovanovich, 1971) 185-298; **P. W. Skehan,** *Studies in Israelite Poetry and Wisdom* (CBQMS 1; Washington, DC: Catholic Biblical Association of America, 1971) **Z. Stefanovic,** *The Aramaic of Daniel in the Light of Old Aramaic* (JSOTSup 129; Sheffield: JSOT Press, 1992); **M. Sternberg,** *The Poetics of Biblical Narrative* (ILBS; Bloomington: Indiana University Press, 1985); **C. Sticher,** *Die Rettung der Guten durch Gott und die Selbstzerstörung der Bösen: Ein theologisches Denkmuster im Psalter* (BBB 137; Berlin: Philo, 2002); **S. Talmon,** "'Wisdom' in the Book of Esther," *VT* 13 (1963) 419-55; **J. P. Tanner,** "The History of Interpretation of the Song of Songs," *BSac* 154 (1997) 23-46; **X. H. Thi Pham,** *Mourning in the Ancient Near East and the Hebrew Bible* (JSOTSup 302; Sheffield: Sheffield Academic Press, 1999); **T. L. Thompson,** *The Historicity of the Patriarchal Narratives* (BZAW 133; Berlin: de Gruyter, 1974); idem, *The Origin Tradition of Ancient Israel* (JSOTSup 55; Sheffield: JSOT Press, 1987); idem, *Early History of the Israelite People: From the Written and Archaeological Sources* (SHANE 4; Leiden: E. J. Brill, 1992); **R. C. van Leeuwen,** "Building God's House: An Exploration in Wisdom," in *The Way of Wisdom: Essays in Honor of Bruce K. Waltke,* ed. J. I. Packer and S. K. Soderlung (Grand Rapids: Zondervan, 2000) 204-11; **J. van Seters,** *Abraham in History and Tradition* (New Haven: Yale University Press, 1975); idem, *In Search of History* (New Haven: Yale University Press, 1983); idem, "The Historiography of the Ancient Near East," in *Civilizations of the Ancient Near East,* ed. J. M. Sasson (4 vols.; New York: Scribner, 1995) 4.2433-43; **K. R. Veenhof,** *Geschichte des Alten Orients bis zur Zeit Alexanders des Grossen* (GAT 11; Göttingen: Vandenhoeck & Ruprecht, 2001); **B. L. Visotzky,** *The Midrash on Proverbs* (YJS 27; New Haven: Yale University Press, 1997); **B. K. Waltke,** *The Book of Proverbs: Chapters 15-31* (NICOT; Grand Rapids: Eerdmans, 2005); **F. S. Weiland,** "Historicity, Genre, and Narrative Design in the Book of Esther," *BSac* 159 (2002) 151-65; **C. Westermann,** *Genesis 1-11* (CC; Minneapolis: Fortress, 1994); **N. Winther-Nielsen,** "Fact, Fiction, and Language Use: Can Modern Pragmatics Improve on Halpern's Case for History in Judges?" in *Windows into Old Testament History: Evidence, Argument, and the Crisis of "Biblical Israel,"* ed. V. P. Long, D. W. Baker and G. J. Wenham (Grand Rapids: Eerdmans, 2002) 44-81; **E. M. Yamauchi,** *Africa and the Bible* (Grand Rapids: Baker, 2004); **G. A. Yee,** "The Theology of Creation in Proverbs 8:22-31," in *Creation in the Biblical Traditions,* ed. R. J. Clifford and J. J. Collins (CBQMS 24; Washington, DC: Catholic Biblical Association of America, 1992) 85-96; **E. Zenger,** "Ritual and Criticism of Ritual in the Old Testament," in *Liturgy and Human Passage,* ed. D. Power and L. Maldonado (Concilium 112; New York: Seabury Press, 1979) 39-49.   G. A. Klingbeil

WISDOM AND PROPHECY

Wisdom and prophecy are presented in the OT as two significant aspects of life in ancient Israel. They are depicted as both complementing one another and conflicting with one another, and are described positively only when they are founded on the *law of God. This article examines various aspects of the relationship between wisdom and prophecy.

    1. Definitions
    2. Wisdom and Prophecy
    3. Literary Features of Wisdom and Prophecy
    4. The Relationship Between Prophets and Sages
    5. Conclusion

1. Definitions.

1.1. Wisdom. The broad semantic range of the Hebrew term *ḥokmâ* ("wisdom") presents some difficulties in the attempt to define wisdom precisely, let alone its relationship to prophecy (see Whybray, 181-83). The term itself refers to any form of skill: "all those skilled in some trait or profession possess wisdom of a sort: the craftsman, the potter, the builder, the farmer" (Grabbe, 162-63). Kings were given wisdom by God in order to rule (e.g., Deut 34:9; 1 Kings 3:12; 5:12; Is 11:2); others were given wisdom for specific tasks, such as the skill required by Bezalel to construct the tabernacle (Ex 31:1-5). Wisdom also appears in different guises: proverbial wisdom (as found in much of *Proverbs); mantic wisdom, involving divination and largely confined to foreign *sages; or speculative wisdom, such as that found in much of *Ecclesiastes. So although Daniel is declared to be wise, his wisdom rests, at least in part, on direct revelation from God (Dan 2; cf. Joseph in Gen 40—41). Thus Daniel's wisdom has more in common with prophecy than it does with the speculative wisdom of *Qohelet (*see* Wisdom and Apocalyptic).

Further complicating the tasks of defining wisdom and understanding's relationship with prophecy is the evolution of wisdom through history. R. Whybray (195) noted, "[That] wisdom ideas or theology underwent great changes during the OT period ... is obvious.... There are tremendous theological differences between the older elements in Proverbs and the later ones, between Proverbs and Job, between Job and Ecclesiastes." Beyond this, the speculative wisdom of Ecclesiastes seems to have given way to a form of wisdom that found its basis in the law by the time of Ben Sira (see Sir 24:23), and the evolution did not stop here, for later wisdom texts suggest further development (see Aitken, 181-93).

These vagaries should not, however, obscure the fact that the bulk of the biblical treatment of wisdom and its interaction with prophecy is focused on the intellectual aspects of wisdom, as noted by L. Grabbe (179): "There is a special sense in which wisdom was applied to intellectual characteristics, especially those gained or developed by formal learning, education, and study." The task of these sages is well described by J. Crenshaw (1993, 6): "The sages ... insisted on the intellect's capacity to assure the good life by word and deed. By using their intellectual gifts the sages hoped to steer their lives safely into harbor, avoiding hazards that brought catastrophes to fools." Moreover, outside of the Wisdom literature, references to the wise frequently focus on their role as royal advisors in Israel and beyond. Thus, when considering the relationship between wisdom and prophecy, the biblical text concentrates on the intellectual stream of wisdom frequently manifest in advisors who sought to influence the course of government.

1.2. Prophecy. The literary records of prophecy preserved in the OT are somewhat more uniform than the wider phenomenon of prophecy in ancient Israel appears to have been. The existence of bands of prophets pronouncing ecstatic utterances (e.g., 1 Sam 10:9-12) and indications of the existence of institutionalized prophets (e.g., 2 Kings 6:1; Amos 7:14) reflect aspects of prophecy that are largely unrepresented among the prophetic books. Precisely how these prophets operated is not entirely clear, and because of the very limited information on them and their activities, any informed discussion of prophecy and wisdom must confine itself to the form of prophecy recorded extensively in the biblical text itself.

Consequently, for the purposes of this article, the definition of a prophet by Grabbe (107) is sufficient: "The common denominator ... is that the prophet is a mediator who claims to receive messages direct from a divinity, by various means, and communicates these messages to recipients." It thus follows that a prophecy is the message received and transmitted by the prophet.

2. Wisdom and Prophecy.

Wisdom and prophecy are depicted both favorably and unfavorably in the OT. False prophecy is prophecy not arising from the God of Israel; false wisdom is wisdom that is not founded in the fear of Yahweh (*see* Fear of the Lord). True prophecy reflects God's desire for his people and so reflects his will as revealed in the law. True wisdom is defined within the law as obedience to the law (see Deut 4:5-6). It is this link to the law that is the touchstone for both wisdom and prophecy, and against which they are each assessed by the biblical authors.

The fundamental difference between wisdom and prophecy lies in the nature of wisdom as a skill or the ability to live well, whereas prophecy conveys direct and specific information from God addressing a particular situation. As such, although the intellectual acumen that constitutes some examples of divinely given wisdom—that of *Solomon, for instance—may be said to come from God, there is no implicit guarantee that the results of the application of wisdom also carry divine authority (see Scott, 11).

Solomon is a prime example of this distinction, for in spite of the divine origin of his wisdom, he employed it to make strategic alliances through marriage and subsequently introduced idolatry into the very center of the kingdom. Unlike the prophets, whose words often are presented as direct quotations of God's words to them, the sages' insights are their own even if the intellectual capacity for reaching their conclusions was God-given.

Consequently, the authority of the sage differs fundamentally from that of the prophet: "[That] priest and prophet were regarded as speaking with divine authority is clear. It is less certain that the same can be said of the 'counsel' of the wise man and the elders" (Scott, 3). The criticism of this distinction by B. Gemser (208-19), arguing that "counsel" (ʿēṣâ) is presented as bearing equal authority to the word of the prophet (cf. Crenshaw 1971, 119), requires significant qualification. Gemser correctly notes that this counsel derives its authority from its relationship with the Torah; however, he fails to account adequately for either the evolution of wisdom through history or the frequent assertions within the OT text that the wisdom of the sages had become disconnected from the law and thus had lost its authority (cf., e.g., Is 5:21; 19:11-12; 47:10; see Shields, 7-19). Where wisdom derives from and expounds God's revealed instruction and calls for an obedience to those instructions founded in the fear of Yahweh (see Deut 4:6), it is favorably depicted in the OT. Wisdom that ignores God's word—that of Qohelet or of Job's counselors, for instance—is condemned.

3. Literary Features of Wisdom and Prophecy.
Scholars have recognized that the various types of literature present in the OT are frequently characterized by specific literary forms. The proverb, for example, is generally recognized as a feature of wisdom. It is therefore significant to note instances where forms typically associated with one genre occur in literature of another genre. The appearance of wisdom forms in prophecy or of prophetic forms in wisdom is often construed as revealing something of the relationship between wisdom and prophecy.

3.1. Prophetic Features in Wisdom Literature.

3.1.1. Proverbs. Both Agur and King *Lemuel label their sayings as maśśāʾ (Prov 30:1; 31:1; [traditionally, "oracle," but *HALOT* suggests

"pronouncement," while others prefer "burden"]). As a description of speech, this term is elsewhere exclusively associated with prophecy (e.g., Is 13:1; 14:28; 15:1; 17:1; 19:1; 21:1, 11, 13; 22:1; 23:1; 30:6; Ezek 12:10; Nah 1:1; Hab 1:1; Zech 9:1; 12:1; Mal 1:1). In fact, so anomalous does its use in Proverbs appear to some scholars and translators that they understand the word to be a place name rather than as a claim that the words that follow are in any way akin to a prophetic pronouncement (see *HALOT;* cf. Gen 25:14; 1 Chron 1:30; Ps 120:5).

B. Waltke (81-82) claims, however, that the use of the term here affirms the inspired status of the utterances of the sages, and that the wisdom recorded in Proverbs is founded not merely on intellectual analysis of the natural and social world but rather on special divine revelation. The only other use of *maśśāʾ* in the Wisdom literature (Job 7:20) clearly does not include the notion of revelation, but the fact that Proverbs 30:1 also uses the term *nĕʾum,* which *HALOT* describes as "an almost completely fixed technical expression introducing prophetic oracles," strengthens Waltke's case.

However, there are grounds for caution before claiming too much based on the use of these terms alone. In spite of Agur's and Lemuel's use of this distinctively prophetic language to introduce their words, the form and content of those words remains distinct from the prophetic utterances elsewhere associated with these terms. Furthermore, these terms are not explicitly applied to all of Proverbs, let alone all the Wisdom literature, and if the use of these terms in Proverbs 30:1; 31:1 is intended to ascribe to the words of these sages prophetic authority, it is quite clear from the perspective of *Job and Ecclesiastes that this ascription cannot be extended to all wisdom, for both these works denounce human wisdom and contrast it with direct revelation from God.

3.1.2. Job. The book of Job, which records God's direct intervention and speech to Job and his counselors, has long been recognized as reflecting some degree of prophetic influence. For example, Crenshaw (1971, 108) argued that "the continuity between Job and prophecy cannot be denied" (cf. Snaith, 33).

Job represents an interesting blurring of wisdom and prophecy, but one that ultimately undermines the wisdom presented by the human sages, Job's "friends" (cf. Job 5:13; 12:17; 38:2).

Unlike Proverbs, which contains material that balances the tendency to read its wisdom as endorsing a purely retributive understanding of the world (e.g., Prov 10:2; 16:8, 19; 17:1; 19:1, 22; 22:1; 28:6), the book of Job does not resort to wisdom to counter the arguments of Job's acquaintances. Rather, the ultimate corrective to their wisdom comes in direct special revelation from God (see Job 38—42), a mode more akin to prophecy than wisdom. In thus resorting to special revelation rather than wisdom, together with the expression of wisdom's limitations (Job 28), the book highlights wisdom's inadequacies and the ultimate role that prophecy plays in understanding the world in which we live.

3.1.3. Ecclesiastes. One portion of the words of the epilogue to Ecclesiastes (Eccles 12:11-12a) is often understood to affirm the divine origin of the biblical Wisdom literature. The basis for this understanding is the apparent assertion that the words of the wise are given by the one shepherd, widely understood as a reference to God. This understanding is reflected in most modern English translations. For example, the ESV reads, "The words of the wise are like goads, and like nails firmly fixed are the collected sayings; they are given by one Shepherd. My son, beware of anything beyond these." G. Ogden (210) endorses this interpretation of the passage, stating that the epilogist, in writing these words, is "claiming that the observation-reflection method typical of the sage ... qualifies as a method by which the divine will and purpose may be ascertained. This then gives the sage's words an authority as revelation, as scripture."

There are, however, a number of significant problems with this understanding of the epilogue to Qohelet's words (see Shields, 69-92). The identification of the "one shepherd" as God is dubious. When God is described as a shepherd elsewhere, the identification is always explicit and unambiguous, and since others are described as shepherds of the people (e.g., Ezek 34:23, which uses the phrase *rōʿeh eḥād* ["one shepherd"] found in Eccles 12:11), if the shepherd here is to be understood metaphorically, then it is not immediately clear how that identification ought to be made. Further, these words claim far more than most would be happy to affirm, for they do not restrict the assertion made regarding the words of the sages to the words of Qohelet, nor even to the canonical Wisdom literature, but simply to all the words of the wise,

without qualification. Yet few would claim that all words from all sages have a divine origin.

Instead, it is better to read these words of the epilogue as a warning against the wisdom of the sages rather than an endorsement of it. As such, they can be translated thus: "The words of the wise are like goads, and like cattle-prods are [the words of] the masters of collections, those which are used by a lone shepherd. In addition to these things, my son, beware of making many texts...." As a lone shepherd must employ painful goads to direct his flock, so the wise use their words to manipulate and coerce their students. Furthermore, warns the epilogue, beware of being consumed by the literary activities typical of the sages, for such tasks are pointless.

If these words do not affirm the divine origin of the wisdom of the sages, then there is little to indicate any prophetic influence in the book of Ecclesiastes. Qohelet reaches his conclusions without ever appealing to special divine revelation; indeed, it may well be that he actively repudiates any notion that such information can ever be reliably discerned and distances himself from any who would claim to have access to such information (see 4.2 below).

3.2. Wisdom in the Prophets. The prophetic books of the OT occasionally employ wisdom language and forms, as R. Scott (4) notes: "Isaiah and Jeremiah scorn the wise men of their time, yet they themselves adopt some of the language, forms, and ideas of the wisdom teachers." J. Lindblom (201-2) identifies a number of instances of wisdom forms used in prophetic literature (e.g., Is 5; 10:15; 28; Hos 7:4-5; Amos 3:3-6; 6:12), together with prophetic use of aphorisms (e.g., Jer 31:29; Ezek 18:2 [although both in reference to aphorisms that will no longer be used]; also Is 65:8; Jer 8:4; 13:12; 15:12; 23:28; 49:24; Ezek 11:3; 16:44). He further identifies rhetorical questions with a specific didactic intent that resemble wisdom utterances (e.g., Is 10:15; Jer 23:28; Ezek 15:2-8; Amos 3:3-8; 6:12; 9:7; Mal 1:6; 2:14-15, 17; 3:7-8, 13-14).

The appearance of such wisdom forms within the prophetic books has prompted a number of explanations from scholars. In the mid-twentieth century some such as J. Fichtner suggested that they indicated that these prophets were once numbered among the sages. Others suggest that the broad distribution of wisdom material throughout the OT can be attributed to the activities of scribal sages who were responsible for the compilation and transmission of the texts preserved as the OT, and that the wisdom forms embedded in the text can be traced, at least in some instances, to their hands. For example, R. Van Leeuwen (1993, 49) suggests that "the end-redaction of the *Tanakh* as a whole was the work of scribal sages who were forerunners of Ben Sira."

Both of these explanations are founded on uncertain presuppositions. No prophet ever claims to have been previously counted among the sages, and so to suggest that several of them were is based entirely on a speculative assessment of the significance of wisdom forms among their words (see Lindblom, 197; Van Leeuwen 1990, 297-98).

Similarly, the suggestion that wisdom language and forms can be attributed to later editorial work by *scribes imposing their own agenda upon the text, though impossible to exclude in every instance, is founded on no manuscript evidence and supposes that the use of wisdom language either would have been inappropriate for the prophet or does not cohere with the work's message. Yet, if some wisdom originated in the home and so was shared in by most of the population—as seems likely, given the subject matter—then it would hardly be surprising that wisdom forms and language should be found throughout the OT. Furthermore, if the observation by M. Sato (142) that "to *propheticize* non-prophetic genres of speech, is in itself a characteristic of prophetic-inspiratory dynamism" is correct, then the presence of wisdom forms and language in the prophetic books ought to be even less in need of special explanation.

Identification of wisdom language in the prophets is also complicated somewhat by wisdom's frequent use of examples from everyday life. In spite of the tendency of some scholars to see in such illustrations dependence of the prophet upon the wise, such connections are almost always unwarranted by the evidence, for to make such a claim ascribes to the sages a monopoly on using common language for their ends. As Crenshaw (1969, 134) says, "The mere use of wisdom phraseology by a prophet does not make him a sage, for his meaning may be completely alien to wisdom thinking" (see also Murphy, 104; Reventlow, 381-82).

3.2.1. Isaiah. Isaiah contains a number of passages that employ wisdom language and forms (e.g., Is 5:21; 29:13-16). The prominence of wisdom themes in Isaiah led Fichtner to argue that Isaiah once a sage who had turned against the wise upon recognition that their wisdom had departed from its roots in the law (cf. Is 6:9-10). Few scholars go so far as Fichtner, recognizing the degree of speculation involved in so identifying Isaiah with the wise, but a number of scholars (e.g., Whedbee; Jensen) do nonetheless acknowledge the significance of wisdom language for Isaiah, particularly when addressing those who claim to be wise (cf. Is 10:13; 19:11-12; 44:25; 47:10).

J. Whedbee helpfully suggested some means to limit speculation as to the extent of Isaiah's dependence upon wisdom by proposing that the identification of influence ought to be restricted to those sections where there is a conjunction between wisdom form and content, pointing to the parables of Isaiah 1:2-3; 5:1-7; 28:23-28, the proverbial material in Isaiah 10:15; 29:15-16, and the "summary appraisals" in Isaiah 14:26; 28:29.

Van Leeuwen (1990, 299) argues that Isaiah's criticism of the sages reflects that of Proverbs itself: "That Isaiah used the wisdom of Proverbs to attack courtly wisdom probably means that the sages were not true to their own wisdom, or that there were conflicting factions in the court, some of which, at certain times in his lengthy career, Isaiah attacked. Unfortunately, the limited data leave uncertainty in these matters" (cf. Collins, 10). This note of caution is certainly warranted, for even the claim that Isaiah used the wisdom of Proverbs is speculative.

The presence of such material in Isaiah, however, has not convinced more careful scholars that Isaiah has been significantly influenced by the wisdom movement (see Whybray; Crenshaw). In light of the apparent ubiquity of wisdom in some form at all levels of society, it seems likely that Isaiah at least shared some degree of familiarity with wisdom and so could employ wisdom forms and language to his own ends without having to have ever himself been a sage.

3.2.2. Jeremiah and Ezekiel. Jeremiah and Ezekiel share with Isaiah their general disdain for the sages while occasionally adopting wisdom forms and language. The book of Jeremiah, in particular, recounts details of the prophet's conflict with royal advisors when seeking to guide foreign-policy response to Nebuchadrezzar (although see Jeremiah's letter to the exiles in Jer 29, at which point Zedekiah would appear to have been in agreement with his advice [see McKane 1995, 150]).

Both Jeremiah and Ezekiel employ aphorisms, perhaps most famously Ezekiel 18:2 (cf. Jer 31:29-30): "Fathers have eaten sour grapes, but the teeth of the sons have been dulled." This aphorism bears all the hallmarks of a wisdom saying, but it is quoted by the prophets to refute its teaching, for they wish to make the opposite point. Jeremiah goes so far as to offer an amended version of the proverb: "Every person who eats the sour grapes, his teeth will be dulled" (Jer 31:30). Thus, although both Jeremiah and Ezekiel employ wisdom language, they self-consciously do so in order to undermine the sages. We will examine this conflict in more detail later (see 4.1 below).

3.2.3. Hosea. The extent of Hosea's acquaintance with wisdom is not entirely clear. Hosea does draw on the natural world for some metaphors (cf. Hos 9:10, 13, 16; 10:1; 14:6; 4:16; 8:7; 10:4; see Macintosh, 129), as the sages also frequently did, but this alone is not sufficient basis for claiming any significant interaction with the sages on Hosea's part. Likewise, although his use of aphorisms does suggest at least some passing familiarity with wisdom, given the likely ubiquity of wisdom in some of its forms, this cannot be construed as indicative of any special connection to more formal wisdom or the sages who promoted it (Macintosh, 125).

Nonetheless, the final verse of Hosea does stand out for its appeal to wisdom: "Whoever is wise, let him discern these things. Whoever is discerning, let him know them. For the ways of Yahweh are straight, and the righteous walk in them, but those who are disloyal stumble in them" (Hos 14:9). Van Leeuwen (1993, 36-39) sees this final verse as evidence of the activity of a scribal redactor shaping the Book of the Twelve to function as a *theodicy and overlaying the prophetic material with a decidedly wisdom agenda. However, the appeal made in this verse is not wholly foreign to Hosea, who has referred to those without wisdom (Hos 13:13) and to those without understanding (Hos 4:14). As such, this closing appeal, although clearly couched in wisdom terms, reflects the prophet's own concerns and need not be read as evidence of later redaction.

3.2.4. Amos. Numerous features of Amos have prompted scholars to identify links with wisdom of one form or another: his use of sayings introduced by sequential cardinal numbers (Amos 1—2 [see Lindblom, 202; although, the connection of these with wisdom has been refuted by Soggin, 120-21]), theological emphases, special vocabulary and rhetorical devices (such as the "woe" sayings). Although these have prompted some to speculate about Amos's links to the sages, these do not make a compelling case for any close association, as J. Soggin (120) has noted: "[A] biblical author ... writes in his own style, and uses particular devices for expressing himself. In our case, these could incidentally have been borrowed from wisdom. But such a stylistic analogy does not turn a writing into a text dependent upon wisdom" (cf. Crenshaw 1969, 134; Whybray, 188).

3.2.5. Jonah, Habakkuk, Malachi. Any unequivocal connection with wisdom in the remaining Minor Prophets is difficult to establish. Some have suggested that Jonah and Habakkuk are in some way connected with wisdom because both are understood to address the problem of theodicy on some level (see Crenshaw 1998, 29; Gowan). Furthermore, some scholars suggest that Jonah is a *māšāl* ("proverb") [although, the Hebrew term describes a more diverse range of literary forms than does the English "proverb," including "parable"]) and as such is of a form more at home among the sages than the prophets (Landes; Crenshaw 1998, 29). The appearance of *disputations, particularly in Malachi, has prompted some to suggest wisdom influence also in that book. Yet the appeals to such features overlook the significant differences between the prophetic use of disputation and those found elsewhere (see Crenshaw 1969, 134). In the end, it is difficult to claim any more than a conscious borrowing of wisdom language and forms by the prophets, who turned these facets of wisdom to their own ends and employed them in the service of their own prophetic, not sagacious, message.

4. The Relationship Between Prophets and Sages.

Any discussion of the nature of the relationship between sages and prophets turns not only on the definition of wisdom and prophecy but also on the identity of the sages and prophets themselves. Whybray, for example, has argued that there never was, in ancient Israel, a class of specialists known as "the wise," and so the notion of conflict between prophets and the wise "falls to the ground" (Whybray, 193). Most scholars, however, think that Whybray goes too far in totally rejecting the existence of an identifiable class of wisdom professionals (e.g., Blenkinsopp, 11; Shields, 43-45).

There is evidence that both prophets and sages occupied positions in the *royal courts of Israel and other nations, testifying to their "specialist" status (e.g., 2 Sam 24:11; cf. 2 Sam 16:23). Aside from official court positions, there are also reports of prophets seeking to influence the decisions made by the king. As such, they would have found themselves competing with royal counselors whose advice would have been founded more on principles of wisdom than immediate divine revelation (see 2 Chron 25:14-24; and perhaps the ultimate example is 1 Kings 11:29-39, where the prophet Ahijah opposes Solomon himself).

In light of the competing interest of prophets and sages in the royal court, it is unsurprising to find indications throughout the OT of enmity between the two groups. W. McKane (1965, 48), for one, concluded that "there was constant tension between [prophets and sages] since the wise men did not permit themselves the luxury of religious or ethical assumptions, their task being to advise the king on matters of statecraft."

4.1. Prophets' Attitudes Toward the Sages. The prophets whose words have been recorded in the OT clearly did not have high regard for the sages. Van Leeuwen (1990, 306) notes that "the sages (hkmym) explicitly mentioned in the prophetic texts are almost always opponents of the prophets. Such wise men, as domestic or foreign royal courtiers, stand opposed to the prophets with regard to justice and political guidance. These sages are not false per se but only as they forget the human limits of wisdom (according to the criteria from Proverbs) and defy the word of Yahweh's messengers" (cf. Scott, 3; McKane 1995, 142; 1965, 65-91; Dunn, 7).

Although it has been common to identify this conflict as arising out of the distinction between "sacred" prophecy and "secular" wisdom (e.g., McKane 1965), the reality appears somewhat more nuanced than is reflected in this disjunction. Wisdom cannot be depicted in monolithic terms, and the criticisms leveled against the sages by the prophets reflect warnings already present within the book of Proverbs (see Van Leeuwen 1990, 300). As such, the prophets

are critical of those who deviate from the law, including priests and other prophets, not merely those who employed a form of wisdom that neglected God's revealed will. So their condemnation is not reserved merely for the royal advisors but rather is directed at all in leadership roles who would flout God's law.

4.1.1. Isaiah. Isaiah's antagonism toward the wise is readily apparent in many passages (e.g., Is 5:21; 19:11-12; 29:14; 40:20; 44:25; 47:10). Of these, Isaiah 19:11-12 is particularly significant because of the explicit link that it makes between wisdom and the counselors who functioned in the royal court: "The princes of Zoan are nothing but fools; the wisest advisors [y's] of Pharaoh give stupid advice ['ēṣâ]. How can you say to Pharaoh, 'I am one of the sages, a son of kings of old'? So where are your sages who can tell you and who know what General Yahweh has planned [y's] against Egypt?" Isaiah notes that the diplomatic plans ('ēṣâ [cf. Is 30:1-5; 31:1-3]) of the royal counselors consistently elevated human wisdom over Yahweh's plan, and so their plans would be thwarted (cf. Prov 19:21; 21:30-31; see Van Leeuwen 1990, 302). For Isaiah, true wisdom lies with God alone, and those who are truly wise derive their wisdom from him. This is apparent in the descriptions of the ideal coming ruler (Is 9:6; 11:1-9; cf. Is 33:6).

4.1.2. Jeremiah. One characteristic of Jeremiah is the frequent opposition that he faces as he seeks to fulfill his commission to speak God's word to God's people. This opposition sometimes comes from the wise or those described as advisors (see Jer 18:18-23 [particularly note v. 23, which refers to the plans of his opponents using the plural of 'ēṣâ]), although Jeremiah faced opposition from all quarters, including from other prophets. Jeremiah in turn announced God's opposition to the sages and advisors of his day, as can be seen in numerous passages (e.g., Jer 4:22; 8:8-9; 18:18; 49:7; 50:35; 51:57). As with Isaiah, the only wisdom viewed positively by Jeremiah was God's own wisdom (see Jer 10:12; 51:15).

4.1.3. Ezekiel. Ezekiel has less to say about sages or advisors than does either Isaiah or Jeremiah, but all that he says is negative. The most exalted wisdom language is reserved for the ruler of Tyre (Ezek 28), who stands in opposition to God and whose wisdom and other virtues are thus ultimately abhorrent. Aside from this, Ezekiel only makes brief mention of those who give evil advice: "The Spirit lifted me and brought me to the eastern gate of the House of Yahweh, which faces eastward. There were twenty-five men at the entrance to the gate, and among them were Ya'azaniah son of Azzur and Pelatiahu son of Benaiahu, leaders of the people. Then he said to me, 'Son of man, these are the men who plot iniquity and who advise [y'ṣ] evil advice ['ēṣâ] in this city'" (Ezek 11:1-2 [cf. Ezek 7:26]).

4.1.4. Summary. The prophets unequivocally condemn the sages and their wisdom for their departure from true wisdom, which was founded in obedience to God's law—a feature of wisdom reflected in Proverbs but absent from the sages, whom the prophets opposed. This condemnation, however, does not extend to all wisdom, for they recognized that true wisdom comes from God and is expressed in obedience to him. Furthermore, although the prophetic condemnation of the sages is unrelenting, it is not exclusively directed at the sages, for the prophets are also critical of priests and even other prophets.

4.2. Sages' Attitudes toward the Prophets. There appears to be little direct information regarding the attitude of the sages toward the prophets in the OT (see Scott, 3). Proverbs 29:18 could be a reference to the prophets, as it contains one of the few words frequently associated with prophecy (ḥāzôn ["vision"]) to be found in the Wisdom literature: "When there is no vision, the people are unchecked, but the one who keeps the law, he is happy." The parallelism of the aphorism links vision (ḥāzôn) with keeping the law (tôrâ) and reveals approval for both vision and obedience to the law. Proverbs 30:1; 31:1 (see 3.1.1 above) also use language more commonly associated with prophecy (and found nowhere else in the Wisdom literature of the OT). These passages, however, reveal little of the sages' attitude toward prophets or prophecy, except perhaps to indicate that some sages sought to attribute to their words an authority on par with those of the prophets.

In light of the scathing assessment of wisdom and the wise recorded in the prophets outlined above (and, indeed, throughout the remainder of the OT [see Shields, 7-20]), it might be expected that the Wisdom writings may reflect some enmity directed back toward the prophets. There is no sign of this in Proverbs, but there may be some echoes of such enmity among the

words of Qohelet recorded in Ecclesiastes.

Aside from reaching conclusions that placed Qohelet in direct contradiction to the prophets (e.g., Eccles 1:10; cf. Eccles 3:14-15, where he claims that there is nothing new, whereas the prophets consistently taught that God was about to do something new [cf. Is 42:9; 43:19]), some of his words may represent a direct attack on the prophets and other religious officials in ancient Israel. In Ecclesiastes 8:5-7 Qohelet says: "[Regarding the] appropriate time and a just outcome, a wise heart knows that for every matter there is an appropriate time and a just outcome, . . . that no one knows what will happen; and that when something will happen no one can tell." Here and elsewhere (cf. Eccles 3:22; 6:10-12) Qohelet affirms that no one knows what will take place in the future, whereas the prophets consistently announce the impending arrival of God's judgment or other events.

In Ecclesiastes 5:1-7 Qohelet condemns those who utter many words in God's house. Although the reference is somewhat ambiguous, it could be that those who spoke many words in God's house were either priests or prophets. Given that Qohelet also makes reference twice in this passage to dreams, and that dreams in the OT are frequently modes of divine revelation (e.g., Gen 20:3; Num 12:6; 1 Sam 28:6), it is quite possible that he directs his words at the prophets who expounded their visions in the precincts of the temple.

Finally, Qohelet may have sought to belittle prophecy by seeking to imply wisdom's superiority, at least in some ways. For example, prophets were known to announce the destruction of entire cities (e.g., Jer 26 [see McKane 1995, 144-45]; Mic 3:12). Qohelet, on the other hand, presents a parabolic tale of a small, relatively defenseless town faced with destruction that could have been saved had the rulers of that town listened to a poor sage (Eccles 9:14-15). Although prophets may have announced destruction, a sage could offer salvation in the face of overwhelming odds.

5. Conclusion.

True prophecy and wisdom are rooted in exposition and application of God's law to God's people. Prophecy proclaimed divine application, whereas wisdom appealed to the human intellect shaped and guided by the fear of Yahweh. In this form both shared the same authority and goal. Furthermore, wisdom's reach extended through all levels of society, such that prophets could readily employ the stylistic characteristics of wisdom when expounding their message. Yet the sages in Israel consistently departed from this ideal and found themselves in conflict with the prophets, who pronounced God's condemnation of the wise.

See also LAW; WISDOM AND APOCALYPTIC; WISDOM THEOLOGY.

BIBLIOGRAPHY. **J. K. Aitken**, "Apocalyptic, Revelation and Early Jewish Wisdom Literature," in *New Heaven and New Earth: Prophecy and the Millennium; Essays in Honor of Anthony Gelston*, ed. P. J. Harland and C. T. R. Hayward (VTSup 77; Leiden: E. J. Brill) 181-93; **J. Blenkinsopp**, *Sage, Priest, Prophet: Religious and Intellectual Leadership in Ancient Israel*, ed. D. A. Knight (LAI; Louisville: Westminster John Knox, 1995); **J. J. Collins**, "Proverbial Wisdom and the Yahwist Vision," *Semeia* 17 (1980) 1-17; **J. L. Crenshaw**, "Method in Determining Wisdom Influence in 'Historical' Literature," *JBL* 88 (1969) 129-42; idem, *Prophetic Conflict: Its Effect on Israelite Religion* (BZAW 124; New York: de Gruyter, 1971); idem, "The Concept of God in Old Testament Wisdom," in *In Search of Wisdom: Essays in Memory of John G. Gammie*, ed. L. G. Perdue et al. (Louisville: Westminster John Knox, 1993) 1-18; idem, *Old Testament Wisdom: An Introduction* (rev. ed.; Louisville: Westminster John Knox, 1998); **J. D. G. Dunn**, "Biblical Concepts of Revelation," in *Divine Revelation*, ed. P. Avis (Grand Rapids: Eerdmans, 1997) 1-22; **J. Fichtner**, "Isaiah among the Wise," in *Studies in Ancient Israelite Wisdom*, ed. J. L. Crenshaw (New York: KTAV, 1976) 429-38; **B. Gemser**, "The Spiritual Structure of Biblical Aphoristic Wisdom: A Review of Recent Standpoints and Theories," in *Studies in Ancient Israelite Wisdom*, ed. J. L. Crenshaw (New York: KTAV, 1976) 208-19; **D. Gowan**, "Habakkuk and Wisdom," *Perspective* 9 (1968) 157-66; **L. L. Grabbe**, *Priests, Prophets, Diviners, Sages: A Socio-Historical Study of Religious Specialists in Ancient Israel* (Valley Forge, PA: Trinity Press International, 1995); **J. Jenson**, *The Use of Tôrâ by Isaiah: His Debate with the Wisdom Tradition* (CBQ Monograph Series, vol. 3; Washington, DC: Catholic Biblical Association of America, 1973); **G. M. Landes**, "Jonah: A *Māšāl*?" in *Israelite Wisdom: Theological and Literary Essays in Honor of Samuel Terrien*, ed. J. G. Gammie et al. (Missoula, MT: Scholars Press for Union Theological Seminary, 1978) 137-58; **J. Lindblom**, "Wisdom in the Old Testament Prophets," in *Wisdom in Israel and in the Ancient Near East: Presented to Professor Harold Henry Rowley in Celebration of His Sixty-Fifth Birthday, 24 March 1955*, ed. M. Noth and D. W. Thomas (VTSup 3; Leiden: E. J. Brill, 1955) 192-204; **A. A. Macintosh**, "Hosea and the Wisdom Tradition: Dependence and Independence," in *Wisdom in Ancient Israel*, ed. J. Day, R. P. Gordon and H. G. M. Williamson (Cambridge University Press, 1995) 124-41; **W. McKane**, *Prophets and Wise Men* (SBT 44; London: SCM, 1965); idem, "Jeremiah and the Wise," in *Wisdom in Ancient Israel*, ed. J. Day, R. P. Gordon and H. G. M. Williamson (Cambridge University Press, 1995) 142-51; **R. E. Murphy**, "Assumptions and Problems in Old Testament Wisdom Research" *CBQ* 29 (1967) 407-18; **G. Ogden**, *Qoheleth* (RNBC; Sheffield: JSOT Press, 1987); **H. G. Reventlow**, "Participial Formulations: Lawsuit, Not Wisdom—A Study in Prophetic Language," in *Texts, Temples, and Traditions: A Tribute to Menahem Haran*, ed. M. V. Fox et al. (Winona Lake, IN: Eisenbrauns, 1996) 375-82; **M. Sato**, "Wisdom Statements in the Sphere of Prophecy," in *Gospel behind the Gospels: Current Studies on Q*, ed. R. A. Piper (NovTSup 75; Leiden: E. J. Brill; 1995); **R. B. Y. Scott**, "Priesthood, Prophecy, Wisdom, and the Knowledge of God," *JBL* 80 (1961) 1-15; **M. A. Shields**, *The End of Wisdom: A Reappraisal of the Historical and Canonical Function of Ecclesiastes* (Winona Lake, IN: Eisenbrauns, 2006); **N. H. Snaith**, *The Book of Job: Its Origin and Purpose* (London: SCM, 1968); **J. A. Soggin**, "Amos and Wisdom," in *Wisdom in Ancient Israel*, ed. J. Day et al. (Cambridge: Cambridge University Press, 1995) 119-23; **R. C. Van Leeuwen**, "The Sage in the Prophetic Literature" in *The Sage in Israel and the Ancient Near East*, ed. J. G. Gammie and L. G. Perdue (Winona Lake, IN: Eisenbrauns, 1990) 295-306; idem, "Scribal Wisdom and Theodicy in the Book of the Twelve," in *In Search of Wisdom: Essays in Memory of John G. Gammie*, ed. L. G. Perdue et al. (Louisville: Westminster John Knox, 1993) 31-49; **B. K. Waltke**, *The Book of Proverbs: Chapters 1-15* (NICOT; Grand Rapids: Eerdmans, 2004); **J. W. Whedbee**, *Isaiah and Wisdom* (Nashville: Abingdon, 1971); **R. N. Whybray**, "Prophecy and Wisdom," in *Israel's Prophetic Tradition: Essays in Honor of Peter R. Ackroyd*, ed. R. Coggins, A. Phillips and M. Knibb (Cambridge: Cambridge University Press, 1982) 181-99.

M. A. Shields

WISDOM OF SOLOMON

Wisdom of Solomon (Vulgate: Book of Wisdom) is an anonymous work written in Greek likely sometime between 100 BC and AD 50, most likely during a period of persecution. It is grouped among the Apocrypha for Protestants and Jews but is considered deuterocanonical for the Roman Catholic and Orthodox traditions. On the whole, the book may be thought of as a paean to following wisdom and a powerful theological treatise on God's faithfulness to his people, both past (especially concerning the exodus generation) and present. The corollary to this is the author's warnings against the dangers of religious syncretism, a case made, somewhat ironically, by employing concepts and modes of expression that were already the fruit of the influence of Greek thought on Judaism during these politically and religiously tumultuous times. The book stands as a testimony of the confluence of Judaism and Hellenism and the degree to which the Jewish faith was able to adapt to changing and pressing circumstances. It is also a wonderful demonstration of the developments in biblical interpretation during the Second Temple period, as many of the author's comments on the OT reflect interpretive practices of the time.

1. Date and Authorship
2. Language and Style
3. Unity and Structure
4. Theology
5. Pseudo-Solomon as Biblical Interpreter
6. Conclusion

1. Date and Authorship.

As with much ancient literature, it is very difficult to pin down with any degree of certainty when Wisdom of Solomon was written and by whom. A date somewhere between 100 BC and AD 50 is a broadly accepted opinion. Arguments from silence must be used with caution, but still it is important to point out that the cataclysmic event of the destruction of the Jerusalem temple in AD 70 is neither mentioned nor alluded to in the book. In fact, in Wisdom 3:14; 9:8 its existence is assumed. Hence, a date prior to AD 70 is favorable (for a summary of arguments, see Lillie 149-79). More precisely, a date during the reign of the Roman emperor Gaius Caligula (AD 37-41) commends itself (Winston, 20-25), since the book evinces a clear undercurrent of strong persecution (see Wis 2:12—5:14), which is consistent with Caligula's reign of terror. Also, the author's vocabulary consists of a significant number of words and usages, some associated with Middle Platonic philosophy, that are unattested elsewhere before the first century AD (Winston, 22-23). All of these factors point to a date of composition in the first half of the first century AD. In addition, the author's diatribe against Egypt, which preoccupies him in Wisdom 10—19, may suggests an Egyptian, perhaps Alexandrian, setting.

Although the original work can reasonably be dated to the early first century AD, the oldest manuscripts are the fourth-century AD Codex Vaticanus and Codex Sinaiticus. Although a fourth century AD date leaves a gap of about three hundred years between the original and the oldest copies, scholars are confident we have a solid and reliable text.

It is not known who wrote Wisdom of Solomon, but the author clearly wishes to identify himself with *Solomon. For example, the author's quest for wisdom in Wisdom 7:1-14 is reminiscent of Solomon's plea in 1 Kings 3:6-9. Also, the author's reference to God's command to build the temple (Wis 9:7-8) can only refer to the Solomon of Scripture. It is a well-attested Second Temple literary device to attribute one's work to a famous figure from the past or some heavenly being. This is not an act of deception but rather a recognized rhetorical vehicle for communicating an important message. Since the author of this work adopts a Solomonic persona, he is conventionally referred to as "Pseudo-Solomon" (Ps-Solomon).

2. Language and Style.

Church fathers and medieval rabbis considered the book to have been composed originally in Hebrew, since it was so closely associated with Solomon. This view has had some proponents in modern scholarship but has been limited to the more "Solomonic" portions of the book, chapters 1—9 or chapters 1—6 (Reider, 22-23). The more dominant view of the twentieth (and into the twenty-first) century, however, which has gained widespread, if not universal, acceptance is that the book was written originally in Greek by an Alexandrian Jew (see Grimm). Arguments for a Hebrew original are based on alleged evidence of Greek mistranslation of Hebrew words and phrases, presence of poetic *parallelism, Hebraic expressions, simple connection of clauses conjunctions, and other elements (Reider, 24-25; Winston, 14-15). These factors, however, do not support an argument for a Hebrew original. Rather, the Greek style of the book simply reflects the mixing of cultures and languages during the time in which Wisdom of Solomon was written, not to mention the influence of the LXX.

Moreover, there are numerous positive indications that Greek is the language of composition. D. Winston puts it succinctly. Agreeing with the judgment of C. Grimm, Winston (15) writes, "Thus the author of Wisd is quite capable of constructing sentences in true periodic style (12:27; 13:11-15), and his fondness for compound words is almost Aeschylean. His manner at times has the light touch of Greek lyric poetry (17:17-19; 2:6-9; 5:9-13), and occasionally his words fall into an iambic or hexameter rhythm."

Ps-Solomon's use of noted Greek style also includes such things as *chiasmus, sorites* (an argument chain in which each successive statement is connected to the one before it, reaching a climax in the final statement), *litotes* (expressing an affirmative by negating its opposite), *hyperbaton* (marked departure from standard syntax for emphasis or poetic effect) and *anaphora* (repetition at the beginning of successive lines). It should be noted that such features (and others; [see Winston, 15-16]) are not the exclusive property of high Greek style (e.g., the use of *sorites* in *m. 'Abot* 1:1; Rom 5:1-5 [see Fischel]). But when one considers in addition to these literary factors the presence of Greek philosophical terminology (see the comprehensive list in Winston, 16), there is little doubt that one is reading a work of Greek composition written by someone well acquainted with Greek thought and literary style. The Semitic markers of the book simply reflect the degree to which Hellenistic Greek was influenced by the LXX, as well as the fact that our author was a Jew well versed in his Greek Scripture.

3. Unity and Structure.
The tendency in nineteenth-century scholarship, reflecting general trends in the study of ancient literature, was to argue for multiple authorship of the book. A prominent reason for such a position is the apparent shift in topic and style from chapter 9 to chapter 10—that is, from the more proverbial chapters 1—9, with their focus on immortality, to chapters 10—19, with their historical retrospective and focus on idolatry. Unity of authorship, however, has been the dominant view of most twentieth-century scholars (see summaries in Lillie, 53-81; Reider, 15-22; Winston, 12-14). An important contribution to the discussion is that of J. Reese (122-52), who argues for the book's unity on the basis of words and phrases that appear in both chapters 10—19 and chapters 1—9, what he calls "flashbacks" (see also Ziener 95-96; Enns 160-68). These flashbacks not only suggest unity of authorship but also indicate the artful and sophisticated manner in which Ps-Solomon communicates his overarching theological message (see 4 below).

Concerning the structure of the book there is less agreement. The discussion essentially centers on whether the book should be considered a two- or three-part work, and where the final division of the book should be made. Advocates of a three-part scheme include P. Heinisch (Wis 1:1—5:23; 6:1—9:18; 10:1—19:22 [Heinisch, xiv; see also van Broekhoven, 87]) and D. Winston (Wis 1:1—6:21; 6:22—10:21; 11—19 [Winston, 9-12]). B. Metzger is one of many who have argued for a two-part division (Wis 1:1—9:18; 10:1—19:22 [Metzger, 68-73]). A. Wright (164-84) likewise has a two-part scheme but makes the division at Wisdom 11:2 rather than Wisdom 10:1. Whether or not one subdivides chapters 1—9, a clear break seems to present itself quite naturally at Wisdom 10:1, since it is here that Ps-Solomon begins his retelling of Israel's history, first from Adam to Joseph (Wis 10:1-14), and then the exodus and wilderness episodes (Wis 10:15—19:22). Although every scheme has its own inherent logic, Metzger's division seems the most straightforward.

4. Theology.
Recognizing a two-part division at Wisdom 10:1 helps highlight Ps-Solomon's overall theological message: as God saved his people in the past (Wis 10—19), he is now also saving his people today—that is, Ps-Solomon's readers who are enduring persecution (Wis 1—9). This theological theme is summarized in the last verse of the book: "For in every way, O Lord, you have exalted and glorified your people. At every time and in every place you have not neglected to help them" (Wis 19:22). To put it another way, Ps-Solomon encourages his readers in chapters 1—9 by way of recontextualizing the exodus.

What binds together the theological message of the book is the exodus theme. The author twice in the first part of the book refers to death as an "exodus" (Gk *exodos* [Wis 3:2; 7:6]). (The *exodos* in Wis 3:2 refers to the faithful who die at the hands of tormentors. In Wis 7:6 the word is used to describe the death of all people. See a similar use of the word to describe Jesus' impending death [NIV: "departure"] in Luke 9:31.) When we turn to chapters 10—19, Ps-Solomon begins to recount Wisdom's acts of deliverance throughout Israel's history, focusing in particular on Israel's exodus from Egypt and subsequent wilderness wandering. Since Ps-Solomon seems to be concerned to give encouragement to a people facing the very real possibility of death (Wis 3:1-9), one begins to see a possible motive behind not only his reference to death as an "exodus" in the opening chapters but also his choice of Israel's exodus experience as a central topic of conversation in chapters 10—19. Israel's historical exodus, its passage from "death to life," as it were, is presented by Ps-Solomon as the prime biblical portrait of what Wisdom is doing now in the lives of these persecuted Alexandrian Jews to whom he is writing: it is their own passage from death to life, their own exodus.

Related to this is the author's use of the Greek literary genre *logos protreptikos*, or exhortatory discourse. This hortatory emphasis is found throughout the book, not only explicitly in the repeated appeal to the reader to follow Wisdom but also in chapters 10—19, where Wisdom's protection of God's people is contrasted to the fate of the ungodly, Egypt and Canaan. The lessons from God's dealings with Israel in the past are applied to Ps-Solomon's readers. God deals with the ungodly and the godly now as he has in the past. The readers are invited to consider the faithfulness and justice of God then as a paradigm for his dealings with themselves.

In addition to this grand theological theme there are a number of other specific theological matters worth mentioning, especially since some elements bear witness to developments in Judaism vis-à-vis its intersection with Greek culture. Perhaps the most important of these is Ps-Solomon's view of immortality, which receives a focus essentially missing on the OT. For Ps-Solomon, the soul seems to have some sort of preexistence (e.g., Wis 8:19-20), although Winston (25-28) argues at length that this view

should be equated not with the Platonic doctrine but rather with that of Middle Platonism, which had already adjusted Plato's pessimistic view of the soul's fall in embodiment. The soul's immortality is hinted at in Wisdom 1:15 and is more explicit in Wisdom 2:23; 3:1-9; 15:1-3. It is the immortal soul, not the physical body, that makes its exodus journey from this life to the next. God's faithfulness to his people is seen not in helping them avoid death but rather in having them pass through triumphantly to the other side.

Another important theological element is the relationship between wisdom and *law. In biblical Wisdom literature the concept of wisdom is more restrictive than we see in Second Temple literature. Whereas, for example, in Sirach 24:19-29 we see the close identification of Wisdom's instruction and law, such an identification receives a passing reference in the OT (Deut 4:6). In a Hellenistic culture, however, where *sophia* and the *logos* were such important concepts, Jewish notions of wisdom were rethought to reflect these developments while at the same time demonstrating their superiority. Specifically, Israel's law was described as rational and philosophical; that is, Torah is Israel's book of philosophy and therefore is worthy of assent and devotion. Such an understanding of law probably was motivated by Jewish apologetic interests, where the narrow scope of Israelite faith could now become a player of more universal appeal in the marketplace of ideas.

As the relationship between law and wisdom is expanded in Wisdom of Solomon, so is the relationship between wisdom and redemptive history. To put it another way, Scripture, specifically Torah, has become the depository of wisdom. During the Second Temple period the role of wisdom, as G. Sheppard (6) puts it, has moved from "mundane advice to Wisdom's recital of her participation in Israel's traditions." In the biblical wisdom books we find scarcely a single, clear scriptural allusion. Starting with Ben Sira's "praise of famous men" in Sirach 44—50 (first half of the second century BC) and Wisdom of Solomon, however, we see books of wisdom that are steeped through and through with references to biblical figures and events. This fact does not make these two books any less a part of the wisdom genre; rather, it is the nature of "wisdom" that has shifted. Whereas the *sages of the Hebrew Bible were concerned with observing patterns in the created order as the basis for godly conduct—"exegeting the world," so to speak—Ben Sira and Ps-Solomon were concerned with observing the nature of God's activity by exegeting the Book; the sage's repertory of knowledge now includes Scripture. Wisdom of Solomon, therefore, with all its attention to Israel's ancient stories (see 5 below), is not a commentary on Scripture but rather is a search for wisdom, for God's overarching, eternal plan, on the basis of Scripture. God's eternal wisdom is to be learned from the Bible, for it is Scripture that is the depository of wisdom. Past events demonstrate the degree to which God's wisdom is connected to the trails of his people. And the heroes of Israel's past are appealed to as models of wise living. This may explain why the individuals in Wisdom 10:1-21 are anonymous: certainly their identities would be immediately known, but by refraining from addressing them by name, Ps-Solomon allows their characters to become democratized exemplars, either for wisdom or for foolishness, for the readers.

5. Pseudo-Solomon as Biblical Interpreter.

An area in which the study of Wisdom of Solomon will bear much fruit is Second Temple hermeneutics. Ps-Solomon's retelling of Israel's history in chapters 10-19 is characterized by a demonstrable familiarity with Jewish interpretive traditions of the time. More specifically, in his rehearsal of Israel's history from Adam to Joseph in Wisdom 10:1-14 (Enns, 17-34) and then his retelling of the exodus story in Wisdom 10:15-21; 19:1-9 (Enns, 43-134), Ps-Solomon's comments on these biblical episodes clearly move beyond the biblical data and incorporate interpretive traditions documented in some form in Jewish literature at various periods of time during the Second Temple period and beyond. This state of affairs suggests that when Wisdom of Solomon was written, there already existed an extensive and well-developed set of interpretive traditions concerning the Pentateuch in particular to which authors such as Ps-Solomon had access and which guided his exposition of Scripture. Fragments and reflections of such exegetical activity can be seen in other Second Temple works, particularly "retellings" or "expansions" of biblical narratives found in books such as Judith, *Sirach, *Jubilees, Book of Biblical Antiquities* and others. Ps-Solomon seems to have been thoroughly versed

in these ancient exegetical traditions.

Moreover, some of Ps-Solomon's comments are in fact among our earliest witnesses to interpretive traditions that are only documented more fully in later rabbinic works. The relevance that midrashic compilations might have for understanding Second Temple texts should not be ignored simply because the dates of these compilations are later than the first century AD. The brevity of Ps-Solomon's references to these traditions militates against any notion of his comments serving as the basis for the rabbinic versions; no line of direct dependence can be drawn. Rather, where we find later rabbinic texts to offer interpretations fuller than, yet similar to, those offered by Ps-Solomon, it is likely that both texts are independent witnesses to interpretive traditions that originated with neither. Moreover, the brevity of these allusions in Wisdom of Solomon indicates how firmly set they were by his time, long before the later rabbinic versions.

The nature of biblical interpretation for Ps-Solomon and his time can be illustrated in the following examples.

(1) In Wisdom 10:5 we read, "And she [Wisdom], when the nations in wicked agreement had been confounded, recognized the righteous man [Abraham] and kept him blameless before God." Here, the tower of Babel incident (confounding of the wicked) is closely connected to an incident in the life of Abraham (Enns, 18-24). In fact, the two are coterminous, even though, according to the narrative in Genesis, Abraham comes on the scene well after the events of the tower are recounted, and with no apparent indication that the two are in any way related. Ps-Solomon's brief allusion to such a scenario is told in much more detail by Pseudo-Philo in *Book of Biblical Antiquities* 6-7 (possibly first century AD), where Abraham is made a contemporary of the tower episode. As the story goes, Abraham and others resist the effort to build the tower (thus being kept "blameless"), are punished by imprisonment and threat of a fiery punishment, but are freed from their cells by an earthquake. It is very unlikely indeed that Pseudo-Philo's elaborate account is dependent on Ps-Solomon's brief allusion. In fact, the latter's brief allusion assumes a general knowledge of a story at least similar to the one we see in the roughly contemporary *Book of Biblical Antiquities*. It is very unlikely, therefore, that there is any de-

pendence of one text on the other; rather, both texts bear witness to an interpretive tradition that existed independent of these sources and was already well known by the time either text was produced.

(2) In Wisdom 10:17a Ps-Solomon reproduces an exegetical tradition that is fairly well attested in later sources (Enns, 53-55). This tradition concerns Exodus 12:35-36 (also Ex 3:21-22; 11:2-3), where the Israelites are said to plunder (Heb *nṣl;* Gk *skyleuō*) the Egyptians, and maintains that the plundering was justified, a payment for years of unpaid servitude. As Ps-Solomon puts it, "She rewarded holy ones for their labors." This interpretive tradition is quite early, appearing in texts that likely predate Wisdom of Solomon: *Jubilees* 48:18, Philo's *Life of Moses* 1.141, and Ezekiel the Tragedian's *Exagoge* 162-166. It seems that a number of ancient interpreters found the Exodus passage problematic (perhaps in the face of anti-Semitic polemics, where the Israelites were labeled thieves [see Winston, 220]) and sought to justify Israel's actions by claiming that it was "payment for services rendered." Ps-Solomon's passing comment in Wisdom 10:17a is another, and fairly straightforward, witness to this exegetical tradition. As with the previous example, this comment is brief and offered without explanation, suggesting again that it was well known by the time Ps-Solomon wrote.

(3) Ps-Solomon's comment in Wisdom 10:19b-20a is an unmistakable witness to a popular exegetical tradition. He says that the Red Sea "cast them [the Egyptians] up from the bottomless depth. Therefore the righteous plundered the ungodly." To say that the Egyptians were "cast up" from the sea is intended, at least in part, to explain how the Egyptians could be plainly seen on the shore by the Israelites (Ex 14:30) when elsewhere they are said to have "sunk like a stone" in the water (Ex 15:5). For the Egyptians to be seen on the shore in Exodus 14:30, early interpreters reasoned that the sea must have cast them up again after they had drowned (see also *b. Pesaḥ.* 118b; *b.* ʿ*Arak.* 15a; *Mek. Shirah* 9:7-15; *Midr. Ps.* 22:39-42). Many commentators on Wisdom of Solomon mention *Targum Pseudo-Jonathan* to Exodus 15:12 in this context, which tells of the sea and the land each refusing to accept the Egyptian dead lest God's wrath be upon them (see Reider, 139; Clarke, 72; Winston, 221; Grimm, 203; Goodrick, 327; Larcher, 2.644-45; Deane, 167). Only after God

swore to the land that there would be no repercussions did it accept the sea's dead and swallow them. This interpretation is meant to reconcile Exodus 15:12, which states that the earth swallowed them up, with Exodus 14:28; 15:1, 4, 5, 10, where the Egyptians were consigned to a watery grave. The order of events according to this tradition seems to be: (1) the sea swallowed the Egyptians (Ex 14:28; 15:1, 4, 5, 10); (2) the sea, not wanting to incur God's wrath, cast them up onto the shore for all to see (the result of which is described in Ex 14:30); (3) after being reassured that it would not be punished, the earth swallowed them up (Ex 15:12). Although Ps-Solomon certainly does have the Egyptian dead cast up onto the shore, visible for all to see, his explanation of the motive is different. The reason given for why they were cast up is not so that the Egyptians might be seen by the Israelites or to obviate God's punishment but rather so that the Egyptians might be plundered ("*therefore* the righteous plundered the ungodly"). The same motive is mentioned in *Mekhilta Beshallah* 7.94-108 (see also Josephus, *Ant.* 2.349). The *Mekhilta* comments on Exodus 14:30 and gives four reasons why Israel is said to see the Egyptians dead on the shore: (1) to prove to the Israelites that the Egyptians did not escape (see also Philo, *Mos.* 2.255; *Memar Marqah* 2:7); (2) to prove to the Egyptians that the Israelites had not drowned; (3) to enable the Israelites to take the spoil; (4) to enable the Israelites to reprove the enemy. Ps-Solomon's comment certainly seems in line with the third reason given by the *Mekhilta* (the other three reasons are not reflected at all in Wis 10:19b-20a).

These examples illustrate the degree to which Ps-Solomon's explanations of OT texts are very much in keeping with how others were addressing those very same issues. Having said this, however, we probably should not understand his comments as deliberate attempts to handle the OT creatively for the sake of it. We must bear in mind the context of persecution into which he wrote. Ps-Solomon was an Alexandrian Jew whose mind was particularly concerned to address the oppression of his people. Biblical exposition was, for him, no mere academic exercise. Yet, in his comments on Scripture he relates not simply Scripture to his readers but rather "Scripture plus." In light of such dire circumstances, it seems somewhat farfetched to think that Ps-Solomon incorporated these interpretive traditions merely to add some flourish or spice to his otherwise drab comments. Wisdom of Solomon was a literary product of some urgency, the purpose of which was to help the people, not to set them on an exegetical adventure. Ps-Solomon was concerned with nothing less than providing scriptural proof that God does indeed deliver his people: he has done it in the past, and he is sure to do it now. It is hard to escape the conclusion that for Ps-Solomon, the interpretive traditions that find their way into his exposition of Scripture actually represent the ways in which he and his readers understood the passages in question. He is, therefore, not so much an interpreter of Scripture; it is not he who is grappling directly with the exegetical particulars of the biblical text. This has already been done for him. Rather, his literary product is an ancient testimony to the state of biblical interpretation in his time and to the degree to which those interpretive traditions informed popular understanding of Scripture. By his time, these interpretive traditions had already become so intimately associated with the Bible that an Alexandrian Jew under dire circumstances was able to retell them succinctly and with conviction as nothing less than the Bible itself and, moreover, to expect to be understood by readers who certainly had other things on their minds than innovative interpretations of biblical narratives.

6. Conclusion.

Wisdom of Solomon is a vibrant example of the development of Jewish thought during the final decades of the Second Temple period. We see the confluence of Judaism on Hellenism in the book's theological and rhetorical dimensions. Ps-Solomon's comments on Scripture evince his deep connection with interpretive traditions well ensconced by his time and that will prove to be influential for the centuries to follow. It is a decidedly pastoral/theological work that seeks to bring comfort to a beleaguered people through the inevitable merging of an ancient faith and contemporary circumstances.

See also SIRACH, BOOK OF; WISDOM, GREEK; WISDOM THEOLOGY.

BIBLIOGRAPHY. **E. G. Clarke,** *The Wisdom of Solomon* (CBC; Cambridge: Cambridge University Press, 1973); **W. J. Deane,** *The Book of Wisdom* (Oxford: Clarendon Press, 1881); **P. Enns,** *Exodus Retold: Ancient Exegesis of the Departure from Egypt in Wis 10:15-21 and 19:1-9* (HSM 57; Atlanta: Scholars Press, 1997); **H. A. Fischel,** "The Uses of Sorites in the Tannaitic Period," *HUCA* 44 (1973) 119-51; **J. Geyer,** *The Wisdom of Solomon* (London: SCM, 1963); **A. T. S. Goodrick,** *The Book of Wisdom* (OCBC; New York: Macmillan, 1913); **C. L. W. Grimm,** *Kurzgefasstes exegetisches Handbuch zu den Apokryphen des Alten Testaments* (Leipzig: S. Hirzel, 1860); **P. Heinisch,** *Das Buch der Weisheit* (EHAT 24; Münster: Aschendorff, 1912); **W. H. Horbury,** "The Christian Use and the Jewish Origins of the Wisdom of Solomon," in *Wisdom in Ancient Israel: Essays in Honor of J. A. Emerton,* ed. J. Day, R. P. Gordon and H. G. M. Williamson (Cambridge: Cambridge University Press, 1996) 182-96; **M. Kolarcik,** *The Ambiguity of Death in the Book of Wisdom 1-6: A Study of Literary Structure and Interpretation* (AnBib 127; Rome: Biblical Institute Press, 1991); **C. Larcher,** *Le Livre de la Sagesse, ou, La Sagesse de Salomon* (3 vols.; EBib 1, 3, 5; Paris: Gabalda, 1983-1985); **B. J. Lillie,** "A History of the Scholarship on the Wisdom of Solomon from the Nineteenth Century to Our Time," (Ph.D. diss., Hebrew Union College, 1982); **B. M. Metzger,** *An Introduction to the Apocrypha* (New York: Oxford University Press, 1957); **H. L. Newman,** "The Influence of the Book of Wisdom on Early Christian Writings," *Crozer Quarterly* 8 (1931) 361-72; **J. M. Reese,** *Hellenistic Influence on the Book of Wisdom and Its Consequences* (AnBib 41; Rome: Biblical Institute Press, 1970); **J. Reider,** *The Book of Wisdom* (New York: Harper & Row, 1957); **J. Schaberg,** "Major Midrashic Traditions in Wisdom 1,1-6,25," *JSJ* 13 (1982) 75-101; **G. T. Sheppard,** *Wisdom as a Hermeneutical Construct: A Study in the Sapientializing of the Old Testament* (BZAW 151; Berlin: de Gruyter, 1980); **P. W. Skehan,** "The Literary Relationship of the Book of Wisdom to Earlier Wisdom Writings," in *Studies in Israelite Poetry and Wisdom* (CBQMS 1; Washington, DC: Catholic Biblical Association of America, 1971) 172-236; **H. van Broekhoven,** "Wisdom and World: The Functions of Wisdom Imagery in Sirach, Pseudo-Solomon and Colossians" (Ph.D. diss., Boston University, 1988); **W. Vogels,** "The God Who Creates Is the God Who Saves: The Book of Wisdom's Reversal of the Biblical Pattern," *EgT* 22 (1991) 315-35; **D. Winston,** *The Wisdom of Solomon* (AB 43; Garden City, NY: Doubleday, 1979); **A. G. Wright,** "The Structure of the Book of Wisdom," *Bib* 48 (1967) 165-84; **G. Ziener,** *Die theologische Begriff-*

ssprache im Buche der Weisheit (BBB 11; Bonn: Peter Hanstein, 1956).   P. Enns

WISDOM POEM

The wisdom poem is in many ways a self-explanatory genre category and as such may initially appear unworthy of individual consideration. As the name suggests, a wisdom poem is a poem (or *hymn) that is rooted in the theology, form and content of Israel's wisdom tradition. What more need be said? And yet the wisdom poem is far from common even within the Wisdom writings, its content and style are not easily defined, and there is much debate among commentators as to which passages may legitimately be described as "wisdom poems." Add to these peculiarities the fact that wisdom poems tend to appear at structurally significant points within their canonical books, and we can reasonably suggest that first impressions have been misleading, and that the wisdom poems are more worthy of consideration than their simple definition would indicate.

1. Wisdom
2. Genre of the Wisdom Poem
3. Content of the Wisdom Poem
4. Creation and Function of the Wisdom Poem
5. Wisdom Psalms
6. Conclusion

1. Wisdom.

Defining what constitutes "wisdom" is an issue addressed elsewhere in this volume (*see* Wisdom Theology), yet in order to understand the wisdom poem, we must make a passing glance at the nature of OT wisdom itself. A cursory overview of the secondary literature will bring up as many definitions of wisdom as there are commentators, yet there are certain recurring themes that inform our understanding of both wisdom as a whole and the wisdom poem in particular. Wisdom has been described as "the art of steering" (Zimmerli, 149). It is all about learning how to live well. "Wisdom in the OT is about how to negotiate life successfully in God's good but fallen world" (Bartholomew, 8). As part of this plan to teach the reader how to live life well, the wisdom authors and editors frequently highlight certain key themes. Chief among these leitmotifs are the consideration of the nature of wisdom itself, creation theology, the meaning of life, *suffering and the sovereignty of God. We

encounter such discussions frequently in the books of the Wisdom literature, and these themes speak to any definition of the wisdom poem because it appears that wisdom poems often focus on or make use of these points, especially wisdom and creation.

2. Genre of the Wisdom Poem.

A. Hill (262) observes, "The wisdom hymn in the Old Testament is an adaptation of the poetic hymn form for the purpose of showcasing one or more of the motifs basic to wisdom teaching." Poetry is the medium of Hebrew wisdom. *Job and *Proverbs are almost entirely written in poetic form (the exceptions to this rule being the narrative prologue and epilogue to Job, along with the prose titles and introductions found in Job and Proverbs). The "autobiographical" style of *Qohelet means that *Ecclesiastes is partly written using proverbial (thus poetic) style and partly written in a type of stylized prose. Therefore, there is a very real sense in which the vast majority of OT wisdom material is "poetic," so why could not each passage be described as a "wisdom poem"?

The wisdom poem is actually a genre category within a broader literary framework. The framework is "poetry," and despite the apparently common implications of its name, the "wisdom poem" is in fact a relatively rare occurrence within this broader form. This, of course, prompts a question: how do we distinguish the "wisdom poem" from the rest of the poetry that so dominates the Wisdom literature?

Wisdom poems, it seems, are best defined by their content and rhetorical function within a book or pericope rather than according to form categories (*see* Form Criticism; Rhetorical Criticism). Some authors see wisdom poems as a specific subset of the poetic "hymn" genre. The hymn in the OT is generally a song of praise directed toward Yahweh because of his character and/or his great works. Commonly it includes an introduction (which announces that praise is to be given and to whom it is addressed), the body (which lists the reasons for praise) and a concluding exhortation to praise. If we apply these characteristics strictly, it is likely that only one of the OT's wisdom poems could be described as a hymn (the praise of the "valiant woman" in Prov 31:10-31). However, although some wisdom poems bear some of the characteristics of the hymn, it seems wiser to suggest that these poems, much like the royal psalms (*see* Kingship Psalms), actually transcend strict genre categories and are better defined by their content and function rather than by their form. Defining wisdom poems as hymns unduly restricts the category and excludes certain passages that may otherwise naturally be considered wisdom poems.

3. Content of the Wisdom Poem.

Given that genre categories are of limited use in this case, we are forced to examine the content of texts in order to establish the definition of a wisdom poem. In order to do so, the best starting point seems to be the examination of those texts that are generally acknowledged to be wisdom poems. Almost universally within the secondary literature Job 28 and Proverbs 8 are taken to be wisdom poems. So, in defining the wisdom poem, it may be fruitful to examine the characteristics that these texts share.

Job 28 comes at the end of the book's speech cycle. Three cycles of debate begin in Job 3 and continue through to the end of Job 27. The debate is becoming increasingly heated, and by this point in the narrative it is certainly producing more heat than light. From the reader's perspective, both sides of the debate (Job, on the one hand, and his friends on the other) seem to be scoring points, and this can cause great confusion. The essence of the debate revolves around two repeated issues: (1) whether or not Job's *suffering is "innocent" suffering (the book's prologue assures the reader that it is); (2) whose wisdom, Job's or his friends', is true wisdom. Arguably, it is this second point that is most open to debate, and this is the very issue that is addressed in Job 28. This conclusion to the debate focuses, appropriately, on the inaccessibility of wisdom itself. In the three major sections of the poem the author focuses on humankind's determined quest for items of great value (gold, precious stones, etc. [Job 28:1-11]), the hiddenness of wisdom within the created order (Job 28:12-22) and, finally, the fact that true wisdom is to be found in God alone (Job 28:23-28). How this impacts the narrative depends largely upon who we understand the "speaker" of this poem to be. There is much debate about whether these words should be read as the words of Job himself or as an interlude from the book's narrator. If the former, then Job 28 probably should be seen as an affirmation of Job's wisdom over that of the

friends, with the conclusion in Job 28:28 echoing the description of Job in 1:1. If, however, the narrator speaks, then the reader is reminded that the wisdom of both sides to the debate is finite and limited because it is human; true wisdom is to be found in God alone, and the only proper human response is to fear God and to reject evil. Regardless of the identity of the speaker in this passage, Job 28 has a key rhetorical function within the book, and we will return to this question below.

Proverbs 8 bears a number of similarities to Job 28: clearly, the subject matter of this poem is wisdom itself, the poem is profoundly grounded in creation language and theology (Prov 8:22-31), and, again, the passage is of some significance in terms of its canonical placement within the book of Proverbs as a whole (Prov 8—9 concluding the introductory section with a strong focus on the essential need to choose wisdom). In Proverbs 8 wisdom is personified (*see* Personification), speaking with a human voice, addressing and calling the reader to follow a right worldview and lifestyle. As in Job 28, the great value of wisdom is emphasized (Prov 8:10-11, 18-19), as are the dual themes of the *fear of the Lord and the hatred of evil (Prov 8:13). So these two wisdom poems show a number of similarities in both language and content.

How, then, do the characteristics shared by Job 28 and Proverbs 8 inform our definition of the wisdom poem in general?

4. Creation and Function of the Wisdom Poem.

In order to define the wisdom poem more clearly, we need to consider how Job 28 and Proverbs 8 are differentiated from the passages that surround them. In terms of its canonical placement, Job 28 concludes the speech cycles and precedes Job's final complaint in Job 29—31. Yet it is clearly separate from each of these broader canonical sections. The tone of Job 28 is markedly different from the preceding (heated and repetitive) *disputation of the speech cycles and from the historical lament and ethical statement that follow. The wisdom poem is a lacuna, a pause, in the intensifying narrative. Its subject matter is central to the big picture of the book but not immediately linked to the surrounding passages. Rhetorically speaking, Job 28 gives the reader pause for thought: the confusion of the speech cycles is brought to a close with a meditation on the nature of wisdom that also serves as an important reminder prior to the resumption of debate in Job's final complaint and the Elihu speeches. So we see the consideration of wisdom, *creation theology and language, and rhetorical significance in Job 28.

Similarly, with regard to Proverbs 8, it is important to consider what sets this passage apart from the surrounding instructions of Proverbs 1—9. Once again the tone is different from the surrounding passages: the familial exhortation of the surrounding passages gives way to first-person speech, the subject matter is wisdom itself, and creation theology is used to paint this vivid representation of Hebrew wisdom.

So we see that, alongside the consideration of wisdom as the subject matter, difference in tone, the use of creation imagery, and rhetorical function are central to the identification of these passages as wisdom poems. These additional characteristics help to inform our understanding of the wisdom poem.

Job 3, for example, fulfills these characteristics. Often described as a "soliloquy," this poem gives insight into the full extent of Job's pain and his internal response. The subject matter of the poem is not wisdom itself but rather Job's deep longing for death in response to the pain of his fate, which sets it somewhat apart from the other wisdom poems that we have looked at, yet the other characteristics seem to be in place. The poem is rhetorically significant because it begins the poetic debate that follows the prose prologue. The tone of the poem is markedly different from the debate language that follows in the speech cycles, and the poem is dominated by creation (or, in this case, "decreation") language and imagery (Job 3:3-10). So should the fact that this poem does not focus its attention on wisdom per se exclude it from the category "wisdom poems"? I suggest that subject matter of wisdom poems should not be restricted to the topic of wisdom itself where other identifying features are present. As suggested above, the purpose of the wisdom poem is to showcase "one or more of the motifs basic to wisdom teaching." Clearly, Job 3 in its consideration of the meaning and purpose of life and existence does just that, thus bracketing the lengthy section of speech cycles that so dominates the book of Job with two wisdom poems. The opening bracket questions the nature of life, and the closing one the

nature of wisdom.

Similarly, Ecclesiastes 1:2-11 probably should be considered a wisdom poem. It too sets the tone for much of the ensuing autobiographical debate while remaining distinct from that narrative. It speaks with the language of creation theology (Eccles 1:4-7), and its introductory status provides a hermeneutical lens through which to read the succeeding sections of the book. Other likely candidates for the category of wisdom poem include Proverbs 31 and the song in praise of the "valiant woman"—a poem that brings the whole idea of walking in the ways of wisdom to life; Qohelet's contemplation of time in Ecclesiastes 3:1-8; the climax of the Elihu speeches in Job 37; and possibly a few other passages as well (e.g., the alphabetized poems of Prov 2:1-22; Job 9:2-24) (*see* Acrostic).

However, the wisdom poem is far from common as a genre category even within the Wisdom literature, and as readers, we should look in particular to the function of these poems within the broader book. They are designed to give the reader pause for thought. In modern terminology, the wisdom poem is a "time out" that encourages us to take stock regarding the key issues of life from a wisdom perspective.

5. Wisdom Psalms.

We should also give brief consideration to one other category of wisdom poem: the wisdom psalm. It is broadly acknowledged that, as with the wisdom poems, the number of wisdom psalms is actually quite few. There is no universal agreement as to the extent of this category, but the most frequently cited examples include Psalms 1; 25; 34; 37; 49; 73; 111; 112; 128. Basically, the wisdom psalms are those poems that focus on the key ideas of wisdom theology and adopt the language of wisdom (e.g., creation, the two ways). R. Whybray (158) suggests, "It would be justifiable to call a psalm a 'wisdom psalm' only if its resemblance to some part of the Old Testament wisdom books—Proverbs, Job or Ecclesiastes—were so close as to be undeniable." So the wisdom psalms echo the style and content of the wisdom poems, but they form individual compositions rather than part of a broader narrative. It is interesting to note that in recent years scholars have frequently pointed out that the wisdom psalms play a significant role in shaping the readers understanding of the book of Psalms as a whole, giving it a more instructional rather than ceremonial final form (*see* Editorial Criticism). Just as the wisdom poems influence our reading of their respective books, so the wisdom psalms shape our overall understanding of the Psalter (McCann, 650).

6. Conclusion.

The wisdom poem is a genre category that is much more significant than the frequency of its occurrence would suggest. Wisdom poems focus on the key themes of wisdom theology, often adopting creation imagery to do so, and they are frequently used by authors/editors to shape our reading of the book in which they occur. Equally, the wisdom psalms are key to the contextual reading of the psalms in the Psalter.

See also FORM CRITICISM; HYMNS.

BIBLIOGRAPHY. **C. G. Bartholomew,** *Reading Proverbs with Integrity* (Cambridge: Grove Books, 2001); **R. J. Clifford,** *The Wisdom Literature* (IBT; Nashville: Abingdon, 1998); **J. H. Eaton,** *Job* (OTG; Sheffield: Sheffield Academic Press, 1996); **A. E. Hill,** "Non-Proverbial Wisdom," in *Cracking Old Testament Codes: A Guide to Interpreting the Literary Genres of the Old Testament* (Nashville: Broadman & Holman, 1995) 255-80; **J. C. McCann,** "The Book of Psalms," *NIB* 4.639-1280; **R. E. Murphy,** *Wisdom Literature: Job, Proverbs, Ruth, Canticles, Ecclesiastes and Esther* (FOTL 13; Grand Rapids: Eerdmans, 1981); **G. T. Sheppard,** *Wisdom as a Hermeneutical Construct: A Study in Sapientializing of the Old Testament* (BZAW 151; Berlin: de Gruyter, 1980); **R. C. Van Leeuwen,** "The Book of Proverbs," *NIB* 5.17-264; **B. K. Waltke,** *The Book of Proverbs: Chapters 1-15* (NICOT; Grand Rapids, Eerdmans, 2004); **R. N. Whybray,** "The Wisdom Psalms," in *Wisdom in Ancient Israel: Essays in Honour of J. A. Emerton,* ed. J. Day, R. P. Gordon and H. G. M. Williamson (Cambridge: Cambridge University Press, 1995) 152-60; **G. H. Wilson,** "The Shape of the Book of Psalms," *Int* 46 (1992) 129-41; **W. Zimmerli,** "The Place and Limit of Wisdom in the Framework of Old Testament Theology," *SJT* 17 (1964) 146-58. J. A. Grant

WISDOM PSALMS. *See* PSALMS 1: BOOK OF; WISDOM POEM.

WISDOM SOURCES

Wisdom includes both the forms of the literature that customarily are identified as Wisdom literature and the content of that literature. The question of sources is a sociological, literary and historical one. Sociologically, the sources of Wisdom literature have been argued as originating in tribal, village and family life, on the one hand, and in courts, royalty and scribal circles, on the other hand. As literary sources, the search for existing antecedents has led to Mesopotamian, Egyptian, Greek and, more recently, West Semitic and Hittite parallels. Related to this is the historical question of the origins of literary forms and content. Behind both lies the question of the forms and their content. Finally, and related directly to the identification of the sources of the content of Wisdom literature, is the question of what is distinctive in Israelite Wisdom literature; that is, what appears in OT Wisdom literature that is not found elsewhere in sources outside the Bible.

1. Social Sources
2. Egyptian and Mesopotamian Sources
3. West Semitic Sources
4. Theological Sources

1. Social Sources.

Wisdom forms include proverbs, riddles, allegories, teaching or didactic narratives, dialogues, hymns and noun lists. All but the last appear in the OT. All may have potential origins in the two traditional places of societal origin: either the oral culture of the village and the family or the written world of the scribal schools and the court. Because the oral culture more easily remembers wisdom material that is pithy and brief, individual proverbs and riddles may have their origins in the villages and their family life. Such wisdom was aimed at informing people of the single goal of the mastering of life. In this respect, the proverbs of Proverbs 10:1—22:16 and Proverbs 25—29 might provide examples of agrarian wisdom (Whybray). Longer wisdom materials may reflect a larger amount of work devoted to their composition, and this naturally points toward a scribal context for their production.

However, these observations are generalizations. If literacy was more widespread than is sometimes supposed, then longer compositions could easily originate in any part of the society. The presence of an abecedary in the eleventh century BC village of Izbet Sartah suggests that education in reading and writing took place in such villages (*see* Scribes). This village, identified by some with Ebenezer of 1 Samuel 4, shares a similar culture with the hill country villages that are generally recognized as Israelite. Therefore, the abecedary was likely used by an Israelite villager who was writing and reading the alphabet. If this could happen in one village in Israel, it could happen in every village. There is nothing to suggest the absence of reading and writing from very early in the nation's history. In Judges 8:14 a young citizen of Succoth, east of the Jordan, is able to write the names of the leaders of his town. A tenth-century BC abecedary was discovered at Tel Zayit, southwest of Jerusalem (Hess 2006). The extrabiblical inscriptions, in addition to those already mentioned, support the presence of some ability to read and write in ancient Israel. In every century, from the twelfth century BC onward, the presence of writing in rural and urban environments and in every major region of Israel attests to the widespread use of this medium of communication. Before the fall of Jerusalem in 586 BC the soldier who authored Lachish ostracon 3 boasts that he reads every letter that comes to him and never receives assistance. If writing was widespread, though not necessarily a skill possessed by a majority of the citizens of Israel, then the production of longer pieces of literary and wisdom works would be possible from any area of society. Of course, such works would have been written on papyrus or animal skin and have not survived.

Court wisdom expressed the power of the elite of the society. It reflected an international context, which by the postexilic period would become available to the general public (Clements). Scribal and royal sources for Wisdom literature are well attested in the Bible. Most often major pieces of literature are associated with *Solomon, directly so for the collection of proverbs (Prov 1:1), where its connection with Solomon is reaffirmed in Proverbs 10:1; 25:1. The attestation is made indirectly for Ecclesiastes 1:1 and Song of Songs 1:1. To the teacher is attributed the composition of many proverbs (Eccles 12:9), which is reminiscent of the ascription to Solomon of a thousand proverbs and even more songs. The biblical connection of Solomon is best known from early in his reign, where he received wisdom as a divine gift, according to 1 Kings (1 Kings 3:9-14). That book goes on to describe his wise decision in the case of the two prostitutes and the disputed child (1 Kings 3:16-

27). 1 Kings 3:28 describes how all Israel heard this and held the king in awe. The Queen of Sheba came from a great distance and praised the king for greater wisdom than she had previously heard (1 Kings 10:1-9; 2 Chron 9:1-9).

Royal origins outside of Solomon's court are also suggested, especially in the book of *Proverbs, an explicitly composite book. Thus Proverbs 25:1 attests to the work of scribes in Hezekiah's court c. 700 BC. They were responsible for collecting Solomonic proverbs in this section, Proverbs 25—29. Although it may be argued that royal proverbs exist in other tribal cultures where they have originated outside the court in the popular culture (Golka), an origin in the king's court is suggested in this introductory verse and is not difficult to imagine. Proverbs 31 begins with the sayings of a King *Lemuel that his mother taught him (Prov 31:1-9). If this is the correct interpretation of the heading, it implies not only a royal source but also one that apparently is not Israelite (or otherwise known). Professional *sages were known from Babylon (Dan 2:12 and passim), Edom (Obad 1:8) and other nations (Jer 10:7). Late in the monarchy Jeremiah knows of Judean sages and lists them with priests and prophets in his indictment (Jer 18:18). By the second century BC Ben Sira (Sir 38:24—39:11) is able to identify the role of the sage as an occupation among the upper classes.

Related to questions of the social sources of wisdom is the role of the family, possibly the royal family but just as likely nonroyal families. Although it is true that references to father-son relationships in the Wisdom literature may correspond to teacher-student relationships in scribal schools, there is little evidence for such schools in preexilic literature (Weeks). Rather, the combination of references to father and mother at the beginning of Proverbs (Prov 1:8) and elsewhere, as well as allusions to a grandfather (Prov 4:1-9), suggest that the primary source of wisdom instruction was envisioned as in the home (Estes; Waltke and Diewert, 308-9). This source as an origin is attested for covenant instruction in general (Deut 6:4-9), although the role of priests seems to play an important part for this sort of teaching in some circles (Lev 10:11).

2. Egyptian and Mesopotamian Sources.

Much of the biblical Wisdom literature has contemporary and earlier parallels in the major civilizations of the ancient Near East. Proverbs are universal. Collections occur in nearby major civilizations with written records. Much of this wisdom is shared between nations. In particular, many have observed the similarity in content between the Egyptian Instruction of Amen-em-opet and Proverbs 22:17—24:22. Although other collections exist from Egyptian sources, this collection is often regarded as a high point in the Egyptian wisdom literature. The extant manuscripts date from a later period, but the text is assigned to the Ramesside period, the thirteenth and twelfth centuries BC. This would predate any of the biblical material that would itself be dated during the Israelite monarchy, but certainty is unlikely. The introduction of the collection describes the purpose to be to establish right relationships, to advise regarding conduct with authorities, to know how to answer and to find prosperity. This is reminiscent of the opening paragraphs of the biblical collection. There too the emphasis is on understanding how to get along in the world and to have success. Nevertheless, the closest parallels remain with Proverbs 22—24. The first three lines of the Egyptian text's first chapter of proverbs have been translated thus (J. Wilson, *ANET*, 421):

Give thy ears, hear what is said,
Give thy heart to understand them.
To put them in thy heart is worth while.

This may be compared with Proverbs 22:17-18a (NIV):

Pay attention and listen to the sayings of the wise;
apply your heart to what I teach,
for it is pleasing when you keep them in your heart.

Other parts of the book do not have such close connections, although parallels with individual proverbs may exist.

On a larger level of formal sources, K. Kitchen (1977; 1998; 2003, 135-36) attempts to relate the form through the comparison of dozens of examples of proverbial instructional literature. He counts some forty such known works, of which more than half are Egyptian. A formal study reveals distinctions between Egyptian collections of the second and first millennia BC. The second-millennium BC forms begin with a short prologue. The style either is exhortational or states an aim (except for the Instruction of Ptahhotep). The dominant form of expression is *parallelism. In the first-millennium BC proverbial collections the Egyptian form changes. Long prologues, rather than short ones, introduce the texts. Rather than exhortations, the presentation is biographical. In place of parallelism the dominant forms are single-line epigrams and short essays. The biblical collection of Proverbs 1—24 begins with a long prologue full of exhortations. Its dominant, indeed virtually only, form is parallelism. Thus it resembles the first-millennium BC instructions in terms of its long prologue. However, its exhortative style and parallel forms make it look like a second-millennium BC composition. Kitchen suggests that this mixture indicates a transitional form, between the second and first millennia BC. He notes that there is no evidence of a prologue ever having been added to an existing composition. Thus the hybrid form agrees with its origins in the period between the millennia. On the other hand, Proverbs 25—29 uses parallelism less and thus appears more like the first-millennium BC instruction texts. Further, Proverbs 1:1 ascribes authorship or at least editorial activity to Solomon. Other wisdom collections of the ancient Near East also contain the names of their authors (Kitchen 1998). The formal sources of the book of Proverbs may thus lie as early as the beginning of the first millennium BC.

The book of *Job partakes of *disputation literature and of literary material related to pious sufferers. The earlier Sumerian texts include the Man and His God composition (*COS* 1.179:573-75), in which a righteous sufferer remains faithful to his god until he is ultimately restored to his former life. Sumerian disputation literature includes The Disputation between Bird and Fish (*COS* 1.182:581-84), perhaps the best representation of this form of literature. It is presented here and elsewhere in the context of a fable.

The earliest Akkadian example of the study of God's ways in the midst of a troubled world is the Dialogue between a Man and His God (*COS* 1.151:485). It considers illness as the context for *suffering. Like the Man and His God composition, it concludes with a restoration. The poem that begins "I Will Praise the Lord of Wisdom" (*COS* 1.153:486-92) explores the questions of *theodicy in a more detailed manner. The Babylonian Theodicy (*COS* 1.154:492-95) represents the Akkadian exploration of this theme in the form of a dialogue, closest to the book of Job. The friend of the sufferer counsels the inexplicable nature of the divine. However, the sufferer concludes with a prayer for the divine Shamash to act as a shepherd. Thus the friend's words are more sympathetic to the sufferer than those of Job's friends. However, unlike with Job, the suffering is not ended. Indeed, the deities come in for their share of blame for the state of the sufferer and for favoring the rich among humanity. Note the final counsels of the friend and the sufferer (R. Biggs, *ANET*, 604):

Friend

"Narru, king of the gods, who created
    mankind,
And majestic Zulummar, who pinched off the
    clay for them,
And goddess Mami, the queen who
    fashioned them,
Gave twisted speech to the human race.
With lies, and not truth, they endowed them
    forever.
Solemnly they speak favorably of a rich man,
'He is a king,' they say, 'riches should be his,'
But they treat a poor man like a thief,
They have only bad to say of him and
    plot his murder,
Making him suffer every evil like a criminal,
    because he has no . . .
Terrifyingly they bring him to his end, and
    extinguish him like glowing coals."

Sufferer

"You are kind, my friend; behold my trouble,
Help me; look on my distress; know it.
I, though humble, wise, and a suppliant,
Have not seen help or aid even for
    a moment.
I have gone about the square of my city
    unobtrusively,
My voice was not raised, my speech was kept
    low.
I did not raise my head, but looked at the
    ground,
I did not worship even as a slave in the
    company of my associates.
May the god who has abandoned me give
    help,
May the goddess who has [forsaken me]
    show mercy,
The shepherd, the sun of the people,

pastures (his flock) as a god should."

The Dialogue of Pessimism (*COS* 1.155:495-96) is also a discussion, in this case between a master and his slave. A similar structure governs each of the ten sections, in which the master proposes one course of action and then argues the merits of the contrary activity. The ten sections themselves may be organized in five groups of two each, so that there are opposing themes. Neither the early forms of Old Babylonian origins nor the later Neo-Assyrian texts achieved the lengthy discussion and dramatic presentation of the book of Job. Nevertheless, the Mesopotamian antecedents and sources provide essential background for basic questions and dialogic discussion of the biblical book.

The sources behind the book of *Ecclesiastes have been a matter of much discussion. S. de Jong suggests that this work should be situated later in the Hellenistic world of Judaism. It criticized the ambitious spirit of Hellenistic life and encouraged traditional Israelite values of modesty and practical wisdom. On the basis of Hellenistic usages of various vocabulary (Rudman) and the presence of a few phrases that are manifest translations from Greek to Hebrew (Buhlmann), some suggest a Hellenistic date with Greek philosophical sources. C. Seow (1996; 1997) argues for a Persian period origin on the basis of Aramaisms and the avoidance of Greek expressions. Others, however, find earlier sources in the ancient Near Eastern world. In particular, T. Longman (1998, 18-20) suggests the genre of the royal testament. In Egypt pharaohs or their viziers collected insights for aspiring young rulers whom they hoped to steer along paths of wisdom. Such instructions could also be expressed in the form of a sage who reviews his search for meaning in life. There is a well-attested genre in the ancient Near East, royal fictional *autobiography. A good example of royal autobiography in the West Semitic world is the fifteenth-century BC story of Idrimi of Alalakh. His story of gaining back his throne is recorded on his statue uncovered at the ancient site. Even closer are the Cuthean Legend of Naram-Sin, the Sin of Sargon, and the Adad-guppi autobiography. Like the book of Ecclesiastes, these conclude with instruction (Longman 1991, 97-129).

However, Ecclesiastes reads less like a biography and more like a series of personal reflections on the meaning and significance of life. In the view of most who study the book, it represents a more pessimistic view of life and the ability to find meaning and success than does the book of Proverbs. Its form as a collection of pithy observations on these fundamental questions brings it closer to proverbial collections than to customary biographical narratives. The Dialogue of Pessimism compares to Ecclesiastes in its pessimism and its concluding counsel of despair (Lambert 1960, 149):

> "Who is so tall as to ascend to the heavens?
> Who is so broad as to compass the under
>   world?"
> "No, slave, I will kill you and send you first."
> "And my master would certainly not outlive
> me by even three days."

The Dialogue of Pessimism, however, is a dialogue, whereas Ecclesiastes is not. A closer example may be the Egyptian Instruction of Any (*COS* 1.46:110-15), a text that likely dates from the New Kingdom, centuries before the Israelite monarchy. Unlike Ecclesiastes, it is written by someone who claims to be a minor official rather than a king. Further, the general presentation of the instruction text is positive with advice from a father to a son. However, at the conclusion the son does not simply accept the advice of the father, as the traditional presentation of such advice would suggest. There are two interpretations of what the son does. One suggests that he humbly confesses his inability to measure up to the demands of his father. Following this approach, the son would affirm the father's expression of traditional wisdom. Another perspective understands the son to take a negative view of following the advice. In effect, he rejects his father's teaching. Although the father has the last word with a set of observations where he criticizes his son, the son's negative view of traditional wisdom would allow for a comparison with the overall negative view of Ecclesiastes.

*Song of Songs represents erotic love poetry. Its role as wisdom literature is suggested by its connection to Solomon in the opening title (Song 1:1). Its origins lie with love poetry. In many cases there are parallels with Egyptian love poetry, although this genre is found among Mesopotamian texts as well (*see* Wasf). However, the Egyptian material bears a closer resemblance in its subtlety of expression and in its use of related metaphors. Nevertheless, many of the parallels are not limited to Song of Songs and Egyptian literature but rather are part of the universal nature of love poetry. J. White (162) observes,

> Not only does the Song's rustic imagery betray a close association with the ways of expressing love in Egypt, but the commonality of love-language denotes archetypal vehicles through which human, sexual love was celebrated in the ancient world. Thus, it is not surprising that specific topoi be common to both Hebrew and Egyptian love literature. The fragrances, sight of the love partners, embracing and kissing, friends and enemies of the lovers, and even specific parallels (scent of garments, the mother figure, love under the trees, gazelles, etc.) denote the Song's participation in the world of human love expression.

Thus there is a common origin to love poetry, biblical or otherwise. What is distinctive about Song of Songs is its length, much greater than other extant love poems. However, the same is true of the book of Job in comparison with other disputation literature. In itself, such length does not prove a composite origin, deriving from discrete poems that were joined together. After all, the genre of love poetry certainly produced many more oral compositions than the written ones that are extant. Indeed, this is the only example of erotic love poetry in the West Semitic world from the biblical era. This raises the question of West Semitic literature as a wisdom source.

3. West Semitic Sources.
Although the sources of wisdom literature have traditionally been located in the great civilizations along the Nile, Tigris and Euphrates Rivers, sources within the West Semitic world have demonstrated the existence of wisdom literature and literary forms.

Perhaps the best-known pre-Hellenistic wisdom source outside the Bible is *Ahiqar*. This collection of Aramaic proverbs combines both narrative and proverbs into a single composition in all extant copies. The earliest version occurs at Elephantine at the site of a Jewish mercenary colony in Upper Egypt in the late fifth century BC. Since the narrative mentions the king Esarhaddon from the early seventh century BC, the text as it occurs in existing versions must date after that time. Although some argue that proverbs predate this period, this is disputed, and it remains likely that in large measure *Ahiqar* dates later than the biblical collection in the book of Proverbs. Furthermore, there is extant evidence of written proverbs in Palestine before the arrival of Israel. Thus Labaya, leader of Shechem, writes to the pharaoh an Amarna letter from the mid-fourteenth century BC and uses what appears to be a proverb about ants as a means to justify his retaliatory measures against his enemies (Hess 1993, 95-96): "When an ant is swatted, does it not fight back, and bite the hand of the man who swats it?" Ants are sources for proverbial wisdom in Proverbs 6:6; 30:25.

A Sufferer's Salvation (*COS* 1.152:486) represents an exploration of theodicy from Ugarit. It describes a sufferer who experienced some form of illness that no omen, divination or sage's wisdom could resolve. However, the deity Marduk enabled the author to recover. This is described as the return of life from the dead. Praise of Marduk as personal god and goddess follows. However, Marduk is credited with both punishment and salvation. In a series of comparisons reminiscent of Ecclesiastes 3 the writer outlines how "he struck me and showed me mercy," "he scattered me and gathered me," and so on. Thus the deity is as responsible for the bad as for the good. Although the text does consider theodicy, its content and the effect of its style are closer to a psalm of praise for the salvation of the psalmist from illness and death.

Of even greater interest from the West Semitic world, and in copies only from the Late Bronze Age (c. 1550-1200 BC), is the wisdom instruction given to *Šūpē-amēlī*. The texts of this form occur only in the West Semitic and nearby Hittite world and are found there in three locations: Emar, Ugarit and the Hittite capital of Hattusas. M. Dietrich (1991; 1993) presents an edition incorporating these three texts. It predates the biblical Wisdom literature that it most closely parallels, Proverbs and Ecclesiastes. *Šūpē-amēlī* takes the form of a conversation between a father and his son. Like the wisdom of Proverbs, the father's exhortations, which dominate the collection, encourage success in life. Many specific proverbs have direct parallels with those in the biblical collections as well as in other wisdom collections from the ancient Near East. Consider the following chosen from throughout the collection (Dietrich 1993, 58-61):

> My son, with evil doers do not plunder an equal for your own gain!
> . . . with a bully you should not wish to fight
> . . . abandon bitterness of expression, do not admit (it) either!
> . . . Give no-one advice for a price . . .

The response of the son provides a viewpoint different from that of the father. Note the opening statements (Dietrich 1993, 61):

> The word of my father, the counsellor have I silently heard, now I shall say a word to you!
> We are doves, birds that sqawk—the most restless of powerful oxen, fierce sky-oxen—, Mules are we!
> My father, you have built a house: You have made the gate high,
> 60 ells is the breadth of the storehouse— what have you taken with you?

The impression is completely different. The pessimism expressed by the son is reminiscent of the spirit that many find in the main body of Ecclesiastes (Hurowitz 2007). Just as the positive exhortations of the father are followed by the dubious pessimism of the son that questions the father's values, so the rules for success in the longer collection of the book of Proverbs are followed by the shorter challenge to this wisdom in the book of Ecclesiastes. Unlike most of the other West Semitic wisdom literature outside the Bible, wisdom is criticized here. The forms resemble Proverbs 22:17—24:22; 28—31. The dialogue is between the father and the son. Like the view of the book of Proverbs, the father encourages success in life. Like Ecclesiastes, the son challenges materialistic values. Thus this book provides a unique antecedent to Ecclesiastes (and Ps 49) as well as Proverbs. It was widespread in the West Semitic world several centuries before Solomon's traditional dates. This remarkable example of West Semitic wisdom literature not only predates the biblical material but also demonstrates how forms of critique of the popular wisdom tradition appeared already in written form a thousand years before the Hellenistic era. Thus the origins of a type of literature such as Ecclesiastes may be identified as native to the West Semitic world in the same manner as the origins of Proverbs.

4. Theological Sources.

The wisdom literature of the Bible participates in forms and in some specific content with the wisdom literature of the West Semitic world and of the greater ancient Near East. However, the canonical text of the OT provides a distinctive source for important theological distinctives that do not occur elsewhere. This is not to suggest that the mere presence of a deity in the Wisdom literature is somehow unique. Rather, the presence of the divine can be found in many wisdom sources. No culture of which the biblical literature shares common aspects was without a significant religious element. Indeed, the presence of one or more deities is customarily acknowledged and referenced in the Wisdom literature. There is little evidence for truly secular wisdom literature in the ancient Near East. Nevertheless, there remain distinctive elements.

The most distinctive element in the biblical Wisdom literature that does not occur elsewhere is the emphasis on the fear of Yahweh (yir'at yhwh) (see Fear of the Lord). Although other ancient Near Eastern (including West Semitic) sources do stress the importance of reverence and honor before the divine, nowhere else does this theme occupy such a prominent position so consistently and in so large a body of wisdom literature. Of the twenty-one times that the expression occurs, twenty times it does so in poetry (2 Chron 19:9 being the sole exception). Elsewhere it occurs three times in Isaiah (Is 11:2, 3; 33:6) three time in *Psalms (Ps 19:9; 34:11; 111:10), and fourteen times, all the remaining occurrences, in Proverbs. All the appearances in Isaiah are explicitly associated with wisdom and understanding. All the occurrences in Psalms are in wisdom psalms. Indeed, at Psalm 111:10 there appears the expression "The fear of the LORD is the beginning of wisdom." This is similar to Proverbs 1:7, where "The fear of the LORD is the beginning of knowledge." This is a key theme for the entire book, positioned at the beginning to suggest its importance. Proverbs 9:10 says something similar: "The fear of the LORD is the beginning of wisdom." Elsewhere in the book it is associated with long life (Prov 10:27), a secure fortress (Prov 14:26), a fountain of life (Prov 14:27), learning wisdom (Prov 15:33),

avoiding evil (Prov 16:6), life and rest (Prov 19:23) and wealth and honor (Prov 22:4). The repeated occurrences of this theme of fear toward God tie the book together as a distinctive whole. They also may explain why the writer can be so optimistic. The author believes that the placement of all wisdom into the context of the fear of Yahweh will truly bring about prosperity and success. This is different from other forms of ancient Near Eastern wisdom literature. Although the fear of the gods is counseled elsewhere, it does not provide the security for the disciple nor does it function as a summarizing theme for the whole piece. The admonition appears also in the heart of the book of Job. In Job 28, Job's great poem on the search for and value of wisdom, we read, "The fear of the LORD [yir'at 'adōnay], that is wisdom; and to shun evil is understanding" (Job 28:28). In Job too this theme stands at the center of the book and provides a key to wisdom. This is true despite the role of Job as protest literature against the traditional wisdom theology. The command to fear God occurs at the end of the book of Ecclesiastes (Eccles 12:13) as well. Ecclesiastes is also a form of protest literature that more radically questions the entire pursuit of wisdom.

Not only does the fear of the Lord provide a uniquely important theme for the integration of biblical wisdom but also it points to the ultimate source of wisdom as lying within the context of biblical revelation. Wisdom psalms may have parallels with other poetry outside the Bible. However, a closely related form of psalm is that of the Torah psalm. This approach, which praises the source of wisdom and success in the study and obedience of God's revelation and covenant, has no known antecedent in the world of wisdom. Here the source of wisdom lay not in any human understanding or production; rather, Torah psalms such as Psalm 1 and Psalm 119 point to the origins of true wisdom in the Torah, seen as God's revelation to Israel. It is this covenant document that forms the basis for a unique relationship with God that no other wisdom source can reach. It is for this reason, as well, that the Israelite Wisdom literature ignores the arts of divination and omen-reading that occupy so many texts among Israel's neighbors. The will of Yahweh is not divined, nor are omens the source of divine guidance. Instead, the unique covenant that God makes with each citizen of Israel provides a true means of direct access to the divine will.

This means of access is available to all. For this reason, as Israel's history moves forward into the Hellenistic and Roman periods, wisdom collections such as *Wisdom of Solomon, *Sirach and Baruch stress the revelation of God's word more and more powerfully. This alone provides a true source of wisdom for the faithful believer. In the form of reason and word, the source of wisdom becomes a hypostatic *personification in Philo's thought and associated with the Son of God as the *logos* in the Gospel of John. Countering secret revelation and wisdom from hidden sources, the connection between wisdom and Jesus Christ reaches a high point in Colossians, where he is the image of the invisible God (Col 1:15). Thus the fear of the Lord as access to Torah wisdom becomes in Christianity the true source of wisdom only as it is received through the mediation of the Son of God and his new revelation.

See also ECCLESIASTES 2: ANCIENT NEAR EASTERN BACKGROUND; JOB 2: ANCIENT NEAR EASTERN BACKGROUND; MAAT; PROVERBS 2: ANCIENT NEAR EASTERN BACKGROUND; SONG OF SONGS 2: ANCIENT NEAR EASTERN BACKGROUND; WASF; WISDOM, GREEK.

BIBLIOGRAPHY. **A. Buhlmann,** "The Difficulty of Thinking in Greek and Speaking in Hebrew (Qoheleth 3.18; 4.13-16; 5.8)," *JSOT* 90 (2000) 101-8; **R. E. Clements,** *Wisdom for a Changing World: Wisdom in the Old Testament* (Berkeley Lectures 2; Berkeley, CA: BIBAL Press, 1990); **J. L. Crenshaw,** *Old Testament Wisdom: An Introduction* (rev. ed.; Louisville: Westminster John Knox, 1998); **S. de Jong,** "Qohelet and the Ambitious Spirit of the Ptolemaic Period," *JSOT* 61 (1994) 85-96; **M. Dietrich,** "Der Dialog zwischen Šūpē-amēli und seinem 'Vater': Die Tradition babylonischer Weisheitssprüche im Westen," *UF* 23 (1991) 33-74; idem, "Babylonian Literary Texts from Western Libraries," in *Verse in Ancient Near Eastern Prose,* ed. J. C. de Moor and W. G. E. Watson (AOAT 42; Kevelaer: Butzon & Bercker; Neukirchen-Vluyn: Neukirchener Verlag, 1993) 41-67; **D. J. Estes,** *Hear, My Son: Teaching and Learning in Proverbs 1-9* (NSBT; Downers Grove: InterVarsity Press, 1997); **F. W. Golka,** *The Leopard's Spots: Biblical and African Wisdom in Proverbs* (Edinburgh: T & T Clark, 1993); **R. S. Hess,** "Smitten Ant Bites Back: Rhetorical Forms in the Amarna Correspondence from Shechem," in *Verse in Ancient Near Eastern Prose,* ed. J. C. de Moor and W. G. E. Watson (AOAT 42; Kevelaer: Butzon & Bercker; Neukirchen-Vluyn: Neukirchener Verlag, 1993) 95-111; idem, "Literacy in Iron Age Israel," in *Windows into Old Testament History: Evidence, Argument, and the Crisis of "Biblical Israel,"* ed. V. P. Long, D. W. Baker and G. J. Wenham (Grand Rapids: Eerdmans, 2002) 82-102; **V. A. Hurowitz,** "The Wisdom of Šūpē-amēli—A Deathbed Debate between a Father and Son," in *Wisdom Literature in Mesopotamia and Israel,* ed. R. J. Clifford (SBL Symposium Series Number 36; Altanta: Society of Biblical Literature, 2007) 37-51; **T. R. Kämmerer,** *Šimâ milka: Induktion und Reception der mittelbabylonischen Dichtung von Ugarit, Emar und Tell el-'Amarna* (AOAT 251; Münster: Ugarit-Verlag, 1998); **K. A. Kitchen,** "Proverbs and Wisdom Books of the Ancient Near East: The Factual History of a Literary Form," *TynBul* 28 (1977) 69-114; idem, "Biblical Instructional Wisdom: The Decisive Voice of the Ancient Near East," in *Boundaries of the Ancient Near Eastern World: A Tribute to Cyrus H. Gordon,* ed. M. Lubetski, C. Gottlieb and S. Keller (JSOTSup 273; Sheffield: JSOT Press, 1998) 346-63; idem, *On the Reliability of the Old Testament* (Grand Rapids: Eerdmans, 2003); **W. G. Lambert,** *Babylonian Wisdom Literature* (Oxford: Oxford University Press, 1960); **T. Longman III,** *Fictional Akkadian Autobiography: A Generic and Comparative Study* (Winona Lake, IN: Eisenbrauns, 1991); idem, *The Book of Ecclesiastes* (NICOT; Grand Rapids: Eerdmans, 1998); **D. Rudman,** "A Note on the Dating of Ecclesiastes," *CBQ* 61 (1999) 47-52; **C. L. Seow,** "Linguistic Evidence and the Dating of Qoheleth," *JBL* 115 (1996) 643-66; idem, *Ecclesiastes* (AB 18C; New York: Doubleday, 1997); **B. K. Waltke and D. Diewert,** "Wisdom Literature," in *The Face of Old Testament Studies: A Survey of Contemporary Approaches,* ed. D. W. Baker and B. T. Arnold (Grand Rapids: Baker, 1999) 295-328; **S. Weeks,** *Early Israelite Wisdom* (OTM; Oxford: Clarendon Press, 1994); **J. B. White,** *A Study of the Language of Love in the Song of Songs and Ancient Egyptian Poetry* (SBLDS 38; Missoula, MT: Scholars Press, 1978); **R. N. Whybray,** "Yahweh-Sayings and Their Contexts in Proverbs 10,1-22,16," in *La sagesse de l'ancien Testament,* ed. M. Gilbert (BETL 51; Gembloux: Duculot; Leuven: Leuven University Press, 1979) 153-65.   R. S. Hess

WISDOM THEOLOGY

The distinctiveness of the biblical Wisdom literature, with its interest in individual experience and behavior rather than in Israel as a nation with its history, cult and covenant relationship with Yahweh, has been found problematic by scholars concerned with OT theology. As a result, some have more or less ignored these books, and a few have questioned whether they have any contribution to make to OT theology. However, during the last few decades there has been growing interest in the Wisdom literature and the recognition that the distinctive theological emphases found in it make an important contribution to theology, providing a valuable complement to what is found in the rest of the OT.

After a brief consideration of the nature of wisdom as it appears in the Wisdom literature, this article surveys some of the major theological themes found in the books of *Job, *Proverbs and *Ecclesiastes and the debates that have taken place about them.

    1. The Nature of Wisdom
    2. The Problem of Wisdom Theology
    3. A Creation Theology
    4. The Personification of Wisdom
    5. The Fear of the Lord
    6. The Two Ways
    7. The Act-Consequence Nexus
    8. God
    9. Humans

1. The Nature of Wisdom.
In the OT in general "wisdom" refers to particular skills, both physical and intellectual. People who possess these skills are described as "wise." So, in the account of the construction of the tabernacle God says to Moses, "I have given wisdom to all the wise of heart, so that they may make all that I have commanded you" (Ex 31:6). These skills include artistic design, metalwork, work with precious stones and woodwork (Ex 31:3-5). They also encompass spinning, embroidery and weaving (Ex 35:35). Elsewhere it is used of cunning or craftiness (2 Sam 13:3), political pragmatism (1 Kings 2:6), professional mourning (Jer 9:17), sailors and shipbuilders (Ezek 27:8-9).

Within the Wisdom literature the meaning of "wisdom" becomes somewhat narrower. Speaking of the book of Proverbs in particular, R. Whybray (1994, 4) observes, "Elsewhere in the Old Testament ḥokmâ means something like "skill": practical knowledge in any sphere, from

that of the artisan to that of the politician. But in Proverbs ḥokmâ is always *life*-skill: the ability of the individual to conduct his life in the best possible way and to the best possible effect."

Alongside this narrowing of meaning there is another one. In the Wisdom literature "wisdom" is often coupled with other words meaning "understanding" *(bînâ, těbûnâ)* or "knowledge" *(daʿat).* This gives it a more "intellectual" slant. As a result, wisdom is seen as "an intellectual quality that provides the key to happiness and success, to 'life' in its widest sense" (Whybray 1974, 8). This is a narrowing of meaning, not a change in meaning, as is shown by the idiomatic phrase "wise of heart," noted above, in texts outside the Wisdom literature. In Hebrew the heart is primarily the center of reasoning and the will rather than, as in English, of the emotions.

2. The Problem of Wisdom Theology.
The writers of OT theologies have found it difficult to incorporate the Wisdom literature into their theologies. One reason for this is given by G. Wright (103): "In any attempt to outline a discussion of Biblical faith it is the wisdom literature which offers the chief difficulty because it does not fit into the type of faith exhibited in the historical and prophetic literatures." This assumes that Hebrew theology ought to center on Yahweh's acts in history and the interpretation of and response to these acts. One of the characteristics of the Wisdom literature in the Hebrew *canon is the lack of reference to Israel's historical traditions, including the fundamental ones of the exodus from Egypt and the establishment of the covenant at Sinai. In addition, whereas theology based on historical traditions naturally leads to an emphasis on Yahweh's relationship with the nation, the emphasis in the Wisdom literature is on the individual. Wright (104) concluded that the material in the book of Proverbs in particular "remains near the pagan source of wisdom in which society and the Divine work in history played no real role." This highlights a common assumption that wisdom in Israel was not "homegrown" but rather was appropriated from the international pool of wisdom in the ancient Near East to which the literatures of Egypt and Mesopotamia bear witness. As a result, W. Eichrodt (81) held that wisdom in Israel "has a strongly secular flavour, and is only loosely connected with religious faith." This wisdom was mainly concerned with the skill in

practical matters that is the basis for success in daily life. It was only gradually integrated into Hebrew Yahwism.

A few scholars have questioned whether that integration ever really happened. Most notably, H. Preuss argued that the teaching of Proverbs 10—29 is entirely in accord with that of international wisdom and, despite appearances, is alien to the faith of Israel. Although the name "Yahweh" is used and there are admonitions to fear and trust Yahweh, the characterization of Yahweh as the guarantor of the moral order and the assumption of the principle of *retribution put him on a level with the gods mentioned in other ancient Near Eastern wisdom literature. Preuss's argument has not convinced many. As Whybray (1995, 127) has said, "His extreme position leaves it unclear how the retention of Proverbs as Jewish scripture is to be accounted for and why its authors gave their god the name of the God of Israel."

R. Murphy has argued that the perceived problem of integrating wisdom with Yahwism is the result of a methodological error. It arises because it is assumed that God's revelation in history is to be given priority. Murphy (1996, 124) remarks, "This view is biased. Rather, one should look directly at the wisdom experience (which is also historical!) that the worshiper of the Lord actually had. What is the religious dimension of this wisdom experience? It is an appropriation of the lessons that one can draw from day-to-day living, from the realm of personal intercourse and the surprises of creation. The dialogue between the Israelite and the environment was also a dialogue with the God who was worshiped in Israel as creator and redeemer."

Here Murphy is arguing that, unlike most of the rest of the OT, the theology of the Wisdom literature is centered on creation rather than redemption. Instead of taking only one perspective as determinative for Israelite thought, both ought to be taken into account as aspects of a single worldview.

3. A Creation Theology.

3.1. Introduction. In a seminal article published in English in 1964, W. Zimmerli (148) argued, "Wisdom thinks resolutely within the framework of a theology of creation" (*see* Creation Theology). He noted that in the Wisdom literature there is no appeal to God's relationship with Israel through their history or through the covenant. God is spoken of as "Maker" (Job 4:17; 32:22; 35:10; Prov 14:31; 17:5; 22:2) or "Creator" (Eccles 12:1) but never as the "God of Israel." The teaching of the *sages, whether expressed as a statement *(Aussagewort)* or an admonition *(Mahnwort)*, is presented as "counsel," not as commandments of the lawgiver of the covenant. It is based on observation and understanding of the created order. "Wisdom shows man as a being who goes out, who apprehends through his knowledge, who establishes, who orders his world" (Zimmerli, 150).

The theme of creation does have a significant place in each of the wisdom books. There are many allusions to creation in Job, and the theme comes to the foreground in Yahweh's speeches (Job 38—41). Proverbs twice refers to the creation of the world (Prov 3:19-20; 8:22-31) and makes several mentions of Yahweh as the creator of humans (Prov 14:31; 16:4; 17:5; 20:12; 22:2; 29:13). Ecclesiastes opens with a cosmology that is the grounding of the teaching of *Qohelet (Eccles 1:3-15). The frequent references to God "giving" things (Eccles 1:13; 2:26 [2x]; 3:10, 11; 5:18-19; 6:2; 8:15; 9:9; 12:7) are a constant reminder of God as the Creator and Sustainer of the world and of humans in it—hence the concluding exhortation, "Remember your Creator in the days of your youth" (Eccles 12:1).

3.2. A Classification of Approaches. Various scholars have developed this understanding of wisdom theology in different ways. L. Perdue (34-48) discerns four main lines of approach.

3.2.1. Anthropology. Some scholars understand the Wisdom literature as being concerned primarily with human nature and behavior. One of the most thoroughgoing expressions of this approach is W. Brueggeman's study *In Man We Trust.* He argues that in the Wisdom literature the goal and meaning of existence is a this-worldly life of joy and wholeness. It values the human ability to discern what is good and true in a world that is the good and ordered creation of God and so legitimates social knowledge as the ground for *ethics.

3.2.2. Cosmology. Other scholars emphasize the idea of an ordered cosmos as the focus of the Wisdom literature. H.-J. Hermission has developed this kind of approach. A study of the wisdom saying (Hermission 1968) led him to conclude that wisdom thought was concerned with recognizing, transmitting and creating an order of life. In a later article Hermission made a more comprehensive statement of wisdom theology, arguing, "Wisdom searches for the knowledge of order, or, for those to whom this seems too rigid, for a certain regularity within the diversity of the phenomena of the world. This world, however, is *unitary*" (Hermission 1978, 44). By the "unitary" nature of the world he means that wisdom does not distinguish in principle between "nature wisdom" and "culture wisdom." Hermission (1978, 44) argues that Proverbs 8 depicts wisdom as "present in the created world as regularity, purposiveness, and therefore also as beauty. Thus Proverbs 8 talks about creation when it talks about wisdom: about creation with respect to its intelligible orders, to which man is to adapt himself." In his view this theology underlies the sentences in Proverbs 10—29, though coming to the surface only in the few that mention God as "Maker." The speeches of God in Job 38—41 present this order with a different slant: "For the good order which the creator gave to the world is not limited by man's not understanding it. What is hidden from him are the origins, the interrelations, the background; but there remains his amazement at that which lies before him as a result of the wise creator's activity" (Hermission 1978, 52). Ecclesiastes shows that "not all wisdom managed to resolve the perplexity over the good order and incomprehensibility of the world and the aloofness of the creator God" (Hermission 1978, 54).

3.2.3. Theodicy. J. Crenshaw has been a strong advocate of the view that *theodicy is the major theme of the Wisdom literature. He accepts that creation is central to wisdom thought but argues that the distinctiveness of the wisdom approach to it is that the sages took seriously the experience of *chaos and its continuing threat in all areas of life. It was the need to deal with the question of God the Creator's relationship to chaos as it appeared in nature, society and moral life that prompted them to defend divine justice by presenting their understanding of creation (Crenshaw 1976). They developed their creation theology in order to articulate a doctrine of theodicy (Crenshaw 1977).

3.2.4. Anthropology and Cosmology. Some scholars have seen a creative tension between anthropology and cosmology in the Wisdom literature. Murphy (1996, 111-49), for example, speaks of two ways in which creation is viewed in the Wisdom literature: as "origins" or "beginnings" and as the world in which humans live, react to and learn from. Creation as origins is most clearly presented in Proverbs 8:22-31 and Job 38—41. The concern of such passages is not origins in itself but rather to locate wisdom at the beginning of the creation of the world and therefore as the means of understanding the nature of the world. Murphy, however, disagrees with those scholars who see the prime concern of wisdom as a search for a cosmic order "out there." The sages were aware of and looked for regularities in nature and human activity, but Murphy does not think that they conceptualized this as an all-embracing "order." He argues that in the thinking of the sages there was no separation of world from the Creator, as if the cosmos was a machine wound up at creation and left to run on its own. Rather, the Lord was understood to be active in the world at all levels. Murphy quotes with approval these words of G. von Rad: "The experiences of the world were for her [Israel] always divine experiences as well, and the experiences of God were for her experiences of the world" (von Rad, 62). This meant that God could be met within, and be revealed in, experience of the world. This view is articulated in the *personification *Woman Wisdom. She is more than a personification of the order of creation because her call is the voice of the Lord: "Ultimately the revelation of creation is the revelation of God. God speaks through wisdom/creation, which is turned to human beings and speaks in the accents of God. Such is the thrust of Prov. 8" (Murphy 1996, 139).

3.3. Conclusion. Each of the first three approaches discussed above highlights an important aspect of wisdom theology. On the surface, much of the Wisdom literature is anthropocentric, concerned with human beings and their behavior. However, underlying this is the assumption of a cosmic order of some kind that seems to be an essential element in the worldview of the wise. Theodicy is an important theme in Job and Ecclesiastes. The justice of God seems to be basic to wisdom theology, the basis for the belief in a moral order. It is more likely that theodicy arose as a subsidiary issue in wisdom theology in response to experience that raised questions about this justice than that it was the basis of wisdom theology. The fourth approach, which sees an ongoing tension between the anthropological and cosmological themes as constitutive of wisdom theology, seems to describe best what we find in the Wisdom literature. It provides a corrective to possible extremes. An excessive stress on the human-centeredness of wisdom teaching has led some scholars to see it as essentially "secular," with little place for God. This is hard to sustain in the light of the evidence that wisdom in the ancient Near East in general was always grounded in religious beliefs (Weeks, 66-69). It also does not do justice to the theme of *"the fear of the Lord" in the Wisdom literature (see 5 below).

An overemphasis on wisdom as the search for an overarching cosmic order can lead to a presentation of it that is rather like some Greek philosophy and at odds with the practical teaching based on the observation and experience of everyday life that constitutes much of the biblical Wisdom literature. It can also lead to a mechanical understanding of the relationship between deeds and their consequences, especially in Proverbs, which is not supported by a careful study of the book (see 7 below).

4. The Personification of Wisdom.
In Proverbs 1:20-33; 8:1-36; 9:1-6 wisdom is personified as a woman. There has been a great deal of debate about the origin and significance of this personification.

4.1. The Origin of the Personification.
*Maat, the Egyptian goddess of truth and justice, is quite often suggested as the prototype for personified Wisdom. M. Fox (1995) has presented a strong critique of this suggestion. Among the points that he makes are the fact that there is no recorded speech by Maat, and that she never became a popular or well-known goddess in Egypt, let alone outside. Whybray (1965, 83-87) has shown the weakness of the evidence put forward to support the claim that behind the personification of Wisdom stands a Canaanite goddess of wisdom. He points out that there is no known Canaanite goddess of wisdom. To this can be added the observation that personified Wisdom shows none of the characteristics of the known Canaanite goddesses (Fox 2000, 335). B. Lang's suggestion that the origin of the figure of personified Wisdom is an Israelite goddess is a hypothesis that rests on virtually no evidence. Some similarities have been noted between the speeches of Wisdom and hymns praising the goddess Isis. However, Isis worship began to spread widely in the Near East only in the late third century BC, and the hymns are not attested

before the first century BC.

The origin of the personification might be much more straightforward than any of these hypotheses suggest. Personification is quite a common literary technique, especially in poetry. It is very probable that the feminine gender of the noun "wisdom" in Hebrew *(hokmâ)* led to the personification of Wisdom as a woman. This would have been helped by the reality of "wise women" in Israel and the fact that in Israelite society *women fulfilled various roles that could appropriately be assigned to Wisdom (Camp, 90-109). As a literary construct, Wisdom is able to combine different roles that might never be expected to be found together in any one human person.

4.2. The Role and Significance of Personified Wisdom.
More important than the origin of the figure of personified Wisdom is her role in Proverbs 1—9 and the theological significance of that role. Proverbs 8:22-36 is the key passage for understanding her role. There are two notable exegetical issues in this passage. The first is whether the verb *qnh* in the opening clause of Proverbs 8:22 should be understood in the sense "begot" (ESV mg.), "acquired/possessed" (NASB) or "created" (NRSV). The second is whether the word *'āmôn* in the first clause of Proverbs 8:30 means "master worker" (NRSV) or "little child" (NRSV mg.) or possibly "counselor." Even if these two issues remain unresolved, certain things are clear about Wisdom in this passage. She has a divine origin (the natural way to read Prov 8:24-25 is that the Lord was the one by whom she was "brought forth") before the creation of the earth (Prov 8:22-26). She was present at the creation of the earth, even if her role is unclear (Prov 8:27-30a). In Proverbs 8:30 she is depicted as having an intimate, joyful relationship with God, and in Proverbs 8:31 she expresses her delight and interest in the world and its human inhabitants. In Proverbs 8:32-36 she calls on humans to listen to her and to heed her instruction because it will give them "life."

The claims that Wisdom makes in Proverbs 8:32-36 are far reaching. Von Rad (163) says of Proverbs 8:35, "Who, apart from Yahweh, can say to man, 'Whoever finds me, finds life'?" This may suggest that here Wisdom is a hypostasis, a divine attribute envisaged as a separate divine being. However, the preceding verses make clear that, unlike Yahweh, Wisdom has an origin, like the world. There are no clear grounds in the text for regarding the figure of Wisdom as anything more than a vivid poetic personification. But of what is she a personification? What is said of her presence before and at the creation of the world, taken together with Proverbs 3:19-20, makes it clear that it was through Wisdom that God created an ordered world. This might be taken to imply that Wisdom is a personification of the order inherent in the created world, a personification not of an attribute of God but rather of an attribute of the world (von Rad, 156). This, however, seems an inadequate interpretation of some of what is said of Wisdom: her origin before the creation of the world, her intimacy with God, the way in which she seems to be a mediator between God and God's creation, and the claims she makes for herself. These suggest that "Wisdom is somehow identified with the Lord" (Murphy 1996, 138). In fact, it is unnecessary to choose between Wisdom as a personification of an attribute of God and of an attribute of the world. If she is a personification of the Creator's wisdom, then it is that wisdom which is seen in the regularities that are experienced and observed in the created world. Wisdom both transcends creation and is immanent in it.

4.3. Wisdom and Revelation. Whereas the prophet asserts, "Thus says Yahweh," and the Torah is rooted in the revelation of Yahweh at Sinai, the sages do not make an explicit claim to be imparting divinely revealed truth. What, then, is the relationship between wisdom and revelation? One the one hand, wisdom is acquired by observation and experience (Prov 24:30-34). It can be passed on by instruction (Prov 4:1-6). Even mistakes can lead to an increase in wisdom if one is willing to receive correction (Prov 10:17). On the other hand, wisdom is presented as a gift from God. To begin with, even the ability to observe and experience the world comes from Yahweh (Prov 20:12). More than that, "Yahweh gives wisdom; from his mouth come knowledge and understanding" (Prov 2:6). That is why "The fear of Yahweh is the beginning of wisdom, and the knowledge of the Holy One is insight" (Prov 9:10). Human effort alone can lead to increased knowledge but is not enough to possess wisdom. However, the person who observes and experiences the world receives instruction and correction, while the person who truly fears Yahweh will receive true wisdom from him. There is no contradiction here between human effort in acquiring wisdom and receiving it as a divine gift.

5. The Fear of the Lord.

Each of the wisdom books asserts the importance of fearing the Lord (Yahweh) or *God (Prov 1:7; 9:10; 31:30; Job 28:28; Eccles 12:13). Fear of (the) god(s) was a concept widespread in the ancient Near East and is quite common in its wisdom literature, and, as M. Barré has shown, it refers to worship of (the) god(s) in the full sense, not just to moral behavior. References to "the fear of the Lord" are strategically placed in Proverbs, providing an *inclusio for Proverbs 1—9 (Prov 1:7; 9:10) and for the whole book (Prov 31:30). This shows the importance of the concept in the book. It is significant that the personal name of the God of Israel is invoked, showing that the sages considered themselves to be working within context of Israelite Yahwism. Proverbs 2:5; 9:10 suggest a relational meaning for "the fear of the Lord," since "knowledge of God" is understood in relational terms in the OT. Proverbs 15:33; 22:4 put "humility" in parallel with "the fear of the Lord," indicating an attitude of reverence toward God. In Proverbs 8:13 the fear of the Lord is equated with the hatred of evil, with moral living. The designation of the capable wife as "a woman who fears the LORD" (Prov 31:30) shows that the fear of the Lord has to do with everyday human life and behavior, not just religious observances.

The fear of the Lord is said to be "the beginning of knowledge/wisdom" (Prov 1:7; 9:10). There has been debate about how best to translate the Hebrew word *rēʾšît* in Proverbs 1:7: "beginning," "best part," "principle," "sum." The parallel word in Proverbs 9:10, *tĕḥillat*, unambiguously means "beginning," and that makes good sense in Proverbs 1:7. "Beginning" in this context does not mean a starting point that is to be left behind; rather, "What the alphabet is to reading, notes to the reading of music, and numerals to mathematics, the fear of the Lord is to attaining the revealed knowledge of this book" (Waltke, 181).

In Job 28:28 "the fear of the Lord [ʾădōnay]" is equated with wisdom. Elsewhere in Job the phrase is "the fear of God/the Almighty" (Job is not an Israelite), and it is used in contexts that put the emphasis on shunning evil, on moral behavior (Job 1:1, 8; 2:3; 4:6; 6:14). Ecclesiastes concludes, "Fear God and keep his commandments; for that is the whole duty of everyone" (Eccles 12:13). This is a call to honor and *worship God. The context of references to fearing God earlier in the book (Eccles 3:14; 5:7; 7:15-18; 8:12-13) gives it the sense of awe, even terror, before a powerful and inscrutable God.

6. The Two Ways.

The emphasis on the fear of the Lord as the beginning of wisdom assumes that other beginnings might present themselves as real possibilities. For this reason, the ideas of the two ways has an important place in the theology of wisdom.

N. Habel has argued that "the way" is a "nuclear symbol" in Proverbs 1—9, with a "satellite system of images": the two hearts, the two companions and the two houses. In Proverbs 4:1-19 the "way of wisdom" is paralleled with "the paths of uprightness" (Prov 4:11) and is contrasted with "the path of the wicked" and "the way of evil men" (Prov 4:14). The effects of a "perverted heart" (Prov 6:12-15) can be avoided by taking to heart wise teaching (Prov 6:20-22). The two companions are Wisdom and "the strange woman," each of which has her respective house. This symbolism of the way is also used in Proverbs 10—29. The word *derek* occurs seventy-five times in Proverbs. The contrast between the two ways underlies the frequent antitheses between the wise and the foolish and between the righteous and the wicked.

The use of the symbolism of the two ways, and its satellite images, might seem to give the teaching of Proverbs a rather simplistic appearance. It results in the presentation of strong black-and-white statements without allowance for shades of gray. It is important to recognize that this is a limitation of the symbolism used, and that the statements are not intended to define hard-and-fast categories. The didactic intention of the symbolism is to set out clearly the differences between wise/foolish and righteous/wicked behavior and the consequences of each. Once these basics have been grasped, one is better placed to deal with the complexities of life.

7. The Act-Consequence Nexus.

7.1. Introduction. In 1955 K. Koch published an influential paper in which he argued that there is in the book of Proverbs, and elsewhere in the OT, the assumption of an act-conse-

quence nexus. It is assumed that wicked actions will result in disastrous consequences, and that good actions will result in blessing. In support of this he quoted a number of proverbs (e.g., Prov 26:27; 28:10, 18). Koch argued that what is being presented in such proverbs is the inevitable outcome of the actions themselves and not the result of God stepping into administer punishments and rewards. His main reason for saying this is that, in his view, there is no hint of any "judicial process" whereby God weighs up the actions according to an established norm and administers the appropriate punishment or reward. He concluded that the Hebrew sages held the conviction that Yahweh does not intervene directly but rather maintains the act-consequence nexus and, where necessary, ensures that it is "completed."

Some scholars have disagreed with Koch's conclusion, arguing that the distinction between an impersonal "nexus" and the personal action of Yahweh would not have made sense in ancient Hebrew thought, which regarded the activity of Yahweh as all-pervasive in human affairs (Murphy 1998, 264-69). Others have questioned whether the sages behind Proverbs really did assume that there is a more-or-less mechanical act-consequence nexus at work (Van Leeuwen).

7.2. The Complexity of Life. Those who question the mechanical act-consequence nexus point to evidence in Proverbs that life is more complex than it at first seems. There are examples of proverbs that contradict one another. The classic example is Proverbs 26:4-5: "Do not answer a fool according to his folly, or you will be like him yourself. Answer a fool according to his folly, or he will be wise in his own eyes." The fact that the sages created or collected such "contradictory" proverbs shows that they were well aware of the complexities of real life. Also, the fact that the compiler of the book sometimes deliberately put them together suggests that the reader is being warned against any mechanical application of proverbs.

There is one distinct form of proverb that occurs several times in the book of Proverbs that clearly recognizes the complexity of life and, in particular, that a simple act-consequence nexus does not always hold up. These are the "better than" sayings. A few of them simply say that "A is better than B" (Prov 16:16). Most are more complex than this, having the form "A with B is better than C with D" (Prov 16:8, 19). These proverbs clearly imply that the righteous do not always prosper and the wicked sometimes do. There are a significant number of other proverbs that assert or imply that sometimes the wicked prosper and the innocent suffer (Prov 11:16; 13:23; 18:23).

A small group of proverbs about what is not fitting/becoming also imply a recognition that the act-consequence nexus does not always work out; otherwise there would be no need to brand these situations as "not fitting" (Prov 17:7; 19:10). Even more extreme is a "number proverb," which recognizes that sometimes things go seriously wrong (Prov 30:21-23).

Given this evidence that the sages realized the limitations of the act-consequence nexus, why is it that so many of the proverbs do seem to presuppose it? Two kinds of consideration have a bearing on this. First, the fact is that the act-consequence nexus is often a good approximation of what actually happens. If this were not the case, proverbs would not have the place that they do in most cultures. Second, the very form of a proverb as a short, pithy statement makes it a black-and-white declaration.

7.3. The Role of Yahweh. There is plenty of evidence in the book of Proverbs that the sages did not regard the act-consequence nexus as rooted in an impersonal "order"; rather, it is rooted in the character and will of Yahweh. Evidence of this is seen in the "abomination" sayings. Most of these contrast something that is an "abomination to Yahweh" with what "delights" him (Prov 11:20). This rooting of the nexus in the character and will of Yahweh is why "The fear of Yahweh is instruction in wisdom" (Prov 15:33). It is also why there are limits to the human understanding of how the nexus works out in real life: "Many are the plans in a person's mind, but it is the purpose of Yahweh that will stand" (Prov 19:21). That purpose is not always readily accessible to humans (Prov 25:2), not even to the sages (Prov 20:24). That is why, in the end, the sages accept that "No wisdom, no understanding, no counsel can avail against Yahweh" (Prov 21:30).

In the book of Proverbs, as elsewhere in the Hebrew Bible, there is an unresolved tension between human freedom and responsibility and divine sovereignty. The earnestness, and at times urgency, with which the sages urge people to follow the paths of wisdom, *righteousness, honesty and diligence rather than give way to *folly, wickedness, lying and laziness only makes sense if the destiny of humans rests to some extent in their own hands. Yet, as we have seen, there is also the recognition that the overarching sovereignty of God puts limits upon human understanding and actions. Perhaps the point of balance is expressed in this proverb: "Commit your work to Yahweh, and your plans will be established" (Prov 16:3).

7.4. Conclusion Regarding Proverbs. In the light of this discussion of the evidence in Proverbs 10—29, it seems reasonable to conclude that the sages were well aware that the act-consequence nexus was only a "rule of thumb" with regard to developing skills for living, with many exceptions. They saw it as pragmatically useful as a teaching "model" at the early stages of learning such skills. Moreover, it was theologically justified because it was rooted in the character and purposes of Yahweh. This provided some explanation of why it was only a "rule of thumb." Human beings should not expect to understand Yahweh's purposes fully. However, it also provided grounds for the expectation that "in the end," whenever that might be, the righteous would be vindicated and the wicked punished, for Yahweh is the upholder of righteousness (Prov 11:21; 24:19-20).

7.5. Job. The book of Job is a protest against a dogmatized misunderstanding of the act-consequence nexus. Job's friends are examples of those who ignore the recognition, seen in Proverbs, of its limitations and simply read off a person's spiritual state from that person's circumstances. Whereas in Proverbs the reasoning is from cause to effect (a certain situation or action is likely to lead to a particular outcome), they reason from effect to cause. Since Job is in a desperate state, he must have committed some great sin. Job accepts the act-consequence nexus in principle, but he knows that he is innocent of any great sin. He therefore concludes that God is making a mockery of righteousness (Job 9:22-24).

The message of the first divine speech is that God has created an ordered world, but since Job was not present at creation, he has only a limited insight into its order that only the Creator fully understands (Job 38:4-7). In the second speech God presents Job with the forces of evil and chaos, symbolized by Leviathan and Behemoth. No mortal, only God, can control them (Job 41:10-11). Since Job cannot understand or control these forces, he is in no position to question God's rule over the world (Job 40:6-8). The message of these speeches does not deny the act-consequence nexus. It does, however, assert that full knowledge of how it works belongs only to God, and that humans cannot fully understand it.

7.6. Ecclesiastes. Qohelet, the spokesman in Ecclesiastes, is distressed by the fact that his experience runs counter to the act-consequence nexus (Eccles 8:14). He believes in an ordered world (Eccles 1:5-7) in which there is a right time for everything (Eccles 3:3-8). There is a sovereign God, who has a plan for everything, but the problem is that God does not reveal this plan to humans (Eccles 3:9-18; 6:10-12; 7:13-14; 8:16-9:1). Humans therefore are left uncertain about what to do and when to do it. All they can be sure of is death, which comes to both the righteous and the wicked equally (Eccles 9:2-3). Faced with the injustices in life, Qohelet speaks of the judgment of God (Eccles 3:17; 9:1; 11:9); however, since he has no certainty about the *afterlife (Eccles 3:18-21; 9:3-6), it is not clear what this means. The person who compiled Qohelet's teaching points to a final judgment by God (Eccles 12:13-14) (see Longman, 37-39).

8. God.

8.1. Monotheism. Nearly all the more than ninety references to *God in Proverbs use the personal name "Yahweh," by which God was known as the one in covenant relationship with Israel. Two of the three occasions when the general term *God* is used without clear reference to Yahweh are in a section attributed to a non-Israelite (Prov 30:5, 9). In the prologue and the epilogue of Job the narrator uses the name "Yahweh." It occurs only once in the dialogues (Job 12:9, which may echo Is 41:20), where the speakers, who are not Hebrews, otherwise speak of "God" or "the Almighty." In Ecclesiastes the deity is always referred to as "God," which contributes to the sense of God being distant that the book conveys. In all three books, whatever terms they use, there is an implicit monotheism. No gods other than Yahweh are ever mentioned or alluded to.

8.2. God as Creator. This theme was covered earlier in the discussion of creation theology (see 3 above).

8.3. God's Transcendence. The understanding of God as the sole Creator leads naturally to the idea of God's transcendence. This is expressed in a number of ways in the Wisdom literature. In the prologue of Job God is located in a transcendent heaven, and Ecclesiastes 5:2 stresses, "God is in heaven, and you upon earth." Anthropomorphisms are rare. In neither Proverbs nor Ecclesiastes does God address humans directly. In Proverbs 1—9 it is personified Wisdom who speaks to people on Yahweh's behalf. When God comes to speak to Job, it is not in an ordinary conversation but rather in challenging speeches delivered from a whirlwind.

Job 26 speaks of God's omniscience and omnipotence as the Creator, and this is expressed at more length in the divine speeches. There are proverbs that assert that God knows everything that happens (Prov 5:21; 15:3), even knowing a person's innermost thoughts (Prov 15:11; 24:11-12) and motives (Prov 16:2). Ecclesiastes warns that because God is in heaven, God is aware of every word that is spoken (Eccles 5:1-6). In Ecclesiastes God is the omnipotent Creator, who has a plan for everything, but the problem is that God does not disclose this plan to humans (Eccles 3:9-18; 6:10-12; 7:13-14; 8:16-9:1). The ultimate incomprehensibility of God's ways is recognized in Job 26:14 and Proverbs 20:24; 25:2.

8.4. God's Immanence. In the OT in general there is a tension in the understanding of God. On the one hand, God is transcendent, wholly other than humans, and God's ways and thoughts are beyond human understanding (Is 55:8-9); on the other hand, God enters into a covenant relationship with Israel, can be met with in worship, and seeks a love relationship with people. In Ecclesiastes the transcendence and otherness of God are stressed to such an extent that it might seem to imply that God does not relate to humans in any way. Ecclesiastes does, though, sometimes speak of God relating to humans, most often by speaking of what God "gives" to humans. God gives to them the gift of life (Eccles 5:18; 8:15; 9:9), though eventually he takes it back again (Eccles 12:7). Those who please God are given wisdom, knowledge and joy, while sinners are given "the work of gathering and heaping, only to give to one who pleases God" (Eccles 2:26). To some, God gives wealth and possessions and the power to enjoy them (Eccles 5:19), while others are given these but are not enabled to enjoy them (Eccles 6:2). The references to God as the giver of these gifts certainly emphasize God's sovereignty and human dependence on God. However, the majority of the references to God as giver are in passages that contain an admonition to enjoy life. This may indicate that God has a personal, and positive, interest in human welfare.

The transcendence of God is to the fore in the dialogues of Job because of Job's sense of alienation from God as a result of his *suffering. However, at the end of them Job finds a deeper, personal relationship with God (Job 42:5). The God who is transcendent in heaven in the prologue appears in the epilogue speaking to and blessing humans on earth.

There are a number of proverbs that depict Yahweh as a God who relates personally to individuals and is concerned about and active in the world. It is a characteristic of Yahweh in the Law (Ex 22:22-24; Deut 10:17-18) and the Prophets (Is 1:23; Ezek 22:7; Mal 3:5) that he is the defender of the widow, the orphan and the alien sojourner. In Proverbs Yahweh is said to be the defender of "the poor" in general (Prov 19:17; 22:22-23), with the widow (Prov 15:25) and the orphan (Prov 23:10-11) being mentioned specifically. Yahweh's wider concern for social justice is expressed in some sentences. One issue that is referred to several times is that of accurate measures (Prov 11:1; 16:11; 20:10, 23). Again, there is a parallel with the Law (Lev 19:36; Deut 25:13-16) and the Prophets (Amos 8:5). Yahweh is said to have a special relationship with those who are *"righteous." L. Boström (213-25) argues that in Proverbs the term *righteous* (which occurs about sixty times) always denotes both correct behavior (as taught by the sages) and obedience to Yahweh; the "righteous" are those who live rightly because they are obedient both to Yahweh and to the teaching of the sages. The righteous person is described in a number of ways, the most promi-nent being one "who fears Yahweh." There are a number of sayings that depict Yahweh as the protector of the righteous (Prov 2:5-8; 18:10; 29:25) and as the one who grants them success and well-being (Prov 3:5-10, 33-34; 10:3; 16:20; 28:25). Yahweh's relationship with the righteous is expressed in terms of friendship (Prov 3:32) and love (Prov 3:11-12; 15:9).

9. Humans.

9.1. Creation and Fall. The recognition of God as Creator entails that humans are understood as created beings that are answerable to their Creator. In all the wisdom books God is the sovereign Judge (Job 23:1-7; Prov 2:6-8; Eccles 3:17). The fact that there is wickedness and folly among humans implies their fallenness. Ecclesiastes refers to the creation of humans from the dust (Eccles 3:20; 12:7) and says that although God created them "upright," they now devise "many schemes" (Eccles 7:29). As a result, no humans are free from sin (Eccles 7:20).

9.2. Human Constitution. In the OT the human being is conceptualized as a psychosomatic unity resulting from the "dust of the earth" being animated by "the breath of life" given by God (Gen 2:7). This view is expressed in Ecclesiastes 3:20-21; 12:7. It also lies behind Job 34:14-15. A variety of Hebrew words are used to refer to different aspects of the human psyche. All of them have a range of meaning, and none can be represented in its range of meaning by just one English word.

In the verses quoted above the word *rûaḥ* ("spirit") is used for the animating "life force" (in Job 34:14 it is used in parallel with *nĕšāmâ* ["breath"], the word used in Gen 2:7). The same word can be used of a person's entire disposition (Job 7:11; Prov 16:18-19; Eccles 7:8-9) and thus is not to be related to physical life alone.

The word *nepeš* has traditionally been translated as "soul," but this is misleading in view of the common English meaning of "soul" as the immortal spiritual component of human beings. It can be used to refer to the animating force (Job 12:10), but generally it refers more widely "to the passionate drives and appetites of *all* breathing creatures, including their hunger for food and sex" (Waltke, 90) (see Prov 6:30; 12:10; 27:7; Eccles 6:7). It often stands for the whole self (see Job 16:4: "if your soul were in my soul's place," meaning "if you were in my place").

The traditional translation of *lēb* as "heart" can also be misleading because in English this word is usually associated primarily with the emotions. In the Wisdom literature the "heart" is the center and wellspring of the inner life, which is why it must be carefully guarded (Prov 4:23). The nature of the *lēb*—for example, whether it is wise (Prov 14:33) or perverse (Prov 17:20)—governs a person's actions. In modern English versions of the Bible *lēb* is often translated as "mind" or by words relating to mental activity because, in the Wisdom literature in particular, it is primarily the center of thinking, memorizing, deciding and willing (Job 1:8; 8:10; Prov 2:2; 16:10; Eccles 8:16; 9:1).

9.3. Human Responsibilities. It is an underlying assumption of the Wisdom literature that humans have the rational ability and the responsibility to reflect on experience and the observation of the world so as to come to understand the order that there is and to live wisely in the light of this. Even in Ecclesiastes, where the limitations of the human ability to understand are stressed, human wisdom is seen to have some practical value (Eccles 2:13-14; 7:11-12; 9:16-18; 10:12), so that wisdom is to be preferred over folly (Eccles 2:13; 7:5-7; 10:1-3). As noted earlier (see 5 above), a prime duty of human beings in the Wisdom literature is to fear Yahweh/God. In Proverbs those who fear Yahweh are correlated with those who are righteous and are contrasted with the wicked (Prov 10:27-28). Ecclesiastes 8:12-13 contrasts those who fear God with sinners, who do evil, and Ecclesiastes 12:13 correlates the fear of God with keeping God's commandments. In Ecclesiastes the fear of God seems more like terror than reverence, but it is balanced by a repeated call to enjoy life (Eccles 2:24-26; 3:12-13; 3:22; 5:18-20; 8:15; 9:7-10; 11:8-10). There is debate as to whether these passages amount to a positive affirmation of life (Whybray 1982) or an attitude of resignation (Murphy 1996, 54-55).

9.4. Human Destiny. As far as Ecclesiastes is concerned, what blights life is that death comes to all as the great leveler, and all that lies beyond death is the realm of the dead, which seems in fact to be an absolute end (Eccles 3:18-20; 9:1-6). The destiny spoken of in Proverbs is Sheol or "the grave." It is the destiny of everyone (Prov 23:14), the innocent (Prov 1:12) as well as the wicked (Prov 9:18). Elsewhere in the OT Sheol is a realm of shadowy existence. Although most scholars conclude that there is no concept of life beyond death in Proverbs, a few see intimations of it in some proverbs (Prov 11:21; 12:28; 14:32; 15:24; 23:17-18; 24:19-20). In Job 14 Job laments that although a tree stump can sprout again, death is the end for humans. There are major textual difficulties in the famous and much debated passage Job 19:23-29. The debate rages over whether Job expects vindication before or after death, and if after it, whether resurrection is in mind. It seems best to conclude that he expects somehow to be conscious of his vindication even if its does come after death (*see* Afterlife).

See also AFTERLIFE; CREATION THEOLOGY; FEAR OF THE LORD; GOD; RETRIBUTION; RIGHTEOUSNESS; SUFFERING; THEODICY; WISDOM AND APOCALYPTIC; WISDOM AND BIBLICAL THEOLOGY; WISDOM AND COVENANT; WOMAN WISDOM AND WOMAN FOLLY.

BIBLIOGRAPHY. **M. L. Barré,** "'Fear of God' and the World View of Wisdom," *BTB* 11 (1981) 41-43; **L. Boström,** *The God of the Sages: The Portrayal of God in the Book of Proverbs* (ConBOT 29; Stockholm: Almqvist & Wiksell, 1990); **W. Brueggemann,** *In Man We Trust: The Neglected Side of Biblical Faith* (Atlanta: John Knox, 1972); **C. Camp,** *Wisdom and the Feminine in the Book of Proverbs* (BLS 11; Sheffield: Almond, 1985); **J. L. Crenshaw,** "In Search of Divine Presence," *RevExp* 74 (1977) 353-69; idem, "Prolegomenon" in *Studies in Ancient Israelite Wisdom*, ed. J. L. Crenshaw (New York: KTAV, 1976) 1-45; **W. Eichrodt,** *Theology of the Old Testament*, vol. 2 (London: SCM, 1967); **M. V. Fox,** "World Order and Ma'at: A Crooked Parallel," *JANES* 23 (1995) 37-48; idem, *Proverbs 1-9* (AB 18A; New York, NY: Doubleday, 2000); **N. C. Habel,** "The Symbolism of Wisdom in Proverbs 1-9," *Int* 26 (1972) 131-57; **H.-J. Hermission,** *Studien zur Israelitischen Spruchweisheit* (WMANT 28; Neukirchen-Vluyn: Neukirchener Verlag, 1968); idem, "Observations on the Creation Theology in Wisdom," in *Israelite Wisdom: Theological and Literary Essays in Honor of Samuel Terrien*, ed. J. G. Gammie et al. (Missoula, MT: Scholars Press, 1978); 43-57; **K. Koch,** "Gibt es ein Vergeltungsdogma im Alten Testament?" *ZTK* 52 (1955) 1-42; ET, "Is There a Doctrine of Retribution in the Old Testament?" in *Theodicy in the Old Testament*, ed J. L. Crenshaw (London: SPCK, 1983) 57-87; **B. Lang,** *Wisdom and the Book of Proverbs: An Israelite Goddess Redefined* (New York: Pilgrim Press, 1986); **T. Longman III,** *the Book of Ecclesiastes* (NICOT; Grand Rapids: Eerdmans, 1998); **R. E. Murphy,** *The Tree of Life: An Exploration of Biblical Wisdom Literature* (2nd ed.; Grand Rapids: Eerdmans, 1996); idem, *Proverbs* (WBC 22; Nashville: Thomas Nelson, 1998); **L. G. Perdue,** *Wisdom and Creation: The Theology of the Wisdom Literature* (Nashville: Abingdon, 1994); **H. D. Preuss,** "Das Gottesbild der älteren Weisheit Israels," in *Studies in the Religion of Ancient Israel* (VTSup 23: Leiden: E. J. Brill, 1972) 117-45; **R. C. Van Leeuwen,** "Wealth and Poverty: System and Contradiction in Proverbs," *HS* 33 (1992) 25-36; **G. von Rad,** *Wisdom in Israel* (London: SCM, 1972); **B. K. Waltke,** *The Book of Proverbs: Chap-*

ters 1-15 (NICOT; Grand Rapids: Eerdmans, 2004); **S. Weeks,** *Early Israelite Wisdom* (Oxford: Clarendon Press, 1994); **R. N. Whybray,** *Wisdom in Proverbs* (London: SCM, 1965); idem, *The Intellectual Tradition in the Old Testament* (BZAW 135; Berlin: de Gruyter, 1974); idem, "Qoheleth, Preacher of Joy," *JSOT* 23 (1982) 87-98; idem, *Proverbs* (NCB; London: Marshall Pickering, 1994); idem, *The Book of Proverbs: A Survey of Modern Study* (HBI 1; Leiden: E. J. Brill, 1995); **G. E. Wright,** *The God Who Acts: Biblical Theology as Recital* (London: SCM, 1952); **W. Zimmerli,** "The Place and Limit of Wisdom in the Framework of Old Testament Theology," *SJT* 17 (1964) 146-58. E. C. Lucas

WOMAN FOLLY. *See* WOMAN WISDOM AND WOMAN FOLLY.

WOMAN WISDOM AND WOMAN FOLLY

One of the most striking features of the book of *Proverbs is the role played by Woman Wisdom and her rival Woman Folly. They both appear Proverbs 1—9 but not in Proverbs 10—31. Indeed, Woman Folly only appears in Proverbs 9 as a counterpart to Woman Wisdom. Many questions surround the role that these figures play in the text, and mystery cloaks their origins. Interest in them is heightened by their later description in select books of the intertestamental period, in the NT, and by theologians of the early church. Furthermore, Woman Wisdom has resurfaced in recent times as an important concept in feminist theology.

    1. Development of the Metaphor in Proverbs
    2. Origins
    3. New Testament Appropriation
    4. Other Post-Proverbs Developments

1. Development of the Metaphor in Proverbs.
1.1. The Main Texts. Any discussion of Woman Wisdom and Woman Folly begins with the book of Proverbs. They make their first appearance in the discourses of the opening nine chapters of the book.

Woman Wisdom appears first in Proverbs 1:20-33, where she delivers a burning denunciation of those who reject her call but at the end of her speech promises safety to those who respond positively. P. Trible (509) comments that right from the start, we recognize her as "a poet, who preaches, counsels, teaches, and prophesies." We also hear her voice in Proverbs 8 as well as climactically in Proverbs 9:1-6. The majority of the rest of the discourses of Proverbs 1—9 contain the instructions of a father to his son. In a number of these the father describes Woman Wisdom to his son and urges him to develop an intimate relationship with her (e.g., Prov 4:1-9). Sometimes it is difficult to determine whether the father speaks of wisdom as a concept or as personified in Woman Wisdom (e.g., Prov 3:19-20).

Woman Folly only appears in Proverbs 9:13-18. However, though she speaks only this one time, we will see that she plays a pivotal role in the presentation of the theology of the book of Proverbs.

1.2. The Ultimate Choice (Prov 9:1-6, 13-18). Even before exploring the identity of these women further, we do well to recognize the climactic role that they play in the development of the final form of Proverbs. Proverbs 9 is situated at a key juncture in the book, bringing to a close the discourses and immediately preceding the proverbs per se (Prov 10—31). The significance of this chapter is underlined by the fact that the young men are required to make a choice. The young men (and in other discourses, the son) are the implied readers of the book. To read properly, the later interpreter must assume the place of the implied reader. Thus, readers of the book are implicitly called on to make a choice: will they dine with Woman Wisdom or with Woman Folly?

Both women call down from their homes on high to the young men going by on the path in order to invite them to a meal. Woman Wisdom sends out her maidens, who say, "Whoever is simpleminded, turn aside here. . . . Come, eat my food, and drink the wine I mixed. Abandon simplemindedness and live. March on the path of understanding" (Prov 9:4-6). On the other hand, Woman Folly calls out, "Whoever is simpleminded, turn aside here. . . . Stolen water is sweet, and food eaten in secret is pleasant" (Prov 9:16-17). Both women address the same group: the simpleminded. And both issue an invitation to a meal. The reader, who identifies with the addressees, must decide between these two women.

1.3. The Identity of the Women.
1.3.1. Woman Wisdom (Prov 8). Woman Wisdom appears in both Proverbs 1 and Proverbs 9, but the reader gets the fullest description of her

in Proverbs 8. The chapter begins with a narrator's (perhaps we are to think of the father) introduction. He calls to get the attention of the men whom she will address. He draws attention to her as she speaks from the high places on the path, at the crossroads, by the gate. The first thing to notice about these locations is that they are crowded public places. What Woman Wisdom offers is not esoteric; it is open for all to hear.

Woman Wisdom herself begins to speak in Proverbs 8:4. She urges the young men to pay attention to what she says. She characterizes her speech as prudent, true, righteous, straightforward, noble and virtuous. It is far from perverse, wicked or twisted (Prov 8:5-9). For this reason, it is of inestimable value (Prov 8:10-11).

She has much to offer those who listen to her, particularly rulers (Prov 8:15-16). She is the very epitome of wisdom as spelled out in the motto of the book (Prov 1:7), for she fears God and shuns evil (Prov 8:13) (see Fear of the Lord).

Perhaps the most debated part of this chapter, if not the book of Proverbs, is the unit Proverbs 8:22-31, which associates Woman Wisdom with God's act of creation. However, the issues are not all present at first reading but rather are heightened by the development of this chapter in the NT (see 3-4 below). Proverbs 8 presents Wisdom as the firstborn of creation. Wisdom witnessed and perhaps participated in the creation of the cosmos. The intent of this section is to remind readers that if they want to know how the world works, they had better know Wisdom, who was there from the very beginning. Her connection with God at the time of creation is also the apex of her argument for why the young men should accept her invitation to join with her. After all, she is with God from the beginning, the "artisan" (ʾāmôn) at his side, laughing before him and dancing before humans (Prov 8:30-31).

The chapter ends with a final exhortation to choose wisdom. Those who do so will get a great reward, and those who do not will be punished.

Who, then, is this woman? Clearly, Woman Wisdom is a *personification of God's wisdom. However, T. Longman goes further and suggests that Woman Wisdom is none other than Yahweh himself. The clue to this interpretation is the location of her house on the highest point of the city. In the ancient Near East and ancient Israel only one house occupies the highest point, and that house is the temple. Thus, the invitation to become intimate with Woman Wisdom is an invitation to become intimate with God.

One might hesitate to adopt this view based on the fact that Wisdom is said to be the first thing created by God. How could God give birth to God? The problem, though, arises only if one forgets that this is a poetic personification, and like all metaphorical language, of which this is a type, it should not be pressed in literalistic detail. The question, after all, would still arise if the reader simply settled for the idea that Wisdom is a personification of God's wisdom. What would it mean to say that God created his wisdom? Was he not wise beforehand?

1.3.2. Woman Folly. The identification of Woman Wisdom also raises the question of the identification of Woman Folly. After all, in her single appearance in the book, she too is said to speak "on a seat at the heights of the city" (Prov 9:14b). For that reason, this personification likewise must represent the divine realm, but in this case the realm of false gods and goddesses. In other words, Woman Folly stands for Baal, Asherah, Ishtar, Marduk, Anat—all the deities that the Israelites were tempted to worship.

1.4. The Consequences. The text is clear as to the consequences of the choice. The choice is between wisdom and *folly, now recognized as the worship of Yahweh versus the worship of false gods. Wisdom and folly in this way become more than mere skill of living, more than navigating life; they are theological principles, and this idea permeates the whole book. This affects the interpretation of wisdom and folly throughout the book, including its second part.

For an example, we take the first proverb of the second part of the book, Proverbs 10:1, which states, "A wise son makes a father glad, and a foolish son is the sorrow of his mother." In light of the development of the metaphor of Woman Wisdom and Woman Folly in Proverbs 1—9, this verse should be understood as saying that a son who makes his parents glad is wise, which means that he is acting like one who worships Yahweh. On the other hand, a son who makes his parents sad is a fool; that is, he is acting like an idolater. Thus, the call to the young men (the reader) is to offer worship to God through a lifestyle that wisely considers the proper act at the proper time.

When the text is understood in this way, the reader recognizes why the one who accepts the invitation of Woman Wisdom "will live" (Prov 9:6), while the one who accepts the invitation of

Woman Folly will die. After all, the simpleminded who go to her "do not know that the departed are there, that those invited by her are in the depths of Sheol" (Prov 9:18).

1.5. The Wise Woman and the Foolish Woman. The book of Proverbs also describes and evaluates human women. In typical wisdom form, it does so by describing the wise woman and the foolish woman. The following are some examples.

"Wise women build their house, but dupes demolish it with their own hands" (Prov 14:1). What is interesting in terms of our present focus of study is that these women reflect the characteristics of Woman Wisdom and Woman Folly. A close reading of Proverbs 31:10-31 illustrates this, since the noble woman there is described as industrious and not lazy, generous, wise in speech, strong in confidence.

The effects of becoming intimate with a human noble or wicked woman is the same as aligning oneself with Woman Wisdom or Woman Folly: "A noble woman is a crown for her husband, but like rot in his bones is a disgraceful woman" (Prov 12:3); "The mouth of strange women is a deep pit; the recipients of Yahweh's wrath fall into it" (Prov 22:14). Thus human women reflect the characteristics of Woman Wisdom or Woman Folly. Young men are advised to form an intimate relationship with a woman who is wise and to avoid all foolish women.

2. Origins.

2.1. Ancient Near Eastern Background. What is the origin of Woman Wisdom? What gave the poet the idea to personify God's wisdom in the form of a woman? It is not surprising that some scholars believe that the inspiration came from outside of Israel. Since Wisdom is female, scholarly attention has been directed toward goddesses from the nations that surround Israel. Isis, Asherah (Smith, 133-37) and even an unattested Canaanite deity named Wisdom (Lang) have been proposed as candidates, but the most promising comparison has been made with the Egyptian goddess *Maat* (Kayatz).

There are two main reasons for this. First, *Maat* is an Egyptian deity (Assmann), and Egyptian wisdom literature has been thought to influence the book of Proverbs in a special way (*see* Proverbs 2: Ancient Near Eastern Background). Second, *maat* functions much like wisdom in Proverbs. *Maat* is a concept that is important not only to the Egyptian Instructions but also in Egyptian thought generally. *Maat* refers to the order and harmony of creation; its associated ideas are truth and justice. A rupture in harmony, truth and justice of the creation is an assault against *maat*. *Maat* is often presented and seems to be seen as an impersonal concept, but is also represented at times as a goddess.

Maat is the Egyptian concept most similar to the Israelite idea of wisdom. It is the order of the universe; it is what the sages seek. Indeed, the fact that *maat* is pictured as a goddess shows a close connection between religion and wisdom in Egypt. *Maat*, even when not deified, is understood to be established and upheld by the gods.

Nonetheless, even though there are similarities, it is unlikely that we should equate *maat* and Woman Wisdom. For one thing, *maat*, though at times mentioned as a goddess, never is given personality in Egyptian literature. *Maat* never speaks, for instance, and is more like an abstract quality. And if the goddess *Maat* does not offer a certain background for the personification of wisdom in Israel, neither do any of the other deities that have been suggested.

2.2. Etymology. So what encouraged or suggested the idea of the personification of wisdom? It may not be irrelevant that the Hebrew word for wisdom (*ḥokmâ*) is itself feminine. Further, though, the gender of relational metaphors of God are often related to whether a role was more commonly associated with males or females in ancient Israelite society. Thus, ruling and warring are associated with the male king and warrior, while nurture and compassion go with the female metaphor of wife. Of course, we have examples of both male and female wisdom figures in the OT (for female, see the wise woman of Tekoa in 2 Sam 14), but perhaps women were more naturally associated with the role of counselor or adviser (for extensive ancient Near Eastern and anthropological arguments, see Fontaine).

In the final analysis, the reason for the creation of the figure of Woman Wisdom is hidden from us. After all, we have no independent access to the thinking of the poet(s) whose imagination produced her.

3. New Testament Appropriation.
It is widely recognized that the NT authors viewed Jesus Christ as the epitome of the wisdom of God (Witherington). The Gospels, for in-

stance, say that Jesus was wiser even than Solomon (Lk 11:31). In Colossians 2:3 Paul proclaims that in Christ "lie hidden all treasures of wisdom and knowledge." And in 1 Corinthians 1:30 he states that "God made Christ to be wisdom itself."

Given this background, it is not surprising to realize that the NT authors occasionally associate Jesus with Woman Wisdom. In Matthew 11, for instance, we read that Jesus' opponents complained about his exuberant lifestyle while at the same time criticizing John the Baptist's austerity. Jesus replied, "For John came neither eating nor drinking, and they say, 'He has a demon.' The Son of Man came eating and drinking, and they say, 'Here is a glutton and a drunkard, a friend of tax collectors and "sinners."' But wisdom is proved right by her actions" (Mt 11:18-19 NIV). Notice how Jesus styles his actions as the actions of Woman Wisdom. Indeed, in the last sentence of Matthew 11:19 "wisdom" would appropriately be capitalized.

In the overview of Proverbs 8 we noted that it was by Wisdom that rulers ruled. Furthermore, we saw that Wisdom was the firstborn of creation. Colossians 1:15-17 echoes both these themes in relationship to Jesus: "He is the image of the invisible God, the firstborn over all creation. For by him all things were created: things in heaven and on earth, visible and invisible, whether thrones or powers or rulers or authorities; all things were created by him and for him. He is before all things, and in him all things hold together" (NIV). Although this is not a citation of Proverbs 8, anyone reading Paul who knew the OT would recognize that Jesus occupies the place of Wisdom. Paul was inviting a comparison: Wisdom was firstborn in Proverbs 8; Jesus is firstborn in Colossians. Wisdom is the agent of divine creation in Proverbs; Christ is the agent in Colossians.

In addition, the renowned opening to John's Gospel also resonates with concepts from Proverbs 8. The Word of God (the *Logos*), who is God himself (Jn 1:1), was "with God in the beginning. Through him all things were made" (Jn 1:2-3). Jesus is the Word, and the association with language reminds the attentive reader of Woman Wisdom in Proverbs 8.

Finally, the author of Revelation also provides a subtle connection between Jesus and Proverbs 8. In the introduction to the letter to the church at Laodicea we read, "The words of the Amen, the faithful and true witness, the beginning of God's creation" (Rev 3:14 RSV). The phrase "the beginning of God's creation" *(hē archē tēs ktiseōs tou theou)* is reminiscent of Proverbs 8:22-30 (cf. LXX Prov 8:22-23). In particular, the phrase may represent the meaning of that difficult word in Proverbs 8:30, *'āmôn,* as the "architect" of creation. The allusion is subtle but clear: Jesus stands in the place of Woman Wisdom.

4. Other Post-Proverbs Developments.

4.1. Sirach and Wisdom of Solomon. The NT was not the only or the earliest post-Hebrew Bible writing to further develop the metaphor of Woman Wisdom. She plays an important role in two major intertestamental books: *Sirach and *Wisdom of Solomon.

Sirach is known from a Greek translation (c. 130 BC), which is based on an earlier Hebrew composition (c. 180 BC). It is a prominent member of the Apocrypha. Sirach 1 introduces the figure of Woman Wisdom: "Wisdom was created before all other things, and prudent understanding from eternity.... It is he who created her; he saw her and took her measure; he poured her out upon all his works, upon all the living according to his gift; he lavished her upon those who love him" (Sir 1:4, 9-10 NRSV).

One of the most interesting developments of the Woman Wisdom figure in Sirach is the explicit connection drawn between her and the *law of Moses. Most scholars believe that in the book of Proverbs wisdom and law are two separate categories, but in Sirach 24 the two are equated: "Then the Creator of all things gave me [Woman Wisdom] a command, and my Creator chose the place for my tent. He said, 'Make your dwelling in Jacob, and in Israel receive your inheritance'" (Sir 24:8 NRSV); "'Whoever obeys me [Woman Wisdom] will not be put to shame, and those who work with me will not sin.' All this is the book of the covenant of the Most High God, the law that Moses commanded us, as an inheritance for the congregations of Jacob" (Sir 24:22-23 NRSV [see also Sir 15:1; 19:20; 33:2]). In this way, Sirach further develops the metaphor of Woman Wisdom in the direction of Jewish particularism (Snaith).

In Wisdom of Solomon (see Enns), another prominent book of the Apocrypha, dated between 50 BC and AD 100, the figure of Woman Wisdom is used to assimilate Jewish and Hellenistic wisdom, in particular a Stoic and Neoplatonic mindset: "She [Wisdom] is an exhalation from the power of God, a pure effluence from the glory of the Almighty; therefore nothing tainted insinuates itself into her. She is an effulgence of everlasting light, and unblemished mirror of the active power of God, and an image of his goodness" (Wis 7:25-26 [translation in Winston, 184-87]).

4.2. Arius. Arius (AD 260-336) was a popular preacher and theologian in the early church. He and his followers exploited the connection between Woman Wisdom (particularly from the Greek text of Proverbs 8) and Jesus as developed in the NT to argue that since Wisdom was created, Jesus was a created being and therefore not God.

Athanasius (c. AD 296-373) led the charge against Arius. The controversy allowed the church to further reflect and define its understanding of the nature of Christ and the Trinity. The controversy led to the production of the Nicene Creed, which asserts the following about Jesus, making it clear that the implications that Arius drew from Proverbs 8 were wrong-minded: "We believe . . . in one Lord Jesus Christ, the only begotten Son of God, born of the Father before all ages, light of flight, true God of true God, begotten not made, consubstantial with the Father, by whom all things were made."

Although the Catholic, Protestant and Orthodox churches followed Athanasius in this regard, the teaching of Arius is not dead. It is found among groups such as the Mormons and Jehovah's Witnesses, who deny that Jesus is fully God as well as fully man. In their understanding, Jesus is a created being, and again Proverbs 8 is a proof text for their belief.

4.3. Modern Feminist Interpretation. Some proponents of modern *feminist interpretation (e.g., Johnson; Schüssler Fiorenza) have used Proverbs 8 to forward their agenda to depatriarchalize the Christian religion. The NT presents a masculine savior, but these interpreters use Proverbs 8 and its connections in the NT to provide the basis for the worship of Sophia (*sophia* is the Greek equivalent of *ḥokmâ*, the Hebrew word for "wisdom"), a female picture of God. Such a view, like that of Arius, treats the description of Woman Wisdom as literal rather than metaphorical. It takes the metaphor too far and in a way that contradicts other Scripture (Jobes).

See also. FEMINIST INTERPRETATION; MAAT; PERSONIFICATION; PROVERBS 1: BOOK OF; WIS-DOM THEOLOGY.

BIBLIOGRAPHY. **J. Assmann,** *Ma'at: Gerechtigkeit und Unsterblichkeit im alten Ägypten* (Munich: Beck, 1990); **C. V. Camp,** *Wisdom and the Feminine in the Book of Proverbs* (BLS 11; Sheffield: Sheffield Academic Press, 1985); **P. Enns,** *Exodus Retold: Ancient Exegesis of the Departure from Egypt in Wis 10:15-21 and 19:1-9* (HSM 57; Atlanta: Scholars Press, 1997); **C. R. Fontaine,** *Smooth Words: Women, Proverbs and Performance in Biblical Wisdom* (JSOTSup 356; Sheffield: Sheffield Academic Press, 2002); **K. Jobes,** "Sophia Christology: The Way of Wisdom?" in *The Way of Wisdom: Essays in Honor of Bruce K. Waltke* (Grand Rapids: Zondervan, 2000) 226-50; **E. A. Johnson,** "Wisdom Was Made Flesh," in *Reconstructing the Christ Symbol: Essays in Feminist Christology,* ed. M. Stevens (New York: Paulist Press, 1993) 99-102; **C. Kayatz,** *Studien zu Proverbien 1-9: Eine form- und motivgeschichtliche Untersuchung unter Einbeziehung ägyptischen Vergleichsmaterials* (WMANT 22; Neukirchen-Vluyn, 1966); **B. Lang,** *Wisdom and the Book of Proverbs: A Hebrew Goddess Redefined* (New York: Pilgrim Press, 1986); **T. Longman III,** *Proverbs* (BCOTWP; Grand Rapids: Baker, 2006); **M. S. Smith,** *The Early History of God* (2nd ed.; Grand Rapids: Eerdmans, 2002); **J. G. Snaith,** "Ecclesiasticus: A Tract for Our Time," in *Wisdom in Ancient Israel,* ed. J. Day, R. P. Gordon and H. G. M. Williamson (Cambridge: Cambridge University Press, 1995) 170-81; **R. E. Murphy,** "Wisdom's Song: Proverbs 1:20-33," *CBQ* 48 (1986) 456-60; **E. Schüssler Fiorenza,** "Wisdom Mythology and the Christological Hymns of the New Testament," in *Aspects of Wisdom in Judaism and Early Christianity,* ed. R. L. Wilken (Notre Dame, IN: University of Notre Dame Press, 1975); **P. Trible,** "Wisdom Builds a Poem: The Architecture of Proverbs 1:20-33," *JBL* 94 (1975) 509-18; **D. Winston,** *The Wisdom of Solomon* (AB 43; Garden City, NY: Doubleday, 1979); **B. Witherington III,** *Jesus the Sage: The Pilgrimage of Wisdom* (Minneapolis: Fortress, 1994).

T. Longman III

WOMEN

Women in the literature covered by this *Dictionary* mirror the extremes of the genres. Portrayed in hyperbole, they range from *Woman Wisdom to Woman Folly, the seductress to the virtuous wife, the adulteress to the mother. They include the lazy gossip and the woman so industrious that "her lamp does not go out by night" (Prov

31:18). Sometimes they come in groups, like the Daughters of Jerusalem. As independent women, they also portray aspects of stereotypical norms: *Naomi as the widow; *Ruth as the dutiful, loving daughter-in-law and humble proselyte; *Esther as the savior queen. Some break stereotypes, for the lovely shepherd maiden in *Song of Songs actively pursues her beloved and is his equal in love's emotional and physical aspects. This literature presents its women as no more or less virtuous than are its men. Instead, these women come through as real people living in a believable marketplace, as real human beings moving through stages of life that provoke public comment and observation.

1. Women in Ecclesiastes
2. Women in Job
3. Women in Lamentations
4. Women in Song of Songs
5. Women in Psalms
6. Women in Proverbs
7. Women in Ruth
8. Women in Esther
9. Conclusion

1. Women in Ecclesiastes.

Complex and at times grim, the book of *Ecclesiastes nevertheless offers insights not only on seasons in life (Eccles 3:1-8) but also on temperaments in life; it balances aspects of the book of *Proverbs. Whereas in Proverbs wisdom is personified as a woman who is accessible, just and loving (Prov 8:1-8), in Ecclesiastes wisdom is remote (Eccles 7:23-24) (Fontaine 1992a, 153). Whereas in Proverbs the search for wisdom leads to an ordered life marked by prosperity and longevity, the search for wisdom by the writer of Ecclesiastes leads him—at least for a season—to hate his life (Eccles 2:17).

The writer calls himself *Qohelet, the teacher, son of *David, king in Jerusalem (Eccles 1:1). Qohelet evaluates all aspects of life, including women, from a distance. He views women dispassionately and somewhat selfishly. His observations, however, lead to the conclusion that women—or at least companionship—help out in life. Ecclesiastes 4:11 may refer to the *marriage relationship because a wife can provide aid, warmth at night and protection, but the next verse, Ecclesiastes 4:12, stating that a threefold cord is not easily broken, probably speaks of friendship rather than marriage because the context of the passage (Eccles 4:9-12) stresses

mutual help. The passage advocates a plurality of work, mutual help and jointly fending off shared enemies rather than an attitude of individualism and going it alone (Murphy 1992, 42). Lives entwined in mutual help produce a strong and enduring community (Provan, 106).

In addition to a kind of objectivity and to advocating an arm's-length approach, Qohelet sees life in terms of contradictions and philosophizes about life's alternatives and twists and turns. His advice is to enjoy life to the fullest, and that includes enjoying women! A possible reference to sexual intercourse is "a time to scatter stones and a time to gather them" (Eccles 3:5), according to some readings, including the *Midrash Rabbah* (Murphy 1992, 33). If indeed sexual intercourse is the meaning, then it fits with the sense of the verse, which condones both a time to embrace and a time to refrain from embracing (Eccles 3:5). Yet the meaning also may be blurred to a literal meaning, simply considering the prevalence of stony fields in Israel.

The writer values women in terms of what they can do for him in traditional roles: women provide sustenance, entertainment and sexual pleasure. In short, they are necessary for his enjoyment of life (Fontaine 1992a, 154). Women also engage in other activities, he notes. Ecclesiastes 12:4 refers to women as "the daughters of song." In keeping with the Israelite tradition of women singing, these "daughters of song" may have performed funeral dirges (cf. Jer 9:20) (Carter 2002, 305). Another tradition views "daughters of song" as the birdlike sound of a human voice (Murphy 1992, 119) or a poetic description of birds (Longman 1998, 271).

In step with his time, the writer of Ecclesiastes includes some derogatory sayings about women. In Ecclesiastes a woman is a snare, and such a woman is more bitter than death; her heart is a trap, and her hands are chains (Eccles 7:26a). But the writer offers a way out of entrapment. In contrast to the ensnared sinner, the man who pleases God will escape her (Eccles 7:26b). With the use of the definite article, "the woman" specifies for Qohelet a particular woman, probably akin to the seductive adulteress or strange or foolish woman of Proverbs and the antithesis of wisdom (Prov 2:16-19; 5:3-6; 7:6-27; 9:13-18) (Brown, 83). Fearing this woman, Qohelet says that pleasing God amounts to escaping her; disturbingly, in contrast to Proverbs, this woman looms larger than does Woman Wisdom for the teacher (Brown, 84).

Sadly, in all his searchings the writer of Ecclesiastes has not found one woman to meet his standards, and only one man in a thousand is upright. However, he fails to specify his grading scale (Eccles 7:28). His observation is merely that—an observation that satisfies him but may leave his readers unsatisfied. His statement may show his true colors: he is a misogynist, and his views are inconsistent with the rest of Scripture (Longman 1998, 206-7). The NIV translation clarifies this verse by adding the adjective "upright" before both "man" and "woman." Indeed, upright women abound in the biblical text: Ruth, Sarah, Esther, Miriam, Huldah and Deborah, to name some of them. A gentler verdict on Qohelet sees him as sadly surveying the multitudes of men and women whom he has known and finding that all, in both genders, lack virtue. Yet if the writer is *Solomon, then this statement also could mean that his lifelong pursuit of women produced a negative effect on his reputation and life (Schwab, 23).

However, the writer of Ecclesiastes also admonishes his readers with more positive sayings. He encourages joyful expression in dress and grooming: "Always be clothed in white, and always anoint your head with oil" (Eccles 9:8). He advises a man to enjoy the life that he's given with his wife, even though the days are meaningless (Eccles 9:9). With this statement, the writer emerges as a person of his times, for he presents women via extremes. He rattles off a conventional view of woman as snare and seductress and then rousingly advocates celebrating life with one's mate and family.

2. Women in Job.
The book of *Job contains women in secondary roles. The number of women depends on whether Job had one wife or two, and how many sisters he had (Job 42:11). What is known is that he had six daughters; of these, three were killed with their brothers in a freak wind accident (Job 1:18), and three were born after God restored Job's fortunes (Job 42:13-15). According to Jewish tradition, the wife who gave him his second set of children (Job 42) is Dinah, the daughter of Jacob (*EncJud* 10.124).

When misfortune strikes Job, his (first and only?) wife speaks these words: "Are you still holding on to your integrity? Curse God and die" (Job 2:9). Interpretations of her words run the spectrum from Augustine's view of her as an "adjutant of the devil" to the idea that perhaps her words offered Job a way out of his suffering (Deen, 333). Perhaps she berates her husband for his integrity (Blessing, 278). Job replies by saying that she speaks like a foolish woman, and he encourages her to see their predicament as he does: it is part of life. As a couple, their response should be to accept the bad from the hand of the Lord as well as the good (Job 2:10). Although she too lost everything along with Job, the text from here on muzzles her; Job's grief and misfortunes, not hers, receive textual consideration and analysis. Her next mention is in Job 19:17, where Job comments that his breath offends her.

The three daughters born as part of Job's restoration are named (unlike their deceased siblings and Job's sisters, wife or wives). The daughters are called Jemimah (dove), Keziah (cinnamon or the perfume of a flower) and Keren-Happuch (container of antimony, an expensive black coloring used in eye makeup) (Gardner, 399). In addition to providing the names of these new daughters, the text awards them this accolade: "Nowhere in all the land were there found women as beautiful as Job's daughters" (Job 42:15). The daughters also receive an inheritance along with their brothers (Job 42:15).

Perhaps in giving them an inheritance, Job exemplifies that he learned a bit about the wonderful grace of God. His fortunes are restored and doubled (Job 42:10) because of God's gracious action (Flesher 2002a, 287). Job passes on this gracious bounty by including his daughters.

3. Women in Lamentations.
The "Daughter of Zion" in the book of *Lamentations, a metaphor throughout Lamentations 1, is depicted in horrific terms. She is Yahweh's daughter (Flesher 2002b, 392). Now like a widow, the Daughter of Zion, bears the worst of fates. Once a great queen among the nations, now she has become a slave (Lam 1:1). Once full of sons, she now is deserted, and her fate is exile. Her foes now master her, her glory is departed, and the world mocks her. Shamefully exposed with filthiness clinging to her skirts, she cowers, despised and naked, and none comfort her (Lam 1:8-9). In Lamentations 1:12 the poetry goes to first person, and Jerusalem laments her suffering herself. Jerusalem blames God for making her

desolate, for handing her over to those whom she cannot withstand and sapping her strength (Lam 1:12-14). However, she repents, acknowledging the righteousness of the Lord and her rebellion against his command (Lam 1:18).

*Zion has become like Babylon in Isaiah 47:1-15 (Dearman, 430). Jerusalem has been forsaken by her lovers—a sexual metaphor common in the prophets (Ezek 16:36) that can indicate either the other gods that she pursued or her unfaithful neighbors (Dearman, 443). The image of the widow is used throughout prophetic literature to shame Israel into repentance (Flesher 2002b, 392). A biblical principle, however, is that God's purpose in rendering shame or punishment is restoration and repentance.

The speaker in Lamentations holds God accountable for his severe parental discipline brought to bear on his weak virgin daughter. The literary tendency of Lamentations to contrast female metaphors seems to petition God to redeem and restore (Flesher 2002b, 393). Actually, Jerusalem must be restored because of the character of God; Jerusalem belongs unequivocally to God, and that is the legal ground for her cry for ultimate restoration (Lam 5:21).

4. Women in Song of Songs.
The presence of Song of Songs in the Bible presents a surprise, for the set of poems comprising this short book runs against the emphasis on restraint in female sexuality elsewhere in the biblical text. Instead, the woman often pursues the man whom she loves, often instigates lovemaking, and is by far the more talkative of the pair. For centuries Song of Songs was interpreted as "an earthly symbol with a heavenly meaning, an allegory throughout" (Stuart, 4). The allegorical interpretation by the Jews was that the book represented God's love for Israel, and by the Christians that it represented Christ's love for the church. Recently, however, these allegorical interpretations have increasingly fallen on hard times, and Songs of Songs is read more literally as a set of poems that explore frankly and forthrightly the love between a man and a woman (*see* Song of Songs 3: History of Interpretation).

The modern tendency and preference to interpret Song of Song's poetry straightforwardly and literally were seen as early as Theodore of Mopuestia (AD 350-428) and later by S. Castellio and J. Calvin (Longman 2001, 38). Writing in the nineteenth century, F. Delitzsch considered the lovely Shulammite to be a real person, virtuous, and possessing "a beautiful soul in a body formed as it were from the dust of the flowers" (Delitzsch, 3, 5 [see Longman 2001, 40-41]). M. Pope, a twentieth-century commentator, noted the growing tendency of scholars to reject an allegorical interpretation of Song of Songs and to read the poetry as applying "to human physical love" (Pope, 17).

Truly, Song of Songs celebrates human sexuality. It bypasses cultural norms by insisting on the right of the woman to love another of her own choosing; the man likewise enjoys that right (Weems, 156).

The positive dimensions of love portrayed in Song of Songs give clues to the Bible's view of molding a strong bond between a woman and a man (Hill and Walton, 381). The Shulammite maiden models for her shepherd-lover, and he for her, a genuine love that shows its sincerity and fidelity by strength of character and by passion. Their love for each other exudes faithfulness, integrity, spontaneity, loyalty and commitment (Song 4:12-16; 7:11-13; 8:10-12).

The Shulammite is the only unmediated female voice in Scripture (Weems, 156). Her feelings, thoughts and desires are conveyed in monologues and not, like the thoughts of Ruth and Esther, via a narrator's voice. Consequently, the young woman's presence dominates the book.

The poems describe love via poetic images and comparisons. The out of doors captivates the lovers, and sensory delights augment their love. The senses of smell, touch, sight, taste and hearing help the lovers to describe one another. The shepherd-lover describes his darling as overwhelming him with her eyes. Her hair is like a flock of goats; her teeth like sheep coming up from a washing; her temples behind her veil like halves of a pomegranate. Truly, his beloved is lovelier than sixty queens and eighty concubines (Song 6:4-8). The Shulammite exults in her power and influence over her lover. Clearly, this shepherd maiden is a sensual woman in touch with her sexuality (Weems, 158).

The voices in Song of Songs offer multiple interpretations and demarcations for biblical editors. For example, the TEV has it that there are six songs (Song 1:2—2:7; 2:8—3:5; 3:6—5:1; 5:2—6:3; 6:4—8:4; 8:5-14). The NIV calls the woman "the beloved," and the man "the lover"; a group called "friends" also speak in Song of Songs 1:4b, 8; 5:1b, 9; 6:1, 10, 13; and 8:5, 8-9.

The Shulammite, however, refers to them as "daughters of Jerusalem" (Song 2:7; 3:5; 8:4). She wisely tells them not to rush into love but rather wait for the right moment—a moment that she enjoys finding again and again (Longman 2001, 131).

5. Women in Psalms.

It is entirely possible that women, although excluded from the priesthood in Israel, participated in the worship of Israel as musicians and as part of the singing community (Num 10:35-36; 2 Sam 6:12-15; Ps 68:24-27) (Kroeger, 297). Likewise, it is possible that they were employed as performers in the temple as liturgical musicians and singers (Carter, 305). Women initiated or joined in the praise of the Lord as victor, as creator, and as one who is a father to the fatherless and a defender of widows (Ps 68:5).

The book of *Psalms underlines the faith and influence of women. In Psalm 35:14 the psalmist speaks of a child's love of the mother, mourning her death. The psalmist describes himself in these terms of honor: he is the Lord's servant and the son of the Lord's maidservant (Ps 116:16).

In Psalm 45, a song of praise for a king on his wedding day, women figure in the wedding party. Daughters of kings and honored women accompany the bride (Ps 45:9). The royal bride receives some advice from the psalmist: she should forget her people and be encouraged because her beauty enthralls the king (Ps 45:10). Her wedding night will be successful because sons will become princes throughout the land (Ps 45:16).

Individual women and their concerns receive mention in the psalms. Fear of God makes people tremble like a woman in labor (Ps 48:6). Daughters are renowned for their beauty. The daughters of covenant Israel will be like pillars carved to adorn a palace (Ps 144:12). The Lord honors the barren woman with a home of her own and makes her the happy mother of children); this public miracle leads the community to praise the Lord, a fitting conclusion for the psalm (Ps 113:9).

The birth process, a rich motif in the psalms, has both physical and spiritual dimensions. Psalm 22:9-10 declares that the Lord brought the psalmist from the womb; simultaneously with nursing at his mother's breast, the psalmist learned to trust in the Lord. "From my mother's womb you have been my God," (Ps 22:10) he acknowledges.

6. Women in Proverbs.

Proverbs presents a multitude of character stereotypes. Drawn in exaggeration, they show the extremes of habits, patterns in life and choices in life (Branch 2005, 57). Proverbs equally presents men and women in good and bad lights. Male characters include the father, husband, king, son, drunkard, sluggard, stubborn man and violent man. Female characters include the mother, noble wife, queen, gossip, adulteress, strange or foreign woman, Woman Folly and *Woman Wisdom.

The roles of father and mother are equal in Proverbs; the mother as well as the father is honored and is a source of teaching and instruction (Prov 1:8). A concept in Proverbs is that correct teaching from parents can save a young and simple man from the adulteress, from the loose and foreign woman with her seductive words (Prov 2:16) (Whybray, 22; Branch 2005, 64).

Scholars debate the identity of this seductress (Prov 2:16-22; 5:1-14, 15-23; 6:20-29, 30-35; 7:1-23, 24-27). Is she a foreign and secular harlot, a foreign devotee to a foreign god, a foreign goddess, a social outsider, a native prostitute or another man's wife (see Fox, 134)? The scholarly consensus is that she probably is an adulteress, a woman far away from her husband or whose husband is away (Miller, 317; Branch 2005, 64).

Questions likewise surround the character Woman Wisdom (Prov 1:20-33; 3:13-20; 4:5-9; 7:4; 8:1-36; 9:1-6). Is she a goddess? Does she express the feminine side of royalty and divinity? She may have a parallel with the Egyptian concept of justice (*maat), but she also appears to be distinctly Hebraic and a new, unique contribution to Wisdom literature (see Murphy 1998, 279). On the human side, she may represent a synopsis of the positive roles played by wives and mothers in Israelite society (Fontaine 1992b, 146). She confidently addresses men and women in a busy part of the city, a place of power (Branch 2005, 59). On the divine side, Hildegard of Bingen linked Woman Wisdom to beauty and a high regard for the aesthetic life; she saw Woman Wisdom as combining both a menacing strength and a soft goodness (Fierro, 26).

Woman Wisdom's opposite is Woman Folly, a loud, brash woman, sloppy in bearing yet brazenly attractive (Prov 9:13-17); she displays an open dislike for Woman Wisdom (Branch 2005, 58). Her lifestyle and her home entice the simple to the realm of the dead. Choosing her lifestyle leads slowly not only to sexual seduction but also to seduction by an alien religion (Perdue, 148). Woman Folly presents an open threat to family, society and God's covenant.

Continuing in a negative light, the seductress, adulteress and the strange or foreign woman present a composite of male fears about female temptation: the ways of these women lead to death—actually to Sheol (Prov 2:16-19; 5:3-6; 7:6-27; 9:13-18). Casting wide her net of charms, the adulteress captures a simple youth and leads him to death like a bird in a snare (Prov 7:23); she entices a silly, deceived adult man, and his life ends in shame (Prov 6:32-33) (Branch 2005, 65). The adulterer brings not only ruin on himself but also the physical blows and fury of the betrayed husband who refuses to be compensated with a bribe (Murphy 1998, 39).

However, even with these negatives, women receive much strong, positive affirmation in Proverbs. A man is commanded to rejoice with the wife of his youth (Prov 5:18). A good wife is considered to be a gift from God, and he who finds a wife finds what is good and receives favor from the Lord (Prov 18:22).

Proverbs ends with an *acrostic poem about the ideal wife or woman of worth. She may reflect the socioeconomic realities of women living in the Persian period (Yoder, 428). This paragon of virtue and industry gets up before dawn, supervises her household, makes quilts for her bed, gives to the poor, buys a field on her own initiative, and raises grateful children. Her husband, after years of marriage, is still in love with her. The poem, written from the perspective of an observer who probably is male, notes the economic initiative and business acumen of the woman (Schüssler Fiorenza, 109).

But the poem also gives a glimpse into a successful, working marriage (Branch 2003, 20). The speaker of the poem is not the woman, for a woman of such high caliber would not praise herself. Instead, the speaker seems to be one who has observed the marriage over a long period of time. This marriage is a marriage of different individuals, each permitting the other to excel according to his or her abilities. The partners then bring back to their marriage and family the results of their industry. They share the joys of their daily endeavors. The picture presented in the acrostic poem is one of life, happiness, confidence in the future, industry and respect. The poem gives many clues about what the partners contribute to the marriage. The husband publicly praises his wife, and he does so again and again (Prov 31:28-29). The wife's industry makes the husband's life one in which he can excel as a magistrate at the city gate (Prov 31:19, 23). Their marriage shows a partnership of diverse equals, one in which the wife invests in real estate without seeking her husband's input, sanction or approval (Prov 31:16). The partners exhibit integrity and trustworthiness, but the wife is singled out as the depository of her husband's whole confidence and trust (Prov 31:11). His praise seems to make her thrive and she decides to do even more (Branch 2003, 22). She directs her handmaidens early in the day and provides a good breakfast for all her employees. This woman enjoys work, and the whole family profits by her industry. She sews her bed linens and clothes in the richest of all colors, purple (Prov 31:22).

This truly remarkable woman must be honored publicly, and Proverbs ends with giving her a place at the city gate, perhaps alongside her husband (Prov 31:23, 31). This woman behaves in such a way that all know that she is a woman who fears Yahweh. The poem, which ends the book of Proverbs, shows that such excellence of character can come only from a firm religious faith (Whybray, 187). An *inclusio, the *fear of the Lord, brackets the book (Prov 1:7; 31:30).

Why does the book of Proverbs end with a poem emphasizing a woman and pointing toward the qualities of an ideal wife? The authors and compilers of the book do not say. Perhaps it is because a goal of Wisdom literature is a life well lived, and part of having a well-lived life is having a happy marriage. The book begins with advice from a father and mother to their son (Prov 1:8) and ends with perhaps their benediction on this son: their wish for him to find an exemplary wife who will bless him all her days (Prov 31:12), provide him delightful children (Prov 31:28), and join him in fearing the Lord (Prov 1:7; 31:30). In living a life hallmarked by wise choices, the woman of Proverbs 31 becomes herself a model of Woman Wisdom. Significantly, both Woman Wisdom and a noble wife are sought and found (Prov 8:35; 18:22).

The noble wife and Woman Wisdom merge on several levels. Each is practical; each is a faithful guide and lifelong companion. Although the origin of Woman Wisdom is God (Prov 8:22-30), her home is this world (McCreesh, 46). Although Woman Wisdom may be abstract, the noble wife of Proverbs 31 is a believable, confident, real woman contributing to the needs of her community and thoroughly enjoying the life she lives. The noble wife serves as a concrete example of Woman Wisdom.

7. Women in Ruth.

The women in the book of Ruth are Naomi; her two daughters-in-law, Orpah and Ruth; and the anonymous women of Bethlehem.

The women of Bethlehem greet with consternation the return of Naomi, accompanied by her daughter-in-law Ruth, a Moabitess (Ruth 1:19). Months later, the women of Bethlehem again figure importantly in the story after Ruth and *Boaz marry and their son is born. The women prophesy and bless Naomi. They point out that Naomi now has a *kinsman-redeemer. They pray that the baby will become famous throughout Israel. They prophesy that the baby will renew Naomi's life and sustain her in her old age. They point out to Naomi that Ruth is better for her than seven sons (Ruth 4:14-15).

The book develops the character of Naomi via her hardships. She faces famine, the journey to Moab, the deaths of her husband and two sons, the travel (probably by foot) back to Bethlehem, and a bitter life as a poor widow surviving on the subsistence gleanings of her daughter-in-law Ruth. Naomi's name means "pleasant." When the women of Bethlehem greet her, however, Naomi tells them not to call her "pleasant" but rather "bitter." She adds her own reason, blaming God: "The Almighty has made my life very bitter. I went away full, but the LORD has brought me back empty.... The Almighty has brought misfortune upon me" (Ruth 1:20-21). The book chronicles both Naomi's grief and her recovery.

The book also chronicles the story of Ruth, a Moabite proselyte who leaves her homeland because she loves her mother-in-law. Ruth wins the hearts of all who see her. People notice her faithfulness to her mother-in-law, whom all in Bethlehem seem to know as a loveable but crotchety widow. Likewise, Ruth's chastity as a widow (Ruth 2:11, 23) earns her their esteem (Ruth 2:23; 3:10).

Modest, meek, courteous, loyal, responsible and gentle (Deen, 82), Ruth nonetheless knows her own mind and sets goals. She knows that she must have a husband to ensure her standing in the community and to provide safety for herself and her mother-in-law. Ruth displays her decisiveness in words twice in the book. First, she firmly refuses to leave her mother-in-law and let her journey unaccompanied from Moab to Bethlehem (Ruth 1:16-18). Second, she proposes to Boaz. In the intimate scene at the threshing floor, she describes herself an ʾāmâ, a servant—yes, but a servant who can be taken as a wife (Roop, 61), and she commands Boaz to spread his garment over her, clearly a proposal for marriage (Ruth 3:9)!

Earlier, Ruth had displayed her flirtatious side. While gleaning in a field that turns out to belong to Boaz, she catches his eye. Singling her out as the new person in town, he praises her publicly, thereby providing her protection (Ruth 2:9). When he prays that she be "richly rewarded by the LORD, under whose wings you have taken refuge" (Ruth 2:12), she replies, "May I continue to find favor in *your* eyes, *my lord*" (Ruth 2:13 [italics added]).

Boaz, ironically, becomes the vehicle for answering his own prayer. He is the kinsman-redeemer. Through a levirate marriage he marries Ruth and takes control of the property of Elimelech, Kilion and Mahlon (Ruth 4:9), thereby providing for her and her mother-in-law (Weisberg, 426).

8. Women in Esther.

The book of Esther contains three named women: *Vashti, queen of Persia; Esther, her successor; and Zeresh, wife of the villainous Haman. Anonymous female characters include a group of young women candidates for queen, and a general category of maidservants of Esther the queen. Only the named women speak.

According to haggadah lore, Vashti, daughter of Belshazzar and granddaughter of Nebuchadnezzar, loved her acclaimed position as the most beautiful woman in the world (Rappoport, 247-48). The story opens with a prolonged banquet that King *Ahasuerus (Xerxes) held for his governing nobles. In a state of drunkenness, he tells his governors of Vashti's excellent beauty. His drinking partners ask to see her. But more than that, they ask to see her naked. Xerxes approves, ordering her to appear wearing only her crown (cf. Esther 1:11). Vashti, according to Jewish interpretation, was no prude and was vain to the core. But while preparing to answer the king's summons, she discovered that she was leprous on her forehead and body. Her leprosy could not be disguised by cosmetics. So she hid behind a false modesty in her response to her husband; she belittled him publicly. She sent him a flippant, surly note proclaiming him a fool, liar, madman and boaster (Rappoport, 248). Because of her impudence, she was condemned to death. In haggadah Vashti joins Jezebel and Athaliah, two other biblical queens (2 Kings 9:30-37; 11), and Semiramis, wife of Nimrod and queen of Babylon, as one of four women who achieved power in the world (*Enc-Jud* 3.814).

The biblical text quickly shifts from Vashti to the drama of choosing her successor. By edict of the king, Persia's virgins are rounded up and taken to the palace for instruction in grooming and court etiquette. Esther, a Jewish maiden, wins the favor of Hegai, the one in charge of the harem, and he assigns her extra beauty treatments, special food and personal maids (Esther 2:8-9). It would seem that Hegai also controlled the time when Esther went to the king to spend the night (Esther 2:15). Indeed, Xerxes chooses Esther as his queen. Significantly, the text says that she wins the favor of all who saw her (Esther 2:9, 15, 17).

But the king's chief advisor is Haman, an Agagite, a designation that probably shows him to be a descendant of Agag the Amalekite; the Amalekites are hereditary enemies of the Jews (1 Sam 15:6-32). Haman hates the Jews and seeks to destroy them. The king gives him a free hand. Time and date are set for their extermination. *Mordecai, a relative of Esther, realizes that she will not escape the destruction just because she is in the king's palace. He persuades her to go to the king for the lives of her people (Esther 4:12-16). Esther agrees. With the words "If I perish, I perish" (Esther 4:16), Esther emerges as a woman and assumes her destiny. She decides to speak out, even if it means her death. Her decision combines courage, humility and piety; she seeks God via fasting and solicits like support from her community (Bechtel, 50).

Esther seems to think through the ways open to her. She sets a course and keeps to it. The course involves calculation and manipulation. She knows the king, and she uses this knowledge to her and her people's advantage. She fights for the lives of her people and for herself.

Courageous, and using her beauty and her status as wife of the king to her advantage, she comes to the king, defying the decree that those who enter his presence uninvited be killed (Esther 4:11). Dressed in her royal robes and risking her life, she enters the throne room, but he extends his scepter to her, thereby sparing her life (Esther 5:1-2). She requests his attendance, and Haman's, at a banquet that she will give that day. The king and Haman come to her private banquet.

Mysterious and gracious, she refuses to tell the king her request until the following day at another intimate banquet. Meanwhile, Haman erects gallows to hang Mordecai. But the king endures a sleepless night and works at his books. He finds that Mordecai has not been rewarded for earlier saving his life (Esther 2:21-23; 6:1-4). The king commands that Haman honor Mordecai by leading him mounted on a horse throughout *Susa and proclaiming that this is how the king honors one who serves him (Esther 6:11). Humiliated, Haman goes home, where his wife, Zeresh, and friends predict that Haman's downfall in front of the rise of the Jew Mordecai is immanent (Esther 6:13). Zeresh's words ring prophetically true.

Guards escort Haman to the queen's second banquet. There, Esther reveals that she and her people have been targeted for extermination by the evil Haman (Esther 7:1-6). The king leaves in a rage. He returns to find Haman, as he begs Esther for his life, throwing himself on the couch where she reclines (Esther 7:8). The king interprets this as an attempt to ravish the queen in his presence. Haman is taken out and hanged on the gallows that he built for Mordecai.

But the lethal legal difficulty—the king's irrevocable extermination edict—remains. Mordecai and Esther advise the king to send new documents, with the king's signature, allowing the Jews to defend themselves. They do, and many of their enemies are killed.

Esther's life and position enable a reversal of her people's status in Persia. Oppressed, they nonetheless stand up to their adversaries and earn the respect of their former persecutors. Both Esther and her people now are powerful and respected. Esther became a hero for the Diaspora Jews in her lifetime and subsequently. Esther's influence combines both strength of character and faith. She serves as a model for persecuted Jews and Christians throughout the centuries.

9. Conclusion.

Women in Wisdom literature provide a fascinating array of lifestyles pertinent to both genders. From queen to commoner, wise woman to foolish slut, faithful wife to insensitive gossip, young woman in love to widow in grief, covenant believer to alien apostate, women are presented in a full range of personalities and functions. Often using hyperbole to make a point, Wisdom literature teaches the consequences of life's choices via exaggeration. Wisdom literature in particular seeks to influence youths to choose wisely and adults to continue along a wise path. Truly, the young woman in Song of Songs points to the ongoing delights of love (and wisdom) when she urges her lover to come away "and be like a gazelle, or like a young stag on the spice-laden mountains" (Song 8:14).

See also ESTHER 1: BOOK OF; ESTHER 6: PERSON; FEMINIST INTERPRETATION; HONOR AND SHAME; KINSMAN-REDEEMER AND LEVIRATE; MARRIAGE AND SEX; NAOMI; RUTH 1: BOOK OF; RUTH 4: PERSON; SONG OF SONGS 1: BOOK OF; VASHTI; WASF; WOMAN WISDOM AND WOMAN FOLLY .

BIBLIOGRAPHY. **C. M. Bechtel,** *Esther* (IBC; Louisville: John Knox, 2002); **K. A. Blessing,** "Job," in *The IVP Women's Bible Commentary*, ed. C. C. Kroeger and M. J. Evans (Downers Grove, IL: InterVarsity Press, 2002) 273-87; **R. G. Branch,** "Spreuke 31:10-31: 'n Bybelse model vir die huwelik," *Die Kerkblad* 106 (2003) 20-22; idem, "Teaching the Old Testament Book of Proverbs via a Play," *Christian Higher Education* 4 (2005) 57-69; **W. P. Brown,** *Ecclesiastes* (IBC; Louisville: John Knox, 2000); **P. Carter,** "Women as Psalmists," in *The IVP Women's Bible Commentary*, ed. C. C. Kroeger and M. J. Evans (Downers Grove, IL: InterVarsity Press, 2002) 305-6; **J. A. Dearman,** *Jeremiah, Lamentations* (NIVAC; Grand Rapids: Zondervan, 2002); **E. Deen,** *All the Women of the Bible* (New York: Harper & Row, 1955); **F. Delitzsch,** *Proverbs, Ecclesiastes, Song of Solomon* (Grand Rapids: Eerdmans, 1975); **N. Fierro,** *Hildegard of Bingen and Her Vision of the Feminine* (Kansas City, MO: Sheed & Ward, 1994); **L. S. Flesher,** "Job," in *The Women's Bible Commentary*, ed. C. A. Newsom and S. H. Ringe (Louisville: Westminster John Knox, 2002a) 273-88; idem, "Lamentations," in *The Women's Bible Commentary*, ed. C. A. Newsom and S. H. Ringe (Louisville: Westminster John Knox, 2002b) 392-95; **C. R. Fontaine,** "Ecclesiastes," in *The Women's Bible Commentary*, ed. C. A. Newsom and S. H. Ringe (Louisville: Westminster John Knox, 1992a) 153-55; idem, "Proverbs," in *The Women's Bible Commentary*, ed. C. A. Newsom and S. H. Ringe (Louisville: Westminster John Knox, 1992b) 145-52; **M. V. Fox,** *Proverbs 1-9* (AB 18A; New York: Doubleday, 2000); **P. D. Gardner,** ed., *New International Encyclopedia of Bible Characters: The Complete Who's Who in the Bible* (Grand Rapids: Zondervan, 1995); **A. J. Hill and J. H. Walton,** *A Survey of the Old Testament* (2nd ed.; Grand Rapids: Zondervan, 2000); **C. C. Kroeger,** "The Relevance of Psalms for the Everyday Lives of Women," in *The Women's Bible Commentary*, ed. C. A. Newsom and S. H. Ringe (Louisville: Westminster John Knox, 2002) 297-99; **T. Longman III,** *The Book of Ecclesiastes* (NICOT; Grand Rapids: Eerdmans, 1998); idem, *Song of Songs* (NICOT; Grand Rapids: Zondervan, 2001); **T. P. McCreesh,** "Wisdom as Wife: Proverbs 31:10-31," *RB* 92 (1985) 25-46; **J. W. Miller,** *The Believers Church Bible Commentary: Proverbs* (Scottsdale, PA: Herald Press, 2004); **R. E. Murphy,** *Ecclesiastes* (WBC 23A; Dallas: Word, 1992); idem, *Proverbs* (WBC 22; Nashville: Thomas Nelson, 1998); **L. G. Perdue,** *Proverbs* (IBC; Louisville: John Knox, 2000); **M. H. Pope,** *Song of Songs* (AB 7C; Garden City, NY: Doubleday, 1977); **I. Provan,** *Ecclesiastes, Song of Songs* (NIVAC; Grand Rapids: Zondervan, 2001); **A. S. Rappoport,** *Ancient Israel: Myths and Legends,* vol. 3 (London: Senate, 1995); **E. F. Roop,** *Ruth, Jonah, Esther* (Believers Church Bible Commentary; Scottdale, PA: Herald Press, 2002); **E. Schüssler Fiorenza,** *In Memory of Her: A Feminist Theological Reconstruction of Christian Origins* (New York: Crossroad, 2000); **G. Schwab,** "Woman as the Object of Qohelet's Search," *AUSS* 39 (2001) 73-84; **A. M. Stuart,** *The Song of Songs: An Exposition of the Song of Solomon* (Philadelphia: William S. Rentoul, 1869); **R. J. Weems,** "Song of Songs," in *The Women's Bible Commentary*, ed. C. A. Newsom and S. H. Ringe (Louisville: Westminster John Knox, 1992) 156-60; **D. E. Weisberg,** "The Widow of Our Discontent: Levirate Marriage in the Bible and Ancient Israel," *JSOT* 28 (2004) 403-29; **S. A. White,** "Esther," in *The Women's Bible Commentary*, ed. C. A. Newsom and S. H. Ringe (Louisville: Westminster John Knox, 1992) 124-29; **R. N. Whybray,** *The Book of Proverbs* (CBC; Cambridge: Cambridge University Press, 1972); **C. R. Yoder,** "The Woman of Substance: A Socioeconomic Reading of Proverbs 31:10-31," *JBL* 122 (2003) 427-47.

R. G. Branch

WORDPLAY

Wordplays are playful but significant uses of one and the same word or phrase with different meanings or of different words or phrases with the same meanings. Such imaginative, exciting and surprising uses of words or phrases can operate on the level of sentences, paragraphs or whole poems. The term *wordplay*, used here as elsewhere interchangeably with the designation *pun*, is a general one for several related but distinct literary devices.

1. Definitions and Terminology
2. Forms of Wordplay
3. How Puns Work: Technical Aspects and Examples
4. Functions

1. Definitions and Terminology.

Wordplays can be distinguished from sound plays (*see* Sound Patterns), which play on how words sound rather than on how they are written. There is, however, considerable overlap between the two, as words that sound similar often look similar. Wordplays come under the general category of *ambiguity, which is, among other factors, caused by polysemy or homonymy. The term *polysemy* identifies words that have two or more related senses, while the term *homonymy* identifies words that have two or more unrelated senses.

Occurrences of words with unconnected senses usually are treated as occurrences of different words, but sometimes it is difficult to decide between polysemy and homonymy. In many contexts ambiguity is a problematic textual feature. Where it is unintentional, a vague or equivocal expression occurring when precision and particularity of reference are needed leads to misunderstanding. Where intentional, an oblique or evasive expression can be misleading and even deceptive. However, ambiguity is also a deliberate poetic device, usually marked as such in the context. The use of a single word or expression to signify two or more distinct references, or to express two or more diverse attitudes or feelings, makes it possible to say much with few words (Empson; Abrams, 10-11). Polysemy can hint at the complexity and multiva-

lence of apparently simple ideas, and homonymy can signal connections between apparently unrelated ideas.

Wordplays, one of the main manifestations of ambiguity, can surprise, amuse, delight, invite curiosity and prompt active reader involvement while communicating serious, complex and significant information, and they can do so in few words. The terms *denotation* and *connotation* describe how polysemy works. The denotation of a word is its primary meaning or the entity to which it most commonly refers. Its connotation is the range of secondary or associated meanings and feelings that it usually suggests or implies. "The connotation of a word is only a potential range of secondary significations; which part of these connotations are evoked depends on the way the word is used in a particular context" (Abrams, 46). The potential of words and expressions to have various connotations is exploited in polysemous wordplays.

The term that was used to designate Wordplays in classical rhetoric is *paronomasia*, which then was used to describe words that were in some way marked as ambiguous and therefore invited the search for meanings beyond their denotation or most obvious connotations. In many modern studies of Hebrew poetry the term *paronomasia* is used more loosely to describe a combination of words that are similar in sound. A popular form of paronomasia is alliteration, the repetition of the same sound, usually initial consonants of words or of stressed syllables, in any sequence of neighboring words and even sentences. Paronomasia in this modern sense is used mainly for aesthetic effect, sometimes to combine otherwise unrelated statements into loose contexts.

2. Forms of Wordplay.

At the most basic level, there are two kinds of wordplays, homonymic puns and polysemantic puns.

2.1. Homonymic Pun. The homonymic pun uses different words that are pronounced and/or spelled in identical or similar fashion. The homonymic wordplay often is contrived and farfetched. The connection between the expressions that are brought into play is obtrusive and generally light-hearted because it appears accidental, a matter of sheer chance (Leech, 209). The extreme example of the homonymic pun "jumps out of its setting, yapping, and bites the

Master on the ankles" (Empson, 108). Examples range from the funny to the ridiculous, but they can serve useful purposes. The preposterous and ridiculous nature of such wordplays makes them stand out and hard to forget.

2.2. Polysemantic Pun. The polysemantic pun is more subtle and subdued. "Because of the resemblance between the senses, their collision is less violent" (Leech, 212). Expressing two meanings through the same occurrence, it "gives two meanings for the price of one, and so adds to the poem's density and richness of significance" (Leech, 212). Polysemantic wordplays carry a family resemblance to metaphors and metonymies. Often correspondences are conventional. Puns do not arbitrarily create such correspondences but rather express associations that are already manifest to the poet, who wants the audience to discover them as well. The correspondence is not contrived but rather is derived and/ or discerned.

3. How Puns Work: Technical Aspects and Examples.

Because they exploit ambiguity, puns are not always obvious. Many technical treatments of puns (e.g., Empson; Leech; Su) suggest that wordplays are always marked as such. The three main markers usually listed are (1) the presence of a double context, with each offering support for one meaning or a single context that can support more than one meaning; (2) the homonymous or polysemous nature of words or expressions; (3) the presence of a "trigger" that "calls the hearer's or reader's attention to the double meaning" (Su). However, the first and second constitute "marks" of wordplay, while only the third refers to "markers" of wordplay. The first and the second do not enforce or reinforce implicit similarities; they only make double meanings possible and likely. The conditions for punning are latent but are not enforced. To demonstrate this, we will look at some examples that display combinations of the three.

3.1. Unmarked Puns. Proverbs 5:3 offers a double context and polysemy. It employs two traditional techniques of punning, equivoque and double entendre. The term *equivoque* describes "the use of a single word or phrase which has two disparate meanings, in a context which makes both meanings equally relevant" (Leech, 213; Abrams, 253). (Sometimes the term

is erroneously used interchangeably with "pun" or "wordplay.") *Double entendre* is a French term meaning "double meaning," and it refers to a wordplay in which a word or phrase has a second, usually sexual, meaning. Proverbs 5:3: "For the *lips* of a strange woman drip honey, and her *palate* [*ḥikkâ*] is smoother than oil," is a good example. On the face of it, the words seem to refer to the "strange" woman's seductive speech (cf. NRSV: "For the lips of a loose woman drip honey, and her *speech* [for *ḥikkâ*] is smoother than oil"). Yet an Akkadian text suggests that "lips" here plays on the lips of the mouth and the lips of the pudenda: "May my *lips* be lallaru-*honey*, may my hands be all charm, may the *lips of my pudenda* be *lips of honey*" (Watson, 247). In Song of Songs 2:3; 5:16; 7:10 the palate *(ḥēk)* refers to the inner mouth, the place of intimacy and the most erotic of kisses. Thus the wordplay in Proverbs 5:3 may evoke the vagina, a more intimate place even than the pudenda, with dripping honey and oil suggesting bodily fluids produced during sexual intercourse.

Especially the more daring puns, such as double entendre, are often not marked as such, as in Proverbs 5:3. Puns like this, which function in the context of cultural taboos that inhibit sexually explicit language in public discourse, leave the initiative to detect the wordplay to the reader or listener, who can choose to take this road or not. If charged with impropriety, the poet may protest innocence. Responsibility lies with the reader, not the poet. It is to be expected that there are many "daring" wordplays in the OT that were left unmarked for similar reasons. This would include puns that imply a critique of authorities, opponents and enemies. Detecting such puns remains difficult, but growing knowledge about the cultural background of the ancient Near East will facilitate the discovery of more puns (see, e.g., the essays in Noegel on Egyptian, Mesopotamian, Ugaritic, Syriac and Arabic puns). Knowledge of traditional punning techniques makes the detection of unmarked puns possible, but most of these techniques do not impose the recognition of such puns.

Another unmarked pun is the following wordplay, a so-called amphibology. In puns of this kind the meaning of an entire phrase is doubled through polysemy. In Job 15:13 the phrase *tāšib ʾel-ʾēl rûhekā* means "you turn your fury against God," but it can also mean "you return your breath to God" (Alonso Schökel, 29).

Since the idiom signals "you will die," the amphibology turns the phrase simultaneously into a factual statement and into a warning or threat. Amphibologies are thought to be rare (Greenstein), but it is likely that many examples simply have not yet been identified (e.g., Prov 10:6b par. 10:11b; 10:29; 13:2).

3.2. Marked Puns. Usually, however, wordplays are a foregrounded feature of language and marked as ambiguous. Typical techniques, sometimes called "triggers," aid the detection and interpretation of wordplays in the OT. Most work on the basis that an expression does not seem to fit the context in which it occurs. Its denotation or initially most natural connotation does not fit. The resultant mismatch creates ambiguity and provokes the search for a different meaning for the expression—the point of the pun. The most important are listed here.

3.2.1. Punning Repetition ("Antanaclasis" in Classical Rhetoric). A double meaning can be brought to one's attention via a repetition of the same sequence, first in one sense and then in another (Leech, 210). An example is Proverbs 19:16a: *šōmēr miṣwâ šōmēr napšô* ("he who keeps [= observes] the command will keep [= preserve] his life"). The direct connection between deed and consequence is suggested by the identity of the language used to express their correlation. A special case in point, frequent in Hebrew poetry, is the poetic device of verb gapping, as in Proverbs 7:2a: "Keep *[šĕmōr]* my commands and live, [ellipsis] my teaching as the apple of your eye." There is a play on the verb *šmr*. Although the verb is gapped in the second half-line, it needs to be understood there, and with the simile "as the apple of your eye" it can only mean "guard" rather than "keep" in the sense of "observe," as in the first half-line.

3.2.2. Zeugma ("Yoking") and Syllepsis ("Taking Together"). These two types of pun, where two identical or very similar constructions are collapsed together so that one of the crucial items of the construction needs to be mentioned only once, occurs frequently. The difference between zeugma and syllepsis is that in the former the gapped element carries the same meaning in both constructions, whereas in the latter the likeness between the two similar constructions is superficial, so that the gapped item is understood in disparate senses in the two constructions. (In the literature, the meaning of these designations is sometimes reversed.) The most common form of this ellipted form of punning through repetition is verb gapping, but other elements of the sentence can also be gapped. Hebrew even has backward gapping of the verb, usually when the verb is in final position of the two halves of the poetic line (Miller). A rather unusual instance where a play on antonyms is combined with syllepsis is Proverbs 23:17: "Do not let your heart be envious *[ʾal-yĕqannēʾ libbĕkā]* of sinners, but [ellipsis] the fear of the LORD." The verse is often seen as corrupt, but more likely it uses a compound pun. Having been gapped in the second half-line, *yĕqannēʾ (libbĕkā)* serves double duty for both halves of the verse. The reader has to supply it, but with a different meaning ("become excited about") and without the negative particle (*ʾal*). The opposition between the antithetical statements and the *parallelism between the half-lines suggests that the same verb needs to be supplied, without the negation. But the contrasting direct objects in the parallelism (nondesirable in the first half-line, desirable in the second) suggest that the verb has another meaning in the second half-line. This is a complex pun that demands much cooperation from the reader.

3.2.3. Asyntactic Pun. Here the denotation (the most frequent meaning) of a word or its expected syntactic relations or the part of speech as which a word is most frequently used does not fit into the syntactic context in which it is used. An elaborate example occurs in Proverbs 29:6a: *bĕpešaʿ ʾiš rāʿ môqēš* ("in an evil man's transgression is a snare"). This half-verse is a variant repetition of Proverbs 12:13a: *bĕpešaʿ śĕpātayim môqēš rāʿ* ("in the transgression of lips is an evil snare"). The sequence of the words *môqēš* and *rāʿ* has been reversed. This initially creates an element of confusion and surprise, since readers who know Proverbs 12:13a would expect that here too the combination of *môqēš* and *rāʿ* means "evil snare." However, the sequence *rāʿ môqēš* is asyntactic and does not mean the same thing as the sequence *môqēš rāʿ*. Only further reflection will enable readers to discern that the adjective *rāʿ* ("evil"), which qualified the word *môqēš* ("snare") in Proverbs 12:13a, has been transferred to qualify *ʾiš* ("man") in Proverbs 29:6a. The word order reversal creates an asyntactic pun that draws attention to the similarity between the two variants and prompts readers to reflect carefully on the precise meaning of the two verses and their rela-

3.2.4. Etymological Pun. Some wordplays bring together an etymological, now obsolete meaning with a current meaning of the same word. Name etymologies, of proper and common names, are also popular. For example, in Job 13:24, Job (*'iyyôb* [last mentioned in Job 12:1]) may be interpreting his name in the light of his experience when he accuses God of regarding him as an enemy (*'ôyēb*) (Greenstein) (*see* Job 4: Person). In classical rhetoric such puns have sometimes been called *nomen omen*—the name signifies the destiny (Alonso Schökel, 30). In the so-called *figura etymologica* (sometimes also called "turn"), words formed from the same Hebrew root are repeated in close sequence, usually to intensify what is being said. Often a verb is supplied with a direct object formed from the same Hebrew root (Esther 2:3). Examples include Proverbs 7:14; Psalm 35:1, the latter expressing "poetic justice."

3.2.5. Juxtaposition of Polysemous Words with Overlapping Connotations. A special but frequent type of pun that is not captured by many of the customary definitions of wordplay involves cases where different polysemous words, some of whose connotations overlap, occur close together. Here the context of each decides which connotations are evoked, and how these relate to each other. In Proverbs, for example, there are numerous instances of such wordplays with the two verbs *nṣr* and *šmr*. Both can have three related meanings that can be expressed with the English verb *keep*: (1) in the sense of "guard, protect"; (2) in the sense of "comply with, observe"; (3) in the sense of "preserve, save." The first two of these senses are exploited in Proverbs 3:21, 26; 6:20, 24. The first and third of these senses are employed in Proverbs 13:3 in an example of multiple wordplay: *nōṣēr pîw šōmēr napšô* ("he who guards his mouth protects/saves his throat/life"). The polysemous *npš* literally refers to the "throat" (denotation) but metaphorically is used for "life" (connotation). Puns like this slow down the reading process and prompt deeper reflection.

4. Functions.

The functions of puns operate on macrolevels as well as microlevels.

4.1. Macrolevel Functions. On the macrolevel there are at least three main functions. First, puns demand attentiveness. Genre expectations (e.g., the high frequency of puns in certain kinds of discourse, such as poetry) and the presence of puns near the beginning of a discourse raise the anticipation of more puns. Even when readers settle into a more cursory reading routine, a wordplay creates ambiguity and makes reading more difficult. The problem in the text stirs readers out of complacency. Puns slow down the reading process and prompt deeper reflection in order to process the reading (pardon the pun). Second, puns can change readers' perception of the world—a related but distinct function on the macrolevel. This can happen in two ways characteristic of the major types of punning. The homonymic pun makes readers aware of new connections between ideas that were not previously recognized as connected. The polysemantic pun makes readers aware of the multivalence and complexity of ideas that had previously been thought to be simple and/or one-dimensional. Third, wordplays can surprise, amuse, delight, invite curiosity and prompt interest and active reader involvement while communicating serious, complex and significant information, and they can do so in few words. Punning encourages readers to view apparently ordinary things, concepts and ideas in more imaginative ways. Through these three related but distinct macrolevel functions, sustained punning infuses a sense of surprise and discovery, of fun and curiosity. It alerts readers to deeper connections. It makes them engaged and involved readers.

4.2. Microlevel Functions. On the microlevel there are as many functions as there are wordplays. I will mention five. First, many wordplays are simply funny. The humorous function of puns divides into at least three subcategories. (1) Humor can be a worthwhile aim in its own right. (2) Humor can range from light-hearted playfulness that delights and encourages to having fun at the expense of others. If the contrast between the two meanings of a pun is more striking than their similarity, its purpose probably is ironical (Leech, 213). The spectrum ranges from irony to sarcasm, ridicule and mocking. (3) Because witty puns amuse, they entertain and sustain interest, encouraging readers to read on and pay attention. Second, wordplays can function like metaphors, especially if the similarity between the senses of the wordplay is striking. Sometimes such puns can breathe fresh life into dormant metaphors (sometimes falsely called "dead" metaphors). Third, wordplays can allude to wider contexts (including intertextual ones), infusing the text with connotations above and beyond the surface level meaning expressed by the individual words, their grammar and syntax (Hurowitz). Fourth, word plays can have aesthetic functions, making the text cohere on the visual level as well as the auditory level. On the visual level, puns can link different parts of a text. Written text also benefits from sounding pleasant, since reading is often done aloud, whether in company or alone. Readers do not only see their texts; they hear them as well. Fifth, word plays can add emphasis.

If texts are "language games," then word plays are like particularly smart moves in a game of chess. The various pieces (= words) can make certain conventionally predictable moves on the board (= in the text), and the freedom with which these moves can be made changes depending on the progress of actual play and the context in which the pun appears. The basic rules of text production are fixed, but puns apply them in ever-new ways. There are so many different combinations of moves that words are allowed to make, and there are so many different contexts in which these rules can be actualized in every new text, that it is impossible to describe them all. Word plays convert texts into particularly exciting communicative games, with surprising moves at every turn. They invite readers to play an active part in creating meaning. Word plays are very frequent in the wisdom, poetry and writings of the OT, as in ancient Near Eastern literature generally (Noegel). Yet many word plays go unrecognized. Two obvious examples are asyntactic puns and amphibologies, discussed above. Further systematic study is necessary to develop a fuller understanding of the texts in which the many different kinds of word plays appear.

See also SOUND PATTERNS.

BIBLIOGRAPHY. **M. H. Abrams,** *A Glossary of Literary Terms* (7th ed.; Boston: Heinle & Heinle, 1999); **L. Alonso Schökel,** *A Manual of Hebrew Poetics* (SubBi 11; Rome: Editrice Pontificio Istituto Biblico, 1988); **I. M. Casanowicz,** *Paronomasia in the Old Testament* (Boston: Cushing, 1894); **W. Empson,** *Seven Types of Ambiguity* (2nd ed.; London: Chatto & Windus, 1947); **E. L. Greenstein,** "Wordplay, Hebrew," *ABD* 5.968-71; **V. A. Hurowitz,** "Alliterative Allusions, Rebus Writing, and Paronomastic Punishment: Some Aspects of Word Play in Akkadian Literature," in *Puns and Pundits: Word Play in the Hebrew Bible and Ancient Near Eastern Literature* (Bethesda, MD: CDL Press, 2000) 63-87; **G. N. Leech,** *A Linguistic Guide to English Poetry* (English Language Series; Harlow: Longman, 1973); **C. L. Miller,** "The Relation of Coordination to Verb Gapping in Biblical Poetry," *JSOT* 32 (2007) 41-60; **S. B. Noegel,** *Puns and Pundits: Word Play in the Hebrew Bible and Ancient Near Eastern Literature* (Bethesda, MD: CDL Press, 2000); **G. A. Rendsburg,** "Wordplay in Biblical Hebrew: An Eclectic Collection," in *Puns and Pundits: Word Play in the Hebrew Bible and Ancient Near Eastern Literature* (Bethesda, MD: CDL Press, 2000) 137-62; **J. M. Sasson,** "Wordplay in the OT," *IDBSup* 968-70; **S. P. Su,** *Lexical Ambiguity in Poetry* (Studies in Language and Linguistics; London: Longman, 1994); **W. G. E. Watson,** *Classical Hebrew Poetry: A Guide to Its Techniques* (2nd ed; JSOTSup, 26; Sheffield: JSOT Press, 1986).
K. Heim

WORSHIP

Although the OT never defines worship, it does provide clues about its understanding of the topic. Its narratives tell of people engaged in various acts of worship, highlight aspects of worship that were directly or indirectly instituted by God, and enumerate cultic actions with which God was pleased or which he rejected. Its psalms were written and used for individual and corporate worship of Yahweh by people subject to different moods or needs during various seasons of life. The rich vocabulary of worship used in its pages indicates that the essence of biblical worship is a proper response to God's person and actions that leads a person to fall or bow down before him in humble submission, express fear or reverence, and serve him in the cult and all of life. This article overviews the biblical vocabulary for worship, and then examines the theology of worship as developed in the OT writings covered in this dictionary.

1. Vocabulary of Worship
2. The Psalms and Worship
3. Wisdom and Worship
4. The Writings and Worship

1. Vocabulary of Worship.
Many discussions of worship trace the etymology of the English term to a word meaning "worthship" or "being worthy." The OT authors would agree that Yahweh is worthy of worship,

but they never use such terminology. (Even though many English versions of 2 Sam 22:4 and Ps 18:3 say that Yahweh is "worthy of praise," "worthy" is not found in the Hebrew. The word is similarly missing where the NIV says that God is "worthy" in 1 Chron 16:25; Ps 48:1; 96:4; 145:3.) To find this terminology used for God the Father or Son, one must look to the NT, where it is found in only four places (Heb 3:3; Rev 4:11; 5:9, 12). To discuss worship in the sense of God's worthiness can therefore be misleading. Thus it is essential to examine the terminology used by biblical authors in order to understand their thoughts about the worship of God.

1.1. Bow Down. The most common Hebrew word for worship in the OT is *ḥāwâ*, which carries the basic meaning "bow down" or "prostrate oneself." As it is frequently concerned with one's inward religious attitudes and actions, it can rightly be translated "worship" or even "pray." Found some 170 times in the OT, it is almost universally translated by *proskyneō* in the LXX. While *ḥāwâ* could be used for a secular greeting in which one person bows to the ground before another out of respect or to acknowledge submission, it is more frequently used for bowing before God or idols as a sign of surrender and submission. The Bible usually mentions people bowing to Yahweh in response to his appearance or to something that he has done. Since Yahweh is the only proper object of worship, Israel is routinely instructed not to bow down before any other gods. Frequently, *ḥāwâ* is paired with one of the other words for worship that will be discussed below.

The Hebrew word *sāgad* and its Aramaic cognate *sĕgid* are similar in meaning to *ḥāwâ*, being used of those who bow down in submission to another. The Hebrew form of the word is found only in Isaiah 44; 46, where it is used in conjunction with people falling down before idols. In the book of Daniel the Aramaic term is used when all the people in Nebuchadnezzar's kingdom were commanded to fall down and worship the golden image of the king (Dan 3:5-7, 10-12, 14-18). When Shadrach, Meshach and Abednego refused to fall down and worship the image, they were thrown into the blazing furnace. After they were rescued from the furnace, Nebuchadnezzar praised their God for rescuing them, since they refused to worship any god except their own (Dan 3:28).

1.2. Fear. Like *ḥāwâ*, the semantic range of *yārē'* is quite broad, ranging from a fear of everyday threats, such as animals, enemies, punishment, sickness and death, to a fear of the unknown and fear of God. The fear of God/Yahweh is a concept that ranges in meaning from being afraid of God's power as judge to reverential awe due to his power to deliver (*see* Fear of the Lord). Thus those who are outside the covenant are terror-stricken when they realize that Yahweh personally leads his people and fights for them (Ex 15:13-16), while those in covenant relationship with Yahweh experience the fear of God as a proper reverence based upon the recognition that he is the rightful judge, the one whom they can trust for deliverance. In many contexts the word *yārē'* approximates worship and emphasizes the need for a proper relationship with God. Its frequent use in conjunction with *ḥāwâ* and *'ābad* (see below), places it firmly within a worship context, particularly as Israel is regularly given the choice of fearing and bowing down to or fearing and serving either Yahweh or other gods. In the Wisdom literature particularly, fearing God parallels knowing him experientially (Prov 9:10). It thus becomes virtually synonymous with righteous living or religious piety. Occurring some 435 times in verbal, adjectival and nominal forms, the word is usually translated by *phobeō* in the LXX.

1.3. Service. A third major verb expressing worship is *'ābad*, which is found some 290 times in the OT. Noun forms include *'ebed* in reference to a servant, slave or worker (800x), *'ăbôdâ* in reference to work, service or bondage (145x), and several other forms. In the LXX the word is variously translated by words related to *douleuō* when referring to slavery, *ergazomai* when referring to work, and words from the *latreuō* group when referring to the cultic service of the priests. Like the terms already discussed, *'ābad* has a broad range of meaning. It is frequently used for someone who serves another human being, such as a slave serving a master, a worker serving an employer (Gen 29:15), a courtier or subject serving a king (1 Sam 11:1), or one nation serving another (1 Chron 18:2, 6, 13). When used in conjunction with the spiritual realm, the term can indicate service of gods, idols or even heavenly bodies and other created things. Israel was specifically called out of Egypt so that they could "serve" Yahweh (Ex 3:12; 4:23; 7:16; 8:1;

10:26), and frequently they were given the choice of serving Yahweh or other gods (Josh 24:14-24)—that is, acknowledging one or the other as lord.

As 'ebed basically points to someone's relationship with a lord, those who serve God acknowledge him as lord and live their entire life in obedience to him. In contrast to a human master who may treat a servant harshly, God is always a good lord (Westermann, TLOT 2.826). Whereas serving God can simply indicate relationship with him, it often points to the performance of cultic rituals (such as offering sacrifices, engaging in other religious rites, or taking part in the appointed festivals) and other types of service for God. Thus the Aaronic priests served by offering sacrifices in the tabernacle and later the temple, other clans of the Levites served by bearing burdens and taking care of the items of furniture found at the tabernacle or by writing and performing music, and the people as a whole served by uniting to celebrate the Passover. The Levites took part in the Lord's worship by literally "serving in the service of the tabernacle" (Num 3:7-8).

Another Hebrew word used for service is šārat, which is used ninety-seven times in the Hebrew Bible (always in Piel); twenty of these times it is a participle acting as the noun "minister." In ritual settings it is regularly translated with leitourgeō in the LXX. Whereas 'ābad can be used in reference to menial labor, šārat refers only to a higher level of service. It can be used to indicate personal service to an important person (e.g., Joseph serving Potiphar [Gen 39:4]; Elisha serving Elijah [1 Kings 19:21]), but usually it is used of cultic worship performed by a priest or Levite at the tabernacle or someone else who has a special relationship with God (including angels [Ps 103:21]). While it would naturally be used to refer to the ministry of sacrifice, šārat could also be used of people engaged in the ministry of song and praise (cf. 1 Chron 6:32; 16:4, 37).

2. The Psalms and Worship.

The great biblical repository of the praises of ancient Israel is the book of *Psalms. In Hebrew the book is called tĕhillīm—"songs of praise," or simply "praises." Even though not every psalm is a song of praise, the book as a whole is designed to lead God's people into praise and worship. Although the psalms show that Israel was pre-

pared to encounter God during any season in life to express praise, trust or delight, to confess sins, and to pour out laments as they faced various problems, it is clear that their final goal was to praise the God who had called them into existence as his people. This is seen both in the way individual psalms are written and the entire Psalter is shaped, with more laments toward the beginning and more psalms of praise toward the end (see Westermann 1981, 250-58).

Since its final compilation took place after the rebuilding of the temple, the Psalter is often referred to as the hymnbook of the second temple. This designation is accurate insofar as the psalms were used in temple worship. Even so, it could be misleading, as many psalms were written at a much earlier period and are suitable for use in different ages and various settings as God's people encounter him. Since their contents rarely tie them to specific historical references or to specific temple rituals, they remain useful for multiple situations. The psalms are thus equally at home in temple, synagogue, church and home.

The psalms are connected to temple worship by the headings attached to some psalms and by their content (see Psalms 4: Titles). Debate continues as to their origin and reliability, but the headings clearly give information about the use of the psalms in the cult, even though some terms are obscure to modern readers (see Cult, Worship: Psalms). Some headings point to specific worship occasions when a psalm would be used (Ps 30; 92; 120—134). Although titles in the MT only assign Psalm 92 for use on a particular day (the sabbath), many titles in the LXX assign psalms to the different days of the week. The Songs of Ascent are generally considered to have been used by pilgrims on their way to Jerusalem for one of the feasts or while climbing the temple mount to worship. The title of Psalm 100, "A psalm of thanksgiving," possibly indicates that the psalm was to be used by a person sacrificing a thank offering. Similarly, the titles of Psalm 38 and Psalm 70 may indicate that they were used in conjunction with a memorial offering (cf. Lev 2:2; 24:7) or simply that they were used by those who wanted God to remember their difficulties.

A total of fifty-five psalms appear to refer to an individual involved in leading worship—the "director of music"—whatever his exact function may have been. Fifty-seven titles identify a *mizmôr* ("psalm"). Twelve psalms are classified as *šîr* or *šîrâ* ("song" [Ps 18; 30; 48; 65; 66; 67; 68; 76; 83; 87; 88; 108]), one as a *šîr yĕdîdōt* ("song of love"), quite possibly a wedding song for a king (Ps 45). Another psalm is called a *tĕhillâ* ("song of praise" [Ps 145]), and several more are identified as *tĕpillâ* ("prayers" [Ps 17; 86; 90; 102; 142]). One is said to have been sung (Ps 7). Other headings refer either to instruments used to accompany a psalm (Ps 4; 5 [?]; 6; 54; 55; 61; 67; 76) or to the melody used when a psalm was sung (Ps 9; 22; 45; 56; 57; 58; 59; 60; 69; 75; 80; 88 [?]). At least one title may denote that the singers are women (Ps 46). A number of terms that are of uncertain meaning but presumed to relate to music include *šĕmînît* ("according to the eighth"—octave? eight-stringed instrument? [Ps 6]), *gittît* (Ps 8; 81; 84) and *māhălat lĕʿannôt* (Ps 88).

In addition to the information found in titles, the contents of many psalms indicate they were intended for temple worship. Some specifically mention the singer's desire to worship at the temple, the altar, God's house or his courts (Ps 5:7; 23:6; 26:6, 8; 27:4-6; 42:4; 65:4; 138:2), or they recall the gates through which the worshiper enters the temple to worship (Ps 24:7, 9; 100:4; 118:19-20). Others identify the temple as the place where Yahweh dwells (Ps 11:4; 18:6; 74:7; 132:5). Frequently the psalmist states his desire to worship (Ps 42:1-2; 63:1-8; 84:1-2) or calls others to worship God (Ps 95:1-2, 6; 96:1-3, 100:1-4). Specific worship acts are mentioned, including offerings and sacrifices of various kinds (Ps 50:5, 8-14, 23; 54:6; 56:12; 66:13-15; 116:17; 118:27) and the payment of vows (Ps 22:25; 65:1; 116:18). Following S. Mowinckel, who speculated from the existence of a Babylonian New Year's festival that Israel celebrated the enthronement of Yahweh as king every year during the Feast of Tabernacles, a number of scholars have attempted to show that the psalms were connected with this or some other feast. It is likely that psalms were recited during the Feast of Tabernacles and other feasts, but it is no more likely that the psalms were specially connected to one festival than it is for Christian hymns to be associated with only one holiday (Goldingay, 54).

The contents of the psalms enumerated many reasons for God to be worshiped. He is the Creator and Sustainer of people and of the rest of the physical world (Ps 8:3-5; 24:1-2; 33:6-

9, 15; 104:2-30; 136:4-9). He acted on Israel's behalf for deliverance in history, both from their enemies (Ps 18; 77:11-20; 78; 106; 136:10-24) and from their own sin (Ps 32:1-7; 38; 51; 106). Deliverance is the major motive given by psalmists for offering sacrifices, which usually are presented in the form of a thank offering (Courtman, 40-44). Yahweh was also recognized as Israel's king (Ps 10:16; 24:8-10; 29:10; 47; 95:3; 97:1-6; 99:1-5) and as the one who established the rule of the Davidic dynasty (Ps 2; 18:50; 78:68-72; 89:3-4, 19-37; 132).

In the psalms worship is an activity to be engaged in by individuals and groups of people who enjoy covenant relationship with God (Ps 50:5). No matter whether times were good or bad, God's people can and should focus upon God and arrange their lives around him. No topics were off limits as they approached Yahweh. When they doubted, they said so. When they sinned, they confessed. When they suffered, they pleaded for deliverance. When things were going well or deliverance was granted, they thanked God and praised him for his abundant blessings. And through it all they encouraged one another, the rest of humanity, indeed, the whole of creation, to praise the Lord. Worship is therefore not limited to the covenant community. All the people of the earth are either charged or said to worship Yahweh (Ps 22:27; 66:4; 86:9; 96:9; 98:4-6). The "heavenly hosts" (Ps 103:21; 148:2) and the "sons of God" (Ps 29:1-2) are entreated to worship Yahweh (*see* Divine Council). Both of these terms evidently refer to angelic beings falling down before God. But the community of those who bow before Yahweh is not limited to benign spirits. After proclaiming the worthlessness of idols and the shame that comes upon those who bow before images, Psalm 97:7 issues the command "Worship him, all you gods!" Even the foreign gods are to prostrate themselves before Yahweh. Indeed, all of creation is charged to worship Yahweh as the one who created all and who reigns over all (Ps 69:34; 98:7-9; 148). Since Yahweh is the only proper object of worship, the psalms exhort Israel not to bow down to foreign gods but rather to listen to the Lord (Ps 81:10; 115:2-8).

From the time of H. Gunkel, scholars have discerned a number of different types of psalms in the Bible. Not all scholars use exactly the same categories, but the following represent the genres that have been discussed: (1) *hymns (psalms of praise), (2) psalms of *lament, (3) psalms of *thanksgiving, (4) psalms of *confidence (or trust), (5) psalms of *remembrance, (6) *wisdom psalms, (7) royal (*kingship) psalms. Although earlier studies attempted to identify fixed forms for these types, it is clear that psalm genres are actually fairly fluid. Few psalms exhibit all the distinctives of their supposed type, and quite a number display characteristics belonging to several genres, making them difficult to categorize. Although not free from problems, form-critical studies of the psalms are valuable because they demonstrate that individual psalms often were shaped by their use in the cult (see Form Criticism). Identifying the way psalms were used in the worship of ancient Israel provides models for their use today. Since lament is the most common genre of the psalms, it is clear that worship involves more than celebration and praise; God's people can engage him through all of life's joys and pains.

3. Wisdom and Worship.

Although it was once argued that Israelite wisdom resembles other ancient Near Eastern wisdom by being purely secular literature devoid of religious content, the biblical texts urge the contrary conclusion. Biblical wisdom is inherently religious, the key phrase being "The fear of the LORD is the beginning of wisdom, and knowledge of the Holy One is understanding" (Prov 9:10; cf. Job 28:28; Ps 111:10; Prov 1:7; Eccles 12:13). As mentioned previously, fear is one of the major OT terms in regard to worship. And even though wisdom writers say little about cultic activities, they are concerned with one's knowledge of and worship of God, actions that make themselves known in the everyday affairs of life (Prov 8:13; 14:27; 15:16, 33; 19:23; 22:4; 28:5; 31:30). From the perspective of the *sages, wisdom cannot exist where practical piety does not exist. The title character of *Job serves as a prime example of a man who "feared God and shunned evil," living a "blameless and upright" life (Job 1:1, 8; 2:3). Job's fear of God is lived out as he acts as a priest for his family, purifying his children and offering burnt sacrifices for them in case they had sinned (Job 1:5). His piety led to prayer for his own physical condition (Job 6:8-9), confession of his sins (Job 42:3, 6) and intercession for others (Job 42:8-9). After his children are killed and his property destroyed or stolen, Job falls down and worships, expressing trust in Yahweh and blessing his name (Job 1:20-21). The book specifically informs its readers that Job's sacrifice and prayer for his friends were accepted by the Lord (Job 42:9).

In Proverbs 8 *Woman Wisdom is expressly connected with Yahweh, who possessed and used wisdom from before creation. After expressing joy at God's work in creation, she invites young men to listen to her in order to find life, promising that all who find her will obtain the Lord's favor. Woman Wisdom's function is to attract people to Yahweh, to bring them into relationship with him. In Proverbs 9 the contrast between this *personification of wisdom and Woman Folly alerts readers of their need to choose between the worship of Yahweh and the worship of other gods. Woman Wisdom builds her bayit (her house or, possibly, temple) with seven pillars (cf. 1 Kings 7:17, which describes Solomon's temple as having seven pillars) at the high point of the city. Similarly, Woman Folly sits at the doorway of her bayit, which is also at the high place of the city. From their vantage point they call out to the naive and those lacking understanding to turn to them and receive what they have to give, whether positive life-giving gifts or negative death-dealing gifts. Since hilltops often served as sites for temples or cult shrines in ancient Palestine, the situation of these women's houses provides a strong clue that worship is in view. The implication may be that those who follow Woman Wisdom are devoted to the worship of Yahweh, while those who follow Woman Folly pursue other deities. Readers are exhorted to choose the way of life by worshiping Yahweh or death by rejecting him.

The sages echo standard biblical teaching that God is not pleased with cultic actions divorced from piety, and that the condition of one's heart is more important than simply engaging in religious activities. This usually is discussed from a negative standpoint. *Qohelet warns his readers to watch their steps when going to God's house, being careful to listen (i.e., obey) rather than offering the sacrifice of fools who do not even realize that their actions are evil (Eccles 5:1). He further cautions readers not to say too much in prayer or make hasty vows, as that is seen as foolishness if not sin (Eccles 5:2-6). The book of *Proverbs informs us that when carried out with wrong motives, any religious act

933

can be considered an "abomination," a word carrying clear cultic significance. Thus, both the sacrifice of the wicked and the prayers of those who reject God's instruction *(tôrâ)* are viewed as abominations (Prov 15:8; 21:27; 28:9). By contrast, Yahweh delights in the prayers of the upright (Prov 15:8, 29). An example of someone who treats sacrifice with contempt is the rebellious woman in Proverbs 7. She seduces an undiscerning youth by boasting that she had presented peace offerings and paid her vows (Prov 7:6-23). Since the meat from a peace offering was to be eaten by the one making the sacrifice, the woman is inviting the youth to share a feast with her. By accepting her offer to partake in this religious meal, the youth joins her rejection of true worship and is himself led off to slaughter; the bed, linens and spices that were introduced as a sexual enticement end up taking on the odor of death (Clifford, 89) and leading to Sheol, the place where a person can neither praise nor worship God (Ps 6:5; 115:17) and where wisdom cannot be known (Eccles 9:10). An improper attitude is denounced with regard to those who make a vow rashly and only in retrospect investigate the propriety of it (Prov 20:25). Similarly, treating a vow made to God so lightly as to never get around to paying it is reckoned as foolishness (Eccles 5:4-5).

4. The Writings and Worship.

As we have seen, Psalms provides the language to be used in public and private worship, and the wisdom books usually view worship in terms of practical piety. Considered in a broad sense, the Writings—particularly Chronicles, Ezra, Nehemiah—often center worship in the temple cult as developed by *David and *Solomon. The narrower delineation that this dictionary gives to the Writings, however, leaves us with books that add little to our theology of worship, as their authors were concerned with other issues.

Through its delineation of God's providential care for normal people, the book of *Ruth shows how a foreigner can become one with God's people (Ruth 1:16) and be recognized as an equal with Rachel, Leah and Tamar (Ruth 4:11-12). Even so, although the characters refer to Yahweh in prayer, greetings and blessings, no explicit acts of worship are detailed. The only worship act that may be discernable in the book of *Esther is fasting, as elsewhere in the Bible this act usually accompanies prayer to God (Es-

ther 4:3, 16; 9:31). The only other link to Jewish worship is found in the book's introduction of the Feast of *Purim, which was added to the other festivals at this point in Israel's history (Esther 9:20-32).

Read as poetry about the love between man and woman, *Song of Songs says nothing about the worship of God, whose name is never mentioned in the book. The only possible way to derive teaching about worship from this poem is to treat it as an allegory about the love between Yahweh and Israel or between Christ and the church—an approach that finds few followers today. Those who use the allegorical approach are left to speculate whether worship or some other aspect of the relationship between God and his people is in view.

Bemoaning the destruction of Jerusalem and Judah's loss of sovereignty as a people, the book of *Lamentations responds to the end of the worship of Yahweh in the land. Foreigners who had been forbidden a part in the assembly have entered the sanctuary and carried off its treasure (Lam 1:10). Pilgrims no longer come to Jerusalem for the appointed feasts (Lam 1:4). The Lord has himself destroyed the temple, allowing foreigners to shout there as Israel had on feast days (Lam 2:6-7). Priests and prophets have been murdered in the sanctuary, in at least some cases because of their own sin (Lam 2:20; 4:13). At a time when the cultic worship that they had known was no more, Lamentations gives the Jews a means in which to cry out to Yahweh for help and express hope that he would yet have compassion on them (Lam 3:21-26, 31-32). It encourages its readers to examine their ways, confess their sin and rebellion, and return to the Lord (Lam 3:40-42). In this way, it witnesses that worship should not be simply equated with praise and joy. There are times for God's people to approach him in a somber mood, singing songs in a minor key as they acknowledge their sin or face desperate economic or political situations.

See also CULT, WORSHIP: PSALMS; CULT, WORSHIP: WISDOM; DIVINE PRESENCE; FORM CRITICISM; MEGILLOT AND FESTIVALS; MUSIC, SONG.

BIBLIOGRAPHY. **R. J. Clifford,** *Proverbs* (OTL; Louisville: Westminster John Knox, 1999); **N. B. Courtman,** "Sacrifice in the Psalms," in *Sacrifice in the Bible,* ed. R. T. Beckwith and M. J. Selman (Grand Rapids: Baker; Carlisle: Paternoster, 1995) 41-58; **E. M. Curtis,** "Ancient Psalms and

Modern Worship," *BSac* 154 (1997) 285-96; **J. Goldingay,** *Psalms, 1: Psalms 1-41* (BCOTWP; Grand Rapids: Baker Academic, 2006); **H. Gunkel, with J. Begrich,** *Introduction to Psalms: The Genres of the Religious Lyric of Israel* (Macon, GA: Mercer University Press, 1998); **H.-J. Kraus,** *Worship in Israel: A Cultic History of the Old Testament,* (Richmond: John Knox, 1966); **P. D. Miller,** "Enthroned on the Praises of Israel: The Praise of God in Old Testament Theology," *Int* 39 (1985) 5-19; **S. Mowinckel,** *The Psalms in Israel's Worship* (Grand Rapids: Eerdmans, 2004); **R. E. Murphy,** "The Psalms and Worship," *Ex auditu* 8 (1992): 23-31; **W. Riley,** *King and Cultus in Chronicles: Worship and the Reinterpretation of History* (JSOTSup 160; Sheffield: Sheffield Academic Press, 1993); **A. P. Ross,** *Recalling the Hope of Glory: Biblical Worship from the Garden to the New Creation* (Grand Rapids: Kregel, 2006); **H. H. Rowley,** *Worship in Ancient Israel* (London: SPCK; Philadelphia: Fortress, 1967); **C. Westermann,** *Praise and Lament in the Psalms* (Atlanta: John Knox, 1981); idem, "עֶבֶד *ʿebed.* Servant," *TLOT* 2.819-32.

W. McConnell

X, Y, Z

XERXES. *See* AHASUERUS; ESTHER 2: EXTRABIBLI-CAL BACKGROUND; VASHTI.

ZION

Zion, a place name often synonymous with *Jerusalem,* is located on the south side of Jerusalem and typically is associated with the Temple Mount. Zion often represents the location of the sanctuary situated on an elevated location in southern Jerusalem. The term occurs thirty-eight times in *Psalms and once in *Song of Songs; otherwise, the word is noticeably absent from the wisdom writings of *Job, *Proverbs and *Ecclesiastes. In prophetic poetry, Isaiah employs the term frequently (47x), and, combined with a number of occurrences in Jeremiah and *Lamentations (32x), it clearly denotes the preferred status of Zion and the theological significance of the designation to the southern kingdom. The construct chain *har ṣiyyôn* ("mountain of Zion") refers to the Temple Mount itself, where God dwells, while the singular phrase *bat ṣiyyôn* ("daughter of Zion") figuratively denotes God's people, as the inhabitants of the holy city. The plural form *běnôt ṣiyyôn* ("daughters of Zion") is another designation for the virgins or women of Israel who compose a wedding processional following King *Solomon in anticipation of a royal wedding.

1. Etymology and Location
2. Inviolability of Zion
3. Zion as a Political Entity in the Psalter
4. The Symbolic Significance of Zion in the Psalms
5. Zion in the Songs of Ascent (Pss 120—134)
6. Zion in Psalms of Exile and Restoration
7. Zion in Lamentations

1. Etymology and Location.

The etymology of the name is uncertain. "Zion" may derive from the Hebrew root *ṣiyyôn* ("castle"), from Arabic *šanâ* ("protect" or "citadel") or from the root *ṣiyyâ* ("dry land") (*HALOT,* 1022). The earlier formulation of the term in the biblical text identifies Zion in terms of a stronghold or fortress (2 Sam 5:7) and connects it with the Jebusite fortress southeast of Jerusalem, below Ophel, probably reinforcing the notion of a place of protection.

2. Inviolability of Zion.

In the Psalter the designation *Zion* often occurs in parallelism with *Jerusalem,* reinforcing the notion that the Israelites understood the two as synonymous. However, L. Hoppe (24) notes distinctions between the two designations: "Jerusalem refers to the royal city of the Davidic monarchy, which includes the Temple. Zion specifically refers to the mountain of God's temple. The two terms encompass the city's role as the political and religious center of Judah." In some poetic texts *Zion* refers to the entire city of Jerusalem, and in several instances to those who inhabit Jerusalem. First and foremost, then, *Zion* denotes the location of Yahweh's dwelling place and immediate presence, symbolizing a place of security or safety (Ps 46:4-5; 76:2-3). Consequently, the inviolability of Zion serves as a hallmark feature of the Zion tradition (Hayes, 419-20).

The concept of Zion's inviolability claims that as the location of Yahweh's presence, Zion is exempt from domination or conquest by foreign leaders (Ps 46:5-6). The belief in Zion's inviolability affected the military and political decisions rendered before the exile. Yahweh will not allow his holy city to fall into the hands of Israel's adversaries (Ps 46:8-11; 48:4-8; 76:4-9). When enemies recognize Yahweh as the defender of Zion, they retreat (Ps 48:4-8). Psalm 76, a poem that describes the victories of Zion's king, depicts Zion's impenetrability in terms of Yahweh's destruction of battle equipment, followed by his subjugation of nations threatening Jerusalem (Ps 76:2-3). In Psalm 76:3 the poet declares that Yahweh destroyed the "weapons of war," metaphorically conveying the totality of God's victory over Zion's enemies. Many of the community *lament psalms (Pss 50; 75—78; 80—83) that address national defeat depict Zion in its military context, expressing confidence in the Lord's victory over the adversaries that have persecuted and oppressed the nation. All opposing forces are rendered impotent against the city defended by Yahweh, establishing God's reputation among the potentates of enemy nations as "one to be feared."

3. Zion as a Political Entity in the Psalter.
Psalm 2 depicts the threat of foreign nations gathered against Yahweh's divinely appointed king. Yahweh anoints his earthly king and enthrones him in Zion (Ps 2:6), Yahweh's "holy mountain," and accomplishes victory by means of an earthly king. Zion ultimately denotes the "dwelling place" of Yahweh, but it may also indirectly signify the throne of an individual through whom Yahweh effects his will. The poet of Psalm 20 characterizes Zion as the source for help and support by means of an earthly king (Ps 20:2-3, 6). Yahweh's anointed serves then as a conduit through which flows Yahweh's help. In addition, the psalmist describes Yahweh as a refuge for the oppressed who "reigns on Zion," avenging the blood of society's marginalized and executing *righteousness for the weak and vulnerable (Ps 9:9-12; 10:14).

4. The Symbolic Significance of Zion in the Psalms.
Although Zion's altitude does not exceed other locations surrounding Jerusalem, the concept corresponds with the ancient Canaanite belief that the mountains were the home of the gods. Mount Zion is associated with Mount Zaphon (Ps 48:2 NIV), the mythical mountain upon which the Canaanite deity Baal dwells. The correspondence denotes Yahweh's cosmic and earthly conquest over chaos, just as the enthronement of Baal symbolized his cosmic victory over Mot in Ugaritic texts. The transformational significance of equating Mount Zion with Mount Zaphon asserts Yahweh's superiority

over all other gods and places him in the position of authority in the ancient Near East. In addition, the Gihon spring running through God's city (Ps 46:4) reflects another mythical motif common in Canaanite iconography, since Genesis 2:13 identifies Gihon as one of four rivers that feed into Eden. Thus Israel integrated and adapted the ancient Canaanite imagery in its conceptual formulations and expressions, applying the ideology to cultic language describing Zion in illustrious terms but without appropriating the theological significance.

Furthermore, the idea that the ark of the covenant represented the throne of Yahweh originates from the Canaanite concept of El seated on a throne surrounded by cherubim, typical imagery in the ancient Near East. Psalm 99:1-2 reflects the link between the Israelite cult and Yahweh's kingship, describing Yahweh as "sitting among the cherubim" in Zion. The psalmist describes the royal role of Yahweh, who dwells in Zion, as one of creator and defender (Ps 65:1, 6-7). Psalm 78:54 reaffirms the central claim that Yahweh established the borders of the "holy land," while Psalm 78:60 asserts Yahweh's election of Judah as the place where he erected "his sanctuary," comparing his creation of Zion with the creation of the world (see Creation Theology). Psalm 50:2 expands the concept of Zion, which further symbolizes the ideal of creation "perfect in beauty" and from which Yahweh's presence shines forth (see Divine Presence). Ultimately, Zion becomes the place from which Yahweh's blessings and judgments flow, and as such, Zion is depicted as the center, or "navel of the earth."

B. Ollenburger (15) maintains that the development of Zion as a symbol derives from early associations of the place with the kingship of Yahweh and the ark of the covenant rather than deriving from a Davidic royal ideology, and that *David became associated with Zion later in Israelite history. Consequently, the development of the Zion tradition emanates from earlier Israelite conceptions concerning the ark at Shiloh and its subsequent transfer to Zion. Ollenburger bases this argument on multiple linkages between the themes of the "enthronement psalms" (Pss 47; 93—99) and Yahweh's presence in the holy city.

In addition, Ollenburger (41) examines phraseology such as "Yahweh of Hosts" and "God of Jacob" as formulations connected to the ark tradition, observing that the employment of these designations by David in Jerusalem seems unlikely, so their usage affirms the preeminent and central role of the ark related to Zion. Ollenburger (64) contends that the "symbol of Zion was employed in utter detachment from the earthly king," and that Psalms 46; 48; 76 do not mention the monarchy or David. Clearly, the Zion psalms mention a human king infrequently in order to emphasize the kingship of Yahweh. Moreover, whereas the psalmist refers to Zion as the "city of God" in Psalms 46:4; 48:1, the book of 2 Samuel identifies Zion as the "city of David" immediately after the ark is established in its permanent central sanctuary in Jerusalem (see Ollenburger, 63).

S. Gillingham (316-17, 323) appeals to a variety of Zion markers in her identification of psalms that advance the Zion tradition. Among these markers, monikers such as "the mountain of the Lord," "my holy mountain," "holy place," "dwelling place," "sanctuary" and "city of God" represent characteristic features consistent with references to Zion, even if the enveloping poem does not explicitly refer to Zion. Linguistic criteria alone cannot determine whether certain psalms that omit the designation "Zion" advance the impetus of a well-developed Zion tradition, although in some cases conceptual ideas informing the connections between Jerusalem, the temple and Zion create an integrated network of semiotic ideas present in Israel's early history.

Furthermore, Psalm 65 relates Yahweh's redemptive activity with his presence in Zion. The community seeks to praise Yahweh because he "forgave our transgressions" and prospered Zion (Ps 65:3). In addition, Psalm 102:13 expresses confidence that Yahweh will "show favor" and "have compassion" on Zion through the reconstruction of the devastated city. He sends forth his support and help from Zion (Ps 20:2) through the "mighty salvation of his right hand" (Ps 20:6). The poet laments in Psalm 14:7 (cf. Ps 53:6), beseeching Yahweh to "restore the fortunes of his people." In anticipation of Yahweh's rescue, the psalmist gives voice to his hopes for Israel in Psalm 69:35, confident that Yahweh "will save Zion" and "rebuild the cities of Judah," so the displaced people may return and settle there. The poet understands that only Yahweh can prosper Zion and build up its walls of protection (Ps 51:18). The restoration of Zion allows Yahweh to dwell there once more (Ps 102:16) and exalts Yahweh as deliverer and protector, bringing glory to his name (Ps 102:21).

Zion typically represents the dwelling place of God among his elect people, but in Psalm 87 the poet acknowledges *worship of Yahweh on Zion in cosmological terms, envisioning the procession of foreign nations to Zion to worship Yahweh. All the nations of the world will find refuge and strength in God's sanctuary if they are obedient to him. The exclusionary view of Yahweh as Israel's God finds expanded expression in this unusual psalm, eschatological in nature, which claims that people from all over the world can identify Zion as their place of origin. The worldwide dimensions of Yahweh's rule and authority ensure his mercy and compassion on all of his creatures. The universal scope of the psalm is atypical of the collection, though the concept finds development in Isaianic prophecies (Is 2:2-4; 49:6; 54:1; 55:5, 11). Concomitantly, Gillingham (328) would like to claim that Psalms 93—100, which herald the kingship of Yahweh (*see* Kingship Psalms), send a message of reassurance to a disheartened postexilic community that Zion will be the place of reunification with God. D. Howard disagrees, arguing persuasively for an overall preexilic provenance for the collection, based on linguistic, conceptual, thematic and historical criteria.

Gillingham (311) argues that the redactional activity by temple personnel is apparent in the "didactic concerns" of the editors to educate an illiterate population and explains the eschatological tone of poems as an intentional means of associating the return of God to Zion with the cosmological scope of his reign. K. Seybold and others affirm the northern provenance of many psalms, suggesting a lack of connection to the temple cult. Gillingham (312) acknowledges that the Zion tradition does not permeate and govern all of the psalms, but she believes that the emphasis on Zion superintends the final editing of the Psalter.

Zion is the place where heaven and earth meet. Consequently, Zion serves as the place where Yahweh encounters his people. Hoppe (29) observes the contrast between Exodus 19, which depicts Yahweh as unapproachable on Mount Sinai, and the accessibility of Yahweh at Zion, where his presence dwells among his people. Israel made regular pilgrimages to the religious shrine of Zion to worship Yahweh (Ps

84:7), bringing gifts of thanksgiving or offerings to accompany specific requests. Three times a year the male population was required to make a pilgrimage to Jerusalem, but the journey was seen as a source of rejoicing rather than a burdensome obligation.

5. Zion in the Songs of Ascent (Pss 120—134).
P. Satterthwaite (106) observes that the "restoration of Zion and Yahweh's purposes for her" unify the Songs of Ascent, each psalm casting a distinctive light on the significance of Zion for the faith community. Although not every psalm in the collection uses the designation *Zion*, the underlying themes of the poems clearly underscore the emphasis on Zion, first as the place to encounter Yahweh in worship, and second as the eschatological expectation as the location of the ideal kingdom. Zion is a center of peace, and the absence of warfare language minimizes Zion's political significance in the ancient Near East. The Songs of Ascent reinforce Zion as the place from where Yahweh's blessings emanate, thus associating prosperity centralized in Zion with the pilgrimage to Jerusalem.

In the Songs of Ascent Zion continues to serve as the focus of Yahweh's protection and provision for his people despite the community's fears that Yahweh has abandoned them. In the face of national dispersion and disaster the psalmist envisions Zion as the official place of worship for a unified Israel. The people will enjoy blessing corporately and individually if they seek God's presence in his sanctuary. The poet builds the anticipation of a discouraged nation, directing their hopes toward a future fulfillment of Yahweh's promises and undergirding his original commitment to them.

Psalm 122 appeals to Yahweh to remember Jerusalem as a place of safety, placing the hopes of Yahweh's people in the restoration of Zion as their haven of refuge. At this point in Israel's early history Jerusalem and Zion have become inextricably linked as one entity. Gillingham (320) suggests that the intermittent mentions of Zion in the Songs of Ascent have been strategically located in the middle of each of three separate collections (Pss 120—124; 125—129; 130—134) as a governing device that enables the reader to apprehend the central theme of Zion's restoration.

Psalm 125:1 depicts Mount Zion as immovable and established in eternity, associating the omnipotence and eternality of Yahweh's kingship with the imagery. The emphasis in Psalm 125:1-2 centers on Yahweh's power to protect his people rather than his military might. Similarly, the overall tone of the Songs of Ascent contrasts with that of other "Zion psalms" (Pss 2; 46; 48; 96; 97; 99), the former reinforcing Zion as a place of restoration and security, the latter underscoring Yahweh's rule over the nations (Satterthwaite, 121). In particular, Psalms 2; 46; 48 describe the threat of foreign attacks against Zion and Yahweh's swift response of victory (Satterthwaite, 122).

Psalm 126:1 recollects the return of the captives to Zion, both as a physical location and as a metaphorical state of security and prosperity. The joy that pervades the community permeates the hymn, which praises Yahweh and seeks his continued provision. The song poignantly expresses the mourning of God's people and their subsequent return to the land as a fulfillment of their hope in Yahweh's deliverance and the tangible realization of their return as a manifestation of their special relationship to God as his covenant people.

Psalm 128 envisions Zion as the source of Yahweh's blessings and as the center from which Yahweh's prosperity originates. The pilgrimage to Zion serves to praise Yahweh for his intervention on Israel's behalf while concomitantly guaranteeing the continued fecundity of the land and the proliferation of descendants. The blessing of eternal life through the filial dynasty emanates from Zion, which is characterized as the place where the "dew of Mount Hermon" falls (Ps 133:3).

Psalms 132—134 solidify the connection between the ark tradition and the Davidic dynasty. Psalm 132 depicts the first procession of the ark and the ushering in of Yahweh's presence in Zion, led by David. The poet recollects that initial procession as the catalyst for national hope (Ps 132:9) and the restoration of a Davidic descendant on the throne (Ps 132:10). The second half of Psalm 132 articulates the divine response, reasserting Yahweh's faithfulness to his promises to Zion and David while concomitantly affirming Yahweh's election of Zion and the Davidic lineage. The psalm represents a further theological development, inextricably linking Davidic rule with Zion as Yahweh's resting place (cf. Ps 78:68; 1 Sam 7). Whereas Psalm 89 articulates God's promise to the perpetual reign of David's posterity, Psalm 132 associates Davidic reign with obedience to the Torah (Ps 132:12).

6. Zion in Psalms of Exile and Restoration.

Several psalms derive from the exile or the post-exilic period and express the disappointments and despair troubling God's people following the captivity. Since Judah associated Zion with security and protection, the destruction of the city and the desecration of the temple evoked a sense of abandonment and fear. One exilic poem, Psalm 74, begins by rousing Yahweh to remember his people as the "tribe of his inheritance" and to recollect Zion as his dwelling place. The nation was disillusioned after the Babylonian invasion of Judah and perceived the defeat of Jerusalem and Zion as representing the departure of Yahweh from among his people and his rejection of them. The poet describes in detail the pillaging and violence exacted in the sanctuary and then appeals to God as creator and great victor over the evil forces of chaos, employing the motif of the divine warrior. On the basis of Yahweh's previous intervention on their behalf, the community beseeches Yahweh to aid them by eliminating their oppressors and restoring Zion (Ps 79).

The despair of Yahweh's people in the foreign land of Babylon receives its clearest expression in Psalm 137, which describes the deepest grief and longings of the exiles, who were taunted by their captors to sing "songs of Zion" that exalted Yahweh and his compassion toward his people and that highlighted the superiority of God and his election of Israel. The departure of God's presence and the separation of the captives from their homeland are juxtaposed with the call for vengeance upon the adversaries that decimated Jerusalem and defiled the temple.

Psalm 147 celebrates the rebuilding of Jerusalem and the return of its inhabitants. Depicted in terms of healing and forgiveness, the remnant of Israel expresses a renewed sense of God's providence through the regathering of their people in their homeland. The poet draws on a phrase from Isaiah 40 to acknowledge that Yahweh has not abandoned his elect, and that he will allow none of them to evade his grasp. The supply of rain for Jerusalem is significant because the city has no regular water source for irrigation and relies solely on the elements for the production of crops. Following their release

by Persia, the community reaffirms their trust in Yahweh and praises his deliverance. God is strengthening the protective bars of the gates of Zion (Ps 147:13), figuratively denoting the restoration of security to the precincts of Judah and especially of Jerusalem. Peace attends the city and the return of Yahweh's presence among its citizens. The concluding poems of the Psalter rejoice in Yahweh's eternal reign in Zion (Ps 146:10; 149:2).

7. Zion in Lamentations.

The book of Lamentations, an extended funeral dirge, mourns the capture and devastation of Jerusalem, the temple and the surrounding areas of Judah. Zion appears twice as the location of cultic worship and practice (Lam 1:4; 2:6). Zion no longer serves as the central gathering location for national cultic celebrations and sacrifices following the destruction of Solomon's temple and the subsequent departure of Yahweh's "glory" from his dwelling place (Lam 1:6; 2:1).

In a few instances the writer addresses Jerusalem affectionately as a mourning "daughter" (Lam 2:15, 18) who has suffered the loss of her children (Lam 1:15-17) and currently experiences punishment for her disobedience (Lam 4:22). The "elders" of the city sit silently (Lam 2:10). In addition, the "daughter of Zion" specifically refers to the city of Jerusalem, the walls that have been compromised (Lam 2:8; 4:11; cf. Lam 2:18), leaving the political and religious capital vulnerable. The violation of women in and around Zion reflects the danger to those citizens left behind (Lam 5:11). The single mention of "Mount Zion" (Lam 5:18) as a desolate haunt for wild animals reinforces the notion of abandonment.

Lamentations 3, sung from a male perspective, does not refer to Zion, while Lamentations 4 contains the only mention of "sons of Zion" (Lam 4:2), a metaphor depicting the desperate circumstances of Yahweh's people as starving "children" born during Jerusalem's invasion. The hopeful conclusion of the book anticipates the deliverance of the "daughter of Zion" from captivity and envisions her eventual restoration (Lam 4:22). Nevertheless, the writer admonishes the people to remember that the exile represents God's judgment for Israel's sin.

See also ARCHITECTURAL IMAGERY; CONFIDENCE, PSALMS OF; DIVINE PRESENCE; MOUNTAIN

IMAGERY; PROTECTION IMAGERY; WARFARE IMAGERY.

BIBLIOGRAPHY. **S. Gillingham,** "The Zion Tradition and the Editing of the Hebrew Psalter," in *Temple and Worship in Biblical Israel,* ed. J. Day (LHBOTS 422; London: T & T Clark, 2005) 308-40; **J. H. Hayes,** "The Tradition of Zion's Inviolability," *JBL* 82 (1963) 419-26; **L. J. Hoppe,** *The Holy City: Jerusalem in the Theology of the Old Testament* (Collegeville, MN: Liturgical Press, 2000); **D. M. Howard Jr.,** *The Structure of Psalms 93-100* (BJSUCSD 5; Winona Lake, IN: Eisenbrauns, 1997); **A. G. Hunter,** "Yahweh Comes Home to Zion: The Psalms of Ascent," in *Psalms* (OTR; London: Routledge, 1999) 173-258; **W. H. Mare,** "Zion," *ABD* 6.1096-97; **D. C. Mitchell,** *The Message of the Psalter: An Eschatalogical Programme in the Book of Psalms* (JSOTSup 252; Sheffield: Sheffield Academic Press, 1999); **B. C. Ollenburger,** *Zion: The City of the Great King* (JSOTSup 41; Sheffield: Sheffield Academic Press, 1987); **T. Renna,** "Zion and Jerusalem in the Psalms," in *Augustine: Biblical Exegete,* ed. F. Van Fleteren and J. C. Schnaubelt (Collectanea Augustiniana; New York: Peter Lang, 2001) 279-98; **J. J. Roberts,** "Zion in the Theology of the Davidic-Solomonic Empire," in *Studies in the Period of David and Solomon: Papers Read at the International Symposium for Biblical Studies, Tokyo, 5-7 December, 1979,* ed. T. Ishida (Winona Lake, IN: Eisenbrauns, 1982) 93-108; **P. E. Satterthwaite,** "Zion in the Songs of Ascent," in *Zion: City of Our God,* ed. R. Hess and G. Wenham (Grand Rapids: Eerdmans, 1999) 129-69; **K. Seybold,** *Introducing the Psalms* (Edinburgh: T & T Clark, 1990). S. L. Klouda

Scripture Index

Old Testament

Genesis
1, *47, 48, 53, 54,*
69, 70, 194,
248, 304, 602
1—2, *274, 855*
1—3, *62, 816,*
872
1—11, *857, 876*
1:1, *464, 502, 796*
1:1—2:3, *69, 228*
1:2, *48, 51, 771*
1:4, *194*
1:6-7, *502*
1:6-8, *321*
1:7-8, *43*
1:10, *194*
1:12, *194*
1:18, *194*
1:20, *431*
1:21, *46, 194*
1:25, *194*
1:26, *196, 814*
1:26-27, *194, 312,*
856
1:28, *457*
1:31, *69, 194*
2, *68, 195, 872*
2—3, *68, 194,*
195, 211, 456,
768
2:4, *676*
2:6-15, *113*
2:7, *431, 910*
2:9, *433, 872*
2:13, *937*
2:15, *196*
2:18, *457*
2:18-25, *456*
2:24, *451, 452,*
454, 680
3, *141, 195, 202,*
254, 433, 813
3:1, *68*
3:6, *857*
3:14-19, *680*
3:15, *820*
3:16, *680*
3:18, *68, 69*
3:19, *432*
3:22, *195*
5, *676, 680*
5:1-32, *693*
5:21-24, *676, 680*
5:22, *679, 856*
5:24, *102, 679,*
726, 856
6:2, *113*
6:4, *113*
6:9, *856*
6:22, *195*
7:2, *159*
7:5, *195*

7:9, *195*
7:11, *47, 321*
7:16, *195*
7:22, *432*
8:2, *47, 321*
8:21, *382*
9:4, *431*
10:9, *534*
10:23, *371, 428*
10:25, *676, 680*
11:4, *196*
11:10-26, *676,*
680, 693
11:18-19, *676*
12, *698*
12:1, *680*
12:2-3, *701*
12:3, *734, 857*
12:4, *196*
12:10, *680*
14, *372, 469*
14:18, *122*
14:18-19, *407*
15, *258*
16, *209*
17:1, *856*
17:23, *196*
18, *196*
18:17, *196*
18:19, *196*
19:1, *732*
19:19, *248*
19:30-38, *680*
19:37, *330*
20:3, *883*
20:11, *860*
21, *685*
21:4, *196*
22:17, *23*
23, *730*
23:7, *479*
24:27, *680*
24:28, *213*
24:60, *23*
25:14, *264, 428,*
429, 867, 878
25:23, *315*
26:1, *680*
26:5, *196*
26:24, *815*
27, *315*
27:12, *159*
27:29, *479*
28, *228*
28:20, *159*
29—31, *206*
29:15, *930*
29:33, *206*
30:3, *426*
30:3-4, *691*
30:6, *206*
30:14-16, *222*
31:13, *683*
31:27, *618*

31:40, *159*
31:42, *201*
31:53, *201*
32:22-32, *315*
33:3, *479*
33:13, *12*
33:19, *344*
35:19, *679*
36, *363*
36:10-11, *371*
36:28, *371*
37—50, *206, 678*
38, *213, 240, 379,*
519, 693, 698
38:8, *680*
38:11, *21*
39, *544*
39—41, *320*
39:4, *931*
40—41, *877*
40:15, *321*
41:37-45, *624*
42:7, *159*
43:32, *159*
48:7, *679*
49, *506*
49:8-10, *693*
49:8-12, *467*
49:11, *510*
49:25, *44*
50:20, *256*

Exodus
1, *261*
2:24-25, *646*
3:1—4:17, *396*
3:11, *166*
3:12, *930*
3:21-22, *889*
4:10, *166*
4:13, *166*
4:23, *930*
5:22—6:8, *396*
6:1, *428*
6:7, *701*
6:12, *166*
6:30, *166*
7:9-12, *46*
7:16, *930*
8:1, *930*
9:20, *365*
9:30, *201*
11:2-3, *889*
12, *458*
12:21-51, *459*
12:35-36, *889*
12:36, *166*
13, *459*
14, *459*
14—15, *51*
14:5, *867*
14:28, *889*
14:30, *889*
15, *50, 230, 231,*

260, 261, 262,
506
15:1, *618, 889*
15:1-18, *619*
15:2, *762*
15:3, *831*
15:4, *889*
15:5, *889*
15:10, *889*
15:11, *115*
15:12, *889*
15:13, *382*
15:13-16, *930*
15:14-15, *166*
15:17, *328*
15:21, *618*
17:7, *714*
17:8-16, *165, 463*
17:14, *463, 477*
18:21, *201*
19, *218, 938*
19—20, *460*
19:1, *460*
19:6, *22*
19:7-8, *460*
19:8, *196*
20, *231*
20—24, *228*
20:3, *199*
20:5-6, *434*
20:17, *199*
20:18-21, *861*
20:22—23:33,*
196
20:26, *620*
21:12-14, *389*
21:13, *321*
21:13-14, *525*
21:17, *316, 422*
22:16-17, *424*
22:22-24, *910*
23, *581*
23:14-19, *459*
23:16, *74, 461*
23:20-33, *114*
24, *113*
24:7, *196*
24:10, *114*
25:6, *466*
28:41, *466*
29:7, *466*
30:23, *221*
30:30, *466*
31:1-3, *872*
31:1-5, *877*
31:3-5, *902*
31:6, *902*
31:14, *317*
32:1—34:35, *396*
32:6, *455*
32:10, *328*
32:12, *328, 395*
32:18, *871*
32:32-33, *6*

33:3, *328*
33:12—34:26,*
459, 462
34, *581*
34:6-7, *408, 434,*
817
34:24, *74*
34:26, *113*
35:30-31, *872*
35:35, *902*
40:15, *466*

Leviticus
1:3, *14*
1:10, *14*
1:14, *14*
2:2, *620, 931*
2:9, *620*
2:16, *620*
5:4, *424*
5:12, *620*
7:11-18, *73*
7:12, *73*
8, *139*
8:12, *139*
8:15, *527*
10:11, *895*
11:7, *17*
11:44, *197*
12:1-4, *732*
12:3, *616*
14:2-7, *617*
15:19-30, *214*
16:8, *617*
16:18, *527*
18:16, *454*
19:2, *857*
19:9-10, *680, 691,*
702
19:18, *194, 199*
19:36, *197, 910*
20:9, *316*
20:24-26, *49*
22:13, *21*
22:26—23:44,*
462
23, *139, 581*
23:9-22, *459*
23:15-21, *680*
23:22, *691*
23:23-44, *74*
23:24, *616*
23:39, *461*
23:42-43, *462*
24:7, *620, 931*
24:12, *320*
25, *379, 380*
25:3-4, *618*
25:23, *692*
25:23-28, *425*
25:25, *454*
25:25-28, *379,*
380, 680, 685
25:29-31, *379*

25:47-49, *379*
25:47-50, *680,*
685
26, *461, 535*
26:12, *762*
26:14-39, *316*
26:19, *159*
26:19-20, *681*
26:38, *100*
26:40-41, *408*

Numbers
3:1, *676*
3:7-8, *931*
5:8, *379*
5:11-31, *76*
5:12-15, *509*
6:4-5, *712*
6:22-26, *458, 460*
6:22-27, *796*
6:24-26, *526, 528*
6:25, *117*
10:4, *428*
10:9-10, *616*
10:35, *72*
10:35-36, *72, 920*
10:36, *72*
12:3, *614*
12:6, *883*
12:8, *712*
14:18, *408*
15:34, *320*
15:39, *141, 637*
16, *26, 234*
16:30-33, *100*
16:32, *26*
21—25, *700*
22, *716*
22—24, *315*
22:1-6, *490*
22:22, *714, 715*
22:32, *714, 715*
23, *261*
23—24, *506*
23:7, *158*
24:17, *467*
25:1, *455, 490*
25:8, *455*
26:9-11, *234*
26:33, *381*
27, *209*
27:1-11, *381, 692*
27:21, *850*
28:16-25, *459*
28:19-25, *459*
28:26, *459*
28:26-31, *460*
29, *461, 462*
29:12-16, *462*
29:35, *462*
29:35—30:1, *463*
30:16, *21*
35:9-34, *321, 389*
35:10-34, *525*

35:19, *379*
36, *209*
36:1-12, *381*

Deuteronomy
1:1, *241*
1:1—21:9, *863*
1:2-5, *241*
1:6, *241*
1:25, *195*
1:34, *195*
1:35, *195*
1:44, *843*
2:25, *201*
3, *859*
3:25, *195*
4, *115*
4:5-6, *877*
4:6, *845, 878, 887*
4:6-7, *725*
4:9-10, *861*
4:10, *541*
4:12, *712*
4:15, *712*
4:19, *117*
4:19-20, *114, 115*
4:35, *115*
4:39, *115*
4:41-43, *389*
5, *231*
5:11, *22*
5:29, *201*
5:31, *421, 541*
6:1, *421*
6:4-6, *725*
6:4-9, *855, 895*
6:5, *194*
6:20-24, *231*
7, *490*
7:1-4, *190*
7:3-4, *680*
7:11, *421*
8:6, *861*
9:26, *617*
9:26-27, *183*
10:12-13, *725,*
861
10:17, *115*
10:17-18, *910*
11:1, *421*
11:19, *541*
11:22, *861*
12:3, *213*
12:12, *684*
12:18, *684*
13, *194*
14:1, *410*
14:11, *18*
14:22—16:17,*
459, 463
15:4-6, *421*
16:9-12, *459*
16:13, *731*
16:18, *389*

16:20, *684*
17:3, *114*
17:7, *159*
17:8-13, *75, 389*
17:14-20, *377, 378*
18, *850*
19:1-3, *321*
19:1-13, *389*
19:4-7, *379*
19:14, *382, 422*
20, *194*
21:1-8, *75*
21:10-14, *684*
21:18-21, *684*
22:5, *633*
22:21, *21*
22:28-29, *424*
23:3, *33, 330, 493*
23:3-5, *680*
23:3-6, *40, 490, 684*
23:4, *490, 694, 695*
24:1-5, *684*
24:19, *680, 691*
24:19-22, *702*
25, *379, 380*
25:1, *379*
25:5-10, *240, 379, 425, 454, 680, 684*
25:6, *379*
25:7, *379*
25:8-10, *692*
25:9, *379*
25:11-12, *842*
25:13-16, *910*
25:15, *422*
25:17-19, *165, 477*
26:1-11, *393*
26:5, *231*
26:16-17, *421*
27—28, *535*
27:11-26, *316*
27:16, *316*
27:17, *382*
28—29, *813*
28:1-14, *421*
28:15-48, *32*
28:15-68, *316, 421*
28:16, *796*
28:20, *100*
28:23-24, *681*
28:37, *532*
28:54, *12*
28:63, *100*
29:25, *114*
29:29, *816*
30, *813*
30:1-4, *408*
30:11-16, *725*
30:11-20, *725*
30:15, *226*
30:15-20, *861*
30:17-19, *316*
31:10-13, *462*
31:18, *160, 188*
31:19, *619, 620*
31:22, *620*
31:27, *382*

31:30, *619*
32, *115, 218, 260, 261*
32—33, *506*
32:1-44, *619*
32:8, *116*
32:8-9, *113, 114, 115*
32:10-12, *525*
32:12, *115*
32:13, *159*
32:17, *114, 115*
32:33, *46*
32:35, *117, 318*
32:39, *115*
32:43, *113, 114*
33:1, *328*
33:1-29, *619*
33:16, *261*
34, *241, 614*
34:5-12, *579*
34:9, *877*

Joshua
1, *232*
1:5, *119*
1:8, *420*
1:9, *119*
1:14, *32*
2, *32*
5:2—6:1, *459*
6:24, *614*
6:26, *316*
6:27, *459*
7:13, *831*
10:1, *122*
11:23, *687*
20:1-9, *321, 379, 389*
23, *232*
24, *75*
24:2, *231*
24:14-24, *931*
24:32, *344*

Judges
1:1, *687*
3:7-11, *687*
3:12-30, *694, 697, 700*
4—5, *51*
4:14, *831*
5, *230, 261, 262, 506, 536, 808*
5:7, *265*
5:12, *618*
6—9, *678*
6:37, *159*
8:2, *534*
8:14, *718, 895*
8:21, *534*
9:15, *527*
12:8-10, *694, 697*
14:5, *311*
17, *374*
17:1, *679*
17:7-8, *679*
17:7-9, *679*
18:30, *795*
19:1, *679*
19:2-3, *21*
19:16, *730*
19:18, *679*

21:19-24, *240*
21:25, *490, 681*

Ruth
1, *217, 454, 490, 491, 492, 678, 694, 700*
1—3, *699*
1:1, *32, 490, 673, 677, 679, 680, 681, 687, 694, 700, 822*
1:1-2, *494, 678, 686*
1:1-3, *494*
1:1-5, *676*
1:1-6, *54, 96, 800*
1:1-12, *96, 800*
1:1-13, *683*
1:1-18, *703*
1:1-21, *686*
1:2, *481*
1:3-5, *434, 686*
1:4, *494, 680, 682, 694, 822*
1:4-4, *683*
1:5, *695*
1:6, *32, 119, 491, 680, 681, 682, 702*
1:6-18, *684, 686*
1:8, *21, 213, 258, 490, 686, 696*
1:8-9, *258, 491, 683, 701*
1:9, *21, 682, 800*
1:11, *379*
1:12, *381*
1:12-15, *800*
1:12-16, *96*
1:13, *258, 494, 682, 683*
1:14, *454, 695*
1:15, *117, 379, 680*
1:16, *117, 258, 695, 701, 934*
1:16-17, *460, 494, 675, 683, 694*
1:16-18, *730, 922*
1:17, *316, 677, 789*
1:19, *696, 922*
1:19-21, *678, 684, 686*
1:20-21, *434, 494, 681, 682, 683, 922*
1:21, *33, 258, 381, 491, 676, 814*
1:22, *219, 381, 460, 491, 673, 678, 680, 694, 789, 822*
1:22—2:1, *686*
1:22—2:23, *686*
2, *32, 258, 491, 494, 677*
2:1, *32, 494, 678, 683, 703*
2:1-7, *680*
2:2, *673, 680,*

683, 690, 691, 702
2:2-3, *684, 686*
2:3, *681, 702*
2:4, *258, 454, 682, 683*
2:4-16, *684, 686*
2:5, *33*
2:6, *673, 680*
2:7, *800*
2:8, *33*
2:9, *922*
2:10, *33*
2:10-11, *695*
2:11, *680, 683, 789, 922*
2:11-12, *258, 494*
2:12, *18, 33, 118, 258, 525, 526, 527, 681, 682, 684, 702, 922*
2:13, *33, 691, 922*
2:13-23, *800*
2:13—3:8, *96*
2:14, *219, 220, 696*
2:15-16, *299, 680, 731*
2:17, *219, 691*
2:17-23, *686*
2:18-23, *684*
2:19-20, *491*
2:20, *258, 379, 380, 516, 678, 680, 682*
2:20-22, *678*
2:21, *673, 680*
2:23, *219, 691, 822, 922*
3, *491, 679, 703, 732*
3:1, *683*
3:1-4, *679*
3:1-5, *380, 686*
3:1-6, *684*
3:1-7, *683*
3:1-8, *800*
3:1-9, *680*
3:1-18, *686*
3:1—4:22, *34*
3:2-3, *732*
3:3, *493*
3:4, *380, 454*
3:4-14, *682*
3:6-15, *684, 686*
3:7, *696*
3:7-8, *454*
3:7-9, *299*
3:8, *789*
3:9, *380, 493, 680, 683, 691, 922*
3:10, *258, 380, 494, 683, 922*
3:10-13, *299*
3:11, *679, 681, 683, 693*
3:12, *379*
3:12-13, *380, 680*
3:13-18, *96, 800*
3:14, *299*
3:15, *454, 691, 694*

3:16, *683*
3:16-18, *684, 686*
3:17, *33*
3:18, *679, 683, 824*
4, *212, 381, 382, 401, 425, 454, 673, 682, 684, 692, 693, 697, 698, 699*
4:1, *381, 682, 800*
4:1-2, *380, 682*
4:1-6, *425*
4:1-10, *684*
4:1-12, *380, 677, 686, 730*
4:1-13, *676*
4:1-17, *686*
4:3, *380, 381, 425, 426, 692*
4:3-4, *96, 800*
4:3-6, *680*
4:4, *380, 425*
4:5, *379, 380, 381, 425, 454, 673, 680, 821*
4:6, *101, 380, 381, 425, 682*
4:7, *265, 673, 674, 675, 677, 698, 789, 800*
4:7-8, *692, 693*
4:7-10, *680*
4:8, *696*
4:9, *380, 922*
4:9-10, *380, 381, 679, 680*
4:10, *212, 379, 380, 381, 673, 680*
4:11, *21, 22, 683*
4:11-12, *380, 679, 684, 730, 934*
4:12, *21, 258, 683, 693*
4:13, *258, 454, 679, 680, 681, 682, 684, 702*
4:13-17, *676, 686, 692*
4:14, *258, 299, 381, 683*
4:14-15, *679, 922*
4:14-17, *684*
4:15, *679, 683, 703*
4:16, *426*
4:17, *299, 381, 426, 674, 676, 679, 682, 698, 703*
4:17-22, *674, 822*
4:18, *680*
4:18-22, *490, 673, 676, 686*
4:21, *32, 694*
4:22, *299, 789*

1 Samuel
1, *374, 401*
1:9, *614*
1:9-18, *76*
1:11, *430*

2:1, *385*
2:1-10, *385*
2:6, *649*
2:6-10, *871*
2:10, *681*
3:1-3, *685*
4, *895*
6:9, *681*
7, *939*
9:1, *477*
9:21, *165*
10:1, *467*
10:1-2, *687*
10:5, *616*
10:9-12, *877*
10:11-12, *531*
10:12, *530, 534*
11:1, *930*
11:7, *201, 316*
12, *232*
12:3, *467*
12:5, *467*
12:14, *201, 302*
12:24, *201*
13:8-15, *469*
14:51, *165*
15, *165, 240, 477*
15:1-3, *165*
15:6-32, *923*
15:7, *467*
15:8-9, *463*
15:22, *870*
16, *467*
16:13-14, *118*
16:14-23, *579, 614, 669*
16:16-23, *616*
16:18, *32, 674*
17, *840*
17:12, *679*
17:43, *314*
18:10, *616*
18:14, *674*
18:14-15, *618*
19, *209*
19:9, *616*
19:24, *531*
21:10, *614*
21:12—23:1, *614*
22—24, *525*
23, *850*
24:8, *479*
24:13, *429, 529, 534*
25:16, *528*
26:10, *619*
26:19, *316*
27:1-3, *614*
28:6, *850, 883*
28:17, *118*
29:4, *714*
30:22, *157, 159*

2 Samuel
1, *579*
1:17-27, *384, 400, 401, 669*
1:19-27, *72, 476, 620*
3:33-34, *400*
5:6-7, *23*
5:7, *407, 936*
5:10, *119*

5:17-25, *674*
6, *73, 579, 620*
6:10-12, *616*
6:12-15, *920*
6:15, *73*
7, *326, 452, 468, 470, 685*
7:5-16, *127*
7:9, *734*
7:10, *326*
7:11, *734*
7:13, *734*
7:14, *326, 468*
7:14-17, *326*
7:15-16, *469*
7:16, *734*
7:19, *676*
11—12, *398*
12, *76*
13, *455*
13:1, *736, 741*
13:3, *902*
14, *209, 914*
14:2, *536*
14:4, *479, 710*
14:11, *379*
14:20, *734*
15—17, *671*
15:10, *302*
15:20, *561*
15:31, *671*
16:23, *882*
18:28, *479*
19:23, *714*
19:30, *380*
19:40—20:2, *673*
20:3, *321*
22, *614, 797*
22:1, *615, 734*
22:3, *527*
22:4, *930*
22:11, *527*
22:12, *262*
23, *91*
23:1-7, *614*
23:5, *326*
23:14, *525*
23:17, *234*
24:11, *882*
24:22, *731*

1 Kings
1—2, *674*
1—11, *671, 733, 737*
1:11, *302, 303*
1:13, *302*
1:16, *479*
1:18, *302, 303*
1:40, *616*
1:50, *527*
1:50-51, *527*
1:50-53, *525*
1:52-53, *733*
2:6, *733, 902*
2:9, *733*
2:13-23, *209*
2:28, *527*
2:28-34, *525*
3, *787*
3—11, *868*
3:1, *537, 733, 735*
3:1-3, *733*

3:1-15, *539*
3:4-28, *236, 849*
3:5-6, *537*
3:5-15, *733*
3:6-9, *885*
3:6-28, *734*
3:7, *737*
3:9, *734*
3:9-14, *895*
3:12, *877*
3:16-27, *895*
3:16-28, *238, 733*
3.28, *895*
4—6, *872*
4:21, *734, 866*
4:21-28, *636*
4:24, *734*
4:25, *464*
4:29-30, *545, 872*
4:29-34, *537, 539,*
 636, 671, 733
4:31, *619*
4:31-34, *530*
4:32, *539, 619,*
 669, 733
4:34, *872*
5—7, *733*
5:4, *714*
5:5, *326*
5:7, *733*
5:9-14, *236, 239*
5:10, *429*
5:12, *733, 872,*
 877
6:11-13, *733*
7:17, *933*
7:19, *617*
7:22, *617*
7:26, *221, 617*
8, *232*
8:1, *123*
8:1-2, *736*
8:2, *461*
8:2-21, *462*
8:10, *113*
8:10-11, *21*
8:22, *123, 736*
8:29-30, *393*
8:31-32, *75, 389*
8:33-36, *393*
8:35, *393*
8:46-51, *408*
8:50-53, *326*
8:54-66, *463*
8:55, *736*
8:58, *421*
9:1-9, *733*
9:7, *532*
9:10, *733*
9:16, *537*
10:1-9, *895*
10:1-13, *236, 239,*
 671
10:1-22, *733*
10:5, *636*
10:7, *872*
10:14-22, *733*
10:19-20, *620*
10:24, *733*
11, *716*
11:1-5, *239*
11:1-8, *735*

11:3, *456, 636*
11:3-8, *733*
11:9, *733*
11:9-13, *225*
11:11-13, *733*
11:13, *116*
11:14, *714*
11:23, *714*
11:25, *714*
11:29-39, *882*
11:41-43, *733*
12, *674, 733*
12:32-33, *620*
14:26, *733*
15:13, *64*
15:23, *871*
16:5, *871*
16:11, *379*
16:23, *302*
16:27, *871*
16:31—21:29,
 209
17—18, *869*
17:6, *18*
18, *236*
18—20, *23*
18:19, *64*
18:39, *114*
19:2-3, *656*
19:21, *931*
20, *865*
20:11, *281*
20:32, *159*
22, *114*
22:10, *691*
22:27, *320*
22:46, *871*

2 Kings
1:1, *687*
2:10-11, *102*
3:4-5, *831*
3:4-27, *687*
6:1, *877*
6:8-23, *831*
8:1-6, *381*
9:13, *302*
9:30-37, *923*
11, *923*
12, *671*
13:21, *724*
15:3-5, *469*
17, *232*
17:37, *421*
18—19, *238*
18:3, *674*
18:4, *19*
18:7, *674*
18:8, *674*
19:14-19, *724*
19:35-37, *724*
21:7, *733*
22:8—23:25, *35*
22:19, *675*
23:1-2, *620*
23:8, *623*
23:13, *675, 733*
23:21-22, *459*
23:25, *675*
24:8-16, *477*
24:13, *733*
25:1, *402*
25:3-7, *402*

25:8-9, *460*
25:8-12, *402*
25:16, *733*
25:25-26, *402*
25:27, *321*

1 Chronicles
1:17, *371*
1:30, *264, 428,*
 867, 878
1:42, *371*
2:3-15, *673, 676*
2:6, *619*
2:11, *32*
2:11-12, *685*
4:17, *619*
6:10, *733*
6:22, *26*
6:24, *24*
6:31, *614*
6:31-48, *24*
6:32, *733, 931*
6:33, *24, 26, 619*
6:39, *234*
6:44, *619*
8:33, *477*
9:19, *26, 234, 620*
9:23, *114*
9:31-32, *620*
11:5, *407, 525*
12:1, *620*
12:6, *620*
15—16, *76, 386*
15:1—16:36, *73*
15:16, *614, 618*
15:16-17, *619*
15:17, *24, 619,*
 620
15:19, *24, 386,*
 619, 620
15:20, *616*
15:20-21, *73, 386,*
 616
15:21, *615, 616,*
 617
15:22, *619*
16, *229, 234, 499*
16:4, *931*
16:5, *24*
16:7, *73, 386, 614*
16:8-22, *325*
16:8-34, *73*
16:8-36, *325*
16:23-30, *325*
16:25, *930*
16:31-34, *326*
16:35, *326*
16:37, *24, 931*
16:41-42, *619,*
 620
16:42, *618*
17:3-15, *326*
17:13, *326*
18:2, *930*
18:6, *930*
18:8, *733*
18:13, *930*
21, *716*
21:1, *714, 715*
22:5-7, *733*
22:9, *733*
22:17-19, *733*
23:1, *733*

25, *24, 636, 669*
25:1, *614, 620*
25:1-2, *620*
25:1-6, *619*
25:1-8, *487*
25:3, *620*
25:6, *620*
26:1, *234, 620*
26:1-2, *26*
26:1-19, *26*
26:19, *234, 620*
27:27-31, *30, 636*
28, *733*
29:22, *736*
29:25, *122, 123,*
 636
29:30, *614*

2 Chronicles
1—9, *537*
1:1, *736*
1:7-13, *236*
3:17, *685*
4:5, *617*
5:11, *21*
5:12, *25, 620*
5:12-13, *619, 636*
6:40-42, *326*
6:42, *467*
7:3, *479*
7:6, *618, 619*
9, *733*
9:1-9, *895*
9:1-12, *236, 239*
9:18-20, *620*
11:17, *733*
12:9, *733*
13:6, *736*
14:7, *23*
15:11, *869*
16:10, *320*
17:10, *201*
19:7, *201*
19:9, *900*
20:5, *393*
20:9, *393*
20:14, *25*
20:19, *26, 234,*
 620
20:29, *201*
22:3, *209*
23:11, *467*
24:21, *37*
25:14-24, *882*
28:27—29:3, *97*
29:5, *21*
29:7, *21*
29:12, *26*
29:13, *25*
29:25-28, *619*
29:29, *479*
29:30, *25*
30:13-27, *459*
30:24, *869*
30:26, *733, 736*
31:4, *167*
33:7, *733*
34:12, *26, 618*
35:1-19, *459*
35:3, *733, 736*
35:4, *733*
35:5, *21*
35:15, *25, 620*

35:25, *236, 399,*
 400, 410
36:23, *171*

Ezra
1:1-2, *171*
1:1-4, *782*
2:1, *620*
2:41, *25*
2:55, *635*
2:57, *635*
2:58, *733*
2:63, *850*
3:8-9, *615*
3:10, *25, 614*
4:2-6, *97*
4:9-10, *782*
4:9-11, *97*
5:17—6:5, *97*
6:19-22, *459*
7:9, *620*
7:14, *845*
7:25, *845*
9, *270, 402, 404*
9—10, *207, 240,*
 454
9:1-2, *190*
10, *673*

Nehemiah
1, *402, 404*
1:1, *781*
3:15, *620*
5:1-5, *136*
7:44, *25*
7:57, *635*
7:59, *635*
7:60, *733*
8:8—10:36, *35*
8:15, *188*
9, *398, 402, 404*
9:6, *114*
9:6-37, *722*
11:7, *867*
11:17, *25*
11:22, *25*
12:24-47, *614*
12:36, *618*
12:37, *620*
12:45, *733*
12:46, *25, 486,*
 619
13, *207*
13:1-3, *454*
13:23-27, *107,*
 190, 673
13:23-28, *240*
13:26, *733, 735*

Esther
1, *173, 186, 188,*
 205, 216, 467,
 492, 789, 790,
 827, 828
1—2, *163*
1:1, *172, 174, 186*
1:1-2, *178*
1:1-3, *172*
1:1-6, *782*
1:2, *171, 781*
1:2-8, *295*
1:3, *9, 161, 164,*
 189, 827

1:4, *826*
1:4-5, *426*
1:4-12, *174*
1:5, *164, 781*
1:7-8, *173*
1:7-10, *220*
1:8, *265*
1:9, *176, 828*
1:10, *821*
1:10-12, *215, 455*
1:11, *178, 265,*
 827, 922
1:11-12, *827*
1:12, *164*
1:12-15, *176*
1:13, *704, 729*
1:14, *173*
1:15, *265*
1:17, *295, 455*
1:19, *426, 719,*
 827
1:20, *295*
1:22, *21, 426,*
 719, 827
2, *162, 183, 217,*
 789, 790
2:1, *189, 265, 644*
2:3, *478, 781, 928*
2:3-15, *321*
2:4, *163*
2:5, *165, 463,*
 476, 477, 781
2:5-6, *162*
2:6, *476, 477*
2:7, *163, 186,*
 188, 426, 478
2:8, *188, 781*
2:8-9, *923*
2:9, *295, 923*
2:11, *188, 478,*
 493
2:12-14, *426*
2:13, *189*
2:14, *189*
2:15, *923*
2:16, *171, 189,*
 478, 827
2:17, *162, 826,*
 923
2:18, *321*
2:19, *783*
2:20, *186*
2:21, *783*
2:21-23, *494, 923*
2:22, *190*
2:23, *719*
3, *8, 183, 188,*
 216
3—8, *163*
3:1, *164, 463*
3:2, *296, 478, 479*
3:2-4, *479*
3:5, *296, 479*
3:6, *296*
3:6-13, *101*
3:7, *166, 478, 631*
3:7-14, *173*
3:8, *179, 191, 265*
3:8-9, *173, 426*
3:9, *174, 191, 719*
3:10, *164*

3:12, *166, 173,*
 708
3:12-14, *426, 719*
3:13, *173, 191,*
 480, 493
3:15, *173, 479,*
 781
4, *173, 175, 185,*
 187, 661
4:1-3, *477*
4:3, *934*
4:4, *493*
4:5-16, *494*
4:7-8, *101*
4:8, *719*
4:10-14, *166*
4:11, *164, 173,*
 265, 426, 923
4:12-16, *923*
4:13, *477*
4:13-14, *167, 190,*
 215, 477
4:13—5:2, *656*
4:14, *101, 166,*
 190, 192, 256,
 480, 823
4:15-17, *183*
4:16, *191, 820,*
 923, 934
4:17, *477*
5, *169, 174, 175,*
 181, 216, 296,
 863
5:1, *732*
5:1-2, *923*
5:2, *184*
5:4-8, *164*
5:9, *783*
5:9-13, *296*
5:10—6:3, *479*
5:13, *783*
5:14, *163*
6:1, *168, 493, 646*
6:1-2, *719*
6:1-4, *923*
6:1-11, *173*
6:2, *182*
6:4, *164*
6:6-9, *494*
6:6-10, *296*
6:8-11, *15*
6:10, *783*
6:11, *164, 923*
6:13, *296, 704,*
 923
7:1, *164*
7:1-6, *923*
7:4, *101, 191,*
 265, 493
7:5, *492*
7:6, *191*
7:8, *21, 22, 923*
7:8-10, *296*
7:9, *163*
7:10, *426*
8, *183, 874*
8:1-2, *21, 166*
8:2, *479*
8:3, *187, 192*
8:5, *265, 719*
8:8, *186*
8:8-10, *719*
8:9, *708*

8:10, *15, 163, 173, 874*
8:11, *101, 192, 480, 493*
8:13, *719*
8:14, *15, 781*
8:15, *479, 493*
8:15-16, *463*
8:16, *431, 493*
8:17, *186, 187, 821*
9, *480, 631, 661, 917*
9—10, *163, 181*
9:1, *164, 168, 493*
9:1-17, *829*
9:2-3, *166*
9:3-4, *479*
9:4, *21, 296*
9:5, *192*
9:5-10, *165*
9:6, *192, 781*
9:6-10, *192*
9:7-10, *463*
9:11, *781*
9:12, *192, 480, 781*
9:13, *162, 186*
9:13-14, *296*
9:13-15, *631*
9:15, *192, 480*
9:16, *192*
9:16-17, *426*
9:16-18, *192*
9:17-18, *633*
9:18-19, *164*
9:19, *167, 186, 493*
9:19-31, *177*
9:20, *161*
9:20-28, *101*
9:20-32, *719, 934*
9:21-22, *463, 631*
9:22, *164, 493, 633*
9:24-26, *631*
9:24-28, *823*
9:26, *186, 631*
9:26-32, *186*
9:28, *177, 631, 645*
9:29, *631*
9:31, *631, 934*
9:32, *164, 631*
10:2, *719*
10:2-3, *296*
10:3, *164, 463, 480*

Job
1, *367, 372, 664, 831*
1—2, *66, 82, 110, 238, 246, 252, 253, 340, 374, 714, 715, 778, 779, 812, 869, 871*
1—3, *334*
1—20, *345, 383, 668, 816*
1:1, *198, 250, 253, 264, 361,*

365, 369, 371, 667, 779, 859, 865, 866, 906, 933
1:1—2:12, *242*
1:1—2:13, *361*
1:2, *372, 453*
1:2-3, *203, 372*
1:3, *14, 15, 372, 867, 869*
1:4-5, *869*
1:5, *203, 349, 372, 730, 933*
1:6, *113, 253, 382, 715, 785*
1:6-7, *6*
1:6-12, *114*
1:7-12, *818*
1:8, *198, 203, 253, 361, 364, 372, 667, 812, 906, 910, 933*
1:8-9, *250*
1:8-12, *779*
1:9, *203, 253, 652, 812*
1:9-10, *66, 777*
1:9-11, *372*
1:10, *14, 364, 528, 776, 778*
1:11, *117, 210, 422, 778*
1:12, *117, 716, 778*
1:13, *220, 869*
1:13-19, *373, 777*
1:13-21, *656*
1:13-22, *108*
1:14, *15*
1:14-17, *869*
1:15, *336, 429, 869*
1:16, *14, 869*
1:17, *15, 336, 869*
1:18, *220, 918*
1:18-19, *869*
1:19, *453*
1:20-21, *777, 933*
1:21, *66, 253, 434, 512*
1:21-22, *210, 778*
1:22, *203*
2, *108, 335*
2:1, *6, 113, 382*
2:1-6, *114*
2:3, *198, 203, 210, 250, 253, 667, 716, 906, 933*
2:3-4, *361*
2:3-6, *818*
2:4, *373*
2:4-5, *777*
2:5, *117, 210, 422, 778*
2:6, *365, 778*
2:7, *465, 869*
2:7-8, *777*
2:7-10, *108*
2:9, *210, 778, 918*
2:9-10, *453, 777, 778*
2:10, *203, 210,*

253, 254, 373, 434, 649, 812, 918
2:11, *264, 786, 866*
2:11-13, *108, 373*
3, *108, 242, 254, 333, 335, 355, 371, 373, 435, 714, 778, 892, 893, 917*
3—25, *243*
3—27, *238*
3—37, *66, 243, 659*
3—42, *242*
3:1, *778, 821*
3:1-10, *778*
3:1-26, *254, 316*
3:1—31:40, *361*
3:1—40:6, *252*
3:2-13, *354*
3:3, *367*
3:3-10, *893*
3:3—40:6, *812*
3:4, *431*
3:5-6, *94*
3:5-9, *799*
3:6, *821*
3:8, *19, 47, 63*
3:9, *19*
3:11-23, *322*
3:11-26, *778*
3:14, *867*
3:15, *22*
3:17, *786*
3:17-20, *5*
3:18, *355*
3:19, *465*
3:20, *431*
3:20-22, *355*
3:21, *778*
3:23, *60, 322, 431, 528, 776, 778*
3:23-26, *779*
3:24-26, *778*
3:25, *812*
3:26, *67*
4, *108, 201, 203, 363, 928*
4—5, *110*
4—14, *334*
4—27, *108*
4:1, *296*
4:2-5, *296*
4:3-5, *359*
4:6, *203, 250, 253, 906*
4:6-7, *652*
4:7, *644, 812*
4:7-9, *66, 100, 667*
4:7-11, *109, 373*
4:7—5:4, *94*
4:8, *779*
4:9, *261, 431, 505, 871*
4:10, *15, 16*
4:10-11, *869*
4:11, *16*
4:12-16, *346*
4:15, *118*

4:16—5:4, *799*
4:17, *659, 903*
4:17-19, *667*
4:17-21, *69, 347*
4:18-21, *653*
4:19, *19, 22, 869*
4:19-20, *432*
5, *82, 205, 288*
5—27, *355*
5:1, *6, 114, 382*
5:2, *659*
5:3-4, *297*
5:4, *528*
5:5, *222*
5:5-7, *109*
5:8, *337*
5:8-16, *653*
5:9, *368, 616*
5:9-16, *350*
5:13, *878*
5:15, *829*
5:17, *297*
5:18-27, *6525:17-27, 109*
5:19, *511*
5:19-22, *534*
5:20, *869*
5:22, *13, 869*
5:23, *13*
5:24-25, *453*
5:25, *222*
5:26, *731*
5:27, *297, 362*
6—7, *334*
6:2, *659, 818*
6:2-13, *355*
6:4, *776*
6:5, *15, 222, 869*
6:6, *222*
6:8-9, *933*
6:14, *203, 297, 906*
6:15-18, *100*
6:18-20, *346*
6:19, *865*
6:23, *528*
6:24, *818*
6:24-26, *297*
6:24-30, *109*
6:30, *818*
7:1, *867*
7:1-3, *60*
7:2, *867*
7:5, *19, 869*
7:6, *822*
7:7, *646*
7:7-9, *432*
7:8, *786*
7:9, *5, 382*
7:9-10, *22, 52*
7:11, *910*
7:12, *20, 46, 63, 321*
7:17, *69*
7:17-18, *361*
7:17-19, *776*
7:19, *69, 361*
7:20, *878*
7:21, *60, 815*
8, *110*
8:2, *109, 352*
8:2-3, *254*
8:3, *652, 667*

8:3-4, *109*
8:3-7, *66*
8:4, *652, 779*
8:5, *337*
8:5-7, *109, 337, 652*
8:6, *344*
8:9, *561, 822*
8:10, *910*
8:11-13, *100*
8:11-15, *22*
8:14, *19, 869*
8:15-17, *94, 799*
8:16-19, *22*
8:20-22, *653*
9, *48, 52*
9—10, *82, 334, 667*
9:2, *667*
9:2-24, *893*
9:2-35, *361*
9:5-7, *482*
9:5-9, *869*
9:5-13, *350*
9:8, *44, 45, 48, 63*
9:9, *17, 346*
9:13, *20, 45, 48, 63*
9:14-21, *330*
9:15, *297, 436, 668*
9:15-31, *109*
9:17-18, *831*
9:17-19, *776*
9:20, *668*
9:20-23, *778*
9:21, *337, 435*
9:21-24, *109, 203, 373*
9:22, *358, 362, 432, 776, 812*
9:22-24, *908*
9:23, *659*
9:24, *67*
9:25-26, *432*
9:26, *17*
9:27, *94, 799*
9:28, *370*
9:30-31, *354*
9:33, *6, 7, 382, 471*
9:33-34, *278*
9:33-35, *109*
10, *62, 63*
10—11, *228*
10:1, *435, 776*
10:1-7, *67, 109*
10:1-22, *818*
10:2, *365*
10:2-7, *422*
10:5, *825*
10:7, *338*
10:8-11, *431*
10:9, *432, 646*
10:12, *254*
10:13-22, *254*
10:16, *16*
10:18, *254, 431*
10:21, *52, 382*
10:22, *52*
11, *110*
11:2, *109, 668*
11:3, *659*

11:3-6, *296*
11:6, *109*
11:7-9, *653*
11:7-11, *350*
11:11, *652, 814*
11:12, *15, 109, 347, 373, 869*
11:13, *337*
11:13-14, *779*
11:13-15, *344*
11:13-20, *66, 109, 373*
11:14-20, *337*
11:16, *644*
11:17, *433*
12, *253*
12—14, *334*
12:1, *928*
12:1-3, *373*
12:2, *109, 659*
12:4-5, *297*
12:4-6, *109*
12:7, *14, 17*
12:8, *18*
12:9, *252, 253, 718, 909*
12:10, *13, 432, 910*
12:12, *109, 373*
12:13, *814, 871*
12:13-25, *653*
12:14, *871*
12:14-25, *350, 358*
12:17, *867, 878*
12:18, *867*
12:25, *771*
13:1-2, *109*
13:2, *297*
13:3, *61, 109, 382*
13:4, *94, 799*
13:12, *109, 373, 646*
13:13-28, *361*
13:15, *117, 362, 364, 799*
13:18, *668*
13:18-20, *94, 799*
13:19, *338*
13:22-27, *109*
13:23, *338*
13:23-27, *94, 799*
13:24, *61, 117, 372, 526, 815, 928*
13:26, *719*
13:28, *19*
14, *524, 911*
14:1-2, *432*
14:4-6, *94, 799*
14:6, *821*
14:7-9, *524*
14:7-10, *432*
14:10-12, *524*
14:11-12, *432*
14:12, *382*
14:13, *5, 526, 528*
14:13-15, *355*
14:13-18, *94, 799*
14:14, *363, 824, 846*
14:15, *869*
14:17, *368*

14:18-20, *482*
15, *110, 352*
15—21, *334, 352*
15:1-13, *109, 373*
15:2, *109, 659*
15:3-5, *109*
15:4, *203*
15:5-6, *254, 517*
15:7, *481*
15:7-8, *346*
15:7-9, *109*
15:7-16, *653*
15:8, *114*
15:9, *297*
15:13, *926*
15:14, *667*
15:14-16, *69*
15:20-35, *652*
15:23, *17, 821*
15:24, *867*
15:28, *22*
15:32, *821*
15:33, *220*
16—17, *334*
16:2, *109*
16:3, *352, 659*
16:4, *297, 910*
16:6-14, *254, 667*
16:8, *347*
16:9, *776*
16:9-14, *867*
16:11, *776*
16:12-14, *831*
16:15-16, *349*
16:18, *516*
16:18-20, *278*
16:18-21, *382*
16:18-22, *361*
16:19, *6, 7, 382, 780*
16:19-21, *114, 471, 667*
16:20, *297*
17—42, *799*
17:2, *297*
17:6, *297*
17:7, *56*
17:11, *821*
17:12, *820*
17:12-13, *431*
17:13, *22*
17:14, *19, 516*
17:16, *5, 52*
18, *110*
18:1-4, *109*
18:3, *14, 869*
18:5-21, *109, 652*
18:8-10, *346*
18:9-13, *52*
18:11, *869*
18:12, *100*
18:17, *100, 646*
18:17-18, *60*
18:18-21, *431*
18:19, *453*
18:21, *254*
19, *334, 382*
19:3, *297*
19:5, *297*
19:5-6, *297*
19:6, *254, 382, 653*
19:6-7, *422, 667*

19:7, *818*
19:7-12, *776*
19:9, *297*
19:11-12, *831*
19:13-19, *348, 382*
19:15-27, *61*
19:17, *918*
19:18, *786*
19:23, *719*
19:23-24, *6*
19:23-27, *361, 471*
19:23-29, *911*
19:25, *6, 382, 383, 422, 427, 780*
19:25-26, *437, 780*
19:25-27, *6, 7, 53, 278, 383, 667*
19:26, *382, 815*
19:26-27, *7, 383*
19:28-29, *6*
20, *110*
20:3, *297*
20:4-9, *100*
20:4-29, *109, 652*
20:8, *432*
20:12, *60*
20:14, *19*
20:16, *19*
20:17, *220*
20:20-22, *60*
20:24, *829*
20:29, *254*
21, *334, 353*
21:3, *297*
21:4-16, *109*
21:6, *644*
21:7-13, *67*
21:10, *14*
21:13, *821*
21:19, *353*
21:22, *871*
21:22-26, *353*
21:26, *19, 432*
21:30, *100*
22, *110*
22—27, *109, 334*
22—31, *205, 374*
22:2, *618*
22:2-12, *109*
22:3, *344*
22:4, *203*
22:4-11, *254, 423*
22:5-9, *337, 653, 667*
22:5-11, *779*
22:6-11, *109*
22:9, *867*
22:12, *350*
22:12-14, *653*
22:14, *46, 725*
22:15-20, *652*
22:21-25, *346*
22:21-30, *109, 337, 353*
23, *359, 667*
23—24, *334*
23:1-7, *361, 910*
23:1-10, *818*
23:3-10, *6*

23:7, *436*
23:8-9, *350*
23:9, *61*
23:10, *382, 435*
23:10-12, *667*
23:11-12, *338*
23:12, *219*
23:13-14, *350*
23:15, *61*
23:17, *61*
24:1, *815*
24:1-17, *358*
24:2, *14, 382*
24:3, *15, 867*
24:5, *15, 869*
24:12, *653*
24:13, *431, 786*
24:15, *453, 526*
24:20, *19, 645*
25, *110*
25:1-6, *254*
25:2, *653*
25:2-6, *350*
25:3, *431*
25:4, *667*
25:4-6, *69, 653*
25:6, *19, 435*
26, *48, 52, 60, 909*
26—27, *334*
26—32, *254*
26:2-4, *109*
26:5, *52*
26:5-14, *254*
26:6, *5, 53*
26:7, *61*
26:8, *321*
26:10, *62, 321*
26:10-14, *60*
26:12, *20, 45*
26:12-13, *45, 48, 63*
26:13, *19, 45, 46*
26:14, *909*
27, *108, 109, 203, 333, 343, 717, 892*
27:1-6, *330, 338*
27:2, *667, 818*
27:2-4, *355*
27:3, *431*
27:5-6, *667*
27:6, *667*
27:8, *435, 436, 824*
27:12, *779*
27:13-23, *110, 254*
27:18, *19*
28, *60, 110, 111, 112, 204, 205, 210, 238, 333, 334, 335, 338, 341, 343, 345, 373, 374, 482, 519, 641, 643, 814, 849, 879, 892, 893, 900*
28—31, *109, 333*
28:1-2, *346*
28:1-11, *346, 708, 869, 892*
28:7, *17*

28:8, *16*
28:9-10, *481*
28:12, *643*
28:12-22, *892*
28:14, *44, 516*
28:16-19, *346*
28:19, *865*
28:20, *643*
28:21, *13, 18*
28:22, *101, 516*
28:23, *643, 779*
28:23-28, *892*
28:24-26, *869*
28:28, *198, 204, 250, 253, 254, 325, 816, 859, 892, 900, 906, 933*
29, *66, 338, 349, 351, 433*
29—30, *255*
29—31, *82, 110, 111, 204, 333, 334, 349, 359, 373, 892*
29—37, *238*
29:1-17, *330*
29:2-10, *297*
29:3, *431, 528*
29:4-5, *862*
29:6, *220, 433*
29:7, *23, 865*
29:8, *465*
29:12-17, *667*
29:13, *433, 867*
29:14, *198*
29:15-17, *359*
29:16, *528*
29:17, *528*
29:20, *453*
29:21, *297*
29:25, *70, 867*
30, *338, 348*
30:1, *16, 297, 869*
30:1-15, *348*
30:3, *869*
30:4, *222*
30:7, *222*
30:9-10, *297*
30:15, *297*
30:20-21, *776*
30:23, *22, 437*
30:25, *867*
30:26, *435*
30:29, *16, 17, 66, 869*
31, *119, 198, 199, 200, 255, 316, 333, 338, 341, 351, 433, 653, 667, 779*
31:1, *199, 453*
31:1-4, *119*
31:1-12, *198, 199*
31:2-3, *100*
31:4, *199*
31:5-8, *316*
31:6, *6*
31:9, *199*
31:9-10, *210, 214*
31:9-12, *453*
31:10, *94, 453*
31:13, *867*

31:13-15, *198, 199*
31:13-23, *359*
31:14-19, *94, 799*
31:15, *199, 431*
31:16, *867*
31:16-22, *316*
31:16-23, *198, 199, 667, 861*
31:17, *219*
31:18, *199*
31:19, *867*
31:20, *14*
31:20-21, *94, 799*
31:21, *23*
31:23, *119*
31:23-24, *198*
31:26-28, *82, 199, 344*
31:29, *297*
31:29-30, *198, 199*
31:32, *729*
31:35, *6, 382, 719*
31:35-37, *109, 361, 667*
31:35-40, *373*
31:37, *373*
31:38, *516*
31:38-40, *316*
31:40, *219, 222*
32, *254, 423*
32—33, *255*
32—37, *94, 110, 243, 252, 334, 340, 343, 373, 650, 663*
32:2, *668, 866*
32:3-4, *94, 799*
32:4, *297*
32:6-9, *110*
32:8, *110, 373, 431*
32:9, *297*
32:11, *297*
32:11-12, *297*
32:15-16, *297*
32:18-20, *357*
32:22, *903*
33:4, *118, 431*
33:4-6, *869*
33:6, *432*
33:8-21, *110*
33:9, *667*
33:10-11, *94, 799*
33:14-15, *534*
33:19-28, *73*
33:23, *382*
33:23-28, *6, 471*
33:24, *511*
33:24-26, *94, 799*
33:28, *528*
33:28-30, *94, 431, 799*
33:31-33, *297*
33:33, *297*
34, *255, 334, 423*
34:5-20, *110*
34:11, *373*
34:14, *431, 432, 910*
34:14-15, *910*
34:15, *432*

34:17, *668*
34:22, *53, 526*
34:25, *264*
34:25-27, *373*
34:27, *845*
34:29, *117, 815*
34:36, *786*
34:37, *373*
35, *334*
35—37, *255*
35:10, *487, 903*
35:11, *17*
35:16, *94, 799*
36:4, *110, 297*
36:7-11, *94, 799*
36:8-13, *322*
36:13-17, *94*
36:13-27, *799*
36:14, *869*
36:24—37:13, *350*
36:29, *814*
36:32-33, *94, 799*
37, *893*
37—39, *862*
37:1-5, *94, 799*
37:3-13, *869*
37:5, *814*
37:8, *13, 526*
37:10—42:11, *94*
37:11, *46*
37:14-15, *94, 799*
37:24, *203, 297*
38, *209, 252, 430, 243, 252, 334, 340, 343, 373, 650, 663*
38—39, *706, 814*
38—41, *20, 47, 48, 60, 61, 65, 69, 112, 255, 334, 335, 341, 812, 816, 849, 903, 904*
38—42, *204, 210, 238, 253, 879*
38:1, *252, 373, 817*
38:1—39:30, *339*
38:1—40:2, *779*
38:1—40:5, *874*
38:1—42:6, *110, 361*
38:2, *297, 350, 358, 779, 878*
38:4-7, *818, 908*
38:4-38, *339*
38:7, *65, 67, 94, 113, 487, 516*
38:7-8, *114*
38:8, *67*
38:8-11, *45, 48, 50, 63, 64, 321, 818*
38:11, *64, 67*
38:12-15, *818*
38:13, *69*
38:15, *100*
38:16, *818*
38:16-17, *52*
38:17, *23, 52, 818*
38:18, *818*
38:19-21, *818*
38:22-23, *818*

38:22-30, *869*
38:23, *821, 822*
38:24, *818*
38:25-26, *69*
38:25-27, *342*
38:25-30, *818*
38:29-30, *60*
38:31, *95, 321*
38:31-32, *346*
38:31-33, *818*
38:33, *62*
38:34, *46, 818*
38:34-35, *869*
38:35, *516, 818*
38:36, *818*
38:37-38, *818*
38:39, *15, 16, 869*
38:39—39:30, *346*
38:40, *526*
38:41, *18, 431, 869*
39, *818*
39:1, *14, 16, 869*
39:1-2, *822*
39:1-4, *818*
39:5, *15, 869*
39:5-8, *482, 818*
39:6, *865*
39:7, *65, 69, 70*
39:9, *15*
39:9-12, *818*
39:13, *17, 869*
39:13-18, *818*
39:15, *13*
39:18, *15, 65, 70, 516, 869*
39:19, *15*
39:19-25, *818, 869*
39:20, *18*
39:22, *65, 516*
39:24, *13*
39:26, *17, 818, 869*
39:27, *17*
39:27-30, *818, 869*
39:28, *526*
39:29, *869*
39:30, *69*
40, *252, 818*
40—41, *840*
40:1, *252*
40:1-2, *818*
40:1-5, *668*
40:2, *252*
40:2-5, *374*
40:3, *252*
40:3-5, *779, 818*
40:4, *297*
40:4-5, *110*
40:6, *252, 817*
40:6-7, *818*
40:6-8, *909*
40:6—41:34, *779*
40:8, *340, 653, 668, 816*
40:8-14, *342, 818*
40:15, *20, 60, 70, 869*
40:15-24, *45, 818*
40:15—41:34,

34:17, *668*

38:22-30, *869*

339
40:17, *222, 840*
40:19, *20*
40:20, *13, 65, 482*
40:22, *222*
40:23, *865*
41, *46, 48, 708, 818*
41:1, *18, 19, 45, 60, 818*
41:1-10, *818*
41:1-34, *63*
41:4, *818*
41:5, *17*
41:10-11, *64, 908*
41:11, *60, 342, 818*
41:12-34, *818*
41:18-21, *46*
41:21, *431*
41:26-29, *829*
41:29, *65, 70*
41:30, *732*
41:33, *64*
41:34, *64, 70*
42, *252, 334, 918*
42:1, *252*
42:1-5, *374*
42:1-6, *110, 243, 668, 779*
42:2, *857*
42:3, *814, 933*
42:5, *61, 910*
42:5-6, *297, 819*
42:6, *350, 812, 933*
42:6-17, *110*
42:7, *779, 780, 812*
42:7-8, *243, 338, 396, 668*
42:7-9, *297, 819*
42:7-12, *252*
42:7-17, *110, 242, 246, 361, 374, 382, 383, 437*
42:8, *14, 423, 779, 869*
42:8-9, *933*
42:8-10, *82*
42:9, *933*
42:10, *364, 918*
42:10-17, *82, 243, 780*
42:11, *95, 336, 344, 423, 812, 867, 918*
42:11-17, *435, 824*
42:12, *14, 15, 364, 869*
42:13, *453, 679, 867*
42:13-15, *918*
42:14, *867*
42:14-15, *210*
42:15, *381, 918*
42:16, *453, 867*
42:17, *363, 371, 846*

Psalms
1, *84, 92, 100,*

150, 235, 314,
  377, 585, 611,
  621, 659, 893
1—2, 150, 151,
  152, 155, 442,
  581, 589, 590,
  593, 611, 681
1—41, 234, 325,
  714, 935
1—50, 4, 27, 258,
  267, 287, 398,
  593, 612, 774,
  820
1—59, 593, 613,
  714, 808
1—72, 59, 90,
  258, 305, 613,
  621
1—81, 607, 613
1—89, 89, 92,
  580
1—100, 92
1—150, 781
1:1, 150, 152,
  224, 324, 433,
  452, 535, 589,
  600, 665
1:1-3, 289, 293
1:2, 150, 152,
  249, 432, 589,
  729, 821
1:2-3, 378
1:3, 432, 433,
  434, 522, 589
1:4, 435
1:4-5, 435
1:5-6, 421, 435
1:6, 100, 152,
  324, 586, 589,
  811
2, 61, 74, 76, 89,
  99, 150, 235,
  375, 377, 378,
  445, 470, 584,
  590, 592, 593,
  671, 932, 939
2—89, 593
2:1, 150, 152, 589
2:1-2, 517, 615
2:2, 467, 803
2:3, 321
2:4, 249
2:5, 817, 819
2:6, 483, 785, 937
2:7, 584, 606, 803
2:7-9, 451
2:7-12, 249
2:8-9, 592
2:9, 819
2:10-12, 820
2:11, 205, 606
2:12, 100, 118,
  150, 152, 378,
  589
3, 75, 150, 246,
  388, 467, 485,
  641
3—7, 235
3—41, 581
3:1, 87, 591, 669
3:1-2, 711, 712
3:2, 485
3:3, 86, 119, 526,

711, 714, 830
3:4, 86, 393, 483,
  711
3:5, 86
3:5-6, 711
3:6, 773
3:7, 86, 87, 528,
  591, 711, 817,
  819, 831
3:8, 711, 714
4, 58, 71, 75, 260,
  386, 388, 616,
  734, 931, 932
4:1, 73, 86, 387,
  421, 486, 669,
  811
4:2, 87
4:3, 86
4:4, 773
4:5, 663
4:6, 117, 389
4:7, 220
4:8, 118, 616
5, 73, 75, 86, 223,
  234, 281, 389,
  485, 607, 669,
  932, 936
5:1, 73, 440, 616,
  618, 669
5:2, 87, 421
5:5, 87, 293
5:5-6, 317
5:6, 100
5:7, 21, 932
5:9, 100
5:9-10, 317
5:11, 87, 118, 526
5:11-12, 665, 811
5:12, 119, 421,
  526, 815
6, 201, 386, 388,
  389, 390, 601,
  775, 891, 917,
  932
6:1, 73, 439, 486,
  617, 775
6:2, 87, 527, 582
6:3, 226, 811
6:4, 811
6:4-5, 711, 713
6:5, 5, 52, 646,
  713, 812, 934
6:5-7, 712
6:6, 87
6:7, 87
6:7-8, 712
6:8, 87
6:8-10, 388, 817
6:10, 289, 591,
  619, 714, 819
7, 75, 228, 388,
  619, 932
7:1, 86, 118, 591,
  664, 666, 712
7:1-5, 830
7:2, 15, 712, 830
7:3, 86, 664
7:3-5, 389, 713
7:4, 87
7:5, 289, 434, 591
7:6, 420, 528,
  811, 831, 832
7:6-7, 712

7:6-8, 710
7:6-13, 830
7:6-16, 616
7:7, 87
7:8, 528, 665,
  713, 811
7:8-11, 421
7:9, 87, 421, 664
7:10, 86, 119,
  526, 713
7:11, 86, 249, 528
7:11-16, 665
7:12, 527
7:12-13, 831
7:16, 54, 262
7:17, 54, 55, 87,
  247, 664, 714
8, 235, 290, 583,
  617, 641, 932
8:1, 323, 486, 588
8:2, 606
8:3, 62
8:3-5, 932
8:4, 69, 646, 822
8:4-5, 69
8:5-8, 814
8:7, 13, 14, 15, 18
8:7-8, 60
8:8, 17, 18, 69
8:9, 323, 588
9, 2, 3, 100, 617,
  664, 805, 932
9—10, 3, 235,
  263, 390, 391,
  399
9:1, 87
9:2, 87, 247
9:3, 87, 100, 665,
  387
9:5, 100, 101, 436
9:5-6, 100, 289,
  665
9:6, 87, 100, 101,
  646
9:7, 3, 591, 825
9:7-8, 811
9:8, 436
9:9, 23, 198, 483,
  586
9:9-12, 937
9:11-14, 392
9:12, 646
9:13, 23, 52, 819
9:14, 23, 290, 617
9:15, 263, 591
9:15-17, 665
9:16, 617
9:17, 322, 421
9:18, 618
9:19, 87, 400, 831
9:20, 87, 665
10, 2
10:1, 387, 811,
  815
10:1-11, 434
10:2, 87
10:2-6, 3
10:4, 293
10:6, 591
10:7, 420
10:9, 15
10:10, 3
10:11, 400, 645

10:12, 817, 819
10:14, 117, 937
10:15, 75
10:16, 87, 100,
  117, 825, 932
10:16-18, 811
10:17, 819
10:18, 528, 811
11, 58, 75, 87
11:1, 17, 118,
  482, 591
11:2, 87, 526, 527
11:4, 21, 116, 932
11:4-5, 435
11:5, 431
11:6, 76, 87, 665
11:6-7, 435
11:7, 76, 86, 117
12, 56, 235, 386,
  391, 712
12:1, 439, 617,
  710, 713
12:3-4, 317, 714
12:7, 118
12:7-8, 711
12:8, 591
13, 235, 388, 651
13:1, 88, 117,
  226, 387, 395,
  526, 776, 815
13:1-2, 524
13:2, 87, 387, 775
13:3, 86, 384,
  387, 392, 528
13:3-4, 524, 830
13:4, 387, 591
13:5, 87, 387
13:5-6, 524, 780
13:6, 387
14, 235, 247, 391,
  797
14:1, 223, 225,
  226, 591, 814
14:2, 618
14:3, 811, 814
14:4, 87, 219
14:5, 118
14:6, 118
14:7, 87
15, 235, 236, 389,
  665
15—24, 151, 442,
  445
15:1, 289
15:2, 395
15:4, 204, 289
15:5, 420
16, 58, 263
16:1, 58, 59, 118,
  591
16:5, 76, 166
16:5-6, 263
16:8, 118
16:8-11, 53, 606,
  615
16:10, 53, 87,
  100, 101, 436,
  614
16:10-11, 5, 437,
  824
16:11, 61, 118,
  119
17, 75, 235, 388,

932
17:1, 421
17:1-2, 666
17:2, 87, 712
17:3, 421, 435,
  713
17:5, 666
17:6, 86
17:7, 118, 712
17:8, 18, 221,
  525, 526, 527
17:8-9, 711
17:11-12, 711
17:12, 830
17:13, 75, 87,
  817, 819
17:13-14, 831
17:15, 71
18, 30, 235, 378,
  584, 602, 614,
  711, 805, 819,
  932
18:1, 619, 712
18:1-2, 525, 819
18:2, 15, 23, 86,
  118, 119, 481,
  483, 526, 527,
  712, 830
18:2-5, 61
18:3, 86, 819, 930
18:3-19, 50
18:4, 52
18:4-5, 713, 819
18:6, 5, 21, 86,
  247, 666, 819,
  932
18:7, 482, 814,
  817
18:7-15, 62, 591,
  711
18:8, 46, 520, 817
18:9, 817, 819
18:10, 46, 527,
  817, 819
18:11, 262, 817
18:12, 817
18:12-19, 831
18:13, 817
18:14, 527, 817,
  829
18:15, 431, 817
18:16-19, 713
18:17, 87
18:18, 76
18:20, 665
18:20-24, 713
18:21, 247
18:22, 666
18:24, 117, 665
18:25-27, 713
18:27, 293, 729
18:27-28, 805
18:28, 86, 528,
  714
18:29, 714
18:30, 526, 712
18:30-31, 119
18:31, 483, 526
18:31-42, 713
18:33, 16, 714
18:34, 831
18:34-42, 714
18:35, 526

18:35-36, 528
18:41, 811, 812
18:42, 713
18:43, 714
18:43-45, 714
18:46, 86, 526
18:46-50, 714
18:47, 434
18:49, 87, 290
18:50, 87, 467,
  932
19, 49, 84, 235,
  378, 583, 585
19:1, 60, 67, 68,
  290, 487, 591
19:1-6, 51, 60, 62
19:4, 487
19:7, 224, 249
19:7-10, 729
19:7-11, 289, 432
19:8, 528
19:9, 86, 198,
  325, 900
19:11, 88
19:13, 87, 88
19:14, 86, 87,
  117, 440, 483,
  526, 616, 711
20, 235, 378, 584
20—21, 151
20:1, 713
20:2, 21, 938
20:2-3, 937
20:6, 467, 711,
  713, 937, 938
20:7, 15, 591, 645
20:7-8, 291
20:9, 713
21, 235, 378, 584,
  617, 832
21:1, 324, 714
21:4, 434, 821
21:4-7, 432
21:5, 289
21:8-10, 100
21:8-13, 819
21:12, 829
21:13, 324
22, 235, 388, 393,
  592, 617, 932
22:1, 73, 153,
  308, 592, 651,
  664, 812
22:1-2, 392, 394,
  776, 811
22:1-10, 388
22:2, 86, 392
22:3, 117
22:3-5, 776, 777
22:4-5, 713
22:5, 714
22:6, 19
22:6-8, 289, 606,
  776
22:7, 592
22:7-8, 713
22:8, 592
22:9, 528
22:9-10, 388, 431
22:9-11, 776, 777
22:10, 920
22:12-13, 591,
  713

22:12-22, 832
22:13, 15, 830
22:14, 311
22:14-18, 713
22:17, 16
22:18, 592
22:19-21, 710
22:20, 16, 434
22:21, 15, 528,
  606
22:21-22, 290
22:21-31, 714
22:22, 87
22:22-31, 780
22:23, 204, 205,
  395
22:25, 932
22:27, 645, 932
22:27-28, 62, 824
22:28, 87, 116
22:29, 101, 479,
  824
22:30, 824
23, 58, 75, 528
23:1, 14, 58, 153,
  522
23:3, 663
23:4, 118, 119,
  516, 815
23:5, 76, 591
23:5-6, 525
23:6, 76, 87, 400,
  821, 932
24, 235, 236, 389,
  585, 620, 641
24:1, 14
24:1-2, 60, 290,
  932
24:1-6, 713
24:2, 48, 62
24:3, 620
24:3-5, 289
24:4, 420
24:5, 247
24:6, 117
24:7, 23, 641, 932
24:7-10, 72, 87,
  290, 591, 713
24:8, 61, 117, 641
24:8-10, 932
24:9, 23, 641, 932
24:10, 61, 117,
  641, 831
25, 2, 235, 388,
  893
25:2, 86, 87, 289,
  712
25:3, 289, 824
25:4-5, 397
25:5, 86, 88, 713,
  824
25:6, 87, 646, 815
25:7, 397
25:8, 86
25:8-9, 397
25:8-10, 389
25:10, 86, 87,
  392, 397, 421
25:11, 397
25:12, 397
25:12-13, 205
25:12-15, 389
25:14, 204, 392,

397
25:16, 117, 777, 811
25:18, 87, 397
25:19, 830
25:20, 87, 118, 250, 289, 714
25:21, 88, 824
25:22, 389
26, 75, 235, 389
26:1, 87, 421, 433, 811
26:2, 421
26:4-6, 433
26:5, 591
26:6, 932
26:7, 87
26:8, 21, 114, 932
26:10, 731
27, 58, 75, 388
27:1, 23, 58, 434, 526, 528, 714
27:2, 87, 591
27:3, 58, 591
27:3-9, 832
27:4, 525, 821
27:4-6, 393, 932
27:5, 483, 526
27:6, 289
27:7, 59, 811
27:8-9, 117
27:9, 86, 117, 526, 712
27:10, 249
27:12, 87, 420, 729
27:13, 58, 61, 62, 305
27:14, 59, 88, 388, 389, 434, 712, 824
28, 235, 389
28:1, 86, 321, 483, 526
28:1-3, 322
28:2, 21, 87
28:3, 87
28:6, 87
28:7, 86, 87, 119, 517, 526, 713
28:7-8, 714
28:8, 23, 118, 467, 526
28:9, 528, 711, 815
29, 46, 235, 262, 263
29:1, 487
29:1-2, 263, 819, 932
29:3, 61, 247, 627, 628
29:3-4, 819
29:3-6, 627
29:5, 222, 629
29:5-6, 819
29:6, 628
29:7, 603, 629
29:7-8, 819
29:8, 629
29:9, 819
29:9-10, 814
29:10, 44, 87,

117, 324, 601, 819, 825, 932
29:10-11, 302, 304
29:11, 324, 815, 819
30, 235, 584, 620, 805, 931, 932
30:1, 87
30:1-3, 77
30:2, 392, 527
30:3, 321
30:4, 87, 646
30:5, 61, 517, 815
30:8, 87
30:9, 52, 290, 321, 322, 812
30:11, 77, 301
30:11-12, 392
30:12, 77, 86, 87
31, 235, 388, 592
31:1, 87, 664, 714
31:1-4, 118, 525
31:2, 23, 483, 526
31:2-3, 23, 483, 526
31:3, 86
31:4, 23
31:5, 86
31:6, 87
31:6-8, 711
31:7, 117, 250
31:7-8, 805, 830
31:9, 87, 811
31:9-10, 712
31:10, 87, 435
31:11, 87
31:12, 432
31:13, 434, 713
31:14, 86, 87, 392
31:14-16, 712
31:14-24, 435, 651
31:15, 822
31:16, 88, 117, 528, 711
31:17, 87, 289
31:18, 87
31:19, 204, 665
31:19-24, 805
31:20, 118
31:22, 87, 117
31:23-24, 388, 389
31:24, 87
32, 30, 235, 389, 584, 805
32:1, 806
32:1-2, 289, 535
32:1-7, 932
32:3-4, 775
32:5, 87, 811
32:6, 76, 87
32:6-8, 806
32:9, 15, 806
32:10-11, 436
33, 3, 235, 582
33:1-3, 439
33:2, 87
33:4, 62
33:4-7, 49
33:5, 86, 87
33:6, 114, 249,

431, 517, 520, 583
33:6-8, 60
33:6-9, 48, 932
33:8, 87, 204, 205
33:9, 586, 825
33:12, 421
33:13-17, 711
33:13-18, 117
33:15, 932
33:18, 204, 205, 434
33:18-22, 830
33:20, 119, 526, 830
33:21, 249
33:22, 87
34, 2, 204, 235, 805, 893
34:2-22, 250
34:4-10, 713
34:5, 289
34:6, 777
34:6-9, 805
34:7, 204, 831
34:8, 86, 815
34:8-9, 289
34:8-10, 665
34:10, 16, 205
34:11, 325, 900
34:11-22, 432
34:13, 322
34:14, 665
34:15, 117
34:16, 117, 646
34:18, 118, 712
34:19, 434
34:19-20, 665
34:19-22, 712
35, 235, 388, 619
35:1-2, 830
35:1-3, 384, 831, 832
35:2, 526
35:3, 527
35:4, 289, 434
35:5, 384
35:6, 384
35:7-8, 384, 591
35:8, 100
35:10, 384, 777
35:11, 384
35:11-16, 384
35:13, 384
35:15, 384
35:15-16, 289
35:17, 117, 384, 434
35:17-19, 290
35:18, 393
35:20, 384
35:22, 117
35:23, 86, 528, 812
35:23-24, 384, 811
35:24, 86, 197, 811
35:26, 289
35:27, 88
35:27-28, 290
35:28, 664
36, 235, 263, 389

36:5-6, 60
36:6, 14, 481, 711
36:6-7, 588
36:7, 18, 525, 526, 527
36:8, 21
36:9, 117, 118, 264, 431
36:10, 711
36:11, 87
36:12, 87
37, 2, 3, 235, 585, 651, 665, 811, 893
37:1, 435, 810
37:3, 665
37:5, 665
37:6, 665
37:7, 88, 118, 435, 653, 824
37:9, 23, 824
37:11, 606
37:12, 434, 729
37:13, 117
37:14, 434, 527, 729, 829
37:14-15, 2, 830
37:17, 421
37:18-19, 289
37:19, 434, 822
37:20, 100
37:21, 665
37:25, 219, 653, 810
37:25-26, 2
37:26, 665
37:27-29, 826
37:28, 2, 86, 811
37:28-29, 823
37:30, 585, 665
37:30-31, 249
37:31, 665
37:32, 434
37:34, 824
37:38, 100
37:39, 2, 483, 526, 822
37:40, 711
38, 3, 235, 388, 932
38:1-8, 831
38:3, 87
38:5, 225
38:10, 528
38:12, 100, 434
38:15, 86, 88, 392
38:16, 289
38:18, 87
38:20, 714
38:21, 86, 651
39, 235, 388
39:1, 322
39:4-5, 821
39:5-7, 822
39:7, 88
39:8, 225, 289
39:9, 824
39:11, 19
39:12, 87
39:13, 824
40, 235, 388, 584, 797
40:1, 88, 117

40:1-12, 805
40:2-12, 805
40:3, 290, 389, 487
40:5, 86, 389
40:6, 75
40:8, 8640:7, 6, 719
40:10, 248, 664
40:11, 87, 811, 815
40:14, 434
40:14-15, 289
40:17, 86, 88
41, 235, 273, 527, 805
41:1, 199
41:4, 87
41:5, 289, 591
41:6, 87
41:9, 219, 775
41:11, 87
41:12-13, 826
41:13, 234, 825
42, 24, 234, 470
42—43, 26, 27, 71, 235, 642, 774
42—44, 26
42—49, 26, 76
42—59, 643
42—72, 234, 581
42—83, 234, 247
42:1, 587
42:1-2, 932
42:1-5, 642, 774
42:2, 61, 382
42:3, 72, 87
42:4, 393, 642, 645, 932
42:5, 642, 711, 774
42:6, 86
42:6-11, 642, 774
42:7, 26, 44, 312
42:8, 487
42:9, 86, 87, 815
42:10, 72, 87, 289, 290
42:11, 642, 711, 774
43:1, 582, 811
43:1-5, 642, 774
43:2, 23, 483, 526, 811
43:3-4, 26, 393
43:4, 86
43:5, 642, 711, 774
44, 235, 390, 391, 398, 582, 651, 830
44—49, 24, 234
44:1-3, 391, 392
44:1-8, 713
44:2, 117
44:3, 117
44:4, 87
44:6, 829
44:6-7, 711
44:8, 87
44:9, 289, 831,

832
44:9-16, 391, 811, 823
44:10-11, 397
44:11, 14
44:12, 395
44:12-13, 397
44:13-16, 289
44:17, 392, 645
44:17-19, 27
44:17-26, 289
44:19, 527
44:20, 645
44:21, 421
44:24, 117, 395, 397, 400, 651, 815
44:24-25, 391
45, 21, 221, 235, 263, 451, 584, 612, 615, 616, 617, 741, 932
45—48, 27
45:1, 73, 439, 486, 707
45:1-5, 830
45:2-5, 27
45:3, 527
45:3-4, 830
45:4, 665
45:5, 527
45:6, 117, 820, 824
45:6-7, 606
45:7, 289, 467, 468, 665
45:8, 21, 22
45:9, 920
45:10, 21, 920
45:11, 451
45:15, 21
45:16, 452, 920
45:17, 289
46, 62, 235, 386, 583, 616, 641, 932, 938, 939
46—48, 27
46:1, 119, 439, 486, 526, 617
46:2-3, 482
46:2-4, 60, 249
46:3, 60, 483
46:4, 117, 247, 937, 938
46:4-5, 482, 483, 583, 936
46:5, 117, 583
46:5-6, 936
46:6-7, 583
46:6-8, 419
46:7, 23, 117, 642
46:8-11, 936
46:9, 100, 527, 583, 831
46:10-11, 290
46:11, 23, 117, 483, 642
47, 235, 290, 499, 932
47:1, 71
47:1-2, 824
47:1-9, 249
47:2, 87, 117,

247, 303
47:3, 584, 832
47:3-4, 303
47:4, 304
47:5, 13, 303
47:7, 87, 618, 619
47:8, 87, 117, 303
47:8-9, 525
47:9, 303
48, 89, 235, 583, 932, 938, 939
48:1, 117, 483, 664, 930, 938
48:1-2, 113
48:1-3, 61
48:2, 51, 87, 483, 583, 937
48:2-9, 419
48:3, 23, 583, 830
48:3-8, 831
48:4-8, 936
48:6, 920
48:8, 664
48:10, 664
48:10-11, 61
48:12-13, 830
48:12-14, 24
48:13, 23
48:14, 617, 618
48:49, 89
49, 100, 235, 585, 811, 893, 899
49:3, 585
49:4, 585
49:5-6, 291
49:5-9, 100
49:5-15, 53
49:7-15, 102
49:10, 224, 225
49:12, 642
49:14, 14
49:14-20, 437
49:15, 102, 436, 781, 824
49:16, 21
49:16-20, 291, 665
49:19, 113
49:19-20, 436, 824
49:20, 642
49:20—79:11, 579
50, 24, 76, 234, 235, 386, 612, 665
50:1-3, 817
50:1-6, 811
50:1-15, 819
50:5, 664, 819, 932
50:6, 436, 664
50:8-14, 932
50:9, 14, 21
50:10, 13, 14
50:10-11, 482
50:11, 18, 481, 482
50:13, 14
50:14, 75, 87, 247
50:14-15, 805
50:15, 290
50:16, 664

50:16-23, *819*
50:23, *713, 932*
51, *235, 389, 393, 775, 932*
51—72, *613*
51—100, *78, 88, 259, 287, 445, 593, 714*
51:1, *87, 248, 811, 815*
51:2, *87, 711*
51:2-4, *578*
51:3, *87*
51:4, *87, 117, 811*
51:5, *433, 713*
51:6, *395*
51:7, *517, 711*
51:8, *517*
51:9, *711*
51:10, *711*
51:10-12, *713*
51:11, *398, 775*
51:12, *87*
51:14, *86, 87, 664, 710*
51:15, *3*
51:15-17, *75*
51:17, *398, 713*
51:18, *938*
51:18-19, *393*
51:19, *14*
52, *235, 389, 617*
52:1-4, *517*
52:2, *100*
52:3, *87*
52:5, *61, 62*
52:7, *23, 526*
52:8, *86, 87, 117, 220*
53, *235, 247, 263, 391, 617, 797*
53:1, *223, 225, 263, 485, 486, 586*
53:4, *87, 219*
53:6, *710, 938*
54—59, *235*
54:1, *73, 486, 711, 811*
54:3, *434*
54:4, *119, 388, 434*
54:5, *87*
54:6, *87, 393, 932*
54:7, *712*
55, *617*
55:1, *73, 87, 486*
55:1-2, *421*
55:2, *87*
55:6, *617*
55:6-7, *615*
55:6-9, *206*
55:7, *615*
55:8, *615*
55:12-14, *206*
55:13, *775*
55:14, *393*
55:15, *206*
55:16, *86, 247, 587*
55:17, *712, 821*
55:17-19, *206*
55:18, *591*

55:19, *117, 205*
55:19-20, *616*
55:22, *388, 651*
55:22-23, *206*
55:23, *87, 100, 101*
56, *617, 932*
56:1, *18, 73, 615*
56:2, *87*
56:3, *87*
56:4, *87, 642*
56:6, *434*
56:8, *6, 87*
56:9, *119*
56:10-11, *642*
56:11, *87*
56:12, *932*
57, *75, 932*
57:1, *87, 100, 118, 393, 439, 486, 525, 526, 527, 614*
57:1-3, *118*
57:1-6, *712*
57:3, *86*
57:4, *829*
57:5, *642, 711*
57:9, *87*
57:11, *642, 711*
58, *263, 316, 391, 932*
58:1, *486, 665*
58:2-5, *665*
58:3, *433, 821*
58:6, *16, 528*
58:6-11, *665*
58:9, *222*
58:11, *811*
59, *617, 832, 932*
59:1, *86, 87, 486*
59:1-2, *586*
59:2, *711, 712*
59:3, *434*
59:5, *247*
59:6, *16*
59:8, *248, 249*
59:9, *23, 86, 526*
59:11, *389, 526*
59:11-12, *831*
59:13, *87*
59:16-17, *526*
59:17, *23, 86, 526*
60, *221, 235, 391, 616, 617, 620, 932*
60—150, *593, 613, 808*
60:1, *87, 486, 831*
60:1-5, *823*
60:3, *220*
60:4, *205*
60:5, *249, 711, 713*
60:6, *21*
60:6-12, *823*
60:7, *23*
60:9-12, *830*
60:10, *831, 832*
61, *235, 616*
61:1, *73, 486*
61:2, *61, 525*
61:3, *23, 87, 118, 830*

61:4, *525, 527*
61:6, *434*
62, *58*
62:1, *620, 711*
62:1-2, *58, 711*
62:1-7, *61*
62:1-12, *23*
62:2, *86, 118, 483, 526, 830*
62:3, *23, 59, 811*
62:6, *86, 483*
62:6-7, *526*
62:7, *86, 483*
62:8, *59*
62:10, *420*
62:11, *511*
62:12, *86, 87*
63, *75*
63:1, *517*
63:1-8, *932*
63:2, *21*
63:6, *645*
63:7, *118, 525, 526, 527*
63:8, *588*
63:9, *100, 434*
64, *235*
64:1, *87, 434*
64:2, *87*
64:3, *829*
64:3-4, *829*
64:4, *393*
64:7, *829, 831*
64:10, *389*
65, *235, 808, 932*
65:1, *932, 937*
65:3, *938*
65:4, *21, 525, 932*
65:5, *664*
65:5-8, *712*
65:5-11, *481*
65:6, *481*
65:6-7, *60, 814, 937*
65:7, *45*
65:7-9, *60*
65:12, *482*
65:13, *14*
66, *235, 584, 805, 808, 932*
66:4, *824, 932*
66:7, *825*
66:8, *824*
66:10, *435*
66:10-12, *76*
66:11, *526*
66:12, *814*
66:13-14, *805*
66:13-15, *235, 805, 932*
66:13-20, *805*
66:15, *14*
66:16, *290, 805*
67, *391, 773, 808, 932*
67:1, *73, 117, 486, 528, 815*
67:1-2, *290*
67:1-7, *824*
67:3, *524, 642*
67:4, *811*
67:5, *524, 642, 773*

67:7, *205*
68, *235, 236, 440, 483, 602, 625, 932*
68:1, *72, 831*
68:1-2, *118*
68:2, *100*
68:4, *47*
68:5, *199, 249, 528, 811, 920*
68:5-6, *321*
68:6-7, *321*
68:7, *774*
68:7-8, *616*
68:8, *61*
68:8-10, *831*
68:13, *18*
68:14-17, *61*
68:15-16, *516*
68:16, *117*
68:17, *527*
68:21, *832*
68:24, *87*
68:24-27, *920*
68:26, *439*
68:30, *14*
68:31, *13*
68:32, *773*
68:32-33, *616*
69, *221, 235, 393, 592, 615, 932*
69:1, *73, 486, 712*
69:2, *582*
69:3, *824*
69:4, *382, 712*
69:5, *225*
69:6, *290*
69:7, *824*
69:7-9, *290*
69:7-12, *382*
69:10-12, *289*
69:13, *247, 712*
69:14-15, *52, 528*
69:15, *52, 582*
69:16, *87, 815*
69:17, *815*
69:18, *382, 712*
69:19, *117*
69:19-20, *289*
69:19-21, *712*
69:20, *812*
69:21, *220*
69:22-28, *713*
69:28, *6, 436, 719*
69:29, *290, 711*
69:30, *87*
69:30-31, *487*
69:31, *15, 75*
69:33, *117*
69:34, *18, 60, 932*
69:34-36, *393*
69:35, *712*
69:35-36, *713*
70, *235, 797*
70:2, *434*
70:2-3, *289*
71, *235*
71:1, *118, 591*
71:1-6, *711*
71:2, *664, 711, 811*
71:3, *526*
71:6, *290, 431,*

433
71:8, *290*
71:9, *821*
71:10, *434*
71:13, *289, 714*
71:14-24, *714*
71:15, *664, 714*
71:19, *388*
71:21, *289*
71:22, *248*
71:24, *289*
72, *61, 235, 273, 584*
72:1, *733*
72:1-2, *588*
72:1-4, *712, 734*
72:1-10, *830*
72:2, *198, 665, 777, 811*
72:3, *482, 483*
72:4, *528, 711*
72:6, *589*
72:9-11, *289*
72:10-11, *734*
72:12, *528*
72:13, *712*
72:14, *382, 528*
72:15, *734*
72:16, *482, 664*
72:17, *289, 734*
72:18-19, *234*
72:20, *734*
73, *29, 30, 58, 61, 85, 235, 432, 585, 805, 811, 893*
73—83, *24, 25, 76, 234, 386*
73—89, *234, 581*
73—150, *258, 613, 621*
73:1, *324, 776*
73:2, *264*
73:3, *118*
73:3-5, *665*
73:3-9, *435*
73:7, *23*
73:8-9, *517*
73:12, *665*
73:12-14, *396*
73:13, *776*
73:13-14, *46*
73:15-20, *71*
73:16, *776*
73:16-27, *436*
73:17, *21, 61, 118*
73:17-18, *117*
73:17-20, *435, 824*
73:18-19, *100*
73:20, *291*
73:21-22, *811*
73:21-28, *61*
73:22, *14, 224*
73:23, *118*
73:23-26, *396*
73:23-28, *117, 812*
73:24, *53, 824*
73:25, *61*
73:26, *526*
73:27, *100, 824*
73:28, *59, 118,*

324
74, *62, 64, 235, 263, 391, 832*
74:1, *14, 811*
74:1-8, *832*
74:2, *392, 646*
74:3-8, *397*
74:6-7, *582*
74:7, *21, 114, 718, 832, 932*
74:10, *291, 382, 819*
74:10-11, *815*
74:11, *819*
74:12, *49*
74:12-17, *48, 50, 392, 711*
74:13, *19, 46, 819*
74:13-14, *62, 64, 591*
74:13-15, *45, 46*
74:14, *19, 819*
74:15, *60, 814*
74:16-17, *62*
74:18, *224, 225, 291, 382, 832*
74:19, *263*
74:20, *392*
74:21, *382, 391*
74:22, *224, 225, 291, 382, 819*
75, *808, 932*
75:1, *73, 118, 486*
75:2, *436*
75:2-10, *71, 73*
75:4-5, *527*
75:7, *811*
75:8, *220, 718*
75:10, *527, 528*
76, *89, 235, 583, 932, 938*
76:1, *73, 439, 486*
76:1-2, *117*
76:1-3, *831*
76:1-6, *831*
76:2, *483*
76:2-3, *936, 937*
76:2-7, *419*
76:3, *527, 583, 829*
76:4, *482*
76:4-9, *936*
76:5-6, *583*
76:9, *712, 811*
77, *52, 62, 235, 386, 393*
77—78, *89*
77:1, *620*
77:3, *645*
77:4, *264*
77:8, *248*
77:9, *815*
77:10, *26*
77:11, *645*
77:11-20, *932*
77:16, *20, 44*
77:16-19, *60, 62*
77:16-20, *51, 811*
77:17, *829*
77:16-20, *50*
77:20, *14*
78, *235, 281, 722, 932*

78:1, *585*
78:2, *585*
78:4, *303*
78:5, *304, 421*
78:5-8, *821*
78:10, *421*
78:13, *304*
78:14-16, *304*
78:15, *262*
78:15-16, *482*
78:20, *14*
78:23, *46*
78:25, *219*
78:35, *483*
78:38, *100, 815*
78:38-39, *249*
78:39, *646*
78:41, *248*
78:42, *645*
78:44, *264*
78:45, *18*
78:47, *220, 814*
78:48, *14*
78:52, *304*
78:54, *117, 481*
78:55, *304*
78:60, *117*
78:61, *815*
78:62-64, *832*
78:66, *118*
78:67-72, *668*
78:68, *483, 939*
78:68-72, *932*
78:69, *21, 60, 483, 872*
79, *235, 316, 391, 617, 940*
79—80, *25, 26*
79:1, *21, 116, 117, 248, 291, 392, 397*
79:1-3, *832*
79:1-5, *832*
79:2, *13, 17*
79:3, *117*
79:4, *289, 390*
79:6, *591*
79:6-7, *775*
79:7, *397*
79:8, *397, 646*
79:8-13, *712*
79:9, *591, 711, 775*
79:9-10, *291*
79:10, *291, 393, 832*
79:11, *320, 321*
79:12, *291*
79:13, *14, 391*
80, *221, 235, 391, 615, 617, 713, 831, 932*
80:1, *14, 117, 390, 391, 486, 528*
80:1-3, *390*
80:3, *117, 524, 528, 642, 711*
80:3-16, *100*
80:4-6, *390*
80:6, *390*
80:7, *117, 524, 528, 642, 711*

80:8-11, *390, 392*
80:10, *222, 482*
80:12, *23, 528*
80:14, *390*
80:15, *390*
80:18, *390, 391*
80:19, *117, 524,*
528, 642, 711
81, *90, 235, 932*
81:1, *486, 526*
81:1-2, *71*
81:2, *798*
81:2-3, *71*
81:6-16, *73, 76*
81:9, *420*
81:10, *932*
81:11-12, *823*
81:16, *219*
82, *114, 235, 391,*
421, 591
82—83, *25*
82:1, *117, 421,*
587
82:2, *811*
82:2-3, *665*
82:2-4, *665*
82:3, *528*
82:5, *115*
82:6-7, *665*
83, *235, 316, 390,*
391, 932
83:3, *264*
83:4, *645*
83:7, *798*
83:9-12, *392*
83:13, *435*
83:13-18, *831*
83:14, *482*
83:14-18, *100*
83:15, *118, 817*
83:16, *319*
83:16-18, *290*
84, *61, 235, 525,*
583, 599, 651,
932
84—85, *24, 234*
84—88, *26*
84—89, *76*
84:1, *486*
84:1-2, *932*
84:2, *118, 250,*
517
84:3, *117, 526,*
527
84:9, *27, 467,*
468, 525, 526,
830
84:10, *118*
84:11, *815*
85, *235, 391, 713*
85:1-3, *710, 815*
85:2, *711*
85:2-3, *616*
85:4, *713*
85:6, *798*
85:7, *713*
85:8, *225*
85:9, *117, 205,*
713
85:10, *517*
85:12, *664*
86, *26, 89, 90,*
235, 408, 588,

932
86:1, *88*
86:2, *86, 88, 711*
86:4, *88*
86:5, *86, 87, 815*
86:6, *87*
86:7, *86, 824*
86:8, *115, 249*
86:9, *62, 932*
86:9-10, *290*
86:12, *86, 87*
86:15, *86, 87*
86:16, *88, 117*
87, *235, 583, 617,*
932
87—88, *24, 234*
87:1, *483*
87:1-2, *483*
87:2, *23*
87:4, *45, 50, 483*
87:6, *719*
88, *235, 373, 386,*
421, 617, 619,
812, 932
88:1, *263, 321,*
486, 780
88:2, *776*
88:3, *582*
88:4, *321*
88:5, *5, 52, 322,*
646
88:6, *321, 793*
88:7, *26*
88:8, *321, 322*
88:9, *776*
88:10-12, *290*
88:12, *52, 321,*
322
88:14, *117, 387,*
815
88:18, *322, 776*
89, *64, 114, 235,*
273, 386, 390,
391, 584, 619,
824, 831
89:1, *248*
89:1-2, *392*
89:1-31, *50*
89:2, *825*
89:2-39, *74*
89:3, *326, 421,*
664
89:3-4, *392, 932*
89:5-8, *715*
89:5-12, *61*
89:5-18, *392*
89:7, *117*
89:8-10, *45*
89:8-18, *49*
89:9, *45*
89:9-13, *20*
89:9-14, *48*
89:9-18, *62*
89:10, *64*
89:11, *60, 62*
89:11-14, *811*
89:12, *516*
89:14, *197, 249,*
327, 664
89:15, *117, 528*
89:17, *527*
89:18, *248, 525,*
526, 830

932
89:19, *289, 327*
89:19-37, *392,*
932
89:20, *248, 467,*
468
89:22-23, *326*
89:24, *289, 327,*
527
89:25, *50*
89:26, *249, 483,*
528, 712
89:27, *247, 289,*
329
89:27-28, *249*
89:28, *664*
89:30, *326*
89:32-33, *248*
89:33, *327*
89:33-34, *249*
89:34, *664*
89:34-35, *326*
89:37, *329*
89:38, *467*
89:38-39, *327,*
777
89:38-40, *390*
89:38-45, *832*
89:39, *151, 326*
89:40, *23*
89:41, *289*
89:42, *387*
89:45, *289, 327*
89:46, *327, 811*
89:47, *646*
89:48, *52*
89:49, *326, 327*
89:49-50, *329*
89:50, *327, 646*
89:50-51, *290,*
327
89:52, *234*
90, *58, 235, 619,*
932
90—106, *234,*
581, 590
90:1, *118, 328*
90:1-2, *328, 825*
90:2, *53, 62, 481,*
516, 825
90:3-12, *328*
90:4, *561, 825*
90:7, *328*
90:7-8, *327*
90:9-10, *822*
90:9-15, *821*
90:10, *327, 432*
90:11, *327, 821*
90:12, *822*
90:13, *327, 328,*
811
90:13-17, *328*
90:14, *151, 327,*
822
90:16, *327*
91, *58, 236, 247,*
830, 832
91—118, *90*
91:1, *118, 526,*
527
91:1-2, *830*
91:1-7, *831*
91:2, *58, 250, 526*
91:4, *118, 525,*

526, 527
91:7, *832*
91:9, *247, 526*
91:11-12, *606*
91:13, *16, 46, 830*
91:15, *118*
92, *89, 235, 585,*
620, 805, 931
92:3, *616*
92:5, *814*
92:6, *224, 225*
92:7, *100, 101*
92:9, *100*
92:10, *527*
92:10-11, *832*
92:12, *222*
92:12-14, *665*
92:13, *21, 117*
92:15, *483, 526*
93, *71, 235, 499,*
620
93—99, *581*
93—100, *155,*
938, 941
93:1, *74, 249,*
329, 584
93:1-2, *584*
93:3, *44*
93:3-4, *60, 516,*
584
93:4, *439*
93:5, *21, 400*
94, *3, 89, 235,*
316, 620
94:1-2, *817*
94:2, *293, 811*
94:3, *811*
94:4, *293*
94:6, *420, 702,*
729
94:8, *224, 225,*
226
94:9, *62*
94:12, *585*
94:18, *528*
94:21, *434*
94:22, *247, 483*
95, *62, 73, 235*
95—96, *89*
95—99, *71*
95—100, *235*
95:1, *483, 526,*
714
95:1-2, *932*
95:1-5, *61*
95:3, *115, 249,*
290, 329, 932
95:3-5, *290*
95:4, *482*
95:5, *44, 62*
95:6, *932*
95:7, *14*
95:7-8, *615, 823*
95:8-11, *714*
96, *67, 234, 499*
96—99, *664*
96:1-3, *932*
96:3, *290, 584*
96:3-5, *290*
96:4, *115, 249,*
930
96:9, *932*
96:10, *198, 249,*

290, 329, 584
96:10-13, *664,*
811
96:11, *18, 60*
96:11-12, *516*
96:12, *67, 516*
96:12-13, *68*
96:13, *67, 290,*
436, 664, 812
97:1, *74, 290,*
329, 516, 591
97:1-6, *932*
97:2, *46, 117, 664*
97:2-5, *817*
97:3-5, *831*
97:4, *61*
97:5, *61, 198, 482*
97:6, *584, 591*
97:7, *115, 289,*
290
97:9, *247, 584*
97:12, *646*
98, *67, 714*
98:1, *248, 487,*
712, 793
98:1-2, *584*
98:1-3, *61, 290,*
774
98:1-9, *516, 811*
98:2, *664*
98:3, *22, 646, 664*
98:3-6, *61*
98:4-6, *774, 932*
98:4-9, *664*
98:6, *61, 329*
98:7, *18*
98:7-8, *67*
98:7-9, *61, 774,*
932
98:8, *482*
98:9, *61, 67, 198,*
249, 290, 664,
812
99:1, *74, 117*
99:1-5, *290, 487,*
932
99:3, *249, 642*
99:4, *329*
99:5, *117, 642,*
664
99:9, *483, 642*
100, *582, 585,*
620
100:1-4, *932*
100:1-5, *516*
100:3, *14, 62, 249*
100:4, *23, 87,*
117, 932
100:5, *248, 815,*
825
101, *235, 289,*
584
101—150, *258,*
287, 305, 325,
593
101:1, *86, 87*
101:2, *22*
101:3-7, *588*
101:7, *22*
101:8, *87*
102, *235, 393,*
619, 932
102:2, *117, 775,*

815, 821
102:3, *582*
102:8, *87*
102:9, *87*
102:11, *527, 821*
102:12, *646, 825*
102:12-22, *393*
102:13, *824*
102:15, *205*
102:15-16, *824*
102:16, *824, 938*
102:18, *719*
102:19-20, *321*
102:20, *320*
102:21, *938*
102:21-22, *824*
102:25, *62, 825*
102:25-26, *100*
102:25-27, *606*
102:26-27, *825*
102:27, *826*
102:28, *651*
103, *3, 805*
103—106, *235*
103:1, *249, 324*
103:1-2, *290*
103:3, *87, 527,*
664
103:4, *87, 101*
103:5, *17*
103:6, *86, 664,*
811
103:8, *86, 87, 815*
103:8-11, *248*
103:10, *664, 815*
103:11, *205*
103:12, *664*
103:13, *86, 205*
103:15, *222*
103:17, *205, 664,*
823, 825
103:17-18, *434*
103:18, *421, 645,*
664
103:19, *87, 824*
103:20, *487*
103:20-21, *302*
103:20-22, *304*
103:21, *931, 932*
103:22, *249, 324*
104, *60, 602*
104:1, *324*
104:1-2, *48, 303*
104:1-3, *817*
104:2, *61, 583*
104:2-30, *932*
104:3, *44, 46, 527*
104:3-18, *48*
104:4, *606, 814*
104:5, *62, 583*
104:5-6, *60*
104:5-9, *50*
104:6, *44*
104:6-10, *481*
104:6-12, *60*
104:7, *814*
104:8-9, *62*
104:9, *44, 814*
104:10, *60*
104:10-11, *431,*
481
104:10-13, *65*
104:10-18, *482*

104:11, *13, 15*
104:12, *17, 60*
104:13, *47, 482*
104:14, *14, 431*
104:15, *65, 219*
104:16, *222*
104:17, *17, 222*
104:18, *14, 17,*
481, 482, 526
104:19-23, *47,*
821, 822
104:19-24, *48*
104:20, *13*
104:20-26, *603*
104:21, *16, 311,*
431
104:22, *526*
104:24, *48, 62,*
481, 814
104:24-30, *46*
104:25, *13*
104:26, *45, 62,*
64, 583
104:27-28, *431*
104:27-29, *603*
104:28-30, *48*
104:29, *431, 432*
104:30, *13, 118*
104:31, *65*
104:32, *482*
104:34, *440*
104:35, *304, 324,*
482
105, *73, 234, 281,*
619, 722
105:1, *304*
105:3, *249*
105:5, *645*
105:7, *249, 591*
105:8, *646*
105:17-21, *320,*
322
105:18, *320*
105:19-20, *322*
105:20, *321*
105:20-22, *322*
105:22, *321, 322*
105:23-45, *823*
105:26-27, *304*
105:27—137:6,*
579
105:29, *18*
105:33, *220*
105:37, *321*
105:39-42, *304*
105:40, *18, 219*
105:41, *482*
105:42-43, *646*
105:43, *321*
106, *73, 234, 273,*
281, 324, 722,
932
106:1, *248, 815,*
825
106:2, *303*
106:4, *646*
106:4-5, *646*
106:6, *397, 710*
106:7, *645*
106:8, *710*
106:8-11, *304*
106:9, *50*
106:10, *710, 711*

106:10-11, *831*
106:17-18, *100*
106:20, *15*
106:21, *710*
106:23, *100*
106:33, *397*
106:43, *710*
106:44-46, *249*
106:45, *392, 646*
106:47, *249, 391, 397, 710*
106:48, *234, 397*
107—*145, 581*
107—*150, 234*
107:1, *248, 808, 825*
107:1-2, *808*
107:2, *225*
107:4, *713, 808*
107:6, *642, 713*
107:8, *642, 808*
107:10, *527, 808*
107:10-11, *713*
107:13, *642, 713*
107:14, *527*
107:15, *642, 808*
107:17, *225, 808*
107:17-18, *713*
107:18, *52*
107:19, *225, 642, 713*
107:21, *642, 808*
107:22, *808*
107:23, *808*
107:25-27, *713*
107:28, *642, 713*
107:29, *814*
107:31, *642, 808*
107:32, *793*
107:33, *814*
107:33-34, *432*
107:38, *14*
107:41, *14*
108, *235, 932*
108:3, *87*
108:6, *249*
108:9-13, *823*
109, *235, 316, 651, 712*
109:4, *714*
109:6, *714*
109:9, *60*
109:12-14, *434*
109:13, *289*
109:14-15, *645*
109:15, *289, 646*
109:17-20, *317*
109:20, *714*
109:21, *811*
109:22, *88*
109:23, *18*
109:29, *289, 714*
109:30, *87*
109:31, *712*
110, *74, 235, 407, 584, 592, 612, 671*
110:1, *289, 606, 614, 615, 786*
110:3, *820*
110:4, *469*
110:5, *119*
110:5-6, *249, 830*

110:6, *812, 820*
111, *2, 61, 235, 893*
111—*112, 234*
111—*117, 154*
111:4, *646*
111:5, *205, 646, 664*
111:7-10, *249*
111:9, *249, 664*
111:10, *325, 432, 816, 900, 933*
112, *2, 235, 289, 536, 585, 893*
112:1, *204, 205, 665*
112:1-2, *535*
112:2, *823*
112:2-5, *433*
112:4, *528*
112:5-9, *730*
112:6, *646*
112:9, *433, 527*
112:10, *100*
113, *154, 235, 324*
113—*118, 485*
113:2, *826*
113:4, *249*
113:5, *261*
113:6, *261*
113:7, *261*
113:7-8, *293*
113:9, *261, 920*
114, *154, 235, 601*
114:1, *22*
114:1-2, *304*
114:1-4, *482*
114:1-8, *51*
114:2, *21*
114:3-6, *304*
114:4, *14*
114:5-8, *60*
114:6, *14*
114:8, *304, 482*
115, *58, 235*
115—*116, 90*
115—*117, 619*
115:1-2, *291*
115:2-8, *932*
115:9-11, *59, 72, 119, 830*
115:10, *22*
115:11, *205*
115:12, *22*
115:14-18, *60*
115:15, *249*
115:17, *52, 290, 934*
115:18, *826*
116, *39, 235, 263, 805*
116:1-4, *713*
116:1-11, *73*
116:3, *5, 52*
116:6, *224*
116:9, *61, 62*
116:12-13, *713*
116:12-19, *73, 235, 290*
116:14, *805*
116:16, *920*

116:17, *932*
116:18, *932*
116:18-19, *584*
117, *235, 582*
118, *235, 236, 378, 585, 592, 668, 711, 825*
118—*119, 154*
118:1, *72, 248, 324, 588*
118:1-4, *71*
118:2, *72*
118:3, *22, 72*
118:4, *72*
118:5-18, *324*
118:10-18, *832*
118:12, *843*
118:14, *526*
118:16, *608*
118:18, *815*
118:19, *23*
118:19-20, *932*
118:19-29, *235*
118:22-23, *606*
118:25-26, *606*
118:27, *71, 117, 932*
118:28-29, *805*
118:29, *72, 248, 324, 588*
119, *2, 4, 89, 155, 235, 378, 432, 585*
119:1, *90*
119:1-8, *289*
119:8, *588*
119:31, *289*
119:34, *420*
119:50, *815*
119:51, *289*
119:54, *487, 509*
119:63, *204*
119:73, *62*
119:74, *205*
119:75, *811*
119:80, *289*
119:84, *811*
119:90, *62, 248*
119:92, *100*
119:94, *712*
119:105, *528*
119:114, *118, 526*
119:117, *712*
119:130, *224, 528*
119:132, *815*
119:135, *117*
119:143, *815*
119:146, *712*
119:149, *249*
119:151, *118*
119:154, *421, 528*
119:164, *616*
119:176, *14*
120, *235*
120—*134, 73, 77, 154, 234, 485, 620, 931*
120:1, *439*
120:1-4, *517*
120:2, *729*
120:4, *829*
120:5, *878*
120:5-7, *830*

121, *58, 73, 620*
121:1, *59*
121:1-2, *61*
121:2, *825*
121:3, *58*
121:4, *58*
121:5, *58, 526, 527*
121:6, *135, 158*
121:7, *58*
121:8, *826*
122, *235, 583, 668*
122:1, *118*
122:4, *620*
122:5, *22*
122:7, *588, 830*
123, *58, 235, 391, 798*
124, *58, 808*
124:2-3, *831*
124:2-5, *52*
124:6, *528*
124:7, *17*
124:8, *249, 825*
125, *58*
125:2, *58*
125:4, *815*
126, *58, 391*
126—*128, 90*
126:5, *812*
127, *235*
127—*128, 452, 453*
127:1, *452, 733*
127:1-2, *734, 814*
127:2, *249*
127:3-5, *734*
127:5, *289, 385, 452*
128, *235, 585, 893*
128:1, *205*
128:3, *21, 220, 452*
128:6, *452*
129, *235, 808*
129:1, *77*
129:1-5, *730*
129:5, *289*
130, *235, 389*
130:2-3, *421*
130:5, *824*
131, *58*
131:1, *814*
131:2, *58, 821*
131:3, *59, 826*
132, *235, 236, 468, 584, 932*
132—*133, 263*
132—*134, 939*
132:4, *263*
132:5, *932*
132:6, *481*
132:7, *71*
132:7-8, *116, 117*
132:8, *72*
132:9, *939*
132:10, *117, 467, 468, 939*
132:11, *326*
132:12, *664, 940*
132:15, *665*

132:16, *665*
132:17, *467, 468, 527, 528*
133, *234, 235, 289*
133:1, *379*
133:2, *379*
133:3, *60, 61, 939*
134, *235, 582*
134:1, *21*
134:3, *249, 815*
135, *234, 235, 722*
135:1-2, *21*
135:3, *301, 815*
135:5, *115, 249*
135:5-21, *290*
135:6, *45*
135:8, *118*
135:10, *118*
135:10-12, *831*
135:13, *825*
135:14, *812*
135:19, *22*
135:19-20, *72*
135:20, *22, 205*
136, *72, 235, 641, 722, 724*
136—*137, 154*
136:1-3, *487, 642*
136:2, *115*
136:2-9, *60*
136:4, *304*
136:4-9, *487, 932*
136:5-9, *304*
136:10-22, *304*
136:10-24, *487, 932*
136:11, *321*
136:25, *13, 431*
137, *235, 279, 316, 625, 775*
137:1, *318, 644*
137:1-3, *793*
137:2, *222*
137:3, *318*
137:5-7, *318*
137:6, *644*
137:7, *646, 823*
137:7-9, *317*
137:8, *317, 589*
138, *235*
138:1, *87, 115*
138:2, *21, 87, 249, 932*
138:6, *293*
138:8, *249*
139:1-18, *822*
139:6, *814*
139:7, *118, 397*
139:7-12, *116*
139:8, *5, 53*
139:12, *47, 821*
139:13, *431, 433, 434*
139:13-16, *62, 433, 821*
139:18, *118*
139:19, *87, 118*
139:19-24, *317*

139:23-24, *397*
140—*141, 263*
140—*143, 235*
140:2, *821*
140:3, *19, 264*
140:6, *87*
140:7, *118, 526, 714*
140:12, *86, 528*
140:12-13, *665*
141:3, *322*
141:3-5, *397*
141:4, *87*
141:5, *250, 787*
141:9, *87*
141:10, *87*
142, *62, 932*
142:1, *87, 614*
142:5, *61, 62*
142:6, *830*
142:7, *321*
143:1, *87*
143:1-2, *664*
143:2, *88, 421, 811*
143:3, *87, 434, 832*
143:5, *645*
143:7, *117, 811*
143:8, *86, 87*
143:10, *118, 397, 398*
143:11, *290*
143:11-12, *421*
143:12, *87, 88, 100*
144, *62, 235*
144:1, *86*
144:1-2, *483, 591*
144:1-11, *584*
144:2, *86, 526*
144:4, *129, 432*
144:5, *482*
144:5-8, *817*
144:6, *527*
144:8, *87*
144:9, *71, 482*
144:10, *88*
144:11, *829*
144:12, *21, 62, 920*
144:12-15, *398*
144:13, *14*
145, *1, 2, 300, 619, 798, 932*
145—*150, 235*
145:1, *87*
145:3, *930*
145:7, *646*
145:7-9, *664*
145:8, *86, 87*
145:9, *86, 87, 814*
145:13, *86, 798, 825*
145:13-21, *711*
145:14, *528*
145:15, *822*
145:15-16, *431*
145:16, *13*
145:17, *2, 86*
145:20, *100*
145:21, *249*
146, *582*

146—*150, 155, 234, 324, 581, 589, 590, 780*
146:1, *324*
146:4, *100*
146:6, *18, 44*
146:7, *86, 811*
146:7-8, *320*
146:7-9, *665*
146:9, *729*
146:10, *324, 825, 940*
147, *39*
147:1, *324, 619*
147:3, *87, 398, 527*
147:5, *814*
147:6, *88*
147:7, *71, 87*
147:8, *482*
147:9, *14*
147:10, *15*
147:11, *824*
147:12, *117*
147:13, *23, 940*
147:14, *219*
147:15-18, *517*
147:19-20, *824*
147:20, *324*
148, *290, 932*
148:1, *302, 324*
148:1-5, *114*
148:1-14, *60, 516*
148:2, *487, 932*
148:5, *249*
148:5-6, *67*
148:7, *46, 249, 302*
148:7-10, *482*
148:8, *482, 814*
148:8-9, *482*
148:10, *13, 14, 18*
148:13, *67, 249*
148:14, *324, 527*
149:1, *324*
149:2, *117, 940*
149:3, *71*
149:4, *88*
149:5-9, *830*
149:6-7, *832*
149:8, *320, 321*
149:9, *324, 719*
150, *300, 301*
150:1, *21, 324*
150:1-6, *234*
150:3-5, *71, 439*
150:6, *324*
151 (LXX), *39, 234, 614*
151—*155 (Syriac Peshitta), 234*
151:1 (LXX), *614*
154 (Syriac Peshitta), *234*
155 (Syriac Peshitta), *234*

Proverbs
1, *54, 55, 209, 428, 471, 536, 912*
1—*9, 24, 63, 70, 102, 104, 105,*

106, 107, 108,
152, 197, 205,
207, 208, 216,
217, 218, 224,
227, 237, 243,
245, 443, 533,
534, 536, 538,
541, 542, 547,
548, 549, 551,
552, 555, 558,
559, 565, 572,
574, 575, 576,
657, 658, 662,
663, 735, 736,
737, 803, 810,
858, 859, 861,
893, 901, 905,
906, 907, 909,
911, 912, 913,
924
1—24, 552, 555,
559, 896
1:1, 236, 243,
283, 428, 537,
540, 704, 708,
733, 735, 736,
867, 895, 896
1:1-6, 563
1:1-7, 197, 202,
540, 546, 552,
554, 657, 844,
859
1:1—9:18, 518
1:1—22:19, 561
1:1—24:34, 575
1:2, 201
1:2-6, 666
1:2-7, 324
1:3, 197, 198, 372
1:4, 224
1:5-6, 735
1:6, 542, 704, 729
1:7, 198, 201,
202, 204, 223,
226, 228, 243,
250, 251, 324,
325, 372, 432,
452, 535, 539,
549, 667, 725,
734, 810, 816,
844, 857, 859,
860, 900, 906,
913, 921, 933
1:7-8, 435
1:8, 102, 107,
193, 207, 433,
534, 542, 657,
666, 851, 895,
920, 921
1:8-9, 657
1:8-19, 102, 103,
106, 107, 243,
534, 545, 657,
658
1:8-33, 106
1:8—9:18, 102,
104, 106, 540,
552
1:9, 534
1:10, 657, 666
1:10-15, 549
1:10-16, 534
1:10-19, 54, 56,

224, 519, 529,
657, 729, 831
1:11-12, 658
1:11-14, 657
1:12, 7, 52, 321,
911
1:13, 56, 658
1:14, 658
1:14-15, 56
1:15, 56, 658
1:15-18, 657
1:16, 56, 658
1:17, 18, 56, 531,
534
1:17-18, 658
1:17—2:1, 95
1:18, 531
1:18-19, 534
1:19, 56, 57, 657,
658
1:20, 5, 103, 533,
735, 865
1:20-21, 55
1:20-33, 55, 57,
100, 102, 105,
106, 243, 516,
534, 542, 574,
657, 658, 905,
912, 916, 920
1:21, 23, 865
1:22, 55, 223,
224, 226, 811
1:22-27, 55
1:22-33, 55, 56
1:24-26, 103
1:24-27, 775
1:26, 533
1:26-27, 100
1:27, 55, 56
1:27—2:1, 799
1:28, 316
1:28-33, 55
1:29, 202, 223,
226, 250, 372
1:29-33, 810
1:30, 293
1:31, 775
1:32, 95, 224,
226, 775, 800
1:32-33, 55, 103
1:33, 55, 56, 433,
778
2, 3, 22, 103, 197,
202, 451, 515,
542, 545, 571,
574, 706, 912,
914
2:1, 107, 199,
534, 542, 657
2:1-6, 518
2:1-22, 103, 104,
106, 243, 534,
893
2:2, 910
2:4, 244
2:5, 202, 250,
251, 372, 810,
906
2:5-8, 910
2:6, 251, 534,
734, 814, 906
2:6-8, 910
2:7, 119, 372, 526

2:7-8, 118
2:9, 197, 198
2:10-16, 519
2:10-19, 225
2:11, 527
2:12-15, 519, 549
2:12-19, 542
2:13, 549
2:14, 810
2:15, 549
2:16, 207, 225,
452, 563, 843,
920
2:16-17, 452
2:16-19, 519, 729,
769, 917, 921
2:16-22, 920
2:17, 225, 559
2:18, 7, 22
2:18-19, 435
2:19, 61, 432
2:20-22, 542
2:21, 372
2:22, 775, 778
3, 201, 223, 664,
872
3—4, 432
3:1, 107, 193,
199, 534, 657
3:1-12, 103, 106,
243, 534, 855,
858
3:1-20, 106
3:1—8:36, 106
3:2, 61, 534, 811,
821
3:2-4, 433
3:3, 719
3:3-4, 292, 534
3:4, 117, 778
3:5, 202, 251,
531, 534, 811,
854, 857
3:5-6, 780
3:5-10, 910
3:7, 202, 250,
251, 372, 571
3:8, 433, 778
3:9, 251
3:9-10, 82, 85,
292, 534
3:10, 220
3:11, 297
3:11-12, 66, 252,
293, 534, 569,
734, 815, 910
3:12, 106, 544
3:13-16, 294
3:13-18, 105, 244,
518, 519
3:13-20, 103, 104,
106, 243, 534,
534, 872, 874,
920
3:15, 536
3:16, 61, 778, 779
3:16-18, 433
3:18, 61, 432,
780, 781, 872
3:18-20, 62
3:19, 62, 66, 251,
854
3:19-20, 49, 62,
84, 85, 106,

197, 245, 519,
547, 869, 872,
903, 906, 912
3:21, 928
3:21-35, 103, 106,
243, 534
3:21—6:19, 106
3:25, 778
3:25-26, 433
3:26, 928
3:27, 563
3:27-35, 849
3:31, 810
3:31-35, 810
3:32, 251, 910
3:33, 21, 421, 544
3:33-34, 910
3:34, 224, 226,
293, 569
3:35, 103, 226,
292, 704
4, 150, 242, 428,
529, 532, 553
4:1, 102, 199,
207, 534, 657
4:1-5, 730
4:1-6, 906
4:1-9, 103, 106,
243, 534, 895,
912
4:1-19, 907
4:2, 102, 193
4:3, 102
4:3-4, 529
4:3-9, 28, 30, 722
4:4-6, 527
4:5-7, 518
4:5-9, 920
4:6, 102, 224
4:6-8, 105
4:6-9, 519
4:7, 541, 800, 854
4:8-9, 294
4:10, 61, 657, 811
4:10-19, 104, 106,
243, 534
4:11, 907
4:13, 432
4:14, 907
4:14-16, 534
4:14-17, 519
4:17, 219, 220
4:19, 103, 435
4:20-27, 103, 104,
106, 243, 534
4:21-22, 534
4:22, 432
4:23, 61, 322,
432, 534, 571,
910
4:23-27, 103, 106
4:27, 103
5, 3, 199
5—7, 544
5:1, 104, 518,
534, 657
5:1-6, 225, 519
5:1-14, 920
5:1-23, 103, 104,
105, 106, 243,
452, 519, 534
5:3, 207, 220,
225, 452, 534,

926
5:3-6, 729, 917,
921
5:3-20, 870
5:4, 222
5:5, 7, 435, 452
5:5-6, 7
5:6, 432, 436
5:8, 22
5:8-9, 292
5:8-14, 534
5:11, 452, 824
5:11-12, 293
5:12, 226
5:14, 452
5:15, 531
5:15-19, 452
5:15-23, 920
5:16, 865
5:18, 921
5:18-19, 105
5:18-20, 421
5:19, 16, 567,
568, 745, 870
5:20, 207, 225
5:21, 117, 251,
292, 861, 909
5:22, 322
5:23, 226, 452
6, 421
6:1, 466, 657
6:1-5, 105
6:1-19, 105, 106,
243, 534
6:5, 16, 17, 870
6:6, 18, 854, 870,
899
6:6-8, 105, 568
6:6-11, 51, 66,
421, 729, 854,
857
6:7-8, 854
6:8, 843
6:9, 811
6:9-11, 105, 854
6:10-11, 540
6:12-15, 100, 105,
519, 907
6:16, 251, 431,
511
6:16-17, 531
6:16-19, 105, 106,
534, 729
6:17, 202
6:19, 549
6:20, 102, 193,
433, 511, 928
6:20-22, 907
6:20-24, 519, 527
6:20-29, 920
6:20-35, 104, 105,
106, 199, 243,
452, 534
6:20—8:36, 106
6:23, 61, 293,
432, 436, 528
6:23-29, 519
6:24, 207, 225,
452, 928
6:24-35, 870
6:25, 435
6:25-26, 534
6:26, 207, 219,

421, 435, 868
6:29-35, 452
6:30, 910
6:30-31, 292
6:30-33, 292
6:30-35, 920
6:32, 100, 226
6:32-33, 292, 921
6:34-35, 421
7, 199, 207, 208,
211, 216, 217,
452, 542, 917,
934
7:1-5, 542
7:1-17, 452
7:1-23, 920
7:1-27, 82, 103,
104, 105, 106,
243, 534
7:2, 193, 221, 927
7:3, 719
7:4, 843, 920
7:4-5, 519
7:5, 207, 225, 843
7:5-23, 870
7:5-27, 209
7:6-20, 30
7:6-23, 102, 542,
934
7:6-27, 519, 729,
917, 921
7:7, 226
7:8, 22
7:9-11, 95
7:10-18, 868
7:12, 865
7:12-15, 562
7:14, 207, 560,
870, 928
7:16, 511, 560
7:17, 188, 207,
221
7:21, 452
7:22, 15, 16, 435,
870
7:23, 17, 921
7:24-27, 542, 920
7:27, 7, 21, 22,
452
8, 30, 48, 64, 65,
84, 197, 207,
208, 209, 452,
481, 529, 550,
551, 569, 570,
574, 575, 577,
725, 849, 862,
872, 892, 893,
904, 912, 913,
915, 916, 933
8—9, 335, 559,
565, 892
8:1-8, 917
8:1-11, 3
8:1-16, 519
8:1-36, 105, 106,
243, 534, 542,
905, 920
8:1—9:6, 843
8:1—9:12, 432
8:2-11, 84
8:3, 23, 865
8:4, 913
8:4-36, 30, 516

8:5, 224, 226
8:5-9, 913
8:6, 198, 372
8:9, 198, 372, 562
8:10-11, 518, 892,
913
8:11, 536
8:12, 209
8:12-21, 3, 84
8:13, 202, 203,
250, 251, 293,
372, 892, 906,
913, 933
8:14-16, 209
8:15, 666
8:15-16, 199, 551,
913
8:17, 844
8:18, 294
8:18-19, 544, 892
8:22, 64, 251,
533, 570, 905
8:22-23, 915
8:22-25, 844
8:22-26, 905
8:22-29, 666
8:22-30, 551, 915,
922
8:22-31, 3, 30, 49,
62, 64, 84, 106,
109, 278, 547,
550, 814, 855,
869, 876, 892,
903, 904, 913
8:22-36, 519, 905
8:23-26, 825
8:24, 64
8:24-25, 905
8:24-29, 481
8:25, 481
8:27, 62, 321
8:27-30, 905
8:28-29, 45
8:29, 48, 62, 321,
814
8:30, 64, 278,
551, 569, 905,
915
8:30-31, 65, 913
8:31, 64, 905
8:32, 535
8:32-35, 3
8:32-36, 84, 905
8:33, 541, 800
8:34, 23, 535
8:35, 61, 252,
432, 433, 905,
921
8:36, 226, 435
9, 209, 224, 225,
518, 549, 843,
912, 933
9:1, 22
9:1-6, 22, 224,
542, 872, 905,
912, 920
9:1-12, 106
9:1-18, 3, 105,
243, 534
9:2, 220
9:2-5, 570
9:3, 224, 550, 868
9:4, 226, 518,

531, 799
9:4-6, 550, 912
9:5, 220
9:6, 518, 913
9:7, 224
9:7-8, 293
9:7-12, 106, 518
9:8, 224
9:9, 223
9:10, 198, 202, 204, 223, 250, 251, 325, 372, 432, 537, 810, 816, 845, 854, 859, 900, 906, 930, 933
9:11, 61, 433, 811, 821
9:12, 224
9:13, 207, 224, 225
9:13-17, 920
9:13-18, 106, 224, 225, 542, 729, 912, 917, 921
9:14, 224, 913
9:16, 224, 225, 226, 518, 531, 799
9:16-17, 550, 912
9:17, 224, 519
9:18, 7, 518, 544, 775, 843, 911, 914
10, 224, 453, 901
10—12, 652
10—15, 224, 576, 778
10—22, 529
10—24, 552, 555
10—29, 102, 107, 152, 243, 529, 532, 536, 538, 573, 575, 657, 658, 772, 903, 904, 907, 908
10—31, 108, 542, 548, 549, 849, 859, 912
10:1, 224, 236, 283, 529, 530, 531, 532, 533, 537, 540, 542, 543, 550, 552, 555, 666, 733, 734, 867, 895, 913
10:1-22, 539, 901
10:1—22:16, 155, 197, 532, 534, 538, 540, 552, 572, 659, 662, 894
10:1—24:22, 237
10:2, 532, 540, 666, 879
10:3, 252, 529, 544, 568, 652, 666, 910
10:4, 201, 203, 421, 530, 531, 810
10:4-5, 729

10:5, 224, 293, 541, 618
10:6, 531, 537, 927
10:6-7, 845
10:6-11, 537
10:7, 292, 463, 646
10:8, 226, 421, 529
10:9, 532, 652, 810
10:10, 226, 572
10:11, 433, 517, 531, 537, 543
10:12, 530, 532, 533, 569
10:13, 226
10:14, 226, 517, 533
10:15, 845
10:16, 539, 652, 810, 901
10:17, 293, 533, 906
10:18, 226, 517
10:19, 224, 533, 618
10:20, 529, 533
10:20-21, 225
10:21, 223, 226, 517
10:22, 778, 845
10:23, 223
10:24, 652, 666, 780, 810
10:24-25, 421
10:25, 652
10:25-26, 536
10:26, 533, 729
10:27, 202, 203, 250, 251, 372, 433, 652, 778, 779, 900
10:27-28, 911
10:28, 100, 666
10:29, 23, 252, 526
10:30, 117, 652
10:31, 666, 810
10:32, 517
11, 532
11:1, 197, 251, 421, 422, 535, 543, 731, 910
11:2, 102, 202, 293
11:3, 372
11:4, 294, 666, 780, 821
11:5, 652, 666
11:6, 372, 652, 666
11:7, 100, 567, 780
11:8, 666
11:9, 100, 531
11:9-10, 532
11:9-14, 153
11:11-14, 831
11:12, 226
11:13, 531
11:13-14, 562

11:15-21, 153
11:16, 294, 908
11:18, 652, 666
11:19, 652
11:20, 251, 372, 535, 861, 908
11:21, 652, 666, 908, 911
11:22, 17, 435
11:25, 731
11:28, 666
11:29, 810
11:30, 781, 872
11:31, 569
12:1, 293
12:2, 652, 778
12:3, 914
12:4, 453
12:5, 666
12:6, 372, 567, 831
12:7, 652
12:8, 292
12:9, 294, 535
12:10, 14, 666, 910
12:11, 226
12:12, 666
12:13, 666, 927
12:14, 531, 845
12:15, 224
12:16, 226, 293
12:17, 421, 666
12:18, 531, 533, 829
12:18-19, 536
12:21, 421, 652, 666
12:22, 251, 810
12:23, 223, 225, 226
12:24, 845
12:27, 845
12:28, 7, 666, 781, 911
13, 573
13—15, 95
13:1, 224, 293, 433, 573
13:2, 573
13:2-3, 536
13:3, 322, 527, 573, 928
13:4, 435, 517, 573
13:5, 292, 573, 658, 666
13:6, 372, 573, 666
13:6-9, 95
13:7, 533, 571, 573
13:8, 573
13:8-9, 562
13:9, 528, 573, 824
13:10, 573
13:11, 432, 567, 573
13:12, 573, 872
13:13, 293, 421, 573
13:14, 7, 52, 433,

530, 573
13:15, 573
13:16, 223, 573
13:17, 573, 771
13:18, 293, 573
13:19, 223, 573
13:21, 573, 666
13:21-22, 536
13:22, 435, 573, 666
13:23, 776, 908
13:25, 810
14:1, 22, 518, 872, 914
14:2, 202, 203, 250, 251, 293, 372
14:4, 15
14:5-10, 95, 562
14:6, 224
14:8, 223, 226
14:9, 226
14:10, 466, 517, 531
14:11, 21, 100, 372, 810
14:12, 226, 531, 540
14:12-13, 95
14:13, 533
14:14, 810
14:15, 224, 530
14:16, 226
14:17-18, 562
14:18, 224
14:19, 23, 666, 865
14:21, 861
14:24, 223, 704
14:25, 421
14:26, 202, 251, 372, 900
14:26-27, 536
14:27, 52, 202, 203, 372, 667, 900, 933
14:28, 868
14:31, 199, 293, 421, 776, 861, 868, 903
14:31-35, 95
14:32, 7, 526, 811, 911
14:33, 910
14:34, 95, 293, 560
14:35, 294, 618, 671, 868
15—16, 535
15:1, 505
15:1-8, 95
15:2, 223, 225
15:3, 251, 292, 666, 814, 909
15:4, 433, 870, 872
15:5, 293
15:6, 250, 666
15:7, 225, 704
15:8, 39, 82, 85, 372, 870, 934
15:8-9, 535, 810, 845

15:9, 251, 535, 666, 910
15:10, 226, 293
15:11, 7, 53, 251, 814, 909
15:12, 224
15:13, 532
15:14, 223, 225
15:16, 202, 251, 372, 575, 933
15:16-17, 535, 810
15:17, 15, 575
15:19, 222, 570
15:19-31, 95
15:20, 226, 293, 531
15:21, 223, 226
15:23, 543, 821
15:24, 7, 436, 618, 811, 824, 911
15:25, 21, 202, 252, 531, 868, 910
15:26, 251, 810
15:27, 730
15:28, 95, 225, 666, 799
15:29, 82, 85, 252, 535, 569, 666, 934
15:30, 569, 572
15:32, 293
15:33, 202, 251, 293, 372, 432, 900, 906, 908, 933
15:33—16:9, 535, 548
16:1, 251, 541, 800
16:2, 251, 909
16:3, 251, 541, 800, 908
16:4, 251, 810, 814, 903
16:4-5, 810
16:5, 202, 251, 293, 544
16:6, 202, 203, 250, 251, 372, 900
16:7, 252, 532, 814
16:8, 95, 535, 666, 779, 810, 879, 907
16:9, 251, 537, 810, 814, 857
16:10, 910
16:10-15, 535, 548, 671
16:11, 197, 251, 422, 910
16:12, 199, 294
16:12-13, 536
16:13, 199, 372, 666
16:14, 549
16:14-15, 200
16:15, 532
16:16, 907

16:17, 527
16:18, 100, 202, 293
16:18-19, 910
16:19, 202, 879, 907
16:20, 251, 618, 910
16:22, 226
16:23, 225
16:24, 531
16:25, 226
16:26, 517, 868
16:27, 531
16:28, 532
16:31, 293, 666
16:33, 82, 84, 251, 778, 810, 814
17:1, 82, 294, 879
17:2, 292, 618
17:3, 251, 435, 857
17:5, 251, 293, 903
17:6, 293
17:7, 224, 908
17:10, 226, 560
17:12, 16, 66, 223, 226, 870
17:13, 21
17:15, 294, 810
17:18, 226, 574
17:20, 910
17:21, 226
17:22, 532
17:25, 226, 529
17:26, 535
17:28, 421
18:2, 224
18:4, 433, 533
18:5, 535, 563
18:6, 544
18:6-7, 54
18:7, 225
18:8, 533
18:10, 24, 118, 252, 525, 533, 666, 830, 910
18:10-11, 536
18:11, 23
18:12, 100, 202, 293, 421
18:13, 226, 292
18:17, 421
18:22, 252, 453, 519, 921
18:23, 908
18:24, 560
19:1, 372, 529, 534, 545, 779, 879
19:3, 226, 435, 517
19:4-5, 868
19:5, 531
19:6, 731
19:9, 100, 531
19:10, 868, 908
19:11, 293, 549
19:12, 15, 533, 549, 868
19:13, 100, 226,

453
19:14, 453
19:16, 527, 927
19:17, 199, 868, 910
19:18, 226
19:19, 549
19:20, 560
19:21, 251, 778, 810, 882, 908
19:22, 731, 879
19:23, 202, 203, 250, 251, 372, 900, 933
19:24, 531
19:26, 293
19:27, 558
19:28, 421
19:29, 226
20:1, 220, 516
20:2, 15, 66, 537
20:3, 226, 292
20:4, 435
20:6, 571, 731
20:7, 372, 666
20:8, 537
20:8-11, 537
20:9, 814
20:10, 251, 910
20:10-23, 731
20:11, 372
20:12, 251, 903, 906
20:13, 567
20:14-19, 541, 800
20:15, 533
20:16, 225, 452, 868
20:19, 226
20:20, 422, 528, 810, 824
20:22, 251, 810, 811, 824
20:23, 251, 421, 910
20:24, 251, 810, 814, 854, 857, 908, 909
20:25, 82, 934
20:26, 849
20:27, 251, 528
21, 537
21:1, 251, 810, 814, 857
21:1-31, 535
21:2, 251, 372
21:3, 82, 85, 251
21:4, 202, 293
21:6, 432
21:7, 85, 544
21:8, 372
21:9, 453
21:11, 224
21:12, 618
21:17, 220
21:19, 549
21:20, 226, 704
21:21, 292, 666
21:22, 831
21:23, 421, 527
21:24, 202, 224, 293

21:25-26, 536
21:26, 666
21:27, 82, 845, 870, 934
21:28, 100, 810
21:30, 251, 908
21:30-31, 814, 882
21:31, 15, 251, 870
22, 224, 530
22—23, 452
22—24, 534, 562, 896
22:1, 294, 569, 879
22:2, 251, 868, 869, 870, 903
22:4, 202, 203, 250, 251, 292, 372, 421, 667, 900, 906, 933
22:5, 222
22:6, 545, 569
22:7, 731, 868
22:9, 421, 535
22:12, 251, 814
22:13, 16, 531, 865
22:14, 225, 868, 914
22:15, 224, 226, 322
22:16, 868
22:17, 539, 552, 555, 556, 562, 704, 734
22:17-18, 562, 896
22:17-21, 546, 561, 563, 706
22:17—24:22, 28, 39, 237, 264, 429, 534, 574, 575, 809, 896, 899
22:17—24:34, 539, 548
22:19, 251, 562
22:20, 555, 560, 561, 562, 565, 574, 719
22:20-21, 570
22:20—24:22, 563
22:21, 562
22:22, 23, 546, 561, 562, 865, 868
22:22-23, 563, 810, 910
22:22—24:22, 561, 562, 565
22:23, 562
22:24, 562
22:24-25, 564
22:25, 3, 562
22:26-27, 562
22:28, 382, 422, 562, 564
22:29, 546, 562, 564, 571
23:1-3, 541, 562,

563, 574
23:2, 533
23:4-5, 546, 562, 563
23:5, 17, 870
23:6-7, 562
23:6-8, 563
23:7, 372, 568
23:8, 562
23:9, 562
23:10, 422, 868, 870
23:10-11, 381, 534, 546, 563, 564, 810, 910
23:11, 421
23:12, 561
23:12—24:10, 563
23:13, 226
23:13-14, 322, 547
23:14, 7, 824, 911
23:15-16, 561
23:16, 372
23:17, 202, 203, 250, 292, 810, 927
23:17-18, 824, 911
23:19, 561
23:20, 220
23:22, 293, 563
23:22-25, 207, 730
23:24, 223
23:26, 561, 572
23:27, 207, 225, 563, 868
23:30, 220
23:31, 220
23:32, 19
24:1-2, 292
24:3, 22
24:3-4, 872
24:5, 704, 830
24:7, 23, 226, 865
24:11, 563
24:11-12, 814, 909
24:12, 569, 811
24:12-22, 563
24:13, 558
24:14, 824
24:16, 544, 815
24:17-18, 251
24:19, 292, 435
24:19-20, 815, 908, 911
24:20, 528, 824
24:21, 202, 203, 250, 372
24:21-22, 100
24:22, 541, 568
24:23, 236, 539, 552, 555, 556, 562, 734
24:23-34, 28, 39, 534
24:23-34, 237
24:24, 845
24:28, 574
24:29, 294

24:30, 226
24:30-34, 30, 722, 857, 906
24:31, 23, 222
24:33-34, 435, 810
24:34, 568
25, 708
25—26, 535
25—27, 156, 537
25—29, 197, 237, 534, 552, 575, 894, 895, 896
25:1, 200, 236, 283, 536, 537, 540, 554, 671, 704, 719, 733, 734, 735, 867, 895
25:1—29:27, 39, 540
25:1—31:31, 575
25:2, 200, 573, 811, 908, 909
25:3, 200
25:4-5, 200
25:5-6, 202
25:6-7, 200, 293
25:8-10, 570
25:9-10, 292
25:11, 220, 571
25:15, 12
25:16, 220
25:17, 572
25:18, 829
25:19, 822
25:21-22, 569
25:23, 549
25:26, 66
25:27, 202, 220, 293, 294
25:28, 23, 535
25:28—26:2, 535
26, 535
26:1, 292
26:1-2, 66
26:2, 17, 317
26:3, 15
26:4, 39
26:4-5, 13, 223, 224, 254, 535, 543, 638, 810, 907
26:5, 39
26:6, 226
26:7, 226, 530, 543
26:9, 222, 530, 543
26:10, 226
26:11, 16, 223, 535, 569
26:12, 202
26:13, 16, 865
26:14, 435
26:15, 435
26:17, 16
26:18-22, 569
26:21, 535
26:23, 535, 799
26:27, 907
26:28, 854
27:1, 558

27:2, 293
27:3-4, 549
27:6, 14
27:7, 220, 910
27:8, 17
27:11, 557
27:13, 225
27:15, 543
27:15-16, 536
27:17, 569
27:18, 220, 292
27:19, 226
27:20, 5, 7, 52, 101
27:21, 293
27:22, 226
27:23, 14
27:24, 532
27:26, 13
27:26-27, 870
27:27, 13
28—29, 537
28—31, 899
28:1, 15
28:2, 517
28:4, 292, 845
28:5, 251, 933
28:6, 372, 879
28:7, 293, 729
28:9, 82, 85, 934
28:10, 372, 907
28:14, 201, 202, 372, 535
28:15, 15, 16, 870
28:18, 372, 907
28:21, 219
28:25, 251, 910
28:26, 224
28:28, 667
29:1, 100
29:3, 100, 868
29:6, 666, 927
29:7, 666
29:8, 549
29:9, 226
29:10, 372
29:13, 251, 814, 903
29:15, 322
29:16, 667
29:18, 535, 567, 568, 729, 883
29:22, 549
29:23, 202, 293
29:25, 202, 251, 372, 910
29:26, 251, 252
29:27, 845
30, 237, 269, 429, 430, 552, 708
30—31, 152, 197, 243, 264, 427, 428, 542
30:1, 237, 264, 283, 428, 429, 530, 540, 708, 734, 867, 878, 883
30:1-4, 202
30:1-9, 30, 430
30:1-14, 39, 568
30:2, 224
30:2-3, 814

840
30:2-4, 429, 430
30:2-9, 428
30:4, 62, 429, 430, 431, 571
30:5, 119, 526, 830, 909
30:5-6, 430
30:5-9, 429, 430
30:7-9, 430, 534, 723
30:8, 219
30:9, 251, 909
30:11-14, 103
30:13, 202
30:15, 19, 511, 534
30:15-16, 52, 516, 534
30:15-30, 430
30:15-33, 39
30:15—31:9, 568
30:16, 7
30:17, 17, 18, 293
30:18, 511, 534
30:18-19, 534, 814
30:18-20, 237
30:19, 17, 19, 534
30:20, 543, 771, 868
30:21, 511
30:21-23, 534, 908
30:22, 810
30:23, 453
30:24-28, 66, 704
30:24-31, 706
30:25, 18, 899
30:26, 17, 870
30:27, 18, 870
30:28, 19, 21, 870
30:29, 511
30:29-31, 529
30:30, 14, 16, 870
30:31, 14, 19, 430, 870
30:32, 224, 293
30:33, 535
31, 209, 237, 243, 269, 433, 453, 533, 536, 552, 575, 661, 681, 753, 840, 893, 895, 921, 922
31:1, 207, 237, 264, 428, 530, 540, 708, 734, 735, 867, 868, 878, 883
31:1-9, 39, 104, 207, 209, 430, 529, 534, 895
31:1-31, 2
31:2, 82, 104, 264, 558, 735
31:2-3, 560
31:3, 264, 453
31:4, 220, 511, 793, 867
31:6, 220
31:8-9, 534, 666
31:10, 244, 536, 679, 681, 693,

840
31:10-20, 2
31:10-31, 2, 4, 39, 104, 105, 199, 205, 207, 237, 243, 245, 294, 403, 452, 519, 524, 529, 534, 536, 538, 539, 571, 575, 577, 681, 693, 731, 755, 840, 891, 914, 924, 925
31:11, 921
31:12, 199, 921
31:13-18, 199
31:15, 199
31:16, 921
31:17, 840
31:18, 917
31:19, 921
31:19-20, 840
31:20, 199, 433
31:22, 921
31:23, 23, 453, 575, 732, 865, 921
31:24-27, 731
31:26, 199, 207, 433, 840
31:27, 219, 575
31:28, 199, 433, 921
31:28-30, 29#431:28-29, 921
31:29, 453
31:30, 2, 202, 205, 243, 250, 325, 372, 535, 840, 859, 906, 921, 933
31:31, 199, 294, 865, 921

Ecclesiastes
1, 453, 862
1—2, 29, 636, 637
1:1, 122, 124, 143, 239, 283, 324, 471, 636, 637, 734, 736, 865, 868, 895, 917
1:1-2, 125, 244
1:1-3, 147
1:1-11, 124, 126, 204, 676
1:2, 12, 66, 124, 130, 324, 432, 638, 643, 776, 777, 813, 814
1:2-3, 239
1:2-11, 893
1:2—12:8, 635
1:3, 126, 130, 135, 637, 638, 643, 813
1:3-11, 129, 244
1:3-15, 903
1:3-16, 435
1:3—3:9, 660

1:4, 130, 821
1:4-5, 822
1:4-7, 893
1:4-11, 239
1:5, 66
1:5-7, 126, 870, 909
1:6, 66, 130
1:7, 130
1:8, 130
1:9, 66, 130, 131, 135, 330, 636, 822
1:9-10, 822
1:10, 128, 130, 883
1:10-14, 95, 801
1:11, 137, 645, 646
1:12, 122, 124, 134, 142, 283, 636, 865
1:12-13, 736
1:12-17, 734
1:12—2:16, 123
1:12—2:26, 30, 137
1:12—11:6, 239
1:12—12:7, 124, 146, 147, 204, 324
1:13, 130, 137, 255, 637, 777, 813, 903
1:13-17, 636
1:14, 130, 131, 133, 135, 643, 779, 813
1:15, 813, 814
1:16, 122, 123, 130, 134, 137, 283, 294, 636, 637, 736, 865
1:16-17, 868
1:17, 128, 130, 133, 137, 223, 225, 294
1:17-18, 637
1:18, 130, 531, 638, 639
2, 225, 636, 917
2:1, 130, 131, 134, 137, 643, 868
2:1-23, 435
2:2, 130, 131, 141, 142
2:3, 130, 223, 225
2:4-6, 870
2:4-7, 30, 636
2:4-16, 736
2:5, 124, 130, 266
2:7, 14, 122, 130, 294, 636, 865, 870
2:7-10, 636
2:8, 636, 865, 870
2:9, 122, 130, 865
2:10, 128, 130, 131, 295, 639, 776
2:11, 130, 131, 133, 135, 294,

471, 643, 776
2:12, 130, 223, 225, 734, 868
2:12-17, 639
2:13, 130, 223, 225, 911
2:13-14, 638, 776, 911
2:13-16, 637
2:14, 130, 435
2:14-16, 127
2:15, 128, 130, 134, 137, 643, 776
2:15-16, 639, 813
2:15-17, 777
2:16, 66, 130, 821
2:17, 130, 131, 135, 637, 643, 813, 917
2:17-18, 7, 776
2:17-26, 722
2:18, 130, 131, 135, 435
2:18-23, 639
2:19, 128, 130, 131, 223, 225, 643
2:20, 130, 131, 813
2:21, 128, 130
2:21-23, 813
2:22, 130, 131, 638
2:23, 128, 130
2:24, 66, 126, 128, 130, 135, 137, 255, 295, 639, 788, 813
2:24-25, 62, 256, 462, 639
2:24-26, 140, 638, 643, 911
2:26, 128, 130, 131, 435, 643, 903, 909
3, 121, 123, 822, 899
3:1, 66, 130, 143, 789, 822
3:1-3, 543
3:1-8, 130, 454, 466, 638, 660, 813, 870, 893, 917
3:1-9, 126, 214
3:1-15, 822
3:2, 7, 127, 135, 462
3:2-8, 821, 822
3:3-8, 909
3:5, 214, 454, 789, 917
3:5-6, 214
3:6, 130
3:9, 126, 130, 638, 643
3:9-18, 909
3:10, 130, 255
3:10-11, 813
3:10-15, 126
3:11, 66, 127, 130, 255, 256,

638, 660, 777, 821, 822, 870
3:12, 126, 130, 131, 137, 535, 639, 813
3:12-13, 7, 62, 126, 295, 911
3:12-14, 140, 643
3:13, 66, 125, 126, 127, 128, 130, 255, 462
3:14, 124, 130, 204, 250, 256, 814, 860, 907
3:14-15, 126, 135, 883
3:15, 126, 130, 636, 815
3:15-17, 813
3:16, 130, 131, 137, 423
3:16-21, 813
3:16-22, 642
3:17, 8, 130, 134, 256, 435, 436, 667, 871, 909, 910
3:17-18, 137
3:18, 130, 134, 435
3:18-20, 911
3:18-21, 14, 129, 813, 909
3:19, 66, 127, 130, 431, 432, 643
3:19-21, 7, 127, 431, 824
3:19-22, 126
3:20, 66, 130, 432, 910
3:20-21, 910
3:21, 130
3:22, 62, 126, 130, 131, 137, 140, 295, 535, 639, 643, 813, 883, 911
4, 223, 288, 664
4:1, 130, 131, 136, 812, 813, 868
4:1-3, 423, 636, 861
4:2, 637
4:2-3, 127
4:3, 130, 131, 436, 535, 813
4:4, 128, 130, 133, 435, 643
4:5, 130, 226
4:5-6, 531
4:6, 130, 535, 643
4:7, 130, 131
4:8, 128, 130, 435, 517
4:9, 130
4:9-12, 454, 917
4:11, 917
4:12, 144, 917
4:13, 130, 225, 638, 704, 868
4:13-14, 322

4:13-16, 123
4:15, 130, 131
4:15-16, 295
4:16, 128, 130, 131
4:17, 130
5, 201, 242, 641
5:1, 130, 225, 226, 933
5:1-3, 777
5:1-6, 909
5:1-7, 82, 83, 256, 652, 870, 883
5:2, 130, 909
5:2-6, 933
5:3, 130, 226
5:3-4, 225
5:4, 130, 226
5:4-5, 462, 934
5:4-6, 424
5:5, 130
5:6, 100, 130, 204, 256, 517
5:7, 130, 250, 256, 777, 860, 907
5:8, 130, 813, 865, 868
5:8-9, 636, 861
5:9, 123, 128, 130
5:10, 130, 435, 643
5:12, 130, 131, 729, 868
5:13, 130
5:13-17, 95
5:14, 130
5:14-18, 801
5:15, 128, 130
5:15-16, 7, 127
5:16, 130, 638, 643
5:17, 130, 137, 435, 813
5:17-18, 639
5:17-19, 136
5:18, 126, 128, 130, 131, 295, 462, 909
5:18-20, 62, 140, 643, 911
5:19, 125, 126, 127, 128, 130, 131, 255, 909
5:19-20, 256, 813
6:1, 95, 130, 131
6:1-2, 7
6:2, 128, 130, 255, 295, 435, 639, 813, 871, 909
6:3, 130, 435, 436
6:3-6, 127
6:4, 130
6:5, 130
6:6, 130
6:7, 130, 910
6:8, 130, 225, 868
6:9, 128, 130, 643
6:10, 130
6:10-12, 883, 909
6:11, 7, 130, 638, 643

6:12, 130, 131, 527
7:1, 55, 130, 295
7:1-2, 127
7:2, 22, 125, 127, 128, 130, 295, 772, 870
7:2-4, 7
7:3, 130, 141, 142
7:4, 127, 130, 226
7:4-5, 225
7:5, 130, 638
7:5-7, 911
7:6, 95, 128, 130, 221, 643
7:7, 95, 130
7:8, 130
7:8-9, 910
7:9, 130, 225, 226
7:10, 130, 636, 821
7:10-12, 330
7:11, 130, 637
7:11-12, 638, 911
7:12, 130, 527
7:13, 130, 225, 256, 814
7:13-14, 813, 909
7:14, 130, 131, 134, 255, 434, 649
7:15, 130, 137, 423, 432, 435, 667, 780, 813, 821
7:15-18, 813, 907
7:16, 130, 637, 638, 639, 667
7:16-17, 534
7:17, 127, 130, 223, 225, 226, 821
7:18, 66, 130, 204, 250, 667
7:19, 130, 637, 638
7:20, 130, 141, 667, 910
7:21, 130
7:22, 130
7:23, 128, 130, 134, 638
7:23-24, 917
7:23-29, 137
7:24, 813
7:25, 130, 223, 225
7:25-29, 214
7:26, 52, 127, 130, 214, 322, 453, 917
7:27, 124, 128, 130, 244, 635
7:28, 130, 918
7:29, 128, 130, 256, 814, 910
8:1, 130, 638, 704
8:1-4, 671
8:2, 130
8:2-4, 123
8:3, 130
8:5, 130, 638, 821
8:5-7, 883

8:6, 130
8:7, 130
8:8, 127, 130, 870
8:9, 128, 130, 131
8:9-10, 295
8:10, 128, 130, 137, 643
8:10-14, 813
8:11, 124, 130, 266, 424
8:12, 130, 204, 256
8:12-13, 66, 250, 256, 652, 860, 907, 911
8:12—9:4, 652
8:13, 130, 667
8:14, 128, 130, 432, 643, 652, 667, 776, 813, 909
8:14-17, 423
8:15, 62, 66, 126, 130, 131, 137, 140, 141, 142, 255, 295, 462, 643, 871, 909, 911
8:16, 130, 137, 910
8:16-17, 134, 137, 638, 777
8:16—9:1, 909
8:16—9:10, 134
8:17, 130, 131, 255, 638, 652, 813, 814
9, 130
9:1, 130, 137, 223, 255, 813, 814, 909, 910
9:1-2, 777
9:1-6, 813, 911
9:1-10, 7
9:1-12, 642
9:2, 130, 652, 667, 813
9:2-3, 637, 909
9:2-6, 870
9:2-12, 127
9:3, 128, 130, 131, 225, 639
9:3-6, 909
9:4, 16, 130, 660
9:4-6, 637
9:5, 130, 295, 646
9:6, 130, 131
9:7, 130, 131, 220, 256, 462
9:7-9, 134, 137
9:7-10, 62, 140, 295, 643, 911
9:8, 130, 918
9:9, 130, 131, 214, 453, 643, 776, 909, 918
9:10, 52, 130, 934
9:11, 130, 131, 638, 813, 820, 821, 822
9:11-12, 12
9:11-18, 12
9:12, 18, 52, 130,

526
9:12-13, 531
9:13, 128, 130, 131
9:13-16, 12
9:13-18, 831
9:14-15, 704, 883
9:15, 130, 295, 638
9:16, 130
9:16-18, 637, 911
9:17, 12, 130, 225
9:18, 12, 100, 130, 638
10:1, 18, 130, 223, 225, 638, 660
10:1-3, 225, 911
10:1-15, 637
10:2, 130, 226
10:3, 130, 223, 225
10:5, 130, 131
10:6, 223, 225, 810
10:6-7, 137, 295
10:7, 15, 130
10:8, 19, 23
10:10, 130, 638
10:11, 19, 130
10:12, 100, 130, 911
10:12-15, 225
10:13, 130, 223, 225
10:14, 130, 223, 225, 226
10:15, 130
10:15-16, 868
10:18, 130
10:19, 130, 131, 220
10:20, 18, 123, 130, 424
11, 814
11:1, 219
11:2, 130, 462, 511
11:4, 130
11:5, 130, 255, 813, 818, 869, 870
11:6, 130
11:7, 130
11:7-8, 137, 436
11:7—12:7, 239
11:8, 127, 130, 131, 643
11:8-10, 911
11:9, 8, 130, 131, 141, 256, 423, 637, 871, 909
11:9-10, 137
11:10, 130
12, 255
12:1, 130, 637, 645, 813, 814, 821, 869, 870, 903
12:1-7, 642
12:1-8, 7
12:1-14, 252
12:3, 22, 130

12:3-7, 22
12:4, 17, 917
12:5, 18, 130, 220, 221
12:5-6, 127
12:7, 124, 130, 255, 432, 909, 910
12:8, 12, 124, 130, 143, 239, 324, 635, 638, 643
12:8-14, 124, 125, 145, 204, 244, 676
12:9, 128, 130, 635, 636, 895
12:9-10, 637, 704, 734, 736
12:9-11, 128
12:9-14, 239, 252, 330, 736
12:10, 130, 719
12:11, 129, 130, 471, 635, 813, 879
12:11-12, 879
12:12, 130, 143, 204, 718, 735
12:12-13, 128
12:13, 66, 123, 125, 126, 127, 128, 129, 130, 131, 193, 204, 250, 256, 295, 325, 535, 640, 813, 816, 859, 860, 861, 900, 906, 907, 911
12:13-14, 124, 125, 128, 142, 204, 244, 423, 667, 737, 780, 909
12:14, 8, 128, 130, 256, 295, 436, 813, 815, 871

Song of Songs
1:1, 239, 265, 439, 735, 748, 761, 868, 898
1:1—3:8, 764
1:2, 220, 242
1:2-4, 68, 748
1:2-12, 748
1:2—2:7, 239, 919
1:2—8:12, 748
1:4, 220, 645, 868
1:5, 734, 743, 866, 868
1:5-8, 748
1:6, 265, 424, 742
1:7, 14, 643, 741, 755
1:7-8, 757
1:8, 14, 870
1:9, 870
1:9-12, 748
1:10, 428
1:12, 868

1:13, *221*
1:13—2:3, *748*
1:13—2:7, *748*
1:14, *866*
1:15, *18*
1:17, *222, 265*
2:1, *866*
2:1-2, *617*
2:1-13, *68*
2:2, *221, 222*
2:3, *220, 526, 527, 748*
2:4, *22, 743, 866*
2:4-6, *838*
2:5, *220*
2:6, *643*
2:7, *452, 481, 517, 748, 749, 758, 866, 868, 870, 920*
2:8, *23, 481*
2:8-9, *325, 482, 748*
2:8-17, *748*
2:8—3:5, *239, 919*
2:9, *68, 459, 870*
2:10-15, *748*
2:11-12, *68*
2:11-13, *68*
2:12, *221, 487*
2:13, *68, 220*
2:14, *18, 482, 870*
2:15, *101, 870*
2:16, *221, 300, 617, 841*
2:16-17, *748*
2:17, *325, 482, 870*
3:1, *298, 746*
3:1-2, *69*
3:1-4, *748, 758*
3:1-5, *748*
3:2, *866*
3:2-3, *866*
3:4, *22, 213, 298*
3:5, *452, 481, 643, 748, 749, 758, 866, 868, 920*
3:6, *221, 743, 746*
3:6-11, *748*
3:6—5:1, *919*
3:6—5:8, *239*
3:7, *868*
3:9, *265, 734, 866, 868*
3:10, *866, 868*
3:11, *734, 868*
4:1, *14, 18, 68, 837, 866, 868, 870*
4:1-7, *748, 752, 835*
4:1-8, *239*
4:1-16, *68*
4:2, *14, 870*
4:3, *68, 220*
4:4, *22, 866, 868*
4:5, *68, 221, 617, 839, 870*
4:6, *221, 482*
4:8, *16, 482, 526,*

801, 866, 870
4:8-11, *748*
4:8—5:1, *748*
4:10, *220*
4:12, *68, 452*
4:12-14, *871*
4:12-15, *755*
4:12-16, *919*
4:12—5:1, *748*
4:13, *68, 220, 265*
4:13-15, *68*
4:14, *221*
4:15, *452*
4:16, *68, 741, 750*
5:1, *68, 220, 221, 298, 730, 743, 748*
5:1-2, *519*
5:2, *18, 746, 870*
5:2-6, *298*
5:2-7, *298, 748*
5:2-8, *748, 758*
5:2—6:3, *69, 919*
5:5, *757*
5:5-7, *743*
5:6, *298*
5:7, *866, 868*
5:8, *748, 758, 866, 868*
5:9, *762*
5:9-16, *748*
5:9—6:3, *748*
5:9—8:4, *239*
5:10-16, *96, 239, 835, 837, 839*
5:11, *18, 871*
5:12, *18, 870*
5:13, *221, 617*
5:13-16, *871*
5:14, *840*
5:15, *68, 222*
5:16, *837, 840, 866, 868*
6:1-3, *748*
6:2, *68, 221*
6:2-3, *617*
6:3, *221, 839*
6:4, *746, 866*
6:4-7, *835*
6:4-8, *919*
6:4-10, *748*
6:4—8:4, *919*
6:5, *14, 211, 866*
6:6, *14*
6:7, *68, 220*
6:8, *868*
6:9, *18, 433, 868, 870*
6:11, *220*
6:11-13, *748*
6:11—7:12, *748*
6:12, *801*
6:13, *866, 868*
7:1, *868*
7:1-6, *748*
7:1-10, *239, 835*
7:1-13, *68*
7:2, *220, 221, 617*
7:2-8, *211*
7:3, *870*
7:4, *22, 738, 866*
7:4-5, *211*
7:5, *837, 866*

7:7-8, *222, 738*
7:7-10, *748*
7:8, *220*
7:9, *220, 868*
7:10, *801, 868*
7:11-12, *748*
7:11-13, *465, 919*
7:12, *220*
7:13—8:3, *748*
7:13—8:4, *748*
8:1-2, *298*
8:1-3, *298*
8:2, *22, 213, 433, 866*
8:3, *643*
8:4, *517, 643, 748, 758, 866, 868, 920*
8:5, *433, 738, 866*
8:5-7, *748*
8:5-14, *239, 919*
8:6, *8, 194, 246, 256, 433*
8:6-7, *517*
8:7, *748*
8:8, *298, 838*
8:8-9, *298, 748*
8:8-12, *748*
8:9, *222, 424*
8:9-10, *23, 866*
8:10, *22, 298, 748*
8:10-12, *919*
8:11, *265, 866, 868*
8:11-12, *734, 739, 748*
8:12, *265, 868*
8:13-14, *242, 748*
8:14, *482, 870, 924*

Isaiah
1, *861*
1—39, *229*
1:2-3, *880*
1:15-18, *870*
1:21, *159*
1:21-23, *400*
1:23, *702, 910*
1:27, *156, 157, 158*
2:2-4, *938*
4:3, *6*
5, *879*
5:1, *527*
5:1-7, *880*
5:5, *528*
5:6, *618*
5:8-10, *692*
5:14, *52*
5:21, *878, 880, 882*
6:9-10, *880*
7:14, *119, 796*
7:18, *843*
8, *476*
8:1, *6*
8:5-8, *50*
8:13, *201*
9:6, *882*
10:1-2, *702*
10:13, *880*
10:15, *879, 880*

10:32—12:6, *459*
11:1-9, *882*
11:2, *877, 900*
11:3, *900*
12, *230*
12:4-6, *401*
12:6, *401*
13:1, *878*
13:12, *618*
14:4, *532*
14:4-21, *400*
14:12-15, *321*
14:13, *113, 114*
14:26, *880*
14:28, *878*
15:1, *878*
16:1, *696*
17:1, *878*
17:13, *158*
19:1, *878*
19:11-12, *878, 880, 882*
20:4, *465*
21:1, *878*
21:11, *878*
21:13, *878*
22:1, *878*
22:12, *400*
23:1, *878*
23:1-14, *400*
24—27, *50*
24:22, *321*
25:8, *53*
26:19, *5, 382*
27:1, *45, 46, 50, 51*
28, *879*
28:15, *53*
28:16-18, *53*
28:23-28, *880*
28:29, *880*
29:13-16, *880*
29:14, *882*
29:15-16, *880*
29:16, *255*
30:1-5, *882*
30:6, *878*
30:7, *45, 50, 51*
30:29, *616, 787*
30:33, *561*
31:1-3, *882*
32:1-2, *527*
33:6, *882, 900*
33:10-13, *388*
33:20, *114*
33:20-22, *113*
35:1, *221*
35:1-2, *67*
36—37, *238*
36—38, *23*
37:17, *382*
38, *76, 615*
38:9-10, *615*
38:20, *615*
40, *524, 940*
40—55, *277, 397, 400*
40—66, *74, 75, 115, 332, 874*
40:1-2, *115, 415*
40:1-8, *115*
40:2, *415*
40:3, *331*

40:10, *74, 329*
40:18, *113*
40:20, *882*
40:22-26, *115*
40:27, *832*
41:7, *157*
41:20, *909*
41:21, *329*
41:22, *330*
42:7, *320*
42:9, *883*
42:22, *397*
42:24, *397*
43:12, *113*
43:15, *329*
43:19, *330, 883*
44, *930*
44:6, *329*
44:23, *74*
44:24, *48*
44:25, *880, 882*
44:28, *171*
45:6-8, *47*
45:7, *47, 649*
45:18, *114*
46, *930*
47:1-15, *919*
47:8, *115*
47:10, *115, 878, 880, 882*
48:6-8, *62*
49—54, *239*
49:6, *938*
49:13, *67, 74*
49:14, *397*
49:17, *397*
49:19, *397*
49:23, *159*
50:1, *397*
51, *48*
51:9, *45, 46*
51:9-10, *45, 48*
51:9-11, *50*
51:12, *327*
52:3, *397*
52:5, *397*
53:10, *811*
54:1, *401, 938*
54:5, *680*
54:8, *680*
55:1-5, *329*
55:3, *329*
55:3-5, *329*
55:5, *938*
55:8-9, *909*
55:11, *938*
55:12, *74*
55:13, *188*
56—66, *849*
56:1-8, *258*
57:13, *12*
57:15, *398*
59:4-15, *391*
59:7, *56*
59:19, *74*
60:1, *74*
60:2, *158*
60:6, *429*
61, *22*
61:1, *119, 398*
62:3-5, *762, 768*
62:4, *455*
62:11, *74*

63:7—64:11, *398*
63:7—64:12, *398*
63:10-11, *398*
63:14, *398*
65:8, *879*
65:17-25, *62*
66:2, *398*
66:22-23, *67*

Jeremiah
2, *239*
2—25, *266*
2:1-2, *453*
2:2, *459*
2:13, *520*
2:15, *311*
2:18, *399*
2:22, *618*
2:36, *399*
3:1-5, *762*
3:9, *225*
4:22, *882*
5:22, *201*
5:24, *201*
5:31, *399*
6:6, *136*
6:25, *399*
6:28, *225*
7, *861, 870, 875*
7:1-8, *875*
7:1-15, *408*
7:3, *875*
7:6, *136*
7:9, *400*
8:4, *879*
8:5, *615*
8:7, *51*
8:8-9, *882*
8:18—9:1, *389*
9:10, *400*
9:14, *399*
9:16-21, *400*
9:17, *400, 410, 902*
9:17-22, *400*
9:20, *917*
10:7, *895*
10:10, *114*
10:12, *49, 882*
10:23-25, *389*
11:18-20, *389*
12:1-4, *389*
13:12, *879*
14:1—15:4, *402*
14:2-9, *391*
14:17, *399*
15:12, *879*
15:15-18, *389*
16:5, *743*
16:6, *410*
16:8, *22*
17:9, *857*
17:14-18, *389*
18:18, *882, 895*
18:18-23, *882*
18:19-23, *389*
20:7, *399*
20:7-12, *389*
22:13-17, *22*
22:17, *136*
23:15, *399*
23:28, *532, 879*
24:7, *398*

25:20-21, *865*
26, *883*
26:4-6, *399*
26:18-19, *408*
26:23, *37*
27, *850*
29, *881*
29:1-2, *477*
31:29, *281, 400, 532, 879*
31:29-30, *881*
31:30, *881*
31:31-33, *815*
31:31-34, *398*
31:35, *45*
32, *380*
32—33, *320*
33:10-11, *73*
33:11, *73, 77*
36, *794*
37:5-10, *399*
38:6, *321, 399*
38:22, *400*
39, *320*
39:1, *402*
39:1-10, *402*
39:5-7, *526*
41, *402*
41:1-3, *402*
41:4-9, *402*
41:5, *236, 393, 410*
48:36, *616*
49:7, *346, 372, 429, 882*
49:20, *372*
49:24, *879*
50:34, *382*
50:35, *882*
51:15, *882*
51:34, *46, 51*
51:38, *311*
51:57, *882*
52:6-11, *402*
52:12-13, *460*
52:12-16, *402*

Lamentations
1, *97, 214, 228, 236, 316, 393, 399, 400, 401, 403, 404, 409, 524, 773, 918, 936*
1—2, *399*
1—3, *403, 661*
1—4, *2, 97, 399, 403, 524*
1—5, *4*
1:1, *40, 291, 404, 414, 417, 455, 517, 788, 833, 918*
1:1-2, *517*
1:1-7, *730*
1:1-11, *401, 404*
1:1-16, *801*
1:1-18, *96*
1:1-22, *98*
1:2, *327, 404, 406, 417, 812*
1:2-4, *788*
1:3, *406*

1:4, *417, 516,*
934, 940
1:5, *214, 257,*
404, 407, 419,
775, 813, 832
1:6, *291, 404,*
517, 940
1:7, *644, 813*
1:8, *214, 291,*
415, 417, 419,
813
1:8-9, *404, 407,*
424, 918
1:9, *214, 257,*
327, 404, 406,
518, 812
1:9-10, *834*
1:10, *21, 399,*
404, 517, 934
1:10-12, *96, 801*
1:11, *219, 257,*
404, 407, 432
1:12, *257, 278,*
405, 407, 518,
813, 823, 918
1:12-13, *214*
1:12-14, *919*
1:12-16, *401, 404*
1:13, *403*
1:13-14, *776*
1:14, *257, 407,*
813
1:15, *257, 407,*
517, 813
1:15-17, *940*
1:16, *16, 327,*
406, 407, 417,
518, 833
1:16-17, *517*
1:17, *214, 327,*
401, 404, 407,
455, 517, 813
1:18, *257, 407,*
419, 424, 665,
813, 919
1:18-19, *404*
1:18-22, *401, 404*
1:20, *257, 407,*
417, 436
1:20-22, *404*
1:21, *327, 404,*
407, 813, 821
1:21-22, *316, 407*
1:22, *403, 407,*
415, 775
2, *236, 400, 401,*
403, 404, 524,
664, 773, 832,
833
2—4, *3, 97, 101,*
399
2:1, *117, 257,*
291, 400, 406,
517, 823, 940
2:1-2, *417*
2:1-10, *404*
2:1-12, *401*
2:2, *100, 257,*
424, 483, 517
2:3, *400, 403, 813*
2:4, *400, 517,*
813, 829
2:4-5, *776*

2:5, *23, 96, 100,*
101, 400, 476,
483, 517, 801,
813, 831
2:6, *101, 406,*
517, 940
2:6-7, *934*
2:7, *21, 23, 257,*
406, 776, 813
2:7-8, *23*
2:8, *101, 257,*
517, 940
2:9, *100, 406*
2:10, *404, 517,*
833, 940
2:11, *101*
2:11-12, *404, 518*
2:11-13, *436*
2:12, *219*
2:13, *100, 517*
2:13-19, *404, 518*
2:14, *399, 407*
2:15, *517, 940*
2:15-16, *291*
2:16, *407, 821*
2:17, *257, 407,*
424, 813, 831
2:18, *23, 257,*
407, 517, 940
2:18-19, *404, 405,*
407
2:19, *407, 436*
2:19-20, *518*
2:19-21, *833*
2:20, *21, 37, 257,*
405, 407, 424,
436, 518, 776,
934
2:20-21, *407*
2:20-22, *213, 401,*
405
2:21, *424, 465,*
813, 821
2:21-22, *823*
2:22, *399*
3, *1, 236, 260,*
278, 281, 288,
389, 391, 393,
399, 400, 401,
402, 403, 405,
408, 409, 424,
451, 517, 518,
524, 773, 813,
940
3—4, *832*
3:1, *400, 405*
3:1-17, *405*
3:1-18, *257*
3:1-20, *257, 405*
3:1-24, *458*
3:1-40, *403*
3:2, *400*
3:4, *400*
3:5, *400*
3:6, *320*
3:6-9, *320, 321*
3:7, *320*
3:8, *407, 425*
3:9, *320*
3:10, *15, 16*
3:11, *16*
3:13, *829*
3:14, *291, 399*

3:15, *222, 399*
3:17, *661*
3:18, *100, 257,*
291, 776
3:18-20, *405*
3:19, *222, 399*
3:19-30, *407*
3:19-39, *407*
3:20-26, *824*
3:21-22, *436*
3:21-24, *405*
3:21-26, *934*
3:21-33, *405, 408*
3:22, *405*
3:22-23, *780, 823*
3:22-24, *3, 330*
3:22-27, *777*
3:22-33, *814*
3:23, *405*
3:24, *257*
3:25, *405, 815*
3:25-26, *257*
3:25-39, *405*
3:26, *405, 824*
3:27, *405, 821*
3:28, *405, 417*
3:29, *405*
3:30, *405*
3:31-32, *417, 934*
3:31-33, *56, 436,*
813, 824
3:32, *405*
3:33, *405, 408*
3:33-38, *405*
3:33-39, *408*
3:34, *417*
3:34-36, *408*
3:34-38, *407*
3:35, *425*
3:36, *257, 425*
3:37-38, *405, 408,*
813
3:39, *405, 407,*
408
3:39-42, *407*
3:40, *257, 403,*
405, 407, 408
3:40-41, *436*
3:40-42, *407, 934*
3:40-47, *401*
3:41, *405*
3:41-47, *405*
3:41-66, *403*
3:42—5:22, *436*
3:43, *424, 813*
3:44, *425, 813*
3:45, *291, 813*
3:47, *100*
3:47-48, *405*
3:48, *101, 405*
3:48-51, *399, 401,*
405
3:49, *405*
3:50, *257, 405,*
661
3:51, *405*
3:52, *17*
3:52-58, *405*
3:52-66, *405, 407*
3:53, *399, 417*
3:53-62, *96, 801*
3:55, *425*
3:55-56, *407*

3:56, *425*
3:57, *425*
3:58, *257*
3:58-59, *382, 425*
3:59, *407*
3:59-66, *405, 813*
3:61, *291*
3:62, *616*
3:63, *291*
3:64, *257*
3:64-66, *407*
3:66, *101*
4, *236, 399, 400,*
401, 403, 405,
524, 661, 773,
917, 940
4—5, *403, 404,*
661
4:1-6, *401*
4:1-10, *406*
4:2, *940*
4:2-4, *518*
4:3, *16, 17, 406,*
528
4:4, *436, 833*
4:5, *96*
4:5-8, *801*
4:6, *406, 455, 833*
4:7-8, *436*
4:9, *436*
4:9-10, *518*
4:10, *101, 406,*
436
4:11, *257, 813,*
940
4:11-16, *406,*
801
4:13, *406, 407,*
424, 665, 813,
940
4:14, *406*
4:15, *400*
4:16, *291*
4:17, *399, 403,*
406
4:17-20, *96, 399,*
406, 801
4:19, *17*
4:19-22, *801*
4:20, *406, 416,*
418, 526, 527
4:21, *371, 865*
4:21-22, *401, 406,*
407, 517
4:22, *400, 517,*
813, 940
5, *3, 236, 391,*
399, 400, 401,
403, 406, 407,
424, 476, 518,
661
5:1, *257, 406,*
407, 813, 815
5:1-13, *801*
5:1-14, *291*
5:2, *406, 407*
5:2-5, *406*
5:3, *528*
5:6-7, *406*
5:7, *400, 407, 424*
5:8, *406, 407*
5:11, *455, 833,*
940

5:12, *291*
5:14, *403*
5:15, *403*
5:16, *406, 407*
5:16-17, *801*
5:17, *96, 403*
5:18, *16, 483, 940*
5:19, *257, 406,*
407, 483, 813,
825
5:19-22, *258*
5:20, *406, 407,*
424, 813, 815
5:20-22, *777*
5:21, *257, 406,*
407, 461, 775,
919
5:21-22, *776,*
815
5:22, *406, 407,*
461
8, *205*

Ezekiel
1, *569, 624*
1:1-28, *460*
3:12, *460*
6:9, *225*
7:26, *883*
9:6, *465*
9:9, *534*
10, *408*
11:1-2, *883*
11:3, *879*
12:10, *878*
13, *850*
14, *374*
14:12-14, *362*
14:14, *336, 371,*
374
14:20, *336, 371,*
374
15:2-8, *879*
16, *239, 453, 834*
16:8, *380*
16:10-13, *835,*
837, 839
16:15-34, *836*
16:25, *762*
16:35-42, *455*
16:36, *919*
16:44, *879*
17:1-10, *532*
18:1-20, *238*
18:2, *400, 534,*
879, 881
18:20, *362*
18:25, *534*
18:29, *534*
19:1-9, *400*
19:10-14, *400*
20, *453*
20:45-49, *532*
22:7, *910*
22:25, *311*
23, *453, 834*
23:14-15, *624*
25:13, *372*
26:17-18, *400*
27:2-36, *400*
27:8-9, *902*
28, *882*
28:2, *113*

28:11-19, *400*
28:13-16, *113*
29:3, *46, 50*
32:2, *46, 50*
32:12-16, *400*
32:16, *400*
33:21, *461*
34:23, *879*
36:24-32, *398*
36:27, *398*
37:1-14, *459*
38:18—39:16,*
463
40:6, *620*
40:22, *620*
40:26, *620*
40:31, *620*
40:34, *620*
40:37, *620*
40:49, *620*
43:17, *620*
45:10, *731*
47:1-12, *113*

Daniel
1, *851*
1—6, *181, 240,*
427, 873
1:1, *873*
1:2, *178, 871*
1:8, *178*
2, *839, 851, 877*
2—6, *851*
2:1, *873*
2:12, *895*
2:21, *871*
2:31-33, *616*
2:38, *178*
3:5-7, *930*
3:10-12, *930*
3:14-18, *930*
3:28, *930*
4, *851*
5, *851*
6:8, *426, 875*
6:20, *875*
7, *50, 51, 851*
7—12, *850, 851*
7:1, *873*
7:10, *6*
8, *851*
8:1, *873*
8:2, *781*
8:16, *781*
9, *402, 404, 851*
9:1, *873*
9:2, *35*
9:24-25, *873*
10:1, *873*
10:10-21, *852*
10:13, *115, 382*
10:20, *115*
10:21, *6, 382*
12:1-3, *382*
12:2, *5, 6, 53*

Hosea
1—2, *453*
1—3, *211, 239,*
739, 762
1:2, *225*
2, *211, 834, 835*
2:6, *528*

4:14, *881*
4:16, *881*
6:6, *870*
7:4-5, *879*
8:7, *881*
9:1, *401, 491*
9:10, *881*
9:13, *881*
9:16, *881*
10:1, *881*
10:4, *881*
11:10, *311*
13:13, *881*
14:5, *617*
14:6, *881*
14:9, *330, 881*

Joel
1:13-16, *393*
2:15-17, *393*
2:21-24, *401*
3:13, *616*
3:18, *113*

Amos
1—2, *534, 881*
1:2, *311*
1:12, *372*
2:6-7, *136*
2:6-16, *228*
3:3-6, *879*
3:3-8, *879*
3:4, *311*
3:8, *311, 312*
3:14, *527*
4:1, *136*
5:2, *400*
5:8, *47*
5:21-24, *14*
5:21-26, *75*
6:1-7, *750*
6:5, *618*
6:7, *743*
6:12, *879*
7:14, *877*
8:5, *910*
8:14, *113*
9:2, *53*
9:7, *879*

Obadiah
1:8, *895*
9, *3728, 346,*
429

Micah
2:1-2, *692*
2:4, *532*
2:8, *561*
3, *850*
3:12, *408, 883*
5:2, *673*
5:5, *511*
6:6-8, *14*
6:8, *196*
6:9, *201*

Nahum
1:4, *44*
1:10, *771*

Habakkuk
1:1, *878*

1:2-4, *389*
1:6-8, *16*
1:12—2:1, *389*
2:5, *52*
2:6-8, *532*
3, *230, 486, 615,*
734, 774
3:1, *615, 619*
3:3, *616*
3:8-9, *44*
3:9, *616*
3:10, *44*
3:13, *616*
3:19, *486, 615*

Zephaniah
3:3, *311*
3:14, *401*
3:14-20, *239*

Zechariah
1—8, *409, 717*
1:1, *37*
3:1, *714, 716*
3:1-2, *714, 715*
3:1-5, *382*
3:2, *716*
7, *402*
7—8, *402*
7:3, *402*
7:3-5, *236, 393*
7:5, *402, 460*
7:12, *35*
8:18-23, *393*
8:19, *236, 402*
9—14, *264, 611,*
849
9:1, *878*
9:9, *401*
11:3, *309*
12:1, *878*
14:1-21, *462*
14:8, *113*
14:16, *462*

Malachi
1:1, *878*
1:2-5, *108*
1:6, *879*
1:6—2:9, *108*
2:3, *71*
2:10-16, *108,*
207
2:14-15, *879*
2:17, *879*
2:17—3:5, *108*
3, *218, 861*
3:5, *702, 910*
3:6-12, *108*
3:7-8, *879*
3:13-14, *879*
3:13—4:3, *108*
3:16, *6*
4:5-6, *724*

Apocrypha

Additions to
Esther
12:3, *426*
13:1, *719*
13:8-17, *296*
14:9, *21*

Baruch
3:9, *424*
4:1, *424*

1 Esdras
4:48, *222*
5:55, *222*

2 Esdras
14:45, *37*
16:32, *222*
16:77, *222*

4 Ezra
1:1, *848*

Judith
4:9-15, *582*

1 Maccabees
1:56, *36*
4:36-61, *620*
7:26-50, *632*

2 Maccabees
2:13, *36*
2:14, *36*
2:26-27, *184*
10:1-9, *620*
15:36, *186, 632*

4 Maccabees
1:16-17, *845*

Sirach
1, *915*
1—43, *722, 723,*
724
1:1, *723, 725, 726*
1:1-10, *84, 723,*
724
1:1—23:28, *723*
1:1—43:33, *723*
1:3, *723*
1:4, *723, 725, 915*
1:8-9, *725*
1:9, *725*
1:9-10, *915*
1:11, *723*
1:11-20, *725*
1:11-30, *723*
1:11—2:17, *723*
1:14, *725*
1:16, *725*
1:17, *22*
1:18, *725*
1:19, *723*
1:20, *723, 725*
1:26, *725*
2:1-6, *725, 726*
2:7-17, *722*
2:12-14, *722*
2:15-16, *725*
2:16, *725*
3:1-16, *723*
3:9, *22*
3:17-29, *723*
3:30—4:10, *723*
4:4-5, *726*
4:7, *722*
4:10, *726*
4:13, *723*
5:9, *732*

5:11-12, *727*
6:5-17, *723*
6:24-28, *726*
6:37, *725*
7:10, *726*
7:14, *722, 726*
7:29-31, *82*
9:1-9, *723*
9:9, *220*
9:12-13, *723*
9:17—10:18,
723
10:5, *719*
10:19, *725, 726*
10:19-20, *723*
10:26—11:6, *723,*
725
10:27, *219*
12:4-7, *726*
12:5, *219*
13:15-24, *723*
13:25—14:10,
723
14:1-2, *535, 722*
14:11-19, *723*
14:13, *726*
14:20, *722*
14:20—15:10,
722
14:24, *23*
15:1, *725, 845,*
915
15:11-20, *723*
15:14-15, *725*
16:5-14, *723*
17:1-24, *84*
17:22, *221*
18:1-14, *84*
18:15-18, *723*
19:2, *220, 723*
19:4-17, *723*
19:20, *725, 915*
19:20-30, *722,*
723, 726
20:1-8, *723*
20:18-26, *723*
20:20, *226*
20:31, *722*
21:1-10, *723*
21:4, *22*
21:11, *725*
21:11—22:2, *723*
21:15, *724*
21:18, *22*
22:7-18, *723*
22:17, *23*
22:19-27, *723*
22:27—23:6, *723*
23:7-15, *723*
23:11, *22*
23:16-17, *534*
23:16-18, *722*
23:16-27, *723*
23:18, *23*
23:22-26, *723*
23:27, *725*
24, *82, 725, 846,*
915
24:1-34, *84, 723,*
724, 725
24:1—43:33, *723*
24:2, *725*
24:3, *723*

24:3-17, *725*
24:4, *725*
24:5, *723*
24:5-6, *725*
24:7, *725*
24:7-8, *725*
24:8, *725, 915*
24:8-9, *725*
24:9, *723*
24:9-12, *471*
24:10, *725*
24:13, *222*
24:13-17, *219*
24:15, *221*
24:16, *723*
24:19, *726*
24:19-29, *887*
24:22-23, *915*
24:23, *422, 725,*
877
24:23-27, *725*
24:23-29, *725*
24:30-34, *725*
25:1-2, *722*
25:1-11, *723*
25:7-11, *722*
25:8-9, *722*
25:16-26, *723*
25:24, *723*
26:1, *722*
26:5-6, *722*
26:10-16, *294*
26:28, *722*
27:1-3, *22*
27:4-10, *723*
27:11-21, *723*
27:22-29, *723*
27:30—28:11,
723
28:2, *726*
28:12-26, *723,*
727
28:14, *22*
28:24, *222*
29:1-7, *731*
29:1-28, *723*
30:1-17, *723*
30:18-25, *723*
30:19, *725*
31:1-11, *723*
31:8-10, *725*
31:10, *725*
31:12—32:2, *723*
31:25-31, *220*
31:28, *220*
32:3-13, *723*
32:5-6, *220*
32:14-17, *723*
32:15-16, *725*
32:18—33:3, *722*
32:23-24, *725*
33:1-3, *725*
33:2, *915*
33:14-15, *726*
33:16-17, *220,*
722
33:16-18, *721*
33:20-24, *723*
33:24-31, *723*
34:1-11, *723*
34:8, *725*
34:9-12, *721*
34:14-20, *723*

34:21—35:13,
723
34:22-23, *725*
35:1, *725*
35:1-13, *725*
35:8, *725*
35:11-13, *731*
35:14-20, *723*
35:20, *725*
36:1-22, *723*
36:13, *21*
36:14, *21*
37:1-6, *723*
37:16-26, *723*
37:27-31, *723*
38:1-15, *723*
38:9-15, *727*
38:16-23, *723*
38:24, *721*
38:24-25, *721*
38:24—39:11,
895
38:24—39:35,
722
38:34, *422, 844*
39:1-2, *725*
39:1-5, *721*
39:1, *721*
39:5-6, *82*
39:12-35, *84,*
723
39:14, *221*
39:15, *84*
39:15—40:8, *720*
39:16-34, *85*
39:26, *219, 220*
39:35, *85*
40:10, *723*
40:19-26, *535*
40:20, *220*
40:28, *722*
40:28-30, *723*
41:1-4, *723*
41:8, *722, 725*
41:8-9, *722*
41:11-14, *723,*
725
41:14, *725*
41:15—42:8, *723*
42:1-5, *731*
42:2, *722, 725*
42:9-12, *294*
42:9-14, *723*
42:10, *21*
42:13-14, *723*
42:13—43:33, *84*
42:15—43:33,
723
44—49, *722, 725*
44—50, *727, 887*
44:1-15, *724, 726*
44:1—49:16, *723,*
724
44:1—50:24, *723*
44:3, *724*
44:3-6, *724*
44:16, *724, 725,*
726
44:16—45:26,
724
44:16—49:16,
724
44:17, *725*

44:20, *724, 725*
45:1-5, *724*
45:2, *724*
45:4, *725*
45:6-22, *724*
45:7, *724*
45:12, *724*
45:14, *725*
45:23, *724, 725*
46—51, *82*
46:1, *724*
46:1—49:16, *724*
46:2, *724*
46:4-6, *725*
46:8, *220*
46:11, *725*
46:11-12, *724*
47, *579*
47:3, *724*
47:8, *579, 725*
47:8-10, *614*
47:11, *724*
47:12-21, *726*
47:13, *21, 726*
47:14, *726*
47:17, *761*
47:19, *724, 726*
47:21, *724*
48:10, *724*
48:13, *724*
48:15, *21*
48:17-22, *724*
48:20, *724*
48:21, *724*
48:22, *725*
48:23, *724*
49:1, *220, 724,*
725
49:9, *39*
49:10, *724*
49:12, *21*
49:16, *724*
50, *720*
50:1-4, *724*
50:1-24, *724*
50:1-26, *82*
50:1—51:30, *723,*
724
50:5, *724*
50:5-21, *724*
50:8, *221*
50:10, *220*
50:12, *222*
50:15, *220*
50:25-26, *722,*
724, 726
50:27, *720, 721*
50:27-29, *725*
50:28, *725*
51, *91*
51:1-12, *723, 724*
51:1-30, *724*
51:12, *724*
51:13-16, *722*
51:13-20, *723,*
798
51:13-30, *2, 4,*
234, 724
51:15, *82, 84*
51:23, *706*
51:23-27, *726*
51:23-30, *721*

51:30, *720*

Tobit
3:8, *715*
3:17, *715*

Wisdom of
Solomon
1—5, *852*
1—9, *886*
1:1—5:23, *886*
1:1—6:21, *886*
1:1—9:18, *886*
1:4-5, *852*
2—5, *852*
2:7, *220*
2:12—5:14, *885*
3:1-8, *846*
3:1-9, *887*
3:2, *887*
4:1, *844*
4:7-17, *7*
4:10-14, *726*
5, *852*
5:13, *844*
5:15-16, *846*
6:1—9:18, *886*
6:14, *23*
6:22—10:21, *886*
7:1, *83*
7:6, *887*
7:22, *64*
7:25-26, *845, 916*
8:7, *844*
8:16, *22*
8:17, *852*
8:19-20, *846, 887*
9:5, *83*
9:7-8, *885*
9:8, *846*
9:18, *852*
10, *726*
10—19, *886*
10:1-14, *886*
10:1-21, *846*
10:1—19:22, *886*
10:15-21, *727,*
890, 916
10:15—19:22,
886
10:19, *889*
11—19, *846, 886*
13—15, *82, 84*
13:10, *844*
14:4, *844*
16:13, *23*
16:16, *846*
16:18, *846*
16:20, *219*
17:7, *844*
18:4, *845*
19:1, *846*
19:22, *886*

New Testament

Matthew
1, *472*
1:1-17, *677*
1:1-18, *695*
1:3-6, *683*
1:5, *32, 33, 40,*
673, 685, 700

1:5-6, *299*
4:6, *606*
5:3-11, *535*
5:17, *36, 738*
5:22, *226*
5:39-41, *319*
5:42, *726*
5:43-46, *194*
5:43-48, *199*
5:44, *398, 726*
5:44-48, *294*
5:45, *726*
6:7, *726*
6:12, *726*
6:23, *726*
6:28, *617*
6:29, *733*
7:26-27, *226*
8:23-27, *45*
9:15, *764*
10:16, *735*
11, *915*
11:18-19, *915*
11:19, *551, 915*
11:28-30, *726*
12:41, *737*
12:42, *733, 737*
13:52, *719*
14:22-34, *45*
15:18, *100*
16:27, *569*
21:9, *606*
21:16, *606*
21:18-22, *317*
21:42, *606*
22:29, *36*
22:32, *811*
22:41-46, *615*
22:43, *606*
22:43-45, *606*
22:44-45, *606*
23, *41*
23:21-22, *119*
23:35, *37, 41*
23:37, *525, 527*
23:39, *606*
25:1, *764*
25:1-13, *227*
25:5, *764*
25:33-34, *608*
27:35, *592*
27:39, *592*
27:43, *592*
27:46, *408, 592*

Mark
1:1—3:12, *875*
1:7, *696*
1:11, *469*
1:21-22, *550*
6:2, *550*
9:2-8, *820*
10:33, *620*
11:9, *606*
11:12-14, *317*
11:20-25, *317*
12:10, *606*
12:28-31, *194*
12:35-37, *86, 614*
12:36, *606*
12:36-37, *606*
15:24, *592*
15:29, *592*
15:34, *408, 592*

Luke
1:26-38, *685*
2:4, *620*
2:40, *550*
2:41-51, *550*
2:52, *550*
3:16, *696*
3:32, *40, 299, 685*
4:10-11, *606*
4:16-21, *378*
6:27-31, *194*
6:28, *317, 319*
9:31, *887*
11, *41*
11:31, *733, 737, 915*
11:50, *41*
11:51, *37*
12:27, *617, 733*
13:1-5, *654*
13:34-35, *408*
13:35, *606*
18:1, *726*
19:38, *606*
20:17, *606*
20:42, *86*
20:42-44, *606*
23:34, *592, 726*
23:35, *592*
24:27, *738*
24:44, *471, 578*
24:44-46, *815*

John
1:1, *197, 915*

1:1-3, *551*
1:1-18, *845*
1:2-3, *915*
1:4-5, *47*
1:10, *551*
1:14-18, *860*
1:27, *696*
1:41, *466*
2:19-21, *458*
3:2, *119*
3:29, *764*
4:12-14, *737*
4:21-24, *119*
4:25, *466*
5, *632*
5:1, *632*
5:30, *378*
7:39, *118*
8:10, *317*
8:12, *47*
8:53-58, *737*
9, *342, 654*
9:1-3, *654*
10:10, *305*
10:22, *620*
10:34, *36*
10:35, *36*
12:13, *606*
14:17, *118*
15:25, *36*
19:24, *592*
19:36, *36*

Acts
2:24-36, *86*
2:25, *606*
2:25-28, *606*
2:25-29, *615*
2:27, *470*
2:29-36, *614*
2:30, *606*
2:31, *606*
2:34-35, *606*
4:10-11, *606*
4:11, *606*
4:23-31, *469*
4:24-26, *592*
4:24-28, *377*
4:25, *606*
4:25-26, *468, 615*
4:27-28, *169*
7, *722*
7:47, *733*
10:4, *620*
10:38, *119*

13:15, *36*
13:25, *696*
13:32-33, *377*
13:33, *469, 592*
13:35, *470*
13:35-37, *614*
18:24, *36*

Romans
1:4, *36, 469*
2:6, *569*
2:28-29, *685*
3:4, *606*
3:10, *141*
3:10-18, *606*
4, *698*
4:7-8, *606*
4:16-17, *258*
5:1-5, *886*
8:9, *118*
8:18-25, *62, 141*
8:19-22, *69*
8:20, *141, 813, 814*
9—11, *278*
11:9-10, *606*
12:14, *317, 319*
12:17, *294*
12:19, *318*
12:20, *569*
12:21, *294*
13:1-7, *526*
16:20, *50*

1 Corinthians
1, *569, 570*
1:17-31, *569*
1:18-25, *227*
1:18-31, *727, 858*
1:24, *519, 569*
1:30, *550, 816, 915*
3:16, *118, 119*
6:19, *118, 119*
10:6, *737*
10:11, *737*
13:12, *816*
15:25, *469*
15:54, *53*
16:22, *317*

2 Corinthians
1:20, *738*
5:17, *62*

Galatians
1:8-9, *317*
2:9, *119*
3:6-9, *258*
4:26, *483*
6:7, *654*

Ephesians
2:19-22, *119*
5, *764*
5:8-14, *47*
5:18, *808*
5:19, *485*
5:19-20, *592*
5:24-33, *745*
6:16, *526*

Colossians
1:15, *901*
1:15-17, *519, 551, 845, 915*
1:15-29, *62*
1:16, *551*
1:16-17, *48*
2:1-8, *858*
2:2-3, *519*
2:3, *550, 915*
3:16, *592*

1 Thessalonians
5:13, *808*

1 Timothy
2:1-2, *526*

2 Timothy
3:14-17, *467*
3:15, *36*
3:16, *865*
3:16-17, *738*

Hebrews
1:1-2, *853*
1:3, *469*
1:5, *469, 592*
1:5-13, *606*
1:8, *741*
1:14, *114*
3:3, *737, 930*
3:7, *823*
3:7—4:13, *606*
3:13, *823*
3:15, *823*
4:7, *615, 823*
5:5, *469, 592*

5:6, *469*
7:1—9:28, *408*
7:17, *469*
7:21, *469*
10:30, *318*
11, *176, 722*
11:3, *48*
11:35, *37*
12:5-6, *569*
12:22-23, *408*
12:22-25, *483*

James
1:2-4, *726*
1:5, *726*
1:19, *727*
3:1-12, *727*
3:1-18, *330*
3:9, *318*
3:15-17, *726*
5, *366*
5:7-11, *362*
5:11, *330, 336, 362, 366, 371, 374, 812, 824*
5:14-16, *727*
5:20, *530*

1 Peter
1:3-5, *33*
1:10-11, *467*
2:5, *119*
2:13-17, *526*
3:9, *294*
4:8, *569*
4:18, *569*
5:5, *569*

2 Peter
1:17, *469*
1:20, *36*
2:22, *569*

1 John
3:2, *816*

Jude
9, *37*
14-15, *37*

Revelation
1—3, *820*
1:3, *848*
1:5, *329*
1:8, *2*

1:13-16, *838*
1:17-18, *169*
3:12, *119*
3:14, *551, 915*
4:2, *592*
4:9, *592*
4:11, *930*
5—8, *820*
5:1, *592*
5:7, *592*
5:9, *592, 930*
5:12, *930*
5:13, *592*
6, *852*
6:10, *317*
6:16, *592*
7:10, *592*
7:17, *592*
8—11, *820*
9:11, *101*
11:17, *50, 303*
11:18, *469*
12, *53*
12—13, *51*
12:3, *46, 50*
12:9, *46*
12:15, *46*
13:1, *46, 50*
14:3, *592*
14:8, *318*
15—16, *820*
16:19, *318*
17—18, *820*
17:3, *46, 50*
18:2, *318*
18:21, *318*
19—20, *820*
19:1, *592*
19:3, *592*
19:4, *592*
19:6, *50, 592*
19:19, *469*
20, *50*
20:2, *46*
21, *408, 764*
21—22, *820*
21:1, *47, 50*
21:4, *53*
21:5, *592*
21:9—22:5, *592*
21:25, *47*
22:3, *319*
22:13, *2*

Subject Index

abomination, 251, 294, 529, 534-35, 543-44, 675, 908, 934
accentual meter, 473-75
Accuser, 108, 114, 210, 340-41, 422-23, 715
acrostic, 1-4, 97, 104, 199, 207, 228, 236-37, 260, 352, 397, 399, 403, 406, 440, 452-53, 464, 499, 523-24, 529, 536, 575, 585, 601, 659, 661, 679, 681, 723-24, 773-74, 780, 921
act-consequence nexus, 907-9
Adad-guppi Autobiography, 134
additions to Esther, 176, 182
admonitions, 82, 103, 108, 127, 152, 201, 205, 243-44, 256, 324, 428, 533-34, 539, 542, 549, 554-56, 561, 574, 695, 729, 731, 832, 845, 900, 903, 910
Admonitions of Ipuwer, 354-356, 574, 809
Adversary, 278, 336, 717
afterlife, 5-8, 101, 111, 129, 354, 359, 370, 436-37, 449-50, 597, 650-51, 710, 712, 781, 825, 846, 909
Agur, 236, 264, 269, 427-30, 537, 540-41, 548, 552-55, 557-60, 562, 564-65, 708, 800, 867-68, 878
Ahasuerus, 8, 9-10, 101, 161, 163, 172, 176-81, 183, 185, 189, 215-16, 240, 275, 295-96, 321, 455, 476, 492, 644, 781, 826-27, 922
Ahiqar, 135-36, 335, 430, 529, 547, 552-55, 557-58, 704, 731, 898-99
Akitu festival, 74, 581
Akkadian, 29-31, 42, 80, 85, 111, 134, 139-40, 161, 171, 335, 346-48, 351, 360, 403, 413, 450, 481, 553-55, 557-58, 561, 574, 595-96, 599, 600-601, 605, 618-19, 636, 640, 655, 688-90, 704, 708, 750, 756-59, 767, 782, 841, 850, 865, 875, 896-97, 901, 926, 929
alef-bet, 2-3
allegory, allegorical interpretation, 40, 144, 211, 229, 231, 237, 239, 257, 271, 306, 310-11, 344, 428, 456, 459, 472, 488, 532, 536, 570, 606-8, 680, 696-98, 738, 740-42, 744, 760-69, 845, 894, 919, 934
alliteration, 348, 439, 512, 521, 523, 543, 588, 656, 770, 772, 925
alphabet, 1-4, 37, 97, 199, 228, 236, 260, 399, 524, 536, 541, 601, 705, 706-7, 718, 895, 906
ambiguity, 11-13, 62, 91, 161, 261, 276, 326, 375, 378, 444, 493, 495, 504, 545, 660, 670, 678, 792-94, 809, 925-27, 928
Ambrose, 144, 367, 371, 417, 571, 696-97
Amenemope, 264, 529-30, 534, 538, 541, 545-47, 552-56, 558, 561-66, 574, 708, 809

Amestris, 10, 162, 172-73, 189, 826-28
angel of Yahweh, 114, 118
animals, 7, 14-15, 19-20, 82, 127, 129, 134, 312, 346, 431-32, 482, 526-27, 591, 617, 625-26, 628-29, 818, 830, 838, 869-70, 895, 13-19, 21, 45, 65-70, 127, 129, 159, 211, 219, 239, 318, 352, 372, 384, 431, 433, 466, 482, 487, 516, 583, 598, 617, 639, 666, 704, 711, 744, 813, 822, 869-70, 930, 940
anointed one, 278, 416, 466, 469, 670
anointing, 27, 118, 137, 278, 327, 351, 375, 390, 416-17, 466-72, 507, 517, 526, 592, 670, 685, 727, 752, 819, 918, 937
anthropology, 80-81, 111, 133, 136, 206, 230, 233, 288, 294, 299, 327, 507, 856, 872, 904, 914
anti-Semitism, 476, 479, 874
antithetic parallelism, 503, 505, 521, 543, 586
aphorisms, 102, 107, 254, 277, 532, 558, 565, 569, 573, 575-76, 656, 658, 722, 879, 881, 883
apocalyptic, 5, 35, 50-51, 93, 160, 182, 185, 711, 846-53, 873
apostolic fathers, 606, 612
apostrophe, 306, 404, 589
Aqiba, 740, 761-63
Aquila, 36, 618, 797, 799, 801, 803-4
Aquinas, 369-70, 417
Aramaic, 1, 39, 91, 93-94, 97-98, 123-24, 132, 135-36, 149, 175, 178, 184, 218, 227-28, 260, 263-68, 271, 273-74, 284, 414, 419, 430, 481, 547, 552-54, 557, 560, 565-66, 568-69, 574, 577, 598, 614, 674-75, 694, 698, 700, 704, 708-9, 763, 784-87, 789-91, 797-99, 802-4, 828, 873, 875-76, 897-98, 930
architecture, 22-24, 133
aromatics, 221
Artaxerxes, 8-10, 37, 162, 170-71, 174-75, 185, 189, 783, 827
artisans, 157, 499, 902, 913
Asaph, 24-27, 73, 76, 102, 234, 263, 386, 486, 499, 608, 611, 619-20, 672, 713, 734
ass, 15, 69
assonance, 439, 512, 521, 588, 770-72
Augustine, 38, 367-68, 371, 473, 512-13, 515, 570-71, 696, 918, 941
authorship, 40, 86, 92-94, 122-24, 145, 147, 206-7, 209-10, 212-13, 229, 234, 237, 269-70, 272, 281-85, 327, 399, 418, 456, 468, 540, 548, 555-57, 572, 579, 607-10, 612, 614-15, 619-20, 636, 668-69, 672-73, 694, 733-36, 738, 767-69, 786, 800, 867, 870, 886, 896

autobiography, 27-30, 134, 146-47, 324, 331, 636, 724, 864, 897
Baal, 18, 42-49, 51-54, 113-15, 236, 263, 439, 455, 483, 551, 583, 598, 600-604, 619, 744-45, 866, 869, 876, 913, 937
Babylonian Theodicy, 1, 81, 84, 111-12, 335, 346, 351, 601, 809, 896
Balag, 413, 595
battle imagery, 831
bears, 16-17
beatitude, 105, 199, 534-35, 806
Behemoth, 20, 45, 60, 65, 67, 69, 70, 222, 339, 818, 840, 908
ben Sira, 36, 720, 727
benevolence, 351, 359, 808, 815, 862
biblical theology, 119, 231, 249, 325, 328, 445, 654, 817, 825, 855, 858
bicolon, bicola, 2-3, 473, 502, 512-13, 520-24, 532, 534, 542, 558, 574, 600
birds, 17-18, 60, 67, 69, 354, 466, 525, 527, 531, 534, 563, 658, 752, 758, 838, 870, 899, 917, 921
bless, blessing, 2, 5, 14, 21, 22, 25, 32-33, 44, 60, 76, 81, 83, 85, 108, 117-18, 150, 152, 167, 195, 203, 205, 210, 220, 235, 247, 250-51, 253, 258, 289-90, 301-2, 304, 314-15, 319, 342, 348, 350, 353, 372, 374, 391, 418-19, 420-21, 427, 433-36, 452-53, 456, 461, 463, 491-92, 521, 528, 535, 543-44, 585, 633, 646, 650, 664-65, 676, 679, 681, 683-85, 701, 711, 713-14, 717, 724, 730, 754-55, 777-81, 814-15, 819, 822, 824, 826, 845, 857, 867, 907, 910, 921-22, 932-34, 937, 939
boars, 17
Boaz, 32-34, 212-13, 219, 240, 258, 275-76, 299, 379-81, 425-26, 454, 490-94, 516, 673-86, 691-98, 701-3, 730-32, 789, 922
breasts, 16, 22, 220-21, 392, 528, 567, 595, 738, 751-53, 757, 760, 764, 835, 838-39, 841, 920
caesura, 506, 520
Cairo Love Songs, 752, 759
Calvin, John, 161, 370, 417
canon, canonicity, 35-41, 89, 91-93, 95, 98, 118, 141-143, 146-149, 160, 163, 164, 169, 177, 180, 211, 212, 254, 256, 257, 273, 274, 283, 284, 327-31, 362, 427, 452, 455-57, 499, 500, 513, 514, 570, 633, 660, 673, 680, 681, 696, 719, 721, 723, 738-40, 744-45, 750, 760-61, 765, 768, 769, 788, 854, 856, 863, 864, 902
canonical approach, 153, 154, 283-84, 328, 376, 470, 580
canto, 140, 772-73
cattle, 14-15, 21, 67, 165, 193, 337,

344, 357, 431, 466, 636, 869, 879
chaff, 158, 432, 435, 659, 731, 811
chaos, 19-20, 41-52, 60-64, 67, 81, 83-84, 237, 249, 304-5, 357, 448, 481-83, 536, 563, 584, 591, 602, 626, 675, 700, 745, 780, 830, 904, 908, 937, 940
Chaoskampf, 42, 44, 46, 48-49, 51, 54, 63-64
chiasm, 54-56, 106, 261, 532, 536, 588, 656-57, 718
church fathers, 35, 38, 176, 366, 416, 455, 485, 570, 606-7, 612, 696, 797
city dirge, 401-2
clause predicators, 261, 522
Code of Hammurabi, 231, 688-89, 692
colon, cola, 2, 51, 252, 323-24, 465-66, 473-75, 502, 509, 512, 520, 521-23, 531, 600-601, 643, 792-94
community lament, 235, 282, 400-401, 403, 406, 410, 580, 582, 591, 595-96, 813, 831-32, 937
comparative studies, 132
complaints, 26-27, 33, 62, 66, 74-75, 108, 137, 203-4, 228, 230, 235-36, 348, 356-57, 360, 366, 370, 373, 375, 384, 386-87, 394-97, 405, 407-8, 410-11, 413, 421, 434, 436, 528, 582, 599, 651, 670, 689, 712, 774, 793, 809, 862, 892-93
Complaints of Khakheperre-sonb, 137, 354, 356
confidence, 5, 57-59, 75, 235-36, 248, 251, 256-57, 266, 268, 289-90, 328, 344, 350-51, 359-60, 363, 370, 373, 383, 386, 390, 399, 408, 419, 425, 437, 467, 470, 500, 528, 540, 603, 642, 659, 711-12, 774, 780, 810, 812, 814-16, 854, 914, 921, 937-38
consonance, 512, 770-72
corporate laments, 384-85, 387-88, 390-94, 396-97, 596
cosmetics, 186, 923
cosmic battle, 60-61
cosmogony, 43, 60, 62, 481
cosmology, 42, 48, 51, 69, 80, 343, 852, 903-4, 938
Counsels of a Pessimist, 134
covenant, 25-27, 32-34, 49, 53, 63, 75, 90, 100, 116, 118-19, 127, 150, 160, 164-68, 174, 183, 185-86, 196-97, 204, 223, 225-26, 229, 236, 246, 249-50, 252, 258, 268, 288-91, 316, 326-29, 344, 364, 372, 376-77, 390, 392-93, 397-98, 405-6, 408, 418-19, 421, 433-34, 436-37, 444, 449, 452-53, 455, 468-69, 470-71, 478, 484, 487-88, 491, 493, 495, 528, 533, 535, 549, 559-60, 565, 576, 579, 581, 590, 599, 610-11, 616-17, 641-42, 645-46, 650-51, 664, 668, 670, 675-76,

680-85, 695, 699, 701, 703, 711, 725, 729, 733-35, 738-39, 769, 776-78, 790, 806, 809-13, 815-16, 819, 824-26, 839, 852, 855-64, 869, 871, 895, 900, 902-3, 909, 915, 920-21, 924, 930, 932, 937, 939

covenant festival, 75, 806

creation, 6, 11, 13-14, 18-20, 30, 33, 42-43, 46-51, 60-70, 79-81, 83, 85-86, 89, 93, 100, 102, 106, 114, 116, 118, 144, 194-95, 197-98, 201-2, 213, 228-30, 235, 237, 249, 251, 253, 255, 257-58, 290, 302-4, 323, 325-26, 328, 330, 335, 368, 371, 391, 417, 431, 481-83, 487, 498-99, 502, 508, 516-17, 519, 531, 533, 547, 550-51, 570, 576, 583, 588, 591, 597, 601-3, 637, 642, 666, 672, 694, 704, 706, 745, 767, 774, 779, 786-87, 789, 811, 814-15, 821, 823, 825-26, 838, 844-45, 854-55, 857-58, 862, 869-72, 891-94, 903-6, 908-10, 913-15, 932-33, 937

creation imagery, 60-62, 583, 591, 893-94

creation theology, 60, 63-65, 68-70, 854, 862, 870, 891, 893, 904, 909

Creator, 14, 20, 62-63, 65, 67-68, 71, 80, 91, 194-95, 197-98, 201, 226, 243, 249-57, 304, 359, 481-82, 580, 583-84, 591, 600, 645, 738, 744, 778-79, 854, 856, 859, 862, 870-71, 876, 903-4, 906, 908-10, 915, 932

cult, 25, 52, 71-84, 127, 150, 196, 209, 225, 230-32, 235, 282-83, 286, 329, 346, 349, 375, 447-49, 484, 525, 527, 556, 559, 576, 578-81, 584-85, 595, 604, 609-11, 616-17, 619, 623, 629, 648, 650, 665, 710, 733-34, 743-45, 750, 753-54, 756-58, 767, 806-7, 842, 846, 859, 869-70, 902, 929-31, 933-34, 937-38, 940

cultic poetry, 230, 235

curses, 32, 68, 75, 88, 117, 203, 210, 222, 238, 289, 314-19, 337, 349, 362, 406, 433, 435-36, 453, 543-44, 650, 681-82, 731, 777-79, 813, Cuthean Legend of Naram-Sin, 897

Dahood, M., 5, 56-57, 135, 138, 156, 160, 263, 267, 499-500, 599, 604, 610, 612, 619-20

Daughter of Zion, 409, 413, 605, 834, 918

David, 3, 14, 22, 24-26, 30-34, 36, 50, 72-73, 76, 86-93, 98, 101, 115, 118, 122, 124-25, 142-43, 151, 229, 234, 236, 238-40, 265-66, 269-70, 272-76, 280, 282-83, 286, 299, 301, 325-27, 329-30, 371, 375-78, 381, 384, 386, 407, 429, 455, 460, 467-72, 483-84, 486-87, 490, 493-94, 525, 539, 552, 560, 578-80, 592, 606-10, 613-20, 636, 640, 664, 668-69, 671, 673-82, 684-85, 692, 694-95, 697, 703, 710-13, 718, 724-25, 733-34, 736-37, 777, 783, 787-88, 794, 798,

811, 819, 824, 838, 859, 866-68, 917, 934, 937-39, 941

Dead Sea Psalms scroll, 89-93, 579

Dead Sea Scrolls, 36, 41, 88-99, 124, 169, 180, 541, 560, 579, 580, 632, 728, 761, 763, 795-96, 802, 851, 874

death, 5-8, 10, 19, 22-24, 41-43, 52-53, 66, 81, 83-84, 101, 104-6, 111, 125-30, 133-35, 137, 163, 165-66, 168-69, 173, 177, 190-91, 194-95, 206, 209-10, 214, 220, 226, 230, 236, 239, 241, 243, 257-58, 276, 290, 292, 295, 308, 316, 322, 349, 354-55, 358, 367, 371, 373, 381-82, 387, 390, 392, 396, 400, 416-17, 426, 431-32, 434-36, 450, 452, 458, 470, 472, 479, 490, 494, 517-18, 521, 524, 526-28, 544-45, 547, 549, 576, 592, 596-97, 600, 603, 606-7, 617-18, 637-39, 642, 645-46, 650-52, 654, 666, 687-89, 695-97, 700, 711-13, 719, 723-24, 726, 729, 743, 751, 754, 761, 765, 775, 777-78, 780-81, 789, 808-9, 811-13, 815, 818-19, 821-22, 824, 832, 854, 861, 870, 887, 893, 899, 909, 911, 917, 920-21, 923, 930, 933-34

debate, 9, 20, 38, 40, 64, 72, 74, 95, 108-12, 123, 128, 141-42, 144, 147-48, 169, 201, 203, 238, 247, 266, 268, 276, 297, 315, 325, 351, 360, 367, 373, 375, 423, 429, 453-56, 472, 502, 510, 518, 520, 523, 552, 580, 622, 638, 643, 667, 672, 722, 761, 772, 779, 780, 789, 795, 821, 860, 863-64, 891-93, 905-6, 911, 920

deer, 16, 73, 312, 567, 587, 643, 870

defeat, 8, 23, 42, 44, 48-50, 64, 83, 170-71, 174, 206, 269, 291, 316, 326, 328, 393, 401, 404, 421, 585, 602, 631, 713, 724, 819-20, 829, 831-34, 937, 940

deliverance, 5, 23, 27, 50, 58, 88, 93, 101, 163, 166, 168-69, 175-79, 183, 186, 190, 204-5, 226, 235, 240, 250, 271, 274, 290, 303-4, 328, 330, 346, 350, 360, 376, 388, 391-92, 396, 405, 410, 418, 472, 477, 480, 482, 492, 495, 584-85, 588, 590-91, 596, 618, 620, 633, 644, 646, 651, 664, 669, 698, 710-14, 724, 727, 776, 781, 805-8, 819, 823, 830, 832, 887, 930, 932, 939, 940

democratization, 376-77, 669-70, 672

destruction, 6, 8, 16, 19, 25, 52, 64, 82-83, 89, 97, 99-102, 106, 119, 166, 168, 176, 191, 236, 254, 271, 278, 285, 390, 392-93, 399-403, 405, 410-12, 414-18, 424, 436, 459-61, 465, 472, 485, 517, 576, 582, 590-91, 595-96, 633, 644, 652, 667, 780, 783, 788, 795, 814, 829, 830-34, 857, 883, 885, 923, 934, 937, 940

Dialogue of Pessimism, 81, 83, 134, 335, 353, 430, 809, 897, 898

diaspora, 470

didactic narrative, 229, 238-40, 894

didactic wisdom, 2, 281

dirge, 236, 348, 400-401, 410, 439, 475-76, 619, 917, 940

discipline, 4, 15, 66, 79, 188, 193, 201-2, 226, 228, 234, 252, 255, 282, 293, 297, 322, 324, 396, 404-5, 407-8, 435, 495, 533-34, 549, 572, 623, 666, 713, 723-34, 815, 823, 859, 919

discourse, 12, 79, 80, 102-3, 107, 125, 134, 207-8, 237-39, 288, 292, 308, 328, 331, 333, 335, 338, 342-43, 438, 420, 423, 441, 444, 451, 507, 542, 544-45, 548-49, 571-72, 574, 576, 651, 657, 661, 729, 791, 808-9, 834, 864, 887, 912, 926, 928

disputation, 108, 110-12, 203-4, 228, 232, 238, 252, 369, 373, 657, 881, 892, 896, 898

divine presence, 116-17, 119, 235, 433, 436, 826

divine sovereignty, 52, 396, 491, 499, 834, 908

divine warrior, 469, 591, 776, 831, 832, 867, 940

dogs, 16, 285, 337, 348, 353, 528, 569, 869

donkeys, 15, 65, 70, 109, 165, 358, 690, 818, 869

doves, 18, 68, 348, 482, 486, 615, 617, 735, 758, 837-38, 840, 871, 899, 918

drama, 7, 44, 110, 126, 128, 239, 242, 283, 325, 340, 440, 442-43, 455, 488, 518, 568, 633, 643, 656, 673, 679, 685, 742-43, 746, 752, 764, 767, 923

dramatist, 745

dreams, 75, 79, 182-83, 206, 298-99, 337, 350, 432, 600, 723, 733, 738, 746-47, 758, 839, 849-52, 883

eagles, 17, 69, 432, 546, 563, 818, 869, 870

Early Biblical Hebrew (EBH), 262, 266

early Christianity, 91, 93, 143, 148, 176, 288, 329, 366, 377, 390, 416-17, 443, 470, 473, 485, 488, 570, 592, 606, 721, 763-64, 797, 846, 912, 916

Ecclesiastes Rabbah, 458

Ecclesiasticus. See Sirach

editorial criticism, 149-56

education, 132, 171, 209, 229, 270, 329, 430, 704, 705, 707-9, 768, 843, 854, 877, 894

Edwards, Jonathan, 566, 571, 577

Egypt, Egyptian, 1, 8-9, 18, 20, 29, 42, 43, 45-50, 52-53, 60-61, 65, 70, 77, 80-82, 84-85, 87, 107, 111-12, 127, 131-32, 136-38, 140, 145, 147, 159, 166, 174, 183-84, 202, 207, 218, 220-21, 229-31, 237, 239, 264, 270, 283-84, 304, 321-22, 335, 346, 354-61, 363, 365, 389, 392, 429-30, 439-40, 445, 447-52, 458-60, 482, 488, 511, 522, 529-31, 534-35, 537-38, 540-41, 545-47, 549, 552-55, 557-66,

572-77, 583, 590, 593-94, 597, 599, 602-3, 605, 607, 615, 623-26, 628, 640, 642, 646, 648-50, 654, 671, 687-88, 690, 704-10, 718, 720, 722, 725, 727, 730, 739, 743-44, 746, 749, 750-54, 758-59, 767, 769, 782-83, 787, 809, 830-32, 838, 840-42, 846-48, 855, 864-67, 873, 876, 882, 885, 887, 889-90, 894-98, 901-2, 905, 914, 916, 920, 926, 930

Elamite, 162, 171, 411, 632, 688, 782

Elihu, 6, 94, 101, 110, 112, 203, 238, 243, 252, 255, 277, 296-97, 322-34, 337-43, 346, 350, 357, 372-73, 423, 650, 653, 660, 662-63, 668, 866-67, 875, 893

ellipsis, 156-60, 260-61, 465, 503, 511, 520, 522, 599, 793-94, 927

Eloquent Peasant, 107, 137, 358, 574

empathy, 29, 397

enemy, enemies, 5, 14-17, 19, 22-23, 25, 50-51, 59, 71-72, 74-76, 82, 87-88, 100-101, 118, 165-66, 170, 172, 174, 180, 185, 190-92, 194, 198-99, 201, 228, 235, 252, 256-57, 289-91, 314, 316, 318-19, 324, 348, 356-57, 362, 372, 376, 382, 384-85, 387-91, 393, 397-98, 401, 404-7, 413, 434, 436-37, 455, 463, 467, 469, 480, 517, 526-528, 532, 580, 583-85, 586, 588, 591, 594, 596, 601-2, 619, 625-26, 629, 631, 642, 645-46, 651, 659, 664, 670, 710-14, 717, 719, 721, 726, 730, 757, 775-76, 813, 817, 819-20, 823, 829-33, 840, 889, 898-99, 917, 923, 926, 928, 930, 932, 936-37

Enheduanna, 440, 594-95, 605

enthronement, 49, 50, 74-5, 77, 376, 499, 528, 580-81, 583-84, 590, 592, 603-4, 610, 668, 932, 937

enthronement psalms, 74, 77, 499, 583, 584, 590, 592, 937

entrance liturgies, 580, 641

Enuma Elish, 42, 44, 47, 49, 62, 230, 601-3, 718

envelope structure, 323, 641

equity, 197-98, 450, 664, 666, 844

eroticism, 40, 68, 452, 456, 660, 735, 738, 740, 744, 747, 754-55, 757, 760-61, 765, 767, 836-37, 841, 898, 926

Ershemma, 595

Esther, 160-92

Esther, Greek versions of, 173, 176

eternity, 47, 66, 256, 327, 359, 660, 820, 825-26, 915, 939

ethics, 48, 75, 79, 106, 159, 171-72, 175, 180, 193-200, 203, 207, 242, 287, 299, 319, 337, 344, 392, 442, 449, 492, 534, 537, 559, 572, 575, 585, 606, 642, 647, 649, 655, 684-85, 696, 706, 724, 760, 821, 833-34, 843-44, 846, 852, 856-57, 861-63, 866, 871, 882, 892, 903

evil, 19, 47, 49-51, 61, 64, 82, 85, 102-4, 125, 130, 152, 162-63, 166,

176, 191, 194-95, 198, 200, 202-4, 207-8, 219, 223-24, 251, 253-54, 256-57, 316, 321, 336-37, 350-51, 353, 368, 370, 372, 385, 395, 397, 415, 434-35, 448, 482, 491, 493, 517, 519, 531, 539, 542, 544, 567-68, 576, 578, 586, 600, 645, 647-49, 665, 667-68, 672, 681, 688, 710, 712, 715-17, 724, 726, 729, 771, 777, 808-10, 812-14, 818-19, 823, 829, 830, 834, 843, 846, 853, 856, 859-60, 883, 892, 897, 899-900, 906-8, 911, 913, 923, 927, 933, 940

exile, 1, 24- 27, 74, 93, 123-24, 127, 136, 146, 160, 162, 165-67, 188, 232, 256, 262, 264, 269, 276, 279, 282, 285, 291, 328-30, 343, 386, 391-94, 397-400, 402, 404, 406, 408, 414, 417-18, 426, 436, 459, 461, 476-78, 494, 518, 528, 560, 590, 608-9, 617, 625, 674-75, 683, 763, 787, 788, 808, 831, 861, 872, 918, 936, 940

eyes, 1, 3, 13, 18, 22, 56, 59, 64-65, 69, 84, 104, 119, 141, 144, 194, 202, 206, 213, 221, 224, 242, 251, 268, 279, 285, 292-94, 296, 298, 309, 348-49, 384, 387, 395, 420, 426, 433, 448, 453, 470, 488, 517, 543, 546, 558, 571-72, 600, 655-56, 691, 702, 712, 716, 729-30, 741, 752, 756, 758, 794, 810, 814, 822, 837-41, 907, 918-19, 922, 927

family, 21, 22, 66, 76, 95, 104, 106, 114, 134, 144, 190, 203, 205, 207, 209, 212-13, 229-31, 240, 250, 270, 275, 294, 298, 322, 330, 344, 347-48, 350, 358-59, 372, 379-81, 421, 424-25, 432-33, 435-36, 449, 451, 454, 477, 489, 495, 525, 536, 541, 545, 547, 554, 572-73, 598, 657, 661, 671, 673, 675, 677-84, 687-90, 692, 700-701, 708-9, 724, 729, 730, 733-36, 751, 758, 796, 812, 827, 832, 862, 864, 867-68, 872, 894-895, 918, 921, 926, 933

fear of God/Lord/Yahweh, 78-79, 105, 119, 128, 142, 197-98, 201-5, 223, 226, 243, 250-51, 253, 292, 295, 325, 372, 432, 434-35, 537, 549, 585, 667, 706, 723, 725-26, 777, 779, 810, 815-16, 844, 854, 857, 859, 860-61, 877-78, 884, 892, 900-901, 905-8, 911, 921, 930, 933

Feats and Exploits of Ninurta, 42

feminist interpretation, 190, 205-16, 277, 279, 699, 703, 828, 912, 916

fertility, 15, 68, 82, 107, 220-22, 236, 240, 257, 379, 617, 628-29, 697, 743-45, 750, 754

fertility cult, 743-45

festivals, 39-40, 74-75, 80, 82, 135, 143, 150, 154, 162-63, 166-67, 169, 175, 190, 207, 229, 234, 238-40, 271, 282, 399, 415, 457-64, 480, 494-95, 499, 579, 581-85, 604, 610, 614, 631-33, 680, 693, 752, 784, 788, 790, 806-8, 823, 931, 932, 934

fish, 1, 18, 45, 69, 348, 355, 705, 758

fool, folly, 7, 12-13, 15, 22, 55, 66, 80, 82, 100, 104-5, 112, 127, 129-30, 144, 178, 201, 222-27, 239-40, 243, 251, 289, 292-93, 296, 352, 381, 432, 435-36, 518-19, 530, 533, 535, 544-45, 549-50, 569-70, 586, 638-39, 723, 726, 733, 735-36, 775-76, 779, 810, 814, 830, 854-55, 857, 888, 907-8, 910-11, 913, 923, 933-34

form criticism, 146-47, 227-28, 231-34, 263, 384, 451, 499, 580-81, 609-12, 655, 807, 933

fortress, 23, 58, 86, 119, 407, 468, 482, 525-27, 589, 591, 642, 712, 798, 819, 836, 900, 936

foxes, 16, 101, 871

frame narrative/narrator, 30, 124-26, 128-29, 137, 147, 204, 241-44, 324, 361, 635, 637-39, 813

futility, 12, 109, 127, 133-34, 137, 239, 316, 434-35, 509, 638

gapping, 503, 511, 522, 927

gates, 23, 72, 199, 296-97, 347, 350-51, 380, 385, 426, 478-79, 546, 623, 682, 684, 691-92, 703, 732, 782-83, 839, 865, 883, 899, 913, 921

gazelle, 16, 68, 325, 481-82, 568, 643, 746, 753, 758, 838-71, 898, 924

genealogies, 26, 34, 258, 330, 371, 472, 477, 490, 493, 673, 676-81, 683, 685, 692-93, 695-96, 703, 822

genre, 1, 27-31, 35, 51, 54, 57-59, 62, 72, 84, 93, 107-8, 134, 137, 145-47, 150-51, 153, 180-81, 227-28, 230-39, 242, 246, 262, 266, 276, 281-82, 284-86, 300-301, 325, 329, 335-36, 346, 354-55, 374-75, 384, 386, 388, 394, 400-401, 411, 418, 420, 436, 438-40, 442, 454, 470, 474, 476, 484, 488, 492, 494-95, 504, 531-33, 535, 542-43, 545-48, 581, 595-96, 615, 636, 652, 655, 657, 665, 676, 694, 722, 726, 740, 754, 758-59, 761, 767, 769, 774, 778, 791, 805-9, 811, 813, 827, 833, 835-40, 846, 848, 850, 852, 863-65, 869, 872, 878, 880, 887-88, 891-94, 897-98, 916, 932-33

God, 246-59

goats, 13-14, 16, 68, 485, 756, 818, 837-38, 869-70, 919

god, gods, 19-20, 42-44, 46-52, 63, 78, 80-82, 84-85, 111-17, 133, 135, 137, 162, 166, 171-73, 179, 202, 213, 230, 236, 248-50, 271, 290-92, 303, 314-15, 317, 337, 344-357, 360, 392, 401, 410-13, 420, 448-50, 490-91, 527, 547, 550-51, 559, 583-84, 587, 593-604, 617, 621, 625-26, 628-30, 632, 647-49, 688, 695, 740, 743-44, 752, 757-58, 762, 767, 778, 782, 798, 809, 827, 831-33, 841, 860, 862, 896-97, 899, 900, 903, 906, 909, 913-14, 919-20, 930-33, 937

goddess, goddesses, 42-44, 47, 49, 64, 80, 83-85, 107, 112, 136, 162, 188, 207-9, 236-37, 348, 352-53, 401, 411-12, 447-50, 547, 550, 559, 565, 574-76, 595, 598, 743-44, 751, 754-57, 833, 897, 899, 905, 913-14, 920

grammar, 13, 54-55, 86, 94, 114, 124, 177-80, 233, 260-62, 264, 307, 323, 388-89, 391, 417, 474, 499, 502-4, 506-8, 516, 520-22, 587-88, 600, 607-9, 652, 660, 696, 706, 766, , 770-71, 795-97, 799, 802-3, 929

grammatical parallelism, 521, 600, 770-71

Great Hymn to Aten, 597

Greek wisdom, 842

Gregory the Great, 368, 765

Gunkel, H., 42, 53, 59, 72-75, 77, 146-47, 150, 229-30, 240-41, 270-71, 280, 282-84, 287, 305, 375-76, 378, 387, 398, 400-401, 409, 497, 500, 580-81, 584-85, 593, 609-10, 613-14, 616-17, 621, 625, 655, 670, 676, 686, 698, 700, 805-8, 932, 935

hair, 14, 18, 220, 412, 568, 625, 628, 752-53, 756, 837-41, 919

Haman, 10, 101, 161-67, 171, 173-75, 177-79, 181-83, 190-92, 215-16, 240, 275-76, 278, 295-96, 426, 463, 472, 477-79, 492-94, 631-33, 719, 922-23

hemistich, 520

hermeneutics, 40, 51, 121, 146, 168, 216, 267-69, 272, 274-75, 279, 367, 415, 444, 510, 549, 567, 570, 606-8, 621-24, 698, 724, 760, 765-69, 795, 815, , 836, 865, 888, 893

Herodotus, 8-11, 21, 162-63, 170-75, 180, 189, 781-83, 827, 864

Hezekiah, 25, 76, 190, 234, 236, 459, 536-37, 540-41, 552, 555, 575, 671, 674, 704, 708, 719, 724-25, 735, 743, 800, 867, 895

Hippolytus, 570, 764

historical allusions, 673, 865, 869-71

historical criticism, 145, 227, 281, 283, 285-86, 327, 417, 637

historical narrative, 168, 231, 240, 329, 495, 531, 585, 668, 734, 869, 873

historiography, 172, 281, 676, 722, 863-64, 871-73

Hittite Laws, 690, 693

Hittite prayers, 598

honor, 6, 10, 21, 68-69, 80, 83, 85, 103, 167, 173, 177, 180, 203, 251, 263, 287-303, 331, 338, 347, 349, 352-53, 359-60, 362, 364-65, 376, 381, 386, 423, 433, 452, 469, 478-79, 494, 544, 556, 591, 658, 666, 670, 673, 677-78, 708, 713, 723, 726, 729-31, 744, 780, 834, 871, 875, 900, 907, 920, 923

honor challenges, 291, 293, 295-96

horses, 10, 15, 70, 137, 142, 158, 163, 173, 296, 337, 479, 516, 532, 591, 627, 711-12, 753, 818, 869,

870, 923

hospitality, 365, 690, 730

house, 21-23, 43, 59, 72, 100-101, 104-5, 113, 117, 127, 189-90, 196, 202, 210, 213, 220, 222, 224, 243, 300, 302, 306, 329, 353, 363, 366-67, 373, 377, 379, 393, 402, 411, 436, 451-52, 469, 477, 490, 492-94, 518, 523, 544, 546, 550, 584, 594, 614, 616, 620, 664, 674-79, 682, 688-89, 694-95, 705-06, 734, 743, 746, 751-52, 756-57, 772-73, 785, 787, 790, 827, 835, 863, 866, 872-73, 883, 899, 907, 913-14, 932-33

household, 21, 24, 105, 189-90, 196, 213, 243, 293-96, 426, 433, 453, 684, 688-89, 729-31, 921

Hugh of St. Cher, 697-98

human body, 22, 105, 570

humanity, 60, 62-66, 68-70, 79, 105, 126-27, 133-34, 138, 144, 194-96, 198, 277, 328, 364, 368, 370, 378, 407, 431, 437, 512, 569, 646, 676, 685, 698, 738, 760, 764, 768, 809, 813-14, 818, 820, 822-23, 833, 854, 856-57, 869, 873, 897, 932

Hymn to Aten, 602-3, 605

hymns, 2-3, 37, 39, 48, 57, 59, 80, 84-85, 105-6, 150, 194, 230, 232, 235, 238-39, 247, 250, 253, 263, 282, 300-305, 324, 326, 329, 333, 341, 343, 346-48, 350, 360, 385, 387, 391, 393, 412, 448, 468, 470, 487-88, 499, 506, 559, 580, 582-83, 592, 594-600, 602-3, 614-15, 619-20, 642, 664, 669, 670, 705, 708, 722, 724, 738, 752, 761, 774-75, 780, 793, 805-6, 808, 891-92, 894, 905, 932, 939

hyperbole, 240, 468, 656, 671, 916, 924

I Will Praise the Lord of Wisdom, 84, 346, 348, 809, 896

iambic meter, 523

iconography, 229, 310, 486, 621-26, 628-30, 830, 832, 937

Iddin-Dagan of Isin, 756

image of God, 58, 69, 394, 434, 488, 856

imagery, 15, 17-21, 23-24, 26, 41-42, 44-51, 53, 58, 60-62, 66, 68, 99-101, 118, 134, 149, 206-8, 211-12, 214, 218-19, 224, 276, 306-11, 313, 320-22, 327, 330, 346, 354, 384-85, 398-99, 420, 424, 431-32, 436, 441, 464, 481-82, 517, 520, 522, 525, 527, 543, 578, 581, 583, 594, 599, 600-602, 604, 617, 621-25, 627, 629-30, 660, 670-71, 710, 738, 744, 749, 753-56, 758-60, 763-65, 767-68, 791-92, 794, 817, 819, 829, 830-34, 836-38, 840-41, 852, 893, 898, 937, 939

imprecation, 100-101, 219, 314-19, 411, 619, 651, 774, 779, 833

imprisonment, 320-22, 888

Inanna, 81, 236, 410, 412, 595, 605, 751, 753-57, 759

inclusio, 2, 150, 152, 154, 202, 239, 323-25, 348, 524, 532, 535-37,

589-90, 641, 656, 659, 678, 723-24, 733, 735, 746-47, 749, 773, 906, 921

individual laments, 3, 235, 282, 384, 386, 388-98, 400-401, 451, 580-81, 584, 596, 665

innerbiblical exegesis, 325-26

instruction, 23, 26, 29, 75, 78, 84-85, 100, 102, 134, 152-53, 159, 193, 197, 200, 202, 207, 209, 219, 226, 229, 231, 237, 239, 249, 293-94, 296, 320, 329, 330, 335, 351, 353, 355, 377, 379-80, 384, 389, 397, 420, 422, 430, 433-35, 477, 491, 493, 506, 518-19, 527, 529, 534-35, 545-47, 549, 553-54, 556-58, 564, 572, 585-86, 589-90, 608, 611, 620, 635, 666, 676, 679, 684-85, 694-95, 697, 706-8, 718-19, 725, 735, 741, 806-7, 810, 844, 846, 851-52, 859, 878, 887, 893, 895-99, 905-6, 908, 912, 920, 923, 934

Instruction for Merika-re, 29, 80, 81, 84, 430, 553, 574, 688, 809

Instruction of Amenemope, 237, 452, 539, 541, 574, 671, 804, 817

Instruction of Any, 708, 898

instructional wisdom, 552-53, 555, 559, 564

international wisdom, 563, 572-73, 576, 815, 903

intertextuality, 206, 211-12, 277, 325-27, 331

irony, 53, 62, 108, 137, 163-64, 181, 198, 244, 253, 276, 354, 479, 493, 504, 620, 656, 658, 671, 827, 928

jackals, 16, 66, 483, 869

Jamnia, 35, 38, 142, 169

Jerome, 37-38, 40, 142-45, 148, 176, 182, 185, 364, 366, 417, 473, 570, 607, 618, 695-97, 765, 797, 799, 802

Jerusalem, 14, 16, 24-27, 50, 53, 58, 71, 73, 75, 93, 97, 100-101, 113, 116-19, 122-25, 136, 142, 160, 165, 169-70, 181, 184, 213-14, 222, 228-30, 234, 236, 238-40, 262, 267, 269, 270-72, 276, 278-79, 285-86, 290-91, 294, 311, 314, 318, 325, 327, 346, 367, 374, 386, 390, 393-94, 397, 399, 400-403, 407-9, 411, 414-19, 424, 430, 436, 455, 460-61, 464-65, 468, 471, 476-77, 483-84, 516-19, 563, 566-67, 569, 570, 579, 584, 610, 612, 620, 632-33, 636, 643-44, 663, 669, 675, 687, 707, 709, 717-18, 720, 722, 725, 727, 730, 734, 736, 743, 746-47, 757, 762-64, 775-76, 780-81, 783, 788, 801, 813-14, 819, 831, 833-34, 837, 843, 865-68, 885, 895, 917-20, 931, 934, 936-41

Job, 333-74

Josephus, 37-38, 40, 174-76, 181-82, 461, 473, 484, 614, 632, 681, 694, 697, 700, 761, 889

justice, 21, 22, 25-26, 49, 65, 67, 71, 78, 80-82, 85, 107, 112, 118, 129, 136, 156-57, 166, 196-98, 201, 228, 236-37, 249, 252, 254, 285, 291-92, 317, 338-42, 344, 347,

349, 352, 356, 358-62, 367, 369-71, 403-5, 414-15, 420-24, 426-27, 430, 433-34, 436-37, 447-50, 453, 481, 511, 528, 535, 537, 544, 547, 559, 574, 596, 598, 638-39, 647-54, 664-667, 688, 690, 695, 711-12, 714, 716, 724, 730, 775-76, 778-81, 808-12, 814-18, 824, 844-45, 855, 857, 861-62, 882, 887, 904-5, 910, 914, 920, 928

kingship, 18, 34, 42, 49, 60-62, 74, 86-87, 93, 118, 122-23, 165, 230, 234, 247, 302-4, 321-22, 324, 328-29, 375-78, 391-92, 407, 467-69, 471, 481, 483, 499, 525, 548, 581, 590-92, 605, 642, 648, 664, 669, 671-73, 679, 695, 811, 933, 937-39

kinship, 379, 421, 730

Korah, 24, 26-27, 102, 234, 263, 386, 486, 499, 611, 620, 734

Lamentations Rabbah, 414-15, 458, 461, 788

Late Biblical Hebrew (LBH), 262, 264-67, 674-75

Latin versions, 797

law, 2, 9, 32-33, 36, 40, 49-50, 65, 79, 80, 81, 108, 117, 128, 150, 160, 163, 179, 185-86, 191, 193-96, 204-5, 212, 219-20, 230-31, 240, 258, 289, 292-93, 304, 320, 356, 364-65, 367-69, 377-81, 384, 396, 420-27, 432-34, 447, 450, 453-54, 460, 471, 480, 485, 490-91, 503-54, 506, 513, 528, 550, 567-68, 576, 589-90, 598, 606, 620, 653, 664, 666, 670, 673-74, 677-80, 682-85, 688-90, 692, 695, 697-98, 700-704, 724-29, 732, 736, 744-45, 760, 773, 786-87, 789-90, 795, 797, 845, 851, 855, 857, 861, 876-78, 880, 882-83, 887, 915, 917, 922,

Laws of Eshnunna, 688-89

Lemuel, 2, 104-5, 207, 237, 264, 269, 427-30, 453, 511, 537, 540-41, 548, 552-55, 557-59, 562, 564, 661, 666, 708, 735, 793, 800, 868, 878, 895

leopards, 16, 871

Leviathan, 19-20, 42, 44-46, 50, 53, 60, 63-65, 67, 70, 339, 392, 583, 591, 602-3, 708, 818-19, 829, 840, 908

levirate, 32, 40, 240, 299, 379, 380-81, 425-26, 454, 490, 492, 495, 680, 684, 690, 693, 697-98, 702-3, 922

lexical parallelism, 521

light, 22, 28, 38, 45, 47-48, 50-51, 58, 62, 72, 74, 89-90, 93, 101, 104, 115, 117, 123, 125, 128, 141, 145-46, 152, 174, 183, 192, 210, 214, 225, 229, 242, 250, 257, 263, 265, 267-68, 271, 276-79, 285, 293, 295, 303, 308-10, 317, 325, 327-29, 344, 351, 363, 376-77, 380, 384, 387, 391-92, 405, 413, 422, 431, 436-37, 442, 448, 467, 469-70, 484, 486, 499, 514, 528, 530, 532, 537, 539, 543, 546-47, 553, 587, 593-97, 602, 604, 608, 611, 626, 633, 646, 658, 672, 679-

80, 683, 685, 691, 712, 714, 720, 723, 725, 728, 736, 739, 743-44, 764-67, 780, 799, 805, 808, 818, 820, 839, 843, 845, 880, 882-83, 886, 890, 892, 905, 908, 911, 913, 916, 921, 925, 928, 939

lions, 15-16, 19, 264, 308, 311, 352, 431, 505, 528, 595, 603, 712, 724, 782, 830, 836, 869-71

literacy, 309, 541, 569, 718, 894

literary theory, 325, 327

liturgical interpretation, 271

liturgical reading, 161, 460-62

logos, 655, 658, 660, 844, 887, 901

love, 8, 17, 21, 23, 33, 68, 72-73, 79, 87, 118, 162, 188, 194, 197, 199, 204-06, 211, 214, 221-22, 239-40, 248, 252, 254, 257, 274, 278, 293, 298, 301-2, 324-25, 327, 329, 357, 364-65, 433-37, 440, 452-56, 465, 468-69, 483, 487-88, 516-17, 519, 524-25, 528, 532, 567-68, 570, 582, 588, 595, 617, 642-43, 657, 660, 664-65, 677, 682-83, 693, 695, 711, 723, 725-26, 735, 738-47, 750-62, 764-69, 777, 811-12, 815, 819, 823, 826, 835-38, 840-41, 845, 861, 866, 868-69, 898, 909-10, 915, 917, 919-921, 924, 932, 934

love charm, 757-58

love lyrics, 440, 739, 742-44, 756, 758-59, 840-41

Love Lyrics of Nabu and Tash-metu, 757

Love Lyrics of Rim-Sin of Larsa, 757

Love Poem of a Faithful Lover, 757

love poetry, 239, 643, 743, 750, 759-61, 767, 898

Love Song of Nanay and Muati, 757

Lowth, R. 440, 445, 474, 498-99, 503-4, 506-10, 515, 521, 525, 532, 585-87, 608, 613

Ludingirra, 754-55

Luther, Martin, 144-145, 147, 161, 169, 179-81, 370, 608, 613, 698, 700, 765-66

LXX. *See* Septuagint

lyric poetry, 437-45, 708, 837, 886

lyricism, 438, 444

maat, 49, 65, 80, 107, 360, 447-51, 536, 547, 559, 565, 574-76, 649, 809, 905, 914, 920

Maccabees, 36, 145, 161, 180, 184, 240, 632

magic, 79, 84, 756, 758, 809

Maimonides, 161, 369, 763

Man and His God, 335, 346-47, 351, 361, 392, 809, 896

mantic wisdom, 846, 849, 850-51, 877

marriage, 9-10, 21, 32, 40, 62, 107, 171, 174, 180, 186, 190, 206, 212-13, 225, 239-40, 242-43, 270, 299, 365, 379, 380-81, 400, 424-25, 433, 451-57, 488, 490-92, 495, 679-80, 682-84, 688-700, 702-3, 715, 729, 738-39, 741, 743, 753-58, 761-67, 783, 786, 835, 839, 878, 917, 921-22

meaninglessness, 129, 141, 148, 776

medieval period, 143-44, 178-79, 181, 192, 361, 369, 417, 419, 428, 458, 561, 570-71, 606-8, 612-13, 618, 633, 696-98, 740-41, 763-67, 785, 790, 796, 802, 885

memory, 5, 62, 100, 127, 137, 165, 167, 170, 172, 174, 189, 301, 377, 393, 463, 477, 480, 484, 488-89, 495, 498, 610, 642, 644-46, 655, 795, 837

merism, 464-66, 588

Mesopotamia, 1, 42, 47, 52, 61, 76, 80, 82, 132-35, 138, 147, 202, 236, 287, 322, 345-46, 348, 351, 353, 360-61, 401-2, 411, 413, 422, 426-27, 430, 439, 481, 488, 517, 541, 553-54, 557-58, 563-66, 572-74, 581, 593-95, 599, 604-5, 610, 623, 629, 648-49, 654, 687, 688, 691, 693, 709, 715, 717, 739, 750-51, 753, 758-59, 782, 809, 833, 849-50, 855, 864, 873-75, 894-95, 897-98, 901-2, 926

messiah, 93, 247, 249, 329, 408, 466-67, 471-72, 605-6, 612, 762-63

metaphor, 14-15, 18, 23, 52, 62, 68, 108, 115, 118, 130, 133, 149, 206, 208, 211, 213-14, 220, 222, 237, 239, 291, 306-9, 312, 318, 323, 343, 355, 380, 382-83, 397, 422, 424, 431-32, 438, 440, 442, 452-53, 455, 464, 482, 504, 514, 516, 518, 522, 524-26, 528, 531, 533, 536, 542-43, 549, 550-51, 571-73, 575, 587, 591, 601, 621-23, 656, 659, 719, 741-42, 745, 753, 758, 762, 764, 767-68, 781, 792, 829-30, 834, 838, 846, 866-67, 881, 898, 913-16, 918-19, 926, 928, 940

meter, 97, 236, 260, 271, 439, 464-65, 472-76, 499, 503, 506, 521, 523, 585, 656, 661, 677, 791

metonymy, 105-6, 117, 464, 487, 792

Middle Assyrian Laws, 688

midrash, 326, 363, 365, 414-15, 541, 614, 616, 785, 867

Midrash Rabbah, 192, 458, 480, 539, 917

Moab, 32-33, 158-59, 212-13, 240, 275, 330, 380, 425, 481, 490-91, 494, 675, 678, 681-82, 687, 696-97, 700-702, 789, 831, 922

monotheism, 80, 114-16, 250, 316, 344, 360, 363, 449, 575-76, 597, 630, 647, 649, 745, 848, 855, 909

monsters, 19, 20, 44-48, 50, 64, 602

Mordecai, 101, 160-68, 170-71, 173-75, 177, 180-83, 185-86, 188, 190-92, 215-16, 240, 256, 275-76, 279, 296, 426, 463, 476-81, 493-95, 631-33, 644, 661, 719, 783, 823, 874, 923

Mot, 43, 49, 52-53, 339, 364, 600, 937

Mount Zion, 51, 113, 311, 382, 393, 481, 483, 527, 602, 937, 939-40

mountains, 14, 16, 23, 44, 50-51,

58-62, 64-65, 67, 113, 117, 158-59, 219, 325, 384, 395, 412, 466, 468, 481-83, 498, 522, 526-27, 591, 594, 602, 628-29, 664, 681, 711, 746, 782, 817-18, 820, 836-37, 839, 841, 866, 869, 924, 936-38

mules, 15

music, 71, 149, 438, 445, 483-85, 487-89, 499, 734, 805

myth, mythology 19-20, 42, 44-51, 60, 62-65, 67, 69-70, 80-81, 87, 152, 209, 229-30, 249, 257, 308, 327, 411, 481, 559, 598, 600-602, 610, 626-28, 649, 705, 718, 745, 752, 758, 809, 830, 852

Naomi, 32-33, 117, 212-13, 219, 240, 258, 270, 275-77, 279-80, 299, 330, 379-81, 425-26, 434, 454, 460, 490-94, 516, 673-74, 676-79, 681-86, 688-92, 694-703, 730, 917, 922

narrative, 9-10, 29, 40, 51, 56-57, 62, 65, 76, 82, 151-52, 159, 164, 168, 171, 175, 177-78, 180-82, 187, 189, 192, 194-96, 206, 210, 212-13, 215-16, 228-32, 238, 240-44, 265, 269, 273, 275-76, 283, 288, 295, 320, 324, 326, 328, 330, 333, 335, 343-45, 351, 356, 360-61, 366, 376, 379, 380, 390, 402, 417, 420, 425-26, 431, 437-39, 441-55, 459-60, 471, 476-77, 480, 492-95, 498, 513, 544, 550, 554-55, 557, 565, 576, 578, 584, 592, 598, 604, 607, 615, 641, 655, 657, 660-61, 671, 673-74, 676-78, 680-81, 683-85, 692, 695, 698, 707, 715, 730, 736-37, 744, 754, 757, 758-59, 761, 767, 813, 817, 822, 829, 848, 851, 855, 864, 866-67, 869, 872-73, 888, 890-92, 893, 898, 929

navel, 481, 839, 937

Neo-Babylonian Laws, 689

New Testament, 36, 41, 98, 113, 115, 120, 131, 141, 148, 223, 226, 279, 300, 320, 332, 399, 408, 472, 513, 550, 569, 578, 592, 605-6, 686, 693, 695, 720, 726-27, 804, 912, 914, 916

New Year, New Year festival, 74-76, 230, 238-39, 282, 581, 604, 610, 632, 754-57, 806, 932

Nicholas of Lyra, 607, 697

Ninth of Av, 236, 271, 416, 457, 460-63, 784, 788

nonalphabetic acrostic, 3

noncanonical psalms, 91-92

nose, 22, 117, 738, 752, 835-37, 839

novella, 240, 286, 494-95, 677, 698

numerical sayings, 231, 237, 239, 529, 534, 722, 724

Old Persian, 171, 173, 188, 782

onomastica, 534, 553

onomatopoeia, 228, 588, 770, 772

oral culture, 237, 497, 894

oral poetry, 465, 497-500

orality, 60, 146, 213, 227, 229-30, 232, 263, 284, 311, 497-500, 531, 540, 581, 656, 698, 705, 718, 785-86, 790, 898

Origen, 37-38, 143-44, 176, 278,

366, 456, 473, 488, 570, 655, 696, 740, 742, 749-50, 764-66, 799, 845-46

Orpah, 54, 117, 212-13, 217, 379, 454, 490-92, 695, 697, 699, 700-702, 922

oxen, 14-15, 173, 350, 373, 435, 440, 528, 535, 754, 818, 869-70, 899

palaces, 9-10, 19, 21-22, 24, 43-44, 49, 100, 113, 161, 163, 176, 189, 190, 295, 392, 478, 547, 625, 706, 732, 781-83, 826-27, 920, 923

Papyrus Chester Beatty I, 752

Papyrus Harris 500, 751

paradise, 68-69, 437, 739, 863, 870, 872-73

parallelism, 1, 3, 7, 11, 55-56, 260, 263, 276, 307, 420, 464, 472, 474-75, 481, 498-99, 502-14, 520-21, 523, 533, 542-43, 558, 565, 573-74, 585-88, 594, 599-601, 608, 622, 722, 770, 791, 866, 883, 886, 896, 927, 936

Passover, 166, 229, 239-40, 271, 457-60, 462, 464, 485, 680, 694, 763, 784, 787, 931

patience, 12, 79, 248, 328, 330, 362-64, 366-68, 371, 698, 728, 824

patristic interpretation, 38, 40, 144, 176, 367, 416-17, 569-70, 606-7, 696-97, 741

Pentecost, 219, 271, 457, 459-60, 680

peripety, 164, 168

Persia, Persians, 5-6, 8-11, 21, 37-38, 41-42, 97, 107, 124, 135-136, 141, 147, 161-176, 178-181, 183-186, 188-189, 191, 215, 229, 240-241, 265-266, 268, 275-276, 279, 284-285, 398, 402, 422, 426, 450, 455, 476-478, 492-494, 610, 616, 625, 632, 644, 661, 674, 708, 716, 719, 739, 781-783, 807, 826, 848, 865, 872-873, 897, 921-923, 940

Persian court, 9, 161, 163, 173, 180, 275, 476-78, 492-94

personification, 43-44, 46, 52, 82, 101-2, 105, 107, 213, 225, 243, 306, 382, 400, 402, 440, 448, 451, 516-19, 533, 550, 559, 565, 575, 755, 872, 901, 904-6, 913-14, 933

petition, 5, 33, 59, 71, 137, 287, 290, 327-28, 353, 358-59, 384, 386-89, 391, 394-98, 421, 424, 434, 436, 596, 598-99, 601, 604, 607, 618-20, 713, 786, 919

Philo, 36-38, 367, 473, 484, 614, 686, 726, 804, 843, 845-46, 876, 888-89, 901

pigs, 17, 337, 569

plot development, 396, 443

Poem of the Righteous Sufferer, 335, 348, 350, 708

poetics, 11, 152, 306-7, 323, 472-73, 498-99, 559, 572, 659, 864

poetry, 1-3, 5, 11, 13-15, 17, 20, 44-45, 47-48, 51-52, 54-57, 60, 74, 77, 82, 84, 86, 90, 94-95, 97, 101-3, 146, 149, 150, 152-53, 155-59, 210, 218-20, 222, 230-31, 235-36, 239, 242-43, 246, 248, 252, 260-

65, 270, 276-77, 283, 286-87, 304, 306-7, 311-12, 316, 320, 323-24, 326, 328, 343, 348, 358, 361-63, 366, 374, 384-85, 400-402, 420, 424, 433, 437-45, 464-66, 472-76, 481, 484, 487, 497-500, 502-14, 516-17, 520-23, 532-34, 536, 542-43, 550, 558, 560, 562, 565, 578-79, 581, 583, 585-88, 591, 593, 597, 599, 600-601, 603-4, 608, 610, 614, 617, 619-22, 625, 641, 643-46, 657, 659-60, 668, 672, 674, 676-77, 698, 704, 707, 711, 717-19, 722, 728, 738, 743, 747, 749-51, 755, 757-58, 767-74, 791-94, 798, 802, 807, 812, 829-32, 834-36, 840-41, 843, 864, 867, 886, 891, 893, 898, 900, 905-6, 913, 917-19, 925, 927-29, 934, 936

polytheism, 80, 114-15, 135, 360, 745

postexilic period, 5, 26, 73, 122-24, 127, 129, 136, 141, 146, 160, 165, 167, 193, 196, 199, 231, 260, 262, 264, 268, 270, 274, 282, 286, 343, 376-77, 386, 388, 392-93, 397-98, 420, 426, 454, 484, 495, 552, 559-60, 572-73, 579, 609-11, 620, 673-75, 698-99, 807, 849-50, 865, 872, 895, 938, 940

postmodern, 146, 277, 529, 612, 656, 661

postscript, 154, 339, 615-18

poverty, 83, 112, 201, 203, 220, 352, 381, 421, 430, 687, 723, 845, 851

praise, 2, 4-5, 14-16, 25, 27, 46, 52, 61, 63, 65, 67-68, 71-73, 78, 80, 82-83, 85, 87, 100, 104, 111, 113, 115, 117, 150, 199, 205-6, 215, 228-29, 232, 234-35, 247-50, 253, 269, 271, 273-74, 278, 290, 292, 294-95, 299-304, 323-26, 328-29, 346-48, 350-51, 360, 365, 375, 381, 384-85, 387-88, 390-93, 396, 412-13, 433, 439, 442, 449, 466, 473, 482, 484, 486-88, 499, 516, 521, 524-26, 571, 575, 578-79, 582-84, 590, 592, 595-99, 601-2, 605, 607-8, 610-11, 619, 642, 645-47, 664, 669-70, 682, 685, 697, 703, 710, 712-13, 722, 724, 753, 755-56, 773-75, 778, 780, 793, 805-6, 808, 819, 825, 831-32, 836, 845, 855, 887, 891, 893, 899, 900, 920-22, 930-34, 938-40

prayer, 7, 25-27, 33, 62, 71, 76, 80, 82, 84-87, 89, 94-95, 97, 108, 112, 118, 160, 166-67, 175-77, 183, 185, 194, 206, 231-34, 248, 252, 269, 273-74, 278-79, 288-89, 316-18, 324, 326, 328-29, 349-50, 364, 373, 384-87, 389, 391, 393-98, 401-2, 405-8, 413, 420-21, 425, 430, 470, 482-84, 487, 490, 549, 569, 590, 592-94, 596-99, 605, 607-8, 611, 615-16, 618, 669-70, 672, 702, 705, 708, 710, 723-24, 726-27, 734, 757, 776, 786, 788, 805-7, 812, 815, 819, 825, 830-31, 833, 851, 855, 870, 897, 922, 932-34

prison, prisoners, 232, 294, 320-23, 417, 713

Prophecies of Neferti, 354, 356-57, 708

prophecy, 73, 193, 278, 329, 414-15, 417, 545, 606-8, 696, 724, 788, 847-50, 855, 876-79, 881-83, 922, 938

protection, 17-20, 23-24, 66, 76, 87, 100, 118, 166, 205-6, 220, 228, 230, 321, 328, 417, 419, 433, 470, 480, 493, 525-28, 533, 596, 618, 631, 648, 652, 684, 688, 711, 787, 830, 832, 870, 887, 917, 922, 936, 938-40prophets, 36-37, 39, 50, 73-76, 78, 83, 92, 100, 108, 114, 143, 165-66, 180, 193, 196, 199, 206, 225, 228, 236, 268, 272, 281, 286, 316, 320, 327, 329, 330, 345, 364, 366-68, 393, 399, 400, 402, 404, 406, 408, 414-16, 418, 449, 456, 459, 464, 471, 483, 504, 533-34, 565, 567, 569, 578, 602, 606-7, 611, 616, 620, 644, 650, 665, 670, 687, 695-96, 709, 719, 724, 726, 739, 741, 743, 762, 784, 848-49, 852, 855-57, 877- 84, 895, 906, 919, 934

Protests of the Eloquent Peasant, 354, 358

proverbs, 7-8, 12-13, 83-84, 102-7, 133-34, 147, 152-54, 197, 199, 201-2, 219, 222, 224, 226, 228, 231, 236-37, 239, 243, 254, 269, 281, 285, 292, 294-95, 297, 324, 335, 373, 428-30, 517, 528-37, 539-45, 547-50, 552, 561, 563, 567, 570-76, 585, 652-54, 666, 671, 677, 705, 719, 722-23, 735-36, 761, 770-71, 778-79, 810, 852, 859-60, 866, 868-70, 877-78, 880-81, 886, 891, 894-96, 898-99, 907-13

providence, 167, 169, 256, 269, 368-70, 434, 491, 685, 813, 822-23, 857, 940

psalm titles, 73, 282

psalms of confidence, 57-59, 812, 933

psalter, 324, 578

Pseudo-Solomon, 885, 888, 890

pun, 71, 440, 925-29

punishment, 5, 66-67, 81-83, 100, 141, 186, 210-11, 222, 228, 232, 236, 238, 257, 292, 314, 317, 320, 326-27, 339, 346, 353, 359-60, 365, 399, 406, 420, 422-24, 436, 449, 517, 544, 576, 596, 598, 645, 650-52, 654, 665-66, 695, 697, 714, 716, 787-89, 809-11, 813, 815, 825, 828-29, 832-33, 888-89, 899, 907, 919, 930, 940

Purim, 40, 97, 101, 162-64, 166-70, 173, 175, 177, 181-83, 186-87, 190, 240, 271, 286, 455, 457, 461-64, 480, 495, 631-34, 680, 784, 790, 823, 934

Qinah, 236, 473, 475-76, 661

Qohelet, 8, 11-12, 28-31, 40, 66, 82-84, 121-33, 138-49, 193, 204-5, 238-39, 244-45, 269-70, 273, 294-95, 324, 330, 332, 427, 464, 543, 635-40, 642-43, 660, 662,

667, 676, 722, 736, 776-77, 779-80, 788-89, 791, 813, 816, 821-22, 860-62, 870, 877-79, 883, 891, 893, 901, 903, 909, 917-18, 924, 933
Qohelet Rabbah, 123, 789
quantitative meter, 475
Qumran, 35-36, 39-41, 85, 88-99, 102, 113-15, 141, 149, 161, 169, 228, 234, 282, 287, 459, 552, 580, 618, 632, 680, 719, 721, 761, 786, 791, 796, 798-802, 804, 874
rabbinic interpretation, 143, 177, 364, 428, 787
Rahab, 19-20, 32, 45-46, 50, 60, 64, 678, 683, 685, 695
reciprocity, 728, 730-31
redemption, 3, 33-34, 40, 60, 62, 80, 84, 101-2, 158, 168, 195, 211, 248, 258, 299, 302-4, 340, 357, 366-68, 379-80, 382-83, 421, 425, 461, 463, 472, 482-83, 487, 492, 495, 591, 616, 665, 680, 685, 694, 698, 710-11, 713, 736, 821, 826, 834, 903, 919
Reformation, Reformers, 140, 142, 144, 147, 169, 175, 179, 362, 370-71, 417-18, 605, 607-8, 640, 693, 698, 721, 741-42, 760, 765, 767
refrain, 101, 148, 239, 298, 323-24, 404, 443, 454, 523-24, 641-43, 667, 681, 773-74, 777, 789, 917
refuge, 7, 19, 23, 33, 58, 59, 117-19, 151-52, 204-5, 247, 250, 252, 320, 328, 390, 396, 442, 456, 470, 482-83, 525-27, 589, 591, 665-66, 680, 682, 684, 712, 819, 922, 937-39
religion, 35, 49, 78-84, 112, 114-15, 119, 135, 145, 175, 179, 193, 196-97, 208, 212, 230, 247-48, 269, 283, 308, 311, 344, 366-67, 392, 430, 445, 449-50, 506, 559, 597, 609, 694, 740, 745, 750, 806-7, 849, 855, 914, 916, 921
remembrance, 66, 137, 289, 292, 295, 460, 521, 620, 642-46, 823, 933
retribution, 67, 81, 109-10, 137, 203, 315, 335-37, 339-43, 351-53, 360, 370, 373, 408, 423, 434-36, 463, 544-45, 576, 598, 647-54, 660, 667, 717, 778, 786, 810, 815, 823-25, 846, 854, 856, 903
rewards, 67, 108-9, 128, 173, 203, 238, 254, 258, 316, 337, 338-39, 341, 346, 353, 360, 364-66, 369, 421, 434, 436, 479, 539, 544-45, 650, 666, 680, 682, 694, 713, 715-16, 776-77, 781, 786, 809-13, 825, 907, 913
rewritten Bible, 88, 722
rhetoric, 31, 55, 104, 129, 138, 172, 183, 227, 232, 244, 263, 294, 306-7, 323, 325, 328, 330, 336, 340, 343, 359, 388, 394, 395-96, 402-3, 453, 468, 479, 507, 510, 513, 516, 519, 523, 569, 622, 627, 643, 655-61, 690, 702, 752-55, 757, 773-74, 819, 830, 833-34, 836, 843-44, 879, 881, 885, 890-93, 925, 928
rhetorical criticism, 227, 232, 336, 655-56, 661

rhyme, 506-7, 512, 521, 523, 770-72
rhythm, 126, 202, 304, 439, 473, 475, 521, 523, 618, 661, 763, 886
righteous, righteousness, 7, 15, 21-24, 49-50, 61, 66-67, 80, 82-84, 86, 100, 109, 117-19, 130, 141, 150, 156-57, 159, 175, 177, 185, 196-200, 204, 210, 223, 225, 228, 234, 237-38, 248-49, 251-52, 254-55, 289-90, 292, 296-97, 322, 330, 336-44, 352-53, 361-65, 367, 368-71, 374, 386, 389-90, 395, 398, 414-15, 420-22, 432-37, 447-50, 453, 463, 481-83, 486, 493, 504, 517, 519, 529, 533, 535, 543-44, 551, 567-69, 571-72, 585-86, 588-89, 591, 606, 608, 639, 646-47, 650-53, 658-59, 663-68, 670, 672, 679, 683-85, 698, 711-17, 730, 734, 738, 744, 775-80, 786-87, 809-13, 815, 818, 823-24, 843-45, 851-52, 854, 857, 862, 872, 881, 888-89, 896, 907-11, 913, 919, 930, 937
rock, 18, 23, 58, 86, 118, 151, 159, 382, 388, 432, 481-82, 485, 525-27, 589, 591, 696, 712, 714, 819, 830, 870
royal court, 190, 199, 236-40, 270, 530, 557, 573, 668-72, 704, 742, 781, 828, 882
royal ideology, 49, 408, 430, 669, 937
royal love songs, 755
royal palace, 21, 50
royal psalm, 74, 76-77, 151, 230, 235, 282, 330, 375-78, 391, 393, 451, 469, 580, 581, 584-85, 590-91, 610, 668-71, 830, 832, 892
Ruth, 672-703
Ruth Rabbah, 458, 695, 789
sages, 7, 29-30, 55, 61, 65-66, 78-82, 83-85, 107, 135, 142, 193, 202, 209, 219, 222, 244, 251, 330, 335-36, 338, 346, 355-58, 360, 372, 415, 427-30, 436, 471, 481, 529, 532-33, 535-36, 539-40, 543-44, 550, 556, 568, 574, 576, 585, 619, 633, 635-39, 658-60, 670-72, 676, 704, 719, 721, 729, 784, 787, 789, 810, 813, 846, 851-52, 854, 856-57, 859, 860, 877-84, 888, 895, 897, 899, 903-4, 906-8, 910, 914, 933
salvation, 23, 58, 61-63, 65, 81, 84, 86, 88, 118, 168, 204, 212, 232, 247, 250, 281, 303, 326, 329, 367, 388, 393, 397, 405-6, 431, 434, 459, 472, 483, 494, 525-27, 608, 664, 665, 710-14, 725, 738, 741, 760, 763-64, 778, 780, 807, 811, 819, 823-24, 848, 852-53, 855-56, 858-59, 861-62, 883, 899, 938
Satan, 46, 67, 108, 110, 114, 117, 177, 203, 238, 253-54, 336, 339, 350, 359, 363, 365, 370, 372, 382, 422-23, 435, 528, 571, 652, 714-17, 776-78, 785, 812, 818
schools, 4, 39, 72, 74, 84, 133-34, 229, 232, 270, 284, 286, 470, 506, 530, 540-41, 572-73, 575, 609, 623-24, 627, 671, 688, 704-9, 767,

785, 850, 872, 894, 895
scribes, 2-4, 37, 39, 78, 80-81, 84, 94-97, 134, 150, 176, 179, 209, 284, 355-56, 386, 399, 410, 430, 449, 499, 530, 540-41, 546, 553-57, 561, 578, 681, 704-9, 717-19, 721, 739, 743, 753-54, 794-95, 802, 850, 858, 868, 880-81, 894-95
sea, 9, 13, 16, 18-20, 42-52, 61, 63-65, 67-68, 70, 100, 150, 249, 321, 392, 431-32, 466, 482, 487, 516, 520, 591-92, 602-3, 664, 713, 725, 758, 817-19, 889
sea monsters, 16, 19, 42, 45-46, 63-64, 67, 70, 249, 321, 602
Second Temple, 8, 35-36, 77-79, 89, 91-92, 115-16, 149, 181, 240, 268-69, 400, 424, 427, 457-59, 463-64, 485, 567, 632, 719-22, 728, 733, 744, 786, 817, 846-48, 850-53, 885, 887-88, 890
secular wisdom, 900
semantic parallelism, 474, 508, 521, 600, 770
Septuagint, 2-3, 7-8, 17, 26, 35-41, 91-93, 95, 97, 99, 113-15, 121, 174, 181-82, 184-87, 216-18, 228, 234, 241, 270, 301, 317, 324, 362-64, 366-67, 371, 379, 416, 427-28, 468, 485-86, 526, 528, 536, 538, 540-41, 552, 561, 566-68, 570, 577-79, 606, 614-20, 631-32, 635-36, 685, 694, 720-21, 728, 733, 764, 785, 795, 797-804, 813, 842-47, 874, 886, 915, 930-931
sex, sexuality, 15, 23, 107, 207, 210-12, 214, 229, 257, 421, 424, 426, 451-57, 488, 568, 738, 740, 744-45, 750, 754, 757, 760, 762, 764-65, 767-69, 834, 910, 919
shame, 21, 118, 214, 226, 288-89, 291-94, 296, 298-99, 355, 379, 454, 456, 584, 592, 714, 723, 729-31, 792, 813, 819, 915, 919, 921, 932
sheep, 13-14, 16, 165, 337, 350, 373, 562, 756-57, 792, 838, 869-70, 919
short story, 495, 677-78, 728
Shuilla, 596
Shulgi of Ur, 755, 759
Shu-Suen of Ur, 756
similes, 14, 108, 219, 239, 306, 455, 465, 522, 524, 533, 535-36, 587-89, 656, 751, 758, 927
sin, sinning, 21, 23, 68-69, 80, 82, 87, 95, 109, 119, 141, 165-66, 168, 179, 186, 195, 204, 213, 224-25, 236, 238, 250, 253-55, 258, 278-79, 281, 293, 296, 322, 326, 328-29, 337, 339, 347-48, 350, 360, 362, 363, 368, 372-74, 390, 395, 397-98, 400, 404-8, 414-17, 420, 423-24, 428, 432, 435-36, 455, 517-18, 533, 536, 578, 596, 598, 607, 625, 645-46, 648, 650, 653-54, 664, 666-67, 682, 710-11, 713, 716-17, 723, 727, 741, 774-76, 779-80, 788-89, 811-12, 814, 821, 823, 834, 854, 858, 908, 910, 915, 931-34, 940,
sinners, 12, 80, 109, 292, 296, 361,

368, 370, 373, 435, 726, 917
Sirach, 36, 38-39, 41, 82, 84, 91, 141, 145, 219, 220-22, 234, 281, 294, 298, 330, 422, 427, 471, 519, 541, 572, 576, 579, 706, 719-28, 731, 761, 798, 843, 851-53, 887-88, 890, 901, 915, 916
social science, 270-71, 728, 732
social space, 732
Solomon, 25, 28, 30, 39, 40-41, 77, 82-83, 107, 122-24, 138, 142-45, 147, 149, 199-200, 236, 238-39, 250, 267, 269-70, 272-74, 283, 285, 287, 324, 326, 330, 393, 427-29, 440, 456, 461, 464, 467-68, 470-71, 484, 535, 537, 539-40, 542, 545, 550, 552-65, 571, 575, 578, 614, 619-20, 636-37, 666, 668-69, 671-72, 674-75, 681, 704, 708, 712, 719, 724, 726, 733-37, 739-40, 742-44, 746-47, 749-50, 759, 761, 764-66, 787-88, 836, 840, 842, 847, 852, 866-68, 872, 874, 876-78, 882, 885-90, 895, 896, 898-99, 915, 918, 924, 933-34, 936, 940-41
Song of Songs Rabbah, 458
Songs of Ascent, 24, 77, 90, 151-52, 154, 234, 442, 452, 931, 936, 939, 941
Songs of Zion, 235, 320
Sons of Korah, 24-27, 102, 234, 263, 386, 499, 608
sound patterns, 439, 523, 533, 770, 772
sovereignty of God, 778, 814
Standard Biblical Hebrew (SBH), 262, 264-66, 673-74
stanza, 1-3, 90, 236, 323, 352, 403, 406, 412, 465, 468, 523-24, 594, 601-3, 616, 641-42, 725, 751-53, 770, 772-74
storm imagery, 42, 44, 46-47
story, stories, 8, 10, 42-43, 45, 48, 51, 65, 68, 70, 105-6, 160-69, 171-76, 178, 181-87, 189, 193-96, 213, 242-43, 265, 269, 270-77, 279, 283, 286, 296, 299, 310-11, 322, 325, 328-30, 351, 353, 360, 364, 369-70, 372-74, 379-81, 394, 422, 425-26, 428, 434, 438, 441, 443-44, 455, 469, 472, 478, 491-92, 494-95, 498, 528, 537, 544-45, 547, 555, 569, 572, 590, 611, 631-33, 639, 661, 674-79, 681, 684, 688, 694-99, 718, 733, 738, 740, 742-44, 747, 755, 758, 781, 822-24, 829, 858, 864, 866, 869, 872, 888-89, 897, 922
stronghold, 23, 58, 388, 461, 525-26, 586, 712, 819, 936
strophe, 54, 465, 508, 523-24, 641-42, 770, 772-74
suffering, 4-5, 19, 60-62, 82, 84, 104, 108-12, 141, 177, 203-4, 206, 209-10, 213-14, 236, 238, 242-43, 253, 255, 257, 274, 278-79, 293, 297, 321, 328, 330, 333, 335-36, 339, 341-53, 355, 359-60, 362-63, 365-67, 369, 372-74, 382, 388, 390, 395, 397, 399, 403-8, 412, 416-19, 422-24, 435-37, 460-61, 495, 517-18, 576, 592, 596, 598,

611, 647-51, 653-54, 667, 717, 738, 775-81, 809, 811-12, 815-16, 824, 832-34, 853, 860, 891-92, 896-97, 899, 910, 918

Sumerian city laments, 286, 410-12, 595

superscriptions, 73, 77, 86-87, 91, 93, 150-52, 154, 234, 236-39, 281-82, 285, 324, 328, 375-76, 386, 399, 451-52, 471, 485-86, 537, 539, 540-41, 578-80, 590, 607-12, 615, 617, 619, 669-70, 712, 798, 819, 868

Susa, 9, 161, 164, 166, 170, 173, 190, 192, 276, 476-79, 481, 494-95, 631, 688, 781-83, 826-27, 923

syllabic meter, 473-75

syllepsis, 927

symbolism, 15, 20-21, 46, 51, 127, 206, 208, 211, 307, 314, 479, 483-84, 516, 519, 526, 550, 691-92, 696-97, 731, 761-65, 768-69, 783, 830, 839, 848-49, 907

Symmachus, 797, 799, 803

synonymous parallelism, 166, 252, 503, 521, 574, 586, 718, 843

synthetic parallelism, 504, 508-9, 521, 586, 608

Syriac, 2, 7, 91, 95, 218, 228, 234, 443, 541, 547, 568, 613, 720, 728, 787, 791, 797-803, 926

Tabernacles, Feast of, 143, 457, 459, 461-63, 614, 616, 632, 680, 932

Tale of the Eloquent Peasant, 361, 690

Talmud, 35, 37-38, 40, 101, 142-43, 145, 160-61, 167, 177-78, 181, 363, 415, 455, 457-58, 460-63, 568-69, 579, 633, 673, 680, 693-94, 696, 740, 766, 784-87, 795, 827

targum, targumim, 99, 784-91

Targum Canticles, 784, 787

Targum Esther, 784, 789, 790

Targum Job, 93, 784-86

Targum Lamentations, 414-15, 784, 788, 790

Targum Proverbs, 784-87

Targum Psalms, 784-86

Targum Qohelet, 784, 788-89

Targum Ruth, 784, 789

temple, 21, 24-25, 27, 61, 64, 71, 73-82, 84, 113, 116-19, 151, 154, 160, 165-66, 178, 183, 229, 231, 234-40, 248, 262, 269, 271-72, 282-83, 291, 326, 329, 350, 352, 356, 376, 385, 389-94, 397, 400-402, 408, 411-12, 416, 428, 435, 485, 486-87, 517, 525-27, 533, 540, 547, 549-50, 556, 559-60, 569, 582, 583, 585, 593-94, 597-99, 611, 614, 617-20, 626, 629, 633, 641, 665, 668-69, 708, 710,

721, 725, 733-34, 737, 751, 755-56, 763, 775, 788, 795, 805-7, 819, 827, 832, 859, 872, 883, 885, 913, 920, 931-34, 936, 938, 940

temple hymns, 440, 594, 599

terseness, 152, 159, 261, 464-65, 475, 502, 520-23, 542-43, 585, 594, 599-601, 791-94, 800

Testament of Job, 363, 371

tetracolon, 520

textual criticism, 55, 89, 176, 227, 233, 499, 504, 609, 794-95, 797, 799, 801

thanksgiving, 2-3, 5, 25, 57-59, 73, 77, 84-85, 90, 229-30, 235, 247, 250, 263, 282, 300-301, 324, 375, 387-91, 393, 396, 405, 420, 449, 473, 488, 580, 584, 588, 607, 620, 646, 655, 713, 722, 724, 805-8, 823, 832, 931, 933, 939

theodicy, 60, 61, 85, 237, 342, 349, 647-54, 708, 809-11, 813-16, 854, 856, 881, 896, 899, 904

Theodotion, 797, 799, 803

theophany, 46, 60-61, 79, 335, 339, 482, 806, 817-20, 838

thighs, 752, 758, 839-41

Torah Psalms, 155, 585

tower, 22-24, 118, 196, 302, 533, 588, 691, 738, 783, 830, 836-40, 866, 888

trees, 17, 60, 62, 65, 67-68, 70, 121-22, 159, 194-95, 202, 219-22, 306, 352, 432-34, 464, 466, 477, 486-87, 516, 522, 524, 606, 659, 723, 738, 753, 755, 760, 780-81, 840, 870, 872, 898, 911

tricolon, 2, 55, 468, 473, 511-12, 520, 542, 600, 603

triumph, 171, 185, 592, 625, 712, 831-32

Turin Love Song, 753

two ways, 104, 106, 152, 215, 304, 308, 432, 589, 811, 861, 893, 904, 907, 928

Ugarit, 43, 53-54, 76, 113-14, 135-36, 139, 283, 313, 345, 347, 409, 439, 451, 484-86, 500, 505-6, 553, 559-60, 598, 610, 627, 654, 687, 690, 705, 708-9, 718, 758-60, 774, 899, 901

Ugaritic, 1, 2, 42-46, 49, 52-54, 61, 113-16, 160, 224, 262-63, 283, 287, 313, 339, 344, 403, 410, 450, 452, 498-500, 505-6, 515, 560, 588, 598-604, 610, 614, 619, 621, 626, 628, 688, 705-6, 717-18, 758, 841, 926, 937

vanity, 12, 66, 129, 141, 144, 146, 255, 294, 432, 539, 570, 638, 779, 788

Vashti, 10, 161-64, 171-74, 176-78, 180, 189-90, 215-17, 275-77, 295, 455, 493-94, 632, 644, 826-28, 922-23

verset, 502, 509-10, 520

vindication, 6-7, 61, 75, 102, 288-91, 338, 340, 342, 355, 361, 366, 369, 382-83, 390, 421, 425, 435, 437, 447-48, 450, 528, 568, 582, 585, 651, 665, 667-68, 711-12, 779-80, 788, 812, 816-17, 819, 852-53, 908, 911

violence, 54, 162, 190-91, 214, 249, 262, 318, 366, 390, 493, 537, 543-44, 657-58, 665, 711, 832-34, 940

virtuous woman, 22, 533, 536, 571, 575, 693, 843

wall, 9, 23, 59, 101, 298, 349, 356, 448, 525, 597, 707, 714, 782, 832, 838, 845

warfare, 415, 517, 626, 629, 687, 829, 830-34, 870, 939

warriors, 32, 69, 162, 166, 172, 206, 353, 392, 397, 403, 469, 487, 507, 580, 598, 641, 711, 713, 729, 820, 829-33, 838, 867-68, 914

wasf, 211-12, 239, 743, 835-41

weapons, 42, 70, 353, 527, 583, 626-29, 714, 730, 829-31, 840, 937

Westermann, C., 150, 156, 232, 241, 300-301, 305, 333, 346, 388, 396, 398, 400-403, 410, 419, 530, 539, 541, 552, 584, 610, 613, 775-76, 781, 805-8, 872, 876, 931, 935

widow, widowhood, 7, 33, 189, 199, 213, 258, 359, 379-81, 400, 414-15, 420, 425, 430, 433, 454-55, 517, 546, 661, 678, 680, 682, 685, 687-92, 696, 698-99, 702, 729-30, 788, 861, 867-68, 910, 917-20, 922, 924

Wilson, Gerald H., 27, 59, 93, 99, 150, 153, 156, 234, 241, 332, 376, 378, 446, 470, 472, 489, 502, 515, 528, 532, 539, 580-81, 593, 611, 613, 672, 737, 894

Wisdom of Solomon, 36, 40-41, 64, 82, 84, 141, 229, 281, 519, 842-43, 845, 852, 885, 886-90, 901, 915-16

wisdom poems, 2, 102-3, 238, 723-25, 814, 859, 891-94

wisdom psalms, 2, 6, 27, 30, 72, 84-85, 92, 100, 205, 247, 335, 535, 580, 585, 651, 672, 842, 856, 865, 868, 893-94, 900, 933

wisdom theology, 408, 854, 893-94, 900, 903-4

woman, women, 7, 10, 16-17, 22-23, 32-33, 68, 76, 83, 87, 102-7, 144, 163-65, 173, 176, 188-89, 191-92, 198-99, 202, 205-16, 221-22, 224-25, 237, 239-43, 258, 274-77, 279, 288, 294-95, 298-300, 322, 330, 350, 353, 356-57, 380-81, 400-401, 403-4, 410, 412, 421, 424, 426, 433-35, 452-56, 465-66, 472, 478, 480, 488, 490,

493, 517-19, 521, 536, 542-43, 547, 550, 563, 567, 571, 574, 575, 588, 595, 600, 616, 643, 658, 672-74, 676, 679, 682-85, 687-92, 695-97, 699-700, 702-3, 723-24, 726, 729, 735, 739-40, 742, 744, 752-59, 761-63, 766-69, 771, 789-90, 823, 826-27, 833-41, 843, 859, 868, 891, 893, 905-7, 912-14, 916-24, 926, 932-34, 936, 940

Woman/Lady Folly, 55, 102-3, 105-6, 202, 207, 209, 224-25, 237, 243, 335, 452, 471, 518-19, 537, 542, 544, 550-51, 657, 912-14, 916, 920-21, 933

Woman/Lady Wisdom, 55, 64-65, 70, 82, 84, 102-3, 105-7, 109, 202-3, 207-9, 217, 224, 237, 243, 335, 432-33, 436, 452, 471, 481, 516, 518-19, 534, 536-37, 542, 544, 547-51, 569-70, 574-77, 657-58, 725, 735, 904, 912-16, 918, 920-22, 933

word pairs, 2, 158-59, 465, 492, 498-99, 508, 521, 533, 588

wordplays, 191, 228, 678, 770, 929

worship, 15, 24-25, 71-74, 76-85, 115, 119, 149-50, 175, 201-2, 204, 207-9, 235, 247, 268-69, 271-72, 282, 288-91, 301, 317, 324-25, 329, 360, 372, 376, 378, 382, 386, 393-95, 420, 449, 468, 479, 485, 488, 516, 549, 578, 584-85, 592-94, 597, 602-4, 616, 620, 645, 668-70, 680, 684, 716, 731, 733, 743, 745, 751, 777, 805-7, 819-20, 824, 851, 856, 897, 905-7, 909, 913, 916, 920, 929-34, 938-40

writing, 1, 2, 4, 28-30, 97, 123, 132, 136, 143, 150, 161, 181, 231-32, 274-75, 281, 286, 326, 331, 363, 368, 422, 430, 441, 444, 485, 489, 497, 516, 529, 544, 553, 557-58, 561, 564, 571-72, 594, 603, 606, 618, 623, 636-37, 661, 668, 670, 685, 692, 696, 704-9, 717-19, 722, 734, 767, 785, 789, 794, 822, 835, 864, 871, 873, 879, 881, 887, 894-95, 915, 931

Xerxes, 8-10, 37, 161-62, 170-75, 183, 189, 190, 240, 476-79, 494, 781, 783, 826-27, 873, 922-23

Zaphon, 51, 407, 483, 602, 626, 937

zeugma, 927

Zion, 27, 53, 61-62, 91, 92, 113-14, 117, 156-58, 214, 217, 235-36, 316, 318, 377, 382, 391-93, 401-2, 404-9, 419, 468, 481, 483, 516-19, 525, 580-81, 583, 592, 599, 602, 610, 612, 664-65, 668, 713, 730, 793, 801, 830, 832-33, 868, 918-19, 936-41

Articles Index

Acrostic, 1
Afterlife, 5
Ahasuerus, 8
Ambiguity, 11
Animal Imagery, 13
Architectural Imagery, 20
Asaph and Sons of Korah, 24
Autobiography, 27
Boaz, 32
Canon, 35
Chaos and Death, 41
Chiasm, 54
Confidence, Psalms of, 57
Creation Imagery, 60
Creation Theology, 63
Cult, Worship: Psalms, 71
Cult, Worship: Wisdom, 78
David, 86
Dead Sea Scrolls, 88
Destruction, 99
Discourse in Proverbs, 102
Disputation, 108
Divine Council, 112
Divine Presence, 116
Ecclesiastes 1: Book of, 121
Ecclesiastes 2: Ancient Near Eastern Background, 132
Ecclesiastes 3: History of Interpretation, 140
Editorial Criticism, 149
Ellipsis, 156
Esther 1: Book of, 160
Esther 2: Extrabiblical Background, 170
Esther 3: History of Interpretation, 175
Esther 4: Additions, 181
Esther 5: Greek Versions, 184
Esther 6: Person, 188
Ethics, 193

Fear of the Lord, 201
Feminist Interpretation, 205
Floral Imagery, 218
Folly, 223
Form Criticism, 227
Frame Narrative, 241
God, 246
Hebrew Language, 260
Hermeneutics, 267
Historical Criticism, 280
Honor and Shame, 287
Hymns, 300
Imagery, 306
Imprecation, 314
Imprisonment Imagery, 320
Inclusio, 323
Intertextuality, 325
Job 1: Book of, 333
Job 2: Ancient Near Eastern Background, 346
Job 3: History of Interpretation, 361
Job 4: Person, 371
Kingship, Psalms of, 375
Kinsman-Redeemer and Levirate, 378
Lament, Psalms of, 384
Lamentations 1: Book of, 399
Lamentations 2: Ancient Near Eastern Background, 410
Lamentations 3: History of Interpretation, 414
Law, 420
Lemuel and Agur, 427
Life, Imagery of, 431
Lyric Poetry, 437
Maat, 447
Marriage and Sex, 451
Megillot and Festivals, 457
Merism, 464
Messiah, 466

Meter, 472
Mordecai, 476
Mountain Imagery, 481
Music, Song, 483
Naomi, 490
Novella, Story, Narrative, 492
Oral Poetry, 497
Parallelism, 502
Personification, 516
Poetics, Terminology of, 520
Protection Imagery, 525
Proverb, Genre of, 528
Proverbs 1: Book of, 539
Proverbs 2: Ancient Near Eastern Background, 552
Proverbs 3: History of Interpretation, 566
Psalms 1: Book of, 578
Psalms 2: Ancient Near Eastern Background, 593
Psalms 3: History of Interpretation, 605
Psalms 4: Titles, 613
Psalms 5: Iconography, 621
Purim, 631
Qohelet, 635
Refrain, 641
Remembrance, 643
Retribution, 647
Rhetorical Criticism, 655
Righteousness, 663
Royal Court, 668
Ruth 1: Book of, 672
Ruth 2: Ancient Near Eastern Background, 687
Ruth 3: History of Interpretation, 693
Ruth 4: Person, 700
Sages, Schools, Education, 704
Salvation and Deliverance Imagery, 710

Satan, 714
Scribes, 717
Sirach, Book of, 720
Social-Scientific Approaches, 728
Solomon, 733
Song of Songs 1: Book of, 737
Song of Songs 2: Ancient Near Eastern Background, 750
Song of Songs 3: History of Interpretation, 760
Sound Patterns, 770
Stanza, Strophe, 772
Suffering, 775
Susa, 781
Targumim, 784
Terseness, 791
Text, Textual Criticism, 794
Thanksgiving, Psalms of, 805
Theodicy, 808
Theophany, 817
Time, 820
Vashti, 826
Warfare Imagery, 829
Wasf, 835
Wisdom, Greek, 842
Wisdom and Apocalyptic, 847
Wisdom and Biblical Theology, 853
Wisdom and Covenant, 858
Wisdom and History, 863
Wisdom and Prophecy, 876
Wisdom of Solomon, 885
Wisdom Poem, 891
Wisdom Sources, 894
Wisdom Theology, 901
Woman Wisdom and Woman Folly, 912
Women, 916
Wordplay, 925
Worship, 929
Zion, 936